# *Windows of the Soul*

# WINDOWS
# OF THE SOUL

*The National Library of Poetry*

*Cynthia A. Stevens, Editor*
*Nicole Walstrum, Associate Editor*

# *Windows of the Soul*

Library of Congress
Cataloging in Publication Data

ISBN 1-57553-002-3

Manufactured in The United States of America by
Watermark Press
11419 Cronridge Dr., Suite 10
Owings Mills, MD 21117

**Cover Artist:** Tracy A. Hetzel

# *Editor's Note*

***Windows of the Soul*** is a wonderful poetry collection which includes an interesting variety of styles and topics. The broad assortment of poems presented here is deeply enthralling. Each of the poets featured within this anthology has succeeded in crafting a true work of art. As one of the editors and judges of the contributing entries, I had the rewarding opportunity to review and ponder the many pieces presented within this anthology. There are several poems, however, I wish to honor with special recognition.

For exquisite description and a distinctive theme, "Aphrodite's Breath" by Joanna Koutsis (p. 1) was awarded the grand prize. The persona of the poem suggests that she is currently involved in a monotonous task late at night *"under the hard, dusty lamplight."* Perhaps processing divorce papers; *"I soften the heavy blows with purple lids."* The persona closes her eyes to envision a time in her past when she was with Aphrodite (the love goddess born from the sea):

> *Roundmoon-lightspill once occupied my blue limbs*
> *in that ancient land of Aphrodite and her baths.*
> *My journeys, so moist, distant in those eyes,*
> *eyes of antiquity and yellowed marble tombs.*

The persona seems to be searching for more fulfillment from life. There is no love in her present situation; her world has become cold and mundane in meeting all the responsibilities to survive. She needs to "venture" again:

> *After all, the goddess shares her secrets with those*
> *who venture into the silver waters at the dawn,*
> *and the foamy warmth becomes yet another womb*
> *from which a daughter, a lover is born.*

Love has been pushed aside -- *"ancient and frail as she is/...."* And, after all her past journeying which may have caused her to become emotionally distant and depressed, the persona comes to realize that there is still love to be found:

> *Yet, withstanding the wind from the North,*
> *the goddess whispers through the trees, "I Live."*

This revelation ultimately brings the persona to tears, *"Her breath, salty and warm, fingers my eyes and fills them now."*

Another highly outstanding piece is "Hieroglyphic," by Heather Lee (p. 234). This poem is full of interesting images which implicate that we are all blind to the messages sent from past generations. My favorite image is that which launches the poem, *"We ate our life and spit out the bones."* Most of us do accept life for what it is instead of taking time to decipher it.

Lee is informing the reader that no matter how much a past generation may try to influence a new age, it is not an easy task because the younger generation is not always willing to see:

> *My feet trip into the remnants of another time,*
> *small dents along a scapula*
> *spell out meaning I cannot decipher.*
> *I do not touch the Braille,*
> *blinded by this hieroglyphic.*

Many generations are blind to their elders' messages, mainly because they choose not to probe into the past as in the line, "I do not touch the Braille." How else can the blind read Braille without touching it?

Maybe we all should make more of an effort to look deeper into history for answers to solve today's problems instead of just looking toward the future as *"the next unsuspecting creatures...."*

> *Their eyes turn from the walls, look into the future*
> *and when they lean their ears into the warning*
> *the echo of our voices cannot save them.*

Also in haunting reference to our past is "Reincarnation (The Base Cannot Be Diffused)" by Maria Josephine Wolff (p. 582). This verse is brought to life by the fascinating descriptions found within, such as those presented below:

> *History's revenge tugs at rampant souls*
> *whispering to us through the tattered pages of dead men's ink*
> *as vinegar tears preserve the spirits in a bottle cast off to sea.*

Wolff's poem suggests that no matter how innocent we may believe all newborns to be (or even ourselves) -- evilness is part of human nature carried over from one generation to the next:

> *And you--you fell without a care from your mother's womb*
> *on the day of the eclipse*
> *refreshed and new after a centennium's sleep*
> *there again to be touched and molded*

*(so they thought)*
*but the soul remains deliciously tainted...*
*deliciously tainted...*

Another noteworthy piece is "The Woman That I Am," by Bonnie Bevel-Maddox, a momentous tribute to women which reveals their immortality. Bevel-Maddox substantiates this claim through various significant impressions as in the example below:

*I am a woman who stands at the portals,*
*Of both life and death.*
*First with the babe, last as she closes the eyes of the dying.*
*For through my hands in this existence, both have passed.*

*There is no death of the temporal in my household*
*For I sew it into the quilts that last for centuries,*
*Warming new generations; bearing witness to both past and present.*
*To be woman is to stand with one foot in that which is eternal.*

The poem, "Ophelia," by Dymphna McAree (p. 271), takes a fresh look at the character Ophelia from Shakespeare's **Hamlet**. Through picturesque description, McAree summarizes the overall sadness of Ophelia caused by her hunger for Hamlet's mere attention. I particularly enjoy the allusions presented throughout this piece.

Several other prominent poems you won't want to miss: "In August" by Kate Bell (p. 97); "Not Greek at All" by Peachy Ragasa Carmona (p. 595); "The Shaly Soil" by Elroy Meyer (p. 251); Sara Rowen's untitled piece (p. 641); "Somatic Adaptation" by Alvin A. Sims (p. 502); "Efficacy" by Laurel Sneed (p. 153); and make sure to look up all of our third place winners.

Although I do not have the time or space to individually critique every eminent poem appearing within **Windows of the Soul**, you will notice that each piece of artistry is an admirable contribution. May all of the artists within this anthology be renowned for their talents and efforts in creative writing.

*Cynthia A. Stevens*
*Senior Editor*

# Acknowledgments

*Windows of the Soul* is a culmination of the efforts of many individuals. The editors are grateful for the contributions of the judges, assistant editors, graphic artists, layout artists, office administrators, and customer service representatives who have all brought their talents to bear on this project. We would also like to give a special thanks to our cover artist, Tracy A. Hetzel.

**Managing Editor**
**Howard Ely**

# Winners of the North American Open Poetry Contest

## Grand Prize

Joanna Koutsis / Denver, CO

## Second Prize

Kate Bell / Stockbridge, MA
Bonnie Bevel-Maddox / Thomaston, GA
Peachy Ragasa Carmona / Hayward, CA
Heather Lee / Berkeley, CA
Dymphna McAree / Bogota, NJ

Elroy Meyer / East Aurora, NY
Sara Rowen / Albany, NY
Alvin A. Sims / Detroit, MI
Laurel Sneed / Spring, TX
Maria Josephine Wolff / Woodbury, CT

## Third Prize

Patricia P. Adam / Ocala, FL
Judith Pike Boos / Middletown, CT
Elva M. Brakefield / Wilmington, CA
Tara Bruckler / Wescosville, PA
Constance Carmody / Long Beach, NY
Krisha Shaun Carter / Augusta, GA
Deborah Carver / Garnerville, NY
Gregory Case / Ellicott City, MD
Wyeth Chandler / Bartlett, TN
Mary S. Chevalier / Joaquin, TX
Nina Cicero / Warner, NH
Adam Coben / Elkins Park, PA
Dan Conlin / Sault Sainte Marie, MI
Douglas Conroy / Poughkeepsie, NY
Victor David / Berkeley, CA
Samson Denis / Fort Lauderdale, FL
Beverly Dillon / Cookeville, TN
Quoc-Bao Do / Southfield, MI
D. Medb Duffey / Chicago, IL
Dennis M. Fahey / Shrewsbury, NJ
Janice W. Fernheimer / College Park, MD
Fannie Fiore / Webster, NC
Raynelle J. George / Lenore, ID
Lee Harris / Los Angeles, CA
David Hylton / Anaheim, CA
Theodora Kinder / Los Angeles, CA
Esaku Kondo / Bloomfield Hills, MI
Betty Leonard / Durango, CO
Brandon Lewis / Westland, MI
Judith A. Litchfield / Portland, OR

Jana Maddox / Pasadena, CA
Anthony T. Marconi / Phoenix, AZ
Gail McCabe / Palm Springs, CA
Bob McGrath / Forest Hills, NY
Brian McLeod / Enfield, CT
Allison Merriman / Grand Island, NE
Gary L. Morrison / Kaneohe, HI
Loreta Muskardin / Brooklyn, NY
Jennifer Myers / Waterville, OH
Carolynne Nix / Mineral, TX
Karen Wilcox O'Connor / Medfield, MA
Jamie Patricia / Ivanhoe, MN
Barbara Prudhomme / Plano, TX
Rachel Raybourn / Pensacola, FL
Esther Roberts / San Francisco, CA
Ronnie C. San Jose / South San Francisco, CA
Auriel Sandstead / Sterling, CO
Shuvendu Sen / Edison, NJ
Jessica Dawn Smith / Provo, UT
Gerald A. Somers / Green Bay, WI
Bill Standridge / Redan, GA
James Lawrence Thibault / Philadelphia, PA
Danielle Turns / Borden, IN
Allison K. Urias / Albuquerque, NM
Brian Vigorito / North Haledon, NJ
Jessica Wangsness / Saint Paul, MN
Dale D. Wideman / Bear, DE
Eleanor Williams / Milton, FL
J. S. Winston / Minneapolis, MN

## Congratulations also to all semi-finalists.

# Grand Prize Winner

### Aphrodite's Breath

*Under the hard, dusty lamplight*
*corporate pragmatism drones in front of me now.*
*I soften the heavy blows with purple lids.*
*My journeys, so moist, distant in those eyes,*
*eyes of antiquity and yellowed marble tombs.*
*Roundmoon-lightspill once occupied my blue limbs*
*in that ancient land of Aphrodite and her baths.*
*After all, the goddess shares her secrets with those*
*who venture into silver waters at the dawn,*
*and the foamy warmth becomes yet another womb*
*from which a daughter, a lover is born.*
*At the edge, I elevated my head to see the singer's*
*melancholy dance on the black sand*
*those rugged men who dream of ships - they dance for her:*
*The goddess of the land; not to please her*
*but for her sake, ancient and frail as she is*
*crumbling like the rotted stones of Pericles in that other city.*
*Yet, withstanding the wind from the North,*
*the goddess whispers through the trees, "I Live."*
*Her breath, salty and warm, fingers my eyes and fills them now.*
### Joanna Koutsis

## "Secret Pal" Cake

3 Cups mysterious friends
1/2 Cup hidden name
1 Tablespoon flavoring of heart 'n' soul
1 Cup Agape love
1 Cup Fruits of the Spirit
1 Cup encouragement
1 cup prayer

Mix together 3 cups mysterious friends with 1/2 cup hidden names; add
1 tablespoon flavorings of heart and soul intertwined with Agape Love.
Mix thoroughly with the Fruit of the Spirit, Love, Joy, Peace,
Patience, Kindness, Goodness, Faithfulness, Gentleness and Self
Control. Fold in encouragement. Pour into the heart of a person.
Prepare spirit of the Secret Pal to accept the keepsakes presented to
them. Serve with a sweet spirit sprinkled with the Joy of the Lord
in your heart. Drizzle with Prayer.

*Jodi Williams*

## I Was Assaulted

I owned a store, a luncheonette and coffee shop in 1987.
3 weeks after the take-over, I was assaulted with a weapon.
When I bought the store, I kept the cook and the Deli man.
I wanted them to train me.
So, I could learn the business the best that I can.
That morning prior to the assault, Marsh, the cook
started an argument with me, then he threatened
me with a knife, he wanted to fight.
After the argument, to release some steam, I went to the store.
When I returned Marsh, was hiding outside behind the wall.
Then he called me outside, his tone of voice sounded apologetic.
Instead, he struck me with a spike across my mouth.
   I will never forget it!
He cut my bottom lip open and punched out 3 front teeth,
   I went into shock.
After he assaulted me he fled up the block, he went so fast,
   he never stopped.
My vanity was gone, it was my teeth!
So beautiful they were white, clean, straight and neat.
I still haven't recovered from that tragic day at the store.
Flashbacks continue to haunt me, my beauty is gone, "Forever more."

*Fidelita Nina Lloyd*

## Beautiful Butterflies

What is as pretty as a butterflies wings?
A beautiful garden filled with flowers,
A white curtain with sunlight coming through,
And a sculpture of Michelangelo.

What is as pretty as a butterflies wings?
A starry night,
A tropical rain forest,
And a beautiful scene of the Virgin Islands.

What is as pretty as a butterflies wings?
A necklace shimmering with diamonds,
An underwater exploration of the sea,
And a cruise on the ocean at sunset.

*Christina A. Mammen*

## It's A Four Letter Word

One day you'll look for me
But I'll be gone
Like the words of a half forgotten song.
In the melody of love where once we met.
You touched a cord in me I can't forget.
For you will always be a gleaming part
In all the precious corners of my heart.

*Janet Washington*

## Visions

I had a vision in my sleep last night
A beautiful woman was dressed in white.
Down an isle of flowers she did walk
Not a word was spoken, no one did talk.

I stood in amazement as my eyes did see
This woman walking to marry me.
In God's eyes we were going to become
A single unit of love and peace known as one.

"Let no man put asunder" everyone was told
So I took her hand to have and hold.
The future looks brighter now day after day
Because no one can take this woman away.

Her love comes from deep in her soul
And to my heart it has taken a hold.
For no woman in the world could take me away
From the woman I have married on this day.

*Jimmy Lee Akers*

## The Gloves

Harsh gloves cover Estonia.
A blanket of dark, wet and cold
Covers its plains.
Murky buildings look out with hopeless eyes.

Gloves with holes worn by penniless peasants
Hide weathered, thin hands.
Children desperate, steal to eat.
Bands of youths drink and smoke.

A gift of gloves
So lovingly knitted.
Intricate designs, fragile and delicate
Given in friendship to a stranger.

A pair of gloves bind two different worlds
Threads so fine reach out to hold me.
Cold memories warm and melt the vision
Because of kind hands and hearts that touched me.

*Heather Graham*

## Not For The World

On the Twentieth of December in Nineteen Fifty-Eight
A boy and girl said "I do," and turned a new page of fate.
They started out small with enough to be eaten.
But they had each other, it was all that they needed.

They worked hard for each other, the worked harder and longer.
And each day that went by, their love still grew stronger.
Their love showed in their eyes, then shown by three little tots,
Whom they loved and nurtured and taught right and not.

I remember the moves, new towns, new places.
I remember the smiles and tears on our faces.
I remember the lessons and I remember the fights.
I remember hugs and kisses and Christmas tree lights.

And the hardest times, it seems, were the times I had to go.
And on your special day, I'd like you both to know,
That I still see the boy and I still see the girl.
I wouldn't have missed a minute of it, not for the world.

*Brian R. Williams*

## Sleepy Head

The stars are so bright in the Heavens tonight,
But the moon on the right is so out of sight,
wake up you Sleepy Head and send your rays
to the earth below, before you go back to bed they said.

*Josephine M. Hayes*

## The Journey Through Life

Life is a gift sent from God above,
A child is born to nurture and love
A Miniature Image of Mother or Dad.
A more precious gift no one ever had
The most beautiful sight you will ever behold
More precious than all the silver or gold
To you is given this child to raise
Be thankful and to God give all your Praise
The Bible should ever be your rule and guide,
To His teachings your family should ever abide
Follow his commandments day after day,
To do his bidding there is no other way
To your care has been trusted a gift of life,
Someday to become a Good Christian Husband or Wife,
As time passes and older we grow
The lives that we lived in our children will show.
When our children are married and Grandparents we will be,
More names will be added to our family tree
Since time began it has been that way,
God guides our path to that Eternal Home someday.

*Carl R. Williams Sr.*

## Passerby

Grasps tighten around purses as I walk by.
A city street is where I walk.
I am neither black nor white, male or female.
I am neither old nor young.
It is not a matter of importance, for I am only noticed as a
presence.
I am only something that, no matter how naive I seem, could
endanger their lives or take their money.
I do not exist in their lives, except as a passerby.
I am not a threat, yet who is to know?
I am the same as thousands of others.
We are The Passersby.
We are not criminals, and yet we are carefully watched, maybe
even feared.
We even do a little watching ourselves.
Because who is to know who is a criminal, a mugger?
Walk assertively and confidently, always look like you know
where you are going.
This is the oath of the Passerby.
Sound familiar? Of course it does.
I am a passerby, as well all are in life.
Be assertive, be confident.
Always know where you are going.
Take the oath of the passerby.

*Elizabeth King*

## The Silent Cry

A silent cry echoed through the night,
A cry that trembled full of fright.
"Our love is dying," it tried to say,
But nary an ear would turn its way.
"Help me please," it begged and cried;
"I know she loves me," to himself he sighed.
But the silent cry she could not hear
Would once again not reach her ear.
And so they both go silently crying,
While deep inside they're silently dying.

*Dennis L. Mullen*

## Africa's Gift

A hundred years ago ... and more,
    a cultural gift America would receive.

For from a nation of little-known lore,
    would come forth a music to perceive.

Music ... a culture's way of communication,
    would be given birth by slaves in fields.

Jazz came forth in this new nation,
    as drums beating out polyrhythms began to peel.

Time passed ... Jazz unfurled and soon flourished,
    as America listened with ears intent.

America's people were soon to be nourished,
    from music of people's discontent.

This continent received the soul of a poor, humble nation,
    through African slaves struggling to survive.

For riches received through slavery's ugly creation,
    ... JAZZ, BLUES, SOUL, etc., were all soon to arrive!

*Cathryn Heinrich*

## The Owl

High among the fir branches
    A darker bulk against the leaden sky,
The great owl turned her tufted head,
    To regard me down below.

A minute passed as she gazed,
    Round yellow eyes set in round dark head;
Unblinking, her eyes meant mine,
    Another minute and she turned away.

Ruffling her soft feathers, back and tail;
    She settled herself once more.
Content that I posed no problem,
    She gave herself back to sleep.

*Carol Kinch*

## "I"

Sometimes, I forget that I am beautiful. Walt - let me say that
a different way - often, I fail to remember that I am not here.
See those daisies growing in the middle of this grassy path?
That's me!
Yes, I live only to be stepped upon, but watch
the life within me spring forth between the footsteps.
Over and over.
Trampled fibers and petals will finally yield to the life itself
- also in those footsteps - despite their resiliency,
and "I" becomes a tree, or a river, or a fish, or you.
I like being you. The look in your eyes in deep meditation or love
or laughter. The curve of your neck while lost in sleep and dreams.
Your fingertips full of play. Your tongue tied with talk, your lips
laced with kisses. Your tears only give me strength, breaking through
the clouds like thunder clearing the sky I am that.
I do not fear our anger - you see, there I live, too.
Yell, and I am heard. Cry, I am seen.
Smile, and I am free.

*Jenine de Shazer*

## Anger

Poverty laced our lives;
a gaunt wolf lapping blood,
although we struggled
toward the oasis
on the hot deserts of life,
the predators won,
in the cold capture of the world.

*June Baugher Deaton*

## AIDS

Something has finally caused this world to come to its senses.
A disease that kills faster than it convinces.

It has over-shadowed our youth,
Forcing us to deal with the truth.

It creeps on you slowly, then kills you fast.
Trust has become our enemy and AIDS hits us with a "Blast!"

Sad but true, we all know someone who died of the cause.
Watched them age before our eyes; death did not pause.

AIDS is just another way of showing, its all coming apart.
Death is all around us putting fear in our hearts.

AIDS is not "choosey" and it doesn't judge.
It thrives on carelessness and kills without a grudge.

Resulting in death..... and maybe even a soul unsaved.
Its all because of the actions we took or the way we behaved.

I know, sometimes the truth is too "deep."
Be careful what you sow now, so later you won't have to weep.

Be careful who you love,
Seek counsel and guidance from up above.

And just keep in mind, we can beat AIDS if we're smart.
Not taking any chances and choosing God is a good way to start.

*DeLayna Brady*

## A Mother's Grief

I once had a dream.
A dream about a baby,
A dream that was shattered one day.
I don't know why.
Why things happen this way
At times , life is so cruel.
Now for as long as my heart shall beat,
I shall grieve.
I will never feel her touch,
her soft skin next to mine
I will never experience her first tooth,
her first word, her first step, so many firsts.
Everyday I grieve for that dream
and all that I shall miss.
But most of all, I grieve for
That baby dream that should have been
More than just a dream
I know though, deep in my heart
She's up in the Heavens' with all the other
dream baby's cradled in God's warm embrace.

*Christina Xidas*

## A Dream

A dream is something you hold in your heart,
A dream means everything,
Something you know could never part.
For only a dream; a dream is found in your heart.
A dream is something that makes you smile on a rainy day,
A dream is something that will tell you you'll be okay.
Though there are days that it seems like your dream will never come true,
If you wait; wait for that special day,
The day when someone will finally hear you.
That's the day; the day your dream will come true.
In the days of tears, and the nights you spent crying,
And all your fears were inside of you, and you felt like dying,
It seems like no one cares when you were crying,
It seems like your dream;
Your dream will never come true.
Until that day that very special day it finally came.
The day your dream; your dream came true,
And all because you never gave up,
And all because you listened; listened to your heart.

*Dasha Sleza*

## Teardrops

A teardrop slowly makes its way down my face,
a face of miserable sadness,
what ever happened to all my happiness,
was it lost when I was lost,
or has it always been there,
not yet discovered, kind of like a ghost.
My eyes look deep into a mirrored image of my face,
if I look deep enough I can find my way back to happiness,
deeper and deeper I go exploring my broken heart,
I have found the reason it aches,
it is empty and needs someone to fill it with love.
My mind travels far away form reality,
it thinks about the life I dream of at night,
it is a fantasy life where there I'm never sad,
it is a life I only dream of,
at least there I can be happy.

*Jennifer Thorpe*

## Heaven

I glance in the mirror, and what do I see
A face of sorrow with no tomorrow
I look deep in the mirror with a raven of fear,
What will become of me
I ask the stranger please help me
He turns to me and stares within,
A shadow hangs over through the fright
I see the flashing screen of night
There is a rush and a shove
Through it all I stay above
In the morning I awake, with the sun beaming bright
So lightly do I hear the bells
The careless odors and the smells
The peace has come to me at last
The gates and clouds of white,
The heavenly swans, the dinging dongs
The harps the beat and I'm the drum
The angels dance and sing for fun
I lay on a cloud and fall asleep
For now life has just begun

*Camille Haburt*

## And The Angels Cried...

A broken toy, A mother's tear
A father's grief, a nation's fear

A lawman's wrath, a doctor's care
A fireman's sigh, a minister's prayer

Lives were taken, Dreams destroyed
The voices are silent....of the girls and boys

"The itsy bitsy spider went up the waterspout"
In went the children but they never came out

Lord, give us the grace to understand and forgive
To treasure each moment, Each day that we live

Their wee souls went to Heaven on the day that they died
God help open His arms......And the angels cried.

*Cheri Wickwire*

## Beauty

Beauty in most eyes is only skin deep,
But beauty comes from within,
We all have the beauty from within,
But a lot of people don't want to show it,
But I say let it out,
Because your beauty from within,
Could make some one happy
And that person could be you!

*John S. Roblyer*

## In Quiet Wonder

As I fished and watched in wonder
A flock of Pelican o'er yonder.
  Huddled there, they looked a dowdy group.
Had the bleakness of the morning added to their dismal stoop?
  I pondered of the service rendered.
Do they help or maybe hinder?
  With the sun rays came a clearing
And a gentle stir of rearing.
  Now, before my quizzical eye
Appeared a performance in the sky.
  Soaring, gliding, climbing, folding
With blended gender great beauty showing.
  Wings spread wide, they tipped and turned.
Reflecting light their feathers spurned.
  With precision timing, grace and form,
They glided down to resume their norm.
  By seeing this, my spirit swelled.
No greater show, had I beheld!
  Now, I knew the reason why —
Our creator to glorify.

  *Erma M. Zwart*

## The Fall

With a glance,
a fold up table breaks into the my memories
and pulls out my worst nightmare.
Many kids swarm into the room
in my flashback to watch.
To watch workers sift through Diamond Almonds
for the rejects.
The moment comes back,
as a horror movie in my head.
Dizziness thrusts its way
into the room.
I feel it all,
the noisy room,
the rocking,
the crash,
the sudden silence,
the floor,
the screams,
the rising kids,
my ankles helplessly glued to the ground.

  *Emily Sopp*

## A Friend

A friend told me it's good to be you,
A friend showed me that friendship is true,
She told me the truth was best to tell
And if I was sick,
She told me I'd be well.

She said "Don't worry it's alright,"
It was those words that took away my fright.
A friend is someone who deeply cares,
One who is loving, giving, and prepares.
So each passing day,
I realize how lucky I am in each and every way.

  *Jamie McNamara*

## Friendship

Friendship is when you feel down inside and
a friend comes along to build up your pride,
Friendship is when your whole world falls apart and
a friend comes along sharing with you their heart,
Friendship is when you share laughter and tears,
Friendship is when you comfort each other's fears.
Friendship is when you don't become jealous and make a big fuss,
Friendship started when God created us!

  *Jennifer Downward*

## Hands

Hands, seeming so simple at a glance.
A gadget - A device - a contraption - a weapon
No, the ultimate invention.  Bending and twisting
Wires of sorts.  Building and sculpting, it's never
too much

Tools are choice, not saying otherwise, but to pick
Up a child puts heaven in your eye.

Building the world is surely one thing.  Using the
This and that - that man has made.

But picking up a book and curling on your side,
Learning the heart of another reach you in your mind.
Stretching forth your hand across nation and globe,
Understanding their lives and even the giving of your
souls.

Tools and such are choice for sure, but hands, great
hands are eternal they endure.

  *brook susan parker*

## Escape

Tired and worn, unbearable pressure builds within,
A great feeling of dejection overwhelms me.
Looking for peace, forget the past, forget the sin.
I walk through the doorway and exit reality.

Dwelling in an existence of my creation,
Finding relief from pains and sorrows will it last?
My mind explores past normal imagination,
I exist as I want, reality fades fast.

But wait, a familiar glimmer in the mind's eye.
A faint scent?  Perhaps a face long since forgotten.
I betray myself; I won't let me live this lie.
Pulled from my escape, time expired, no more to lend.

Nothing is permanent in a life of trial and pain,
Nothing but the eternal rest I hope to gain.

  *Alexander Knight*

## Mommy

Sometimes in a dark time,
A hard, lonely time, a time of pain,
Something within me seeks, cries out instinctively,
"Mommy!"

I'm reaching for the edge of a memory,
The wish to be cradled, rocked, and loved,
Held securely in a place of comfort where nothing can touch me,
Where all is warmth and love and utter contentment.

I'm reaching for you.

Those days will not come again for you and me.
I am too big to rock, too far away to cuddle.
They are part of a host of things, forgotten,
Yet not really forgotten, woven into strength
So I can rock my little ones, and be their comfort.

On Mother's Day I remember things to thank you for.
This year I thank you for what I do not remember,
The edges of memory, the forgotten sacrifices, the time-blurred
  delight.
These are the foundation of my happiness,
The building blocks of my children's future.

I love you.

  *Diane Scudder*

## Guardian Beloved

Dear Lady, you're treasured, truth without lies,
A heart made of gold, endowed by my eyes,
Good fortune past found, your presence by fate,
Providence smiling, views blessed to relate.

My son you have held, safeguarded by love,
Mother's pure shelter, warmth found from above,
Birthed by your caring, my boy left alone,
Guided with passion, his castle your home.

May God be with you, this thought now bestowed,
My search to repay, a debt ever owed,
Bill everlasting, secured by your time,
Priceless in nature, a pleasure all mine.
    *Daniel C. Leesburg*


## To Enter Leaving

Entrance  Now it begins and life unveils
        a heart's nuance,
        and so we dance to the chant
        of fate
        filled with dread or hope of assurance.

Prayer    May this cadence new and bold
        endure pangs of change
        it needs to frame so few days as
        deity calculates;
        propelling swiftly through corridors waning.

Rebuke    In leisure we evade the gospel
        of bastions passed,
        forgetting, casting precepts
        to waste;
        donning frivolity as if nothing matters.

Resolve   With freewill a gift of profanity
        we fashion our choices
        a path to remorse or glory
        and wait;
        pulse languishing, time ceases with no recourse.
    *Emma Faith Mayo*


## The Fading Stranger

Fading away into the night,
A loner who loves it yet he is not alone
He walks silently like an indian
Would in the woods,
He is an eagle unable to be tied down
Yet somehow he is tied down in his heart
He has lots of friends yet I see
Him as a loner-one who goes
Alone unless he wants companionship
Fight describes his anger,
Fearless describes his happiness.
Unknown yet known.
Whether he is going or staying you never know.
he comes creeping up on you like a creature at night
He comes silently but sometimes,
Not always, loudly.
You've just got to learn to
Expect the unexpected by the
Fading stranger.
    *Alison E. (Lewis) Johnson*


## Life's Treasure

All my life, I dreamed that I might find,
A love as pure as snow, to be only mine.
One so sweet and more beautiful than flowers,
One I would posses until my last hour,
One that no other ever touched or could say,
They took possession of it for just a day.
A love so kind and gentle, taking my heart to keep,
Crowning me with happiness, making my
life complete.
Tears fall quietly, as my life comes to a close,
Because of such a love I will never know.
Life is filled with beauty, delight and pleasure,
But to know true love is to posses
life's treasure.
    *Juanita Brannen*


## My Love For You

I have this special love for you,
A love that grows from day to day.
A love as fresh as the morning dew,
A love that will never fade away.

Sometimes I find it hard to express,
This love I have for you.
But it's a love, I must confess,
That is only shared by few.

This love of mine that I feel for you,
Is one I have never felt before.
I guess it's all the nice things you do,
That make me love you that much more.

So just remember this one thing;
I love you with all my heart.
And as long as you wear that diamond ring,
Nothing can draw us apart.
    *Bob Sanders*


## A Father's Goal

A father should be what my Dad has been to me.
A man of kindness and tenderhearted,
One of whom God has not departed.
A friend in time of need,
As well as a guide whose advice I can heed.
A man who goes the extra mile,
So he can see me lift my head and smile.
A comforter in sorrow,
As well as a provider for all of us tomorrow.

A father should be what my Dad has been to me.
A man who will not allow his faith to yield
To the temptations that the world may have to wield.
A man who takes his family to the Lord,
And uses his Bible as his only Sword.
A man who invites his family to the Word of God,
So they may receive Him and be shod.
A man whose character is that of Christ,
So the world may see the cross and not pay the terrible price.

Fathers, you should follow this example too,
And Dad, I want to say, I love you!
    *David A. Deighton*


## Bonfire

Dancing flames leap to and fro
Casting all around a glow.

Crimson coals burn hot and bright
In the darkness of the night.

Shooting sparks fly high and low
Up and down and 'round they go.
    *Donna Topper*

## Findings Happiness

Seems all mankind is in
A most desperate pursuit
To find happiness most anywhere
However, discovering it and retaining it
Seems like a most difficult thing to do
And thusly we go on searching in vain
When I have found happiness
Is just within our very reach
For it is just a positive state of mind
If you will just take time to be patient and kind
And that by making one another happy
We can all be happy too
For the happiness you give away
Will return over and over again to you

*Coletta Mizlock*

## The Surrealist

My mother in exotic display
A mother whose life work is a creative play
In which she rules and preens and spurns
Those who love and woo her yearn
And those who near her fire do burn
And thirst and pine in turn.

Mother gorgeous through her years
A life devoid of thorn and tears
And on she dances, twirls in graceful glide
Her tears are covered deep inside
And some who find them are denied
Placate and comfort, hearts opened wide.

Mother has her many faces
Frilled trimmings, baubles, social graces
And on she searches high and low
Tossing her heart to and fro
And those who have her heart to hold
Have hearts of, pockets with, solid gold.

*Jan Keck*

## The Most Beautiful Sights In The World

A child at play
A mother's prayer
A Daddy's hug
A teddy bear
A sky life storm
A bird in flight
From one you love - a kiss goodnight,
The moon coming up stars shining bright
A bride and groom.
What a beautiful sight
The sadness of all as they say goodnight.
To watch one ride his first bike
Times when you knew, your children were right.
The world keeps turning everything seems bright.
Just knowing, how you have helped me to see
The most beautiful sights
In the world tonight.

*Billie G. Herndon*

## Violence Everywhere

Guns and gangs fill the streets
Drugs and rape are all around
Not all violence has a sound
No place is safe to raise little children
They are our future generation
Do you want them growing up with that kind of hate?
Please don't let it be too late!

*Jenny Marsh*

## Ibara Village

Below the steep, dark thickly wooded mountain sides of Ibara Village.
A narrow road traverses long green valleys where sparse Hamlets
emerge to greet the weary traveler. It is a lonely, silent, isolated
world. Where once remnants of the defeated Heike clan dwelled. Once,
while walking along one of its footworn paths, I had a strange
experience. Leaves were just changing into garments of autumn colors.
In the sunlight, green fields were now bathed in gold. Where radiant
rays seeping through clusters of leaves fell, a small murmuring stream
sang with the joy of the wind. Sitting to rest for awhile upon a rock,
I closed my eyes and felt a deep sense of happiness. Suddenly, in
rising, falling, floating waves, the musical notes of a flute wove a
spell. Opening my eyes, I gazed about trying to find its source.
But, found only the vast blueness of the sky above and flaming hues of
leaves falling across a path of sunlight.

*Alfred Valencia*

## The Fires of Autumn

Just walk with me, that is the start —
a new beginning to something wonderful in our lives,
as we approach the years of autumn.

We will scuffle through the fallen leaves of time,
hearing them rustle and crunch.
We will smell the fragrant smoke of the autumn fires
as old logs are turned into new ashes.

This is what we will do today.
And tomorrow, who knows?
We may touch shyly but tenderly.
Until, in a sudden moment,
we will need to cling,
knowing our bodies have re-awakened.
This we can do for each other,
that we may have many new tomorrows.

Let us be together.
You may find solace from your old grief.
I will be closing the door on old memories.

*Jo Piper*

## The Rose

The rose is a creation of beauty fair,
A part of God's great love and care.
The very formation of each precious rose
Resembles life, in the way that it grows
A tiny tight bud, like small precious babies
Bring to mind daydreams and a great many maybes.
The bud starts to loosen and then partly gaps
As full of wonder, as a toddler that naps.
The brightness and color of that first open day
Has the freshness of a young teen, finding their way.
A full open rose with all its splendor showing,
So much like a young mother, radiantly glowing.
Yes, roses are special and each one unique
Like all individuals, the strong and the weak.
They're all very different and pretty to see
Just the way God intended us to be.
So when in the garden of life each day
And questioning problems along the way
Remember the rose, how its beauty adorns
Is seldom, if ever, without any thorns.

*Everyl Clinkenbeard*

## Time

I have only just a minute, only sixty seconds in it,
forced upon me; can't refuse it; didn't seek it,
didn't choose it; but it's up to me to use it;
I must suffer if I lose it; give account if I abuse it.
Just a tiny little minute - but eternity is in it.

*Bennett C. Oelheim*

## In Respect for Kipling's Wisdom,
## Or, Sonnet of East and West

When in the grip of youth's all-knowing spring,
A Persian prince and I met face to face,
We scorned, then shunned, each person, sign, or thing
That dared suggest our worlds could not embrace.
What more romantic bond could God decree
Than two hearts joined from distant fabled lands;
My world, caressed by prairie breezes free,
His, hewn from winds off sultry desert sands.
But that was spring and time was on our side,
While days and nights have passed to prove us wrong.
Between his world and mine's a great divide;
Our love, the bridge, could not suspend it long.
    We wonder now what quirks our minds possessed
    To make us think that East could merge with West.
     *Carol A. Nader*

## Longing To Belong

All my life, I've searched for a place.
A place I could call my home.

I've longed to have friends.
Friends, that I could call my own.

I've looked for a family,
Family that I could say was mine.

Hungered for a father.
A father that could stands the test of time.

Now I know, what I did not know.
I know the love of Jesus.

Now, I have a house, a house to call a home.
It's always been a part of me, but not a place I've known.

Now, I have a father, who not only loves me.
But, teaches me to love.

Now, I no longer, long to belong.

For he fulfills all hopes and dreams.
He completes all families.

I have a father that writes the test of love, that only the can pass.
And I'm glad I know him now, for, he completes my past.
    *Cheryl Dodd-Ray*

## A Special Gift From God

A child is a special gift from God,
  A precious personality to be loved and nurtured
And encouraged to develop and grow
  Like the flowers of spring that color the landscape.

And, as with all the beauty that God can give,
  So too, can He take it away, at His will.
We do not understand the time frame
  Each of us is allotted upon this earth.

But the length of time we are here
  Is defined by parameters beyond our comprehension,
Controlled by a schedule we must accept
  How unfair or ill-timed it may seem.

And so it is that the message of life
  Your daughter brought to you was fulfilled
And God called her to step over to the other side
  To the next life that awaits us all.

Her beauty and spirit are the legacy
  Her life was meant to bring to this space and time.
While our wish is that it might have been longer.
  We are grateful for the time she had.
    *Dorothea S. Mosby*

## Danse Macabre

I wish that a wish were more than a wish,
A promise more than a word;
The pass of a promise like curtains that swish,
The promise—the wish—like suds
With bubbles that break, and buds that are flowers,
That wilt and fade, pressed in books.
(Hurry—throw it on the rubbish heap
before some one see the kind of place we keep.)
Break the promise wholly; count the wish as folly,
like the Christmas dolly thirty years after:
lost teeth, and running wax features
(whatever did the First Cause intend
with such creatures?)
For a promise begins life,
but Death's dirty old knife cuts off the last wish,
which is not to end a broken dish,
a wilted flower, a blown-far bubble.
What does Death do with the house He keeps?
Does he throw the parts on His rubbish heaps?
    *Elizabeth June Duykers*

## My Life

My life is a, A question
A question of what to do and what not to do
A question of who to see and when
A question of what to say and what not to say

My life is a pile of choices
A pile of choices with no manual on how to live
Choices that don't tell me what to do when the new arise
And when the choices are made they will return at me
Return at me with the good or bad results
And the result will be my fault whether good or bad

And yet my life is like a river
A river that is sometimes deep
And sometimes warm
A river that is at times, ruff and coarse
But do not misunderstand me, my life is also gentle and soft
But not like some rivers my life will one day perish
And then I will flow into another land
And hope that there my life will wither in the mist with
the Angels
    *Aja Javae Anderson*

## Reality Revisited

To turn forty years old, but to really be twelve.
A shocking development, not handled real well.

So absorbed in oneself, not to see past your dreams.
Looking only at others, to assist in your schemes.

Should a man so uncaring, and so full of pain,
Be allowed to return to the world whence he came.

This question has been answered, by many a soul.
Who were brought into the light, to assume a new role.

Allowed to regain, that dignity they had lost.
To be so grateful and unsure, to endure at all cost.
    *Gregory Mulvaney*

## Seasons

It was a warm summer day
As the white snow sprinkled
The brown autumn ground.
As the turning leaves of the evergreen
Fell to their sweet oblivion,
Beautifying the landscape.
-Valley of the Pigs
    *Julia Wright*

## Annie's Gone

Just as she began to blossom and bloom,
A sickness came over her, a terrible gloom.

The doctors tried hard to find
Something to restore her once strong mind.

Reluctantly, she was sent far away,
Many tears were shed on that dreadful day.

"They will find a cure for her real fast,
And soon she will be home again at last."

Every day her parents would pray and pray
That she would be coming home soon one day.

Then after she turned fifty seven,
The angels escorted her back to heaven.

They never told her aging mother that
She would be back no more,
But was waiting for her at heaven's door.

**Edna Carpenter Staton**

## Web And Moonlight

The moon beckons me into the marrow of midnight.
A silver spider — only he knows the course,
spinning silk in its glands, secretions that crystallize
into filigree and then laid, like a shivering egg,
to unravel in the opulence of midnight's delirium.

A web now not to entrap but to seduce,
liquidating the licentious beasts as it curls out,
consciously, like a snake amidst the jungle's chaos,
hypnotizing plants, glazing the river into oblivion,
mesmerizing each article of creation that crawled or sprouted
from the garden of tears.

An arcane calligraphy, luminous as squeezed mercury,
is prancing into time — a messianic latticework.
Is this the design that was spoken of?
The Unmoved Mover, the Still Center of the Turning World
in the body of spider?
The moon is transfixed this night
and will yield no moon.

**Jenny Lenore Rosenbaum**

## Untitled

The poem it does so seldom spring
A song I find so hard to sing
Empty pages, darkness, fire
A man in my head screams "Liar, liar."

I ache to tell you all I know
Honest as sh** and pure as snow
These green eyes look and sometimes see
Much more than some philosophy

Doors opened inside my head
"No exit" is what they said
But I'm a lover, not a crier
A man in my head scolds, "Liar, liar."

I wanted all things to make clear sense
So I could climb down from the neutral fence
To say what I mean, mean what I say
Hypocrisy can't be the way.

I flap my arms but cannot fly
Visions thrust into the sky
Freedom is to make a choice
Sweet wisdom is to find a voice.

**Bob Gibson**

## Jesus Is The Answer

For every question there's an answer.
For every answer there's an explanation.
For every explanation there are two sides.
For every side there's a different point of view.
For every point of view there is a unique individual.
For every unique individual there is Jesus.

**Diane Partlow**

## The Gentle Cord of a Mother's Love

A mother's love is a gentle cord
A special gift from above.
It will stretch from here to eternity
As you travel in search of love.

As you spread your wings and open each door,
As your quest for love continues,
That gentle cord will be there for guidance
To the best that is there within you.

When each path seems to lead to deep sorrow and tears,
And all doors appear closed forever,
The gentle cord of your mother's love
Will protect you from pain and all fears.

As you follow your dreams, looking for your star,
And your journey is finally over,
The gentle cord of your mother's love
Will lead you back from afar.

No more will you suffer, never more will you roam.
Your mother's heart knew all along
That all you desired, all the love that you craved
Were waiting for you here at home.

**Josephine Knight**

## Sunset Portrait

I watched the boat sail down the bay
A spectacle in white,
Surrounded by the blue of sky
And shadows of the night.
Golden sunset in the west made the waters gleam,
Bathed this scene in flaming hues
And made this study seem
As though the nighttime would appear
And cover without sound this perfect portrait
Much the way a lady does a gown—
Silently, too quickly, and then appears the night
The lady's cape—to hide from view
An ever lovely sight.

**Camille V. Bailey**

## What's A Lie

A lie is anything you say false
A statement that's made untrue
After telling one you feel like a wasp
Has put a bad sting on you

All are liars, says the Bible
Because no one is good
They sometimes hurt you more than a rifle
They could do more than that, they could

Don't think because a man's a preacher
That he won't tell a lie
And just because you've been born a new creature
You're always trying to get by

Many times people try to get by
The truth they will fail it
But you must remember a lie is a lie
No matter who tells it

**Dwight Conway**

## Light Time

An air of cold, and darkness clear,
A stillness bold, the time is near.
It came at once, and with no warning.
I blame a hunch, for now is dawning.
Future when, past is coming
Present then, the moment numbing
Forever gone, forgotten shadow
The image strong, your spirit shallow
These lines above, not near the feeling
A memory of sometime revealing.
You're out of reach, I yearn to clasp.
There'll be a time, of points converging
Where all will rhyme, and light emerging

*Douglas Valenti*

## Tears for Mother

Mother left us unexpectedly last November
A sweeter face I can't remember
A princess or corporate executive she was never to be
Her calling in life; wife, mother, taking care of me
Two loving arms
A golden heart
Hard working hands that held us tight
Her greatest gift; she gave us life
Her home is now in Heaven
Still watching us with loving eyes
We miss her so
It's hard to let her go
Our grief is immense
It makes no sense
Time will dry our tears
Wonderful memories will fill our years
Beautiful thoughts fill our hearts
Of a loved one who is now gone
We love you mom
Your love will always live on

*Barbara Weaver*

## Nature's Greatest Show

I have seen tumultuous rivers running!
A tropical singing rain forest adorable!
Marvelous rare birds in jungles whistling...
And much more to me memorable!

A bee jumping from flower to flower...
Or a humming-bird backwards flying...
Make me lose my power...
And almost hypnotized I start crying!

I climbed murmuring mountains but I'll tell...
Not yet the wonder top of the world, the Everest!
The noise of the oceans is another marvel!
For the beauty of gems I mined style old west!

The delicacy of an orchid or of a butterfly the divine reaches!
Sunshine, whispering wind, moonlight are enchanting!
The rainbow is spectacular but in my mind persists...
A phenomenon that is the most brilliant!

I will bet no one suspects what I guess...
Which is, to me, NATURE'S GREATEST SHOW!
It is wonderful but also terrifying and impresses!
It is the white ghost, the falling and fallen SNOW!

*Henrique De Paula*

## Charmaine...

5:23 A.M......... 1953
A wonderful gift from God was given to me...
When I think about 'Miracles'...along the way...
One's name is Charmaine... What more can I say.
The journey through life - Has many roads and turns...
Lots of lessens to be learned.
One true lesson of "LOVE" - Was given to me...
When presented a daughter ...
For the world to see.

February 8th...(40) years have passed...
Through God's help I'm fulfilling my task.
A mother/daughter bond...
Cannot be measured...
Through the eyes of God...
I have a treasure.
I knew... and I know...
How precious you are...
You are my bright and shinning star.
Love....Your Mother

*Jo Ann B. Cordova*

## Mirror's Image

I look in the mirror and what do I see,
A wrinkled up face, just starring at me
I'd like to say this, If I'm not too bold
I'm certainly glad, I don't look that old.
There are bags under her eyes, or it seems to be,
Why, she doesn't look a bit like me.
There's a roll of fat here and there,
It's as though she doesn't care,
I'm not as fat as that woman, you know,
And if I was, I'd feel mighty low.
She looks like it would hurt her to bend,
And she has age marks on her skin,
Her skin looks rough like an orange ring,
It's not nearly as smooth as mine.
There's no way, we are one and the same,
So a faulty mirror will get the blame.
The mirror is an image, or its supposed to be,
But there's no way that this person is me.
But they say the mirror is accurate, it has to be,
I guess the fat, wrinkled old lady, just has to be me.

*Betty S. Hall*

## Women's Role In Life

Today's working women are concerned,
About their role in life,
Formerly, they had been cast,
As homemaker, mother and wife.

This is a noble way for a woman to live,
To raise the family in a conventional way,
To stay within her husband's means
And create family happiness day by day.

Yet, drifting away happens in many homes,
It is prevalent in futile dismay
When sadly deprived of money or care,
Women were determined to have their say.

Women's role has made a dramatic change,
When working outside of the home,
Adjusting to two roles instead of one,
And in some cases doing it alone.

Today they prove their way in life
Depending on their own responsive ways
To bring back harmony into the home,
Sharing with family makes happier days.

*Gladys I. Swanson*

## A Picture Of Her Pain

The canvas lies there blank as she splashes the color black
across its face, then the red to show the rage is in its place,
fillers of dim and dreary colors fill in the other space as
if to show the confusion that's interlaced, the mountains peaks
and the valleys lows somehow demeans the picture that she shows.
The ugly that lies just below, how she wishes it would go.
Oh! To bring the beauty to this place.
Oh! To draw the beauty across its face.
With no more confusion or suffering to embrace, just that solemn,
quiet beauty in its place.

*Carrie Greer*

## The Photo

Your picture sits on my nightstand still,
After all these many years.

At first you were there to remind me,
Of where I had been, and how far I had come.

And then you were there as a promise,
That our lives would forever touch.

So many nights your eyes kissed mine,
As I reached to turn out the light.

And your ageless face smiled back at me,
Of a time that was yet to be.

But now the memories slowly dim,
And sadly the photo fades.

And I wonder if what we seem to have lost,
Perhaps we never had....

*Julie Morrison*

## Night

When the sun meets the mountains
after the fountains of color
disappear behind a block of
dark, suddenly the air becomes
damp and heavy, the grass becomes
cold and wet beneath the feet of animals.

In the distance, the sound of
wind in the trees and pine cones
falling to the ground with a thud.
Listen hard, and hear the
whispering of the night creatures on the wind.

The night air becomes cooler and
crisper. It's easy to spot an
animal, just look to the ground and
see puffs of white steam rising to the occasion.

But all good things must come to an
end. The sun is rising and with it
brings morning. The night creatures
scamper off to their cozy dens to
make room for the day animals.

*Aleasha Weimer*

## To Someone Very Special

To the girl who has come a long way
And inspired mountains and blue sky
In my heart so heavy with reflection
I send you my warmest recollections.

You are soft and firm like the shoreline's powerful reef,
You are gentle but judicious in your sly encouraging belief,
You are petite though strong shining your love light's rays,
You are innocent yet sultry and I will want you always.

*James Morett*

## Let Me Out

The BODY stands:  Five-Foot-Two, overweight, growing wrinkles
Aging...awaken at night's—dozing day time; legally maturing
"That couldn't be Me:  The living s o u l—has no age, there is
A cry in my heart—but You still give the day-by-day aging
Body Your attention and love—send flowers and gifts on —
Mother's Day...but the same time, pretend not to see the real
ME, appreciate my creativity—"Let Me Out," accept my s o u l
Discover the beautiful:  Breeding, feeling, creating p e r s o n
Inside of me—don't let it d i e...forever unknown to You—
Let-me-to-be-ME...the mother I would like to be for thee-
Get to know my—creative living soul, before it's gone for—
Ever:  A soul who appreciates the surrounding beauty of the
World, and is trying very hard to resolve the mystery of
Life:  Why are we here?  — And when one-day we have to GO...
What is waiting us t h e r e..."Let me out." — Don't censor-
My creativity—my living SOUL.  Accept ME-to-be-Me:  Love me
The beauty and creativity inside of me...legally maturing-
Don't let it be the only thing You'll see—of m e:
"LET ME OUT" — to be the r e a l mother for Thee.

*Aino Kabe*

## "Psychiatrists Or What Do You Think?"

I had a problem so I went to a shrink.
All he would say is "what do you think?"
I paid $100.00 for a 50 minute deal.
Was he a doctor, was he for real?.
When I asked him more questions he didn't blink
He looked at his watch and said,
"What do you think?"
If I could answer that question,
I wouldn't be here.
I'd be in a place where they served cool beer.
After 49 minutes he was kinda' abrupt
I'm sorry Mr. Fisher, but your time is up!

*Harold Fisher*

## In The Woodwork

I wish to speak to you - if you would understand.
All my people are now gone.
Wind has blown and they have answered with their wings.

Though their flight gives cause for joy -
    they come and go.

I'm alone.

You have come now to these woods.
Will you stop to think on them?
Peaceful? Plain? Weak? Dark? Distant? Heavy? Blunt?
No telling what you see.
Don't be fooled by what is seen.
This frown comes from weathering.

If you can find me -
    ask, and I may have some things you need.
I've stored them in my home, all safe.
(only I can find it)

You must give me chance enough.
You'll see - I can find it.
Just please don't leave.
I'm alone and I like it; still -

I'm alone.

*Jennifer Hodges*

## My Grandpa......My Gido

Early memories, a fun filled kitchen; an old man playing the fiddle
all of us dancing, happy moments to treasure... grandpa's friend so
talented, made my heart and feet sing to his music;
my grandpa so proud....

Memories of him placing me on horseback and walking me round
the farm.
Christmases at the farm where we all gathered to be together.
The look of love in his eyes as he gazed at yet another grandchild.

Or him so proud bearing his citizenship for us to see...
A struggle to climb three flights of stairs with stiff and tired legs.
I saddened as the years passed seeing this once agile man grow clumsy
with age.

On occasion seeing him struggle with nails and hammer as
he laid linoleum stripping, bringing tears to my eyes.
My grandpa, Gido as I called him, a sweet proud and handsome man,
how I loved and miss him.

*Evelyn Solomon Fields*

## The Search Is Over

The heavens beckon with but a simple kiss,
All that is good runs through my body like water,
Oh to feel this much emotion must be sin!

I search for her body to caress,
And find velvet pales in comparison,
The eyes hold my heart prisoner,
I find my will has spent itself needlessly

The embrace binds me in chords of desire,
I stare into eyes which promise much passion,
And know that rational thought beckons not—
I could no more hold back the wind!

Moist lips join softly weaving souls together,
Hearts melt into ecstasy revealing all,
Two become one as love descends softly,
Uniting both for all eternity

*Joe Oven*

## Take My Hand

Take my hand, I'll guide you through
All the glorious things in view.

Take my hand and follow me
down life's road - there's so much to see.

From the colored sky, down to the ground
Just take an extensive look around.

The birds are taking off in flight,
or a rainbow may show ever so bright.

The trees are as green as green can be
and the flowers are in bloom for all to see.

And do you hear the child's laughter so clear -
It truly is music to the ear.

People of all ages are walking hand in hand
All around this wonderful land.

So take my hand and we will explore
The many things we've never seen before.

*Arlene A. Fickett*

## Soldier

The soldier's woman needs to understand,
 all the things that make up this man.
The bits of hell that cause the sorrow,
 sew the pieces for tomorrow.
She must know the things which his spirit bleeds,
 Stand by him silently when he needs.
Be his right hand when he needs a lift,
 the bonds which are built will be a special gift.
She must be strong when he must be apart,
 she'll be the refuge he seeks in his heart.
Be compliant when he needs his brother,
 be his best friend, his confidant, his lover.
She will bask in the fire that burns deep inside,
 and to that desire she will abide.
Arise - tall and proud, yet meek as she stands there,
 for this is the man known as the Soldier.

*Debbie McKinney*

## Damaged Woman Blues

You offered your hand. I gave you mine.
All the while explaining that I'm not fine.
Just like a can that's dropped and dents in the same spot each time
So am I also bruised and dented, my own fault from being blind
Oh, I'm damaged goods, baby. That's what I am.
I'm a woman in pain. Do you still want to be my man?

Memories resurfaced with every familiar mistake you made.
Reminding me of the others, not allowing my hurt to fade.
Sore from bad choices and being handled by the wrong hands,
I try to drop the excess baggage and can't. Can you understand?
I've told you I'm damaged goods. There's nothing "good" about it.
If I could bare my scarred heart you could never doubt it.
I too long for love that's easy, soft and slow.

I ache for a tender heart in order to show
That I'm human and I'm real.
To show my sensitivity and let you know that I feel.
But I'm damaged goods, sugar. Damaged to the bone.
I'm flawed and faulty but please don't leave me all alone.

*Irma M. Taylor*

## Lost Time

I forbid you to get old, to grow older each year, to age, I will not
 allow.
It's not you that ages, your face forever young in my soul
Your eyes ever luminous. It's not your spirit, nor your style.
It's age robbing me of your time. Age taking away my chances to
 create memories.
A life time of treasures never found, instead, forever lost in time.
I curse my inability to capture the past for I was not a part of it.
The lack of time to renew the present because the present has not yet
 been found.
And my hope for a future is threatened because time steals your
 presence.
My youth is lost in longings of age
My age dissolved in no memories, no sharing.
An existence without you, intolerable. A future inconceivable.
A present wasted in regret.
Age, tread not here, leave me my moments of peace,
Allow me to find my memories,
Permit me time,
Deny age.

*Carla Ann Thompson*

## Can I Trust You

Can I trust you, that is the question
Almost everyone I meet I can never seem to trust
In my past, I was hurt real bad
The past makes me keep on running down this long dark road
Unknowing what is in store for me
Still, I wish that there was someone
Someone that I knew inside my heart I could trust.
Yet, there is still this pain that holds me back
Only to make me wish that I could crawl under a rock and hide
Please be honest and tell me truthfully...
Can I trust you?

**Donna Bulger**

## Alzheimer's

I am familiar with the tears of sorrow,
although I cannot tell you the difference in the saltiness.

There is a difference.

There are the tears at the beginning of loss of memory
and forgotten togetherness:
    "Remember When...No?"
    "Remember we went...No?"
    "Remember we met them and did...No?"
    "Remember...No?....No."

There are tears at loss of person:
    "Remember yesterday I did...No?"
    "Remember my name....No?"
    "Remember me?  Oh, remember me!....No?....No."

There are the lonely tears from the overwhelming of
singular remembrance:
    "When we...."
    "What we said...."
    "What we did...."
    "How we laughed.... Oh, how we laughed!"

There is a difference in the saltiness.

**Ina Taylor Hartman**

## The Man of Evermore

   Through all time, has he walked,
always deep in thought;
   He has seen the future, he is the ancient past,
all of time has felt his icy grasp;
   In pharoah's day he was a slave,
in Shakespeare's time he was a knave;
   Norsemen worshipped him as a God,
but later labeled him as a fraud;
   He lived as a brother to natives in an undiscovered land, and
thought his soul appeased,
yet a foreigner came to the land and killed his brothers with disease
   In a fierce battle of a little big horn,
it was a celebrated general that he slew;
   In Borneo he was a wild man,
In Jersey, a devil;
   Yet, still walks through time,
Unscathed, unaged;
   Forced to walk through the sands of time for a crime unholy,
So does, the man of evermore

**Brandon Lewis**

## Darling Amanda

   Dear Darling Pam.  Why the troubles in life God has
given us both so much.  If it was not for MS I would have
been working.  I think you left me because you wanted a
working husband.  Well guess what I'm applying for jobs.
I feel I can handle it with God's help.  Remember our
wedding vows.  I can forgive you can you forgive your self.
Think of Amanda

**Dan Brower**

## My Flashlight

In the darkness of my life, I have a flashlight.
Always to separate the way.
He is my Bishop and brother pointing
to the stronger light that isn't so far away.
This beacon is giving still
to another who is brighter.
On to another to the greatest light at last.
Giving direction and hope to hold on fast.
This one says to you and to me,
"I will make you fishers of men, come and follow me."
This is my dream, my reality.  One that is of truth.
But who are these fishers of men?
What is their purpose?
The light said to me, "These are my chosen.
To them, I have given a portion of my light,
always to separate the way."

**Jeffrey D. Pope**

## Sadness And Sorrows

Amigo mio, you are not having sadness and sorrows,
Amigo mio, because our Lord, is been good to you, in your life,
Amigo mio, because our Lord, does know what is in your heart, for
   him,
Amigo mio, then in his greatest love for you, he did send his gold
   heart,
Amigo mio, in your existence, you did give to our Lord, your
precious
   heart,
Amigo mio, ardently you are living, your faith to our Lord,
Amigo mio, your love to our God it is in yours prayers,
Amigo mio, eloquently it is your voice in fervent prayers.
Amigo mio, sadness, and sorrows are not in your heart,
Amigo mio, your paused, and wait, and is a rare privilege,
Amigo mio, do your compassion is fragrances?  Yes!
Amigo mio, your quietly caring, is the key of not having sadness and
   sorrows.

**Dolores Maria Bolivar-Brauet**

## A Walk In The Park

We came to the park looking for a day of fun
among the children playing.
A day to enjoy the cool breeze
as our faces were warmed by the sun.
Throwing the frisbee across an open, lush field
gliding a hovercraft sailing freely through the sphere
on waves of silky, lofting air.

But then we really came to the park.
A place where no children played
or were not allowed to play.
Instead, we came upon men
whose faces looked much older
than their actual years.
They asked us "how much?"  We wanted
and laughed at the puzzled look on our faces.
Instead of an open field
to let our imagination take flight,
we found nothing but empty wine bottles and dirt.
A place where no blade of grass would even dare to grow
among the syringes and tiny ziploc bags.

**Derek J. Vander Schaaf Jr.**

## The Cost Of Knowing

Eyes staring back from the mirror behind a smoke filled bar,
an aged face in the rain stained window of a passing car,
a shoulder brushed on a subway stair,
It doesn't matter - they are everywhere.

Bonded by a common memory,
a childhood's dream,
the fathomless ache for home, a wish without a name,
It doesn't matter - the loss is all the same.

Why did we come?  The farthest star was home...as earth could
never be.
The mote of memory is borne away,
we pass as strangers,
silent and resigned like the rivers flowing.
It doesn't matter - it is the cost of knowing.

*Gail McCabe*

## The Dream

A dream at night
An armadillo troll who lusts and speaks sharply with biting words
Wise and fear-inspiring.
The sagely creature with an ominous aura
Soft reds, browns, jet black - creature of passion
Higher intellect as yet unknown to the recipient
Biting words clawing at the throat
Putrid odor of urine
Unbearable..
Rapid, scurrying movement - spontaneous
Awestruck with morbid fascination
Black eyes of a serpent
He knows her
A savage bite of the forbidden apple.
The recipient runs, frightened, terrified
Not of the creature - he inhabits the mind
Afraid of the realization...
A mirror shatters instantaneously
7 years bad luck have passed in a moment of profoundness.

*Janice W. Fernheimer*

## A Man, A Husband, A Father, A Grandfather

Big, strong and kind,
  an incredibly strong mind and
    hands that were wise.

A heart that was good
  and as big as the sky.

Always first to offer a helping hand
  to young and old, come rain or shine
    even if it left him in a bind.

Fishing, hunting and cooking
  were hobbies at best, but
    not much topped TV, a good meal and rest, rest, rest.

A dreamer he was, some would say, but
  a man who does not dare to dream
    may wither away someday.

A wealthy man he was not,
  measured in a monetary way, but

Our Dad's riches will always lie in
  the man he was, the father he became and in the memories that are
    stored in the hearts of the family who will love him forever.

*Denise A. Shaw*

## An Innocent Victim

I was hurt at work, that was when I taught,
An innocent victim of a crime for which I now pay.

I've lost all hope - I only feel pain,
I see lots of doctors and all they say is...
It will get better some day.

I can't sleep at night - I can't play with my child,
Their doctors say I can work when my memory is gone,
I feel all alone but I'm getting better they say.

I try very hard to think straight and when I talk,
But I know at times it comes out all wrong.
There must be a way.

I've lost the life I once knew,
I'm someone else but they say it's you.
I don't understand what they're trying to say.

I get help from my family and also the neighbors,
I'll not let them lick me or even trick me,
For it can't go on this way.

But I know I have the courage,
My truth will be heard-their lies will all wither,
and I'll see the dawn of a new day.

*Elizabeth Scollon*

## Solitude

Loneliness wraps its chilly arms around me
and I long for the warmth of your love...
The love we shared.

But now you are gone
and I can only embrace the memory of that love.

Yet if I close my eyes,
I can see those happy days come rushing back
to bring me comfort in my solitude.

Thus, I am never alone...
Not as long as I can remember.

*Dolores Karides*

## My God

Sanctuary, Goodness, Strength, Friend To Me.

Nondenominational, Encompassing, Angry,
RULING OVER
the rigid, narrow-minded.
The Light at the end of the tunnel. HOPE for a brighter tomorrow.
Where the "dead" can live again from a "once upon a time...,"
when there is FAITH TO BELIEVE.
Where a "religious" statue can crumble,
or a "holy house" fall to ruin through ages of decay,
... and I can be guilt free!
I, still confident; because I had the guts to be different!

When science makes sense and philosophy fits puzzle pieces
securely-
politically, into just the right places
If a goodly conscience is followed.

Within wonderful universal spaces
Time flowing smoothly, diminishing fears....
LOVE abounding
An abundance of happiness.

Where the unknown becomes known to me and I find INFINITE
PEACE.
Brilliant colors of a beautiful spectrum
As I view life
Once more.

*John Laffey*

## Visions of Life

Visions of a darkened room and a rocking chair
An old woman slouched, with loosely braided hair.
She stares out the window, a tear in her eye
Remembering, long ago, a little baby's cry.

Visions of joy, as it lies in its bed
Never wondering for a moment, what lies ahead.
Many years have passed, now she sits all alone
Knowing each breath, takes her further from her throne.

Visions of her youth seem so far away
Struggling for strength each and everyday
Now, the room is brighter, as she hears that baby's cry
With a smile on her face, she's not afraid to die.

Visions of a darkened room and a rocking chair
Vanished from the universe, and is no longer there.
Mysteries of life begin with a baby's first breath
Visions of life are yours till the last sigh in death.

*Frances A. (Damico) Hall*

## Beast of Burden, Boy of Beauty, Bird of Flight (A Dream)

I became the beast of burden that trod along,
An ox with great strength, a boy with his song.

I watched as they tried Him; I watched as they jeered;
I carried His body: I felt what they feared.

I soared as a bird and viewed like a play
Each step that He took on that awful day.

As an ox, His beast of burden; a bird; a boy,
A guard for His beauty, all in wild fits of joy.

Each part that I played had an ecstasy its own
As I was allowed to view it all from the throne.

His beauty, His strength, tumbled walls with a glance,
Telling the evil one, "You don't have a chance!"

O ox with great burden trudging tapestried hall,
Lean your head on the door frame lest from burden you fall:

Your nostrils on fire, your back nigh to break,
You must carry your burden for humanity's sake.

Dear boy of beauty, I joined you as one.
We sat on His knee as His works they were done.

Then winging the heavens, O great bird of flight,
We watched as our Saviour showed Satan His might.

*Hilda Gaw Payne*

## The Redoubt

The river winds below a limestone bluff,
And all along its course is boulder-strewn;
Against the cliff stand outcrops tall and rough,
Rectangular, like ancient forts in ruin.

Atop the largest of these giant blocks
My love and I once spent an afternoon;
Like lookouts posted at a sentry box,
We lay in clefts the wind and rain had hewn.

It rained that day; we never left our lair;
Not when the sun made ovens of our rocks,
Nor when a passing workman stopped to stare,
Or when we heard the nearby quarry's shocks.

At dusk of course we had to separate,
Then face harsh words for getting home so late.

*James Clark*

## Remembering

It is the end of World War 2
and all of the countries solemnly swear,
that the Holocaust horrors will never recur
because people have finally learned to care.

It is the end of the 20th century.
In Bosnia different groups are killing
each other just because they are different
to fight to their deaths they seem to be willing.

In Rwanda innocent people died
because of brutal tribal fights.
People were left without any home
to travel to countries where they had no rights.

Many small counties wanted democracies.
But people found that if they would try
to speak against their present governments
they and the ones they loved would die.

People talk about the Holocaust,
not knowing that in a smaller way,
with political persecutions and ethnic cleansing,
the Holocaust is happening again today.

*Adriana Leigh*

## "The Murder Of Katherine By The Sea"

She walks alone daily by the sea,
and all who know of Katherine
preach often of her beauty
like a vision holier than Thee
  Her hair, is golden as honey
  Eyes, richer than the rarest sapphire
  With a smile, envied by heaven's angels'
That is Katherine by the Sea.

And when a week had come and past,
not a soul could remember when she had walked last
The skies, suddenly grew dark and stormy
and the sea wept mournful tears
'Twas only after that time
did Katherine's body appear
And when all those who admired her
had come to see her laid to rest
A single tear amongst them all, was shed at the very best
And without a hint of sadness proudly they all did state,
"That the flaunting of Katherine's beauty
led to her justly, but untimely fate.

*Elaine Okawa*

## Night Song

When I see the darkness of the night
and feel the gentle breeze.
It is time to put away the work tools
Hope for peace and feel
the quietness of the night.

Even birds and animals seem to know
another day has ended.
As everything listens to the night sounds.

To be awakened with the morning light
another day has started.
Then another night.

A new day, a new beginning.
A new night, anew peace.

*Frances V. Caffey*

## University Interlude

Solitude was our most valued friend,
and ally; alone, or amongst others.
It provided protective sanctuary for the
liberation of our thoughts,
and the sensual which consumed us.

Your sentient, involute hips, embodied the
eternal metaphor of the transcendent.

Love, not supplication, was our offering.
So little room we needed
to ensconce, and commingle,
as we became one being
for our divine gift.

It seemed preordained that we
succumb to our burning
mutual carnal desires
and needs, during then, our summer of '71'.

In silence, and with inner warmth,
will I reminisce, and envision
dreams too blissful,
to attempt sharing with others.

**Bill Schauer**

## Empty Eyes

Empty eyes stare from the little girl you run to hold
and as they close you feel her body turn cold
I sat insider her -
watched you crawl and plead
her pain made you cry, her words made you bleed
This little girl can't get what she needs
Empty eyes with no explanation
Empty eyes nowhere to go
One little girl with no one to hold
She makes you laugh and you always cry
you hold her close without any clothes
this isn't dirty - she's over halfway to thirty
she rolls over she sighs
What's hidden inside empty eyes
from a little girl you run to hold
but you see you're too late
her body turns cold.

**Dawn Stanek**

## Love

I have Mexican jumping beans in my belly,
and butterflies behind my eyes
The beans bubble and bump with delight
Boiling with my excitement
While the butterflies cascade past my eyes,
And become entangled in the lashes,
Filtering the world to a ravishing spectrum
Of saffron glitter and rosy dewdrops.

There are sea gulls in my toes,
And wind chimes in my tongue,
Gulls soaring high above my crashing blood
Beating, Fluttering, Diving
Curling my toes with ticklish breeze,
While chimes ripple and purr,
Dripping sun-sugared nothings off of my teeth,
And misting the air with silvery scent.

There are lions in the darkness over there,
But they are afraid of me.
I am a goddess,
And I can eat the moon with a spoon if I want.

**Allyson Coffey**

## Looking Forward, Looking Back

I sighed for what was not
And cried for what will never be
I remembered what had been
And pondered a future I could not see

The tide rolled in, The tide rolled out
As I sat and thought about
What was or what will never be
Chances past, a missed opportunity

And my tears slowly stopped
For the more I sat and thought
I realized the past is simply that
Time gone by cannot be bought

So I looked back through the halls of my memory
And saw through the eyes of a believe
That in all I had done I had been myself
And in that I had been an achiever

So with a new and clearer vision
I took the hand of Destiny
And walked into the future
With my past for company

**Brooke Garten**

## "Spring"

The Sun is good!  It's warm fingers circle
and embrace me, while I kneel in delight.
Pushing through earth still swollen from the
snows now past; I see the pointed spears
of crocus leaf with Easter's purple mourning
and golden joy in her opening blossoms.

Spring!  Her new beginning stirs something
within me like the fluttering of a babes
first movements beneath his Mother's breast.

I feel my spirit singing and my heart swells
with the joy of being a living thing.
Sharing the creation with my senses and my being.

For a whisper of a moment, all worldly cares,
leave me in tranquil peace and
like the warming sunshine, it is good.

**Francesca A. Lavertue**

## Wishing

I wish I could fly just like a bird
and float upon the clouds with feathered wings
I'd listen to the wind so seldom heard
and all the magic melodies it sings

I'd float and glide and drift...

The people on earth would look
they'd see the beauty in me
and how the new me defies gravity
as to the air I took

But soon I'd fly
and have no eyes upon me when I glide
they'd all be busy doing things
and being things which now I cannot be

And thus I'd wish for hands instead of wings...

For now I'd wish to be on land
So I could think and be like man.

**Brian Kendall**

## Carapace

A tortoise stretched green
and folded flesh over the
chipped, clay soil.

Brown winds gust across the shell,
chiseling away the smooth surface.
He seeks no shelter for his shelter.

Weakening.
Desert bugs and parasites
crawl in the shell;
they want control of the
body that is his to carry where he wants to
take it.

Lying on his back and trying to push himself
back to his feet, he feels the warm finger
of fire angels, who stepped out of the sun,
purge past parasites from his shell.

*Gregory Case*

## Angel

You watched over me, like an angle from above,
and gave me your strength and love.
You always knew what to say,
And said you'd be there for me, day by day.
You were always standing by my side,
a person in which I could confide.
You were an angle sent to me,
you could only see the good in me.
You were my guardian angle,
you saw me from every angle.
To me you never lied,
and were always there to console me when I cried.
You stuck by me through and through,
through times when I was happy and blue.
Not every one was lucky enough to have a person like you,
honest and true.
I didn't have a father or brother,
you shared my sadness,
your name?
Mother.

*Caitlin Hannah*

## The Old Rocking Chair

The old rocking chair is empty,
and grandma is no longer in it.
She's off to her bowling — that gal
is busy every minute.
No one shows grandma around for she's
forceful and dynamic.
That's not a pie in the oven,
my dear — she's firing her own ceramics.
You won't see her in bed early
tonight cause she picked up
her paints and she is painting.
She practices the organ and plays
fun tunes and never has time for complaining.
Grandma never looks back in the
past to suggest that her age is advancing.
She won't tend to your babies
anymore 'cause grandma has gone out dancing.

*Emma L. Grav*

## He Will Always Be In My Heart

Even though his body is gone his spirit lives,
he had some work undone and more love to give.
I know him and I will never part because
he will always be in my heart.

*Jessie Zahn*

## Virtuous Woman

Wives, support your husbands and the things that are true,
　　and he will cherish you.
Always respect your man,
　　and help him as much as you can.
Do not provoke him to anger,
　　or put your marriage in danger.
When he gets home from work
　　and his muscles are sore and they hurt,
　　get him a seat, and something to eat.
And when he invites his friends over for a game,
　　be courteous, and glad they came.
And should be decide to wage a small bet,
　　don't get upset.
If he wants to go on a fishing trip,
　　don't get angry and poke out your lip.
Wives, if you follow these instructions with care,
　　your mate will always be there.
When you lay your head upon his chest,
　　and he caresses your breast,
　　then he will confess that it is he whom God has blessed.

*Edward D. Williams*

## Untitled

On summer nights the paths I trod...
And hear myself not.

On starry skies with misty eyes, I search...
And find myself not.

In empty, gloomy naves of church,
My soul doth pray...
And it believes not.

Eternal craze to know myself,
To see myself, to hear myself

It shall succeed not.

*Fred Deza-Luis*

## When I Think About You...

When I think about you I close my eyes, hold my breath,
and hope that every fantasy comes true.
Though I think of you non stop I never love you any less.
When I think about you I hold my pillow tight,
wishing it were you.
I sit and wonder still knowing you're the greatest sight.
When I think about you I think so hard I sometimes cry,
knowing you'll never be mine.
Nevertheless I always seem to try.
When I think about you I wonder what she has that I don't;
you, I softly say to myself.
Twice I shove you aside, but I know she won't.
When I think about you I feel everything is so dear,
just like the love we used to share.
Looking into your crystal blue eyes I certainly have no fear.
When I think about you I know I may never wake up knowing
you're mine,
but of course there is no harm in trying.
I know you'll never feel the way I feel about you,
but I can't ever seem to get the thought of you out of my mind.

*Amanda Taylor*

## Two Little Gems

Recently I was delighted to meet a sweet, little girl named Molly.
And I am sure if you could meet her you would certainly agree she is quite a dolly.
With big, blue eyes and a cute little nose, and "two strings of beads" that just happen to be ten perfect toes.
So warm and cuddly and pink in hue, it almost makes me wish I had one, too!
We can't forget her dear little brother, who is still very much dependent on his mother.
Bryan has big, blue eyes and a brown head of hair, and gorgeous eyelashes and a complexion as fair.
He will capture your heart with just his smile.
Even if you are with him for a short little while.
His antics are funny and he's a pleasure to be around, and he can fill a room with laughter by merely just a sound.
I surely do miss them because they are so far away,
After all, I am their "Nana"
So what more can I say.

**Carolyn Lehman**

## Untitled

As we lay against this earth the silence plays her music,
and I am surrounded by starlight dancing in your eyes...

the heavens adorn the song, while moonbeams give light
to our hearts orchestration.

Moving in rhythms of beauty, you swirl me around like the sea—
lulled by the warmth of your smile, compelled to swim in your gaze...
we've traveled as such for centuries, staying the path of the skies;
and I am guided, as always, to find myself here by your side.

I breathe you as breathing the air, feeling you stir within me...
our souls dancing high above all the clouds
as our hearts beat melodic accord.

Adrift in the seas of the starlight, the call of you draws me near
an I'm graced by you life after lifetime.

What man is this who has touched me?
Are you real?  Have I found you at last?
It is you who has captured the starlight, placing it here in my hands.

You've brought me a small piece of heaven,
where time exists without meaning;
my souls has settled to rest — finding home,
once again, in your heart.

**Jennifer Gessner**

## I Stood There

I stood beside His mother
and I did not know His Father.
We were walking up a hill,
to see this man be killed.
He knew that this would come to happen,
I know He wishes this a dream to only be awoken.
And as I looked at her I could see only
that she loved Him.
And as she looked beyond to her son,
I knew she wanted to be with Him.
And help Him with the pain....
And suffering
but she knew He would not let her....
For this, was His call,
to serve and loves His Father.....
So the world would not fall.

**Charmaine Racquel Turbitt**

## Untitled

There's a place in my heart, where there is enough love for an army
And I don't have anyone to share that love with, except myself and I can't keep all of that love for myself.  It's hard to find a person that would love you like you love them if you don't have a boyfriend in school and you see all of the girls that have a boyfriend.  The other but I can't get a boyfriend because none of the boys at school would go with me because they think I'm "ugly" but then "prettiness" is only skin deep.  What boys look at is the body and the way they dress!  The girls that have the looks and what the boys look for, they do not have the love it takes — the love of girls like me, and I'm sure that the boys would appreciate.
(And that goes for the boys what don't look for what the other look for!  But they look for love too.)
But not only those who have love and they need to give it to someone who would take it — and maybe give it to someone who deserves it like me.

**Julie Pickens**

## Untitled

You are my canvass
And I, your brush...
Allow me the joy to color you with trust.
Your grey's, your blues
Your violet's and pinks...
These are the color's, you make me think.
They are brilliant, so strong, and bright
I long to color your world, each nite...
My passion for you, will grow with great flight
To live and love and just be again.
Your canvass will never be "Just White" again.
For each stroke of my brush, you allow me to reveal,
An inner most depth, I so long to feel.
As any true artist that knows what is real,
Its simplicity and truth I don't want you to fear.
Just let me paint you, and don't ask to see,
The most beautiful canvass, you are to me...

**Dennis M. Hickey**

## April Storm

When the storms raging force shakes my windows
and intensifies with each angry blow, I sometimes
fear for my safety and all of God's creatures here
below.

Strong winds can oft' pluck giant oak trees
from their resting place deep in the earth and
forcefully lift them upward and deposit them
far from their birth.

Lightning is brilliant but deadly as it dances
over a sky of grey, with fingers stretching out
through the horizon, it searches for a place
to play.

As the raindrops dance gently on the rooftop,
my thoughts become focused on spring.  My
fears turned to anticipation of the beauty
this new season will bring.

So gently roll back the curtain of darkness
into the furthest corner of the sky and
punctuate it with a kaleidoscope of color,
accentuated with a lone butterfly.

**Fannie I. Hyde**

## Stage 37

As I pass through an age so I pass through a stage
and into the next, so much alike.
The future.  It is the time that comes, or is it the time that
returns?
Circular in it's motion.  It is good!  It is best!  It is bad!  It
is worst!
Is it the past that returns or is the time that comes?
Is each stage different, or is there only four that repeat?
Over and over again.
Well, there's no stopping it, so I'll just hang on to the good and
enjoy it when it's best.
Deal with it when it's bad and hope the worst is short before it is
good again...

**David John Wall**

## The Sunset

You are like the sunset.  The colors are your moods
and it's so beautiful everyone wants it.  But everyone's
to afraid to ask.  Afraid it will not let them have it.  So
everyone admires if from afar.  And they hope it will come
to them.  But no one gets it, because the sunset will not
ask anyone to take it.

I am like a tree.  One of many who admire it.  They live
for the sun and the sunsets.  They need it everyday.
And when it's not there the trees are sad, and settle
for the rain.  But the rain is not what they want.  So
they long for the sunsets of the sunny days.

**Corissa Johnson**

## Itching Powder In His Sandals

I've pondered the concept of "Original Sin"
And I've been kept awake nights trying to think of an original sin;
A true innovation that would qualify, not necessarily by its magnitude
But by its fresh approach; its initiative.
Something vile enough to elevate it above petty pranks,
But not so big as to rank it with the despised and rather overworked
"Crimes Against Humanity"
Something to pique the interest of both those searching for a
refreshing new diversion and those who would pray to overcome it.

So somewhere in the armor of righteousness there must be a spot worn
thin enough by the eternal onslaught of all the old and un-original sin
sins;
Someplace where a determined and well-managed transgression of
original design could break through into infamy if only in a small way.

But where in that ten-fold, iron-clad menu of shalts and shalt-nots
Have they left room for a little honest knavery to creep in?
I'd just like to create some original mischief for the sake of variety
Some small pain in the butt of Creation that might possibly
Catch the attention of God, but not make me a permanent hash-brown
In His skillet of retribution.  Maybe just something————annoying.

**Dave Gifford**

### It's Fall Again

The Smell Of The Air, The Caress Of A Breeze
It's Fall Again
The Sun Warm Upon My Face, Another Embrace
The Sky So Blue Filled With Puffs Of Whitest Clouds
You Can See Forever
The Trees Are Changing Colors, The Mountains Will Soon Be
Ablaze
God With His Magic Pallette Has Done It Again
I Feel My Pulse Race, I'm Rejuvenated
Can My Eyes Withstand Such Beauty
Grateful For My Eyes Am I
For They Are The Mirrors Of My Soul
It's Fall, Beautiful Fall, It's Fall Again

**Allice Requena**

## They Say

They say, I am shiftless, to go for a walk
And leave dishes stand all about.
A better housekeeper would sail in, they say,
And wash them before she went out.

They say, I am lazy...my beds aren't made,
But I've climbed to the top of the hill.
To feel the soft rush  of the wind on my face,
And to listen to wood thrushes trill

They tell me that "Morning's the best time to work.
To clean, or to bake, or to sew."
But I slipped away as the sun topped the hill,
To find where the trilliums grow.

My floors aren't swept, for I've been out since dawn,
Perhaps I should care...but I don't'
For house-work will wait 'til I come back, you see;
But dew on a spider web...WON'T!

**Clara B. Salzman**

## To Pat On His 16th Birthday - A Motor Cycle

Pat's 16th birthday has came and gone
   and life will be different from now on
with driver's license and all that fun
   you'll plug your ears or learn to run.

When he hit the saddle of that savage beast
   that was the end of peace and rest;
it roared so loud it broke the eggs
   and blew the chickens off their nest.
The cats leaped up and tore the grass
   baby robins fell out of their nests,
the old shed shook till the slats fell off
   as that horrible rocket reached its crest.
The air was vibrant and smoky blue
   the very worms recoiled in fear
as they squinted up from the rocking earth
   to tell each other that Pat was here.

The grass lay flat as he forged ahead
   the curls lay straight atop his head
as down the road to the store he sped
   to get his mother a loaf of bread.

**Evelyn E. Bacon**

### The Price Of "Old Glory" On Iwo Jima

To some of us, it was but a picture the national news displayed,
to others, a "patriotic" gesture - a "good shot" Rosenthal made.

Have those of us here at home truly earned the right
to gaze upon this waving legend of freedom won by fight?

As those eager hands worked as one to hold
the staff of freedom as our flag unfolds

Giving of their strength so we may stand
as brave as those men in that foreign land.

Tired, worn, in jungle green, they now proudly lift
the priceless fibers waving clean

No, we at have not won that right - by far,
it belongs to those who hold in their hearts a scar

But I shall frame that picture with love and a prayer
for those who gave their best "over there"

And for those who have earned their eternal peace and rest,
I pray the price of "Old Glory" on Iwa Jima,
be always remembered
and their loved ones
be eternally blessed

**Gramma Wagner**

## Hunter's Moon

Come walk with me in the Hunter's Moon,
And listen to the hunter's sound:

The snap under boot,
The tread of the hoof,

The bark and the bay of the hound;

Come walk with me in the Hunter's Moon,
And look in the hunter's light:

The bare, black trees,
The crackled leaves,

The frost falling down through the night;

Come walk with me in the Hunter's Moon,
And taste of the hunter's wine:

The feel of the whole,
The still of the soul,

The night and the self all entwined;

Come walk and listen, look and taste;
Hunter's Moon's a rare, rare time:

When the heart's lonely quest
May also find rest,

And new hope in the hunter's mind.

**Evelyn J. Dallas**

## The Magic Pool

A little Fat Grandma sat on her stool;
and Lord, how she wished for a pretty pool
With lattice and deck and pretty plants and such
The wish was a dream, the cost was too much!

But Fat Grandpa heard her wishing so;
So down to the store he did go
He got the lumber and posts and nails
And went to work each day without fail.

He labored long and he labored hard;
He hired some help to clear the yard.
He dug up the dirt and tore down the trees;
He chased the mosquitoes, the bugs and the bees.

He put up a pool and he built a deck;
Worried with money, a nervous wreck!
But he built the pool with waters of blue;
And a pretty deck for her dream to come true.

Now Fat Grandma doesn't sit on her stool;
She's laughing and splashing in her Magic Pool.

**Dale Wederbrand**

## Mystical Regeneration

Insects in pagan pitch dance in the moonlight
and make love beneath the grass.

An ocotillo standing tall and proud,
spreads its thorny fingers in hushed silence
...as ancient hill-shadows advance.

Clouds sweep through the Southern sky -
the monsoonal sauna slowly lifting its
heavy hand in relief.

Lazy thoughts and a leadened heart rejoice in
this undersong of creation;
a cosmic breeze slowly etch-a-sketching
a heart clean.

**Beverly Fox**

## To My Wife

Forty seven years ago God in His infinite wisdom created a goddess
and molded it into your likeness.
When I am with you, the hours, the days, the very minutes evaporate as
the sea upon the sands of time.
Apart from you I am nothing, a nonentity wallowing in an eternity of
squalor and misery.
I am not worthy of you, as I am a mortal being, and whom but the very
Gods themselves should love a goddess?
You are the sun and the stars that my private world revolves around.
Without you my world would sputter and die as a meteor that appears
briefly in the heavens and the passes into oblivion.
To me you are as a golden idol which belongs in a sacred temple,
my heart.

**Albert Cheraskin**

## Only In My Dreams

All of a sudden the world is blind to me
And my dream has become a great reality:
No more crime,
No more discrimination,
No more hate,
No more disillusion,
No more stereotyping,
Just a perfect world, with no problems to see
But only in my dreams can I find that reality.

**Darren Harris**

## Untitled

With the pain in the window, it only reflects
and never shines.  The images, dull and grey,
move with no style or grace; just rust colored
movements of horrifying squeals and grinds.
It brings one's mind to rest on an unrested
soul trying to feel its way to the emptiness.
But the window never shines, it only reflects.
Looking in or out, it makes no difference for
the scenery is always the same, never different
but always changing.  Clinging and grasping will
only leave streaks of empty desperation that
disfigures one's view from the window.  Slowly
the images dance closer and grow louder only
to disappear into the window that reflects but
never shines.

**Jason Silvashy**

## A Miracle

There will never be anything quite like it
And now upon us
we see a new bundle of joy
is about to enter its new world

After all those months of waiting
The little thumps and movements
It looks like baby's trying to tell us something

And after all the pain has gone
we will remember
that we have taken part
in one of God's most precious gifts of all,
the gift of life

Skin so soft and wrinkled,
their tiny little hands and feet
Oh look!  There's a little smile too.
Now the joys of being a new mother
are now complete

And a new chapter in our lives
has just begun

**Jackie Simao**

## Untitled

Sheathe the word with a lock of your hair
and offer your plush body to my longings
breasts hang upon my lips
kiss this soul with the meadow between your
thighs—
   as a pheasant flies up

**Christopher Steele**

## The End

Another dream gone,
   and one more time my heart is broken.
How many times have I seen me this way,
   with no one to hold, with nothing to say.
Alone with my dreams,
   just wishing they were true;
   and praying for the night
   that I'll be with you.
Such a fool to fall in love,
   not watching where I go;
Such a fool to fall in love,
   not seeing she'll say no.
I find myself now crying
   in this lonely, dismal place,
   with no one there to hold,
   just an image of her face.

**Joseph Dean Schwierking II**

## A Far Cry

O'er desperate rows of settlement
   And parched-plot afternoon,
I light on billboard avenues
   Through suffocating hues...
Crossed and running ribbons track mindless
   through the squall;
To each his own locked prison,
   Periphery be gone.
And to the lapis reverie
   And palm-lined brick facade,
An exploitation's manifest rolls, stricken,
   On and on...

**Grey C. Halvorson**

## Give Honor Where Honor Is Due

God's word says give honor, where honor is due
And pastor we know, this is certainly you
As shepherd of his flock, you work and you pray
But you'll be rewarded in Heaven someday

I thank you for all those long nights on your knees
You could have been sleeping, not praying for me
The times that we've called you, when things had gone wrong
You wept then, and prayed with us, there on the phone

You can't plan your hours, our needs must come first
From a marriage to perform, to following a hurts
A call to the hospital, any hours of the night
We rely on you heavily, ever battle we fight

You're running this race here, with patience and pride
And it's very obvious, God's by your side
Your life is a beacons, it's shining so clear
It's drawing the sinners, from far and from near

So let us give honor, where honor is due
We want you to know, we'll be praying for you
May God's richest blessing, flow down from on high
And stay with you here, till the day that you die.

**Joan Walker**

## My Tree

I rested beneath the voluminous tree, partaking of its shade,
And pondering over the creature that had, this majestic tree made.
I listened to the songs of the birds, enchanted by their beauty,
And wondered what the songbirds, through their melodies,
   wished to tell me.

How glorious were those days, those summer days of my youth!
I was a lad then, ignorant of many things and slightly uncouth,
But how did I revel in the simplest of Nature's pleasures,
Until the day that marked the end of these divertive measures.

I went to war in the summer of nineteen hundred and forty three,
To see a removed Europe that had been quite unknown to me.
What I saw and experienced transformed my body and mind,
So that in introspection I was terrified of what I might find.

From thence, gone were the summers of simple delectations,
And gone was the ability of my favorite tree to evoke elations.
I was a youth no more, but a man hardened by war.
And now, I wonder, to where has my tree gone forth.

**John Lee**

## Heartstrings:  Tony and Dorinda

*By your loving mother; also loved deeply*
*by your brothers, Brandon and Todd*

Rarely is a heart so pure
   and precious as tonight.
A beat of innocence so sweet,
   perfection is the sight.

Two tender lives.  A world sublime,
   on this, your wedding night.
A symmetry of love will be,
   unique, as you unite.

Tradition's old.  The future's new.
   May time that's borrowed never be blue.
Good luck and wishes are hoped for you.
   Just like a sixpence in her shoe.

May your marriage be made in heaven.
   Another sweetest, story told.
One that's blessed by man and God,
   and shines like red and gold!

**Fran Crawford Dyer**

## Community

If I was to take you into my arms,
And pull you close to me,
I feel that there would still be space between us.

If you were to talk with me,
Tell me the ways of your people, your family, your life,
And I was to listen,
The space would grow smaller.

If I explained who I am,
Where I come from, where I am going,
And you were to begin to understand,
The space would decrease.

If we were to respect all that we learn of each other,
Teach our children and their children to do the same,
And continue to talk, listen and live amongst each other,

   Then I could take you in my arms,
   Pull you close to me,
   And the space would no longer exist.

**Catherine L. De La Mare**

22

## V-J Day Memories

We were lifted up into the air
 And put back down with care.
A few messed up our hair.
 Oh! What an evening to share!
My father disappeared from sight.
 Into my heart came fright.
Suddenly, before me, in the night,
 Was a hometown soldier I liked.
Milton Gould became my protector.
 He guided me to a quieter sector.
We embraced at a church door.
 It wasn't our first time together.
However, it was destined to be our last.
 He wanted to revive our past.
"May I take her home?" Was his request.
 Daddy refused to let me leave his nest.
 ***Gladys Scott Henderson***

## Frosts Autumn

When golden summer sun reflected in the stream.
And quietly remained 'til an autumn frost,
The trees above took on the golden hue,
And kept it, 'til each golden leaf was lost.

The orange and red of sunsets all year thru,
Crept silently into each leaf of green
and waited, for the autumn's gentle frost,
to change the forests very mein.

On hill and valley, green with Spring's soft rain,
The frosts of Autumn spread a blanket bright,
A master piece that changed with every fleeting day,
But kept it's warmth thru, every winter night,
 ***Dorothy H. Edmonds***

## Thursday Morning Road

In Dark thunder somewhere I heard an old song
And saw a round cobweb the spider built wrong
I swear it was square and it hung in a tree
Which was leaning to earth, for the sky wasn't free.
All the hot little shacks I could see in the glare
With hummingbird feeders and rickety chairs
Were a long way from anywhere that I could see
And sat in the heat wave a-comin' at me.
Out there on the summer roads shadows were blue
The middle of nowhere was peaceful and true
That winding old road doesn't call days by name
So Thursdays and Sundays are one and the same.
For clocks are synthetic but sunshine is real
And days are for living whatever you feel,
Sweet summer perfume's on a fancy-dressed toad
And I'm going dancing down Thursday morning road
The bright dust will settle into the old weeds
And Monday won't matter to windblown young seeds
I'm free as the river, I'm young and I'm old
And following summer so green it is gold.
 ***Joyce Griesmann Carter***

## The Beating

Under the lunch table,
Her frail limbs flying,
My kicking feet and pinching fingers,
The hatred flowing like blood,
Her breathless body
Struggling, gasping for life,
Laughter.
 ***Jennifer Whelpley***

## Summer Child

Summer child of mine come look
 And see you image in the brook.

Come summer child on brown bare feet
 Through the swaying field of wheat.

Make soft tracks on dewy grass.
 See the brook shining like glass.

Come see your eyes mimic the hue
 Of summer skies, gold and blue.

Your hair like strands of summer light
 Golden yellow, platinum white.

Come through the wild flowers and the dew.
 To see the gift God gave to you.

Come summer child of mine and look.
 Come see your image in the brook.
 ***Alycia Hawk***

## Untitled

The old one sits inside a ring of stones
and sees into the ring of ancient fires.
He begins to beat a seal skin drum
chanting for the spirits of his brothers,
the caribou, asking them to come.

Such are we now,
from technologies created by our hand,
that we can look into the ring of ancient fires
of stars whose light has journeyed far
seeking to understand in our minds
the eternity of the creation
in the light from the ring ancient fires.

The old one sits inside his ring of stones
chanting to the spirits
through the beat of his medicine drum
and watches the stars of the Arctic night.
He sees the beginning without an end
inside the ring of stones.
 ***John Fischbach***

## The Stranger Within

The stranger within me is calling my name,
And so I must answer once more.
I cannot deny her for she is my friend.
Has she ever failed me before?

This stranger within me is bidding me go
To search for new strength in my life.
Oh, she is much wiser than I'll ever be;
She is so aware of my strife.

The stranger within me is someone I trust.
She's been there forever, it seems.
She's laughed with me; cried with me; kept me so safe
While sharing my hopes and my dreams.

I just can't deny her or turn her away.
She's where all my living begins.
For we share a secret. I'll tell it to you:
I am the stranger within.
 ***Jo Piper***

## Life's Road

We all have our names upon this road,
and sometime in the end we are proclaimed old.
The beginning of the road is as fine as sand,
and as we walk on further it turns to rocky land.
Yet still we travel weary with eyes covered over.
As the road widens we lose that cover.
The road is busy and full of trials,
Then we are faced with maturity, facts, and denials.
All too soon the road becomes gravel, then turns to clay.
At the end of the road we all fade away.

*Cindy Dawn Berkovich*

## Darkness-Bellows

Sometimes the darkness bellows to me,
And sometimes I want to see,
What's behind the walls of darkness,
That I can not seem to see.

And sometimes I leave it waiting there,
To see I have no need,
But mostly I see no ugliness, deep into the dark,
It's just a sea of blackness through a beautiful cloudy park.

Why would people fear it,
When it's as much a part of us as the light,
Unless they need to hide that part of them,
That doesn't feel quite right.

But me, I say the fear of it,
Comes from fear of you,
But I only see it as,
A deeper shade of blue.

So wrap the darkness in your arms,
And cherish it like the light,
And then you will watch the darkness,
Make rainbows in the night.

*Joyce Ambrose Wiseman*

## Touch Me

When the pain is perpetual
And sorrow is sanity
When hurting is all that can move you
It's hard to trust
If your eyes are jaded
Your ideals sacrificed in vain
Morose becomes normal, your companion is pain
People walk through me, afraid to touch
Perhaps frightened to awaken the doubts that lie within themselves
If only one would cease their charade a moment
And share my soul
My hopes and dreams are filled with grandeur
Still I remember how to love and cry
Alas, no one feels me as they pass me by...

*Brett Matthew Lassek*

## The Pain Of Sexual Harassment

I feel like a ship in a bottle, that cannot be free —
all this pain and mixed emotions wrapped up inside
of me. My respect no longer exists, someone took it
away; only God himself can restore it someday. God's
the only one that can give you self-control, because
He knows all the hurt that's in your body and soul.
Sexual harassment is not funny my friend, it's a pain
inside it has no end; the tears always fall like
rain, because there's so much pain. Until we are all
able to be bold and come fourth, sexual harassment
will always be out of control!

*Donna S. King*

## Untitled

I happened down a country road,
and stopped to rest awhile,
across a broken fence, of wood
a Church decayed in silence stood.

I saw a ray of sunlight shine
through a broken window pane,
its shown upon an old sign
where faded words remained.

It read, "I came in life, I'll come in death
and take you home with me".
"For there you'll live everlasting life,
just believeth ye, in me.

The old Church somehow beamed,
with gossamer and gold,
God changed my life that day
With faded words, on the old country road.

*Henrietta Peterson*

## Night Delight

Stars blanketed the Heaven on a glorious night,
And surround the earth with a mysterious light,
Behold! Another wonder has come into my sight,
A lovely unicorn dancing with delight.
I watched in silence so not to cause fright
To this graceful vision of strength and might,
All at once she breached as if in plight,
Reared up toward Heaven and swiftly took flight,
Her shadow crossed a moon of white.

*Betty Jo Beheler*

## Remembrance

We used to gaze at wondrous stars at night
And talk 'til dawn would make the heavens glow.
We always used to hold each other tight,
And think our love would always change and grow.

Then something seemed to happen suddenly —
Like nature seems to change when there's a storm.
We fought to stay together violently,
And then our love just seemed to turn lukewarm.

The wind was blowing softly through the trees;
The air grew still as lightning split the sky.
Our love seemed made for nighttimes such as these
Without our ever really knowing why

We always have to hurt each other, then
We always come together once again.

*Debbie Wentworth*

## Travellin' Woman

I've had many a house, but never a home,
And that's what I wanted the most.
I've lived in the valleys, and up on the hills,
And travelled from coast to coast.

Only a home with my roots in the ground,
And friends who grew older with me.
Now I'm ailing and the time is all gone
And I know it is never to be.

A few years here - a few years there,
And thousands of miles on the way.
I'm very tired, I have to pack,
and then I'll call it a day.

*Audrey Cafaro*

## What Can I Give

If I take away your sky of blue
   and the caressing wind akin to love,
If I destroy the fragrance of the rose,
   and silence the cooing of the dove.

If I tell you there is no God,
   that miracles are a thing of the past
If I tell you there is no heaven and only
   death will claim you at last.

When I take away all these thing's
   that within your heart does burn
My God, what do I have to offer
   you in return.
     *Bonnie Durham*

## Your Golden Heart

As memories grow faint and restless
And the depth of mind and soul departs
I search for words of warmth boundless
In peerless beauty of golden minds and hearts.

In the quiet peace and comfort of your bosom
Lie the soothing balm of love's constancy
And the angel face no one can fathom
Cannot but be in infant's fancy.

In the wake of misfortune and discontent
When friends flee and desert a poor soul
Where else can I turn like a lost penitent
But to the everlasting warmth the gods console.

For in the midst of my mind's brew
Where oft springs tyrants in my heart and soul
The thought of the smiles that your heart drew
Soothes the aching wounds of my being whole.

I looked for passion in beings tender
In cathedral mountains of remembrance lame
I know now dwells a heart kinder
Than any mother could hope to claim.
     *Expedito A. Ibarbia*

## Fact Through Fiction's Form

A sunset reversed to be the earth
And the sea overturned, the sky to birth.
A visual grasp of reality in halves.
Half in knowing and desire in half.

Perceiving the future as the past once dealt
Now to be present, prolonged in death
But to come alive, abroad, astride;
Ample yet forsaken, memory deprived.

Unconscious belief of truth now slain.
Protruding as half to baffle the flame.
Ghastly the approach of the heralded sign
of life received, in vain to draw nigh.

Funeral scars as a drying fragrance
yellow and bloodless, a corridor sourceless.
Shaken as leaves, with their vegetation fury,
imprisoned by all; your soul so blurry.

So come to the endless fall of retreat.
A measureless dream, fully incomplete
Of neutral doves floating the silence aloft,
to vanquish the subtle lament of life.
     *John Hill*

Chance,
and the terrible risk of losing you can no longer silence me.
No matter the price, if it should last an hour,
however it ends, an hour will be enough.
I no longer exchange gifts.
The ritual of reciprocity expired with my youth.
And if you should answer that it is already over,
I'll forever be grateful that you were there to love...
     *Ace D. Lynn*

## To Ask What I Believe

I believe in the sunrise
And the walk of the killer
I believe in the sadness of the mother
I believe that the most sincere thing
Is the child's eye
I believe in the power love
And of hate
And the good guy and bad guy
But most of all I believe that the greatest
Thing that one can have is
A malignant humor for life
     *Douglas Stephan Bushong Jr.*

## Family Closeness

You start life with your family
   and then fall in love and leave
And then you start your own family
   and have children and then they leave
to get married and watch their children leave
And then the ones who started
   the family leaves
A gap impossible to fill

The pain of absence is almost unreal
   it hurts to talk, but helps
Friends come and leave
   relatives come and leave
and then you realize you are not alone
   they too have started with a family
and fell in love and leave
   and then they had children
and watched their children leave
   to get married and watch their children leave
and then one who started the family leaves
   one day you'll leave.
     *Bettie Norman Noble*

## Winter's Nights

There is frost on the grass,
And there is snow on the trees.
Snowflakes all pass,
With the cool winter breeze.

As the children of all around gather and play,
"Christmas is here," they all would say.
They would build snowmen, they would build balls,
As their parents begin decking their halls.

The families get together and watch through the night,
Watch and singing the carols under the lighted lamplight.
The night is all cozy and abundant with joy,
As the child eagerly waits to open his new toy.

All through the night is as quiet can be,
As the lights light-up the Christmas tree.
Presents all stacked and bundled across,
And the house tucked in with the soft fluffy frost.
     *Anthony Tang*

## Grandma's Thoughts

I walk along the grass so green
and think of years gone by,
when the children were much smaller
and how the years did fly.

The grass was not as green then
but patchy, brown and torn,
because the little feet would run
and play 'til it was worn.

The swings, the balls, the catching games,
each day was something new,
the pleasures, hurts, and sometimes tears
were part of how they grew.

But now they have their grown up lives,
they watch their own ones grow,
and I'm alone with thoughts of them
the Lord has made it so.

So though the grass is green again
and my little ones have gone,
I'll always have my memories
to help me get along.

*Fay A. Galvin*

## "Once A Year"

I would like to shoot a buck
and this year I've had no luck
but it's O.K. that I have none
'cause the scenery was great and company fun
just us men all fooling around
I even four-wheeled to leave tracks on the ground
the point of the trip was to be hunting a deer
but there's many other things that I've enjoyed here
like spending time with my brothers the three of us together
all the great things we did I'll always remember
I'm not that upset for not getting a deer
'cause I've got some memories and

I Can't Wait Till Next Year!!

*Jessica Patterson*

## Dwelling

This place is held together with tape and wire
and thoughts too old to remember
The ceiling's cracked and peeling layers of paint
form a three-dimensional map
of lands far away
perhaps long forgotten
or yet to be discovered.

The north wind whistles through the window
and shakes the glass panes
'til they rattle in response.
The drip, drip, drip, of the bathroom faucet
the only other sound
in these rooms of passed time

Where a woman sits silently
a glass of dry sherry
her sole companion
She ponders days gone by
and days to come.

*Elizabeth A. Wojcik*

## The Shape Of Love

Rest lightly on my heart, my love,
And throw away the demons of demise -
The lumpish clay is now again
The artist's mirror of disguise -
The wheel will turn - the potter's centered hands
Will shape once more a vessel of surprise.

Rest easy on my heart, my love,
And let your shadows jostle into free -
The whirlwind clay can do no more
Than what the potter's eye can see -
And if perchance it skews itself again,
It can't destroy the potter's memory.

*Celine McInerney*

## Little Sister

When you were a baby I loved to watch your little toes wiggle
And to hear you softly giggle
When you were a toddler I loved to listen to you as you
began to talk
And to watch you explore while around the house you would walk

When you were a child I loved to watch you bring so much
happiness in
so many ways
And to dress in matching outfits on those special days

Now as a young woman I love everything about you
Your strength, support, beauty and love

I love the thought of knowing
Our friendship will never stop growing

Most of all I love to know that I'm the lucky one to have you as my
Little Sister

*Jennifer C. Ripper*

## Hurricane

A banshee wind that weeps and wails —
And vents its fury like a jealous woman
By her lover scorned!
With taloned claws, it tears, uproots - destroys
And slaps the raging waters,
With obvious delight!

Clothed in grey, the angry ocean swells
In pregnant fullness to screech defiance to the wind!
Her whitecapped waves rise up to awesome heights
And play leap-frog, in their hurry
To batter down the dunes that would restrain her

Spawned by the rage, the Heavens weep —
With torrential rains, as tho to cool —
The frenzy of the battling foes!
As slowly as it built, it calms,
The rains stop, and the wind becomes once more
A brisk, but gentle breeze!
The ocean kisses the shore with tenderness
And all three, with shamed innocence,
Behold the havoc they have wrought!

*Faye Keene*

## Mother's Day

Not quite a year ago my mother passed away,
And I've grieved and mourned for her in almost every way.

For her a spring bouquet decorates my home,
While my memories and I celebrate Mother's Day alone.

*Carla Lopez Duerksen*

## Ode to the New Year

As the old year fades into memory
and we think of the days that are past
as we rode the waves of life's stormy sea
and sailed into the harbor at last
each new year starts a page in our book of life
hopes are high as the chapters unfold
for a bright new world undimmed by grief and strife
and a share in the joys life can hold
so we great each new year with a joyful shout
and we sing as the glad bells ring out
happy new year to all echoes through the air
and Gods blessings to all is our prayer.

**Dorothy Armour**

## "Spirits That Bond"

I gazed at you, and you, at I,
And we were different, so we thought,
Not just externally, in spirit and thought.
In the silence we stood, glaring at each other,
Until we heard, cries of the winds, as the sky turned dark,
We both felt FEAR, we grasped each other, holding dearly,
As objects flew by, whistling winds, Earth shattering sounds,
Crashed from the sky, yet we ride the storm, just you and I,
SUPPORTING Each other, wanting to LIVE, to afraid to DIE,
Then the silence returned, as the storm drifted away,
We CRIED.
We LAUGHED,
We became FRIENDS, on
That GOD Fearing Day!

**Denise Thornton**

## Truth

It seems all we do is roam around in confusion
And when our paths cross it's only regarded as an intrusion.
Always on the way to somewhere, be it work home or anyplace in
between
Moving constantly on what seems to be our last breath
We can't even enjoy something as important as watching our
children
   grow up
Or something as simple as a sunset.
And we may wonder if we'll live only twenty or all the way to
ninety
   years
Nothing may seem certain, but there is one thing that's clear.
It's that all this uncertainty will leave when it's washed away by
   God's tears
And then the truth will be no mystery, for it will be proclaimed for
   all to hear.

**David Paz**

## "Perfect Creep"

when i saw You, i said to myself, "He is so Beautiful!"
and who ever said that nobody's perfect was a fool,
because i have found in You the perfect guy,
You're the angel to whom i'll never say goodbye.
God had indeed created a flawless creature...
and so i thought.

that night, You showed me a totally different side
You took away my dignity, my purity and my pride.
Your perfection completely vanished on the bed;
reoccurring dreams will haunt me till i'm dead.
i didn't think God can create such a horrible creep....
i thought wrong.

**Daynabelle Santos**

## My Poet's Heart

May nature grab my poet's heart
and wring it 'til it weeps
words like raindrops upon each page
the untold secrets that it keeps.

One nite when the moon was full
and the nite was very still
she pierced my poet's heart
with silver arrows sure and deep.

There by the river path she grabbed my poet's heart
and clutched it to her breast,
the wind sighed and the willows wept
while moonbeams danced upon the river's crest.

The yearning in my poet's heart
weaves tales in my sleep.
I dreamt it spoke my poet's heart
filled pages with its words

a soothing balm my heart did calm
unlocked at last its truth and love,
who knows the hearts yet locked to touch
with echoes from above?

**Beverly Jo Valentine**

## To See Your Crown

Sweet Jesus, reach down and squeeze me tight
And wring out all my sin and spite.
Cleanse my heart of hurt and pain
And make me ever whole again.
Take it all, each tiny bit,
All my sin, get rid of it.
And when you're through
Don't put me down.
Just let me see
Your shining crown.
And, Lord — when I happen not to sin,
Just pick me up and hold me again.
I don't need a crown for my head,
Just let me look at Yours instead.
For just to see Your glowing face
And feel Your gentle, sweet embrace —
That's enough reward for me,
To see Your crown is all I need!

**Julie A. Magee**

## While You Were Sleeping

In a deep sleep, our thoughts blacken.

Color appears in a fuzzy, cloudy sketch,
and you are now entering the fantasy world of the untouchables.

As you enter,
you see yourself appearing only as a moral,
and you walk blissfully along the path your mind has chosen.

It's roads may be black, or maybe a mysterious white.
The fear that lies ahead is soon to appear,
as you probe along then dusty path of the untouchables.

Fear-stricken, and not able to voluntary act,
you run faster, and faster until you are at the beginning of this
never-ending mission.
The cliff is at your feet, and you jump.
Unable to hear, or see anything but the rocky ground,
you open your eyes only to find yourself awake in your bed.
In your dream you died,
and in reality, you're still alive.
Isn't that what we all think?

**Danielle L. Forshee**

## Go Where You Want To Go

You must live your life
and you do have a choice.
Decide from choices
which you value highly
You deserve respect
as you also want to give it.
What you will do is an exchange of many days
of preparation.
As growing from infancy.
Do not hesitate to take that step
do not give up there is so much you can do
Reach for the top.
There is a risk to the very existence of the next day.
When You wake up, the day is there
You have a challenge to use the time
to benefit or to waste.
The days will keep going and your time will count.
Gain as much knowledge which will help you reach
your place among others.
You'll find you're not alone, the world awaits for you.

*Gregoria Vela Torres De Avila*

## Ode to Margaret

You gave us music, you gave us laughter
And your wisdom touched our souls.
Like the trails through Yosemite,
You have bound us forever more.

We slept like children, we swam like mermaids,
And the stories were divine.
But the richest of our memories...
The flute at dusk will outlast time.

The river poems, the morning songs,
We close our eyes, the light still glows..
And we long, if for a moment,
To be near the Mousetail Rose.

So many switchbacks, so many miles,
Pluto Rock calls to us still.
Drunk from overwhelming beauty,
And the meadow's early chill.

Through the rivers, and the forests,
And the deserts of our Earth,
We're connected, not divided...
Shooting star ....we feel re-birth.

*Barbara Prudhomme*

## Another Man Dead

As another bird in the sky will fly
Another man on the streets will die.
Do not drive at night all alone
Or from your car you will be thrown.
Beat down and shot in the head,
But no one cares; it's just another man dead.
You can call the cops or the FBI,
But it doesn't matter; more men will die.
The news of murder fills our head
While another man in the street lies dead.
The top headlines on the newspaper page
Read another man dead by a Winchester 12 gauge.
All the crying and all the sorrow
Will last much longer than today or tomorrow.
You might hear gunshots one night while in bed,
But don't worry it's just another man dead.

*Chad Martindale*

## ER

Cotton swabs and alcohol, a prick they test your blood.
Another prick the IV's in. It drips. It's not a flood.

A baby cries, his throat is blocked. The sirens scream and wail.
An old man gets his weekly shot so his heart won't fail.

Ear, infections, heart attacks. Their beds are side by side.
A young man's fever shoots too high. He is his mother's pride.

From hour to hour they play with life, the doctors and R.N's
Who work the E.R. room in town. The drama never ends.

We sit at home and watch TV wrapped in our own cocoon
While every minute life can end in an E.R. room.

The heroic men and women there help strangers every hour,
Frantic mothers, sons, and wives who fear their lives have soured.

Many patients leave complete with full years left to live
All because these E.R. teams have so much to give.

The world is run by thugs today from sea to shining sea
With drug abuse and gun attacks that could hit you or me.

But people who still care and hope work in these E.R. rooms
And try to resurrect the good and take away the gloom.

My hat goes off to every one who works till 4 a.m.
To save a life or fix a bone. I say "amen" to them.

*Janet H. Driegert*

## Just A Few Words

Just a few words "Well spoken
are like apples of Gold.
In silver pitchers if given"
occurring to our God above.
And written through with God's great love
"To help someone on to Heaven above"
'Tis not the great things we may do.
Only just a word or two.
Can bring happiness to
perhaps more than one or two.
So let us watch out..
Whatever we may do
Just trust our God to see you.
Through He will teach us.
And show us what to do.

*Erma Dewar*

## The Rocking Chair On The Front Porch

Many hours on as many days,
are spent rocking in this chair.
Over one year ago,
it found its home.
But not alone, on the front porch.

Visitors, friends and family all have shared,
the pleasures of the wonderful chair.
Treasured stories of past, present and future dreams,
rocking there, under many star beams.

It's old brittle wood now.
Painted white and withering with age.
Oh, the stories it could tell.

A solitary place on the front porch,
for, the rocking chair.

*Ginger C. Thornburg*

## Buried In Your Past

What ya doin' to better yourself
  Are ya learnin' anything,
Are ya workin' to get your share of life,
  Or just gettin' what it brings,
Are ya makin' things happen,
  Or acceptin' what there is,
Are ya keepin' up with the Joneses,
  Don't ya believe it's better than this,
Are ya feelin' like you're content,
  And satisfied where ya are,
Are ya thinkin' this is all there is,
  And you'll never get very far,
Are ya dreamen' about the things you want,
  Or ya makin' them a goal,
Are ya ever gonna get ahead,
  Or ya gonna just get old,
Are ya livin' in the future,
Or ya buried in your past,
Are ya ever gonna teach your mind,
  There's more than being last.

**Billy Dee Hicks**

## One

All notes in their perfect destination,
are yet blended into ONE.
One central tonic note that is unheard
and unuttered
To this, every other sound ascends or descends,
To which every other meaning aspires to know
its true fulfillment.
To ask when the note will sound, is to lose
the afternoon;
It has already sounded, and all things now hum
with the resonance of its ringing.

**Elizabeth L. Andrews**

## I'd Rather Not

I'd rather not be tall,
around seven foot two.
Because when you're this tall,
all the girls laugh at you.

When I walk in my house,
I'd be as tall as the ceiling.
And when I walk down the street,
people would make fun of me without feeling.

I could step over people,
or maybe even a car.
And when I stand next to a building,
the roof won't be that far.

So as far as you can see,
being at this height is not a ball.
So before I go to bed I thank the Lord,
"Thank God, thank God," I'm not this tall.

**Charles Boyce**

## Contests

Contests all consist of
completing with maybe another team.
I usually play alone or with a
friendly foe.
What really interests me is
dominoes, yacht, and pachisi,
chess, checkers, chutes and ladders too;
what many amusing games to
play with the crew.

**Jennifer Stone**

## Golden Memories

On this day you began a brand new life
as a devoted husband and loving wife.

Sharing the good times and the bad
mostly happy, but sometimes sad.

Gaining more knowledge every day
with faith to guide you along the way.

Then children were added to your joy
a beautiful daughter and handsome boy.

When they were little you calmed their fears
bandaged their knees and dried their tears

The teenage years were another story
of sleepless nights and endless worries.

Next came the grandchildren, something new
for you and Bob to cuddle and coo.

Friends and family gather to be
with you on your Golden Anniversary.

We offer a prayer to the good Lord above
for many more years of abiding love.

**Grace McGuire-Boyce**

## An Exquisite Loneliness

A smoky gray mist merges toward a blue haze
As Blue Ridge marches toward North.
And travelers sweep through the marvelous scenes
Enriched as they venture forth.

I skimmed along once as the dusk turned to dark
The mountains towered left: purple; lavender; black!
A vastness of emptiness far to the right;
With pinpoints of light, way off to the back.

An exquisite loneliness keened through my soul
And pinpricks of tears touched my heart.
I felt stripped, and alone; a beautiful pain;
A sharp, utter ripping apart.

I longed for my home; for a place that was safe.
Felt sadness; a poignant loss!
Then I felt cleansed; refreshed and restored;
Full of awe and a sense of the cross.

That night as I looked in the face of God
No question was left unasked!
The Power; The Glory; The Reverence; The Love!
All whirled; then resolved to my task!

**Ellen M. Smith**

## A Touching Goodbye

The old man softly cries
As he watches the life of his wife pass by.
He gently holds her head in his hand
Trying to stay calm - the ideal man.
All the years - is it really time to say goodbye?
He is doing everything he can not to break down and cry.
Together as one - it's as if half of him leaves.
This feeling is unreal, hard to believe.
As her life is slowly being taken away
He knows she'll be in heaven by the end of the day.
A safe yet sad, empty feeling comes to his mind
As he whispers "I love you.... what we have is divine."
She squeezes his hand, as to say goodbye
And softly silently closes her eyes.

**Amber English**

## Ode to Leroy

The bough of the tree bends slowly with the passage of time
As each year passes - it's arc becomes more pronounced
The color, once such a sturdy dark brown is now a lighter shade
And the leaves have lost their luster and bright green gives way to
    tan

Then winter comes and the snow falls on the bough and the leaves
The top of the bough bends further to touch the ground below
And the wind comes and the leaves start to fall and the bough bends
In the dead of night the snow freezes and grows heavy

And the winter days increase and last long, bringing more snow and
    wind
The bough is now very bent and its leaves are gone to the earth below
In the very still quiet of the morning - a crack is the only sound
Then all is still.
The bough has fallen heavily to the ground
Life is gone.

Such was your life, so hard and heavy with the snows and winds of a
    nature you could not fight
And finally, the forces of that nature broke you and freed your soul
You are free of this world now - to rest and take care - no more
    snow, no more wind, no more freezing

*Joan E. Chubb*


## Mothers

God made the Mothers, to express His love,
    as He looked on earth, from His throne above.
God gave the Mothers, a special kind of heart,
    a heart that's so strong, their love will not depart.

Mothers are the ones, sitting up all thru the night,
    Mothers will stand by us, whenever wrong or right.
Mothers are never hungry, until each child is fed,
    Mothers are understanding, encouraging words are said.

And as we grow older, problems we face each day,
    Mothers sense we're hurting, she then begins to pray.
When we make mistakes, Mothers are forgiving,
    teaching us God's word, in the life that they're living.

Mothers will never forsake you, her support is always there,
    always caring for you, your problems she'd gladly bear.
So let us thank our Father, for the Mother in our life,
    it's the prayers of that Mother, that gets us thru our strife.

Thank you Heavenly Father, for the Mothers that we love,
    teaching their children of you, leading to heaven above.
Thank you Heavenly Father, for each Mom that leads the way,
    so in heaven we'll be with you, forever with Mom to stay.

*Carla Bell*


## A Dream Of Cinema

"The movie will start in five minutes," said the voice
As I sat in the dim, artificial evening of the dingy theater
I wondered where the voice came from
And as if he had read my mind, the voice said:
"I am the voice of all your idols
I am the myths you believed as a child
And I am your lone sustenance now."
I pondered his words as I dropped another piece
Of popcorn down my throat
And decided that I was imagining things
But then wonderful things began to happen
As the voice showed his might in demonstrating to me
That he was, in fact, telling the truth
I saw my idols leap from celluloid stupor into full mortal glory
I saw William Holden and Humphrey Bogart and Chow Yun-Fat
All parading before me, displaying their celluloid bravado
And acknowledging my existence, surprisingly enough
After I'd idolized them so, I wondered if they's notice me
And they did, which made me happier than you could ever know.

*Daniel Bowes*


## My Cowboy Joe

I do not grieve my cowboy Joe...
as he was born for the saddle;
got his first horse at the age of five.
Rode him to his grandparents ranch two miles
down the road.
At that age it was quite a tour!

To Joe, the range was home
with the smell of sagebrush
and the sound of cows bawlin' for their young.

Joe liked to sit in the saddle when he rode
to the top of ole' Squaw Butte Mountain
and looked around.
There was beauty there and he'd say "God is good".
He had learned that
long ago in his first Sunday school class.

However life must be, good or bad
All things must come to an end;
but when he lived, it was when he was
in the saddle atop old Squaw Butte
my cowboy was content.
*(September 6, 1995)*

*Josephine Keith Cunningham*


## For the Glory of God

Divine inspiration it came to me
As I fell out of the maple tree
God said to me, "GO FORTH AND KILL"
But my mind can't stand the thought, still
I will go and mutilate and desecrate
For I am a killer with thirst to sate
My hands are covered with the blood of my latest victim
All that comes to me is my favorite dictum
"GO FORTH AND KILL," God whispered to me
But I will not worry for my mind is free
For if I get caught, I will achieve fame
But rotting in a jail cell is not the life I want to claim
Hanging myself with a length of piano wire
That should be the gory end the police desire
But watch out my spirit will roam Heaven free
Since God himself has sent me on my spree
Burn in hell, people have said
But I will experience the glory of heaven instead

*Jeremy Peterson*


## Memorial Day

Rain-worn rose petals fall on your ash-grave
As I stand on the memorial dawn, a gentleman caller
For yesterday's parade.

I call out, but you don't answer; I knock,
But you pretend not to be there as I write a love note in the
salt-wind.

Is it possible to rest my spirit in the granite-day of your
memory? I love you.

How could suicide have been an option?
Time has been the universal anesthesia, but why not just an
explanation?

Rain-rust patches of sunlight wrap around me and I leave you
Not answering, not seeing me this
Memorial Day.

*Gary Elkins*

## Solitude

The Blackness of the room surrounds me
　　as I stare into the night.
I see nothing—
　　nothing but the ethereal glow of a streetlamp.
The gleam pierces the darkness—
　　I shudder.
Slowly, I rock back
　　and forth
　　back
　　　and forth.
I see nothing, feel nothing—
　　nothing but the luminosity from outside.
It threatens to filter through the glass,
　　but the pane protects me.
A lonely tear reflects the light
　　as it slides down my face.
Disappearing into the Blackness.
I see nothing, feel nothing—
Am nothing.

*Darcey Jean Livingston*

## "The Washing Of The Water"

Clear pure salty water licked my toes
as I wandered in and among the breakers
that crashed on the glittering quartz beaches
my feet were dirty with guilt
ruby red drips slid off my fingertips
guileless to the knowledge of wrong and right
they responded to gravity
as did my heart

Shamefully I let the waves surround my ankles with a vengeance
pull me in
trying to send me scurrying out again with a rush of sand and shell
angrily the green water washed the guilt from me
in turn blushing itself a rich scarlet
my body was clean but my soul
it was streaked with guilt
and the water rushed back to my feet
leaving rings of blood on my ankles
burning crimson tide
fled back to the depths of the ocean
to hide from the light

*Jocelyn Delmar*

## Men Are Like Gods-And People Begotten

I was wondering about the Gods
As I was walking down Constitution Avenue
For always since I was a boy
I was conscious of the gods in the offing,

Always off there somewhere in the air,
Never immediate and satisfactory,
Yet indubitably the master stuff
And living and seeing of our being,

And now here on Constitution Avenue,
With memorial buildings austere and white
I vacillate about the Gods of the world,
Their existence, their glory, and their authority.

The gods were so plural and so vague,
Yet so powerful and so composite
That I was perplexed on Constitution Avenue
Even as I had been perplexed as a boy

And nurture this poem about the Gods,
Who spring and leap out of our blood,
As one still seeking for definition
At odds with, but admitting the Gods.

*George John Guerin*

## Joe

We were together but never touched
As if we are from two different planets
Our warmth becomes even further apart
Looking at each other with hungry ways
Searching for a means to communicate feelings
There has been too much pain from the past
Blocking all that we feel deeply inside
Every emotion comes through with a tear
So we laugh and wear the mask of a fool
Just to be sure that no one ever gets into
Places within our soul where a cloud covers
The joy and love we cry to extend and share
So we continue to sit and look at each other

*Jeannie Keene*

## The Storm

December, it came, snow; freezing rain
As it formed beautiful lights—on trees, on fences
On anything that stood still
The lakes lay long and crystal, as nature looked silently on
And seemed to whisper.... "This is beauty."

February the heavens seem to want to bless mankind again
And emptying out its whiteness, we stand in awe and gaze
upon its brightness
Would there be an end to this seemingly awful storm?

Listen!  As we travel to and fro and manage to survive
Could we pause for just one moment.........
"God is good"!  And we are lucky to be alive.....

Some men may ask could this be God's punishment
For this sin-cursed earth?
But alas!  Let me say!  This is only a drizzle of what is to be...

*Celia Pompey*

## Mortal Man's Bed

Fumes of flowers rise in air,
As mortal man lies in his bed.
Mourners weep at the sight,
As the handkerchief rises to the eye.
They walk up the path, that leads to mortal
　　man's bed.

Slowly they kneel,
And say goodbye.
Then rise and drift away,
And turn for one last glance.
For this is the last time they will see,
The mortal man in his bed.

*Jean McGloin*

## King Won't Be King Anymore

Oh!  Prince Charles won't be king anymore,
As Princess Di put a lock on her door.
He thought, that he'd be her lover, for life,
Now he's only, the sweet pea rolling of her knife,
Princes Di looked in his pockets and saw
Camilla's stocking, she always wore.
It was then Princess Di smacked Charley in the eye.
Oh The King, Won't Be King Anymore.

*George E. Neubauer*

## Satan's Lies

Please don't let Satan tell them lies,
It's very sad when you look into their eyes.
Children not knowing if they're loved,
Wondering if it would be better to be up above?
Children are beaten black and blue,
Parents treat them like they live in a zoo.
Some children sit locked up in their rooms,
Trying to get high and escape those lunes.
Every second a child is getting beat,
Because of their homes they live on the street.
My friends tell me they want to die,
They can't get rid of the pain hidden inside.
Others turn to alcohol or drugs,
Just because they never get hugs.
Just reach out and give me your hand,
I promise I'll help if I can.
Either way you look at it, it's black or white,
Why don't they know what's wrong or right.
As another second passes by,
One more child is beat and maybe dies.

*Amy Olar*

## Josue

Josue washes over me like a warm river.
Josue is a feeling in a touch, a daydream
within a dream. Saying, experience me,
feel my heat. Whispering in the wind the
language of love that caresses my body
with soft breezes.

Josue's love is but a breath away. Sighing
and moaning, please stay, please stay.
Tomorrow's sunshine brings love renew.
Soft lips touched with the morning dew.
Tomorrow night is a different story, with
Colombian moon light and all it's glory.
Josue's love is but a breath away. Sighing
and moaning, please stay, please stay.

*Anna Kuenstler*

## Do You Ever Lose Someone You Love?

All the memories come back,
  Just like the waves on shore.

The precious shells that the sea has cast
  become the special memories you have built within me.

As I find peace within the beauty of the sea,
  I firmly believe you are helping to create that same
  beauty within me.

You gave me so much.

You found faith in me,
  when I couldn't find it in myself.

You gave me the strength,
  to know I could take care of you.

Just like you had taken care of me,
  so many times, so many times.

You gave me an everlasting gift.

You fell into eternity,
  Into the hands of God.

I'll always love you,
  for everything you've been and
  for everything you will always be to me.

*Ann A. Norman*

## A Salute To Independence Day

Yes that's right it's the fourth of July,
  look our limits are the sky.
Red, white, and blue that's our cue,
  to liberty and justice for all, not just a few.
Freedom and peace guide us all,
  with a salute to the flag, flying proud and tall.
Memories arise on such an occasion,
  to give us hope and determination.
Children of all ages watch the parade by day,
  and at night the fireworks end the big display.
Get out the champagne, let's have a toast,
  to the best country from coast to coast.
With this last phrase we'll end the day,
  "GOD BLESS the U.S.A."

*Andrea Derpinghaus*

## Allusions

Let me take you on a journey
maybe not as exciting as Thoreau, but not as crazy as Poe
no just a journey inside me
to show you what I see:
A lot of pain and tears
lots of qualms and fears
low, low self esteem
sadness is the hearts stream
but in a far away place in a small tiny space
glows a light, oh so dim
waiting to burst over the rim
like Phoenix coming out of the fire
only to soar higher and higher
springing forth to life with powers
no more rainy showers
happiness soon to be at it's finest
glowing through it's kindness
hopefully springing others inside
and in them I'll abide
remembered forever - inspirational

*Angela Macy*

## Hope

  It is over
Death has taken you on a far journey
My heart is barren as the winter trees
Scraping their leafless branches in dark tracery
against a leaden sky
Time passes
I walk through empty days of sorrow
But then - the branches stir in new born beauty
Softly swelling buds cloaks the trees in profusion
as their fresh leafy branches
seem to bend down and enfold me
in their cool green comfort
There is room in my empty heart
For the sweet rush of spring and hope
And I can live once more

*Anna K. Hilliard*

## Reoccurring Labyrinth Dream

Drizzling nightdrops of
Passive emotion;
On tireless eyelids
chaos's dreams dance,
Naked from daylight,
And drenched in slivers
Of sleepy reality.

*Amy Denfeld*

## Mother's Day

Breezes blow through trees like traffic in the distance,
The sun seeks places it has never seen.
I lay stripped of all boundaries;
Time. Place. Duty.

Nature nurtures a new child's mother,
I bask in the warmth of memories and horizons.
Like a rock, I hold heat against the chill of night;
Quiet. Waiting. Ready.

I imagine the trip home for Mother's Day,
It is filled with hugs and tears for times that have past.
I girl - talk with grown daughters;
Easy. Happy. Knowing.

We get ready for bed, they stare and whisper
*Mother, you have no tan lines.*
I whisper back *I don't need them anymore.*
Sure. Loved. Loving.

    *Anne C. Schneider*

## Untitled

Gray mountains stood before me on my path,
The walk around them seemed endless and far,
Though blocking me, I felt no sort of wrath,
Instead, I gazed upon a guiding star.

It beckoned me to climb the rocky face
And conquer all the steep and jagged cracks,
The base was rough but soon I found my face
While leaving many disappearing tracks.

I reached the top and eagerly viewed round
Nothing all the places unexplored,
I realized what it was that I had found
And why this long struggle I had endured.

Down, I climbed, much easier than first;
My path made clear and smooth by those before,
Reaching the base I saw the guide-star burst,
But found my path despite my short detour.

    *Amy Snow*

## Falling In Love

I never thought it would happen to me,
to fall in love; to be happy and free.
But now looking into your eyes as our hearts beat as one,
I can understand our passions have just begun.

We used to only be friends,
but not now; not with the message my heart sends.
It sends a message in which no satisfaction could ever match.
It throws my emotions into an eternal breeze for you to catch.
You catch them and embrace them close to you,
As I once wished for you to do.

I never thought it would happen to us,
I feel my heart is going to bust.
We sit and watch a pure and innocent dove,
We sit in the daylight and we fall in love.

    *Anna Carpenter*

## The World

The World is full of hatred,
I, myself should know.
The World is full of hatred.
Every day and every night,
the World is full of hatred.
Nor man, nor beast is full of love,
the World is full of hatred.

    *Amy Cooksey*

## A Teenager In The Sixties

As a teenager in the sixties, with his dreams so fresh and new
was called to serve his country, swore allegiance to be true.

To defend this land he loved, was an honor he held high.
One he must fulfill, even though he could die.

He shakes his father's hand, hugs his mother, and wipes away her tears
Turns to the girl he love, kisses her lips, and tries to calm her fears

I'll be home when its over, his voice echoes down the hall,
one more turn to wave good-bye, and a smile he gave to all.

A teenager of the sixties, no longer a carefree boy
marched away to victory, one he would never enjoy.

For when the battle had ended and all the smoke had cleared
a teenager of the sixties had sadly disappeared.

He gave his life for freedom, a higher price could not be paid,
The honor and respect he died for, and the allegiance that he made

Will make this country stronger as the years go swiftly by,
If we take the time to thank those, who gave their lives and died

This wall has his name on it, as well as many more
Who gave their lives so bravely, during the Vietnam war.

    *Anita Lacy*

## 'Us'

We all look alike————us.
We with the skin of many hues.
Shades of charcoal and mocha,
Tints of yellow and blue, us. Us.

We all look alike————us.
We with the hair of many colors and textures;
Kinky, curly, long, short—
A mixture, us. Us.

We all look alike————us.
We whose fore mothers suffered many nationalities;
Red, yellow, black, and white. Yet . . .

We all look alike. Us.

    *Anita D. King*

## A Letter From Jesus

Welcome back my friend, I am glad to see you here.
Welcome back my friend, I am here to rid your fear.
May the road be lit before you, as you travel back to me.
May the love that I have for you, be the light by which you see.
May the obstacles in your life, be less burdensome to you.
May you understand the things in life, that I want you to do.

May you find my strength inside you, when difficulties you do face.
May the pain that life has given, be less harsh with my embrace.
May the answers to your questions, find themselves within your heart.
May you turn to me my friend, when you feel so torn apart.
And just know that I am with you, if you'll only call my name.
For no matter how long you've been away, I love you just the same.
So take it slow on your way back, and know you're not alone.
For your return, "Let's Celebrate"; thank you for COMING HOME!

    *Anna Marie Reilly-Bosna*

## Sad

Sad is a poem that describes
The way you feel when you
Lose a loved one, the way I
Felt and still feel to this
Day over losing my grandparents
And my rabbit walnut.

    *Anne Bartlett*

## "A Child's Christmas Dream For 1994!"

"Santa,——is that you? An "excited" young child whispers
as she examines their "family Christmas tree," presents precariously
stacked beneath! Some large, some small, some hidden from view!
Dazzling and delighting the senses, dressed in dancing colors
of jolly red, mint green, and heavenly blue!"

Yet—across to the poorer section of town, a soft, sobbing,
child's crying is heard! "It's another Christmas God, and my mommy
and daddy are arguing they don't know what they are going to do?
They fight more often now, it makes me quite sad, tell me dear God—
does it make you feel sad too?"

No gifts lay under "their" christmas tree, as only "paper"
decorations adorn its outer beauty—made from the hands and
heart of this small, loving, innocent child, whose questioning
prayer brought even a tear to me! God promises us that "He"
watches over even the tiniest of sparrows—may we pray that "He"
intervenes this Christmas season, and showers "his" gifts of love
and laughter to the "broken hearts" of all these families!

"Yes, Virginia, there is a "Santa Claus," and there's a God who
lives in Heaven, where miracles are done! This tiny child, who prayed
to God, he heard her prayer, and at Christmas her wish was won!"

*Cynthia Nazworthy*

## Sam

Sam has eyes so big and brown;
As she stretches upon the ground.
Sam has a tail so curly;
And her teeth are white and pearly.
Oh, she has many a colour hair;
She sleeps most often in her lair.
Sam has big floppy ears;
She has eyes as gentle as a deer.
When she sleeps she looks like an ole log;
You might not know it, but she's my dog.

*Alexandria Perkins*

## Exam Week

"When will it all stop?" I say,
As sleeplessness starts to reign.
The anxiety, pressure and fatigue set in,
While the school controls me again.
"You WILL want this paper. You WILL write it now."
"You'll be miserable until it is done."
"But you will graduate; just think of this May."
"And THEN you can start having fun."
Irrational thoughts spin through my mind, as anger starts to set in.
The stress is non-stop, anxiety prevails,
and I know that I just can't win.
Always on the go. So tired, I see three.
I'm going through withdrawal; the tension overwhelms me.
It'll all be over soon, I keep telling myself.
No more papers to write. I'll put my books on the shelf.
Summer will arrive, and all bad thoughts will be done.
School will be over, and then starts the fun.
I won't remember this paper, or the others that I wrote.
I won't remember how to footnote, or even how to quote.
Just a few more lines to go. The finish is definitely near.
Bringing a sigh of relief, contentment,
and the end to this wonderful year.

*Denise M. Panfil*

## "Beautiful, That's Me!"

I wake up and look in the mirror and say to myself "I am as beautiful
as the eye can see, beautiful, that's me!"

I get downstairs and say "let them see the beauty that lies in me, beautiful, that's me!"

I walk down the street, heads turn and stare. I say to myself "they can see the beauty in me, beautiful, that's me!"

I go to a party, they like my style. I walk in grace and a pearly white smile. I say, "They can see the beauty in me, beautiful that's me!"

Now I might not be Miss America and all that, but the beauty in me is definitely not whack.
So I walk with style, I walk in grace and I let them see my beautiful African American face.
I let them see the beauty that's in me, beautiful, that's me!"

*Ebane' A. Smith*

## My Windowpane

The rain pours down the windowpane
as the tears pour down my face.
Life and the weather are so alike yet so different.
As they say, "When it rains it pours," and so it does.
But why not, "When the sun shines it does so brightly," as it does?
The weather of my life constantly changing, earning,
turning, exploring, as does every ones.
Presently my life is forecasted as
"Heartbroken with a chance of rain."
But then over will my troubles pass and out will rise
my sunshine of goodness.
Then upon my windowpane will the sunshine over so brightly,
and the birds will sing, and the flowers bloom
and life, such sweet sorrowful life, will once again
turn around for the better or for worse.
I can only wonder what will become of my Windowpane of Life.

*Doreen M. Ziemann*

## The New Breed

They no longer have their burros,
   As they go up in the hills,
Most everything they drive today,
   Come equipped with four wheels.

The modern day wenches
   Are no longer in saloons,
They're bolted to their four-wheel drives,
   Or buggies... used on dunes.

Some may use detectors,
   Others....have a dredge,
They all love the excitement,
   Of living on the edge.

There's some ole time prospectors,
   With a gold pan in their hand,
Looking for a big nugget,
   In the midst of that black sand.

One thing I know for certain,
   There's some gold to be found,
And I hear in California,
   It's just laying on the ground.

*Chuck Hann*

## I Couldn't Live Without You

I couldn't go on without you
I couldn't breathe without your love
I couldn't see without your touch
I couldn't hear without your voice
I couldn't taste without your kiss

*Jeni Foskey*

## Island Sun

A gentle breeze swiftly passes against the white sail
as we drift closer to the landing
of the coconut palm covered mass in the corner of the sea.
The waves cradle us as we see the island grow.
With one puff, our boat leans on the white sand
and we anchor our float.
We kick our heels along the ocean's surf.
My white dress flutters with the wind.
As you climb trees bringing fruits,
I glance above to see the blue skies
with cream clouds like pillows.
I dip my fingers in the warm water that froths
with every shell bringing wave.
I run along the ocean shore and feel the water between my toes.
I kick my heels into the sand and stare beyond.
You give me a hug and together we get tossed
and ride with the current.
Kicking and fluttering, we are flustered
in the moment of truth.

*Janice M. Chang*

## The Clock

And the clock struck a sour note
as we glanced up to see
and glanced down to not see
because we couldn't bear to see it
the ruins of time lay bare there
was all the strength upon our backs
to take it from the wall asobbing
put it outside to dwell forever
for there is no time out there
we figured to leave it a week or so
for a mere small vacation from it all
yet when we went out to bring it in
a small pile of dust was in its place
and the hands of gold were not to be found
having run away to a safer place
we toasted our cups over the coffee break
and wished them happy in their journey where.

*Carla Richert*

## My Two Loves

I wonder if a certain lane so happily is faring
As when my first love, Ellen Jane, there took her daily airing.

My lollipops I shared with her, and, daintiest of misses,
For every sweet, without demur, she paid me off in kisses.

My latest love is Eleanor, by her, I am now chided,
And though I still divide with her, my pay is undecided.

Sometimes when sweets and flowers most rare I on her shrine
am showering,
Her smiles with sunshine fill the air, but, ah! too oft she's
lowering.

No matter how I strive and woo, no more for me such bliss is
To see her — as she used to do — put up her lips for kisses.

Sweet Eleanor, though in love are we, my heart feels more of pain,
Than when your summers numbered three, and you were Ellen
Jane.

*John Rowland*

## I Miss You, Now

I miss you, now,
As you depart
To wander trails of an aching heart.
I stand alone, my soul bereft
When you are gone there's nothing left.
Is this the nightfall of our togetherness?
Must I feel my heart's distress,
In this the moment of your passing?

I miss you, now,
In the quietness of nightfall's
Ever seeking nature calls,
Loon's empty painful echo wails,
Clearly speak souls' searching tales,
Ever seeking one serenity;
Needs fulfilled for all eternity
When two spirits join.

I miss you, now,
As I skyward turn;
Glories born of a sunset's burn,
Promises of your return.

*Daniel S. Konieczko*

## Control

All I really want to be is a lovely shell
as You shine through me
but ego, anger, worry, pride
take up so much space inside
the places where You'd love to dwell
I cling to my private little hell
of analyzing everything
resisting all the peace You bring
holding on, holding in, clinging blindly to my sin
do it myself! keep control
dig a blacker, deeper hole
but when, in my futility
I fall exhausted on my knee
I cannot do it, God, help me!
Your love breaks through and shines on me
a vision of how life could be

*Christine Powell*

## At Cool Park—July 3, 1994

Standing before the Copper Beach...an arm away from etched
attempts
at immortality...initials, like fingerprints of the "travelled people"
as William Butler was wont to call this Aesir, these Gods of Irish
literature, plush and green is the very spot where at Lady Gregory's
Estate, Cool Park, Gort, County Claire — O'Casey, Yeats, Joyce,
Shaw, Synge, Hyde and the
friendly cycle goes on about the trunk...
carved their letters in this famous "autograph tree" to seal their
dedication in small piles of wood chips.

"Here I stand"—no Luther in defiance,
But a worshiper, in awe, where finally
That word deserves its intention,

Lover of literature,
Irish-descended American come, to
honor names I have only read or taught, now, for tangible joy
so close to me I can imagine
on this almost hot day
away form the wandering tourists off about the woods,
These dead spirits materialize for just that
Brief epiphany.

*Joseph W. Mahoney*

## The Stranger

I met a stranger, while walking one day. He smiled
at me, but I quickly turned away. His countenance of
love was on his dear face, his eyes were so steady as they
followed my pace. He watched me and waited for me to
retreat, and oh what compassion, when I saw his dear
feet. The stranger said "Go ahead, touch them and feel
the pains and sufferings of a whole world to heal." The
moment I touched them I shuddered and shook because of
this feeling the stranger said "Now look, my hands are
the same and so are my sides and for you my dear friend, I
was tortured and tried." My eyes filled with tears, my
soul felt so free, because this stranger had prayed just
for me. I'll never forget the smile on his face as he
touched me and said "Now walk with my grace, when
walking life's pathway's with trouble you'll meet." Take
heed of the stranger who has special feet.

*Juanita Patterson*

## Searching

I'm sailing away on a sea with no sound,
  At the river there is a hush,
  And no one is ever around.
I don't know where I'm going,
  Or whom I may find,
  I'm trying to find someone that will be kind.
He knows not if I'm coming,
  Or if I'll be meeting him at all.
But I'll search for him forever,
  Winter, Spring, Summer, Fall.
And if I'm unable to find him you will know not
  What I'll do,
  But I'll no longer roam this earth
  But walk the heavens blue.

*Jill Byrnes*

## Sorrow

  Your mind, it starts to float,
Away
Far away.
And you feel a remembrance of this sorrow,
It hurts
Badly.
It makes you think,
Think about your life and its greatness.
It will happen many times,
But you must learn,
Learn to get over the pain,
The pain of sorrow.

*Alex Baxter*

## Alone At Night

No one exists but me. All are asleep far
away from me. I am alone. I touch the night
as it creeps in through the open windows,
floating over me, bringing with it the smells
and sounds that hide during the day. It
strokes my skin with gentle hands, soothing
and hypnotizing me. The heat and sweat of the
day disappear, leaving behind balm to the body.

Listen carefully. Hear the insects as they
meet and mate, singing their tinny songs of
life - joy of just being, with no particular
purpose in their lives except to exist and sing.
The world is theirs now. Theirs and mine.
They share it with me. There is no sadness
in their voices, no strife. There is no fear
of the future. There is only here and now.

*Betty Carol Mayo*

## In The Shadow

Their playground was a sidewalk in a ghetto.
Bare feet, bare tops and rags on their bottom,
Graffiti and crackhouse rubble bloomed in their junkyard
meadow.

I kicked a piece of junk yard chain - deja vu,
And loosed images of hand-me-down crutches
Crafted with guilt and quotas bonded by
bureaucratic glue.

Bland black faces stared at me with apathy.
They had never before seen me I'm sure.
At ages three, theirs was already a programmed
destiny.

The right to run doesn't come with a right to win.
Crutches and quotas don't inspire a crown.
Quality, quotas counterpoint; one looks up, one
down.

Bare feet, bare tops and rags on their bottom,
In their Olympiad ghetto meadow,
They trained in an August sun under a lengthening
shadow.

*Jay Walsh W.*

## Untitled

  In drive on teenage roads in dreams
bathing in the illusion of something that doesn't belong anymore
  where did those days of hapless wandering down the dry roads of
america go? When you could strap into friend's 350 with the
headers
  and the multiple carburetors and the fat seatbelts of detroit
speed-lust with the spring sun of our young lives
  shining down into our heads and into our hearts
becoming the strange fuel in that fire that is young.
  The threat of death made us laugh and drive still faster
racing each other on bumpy country roads
  the likes of which have never seen a speed limit sign
and the wind whistles thru with fury and exhilaration
  it almost takes on a life of it's own, picking up all loose paper
tossing it out the window or bunting it around some corner of the car
  resembling tiny tornados, the wind at 110 mph...roaring in your
ears the symphony of adventures-lust, that drove our young appetites
  to the brink of annihilation.

  Some days I remember these things
and the chair of life feels just a little more uncomfortable.

*John Halicki*

## In The Early Morning Rain

In the early morning rain, you see him standing on a hill
Battle scarred and freshly wounded this young man was trained to kill
Kill all that comes before him to challenge his great pride
A pride that's in a country for which many men have died.
In the early morning rain, that young soldier falls to death
Thinking of his country while he breathes his final breath
A country which he died for, he's shown no selfishness
His life has ended for our freedom so sadness we suppress.
In the early morning rain, memories we recall
Of that soldier and the devotion that he had for us all
A devotion he felt inside and knew his life he'd give
Not just for people and their lives but also how we live.
In the early morning rain, we all must understand
He was fighting for ideas and rights not fighting for our land
For lands the same the world around no matter where it be
That soldier really gave his life to save democracy.

*Christopher R. Wills*

## My Bear

Every honey out there has a bear.
Be it a brown, beige, or white
they are all a delight.

My bear is a brown bear
He's strong, hard and bold
But most of all he's mine to hold

My bear is a trucker so when he is a way
I continue to love him and not
go stray

My bear is my life band I will always
be his wife

Continue to love me my bear
and I will always be here

Because in our love there is no fear
**Barbara M. Williams**

## I Love You

When you say the words I love you
Be sure you know what you say,
For love can be everlasting
Or may only last a day.

Love can soar you up to the heavens
And land you on a distant star,
Make a weed patch into a flower garden
Or the breeze sound like a thousand guitars.

Love is such a delicate feeling;
There is only so much it can stand.
It's power can topple mountains
But can be shattered by a grain of sand.

So when you say the words I love you
Be sure you know what you say
For love can be everlasting,
Or may only last a day.
**Julie Ann Sylva**

## Gone But Not Forgotten

I know you're dead, but you will always
be with me for you will be in my
thoughts and heart forever.  If I keep
you there, I will be able to face the
lonely days and nights ahead.

You were everything I wanted or
needed for my life to be complete.
You showed me what true love, and
happiness is.  Our love, happiness and
closeness was very special.

I will treasure the memories I
have of you, your sweet love, and the
times we were together forever.
Because of you, I can truly say I was loved.

Thanks for the memories,
I will go to my grave loving you.
**Doris Tyner**

## Tough Love

My love is tough enough;
I avoid the softer stuff
The words are gruff and bluff,
Made of sterner stuff;
My love is rough enough.
**Donald J. Kennedy**

## Forgive Me

My great cries out in pain
Beating with love nd trust in you
I am the one to blame
I love being with you every minute of the day
And when I can't see you
I can't hide the pain
My love for you is stronger than you know
I wish you could just see how much I care
I hope and pray you feel the same
I have all my trust in you
Please don't hurt me
And leave me to die
And wither in sorrow
And shame with no pride
**Christina R. Lovett**

## Beautiful Heart

Catch the beauty of the moment
Beautiful heart has no need for
perfection equal opportunity competition
should be with ourselves process of change
creates beautiful heart sharing listening
to each other feeling achievement incredible
virtue experience freedom motivation patience
Beautiful heart capacity potential energy
Exciting adventure live in love vulnerable
growth tenderly respect dynamic
Knowledge insight reinforce immersion
flexibility endeavors uniqueness personal
challenge intellectual exchange love eternally
Beautiful heart
**Barbara Thomas**

## Boo's Secret Song

Oh, they think I never change
because I never re-arrange my smile
when company comes to watch or listen.
But, Yes, I know, I expect, I plan and I perceive.  AND, I remember.

While they imagine I sulk and grieve
for lost, and never-coming lovers, and all sorts of others
that march in similar categorical disarray, I see and I remember.

The sky is gray when Christmas comes in December,
but listen to your values, my darling.

Time is a thoughtless silly starling, not an eagle;
never a swooping, clutching condor,
or a silent, suspended hummingbird.

While it wings and weeps and starves and eats, I remember.

How mediocrity delights us all,
blindly guiding our sweating days and melting nights.
And, as I clutch the fleece of a golden thought eternally,
I remember, the life I didn't live, and I am safe.

Do-wack-a-do.  Ditty, ditty.
**Dennis M. Fahey**

## Onward Great Eagle

Fly, oh fly onward great eagle,
as I sit here securely on the earth.
Soar to great heights amongst the clouds,
trying to touch each for what it's worth.

Let the warm wind run through your feathers
as I watch from far below.
Glide for miles caring only for yourself.
What a botherless life I'd like to know
**Christen Lee Pfaehler**

## Happiness In Absence

She smiles at anything, everything, and nothing
Because she remembers the smile from you

She performs the monotonous duties willingly
And does her best for you

She sits alone gazing at the stars
Whispering the name of you

She sheds tears in the rain
For the happiness brought by you

With tender hands she gathers yellow flowers
Remembering what she gathered from you

She looks in the mirror and smiles,
For she sees the face of you

Why is she happy in your absence
In a world that craves the tangible?

***Deanne Winterton***

## Lovely Summer

The summer is a perfect time for love
Because the body chemistry is warm.
Awaiting for her mate the pure white dove
Will nod her head, accepting love's sweet storm.
Because the summer is a time for fun
Go boating, swimming, walking in the wood
And bask on beaches in hot summer sun.
Ignore your love! as if you really could?
Combine them both, I'm sure they will agree
For summer fun and love go hand in hand.
Remember how the body chemistry
Is at its zenith on hot summer sand?
    As summer also helps the world go 'round
Then that is why with love it's tightly bound!

***Dorothy Delaney Roberts***

## The Starry Stardust Sign

There will be no shining daystar when she shyly wanes
because there is plenty of sadness with her gaining pain.
The brilliant stars will tingle as they shootingly fall along
with the closing eyes smiling for all things gladly gone.

Hope for no good or evil.  Hope for no sadness or gladness.
Let there be nothing to scare the solemn soul of gold;
Only peaceful sleep that gives a pleased place of graceness
knowing that living on earth was a worthy goal of old.

No more heavenly hail storms of wailful icy tear drops
that breaks the brace spirit and makes the whirling world stop;
Only to release the winged courage to the wild willing wind
as a bright inspirational force in a breathless javelin spin.

***Bonita L. Andrade***

## Lights Of Heaven

    Once I asked the Lord to take me to his
heaven.  I wanted Him to take my life, as well as
he has taken my son, and let us walk in his
light of heaven forever, together.
    I begged of him, to take me.  For as
I believed my life had ended without my son.
Today he has given me a chance to begin again.
    Although, he has taken my son upon his
worldly heaven, he has given me a reason to stay
in this life.  For my precious, most dear baby girl.
    Someday when he takes me, I will have
had a chance, to have a life here with my baby
girl; and then eternity, in the lights of
heaven with my son.

***Joyce M. Reifsnyder-Lukins***

## The Caretaker

We love you our dear heavenly Father and Mother, and we need you
because we love you, and we need and love you most of all because you
are our Lord, you are our creator, you are our savior, and you are God
of all creation.

We believe in you and in your wonderful ways, in your creation of life
and the life here after, in your resurrection and ascension into
heaven, and in your heavenly spirit.  We pray that our actions,
thought, words and life will be worthy of your forgiveness, worthy of
your mercy, worthy of your consideration, and most of all worthy of
your divine love.

We are grateful for your sharing this day with us.  Thank you for
allowing us be a part of it and thank you for allowing our family
and friends be here at this moment.  You are most kind and we
appreciate it.

***Joseph B. Miglizzi***

## Find Strength In Your Memories ...

Find strength in the memories you hold dear to your heart,
    because with those sweet memories your healing will start.

Your mother was special and dear to us all,
    but the loss that you feel leaves you empty and small.

Please remember the good times you two shared in the past,
    for with God's precious love your aching will pass.

Your mother is no longer in need of your touch,
    but remember while living she loved you so much.

The loss that you're feeling, will go dimmer each day,
    as the memories inside you start to show you the way.

Our lives here on earth, are like the flame on a candle,
    God will only give us what he knows we can handle.

Your mother is now living in her home up above,
    and her heart beats as graceful as the wings of a dove.

These are just words that I've written on paper,
    while praying and asking God why he would take her.

As your days turn into weeks, and your months into years,
    happy memories will embrace you and replace all your tears.

So find strength in new memories, as you find them each day,
    and remember your mother, she'd want it this way.

***Barbara Prather***

## Vision Through A Cloud

You don't understand and you never will
because you won't open your mind
look in my eyes
not at them
in them
see the gray cloud circling inside
it rains on me more often now
it was never in there before
but because of you
this gray cloud is stuck inside my eyes
I wish I could see clear again
but now I only see hazy
Do you know what it's like looking at life through a cloud?
And not even one of those white ones where the angels lay their
heads
but one that brings showers of rain, lightning, and thunder
but you don't care or understand and you never will
because YOU go through life
protecting YOUR eyes
by keeping them securely closed.

***Charity Latham***

## Irreconcilable Differences

With my signature on the paper, the meaningless form
Becomes a compelling force changing my life and his.
"Irreconcilable differences," it says, but I remember the years
We walked comfortably in step with my hand clasping his.

We knew the excitement of adventure, of fun and laughter,
Touching, cuddling, sharing love in inexpressible pleasure.

Sadly I look at each object in our once delightful home.
Is it his or mine, where will he take his things, or I move mine?

There is no protocol for breaking up a marriage.
Moving through dismal days, I resist the immobilization of despair,
Courageously facing decisions. When to discontinue hugs and kisses?
When to move to another bed, and how and when to tell our friends?

Slowly and painfully I move through the stages of grief —
Denial and anger, guilt and numbness until I attain acceptance.

I have lived long enough to know that today is not forever.
Sometime this throbbing grief will no longer torment.

Gone is the gold band I wore, but its mark still circles my finger.
It will disappear in time, but my scarred heart will long regret,
Not just the loss of a special person, but the end of a way of life
That provided comfort, contentment, and security.

*Clela Fuller*

## By the Sea

There is a place where I can stand by the sea.

I can stand there and watch my life pass
before my eyes.

I can see times when I was a child, so happy
and so full of jubilant energy, with loving
parents to teach me right from wrong.

I remember times going out with my friends or
just sitting and talking about what was new at school.

The best times were when my whole family
gathered together at holidays or family gatherings.
Now, I am watching the sadder scenes of my
life, when times weren't so happy.

When my grandfather died, and when a friend
rejected me.

At these times my family, especially my mother
and father, were there to help me.

The most important thing was that I could
always feel the Lord seeing me through the storm.

Now, the sun is setting on the sea, and this
is one of the happiest times of my life.

*Janeel Ramsey*

## Circle

I went for a walk and became a line.
I curved and twisted, I even intertwined.
Life was so simple it was nearly divine.
But I made a few quick turns and became kind of square.
So I pushed in a couple corners, then I was a diamond.
"Too ostentatious," I said. But from there I shined on.
I bulged out my sides and became rather oval.
I seemed kind of odd, I fell over.
So I squashed myself in and then I was a circle.
I ran around and around myself.
Life and I were somewhat normal.
Life

*Jeff Fischer*

## My Mother

She started out young, sixteen was her age,
Before she turned around, four children to raise.
A wife, a mother and a homemaker was she,
Then took on a job, to help pay bills, you see.

When asked a question, with an answer you would leave,
She must have had them all hidden up her sleeve.
And her kiss was as magic as any magician,
When she kissed away pain, you didn't need a physician.

The four children she saw to be grown and married,
Her grandchildren now in her brag book she carried.
Still cleaning, washing and cooking everyday,
Loving each of us in her own special way.

She worked long and hard for most of her life,
Some pains she began to suffer, from fighting the strife,
For her husband had died and left her alone,
She now was getting weary, down to the bone.

She slowed down a lot in her later years,
And you could see her eyes shed many more tears.
So God looked down and said with a smile,
"Mama, it's time to rest for a while".

*Evelyn Pickelsimer*

## Seasonal Transitions

Beating a rhythm, hail drops from the skies
Before the silence of falling snow,
An eerie quiet over a white carpet lies,
Early flower blossoms no longer show.

Gusting winds whistle through mighty oaks and pine,
Constant rain pounds on window-pane,
Sleeping dog by crackling fire of flames that shine,
Fog swirls around the weather-vane.

Waterfalls appear, splashing over grey granite rocks,
Creeks flow noisily ever on downhill,
Rushing waters rise, flowing past dams and locks,
As rivers, lakes and valleys overfill.

Long awaited, with anticipation Spring's timely arrival,
When Nature re-emerges for another year's survival.

*Jane Gary*

## Subtle Lesson

Life lessons some will call it
being stressed out and pushed to the limit
helping one out is now a thing of the past
Facing reality - Steering life in the face
is part of the pace
for one to take in
for one to walk in

H'mm - Reality - is something else
It becomes really scary sometimes
Body, Soul, and Spirit - one's self
Taking life at face value only last for a time
For one can pass
For one can last

I like to provide all things honest before all men
So they can see you for what you are
So they cannot take you at face value
So they can have a lasting true knowledge of you

*Cynthia Peets*   .

## I Found You

We met on an April nite
Beside you I sat in the dim light

We spoke as if we heard no others
Our hearts knew we would be lovers

We felt our souls bonding together
As if we had known each other forever

You are the man that women dream of
In hope of finding true love

I heard of such men so wonderful and true
And there you were, I had found you

*Donna D. Sleeman*

## "Do Fence Them In"

Gangmembers, Paramilitar "Patriots",
Better yet, misfits, losers, and traitors,
The devil's disciples,
The arms dealer's flunkies
Who scatter hatred far and wide
Affecting the smallest to the oldest:
Too bad, you hoodlums, illiterates, and bigots;
You lose in the great scheme of things,
Because in America the Beautiful
The majority rules; the melting pot is "Cool,"
And co-existence is alive and well.
Warmongers, go the Bosnia, Rwanda, and Iran;
Fire at the "other" bad guys, because
Here in the U.S. you don't belong;
Your ugliness and stench must be washed away;
They must be slain,
And you,
Fenced in together,
Can have the honor.

*Barbara J. Belisle*

## A Down to Earth Tale

The brown and red Grand Canyon is quite a
big beautiful sight. There, an artistic Arizona
Native American, named Blue Sky Butterfly
flew a kite that was white. Yellow feathers
and fluffy cotton were attached to the kite
being bright. A gliding bird made of cloud
puffs was the shape of the kite in flight. Later,
Blue Sky Butterfly let go, of the spool and
the string that ran way, way up to the kite.
It was a mystery why, so then in the wind,
the kite glided to a far away forest's play
ground park from some canyon's heights. Then
the kite safely landed on a Native American
designed trampoline of recreational delight.
Nothing broke and every life was all right.
Later, it was a quiet night.

*Jon Alan Jarvis*

## The Question

Why are all women,
Bit-es or 'hoes,
Why is it what men says goes?

Why do we have to be stupid, horny, or grotesque,
why can't we be women,
nothing more nothing less...?

I have all these unanswered question to my mind,
but I will find the answer,
that I will find.

*Charmel Gaulden*

## It's How the Shadows Fall

Designs of mesquite in arabesque forms drop their silhouettes,
black and exquisite
upon the green velvet earth in artistic hieroglyphics
and the clock inside my chemistry strikes 1949,
for in some strange manner it's turned back the hands of time.
For today's calendar sports 1995, and I know I'm me and I know it's
    now and I know that I'm alive.

But there's something in the light; it's in the aura there;
it's how things look and how they smell; it's in the very air.
It's how the shadows fall that moves the invisible wall
dividing now and then.
How is it I'm there and yet I'm here, I'm an adult.
    Yet I'm a child again?

It brings two words together, yesterday and today.
It brings to present old times and old friends and makes me want
    to run and play
and stand by that white stucco wall staying out of the wind...
    just staying out of the wind.
All because of how things look and how things smell
and how the shadows fall. It's how the shadows fall.

*Carolynne Nix*

## Untitled

Pinks and reds, blues and purples.
Blending, changing, fading into black
Blackness. Deep and unending.
The blackness, a shroud, surrounds us,
engulfing, suffocating.

A silver crescent.
Large and bright, it sheds light, and turns
black into purple and deep blue,

A point of light.
Small and ineffective, alone and weak.
Another point, and another, breaking through
and putting holes in the blackness.

Together, millions of tiny points fill the blackness,
and light the way.
The silver crescent, a seeming leader,
a million points of light.
Together light out path,
and guide us home.

*Dijah Hall*

## The Straight Edge Of A Sphere

Against a wall
Books laid open on the ground
Knowledge of years in front of his eyes
Accumulated after being spun
By the winds of truth and lies, and right and wrong
and the dizziness that ensued

But the facts and figures in which he trusted
to lead him through the Garden's maze
speak the truths of times gone by
And black and white is overpowered
by the grey in between

What do you do, when one and one isn't two,
when grass isn't green and skies aren't always blue,
like they're supposed to be?

Scribbling numbers against the wall
yet none equal a way around
The scientist frantically searches for the answer
And there he'll stay until he figures out how to overcome

Because it's hard to see when you're up against
the straight edge of a sphere...

*Ben Pastore*

## Lady In White

For my sister Elizabeth Lena Hopkins
Born October 7, 1966-death December 7, 1994

The lady in white free spirit upon the earth,
an angel in the heavens.
    It come to pass that you are gone
And I am left behind.

Like a dove of white you have soared to the
heavens leaving behind a blue eyed child of thee.
A reminder of what was and shall never again be.

Look into those eyes you will see a child
Who doesn't wish to see.
For in those eyes the color and light in the same as thee.

The lady in white shall always be within
and part of thee, those who really see look into his eyes you
can see the spirit of the dove to never die,
for it is the power of a mothers love.

The lady in white left behind the greatest
gift of all life a youthful version of herself
within a blue eyed child of thee.

**Dorothy Genton**

## The Bright Blue Sea

There's a place I would like to be it's the
bright blue sea.
Shining bright about the land there's no place
I'd rather be then the bright blue sea.
Lots of people like it there shining bright everywhere.
The only place I'd like to be is the bright
blue sea.
It's like a second home to me.
It's the bright blue sea.
I would stay there anytime.
But maybe not at winter time.
The only place I'd like to be is the bright
blue sea.

**Jennifer Lee Newton**

## A Sensory Excursion

I behold with my eyes myriad sights,
    Bright sunshine, blue skies, and darkening nights.
A paean of music I hear with my ears,
    The cadence of a waterfall and the sadness of tears.
I touch with my hands a multitude of things,
    A lamed and frightened bird and the flutter of its wings.

Loud flame of color burnishing the autumn hill,
    Quiet gray of water flowing under the mill,
Pristine gleam of dust motes filtered through sunlight,
    Arrogantly quilted patterns in the world of sight.

Swift flight of laughter darting across the room,
    Low lilt of music piercing the silent gloom,
Soft rush of rain flung against the ground,
    Lovely echoing gradations in the world of sound.

Feathery feel of snow drifting across the land,
    Pulsating beat of breakers blending with the sand,
Clean cut of scalpel touched with tender healing,
    Many faceted mirrors in the world of feeling.

**Ginevra Ginn Tidman**

## Growth

Where does the pain, the pain of the soul come from?
Broken promises, broken trust, broken dreams,
broken mind and broken spirit.
Where does the love, the love of the soul come from?
Promising me, knowing me, liking me, nurturing me
and accepting me.
The pain of the soul was born in the past, lurks in the
present and threatens the future.
The love of the soul was nonexistent in the past, was
born in the present and is shining in the future.
As the pain fades, the love explodes in colors of beauty.
The beauty of a family protected, a family nurtured, a family
respected, a family promised and a family loved.
A family LOVED:  through me, by me, because of me.
The love of myself shall conquer all because of my
STRENGTH, KNOWLEDGE, COURAGE, TRUST and
WILLINGNESS TO SAY IT WILL BE!
The love we acquire through our own strength will be of
comfort to us everyday and our future shines with the
promises that we have made, to overcome it all.

**Jennifer L. Brewer**

## The Art of Dying

Whispering willows brush my hardened and weathered face, as she
brushes passionate delusions of permanence through mythical halos of
grace. Thanatos laugh with disdain as I refrain in the echoes of the
burdens of life's frame,limits set by the lines and angles painted by
the carnage of untouched dreams while childhood schemes pummel through
the arthritic pains of aging bones inflamed, so lay waste the buoys of
the ports of my wayfare on life's express of an endless sojourn, from
the trauma of birth to the trauma of life. I have come to my final
countenance, the mirror of an abyss, where the answers of life and
love, shower the stream of consciousness like empty carapaces, that
crack along the dried shore of Aegean ideals in Platonic coves of
surreal forms, an armour of inspiration that reaches to the sky
disappearing in the looming storm of fright, of the unknown tempest
that awaits the next plight, unfurl into the maelstrom without time
nor space, down the spiraling fractals like a nautilus unwound, or
will I fade into obscurity, marked by a word, a poem or book in the
dreamy eye of youth unscathed, of an inert catacomb in the earths
womb, not warm and comforting, but still in times expanse, no
different than a fly in an amber cell, without mind, or a hand to
hold. Is this existence but a shared dream? Have I drank of the
penchant of my desires, did I not walk upon the peak of flames of
passions afire?!? I dive in an act of faith, creator cease not the
stirring of my soul, like the winds unfurl your timeless folds!

**Daniel C. Rudofossi**

## Shoen

I slide out the door
    Buckle on my canteen
And check the lunch in my pack
    The miles slide by in silence
Each turn in the trail brings a new sight
    A moose with her calf
A buck sliding out of sight in the quakies
    A clear mountain lake
With its blanket pulled up to the shores
    The scream of a cougar
My snowshoes pack the snow beneath my feet
    Leaving an eerie trail behind me
And I feel God's own sweet breath upon my soul.

**Jon Klopfenstein**

## I Feel The Emotions Of Wind

Winds behavior I find
buggles my mind.
Often suggestive of a manic depressive.
An ill wind seems to do so good
slinging, blowing throwing
trees it cleans out doing spring cleaning
no doubt

Why doesn't she behave as she should?
With points good or points bad
I still love her a tad and
welcome her in my hair
whether witch or princess debonair.

*Clara Sandridge*

## Untitled

A child nor woman am I,
but a teenager full of dreams as high as the sky!
As I sit in class and learn of poems,
I secretly dream of building my life.
With mixed emotions, I sit and wonder of the coming events I
will encounter.
Will they be good or bad,
happy or sad?
Will I marry and give birth?
In seventy years will I still be here on earth?
Will I find out none of my dreams came true?
Will I shrivel up my dreams?
Will I prove the future wrong?
When I wake from my dream,
I'm confused and afraid,
angry and enchanted,
hurt and jealous of those who succeed.
A child nor a woman am I,
but a teenager full of dreams as high as the sky!

*Jennifer Potts*

## Titus 3:5

Not by works of righteousness which we have done,
but according to his mercy he saved us, by the washing
or regeneration and renewing of the Holy Ghost.

Not by the work of hands
It shall be by GOD's plans
Whether Good or Evil
It shall be by GOD's upheaval
From start to end
Christ shall be our friend
The spirit may come and go
But when the End shall come, only GOD will know

*Edward L. Jones Sr.*

## The Shower

Water that falls.
Bodies that move against the cold tiles.
Thirsty mouths drinking off the water that
runs down the bodies.
Refreshing.
Water that runs fast disappearing
somehow, somewhere.
Hands that hold. Mouths that kiss.
Ecstasy.
Two hearts beating fast
afraid of an end to come.

*Jairo M. Moises*

## Remembering My Dad

I remember a man with little to say,
  But at times, he could be funny.
He was tall and slender, with wavy hair,
  Dressed well, but not free with his money.
He stayed an independent man.
  Always doing for himself.
How sad it was to see the day,
  Things were done by someone else.
He went from man to little child,
  Someone I didn't know.
And then one day I got the call,
  Death had struck its painful blow.
Now, I look forward to the time,
  Of which the Bible speaks.
The resurrection of the dead,
  To a paradise earth, many seek.
There'll be no pain or sickness there,
  No reason to ever be sad.
My tears, will then be tears of joy,
  When once again, I can see my dad!

*Alice Pelletier*

## I'm Here

Some say my life is over, my time on earth is spent
But hear me when I tell you, I've not yet made a dent

My body may be tired, my legs no longer run
My spirit still climbs mountains, my mind still longs for fun

I have so much to offer, my years have taught me well
Just take the time to listen, I have a tale to tell

Give me but a moment, we'll both be richly blessed
And if the chance be given, I can pass the test

Like fertile ground unplanted, I need a willing hand
With your consideration, again I'll proudly stand

Don't pass me by so quickly, inside a fire still burns
Give me just your loving touch, for which my heart so yearns

I'll share with you the joys I've known, I have so much to give
God meant our lives to intertwine, in this world in which we live

Together we'll build bridges, between your years and mine
I'm waiting here with tools in hand, give me but a sign

*Cari Whitaker*

## Little Friend of Mind

There's a friend of mine; he's only nine
But he's already paying his dues.
His father left him when he was five.
He cried when he heard the news.

He's still in school but he follows no rules.
His anger is bringing him down.
His mama is drunk most of the time,
Hell, she doesn't even know he's around.

The child's body is so tender and frail;
His heart can be easily tattered.
The dreams that carried him, through the night
May very well be shattered.

You just may know of a girl or a boy
Who's living in such dismay.
Take a stand and extend your hand,
And with all your heart you must say:

Hey, little friend of mine, where do you belong?
I do believe I have some time, Why don't you come along.
Together we can share our dreams as we while away the day.
I'll try my best, you must do the rest, to ease the pain away.

*Dee J. Tyler*

## Who Am I?

I am a King
But I don't have a court or a diamond ring
I am a black man
Not to be judged by my dark tan
I am wise
In bad situations "still I rise"
I am debonair
Not just nappy hair and a frightening stare
I am NOT a statistic
I live for more than a punch or a kick
Or to make a buck on pure luck
Or to have a love span of a one night stand
Because I am a man
A BLACK man

    *Glenn Curtis Jr.*

## Progress

They say progress is necessary for the future of man
But I hate it
For it leaves in its wake
Strings of nothingness
And destroys that which
Will never again be part of my life.
And it relegates to past
And forces happy times of youth into memories
Into dreams
To be spoken of in quiet moments
Into times in gathered company
When all who witnessed it can say
"I remember."

    *Denise Granger*

## Dad

Dad is a person who you look up to
but I have to look beyond the sun and stars to see mine
The time we had together was so short
but oh so fine, oh so fine
A father and son go together like the good and bad, the stars and
moon, the sun and sky and all I ask myself is why oh why
It could have been just him and I
and I wouldn't have to ask why, oh why
Till the first time I said hello
till the last time I said good-bye,
I could still see his smile
that went with his blue, blue eyes
He'll be by my side forever and ever
for that I do know, I do know
But don't know why, oh why God took him away
I miss him everyday, everyday
in oh such a special way, oh such a special way

    *James P. Savino*

## Au Revoir

He was doing the dying,
But I was right beside him, death defying.
But death had his way,
Said to me: "I'll get you another day."
"Please take me," I cried, "now...too?"
"Nope, I'm not ready for you,
For you still have work to do."
  So, now, my life is a bottomless black hole,
And I am no longer whole.
I am bits and pieces of torn memories.
But, in my reveries, I put them all back together
And they are mine forever!
They renew my soul, and once again
—I am whole.

    *Gloria R. Barron*

## I'm So In Love With A Shadow Man, Is It You?

I would love to fall in love and take the chance.
But I only see a glimpse of his romance.
He catches me when I am unaware.
He's practically invisible, but I feel him there.
Beside me I feel his love only at a glance.
Will he ever find me?
He's always hiding beside me.

And though whenever he's there,
We're hiding in the dark of the night.
We're shy and yet we know that since we've met
That it is love, in a way it's love at first sight.
But who is he is it you?

Now he came to me in the night.
And I worship him in the moonlight. He touches me so deeply.
He says he'll always be in love with me he's the only one form.
And I feel his warmth.
And we dream our dreams,
When we are sleeping.
I'm so in love with a shadow man. Is it you? Is it you?

    *Eileen Bonnie*

## Bird on a Limb

I'm a little bird out on a limb,
But I'm praising God and singing to Him.
My feathers are ragged, my wing is torn,
For during the night there was a terrible storm.

Now the storms may descend and shake my tree,
But I have a God who watches over me.
He clothes the lilies and flowers in the fields,
He knows each pain and heartache I feel.

But God gives me hope when I feel low.
He watches over me on the dark valley slopes.
When I need Him most, He is always there,
To see me through storms of dark despair.

I'm a little bird out on a limb,
But I'm praising God and thanking Him,
For He feathers my heart with peace and love,
When I accepted His Son from heaven above.

    *Julia A. Haun*

## Things Money Cannot Buy

We all work hard for money earning all we can.
But it usually shows the foolishness of man.
As we go through life and the years go flying by
We learn as we go just what money cannot buy.

You cannot buy daylight when night is flying by.
You cannot buy moonbeams with black clouds in the sky.
You cannot buy youth when your life is nearly gone.
You cannot buy happiness with money alone.

You cannot buy contentment though you may try.
You cannot buy sight when you're blind in the eyes.
You cannot buy beauty that we see every day.
Your filthy lucre only gets in your way.

You cannot buy sunshine or rain to make crops grow.
You cannot make companions of folks you do not know.
With silver or gold no matter how hard you try
I've listed a few things that money cannot buy.

We all hope for heaven when it's our time to die
But that is one place our money cannot buy.

    *Joe Harrison*

## Autumn Soul

Occasionally, a warmer day
But mostly, a cold brisk wind
Blows restlessly, carelessly
Through my Autumn Soul

Causing a shiver to my Spirit
Which endures, until the changing colors
Of love releases it
To a warmer day

Lately, winter comes early
And a thick frost forms
Chilling my bones
Shocking my mind with icy bitterness

Please God, no more snow...
Send a warmer day
I haven't felt the sun
In such a long time

*Cheryl Lynn*

## Untitled

From youth we are taught that man is king
but not just giving orders will this role bring
the physical chores, now the lawn, paint the house
the lads are given the test are you a man or a mouse
a bully has chosen your sister as prey
Now stand up and defend here even if everyday
High School and dating, peer pressure and all
Drugs, gangs and loose women, your taught resist and stand tall
Soon you are working, getting married in love,
Mortgage, insurance, investments to take care of
Your wife you must cherish, bring her joy, happiness
Console her of troubles, be her strength show no weakness
To hard to cry, no sad songs to sing
Please never say it's easy being a king

*John Castro*

## Apparition?

Out of the past you came ... silently;
But, oh, that look of radiant love
Emblazoned the room with such a glow
    of brilliance, that I saw you
Standing there, so close, and yet so far...
How, then were you able to move my soul?
And compel me to return to you
    that same look of love that I've withheld so long?
It's because my love, time cannot erase
    the oneness that we became
    so very long ago.
The look was enough;
No words, no tears are necessary,
    ever, for us.
The nod, the smile and the twinkle;
    say it all; wherever we are.

*Gerri O'Brient Gregory*

## Untitled

Dear God,

    Forgive an angry soul for hoping to find love within a
heart of stone and trust in mankind.  Priorities of mankind
bring hopelessness to part from guiltful minds and broken
hearts.  Conceit destroys the feelings.  The hateful heart has
searched to find.  Selfishness and greed can kill when an
angry hand destroys the mind.  There can be found peace
only in nature not in the heart of man.  There in lies only
ruination from a hateful hand...!

*Hazel Froemming*

## Springtime's Embers

A sunrise sees the flowers grow,
but only in God's time we'll know.
If springtime's embers once full aglow,
are to be rekindled but again.

A rushing river or mighty sea,
With a wave of God's hand they could cease to be.
And what of my prayers and His promise to me?
"I'll rekindle then but again."

But the serpent's whispered lies received,
Twist the facts that we perceive.
And makes his promise hard for us to believe,
that they could be rekindled but again.

Rather lean thee on the Rock my dear,
shunning the lies whispered in your ear.
And find God's love will make it clear.
He can rekindle it but again.

So when springtime's embers again burn bright,
forget not who made it right.
For only God's grace has the might,
to rekindle our sweet love but again.

*Bruce C. Cameron*

## Zellie Mae

She's my neighbor who lives in the white house over that way.
But she'd rather live on a farm having to bale hay!

She's so jolly, hard working and kind.
I really don't know how she finds so much time.
So busy tending to her flowers, bushes and vines.

But the large pumpkin patch is best of all!
It creeps over the back doorstep, so watch that you don't fall.

Then it's cleaning her pool, saying, "come over for a swim."
Oh, where's my bathing suit—so I can jump right in.

Off she goes taking son to school
In her Bronco transportation tool.
Always a wave and a smile
Only wishing it was a trotting horse going 55 mile.

Then there's more time for care and feeding of her many pets.
Gee, she'd make a darn good Vet!
But, being my greatest friend is really what she does the best.

We share many interests, laughs and cries,
Even recipes on baking different pies.

Her enjoyable company brightens many a day.
And no one else in the neighborhood could take the place of our
    Zellie Mae!

*Joann Knapp*

## Battle Cry

The battle has yet to be won
But those who have given their life for this country
May disagree, that the battle is won and all is not lost
For to give up one's life in war for all others to go free
Is the greatest American heritage
One by one they sleep in the grave, so the red white and blue
May fly freely in the wind
And we Americans can have honor and dignity within
They are gunned down and blown away, many injured beyond
Recognition, but still they sacrifice for you and me
That we may go on living in the land of opportunity
Old glory is still here today
And forever will be as long as others are willing to lay down
Their lives for freedom and liberty

*Carolyn S. Andrew*

## I Must Be

I'd searched in vain for the book of pain that surely must be penned,
But soon I'd see that I must be the means unto its end.

To write for those with burdened souls unsure of their tomorrows,
To show they're not alone in thought, alone in counted sorrows.

I am like the open wound, my blood flows through my pen.
As many times my life seems ruined, I'll ink the page again.

So now I see that I must be the rhyme in your unreason,
A poetic sea of agony, where lonely souls are freezing.

I am like a part of you, I know your soul is crying,
I can touch the heart of you and feel your fear of dying.

Your reality is mine, it bears a crushing weight,
You fear the dreaded box of pine that guarantees your fate.

So you will read this poetry and you can rest assured,
You're not the only one that's lonely in the pain that you've
endured.

*Jayce Robinson*

## Self Fulfilling Prophecy

I wanted to write you a poem my dear.
But the more I thought about it, I feared
that I could never assemble my words
in the correct fashion and you'd be bored.

I started a poem with "Roses are red,"
but it was winter and the roses were dead.
So I tried again on another day
with, "How do I love thee? Let me count the ways,"
but I couldn't think of all the numbers
and needed them all to give my answer.

I thought about becoming a robber
to steal your heart with words of another.
But then I realized it wouldn't be me
and you would find out eventually.

I sat down with a blank sheet of paper.
I hate to tell you I failed my lover,
but the pen would not translate my feelings.
I am the poem I wrote to you called, "Nothing."

*Jason Eric Berthiaume*

## Life, Love, and Not Much Happiness

You used to hate the country, you used to think it was dumb,
but then you learned to love it with a snap of your finger and thumb.
Then all of the sudden you moved, and left everything you loved
behind, to where you think you may never have again what you had
to leave behind.
You left your best friend Susie, and also your loving Dad.
You left your cats, your dogs, your horses, and last but not least
your house.
You now live with only your mother and sisters, which you love with
all of your heart, but every night you lay wishing that you hugged and
kissed your Dad goodnight.
You used to see him every day, but now maybe once a month.
Sometimes he may be gone or working till who knows when, and
he may never be thinking about when he'll see you again, but at least
you have your Mom and sisters that when you need them they'll be right
there, but then again you wish your Dad would just magically appear.

*Jessie D. Antisdel*

## No Bike

Dad had a bike for Pat, Joe and Clay,
but there was no bike for me.

I thought of nothingsville and went out
back under a large oak tree.

I thought why, why, why, and that word kept
haunting me.

Dad hollered that I would get mine in due
time, and to tough it up, act like a man!

Sure Dad, whatever—but deep down inside I
really didn't understand.

Bikes, bikes, bikes, I tried other ideas
but I could think of only one thing.

As I watched my brother's bike come together,
I walked the yard and settled on a swing.

I flew back and forth and felt just like a
kite, and a voice sung softly inside.

"I'm the only one in the whole world without a
BIKE."

*James R. See*

## Angela Marie

Dear Lord I never ask for much, and nothing never seem's to go my way.
But this is one time I'm asking you Lord, will you just listen to
    what I have to say?
Heavenly Father I love her, and I don't know what to do.
I want what's best for Angela, that's why Lord I'm turning to you.
I guess it's best this way, the way it has to be done?
Oh how I'll never forget her, Angela Marie my little one.
Watch over her Lord, cause that's something I won't be able to do.
Place her in a home of love, and where she's cared for too.
I guess I could never give her, the kind of life a child should have.
This way she'll have everything, a home, love, and even a Dad.
Now she's gone from me, my little girl I'll never know.
But in my heart she'll always be, oh how I love her so.

*Barbara Ann Voiles (Greene)*

## My Mother's Daughter

I have my mother's eyes,
   but we do not always see things in the same way.

I have my mother's voice,
   but we do not always speak the same language.

I have my mother's laugh,
   but we do not always find humor in the same things.

I have my mother's ears,
   but we do not always hear the same sounds.

I have my mother's quiet gentleness,
   but we do not always find comfort in the same things.

I have my mother's strength,
   but we do not always draw strength from the same things.

I have my mother's patience,
   but we do not always find reserve in the same place.

I have my mother's love and she has mine!
   I AM MY MOTHER'S DAUGHTER.

*Cheryl Lea Todd*

## Loving Request

Should I become not what I am or was to you,
    but what I might then appear to be,
I would ask of you to look past or deep beyond
    my changed mask,
and see me as what you best remember me;
    not for my sake, but for whatever good you are
in God's eyes because of me.

**Don Bodine**

## Our Country

What is happening in this country is really a shame
But who is at fault, who is to blame
There are those people who are honest and good
Some have had to put up with more than they should
Parents abusing and killing their kids
Loved babies who died of what is called Sids
Teenage pregnancies each and everyday
The poor children suffer, they're the ones who pay
There is over crowding in the prisons and jails
Drug dealers who have no problem posting their bails
A bombing of the building where so many died
All the people who watched and oh, how we cried
We must stop the violence, the killing and shove
What this country needs is to show more love
Everyone should be feeling happy, not feeling sad
I wish for there to be only good and to stop the bad.

**Janice J. Gitschier**

## Mom And Dad

Mom and Dad, you were suppose to drive me to school in the morning
    But you didn't.
Mom and Dad, you were suppose to feed me
    But you didn't.
Mom and Dad, you were suppose to shelter me
    But you didn't.
Mom and Dad, you were suppose to cloth me
    But you didn't.
Mom and Dad, you were suppose to kiss my bruises when I fell
    But you didn't.
Mom and Dad, you were suppose to tuck me in at night
    But you didn't.
Mom and Dad, you were suppose to read to me at night
    But you didn't.
Mom and Dad, you were suppose to talk to my teacher to see if I was
talkative or bad
    But you didn't.
All these things you were suppose to do,
    But you didn't Mom and Dad.

**Ashley Jenkins**

## Lost Love

It was in your arms,
But you gave it up,
And you hate to admit it,
But you wish you had it all back,
All the lovely candlelight dinners,
The walks in the park,
Going to the movies,
But the part I miss most is just talking,
Now it's not going to happen ever again,
Because you lost the wonderful you,
And I'll never forget you,
You know I'll never find a love as wonderful as you.

**Jennifer Hill**

## Despair

I open my heart and come to you
But your still shoving my face in the things I didn't do,
For over six years I have been by your side
Knowing you would never marry me yet closing my eyes and remaining
    blind,
Is this love is this how it is suppose to be
Everything comes first except for me,
I just got off the phone with you
And I'm hurting so bad I think my heart just broke in two,
Whatever I do whatever I say
In your eyes I never do it the right way,
My Grandma has cancer and her life is coming to an end
Why is it so foolish to expect you to understand and be my friend,
Why is it so crazy for me to say
I need you to support me and help me make it through another day,
You say you love me and claim you care
But I need you physically to be there,
So one more night alone I look into the sky
Wishing upon a star and trying not to cry,
Finding my own strength to make it through another day
Making excuses to myself for the things you didn't do or say.

**Joanne M. Jones**

## Monuments

Building monuments around us
Buying many splendid things
Caring little what's inside us
Or what the next life brings

What do we show our maker
When it's time to call it a day
Are we left with any substance
When they carry our body away

Our monuments should be eternal
Nothing we can buy
Our best deeds and energies
Expended for the other guy

**Frank E. McGinity**

## Looking Back From Dying

Blissful last gasps are usually preceded
by deep sighs, heavy breathing,
while, interrupting that deadly sense
of Sysiphusean futility,
we strive for a resurrection of time and truth
to discover life's meaning —
as if there were that exactly.

And so a fragile idea — sight, sound, shape —
is captured passionately
to be composed into a mind-lit symphony
of gentle whisperings
or sculpted with an all-consuming caring touch
into "a thing of beauty"
a psychic diamond, shimmering,
displayed under a no-longer godless moon
for the soul's searching.

**Elizabeth Lansing Holmes**

## Music

I hear music in a gently falling raindrop.
I see music in a rainbow overflowing with colors.
I feel music in a hug with a friend.
I taste music in a cup of lemonade on a boiling day.
I smell music in a shady pine forest.
I sense music all around me.
Do you?

**Jenny Paget**

## A Soldier's Lot

Though I deserve death, hell, and the grave,
By His grace and Son, I shall be saved.

A soldier's lot is no excuse
To live a life of coarse abuse.

God has spared me once again,
Despite this yoke of mortal sin.

What a wonderful thing to serve the king;
You know His praises I will sing.

I have been kept safe in His hand
While serving off in a foreign land.

Death and famine lay all around;
The suffering of man did in fact abound.

The children here knew no happy sounds,
But knew too well the burst of mortar rounds.

Why then is it me, I thought,
My soul to save that He has fought?

What have I done to merit this
While others suffer in this abyss?

Though I deserve death, hell, and the grave,
By His grace and Son, I shall be saved.

**Glenn L. Husted III**


## The Breath Of My Soul

She, the breath of my soul,
by the same powers,
to me, borne
that shed the gleam of a morning dew,
that shed the hue of a mount, purple and rose,
that shed my smile, gladdened by the sun, warm and bright.

She, the breath of my soul,
grants powers, omnipotent,
to me, unaware
to share a moment, by her presence, joyful and loving,
to share a decision, by her beliefs, made confident and sure,
to share a lifetime, by her smile, buoyant and sparkling.

She, the breath of my soul,
with powers, gentle,
to me, unites
to know a butterfly, captured by a child, yet unborn,
to know a couple, remembering a life, yet unlived,
to know each other's heart, with passion and hope, shared.

**Gary J. Tromp**


## Untitled

On a Monday dark and dreary while I thought teary,
came a tapping almost rapping at my classroom door,
'tis a jerk and nothing more.
Again that hour came a tapping, tapping at my classroom door,
to the door I ran, and nothing more.
With the door unfolding came a look at this usual wisdom,
empty halls and nothing more.
Still I wondered what would lie beyond the door,
maybe some forgotten lore.
Then came a ringing, a sweet ringing of bells of a new beginning,
'tis not my problem any more, off to class forevermore.

**Jeff Donofrio**


## Can You?

Can you tickle a pickle for a nickel?
Can you kiss a lime for a dime?
Can you squeeze a sneeze or sit on a flea's knees?
Can you cool your tea with the wing of a bee?
Can you share a pear with a hunger bear?
Can you bake a cake for your favorite snake?
Can you buy a hat for a poor alley cat?
Can you watch a fat frog fall on a log?
Can you find a bug on your rug and give it a hug?
Can you make sure it's dark to bark at a shark?

**John Lawler**


## Flashback In My Mind

Seeing people, or doing thing's,
Cannot erase you, and love in all it's passion.
A flash soon brings your face in view,
I try to blink my eye's, hard to block the vision.
The fire keeps burning from within,
Then many sees us embrace, with a love divine.
Oh mind, please forget thing's of past,
To be so unkind, to send flashback in my mind.

If only I could get over you,
The memories wouldn't haunt my mind.
Maybe I would be free to love again,
If vision's could be left behind.

The ecstasy of wanting you,
To touch and feel your lips on mine, softly  blending.
Of only this could all be dreams,
To awaken dreams fade, but flashback no ending.
To lose love means an aching heart,
Cupid dart turned out instead, a stab of no bind.
Oh mind please forget things of past,
To be so unkind, to send flashback in my mind.

**Beverly J. Hutton**


## The Persimmon Tree

When the persimmon's mellow sweetness permeates into my tongue,
Capillary vessels carry my mind back to Japan's cozy childhood:
  An aged giant persimmon tree thickly covered with foliage
  Hugged a black tile roof house I was born under the shadow.
  While my mother retailed tobaccos, charcoals, stick incenses,
  My father commuted on foot to a mountain school for teaching.

When the persimmon's greenish tannin benumbs over my tongue,
Alert signal drives me to indulge in the hard old days pathos:
  Opposite edge of the branches leaned against a thatched roof
  Where a strolling vaudevillian family stayed for a festival.
  While a wretched husband and wife team entertained people,
  A thin girl in my age of the couple played hopscotch with me.

When the persimmon's red fruits are spotted in the video screen,
A sentimental scenery crosses vividly throughout my meditation:
  Brittle sprigs spread in the sky hung juicy lanterns sparsely
  Among the survived orange leaves reflected on the setting sun.
  While all silhouettes were stretched eastward in late fall,
  Ravens flew to their nests as temples' bells tolled in the dusk.

**Esaku Kondo**


## Corner Of My Eye

Side glances see all.
But to the mind a swirling blur.
That holds colors and shapes.
In a restless turmoil of half understood events.
Compressed into incomprehensibility.
And forgotten.
As if it had never occurred.

**Bradley S. Tice**

## The Rosebud

*(In dedication to my friend, Lisa G. Martge, and to
her two precious daughters, Katherine and Rebecca.)*

The precious rosebud
Carefully dusted with tears
Lies upon the grave
Knowing it will never bloom
Yet understands the sorrow

Words never spoken
Carefully carved in his heart
Feelings never felt
Denials of emotion
Killed all but the strongest love

A silent knowledge
He knows, yet frustration builds
Realization
The key to all happiness
He knows all but the answer

Moist tears of sorrow
Furrowing down the petals
From the sweet rosebud
On his grave of emotions
Never to bloom in his heart.

*Angela M. Olsen*

## No Doubt!

No doubt!  No, not a shadow of a doubt!  That every shadow ever
cast, is anything more than, a silhouette.  No doubt!  That every
silhouette filled, is anything less than, a shadow.  Ancient
are the shadows in the night, silhouettes they are, to star-like
eyes of mine.  I am as if a shadow, filled in a silhouette's
form, seeking only the company of a warm fiery candle, to
announce my cool and shady ways.  No doubt!  No, not a silhouette
of a doubt, that every reflection ever cast, is anything more
than, a silhouette.  No doubt!  That every silhouette filled,
is anything less than, a shadow or mirrored reflection.  I am
as if a shadow, filled in a silhouette's form, seeking only
the company of a warm glowing candle, and a mirror, please,
to announce and reflect my many ways.  No doubt!  No, not a
reflection of a doubt!  That every shadow ever cast, is anything
more than, a silhouette.  No doubt!  That every silhouette filled,
is anything less than, a reflection.  I am as if only a dark
and lonely image, created to stand upon a lighted stage, or
sit and mingle with an audience, there, in the crown of darkness.
No doubt!

*Jamal S. Jailawi*

## Daddy's Job

A daddy is a special job, that is sometimes over looked.
Cause when you need to talk to dad, he is simply never booked.

He's always there when you need to talk or need to be held tight.
He tucks you in with a teasing kiss and dims the bedroom light.
He always makes you feel extra special, each and every day,
And calls to say he misses you when he has to be away.
He welcomes all your friends, who think that he is really funny.
He works hard to save for college, which takes a lot of money.
When he worries someday you won't need him, give it all you've got,
And remind him that you'll always love him more than just a lot!

*Amanda Yoshida*

## Salem Witchcraft Trials

Witches are thought of as black not white,
Causing mischief and mayhem, flying at night.
I, of course, know these things are not true,
The Salem witchcraft trials were held in 1692.

19 men and women were convicted and hanged,
While children cried and Samuel Parris sang.
He lead the witch hunt in Massachusetts Bay
Where now Danvers stands today.

Suspicions arose and convictions came;
Parris had innocent people burned and hanged.
The ignorant farmers followed his plan,
Like a pack of wolves after a lamb.

For over a year they would torture and kill
The people who opposed Parris's will.
Until many menacing ministers answered the cries
Of the incarcerated villagers waiting to die.

Witches are thought of as black not white,
Causing mischief and mayhem, flying at night.
I, of course, know these things are not true,
If you lived at that time, it could have been you!

*Alicia Legato*

## Divine Province

The median of life's accomplishments evokes
    changes good and bad.
A cruel glimpse of fate, twice turned, may leave
    you feeling sad.
Look above to judge yourself,
    lifework in clear perspective.
Alteration of mirrored memoirs
    may deem you resurrected.
In absence of metamorphosis,
    regrets are all you yield.
Kneel to divine province, thus,
    to reap your life span's field.
Knowledge sought, directions clear,
    they're all divulged to you.
Don't turn from grace or guidance,
    these two will steer you through.

*Candace Morimoto*

## "The Spirit Of America"

The spirit of America in all its people is found. . .
    Cherished within the minds and hearts of the young and the old,
Nourished by those in whom vitality and strength abound. . .
    Cared for by men and women who will not see it grow cold.

If this to skeptics may seem to be just a little strange,
    One has only to reflect on the beauty of this land. . .
And to ponder how so many races can still arrange
    To find enough room in their souls to love and understand.

This great land of ours has overcome challenges before. . .
    This is a country in which the weak and the strong
Find common ground. . . on what used to be a forbidding shore;
    No matter what their station now may be. . . here they belong.

There is no gain to be made in dividing one from all;
    There is no need to seek or wish the death of unity. . .
When there is still found such a strong response to freedom's call
    In the minds of all our people in love with liberty.

Take a look about you, and see that you are surrounded
    By every race under the sun. . . those who now are free.
Let all put to rest the many fears that are unfounded. . .
    For how can a nation once united. . . lose it's liberty?

*Bob Wangler*

## America 1995

Garbage strewn along the road,
Children on corners barely clothed.
Hatred, addiction, grieving moms,
Next door neighbors making bombs.
High rise buildings, caviar,
Corporate parties, pools and spas.
A hand reaching out to another with hope.
A desperate young woman at the end of a rope.
A hungry young man with a gun in his hand,
Took away "Freedom" from all in the land.
Computers, car phones, mansions and riches,
Unfortunate people living under bridges.
Technology taking us places unknown.
No cure for Insanity, AIDS, Foster Homes.
Natural disasters, war, fear in our eyes.
Who's telling the truth? Who's telling us lies?
Battered women, shelters, child support and abuse,
Over crowded prisons; Satan's on the loose.
People gathered together to pray,
Faithful to their God, there will be a judgment day.

*Brenda Farmer*

## A National Cemetery

Pure squares of stone before each gentle mound,
Cold white hands proudly raised above the ground,
Joined in silent chorus, ranks by Pluto caught
At attention on the green echoing— "we fought!"

General Johnson lying beside Private Town,
Their heads boast the same, neat marble crown.
The five-star man was an order-caller—
His tombstone stands a half-inch taller.

Misty morning, sunny noons, dusky eves,
Pallbearers trample through the crackly leaves—
Transporting sadness into infinity,
Hiding "these honored dead" beneath the lee.

Until the tardy rain threads by in lower gear,
Perhaps a widow straggles by during the year,
Grass sea of non-existence, boxes of steel—
Survive in tidy rows the boredom of the hill.

*Janie Watts Spataro*

## Apartheid

Indians to front!
Colored's to the left!
Blacks to the rear!
White police scream "separation, segregation".
Burning fear in the eyes of the oppressed.
Lingering disgust in the mind of the oppressors.

Hunger in the stomach,
Hunger in the mind,
Hunger in the soul.
Starved of life and dignity, retreating to within.
Hunger pangs in the lives of the depressed.
Bloated stomachs over the belts of the depressors.

Wonder in a child,
Sadness in an adult,
Hopelessness in the old.
Thoughts and feelings hidden under black smiling masks.
"Yes baas" from the suppressed.
"Lazy Kaffir!" from the suppressors.

The cycle continues, life after life and mind after mind.
Time and again cast into the white hole of repression, until death.

*Casie Schmidt*

## Alone

All of your life you pray for someone to
come along and take away the heartache.
The longer you wait, the stronger the
loneliness and emptiness becomes.
You believe no one can understand the
pain and anger that you have buried
inside of yourself.
One day, the feelings begin to escape.
You try with all of your strength to keep
them buried, they can not be stopped.
You find yourself believing no one will
be there to help you sort through the
feelings and confusion you endure.
As every minute goes by, you find it
getting harder and harder to hold on to
the dream of being free of loneliness.
When your dream of freedom begins to
fade, the strength you need appears.
Do not give up on your dreams of freedom,
some day it will come true.

*Adrianne Mielnik Gammon*

## Heart Tears

The tears I shed
Come from my heart
The words I speak
Are only part
Of the pain that comes from within my soul
The songs I sing
Will make me whole.

*Juanita Marble*

## Gisela

In magic summer
    comes August with its heaviness;
    and on a certain night
    Gisela comes to dance beneath the stars.
Two hundred years are in the face that tilts heavenward;
    the smooth bronze cheeks are wet with tears.
    Thousands of miles the feet have trod
    that now glide softly on the carpet of moon flowers.
Such hidden pain in the hands
    whose wrists like willow fronds
    bend exquisitely
    in the midnight breeze.
She twirls and the gossamer gown
    caresses her body like angel's wings.
    Gisela, spirit of the earth.
    Gisela, my mentor, my love.
And with the fading of the starlight there remains
    only a shimmer in the glen where she once was;
    a thousand tiny raindrops suspended in the air,
    and the fragrance of trampled flowers.

*Dale D. Wideman*

## Winter

The crashing ocean comes to a freeze
Cold winds left behind the gentle breeze
Gone now are the colorful leaves
Standing bare are the lonely trees
The wind cries a sad song
A blanket of snow covers the ground
The scent of pine carries along
People are happy, like the joyful songs they sing
They know that after every winter, there's always spring

*Cheryl Bennett*

## Untitled

And in the package of life it seems,
Comes your wants, your truths, and dreams,
The basis of the struggle,
Is to have a peaceful mind,
No worries of the future
No worries of any kind,
But this is the paradox,
This package isn't real,
What is, is now and how you feel,
The values of society
The conflict to conform,
The questioning of beliefs,
Of yours and of the "norm,"
Can never bring you fulfillment
Of you and who you are,
Those beliefs only create,
A common human scar,
Allow yourself the freedom,
To think the thoughts you do,
Ultimately, it all relates to you.

*Chelsea Tait*

## Alone in a Crowd

Traffic lights and traffic lights with cars passing by,
Concrete below, concrete beside-alas the smothered sky.
Shimmering heat rising up, foul smells, passing sighs,
Bright clothes, dull clothes, raggy clothes, rich clothes.
Young and old striding by-two by two, one by one; heads
Back and forth, up and down, to and fro, across and back.
Loud talking, soft talking, mumbling and whispers,
Carbon monoxide, undigested foul-smelling fuel abound; "Mr
Do you have the time?"-nay, never an answer around-err
Am I running late or early - O where is the silent country.
Cafe's smells, hot dog stands, horns, shouts-still cars passing.
People alone, people bunched or huddled at non-descripts-standing.
Waiving, gesturing, dancing-some singing at bus stops waiting.
Screeches, thumps-sirens echoing through the boulevards.
Bumping, pushing, pressing, hands help out from life's too hard.
Do I see anyone, does anyone see me walking around-
Haplessly approaching my destiny up ahead amid mingled sounds;
Soon to reach my destination-my perch for the day,
And soon enough I will be traversing the other way,
With traffic lights, and traffic lights, and cars...

*Bill Standridge*

## Aphrodite's Breath

Under the hard, dusty lamplight
corporate pragmatism drones in front of me now.
I soften the heavy blows with purple lids.
My journeys, so moist, distant in those eyes,
eyes of antiquity and yellowed marble tombs.
Roundmoon-lightspill once occupied my blue limbs
in that ancient land of Aphrodite and her baths.
After all, the goddess shares her secrets with those
who venture into silver waters at the dawn,
and the foamy warmth becomes yet another womb
from which a daughter, a lover is born.
At the edge, I elevated my head to see the singer's
melancholy dance on the black sand
those rugged men who dream of ships - they dance for her:
The goddess of the land; not to please her
but for her sake, ancient and frail as she is
crumbling like the rotted stones of Pericles in that other city.
Yet, withstanding the wind from the North,
the goddess whispers through the trees, "I Live."
Her breath, salty and warm, fingers my eyes and fills them now.

*Joanna Koutsis*

## Life's Journey

Darkness and warmth and moisture surrounds
Contentment and a sense of security abounds

Suddenly! Light and sounds invade my ears and eyes
And the joy of those around, overshadow my cries

I see and smell and taste and touch
And snuggle to my mother, whom I love so much

I have begun this journey, this life of mine
To its challenges and joys and sorrows, I resign

So much to learn and do, so many things to accomplish,
To succeed with all, and fail with none, is what I wish

At every crossroad a decision must be made
So I trust in the foundation that my mentors have laid

My productive years are met with much determination,
To be the best I can for my family, church and nation

But the time will come when my declining years,
Will give me cause to recollect my joys and my tears

Then when my days I've lived are done,
To old age or illness, I will finally succumb

The sounds and feelings and light begin to fade,
And by family and friends, to rest, I'm laid

*Glenn L. Debban*

## The Trunk in the Attic

The trunk in the attic is covered with dust, it's hinges are orange, corroded with rust.
But the memories inside still live as of old in the stories that dear Grandmother told.

There's an old button hook that's tarnished and black, a picture of Grandpa and the glass has a crack.
An old cloth purse that smells musty with mold, someone's ringlets wrapped in a paper of gold.

I see a black Bible whose pages are worn, a wedding dress that's yellowed and torn.
A tiny glass doll that was treasured and kept and a diary that's blurred from tears that were wept.

Two little gray mittens tucked neatly away - moth holes in the fingers and worn from play;
Knitted for some little boy in the past and kept through the years so the memories would last.

There's the little worn shoes of a dear little heart that trudged slowly behind a push hand cart.
I've been told they took turns carrying the child, till one day a small grave was left in the wild.

Yes, the trunk in the attic is old and antique, it calls to me often, and I must go peek
At the memories inside, still alive as of old, in the stories that dear Grandmother told.

*Elizabeth E. Stout*

## A Feeling Of Spring

There's a time every year when new life is born.
It comes after winter when we're weathered and worn.
It comes with sunshine and long drenching showers.
It comes with warm weather and beautiful flowers.
The birds and bumblebees float on the breeze,
Wind rustles the blossoms just bloomed in the trees.
A feeling only God and nature can bring—
A feeling and season that people call Spring.

*Jason Unterbrunner*

## Today and Today

Life to-day is a frivolous thing, and yet, and yet -
Could there be hope for those who dally in life;
Who soar on, on - on, with very few
Fruits exchange for ones strife.

Yet, on and on - like birds with-out wings,
We'll destroy the beautiful; the monster create -
Could it be that I too am one of these things?

We've been molded and tempered; our minds
Destroyed, no time to grasp, take hold of
The beauty of life - no! no! no! on ever
Onward with our terrible strife.

To be like a child would be an asset indeed,
Many have pleaded this call, but who I ask,
Who, can pull up from this downward fall?
So we'll continue our plunge down whoredom's
Hall - so is the way of today, and today,
And today.

*James P. Rose*

## Six Cowboys in the Night

One lonely fall night, there sat six
cowboys all dressed in black.
They were all dingy and dirty,
They had been up all day, and all that night,
The cowboy's names were Lucas, Larry,
Jack, Randy, Handy and Pat.
They looked like they had climbed a chimney, which made them sootier
and black.
The moon was full that particular night.
All you could hear were their horses,
hoofing and wolves hollering
The cowboys seem to be brave, until
bats and eagles started soaring their camp.
The wind was so strong it blew out their lamp.
From their long journey, they became hungry and tired.
So they began to huddle around the fire.
At long last the night had come to an end.
They started singing one of those cowboy hymns

*Jackie Savage*

## Mind of War

Fears and shadows cast the walls
Cracked and broken, yet to fall
The missiles sieged throughout the war
The tears, the tears
Brought tears no more

In search of a soul
That abolished such law
Rebellion, rebellion
I need you no more
Your destruction awaits me, at the door

Unwelcomed by night, the demon came
No entrance here, in Jesus' name
The castle walls have been reclaimed
And truth has mastered your foolish game

So the fallen kingdoms with their chains
Sought out other lands to claim
And I knelt in prayer for all the world
The lost, the weary, the traumatized
And whispered, "Let Freedom Reign"

*Elizabeth Marx Giovelli*

## Raping of the Environment

In the beginning, I was a wondrous breath of infinite purity
Cradled by mother in her earthly arms ever so lovingly
Resting on her breast, I suckled the clean waters of the rivers, and seas
Basking in the warm sun, and playing in the luscious fields

It was such a beauteous sight then to behold
The environment ever clean and safe a treasure untold
The birds, the trees, the animals blossomed with desire
And man happy, as he too lived free of mire

Then one day disaster struck, as man ambitiously proposed
He wanted progress, and dramatically changed natures clothes
He made his bombs, his engines and his chemicals with such delight
Polluted the air with his explosions, and dumped his wasted on any sight

Now I am broken hearted, stripped forever of my dignity
Defiled, unclean, quivering in the dust, and smoke of iniquity
No longer can I see the greenery or drink the waters full of impurity
The smokes have drowned my soul, and left me naked mercilessly

Slowly I am dying amidst the abyss of endless fear.
The pollution, the oil slicks, the bulldozing of the mountains
I cannot bear
Help! Help! I cry please stop the raping of the environment so savagely
I am smothering in despair and cannot breathe, will someone have pity

*Joan Manzano*

## Winter Run

Out from Maple Street I discovered the
crisp wintertime I ran through the sullen
streets I was a bird screaming in the
night I was a freight train unstoppable I
Flew The night was a part of me the stinging
cold air in my lungs the snow in
my hair my eyes went dry as I ran on
smashing the snow into dirty tainted
footprints I ducked under the frosty white
bush past the skeleton trees my feet bruised
the pale innocence of the snow but I would
not stop I could not stop I was
a bird screaming in the night I was a
freight train unstoppable and I was the
burning cold of the winter night
flying through the streets

*Christina Bendel*

## The Dance of the Universe

Long ago when time was new, the black, sheer
Curtain of night lifts, as the Master Choreographer
Begins the beat.

The stars are klieg lights revealing dust dancing in
Their beams. Hasty comets rush ahead, streaking, cuing
The slow, large lumbering planets, that now begin to move.

The moon: ebbs, waxes, wanes and pulls the tide to find
Its footsteps, and responds in highs and lows.

Each planet spins to the rhythm: small ones
Hurry in their path to keep cadence.

The sun heats: the wind rustles, howls and roars over
The loud, clumsy steps of booming, bashing, banging thunder.

Mountains heave, jerk, pulsate.
Rivers pulse, quiver, surge.

Man steps humbly on the cosmic stage, and is forever awed
By this divine, graceful dance.

Reverently, he knows his part is
To applaud.

*Jackie Brown*

## A Letter to Daddy

Dear Daddy,
Daddy don't you love me?  Can you hear your child say?
Daddy don't you love me?  Why did you go away?
Was it really that important, to find another bride?
To give those up, who loves you most, because of selfish pride?
Mommy worked so awfully hard, to raise me as she did,
Scrubbing floors, washing clothes, since I was a little kid.
To me, she was both mother, and father, because you weren't at home.
No one could have done a better job, then she did all alone.
While Mommy went out, to work each day, with me Grandma took care.
Outside of Mom, there was Grandma's love, 'twas all I had to share.
For you weren't here, to show that love, as a Daddy should.
I guess today, would be a little late, even if you could.
Because of you both breaking up, that's when my love was torn.
I'm sorry if it had to do with the day that I was born.
Maybe it was back then, when I became not that little boy,
But today it really doesn't matter, for I'm still my Mama's joy.
Through all this, I've learned a great lesson, I'll remember for many years.
So, Daddy, if you have any concern, give with an open ear.
When I grow up, and find my love, with a future I'm to make,
I'll review back over my mother's choice and make not the same mistake,
Good-by Daddy, I love you.
*From your daughter Joan,*

**Joan Marie Harvey Reid**

## Tribute

Forgotten stones 'neath trees in graveyards lie,
Dark granite, gloomy, covered by the weed,
These stones a monument, to those who die
For those oppressed and waiting to be freed.
They fought for country bravely and for lives,
Their own and those devoted to their cause,
For freedom justice, peace for those whose cries
Made heroes of their lives;  their deaths, drawn straws.
None yet remembers soldiers, heroes old,
And here interred with bones of soldier are
The memories of action past and bold,
The hardship and the triumph of the war.
  Now buried here beneath six feet of dirt,
  Lay all forgotten glory, blood, and hurt.

**Dan Conlin**

## Your Sins Outnumbered Your Good

Last night I dreamed I was dying
Darkness was all I could see
I cried out to my God in the heavens
I've been good so you must set me free.

But my cries seemed so low and so hopeless
My heart welled up in despair
I felt I was sinking in darkness
I cried out, Oh God hear my prayer.

The gates to heaven were open
For a moment I felt great relief
I was about to enter that haven
Where your heart will feel no more grief

But Lo— a voice called out clearly
You didn't do all that you could
And the gates slowly closed as I stood there
Your sins outnumbered your good.

**Gladys Zellgert**

## The Bottom Of The Barrel

Crawling on the floor, trying to find an opening
day after day nothing in sight.
I crawled the wrong way, which you told me was right.
Depressed and oppressed, by what I feel and see
If I stay here, it will suffocate me.

Trying to get a better job, I was pushed back.
You'll never amount to nothing, your skin is black.
Pounding my chest, with a furious beat, am I suppose
to hate me?

Come touch my black skin, look in my dark eyes.
They cry, "I have life inside."
I'm trying to crawl away for a better day.

As a man, I can't walk upright, I'm beat from all sides of life.
I want a future, a wife and children that can carry on.
I don't want to go to prison for doing wrong.

I'm trying to crawl away for a better day
As a man, I can't walk upright, I'm beat from all sides of life.
Give me a chance let me walk as a man.

The bottom of this Barrel, I'm crawling in;
I'll crush it and new life can begin.

**Betty J. Garner Johnson**

## Is This Love?

What else could possibly feel this good?
Days are cluttered with people that don't matter and tasks that seem mundane;
Just a few quick seconds to ponder — I think back to a tender moment
shared with you.....and it brings a glowing smile to my face;
Thoughts of you make each of my days so much easier to get through —
somehow, you make it all worthwhile.
Anticipating the end of the day; it seems to move so slowly —
dragging on, and on, and on.....
Will I ever escape this world full of superficial experiences and insignificant persons so that I can return home to the one person that I so long to be with?
Finally, it is here — end of day!!
The excitement and anticipation inside me builds as I near the safety and shelter of your bosom; tenderness and softness, calm and collection, all in one petite and beautiful presence.
Intimacy... closeness... companionship... loyalty—
I have them all as I step through the threshold and enter my safe haven to find you there.
No more outside entities for which I have so little accord — just you and I... one on one
You are my world; you are my all that matters
This is love!!

**Brad Weeks**

## Walking Home During Rush Hour

On the horizon a purple line.  Birds.
Deep blue branches and wings.  A white haze
above the trees.  The red light turns
green.  And all the way down route one
windows between yellow leaves
go dark.

November.
Each day is the same:
headlights in a long line, leaves burning,
a fire in the glass, and the blue sky opens
into stars.  Stars, so many stars
they line my dreams.

It used to be so easy to be happy
to be going home.

**Diana Patricia Vance**

## Injustice, my Andrea

Back twenty-five years I stood at the White House
demanding the answers to questions that May.
Why are they dying?
Who is the blame for?
What is the truth?
Can you explain?

Years have passed.
My questions have mellowed.
My youth forgotten, desire decayed.
Its your turn now to fight for the answers.
Different issues, but questions the same.

Now you want to know,
Why was he dying?
What is the truth?
Why won't they explain?
Your legacy is finding solutions.
With struggles and searches, life cycles your way.

*Florence Dilworth*

## Nature's Cry

If there's one thing that God would say, its stop
destroying what I have made.
He made a place for all to live—it's not for man to take or give.
Man takes credit for things he has found, like planes
that somehow leave the ground.
But going back there must have been a bird flying even then.
People travel everyday in machines that man has made.
When looking out along the way, I hope they see what
God has made.
Now looking back, some may recall when lakes were
clear, and trees grew tall.
Man has taken through the years, and now the rain is
nature's tears.
So to close, I wish to say the time has come to change
our ways!

*Dan Blanton*

## The Tree Of Life

On top of the tree of life grow
Diamonds wet an wild among the leaves.
Life exposed to the open sky.
Twinkling
Each vivid stone formed of coal at the roots.
New beginning of time.
Dust of before grows slowly up the tree of life,
To change, to achieve.
To form that perfect diamond wet an wild among the leaves,
On top of the tree of life

*Judith E. Burgess*

## Bradenton

Just you and I at Bradenton as the waves
  did gently roll
We laughed, we played, we picked up shells
  as we took our little stroll
I love you more than each grain of sand
  on a beach without an end
My prayer is for a rich long life
  with you my love to spend
So take my hand and dream with me
  and breathe in all its splendor
The times we spent at Brandenton
  I always shall remember!

*John Turner*

## Jesus

Did he die for all my sins?
Did God let the devil win?
But we know Jesus rose from the dead
And stomped upon the devil's head
Then Jesus went to heaven to be with his dad
And all his people were very sad
But we know he lives in our hearts and in
our minds
He never really left us behind
For those who love him will be blessed
For those who don't, will never rest
Don't let the devil have your soul
Go to Jesus and you'll be bold
Stand up against the demons of the night
With Gods power you'll be alright
So go to church, and learn his ways
He'll make you happy for the rest of your days
And in the end you won't have to worry
You'll be with Jesus in a hurry!

*Dyana Hollenbach-Bailo*

## Make Someone Happy

Have you paused to make someone happy?
Did you smile at a stranger today?
Was an old man or woman in tatters
Given kind words to make their day?
Have you paused to make someone happy?
A child with a dirty face
Did you give him a hug or a cookie
Did his face light up and make him feel part of the human race?

It doesn't take much effort
To make somebody else's day,
Just smile and ask "How are you,"
Happy is one smile away!

*Emily J. Nesvacil*

## Unconditionally...

To know you has caused me to look at things
differently; without having met you, you have accepted me
unconditionally.

Without conditions-

You are accepting me as a human being, making mistakes along
the way. You are accepting me as a woman, with strengths
and weaknesses. You are accepting me as a soul, that needs
to be loved and nurtured. You are accepting me as a love,
that warrants trust and respect.

With conditions-

I am giving all of me that I can give, without losing
myself. I am willing to be the strength or weakness, as you
need. I am catching your soul and love with my heart,
hoping that trust and respect will nurture us both.

Unconditionally, we have the beginning of something good.

*Imy Daniel*

## March Capers

The wind is up to its tricks this morning.
It has found that tear in the patio awning!
Bet you six to one my canvas will be sailing
To the very tune that wind is wailing.

Across the front yard, and over the street
To some astonished pedestrian it's bound to meet.
I pray all goes well, it's hard to tell
Until I answer that urgent doorbell.

*Jane M. Pickering*

## True Love

Now in the sunset hour of life,
Cruel winds chill our fragile frames.
You're but a shattered semblance of yourself,
While I, entrusted with your care,
Sobbing silently within,
Am blessed by God with strength and grace
To love more deeply than before.

**Dorothy Stern**

## The Attic

What fascination lies therein, of things grown old, their brightness dim.
The timelessness of each must hold, stories often times untold.

The pervading scent of mustiness creates its spell of charm.
Where one can view the dustiness, without undue alarm.

Ahh! Come with me and let us browse until we find a treasure,
Here's a rocker where one might drowse, or read, or muse with pleasure.

We find a table with lovely grace, it once held silver, china, and lace.
What loving hands had shown such care, to rub it to patina rare?

Lets look beneath this sloping beam, and push the webs away,
The eerie light lends a ghostly gleam, but we are won't to stay.

A delighted sigh escapes our breast, what does that light reveal?
The beauty of an old carved chest, at which we pause and kneel.

Herein we find a lovely urn, such gentle hands have wrought.
Thru generations of father and son this beautiful art was taught.

One more step, and then we see, a handsome lamp of pewter.
Perhaps one time, it lent its gleam, lighting the way for a suitor.

With a lingering glance, we leave at last.
These cherished objects from the past.

**Dorothy Saulten**

## The Waiting Room

The ICU Family waiting room echoes with voices
discussing loved one's conditions
while many recline in uncomfortable chairs
in strange contorted positions,
yet nevertheless tho sadness prevails, the love that shines thru
brings comfort, hope, and compassion;
and we are all touched by the hand of that love,
so difficult to put into expression.
And so may the Lord bless us and keep us always
along the bright pathway of family devotion;
And may we all never ever forget
the love that shines thru in times of distress
like a wonderful, soothing, sweet lotion.

**Jason Moore**

## As We Pass By

Do you see me when you pass by
Do I see you?
Do you look at me or is it the surface.
What is it? What is there?
Do you know?
Sometimes even I wander.
The secret most inner parts of us all,
Only we and God do know.
What is it about us that really shows.
Do you have a fleeting thought as you pass by.
Do I really see you or like you with me do we see.
Do we really care.
Should we trust to speak to one another to stop and share,
do we dare to think and take a moment in
time to smile and say (Hello)

**Eddie M. Messer**

## Ode to Husbands

Momma done told him in so many words:
"Do not trim while I'm away!
Remember the buddy system—it works!
Put off that job another day."

When momma got down the road a piece—
Poppa said: "Oh, what the heck!
There's no danger to trimming trees.
I will keep everything in check."

So poppa with chain saw, ladder and all,
Set to work on trimming a tree.
But misfortune prevailed and poppa fell—
So now he has a busted knee.

Poppa, while in much pain,
Is in a very remorseful mood.
Poppa learned the hard way —
Momma's advice was good!

**Edward R. Raasch**

## My Daily Best

While we live from day to day,
Do we always think to pray?

To thank our Lord for his love and care,
For the abundance of blessings we can share.

Is our day complete at night?
Have we lived the hours all right?

Will he be pleased when we lie down to rest?
Can we say, dear Lord, I've done my best?

**Janis B. Drinnon**

## Questions

Is a sunset wasted on a cow?
Does a cat mean "Yes" when it says "Meow"?

Does the mantis hear the mocking bird?
Or are his notes not even heard?

When a puppy dies, does he go to heaven?
I wondered about these when I was seven.

Is a weed sad when you pull it up?
Does it hurt when you pick the buttercup?

How in heaven above
Does a chigger know how to make love

To another chigger?
I'll bet he wishes he were bigger.

Are plants and animals related?
The story of their lives, X-rated?

Both grow and die and reproduce—
That is they do, if they seduce.

When God created the universe
It must have been for "better or worse."

What a job it must have been!
How did he know where to begin?
And who made him?

**Eleanor Obert-Westgate**

## Creature of the Night

Calling...calling out to whom?
Does anyone listen?
Does anyone really hear?
By the heat of the day, you are still.
But as the burning rays race to the west.
Then the land will start to cool.
This is the time of much unrest.
Do you call me?
Many times before I have heard this hail.
As you summon through the long bleak nights.
Your message is still confusing.
Hear you I do and hope to understand your call.
To feel the meaning within each little sound.
Let me hear the echo of joy, hope and love.
Trumpet a testimonial for all to hear.
No wait.
End this harmony.
For I believe, I am the only one listening.

*Bonnie Biesterfeld*

## Love And Life

Twenty-two years, they've passed so fast.
Does the end start here or will it last?
What made things change so much this year?
What brought the problems we have to fear?

The trials, the dreams, the good, and the bad.
Why does it end now?
Look at everything we had.
To love and to cherish till death do us part,
what does that meant?
Did it ever start?

Things will change if time permits.
Life has to end starting bit by bit.
Love and life must mean the same,
Life must hold much love to gain.

Live together in marriage for years,
Now things changed—we must fight the tears.
If life could last forever and ever,
Then we'd have love today and be together.

*Cynthia R. Jackson*

## For Whom the Clock Ticks

"For whom the clock ticks," I always say,
Doesn't it just tick anyway,
Or is time out to charm us?

For whom the clock ticks, I always wonder,
What about those people who are six feet under,
Is time really out to harm us?

Time will be forever,
It's all in a matter of time,
But why is time so everlasting,
When everything has an hour glass,
It's kinda confusing when you have a watch,
But yet amusing the batteries won't last,
So I guess even clocks have an hour glass.

When the last grain of sand hits the bottom of the top,
The thing that lasted can always stop,
For whom the clock ticks?

If you really notice, time comes with disaster,
Or it may come with pleasure,
But everything happens thereafter,
So time is impossible to measure.

*Brent Plott*

## A Pure Thought

One white kid doesn't know any better,
doesn't know any worse
plays with a black kid
same age, same discourse
first kid says "you're white"
other kid says "you're black"
both of them wonder, what's that mean?
first mom says "they kept us down"
other mom says "they can't be trusted"
black kid says, "I like you"
white kid says, "I like you, too"
"we could have fun together", they said aloud
"we could be friends"
but their parents thought twice
"you have many friends at your school", they said
not like him, they thought

twenty years later
the white man sees a black man
says "he looks familiar"
as he reaches to lock his car door

*Derek Korn*

## On The Other Side

I heard someone say - it's better - on the other side
don't laugh - pretend - until you get there.
Choose for today - or you will lose at your tomorrow.
Wisdom plus courage = freedom
Help lead your soul on.
You need not wonder - who will be there to catch your fall.
You need not wonder - who's behind you
when your back is up against the wall.
Love and happiness is his quest,
It's true he loves you the best
So wipe away, your tears of fear
And allow him in, to show you the rest
My savior is my friend, and he's part of me
And I give myself to him,
Bet you never thought to do that,
please pass it on - to the rest,
Love and happiness
This is my quest, and I get that from
My Jesus, my best friend, Amen

*Eugenia Dunn-Belcher*

## The Cure

Are you happy?  What makes you smile?
Don't rush your answer, think for a while.
Little credit is given when credit is due
to the subtle beauties which surround you.

The song remains the same from dawn until dusk
but soon it will be over as all songs must.
So don't waste your time being angry or aloof
a smile is contagious.  Just do it if you want proof.

I have a theory, a way to change the whole world
it begins with the smile of an anonymous girl.
She smiled at me I couldn't help but reciprocate
no words, just a smile, I suddenly felt great.

If people would smile more of the time,
"How are you?" would be answered with more than just "fine."
A smile is contagious I said it before
try it with your neighbors go knock on their door.

And if it's a stranger who you should then meet
look into their eyes and smile instead of down at your feet.
It's only a theory and it might not be right
but if it is true we'll all sleep better at night.

*Jeff Sidlow*

## Gripe Gripe

Gripe, Gripe, and I hear.
Dope, wild women, whiskey and beer.
Gripe, Gripe all I hear.
Trouble, Trouble no cheer!

Problems, Problems, men say.
Boast, Boast, big ego, I say.
Young men, old men, what is wrong?
You need a new song?

I know you work hard, sweat, toil, and strain.
This kind of life will tear you in twain.
Come, come, gather all around to hear me.
That is not the way it has to be!

There is a better way to live, and greater to be.
You will reach life's potential, what is hid in thee.
You are of great value, more than gold.
But you can't know it unless you are told!

Jesus Christ, the truth, life and the way!
Learn all the aspects of His life today.
Read the great book, He gave to see.
How much God loves both you and me!

**Howard Nicholson**

## Certain Times

I wish I'd written
down certain times,
moments of memories
still ticking in my mind

An alarming antic
of a smitten soldier
who, by hanging a tree full of mistletoe
over my head, hoped to melt my cold shoulder

The fast-beating tempo
of a confessed enamored heart
by envisioning me, drove through traffic lights
signaling stop, not start

Precision movements of a waitress
sent on a mission with a note
that read "TO:  You're beautiful"
found it later in the pocket of my coat

I wish I'd written it all down
each savory second
Date:  Day:  Time:

**Dana Welch**

## The Prince

Time ticks once -
Dreamers are a casualty.
Celebrity's a must in this passage -
the waves and walls are closing in
and the summer haunts what could have been,
what should have been.

And so to the unwoven one
whose head gives in to the unsynchronized filly
Do not die through the decades
from duty, but touch a heart, scarred
And weave a tapestry golden,
a rhythm bonded in spirit,
that only the prince would know.

And so she leaves her bleeding one, bewildered.
Time's ticking -
His turn to grace the road of challenge,
To enter the laughing sea wall
of a flooded cyclorama of adventures.
Will the heart die weary before the walk is done,
or will the prince find his Camelot, and tower of kin?

**Julie-Anne Breen**

## For Family

The young man runs along the shifting sand,
Dreaming of the riches of the life he's planned—
Money, fame, travel, honors—
And he gives no thought to finding time
    For family.

The middle-aged man strolls his glorious land,
Enjoying the riches of the life he planned—
Money, fame, travel, honors—
And he pushes back thoughts of finding time
    For family.

The old man hobbles, a cane in his hand,
Bored with the riches of the life he planned—
Money, fame, travel, honors—
And he tearfully laments not finding time
    For family.

The withered man lies in his coffin grand,
While strangers steal the riches of the life he planned—
Money, fame, travel, honors—
And he is soon forgotten, leaving nothing in time
    For family.

**Judy A. Peterson**

## "Lock Down"

It's all the same when I close my eyes,
dreams and thoughts stay enclosed behind
the words and locked doors, so much and so
little to find what's there within itself, the
smiles and laughter aren't the same just
another emotion threw out daily lives,
green grass, pine trees, growing, watching,
listening and nothing can be said as to
what's learned for us to be taught,
nobody wants the truth, only this an than,
I see this light like I see this daily but
nothing can be done to let the words follow
the wind with these lungs of mine,
everybody has something to show, something
to let be hearted, no sense in them when their
eyes show emptiness, me,
I just lost my eyes it's all the same.

**David Lone Wolf**

## Untitled

You insist on being dismal when it rains
Drowning in its puddles, belaboring your pain
Yet you say you love flowers
Reveling in their beauty, possessing it as your own
Have you so easily forgotten that it's April showers which bring May
    flowers?

Why do you fear the face of truth?
Avoiding your own wounds, refusing to heal
Yet you begged me for roses
Desiring their openness, spreading in full bloom
Don't you know that the rose you held came from a bush of thorns?

How pensive you were when she passed away
Angry at your Maker, losing your faith
Yet you wonder at Nature's marvels
Gazing at its sunsets, meditating upon its shores
Have you ever realized that what the caterpillar calls death the
    Creator calls a butterfly?

If we could only learn now from what we didn't know then
Pouring rain nourishes the seed God planted
Piercing thorns yield blooming roses
And dying prisoners are set free, receiving wings to soar in flight
We would've known that only after we survive a storm can we blest
    with a rainbow.

**Brian Vigorito**

## Darkness

The two separate rails become one in the distance
Each anticipating their future existence

I soon realize that the rails never meet
The only connection lies under my feet

The once easy steps are tougher to reach
As the distance continues to grow between each

The next step seems impossible to achieve
Just too many fears that I must heave

But I lean forward and leave my thoughts behind
Incessant desire is all that I find

The sun seems brighter and ire sets in
Radiating the beauty of unleashed passion

But traditional clouds linger in the distance
They're full of hostility, I must be cautious

The odious storm releases its wrath
Turning crossroads to crossbones and all in its path

The desired dusk soon fell to darkness
And desire itself now fails to surface

No steps and no rails to complete my plight
My elusive fate still searches for light.

**Carrie L. Wood**

## +1 + -1= 0

Two men fought over our mother's hymen
    each claiming it belonged to them.  They
pulled and clawed and tore the cloth.

    A man rose up and claimed he knew
        the answer, but he would only give the
    answer to the man who bought him the
        biggest and best lunch.  He ate at one table,
    belched loudly, and then ate at another.

As the sun set, the silhouette of a little
    man appeared in the distance on a small
knoll.  After a while he crept up to the
    men tearing the cloth and the man eating
lunches.  When he got close he whispered
    jobberwocky in their ears; and, as he
said mounds of nothing, with no one noticing,
    he put shackles on their hands and feet.
Satisfied with what he had done he smiled
    and he grabbed our mother's hymen and put
it in his pocket and walked away whistling.

**Gary Akers**

## Day by Day

Time passes like sand through the fingers of a hand
Each day different as you get by the best you can
There are those with dreams and visions that often seem
hard to reach
Then there are those just looking for happiness and that's
all that they seek
We shouldn't take time for granted, don't let a bad situation
keep you stressed
Live each day to its fullest because we're not promised the next
Dreams will keep you motivated, your hopes should always be high
Keep striving for your goals, they can be reached if you try
Always believe in yourself, never doubt what you can do
Anything is possible when you believe in you

**Glenn Flowers**

## Father of Mine

Life has many ways of telling our age
Each more interesting with each new page
But in my heart you will never grow old
Dear father of mine with many stories to be told

With patience and love you guided me
Bringing me up - to the best I could be
You worked hard and long - even after I was grown
Thank you dear Father for the love you have shown

So much to be learned from your experience
All you went through all your endurance
I will always "treasure" what you have done
Dear father of mine - your number one

So often this child - has failed to say
How much you're loved - each passing day
And I thank God - he picked you to be
The greatest father ever for me

**Betty Halverson**

## Feather On The Wind (Little Happenings)

Life is like a box of chocolates...
Each representing a friend...

Or a series of little happenings...
Like a feather on the wind!

You never know what to expect...
Nor yet—just what to do!

But most of us would simply reject...
The path we didn't want to pursue!

So accept it with a feeling...
Give it an affirming nod!

Life is like a box of chocolates...
Each moment a confection of God!

Each experience coated with bitter chocolate!
But oh how sweet the cream inside!

Yet like a feather on the wind...
There's nothing to fear or hide!

A spirit that's loose and whimsical...
That can never be stilled and yet...

Life is like a box of chocolates...
You never know what you'll get!

**Dennis Dale Popham**

## Life in the Country

A walk down the lane, our mail to retrieve
Eases strife from my heart, peace, and joy to achieve

Where the squirrels scamper among the trees in play
Stealing our pecans along the way.

One early morn not long ago
I glimpsed a weasel, flitting to and fro,

Then a black snake slithered amid the grass half way
No doubt searching coolness on a hot August day

By eve a bull frog croaks by the pond
Near the gentle wave of a tall slender frond,

I oft dream of a life that would be less toil
To save the back, and the hands never soil.

But a life in the country, on a lane strewn with gravel
Is a peaceful way life's path to travel.

**Carol Elizabeth Spears**

## Animal Kingdom

The chain of life sustains innumerable variations.
Each species guided by genetic marvel
knows its place of action -
driven by survival and propagation.
Touched into presence by strong forces,
its only goal unknowingly fulfilling.

Crowned are the glories of nature,
for human beings appeared at the highest
ranking level.
Possessing the power of reason and communication
through language -
triumphantly ruling the world.

And yet - a fine line separates our kingdoms:

Animal instinct lets the herds watch in silence -
while quarrels are fought one on one -

Human intelligence provides rulers with
unlimited power -
and millions are losing their lives.
How rational we are!!

### *Heidi Rimanich*

## She Is

She is like a field of daisies, she is.
Each with its small sun; "days-eye" called by the ancients.
Like a daisy, she opens to a sunny day.
Clean and bright and filled with quiet patience.

She is like a snowfall deep in the woods, she is.
With reverence covering unpleasantness left by the growing year.
Like a snowflake, she is heaven sent.
Fragile and unique, snowflake-like she can melt into a tear.

She is like moonlight on Lake Superior, she is.
The percussion and shimmer of the waves is enchantment.
Like this great lake, she is deep and clear.
Fresh air on fresh scent.

She is like a field of daisies, she is.
Some search for beauty, and this flower shows them how.
Like a daisy, beauty should be free;
and felt with grace to bestow.

### *Gerald Koos*

## Evening Interlude

From the sort of light, and sort of dark
Echo muted sounds from a nearby park,
The moon is softly showing light
The day is gone - how sweet the night.

A breeze is gently blowing now
And mingled with the trees, shows how,
The branches offer out their leaves
And play with fancy one conceives.

There on the floor, the shadows fall
And climb my leg and up the wall.
The moving leaves form more than lace
A babe in arms - an old man's face,

Two lovers kissing at a gate
And soldiers marching, tall and straight,
Some puppies playing in a field
Long rows of corn that cannot yield.

Like fingers, touching, parting then
They reach and close as one again
But clouds erase the glowing moon
And pictures vanish - much too soon.

### *Grace Brooks Johnson*

## The Admirer's Poem

In the midst of the cool clear night, I hear her name
echoing in the halls of my mind.
Over and over, softly ringing like wind chimes when the
winds blow. Imprisoned is how I feel when she casts her
beautiful almond shaped eyes my way. I watch her
moves...and gracefulness dominates her every sway.
I hear her voice and it bonds my heart with the chains
of it's sweet melody.
I watch her as she gently brushes her hair from her
face. Her face. How could something appear so beautiful and
delicate, yet possess such strength?
Her scent, so enrapturing, my heart seems to dance
when a single rush of air drifts by. So radiant, she
resembles a flower....and I am the bee.
I catch myself whispering her name and wonder..... could
it ever be?

### *Charles T. Stansell*

## Pondering Life's Mystery

Soft cool breezes on flowers dancing, their essence spreading and
enhancing blue skies and an azure sea, reflecting on the melody
of being alive.

Who are we - from whence did we come, where will we go, when all
this is done? What was our mission when sent from afar to this
strange land warmed by the Sun? Were we handed Earthlife like
potters clay, with "Here dear one - mold it your way?"

Would we never have learned how wonderful it is, to live forever in
celestial bliss, unless first we'd been touched by Earth's
worrisome kiss - where weeds grow wild without toil or care
but it takes love and effort to grow a flower.

God asked Job this question centuries ago - "Where were you when I
created the Earth, and all my children shouted for joy at its
birth?" Job couldn't answer, but we understand, if he couldn't
remember his part in the plan.

The message to all of us, sweetly told, is "Earth is your classroom
go forth and be bold." "You're pure in essence, but without
experience. So, seasons of time will pass 'til you gain it."
But never shall you learn those lessons alone, for angels stand
watch until you come home.

### *Janette Kirkland*

## My Life as a Farm Wife

I climb on a tractor in early morn preparing fields for beans and corn.
Enjoy mother-nature throughout the day, when time is right I help make
hay. Mowing the lawn, a change most pleasing, vegetables ready for
canning and freezing. Chores all finished, I did my best, hardly had
time to stop for a rest.

Meal times I hurry to the house, prepare hot foods to nourish my
spouse, After eating his fill he sneaks out the door, I do dishes,
laundry and the floor. Days when book-work and house-work are
  done, I
take time to walk not run. Attend to tasks of things that don't show,
buttons to replace, patches and mending to sew.

Once relaxed in out of the sun, I hear a familiar voice say, "Hey Hon"
I need repairs run into John Deere get new parts for the tractor,
Dear. That suddenly ends my plans for the day, I quickly change get
on my way. A lot of changes in this life, I'll never change from
being a farm wife.

If ever there's time for relaxation we may just take a needed
vacation, get away for a while, be nice, that's for sure, return to a
barn full of manure? I'm thankful to God for giving me this life,
being on duty as a "Farm Wife". It's most satisfying to toil all day,
your spouse beside you all the way.

We had two children which was a thrill, first a boy then a girl,
Soon they grew up and on this ways, we'd love to relive those precious
  days.

### *Georgie E. Hobson*

## Wakeup

Enter into existence, encountering establishing ideas, goals,
Enter into existence slow match damnation, kazoo, wizard of oz
It's amazing how life pass and there's no harness on time
A Robin sings, a woody pecks - the polar bears the loneliness,
An elephant has its day lying in the mud-while Jonah rested
in the belly of fish, largest ever -
You're down, one foot to go on the one yard line
Your family tree? by the way did you get your degree?
Are you sleep? everyone has a god - "What's that white powder"?
Who's your hero?

*Howard R. McClain*

## Mystique of Put-In-Bay

One single sliver of celestial earth,
    enveloped by placid waters,
stretches beyond a sphere of time,
    drawing humankind toward its tranquil shores.

The towering monument of battle beacons,
    as winds whisper an ancient victory cry.
Waves caress veiled secrets of history,
    eternally entombed beneath their frothy crests.

Ashore, a whirling carousel of jubilant creatures revel
    in whimsical tourist fantasies.
Pagentries of adventurers roam about an island stage,
    like puppets, entwined in vintage history.

Caught in time, a tiny Erie island
    plays host to past and present.
Forever, ensnaring its willing prey
    in the mystical charm. . . of Put-In-Bay.

*Denice L. Baldetti*

## Cappuccino

The scent the aroma
escapes past today
and finds itself knocking at yesteryears door
snowy winters
the fireplace the Duralogs
Michael and Danny
the water hole
Witches Pond
Killer Hill on homemade sleds
the indian reservation
fishing poles of broken sticks
water fights Ralevio
the ferris wheel bumper cars
my little brother in his little striped shirt
with a bigger smile and a bigger heart
than he could've ever grown into
my hands are warm
wrapped around this coffee cup
but my heart is warmer...
wrapped around these memories

*Dina J. Lauze*

## Do I Love You?

I love you as the sky is above.
I love you as the sea is blue.
I love you as the sun is above.
I love you as the Moon shine.
I love you as there is Fall and Winter.
I love you totally as sure as there's a
God Above.

*Addy Cox*

## Today I'll Cry

For all the babies who'll never see,
Even one day of the lives God meant them to have.
For all the first steps never taken and first words never spoken.
For all their tiny dreams that will never come true.
For all the good things they would surely have done for us.
For all the joy they could have brought to such a sad world.
For all the mothers who made this most terrible mistake.
For all the children who'll never hold their little sibling.
For all the doctors who promised only to help and to do no harm.
For all the people who stood silently by and let it happen.
For all of us who now grieve for them,
For all the sweet precious new angels,
that God will forever hold close in his tender love.
Tonight I pray.

*Janice Rose Smith*

## God's Hand - Maiden

Ever feel that your footsteps are dragging?
Ever feel that your head wants to nod?
That's the time to talk to the savior
And get that "Pick up" from God.

Ever feel that you're gloomy or grouchy;
That most people are surely a bore?
That's the time to replenish your treasures
By shopping at God's grocery store.

When your heart feels mostly down-hearted;
Even notes you sing sound like they're flat,
It's time to surrender your ego
And sit down with God for a "Chat"!

Hold on to His hand real tightly;
Just feel his working in you!
Then smile love and lift your dear neighbor
and share Him in all that you do.

*Dorothy L. Allen*

## Grandma Received Her Angel Wings

In days of old it has been said
Every time a church bell rings
An angel gets their angel wings
This being so, sure as God is in heaven

"Grandma received her angel wings"
As the church bell did ring
This lady so precious and dear to me
As the church bells began to ring

A choir of angels began to sang
Their voices so calm and clear,
For every one present to hear
There was such a calm such a hush

As the bells rang "Grandma received her angel wings"
Then you could hear Grandma and the angel choir sing
"Hold my hand precious Lord", "Just a closer walk with thee",
"You are my everlasting grace", and "You are my sunshine"

Everyone present shared that moment so special, so rare
As the angel choir sang, as the church bells rang
"Grandma received her angel wings" then she began
With God in heaven and his new angel choir

*James L. Nelson*

## My Museum

This awesome building spills onto the street,
My museum of arts so filled with mystery.
I climb the stairs to get to my retreat,
Prepared to take a walk in history.

And now the question of just where to start,
There is so much I always want to see.
Let Pablo's Weeping Woman break my heart,
Or be amused with Warhol's foolery.

Quickly, I bee-line to the second floor,
Then start to slow a bit before I pause,
To view once more all the paintings I adore,
And thrill again to Paul Cézanne's Sous-bois.

Devoted, I sit, while Rembrandt stares at me,
My day complete, I leave - reluctantly.

*Anita Kingsley*

## Untitled

There are so many obstacles in life,
    ones that must be faced,
    faced to the end -
Even if there is fear of losing or getting lost,
    we must be brave and we must have faith.
If we have no faith in ourselves to overcome these obstacles,
    there is no hope -
No hope for anyone who is scared and lacks determination -
No one knows why life can't be perfect,
    why everyone can't be happy -
There must be a reason...
    a lesson in all of this -
But until we find an answer,
    we must move forward -
Live each day to the fullest,
    and try not to look behind us at the dark and dismal past.

*Amy Prentice*

## The Lonely Little Fir Tree

The lonely little fir tree, standing in the cold
Said no one loves me, so I'm told
I bow my limbs and feel so sad
Won't someone love me, and make me glad
The forest Angel heard and behold
The tree lit up in silver and gold
"Don't be frightened" a voice softly spoke
I live in the forest, by that big Oak.
She bowed her head and blinked her eyes
Out of the woods came joyful noises and cries
All the animals and birds started singing
Many bells and chimes were ringing
We of the forest need Christmas too
We all came out to share with you
Laughing and dancing to their delight
We praise His birth, this special night.

*Angeline Shannon*

## The Love Bug

The love bug is a lusty beast,
Sex to him is one big feast.
    Emerging from a leafy mould,
    On just one thing his mind is sold;
To find himself a willing mate,
And settle down to procreate,
    He sees the apple of his eye,
    And quickly spears her on the fly.
They'll buzz around in this position,
Till they come to their perdition.
    In a word, they're overcopulous.
    No wonder they're so populous!

*Andrew R. Johnson*

## Now And Then

I really did love you and in some ways
Still do when I remember how you held my hand
until we were warmed and stuck together
when we walked or the way you hugged me tightly
when I was frightened, as if you could squeeze all
my fears away; and I still love
to love you when I remember how you would get
that little lost boy on your face
when you were slightly angered with me,
but all that changed when you lied to me
so I have to wonder, Did you hold her
the same way you held me or did you make her think
she was the"other" greatest person in your eyes;
Are you raising the family with her
that you said would be mine,
but now all I want to know is when you feel
you have been betrayed or when you experience
a sensual moment, I hope you think of me
because I will be thinking of you.

*Amy Craft*

## Untitled

The stormy winds of ungailed ghosts
Stride forcibly through the souls
of the unwarned.

To reek havoc in their wake,
Stealing precious moments of days a gone
for pleasureless torments of you and I.

Speak soft, not to wake
The still sleeping tales of past
and then only.
To warn us of the danger

The untouched stone, subjects of silence,
Known only through the unspoken agreement-
lies to the deaf ear of the psych.

Knowing full well,
The impact of the tale.

*Angela Olivier*

## One Mile From Home

One mile away from Home
    The car just stopped and I am alone
    The sun is setting and its getting dark
    And here I am alone and parked
    One mile away from home.

Some one will miss me and try to find
    Just where I am and save my mind.
    Thoughts, thoughts where shall I turn
    What shall I do one mile from home.

Cars go by with people in them
    They won't look my way - they don't want to stop,
    Who knows who I am or what trouble I might bring.
    Can't blame them - I've done the same thing
    Now I am alone and one mile from home.

It's getting late and it is dark.
    I should of walked and left the car parked.
    I am all alone, I'll just sit here with my eyes closed.
    I'll just wait one mile from home.

*Ann Brock*

## He Beat Me, And I His Wife

I was forced back in past as my thoughts unchurned.
The present is near, but not well learn'd.
Loneliness is:  A bitter feeling I share;
A hole in my heart-there's nothing there.
A space so needed to be filled with hope,
But too much care has tightened the rope.
The rope squeezes my heart, and it's left uncleansed—
There's a circle-burn left, pulled by lassoed hands.
His fists were clinched as they popped the burn;
Then, my cold, red face would quickly turn
To see his eyes filled with that hateful lust.
He didn't know that blood colored rust.
While I lay to the ground, face buried in dank
It's my courage he took, and my heart he sank.
I remember the words he spoke to me, in rasp.
They left me to, quickly, look in past.
I was forced back in past as my thoughts unchurned,
The present is here, and now I have learn'd.

*Andrea Nail*

## Up I Must Go

   Flowers above so far I can't see,
up in the sky is light for me.

   The birds in the sky above in the clouds.
I wish I were up to look in the crowd.

   Gleams of sun shining gleaming through air.
Love of beauty is where I must bear.

   I wish I were up, up in the sky,
all of the stars floating right by.

   One day I'll see how it is to be free,
like all the waves that come from the sea.

   I must not stay, I don't belong here,
it is the world I live in such fear.

   Now I must go, I'll see you someday,
up in the sky so far and away.

*Amy Gomez*

## Vietnam Veterans Memorial Wall

The other day I saw the 58,106 names of those who in the war had died
   When I saw this wall I was very proud and I sighed
It doesn't look as if many had a chance to live
   But they sure gave us much as they could give
It made me really stop to think, and also wonder
   How they felt hearing the guns roaring thunder
Some will never get a chance to see the tomorrow
   As there torn loved ones gathered and wept in great sorrow
Along this spiritual wall were proudly standing red, white,
and blue flags
   Some sat holding the soldiers warfilled dog tags
Seeing this wall was depressing and ripped me apart
   These unforgotten soldiers I shall remember in my heart
And as for the missing and unidentified soldiers we should pray
   Because as for us we get to live life to its fullest on this day
We should all also be happy and share our powerful love
   For me I am very grateful to God who drifts up above

*Angela Lueddeke*

## "Open Grave"

Here I lie in an open grave.
Where time stands still for those who pray.
The midnight hour close in hand.
As shadows fall across the land.
My blood boiling in this grave,e
A lonely hell where no-one is saved.
My mind wanders far and wide,
To where Eagles sore and cry.
As I still lay,
I wander for help.
Though my bodies just a crocus now.
Feeling of death and diseases.
Life its - self flies away from me.
Pain in my heart,
Tears in my head,
You know sometimes your better off dead.

*Amy B. Stogsdill*

## Uplifted

Say to yourself: "I am me.
Whoever that is — that's who I'll be.

I was created by my heavenly Father and sent here for a reason.
To that purpose, I must be true from season to season.

I know the road He paved for me will not be one that's easy.
If I stumble, I'll take hold His hand.  I know he'll never leave me.

There will be many questions I'll have to ask.
Many prayers I'll have to pray.
My faith will answer each one, though,
With each passing day.

My friends may not understand my will to complete the task before me.
For them, I'll hope and pray that they, one day, will join me.

I must remember I'll never be perfect or better that those I'm around.
Must never place myself on a pedestal, then in my brethren look down.

I will speak what I know is truth and live my life in that way.
Let the entire world know that I mean what I say.

Even if another's success seems a little more than mine,
I'll be satisfied and press on believing I'll get more in time.

My life I trust with him who created it — Strong and Gifted.
Because of him, I am inspired to Aspire and be Uplifted."

*Andy R. Williams*

## Many Things In Life I Don't Understand

Why some babies die and others live.
   Why some people are genius and others are retarded?
Why some love and others hate?
   Why some get cancer and die young?
Why some people die in fires and accidents?
   Why some people get along and others don't?
Why some live through war and others die?
   Why earthquake, hurricane, tornadoes and floods?
Why some live to be old and others die younger?
   Why some are so mean and others are so kind?
Why some live in sickness and pain and others are so healthy?
   Why some are blessed with plenty and others have none?
Why do some die of starvation while others throw food away?
   Why some live in a mansion and others live on the street?
Why life is easy for some and hard for others?
   Why some care about many, while others are selfish?
Why some are abused and others are protected?
   Many things in life I don't understand.
One thing I do know is that life is precious.
   I will live life each day to its fullness.

*Annette Rodriguez*

## Ahhh...Life

...”Is what you make it,” they say
everybody’s enjoying and gay
whether it be good or bad during the day
ahhh...life, just go on your way...

It’s very precious for God created this
and He wants us all to be in peace
but why should others fight in risk
ahhh...life, where’s justice?

Different people have different signs
sometimes strong, sometimes weak, it’s all in their minds
worries...we can’t read between each lines
ahhh...life, you’re one of a kind...

Love binds us everywhere
in our hearts we always share
feel and spread our care
eternal, we’ll live and die fair...

**Ermigarda S. Rosal**

## An Old Fashion Christmas

An old fashioned christmas where folks sing with glee,
Everyone happy with faces that beam.
Children excited awaiting the sleigh of old Santa Claus and his team.

Mama’s and Papa’s so tired from the rush,
Hoping the presents all fit and aren’t crushed.

Smoke on each house top and tinsel trim trees
That’s an Old fashion Christmas to me.

Sleigh bells ring carolers sing,
Music fills the air.
Friends you meet all stop and greet
Lots of love is everywhere.

Holly and mistletoe green and bright
Lovers enchanted this special night

Everyone happy and so care free
That’s an Old fashioned Christmas to me.

**Betty A. Welch**

## Don’t Be Afraid

“Don’t be afraid” I heard her say
Everything will be okay
She never complained, and she never cried
For she had faith that reached to the sky

She had a heart full of love
She had a spirit full of laughter
She had faith sent down from above
She had hope like no other

Ever so brave, ever so strong
For he knew where she belonged
In the hearts of every person she met
There she would stay, where no one could forget

Take her love and spread it around
Take her faith and make it renown
Take her words and make them be known
Take her hope and let it be shown
And in whatever you do remember what she said
Please have strong faith and “don’t be afraid”

**Dana Dunn**

## A Mother’s Only Son

*Dedicated to my son Trey Marcell Portrym*
Son what this world has to offer you is
everything you say and do...

I’ve tried to start you out with everything to know.
Little things to guide you wherever you might go...

It hasn’t always been easy for me to
meet your every need but you have inside
your heart my son the desire to succeed....

The world is out there waiting for
all you have inside...

Just touch the lives around you dear
and always look with open eyes...

I will leave you with this message
and in this, you can believe,
trust in our father up above that
you will always have your mothers
love.....

**Fayna Annette Portrum**

## Past, Present, Future

I look at my grandma’s legs and my greatgrandma’s
face, they all seem to move at a slow pace.
There are so many years of horror, tragedy, and
oppression.
You can see it in the way they move and in their
expressions.
They’ve learnt a lot of things as the years past;
about themselves, their people, and how the world moves so
fast...
Yet, they seem so calm, peaceful, and full of
memories,
I wonder...what will my grandchildren and great-grandchildren
see in me, in the next century.

**Cari Lynn Crawford**

## Memories Of You

Broken down and beaten, trying to find a spark of hope,
Falling fast, hanging on to the end of my rope,
His hands wrapped around my neck, gasping for air, my face
turning red,
I think to myself kill me already, I wish I was dead,
He finally stops but only for that night,
I know it will happen again so I live in fright,
I want to run and be free like wild horses,
But I live in hell under his unruly forces,
Day after day I live in my pain,
If I don’t leave I’ll go insane,
Kicked in the head my face full of blood,
Tell me again that this is love.

**Debi Leiter**

## Blue Solitude

Quiet solitude while on the stair
Fibers studied with great care
Woven tightly blue enmeshed
Entwined but separate together pressed
Soft and quiet lay your head down
Smell the fragrance of fibers bound
Purposes two fold not just one
An adult necessity becomes children’s fun
Solitude peace with each graduation
Advance to the top for sweet imagination

**Elizabeth Jane Songer**

## When the Master Calls

There's a brief splash of radiant light before the darkness finally
    falls
And the mind flashes infinite messages within the closing walls
Are you sure you want to go there, are you sure you wouldn't rather
    stay
And the light keeps glowing brighter that guides you on your way
You begin to walk that trodden path, you're so curious so distraught
Could this realm in which you're entering offer more than you had
    thought
Could the beauty that you see ahead be what this life portrays
And the vivid golden peaceful light holds your being in a daze
There's a fleeting glimpse of happiness, more pure than life has sown
And you meet yourself - the real you, the self you've never known
You're entranced in magic lilting flight and you only catch your
    breath
When you realize the light ahead is leading you to death
There's a brief splash of radiant light before the darkness finally
    falls
And the mind doth work such infinite schemes before its Master calls

    *Deborah L. Darling*

## Music of the Wilderness

Listen to the music of the wilderness.
    Far away from all the crowds
The whisper of the lonely trees
    The darkness of the rolling clouds.

Wild country lies beyond each trail
    There are rushing rivers all about
Where anglers go to try their luck
    For Rainbow, Lake and Speckled Trout.

Other wild life thrive as well, and yes
    There are wild geese, ducks and waterfowl,
Beaver, Rabbits and small red squirrels, while
    At night in the distance a Coyote's howl.

The sweetness of the Mountain air
    The breezes weave a melody,
In the language of the forest night; and
    In the silence there is music there for me.

The Forests have an abundance of flowers.
    Nature rules and wild life runs free.
The plants and flowers breath Mountain air,
    While nature whispers songs of serenity.

    *Afton A. Ruffin*

## The Night Cat

The night is my home
Fear is my food
I see them... but do they see me?
I hide in the shadows watching for a meal
My heart's pounding is the only sound made
My burning eyes watch for the small and weak
My body says hunt to eat... my heart says hunt to kill
Many have tried to end my madness... they have failed
The penalty must be enforced
Mercy is withheld
Ending lives is my job... and I do it well
My muscles ache as I run through the darkness
I must make the kill before light
The kill is made... and I am weak
The light is shining through the trees
I must find my home before morning
I make the long jump for the darkness
I must remain here until it is again time for... the night cat

    *Gretchen Seagraves*

## Just Sitting

Watching life through the emptiness of time.
Feeling the wind as thoughts float by.
Knowing that trees outlast one's own eternity.
What was made to last?
Wishing, wanting, hoping, doesn't happen anymore.
It's too late for that.
Waiting for the sun.
Waiting for winter to make its bite.
Spring is here.
The flowers bud.
The sky is blue.
Warmth happens. So what!
So what.
Needing to care.
Needing to be heard and listened to.
Nobody does or wants to.
Just sitting.

    *Jeff Edmond*

## Feelings Are

Feelings are great when someone loves you
Feelings are heartbroken when no one cares
Feelings are happy when you do something good
Feelings are sad when you cry
Feelings are touching when you are having fun
Feelings are confused when you don't know what to do
Feelings are cheerful when someone smiles
Feelings are scared if you don't know the answers
Feelings are brighten when they are there for you
Feelings are bummed when they want to take away everything
Feelings are wonderful when you laugh
Feelings are hurt when someone says good-bye to you forever
Feelings are terrific when you have something for always
Feelings are depressed when there is nothing left
Feelings are excellent when you live the life you want to live
Feelings are sorry when you have done something wrong
Feelings are hopeful when there is hope for someone to come back
Feelings are cold when there is no one to talk to
Feelings are like the world changing and bringing new ideas
everyday,
but nowhere to go ever.

    *Jamie Anderson*

## The Fire Of Life

A passion for life, raging bright and hot
filled with wonder, rebellion, innocence
the magic of being
a bonfire

Mellowing to a golden glow of quiet strength
surviving the winds
of sorrow, pain, and disappointment
calming to the comfort and warmth of love

Minutes of blinking embers, flashes of years
hazy wisps of memories drifting up in smoke
carry sparks of joy and laughter
leaving ashes of hurt and tears

Diminished to a flicker, a faint crackle
of fading beauty and wildness
a wistful whisper of
the fire of life.

    *Carol Flores*

## Spawning Waters

The rustling brook as I sit here
Fills my ear with the sweatiest song
One would want to hear
As I watch the fish swimming along

Small and big fish are at my feet
Going up the brook to lay eggs and spawn
A sign beside this place I sit
Tells me that fishing here is wrong

I gaze dreaming at the water
As it runs past my feet
Knowing sometime later
The warm waters will be a treat

Oh summer, oh summer I've waited so long
You bring so much joy even the birds sing a song
You bring flowers for the old and young to behold
Yes we even forget it was once cold

*Floyd Elton Duff*

## Conscience

A leaf falls gently to the ground, beyond it, an animal emits its
final breath. An arrow severed both the life line of the leaf and the
heart of a beast. Was it for food or just for sport?

The air is suddenly pierced by a high pitched squeal,
beyond it an animal falls to its death.
A bullet split both the air and the life sustaining pump of a beast
Was it for food or just plain sport?

A city sleeps while children starve and get neglected,
beyond them a prison dinner is being served.
The feeding gun had missed, killing both the children and
    society's desire for freedom.
Was it for fun or just sporting pleasure?

A laser light shatters the night time darkness, (eyes for the rocket)
below a sleeping tribe's dreams are snuffed.
A bomb crushed the lives of some and the hopes of others.
Was the finger responsible or just the hair pin trigger?

A leaf falls gently to the ground, beyond a woman kneels weeping over
her husband. The tax snake had squeezed both the husband's life and
the woman's future. The ground hasn't moved yet the death leaf
continues to fall

*Dennis P. Valliere*

## We Three

We bob about on a turbulent sea
Flotsam, Jetsam and I make three
Tossed by waves and beginning to drown
We cling together ever shoreward bound.

Ashore at last - on the sand, in the sun
While waves recede in a foamy run
We laugh with delight in a spate of glee
Victors once more over adversity.

We bask in the warmth; the sea seems to sleep
But we know full well what lies in the deep
That craven leviathan of adversity
Crafting his next move with artistry.

Only God knows what tomorrow will bring
Our faith wavers, but tightly we cling
Flotsam, Jetsam and I - we three
Together we stand indomitably.

*Elaine E. Kelso*

## Our Children's Blood

The red tide of humanity,
Flows with the blood of our children.
Death and carnage caused by our children.
The value of life is worth nothing,
In a world of violence and guns.
Can we live with our own stupidity and ignorance?
Can we ignore the pleas for help?
Or do we band together.
And demand enough is enough!
Life is to precious,
To be taken so easily.

*James H. McCrea*

## My Friends Return

Guess who woke me up this morning, a - pounding on my tree?
Flung wide the drape, my red-headed friend,
Was looking straight at me!

Yes, he's back! My favorite bird, spring has come to be
Again in this place, a joyful sound
A beautiful sight to see!

I also hear another sound and look in my yard out there
And see the Mourning Doves back again,
with two Robins bright and fair.

The Blue-Jays still fighting to get their space,
At the feeder they must share,...
And the Chick-a-dees finishing the suet,
Left over from winters fare. The older I get, I'll never forget
The sounds and the sights always pleasing!
The sounds of the morning, very precious to me
As SPRING'S still my favorite season.

My mind gets a "rush," my ears fill with tunes,
My eyes see the gifts of this season.
The Miracle comes, softly gently creating,
My feathered friends are back for a reason!

*Coralie George*

## Wings of Spring

Something about a butterfly
fluttering around in a colorful array.
Seems an inseparable part of Spring,
especially on a sunny day.

The hard working caterpillar
eats, and eats, and eats all day.
When he reaches adults size,
he creates a cocoon for a stay.

A miraculous metamorphosis takes place
as the caterpillar works out his way.
God's most beautiful insect is born
to find flowers for eggs to lay.

The adult butterfly feeds on nectar,
as God's fairies pollinate the flowers of May.
Spacious gardens will soon be a majestic party,
Before the cool fall winds chase them away.

*Jennifer Reeder*

## Colorful Bird

Bird, bird, bird
fly for me, only for me.
You have colorful wings,
you fly real good and you make
me feel happy. I love to watch
you fly because you fly fast and
I Love playing with you; colorful bird you.

*Erika Conner*

## For a Moment

For a moment, I thought I could forget you
For a moment, I thought I could keep still the restlessness
in my heart
I thought the past could no longer haunt me nor hurt me
how wrong I was..

For the past, no matter how distant, it has become
so much a part of me as life itself
So much so that every words and every thoughts
are coming back no matter how I try to forget.

Yesterday is gone and tomorrow may come
Another love, another heart this time
But the love that we have shared so much together
Will never be forgotten no matter how much I try

How can we be together again
to continue love's precious moment
All the past sweet memories keep haunting me
Memories that will linger on through all ETERNITY.

*Frances G. Vicente*

## Through Him I See

When all seems lost, my love I turn to you
For, even in desperation, the heart knows that which is true

All doors seem closed, not even a window for light
I become so still, so silent this fear to disquiet

I listen; tho' far away I hear your voice  that gives me sight
Oh, yes here is my hope, filtering through this terrible fright

Then, alas, you are once again close by my side
Holding me, comforting, serenely loving that my heart opens wide

I begin to speak, expelling all to you as I almost fall;
Gently, ever so gently you speak, "Don't miss the point of it all"

Our love together is here, is now, "You I shall never leave"
We've spoken before of our struggles; the times to grieve

So safe, so secure, you wrap me close in your arms
Again, made known it is you, my love, that keeps me from harm

Now, and into eternity forever this it shall be
For, when with you, hearts beat in rhythm and it is through
  Your eyes I see-

*Frances Anne Emmert*

## Nightmares That Steal La Luz

It's hard to ponder the years that bruised,
for fears of truths,
lies turned real.
Nightmares stealing la luz.

For dread of tears that hide;
Revealed by trembled words or
Opaque drops of blue.
Revealing secrets that torture souls.

For speeding sounds that pierced the haze
Removing friends moments old.
Stealing love of
years evolved.

A multitude of lives flash by.
Ephemeral innocence enduring darkness.
Does it matter?
In nightmares that steal la luz.

*Gordon P. Hellstrom*

## A Simple Message

I'll say it in verse, this message I send,
For I believe poetry has much sweetness to lend
To a heart that is drooping or weighted with care,
So lonely and burdened and filled with despair.

Though weak and uncertain in life's game of chance,
Our God is aware then we give Him a glance
And ask for His mercy and wisdom and grace
And look for His Presence in those whom we face,
In our everyday walk when we meet on the street,
Or sitting to dine with some one we meet.

By asking God's blessing as we face each new day,
Our burden are lifted whenever we pray,
And the heart is made joyful, turmoils then cease,
And God crowns our day with infinite peace.

*Eunice Lucas*

## An Inspirational Moment

I had a frightening dream last night
For I saw the world in a state of fright.
I saw a group of people running for their lives
While others were chasing with guns and knives.
The world seemed miserably corrupt and gray
But then I saw people kneeling to pray.
Suddenly the darkened sky seemed to brighten
Then I heard a voice say "I'm here to enlighten"
As I awoke, I began to pray
For I knew in my heart what God had to say.
While we're here on earth, we have the right to choose
Which way to go, whether to win or to lose.
If we choose to win, we can walk in the light.
Our comforter walks with us both day and night.
If we decide to lose, then darkness is the gift.
For there will be no light around to uplift.
I know with out a doubt, this dream was meant to be
So that I could share it and help others to see
That God is always here to light up our path.
But if we wait too long, we will suffer his wrath.

*Frances Seymour*

## Love And Friendship

I know what mere friendship can be
For it has brought such joy to me
It makes me laugh when I wish to cry
It makes me sing when I wish to sigh
But till I met love I could not see
How plain that mere friendship can be
For friendship is but buttered bread
Love is Jam, Jelly, and Honey spread

If friendship is a flower love is a rose
While friendship maintains love it grows
If friendship is a candle love is the sun
If friendship is joyous love is fun
If friendship is a strong wind love is a gale
If friendship is a fish love is a whale
Friendship is of earth so sweet and fine
Love is of heaven and so divine

*Barrington Barnswell*

## Brotherhood

He who shoots his arrow from the tree of a distant hill
Knows not what his arrow will kill
Upon a closer glance the righteous archer paused
He was astounded at all the pain he caused
For his arrow did meander in its weakness much to his dismay
And strike old forgotten wounds of yesterday.

*John R. Dodds*

## Soft Wishes

When I look at your son he's not all that I see,
For me heart places him where I long you to be.
I watch him run to you, your arms open wide,
You gather him closely with  motion of pride.
There is a feeling of realness from the heavens above.
You have been given a way to show him your love.
You can be here to dry tears if he's hurt
while at play,
And there is laughter of love for his comical ways.
I believe any moment you can reach out your hand,
And touch his head gently as part of God's plan.
The warmth of your happiness can be seen every day,
And it is shared by your son in so many ways.
You are part of his heaven, he is part of your earth,
Joined together for eternity on the day of his birth.

*Helen Madge Clark*

## Hole In My Heart

I host a hole in my heart
momentarily mended, last night
when I spoke with you.

A mountain of memories
came crashing down, on the wall
that you broke through.

The sweet sound of your voice
softly soothed, my dull ache
carried in a crevice of my heart.

Heavy haze of remembrance
partially parted - for a moment,
one last longing look at you.

*Ann Gaunt*

## Mother's Day — Sunday May 14th 1995

Today is Mother's Day.
For me, it's sad as I knew is would be.
But I'm thankful for my mother God so proudly shared with me!

She had a beautiful personality
A heart full of love and so very kind
And when I wanted a kiss or a hug, she never seemed to mind.

She was a beautiful mother,
With so much beauty within.  Not only was she my mother,
She was also my best friend.

On Sunday, March 12, 1961,
When God came and made his call,
She just smiled and closed her eyes,
As she said good-bye to all.

My praise and greatest thanks
Go out to God above.  For giving me such a beautiful mother,
And one so full of love.

Mother I love your dearly,
As I have always from the start.
The love you gave me, and my precious memories of you,
Will always linger in my heart.

*Bessie Lucille Cockfield*

## Thunder In My Soul

Thunderous, rhythmically
my soul began to stir.
Calling out to me like thunder lion roar.
Deep within my desire, like leaves in the wind they blew,
upward from their buried state, to my waiting soul.

*Gail Montgomery*

## That Special Day

On the day I was born she must have cried
For she certainly did not want any child by her side

Days, months and years past
But her hate for me continued to last

It was so hard growing up and learning  to love
When a hug to me was just a big shove

Determine I was, that I would never be
Like the woman, who gave birth to me

Four children, Jerri, Tammy, Billie and James, are my
Greatest life's treasure
So much love I have for them that I cannot measure

It is because of them that I want to say
Thank you for that special day
The day that I was given life
And a chance to rise above all the abuse and strife.

*Glenda J. Weatherman*

## Who Am I?

Some try to speculate on my return
    for shows have proven so.
No one plays me better than I.
    The audience flutters when I materialize.
My presence is met with a gentle roar,
    like the shutting of a door.

Crevices open to feast on it's prey,
    not being picky, just what's in its way.
An array of edifices quality,
    and lemons satisfy.
Levees don't do their job,
    so drivers begin to bob.

Rick Tor-rents is the judge that supplies the evidence.
    His scale starts level and goes to intense.
The drum doesn't beat,
    but it keeps track of the heat.
The needle won't cut,
    like a scalpel would.

The vote is in, and I win,
    with a ride down a landslide!

*Denise Jacques*

## The Christian Walk

We need God's Word in our hearts
For the christian walk as we start.
I wish that everyone could see
His Word's the map to eternity.

There are only two roads in which to go;
One is to heaven, the other below.
The narrow one to Heaven leads,
And is paved with our good deeds.

Read God's Word' you'll find He loves us so much.
Look to him, daily, for a brand new touch.
Our tests and trails are often quite hard.
Satan is waiting to catch us off guard.

God gave His Son as a gift to one and all,
Some trampling under foot, refusing His call.
He loved us when we were unlovely, too,
Tho He didn't love the sin we would do.

His heart was broken as He hung on the tree
For sins committed by you and by me.
We were made in His image, yet marred by sin,
But He provided the way of return—by accepting HIM.

*Beulah Sapp*

## The Enemy

Mothers, teach your daughters well
For the enemy is lurking around,
To make your life a living hell
And to tear your girls to the ground.

He comes with smiles and dazzling eyes
To deceive the innocent prey,
His tongue is filled with polished lies
And he knows just what to say.

"I'll give you the moon, the stars," he says,
"What ever you want you will receive."
The poor inexperienced girl these days
Most likely would believe.

Hooray! He'd shout and gallivant
Scandalizing the poor girls name,
After the kill he'd joyfully chant
Another one yet to defame.

So mothers teach your daughters pride
Let them know that they have worth,
Show them love and be their guide
So they can face the men of this earth.

*Juliet R. Jordan*

## The Proposal

Are you willing to walk with me, my love?
  For the road will often be hard, the path rocky, and moving
  steadily uphill.
Are you willing to walk with me, my love?
  For the rewards won't be that the road grows smoother, or the path
  becomes level, and easier to make progress over.
Are you willing to walk with me, my love?
  For the very thing we will look to, to save us, to give us strength
  to keep on walking, will be the thing that causes us to turn and
  run the other way, countless numbers of times.
It is the infinite and shining beauty of the love that is shared by a
man and a woman,
  the love that is you, expressed by your man's body and mind
  the love that is me, expressed by my woman's body and mind.
It is this beautiful and terrible love, so overwhelming in its power,
  that will cause us to stop and want to go back, that will make us
  go numb with fear, and cold in the denial of our longing for it.
But, in the midst of my fear, I reach out, choose to listen to my
  heart, and reach out of myself, to touch you and ask....
Are you willing to walk with me, for I want to walk with you.

*Diane Miether-Malachoff*

## "A Woman Clothed In Blue"

She must have been very beautiful as she walked across the land
For the service she fulfilled held a baby in her hand
That beautiful baby that she bore, would become a kingly man he will
rule the world with honor and with his scepter on his throne
And throughout the world and heavens he will become well known
His name is known as Jesus and he is the Christ child from Mary's
womb.
And when he comes back to rule the nations, there will be no more
heartache and gloom
For every one and everything will be transformed in an instant time
And there will be no more sadness and crime.
Because everyone will be filled with love, and compassion will abound
And all God's creatures and animals will be gentle and profound
We must give thanks to a lovely lady "A WOMAN CLOTHED IN
BLUE"
For having brought the child Jesus into the world, the main one
of a chosen few
God chose this special lady to give birth to a special king
And he will rule with God, the father, all nations supreme
But his adoring mother should be given glory too
For she does reign a queen and she is "A WOMAN CLOTHS IN BLUE"

*Glenna Mann*

## Song For Aunt Marjorie (92 at Pierce)

A tent is pitched near Somersby, where Tennyson was born,
for there lives Lady with like name, and I've been rightly sworn
to code a bar of poetry, to ease uneasy game.
  The skirl of pipes is fainter now,
  displaced by welcome draft,
  as Lady fathoms why and how
  Lord Tennyson plied craft.
  Like his, her skiff was honed to stand
  swift currents of the sea,
  but mainly sailed in sight of land,
  in view of family
  so came the time — time on the wane—
  prime barque might come to rest
  beyond the reach of skirling pain,
  to dock at Endo' quest.
Come, light a pipe near Somersby where lords and ladies bide.
Come raise a glass to cherished name, occasioner of pride,
and Lady — known as Marjorie — at ease with waiting game.

*Judith Pike Boos*

## Love the Children

Love the children
For they are our tomorrows
Reach out your hand, guide their way
Give them understanding, give them praise
For they fill our lives with sunny days.

Love the children
Teach them to stand tall
Teach them the values of right and wrong
Teach them to carry their dignity with pride
And not lose it when things subside.

Love the children, when they cry.
Caress them softly, show you care
And if you ever feel sad when old and alone
Think back of a time when you were small
Think of love as in a song.

Their reaching out with their small grown up hands
They've learned understanding, they've learned how to stand.
So love the children
And give them praise
For they fill our lives with sunny days.

*Cheryl Regina Miller*

## The Warlord

He's got a hatred for mankind,
for what they've done to his mind.
He blames civilized humanity
for his life's insanity.
One just finished, he hopes for more.
The Warlord hungers for a war.
He's got a desire to grow in power,
from his enemy's he'll never cower.
To look at him he looks so sad,
but his closest friends say he's mad.
Watch him work he's not lazy,
but see his plans, and you'll know he's crazy.
The Warlord trusts no one with his life.
He's even scared to take a wife.
One just finished, he hopes for more.
The Warlord hungers for a war.
He leads his men dressed in black.
With the rising sun he makes his attack.
He's got a hatred for mankind,
for what they've done to his mind.

*Brett L. Hawks*

## Never Alone

Lord, how can I thank you and possibly say
For what you have given me today
With all my heart I hope and pray
That others somewhere along the way
Can open up their hearts and say
Lord, within your arms I will stay

When others around me are full of sorrow
Many who worry about tomorrow
Just look to the Lord and you will find
That wonderful joy and peace of mind

No matter what the future has in store
The Lord will never close his door
He always listens to our heart
And from our side he will never part

*Joyce Scales*

## "Never Make A Promise You Can't Keep"

Never make a promise you can't keep,
For you never know the seeds you may reap!

For those little ones at your side they stand,
Will one day become a woman or a man.

Held within that sacred vow
Is the promise you gave them here and now.

A bonding of trust either broken or built within
The journey of their lives as they begin,

To form principles honest and true
For their integrity started with you.

Never make a promise you can't keep,
For you never know the length or how deep

That promise is taken to the very heart and soul
Of where it will end and what will be their goal.

*Joyce A. Leonard*

## Remember Him

Cry not for your own good,
For your sweet Lord was nailed on wood.
Do not cry, and do not fear,
Remember Jesus is always near.
Do not hurt others for personal gain,
For the Messiah would not live in vain.
Do not murder, and do not sin,
Remember whose world you live in.
Try your best, with all your heart
For Jesus made the river part.
Love each other with all your soul,
For it is the Almighty that makes you whole.

*Alison E. Smith*

## Janaranya (Sanskrit, Meaning "Jungle Of People")

The thick, dark and gloomy equatorial forests
flash in my inward eye,
Where creepers and trees vie for the
same brilliant sunshine,
The tall outgrowing ones are lucky
leaving the rest under their shade below;
Some thrive, some survive in the perennial shade
while a few perish cruelly,
their desires unfulfilled.

*Chandrashekar A. S. Tamirisa*

## The Photograph

Women and child
Forever captured in a photograph; never aging
While their counterparts change; growing older and maturing
The child now grown, a life of its own
The woman, older, fretting night and day
Days pass into years and time whispers it death
The photograph
Though yellowed, torn and well worn
Keeps its images prisoner, and alive
Withered hands trace the two
The child, now much older, holds memories in her hands;
and in her heart
She whispers softly and puts it away
The whisper creeps around the room; to land on silence
A small child's giggle ghosts by
"I love you, Mother."
A memory taken in an instant lasts forever in its gaze
Forever caught in love; in silence; in memory
In a photograph long past
A woman and child, a mother and a daughter.

*Jessica L. Josephson*

## Forgiven?

"Let's forget it, I forgive you"
Forgive what?
What I just told you.
How you look and took from the folks
all those years
They paid for your two divorcees
and you lived there with your three kids
  "I paid my way" "I can't believe you
have held that all in for all these years"
  It was a very emotional time
going through the last sale of dad's
belongings.  Having a friendly drink.
  the hardest to hear that I had taken
every thing but the kitchen sink to take him
to my home to take care of him.
  "You had said one time you would like to get good
and drunk so you could tell somebody off.
  Now we are all that's left
I've tried to treat you like a real sister
  Can I trust you?

*Doris Capp*

## Mobius Trip

To begin, relinquish what must be
  forgotten , left behind in the
Bardo just before birth, just after...
  It is all flux, as one master
Has said, though also a stillness,
  a dance of utter wakefulness
Folding into sleep.  Take Escher,
  for another, who used queer
Mathematical scripts for overlaying
  meaning onto life.  Even in the saying
He knew nothing solid would arise
  from the karmic drama right before our eyes.

Alums of the NDE forthright assert
  presence, entities, an orbed light inert
And welcoming and warm as, reclining,
  they floated into it dismissing
All prior notions regarding reality.
  Can we afford to doubt epiphany?
Or shall we defy all science, suspend
  disbelief and embrace living end?

*Durren Anderson*

## The Human Heart

So easily broken, so easily appalled,
Fragile and so sensitive, easily hurt and scarred.
Pitter patter moves my heart, as it cries out for love
And attention.
To get affection and security is like a competition.
A heart is shattered so quickly by lies and deception.

The human heart is amazing, complicated like a puzzle.
But how to win one is confusing and so much trouble.
Unsure of what you think - I don't want to turn you away,
So instead of speaking to you, I ignore you and just stay.
Wishing I could make you mine, if only there were a way.

Maybe I should move on, and forget you were ever there,
But feelings deep within me, bind me here.
Unwanted good-bye's tear this mind apart;
Ripping in pieces, this human heart.

*Casey Tindle*

## Ode to an Orca

Mammal majestic, aged million year, deep in the ocean, frolicking and
free; land-dwellers in their boats, drawing you near, completely for
the sake of some money. To levels low have we sunk human life, that
we enslave, we kill such loveliness, all in order to dominate the
world. While we in separate factions meet in strife, you join with
family in happiness and frolic and fish in the waving curl.

Long-living animal, magnificent, bowing to you, strange-eyed, is how
it ought, as your race will go on when ours is spent by way of killing
all that nature has wrought. Teach us to nurture, thou of black and
white; as humans, we destroy all that we touch; we call it progress.
Nature calls it death. God of the fathoms, o creature of might,
advise us, so we cease destruction such, making thou certain not to
breathe last breath.

O Orca, you have seen us through it all; if only we could see through
your strange eyes, how every time we try to rise, we fall. We know
you witness it, but we ignore your cries of warning, as nothing to us
they mean. Our search, our thirst for total and complete power and
domination is hurting your world. You beautiful majestic creature,
seldom seen, whose world is delicate, just like a flower; I'm sorry
for your flag of pain, by man unfurled.

*Jennifer Sifuentes*

## Freedom

From the first time you see the light, to the last,
freedom.
When the world you once knew is gone, Heaven is
freedom.
To fight for your country, and die for your country,
freedom is what you gave to millions.

Love is freedom in a world with hate and war.
Freedom.

*Joey Kuba*

## Friendship

When the squirrels are still and birds don't fly away.
Freedom is yet to come.
You can hear the birds singing in the trees.
And people are nice to each other.
And when you're feeling blue, you always have a person to look up to
and to
help you through.

*Allicia German*

## The Love of Books

It was through the love of books I found a
friend - it was through the love of books
I reached to heights I only dare to dream.

It was through the love of books I climbed
to heights above my peers and threw off the
scales of darkness, and shackles of poverty
that just seek to keep me bound in weights
of ignorance.

I see a new day dawn as the night vanishes
as it sees the light. So did my mind see
clarity as the shadows melt away. It was
through the love of books I finally found
my way.

*Elizabeth Clarke*

## Departed Friends

Friends I have known,
Friends who have gone...
The memory of them still lingers on,
Sweeter than nectar or honey cone
More esteemed than jewels or any precious stone;
They're all locked in my valued treasure of thoughts
To nurture and last as they really ought...
AND - to be a part of me - predestinely.

*Ida Mae Gurley Miller*

## Pilgrimage to the Heart

Hope
From dark caverns and eery tunnels a faint cry of the soul
Treasures live which yearn for speech
Turmoil asunder as blinded eyes grope for light
Bound in chains of fears, voices muted in hues of gray
Succumb to his hope, placed delicately live a prayer
The pain of struggle in search of a song.

Inspiration
Awake and breathe oh tender spirit
Imagination rests in the heart
Dreams of winged creation, grounded in the secret of humanity,
Swept up in a tale of inspiration
Boldness releases a journey of a thousand faces
Ripped from the head, nurtured in the soul,
Enthralled in safety, dares to summer magic.
Lodged in the stillest center of love
To thine own self be true.

*Elizabeth Anne Bowen*

## His Last Rodeo

He's on a rode that will take him a thousand miles away
from his friends and the only woman he love's and he wonder's
if he's doing the right thing. A thousand miles back they sit
and wonder where their friend may be on his rode to Texas. She
sits there wondering about him and why he had to go. He was her
everything. She'll die if her cowboy doesn't return from his Rodeo.
Two thousand miles away he's still driving and their song comes on
"The dance," then "If tomorrow never comes," and they make him think
about her. 1,2,3,4,5,6,7,8, he rides on his Rodeo and down he goes
this is one cowboy who won't be forgotten.

*Jennifer S. Combs*

## Tenses

My country's face was beauty, and
from it came that glow, where faith
and hope are nourished, that
charity might grow. Held high its
torch of freedom, to those from
every shore, that they might know
abundance, they had never known before.

My country's face a stranger,
ominous to eye. It lurks in those
dark shadows where hate and vengeance
lie. It laughs at immorality, and
glorifies its lust. It scorns the
light of heaven, and chides the moral just.

My country's face shall ashen, and
struggle for its breath. Its
countenance of beauty, will become its
mask of death. It traded its true
freedom, for the abortive seeds of
hate. Now only "God" can save it,
from its moribund state.

*Anthony T. Marconi*

## Spring Catalog

When April comes I no longer can see the Arch
From my window as the elms and maples foliate
Blocking the view, and the earth begins to melt and march
Out of winter's lockstep, or stirs once more to mate

By the rosebuds: squirrels, rabbits and everything
Airborne: doves, jays, robins. Soon there will arrive
New hybrids to plant. Yet the taste of this cold Spring
Is bittersweet with the uncertainty of what's still alive.

If to believe that what lies dead will be deployed
In some dimension again, alive and growing
Invisibly, or in white or brown or green,

Is beyond our reason, yet surely if it isn't destroyed
It must be inviolate, like the pain and peace in knowing
That what we may see isn't what we have always seen.

*Charles Guenther*

## The Green Evil

The freedom of the mind, to wander, to roam endlessly floating
From one cloud of thought,
    To another of perception.
My mind as it roams discovers the insecurity of myself,
    My paranoia trapped within.
    Within a body lost of its cause,
    Of its inspiration,
        Its being.
My surroundings unknowingly sequester
    Me
    To my thoughts,
    My perceptions,
Misconclusions.

*Anthony Risko*

## Untitled

Have faith dear friend,
    For the Lord is here.
So tell the truth for all to hear...
Repent your sin, for he alone...
Will listen and forgive
    the wrongs you've done.
So fall to your knees, oh sinner fall...
For the Lord will hear your plea and call.

*Ericka L. Norquest*

## Brave GIs of America!!

Brave GIs of America, we're proud of you today!!
From rank and file to officer, marines and green berets.
For standing by your country true and fighting to the death
To honor well your country's pledge
More sacred than life's very breath.

To all of you who sail the seas to fight by land or air,
Who sacrifice for "blood and tears" your comfort, home and ease,
We hold you all in deep respect our gallant servicemen
Who hear the call of "duty" stern
When aggression's dark red light does burn.

For fallen lives we ne'er shall know
In freedom's cause so brave
The "Everlasting Flame" does glow
At the "Unknown Soldier's" grave.

And we for vet'rans all do share
Our warm and earnest prayer
For God to bless and honor you
BRAVE GIs OF AMERICA!!!

*Helena H. Butterfield*

## Oh, How I Yearn To Be Free

From apathy
From sadness, hopelessness, and despair
From hatred, war and starvation
From the unsmiling stone faces that walks pass me
From a society's lust for power, greed and domination
From man's destruction of Mother Earth

To see everyone have compassion for one another
To be jubilant, optimistic, and peaceful
To love unselfish, love thy neighbor, share thy bread
To smile at others and genuinely receive it back
To be in a society that recoils from man's devices
In a world that loves and respects mother earth
Oh, how I yearn to be free

*Deborah A. Connell*

## Impact By Divine Pursuit

Where is the bliss, calm, or still
From shadowy darkness and the unknown?
Relentlessly helpless, all nerve ends bend
Oppressed, vehemently shattered and broken

Anxiety heightens, out of control
A sight of clamoring in hopelessness
Pangs of infruition throb the emptiness
Nowhere to go, no one to care

Then alas intent and openly listening -
Pleading innermost, but humbly seeking
The soul beckons for change
Divine power claims then its own
To rid ravage gregariously from the soul

Hope arise; the spirit lifts
Wisdom emerges; then love,
Immeasurable healing, peace and trust
Joyously fortified by divine pursuit
Indeed now, unafraid nor alone
A whole being reconciles anew
By divine impact of grace in the soul

*Jeroline D. McCarthy*

## The Painting

My eyes watch each drop of rain
From the cafe I see
The sorrow eyes of walker by's
With their heads lingering under
Great black shields
My wandering eyes search for new prey
The bartender makes his art forms
For loyal customers
Sucked into his society of insobriety
The fidgety dame puffs away
While the light reflects on the silver lighter
She twirls through her fingers
My mind is challenged to see
How smoking can be so clumsy
Thoughts drive though my blockade
Of others lives
While my reality comes back
I wish James Dean was still at the show
That the king is still rockin'
And Marilyn Monroe was still turning heads.

*Dwayne A. Sills*

## The Colors Of Nature, The Nature Of Colors

Perhaps a rose is the shade of red,
From the dripping blood that had been shed,
As an innocent hand was once intervened,
By the guardian thorn; instinctively mean.

Perhaps the sky is the color of blue,
From the loneliness that it feels too,
When its nearest companions are miles away,
And whatever travels through can never quite stay.

Perhaps the grass is painted green,
By an unseen brush which can't be cleaned-
-of its bugs and its life, no matter what's used,
By the keepers of land and their hard attitudes.

Perhaps the clouds are unpompous and white,
Upon constantly losing each futile rigged fight.
They grow sordid and sick from pollution and smoke,
Turning rancid and black as if ready to choke.

Perhaps there's more here than what reached our eyes,
These things are facades; objects in disguise,
In a world with experience far greater than ours,
That conceals its harsh lessons within its sweet colors.

*Bryan Lopper*

## Bingo Night at the Marcy St. Retirement Home

On Wednesday nights they pull the pin
from the gate and the old boys
don't worry about gummin' their chow,
the bags at their sides or who's got B5.

Tonight, Whitey, Shorty and Bob spin
from the chute without making noise
and stride toward picnic tables out back.
While white, numbered balls spin inside

They hitch up their redwood ponies,
remember Pendleton, Cheyenne
and Calgary, the busted-out teeth
and punctured lungs. Drunk on the night's
Cold air, they're herded back at ten
to dream of horses and whiskey again.

*Joseph Ivey*

## Christmas 1994

Where have all the children gone
from where has come these unhappy cities
where these lands groaning under
deficits and hate and immoralities
have we never learned the lessons
of Sodom and Gomorrah destroyed
because God could not find ten good men
within them worth saving
Lord you have sifted us about like wheat
promising the reaping of the good and bad
and then the separation
at Christmas we kneel to look upon
the Child of our salvation
who came to give good men to every city
revive our heart oh Lord
se we can shed abroad your light
and raise new souls to stand
joyous and free in every marketplace

*Joan Arrivee Wagenblast*

## Behold, A Pale Horse

Behold, a pale horse, the flower bed he crosses will bare fruit no more,
have mercy on his soul, as he stands before death's door.
Have pity on this being, that has known only tragedy and sorrow,
this instrument of doom, alone against tomorrow.

A heart made of ice, a body as warm as a shell,
a mind full of illusions, a place where demons dwell.
One step from the grave, a hand reaching for tomorrow,
this creature from hell, a sympathy of sorrow.

Yet, he walks with grace, symmetry and perfection,
a lethal power of persuasion, no need for correction.
Born to be a prophet of man, but something went tragically wrong,
slaughtering through the ages, on a world he doesn't belong.

Behold, a pale horse, the people he touches will live no more,
who has caused him to escape, from the realm beyond death's door.

Have pity on this being, that has known only catastrophe and sorrow,
for he must forever shun the friendship of man, alone against
tomorrow.

*Jotham R. Austin*

## Mean A Heart

You came in my life away that
   fulfilled so much

You walked with me in away that
   taught so much.....

You lived within me away that
   gave so much.....

You loved me in away that never before
   meant so much......

So I give to you my mine
   body and soul to you today.......

For tomorrow is not promise
   to no one.....

For today I was bless with loving
   children boys and girls.....

For today...tomorrow ...next week...even next month....
   and as the years rolls around...

I told you my heavenly Father
   my mine... body... and soul....

*Jacqueline Evon Nelms*

## When Doubt Creeps In

Plans for happiness and
Fulfillment of dreams to come,
Gladden the spirit for those joyous plans
But they were swiftly turned to nought,
When doubt suddenly knocked at the door.

A conflict ensued for doing the right thing,
But the battle continued for hours to come;
It even dragged on, for days on end;
Then sure enough, the conqueror
Claimed victory once again, and stood as before
With strength and optimism.

Then on intent, to reclaim its status,
Doubt knocked again to ensue the battle.
Perhaps it was right in sending its message
So put the battle on hold
And review your plans,
Because this, may have been the reason,
Why doubt crept into your plans.

*Joan E. Gettry*

## "The Golden Years" -

## An Incest Survivor's Right To Embrace Life

To live life to some is dark and despair; to ponder life is such futility; but fear not, to embrace life is work, experience worry, joy and love.

Ah, to ponder old age after work is finished, to worry about your life and the despair you have suffered is futile; to embrace old age is to embrace love, understanding of your goals in life, commitment, work, and love.

I ponder life daily, wondering why am I here, why did things happen to me that I had no control over. Why am I filled with so much hate, but at the same time so much understanding and love. Mine is not to ponder why, but to embrace life, use what I have learned and finish out life with gusto, understanding and love.

What is love? I do not know, but enjoy it, revel in it, become part of it.

The "Golden Years" is a time to enjoy, remember not the past, but the future, not despair, but love, not fear, but understanding. Enjoy what you have and forget about the past and the despair of your younger life.

With remembering comes pain, agony, fear, despair, but to go on takes love and courage.

Remember not what happened, but what will happen and can happen in those glorious "Golden Years."

*Colleen Young*

## All Dressed In Yellow

The sun caressed her as she moved past a flower
garden and up the red brick walk to the fountain.
She stopped for a drink, barely touching the water.
A warm spring breeze blew soft white marshmallow
clouds over the baby blue sky.
She completed the summer time picture
As I sat in the shade waiting, watching, I asked myself,
would she come this way?
She turned around, something changed her mind.
A breeze, a smell I couldn't tell what.
I waited, watching hopefully.
Would she continue on toward me?
She was beautiful.
I was barely breathing as she came closer.
She was radiant in the bright sunlight as she
lifted one wing after the other.
A yellow butterfly was captured in my heart, not a net.

*Dorothy Dandron*

## Lord Help Us To Be Just Like Him

With each ending a new start begins not knowing what God in our future may now to us extend;
But with a purity and a newness of heart, we can simply ask for His leading to immediately start.
First in obedience in seeking His will that only His desires in us He will begin to instill;
that we may become evermore just like Him, for He is our Savior, our Creator, our Master and our Friend!

Thank you Lord for the hurts we suffer through, for through these sufferings we learn and know more of you. Heal us, restore us, help us to grow; that through our outstretched arms to others your love we may bestow. In helping others through their hurts and despair, let us minister with an acknowledging hug, a warm smile, a comforting word and then a sweet simple prayer.

We love you Lord for all that you gave, when your son died on that cross so very far away. "How much do you love us?", we so often reply and Jesus simply stated "This much" as he opened up his arms and then died.

He sent forth his spirit in each of us to abide; If we will simply ask Jesus to enter our hearts and reside. Lord teach us your son's humility and to be servants to all; trusting you completely if and when we may fall.

Let us thank you and praise you in all that we may think, say and do, that through all of life's circumstances may the light of your son Jesus always shine through. We love you Lord, Amen.

*Cynthia Rhudy*

## Mary's Lullaby

Her gentle hands, adorning eyes are
    gazing down from heaven's skies.
She whispers sweetly in each child's ear,
    calms their hearts and soothes their fears.

My little ones I am at peace,
    my earthly state is gone.
Father and mother here on high
    want me to carry on.

In Gods Kingdom here on high,
    sweet music fills my ears.
I'll watch you grow and see your trials
    and you will know I'm near.

A mother's love is always nigh,
    it stretches broad and far.
Love floats, from here and radiates on
    a twinkling star.

Rejoice in life and living and when
    the day is through.
Lift up your prayers to heaven,
    and I will be with you.

*Diana K. Thacher*

## Life

Life is the best thing I was ever given.
Life is so full, I have so much to look forward to.
Unlike my friend I loved life, she despised it.
I wish somebody had listened to her.
She was telling the truth.
One day she went to far.
She ended the best thing she was ever given.
She put her family and friends through it all.
Our church was never fuller, everybody loved her.
    Except her!

*Gilienne Roher*

## Nevada

WITH HORSES ROAM THE DESERT THEY HAVE NO HOME
Geese and Ducks fly overhead calling out
Their demands looking down at the land.

The air is so clean and air is dry, I just said Bay Area Good-bye.

I started having eye trouble, went to an eye doctor, went and got
glasses; asked what was wrong, as it was getting hard to see

He said, "You're getting old-89 and you are fine."
When I was 90 I was told I have cataracts in both eyes.

I called a Cataract Surgery Center and told them, "I'm going on
91 years old. Can you do anything for me?" "Come on in we will see."

I met Doctor Paul, he examined my eyes said, "Yes, I can remove them
but it'd be one at a time; it takes 45 minutes and after the surgery
you go home. Bring someone with you; don't be alone."

When I came to O'noops Cataract was gone.
Next day, bandages were taken off; I could see.
20/20 vision, yes this was me.

Doctor Paul gave a living life back to me
I can go back to writing poetry.

*Esther Lafaye Pohlman*

## Things I Wouldn't Want to Happen

Some things I wouldn't want to happen are like
getting hit by a car
and landing on a bar.
Or a gun up to your head,
then you would be dead.
Your head cut off,
a car accident,
a heart attack,
or die at a young age
that all would be a rage.
If your friend is dead,
well, let's talk about something else instead.
These are some things I wouldn't want to happen.

*Camila Klinger*

## The Souls Aloe

The plant of aloe
Given from nature itself;
That is said to heal
The physical scrapes of life.

What then has nature provided
For the souls scrapes in life?
The aloe for my soul
I believe, would be to love.

I will therefore search this day with nature
To seek the power of love.
For to heal any wound
One need only to apply.

As I apply the aloe for my soul,
And all healing becomes more complete
Let me embrace each day
And give a part of it away.

For love is like the aloe.
The piece you give away
The break itself will heal
For yet more another day.

*Catherine M. Bokach*

## Father Phil

Father Phil, I hold a cross-
given in a parking lot that I hold
    closest to my heart there is no loss-
I can dance around the world but I can't dance around you-
    You are my friend- enough said-
I think with two hearts, I hear, this eternal thing-
    I'm not prepared for
But I accepted-
    I need to be held-
As equally as you
    need to be felt
I speak to two hearts here
I hold- I feel- I sink-
    I will not drown-
In you my father a godly priest
    There is no Corporal-
That could make me sink
    No, not in the least
Suess, my friend

    I think I can finally sleep- So sad-

*Cliff Donaldson*

## Paradox Ultima

"If I am to experience love in all its righteous and terrible
glory, let it be with you:
    Allow me to taste ultimate agony and never ending bliss in your
lips as sweet as dew.
    Let me touch Hades and Paradise in your skin:
    My quest and mission always being, your heart to win.
    Many times have I said,
'Logic is the downfall of all great dreamers,
    But now let me add unto this phrase,
'Love being their torture, solace and redeemer.'
    For all this which I say here is true.
    Since I do not have the power to lie before the total beauty I find
in you.
    I have found true beauty and it is life...
    ...Be it known, I will always love you, through peace and
happiness,
war and strife."

*Artur Prejna*

## Joined Together By Providence

Joined together by Providence
Go on your journey with confidence
Endurance and patience
Have been duly recompensed.
Not yielding to reckless abandonment
You instead chose obedience and common sense.

Life's dance will no longer be solitary
Its choreography will be that of two
Hearts that are merry
So much to share both the sad and the cheery
Love's protective instincts will
Refuse to be weary.

With tender care and sincerity
Woo each other for eternity
And when there comes the time for debating
Retrain from word that triggers hurting
Love and honor till death do you part
Should be indelibly printed upon your heart

When you go to sleep at night
Embrace and hold each other tight
Comfort, encourage, communicate
And leave the day's turmoil outside your gate.
With peace and harmony reigning inside
You welcome the Savior to come and abide.

*Barbara Eliane Isaacs*

## "The Throne Is His"

My Jesus came to earth just for us.
God created and sent him, and the death Jesus died, God said was a must.
He died the most crucial death known.
Now he sits on the highest Golden throne.
He came to earth to show us the way. He showed and told everyone about
His father in heaven in any way he could say.
Jesus proved he could die, and rise again.
Who could not believe in him, I'll never understand why.
But when God said Jesus had been here as much time as he could spend.
He took Jesus to his beautiful Golden Throne.
And said, I love you so much my son, it's time for you to come home.
The people had drug him and hung him to a cross, drove nails through his hands and feet.
I know in my heart those cold, cold hearts are forever lost.
But for those who worshipped and followed, and believed in Jesus.
Next to his Golden Throne will always have a seat.

*Joyce Ann Lambeth*

## Awaken

Go deep within and look inside
God is there, besideS
You just might see
Where you have been and are now meant to be
Yesterday has now become the past.
Let no one evil cast
Listen to what God has to say
Then the lessons will stay
Today is in the making
open your heart and soul to your awakening
Tomorrow is yet to be
I am looking forward to see
the love, truths and wisdom it shall bring
So my joyful heart can sing
How wonderful it is to be
Me
And God will show me what to do
To always see
How wonderful it is to be
You

*Betty Ann Bradley AKA Moonlight*

## My Mother, My Friend

She has now departed, her life on earth,
God saw fit to give her new birth.
Her life while with us, she gave so much,
From her smile, I could feel her touch.

Her guidance and love, an abundance of all,
She was always there, she stood very tall.
Through good and bad, she never let go,
It was an honor, this woman to know.

When I needed her to listen, she found the time,
Her words of wisdom, brought the sunshine.
Through many struggles, she was by my side,
My mother, my friend, my head I hold high with pride.

I know she is with me, each and every day,
She watches over me, as I continue on my way.
If ever I need to talk, she's not far away,
She's in my heart and there she'll always stay.
I love you very, very much Mom.

*Denise Lynn Kotowski Fincham*

## Untitled

At Four O'Clock
A Hawk
chased a Gull around the Moon
and chase them all
did Afternoon.

*Jennifer M. Noren*

## God's Child

I still remember taking you from that doggie bed
God spoke to me and this is what he said
I give to you the best gift that I can give
A child to hold and love and show her how to live
Freely giving hugs and kisses and a warm embrace
We would get a beautiful smile when looking at your face
Grandma would change your wet, and dirty things
You would listen so intently to the lullabies she sings
You have learned to walk and talk, and even run and play
You bring unto our hearts and lives, sunshine everyday
Going to school now you are learning to read and write
Grandma helps with your homework, almost every night
I pick you up at school each day bringing you a treat
Before going home you get an ice cream cone to eat
You are growing up and your attention now is clothes
I would like to say this before I must close
To express how much I love you I am at a loss
How true it was and is when you said I am the boss
I thank the Lord God in heaven up above
For the beautiful children he has sent for us to love

*Donald H. Elfreich*

## God's Special Union

To my new Son and Daughter's union:
God will forever bless you from this loving
nineteenth day of May
Throughout the eternal years
together you will stay.
Love each other and greet each other
with a morning kiss
So your Godly union
will never be amiss
Our eternal love also bless you from above.
Mom and Dad

*Betty J. Diggs*

## Night And Day

The moon has waned the sun is up
God's dew is on the buttercup;
The nocturnal creatures on each pretty flower
Have gone to sleep 'til the twilight hour.

The dazzling sun with it's healing rays
Casts a magic spell over long summer days;
The Robin, the Chickadee, the lazy old grouse
Come alive to the sunshine which has entered
their house.

When the sun will have hidden his big shiny self
Beyond the horizon 'neath earth's crusty shelf;
Then will the moon rise in her mesmeric glow
Lighting the pathway soft as new fallen snow,
And they of the night, and we of the day
Will know it is God who is holding full sway.

*Dorothy Marple*

## Life is like a Mountain

Life is like a mountain
going tall and wide
and once you reach the middle
there is nowhere to hide.
The way is rough and rocky
the trip is tough.
It is a struggle for soul and mind
if you try hard enough, you can benefit man kind.
Don't ever give up.
Keep trying.
Don't worry about crying.
When you get to the top.
Try to think and stop.
You have conquered the mountain.
Now quick, run to the water fountain.

*Amanda Ploegstra*

## The Fourth Wall

The value of life. Never appraised like diamonds or weighed like
gold. Never watered like young plants or drunk like expensive wine
only wasted like bruised fruit and sold as slaves for souls.

Whoever invented the fourth wall was the executioner of human
empathy. See I understand, I truly understand the need of a third
wall, the wall that helps hold up the roof and we need roofs I know
that, I understand that but the fourth wall, the wall that everyone's
t.v. sits in front of, the wall that dusty literary classics sit upon,
the wall that breaks the thrown dishes, the wall that separates me
from my unknown neighbor my possible hero my possible saviour.
This wall I do not understand. This wall I pray would collapse and
crumble before my lead filled eyes then I could see my neighbor my
possible saviour sitting at their table eating a chicken sandwich or
solving a puzzle or maybe watching me as its t.v. replacement.
    Maybe my
neighbor my possible saviour would know what to say to me or perhaps
put on a record and dance with me. Both these things could save me.
Both these things would sooth me.

The fourth wall is for privacy and my private life is killing me.

*Bruce Ramsay*

## Untitled

She is a leaf on an autumn day,
    gracefully falling, yet not ready to touch down,
    lightly floating, yet in control of her movements.

She is a fox in the winter snow,
    a thing of beauty, yet a sharp wit underneath,
    a nocturnal stalker by nature, yet ever so soft of heart.

She is a bird on a spring evening,
    singing an exuberant song with pride, yet quiet and hidden,
    spreading her wings without care, yet humble and kind.

She is herself on a summer lawn,
    her laughter carrying too easily,
    yet setting all that hear it a light,
    her smile is given freely,
    yet is as sincere as her wonderful spirit.

*Alex Wobbema*

## Soliloquy To Great Grandmother

You're sweet like honey
nice and funny;
You're all I need
Love grows like a seed
Between you and me.

*Amanda Maples*

## Burning Innocence

My life, my dreams all vanished in a moment.
Grandma's brooch, a treasured piece of my family's heritage-
Ripped off my blouse and tossed in the mud with other
    family's treasures.
My crowning glory - the auburn hair that I would sit and brush
    for hours - chopped off in a moment.
Every shred of my dignity stripped away as my clothing was
    torn from my back.

What did we do wrong? Where did this injustice come from?
Only because of the star we wore on our arm.
All that we lived for, worked for, believed in, burned away
    as the ashes floated through the sky.
The jewelry that I wear now is the tattoo on my wrist.
    Do we have any hope...

*Elizabeth Sewell*

## Better Than Before

My farewell days have motioned themselves to the
grassy fields where forgotten about memories
are stored and kept under key.
As the river runs deep, I today, with each maneuvered
breath, have learnt to better my ability to shoot
up and become a rock.
A hard, solid, steady, and powerful devise-able to
deter that latching hate that at times attach itself
to the pith of my back.
Clawing at my open wounds and desisting me from sprouting
up tall like the yellow Sunflower in fighting those
persistent mortals, who with the nerve, have took one
too many dismal steps toward my inner space.
But, through the horror, the green spot that have
presented itself, still, my mind is set and the rhythms,
I move in are flowing like the river deep.
So, Yes!
I am truly, better than before.

*Davied J. Peoples*

## To My Maltese

I love walking Freddie in the morning, when the meadow is fresh
with
    green,
Before long flowers will fall and leaves wither.
It is a sight indeed watching him in and out of the first thick snow,
    leaping.

From Malta Island did he come,
A silky silver ball, with dark eyes, tiny lips and a nose nutty brown.
Passers-by would greet him with smiles and shower words to his
praise.
"Is he real? Is he real?" school children'd stop, feel his pulse with
    wonder, and move on.

A "Toy Dog" is he, dancing on his hind legs to the turn of com-
manding
    fingers round and round.
"Freddie, sit!" with military precision he'll quickly respond.
A living act each morning as he chases and fails to capture running
    squirrels across his walk
Watching the dark moving images disappearing up the trees,
    he looks bewildered and forlorn.

Alert, fearless and commanding,
He guards the house with full devotion: At the faintest noise from
    afar he would bark,
Barking but jumping with joy at his master's homecoming.

A toast to Freddie, our Fountain of Delight!
You are the perfect baby who does not cry.
You've added years to our lives,
In rain or sun, your beauty will shine through, forever bright.

*Grace Chin*

## Mother Earth, Will It Stay?

Blue skies above us.
Green grass below us.
Isn't the world a beautiful place?
Wolves howl loudly.
Weasels stand so proudly.
Isn't the wilderness pretty?
Small, fluffy cats.
Big, fuzzy dogs.
Aren't animals lovely?
Beautiful flowers.
Gorgeous trees and plants.
How did we get all these Amazing things?
The one thing I know is that I love it here, on
This beautiful place called earth.
But alas, we are destroying it all.
Cutting it down, and killing it!
Why can't we just leave it alone and let it grow wildly
Once again?  Are we just lazy, or do we not know how?
If we do not leave our home alone, this will all
Disappear very soon, along with the sun and the moon.

*Erin Poulson*

## Our Place

This amazing place, full of living things;
growing, crawling, climbing, swimming,
flying, and microscopic living things;
Plus even us, the great human race.
We walk, we talk, and claim a soul.
Why is it we don't understand our role?

This incredible world, so colorful and varied,
with oceans, rivers, forests, mountains,
deserts, and frozen places;
Plus man's construction on every landscape.
We have machines, wireless transmissions and high towers;
How is it we are so unwise with our powers.

This deteriorating place full of harmful creations,
like acid rain, oil spills, killer bees,
man-made disease, and nuclear accidents.
Put the blame on misguided views.
Veiled under the guise of what's best for mankind.
When it's for economic gain, most eyes are blind.

*Gerald Green*

## A Mother's Job

If there is one thing I've learned,
   growing up as I did,
It's to be there for my children.
I'll be a bowl without a lid...

   "Always Open."

I'll teach them all the good things.
   I'll never be too tired.
I will help, no matter what.
   I'll be the fry pan, without the fire...

   "Easy to be Close to."

I'll always make them feel special
   throughout their lives,.
Unique each one of them and loved.
   They will be my fork and knife...

   "Both different-Both needed."

This is the life I choose.
   The basket I have woven.
They will be the bread.
   I will be the oven...

"There with warmth 'til the job is done."

*Jeanene Zielinski*

## Tonight

Hot and wild and sultry, the indigo African night.
Gun-fire, on the burning wind fills my heart with fright....
Palm-fronds slap against the fragile window at my side.
I lie, perspiring, wondering, how many friends have died.
Tonight?
A Horn-bill, lost and lonely, takes flight across the sky.
Silhouetted by the moon, it screams, as it goes by.
The sad and wandering spirit of a murdered Zulu bride
Searching for the lover who should be by her side.
Tonight?
Death, is all around me, I feel it in my soul...
I wonder if it's waiting, that deep eternal hole
Dug for me in the red soil of this tormented land?
Is it reaching out, to grab me - a rifle in its hand
Tonight?

*Christine Ann Vickery*

## Hospital Trip

Outside icy blackness, inside warm light
Halls of the hospital twisted and turned
like the tunnels in an ant farm

Bumps in the floor slow
down wheels of the wheelchair

Dull yellow blanket contrasted dark red-tan floor
Nurses with needles must have thought
my arms to be pin cushions
Sharp pain with each needle poke

She stuck it in my left arm and moved it to leave a BIG BRUISE
I. V. machine was angry,
when it was turned on without being hooked up
At last:  left alone to sleep.

*Gwyn Gamsby*

## Mother Earth's Cry

This planet called Earth we all know as home,
has an increasing hole in its layer of ozone.
If we refuse to listen to Earth's painful cry,
all life as we know it will surely die!

No soft grass of green to walk barefoot in,
no roses to bloom after cold winter's end.
No birds to gracefully soar up above,
no sweet newborn babies to cuddle and love.

It would be much too late to ask ourselves why,
we let all our chances slip right on by.
Our world would become an empty waste land,
all through the carelessness of modern man!

*Elizabeth Bodden*

## Tears

The white man has come he brings guns...colonization.
   He creates a new state system a new government
      the apartheid regime begins.
   Torture and misery for me because I ask questions
Look at us look at him the man in jail...it is Nelson.
   How we all try to fight apartheid
   A Tutu on the horizon.  The struggle continues.
   27 years the man is free but perhaps worn out?
      Tears
      The fight is still in him!
         The regime crumbles.
   I am to vote...will there be more violence.
I cast my vote Nelson casts his vote...Nelson is president!
      A new South Africa is born
         Tears
My mother's and father's dreams have at last come true.

*Joanne Wambaa*

## My Venus

My love's soft green eyes that change as the sky
Has skin that is soft as an angel's sweet sigh;
And breasts as a delicate mention of love,
In voice as the calling and cooing of doves.

My love for her is as new life in spring,
And I long to tell her of these private things.
Sharing such love is intoxicate bliss;
Holding her closely; sharing a kiss.

The warrior in me caresses her neck
And whispers, "Dear one, 'tis you I protect".
My quest is complete with my dream in my arms;
The bride of my life; her manifold charms.

My feelings - ecstatic at her tender touch —
Would that I could, boldly tell her of such.
My life is transformed. She's what I hold dear.
The ultimate joy is having her near.

I silently watch her performing a task;
Those love laden gifts she gives 'fore I ask.
I marvel. Did God make this goddess for me?
And vow that my love will eternally be.

   *Dave O. Mumaugh*

## What If

I often wonder how many people
Have really experienced love in a pure
Form, and not only in apparition. How
Many souls have lingered in the white
Moonlight, and felt their souls being
Touched by an angel?
But with all the good some evil must rear
Its ugly head. Satan's fingers have stroked
Far more souls than the fingers in which
The Angels own. They say to live is to
Die, but what if life has not yet graced
Your path? What if?

   *Derek Taylor*

## Questions

Have the land dwellers noticed all the road kill they produce?
Have the scientists given up the shark and cancer they induce?

Have the oceaners and fishermen stopped steeling fins from sharks?
Have you gone down to the pound and heard the innocent puppies bark?

Has the power of mankind become so selfish as not to care?
Have men and women learned to coincide and not strip each other bare?

Have the people that kill the seal stopped leaving bloody pools?
With the knowledge, science, and power we have we should protect
   all the world.

The balance is so crucial to every aspect of the life.
If one is gone another in turn is surely to over thrive.

Can we not see our trees and wreaths protect the land, animals and
   seas?
If God were looking down on this what would he conceive?

With the life we take day in and day out does mankind have a worth?
All this makes me wonder is there intelligent life on earth?

   *Donna Davison*

## Life's Highway

Life is a highway - with many abstruse roads
Hazardous paths to off set your goals
Twist and curves seem never to end
Unexpected danger lies around the next bend
Worn out trials indicates where many people travel
Their prints still mark the pavement and gravel
You're not the only one traveling winding roads
Many others experience similar loads
Keep your mind stead fast -
   you'll reach your destiny at last
Then life's disappointments will be part of your past.

   *Dennis Anders*

## Trembling Innocence

With every touch I metamorphose into perfection
he cradles my breasts affectionately
embracing my insecurities
as they fade into the limelight
melting into strengths
blossoming in the palm of his hand
with every caress
I become a woman
he uncovers the beauty
I had camouflaged with disbelief
I now remain stained with the tenderness
of my femininity

   *Julie Silver*

## Supper

Grampa, grampa get your gun
he got his gun and away we run.
Grampa, grampa do you see,
see that squirrel atop that tree.
Grampa saw and with dead-eye aim
he shot that critter, down he came.
I grabbed that squirrel and home did trot.
We threw him in a stewing pot
that was the best sup I ever had
squirrel and noodles with old granddad.

   *Donna Reynolds*

## He Will Always Be In My Heart

Even though his body is gone his spirit lives,
he had some work undone and more love to give.
I know him and I will never part because
he will always be in my heart.

   *Jessie Zahn*

## My Son

My son loves me don't you know;
He hugs me when I see him and he tells me so.

His mom and I have grown apart;
My son feels that it's his fault, though we tell him it's not.

He wouldn't understand that it was mom's idea for me to go;
That she just doesn't love me anymore.

I won't tell my son that, he wouldn't believe it anyway;
He would blame himself and run away.

So I just tell him that we love him and moms and dads need time apart;
To think about life and what's in our hearts.

   *Danny L. Meade*

## The Narrative Poem

There was a boy who sat in his home,
He just couldn't write a narrative poem.
He thought and thought and thought some more,
"I just can't do it" and he fell to the floor.

The wheels in his head started turning and he finally started to think,
He said, "I got it," and he went to get some ink.
He scribbled and wrote for over an hour,
The ideas flowed and they were far from sour.

He wrote and wrote admiring his poem,
The lines kept flowing like ocean foam.
When he got stuck he would walk around,
He would get a new idea then sit back down.

Soon his hand begun to cramp and his pencil ran out of lead,
He said to himself, "If I don't stop soon I might be dead."
But he knew he had to finish, he couldn't give up then,
After all he'd come so far he had it all in pen.

Now just to revise it and copy it over neat,
After that he would be done and he was not yet beat.
The poem started out about a boy in his home,
And that little boy couldn't write a narrative poem.

*Garrett Henderson*

## Song of the Mighty Warrior

I've heard the song of the mighty warrior,
He sang last night to me.
He brought forth a vision,
So that I might see.

He sang of the buffalo,
Many years ago.
Of how his people needed them,
To help the children grow.

He sang of his people,
Mighty, strong, and brave.
He sang of how the white men,
Would put them in their grave.

He sang in the moonlight,
His eyes were full of pain.
He knew the battle he had fought,
Had only been fought in vain.

I can here the drums,
In the distance over there.
Where once stood a mighty nation,
Was only vast and bare.

*Georgia Cox*

## Hate Then Love

A man who hates, hates the whole world and everything about it.
He sees no beauty in any thing.
He grows old before his time,
and nothing to say good about any man,
or this land or anything in it,
He cripples his body and mind and soul
to where no one wants to go around him,
and he walks for miles to dodge a man to keep from greeting them
and when he arrives home, his family tries to avoid him,
and tries not to see him,
with this slapping and mocking them about.
And no love in his heart, how can anyone stand him,
only to know he was the bread winner of that family,
so that's why they tolerate him with no other way to survive.
With his big gruff voice and his husky hand you dare not mind him.
Oh! How nice he was, when he turned his hare to love,
everyone would say how nice it was to see him that day.
He works his heart out with a smile upon his face
with no hate about him.

*Eunice Arnold*

## A Woman's Wish

A Woman can tell when a man really cares.
He treats her with love and all things he shares.

His voice when he speaks is so warm and so tender.
You know it's for sure he's not a pretender.

The gift that he offers is better then gold.
The gift of love is more precious I'm told.

He's honest he's truthful, he's giving and kind.
Where is this man that I'm wishing to find.

I know that I'm dreaming, for this could never be.
For there is no such man on this earth you see.

For all of the wishing a woman can make.
The wish of all wishes, that her man is no fake.

*Carmadean Vega*

## God Bless Little Michael

God bless little Michael, hold him ever so tight, keep him safe when he turns out the light. Wrap him up with your warm sweet love, protect him with your angels sent down from above. Let them rock him and protect him too from goblins and danger his whole life through. Take his worries away so he'll have time to play. Let him know that he's special a child so bright, that a special star shines in his honor each and every night.

Let him know he's worthwhile and loved ever so much, that he's bright and creative, and that he has that loving touch. That no matter how he feels, no matter what he thinks, he's a bright angel a priceless keepsake.

Let him know that he deserves the best, that the stars hold no limits he is the best. He can create rainbows and sunshine, that he's capable and always worthwhile. Let him know when he's down that your right by his side loving and guiding him, and that your love will never subside.

That his dream can come true, that they'll be answered by you. God bless little Michael, he's such a sweet boy, full of laughter and love a sweet, sweet boy. Let no harm come to him, only rainbows and love. Fill him with warm sweet dreams of tomorrow, fields of flowers, rainbows of love, friendships that last forever, and angles from above.

Tuck him in with his teddy, kiss his forehead. God bless little Michael forever Amen.....

*Ginny Cerar*

## The Living Watch

Once there was a living watch;
He was a very nice Swatch.
People would stare and people would talk
But he still went on his merry little walk,
Until the watchmaker took him apart
And broke his little tic-toc heart.

The living watch's family was caring,
And with all their love they were sharing.
Who would tell his loving friends?
Who would be the one to make amends?
Then up came the living watch's boss,
He said he'd tell the family about the sad loss.

His family of little watches were brokenhearted
Because their father was unfairly taken apart
The little ones cried,
The older ones sighed,
Until it looked like they'd be sad forever,
But the watchman came back and put him together.

*Dustin Abanto*

## The Joy Weaver

There was a dear old man who lived in Heavenly Wood
He was a teller of stories that would make you feel good

He knew how to weave hope through each story's seams
And the pictures he painted could brighten your dreams

The man was a poet, Jacob was his name
He didn't seek riches, he didn't seek fame

He just had a wish to give people joy
And bring a big smile to each girl and boy

The people all came from far and from near
Each wanted a special story to hear

And Jacob would tell them night after night
To ease all their fears and to make their thoughts bright

He told me a story I'll never forget
About a prince and a princess and the world where they met

And all of the beauty there was there to see
And he said the princess looked a little like me

He lifted my spirits and lessened my pain
He made me feel pretty, not simple and plain

But I knew that Jacob was just being kind
He only saw goodness, for Jacob was blind

*Espree Devora*

## Lost Love

My brother, my friend, my lover, my life
He was all of that
yet, I never became his wife.

His love like blood, through my body flowed
and everything about me
only he will ever know

My most intimate connections
were made with him,
now without him life's pretty grim.

He taught me how to laugh
and oh yes, how to love.
He treated me like a queen
for me he placed no one above.

Again I long for that kind of
warmth and security
I need that person who has eyes—eyes
for only me.
That person who will help make me feel complete.
Together — every obstacle faced — we will surely defeat.

*Debbie Waugh*

## An Elderly Lady

Each evening I see her sitting there,
    Heavenly still in her favorite place,
The stardust that glimmers through her hair,
    Shines in beauty around her face.

Oh what are the things she's thinking of,
    Have all of her dreams faded away,
Perhaps she remembers her young love,
    And a world more beautiful yesterday.

Gone are the days of great desire,
    When someone worshipped her lovely face,
No more is there the same warm fire,
    In the house she made a holy place.

Oh I would like to take her hand,
    And somehow let her know,
That I think I understand,
    And with all my heart, I love her so.

*Jack Lynn Schroyer*

## Words From A Heart

A broken glass does not share much water.
I have yet to cry.

*Charlie Keener*

## Figueroa Street Tunnels, Circa 1938

The old black coupe belonged to my brother Baxter.
Headlights mounted on fenders -
running boards.
The magic plane, my place,
was the deep well in back, a rumble seat.

One foot on the running board,
another on the special place built into the rear fender -
up I went
into a cocoon of blankets,
to keep me warm? Or in?

How I loved it
when he would drive toward L.A. -
when I could see the gray stone outline of the tunnel ahead.

Inside then out again,
inside and out again.
Horns blaring! Noisy!
I put my hands over my ears.

He laughed!

*Carol Marshall*

## Christmas Day

Crinkle, crackle, crinkle, crackle.
Hear the gift wrap come to life,
Watch the boys play their fife.
"Hooray! Hooray!" The father did say,
"Today is Jesus' birthday!
Now gather 'round
And hear the sound,
Of the carollers at our door.
They sing of pleasure even though they're poor.
Come, Dear, come!
And let us sing to the world with some
We sing of Jesus this day,
And hope all will pray.
Sir! Miss!
Will you sing in our bliss?"
"Thank you! Thank you! We hoped you would ask,
But first let us finish this task.
It's a gift for our boy,
Oh, he will enjoy
This holiday gift today!"

*John Esler*

## The Beholder

    The voice of a little man can make a
difference. The delighted sight to see the
color of a groomy thing. To have an open heart
of ever lasting love. He feels that to help is to be
there. To see this world full of violence is a crime.
To do it, in itself is a death wish. To hold a
helping hand he is the angel one would
call lost. For everything has it flaws. The bright
hearted man been turn away and laughed at.
Deep down more pain he does not share as
would anyone would. Alone you die and alone
you are born. But it takes love to live on
the earth. Just to see the smile of someone is
the world at the palm on his hand.

*Arlee Morgan Jr.*

## The Sounded Silence

Dead leaves whistled softly on the trees
And drops of water dripped from icicles,
As the cold winter wind blew softly on...

A lonely face stared out the window,
A thoughtful eyes glanced around,
A tired smile formed the lips.
Hair, color of the darkness
Was brushed by someone's rough hand,
The pounding silence was broken by -
A kiss that slowly cried and died.
The stillness seemed to become alive
And forgiveness was given without a word.
At last; a broken heart was mended.
And things continued as they were when:

Dead leaves whistled softly on the trees
And drops of water dripped from icicles,
As the cold winter wind blew softly on...

**Kathleen M. Casamasima**

## The Stranger Of The Night

The stranger of the night walks and holds his breath,
And he knows what is coming and can smell death.

The friend of night has red eyes glowing bright,
And his teeth are showing fangs of white.

The stranger of the night his eyes gleaming yellow,
Sounds a sound, a bellow.

The friend of the night sounds a deep cry,
Like saying stay away or I will make you die.

Finally they meet each other and seem like an enemy,
But a light shines upon them and they look and see.

Dawn is here, and day must be,
And both see they can live in perfect harmony.

God had said in the end,
If you were old enemies become a new friend.

**Kristin McKenna**

## Dreams

When the day is plain
And voices are irritating,
My eyelids slowly close.
Beyond what I can see
Is a world with no boundaries.
It sneaks through the cracks
And opens up my imagination.
Wonderful, happy thoughts run by
Some passing, others pondered.
What seems forever, lasts but a second.
Others do not notice
While I am in outerspace.
Sometimes I smile, laugh, or cry
Other times I show no expression
A loud sound quickly opens the lids that create darkness,
And I come out of my daze
From the crazy world of dreams.

**Kristin Stephens**

## The Search for Peace

On this sleepy morning
My thoughts had not the strength to wander far
They stayed close to home
And there, found true peace and rest

**George R. Swieringa**

## Down Home

"We're going down home," Mom used to say, "we'll see how Grandpa's
    doing today."
Down home, you know, was that little farm that Grandpa kept with all
    its charm.
An' Grandpa was that great big guy with a heart of gold named Zenas
    Fry.
On the farm, Grandpa had pigs, an' chickens and a horse; he had bees
    in the orchard and a cow, of course.
In the barn were two buggies, in the front a straw stack, on the side
    was a chicken house with melons growin' in back.
A creek ran through where we used to play, an' just east of the creek
    Grandpa made his hay.
I remember the wooden pump and the big grape vine near the large tree
    Mom planted when nine.
I remember the crackling on butcherin' day, the making of sausage and
    hams smoking away.
I remember the fried chicken, and that we never broke bread until
    Grandpa's prayer of thanks was said.
Oh the memories are great from that little old farm that Grandpa kept
    with all its charm.
And it all started out in about 1880 when Grandpa built the house and
    married his lady.
Nine girls and two boys God blessed them to raise and they never
    forgot to give God all the praise.
So don't let us forget what this family's about, out heritage is
    great, so let us all shout:
"Hurrah for Grandpa and Grandma too, their prayers and their lessons
    have carried us through."

**Donald G. Henkel**

## Love

How would I describe Love? Love is the strongest
force we feel within. The shapes and shades of color love has, to
    describe, one can't begin.
The height and depth and length and width are too great to comprehend.
It is more than one can fully understand or grasp, to try is to
    pretend.
Love can make one's heart beat faster, it makes one's eyes become
aglow. Love is beauty and disaster, needing time and nurturing to grow.
It makes you feel like you can walk on air and soar with birds on high
Love can hurt like nothing else on earth, it makes us laugh and makes us
cry. Love is always testing while at the same time feels so secure.
It makes one wonder if it's really here or there, but ever always it is near.
The fear one feels when reaching for love comes at time from those we
    hold most Dear.
Sometimes, one wishes not to love or be and if one had the choice to
choose so, would only very soon discover no one ever should.
Love is that which gives life meaning, true heartfelt concern
And to live one's life without it, for love ones' heart would ever yearn.
Real love is something un-conditional and
above all else, this, one must accept, or, at least, attempt to learn.

**Elizabeth Ann Moritz**

## Southern California Dreams

User friendly shopkeepers and laid-back waitresses
Foreign tourists speak in tongues among surfer dudes
The marine layer creates sunless days and starless nights
Wind swept torrey pines and tall palm trees
Pounding surf and salt air breeze
Hillside awash in colours of ice plant and sea lavender
Grace this quaint seaside town
A sandy beach gives way to distant cliffs rising from the shore.
Who could ask for more?

**Karen Johnsen**

## War

A dreary night I believe it was. No bird quoth "chirp", no bee quoth "buzz". A silent night for man to hear, while fear of the dreaded war comes near. Although it's said we shal'st succeed, I wish no great king for his country to plead.

Some say life's too short to be infernal but either way, death's eternal.

From war a man's soul has gone insane, wondering why his death hath gone in vain. For he believes that life's too short, to bother oneself with gun or fort.

And when this great king of whom I spoke, had been slashed and run through, I believe his terminal phrase should be, "Why?" and not, "One reason I hate you..."

You see our last war was genocide, many-a-man did suicide. And how can I say that he's to blame, when one must hang his head in shame, when a farmer's field becomes a grave for men who have wounds that make them all look the same, and a field of grass that was meant for cattle, turns from that into one of battle, and death results from someone's birth, and rulers must question winnings worth.

From now until the day I die, I shaln't forget that war colored sky, red from the fumes of blood and a bullet fest, and souls that were never laid to rest. So when your enemy makes you mad and sore, remember my sad tale of war.

*Jason Blinder*

## Grandmother

Forget me not when I am gone, I am not here but, I live on.
I'm lost in time in a forgiving place; you can't see mine,
but I can see your face.
Forever shall I look over you to keep you safe and see you through.
Never forget the times we had when we laughed and when we were sad.
I'll forever remain inside your heart and last for all time,
we will never part.

*Danielle Trittenbach*

## From Fear To Freedom

Darkness filled with muffled sounds; twisted shadows on the ground.
Fear filled my head - Night after night, alone in my bed. Mama! I'd
Mama! I'd cry, and my rescue was sure; she'd come to me or I'd go to her.
Though the danger still there, in her arms I was safe - In her warm
  side I'd bury my face.

Time went on, both of us aging; childhood memories gently fading.
Cries for Mama, I no longer made - I had to grow up and stop being afraid.
But pretending you're safe, with a heart full of dread; does nothing
  but move the battle, into your bed.
As a child you're safe with blankets over head - As an adult, fear
  joins you under your canopy of sheet, blanket and spread.

Left to themselves, and over time; safe day light hours weren't even mine.
Uninvited they came, but I'd let them stay - Cowering in fear,
  entertaining them, in a way.
To whom could I cry; who could rescue me now?
On Him, I called, though fear all about - God came with His angels to
  to guard me and my house.

How true I've found His word to be; Thou wilt keep him in perfect
  peace, whose mind is stayed on Thee.
Fear may try to raise it's head - But with one word, "Jesus!" that
  fear is dead.
Where it began, at night, alone in my bed; it came to an end, there's
  no more dread.
God, laid the ax to the root, of all my fear, saying it is done - He
  brought me from fear to freedom!

*Joann De Lugt-Price*

## Selfish Kings

A tattered soul left to die alone
A king sits surrounded at his throne
A poor man weeps for his hungry child
In a place where nothing is wild

A mother fears for her child inside
When It enters the world she's unable to provide
A child looks through the window of despair
Realizing no one has the ability to care

A score and a half and your on your own
And the king still sits at his miserly throne
Standing on the corner in the winter cold
There dies another lonely and tattered soul

For the ones who manage to survive
They live only for a war to unjustly die
And the king gives orders from his throne
For the homeless souls to die alone

A poet writes of the unjust and sorrow
Of time so costly to be borrowed
And the king sits with wealth at his throne
As a child shivers, cries and moans

*Kelly Haskell*

## Shed Some Light

The simple acts of life are tired and mundane
A struggle made strife as only obstacles remain.

I no longer move in strides without doubt
but rather question my decisions thoroughly inside out.

My head is above water, barely these days
seems tides keep on flowing, making bigger waves.

Just when I'm able to try and stand
slowly slips the sand melting through my hand.

If I squeeze a little tighter, faster it flows
leaving me in water, where no one goes.

I've dug my own grave and tortured myself
am I worth the save, should I cry for help?

Surrounded by blue and the cold salty air
traveling less than two and going nowhere.

Seemed the sun Shed Some Light on my face today
and gave me the strength to fight the water away.

Soon I'll be able to stand on my own
starting from bottom I will build a throne.

Always I will remember that familiar salty air
Never ever forgetting what it is like to be there.

*Kimberly Ann Johnson*

## Mama Pauline

M is for motherly
A is for an angel of a grandma
M is for mama's mud pies
A is for never being angry

P is for paying attention to me
A is for always being able to help me.
U is for always understanding
L is for always loving me with all your heart
I is for an intelligent grandma
N is for never saying NO!!
E is for being an excellent grandma!!

Happy Birthday, mama!

*Krissy Calandro*

## Not So Mary

Yesterday Mama made us watch
that Mary Poppins movie.
I hated it.
She flew on an umbrella
while we'z walk in the rain.

That rich boy used his savings
to feed sum ugly ass birds.
Them kids got sugar
with their medicine.
All we'z gets are shots in the butt.

Supercalafra...what?

They all happy about flying kites.
My big wheels busted,
someone broke the hand brake,
Miss Poppins had that nice Chimney
Sweep.
None uh Mama's men ever nice or stay.

And at the end
she said she'z gonna help some other
family.
I ain't seen her ass yet.

*Andrew Kaplan*

## Fragile Rose

Love is like a fragile rose
starting from a tiny seed.
As she grows, a bud is formed
which opens for all the world to see.
The beauty of her crowning glory
emits a lovely scent.
She makes all the ladies swoon
when given by a gent.
Given time and nourishment,
a fragile rose will bloom.
She is a star upon the midnight sky
shining through the gloom.

*Angie Foreman*

## Where

I feel like there's no hope for my life
Seems like everything's been stolen
The pages have been ripped out
My heart is fully broken
The grief and sorrow flow from me
Time has left me behind
I try to do everything I can
Nothing works or fits in my mind
These raggedy scraps of who I am
Are worth nothing in time
Could be burnt up in a second
Not even worth a dime
Which way does one go
When they can't find their heart
At which place do you arrive to
When you finally start
Where am I, where am I
Why
Can you find me, can you find me
Just cry cry cry.

*Shannon Leigh Wade*

## As The Darkness Sighs

I lie awake at night listening to the sounds above my bed, sounds in
    my head.
As the darkness sighs, what a troubled life.
I walk the days in a dim lit haze, my imperfections go unknown, in my
    head all knowing is dead.
As the darkness sighs, what a troubled mind.
I talk in words that mean what no one else knows, I follow dreams into
    the darkest holes.
As the darkness sighs, what a troubled soul.
I feel my heartache everyday I wake, I wonder about a love I once knew
    and listen to the sounds above my bed,
    demons living in my head.
As the darkness sighs, what a troubled heart.

*Andrea Ziccarelli*

## Christmas Lights

Will shine on the path, and show the
Shepherds their way through the night
and into the day!

Will shine, on the kings and show
them the way!

Will shine, on the babe, and lead thee
kings, too bow on there knees, and the
shepherds too quake, with Joseph and Marry
and the animals, all gathered around!

Will shine all you Christians on your way,
to light your path and show you the way,
to Heavens pearly gates, and Christ light that
showed them the way! On that Christmas Day!

*Andrew J. Perricone*

## Grandpa's Old Rocking Chair

Grandpa used to rock in his old rocking chair,
With his old brown pipe and white locks of hair.

On that old front porch, I used to swing,
And together, we'd discuss the oncoming spring.

I remember his clothes, and even his smell.
The old cigar smoke, and the stories he'd tell.

I remember most that he used to draw.
And as I watched, I was completely in awe.

Sometimes I wished we could sit and rock again.
Maybe I could reach out and just touch his hand.

Or smell his cigar or old pipe smoke,
Or hear him tell stories of all "the old folk".

My memories are vivid, so they will carry on.
And I will tell those tells to my own son.

Maybe one day, with his Grandpa he'll sit,
On their front porch and talk a bit.

Maybe, he'll too, remember Grandpa's smell.
And also have his own stories to tell.

Then, because of his memories his Grandpa will live on,
As my past lives with the FUTURE of my son's, son.

*Amy E. Loftis*

## Friends Again

Since I started talking to God again,
I have discovered a long lost friend.
As silent as he may be,
There is always a sign to see.
I had to wipe my eyes of the devil,
And take myself back to God's
level.
Now I try to talk to him everyday,
Looking for the signs of His way.
Even if life begins to look dim,
I must remember to keep faith in him.

*Norma Jean Avery*

## My Special Friend

You're such a special person
Know words can be compared
The thoughtfulness and kindness
A great person like you
has shared.

I thank you for the confidence
In loving my Lord on high
You've brought the many happy
things God gave us from the sky

Whenever you are down
And need a friend close by
I'm here with an open heart
with God by my side

I hope these many simple words
have brought some little joy
your way

For you my friend your in my heart
And there you are to stay.

*Ann LaDeen Blanshan*

## Find The Silence

Gentle flowing, blowing corn
In the flat fields far away
Where the pace is slow and easy
Where the soul has room to grow

In the land of tall, glass buildings
Cars and people—hurry, hurry
Always doing, never being
Always searching, never finding

Listen, listen, find the silence
You can hear it if you try.
Leave the land of constant running
Drink the silence of the soul

*Ann Milvenan*

## Slow

I'm raw from feeling.
I'm dry from remembering.
I'm numb from understanding.
Disappointment is my shadow.
I am out of reach.
An aura of nothing
Has enveloped everything.
I scream for comfort,
But I can't speak.
I lust for answers,
But I can't hear.
I search for hope,
But I can't see.
I live for you,
But I can't breathe.

*Angela Deeter*

## Untitled

As the spring brings blossoms new.
Like a flower I think of you.

Though life has dealt us different hands
In it's garden once thought planned.

So let us try then we'll know,
If our garden will ever grow.

*Andy Burch*

## Excalibur

*For Robert*
Mystic excalibur, sword of the ages
I speak the spell to call thee forth
Dwarf forged of the lady's silver
Merlin's gift to Arthur's hand
Spell bespoke in crystal caverns
Grails mate in legends old
The Lakes Lady keeps you safely now
Deep hidden in timeless time
For the king from time before,
Will be king in time to come.

*Rhiannon ap Griffith*

## "Moses Loves The NRA"

Moses loves the NRA
I saw him just the other day
shooting words about your rights
to partake in firefights.
Think what Pharaoh might have said
with an Uzi at his head:
'Yes, I will let your people go.
As it's written, now it's so.'
Yes, Guns and God go hand in hand
straight into the promised land
for 'they are different's' at the core
of every bloody holy war.

*Andy Stanfield*

## Kristi

They do not stay where they belong,
I can't put up with them for long.
I've seen them stare, their evil blink,
I've been exposed to their raw stink,
I've seen then scratch and claw a chair
Our love seat now is full of hair.
They always do what I most hate,
They always jump across the gate
They knock our stuff down to the floor,
For this, they must be shown the door.
I've seen them prowling here and there,
I do not wan them anywhere
I have not seen them catch a mouse,
I do not want them in my house
I do not like the sight of them,
I do not want them, Sam I am.
Even though I've had my fill,
I cannot bring myself to kill.
I cannot deal with cats real well -
Please rid us of these beasts from hell.

*Andrew Holub*

## Once Upon A Mattress

Once upon a mattress
High in a tree
There sat Santa Claus
As cute as can be
A bundle of tons
Upon his back
But you he isn't there
To take away
He's yelling for panner
And Blitzen too
He's telling them all
He's got a job to do.
As He boards his sleigh
He knows the right way
To take the toys to me and you

*Ann M. Smith*

## Oath To A Star

Star light, star bright
First star I see tonight
I wish I may, I wish I might
Wish upon this star tonight

With all my might I wish I do
Wish this wish uponest you
That my beloved, my love true
Would see the lights guided by you

To stay away from drugs and beer
From all the dangers steering clear
For this is most my greatest fear
That I should lose a loved one dear

So by this power, by this might
I'm giving you eternal fight
To keep my loved one safe tonight
I wish I may, I wish I might

*Amy Redmond*

## Traveler

I stare at a picture of your face
And I long to dream at night
To be an eagle of the sky
And slowly I take flight

I soar over the tops of mountains
And down to the bottoms of trees
Low over the nothingness of valleys
And high over the unforgiven seas

The lonely winds take me places
I wish to never go
To places where darkness dreads
And rivers never flow.

Slowly I'm brought back
By the gentle touch of your hand
To never be an eagle of the sky
But a traveler of the land.

*Amy Northam*

## #12

I scream, but no one hears,
I speak, but no one understands.
I cry, but no one sees.
I die, but no one weeps
for me.

*Anitra Novy*

## One

One had creativity to the max,
One a range like the mountains,
One had personality like Mother Nature,
One had a thing for rings.
They are one forever and always.
May I present to you The Beatles.

   *Erin Spainhour*


## Freckles

I am not positively sure,
Although, of course, there's always hope,
That, for freckles, there's a cure.
With freckles I can barely cope.

Freckles fade and reappear.
Freckles will nest on any fellow.
They could live anywhere 'round here,
Freckles, red, brown, pink and yellow.

Never go out into the sun,
Never try to catch a tan,
If you do they'll jump the gun.
You'll want to fry them in a pan.

I can't help it if people smile,
I inherited freckles from my dad.
My freckles will be here for quite a while,
And freckles aren't quite that bad.

Still, I am not positively sure,
No matter what my history,
That, for freckles there's a cure.
To me, freckles are a mystery.

   *Kea Gilbert*


## The Pumpkinseed

Went fishing today, my father and me,
   and I caught a fish — it's called a Pumpkinseed.
You can't imagine how proud I felt,
   and I couldn't wait to share my wealth.
I took it home and showed my mom,
   she asked where I caught it, I said the pond.
I showed my brothers and they grinned,
   you can't eat it cause it's too thin.
I went outside in the back,
   and buried the fish all snug and intact.
I knelt and prayed and asked for forgiveness,
   for who am I to obstruct your business.
The poor little fish, please send it to heaven,
   and forgive me LORD cause I'm only eleven.
The lesson I've learned is all too great,
   I'll think of life first before it's too late.

   *Karen M. Rock*


## Second Best (A Grandchild's View)

She used to be always there
and now it seems she doesn't care.
It was easier when we were little
I guess our feelings were not so brittle.
She might think we can't feel pain
she might even think it's another game.
Just incase they don't do great
she knows were here to congratulate.
God forbid were not in first
were the one's that would get the curse.
This is how it is and probably always will be,
unless one day she happens to see,
how mentally she hurt both him and me.

   *Kerri J. Wood*


## The Island

An Island — thrust from the Oceans Deep — upheaved from the Waves for the Sun to keep — Fire in it's Belly and Ice on it's brow, MAUI-the Land as we know it now. Much of it green, some of it dry — with Valleys deep and Mountains high, caressed by the Rain that greens it's fields, scoured by the Wind that never yields.

Each Dawn the Sun, by Creators command. Arcs through the Sky o'er this Blessed Land. Warming, scorching, burning it's way, Monarch of the world by day. Then comes the wind and storm-tossed Clouds, rolling in like a Mountains Shrouds. Rain-swept Valleys, wind-scarred Peaks, scorning the blasts on their battered cheeks.

But — when Sunset comes — and the Sun departs, softening the Land in Shadows dark, over the waters, Valleys and Peaks — a Silence descends that the whole World seeks, a breathing space 'tween Day and Night, when the Sun takes it's rest and out of sight, goes on it's way and leaves the Land — to the Night and Gods other Hand.

Slowly rising — the Silver Orb, reflecting the Light it can't absorb — Sheds a cooling light on the world below, sans the burning heat of the daytime glow. When the Moon rides high, in a Star-studded Sky, and the Earth below shimmers with Light — Then the Wind and the Sea both whisper to me — that God's very near in the night.

   *Frank E. Wherley*


## The Christmas Gift

This is a day I shall remember.
A day never to forget.
A day I can look back on and never will regret.
Accepting a gift I received but had
to go and get.
I asked if she'd do me a favor.
Her face filled with surprise.
After granting my wish she saw a certain
look in my eyes.
My eyes almost watering, my voice it could not speak,
But somehow a thank you, I managed to squeak.
The pain inside of me she somehow must have felt.
She asked me what was wrong but I really couldn't say.
She asked if I'd be alright, I said yes somehow, someway.
The simple gift she gave me, it did not cost a cent.
To me it was priceless, and you might say heaven sent.
It was the best gift I've
received throughout my christmas years.
It was a warm loving hug,
that filled my eyes with tears.

   *Kevin Jacobson*


## Stars Smashing Moons

Out of a vision you appear,
a glowing, gyrating, sphere of comprehension,
baptized in emotion,
confirmed in bliss secreted from the heart.
To perform the matrimony of souls,
inspiration.
As if to say "take her, she's yours"
a cry echoes through the long halls of night.
To me it is the symbol of the trumpets' lead,
significance of the beginning of the end.
We converge in a blaze of light
smashing stars against moons,
scattering planets to distant galaxies,
The consecration of holy souls.
Death calls out its helpless, pitiful, cry,
it has lost the battle,
only in the consecration can love sustain life.
A higher existence,
led by pure emotion,
where belief is our only God.

   *Katherine Geragi*

## Grandma

Mom came with bad news today
A greatly loved family member has passed away
Mom said it would hurt
That it was o.k. to cry
But why did this have to happen to me why?
I miss her so much
It's like a piece of me is gone
But I must go on
I will never forget her
I don't know how I could
I will love her forever
And she will be a part of me till
I'm gone

***Kelli Morgan***

## Salvation Of A Heart

Step by lonely step, in-shadowed by dark clouds of despair,
a heart's feet shuffled aimlessly, of his destiny, unaware.

Through time's maze corridors that corner, curve, and twist,
and weave their web of seconds to days to years in blinding mist,

the journey this heart had set upon continued to reveal
the sights and sounds and smells and tastes that life, to each heart,
deals.

Yet somehow, with each new encounter, his loneliness only grew;
steps shared with other hearts most often left him sad anew.

And just when hope for life-sustaining love seemed at its end,
a love he never could have fathomed, upon him, God did send.

The first embrace collapsed the labyrinth's walls and dried the mist;
all clouds dispersed and sun broke through to shine upon such
bliss.

Now hand-in-hand and heart-to-heart, their separate courses, one;
their friendship, love, life, and journey together has begun.

***Kenneth Vickery***

## Untitled

I sat at the edge of the wood
About the time when night slowly stalks day
And day makes an honorable retreat.

I sat and observed our country's flag,
Slowly merging with the shadows
Of the trees.

The distinct rumble of thunder,
Accentuated by lightning, prophesied a storm.
The splintered sky hemorrhaged.

The flag looked sinister betrayed
Amongst the shadows in the sporadic light.
Strangely it did not stretch proudly in the wind,
It hung limply, tattered, faded.

I ran to it,
But by the time I had arrived it had fallen.
I looked upon it, crumpled in the mud, soaking up
They sky's blood.
And I wept.

***Kevin Burgun***

## Fear

Tastes like the breath you cannot take.
Looks like the horror you cannot see.
Feel like the enemy you cannot feel.
Smells like the fire you cannot stop.
Sounds like the scream that cannot come.

***Elizabeth Gwynne Beene***

## Nightmare

At night, when sweetly dreams do feign to soothe
And ready mind and soul for morrow's break,
Extreme sensations breach my sleep and quake
My frail foundation.  I can not remove
The sounds of monsters grunting close behind,
Nor tastes of screams that would not pass my teeth;
I trip on twigs and rocks beneath my feet,
Inhaling fear — no shelter can I find...
And then comes dawn, when sunbeams warm the air,
Illuminating all that can be seen;
My refuge found where nightmares had just been —
Once dread, now peace resides within my lair.
My sheets and pillows glow amongst the light,
And I can overcome my fear of night.

***Katherine Palley***

## Growing Memories

The first thing I remember, is my mother reading to me,
and teaching a prayer and table grace when I was three.
She read me Bible stories of God and His love,
and how he sees and cares for us from heaven above.
How Jesus came into the world and of His lowly birth,
how he gave his life down here to save the men on earth.
There was Noah and the ark and just his family to tell,
how God had kept them safe from all the rain that fell.
And when the flood was over and all the land was dry,
they saw the promise of God, a rainbow in the sky.
The story of Moses as a babe and how he grew to be a man,
Then God chose him to lead the children of Israel to the promised
land.  I liked to hear the stories, the good and the bad.
But the one I liked the best was about David as a lad.
With his harp and his sling, I could plainly see,
he must have been a boy about the size of me.
I could see him as he watched the sheep a way up there,
how he killed the big old lion, then he killed a bear.
Then when the day came, his strength was put to test,
he took a rock and his sling and trusted God to do the rest.

***Katie Shelley***

## The Blood Engulfed the Sheets

Despondency webbed closely like dark ivy to a cool wall
    as footsteps echoing into Hell approached the drafty hall.
My entrails deflated as the doctor assured
the garbled words of truth I never really heard.
My heart stiffened in its stagnant pool of blood
while death raped our life, and sadness began to flood.

I steadied then stumbled to the bed of his pain
where the emaciated body and crumpled frame
tangled in a net of wires and plugs.

There lay my dad, whom I ached to hug.

Sensing my palm, he gave an undetectable squeeze,
and said not to cry, while in slow motion I sobbed to my knees
    as the blood engulfed the sheets.

My hand sadly slipped from his cold one as his stream evaporated dry,
while staff in white and mint green streaked quickly by.
"I love you..." I screamed with the voice inside my head,
but the fate I'd been dodging was now the reality I had to dread.

I found my head on my mother's lap for the first time in years,
her familiar hand stroking my aching forehead, wiping away the tears.

***Kerry Donoghue***

## I Used to Have Faith

I feel so often
as though I've lost my rhyme.
So much goes on so quickly
each day I lose more time.
My youth is slipping away
as my beliefs fade into lies.
I use to have faith in God
but he is no longer part of my life.
God is for the weak:
for those unable to conquer their fears.
I believe in morals but give me a few years.
Time has a funny way
of changing ideas.
Through the knowledge I gain
I lose faith through tears.
History and proof-
it's all I need to hear.
It's sad how much time
I wasted on faith throughout the years
But even sadder that I have no faith to pass to my peers.

*Kelli Dunaway*

## The Sprinter (alias Kristy)

Sinewy muscles, taut and anticipating,
As you coil into the starting block.
Nerves wound as tight as your tensing body,
Yet molded and trained to be hard as a rock.

You crouch down, waiting what seems terminal moments,
As the starter raises his gun up high.
Then he says, "Runners on your marks, get set..."
And the taunting pause as your life ticks by.

The gun goes off with a bang, launching you forward,
Like a freed spring, you explode from the start.
You slice the wind like a well-aimed missile.
A race can be lost by a timid heart.

The runners in the heat are not your opponents.
It's the physical stress to find more speed.
"Breathe!" the mind tells a dutiful body,
And commands of form it also must heed.

Trained to push the limits of your endurance,
Beating the clock proves the battle is won.
One last thrust as the finish line passes.
Tenths of seconds faster, one more race run.

*Kate Guesman*

## Our Little Fighter

Come on little fighter hang in there tight.
Because pretty soon you'll be a beautiful sight.
You shook us all up, you gave us a scare.
But it worked out O.K. Because your Mommy
was there.
Your Daddy was with her all the way through
and they always will be there because they love you.
We've all wanted to hold you and show
you we care, we've wanted to touch you but
you're still not there
We've waited to love you and rock you to
Sleep, but you're always so quiet not even a peep.
So rest little fighter and get very strong
And we'll see you soon, it won't be to long.

*Kim Montgomery*

## I Remember

I remember you and I
Both of us pinecones amongst the rocks
Sitting on the roughness of the cement
We made the life that never passed by

The only ones that were left of our kind
Fall and winter had already passed
Blowing away everyone else
Leading us to be left behind

The summer brought contentedness in the air
As the rain danced upon our heads
Thinking the happiness would always stay
There wasn't a thoughts we wouldn't share

But as the trees began to sigh
Disdain was staring us in the face
So you blew away from are content
Yes I remember you and I

*Kristie Reiprich*

## Destiny's Cry

Pearls of sand gaze up through time
Breaking cruel barriers; buying no crime.
Yet, ruthlessly emblazing the status quo
Where friend, fiend, or horror dare not go.
Magic bedazzles the dauntless few
Waiting on venom and hatred to chew.
Mean winters ride the lengths of the tide
Sarcasms quick the mockeries they chide.
Blow by blow we trudgingly show,
Despising our own blood of the ones we know.
Torn and dismembered in silken crimson haze,
Burning our flesh by riding tormented heats of the blaze.
When will we retire this mean-spirited desire,
Giving ourselves hope with the flame of our fire?!

*Kari Anne Wick*

## Don't Lie

You asked me out during the show,
but my answer was "I don't know".

My life is such a mess,
I wonder if I can make it through the stress.

You popped the question so fast,
that I couldn't help but remember the past.

It's only been a few days since that other guy,
I made you promise and I hope you won't lie.

I hope you understand how I feel,
and understand this relationship is real.

I know we've only had our first kiss,
but you are so hard to resist.

My friend told me not to go out with you,
I just hope you feel in your heart the way I do.

Please don't treat me like the other guy,
I don't know if my heart can stand another lie.

*Kimberly Jantz*

## Curiosity

Going through life wondering what will be,
As the future becomes the past,
You try to make every moment last,
As days become longer and breaths become harder,
You realize you can't go any farther,
Then you begin to think what will happen when you die,
Will you end up in that big city in the sky,
You will just have to wait and see what is meant to be.

*Kimberly Tobey*

## Potash Prospectors

We've found a mass of polyhalite,
But will it see this side of daylight?
Our crop growth testers in Hawaii,
Sometime spoke of it quite highly.

Now sulvinite it's nemesis,
Puzzles us it's genesis,
And even more elusive still,
Is it's location when we drill.

Tucked a thousand metres down,
Seismic shocks our hopes surround,
But certainly at quarter stuck,
What we really need is luck!

"What! Just one hole that's much too tough
Our million eights just not enough!
We'll drill four holes," says David grandly
"But where's the cash?" Says Patrick blandly.

So back to H.Q. rushes crew,
Testing friends, much tried, but true
Where talk and fuss and byte display
Make clear to all our latest play!

*Kerry J. Stanaway*

## The Quickening

Not forward, nor backward, in a circle well closed
Can vision escape as intellect grows.
But locked inside walls cemented with age
Life becomes death and living a cage.
Rules, regulations, and patterns cut tight
Shut down the mind and blind out the sight.
Moment by moment, and year after year,
All the denial's compacted by fear.
Like nitroglycerin, unbalanced, will blow;
Emotions all mixed up, ignite and let go.
Inside the circle the cells start to simmer
As vision and intellect's walls become thinner.
Out of the mist awareness awakens
While all the belief system structure is shaken.
Now forward and backward the circle will bend
As rigid closed mindedness comes to an end.
In through the cracks new messages seep.
Death becomes pain as the soul starts to weep.
All through your being light glitters and shines,
Life is now limitless and undefined.

*Kathy Hudson*

## A Conversation

I once met a blind ol' man. He told me,
"Come, make a stand."
"A stand for what?" I asked him proudly.
"A stand for our Father." He answered loudly.
"Do you not know the Father above?
The one so beautiful like wings on a dove."

"How can you see this?" I asked the ol' man.
"I feel it in my heart, it's his gentle hand.
Listen closely and you will hear his soft singing
Voice whispering in your ear. These are the words
Of our Father above. The words he speaks
Are only of love."

"I can hear them." I said to the ol' man.
"He has opened me heart. I shall take a stand!
It was not you who could not see..but..now I realize,
That it was me. I thank you for opening my eyes.
May the Lord have for you a wonderful surprise."

The ol' man answered with a smile on his face,
"He has already blessed me with his grace."

*Kimberly Dianne Harden Carroll*

## A Girl's Love

It is obvious that a girl's love,
Could only be from the heavens above.
It is something that a man keeps searching for,
A girl that he will love forever more.
Her emotions and feelings he tries to understand,
While all he wants to do is hold her gentle hand.
Her care and understanding he wants from the start,
And at the end, he would want her forever in his heart.
He wants her to feel safe and secure,
And prove his love will forever endure.
If he could only have one single wish,
It would be for him to receive a gentle kiss.
After looking in her deep brown eyes,
He could never tell her a lie.
The emotions of men with a girl's love are high,
While those without it want to shrivel up and die.
I can say there is no treasure I can think of,
That can equal or challenge the value of a girl's love.

*Kevin Stanton*

## Listen....Listen....

As silence fills the air,
    Darkness has brought upon sadness,
        Wishing upon a star.

As a baby cries, a man dies,
    Life as we know - has fulfilled mankind,
        And
            It's destiny of creation.

Waiting for life again,
    Finally
        The sun brings brightness upon the earth.
A chirp of a bird, a scream of a child,
    Only as this brightness appears,
        It fades into thin air.

Silence once more,

    And if you listen carefully you may even hear a
baby cry.....

*Kalei Chan*

## Planting Flowers Out of Season

She knew where she wanted
each plant. She had carefully
selected each from the meager
assortment offered at
the hardware store this year. She stood
over ninety-three years, and a
grandson, enlisted to
dig and deposit where pointed.
She thought about these
impulsive youths as she watched him
dig. It had been hard to get him here today
to help her plant her flowers. She wished she
could get down on her hands and knees
for an hour or two: feel the
boundless energy of soil cascading
between her finger-tips; or the
dampness creep into her being through
knees that could develop roots all their own.
Roots would support her aged frame- comfort
her swaying in each gentle rainstorm.

*Kathleen Bernal*

## One More Day

My feelings have grown stronger
for the one that's loved by two
I keep trying to stop the power you have on me
But there's nothing I can do.

I miss you much, just like you said
some might say I was mislead
But I now know that's not what was meant
closer we grew, more time with each other we spent

Change has went though us both
we have to admit
the feelings we have for each other
I can't seem to forget

We just can't deny, when we look in each other eyes
The way we feel inside
we know it's there
and to both of us it isn't fair
I wish it were different, would we stayed the same
Before we had to come back to reality
Then go our separate ways
If together we could have one more day

*Kara Dodson*

## Two Hitchhikers

We were there someplace, with our thumbs jutting out
For what seemed like a short time, but the seasons
Said differently, as we jostled and shuffled about,
Seeking no purpose, no distance, no reasons...

Along came the van, and we cluttered on board
All in the back seat, not caring who drove,
Nor what direction we were headed toward
Nor if we were changing, nor how long we had loved.

But we could sense movement from that moment on
And we told the driver never to stop
To pick up another, like us, to sit down
In the space between us, where the armrest should drop.

And so ... so far, we two travel alone,
The relationship must hitch a ride of its own.

*Ken Lovette*

## Ocean Water

Ocean water speak to me, can you tell me my destiny.  Will
good things come my way, or will sadness fill my day.  Ocean
water speak to me, calm my mind and give me peace.

Ocean waves rush on in, just to roll back out again.  Will
my future be as steady and if not will I be ready.  Give me
the courage to continue on, and the strength to handle things
gone wrong.  Ocean water speak to me, safe and sound is where
I want to be.

Ocean water blue by day, I want to know what you have to say.
There are things I don't understand, Tell me about the Master's
plan.  Was I destined to play a big part, in his vision from
the start.  Ocean water speak to me, free my spirit so I can
see.

Ocean water God made you, and all that's beautiful he made too.
Ocean water now I hear, what you're whispering in my ear.  No
need looking past today, and let the Master guide my way.  Ocean
water smiled on me, now I know my destiny.

*Kirk Harris*

## The End Of An Era

The young may, but the old must!
Grandma was speaking of the end of an era!

Pick their brains
Absorb all the knowledge you can from their experiences!
For when you least expect it-it's the end of an era!

Make the time!
Give the sacrifice it takes to spend with the elders!
Cause they will become the end of an era!

Live for wisdom!
Then pass it on!
God only gives us one day at a time!

Don't waste it!
Life is too short!
You too-will become-the end of an era!

*Kathi Dian Gibbons-Rainey*

## Unrequited

For love bittersweet doth my broken heart mourn;
Having not yet healed doth my weaker half sojourn.
A lesson failed in learning thus will itself repeat;
And to the teacher of this lesson doth my heart now entreat.

Ill advised, ill advised doth my greater half proceed;
Refusing recognition of the latent deed.
Harkening unto the sickened soul of weary plight
Doth my tender foot hasten on this lonesome night.

Anon, cruel teacher thou shalt see my best!
One thousand and one trumpets sounding in my breast!
Though smitten and burned, taunted and torn,
Fierce desire treks ever onward to the scorn.

Behold, I am here, in bewilderment of thy charms.
Too late to take notice of thy unopen arms.
Even now I realize and in this I trust,
Futile are my attempts to retrieve thy heart from the dust.

O thou bold naive!...Once more thou hast been scorched.
Unloved and unwanted by the one for whom thy carrieth a torch.
Shall thy let the flame dwindle and peter away?
Alas, not so wise, thou shalt once more journey this way.

*Krisha Shaun Carter*

## My Brother And I

My brother and I, it has always been.
I could share anything with him.
He was my best friend.
I never thought I'd see this day,
When God decided to take him away.
I loved him so much you'll never understand,
I just want to reach out and be able to hold his hand.
Just one last time, I wish I could say,
"I love you so much and I want you to stay".
Tears run down my face and sadness fills my heart.
We will always be brother and sister,
Even though we're apart.
I wish I could go with you and be by your side.
My life will never be the same and part of me has died.
You'll always be with me wherever I go.
My brother, your love made me human and whole.
Today, I must let go and kiss you goodbye,
But someday, very soon, it will be

My Brother and I.

*Kelly Bryce*

## Verbal Motions

The once silenced voice no longer quiets.
I enter reality, afraid, and unsure.
I face the verbal motions
They burn, and hurt, although we do not
I turn away, they follow
I cannot escape from the verbal motions

I ponder the motions not knowing what to do
They lash at me unmercifully
They grab at uncaringly
They have no cares, only to disturb you.
I escape reality, the verbal motions enter
They lash out and knock me down.

The once disturbed voice no longer speaks
It grows quiet, I recover
Who can heal my pains, and disillusionment?
I reach out and find no-one.

*Karen Karlicek*

## A Mother's Fear

Baby boy lying in my arms so dear,
I love to have, and keep you near.
As I hold you so close to my breast,
I pray you'll only see the very best.

Your precious new life has only just begun,
and I'll always try to make it a happy one.
But it's hard to dismiss the reality,
percentages, averages, that say what maybe.

Chances are before you know your tables,
someone will classify you learning disabled.
Odds are by the time you are ten,
exposed you'll have been to crack, and heroin.

Perhaps handcuffed they will take you away,
before you've reached your eighteenth Birthday.
Possibly before you reach age twenty nine,
your funeral I will have attended by this time.

Hush little baby don't shed a tear,
this is only a mother's fear.
A fear based on statistics and facts,
which were given for most male blacks.

*Kathleen Gordon*

## Sonnet on the Night

Reposed in the magic of a woodland dell
I sat alone with the peaceful woods and sky.
The darkling forest and fading light wrought a spell
As we tarried there - the sky, the woods and I.
Chapel quiet it was, all totally hushed
As the blue of the evening pinioned my soul.
And then, as I with holy quietude was flushed,
The black of night suddenly upon me stole.

Disquiet replaced the calm of my forest church
And strange nocturnal cries and the whir of wings
Took away my peace and my heart gave a lurch.
Evening gone, night was come, full of unknown things.
The dark holds much that's inimical to man
So, frightened and unthinking, I turned and ran.

*Kenneth F. Wainner*

## Self Portrait

When asked to write a portrait of myself,
I sat stunned at virgin page.

No paints of color to sweep canvas,
No shadows of detail for my face.

My only instrument, my pen.
Mere words to fill the page.

I began a thousand times
To find others in my place.

I began a thousand more,
Placing strangers on my stage.

And at the end of this,
The knowledge that I gained,

Was that the portrait of myself,
Left me stunned by empty page.

*Karen Lovell*

## Treasured Friend

Because finding one special friend is so hard to do,
I thank the Lord for blessing me with a friend like you.

I know it had to be the Lord who sent you my way.
You're always an encouragement with kind words to say.

There was a special reason He brought you into my life.
He knew I needed a friend willing to help bear any strife.

When I need someone to talk to, you're always there
To patiently listen and show how much you care.

Thank you for being exactly who you are.
When I need a friend, you're never very far.

I asked the Lord for a very special kind of friend.
And I know you are the very best He had to send.

I know the Lord really does answer every prayer,
Because He gave me a friend that's so special and rare.

You bring so much goodness into every life you touch.
And having you as my friend means so very much.

Compared to other friendships, no other can measure
To my friendship with you that I will always treasure.

*Kim Polina*

## My Shepherd

Your fur is soft as velvet.
I trace your face with my fingers,
and sense the kindness in your heart.
Together we walk, I follow your gentle lead.
Strong and devoted,
willing to sacrifice your life for mine.
Your eyes are mine,
but we share more than your sight.
You are more than a guide dog.
You're my friend,
and have given me new life.
When we walk and I hear the rustle of leaves,
smell the fragrance of spring flowers,
or feel the warmth of the sun on my skin,
you brings me joy.
When I feel a playful nudge of your nose
against my hand,
I know you are content.
and it bring a smile to my face.

*Kathy A. Dumont*

## My Pain

I guess I kind a feel like it's tearing us apart.
I wish all these problems would have never had to start.
I believe it's a day by day struggle.
Just keeping us all together.
Feelings are hurt and trust is betrayed.
It seems as if all of our loves are now frayed.
Praying to God - hoping this pain will one day come to an end.
This time finding out when a friend is really a friend.
We all have problems - some just worse than others.
I think being here we all seem a little smothered.
Sometimes we all just need to get away
Hoping that tomorrow will be a better day.
I usually just put all the hurt and pain aside.
Because these are the feelings that I went to hide.
But just remember I will always love and care about you.
No matter what you do.
And I know you feel the same.
So can we please try to solve all our problems and get rid of all this pain?

### *Kimberly Ann Carlin*

## I Wish......

I wish I lived in a mansion
I wish I had a great job
I wish I had lots of money
I wish I were rich and famous
I wish evil things would come to an end
I wish people were kind and sweet
I wish world peace would last eternally
I wish happy dreams would come true
I wish for an everlasting life
I wish for peace
I wish for harmony
I wish for everyone to have sympathy
I wish I could escape from evil
I wish that wishes come true
I wish that happy endings in stories come true
I wish for peace to come among the earth.

### *Kimberly Rose Veltre*

## Help

Life would be better
if all the violence and killing would stop.
The gang killing,
and the children dying,
I wish someone would help me.

The children could play and have fun
without fear of gangster near,
children would live to see 22,
instead of barely living through,
the childhood fun and teenage years.

Crack babies born.
They won't see 2,
and if they do,
well, they're just a few.

We live to die
or die to live.
In this hell, which we're trapped within.

All I ask, is if we could,
change the past, make the world a little better.
With everyone's help we could put, OUR world back together.

### *Katina Edwards*

## A Fox Tail

If emotions give life, then you are my breath.
If heartache can kill, then you are my death.
If eyes can burn fires, then you are my flame.
If words can ignite, then call out my name.
If kisses sing love, then you are my song.
If desire is sin, then you are my wrong.
If darkness can seduce, then you are my night.
If laughter can shine, then you are my light.
If following is leading, then you are my sight.
We shall uncover in time we were always right...

### *Kellee Ann Huron*

## I'm Glad You're Here

You are my friend - I value you,
I'm glad you're here today.
Your smiling face and helping hands
Help get me thru the day.

And though I never tell you just
How much you mean to me,
I'm GLAD you're here! I'm GLAD you're here!
For me to know and see.

This is a poor attempt to rhyme
My feelings felt for you,
When all I really want to say is
GOD BLESS YOU!

### *Kay Hunt*

## Untitled

As tears are falling upon my face
I'm wishing you are in a wonderful place.
You weren't as perfect as I wanted you to be,
But I always knew that you cared for me.
Now you've gone into a silent land
Where I can no longer hold your hand
I can only talk to you through my prayers,
I can no longer tell you all my worries and cares
You left so fast, before I could blink my eye,
So now its my turn to say goodbye.

### *Kristy Wilson*

## Windows Of Her Soul

One that has brought light from beyond the void
into the eternal creation of life. She dances with
the illumination of what is and forever will be.
Having many faces, but one true self
Sharing with none, the sacred Heavenly Union
foretell, the Child knows the Mother of many faces.

Unfortunate are the children of earth, to them
that do not know. The Mothers great love in abundance
doth flow. With never changing eyes, but windows of her soul;
to ever changing names as do the centuries toll.
Always the Old One, forever the Goddess;
behold the majesty as the Blessed Mysteries unfold.

For into the womb of endless time, brought forth
the birthright of the divine. Back to their homage
of eternal life, passing through the mist of illusion;
the veil is unknown. Hers is the love of the true Mother,
known from an earthy heart, enthroned with
the Living Breath; of the undying Goddess.

### *Kimberly Ward-Wyman*

## Fall Floats In

Fall floats in
Leaves are falling, wind is blowing
Running between summer and winter
Catching up to the coldest nights

*Daniel J. Ruben*

## Ragged Doll

She used to have a ragged doll, she held to fill her nights.
It scolded beasts, and gave her peace, and made the world all right.
When her friends became to much, her doll still knew the best.
All she needed was some time to dwell in loneliness
It followed her across the globe and even across the room.
It told her secrets she couldn't learn from any friend in school
Now, it sits within the box in an attic room.
Forever stuck, with clothes and toys, inside a memorial tomb.
If you listen close at night, she weeps, for she's alone.
What ever shall become of me now that my friends has grown??

*Kenneth G. Hobert Jr.*

## Death

No one known when their day is coming.
Just be ready and steady, when he comes
Church is a wonderful place in life.

I can see you now breaking your neck going to a party.

Not being able to wake up on Sunday
morning to go to church.

Death is a time of rejoicing.
Not a day of moaning and groaning.
We should be happy, because God has added one to his flock.

When death comes, you'll see all
relatives coming out the woodwork.

Coming to take things, such as clothing,
Furniture, money etc.
And you haven't seem them for years.

Every knee shall bow, and very tongue shall confess.
That Jesus is the "King of all Kings,"
The "Lord of all Lords,"
Those who are going through an eye
of a needle, will be saved.
Wide is the gate leadeth to destruction.

*Karla Ellis*

## The Beach...The Sea...

The beach...what a lovely, lively scene...
Late in May, on a gorgeous Sunday.

Waves caress across gaudy colored suits
Of children running to put the top on the castle.

The sun still peeps and the sea gulls dart over my head..
Where are you flying, I've forgotten to bring bread.

And, the baby kiwis, heads down, scurry to and fro..
Back and forth and then again...why...does anyone know?

And out on the water there's a ship or two...
Going far away...?  One thinks inside, "Take me with you."

But even this calm, sandy beach drowns out the chaos...
And fills one with a serene sense of wonder and of life.

God, in his nature...in his order and in the beauty bestowed...
Transcends all of life's turmoil, our souls are restored.

Why do we ever question His ever loving trust...
When beaches...seas...everything...speak of his love for us.

*Kathleen K. Bevans*

## Progress

Indifferent mist on an ocean shore
    laying its weightless body upon the quiet
    beach.
Sightless eyes searching each grain of sand,
    roaming forever across bleached
    wilderness.
Hands without touch unsparingly
    molding to the curvatures of shells lying silently
    in rest.

And last...

Tasting without a mouth, the bitter evidence
    of man.  A dark suppressing cape of crude
    rolling along waves cluttered with sea life

No longer living...

...And we dare call it progress?

*Kevan S. Beijan*

## The Changing Seasons

The wind snapped at me like an old grouchy man as I watched the leaves play,
On the cold Autumn day.

The leaves were turning red, orange, yellow, and brown,
As they leaped from the tress and floated gently to the ground.

The joy and laughter that once filled the air,
Will soon give way to winter's cold stare.

Soon it will resume again with the freshly fallen snow,
Creating bliss for everyone we know.

But soon the winter will melt away,
And we'll see life in a brand new way.

Say good-bye to winter and hello to spring,
And all the joy that it will bring.

All is well and has to end,
So it can start the cycle of life all over again.

*Kim Strecker*

## Untitled

My friend it is your turn now,
life has played with you
now it is you; go on and play with life.
This is your chance, prove that you can,
love awaits, it is knocking at your door,
at the door of your heart that...
...it has so many feelings wishing to be set free.
Open the door answer its call;
let those feelings free
its your destiny, go on take it!
Don't let them tell you wrong,
let them dress you with sweetness,
with joy, with passion,
specially with love; which its eternal.
This is your chance and it is real,
not just a dream, not a make believe.
This is true, it is yours to be.
Touch it, that is how real it is.
Take the call and be happy, give it a chance to be
and let it nile your destiny.

*Karen Sanchez*

## Natural Harmony

The winter is near, a breath away
  like a thief who lurks and waits
For stumbling prey, lost and alone
  In a homeless nightmare
   UN-decent and undeserved,.

How many will the beast swallow?
  Those, by circumstance divided,
Separated from mercy and God's grace
  And tumbling down an unending void
A maelstrom of loss and horror.

But the sea waits and tests and waits some more
  Where will that new moon rise?  And when?
Day from night, light from dark,
  And end to trouble, and heartache's pain

No matter demands, winter must end.
  And spring brings new life
From death and dying, misery and despair.
With new born hope for eternal balance
Crowned with love, surrounding love
Internally, eternally within..

  *Kurt Soller*

## Me

Me!  What a word!
Me!  I am glad
Me is what I am!

Come let me show you me, my life, my hope,
my destiny, is to be a better Me.

Me!  What a word it can be
used for so many things,
Me!  A great word to use.

Me!  I am glad,
I am able to use Me.

  *Karen English*

## Deep In My Soul...With All My Heart

Time is short, the years rushed past...
Me, your little girl, all grown,
To your surprise, it went by fast.

My secrets I shared with you at night,
My fears you soothed with such might.
You tiptoed softly out the door,
I waited to see you stay a minute more.

No more good-night kisses
No more prayers to hear
Mother, for all this belongs to yesteryear.

Your job with me is completed,
with a loving heart, you have seeded.

I hear the prayers,
I kiss good-night,
I tiptoe softly to the door,
I always stay a minute more.

For this time is short, with years that past,
To my surprise, my little girl,
is growing up too fast...

  *Katherine M. Floravit*

## Fly Wind Fly

Listen now to whispering wind.
Mostly its just our secret heart with in.
Violins play with ancient bow,
While softly strewn lays new fallen snow.
Our souls knows no bound
While our love is all aglow
Sing gently wind song
Caress the ground gently,
As peacefully you fly.  Shake your magic carpet
Softly through the leaves.
Lift them too the sky.
And with our soul aloft, send them with our hearts
To him who rules the sky.

  *Kathryn Granger Smith*

## The Lady of Twelfth Street

"Mama, who's dat lady?" the little boy asked.  "Hush yo'
mouth, child and turn yo' head," Mama said.  "But, mama, why
she satshayin' up and down the street?"  'Cause she's, the
lady of 12th Street!"  Mama said.  "Why she walk like dat?"
said the wide eyed child.  "Cause she turns many a man's head
and breaks a many woman's hearts, and take a home turns it up
side down," cried Mama.  "Cause she's the lady of 12th
street," said the child.  "Wicked come and sin behold, Lord,
Sweet Jesus, come take me home," shouted Mama.  Now, the child
was frightened and despaired.  For the people on the street
gathered for mama's fanfare.  Look at the painted face, and
fancy grin, that why our men sin.  You take them where we
won't go, but they don't come home.  "Oh! Hush silly woman,"
cried the lady.  "I try's to have little fun," said the lady
of 12th street, in pure fun.  "I does no harm to yo' soul and
mine.  But, sho's gits a kick out of havin' a good time.
I's think I tired now," she says with no regret, "But, watch
out, she'll get yours, yet."

  *Kim Edwards*

## My Father's Parents

They didn't know my favorite color
My favorite food, movie nor song
They never could remember my age
They always spelled my name wrong

I longed so desperately to once
Hear their reluctant voices calling for me
Feel her unyielding hand clenched onto mine
To be bounced upon his knee

I tried to drill into my head
That Father's parents loved me too
And the reason they never told me so
Was because they thought I knew

Through years their feelings became transparent
The truth I was destined to find
I realize now they never truly cared
I was abandoned in their minds

My love-starved heart was fed leftovers
Morsels stale from a table selfishly occupied
I devoured the bits one by one
Until my unnourished dreams died

  *Katina Renee Frye*

## My Hand

A wondrous thing my hand is
my hand has rippling wrinkles
as a wind blown lake
my hand has felt intense burning
as a rapid forest fire
sometimes I think my hand will scream
when it starts to panic
as I draw near to touch a man
I can feel my heart beat racing in my hand
when I am finally with that man
awh, but at last my hand feels blackened as I drift
asleep

   *Kelli J. Warnke*

## My Garden

   My garden has been my life.  At times I have let it go, how I have
neglected it with bad thoughts and blame.  I felt the shame.  My
special spot of once carefully tended soil has gone to seed.
   Thank heavens I have finally dug deep within my garden, so deep
that Thistle no longer grows and Itchweed screams as I approach
knowing it will be yanked straight out and not allowed to fester.
   Joyous is my garden now, the birds are heard their song
majestic praising.  "Open hearts, keen minds, clear vision."
Happy are the pheasants roosting by my creek.  They've come to
stay,
make a nest, and raise their young.  They know they will be fed
because my garden is bountiful, full of love, food, and beauty.
   I hope weary souls will come and rest and partake of heaven's
air.  To calm the soul's unrest and send them on their way.

   *Katharine Kivett*

## Reaching Beyond The Horizon

I've reached the horizon yet life is just beginning, opportunities
never-ending, aspirations all unfolding.
I've reached the horizon now I'm living in the future, the past was an
adventure, the present here to nurture.
I've reached the horizon life seems to be all a game, how shall I help
my fellow man ease so many years of pain?
I've reached the horizon my career's about to start, but I'm quite
undecided and it's tearing me apart.
I've reached the horizon will I be a lawyer or a doctor, a judge, no
a machine operator, or maybe even an....... engineer?
I've reached the horizon and the world is mine to conquer, having new
hopes to surrender and lost dreams to recover.
I've reached the horizon and there is so much I can do, so many doors
are opened it's only up to me to walk right through.
I've reached the horizon, yes I'm proud enough to say it "hitch your
wagon to a star" and the sky will be your limit!

   *Kpana Kpoto*

## No Alters

I build
No alters
Or throw not stones
What is my nature
Is mine
Alone
I build
No alters
And eve
Did not falter
Nor have I
We both have seen the earth and kissed the sky
And yet
We are shunned
No alters here
No alters.

   *Kimberly Ann Blanchette*

## Friends Forever

The best things in life are the friends that you have,
No matter where they live on water or land.

Through thick and thin, they will always be there,
No mater what the topic, they always care.
They give you help when times are rough
Or when situations are fairly tough.

They hurry to your side when you let out  moan,
And they always put up with your awful groan.

Friends are nice to comfort whenever they're sad.
They stick by your side whenever you're mad.

There's never a time when a friend lets you down,
Even when things are downer than down.

Friends are the most valuable thing in the world,
They guard and protect you more than the sharpest sword.

With friends by your side every day and every night
You'll be glad to hear that things will always be right!

   *Katie Homan*

## No More Tears

I'm tired of all the depression and I'm not lying
No more tears, no more crying

No more pain and no more tears
No more frowns and no more fears

No more tears - I'm on my way
"On my way, to a much brighter day"

No more tears and no more strife
No more tears, in my life

No more tears, because of things I lack
"No more tears and I'm never turning back"

No more tears, believe in me
No more tears, you'll see!

No more tears - I've got to go on
I'm through crying and now I'm strong

No more tears and no more pain
No more tears and no more rain

No more tears - I'm alright
"No more tears, day or night!"

   *Kenneth Blount*

## Peace, Love, and Harmony

If all the countries could agree
No nuclear war was to be
If all the presidents could see
How mother earth would suffer tragically
For the decisions of power to be
Peace, love, and harmony
Is what the world really needs
Not cruise missiles overseas
Are long range titans our destiny
To destroy mother earth unmercifully
What the world really needs is peace, love, and harmony
Care more about the hungry and the poor
Instead of some damn presidential war
Put third world countries on their feet
I'm sure nobody wants nuclear defeat
Bring the world a little closer with
Peace, love, and harmony
Would surely make the world a better place to be
We're all God's children, I'm sure you'd agree
To·live in peace, love, and harmony

   *Keith Alan Armstrong*

## The Buck

The snow had fallen, casting shadows in the glen.
No sound was heard, all nature was in slumber.
The thick blanket lay undisturbed by God's creatures,
While in the distance was heard the warning sound like thunder.
Suddenly ears perked and turned toward the invading noise.
Startled, somber eyes searched the darkness.
Dainty black hooves scattered the covering of white.
No longer would the forest its creatures caress.

The thunders grew closer as daylight approached.
Imminent danger hung in the breeze as animals took flight,
Their sanctuary of darkness gone as night turned to day.
Death looming ahead would be their certain plight.
An explosion of fire echoed through the trees,
Still, brown eyes no longer held the promise of a new day.
Now, as before, the earth was quiet, all sound was hushed
While the soft snow again cradled the buck where he lay.

*Kris Anderson*

## A Little Smile

The touch of age has crossed over
Now you find you have grown old
Seems like all of your loved ones
Won't come home for you to hold.

Your face has signs of many wrinkles
The color has been replaced with gray hair
Trembling hands pick up the bible
While rocking in your old rocking chair

Loneliness in the heart has come calling
But somewhere you now find a smile
Because the words you find you are reading
Makes your pain seem to feel worthwhile.

Soon the bible says Jesus will be arriving
And on a long journey you will go
To a place that is called Heaven
Where angels wait to embrace you so.

All the hurt seems to have slowly faded
A sweet smile has come upon your face
Soon this unhappy life will be traded
For eternity at the golden Heaven gates.

*Karen Hockett*

## Being True

If JESUS above we wish to see
Obedient to Him we need to be
Confessing of our each and every sin
Opening the door of our hearts for Him to come in
His loving hand we need to receive
And in His name trust and believe
Following in His steps each day
Allowing Him to lead the way
Reading His word, applying it to our life
Using it when satan tries to bring strife
Sharing our needs and burdens in prayer
Knowing that JESUS will always be there
Telling others of that special story
That to Him we would bring honor and glory
Doing and saying the things we should
Without Him we know we never could
Living the lives He would have us to
And to our Saviour being true

*Kathy Glenn*

## Blue Skies Falling

Blue skies falling through time like splashes of water in an endless ocean. Unborn babies wailing silent tears to almost mothers who will not hear. A social correctness that knows no morality. Churches that grow like weeds, but know not the Christ of whom they preach. Christians who boast their Christ-like stewardship for a Lord who humbled Himself for humanity. A government of the people, for the people, by the people, that does not even know it's people. A person having more friends than a phone book can hold, but yet still alone; alone on a field of blue skies falling through time like splashes of water in an endless ocean.

*Kevin F. McHugh*

## Fear

Fear.
Of being alone.
Never feeling that body pressed against mine, molding to every curve.
A perfect fit.
Holding me so tightly there is no space between us.
Flesh on flesh.
Security.

Fear.
Of never feeling those lips pressed against mine.
Warm, soft, tender; gently caressing.
Kisses so intimate, so meaningful, they make my whole being
Weak.

Fear.
Of never hearing those words.
Words that stir the soul with a single whisper.
Words that make me feel wanted, needed,
Whole.

Fear.
Of being alone,
With myself.

*Kristi Ross*

## Let's Hear It for the "Little Ones"

Children are a foundation
    Of faith and hope and love;
They possess the ability to strengthen
    The weaknesses we, as adults, often do not see.

We are their "pillars" — the mountains
    And ladders they strive to climb;
Within their grasp but often out of reach —
    They search, in constant need to find...

Always in awe and wonderment —
    Each issue becomes a "WHY?"
It is hard to imagine we too
    Began our lives this way;
Each moment a curious adventure —
    A word, a look, a sigh.

Yes, children are the picture —
    Of innocence: kind and sweet;
A gift of God and reflection of ourselves —
    The future of tomorrow,
    In whose eyes the world is unique!

*Karen Visone*

## Our Flag

Our flag flies gentle in the breeze
Oh how hard it tries to please
It flies so proud at ever important occasion
Telling everyone it's there for our nation
It flies for you and for me
Hoping there it will always be

Our flag flies gentle in the breeze
Oh how hard it tries to please
Sometimes it's ragged and worn
From the many battles into which it was borne
And sometimes it hangs at half-mast
Because someone great has away passed
In the cemeteries above the graves
It flies over a veteran brave

Our flag flies gentle in the breeze
Oh how hard it tries to please
And if by chance a hard wind blows
It's stars and stripes stand out real bold
To show it's colors true
Of red white and blue

*Kathleen Greenslaugh*

## Transition

The predawn mist that leaves the dew
On peaceful meadows of lavish hue
Where blossoms of gold and crimson and blue
Grow free from human hand

Is sent to shroud the early morn
From midnights passing to daybreak's scorn
(The hour when night and day are torn)
And stillness rules the land

But sunlight comes to call the day
And slowly sends the dew away
And the breeze begins its rhythmic sway
As mist and earth disband

And moment by moment tranquility lifts
From dawn to day the power shifts
And respect is lost for nature's gifts
As the day belongs to man

*Kelly L. Phillips*

## Alabaster Darkness

Dusk comes sooner,
Once the snow begins to fly.
The landscape once full of Autumn's radiance
turns white and shuts his eyes.

A serene time to feel the lastingness
To contemplate one's self and begin to learn
Quiet disciplines never mastered in school
Meant - meant - to last a lifetime.

Drum - drum - drum
Pound the yearnings of your heart
Tick - tock - tick
Waste not the moments of your life

Do it now - do it later
How much time is allotted a soul till
Till the turning of the white
the shutting of the eyes?

Dawn comes later,
After the frost has formed.
Naked trees with vacant arms of alabaster,
Wisely - wait for the time to be reborn.

*Kellyanne Taylor Gottschalk*

## One Last Moment

One last moment, one last night
One endless dream in the pale moonlight,

Our eyes set on the future, our hearts set on the past
Our dreams set on the moment that the moonlight has cast,

The soft sound of music that brings inner tears
Knowing that this moment will remain with us for years,

The moon that was above in the dark shimmery sky
Is now falling slowly as the music begins to die,

The ending of our moment in this one last night
Is now our endless dream in the pale moonlight.

*Kimberly Cilluffo*

## The Kiss

Soft as a teardrop resting lightly upon my cheek
Or strong and powerful as a mountain's peak
It starts with her eyes as they lock onto mine
And grab hold of my soul and grab hold of time
If I could freeze that moment my heart would be glad
But equally so my lips would be sad
Because what comes next leaves mere words wanting
And in the days that follow it continues haunting
As slowly she leans forward never breaking her stare
Till our lips gently touch in that still quiet air
So tender and sweet is that moment they meet
With their bodies pressed firmly, two hearts with one beat
Now the intensity rises like a great ocean's tide
And my emotions race furiously till the waters subside
I laugh and I cry while my brain shakes its fist
In a vain search for words which do not exist
How then can I expect this pen to succeed
To capture on paper what my brain must concede
But perhaps the answer lies between the lines of this paper token
Because sometimes the clearest pictures come from words never spoken.

*Kevin Hebert*

## The Changing Winds

As we go through the hills of time,
Pondering the valley below
We wonder sometime where the wind comes from,
And when it leaves, where does it go!

It blows in cold from the East
Then changes suddenly to the West.
But of all the winds that come to us
We love the south wind best.

For when we feel its gentle touch
It's always soft and low.
We know that spring is very near,
And the wintery winds must go.

The wind, that ever changing wind,
Where does it get its force?
What gives it so much power
When it abruptly changes course?

Much like our God who rules it all,
The wind we cannot see,
Only the effects, be it great or small,
And so shall it ever be!

*Kathleen W. Thomas*

95

## The Lake

You are like a lake,
  reflecting everything in nature.
You reflect the rocks that line your shore,
  but even they are not stronger than you.
You reflect the trees that seem to tower overhead,
  yet you are much taller than they are.
Rays of sunlight pour down on you,
  and you shine them on all who pass by you.
If you look hard you will see two flowers,
  a yellow rose and a red rose that I planted along your bank.
  The greatest gift you have given me is my reflection in you.

  *Katie M. Butler*


## Untitled

I wish the tears I could take away
Remove all pain felt inside
You hold so much kindness for others
If only your face and heart smiled
Giving all to everyone around
never fulfilling your own needs
Thinking there are none to fulfill
If only I could show how wrong you are
There is so much out there
Reach, it is yours
If only you could see
You blind yourself from all life has to offer
Afraid of happiness, loving
Not wanting your heart ripped out again
I would give you happiness if only I could
I shall hope, wish, pray
But only you can make happiness come your way

  *Kelly Anne McCarthy*


## Run Away's

Sometimes you run away, because your parents make you pissed.
Runaways are made, hurt and worried
They don't know where they are going to live.
Sometimes they live on the streets.
To make money, some of them sell drugs, or sell their body.
Half of them go back to their families,
the other half die on the streets.
Some of them die of AIDS, a drug over dose of someone shot them.
You think at that moment it seems right but you regret it years later.
I know how you feel trust me I know, I was once a runaway.
Now I know I was wrong, but at the time I was right.
Remember this your fears are going to follow you no matter where you
go.  You can't runaway from your problems.
I know what your thinking and why should I stay no one likes me.
But believe it or not, they do love you.
You think that everyone hates you what do you have to live for,
is that what you are thinking, because I know you are.
I know what you are going through please get help before you
runaway.

  *Kate Tricarico*


## Love, Joy And Peace

"What is Love?" asked the young of the old
"Love, is putting yourself aside for others.  Or so I've been told."
"What is Joy?" asked the young of the old.
"Joy, is wanting only happiness unto you.  Or so I've been told."
"What is Peace?" asked the young of the old.
"Peace, is wishing only grace to your friends and enemies.
  Or so I've been told."
"How do you know?  Who told you so?" asked the young of the old.
"The Lord, has told me so."

  *Kristen Allison*


## I Hate TV Sports!

I really hate watching football, and I hate watching baseball too.
Running up and down a court is a really dumb thing to do.
Big and strong and muscled men who always eat their Wheaties.
Helmets on their little heads and spiked shoes on their feeties.

Bruised up bodies, padded knees, dribbling on the floor.
When they collide and 'bout kill themselves, my husband yells for
  more.
The broken ribs and banged up heads, when their vision starts to fade.
"Never mind them being carried off the field, did you see the play
  they made?"

I can never get hubby's attention, no matter what kind of scene I've
  made.
He just sets in front of the TV set with his popcorn and Gatorade!
I can kiss him on the ear lobe or run my fingers through his hair.
But this thing he has for TV sports is like a love affair!

I try to lose the remote control, or hide the TV guide.
He knows this and keeps them neatly tucked securely by his side!
My husband dearly loves it, nothing I can do you see.
When he cheers about shooting a basket I'd like to shoot the
damned TV

  *Kristie E. Ferrell*


## Grandma

Her rickety chair creaked to and fro.
She was curled over even so.
Her dull grey locks sprung out everywhere.
But she never gave a care to her hair.
Her teeth were in a glass on top of the t.v.
Her glasses she couldn't find to see.
Her worn bones groaned and moaned
as she counted the money she loaned
every so often for me to use.
A payback she always refused.
She then leaned back and fell asleep.
Her slumber was so very deep.
She started snoring.
Soon it got boring.
So I tiptoed out.
But she never found out.

  *Kristen Willey*


## What Is A Mother

A Mother is everything; everything to everyone.
She's doctor, a nurse, an advisor a lover.
And most of all the's a comforter.  A comforter for all.
A comforter, a teacher; an all around help.
She's always there when you need her.
She's someone you can count on in times of trouble.
She's someone you want to be with all the time.
She's someone who's special all year through.
She's someone who's special, to everyone, including you.
She's the only one, who can give birth, she can give you life.
She's someone who earns your respect and love.
She's someone who is picked by God above.
She's picked by God above, because she's full of love and compassion,
She's a nurse, a teacher, an advisor and a friend.
She's always there, her love will never end.

  *Kim Kelly*

## Dear Mom And Dad

Dear mom and dad, I wish we could talk
Since you both passed away, I do miss our walks
Lots has been happening on earth since you died
Nicole Brown Simpson was murdered, O. J. S. being tried.

Bill Clinton is president, the economy is still sad
Government and politics, the shape of congress is bad
There are dozens of talk shows, and all different hosts
They cover every subject from sex changes to ghosts.

Nothing is sacred or holy or right
They want God out of everything, while they push civil rights
They're passing out condoms in elementary school
A disease called AIDS is killing millions, but safe sex is cool

We have gays in the military, and computers have gone far
Forrest Gump was best picture, Tom Hanks was the star
They recall everything from breast implants to baby food
People are depressed and they take Prozac to help their mood

As for our family we are all well
Everyone is still working the kids are doing swell
I miss you both so much and you're deep in my heart
Writing is still my dream, which you will always be a part

***Kelly Hyler***

## In August

The hayscent of summer ferns lingers like the
smell of the secret parts of my lover's body.

Pressing my face forward, leading with lips
and nose, I close my eyes and let the
sunlight settle all worries, a warm unexpected
breeze reminds me of summers past, life times
ago when the world was just as cruel but I
was not yet conscious.

Now I am mourning my sisters in Sarajevo
my battered and broken mother in Rwanda, and
all of my crucified cousins who have died in a
circle of fear.

Sunlight shifts in a faraway country,
the odor of blood burns over blue lakes
ancient hearts buried in the earth heal
but can't explain why we must face
the dark side of ourselves to survive.

***Kate Bell***

## Alone

The frown on my heart arched great as you left; left me free
So painful was the ache of my sorrow
From the broken chains which bound me to hell
It spreads through my limbs like the darkness of blood
Dark from the silhouette of my soul
The soul which tugs with a force of 10,000 men
Trying to revive my being
The forged light which had led me so far into nothing
Has faded and flown away on wings of coal
The want to trail it is strong, but I cannot be blinded by what is
artificial. A bright light will come
One of a great, incandescent flame that burns with a life
I will follow that flame when it's heat warms my heart
Away with it I'll fly on the strong wings of fate
My spirit will lift to the heavens and spread to all around me;
Because I.. I am One,
One of confidence,
One of pride,
One of knowledge,
One who stands alone.

***Kenneth Heistuman***

## Waitress Blues

Here I sit with the Waitress Blues.
Sore feet in my very old shoes.
An old uniform that needs repair;
I need a hairdresser to fix my hair.

When I get home I soak my feet;
I throw my tattered body between cool sheets.
My tattered uniform is washed everyday;
I am always broke before I get my pay.

I need more money to run around;
I need a man- not a clown.
A simple raise is all I need.
I have a few hungry mouths to feed.

Still, I sit here with those waitress Blues.
With overdue bills and medical dues.
I need to get out of this rut...
And maybe go to school, but...

***Kimberly Parrish***

## The Scent Is No More

Words of time past being fulfilled,
Still you seek the wrong path.
You have become prisoners of yourselves
And enemies of your kind.
Given the sweet fragrance of illusion
Lulling you into the apathy of destruction.
You have become the deceived as well as the deceiver.
Lost truth, wisdom of fools consumed by the fragrance.
Tunnel vision of self fills the spirit within.
Extinction is from your iniquities,
Your iniquities from your blindness
Your blindness from your choice of selected knowledge
Ignorance is rampant.

Prophecy fulfilled, the storm of truth breaks through.
The prison is no more, the heavens roar in praise to the Lord.
The breeze of silence sweet to the taste
Sweeps over this lost place.
Those who followed the narrow path of truth
Unspeakable joy engulfs for the scent is no more....

***Karen R. Ayer***

## The Pace

Slow down the pace.
Take time to think.
This isn't a race.
Sip a cool drink.

But life passes by before we even realize.
Changes occur as each day ends.
We've got to adjust, not to idealize.
The time has come to make amends.

As we get closer to meeting our Maker
Each passing moment can make a difference.
And deciding to be a giver, not taker
Is the only choice that truly makes sense.

For whether you believe in one true God
Or whether you don't even care,
To give to others is not at all odd
Considering the love you can share.

So slow down the pace.
Take a deep breath.
Each soul has its place.
Be at ease with Death.

***Kathy E. Henry***

## A Closed Door Has No Key

There is nothing sadder to hear...
Than a child's muffled cry...
Does anyone ever stop to wonder why...
"I'm only eight years old" she sobs, in the quiet of her room...
"How come mom and dad don't know, Uncle Bob will be here soon...
When you see a change come over her, the difference of night and day.
Stop and ask yourselves - what makes her act that way...
Gather her in your arms so close and tell her it's all right...
'Just let us know what's happened to you at daytime or at night'...
A child is so precious, so young for a short time...
So innocent and giving, I know for she was mine...
Things are getting better now, we can finally close the door...
Because...
Uncle Bob won't be here any more...

*Anna Larson*

## My Message to You...

The "Oklahoma Blast" has hit us all hard,
that is the reason, I must send this card.
As I sat and I watched the t.v. today,
I just can't believe it - as I cry, as I pray!
The fire fighter carrying baby Baylee, just one
and the family embracing, they just lost a son.
Why did it happen? How could this be?
These questions are asked, not only by me.
The victims are more then the bodies they'll find,
for how can this image, leave a child's mind.
We watch, we mourn, we want to help "mend"
you can do this today, just hug a friend.
Don't put off 'til tomorrow, what can be done today
do what you must do, say what you must say!
My message to you is simple and clear
Remember I love you, remember I care!

*Kim O'Keefe*

## On the Precipice of Tomorrow

I heard the sounds of pain and sorrow,
That swept across the land stretched wide.
I felt the haunted eyes of fear,
And found nowhere to hide.

On graveyard walks they passed by me,
Heads bowed down with minds that know.
Is man capable of this but once,
Or twice as history shows?

I listened to their silent prayers,
Their courage filled my heart.
I smelled the darkened chamber air,
Hope's breath did not depart.

Not for those who once were witnesses,
This monument cold and gray.
Instead it beckons for all who pass,
To help them walk your way.

As I stand on the precipice of tomorrow,
I vow life's lessons will never cease.
Do not forget but dare to remember,
So all might live in peace.

*Karen Wilcox O'Connor*

## Comatosity

Comatosity, living in this great city.
In a deep sleep, I do not make a peep.
My eyes are open yet I do not comprehend,
What is this world around me
And when will I descend?
Comatosity, in a mellow state of mind.
Comatosity, when will I meet others of my kind?

*Kathleen Stupec*

## I Am Home

I knew, the minute we met, we had been lovers before.
That was the easy part — the part I knew.
The list of what I did not know continues to grow.
The revelation came early, unfortunately.
To stave it off would have been kinder.
Maybe you're right.
Maybe I am your punishment, but together - the light nearly blinds me.
I revel in the significance, unlike me heart.
It has become manic/depressive.
How many years must I wait?
If we chose now there is a reason
It must be worth it.
Step out of linear time — we are already there.
My God, my God, was it really that simple?
I must be in Oz.
Thank goodness I bought those red shoes,
but I won't be needing them now, for I am home.

*Kelly K. Baca*

## Black

BLACK is for death, the second hand beyond life:
The BLACK light from destiny slowly becomes white:
The holy BLACK is for the past, present, and future
Suffering.
Intuitive BLACK of the night;
The stream of BLACK tragedy running through the veins of
Passion;
BLACK is for loneliness of the crying eyes;
BLACK runs beyond where the eye can see;
BLACK shall sit through death with a tiny chuckle of a
Laugh.
BLACK hammers into the heart to stop the silent beat.
BLACK runs with the sound of THUMP THUMP, THUMP
THUMP
And then it
  STOPS!

*Kristie Pesce*

## Perfect Integration?

Once upon a time ...

At the feet of the Himalayan Mountains
the Mandarin sat down in tranquillity,
so in harmony and continuity
comes the time for perfect meditation
on integration of pandas, his subjects
into the existential framework of bamboo ...

Along with a sparkling mountain stream
with fuzzy limitation invisible as reality
the bamboo forest beauty is a miracle dream,
majestically flows down, as silk tapestry green
so it never becomes a perishing vanity
for his subjects, the pandas ...

Look into the image of a shiny silk mirror
see the moving imperfection's beauty
graceful as the pandas, black and white
subjects of the Mandarin of Mountains.
The pandas give beauty to the silk carpet green,
but if they vanish, where be the life within?

*Kris S. Teski*

## Dear Lord

Lord I want to thank you for every waking day.
The miracles you've showed me your help along the way.
Why you chose to save me when I fall short every day.
What a wonderful merciful God you are to say that it's O.K.

The world is full of destruction and sorrow,
The time we are here is only borrowed.
When I forget to thank you for my health and happiness.
Please forgive me for my selfishness.

Lord thank you for your walk with me each and every day
The course has not been easy but you've been there everyday.
No life has not been easy the trials big and small,
But with your words and guidance we come out standing tall.

I have been blessed with the joy of a baby
Who brings much love into my life daily.
Sometimes I want to end it all, but then I think of my baby
And who would tell her about you Lord all the joy and love you
gave me

So each day I stomp the devil under my feet and say another day
you won't get your way for with the Lord I claim your defeat.

So if I forget to thank you Lord for all that you do,
Please know in my heart that I will always love you!

*Kimberly Putterbaugh*

## The Halls

The bell summons.
The once silent and empty hall
Now swarming, they are free.
Free but for four minutes
But free from the expectations and requirements.
Rushing, rushing as if life itself depended on it,
Carelessly pushing their way through the crowds
The drone increases.
Louder and louder, overwhelming
As if it itself could consume everything.
Frantic shouts of forgotten assignments float aimlessly.
Gossip traveling quicker than they can,
It bounces its way from person to person
A little lost each time in the translation.
Metal against metal echoes endlessly.
Materials carelessly discarded,
As if never to be thought of again.
Slowly they disperse
Going their separate ways
The bell shrieks, the doors close, silence.

*Kristen McHale*

## Greetings of the Hearts

The beauty of your eyes reflect
  the warmth of your smile
The kindness of your greeting character
  a genuine style
You enhance desire to express my notion
Of your everyday presence -
  like poetry in motion
The proximity of you is inviting and alive
  for that which makes our hearts subscribe
Of a look that you and I must "sigh"!

*Kwaku Bilal-Shabazz*

## The Flower on the Mountain

Together the flowers bloomed. In unison
their beauty sang. Throughout the giant
valley, their vanity constantly rang.
Far off, in the distance, an unusual
flower grows. It blossoms till its power,
begins to overflow. The flowers in the
field are ruthless and care-free, the
menacing world around them their eyes
do fail to see. The flower on the mountain
is choked with a feeling of grief. It mourns
the meadow below it, with sorrow and
disbelief. Within the mighty flower, this
painful anguish glows, it feels as if it is so
tiny and the others are fully grown. But then
the flowers sees in some unnatural sign, that
its eyes are widely open and the others are
pitifully blind.

*Kathryn Frantz*

## "Glimpses Of Forgotten Dream"

I sometimes have glimpses of my Forgotten Dreams
Then I pinch and shake myself into reality
Oh! How different does this world look?
From the Beautiful dreams ...

Was I much drunk with the power of my dreams?
to make me feel so tipsy?
To forget that I belonged to this Mortal World?
Still I have Glimpses of my Forgotten Dreams

I feel my life slightly, delicately tinged with
  the enchanting dreams
Am I obsessed with these gullible dreams?
Though I awake from my Dream Visions
And try to relate one, only the Shadows remain ...

*Kuchakulla S. Reddy*

## Faded Memory

In my mind's eye I see
there's someone looking back at me.
His dark brown eyes are filled with passion
as he holds me close with much compassion.
His skin feels soft and very smooth
while making his slow, sensuous moves.
He caresses my face with his gentle hands
like the motion of water on the sand.
As he leaned himself a bit further toward me,
the next thing that I could barely see.
This handsome guy slowly lifted my chin,
and the next thing I knew, I was in heaven!
I've never experienced such a tender moment.
I'll remember to make a special note of it.
To feel something so innocent and so new
makes me feel happy and very subdued.
To be able to love and to also be loved
is the one thing that everyone surely dreams of.
What a most pleasant and wonderful dream
ending like a faded memory.

*Kimberlee A. Gersaba*

## Hope

A summer rain
of sky pregnant with cloud
Catching swollen drops on my tongue
Grass tickles a boy's
naked, rekindled smile

*Devon J. Platte*

## Children

As the boys and girls run and jump around,
They bring joy to many people's faces
By having fun in different places.
Their acts reveal that they are not bound
By string, rope, nails, or tape to the ground.
They go to the park, where they have races;
Watching television, they see car chases.
Then they go to bed to be safe and sound.

They go to their schools everyday but two.
At school they see their friends and their teachers;
They gets lots of assignments to do.
They also go to mass and hear preachers.
Their lives include schoolwork and time with friends.
They have tons of fun, hoping life never ends.

*Karim Shanahan*

## Changes

Changes in life generally do not occur with ease,
They can be violent like an earthquake,
Or as gentle and refreshing as a summer breeze.
   For most, it takes someone special
   To bring a change needed or not.
For me, it took you to bring those changes to my heart.
You made me realize what was wrong with my life,
And some of those realizations cut like a knife.
These changes were necessary for body and soul.
These changes you have instilled, made me whole.
   The renewed life you have brought to me;
is like the rain to a dry and dying tree.
How do I repay all the gifts you are giving,
or is it possible to repay someone
when the gift they are giving is living?
   So to you, Cary, I do vow
To try and repay your gifts of love somehow.

*Karen M. Dupoise*

## Dreams

*Dedicated to Rhonda*

Dreams are wishes from your mind,
they rarely come true, I think you'll find.
They come from within, wants and desires,
could be fame or fortune, whatever you aspire.
My dreams are about lovers, you and me,
living together, in peace and harmony.
In these dreams, your love for me is sincere,
you're beautiful, happy and smiling when I'm near.
And I'm a strong person, loving and caring,
offering a lifestyle, you wouldn't mind sharing.
Alas these thoughts are just a dream,
then I wake up alone, wanting to scream.
I'm doing the things to improve my life,
someday you'll want me, and be my wife.
All these thoughts and dreams are true,
And I'll never love anyone as much as you.
But don't let these dreams make you fret,
because if I'll love another more, I haven't met her yet.
Your love was glorious, your love was fine,
and I'll keep on dreaming of when you were mine.

*Kendall Smith*

## fogMaker

He only appears in summer;
this safe man from government.
His man-made fog, cousin to agent
orange, is good for us we're told.
It destroys mosquitos and greenheads,
yet is safe for children.

The fog moves deftly from Kennedy,
to Johnson, and to Nixon;
it circles, engulfs and fogs the vision.
Peak to valley it flows like the serpent
for it can create shape with fluid despair.

Summer is the sixties, the fogMan looms—
his latex fog of water, oil, and DDT
infiltrate the air of innocence; the children
rally in a totality of ignorance.
Hurry! it's the fogMan; the one who kills.
The fog is thick and white and blue; it collects
children riding bicycles like bugs to poison.
The young legs peddle ferociously in the wake of pestilence
and follow the fog of propaganda.

*Kevin Murphy*

## Feelings of Hurt

Alas I have awakened from my fantasy yet
This was the clause I had hoped to elude
I had heard all good things come to an end
But for us I never considered this

This impeccable relationship shall be no more
With you I had found happiness unparalleled
One day you too shall awaken and realize that
No other will suit you as well as I do

Once and for all the magic expired
The fascination having run its course
The desire being brought to an end
I guess you have had your fill of me

Never able to replace what has just slipped away
Just as the scars on my heart will never heal
Our time together nothing more than memories
Memories of utopia never to be felt again

Like they were felt with you.

*Kenneth S. Williams*

## The Invite

You entered my life and caught me unawares
Though not like a thief, did you
invade my heart-
But, with a tender and loving breath,
you whispered my name,
And the call, such an aching sweetness,
your arms extended - I ran toward your embrace
With hearts entwined, the journey
began-with Grace by my side.

*Kay Stephens*

## It Began as a Whisper

"What does love fell like?" I whispered.
Thoughtful quiet followed; then the response,
"Well, I think it feels..." murmured another
Unsure of the answer.

"What does love feel like?" I murmured.
The bustle around stilled in mocking surprise.
"Physical attraction, excitement and fun."
The world and its driving Force hollered back.

"What does love feel like?" I shouted to the sky.
No answer. Nothing.
The great expanse of deep blue dotted with distant suns, moons and
    planets stared down at me, repeating my question back to me.
"What does love feel?" I felt the stars shudder.

Humbly genuflecting, I asked again with folded hands,
"What does love feel like?" I felt the stars shudder.
The Blessed silence was filled with the Light's sweet warmth.
His arms enfolded me as He whispered His answer gently into my ear,
"Why, my dear child, I am Love."

*Kristina Hodson*

## A Tired Phrase

Nothing special 'bout the phrase, it sounds so simple
Three words often over-used - they lose their style.
"Have a nice day" gets abused - it gets so tired;
And "How are you" with a true response unheard.

At a loss for better words that have more meaning;
With a burning in my heart that can't be found;
No allowance for these feelings to be spoken
That tired phrase the only words I ever find.

Because I do love you - you are the reason
That this love inside of me is much too strong
How much I do love you — I want you to know
And the only way to say it — "I love you".

A tired phrase can still be special when you feel it.
But then again this feeling just can't be explained.
An emotion I discovered when I met you
And it's growing stronger every time you're near.

By any method it's impossible to measure;
But it can't go on the way that it has been.
Somehow I know I can't contain it any longer.
If I can't say it — then I'll find another way.

*Kathy L. Roe*

## Flies

They feast upon things I will not mention
To make me ill is their one intention.

They tickle my nose while I'm sleeping
Across my plate I find them creeping.

Unwanted guests at picnics and parties
Just try to catch those elusive smarties.

Every time I spot a squatting fly
I grab a paper and swatting try.

Just a flick of the wrist with motion so swift
There'll be one dead fly when my weapon I lift.

To no one's surprise the fly has long flown
Another execution that I've blown.

Of all God's creatures in earth and sky
I often wonder why He made the fly.

*Ken Wilkins*

## A Mommy Is There...

A mommy is there to answer a cry.
To feed you, to dress you,
to sing a lullaby.

A mommy is there to laugh and to play.
To bathe you, to care for you, to teach you to pray.

A mommy is there to nurse you when blue.
To rock you, to hold you, to kiss a "boo-boo."

A mommy is there to read to you,
about animals, nature, and Moses too.

A mommy is there to be your #1 fan,
at ballet recitals or in the baseball stands.

A mommy is there to be a friend of yours.
To bake cookies, to build snowmen,
to take you for walks outdoors.

A mommy is there to teach you of love.
To teach you of service, of sacrifice,
and God and Jesus Christ up above.

A mommy is there for your every endeavor.
She'll love you, support you, and be your
Mommy forever.

*Kristi Hamilton*

## Untitled

Turtle, raise your weary head
    to Night's unpredictable glow;
    the moonlight caress
    washes through the deep crevices
    of your cold, beautiful heaviness.

Turtle, dare to stretch your lonely neck
    into that Unknown,
    perhaps to catch a glimpse
    beyond the dark branches
    flickering shadowy bars
    across your back...

Turtle, do you feel trapped inside that armor—
    ever restless of your safety?

*Kelly Wilson*

## Oh, Precious Time!

When I was little time was for wasting...carelessly exploring...
touching...and tasting. Everything was like new and so very
interesting to me...my how large everything seemed to be. Oh,
what a precious time!

Soon I was bigger, still fascinated by all that was new...seemed
time was never enough...each day just flew.

So methodically, so as not to be wasting precious time, I grew
and
I knew...

The older I became, the more hurried the pace, never enough time
to savor what time would soon erase.

So, when you get caught up in the turmoil of time...find yourself
a quiet place, close your eyes and try to remember when time was for
wasting...spent exploring, touching and tasting. Oh, precious time!

*Kitty J. Land*

## Time and Again

Time and again we take for granted, the life we are given to live.
We don't open our hearts to let our loved ones in.
Time and again we sit back and say what we should have done...
Tell them "I love you"
Pick up the phone
Instead we always run.
Taking for granted the memories that we have,
    not attempting to make more.

Time and again I kick my self for all the things I could have done.
Instead I fell into the pattern to always have to run.
We take for granted things we have, for,
    we think they'll always be there.
Time and again we must realize how true, that life is so unfair.
Now, I find myself sobbing because you're not here.
And all the hours, minutes, seconds, I could have been doing,
what should have been done,
To make one more memory, a little more clear.
If only I had time...again.

*Kelli Regan*

## Mom

Mom, you are really great to understand me, because sometimes
we just don't agree.
On clothes, on hair, even on shoes that I wear.
But sometimes Mom I think to myself of all the things I wouldn't be.
I'd just be a book on a plain, dusty shelf.
But Mom I'm not!  You taught me to stand out.
And when I am down you told me not to pout.
"Go, go!" you shouted at my game.
Even when I missed the ball and felt really lame.
You soothed me and told me to do my best.
You told me I was beautiful when I was a mess.
So you see Mom I wouldn't have anything to say.
About the best Mom anyone could get.
I hope this Mother's Day is the best one yet.

*Katelynn E. Knutson*

## Evening Shadows

Evening shadows enfold the earth
When Day is called to rest
And Night tends her wandering children.
The closing day reveals to us
The mountains standing firm and proud
And trees whose arms are lifted high
In thanksgiving at eventide.
Thus Quiet walks near ponds and streams
Where fish and foul have taken rest.
The fragrance of each morning bud
Still lingers in the heavy air
Reminding us that morning, not long past,
Is still not long to come!
And as we watch the sun's last rays
Fade calmly in the arms of Night
We hear the wind call out to God:
"All is calm; all is quiet."
And God replies: "All is peace."

*Kenneth R. Van Gilder*

## A Friend

A friend is someone who will help you through the rough times.
Yet never pries to see what is on your mind.

A friend will never laugh at the mistakes you make.
They will steer you toward the right road to take.

In a lifetime a friend as good as this is hard to find.
So if you have one...hang on.
It will give you a peaceful state of mind.

*Karen Petersen*

## Unreturned Love

I say I love you, but how could that be true
When I say I love you, you can't say "I love you too"

Love is a feeling
Love is touch
Love is a hug when everything becomes too much

Love has nothing to do with money
Love isn't often funny
Love hurts on and on until your heart has no tears left
to cry
Why, you ask yourself, why

Love is the answer
Love is the question

Does he love me?
Probably not
Do I love him?
How could I not.

*Keri L. Scheer*

## Good-Bye Dad

I know the day is coming
When we will have to say goodbye
I just want you to know,
That I love you so.
My heart has always known this
Yet the words were hard to say.
You were there to hold my hand
The day my life began
Now it's my turn to hold your hand
When it's time for you to go.
It's so hard to let you go and say goodbye
but it's time.
Always know you will forever live within your children
and your grandchildren.
You'll always be with us
You'll always be remembered,
You'll always be loved.

*Kristine Stewart*

## Lady Quixote

Welcome my fragile heroine of yesterday
    when you slew my dragons of fear
    and jousted with my windmills of doubt
Was it only yesterday...
    we fearlessly rode into the realm of adventure
    teasing mortality while looking for immortality
Was it only yesterday...
    we undauntingly strode into the realm of hell
    playing time and searching for eternity
So welcome my friend
    the dragons now listless and ghostlike
    the windmills rusted and broken
    defeated by eternal time
Was it only yesterday, my dear friend
For now our tomorrows have come
    our days are shorter
    our nights longer
Yet our spirits remain
    to once again embrace
    the young fearless dragon slayers of tomorrow

*Karin Mandradjieff*

## Untitled

I saw a gull once, late at night
while I sat on the beach in solitude.
As I've grown older my thoughts have returned
to that wild yet gentle gull.

I've seen him flying close to the water,
suddenly diving down,
splashing through the surface.
Every time returning
with a bit of his night dinner
and going back for more.

I think love is like that bird;
moving steadily then taking a headlong fall,
crashing to bits in temporary defeat.
Yet, returning to try again
with more knowledge after each fall.
Moving steadily again, never quite satisfied.

**Kathy Muggy**

## If Only You Could See

I suffered long, I finally go home
Who is welcoming me, a family member I see
Peace and love overwhelmingly, a dip in the river of life
I walk out pure and dry, like I can fly, velocity
Place to place such enchantment; if only you could see
Jeweled fountains, bright scented flowers surround me
Twelve fruit trees, everyone gowned in pure satiny white
He said "follow me" everyone smiles so happy
If only you could see, all are glowing, busy or chatting
Death was my beginning and I took with me skills and tastes
And my desires, on paths of pearl we walked happy and smiling as He
    talked

**Karen Ann Saffa**

## My Father Who Art In Heaven

It was my father when I was young
Who taught me how to have some fun
He gave me strength to do my best
Even though sometimes I failed
I always seemed to pass his test.

I can't remember when my Dad
Didn't have time to spend with me.
Sometimes we would play
Sometimes we would work
Just the two of us, together we'd be.

As I grew older, life grew clearer
He reflected his wisdom like a shiny new mirror
It was my father who showed me the way
To become the man that I am today.

Though my father's time has come to pass
My love for Dad will last and last
I want to tell, all that I can
My father was one great man.

**Kenneth Scott Lutz**

## LOVE!

What "is" LOVE?
People say LOVE can hurt;
People also say LOVE is special!
I always wonder - Is LOVE thunder?
I don't know - I don't know
Will I ever know?
    What "is" LOVE?

**Crystal Galbiso**

## The Beach

At the beach is where I run,
play in the sand and just have fun.
Under the umbrella I hide from the sun,
I play and play until the day is done.

**Christopher Pilla**

## Reunion

There once lived a man name of "Ol John Hash"
Whose time on this earth has long since passed.
For time moves on like dust in the wind,
Generations must go and new ones begin.

Children must carry deep in their heart
The memories of family and where they did start.
Down through the ages they'll gather to share,
Their tales and stories, their joy and despair.

Remember the old ones along with the new.
Like "Ol John Hash, they'll remember him too!
Grand-daddy to us all each daughter and son
And through all of us here, "Ol John" lives on.

**Kimberly Pour**

## Dreamer

Oh Dreamer, Oh Dreamer
Why do you dream so much?
You dream of things nobody else can touch.
Your fantasies go on from day to day,
Leaving you with nothing to say.
Oh Dreamer, Oh Dreamer
Where are we going?
If only you could see the tears I'm showing.
I'm leaving this world that I know,
Can't you see the winds blow?
Oh Dreamer, Oh Dreamer
It is I in the sky above,
Looking down on all the things I love.
Where did you go, I can not see?
Are you saying that you are me?
Oh Dreamer, Oh Dreamer
I don't understand the things you say,
Please come back to me and stay.
Why do you dream the things you do?
Where ever you go take me too.

**Kelly Fitzpatrick**

## Bearing Walls

These stones hold the secrets of generating long past,
Yet, they remain strong and bold, inspiring forever...
The young listen to try to hear
The secret sounds from yesterday,
To catch a glimpse of visions past,
To move forward from their visions last.
Sitting still the minds race
To capture the flag of another's dreams.
But, the fervor dies when the banner appears
In the vaults above on the field of beams.
There have been like you,
There will be many more.
They'll neither discern my grandeur
Or repeat it nor.
It's an intangible pursuit, a yearning at best,
A journey to discover, or better, a quest.
Your drive instilled, must the future seem distant.
My foundations are sturdy.
I'm the keeper of the secret,
And I'll live forever.

**Kevin De Leon Ammons**

## My Sweet Baby Girl

The waiting is over, your face is beautiful.
You cry because you're mad; I, because I'm happy.
I cradle you in my arms to comfort you, saying,
"Everything's all right, mommy's right here."

My sweet baby you'll never know how much I love you.
I'll always be here for you; to protect, guide, and
Teach you about life and love.
You need never feel alone or scared.

All too soon you're taken from me; no good reason.
"God's will," they say. No more "us."
Only a mommy with a broken heart, empty arms,
And two months of beautiful memories.

Memories last a lifetime and so does a mother's love.
Don't be afraid, my precious one, for mommy will
Be with you again someday and then we'll never
Have to part again. Mommy's right here, my sweet baby girl.

*Karen S. Miller*

## The Most Special Part

You're the most special part of being a mother
You make me smile in one way or another
You're forever keeping me on my toes
But I guess that's the way motherhood goes.

You're the most special part of each new day
With your new antics and winning ways
Each new discovery that you find to do
I find I'm discovering how much I love you.

You're the most special part of all my dreams
You keep away my nightmares or so it seems
You're such a joy to have in our house
And when you're sneaky, you're quite as a mouse.

You're the most special part of learning and growing
Your love of me never stops showing
And on this special day you're one
And the most special part has just begun.

*Kimberly Graves*

## The Path of Life

Down the well worn path where we first met
You were so handsome I'll never forget
The woods were so pretty — full of cheer
With snow drops and violets here and there
Down the well worn path we used to walk
We were so happy — there was no need for talk
Streams of white water tumbling down
Squirrels and chipmunks scurrying around
Down the well worn path where we first met.
Birds sang in tree tops, melodious songs
Leaves and sweet blossoms danced along
Laurel and evergreens laden the ground
Berries and mushrooms abundantly found
Leaves are now turning red, yellow and brown
Silently cascading to the nearby ground
The well worn path where we used to go
Is now covered with footprints on a
Blanket of snow.

*Kay Wood*

## Rose Blossoms

There was a time when I sat, blurry stare at the blossom held before me.

There was a time when I clasped my treasure, hopefully holding
it out to everyone.

There was a time when I carelessly ripped it from it's branch as I ran
in abandoned games of youth.

There was a time when I held them cradled in my arms, entwined in
baby's breath as the linen and lace trailed behind, filmy veil
blurring my view.

There was a time when I lovingly laid them to final rest in a
field of granite and tears.

Now I stare, blurry eyed, at the virgin petals, drinking in the
fragrance of memories too precious to forget, too painful to remember,
the tiny hand, carefully clutching her treasure
for the two of us alone to share.

There will be a time when you cradle them in your arms,
as linen and lace trail, blurring your view, thinking of me,
and as you lay them lovingly among my field of granite and tears
drink in the fragrance and love.

*Karen M. Flack*

## Whispers

Whispers of the past brushed against my skin
And a chill froze me for that second.

Time only heals when I unclench my hand,
Breathe deeply and slowly of the aroma of a new day.
The longer I stay away from the shadows,
The sun creeps stealthy across with promise and warmth.

The pain of child birth screams through a woman's body,
Yet on the birthday there is great joy and thanksgiving.
The pain of a death wrenches the heart like a wet towel wrung of water,
Yet on the anniversary the inner voice is quieter and in a
recessed place.
The tears become part of the day instead of an intrusion of misery.

If you could make the young see that tomorrow the clouds might be
lighter gray,
Next week the torrent of emotion may break over the rocks,
And the rapids slow to a trickling stream of cool, calm, water,
Next season the answers are more clear and touchable.

The cold winds stall to a whisper, a painting still frozen, but
somehow brushed vague from the mind.

*Kim Grimes*

## The Feeling of Being Unloved

I know mother you never wanted me. You told me that once, while you
were overwhelmed with anger. I already knew that deep inside myself.
Did you know something has always been missing in me, in my life,
that security a child feels because of the bond with their mother,
only you could of provided me with that security, with that bond.

When I was a child I felt so sad and empty, so alone. When I was a
child I felt rejected, that no one cared about me. When I was a
child I felt scared and fear death. When I was a child I yearned
for love.

Mother, you use to say, "Why can't you be happy like other kids?"
I did not know why, I just felt different. When I grew I searched
for a man that would love me.
I wanted to show you I was worth something. To show you
somebody love me, all of me, to show you I was important to somebody
that He saw in me what you never looked for. You never took the time to
know your own child. I am still that child now with the appearance
of a woman.

*Karen R. Julian*

## A Banner for Our Country

When Betsy Ross was asked to sew
A banner for our country,
She smiled and 'visioned how we'd know
A sign of peace and freedom.

Then she pondered.

How shall it be designed?
What shall the colors be?
Maybe white - with red
Perhaps a patch of blue?

So she took some white, for purity,
Some red, for blood shed freely-
And then some blue, for courage true,
And stars for states, she added.

When Betsy put together
These colors we all love so
She foresaw men of stature fine
Who'd die for their country's honor.

So we today, as Betsy did, respect and love
that banner
By thought, and word, and deed alike,
In awed and reverent manner.

*Hazel Peterson Ecker*

## Falling Leaves

A leaf that falls from tree ablaze
A beauty to behold
Though dying still remembered
Long into winter's cold

So, to leave one's mark on earth
A loving memory still
To touch a heart with gentleness
A void in life to fill

In this quiet passing
A soul may touch a soul
And with this simple act alone
Another life made whole

*Bill Mathers*

## Happiness Cake

A big kiss each morning.
A big kiss each night
A heap of loving to
Make each day be bright!
A lot of understanding
Mix with tenderness and love.
A world of faith and helpfulness,
And prayers to the "One Above"
A dash of humor when things are grim.
A cheerful smile if the light gets dim.
Mix well with:
Much encouragement
In all that is worthwhile.
Some praise for things well done.
Will feed you in good style!
Frost with topping
Made with kisses every morning.
More kisses every night!

*Eloise M. Lee*

## A New Beginning

Absence of happiness with vanity
A breath by negative pressure
Living for others to live again
Redemption of the soul

Cleansing of the storm
The start of a separation
Embarking on the future
Ability to see the light

The gift is endless
Limits are unknown
Change is inevitable
A New Beginning.

*Jihan Murad*

## Introspective

In black of night
A bright star radiates
   To guide my soul.

Within the blue vault of sky
A warm sun sympathizes —
   I give gentle humanness.

Under a soft rain
The green earth thrives —
   I grow in life experience.

As the white dove
Rests within this quiet self
   I gain an inner freedom.

*Georganne G. Tiemann*

## Sara

Pale glowing skin,
A chin protruding in deep thought
Punctuated by a ruby red pucker.
Piercing blue eyes
Like her aunt.
She is an amazing being
Who never existed
Until just the other day,
Who only exists in my memory
Because by now
She is another child.
But I have seen the layer
Upon which her life will build.

*Gertrude Weber*

## The Tree

A majestic sentinel, the tree
A friend among all friends,
As it stands with dignity
Much in life on it depends.

In its carriage there is grace
When it gently sways and bends,
As it firmly stands in place
Regal government it lends.

With-in all of nature's realm
Unanimity is found
But the tree stands at the helm
With roots creeping under-ground.

There's a lesson to be learned
As we look up at the tree,
Before life is fast adjourned,
We must stand with dignity.

*Juanita Derringer*

## He's Comin'

One day he's a comin'
a comin' back again.
Gatherin' all His children;
from a world dark with sin.

Trumpets will be soundin'
angels singin' near.
He'll be callin' out the roll,
so listen carefully my dear.

Do you know what He'll say?
As your name is called from the roll.
Will He look and shake His head
for things you should have done.

Or will he look and smile
and then begin to say.
My child you have done well;
good works you've done today.

Your ticket you've well earned,
to leave this world of strife,
For now you have received
the gift Eternal Life.

*Gloria L. Williams*

## Our Moment of Life

You're a streak across the sky
A falling star is what you are
No matter what you do or say
Life's not easy come what may
You think that you will never die
But death can hit you like a sigh
Do good to every one you know
And God will bless the love you sow
Now pray to God with all your mind
That in some way you'll help mankind
Then lift your head and look up high
And God will bless you by and by

*Geneva Wilcox*

## A Doll Named Lorinda Elaine

Cherubic mocha face,
A hint of blush within the cheeks.
Lips red as a spring rose
And sculpted to a delicate pout.

Eyes like a dark sea of chocolate
Shadowed by long dark eyelashes.
So alluring and hypnotic
A person could drown in their splendor.

Hair parted straight down the middle
And fixed into two high ponytails.
Dark tresses, crescents of waves,
Held by curly pink and blue ribbon.

White frilly lace collar
Of the pastel blue and pink dress.
White stockings with a ruffled panty.
Black Mary Janes with silver buckles.

A perfect doll, a perfect friend,
A little girl's fantasy.
A never ending bond to develop within
Two hearts: One beating and one still.

*Amber Lawrence*

## Rush

A little here
  a little there;
It seems we're running
  EVERYWHERE!

The RUSH of day,
  the HASTE of night,
Working through
  the dark and light!

Just where do we run to,
  Onward every day
that we do not STOP...and PONDER
  the true value of TODAY?

Tomorrow may bring sorrows
  or opportunity...
If all we have HERE...TODAY,
  When will we stop!....and SEE?

   *Deborah Michael Skergan*


## "Thoughts"

A restlessness invades my day,
A need for time alone.
I turn my back on endless tasks,
And ringing of the phone.
Shadows cast by tree tops tall,
Upon the path I walk.
No comforting hand to hold in mind.
Nor insignificant talk.
Just thoughts that seem to come alive,
Persistently they cling.
Reminding me of others days,
Unique and timeless things.

   *Jean Tooley*


## You're My Child

From the moment that you came to me
A new life born from mine
I promised that I'd care for you
To help you grow through time

But time has passed too quickly
You're leaving my world for your own
Wanting to break free from me
This family, your home

I want to keep you here with me
Safe and close and warm
There are demons to be wary of
Who will guard you from the harm?

I must accept your going
I understand your need to fly
Now you must make a promise
Not to let my ribbon of family untie

You're my child
I've done the best I could
You've grown so strong and beautiful!
But then, I always new you would

   *Cinda Tietjen*


## Witch's Brew

A bit of this,
A pinch of that,
An old dried wing,
Of a long dead bat.

Eye of lizard,
Heart of stone,
Dead man's gizzard,
Graveyard bone.

Powdered spider,
Pumpkin seeds,
Apple cider,
Thistle reeds.

Now this is a magic brew,
Also known as ...
VEGETABLE STEW!

   *Alexa Roney*


## Our World In Which We Live

Our world in which we live
A place of many things
  Our sea and sky
  And birds that fly
A place for everything.

Our world in which we live
A place to sing and pray
Our children, dear
So far and near
We hope they never stray.

Our world in which we live
A place of dread and fear
  Our safety not so sure
  Only when we hear
In Gods hands you are secure.

   *Elizabeth Faust*


## The Promised Land

Oh!  Give me a land for my own
A place where I'll run wild and free
I'm God's chosen one so I'm told.
Oh! give me a land to grow old.
From Elat, Haifa, Jericoh,
Jerusalem to Tel-A-Viv
I've waited so much and so long
For a place truly to belong
I've smelled ovens burning of flesh
Heard cries from the showers of smoke
I'm no longer a vagrant, you see?
This land was once promised to me.
I'll make flowers grow in the sand
Make sweet water from salty seas
I'll fight and die if I have to
For this land that God gave to me
So give me the right to be here
I want to live in peace, can't you tell?
I will even share it, I will
My sweet promised land of Israel.

   *Antoine DeSouza*


## The Coming

In the dawning of a new day
A single seed manifest itself
Through love into a "being".

Thrusting against flesh
To set it trembling, oozing
The claret flow of life.
Dancing in rhythmic measures.

Elation ... fear ... joy ... pain.
Ponder this mystery hidden in mystery.
The miracle of life
Rising to see, to be, to know.

   *Dolores M. White*


## A Baby's Breath

A baby is a blessing,
a special gift of love.
A miracle sent from heaven,
as we praise our Lord above.

Our beautiful little bundle,
as precious as can be,
will bring our lives much happiness,
shared by you and me.

A baby's breath is peaceful,
soothing for one to hear,
A beautiful little treasure,
sleeping, oh so near...

Yes, a special gift from heaven,
God's given us to share,
as we give Him thanks,
for this blessing in our care.

   *Jerry Mann*


## "The Fear Of Life"

I failed in life and life failed me
A spoonful of love, a taste of hate
A mouthful of anger;

Finding myself stuffed with fear,
I washed it down with a cup of blood
That was sitting near;

Blood spilled from the wounds of my
Fellowman who fought so courageously
At my command.

How foolish of me to think success in
A senseless war, that ends with a
Tombstone at our own backdoor

My cry for mercy fell upon deaf ears
Who am I to kill my own peers

Now wishing I could reach back in
Time and start anew, realizing I
Have bitten off more in life than
I can ever chew.

   *Clarence Hester*


## "America The Best"

There's something so warm in America
  A country, that really does care
Just knowing, whatever happens
  Our burden's and sorrow's we share
A feeling of love and assurance
  With peace in which we can rest
Had I, all countries to choose from
  America to me is the best.

   *Bonnie J. Riffle*

## Tomorrow Is Another Day

A day of rejoicing
A time to cry
This day is closing
I say goodbye
For the time has come
As most times do
For us to part
And say, "I love you."
The sun is setting
The moon is near
I become lonely
I wish you were here
Tomorrow will come
Another day
To be apart
And for me to say,
"I'll try again
As I always do
With all my will
To see you."

*Christine Lynn McClevish*

## Ben's Den

Acres of trees on a countryside
A timeless haven, a place to hide

Dawn arriving with a chill in the air
A warmth inside forgotten and rare

Long treks tiring the durable two
Through forests of snow, skies of blue

Laughter and silence filling the day
Wanting so much, letting come what may

Evening stillness with fire as light
Deer coming close then into the night

A struggle to free fears of old
Accepting dark thoughts left untold

Side by side with secrets held deep
Wanting to touch, afraid to keep

Peace to be found, still an unknown when
A place to start, this man's den

*Juli A. Pionk*

## Friend

In my hour of sadness
A wall clock ticks
Slowly but surely
Can you hear it click?
My heart feels anger and hurt and pain
For you left me alone
With nothing to gain.
Alone in a room with a handful of dust
We cannot be friends
For there is no trust.
A stranger enters
And I hear a voice
It sounds so familiar
I must rejoice.
It is you my friend
The one I adore.
You entered the room through that door.
Will you forgive me?
I've been so wrong.
May we be friends, forever on?

*Danielle Boyd*

## "His Eyes"

His eyes caress me
A wave fondling the sands
Undulating
Shifting
Moving my soul.

His eyes absorb me
An artist seeing creation
Stroking
Touching
My beginning, my end.

His eyes love me
And reach inside my soul
Beauty mingles
Melds
And is.

*Lane*

## Twentieth Century

"We are all created equal,"
a wise man once said.
but now like all wisemen,
that man is dead.

They've taken their lives,
as they've taken their hope.
Now kids only heroes,
are the guys selling dope.

The only things left,
are anger and fear.
Another man dies
no one sheds a tear.

The almighty dollar,
is mighty indeed.
It's too bad our children,
barely can read.

The pollution chokes us,
from way up above.
It's just too bad,
All this world needs is love.

*Abdalla Awwad*

## Awaiting Peace

How could people ever know
About the fire that burns within
me so slow
When all I do is try to hide
The pain, that flame that burns
inside
Holding it in can take a turn
for the worst
Could only mean one thing, soon
I shall burst
A picture is what I see and
is where I'll stay
When the fire extinguishes and
turns to grey
Fire can't burn forever one
day it has to cease
And when it does, that's when,
I'll be at peace.

*Eric Pastor*

## The Storm of Time

The lighting seconds flash
Across the firmament.
Sparks leaping from with out
The minutes clouded flint.
Condensing clouds darken,
Changing into showers;
Plunging through the distance,
Profusely spilling hours.
Steady motion as the
Liquid hours fall away;
Collecting drops splashing
Into fast pools of day.
The sun evaporates
All of the puddles dry,
Vaporizing years back
Into the static sky.

*Brian Pass*

## A Second Answer

The gale winds sweep
across the sun-bleached dunes
A sandstorm roams like
a destructive child
Then dies...
And across this barren wasteland
there is no life to be found
A single misplaced seed
Grew...
Far past the boundaries
Which sane men do not cross
There lies
a single
pink
flower.

*Joe Harlin*

## The Open Meadow

The open meadow
  Across the way
The new mowed fields
  The smell of hay

The stone wall fences
  Close at bay
Where chipmunks run
  And chirp and play

The summer sun
  The blue sky above
And off in the distance
  The call of the dove

Up in a tree top.
  The hawk waits its prey
As the birds fly free
  Through another day

And as I watched
  I wondered why
I felt so lonely
  Deep inside

*Jennie Williams*

## You, Too, Alverez-Machain

Medusa are most commonly found
Aimlessly bobbing up and down
In turgid waters with their brethren
Trailing tentacles of dissuasion
Sensing light but lacking vision
Wanting heart and spinal column
Swept by currents of derision
Flaccidly finding some blurred position
To maim by mindless determination.

*Alexander W. Malick*

## Keep Smiling

We see signs from heaven
All around us today.
Many smiling faces
Keep life peaceful this way.
Our minds enjoy good thoughts
Which crowd out all the rest
As acquaintances here
Help to bring out our best.
God is each soul's lover
And controls faith - filled lives.
But married or single
Our Lord's plan includes all.
We've reason for smiling.
We're fulfilling God's call.

*Eileen R. Hallahan*

## Life

Life isn't like a dove,
all full of friendship and love;
It also has it trials,
that don't always end in smiles;
For the bad times there are good,
For the good times there are bad;
For some people life ends tragically,
For others life ends majestically;
Be happy that life was granted to you,
even though it isn't always a rendezvous.

*Ashleigh Batton-James*

## If

If
All that is and
All that was and
All that ever will be
Should be terminated,
Disintegrated, destroyed
Finished and forgotten
If
The fates are allowed to
Take over and yet are
Overtaken
If
Destiny's own is decided
What will become of us?
What be our fate?
Our destiny?
What of eternity?
Be it known to all:
Peace.

*Jeanne Grossheim*

## Thoughts Of Home

Do you remember when we were kids,
All the crazy things we did?
Swinging from the trees like Apes,
Falling down and getting scrapes.

Mother and Dad were seldom home,
So we were kind of on our own.
But Mom and Pop were always there,
With their tender, loving care.

Waking up to pies and cakes,
That Mom would start when she'd awake.
Pop, peeling apples for her pies,
Then playing games with the little guys.

Sometimes when I get tired and pained,
I think of Mom, who never complained.
I think about Mother and Dad,
And how hard they worked for what we had.

The time has gone so very fast,
And though our parents all have passed,
They're in our memories and our hearts,
And nothing will ever break us apart.

*Jeanne Jeffries Fox*

## Why?

I thought, I sighed, I wondered why
all those children had to die.
They came to sing and laugh and play.
This was just anther day.
And then the bomb went off!

I thought, I sighed, I wondered why
all those children had to die.
Their mothers left them in good care.
No one told them to beware.
And then the bomb went off!

I thought, I sighed, I wondered why
all those children had to die.
I pray that I will understand
what was God's eternal plan
the day the bomb went off.

I thought, I sighed and then-I cried.

*Betty Kallsen*

## Pathos

When the world comes to an End
all will be Told
muddy rivers contextualized to Blood
our enigmatic God
will show His Face
or Not

Sudden realization will dawn upon Us;
the ruins we have Created
alternative paths Ignored
sanctity of life Muddled
   by the greed of us All

Visions of our Forefathers,
wrought by blood and Ingenuity,
end in the destruction by us Fools.
then it is too Late
too Late

To remember our Wrong Doings

*Jennifer Scharn*

## The Pinewood Walk

Today I walked beside the pines
Along a path that gently winds
Around a hilly curve, and then
Suddenly straightens out again.
On to shady lanes ahead,
My feet on Mother Earth did tread.
On I strolled beyond the bend
Not caring where the trail would end.
An old short stump stood by the way,
"Come sit awhile," it seemed to say.
"Of course I shall", I said aloud,
And thanked it kindly as I bowed.
Here and there I paused to touch,
A branch, a limb, the bark and such.
At last I turned to trace my steps
When evening duties called.
Beneath a pine I almost wept,
I still was so enthralled.
I stopped to kiss one old pine tree,
And blessed his heart for checking me.

*Jessie Killingbeck*

## Path Of Love

By the brook
along the path
we tell some jokes
and have a laugh
we swing our arms
and hold our hands
we put our minds in wonderland
at the bridge
along the stream
there's a waterfall
the first we've seen
we feel the air
a real cool mist
there's a casual touch
a casual kiss
you're the one that makes my dream
the girl I loved
down by the stream

*Earl G. Panaro*

## Lacewings

Am I pretty
Am I holy
Yet God's
creature
they say
And mysteries
are sevenfold
Dare I give
one way
Perhaps already
the one you
know
Lacewings never
tell
When I come to
you but after
Yourself in better
dell

*Donnell W. Partin*

## Nebraska

Nebraska is
an ancient
tribeswoman

You can
graze her fertile hills

You can
explore her fertile valleys

or

penetrate
her golden grasses

But

you cannot
steal
her
virginity.

*Helen G. Crosswait*

## Sextistical Dilemma

For every woman there's a man.
An ancient proverb tell us so.
But, now, females outnumbers males
By millions, and the surveys show
Straight men are in such short supply
3 gals may have to share 1 beau.
Does half a love beat having none?
My head says yes.  My heart says no.

*Alice Hausman-Herman*

## Newborn

They come from a great void
An emptiness
A black hole
Catastrophic events begin
Upheavals
Chasms
Scarring
Creating the precious
Semi-precious
Tears come
Joy comes
At deliverance
A great hunger
Suddenly
A spark appears
A star orientation
Aligned
The rock cleaved
And one song
Warms a planet
STARBIRTH

*Carolyn Hull Schurmann*

## Untitled

The queen's black carpet
Rolls across the sky
   As thunder cracks
You begin to cry
   As the queens's black
Carpet covers the sky
   The wind blows hard,
Hard against the glass
   You say somebody
Save me, save me at last

*Jonathan M. Weaver*

## Poems

A lifeline to some,
an escape route to others.
Expressing oneself can seem
so difficult,
as if there were a rope holding
back all your emotions.
They come together
in one confused knot.
But soon, the words attenuate
and the boundaries become
endless.
Your tool flows across
each line and the emotions
are eternal.
Poems are not thrown together, but
a mixture of multi-colored clay
carefully molded together
to form a sculpture
of oneself.

*Jennifer L. Kalbaugh*

## Past, Present And Future

A dimple was a cheeky thing
And a bold exclamation
Of cuteness, of
Mystery and subtle flirtation.

Now—more of a hiatus,
Hiding place for worms
Whose castings fill it up
And overflow

Fertile ground for planting
Seeds of new life
Cleaned
And cleansing.

*Barbara A. Talbert*

## A Grandmother's Love

There's a time to love,
and a time to believe,
and a time to know
when it's time to leave.

The love of family and friends
holds you near.
You're quietly waiting
you've nothing to fear.

Sometimes we know,
sometimes we cry,
sometimes we struggle
with the final goodbye.

Then time again will come and go....
And love withstands all time we know.
So your gone away,
but not from my heart!
Bodies leave, Souls never part.

*Cayenne Barnes*

## Let The Trumpets Sound!

Let the trumpets sound!
Played at the palace, heard all around!
Let the trumpets song fill the air,
Let people rejoice everywhere.
Let the trumpets play all day long,
Play it loud and play it strong
Play a song on a very bad day,
To help chase all the gloom away!

*Jonathan Anthony Kozaczuk*

## "Heart And Soul"

Put your heart and soul in what you do,
and always follow through.

You have to stand up and be bold,
because all you have is heart and soul.

When there are obstacles in your way,
take a little time to pray.

Sharing problems everyday,
can always help someone along the way.

God wants to be in control,
of our very heart and soul.

A clean heart and soul stands out,
so everyone knows what it's all about.

Heart and soul is like a light,
that shines very bright.

So always be in control,
of your very heart and soul.

*Doris Mae Brooks-Brewer*

## The Day I Talked With God

I walked alone beside the sea,
and as I walked there seemed to be,
an unseen Friend walked by my side
as I wondered at the changing tide.

He rules the sea, the sky, the land,
the moon and stars hear His command.
All else but man, joins his melody,
of love and faith, and harmony.

His gentle voice spoke from the sea,
"Be not afraid, just follow me."
I noticed not the time nor way
as we walked and talked that day.

I lingered there until the sun,
dipped in the sea, and day was done.
My cares, my fears all slipped away,
because I walked with Him that day.

I hurried home, my duty called,
all seemed right, there-in walled,
my hope renewed, fears washed away,
Because I talked with GOD that day.

*Charles V. Hearn*

## Untitled

The world goes round and round
and carries us without a sound
We are joy riders here
knowing not that we have only
ourselves to fear
Sounds and lights abound
We know not what we've found
With everything there is a cost
We'll never know just what we've lost
We move forward daily
knowing not where we head
not paying too much attention
to where we tread
Days lead to months
and months to years
and We become ancestors
who father tears

*Elizabeth DeOliveira*

## Oneness

I am every man
And every man is me.
I am father to every child
And every mother is mine.

Every hungry one is my trust
And any man's wound, wounds me.
Every tear is salt on my tongue
And every smile a light by the sea.

Every birthing cry is mine
And in very death dies me.
Before the mercy seat of God, stand all
And each being judged is me.

Take care my friend,
For I am you,
And you are me.

Oneness is the door to heaven
Decreed by the source that said,
   "Be".

*Del Wells*

## Alan K. Bland

Your smile from Britthaven doorways
and everywhere I walk and roam-
You are there for me.  Thank you!
Our four a-glowed and arrayed—-

Pink rescuing angelic roses.  PTL!
Upon the sanctuary of rest and solace-
It doesn't matter that your
only means of mobility is your
'Electric Wheelchair' of charm and grace.
I love you Alan from the heart.

*Bert Rivett*

## God's Gift

As we run through the meadow,
And feel the warm summer breeze,
Our laughter fills the air,
Happy to be free.

Our hands holding as we run,
Not knowing where we'll go,
But when we're together,
Loneliness, we'll never know.

The sounds of nature, is a gift from God,
And the love that we share,
Are unseen miracles,
Just knowing that you care.

I'll do my best to make you happy,
And to make God so very proud,
For when he gave your Love to me,
My life, it turned around.

Now I know what caring is,
For its something that one feels,
Yes, all God's gifts are miracles,
Something, no one can steal.

*Darrell W. Cook*

## My Flute

I brought the mouth piece to my lip
and blew as hard as I could.
I looked at my music,
And heard how beautiful it sounded.
My flute is a precious instrument,
and what I always wanted.

*Jaclyn H. Laufer*

## It Takes More Than One

Why are people evil
and fight for no reason.
They don't just do it now,
they do it all through the seasons.

Sometimes for your color,
or the color you're wearing.
Sometimes it's only
just for staring.

Wouldn't it be wonderful
if there was world peace?
All of us acting
almost like priests

Instead of gunshots,
handshakes would be there.
Instead of killing,
friendship would be fair.

But too bad it's only
my imagination.
It takes more than one
to solve our situation.

*Daphne L. Charles*

## Thinking Of Old And Gray

I sit in a chair, of black
and gray.  Wondering what will
become of me.  As I sit here,
time ceases to exist.  But around
me, time drearily ticks by.
The colors of the world are
bright and lively.  But the
colors of myself are dark
and deadly, oh why oh why me.
I'm sitting in my chair
wondering what will become
of me.  Got nothing to finish,
no deeds to do.  Just sitting in
my chair wondering what will
become of me.

*Julie Ritchie*

## He's Gorgeous

I saw him from afar,
And I didn't know his name,
But I thought to myself,
He is gorgeous!
He must be conceited,
As handsome as he is,
A Greek; God; standing.
He must be aware he is flawless.
Then, I spoke to him one day.
I stared, deep, into his eyes,
And here is, what, I saw.
A man unaware, of his beauty.
So this is what I wished for him.
May life's tricks leave you unscathed,
Your beauty stay inside and out,
Your lips always turn up with a smile,
The twinkle stay forever in your eyes.
Because, you are truly gorgeous!

*Beverly Stanczyk*

## Wedding in the Sky

There will be a wedding in the sky
And I know the reason why
When I'm tested and I'm tired
I'm being made ready to be the bride
For the wedding in the sky
   For there's a preparation
   For that glorious celebration
   For the wedding in the sky

There will be a wedding in the sky
And I know the reason why
That my saviour's returning soon
It may be night or noon
He is coming to take his bride
To the wedding in the sky
I'm being made ready for the wedding
The wedding in the sky
I wonder why, when I've learned how to love.
Him then I'm lasted and I'm tired oh now,
I know the reason why!
I'm being made ready for the wedding in
the sky!

*Iris Eileen Jones*

## The Wind Has Done Its Dusting

The wind has done its dusting
And I must see to mine.
Remove the grit throughout my house
And make the tables shine.
Times past this job was given
To children very small;
And if they left some streaks or grime
No one cared at all.
The wind would do its dusting
Again another day,
And the children grew from helping
Before they went to play.
Now pictures of these children
No longer young nor here
Fill every table top they shined
With images most dear.
So family portraits standing
Where they have always stood;
My mind goes dusting memories,
My hands still dusting wood.

*Ardith M. McBride*

## A Penny in the Fountain

There's a penny in the fountain,
   and I tossed it there you see.

I thought I had to make a wish,
   a wish for you and me.

A penny in the fountain, the penny
   that I threw.

A wish for you and me, I hoped
   it would come true.

But pennies in the fountain, are
   wishes but in vain.

For fountains cannot grant our
   wishes, to ease our fears or pain.

A penny in a fountain is a foolish
   attempt by man, to get our wishes
   granted without following the
   Master's plan.

*Joe Matthews*

## "Old"

I'm old and I'm tired
and I want no more.
Won't somebody please show me the door.

I'm old and I'm tired
and I'm over the hill.
Won't somebody quit handing me a bill.

Yesterday's gone
and tomorrow is today.
Won't somebody please show me the way.

Somebody who?
you old fool.
Pick up your cane and get off your stool.

Stumble and grumble
but open your eyes.
It was all there in one of your lives.

*Jo Price*

## A Rose

A Rose to me is many things.
And I will tell you.
A Rose is Happiness.
When you I get a Rose from you.

A Rose is a beautiful flower.
That stands out among the rest.
A Rose is hard work.
When you have done your best.

A Rose means I love you.
When it is set apart.
You are a Rose.
A Rose in my heart.

*Jeanette Stamper Huff*

## After Everything Else

I lied to you,
and I'm sorry.

I promised you something,
I could not deliver,
and it hurt you,
and me,
and I'm sorry.

I can think of nothing I'd like more,
than to hold you,
but that seem so out of the question,
I wish I could still ask it,
but there's nothing left to ask,
I'm sorry.

I've tried every person,
every thought,
every angle,
I wish there was more I could say,
but all I can do,
is bow my head,
and softly say, I'm sorry.

*Carmen Pardel*

## Rumors

We hear things but do not listen
And do not consider others feelings
Instead we just pass on the message
Even though it may not be true
But when it comes to me and you
We may get our feelings hurt too
In this social game of rumors

*Cristine Guevara*

## The Mask

Cold hard faces,
And indifferent stares,
Vast empty spaces,
Where nobody cares.
Fantasy is a lie,
Dreams is a joke.
You can't even cry
Where there is no hope.
An unwritten creed-
Own no tender heart,
Love becomes a need,
That will rip you apart.
So you put on the mask,
And wear it with the best.
You have a cold hard face,
Just like all the rest.

*David Bishop*

## Untitled

We must cherish every day,
And live for what we have.
For the hands on the clock,
Are ticking by and won't stop.
A dear friend has passed,
And we all feel the sorrow,
Some didn't know him,
But still feel this pain.
With his passing we learn,
We learn that we must try.
Try to live for what we have,
And not for what we want.
Try to grasp our joy,
And not our sorrow.
We must hold onto life,
And cherish our friends.
We live on and grow,
Even when we lose someone we know.

*Erin Green*

## God

The power that causes sun to shine
And makes the smiling flowerets nod,
When winds are gently told to blow—-
That force is what I call my God

The rootlets in the warm moist earth
Will never grow the golden rod
If pansy blossoms come instead.
Because of what I call my God.

Why grow the grasses always green,
Instead od red or purple sod,
And what controls the fleecy clouds?
The something that I call, my God,

The birds, on wings of song, my God
And open silent dully plod;
Each makes his way through earthly life
Decreed by what I call my God.

And when I stand upon a hill.
And look back down the way I trod.
Or turning upward, see the sky
I think that I should thank my God

*John Dresser*

## Lifetime Moments

I will have my few great moments
and most of all
I will have you.
And when I die,
I will be remembered
for some of these moments
but hopefully
mostly remembered by you.
You have become
my second nature,
my one true sign
of living.
And within all of my great moments,
the greatest of all
will have been
the day we said,
"I love you."

*Grisel Marino*

## Over the Hill

When my teeth begin to rattle,
And my knees begin to shake,
My hands are growing unsteady,
And my heart begins to quake,

When the kids call me "old lady",
And neighbors look the other way,
I keep my eyes upon the ground,
As I toddle on my way.

My height is getting shorter,
And my eyes are growing dim,
My hair has turned to silver,
And my disposition's grim!

Do not pity me, my darlings,
For my soul is rich within!
I have a storehouse of joys
To last me to a hundred and ten!

*Edna Blythe Elwell*

## Dark Clouds

Sometimes dark clouds roll in,
and my light is left behind.
Can I walk through that cloud?
Can I make my own sunshine?

When the clouds come over my head,
and sometimes bring the rain.
Can I walk through that cloud?
Can I pray to ease the pain?

In every life these clouds do come
but yet I can stand tall.
I can still walk through that cloud,
and yet, let nothing fall.

When I was in that dark cloud,
my praying never ceased.
A special calmness came in me,
and my spirit kept that peace.

*Carolyn Richardson*

## The Hunter

Strange the lion that stalks by day
And roaming, hunts his hidden prey.
How graceful he does step and scent
Upon unsuspecting death, intent!

Although I do not understand
His scheming method, nor his plan;
With compassion I am filled
For the hunter, rather than the killed.

*Barbara R. Reid*


## "Morning"

Go find the Rose within your Garden -
    And see the dewdrop there.

It's me - take a moment -
to watch it gently fall away -

    Just like the dewdrop every
    morning - I too shall always
    reappear - ....

*Eva E. Hannig Hendricks*


## The Valentine

Some are calling the day Black Tuesday.
And that is what it is,
if viewed from lonely eyes
who have no one "special"
Who miss receiving a gift.

But, what if we look from
caring eyes upon those we love,
and think of the gifts that can be given,
instead of those we do not get.

Yet, best of all
let us look from upturned eyes
upon Him
Who gave a gift to all.

A Valentine of love
Three colors of a Heart
Red for the blood that was shed.
White for the purest cleansing.
Pink for the blush of excitement felt
when we accept this Valentine of Love.

*Elizabeth Applegate*


## On the Limb with:

## ONCE! DON'T 'CHA KNOW

Once in a lifetime a person comes by
And the chemical values hold.
Attention is swift, elation a stun
Deeds do occur, emotions are shared
    as chemical values endure.
Memories are massive, never passive
Never forget, never regret.
Once in a lifetime for sure.
Never forget, never regret, Once!
Don't 'cha know?  On the limb

*Jersey Jim*


## Blood-Filled Tears

As the wind falls,
    and the clouds close out my world,
    lightning thrusts against the skies,
    and I remember.
Flesh against flesh,
    but one of us trying to survive.
One with tears,
    the other, just fighting.
But then,
    something stabs,
    and only one lives.
The mind fights to keep the terror away,
    for if neither had died,
    I'd be here, holding her,
    and whispering and singing...
    I'd hear her laugh and see her smile.
But why should I even think and remember?
For the terror, will always by my side.

*Juliana Quintanilla*


## The Soldier's Lament

For above you the battle rages,
And the lights go out one by one.
At last you are alone with your thoughts,
But the tears won't come.
Cause your song is sung.
So you bow your head,
and know you are dead.
It matters not how hard you fought,
how clean the fight,
nor who has won,
'cause when the lights go out,
you know it is night,
and you are done,
and your song is sung.

*Elfreda M. Almgren*


## America Wake Up

The days don't seem as long no more,
And the nights seem shorter too.
The world is spinning twice as fast,
And who knows what to do.

The Ozone every year gets worse,
And few folks seem to care.
Some parents don't teach right or wrong,
And AIDS is every-where.

The world is in a terrible fix,
Seems life don't have much worth.
The abortion clinic slaughter house,
Kills babies before their birth.

Guns they used to take to war,
But now kids take to School.
I think we better all wake up,
And teach the Golden-Rule.

Who are we to change God's Law;
He made them for us all.
Right and wrong are still the same,
How far will people fall?

*Estella Bauman*


## Winter Is Coming

The leaves are falling,
    and the winter wind blows -
    the remaining leaves,
Whispering - winter is coming.

The sky is over-cast,
    with touches of blue,
    here and there -
Whispering - winter is coming.

The woodstove radiates heat -
    as I sit nested in my chair,
    while outside it is dreary,
Whispering - winter is coming.

I sit with cat purring on my lap,
    making me enjoy the warmth and,
    coziness of home, while outside it
Whispers - winter is coming.

Time for peace and thankfulness to come
    and leave the winter outside,
Whispering winter is coming-coming,
coming.

*Jessie M. Combs*


## Living

The great complexities of life
And things called commonplace;
The many mediocrities
Lead us to seek God's face.

The great twisters of yesterday
And storms the day before —
Tornados that have come our way
Make us just seek Him more.

The wars and rumors of the same
That puts us so on edge
Encourage us to call God's name
And allegiance to Him pledge.

Our loving Father is above
And sees us, every one;
He'll take the load and lead us to
Salvation through his Son!

*Joyce A. Bratten*


## Eternity's Chance

With shadow-closed eyes,
and truth in your lie,
I fall swiftly to tears,
as you whisper good-bye.

In a moonlit hour,
with darkness from day,
and a bitter-sweet smile,
you turn sadly away.

My heart breaks in two,
as you walk through the door.
Looking for less,
we're finding but more.

With a tear on a rose,
and a final set glance,
we separate wishing,
for eternity's chance.

*Cara Levine*

## Farewell to the Homestead

The day we left the Homestead
And turned to say good-by
It left a queer sensation
And a tear within my eye.

Words to tell you how I felt
I know I'll never find,
I was thinking of our home and friends
That I had left behind.

And all those happy memories
of the years that have gone by,
I know will dwell within me
Until the day I die.

*Frank G. Keller Sr.*

## A Mother's Way

I look to my mom
And what do I see
Her open arms
Waiting for me

I listen to mom
And what do I hear
A beautiful voice
That is always near

I reach for my mom
And what do I feel
Her sweet little kisses
That make boo boo's heal

I look at my mom
And what do I see
All the love in the world
Shining back at me

*Caroline L.K. Uribe*

## Me

I look in the mirror
And what do I see,
I see a little girl
I'd like to call me.

Though me may not be perfect
Her hair might be dry,
On the other hand
She has a sparkle in her eye.

Me isn't bony
And me may not be fat.
Maybe she's round,
But she's loveable like a cat.

Me isn't short
And me isn't tall,
Actually she's the perfect size
To play on a seesaw.

Me may not be a model
And may not be pretty,
But one thing's for sure
Me isn't dirty!

*Danielle Martlock*

## Untitled

She looks into my eyes,
and wonders what I see.
A child beyond her years.
A child full of fears.
Seeing more than she thought I'd see.

The time we spent together.
Trading memories, one after one.
Strange how moments pass.
Every feeling clear as glass.
Till morning came with the sun.

We go through our lives.
Searching for one who is dear.
Always hoping and praying.
Wanting the chance of saying.
The words we all want to hear.

*Chris Suwanski*

## Mystery

I search for thoughts
And words and writings,
And scan the skies
For wondrous sightings.

I probe the seas
To depths unknown,
And trace the flights
Where birds have flown.

But I fail to reach,
Deep within,
Where there to find,
Lies peace of mind.

*Charles J. Fitti*

## Hurt

Just a wisp, that inside feeling,
   And you know that something's wrong.
Then the words that send you reeling
   From the lash of someone's tongue.

Now you feel retaliation,
   Deep within, you feel the urge
To strike back, without hesitation,
   "Go on, go on" your instincts urge.

Oh! But stop and think it over,
   Is it worth where it could lead?
Separation from a loved one,
   And the hate that it could breed.

*Ermine Kazor*

## To My Dog Fluffy

I looked into a box one day
   and much to my surprise,

I saw a ball of curly fur
   a head with two bright eyes.

It sat right up and gave a bark
   my heart beat fast and then,

I picked it up and all fear left
   as love came flooding in.

*Dlorese Lovison*

## The Art of Living

There's a special art to living
and you need a frame of mind
that can overlook the showers
'til the sun begins to shine,

To develop to the fullest
you have to understand
that things don't always function
in the way that they were planned,

There's a special art to living
and the challenge must be met
but the longer that you try it
why the better you will get,

Don't waste your time in waiting
for the world to come to you
you have to climb the mountain
to appreciate the view,

So on those days you're tired of everything
especially tired of always giving
tell yourself I'll be better tomorrow
it's all part of "the art of living"

*Adriana Romero*

## Dare to Discover

If I gave you a dare,
   and you took it.
What would you discover?

If I dared you
   To find a heart,
Would you discover LOVE?

If I dared you
   to find a flower,
Would you discover BEAUTY

If I dared you
   to find an eagle,
Would you discover FREEDOM?

If I dared you
   to find a baby,
Would you discover TRUST?

If I dared you
   to find a brain,
Would you discover KNOWLEDGE?

And if I dared you
   to find all these things,
Would you discover HAPPINESS?

*Joseph Bisbee*

## The Seasons Of Life

The Seasons of Life
are sorrow and pain,
from love to hatred
to going insane.

Like summer and winter
are the seasons of life,
live for tomorrow;
don't live for the strife.

Life's to be lived,
so live it—for reasons.
Don't go through the motions;
Live life's many seasons!

*Jason Freitas*

## Reflection

Another day has come and gone,
Another chance to sing a song,
Another path to go along,
Another day has come and gone.

One more chance to help a friend,
One more journey that may end,
One more memory that we'll make,
One more chance for us to take.

A chance to cherish someone dear,
A chance to brush away a tear,
A chance to help someone in need,
A chance to be a friend indeed.

Did I let a day slip by?
Did I wonder at the sky?
Did I show someone I care?
Did I help by being there?

Another day has come and gone,
Another chance to sing a song,
Another path to go along,
Another day has come and gone.

*Becky Nanninga*

## Christmas Greeting To My Sister

Another Christmas links our years,
  Another thought of love is nigh
As gratitude Divinely steers
  Its beams across our sister-sky.

This love that lives within my heart
  To reach you in a single whisper
Gains volume from its counterpart
  In love from you, my sister.

*Gladys Rhein*

## Above It All

Oklahoma cries
April nineteenth, ninety five

Scenes of horror, edged our core
Voices screamed, on hypnotic screens

Lines moaned, please call home
Hearts raced, in need of space.

Mountains of rock moved, lifting moods
In the head count, some were found

We cheered, then the rain brought tears
A singing bird, announced June 23rd

With man's help, building's melt.
Pale smoke rose, eyes upward froze

Heaven gently spoke, we awoke
Loved one's set free, with golden keys

*Doris Denton Carr*

## The Pack

Wolves, modern day raptors,
are swift and keen.
They hunt in groups and circle there prey,
but their young just like to play.

But the adults make the kills,
with blood here and bones there
They have made a kill,
so beware, the pack,
they will kill some more.

*David Bates*

## A World Of Dreams

A world of dreams is where desires
  are found, where your own illusions
  become reality;
Is where your mind is set free,
  and your soul wonders in a heaven
  of your own;
Is where you have control over time,
  and not time over you;
Is where you can be as one with
  yourself and not worry about the
  famine that surrounds you in this
  reality that we live in,
This place is where feelings are
  not hurt but understood,
Though a dream doesn't always seem
  to be as kind as others,
We are left to have our imagination
  take control over our continuousness,
We have become addicted to this world,
This world we call dreams.

*Antonio A. Martinez*

## Games Children Play

Games children play
are in a circle -
stand by me.
Ring around the rosy - pick me.
Duck duck, grey duck - take my hand.
Drop the handkerchief - choose me next.
A circle keeps the ball
inside the dodge ball game.
A circle of friends keeps
the unwanted out.
Round and round the children play.
Make a circle
the teacher will say.

*Barbara Strommer*

## Secret Love

My hopes and dreams
Are in a secret place
Along with the memories
Of a kiss, an embrace
There also are pictures
Of hands and of eyes
There are poems and letters
There also are lies
There before
Has my heart filled my head
With feelings and questions
And things left unsaid

*Angela Olsen*

## Untitled

The hearts of men
are not so darkened
as Jim Morrison
would have us believe.
"Riders on the Storm"
fighters of the norm
usually swallow
their own swollen tongue.
Vomit. What a way to go!

*Dennis J. Blauer*

## A Lesson

I watched a little sparrow
As busy as can be,
Preparing her future home
High in a stately tree.

Some power seemed to drive her
Toward her final goal,
To build a safe haven
That would satisfy her soul.

The early morning chill
Of spring breaking day,
Seemed only to inspire her
Along her solitary way.

She seemed to sense that time was short
Each trip she made with haste,
Until her job was done
And home was well in place.

From this a lesson can be learned,
Do not let time pass you by.
If a little sparrow can do it,
So can you and I.

*Carlton Buddy Barricks*

## My Happiness

Today the sun shown on my head
As I awoke upon my bed
There beside me I had found
The one to who I have been bound.

I love this one with all my heart
Never a fight did we start
He is the one to whom I tell
All my troubles as they swell.

Our life is full of happiness
And I can be a loving wife
Because in me there is no stress
To him I vowed my very life.

The joy we've shared for years
Has covered over smiles and tears
I'd never ask for less
Because this is my happiness.

*Frances R. Scholze*

## Fire

I see the fire in your eyes
As I see your rage fly.
You yell, scream, and spit,
You whack, pound, and hit.
You told me once, you told me twice.
Your eyes turned as cold as ice.
You kept me there for almost an hour.
Now it's your turn to quiver and cower.
You yelled and screamed and didn't tire.
Now it's my turn to return the fire!
Shut up and listen, listen good.
I think you will, I think you should.
If I told you once, I'll tell you twice,
Now my eyes are as cold as ice!
You hear the fire in my voice
Hey, you have no other choice!
Now leave me alone before
you get hurt.
Leave me alone or I'll shove you
in the dirt!

*Christine Ostapiuk*

## Follow Me

Still they listen.  Even now.
As I speak
From the deepest, darkest spot.
From the very center of the
Inferno, searing hot, yet cold
Beyond all endurance.
Here in the third mouth of
That old dragon, being ripped
And torn asunder through-out
All eternity.
I have replaced Brutus
That betrayer of friends.
My followers; no my children
Still hear my message of hate
And destruction.  And let no
One deny them their right.
For they should join me.
I would should have ridden to valhalla in
the arms
Of a valkerie riding a white steed.
They should join me.

**Jerome Hickmond**

## eventide

"The mountain covered my sun,
as it sank into my sea,
the flowers have scattered my sky,
and the moon has smiled at me,
my hands of pale - blue - green,
my lips of rosy red,
its time that I make peace,
its time that I take bed."

**Breeane Diaz**

## Fallen In Love

Oh God why do I love him
As much as I do
I try to make believe I don't
But now I know it's true.

I think about him always.
Every night and day
I think of how I love him
And how I'd wish he'd say

Those three special words
That I long to hear
I hope he says "I love you"
And shows he means it with a tear.

Then soon after we will kiss
The kind that we all dream of
Then I'll know that we
Both have fallen in love

**Amanda Hoffmann**

## Touch Me

You touch my mind
   And I am intrigued

You touch my heart
   And I am in love

You touch my lips
   And I am weak

You touch my soul
   I am yours forever

**Garneta Lokken**

## Hope

A lonely star shines at night
As the white snow flakes dance
about the night

The stillness of the winter cold,
no shelter for some I'm told

But still they go on, as they
grow old and bold

Looking, for hope somewhere down
the road.

Sometimes feeling, that they've finally
come to the end of along lonely rope

In a warm and gentle sadness,
that there still is lasting hope.

**Bonny Pritts**

## Seasons

It was a warm summer day
As the white snow sprinkled
The brown autumn ground.
As the turning leaves of the evergreen
Fell to their sweet oblivion,
Beautifying the landscape.
-Valley of the Pigs

**Julia Wright**

## Thoughts

What do old men think about,
As they sit there in their chair,
Do they drift back to days of yore,
Recalling times and desires
   that are no more?

Does he see the grandchild
standing there; does he hear
her ask, why, grandpa,
was this something you did,
   when you were a kid?

He sits and stares ahead,
No outward interest there,
He's already in another world,
Forgetting those who care,
   and times they used to share.

Perhaps you've already left us,
It's hard to know, as you
sit there thinking, looking
here and there, without a plan.
   We miss you, old man!

**Eva Deeb**

## Here/There

A touch is remembered
as Time stand still
A voyage of Ecstasy
A memory Relived....

   Awake... there is nothing
   A dream has disappeared...
   Uncertain Discovery
   When is real... Real?

**John Tillman**

## We

Many things are different
as you can plainly see
blacks, whites, many races
all as you and me can't you see
that we can be one big community
hearts together
friends forever
just like you and me.

**Jennifer Tidwell**

## Untitled

Ring morning from your nightbell
As you would pound a gong
The day is coming near
When the drawings on walls
Echo the singing of times
Humans and beasts talk
This is being awake.

**Charles Maden**

## Mother

You are a special mom you see,
At least to me you are,
Because your the kind of mom for me.
In life you will go far,
You always stood by your family,
In times of good and bad.
And always tried to cheer me up,
When I was alone and felling sad,
But there aren't to many moms like you
In that big world out there,
Though always had the time for me,
To show how much you cared.
You always tucked me in at night,
And taught me how to love,
But now I know deep in my heart,
I was blessed from God above,
So now I'm grown and on my way,
To live my life you see,
Cause your the best that ever was,
And forever mom to me.

**Edward Manning**

## "You Are With Me"

Seeing you lie there
At peace with yourself
Silent to all the world
Your inner soul floating
Around in the air
Your body so stiff
Yet the angel's face
Lie upon you
The tears of the angels mist the room
As we gaze upon
Your heavenly sent body
We gaze as though you
Were the one and only
Because you were
He made you different
To the sounds of the heavens
And the angels of the seas
God be with you
Because he is with me.

**Deborah Penn**

## The Sandman

Quiet and still the songbird lay
At the close of another day.
Trees rustle through the breeze
Catching the wind upon its leaves.
Laughter of children is gone
With no one left to carry their songs.
The Sandman comes on winged flight
Bringing dreams to stay the night.

The ground so frozen and white
Sends cold shivers through the night.
Shooting stars flash in the sky
Carrying childish wishes high.
Moonbeam's incandescent glow
Patterns reflections in the snow.
The Sandman comes on winged flight
Bringing dreams to stay the night.

*Carol Marie Olejnik*

## Sunset

Standing on the dock
At the end of the day
You can hear the music
The sailboats play.

The wind in the rigging
Makes a lonely sound
Like wind chimes do
When a breeze stirs them 'round.

The boats gently rock
As waves wander by.
Masts silhouetted
Against the darkening sky.

Take a long look
But then turn away.
You can't find tomorrow
If you're lost in today.

*Jeff A. Horne*

## Alone

In the night
At the ocean
On a rock
In the sand
Sitting alone
On the moonlight
In the loneliness
By myself
Out of the love
Walking the mile
Seeing the strangers
Talking to no one
Under the tree
Watching the world
Into the darkness
Out of the light
Watching the freedom
Seeing the light
Watching them go by,
I'm so alone.

*Jolyn Landrie*

## Venus Fly Trap

Ominous jaws quivering,
Awaiting a midnight snack,
A voice inside should warn him,
"Get Back!  Get back!"

But he does not listen.
Instead, he wanders astray,
Towards the waiting predator.
He has now become the prey!

A careless step and then a pause...
Into the open, hungry jaws.
Slowly, silently, they open again
Patiently awaiting another friend.

*Benjamin Lewis*

## "Paradise"

It's solitude, pain free,
awareness, comfort and trouble free.
It's happiness, joyful and
caring feelings.
Singing, rejoicing, and dancing all
in one beat, go hand in hand.
Trees are green, brooks are clean
and cool.  It will soon be
discovered at the end of time.
Judging of all kinds;
blacks, whites, Asians, and
every race, creed, and colors,
and beliefs.
We'll love, care, and watch
over everyone.  We'll be caretakers
of such beauty which will
be an honor.

*Damita Robinson*

## Slowly

Slowly rocking
Back
and Forth...
Back
and Forth...
Her quiet breathing
rhyming with the silent breezes
brushing across the meadow.
Overlooking the valley below
from the serene hilltop,
The sun glinting off
her bifocals,
sleeping peacefully,
Grandma.

*Elizabeth Darcy Lewis*

## Peace

Take some pills
Be in peace
Without my love
Here by myself
With no one
By myself
The only love
Gone
Today I am nothing
By myself
Tomorrow
I am with her
In heaven
Out of this hell
Forever.

*Gary Sellers*

## Rain

Rain is such a pleasant sound
beating on my roof.
Splashing on my window pane.
It beats upon the earth
and washes all the trees.
The grass becomes a luscious green
so beautiful to see.

The worms come out upon the ground
a harvest for the birds.
The babbling brook becomes a stream
for animals to drink.
Fawns wade and frolic on it's banks,
a pleasant thing to see.

All nature comes alive anew
with boundless energy.
What a privilege for me
to enjoy God's menagerie!

*Dorothy Jefferson*

## She

Born a child;
Became wild.
Grumpy with a frown:
Became her adorning crown;
Sassy and explosive;
Became lovely and inclusive.

Set a goal;
Became a requiting soul.

She teased;
Yet wanted to please.
She smiled;
Became one of style.
She cried;
Never admitting she lied.

She deceived;
Yet yearned to be received.
She stood out above the crowd;
Made everyone proud!
She laughed, loved and lived;
So to others she might give.

*Faye Garrett*

## Peaceful Fishing

At three in the morning
before anyone is awake,
I grab my cap, my fishing pole
and head out to the lake.

I need a day of peace and quiet
And yearn for total relaxation,
if I could do this everyday
life would be one swell vacation.

Bait my hook, get all set
then leaning back, pull down my cap,
the sun feels so nice and warm
maybe I could have one little nap.

Fish not biting?  Doesn't matter!
I still have a goal,
I'll be back another day
to rest my weary soul.

*Edith Piercy Zimmer*

## My God The Creator

Among the starry heavens,
beneath the apple tree,
my God the creator there He will be.

Along the narrow paths,
inside horrid dungeons,
my God the creator there He will be.

Through times and tribulations,
the depths of the sea,
my God the creator there He will be.

His majesty beholds all forces,
his face too bright to see,
my God the creator lives inside of me!

*Elizabeth Branan*

## Just Lookin'

Looking for the spiritual distance
Between my lonely heart and soul
Looking for a certain kind of romance
That of my life would take control

Looking for the best direction
That would lead me to your town
Looking for your gentle affection
Every day after sun goes down

Looking for my long lost friend
You know, the one turned local hero
Been looking for a gracious dividend
But all I come up with is zero

Looking for my one lucky day
The one I forever dream about
Looking, but I know there's just no way
I'm gonna find myself an easy way out

Yes, looking for my way out of hell
Guess that's been my whole life's story
Looking for someone I could tell
But it all may seem too derogatory!

*Henry J. Nunez*

## The Kiss

You cupped my face
between your hands
and touched me
with your tenderness
your eyes met
and locked with mine
and sealed upon my lips
the Kiss.

*Deborah Hahn-Wade*

## Black Woman

Black woman so strong and true.
Black woman with heart so blue.
Black woman with heart of stone.
Black woman with mind so bold.
Black woman with skin so gold.
Black woman she carries the weight.
Black woman I know your hell.
Black woman I know so well.
Black woman I know your pure.
Black woman I know your sure.
In my mirror I see your face,
And in your heart I see the trace.
Black woman you are you.

*Barbara Reaves*

## Shadows

Images of dark and light,
Blocking what could be.
Hidden wrongs from their right,
Blinded by what there is to see.

My shadows name is love,
The darkness is only to gain.
For past is here only to shove,
Bringing up its forever pain.

The pain we refuse to forget
The memories of it held so tight.
The passage of a new love only to fret,
Making one feel it could never be right.

Cast the shadow away,
Let your heart open once more.
Have again love make its way,
Push the yesterday out the door.

Goodbye to the shadows yesterday,
Let the light shine through once more.
Let the light make its way,
And love again be adored.

*Doreen Webb*

## Believe

Run barefoot through tall grass.
Blow dandelion seeds.
Howl with the wolves.
Laugh with the waves.
Dance with the trees.
Walk among brothers.
Hold hands.
Listen to pain
Talk to the wind.
Reach for the stars.
Believe.

*Dana Lyn Gauthier*

## Holocaust

Pitted sheds, a barbed-wire fence;
Bodies in the ground—they lay so dense.
A silence fills the morning air—
Pain etched in the faces gathered there.
A starving boy with an empty bowl,
His family gone—a tortured soul.
A line of broken bodies stands
With tattered feet and calloused hands;
Battered, weary—too weak to cry...
Almost wishing that they could die...
And as the guns begin to blaze,
The others...they just stand and gaze.
No refuge in these camps of death...
A final shot, a final breath.
Darkness falls on this bloody scene—
Maybe it was all a dream...
But in the morning there's death once
more—
Weaponless...they fight this war.
A silence fills the morning air...
The faces are no longer there.

*David Brown*

## At LaPush

Rock and wood become
bone in surf shaped into
muscle and form-
bending into graceful wrists
and flesh folds around waists
is bleached wood in the sun.
Toes bury in the sand and stay
as the Douglas fir waits in
all tides, branches here bone
of old twisted hands where
Madrona red lends an
Indian's bicep bulging and wet
from hauling in fishing nets.
So ghosts of stories
and specters in mist climb
into the driftwood and sit
waiting for a walker's imagination.

*Camie F. Sands*

## Maya Angelou

A prize and jewel
born in pain,
shocked to silence,
but her gain
was a thoughtful,
meditating, thinking brain
that emitted elegance
once speech came.

A joyful face
in God's bouquet
a leading poet
in the world today;
a voice with power
to touch and teach
all God's children
within her reach.

*Edith Bustle*

## O Universe

O universe!
Boundless contained space
That turns in on itself
And explodes:
Dimple; pimple
Endlessly
Contracting, expanding,
Breathing in, breathing out,
Are your boundaries
Merely another illusion?

*James W. Cole III*

## The Horse of Troy

Red and yellow flames dancing all around
Burning, flaming, terrible light
Razing the city to the ground
And in the midst of flames
...a wooden horse...
Standing tall and proud
Its shadow looming over the doomed city
Like a dark and gloomy shroud
Hail, great Odysseus!
The city is burning
The battle is won
The siege is through
And the horse still stands
Tall and proud.

*Bruce D. Vail*

## Wildflowers

Swaying softly in the
breeze wildflowers awaken
to beautiful sunset far off
on the horizon

Purples, greens, yellows, and
oranges blend together in
one magnificent scene

A long day goes by and
before too long the moon
comes out and down goes
the sun

The shadows fall across
the field and stars begin to
light up the sky as the
flowers begin to close
their eyes.

*Courtney Graves*

## Sean,

The day you were born, you
brought joy, peace, and a new
understanding to the meaning of
life. I didn't quite understand
it, but when I reflect back to
that day joy and peace returns to me.
It lets me know that there
is a God and that you are a
Blessing, a gift to me from God.
You are special to me, I'm proud of
you and I love you .

*Daddy (Jacob)*

## Waiting Patiently For The Breeze

"Is that you, Chad,
brushing up against me?"
I hope so because
it sets me at ease;
with each touch
my soul tingles.
I realize you haven't
left me, you only
departed and have come back
to comfort my aching soul.
But I call to you
it is not I
who needs it most.
It is the people like your mother,
your father, your brother,
Traci, Tracey, Nanny,
Papa, Mama, Pa Pa
who need it more.
I ask you to comfort
them first, I can wait.

*Jason Lipscomb*

## Untitled

I dreamed I walked on
silken sands,
and heard the music of
the sea.
I knelt and touched them
with my hands,
And they became a part of me.

*Elizabeth G. Martin*

## Child Without A Name

He feels sharp pain,
  burning the souls of men.
He hears cold words,
  destroying hearts again.
He creates inner destruction,
  ripping them apart
He administers hatred,
  exploding their hearts.
He says racist remarks,
  slicing some in two.
He uses harassment,
  making them blue.
He wants revenge,
  so sweetly wrong.
He needs hope,
  separating the weak from the strong.
He gets death,
  ending all his pain.
The child no longer suffers,
  he died without a name.

*Gabriel Sifuentes*

## Burnt By Love

Ashes upon the butterfly's wings
burnt by love's dream.
No more to flutter here and there
Just this silent knowing of nothing
coming, nothing going.

So sad love's dream, it takes so
much and leaves so little.
To soar never more
Wings of ashes . . . . . crash!

*Diana Dolhancyk*

## Colours

I see no colour
But a light within
Shining brightly
Surrounding me

I see no creed
But compassion for all
Touching many
Touching me

I see no religion
But a soul so beautiful
Radiating love
Loving me

I see no race
But skin so warm
Worn a proud cloak
Accepting me

What then do I see?

I see a beacon in the darkness
A lamp to help guide my way

My friends are the colour of LOVE

*Carole Emilie Fellows*

## Spiraling Down I Grasped

Spiraling down I grasped for something,
but came up with nothing.
The stairs that lined the walls
I couldn't reach as I spiraled down.
Around and around I went
faster and faster until everything
was a flash of light.
The tunnel had no end and no beginning,
It went on forever,
The darkness, the blackness,
pushed me as if to hold me still.
The smell was very strong,
mingled with the bad things in life.
The heat, a furnace blowing
its breath to scorch the mind
and burn the soul as I spiraled down.
The bad memories hit me like stones
and then I understood,
    This is life.

*Erin Jensen*

## Different

I may have a disease
but I'm not any different
I feel on fire
I can do what anyone can do
and I can't do anything
I don't have a chance
My blood is different
I'm supposed to be different.

*Frankie Keller*

## The Light

It was a light in the distance
  But its light shown warmth
It was a light in the distance
  But no matter how far away
  they always could see it
It was a light in the distance
  But no matter how far away
  they always knew it meant
  they would see each other
  someday.
It was a light in the distance
  But its light shown warmth.

*Heather Marie Unglesbee*

## Never Alone

The door is standing open,
  But I've yet to climb the hill
That leads to life eternal,
  Though I know someday I will.

As I gaze into the valley
  Of times so long ago,
The winding path that brought me here
  And friends I used to know—-

My heart fills up with love and joy,
  Alone I'll never be,
For all who ever touched my path
  Will climb the hill with me!

*Isabel Muterspaw*

## Broken Heart

She's gone
but matters
of the heart
need attention.
She gave
her all
for a while
but found
stronger love.
Be free
keep eyes
open wide
travel within
destiny Paradise
where love
heals hearts.

*Carl R. Miller*

## Tracy

Woman a rose is very beautiful
but not compared to you.
Your body more breathtaking
than an Eiffel Tower view.
When west wind zephyrs warm air blows,
the sunset catches your golden hair.
There is nothing one can do,
but simply stop and stare.
Your smile bright like fallen snow,
that drifts across Nebraska plains,
the sound of your voice, or your laugh
can drive away the rain.
The memory of you burns in my mind
like Aurora borealis.
With smooth as porcelain skin
and satin lips I long to kiss.
Those blue eyes by candle light
put full moons to shame.
Your beauty is unmeasurable.

Love, James.

*James Derek Safrans*

## Untitled

I hear you calling me
But sometimes I don't answer
I feel you touching me
But I just pull up my covers

I hear your voice, I feel your touch
But sometimes it's a bit to much
I hear your voice, I hear you calling
When I answer, I feel i'm falling

Your whispers calling me
It scares me half to death
Could it be beer or wine
Or was it crystal-meth

I hear your voice, I feel your touch
The reaper's upon me, it's a bit too much
I hear your voice, I hear you calling
You bring me deeper, I feel I'm calling

Falling into darkness
Falling into hell
Falling into darkness
Hopefully it's only a wishing well

*Jason Michael Masuko*

## A Psalm Of Christina

Lord, help our light to shine through,
but the only way is through you.
Lord, let our minds and hearts open
to others,
So we can help one another.

Lord, let everyone be like you,
So we can see you.
Lord, be our Saving Grace,
So we can see you face to face.

*Christina Marie Warren*

## Your Heart

It's locked,
But there's a key.
I've tried hard to find it.
I know it's there.
You keep it hidden well.
Maybe just from me.
I guess I understand.
My key's hidden too.
But if you asked,
You could have it.

*Amanda Jo Geaslin*

## Eternity

Eternity is our goal
But time is our enemy.
Each moment we are together
Seems to last forever
Yet I can feel the minutes
Growing shorter
Till you have to go.

My love grows each time you hold me
And threatens to control my mind.
When you leave
My thoughts are of you.
My smiles remembrances of us
My eyes are mirrors of emotions
And the only words I know.
The only words I feel
The only words I can say...
I miss you
I need you
I love you
For eternity.

*Adrienne Hudson*

## My Bother

He was lonesome as a lonesome dove.
But to me he was my brother
with lots of love.

He worked real hard in what he did
But now, his time had to end.

There were so many things that
I did not say, but I hope he knew that
I wished he could have stayed.

*Helen Roseberry*

## Plain and Simple

Call me kike
Call me nigger
Call me chink
Call me dot head
Call me spic
I've heard them all
I've felt it all
The hate
The fear
The frustration
For I am you
I am your brother
I am your sister
I hate
Because of you
I kill
Because of you
I have no peace
Because of you

*David Doljan*

## Daisies Cry Too

And they played a game
Called he loves me, he loves me not
And each petal was slowly plucked
Until its face was stripped and bare
And as the dying flower was placed
Upon the earth I touched its face
Which was soggy and wet then
Suddenly I knew that daisies cry too.

*Joan E. Prussia*

## Axis

The illusions we create
Can balance our universe
We are worlds apart
Passions so intense
Open narrow spaces

The wonders of existence
Take many paths
Beauty of beginnings
Struggle of balance
A world is harmony

Objects of love surround us
Unifying the earth
Contrast and shape in opposition
Struggling harmoniously together in time

*Claire Marcus*

## Thoughts

The wings of swallows flying to the sun
Cast dark shadows upon my soul
A blanket of leaves is covering my mind
Under the stars I'm walking alone.

It's raining outside and in my soul
Dark clouds are covering the horizon
Your promises with empty words
Ring so dark and hollow.

I'd love to fly but I've no wings
My thoughts are gray and rusty
I beg, I cry, but no one hears
My love is drowning in the night.

*Corina Szori*

## "The Window"

Pearl-rayed moon,
casting shimmering shafts of light,
through a diamond paned door.
Gently she leaves her husband's side,
through night's soft eternal blackness.
She walks the long hall,
drawn inexorably as the tide.
The vast silver ocean reflected beneath,
piercing her heart.
Silently to bed.

*Antoinette Anderson*

## Search

A soul is a lonely thing
Caught in a human frame.
It grows by giving of itself,
Fades with what it takes.

And yet, sometimes,
There is a meeting -
Soul with soul;
And the giving light
One to the other
Catches and holds.

Song blends with song;
Light with light;
Color with color;
And in the mingling
Some small bit of heaven
Hangs suspended there.

A soul is a lonely thing
Caught in a human frame.
And yet, sometimes, dear God,
There IS a meeting - isn't there?

*Eleanor Hayes Chandler*

## "Dance Of The Stars"

The sky calms me,
'cause I know the stars
are my loved ones who've gone to heaven.
Though I miss them,
though I may have never known them,
they are in the sky,
as stars,
to remind us all
to remember them.
Sometimes they shine brighter
than other times.
Don't feel sad, the stars aren't lonely.
They have each other.
They shine through.
Most times they dance.
Whenever I see the stars,
amidst the black backdrop,
I remember the past, and
the memories of times long gone come back
to me.

*Ashley Wetzel*

## Mental Intrusions

Noisy utterances
sink into the depths of my thoughts.
Without consciousness, I allow them to
infect my emotions
until I am nothing more than a
victim of my own disturbed visions.

*Candace Adams*

## Directly from His Heart

Snowflakes are like babes
Masterpieces of God's art
Each wrought in His heart

*Hadwin Alsever II*

## Running From Darkness

So empty inside, feeling like dying,
cause there's nowhere to run, and hide.
No friends, no family, no one to turn to,
in need of someone to count on.
The search has been long, and in vain,
always choosing the wrong path.
Forever roaming in the dark,
so lonely, so cold, so empty.
No faith, no hope, no trust,
beliefs I have none.
So confused, uncertain,
afraid to live, afraid to die.
Where do I go from here?
Please leave me alone,
I need no one, not him, not you.
I'll find my own way ... someday.

*Gail Neuendorf*

## The Monotony of Sin

People say they need love bad
Chances are it won't be had
For in love to be a thing, a little
Love you have to bring.
Go ahead do your sin go
And let the devil in.
See him laugh never cry
Your about to die.
Controlled by powers of temptation
You grieve for love and lust,
You'll never find it in his station
Your mind will turn to dust.
Try and hit him with your fist,
Throw him against the wall, he'll
Bounce off with the greatest ease
And then you'll start to fall.
God will be there watching when you
finally lose,
Cry he may but he will say, that you have
paid your dues.
The only way not to lose is love just not
yourself
God will see you through his tour, with love
nothing else.

*Chet Austin*

## Our Devastations

The world around us is cold.
Children are being bought and sold!
Parents only want to scold.

What happened to love?
Where is respect?
It was all replaced by sex.

Trust is gone,
Children are torn,
Discipline has faded,
Society is devastated!

Parents stopped caring,
Children stopped hearing,
And now the world is fearing!

*Bobbi Huber*

## Shadows In My Mind

Nostalgia crawls up the spine
Chilling the soul's bones.
Memories of things gone by
Reminds me of my aging mortality.

The Beatles of 1965
Sing songs of my youth,
And now John is dead
And Paul is older than I.

I can't bring the past back
Or fix the wrongs I've done;
I can only fear growing old
And feel saddened for times lost
Or for friends now gone.

Sometimes when I hear an old song
I dwell on the might-have-beens
And the never-will-be's.

But, when you are here with me
I'm filled with now
And leave behind
These shadows in my mind.

*James C. Shearer*

## Ireland's Corners

My shadow saved me from the burning
    city's death.
People running scared, red terror fills
    streets, the thought of roses
rising to save us betrayed by anger.

The hills have the answers but you
    can not hide anywhere,
and no love is as selfish as ones.

Eyes melt from reading the next
    chapter, no safety from the apple.
Easy access to pain, indulging with
    laughter.

Where have the years taken us,
    will we see who lives behind
the SON? The back of a hand
    does not teach discipline...
only in death will that occur.

*Gregory Aidala*

## Clouds

Clouds of doubt,
Clouds of fear,
Clouds of sickness
Oft appear.

Clouds of sorrow,
Adversity,
May veil the glory
Of God from me.

But, through those clouds,
God's presence still
Shines in my heart,
My life to fill

With light of faith,
Love, health, and joy,
Abundant life
Without alloy.

Into each life
Some clouds must come,
But they're dissipated by
The light of the Son.

*Doris L. Morris*

## Spirits Flow

Spirits flow
Come and go, don't you know?
Round and round, then down again
Can you see them?
Touch them, smell them, feel them
Down again, round again
Enter me, enter you
Can't you feel them when you're blue?
I can feel them through and through
Do not clinch your soul untrue
Let your spirit fly with you

*David Bedell*

## Stupidity

Dark corner, trapped.
Coming closer, her.
Standing between, him.
He's gone, I'm on my own.
Departing words, carved in my memory.

Deception, naive acception.

Black hole, blind.
Buried by hate, her.
Watching over, him.
He's gone, I'm on my own.
Telepathy, stamped on my forehead.

Deception, naive acception.

Dead coffin, hurt.
Laughing hysteria, her.
Finally realizing, him.
He's gone, I'm on my own.
Beautiful roses, kissing my grave.

Deception, naive acception.

*April Garvey*

## Silver Rain

Silver Rain—
Coming down in white streaks
Forming diamond droplets
Hanging from the green shrubs
Puddling in the street.

Silver Rain—
Making a peaceful sound
Entering my consciousness
Soaking white sidewalks
Singing its tinkling song.

*Jeanne Mason*

## Reasons Why

I see the raindrops coming down.
Coming down upon the ground.
I see the clouds overhead.
My eyes, my thoughts, filled with dread.
I know the reason people kill.
It's not for laughs or a cheap thrill.
I know the reason people die.
I'm sorry I can't tell you why.
I see the hurt in people's eyes.
I know the pain, and why they cry.
I know the reason people weep.
It's for the loved ones they can't keep.
I know the reason,
reason why.
So now you can wipe your eyes dry.

*Jenna Masucci*

## The Wall

In life there is a wall —
complete, yet missing one brick,
if the wrong brick is chosen,
the wall may fall.
Finding the perfect brick is the trick,
because some bricks almost fit.
Some bricks don't fit at all.
But, the perfect brick won't move a bit,
so the wall stands sturdy and tall.
I thought you were the perfect brick,
but I was mistaken.
Because when the wind blew,
the wall of my heart was taken.
Now there's nothing left for me to do,
except rebuild the wall.
Making sure every brick is a perfect fit
and making sure there are no loose
bricks at all.
So when the storms of life come,
the wall won't move one bit.

*Charlene Wilson*

## Reflection

Fading voices
confusion screams
Knowing choices
with similar dreams
Calling emotions
never ignored
Certain notions
wrongfully poured
Forming habit
between lines
Snug the fit
nothing declines
Dreaming of
desired perfection
Falling in love
with no reflection

*Jenifer Barnes*

## Gun

Fear-marked sensibilities rule,
convictions entombed in rhetoric.
Projectiles coming from mania.
Bystanders, face down on the walk.
Images of homages to enforced power.
Man is a biped.
not meant for crawling.
The inadequacies creep up behind,
ranting in the inner ears,
having the last, explosive say.
We are locked and loaded.
Standing in the cross hairs
on the inner city precipice.
Fear governs the neighborhood.
Arming our children to frightened study,
without consideration for our own stale
teachings.
Look down on us again,
all you brave, lone stars.
Shed a little cold light, please.
Put some sunshine on the metal.

*James E. Danielson*

## Untitled

I could hear him out there,
cool night, cruising the boulevard.
His engine screamed,
as he drove it hard.

I sensed his presence,
his heart is young and his soul free.
His tires peeled rubber,
as he roared past me.

I could see it in his eyes,
I know how he feels.
He's on top of the world,
driving the meanest iron on four wheels.

I know this boy and his first car,
he became a man seldom seen,
as he taunted the rest of us,
in his awesome driving machine.

Now, I cruise the empty darkness,
listening, as I did many nights before,
knowing the warrior and his might chariot,
won't be out there anymore.

*Hallette Dawson-Day*

## Autumn

I feel a hint of Autumn in the gentle
cooling breeze —
The rustle of the cornstalks, the
baring of the trees.

Some people think of Autumn as the
beginning of the end.
The fun of summer's over; Winter's cold
lies 'round the bend.

But Autumn's just a lullaby which
Mother Nature sings
To bring the earth to a wintry sleep
To wake refreshed in Spring.

She even paints the hillsides in
multi-colored scenes
To give us beauty while the earth sleeps
And dreams her golden dreams.

*Jo Anne Posey Liles*

## The Cord of Life

I knew about cord
Cord was for tying
Packages and flying kites
I knew no other
Later came blue red
And green for weaving
I heard of under water
Cords for rockets
I become pregnant
I heard of umbilical cord
Life cord for fetus
Connecting placenta to
Embryo-
My son was born
Grateful forever to the
Cord of life.

*Alice Miller*

## The Basics of Life

I'd like to be free.
Create without desires of fame,
let my art be me.

I like the honesty of now,
it can be touched.

Love is the expression of
good news I want to hear.

It's going to have to get a
little bit crazy, for life
to feel free.

It's going to have to get a
little bit crazy, to smile.

Life is a personality,
always a surprise.

Sometimes, we get caught
up in lies, and must laugh
our way through.

Sometimes we just have to quit
to get what we want.

*George E. Porter Jr.*

## Precious Hands

Tiny fingers, wrinkled and pink,
curled lovingly 'round my heart,
even as they clutched my thumb
lest we should ever part.
I gazed in awe at the precious gifts
the Lord had bestowed on me,
but knew not then what treasures indeed
my children would grow to be.
Years have passed since those days
when I cradled them in my arms,
yet their hands, now large as mine,
still 'round my heart entwine.
And ever will I thank the Lord
for the gifts He's given me —
for in my children, I have found,
I'm blessed as one can be.

*Frieda D. Klotz*

## To Ann

Your eyes, bright as flame,
Dance in mine and call my name;
Your smile, soft and warm,
Creeps into my heart and calms its storm.

Oh Ann, you awaken life in me
Where life has long been still;
You bring new strength and joy to me
I know you always will.

Your arms hold me fast
And, as the day hurries past,
The touch of your hand
Lingers on my skin like grains of sand.

Oh Ann, you waken life in me
Where life has never been,
You fill my night with ecstasy;
My day is bright again.

Your love, sweet and true
Fills my soul with love for you
My love grows each day;
You are in heart and there you'll stay.

*Byron Friar*

## Visions

Visions of you
Danced in my head
As I laid there
Asleep in my bed

Visions of you
That felt so right
Because of the way
You held me tight

Visions of
The love in your eyes
Its beauty
Like a sun rise

Visions of
Your tender touch
Oh, how it did
So, so much.

Suddenly I awakened
With a gleam
Only to realize
It was just a dream

*Charlotte J. Jennings*

## Darkness

What I see, I see forever
darkness a wound they do savior
I say hello but know one
hears me
in my heart it would pierce me,
now only darkness is what I feel
when I think it makes me I'll
all darkness is a different thing
called by darkness they do sing
a screeching melody of the mind
were lost soles are left behind

*Jennifer Switzer*

## Footstep

The sun has set
Darkness is now before me
I am anxiously awaiting the dawn
Of a new life
Apprehensively stepping forward
Yet always looking back
At the weatherbeaten path
Behind me
I have your supportive footsteps
Paralleling mine only to a point,
The point of the present
I turn back to the future
And make my tracks alone
Waiting and knowing that
I'll back to see the one
Who helped me make that
First footstep

*Carrie Quantock*

## The Marionette

She was a beautiful puppet,
And he used her so well,
Most people believed she
Could almost be real —
Except for those strings he
Kept tight in his hands.
She laughed and danced,
But mostly, she cried.

*Jamie Patricia*

## Fifty-one Syllables Of Spring

Vernal equinox,
Day and night of equal length,
One more winter ends.

Through the ice and snow,
Come the sights and scents of spring.
Needle translations.

Continuous thread
Marks early bulbous beauty,
Tulip borders bloom.

*Auriel Sandstead*

## The Tower Of The Sun

God bless man who made it so
Day by day we watched it grow
Now at last it is complete
It's beauty in your heart we'll keep
The Tower in its splendor gleams
Amidst the flowers an Isle of Dreams
The lights are soft, the music low
The sights you see forever glow.

*Aurora Montesano*

## Promises

The nights are far gone and the
days are spent at hand planning
for tomorrow's promises.

Missed out on opportunities that
are at reach, goals that are
strived for and yet we have not
reached our mark.  Stepped on
by lack of knowledge.  Subdued in
a society of economical handicap
and resources.  Mislead by who
we can trust and political promises
that are never kept.

Subject to ridicule by discrimination
of some means of one kind of another.
In a overrated commercialized society.

*Deborah Railey*

## Today

Come - run with me
  dear child of mine.
Quickly pick up speed.
No time to chase a butterfly,
  nor to stop and dream.

No time to pick a daisy
  not today, dear child of mine.
For we are chasing rainbows,
  and there's very little time.
No time today to sing a song
  or wiggle our toes in a stream
Pandora's box is just ahead
  and tomorrow is just a dream.

*Beverly B. Turnmire*

## My Husband, My Friend

To the one I love
Deep in my heart.
Bonded forever
Never to be apart.
You are my sunshine
Filling my life with light.
You are the star
Shining bright in the night.
You are my guardian
Keeping me from harm.
Together in happiness
Forever arm in arm.
You are my husband
And my best friend.
I love you to death
Forever, until the end.

*Denise James*

## Border Crossings

Gifts unsought from my neighbor's garden
Defying fenced-in order.
Riots of color in purple violet
Disturb the ordered plan of
Hues subdued.

Through unseen rifts in walled-in space
Tendrils creep o'er tilled earth
Embracing roses, adding vibrant green
To pastel shades of muted
Elegance.

Thus colors blend in worlds unplanned
Merging riches crowding
Best-laid plans of men and states
Creating tapestries of
Wild surprise.

*Barbara Stewart*

## Each Star Would Be A Note

Somehow I let night
Descend upon my life
And put on the garment of darkness,
But even in the heavy blackness
Are stars by the billions
Punctuating the lonely, loveless hours.
If somehow, I could pull down
At least one constellation
Maybe I could find my way.

Sunrise is coming,
It always does.
If only I can endure the wait,
Would I compose a symphony
For its arrival!
Each star would be a note
In my song, my beloved piece
All played,
A new life,
A new day begun.

*Gregory J. Nuno*

## It Can't Rain All the Time

I'm gonna keep my heart open
despite the pain
I'm gonna let myself feel
my tears fall like rain
all colors can change
including blue
maybe soon it will brighten
and enlighten my view
as anger turns
from red to white
when forgiveness
smiles in your sight
my dark cold clouds
of fears and whys
might soon leave
my troubled eyes.

*Bonnie Porter*

## Moving

Why do you have to move?
Did I do something?
Are you mad at me?
If I told you not to...
Would you listen?
I know!
You could live with me!
Oh yeah,
You'd miss your parents.

I'm going to miss you.
True...I can always call you.
And we can write.
But it's not the same.
I guess I have to face the fact
That people grow up and move away.

*Erin Edwards*

## "Why Daddy Why"

Why Daddy why
Did you make your little girl cry
Why daddy why
Did you make my heart sigh
Why Daddy why
Did you suddenly say goodbye,
Why Daddy why
Did you have to lie, to Mommy and I
So tell me Daddy,
Why Daddy why?

*Elizabeth Belcher*

## Stephen

The sun arrived that day in May,
Distraught it was to find,
That you, my son, had flown away,
Left it and us behind.

A thousand times since, in despair,
It 'round the world has gone.
It cannot find a thing so fair,
To shed it's light upon.

Sometimes when overcome by grief,
Behind a cloud 'twill go,
In solitude to seek relief,
Where sorrow does not show.

And when it cries, its teardrops flow,
To mingle with the rain,
And only those who share it know,
It still feels so much pain.

*Daniel M. Sullivan*

## The Widows' Three

We are the widows three
Do not be fooled by our
  looks of glee

The singles clubs simple
  won't do -

He must have charm but
  money too

So here we sit and sip
  our drink

but not without that
  welcoming wink.

*Florence R. Alderman*

## "They"

"THEY" say that the brave
Do not cry,
And it's only the weak
Who show a wet eye.

But "THEY" know only
Of what "THEY" can see.
What do "THEY" know
Of you, or of me?

"THEY" perhaps, are
Too blind to know
Of sadness in others
Or, their hidden woe.

So while I laugh and talk
And show no fears,
Its my heart that cries
With unseen tears.

So "THEY" cannot know
If one's eyes are dry,
That one's heart may weep
when one must cry.

*James F. Preble*

## Lost Friend

I miss her, but I
do not miss the pain.

How do I deal with the loneliness
that fills my heart and soul again.

I have no hate towards her.
Just sorrow of blindness
she has for love.

I shed to her a tear,
Is she blind to what I have
A gift of life,
I've starved my self of,

Unselfish ruling of love I give,
I wanted to share with her.

Does she hate me for
what someone else has done?
Why? Will she ever love me
like the one who hurt her most?

Not me, nor our child deserve
what we have gotten, blindness of pain,
forever it will rotten.

*John R. Leniger*

## What Is Love?

How do we know when we are loved?
Do we really know when we're in
love or do we just mistake love for lust.
Love, reaches out and wants the
best for someone always.
Does anyone love you?
Does anyone really love me?
Does people who say they love you
really mean it?

**Joseph Finders**

## Purpose?

In a world so big and brutal
Do you feel your life is brutal
Force yourself to find a purpose
Bake a cake, plant a flower
Read a book, take a shower.
Move your boy, use your mind
There are others you will find
Who see your spirit and will cry
If he can do it so can I.

**Berniece Miller Vaughan**

## Does It Make You Wonder?

When you hear the roar and thunder.
Does it make you wonder?
Do you still have your doubts?
That beyond the dark clouds.
Above the bolts and lightening.
That is sometimes quite frightening.
To hear the roar and crash.
To see the bright, white flash.
Does it make you wonder?
If the Angels are up yonder.
With ball in hand.
Do they sail it down the lane?
Will they make a strike?
I wonder what it is like.
To hear the birds shouts and cries,
As the Angels bowl in the skies.

**Jenny Pigg**

## Have A Heart

Don't be cruel
Don't be mean
Keep a song in your heart
Because that's what is smart

The ways of the world
Can turn you bad
Know adventures of caring
Of sharing and daring

Isn't it exciting?
To be so involved?
Instead of mundane ho-hum,
Rather forward and from

**Bernadette Sievers Gannon**

## Expose

When the heavens rain
God is crying
His children are dying
Only Peace on Earth
will comfort him

**Billy Rodriguez**

## A Selfish Mood

I don't drag these tears
down my cheeks
because I like their taste,
as they tentatively,
touch my lips:

It's all a pearly mystery to me.

I'd rather be touched,
be cursed and cradled,
looked upon with eyes
that fasten to my flesh
like light, like a lover's lips,
fingers, identities;
made a guardian of sacred secrets
that bear down on me with sharp pain
for another
who trusts me more than others
but only with whispered things,
whose divulgence half skips, half crawls
through my bones, to touch me
touching me (more than I think).

**David P. Gesser**

## Joseph's Coat

In the days of old a coat was made.
Down through the years this story
portrayed, a symbol of love from
Father to Son, because He was the
blessed one. Coat of many colors
climbing up the wall, bless the one
who possess you, give them strength,
love and patience through it all.
Blessed is the man whose strength is
in thee.

**Harriet A. Sims**

## My Good Night Prayer

When I lay me
down to sleep,
I pray your love
is what I keep.

If I should be waken
at night by fear
I pray it is your voice
that I will soon hear.

But, If I should dream
with a smile upon my face
know my dreams are of you
and hold me in your embrace.

**Amanda Kelley**

## The Orb Of The Night

The pale crescent shape,
Drifts nonchalantly,
Amidst a pool of bright stars,
Benevolently bequeathing luminosity,
As the time goes by,
The shape sinks below
Into the sea,
That was once filled with stars,
Awaiting for the sea to be recreated,
So it may sail again,
Flashing its brilliance.

**Asha Balakrishnan**

## Untitled

It's early
Dust settles in
Sounds bounce wall to wall
Sunlight slivers through window's edge
Thoughts creep slowly
Making pursuit of consciousness
'Til gaining a glimpse of recognition
Eyes whisper to be open
Soft compression of air drifts
Calling to see color of the day
Tingling sensation everywhere
Motion comes from rising sun
Scaling upward note for note
Brings smile of wonder each time.

**Brian McLeod**

## Sharon

A daughter of Erin, from the
Emerald Isle -
Winsome of figure with an
impish smile.

Shy as a flower with the
first breath of spring -
but restless of spirit as
the birds on the wing.

Conscious of time, like a
clock on a shelf -
Yet savors the hours that
she spends by herself.

An essence of innocence, as
the first flake of snow -
but the strength of resolve, in
her desire to grow.

An enigma to many,
a window to few -
To those who love her,
is to cherish the view.

**Clark Beardslee**

## She Is

She is the little devil on my shoulder,
enjoying embarrassing me when possible.
She is the humor,
making me cry tears of laughter.
She is the flashlight,
showing me the way through darkness.
She is the compass,
guiding me in the right direction.
She is the bridge,
helping me to cross tortuous rivers.
She is the angel from up above,
sent down to watch over me.
She is the diary,
letting me tell her my secrets.
She is the best friend,
giving my life meaning.
She is many things to me;
she is my mother.

**Allison K. Urias**

## Colored...!

Life is fun!
Entertainment everywhere...all kinds;
Color it blue and green
Politics, the garlic of life;
Color it red and yellow.

Sports for flavor and excitement...
For young and old;
Color it orange and black.
Business for fibre and strength,
The infrastructure;
Color it green and gray.
People, what life is about;
You have to be colorblind
To see them...!

**Edwin D. Arsht**

## Summer

Ah, the sweet summertimes of old,
Every day worth its weight in gold.
Come sit under the old shade tree,
Walk down memory lane with me.

Remember swinging to the leaves?
Climbing trees and skinning our knees?
Shedding our clothes, baring our toes,
Squirting each other with the hose?
Mom's biscuits with strawberry jam
Or a slice of Pa's country ham?
Catching crawdads, jumping the creek,
Dodging cowpatties at our feet?
The swimming hole and sliding rock?
Cold enough to make your knees knock!
Kicking the can and hunting snipe?
Picking blackberries plump and ripe?
Catching lightning bugs in jars?
Ghost stories told under the stars?

Though summer comes and goes each year,
None can equal those days so dear!

**Donna W. Brenner**

## Feeling Love

The flowers have bloomed:
every thing is music, and color
every thing is pink and blooming

The girl sees herself in
the mirror, and smiles
as if she were a flower

By the rays of the sun
she sings to her bird:
and the bird sings back

Feeling the love, everything
is rushed every thing is giggles
everything is like a flower

The girl awaits, morning
because early in the
morning she will put on

Her long dress, with her
shoes that are pink, everything
is so pink in her dream, of
Illusion:

**Cristina La Paz**

## Free Will

Free Will with lack of Wisdom,
Evicted Eve and Adam.
Then Cain the blood of Abel spilled,
And severed Brotherhood.
Christ, praying in the garden,
Saw the present, past and future.
Free Will chose Power, Pride and Greed,
And shattered Brotherhood.
Christ's agonizing tears of blood,
Enriched Gethsemane;
As He prayed for PEACE and BROTHER-
HOOD.

**Beulah Thacker**

## Midnight Rain

Drizzle drizzle, drip drop
Falling gently from clouds
Ping-pang, splish-splash
Drinks the dry earth

Pitter-patter, clickity-clack
Raining, pouring, steadily falls
Ting-tang, clink-clank
For days it falls

BOOM, rumble, roaring, CRACK
Strikes lightning, thunder rolls
CRASH, BANG, rolling, CLANG
Wakes all, violent rain

Ting-tang, clink-clank
Hard, soft, all day
Pitter-patter, clickity-clack
Slowly falling, quietly rains

Ping-pang, splish-splash
Day in, day out
Drizzle drizzle, drip drop
Never stopping, PLEASE STOP!

**Erin Welton**

## Prayer

God's love though never
far away
Is closer still each time
we pray.

God's light and warmth
give us the peace
To humbly walk
and serve and reach

His children He longs
for everywhere
We need to tell them
God answers prayer.

**Clarice Page**

## Time

Through the shadows
And thickened walls
I felt time pass
Time so shallow
It could be cut
With a single blade
But then morning came
The walls crumbled
And the shadows fell

Time...

**Jenny Lynn Durst**

## Permute Stage Prop

Quick!
Fascinating!
I am disassembled,
Like stage prop stairs,
Debolted —
Stored —
After the final performance
Until
My friends
Power up my assembly line,
Retooling my similes and motifs —
Resecuring my bolted banisters,
And I am made whole —
Step by step —
As a way for the
Feet of my poetic essence
To impulsively climb
A non-ramshackle lexicon
To jump,
Skywardly mobile.

**Irene Lillian Evans**

## Sorry Yet Sad

People are afraid to love children,
Fear feeling guilty once that child
becomes an adult.
I'm not blind yet can't see.
Open your eyes, sorry yet sad.

Life is no good when ever
society pulls our plug.
Only when you gain respect,
People become eager and open minded.
Take your time in growing my child,
This is L-I-F-E, sorry yet sad.....

**Darwin D. Smith Sr.**

## The Gift

As I sit here alone
Feasting on still and quiet
I wonder of others
With the same daily diet.

There is much to be said
For being alone,
The time that you have
Is entirely your own.

To some it's a bore,
To others a fright.
To me, it's a window
That offers new sight.

You may sleep, or dream
You may work or play
And then you give thanks
God gave you the day.

**Betty R. Pierce**

## "Only One"

In this life, it's been told
Only one true love
Only one to touch the soul

Some will never know
Others will let go

Blessed are they that
have and hold.

**Joan Bishop**

## Destiny

Knowing each other for so long,
Feelings becoming uncontrollable strong,
Acting on an impulse they are known,
And for a time even shown,
But it's soon in the past,
Both moving on,
After believing the feelings are gone,
The friendship again becomes strong,
A situation arises and fate steps in,
To see them through
And rekindle a love so true,
Because this is their destiny.

*Jennifer Brown*

## Untitled

Drew the lines
Felt it drip away
Crossed the line
Felt me drip away
Mouth parched
Baking in the steam
Drank a pool of cold water
Let flow a stream
Rolling around
Trying to get cool
Face on the ground
Hot
Like in wool
Tingling in my hands
Pins in my fingers
Tried to fade away
But still I stayed and lingered

*Ian Birdwell*

## I Dreamed of You in Childhood

I am your Broodmare.
Fill me with the "Howl"
you keep zipped behind your pants.
Mark me
with your spurs.
Every wound
bears your name.
I have kept all that
you have whispered to me
sealed in fire.
What were the chances
we'd both be
"living in the light."
The embroidered "Welcome" sign dangles
above the main entrance.
Inviting you in,
I take your arm
as we hesitantly
move forward.

*Alice Louise Long*

## Delusion

I follow
   and see
      and hope
         and deny.

Till you are
   not you
      but me
         in my eye.

*James Fleetham*

## A Child Called It Blue

A child called it Blue...
filled with pain and questions.
Questions without answers,
Pain without reason or relief.

A child called it blue...
Tears wailed up in her eyes
As she stares helplessly to the sky.

A child called it blue...
The fear and sorrow showed on her face
There beside her, her brother lies
in a puddle of blood...
His own blood.

A child called it blue

*Chriss Johnson*

## Untitled

light
filters
deep into the coolness
of the forest

softly playing with the wind
dancing downward
through the trees

full
green and lacy
lucent

speaking with the
whisper of a lover
down to where
i have come to sit
upon the cool red clay

*Carole R. Pratt*

## Old Friends

Old friends are like
findings in pockets
we've stored;
like memories
we've chosen to
cherish and hoard.
They lay in
the cracks of
such busy minds
and when we
relax, they're
such precious finds!

*Jann Mattson*

## A New Baby

He's safe and sound
five pounds, eight ounces.

We all, his aunts and uncles,
grandparents, wait to hold
the little fella.

Things are different
in our family.

The world has changed.
We have a new baby.
The universe is different.

*Allan Nixon*

## To Grandmas

I love to go Grandma's house
she is so nice to me,
she makes such good food
and always has some tea.

*Jake Wilson*

## Drifting

Drifting thoughts,
   fleeting images in my mind,
      of memories I can't forget.
I wander aimlessly,
   not knowing, or caring, where I am.
      For there is nowhere only.
My travels take me everywhere,
   up, down, around,
      but really nowhere.
Is there an answer, I question;
   there is no reply,
      but the echo of silence.
Perhaps that is my answer,
   to be only nowhere,
      always wandering,
         questioning.

*Charles E. Reardon Sr.*

## The Spider's Web

The gossamer threads
float in the wind...
not yet anchored to reality.

Soon a web of illusion will form;
its inherent strength belied by
a appearance of tenuousness.

Entrapment will occur;
struggle will be fruitless.
Another victim will succumb
to natural law.

*Elizabeth Miller Harris*

## Gone

Leaves fall around your head,
Flowers heaped about your bed.
In the grass I sit and weep
I hurt so much because you sleep.

I got to kiss you one last good-bye,
I stood up strong so not to cry.
I remember the times that we once shared.
I remember the times that you had cared.

I'm happy that you got your way.
Now I sit and smile at where you lay.
I'm glad your pain is over and done,
Now life's victory you've already won.

*Charo Garlitz*

## Untitled

An inner river of me
   flows in mist colored solitude
Currents of homesickness
   with no home in mind

Unreachable,
   Unspoken,
      small desolations
         wavering in velvet forest waters

*Helen Gouvert*

## Hawk In The Sky

There's a hawk in the sky
Fly away fly
On top of the hill
Stands an old tree still
All on its own
Don't cry, you're not alone
Fly away fly
Hawk in the sky

Leaves in the wind
Lost like an old friend
In the seasons that twist
Swept off by one kiss
There are tears in your eyes
From a heart that cries
Did he fly away fly
Like the hawk in the sky

*Gypsy Barrier*

## Moon and Sky

See moon and sky
Fly high
As you can
To where the universe began
Past gently spinning bars
Of dust
Oh you must
See...wind and wings ah!
Things without a flaw
Light
Shining white
The milk
Of galaxies smooth as silk
Oh you must see
What it is to be
Flying past on silver wings
A shooting star!

*Ellen McGehee*

## Spirit, Heart and Soul

As an eagle strokes its wings
Flying high in the sky
Our spirit yearns to fly
Along side

As we watch a mother bear
Tend to her cubs
Our hearts long to give that
Much love

As a wolf howls in preparation
For a Hunt
Our soul cries to run
Along side

For within nature each creature
As spirit heart and soul
And in order to experience nature
We ourselves must share our
Spirit hearts and soul

*Christine E. Sperry*

## Letting Go

The roses have withered;
Our hearts did cry;
Time to move on;
The love must die.

*Elizabeth Kovich*

## Oh, To Fly

I'd like to be a kite
   flying over the trees,
   gliding out of sight
   on a warm summer breeze.
I'd ask a butterfly
   to perch on my tail,
   and into blue heavens
   we'd happily sail.
We'd look at the birds
   see how they fly,
   and meet God's Angels
   as we soar on high.
I'd ask directions
   to Heaven's door,
   peek in the keyhole,
   and see "evermore."
When a jerk on my string
   brought us earthward at last,
   we'd rejoice in our trip,
   and the memory's past.

*Diane Carrick*

## "An Unloved Poem"

For lack of love I should be blue
For all the things that you don't do
I could just mope around all day
Be discontent while you're away.

There are things I cannot do
That I could, when there was you.
But there are things I'll do alone
I cannot do when you are home.

I won't feel sorry for myself
And sit at home upon a shelf.
I will go on with my life,
With all its ups and downs and strife.

The sun will rise and the moon will shine,
Whether you are or are not mine.
Time will always come and go.
What life bring we cannot know,

So I will hold my head up high
And if your love has passed me by
I'll mourn awhile for what might have been,
Then live and laugh and love again.

*Gaye Ohlinger Cheshire*

## Summer's Calling

Summer's calling from the wind. I long
for blond. Breezing in the sunrise.
White sands, blue skies, warm seas.
But only stormy seas, gray skies,
and black sands. I call to the clouds,
come fly me for a spell, so I can feel
the luminosity of golden rays around
my cloud. I miss knowing the treasure
of my patron, and long to share clouds
with light wings, that take flight high
above our golden clouds.
Faraway thoughts of summer calling from
the wind, I long for blond. Golden,
wheat blowing from the wind. Fresh
air when we take flight, higher than
the clouds. Drifting sadness when we
miss flight every sunrise. Sedate my
desire for blond. It hurts when summer's
calling from the wind.

*Darylyn McKinney Rose II*

## Thank You Mr. Policeman

Thank you Mr. Policeman,
For finding my lost dog.
Your search was very successful,
In spite of all that fog.

Thank you Mr. Policeman,
For climbing up that tree.
You saved my cat, Samantha,
Although she clawed your knee.

Thank you Mr. Policeman,
For reviving the animal that sunk;
My pool was full of toys,
And I had no idea it was a skunk.

You know something Mr. Policeman
You don't even need a gun;
I've changed my mind from being a vet,
To a policeman who just has fun.

*Darlene D. Hunter*

## Untitled

Leave me alone all on my own
for just a while, so I can smile
without your pain so I can gain
something of mine, and I can shine
where I am me, and I feel free
from all of you, its sad but true,
its time to be just there for me
its hard enough, so very tough
to make it through, and care for you.
It's supposed to be you're there for me
to hold my hand and understand
and help me see how things should be
but what's worse, its in reverse
and I can't stand to hold your hand
and light the way, find words to say
and let you know how things should go
and calm your fears, hold back my tears
and smile bright, turn wrong to right
and keep me strong while all along
I am weak, and what I seek is someone who
replaces you.

*Christine Ruisi*

## Prejudice

When a man hates a man
For no special reason,
No special place,
No special season.

When fear arises
With the sun, moon, and stars,
We are locked
Behind imaginary bars.

It's when the truth is found
In the dark dim grey,
And every one has
Not a prayer left to pray,

That's when everyone strides
To stop its existing,
Back is the hope,
Freedom's club is enlisting.

*Jenna Harjani*

## Untitled

I cry with a sigh
for one day I'll die
I have a disease
not the measles
The name is cancer
For which there's no answer
I look in the mirror
reflection, there's no cure
This is no Joke
for there is no hope
Cancer has won
So I am done
salute my dear friends
for so here is the end
I will not though go without a fight
which I'll do in all my might
Give money with all your heart
So maybe no more will depart
For one day there will be a cure.

SO DON'T DESPAIR

*Jean Stovall*

## Lonesome Teddy Bears

The lonesome Teddy Bears are weeping.
For the children who are sleeping
In the arms of a loving God.
Nineteen lay buried under the sod.
After the terrorist bombing day,
April 19, sent 169 on their way,
To heaven where angels say,
For this tragedy Satan will pay,
And love will find a way,
In Oklahoma Heartland U.S.A.

*Daphne Van Nort*

## Kitchen Dance

Mother clips purple lilacs
for the vase in her kitchen.
She likes the fragrance of summer
to waft mysteriously about.
When I was a little girl, mother
would dance with me in her kitchen.
We did the Charleston until our
faces were wet, sweet wet.
Once she did the tango
with a long stemmed rose in her mouth.
She said roses were for winter,
lilacs for summer.
Mother was a good dancer,
she felt the freedom of movement.
I can still smell the scent of
lilacs in mother's kitchen.
The smell dances mysteriously,
like her movement.

*Becky Ruden*

## Manatees...

M - is for magnificent.
A - is for animal.
N - is for no motor boats.
A - is for amazing.
T - is for terrific.
E - is for excellent.
E - is for endangered.
S - is for sweet.

*Chris McCarty*

## I Am As I Am

I am as I am
For who else could I be
I am not you
And you are not me

I am not as I was
Nor as I shall be
I am as I am
Can you accept me

I am as I am
Not an advocate lying
Neither to condemn
These people for trying

I am as I am
Come what may
I am as I am
As I am today

*Eugene B. Wilkinson*

## When You Say

## Good-bye To Tomorrow

Will the world be a better tomorrow,
For you having been here today?
Will some child look up with wonder,
For something you might say?
Will your life be an example
To show another the way?
Will you have that peace on leaving
That your best has been done,
That your mission here has been
accomplished, and know Victory
has been won?
When you say good-bye to tomorrow,
And step over into eternity,
May you hear that still quiet voice
saying, Welcome, Come with Me.

*Flaye H. Lehman*

## "Forget"

Forget his name, Forget his face,
    Forget his kiss, his warm embrace.
Forget his love, that was true,
    Remember there's someone new.

Forget you memorized his walk,
    Forget the way he used to talk.
Forget the times he made you mad,
    Remember now he's happy, not sad.

Forget the thrills when he walked by,
    Forget the times he made you cry.
Forget the way he spoke your name,
    Remember they aren't the same.

Forget the times that went so fast;
    Forget them all, they're in the past.
Forget he said he would never leave,
    Remember now . . . he's gone and
relieved.

*Adam Foster*

## June

One time in June
I bought a balloon
It started to glow
So I let it go.

*Jayme Trujillo*

## A Pen

A pen is freedom, freedom to write,
Freedom to condole, freedom to fight.
A pen can create, a pen can destroy;
A pen can fulfill, a pen can annoy.
If only the ball at the end of a pen,
life would flow free;
Destiny would be certain, things would
just be.

*Elizabeth R. Iacona*

## A Porcelain Doll

A desperate call,
From a porcelain doll.
A shot rings out,
There is not doubt.
A life now gone,
Other faces drawn.
They looked right through,
A face they knew
So unable to ask,
For a hand to grasp.
They did not hear,
The cry of fear
Of the one in need
A sad WHY? They heed.

*Dawn M. Kilgore*

## The Key

I set my sail on silver ships
From harbours draped in lambent light
In hopes that I might loose my grips
And rest my foundered dreams from sight

Imperfect colors fill my head
The somber colors of the deep
The hues by which my thoughts are bled
That cradle me in anchored sleep

For time no longer plays a part
In this abyss which draws me near
So let the artist mold my heart
Endorse the prophets of the seer

The strangest voice now beckons me
The door is locked you have the key

*Craig Smith*

## August Surprise

Oh, it has come
    from the far North
Promise of respite
    on August fourth.

I turn off manufactured
    cooling air.
A night in August
    that is rare.

I open the windows
    and feel the cool breeze
brush my face and listen to
    leaves whispering in the trees.

I shall sleep well
    tonight under a cover,
as coolness sweeps across me.
"Please stay here until summers over."

*Donna M. Spencer*

## Earth's Awakening

I was witness to them
gathered on an open field,
their breasts proud orange swollen—
first harbingers of Spring.

The trees were revelling
as they danced, blushed
with new found color.

Grey laden clouds
hung heavy in the sky,
promising nourishment
for Earth's awakening.

Nature pregnant with Hope
I joined the chorus,
seeds long dormant—
Now would bear fruit.

*Janet Kae Jacobson*

## Bioscope

Made of sand the lens
gave insight on life unknown
made of sand it guided man
to see new ways alone

Where is the lens for to-morrows
that holds from sphere to sphere
the flow of life in the universe
from yesterdays through here

Wonder bestowed the seeker
humbly gives thanks for each day
through timespace ever growing
spirit the lens shows the way

*Charlotte Cramer*

## Tee

This beautiful woman
Gets all of my love
I think she was sent
From the heavens above
She has the face of angel
Eyes of blue
My love for her
Runs deep and true
She is all I can think of
Twenty four hours a day
To be with this woman
There has got to be a way
When I'm with her I feel
Like I've never felt before
Whenever I'm with her
I know I love her more
I love her so much
I sit and prey
That this beautiful woman
Feels the same way

*Daniel R. Healy*

## My Child

In-all-the-dictionaries
  Ever-compiled;
I'll-not-find-the-words-
  To-describe-
  My-child.

*Bob McGrath*

## Autumn Song

Aspen's golden standing tall
Gild the path at eventide
Dark shadows dance in windswept glee
And gently move in patterns wide

As leave in beauty rarely seen
Fall soft and gentle all around
A carpet laid in nature's gift
Of golden nuggets on the ground

Along the distant mountain rim
In deepest red proud maples peak
Throughout the dell a winding stream
In endless quest, its way to seek

In the raveled look of the woodland
Faced down with graying rails
Sweet birdsong heard in happiness
Lures us on to walk the trails

*Betty Cable Juelfs*

## Anita The Spartan

Dear Anita, Spartan tour guide
Glib in English, French, and Greek
Three tongues, all sharp
Did you know we laughed at you
When you said farmers
Were making manifestations
Blocking our road with tractors?
We at last decoded:  demonstrations.
You bragged about Sparta constantly
As if war with Athens had never ended
We listened with a smile
Till the last day when we were
Almost back to Athens.
Passing a beautiful beach
You said Yes, but not as beautiful
As the ocean near Sparta
We hooted, seeing the ocean on the map
Fifty miles from Sparta.
Finally you laughed at yourself
For this most outrageous chauvinism.

*Barbara R. DuBois*

## Promises

I promise you I will not
go back in time to take
the chances I have lost,
unearth the dreams I have
buried and thwart the
decisions I have made.
I promise you I will not
live in the past of what
might have been or dream
of the hopes of yesterday.
I promise you I will not
blame you for the pain.
Yet, I cannot promise that
I will not hold you in
my heart for always,
or that in the silence of
the moonlight, that
I'll not think of you again.

*Emily M. Jackson*

## Words of Inspiration

As you go forward with life
Go not only with your mind
But also your heart
For you know not what lies ahead
But you can always look back
To see where you came from
Though times might get tough
And you might be brought down
It takes a strong person
To pick themself up off the ground
So find new friends
And enjoy new experiences
But don't forget the old ones
Because like me
They'll always be
The one's who will listen
When you're ever in need

*David C. Fisher*

## Winter's Snow

Snow snow
Go on and blow
Fill the day
And fill the night
With a white
Beautiful sight
Winter, winter
Where are you?
All I see are skies of blue
Days so warm
Not a storm

*Christopher Sorenson*

## I Love America

America, the land of the free
  God has given to you and me,
We must fight to keep it this way
  Daily to God we must pray.

I love your country and mine
  As we serve our God, so Divine,
The "Land of the Brave", we enjoy
  So let's shout it, Ahoy!

I love this land of Liberty
  God provides for you and me,
So, to the red, white and blue
  Let's salute it with pride, be true.

Be proud always, to all
  Keep it free, don't let it fall,
To anyone who would delight
  To put us in such a terrible plight.

*Gladys Lumsden*

## Miracle Butterfly

The chrysalis broke and a new life is out.
"God's miracle," we shout
He changed from a color green
Now a color black and orange is seen.
One wing he lifts to try
Then the other moves straight to fly
What a joy it is to see
Him flying so brightly by me.
People sometimes come into life
When their chrysalis is broken
They become very, very out-spoken.

*Helen A. Nagy*

## In His Garden

In his garden
God's women are nurtured.

Our gifts cultivated by
the gentle Gardener's hand.

We take root in the rich,
fertile soil of His love,

And bloom in the season of
His favor, according to
"Father" nature's timetable.

His own arrangement,
we are the centerpiece of our homes.

Our fragrance rises to caress
the nostrils of our Creator

And He is pleased to pick
us one by one.

*Dee Griffith*

## 9 x 18 Feet

My world consist of bars of steel,
gray floor of cold concrete;
    It's contained within a cell block,
    which is nine by eighteen feet.
    To some it's called a "catwalk,"
but to me it's just a "space,"
    to indulge in daily functions.
    Such as eat, and sit, and pace.
    No easy chair or sofa,
no plush carpet 'neath my feet;
    the decor is, bench and table,
    for my nine by eighteen feet.
    I must admit, it's adequate,
even tho' it's cold and plain;
    my remarks: to the inventor,
    "you must have been insane!!!

*Clarke A. Watkins*

## A Christmas Message

C hristmas is for carols and
H oliday cheer,
R inging of bells
I ncredibly clear.
S tuffing the stocking with
T oys galore,
M istletoe, holly and much much more.
A nticipation and wonder as
S anta is due,

H ope love and laughter all sent to you.
O ur greetings come warmly to
L inger and last
I ntended for now and memories past.
D elivering this message to
A ll family and friends,
Y ou are thought of this
S eason, with love 'til it ends.

*Barbara A. Akehurst*

## Old Friends

As the neverending
Tide washes upon
The shores of time,
The memories
Of true friendships
Never fade.

*Jacqueline Ingersoll*

## Untitled

I stand in dew-wet green,
hair blowing, skirts whipping my ankles,
and I tread
past tricycles, and discarded shovels,
until, I find him, and with a
bear-like grasp, I rescue my
little sailor, yellow curls matted.
His treasures in pockets, tear-stained
face, pointing to scratched knee.
A peppermint, and several
tender kisses late, all is calm,
and I retreat, leaving him
to again tend his castle.

*Beth Ford*

## Untitled

Walking
hand in hand
upon the road,
with the sun at our backs,
and a song in our hearts.

You turn to me
smile,
I am so happy,
so content.
Your smile is the key
unlocking the door to my heart,
the journey has just begun....

*Deborah L. (Singer) Swiss*

## Song of Spring

Softly seeking, spring
has come alive.
Moon-light blossoms
touch the velvet sky.
Crescent gardens blushing
pink imply.
Rustic splendor to an
inspiring eye.
Oh, to see sweet gathered
petals, etched separately divine.
Denotes an order we
have failed to define
Love truly chose
its proper place in time.

*Catherine Robards*

## Which Way

He was a boy.
He started young and was quick to excel.
His chin up, his chest out.
He was quick to rebel.
He swallowed it all,
said he'd never give in.
But as he aged,
knew he "could" not win.
No way out -
He didn't know what to do!
He had been there too long,
it was all that he knew!!
You see, I am that he that I've
Tried to describe.
And it's me and alcohol
That's been taking this ride!
I've finally hit that big time low!!
I've murdered my pride!
"Which way do I go?"

*Charles D. Tucker Jr.*

## A New Dawn

A hearts once broken
Has now begun to mend,
An eternity of pain
Has now come to an end.
A world of grays
Now allows colors to blend,
The stony path once trod
Is left beyond the last bend.
A world once lost in chaos
I can now comprehend.

The dawning of a new love
Has washed away my tears.
The rising of a new hope
Has thrown away my fears.
A new desire to live life
Makes me look to the coming years,
Melodies of joy and ecstasy
Are sounds again my soul hears.
You are a love
My heart and soul endears.

*Daniel J. Lammers*

## The Difference

"Home is where the heart is"
Has so often been declared
But what if there is now...
No other heart to bare, share, care?

One lonely heart with none to care
To share the heart's emotions,
With so much love locked within
To give in complete devotion.

Where love once reigned
When hearts were shared
The familiar step along the hall
Familiar voice beyond recall.

Where no longer the anticipation
Of much loved voice to speak your name
Two arms reach out in love's invitation
Showing she is here again.

Such the joys to make house the home
And is love's epicenter
If that departs what remains
To continue love's adventure?

*Edwin P. Spivey*

## Friends

The blessings of our Lord above,
Have come to me through you.
The love I feel within my heart
I send to all of you.
I came to help the best I could.
To lighten your heavy load,
And in the return he gave to me.
Special friends with hearts of gold.
No matter what I do for you,
It could never quite compare,
Because these friends he gave to me
Are the friends that truly care.

*Claudia Rodrigues*

## Untitled

When life ends
there's nothing else
but the lonesome thoughts
of what could have been.

*David J. Gabanelli*

## Night

The night sweeps down,
To cover the small and sleepy town
The town of Hearlad's Down.
By Burnside Sound.
Night falls all around.
Surround the world in a shroud.

*Eric Ramsby*

## Mirrors

Tiny pieces of broken glass
Have held your image
throughout the past.
A fleeting glimpse of your inner soul
And of the ranging emotions to behold.
This self is not in public seen,
Only inside of your closest dream.
Some see you as a child all day
Yet, others know it for a role you play.
Always afraid to show what is inside
You live out a set of desperate lies;
Hiding from your own reflection
And on the run from everyone.

*Cin Griffiths*

## Eternity

When wind and wave and weather
Have worn the world away
And time and tide together
Too tired to rule the day
Have ceased their ceaseless motion
And no more ages keep
The roaring rolling ocean
Has rocked her self to sleep
When magic flashing fountains
Their last sweet sprays have thrust
And misty mighty mountains
Have crumbled into dust
When all the earthly mortals
Have withered and are gone
Serene on heavens portals
God's love will stand alone

*Fred Brown*

## A Magnetic Friend

Friends stick together for sure
Having a bond that's a rare treasure
Loyal and most trustworthy
Sharing love in good times, bad times
Listens and cares, rain or shine
The silence of the magic words,
amazingly can be heard.

Oh the simplicity of a friend
When in need, you can depend
On loving kindness that mends
The passing of time and days gone by
Brings special memories magnified
These golden remembrances never die.

The warmth and wealth of a friendship
Is a true blessing in companionship
It is a cherished, precious love
Sent from heaven above.
"Friends are like human magnets
Forgetting what they give,
they get back."

*Helen Lanham*

## Happy Valentine's Day to You

He loves you ...
He adores you ...
He's longing to hold you
right forevermore ...
Girl, why don't you make
that phone call away
and say you care ...
Give him a hint of what you're feelin'
right now ...
For he loves you,
he's going to purpose that special word
your longing to hear.....
Dreams fulfilled, dreams coming
true ...
Make that phone call away and say
Happy Valentine's Day to you.

*Evelyn H. Yadgar*

## "The Obstacle"

Who is this little boy?
He does not belong to me.
He cries, he whines, he wastes time,
and all for no love of me.

His mother she is beautiful.
Of her, I wish I could!
But he..., of him I've had my full.
He..., He is made of wood.

*Anthony Repici Jr.*

## The Personality Clash

She hated him,
He hated her.
She pinched his chin.
He pulled her curl.
She felt so blue.
He laughed with glee.
She was only two.
And he was only three.

*Dorthy L. Webb*

## From Slave To Servant

Once I was a slave to satan,
    He kept me in bonds and chains;
I was made to do his bidding
    And forced to give him my gains.

Then one day I met my Saviour,
    He paid sin's price for my soul;
He took away the bonds and chains-
    Set me free, and made me whole!

Now I am no longer a slave,
    And even death has no sting;
I am free to go, but I stay-
    I'm a servant of the King!

From wretched slave to a servant,
    He lifted me from the mire;
I'm free to go, yet I remain-
    For His will is my desire!

Free to go, yet I stay and serve,
    As He sends strength from above;
I dwell in His mercy and grace -
    Bound only by chains of love!

*Eileen Howell*

## "In The Beginning"

God made man and breathed into him life;
He realized he needed a helper
So he made for him a wife.

They lived together for many long years;
They shared their happiness
They shared their tears.

Life is a pathway we each one must trod;
It isn't so bad if you only trust God.

Ladies take care of your husbands,
And tell him to his face;
How much you love and appreciate him,
Because he would be hard to replace.

*Edith Wampler*

## Creator Of The Universe

He makes the clouds up in the sky,
He shapes each tuft and swirl,
He chooses colors and design
This artist who covers the world.

Purple and pink and yellow and gray,
Salmon and orange and blue,
White and fluffy, or gold and black,
He paints the clouds over you.

He makes the stars and sets them where
They're seen from near or far,
He places moons and suns above
To light up wherever you are.

Twinkle and sparkle and shine and glow,
Do it both day and night.
Glitter and glimmer and flicker and twirl
He makes such a glorious sight.

Stalks and stems, or legs and arms,
He creates all that is;
And when He's finished, in His arms
He holds us, because we are His.

*Jan Harris*

## My Love

We were married when we were young
He was loved more than he knows
He left me, and he hurt me so
I saw him with a girl or two
He didn't know he made me blue

The radio played our favorite song
When I heard it I cried all night long
He was my husband and I loved him so
I wish he hadn't gone away
One day I asked why he left

He said "I'm sorry I couldn't stay
I thought I was in love with another
But that didn't last
So I said to him fast
Let's give it another try
He replied "yes! This time I'll
stay till I die

*Betty J. Young*

## Why?

Running.
He was running.
He came up to a man.
Money?
NO!
The words flew from his
mouth like flames from a lighter.
The running man sat.
I pressed my nose against the window.
I wanted to cry.
I stopped myself.
Why?
Why doesn't anybody care?
I feel his pain.
I care.
They won't do anything.
Let me help him!
Do
Something.
Why?

*Brian Ziff*

## Charles B. Schockey

He took his life,
He went away,
I kept asking,
why he didn't stay.

He meant so much to me,
I didn't understand,
Why he didn't ask for help,
I would have held out my hand,

It's been a year,
and all forgotten,
of course not for me,
I cry quite often,

He was easy to talk to,
A really great friend,
and all of a sudden,
It came to an end,

The day he was gone,
I felt nothing but pain,
I thought that soon,
I would be going insane.

My friends helped me through,
And to them I say,
Thank you so much,
for that awful day.

*Carrie Pontius*

## "Your Sweet Love"

When I go through the
toughest of times,
Your sweet love is always near,
Comforting all my tears
that I cry.

As time passes by,
Your sweet love continues
to warm my heart,
Like the sun shining high
in the big blue sky.

My dear, your sweet love
Will be my treasure,
Everlasting in my life.

*James C. Hovis*

## Janice Lee Ann

One day I had a little girl
her names was Janice Lee
she was the sweets little thing
that you ever did see.

I didn't have her very long
God wanted her you see.
But, oh! how my heart does long
for my little Janice Lee.

Our dear Lord sitting on his throne
gazes down on one sweet face,
'tis a little angel standing there
waiting for her place.

Now the saints all gather round her
with eager arms lift her to him
he places her so everyone can see
his favorite is angel Janice Lee.

*Helen Legassie*

## Once

In the beginning,
Her song was sweet,
But now, in the end,
She suffers from defeat.

Her beauty once graced,
The pictures of my mind,
But now, in the end,
She has yet to unwind.

Her heart was once loving,
Very big and strong.
But now, in the end,
She knows not right from wrong.

She was once a recourse,
And would always listen,
But now, in the end,
Her ideas all but glisten.

In her mind,
I once found love,
But now, in the end,
She does not and will not stand above.

*Erica Powell*

## A Smooth Tongue

Her tongue is smooth as polished glass;
　Her voice is soft and sweet.
But, great care must be exercised
　In whate'er you repeat.

She has puppets that she uses
　To mimic every word.
Now, when her stories are passed on,
　You'd think 'twas truth you'd heard.

'Tis easy, though, to recognize
　The fables and the facts.
Fables stir up a lot of dust;
　While truth controls our acts.

*James M. Wynn*

## Football

Football,
a contact sport,
maybe too rough for some,
but for others it's not enough.
My sport.

*Justin Myrick*

## My Grandpa

My Grandpa means the world to me.
He's just as friendly and kind
　as he can be.
He helps me when I'm feeling down
　and puts a smile on my face
　instead of a frown.
He's the best friend I have to show.
　and he loves everyone he knows.
As a young man he fought for his
　country.
　So his grandson could live in the
　"Land of the Free."
He is courageous, smart and kind.
　No greater grandpa you will find.
GOD gave me the best Grandpa there
　could be.
When they finally have to bury him,
　they'll take a part of me!

*Chris Godwin*

## I'm Not Even There

She comes home and walks in the door,
He's right there behind,
And I'm not even there.

The room is filled with music
And the music's playing here,
I'm not even there.

There are three of us,
Always fighting,
I'm not even there.

She doesn't care
When he's around,
And I wish I was there.

Many things come and go,
And I wish I were there.

*Carrie Ann Schutz*

## Inside of You

Inside of you,
Hidden within,
Are joys and hurts
Of where you have been.

There are unsolved mysteries
And there are secrets too;
They are all locked up
On the inside of you.

Inside of you
Are God's hidden treasures,
Inside of you
Is God's full measure.

There is untapped potential
That you could never dream,
Love, joy and peace
Like you have never seen.

Inside of you
Is God's very best,
Love, joy and peace
And sweet, sweet, rest.

*Dwarline Jean Rutherford*

## A Gift Worth Fighting For

As we contemplate the world's
horrible realities without being
turned to stone.  Since sweets
and beauties must themselves
forsake and die as fast as they
see others grow.  They died
of a rose in aromatic pain,
let the children go in peace as
cosmic orphans, for this brute
and harsh world is no place
like home.

*Julio E. Castillo Jr.*

## Untitled

I often wonder
how life would have been
with you by my side
the possibilities were endless

We were such a great team
when you were a live
nothing could keep us apart

Everything we did
we did for each other
with unconditional love
no question asked

Now that you're gone
and in a better place
I often wonder
how life would have been

*Daphne McNulty*

## Snappy Answers To Stupid Questions

Question:
  How was your week-end?
  Where did you go?
  What is the number for 9-1-1?
  And is that a carnival dog
    in the sky?

Answer:
  My week-end was fine
  Since when did you care
  The number is 9-1-1
  And no that is superman making
    love to a fly

*Jose Hernandez*

The corner store
Huddled round
The corner poor.
The heat,
Cold.
The clothes,
Old.
Stories told
Of days gone bye,
Stomach's filled
With hate and lies,
Life of living
Cheating fear,
One foul turn
Wound up here.
The corner of the year.

*Bryan Hurst*

## Untarnished

I look into your eyes of aquamarine
I am lost in their beauty
I feel the crashing of the ocean waves
I dare to hope it's not a dream.

I kiss your lips formed by rose petals
I touch your skin of silk
I feel joy in your beautiful perfection
I dare to hope the dream comes true.

I see rays of golden sunshine
In the highlights of your hair
In the rich warm glow of your skin
I dare to hope you're still mine.

You speak words of love
With your voice mellow and strong
I feel so loved and cherished
I dare to be sure.

I feel pride because of your dignity
The character in your finely chiseled
features
You reach out and touch my hand
I dare to hope it's forever.

*Catherine G. Wiley*

## Perfect Notice

i am yours
i am one with your
slice of heaven
that crackles under
your breath

i am your soapbox derby queen
i am loud

i wish i could keep you running
i wish i could keep you coming

crutch speech
slip reach
I am

below the awning
a couple is sunning

even moments,
perfect notice...

lotus lotus lotus

*Jessica Wells*

## An Invitation

I believe in inspiration
I believe in mystery
Set free your imagination
Take a wild walk with me

Look again at those around you
Stone cold eyes and hearts of steel
See in my eyes freedom has found you
My heart is warm, and yours will heal

Walk with me, or you will chase me
I can fly beyond the stars
Don't try to hold me just embrace me
Know me, for what I am you are

*Carisa Battin*

## Inside My Mother's Womb

Inside my mother's womb
I can do no harm
I can see no evil
I can hear no violence

I can feel the love of
my mother's hand
and I know I can always
count on her
I can see all this inside my
mother's womb

But no matter if I'm out
of my mother's womb
I know she'll always keep
me safe.
She'll never let anything happen
to me
As long as I'm ...
Inside my mother's womb

*Erana Hodges*

As I walk
I can feel the bright
Searing sun on my face
I can see the beautiful
Blue sky with patches of white
Above me
I listen to the birds sing
And watch the ducks
Swim thru the water
and I'm thankful to God
That I'm here to
Witness such a beautiful day
Of His Creation
Thank Him that I can be out
2 enjoy it
And then I thank Him for u
And I wonder when we'll
Be sharing such beautiful days
Like this one
Together

*Erika M. Bryant*

## Gently Missing

I miss you gently.
I can miss you gently because I know
that I will be with you again shortly.
I will feel you around me.
Knowing this I can miss you gently.
But, should my time with you be torn
from me,
I would miss you with a pain that knows
no gentleness.

*Gayle F. Stowe*

## My Am

Although my am
Ain't worth a damn
There's a me
I hope to be
Who is!

*Geraldine R. Carter*

## Little One

You start inside, so small and weak
I cannot tell you're there.
Your beginning to form hands and feet,
your nose, your eyes, your hair.
And soon time goes and I can feel
A kick, a turn, a cry.
Your dad and I wait patiently
as months and months go by,
and suddenly the time has come
for our little one to appear
I gladly take the task at hand
the excitement and the fear,
and all at once you're here with me
a perfect little one
I can't believe how I am blessed
I have a little son.

*Diane Cioffi*

## Untitled

Since we broke up
I can't stop thinking about you
I'm like a long lost pup.
Wondering around the zoo.
I really wish we could get together
But I guess my wish will never come true
the only thing I'd like to say
is I was falling in love with you.

*Becky Leonard*

## Way Back When

Now I'm here all alone
I close my eyes and go back home
where I was as I was raised
way back when, the good old days
though I'm young, I reminisce
and think of all the things I miss
running from the water hose
wearing my sisters clothes
making food out of moss and dirt
tie dying a plain old shirt
washing cars with my cousin Brian
watching all the airplanes flying
catching all the lightning bugs
giving pappy great big hugs
listening to grown ups talk
coloring the sidewalk
hear the bells of the ice cream man
making voices in the fan
these are things that I did
when I was a little kid.

*Amy Arnold*

## Which Way Should I Go?

Left or right?
I don't know.
Where ever I go, nothing left.
But sadness and greed
Where should I go?
People crave for love, but how to give,
They don't know.
I do need love to:  Where should I go?
I don't know.
What is left?
I better go.

*Julianna Forest*

## The Cross that Crowns Forever

The one who did come
I dreamed about this man
I dreamed about perfection
...in a son...and, in a plan.

I dreamed about souls
I dreamed about redemption
I dreamed about sins
all covered by Salvation.

I dreamed about a crown
I dreamed about submission
OH!  He wouldn't come down
but, yielded to His condition.

I dreamed about Heaven
I dreamed about love
I dreamed of a cross
made beautiful by the blood.

I dreamed of Eternity
I dreamed of a Saviour
touched by a cross
the cross that crowns FOREVER.

*Helen Roark*

## Solitaire

I waken a meaningless forlorn day
I fall asleep for no reason
Until the cold defeats my body at dawn
Especially during the winter season.

The family I love is gone
There is no lover to understand
The job, the food I eat are gone
Will anybody hold my hand.

Society, a game of solitaire
I fight for my life everyday
I walk alone habitually through the park
This day is no different from yesterday.

Tomorrow hell facilitates life
It is a blessing, nothing less
I live a life of solitaire,
For I am homeless.

*Charles C. Barowicz*

## Fear

Other people fear of death.
I fear of beauty.
For beauty comes with pain
Like the inseparable twin.
Beauty comes with a dagger
To pierce one's soul.
Beauty comes with her "weight of glory",
To break the hearts of us all.
I fear thee, beauty
Yet I welcome thee!

*Celia Yu*

## The World

I don't believe the old saying that
"love makes the world go round"
I think violence and hatred and
anger is what makes it spin
Why do I think this - you ask
because there is twice as much
of it in the world.

*Jennifer Caudill*

## Wake Up!

Looking into the hazy forest,
I feel its strengthening power.
My watch melts off my wrist.
Halting time freezing the hour.
Two steps I'm deep inside,
it knows I'm here.
The trees create a path,
to bring me nearer.
The Master summons me,
I beckon the call.
The world beneath him,
he offers all.
When standing before him
my head falls low.
Submitting to the power,
I help it grow.
The gift is immortality,
or curse as we shall see.
Lost in reality,
I can't be me.

*Julio Galarza*

## Reflections

I look far into the distance,
I feel you in the night.
The reflections of your presence,
In the shimmering horizons light.

I know you're out here with me,
I hear your song of dreams.
It echoes through the forests,
And flows down every stream.

Every night you're closer,
I sense it in the air.
And every day when you're away,
I wish that you were there.

*Dan K. Tibbitts*

## Together

I hear your breath so close to me.
I feel your soft, smooth lips
Touch my lips.
Together we, we are in love.
Love and peace
We cannot be broken apart.
The love of us,
Together is not enough.
With peace
We are united together.
We love each other dear.
We are one together.

*Crystal Spracklen*

## With God With You

I caught the wind
I felt you near
I caught the dew
And it was you
I searched and found you
Oh, that I could hold the wind
And night's stars
I walked on mountain tops
On life's roads
Reaching for the heights
Shooting for the stars
I caught them
I have them
With God
With you

*Bess H. Haney*

## A Tribute

Though steep is the path
I follow today, the foot prints
of time will show me the way.
For many have traveled a
similar road and carried an
equal or heavier load
no, trouble I face are new
to this earth.  The route has
been charted.  The road has been
paved by other who were brave
their steps never faltered,
nor courage grew dim for they
trusted the Lord and let him lead them.
If my faith remain stead
fast and true.  God will guide
and protect in all I do.
Yes, I'm grateful for God's
guiding love and grateful
for the life (dear husband)
we have known and loved.

*Ellen Holmes Crawford*

## One Misty Morning

One misty morning
I found a child alone.
One misty morning
No one to call his own.
One misty morning
I found him by the bay.
One misty morning
He shall be mine today.
One misty morning
He now has a home
One misty morning
and someone to call his own!

*Christina Fox*

## My Best Friend

Thank you Lord for loving me
I give all my praise to Thee
The gift of life to us you gave
A life to take beyond the grave

You ride the clouds and walk the wind
I know that grace to me you send
You are so close and yet so far
And stand so tall above the stars

I feel such love when you attend
No greater one has ever been
I wait upon you my best friend
I praise your name my Lord Amen.

*Fannie Logan*

## All Alone

I look up at the sky,
I see birds flying high,
It's getting ready to snow,
All my friends have to go,
I'm high on the hill,
Standing very still,
I'm all alone,
Feel like I'm in a different zone,
The wind in my hair,
The snow in my eyes.

*Jeremy D. Bettis*

## Chicken!

It flies effortlessly
Carrying its human cargo,
Among them me.
Why must I agonize?

*Jean T. Hughes*

## My Friend Jewel

When I was just a little girl,
I had a friend, so dear,
She lived just down the block from me,
A little older, maybe a year.

I didn't have a pair of skates,
But she would share with me,
Her on one and me on the other,
Or she would borrow her brother's, Dee

Sometimes I'd have to run away,
Then I'd get a spanking, hard,
But I'd take almost anything,
To play in her front yard.

Now we're many miles apart,
Senior citizens and getting gray
What I'd give to turn back the years
And could play with her today.

*Frances Terry-Brandon*

## The Wind Blows

The wind blows
I know I hear my name
Who is calling me in the wind
Is it you my friend
I know I hear a voice
I must know that tune
For I have heard it before
Was it the Lord who calls
Before I thought it was you
My angel who brought me fourth
To this world we call existences
I know you have a hold on me
In the wind it echoes my name
I shall find you,
I thought it was you calling me,
I know it is him sending me your way
Until we meet again
I'll send my love
Through the wind.

*Darlene Judge*

## Orpheus

He sleeps the long sleep, my brother —
I know that sleep, the cold embrace
Of death, the snap of icy breath,
Dread secret of the human race.
He sleeps that sleep, and I remain
Reclaimed, that place is not my place,
At least not yet.  As in a dream
I see the phantom of his face.
He dreams the long dream, my brother,
Transported to another place,
A traveller, Marco Polo
Of the shadows, an empty space.
He dreams that dream, and I remain
Transfixed, having not long retraced
My steps from that dim underworld,
I know that dream, I know that place.

*George N. Braman*

## When The Sun Goes Down

When the sun goes down
I know you'll be waiting there for me
To comfort me once again
Through all eternity

When it's time for me to go
You'll be there to see me through
To ease the pains and fears
Of letting me go

Safe in your arms once more
Hand in hand together we shall go
Never to walk alone again
We'll start a life that's free

Full of hope, love and peace
For those that we have left behind
To greet the sun again
As it goes up once more.

*Helen V. Ignacio*

## Untitled

I needed you once.
I leaned to you for strength.
Defiance is not easily undergone
And individuality not easy alone.
I clung to you at night
with the fear of somebody being alone,
but now I've grown,
or shrunk,
(I don't think it matters which)
And you prove to me now useless.

I'm proud to stand atop the hill alone-
let them look to me in awe
or curses-
let them send me to Hell.
Dress as I choose and act to lose.
I'm proud enough for me now
and your shoulder is a crutch
I'd sooner not touch.

*Jason Oldham*

## Hearing My Master's Voice

In the stillness of the night
I listen to my Master's voice
This time we spend together
Is a time in which we both rejoice.

He teaches me His wisdom
At a time of no distractions,
He fills me with His love and care,
And to me, brings gentle satisfaction.

The quiet time we spend alone
We cherish - oh, so great,
I know I'm walking in His Kingdom,
He's opened wide the gate.

I hear his voice much clearer
In the still and dark of night,
I walk and talk and pray with Him
He makes everything seem right.

All the words that I have written
Of his wisdom and his love,
In the stillness and the darkness,
He has sent me from above.

*Esther G. Underwood*

## Is Love Real

I say out loud.
I look and see a person that's me
I am lost I can't recall my name
I feel no pain
Yet I cry with a cry
Who am I
I don't remember
What it was this thing
called love
Is it real
What is this that I feel
sometimes I feel something within
I can't replace the feelings I trace
For I'm feeling blue.
I wish I knew
If my feelings are true
Just one answer
Someone say
For my heart aches everyday
I ask is love real

### *Juliana M. Burns*

## Wings of Love

Through the window,
I look to see
A fluttering brown sparrow land in a tree.
Upon a branch
Does a fancifully dance like thee
After which I knew it had come by as you
For me.
Oh sparrow, brown sparrow,
Come rest on my knee,
Bring me again
The love song of he!

### *Anne Moore*

## Among The Trees

Among the trees
I love-love thee
Birds and bees
Singing sweet melodies
glove - love to me
Among the trees
Makes my life complete
In the brown leaves
Clinging to my feet
In the morning air
Will be there
Among the trees
The red roses grow
Far me there
The birds and bees
Sing sweet melodies
Of love-love to me
Now and then
I wait and see
Among the trees

### *Ethel Sebastian*

## Untitled

There once was a lady quite fat.
Who had a little black cat.
Until one day,
There he lay,
Under the place where she sat!

### *Carol Bender*

## Silhouette

Even tho, I met you a year ago.
I met you by sight.
I've failed to introduce myself.
Because you really don't know
how bright you shine.
Finally a year had passed.
I still don't know you.
How can one describe one star
among stars?
When I've not glimpsed you face.
But finally, our eyes twinkled
and met to say, "hello."
Hello, my shiny star.

### *Elizabeth Perkins*

## To Know

To know me,
  I must know You;
To know love,
  I must know hate;
To know hate,
  I must seek peace;
To find peace,
  I must feel storms;
To feel storms,
  I treasure joys;
To treasure joys,
  I give thanks.
To know life,
  I must know death;
In knowing death,
  I find Life.
In finding Life,
  I know me.

### *Beverley W. Wicks*

## Untitled

In the seat in the heat
  I no you are very neat

In the morning in the noon
  I hope I see you very soon

In the sun in the cloud
  I hope you speak very loud

In the front at the back
  you surely look like a sack

If your short if your tall
  I hope you don't hit the wall

### *Barbara Bell*

## Comrade Of Heart

I know you,
I reflect life from you
through aged shields - of veils,
your sorrows echo through.
You think that I can't see your pain,
nor bleed upon your lies,
transparent are your weeping lids,
though smiles fill your eyes.
'Tis you, I know your rage with fate
and all the dreams therein.
Through thick of skin we sometimes seem,
our shield from pain is thin.
Within your reach, you have the gift,
you need not look too far.
Comrade of heart, look to thy face,
'tis all of what you are.

### *Georgia Lynn Munson*

## First Separation

When I leave home
I run back into my mother's arms,
hoping this moment will never end.

Watching me, you know I cry,
you wave a kiss to say goodbye.
I can't stop this pain inside myself.

All I am
is a child with promises.
All I have
are miles full of promises of home.

If only I could stay with you.
My train moves on, you're gone from view.
Now I must wait until it's over.

Days will pass, your words to me,
it seems so long; eternity,
but I must wait until it's over.

### *Adam Alexander*

## Untitled

Once upon a rainbow day
I saw the sky cry blue
And where the colored raindrops
fell a rose did bloom
with petals made of satin
And a color never dreamed
And to this day the rose
is beauty
In a land called fantasy

### *Dara Lee Martin*

## Never Letting Go

Whenever I look at you
I see all the things I always
wished in someone...

But never thought I would find them
It seems to me that finding
a person, who could hold all
those wonderful things
was just a crazy dream...

And then after I
got to know you
I found those things in you
That I couldn't ever dream of having...
I thought never existed...

And now that I have them
I know I could never do without them
or without you, my true love...
Now I know to NEVER LET YOU GO...

### *Carmen M. Robles*

## Sparkle, My Pig

I have a pig named Sparkle
He's very fond of the mud
I have a pig named Sparkle
He scratches up against the gate
I have a pig named Sparkle
He bites my sister's butt

### *Jessica Glade*

## Immobilized By Love

I see reflections on the water.
I see reflections of the sky.
As I sit and ponder,
I have to wonder why.

Why is love so elusive?
Why are you not the one?
Why is the only one I love,
someone whose love for me is none?

What I can't have more than friendship,
from feelings so intense,
leaves this love so deep inside me,
in a fog so dense.

A fog that covers all reflections,
that blocks the water from the sky.
A fog that stands so still between us,
and leaves me with no place to fly.

**Jamie Baker-Parsons**

## My Best Friend

Oh, sweet memories of days gone by
I sit and think
But yet I cry.

Why has life dealt this terrible card
It is suppose to be easy
Not this hard.

There's a void, an empty space
At home, at church, at school
In every place.

I guess his work on earth was done
But to so many
It had just begun.

We are not to question, or even doubt
"His" great plan or what it's about.

How can I say good-bye to you
Unfinished dreams
Are left to do.

Let's not think that this is the end
You'll always be
My best friend.

**Donna Lucas**

## No Escape

The fan oscillates
I sit squinting at the afternoon
the willow still hangs
over the porch
where you left me standing
cut off
like a diseased arm
the winter was blank
in the spring I dug and planted
trying to get the taste of you
out of my mouth
But there you are
standing in front of me
I can't escape
a bug in a mason jar

**Eleanor Williams**

## The Man Next Door

I see you in the morning
I sleep with you at night
I feel so all alone, when I
lie to sleep at night, for there
is no holding you throughout
the night.
If I only got to hold you,
the moon would shine so bright
so, until the two shall meet,
the man next door I still shall be.

**Barbara Ovens**

## You Remain

I cannot forget you
I still can see your face
The way you looked into my eyes
Your touch and your embrace

My heart now lies here broken
With no hope that it will mend
You want no part of my life
Not even as my friend

My loneliness grows daily
The emptiness inside
The love I want to show you
Once again denied

But in my heart you're with me
No need for me to grieve
In my dreams you come to me
And promise you won't leave

For you I'll cry no more
No more tears to shed
We'll always be together
If only in my head

**Jessica Salyers Bacon**

## Mirror

You say, "I don't understand"
I tell you
words fall out
unconsciously heard
I see me

**Irene M. Pronschinske**

## Suicide

The first time I saw you,
I thought you could be mine.
I kept my eye on you all the time,
I thought you were something special.
But when I got to know you,
my whole view changed,
you turned out to be a real snob.
When I think of how I loved you,
I feel like suicide.
You ripped my heart out,
it's like you didn't even care.
You made me feel like dirt,
that's why I took this dare.
   Suicide

**Christian Kimmel**

## Nostalgia

Today I rode Nostalgia
I traveled across
the plains of the mind
to where we lay in the moss.

Our laughter was like
a gurgling brook
and I loved you
in this wooded nook.

As time passed
we drifted apart.
I have often wished
to go back to the start.

Can we bring back
what we thought would last?
Or is it lost forever
somewhere in the past?

**Carol J. Monaghan**

## Why

The past is behind me.
I want to forget,
but the memories still stay
vividly in my mind.

The present is here.
I'll live for today,
trying to make it through,
somehow, someway.

The future will come.
What's in store for me?
Will it be bright,
or will it fade away
like memories?

**Jennifer Langholz**

## Seeing You

Every day I know you
   I want to know you more.
Your thoughts and talents amaze me
   Cause my mind to soar.

I try to use words to describe
   The beautiful man you are to me
But others may never realize
   Things the eyes of love can see.

With you I see the thoughtfulness.
   The tenderness you try to hide.
While others may see the macho man
   I see the loving side.

It's so easy to get used to you
   It's good to have you around.
If you were measured in decibels
   You would be the ultimate sound.

The sound my heart keeps hearing
   When I try so hard to sleep.
Is the sound your heart is sending
   And mine is trying to keep.

If love had a face.  It would be yours

**Evelyn Garrison**

## My Quest

I want to write something beautiful
I want to sail away
Upon these very pages I write
To a most unusual day
A day where only I can glide
Upon my souls own wings
Within these pages tears I've cried
Where my own sorrow sings.

Over the mountains of my mind
And to the seas I'll go
My wings will carry me far to find
A place I need to know
This place that I can call my own
Where my spirit is truly free
I'll find the peace that I have sown
And give some back to me.

*Cammie L. Hall*

## Untitled

June twenty-sixth,
I was brought to life;
by an unfaithful husband,
and an endless forgiving wife.

At the age of six,
my father said goodbye;
to me, my mom, and my brother,
leaving us there to cry.

Alone but determined,
our mom was our dad;
giving us her best,
because that's all she had.

Every hard earned penny,
was spent to create a smile;
the enjoyment of her children,
was definitely worth her while.

She survived as a woman,
and provided as a mother;
she painted our hearts with gold,
and this is why we love her.

*Jeny Counter*

## Beside A Stream

Beside a Stream
I watch my life flow.
Over boulders
Around trees,
But most important...still flowing.

Quiet, contemplating
Waiting, ever silent,
The stream flows on
Just as my life.
Waiting for someone like you
To share it with.

*Bonnie Garcia*

## Untitled

How kind our Father was
In giving us the time of day:
Giving sights precious gift,
A way, to nature's paradise.

How kind of Father too -
To create such lovely blue skies -
Sparing us, for a time,
Infinities twinkling eyes!

*Ed Rowland*

## Over the Mountain

Over the tall grassy green mountain
I wonder is there a cruel place
or a glorious place.
   I do not know whether to climb
the grassy green mountain or stay to
never find out!
   Do I stay or do I climb?
If there is a cruel place I do
not want to get hurt, but if there
is a good place I won't have to
worry.
   I guess I shall never really
know what is over the mountain

*Jessica Carlo*

## Lily

The sky is perfect blue;
I would have it no other hue.
The grass is lovely green;
Lord, You've seen — to everything.

Lily is dazzling in her dress!
I've considered her and —
Yes, I'm quite impressed.

If You so arrayed the lowly weed,
How much more will You
Tend to — my every need!

*Daisy Onate Sohne*

## Love Again?

   You would come with a different face,
If I would love again;
   In just one moment there you would be
Standing right in front of me;
   I still faintly trace memories
Of things I remember and cherish well.
   If you spoke to me I even know
What you would tell;
   The sound,
The warm feeling,
   When love matters most.
There's so much to hear
   When love is near,
Around you, a part of you
   Flowing and new;
It would be the same,
   Only you'd have a different name.
Love becomes love,
   Stays awhile,
Lingers, and always..waits.

*Betty Reining*

## Part Of Me

Part of me, your gone now
I'm so sorry, please forgive me,
Part of me, I didn't care,
I was blind, you deserved more
Part of me, I was scared,
I was alone, I was wrong
Part of me, I hurt you,
I hurt myself, you didn't live long
Part of me, I touched you,
You touched me, I should of held on.
Part of me, your gone now,
I'm sorry, please forgive me.
I love you.

*Jennifer Buchta*

## Love?

Do I love you? I don't know.
If joy is love, then maybe so.
I know you made the morning sun
Shine brighter than it's ever done,
And roses grow in frozen ground,
And music stir the night with sound,
And rainbows follow every storm,
And me feel warm...

But if love's joy, then why this pain
This hopeless hunger once again
To hear your voice and touch your hand?
This silent screaming in my brain
That can't forget or understand,
And will no longer trust or blame,
But waits in wasted, wordless prayer
To see you there?

Or is love strength to carry on,
To realize you're really gone,
And keep the best of what I miss?
I think love's all of this.

*Carol A. Taylor*

## Retaliation

Would you be discontented
if the smoke filled sky said to you,
"I've decided to disintegrate
I'll take no more abuse from  you."
Would you be discontented
if the mud brown sea, once blue,
said, "I've decided to evaporate
you've made me garbage stew."
Would you be discontented
if mother nature said, "Goodbye.
Your money will not help you now
there's nothing left to buy
the poisoned air will choke you soon
so just sit there and cry
the dollar sign within your mind
was the price for which you sold your world
Goodbye."

*Frank R. Kowalski*

## "A Better World"

Wouldn't it be great
If the world wasn't full of hate

If the color of our skin
Wasn't important as the person within

If people helped one another
For everyone is our brother

If people wouldn't fight
And instead they'd unite

If people would stop being greedy
And instead they'd help the needy

If violence would be put to an end
Then everyone would be our friend

If the world will become a better place,
And love will be present in every face

All this can come true
How? Well that's up to you!

*Bette Anne Yap*

## My Advice

If you won't worry about yesterday
If you won't care about the morrow.
If you won't fret about the way.
Someone looks at you to stay
"With you, I don't want to play"

If you won't regret,
The things you've done;
and if you won't fret,
But look towards the sun
At the man in the sky.

Don't ask him the cause,
But without a tear in your eye
Without any pause
Ask him to show
you which way to go.

After you've been told
And you know how to find
That city with streets of gold
Then, my friend, you will have PEACE OF
MIND.

*James R. Densman*

## Distance

Distance between us is long and wide
I'm always hoping to reach your side
The undeniable chemistry is thither
Your touch invariably makes me quiver

The reflections of you make me smile
Are you willing to try the extra mile
Retort and see
What your destiny could be

*Cheryl T. Gervais*

## Delicious Spaghetti

My name is spaghetti
I'm delicious
When it's dinner time
I drop from the tips of a fork
And land on top of your plate
So be ready to eat me!

When you do
Just don't slurp me down
I despise that!
Everything else you do to me
Is fine

*Brett Rehfeld*

## Untitled

You may add this poem, to your book,
I'm honored that you like my work.

For any talent, that comes through,
The inspiration comes from you.

If I am able, to write more,
You know it's you, I'm writing for.

All I need, for you to say,
Is write me something, every day.

The words come easy, that is true,
When I write, I write for you.

You are the one, I'll try to please,
When I write, my masterpiece.

*Don Vigue*

## Ms. Marsil

Ms. Marsil,
I'm leaving for my hometown
I know I should leave quietly
Crying for you let me down.

I wonder how much you gained
For lying to me all this time
You've made me unhappy
What a shame! What a crime!

You can even say it was my fault
But it was your fault too
For no one would ever say
I couldn't fall in love with you.

Then, why didn't you tell me
You had a whole bunch of men
Who met you after dinner, or work
God knows when.

Listen, perverse Ms. Marsil
I'm really going back to my hometown
Keep meeting those who cheat you
Until the guilty one will be unknown.

*Jovelino Dos Santos*

## 1990's?

Trying to be strong
In a time of weakness
A shakable reality
Questioning past and present
With an unthinkable,
Unimaginable future.
Is it sickness?
The rotting care of the soul
As piece by piece by piece
Torn off
For a gratification;
A saneness.
Or is it society?
Ravaged by desires
Meritable wants and costly needs
Ripped apart by anger
Searching for an understandable meaning
A dying purpose
Hitting an unbearable low
Reaching for an unsurmountable high.

*Jamie Stinger*

## Immortality, Of A Sort

Bury me not too deep.
In a wooden chest.
And place a pine cone,
Upon my breast.

So that back to earth.
I may soon return.
And youth a lesson,
From me may learn.

That when one leaves,
This earthly strife,
He is not dead,
Who gives birth to life.

*John A. Wilson*

## Patricia's Symphony

This life I have created
in concert with my love,
is the most astounding gift
a Symphony from above.

The Melody is mine to write
I pray God guides my hand
to mold this new and precious life
into a song that's grand.

Each movement is of great import
indeed each note as well
and as the Guest Conductor
my Baton directs each swell
of the Music of the Master
played by woodwind, harp, and bell.

And if at times the symbols crash
or drums their thunder roll,
may He help me to remember
His Lullaby in my soul.

*JoAnn Martin*

## Caged

My little canary is singing
In his tiny cage,
With abandon and artistry
As if it were a stage.

There's pathos in his singing there
Day after day
That makes me start to open the door
and let him fly away.

But sound reason comes to tell me
His idle wings aren't strong,
And some cat would end forever
His clear sweet song.

Does he long for the door to open,
The bears dissolve away?
Does he dream of a utopian freedom
That may be his some day?

I cannot know for when I ask him
He lifts his downy throat
And all that comes to my listening ears
Is a brave and perfect note.

*Janice D. Onion*

## Untitled

Where does my heart lie
In mind fields of sun blinded love
Amid flowers trampled yet still exuding
Perfumes so sweet of memories
Captured somehow today again in meeting
Lingering still and there as before
Yet not understanding why changes are so
Apparent and final feeling.

*Elizabeth Anne Anderson*

## Look For It

Look to the past for
What your heart seeks,

Look way back,
Then way, way back.

If you don't find it,
Then look here,

Where eternity meets now.

*Gregory J. Maeder*

## Untitled

Seeing her face searing deep
in my mind.
I'll never forget she was so unkind.
Now trapped in death for all to
see, an accident fell unto me.
Before the end there was much
joy, how could she treat me
like a child's toy?
I could not see her stealthy
way, it seemed to me she'd
always stay.
Yet soon the end, it came
along, as she had said I'd
been all wrong.
She took my heart and ran
it through, watch out my
friend she'll come for you...

*Jeffrey A. McMahon*

## Love Plays Its Game

I see your reflection in my dreams.
In my thoughts, your voice is clear.
In your eyes, I found love.
Now when I need you, love plays its game.

It seems like yesterday you were here.
In your arms I felt so safe.
In your eyes, I found love.
Now when I need you, love plays it game.

I'm feeling this emptiness in my heart.
A space only your touch can fill.
In your eyes, I found love.
Now when I need you, love plays its game.

*Julie and Russ Waha*

## President F.D.R.

The date was April twelveth
In nineteen forty-five
When we received the tragic word
That our president had died.
The sky was angry at his death
It roared and lit up bright
And after this was over
It rained with all its might
His death has caused a dark cloud
One that will always be
For the world has lost a great man
A friend to all was he.

*Joyce McPherson*

## A Thousand Deaths

I have suffered a thousand deaths
In one moment of hate
And I've been reborn a hundred times
Because of careless fate

Life has won the battle again
Over death's evil grasp
I sometimes wish I could sink to hell
And leave life's unending task

The world has torn me inside out
With the vengeance of her greed
But I have sewn the pieces back
When I should have let them bleed

Let me sleep a million years
In sweet death's grip
For I've been awake far too long
Traveling life's wayward trip.

*Brandy Bennett*

## Give Thanks for Liberty

Give thanks for liberty
In our great land.
Let's preserve it
And deserve it.
May our liberties never be banned
For free speaking,
For religion,
For our other liberties,
Thank God for all of them
In our great land.
Thanks be for liberty
In our homeland.

*Irene Rector*

## The Eyewitness

There are many eyes of nature
In some which we do see,
From the knots onto the trees
To the stinger on a bee.
For they are watching what we do,
"So please don't hurt the land."
From the everglades and mountains,
To the footprints in the sand.
For they are watching every step
And every breath we take,
From every creature we disturb,
To every branch we break.
So let us surrender and listen,
To nature's only task,
And that is the only thing from us,
That nature does even ask.

*Dawn Marie Ingraham*

## The Promise

Safe and warm, but restless
    In the cabin,
I stir the fire, then steal a
    Glance outside.

The shimmering snow reflecting
    Ice blue sky
Embraces rabbit tracks and
    Man-made hollows.

The icicles like daggers
    Pierce the cold
Above the pane with threat to
    Slash my view.

I've seen this scene a thousand
    Times or more,
But never cease to marvel
    At spring's promise

When all snow-tipped tree tops
    Become sun-kissed,
And earth begins to swallow
    Winter's art.

*Gloria Peabody Gallagher*

## Kind Words Are Like Honey

Kind words are like honey,
    so sweet to the taste.
They make the day sunny.
    They stick like a paste.

*James I. Morgan*

## Morning Glory

Look to the east
In the early spring morning
When first light shines past
The dew covered awning

The suns new position
Gives bright warming pardon
Long fingers of pearl
Touch deep in the garden

Bolder each day
The rise marches north
Its power declared
As green buds show forth

In late May the journey
Is almost at reach
Crossing painted terrain
till summers peak

The time spent to warm
And nurture the earth
Gives rise to the glory
That's happened since birth

*David Henry Syrett*

## Summer's Treat

Ninety degrees
In the high noon heat.
Tan bellies and bare feet.

Remember
Where we used to meet?

Counting the minutes
we stole.
We kept inside
our lonely souls.

Don't come September!
Loving you
In the high noon heat.
My sweet summer's treat

Remember
The end of our street?

*Joy C. Johnson*

## The Pilgrim

You seem to know where you are going
In the hills and valleys
You know your way
You seem
    to know where you are going
Don't listen
    to what
We say

Send news
    of the trip
You take
Don't stop
    for our sake

You seem
    to know where you are going
Please stop and pray along
The Way
We wish you all the best
    and guardian angels
    where you rest.

*Alice Z. Quinn*

## I Believe

I believe.
In the moon and the stars.
In heaven and earth.
In God and angles.
In good and evil.
In right and wrong.

I believe.
In hard work.
In good times.
In laughter and tears.
In sunshine and darkness.
In caring and sharing.

I believe.
In daydreams and night dreams.
In friendly "other beings".
In family and friends.
But most of all,
I believe,
In me.

*Judy Marie Wilson*

## The Stone

You put a pebble
In the palm of my hand.
It was a stepping stone,
Something I'd later understand.
But at the time,
It was to comfort me.
Something tangible to hold
When I set you free.
It held the warmth
Of your lingering touch
You knew it meant something;
But did you know how much?

*Cheryl Wilcox*

## Solitude

Alone with my book
In the shade of giant trees
Shadows lurk around me
Weird, long and lanky
Fingers pointing to the sky
My thoughts are on nothing
I only wish to be alone
To unscramble the madness of the day
The birds sing softly
As a gentle breeze ruffles past
A saucy squirrel pauses
Only for a moment and scampers on.

Evening is near at hand
These moments of solitude
Quiet my inner spirit
And my body slowly gives
Into a feeling of utter peace.
Nature, a balm for the weary
soul, a healing for the hungry spirit
God's gift to man.

*Flora Brown*

## Paper Airplane

Savoring the firm young grasp
Intense with anticipation
Flinging a pathway in air   while
Laughing upward.

Whispering a streak of nothing
Maneuvered by invisible forces
Suspended in a breath   then
Singing downward.

Sighing back to earth.

Fetch me, child, fetch me.
Let's fly together again.

*Harleen Pepler Putnam*

## Together

The stars may glide
into the dusk without any pride
But as long as we are together
We are like a feather
blowing along, without any wrong.
The sun will seep
through the deep leaved trees
as the breeze still carries
the feather along.  We are
like a rose pedal,
always together.

*Bridget Grumley*

## Here's Lookin' At You

Lord rest his soul
   into this bluelit morn
There is nothing to fear
   nothing to sorrow
Give him a still blue lake
for his soul
   to float awhile
Grandpa.
I watch the reflection of his roads
There   in the dispersal of his waves
caught in A moment of day's length
the resonant echo of water
   lapping beneath the pier
So   seeing his boat is in order
He fires up his outboard
in two cranks
And heading towards another shore
   cuts a wake into the ethereal
   as he always will.

*Art Howard Hartney*

## Being "Real"

The fun in being real
is
you surprise yourself
in
Oh, so many, many ways,
no matter how far,
you seek
nor, how hard you search
no one
will be like you, although,
many will feel like you..do.

*Fred Weaver III*

## Time

A thousand years as one day -
   Is a day as a thousand years?
Our days - so bound by time -
   God, yours are not.
Work, rest, scurry, fret
   For time - for what?
Race the clock and never stop
   To smell a flower, much less think
Of God's time.  We run -
   To make our mark, a valid one -
To be remembered - but -
   Each life a flower, just one -
In the multitude it withers and dies -
   And no one remembers - but -
Though not our importance -
   God remembers!

*Jeanette Carlander*

## Judgement Day

The day has come when man
is done and he is judge by the Son.
The oceans rise and the land
dies and the wind becomes great
and then nothing flies.
The ground will crack and buildings
will fall and then great fire will
cover us all.  When everything is
gone a white dove will sing a song
and trumpets will sound and then
the water will go down.  The land
will rise and the Son will come
down to revive our lives and a
great kingdom will arise before
our eyes.  The air will be clean
and the water will be pure and
the land will be beautiful all over the world.
The Son will raise, His arms in the sky
and birds and animals will appear
before our eyes.

*John Kusmirek*

## Crystal Branches

The world outside my window
Is like a storybook to me
It makes me feel as tho' I've traveled
To a distant land beyond the sea.

The trees and shrubs are made of glass
They look as fragile as a china vase
Each branch is drooping toward the earth
As tho' they're wearing a mournful face.

Soon the world will be warmed by the sun
The snow and ice will melt away
Everything will come to new life
All will be glad for a sunny new day.

*Alice Rogers*

## The Shadows of Love

The shadows of love
is like another God from above
your scared to face it when it's there
But be careful and be aware
The shadows of love are always there

*Brandi Burton*

## The Sky Crystal Blue

The sky, crystal with its blues,
is not appreciated its truths.
It expresses anger and pain,
and tears with falling rain.
Its joy shown with clear
blue skies;
and hate with loud,
thunderous cries.
It can be gentle and soothing
on a summer breeze,
or have war-like destruction
and bring the day to its knees.

And God's grace resides
above those skies;
He controls them thoroughly
in His warm, gentle eyes.

### *B. M. Spencer*

## Why

Sometimes the morning
   is the dawning
Sometimes the day
   shows the way
Sometimes the night
   feels just right
Sometimes the cloud
   calls aloud
Sometimes the rain
   can explain
Sometimes the snow
   lets me know
Sometimes the moon
   plays the tune
Sometimes the sun
   makes it fun
Sometimes the sky
   tells me why

### *Allen Aherne*

## The Great In Grandma

The pain you have
Is the pain we share
In this time of need
There are so many who care
We love you so much
For the times you have shared
As our friend...
   our sister...
   our mother and grandmother...
And yes, the GREAT of great-grandmothers
You have touched us all
From every stitch you have sewn
Every rag you made to riches
Every hand you lent
Every story you told
Every smile you shared
Every memory you let us have
For all these and many more things
Thank you Grandma
For the memories

### *Brenda Fogarty*

## Untitled

To be free
is to have your life back
from whatever bound it up,
to sing the colors of a mountain sunset,
to dance on the sparkling surface
of a mountain lake,
to open your arms
to the whole universe,
wrapping your arms around
the wonder of being,
to be generous in temptation,
giving another the sweet taste
of rescue,
to know that the Adversary
is not going to rest
until your life is espaliered
and pleached and knotted and choked,
ravished and limp.
Well, s--t happens, Beelzebub!

### *Charles Dukes*

## Dear No One

Dear no one,
Is what all my letters say.
At the heading, I write no one's name.
No one's there when I help,
No one's who I have to blame.

Dear no one,
Is becoming normal to me.
No love, no happiness, no somebody,
Nothing around but silence.
No one around that I can see.

Dear no one,
Was all in yesterday,
Because I finally learned someone's name.
The name I've learned to trust and see,
I learned that someone was always me.

### *Jennifer N. Ball*

## Liquid Mirror

I look in the mirror a face appears
it asks me why I am here
I ponder this question everyday

Wondering what I'll become

I hear voices telling me things
I don't want to hear
they talk of a place this horrible place

As I am sitting alone
I think of such things:
The face, the voices
then I wonder is it me?

Am I the answer to life's problems.
Do I have the power to stop it all

HELP

I am afraid of what my true inner-self
is capable of

As I take another trip (in my mind)
I see things clearly
and once again,
I am free

### *Bianka Balisinski*

## In Memory of My Sister, Lisa

Death is like a blanket,
It blackens all in sight,
Death is sometimes pleasant,
But death is never right.

It saddens our hearts
And brings hurt to our mind,
But a deeper love
Is left to find.

For when a loved one dies
Our hearts grow fonder,
And we never forget
The one who has left to go yonder.

We know we will see them again
When our life comes to an end,
And when we meet at the gate
A broken heart will mend.

### *Julie Callaway*

## Love

Love are you so blind when
   it comes to me?
Can love see that I do

   want in?
Love, can you hear my heart
   cry out for you?
I need to be near you
   love.
Can you talk to me
   please, love?
I know you can see me talking
   to you.
Love, please help me to
   understand what is
   going on.
Once I cried out for you
   love, to help, but
   no more.
Love, now it's your turn
   to cry out for my soul.

### *Cora J. Hall*

## Dark Whispers

Death is near.
It gently whispers.
Listening closely, I can hear it.
It's waiting for me,

Calling me in little whispers—
whispers as quiet as the calm sea,
as sweet as candy, as salty as tears,
and dark as the sun-less sky.

After death there is nothing—
nothing more to come,
nothing more to see.

Death often whispers
little winds that form
circles around my head.

It whispers gently,
in a soft voice,
sweetly beckoning
with welcoming arms.

### *Hrisoula Mihelis*

## The Quiet

It is overpowering the quiet
It is deafening the quiet

My heart will burst
My head explode

It is threatening, the quiet
It is heartbreaking, the quiet

Time seems endless
My loneliness magnified, it is so quiet

*Helen Kobasa*

## Untitled

Life is so fragile.
It is like a teardrop,
Bittersweet with sadness
And joy.
It is the glory
Of the sunrise,
And the serenity
Of a full moon
Floating in the dark sky.
It is time,
Fast fleeting,
Soon gone.
Life is so fragile,
Its only strength
Is love.

*Joanne Zumpe*

## Oh Wondrous Tree

A tree is such a lovely thing.
It makes a home for birds that sing.
It shades us from the summer sun,
while climbing branches just for fun.

In winter such a wondrous joy,
for every little girl and boy,
to see the snow on branches high
that build a tower to the sky.

And Christmas wouldn't be complete
without a tree and Christmas treat.
Oh tree with all your lights and toys
you fill our heart with lasting joys.

*Eileen Candy Gould*

## The Leaf

A leaf is like a person.
It must fall and fall again.
During autumn it glides to the earth.
But it soon rises back to the tree.

Life is a leaf.
It's very alive.
That life lives within us.
Just as you fall, you also get up.

Live life like a leaf.
If you fall and you will.
Get up and rise just
Like a leaf would.

*John Stilwell*

## Innocence Is Ending

Innocence is ending
It slips through time's
fine sands
it's lost forever
like virginity
it's cradled in your hand
Some choose, early, to cast it out
others hold it dear
but eventually it fades away
and becomes replaced by fear
and hatred and lust
and pride and glory and need
until it's long since
withered away
and never gone to seed.
For innocence does not return
when last it goes extinct
and soon becomes what you
desire
more than anything.

*Erin Ramage*

## God and the Wildflowers

When God created wildflowers
It was the best He ever did
He showed His gift of love
in all He had to give

I love to look at wildflowers
Blowing in the wind
They never need a bit of care
and come back again and again

To walk in a field of wildflowers
You can have such peace of mind
It's like walking next to God
and being in a different time

Wildflowers look like rainbows
Different colors after a shower
He made them in His glory
the prettiest of all the flowers

When I die and go to heaven
I know just where I'll be
Very far up in the sky,
God, the wildflowers, and me.

*Helen Polston*

## Keep It

Keep it.
It's as much mine
As it is yours.
This was no accident.

A divine plan—
If you destroy it
You know we're all
Going to hell.

It was just meant to be.
You'll just have to
Endure the suffering,
And no one can help you.

God and I agree.

*Christopher Fortin*

## The Tormentor

It never goes away
It's here to stay
Therapy is temporary
There is always recession
The mind recesses deep
Into the soul
To find the tormentor
The tormentor comes
Again and again
Good times are brief
Now the tormentor
Is ever so dominant and present
It never leaves for good
It's always lurking
Behind the next second
Just waiting to jump
Out like a child
Playing Hide -n- Seek
It's here to stay forever.

*Dianna Michelle Cook*

## Heaven's Dream

I hear a whisper soft and sweet.
Its incantation as angels keep.

The sky's gray hues draw doves
of lore, to grant us peace at
heaven's door.

All burdens held in captivity
restores the reason for nativity.

Extrinsic values put to rest,
concludes our principles put to the test.

No more needless craving as all
creatures enter in, to claim their
final dwelling amid the cherubim.

*Barbara G. Cascone*

## A Winter's Muse

Wrapped in silvery silence,
Its music hushed by shimmering snow
The fir tree stands in quiet harmony
With Earth.
While blanketed beneath the sod,
Lie those who once the Earth did trod.

Yet do not mourn mortality,
Nor chafe at life's inequity,
For towering high o'er Earth and tree,
Are countless thousands souls now free.

*Helen A. Osborne*

## Yellow

Yellow is always bright
It's really light
The color of most kites
And stars in the night
You on your flight to see a sight.
Yellow is the light of day
That makes you want to stay
Just one more day.
Yellow is the color of honey
Or maybe even money
Or just something funny.
Yellow is like a daisy.
It's the blazing fire in the meadow.

*Jon Mikel Walton*

## The Mixed Up Poem

Mary had a little ham,
Its skin was as brown as snow.

Everywhere that Mary went,
The ham was there to go.

It didn't follow her to school one day,
In the brown snow.

Because the little ham,
Was eaten by a big brown wolf.

**Brian J. DeVoe Jr.**

## Love Is Not

Love is not a color, but
It's what makes all the colors bright
Love is not the picture, but
It's what gives the sight

Love is not tangible, but
It can always touch
Love is not something to buy, but
It gives so much

Love is not a song, but
It's the force that makes you sing
Love is hard to notice, but
It's everything

Love is not the healing, but
It's what makes it possible to heal
Love is not a dream, but
Something very real

**Joan Sullivan**

## Knowledge

The phone rings.
It's you, concerned about me.
"Who else cares for you as I do?"
You inquire.
"No one," I reply, "no one."
And I smile with the knowledge
that I am loved.

**Bonnie Strum**

## You'll Never Know

You'll never know how many times
I've asked our Savior, why?
Why did he have to take, so young,
The keystone of our lives.

A loving wife and mother
Our blessing in disguise,
The pain withstood with no complaint
Shone through her saddened eyes.

And then one day He answered me
A message sent with love.
"Her work's complete on Earth,
I need an angel up above".

**Janice L. Rowland**

## Sun Temple

Surrounded by glaring white pillars
Laid out on a marble slab
My wrists slashed and bleeding
In the temple of my familiar
Ghosts swim past glassy, dying eyes
Like clouds in the vast blue sky
I await resurrection

**Elisabeth Mari Coppola**

## Rain Drop

Single drop of rain
falling slowly to the ground
landing with a splot

**Jill Armstrong**

## Teach My Children

In my heart God told me,
I've got a task for you
And in this new adventure
You'll find a lot to do.

As most folks do, when God speaks
I too made a humble plea.
Oh, dear God, please, please, please,
Don't give this job to me!

God has a special plan for all
Because he sees ahead
He took the doubt and fear within
And stirred up faith instead.

He placed me in the middle
Of a very chosen few.
In my greatest time of need
He always pulled me through.

God said, teach the children,
Teach them how to pray
Love and hug and give a smile
Then send them on their way.

**Joyce Murry Zaharsky**

## Love Grows

Stronger each day
I've watched you grow.
More enormous today
than ever before.
Reaching out from body and soul,
taking what's needed to keep you whole.
Reaching, never failing.
Taking, never trailing.
From my needs you never stray.
In my life you'll always stay.
Growing, growing, in every way.
Within me, forever be.
My love, you are the heart of me.

**Debra Decarne**

## Let Not Your Heart Be Troubled

Let not your heart be troubled;
    Just close your eyes in prayer.
Our blessed Savior waits for you
    To bring Him all your cares.
Tell Him what is on your heart;
    Your burdens and your fears.
He will hold you in His loving arms
    And wipe away each tear.
No matter what you're facing;
    He will never leave your side.
Whatever road you travel;
    He will always be your guide.
If you have sorrow now;
    You will know joy again.
He loves you with a perfect love;
    That will never ever end.

**Janet Lee**

## Why Is The Sky Blue?

Why is the sky blue said he.
Just like a lake or the sea.

Why couldn't it be green,
Just like a window screen.

Why couldn't it be gold,
Just like the rings being sold.

Why is the sky blue said he,
Just like a lake or the sea.

**Ashley Elizabeth Decoteau**

## Nightmare

I look outside my window
Just to remind myself there's rain.
It's just a small reminder
There's no comfort from the pain.
I sit inside my cabin,
To tired to really sleep.
The nightmare comes to haunt me.
Inside my head the monsters creep.
As sweat runs down my face,
I look up and see a light.
Then my eyes they close again
And in my head it's night.

**Emily Nelson**

## The Musings of Growing Old

Here I sit a wondering
Just what I'll do today.
It may be something pondering,
As I wander along life's way.

There is one thing I'd like to get
Out of my mind and off my chest,
And that is that life itself
Is just too short to play chess.

I've wandered through life
With sickness and with health,
But never have I found
Great riches and wealth.

N'er I scaled the highest mountain,
Nor plumbed the deepest sea
But I did quench my thirst
At life's eternal fountain.

And now as life grows very short,
Like waning days in December,
Life's been good to me.
It's good to remember.

**Dale Sprague**

## My Dream

I dreamed with you
Last night
During the dream
You kissed me
And was so real
I swear for God
That you were there
With me
When I wake-up
What's a surprise
I had my lips wet
With the flavor
Of your kisses.

**Felix O. Hernandez**

## Drumbeat

One day we will visit,
  laugh,
  part,
  wave goodbye....
And then no more.

One or the other
  will be called.
  It may be you....
  It may be me....
Who is to know?

There are two friends:
  One goes,
  One stays
  to weep....
  to mourn....
  and to remember
  with warm thanksgiving.

This is the way the drum beats....
This is the kaleidoscopic pattern
  of life.
  *Della A. R. Meadows*

## "Mother Is A Person"

Mother likes moonlight and sunset
  Laughter and dancing.....sometimes
    Mother has sorrows and regrets
    Scars on her heart
      Secrets on her mind

Mother is a person
  You could tell your troubles to
  right or wrong
    she'll bear your burdens
      never leaving you

Mother rejoices, sings, and cries
  Like the green leaves in Autumn
    One day too soon
    She'll say goodbye

Surely you can see
  She's like you and me
    And that's for certain
    "Mother is a Person"
    *Elaine Brown*

## Ain't Life Funny!

It changes it's path from day to day
leading us sometimes far astray.

It creates bitterness and sorrow,
just to swirl around and give us
laughter tomorrow.

Ain't life funny!

It tears down our self-esteem.
Then bounces us back swinging
on moon beams.

Through it all, we will endure.
Because the "Lord" above will insure.

Ain't life funny!
  *Connie Tilson*

## Nothing But Love

I walk down the boardwalk,
leash in my hand,
with my guy at the end.
He's got little black spots,
that cover his ever so soft white fur.
He likes to bark,
at the passing car tires,
and the people.
This little kid comes up,
pats him
on the
head,
then walks away.
His little tail wags,
while he smells the popcorn, hot dogs,
hamburgers and cotton candy.
He's so adorable, we can't leave without
his hot dog.
I love him, he loves me,
nothing but love!
  *Jennifer Grindrod*

## The In-Between

On a pathless journey,
leaving no footprints, they walk.
Like leaves spiralling ever closer
to the ground, they descend.

Specters existing between the
world of more is too little,
and the one where nothing is enough.

As flickering images of conscience,
they appear.
Substance and form without matter.
Like the hidden embers of a
forgotten fire, they are forsaken.
  *David Hylton*

## Prayer For Mom

Dear, God, please hear my prayer,
Let it not be in vain.
Bring good health back to Mom, God,
And give me all her pain.

To know that she is suffering more,
It makes me feel ashamed;
Why, not for her, just happiness;
Let me be the one that's lamed.

I love her, God, with all my heart,
She may, or may not, know it;
Seem's I've always done the wrong thing,
And haven't taken time out to show it.

Dear, Lord, If there is a way
Of whispering in her ear,
Say, She is very sorry, Mom,
And she loves you, Do you hear?
  *Jean Barlow Spires*

## Japanese Haiku

Cool crystal waters
unwinding like a ribbon
skip o'er stony beds
  *Deanne C. McCurdy*

## Transcending

Dispel my heart of fear.
Let me be the aroma of incense
in your hearth,
the sweet-smelling incense
of a life well-lived
not by appearance
but by the tedious bargaining
of the mundane for the eternal,
a conflict of premium importance
if I am to shed what keeps me apart
from Your enveloping and transcendent
Presence in my life.
  *Elizabeth Morales*

## Where Has Spring Gone?

Let it be spring again
Let the sun warm my soul
Let me be young again,
the carefree world of life to unfold
Hold my hand just a little while
Be patient and caring if you can
And I will give you a smile
To Thank, You, because you understand.
  *Cathy Volenec*

## Letting Go

Let me
  Let you go...
    With all the grace, love, and peace
    I held so dear
When near the light of your open heart.

Let me
  Let you go...
    With sweetness, not tears,
And know that through the years,
  I am yours.
  *Barbara J. Cooke*

## To Live Is To Die

I tried to live this side of the grave
Life somehow eluded me
Now I'll pass to the other side
Death won't elude me
It is there I'll surely find my life
My spirit is the who that I am
I belong in the heavenliness with Him
Open now your doors of life
My God, My Maker, My Father
I'm on my way
I'm coming home
  *Janis E. Belk*

## Leaves

From the sky the leaves are falling.
To the ground but not to die.
Mother Earth her arms enfolds them
Safely, gently lets them lie.

Softly sleep with rains calm voices,
Merge with ground to profit all.
Life to death to life unfolding
Go the loving leaves of fall.
  *Duane A. Chaffee*

## A Breeze

A stiff breeze
lifts the towel on the line
fills it with air...
how it billows out,
how it moves.
Then you hear it snapping
over and over
in the movement of a wild dance.

In an instant
I feel it too.
Like the towel
filling with air
I twist, move
and find myself snapping.
But unlike the towel
I react
to a breeze within.

*Adelaide Hartung*

## Far Away Lights

The light in the darkness,
light far away on the hillsides,
light of the world.
That light shows the beauty
of another time, another place
that I am pulled to —
hoping and wishing
you are dreaming the same
that I do,
hoping you will not see
the darkness tonight.

*Jamie Yinger*

## The Dreamer

I'm flying high
Like a kite in the wind,
On a fluffy, puffy could
Like a bird and his friends.

The higher I go
The freer I feel;
My spirit gets lighter
No trouble seems real.

I'm flying high
Like a ten year old boy,
A cape and a dream
Heart filled with joy.

The wind at my back
Better days I've seen;
If only I could fly.
What an incredible dream!

*Antoine Peterson*

## Windows of Love

The stars are the windows
Looking down from above.
Casting a glow of beautiful love;
To you and to me it is given with ease
May it continue to give
Never wanting to cease;
In this life with its cares
A light I can see,
And it will always be there
For you and for me.

*Edna Ellis*

## The Old Cotton Gin

The old cotton gin just stood there
like an old woman, waiting to die.
Her boards were gray and wrinkled
the roof sagging down on one side.
She stood, there, abandoned, alone
forgotten, and falling down...
Until one day, the children came
to play within her...arousal, sound!
She came alive again with laughter
shouts, and fun...as the children
played within...until the day was done.
She kept them safe and warm...
dry, from the falling rain.
No more forgotten nor alone
but useful, once again...
Life, like the cotton gin,
Tho old, wrinkled, and gray
All, stand useful to someone
some thing...till there is no
more day...

*Frances Morris*

## Thanksgiving

Thank you for all my hands can hold-
Like baby puppies with hearts of gold,
Kittens as soft as pom pom balls,
And a friends hand as sweet as can be.
Thank you for all my eyes can see-
Like running horses in the evening sun,
Miracles that happen day and night,
And rain drops on windows,
Thank you for all my ears can hear-
Like crackling of fire,
And crashing of waves.

*Allison Brestel*

## BEHOLD

All life seem to bubble,
like liquid in a cauldron.
Steaming, churning, burning,
the mixture ever turning.

Approach not in fear.
Shed only a relegate tear.
the hour of cooling is near.

The joy within you shall spread,
as recognition clears your head.
A sight more beautiful,
no words can be told.

In God's image is you,
BEHOLD!

*Deidree Ann Curci*

## Josh

To hear your voice makes me
melt where I stand.  To see your
face is like seeing the face of a God.
I look into your eyes and sense
the pain you're feeling, the problems
you're going through, the sorrows
you're sensing.
If only you would share
your sorrows and share your pain.
And let me, in return, hold you
and tell you that everything will
be okay.

*Heather Farmer*

## No Longer Homeless

Have you had that homeless feeling
Like you really do not belong -
Even with parents who did care
There's a sense that something is wrong.

With a vacuum of emptiness,
The true God takes away sorrow -
There can be real purpose in life
As each one faces tomorrow.

All gratitude to the Giver
Who has given eternal life,
We can know to Whom we belong
When we turn from our sin and strife.

"The fruit of the spirit is love" -
God's children should love each other,
Perhaps you've heard someone comment,
"She's my sister — he's my brother."

God's family is wonderful
Christ's compassion each will display -
Awaiting our Father's return
To dwell in HIS home every day!

*Carolyn F. Marquis*

## Untitled

Pressed flowers,
Locked between the pages,
Of a brittle, yellowed tome.

Dead roses-
Time capsules.

Phantom fragrances,
Fill my senses,
With the sweet,
Aromas of the past.

*Debbie St. Jean*

## Of Tears

Tears of sorrow
Lost tomorrows -
Tears of pain
Pour down like rain.

Tears of fright
Exist in the night -
Tears of rage
Calm with age.

Tears from no sleep
Bring on the sheep -
Tears from grieving
Somebody's leaving.

Tears of hope
Means you can cope -
Tears of love
Rise far above.

Time moves on
Through tear filled ponds -
Faith is strong
My tears are gone.

*Jillian Reis-Matz*

## Love 16

Love can move mountains.
Love can crack the sky.
Love sends light from sounds.
Love will never say good-bye.

Love will tear you up.
Love will let you down,
Love will then find you,
Love will never say good-bye.

Love can make mountains.
Love holds up the sky,
Love stars of light fountains.
Love will never say good-bye.

Love will fill you up.
Love will light your town.
Love will then find you.
Love will never, ever, say good-bye.

**Uriah**

## Love

Love, love love, makes people happy;
Love, love, love, makes people free.
Love, makes people do..the things they
know they ought to do,
Love is doing things for you and me.

Love, love, love, makes people friendly;
Love, love, love, makes people kind;
Love makes people do..the things they
know they ought to do.
Love is helping those who fall behind.

Love, love, love makes people thank-ful;
Love, love, love makes people share.
Love, makes people do..the things they
know they ought to do,
Love is showing others that you care.

**Gail Jiron**

## And Still I Sleep

Battered by the sea!
Lying helplessly in the sand-
Thinking...
But only momentarily.
The warmth of my inner feelings
Nestled deep within my breast...
Leaves me sleeping.

While the thought of bygone
Days hurl themselves-
Shattering into thousands of
Pieces against the walls of
My mind...
And still I sleep!

And in the background-music!
Fiddling through my scalp.
Twisting around every hair...
Dancing,weaving and sliding
Onto my shirt and down into my lap.

And Still I Sleep!

**James Michael Ivester**

## Heaven or Hell

In this weird world of being
Mankind repeats without seeing
That each life must be conclusion
Heaven or Hell just an illusion

There could be no other way
To control earth's rules of play
Nothing is from whence we came
Return to nothing is the same

As blades of grass we come and go
Renewed each year by rain or snow
Splendid, Intended, one season's worth
Heaven or Hell right here on earth

For if we were not swept away
There'd be no room for life to pay
And we would still amoebas be
No Heaven or Hell dreamed up to see

We must learn each life or death
Is nature's rule to bring new breath
To creatures strange as those gone by
Heaven or Hell is not when you die

**Elmer G. Coffey Sr.**

## Passages

Glacial remnants
Melt in upland streams
While crocuses dance.

  The lazy river
  Laps at its banks,
  Pesky mosquitoes buzz.

Quakies flicker
In golden splendor,
As chilled winds blow.

  Frigid air streams
  Over white peaks and prairies,
  The Snowman stands watch.

**Betty Leonard**

## In Loving Memory

As the years pass by,
Memories will never die.
Remembering that special someone,
In loving memory, to a loved one.

Putting a candle in a window,
Its flame flickering in a shadow.
Reflecting back to yesteryear
With eyes filled with tears.

Eyes that cry are a heart that feels,
Sadness that so very real.
Never knowing never asking why,
A loving memory will never lie.

**James Belcher**

## David

We left him there on the sunny slope
Under the sky and the sod
Among his silent neighbors
But not alone—for he's with God.

His favorite chair is now vacant—
His gentle smile no longer we'll see
Still he'll be with us forever
Etched in our memory.

**Dorothy L. Watts**

## Away

Life it seems to fade away
misery and hate seems to run away
I seem to brake away
while you just seem to go away.

Death is I know it on the way
what to do I asked you
your face lighted right away
while mine just faded away.

Death has come I flew away
your face is still lighting why is that?

Your place is burning
it hurts I know it
if I could rescue you I'd do it!

**Biljana Kvalic**

## Weather Haiku

Rains come down and fall.
Moisten the dirt on the earth.
We depend on you.

Clouds come towards us.
We like to see your nice shape.
Your shapes are the best!

Winds come to us soon.
Send a breeze to cool us down!
Your nice breeze is great!

Snows come down and fall.
Bring your whiteness to the earth.
You make the world white!

**Christine Simone**

## We Didn't Die In Vain

Mommy, Mommy, please don't cry for me
  Mommy, mommy, please try and see
I had to die and come up here,
  Causing my BROTHERS to see real clear
The need to help each other
  No matter one's color

Oh Daddy, I miss you, that is true
  But God had something for us to do!
My friends and I, we couldn't stay
  We were all quickly whisked away
Though the hurt is hard to bear,
  And I know it seems unfair,
Our untimely deaths caused there to be
  An awakening of real unity!

Now our country is able to see
  The existing factors of disunity
Hopefully our deaths have ignited the
"flame"
  Of LOVE and unity again!

**Barbara Inez Callari**

## Growing Old

A garden full of flowers,
is symbolic of the years.
In youth, the blooms are plentiful.
With age, they disappear.

It seems like only yesterday,
my youth was in full bloom.
The petals wilt, the blossoms die,
today has come to soon.

**Dorris O'Brien**

147

## Longing

Longing to be at sea
Most all would agree
One of life's pleasures
No ruffled feathers
Stop where you want
It's always your jaunt
Fish for your food
Never in a bad moon
Wind always free
Never a fee to me
Sea smooth or bumpy
Never will I be grumpy
The sea birds cry
I don't know why
If only we could fly
Across the blue sky
Surf the clouds
Never in a crowd
Out in the open sea
Forever we could be free!

*Craig Eiszele*

## The Mountains

Mountains are beautiful
mountains are high
mountains are always
way up in the sky.

From mountain to mountain
the sun will be there.
If the lowland is dry
the rain will take care.

Sometimes I know
the mountains are white.
It is the snow
that makes them look bright,

*Gina Donato*

## In The Twinkling Of An Eye

The hands upon my old clocks' face
move 'round and 'round with ease,
clicking off the minutes,
first one, then two, then three.

Each minute, sixty seconds.
Each second - surely gone.
Each hour slips away of me,
as time goes on and on.

Now that I am older -
The decades slip away.
Sometimes so much faster, now
then I would like to say.

I think of time in many ways,
both the larger and the small.
I think about eternity.
and God - and us all.

How long it takes his eye
to twinkle -
And will I
rise, or fall.

*Bruce Casper*

## Instead

I will let
musicless evil spirits
get their
hooks
in me
no more forever

they shall not drag me
        d
         o
          w
           n

Instead I think of you
and of the magic country
where we dwelt awhile
and
the happy thought
peterpans
me into
flights of rhythmic ecstasy

*Fred Wind*

## Home At Last

Tear-blinded beaten by the breeze
My blood runs hot and cold
Like currents warm through icy seas -
Behold the blue and gold!
    Soft joyful sobbings beat
    on paralytic ears
    Staccato marching feet
    Storm of elated tears
Through waving caps came forth your face
Benevolent and kind
As arms reached for a long embrace
Thoughts lingered in my mind
I was at peace, I stood at ease
Cheers for the battles won
So many months on open seas
Back home at last - my son!

*Clara Evelyn Clark-Cummings*

## A Beat

A beat besides the silence
My eardrum's pounding wild
Sounds of nature fill me
I feel like I'm a child
Twisting through the currents
Flowing through with ease
The surroundings now become me
As if I were diseased
Winds are whispered to me
Sweet secrets in my ear
One with the environment
Is dancing with me dear
The atmosphere's the center
Of all that's going around
A clashing point of instance
Recurring is the sound...

*James Breton*

## Mind Over...

Crammed in a cold crate
With strange, grey figures - I float
Free on sun-warmed sand.

*Joanne E. Donovan*

## Elaine

She's passed away.
My friend.
Elaine.

She's passed away
And I am
Sad.

Yet, awfully
Glad...

She
passed
MY
way.

*Joyce Bierman*

## My Gargoyle Rose

I woke to feel
my gargoyle rose
uncoiling from my dreams.

Frozen, mute,
with mummied breath,
within my iron skin

I watched the unwinding plant
vein the early light
with criss-cross shadows

That blessed my eyes, my breast,
my solar-plexus self
to release my exhaled Mary's.

The room grew choked
with hungry roots,
the vine reached outer space

Where that ravenous rose
frightened the stars
and ate the eyes of God.

*James C. Hawkins*

## Child to Woman

"I hate you," she screamed.
My heart broke in two.
I hoped that she didn't mean it,
That it couldn't be true.

You raise a child
The way you think is right.
Then she becomes a teen
And nothing is right.

You just can't seem to get through,
Everything you say to her is dumb.
You try so very hard
You begin to feel numb.

After years of struggle
That you thought would never end,
You begin to see an ending,
Your heart begins to mend.

She's grown into a woman now
With a child of her own to tend.
You can hardly believe it,
She is now your friend.

*Bobbie Tait*

## Darkness Came

The darkness came without
my knowing took me away
Left me alone, empty astray
I lost myself in the night
bowed down to the neon lights
Naked under a full moons light

I gave away my fears for -
gotten tears
Don't want to be there don't
want to be here
Haunting echoes in my head
things I did, things I said
so alone, so alive, so dead.

I'll keep looking to the skies
waiting for a new sunrise
To dry those tears from my eyes
lay me down to sleep
Pray the Lord my soul to keep

*George Cabrera*

## Jesus You Are

You are my world that keeps,
my life turning.

You are the sun brightens up
a gray gloomy day.

You are the unreachable star
here in my heart to have and to hold.

You are the light at the end
of the blackhole

You are the truth
as all else is a lie.

You are life
when death knocks at the door.

You are laughter
when sadness overtakes my being.

You are a summer nights breeze
in a cold winters night.

You are the future.
that got rid of the past.

You are you,
and in you I exist.

*Irma Miranda Baez*

## Candy Bars

As I looked into the case,
My taste buds began a merry chase.
Round and round they went,
Until my appetite I must vent.

Clark and Hershey caught my eye,
No, too fattening, I emit a sigh.
Twix and Crunch, my taste buds shudder,
No, no, my mind permits me to utter.

Black Cow is near Fifth Avenue,
I still think Clark is a better chew.
Should I try Snickers or Crunch,
But that's too many just before lunch.

A number of bars between Twix and Clark,
I will try a Zero for a lark.
Three Musketeers pass my way,
As I search for another Milky Way.

*Frank A. Robison*

## The Passing

You knew I would die,
my time had come,
with ebbing night,
and waking sun,
I have always been here,
never will be gone,
Flesh to dust,
and soul to home.
I left without a sound,
stealing through the night,
Like a whispering wind I traveled,
burdens all left behind.
Stretching my wings for flight,
wind beneath the membrane,
Fleeing for distant shores,
shadow of the evening.

*Jonathan H. Cole*

## View From The 19th Floor

A 'northeaster' snow storm raging
  nearby buildings barely visible
then clusters of snowflakes
  began hitting the windowpane
    staying and slowly separating
into single snowflakes, delicate, lovely
  time
    after time
  after time
all through the snow storm.

*Elizabeth G. Hudspeth*

## Grandparents

Now that we are grandparents, we
never knew before how great it
would be.

My husband grandpa oh what a
change.  Before with our own children
impatience and rage!!

Now all has changed.  Time is of the
essence.  If we only knew before
when we were young we would of
sung a different song!!

Experience of family life.  Happiness,
sorrows, yes! Even strife!

Grandparents have a second chance.
How our hearts dance!!

Our hearts are happy so glad inside.
Feelings of ecstasy that can't hide.

We can never return.  Never turn
back the clock.  Our feelings grow
and deepen and lock!!

*Emma Martinez*

## Feelings

All kinds of feelings bundled up inside,
Not one single soul in which to confide.
Memories galore of days gone past.
Oh how I wish those
feelings had last.
Got to keep hoping for
things all a new.
And maybe some more
beautiful feelings too.

*Donna J. Hayes*

## "And Airplanes And"

Architecture
Never teaches
The wonderful quality
Of see-out-ness

Bricks and steel
Are taught from
Iron podiums
  Of devoutness

Incredibly shifting
Look - forward - to
Wallpaper
  (More than decoration)

While iron is
  Magnets
And airplanes and
Subways the window
  Is realization

*Jason Morgan*

## Daybreak

If I listen I can Hear the silence of
night and watch the stars quiet
departure from the sky.

If I listen I can hear the graceful
fall of petals on grass thick with
moisture.

When I can see the dew of morning
sparkle with the first faint rays
of dawn, I know the day has
called me.

*Betty A. Clement*

## Dark As Night

In my room, in the middle of the
night, lying in my bed with chills and
fright, lying in my bed in a room dark
as night.

Teeth chattering, wearily glancing
around, afraid to move or make a sound.
Shivering while the wind blows around,
wondering if ghosts might be waiting on
the ground, on the ground in a room dark
as night.

Wolves, witches, vampires too, ready
to scare me and you.  Owls give a sudden
"Who" outside windows startling you,
while you lay in a room dark as night.

Shutters rattle and blow in the wind.
Trees make shadows in the room that you're
in.  The witching hours are almost gone,
then you'll know in will soon be dawn.
It's time to relax and say "Goodnight"
to your room so dark, so dark as night."

*Gavin G. Roberts*

## Jack Frost Went Up The Hill

Jolly Jack's jading Jills,
   Nipping nails,
    Painting pails,
Hitting hapless, helpless hills.

Frosty fingers freezing fields,
   Wilting weeds,
    Spoiling seeds,
Yellowing yester-season's yields.

Coyly cracking crinkly cabbage
   Stopping sands,
    Lacquering lands,
Lazily lathering leather luggage.

Primping padlocks, popping posts,
   Inching icicles,
    Burdening bicycles,
Ghoulish glidings, growing ghosts.

Painting prankishly on glass,
   Slick'ning sleets,
    Shaping sheets,
Grossly glaring gilted grass.

*Elva M. Brakefield*

## Yolanda

A smile for all seasons,
No other was the same
A breath of fresh air,
In every room she came
Like a ray from the sun,
There wasn't one lighter
On a falling star,
You couldn't wish for one brighter
Her essence so sweet,
Truly a blessing from above
Her presence so warm,
Her heart full of love
A gem so rare,
So beautiful to see
So precious to us all
Another?
There will never be
Like all of God's creations
We must leave as we came
Yolanda, well miss you
But love you just the same
Oh What A Smile!

*Darnell Carter*

## Untitled

Mourn not my passing —
Nor despair for what we no longer share.
It is your grief that shackles my soul,
and makes me a prisoner of sympathy
For I have not the heart to leave you
so —
Let go — sweet light, twin flame.
Serve your destiny,
As we were bound to,
But remember the way —
For we have traveled it before
You & I
And together we will be
for all eternity,
Somewhere in time.

*Christina Bistodeau*

## Wherever You Are

The roads are lonely
Nobody stops to look around
I lost love and so lovely
And nowhere he can be found

I know it's gone
And I don't know where
I'm all alone
Looking for him somewhere

Turn back wherever you are
It's you that I'm needing
Shine again in my star
And stop this lonesome pleading

As the wind kisses the rain
Love keeps me seeking
I'm trying to forget the pain
That my heart is always feeling

At the end of the rainbow
There's a pot of gold
Maybe that someone I love
Will be waiting for me to hold

*Joe Fernandez*

## My Face

Love me not for my outer grace,
Nor the beauty of my face,
But love me for my love's embrace.
For if those things should turn to ill,
You must vow to love me still,
For the love my heart and soul's provided
And not what others have decided.
My beauty you will have to seek,
For it lies not in my face.
But lingers amidst the words that I speak.

*Jamey Waters*

## Her

Who is to blame
not I, I say
for my foolish ideas
my mind went to play
a fondness I have
as I blow off the dust
of memories of her
the anger a must
the confusion I have
it's the only thing clear
I can't sleep at night
without her I fear
but what did she do
to make me so mad
to say goodbye
it wasn't that bad
so to her I write
as I fall apart
I love you and miss you
with all of my heart

*Jeffrey T. Androsac*

## Grandpa

I love my grandpa very much
Now I can't keep in touch
Now that he has past away
I miss him much day by day
I miss his smile I miss his laugh
I miss his stories of navy past
His nick-name was Grandpa Bean
The funniest Cajun I've ever seen
So Grandpa if you're looking down on me
I hope you're proud of what you see
I loved my grandpa very much
And now I can't keep in touch.

*James Clark*

## My Lovely Valentine

T o my precious Valentine
O ur true love's doing fine.

M aybe we should celebrate
Y ou can be my special date.

L asting love's now in store
O nly you can please me more.
V ery exciting feelings are
E ntering in my heart so far.
L iving in a word of dreams
Y esterday was good it seems.

V alentines are made for love
A lways blessed by God above.
L eaving happiness in the air
E njoying love that is there.
N othing ever cheers me more
T han the charms that I adore.
I love you proudly every day
N o part of me will go astray.
E xciting pleasure is all mine
   Knowing you're my Valentine.

*Howard Golley Jr.*

## The Wind

Softly blows the evening breeze
O'er the fields and thru the trees.
From whence it comes no one knows.
Nor do they know just where it goes.

It touches each and everyone from dawn
to setting of the sun.  Sometimes a
message it will bring.  So happy
that our hearts will sing.

From hills to valleys it travels on.
Sometimes a puff and then its gone.
But back again to blow real hard,
to send dust devils across the yard.

I wonder if the wind that blows today
Will help some sailors on their way.
For ships with sails will need the wind
to take them to their journeys end.

Just imagine the soft and gentle breeze
that blows so softly thru the trees,
can take you to a distant land,
then bring you safely home again.

*Bennie J. Humphries*

## Happiness

Dancing around the waters
Of a cool, moonlit stream
Taking people's compliments
For what they really seem
Laughing at life's silly things
And smiling when you're mad
Gently telling someone
When you think that they've done bad
Crossing a wide open field
With dandelions in your hair
Watching a lion play with his cubs
Near his snug and cozy lair
Doing nice things for people
To make their life worth living
Receiving love from someone
And in return love giving
Happiness is pink, purple,
Yellow, orange, and red
But most of all it's loving
Even when it is not said

**Elizabeth M. Spang**

## Shoganai

Eyes staring in numb acceptance
of fate's cruelty.
Flashbacks of same destruction
in her country when she was a child.

A middle-aged woman sitting
amid quake death and destruction,
tells a reporter she is alone
and has nothing left.

A witness of man's bomb and
nature's restlessness gives
her knowledge of pain and loss,
wondering once again why she lived?
Kobe, Kobe....another Phoenix?

**Jean Slaughter**

## Our Son

I have a favorite memory
Of going with my son,
He would find a hill top
There gather one by one,

Precious little belly flowers
A bouquet just for me,
And we would scan the horizon
As far as we could see.

A son like Tom is special,
His father knew it too.
With life's many problems
Tom worked out what to do.

Gets busy then, and does it.
Helps others on their way.
I pray God help this son of ours;
What else is there to say.

**Charlette A. Payton**

## One Summer Day

One Summer day as it was hot
The earth was like in a boiling pot
I dreaded to go to work that day
But read and sleep on the lofty hay.

**Joseph Polizzi**

## Tears

Tears are a sign
Of happiness and joy
Like the arrival
Of a girl or boy

Tears are a sign
Of sorrow and pain
When you feel you
Have nothing to gain

Tears can come and go
Like a river that flows
Tears feel good
To just let go

**Elsie Narvaez**

## Living The Dream

The dream
of hope
The dream
of opportunity
The dream
of freedom
The time is now!
To pull our nation
out of the quicksand of
racial injustice
The solid rocks of
brotherhood must be incorporated
within ourselves
To settle our differences
Love is evident for each other
Make choices
Make a difference
The time is now!

**Jennifer James**

## Listen

Amid the noise
of life,
take time to listen
to the sounds
within yourself.

Record these sounds
of hope, fear,
joy, love and hate —
bring them to the
surface of your being.

This is you —
A human with feelings
among a world that
sometimes appears to
have grown cold and callous.

**Brenda Wells**

## As Long As The Flowers

As you walk through the garden with me,
You see a small baby tree,
Who's leaves are growing and springing forth,
While its mother holds a fragrant
torch of flowers and fruit
You'll see,

Baby, I'll never leave you,
Darlin', I'm yours for now,
Honey, we're here together,
and this is my vow

**Jessica Petersen**

## Searching

I've searched the far corners
   of my mind and pulled out every
memory I can find and still
I can't find you.
   Traces of love fill my heart
and for every day that we're
apart my soul cries out, and
still I can't find you.
   Spring fills the air with warm
sunshine and the birds sing,
but I look for you in the
shadows of my dreams and still
I can't find you.
   I've walked the paths we
used to walk and looked
behind each and every rock
hoping to catch a glimpse of
the love we shared and
still I can't find you.

**Carol Donaldson**

## Untitled

Clearing out the closet
   Of my very cluttered mind.
All the shelves and boxes,
   And the treasures there to find.

An idea put here yesterday,
   A dream is set aside.
A half remembered love affair,
   A moment out of time.

And there behind a pile of junk,
   A package wrapped with care
A very special memory
   With only you I'll share.

It's nothing bright or fancy
   No one else would make a fuss
But I couldn't bear to part with it
   A memory of us...

**James V. Huddleston**

## Tense

Yesterday I thought
of people
I had known -
thru childhood,
years at school,
years at work,
the facets of
family and worth
personal, impersonal,
with days of
laughter and strife,
those in hardship
others in wealth,
facing challenges
of life
today I am here
the others
are gone -
tomorrow is
another dawn.

**Irene Robin Hall**

## Untitled

It hurt when you accused me,
of something I didn't do.
I don't understand,
why you don't trust me.
I feel like you are blaming me,
for someone else's actions.
I didn't do anything wrong,
why don't you trust me?
You never asked for my side,
you just believe your friends.
I guess I'm trying to say,
WHAT DID I DO?

*Jill M. Schum*

## Untitled

At Christmas time I reminisce
Of times so dear to me.
When Santa left my presents
Underneath the Christmas tree.
When Christmas pageants at the church
Were never to be missed,
And mistletoe was special
'Cause it meant I might be kissed
Christmas cookies baking,
Pine boughs to decorate —
Filled the house with glorious scent.
No one can duplicate.
People, oh yes. People -
Relatives I loved so much,
Mostly gone, but not forgotten
Have forever left their touch.
Friends, known for such a short time
Others always here and true,
I am grateful to have known them and I am
Including you!!!
Merry Christmas and a Happy New Year

**Betty Bacon**

## Meadow Brook

Meadow Brook is an endless stream,
Of years gone by and a broken dream,
Reflections from its flowing face,
Reach out for love with an embrace -

Old water flows beneath a bridge,
A Meadow Lark sits upon the ridge,
Cattails grow along its base,
Meadow Brook is an endless place -

The lonely wails of a silent train,
That can be heard yet feels the pain,
If you believe right from your heart,
Meadow Brook and I shall never part -

If it could speak what would it say,
Of things gone by and yesterday,
Meadow Brook is the place to be,
For broken dreams of you and me.

**Dennis J. Carpenter**

## Life Or Death

Maybe it seeps into the ground
On a rainy and windy day?
Does it rise into the heavens
And watch upon the world.
Maybe it just sits there rotting away
Or does it come back to haunt the living.
What if it does nothing.
Like an owl on a moon filled night
Or does it lie there six feet under.

*Jeremie Schaub*

## Chincoteague Island

There lies a small island
Off the Coast of Virginia,
Chincoteague Island
Where horses run wild,
As free as the wind.
And the deer in the forests
Stand tall in the clearings,
And everywhere around you
The birds sing their lullabies
On the long, summer days
To the lovely blue sky.
The ocean is gorgeous.
A deep, vibrant turquoise.
Whose great waves are crested
With on ivory foam.
The waves roll to the shore —
Towering walls of water —
Then fade to mere ripples
In the powerful sea.

**Amanda Scott**

## Words That Meant Nothing

You told me that you loved me,
Oh, so long ago.
I wish you would have meant it,
because I loved you so.

When you said those words,
They replenished my heart with joy.
It was like a little child,
getting a new toy.

Whatever happened,
to those words you used to say?
All of a sudden, they turned to anger,
and where suddenly swept away.

Instead of saying, "I love you,"
you said there was someone new.
What is there left to say
and what is there left to do?

You were so deceiving
and your love for me was untrue.
I guess you'll never know
exactly how much I loved you.

**Candice Duke**

## Treasures Found

A lonely street, mid cities din
Old and worn, it beckons in
A quiet church, a house of prayer
for troubled souls, there's solace there
As candles flick, their burning light
A cross of wood, a hope so bright
That only he, can ease the pain
Just to ask, to call his name
Then without, a reason sound
Peace of mind, is all around
Logic gone, a friend to see
For a time, to dwell with thee
Then in a while, we take our leave
And pity those, who can't believe

**Bob Kenny**

## Through A Child's Eyes

Outside there is lots of rain
On a child's cheek lies a tear
This lone child is experiencing pain
Because of the thunder he fears

He is looking out the window
The hazy moon overhead
He is wishing the sun would glow
But there is lightning instead

For him the world is gloomy
But across the street and only here
There is a party
While sorrow is so near

This happy house is full of light
Everyone is so excited
There faces are glowing bright
They are all so delighted

Here the people dance
They are happy and warm
The lone child wishes he could have that chance
But there is only pain for this child called Norm

**Amanda Headworth**

## Moon Flowers

I've seen moon flowers flourishing
On Loyal Hanna Street,
Glowing in pristine white in the
middle of summer's heat,
Each blossom draped, endowed by
Nature, with queenly grace,
Shade and shadow drinking in the
beauty of each face.

When night shall follow after,
extinguishing the sun,
the moon, seeking her own, shall
re-light the flowers,
one by one.

*Cyra G. Renwick*

## The Window

Looking through the window
    On such a cloudy day
It feels as dreary as the loneliness
    Passing by my way

Looking out the window
    I see cars and trucks go by
Traveling on streets, going on highways
    Their destinations are nigh

Looking out the window
    The sky still looks blue
As pretty as a painting
    It's beauty captivates you

Looking out the window
    I hear the familiar "chime"
Racing faster and faster toward me
    I'm speaking of "father time"

We feel happiness, sadness, love, hurt and
badness
    Until one day, it all just stops - with no
thought of you
    Just
        Looking out the window

**Diane Johnson**

## Send Me Some Clowns

Send me some clowns they wear no frowns.
Send me some clowns they always cheer up the crowd, make them laugh
loud.  Send me clowns when they come to tame the town.
Send me some clowns I need to see their sunny funny faces.
Send me some clowns they'll turn your frown up side down.
Send me some clowns I know there is still some around they will
comfort me.  Send me clowns dressed in all the colors of the rainbow
make those clown colors
Flash and clash so rhythmic it's true.
Send me some clowns it's laughter I'm after raise it to the rafter.
Send me some clowns the worlds much too serious and furious now send
me some clowns.  Send me some clowns they really can brighten and
lighten the day.  Send me some clowns let them bring the circus along
as long as they send me some clowns.
Send me some clowns bring peanuts, popcorn and monkeys along but lend
me some clowns.  Send me some clowns let their oversize shoes shoo the
blues away today, then say hurray.
Come on now it's a charade.  Send me some clowns, come on now where
is the parade.  Send me some clowns I know now you need some too so
cheer up my friend I'll share them with you.

*Kenneth D. Patton*

## Efficacy

Self-pity, Honey, is getting you old; the bitters don't ever get sweet
There's a gentle someone I am told; see the mirror where you will meet.

The years will not be graceful passing as long as you keep looking back.
Your pain will be yours everlasting because you keep on keeping track.

Self isn't something you search for in tapestries you fabricate.
The journey to whole is made up of the choices that only you make.

Rich isn't something you harvest and love's not a favor you trade.
Anger is only a cry in the void the beast of ambition creates.

Everything happens for reasons often beyond our control.
Every time there's a cycle of seasons, there is a spring and a fall.

We're blessed with the vision of yesterday...gifted with the miracle
 of now.
Humbled with the quest for tomorrow...we grow from seeds that we plow.

God gave us the chance of purpose; He trusts us to grow from belief
A life with the strength of a forest; a death with the grace of a leaf.

*Laurel Sneed*

## Chris Buchanan

She was my second mom; she dreamed of her daughter going to the prom
Her daughter, Angie, was my best friend; we stuck together through the end
Elementary school class was where Angie and I met;
 Poncho was the family cat, their beloved pet
When I first met Chris, I knew that she deserved fame;
 with Angie and I she played piano, dolls, and a card game

She wanted Angie to be on pom pom; then off went the bomb
A job transfer came and off to Dubuque they went; many letters were sent
Sometimes we traveled there for fun - filled weekends of skating and
 playing four - square
Sometimes they traveled here where swimming and Putt-Putt were dear

Visits were special, usually once a year; soon, however, came fear
Fate had turned; nothing good lasts forever as we learned
Chris was sickly; cancer came over her and spread quickly
Now visits became treasured; as time became measured

Early one morning, we received the news;
 soon we were all seated in church pews
And as they played the songs, I wished her life would have been long
Although to an extent it was a relief, her life was far too brief
We all loved her so and did not want to see her go.

*Katrina Mahan*

## Untitled

It's cold here
on this mountain,
the wind blowing
  Always against me.

Sometimes I can
tuck myself away,
stay warm,
  Gather strength.

But mostly I try
not fall over
  The edge.

I promise myself
I'll make it to the top-
  And soon.
Then I slip.

*Bridgette Janette Taylor*

## Braces

Are looks really worth all this pain?
Once a month they make it more tight.
I don't know how I will sustain.
What can I do?  How can I fight?

They never warn you of what's near.
Of all the hell you must endure.
I know the pain, I know, my dear.
For all this suffer, there's no cure.

Whose fault is this, it is not mine.
Those dentists, everyone can tell.
It's a sin, to mess God's design,
So all of them will go to Hell!

What is the outcome of all this,
A better look, a better smile?
Or lots of pain you will not miss,
Painful memories for a while.

Why must we go through this horrible fate?
Do people really care if my teeth are straight?

*Gil Peles*

## On the Invasion of Poland

Poland, hapless Poland,
Once again was torn in two.
Invaded from the East and West
There's little she could do.
An un-armed man lay dying
Where a Nazi shot him down.
A woman stood by crying
In a ripped and tattered gown.
No one could imagine
The carnage that began,
"Kill all of them,"
Der Fuhrer screamed,
"They are not Aryan."

*George Roy Hurlburt*

## A Sunny Day

I woke up very early,
One bright and sunny day;
The day was surely sunny,
In every single way.
The sun was shining brightly,
The birds were sweetly singing
A song that made me smile,
And stop and listen for a while.
If only I could sing as they,
Then I could help brighten every day!

*Julie Taylor*

## After The Rain

Outside the rain is falling, making its way to the stream
Flowing gently to the valleys, heading for the seas.
And as the cool water passes, it kisses the dry, thirsty land
Bringing life to desert places, growing flowers in the sand.

After the rain there'll be singing and after the clouds are gone,
Sunshine will break its way through darkness,
Night only lasts so long.

After the rain there'll be laughter. My heart will sing a new song.
Skies will be clear, He will be near,
After the rain is gone.

Clouds sometimes come on the inside, sometimes they darken the day.
And like a raindrop, tears of sorrow fall along the way.
But tears are the seeds of the morning, clouds are the signs of spring,
And like a cool, refreshing shower,
Hope will make me sing.

*Marilyn V. Ropp*

## Diversity

The fall tree blows with multicolored leaves.
Red, brown, gold, and green.
A beautiful arrangement unified by limbs and branches.
Separate, but together. Different but unified.
Bonded by the roots of life and creating a natural beauty.
Is this not true diversity?
Is this not what humans aspire to?
Respect, listen, and learn from each other.
Strength and success is in unity not division.

*T. Eugene Munson*

## The Desert Is Alive!

There is nothing quite like
A beautiful bouquet;
That is carried by a bride
On her Wedding Day!

Pure white calla lilies —
Radiates her happy face.
Frames he heir-loom gown;
Trimmed with hand made lace.

There is nothing quite like —
A deep purple, lilac bouquet;
Its fragrance celebrates Spring
In a breath-taking way.

But when you see a Palo Verde tree;
With a thousand tiny blossoms, strive
To light an April day with its golden glow —
Then you know, THE DESERT IS ALIVE!

*Nita D. Schlickman*

## A Portrait

Her figure outlined in the shadows' gray
A beautiful sight to behold.
Her arms outstretched as if to pray
Her hair a banner of gold.

The breasts of the model were
pears of white
The nipples as dipped in wine
Her legs were such a lovely sight
Not old and feeble like mine.
And yet something was missing
From this beautiful portrait divine.
It seemed to lack the most important thing
This old experience of mine!

*Penny Davis*

## The Beauty Of A Woman

There is nothing under creation more beautiful than
a beautiful woman,
    She is most magnificent of all God's creations,
Her beauty radiates forth like a burst of bright sunlight
or the brilliant glow of a full moon, with majesty and
grace.
    She is the utmost species and the most glorious of
all mankind,
    Her glory, grace and elegance portray her beauty more
than any other creature,
    Her beauty, Her smell, and Her touch will send your
senses reeling like a whirlwind and set your heart afire,
    To see and know a woman is to have seen and touched the
finest of jewels,
    Her radiating beauty, composure and grace is the most
priceless of all gems.

*Lloyd Croft*

## Charleston Flower Child

Hey little girl a strolling like the wind.
A begging them to buy your flowers.
Charleston child you can't be more than ten,
A running these old streets for hours,
In the sun, the cold, the showers,
A staring up at ivory towers.

She spotted my car,
Came over to the window,
This is what she said to me.

Hello Mister, does ya -
Want to buy a bunch of flowers for a quarter?
Hello Mister, does ya -
Want red or yella?
Hey Mister, just take them -
Home and put them in the water.
Hey, your lady friend will loves you tonight.
Hey, everything will come out all right -

A quarter please,
Or does you want two?

*Rayberry*

## Evil Kneivel

Experience in his lifetime of connivance hovers near
A bold, colorful thief tormented by lack of fear
Survives on a harsh diet of vodka, tomato juice and beer,
But mostly survives on evil.
Projects glamour and excitement to his profession of choice
An artist for design;
A legend in time
A swashbuckler? A fool?
A man not content with mere being
He will love and be loved and know life.

*Marilee Brown*

## The House Of The Lord

We pray that one day in December,
A day that is wondrous fair,
A great host of people will assemble there,
This chosen spot in woods serene,
Where Christian hearts will care.
And the love and faith which built this church
Will be for all who enter there.
Where happy children will laugh and play,
And each of us in thoughts rejoice.
For this day God brought to us
To hear—a reverent voice,
    "Let us go into the house of the Lord."

*Virginia B. Brainard*

## Tears in My Eyes

There are tears in my eyes today.
A boy and girl are throwing their life away.
Home, life isn't any fun, so clinging
together they are on the run.
No one ever understands they
Can't live up to people's demand's
Two young people floundering
in the dark, determined togetherness
in life will embark
Now life hasn't taught them how
rough it can be.  Out on the streets
with no place to retreat.
Along comes a man in a big limousine
looking for girls for trick's and a fling.
She hesitates but not for long, she
hasn't eaten and neither has he.
She take's the first step, no turning
back, drugs and fast living they now call home.
If only they had listened to Mom and Dad.  Things
Would have been different.  Oh how sad.

*Mildred Ransom*

## Expressions of a Game Lost

The players' glistening sweat attests to the energy spent this day
A brave last ditch effort to avert defeat just barely goes astray,
After reality suddenly unfolds before us with its familiar clarity
One team claims victorious glory, the other only words of charity,

Leaving the field at contest end, this game now quite done
The winning team is exuberant for the victory they have won,
But of their defeated opponents, it can only be said
There was total dejection and emotionless expressions of the dead,

For the vanquished, it's the platitude of how you play the game
But of great effort without triumph, there is only despair and blame,
Mental accusations of others' errors dominate your every thought
Without fully realizing that your team has simply been outfought,

As the sun casts its last slivers upon the empty field of play
It may be of some small comfort to focus on tomorrow's day,
Just remember to keep a positive attitude and surely one can see
The joy of life and yet another chance—that's the hopeful key,

All who live and compete are aware of the moral to life's story
Oh, how fleeting a moment is each death and victory with its glory,
So my wounded warrior, soothe thyself, and rest this very night
It's the end of just one battle, and there are so many more to fight.

*J. C. Sherman*

## The Tomb

It stands among the rubble, a silent ghostly tomb
A casualty of the ravages of tragic senseless acts
It holds the innocent victims who never had a chance
They lost their lives in an instant, their innocence still intact.

The prevailing winds of love and hope, concern and care
Blow softly and gently, creating a stir among the debris
Allowing a glimpse of a crayon drawing or a teddy bear
Opening wounds, bringing forth tears and silent desperate pleas.

Occasionally the winds of doubt and anger blow cold and harsh
A chilly reminder that evil and hatred still remain
Bringing with them destruction and filling our souls with grief
And an overpowering sense of helplessness and pain.

After we've buried our dead and paid our final respects
We'll take the time to heal and let our bodies mend
We'll denounce the forces of evil and embrace the bonds of love
Lest they died in vain, our family and our friends.

The peace of the Heartland was broken, our hearts are torn in half
But our spirits are undaunted and our faith is ever strong
Our lives and our city will be rebuilt from the ashes of death
For the Heartland of Oklahoma is where our hearts belong.

*Sherry D. Hillemeyer*

## Faith Without Works

To turn the eyes of the surgeon's spear away from the smoke and blaze
A child's brought down by senseless war
Life red in the crimson haze

To which the end I see not near for fallen fruit of wombs
'tis death enough, a cry, a gasp
And last before the tomb

This child of 5 or 3 or 2 speaks loudly from the grave
through mother's eye and wailing cries
And fields that hope can't save

So when it's over and when it's done to which the world will say
We spoke of peace and acted not
to save this child that day

*Robert L. Blue*

## A Child's Dream

A dream that is the middle of the night,
A dream to behold.

On a spaceship in the middle of the night.
And the new creatures give you such a fright.

To sail the seven seas would be great,
But I have to get up at eight.

Now the work is done,
And we had a lot of fun

A dream with imagination,
And a lot of fascination.

This could only be one thing -
A CHILD'S DREAM.

*Michelle Shuman*

## Circle of Life

Thunder and lightning, such an awesome sound
A flood of raindrops fall all around
To bring new life from this sacred ground.
    Hoka Hey!  It is a good day!

A hot summer day, with a clear blue sky
The dancers in tune to the eagle cry
As the sundance raises the spirit high.
    Hoka Hey!  It is a good day!

The goose's call to flight, it echoes!  There!
Busy beavers are working everywhere
It is harvest time in the crisp fall air.
    Hoka Hey!  It is a good day!

The gentle, healing snows have come at last,
To soothe the land scarred from the year just past.
As the icy winter spell is being cast
    Hoka Hey!  It is a good day!

Grandfather has called me so I must go.
I will miss the joys of this life.  That's so.
Tomorrow's promises I will not know.
    Hoka Hey!  It is a good day!

*Steven C. Hedden*

## Golden Days

Oh the days!  The golden days!
When we were all once young.
Oh the days!  The golden days!
Of good times and fun.
Oh the days!  The golden days!
Of youth at its highest peak.
Whatever happened to the days the golden days
When we were all once young?

*Jessica Ergle*

## Flutter

What makes your heart flutter?
A scare, waves crashing the shoreline, beautiful sun rises
or sunsets, maybe its the mountain or a memory that lives
in your heart? Everyone has a different reason, but each
has a flutter once in a lifetime. Mine is all that I am, everything
around me is a flutter. I want to take all that life has to give
me and store it to memory. I want to awaken others to this
gift we have for free. Appreciate all that is given and all
that is lost, for someday it may be gone in a flutter!

*Tracey A. Mathews*

## My Soul Like A Garden

Of all the places that I ever go,
a garden most closely resembles my soul;
birth and death and resurrection within
giving meaning and comfort to my life again;
and if you watch closely, in the garden you learn
great lessons involving life's every turn;
you plant many seeds and give them great care
and patiently wait for what soon will grow there;
and then sometimes a unique little plant
will emerge from the ground with particular slant;
its disrupts the order that you worked hard to own
but you make a decision to leave it alone;
and that little plant begins to blossom and grow,
that beautiful flower becomes part of the show;
and if you're lucky it may happen within you,
something will grow from where you haven't a clue;
and when it sprouts up you better address,
the things that matter, down there deep in your breast;
its scary for sure, but your alive and your whole;
its a garden in miniature, deep in your soul.

*Randy F. Hudson*

## What Is Love?

What is love?
A gift from God enabling me to see
the best in you
no matter what your iniquities.

What is love?
Enduring acts, patient and always kind.
It never fails
For love prevails, to wrong it's always blind.

What is love?
Unselfishness - always willing to share
without complaint
or self restraint, just the will to care.

What is love?
Hugging someone, letting them know you're there
at anytime
come rain or shine, their cross to help them bear.

*Lisa Guthrie*

## A Blue-Eyed Dreamer

Baby blue-eyes, baby blue-eyes how do you sleep?
  A giggle, a sob and then not a peep.
Visions of clear skies, of clouds and much more.
  Lions and tigers who know how to soar.

Mystical places and magical moods
  and grassy green fields so soft and so smooth.
The oceans are blue and the world is green,
  but to you my dear baby, these mean not a thing.

You're looking through glass which hasn't a tint
  and oh what a view you must have through it.
Baby blue-eyes, baby blue eyes, the dream has to end.
  Wake up sweet babe 'til its bed-time again.

*Larry Crist*

## Arousal

It had been a long cold winter.
A grizzly bear coming out of hibernation,
I scanned the horizon, the sensation
of something flitting by hit me:
a sprinter deer's shadow on the snow...
I do not know.

Heavenly, I gazed day-dreaming.
Suddenly you were there,
appearing from nowhere, within arms' reach,
sitting on my desk, a proper peach:
Your figure full and ebullient in the sunlight;
rubbing your arms sensuously up and down your sides.
Mesmerized, I watched you wiggle your tight behind,
the head toward the feet inclined...

Mr. Cool was losing his mind...
But not his eyes or his desires!
"Oh, you beautiful...!", I exclaimed, amazed.
Then you zipped past my amorous gaze,
buzzing by my eager ear, -the utter disdain!-
and landed... on the window pane...

*J. Paul Lennon*

## Vietnam Veteran

I'm jus' a country boy long since my days at 'Nam
A gun I had, a party toy and shot a little man.

Didn't have much learnin' did no good at school
Killin' ain't my yearnin' ain't no fightin' fool.

Lord, Lord, gimme one mo' chance.

Lately I've been dreamin' little man I killed
Wake at night jus' screamin' for the blood I spilled.

Pleadin' eyes now haunt me eyes I shot away
Squintin' eyes that taunt me eyes that seem to say,

Lord, Lord gimme one mo' chance.

Little man, let me be shut yor eyes and sleep
Turn away, don't look at me my head's about to leap.

Drinkin' booze and smokin' pot makes you go away
Little man, I know I shot leave me 'lone today.

Lord, Lord, gimme one mo' chance
Please Lord... Gimme one mo' chance.

*Victor E. Legaspi*

## The Survivor's Truth

All wounds heal in time;
a jaded phrase of little comfort.
Advice that is often given
by those without the scar.

They know not of the sleepless nights,
cuddled only by the fear.
Starting at the slightest nose
imprisoned by the terror.

Time in reality, is like a cloud.
It will cover and even shade the pain,
but never fully block it out.
Pain can easily break through like the sun's rays.

Only the strong can bear a sunny day.
This strength can only come from within.
A tough heart and a brave soul
are what will push you through.

After the clouds have formed
there are days that are wonderfully stormy
and also days of hideous sun.
Endure the sun, and live for the thunder.

*Megyn Byrnes*

## My Dear Mother

Who can cast away a mothers special treasure,
A love so endless it's useless to measure.
A love so precious and truly divine.
Keep others wondering how it became mine.
But a mother so loving is an invaluable gift
You strengthen bad days and give them a lift.
No one can compare to a mother of gold
Who held her child close when the world was cold.
Long life to mother my continuing friend
may our love continue to grow forever and again.
And long lives the woman who bears a child
And makes them feel loved even with a smile
It's hard to day I love you and thanks for all you've done.
But you mean more to me now than the rising of the sun.
You gave me a life to give onto another
and no one is more precious then my Dear Mother.

**Shirley Diana Worelds**

## Faded Memory

I remember clearly the night we met,
A midnight blue sky, the thousands of stars
and a silver moon behind the oak tree.
We walked along the dew drenched grass,
you touched my hand and we kissed.
You sweetly whispered "forever"
and I silently agreed.
But when the blue sky turned red,
the stars faded away and the moon dipped
daintily behind a fire like sun,
I was left with nothing more
than a faded memory.

**Nicole Leigh Sasso**

## "The Child"

A child's voice you hear crying for help
A mother's love tries to heal the crying pain
A father without a soul, yet with a kind gentle heart,
tries to reach out to the crying child

The child cry's, cry's louder still but the mother or father
never hear it out of her mouth.

Hurt and alone, the cry's for help are heard only by clouds and wind.
There the child's sits and cry's for help, no one comes.

The child sits and with one more breath, it fades; it cries
one last time and no one hears.
A year later flowers cover over where she has cried and is no more.

The child's mother and father loved and cared but could
not hear the crying, the deep crying.

**Leslie Ann Sturm**

## The Last Slurp

His head arose from just-trembled mountains—
A naturally desired disaster
Erupted,
Spilling forth precious fluid.
The taste of blood
Swirled around his vibrating tastebuds.
This new flavor he liked much.
Prey tamed and conquered
With a most potent weapon.
Solidness gave way and exploded.
His probe forced wide open gates
Held fast
By lunar forces,
Choking the moon
Until the redness oozed
And mixed with her love.

**Maria Elizabeth Walinski**

## Blue-Green

I put on a blue shirt and
a neat blue tie and then

Began writing with a pen that had
the smell of time, the odor

Of light, but now while all the paintings
in the house are turning blue,

I stand disconsolate before a window
and look at the city below

That January has captured, gloomy with
an infinite rain, and I think

Of that green pen on the desk, pen green
with time and death,

**Sumio Matsuda**

## My Night Companion

I long for a night of dreamless sleep,
a night without you hovering at the edge
of my semi - conscious mind.

Stealing your way into my peace,
bringing the ultimate pain that wrenches
at my once healed heart.

Widening the crevice, spilling out the contents.
Once again, needs unanswered.

Drifting into my wakefulness,
leaving frustration, devastation,
pieces to hold together.

No shoulder to cradle my head.
No rest upon my bed.

**D. L. Schnackenberg**

## Babies

Shall I compare thee to the clouds
A package so small and frail,
A bundle of dynamite so loud,
A fragrant rose so sweet to smell.
Your the apple of your parent's eyes.
A blanket of pink or blue,
A bed of slumber; your satisfied,
A bud in the springtime coming anew.
From heaven you came from the arms of God,
A miracle indeed,
Your substance He did laud,
Before you were a seed,
Even the hairs of your head He numbers,
God's eye on you never slumbers.

**Tara Turnbull**

## A Quiet Man

A quiet man with simple tastes
A patient man - does nothing in haste
He made his mark in the profession he chose
And fought some struggles that only he knows
Has a genuine affection for his fellow man
Spreads goodwill wherever he can
Fathered three children, a daughter two sons
And cared for their mother 'til her life was done
His demeanor, his touch, his language is kind
A true gentleman in all ways defined
Lady love came again - second time around
A marriage so right, so fine and so sound
Two lives fit together - a near perfect blend
He's my gentleman husband, my love and my friend

**Leona D. Nash Hunt**

157

## Wet Dream

Stimulating, squishy sounds of ecstasy, accents every move.
A periphery of passion pervaded perspiration leaves nothing to prove.
Undulating bodies, sway to the sweet a cappella, of grunts and groans.
Let love last, is uttered endlessly, in the midst of moans.
Careless kisses, unveils hidden desires.
Come, let's come together. My body is on fire!
Savage screams, precede the sedative of our seething release.
Fear not my love, fear not. I come in peace.
The persistent, pitter-patter of rain declares itself.
I reluctantly pull away, from her wanton self.
Hypnotized, I stare at the rain.
I'm glad I came, I'm glad I came ———
If only to delight in the boudoir's succulent eclair.
I rouse, from a sleep of which I was unaware —— wet!?!

### *Mark A. Seaton*

## Untitled

When love dies...
a rose crumbles
a heart breaks
snow falls.

When love dies...
time stands still
music stops
winter comes.

When love dies...
there's fresh earth on a new grave
all colors turn to shades of black and grey
the sun ceases to shine.
When love dies...

### *Rachel Harris*

## Does She, Or Doesn't She?

Life is nothing but maintenance,
a series of fixings and woes.
When I'm not cussing my car out,
I'm chasing the runs in my hose.

The light is out in the hallway,
the kitchen sink's drip, drip, dripping;
I'll have to tend to them later -
my fingernails all need clipping.

My husband's trying to push me,
the children are trying to pull,
the refrigerator's almost empty,
the baby's diapers are full.

The bills that lay on the table
wait for organizational stacking,
while vacation clothes still in the suitcase
beg me for their unpacking.

In time I can handle it all,
but one thing that tends to irk
is my husband answering, "No,"
when asked, "Does your wife work?"

### *Stefanie Drown*

## The Old Bedroom

The dust gathers around the memories I once had.
The coldness of my old bedroom, is where I stand.
The coldness felt as if no one had lived in this room before.
The memories, I remember I had in this room.
I slowly think of the time I first moved in this beautiful room.
But now I start to think, it's not so beautiful no more.
As I turned to leave the room.
I wiped the dust of the shelf that once held my teddy bears.
And then I walked out, the door closing behind.

### *Sweet Justice*

## Sweet Sorrow

Lay me upon that sweet sorrow, which I
will love until tomorrow, now bless each side and
reach with pride to lay upon that Sweet
Sorrow that I will love unto tomorrow.

### *Jacey Christiene Terrill*

## The Birth of a Bag Lady

She can be seen wandering the streets;
A shopping bag dangling from her weathered hand.
Pondering her reflection in a glass storefront,
She pulls her limp hair back with a simple rubberband.

Wonder what could have happened to her,
What circumstances might have brought her to this?
Did she have a wonderful love,
Someone with whom she shared passion and bliss?

Does she have hidden pain,
Something of which she has never spoken?
Did he leave her for another,
And is her poor heart broken?

Could she have been callously abandoned,
Left alone and forlorn?
Trying to escape her pain by wandering the streets,
Was another Bag Lady born.....

### *Lea Roth*

## The Lull Before the Storm

'Twas a new day dawning, tiptoeing into the day
A single, subtle warning of what soon comes our way
I should have seen you coming, with skies so dark and gray
Instead, I sat there yawning, your cool breeze upon my face

You have lulled me into slumber as you cast your magic spell
I can barely hear the thunder, like a secret not to tell
And as I lay here napping, never knowing what's in store
The drops become a rapping on my windows and my doors

My house, they have surrounded, like an army waging war
Their relentless, charges mounting, growing larger by the score
I'm awakened by the thunder and now am quite amazed
as the lightning strikes I ponder at the fury and the rage

I revel in its beauty and then am led astray
by the fear that now instills me, on this dark and dismal day
As slowly as it came, it draws its final breath
I swear, I heard it call my name with a low and grumbling gasp

Now, I know the meaning of "The lull before the storm"
It lulls you into sleeping so as not to show its form
And while you lay there dreaming of a fine and sunny day
It brings its secret vengeance in its unexpected way

### *Steve J. Miller*

## Winter Icing

It's a Christmas type of morning -
A soft, snow-fall type of morning
That arrived with no forewarning
    To enhance our sleepy world.

Proud, tall evergreens in icing;
Chickadees "at bath" in icing;
Winter landscape so enticing
    Mother Nature has unfurled.

Even the flowers, long since done blooming,
Seem to come once more to blooming -
They respond to magic grooming
    Wearing lovely cloaks, snow-pearled.

### *Loraine O. Funk*

## If Never Ever Comes

Looking for a little spark,
A spark from your eternal fire,
One spark to fuel the flame,
Just enough to send me higher.

You make me feel invisible,
Treat me as if I wasn't there,
Seeing you with all the others,
Makes me wish I could vanish in thin air.

Then one day you spoke,
With words intended for the meek,
"Wouldn't be caught dead" with me,
Not tonight, tomorrow, or even next week.

Said I'm not your "type,"
Hidden in words so clever,
We can't be a couple,
Only in "your dreams"...never.

Well, if never ever comes,
I'll be there by your side,
To help you pick up the pieces,
Scattered along life's bumpy ride.

*Randy Overton*

## "A Lonely Tree"

Christmas comes once a year,
A time of joy and of good cheer.
There stood in the woods a sad little tree,
Begging everyone to please, take me.

Saying, I want to shine with light so bright,
making everyone happy Christmas Eve night.
I want to be there just santa and me,
When he comes with toys for me to see.

When families gather and began to sing,
When children laugh and bells begin to ring.
When on this night of Christmas Eve,
Appears a jolly old man whom they believe.

I want to be there looking for a glance,
To see Santa and his Reindeer, how they prance.
As they glide through the night with his sleigh,
Bouncing over roof tops on their way.

As the morning sun comes shining so bright,
Children all around me with great delight.

*Lealon R. Tate*

## "Time"

A time to love, and never hate.
A time to be prompt, and never late.
A time to sorrow; a time to be sad.
A time to be happy; a time to be glad.
A time to be silent; a time to speak.
A time to be strong, and help the weak.
A time to be alone, or be in a crowd.
A time to be humble; a time to be proud.
A time for tears; a time to smile.
A time to forgive, and go that extra mile.
A time to miss our loved ones.
A time for sweet memories, too.
A time to look forward to a great reunion with you.

*Ruby Whisenant*

## Clouds

There was a time when I was high
a time when gold dripped in the sky.
I was alive, so full of life then
but when you came so did my end.
I walked off my clouds so precious in flight
leaving my skies meant leaving my light.
My steps so small and so unsure
led me through darkness- a frightening blur.
I reached out for your hands to hold onto me
but I kept slipping and you just didn't see.
I've been here, so alone- chasing my tail
wandering too far, leaving my given trail.
Spinning in circles, passing the time now
time leaves me clinging to a broken tree's bough.
Unaware of my grasp to rotting, dead wood
your words spoken so clear, so misunderstood.
How I dream of my clouds above my head
my safety, my life which I have fled.
I can never reach them, not in my years
I'm here still, chasing you through my tears.

*Melissa Stagner*

## The Little Dragon Fly

A buzzing noise from the mountains coming
A tiny little dragon fly with hills, mountains in his eyes
he has tasted the fresh water from the streams
The trees, plants where he has rested
I smell what he has smelled
I am calm, happy, peaceful
Why can't everyone smell, touch, see the little dragon fly?
Taste fresh water, hear calm sounds of nature?
Why can't everyone be a little dragon fly.............
Live in a world of buzzing harmony?

*Lynn McCormick*

## The Talent Show

I looked at the things hanging above my head,
A trophy, and ribbons of white, blue, and red.
Then on the table, pictures, poems, stories GALORE!
I got halfway through, but there was so much more!
Pictures to see, poems and stories to read,
And beautiful dresses with thousands of beads!
Bread to taste, songs and music to hear,
I won't be able to finish, I fear!
Then a man said a name, he held a ribbon - white,
"Third place goes to you for your picture of night"!
Then on to another, this time a ribbon of red,
"Second place goes to you, for your baby-blue spread".
A smile came to his face as he took the ribbon of blue,
"For the one who sings like a dove, runner up goes to you"!
Then down came the trophy, polished to a shine,
"To the one who writes like no other," I wish this were mine!
Every one cheered, as they clapped their hands,
Then the crowd danced to the beat of the band.
But all I could do was stare at the hole in my shoes,
And hope that some day I'd be in the talent show, too!!!

*Rachael L. Houchin*

## Welfare Lady

I got five kids and I live in the projects and I'm married to welfare. Sometimes he don't come on time and we go hungry, or sometime not at all, he fuss with me about me not having enough bedrooms for all the kids, and my papers not being right.
So I just wanna say to all my lil sisters out there, if you ever get to feelin' cool or high and think you can take advantage of the system by havin' a baby, think again sister about the welfare lady.

*Julie Curry*

## Wishes

A tune, a melody, a beat
A variation of a familiar sound
One that is sung year after year
But this year is sounds so good...
Where have the years gone by?

Sing it to me one more time
That is my wish for you; to enjoy
Those things we take for granted.
Remember the smile that crept from the heart?
The packages wrapped in ribbons and the smile
On grandma's face...the anticipation of, "What I got."
Let's have cake and ice cream; and the games
We played...where have the years gone by?
Sing it to me one more time.

**Ramona Therese Dolega**

## A Mother's Voice

Listen, hear the sound, it overwhelms
A voice from the past rebounds
Echoes within the mind, memories to dwell
Sound continuing to bind
Releasing a word so profound
Whispered, conquers the mind
Tone commands the moment in time.

A plea for help, tears now quelled
A voice to soothe the hurt, to expel
Musical sound known so well
Loving trust, projecting strength so vast
Whispered words, seemingly present, yet past
A voice, patterned to task.

A mothers voice breathing time
Dwelling with realms of mind
Listen, hear the sound, 'tis divine
The musical sound, oh so very dear
A mothers voice forever near
Listen, hear the sound, memories do appear.

**Mary Ann B. Mistric**

## Sermon of the Divine in Green Vesture

Does your soul cherish the joy of spring?
A whisper of warmth informs the morning air
That something exquisite is happening -
A hushed imminence stirring everywhere.

Have mundane cares desensitized your eye?
Then "stop, look, and listen" like a child
At roadway's edge, as seasons wending by
Bear miracles - just seeming to be mild.

Blossom-laden branches sweep the sky
As nesting robins chirp laconic praise
In trees whose sinewed arms are lifted high
To thank the Power behind the warming days.

The sun prolongs its silent trumpet call
And sprigs of green awake from carcass-pods,
Reaching up for life lost in the fall
From their sullen grave of earthen clods.

Can you discern the master metaphor
And thrust through soil of selfishness and rise
Above the ravage of the Fall, and more -
Gain glory with the Sovereign of the skies?

**Ralph Sheffield**

## Death And The Dragon

The deaf mute death rides a dragon,
Whose nostrils breathe red flame.
But the eyes of the rider are calm and kind.

They sail beyond jet trees of twilight,
Dwindle in significance against the heavens
And hide, like a bee, in the sky's grey flower.

**Genevieve F. Miner**

## Make Me A World

Make me a world unshackled.
A world free from the hindrances of arbitrary rules
binding arbitrary players.
A world in which love and kindness take precedence.
A world in which the universal goal is to love
blindly and without fear of reprisal.

A world in which gentleness and caring
aren't manipulations for personal gain.
A world in which power is used only to strengthen
our thoughts, feelings and actions toward others.
Make me such a world and I'll hand it back to you...
with love..

**Pat Plummer**

## "Dare To Discover"

Dare to Discover the unperceived,
A world that is to be believed.
A place filled with happiness and love,
But only through faith in God above.

Having problems with pressure or stress,
Then take a moment to think and confess.
Then cast your cares on the Lord above,
For he'll bring you righteous answers with love.

Being true and loyal day by day,
Showing his love in every way.
God is Holy, Righteous, and Pure,
Bringing everyone his eternal cure.

The Lord's precious word cannot fail,
His love and mercy shall prevail.
So Dare to Discover the one above,
And I guarantee you'll find eternal love.

**Tiffany Crook**

## Blue Sky

Have you ever wondered,
about our bright blue sky?
It holds lightning and thunder,
but can you tell me why?

A lot of people are concerned about our planet
because their worried about pollution.
We still take things for granted,
though they haven't found a solution.

Instead they keep talking about space.
and putting things up there.
I guess they want to help the whole human race
but I wonder if anybody cares!

While we're on the ground,
shouldn't we take a look around?
And enjoy all there is to this,
before we sail away into emptiness?

Take a look above you,
and tell me what you see!
under a sky that's blue,
that's the color of the sea.

**Tom Jackson**

## Books As Life

Don't talk to me
about people who are young and alive,
because, though I may only be twenty,
I'm quite bored already.
Step into my shoes
and see the world through my eyes:
- the suffering, the pain, the mentally deranged -
(oh, and these are the good sides of life).
So, though the tears say otherwise,
I've committed to a peaceful life
I've resigned to a lonely life
with every day ending in the same fashion:
- me reading some book on love, desire, and passion -
and though I've yet to experience these emotions
the "printed pages" have quelled those notions
and has left me quite filled
though perhaps a little unfulfilled in the eyes of some
and literate in the eyes of others.
So don't feel that I need convincing
because I have chosen books over living.

*Swearingen*

## Twice Blind

Two blind men sat in quarrel
About the rising sun.
One said, "Yes, I think it does,"
The other, "There is none!"

Now, while they mulled their variance,
The sun began to rise;
Then, moving toward high-noon's full light,
Pressed on toward ev'ning's grandeured skies.

O twice blind men! They could not see
The sun in circuit wend;
Nor wait — their quarrel to finally cease —
To be the sun:
To rise, and set again!

*M. E. Wilson*

## The Last Gull

It came as quickly as it left,
   Across the empty fingers of a tree,
   And quick against the cold, blue sky...
      It was the last of the evening;
      It was the last of the gulls.

Somewhere, hidden from any eye, save one,
   Its wings were folded in a nighttime place.
   And this distant, unseen place of rest;
      Was somewhere, soon to sink in evening shadow
         Thus, was gone the last of daytime's movement;
            Thus, was gone the final flying gull.

*Walter Dennis*

## The Needs of a Child and a Parent

A child needs to know they are loved, a hope, a faith, a dream
A child needs a hand to hold, a neck to hug and a shoulder on which
   to lean
A child needs to learn patience, discipline and respect
A child needs all of these to have a life that is a success
A parent needs to take the time to guide a child through their life
A parent needs to teach a child all they need to know and shield them
   from strife
A parent must be there for a child's needs both big and small
A parent is the rock on which a child will stand tall or fall
To do all this a parent needs a strength that can come only from
   the Lord above
A parent needs to know that they can do it all with LOVE

*Louise Patterson*

## Daughters Of America

Daughters of America arise and let your love show
Adorn yourselves and bloom in beauty,
Your men in silence wait to receive you in their loving arms.
A place in your heart they seek.
In the summer's heat your coolness they ensure.
Freezing winter's persist but you they touch not,
   for your men an insulation be.
Daughters of America let not your men their shadows be.
Your femininity a weapon be, today and tomorrow
   your respects demand.
In every area your rights fight, the world a man's
   was, now you share.
Your civil rights demand yet your sweetness lose not.
Daughters of America fly your colours and side by
   side stand with your men.

*Peter Gaskin*

## Wonder of America

Our American essence, once vital, now so beaten and worn.
Advances for the good of man; yet genuine progress not borne.
Freedom our forefathers structured, but liberties we've kept taking.
Hard work built roads and parks, for the convenient lives we're now
   making.

Miracle drugs help heal, techno-gadgets abound in our domain.
Well-intentioned inventors have solved problems but grave ones remain.
Culture changing slickly, so little to inspire and beautify.
Instant art everywhere, for our tastes, not much to amplify.

Craftsmanship lost for the ages, new buildings of concrete and glass.
Apprenticeship all but gone, leaders slogging through social morass.
Leisure time fought hard for, uncommitted time we humanly waste.
Self-study and interaction performed with unfortunate haste.

Consumers less discriminate, advertisers making bold claims.
Scientists are unknown, sports stars and entertainers are the names.
We didn't earn our freedom, how could we hope to appreciate?
Witness the gratefulness of the fortunate souls who immigrate.

America's still the promised land, what promises must we make?
To care who we are and for others, to think what's really at stake.
To contribute to home, work and beyond in valuable ways.
To forge a new America and rocket through this passing phase.

*Simon A. Snyder*

## The Butterfly II

At the end of an ever-long Winter's night,
After struggling with the cold,
While the stars, they held their place just right
In the sketches of heaven old,
The rose bowed his weary head
And drifted off to sleep,
Dreaming upon his lonely bed
Of fields rich and deep.
Then dew from an early Springtime morn
Awakened the sleepy rose
To gesture toward the newly born
Rays and hopeful glows
Of the coming glory in the air
To warm the rose's chill,
And cast the weary rose's stare
Upon the lighted hill,
Where the love God has sent, through wisdom spent,
Along her gentle way,
A butterfly to happen by
And whisk the rose's dreams away.

*Tim Larsen*

## Now We're Here

As the shadows fall,
against the trees so tall,
I wonder how I got so small.

Wondering an weaving,
daring an dreaming,
conning scheming not even living.

Onward I go, bound to put on a show,
but truly not knowing where the last stop will go.

I am that, what I am.
Why didn't I see what a damn.
I went on by not using the master plan.

So now in this I dwell,
realizing I didn't do so well.
praying and paying through a state of hell.

So to the last I will stay,
even if it's a long day.
In a brighter way is what I pray.

So my father up above,
answers gently like a dove,
creating a world for us to love.

### *Mathew George Owens*

## Justice

Said Mattie to the Judge "Yo honah it is tru,
Ah hit with wif da rollin' pin until I knowed he's fru!"
"But Mattie,..." said the Judge "...it's why I want to know.
What had he done to make you think that you should hate him so?"

Said Mattie to the Judge "Yo honah doan you see?
He tole me dat we boff was fru, dat he was leavin' me."
"But Mattie.." said the Judge "...he'd have to file a suit
And once the cost got through to him he'd be back on your stoop."

Said Mattie to the Judge "Yo honah dat ain't so,
We nevah did git wedded so he was free ta go!"
"Well Mattie..." said the Judge "...for crime to you always pay.
I fear that we must lock you up, have you anything to say?"

Said Mattie to the Judge "They is jest one mo' thing,
I wondah if ah'd be allowed to buy a weddin' ring?"
"But Mattie..." said the Judge "...you say you never wed,
What makes you want a wedding ring especially when he's dead?"

Said Mattie to the Judge "Yo Honah doan you see?
Ah nevah was so sho befo' dat he belong to me!"

### *Ginger Gordon*

## I So Fine

I is as pretty as a summer rose
Ain't no need being modest cause everybody knows
I is got eyes that sparkle like the stars at night
My lips are full and red like an apple that's ripe

I is got skin so bronze you could swear it shines
Child it ought to be a crime to be this fine
I is got a waist so small and my hips are round
That's why all heads turn when I strut downtown

My legs are long and I'm bosom strong
I is swear I can't find nothing that's wrong
People envy the stylish clothes I wear
I ain't at all surprise when people stop and stare

I is got hair that's long and feels like silk
These teeth are as white as any cow's milk
I is like a work of art when I strike a pose
I is just that fine and everybody knows

### *Mona Lisa Bass*

## Get Up Brother

Rise above your feelings
Ain't no use wearing that frown,
Look at the sunset
Its all good.

Keep a straight head not a straight face
Smile sometimes and give your face a rest
Never let your face express your true feelings.
I know what you are feeling
Because I am feeling it too.
But you always see me smiling
It may seem confusing.
But they don't know what I am thinking.
I am in this game to
And I am long ways ahead of you
Keep Stepping
its all good

### *Martin T. Wood*

## The Dandelion

Poor little despised fellow
All dressed in a coat of yellow
With a quaint little hood of green
Saying "Hello" in early spring

If it weren't for you said a lady gay
I could take life easy today
But with you bobbing your heads in sight
I'll have work to do from morning until night

So she cut and dug from dawn till night
Until not a dandelion was left in sight
And now said she as she chuckled with glee
I'll not be pestered with you you'll see

She was tired and slept quite late
Awaking when the postman came through the gate
Hurrah! Hurrah! my work is done
This is going to be my day for fun

She went to the window and looked out, upon the lawn
Her hands went up in horror at the sight she gazed upon
All her work seemed to have been done in vain
For lo! all the little fellows were back again.

### *Winifred Genner*

## Life Review

Deeds undone and done
all here for me to blush again

Words unspoken and spoken
all here to haunt my memory

Unfinished business with the dead
but none that I can finish now

Some place within must hold a court of mercy
where I may plead my case
and grant us all forgiveness
the dead for doing what they did
me for not letting it die with them

### *Michael Erlanger*

## Friendship

Friendship is loving and caring
When your friend is down you feel down to,
When your friend is happy you try to be happy with them,
When your friend is hurt you feel hurt too.
When your friend is sick you feel sick too.
When your friend needs a friend you're there for them.
That's what I call friendship.

### *Gena Moore*

162

## Untitled

I look forward to my lonely years,
That, in time, will give me
So much more to love about the past.

*Jana M. Thompson*

## Funny, Funny, Hop Along Bunny!

Funny, funny Bunny,
All I do is laugh with you,
Oh, funny, funny Bunny,
Look at the way you hop and jump

It is so pleasing to me, my funny little Bunny,
The way you hop and jump.
I watch day and night out of my little two by two window;
To see you hop and jump.

Could you come to my window?,
Would it be OK for me to make believe I can hop with you?
For I cannot walk,
Though if I could, I'd surely walk with you.

Oh funny, funny Bunny would you be my friend?
Be my hop along buddy, funny, funny Bunny.
For if wishes were to come true, I wouldn't ask for much; only,
For you to be my to be my funny, funny, funny, hop along bunny.

*Shawn Milne*

## I Apologize

As still waters do run deep
all my promises I try to keep
for any promise that I break
please forgive me for the right sake
I made you a promise with all my heart
breaking it was not intentional on my part
though my promise is kept in belate
please never never do me berate
I'm sorry if I caused your heart any kind of pain
I apologize profusely, let our friendship still remain
I made you a solemn promise
that on me you could depend
the promise was straight from the heart
'cause I cherish you as my friend
I'll continue to make sincere promises
that are straight from the heart
but if for some unknown reason
I can't keep them
may our friendship never depart.

*Sharon Wheeler*

## Fright Night

Witches and goblins will come out on Halloween Night,
All scary things imaginable are in sight,
Filling your head to the brim with fright,
That's what happens on Halloween Night.
First you can only see the eyes of an owl,
Then you will hear a hungry wolf howl.
Jack-o-lantern eyes will glow in the dark,
As wild dogs begin to bark.
All of a sudden a mist starts to rise,
And then you start to realize,
That you're alone, all alone,
And then you hear a frightening moan.
So you scream and run to someone's door,
But all you hear is a scary roar!
Then you start to see more and more,
And then you realize that you're done for!

*Taryn McMahon*

## For Bob and Lisa's Kids

Have you ever seen a cloud
Aloft upon the wind
with fluid grace and form untrue
waiting for a child's game?
Can it be a pillow
So the birds at night can rest
or a long grey beard for the mountain king
to warm his chin at night
We all have eyes to see these things
to feel so young again
its up to you just lift your head
there's no telling what comes next

*William C. Obst*

## Loneliness

Nothing is more lonely than always being alone,
. . .alone and depressed you tend to follow,
a path of careless footsteps,
that leaves you broken and hollow.

Being alone at times does have its good qualities,
as long as you can drift away in dreams,
away form life's realities.

But being lonely is one of
life's useless components,
the time seems to stand still
with each depressing moment.

How we all dread it
when this feeling comes around,
you stay gloomy and depressed
without making a sound.

Still in more ways than none,
you experience life's pleasantness,
when you've got family and friends
away from the misery of loneliness.

*LaVonya M. McConneaughey*

## The Path Of Unintent

How many years I've wandered on
Along the Path of Unintent;
How many times I've said a word
Then stopped to say instead "I meant".

I did not mean it as it sounds
I've said a hundred times or more;
But once it's spoken, things somehow
Are never as they were before.

My face still smarts from branches flown
Back into it along the way;
There is no doubt that as I walked
I tossed them out quite carelessly.

But now, it seems, at fifty-eight
A bit more hope for me I see;
I choose a path through garden blooms
To stay away from bushy tree.

For if there's one thing I have learned
Along the Path of Unintent,
If you throw blossoms on the way
You'll never have to say "I meant".

*Ruth Charlton-Thurman*

## Ho-Rain Forest

The sound of my footsteps break the silence
along the rain forest floor
Trees growing for centuries
towering dramatically above the earth
Convoluted tree roots exposed on the surface
curled and twisted, over and under
Fallen trees weathered by the seasons
nurture the seedlings for reproduction
Giant maples draped in moss cast shadows onto the path below
The forest floor laden with ferns
fan upward, swaying in the breeze
Fresh footprints in the soft dirt
signs of wildlife roaming free
Staircases of rock and roots etched by winter run-off
White water gushing from the hillside above
echoing the splashes on the rocks below
Ground cover cluster's making a silhouette
soft green leaves reaching skyward
The rain forest, warm and whimsical
radiating energy without invasion

*Patricia A. Holbrook*

## Water Free

STOP, THINK about how much I mean to you,
Also you to me.  I quench your thirst.
I provide for all people, places and living things.
You use me in some kind of way.
I help flowers blossom, like the birds, the fish, the tree.
These are just a few ways I can make you see, clear enough.

So you will stop taking advantage of me.
There are people out there killing all of us, especially me.
There Dumping Chemical waste into our oceans lakes
And streams so please stop don't kill me.
For I am also a living thing.
Help run, help me run free.

*Tamara Hileman*

## The Winds Of Faith

It's true, I can induce some entities to stay,
Although some parts of me have gone away.
I do not laugh at things light-hearted humor brings to you and you.
My humor, born in pain, discovers jokes anew when day is through.
No longer shackled by fickle extremes of haughty youth,
I play at "hide and seek" like a challenged, wise, dedicated, sleuth.
There are no dreams of "droves that morn" when earthly time is done.
Friends are counted in increments of one.
Away from sea or cloistered room I fly (no eagle ever flew so high),
And dip my wings as each cloud passes by,
To signify the times I've questioned "Why?"
In this release from earthly bonds, I find...
No sun, or moon, or stars, to soothe my mind.
Only revelations in "spirit-flight" its self, evolved.
Mysteries confinement never could have solved...resolved!
No day's too dark or night too bright, that I can't trust my sight.
No pain's so great that I can bear no more...on winds of faith I soar.
So, if I lose more parts of me - and almost disappear - as that may be,
...and some might wonder what's left in life for me...
I'll play music in the darkest of dark...or listen to a meadow-lark.

*Marjorie Foster Fleming*

## Friends

   Friends are always there to lean on, to lend a helping
hand, and just to talk to when times get rough.  Sometimes
I wonder why they stick around.  We unload all our problems
and worries on them and they listen faithfully without
expecting anything in return for their time.  They are remarkable
people.  I hope I have them forever!

*Lauren Elizabeth McWhorter*

## The Answer to Chronic Complainers

I'm a very healthy specimen, never have a pain.
Although the years have rolled around again and again.
My feet never hurt, oh no not mine.
Because I've kept my figure, I'm thin as a dime.
Troubles don't bother my nerves, I'm calm as can be.
High blood pressure is a medical term, never applied to me.
Arthritis is a disease of the elderly, I'm not that old yet.
And my childhood diseases, I've been taught to forget.
My heart keeps pumping, vim and vigor to every vital part.
I never have any symptoms of diseases of the heart.
Haven't had a headache in I don't know when.
All these aches and pains are for older men.
And if I live to be one hundred, I'm going to stay this way.
Cause how I hate to hear complaining day after day.
We know when someone asks, how are you?
They're only being polite, and don't want to hear what's true.
So smile and say, "just fine" and I'll do the same.
And everyone will follow suit and play our little game.
Then we'll all feel better, the world will be a brighter place.
If we take our pills each morning, then put a smile upon our face.

*Leona Barnes*

## World of Strangers

Here I am, a person in a world of strangers.
Always seems like in it, I find only dangers.
People seem to be grinding me down with words and actions.
I really wonder if they're looking for some sort of reaction.
Seems like no one understands what I'm going through.
What can I do to send them a clue?
All these feelings bouncing inside of my head.
Sometimes I wonder if people ever listen to what I have said.
Time passing by ever so fast, I really wonder if I,
My body and soul, will last.

*Randi Hanson*

## Now On Your Own

You are now like a bird, with your
    ambitions, soaring high in the sky.
      No longer can I help or
      participate; I can only
      wait and stand by.
I miss helping you and being an
    active partner in fulfilling your dreams.
      Now, while planning your own
      destiny, your face, like a
      halo, beams.

I know you must seek success while your bright,
    shining star is at its highest.
As you leave, my loving heart aches,
    and my eyes will not be the driest.
I can only hope, when your quest is over
    and your dreams are fulfilled,
      we shall still be close, the best of friends,
      and always will.

*J. P. Kennedy*

## Night

Oh, would the night were come on blackened wings
To shroud the face of this my troubled form
For lo, the storms and strife this day have raged
Around my weak and weary soul forlorn.

Blessed night, my haven and my shield
Swaddle me, in peaceful darkness borne,
Hold me to thy sheltering breast
Till my spirit wakens to a brighter morn.

*Janet F. Whiteaker*

## The Sentinel

There at the gate, a dark foreboding figure,
An ashen pallor, colder than a stone.
With eyes like glints of steel he scans the foothills,
Lest some unwitting stranger this way roam.

How many foolish souls have tried to pass him?
How many anguished cries were quickly stilled?
Compassion is a thing he's unaware of,
So unaffected by the blood he's spilled.

His purpose here is singular and final,
Born of my fear, and nourished by my pain.
From some ancient despair his form was fashioned,
And tears, not blood, pulsate through every vein.

This Warrior, he throws a deadly shadow
Upon the fortress walls this weary night.
Eternal wakefulness, he never slumbers,
His gleaming armor casts the only light.

A feeling of uneasiness surrounds me
In gazing at the unmarked graves below:
So well protected, I am now the Prisoner.
The Sentinel will never let me go..

*Nancy Coffey*

## Alongside Me

Since you died
an emptiness moves alongside me
wherever I go, like a wake in the air as I move
but not behind me, a space alongside me.
The space you once filled.

People rarely speak of this absence at my side,
They fear it as they feel it pressing on their future.
They only see me once in awhile,
with my new space next to me.
But me, I have this emptiness
by my side all the time.

It has impenetrable bubble-like walls.
I can gaze in, but I can't enter it
yet, it stays with me, a part of me.

It is the space you once filled
It is what is left of you outside of memory.
It is the essence of you, still
left behind
empty, yet palpable
a nothingness of real proportion.

*Richard Spiegel*

## Liquid Time

Liquid time flows on by, like
an endless river from which anyone
or anything is unable to find a place to hide.

People like flowers fall and float away,
carrying with them the joy and sorrows
of by gone days.  Never able to scoop it
up or store it away.  Liquid time carries
every fleeting second away, every person
a ripple, some great, some small
But liquid time feels them all.  Aging
memories are clouded like smoke from
the water that puts sight in a haze.
Liquid time carries all away.

*Robert B. Glass*

## The Family Of God

A Family is a Circle...
An uninterrupted Journey of grasping Hands around the World.

All Peoples, all Cultures, United by God
All Friends, all Brothers, all Sisters, all Children.

Our walking and sleeping know not of ending...
Perpetual Life of growing and learning and gaining and losing
    maintains a Balance in the Universe.

Each experience strengthens our Communion,
Each loss enables us to reach out in acceptance of
    Heavenly Works not yet understood.

The infinite number of stars in the sky are as Blessings upon our
    lives.....
Yet we are all of one Body, Heart, Mind, and Spirit
Together in darkness and in the Light of unfailing Time Immemorial.

Though at times we may perceive Brokenness in our Existence,
The Alpha and the Omega are each alike...
Truly the Circle is unceasing.

For we are encompassed by Loving Hands,
Surrounded by Belonging Hearts
And Wrapped in the Wondrous Belief
That we are indeed Children in the Family of God.

*Marianne De Stefano-Hill*

## Girl Playing Pool In Northampton

A thin column of smoke feeds the haze around her face
and a tough black leather attitude gropes her hips.
Arching over down.
Squatting to table level.
Blue explosion!
Lightning crack!
She licks the pouting cigarette between her cheeks and
folds her arms under her sharp chest.
A hairy hand swishes around her lower back and falls
possessively down, rising rough to pinch her neck back
as beer stained fingers pluck the fire from her lips.

*Robert Gardner*

## My Ami Died

When nite draws its curtain of darkness
And all is still and quiet
I am alone with thoughts of you.
My Ami - my own - oh, my darling
Where have you gone, and left me all alone?
This day was never here before
And will never be again
A day that I have lost, my dear
And will never know again
I think of moments we have shared
The ecstasy we have known
Of lips on lips - in bliss
Enfolded in your arms
So safe was I in any storm
Oh, my love where have you
gone, and left me all alone
I feel the pain of a remembered touch
And as the nite moves on
I sigh, I cry, and wish you
could come home.

*Molly M. Clarke*

## September Morn

Dear child, I've watched you leave my house so many times
and always fear reached out and clutched my heart.
"Oh God, please guide her faltering baby steps,
Hold fast her tiny hand while we're apart."
Knowing my faith, so forgiving my doubts and fears,
Always He brought you safely back to me.
And you who had feasted on the joyful day,
Were too tired to vision tears you could not see.

This morning as I watched you leave once more
I felt a loneliness I did not even dare to hide.
Forever gone the child I knew six happy years;
You proudly swung a school-bag at your side.

    *Virginia Windsor Tate*

## Dream of the Brave

I kneel before you with a humble heart
and ask.
I desire with each new day a sense of
self renewed.
To see the light in all that is around me.
I want to feel true joy, a sense of glory
in your being.
The courage and the strength to live each
day ahead.
To not be burdened with despair at the times
to come.
To feel the peace of mind I feel in my dreams
To live my dreams, to manifest them into this
world.
To explore myself and to know myself, to know
just who I am.
And why I am here.
To fulfill my purpose, to help others fulfill
theirs.
To dream, to know my dreams, to live my dreams.

    *Wade Washburn*

## Kitchen Window

Thru the slatted blinds looking out, I see the wall
and beyond that, the vineyard.
Sometimes the rabbits romp there, chasing and mating.

Half a mile beyond, (I know, I measured it once)
stately eucalyptus trees form the horizon,
unmoved except by the wind.

Today it's hazy as I feel this tanka form.
It's fall; the vines are dying.
Overhead, the sky is filled with flocks of starlings.

Irresistibly, the sun is pulled to the south.
Right now it seems to be perched atop a 'phone pole,
and soon will grow large and red.

Dusk comes cool and quick about this time of the year.
The earth is in a hurry to end this cycle,
and speeds on toward winter.

The vines hurry too. Soon only stakes will remain
to return my morning gaze,
seen thru Valley fog, beyond the kitchen window.

    *Weldon Faulmann*

## "Escape"

The chicken escaped from the broken crate
And bidding "goodbye" to his envious mates
Made a desperate dash for liberty
Determined to live this land of the free
The passersby stopped in their leisurely stroll
Amazed as they watched scene unfold
The cats and dogs joined in on the race
They did not know 'twas a deadly chase
From the butcher boy ran with hands outstretched
Determined to capture this defiant wretch
As the poor chick stopped and looked around
Flying feathers hit the ground
As the poor chick stopped and looked around
And in that moment his fate was sealed
For his head was dizzy and his senses reeled
Bewildered, our hero turned and ran
Protesting, into his jailor's hands
Squawking and Squirming and filled with hate
He was hustled off to meet his fate
Soon all that was left of the fighter so true
Was converted into a delicious stew

    *Ruth Glatt*

## Cob Web Cradles, Waco And Oklahoma

Cob web corners are cradles.
And blanket is pillow feather caught
And the baby spiders hurry and scurry
Their just like their mommy, funny and furry.
And while she chord, she sang Indian lullabies,
And friends who live under the bed, are dust puppies.
And man gather dust, ashes to ashes, dust to dust.
For a lady of the house had baby nothing why she loved baby
anything.

And if mention of her cradles, her reply, don't fuss.
Aren't you afraid the spiders will bite?
And a shake of the head, no!
And as summer winds flow into the house, cradles rock.
Children aren't spiders.
But like a spider, they were totally ignored.

No one dare fuss, less your showed the door.
For the least of us, could be a child we hold the door open for.
First they where children, and now the word is dead.
And to all cob web cradles that people ignored.  Amen
  God have mercy.

    *Marjorie Moss Taylor*

## A Long Time Ago

The years have found you and let you grow old,
And blessed you with treasures much greater than gold,
Like the memories you now have to show,
About your childhood days a long time ago.

You now watch the children as you rest in your chair,
Beneath contentment, joy, and soft angel hair.
Retired from exertion that you used to know,
As a struggle through life a long time ago.

The roses around you now bloom on the vine,
As the years that went by you still bloom in your mind.
And though they're behind you the roses still grow,
And so do memories from a long time ago.

You're closer to Jesus, you're an angel on earth,
You've a memorable lifetime and a gold plated birth.
You've outraced life's hustle, now things are slow,
You have time to remember a long time ago.

    *Robert Dale Smith*

## My Precious Granddaughter

You are so very special to me
And everyday I live to see
How very good you are to me
You are very thoughtful in many ways
And I hope I can stay close to you
For the rest of my days.

I remember that May night
When you gave us such a fright
You laid there so very still
I was so very glad that you hadn't been killed

I looked at you
With your face all swollen
And your body so crushed
And I asked God
"Please don't take her from us?"

And now that you have fully recovered
I hope that you have already discovered
How very precious you are to me
So I wait each day so I can see
Your shining happy face in front of me.

*Shirley Ward*


## Child Of Silence

Soft freckles spell out 'boyhood' on his face
And eyes as blue as the deep lagoon... pace
To and fro beneath a pretty brow... but limbs
Hanging limp... can't feel the wind's embrace
Or know the warmth of sunshine's fav'rite place.
To see him laugh at sounds of music played
Is to see the soul of 'Pan' peeking from the forest's
Glade... enchanting those who wish to know... life's
Sweet, solemn kiss.......... an echo played in lost
Harmony... somewhere, slightly out of key... 'Bobby'
This child of silence... time neglects to tell
Just where the fairies hide their wishing well.
He cannot speak... knows not his name... and yet
He laughs... when others cannot do the same....

*Tobi Kumar*


## Thrillseeker's Adventure

You slide into the cool plastic seat
And fasten the belt.
Officials stand by
And give each other hand signals.
With a lurch the cars begin to roll.
Slowly at first, then faster, faster,
Until you're at the summit of a lengthy slope.
Suddenly, an acute turn sends you plummeting
To unknown depths below.
You scream, try to cover your eyes and flee,
But the car sends you into a dark tunnel.
You emerge into daylight again,
Your eyes blinded
As you go around menacing loops
Which make your blood run cold.
Then it's over.
The car has stopped and you
Stagger out, mentally noting
To go on the ride again.

*Marcy Carlson*


## Who Is More Afraid..?

I awaken to the sound of crying
And from bed I rise inwardly trying
To quiet my fears and silence alarms
Until I can fold you into my arms.
Holding me tight you have nothing to fear
For no harm will come so long as I'm near.
To you I possess great strength like an oak
While inside my breast my heart strings are broke.
Your innocent eyes are searching my face
So I pray you won't see even a trace
Of doubts and troubles I carry inside;
You need me strong so my worries I hide.
Begging and pleading you cry out "Don't go."
I must 'cause I work tomorrow you know.
With one final embrace I must now leave
But the look on your face makes my heart grieve.
Reaching out to wipe a tear from your cheek
You seem to me now as fragile and meek;
Though tomorrow you'll be restless and wild.
It's time to sleep now, so rest well, my child.

*Robert M. Rowe Jr.*


## Hardship and Humor

We stand and sit upon ourselves
And gather dust between our cells.
We miss you softly for dinner
And invite shadows to our side.
We calmly shelter the thinner
Of two merciless rides.
what's is it... I said, what is it... I do
How can you be read, how is it...I knew.
Bite only the hand that feeds you
And dinner shall be cripple.
Open your eyes only when you
Want time to form a ripple.
You can't awake if you don't sleep.
Feed your heart and watch what you keep.

*Todd M. Davis*


## A Syndrome Called Love

I look out of my window
And gaze at the crowd below
There I see your face
Among the jostling, mottled race.

I face the typewriter
Vainly putting words to a letter
Words leap out, then freeze in mid-air
Today my mind is just not clear.

When my radio blurts out each night
Musical treasures of classical delight
Wafting lingeringly too in the misty air
Is your voice loud and clear.

If each of these is a tell-tale symptom
That I am ill of a terminal syndrome
That which we call love - let it be so
As long as the cause is you.

*Rodolfo I. Necesito*


## Fond Memories

Pictures of sod homes, ginger bread trimmed houses.
High buttoned shoes, long skirts and frilly blouses.
Handle - bar mustaches, goatee and celluloid collars,
Lord flantalaroy or bow tie and knicker bockers,
Huge canstogas with their white canvas covers.
Pulled by four oxen, sometimes four or six horses.
Sometimes called prairie schoners
Memories are magical when you think of the pioneers.

*Mary Lillian Mason*

## My Gift

Just today, I sent to the World, "The Eternal Bouquet,"
and, glittering within transparent's heart-shaped box,
primadonna's iridescent jewels emblazoned amethyst's prismatic
sparkling stars, showering beautiful magical prisms, delightfully
dancing for several blocks afar; and I prayed that, in
God's unity, goodness' diamond brilliance remains, forever
crowning the Bouquet in rainbow's crystal windowpanes;
that, mercy's luminous silvery stars shimmers purest
water lilies upon the goldspun heart; and, in eternal blessing
that: "Nations, evermore, will live in peace, and the Bouquet
flowers forevermore upon the Heart of Humanity."

"The Eternal Bouquet," sent by first-class mail, this day, will ever
shine tomorrow's night, in day, — that Nations may always see the
starlit promise, and he, evermore, and free; and, upon the
World's front door, forevermore, the Bouquet's majestic grace-filled
flowers will Bless humanity, — and that flaming everlasting star
will be "The Princess," crowned, in "the light of World Peace,"
for all eternity, — my gift, "to all the World," from me.

**Sheila Wainscott**

## She Can't Take Anymore

She asked him to stop, he told her he would
and he really tried, as hard as he could
but the need was there, he wanted it so much
to feel it work, its magic touch
he didn't tell her, so she didn't understand
how hard it is to quit, how far it is to land
because she didn't, understand his pain
he tested her strength, saw what he could gain
but she was getting mad, and she was seeing red
ugly things and ugly thoughts, were going through her head
she saw what he was doing, she saw that it was bad
drugs, and pot and drinking, were the source of fights they had
she told him if he ever, she would finally say goodbye
but every time he did it, she gave him one more try
what he doesn't realize it the pain he puts her through
by lying to her face, and breaking her heart in two
how long will this go on? No one knows for sure
but the hurting will continue, till she can't take anymore.

**Mary Anne Unopulos**

## About Face

I looked upon his face
and he turned away.
I looked upon her face
and she did the same.
I don't know what to do
I can't get through.
While I gave love and compassion,
I was met with indifference and detachment.
And while it may look grim and dim
I know the light in my heart
will help me win.

**Mary E. Gonzalez**

## The Cold Of Winter

The cold of winter sometimes show,
the frozen heart of the lonely as the cold winds blow.
If you listen closely to the breeze as it rushes pass,
you'll hear the cry of the lonely as they learn that they're last.
In a world of millions and thousands, I hate to see the faces,
of those who learned their presence isn't welcome in many places.
So I ask God to take care of them and give them what they crave,
because one day, I'll join their group and become one of the staves.

**Kim Anderson**

## As The Years Go By

As the years go by, we turn around
and, hear a whisper in our ears,
saying "don't go, please don't go!"

Keeping in-touch with one another is hard to do,
but believing in one another,
makes a dream come true;
There's so much we can't discuss,
but remembering does all the rest;

As the years go by,
the world makes its final turn and,
we all lie down to rest.

I'll always remember you,
as the years go by.

Praying to God, to save all the young lives,
even if it means, sacrificing your own life;
just enjoying life as it comes and,
don't let hatred bring you down
'cause, life is too short as, you see it.

As the years go by and,
the world makes its final turn.

**Rachel Johnston**

## The Embarking, the Voyage, the Parting

Her life had been lonely before they met,
And his world had not been carefree.
Slowly, they began a dialogue;
He was nervous, and so was she.

As time slipped by, they found themselves lost
And lonely when they were apart.
Soon, before many, they whispered the vows
That surged from the depths of their hearts.

Proudly he called her the queen of his kingdom,
And she responded by crowning him king.
When they were blessed with two little bundles,
They knew they had everything.

Fifty years later she and their sons
Knelt sobbing at his grave.
"God, change my grief to sweet memories," she prayed,
"Of deep love to each other we gave."

**Margarette Combs Saunders**

## Untitled

I wondered how the end of the road would look
And how I'd feel standing on its path
Gazing back a little I see the winding wilderness
And made me gasp as to how I traversed the same
　　　With its twisted route.

I now envy the traveller who rests without that weary
　　　look on her face
She walks a different pace
And now I ask...could it be I walked "the road less travelled by?"...
If so there are no regrets,
It was still worthwhile reaching the end of the rainbow
Though now I sit without my pot of gold.

**Marylinda Campo-Castillo**

## Please Be Patient

If what you said, I haven't heard
And I ask you to repeat it, word for word
    Please Be Patient

If I walk too slow, when I cross the street
And I can't hurry, because of my sore feet
    Please Be Patient

If when I write, mistakes you see
It's because my eyes, aren't as good as they used to be
    Please Be Patient

If I seem confused, or in a daze at times
And I find if difficult to say, what's on my mind
    Please Be Patient

If now I can't see, hear, walk or think too well
It's part of growing old, I've heard tell
    Please Be Patient
        *Wilma Wilson*

## Raped of Dignity

A pale gray mist envelopes me and begins to choke me,
    and I gasp.
The brightness once there is lacking,
    and I gasp.
Struggling to wade back out,
the shackles grasp my wrists and tighten.
Relentlessly, the mist thickens,
blackens, and deprives me of air,
    and I gasp.
Terror bursts through my veins as I'm secluded from society,
    and I gasp.
Help me, I can't breathe.
One by one, joy, love, friendship, desire and pride are smothered,
    and I gasp.
My spirit has been successfully amputated and asphyxiation creeps
ever so slowly,
    and I gasp.
Depression has raped me of my dignity,
    and I no longer gasp.
        *Lori Butler*

## The Nothing Time

Winter solace has now set forth,
    and I ponder each daily worth.
The dulls and grays of cold air skies,
    leave cataract's haze upon my eyes.
The feelings of these somber hours,
    wash o'er me like their misty showers.
For the dreariness of this time of sorrow,
    burdens every dusk and dawn of morrow.
No lonely echo whisper chimes,
    upon these minutes of nothing time.
        *Wendy Ann Rehm*

## Untitled

I believe that you will never see my smile
And that dreams are the only link we have for now.
You and I could be light years away,
but that won't stop my dreams every night and day,
It makes me sad to know you love someone else.
And that I'll have to face tomorrow again by myself,
together I know we could have been happy,
but that's just a dream and not reality.
Maybe one day I'll wake up and find,
that you're not always on my mind.
But as for now I'll have to say.
I'll love you till my dying day.
        *Krista Cortes*

## A Letter We Should Have Written

When it is over,
And it will be over,
Let us each allow that it was the other who
    could not commit
It will be less than kind.
But easier dealing with the guilt,

When it is over,
And it will be over,
Let us agree it will be without rancor,
A gently parting
With sweet days and nights remembered,
With recollections of tender touchings
    and whispered reassurances,
With memories of those moments in highlight
When if what we had was all there would ever be
It would have been enough...

When it is over,
And it is near my love,
When it is
Let us be kind.
        *Virgil Catalano*

## Look Up to Jesus

When it seems like nothing is going right;
and it's hard to see your way,
Look up to Jesus (The Holy One),
He'll brighten up your day.
He's always there to listen;
No matter what comes up in life,
He'll be right there to comfort you,
In the midst of hatred and strife.
So, when you feel like you're all alone;
And there's no one on your side,
That's when the Master comes to your aid,
Trust God, He will provide.
        *Valerie Jackson*

## Rainy Days

It's dark and raining outside;
And it's the same in my heart and mind.
To see you walking down the street,
Send a shiver from my head to my feet.
But as you come near;
I know I must steer clear.
Because although my love for you is undying,
There comes a time when you must stop trying.
But even as I realize this,
I know what I am going to miss.
Thanks for the good times
Out in the sunshine.
        *Shane DiGiovanni*

## Spring

The snow melts like evil drawn away,
And life begins after death has relinquished the land.
The children are together again,
Watching the Creator at work.
Winter is gone and plants begin to flourish,
And all see the life and rejoice.

Spring time is like a war,
Life fighting the darkness of death and winter.
A war without guns and bombs,
But a war our Creator controls.
And as the day has conquered the night,
Life shall win over death.
        *Maureen Copeland*

## "My Love Is Like A Rose"

My love for you, it grows among the roses
  And like that rose, it grows sweeter
    With each passing day.

The rose lifts its' petals to the sky
  Just as I reach my arms to you
    For your embrace.

Waiting for the morning mist to refresh
  And for the sweetness that brings
    Each new dawn.

I eagerly wait to see you
  So that I too might be refreshed
    As I start my brand new day

My heart it tiptoes
  So that I may not feel
    The thorns that lay within

As refreshing as a summer rain
  That awakens all, that is about

You, my dear, refresh my heart, my soul, my spirit
  And my love lives on
    Reaching for that space beyond

    ***Shirley Morris***

## Reflections of a Vagrant

As I wander thru life and think of the past -
And live thru each day as if 'twere my last,
I remember mistakes I made as a kid,
How I hookied and smoked - almost every kid did,
But the rest married and somehow made out -
But yours truly just wandered about,
Now I am old, lonesome and broke,
I walk down the street, to me no one spoke,
I'm rich with my memories, but poor without friends,
I'm tired of living and hope my life ends,
But before I die I write this poem,
To stop some poor youth who has decided to roam.

    ***Robert W. McNaught***

## "A World Without Fear"

Flowers bloom every spring,
And lovers exchange vows and rings,
A child is born into the world,
And a hero's great tale is told and heard,
In our world there are so many good things,
Like how you feel when a bird sings,
Sadly it is polluted by hate and crime,
If only we took a little time,
We could appreciate all the wonders
that lay near,
And not have to live in a world
full of fear...

    ***Michele K. Leiser***

## That Special One

He is special to me.
He is my secret admirer.
He is handsome with a cute face.
He reminds me of a fudge-overboard with 2 cherries.
He is the one in my dreams.
His way of sense is humorous.
He is a very nice man.
He cares for me specially because he is "The special one."

    ***Sharon Nickol***

## Alex Bay

There is an aching in my heart when you are away.
And my fingers are stilled when they haven't you on which to play.
There is a beautiful song of love played when my fingers touch you,
Alone, I feel the melody, but the sound doesn't come through.

I feel lost at times when you're away, and the night slows into a
  very long day.
I see your face in the sun outside; I'm so full of feelings that
  I can not hide.
I want to transport myself to tomorrow somehow - what I wouldn't give
  to be able to touch you now.

I play the music you left - the part of you I see; still it
  doesn't compare to the songs I hear when you make love to me.
The velvet red rose eases the ache in my heart:

I know I will never learn to do well when we're apart
I miss you -

    *Patricia J. Carlsen*

## One Heart, One Hand

May you never forget, the Love we shared
And never spared each other, the hurt and pain that Love causes..

May you never forget the Love, we shared, that comes from caring...
Instead of two, we were always one, held together with Love...

May you forever remember, the Love affair, that would not die...
And thought our lives may someday change, you will always be..
a special part of me, as I will always think of you..

May it go down in history, as the two hearts that were one...
And the hands that held each other, through all time...
That could never Die...

    ***L. D. Thames***

## More Cliches

Robert's classmates thought he was a bad apple
  and not all there
His neighbors thought he was up a creek
  without a paddle
His teacher thought he was in over his head and
  the odds were stacked against him
His grandmother thought he was too big for
  his britches
His bus driver thought, here today and
  gone tomorrow
His girlfriend thought he was at the top
  of the heap and would never kiss and tell
His minister thought he could be saved
  in the nick of time
His parents thought he was the cream of the crop
  and one in a million
What did Robert think?
Robert thought, that's life!

    ***Marilyn S. Cadzow***

## Pollution

They have invaded my home
The voices and images emanating from the
boxes in all the rooms
Some are pleasurable and fill my life with joy
Others are disruptive and spew forth filth and lies
But I have a power greater than them
I can turn them off
or can I.

    ***Howard T. Mars***

## Now Is The Time To Remember

Now is the time to remember all the love you have known
And now is the time to be thankful, that you haven't been alone
Someone to get up for, to work for and always someone to pray for
Children and grandchildren that fill you with pride more and more
Yes remember a life filled with sharing all that life could afford
yes now is the time to remember, remember to thank our Lord...

This one I wrote for grandchildren as I want them to remember me and, some of things I want them to remember about God, country and family.

"I'll walk with you"
I'll walk with you just take my hand we'll have such fun together
We'll camp or snow-mobile or boat depending on the weather
We'll sing and laugh and play for years and build golden memories
together for memories are built with love and they will last forever
then when I'm gone and things get rough and you don't know what
   to do
just find my hand in memories my love will always walk with you.

**Thomas C. McAlpine**

## Flight

As we choose our paths of travel,
And our yarn of life unravels
Young birds venturing from the nest,
Attempting to accomplish our best,
An open world, like none before
To be experienced and explored.
Opportunities may knock upon the portal,
And we'll respond according to our morals.
Using the tools we've tucked under our wings,
Imbedded in the feathers through which liberty rings.
When the golden days have passed,
Peering nostalgic through the looking glass
reflections of my comrades return.
Memories in the wind will churn,
Stirring the feathers of our hearts,
And tickling us in those special parts;
The laughter, tears, hopes and smiles,
Treasures shared all the while.
Take flight, my friends, into the blue,
To your hearts always be true.

**Theresa Izzard**

## "Juanita"

Juanita is my mother's name,
and out of Buffalo Holler she came.
She grew up eating wild squirrel and possum
And when she was a young girl,
her beauty did blossom.
Then she entered the Army life
She met my father and became his wife.
Her nature is like a glimmering jewel.
But, watch out for she's no bodies fool!
She'll take you under her wing,
and then a soft song she will sing.
She will let you grow your own way.
But she'll be there to help everyday.
I can't put into words how much I love her.
All I can say is I'm glad she's my mother!!

**Lisa E. Greiner**

## Sharing Our Priceless Gift

When we gather as friends to share our life
experiences, there can be no greater joy.
Everyone of us has a special gift to offer.
May we continue to share that priceless gift
throughout our lives.
The reward is great.
Let love reign supreme!

**Winston A. Gordon**

## Reflections

I see the reflections upon the water.
As the leaves fall, I feel the cool breeze.
I see the ripples of peace and
tranquility as each leaf hits the water.
In which comes a new dawning
upon a new morning.

**Linda E. Webber**

## The Neverending Everything

Love casts its shadow on my soul
And over time fills that empty hole.
Though love is sweet, I smell the rain.
Though the sun is shining, I expect the pain.

Tears flow over my tentative smile
But my guard is up all the while
In the winter I learned how to cope
I learned not to have faith and not to have hope.

Hate has come and hate has passed
But this storm won't be the last.
Seasons will change until the day that I die.
The moon will never hear me cry.

The waves crash on me like the rain,
Like my tears, like my pain,
Like the summer, like the spring,
The never ending everything.

**Vanita Soni**

## Our Good Talks

They start from scratch
And quick-silver everywhere.

Like deep draughts of golden wine
Filled with essence.  And effervescence.

Like sudden summer rains
Skittering into unexplored crevices.

Like lilting zephyrs, light-as-feathers,
Riffling in a myriad of unlikely directions.

Like stones, sharp and heavy as pain,
Hurled without warning
Against our most tender places.

And before we know it
Three hours have winged past
Leaving us giddy and dazed
With discovery.

**K. Keaster**

## To My Dad

May the Lord always be in your heart
   and remain there a very big part
Of who you are and what you do
   Just trust in Him to see you through.

There are times that we stumble and fall
   But we must realize above all
That He's there for us just call His name
   Let Jesus in your heart - you'll never be the same.

Just trust in Him and do your best
   And our Holy Saviour will do the rest
You're never alone, He's always close by
   To share in your laughter or be there when you cry.

A friend for always there's no doubt
   Trusting and loving the Lord is what it's all about
Just open your heart to Him and don't ask why
   Jesus will love you forever Dad and so will I.

**Shirley H. Inscore**

171

## If Only I Had Wings

How I'd love to swoop and soar, among the cotton candy clouds
And sail the ocean blue skies, skimming far o'er the crowds.
So close to heaven's gate I join in songs angels sing
And do my loops and turn abouts...
  Oh, if only I had wings

Sometimes when life wears thin, I think a lot about being up there
Intent on riding the windy surf, breaking o'er clouds without a care.
How happy I'd be miles above earth racing angelic windy swings
Up and away with bird-like grace...
  Oh, if only I had wings.

I'd wheel about and fly upside down, from earthly ties forever free
Gliding toward home on an airy slide, fingers tracing each green
  tree.
O'er majestic snow-capped peaks, earth's beauty to my eyes springs
But, recalling now, 'tis only a dream...
  Oh, if only I had wings.

Tho' my flight of fancy is now at end, memories aloft I'll ne'er
  forget
For a moment I sailed above my cares, free for one moment and yet
Deep in my heart I know it's true, God's love to me forever brings
A hope that someday in His time...
  I know I'll have my wings.

*Roger B. Kays*

## Wish Upon a Star

I looked up in the sky tonight
  And saw one star that shined so bright.
Its beauty was by far the best
  Its splendor outshined all the rest.

It held within its silver streams
  The answers to ones' fondest dreams.
I gazed upon its beauty rare
  Then closed my eyes and said a prayer.

Oh please dear star, I wish of you
  To shine upon my friend so true
For she is too a star, you see
  The best by far, if one asks me.

The clouds did try to hide her light
  Upon one dark and stormy night
So shine, oh star, upon my friend
  And comfort her till twilight's end

*Rebecca Harling*

## In My Life Forever To Stay

I wake up every morning with a thought in my mind,
And somehow it is always you that I find.
I go through each day wondering just what I will do,
Hoping and praying for one day it will be you.
I don't know the future or what it holds,
I know that I Love You and to you my heart has been sold.
You are so kind in your each and every loving way,
And each and everything you do and give to me I could never repay.
You brighten my day with your touch and smile,
And all of this has happened in just a short while.
What will we do if it is not meant to be,
I'll tell you what, Friends Forever we will always be.
Who knows but God what the future entails,
I know in His plan He never intends for the outcome to fail.
Our love will grow stronger with each passing day,
And in my thoughts and soul forever you will always stay.

*Melissa L. Davis*

## Together As One

Walk with me to the dawn's end,
and stay to see the sunset.

Let the wind blow through our souls,
and intertwine them together.

We shall be ourselves as individuals
but always together within the heart.

The power of two is only as strong
as the one alone.

Let us not lose ourselves in each other.

We can walk side by side on the path
then we would not be in the way of the other.

At the path's end we will find delight in life's sunset,
whether we be together or apart.

*Sheryl Pownall*

## Thoughts From Auschwitz

The wind blows through thin walls,
And tears at our ragged clothes.
It drowns out the cries of our children
And no one will ever know.

And outside the fence of sharpest wire,
The world rushes by without knowing,
Our insufferable pain is harder to bear
When we are forced to work without slowing.

Death is welcome here,
In these camps of hellish terror.
The cruel "experiments"
Are worse than satan's lair.

Oh, the memories of long ago,
When laughter did abound.
The love that lived in all our hearts,
Kept us safe and sound.

*Rochelle B. Kibby*

## Freedom

Freedom, freedom, the bells will ring,
and that's what the people on the streets will sing.
Freedom, freedom, no more Great Britain,
So let's leave the Declaration of Independence the way
it's written.

Freedom, freedom, that's what I said,
The sad part is so many people are dead.
Freedom, freedom, good thing George Washington lead.
Too bad the Continental Army was so poorly fed.

Freedom, freedom, thank God our forefathers had the insight,
To stand up to the British and put up a good fight.
Freedom, freedom, I almost died,
But because someone believed in me, I survived.

*Michael Medrano*

## The Earth

When the sun rises over the clear morning sky
And the birds soar above the everlasting fields of rye
You may ask yourself one question one time after time
How high does the sky really grow?
How high does the sky really climb?
And when the moon comes out and the stars fall from space
Ask yourself one more question
How do stars know their place?
The earth is a mystery both far and wide
Gods majestic creation
Both in and outside!

*Stevie J. Arroyo*

172

## Crumbs

I do not know where the grey will end
and the day will begin.
I am just a lonely flicker drowning in a bowl
the shadows dawn above my head and hollow out my soul.

Sitting in this dish just waiting to be served
A silent little window seal, I feels is well deserved.
I can hear the babes breathing and feel their haughty breath
I look to stand and raise my hand, but pierced my eyes instead

Just flaking for the moment they cover me in food
Pick me up and take a bite of the crescent moon
I tried to call my mother at her cozy nest
The summons blurred a murmur of the oceans crest

I'm curled up in the darkness trying to kiss my cheek
I'm struggling to touch my body, but I'm tangled in your sheet
Praying for the strength to kick away the stone
Lost somewhere forgotten in this shallow bowl.

*Tammy Kay Miller*

## Nature's Call

The willow tree bows to the winter winds call
And the evergreen stands so majestically tall.
The oak trees are bare, their leaves are all gone
And over the rocks, the creek babbles on.

The rabbit hops through the cold winter snow
Not far stands a buck, at the side of his doe.
A squirrel scampers by, taking food to his nest
The day's growing darker, as the sun sets in the west.

The birds are all flighty, getting ready for night
I'm really happy with myself, everything is alright.
I'm at home with the animals, the tree's and the creek
With the peace that I've found, there's nothing else that I seek.

I may be by myself, but I'm never alone
Mother Nature talks in a language of her own.
But I can hear what she says, it's all very clear
And that special bond that we have, I'll always hold dear.

You too can have peace, it's not hard to find
Just release all your fears, that's clouded your mind.
Then sit and listen to her whisper in the trees above
And wallow in the beauty of her eternal love.

*Linda Fee*

## Retrieval

The long tortuous day and Evening passed,
and the exhaustion enabled my retreat
from the Waking life.  I returned to
that place where I could be undisturbed
and travel great distances, with
no fixed boundaries.

I surveyed the pictures that my
mind's vision bore.  The shadowy
creations were at times barely
perceptible.  My mind began Winding,
twisting and straining 'til the elaborate
Images could be understood.

Yet the night segued into the dawn of a new
day, and I was forced to depart from the
familiar narcotic of the Dream.  Not knowing
how much time I had wandered in the faux
world of spontaneous, effortless images, I
sought to retrieve them as the Sun shone.

*Wayne S. Bell*

## Enduring Love

The essence of spiritual affinity,
and the invisible expression of pure love,
is realized in the ability
to see one another in the light of darkness;
to speak with one another in a dialogue of silence;
to feel one another without touching;
to know one another without asking questions;
to grow through one another without possessing;
to give space to one another without fearing;
to find ecstasy without searching;
to grasp the high without reaching;
to descend into the valleys without accusing;
to rise from the valleys without separating;
to ascend the highest mountain without forgetting.

*Lance Watson*

## I Have Missed You

I have missed you
And the sun has given me no morning light.
I have walked my days
As in a silent night
Flowers that were blossoms
I have held
In the darkness of night
In my stillness
I heard their dry petals fall.
Has one week passed, or
Has it been one hundred years?
Tell me not, for in my silence
There is no hour keeping.
For time has come to be
An eternity.

*Olivia DuVall*

## Our Feathered Friends

At break of dawn, I hear the "pretty, pretty" of the cardinal,
And the "sweet, sweet" of the little goldfinch.
I stop and wonder, am I awake or sleeping?
Someone, please, give me a little pinch.

As I watch these feathered friends
Building nests and keeping eggs warm
While they go busily about their day,
Always trusting His love and fearing no harm.

Such undoubting trust and faith
Of each and every feathered friend
Turns me to God in prayer and thanks
For His wonder and beauty that never seems to end.

If these little ones can have such trust,
Don't you feel that we should, too?
For as He loves our feathered friends,
You know He feels the same for me and you!

*Patricia Ann Coy*

## 1 Ton

Have you ever started to run,
And you felt like you weighed a ton,
It makes you mad,
and sometimes even sad,
sometimes it makes you mean,
And gives you good sensations of being lean,
so next time you go on a run,
be positive you just lost a ton.

*William Tobler*

## I Was Running The Other Day

I was running the other day just trying to clear my mind.
And then I began to think of you. How strange, my mind
Began to cruise through our high school days. Yes! I am
walking you home with a smiling face. Then my mind takes
me to my army days. I am in a dark jungle, it is raining,
and it is cold. I am thinking of the two women in my life,
You and Mom. Then, the sergeant hands me a letter, and tells
me "It's for you Corporal" how strange, even my M-16 is
named like you. Even my parachute is named Laura. Then, my
mind takes me home. There at the airport, you wait for me
with someone new. You tell me he is your friend. My heart
tells me different. Later, you dump him, and bring me back
into your life, then I see you go off to the University,
and four years later see you graduate. You tell me, "Thank
you for everything, you are free to go. Go, believe me, I
won't need you anymore." Then my mind brings me back to my
running yes! Ohh! yes, how much I love You! I am materialistically
a free man, But spiritually your slave. Because of
all the things I am still willing to do. To say I love you.

### *Reggie Rendon*

## I Quietly Knelt to Pray

I dreamed I took a trip to the sky and walked the Milky Way
And there on the path above the earth I quietly knelt to pray
I dreamed I then looked into heaven from the star studded path
that I trod and saw our loved ones together wrapped tight
in the arms of God

I cupped my hands around my eyes, the view was simply grand
Every saint I'd ever known was gathered there in that land
The new bodies they had were magnificent with a beauty so rare
to behold
I saw their mansions God promised and the streets running
by were pure gold

It seemed I could see the strength of His love, it's radiance covered
the place
I heard the celestial band singing, brought home by God's
wonderful grace
Surely my cup runneth over with a joy I never could tell
I'd seen our loved ones with Jesus, God's promises never do fail

With a thankful heart I dreamed I stood and walked the Milky Way
And there on the path above the earth
I quietly knelt to pray

### *Ruth Hales*

## Soul Mates

We have grown together, you and I...
And to think of a world without you...
   My love
For me, would be no world at all.
You are my very best above all things.
   My soulmate for all eternity.

In your eyes I see only gentleness
You have been my strength in darkness
My darling you are my protector...
   To shield me from all harm.
You and I have become one...
   My beloved.

Each day I thank God in his wisdom...
   For this gift.
So hand and hand we walk now tho' at all times...
I can only feel... nothing but inner peace and comfort.
No words could express this love we have shared...
My love, my darling...
   My soul mate for all times.

### *Remick*

## Amo

Thou art fair. Thy beauty fills my body whole
and very softly doth touch my turbulent soul
Calmed by thy caress I can to you express
I give thee love-my love-the love you bless

Thou art clothed in the splendor of the night
Moonlight reflects glory-thine aura in my sight
The universe pulsing to the rhythm of my heart
Forever fearful-dreading-the span we are apart

Love's flame burning-there is no limit-no scope
In light fulfilled, I say thou art my love, my hope
With joy, I dance and swirl to its music's beat
Thou art mine-ecstasy ours when next we meet

Come-Oh!-come beloved and join me in life
To face this struggling-uncertain-earthly strife
One in body-our heavenly rapture entwined
Lord! Give thy blessing-faith-in destiny assigned.
*To my granddaughter with love -- December 25, 1995*

### *Granddad*

## The Privilege of Growing Old

As I approach the autumn years of my lifetime,
and watch the sunset settling down in the sky,
I have to wonder - what happened to all those years,
that so swiftly have rolled on by.
But then I realize - that we are all living on borrowed time,
donated by God, who controls the time
from the date of our birth until the day that we die,
and he makes careful note of how we live our lifestyle.
So I am very proud of growing old,
because I feel I am doing just as I have been told,
for I know God decides who shall inherit the earth,
and how long they shall be here from the date of their birth.
So now that I have reached a ripe old age,
I have earned the right to become the family sage,
and while some of my grandchildren may be a little too young,
to fully realize or understand my tongue,
they will always remember the stories that can only be told,
by someone who has been given the privilege of growing old.

### *Peter F. Gorse*

## White Buffalo

What will happen in this world
And what will the people say?

When our adult populations and so called world leaders
Learn to live with each other as do little children ... when they
play

Somewhere 'tis written ... There will come a day
When the savage lion and peaceful baby lamb
Together will blissfully sleep ... romp ... and play

Can it be that day is now
For the world to spiritually grow?

As true American's, our Indian tribes ... somehow mystically know
Through the birthing of a spiritual

Pure White Buffalo
### *C. W. Bryant*

## To Have Being

Where do I fit into the whole scheme of things?
And why is it that no matter how great things are
There always seem to be something missing?
There is so much to know
And so much more that I'll never to able to figure out
Uncertainty most time is the given.
And time, aah time
Today never changes
Only to realize that so many years have gone by
Where was I when all this happened?
I want so much to be a part of life
To live, to say something, to help someone, to be somebody
I want to laugh, to be happy, to help to make the world
   a better place.
And what if I can't sort through all the why's and reasons?
I'll live and do the very best I can
For such is life.

**Maureen Miller**

## It's Marvelous In Our Eyes...

So the Lord took your loved one,
And you didn't think you'd make it,
You prayed to God each day, for this pain,
Oh God please take it,
The days turned into weeks,
The weeks turned into months,
You got closer to God each day,
And you learned to use more faith,
This is the Lord's doing,
And it's marvelous in our eyes,
Remember when you were sick,
And could not pray for yourself,
The Lord turned the death angel away,
Now look at you today,
This is the Lord's doing, and it's marvelous in our eyes,
This is the Lord's doing,
No need to say good-bye,
This is the Lord's doing,
Wipe the tears from your eyes,
This is the Lord's doing and it's marvelous in our eyes...

**LaMont C. Kidd**

## Walk With Me

Come walk with me my love-
And you shall be my little turtle dove.
We shall go slow-
And savor nature as we go.
Tiny steps run to keep pace
While laughter smothers your face.
Walk along with me my child-
Hear the birds sing in weather mild.
Smell the perfume of flowers everywhere-
As we stroll along without a care.
No need to hurry- we are going no place-
Step lightly now-lest you crush
The violets underfoot-watch the bees brush
And sip daintily from fragrant buds now and then.
Come now walk with me-soon home again.

**Odessa Roberts**

## Untitled

Wash my fears of dread and death
forget myself in a pool of guilt.
Self-pity maybe, pieces of what I thought I became fall around me
blow in the wind.
I fall apart, mind and heart.
If there was a reason, it was you.

**Michelle Smith**

## The Grainy Soldier

A diverse army glittering strong,
Arduous days harsh and long,
A march slowly progressing with time,
Drifting, portraying a silent mime.

Mountains of lifelessness eventually rise,
Lonely winds echo groans and sighs,
Flat footed mammals diligently plod,
In shrinking humps carry food and sod.

A merciless star of scorching heat.
The deserts forever unfailing heartbeat,
An hourglass of time is ceaselessly flipped,
The army disembarks on an unending trip.

**Sheri A. Burnham**

## The Telephone as Instrument of Torture

The three most oft-used words today
Are not "I love you" but "can you hold?"
Spoken into the phone in peremptory assumption
Of an affirmative response.
Sometimes it's "I'm going to put you on hold."
Your blood-pressure rises, your stress intensifies
And seething, you wait and wait, and wait
Then, frustrated, hang up.

When at last God calls me,
I'll answer "Can you hold?"
Then put the phone down,
And quietly assume a second life.

**Miri K. Hargus**

## U.N. Neighborly

A hundred yards from the illustrious U.N.
Are scattered dwellings of derelict men,
Sleeping on cardboard boxes and concrete
Yet all within eyesight of the world's elite,
Unwashed, unwanted, unfortunate, unemployed
Unapproachable dweller's who the city avoid.

From Tudor City you look down on the homeless
Then raise your eyes to a prestigious address
The green, glassy giant; New York's tourist spot
But what of the cardboard residents who are simply forgot.

Bearded, bothersome beggars huddled together
Papers for a shield regardless of weather
Ignored by the eyes of passersby
Who prefer the scenery reaching to the sky

The world's leaders never see the pleaders
For the boxes are moved when the elite are in town
Sadness may view young and old huddled on the ground
But neglect allows them to sleep on a paper mound.

**Stephen Kilpatrick**

## Love's Light

A shaft of light doth light thy path
As ere I walk on yonder green
protecting wings of love unseen surround
Me in a misty hue illumine by a starry
blue
Oh sweetly flowing wind doth blowing
whispering through the trees and lo
A gentle kiss upon my brow move swiftly
Across the stirring sand
I know that I am in thy hands
Will thou listen to this song that dances
Among the stars afar
Oh wonder not this precious gift but take
thy fill of heavenly joy

**Maxine Allen**

## Paradise

The trees, the moon, the white clouds soft as a newborn baby's skin
Are so beautiful, so peaceful, so natural
Like water, falling form a waterfall
A swan graceful floats by
I hear the sounds that express only peace and tranquility
That we so often take for granted
As the birds gracefully spread their wings for flight
Tears start running down my face
At such beauty these creatures are able to create
The sense of togetherness overwhelms me
No racism, no prejudice
They are one, as all of us are under God's guiding light
God looks upon us as a whole
Not individually by color or nationality
For we are all equal upon him
And until we can break the barrier
That separates so many of us
Until we realize unity is the only way
Only then will we be allowed to run free in Paradise,
Forever and a day.

*Nicole B. Soto*

## Reopening Pandora's Box

Lying alone on a twilight field
Arms reaching for the future from afar
Darkness descends upon the silent horizon
As paralysis melts with the first sparkling star.

Trapped in a web of insignificant moments,
Ghosts of the past slowly begin to fade
Daydreaming about the celestial oasis
Keeps me from being cut by each grass blade.

Every storm cloud and rainbow
Connect to build life's mosaic pattern
Doubts at the crossroads and wildflower quicksand
Force the wishing well still to yearn.

Years of minutiae accumulate tonight
Shooting stars of joy, black holes of sorrow
Yesterday's dreams become the reality
Of the chiseled path to tomorrow.

As moonlight casts shadows of memories
Pebbles and violets create my true fantasy
I smile and gaze up at the heavens
One star in one constellation in one galaxy.

*Miriam Hartstein*

## Montana

Sunrise greets the waking world.
Around the mountains mists are curled.
The sky unfurls its purple tones.
Billowing clouds float like islands — alone.

Snow-capped mountains stand silent and high
Etched against the clouded sky.
Rivers wind through valley floors.
Heading toward the ocean's shores.

Trees sway gently in the mountain breeze.
Birds sing sweetly their melodies.
Cattle graze in wide open fields
Where wildflowers their fragrances yield.

Sunset sheds its amber hues.
Meadows grow wet with blankets of dew.
Crickets begin their orchestra sounds.
The meadowlark's lonely calls abound.

Darkness throws its veil of black
Over the world — no crevices lack.
The mountains still stand as sentinels silent
Waiting for skies once again to be violet.

*Lee Beavers*

## My Four Legged Daughter

She joined our family as a tiny creature;
As a dog lover, I accepted her not as a threat,
But more with toleration;
As time passed and she grew larger, we would eye each other daily;
Plotting, strategizing, testing our roles;
It was an interesting game;
She knew the ground rules, I didn't;
I longed for the companionship of a dog who would sit, roll over,
Be my friend; I tried to train her but to no avail;
The web was cast and I didn't know it;
She knew what I wanted;
she slowly trained me to be what she wanted;
My training took patience on her part;
The web grew tighter;
She rewarded me with sign and body English though always remaining
aloof; our relationship grew, we gradually accepted each other;
She played with me, I learned my part;
She would always win;
You are my four legged daughter, I am your pet;
You are a calico cat.

*Robert Alan*

## Power Place

Surrounded by life —
as above, so below.

The rings are the past
    irretrievable, dead
The tree does not dwell on its past
    though it does not forget
Each year recorded in
    the circle of life

A tree is as deep as it is tall
In the forest we are surrounded by life
    feel it
It is not like the city
    here we are not surrounded by
    concrete and frustrations

Here we experience the energy of existence
    still and poignant
    and are reborn

*S. Brook Putnam*

## V. J. Day

This day brings memories of day s in World War II
As American Red Cross workers we'd may things to do.

Sometimes it's fun remembering the may things we'd plan
Serving coffee to a mission on the way to bomb Japan.

Or crouching in a slit trench each time the moonlight shone
Or making Christmas cookies for boys away from home.

Or planning G.I. dancestone band to serve all groups
We taught the Chinese dance steps to struggle with our troops.

Our Red Cross Club in China was the only one in tents
We later had a building the change was quite immense.

At last the war was over, we won and on our way
Aboard a crowded battleship, back to USA.

*Rita Pilkey*

## Rainbows and Four Leaf Clovers

Words of silence echo through this lonely room,
As death slowly seals my doom.
In my prime and life's almost over.
Whatever happened to climbing rainbows and,
having good luck with four leaf clovers.
So much to live for, so many thing to see and do.
But not for some unlucky few.
Please save me and don't let me die.
Why can't I have just one more try.
Try to keep my memory in your heart;
Keep me there and we'll never have to part.
At least I did one great thing.
Into this world new life I did bring.
Tell my son I love him very much,
and my heart he did touch.
Remember family I love you too.
So keep my memory deep inside of you.
When you remember don't be blue.
Because you know if I had my choice,
I'd be right here with you, in rainbows and four leaf clovers.

*Rebecca Marron*

## Feathered Friends

I sat and watched a bird one day
As he searched for straw to build a nest
He picked and scratched as he searched
Until he found the very best

The nest was in lovely apple tree
That bloomed with beauty every spring
He dance and fluttered in the tree
As loudly he would watch and sing

He was looking for a mate
And as the birds flew by
His choice was for a special mate
So he kept a wondering eye

Oh! Here comes a lovely one
She's all decked out in orange and blue
She sat beside him on a limb
As he decided if she would do

Just then the couple flew away
As they went gliding through the air
I felt a warm peace from within
At having known this lovely pair

*Venice Waugh*

## The Truth About Me

It's not easy to know what is true about me.
As I feel, see, and hear I know what to be.
For what I see is how I act.
What I hear is always an unknown fact.

I like to be around my friends, just as everyone does,
I have feelings for people and tend to be in love.
I see my options and know what there is to gain.
I'm not afraid to show my pain.

When anyone's in need, I lend them a hand.
No matter what color, race, or religion, I try to understand.
I see myself like everyone else around.
To me hearing laughter is the happiest sound.

I live my life day by day.
My decisions are made, when they come my way.
To be yourself is sometimes hard to do
I try to listen to myself and feel what is true.

*Tami Kehl*

## Dreams

Deep sleep fails to occur
as I lay distracted by
a spectrum of life's mental images escaping
from my innermost thought chambers

Eventually they will go ignored
and each idea is liberated
Freely floating through the open window of my mind
into the night and beyond

Turbulent, whirling, and spontaneous
the once anomalous reflections
converge and randomly interact
weaving tales for no one

As dawn emerges and darkness dissipates
the newly formed stories unravel
and each thread of thought returns to its origin
forgotten, as I slowly awake.

*Vicki Gorczyca*

## Doubt

My soul in agony wells with tears,
As I traverse on through life by years.
As I keep my grief all tied up within,
And my joy only showing now and then,
I sometimes wonder if in the hereafter
There'll be just gaiety and laughter.
But then, during times of happy bliss
When my Saviour comes to show me that this
My attitude in life is out of accordance
With his divine will, I see in a glance
That life could be sweeter with Him
As my guide and my Lord; so in a harm
I lift up my voice the Him, who is God,
And forward in life with Him do I trod

*Margaret Good*

## I Thought Of You

I thought of you last night.
As I was walking, alone,
Late, in the cool of the evening;

Under a sky so clear.
And so black,
I could almost feel
God looking down on me;

As the cool evening breeze
Touched my face
with its soft sweet whispers,
Penetrating my senses
And the deepest recesses of my
mind and thoughts,
with its scent of the grass, and the trees,
And the day long since gone

And I longed to be part
Of a different reality;

As I walked, alone,
While God looked down, late
In the cool of the evening; and I thought of you.

*Troy Edward Calvin*

## Ostrich

The wind ruffled my feathers,
as it forlornly blew across the plain.

It was calling me in its own subtle way,
willing me to take to the air.

I try with all my heart and soul to answer,
but try as I might, all I can do is attempt to keep up.

I cry out as I am balked once again,
from taking my place in the sky.

The wind is taunting me,
in it own nasty way.

No one can help me,
for evolution has cursed me,
by giving me wings that have no use.

What a cruel joke.

*Michael Fitzsimons*

## The Carousel of Life

The tantalizing beauty of the carousel
As it spins 'round and 'round;
Takes us on the magical journey of life.

As the carousel goes up,
You feel delightful - you're on cloud nine.
People see you differently...
You see yourself as a different person.

Then the carousel travels downward,
You remember sad times, when you've been depressed...
Disappointed.

As the carousel circles, life advances forward
You remember the past as if it happened only yesterday.
You imagine that the future holds greatness
For yourself and loved ones.

Then the carousel stops,
You feel lost....alone.
Friends and family vanished into thin air.

You're still on the motionless carousel, thinking,
"What happened to my life?"
But no one cares.

*Rhiannon LeVeque*

## Awakening

This pain and sorrow tears me apart
As my lonely hand reaches into the dark
At the end of the obscured tunnel of emotions
I see a light
Pandemonium overwhelming me,
As I crawl through the night.

Tears streaming down my face,
He reaches and grasps my hand,
Pulling me out of this odious world
That surrounds me
I step out, now I am able to see
I awake to the same feelings of misery
Only to realize he was a dream
And the cycles of torment begin, again.

*Pamela Dillahunty*

## Forever In A Dream

You are my beginning and my end,
As my search for true love has lead me to you.

A beginning of a lifetime together,
Filled with love, passion and trust.
An end to the heartbreaks and pains,
Of bad judgement and poor choices.

You are the only man I will ever love,
My life is no longer mine, but ours.

When we're apart I feel you surround me,
Enclosing me with your love.
When we're together I feel whole and alive,
I can never be without you again.

Sometimes I wonder if this is real or a dream,
But somehow it doesn't really matter.
For if this is a dream I will stay asleep forever,
Each day loving you more and more.

*Patricia M. Kronske*

## Coca Cola

Enjoy Coca Cola said Lola..
As she gulped the whole can-down-down-down
All that -brown-brown-brown
    syrupy sugar so full of ting
    and zing-sing-zing
Ah!  Just what I crave
    this liquid marmalade...
That's an American Institution
Just like the -the -the constitution
I wonder who invented this beverage?
That has more leverage-
Than real- estate
Or high interest rates
Order me a bushel and a crate!
Go—don't hesitate...
    Commands Lola
Guzzling her COCA COLA....

*Micheline D. Birger*

## The Rose

Maria lays in bed tonight,
as she thinks of the pretty red rose
she got so long ago.
Just like the rose he is gone too.

One spring day he gave her
the rose, to show how much he
loved her, and that was the first
day Maria's best friend told her he loved her.

On a warm spring day, they got married.
And today as she thinks back on years they married.
She believe they were together for twenty years.
And today eight years has past since day he left her.

And today as she stops by his grave,
she lays a rose by it.
To show how much she loved him.

*Mandy Simmons*

## Reverie

Beside myself yet I am not alone,
For memories hold me warm within their arms,
And I am free to travel and to roam,
Among my yesterdays and all their golden charm,
I see your face still young and hear you sing,
The song of youth so full of love and hope,
And I am glad for all of life was good,
Amid my dreams, in memories, beside myself with you.

*Ramona B. Amell*

## Moonlight Soliloquy

I stood enhanced, bathed in moonlight splendor
  As the moon played hide and seek with the flitting clouds
    Like bewitched children of the night.

The concentrated essence of madness for beauty
  Dried up my very soul, as I drank to the loveliness
    Of a moonlight night.

I felt alone in a world of chaos,
  Where man drank his kin's blood, to quench his thirst for reason
    A justice to humanity.

Ah, the vanity of man, jealousy and hatred doomed to decay,
  A confused medley of wretchedness and fear
    Enveloped man's destiny to nothingness.

A wonderfully tranquil night, my thoughts a wander-lust,
  And in my heart, a cloudless pleasure, alive among the living dust
    As I stood alone.

  *Virginia N. Rhoads*

## Rain Storm

A breeze blows gently,
As the sky turns grey.
Rain drops start falling,
Tree limbs swing and sway.

Flowers and bushes quiver,
Leaves shake and prance.
Thunder rings out like the beat of a drum,
While the lightning performs a dance.

Drops of rain are pounding down,
Thunder rolls and then crashes.
The whole sky is lit up,
As a bolt of lightning flashes.

While the storm is raging on.
The winds are twisting and turning.
Rain drops collecting in puddles.
Clouds rolling and churning.

Pounding, raging, and dancing.
Well into the dark of night.
But, as a new day begins,
There's no trace of it in sight.

  *Michelle L. Mientek Solocinski*

## I Go Forth to Move about the Earth

I go forth to move about the earth
as the wolf, protective and strong

I go forth to move about the earth
as the lion, fearless and king of the forest

I go forth to move about the earth
as the deer, majestic and silent

I go forth to move about the earth
as the humming bird, kind and gentle

I go forth to move about the earth
as the bald eagle, freedom and liberty

I go forth to move about the earth
as the wind, free-flowing and wild

I go forth to move about the earth
as the human, polluting our air and
  destroying all life

I GO FORTH TO MOVE ABOUT THE EARTH

  *Texie Lea Pender*

## A World Changed

Here I sit watching time fly by
as the world turns greedy
a tear fills my eye.

Children dying everyday.
Cops are outnumbered
yet continue to fight.
As blue sky's turn grey.

Rain begins to fall,
as hopes of sunshine fade.
I hear a lonely Robin call,
and see the water as it cascades.

I dream of the day, a day to raise kids.
But I hate to think,
of them growing up in this.

This world of nothing but hate and greed.
I do wish I could ride off into the sunset,
just my wife and I on a great beautiful steed.

Into a paradise of so long ago,
that has now been replaced.
As the cold winds of Humanity, continue to blow.

  *Robert Darner*

## Love Is To Be Shared

Each of us has a set amount of allotted time,
As we journey through our world of "Earth",
And we are passing along through present time,
To future time, from the moment of our birth.

The journey is through moments of great joy,
And through heart ache, illness, sorrow and woe.
Hanging onto goals, plans, and dreams,
With every ounce of strength, never letting go.

We know and love first our parents,
Precious mother and father too,
Then grandparents, aunts and uncles, cousins,
Best of kin who cherish and love you.

Venturing out we make acquaintances and friends,
And knowing them we make our lives full,
With shared adventures, missions, and experiences,
Working as a team, our share of the load we pull.

Time is jealous, fleeting, hard to hold,
It runs away on winged feet and is gone.
We must learn to love, to give, to serve,
Seize the day, the moment, traveling toward our heavenly home.

  *Rochelle A. Wright*

## The Innocents

You gave us your great joy and cheery gladness
And nourished our delights with hugs and kisses,
These are not gone by the deeds of men unblessed.
Your lovely chatter will live forever in our lives.
We will not forget you as the focus of our dreams.
I will cry long for what they have done to you
And wish the wrath of God be heaped upon their souls.

I curse these deeds of ignorant and depraved men,
But what do I do to seize the moments of your
Radiance?  Where will those soothing fairy laughs
And dances be if I do not vow to take note of the
Love of all mankind?  I will preserve my love for you
In my love for others and say each dawn a prayer for
All of you in the playland of heaven.

  *Thomas W. James*

## The Children Are Crying

Has the world gone crazy, have the people gone mad
As we see the children crying and looking so sad

When the children are killed and the reason is spite
Then our hopes for the future are not very bright

If we look for revenge and stir up the hate
If we turn from our, God it maybe to late
To turn from the violence and evil we see
To change mans nature and make him agree
That God is the one, whether Christian or Jew
To show us the way as to what we must do

Let us search for the truth and not for the lies
Let us look for the things that bring joy to our lives

Teach the children the lessons that make thing right
Teach them the path that will show them the light
For with understanding and knowledge they will know
That all people are equal and entitled to grow
To see their children grow with hope and with love
To see their future flourish with faith from above
So the children can smile, can laugh and  be free
So they can look back at today and say, thank God it wasn't me

*Marvin H. New*

## Marvelous Wonder

Looking at your innocent face,
As you sleep in this safe place,
Next to my bosom, close to my heart
I've been struck by Cupid's dart.

Littlest Angel, kin of mine,
How can thy fondest wish I decline.
Safe here with me from all the world's harm,
How can I not be ensorcelled by your charm.

Eyes of blue, skin so soft,
To God, my hat I must doft.
How such a perfect creature, could be born,
Without you my heart in two'd be torn.

All the right number of arms, legs, and toes,
When you smile, your face and my heart glows.
May life bring you all that is beauteous and good,
'Cause ne'er a tear would you shed, if help it I could.

Today's the first day of what I hope is a long life.
May the devil keep all his onerous strife.
Laughter, joy, and love may you share,
With all those whom one day you will care.

*Orysia Effler*

## Little Grey Stone

Little grey stone on the mountain top
Asleep in your soft black earthen bed
Covered with sheets of satin leaves,
What secret of bygone quake and fire
Is locked forever in your furrowed head?
I ponder as I look to azure sky
Through lacy curtain of fairy flowers
And then, snatch you from an aeon of sleep.

My saw relentlessly cut you in pieces
And I polished your radiance of gold and red
But now as you grace my table top
And glisten seductively in shadow and light
What right did I have to disturb your bed?
Please forgive the trivial pursuits of man,
Our failure to understand the nature of God's plan,
Little grey stone from the mountain top.

*Phyllis H. Nelson*

## A Field Lost

Gazing through a window
    at a field, torn and brown,
A building soon to rise
    upon the staked and tracked up ground.

A farmer used to work the land.
    His bails of hay all rolled would wait,
Like sentries standing guard
    to the meadows open gate.

Slowly buildings would spring up.
    All the trees seemed to retreat.
The concrete horizon slowly rose.
    The flowers and butterflies knew they were beat.

I wonder how the farmer feels,
    his family lands beneath the stone.
The future of the generations
    lost and fading, he's all alone.

*Roxanne Hull*

## Somewhere Out There

On a gorgeous, hot, August afternoon
at Virginia Beach, VA.,
I really opened my mouth
at the wrong time "literally."
I dove headlong into a wave as I have done since age 5.
Nothing unusual, right?
Until I surfaced and realized-
I had no front teeth.
It's a most peculiar feeling
running your tongue across
your front teeth,
and finding them gone,
Not that I had smacked my face
on the ocean bottom, knocking them out...Oh.no..
My partial plate was missing, simply washed from my
mouth and now a permanent part of the Atlantic Ocean.
Or at least until it washes up
on another beach somewhere out there.
Hopefully whoever finds it will have a good laugh...
At least they'll have the teeth for it.

*Linda Bonebrake*

## In Search Of Balance

If I cry a thousand tears and laugh a thousand laughs,
At what point does my future merges with my past?

If I drive a thousand miles or fly a thousand hours,
At what point do I arrive at reaching a balance of powers?

If I sing a thousand songs or pray a thousand prayers,
Will I reach the point of balance to wipe out a thousand
Failures?

If I write a thousand poems or write a thousand books,
Will I have stated the purpose or simply gained some looks?

If I slept for a thousand days or awake a thousand nights
Will this make the difference in keeping all my rights?

If I raise a thousand children or kill a thousand men,
Will I have learned the meaning of life or simply lived in sin?

If though a thousand trips I make around this planet earth,
When will I the human man, reach the balance of my birth?

Though a thousand questions I may ask,
In seeking the balance within.
But until the journeys taken,
The balance can't begin.

*Ronald Anthony Bolin*

I see you through two eyes.  You see me through
scars where branches could have been, if not for human
intervention.  Four gifted eyes that return my curious gazes
with an air of dignity which accompanies age.  You can feel my
awe-inspired apprehension.  Sense my innate inferiority, for I
am not a true product of nature.  Your sturdy branches mirac-
ulously disperse into countless skinny twigs forming an intric-
ate network too simple, yet incomprehensible for my socially
molded mind.  You are restricted only by limits carefully
set by Mother Nature.  A perennial cycle that provides
you with cool cover year after year.  A being
that is truly free.  My envy is only over-
shadowed by my longing to
understand-
what does
it feel
like to
be free
but in-
capable of
moving
from your
place of birth?

*Martinne J. Geller*

## "Fallen Hope"

We both may hope or wish that we'll
be together forever but only we will be able to tell.
So therefore we have fallen hope.  Our hope is
to be able to help each other reach the stars
and be together.
Our wishes are very similar when neither
of the hopes or wishes come true we have
fallen hope.
Our lives are so similar yet so different we
make a perfect match.  We both hurt so bad the
pain inside hurts more than pain itself.
You mean so much yet I am still scared
so therefore again we have fallen hope.

*Nikie Camerota*

## Hope

Rainbows are beautiful to see
Beaches are like heaven in summer
To get away and dream
To drive away and leave her
Hair shining golden-blond
Sand sparkling with the light
Summer breezing on and on
Helping trees move in the night
Your dreams then come true
Shortly thereafter, they'll be with you
Life is big and health is good
It brings lots of meaning to be understood
To know you have friends who bring happiness to life
Like taking a vacation or loving a wife
And in the dreams the beaches are like heaven
In summer because rainbows are beautiful to me

*Ryan McCleary*

## In A Time

Tear drops fall in a glass of wine.
As we sit around a table and dine.
Back in a time when you were mine.
Bitter sweetness filled a year, and violent
filled sadness has always near.
Love filled our hearts.  Time stood still,
as we took a walk through the
blooming hills.  Back in a time.

*Sheri Buser*

## Sly

We were flying East to West in a gray September sky,
Beads of sweat dripped from my forehead and fell on my thigh,
I tried to think of Mom and her French apple pie,
But I couldn't escape from the thought that soon I might die.
Sgt. Thompson grabbed his M-79 almost in unison with the ship's banked
   dive.
John's M-60 started to buck, full metal jacket began to fly.
This should have brought me relief, but I knew, he always shot high.
Oh, if only I could hear Carol's soft sigh.
We began to hover, and I could think of no lies,
A heartbeat and a jump found my a** in the razor grass, near a sty.
Incoming was shouted, it burst nearby, and then that everlasting,
   grasping cry.
I wanted to hide, I wanted to run, then somebody shouted, it's Sly.
I had no strength and God only knows, how, I found myself holding his
   eye.
Tag it, bag it, there is no time; damn it, this is Sly.
Years have past as time slid by, and my only regret is that I didn't
say Goodbye.

*J. F. Davison*

## The Earth Is Beauty

Beautiful was the forest, before we burned it down.
Beautiful was the land, before it was a town.
Beautiful is the ocean, as she once was.
Beautiful is Mother Nature and everything she does.

Ugly is the car, and the truck and the train.
Ugly is the exhaust, that follows the plane.
Ugly is taking the easy way out.
Ugly is the future, for which there is doubt.

Beautiful is the balance that our planet must hold.
Ugly is the oil, that we've stolen and sold.
Beautiful is the water, and the life that it breeds.
Ugly are the warning signs that nobody heeds.

Beautiful are the pictures sent back from space.
Ugly is the way we pollute this place.
Beautiful are the lakes, rivers and streams.
Ugly is the greed behind some of our dreams.

Think of the time a small cut takes to heal.
It's only a cut, it's not a big deal.
Now think of the time that the Earth must take,
to heal all her wounds, and fix what we break.

*Paul A. Carlin*

## A Gentle Spirit Guarded By An Iron Will

In your eyes I can see,
Beauty the way it was meant to be.
Beyond my shield you will find,
A loving spirit caring and kind.
Tears of pain have hardened my skin,
Through the trenches of hell and back again,
Leaving my heart numb and cold,
Where Faith is weak and trust is bold.
But deep inside love is waiting still,
A gentle spirit guarded by iron will.
So believe in me as I believe in you,
And we'll share a love that is pure and true.
Hold me close and you will see,
The beauty in you is the love in me.

*William E. Hines*

## The Cosmic And I

If I was I, I would be much, much more than I
because I am who I am - and the whole of me likes
me as much as I like me.

If I was me, then I would not worry about me - though
the I in me would wonder why I am who I am - I would
still be me.

The Cosmic is in me - and I am in the cosmic. The
cosmic and I and me become one and the same.
Since the cosmic is in me, then I am the cosmic.
When I am me, I see the cosmic in I as much as in
Me - I then become a reality of that manifestation.

Since I am who I am, then I am the God of my heart
And I dwell within me, and also dwell within the
Cosmic realm.

*Otu A. Obot*

## "Today's World"

Today's world is full of great distress
Because of bad habits and Satanical Express!
How long will this go on and be displayed
To our good people and little children
Who are sorely afraid?

Many answers we seek to find
Of coping with our unsettled minds.
We seek a true feeling of gladness and joy to have.
It is quite possible if we don't become too sad.

Keep on going and keep up our spiritual faith!
And soon again we can become quite safe!
Today's problems are very big and very real!
We must be aware of Satan's many deals!

We can overcome these wrongful temptations!
How?
If we but seek God's loving and divine help
Now!

*Mildred H. Rak*

## "My Very Best Friend"

It is you I have chosen as my very best friend,
Because on you I have grown to always depend.

You have carried me through some of my life's greatest strives,
I'm lucky to have you as part of my life.

We laugh with each other at life's little surprises,
We cry with each other when the need arises.

Our friendship is special and built with unique kinds of links,
Since often we know what the other one thinks.

We tell each other secrets to have and to hold,
Because of the trust between us, they remain untold.

Our friendship has grown strong as the years have gone past,
Ensuring the chance it will always last.

*Leslie Endicott*

## Why Can't I Remember Me As A Baby

Why can't I remember me as a
baby, when I was small and
weak; when I had a pacifier.
Why can't I remember me as a baby
when I had to sleep in a crib.
Why can't I remember me as a
baby when I slept without a
pillow. Oh, why can't I remember me as a baby?

*Nastasha Ostrom*

## Walking With Nature

It's nearly spring and you can hear the serene crackling of ice that's
been smothering the marsh as it begins to release its hold, while
the crisp arousing weather paints a very pleasant picture for our
common soul.

It's at this time of the season when the birds rehearse their
brilliant harmonies, as you eagerly await for what you'll see.

It's at this time of the season when the water begins to fall, and
you can hear the soothing voice of God's fragile wildlife whispering
their call.

As I take my first few steps into these great outdoors, I suddenly
begin to feel secure, and it all appears so overwhelming, this
heavenly sketch that seems so divinely pure.

Where nature surrounds you and cradles your soul, while at the same
time capturing your attention away from a world that's gone so
incredibly cold.

These paths that I follow are carpeted with the earth's immaculate
soil
laid upon the ground that's surrounding our feet, and I take great
pleasure walking
upon those poignant sorrows with flowing sweeps.

It's only here that I suddenly begin to feel some relief, as I walk
over those scattered memories that have caused me such tremendous
grief.

For it's when I walk with nature that I can forget about those I've
cared about, and which I must now face a future that's shared without.

It's when I walk with nature, and only here, that I can forget about
all my debilitating fears, and I can, at last, wipe away all those
many perilous tears.

*Sue Ann Schiely*

## Incomprehensible

Beyond the blue horizons of early times
Before God thought of making earth
Only vapor - Drifting here, and there, and yon -
While God pondered His next move.

Did He wait a day? A month? A year?
How did He measure time?
Was it oh, so far? Or was it near?
Was it done in anger? Or in love?

God is still beyond man's ken.
Still in the blue mists above,
Mysterious - unfathomable —
Maybe God still ponders His next move...

*Ruby Nifong Tesh*

## Untitled

Are you strong enough to be weak,
awake enough to sleep tight in my arms?

Wise enough to hear my voice in the thunder,
quiet enough to accompany my song?

Are you small enough to stand tall on your knees,
slow enough to run beside me?

Can you find me in the center of the storm
and shelter me from the heat?

Are you fierce enough to fight for my heart
and alert enough to recognize love?

*Laura Evans*

## Mother

I saw you wrapped in terrycloth, standing
before the gas stove, cooking lambchops and peas
while eating a potato peel from yesterday's dinner.

I saw you huddled in front of the TV,
sipping coffee from a cracked cup,
your feet covered with your husband's worn socks
and your curled toes sticking out.

I saw you clean laundry on a washboard,
clear snow, mow lawn and shovel dirt.

I felt your muscles and looked at the hair
grow on your legs and under your arms.
You said you had work to do and no one to impress.

I have watched you become older and silent,
your fingernails chipped and dirty,
your breath smelling of cigarettes.

I have watched you become old and more silent,
rotting away like kitchen garbage.

Come home my mother, these arms are open
and women are dancing tonight.

*Tova Vitiello*

## The Wanderer Is Home

For years the wanderer traveled around,
Believing another word could be found.
Looked high and low and acted out.
Believed it was man life was all about.
Made some choices against the grain.
Thought she could never go home again.
Then all was taken away one day
And the wanderer finally knelt down and prayed.
She knew her roots and cherished them
And found the strength to start again.
A church around the corner lay.
She found the courage to go in one day.
She heard a choir of angels sing
And wondered if they would let her in.
They let her sing, though notes did stray.
They strengthened her each passing day.
And now she knows within her heart
That from this group she could not part.
Through their commitment to God's holy way,
They brought her home and she chose to stay.

*Lisbeth Sweet Frank*

## End of a Bougainville Day

Twilight comes to Empress Augusta Beach
  Beneath pale clouds just out of reach;
A melancholy world seems to fade away
  Into the eternity of a war-torn day.

The surf beats angrily against the shore,
  Phosphorescently relentless in its gruesome chore
Of disintegrating Bouganville wave by wave,
  Transplanting her sands to a watery grave.

The sun sinks magically out of sight,
  Leaving me in this forlorn plight
To battle with a muddled soul
  Tormented by the trials of a soldier's role.

*Sgt. Marion E. Willson, USMCR*

## Is She Worth It

It's hard to think straight, see both sides clear, tides of emotion,
betrayal and fear, the casual blanket that covered the affair now
peels away, naked eyes now stare. Sooner or later a quiet question
seeps in, is she worth it, this mess this sin, a dangerous question
this secret one, gone now the laughter, the ease, the fun.
Is she worth it, my heart lurches and reels, I now question what I truly feel,
blame and trust now do battle in the brain, grinding and
twisting like some dark speeding train. My most valued possession,
my most valued gift, ah to trust her, here lies the rift. The norm,
some fiend clashes and screams, often winning, obscuring and mean,
forget what hangs on the family tree, it's mine, my time,
time to fly free. Regret be my devil, often rearing her head, be gone
with this curse for I'd rather not dread, I've heard the dogs barking,
I've cringed and cursed, the wind in the elms, thy leaves be my nurse.
I know this will hurt, I don't think she sees, my burgundy blood,
my heart's pump and please. Aprils are infinite, choices too,
always haunting, maybe true, still, what a package this woman reborn,
with forever eyes and the smile of a storm.  I imagined a softer
inner shell,  one she surrounds like a white wizard's spell. The dust
firmly settled years ahead, what lingered affects hide under my bed,
there with the books, the shoes and the toys, silent now, but I hear
their noise. Is she worth it, I think maybe so, forward I head,
but carefully so

*Scott Benner*

## Spring Jewels

Sun rising on a purple horizon
Blending rays of glorious colors.
Singers of a bird chorus blending praises
Mingling with noises of the world of man.

This my day of spring beginning
Dew glistening with diamond-like rays
A rainbow of flowers softly swaying in whispering breezes.
God gift us with springs to restore our faith.

Animals flirting with grassy meadows
Romping with new found freedom
At last a day in warm renewing sun
Oh! heavenly! Earth! spring has begun.

'Twill be a brief tomorrow
To enjoy this striking array
Flashes, twinkling, brilliant again and again
To give our spirits a renewed praise.

Sing heavenly creatures both large and small
Give God credit for this - overall
Beauty breath-takingly seasonal spectacular
World stand still to let us take it all in.

*Margie Fiebig*

## Worship God

Wider your mouth and lift him.  Articulate who He is.
Bless Him with your praises, and say that you are His.
Speak to Him, declare His name.
Ascribe to Him honor for he is almighty and he reigns.
Glorify His being, His presence, His existence.
Because your life is but a vapor, it's gone in only an instant.
Adore Him for He is sovereign.
See Him for He is everything.
Raise your hands and bow your head considering the
cross where he hung and there bled.
Acknowledge who He is.  Recognize what He does.
Praise Him for His precious love.
Because he is, will be, and He was.
Open yourself to Him.  Give your mind up.
Empty yourself out, yes, empty out your cup.
It's not what you can get, it's now what you can give.
Because He's so great you see, I know that Jesus lives.
So worship the Lord in truth and in the Spirit.
Proclaim His glory with your mouth so He can hear it.

*Tamiko S. Taylor*

## Nature

Amazing is the abundance of nature.
Blissful is its beauty.
Its colors are a marvel of creation, divine in the deep circle of
    life.
Enchantment brings ecstasy to a forest of fantasies.
Nature is God's garden.
A heavenly balm for the heart.
Illuminated by the sun and stars, behold a jungle of joy.
A kaleidoscope and a kingdom of colors, living and full of life.
Mountains standing majestically, so natural and new.
Oceans filled with oysters and pearls.
Quiet and quiet.
Raindrops that turn to rainbows.
Snow bathed in the golden sun.
Trees, tall and graceful, under the umbrella of the blue sky.
Valleys, vales, rivers, islands, and seas that make a world wild and
    great.
A place where animals are not extinct.
A young yard of hope.
And zillions and zillions of reasons to see beauty.

*Nita Sood*

## Island Reflections

Sunshine and a gentle breeze
    blow amidst my hair.
A scattering of raindrops
    falling here and there.

    People of many colors live in quiet harmony.

The sound of the ocean waves
    rushing to the shore;
Fragrant tropical flowers
    orchids and much more!

    Children in colorful clothes laugh and play together.

A bright colorful rainbow
    appears across the sky.
Casts a delightful shadow
    on dark green mountains high.

    Provides a perfect backdrop to gather comforting thoughts.

The sky turns a hazy blue,
    the twilight hour draws near.
My head rests on your shoulders;
    your love so warm and dear.

    Memories of my childhood surround me ...and fill my heart!

*Marilynn Laker*

## Drifting

Drifting in and out of time, never knowing where to land,
Blurring of mind, filled with a muddle of sand,
Get clear, get free, wake up, listen to the band,
Haze fills my eyes as I try to look for a helping hand.

Wobbling head reeling to and fro with no where to go,
Misery stops here, to give its final show,
Like a dandelion flower give it one good blow,
Doesn't matter when your mouth might as well be a toe,

Eyes too heavy to see, won't stay open cannot think,
Move, do something, wake up connect with the link,
Arms too heavy can't be lifted, as I further fall and sink,
Images of fairies dance before my eyes dressed in pink.

What is real, what is fantasy, the veil becomes too thin,
Lucidity is blocked, sliced through with a sharp fin,
Raging beliefs wrong or not become the basis of sin,
Quiet, solace required but hard to find in life's loud, loud din.

*S. C. Moon*

## Untitled

a child walked barefoot across creaking, splintered
boards with no sound following her...the
pattering companion has gone back to the earth
and no other follows...now.

wide eyes stare unseeing into mirror for
tears of grief blind them to the reflection.
the thin chest burns with the dying effort
to continue breathing.

pillow of down and eclipse of sun, let me
know the dark, black peace ... allow me to
hold the worrybeads and clasp the sad relics
so my knotted spirit can drift.

the widow's web sways in the corner
as the plaster departs from the city's wall

*Therese Hoskins*

## Purple

They say Red is the color of love,
bold and burning like a flame at midnight
with penetrating beauty and the passion of blood.
And Blue, Blue is for sadness,
the color of a lover's tears,
or of the lips of a fallen angel.
But, what I feel most is Purple
that brilliant balance of love and sadness,
like the bruise I got last summer
when you closed your front door in my face,
like the bags I found beneath my eyes
when I stayed up all night crying,
or like the color my knuckles turn
as I ball my fists in anger.
Purple, your favorite color.
So when you tell me that you love me
then pretend you never said it,
I start to wonder if you realize that the Purple overwhelms me.
I wonder if you care,
or, is that the way you planned it?

*Marsha Foster*

## What You Are!

Thinking denotes WHAT YOU ARE!
Bright ideas will flourish by far.
Visionary thoughts will inspire you all -
Nothing to fear, continue without a fall.

Seeing what you see is WHAT YOU ARE!
Seeing is believing in what you see.
Illusion and delusion may be confusion.
Discretion should always be in moderation.

Reading what you read is WHAT YOU ARE!
It's a reflection of your own thoughts by far.
A good reading may bring forth an inspiration
That will guide you in your formation.

Saying what you say is WHAT YOU ARE!
Giving a good example is noteworthy.
It brings forth your righteous decision.
One good word will change the nation.

All of these make you a happy person.
Living a good life is lot of fun.
Persevering to the end will really be done!

*Thaddeus Capek*

## Across The Ocean There Came Hell

Across the ocean there came hell
Bringing agony, pain, hopelessness and disease
They brought their lies and christian ways
And drove us to our knees
They killed our game and raped our land
And tried to trash our pride
But our spirit will live forever
In the mountains, trees and sky
The day will come I hope and pray
When the great chiefs will rise again
To correct the wrong that has been done
And take back the stolen land
Take it back and set it free
Just as it always should have been
let the eagle fly with pride
And let us sing again
Across the oceans there came hell
But this they'll never tell
We're all a scream that has no sound, our story gaged and bound
Across the oceans there came hell but this they'll never tell.

*Sean S. Hooker*

## March

March winds blow through the air
Bringing in the spring so fair
It brings its beauty of flowers and trees
Shows its voice as it whispers its breeze
The winds of March they blow so sweet
Bringing young lovers to meet
We think of March as a month of growing
All the time we see it showing
Through small blades of grass and tiny weeds
We know the wind has brought some seeds
I love March windy as can be
It really is the month for me
Of brisk mornings, and sun warm days
Cool crisp nights by the shadows lay

*Vicki J. Hall*

## Mystic Pathways

A gathering of angels where beauty abounds
Bringing sunshine from heaven and warmth which surrounds
All of my being, my thoughts and my bones,
Encompassing love and soft visions of home.
Leading me onward and upward in flight
Face toward the sky looking at a great light.
Not to be blinded or burdened or scorned
But guided to comfort and blessed by the morn.
Questioning life at the moment of birth
Returning to darkness in the texture of earth
Seeing not shadows but brilliant embrace
Feeling the radiant glow of His face
And knowing at once my journey's not over
But rather continues in the color of clover.

*Louise M. Kress*

## October Tosses Colored Leaves

When October tosses colored leaves
Blue Jays bounce back a raucous cry
For acorn cups filled with fire.
Then November sends a heavy rain
To overcome the noisy game,
And the Blue Jays leave a streak of blue
Across the sky from tree to tree.

*Susan Carlton Smith Cavanagh*

## Together Forever In Tears

Please, my darling, don't cry,
But if you do, one tear will be yours
And the other will be mine.
Down your face we will run,
Joining, on your chin, together as one.
And so, remember my darling, the next time you cry,
One tear will be yours and the other will be mine.

*Thomas Hoskins*

## Unbridled

Get the kerosene and the matches.
Burn this old barn down.
Set me free.

Since the beginning of time my heart has cried out for
Understanding, encouragement...love.
Times beyond counting it has received
Scorn, ridicule...apathy.
Like an ancient harness on a tackroom wall
Those parts of me I thought dead, yearn to be reborn.
Set me free.

I pleaded with you for love-or release.
Twenty years of tears and you offer me a handhold in the dark?
No explanations of why you want me to stay?
No words of love to make me change my mind?
The reins are unbound,
There are fences to jump.
Set me free.

The horses are gone, close the barn doors-
Burn it down if you must.
I will be free.

*Zandra J. Kingsbury*

## Sailing

Oh, the sweet joy of sailing! With salt in the air
Burning bright on my breath, and the wind in my hair,
I am strong as the breezes that billow the sails,
Sending foam, fair as snowfall, to flume o'er the rails.
'Though the tide may be turning, my ship seeks the deep
Where the halls of Poseidon wait, haunting my sleep
With their sweet song of silence. My mast scrapes the stars
As I sail from the shores that inflicted my scars.
For the sea holds contentment, the ocean knows peace,
And the waves journey on without rest or surcease;
So I stride 'cross the decks, skimming over the sea,
Searching e'er for the shore where my soul shall be free.

*Stephen A. Cornine*

## The Mask

I have a mask I wear; oh, not one you can readily see;
But a mask I wear upon my soul, one that hides my vulnerability.
I got it some time ago, back when I was very small,
It seems I felt I had to hide away from those who were wiser
   and very tall.

When I got a little older and went off to learn at school
I thought the mask protected me from the teasing and the ridicule.
What I really learned to do was turn away from being me
Living in fear, anger and doubt, I was blinded, just could not see.

Today I took the mask off, and someone dared to look inside!
She said she liked what she saw there, could it be.
   I really don't have to hide?
So this mask I wore for so long, I will proudly hang upon my wall,
A reminder of my inner beauty, and the truth,
   that I never need to hide at all!

*Terry L. King*

## The Martini

I've been a complete teetotaler all of my life,
    but, a very dear one taught me to drink, my own wife.
That was a moment very, very fateful,
    and ever since I have been eternally grateful.
I first tried a martini with a gin called Beefeater,
    it was great, and I was sure that nothing could be neater.
But, then I tried a martini with a gin called Bombay,
    it was so good I tried still another called Tanqueray.
Still not satisfied, I tried yet another called Boodles,
    yes, you guessed it, I drank it, oodles and oodles.
I savored each, and they were truly sublime,
    they were so good, I can't even think of a rhyme.
But a genuine martini drinker I can never be,
    because I only enjoy one...at a time, don't you see.
Ah, but a fine, dry, icy martini has an exquisite taste,
    so I slowly sip and savor and swallow, so as not to waste.
I must confess, this revelation came to me quite late in life,
    so, a toast and thanks to the one who makes them, my loving
wife.

**Mortimer Cohen**

## Alone

They say you can't do everything alone,
But alone is a safe place;
No one is there to hurt you.
Alone is like a shield of armor.
No one makes you cry.
Alone is free from other points of view that disagree with yours.
Alone is never having to say your sorry to someone else.
No one embarrasses you when your alone.
No one infringes on your space.
Alone you can do anything you want.
Alone you don't have to share.
Alone you don't have to care.
They say you can't do everything alone;
No one is there to help you.
No one makes you laugh.
No one makes you think.
No one apologizes to you.
Alone you don't want to do anything.
No one shares with you.  No one cares about you.
They're right.  Alone is Lonely!

**Leilani Dillenbeck**

## Spring

The Lord has given us many thing,
but best of all is the month of spring.
When children laughter filled the air,
as they run and play without care.

Becoming an artist in disguise,
he adds a blueness to the skies.
And fans the suns's golden ray's,
To chase away the chilly days.

Next he sends his angels down,
to kiss flower upon the ground.
Bringing with them the morning dew,
to place upon the plants so new.

Though he works hard, he's not through,
for there is still plenty of work to do.
He makes the leaves for every tree,
And paint the country side for us to see.

And like a miracle, life appears,
Creating music to the ear.
As tiny birds flock to sing, their echo's toward heaven ring.
Thanking the Lord, for the month od SPRING....

**Mary Walker**

## Green Grass And Blue Skies

They talk about "grass" and say that it's "green."
But grass is something I've never seen.
They talk about a "sky" and say that it's "blue."
But I cannot say whether this is true.

A "cloud," they say, is fluffy and "white."
The "sun," they say, is big and bright.
A difference, there is, between day and night?
But I will never see the light.

They talk about my "world" and say that it's "black."
Comprehension of this is something I lack.
They talk about an "apple" and say that it's "red."
But I cannot imagine it in my head.

I can feel the heat of day.
I can avoid obstacles in my way.
I can hear the children play.
But I will never see what they say.

**Mandy Jo Myers**

## Peace Like A Dove

Jesus died on the cross for you and me.
But, He did it voluntarily.
He is so perfect.  We are so wrong.
We are so weak.  He is so strong.
He did it for love,
For a commitment made from above.
They mocked and spat in His face.
They put a crown of thorns on His brow for Him to embrace!
The pain they put Him through is more than I can bear!
That is a sign of His love and willingness to share.

**Nicole Dunaway**

## Wish You Have Been Here

My father was a great fiddler is the story I was told.
But he left this land of ours when I was six years old.
He used to take my hand, walk, and whistle, or he'd sing.
I can't remember this at all, I was such a little thing.

I have been strumming on my guitar quite sometime now,
Wish you could have been around just to show me how.
Heard about the mocking bird song that you used to play.
People said they came out of the violin and slowly flew away.

Dad, I'm now a country singer playing on my guitar.
Looking to make people happy here and from afar.
Wish you could have been around to help me with my song.
You playing your violin and me just singing along.

Dad, you should have been to Nashville. It's really a place to see
When I got there I said "This can't be really me.
If I get on T.V. someday to play and sing my song.
Would you take your violin and please, please play along?

**Phyllis Putz**

## Till Kingdom Come

I can't pull rabbits out of a hat
But I can pull feelings out of a heart
I look to the stars for guidance
And praise to the rays
That plan our fate
Here as well as in a higher plane
Every day more treasured than the previous
Remember those who are a part of our history
As we are theirs
Align our conscience on a straight path
And help those who have taken a turn
Because our hearts reach out for each other
The measure of which is an infinite sum
Till kingdom come

**Victor Young**

## Untitled

I still love you, as I always have
But I guess you didn't know
For I was shy and frightened
I turned away and let you go

You are always in my thoughts, everyday and night
I try to push you out of my dreams, because I know it isn't right
For you belong to another who also loves you true
And I am just a shadow of a memory to you

I guess I shall always love you, to my dying day.
In my mind and in my heart, you refuse to go away.

*Roddie Ruth Bowers*

## Tears In The Rain

My love for you once burned a white hot flame;
But I have found that as the years grind by,
The flame has guttered and ebbed, so that I can't even cry.
Our passions have all been washed away; gone like tears in the rain.

Songs of love once filled my heart with sweet refrain.
Then as midnight was tolled, the music faded away.
Now only silence has lease, empty, hollow, and grey.
All the songs have died; gone like tears in the rain.

Once I vowed that my soul would always with you remain;
Now those words have me trapped as if in walls of stone.
My soul withers and starves, ensnared in this union all alone.
all the words and promises are swept away; gone like tears in the rain.

We have each tried to hold onto the past, yet in vain:
Closing our eyes tightly, blind to our shared pain.
All that was ours slowly slips down the drain,
Leaving only a terrible, awful loneliness; gone like tears in the rain.

*Robert Wilkes*

## You

My heart is reaching out
but I know it's all vain
For you seem to be avoiding me
and I am touched with so much pain.
I think back on all those memories,
we've shared so many times
and few of them we do regret.
You pulled back and try not to
let your true feelings arise to surface.
You're always saying "I am just a friend,"
Well, friends can also be lovers.
So put this heartache of mine to end
the worst thing to happen when friends fall in love
Is a lifetime full of happiness
guided by the Lord above.

*Maia Weir*

## Loss

Death is all around us
but of its face we see only shadowed glimpses
should we condemn death for taking away
the once with whom we shared
our lives and times good or bad
or should we be grateful to death for stealing away
the pain in which our loved ones were caught
should we grieve their loss and
and mourn for them
or rejoice in their release
regardless they should be remembered
and allowed to rest in peace

*Xavier Alexander Robertson*

## A Love For A Loving Mother

Once I knew..... Once I lost..,
But I never lost the love of you.
When I awake to every day I know it's new.
That Love you have for me.

For did you not give me life?
And did you not caress me?
Did you not breast me?

So how can I awake without the thought of
you? Knowing everyday the love you have
for me and knowing my day begins and ends.
For did you not give me life?

My life which starts with love for you...
For all my life did you not give me love?
And at the end of time.

We will see how much all the love God had for you.
For within you comes a feeling that makes
me greater than I AM.

So with this I say........
Oh, how Sweet my Mother is.

*J. G. Davidson*

## Happy Birthday Mom

Today is your birthday and I have nothing to give
But I would like to thank you for helping me live
The life I've lived.
Over the years I've grown and changed
Sometimes I felt a little deranged
But you're always there for me as a friend and a mother
If I had the chance, I'd choose no other
No one could ever take your place, no one of any
Different color or race, because it would be you I
Would miss and if you ever have to leave me remember
This.
I wouldn't be here if it weren't for you, I wouldn't be
Brave or be so cool, I wouldn't be anything nothing at all
If you weren't there to catch me when I fall.
So I want to thank you on this special day for helping me
Lead my life the right way, and thank for everything you've
Done for me, and thank you for making my life happy, thank you
For helping me feel no shame, HAPPY BIRTHDAY MOM, I love
you mame.

*Mary Cleman*

## Condition Of Love

A heart is not a play thing, a heart is not a toy.
But if you won't it broken just give it to a boy.
Boys like to play with things to see what makes them run
but when it comes to loving you they do it just for fun.
When you're choice comes to meet
him your heart begins to dance,
the world revolves around him there's nothing like romance.
You wonder where he's been
in life you wonder if he's true
one moment you'll be happy the next you'll be blue.
Don't ever fall in love my
friend you see it doesn't
pay and though it causes
broken hearts it happens everyday.
my heart would of been yours
forever and I hope you
understand that when I gave
my heart to you I thought
I gave it to a mom.

*Stephanie Daigle*

## Dear Employee

You think us harsh and demanding without a trace of a smile,
But it is in the interest of all that we walk this long mile.
We may seem unjust at times, or look like administrative fools,
But, you'll never know how hard we try to follow our own rules!
There may be times when we're too busy to say you've done a job
well,
maybe, we believe you know it and it was not for us to tell.
Then, shame on us, for it is a need on your part, to hear
our words of appreciation to find loyalty in your heart.
We provide a service to those who need our care, and sometimes
they must be put before our feelings even though it
may be somewhat unfair.
When you entered this world of sickness, and thought to do
everything you possibly can,
You had to know at times it would be thankless and not
everything would go according to your plan.
So, please remember, when you come into this building each
and every day,
That we rely on all of you to give of yourself in the most
honorable and professional way.

*Mary H. Mello*

## Noses

Noses are a funny race, they stand out on every face.
But lately they all look the same, I say is this
   some kind of game?

There's Dr. Straith, the father figure, now
Dr. Jeff is even bigger there's Dr. Davis
   and Dr. Chow, and Dr. Joy and even now
   a Dr. Golden

I'm afraid of this new rage, the same old nose of any age
What next is my chant and cry, I think I do defy.
You lift my breast, you flatten my tummy
You take in my thighs, and make my lips yummy.
You fix my eyes, my chin, my ears, what
else I do in the coming years?
I won't know my age, my face or my image.
And soon I'll be too old for this kind of scrimmage

*Nancy Phillips*

## One And Always Love

A love I have for all things alive,
But my one true passion you can ride astride.

My horse to me is more than my pet,
Such a beautiful animal, you'd never forget.

He's smart, he's funny, he's daring to me,
But the best is to ride, for I feel set free.

Him I love, and have from the start,
Since the day of his birth, he stole my heart.

*Linda Kay Hutchings*

## Never Knew

She was always there
but never knew
How you felt
or what you wanted to do.
Before now, even you
Never knew what to say or to do.
Before now you never knew
the feelings for her in your heart,
But now that you know what is in your heart
With these feelings you must part
For she could never be,
Never would be,
Truly yours.

*Mike Bernardin*

## "Listen"

You say my words mean nothing,
But nothing's what I am now...
Floating above everything,
Please come show me how.....
If you want to race to hell,
I'll give you the head start....
I know that I'll beat you there,
Because you've taken my heart....
Now I'm idling here,
Nothing to do, nothing to be....
After all I gave to you,
This is what you've done to me??

You say I can't cross your line,
You watch so I can't get through...
But if I can't stumble down your weaving path,
I'll never run into you...
You've put up walls to keep me out,
They shun me from your world...

So I fight and I bleed and I scream and I shout,
All just to be heard....

*Matt Plaisier*

## Close Enough For Me:

I wasn't born with a silver spoon in my mouth
But soon as you held me, I knew what love was all about
And since that day you've never let me down
I thank God for giving me a mother that will always be around,
I know you're not perfect, and so, who could be
But regardless to the drama, you're close enough for me
I miss putting proud smiles upon your lovely face
Because there will never be anyone to ever take your place
When God was making families, He would plainly see
He couldn't make us perfect, but close enough for me
When I look at these walls and don't know what to do.
I gain strength and comfort knowing I got my qualities from you.
You taught me to be sensitive and life has made me tough,
So when you feel you're far from perfect
Just remember Mom to me you're close enough!

*Nathaniel D. Carswell*

## The Journey

He approached, from where I did not see.
But, spoken quite clearly were his words to me.

"I've been on a journey, a journey of mine only."
"Won't you now travel with me, for with two we're not lonely?"

At first I was frightened for I did not know him well.
"Sir, please speak to me now and of this journey tell."

"It is alike no other you've traveled I'm sure."
"And each finds it different, all hearts rings pure."

"Some do not like it," he smiled through the tears.
"I believe," he spoke softly, "it could be their fears."

"The heights you reach are of an eagle's soar."
"But once at the bottom only one hears your roar."

He laughed very gently and said to be certain,
"This journey I speak of is to all like a curtain."

"Some days it is open and one's vision is far."
"But, oft' it is drawn like night air filled with tar."

"Do you now understand, I wish to cause you no strife."
"What I speak of, my dear, is simply called Life."

A gasp escaped me when he first uttered the word.
Then I smiled and replied, "To not go is absurd."

*Laura Vodovoz*

## Workings of a Stroke

God forgive the inventor of the vacuum cleaner,
but the broom just won't cut the mustard today,
and pushing the nozzle under your dresser...I unearth your glasses.

I jump when I feel you reaching out for me.
I see your greasy hand-prints on the white door facings
left there from your breakfast buttered skillet toast I prepared.
I see you crumbling the toast in your lukewarm morning coffee,
eating it with a spoon and giggling...calling it "soakie."

Pushed under your bed , I suck up flowered handkerchiefs tied in knots
lost for so long, and you swore to me you had not hidden them there.
You blamed me for most of the antics you pulled, and sometimes I
laughed.

Straightening the narrow black framed piece of paper...parchment,
I take the time to read: We are delighted to send our best wishes
on your 90th birthday...Signed: George and Barbara Bush,
and I drop the stiff end of that vacuum cleaner just long enough
to see you in myself in the photograph propped upon your night stand.

*Mary Ann Gamble*

## Dedicated To The Unsung Heroes Of The Vietnam War

The war is definitely over,
but the deep wounds still remain.
The scars will always be there,
and lives won't be the same.
A war that seemed so senseless,
so hard to understand,
men and women were dying,
in a far away foreign land.

It all was so crazy,
the insane things that were done.
A war that went on and on
and no one really won.

How can one forget?
The nightmares that linger on,
the memories that still haunt them
from the dusk, until the dawn.

I write with admiration
for the ones who fought with pride.
I pray that all the Vietnam Vets,
will find some peace inside.

*Sandra J. Boisvert*

## Kiefer Tyrell

I found out my mom was to have a baby
But the doctors said it would be a dwarf, maybe.
There was even a big change it may die
All my mom said was, "It's all a lie."

I wondered what it'd be like to have a dwarf brother
The thought made me cringe, it made me shutter.
I sat around and pondered and thought
Knowing with his disability, there's lots I'd be taught.

From the beginning all I wanted was a girl
And her long hair I'd get to curl.
but I didn't think once he'd be unhealthy
I guess for others sake I was very stealthy.

Finally the due date was coming around
And from the labor room I heard the sound.
Of the baby's screaming cry on Mother's Day
And the doctor said, "He'll be okay."

My brother was almost as perfect as can be
Except for the little tubes and IV.
On his body there was not "too short" a limb
And I gave a gentle kiss because I love him.

*Lacresha Graham*

## Welcome

'Tis the heart  of joy that welcomes joy
But the heart of pain that prevents it
'Tis the heart of joy that ushers in
the Lover... who awaits steadfastly and whispers
"Receive me and let my longing be brief
Drop then your mantle of grief."

'Tis the heart of joy that engraves the
Divine delight of kings... and beckons the merriment
As the devic force sings
But - woe - the heart of pain kneels
And pummels Sadness... so holds up its hand
To the gentle consort who then does admonish

"Know you that from joy were you strewn...
From magic, from miracles,
From instruments of gossamer tune...
'Tis the heart of joy empowers
the lovers to proceed
Never again to allow pain their
consummation impede."

*Virginia Bari*

## Indeed Not

My!  but hasn't it been cold you say
but the snow is melting today
And so is my heart
Of all the twisted frozen thoughts

About to say
Oh yes the world is good and fine

And so the sun does shine
upon the dripping show
Sending it in whirling puddles
for cars to splash through
And am I blue?

Indeed not! for what do you suppose?
My old winter blues have taken on the form
Of brand new shoes.  A breath of Spring
Yes - new blue shoes so dainty
To take your breath away.

*Laura Doris Smith-Roush-Brack*

## Dance of Stillness

Beauty exquisite I find in the stillness
But the wind whisper to me and invites me to the dance.
The sacred dance calls me with crystalline clarity,
And beckons me to enter into the lyrical flow.
As I answer the call that sweeps through my heart
Creative forces stir in my soul.
I move with the grace of the stillness within
Choreographed by a bright inner light.
The energy takes me to luminous places,
Wondrous ecstasy to know.
Who can believe that the two becomes one
That the stillness becomes the dance
And within the dance is found the stillness?

*Margaret M. Schneider*

## Mother

Blessed are those who shine from above
For the blessed are those who show kindness with love
A smile, a hello, a gentle warm embrace
A kiss, a hug from a gentle mothers grace
Her hand is extended what woes it will take
Dear Mother, Dear Mother your heart I shan't break
Thank you Dear God for this life of her love
Break not her dear heart its the heart of your love.

*Lynn Deckard*

## Death

In a dark room all closed in by walls,
but there are not four walls; it is a circle.
a circle that has no specific start and no specific end
There is no escape, there is no door; just the 1 inch by 1 inch window
close to the ceiling.
But you cannot see it; the ceiling is too high.
you feel as if you could reach higher and higher and higher and never
reach the top
But you know you will.
You also know the circle will come to an end.

*Sari Chait*

## Last Hope

Through the rainy clouds one can see what was once the sun.
But there is no energy left to give life-bringing warmth, and soon the whole earth will be frozen.
The last groups of people shudder in the cold like lost leaves in a blow of wind.
The gray landscape only leaves behind memories of the green hills and long meadows, that once stretched across the rich land.
Food is scarce, and empty eyes are scanning their surroundings for a green leaf.
Most people have no hope left, giving up their bodies to the cold ground only to become one with it once again.
Soon they will be one of the millions of restless souls, searching for an answer which they will never find.
Through the gray fog the last hope that is left can be seen like a bright light, fighting desperately without a chance.
The darkness has it covered like a blanket of evil, wrapping it more and more.
In a last, forlorn attempt a few radiant beams break through the cover, revealing some of what was once a hopeful world.
The two elements collide, unleashing all their power in a bright flash that reaches across the horizon.
A last flicker of hope arises in the hollow eyes of the spectators, just to be crushed again by the endless gray stare.
The blanket has covered their surroundings, leaving nothing but black, infinite darkness...

*Phillip D. Nies*

## Untitled

What I'm going through isn't easy and frustrations have set in fast
    But there's no time to look back and dwell on the past
I hurt and sometimes feel defeated
    I've cried and even pleaded
But I can't quit cause I'm not a loser but a fighter
    I will find a way to make this load lighter
We all have to lose sometimes before we can win
    Regain the strength to start over again
We have to cry sometimes before we can smile
    We may have to struggle but it's all worthwhile
We have to hurt in order to be strong
    Just fight when things go wrong
If you keep on trying and believing now and then
    You will have victory in the end

*Teresa Johnson*

## The Wedding

Your souls are united on this special day
By the love you share and the vows you say
As you stand at the altar and declare your love
Before family and friends and the Father above.

United before God, two become one.
What is truly God's choosing cannot be undone.
Two lives, two loves, two hearts united,
From this day forward, a house undivided.

*Pat Canuteson*

## Behold... I Knock...

He knocked upon a door one day
But those inside said, "Go away!"
"I only wish to sup, and dine."
"We're busy now, we've not the time."

And so He turned, and walked on by
Then gave another door a try.
They looked outside, and said to Him -
"You're not our type, You can't come in."

He tried then, yet anther one -
"If You come in, You'll spoil our fun."
"I wish to make your life complete!"
"We're organized, tidy and neat."

He left, and gave one more a try -
"Will they too, let Me pass on by?"
A child came out, and smiled at Him,
"We love You Lord, won't You come in?"

*Roland L. Crosby*

## Different

I want to be different,
But what is different?
I used to think that
It was being an individual,
But, if everyone is an individual
Doesn't that mean that individuality equals conformity?
And isn't conformity the opposite
Of being different?

Maybe, we are different in being the same,
David Byrne once said that he's the same as he ever was
And people still call him different.
If I'm the same, will I be different?
Maybe similarity breeds differentiality,
For if we are all being different,
Then we are all doing the same thing,
Namely being different!

Nevertheless, I still don't think I'm different,
I guess that just makes me the same as everyone,
Yet different from those being different.

*Mark D. Spratt*

## The Ocean

The others were rivers, streams that would soon end.
But, you are my ocean, a world that goes forever.
I look out to sea, and I see all our possibilities.
Our love is like the ocean, it's beautiful and clear.
A love that shall be forever here.
There are many different things buried in the sea.
Things like the love lying deep within me.
Our love will change, our love will grow.
Just like the currents, moving fast and slow.
Just like the ocean creatures, who have their quarrels,
We'll have our share of problems.
But, we'll always have tomorrow.

*Michelle Ward*

## The Healing Song

Come out of the darkness
Come out of the fear
Years of torment, torture and shame
Come from the shadows
You have finally seen the light
Shout victory that have just been won
Awaken my dear there are no more shame to bear
Look towards the light
That where your future lies

*Pauline Thomas*

## Dirigible

I made something for you today
But you won't ever see it.
I'd filled it full of good advice,
And parables and other hot-air things,
Until it bulged and billowed out......
A logical, dirigible.
A swollen mass of rhetoric,
The thing ballooned and tried to fly,
But when I saw the shape it took
I knew it wasn't right.
Too smug. Too long. An empty bag of nothingness.
The thing I'd built could not transport
My thoughts from me to you.
I sharpened up my pencil point
Harpooned the thing,
Watched it collapse.
Instead of air, I send you this;
I care
I care
I care.

*Richard Klokow*

## A True Friend

When you came along I just wasn't sure.
But your friendliness just led me a lure.
You had an idea that of the life I had lived.
You kept being my friend right up until the end.
You stood by my side, through thick and
through thin.
I just didn't realize you were my true friend.
You made a promise that you could keep.
But now I've gotten myself in to deep.
My life is in your hands now just show me
the way.
And I will make you happy day by day.

*Loveta Mitchell*

## THE WATER

Drowning my troubles in the deep depths of a bath of bubbles
By candlelight I recognize the goddess somewhere in the shadows of
the tub,
trapped in the light of the wax, flickering
It reminds me that there is no beauty like this
For nothing glistens as this golden bronze skin by candlelight
Impression as beautiful as the hills and valleys of the Motherland
dances
Here, bubbles know her as royalty, clinging as devoted subjects
And they pay homage to the Princess within
As the candle burns, and I learn to forgive the black rose for
having thorns,
I pray, take me to the water, take me to the water

*Shena Abercrombie*

## A Fallen Leaf

There are times in which I see myself as a fallen leaf suppressed
by life's tempestuous storms,
Undulating between the wind currents,
Bedridden.
Almost completely disheveled controllable capacity.
Yet there remains a burning desire which you give me an incentive to
fly up again to my original status
Your undeniable strength and pleasant outlook startles me
Your remind me more of a steady surfer, riding the high waves of
life, surpassing every deathly current, and stresses we all are
subject to
Yet an undeniably metaphysical strength
a passion for life's very existence overcomes you.

*Shifra Yael Burstein*

## The Magic of Academics

Ancient desires set abound,
By magic text which hath found,
A mote of light so covered deep,
By life's own troubles and doldrums, Sleep.
Aspired now from tempered pit,
Fire's ready, all but lit,
From mystic voice and cryptic, Tongue,
Should paint the picture to be, Hung.
Eoned flesh the Beast will gorge,
Flesh anew the Storm will forge,
Polished armor to display,
Among the Kings of yesterday.

Never-ending battles cease,
Gold and riches — pseudo peace,
Wisdom given by evoking song,
The lands of youth ye yet still, Long.

Spells now mastered and prodigy.
That wizard's apprentice is the, Key,
To ornate doors of ethereal birth,
Where lay unveiled treasures of, The Earth.

*Richard J. Ruckdaschel*

## What Does It Matter?

Some people just seem to waste their life away,
By spending time worrying about what others say.

When the bottom line seems to be,
What does God will for me?

What does it matter who says or does what each day?
If we were put here to do it God's way.

What does it matter how much we achieve?
If God sees to it, we have more than we need.

What does it matter how much money we make?
If in a fleeting moment the bank could break.

What does it matter what we do each day?
If God takes care of it when we pray.

*Sharyn Harms*

## "Boats To Paradise"

Romance is like a voyage on the waves of love
calm and free spirited like the heart of a dove
An adventure that journeys from here and there
with sensitive emotions towards the one who cares...
Words help describe expressions of the heart
but occasionally silence plays the part
Of knowing this love is tightly embraced
when a warm smile appears on her face......

There's unlimited richness of passion inspired
through mind and body in harmony with desire
An ancient treasure in relation to heart and soul
a pure attribute of appreciation lined with gold.....
One hundred percent of me is what I give
to the end of time together we'll live
Sharing the goodness of each other starting today
and on boats to paradise we'll sail away.....

*William Boyer*

## Winters End

How many winters will I see?
Can I expect bad weather?
Shall my days always be as overcast as this?
When will my days be rewarded with the sight of the mighty sun,
whose mighty rays guide my footsteps and let me see what is good and
what is bad?
If the sun did not shine on me would I eat poisoned berries?
Or could be able to tell good from bad without its light?
If I lived somewhere else would rain still fall?
Would my home be of wood, brick or possibly adobe?
Would the sun look any differently from another land?
Would there be clouds in the way or even mountains who stay forever in
the way? Or maybe man made skyscrapers that stand in front of the sun
whose light is but a vague shimmer of gray?
People say there are many suns, yet they only look like twinkling
stars to me, I only see one sun, which keeps us warm and will always
shine on us. Wherever and whoever you are.

*Mike Dominguez*

## Coming Together

May our world come together, may we all meld as one.
Can we forgive all bad things, anger and hatred have done.
Can we forget all that's happened, in a world so distraught.
Can we forget all good things, that our teachers have taught.
In this world full of anger, and hatred so strong.
We've forgotten our roots, and where we belong.
Let's look to the future, with kindness and peace.
With prayers and hopes, all this madness will cease.
Be kind to all strangers, from near and afar.
For God will be watching, through each shining star.
He looks for all mankind, to share all his wealth.
To live with his love, and thrive in good health.
There's no easy answers, we all have to care.
We all have to take part, of the burdens we share.
If we can give help, to just one friend in need.
Payments are tenfold, for your kind hearted deed.
So look to your neighbors, with kindness and smiles.
The wealth you will feel, spans miles and miles.
So lets come together, for peace all around.
For in God's embrace, his love will abound.

*Shelley Dischler*

## The Chameleon

I am the chameleon.
Can you see American heroes in my eyes?
Do I resemble great musicians?
Look closely, do you see me take on the myths
and legends of people that have gone before me.
I am the chameleon.
Will you not know what name to put on my gravestone?
I bear so many just look into my eyes.
I am the chameleon and I am so good at it that I can
no longer find the real me.
And if I can't find me, then I must be very elusive to your
naked eye.
I am the chameleon and I have taken head-on every life I
could imitate, but I refuse to face my own life.
For I am the chameleon.
Find me if you can.

*Robert E. Hurley*

## Can Sweat Mask Tears?

Solid solutions to liquid problems
cannot avoid the leaks.
And false illusions to hide true feelings
will never soothe the freaks.
In my philosophy, there's no room
for privileged lies,
though often there is time
to hear what another sees.
I'm not asking you to act as someone else,
but I should think you would step outside yourself.
Can sweat mask tears? I've wondered off and on for years.
Vivid discussions to sanctify pain
won't take the truth to task
and repercussions which arise at night
won't help remove the mask.
In my experience, I've met no one built of glowing light,
we only pray to contain the light forever around.
I see no scale to measure closeness to God,
and those who think they're near, are somehow far and gone
can sweat mask tears? Where would we be without our greatest
fears?

*Warren C. Elliott*

## Us

Almost all grown up me and her
Can't believe it
We are like two inseparable burs.
One's happy, one's sad
What's funny will usually always stay that way.
We always make time
Whether it's at home, school, or play.
I consider myself the dull, ugly one
While she's the beautiful swan.
I can't believe we are still together
It's hard to comprehend one day it will all be gone.
When she's gone for good
I know I'll grieve her.
For she's my strength
While I'm her believer.
True friends we are
That's why it lasts.
Someday we'll both look back
And remember each others pasts.

*Mary Anderson*

## Where Treasures Lie

I walked thru the dark green grass,
Carefully seeking not to step on sacred
Ground — ground holding traces of kin,
Some very precious, some just remembered,
  Not for love, but for a hurtful and selfish life.

Carefully reading the words, words engraved
On grey stone — she was a wonderful
Mother, knitting sweaters of goat's wool
And making clothes out of fertilizer sacks,
  Stylish things that I wore with pride.

Beside these mounds were other mounds of green
Holding grandparents who were kind and sweet,
A grandfather who lived a century, fought
In three wars and died of a broken hip.
  He was able to maintain himself to death.

Tears wet my face as I walked away,
Feeling that it was only yesterday when
They were placed there, awaiting
Christ's coming. I'll return again,
  Daring not to tread where treasures lie.

*Rubye Dowlen*

## Moon Magic

I see the clouds trying to hide the moon glows,
casting mysterious but beautiful shadows.

I see the moon weaving in and through,
it works on the mind-the loins, too.

I have a feeling of emotion and romantic inclinations.
I see on the face, all kinds of great sensations.

I feel it pull into a dreamlike way
causes a longing and hunger, for those on our mind today.
Those who are away.

Thinking how nice it would be,
if the I, was we.

*Lawrence*

## Untitled

As I leave to walk down the lonely path again,
Certain private burdens weigh upon my heart.
Only time will tell if it is worth the wait,
Only this time apart.
Will this duration urge me
  To surrender?  To forget?
Or shall I struggle and fight
  Between heart and mind to

Remember the special one

My own personal theory of this
  Period of time will
  Determine for me my future endeavors.

I have the knowledge that the path
  is what I make it.
Whether it be familiar or totally
  unknown...
Is truly a mark of destiny.

*Terri Punziano*

## One Morning

Tears brimming from eyes tumbled down
  cheeks...usual teardrops;
  Wet and moist upon a breast,
They didn't just stop right there though - changed,
Teardrops turned solid shards of ice each
  'bout an inch and a quarter long,
Quickly they entered, deep and clean.
  You ever felt anything like this before?

I cried for a long long time that morning.
  Then, a familiar road - the one - you know,
Where the asphalt's cracked
  And crumbling with grainy chunks worn off the sides yet,
Popping up here and there as if playing a game of hide-n-seek,
  appear the tiniest of green plants -
Fresh, vibrant, hopeful...
  And you just can't help but feel good inside!

*Rebecca Yapuncich*

## Life's Fragrance

The fragrance of life...soft, not overpowering,
Engulfing your very soul, lingering like the
Smell of honeydew, the alluring web of
A spider, pulling you deeper into its tapestry...
A gentle voice whispering sweet memories
Of a lost moment...the twinkle of a star...
The colors of a rainbow...the moisture in a
Droplet...ever so present, but unable to be
Captured...the scent of perfume slowly
Evaporating from your skin...like everything
In life...temporary yet feeling so permanent.

*Patricia Williams*

## Fences

Tops jammed on pens,
Chewing gum plastic wrappers
Side rails on beds
Seat belts on anything
Not enough space inside of or on top of
Sweet 'N Low, creamer packets
Heavy doors with no door stop
No table high enough for wheel chairs
Impatience; no privacy
Church steps; small print
Body unbalanced
Invitations but no way to go
For an elderly woman in a nursing home
Is this all there is?
After a lifetime of love and relationships
Memories and souvenirs of good times together
Children's art and "I love you's" collect in a box
Friends visit, we exchange news of others
Is this all there is now
Memories and fences.

*Virginia R. Lyle*

## Rejoice!

The March winds blow the landscape bare,
Churning and turning and teasing the air.
Thunder then rumbles 'cross the sky,
Awakening the earth, for April is nigh.

Nude branches, weary of winter's strife,
Burst forth with buds of vibrant life,
As tulips and daffodils push through the earth,
Parading their hues in joyous rebirth.

The cardinal, finch, and the chickadee
All chirp and sing Spring's harmony,
Flaunting their colors, they flitter and flutter,
While woodpeckers peck and hammer and stutter.

Earth's abud and abloom in this season of wonder, as
God's creatures arise from winter's cold slumber.
Melodious with song, resplendent in hue,
May the spirit of Spring touch all your hearts, too.

*Virginia Marcelene MontBlanc*

## The Sunken Cathedral

Legend whispers of a great cathedral
Claimed by the tides,
Lost long ago in a sunless valley
Lost to the sea

Lonely it stands, in a haunted garden
Where fishes are
With clangorous bell, it tolls vain summons
Over empty waves

Once I approached it through the gate of dreams,
And heard the carillon
And plucked salt blossoms from their waving stalks,
—But could not stay

Nor take away from the drifting kingdom
A memory even.
Only one note's echo could I steal
Of the bell's song

And now the echo sounds daily fainter,
Engulfed by the light
As the wonderful spires were once overtaken
By a restless sea.

*Patricia Shaw*

## Lost and Found

I found myself in the rain.
Cleaning up the shattered glass with blood then came the pain.
The cold rain dripping from my body.
I found my soul and from there I wasn't sorry.
   I felt my spirit come to me,
It came out from all its years of hiding
My paintings and writing all made sense.
I was here on this Earth for a reason and hence.
I was a single piece in a perfect sphere.
I had nothing now to fear.
I would not and will not be pinned down by my own spear.
All the worries and bad memories just seemed to disappear.

   *Laura DeVito*


## Journey Through The Thick And Thin

I used to run through fields of gold
Climbing oaks thick and bold
I'd play all day and sleep all night
with no fears or worries of a fright
I'd talk to strangers and make new friends,
but now I follow new trends.
I'd walk in the footprints of God himself,
but now I walk soft and watch myself.
I'd run the creeks and explore new lands.
I loved adventure and soft whit sands.
The feel of cold clay between my toes
was ten times better than the shows.
Sometimes these days I seem to find
that I am in a body that is not mine.
I hope and I wish for freedom of mind,
but I have found that the world is unkind.
So now I have to turn my head
to watch for thieves who will steal my bread.
Some say it comes with growing up,
but I believe that society is corrupt.

   *Sean Galewaler*


## Reality Versus Naivety

Reality's rays are invading naivety's shelter,
Clouding dreams, beliefs and goodness.
Naivety's innocence struggles to stay intact,
But confusion's shadow appears.

The shelter of naivety is being invaded by the laughter of reality.
Reality takes the dreams and optimism of youth;
The laughter grows louder.
Bitterness enters and routine replaces child-known freedom;
The rays grow stronger.

Reality's rays have invaded naivety's shelter.
It is dark.
Security has left and innocence is gone.
It is light.
Naive dreams are no longer dreams.
They're realities waiting to happen.

The time is now.

   *Marie Connors*


## Eyes

   You could see it in her eyes. The person in the corner watching
each snowflake fall. Every part of her body was weathered by age.
But her eyes, her eyes were alive. The little twinkle dancing in
her sky blue eyes was the young spirit in her yearning to get out,
wanting to be a child again. Wanting to play in the sunbathed fields.
To the spirit it is within reach, but for the mind, it will always be
a secret wish.

   *Matthew Wetschler*


## Me and My World (A Celestial Message)

Thoughts bustle in my mind
clustered in the depths of my being
exploring my individual world
to find if my life has purpose and meaning.

Why at this stage of my existence
Am I obsessed by that feeling
of altering old personal patterns
that for long made my life fulfilling?

Am I right or am I wrong?
I ask the angelical spirits
that excel in strength and direction
to reveal the truth of my perception.

Winged messengers looking down upon me
whispered in a melodic tone
as your world is in evolution
don't be worried, dear one.

   *Milagros Ramirez*


## Blankets

I lay curled in fetal positioning
cold because the floor
heater, centrally located

heats mostly the center of my house,
my first-

With two good comforters
comforting only each other

Icy against warmth
I recently bring
alone

To the complex equation of eventual slumber
beyond my circumstance

Lulling into see-saw patterns peek-a-pooing
at my consciousness

Beckoning sleep to enter with(in)
the warmth now realized is barely manageable
without

Freeing me momentarily
of my loneliness once more

   *M. Rose Barkley*


## Father's Love

A father's greatest joy in life
comes as his children grow
because of every chance he gets
to let his children know

The most important things there are
for everyone to learn
the how's, the why's those facts it takes
an awful lot to earn

Too many people spend their time
just living day to day
Their parents never told them
never took the time to say

Make the most of all your time
do the best that you can do
and always try the hardest thing
the most difficult for you

And we, too, must remember
to take the time to say
to those we love and care about
"I love you," everyday.

   *H. James Hayes*

## "Discarded"

They sound like whispers,
coming from the gentle lips of angels,
Somewhere in the darkness, a sigh escapes,
like a determined last breath from a tomb-

Soft tears trickle down and melt into my shirt,
a long stream of memories follows suit,
Lingering on my pillow, the sweet scent of her hair,
now, a painful recall-

Dreaming of rest and peace at heart,
a broken dream filled with realities,
Lost and unsure of the way I came,
sitting in the same place for years-

Dawn beats in my window and breaks the glass of my thoughts,
I remember, I remember, I love you-

*Nathan Wilson*

## The Courthouse

Buzzing
continuous buzzing
like a great monster exhaling
then click click click
echoes of stilettos
receding to the end of the hall
sunlight spills onto the floor by the glass doors
turning the marble into a pool
of clear clean water
or ice
slippery surface — mind your step
the warning comes too late
for many who have entered through those doors
a fluorescent bulb signals a final message
in its own secret code
last words before dying
the monster breathes louder
it seems to be sighing

*Zena Khan*

## Nature's Serenity

A blanket of dark blue velvet,
covering the Heaven's with millions of
stars twinkling like diamonds as night
lights of the Angels.
The moon, in its different phases,
casting a watchful eye over all while asleep.
Calm, still waters kissing the shores.
Dark green foliage of the forest protecting all within.
Mother Nature, dressed in her beautiful
white gown of soft, white snow; gently
nurturing all within her whilst they sleep
and prepare for Nature's birth of Spring.

*Sandra Linacre*

## Compassion

Before you judge your neighbor's deeds
Check him out and feel his needs
And before you decide that he's unfit
In his shoes stand and in his place sit
Let your compassion for a fellow human
Guide your steps when approaching him
And then let your compassion for yourself
Keep you from pre-judging anyone else
For if we judge a book by its mere cover
How is it that we shall ever discover
The true treasures that lie gently within
Our pages of life, the ones called friends

*Lawanda K. Braggs*

## Rain

The raindrops are falling on a sleeping town,
Covering the streets with a light gray mist.
The usual noise has abated somehow.
It seems nature is cloaking her tight-clenched fist.

But now, it is nothing like "Singin' in the Rain",
Where Gene Kelly dances without any strain.
If only life could be like one of our dreams,
Where no downpour wreaks havoc
On land and the seas.
And man waves his hand like a wand indeed,
And the wind would cease, and the skies take heed.
And the mud and the storm recede as they go,
Leaving the ground in a warm hazy glow.
And the quiet of the raindrops
Would descend on the earth,
Covering it gently to await its rebirth.

*Marie Finkstein*

## The Ocean

My reverent heart hears the lion-like roar of its power,
crashing against itself, ever so limitless, brutally strong as I
walk along the wet, sandy shore, feeling a oneness with the
elements of ocean saline.

It is in this bright day of blueness that I leave my cares
at home, and lift my thankful heart to God for all the miracles
He has bestowed upon me; my health, saneness, love, healthy
children, steady work, peace, joy, spirituality, good friends,
and the love for Him and His created earth.

I see damaged lands and waters that require a cosmic
healing force, a deep appreciation, A Navajo respect, for earth,
air, water and fire. Consciousness and love have come into my
heart and touched the stone, cold frozen tundra of my existence.

Yes, the glorious sun has melted away the numbness I used to
live my life in, and created a hallowed ground there, where
sea gulls rest their tiny legs and scratch.

*Lucinda S. Cooper*

## Snow Flower

Snow flower, snow flower
Created by a higher power

There is the story of so long ago
In ancient times it was told
A story about romance
And a symbol of the God's love of love

A tale told to all the young
That when your time comes
To fall in love, the seasons will change
A blessing from above

Fear not the change, the young were told
It is a sign to the very old
That a new life has begun
And every one will be young

You will see it twice ways
When you are in love to stay
And when new love is on the way then the day has come to play

The symbol is the flower in the snow
It's fragrance narcissus so the flower is flesh colored
A symbol made of the color of life to all who are husband and wife

*Robert L. Sorensen*

## Smoky Mountain Air-August

Current of sound, the steady hum of the river water;
Cricket music by night, bird songs by morning light.

Fresh, clear, with hint of moss, or mint, or mountain laurel.
Still.  Or gently moving like a humming bird's wings.

Whirlpools of sycamore leaves, early fallers
held in the palm of the draught, the invisible hand of God.

Sometimes in morning mist a wren's bath splatters
into the air where sunlight refracts
making momentary diamonds that brighten our days.
Knitting crowns of precious stones, it halos mountain, bush, and wren.

As if to make windows in an otherwise unseen world
willow boughs collide then part, like curtains drawn to reveal the scene.

Or consider the air as it caresses the skin of a father with a young
child down rivering, tubing.  Or the kaleidoscopic colors of the water
splash, prismed; or the air as it furls and unfurls the flags of the
lower forty-eight rimming round the park grounds, the air like the
sound cadets' rifles make against their uniforms as
they march, frap, frap, frap; or the air expelled in a sigh which is a
silent prayer to say this peacefulness was grace today and the
river-cooled air a breath divine.

*N. A. Runion*

## Abbarit, My Abbarit

The sun, abbarit, is fast setting beyond the
crossroads of Los Angeles—ay, your milky
way... it needs to be my iron rod along the
freeway in bringing home my mission before dusk;

My eyes are enamored with the green fields in
your limas; the aroma of golden grains in your
kabanayan had been long cherished; I wish to
watch all the fishes in your rivulet, I like to
gather the mushrooms under your bamboo trees,
delicacy even corns and watermelons in your
vineyard; watching the colorful birds chirping
up in your uplas tree uplifts my spirit...

I love to listen the whistling of uncle aling
during the dusk while drying Virginia leaves
in your oven; I am unfolded by the melodious
singing of manong boni under the window of
manang paring; and, I wish to be with the children
laughing and playing under the bakkalaw tree...

Ay, ay, abbarit, my beloved abbarit, my
spirit comes to rest under your wings!

*Lorenzo G. Tabin*

## Untitled

Sitting there, in conversation of repressed past
your words ignite my admiration.
With fortitude and seer power of will,
zealously fighting what is wrong
and trying to make it right.
Pain of self expression
and fear from self awareness,
gives way to hope and confidence.
The spirit you have,
to simply embrace the ideals
with the uncertainty of life's experience.
You are commendable.
You carry a great load my brother
and your acknowledgments and self worth
has dignified our siblings wounds,
while giving others way
for an easier journey.

*Kevin Drane*

## Summer's End

Lonely lies the hammock underneath the hill,
Curved between the pines, motionless and still.
Stilled the joyous voices, stilled the happy cries:
"Watch ME everybody, watch the big surprise!"

Only waves are splashing now, only gulls will scream,
And only fish are swimming, was all the rest a dream?
No one sheds a swim suit upon the boat house floor,
No one dashes through the house, no one slams a door.
No one rustles Sugar Pops, or begs a candy bar,
Only Grandpa's left to raid the peanut jar.

Deep inside the toy chest, safety tucked away,
Peter Rabbit and his Friends whisper of the day
When they 11 be free and stream, on to the Meeting Place!

Seven bits of clay left drying in the sun-
Who will come to turn them, to see if they are done?

O baby toads, you may hop in safety among the cool,
green arches of the lily bed.  The Mighty Toad
Hunters have gone home.

*Ruth S. Hudson*

## Man In My Dreams

Dare I tell you of the power you have over me?
Dare I tell you that my heart beats faster when I see your face
flash across my mind?
The winter wind brings with it tales of an untold story
The snowflakes fall from the sky like confetti from a Rip Taylor
Vegas
act;
and make me yearn for the warmth of your touch.
What it is about you that makes me forget my real world and be lost
in
a world of make—believe
which you are a part of
your smile
your laugh
your kindness
your baseball cap turned backwards...
but I must keep my feelings a secret
my hand belongs to one; your heart belongs to another.
What a shame.
I guess you'll never know.

*Velvet Jones Sanchez*

## Unity

The rain blows in like a dream that never ends.
Darken clouds with much desire.
Rolling thunder lighting flash, Will and Spirit Unity
clash.
Mother so angry showing her power, not holding back
a day or an hour.
Father receives this reflection of oppression, hastily
warning this Mother of affliction.
He takes this thrashing...heartily she gives for he
knows it's a life force that lives.
They tumble through creation like a tidal wave in dissension.
Emotions explode creates a new mode.
Tearing eyes meeting in the heart, they know now they'll
never be apart.
The wave dissipates with warm embrace creating an image
for the eternal race.

*Vincent N. Sciarabba*

## "Not Anonymous"

A travelling search; Albeit, a searching travel
Darkness begins to unravel
That which does conceal
Also proves to reveal
One's self.

From the densest matter begin
To the highest mountains within
I find all I'd thought amiss
To be only that which is
One's self.

All that I've termed as either right or wrong
A mere matter of thought all along
This illusion in which I'm sinking
Finds it's origin within the thinking
of one's self.

For life in it's purest sense
Illuminates the matters so dense
Collective freedom so greatly sought
Synonymous with the elevation of thought
of one's self.

*Nicholas Landrine*

## Depression: Not Just A Mood, But A Plea For Death.

Every living thing must die.
Dear God, Why can't I?
Ever since I have been small,
I have been waiting for you to call.

Your teachings say to pray without ceasing.
So each day I ask for my life's releasing.
But instead you just ignore my plea.
Even though I beg on bended knee.

I don't know why I want to die.
I only know that I must try.
Living has not been painful and bad.
There really is no reason for me to be so sad.

The cycle of life continues moving, marching right along.
But life's cycle could still continue, even if I was gone.
Each day upon awakening, I pray for my death.
Then night comes and I'm still hoping to draw my last breath.

If only society would condone my suicidal ideation.
Bring on my death.  End my life.  Terminate my station.
But suicide would hurt my loved ones, so I just continue to pray.
For death will surely come, Please God, make it today!

*Sonja J. Asay*

## I Put You In A Special Place

I put you in a special place in my heart
Deep down inside where my feelings wouldn't be torn apart.
I built a wall so high; a barrier, I thought could not be broken
Secret, silent, desperate longings of a forbidden love was to
be my only token.
I placed you on the highest pedestal, where could be no falls
Reachable only through my dreams, and you would always
answer my passionate beckoned calls.
I put you back in the farthest corner in my mind
Trying to conceal my feelings so no one, not even you,
could ever find.  I had you locked up tight way down deep in my heart.
But with just one touch, you found the key and took a big part.
Your touch released all my feelings, and throughout my body, a
smoldering burning desire.
Yet impossible as it seemed, searching deep within was
the only answer to put out this flaming fire.
No, I can't deny it, for always in my heart, for you, there
always will be plenty of space.
I will just have to work harder, to put you back...
In your own special place.

*Winifred LeBlanc*

## "A World Of Fear"

A world in fear
Descending into a field of dreams
A tear of love cries out
But few have none
The desperado lives alone
In a world few have known
He lives on the edge
And comes from the night
He slithers along the crack of dawn
A world in fear
Where few can survive
Survival's the game and the game goes on
Under the shadow with men that have guns
Descending into the fields of grey
The gun shows the light the light of day
and the guns end the night at the light of a ray
The tear of love cries out again
FOR THE MEN THAT ARE GONE AT THE END OF THE DAY.

*Rick Alfaro*

## To Have Been In Love And I Have Fallen From Love

To be in love is a thing so grand —
description is beyond this world.
To be in love is to cherish a person for
them and never want to fall forth from
its tender and gentle grasp.

To fall from the gentle tender grasp lane
is to be hurt by yourself alone.
To fall from love is to know what you cherished
more than life itself has left from you.

To fall from love is to be left with its memories
both good and bad, and hoping and
longing to be left with at least a friendship
to last through all eternity.

To have fallen from love is to be
grieving a great loss and wanting to fill a newfound
void never before there that seems it may never
again be filled with love.

And to fall from love is to hope to
unfall and relieve your best friend's pain and knowing
that may never be able to be so again.

*Thomas Dumansky*

## Is It Time, O.J.?

Is it time, O.J. to come clean?
Did the Sunday morning sidewalk get to you?
Was there something in that Sabbath that made you feel so alone?
Were you wishing Lord that you were stoned?  Were you?

Is it time, O.J., to admit drugs don't pay
And that money cannot buy everything?
There are things you can't run from
No matter how fast, rich or smart you are.
As you sit in prison,
Will one day you ask the guard, "Is it time?"

Is it time, America,
To change those Sabbaths
Close those malls, dress up,
Examine life on a weekly basis in church?
Take time off, rest, remember, ruminate.
How can we keep the Sabbath holy?

Is it time, World,
To hear the bells of a church chime
To go to God's house in a climb,
To take life in rhythm to His time?

*Margaret Ann Scheffer*

## Did You Ever....

Did you ever like someone, and know that they did not like you
Did you ever feel like crying, but, what good would it do
Did you ever look in her eyes and say a little prayer
Did you ever look in his heart and wish that you were there
Don't you ever fall in love my friend,
You will see that it does not pay
Although it causes broken hearts,
It happens almost every day
Did you ever wonder where they're at or if they're being true
You see you lose no matter what you do
Love is fine, but it hurts so much
The price may be high
If I could choose between Life and Death
I think I'd rather die
So don't you ever fall in love, my friend
You will be hurt, before it is through
I ought to know, because I fell in love with You!

*Pamela S. Green*

## I Hope You Smelled the Roses

I hope you smelled the roses in your immortal souls delay,
Did you linger over petals, velvet, as night sought dawning day.
I hope you walked in sunshine, turned your eyes from sodden skies.
Did you boldly splash thru' murky puddles to claim your conquered
   prize.

I hope the ocean spray refreshed you, giving back the salt of life
The currents did they daunt you as they pushed and pulled reamed,
and lied? I hope you formed a bond, as suckling at maternal breast
as roots down twine, they held? They grew? Bursting forth as nature's
   best.

I hope you grew in wisdom, I hope you found a path
thru each problem and confusion and learned at life to laugh?
I hope your golden years you harvested the labors of your prime
Did you savor each red drop of life, 'til death doth cut the vine?

I hope you were not frightened, your face in peaceful slumber set?
As your soul rushed toward new portals, a life without regret?
I may borrow from you this knowledge, dad, "if" in fact you know at
all, to smell the roses, and hope it's so, that's in fact you knew
   at all.

*Lisa Huddleston*

## To Kyndal

Bright loving eyes that are glowing with smiles,
Dimpled cheek that charms and beguiles.
Innocent trust in an innocent face,
A gift from God, presented with grace.

She gets what she wants because she knows how
To uproot all peacefulness, and yet - we allow,
Because of a silent, unwavering grin
She instills in us all with her quivering chin.

"No - no" it seems she can't understand.
"Night - night" - a word she can't comprehend.
"Go - bye - bye" - that's easy! She answers the call
 And searches her room for sweater and doll.

She sings through her day in her own secret tongue
Bringing memories to all of when they were young.
The melody's directed to the clown on the springs,
And he nods in agreement at each word she sings.

As eyelids get heavy and play days get long,
So little girl's words drop from little girl's song.
The melody slows, it comes to an end,
As it's claimed by that word that she can't comprehend.

*Sue Price*

## Angels

Five little angels in the heavens above
Discuss their work as messengers of love.

Plans were made for all that day
And soon the angels were on their way.

One little angels flew to a school
To teach the children the golden rule.

The second little angel went to a home
To be with an old man who was alone.

The third little angel flew to a dance
There witnessed a Valentine romance.

The fourth little angel went on her way
To be with a sick child through the day.

The fifth little angel, afraid to fly
Prayed for the others as they flew by.

When the angels met at the end of the day
They all had something very different to say.

Messengers of loves is what we are
And we help people wherever they are.

*Lucille Hosek*

## "What Color Are You"

They say that you are without light,
distant like complete darkness, nothing of a
image, a reflection of a shadow.
   Just only a picture that 'tis abstract with no
meaning, or expression, yet you are there in reality
but virtually non-existent.
   Your concerns are of no interest an your
tear's are only wasted fluids that exhaust the pressure.

   What you see is only a illusion so you pretend to be a real
you've been exile from reality.
This has deleted, your senses of acknowledgement,
therefore you know nothing.

   When you seek there is no direction but yet, you travel a journey
without a destination, Constantly confuse but you are here and
yet lost.

   Complexed, to be exempt from all through the pigment of your
flesh, and if confronted through realities concept of realization,
could you tell me,

What color are you?

*Zelt Thomas Minor*

## The Window

When you look out the window do you see the same thing I see?
Do I see the sun and clouds and you see the moon and stars?
Are we so far apart this happens?
Or we so close together when we look out the window we see
the same thing?
When you open the window do you smell fresh air?
And I smell the dairy farm down the street.
When you open the window next time you hear the splash of the
pool, it's your neighbors swimming.
I hear the hail hitting the roof and ground.
Are we so far apart we hear these things so different from each other?
WHY? PLEASE TELL ME.

*Sadie Bodway*

## A Rage of Hearts

Shook, I my fisted hand, at the dark and stormy sky.
Do not intrude the glory of my sun, implored my heart,
Rather pause upon the hill and listen to my cry.
Do not Spread your bitter cold across my growing sorrow.
Scatter no rain among the hours of my long and dreary night.
Go you back to whence you came, nor come again tomorrow.
Leave me consumed within the misery of melancholy tears.
Do not tread within my desolate, though fenestrated soul.
Let me ponder, through dark hours, all my lurking fears.
Flashing rage and growing fury came the quick reply.
Night long, raged the storm's heart upon my raging heart.
Then, I listened to all the storm would or could imply.
Despite my raging heart, the storm would not be stayed,
Until it had finished the work it had been assigned.
Only when nature's voracious demand had been allayed
Could I then begin to know the depths of my own despair
And measure the rage of my heart, against my heart's repair.

*Lavon E. Miller*

## When I Am Gone

When I am gone and you must stay,
Do not weep or mourn, nor waste a single day.
Think of me not as gone, but gone ahead,
Not as gone away, but gone to make the way instead.

Pass your days without me in quite contentment,
Among the special things and loved ones that remain.
Find peace and comfort from past times we have spent,
Knowing soon we will be together once again.

Should a lonely moment ever start
   to find its way into your heart,
Simply smile and remember me,
For surely in your heart,
   I will never cease to be
When you pause to think of me.

*William C. McDonald*

## Searching

Searching - yes searching
Do we not all search - and search
For something to quench our thirst in this life?
And what have we found?
I myself have searched for love
And found love - along with its pain
That I did not care for.
And I've searched for God
And found God - along with tremendous confusions
That I'd never thought of.
Searching - yes I'm still searching
Perhaps we exist to search
And cease to search
When we no longer exist.

*Rachel C. Ean*

## On Maturity

How do you know
Does it ever show
Do actions speak
Or should age determine the beat
Is it 14, 16, 18, 21, 31, 42?
Some still don't seem to know what to do

Decisions, Decisions, Decisions, and so
We want them to be in the know
Eventually they will choose right from wrong
Someone will say, "What took you so long?"
It's all in this marvelous process you see
That we call the age of maturity

*Winniefred A. Jones*

## Untitled

Does the spirit of your mother help to tend your garden?
Does she, part of earth, still bring towards your face the warmth of
     summer sun,
and a soft breath of wind past your cheek?
Her hands against your back
as your nose presses into her flesh.  Then your fingers
move to pluck the blossoms of all that you have sown.

Does she smile gently and step backwards
as you bend slowly away looking out to sea and sky?
Thinking quickly she is briefly known again, you
turn and walk up those wonderful stairs along the side
towards the back door.
Standing, balanced and sure-footed on the sloping deck
you look back into the garden towards the tree.

She is still wish you.
Always,

*Claire Isabell*

## Blessings Beyond Price

I've dwelt in many a place and clime,
Done different things from time to time,
But nothing more precious have I found
Than the love of God which does abound!

A man may possess wealth beyond compare,
Be the richest man known anywhere,
But, in the end, Lord let him see
That his greatest treasure is his family!

If I were richer than any king
And knew I could have anything
I could not ask for more from above,
Than to know for certain that I've been loved!

And when it comes my time to die,
When it's time for my poor soul to fly,
I'll know my God has been good and kind,
Because He has blessed me with peace of mind!

*C. N. Wesson*

## These Words In Silence

As you advance and walk freely towards the road of invincibility,
don't look back, but remember from where you came.

And in that place, the garden of discontent, where dreams await there
escape- there still lies one precious flower, on the verge of
beautiful bloom.
You don't remember, at first, yet she was there the whole time-
learning you, understanding you, defending you-constantly.

Her petals wept, most thought it was dew,
only she knows- they were drops of frustration,
pooling in silent admiration.

Knowing that her road does not lead towards your destiny,
there is no bitterness, just infinite memories
of what was once briefly in her possession.

She will look on...strengthening, growing.
Her only regret is that you will never know
the fullness of her bloom, or the colors of fertile promise.

Before you advance, and walk freely
towards the road that might not bring you back,
Taste the drops, hear the words that have been kept in silence
beside your name for so long.

Keep her silence no more

*Michele Peysson*

## No One Waiting At Home

I didn't come here to talk, I don't have much to say.
Don't tell me your problems, I have my own any way.
Don't ask me what's wrong, you don't really want to know.
Don't promise me tomorrow, I know it's all a show.

Ain't it a shame we have to play this game.

We don't need to worry, no one's waiting at home.
We don't have to hurry, I know were alone.

When I need affection I go looking 'round for you -
'Cuz you know that you effect me, with everything that you do.
I'll never ask for love, it isn't what I need.
I need to be myself, I wanted to be free.

Isn't it strange how some things never change.

It doesn't really matter, no one's waiting at home.
Sometimes it's better, sleeping alone.

*Melissa Rice*

## Dedicated To My Uncle Louie...

I know you're around, just not visibly,
Don't worry you are in my heart.
Precious memories of you will always be with me.
Locked in my heart and mind are the things you used to do.
You guided me through much childhood,
inspiring my growing years.
There is a warm glowing memory in every tear I cry.
Yet it's stronger with each that I hold back
I wonder if you hear me when I pray to you at night,
Wonder if you'll ever appear before my eyes.
Now you can protect me and watch over what I do.
You can be my guardian angel.
I wonder where you are.
On a cloud? Another universe? On a star?
Wherever you are, I hope you're happy!
I love you U. Louie.

*Natalie Sabolewski*

## Journey of the Wind

Through the many voices of the calling wind
Down from the heavens, she has heard his faint whisper.
Wiping away her tears with his velvet hand;
He lies her down on a bed of roses.

Breathless, she soaks up all of his glory;
Holding his hand as she is cradled in his arms.
They flood eternity with a realm of light,
Revealing to all, their infinite love.

The storms of yesterday, leave clouds over today;
On the wings of the tempest he is called to order.
Kissing her as he departs with the wind,
He leaves the sound of his echo.

*Marianne Ware*

## Fitting-In

I wasn't the deepest kid
didn't like school
kept to myself,
parents wanted to send me
to one of those special
schools for dummies, retards
and slows, all the names they called me
at recess, but when I tried to stop the laughter,
break those pointing fingers
aimed at my back, I was the one
left lying in the gravel, only
to be brushed-off and sent away.

*Scott Cohen*

## Gone To Sleep Up On The Mountain

Gone to sleep up on the mountain
Down the road form where we used to live
There's no getting up early in the morning
There I'll sleep all day long.
Gone to sleep up on the mountain.

Sorry I had to leave you
to watch our son grow, up all alone,
But tell him,. "I love him"
And will throughout all time.
gone to sleep on the mountain.

When it come your time
To sheep up on the mountain
Come lay by my side
We will sleep there 'til Jesus comes.
Then we will walk hand in hand
All over glory land
gone to sleep up on the mountain.

*Virginia Loggins*

## "Alone"

Wondering fantasies never let start
Dreamers and schemers not far apart
Seems to be endless addicts in need
Hopelessly dying while broken hearts bleed
Silently crying hiding the pain
Living a lie hating the game
A desire for life to afraid to live
Sick of the deception there's nothing left to give
How could this happen what went wrong
I'm so sick and tired of the same ole song
We've deserted our families, our friends, our homes
Now we're left staring into darkness
We're left standing alone

*Shawn L. Pelz*

## Racism The Person Within

Death become her,
Dust is her only secret.
Hatred and pain is the only thing that could please her.

The love of life wasn't beneath her.
She has no friends, except a perished creature.

Is she a wild jungle beast,
'Cause no feeling runs through her?

The heart that pumps black gold
Is the soul that doesn't reap or sow?

Does she exist, or die?
Risk your soul to racism.
And you shall be Satan's next victim

*Neiketa Harris*

## "Azure Palette"

Distant thunder lulled now still
Dainty raindrops—almost unseen
I gazed at the glorious valley
Framed by hills plush and green.

Muted purple like high peaked mountains
Soft teal of oceans wide
Tender golden crescent of a fading sunset
Heart pounding—I'm mesmerized!

Each hue a billowy haze
Rose danced and bowed across the sky
My soul is in awe!
The artist? JESUS, with His rainbow eyes.

*Mary Ellen Cole*

## Ripples

We sit entranced along the shore of Mirror Lake—
Each lost in thought and daring not the silence break.

There at our feet are two small stones worn smooth and round.
And as we rise, in each clasped hand a stone is found.

Two hands swing out in rhythmic arc—their burdens lost.
Two splashing sounds reveal just where the stones are tossed.

The silence ends, the mirror cracks, stones drop from sight;
Two circles form expanding wheels of dappled light.

Out from the hub the wheels lose strength the more they grow.
Intersecting—touching, crossing—onward they flow.

Men are stones cast into life's pool by some Great Hand
Their waves go out in endless wheels through every land.

Their circles meet in friendship first—hands reach and grasp.
Soon minds embrace and souls entwine; hearts leap and clasp.

Love is the touch of inmost waves close to life's core.
Love is the surge of stones once cast from heaven's shore.

*Myron F. Klinkman*

## A Mother's Day Poem for My Daughters

Life is like a rosebud waiting to unfold
Each petal is a story waiting to be told

The day I had a baby surely changed my life
We were now a family, I was a Mother and a wife.

The growing years were busy, speeding swiftly by
A year of five went past in the blinking of an eye.

The day I had baby two, again changed my life,
We were now a family of four, I was a Mother twice and a Wife.

Hugs and kisses, runny noses,
skinned up knees and trampled roses!  (or Japanese Holly)

Flying kites, jumping rope
pony rides under tree limbs and toys that broke.

Through laughter and tears very very small,
We have seen and done it all!

Now that you have had children you can surely see
Why being your Mother means the world to me.

Thank You Thank You

for making me a Mother!

I Love You Very Very Much!

*Linda Samples Buffington*

## Hearts Beauty of a Song

A robin sings sonata to a sunlit morning's ado.
Early bird opportunists always ahead of me and you.
Hurrying and scurrying before the day draws long,
Who failed to really notice time has no anchor strong.
After the day is over and we all finally settle in,
Did they even stop to notice all the music from within?
Whatever happened to each moment that we spent?
Was a memory imprinted for a quick conscious ascent?
Are all of our senses mechanically wrapped up for display?
Reflecting subconscious behavior robotically traveled each day
So as not to even notice the chrysalis or clover
Traveling so fast now, that our time is almost over
Dusk is upon us with hints of another midnight blue
Just can't wait until tomorrow, to see what else we need to do
Let's all take a second to preserve a moment long..........
Wouldn't you like to join us, regardless of rhythm weak or strong.
Our gentle hearts are thumping to a beat that we create
Don't let its song retire too soon, don't let it be too late
Slow it down a little, then listen right along
There in the stillness is true beauty of a song........

*Raynelle J. George*

## The Home T.V.

The family sits, at home they slouch,
Embedding fossils, on the couch.
Their faces pale, their bodies stout,
Their eyes so wide, they bulge right out!

With no expression, and words so bland,
The hours pass, remote in hand.

The days go by, the months they drift.
The channels change, around they're flipped.

Seeing the violence, dirt and "crud,"
They do not move, they love the blood!

Sex is plenty, they dig the dirt.
Their lives are lazy, they do not work.

The world is dull, there are no hugs.
They go to the corner, and get some drugs.

They end it all, they have no life.
They've seen it all, with gun and knife.
They've learned it all, it's all what they see.
The world of horror, the home T.V.!

*Sandra Gallof*

## My Poem Is Over

My poem is over, but I hate to see it go.
Ending a poem is like ending a relationship.
No one wants to make the first move.  So it must
die a quiet death, unnoticed and obscure.

My poem has ended, and with it a hopeless dream.
Would that I were a part of thee, and thou a part
of me.  I wish these words could draw us closer,
each to the other, through all eternity.

My poem is finished, it has run its predetermined
course.  One word after another brings a message of
love and compassion to ink-stained sheets of paper.
Alas, to no avail.

For when these words disappear, as they must in the
unremitting grasp of time, this paper will return
to a white silence.  To that empty silence which
was there before.

*Leon Katz*

## Why Don't We Care?

Why did we make this world such a mess?
Environmentally speaking, were in severe distress.

The air we breath, is not pure at all.
The o-zone layer damage is no longer small.

The fish are all dying in horrible ways,
Our oceans are dying, day by day.

Children are sick because of the air,
People turn their heads, why don't they care?

If we ignore the problems, like we always do,
Your child may get sick, like the other one's too.

We try to pretend, the problems not there.
In a decade or so, no one will care.

I really don't know, if our world has a chance.
But if we all pull together, we could make a strong stance.

*Susan Kline*

## Mysteries

To have, to hold, means so much,
especially, when you hunger someone's touch,
the ache it leaves, to just desire,
is like, a constant burning fire.

To want, for something you can't have,
is like forcing, you're soul to starve,
when to force it, would bring disaster,
to what is now, and forever after.

So the soul, must find, fulfillment elsewhere,
even though, happiness, may not lie there,
so to survive, and hope for future,
you, must be, you're souls only, tutor.

For if you have, the strength of mind,
fulfillment, for you're soul, you'll find,
for fulfillment, and happiness, do contrast,
only you, can choose, which first, or last.

*Micheal Callaghan*

## Spring

Spring at last is in the air,
Eternal example of His loving care.
Tender shoots and buds so bold,
Dismiss memories of winter's cold.
A new chance to life we are given
A preview, maybe of Gods own Heaven
With Spring comes thoughts of Cavalry,
of my Savior's death and agony.
O Jesus, how much you had to give,
To save my soul, that I may live.
You healed the lame, made the blind to see,
And then, O Lord, you cleansed me.
I want to shout my love for you,
Love for my Jesus, my friend so true.
Spring brings feelings of joy to me,
of my risen Lord from Cavalry.

*Margaret G. Holloway*

## Love Finds A Way

If you don't mind, when I still call you Sweetheart!
even though, for a time, we've been wed.
I love the name given you, but I prefer,
calling you sweetheart instead.

I recall our first lunch together,
seeking out each others traits.
This meeting proved to be very special!
For soon we would meet at the Parson's Gate.

Therefore, we planned an early wedding.
Because, from each other we could not stay!
For there is an old "adage" surely you know,
Love always finds a way.

So, love found it's way my Sweetheart!
With you there's marriage bliss!
In each and every chore we happily do,
always ends up with a kiss.

When I gaze into your eyes, you can not "disguise",
the love you have for me.
I, in return, find the sparkle still there and
all the love that awaits me, I see.

*Lonnie Blankenship*

## Mother's Love

The wind whispers through the trees, as I sit on the dampened ground,
Even though the birds are chirping, my ears can hear no sound,
A shadow falls across my path, but I look up and no one's there,
Your spirit's somewhere near me, although I know not where,
My mind begins to wander, along with the clouds in the sky,
It ponders when you left me, but can find no reason why,
It wanders back to all the screaming, the fighting, and the tears,
And how it all seemed to grow, as I grew up through the years,
My heart becomes so heavy, when I remember back and see,
That all the heartache in your life, was mainly caused by me,
I think of how it could've been, fewer tears to be shed,
Fewer angry punches thrown, in what we did and said,
It's amazing how we realize, too late that it was wrong,
To say we hate each other, when the love we had was strong,
But now you're gone, and apologies no longer mean a thing,
To say 'I'm sorry' to your face, would cause my heart to sing,
And now I finally realize, as I raise my eyes above,
That none of these could ever weaken the strength of mother's love.

*Stephanie Teasdale*

## An Act Of Art

It springs forth in the worst of times;
Even when winter darkens the writer's glow,
That summer's muse hath made divine
Through rhyme and reason of long ago.

Jove's unkind eye winks at the poet's heart
And elicits the sensuous act of art,
Unfurls the soul's mysterious hum,
Then tunes the God's furious drum,

Which beats the rhythm of slate and sand,
Raps out each stroke for every man
Whose fiery breast calls forth Erato
And simmers in her ephemeral glow.

The poet is filled with wit sublime
Thus love outlives the whims of time.

*Lillie E. Bailey*

## My Perfect Love....

Many times I just sit and wonder if I'm
ever going to find that special someone?
That someone to open that locked
space in my heart, with all my most
intimate feelings are put away.
Many have tried, but none have done it.
Maybe I'm just scared to love, but I feel one day
someone will teach me to love.
The kind of love you feel within, the kind that feels
warm and wonderful. Like holding hands and
caressing at the beach, with the moonlight
shining, over us and the stars smiling down.
And seeing that spark in your eyes when
you say I love you. That's the love I will
like to feel, and maybe you might be that
special someone my heart is looking for.

*Virginia Gomez*

## Wind

Run against the force of the wind,
Fly in and out of the whistling existence,
Huddle under shelter,
Jump out and sail again.
Curl under it like a small animal,
Die as it knocks you down,
Swim through its reaching arms.
Land on its softness,
Throw yourself over into the pull,
Release as you spring forward.

*Rachel Fitzgerald*

## Ola Mi Esposa

Jewels rare in this universe
ever pale before you Mi Esposa
as your warm inviting smile shines bright;
nothing I recall or even could
imagine speaks such universal truth,
elicits such enjoyable delight!

Jazz themes echo the melody of you
enrapturing my mind, my brain;
a rhythmic cadence not unlike a beating heart
nurturing, soothing, filling my space
in ways that flood my soul,
enriching the whole, completing each part.

I write this poem to speak
loudly and clearly to those who read these lines
over time, eternity and space;
verily I say unto you,
evermore shall it be that
you will know and believe
our love is firmly in place,
utterly, eternally in place.

*Terrence J. Roberts*

## All Is Said and Done

Everywhere I look, I see your silent face.
Every night I weep to be in your embrace.

If you looked down, deep into my eyes,
The pain there seen should be of no surprise.

You have caused such anguish here, deep inside my heart
That cupid shoots no love arrows, but a painful, strenuous dart.

If I saw you once again, to you I would beckon
Into my heart to stay forever, or just for one second.

My memory, still lured to you, shows me of your face
And of my feelings then for you, of which no pain to trace.

Please come back, come back to me as if there never was
And together we can be happy as most true love does.

Forget the pain; Forget the sorrow; forget, forget it all.
Come back to love; Come back to me; Come to my simple call.

You still ignore; Ignore my plea. In your memory I am lost.
You're over me, but me not to you; To which my heart's the cost.

Come back to me and all's forgiven, but still you are gone.
So this is how my love will end; All is Said and Done.

*Rebecca Boland*

## Blue Rose

Pretty little blue rose,
everyday my love for you grows.

A shade of blue that is very unique,
could only be matched with a scent so sweet.

Among a garden of weeds I found you,
I never thought a love could be this true.

As simple to others it may seem,
Every moment together is better than a dream.

A blue rose is a very rare find,
I knew one day you would be all mine.

You are my blue rose

*Scott Killiebrew*

## Until Tomorrow

It's dark...I'm alone with him once again.
Everyone is asleep and she's at work.
I can't sleep, but he must not know.
My whole body hurts from shaking so hard.
Why me? Why anyone? I'm afraid...I'm so afraid.
Please dear Lord, don't let him come in here tonight.
I'm afraid he's really going to hurt me this time.
I don't hear anything...Maybe he fell asleep! I hope so!
I'm getting tired. I'm fighting sleep but sleep is winning.
Maybe everything is okay...Maybe I can sleep now.
Wait...
I hear him coming. He's opening the door...
Does he know I'm not sleep?
he's coming to the bed...He's calling my name.
I'm not answering...He's just standing there.
Why?...Can he see me shaking?
Wait...
He's leaving! I fooled him...I really fooled him!
Everything is going to be okay...
...Until tomorrow.

*Melissa Webb*

## The Stranger

I am a stranger in this new world
Everything is new and different.

I am a stranger in this new world
I am lost, I am alone.

I am a stranger in this new world
I cannot have what I want only what I need.

I am a stranger in this new world
With curious faces with blond hair and
Blue eyes, staring at my brown hair and brown eyes.

I am a stranger in this new world
I am not like everyone else, I am not one of you, I stand alone.

I am a stranger in this new world
I don't have any friends, I don't fit in.
I am a stranger in this new world
I cannot go back, I have to stay.

I am a stranger but one day, one day
I will not be lost I will not be alone I will fit in.
But this feeling has helped me appreciate
Who I am, and for this I am a better person.
I am no longer a stranger.

*Victoria Nunes*

## Homeless

Do you see that old man, standing in the street
Filthy rags on his cold body, nothing on his blistered feet

He was once a young man with dreams like you and me
Now his dreams are of warm places and where the food is free.

He knows there is no future in begging on the street
There is no hope before him as he walks the same old beat

He stands upon the corner his weathered palm turned up
Hoping some kind stranger will drop money in his cup.

The days go by so slowly when you are no the street
The nights go even slower when there is no heat

He had a home of comfort once, a life of hope and pride
Now he lives with nothing, but the fear inside.

The people all pass by him and look the other way
They don't even realize this could the them some day.

*Susan M. Adams*

## Angles

Lines on a page bond in simplistic kinship.
Expressions are fostered through immediate visibility.

Pulp and resin may formulate the playground but shapes provide
the impetus for true understanding.
Twelve essential vitamins and iron are included.

Beyond what is seen lies alternative interpretation.
Squares or triangles boast impeccable clarity but angles lurk in
opaqueness.

Surroundings may weave the societal fabric of illusion.
Angles dismantle that which is seemingly impenetrable.

A mere glimpse can smooth the shadows before time ellipses the window.
Truth can be seismic but ultimately soothing.

A glance or thought is seasonal in nature.
Angles swirl in convective motions to form a perpetual tool.

Refraction is both a distraction and a distortion.
Foundations are mortified by crumbling integrity.

Objects in mirror are of no consequence.
The wind-blown perspective is more permissive; some assembly
required.

*Richard A. Baird*

## A Mother's Love

From the first moment, her
eyes light up and her face
glows with a radiance that is hers alone.

She gives her all, never complaining,
offering every bit of herself throughout
her life, she gives so much.

She is a very special person, who
never backs down, and never gives up.
Always striving to make things right.

All love is special, but a mother's
love is especially unique. Because that
is where all the pureness of her
heart touches those around her.

Yes, a mother's love is something
to behold, exactly like my mom
whose heart is pure GOLD.

*Wendy Walter*

## Just Want Chance

We are misfits crying for renewal.
Eyes of sorrow stare down new opportunity.
Looks of fearful finding scare the tries
for a new beginning.

Blank out with the feel of fire at your feet .
Remember what you tried to leave
and begin to feel excruciating pain.
The memories pour into your faintness
while the eyes of sorrow give off tears
that the sacred image never forgot.

These tears roll slowly on like life
and move on down to the bottom,
the underworld.

*Renee Rapisarda*

## Bloodshot Eyes

As you can feel bloodshot
eyes watching upon you,
you turn but nobody's there,
you feel as your surrounded in a long
dark tunnel people watching everywhere,
you feel solid, unmovable
unspeakable, where are you,
what are you doing, are you alone.
No, there is someone with you
but who, a person close to you or a stranger.
What is he feeling happiness, jealousy,
or perhaps tragedy, you don't
quite know but you know
deep down that you don't
want to find out.

*Rachel Griffin*

## The Gift Of Faith

Faith is God,
Faith is grace,
Faith is God's gift forever.

Faith is love,
Faith is peace,
Faith is everything.

Faith is life,
Faith is freedom,
Faith is whatever you believe.

Faith is love above with God,
Faith is the sea and sky,
Faith is everything, whatever you believe.

*Rebecca Freedline*

## Whichever Way The Wind Blows

It's cold and lonely and it's dark as sin
Feeling that emptiness trickling in.
Brush past the hedgerow beware of the pain
The wind's picking up and the sun's gone again.

Watching the white sock as it tells me its course
Transformed from a donkey into a white horse.
And from quiet young birds into wild-eyed tigers
It brings out the animal buried inside.

It's all very crazy and mixed up and weird
The cemetery's waiting, the digger is feared.
It's keeping its secret and it won't tell a soul
Transforming the innocent into the bold.

Dust is thrown up and it's blinding the size
I can't see the future I can't use my eyes.
The sign posts are pointing the way of the storm
Flags should be waving but they're shredded and torn.

You can tell the way of the girl
You can see where ever she goes
All the time you know how she feels
By whichever way the wind blows.

*Philip Bryden*

## Mask Of Treachery

At one time or another we have all been
guilty of trying to appear to be something
we're not...
But one night out of the year we're
permitted to adorn ourselves with masks,
in our attempt to deceive.
Some of us just forget to take them off
after Halloween.

*Marie Valquette*

## Unknown Significance

I look out over a field.
Field of dreams of only imaginary.
I am me and you are yourself,
Never knowing if our worlds will collide.

I know that the man leaning against the pole
Only matters to here and now, nothing else.
I will probably never see him again
Therefore his existence matters only to others.

I care for people whom care for me.
That person walking to their car
Has nothing to do with me.
So, unknown significance only pass through life.

Adding bright of dismal colors to the day.
They don't care for me, don't know me,
So be it.
Like them, I am only here to add to the contrasts.

*Tracy Nason*

## On Inner Space

Our moment in time ticks in an empty vacuum,
Filled with silence, loneliness and hate.
While we, afraid we'll face alone a loveless doom,
Live, trembling in this world that we create.

Though it is true that man has solved the puzzling atom;
Unleashed it's deadly power upon the earth.
Yet, if we dare to reach beneath our surface,
Destructive force may soon give way to birth.

To look at self for one unguarded moment;
Suspend the fear of what that search may show,
And lift our eyes to gaze into the corners
May be the greatest challenge man can know.

For while man looks for life on other planets,
And dreams of what we'll find in outer skies,
If we will look inside ourselves for just one minute,
We'll soar in inner space before we die.

*Ruth L. Fellhauer*

## Garden of Desire

She sits alone in her Garden of Desire
Flowers fragrant with hypnotic scent.
Closed eyes remember days gone by
A smile slowly, gently, created by memory.

On her life she reflects with clarity and calm
The good, the bad, the inbetween.
Hopes and dreams fulfilled through love, through devotion
A tear drop forms in the corner of her eye
Falling freely down her cheek.

The nights are long the days very short
She waits alone in her Garden of Desire.
Knowing time and space is running out
Her loneliness soon to be replaced.
"We will be together soon," she says
"Oh how I have missed you, my dear sweet"
Her smile fades, eyes close, peace at last.

*Robert Eisenthal*

## The Will

Give me the sight to see beyond the light.
Give me the strength to carry on.
For I am whom I am...
The guidance, the trust and the will
to survive.
As the tears run down my face, I fight to
stay alive.

*Patricia Bowker*

## Through a Child's Eyes

The world through a child's eyes;
Flowers, rainbows, peace of mind.

Houses made of gingerbread,
Fairy tales longing to be read.

Cinderella's life so real,
Candy is waiting after every meal.

Oz is not a myth-
Smiles remain brightly lit.

Scared of the monsters underneath the bed,
Wondering what the shadows said.

Santa Claus is not a lie,
This is the world through a child's eyes.

*Larisa Barham*

## Epitaph

My life is like a poem.  At times it is long,
flowing, and full; at others it is short, choppy,
and lacking.  Like a poem, my life is there for the
enjoyment of others. It is open for criticism
and for personal interpretation.

Some poems are happy, some are sad, some provoke
thought;  my life is all of these.  It is an
inspiration to all who have come in contact with
my life.

Stories of my life will be passed down to future
generations as the words of a memorable poem.

Some poems are popular and some are forgotten, but
all of them have made an impact — as did my life.

*Maria T. Gonsiorek*

## Angel Tears

Like rain drops on the river consumed,
Flowing swiftly to the ocean free,
One drop so powerless alone,
Is the ocean's power to be.

So fall the cleansing angel tears,
Consumed with grief they see,
Flooding sorrow from my soul,
Where I feel your agony.

The silent dove sitting on a limb
Listening with heart and soul,
Hearing the eternal cooing of her far away mate,
Remembers the joy of being half a whole.

Shining through the darkest night
And even when I cannot see,
I know there's a heaven above
While your star shines on for me.

*Nancy B. Poole*

## An Ode To Stan (Islovs) Circle

Out of the Door from the set of rooms
have coo, woo, and nestling endeavor the audience
response mechanism to the station management.
Incur an avid anomaly into the Future Vents.
Parental tape relay or recordive tract delay,
The habitat facilitator finds perfunctory report
Cleansing attitudes and bodily turn, in line, whence
Of rounds of above social interstices.
The channel bans, groom yeomen he made them both
Gnaws hunger and warmth full circle
pares sixth down from sternum.

*Nancy A. Phillips*

## Seeing the Light

The darkness suddenly filled with the sound of feathers
fluttering ever so gently, in the silence of the room
the Light was off in a distance a mere speck in the night
I strained to see the shadows to cleanse the fear of gloom
"I'm over here" I said "Can't you see me I'm near the light?"

Were they Angels sent to protect and guide me with their hand
or was this a dream in which I would revel in and seek my fame
had I wronged those of the heavens and over the land
and this was the punishment dealt to those you couldn't tame
or was I somewhere else now never to return to what I once had

The feathers fluttered gently and swept against my face
"Look over there," a voice said, "that is forever you"
I looked, seeing the Light and then I felt an unwitting grace
embarrassed, I turned to face my jury of Angels on cue
I whispered, "May I return so I can correct my waste"

"It's not your turn" the deep sounding voice was so strong
its authority was without doubt over anything heard before
"you have one more moment to cleanse what you did wrong"
The Light grew intense, the feathers whispered the silence
then I woke up, alone and well, to change and sing my song

*William Byron Hillman*

## Father Joe - On Father's Day

Some fathers deserve a medal,
For all the things they do.
Others, are worth their weight in gold,
If you multiply by two.
Occasionally, you run across one,
Who seems too good to be true....
Who's simply indescribable,
Someone, just like you.
Your halo always shines brightly,
And your wings are all-a-flutter,
That's because you're so busy,
Going from one place to another.
There's only one thing clouding this picture,
Or so, it seems to me...
that there's only one "Father Joe,"
When we really need two, or three!!!

*Linda Yetto*

## Thank You Lord

I thank you Lord, each and every day
For helping me along the way
When things get tough, and I would frown,
You never, never let me down.
You lifted up my spirits high
And took away the tears I cry.
It made my faith a little stronger
To deal with life a little longer
I'm here to earn my daily bread,
And listen to what he has said.
To pass it on in some small way
And live up to it, day by day
To help out when I can, you see
If someone is in need of me
A smile, a word, a hand to touch
And thus I'm learning, oh so much
So much about the spirit me,
That God intended me to be
And so my life on earth was planned
Because God let me hold his hand

*Shirley Tremblay*

## Endangered

The most endangered species is man, himself, alone.
For he's the only species that makes the others moan.

The water, air and landmass is crumbling neath his feet.
His use, abuse, excuses are constant and repeat.

So stop and reconsider, what efforts we most need.
The one thing that will save us, is to rise above all greed.

Our earth can be a paradise if only we will try,
to live with one another, make love the reason why.

The world abounds with treasures, but we must understand,
if we don't recognize them, we'll lose our wonderland.

The water, air and landmass.  Is home to you and me,
and also to the animals, the paradise is free.

We were made the landlords, the prices we decree,
can crumbled every treasure, given to us free.

*Larry R. Buss*

## Shadows

Shadows, are they shallow, I wonder?
For I am a shadow, and it seems I have no substance.
I disappear at night, only to return in lamplight -
Artificial and just temporary.
I am cloaked in darkness, a part of that which is mystery -
Know myself I do not; feel I will not
Unless it is an emotion or thought that is thoroughly negative.
There I exist in full strength - in that pitch black world of shadows.
No moonlight for me — it is too naturally bright and eternal.
In the world of shadows, objects overlap, are vaguely outlined and
    two-dimensional.
That is where fate placed my being.
I reside there and am a mere subject in a kingdom of dark nature.
Yes, night can be beautiful, but it has an unpleasant by-product -
    shadows.
Shadows are often feared and misinterpreted.
That is me.

*V. Roselyn Savinon*

## The Challenge

Go forth, my friends, but not to 'serve',
For in 'serving' many see connotations of inferiority,
And we have had enough of that.
None can recall the names of those
Who served in the third line of the fifth battalion
At Vichy, or Majuba Cross, or Dien Bien Phu.
All recall those who led, and those whose words told
of leadership, and bravery, and death in the service.
Nor do we know the names of those:
Waitresses, stewards, valets, maids,
Who served in famous houses of bygone years;
But well we recall the names of those who lived there.
If you must serve, let mankind be the beneficiary.
Immortalize your name by uplifting the hopes of the poor,
Cheering the despairing, strengthening the weak.
Create a verse, heal the sick, or ponder quietly
For the benefit of all.
Discoveries are waiting to be made.
So go, my friends, the world is yours, but in your going, remember.
History forgets those who 'serve', those who create are immortal.

*Linda E. Edwards*

## To My Mother

My words for you are many, colorful yet few;
For into every life I walk I think of you anew.

Too many precious memories I cherish in my heart
Of fleeting bygone hours spent together yet apart.

You never tried to mold me into shapes I dare not take;
You never found my words to be meaningless or fake.

So many, they have failed me throughout my careworn path,
But you have merely watched me and wondered at my wrath.

Times have come and times will go stealing us away,
Yet no matter where our souls may drift we'll meet again someday.

*Maria Hess*

## Thank You Lord

Thank you Lord for all you've done,
For leading me in the right direction
when I thought there was none,
For teaching me right when I am wrong,
For easing the pathway as I walked along,
For when there is darkness being my light,
For guiding the way through a scary night,
For forgiving my sins made constantly,
For putting a roof over my family,
For the food on the table and clothing to wear,
For looking over the times we mistakenly swear,
For watching over me while I sleep,
For listening to me as I weep,
For protecting me wherever I go,
For giving me the ability to learn what I yet do not know,
For always leaving open your door,
I thank you for everything and much much more.

*Nancy Garcia*

## "To Be Independent!!"

I cried she was there for me
for my every need.
He would come once in awhile
for he would be tired.
She told me she loved me,
to prove it, I felt it through her touch.
He said he loved me too,
but says there is no time to prove it.
I would feel happiness in the air
when I was falling asleep, in her arms.
He would come and let it escape,
through the wide door, bringing in a drift,
that would scare the sparkle
out of my eyes, and fill them with tears.
One day I never felt or saw either one of them.
That day I didn't care
which one loved me.
For I loved them both
Because I realized you can't live without
Your mom and dad!

*Mike Shakoor*

## Bloom Where Your Planted

In the midst of contradiction,
I don't quite feel at home.

The natural bombarded by man's illusions,
Weathered by the life around me.

The warmth above inspires my instincts,
While civilization deprives my roots.

Crowed by other lives, I endure another season.
My growth has been dictated, but it's the only truth I know.

*Lonna Henderson*

## "Mystery World"

My secret world never again will I share.
For once there was one I welcomed there.
  Experience was my teacher.
  Build my shield and never venture.
Should I fall and loss again, my secret thus would share.
I beware of those who try to enter there.
Lonely I may be, yet never dare.
For my heart will never heal from such a tear.
Twice this hurt, is more than I could bare.
  Experience was my teacher.
  Build my shield and never venture.
One by one those lechers steal and destroy your thoughts and dreams.
Leave you drifting as the summer streams.
  Experience was my teacher.
  Build my shield and never venture.
Not so proud like I just to stand waiting while the world goes around.
Through faith I know someday, what I lost will be found.
  Experience has been my teacher.
  I built my shield, never have I ventured.

*Willie M. Jordan*

## One Love That Would Not Let Me Go

I broke the wishbone and I held on to my half
For One love that would not let me go
I blew the candles out and could not help but laugh
For One love that would not let me go

One love that would not let me go
For One love that would not let me go
And I would give my breath my very soul
For One love that would not let me go

I would pour my heart out like a drink upon the flames
For One love that would not let me go
I'd change my way of thinking and the way I write my name
For One love that would not let me go

All for one stubborn love - one tough love with a heart of gold
All for one stubborn love a hard-headed love that would not let me go

I could be as noble as a knight upon a steed
For One love that would not let me go
I could take my heart and wear it right here on my sleeve
For One love that would not let me go

*Phillip L. Christensen*

## Search For Peace

With all of the fighting going on I feel there is no longer a time
for peace.
A time to love and a time to care,
A time to forgive and a time to share.
We need a time to move on and a time to forget.

I hear stories of people dying.
I ask myself why people are not crying.
If people would just realize many are in pain,
Then we wouldn't have to worry who is to blame.

When we all begin to take responsibility for our actions,
We will have earned great satisfaction.
Then all of the hurting will cease,
Again we will happily live in peace.

*Meagan Hawkins*

## The Dream

I closed my eyes to wait for sleep,
For sweet repose and slumber deep.

But, with that slumber came a dream
Like images upon a screen.

Or, was it real?
I couldn't tell.
I seemed to be in depths of hell.

A view of life so barren and void,
As if our world had been destroyed,
The scene before me was desolation
No voice was heard from nation to nation,

It's not too late, I heard myself say
There time I know for the Son's bright ray.

Let it penetrate to every heart,
An burst with light through the darkest night.

And then I awoke,
And the light filled my eyes,
As I felt warmth and hope from the morning sky.

*Sandra Ferraro*

## A Flower and Life

Life to me is like a flower,
For the bud, is the beginning of a new born.
And the flower, opening is like,
   a birth of a child.
And as the sun, kisses the flower,
The rearing of a child begins.

Then the flower is in full-bloom,
A teenager has emerged.
The beauty-of-the flower grows,
An adult, comes into view.
The flower, doesn't die,
It goes into an endless sleep.

When it grows again,
A new life, will be conceived.

*Ruth Lewis*

## Sleep

With gentle heart face the coming of night
For the day must set happy task aside
To embrace the eventual twilight,
And with good grace in destiny abide.
In dusk we see a dark shadow of fear
Come from those ancient memories of dread
So in night with those old memories near
Refuse to sleep in our natural bed.
The mind, at times, does stimulate the heart
To feel beyond all fact strange emotion,
Strange in that compass and stars do part
As the heart ignores the mind's devotion.
This calm sleep we can not hope to avoid
So we dream of bright lands beyond the void.

*J. W. Nugent CEng MIMine*

## 'Til Death Do Us Part

This promise made does by its very nature bring some tears.
For we were two alone, set in our ways, before we met,
all those years.

And now we are one, facing the problems, the hopes and the fears.

How will we use these opportunities, these tests of our love?

Resolve, through work, through doing, with heavenly guidance
from above.

*Sherry Perry*

## Mother

God bless you, mother
For the happiness your tender ways have brought,
For inspiration, advice and guidance,
For deep concern and sacrifice,
For your wisdom, knowledge and understanding,
For friendship, cheerfulness and strength.
God bless you, mother

God bless you, mother
For your leadership, instruction and chastisement,
For your love, joy, peace, long suffering and gentleness,
And for your goodness, faith, meekness and temperance,
For your patience, truthfulness and compassion,
God bless you, Mother.

God bless you, Mother
For you are the gentle touch,
That blesses your family so much
You are clothed in strength, honor and righteousness,
That is why you deserve warm thanks and blessings,
For all your kind and loving ways,
God bless you, Mother.

*Lillie Burns Davis*

## Flowers

In nature's scheme, the flower came first
For they were placed on earth to provide
Beauty, peace and love.

Strange that such a small form of life
Can mean so much and bring such happiness
To so many.

Their variety of color and form are
Indicative of the vast sea of emotions
That touch all of us each day.

Just as the rose only has a fleeting
Moment to give the world its gift
So has each of us...Don't let this
Gift be wasted.

Flowers draw their strength and
Beauty from other sources.  So do we.
For nothing can survive alone.

But do not fear...flowers will survive
All else.  When other life has passed
Two flowers will remain to start afresh
For the world would perish without love.

*Stafford Werner*

## Untitled

Poems can be shared
For those who dare
Poems can be about anything
Such as love, hope and happiness, schools, and more
Poems are even in song
I bet you didn't know that poems don't have to rhyme
They are just around for people to write other people or for just to
   have
I love writing poems for people
Especially when hooking up people for a soon to be relationship
No one, yet, has became poet in my family, I think
I sometimes just have my friends give me articles about poems and
I take words out of them and make poems for them
Sometimes they don't turn out to well but, oh-well
I'll make them better well, this sums it up because
I just can't stop but it's poems are great!!

*Vanessa Kienoski*

## Strive

Strive to achieve a higher goal,
For to follow in someone's footsteps would lead in the same
direction.
Go further, move upward, push past the obstacles,
For to make your own imprint is truly an achievement.
Surpass what's been and reach for the insurmountable,
For to keep the same pace would be to stand still.
Endure when others have conceded,
For to accept challenge is to accept growth.
Look to the future and seek your success,
For to be content with today means no expectations for tomorrow.
Make an attempt to conquer your fear,
For to wonder what could have been means you never tried.
Set the example for others to follow,
For to create a new vision is to give hope.
Turn corners, climb new paths, where others fear to venture,
For to reach new heights you must face the unknown.
Use patience and wisdom to conquer an injustice,
For to accept defeat means you are content with inequality.
Strive to achieve a higher goal,
For to do anything less means you have lost the opportunity of
    a lifetime full of wondrous achievements.

**Ryan Murphy**

## The Sufferer

You speak of love but know nothing of it,
For you are painfully blind to my feelings for you.
You offer to endure boundless pain for your love
Lest she feel the smallest discomfort.
Still, I wait here with pain you could not know
With pain you could not understand.
You are wicked, for not once in your altruistic heart
Did you find enough goodness to offer to play my part —
The Sufferer.
Oh, you are too wise ... too cruel.
Can you not feel my eagerness?  Can you not taste my pain?
Wretched, wretched fool...
What you search for is sitting here quietly, suffering beside you.
Listening to your heartache and wishing all its bitterness
    would befell herself instead.
I read your every word that blisters with emotion.
I know every knot and groove of your innermost soul.
You bear all your heart and are thankful
For the friend that listens..
But are insensitive to the slave and
Blind to its eternally devout and unreciprocated love.

**Nazanin Lahijani**

## "Psycho"

You can't judge a book, by it's cover
For you may be shocked, to discover.
Be he, stranger, friend or lover.
That he is a modern day, Dorian Gray
With the face of an angel and
The soul of the Devil

A Dr. Jekyll and Mr. Hyde
Concealing the bad -
While professing, a good side

So beware!  Don't jump to conclusions
For you may become disillusioned.
A wolf in sheep's clothing
Sons conscience, he's capable of murdering

He is out to deceive
He would have you believe
That he is man's perfect example.
When in truth, he is -
"The Devil's Disciple"

**Martha L. Sullivan**

## Garden of Eden

We have all walked through the Garden of Eden
Frantically plucking for ourselves the choicest and best.
While our Creator invites us to discover and enjoy
The riches he has placed here in abundance for us,
He cautions us to heed a few guidelines.
A few laws that will help us attain the happiness we want.
We obey and all goes well until one day
We desire something we know we cannot have.
It's then the tempter suddenly appears.
Like a slick salesman, he convinces us we need the "forbidden fruit."
He never mentions the price of it.
"You deserve to have it", he smugly whispers to us.
Like Eve, we give in to his reasoning.
Though not immediately, but eventually
The results of our actions engulf us.
The serpent, now long gone, leaves us alone to our fate.
In desperation we remember our Creator and call out to God.
He gently picks us up and stands us back on our feet again.
Perhaps as if for the first time, we look around us and see
The vastness of all we CAN HAVE in the beautiful Garden of Eden.

**Laura Gamble**

## A Child Of God

I am a child of God, born free—
    free to laugh,
     to run,
      to see;
    free to cry,
     to pray
      to sing—
    free to do most anything!

My Father's house is filled with light:
    endless day—no fear of night,
    Joy engulfed in radiance bright,
    weakness caught in strength and might!

My Father tells me many things
    and I just can't help but wondering
     how such a great good God as He
      would choose to love
       someone
        like
         me.

**Rosemary Sakis**

## Billy The Witch

I saw it fleeting in the night
From house to house with speed of light
Bag and Flash in hand
A mission bent not by plan
A grotesque mask on cherub face
A yellow skirt and golden cape did not hinder
its springy race
On and on through the night
Governed only by the stops in sight
The flash did dim
The bag grew heavy
The mask did fall and the pace slackened
The cape did twist
The skirt kept falling
Its legs grew tired and Mom was heard calling
The night was over
His first Trick of Treat with the gang
Sure did make Mom and Dad's heart pang

**William A. Toomey**

## O God When Does the Pain Go Away

I tried to write a verse
Full of mirth and glee
Words that would lighten up
The hearts of you and me.
The words just would not come.
The sadness still can not be undone.
In fleeting shadows of memory
Light and dark intertwine
The past and present stopping for a time.
So much happiness and love
All of a sudden stolen from above
I cannot take this any further.
For I'm the child - He the Father.
He in his wisdom and I in my sorrow
Together we can make a new tomorrow
But O God when does the pain go away.

*Mary Agnes Costello*

## Anasazi

Beside a thin dusty road,
full of rocks and broken daisy stems,
you wove a cornsilk through an anklet
while I waited for the present
you promised to give to me,
and the ruins looked at us
with ancient unseeing eyes.

You were trying to slip away
somewhere in the desert
through pueblos and kivas, like the Anasazi,
leaving quietly, without any trace,
playing a haunting good-bye
on a pipe carved from a
lightning burned evergreen tree.

I dreamed that I saw you in the desert,
dancing through your ruined kivas.
You were playing hide and seek with me,
dodging my gaze, like a frightened rabbit,
smiling at my confusion, and though
I tried to seek you, I could never catch you.

*Lisa Mayhew King*

## Love

I came to you with a smile and in return you
gave me your smile.

You came to me with roses and in return
I gave you a rose.

I came to you with open arms and in return
you opened your arms.

You came to me with your heart and in return
I gave you my heart.

We came to each other with love and in return
We've fallen in love.

*Rosemary Cavin*

## A Gypsy's Promise

Give me your silver, and I'll turn it to gold.
Give me your warmth, and you'll never know cold.
Give me your youth, and you'll never grow old.
For I know the magic of love.
Give me your hope, and you'll never despair.
Give me your dreams -
They'll come true in my care.
Give me your heart -
And your passion we'll share
For I know the magic of love.

*Madeleine Matthews*

## Pale Moon Singing

As I fall softly, into your trance,
gazing into the depth of your shimmering hazel eyes,
losing all time and space in your embrace.
Memories fill the room, a soft salty breeze, as you tenderly
touch my cheek.
It is a moment in time beckoning me hither.
Of cotton candy clouds so white, so new; the sun spun her
majesty for our
Love so bright and new.

To hear your voice so softly speak... awake my slumbering heart...
Hear the tender tones...
Harps dancing with time and space still a trace of love and grace.

Loves' fire, passion, loves' delight desire burns long through
the night...
fall slumberly to quiet rest.
Walk softly in my dreams, my love... till twilights final hour.

*Pamela Michele Eads*

## Serenity

A rainbow,
gently embracing misty mountains,
Promise,
glistening in the morning sun,
written softly on the rain.

Whispering waters
giggling over rocks.
Joyfully meeting the pond,
awakening the flowers with splashing pearls.
Cascade of light.

Shadowy figure
against the horizon,
belonging,
Peaceful man sharing his world
in oneness with the rainbow.

*Theodor Domay*

## Forgotten Prayers

The light filtered in through panels of stained glass
Gently reminiscing about a forgotten Mass,
The leaflets and missals yellowed with age,
A velvet memory on every dusty page,
The Holy Bible cover cracking and red,
Songs once sung, words once read,
Pooling upon the floor, the sun's dying streams
Fed only by the glimmer of unfulfilled dreams,
The soft steps echoing loudly upon the wooden floor,
Pastel pictures telling stories they could tell no more,
The gentle breeze breathing life under the silver moon,
The heavy oaken doors had closed much too soon,
The life of the chapel has come to its end,
The golden day is over, sleep well, my friend.

*Sheena Mukkada*

## Along The Beach

Along the beach I walk in the sand,
hold small white sea shells in my hand.

I look at the waves in the clear blue sea,
rolling, rolling gracefully rolling toward me.

I like to walk in peaceful places like these.
Nothing but sand, water, and palm trees.

Now you know how precious I hold each,
for some of the most breathtaking sights are
found on the beach.

*Sarah Curtis*

## His Need

In the Spring a young man's fancy
   Gently turns to higher things,
To flowers and trees, the skies and clouds,
   and birds on soaring wings.

To Life and Man in his daily task,
   making the World go 'round,
He sees, he learns and understands,
   his ideals have no bounds.

'Tis then his thoughts are highest,
   when from dull Winter 'roused.
He pushes on, and seeks to gain,
   with ambition long been housed.

Nay! tho troubles 'round him rise and fall,
   his faith shall know no end,
If through his upward battle,
   he has one faithful friend.

     *Leslie B. Stanley*

## Sunny Days

A sunny day on white sandy beaches,
   gift from God, lake blue eyes and golden hair.
Instant warmth, kindred spirits,
   passion mounting, growing care.

A sunny day, a building with spires high,
   gift from God, in white and gold.
Down the aisle on her sire's arm
   Now mine to have and hold.

A sunny day, 'midst five jewels,
   gift from God, with troubled eyes,
courage and hope now fled,
   No help 'cept from God we cry.

A sunny day, we all in black,
   Gift to God, ease our brow
We had your gift so short a time
   Gift to God, guide us now.

     *Rick Wilson*

## Transaction

Wrinkle-clad eyes smiled amidst shelves of dusty memories
Girl woman being offering him the ripest exchange of the season
Glistening white vessels once held ten tiny toes
A single scratch; twirl on cobblestone path,
Romp on Dad's pony-leg
Don't fit anymore
She will tap dance with cement blocks carved cowboy style
Silver spurs will cut through vines of the jungle
A barter of years, he is sweetened by a pair of innocence
An exchange of dreams, sex and power ignite her legs
She digs her heels into the night

City and sky meet on a window sill for their final match
Skyscrapers compete for the moon's attention
Twilight alone knows what the years will hold
And she dances
Thrashing movements of dreams unborn,
Struggling for life in the womb of hope
Still, an umbrella of naivete refuses to fade
Warming her from the tears of an old, vicious city

     *Lindy Amos*

## To All the Street Kids with Love

A little bit of a baby, and just a little more,
Give credit to the streets, for they raised one more.
A little bit of loneliness, to stop it...that depends,
On the quality of man, and the quality of friends.
A little bit of slowing down is always out of range,
Out of sight, out of mind, do you want it to change?
A little bit of happiness by living in the wind,
Satisfied with fantasy, dreams, and with friends.
A little bit of innocence, although its hard to see,
A little bit of wondering who the hell they can be.
So I've seen a little bit, and I've watch some cop a buzz,
And I want to tell them a story of a little bit I was.
Then my heart cries, and I want to hold them a little bit,
And hold them pretty tight,
And promise to them that everything is going to be all right.

     *Zella J. Dunn*

## Shy Laughter

How do I hide my fear, if I touch you
Give my passion and trust, incinerate barriers
And you are not the One.
The burning, intense intimacies would scar me.

Not incinerate leaving a shadow of twinned souls,
joined at the heart
Etched into the stone of time
For all to see, forever
And our journey would be over.

How do I hide my fear
That I'm not he one for
You.

We seek in solitude, breaking trust
Educated in Foolishness
Eye to Eye, I to I
My fear always make me laugh.

     *Michael Richard Raziel*

## By God's Grace

By God's grace my sins are washed away
Given a new life in Christ to live each passing day,
I've been added to His Kingdom, nevermore to roam
to sojourn in His footsteps, to that eternal home.
I have His peace of assurance, that allows me to smile
that will enable me to stand before Him, who went the extra mile.
Had it not been for Him, my soul would ever be lost
But His love is forever, who paid the precious cost.
I shall enter heaven, where there shall be no night
So that I may soar, in His forever brilliant light,
there will be joy and laughter, with no more pain
For this is His promise of Heaven, His everlasting domain.

     *Phillip Headley*

## The Dreamer

Let young men dream dreams while they may
For far too soon they grow old and gray

   Let them be like eagles flying high
   Lest life elude them, pass them by

Let them dream dreams and may they come to pass
Let them be good dreams may they be high class

May their dreams be worthy and true
May their dreams glorify you

   Not just dreams of personal wealth
   Nor of power or glory for himself

May young men dream dreams, oh, Lord I pray
Men wish they had when they are old and gray

     *Patricia Anne Silfies*

## The Giving Trees

Trees, yes trees!  What would we do without your
Giving and soothing breeze.

You help us to live, you help us to breathe
You also shed your golden brown and shining leaves.

You blossom, you bloom and bare us sweet and tender fruit
Make us homes and nest for the birds
And give shade for the ground when it's hot
To keep it cool for us to lie down and rest.

Trees, oh trees!  What miracles you do perform
You give wood to burn to help keep us nice and warm.

So, we thank you, oh trees for the good things you have done
Play hide and seek and all that kind of fun.

"Apple trees", "Cherry Trees", Yum, Yum, Yum
But without you, oh giving trees
There would be "None, None, None"
The giving trees
            *Marvin Phillips*

## Seasons of Orange

Orange arc of early sun
Glorious glow of day begun
Remembering morn meanderings
Parents, earthlings, mortal things.

Father wooed the winter wind
Drew me to the rustic cool
Searched mid tangled fern and peat
Chestnuts, acorns, bittersweet.

Mother savored summer days
Led me to the brick red warmth
Searched among the graveyard stones
Puffs of milkweed, violets, golden clones,

Orange arc of evening sun
Elusive haze - life almost done
Rain cooled woods, steam drenched heat
Parents, earthlings, bittersweet.

            *Nelly Bly Carter Grimes*

## Torment

The man said
    "Go not quietly into the night,
    Rage against the dying light."

But what does the man know?
    The man who's soul is that of snow.

What does the man know?
    Of my innocent lost,
    And of its cost.

What does the man know?
    About one such as me,
    Who only through death can be free.

Does the man know?
    That even in death I shall not be free,
    They will always remember Me.
            *J. Wright*

## My Perpetual Woe

O, stars that shine high in cloudless, clear and the transparent sky
Go tell her, my heart burns - oh, will she ever return to me?

O, radiant moon, queen of the night,
go tell her my life has become dark;
when will she wake me in the spark of love?
For love opens the gates of joy;
and brings the beam of light, in my world of darkness

To the Breeze that blows so cool and soft
Have I not implored - how often?
Go whisper in her gentle ears each lonely day is like a year.

The dreams that were with her at night while she slept
in slumber light, tell her I am still think of her wake and in sleep.

I weep every day on the window sill, my eyes have dried of tears
Every breath cries for her; if she delays my heart will break;

Go tell her I want no wealth nor fame nor greatness
all I want is pure love and devotion, for I am of
the nature of ineffable love and am captured by your heart.

My nightingale, make haste, the flame of life is becoming dim;
every nerve in my body aches for you;
come beloved, Come before death comes to kill.
            *Mrugesh Lala*

## You Need To Pray

Bless thee thy father have made, instead of deceiving all.
GOD is watching over you, no matter how big or small.
A loved home is a happy home that GOD has looked over with care.
A broken, lonely, confused home has loved ones in despair.

Fear not the LORD, HE sympathize to HIS child in care,
For I'm the GOD who created you and where you go, I'll take you there.
For I'm the one who gives you from now still day to day.
And if you despise, within a blink of an eye, I can take my child away.
Not because you stabbed my back, then disrespect me through the evil
satan's ways.
For I am GOD, your father and you're my child,
And to you I might say:
My trust is within my love, and though you disobeyed,
I'm sorry I have failed again and let you go astray.

But I am GOD and so I forgive, but then you, my child I say,
I may forgive for this time, but when next time comes
YOU NEED TO PRAY.
            *Nicole R. Benson*

## Mothers

Mothers are marvelously unique creatures
God made them a very special way
They comfort you when you're sick,
They listen while you pray.

They laugh with you when you're filled with joy.
they cry with you when you're sad.
They praise you when you've done good.
They discipline you when you're bad.

But thru it all they love you!
And when all is said and done-
hey wouldn't trade their place with you
With anyone under the sun

But Mom, you ar my guiding light!
You are my beautiful start
God blessed me more than words can tell
By giving me you as my mother just the way you are!
            *Vivian Jean Leslie*

## Like No Other

He wakes up early in the day
going to work to earn his pay.
He sleeps late in the wee hours of the night
getting up again at first light.

He bears the burden of all
protecting everyone from an unneeded fall.
He always knows what to do and say
showing his ever-caring way.

He is my father, so dear,
Never ever displaying fear.
He is so very special to me
because I love him immensely.

*Suken H. Shah*

## Golf

Time management was always difficult for me,
Golfers can always manage time right to a Tee.
When everything seems to be such a din and clutter,
Golfers just relax and pick up their putter.

When most of us become frustrated and start thinking mean,
Golfers think of a nice playground manicured and green.
Some of us sit and watch television, as the World Pivots,
Golfers are out there making, or replacing divots.

Some of us would like a chaffer to get us there alive,
Golfers solve the problem, just let me drive.
While that might have been a little pun,
An ecstasy of golf, is a hole in one.

Golfers get their pictures made while holding sturdy,
The old time photographers said, watch the little birdie.
Some golfers get their clubs by mail order from Spiegel.
They don't care from whence they come if they can get an eagle.

I am not a golfer myself, I'm not even par,
I can hit the ball, but neither straight nor far.
Though unsolicited, I will give you all advice,
Head down, feet spread wide, club straight, and watch that slice.

*Lloyd L. Pope*

## Morrow

Live for the morrow, for this day has passed,
Gone with it, sorrow, do not hold it fast.
Sorrow is as deep night, - a fearful pit of darkness.
Flee from it to the light, aglow with hope and blessedness.

Beauty's in the morrow,
In every color of the rising sun,
Its peace banishes sorrow
And embraces love for everyone.

With sincere purity and perfection
Weave tender strands of love,
Amid gentle threads of affection
As the nestling Mourning Dove.

Love dwells as the light
Hidden in every quiet place,
Often infinite and out of sight.
In one's heart, never to be erased.

Inner peace and strength as flowers grow
From seedlings nurtured with loving care,
Creating loving kindness which will outgrow
Stinging weeds of discord and despair.

*Vivian Archie Mathews*

## Blue Jay Summers

Tho' they seem to come in droves to where tall
  Grass grows
To eat or drink and flutter or sing,
  While they hop and fly when doing their
Thing.
  So as you see those beautiful Blue Jays hopping
All around,
  Upon the green, grassy ground.
They flop, they flutter, they fly
  they scatter as if to be playing a
Game with one another.
  Those beautiful blue jays birds they come
In bunches ready to gather the days of summer's
  Lunches.
For their enjoyment of this summer
  While watching the Blue Jays play this
Summer, it makes one think and it makes
  Them wonder.

*Muriel L. McClure*

## Doctors

  Great things have been done by famous men,
Great things will be done again and again,
Things filling man with fear-admiration,
Things bringing ruin or aid to creation,

But of all those engaged in the worlds busy strife,
'Tis the doctor alone that saves human life,
He seeks not for worldly power and fame,
But with heavens will his highest aim.

Is to give relief to those whom illness and pain,
have broken and torn-make them whole again,
To give strength to the weak and light to the blind,
To dispel the darkness of some distorted mind.

Sighing when the angel of death draws nigh,
He smiles at a new-born's lusty cry,
Tireless and patient he strives to the end,
He is humanities greatest friend.

*Stella Lazarski*

## Gene Roddenberry

In the past sometime ago, a man was born
Great vision of the future he had, to pass on.
So a fantasy he did conceive.  He placed some
Friends, male, female, all colors, all creeds,
Into his fantasy you see.
To show the world, where we could be many laughed,
And he was scorned they said it couldn't be done
But it grew beyond all belief a legend in his
Lifetime he would be big bird of the galaxy,
He was given a new name.  His life would affect
Many, give many fame.  His last sun set he has
Seen.  The space shuttle carried his ashes
And they floated free.  A quest for space in life,
Only in death did he achieve.
Many friends of Gene, to many to quote by name
Of our friend we say this, let history not
Forget his name or of his Starship Enterprise
Fame, all of us can do one thing
Remember.

*William S. Roe*

## Auras Of Death

Mournful sounds of the forest at morn,
greets me, as I wade through crisp leaves at dawn.
Weeping Willow boughs bent to the earth.
Rhododendrons stiff, near the aura of death.
Mist creeps softly, over tree tops bare.
Golden leaves shiver in the breeze.
Grasses stand silent in the final hours of doom.
Senses of the forest are clothed in mournful gloom.
Scavenger birds soar above my head,
screaming in the breeze, winter's lament,
others settle in a circle on the pond.
Water bangs the ice thin stratum of top.
Raindrops make a circle on still water there.
Sounds of the forest murmur a mournful prayer.
The aura of death hangs heavy over the land today.
Let us bow our heads and pray.

*Marian V. Kelly, O'Shea*

## Daffodil

Her beauty was like a daffodil
Growing in a garden of bright red roses
It stood out from all the rest
Yet she had no idea
And never saw the beauty
Within her lovely self
Her love for animals and the world
Made her caring and full of life
And then one day
All the life was stolen right out of her
Her soul will stay with all her loved ones
And with all who loved her
Someday our paths will cross again
But until then, wherever I am
My love and thoughts
Will be for her
And only her
Always and forever

*Miranda Lemburg*

## Something Priceless

Although I can't see him I know he is there.
Growing inside me every minute, I begin to feel the love we share.
In no time at all I can feel him kicking and thrashing around,
as though to say let me out!
In only nine months the time has come to see my precious little one.
In that moment, I noticed his amazing completeness.
His tiny hands and even tinier fingers covered with wrinkled skin.
His fully formed nose, lips, ears, feet and toes.
Holding something so beautiful, so priceless, and so perfect in my own
hands was joyous, for a second I wondered why no one had told me about
the purity of this moment.
Then I realized that I too would find it difficult to explain.
Though physically complete, our little one was an empty vessel I was
now entrusted to fill with humanity.
He would look to me to learn tight from wrong, to learn compassion
and acceptance.
To gain insight and curiosity, to experience joy and sadness,
It occurred to me that as I guide him and help him grow he will do
the same for me.

*Stacey Gatzke*

## Korea: 1953

The shells scream over, then burst upon the road.
Guns chatter, bullets whistle, my courage to erode.
I check co-ordinates and use the mike,
To call help from up ahead.
But nothing happens to bring relief,
Because now my radio's dead.
The Chinese infantry with bugles blaring,
appear upon the rise.
My mouth grows dry, my hands grow wet,
Is it sweat that's in my eyes?
What to do, where to go, my jeep is now ablaze,
And looking out toward the north, the enemy's within my gaze.
But lo and behold, I'm not lost,
As plunging from the sky,
Our jets drop down to bomb and strafe,
And I feel like I have to cry,
Cry with fear, cry with love, cry with hope eternal.
For once again I've been saved,
Saved from hell infernal

*Milton M. Mendik*

## Affirmation

*To Celeste*

Could we have shaped a life and love—dear heart-
Had we not shared a vision long ago—
Or fought so hard and parried every blow,
And marched, as one, from worlds so far apart?
Could we have come to this, without the might
Of friendships, grown and natured through the years—
Through storm and stress and all the laughs and tears—
Though worlds have changed and loved ones fade from sight?

This life and love of children and of friends—
How will it play—what will be fresh and new,
As a new century looms into view?
Who can foretell—or where and how it ends?

Though vision blurs, and oft all seems askew—
Our book is incomplete—more chapters due!!!

*Leon Kaplan*

## Burning Mammoth Bones

Some eyes bluer than...some...thoughts
Hands smelled some of apple pies
    or even more...her sighs.
Face forget...never forgotten
Hips arranged for hugs..hugged!
All traded for our absence
    in this room...somewhere...

...I try to remember whose were..were you?

I knew...you who were...
I know...who you are
...you can't fool me..you can't.
Maybe jus'...jus' what I been told...
...jus' don't know that ain't so
    'cause Gypsies come to say good-bye
    Gypsies don't come to stay...

..another good-bye...every passing day.

*tobyRAPPOLT*

## Graduation

So now we try to say good-bye!  It is the most
happiest time in our lives but also the saddest.

For we walk off the stage and off the field.
We do not know what lays before us.  Will we
become our parents dreams or will we follow our
own ambitions.  Some will be doctors, some will be
lawyers and some will lay the land.  Only we decide
what will become of us.  For our class is unique
in its own little way.  Right now we look back on
memories that are so near to us.  Time will tell,
people will change.  Friends will be lost, and
those memories will fade away.

And now we say good-bye.  So cherish what you
have now, for it is supposed to be the best time
of our lives!

*Torrie Roberts*


## When The Names Are Gone

We explode here like new born stars.
Happiness, grief, pleasure, fear, all of it
erupts within us and pushes to the surface
demanding attention and compassion
like beggars on the street.

I, for one, am too small to understand it.
I just throw names at it,
calling one event one thing
another some different word,
learned long ago before I knew
that names are not
the thing itself.

When the names are gone, there is only mystery.

We hope for happiness,
suffer the pain, stumble in confusion,
Collapse in chaos, or discover love.
We need friends to travel this way.
How else can we stay upright
in this torrent of experience?

Give me somebody's hand.

*Robert K. Hall*


## Communique

The communication I find most profound
Has one syllable, does not make a sound
It offers safe haven with its calming effect
It's the most successful Band-Aid, I do suspect
It can exit tears; it can dispose of fears
It can give warmth from head to toe
And for as long as it lasts
It will keep you free of woe
Unequalled, there's always a continuous supply
Worth a king's ransom, it is something you never have to buy
On occasion, its spontaneity never lessens its intensity
It's the most obvious gesture of the sincerest love
Truly earthly magic directed from above
Given freely, accepted the same
The Bible failed to give it a name
Although, it could be as large as an elephant, or as small as a bug,
Size was never a factor when God created the HUG

*Mary Lin Burditch*


## Graveyard Poem

Cemetery cool and quiet.
Hate to leave your sacred lay.
Dread the coming of the day.

Tombs of wisdom, tomb of fire...
Tombs of overwhelming desire.

Join the kingdom of darkness, overpowering light.
Grow fearless of the night.
Send me an angel from star-lit night.
In beauty she lies in power of flight.
Holds me in warm summer night.

River flowing not far from here.
Fearful darkness, lonely pier.

Trees swaying in gentle breeze,
Consuming the power of you and me.

Now gently we lie
Beneath the moon-lit sky, unearthly presence unseen.
Animals grazing in meadow of green.
Like water flowing freely to the sea.
Time everlasting for you and me.

*Stuart L. Spanier*


## Rhythms of Sorrow

Beat of ye may wondrums, death Angel
hath hanken thy wake -
Loudly sound the dry of man to silence
the many cries of rain -
Beat slowly, beat steadily the rhythm
Of heavy hearts -
Beat softly, bet sweetly the mute
Sounds of flowing teams -
Be silent, be still - for the angels
have done their tasks
Of serving souls from mortal flesh
Now marked win unmarked graves -
Alas!!!,  A place of rest.

*Wayne Berry Sr. (deceased)*


## The Storm

It's going to storm.
Hats off to the King of the Sky—He is angry with the world today.
It started as a low rumbling, but the thunder is closer now.
Don't be afraid.  I'm not afraid.
Storms roll all the time across the empty desert that is my soul.
It wasn't always this way.
I once knew the warmth of happiness, soft as light, that spread its
wings over the darkness inside.
In the shadow of that comfort, I was free.
Somehow I didn't realize that no spirit with wings could hover forever
and the light that once protected me left my soul
and took to paint the vastness of someone else's internal sky.
Emily said Hope was the thing with wings.
I thought it was love.
Maybe it is different for everyone.
No matter, the storm is coming, fast and strong
To wash clean the sky.
A canvas?
God, is that what You made my soul be?

*Rachel Fairbanks*

## A Sinfonia For Eduardo Mata

A habanera dances across the airwaves in my room, a flute plays
haunting strains of the "Intermezzo" from Carmen.
Eduardo Mata, as you lie dead in Mexico with the earth gently
covering you, these images of your country fill my heart and my
house and I am reminded of your warmth and charm and the
laughter
behind your very blue eyes.
Somewhere in God's great eternal plan we were meant to meet,
meant to learn from each other, meant to share a rhythmical beat.
When I hear a Spanish melody I think of songs that you taught me
and how your music became part of what I now am.
The day the announcement came of your crash in your own
airplane,
it slashed my heart with pain, and I knew what it meant to have had
you as my friend, but your musical memories live on in me and that
is the best part of having known you, for me. From you I learned
that life is a symphony.

*Patricia A. Turner*

## To Education

Have it all been well with you?
Have all been able to go forth from you?
Have there been engraduates as well as outsiders?
Have you been a real joy or just something used?
Have you given all to all, or have you been in bondage to yourself?
O' Education who are thou and truly what are thou to me?
Shall there be glory given to you or shall glory be subdue in you?
Do thou know who thou are, tell me if thou can?
I speak this to you, all is well when it's in the ABSOLUTE
TRUTH.

*Minister Whitelove*

## God Is My Personal Shepherd

I truly believe God is my own personal shepherd.
He is my constant protector and my only strength.
His soft gentle voice is the sweetest I've heard.
To prove his love, he went to such great length.
Each day he guides my way and him I will follow.
He meets my needs and gives me water to drink.
He does not want me in sin to abide or wallow.
He will not let the cares of life make me sink.
God heals me from sorrow when I am down hearted.
Even in my darkest night he sends a great light.
From this great true love we will never be parted.
He lifts me in his arms from many a sad plight.
Sin nor grief can never destroy me with God by my side.
Right and good choices I'll make by obeying his word.
In the cleft of the solid rock I can safely hide.
God cares for all his creatures even a little bird.
Yes, God is my personal shepherd and my dear friend.
I rest in the great assurance his love has no end.

*Wanda Lee Beck Skinner*

## Dandelion

Lovely, stately dandelions
Heads held high in the morning sun.
Surveying the earth till your day is done.
Closed until natures warm embrace
Opens your lovely golden face.
For weeks your golden heads shine bright.
Then it seems just overnight
You are soft and grey,
Ready to fly to the neighboring fields
Where you will lie.
Spring will bring you back again
And I'll remember when,
You raised your lovely golden heads
In Pushkin town.

*Martha-May Woodman*

## Untitled

He is your dad and you love him so,
He is your friend and its hard to let go.
You know he's suffering and that's hard to take,
But you hope in your heart the pain isn't too bad for his sake.
It must be frustrating to watch him change so very fast.
You always hoped his life would last and last.
I can't imagine what you must be going through,
But I would bet this is the toughest thing you've ever had to do.
Life deals us some pretty serious blows,
And we think we have to keep going because others tell us so.
It's okay to let the tears come,
For me that's easier than feeling like I have to run.
Our fathers are always the first love of our life,
That's why others cause us so much strife
Your father will always be a part of who you are.
And no matter where he is, he'll never be far.
I really don't understand how you must be feeling,
I just want you to know I'm here if you feel like leaning.
For you and your dad I'll say a prayer tonite,
That everything for you will be made just right.

*Teresa Sarabia*

## Dreams

As I spoke with a friend about new thoughts on time
He shared with me some dreams that he seemed to find

It set me to thinking, what happened to mine
I know that I had some at another point in time

I started a search I checked the nook in the hall,
Old boxes some albums I found nothing at all

I know when I lost them though I never heard a sound
As they twisted and turned and plunged to the ground

I stood like a child in the wake of that storm
Defiance and indifference took a brand new form

I remember the night the stars fell from the sky
They crashed all around me and I silently stood by

Suddenly my thoughts seemed no longer my own
My dreams seem to shatter like a precious stone

It seems we need a dream to have and to hold
For without them our hearts become barren souls

So just stand beside me don't push me or pull
This adventure is mine and dreams make me whole

*Shannon Davette Hartman*

## Tears

He used to be a friend
He used to be a lover
despite our differences
I could never love another

We played in the snow and in
the rain we danced
We both knew we were taking a chance

Now as I moan
I am on my own

I've taken my last breath
Since his death

I walked away to start a new life
Knowing tomorrow I would have been his wife

*Tamdeka Carroll*

## "A City"

And the young man, he is running from a past:
he wants to hide; prisms crystalline in memory;
while a lady mourns in black.
can't you see?
The wrinkles form creases for the jeweled droplets
to swim down her face.
Keep walking, past the Salvation Army Band-Man
whose face cries out in soft despair;
fountains dance in streaks of reflected glaze.

And the gray-coated businessmen are now rushing home,
marching forward with dazed, pale faces;
read the paper, catch the train;
as the children play their street games
soon to become nightmare of glittering steel
in the cold shiver, gray snow flaking white and black;
monsters with windows for eyes.
Smiles and frowns flash past Coca-Cola signs.
Joe with no leg shines shoes.

Ground into the pavement you can feel
the helpless monotony of endless feet with nowhere to go.

*Patricia McAuliff*

## Bobby and Me

Bobby was a big man, I knew him quite well.
He was a man you'd like to know—he wore a pleasant smile
I never saw him angry at anyone he met.
He was neat, clean, and always kept his airborne boots a glossy
    state.
We went to Vietnam together, where we saw that blood was shed.
He was black and I am white but we saw all blood is red.

It was on a company mission we hit a hot L.Z.
Bobby said "I'll take this chopper top, mine abort you can come after
    me."
He took his last four men with him, to catch the main assault.
But Bobby's plane was late to land, bullets met them afloat.
At this time and place the pilot lost his bearings.
When attempting to land the chopper, green tracers were appearing.

The Viet Cong lay waiting there in the bush below.
They opened fire on Bobby's ship the pilot lost control.
The chopper fell in a ball of fire, all men were killed or burned.
I had to get Bobby's belonging ready for the shipment home.

I've thought about this many times, how that could have been me.
But Bobby took my plane that day where I was supposed to be.
I've dreamed about it many times and sometimes even cried
When I think about Bobby, my best friend who took my place to die.

*Ray E. Poynter*

## "Stop"

STOP.....listen to the power of your breath.
    hear the rhythm of your heartbeats.

STOP.....taste the sweet rain on your tongue.
    see the drops dance in a puddle.

Stop.....touch a tree trunk and feel its strength.
    see one of God's painting in a boulder.

Stop.....feel the wind gently touch your face.
    when it blows hard, let it mess your hair.

STOP.....just because you don't have to be somewhere.....
    or be somebody.

*Robert H. Levine*

## That Magnificent Fighting Machine

Muscled of rump and shoulder expanse,
heavy and thick of neck,
he lifts his handsome curly head
and emits a grumbling, bear-like growl
before he sounds his bovine trumpet call
that warns and chills his advancing foe.
Then with bloodshot, brown eyes rolling,
distended nostrils flaring, dripping,
he paws the ground, gray dust boiling,
and charges forward, madly bellowing,
his ruffled, pendulous dewlap swinging.
What an exciting, magnificent sight,
his sorrel-red body of challenging might!
We watched in thoughtful contemplation
as the macho contenders fought;
beasts of the field, defending their turf,
differed little from us, it seemed,
when faced with a threatening, hostile change
in the status quo of day to day.

*Marguerite I. Wilkinson*

## My Sons

   Growing up is a time of changes, sometimes happy others sad,
heed what I say, my sons, your dad is the best friend you could have.
He can take you by the hand down the road to being a man.
Dad will teach you many things, like catching a fish on a string,
catching a ball, swinging a bat, the love of a dog, the slyness of a
cat.  The day will come, take heed my sons, he'll teach you how to
use a gun, but once you kill the deed is done!
   Never again will that creature run through the grass,
laughing his innocent creature laugh, never again will he drink from
a stream, a nightmare to him, to you just a dream.
   Never again will he run through the snow, never have children
to watch them grow.

   Remember my sons, always try putting your foot in another's shoe
so you'll know for sure what you should do.
   Heed what I say, my sons, the day is near when you'll be a m n,
dad won't be there, to hold your hand.

*Lory Brooks*

## The City And The River

She lies down beside the city's door
Her body twisting, turning in her bed;
Her silent journey halfway to the shore,
From lakes from which her gleaming length is fed.

She carries with her sandy northern soil
Mementos from midwestern towns and farms,
She rushes by her bosom all aboil
And welcomes southern lands with open arms.

She pauses briefly at the bridges span,
She seems to gently throw a loving kiss,
As if the bluff's tall buildings were a man,
As if she were a naive blushing miss.

This love affair has grown as years passed by
As bluff and river melted into one,
As daily down together they would lie
And doze together 'neath the torrid sun.

The city, Memphis, where bolls and blues brought fame,
The broad deep rushing river, "mighty" is its name;
She pauses now again beside the city's door,
Her silent journey halfway to the shore.

*Wyeth Chandler*

## Tribute

When I was young my mom and I'd watch Captain Kangaroo.
Her eyes would get all misty when the piano played this tune.
A little old rag dolly swept up star dust with a broom.
At every chance her heart would dance around the tiny room.

A TRIBUTE TO MY MOTHER, who taught me to believe
In loving that surrounds us.  In love we cannot see.
She gave to me the gift of dreams and helped me understand
That whether near or far away she'd always hold my hand.

Now many years have gone since we watched Captain Kangaroo.
But memories are sweet enough to brighten up the view.
And in my mind that old rag dolly's dancin' dreams came true.
At every chance my heart will dance to memories of you.

**Lauren Lane Powell**

## "Tree In Winter"

Her arms are heavy with the first fall of snow;
Her fingers, tipped with ice.
Frozen in the bitter cold, she longs for her lush green coat she lost
    in autumn.
The rough and tough skin of her bark is the only thing to keep herself
    warm.
She implants her feet in the frozen soil to hold up her massive torso.
Motherly instinct tells her to shelter the animals in the niches of
    her trunk.
She is sad and lonely when she thinks of those days when boys and
    girls climb up her branches and swing from her limbs.
She is hopeful to see those days,
And survives to meet them.
Dancing in the wind, she rejoices- for spring is near.

**Liam T. Dall**

## Moment Of Truth

In the still half dream of dawn
Her hand feels, pleading
For the flutter that means
Life is there
Waiting to be born.

Decisive daylight welcomes pain:
Labor, sure and right
Absorbs the shrouds of Night.
Hope's hard work
Won't be in vain.

Hurry, now! Contractions in a crescendo rise
Beneath bright lights, expectant hush.
A final surge,like a symphony. Oh! God!

Stab of silence
Searing stillness
Still -
Like a stone.

"You knew, didn't you?"
"Yes, I knew, but didn't believe
Life and death are one."

**Mary Brust Heaney**

## A Promise For Today

Today,
I exercise the strength of my intellect;
embrace the essence of my womanhood;
examine the uniqueness of my people; and
expunge the negative energies from my soul.
today,
I expose myself to you for evaluation;
but, you will not decide who I am,
nor what I am to become;
not today.

**K. Denise Adjip**

## My Biography

We watched as the woman staggered down the street.
Her lack of dignity was apparent in her slurred speech.
Her lack of pride was apparent in her shaky hands.
And her selfishness showed in her red, bloodshot eyes.
I listened in horror as the other kids laughed and made
Fun of her.
But me?
I cried.
I had seen someone I loved in another life go through
The same nightmare.
And when the kids asked me what my problem was,
My lack of self-esteem was apparent in my answer.

Silence

**Sadie Warner**

## A Family for My Daughter

I walk past my daughter's room to watch
her sleep under pink canopy; I listen for her humming,
her talking to herself, her calling out, "Mommy, where are you?
Mommy, when will you be done working?"
I spend my days and nights with her father
so she'll have a family to come home to,
though I know we've outlived her.

My husband's arms circle me, pull me down,
and we make love:  I arch against him, help him,
moan aloud - distant - I watch myself lift
and move my hips as he shuts his eyes,
and cries my name; I turn my face away.

While he sleeps, I stand near the bed, and look
at the sheets - rumpled, falling to the floor,
at the pillow pulled into bed's center
to raise my hips, at his wet stain near it.
I turn, walk into my daughter's room, pull back clean
sheets, and slide between the covers.
Watched by the solemn, unwinking glass eyes of her dolls
and animals, I wait for sleep.

**Michelle Messinger**

## My Gram

I miss the joy in her eyes,
Her warm, sunny smile.
The vibrant lady I know
Has been gone for a while.

I miss her great sense of humor the laughter and fun.
A strong shoulder to cry on, and good friend she is one.

Her disposition is colder
Which seems silly to me,
'cause she's just one year older!
She's still bright and attractive
on the outside - no aging
could it be she just doesn't care?
Or her hormones are raging!

Whatever the reason, whatever the fear,
The loving woman I know, is still with us here.
She needs to find her way back, and get into life,
get on the right track her days filled with light.
Get busy - get happy, she's got a long way to go.
We'd be better off without her?
I just don't think so!

**Lisa J. Zahn**

## My Daughter

There's lots of daughters in families
here and there
Each one is different, God gives us to care
When I think of what joy, my oldest has been
I let my thoughts drift, way back when!
A plump little blond, so Happy and bright
Seems she grew up, almost over night
Many trials I had, as I went thru her years
But I knew she had been worth all my tears
I wouldn't trade those trials today
In fact, I'd go back, and to her I would say
"No Sweeter daughter has God put on earth"
From the very day of your wonderful birth
As a Mother, I'm lucky, privileged and blest
Linda! you've been the Perfect BEST

**Millie Knight**

## Our Pledge

On this day, we pledge our love,
Here before witnesses and the Lord above.
Two separate lives, entwine as one,
An endless love we've just begun.
To live together as man and wife,
Loving each other until there's no life,
Sharing our joys and our sorrows,
Endeavoring to seek a brighter tomorrow.

And when this Day has past away,
The memory of our wed shall last always.
This pledge we give shall ever be,
Bound by love and prayer till eternity.
In holy matrimony we will take,
Giving unto the other and all else forsake.
To love, to cherish, till death do us part,
United in love, a new life we will start.
In sickness, in health, for richer, for poorer,
Sacredly, we hold that which God has brought forth.
And this our pledge it shall be,
To love each other until eternity.

**Wanda Diane Hayes**

## My Wish

When they know that I am thru -
Here's what I wish they would do -
Give my sight to a man who has never
seen a sunrise, a baby's face or love in
the eyes of a woman.  Give my heart to
a person whose own heart has caused
nothing but endless days of pain.  Give my
blood to a teenager who was pulled from the wreckage of his car,
so that he might live to see his grandchildren play.
Give my kidneys to one who depends on a machine to exist.
Take my bones, every nerve and muscle in my body and
find a way to make a crippled child walk

Explore every corner of my brain.  Take my cells,
if necessary, and let them grow so that,
someday, a speechless boy will shout at
the crack of a bat and a deaf girl will
hear the sound of rain against her window.
Burn with is left and scatter my
ashes to the winds to help the flowers grow.
If you do all I wish, I will live forever.

**Hobart J. Cree**

## My Husband

Long ago, not far away, I met this wonderful Beast
He's so quite, you'd think he's from the Far East.

Somehow, through the years, I've lost my Beauty
It's seems, he always expects me to be on Duty

Laundry, cook and clean, most of the day
Then, I do as I please, and have my own way.

"He hate's the smell of Pizza, "Says it makes him sick.
I have to sneak, wash the pan, and eat it quick.

The windows I open and turn on the fan.
You'd think, I was trying to kill the man.

He's always the first to get his hand on the remote,
he acts like he's playing the piano, not missing a note.

When we go out, I'm always expected to ride in his truck
but he doesn't know, I'd soon ride on the back of a duck

There's never a dull moment, and thro-all-of this
our marriage is really, "A Happy Bliss."

He's my best friend, my pal, my lover.
And, if I had my choice, I'd have no other.

**Opal F. Kirtley**

## It Gives Me Great Pleasure To Introduce....

He's the giggle in my pocket,
He's the imp in my curled up toes.
He's the good in my soul and the bone of my every ornery deed.
He's my dedication and my sure footedness, my excuses
  and my pout.
He's the bend in my willow, the stubborn in my stride.
He's color stories late at night, bubble gum in church,
and Cracker Jacks in bed.
He's bandaides on my booboos and just enough iodine
to make me tough.
He's a lifetime of memories and an eternity of amazement.
He's my childhood, but more than I yet know - he's
my tomorrows.
He's my pride.
He's my joy.
He's my Grandpa!

**Patricia L. Russell**

## Untitled

Lay my body next to a peaceful stream
High in the mountains where the air is clean.
Let the morning sun filter thru the trees
And lay a blanket of warmth over me.
I'm tired of city life and this rat race
And I would do most anything to get out of this place.
Office politics, back stabbing and lies
Have become part of our daily lives.
It has become hard to sleep at night
And every day I get more uptight.
Blurry eyes, stomach knots and chest pains;
This kind of living is making me go insane.
Weeks become months and months to years;
There's never enough time for those things dear.
So when my time comes I have but one request;
Take me to the mountains so I can rest.

**Les Johnson**

## Man With Voice

I met a man on the bus today; his head wrapped in stone and parapet.
His lips moved with the weight of a drawbridge.
He said he'd like to meet a poet that could speak in a language
   Unknown to rocks and mountains and earth.
He said that he was tired, and I tried my best to understand.
He said, "Look here,
   A tree is burning because the phoenix lives there.
   Tomorrow she'll die. A man can't live like that;
   I've never been in flames, though it feels like I'm going down.
   A man can't live like that..... Over and over, "and over again."
He said his mouth was dry; he said he was thirsty for tears.
He said his phone had been injured in a silent accident.
He said that his son didn't want to learn talk; he said he knew how
   that could be.
He said "Look here. Do you see?"
Then he took a deep breath and sighed without surprise,
"I've forgotten again what I wanted to say."
There was a man on the bus today; He spoke softly,
   but we heard him just the same.
I can't remember his name but I don't think he said it.
I don't think it was important anyway.

   *R. Victor Brand*

## What Did I Hear?

I walked and talked with God today.
His voice was the
   Whisper of pine,
    Rolling waves,
     Birds songs — and I heard Him say

All lovely sounds
   Right the wrongs — of each new day.

I walked on the sand and rocky mound,
Looked at the heavens and felt the ground.
Only then did I understand,
I was not talking —
   Not walking
    With Him today.
But heard and saw this beautiful land
   While standing still
    In the palm of His hand.

   *Mary Jane Johnson*

## Ursa

She ages on, growing older in her untouched berth
Holding to the tapestry in which she exists.
The rich black velvet where her steel pin nose
Pierces that fabric of the dark stasis.
Her glow warms, it guides. Pulses
To those who seek to witness,
Like blind seed pushing up toward the sun.
Through time's tides turning, she grows dim
With the increasing haze of streetlight, light bulb, limelight.
Mask of wrinkles. She is still strong in pallor
Aging gracefully, she is still seen.
The light glints, points to her luminous nose.
Ever twinkling, kaleidoscope smiles,
Guarding from her perch.
She understands in all ways.
Always. It beats. Major, Minor. Pulses.
Universal heartbeat.

   *Sheruni Ratnabalasuriar*

## A Guiding Light

Just a little old lamp
Holds memories I treasure
From my childhood days
The joy, I can't measure.

A guiding light for my mother at night
To help her children when sickness brought fright
She'd climb the stairs with this light in her hand
A smile on her face. Oh! She was so grand!

A guiding light came from Him above
For to help her children she showed her love
By prayer and dedication she honored her duty
As mother to all she was really a beauty.

Now, she is gone and the lamp she carried
Was a gift to me when I got married.
I've carried it from childhood through
It shines in my memory and guides me, too.

   *Virginia Coblentz*

## "The Ever Presence Of A Rut"

It has the capacity to last for minutes
Hours, days, months, or even years,
A rut is a extremely vicious cycle and
can easily bring upon doubts and fears.
No one individual is excluded from its powerful grip,

Your inner and outer thoughts and actions
begin to take you on a very unpleasant trip.
If you refuse to acknowledge it's presence
Then surely you are bound to incur grief,
Only when you diligently deal with it and
Battle can you ever expect to attain relief.
Being in a rut pollutes the thoughts of
Positivity and it eat's away at your will,
It has contributed to the downfall of a many
great nations so be prepared to get your fill.
The appearance of a rut has neither size, shape nor form,
The best way to describe it is to say that
your positive ways are definitely out of the norm.

   *Montgomery Lamarr McCants*

## Winter, Leave

   I see the summers go and winters come.
How brightly the stars glitter, how they flow
Why does the winter cold come calling now?
Snow flakes drop and glow, but I make a vow
I'll halt the winter from coming again!
    How will I stop this winter fiend?
    Again I ask this fatal question.
    Who will help stop Proserpine
    From eating the pomegranate?

November comes and December goes like
The thunderous and rainy storms that strike.
   I think and I think, but never do I find
   A way for a permanent summer, kind
For I wait and wait until winter leaves.

   *A.D. Collyar*

## Jennifer

Can words describe this lovely creature
Light and joy is her greatest feature
Sweet sixteen, but she's always been
So sweet and precious to her kin
Blue eyes sparkling over a freckle or two
I don't know anyone like her, do you?
A beautiful reflection of her dad and mother
A wonderful gift from God, that's "Jennifer."

   *Jack E. Jones*

## Mother

How can the world go on without you, as if they don't even care?
How can the world go on without you, as if you were never here?
How can they just go on day after day,
Not thinking of you one time, in work or in play.
How can they wake up in the morning without you on their mind?
When GOD knows I think of you all the time.
How can they go to sleep at night without saying a prayer for you?
Knowing what it takes to raise four boys by herself, on the welfare too.
How can they just walk around here as if they don't ever care?
Care that I am talking about one of the greatest woman that
ever lived, is now in heaven somewhere.
I just can't figure it out to save my life, how can anybody
forget Louise Schoonmaker, the mother of my life.......

*Rickey Ray Schoonmaker*

## "Memories"

Yesterday, when I was young,
how long ago that song was sung.
What is young, you simply ask,
it's a part of your life that long has past.
The memories linger and bring you joy
as you recall every girl and boy
that touched your life along the way.
Some will go and some will stay,
but they'll leave memories along the way
that will last until your old and gray.

So gather them up, your yesterdays,
and when someone asks, what have you done
you can give them an answer one by one.

When I was young my friends were many.
I valued them all so I had plenty.
Treat your friends like treasured jewels
so that yesterday's memories will be the fuel
that warms your heart and brings you peace
so that in the coming years, your friends increase
and once again memories in store who on earth could ask for more.

*Virginia Warner*

## The Dove

I look at the clock—he's late again
How many times now...I forget.
I keep on sinking into the rut
Of letting him go and do what he must.

Always putting ahead his feelings for mine
Sacrificing wisdom to the tears I've been crying.
Easier it gets to grow away
From the people we were to those we became.

These feelings I've had I don't understand
In my heart there's always been only one man.
Our wings are both flying in opposite ways
We don't see much of each other these days.

I wait in the wings for the next spark that lights
The candle that burns as he turns out the light.
Please don't let go of me or the spark
Please don't keep me locked in the dark.

You must hold on to what you love...
If you set it free, it just might be
You have just let go of a dove!

*Vickie Langowski*

## Release

Loneliness has become my companion.
How pathetic I am to mate with despair.
This is my choice.
This is my existence.
So deep are the scars of my past that they cut through my soul.
I am at one with myself.
Yet not as any whole.
Not as one should be.
My destiny led me to you and each day my memory brings you to
me again.
Fueling my endorphins only for a moment.
Then I relapse back into the familiar.
Into my reality.
Enduring another day of pain.
I wear the face of a clown for all to see.
An expression so empty in a world of fools.
To have and to have lost shall be engraved on my headstone.
A signature to my release.

*Ron Clark*

## Give Us A Song

How shall we lighten the burdens of living?
How shall we shake off the gloom of the night?
How shall we show forth the value of giving?
How shall we strengthen the worth of what's right?

Let us be singing some song that is easy!
Let us delight in the sound of its way!
Let us take heart in the verses so breezy!
Let us rejoice in the words of the lay!

Give us a song we can shout to the heaven;
Give us a tune we can love for its tone;
Give us a rhyme we can chew for its leaven;
Give us an anthem to keep as our own.

Sing it as no one has sung it before us.
Sing it for gladness in lifting the soul.
Sing it, - a triumphant, jubilant chorus!
Sing it, the harmonies making us whole.

*J. Billson Jr.*

## "To Surrender To Life, A Single Man's Life"

It was a cold and windy Southern California day,
How very unusual for the spring month of May,
The day I decided to surrender to life,
To consider to possibly take on a wife.

I'd tasted for years, a single man's fears,
Of maybe's of no's of AIDS and of tears.

I had, as yet, chose to live quite alone,
With nary a woman to call all my own,
Not to worry, to cry or even lament,
For the choice I have made, and I will not repent.

Not to worry again for the fate of a date,
Or whether or not I could possibly be late,

So what do I fear of the court of divorce,
Is that such a terror or omnipotent force?
Though, compared to the bars,
One can't conceive of worse scars.

So alas I'll except the terms of the deal.
Knowing the ceremony will hardly seem real.
This man has chosen his fate is to kneel,
To surrender to life, this single man's life.

*Terry J. Toman*

## Inner Outings

Hello how are you today
How was work
Did you pick up the mail

Words how can I reach you
How can I touch you
Where are you hiding
I feel your presence deep inside
How can I bring you to the other side

I am waiting at the steps of the entrance of your heart
I want to see you

Pressing my hands against a mirrored wall
I feel your presence now a sense of awe
Tears are rolling down my face
Full of reverence for this sacred place
Can we meet halfway and merge our energies
I will show you the world
You can show me my divinity

*Rosalie Ann Galloway*

## Goodbye

I want to write a poem about you,
How you made me happy, how you made me sad.
Something to remember you by,
like lifting my wings learning to fly.

Slowly letting you go, yet not forgetting the past,
Reaching in, pulling out, with something to grasp.

I want to see your face forever in my mind.
How things fell into a place locked in time,

My world was standing still, my heart couldn't be fuller,
Then I suddenly felt pain, telling me it was over.

I want to say goodbye with a smile on my face,
Knowing I did the best I could,
Not wanting to leave, knowing I should.

I want it to end with the perfect touch,
Forever remembering the face of the one
I love so much.

*Laura Brookey*

## Down Memory's Lane

Listen, dear children - if you wish to hear
How your parents arrived at this time, and year;
Fifty years must seem endless to you,
We have been young and we thought so too!

There has been laughter, and also tears
While traveling through these many years,
There has been pain, and there has been pleasure,
So much of worth we shall always treasure.

Sons and daughters - four of each
(One soon went beyond our reach).
We have known failure, and success,
Clouds and sunshine all to bless.

We're making memories, children so dear,
Deeply we love you; it's great that you're here.
Yesterday's gone, and tomorrow may never come,
We have these moments, together - well done!

So here we are - both hale and hearty
Ready to happily enjoy our party
You've warmed our hearts, you've made us glad.
Lord bless you, we love you, your Mother and Dad.

*Pauline M. Brown*

## My Church

It's just an earthly building that's made by
human hands
But it represents Christ's body crushed
beneath a load of sin.

It's spire which points toward heaven is a
beacon of truth and light
That lifts our spirits upward
Like an eagle as it takes it's flight.

I try to picture the cornerstone
Upon which the foundation is laid
And remember the rock of ages
And the price my Savior paid.

Inside we feel his presence
As we sing sweet hymns of praise
And listen to His glorious word
That teaches us His ways.

I go out from this sanctioned house
With visions of a brighter place
And hope that I will be a spark
That brings joy to a crying face.

*Virginia Cruse*

## I Am A Man

I am a man, created in the image of God.
I am a man, driven by a destructive nature that is inherent.
I am a man, though the divine spark of a loving God does glow
within my breast, though with all my heart, soul and mind,
I wish to serve Him.
I cannot, for the war that rages within my heart allows no other god
to rule, save the one that drives me even to the brink of oblivion.
I am a man, with dreams of self satisfying egocentric, divinity!
I am a man, yearning to be free, caught in the iron jaws
of complacency. Seeing I am blind, hearing I am deaf.
I am a man, the ruler of all I see.
The sum and total, the everything.
I am a man, desperately seeking solace in the things that I allow
I am a man, torn by indecision and anxiety,
knowing, not the path that I should take.
Making paths where there should not be paths, I am a man,
strong as any oak, weakened by that very strength.
Molded by what others think of me. I am a man, yet I am a child,
imprisoned by my past. Impoverished by my passions,
incapacitated by my fears. I am a man, in need of the Great I am!

*Robert R. Smith*

## The Entity

The light that was life fades to black
I am drawn deep within myself
Vast darkness surrounds a lonely spirit
In all directions I seek but cannot find the way
Alone, though in the company of many
They cannot see within me
The black hole that was my soul
A ghost of one who once lived
No joy, no hope, no fantasy - aimlessly wanders
Not seeing, not feeling, not experiencing
Living in a mind with no response
A shattered heart bitterly crying
Alone in the emptiness that is my shell
Intense is the pain of what was love
Consolation comes from none
Existing only by necessity
Drawn by those who keep me in their world
Passing through the endless black of night
Waiting, alone, for the light of a new day
That the entity that was me may live again.

*Renee Judkins*

## Untitled

I am lonely in the midst of my chores
I am drowned in the swamp of my mind.
I am lost in the world of confidence
I am drowned in the world of lies.
Empty smiles, silent words pretending love, and all those lies for a
  few cramps of lust.
It is love?
I live and I continue my forced silence.
My silence surprises me.
I miss myself.
The bitterness of a man's whims shadows my light laughs.
Will I ever again listen to love with my heart rushing to my cheeks?
Will I ever again play with silly letters to rephrase the word "love?"
Why don't I get used to the terrors of a mistaken love?
Will I ever be able to get used to broken vows?
Will I one day be able to sit and watch the sky and dream about love?
And inhale the lilies and hear the sweet sound of hungry bees buzzing
  around us.
Me and lilies and bees called "Us" will sit under a blue forgotten
loneliness and will examine the sweet taste of nothingness.
And our laugh will frighten the hungry bees away.
And one more time I will be a lonely woman again, lonely with my heavy
  empty self.

  *Mahshid Noshirvani*

## Are You Here

In every sunrise and sunset,
I am loving you, knowing you'll always be
there for me.
Yet, I'm not sure where you are.
Are you sitting here beside me or are you just
my imagination?
I feel the wind blow in my ear,
I'm wondering if that's you?
Are you reading over my shoulder?
Are you holding my hand right now?
I want to tell you I love you, yet,
I'm not sure just how.
I can feel you wiping my teardrops and
asking me
please not to cry.
But, I'm missing you, loving you so much;
and I'm sitting here wondering why you had to go.

  *Stacey Zachary*

## Untitled

Whenever I speak her name,
I can hardly catch my breath,
The longing is beyond my furthest
  thoughts.

This emptiness I speak of is a loss for me
A fond memory, a friendship never to end,
Its an undying one so I thought.
One that was to keep me warm no matter
  what the weather holds.

I did say my goodbyes and exclaimed
it was for the best...
  not knowing for who's better.

Time passes and heals they say,
I'm waiting patiently for something to heal.
Maybe this hole in my heart will be
  with me always.

For there is no greater love
than that for my mother who is my friend
  She is missed always.

  *Lillian J. Kurek*

## Wrong Justified

I'm not a child; I changed your diapers.
I can hear; I'm sitting right here.
My body is old, but my heart still feels sharp words.
My mind sometimes forgets, but yours did too...once.

I sat with you through many childhood sicknesses.
You send me here; a nurse sits with me.
I held your hand when you were afraid of the dark
Now I face a greater darkness than childish fears...alone.

You say, "Mother, times have changed."
I think, "Not that much", but I do not speak
My heart cries, as you justify your guilt
Wrong justified is still wrong.

Still I am here, and you are there
Here with my outward acceptance.
You there with your justified convenience.

  *C. P. Lanier*

## I Wish I Could Ease Your Pain My Dear...

I have looked upon your gentle eyes so blue
I can not feel the pain for which is so great
yet I can see it within your loving eyes so soft.
I wish so hard that it was not true, but yet I
know that one day soon you will pass to the other side.
The tears flow heavy from my blue eyes like that of a
rushing waterfall as I think of your love that is so dear,
and yet I can not say that I understand your ways.
For soon you will pass away beyond that bright light.
Sadness is upon my heart as I think of your heart
yet I know of our ways, and yet I say; "no way."
I wish you to stay for I love you is so many ways.
I wish I could ease the pain in our hearts, but I
know that you will live and die by your ways which
will always stay...

  *Tracy Christensen*

## Changes of Reality

There is nothing I can do to change the past
I can only began a new day and make it last
The words of my mouth, nor the actions I take
can change the past, or erase my mistakes.
I think not of tomorrow,. but live day by day,
for when I thought of tomorrow nothing ever went my way
I choose not to be bold, reality has shot me down.
I was played like a fool and made like a clown.
I failed to be what I said I was all about.
I locked myself in and can't find the way out.
Reality momentarily left me, but sad I not be,
'cause I'll always have reality, but reality won't have me.
Time will tell of what will come through.
Until then, I'll just wait on what to do.
Getting used to changes is the reality I must face;
when that is overcome the rest will fall in place.

  *Regina K. Peterson*

## Heaven's Blessing

Someone very special is watching today.
He's seated front-center but afar in a way.

Much closer to paradise he's holding our place.
For when we're together again, face to face.

Daddy is the special one I speak of.
He and my mother filled our home with true love.

That love will be carried into our new home.
And the memory of Daddy will forever live on.

  *Rhonda W. Jolley*

## Moon Spores At Night

What, I cannot see. What happened to the light?
I cannot see through this blanket of night.
The sky has changed from azure blue to grey, to black,
and left me with a melancholy winter at my back.

I cannot see. I cannot see without the light.

Something plucks the strings of this moment,
releasing heavenly sounds across the chords of my spine;
vibrations of night music shiver, insistent drums begin to whine
as blindness directs my view inward, and sight opens as my sign,

Now I can see. I can see in this sacred light

Moon colored spores of life yielding substances swaying
like heavy headed grasses, from the grasp of my hand.
My thumb combines them as a family portrait - young siblings,
with heads barely larger than the tops of matchsticks,
reaching up and out from my fingers, creating a broader mix.

Overhead, the watchful moon eye stretches night beams
to this earthly congregation of all but what it seems
and around me the entreating night
envelops everything with lunar light.

Ah, now I see. Now I see with sacred sight.

*Yvonne Vance Devastey*

## Evening Flower

Like the dawning of a new era
I cast out forth my petals to full bloom

And bring forth new life.

Just as the shades of pink and lavender
fall down and cast out upon the open sky.

Each and every day
I rest and rise.

To be the most beautiful and exotic
at full bloom.

Just to drawback back...
to my mother, the earth again each and every day.

*Sandy Gayle Wootton*

## Chains of Love

I chained the unicorn.
I chained her with chains of love.
I beg for forgiveness from the unicorn
For everyone knows she can't be chained for long.
Unicorn, I release you from my chains of love.
Know that though the chains are gone
The love will always live on.
I know, now, that you love me truly,
But your first love is stronger than I ever knew.
You love your freedom and that you now shall have.
Run, run my unicorn for freedom is yours again!
Never again shall I bind you!
Never again shall I chain you with my chains of love!
If ever you should pass my way again,
Stay as long as you would like
And when the need for freedom comes again
Run with it 'till your heart's content.
So long my unicorn 'till we meet again.
I know now that you run not from me, but for the joy of running.
So run, run my unicorn your freedom is yours again!

*Ronald Thomas*

## Melissa

Melissa is a sightless child and she is only three.
I cherish every moment that she wants to share with me.

It seems like we spend hours feeling petals on the flowers,
While I tell her of the colors which I wish that she could see.
Then we talk about the robins and the finches and the doves,
and the squirrels scampering up and down the tree.

"What color is the wind?" Melissa asked one windy day.
I knelt and held her little hand and wondered what to say.

I explained about air currents just as simply as I could,
and then I asked Melissa if she thought she understood.

She said, "I think the wind is like a fairy or an elf;
it flits around from place to place, but never shows itself.

She told me how it felt to be in darkness day and night,
and how she hoped they'd find a way to give her better sight.

And so the day the Lord tells me I've used up all my time,
I hope my eyes go to Melissa and she can see the world
through mine.

*Muriel M. Walters*

## Dare to Discover

I Dare to Discover a place where people don't face pain
I Dare to Discover a place where people don't face hate
I Dare to Discover a place where people don't face prejudice
I Dare to Discover a place where people don't face discrimination
    against one's race
I Dare to Discover a place where people do face love
I Dare to Discover a place where people do face joy
I Dare to Discover a place where people do face respect for one
    another
I Dare to Discover a place where people do face equality
I Dare to Discover a place where it doesn't matter what race
I Dare to Discover
I Dare to Discover
I Dare to
I Dare
I Dare...
I Dare you

*Tyanna Shelton*

## In Retrospect

My hands were busy through the day,
I did not have much time to play
the games you asked I play with you,
were not beyond what I could do.

I'd wash your clothes and sew and cook,
but when you brought your picture book,
and asked me please to share your fun,
I'd say: "A little later, son."

I'd tuck you in all snug at night,
then very quietly switch the light,
and as I tip-toed through the door,
I wished I'd stayed a minute more.

For life is short and years rush past,
and little boys grow up so fast.
No longer are you at my side
with precious secrets to confide.

Your picture books are stored away, there are no longer games to play,
no goodnight kiss, no prayers to hear, that all belongs to yester-year

My hands, once busy, now are still, the days are long and hard to fill
I wish I could go back and do so many things you asked me to.

*Roy J. Champagne*

## Canyon Dream, An Adventure

I didn't know I had a dream,
I didn't know I had a canyon
until the day the dream stood awestruck on the rim of the canyon
and exclaimed, "I didn't know I had a canyon until I gazed upon its
    beauty
and felt its haunting call in the belly of my soul."

And the dream entered the canyon,
at first with measured and carefully placed steps,
watching the colors as light and shadow caressed walls and plateaus
changing the glory and experience of each particle of sand,
each rock and crevice.

And the dream swelled to fill and hug each canyon surface
and was held there as a baby suckled snug at its mother's breast is held,
the suction of each life feeding the other.

And milk poured from canyon walls in a torential stream
and a flood burst from within the dream
and the stream and the flood became one as the Canyon Dream
leaped and swirled into the mystery and stillness of deep space.

**Roe Kienle**

## My Confidant

We have shared many wonderful years together and yet
I discover new things about you everyday
Can we be so strong that we never allow anyone to completely
know us?
Why are we afraid?
Who will ridicule us if we open that secret door within our soul?
Who will understand that even if you love me as you say you do you
will not think that I am not at all what you had expected me to be!
We all have that deep side that no one is allowed to see
Only we have the key to that place where we keep all our secret thoughts
Why are we so afraid that someone, anyone will not approve of how
we feel
Our fears are not just of spouses, lovers and friends but of parents
and family, those we try so hard to get their approval.
If we are not accepted by them, all we have strived for is lost.
So we keep that secret door closed, sometimes forever...
For we may never find that certain someone we can share all our
deepest thoughts with...
So when I pray I tell all to that higher being, for I know that I will
never be betrayed!!

**Rosalie LoCurto-Finkel**

## Untitled

I really do want to go home.
I don't like the place where I roam.
I don't want to be here;
I can't stand the scenes here;
So please, Mom, just let me go home.

I've got friends at home who are waiting,
So Mom, just stop all your debating.
I don't want to stay,
And I don't want to play.
So, Mom, please just let me go home.

The weather up there is quite cry,
But really is very enticing.
I'll play in the snow
With the friends that I know;
So please, Mom, I need to go home!

I'll fly home in a plane in the sky.
Just like all the eagles, I'll fly.
I'm all packed to go,
And I am going; so,
Bye Mom, I am going home.

**Sarah V. Jahn**

## He's In Heaven

Dad died when I was four,
I don't remember seeing him before,
He was six foot three and feet size eleven,
but now I know he's in heaven.
I never had a dream about my dad,
that made me very, very sad.
The closes I came to a dad,
I had a stepfather instead.
He keep us fed and in clothes so warm,
because he was raised on a farm.
Then one day he had died,
I was left without a father at my side.
So I cried and said dad don't go,
because I need a father much more.
I kissed the only man I knew as dad good night,
and watch them lower his body out of sight.
So if you have one love him with all your heart,
because I never had one from the start.

**Shirley Smith**

## Show Me How...

All that I've ever lived for in my life
I don't want it anymore
The way I taught myself to be
I want to change
Because all I want is you
It may sound dumb
But that is it
I lay my emotions
Out on the table
For you to take them
In the past I've loved
Now all I do is cry
I can't tell the difference
Between hate and love
I forgot what it was like to have feelings
Now I come to you
To show me how to feel again
Let me discover the love I once had but forgot about
Let me care, feel the pain when I have to kiss you goodnight
Because all I want is you.

**Michael Miller**

## Reflections

When I was young and the world seemed knew
I dreamed of the things I wanted to do.
So many vocations from which to choose
And years ahead I had nothing to lose.

Now that I am older and reflect on the past
I am reminded of experiences that seem to last.
I recall the good as well as the bad
Experiences and moments that were extremely sad.
Memories I will cherish of friends I have had
Who gave me much happiness for which I am so glad.

Life gave me so much from which to learn
Yet there is something for which I yearn.
That is that some day I will be able to express
My gratitude to God and my Parents
By whom I was so richly blessed.

**Lela M. Cummins (nee: Gallatin)**

## Driving Home From El Paso

For one hour each night
I drive my little blue car
Through the high desert.
Right by the stars
Say hello to Orion
Shaped in that big "Tee"
Or that galactic pan-o-fryin'
Known as the "Big D"
If the wind is just right
You can smell the polluted stench of Juarez
If the wind is blowing wrong
It's just the bovine odor of the dairy ranches.
And the billboards - they talk to you like you were
  their best friend
But all have a common theme - SPEND, SPEND, SPEND!
Approaching EXIT ONE, five minutes from my bed,
Mr. Debussy plays his last song
The one that sticks in my head.

*Michael J. Romero*

## The Blank Picture

A blank picture of what will be
I eagerly watch
To see, what will be
I watch it actively on the happy piano
The piano plays its lively tune

We put on our party hats and swim through clear blue waters
And listen to crackling music on the old radio
Slowly, I watch the picture, to see, what will be

I stumble

The mail comes
The picture falls from the black piano
I cry, expectantly, for a lost me
The music stops, it falls slowly; a nightmare
The frame shatters, we watch, glass everywhere
I pick up the pieces
They watch the picture, me
They look excitedly

I look sadly upon my casket
BUT
The picture is still blank

*Thom Breckenridge*

## Visions of a New World

Beyond this place on an inner shore
I envision a world where less is more

Where love resides in every heart
And the whole depends upon each part

No one is lost or left behind
The acknowledgement of all is what you'll find

The goal is to live for the expression of beauty
In reverence of life enveloped in harmony

Soon there will come a special time
When all the world will be sublime

A world in which humanity
Will be aligned with divinity

*Mildred Gertrude Palmer*

## The Cold Soldier

I walk along the dusty trail of death, searching for a better way.
I feel a strange something looking at me, and the fact is I don't
  know what it is.
But I know he is there, but why is he looking at me?
I feel the presence of the man in me, but why is it in me?
I saw the ungodly sight of a man laying in the dirt staring into my
  soul.
His once blue and gold uniform was more of a pale green infested with
  the hatred of a bullet meant to kill.
As I walk further and further away, I can faintly hear the sound of
  gunshot, the fire of a cannon, or the trot of a horse.
I only see the blackness of the clouds.
The only vision I have in my head is the picture of that cold and
  lonely soldier lying against that tree.
If it was only me instead of him, the burden of war would be vanished
  into thin air.
Only if I could go back and wear that uniform proud, such as he.
I might just have the chance to be that cold and desolate man!

*Laura Marie Tennesen*

## Light for Love

As shades of night softly gather, and daylight hours come to an end,
I feel an overwhelming presence of your love, come to my dreams,
I dream of the happy times and think of the pain
when things tend to tear my world apart.

I love that comfort when you say, "Honey, I love you,"
It seems to melt my heart and I count my blessings when,
I know you will always be my one and only love.

I learn, as time rolls onward, leave the hard times behind.
Many times I will long for my Rose, and I can hide the thorn of pain.
As clouds can cover the sunshine, they cannot banish the sun.
Just as my love for you, Rose, it will shine out brighter every day.

Light is the very strength of LOVE.

*Merrell G. Hill*

## Lifetime

My get-up-and-go has got up and gone —
I feel like I'm over the hill.
I think of how all the years went by,
how I managed my life with a will.

I remember when I was young —
that was a long time ago —
the trees and the leaves I walked among
with the fellows I used to know

Who often asked me out to a dance,
especially a boy named Harry.
For a while it seemed like a great romance
but he never did ask me to marry.

All this time I worked each day
as a packer in a hat factory.
Time came when employers had to say
they thought the work was too hard for me,

So, now I'm retired — serious and solemn —
A "lady of leisure," it's said.
After breakfast I read the obituary column.
Then I go back to bed.

*Peggy Raduziner*

## Will You?

You're never quite sure, 'til you know it's true
I feel so secure, I believe in you
together as two, heading for a ride
forever be true, as one, we're tied

The wonder of the new, on our lifelong trip
My loves only for you, knowing we won't slip
Everyday's a new day, one by one
Our flame stays lit, 'til there is no sun
The heart of truth has been found
strength of honesty, won't let us down

Come with me and I will follow
Everyday is great as is tomorrow
Appreciate our love, know it's power
the one above, knew beauty in a flower

Thoughts I hold deep are now told about
my love's only for you, there is no doubt
Still one canvass remains undone
our official commitment
Its time has come

*Paul Ekstrom*

## Once In Love

When I was young and in my teens.
I fell in love with a man of my dreams.
But problems arose for he and I:
Pop hid my letters and made me cry.
Many years have flown by...
He married and so did I.
It was too much for him and he died:
I was dressed in white, my hand on his coffin;
I looked down at the ashen face of my beloved.
I wished that it were me that died:
Instead of my Love:  Oh, I cried:
I never fell in love again.
My love is beneath the sod ...
There I should be, believe me GOD:

*Nethelia Osgood*

## My Journey To Life

With each new experience I encounter,
I find a new life inside of me;
A totally new facet of myself waiting
To be drawn out and explored.

A certain amount of excitement mounts
With each new situation I'm thrown;
And the changes and decisions of every
Moment of life challengingly awaits.

I've taken the wrong road many times
And managed to find the strength to change;
Yet I must still find the confidence
And ambition to explore and chance another.

No matter how painful some of these
Experiences have been, I must never
Stop searching for that ultimate goal;
Which I think of as my journey to life.

*Pamela Holt*

## A Touch with the Past

As I walk the fields of my father's farm,
   I find arrowheads left by Indians from
hunts or in arms.
   I know they made them with strong and
proud hands.
   I feel like I can go back in time on this
piece of land.
   As I pick up pieces of clay pottery with
their design still clear and held in my hand,
   I know that each piece was made with pride
from this great land.
   As I hold pieces of clay pipe in my hand
and close my eyes and go back in time,
   I can see the Indians sitting around the
campfire smoking and talking about their
days find.
   As I walk through these fields going about
my task,
   I feel a great privilege to have a touch
with the past.

*Linda L. Sawyer*

## Reinvention

Last night, amidst a violent hailstorm,
I found myself inside a shoe-box

And with a morbid detachment, noted that I'd grown yellow
and brittle

Meanwhile, the bookshelf feigned friendship
shouting in the tone of a penny-whistle

"Consign yourself to History!"
"Resign  yourself to History!"

Igniting a single match
and glancing heavenward
I took the next logical step

*Tom Gazdag*

## Wishes

Walking along under the light of the moon
I gaze at a falling star so beautiful it makes me think of you
I wonder if you see the same thing that I see, or if it's just my
   curiosity
But I make a wish, and that wish is to always be with you
And then I wondered if you had made a wish too...
If you did, may your wish come true.

Walking along a beach of warm sand I saw a bottle floating in the water
It had a note written in ink, so I read it and it began to make me think
It was written by the hand of a man who had been lost at sea
The first line read, "...still dreaming of you and me"
It also said, "if I could have only one wish, it would be just to
   hold you"
It made me wonder if his wish had ever come true.

Walking along the street I noticed a magic lamp in a shop
It made me ponder if it still had any wishes to give, so I decided to stop.
I picked it up and looked at it for a while
I thought how wonderful it would be to get a wish...it made me smile
I put it back on the shelf and kept walking down the street
Because in my mind, I already knew
That my one and only wish had come true
My wish was that now and forever I'd be with you.

*Lynn Osmera Jr.*

## A Mental Regeneration

Whenever I feel down in spirit, frustrated, lonesome, or blue.
I give my mind a little vacation, and retire into a quiet
meditation of you.

I'm utterly relaxed, and at peace with the world.
Nothing can touch me now, for I'm with my sweet lovely girl.
For all the fears and worries, I've left behind.
Love has intervened, and taken control of my mind.

For here you are now princess, deep in my mind.
So modest, conspicuously beautiful, for you are one of a kind.
Your beauty is enchanting, your spirit is so high.
Whenever I think of losing you, I have to break down and cry.

Your love is so strong, your smile is so bright.
Your eyes remind me of stars, that shines so beautiful through
the night.
Now I feel hypnotized, intoxicated by the sweet of your love.
I really believe you are a gift, from Almighty God above.

So far away I am, but still in my mind I see.
A little meditation of you each day, makes me feel wholesome,
happy, and free!

**Timothy Jones**

## My Gift of Love

All these things I write from the heart
I give to you when we're apart.
They are not made for the world to see
They're a gift of love to you, from me.

They're words of love that I held in my heart
And they were meant for you from the very start.
Then when many years have all passed by
And I have left for that home on high

You'll someday re-read these old words thru
And know they're my gift of love
That I left with you.

**Marie M. Smorey**

## A Lost Friend

It was a lost love
I had put it as a part of my past
Buried
I feared it
It only would put in front of my eyes pain
How could I begin to believe that it actually
could heal me
Make me whole.

I was inspired then
To challenge my own inhibitions
To stand aside and allow regrowth
Yes, regrowth, for once it abundantly flourished.

The choice.
The choice?
The choice!

Alas, it will be
It will be
me
me, again.

I'm home.

**Rebecca Bargas**

## Our So Called Rights!

Freedom of speech, it's our right!
What we hear, what we say,
What we wear, why do you care?

Why can't I a "person" of 16,
go to see a movie, listen to music,
or even take a drink?

Who are you to tell me what I can
and can't do? Or what I can and cannot say?

Teachers, parents, people everywhere
tell us what to hear, or say, or play.
We have rights, too!

Just because were 15, 16, 17 doesn't mean
we don't care, share, or stare
when things aren't right

Why can't they see
we're humans, too?

**P. A. Stinson**

## A Place for Me

One winter night while sleeping in my bed,
I dreamed of oak trees and the sassafras.
Of each day the stars were shining overhead,
Of the rolling valleys, the lakes of glass.
Of being in the clean, fresh country air,
Where love and happiness run like a stream.
The visions made me wish I were still there,
My heart holds very dear,my endless dream.
Here the dying eagle with grace does fly,
To the sweetest sunset you will ever see.
A threatened hero soars in the spacious sky,
Providing a stirring moment for me.
And as the seasons pass I realize,
My decision to visit here proved wise.

**Randy Etapa**

## Ah, My Love

Ah, my love
I am so glad we met;
The day is long; 'til you come home to your dove.
I was blessed when I bet
That my love would forever, come home to his dove.

You are my treasure
As you give such pleasure;
You are precious to the heart of your dove
And thus, do I wait for thee my love;
To come home and be my dove;
So we may live together as two doves.
Ah my love, it is better then I bet.

**Mary A. Drouin**

## Life The Ultimate Wonder

We are born only to die years later.
I ask, why? But no one answers me.
I ask, what is my purpose?
I do not know.
Am I to question my being
can no one answer me.
Do not the greatest mines know
am I to wait till death to find why
Is it a gift or curse that God gave me,
or is it both.
I fear I will never know
the wonder of life seems to have no answer.

**Tina Pelton**

## Dear Mother

You and I, from the start formed a bond and right then I knew in my
heart, how I felt for you - unconditional love... Me from you, little
miracle, knew only crying but then you held me tight, and then I knew
what you were for - making everything alright. Oh mommy, what's this
around me, won't you take my hand and show me the world? Your heart,
gave mine rhythm, a reason to beat and my soul a reason to feel, I
never hurt so much the first time I saw you cry. Your mind, gave me
conscience, a reason to dream no matter how far out they may be, you
never doubted me and one day we'll both fly... Oh momma, I like what's
around me, won't you take my hand and show me more? And del-sol shines
regardless of how cloudy life gets, God's in the midst of the stars-I
know He's watching you, I am living proof... My soul never believed in
forever, until I heard you pray - and then I knew it must be true,
because what mommy says comes true... Oh mom, I like what I've
learned, won't you take my hand again and explain to me this world?
Your eyes gave mine vision to see the truth and the world as it really
is, sometimes cold and dark - but your sunshine always come through.
And your life gave mine music, a gift to express myself through endless
song, endless melodies, and my angels sing through you. Dear Mother
after all these years please take my hand and lets soar forever

### *Timothy Yeargin*

## Lady

Damn you Disney all to hell, you cast her semblance all to well.
Her smile turned gently at both ends, her subtle curves, a nose which bends.
Her eyes were beauty pooled and damp, which shown so brightly for her tramp.
You brought to life on silver screen my life long quest, sight unseen.

The years wore twenty and six more. I had to find her, to adore
    and coax my heart to beat once more.
I forded rivers in canyons deep and climbed the crags of mountains
    steep and spent my nights in fretful sleep...all for naught.

Then one morn as I hefted my load, a vision softly barred my road.
Birds flew brightly and the sun shone high, my jaw dropped loosely and
    I wet my thigh.
Your "Lady," my vision had come to life, and I knew very soon she
    would be my wife.

I wanted to crone and I wanted to sing, first I was Bob and then I was Bing.
But as I embraced her for a kiss, my lady, your vision
    disappeared and left me this...
"To Tom and Walt, all my best. Look to your heart, imagination rest."

### *Thomas Baumann*

## To A Father Dying

I watch you slowly disappear as you begin to die.
Life's conflicts raging in the aging do not catch my eye.
For now an then your mind meanders to an unknown place,
Yet subtly this same lame frame moves with diminished grace.
But bite by bite both you's are gnawed away perniciously
As time's twin, strange, lethargic beasts feast surreptitiously.

### *Francis J. Manduca*

## Memories of Grandpa

I miss my grandpa, he lived next to me; Whenever I'd go over, he'd be watching T.V.
He sat on his couch, remote control in hand; My grandpa was a very talented old man.
He played his harmonica to help us rest; He was in the service, "the best of the best".
He was proud of what he did in the war; If it weren't for his farm, he'd have been quite poor.
He took care of his chickens everyday of his life; When she was sick, he took care of his wife.
He loved all he had and all he could give; He would have done anything just to live.
He loved to go out and dance on Sundays, I was even taught to polka one day.
We were always together for the holidays... Until Diabetes took him away.
He was rushed to the Veterans Hospital, for he had a heart attack that was unrecoverable.
Grandpa passed away on the morning of October 5th, after telling my mom his last wish.
The following days were quite hard; We all cried with no holds barred.
I really miss him, I always will... but the memories of grandpa are with me still.

### *Mia Smith*

## The Cowboy

The cowboys at the rodeo
He's thinking about his ride
Will he last eight seconds
Or just fall off the side

The bulls nostrils are flaring
As they open up the gate
He prays to God above
That the second hands not late

He wants to be a champion
He's worked hard all his life
As he straps his hands in the rope
He thinks of his children and wife

He's hoping that he makes it through
Though he's tried again and again
He's got sweat on his brow, a smile on his face
When the judge says it's a ten.

### *Jean Sanderford*

## Through His Eyes

Cup in hand, outstretched wide,
His glasses black, white cane tipped red,
A torn, gray suit, dog by his side,
He is that which we all dread.

A vase of pencils does he sell
For whatever he can make;
While busses leap and people yell,
The Lord's protection does he take.

As the day turns into night,
And to his small flat he does drift,
He, without a ray of light,
Still gives thanks for his great gift:

That of LIFE.

### *Gerald M. Warkans*

## Reflections Of The Dearly Beloved

God restored your soul to eternal rest,
His mansion you grace now at your best;
You arrived in water and left in ash
As the door opened to eternity's Mass.

Though your presence is sadly missed below,
Memories yet recall times precious as so;
My heart remains to reflect your image
Till we meet upon the Golden Ledge.

### *Dennis E. Voigt*

## Unspoken

You came to my life ...
quietly ... simply ... tenderly ...
and the world stood still!
I couldn't say a word,
nor, with a single gesture,
show the feelings in my heart!
So, I loved you in silence,
worshipped you from the start...
dreamt of you from afar.
I wanted to say "I love you"
wanted to show I care -
but, I was afraid ...
afraid, you'll only
laugh at me.
In silence then will
I just love you
in silence will I care
forever -

### *Bernardita F. Vera*

## Is There Light?

Darkness covers my mind,
Helping to dull the memories,
That burns deep inside.
It also kills the pain.
It may last for hours or days.
Confusing all who love me.
Darkness covers my mind like a tent,
And there is only one way out.
There's no more light.
Each day is a threat,
And only my friends can help me.
The day grows shorter and the nights longer.
I await the day the lights go out for good.
Knowing I have no real say,
Just knowing that this day will come.

**Heather Maloney**

## A Mothers Rose

At sixty, mother had only a rose in her hand
Her life passed by to quickly to fully understand
Thinking her young life would always roll
Too soon, too late, it took its painful toll.

At sixty, she sat alone watching a rose grow
Wondering what went wrong, never to know
Children and grand children now have grown
While she was so busy on her own.

At sixty, with a red rose in her hand
Sitting in her silk gown-without a band
The younger ones now with a faster pace
No longer hurry home for a loving embrace.

At sixty now with my rose, in my hand,
My life taught me to hold and understand,
But the younger ones I loved so also must go
Leaving only a rose of care and thoughts to show.

**Dorothy I. Brown**

## Caged

Paralyzed, caged, and lonely,
Her restless soul paces in its confinement.
A heart crying out, no words pass her lips.
Her mind races, her body is still.

A yearning so great encompasses her spirit.
She grasps shreds of happy memories
Summer strolls through golden fields of unharvested wheat
A worthless effort to restore an irreplaceable life.

From behind the bars, watchful eyes mourn her loss
Holding back,
A wall of tears
Crumbles, overwhelming with its flow.

Never too bold, never too proud
Almost a defense, another cage,
She is locked within.

**Chapin Faulconer**

## The Rose

I wander through my garden fair
Roses blooming everywhere
The red, the white, the silv'ry blue
The yellow, pink and orange too
I view the beauty of the rose
It's fragrance trickling through my nose
Intricate colors on display
Petals formed in unique array
Oh what beauty God has given
Made to pave the road to heaven

**Judith Lubarsky**

## Twilight

The image of that house, without her, fills my mind.
Her rocking chair before the hearth, stilled,
Pillows all in place, neatly plumped, orderly,
Gone the hollows her thin body had shaped in them,
Smoothed away by my sister's hands
To quickly erase the memories.

From afar, a second image, her resting place,
Her tired body longs to lie beside him there,
To sleep together on that grassy hillside.
The simple, marble headstone, already in place,
Has both their names carved in it.

Her world reduced by pain and fear,
She sits and waits, alone,
Waits for someone else to do the things
Her crippled hands no longer can.
Fragile scrap of humanity, my mother, turning, smiles,
As the setting sun deepens the shadows on the mountains.

**Judith Lee Whitney**

## Tracy

The light glows warmly from her green-gold eyes.
Her smile shines with love for everyone she knows.
She climbs steadily over all life's mountains.
An inspiration to all who come to know her.
Especially to me. The special smile she has
for me turns me from my blackest moods.
The sun brightens the most cloudy day when
she says...I love you. Those words can have
many meanings. When they are directed to me,
I know they mean something very special.
I am the only one who hears those three words
with all their meaning and feeling...

**Benny H. Hamilton**

## The Jane Doe Self Deprivation Blues

Her coffee's growing cold. Her eyes are growing dry.
Her smokes are running low, as she eats another lie.
The pace is quickening. The pain is turning blue.
She sits there wondering, what the hell's inside the glue.

She's got the Jane Doe Self Deprivation Blues

The girl's still very pretty. All her friends, they tell her so.
She always did well in school, though today you'd never know.
Her heart bleeds her sympathy. Her head say's she's a fool.
Just another love addict child, who needs a fix to keep her cool.

Strung out on the Jane Doe Delf deprivation blues

I don't wish to kill the flame of what was a sweet romance.
And I believe people can change, if they're willing to pray for the
   chance.
But outside help is needed, for this situation here.
Because patience is no virtue, when your left with pain and fear.

Stuck in the Jane Doe Self Deprivation Blues.

Her coffee's gone dead cold. Her eyes have both grown dry.
Her smoke just smolder's low, as she digests the lie.
The pace has quickened. Now the pain is BLACK AND BLUE.
He watches reruns on TV, without the nerve to read the clues.

He's inflicted the Jane Doe Self Deprivation Blues.

**James Joseph Byrne**

## Bow Legged Cat

These are the questions that I asked my cat.
Here are the answer he gave me back.
Sneakers! Sneakers! Where are you?
Under the bed inside your shoe.
Why are you walking pigeon-toed and so slow?
I'm a bow legged cat I have you to know.
What did you do when I was away?
I slept all day so tonight I can play.
Where are all the toys I bought from the store?
I hid them so you could buy me some more.
Why are you looking so glum and so blue?
I am trying my best to imitate you.
Why are you jumping like you're on a trapeze?
I thought you would let me do as I please.
Who ask you to cut off the phone?
I was just pretending I was home alone.
All questions answered about this and that.
I still remain your bow legged cat.

*Ida B. Seaborn*

## A Fisherman's Tale

I'm sitting here down by the lake, not even fully awake. I've been
here since way before light; did I even go to sleep last night?
I've got all the latest equipment and the best gear money can buy.
If I don't catch something with all this stuff, I just won't
understand why. I throw out my line into just the right spot, where
I know the fishing should be real "hot." I lean my pole up against a
rock, and kick back in the dirt like a fishing jock. Time passes
slowly as I'm watching my line, when I start to wonder if
everything's fine. So just to make sure I reel it back in, check my
bait and throw it out again. And back in the water it goes once
more, with a fresh worm as the bait. Then once again, as all good
fishermen do, I wait and I wait and I wait. As I'm sitting enjoying
the sight, I'm aware that I might have a "bite." I wait just a tad
to be sure, then jerk on my pole to set the "lure." The fight
begins with that tug on my line and I know I've got the big one this
time. I'm sure it's a whopper, a real giant in size, and I envision
the envy in all my friends' eyes. But as I continue to reel in and
reel in, suddenly the sensation comes to an end. The struggle has
ended and I know when I look, all that's going to be there is one
empty hook. Still I know there's fish in this fishing hole, they've
just been darn good at avoiding my pole. But my fishing day's end
is drawing near, I can tell 'cuz I've just finished my very last
beer. Well I was hoping to catch the big one today, but since that
didn't happen I'll just have to say: "YOU SHOULD HAVE SEEN
THE ONE
THAT GOT AWAY!"

*Barbara Ayers*

## Child on a Wing

*By Daddy*

Fingers up and fingers down
He's not sure where he's bound

One and one ain't two he's up in the morning
as bright as a star. Down at breakfast
he's not sure who you are

Off to school to see Mr. Mike
a superman spin is his delight
Everything jumbled try as he might

When the going gets hard he takes to flight
not by wing and not by song but into a world
where only he belongs

He can't figure out what's wrong and what's right
You got to hug him and squeeze him with all your
might and hope he sees it's alright

*James Sullivan*

## Imagination Vs. Jewels

Poet's views vary, expressed thru his words.
His hand trails the pen with no imitation.
What he cannot portray in an artists way
Is sketched by that pen of his own imagination.

Poets may see the nature of objects
Quite oddly than you or I.
Diamonds, glistening, falling downward,
Are merely raindrops from the sky.

Rocks or boulders in a babbling brook,
Moss upon some that age can deliver.
Sun smittened waters, like mirrors
Reflecting emeralds upon gold, or is it silver?

Quick! The eye catches an object float by.
At first glance, a brilliant ruby of red,
That second look reveals only paper
Or a simple scarlet ribbon floating instead.

Be it a poet or one who is not,
Imagination belongs to anyone...
Jewels of the mind, thinking ever more,
Apparently, this job is never done!

*Dottie Macik Race*

## Ride Of The Black

The powerful black stallion bolts forward with flight
His muscular body contains power and might
Fury and rage with elegance and grace
His long legs moving like free flowing lace
No restraint holds back the stallion's stride
A feeling starts building up inside
His powerful mightiness enters your mind
Around your thoughts it will twist and wind
Now you mentally start to mature
The thoughts and feelings reassure
Another persons talent makes you understand
That life is something wonderfully grand
The sound of the stallion's rhythmic hoof beat
Brings you into the church and off of the street
Reality will get your mind on track
After you've experienced the Ride of the Black!

*Danee Rudy*

## God's Love Is Real

God's love is so real,
His touch I love to feel.
When the storms of life begin to rise,
I just pray and look toward the sky.
Knowing He will answer by and by.
God has never failed me yet, or let me down,
He put joy in my heart, a smile on my face and took away my frown.
He is my Lily of the Valley, My Bright and Morning Star,
He will be that for you, no matter where you are.
His mercy and grace are forever and ever,
He will stand by your side and leave you never.
He loved us so much he gave his life,
To set us free from misery, and strife.
Won't you give your life to him?
He is standing with open arms saying "Come on in."
If we walk with him we will never be alone,
He's gone away right now. To prepare for us a new home.
Some sweet day his blessed face we shall see,
Then there will be happiness eternally.

*Jeannie Coin*

## What Is Black?

Black looks like shiny church shoes and shiny black
horses running through the tall grass.

Metal horses shoes sound like black, black also
sounds like someone crying.
Black is the taste of burned food.
Black pen ink smells like black.
Halloween makes me feel like black.
A dark black room seems black.
Some horses and cows are shiny black.

A dark black hole, a tunnel, and the Grand Canyon
are black places.
Black is what it is at night.

*Heather Klein*

## You Gave Me

How can I begin to describe you to anyone?
How can I speak of your love?
I was as a rose in a dry, parched land that once beseeched
the tender hand of love.

I told you lies; you set me free with truth. The truth that you
gave me once a bitter taste on my tongue now seems as gentle,
cleansing raindrops from heaven.

I, who once looked with eyes twisted and tormented by agony,
have been able to behold the beauty and
splendor of sunrise once more.

Like a solemn knight, I once wore a full armor of strength and you—
you stripped away my burdensome dress; my nakedness was not hidden
in the light of your eyes. I gave you secrets;
you taught me intimacy.

Like a jester with jovial face and frock, I pranced before you and
gave you laughter, then you showed me the ghoulish mask of fear
that lay behind my laughter and brought me to tears.
I was enslaved of my own accord, constrained by self induced
chains of sorrow. You laughed at me and exchanged my shackle of
sorrow with joy.

Were I an eagle I would spread my wings and cry out to the world
about your love for me. I would announce to all of the earth with
a roaring clap of thunder how you have given me dignity.

My soul does cry for wanting you, my heart aches for the love of you,
yet I am comforted by the peace within. I know not how this can be.

In future times, I will look back upon the wondrous feelings I feel
now and grieve not, rather I will find strength in what has been
laid upon me; no doubt the love I feel will be rewarded by the
precious memories of you embedded in my heart forever.

*Jannine Warren*

## "Why"

Why don't people care anymore?
  How can they walk away and close the door?
Does their heart hurt; their tears pour?
  Tell me why they don't care anymore.

People dying on the streets,
  Helpless animals dumped at trash heaps,
Homeless people,
  Babies being beat,
Little children with not enough to eat.

Oh, Lord please help us find a way
  To deal with the struggles we face everyday,
And reunite our world with love.

*Cynthia Morris DeLoach*

## The Color of Pain

How can there be love, when there's none to give?
How can there be peace when hate rules the world?
How can there be light when brown-yellow fills the air?
And how can there be quiet when a child cries alone?

Women should be mothers
Men should be dads
But so often LOVE disappears.

Hate, anger, resentment and fears
Are all they have left to give.....
The child is a nuisance, a bother, a pain.
And the hits come more often so the
CHILD feels the pain.

The yells of anger, of bitterness all flourish and the
CHILD feels the pain.

The sun hidden; the world looks gray,
And the child...
the child...
The CHILD...
will always feel the pain.

*Billie Carlson*

## "Why"

Why do you hurt me;
  how could you say, "I Love You" after you hurt me this way?

Bruises may show, but they'll go away;
  the pain you give me can never fade away.

I've never known anyone to treat me as you do;
  your love hurts so badly, yet it's not like its new.

You use to be so caring, I guess it was a disguise;
  as you treated me so hateful my heart was so surprised.

*Brenda C. Colbert Smith*

## Thoughts On My Ninety-Third Birthday

When friends all ask me, curiously,
How does it feel to be ninety-three?

My ready answer, to tell you true,
Just a little bit better than ninety-two.

A little more time to feel alive,
To be one of the others who have survived,

It's a fine excuse when "No" I say
To what I don't want to do anyway.

A little more pleasure from April sun,
More time to finish what I've begun.

A little more wonder at rising moon,
At morning freshness, at blazing noon.

A little more time to mend my ways
In the next three hundred and sixty-five days.

A happy time for I can't resist
To be an incurable optimist.

But a thoughtful time to anticipate
What lies beyond life's closing gate.

So if anyone wants to ask of me,
That's how it feels to be ninety-three.

*Gladys Lawler*

## Zero - In On The Planets

How great is the creation of the heavens!
How great is the creation of the earth!
Out of the void God created great wonders.
Stars in the firmament obey His command.
Who can ever doubt the majesty of the Lord?

Comprehend the volume and size of the sun
which has given light to all mankind.
Taking twenty-three days to revolve one time.
The moon that rules the darkest night.
Jupiter, Mars, Venus, Saturn and the planets
established among the thousand stars
following His Master Plan of equilibrium.

The earth, as we know it, of land and water,
mountains and valleys, which encompasses populations,
a refuge from the vastness of the universe
where in a tiny place I call my home
a fragment of dust scattered here and there
Finding no place anywhere to be heard.

*Professor John Buckland Erdell*

## Time

The hour glass of time is running, no one can stop or turn back time.
How many soul's have been lost in the hourglass of time because they
did not see and had no more time?
How many souls walk and heed not to God
in time and are lost forever in time?
In your life as the hourglass runs down look
to God through His son Jesus and be saved in time.
When the last grain of sand in your life drops,
then you have no more time and you will be lost forever
and ever in time without Jesus,
But with Jesus your hourglass of time can run through eternity in
heaven where the day has no end.
And God's love you will have for all time.
Caution if Satan has his way you will run out of time
and be lost forever in time.
Eternity is a long time.

*Charles Harvey*

## The Generation Gap

I'm not so old I can't remember how we used the radio;
How we enjoyed the music, or a fascinating show.
We could relate with others with the use of our phone,
But televisions, and stereos were at that time unknown.

Though discoveries in our day were surely made by some,
Electric Blankets, and Air Conditioners were meant for days to come.
Freezers, and clothes dryers were destined for our way,
Contact lenses, Pampers and the Pill would appear a later day.

The Dishwashers that we used were a pair of busy hands,
And "fast-foods" were sandwiches made ourselves, when short times
    made demands.
"Making-out" referred to how you came out on a test,
And "Coke" was just a cold drink people used to feel refreshed!

"Aids" were people who helped others, and worked for modest pay,
And men hadn't walked on the moon, as we know they have today.
"Grass" was mowed, and "rock-music was grandma's lullabies,
"Gay" was just a state of mind, not meant to criticize.

"V.C.R.'s", and credit cards have changed our way of living;
We of the past, enjoy at last the pleasures they are giving!
Our youth's use of words, causes us much concern,
The language that they use is one I've never learned!

*Iva J. Smith*

## Unanswered

I heard the mother whisper, my sweet little son
Hungry for food for I have none.

I'm thirsty too mommy, my throat is dry
Can you go pump the well before I die.

Tell me you love me, tell me again
Touch my fevered brow, with your cool hand.

Why do my stomach rumble, like the roaring of waves
Why church every Sunday, to hear God saves.

For he must've forgotten us, for we still weep
Praying to him each night, before we sleep.

Dreaming of many things, to good to come true
Or maybe a miracle before rents due.

You say I'm supposed to love God, for he knows what's best
Because he puts us through all kinds of test.

But when we go home Mommy, will our miracle be waiting there
Will there be a sign he remembered, and unanswered prayer.

*Joyce S. Bryant*

## And That's Just Fine

I cannot see far, I can see near, and that's just fine.
I am blind in one eye, but I still have the other, and that's just fine.
It's real hard living with just one good eye, but I am sure it's
real hard living with one leg, or one arm, or no eyes like some
people do, and that's just fine.

I never ask, "Why me?", I just say this IS me, and that's just fine.
It is a part of me, God gave it to me, and that's just fine.
I do know it was for a reason, and I believe in my heart that
everything happens for a reason, and that God works in very funny
ways, and that's just fine.

Sometimes I wish I could see a little more, a little clearer, but
then I realize that God doesn't want me to see that far or that clear,
and that's just fine.
He wants me to fight for everything that comes my way.  God gave me
a good eye because He knew I'd be just fine.
Just fine, looking out to Him.

*Jennifer Somogyi*

## Death Cannot Hold Me

Do not stand at my grave and weep,
I am not then there; I do not sleep.
The wind around you sings my songs
I am not here; already gone.

Gone to the place I have longed for so long.
No more suffering, tears, disappointments, bygones.

God sat anxiously waiting so long for me.
Jesus, on his right side, had prepared this place, you see
Just for the ones who accepted what he did on Calvary.
His blood spilled willingly to make us free.

If I could only tell you of this glorious place,
Streets of gold, gates of pearl, everyone praising God for His grace;
But nothing can describe it in this old world,
For this is heaven, all beauty unfurled.

My prayer to you is don't wait too long,
Believe on my Jesus, and what he has done.
His love has covered all your sin; open your hearts and take Him in.

*Betty Lanonne Downs*

## Change

Safe within my cocoon of bark and pulp
I am secure.
There is no need to change, no need to grow.

The sun shines forth with enticements and promises of spring.
A life where breezes blow across my new green dress,
And raindrops feed me through a fragile stem.

Forces push and shove and I explode into a spring I do not want.
Confusion swirls around me as I twist and turn in this new world.
I look and see that I am growing and changing.

Others watch.
Who and what will the new me be?

Something deep inside whispers of courage,
And fear falls away like dewdrops off a rose petal.
So I stretch and open to the sun and wind and rain.

Inside, I am still me.

I investigate: up and down and all around me.
I see with new eyes that cannot see the future,
And with a soul that no longer fears change.

*Charlene C. Lee*

## My Teacher

Today my teacher came to me
I am so happy her to see
Even tho' she's stern with me
She reminds me of HOW GOOD I can be

She instructs Mom and Dad about lots of things
I sure like the treats and toys she brings
I have a big brain in my little head
Really that is what my teacher said!

She orders me to "sit" and "stay"
and tho' I don't care to do it today
I can her in her voice
that I do not have much of a choice

After she tells me "okay!"
I love to hear her say "Yea! Yeah!"
"Come" becomes a lot of fun
for I get a treat when I am done

It is sad to say good-bye
but I am tired and need "shut-eye"
I will now dream of what I did learn
and of ALL the treats I will earn!

*Joan C. Stephens*

## Self Appreciation

I can live with myself.
I am some one of value.
I am good and God loves me.
I can feel His love.
I do not have to be afraid of my failings;
All I have to do is recognize them.
I am sorry for any pain I cause my fellow man;
I ask his forgiveness.
I am not surprised when I am misunderstood;
At times, I do not understand myself.
I do not know what my identity entails,
But I am willing to devote myself to the search.
I thrive on words like:
"Thank you"
"Great job"
"You're wonderful"
I want to be approved and appreciated.
I expand, grow and develop in the presence of love.
I adore my God who gathers around Him all those who love Him!
I pray that I may be one of those loved ones so gathered.

*Arthur J. Smith*

## Hieroglyphic

We ate our life and spit out the bones.
I am stumbling over their hard white surfaces,
noticing how your teeth
fell through that flesh.
My feet trip into the remnants of another time,
small dents along a scapula
spell out meaning I cannot decipher.
I do not touch the Braille,
blinded by this hieroglyphic.

Curving walls enclose this place.
The message is written
in a language we are forgetting:
Words I no longer read, left here
for the next unsuspecting creatures
whose body parts may fall together,
their bones clattering against the dark.

Their eyes turn from the walls, look into the future
and when they lean their ears into the warning
the echo of our voices cannot save them.

*Heather Lee*

## Wherever You Are

Wherever you are Dad, I need you,
I am the infant who needs to be held, rocked and sang to.
I am the child who needs to play and have my "Whys'" answered.
I am the teenager who needs a firm but gentle hand to guide me.
I am the adult who needs to share life's everyday experiences.
I need your love, guidance, approval, acceptance, respect, and
    support.
Wherever you are Dad, I need you.

*Dixie L. Hunt*

## A Tree

I am a tree
I begin as a seed
experiencing and feeling as I grow,
and learning to stand on my own
Against the many forces from all around,
that continually try to keep me down.
On the ground below I now have a firm hold,
What I've learned is mine and I'll never let go

To the world I now reach in every direction,
expanding and grasping for every sensation
As my reach is extended I feel my roots grow,
providing me stronger, more permanent hold
I watch the forces below me once trying to keep me down,
becoming ever so smaller far beneath my crown
With plenty of room now I continue to spread out,
for the dream I once had there remains little doubt

SOMEDAY I WILL TOUCH THE SKY
*Darren Ball*

## Song Of Autumn

O leaves, a-hanging from the trees,
I bid ye change your emerald gowns;
Array yourselves in varied hues,
Be clad in reds or golds or browns!

O fruits, close-clustered 'mid the leaves.
I bid ye ripen in the sun;
For juicy grapes, sweet-kerneled nuts,
Are sought with joy by everyone.

O birds, here do you linger still?
Fly southward, feathered minstrels, go!
Soon winter, following my steps,
Will fill the air with swirling snow.

*Carolyn Siefert*

## Master Of Rhetoric

I'm a Master of Rhetoric, I hope you'll agree
I can charm any word into working for me.
I've found that clauses can often be
Made insubordinate semantically.
And this linguistic phenomenally
Can be explained quite simply.
I massage each sentence individually
Until it becomes perfect grammatically.
There are other syntactic foibles that fascinate me,
Such as verb-particles and where they should be.
Hopefully, it is now obvious for all to see
That language transfixes me metaphorically.
The possibilities go on infinitively.
I end here reluctantly
With the advice that grammar rules must always be
Used with caution and certainty.
If they are, you will be
A Master of Rhetoric just like me.

*Barbara Millar*

## Angel of the Earth

Fairies and Angels are all around you,
  I can feel them every where.

And though I don't often see them
  I know that they are there.

Hovering around you, singing a celestial hymn
  happy to be near you, for you are truly one of them!

Sometimes sitting on your shoulder with a little grin,
  one feelings so at home thinking perhaps you are it's twin!

They may be here to keep you company, or maybe just to let you know-
that you just might be one of them, because you have that inner glow!

Angels and Fairies- I'm sure - send
  Special Prayers to you
for there's really a touch of Heaven
  in everything you do.

There is kindness in your soul and love in your heart
and those of us around you are happy to be a part
  of your daily life upon this earth
and our days so happily spent
with you; so dear and near to us- because you were heaven sent!

*Judy Dandridge*

## Poem of Truth

I can see you in the dark
I can feel you in the day
This sudden silence surrounds you
Whether night or light, and even as you fade.
Scenes of mysterious behavior
And with these memories galore
I feel you presence always
As you speak to me oh Lord
Whispers of sorrow
Whispers of hate
Whispers of knowing
Whispering of fate
Gestures of truth, gestures of obtain
Vision of happiness, vision of gain

These sentences are inscribed
And to all eyes appealed,
Carefully objurgate-for these
Things are concealed

GOD

*Anthony Perry*

## Symbols

Firstborn..
I can no longer often be with you...
  so I have chosen this...
    special gift for you...

A ring of precious metal...
  adorned with a tiny...
    intricately shaped dove...

It is only a symbol...
  of God's Holy Spirit...
    with no inherent power...

I trust that its very presence with you...
  will be a constant reminder...
    of His ever present availability...

The circle itself can signify...
  an unending covenant between us...
    to remember that wherever we are...

When we need confident hope and courage...
  that "greater is He that is within me...
    than he that is in the world'.....

*Deanna Skinner*

## Running From The Blues

They say you can't run away from your problems
I can, or at least defer them for later
I just put on my running shoes, and run
Rain or heat wave, it doesn't matter
Where and how long?  I don't care

Cheap therapy
When I'm sad or want to cry
Over stressed at work, or about a girl I want to meet
If I can make the rent this month
When I'm lonely, all I know I'll feel better when I come back

I stopped at a stoplight
There was a guy in a wheelchair
Tried to make eye contact
It was toward the end of my run
Running from my problems
But I tried to put myself in his shoes
I couldn't
A sentimental feeling came over me
A deep feeling for my fellow man
I guess everyone has their problems

*Jon T. Umeda*

## Voyage Of A Lonely Man

I walk down an empty road with barren ground
I cannot go left nor right; faster or slower
I cannot outrun this feeling, nor can I let it pass
It is like a sound I've never heard
I move my lips but no sound appears
My footsteps make no noise; the wind does not blow
How I long to hear a voice but I do not
There is a mist in the air, but it is motionless
It smells of moldy water;
There is a taste on my tongue I cannot distinguish—
Because I taste no other taste to compare it
There is no light nor dark, it is not like sight
But more of a presence without a definite substance;
There is no night or day that stands still;
I feel nothing, not my legs walking
not the sweat on my face, or the rocks under my feet
My surroundings do not change, colors do not vary;
I am aware, but have no control—
I FEEL LIKE A MAN WITHOUT A SOUL

*Jason Mellin*

## No Key

Every knob I turn, the door is locked,
   I can't seem to find a key!
"Won't somebody please hear my cry,
Open these doors, and set me free!"

When I look to my left, there's the poverty door,
I want out, caus' this ain't me.
I look to my right, there's hatred and death,
"Somebody please help me find a key!"

All in front of me, the future looks bleak,
I can see things that just can't be!
Then when I look back, I can't believe,
I didn't take time to make me a key!

All around me I find, I locked my own doors,
Knowing full well I needed a key.
If I had another chance, I would make a change,
No doors would lock, and I would be free!!!

*Florene Rhoads*

## A Moment Like Me

I babysit sometimes.
I clean up all sorts of grimes.
After my cleaning,
I do something with meaning,
I call it a moment like me.

If only people would see,
The way I am, the way I like to be.
My personality is disguised, it get's resized.
Then I spent a moment like me.

Cleaning up all that grime,
Takes hours and hours of time.
People think I'm not me.
I'm really someone I can't be,
That's when I spend a moment like me.

*Jessica McCollough*

## Havens

   She says — I've found many havens, safe and glorious harbors.
I collect them like the shells upon your beaches, dream within them,
float on my back and look up at the blue blue sky, imagining their
meaning arcing out across the waters, misting out across the land
drops of freedom falling down in sweet, sweet universal celebration.
   Wind and water caress the soul,
little oases, little Casablancas,
Moroccos when the whitecolored lights ignite the sky softly.
   Would that this place expand in width and breath,
extending its heart to others reaching back to it across the sea.
Freedom freedom place, all are welcome here:
place of peaceful hearts and hearts come to seek their birthright peace,
place of shrimp and oysters in a land of seajuice adorning.
   Meet me in Morocco on a day of rainy wind, see the fruition of our
desires forming from the plumes of creation, growth and change.
Bless this place and all who set their feet upon this clay
to live within the jubilation of their hearts and let your
blessing be returned to you a thousand times a thousand times
from a universe that knows only that the singing heart
cannot go unheard.

*Amy Marie Beyers*

## The Son My Mother Never Knew

All your lessons taught, it was not your fault, the college education
   I did not get, the perfect son... a role I
did not fit. Christmas day without one present, Mother's Day gifts
I
   forgot; pretty boxes, empty, tied with
a knot, couldn't buy you a brand new house. Hell, couldn't afford
   that pretty blouse, all the things I didn't
do, but still your love rang true.

Oh! mother you love me a lot, but I'm not the son you begot. All the
   times to stop I have tried, all the
tears you have cried, I could never get it right, so to God you prayed
   with all your might.

All that unpaid, borrowed money, you said, "I still love you honey."
   There you held me by your side, there
still I cried and cried. I'm the son you never knew, it's a crack
   addict that's hurting you. Again you prayed
all through the night, "God, please make my son alright." He wiped
   away all your tears, he even took away
your fears. He sent me away to "SPARC" to calm your bleeding heart.

He knows your love for me runs true, so don't be blue... God will
   bring me shining through. Of all the
lessons you did teach, it's to Jesus I should reach. I'm the son you
   never knew, I'm the son God made brand
new, and the price He said I must pay, it's only to get on my knees
   and pray.

*Curtis Poole*

## I'm Sorry

I'm sorry for the way I hurt you so,
I didn't mean it, but you still let me go.
I wish I could be with you today,
and say the things I meant to say.
But you got a new love, that I know,
But I'm sadder than you'll ever know.
I know I'll never forget your love,
but I took it for granted
and now your gone.
So if you ever read this one
day, I hope you know
"I'm sorry in every way and
I still love you so, and I'm
here every day if you want
to know."

*Amanda Murphy*

## Carefree Youth

In the days of old
I didn't search for gold.

I walked along, kicked a stone,
Climbed a tree, gave my dog a bone.

I wore no shoes, seldom combed my hair;
Just enjoyed nature, the sun, and the air.

I sailed a boat, and flew a plane, and even made a kite;
And Mom and Dad were always there to see that things were right.

Those were the days of carefree youth with happiness untold;
Unconcerned with daily strife and how much goods were sold.

Now, Father Time has aged a bit and life's problems I must share.
I have a duty to perform and a family that needs care.

I enjoy my chosen work and would feel sad indeed
If I could not provide the things that my family needs.

Yet, in the course of daily toil I sometimes feel despair
And long for those youthful days and for that carefree air.

My feeling is I'm not unique, of this I have no proof,
That most grown folks from time to time long for carefree youth.

*Gordon S. Neff*

## Sonnet XX

The problem now to solve is how to wait.
I do not wish for life to pass me by.
The day advances, it is growing late
Indeed for any answer to my cry.
Shall I with dignity and grace serene
And cool pretending of indifference
Await an answer from the great machine
Of life, or speak out in my own defense
And put my case again?  Does no one care?
And would it be unseemly to protest,
To curse and scream and cry and tear my hair
Demanding life to grant my wish at best,
Or tell me firmly, finally no at worst
And send me out, no more with hope accurst.
### *Jan Reagin*

## Live Or Die?

I've never seen the world outside of this little womb.  But
I don't know if I ever will.  I'm only three months old, and
there's talk of aborting me.  I'm not sure what abortion is.
From what I've heard it means killing a baby.  That baby is
me.  I have no way to say, "Hey, I'm alive."  Even if I did, would
they listen?  This answer I do not know.  Because I do not know
how they think.  Do they think I don't want this child, I'm not
ready to care for this unwanted child?  Or are they thinking
this child, innocent and pure, do we let it have a chance at
life?  There's no way for me to know what they decide.  Except
if I live or die.  If I see another day, then there's still a
chance for me.  But if a die today, then none of this mattered.
Not even me.  Let me give this final plead, if you ever have
to decide.  Let the child live, that child is apart of tomorrow.
A tomorrow that may never come, if people continue to kill
unborn babies like me.
### *Jessica Snider*

## Let Me Be!

Let me be a servant LORD and use me every day
I don't know where or how but I'm sure you'll find a way;
Perhaps a lamp lighter I could be to spread your light o'er
    land and sea
Where all may walk with open eyes and arms outstretched to thee.
Let me be a soldier LORD in the army of the right
With you always in my heart, your word my guiding light.
If this should be my lot for here and now——
I'll gladly do them all with you to show me how;
So heavenly FATHER, GOD of all, whatever your plan may be
PLEASE let me be——
    All that you expect of me.
### *Aritha Pinion Thurber*

## The Calling

When I was a child of about seven or eight,
I dreamt of a kingdom with pearly gates.
Fields overflowing with tiger lilies and turtle doves,
Against a backdrop of warmth delicately laced with love.
A place filled with the laughter of people near and far
Glowing with enough energy to light every star.
And as I laid sleeping on that cold, dark night,
I prayed that I could stay there with all of my might.
But alas, I searched yet could find no place for me,
For at that particular time, it just wasn't meant to be.
So now I lay in my bed when I'm tired and alone,
And wait for my Father to summon me Home.
### *Tracy Runnels*

## Myself

I don't understand all these weird feelings,
I don't understand why the world sometime does terrible things
My heart is torn from things that have happened, but I just don't
    understand how to deal with it.
I'm scared to death for fear of my life, fear of family and
    friends as they go out of sight
I don't want anything to happen and I always say I want to be
    first, but what if I'm not,
My heart may just burst.
Its hard to go each of my life, after all the bad dreams that
    fear me from the light.
As I follow this light in my dream, it scares me
    because I'm just a typical teen.
As I walk this light, I knew it was me, because I can see
I don't understand how to let go of people
I know I'm in the real world and I have to deal with it, but why me?
I have all these feelings that I don't express, I just
    keep them inside as they start building stress.
One day, I'll understand and when I do, I'll try
    not to be scared of losing you.
### *Jessica Ryan Florio*

## Lonely Hearts

Last night I dreamed of our good times, that used to be a part of me.
    I dreamed I held you in my arms, the way it was meant to be.
But all at once I woke myself, and came back to reality.
    I didn't hold you in my arms, but only a lonely memory.
My thoughts drifted to our good times, and the way our life used to be
    We were young and so in love, that time was eternity.
I dreamed of our good times, the way it used to be.
    But all I have is a lonely heart filled with memories.
Along the way we broke up the thought occurred to me.  When so
    in love
this wasn't meant to be.
    When I left we drifted apart.  I didn't even leave you a picture of
me.  You found someone else and I became a memory.
    A memory lives in a lover heart.  And you will always be with me.
I will always have you in my heart.  And love you in my memory.
### *Jose Francisco Martinez*

## Please Say You Love Me

Everything I do, everything I say,
I feel as if I'm only pushing you away.
And even if we stay apart,
Just remember you'll always be in my heart.

You come and go as you please,
I know in my heart your not thinking of me.
I know where you are and its not with me,
Please, please say you love me.
### *Jessica Ware*

## Her Golden Wings

As I close my eyes at night
I feel her warmth and her light.
She is the protector of my soul
And she stays close to me I know.
As I drift to sleep there is no woe
but my spirit knows it can go
to heaven hand in hand with her light
it shows like a beacon in the snow.
Alone I'm not ever my angel knows
she protects me from my foes.
Happiness, love and a long life she brings
and God smiles down, I know, on her golden wings!
### *Joanie Zammito*

## Strange Thoughts

It seems that lately my life has come to a halt.
I feel it's the daydreams that are constantly in my head,
that sometimes seem like nightmares instead.

I started feeling this way awhile back, and I'm
certain my mind is still intact, tho hard as I try to
push the thoughts away, still they come growing stronger
every day.

I fear all too soon what I think about will come true.
So, I'm writing this down in hopes that I'll find
it's just my overactive mind, caused by boredom and
too much time.

*Cynthia Louise Hinton*

## I Am The Desert

I feel the windstorm's violent thrust
I feel the desert's wind dust

I feel the animals walk on my body
I feel the Mono River go back and forth on my body

I smell the hot desert air
I smell the fumes from up above

I smell the fresh cactus fruit
I smell the cactus flowers as they open

I see the sunset beyond the Red Rock
I see the hawk with his wings outspread

I see the wet mirage in front of me
I see the snake eating the lizard on the rocks

I taste the rain that falls into my mouth
I taste the dusty sand that blows into my mouth

I taste the cactus fruit as they fall from the cactus
I taste the cactus fruit juice that drips from the fruit

I hear the space shuttle overhead
I hear the coyotes howl from in the rocks

I hear the tumbleweed stampede along the side of my arm
I hear the wind blow through my hair.

*Casey Jenkins*

## My Will of Intangibles

To My Mother with gentle eyes
  I give the never ending skies.
To My Father with stern face
  I give the much needed gift of grace.
To My Brother with good intentions
  I give the many "Thank You" I never mention.
To My Older Sister with silent mouth
  I give the songs the birds sing as they fly south.
To My Younger Sister with unusual ways
  I give the sun that shines on all the days.
To My Grandparents who know so much
  I give the highest mountain peak the clouds only touch.
Most of all to everyone listed above
  I give my everlasting love.

*Christine A. Carlo*

## Untitled

"When we compete in life's big arena
Old Father time will be our foe,
Though we bravely fight with skill and emotion,
We have lost the fight before we know."

"While playing our part upon life's stage
under the master's strict direction,
If we improve our role to the very last act,
We shall surely act with great perfection."

*Hughie Dale*

## The Spotlight

The light shines on me over yonder
I glide across the stage, but the light seems to wonder
I try to catch it, but I constantly miss
And now I hear the crowd, its starting to hiss
I jump into the light, but then it leaves
All I hear now is the crowd heathing
I try to sing to calm the crowd
Oh my god, they are starting to get loud
Maybe if I dance, maybe then they'll relax
Maybe I'm wrong, for not even one clap
Why is it that when the light is so bright
I always seem to miss it and can't dance just right
I'm trying so hard, nobody seems to agree
Thank God it's only a dream, a dream about me.

*Jason Badian*

## "Love Returns"

My heart seemed black, love was war
I had no idea there could be so much more.
How was I to know? How could I believe?
I just couldn't see the forest for all the trees!

In my dreams, one was never so kind
so gentle and sweet as the one on my mind.
Is he real? How can it be?
As I open my eyes, now I can see.

I'm afraid to fall so hard
What if he fades? It would break my heart.
My heart is warm now, soft and tender
I can't help but love, give my soul and surrender.

You see my eyes gleaming, only smiles abound
Darkness is lost and sunshine is found.
The love I feel makes all fears go away
Yes, a bit cautious, but I want him to stay!

*Elizabeth E. Helsel*

## Diagnosis

After careful study and deliberation,
I have come up with this configuration,
That I am happiest when you are around,
Always up and seldom down,
Usually seen with a smile on my face,
Happiest member of the human race,
Walk with a spring in my step,
Comical, lively and full of pep,
There is just one thing I did not figure out,
A little niche in my mind that is shadowed in doubt,
Is if this feeling is because of you,
Or is it the love that I feel for you,
I guess it is a combination of them both,
And this I would swear to under oath,
And if you do not know who I am speaking to,
Just look in the mirror, I am speaking to you.

*Garth Puckerin*

## "Glances"

Back and forth, again and again
Piercing each others' mind
Swimming in oceans of blue-green and brown
Lightning flashes and dances in their reflecting pools
Thoughts are stirred and the temperature rises
A gleaming fire ripples the deep waters
The undertow pulls them under
Drowning in each others' black seas
Begging and pleading for death,
Acceptance, and forgiveness

*Henry DeLeon II*

## Alone

Blackness, dampness all around.
I have the fear that I will never be found.
I wish that someone would have known,
that I was left here all alone.

Some guys dumped me down into this well.
Why they did it I cannot tell.

I sit and scream for someone to help.
I know its worthless, but I took what was dealt.

I cry sometimes, but its all right,
no ones around, no one in sight.

I'm just fourteen years old,
left here alone, cold.

I wish at least someone was here,
just to talk to and share my fear.

I won't die I'm too young,
I need water to wet my tongue.

All I can do is pretend,
I will survive my life won't end.....

**Gala Stephens**

## Garage

As I enter my second domain
I hear the rattling of the big door
The coldness of the bare wind that runs
through the holes that made before I was there.

But soon all this is forgot
Now that I have started to create something.

**Jared N. Thompson**

## Tears From Above

Pitter-patter, pitter-patter
I hear the sounds and want to cry.
Rain reminds me of tears I've shared.
It reminds me of times when no one's cared.
Sometimes I try to laugh away
The tears and pain of yesterday.
Yet I don't always succeed.
And this is why I wish to heed
My own warning on this matter
When the sounds go pitter-patter, pitter-patter.

**Carlea Alfieri**

## I, Superman

Superman was I, so I thought
I jumped off my top bunk
I should've naught
I anxiously awaited to glide through the air
To my disbelief my super powers weren't there
I slammed into the ground, which I fell upon
This confrontation, gravity had won
Yet I wore that cape for what seemed like years
What stopped my reign as superman were my
Mom's razor sharp shears
She would cut off part of my cape from day to day,
for any reason;
Maybe she was embarrassed to be seen with me
Always running and jumping about
With my cape on me but none the less
I wasn't superman or ordinary, somewhere in between

**Edward Baird**

## How Much You Mean To Me

How much you mean to me
I just don't know where to start
My love for you grows greatly from deep inside my heart
You are my everything the woman I adore
For all you have given me I want to give you more
The times we have shared together
Have been the best moments of my life
For I would like to extend them and
Have you become my wife
I give my heart and soul to you and
All the stars in the sky
For you to answer my only wish to never say goodbye
I can't explain in words how much your love means to me
Forever in your heart is where I long to be
Your an Angel sent from heaven a gift from God above
Given to me to share your special World of Love
You are my happy ending my fairy tale come true
Our beautiful future together forever to be with you

**Bob Seidenschmidt**

## Thank You

I just wanna Thank you, "my mother"
I just wanna Thank you, "my father"
Thank you for staying in my life.
When I was sick and it looked as if
I wouldn't get well. I wanna thank you both
for staying in my life.
When I was all alone and friends and
family left me you both stayed by my side.
And I just wanna Thank you.
But most of all I wanna to Thank my
"Heavenly Father" who stayed with me
day and night, through all the pain and
suffering. I just wanna thank "Him" for
being in my life.

**Eldrin Sloan**

## Locked In Crystal

It lay there all shattered, broken and torn apart.
I knew I should not let you play with it, right from the start.

Others had played with it and broken it before.
Now I sit and stare at its pieces, just lying on the floor.

So many times it has been played with just like a toy.
It gave me and others pleasures, into my life brought much joy.

It's been stomped on and walked on, oh so many times.
I'll not fix or put it back together, no, not this time.

But where can I put it, in what will it go?
I'll hide it in something, where it will never show.

Then my eye caught your crystal necklace, and I knew just what to do.
Because I allowed you to break it, I would give it forever to you.

I picked up the necklace, placed every piece inside
Then for hours I just sat there, and I cried.

I only hope you keep it, never give it away.
It's yours now forever, to do with what you may.

Throw it in a drawer, let it just collect dust.
But whatever you do, it's now in your trust.

For you will never know, no matter how far we are apart
That you are the keeper, the keeper of my heart.

**Janice Bryant**

## Gift From God

From the moment you were conceived
I knew You were a gift from God.
The first time I felt you move inside me,
I knew you were a gift from God.
The day you were born and I heard your cry and saw your
pink, round face, complete with dimples,
I knew you were a gift from God.
The first time we nursed and we both fumbled from inexperience,
I knew you were a gift from God.
The first time you looked up and smiled at me,
I knew you were a gift from God.
The first time I heard your musical laugh as I wiped your bottom,
I knew you were a gift from God.
The first time I had to leave you all day
I knew you were a gift from God. The day you were baptized among
family and friends, I knew you were a gift from God.
The day I learned you would be a one and only,
I knew you were truly my special gift from God.
And as you grow bigger, wiser and more loving each day,
I know you are a special gift from God, for all to enjoy.

*Helen M. Ritchie*

## Tears On My Cheek

The day is here to end my life because something's coming over me.
I know that I will not live to see tomorrow.
This is the beginning of the end.
Sweat chilling cold as I make my death unfold.
Wait for the sign to pull the trigger of death.
I know the end is finally here.
The voices have made me commit this sin.
I know the time has come to fill my brain with lead.
My life is finally done.
As I load this clip I think has my life been fulfilled?
Have I completed my dreams?
Then I think of my endless pain and think "AH HECK I CAN'T
STAND IT."
I went and took my gun put it to my head.
I shut my eyes really tight as I think of my last might in this
unforgiving world.
I thank God for a great life and hate him for my suffering.
I shove the clip put the cold steel to my lip.
As I pull the trigger I know I'll live no longer.
I remember my life as it flashes before my eyes.
I see it has been full of lies, no one has loved me, there is no God.
As I hit the floor my love walks in the door, she holds my head as
she realizes I am dead.
For this was my final week. I realize this as a tears fall on my cheek.

*Jon Roop*

## Death! Happiness

He's dead! I moaned.
He's gone my husband, I loved.
So dear and strong, "Oh God," I cry, with sorrow
There can never be a happy tomorrow
A door bangs.
Mom is the cry a runny of feet.
God bless you,
I sigh as I rise to greet my children fair
I will go on I will be strong.
I will care knowing he will watch over us
He will be there.

*Gertrude De Luccia*

## Jungle Gym At The Park

A child asked, "What is in a park?" With excitement I answered,
I know what is in there. I said there are swings, slides, and
jungle gyms. There are birds chirping and kids playing. A breath
of fresh air blowing the wind, tons of trees fill the park field.

There's dirt below me, and beautiful green grass all around me.
There are more swings and a small balance beam, they even have a
workout area. People drive by in their cars, some stop to play
at the park, while others just go right on by.

Sometimes there isn't anyone in the park and it is so quiet,
while other times it is really noisy. It is mostly sunny, and very
hot. Sometimes it is cold and cloudy, while other times it is
stormy and rainy.

People like to have picnics under the pavilion, or sometimes they
like to have them on a blanket sitting on the grass. Children
chase each other around, playing Duck-Duck Goose or Ring Around the
Rosie. You can come when you wish, and stay till hours on end.

As it gets later everyone leaves, I grab my stuff to leave. I
remembered what I had seen, the trees, park equipment, dirt, and
the grass. I heard the birds chirping, I felt the wind blowing.
So, I said again to the child, this is what is in a park.

*Jennifer Williams*

## Unrealistic Goal

Has anyone seen my snowman?
I left him standing here, on the lawn,
Amidst the fallen snow,
With his eyes of coal all aglow.

He had confided his greatest desire,
To bask in the sun until a tan he'd acquire
But, now alas, I do not see him around,
I wish I knew where he could be found.

With his top hat and no attire,
Clad only in a belt, glimmering with fictitious sapphire.
My beloved snowman so big, fat and around.
Did he get his wish and tan to brown?

I wonder where my snowman has gone.
Could he have rolled into town,
Gone astray, or just melted away,
Somewhere on Cape Cod Bay?

*Jennie Sikura Meshulam*

## Flying or Flight of Fancy

I soar above the clouds and think of how
I left the earth as
I left your warm embrace,
It is so beautiful up here in the sky
Aloof, so very high.
But with you on the earth it is warm
It is comfortable.
And sometimes - it is ecstasy.
A thousand white cushions
That is what I see
As I look out of my window.
They look so beautiful.
I wonder how they feel.

*Dolores Burt*

## Moonbeams

When moonbeams shine at the end of the day
I lie awake alone and see your face
I wish you were here with all my might
But I see only shadows in the moonlight

When fall is gone and winter appears
You haven't returned and there is nothing but fear
That you won't return and be only mine
If you would, everything will be just fine

Open her eyes that she may see in my heart
All the suffering I've done since we've been apart
The moonbeams tell me she is suffering too
I pray that she will be returning soon

Open her ears that she may hear
Words of love for her ears alone
Open her heart, let there be no more tears
Let us be happy together for at least fifty years

*Alice Johnson*

## My Own Reason

I like snow, I like flowers planted in a row.
I like flowers for many reasons.

I cut some flowers and placed them in a vase.
I then mixed the flowers so they would look pretty.
I took a petal of a flower and held it in my hand.
It felt as light as a snowflake.
I then watched the petal fade away.
It was so beautiful that it made me sad to see it
depart from it's bouquet.

I sang as I tossed that petal and the rest
of that bouquet into my garden in hope
to see the offspring of that petal grow.

*Frances Dunn*

## My Motorcycle and Me

I fly through the air, not a worry on my mind,
I look for the ground I can not find,
I look to the side of me as my opponent waves high,
I find the ground first, I wave to him bye.

We race to the turn, who will get there first?
My power kicks in, I get there first!
We race through the corners, jumps and straights,
He is on the side of me, I know his face,
I hope my boot does not unlace, because I am about to win the race.
He speeds on the side trying to pass, but it is too late, I have
   kicked his a**!

The race is over, we go home to rest,
My motorcycle and me, we are still the best.
The race completed and we have won,
My motorcycle and me know it was a job well done.

*Aram V. Khatchaturian*

## One More Day

In your absence I sob
my mind filled with questions
lost to truth
hoping your love is true
though my heart becomes pale with memory of love lost
and as I fade to dreams I wish for just one more day
one more day in your arms without fear
one more day without pain
at least one more day with you.

*Brian Ray*

## The Sunset

I love to see the sunset it's pleasing to my eye,
I love to point out all the colors in the radiant, spacious sky.

As I look at the sunset it reminds me of how beautiful heavens
going to be,
When we go there to sing praises to the Lord, and live
eternally.

It's like our lives, it's incalculable, changing all the time,
It makes me feel so good inside to know this life is mine.

No words can explain, no vocabulary you could use,
To describe the colors the sunset yields, the deep greens, bright
reds and many blues.

*Ashley L. LeVeck*

## For My Three Boys

When I was young and not long ago
I never dreamed I'd be the mother of three boys always on the go

I cook, clean and pick up toys
My ears are filled with the never ending noise

There was always time to rock and sing
When they grow up they call you "mean"

The dirty hands upon my neck
The love and sweetness of wet kisses and pecks

Through the tears and fears
The pressure of peers

You know Mom's there with hugs and kisses to give
Always room in my heart to forgive

All that I do all that I say
I'm wishing you'll grow to be good men one day

I wonder where my dreams all went
When all is quiet you know your boys are heaven sent

Never forget there's no love like your mothers
Remember your family, friends and brothers

*Debbie White*

## Why?

"Nobody said it would be easy"
I never said
Anybody said it would be easy
And
I never said
It would be easy
I had always thought it had been easy for me
For a hundred, a thousand, a million others it has been
But in retrospect
What has come to me unearned?

Yes,
At least I have you
And, yes,
At least we have found each other
And, yes,
I love you, too
But
It's terrible that I had to find you
This way.

*Gagendra P. Kampta Jr.*

## The Wall

Weird paint splashed on the wall.
I picture red, green, black, and blue.
I also hear it splat, hitting the wall.

I pick up another bucket
And realize I have four more walls to cover.

Frustrated because of my situation,
Thinking only if I hadn't gone to that costing war
I wouldn't be this way.
Then the thought of guests coming to my house
Appeared in my head.
I didn't care because they would be the only ones to see it,
And I won't, because I'm blind.

*Byron Mitchell*

## Forever Comes Too Soon

I've loved you since I can't remember when
I promised I would love you forever
I never thought forever wouldn't last
Now you have gone and I am left with the past.
My memories are very clear of the first time we met
I was too shy to let you know I cared
Afraid I'd lose you and regret it
Little did I know you felt the same
And was also too shy to admit it
I'd look in your eyes and my heart would smile
I had felt your love for me for quite a while
It took us a long time to say the words
I don't know who said them first
When you told me you would love me always
I thought my heart would burst
We promised our love forever
But forever came too soon
It was like watching the sun come up in the morning
And with a blink of the eye you're looking at the moon

*Betty J. Howard*

## "I Love Not Wisely, But Too Well"

God said; "Take care of house and household".
I reach out my hand, only to find it empty.
Why is my load so heavy, are we not two, am I just one!
Are the answers already behind me?
I love not wisely, but too well!
I eat, sleep, see, and feel; I know how rich God made me.
Where then, is this abundance of love and beauty?
Has it strayed, will it be back, is it gone!
Are we not two, am I just one,
Are the answers already behind me?
I love not wisely, but too well!
Am I the fruit you seek each day, or will you be sorely tempted
To sample the forbidden fruit?
Will your name abandon me, or will you take care of
house and household?
My load is heavy, my hands empty, and I feel so alone.
Are we not two, am I just one,
Are the answers already behind me?
I love not wisely, but too well.

*Doris L. Carol Griffin*

## Helplessness

Unharnessed energy
Rebound... bound... bounding... endlessly...
Searching for a current to direct its charge.

Housed in animality
Contained, no outlet, spiraling...ing...ing...
Building ever upward to explosive limits.

Bang!

*Donna J. Zine*

## I Now Have Mercy From Him

As I lay and wonder what my sanity is,
I realize how slow your mind mends,
yet the mocking heart is no different.
Embedded are terrifying memories he still sends.

The bruises within are creating life long scars.
Beauty finally fills my eyes,
my ears hear no more lies,
my body no longer brutalized,
and my mind no longer hypnotized.

Trust I finally seek.
My love is no longer dim.
My heart finally speaks,
because I now have mercy from him.

*Debra McRaven*

## Happiness

"Hallelujah," sings my soul.
I rejoice, for now I know
I know the secret of happiness.
For now and forever - nothing but pure bliss.

Happiness is you.
Happiness is true,
If you let it be.
Let it shine from me.

It lies inside.
Happiness don't hide.
Come out sing
"Hallelujah!"
Happiness - what a wonderful thing.

*Britta Dahlke*

## Untitled

I remember wooden toys on top of warming radiators.
I remember Crayola crayons in the colors of a rainbow.
I remember chalk boards and cork boards and the smell of Elmer's glue,
I remember my first Stuart Hall notebook,
and how it felt so new.
I remember lunch lines and lunch trays, reusable forks and knives.
I remember Miss Osborne,
and the color of her eyes.
I remember recess and swing sets,
I remember having fun.
I remember all these things,
how could I ever forget,
the good times, the bad times, the special friends I met.
It was my childhood, days I thought would last,
but the days turned into years,
and the years went by so fast.
Now I'm in my adult years, and I really can't complain,
because I can remember,
These memories still remain.

*Jack Tully*

## Visitor

An old man moved inside of me.
Living there aching, complaining
An though I bid him leave, he remains
Saying that he has no place to go.

So here he lives, taking over more each day
Now I cannot make him go.
He looks so much like my father did
That I have made friends with him.

*Daniel Levin*

## Untitled

Just a victim choking on life.
I remember the sound.
I relinquish all my thoughts to you
    even though I am reluctant to do so.
Obsession, compulsion; these are my
    infections festering.
The city of disarray.  I've sucked the poison.
I've tattooed the mosaic to my soul.
So numb, so dumb.
Frozen rain falling like broken glass.
Now it cuts and burns and heals
    the incubus.
I now pronounce you man and life.

*Edward Plank*

## Cry of the Dolphin

Though I'm in captivity I wish I could be free.
I remember when I could look up high and see the
beautiful sky.

Being fed is okay.
But I'd rather hunt for my own prey.

Humans try to make me do right.
I usually try to give them a fright.

Doing tricks for fish all day.
I'd really rather be free and play.

Children tapping on the glass, as they pass class by class.
My closest friend is a whale.
We both feel like we're in jail.

I have to go do tricks right now.
Who knows maybe I'll get free some way, some how.

*Crystal Borelli*

## The Change

I remember the change well.
I remember when I cried 'cause I hurt my knee playing games,
Then I remember when I cried 'cause someone hurt my heart playing
games.
I remember growing up with Daddy.
Then I remember me and Daddy growing apart.
I remember that special pact I made with my best friend that
we'd always be together.
Then I remember when she moved away.
I remember my favorite tree that I'd play in all day long.
Then I remember when they tore it down.
I remember when Grandpa used to rock me to sleep.
Now the rocking chair is empty.
Sometimes I wish I had never grown up.
Then I remember I still have a lot of growing up to do.

*Emily Szopinski*

## Why

Lost summer nights by bright city lights.
I sat by the phone - waiting... for her call home
those wasted days - I waited in vain -
waiting for the call, that never came
I never thought... she would leave me alone -
smashing my dreams, of a happy home.
But left me she has, for another man.
The wound so deep, I thought it might never heal.
She's stolen my zeal I felt for life,
now all I feel is pain and strife
why has she gone and left me like this?

*Colin Scholl*

## Untitled

While waiting on a wharf in Crescent Bay
I saw a great gray whale come up to spray,
And as the crabs were biting slow that day
We spoke awhile to while the time away.

He said, "I've traveled four times 'round the world.
Love echoes in my heart a songsome girl.
I feel her out there, waiting on the waves.
I've chased her over halfway to my grave.

"I hear your sailors sing their songs of land.
Their loving chants I never understand.
I've come to think of swimming up on beach,
In hope to find in death what life can't reach.

"Cast off despair," said I.  "I've felt like thee";
Alone and wand'ring starless in the sea;
And found my love.  She's here in Crescent Bay,
Her sunlit smile now never far away.

"Those sailors whom you've heard, they talk to me
And sing of longing for your salty sea.
Take it from one who knows, take not to shore.
Go swim the wavy waters eight times more!

*Erik Johnson*

## Wondering

Once as I sat near the crashing sea on a lonesome point of land,
I saw a silent ship go by with her sails set to the wind.

She skimmed o'er the crests,
and she dipped to the troughs,
Like a gull gliding high on the wing
And she went with the drift of the stormy waves,
as a paper tossed in the wind.

The wind came up, and the tide dropped down,
and the sky grew black as night.
As the ocean crashed and roared and churned,
and then once more there was light.
The sun shone down, thru a vent in the clouds,
and spread abroad its light.
And the gulls cries sang thru the sunlit air, as they
wheeled in their soaring flight.

And I searched with my eyes the ocean wide, for a
sign of that ship sailing free.
But all I could see as I gazed toward the deep,
was the sun, the sky, and the sea.

*David Michael McRae*

## No Fear

As I catch the inbounds pass and listen to the loud roars of cheers,
I say to myself, "I have no fear."
When I cross the half court line, the defender looks for the steal,
I try to make my move, but it bounces off my left heel.
Loose ball, loose ball, yells the players on the sideline,
I pick up the ball and scream, "Get off this one's mine!"
I look for the pass, the shot, or the three,
Which one should I pick my minds screaming at me!
I get my feet set and just let the shot go
Do you think I have fear?  Na, "I don't think so!"

*Daren Anthony Lake*

## Each Passing Day

Each morning that I look into your eyes,
  I see a beautiful sun arise.
I wear your love, and they say it shows,
  a feeling few people ever come to know.
Being sure this love is for real,
  burns a brilliance impossible to conceal.
I feel your warmth each passing day,
  a pleasure like this was made to stay.
Happiness fills each long day through,
  because I know you love me too.

  *Donna M. Rignola*

## Room Full of Memories

As I walk into my room full of memories, what do I see?
I see mementos from the past, all neatly placed by loved ones
There to remind "remember me."

The doll Dad bought, when I was 40 years old.
Because when I was young, there was no money to hold.
The dishes that my mom, gathered one by one.
Each trip we took, the fun we shared, to purchase just that
perfect stone.  The old fiddle that my dad learned to play.
Lies silent, today.

The echoes of memories of times gone past.
Of the cherry gatherings in the kitchen of holidays last.

All gone now, except for mementos in my memory room.
But precious yet, hoping someday to join them soon.
Birthdays, christmas, holidays cheer.
I'll never forget, for each was so dear.

My memory room is all I have now.
But, they live year to year with me somehow.

The sounds my mind recalls when I listen close...at nightfall.

It pleases me so..when those I love so dear.
Still remain with me in my memory room here.

  *Fran Cook*

## Changes In Views

As I rest beside his sepulcher
I see my Life with a new perspective.
He was a mortal, and I was a mortal,
but now he has gone to eternity
to join the messengers of God, and I am alone.
He was my Life, my reason for existing,
but now he has his seraphim, and I have myself.
But alas!  It is not as foreboding
as I thought it would be.  I feel free.
I can serve myself, instead of another!
I don't have to reach anyone's expectations,
Except mine own!  I may do what I wish,
not what another wishes!  Oh glorious Life!
I am finally free because
He is floating down Phlegethon
down in the nether world,
hand in hand with the Serpent.

  *Allison Wysaski*

## Invitation

Come with me to the roof tops,
Let our feet dance upon the newly-laid shingles
Let the spirit of youth and childhood
Enchant your Heart.
Have the tar squeeze between your toes
And let the heat bouncing off the shingles
Warm your heart.

  *Devin Culbertson*

## "Mourn Of A Tear"

I love and cry with mortal eyes,
I see the lies and I agonize,
but the one hope that I do not see
is when my tattered soul's set free.

I follow my heart with nothing to gain,
with no enlightenment, just driven insane,
And what life has made me realize
is that with foolish hopes I am dehumanized

I struggled with reason my love repressed,
I pray to the God within my breast.
From a wounded spirit worn so thin,
May I please heal the scars within.

Misery lives in thee,
Save me from my own tyranny,
Sanctity let me free,
Let death be my liberty.

With all my lost hopes and all my lost dreams,
May I have just but one of life's redeems.
It is not fame, or fortune, or power I seek,
It is that I find love in this world of the meek.

  *Craig Hewitt*

## I See

I see the sky, the sun, the moon.
I see the shadows of the trees at noon.
I see the ocean, the waves, the sea.
I see the valleys where a sea could be.
I see the mountains the cliffs, the peaks.
I see the caves that people don't seek.
I see the stars, the planets, that darkness of the night.
I see the life God created with little light.
What do you see when you look at our world?
I see the trash that people hurled.
So save our world before it dies,
So our children won't see it with tearful eyes!

  *Chandra Hacker*

## Angels In The Sun

As I look out my window
I see two angels in the sun
Frolicking, bounding having such fun

One is dark and tan
One is kissed by the sun
It would be hard to say who is the favored one

Their voices rise and can be heard by all
Its summertime and they are having a ball

Two free spirits soaking up the rays
We wish this is the way we could all spend our days.

This is a sight I love to watch everyday
My beloved Yorkies hard at play

  *Jan Hounshell*

## Rain

As I sit in the rain, I think of you
Of all the wonderful things we used to do
I think of your hair, your eyes, the way you walk
Your beauty, your charm, the way you talk
And then I think of the time we spent together
Oh God, why couldn't it have lasted forever?
As I sit in the rain, I think I'll never love again
For I'd be thinking of you, and to me that's a sin
As I sit in the rain, it becomes quite clear
That the water on my face is not rain, but tears

  *Dan Schmidt*

## The First Time

The first time your lips met mine
I should have known that what I'd find
Would set my soul free to soar far beyond heavens door.
A passion that burned so hot it could melt the coldest heart.
Time is stopped when I'm with you
Your eyes are all I need to see, and your love is all need to feel.
Your touch is what keeps me warm at night,
And your reality is what me from my dreams.
Each day dawns for you my dear,
Like the night falls so that you will draw me near.
And maybe somewhere behind your eyes I might find
That you felt the same way,
The first time your lips met mine.

*Julie Cotner*

## Time

Time, time, time come heal my wounds
I sit here in this dark cold empty room
The clock is ticking on the shelf
As I sit here by myself

Time, time, time come ease my pain
I've got to get these feelings out of my brain
I remember times gone by
And it makes me just break down and cry

Time, time, time don't make me wait
You've got to help me now 'fore it's too late
Why she left me I don't know
What made her have to go

Time, time, time don't do me wrong
These feelings that I've got are just too strong
I'm waiting until the time when
I will feel complete again

Time, time, time you keep slipping away

*Charles Crandall*

## Anyone

I sit here to ponder, why this hell?
I sit here to try to remove this shell of pain and self-defeat.
The lack of pain is an immeasurable treat
Hell is not some strange place
'Tis here with another face, a new dimension of loneliness
Much like here, without guess; hell is inside my mind
A deep dark corner, far too easy to find
A place of loneliness and fear
A place full of one distorted mirror, of reality led astray.
I retreat there many a day; 'tis no worse than reality.
The pain is in breaking out, in becoming free.
Four walls, ever pressing out all comfort held inside
Yet to this place I come to hide
For it is worse outside, where I am alone to face the mirror
And people who are filled with hate.
Death! Please come to me! Open up you eternal gate!
For here happiness is gone many a day, yet here
I let my mind stray to my hell of distortion and pain
Again, it is an endless chain. I need your help
to break out; hear my beckon, hear my shout!
Anyone!

*Gary D. Feldon*

## Untitled

Dark nights seem endless; for the day holds no light
In the shadow or a broken heart.
The soul weeps for the mercy of time for only time
Can ease the pain, yet the lingering shadow remains.

*David L. Robinson*

## "Copy"

As I sit and watch the river flow
I sometimes wonder where the waters go
Is it up the hill or down?
Does it race thru streets or towns?
Who has control as to where it goes?
Not you or I, I am sure of that
So, it is evident there is some
one greater than me or you.
Let us begin to be basic again
and see the image of God in you and me.
Made in His image there is a
river that flows way, way deep
in the heart of our souls.
Let's open our mind, heart and soul and watch
and wait for the river that flows.
The river of love thru the blood
of Christ that binds us together
so that we might truly become the image of Christ.
So flow on river, river of my soul,
swell and swell that I might grow.

*Gloria Jean Marshall*

## An Ode to Minimalism

Once while strolling through an art exhibit,
I spied a painting of a dot, entitled minimalism.
"Mimimalism?" I asked my artist wife. "Simple,"
She replied, "one dot on a canvass - a lonely pimple."

"It's the least one can paint in a picture," she continued,
"A dot or a line, a minimum of minimums,
Abstract art in a minimal style.
"Stop," I cried, "let me ponder awhile."

I've thought of this dot or pimple, long and hard.
I must lack some aesthetic sense, or worse I think,
I'm woefully missing the point, or pimple, or spot.
Because, it seems, that others get the point of this dot.

I think it would be grand to compose a song,
A melody, a sonata, a suite, or better yet,
A symphony created with one note. "Monomalism,"
I'll call it. One lonely note; music minimalism.

If I could only express myself this way.
What rapture, to create a note or sound;
Just a tiny vibration so pure and sweet.
My own legacy left for generations to expound.

*Jesse Pettey*

## A Grain of Sand

Like a grain of sand in your galaxy
I stand in awe at your majesty,
What you did for me to see.
As a Van Gogh landscape in your artistry
You painted the heavens just for me to see.
Your solar rays, yet so far away
Were beamed on me for my nutriency
just for me you see

The empty void which was so tranquility filled
For every scope of man's will,
And nurtured the earth for us to breathe in
Made just for us, your beings, to be in.

What course to charter for your generous larder
And with you I dare not barter,
For what you did for me, you see
Boggles the mind for all eternity
Through your omnipotence
what you did for me.

*Joseph Nugara*

## When I Think of You

When I think of you alone in my bed...
I think of the smile you once gave me,
I think of the way we were both
trapped by the words I'm falling in love,....
But then I learned of a deep dark secret,...
you never loved me, you loved her and only her.
Why you didn't love me!
that's the question I want answered.
But when I look in your so prefect face,
I see the love you once had for me,...
destroyed by the one girl you love.
When I think of the bad times and the good times we had.
The 3 words I never said to you were... "I love you."
If you only knew how much I cared for you!
Would you have loved me too?

*Brenda Miranda*

## Grandpa

I wanted to see you before you went away
I wanted to say so many things, but I couldn't bare to see you
  that way
I wanted to hug you one last time before your heart stopped
  beating
I wanted to remember all the time we shared, all the times worth
  repeating
I wanted to remember you the way you were before you got sick
I wanted to remember all of the love you gave me,
  but the memories just wouldn't stick
I wanted to say good-bye to you before you closed your eyes
I wanted to be there with you when it was your time to die
I wanted to feel the pain that everyone felt that day
I wanted to know why I couldn't cry when everyone else was in
  their own world far-far away

*April Lawer*

## It Worketh

A most wonderful thing has happened to me.
I was almost blind, but now I see.
God's Word, mixed with Faith, has restored my sight.
It worketh! Praise the Lord!-Darkness turned to light.

Luke 4:18 and Mark 11:22,24 activated this state.
Healing is there ... There's NO mistake.
God is your answer-Take your Bible and read.
What you are doing-You're planting God's Live Seed.

FAITH-ABUNDANCE-JOY and PEACE
Words from GOD ... That never ceases.
Yes! I'm HEALED! God restored my sight.
And He is with me
EVERY DAY ... EVERY NIGHT

Read these Scriptures for yourself.
They work for the POOR-they work
For the WEALTH

Thank you, Father, in Jesus' Name

Healings for the "Who-so-ever"
believeth in His NAME.
AMEN!

*Eugene R. Henry*

## Kaddish

Until yesterday I thought
I was in love with the dead.
Grecian urns and pyramids spoke
Of ancient lore and gods of dread.

Dread—I learned its cacophony today
As museum artifacts turned sour.
The striped shirts and wedding rings
Tell of dead, and dread, and unholy power.

I am not Anne Frank; I survive to tell
Of history that shapes the race.
Fifty years have come and gone.
I never knew, yet always know her face.

No more my legacy the shards of years forlorn.
Memory drives just necessity to mourn.

*Eileen Z. Cohen*

## I Am A Veteran

I am a veteran, I was my country's strength in war,
I was the heart of the fight, wherever, whenever.
I carried America's faith, honor and will to win,
against her enemies. I led the battle cry!

I was what my country expected me to be, in the race
for victory, I gave my life, my heart, my will.
I was swift, determined, and courageous, armed with
America's will to win.
I never failed my country's trust, I always fought on.
On to the objective, I closed with and destroyed the
enemy. When necessary, I fought to my death, surrender
was not in my creed.

My country's freedom was sacred to me, to tyrants, I
didn't bow, where brave men fought, there fought I
I was relentless, I met the enemy face to face, will
to will. I am a veteran!

I was young, but mentally tough. I yielded not to
hunger, weakness, or superior odds. From the Mekong
Delta, through the central high lands, and on to the DMZ,
I fought, I cried, I ached...I'm a Veteran, I am the shield.

*Carlos R. Pino*

## Departure

This was your life's last day
I was watching you in dismay
You were looking at me with a pitiful eye
I was told by Surinder standing near by
The grief was at its peak on that fateful night
Your tongue was struck and I had no eyesight
To say good-bye was not written in our fate
To converse with one another we were too late
Oh my mind why are you so frustrated
In your holy books it is clearly illustrated
Prayer from heart takes you to Gods treasure
Vanishing your grief and bringing you pleasure

*Banarsi Lal Basho*

## City Of Silver

Angel Freefalling,
I watch the fickle mortals from a position high above,
This taking wing and falling is my only love,
I see their blind efforts as I take the dive,
All their petty hopes, struggles, and fears come alive,
While their past, present, and future assimilates my mind.
I'M IN AN ANGEL FREEFALL,
The truth will I help them grasp,
But I reach terminal velocity,
And He pulls me back.

*Dan Weber*

## I Wear Black

I wear black cuz black's been here since my birth.
I wear black cuz it'll be here when I'm goin' six feet below the earth

I wear black on those golden, sunny days.
I wear black on mystical, gloomy nights.

I wear black when I know I needs to pray.
I wear black when that ole' devil says fight.

I wear black when I got somethin' I wanna say.
I wear black when my silence is my might.

I wear black cuz I wouldn't have it any other way.
I wear black cuz black fits me right.

I wear black cuz black's been here since my birth.
I wear black cuz it'll be here when I'm goin' six feet below the earth

*James Ravenell Jr.*

## I Wish

I Wish
I were a butterfly
With many colors grand
And all the little children would hold me in their hand.

I wish
I were a swan
With wings as white as snow
And all my baby swans would follow where ere I go.

I wish
I were a weeping willow
Standing in the breeze
Swaying to and fro in the winds across the seas.

I wish
I were a firefly
Glowing every night
And everyone would see me because I was so bright.

I wish
I were a rose
As red as red could be
With very silky petals for all the world to see.

*April E. Phillips*

## The Fallen Angel

"She wasn't quite the angel I remembered in my dreams"
I will not soon forget
I loved her once I swear I did
But sometimes I think yet,
Who is this girl I say I love
And is she still the same?
She was fun and she was fresh
And I was only plain.
But now she is a different one
That has lost her spark
She is slow and she is cold
And I am on my mark
I appreciate what I learned from her
And will not soon forget
The girl I thought that I loved once
And the angel I had met.

*Jason Authier*

## My Promise

I will live each day with you, as if there will be no tomorrows.
I will share with you all our happiness, as well as the sorrows.

I will listen and learn from you as much as I can,
I will cherish your wisdom and feel the love of a gentle man.

I will journey with you to places only true hearts can go,
I will always be safe within your love, this I know.

I will be there to offer support in whatever you choose to do.
My love is unconditional, my love is true.

I will walk with you through pastures of green and on shores of sand.
And when our time on Earth is through, then too
You will have my Hand.

*Deborah Bridges*

## Did She Know?

On that day Jesus was nailed to the cross,
I wonder if Mary considered His death, gain or loss.

After all, this was her first son,
and the death of a child can't be explained to anyone.

Could you just imagine how she must have felt,
when at the foot of the cross, she knelt?

When she looked up into the face of her beloved boy,
I wonder if Mary knew, that Satan was jumping for joy?

When the nails pierced the flesh of Jesus,
did she know, He was dying for all of us?

Or when the soldier stuck a sword into His side,
I'll bet a little of her also died.

Did Mary even have a notion
that these same nail scarred hands, laid the foundation for the ocean?

As she saw Him hanging there so battered and weak.
Did she know this same man, created the universe, and had only to
   speak?

And as His blood flowed to the ground,
did she know that in 3 days, with glory, He would be crowned?

But whether she knew these things or not,
I'm sure grateful for the Lord Jesus, she begot!

*Howard Clay*

## Lonely Soldier

I am an independent individual
I wonder if people like me
I hear people's negative remarks
I see horror all around me
I want peace and equal opportunity
I am black slave, held down
   by the creed of those who are evil, those white folk,
   which I want to see as my brothers and sisters, but can't.

I pretend I feel nothing, I'm as hard as a rock
I feel hopeless, while bound to these chains
I touch the cuts and lashes from the whip
I worry for my family, my brothers and sisters
I cry when I see my friend die in my arms
I am a black man.

I understand nothing they say or do
I say what I feel and feel what I say
I dream of freedom and of brighter days
I try to understand their reasons for hurt
I hope that they will one day see the pain they have caused
I am a soldier, I am a black man.

*Justin Silva*

## Untitled

I am a teenage girl wishing for more.
I wonder what it would be like to be famous.
I hear the cranking of my brain as I think.
I see my wishes start to come true.
I want the world around me to love.
I am a teenage girl wishing for more.

I pretend that everyone needs me in some way.
I feel the hatred and war around me.
I touch the sky and hope that it doesn't fall.
I worry about the future and if we will be at peace.
I cry at the sight of the homeless people on the street.

I am a teenage girl wishing for more.
I understand that you don't always get what you want.
I say that you're no different than anybody else.
I dream of the world being a better place.
I try hard to see things in other peoples' eyes.
I hope that my future is living.
I am a teenage girl wishing for more.

**Bethany Miller**

## I Am

I am an innocent child who lives in a dark world.
I wonder who will be killed tomorrow.
I hear about people being killed every day.
I see people with no food and nothing at all on tv.
I want to help, but I have little to offer.
I am an innocent child who lives in a dark world.

I pretend that nothing is happening.
I feel that I must do something.
I touch my most inner feeling when I see the pictures of
those with nothing.
I worry about being killed.
I cry for the people that are killed by guns.
I am an innocent child who lives in a dark world.

I understand what has to be done.
I say we should help everyone less fortunate.
I dream of a world in which everyone is equal.
I try to make the world a better place.
I hope that you do to.
I am an innocent child who lives in a dark world.

**Chris Santiago**

## In His Compartment

On a transcontinental train
Ibsen turns his eyes.
His head follows to face a character in a suit of mist,
the skin more mist than flesh.
Ibsen look into those eyes as if into a well.
He knows hundreds of characters.

Ibsen re-reads manuscript pages, thinks,
"I wait a for that bright one, with a face like the moon."
He sees a silver haze sleeve the compartment.
They sit side by side, going far beyond.

**Elaine Dallman**

## "Share A Smile"

A smile is always with you.
It is something that will always be there.
No one can take your smile from you.
Sure you can hide that smile but why hide
Something which by just a simple gesture
Can make someone's day or even their life.
My smile is mine and I share it with you.
Your smile is yours
I hope you shall share it with me.

**Christine Conway Hickman**

## The Ice Storm

I awaken to a world of crystalline beauty.
Icicles hang everywhere - drip, drip, dripping themselves slowly
away.
Branches cover the ground - snapped by an unusual new weight.
Tall pines stand with their heads bowed under the cold, clear
burden
Praying for the warmth of the sun's golden orb.
People hammer at frozen windshields, clinging to any solid object
Trying to avoid a fall on the slick new surface.
Heavy gray clouds meander on ever so slowly
Waiting to empty themselves on further reaches of the cold earth;
Knowing full well that the sun is following close behind
Waiting to turn this icy, cold world into a million sparkling prisms.
Melting warmth begins to drench the slippery earth,
And the icy surface disappears in rivulets and pools —
Making us forget the hazardous beauty of ... The Ice Storm.

**Archie L. McEvers II**

## If I Were A Tree

If I were a tree
   I'd stretch my branches far and wide
      Reaching out on either side

      My leaves would catch the morning dew
         Then the sun would dry them through

   I'd shelter life beneath my limbs
      Embracing nature's finest trims

      Oh!  How great a tree I'd be
         In all of earth's pleasantry

**Denise Dormer**

## Jet Vapor Art

The rumbling sound from the jet is quite deceiving.
If follows behind like a long, long tail of a kite.
The ribbon of vapor will help you into believing
That the speed is faster than the sound of the flight.
White vapor as white as a cloud is streaming out back,
So narrow and straight when it is first released,
But ripples and widens in billowy clouds not exact.
The wind is the artist creating patterns that increase.
At times another jet will enter from the opposite way,
And add to the art work that was made by the first.
The picture completed last only minutes of the day.
Now thinning and drifting until all beauty has dispersed.
You're spellbound for a moment watching the art in the sky
That was created by the wind and the jets zooming by.

**Grace S. Smoak**

## Twelve Oh One

It's twelve oh one and the clock is ticking
I'm all alone
oh what you're missing
to love me and the baby instead of your glass
your friends at the bar won't go far
but still you insist on sitting alone
while I'm by the phone, keeping a vigil
a cup of coffee and your crying baby
waiting for a call that would tell me
all my fear, hope, and misery can be laid to rest
I'm not sure when the call will come
But I'm certain that it will
Because you can't stop
and if you could
you never will.

**Amanda Rosetta**

## When I See An Old Barn

When I see an old barn
I'm drawn within its walls;
I feel the quiet of the inner gloom,
The hush of the empty stalls.
I know there's a room with battered racks,
Holding dry, cracked leather gear;
I know there's a place in the dusty loft
Where my view of the earth comes clear.
I can see the creek down past the field
Where the birds and bullfrogs sing;
I can feel the peace of the quiet pools
And listen to the heavens ring.

**Jearl Nunnelee**

## My Shadow

My shadow always follows me around,
I'm never by myself with my shadow on the ground.
Light and sunshine from the heavens above
    Creates this special creature that never makes a sound
This shadow falls on solid ground -
    Showing all my features in the background.
Never, never be afraid to do that challenging task,
Always be ready when someone stops to ask.
My size is like a grain of sand on earth's vast open space,
Together my shadow and I can make the world a better place.

**Ethel M. Shannon**

## "Mirror, Mirror..."

As I look into the mirror,
    images flash before my face.
They appear as clear as day, for an instant,
    then swirl and fade, disappearing without a trace.

Life can be such a mystery,
    so hard to understand.
As I stare at my reflection,
    I ponder the mysteries of the man.

Can anyone truly see,
    or feel what I truly feel?
I often wonder, as my thoughts wander,
    if anything is really real.

Yet the mirror reflects,
    everything, showing it all.
Some things lead you to greatness,
    some just make you fall.

**Christopher P. Magra**

## Nightfall of Sylvia Plath

Frozen nightingales precipitate in me
Images of a crystal crackling shimmering sea
Of meaningless worlds, reverberating sounds which grow
In silences that echo a footfalling crunch on snow.
Trees shattersplitting, muffled by a lonely night—
No escaping entering light
But falling, calling darkness, a path forbidden,
Hidden,
Obscure and forgotten by some arbitrary choice,
A voice
Crying out words, songs, melodies, a breath
Of cold unsmiling innocence that dies a wintry death.
My soul suspended in nature's glass to jar is never heard
But cracks, shatters, chilled to stillness, still absurd.

**Gary L. Morrison**

## Dozetime Reflections

As the soft light wanes to dim, my mind begins to swim,
Images of the day fly fleetingly past, fueling a fervent hope, I pray
will last.
But old pain-filled scenes rear up fresh,
Causing, a slight shiver, to slither over my goose-pimpled flesh.

My heart cries out, directing my hand,
The stubborn courage shall force a stand,
Against the giant stumbling blocks to come,
There exists my very own dream to fulfill, a hope I grasp and cling
to... still,
So much ceaseless labor to be done.

Every night I lay it all out on the line,
Wistfully imagining the conquering time,
A tear escapes down my cheek,
To overcome strife, smash through all obstacles in life,
Only then may I truly sleep.

**Daniel Aaron Nopar**

## I Never Will

As if it were a mystic star
importing solemn news,
an ill-starred moth of fated flight
hangs brightly dead for contemplation.
What spark, what light,
what influence ill-favored,
induced and trapped you there
in deadly woven shadows?
The threads of Chance
you never saw?
The web of Doom
you never knew?
Beware the Spider's secret art!

But wait, I'm sorry now.
These thoughts seem pointless, after all.

Dear father, poor, fated father,
just rest in peace.
Your death was long — so long — in coming.
It's just,
we never saw; we never knew; I never will.

**Jim Stevenson**

## In the Eye of Decision

Collapsed and broken
In a blind mad man's rage
Mixed in a world of pleasure
Beaten deaf in a thorn bush cage
The oppressor was perfection
I was only half of that
Every time I tried to please him
He knocked me farther back
Till one day I sought him and brought him to his feet
He turned blue and frigid
So I left him in defeat
One day a question I did bring
Down upon myself
If the cage hadn't wronged me
Would he be living in good health

**Jason Beckwith**

## Voltaire's Press

Vain little Voltaire sat in his chair,
In a soliloquy row with God;
His reason made plain that God wasn't there - and so he declared -
That God would soon be forgotten.
So he tho't and he wrote,
And he taught and he spoke
With such smooth words and appeal;
That beyond any doubt he'd reason'd it out:
"That God..." well, he just wasn't real.
He claim'd in half a century on
The name of Christ Jesus would be
Less than a by-word, for reason would triumph
O'er deity's necessity.

But time passed on, and so did Voltaire,
And fifty years after his death,
A Bible society purchased his house -
Printing Bibles upon Voltaire's press!

So let us not mock, nor be very vain,
For we all live under His auspice:  Lest receiving from God
When we're laid in the sod, deity's humor - Poetic Justice!

*Daniel G. Roe*

## Renewed Hope

A release of truth illustrates a poem that's completed
in a tradition with a touching tale of life
insight facts about her teen years
confirm an expression, a relief

When the world was in a turmoil
and no purpose to prevail
defenselessness beyond description
stir up bitter memories of yesteryears

From an extension of a beautiful language
in a quiet mood to set a light
she is gathering the words to work with
the rudiments that still linger in her heart

Her guidance lead to new direction
emphasis was heightened to survive
to find peace of mind, normality perhaps?
Ability to keep her faith alive

Accumulation of tears and tragedy
grieve sorrow and separation unknown to some
with a renewed optimism for now and
a desire for hopefulness is restored again.

*Eva Widawski*

## Observation

Cool, quiet, withdrawn
In control and out, beer in hand, lips in a pout
Waiting for the night to pass, watching for the dawn

Intelligent, but confused, trying to understand the self
Dreaming of future endeavors, hungry for wealth
So handsome and so amused

Laughing on the outside, making fun at the world
White teeth flashing, shimmering like pearl
Smile fading, his mind on a ride

Running through the intricate maze of his brain
Looking for something or someone he can hold on to
Trying to find out what he is or maybe who?

Killing his feelings, trying to destroy all the pain.
Working at staying alive
And fighting to stay sane.

*Brenda Hammond*

## Billy's Hymn

When Billy appeared in the doorway, he was no longer the same
In his very first suit so handsome and blue, a portrait in a
sunlight frame.

Leaving boyhood behind him, daring to feel like a man,
He tried to hide his sensation of pride, wanting not to be vain.
He walked like a soldier, not casting about with his gaze,
Asking within if this was the end of his carefree, childhood days.

His father remembered so clearly the day he wore his first suit,
And the pain and joys that come to boys as they try to follow their roots.

His mother beamed her approval, feeling her life fulfilled,
Praying to spare her child so fair the perils of men strong willed.

The other boys  watched with scorn, feeling somehow betrayed,
Fearing inside that they couldn't hide from a future of dignified ways

The girls with their hidden glances marveled at this new man.
Was this the boy who used to enjoy tormenting them till they ran?

The  choir in the loft was enchanted to see  such a lyrical sight,
And dare say they heard a heavenly host sing a hymn to all that is
right.

*Jim K. Zartman*

## Kevin

Children in wheelchairs, on crutches,
in hospital beds.
No bikes, no skateboards or shining new sleds.

Kevin you touched me deep inside.
You exposed my soul,
I've nowhere to hide.

You showed me my problems were blessings instead,
I'm able to stand up
And walk from my bed.

I took things for granted, like using my hands,
Like swimming and walking
The warm summer sand.

Oh God please forgive me for being so blind
I'm blessed with my body
And use of my mind.

These children, God's children,
Unable to play
Helpless dependent, our teachers, are they.

*Alan Arcieri*

## Our Youths

We look for stars that do not shine
In our sight it's so divine
To see our youths in harmony
And making progress for our community

In them we see our future
Even when their behavior is not in nature
We build on the positive they portray
To make them better..not to go astray

To correct and direct
And show great respect
Our youths of today
Shall pave the way

Our course in narrow
But we will soar like the sparrow
Towards the top
We will not stop

We are all blessed
In our hearts and soul
The ultimate test
Is our major goal

*Alacia A. Harvey*

## The Purity of Artists

The insanity protrudes
in overlapping
and perpetual substances
swirling the demonic
madness
of deafening and piercing tones
thumping heads against walls of recycled life
dwelling on
systematic non-changing reality
set aside
while terrors of the night
skip into my subtle soul
fauceting tears
dripping a wistful existence
show the bleakness of my loneliness
my mind shuts out the logic
and amplifies the madness
into desolate forms
of no escape.

*Gregory Westcott*

## Dear Lady

He dreams of a dear lady
in satin and white lace
magnolia trees will prove shady
as she walks with flowing grace

Born into a paupers life
a man that's seen only pain
he dreamed this dear lady his wife
though a daydream is all that he'll gain

A broken man weathered and worn
aged well beyond his years
with his dear lady a young man is born
and strength will emerge through his tears

He was buried alone in an unmarked grave
final passage is whispered in latin
his dreams he will lose...in his soul he will save
his dear lady in white lace and satin

*Jeffrey A. Rayner*

## Clifford

We nearly lost him — He was home alone.
In spite of the pain, he got to the phone.
He needs help — call 9-1-1.
They come real fast — on the run.
These guys are good — Know what to do.
They know you're sick — take care of you.
Good Samaritan is thirty miles away.
They get him there for a twelve day stay.
The surgeon said, "He may not survive.
He's terribly sick - just barely alive."
I kiss him good-by.  They take him away.
It's a long, long night.  We wait and we pray.
I wasn't alone.  My kids were there.
Loving family — A lot of prayer.
Early in the morning the doctor came.
He'll be okay — he's won this game.
It will take some time to really be well.
Hard work and patience and love will tell.
We can do it.  I know we can.
Thank you, Lord.  I still have my man.

*Barbara Jeanne Felton*

## The Shaly Soil

The bark-faced oak thrust his rooty fingers deep
in the dark earth of October,
for summer's waters fled him level after level
through the hard, shaly soil.
In November he would only have
a withered tree's grasp of a winter's dream;
and senseless, he could not waste watery tears
for his children's autumn funerals,
when grave dancers in somber columns
swept the summer before them
with the harvester's scythe.
His papery leaves were spread like a faded wreath
on that hard land, as he settled to the stern
call of the sky-fallen waters interred below;
that which would slake his finger's thirst
in the cooling, shaly soil.

*Elroy Meyer*

## Creativity - God's Gift

In the fragile wing of a butterfly,
In the grandeur of mountain peaks,
In the beauty that comes from an artist's brush,
In the words that a kind heart speaks.

In the beauty of the sea and shells,
In the hands that mold the clay,
Is the realization of someone's dream -
Finding an answer - a means - a way.

The fulfillment of creating
Is a gift God shared with man -
To see beyond the bud - the flower
And a spirit that says - I CAN!

*Gerry Snyder*

## The Runners

Beyond the heat of the rising sun
In the midst of the cooling winds
Joyous laughter opens a new chapter
In our life together.

Through the waving fields
We ran for years
It must have been miles
Knowing it was love all the while

Catch me lest I fall
Carry me through the fray
Hold me in sorrow
Running till the 'morrow

For time and time again has found us here together
In the shadow of your passion
I run against a feather
Knowing it was love all the while

*Eric Erker*

## Going Away

Moving is such a fuss,
Leaving all the friends I've grown to trust.
Going to a house I'll never call home;
Knowing that my life as I know it,
Will be changed for all the years to come.
So because I'm forced to go
I'll say my goodbyes;
But I'll always know,
This is the only place my heart will
ever truly belong.

*Jessica Marie Grubbs*

## Waves In The Wind

The water in the lake, rippled its waves
In the wind, as the day came to a close,
And they selected the shoreline as their graves,
For the end of their journey of repose.
The water in the lake, spattered its waves
In the wind, as the nighttime appeared,
So silently, but the din was in sprays,
Rounding that shoreline, angry and weird.
The water in the lake, clattered its waves
In the wind, as the sunset settled beyond
The horizon, but the noise was in arrays,
For miles and miles, and it would continue on.
The water in the lake, rippled, spattered, and settled,
Its waves in the wind, as they died, and became, weathered!

*Eva M. Roy*

## Awareness

You thought that life had given you a frame
In which the years would fit with placid ease;
The paths you took would always be the same,
You will grow old among your own loved trees.
For you the tired and broken roads were blast
You had no wish to ever turn aside;
No unknown voice could call you from your rest,
Though others walked where roads stretched far and wide.

You went your way in peace and I went mine
Contentment clothed us both in simple shrouds.
We did not taste loves' sweet or bitter wine,
And were alone although we walked with crowds.
And then one night we stood upon a hill;
Your hand touched mine - the past lay dead and still.

*Bernadette E. Jordan*

## Childhood

To run through a summer lawn
In your bare feet,
licking a popsicle in the summer heat,
Childhood... Building a treehouse
sleeping there all night,
chasing warty frogs through swamps,
itching mosquito bites.
Childhood... Imaginary best friends,
days that never end,
racing away from haunted houses
while playing trick-or-treat,
sneaking around on Christmas Eve,
hoping it's Santa you meet,
Childhood...
girls putting on make up and boys pulling hair,
jumping in swamps and taking double dares,
Childhood...
once in a lifetime!

Childhood...
Once in a lifetime!

*Elizabeth M. Hamilton*

## "River Of Size"

River of size.
Knows no end.
Time her only compromise.
Gently, but inevitably, eroding away the earth , exposing the
very roots of my affection for her.
Will I drown in a sea of loneliness.
Never to drift  on her loneliness.
Never to bath in her waters warm caress.
Or will I sail the beautiful river of size to an endless ocean
of love.

*David E. Hickman*

## A Burning River

Keep in your heart a burning river,
in your eyes a gentle sea.
Such easy strength upon your face,
in languid beauty and simple grace.

As slowly as day does slip from night,
to steal its jeweled crown away.
You have claimed such a right,
my heart cannot return that way.

Keep in your soul the kindness I have given,
the key to chains of mortal skin and bone.
Such is a trait I've not misgiven,
a sign of weakness rarely shown.

(See me then)
a burning river,
a gentle sea,
Kindness misgiven.

(See me then)
a portrait undone,
where there once was a future,
now there is none.

*Ernest Serna*

## Father Figure

There is, in a garage someplace a rope that extends six feet three
inches from end to end with knots on each.
On days of courage I can find this rope in the piles of sacred trash.
Though it is not heavy I carry it in both arms
to feel it against my skin.
In the grass long of uncut I lay myself next to it.
Almost ten years short of his eternal age I am not quite as tall
and never will be, but still I check.
On this vast lawn of green I am only a speck
sinking and sinking into that which is his.
As always the rope is there...
able to find his way to my depths
pulling me with his strength
and holding me tight as he does so.
Now carrying me as I carried him, in both arms,
I find myself in the garage
among the cherished debris,
placing the rope where I will remember...
Always.

How could I forget?

*Jason Michael Fullan*

## Mine is the Darkness

Engulfed by it, seeing no end,
infinity is the darkness.

Hunters seek, vultures prey.
All around me they hover.

A babe alone weeping in the dark;
creatures taunt, the night children dance.

Mine is the darkness for it reveals nothing.
It's true nature hidden, and I hunt.

Prey becomes predator
and the shooting star.
A tear and the sun fall
igniting the black flame.

Made of nothing, blanketing all
I am hunted by one.
The seekers move on
and I am laid to rest.

*Brian Bushnell*

## Oklahoma City

Those roses bloom again, that my lifetime ago,
   Instantly unfurled with flame and shrapnel steel
   Revealing the beauty in the blood of Ethiopian peasants;
The fruits of civilization apple down the air.

Roses of yesterday blossom, blest by neglect
   As stone foundations slump by the hollow of the cellar.
   What treasures in the original of flowers
Cultivated to the harm of wholesomeness and scent.

Then, cultured men (I would be incompatible with them)
   Dithered, for fear that civility, if threatened,
   Would vanish from their circle.
Bullies, for our own good, should be encouraged.

Weeds, unchanged and unappreciated,
Punch through the drift of this year's petals.

   *Eugene W. Foote*

## The Two M's

That which is built in the imagination
Is always beyond compare and expectations
So you will lower the tangerine lights
In order to contemplate another route there

Stretch yourself out and flip the pages
Enumerate what your life was lacked
To grasp a brief interlude of pleasure
Or the constant method of immediate gratification

It can take divergent forms
All you have to do is indulge
And drift away on damp remembrances
Of times that were and hope to be again

Rites of promised passage
Into a supposed adult life
Complete with poignancy and occasional sweetness
Until tender outlets are all stripped from you

   *Carl L. Johnson Jr.*

## "God's Chosen Champion"

   God's chosen champion
Is filled with His Holy Ghost
With His Eternal Salvation Insurance
Protect and guard, that's our reason to boast

   God's chosen champion
Is filled with His anointing power
With His Eternal Salvation Insurance
To keep us everyday and hour

   God's chosen champion
Don't accept defeat from anyone
Keep the faith in God and His word
Because the victory is already won

   God's chosen champion
God has anointed us to live and not die
Just be strong, brave, courageous soldiers
That'll give satan a big black eye

   God's chosen champion
Is bold, never, never takes down
No matter how satan tries to blind us
Keep our eyes on (Jesus) He's the crown

   *Eunicetine Brooks*

## I Know My Jesus Wept

A wonderful thing, I have learned,
Is - for me, Jesus does weep;
With that truth in my mind and heart,
I can have a peaceful sleep.

He knows my heartaches, He knows my pain,
He knows each time that I fear;
He knows each time I'm lonely and sad,
And He knows when I shed a tear.

But, if there be a night, that I lie awake,
At morning time I still haven't slept;
I'll know that He spent the night with me,
And as I cried through the night....
   ....I'll know my Jesus wept.

   *Cledus Kyle Russell*

## Why Do Men Feel the Need to Control?

Why do men feel the need to control?
Is he trying to be the man or just be bold?

You tell me what to wear; you tell me where to go;
tell me, do I look stupid or slow?

If he comes home and I'm not there, he's wondering why.
But, when I take the time to tell him, he only hollers and
makes me cry.

You act like I'm a 16-year-old on her first date.
It seems as though you follow every move that I make.

Whenever, I want to go somewhere, I have to ask your permission.
You treat me like I'm a two-year-old who can't make her own
decision.

Trying to control was played out back in the day.
So, if you can't treat me like a woman, get out of my way!

I'm a grown and independent woman, not a child.
I know everybody make mistakes every once in a while.

It's time to put my foot down, and tell you, I'm not taking this anymore.
If you don't like what I'm saying, you can hit the door.

"Tell me, why do men feel the need to control?"

   *Christina R. Lewis*

## What Is Music?

What is music?
Is it a gift, or an art?
Or is it something we posses, right from
the start?
Is it a challenge, you must reach from
afar?
Or is it something, that can be kept in
a jar?

What is music?
Is it a form of love and joy?
Or is it something you own, such as a toy?
Is it a talent, that can be bought?
Or is it a fight, that must be fought?

What is music?
Is it a prize to be won?
Or is it something to admire, such as
the sun?
Is it a voice wanting to be let out?
Or, perhaps it is a spirit, in each of us.

   *Dawn Marie Tarica-Kemp*

## The Girl Behind the Mask

Who is the girl behind the mask? Does anyone know, will anyone ask?
Is it a girl wanting to stay young? A newborn song waiting to be
   sung?
Is it a woman waiting to be discovered, waiting patiently to find her
   destined lover?
Does anyone know? Will anyone ask about the girl behind the mask?
Who is this girl? What is she about?
No man knows. There is always a doubt.
She is but a lonely lady longing to be loved,
and yet in need of freedom like freedom is needed by a dove.
Will she know what it means to be loved,
Or will she stay lonely till she goes up above?
Does anyone care, will anyone ask?
What happened to the girl behind the mask?

   *Deandra C. Rademacher*

## A Light Will Shine

As I walk down the street, I wonder what people see
Is it someone very weak - what do they think of me
Do they think I have a place - a place called home I have not
Can they see a look upon my face of a family who has forgot
Sometimes I wonder if they know - 'bout all the things inside
Like the places that I'd go or what I have to hide
Go away and never come back
That's what they say - I've done just that
I know that wounds can heal but sometimes words cannot
They truly hurt the way I feel - I'll always have that spot
But it's not like a scar or something you can see
It's something deep down far, far down inside of me
I think it's time for this child to stop being on her own
This world is just too wild for a kid without a home
So I guess it's time for me to return even though I don't know
   what they'll do
Maybe those words will stop their burn -
A light will shine on through

   **Aimee Fisher**

## The Fee

Mother Mother, what is wrong, why are you crying
Is it something I'm too young to understand
But Mother I have eyes too, and they shed tears like you
For Mother, I'm a part of you

Father, Father, what is wrong, why are you quiet
Your eyes tell me things, you never say
They tell me what is life, for an honest man and his wife
In a world where the only sacred thing is money

All you people, you know who you are
You sold your hearts for money and fancy cars
But on your road to success, you didn't look behind yourself
At the honest man and his wife
Who paid your price, with their lives

Now all you people, with plastic hearts
There is one important thing you forgot
That there are millions of people like me
And you will have to meet our fee
For yielding the knife, which killed the honest man and this wife
For yielding the knife, which killed the honest man and his wife

   **Francisco Molina**

## The Rocking Chair

The Rocking sits beside my bed night and day
Inviting me to sit or pray It greets me with willingness and strength.
Offering power beyond extended length
A treasured gift which I adore
Pleasant memories of a gracious presenter
The Rocking chair is mine to keep
With lasting love forever more

   **Irma Hicks**

## Somewhere Out There Someone Loves You

Somewhere out there, someone loves you; that someone's name
is "Jesus."
   J is for Jesus
   E is for His Excellency
   S is for His Saving Grace
   U is for His Understanding
   S is for His Salvation
Somewhere out there you too can know "Him." It makes no
difference who you are Nor where you are. He turned water
into wine, To make others happy at a Wedding Feast.
He walked on water to bring "Faith." He fed five thousand
to show His Compassion. He raised His friend Lazarus from
death; A friend He loved and wept for. Somewhere out
there, someone as fell, He has picked them up and carried
them on. The same He does for All. He never changes, He
is always the same, Yesterday, Today and Tomorrow.
All around us, His beauty prevails.

   *Charlotte M. Ryan*

## Emotions

The idea of a love that doesn't hurt
is like a tear that cannot fall;
An infant that can't cry
or an eye that never saw.

A hand that doesn't move
A head that can't be turned;
These things would just exist
like wood that can't be burned;

What good is a tear that can't be released
at the wails of a baby's sound?
A hand that can't show its signs,
A head that's straight ward bound?
An eye that can't see
when life starts to unwound?

What good is a love that can't touch your heart?
   It could not exist without,
"Emotions" from the start!

   *Barbara A. Joiner*

## To Be

One of the most special gifts one can give another
   is that of yourself...
We truly give of ourselves when we give gifts of the mind
   and the soul: Ideas, dreams, purposes, poetry...

Our thoughts must give peace and serenity within —
Like a warm summer breeze in wide open spaces
Gently caressing my body - my soul
Yet leaving me still to be free.
Free - to meet life's challenge and existence
Free - to feel the meaning of life
Free - to be in harmony and companionship with my true self
To live according to the truths within myself
To learn who I am and why I am here
So I may give the finest gift of time —
The gift of a constructive and creative life.

Awake! Life is beautiful!
Awake! Life is for you!
The conditions?
Peace and love, freedom, courage.

   *Diane Louise Alling*

## Microcosm Of Infinity

The brief microcosm of infinity;
is the chain letter that has yet to be broken.
It passes from him to her to me,
and when it leaves me it will come to you!

It is the petals of a flower in early Spring.
Innocent fresh young life, newborn to the world.
I bring hope, love and joy to the world...
...this young blue, perfectly flawed planet!
It is the bark of a mighty oak in a Summer storm,
that stands strong against this harsh world.
By virtue of strength I survive;
in this intergalactic petri dish!

It is the leaves falling from a lilac bush in Autumn,
growing ever so lovely into another age.
I tire and wish to rest;
under this quiet black speckled forum!

It is the aged corpse in a field of Winters snow.
Time to move along in the natural order.
Now I rest,
and starlight shines down upon me...making me young again!

*James P. Horigan*

## Some Verses For I.P.

The hand that holds the cup of bitter discord
is the hand that once held the flask of dreamy love's scent;
yet, now it wields intemperance's sword;
and passion's fire in drunkenness is spent.

Clear, blue teutonic eyes in sadness mist are drenched.
Tears down her cheeks run a blazing trail.
Crashing to the floor the spirit's vase is sent
as the hand's unsteady grip so suddenly fails.

And her eyes - amethyst stones, blue as the boundless sea -
seethe with the brimstone fire that within them burns
as she looks inward, in ire, into the annals of her memory
and her tortured spirit into a pillar of salt turns.

As I look down at the shards
strewn on the marble floor
I ponder very hard
this thoughts over.
"I'll lend a hand and help steady your step, time and again.
Stand firm for you through endless hours of strife.
Still, can't help but wonder, for all I do for you, my friend:
who'll put together the broken pieces of your life?"

*Gualberto Mendez*

## An Alaskan Christmas

Well, it's Christmas time here in Alaska
Is there anything else like it I ask ya
So many loved ones, so far away
In another world, in Prudhoe Bay
Nevada, Minnesota, and Illinois, too
It's a white Christmas that's tinted blue
Don't get me wrong, there is happiness here
We people are strong on the last frontier
The Santas in malls help cheer lonely eyes
Gaily lit houses prompt jubilant cries
There's hope in awaitin' Santa's reindeer and sleigh
And faith knowing Daddy's on his way from the bay
When he finally gets home the hearts overflow
And that's when the eyes are truly all aglow

*Debbie Whipple*

## The Rose Of My Heart

Your sweet kind words, your soft gentle way,
It all means so much to me everyday.
The care that you've shown helps me to know
That I want what we have to continue to grow.
The Lord opened the door for me to finally meet you,
Someone I'll cherish in all that I do.
With the Lord as my guide and you up ahead
Life has new meaning to ones heart which was dead.
The rose that you gave me still blooms in my heart.
And reminds me of you, when distance keeps us apart.
But since you and I are under God's will,
I know what we have will never stay still.
The Lord will nurture us and give us the love
To turn miles to inches by His Grace from above.

*Becky Mock*

## A Rose's Power

A rose's scent is so delicate and sweet,
It can sweep you right off of your own two feet.
Its petals are like silken velvet,
And its stem is long and slender.

A rose is romantic and full of life;
It has thorns as sharp as a cutting knife.
Its colors are most' anything,
Like the cloak on the back of a well-
   known king.

No matter where I go to look;
A rose is a favorite in my book.

*Jennifer M. Dallmer*

## Where the Willow Weeps

The willow weeps silently that it's hanging on the wall.
It covers the agony filled screams of the girl in the hall.
Lying on the floor filled with pain
blood flowing from all her veins.
Foot steps walking away from the body
and evil laugh sounds as the body of
another victims hits the ground.
Still the laugh gets louder 'till there's not a sound.
Then the sudden crash of glass falls upon the murderer's ears.
For that he flees, for the fear of getting caught he falls to his
   knees.
Then he gets caught by a ghost.
Who is an unpleasant host, she eats him alive.
For she is the victim he let die in the hall where
the willow weeps.

*Heather Smith*

## A Tear Drop

A tear drips from the corner of my eye.
I weep in silence trying not to make a sound.
My cheeks become red and damp.
My eyes wet and blood shot.
I see life past before my eyes.
Knowing how much I can't stand mine makes me sick.
I acknowledge my fear of dying, but yet can't stand living.
I live life one day at a time.
Time, life, and love are not on my side.
They are on the side of the tear.
The tear dripping down my face.

*Jodi Roth*

## The Color Of Love

The color of my love is behind my eyes
it crowds my thoughts
it floods my domain

and only causes me pain

The color of love should be blue with hints of violet
but turns to red in what seems like no time
when the eyes that love are only mine

and my love spills like wine

The color of love is behind my eyes
and never in front of my face
for when my eyes do open

love leaves not a trace

I toss and turn and try to find
the color of love that's in my mind
I look so hard with all my time

its a wonder I'm not blind

The color of love, don't I see
cannot be painted or drawn
its only a fleeting image

that goes with the coming of dawn
### *Jeffrey Dennis Pasternack*

## To Sons — Love Mom

Your lives, a stairway, experience the steps!
It does not matter whether they are spiral or straight.
My sons, you will have to walk carefully, or you will negatively
change your fate!
For opportunity seldom knocks twice!

Some days the steps will have a tack or two,
but don't look back my sons.
Life's too short to be just sitting on the steps!
Walk proud, and look up high to God, sons!
Birthdays, Graduations, years quickly go by.
Someday, you will all grow up, and have family ties.

So, remember, my sons,
Just watch those steps!
They could be slippery sometimes!
Try not to fall back.
Practice what you have learned greatly,
And fortune? There'll be more.
You will all be a success, I'm sure!

### *Janice D. Scaduto*

## A Thousand Years

There is a piece of my heart that can not be mended
It happen the day your life ended.
It seems a thousand years have gone by.
Since you closed your eyes and breathed your last sigh
I miss your smile, your hug, your love.
An angel you are from above my dear precious mom, my best friend
You are always with me now and forever again.
I will teach my children all the good you taught me,
the caring, sharing, ending love as deep as the sea
You are an angel with God way up high
With all of his children in the beautiful blue sky
Not even a year since you said goodbye
A thousand years it seems, and that's no lie
Only ten months that you went to rest
When God took you, He took the best.
I love you so.

### *Barbara M. Brennan*

## Heart And Soul Holds On

You're in my heart and soul, how much you might not ever know.
It happened in early spring one day, you touched my heart, then
made the play.
Oh, what memories we have made, what stories we could tell.
Those stormy nights so snug inside, through porthole views,
those starlit skies.
The echoes of the distant foghorn, the sound of home.
I grew to love you, so innocently, so carefree an willing.
The sound of your voice like a raging sea, my heart
pounding so hard, I could barely breath.
Hand in hand you and me. your tender touch sparks the flame you
see?
I'm lost and so scared, can I ever be freed?
Were we loving laughing and crying;
was I really then could it really be?
My heart it has betrayed me reaching for you again. Will it ever end?
Now here we are, but how do we begin; with you in my life again?
Still loving but it's not the same; you're my friend.
My best friend, my life that's ours forever, no matter the strife.
There's a special bond between us,
a special closeness that just grows on.
No matter where we are, no matter where we've been
Heart and soul holds on...

### *Haley Bisconer*

## Love Knows No Season

Love knows no season,
It has no sense at all.
It has grown cold in summer
And torrid in the fall.

Been lacking in a home of plenty,
Gone begging many a lonesome night.
Was headstrong and crazy when you were twenty
And wonderful, when it was right.

Love is stern in its demands,
Exacting - never treat love lightly
Grand for one who understands
False if served to you politely.

Love is a mystery, an enigma.
Heaven bless me with its stigma.

### *Harvey Jurist*

## The Traveller

Taste the life how bittersweet
It has so much to offer
Tempting you with jewels to keep
To treasure and to plunder
With glorious grace we reach to grasp
The boundless sea beyond us
But find ourselves fall short of belief
We then are left to wander
Pull yourself out of this place
This quicksand you've discovered
There is a such
True discovery of which you have not stumbled
Lead the way with heart and pride
For all to see and follow
For the truth of life is getting clear
The sweet exceeds the sorrow

### *Alicia R. Lockett*

## Hurricane

September came more vividly this year. I could feel
It in the tropic air. It was bright and warm and kind,
And sometimes sad with rain, that often gently fell
As tears fell from my eyes. How could I know or mind
That storm clouds slowly drifting to the shore
Would circulate their forces into the cruel, reckless
Power of a full-blown hurricane? And furthermore
Reach into my life, and leave me stunned and breathless
As I felt a strong new wind, a sharp new rain
Upon my face. But then the calm, the sudden blue
Of unveiled skies and sudden blaze of golden sun again!
The pure delight of being on the stage of this impromptu
Drama, starring Nature in her daring little folly.
But soon the storm is gone, and with it bright, warm, kind
September, I wonder what has happened to the jolly
Happy days that I knew then? I wake each morn and only find
The turbulence that whirled mid quiet calm that I remember
Has quelled. I saw September and the a Hurricane depart.
Were you that sudden storm? Or were you sunny kind September?
O quell and flee, fierce Hurricane, that whirls within my heart.

**Fay Harrington**

## Love Without Need

Genuine love is a strong energy that grows and lasts,
It is active and never dormant,
It emanates and is obvious,
Reaching outward, upward and in all directions
It remains complete and is ever anewing,
Stale it does not become;
A pant of need it is not for it is independent,
A complete energy that does not require leaning,
Dependency or fulfillment from elsewhere
It is self-fulfilling, capable, reliable,
Steady, consistent, joyous, exhilarating,
It is not foolish but very aware,
A softness it has yet the softness is strong
And it allows no manipulation, no domination, no abuse, no falsity,
It does not blend with emotions,
It does not come in and go out,
Love does not include sacrifice and partners not with it,
It must be genuinely expressed yet requires no tests,
Live in it and with it and move glowingly,
Make it a part of you and soar limitlessly.

**Guen Chappelle**

## Fantasy

There is a place that I can dream
It is hidden far away.
And I can go there when I want
For a few quiet hours in a day,
'Tis there I find a peace of mind
Away from all earth's strife.
I wish I could really live there
And be happy for the rest of my life.
But this place is only a fantasy
That I see in my mind's eye
The things I see are so beautiful
They are just dreams of things passing by.
If one cannot dream of longed for hopes
Life really wouldn't be worth living.
Those beautiful thoughts down deep inside.
Are for those who are loving and giving.
So clasp to your breast your fantasies
Live life the best you can
For no one else can share those dreams
When you go into Fantasy Land.

**Imogene Landers**

## My Inspiration

In front my window stands an old, old tree.
It is tall and strong and full of dignity.
Its trunk is dark and full and round,
Its branches heavy, knarled and sound.
In winter it stands straight, dark and bare,
Ready for the burdens of Winter to dare.
In Spring, it is a wondrous sight,
Sprouting new buds so full and tight
That suddenly open to the sun's warm light.
That old tree is young again,
In a gown of candlelight!
Oh! What a blessed sight!

**Jane Minzberg**

## Hope

It is the sun shining through a cloudy sky.
It is the oasis sitting in the midst of a barren desert.
It is the rose blooming through a patch of thorns.
It is hope.

It is the calmness of the river after the raging of the rapids.
It is the landing of a plane after flying through a storm.
It is the tasting of freedom after being imprisoned for years.
It is hope.

It is the laughter of a child after listening to it scream.
It is the sigh of relief after finishing the race.
It is the applause of the crowd after performing on stage.
It is hope.

It is our dreams.
It is our visions.
It is our expectations.
They are our hope.

**Dawnmarie Nycz**

## Heart

I come to God, with a heart of clay, I ask him to shape
it, make it better in some way. Free of sin, and
without any hate, full of loving goodness and wrapped
in saving grace. Void of any fear, and strong in faith.
Able to light the darkness as I struggle along the way.
Give it knowledge, to lead the lost to your door step
whatever the cost.
I pray it has wisdom to witness your word, to all
who will listen about your way, so they find joy
and happiness each and every day. Give it courage
in the face of fear, to laugh during sadness, to shed
no more tears. Teach it to love when I have been wronged
make it light of weight and full of song.
And last I ask, that it remain honest 'till my
dying day. Then give it to another, let it light
the path. And show him the way. And give
him life over death. Until he also passes away.
  And the Glory be yours.
  Amen.

**David Gooch**

## Lonely Heart

Lonely heart I cry for you, in the night and in the day.
Lonely heart I hear you cry, I understand what you say.
You are reaching out, I'm hear for you, for I feel the same.
I feel the love within my heart as I whisper your sweet name.
I cry for your caress, your arms around my spine.
Your scent, it smells like heaven, you body feels so fine.
I ache for your body next to mine, it's torture to my soul.
Without you I'm not real, without you I am not whole.
Lonely heart I cry for you, what else is there to do.
Lonely heart I cry for you, for I am lonely too.

**Erica Rockwell**

## Sophisticated

It came from his heart, a note he gave to me
it say's "wife I love you, and always will"
Laced with butterflies; words in red.

It came from his heart, a look he gave to me
as if to say "wife I love you, and always will"
Eyes glowing; elegant grace.

It came from his heart, a rose he gave to me
with meaning "wife I love you, and always will"
Long stems; buds in red.

It came from his heart, a kiss he gave to me
unspoken "wife I love you, and always will"
Wet, passionate; tender too.

It comes from my heart, myself I give to you
I say "husband I love you, and always will"
Creative, poised; sophisticated too!!

**Diana Hancock**

## A Forgotten Friend

Way up on a hill, stood a lonesome pine
It seemed longing for a friend
So I trudged up the hill in silence,
Time at the tree to spend.

I sat on the ground at the trunk and thought
How lovely a tree could be
I explained all my life's problems
And it never once lectured me

But as day by day time passes
And months turned into years
It seems I forgot the pine tree
And how once to me it was dear

Years passed and I came to see
The tree, but it couldn't be found
But I could see the traces
Where the wind had blown it down

I kind of felt deserted
But the fallen tree seemed to say
That if you don't nurture friendship
Sometimes it goes away

**Jory Shepherd Triplett**

## Punctuality——punctuality!

Why not make it a reality?
It seems to me that maybe you
Have had some difficulty with punctuality too.

It may not be your fault and yet,
Each time you come it's with regret
That your teacher reprimands you so
And his dislike for you seems to grow.

And in the end you cannot make amends
His patience soon comes to an end.
And then in all formality —
Try to use some punctuality!

And as he seeks to prune and mold
This strange and new personality,
He tries to impart to young and old
The priceless value of "PUNCTUALITY."

**E. Alice Stevenson**

## Our Dream

Once there was a dream so bright,
It sparkled in the broad day light.

A tiny house, some grass and trees,
A place where we could live with ease.

Invoked from Heaven it came to pass,
Born of love and built to last.

There will be storms upon a chart,
And some will spring from hardened hearts.

But dreams, thought fragile and ethereal,
With faith become like tempered steel.

And so, secure we may affirm,
Our dream is real, our happy home.

**Alanna DeWitt Bellflower**

## Love

Love is a difficult thing,
It takes you by surprise.
Love brings on many things and puts roses in your eyes.
We find LOVE sometimes happy, sometimes sad, it even some-
times makes
    us mad.
There are lots of things you can say about LOVE
But one thing still holds true.....
It has a certain bond never lets go of you.

**Jerold Ellis Ford III**

## Journey's End

The spirit soars above the sky riding winds that are unseen;
it travels faster than the eye and goes beyond where it has been.
The spirit sees the distant plains with eyes that need no sleep;
it doesn't feel the pelting rain nor see the surging oceans deep.

The spirit only ventures forth to bring reality into view,
to understand the reasons why the wheel of life is never new.
Life in its ever changing way illuminates the path of life;
we all must travel on our way to rise above our earthly strife.

We must all try to understand that love's the thing that brings us
    home;
to family, friends and all we share back to the heart from which we
    roam.
We cannot leave the things undone, the things we all were meant to do,
until all our earthly travels done, and all our earthly battles
    through.

Our creator made all its plans with only you and I in mind,
to teach us lessons yet unlearned, to urge us on so we shall find,
eternal rest within his arms, and loving peace beyond compare.
With all the wisdom that we need, to justify our being there.

When that day does finally come every living human soul,
will join the things he gave to us, to make each loving person whole.
We will be there in paradise, with God, whose name's eternal love
in peace and joy and harmony, with lights of heaven from above.

**Charles "Don" Crispin**

## Life

Life, is shorter than you think
Life, is not always pink
But when you'll find out the clue of it
You'll be opening the door of it
If you take a wrong step in your way
The door will shut and your dreams will go away
The right step will take you in the right direction
But you have to pay attention
If you take the wrong step at the wrong time ever
You'll be gone forever.

**Azin Rahimi**

## Hercules Cluster

I know I saw him sitting there tattered unwashed clothes.
It was easy to see by his weathered expression,
He had been afflicted with the hardships of our cruel world.
Where was his sanctuary to escape the brutal horders of ghosts, that
Haunted his soul each and everyday.
Red light ahead, no one to stop for so I bust on through.
The early morning moon is surrounded by a crystal mist,
Joined by a mammoth swarm of stars.
I glance over my right shoulder and the tattered man is no longer
   there.
The bus bench is empty, I know I saw Him sitting there.
Tattered man in tattered clothes, lazy man I might, crazy man I'm not.
His grocery cart leans against a pole, filled with odds and ends
That support his vagabond lifestyle.
A comb without teeth, a neatly rolled blanket is his bed and a map of
   the stars.
The empty streets have many ghosts, only he is no ghost at all.
He lives in pain and walks the streets, a star in his dreams and hope
   in his heart.
Tattered man pushes on through, to unite with the hercules cluster.
The bus bench is empty, I know I saw him sitting there.
Tattered man in tattered clothes, lazy man I might, crazy man I'm not.
His wounds have healed, his spirit set free, a star so bright he
   shines through the night.

   *Eddy Taylor*

## An Old Room

It was an old, roomy, romantic room.
It was more of an attic filled with
fruits, grain, and toys to play with,
then anyone's comfortable bedroom.

It had an iron bed in a corner,
next to an off-white painted wall,
and a floor window on the same wall,
and wooden stairs in the opposite corner.

It had a straw-bottomed chair, a night table
with gray and black marble on it,
where, at night, I lit my candle, and stared at it.
It had in the middle a tiny, tiled table.

I ran to that dim, displaced room
to take the sun by climbing on its roof;
to look at the village, the vast valley, the enormous rood;
to glance at the stars, and to see the four faces of the moon.

I ran to that roomy, romantic room
to study, to dream, to sleep or to sweep
and, if unhappy that was the place where to weep.
That old, quiet, overstuffed room is gone. It was my room.

   *Giovanna Minutolo Cicillini*

## Tear of the Wolf

Once so many, now so few...
   It was tiny, transparent
Once quickly, gracefully yet forcefully they ran...
   A tiny transparent rainbow of watery colors
Once is all they mated - for all eternity...
   Slowly the watery colors took on shape
Once life was sweet, the taste of blood warm...
   A diamond shape moving down on rich warm fur
Once cubs played without fear...
   Warm fur now growing cold from approaching death
Once the strong heart of the wolf beat fast...
   Now only a tear stains it, as death enters at last

   *Becky Ann Brinn*

## Battered Women's Anthem

My body will be strong and accept what is about to happen to it.
It will accept the foreign matter with love and trust.
My body will love the new addition and embrace it wholeheartedly.
I will be a better person after all this trauma and I will be
strong and spiritually rise above this plateau of pain and uncertainty
I will become whole again and dedicate my love to life ever after.
My body and mind will be one in rejoicing the birth of a better me.
I will be alright and live my life with a new purpose.
An awareness of what more I can do for me. A purpose to bring
joy and happiness. There shall be no doubt. I have missed
so much knowledge, yet I can seek it out and absorb it,
It is never too late. My body has been violated and
changed forever. The key to change is to have no fear of it.
To face it with truth and faith. I will have no fear
When I face the demon and I shall cast him out with
my sword of belief. My body will be whole again, with
my heart and spirit to follow. The strength of positive
affirmations shall be written stone, never to be worn down,
always to be the strength and foundation of a new beginning.

   *Cissie Cobb*

## Home Team Star

It was the fourth quarter and the game was close
It would come down to who wanted it most
Three minutes left and the home teams down
Their star player was fouled and fell to the ground

He hit the first and missed the last free throw
On the other end of the court he shot his man an elbow
The referee saw it and called a technical foul
On the player's face he wore an intimidating scowl
The teams began to drop in threes
Players began to taunt and tease
When the clock ran out the home team led by one
This game was close but they won

   *Emmanuel DeWalt*

## A Memo from Dwight N Vincent

A family is created from the magic of love
It's all impossible without the perfect mom
I've been around long enough to see
that another family like ours just can't be
All a parent can do is set the right example
then open the doors to the world's tricky angles

We were babied while we were babies
and guided while we were lads
You also let us make our own decisions
whether good or bad
And still you were there when we fell
and needed a hand

Mother you brought me up to be clever
sometimes I may not show it
but to purposely hurt you I would never

Mom I hope someday I find a girl like you
who will be the perfect wife and the best mother too

   *D. N. V.*

## Civil Liberties

Tears flowing down from Americas eyes
If we lose our civil liberties
A bit of America dies
Civil Liberties make America the land of the free
Without Civil Liberties where would we be?
Justice should be served some way
Without all of America having to pay

   *Evette McKinney*

## "Fly"

The sun comes up, the curtains buzz,
it's as sweet a day as ever was.

The air is warm, but hopes and dreams
are barricaded by a screen.

You spent your day on the window sill.
One day of life and now you lay still.

Little man you never flew.
You lived and died and no one knew.

The sun goes down, silence prevails,
No buzzing curtain, no grieving wail.

*Heather T. Green*

## Mom

Losing you Mom was my saddest day, it hurts so much in every way.
It's been 15 years now, that you've been gone, life does go on and on.
I miss you so very much. I miss having a motherly touch.
Our family, you held us together, now you've gone away.
We're lucky, if our family gets together for one day.
I miss the old family ways. I miss calling and coming and gabbing with
    you.
I wish just once, I could talk to you too.
It's been hard not having a Mom, now Dad is getting so sick too.
For Dad breathing is hard to do, soon I fear, Dad will be joining you.
That will be my darkest day, that my last parent goes away.
I'm not looking forward to that day. May that day be far away.
With Dad I got to know him, with Dad I spent time.
Now, me and Dad a good relationship you'll find.
Not having a Mom makes me sad. My kids not having a grandma
makes me mad. Three grandchildren you got from me. A good Mom you
    showed me to be.
Now, I see how being a Mom really can be. You have to live it to
    really see.
It's unfair that you had to go away. I hope we'll meet again someday.
I love you — Love,

*Janet Small*

## The Visit

It's cold in here.
It's been like this for the past fifteen years
Close the door...It's already closed.
Shut the window...That's closed too.
Turn up the heat...It's as high as it goes.
Then why is it so cold..? Surely you know.
I'm not dead am I..? No you're alive and well.
Are you sure I'm not in .....?
No, you're not in hell.
But, I see angry faces...That much is true.
And look! Over there, isn't that Jealousy?
Yes, I see him too.
Envy just winked at me...Maybe you should wave.
But he's standing next to Hatred! Come, you must be brave.
What's Lust doing in here...? You tell me.
I don't like this place...Soon we'll see.
Who are you...come let's depart.
You know I can't leave...I'm the landlord of your heart.
But it's much too cold in here.
It's been like this for the past fifteen years.

*Calvin Gorrell*

## Love—Show Me the Way

This warming smile empowers great, this fragile life of mine;
Its golden glow reveals just below
A seed a'sprout so pure and fine.

Open me onto a world where hope never dies;
Where rainbows sing through angels' wings
And tranquil hues caress in lullabies.

Love—Open me onto your world where tears are streamers on parade;
Where children laugh a mist of happiness
And never a somber glance displayed.

Love! Enrapture me sweet—
Cast away all bitter fruits and weeds of woe;
Be my virtue light to guide me right
To a height divine; through your sight I only know.

Love—Open me onto your world where rivers of peace never run dry;
Where fields of dreams spread forth a harvest green
And compassion a kiss of crimson fire.

Love—Open me onto your world where crystal seas never turn vile;
Where gentle winds a'whisper words of wisdom
And never a soul beguile.

Love—Show me the way!

*Alden W. Domizio*

## The Joys of Life

There's so very many joys in life
It's hard to count them all;
The beautiful fragrant blossoms of Spring
And the dancing leaves in the Fall.

The brilliance of the morning sun
Warming nooks and crannies of the land;
Wildflowers playing peek-a-boo
With shells on the sparkling sand.

Naughty puppies play tug o' war
And chew everything in sight;
Kittens leap from lofty heights
And cuddle in the morning light.

Butterfly wings, Bumble Bee stings; the laughter of a child,
Church bells ringing, choirs singing, animals in the wild.

Rainbows in the misty clouds; a prayer to Heaven above,
But none of these are possible
Without virtue, faith and love.

The joys in life are many, look into the hearts of man;
Find peace of mind and love divine,
Find Paradise in your hand.

*Betty Steeves*

## Why

Why do we seek those who too or African,
it's important for us all to make a plan.
Why do we let them pull us apart,
it's togetherness we need and its time to start.
Black against black is no way to go,
because whites sit back and enjoy the show.
It's time for us to open our eyes and be wise,
because we're killing our dreams and
halting the rise.
Brothers and sisters, we must all unite.
To come out on top and win our fight.
So way do we do this, we all must think,
we can't pull together with one broken link.

*Bobby Green*

## Valentine's Day

To celebrate Valentine's Day is not a joy to me.
It's not like hanging stockings by a mantle
or putting ornaments on a Christmas tree.

To me it's just like any ordinary day,
like the first of September or May.
But Valentine's Day is a day for love;
a day for the Earth and the World above.

To my future Valentine, if not on Valentine's day,
please be mine on the first of September or May.

*Felicia Moore*

## It's Not Needy It's Greedy

First you should know in this world today,
It's not needy that gets help it's greedy.
Once there was a hurricane in a certain
Country and all countries in the world
Came to there aid by giving them
material to rebuild their country
and I was disillusioned. Instead of
giving the material to people who needed
It most, they gave it to the merchants -
The big ones, who are greedy. Speaking
of greedy, it would take me a decade
which is 10 years, did you know
greed. That greed starts at home
then spreads to the wider society.
The only cure for greed is love so,
my love, I leave with love one another -
then all greed will be eradicated.

*Delroy G. Needham*

## Hurt to Feel

I'm sitting in a room with people I thought were friends.
It's nothing they did to make me say that. It's just me.
It's all in my head.
Something makes me second guess what they do.
I even second guess every time I make love to you.
Why do I think so much? I think I'm drowning.
Why do I have no luck? I think I'm sinking.
Why do I suck? I think I'm dead.
Everyone says they love me. Love is all around my body,
But for some reason it won't come inside.
I've forgotten how to ask it in.
I've forgotten how to pose the question.
I've forgotten how to live.
Why do I feel so much? I shouldn't have a heart.
Why do I see so much? I shouldn't have eyes.
Why am I? I shouldn't be.
I've lost the will to live. I've lost the will to die.
I am I.

*Christopher C. Dietz*

## This Day

This day can't last long
It's one more to pass soon
And although it's a puzzle waiting to be put
Together
Make the pieces bigger today

You can show some-one love
Or give a piece of your heart
So next time you say
What have I done with my day
Just think what more you could have done
For the person who came your way

*Darci Huck*

## "Watch For This Light"

He gives us His special light...To see from within.......
It's only thru His special power that we shall ever win!
His light scatters darkness everywhere.....
He helps with our ev'ry care.....
and that's how we know - that His light is always there.
Watch for His light!!! Watch for His Light!!!
He never shuts the door on a single soul.....
and He waits so patiently to make us whole!
You'll never be lonely again....
Jesus will always be your friend....
When you watch for His light
and you find it and let it come in.......
No more questions, no more fears....
No more darkness, no more tears......
Cause God sent His Son...
To show us how to love
Watch for His Light......
Watch for His Light.......
Watch for His Light.......

*Janice Maurine Ames*

## Abolish The Rose?

There is nothing like a rose.
Its praise I can sing from eve tell morn,
It has unforgettable fragrance, boundless beauty,
But alas, it has a terrible thorn.

For all that they tried to change that fact.
Crossing pollens and petals perpetually. I suppose.
If they take away the cruel cutting thorn
How would I know it was a rose?

And so my dear, my truly beloved,
You could be more tender, sweeter, more true.
Though if you were changed, rearranged.
How would I know it was you?

*Edith R. Nichols*

## Eyes Are Closing

My soul is bleeding, crying to be heard,
it's silence, like glass,

A brush of death is felt against my skin,
the touch of God, felt against my soul,
His every breath felt flowing off my face,
His blood, shedding upon my soul,

I am drowning in my own pain,
I scream to find a way out, to regain my conscience,
the one I never had,

The glass encasing me, only cracked,
but I want it shattered,
I lie still, feeling, experiencing nothing more than pain,
Let it end now!
May I be cast into the heavens,
finally free, finally at peace,
finally found.

*Jason Vasquez*

## Me

I am like a flower just waiting to bloom.
I'm like a breath of fresh air on a winter's afternoon.
I am like the first star that twinkles in the night.
I am that lonely star that sees no other stars in sight.
I am like the falling white snow on a cold Christmas Eve.
And on the last day of autumn I'm like the late falling leaves.
I am like a rose that blooms in early June.
I'm like a brilliant colored butterfly that emerges from its cocoon.

*Brandye Williams*

## A Jazz Impression

There's a nice kind of rhythm in Bop;
It's so cool, and yet it's so hot.
It has a heavenly beat and you can feel it—
So open and free, no one can seal it.

You can never be blue with the Blues,
All the hues in the world you can use.
There's no black or no white,
No wrong or no right,
It keeps up with the times like the news.

Like the heaven on high it's above me.
There's no need to have someone to love me.
A fusion of joy and pain — with every refrain...
...it makes you always want to listen again.

*Dennis Greene*

## The Passing of Time

How wonderful each day is.
Its something, you can't bring back
to enjoy more of.  But, you can throw
the moments away
The experience, joys, happiness
The knowing of the sunrise and the sunset.
The feelings of love, contentment,
learning and fulfillment of oneself
Live it to the fullest, for it does not return.
Just memories remain.

*Hazel L. Earl*

## There's Something About You

There's something about you, since the day we met,
It's still a mystery that I can't forget,
There's something about you, can't put my finger on,
At times I think I've got it, and then it's gone.
There's something about you, etched in my brain,
It remains constant like an all day rain.
When will it leave me, never, never, never,
This something about you, will last forever.
Is it the laughter in your eyes?
That somehow seems to hypnotize.
Can it be the sun shining on your hair,
Or the way you seemingly walk on air.
There's something about you, I seem to recall
It's with me winter, springtime, summer and fall.
There's something about you, that I hold dear
There's something about you throughout the year.
When will it leave me, never, never, never
This something about you will last forever.

*Betty J. Miller*

## To My First Son

I can remember where you used to play;
I've gazed intent on scenes your jungle-gym
Aroused.  I can't forget the day I swayed
You on the swing so clumsily:  You brimmed
The vast horizon, then you hit the ground.
Forgive my hands for pushing you toward heaven,
I never meant to let you drop and frown
Among your tears.  You were only seven—
That helped you heal, but did you feel the joy
Of swinging worth the pain?  I hope you did
Because the swinging never changes, boy,
And falling will remain the cruelest bit.
  My son I want you to remember this:
  The hand that raises you will often miss.

*Chris Meyer*

## The Whispering Falls

The Whispering Falls is the only way for man,
  it's the next thing to being free.
We're taking life in our hands,
  to make this journey a reality.

As I listen to the thunder of the Whispering Falls,
  through the silence in the night.
The coolness in the air touches us all,
  since the darkness is taking over the light.

The stars twinkling through the midnight sky,
  while our flame begins to burn higher.
We listen to the birds singing as they fly,
  knowing peace is near the open fire.

In the morning the flame burns low,
  knowing our love has spread this land.
Time after time the Whispering Falls urge us to go,
  crying for one day we will safely have love in our hands...

*James Spigle*

## Laughter from a Child

I've stood on sand at midnight — heard the mighty ocean roar.
I've been atop a mountain — watched the graceful eagle soar.
I've heard the music of the wind — its ranting ever wild.
But none of these can match the joy of laughter from a child.

I've soared in planes, slipped through the clouds — looked down on earth below.
I've watched the moon, the sun, the stars, in great majestic show.
The little streams, the canyons, hill and vale, have me beguiled.
But none of these can match the joy of laughter from a child.

The little bird at twilight, the friends at campfire glow,
Good music, sounds of silence, can peace to us bestow.
The petal from a flower — with beauty undefiled..
But none of these can match the joy of laughter from a child.

*Iris Rose Sherfey*

## From the Mouth Comes Truth

I've never been the prettiest, I've never been the skinniest.  But I've never had to crawl down on my knees.  I'd catch someone before they fall, they take a step and make me crawl.  Then push me down into the deep dark sea.  I try to fight and I try to win, but somehow my spirit just gives in.  I can't struggle, I can't cry, and feel as though I might die.  I try so hard just to be, and then they take that away from me.

All I want, I never got; just someone to love a lot.  No one cares or ever will, that's my picture, so hard to thrill.  I can't keep going on like this, I'm not a mask trying to conceal.

I've got a truth, no one wants to hear, and even if they do, it's not for real.  It makes me mad when I want to speak, and they all just walk away from me.  No one who I want to please ever thinks of what they really see.  They only care about themselves, unless I try to help them out.  Then they think sometimes about me, but only how to help them be.  Soon they stand all by themselves, and only give me grief and doubt.  And if they fall I help them up; they won't help me, constantly stuck.

*Jennifer Hartz*

## Untitled

I wear the red ribbon with pride and compassion
I wear the red ribbon with hope of a cure
I wear the red ribbon with love and determination
that all of us will on day wear the red in celebration
that at long last this menace has been defeated

*Alan R. Kestin*

## Boys

Muddy foot prints on the floor.
Jelly handmarks on the door;
A trail of marbles down the hall
Crayola art work on the wall,
A jillion glasses in the sink —
And not a moments time to think.
Chills and bills and western drama;
Cokes and pokes and cries for Mama!
Dogs and fish and birds to feed;
A stray little kitten — eight eyes that plead;
Bandaged toes and sunburned noses
Indian forts where I planted roses —
Tears, with laughter tumbling after,
Echoing roof and trembling rafter,
A hundred thousand broken toys —
Add these up and you have boys...

But there isn't one that would be sold
For a million tons of minted gold!

**Jeanne Louise Morgan**

## Conjugated

Oh yes, you have a right to strut around
Jockeying for position in your jockeys,
Gut extended over exhausted elastic.

Oh, yes, you have a right to ignore
Me when I tell a story that made me laugh.
Stony faced, you squelch conjugal communication.

Oh, yes, you have a right to explode
Using foul language, throwing up arms
And shouting stubborn offenses; extinguishing enemies.

Oh, yes, you have a right to control
My every move, every thought, giving directions
To my simplest of moves, implying imbecility.

Oh, yes, you have a right to submerge
My soul in scalding oil; then crackling ice.
A master of manipulation; drowning dreams.

Oh, yes, I have a right to curl up,
To curdle with frustration in futile protest
Hugging to my breast, shattering psyche.

Oh, yes, I have a right to turn away, amazed that you think I am
Attracted to you when I lie down beside you, loathing love.

**Elizabeth Righter**

## In Memoriam: Oklahoma City 1995

The vail of tears of a million mothers
joins the gentle rain of spring
in an attempt
to sanctify the rubble that covers
the hopes and dreams of innocent souls
that were blown apart before they
had opportunity to realize the magnificence
of the gift of life.

While Satan quietly slips away saddened
realizing that spirit lives,
a nation begins to pray
as the warmth of the new day's sun
confirms the compassion for those
remaining hearts and pronouncing
I love for the lifeless child
in the arms of a fireman.

**John F. Sobecki**

## Working Mother

In my work there is no ending-no peace.
Just a sameness, forever, eternal,
From morning to twilight, will it cease?
Do they need me, am I merely banal?
There are good days, there are dull ones sometimes.
As a peasant, the wage-earner in strife,
Trapped and tangled so deep in these phone lines
On a word search for humor, wit is the knife!
As I grope through this forest of same words
And phrases, I'm fueled by blue eyes and pink,
Small faces with wide open mouths like birds.
It's for my children that I work, and I think;
  I'm not nothing. They need me. I love them.
  The job keeps them fed and happy, 'round my hem.

**Desiree Fox**

## My Love

He didn't have much to say on that beautiful fall day,
Just a soft humble smile in an easy quiet way,
A ride in the wind, our day in the sun
We knew from the start our lives would be one.

Two little girls and a tiny baby boy,
Our lives together had only great joy.
A drive to the mountains or the beach for a week,
Looking for rocks, flowers, or sea shells to seek.

Our hearts content, with this treasure of love,
it seemed that all God's blessings just fell from above.
Our years together, too short they seemed,
but through all this, that star still gleamed.

Ever leading and guiding and encouraging us on
to the mark of the high calling and a place called
"Eternal Home".

So swift the call from the Master above
and you soared upward like the morning doves.
To receive the rest you so richly deserve,
because you chose our Savior's great love.

**Janie W. Corn**

## The Halloween Pastry

A delicious piece of pastry
  Just didn't know what to do
He sat in the bakery window
  And watched the kids say "boo"

On Halloween night
  when the moon was scary
The pastry dressed up like a hairy blueberry

He was picked up as candy
  And taken away
From his comfy home
  On the bakery tray

He hid in a sack
  And looked out the crack
At a scary old witch
  With a frog on her back

It was then the blueberry
  Just melted and died
And agreed it was better
  Than being pastry-fried!

**John Geimer**

## Black Swan

I saw a most enchantingly beautiful, black Swan:
    Just drifting on a sea of crystal so clear;
    Was it blue? I could not tell, the sea so pure:

She sat the sea so magnificently
Without a care ... it seemed; O what a sight to behold;
Shining so radiant, in the late evening light:

I looked around to share the wonder with anyone!
Such beauty, the works of God:
But no one I saw ... as I looked back to the crystal sea;
She sat still, is she real? Before my thoughts could take shape;
The enchantingly beautiful black Swan, took sail;
Straight toward the bright harvest moon, with diamonds surrounding;
My breath caught!
Then, as if time stood still ... I was in Paradise:

As the enchantingly beautiful black Swan disappear out of view;
    My breathe came again as I whisper;
Sail on enchantingly beautiful black Swan, sail on.

*Doris Marshall*

## Hold On To My Dreams

As time goes by sometimes I feel as if I'm ready to die.
Just lay me down in the depths of God's earth.
Peacefully, gently - the rest I deserve.
It would soon be all over - the pain I feel.
God will lift me into a world that I know is real.
I will be guided and treated with all respect
just let me go now - lay me to rest.
My life you can not hold on to, my memories you can.
Walk along the beaches with my soul, remember, hold my hand.
Your eyes will be my vision to watch over you.
My heart felt dreams will live within you.
I can still hear your tears at night.
That's why you can seem to feel me holding you tight.
I'll continue to hold you in my heart - I promise
Tara - our love will never part.

*Christine Haskett*

## Reflections

The water so still, reflecting the moon,
just like a mirror, in this quiet lagoon.
Clouds drifting by cut off the moons light,
making stars glisten brighter this warm
summer night.
Off in the distance an occasional fish
makes rings on the water, just like a
big dish.
On this quiet night not even a gull,
breaks the silence of this beautiful lull.
I know that morning will change everything,
with the crash of the surf and birds on
the wing.
Just being here in this beautiful place,
makes my heart lighter and puts a smile
on my face.

*Burt Chancey*

## Where's The Barbershop Quarter?

T is for the time we spend complaining
A is for the anger that we spew
X is for the X-tra bills we're paying
E is for the empty pockets too.
S is for the simple life we long for

That we know we never can regain.
Put them all together, they spell TAXES
Which follow us from cradle to the grave.

*Virginia Iaia*

## My Prison

I am locked within a prison the prison of my mind
Just like a ship on stormy seas
My way home I cannot find.

I grabbed on to cold, hard steel
And I looked between the bars,
But all I saw was destruction and death,
I saw the world's eternal scars.

I rested my head against the bars
And I hung my head in shame.
I could hot help the tears that fell,
For we were all to blame.

I'm here to serve a lifetime,
There will never be parole.
I will do what I must to save my tortured soul.

To heal the wounds that torment my heart
I have stayed within my shell,
As I look for some small ray of hope
From my prison cell.

Pain, death, destruction and crime, will it ever end?
In my Prison, I am forced an eternity to spend.

*Elena Van Meter*

## "Wheel of Fortune"

"Wheel of Fortune" - Let the try-outs begin,
    Just tell me now, what to do to win...
They put you on to spin a wheel,
    Boy-oh-boy how exciting that must feel;
A letter you have to pick,
    To make their phrases click,
You picked the right letter Yes, Yes, Yes,
    To the final round you're their guest
So much excitement fills the room,
    A big winner you could be soon,
Only the final puzzle, now you must solve,
    Lots of help they give to make the word evolve;
But, the final letters you must call,
    Here is where you give it your all
You do it, you got it, Listen to the Cheer,
    "Wheel of Fortune"'s big prize is presented to you here,
This is not a dream, for lots of people have seen,
    What fun it is to meet Pat and Vanna, these people of fame,
Now, let it be my fortune to do the same...
    For I am ready to play your game!!!

*Dawn H. Barrell*

## Gentle Hint

Just a little note cause I wanted to say
Just the thought of you makes me happy during the day.
Then during the night when I'm feeling run down,
I remember you and sleep, deep and sound.
Oh so often you see, just a little thought
will bring sweet dreams to me.
So I wanted you to know, I need to say
Just thinking of you makes me jealous in a way.
Cause I can't be there to share each moment of everyday
But I hope it pleases you to know
I'll take you along wherever I go.

*David Graber*

## Schools

When in school are we asked to read a book
just to enjoy it?
  In History or English we are told
"Write five hundred...talk ten...deploy it."
  Judgement is sure - pressurized, testurized.
Graduation a delayed reward.  Or threat.
  Thirteen credit points or else
One more semester will be yours.
  To be enjoyed?  To be deployed?
What happens to the joy, that bubbling ecstatic laughter
  that thrills from a baby?
It is silenced, judged, graded, compared, despaired.
  How sad.
  How sad.
It is found again in a pad,
  released by drugs -
and hugs.
  How sad.
  How sad.
### *Joan Watson*

## Love's First Kiss

Like a snowflake falling gently, softly
  Kissing her cheek.
Both of them like a blush peach wine
  To be savored till it's ready.
He stood there so quietly,
  Wondering if he had a chance.
Shaking like a little boy
  not quite sure whether to ask or take,
Proceeding cautiously so as not to make a mistake.
  Like a little twinkle star
They came together as one.
  The beginning of a bright, vibrant, beautiful
Rainbow, with only the promise of tomorrow.
### *Carol Lee Gavello*

## "Crossroads"

Where am I? I thought as I came to a crossroad; where I am I do not
  know.
To my left is forest which I observed,
But the road is not straight, it is narrow and curved.

To my right is a path narrow and straight.
At the end of this path is a radiant golden gate.

As I look straight ahead, I cannot see
For a vast white mist covers the road before me.

I could always turn around and go back the way I came,
But in my past there is no glory or fame.

I chose to go right because of the golden gate,
But something inside my gut told me to wait.

Then I heard a voice as if from the Lord;
"The hardest path has the greatest reward."

With that in mind, I looked left then right.
Then I looked straight ahead into the mist so white.

I took a step straight ahead.  This was the hardest path for I know
not where it led.  As I walked through the mist it opened before my
eyes and revealed the greenest grasses and bluest skies.

"You have chosen well," said the voice from before,
And I came to a crossroad nevermore
### *Ben Kervin*

## The Front Porch

Delicate trees graced the scene, like ballerinas spinning across the
  lawn.
I sipped my coffee as the sun peeked through the clouds at the break
  of dawn.
I gazed beyond the boundaries of the safe, green yard
And spotted a trio of blue jays, dive bombing, never letting down
  their guard.
Bordered by green and orange honeysuckle vines,
Far from the cities, the violence and crime.
Thunder, lightning on the horizon, with promises of rain.
And off in the distance, the lonely moan of a train.
I recalled colorful, autumn days that became drab by November,
And anticipated snow covered Christmas scenes, as I remember.
But, when the weather is fair and stars sprinkle the skies
The children whisper ghost and chase fireflies.
I soaked up the scenery, awaiting the rain
But, it went on by us, the storm never came.
By twilight, I lit the citronella torch
And just keep right on sitting there on my front porch.
### *Ellen Denton*

## The Curse of Sight

In a dark room, a prison cell
lay two men in this dark hell
together they were for 12 months
speaking and laughing, content in one another's company
they helped each other through the pain
and both remained sane
but they never saw the others face
for the room was dark and light scarce
and so they learned to endure, the fear of the unknown through the
others voice

One day they were freed and brought to light
both saw what he thought was a gruesome sight
both saw the truth hidden by lack of light...
one man was black, the other white
they curled their fingers and held up their fists
they fell at each other and began to fight
they forgot about the many times they'd prayed together hands
  intertwined
and so it often seems to me, that man was cursed with the gift of
  sight
for is it not the truth to be, that in the dark we needn't be remind,
that the color of another is just in ones mind
### *Julie Herrmannsdoerfer*

## The All Knowing Christ

By those mighty powerful hands of God, He guides
Leading all the way through life, none can hide
His Holy eyes, supersedes every earthly creatures
How He longs for mankind return close to His side.

Wide open are his alms, He'll not always chide
Confiding in His beloved children, Christ, is mine
Yet overcoming in stride, from all those evil tides
His loving penetrating, loving eyes, beacons your return

As His Holy Word recorded, true believers His bride
With Christ we'll reign, and forever will abide
Our destination, Heaven where the saints resides
Then, the pride of knowing Christ as King, God had not lied

None can behold the inside, looking from the outside
No wonder, all sorrows, tears and sighs, be wiped away
Outside the Pearly Gates, stand our accuser, spied
Who've defied God's command, whose return denied

Like an angel, whose penetrating vision, sees afar
There aren't any offside, to His boundless grace
This All-knowing Christ, has all the ability to redeem
Would you become His child, accepting all He provides?
### *Alfred W. Parson*

## Yesterday's Tomorrow

Hope for the future comes from yesterday's past,
learn from mistakes and regrets never last.
We're here for a purpose never defined,
a meaning to life to light what is blind.

Is time predetermined? A question to pose.
Explore this idea, but nobody knows.
Goals we set forward from one day to next,
a struggle appears and we soon change the text . . .

Wisdom can come from living, as life was meant to be.
As long as mind is open, then eyes will surely see.
A man is said to prosper by the riches which are earned.
Still others are more wealthy by the lessons they have learned.

Years can mean so little, while a moment is so much.
A simple glance, a familiar scent, or a knowing, loving touch.
Time will pass so quickly, that life is like a blur.
An idea on fast forward as if it never were.

*George W. Noble*

## Nowhere

The sun as it goes back into bed,
Leaves a fresh scribbled like sky,
Like a toddler scribbled on a piece of paper.

I stop to marvel at it,
For almost a second,
Then I feel a slight faint,
Because the marvelous colorful nature of wonderful earth,
Takes my breathe away.

The sky shows me and the world the child's frustrations,
Hopes and fears of his or her life and the dark lines show,
Scary future plans watching the sky and it's colors combined,
Reminds me I'm the child and this my picture so I must.
Be careful how I paint it, otherwise the paint will dry,
Permanently and leave my life, with unfinished marks and
Uneven lines and I'll go nowhere!

*Jacqui Smith (Popeye Leggs)*

## AIDS To Unity

We have had
    Lemonade
    Serenade

    Public aid
    Hearing aids

    Teacher aides
    Presidential aides

    ....we could always do without one or the other.

Now we have

    HIV/AIDS
    AIDS awareness
    AIDS to be comforted
    AIDS to deeper spirituality
    AIDS to heaven-consciousness

    Personal AIDS
    Family AIDS
    Community AIDS
    World AIDS

    ... we are all involved in one way or another.

*Arthur M. Ross*

## Dawn To Dusk

As golden rods pierce through the morn, new
    life is brought into being.
This child: nurtured and cared for,
Understands everything in the simplest form.
Questions neither origin, nor creator, nor self.

Moons turn from new to full.
Much is lost through science;
Innocence, reality, self.
A search begins.

Travels through centuries of history bring only
    more questions.
Young is young; old is old;
Nothing can change the time expired.
Look forward! for the day is almost done.

Every moment is cherished within its own right.
The struggle is over; acceptance remain.
The sun sets upon another life;
As the soul enters into a timeless moonlit night.

*Bettina Lengsfeld*

## A Breathe Away

I breathed in, she breathed out.
Life is forever, or so we thought;
We shared two souls, one precious heart
Nothing but nothing could pull us apart
She was always one thought, a breath away.

Where is my sister, my very best friend?
Lost is the strength which couldn't be bought
Life is forever, or so we thought;
Shared was our childhood, its dreams and tears;
Shared was our laughter and all our fears

I cling to my dreams where she spins for awhile
All of God's plan, His secrets, His style;
She reminds me of good times, all of the mirth
Her foothold's in heaven, while mine's on earth

I study at length my mirrored reflection
Life was hugged with her special affection;
My eyes are hers and I've copied her style
Those are my hands, but that's her smile;
She's only one thought, one memory, a breathe away.

*Jeanne Deroche*

## Growing Old

Age is just a frame of mind,
    Life is good, Life is kind!
If you will only let it be,
    You can grow old gracefully.
When grief and sadness comes your way,
    Convince yourself there's a better day.
If you believe it with all your heart,
    It will be that way from the very start.
Be kind and considerate to those you know,
    Remembering always "you reap what you sow."
Face each day with joy and a smile,
    And you will determine life is worthwhile.

*Clairene B. Young*

## Work Together

As the sound of the rain drop falls,
lightning crashes and thunder rolls,
and the silence in the late night cry,
you think of a lost soul and want to die.

Wishing someone else would really care,
you look at the moon to say a little prayer.
There it goes, the light is gone.
Now you must wait till dawn.

To see the light that lasts forever.
To stop the cries, let's work together!

*Autumn Featheroff*

## Misty Dreams

It was the night of regulus reign in the mid heaven of the wheels of
lights.
That are earth laid dreaming of misty sights.
And sighed "mist be born of dew drops and dreams."
The dew did drop like nectar from heavens lofty heights.
As the moon did lend her silvery rays to each dew drop.
As tenderly as mother earth did weave her spell of mist and dreams.
Her daughter the mist began to rise.
She danced and waved in the starlit fields of her mothers bosom.
Earths daughter the mist brought forth many Misty forms
whenever the moon beams gently touched her.
"Queen of the mist all hail her for she is our mother." sang the
misty forms.
Her mother is the bountiful earth and her sister is the silvery moon.
Her father is the starry heavens and her brother is the bright
morning star.
For they were the cause of this enchantment
Of mist and dreams of mother earth.

*Diana Maria Cruz*

## Unity

Like a freshly fallen snowflake in the middle of June,
like a flower in winter, or the man in the moon,
I stand alone.

Like the blind man who sees,
like the deaf man who hears,
I've stood alone for too many years.

Like the man who buys love,
like the man with no sins,
I stand alone, more losses than wins.

Like the love that makes sense,
like the sun in the sky,
I'll stand alone until the day I die.

Like freshly fallen snowflakes, on Christmas day,
like raindrops in April, or flowers in May,
We stand together in every way.

The stand that I stood, alone and forlorn,
Was inside my soul from the time I was born.
I searched throughout life and now I can say,
we all stand united in love, every day.

*Erik Steven Langhoff*

## White Dogwood

White dogwood petals drifting down
Like snowflakes carpeting the ground,
Reminding me of other SPRINGS
Of youth and love and magical things,
Bridal laces - baby faces
All the songs my heart still sings.
White dogwood petals drifting down
Like snowflakes carpeting the ground.

*Sarah Daniel Vaughan*

## The Dying Art

Writing is a dying art
Like a shooting star or a thought of desire
It's life, in no way, outlives it's death
But, this art isn't dead.
There are some days, some weeks
I wish it was. The longing, the waiting for a response
But this art isn't dead.
It lingers on, fed by my love
My love for it, my love for you.
No one seems to understand.
Why this art isn't dead.
The spoken word is best, some say
No waiting, no longing to read your voice
To hear your words, its my own choice
To believe that this art isn't dead
Don't they know.... when I write to you
It's the me you like, the me I wish
To be. Without this art you'd disappear
And I'd be left with nothing here.

*Jennifer Perkins*

## Scare Trees

Scare trees, let my old golden dreams go.
Like bright yellow kites, they could fly
So high, a la Truman Capote's.
Twisting, soaring, and skimming,
At first they barely skip along
Before suddenly streaming aloft.
Watch them dip and whirl a mad
Polka with the wind.

Some fly so high they melt into the sun,
Small white tails still trying to balance them.
But no line can be seen.
Other dreams, turned to night terrors,
Fly to certain destruction.
Screaming, they try to seize the wind.
They catch on talking lines,
Or wind around tall black scare trees.

*Dorothy V. Pettee*

## yesterday's monsters

bring back yesterday's monsters
like casper and the boogieman
the kind that hide behind doors,
under beds, in closets...then
disappear when mama waved her hand.

bring back yesterday's monsters
today's monsters are too scary
dressed in their everyday people disguise.

masquerading
masquerading as the boy next door
the cute little toddler you used to
baby-sit for.

masquerading
masquerading as the mother of two
what unimaginable horrors she put
her babies through.

so bring back yesterday's monsters
the kind that can be explained away
they didn't wreak as much havoc and
heartbreak as the monsters we have today.

*Carolyn J. Washington*

## A Child.... A Simple Thing (A Teacher's View)

A child is such a simple thing,
like down beneath a sea gull's wing,
or rosebuds kissed by gentle rain......

- eyes searching through a window pane.

They'll find a land of make believe,
Where daisies dance and spiders weave
great castles with their golden threads,
while fairies yawn and scratch their heads.

And in the wind music is heard,
and every toe on every bird
is beating time on swaying trees -
while harmony is kept by bees.

And within the tiny crabs I'm told,
are precious grains of magic gold,
they dust the sands of every beach.....

Is this the kind of thing we teach?

At one time we were simple things,
building castles, riding swings - but, to meet those eyes
across the pane would that mean more for us to gain?

For within a child's simple mind, there's so much more for us to find.
### *Emily D. Franz*

## Spring Song:  With Variations

The rains of April skies that oft the earth caress
Like fumbling hand of child at mother's breast
Awake the many glorious forms of nature's life
To vernal sounds, aromas, sights and colors rife.

The earth in quickening movements swells to help bring forth
The fruit she bears, a sign of spring's seductive court.
And though the darkened skies are heavy now, downcast,
The birth of child by spring, glad joy and great, forecast.

Breathe the redolent air:  see the quickening there.
Bask in the feeling of ecstasy rare.
Hear the quivering song:  hear the rivulets throng.
List to the concord of harmony long.
Sing the beautiful spring:  make your song its praises ring.
Life to the soul, to each natural thing.

Let's live again and love again
Let all our rapture ring.
It's spring again, let's sing again
The happy, blissful spring.
### *Albert P. Okray*

## School

In school you can learn many different things,
Like reading or spelling or how to draw rings!

You get to write stories and sometimes you draw
If you're good, you play games, the best part of all!

Your teacher's a person you can look up to,
For they're very smart, and they care about you!

The best part of school's that you learn every day,
Your teachers help you to learn, in any way!

School is a place where you can get your things done,
But then afterwards, you can always have fun!
### *Erin Slack*

## Epitaph

She reminds me of the essence of springtime,
Like the birds that sing and the sun that shines.
She is like the soothing scent of lilacs,
And the first sign of robin tracks,
She told me something, a time back when,
That all good things must come to an end.
Treat all that you love with undying affection,
Don't regret the days of selfish rejection.
It's never too late to share with her,
As much of yourself you can possibly endure.
Her life I value, more than my own- I must say,
Others couldn't be as lucky, as I am today.
The day will come when her life, time will steal,
I can't even describe how empty I'll feel.
If for my next life, I were to choose another,
I'd have to say, I'd choose the same wonderful
Mother.
### *Dana T. H. Fillion*

## To Reflect and Reminisce

I am undulating, undecided-
Like the breeze, changing direction
Back and forth along the river's edge.

I am the tree branch, adrift in the water's wake
Caught in the rhythm of life.

I understand the forces that surround me, and yet
I care only to skip freely,
Like a dragonfly hovering and skimming the surface.

I care only to glance wide-eyed up at the clouds
Snaking lazily along the horizon.

To feel my feet touching down on the uneven landscape
Just long enough to propel me forward into the afternoon air.

I realize that life is such a serious pursuit,
And there must always be a reason; an explanation;
A purpose for my existence.

But today, I relish only to exist.
To breathe the fragrant remnants of wildflowers-already
beyond the glory of full bloom, as they languish in their demise.

I too, have already given my best, and now wish only
To recline upon the riverbank, to reflect and reminisce...
### *Charles J. Bertolino Jr.*

## The Gift of Time

Time passes silently throughout our lives,
Like waves ebbing against an unseen shore.
Intervals of light and dark, time derives
Until the sun and moon appear no more.

Time, the deep mystery unsolved by man
Its dimension unknown to finite truth.
Through our fingers, it slips, like grains of sand,
While this ungraspable force steals our youth.

Taken for granted, as though not present,
Its value to life is lost forever.
Seized as a choice to be benevolent,
Life is enriched by those who endeavor.

Time, the Creator's unseen gift to man
For each to seek and do His divine plan.
### *Bruce Bunner*

## February Fourteenth

February Fourteenth is a Winter's day.
Likely to be cold with snow or icy rain,
Likely to be chilly,
Likely to be gray
Wind skating through the streets
Dodging white snow flakes
Snow that looks so pretty falling from above
No sooner on the ground than all turned to mush
Painting tall gray buildings with earth's own gray slush
You would think the world was sad and lonely
but-
February Fourteenth is Valentine's Day
Warm though it may snow,
Cozy though it may rain
February Fourteenth is a friendship day
So put away your poems and come out to PLAY!!!

**Jessica Rubenstein**

## Hayride

Bumping along a shaded country road
lined with flowers and wild blackberries,
we share the fellowship of Your family
drawn together on cinctured bales of fragrant hay.

Peace pervades this place amid the lowing of cows,
the whisper of a gentle stream and the laughter of children.
A tousle-headed boy-child snuggles dreamily in my lap
and drifts into quiet slumber.

Shadow and light play tag among the branches overhead
as hints of Your glory sneak through gateways of gold-rimmed clouds.
A gentle, cleansing rain speaks silently of Your mercy,
of life renewed, a second chance.

"How lovely is Your dwelling place, O Lord, God of Hosts"—
in the bond of fellowship and a hayride on a country road.

**Carol Barlow**

## Forever Without You

Sounds, colors, smells . . . . . .
Liquid gold, flowing ice, pearls of amber, rushing ruby
let out by the pop of a cork, the soft grind of a lid.

From the rim of glass to avid lips, the wake of sunny
cool, the frosted glow, the sweet harshness, the infinite now,
the brutal peace that kills the soul.

For it is a dying soul that cries and rages at you.
You lulled, then rocked; you purred, then roared; you
seduced and then betrayed. And amid the solace hid the
fang of destruction that snatched and slowly poisoned.

To thee I say never again, ever so no more. I will be
blind to your radiance; I will forbid your scent, I will
shut out your siren song.

The tattered cloth of my life lies, barely able to
rise on the whispers of hope. As its threads are
weaved again, the song of life soars:

blowing the timid sail
on the uncharted sea
of tomorrow...

**Danielle Turns**

## Untitled

As she sat alone in the dark,
listening to the rain beat upon the tarp,
she thought of when they would meet.
What she'd say,
what he'd do,
wondering when he would whisper the worlds,
"I love you."
Just then the darkness went away,
as the lighting lit up the sky,
and that moment, she knew,
that one day all her dreams would come true.

**Jaclyn Renee Givens**

## Somewhere Over Ohio And Illinois

Man has taken the Holy roundness and turned it into
little building blocks.
What once was Holy in its roundness, a perfect circle
of balance, is now little postage stamps of farms
and ribbons of concrete on the land far below.

The balance is still there, but man has stood on top
of the circle and mashed it flat.
To conform, to what he wants and to forget what God
had created was Holy and sacred and round.

The history of man is conformity, a million monkeys
aping each other.
Beating the roundness flat, beating everything into
conformity with who so ever is the stronger.
God help us all!

**James R. Hoyle**

## Often

Often I dream that can touch the sky,
Live among angels, and perch above rain.
Often I wish for my body to quickly die,
So my soul can soar wildly, above all this pain.

Often I fear that life ends with death.
Life continues moving without me;
Often I dread an eternal black rest,
A place for my dreams to no longer be.

Often I cry when you are not here,
My thoughts becoming my only friend.
Often I think of you being near,
Our love holding strong until the end.

And often I kneel beside your grave,
Praying to join you again someday.

**Alexis Dujan**

## The Wind

It's been a while now since I have seen her
It's been a long time now we've been apart
she gently rests within my memories
and her love lives and breaths inside my heart

Something's slowly dying here inside me
heart aches every night she's been away
the wind softly whispers "she still loves you"
but it doesn't make my heartaches go away

My hands are shaking, tense I seem to be
the absence of her love is all I'm missing
the absence of the love she had for me.

**Gabriel Richards**

## For Sale By Owner

Used to be a Whistle-pig, a quiet little neighbor,
livin' in the field behind my house.
Mornin's I'd rise to pipin' hot coffee
and the Whistle-pig, plumped up on his stump,
both of us awakenin' in the cheery, yellow sun.

We liked it then, in our simple little homes,
the sun warmin' our backs and loosenin' our bones.

But one gray day we couldn't stop a dirty yellow dozer
from pullin' up his stump, snappin' its bones,
chasin' off the whistle-pig from his pretty little home.

Progress set in and the new owner built:

2 story split ranch with lots of country style,
4 bedrooms 2 1/2 baths, skylights to let the sun in,
Full Basement 2 car garage, sitting on a NICE LOT,
Near the BEST SCHOOLS and a PUBLIC PARK,
GREAT for your LITTLE "ANIMALS!"
FOR SALE BY OWNER...

A quiet, little whistle-pig.
### *Jack R. Hayes*

## Kleptomaniac

Being alone makes me a kleptomaniac
Lock me up in a cell...
and I will still be alone...
still a kleptomaniac.
Being in love makes me a kleptomaniac
You tell me you don't love me...
but I still love you...
still a kleptomaniac.
Waiting to hear your voice makes me a kleptomaniac
You say it's best that we never find each other...
'cause in the future we're all lost...
we're all kleptomaniacs.
Losing you makes me a kleptomaniac.
I died when you did...
you took my heart with you...
but I'm still a kleptomaniac.
### *Hannah Quall*

## Joust

The door slams, and leaves a
lonely echo in the kingdom.
A bitter hollow sound, like the guillotine.
He tightens his armor, and we're off.
Not a word exchanged except for
the occasional rattling.
It's the polite way of communication
between noblemen and sires.
I play with my helmet's tassel, single-colored,
as we approach the bridge.  As we cross,
he speaks in his slow and audible fashion
of the morning scroll, similar to the town
crier, whom I despise.  The black fog's thick inside,
oozing its way in as though it were sap
from an exploded serpent's tree, coating us
with unpleasant shields.  We bow to different
kings-his is green, mine's uncolored.
He begins to sharpen his lance, just in case
as we stop and dismount.  The herald's all booked up,
but the day may come if the black fog doesn't lift.
### *Jeff Kelly*

## Lonely Man

Lonely man, overflowing with care.
Lonely man, suffering from solitaire.
Longing to hold, yearning for touch.
Lonely man, needing love so very much.

Afraid to discuss, afraid to confess.
Seeking to share his world of success.
What other greater reward in life?
To have a lover, companion, a wife.

Lonely man, still full of desire,
So friendly and nice, everyone admires.
Full of potential, full of pride.
Just wanting someone to be by his side.

The world is harsh, full of duress.
Love is needed to ease the stress.
One must be patient, confident and strong.
With love, nothing can go wrong.

Lonely man, all you have to do is believe.
Love, you shall one day receive.
Receive in a way you will not understand.
Just another evidence of God's tender guiding hand.
### *James Hague*

## One More Mile

I'm walking thru that lonesome valley,
   Lonesome dear for the sight of you;
There's nothing here but gloom and darkness
   Just one more mile and I'll be thru.

Just one more mile to walk without you,
   Just one more mile to walk alone,
One more mile of groping blindly
   Just one more mile and I'll be home.

Home again to those that love me,
   Your tender arms, your love and care,
May God protect and bless each of you
   God be with you is my prayer.
### *Alpha Jennings*

## The Old Willow Tree

You have stood here
Longer than I remember -
A lonely tree
Gracing a barren, black-topped yard.

Your bushy crown
With slender, drooping branches
Waving like banners-
Was welcome home to many birds.

Your burly trunk
A twisted shape, split through the middle,
Invited children
To explore, have fun and climb.

You have survived
So many storms and winters.
Now you lie dead,
Blown over by a gentle breeze.
### *Erika I. Zettl*

## The Beauty Of The World

Smile in your life instead of complain.
Look at the world different, everyday's not the same.
Never be doubtful that miracles come true.
Always have love for one first, that's you.
Go through life looking but don't ever miss the prettiness
Of a flower or the tenderness of a kiss.
Go through situations positively and don't let negative
Enter or set you astray.
Always be thankful for the good things that happen, and
Don't always cry but continue laughin'.
For life is too short to sit around and moan, but look
At it as a challenge for the person you've grown.
For the world is so beautiful there's so much to see and
The world's what you make it as you want it to be.

*Dollie L. Cecil*

## Love's Second Chance

We are the masters of our fate, the keys to the future
Look beyond the horizon and unfold the many mysteries of life
We are the ones who can shape our future and control our destiny
Our pasts hold untrodden paths-unspoken words- unfulfilled
Dreams and desires
Today is the now of "Another Tome' another place"
Take each tomorrow-embrace and delights each enchanting moment
Add to the joys of yesterdays- revel in the glory of the
Adventure and cherish the feeling with every fiber of our being
Reach in and touch the very depths of our souls an unleash
Our emotions as we sand on the threshold of a beautiful, deep
And abiding relationship
Our paths have crossed again so let us embark on another
Journey into the vast unknown
You alone can make the difference - to enchant - to delight-
Make the most of it as we may never again know the beauty,
The magic and magnitude of togetherness

*Evelyn Jodan*

## I Choke On Gnats

I've made many mistakes as I've travelled life's road
looking for someone to carry my load.
I've cultivated weeds while I plowed under hay,
trying to find clouds on a sunny day.

With my nose in the air, I've trampled on flowers.
While trying to save minutes, I've wasted hours.
I've pinched measly pennies and then squandered gold;
took advice from the young and ignored the old.

I've worn new shoes with a hole in my sock,
as I stepped over diamonds to pickup a rock.
While building my life, I've been the greatest of fools;
because I kept all the scraps and threw out the tools.

I've been too tired for church, too busy for God,
with my nose to the grindstone, all bent up and odd.
There is no excuse for the things I have done;
the heartstrings I've broken, the love that I've shunned.

I'm just very thankful there's God up above,
who is never too tired or busy for love.
Who looks down in forgiveness and helps me along,
as I sing out the cuss words and choke on a song.

*Beverly Dillon*

## Untitled

She sits in her chair
looking out the window
watching the birds fly
and thinks back to when...

They were so free to care for nothing but themselves
To survive what life had in store
Knowing they always had each other.

Then the storms came and they had to fly there separate ways
But always knowing they would fly together again.

The storms of life tore them apart
But they could always pray for the sun
The precious sun that would dry up the rain
And heal the wounds of life they know deep in there hearts
Nothing could replace what they have and nothing will.
It took the storms to realize
That they needed each other — and always will.

She shakes herself back to reality
Knowing life can be so cruel — yet so kind
For she found a friend for life no matter what storms came about.
She sits back in her chair and smiles.

*Denise Martini*

## Ophelia

Ah Ophelia, it was love did burn your soul.
Lost as an echo to the depth, betrayed by seeds your own.
Innocence ablaze scorched thy blossom breast.
On a shining day t'were put to dirt to rest.

Mercy, you cried still the shadows' trembling horror
that swallowed the kindness of faces.
A child soaring upon a grassy hilltop,
you were only picking flowers.
Gracious your gift though not one did invite you.
Yet poised stiff did press their puckered lips
to anoint curses as moist kisses upon your brow.

So as the bee gives honey,
from your nature was suckled fruit so sweet,
as to the ram tastes the pet blood of his orphan lamb.
Not surrendering the thankless succor did damn you.
The cruel amen when in fear you struck to avenge the ill.
Life sought sanction in death, as ye lay defenseless — fleeting —
short of striking distance, plucked of sting.

*Dymphna McAree*

## Hear The Cries (Oklahoma City)

Voices cry out but the thunder rolls.
Lost in the blast, lost in the rubble, lost in the dust.

No cries were heard in the distance.
Lost in the blast, lost in the rubble, lost in the dust.

Cries quieted before the thunder ends.
Before the rubble ends its fall, before the dust clears the air.

Hear the cries.
Not from the blast, not from the rubble, not from the dust.

Hear the cries.
From the fathers, from the mothers, from the children, from the
nation.

Hear the cries.
For the lost, for the dead, for those who survive.

Hear the cries.
See the tears, feel the sorrow, share the grief.

Hear the cries.
From those who care, and share, and search,
And pray, and hope, and hope, and hope, for life.

*Joseph P. Warren*

## This Is Life Eternal

Joy cometh to he who bringest joy.
Love cometh to he who giveth love.
This is life eternal!

If you see a man fall, lift him up.
Give him courage and understanding.

Tell him that God above,
Showers his blessings upon him.
This is life eternal!

Help the sick, feed the hungry.
God will bequeath his blessings upon you.
This is life eternal!

When I was young, I often wondered —
Where is God?  Is He by my side?

As I moved on into this wicked world,
I found that I could smile, in spite of sorrows —
Laugh in spite of tears - live in spite of torment.

It was then that I realized —
God is OMNIPOTENT!  OMNIFICENT!  OMNIPRESENT!
And God is within my heart!

*Alberta Martin*


## Love's Seasons

In the Spring of love all is new
Love encounter reached between two
Blooming colors burst like lightning
Every minute apart is truly frightening

Summer follows with warmth evergrowing
Both are comfortable with their love-knowing
A family grows under the light of the sun
A home is made out of the long days of fun

Then comes Autumn the changing time
The light of love does not as brightly shine
Leaf by leaf the sturdy tree falls apart
Until all is bare in the mind and the heart

Winter blows in with a cold, brutal chill
Both work hard but no longer, have the will
Love has been frozen in an earlier time
Now all that is left is only yours and mine

You may think this the end of Love's Seasons
But Spring comes again and renews the reasons
Why lovers love and become man and wife
Because love makes love in a newborn life

*Dale Walsh*


## I Guess It's Over

You say that I don't care, that I don't
love you anymore.

You say I am not the same, that it is
not the same anymore.

You question my love for you, time after
time, day after day.

I listen to you in silence, without
bothering to answer or explain.

Letting you believe your own words, Mine
would probably not matter anyway.

For I know how much I care for you and
feel you should know this too.

Is it really my love for you that you
only seek answers for, or your love for
me..... that isn't anymore!!!!!

*Edith Lucero*


## Fall Is So Lovely

Light mist touching cool ground
Lovely violet red leaves swaying in soft wind
Sparkling drops of water on long blades of grass
Chirping birds flying in artistic formations
White clouds that look like cotton blankets
Wind blowing silently and making the trees dance
A tiny bird sweetly chirping in the distance
Branches quietly tapping against each other
Fresh grass and evergreen trees which are delightfully piney
Minty leaves at the tree tops
Water from the stream fresh enough to swim in
Feeling free and unlimited in the open
Do whatever you please
Green grass soft enough to sleep on
Comfortable earth feels so wonderful
Fall is so lovely!

*Amreen Quadir*


## Giving Life After Death

They lie waiting in their hospital beds, slowly dying
Machines and medicines can only slow but not prevent the inevitable
Their loved ones, stricken with grief, are languishing and crying
Saviors are plentiful if ordinary people do what is right and
    honorable

No one can deny that there comes a time when we all must say good-bye
That people are buried or cremated with life saving organs makes me cry
Because of these selfish acts, potentially curable people disintegrate
    and die

There is a belief held my many that organs are needed for a
    resurrection
Religious leaders needed to make the appropriate proclamation
That organ donors are not to be considered iconoclast
But as benevolent persons who help make lives last

If religious leaders do their moral part
People will begin to understand how easy it is to be a hero
Then many more patients will receive that life saving heart
As well as that kidney, liver and bone marrow

*Gregg M. Sitrin*


## Life Is Like A Mushroom Field

Winter has prepared the ground for
magic in the early spring.

Ever so softly the night air gently warms the
pail ground and sullen trees.

Light exchanges places with the darkness
filtering through the mist of dawn.

Tiny stems poke their heads through last
years glory.

The mushroom becomes a random part of
the field of living.

What kind of mushroom challenges the
persuasion of God's Creation.

Mushrooms of varying dimensions and colors
are filled with goodness and sorrow.

Transparent to the firmament but opaque
to each other.

Returning to the earth expeditiously as a
river during spring thaw.

Winter has prepared the ground for
magic in the early spring.

*Gary R. Collins*

## Whispers So Soft In My Ear

Whispers so soft in my ear,
Makes me wish that I could have you here.
Each and everyday I cry,
Remembering the day that you said goodbye.
I try to forget and move on,
But the love I feel for you just keeps on growing strong.

Whispers so soft in my mind,
Blows your voice to me
Time after time.
It's hard to say how I feel,
All I know is that I'm in love just so real.
I wish that I could have you now
Because your love is something that I just can't do without.

Whispers so soft in my ear,
So soft to listen to,
But loud enough to hear.
I always wonder why,
Why was I so foolish just to make you cry.
If I could go back to that day,
I would whisper in your ear and try to make you stay.

**Eric Bryant**

## For Richard Wrong

Going forward through your day and your life.
Making choices that free you up and make you clear.
Free and clear and beautiful baby like the jazz I hear.
Blow, Miles, blow! going forward; being present, being past,
    being future, and constantly and beautifully moving forward.
Moving forward in my life not just in my mind.
In my speech and voice not just in my throat.
Going forward, pressing through the white glare of obstacles
    and cold uppercuts of disappointments.
Barreling forward not to lose time, lose purpose or lose heart.
Plunging forward into unknown and letting it fill me up
    and build me up and make me strong.
As Miles plays on, I listen and I hear him and we are
    moving and grooving...forward.

**Alexis Wilson**

## Whispers

divine discontent is breaking my heart
making room for I do not know what

divine discontent is nudging and prodding me
insisting it is time to move on

in panic and denial I try to ignore
the promptings of the still small voice

but divine discontent can not be denied
its call impossible to ignore

so reluctantly I agree to give up control
and follow where spirit may lead

with faith as my compass I prepare to embark
on a journey of transformation

and finally sorrowfully I bid adieu
to the life and friends I have known

trusting tomorrow I give up my life
to become an instrument of God

**Cynthia Carder**

## From The Heart

When I was just a little girl my
Mama said to me -
    As you go out into the world be all
that you can be.
    Just hold God's hand and do your
best and know that He will do the rest.
    Oh - it won't be easy, there'll be ups
and downs
    Lots of joy and lots of frowns.
But in the end - in your old sinful heart
    You'll know that God has done
His part.

**Betty E. Brock**

## "Iron Maidens"

    The orders have been given from the top;
    Man and machine go to battle with the ever present enemy to stop.
    Another day, another job, like a conductor they step into their
space for the day,
All engines started, all blades going, the music of these magnificent
iron maidens, their mission starts this way.

    Each man cautiously approaches his iron maiden for he
knows she demands all respect due!
Even though familiar with magical caresses of his touch alone,
she bids him fair warning too.
His skill has been perfected so she does the bidding of his will.
The uniting of man and machine working against a common enemy of a
unique combination of flesh and steel.

    Wouldn't our ancestors who communicated on the walls be proud?
To hear the unison of the iron maidens as they feel the air musically aloud:
Time is the all consuming enemy, for there is never enough!
The pressman the printers, and bindery workers, all work feverishly to
to polish this diamond of language out of the rough.

**Barb Saveley**

## A Friend Unknown

Old and unused
Marked by years of abuse
Sitting silently by
Waiting to reveal the wisdom of years
And to describe the reason for many tender tears

An old friend that need only to be known
A gallery of beauty
Waiting only to be shown

The world holds many stories to fill ones head
Yet one of the most sad
Is of the book unread

**George E. Cochran**

## Pictures

Pictures are like a lock, a lock on memories.
Locking them safely inside, tucked away
In a golden picture frame.
Waiting for that special moment
When someone catches a glimpse and
Remembers that moment when...
It just takes one look to remember,
A look into the past that dawns on
You now and again.
Take a look at a picture and remember when.

**Heather Nicole Mooney**

## Star Ship - the Woods

An illuminated Star Ship
Marooned on a cloud of memories.
The voices hum in descants,
Rise and fall to a crescendo — then silence.
It's supper.
To break bread together is a sacred rite since man knew man.
A cornucopia of fruits and nuts, balsam, holly,
Pecan and wine on an altar of mums.
The totem pole from the first charismatics.
The menorah of the seven sacred lights.
Incense and wild roses, the holy candles burning.
The prayer flags wave
In the whisper of a southern breeze.
The callous hands offer grace in song
As the fanner bees spray jasmine.
The glow on each face is the glow of kin,
And the vibes of kinship are prayer.
The strains of Mozart's "Magic Flute" fade
As the choir sings, "Te Deum."
The lamplighter is here.

### *Fanny Fiore*

## Untitled

A father says to his son:
"Mature, be a good man.  Ascend to height that I cannot see.
Be the man I cannot be.
Conquer the world-yours for the taking.
Where ever you go, whatever you do, you are my son."

As my father's words, heard on his knee, bade me to
seek what could be.

In truth, a father says to his son;
"I love you, life from me.
I want you to be what you want to be.
Wherever you go, whatever you do,
think of me kindly,
and tell your children of me."

### *Jerry Bannon*

## Bus Station Bench

That flat spot within you of which you spoke
May just be the ground upon which I stand.
Yet, you seem to fear that closeness,
Why is that?

The changes you've seen and kept hidden
May just be the secrets I want to know.
Still, you reject that sharing,
How is that?

All those years left on some Bus Station bench
May just be the memories I need to find.
Yet, you won't search for them with me,
Where are they?

That shadow which makes me want to know you
May just be that something I should live without,
Even so, I reach out to touch you,
Could I love you?

### *Audrey Mowry*

## Sonnet to Dawn

I hope for sleep to keep me till tomorrow
Meanwhile to drown the day that this has been
And bring my soul to morning, fresh and clean
As in the spring with each succeeding furrow
The plow upturns the new earth, brown and mellow
And lays the tired soil beneath to sleep
In undisturbed reposing, cool and deep,
Sheltered awhile from farmer, hoe and harrow,
So come my soul through night's oblivion
To quiet dawn before mankind's astir
When twilight's subtle shapes, still softly drawn,
Subdue day's hard contours, still but a blur.
The East is tinted with incipient dawn,
The West a brave defiance with a star.

### *Harry P. Eldridge*

## Where's Daddy?

She came to this city to find herself, to run away from painful
memories, to find daddy.
Poor pretty girl with dreams so big and sights so high -
she starts to fly so high, so low, wondering where's daddy?
Why'd he go?
Searing scars of yesterday when he went away silently.
She never knew there would come that day when her heart would cry.
He didn't say good-bye or why.
So she packs her bags and runs away to hide - to the big city -
she's looking so pretty.
Such a pity and why? (they wonder) does she repeat the same old song
of lost little girl in need -
always searching for her missing key "Where's Daddy?"

### *Debra Wilder Moulder*

## Nightfall

After a day of laughter and play,
    Mid wandering wonders about me,
Dreams of the night are beckoning to me,
    To come in and rest for a while.

As I drift in a swing, caressing hot cider,
    I replay the hours gone by;
Reliving the splendor and joy of the morning
    And exploring the afternoon sky.

Then as the stars of the midnight hour
    Weave a web of perfect delight,
I lay down my head on a dream-feathered pillow
    To laugh and play all through the night.

### *Allysa Faith Haygood*

## Our Power Within

If we could only find our inner self and put everything out of our
mind and focus on our power and wisdom will we then be in harmony
with ourself.

Intelligence is the key to our inner eye, which is our third eye.
Our third eye is the knowledge into another dimension.

What I mean by dimension is the outer world, a world where
there is peace inside us all.

When we are born, do we have any fears that we really know or
understand?  I don't think so.  We might have had in the past a
sense of something going wrong, but couldn't comprehend the meaning
of it as we do now, now that we have experienced more throughout
our lives.

We have to learn how to react sensibly in certain complicated
situations and strive for relaxation and find purity in life and in
ourselves.  Once we find all that, we will achieve our power within.

### *Danielle Anne Woerner*

## Surprise

Never thought this would happen. Never thought I'd let it, but my mind changed and so did my heart.

I once loved someone with heart, body, and soul, but he had to go. No goodbyes, no answers, only questions. Time after time going out with guy after guy, trying to find the missing link, yet always failing and falling harder then before. But from nowhere came a man, picking me up off the ground and setting me straight.

I listened. I learned.

At first I did not want my heart to change. I always thought my love would come back to me, yet I was wrong. I learned to forget him and give another a chance, a chance he deserved and got.

The chance, I'm glad I gave him, because now my heart is learning how to love another, healing old wounds, never bringing new ones. He's such a person always telling me how beautiful I am, and how much happiness I bring into his life. If he only knew how he does the same for me, letting me live again and enjoy life for what it is and not for what it was.

*Beata Sek*

## Peace

Utter thoughts, Gracious words, like of a lark skyward bound, misfelt, without depth, inward seclusion.

Yet of mountains, tales of myths reaching beyond that of man. Soaring upward, herald, heard on high.

Beauty in landscape, without flaws of earthly realm of injury and harm. Hear, O' my cry, weeping— yearning.

Break the sky, quench my thirst, seeking that which all men seek but never attaining light of life

Wonders ceasing, times of movement, releasing, mind, body and more. Yet without delight, nor peace of mind.

Wishful, grant to him the art, grant glory, honor, wonder, light Crying out, he cries to thee, yet ne'er to be heard.

Within light, a journey long, but toward a simple, common goal nor without, wonders cease, all in peace.

*Cory Peatrowsky*

## The Rose

I have never seen a rose
more colorful and innocent
than the rose I have observed today.
Her color enlightens her surroundings
and her innocence captures my heart.

I have never felt a rose
more gentler and delicate
than the one that I have felt today.
Her soft and tender features
delight and impress her observers.

I have never smelled a rose
more sweet or divine
than the rose that I have sensed today
her scent is unique - and shall always be remembered.

I have never watched a rose
stand tall and stand proud
while being hassled through the rain, sleet and snow,
she has grown stronger and prouder.
She also brightens up the world with her beauty and grace.
She will survive.

*Elizabeth Eilers*

## Mother's Day Prayer

Lord grant each mother on
Mother's day that special blessing
May she find that peace and love
Special things she gave us
Smiles cuddles cares laughter
When we were growing up
Lord Grant her that special day
When we needed her most
Food and guidance prayers each
Day and night
Lord be with each mother on this day
on earth as it is in heaven
may each one say
Thank you so much that you gave us life
hope dream to carry us thru years to come
Someday you'll always be on our hearts today
Happy mother's day.

*Douglas C. Gibson*

## The Big One

Firemen cringed,
Mustaches singed.
Doors unhinged.
Looters binged.

Psyched-out house pets ran amok.
Shattered stucco came unstuck.
Most folks were spared by Lady Luck,
Though some could not Fate's Fickle Finger duck
And were by a plague of ruin struck.

Mere survival instant heroes made.
But unsung rescuers' roles to the hilts were played.
Ironic twists in Buck Helm's fate left many hopes betrayed,
Yet grateful flashbacks to those heroics probably won't fade.

Oh that Black Seventeenth, many were with fitting angst imbued,
When they—by buckles, cracks and jolts—-
Were in a handful of endless seconds screwed.
Still, they didn't see fit just to sit around and brood.
No, THE BIG ONE could not make those gutsy people come unglued!

*Adam Pollack*

## One Less

*(For all our pain Mom)*
You wanted me to be aware of the
mutations that live inside of us.

You started to lift your sweater,
the first thing I saw was what you
called the "The Drain."
Half filled with blood and puss,
the yellowish red mixture was
strapped to your stomach.

As you lifted the sweater higher,
on the skin were blotches of black,
bruises jagged shaped and dark.

It was hard for you to keep your arm up,
but you showed me where they took out
the three lymph nodes, that were positive.
Dried blood was caked in between the stitches.

You pulled your sweater back down to cover yourself.
I got up to hug you and I only felt "The Drain"
up against my stomach and a tear in my eye.

*Bryan White*

## The Eroticism of Touch

Intimately involved in my advances,
 my attention was swept away by his touch,
 his kiss, his teasing advance, then slow retreat.
His tongue lightly dancing on my arm, my shoulder,
 soft touch of lips, not quite a kiss,
 my breast, my stomach,
touching my leg, advancing toward
 my secret place, taking my breath away.
 I am under his spell, his control, wretched slave
craving more and more, pleading 'don't stop,'
 deliriously obedient, abandoning myself
 I am consumed,
my body racked with lightning
 from head to toe.
 I lay motionless, silent and spent
        and
            still.....
                he touches.
*Belinda J. Wilder-Snider*

## The Tree

Alone, like my shadows cast, lost amid the woods
My branches numb from the cold, felt the weight of the frost upon them
From nowhere a mighty blow from the woodsman's axe. Sent me crashing
to the icy ground
The woodsman gathered me up in a bundle
And placed me in a concentration
camp for wounded trees
It was awhile before you came upon me
you gathered me within you arms
you placed me before your fireplace
and within the warm of its
glow the ice around me began to melt
You decorated me with angels,
and filled me with magical
Lights that danced like the stars upon the sky.
You filled me with childhood
dreams, sugar plums and candy canes
You placed gifts of beautiful
colors beneath my branches and filled
my heart with all the colors of the rainbow
and now and forever I will
Always be your Christmas tree!
*Cynthia S. Rothschild*

## Night Shadows

When the dream unfolds in the dead of night
My chest is tight, my breathing labored.
White skin is covered with a sheen of fright,
Trembling, as I toss and turn on a moving bed.

The light so dim, fading, as the shadows streak
Like the phantom stalking its vulnerable prey.
My eyes try to focus yet everything seems bleak
With naught to look forward to on the break of day.

No stars do I see as I slowly open my eyes
To greet whatever awaits me as my fear abounds.
And I try my best not to hope and fantasize,
Yet, muffle my thoughts and night's eerie sounds.

Dawn is breaking, the night fading into awareness
Of the sounds of life, and never ending time.
And so I must rise, the new day to address
As night shadows fade into this future of mine!

*Joan Heinkel*

## Yanked

All about lies a threat.
My ears are stopped by the railing
of the antagonist sweeping overland!
I turn to morning prayers for the innocent;
I plead for restoration and healing of wounds;
but what can I do between the jaws of the wrench
that yank me about with pseudo- sophistry and terror?
Better for me to watch this little tree toad
freely leaping across my path to jump upon a log
and stare like a lost soul, bewildered and agog as I!
*Carolyn T. Abbot*

## Lovely

My husband is my lovely angel:
my friend in all circumstances,
my loyal partner in times of need,
my reason to love at all. . .

My husband is truly sweet:
he almost never "snarls"!
He is even almost sweet
When tired, exhausted, or frustrated. . .

My husband works too hard -
and like most husbands today,
there are very few rewards
for all the sweat, tears, and fears. . .

Lovely is the word for my husband:
if yours is like mine too,
then join me in this poem -
and read it to your husband:

At the end of a long, hard day. . .
*Florence Ann Kelly Stults*

## "The Flag"

As I watch the ole flag, I think to myself
 my gosh how I love what its worth.
It stands for my freedom, it stands for my love,
 and Ms. Betsy Ross gave it birth.

O say can you see by the dawns early light
 is a song that we sing when it's raised
Our hearts we do cross when we say our pledge
 in a sing - song of honor and praise.
It belongs to the people but it flew over there
 where the boys from our country died proud
And the ones that survived to tell about it
 are singing its praises real loud.
So don't run down my flag and don't tear it to shreds
 it always is there for the call
United we stand so lets stick together
 divided we could all fall.
 A Nation, A Town, A Village
*Bonnie Bowman*

## Life

Life is the best thing I was ever given.
Life is so full, I have so much to look forward to.
Unlike my friend I loved life, she despised it.
I wish somebody had listened to her.
She was telling the truth.
One day she went to far.
She ended the best thing she was ever given.
She put her family and friends through it all.
Our church was never fuller, everybody loved her.
 Except her!
*Gilienne Roher*

## Untitled

The loss of my sister fills my heart with pain and sadness tonight
My grief surrounds me like a cloak of darkness, chasing away the light

Alone now I walk among the shadows, seeking comfort from within
Gathering up my memories of her so my healing can begin

I carefully wrap each one in my love, I have to save them all
And accept the bitter truth: I'll never have new ones to recall

I sink deeper into my sorrow, adrift on my own sea of tears
So lost in my thoughts, going back in time, reliving all her years

Then a nudge in the darkness and the sound of a familiar voice:
"It's time for you to leave now, live your life, be grateful for
    that choice

Open your heart, share your memories of me and soon you will see
I'll always be with you, it's just my spirit God wanted to set free.
    *Catherine M. Foster*

## Welcome

Welcome into my space
My heart, mind, soul..... my place
My senses and consciousness have been touched
The sensation is giving me a rush
Feelings have been brought back from the dead
Words that were forgotten are now said
The pleasure of life is once again in sight
Once again there is a light
Thank you for daring to come to this place
Welcome to my space.
    *George E. Jones*

## Spirit Runner

*For Anthony Norcia*
Here in paradise found,
My heart shall dance on hallowed ground.

For I have come home to the mountain
To cleanse the body and allow the mind to remain sane.

That the spirit shall return
To the temple from whence it came.

A safe heaven I have found
Here on enchanted ground.

I praise the great spirit
For the happiness I have found.
    *Gordon Lester*

## The Weekends

The weekends are so lonely
My hearts cries out for you
Hoping for just a little affection for two

Needing some answers not wanting a conflict
I ask my self, "How does a relationship stick
to commitments and promises?"

I've been watching in wonder, can such a union
survive when it's not being nurtured to be kept
alive?

My man keeps a distance and prolongs the day
keeping busy and such and never do we play!
From sun-up to sun-down he's away from my side
he looks on for only a moment keeping me at bay

"Oh," I say to myself, "What do I do, am I expected
to continue to be true?" Our commitments and
promises were once so very new now they are only
sad memories desperately seeking attention from you!
    *Cleona Patterson*

## My Little Doll House

My house is the smallest on the street,
My husband bought it just for me.
We have a new born baby boy,
That gives us lot's of special joy.

The house is the smallest on the street,
It's so snug and tight sitting in a row
Gave mother the proudest she would ever know.
Being so small it was all aglow,
With so much warmth and love you know.
Living with Jesus in our hearts,
Would keep us together and not apart.

This cute little doll house
Is not better by far,
For it is sitting just like the others under the Star.
For Jesus chose this doll house just for me,
For he knew I would love it for all eternity.

For now I'm with Jesus in my Heavenly Home,
And I thank Him every day, for my lovely little home.
    *Barbara Jo Schuckmann*

## Confusion

To pause..with thought,
My imagination spins rapidly
And becomes reality
I see you standing before me
Your bright eyes twinkling
your warm smile inviting me
To fill my thirst with you
So that my soul will be quenched
I rush to embrace you in my arms
So I can press my lips against yours
And suddenly
And completely
You disappear!
And my arms fold encircling only themselves
And I feel the cold rush of air
On my chest
Where my heart is beating ever so loudly
The moment is gone
And I am left,
Wondering?
    *D. Joseph Garrison*

## The Lake

I went to the lake to see my reflection
my life has no point no sense of direction

I've come to this lake to sort through my head
If I find no point to live I'm better off dead

My childhood is gone innocence lost
The border of death and life has now been crossed

I used to see myself for the last time I can
I'll never see me or my family again

I used to love life but that's now gone from me
I've come to the lake in hopes that I'll see

The fun in my life was here now it's not
My family calls for my life I'll miss them a lot

If only I could explain - I can't keep on living
Without any passion and no reason for giving

I wish joy was a virtue I had
Then chances are I wouldn't be so sad

The lake gives an image of a soulless man
I can no longer live - I no longer can
    *Adam Yoe*

## The Woman That I Am

I am a woman born of the earth.
My matrilineal lines reach deep their essence,
Into the sun-warmed Georgia earth,
To touch the roots of the feminine and the finger of God.

I am a woman who stands at the portals,
Of both life and death.
First with the babe, last as she closes the eyes of the dying.
For through my hands in this existence, both have passed.

There is no death of the temporal in my household.
For I sew it into quilts that last for centuries,
Warming new generations; bearing witness to both past and
present.
To be woman is to stand with one foot in that which is eternal.

Through my hands pass lowly vines.
Pulled from the thicket or arbor,
Woven into cradles for future generations or baskets for a harvest
That will last beyond my living.  Is this not immortality?

I count my age, not in years,
But in scars and collected jewels of experience.
For what is the passage of time, but a clock nicking the silence?
I am, and forever will be, but a child

### *Bonnie Bevel-Maddox*

## The Day, I Can't Forget

The day, was the seventh of September, 1994
My mind unforgettably, remembers, embedded there forever more
The morning was clear, the chirping birds, were music to my ears
As I crawled out of bed
I bowed my head
To thank God, for letting me see, another day
As, I prepared myself to be on my way
I didn't have a hint
Of the unfolding, before noon event
That would change my life completely
And touch my soul so deeply
It happened at work
A quick an sharp electrical jerk
It happened so fast
I had no idea, how much time, had past
It was a near death experience
Judging from the afterwards appearances
Still, to this day, I get down on my knees and say
Thank you God, for granting my life, a stay

### *Evelyn Bell Latimore*

## To My Little Stars

It is for you, my Little Stars.
My most precious and wonderful gifts in life.
I wish you the best in the years to come.

Always be smart, be honest,
be good and have a friendly soul.
And remember: dreams do come true.
Just work hard through your life
and you can achieve every goal.

You have a lot of strength and courage
to run your future life the best as you can.
Never forget the meaning of the word LOVE.
And keep this feeling in your lovely hearts everyday.

I'm so proud of you.
You are my PRIDE and JOY.
I love you s o  much;
Like nobody else in the world.

### *Ewa Sekula*

## A Mother's Call

In the meadow, where I use to play
My mothers ghost never fade
Special memories of days gone by
her heart still beats within mine.
I see my daughter
her life such like mine
I know now why mom never left my side
I smile as I sit alone
her voice still echoes from long ago
As the breeze blows gently through my hair
I feel as if she's very near
this must be my mothers call
So as the light goes dim, and reality real
I hug my daughter, so that one day she
could feel - a mothers call.

### *Joanna Ott*

## Life

My days are full of chaos
My nights - I'm never home,
Trying to decide what life's about
On this I am not alone.

Children are a blessing
That I know for sure,
but for all this crazy running
I know of no cure.

We live our life for others
Jesus first, others second, yourself last,
I need to remember that always
Especially when life goes so fast.

Someday the running will be over
I'll have lots of time on my hands,
Wishing for those times of chaos
As quiet reigns throughout the land.

### *Becky Ober*

## Untitled

My soul cries out to me, I cannot please.
My soul cries again louder, harder and in anguish.
I become confused.
For the last time my soul cries in hunger.
Hunger for what? I question.
I sit and ponder.
What is my soul hungry for?
Then it stops.
Love.
I am hungry for love.
O.K. I said. I'll help, but where do I go
And what do I do?
Go to yourself and learn to love yourself
My soul replied.
I can't.
Why?
Because I forgot how it feels to be loved.
Silence is the only reply I receive.

### *Elisabeth Kuisis*

## How Long Would I Love You

For you my heart is full of love.
My stubborn heart can't understand, Love should be mutual.

How long would I love you, I don't know.
How long would I love you, it's up to my heart.

How long would I love you, who knows.
If I love you forever, I blame my stubborn heart.
How long would I love you, I don't know.
How long would I love you, it's up to my heart.
How long would I love you,
Who knows.

*Carmen Feliciano*

## At the Close of Day

As the day draws to a close,
My thoughts often touch upon those things
that only a few hours ago took place.

I ask myself, "How was this day spent?"
"Was one hurt through something said?"
"Was comfort withheld from one in need?"
"Could another have been helped
along the twisted paths of life?"

"Were my thoughts and motives pure,
or tainted with things that should not be?"
"What should have been but wasn't?"
"And what about...?" (There's so much more!)

Alas, this day's done, 'tis true,
But there's no regret nor despair;
Yes, it's gone...now part of the past.

I cannot undo what has already been,
But I can influence what is to be;
And know that good things of tomorrow
Are often birth'd from testings and failures
of today.

*Gale L. Player*

## Divinity

The hurt I hold seems beyond repair.
My torment lingers in the night air.
Others pick at my tortured soul.
Very few mend the wounds.

Glimpses of light swoon by too fast.
Ounces of hope are all that last.
My existence is waning rather thin.
Someone be witness to me here,
before its too late and I disappear.

I don't want handouts, nor do I want charity.
Just give me hope and clarity.
Let the meaning of my being be known to everyone and I.

My being yearns for focus and form.
My heart seeks comfort not scorn.
My mind seeks answers not confusion.
Steer me clear of all delusion.

My soul seeks a bridge between a comforted heart,
and a pristine mind.
Once that bridge is built, then and only then will I be divine.
Then and only then will I be divine.

*James M. Haber Jr.*

## My God and I

My beloved is gone to my God on high.
My trouble and sorrow are but a sigh.
As the mist of time, like cooling rain, falls on my grief and my pain,
I hear God say "These are my tears and your beloved's.
We are crying with you, your grief we share."
And I hear Him say "Be still and know that I am God."

My sorrow and grief have turned to despair.
As I lift up my eyes to the sky in prayer,
I cry out to God' "Do you still care?"
I see the stars, the moon, and a rainbow there,
And I know with His hand God made them with love, and with care;
And I hear Him say "Be still know that I am God."

Each day I say a thank you prayer as I lay my burdens in His care.
As time passes by my love for Him grows;
As His light shines upon me, He tells me He knows,
As I hear Him say "BE STILL AND KNOW THAT I AM GOD."

*Helen Dietrich*

## Cheapskate

I must confess that I got caught
My well meaning efforts all for naught

The girl wanted flowers of red, and white, and blue
Of every size, and name, and hue

She wasn't satisfied with common native flora
She wanted the costly exotic that gave off an expensive aura

They had to be a certain select variety
That said she was the cream of society

So I gave her bouquets of splendid colors
And soon exhausted my hard earned dollars

I found a way to satisfy her demands
By using my head but mainly my hands

To gather bunches at the cemetery I would select the best
And leave those wrinkled and wilted for those who lie there at rest

Flowers are for the benefit of the living
So why complain when love is in the giving?

So I waged the war and loved and lost
The money saved at such a cost

Now I travel through town knowing I misbehaved
But I do it in a brand new car on the money saved!

*Dennis Michael Wells*

## A Meditation On Life

When I was just a little rugged tot, I was with this nice girl, her name was Dot.
She wasn't like the other girls I knew. She talked to boys both in and out of school.
As we grew up our friendship did not end; and in 10th grade we were the best of friends.
We graduated on the 1st of May. I know I won't forget that joyful day.
To college both of us went on from there. Which school? Right then we didn't really care.
Our friendship had survived our hardest years: That time when constantly our eyes had tears.
Together we attended Harvard U.; and finished there to start a life anew.
Surprisingly enough we ended up, together with two kids, a cat, and pup.
Throughout these years I never chose to say, "I love you and I hope you'll always stay."
You've been my friend throughout my changing life, and now you stand
by me-my dear sweet wife.
I hope we are together to the end. Not only are you special, you're my friend.

*Derrick Delmore*

## Unity

Neither Jew nor Greek-Gentile or slave,
    neither Catholic, nor protestant, nor Lutheran made.

In the eyes of God we are all one.
    Because of Jesus, the Cross, His precious Son.

Red, yellow, black, or white;
    we are precious in His sight.

For from my mother's womb, You have known me.
    Fearfully and wonderfully made, that's how it was to be.

You are the Creator, knowing our frame.
    Making man from dust, knowing our names.

So we must all work together side by side.
    For when we get to Heaven that's where we'll abide.

Let us start here, the Father would be pleased;
    because Jesus, Father, and Spirit does always agree.

And when you get up there, the Father will say;
    "Well done" faithful servant, "You've made my day."

### *Janice Howell*

## My Old House

There's an old house in the mountains;
    nestled in the pine.
Waiting and watching for old father time.
The roof is all gone and the grass has grown high
It will never hear a mother voice nor hear a baby cry.
Their's no lights in the windows and no
    foot steps on the stairs.
No children calling through the door;
    mommy are you there?
There were lilacs in the front yard and a dog house too -
Built for my mandy so she could welcome you
There was a garden in the back and clothes hanging on the line.
There was a lot of living in that old house of mine.
They say it is to old and they say it is condemned;
    they say it must come down
I just can't comprehend; it was my humble abode;
My haven from the cold my little nest and my perfect place of rest
Now it's an old house in the mountains
Nestled in the pine;
Waiting and watching for old father time -

### *Dorothy DeVaney*

## God's Angel

Oh, Lord, watch over me,
never let me stray;
You know my wants, You know my needs,
Just lead me day by day.

Make all my problems little ones,
Keep an angel by my side,
And when I slip and start to fall,
Let him be my guide.

Life is never easy,
And things don't always go my way,
But knowing You, dear Father, the way I do,
I know I'll have a better day.

### *Donaldene M. Spring*

## Remembering

She always held me whenever I'd cry,
Never once did I hear her sigh.
She meant so much to me,
Why couldn't anyone see,
She was everything I wanted to be.

She'd tell me to take life one day at a time,
Then I'd think, wasn't my life mine,
To live as I liked,
With all its twists and turns?
But now looking back, I know she taught me a lot that I knew
I must learn.

For more reasons than are stated above,
I will always remember her reigning love.
I will remember her helpful advice,
Which she offered to me, because she was so nice.

She was the one who taught me to "be myself"
Even when she was falling,
She was always right beside me to hold my hand,
I will always remember my dearest aunt, who was right there
    down to the end.

### *Elizabeth Harmon*

## Gossip

As if they stood me up beside a wall and there they shot me dead.
No leaden-bullets did they use, only words instead.
The roster of the firing crew included all I know, who had
sent regrets to everything else to be in on this coup.
It started out so innocently, as if no one had a care;
But a look, a glance, a sly remark was more than they could bear.
The hounds set free, fox-bent trampled truth for news, and
pell-melled vied at tete-a-tetes to air their latest views.
In mattered not the lives they hurt in frothing their ignoble
prose; just catch the victim in the tangled web they wove.
'Tis over now, the actors have taken their last bow.
They have fled the scene to find more fertile fields to plow.
I wonder now, in looking back at the score, whose souls were
scared the most, the prey or predator?

### *Buck Cowart*

## Last Steps

A forest lies in the midst of my path
No light bright enough to span the other side
I have no one's hand to hold
I must face the reality on my own

As I look forward on the universe as a whole
I think back to those towering stones
Who stands so proud and tall
I think of what they overcame to get where they are

I stare across an endless meadow
A thousand years to the other side
A journey into an uncharted land
And realize this trek I must I make alone

Looking over into the vast pit of space
I take a look at the silent seas of light
What can be done to save the stars
How can I change the unknown

Inching closer to the edge of the earth
I reexamine the fields of dandelions
Take a closer look at the past and present
And wonder what to make of these last few steps

### *Jennifer L. Moore*

## Untitled

Memories, oh memories, no longer to build on,
no longer to be.
Hold on, I'll be there.

Precious moments taken away,
stolen forever,
no longer to be.
Hold on, I'll be there.

Life, once lived with abundant spirit, cut off,
no longer to be.
Hold on, I'll be there.

Angels gather, as do I,
to share those last precious moments,
no longer to be.
Hold on, I'll be there.

As final sleep gently slips into the room,
hold my hand and know you're not alone.
Hold on, for I am with you, I am there.

*Barbara Delk Bagley*

## (God) You and Me

In my heart I truly believe you and I were meant to be.
No matter how I try reasoning or try dealing with reality,
it still comes out you and me.

I tried reminding myself that there was someone else in your
life along with an estranged wife.

Then I'd remember my talk with God. I told Him how I'd like
my man to be!! I feel He smiled and said, "Leave it to me."

That's when you showed up at my door and spent two nights talking
with me. As I listened to what you were saying, I truly
began to believe that God had taken the desires of my heart,
wrapped them up in you, and sent you to me.

By the second night I knew I'd lost my heart. It belonged to you.
So I said, "Okey, God, we both agree;" then I thanked Him for you
and me!!

*Bessie Deas*

## Recognition

Recognition should always be given,
no matter how small the deed.
For recognition is the water that moistens the seed.

Praise the seed and it will sprout,
because being honored is what life's about.
Ignore the seed and it will decay.
And there will be no one who will look its way.

Praise the seed with the water of recognition.
It will then fulfill its mission,
to be a flower as it was meant to be.
And to be looked upon by you and me.

Children should be treated just the same.
So one day they may see the light of fame.
Being revered from far and wide,
and it all started from those outside.
Receiving recognition from high and low,
so they may now thrive and grow.

*Joseph D. Wilkins*

## The Indomitable Spirit

When you're down and out, at the end of the rope
No matter what happens there's always hope.
During war and famine, whatever the plight
When hope springs eternal, the burden is light.

If we could harness this natural force,
Without doubt it would be an incredible force.
When futility sets in, and all seems lost,
Why does hope surge and survive at all cost?

In many cases hope gives us life
No matter the problem, no matter the strife.
Hope will always give us a light
At the end of the tunnel, the courage to fight.

If when longing for an answer it eludes us even more,
And the inclination is to ask what is it al for?
Hope will keep us on the track and guide us to the end
On this we can rely and on this we can depend.

*David Manegold*

## "Our Old Battered Car"

No matter where we are
No matter where we roam
Our old battered can never gave up
It always took us home.

The floor boards were rusted out
And you could see the street below
Our car heard children's songs and laughter
And somehow it didn't know.

It knew it was needed and loved
So it never left us down
As it tugged and tugged along
From home to beach to town.

It was a special car
Where its loved ones sat within
As we recall happy memories
Let us once again begin.

Climb into that dear old car
When you feel a little sad
You will find the road to happiness
Love always,
Mom and Dad

*Joan Erickson*

## Street Violence

It can strike at anytime . . .
no matter who you are . . .
no matter where you are . . .

A child playing on a playground . . .
a teenager hanging out on the corner . . .
an adult on their way to work . . .
it can strike without warning . . .

A stray bullet cuts you down . . .
a simple argument ends your life . . .

It isn't one race killing their own . . .
it isn't one social class against another . . .
it's brother and sister spilling each other's blood . . .

We kill our family over material possessions . . .
maybe even a boyfriend or girlfriend . . .

Street violence is a part of life . . .
sadly, it always be will . . .
The question is: How do we stop it?

*Donna DiGiacomo*

## The Reaper

Last night I saw the reaper, I met him eye to eye,
No more was he a story, no more was he a lie.
Many bodies lay around me in the slowly fading light,
And that was when I saw him, wearing black in all his might.
The battle had been bloody, many brave men had been felled,
Many more men had been injured, he came to take these men to hell.
He began to swing his scythe and claim those many souls,
The screams of the men were piercing as they slipped into hells hot coals.
He then walked to where I lay so still and lifted up his blade,
But when I looked up into his face his motion was belayed.
I don't know what he saw in me as he looked from where he stood,
But I know full well what I saw in him as he lowered his blackened hood.
I saw his face, I saw his eyes, I saw the depths of hell,
And realized I must change my ways or I would know that place quiet well.
He passed me over and went to work claiming those who had been damned,
And that was when I felt the touch of a strong but caring hand.
I was taken from the battlefield where so many soldiers lay.
My several wounds were treated I would not die today,
But I know that I will never live life as I did before,
Because the fear of hell will haunt me from this day and evermore.

*Brannon Coker*

## Ode To the Glorious Seven

The silver craft soared through the Florida morn —
No one could know how our hearts would be torn.
At an exploding bright light and a thundering boom,
Our shattered hearts wept at our astronauts' doom.
In an instant it was over for the brave souls on board,
Meeting their destiny, they greeted their Lord.
The great craft exploded flinging itself far,
Fate had stamped "Cancelled" on their quest for a star.
Who knows what happened on their ride into space!
Is this then a signal to end this mad race?
Surely not because these glorious seven,
Gave up their lives on a trip to the heavens.
And so, little children, accept and don't cry,
When destiny calls, we each have to die.
Look to their sacrifice, see the unknown explored,
By all the brave astronauts, the seven on board
  the Challenger.

*Bill Manosh*

## Morphine

No one can see me and I sit alone,
No one ever heard me and now I'm gone.
No hands to catch me when I come undone,
No beautiful face to help me see the sun.
No drug can stop this,
And no loss could top this.
No lips to kiss me,
And no fists to hit me.
Guns can't scare me,
But your eyes always tear me.
I'm so numb, nothing can kill me,
And no one will come.
No syringe in my veins can ease the pain,
Because I can't seem to get out of the rain.
When I see your silhouette walking on the horizon,
I feel all the pain and I know I'm dying.
I see your smile, I feel the tears rising.
I fall into your eyes, I can't stop crying.
I want to kiss your lips and hold your hand,
But the only thing I know is the must of the band.

*Julien de le Mans III*

## The Final Flight

A pigeon flew into our garage one day
  No one knew how long he would stay.
He came to take Jimmy's spirit away.

Together they would fly to Heavens' door
  To be free from troubles forever more.

As he looked back as his friends and loved ones left behind
  He saw his Dad weeping, for he didn't know it was his time.

Jimmy cried out "Don't morn for me
  At last I am happy and my spirit is free - if only I could let
  you see!"

A second chance was given to his Dad to be treasured
  Little did he know the days would be measured.

His Dad believes in God's everlasting love
  And now his son is with him above.

Please pray for him before you sleep at night
  His spirit will return but be gone before light.

So do not worry anymore
  Someday you will see him when you enter Heaven's door.

Please keep your faith, love and a smile
  For the time on earth is only a while.

*Barbara R. Mellas*

## A Letter to My First Grandchild

"Sarah Elizabeth" is the name I gave you,
No one knows this name but me.
My first grandchild, you were given away
But you're in my thoughts each day.

My prayers are for you, my darling
That you are happy and well.
Loved and adored by your "parents" new
Whether Christian, Atheist, or Jew.

My arms will never hold you.
My ears will not hear your cries.
Your laughter is shared in a home somewhere,
At times, the hurt, so hard to bear.

Our spirits can never be stolen,
We are too close, always to share
Our thoughts and our feelings, which will always exist
If known only by the air.

*Betty Mahurin (Garrison) Baker*

## Memories

Soon I will be a man
No one to lead me by the hand
No one to tell me it will be all right
When I hear scary things go bump in the night
No one to tell me right from wrong
Just the memories of the years that were short but long.
Soon my mother and father will pass away
But I will go on living for many days
With only the memories of them by my side
Telling me it's all right, and don't cry
My parents were always there for me
Now all I have is my memories.

*Brennan Mischenko*

## Silence

Sitting in darkness as night passes by
No one to talk to except myself
Time seems to be standing still
No wind, no rain, not even a sound.

Trees are motionless like in a painting on the wall.
I talk to myself as if someone were there.
Ask myself a question, come up with my own answers
Thoughts come and go can't seem to stay on line.

It's almost as though the world has stopped
   in the middle of time
The glow of lights look as if they were stars
We wander alone with the silence, until
The sun comes up to bring us the dawn.

   *Bernard Boisvert*

## The Beginning

In the beginning God had a plan.
No sickness, no pain, no curse upon man.

But evil stepped in and sickness began
to take over the happiness and well being of man

No one knew how to treat the curse,
but God stepped in and created the nurse.

The nurse was created to relieve all the pain.
To comfort, to love and help to regain.

All that was lost in each patients struggle
along life's road and through every puddle.

I am a nurse and with God by my side,
I will nurse the sick and help to guide.

All those in pain and those all alone,
to have a better life until they reach home.

   *Elizabeth Fast*

## Darkness Without Light

I fear darkness without light for it has no shape
no start, no end.
For one can see what one wishes to see.
Long green fields, the woods filled with dragons...
Any imagination of mind.

Yet in darkness you think things out.
Once you lose your fear of what might be around.

And how it must be for the ones
who have never seen the light
not to know the colors or the growing life.

And for those who have lost their sight
what mental pain it must be
not to see what one used to see.

But to this day I fear more
the darkness of light
the thing I see and know nothing about.

But one must realize
that half of ones life
we live in darkness of light
not knowing what tomorrow's life will bring.

   *Julius Garcia*

## This Very Day

A babe was born on this very day,
not a care in the world, just fun and play.
This babe grew to be a sensitive child,
with a nature to be loving and mild.
Into young womanhood now she did whirl,
the stages that make a woman from a girl.
One by one the years pass her by,
and in her mind, she wonders why.
But do not be sad of those passing years,
wipe your eyes dry from sentimental tears.
Seek happiness and pleasure in your own way,
for I your daughter, am grateful, for this very day.

   *Crystal Black*

## Passion

Way down deep is where it lurks inside
Not even the soul knows where it hides

To acquire this taste it doesn't take much
Most may experience it from a touch

Like a raging fire it explodes from within
You hear the devil himself tell you to sin

Your body, it tingles, you love the feel
It's doing all the work, as your lips stay sealed

Pride is not an issue, shame not a concern
You want to see and do it all, cause you want to learn

Nothing's planned out, it's just a chain reaction,
But that's the beauty of it all, when you are touched with passion.

   *Clifton M. Dobson*

## A Valentine's Wish

My valentine wish is that you will love me for who I am,
not for who I know.
A wish that with every fleeting look,
grows dimmer and dimmer.
I'm assuming you don't realize how much you
cared for, how much your loved for.
I love you for you,
and I wish you could love me,
the same way.

   *Amberleigh Covell*

## Alone

The tree standing alone
not friend, not foe
in a field of no great achievement,
and by a lake with much pride in her size,
where no friends come to play,
or come to watch.

He needs no one,
longs for no friends,
for while seemingly alone,
his mind and soul frolic through the world,
and as one might be lonesome,
this tree longs for none.

The lush green of his arms and strength in his bark,
conceals a child who dreams,
and though his dreams are with others,
he needs none other,
and continues to dream... alone.

   *Josh Rubin*

## Evil's Squeeze

Sweet, early in life, innocent
Not knowing Evil is watching
Awaiting its chance to strike
With its nails of flattery,
Its welds of deceit.

Will this young eye see through the camouflage?
Will she emerge with herself,
Or be bandied about from high to low
Till swallowed whole
  used up
    burnt out,
So that sweetness has become bitterness,
Innocence, wrongful knowledge,
And love, rage?

And so it goes,
Evil has absorbed another.

    *John Bedinger Williamson*

## Cry Baby Cry

Cry Baby cry,
Not to suffer
and not to die
your eyes widely open
in the middle of the war,
your standing under shadows, without a reward.
Cry Baby cry,
not to suffer and not to die.
You're surrounded
by your loved ones, that just die.

Cry baby cry,
not to suffer and not to die.
You are surrounded by misery,
without a friend,
you are crying for the war to end.

    *Juan A. Lameiro*

## Uncertainty

Trembling, seeking.....
  nothing, I find.
Encouragement, acceptance.....
  none given, this time... or, ever.
Look!  What do you think?  I made this for you.....
  waiting, hoping,...nothing will do.
Walking away, confusion, alienation,
  alone in my world....warm illusion.

Why do you care?  No one else has....
  leave me alone, just go back!
No, I don't believe you!  Go now, please....

  You're still there, waiting in the trees.
I insist that you leave, get out of my way!!
  What?
You're a part of me?  What does that mean?
  Just then, I turn and your image is gone..
I sent you away...
  Where are you?
  Come, back....
I know now I was wrong.

    *Denise L. Ketcham*

## Big Brother Lost

Once I had a big brother.
Now he's gone.
No longer can I reminisce with him
He always remembered our youth,
Our experiences, our joys, our fears.

We were a team.
Why did he leave me
I still need him.
Many nights after the lights are turned low,
I talk to him.

He does not answer.
Yet I know he's watching over me.
He hears.
He cares.
He protects me with his silence.

    *Helen Shirley Fein*

## Treasure Or Crutch?

The man fell on bended knee
Now reduced to a meek child
Laid down for a moment in silent prayer and asked
God, why did you steal the one treasure from me?
That which made something whole inside.

What had been stolen was buried deep
within a chasm below the heaven's ogling eye
Placed there by one that I don't want to hide behind, God.
Using repetitive words only to twist them into a ploy
the way so many others do for their self-righteous, one-sided views.

All this links to a day's dawn born upon a baby's brow.
Courage, man!  Sink into a silky warm den.
Alone and ignored, all by myself for a brief time
Turns out to be a nightmare on a wild ride that ends
when my treasure is no longer the crutch that I need.

    *Heather Mersing*

## Where Is The Beauty?

Once there was beauty surrounding me.
Now there is nothing but filth.

Where in the sand, and the wind, and the sea?
Where is the beauty that surrounded me?

Is it buried so deep in the earth so far down?
Will we ever be able to turn it around?

Where is the fresh flowers; the clean air that we breathed?
Oh where, oh where can it be?

Are we changing the tides with the time we have left?
Are we mending the damage we've done?

I got down on my hands and my knees, and I prayed that I could
see the beauty that once surrounded me.

And there it was, the beauty that surrounded me.
I had just failed to see.

There were the birds, the flowers , the trees.
The laughter and smiles of the children.

Then all of sudden I knew what was lost,
It was the love in my heart and others I sought.
Where in the sand, and the wind, and the sea?
Where is the beauty that surrounded me?

    *Carol Jessop*

## O Man of Wings

What thinkest thou
O man of wings
When soaring high
In lonely spheres.
Do worldly matters share at all,
Art thou free from earthly tears.
Dost thou feel half mortal man
In that realm of clouds and such
Dost thy spirit not seem light
Beyond all human touch.
Would this were true,
This ecstasy where man could soar into the sun
If only he could but forget
That mortals work be done.

*Betty Forker*

## The Determined Verdict

A call came in
Of a crime, wrought in sin
The police arrived, then came the detectives
There was havoc, misguided directives
A Bronco, given a slow chase
Quick, quick, we've got a case
Time went on and on
The Perpetrator, I'm sure, is gone
At the trial, Jurors got ill
Oh God, who will be there to fill?
The Prosecution wanted electrocution
The Defense cried wrong accusation
The state said this and said that
The Defendant cried, "It's not like that."
All the trials and tribulations
Swept across the nations
And at the end of the trial,
There can be no denial;
"THIS IS A MISTRIAL"

*Harry P. Wachter Jr.*

## "My Message"

We're coming to the bitter end
Of a world my friend that's full of sin
Killing, killing everyday when we all know, that's not God's way
He put us here on earth to enjoy
This world that we have all but destroyed

Things have changed and it's getting worse
For all the inhabitants of this here earth
Crime is at an all time high
People world-wide are barely getting by

Wake up people, open your eyes
Because time is certainly passing by
Look at society and what it's become
A world consumed of drugs and children with guns

What is life but a gift from God to be enjoyed and valued by everyone
You get one and one only to do as you please
Once your life's over that's the end you see

So get it together and do it fast
Or you'll miss out on what will come to be the past
It's a cruel, cruel world that we now live in
And you better wake up, cause it's coming to an end

*JoAnn Graves*

## Me and My Shadow

My Shadow is very small, he's barely 3 feet tall.

My Shadow walks with me, he laughs with me and loves me best of all.

Hundreds of questions he can ask.  Why do birds fly?
Why do bears have paws instead of hands?
When will I be BIG and not so small?

Questions of wonder, questions of why?  How do I teach him?
Will I be able to reach him?  My patience must prevail.
For my shadow I must not fail.

I step back, little toes I step upon.
Beside me walking, always talking this shadow of mine.

Your love and devotion has me in awe.
Not one thing would I change.
Precious memories of all I've learned and all I've gained.

When your scared, from your bed to mine, "Grandma, Grandma,
I'm afraid, can I snuggle with you?  Please can I stay?

Time is passing so fast and each day you grow so tall.
Tomorrow my little shadow will no longer be small.

"Grandma, Grandma", I'm afraid, can I snuggle with you?
Please can I stay?

*Deborah L. Hatt*

## Mandela

Sinewed warrior speaks, to our children's world and time
Of ancient principles cast not in gold nor solitary hue or rhyme
But of individual nobility and impeccable humankind

Hear him, feel in him evolution's design
In him, echoes man's lament
Respect your brother-sister, deny the derd's content

Fools, who deal in petty kingdoms, cannot his song you see
Why shout fanatic dogma or hide in apathy
When what is right, is plain, harmoniously to be

Listen world, of systems suffocation, struggle to be wise
It's in the spirit deep, singular purpose to be prized
It's in our seed, it's fate that calls, ever yearning to be freed

Hear him, feel in him cosmic vibrations
In him, whispers psalms of virtue bold
Salted wounds of slavery's whip will not a passion hold

Give the just fair treatment, let tyrants' voices die
Master the vision of oneness kind people
Hear Mandela's cry.

*Carlos Derr*

## Untitled

I used to live in a castle;
of cool sugar-marble walls and ivory turrets,
with winged horses as my steeds and the winds of angels' sighs.
I had fairies in the garden and forests of unicorn spirals;
winds played with fallen feathers from cherubs' wings,
little tokens of remembrance.
I didn't see the transformation -
from marble to granite stone,
a fortress with iron gates aspired and forbidding.
The grass is turning brown and the angels litter the ground,
storms bordering the skies and rain falling down
as a curtain closes on stage at the end of a play.
Was it all in play?
Well, then I've lost.
And, stupid me, I had tried playing the game again and again.
Even now, with the board gone and the players fled;
I still find myself fingering the pieces.
A king.  A broken queen.  Pawn...
Funny, where are my knights?
I wish I could light matches.

*Irene Choi*

## A Mother

A mother is someone who cares and would go out
of her way for her children.  A mother is someone
who put you on this earth.  Someone who will
be there for you when you are down or upset.

A mother is not just a mother.  She is also
your best friend.  Someone who you can talk to when
your down in dumps, or just need a good truthful,
caring, friend, and who will not backstab your or
be a two faced person.

A mother is someone who needs, wants, and should
get the respect that she deserves.  A mother is someone
who will be there when you get sick.  A mother is
someone will hold you when you need it.

Most of all, a mother is someone
who understands you and your problems.

*Jennifer East*

## "Heart"

Inclusion in my heart
of hopes and dreams and fears
what passed as a boyhood fancy
Has grown to a persistent adulthood ache
Red halves that have broken apart,
Fuse together once more, with the passing of time.

Emotions that pass through
the shining scarlet flesh,
Leave a presence, not of mind,
but of a deeper lasting feeling

Phases enter, grow and depart
from Cupid to lust to love,
As the tide ebbs and flows
Until the silent translucent veil
of an everlasting sleep,
Descends and envelops
the gentle guide
to the final throb!

*Frank A. Klump*

## Memories

As I enter the dawn
of my "40-something" age
remnants of yesterday play
upon my mind's stage

Acting out the memories
I carry deep within;
visions of my childhood
and the child that I had been.

From strolling with my grandfather,
as we walk hand-in-hand,
to building foreign castles
in my backyard box of sand.

As I myself have children now,
I've realized along the way
that the moments that I now share with each
will be treasured memories some day.

So, I strive to fill the moments
for my children, to create
memories of warmth and love
for THEIR "40-something" age.

*Debbie L. Troupe*

## "Oklahoma"

A city of great beauty
of sights to behold
where loving people mingle
with faces all aglow

A place of fun and laughter
of peace and quiet too
with children playing gladly
eating cones and candy too

but then the peace was shattered
one bright and early morn!
bringing pain and great sadness to everyone

Mothers and fathers weeping
even little children too
for their love ones had perished
at the hands of one unhinged

With faith and strength in numbers
they can certainly repair
their broken hearts and spirits
and mold together as one again.

*Helena Patricia Evans*

## Dry Ends

Talk amongst the devils and demons
of sin, sorrow, ills and reason,
while hiding among the chemists salts and solutions.
Fear not! Rise above and toss away the illusions.
Raise your willowed head against the whispers
of threatening ghouls and satanic vespers.
Choose to walk among the happy souls.
And don't give in to devious lulls.
Give up falsehoods and pretentious desires.
Try not to mingle with your period liars.
Trust yourself and your true friends.
And let clean means meet dry ends.

*Hilton Robinson*

## My Favorite Teacher

My memories of school days so long ago
Of teachers and classmates I used to know
Bring mixed-up emotions from out of the past,
Some happy, some sad, but through time they did last.

While students soon scattered both far and wide,
And thoughts of them are like the tide,
The teachers stand out with strong impressions
when one reminisces those high school sessions.

Of all those teachers that would come and go,
There's only one that I used to know
That I now remember as my favorite one
Who still stands out for what she's done.

Her English class was never dull
Nor was there ever a boring lull.
With a friendly smile of encouragement,
In guidance and counsel much time she spent.

Her words to me were a great inspiration
As she once made me feel a great elation
when urging me to goals ever higher.
This teacher could really her students inspire!

*Alice Marie Imig*

## Which Way

You are standing at the crossroad
Of the path you take today,
You turn to the right, or you turn to the left;
You decide the way.

As you decide the future,
As you decide the road;
Will it be the wide easy pathway,
Or the narrow less traveled road.

As you choose your future,
God holds it in His clasped hand;
He loves you and will guide you,
Above; to that bright promised land.

**Charles Ferguson**

## Winds of Longing

Outside, all alone, listening to the susurrus and the feel
of the wind gently caressing my body
Like a lover, whispering how much she needs me.

A chill flows through me as I let my invisible
lady sooth my mind and body,
Almost quivering in anticipation to where she'll touch me next.

She cools me on a hot day and warms me on a cold one,
Yet always eludes me, for I cannot return the gift she gives me.

She always hides when I look, but will catch me when I least expect
it;
I know not to chase, for if I do, I'll lose her forever.

**Brent Wagner**

## Gone But Not Forgotten

Gone but not forgotten are the memories held dear
Of those we have loved and lost over the past years

No matter what the circumstance it's still a very sad day
When someone we care a great deal for goes their own way

But even though they may leave to go onto something new
We still have all the good times shared to always hold on to

For these are the moments that influence our everyday life
And through this experience we learn to take life in stride

**Jaclyn A. Guynes**

## The Wedding Gown

There once was a Love story that should be told,
of two people now, that have become very old.

They are your Grandparents,
Who are special and should be treasured,
For the love they have showered,
Can never be measured.

All through the years they loved and shared,
Always giving to others, showing they cared.

So it was, their pledge of love,
That created this gift to be blessed from above.

May all future grandchildren be Christened in this Satin and Lace,
And know that their Grandparents will always be watching,
Through the eyes of an Angel's face.

May you pass along their story, of their love and their family,
To future generations, whose hearts will be touched warmly.

It was Love that began this special tradition,
And may it be Love that passes it to each new generation.

**Denise R. Parlovecchio**

## Inconclusions (Saying Grace With Every Thought)

grace all your thoughts with the life of your senses,
of walking and talking and moving and sounding,
evoke sensuality with the aspects first noticed,
while venerating venerating all of her essence,
skewer her soul for the need of your verses,
breathing inflating transcending her splendor,
seize upon my eyes and take both my eyes out,
enticing with skin both supple and alabaster,
permeate my mind with passionate outbursts
and christen your thoughts with a liquid fantastic,
of keenness and brightness and fathomless musing,
for twenty-five moons of object singularity,
with picture and painting dividing each page,
wait for anointing with inconclusions of verses,
then question and question the truth from all facts,
and evade all the muck from the muddle of truth.

**Ed Raz**

## The Third Day

Under the hazy sun now, a lavender sky is formin'.
Oh, how I do love this time of mornin'.
Ribbons of mist swirl over the tops of the trees,
while the horse's lazy click is matched by bees.
The very sweet scent of the risin' dawn,
is like music in the distance goin' on and on.
White rows before me slowly do awake.
Their sounds are calm and orderly, for their own sake.
As colors move about round' the scenery;
I lose sight, for they fade in the greenery.
Elements now mix as the air is swayed.
How I do wish they would have stayed.
Brown paths are stamped in the earth,
and now I think of a Richmond hearth.
Far, far away with its beautiful lands;
I can see it all as clear as my hands.
All is at rest, but still .... what sound?
I must now turn around.
For the cannons do cry,
that many a good boy today shall die.

**Jennifer Myers**

## Death Calling

Knock, knock. Who's there?
Oh! It's you, but I'm not prepared.
So why do you follow me everywhere?

Lately I have seen you wherever I go,
And when I just have missed you,
I know that you have been there right before,
Because you have left your message lying
on the floor.

The pain, the sorrow that you have left behind,
It seem to make me lose control, enough to lose my mind.
No, I cannot leave, I told you once, I told you twice
I cannot leave the ones I love behind.
So please just go, I'm not prepared, I told you so!
I told you so I want to see them grow, you know.
So don't come knocking at my door no more!!

**Guadalupe Quintanilla**

## Thoughts About The Passing Of My Mother

Death came to my mother, I was not prepared
Oh the sorrow, do I feel it yet

Shall I wear it, shall I show it
shall I paint it upon my face that all may know it

No

This sorrow is mine, uniquely mine
Within the depths of my soul I will savor it
Its full weight, when on occasion felt, borne alone
Shared, if ever, only with one who knows

This sorrow exists because of its companion, joy

This joy was hers, uniquely hers
From within the depths of her soul it bubbled forth
Its full uplift, frequently felt, warmed us all
Do I share it, as did she, with those who do not know

Yes

I shall wear it, I shall show it
For she molded it within our souls that we may know it

Oh the joy, how I feel it
Eternity came to my mother, she was prepared.

*Joe Thompson*

## Life's Choices

The owl and the pussy cat
Oh what a pair.
One sits on a roost;
The other a chair.
The owl is so wise,
The cat is so sly.
They stare at each other
Not blinking an eye.
Both of them harboring thoughts about mice.
Hunting such prey surely isn't a vice.
The dark of the night is the very best time
To search out a victim and perpetrate crime.
The sleek stalking cat on a serious prowl
Unaware of the quiet and fast swooping owl.
The cat finds the young ones are more to his taste;
The owl likes them plump and more leisurely paced.
The mouse, for his part, doesn't much care
If disaster approach from the ground or the air.

*Dee Ulrich*

## We Once Had No Vision

"...We were resting
...on a wide hill
...in your field one night.
It was 50...55 degrees, with a slight wind, but
we weren't with our coats
just our T-shirts."
            "Any trees?", she asks, eyes closed.
"None that I heard," answering her.
Swayed by her voice, he asks her,
"Did you ever look, kill time, in one of those half-ton world atlases,
and at the beginning, there are photos of galaxies?
That's what you see,
except, waters spritzes and apples-blossom petals, as you stir them all.

"Then—we share occasions
of when we felt perfect.

"But, just off the ground,
there's a thin crack of light.  It's more on your side—
like a part of the curtain not lying on the stage—
remaining from the swarm of blackened-grey.

"The light says, we are flawless."

*Douglas Conroy*

## The Bombing Benediction

  On April 19, 1995, the Alfred P. Murrah federal building in
Oklahoma City was bombed, and a nation came together in glory, in
grief, and in God.

Glory was there.

After a terrible explosion of evil, there came a magnificent
  explosion of good.
All classes and color barriers came down.  People helped people.
The brotherhood of mankind was exalted.

Grief was there.

Who can forget the dead, the wounded, the blood?
Who can forget all of the innocent children and the many caskets?
Who can forget the American flag flying over the rubble?

God was there.

God was on His throne and in the hearts of believers.
He was there to bind up the wounded and heal the brokenhearted.

The bombing benediction is the same one God gave to Moses for the
  people of Israel:
"The Lord bless you and keep you.  The Lord makes his face to shine
upon you and be gracious unto you.  The Lord lift up His
countenance upon you and give you peace."  (Numbers 6:24-16)

*Barbara Holt Merck*

## Hunkapi

I went to the Grandfather.  "Enter the Moon Lodge," he said.
Old man wrinkled skin so worn, and I know him.

"Tell me why the world makes war, Grandfather?"
"My eyes are black - yours are green.  My hands are deep brown -
yours are faded.
My hair is straight and yours is curved.

Take the wounds from 100 years ago, bury them with leaves of gold,"
  said he.
And then he asked me:  "What do you know about the Hunkapi?"
And I do know...

"It's peace Grandfather...making relatives within myself
and outside, it's what we have in common.
Two hearts are the same no matter the color of the blood."

"Go into the world," said he, "Tell them what you know about the
Hunkapi.
Tell them that wasichu knows the Red Way.
Tell them what is in your heart."

"Tell them of the rock which sings the world awake,
of the ground which shook at Wounded Knee
of four who smoked together in the lodge,
of children crying, running, dying."

"Go the way of the Hunkapi."  Grandfather laughed at me.
As I lay chasing to get a vision, with the truth hanging right above
  my head.

*Deborah Martinez Hicks*

## The Poet

The glory of his eyes shined like the
night opening cuts and wounds;
Stood, unbroken on top of his glory;
The night shined images of fierce light
that filled his soul;
The sky shivered at the sight of his golden
heart that moved eternity even more;
In victory waves of winds crashing
stars lighting the way
As he pierced the sky open
Violet screams praised him
He had conquered.

*Carlos DeHernandez*

288

## Confined Within The Innocence

It began so innocently, sweet and foolish love.
On an impossible quest for her majestic beauty.
One that would be found and lost within
The abyss of untamed souls of the heart.
Yet, there in the darkness, lay a single soul
Who may share the anguish of the battered poet.
There she beckons me, with a deliberate yet peculiar call.
Between then and now the innocence was lost,
And the sinful pride gave birth to what is now,
A call of distressful hurt and suffering.
As I wait for my unforeseen climb out of the darkness,
I leave my soul vulnerable to regain the innocence it has lost....

*Frank Artiga Jr.*

## A Father Grieves

What sorrow, sir, to lose your only son!
On blood-soaked fields of rice 'neath hostile gun

This painful message briefly came to say
his soul and body went their separate ways

Deceitful death knocked twice at thy abode;
the sun withdrew and left a darkened road

Sharp steel was driven deeply through your heart;
it buried there with grief and cannot part

Thine eyes are cast with shadows strangely sad—-
how much you loved that brave, courageous lad

Strange warrior he who felt war gravely ill
poor weapon to perform the soldier's will

When twilight falls I see thy downcast head
recalling nights your child was safe in bed

I hear a sigh of woe escape thee now—
behold a look of strain across thy brow

For as you hug and kiss a tattered toy
you think he was a man though still a boy

Deep sorrow fades with passage of the years
yet wish that I could stop thy falling tears.

*Evelyn Olson*

## Untitled

An everlasting tribulation
on morrow, 'I had once thought'
Only a time borrowed,
could there be a higher respect on reasoning
in communion, on souls.
Trust, therefore, our entities,
the good bereaves no essential loss.
We spoke on ways to reach once grace,
we spoke on a developmental of attribute always of understanding,
but however, had it out withstanding the greater cause
of the meaning we sought-
No one in our outermost conspicuousness in dimension.
No. Moreover our bodies pronounced the angular
unrelentlessness time honouring the space of creation.
We've spoken. It was our livelihood -
we triumphed an unintangible asset.
For our love,
there is no greater source.

*Jennifer A. Lee*

## The Battle

The battle began with feelings worn
on shoulders short.
Old man winter and Summer's Spring.
The fight for a period of time, a short time.
Old man winter with his cold harsh
breath and spring with it's polite sunshine.
Flowers are forming, birds are singing,
and lakes are beginning to thaw.
Old man winter is dying, and Summer's
Spring is coming of age.
As the daisies form full and the birds
fly far, the last words of old man
Winter, "I will return!"

*Eric M. Stephens*

## A Walk With God

I met God one morning as I took a early walk.
On the pathway were two robins chirping as if they could almost talk.
It sounded like they were saying,
"Child, let not your heart be troubled or filled with fear.
All you need to do is trust God, and He will take you in His care."

At the edge of the woods was a beautiful sight to behold.
Two deer were looking at me, as if to say "Are you a friend or a foe?"

I tried to get a little closer so I could look upon their faces,
but they jumped and ran so quickly that I knew within my heart
only God could make an animal run with such beauty and grace.

I approached a little clearing in the middle of the woods.
Joy began to fill my heart and the tears began to flow.
As I looked toward the sky there came a peace within.
I began to pray to God who had freed me from all sin.

His arms enfolded me and from my heart He lifted a load of care.
What a wonderful blessing I received that day through just a little prayer.

As I began to walk home, my heart was rejoicing
because a burden had been lifted from me.
once more I was able to sing with the robin
that God put beneath my tree.

*Iris LeVault*

## God Makes His Presence Known

Who was there to hold you, caress and console you,
On those dark nights you thought you were alone?
  Oh no, you didn't see me-
  I didn't let you see me-
THERE ARE MANY WAYS I MAKE MY PRESENCE
KNOWN.

Each morning when you wake-up, sit-up-, and get-up,
I'm there to help you start a brand new day,
  You didn't feel me lift you-
  But I in fact did lift you-
GAVE YOU SOME STRENGTH AND SENT YOU ON YOUR
WAY.

I AM with you in the morn-time, noon-time, and night-time,
I'm with you in wee hours of the night,
  You didn't hear me enter-
  But quietly, I did enter-
I CAME TO TAKE WHAT'S wrong AND MAKE IT RIGHT.

Those times when you feel worn-out, tired-out, and shut-Out,
I'm always there to lend a helping hand,
  If my word you believe-
  Then you will be received-
MY PRESENCE I MAKE KNOWN THROUGHOUT THE
LAND.

*Adella D. O'Neal*

## Again and Again

Once and once again is the way to proceed
Once this is known we can succeed
With a little help we are able to cope
Once this is known we are more grown
This is not spelled g-r-o-a-n
To master that which we must
We have to remove some of the dust
If we don't we might rust
Once we are ahead
There is much to gain
If we do not wane
Often it's a matter of grace
In order to keep a better pace
Once we have learned
It's best to be firm
Rally around to a certain point
If it's in your best interest
To a certain degree
At that point you should be free.

*Edward T. Philpitt*

## Once Was Young But Now Is Old

Once was young, but now is old.
Once was warm, but now is cold.
Once could run, but now is slowed.
Once owned his own home, but now is sold.
Once had a smile, but now a face of stone.
Once had a lot of friends, but now all alone.
Once was strong, but now brittle bones.
Once has a lot od stories, but now all told.
Once could walk, but now being rolled.
Once could hear his laughter for miles,
But now all you here is his moans and groans.
Once could think, but now his mind roams.
Once was friendly, but now is bold.
Once was young, but now is old.

*Corrina Whitney*

## An Unbreakable Love

If ever a maiden so sweet, so frail, so soft, so petite...
One look in her eye, her sweet bluish eye,
Oh! the lust, the passion, the heat.

If ever a man so fine. Oh, how I wish he were mine.
How handsome the hulk, a formidable bulk. If I had
a wish he'd be mine.

But once came a man who was bad. A bad attitude's what he had,
He loved the girl, the beautiful girl,
and he'd kill her true love to get that.

Engaged in a duel were they. Fencing was bad man's forte,
At the very dead end, at the very last end,
the beautiful lass got her way.

When the end of the duel was done, and the lass's love had won,
She gave him a kiss, the world's finest kiss,
on the ground lay the man who'd been "done".

True love was all of their life,
It sheltered them from all of life's strife.
And so they did wed, a beautiful wed, and love made them husband
and wife.

*Amanda Schlager*

## A Secret

I've a secret I've kept for many years.
One that made me feel happy even when there were tears.

I made it a private escape from my daily chore.
I'd lose myself within it, when life was a bore.

It was about two youngsters and a single kiss.
**SECRETS** in the eyes and the touch that I deeply miss.

I wondered often how things would've turned out.
Where he is today, what his life is about?

In my heart somehow I felt that he must know.
I would never forget and my love for him would grow.

"How can this be possible?" Many times I've asked myself.
"Easy", by placing a piece of my heart upon a shelf.

Never forgetting what life's about as I live each day.
Trusting the Almighty to help me find my way.

My best kept **SECRET**, he was, of this I'm very sure.
I hold on to these memories, so sweet and pure.

*Hazel B. Swift-Shannon "Ms. B"*

## In the Oakland Museum of Natural History:

### Two Exhibits, Juxtaposed

The glimpse of a dark bird flutters at the edge of memory
   Only
Because I could not bear to gawk behind the glass on which
   Words
Official in white demanding font expounded a fault that explained and
   Stunned.
Sleep and his brother have not been my friends since.
   Appalled,
First jammed into teeth, knowing then what I had missed.
   Sickening,
My soul withered, my mind scolded. Sooner should life have shouted a
   Warning:
Neither had I created associations by not being eaten; nor had I
   created Associations
by eating and being eaten.
   Not natural.

*Glen Drake*

## To Thee

(Love no longer makes me cry
only eyes full of quiet admiration)

I've never seen a woman as fragrant as you
you have a scent of a tulip.
In you gentle breezes like fall flow.

Your lips are warmer than Spring
purer than a lady of nunnery.

Your smile is sweet as a flute
lighter than a butterfly.

In your trim hair with the fragrant oil of
spike-nard poured
I long to wash my weary soul.

Into your bright eyes that shine like a deer
I wish to dive in - - - -
Like a fish - - - - like a fish.

*Joo Il Pak*

## To Never Reach the End

My head it hurts, I cannot think
only listen to the voice

I shed a tear, but do not cry
as I wait to be told my choice

I have a fear that I already know,
what alternative could there be

The past is gone, the present brings pain
there is no future for me

It has to be done, but I've lost my nerve
I'm weak and shaking and turning pale

My life completely has no worth
when even trying to end it, I fail

    *James F. Bellon*

## Not Much

I ask not much
Only things we all need
The things we all crave, to love, eat, sleep, and breathe
All these things I have to my heart's desire
Except for one and for it I burn like fire
I only want one special man
One that I will love like no one else can
To hear him say "I love you too"
Would make my grayest skies turn blue
To know I'm in his thoughts and on his mind
Would be the greatest joy that I could find
I ask not that his world revolve only around me
But only that he'll be faithful and I'll be the only one he'll need
I ask not much
But still I don't understand
How something so simple has slipped right through my hand
The thing called love
Must only be sent as a gift from above
And so for now I hope and pray
That it will be sent to me someday

    *Jennifer Lowery*

## Okay

I am the one who has no viewpoint, no point of view, and no
opinion of my own. To sway my opinion would be as simple as
simply saying your own. I have some convictions, and I do defend
them really. But, then, your beliefs seem all the more and always
more appealing. I will disagree with you, but say something
strongly and certainly, I will agree with you. What of the sturdy
spine we all should have? Surely, I have not seen mine and
definitely, I have not felt mine. Perhaps, you are just right.
At least to agree would cause no strife. But to believe in
nothing, makes me feel like nothing. But, you could always tell
me I'm something, and then I will absolutely say yes. Perhaps it
is only just lack of self-esteem. You are correct, of course, and
I can change. I have tried change, but to begin, my opinions were
never my own. Borrowed, pilfered, quoted. Everything I believe,
I stole. I am the reflector. I claim bourgeois, prejudiced,
bigoted, snobbish ideals that were never mine, and then I claim
the brilliance of the lies that you say should be mine. I don't
want that to be me. I don't want to be me. Perhaps, that is why,
you see, I am you, whoever you may be.

    *Grace C. Lee*

## Jealous Rage

Does something pull you apart?
Or does love get in the way of your heart?

Do opposites attract?
Or do opposites attack?

When a ring is on your finger
Does it spell danger?

Is you lover a control Freak
To another guy you can not speak?

I will beseech you?
Does he beat you?
What love does not make you scream?
Your love give you bruises because he lets off steam?

I mean does your cosmetics come with black and blue?
Or does your marriage certificate come with a
hammering shoe?

Does your certificate have doom?
Or does it mean it comes with a tomb?

    *Julia Estrada*

## My Little Friends

I'd sit on the patio till after sundown
or early in the morning when the dew is on the ground.
That's when my little friends come begging for food,
they seem to like me, but to each other they are rude.

The first to arrive thought he was king,
chased the others off so they wouldn't get anything.
But I knew I had enough for them all,
even for the Blue Jay's should they come to call.

These little squirrels I gave them each a name,
little Willie would basket catch a nut as if in a game.
Brownie would sit up and try to do the same,
Bubba would get on the table, but wasn't very tame.

We'd share this all summer long,
till days got short and they'd hear winters song.
Saying "gotta gather up things and put them away,
see you next spring if you still want to play."

    *Alven Chitty*

## Sea Gulls in the Sun

The gulls that scream in Summer's happy face,
or in Winter's deep freezing have good reason
to sound the same whatever be the season:
As fledglings from a father flung -
these children of a dying sun
have long forgot the glad elation of earth that's new
and full of delighted expectation: Forsaken, weary in isolation,
scavengers on dusty shores of cosmic seas annihilation.
On fragile wings they soar and scream, souls
caught in clouds on memory's misty peaks left to seek,
to gather, fragments of thin air for novel tokens of a
dying ancient face - lest nothing be left to fill
the void when this sun, his race with time be done,
no longer carves a space for children of the sun.
When all the summer days be cast like droplets from
dangling fingers in a pool that leave no trace of all our
yesterdays and dances in the sun when sea gulls called and
soared over head and wailed and wept to us a last lament.

    *Jillian K. Wall*

## To Jean — My Pledge

I wish not for gold, to fill a selfish till,
Or of fame, as laurel to my crown.
My heart is void of any gain
That might engender world renown.

There is no room in crowded heart,
For things Creosus yearned to claim.
My fingertip must ever touch,
What pulse of love you choose to name.

Now sheared am I of selfish aim,
And in my grateful heart I view,
Those things which sire my happiness,
For all my happiness - is you.

And now with love, I freely pledge
Forever now, God's help I press
My fervent prayer will ever be,
The "touch" to bring you happiness.

For all I am, and all I'll hope to be
With wealth, or naught but paupers strife.
This is all the prayer I give,
"God,....let her love me, all my life."

*Hy E. Zigman*

## Believe In Yourself

Who am I? We sometimes ask ourself,
or what can I do?
Trust me- you are "Somebody,"
Regardless of what you have been through!

People are in your corner much more
than the eye can see...
You must "first" Love yourself
and let "your heart" have its peace;
"Then" your "mind" will become free!

To have money is good, but it's not
Like "Good Health"......
Remember, Please to....
Believe in Yourself!

*Gerard Herriott*

## Anything For You

I don't know what will become of the present
or what the future will bring, I can only hope it's
you. In my dreams I wait for you to come for me, I
watch your every movement, and listen to your every word.
At night when I watch the sunset I think about
how much more beautiful it would be if you were here
with me. I would sit with you all night until sunrise
and all day again until sunset.
I would do anything for you, I would climb the
highest tree, swim in the deepest river, and cross
the longest desert. You don't know how much you mean
to me and you probably never will. I'm sad to think
that the closest I may ever get to you will be in my
dreams. And even if we're never together you'll
always be a piece of my heart.
It seems like I've been waiting for you
forever. Will the day ever come that you feel the same
as I? No one may ever know but I'll always be here
waiting for you. You'll always be a piece of my heart
and you'll never be forgotten.

*Jennifer Keepers*

## "Treasure Each Day"

Have you noticed the flowers in summer and spring?
Or've merely ignored the simplest of things.
Did you happen to glance at the moon, or the tide?
Or foolishly forget, this world has a sky.
If you're fortunate enough to wake up each day,
Then enjoy all the beauty that's coming your way!
Don't take for granted you'll wake up tomorrow.
Don't be so sure, you'll live the next hour!
For today might just be the last day you see,
And tomorrow might begin, with an eternal sleep.
So treasure each day, as though it were your last.
And then might we learn to appreciate our past.
If today you're in love, then express how you feel,
For tonight might you dine, your very last meal!
Say a prayer of thanks, for the loved one you hold.
For before you know, friend ... you're suddenly old.
So next time springs here, and stars up high shine,
Appreciate these things ... appreciate all time.

*Gloria Almeida*

## Window Of Opportunity

I loved your opening, oh yes
our affair, the window to your warmth
the enjoyment we shared, so delicious
the cool, clear glass of our passion
transparent window of opportunity
vulnerable and ajar, how marvelous.

Yet of all the windows I have loved and washed
standing always outside the threshold
yours is one I've wished to step beyond
into the mansion, the house of your being
and that of mine.

To climb aloft to your inspired attics
lie down in damp, crawling basements
dance and laugh in rooms still empty
filling with noonday sun
waiting to be painted, curtains to be hung.
Bold wooden stairways encircling adventure
combined journeys destined to be ascended
together in the house of our tomorrow.

*Gerard Van Gils*

## We Can Make A Difference

What breeds these sounds of violence
Our country has come to feel and know?
These few with their "cause" have chosen to show
The outcome of their deeds is "silence" (death)

Perhaps as parents we could give more time
To our children to listen, talk, and share,
Making them feel important and that we care
And from these actions, they would shine

There are responsibilities as a neighbor and a community
You can show a child your garden and how to plant,
Have a clean up trash day to let them feel "I can", not "I can't"
They need to feel this unity and be given the opportunity

If enough care and love are shown to these few
By all in this country each and everyday,
And we show them that this is a better way,
It just might make a difference to one or two!

*Judy D. Ellis*

## Ode

You have touched me in ways I thought unimaginable
our lives have become intertwined,
We have formed a special bond of friendship
inseparable by space or time.
You been there through the sorrow and through the pain,
through the bitter tears that fell like autumn rain.
You have been there through the laughter and the joy,
like the refreshing innocence found within a little boy.
To fathom the thought of you not there
simply breaks my heart,
There is so much more we have to share
why do we have to part.
But yes you are one of the very few
that have made an everlasting impression,
Like the sight of a rose drenched in the morning dew
and all the other joyful things too vast to mention.
The memories of the times that we shared
will always give me the strength to go on,
You are an will forever be my hope and inspiration
Now and in the times to come.

*Frank Galuszka*

## Some Glorious Day

There is a meeting place somewhere beyond the blue.
Our precious friend Jesus is waiting for me and you.

Our loved ones there will welcome us,
With love and joy unknown.

Just to be united together forever;
In our heavenly home.

God will shower the many blessings,
That we have never known before.

In the beautiful land of glory;
On the blue magnificent shore.

We will have joy and laughter through all eternity.
Jesus will be our guide through the endless time.

Oh! What a glorious time, sharing his love forever more;
On the blue magnificent shore.

We are traveling through this world,
As a spare of moment's time.

Just to spend eternity with Jesus;
Will be a glorious time. PRAISE THE LORD.

*Helen L. Smith*

## Victorious King

I dreamed that I awoke on Easter morning
Our Precious Savior did I behold
Descending from heaven, surrounded by angels
Swathed in white, with a crown of gold

I looked around in utter amazement
At crowds gathering from near and far
And my gaze was drawn to a voice from heaven
To a gigantic twinkling silver star

"Behold my son, the risen saviour
Who from the cross, has set you free
He broken the chains of sin that bound you
and conquered death eternally"

The angels blew their golden trumpets
They spread their wings and began to sing:
"Hallelujah, Hallelujah, he has come for the faithful
Praise the Lord our Victorious King"

I awoke reluctantly from my dream
Peace and joy now filled my heart
And I looked toward heaven and cried aloud
"Oh my God, how great thou art"

*Jean Bell-Chinchillo*

## Starving In the U.S. Of A

### It Shouldn't Have To Be This Way...

Everywhere I look, T.V., newspapers and even magazines.. but mostly in our streets... where I've been since I was a youngin'... I see and have seen people starving... babies crying for a bottle of milk... regular people just like you and me begging for nickels and dimes... cuz they say there hungry and want to get a bite to eat... soup lines soup lines, soup lines... men, woman and children alike lined-up blocks at a time... they say there happy with rice and beans... forget the meat... all I can say folks... is all these people... grown-ups and kids alike being hungry... bottom line... starving in the U.S. of A... it shouldn't have to be this way. We see our government... sending food to far away places... along with millions of tax payers dollars, to China, Cuba, Korea, San Salvador, Panama and Africa and etc. If I had any say so... or (if) I were president... I'd say we should look at our own back yard... the land of the free... the land of liberty... the land of opportunity... Yes! Folks speaking as an American I'm talkin' about the good ol U.S. of A... take a stand people... no more folks and kids being hungry... cuz starving once and for all... pilgrims... shouldn't have to be this way not in the U. S. of A.

*Joe Sandoval Jr.*

## Requiem

How is it we trust and love laying
our very soul and heart beyond the barriers
of ourselves into the care of another
that very risk so consuming only in
equal to the fire of passion allowing
that of gentle flowers petals bloom
fully a will of love carrying with
it all love does, its fears of April's sun
which may burn brightly only to
be clouded by displeasing showers
which carry the cool, crushing, frost
of the moons watchful eye.
Who are to chance but the fool
or the few brave who wish to
drink the warm sun and crystal air
which they perfume with their joy
how is it that they know and I
have only withered and died.

*Guy Gallo*

## I Wish I Could Take Your Pain Away

I see you walk away, my heart cries
out to yours, I wish I could take your pain away!

In my mind I know the truth, I
can only be here with open arms and
ears if you need me

I ask you questions, the answers you do not know.
So I give you a hug and I choose to go

I hope you realize you're in my mind,
heart and soul. But I will give you
your space and stay out of your face.
I'm trying to learn how to let go.

I see you in my mind and heart
knowing that God is in charge of you
and your life, that I don't play that part.
I'm just your wife.

*Darla Sue Baker*

## I Do

Endless nights - strong delights
outside I hear the sirens roar
You've broken the dead bolt of my hearts door
with sweet release - because with
you I am in peace
you brought at the worst yet the
best in me. My love you see;
you've pushed open the gates and
broken all barriers, you are my
strength and now my carrier.
You lift me up when I am down
you help me smile when sadness surrounds.
You are my hopes my dreams
my fire - my one and only true desire.
So to you I vow my love so to you....
    I do!!!

*Janice J. Wright*

## Attending Nature's Production

Expansive distances blew shapeless breezes roaming,
Over life-forms interacting within the watching sun,
Where overcast accumulating settled yet that peaceful eye,
Like clustered thought like dream afore vision limitless.

Image flashed of youthful boy with wonder's open eye,
Coursed in Nature's guidance into funeral shows of death;
Presented frustrations enraged, and vanities ordered by fear:
And come for why but Nature is, and conflict gathered inward:

Fancy, irresolute, rapid-producing, reacting over and onward...
"Everything is indefinite, and disunion inhabits every man"...
In psychic intercourse his very image be composed
And reflexively protected when imposing persons arise —
Disruptions to defend against, to repel and stabilize:
Thus divisions of self contend when threats encountered re-mind...
And memories impatient to memories respond...
Tension sweating restless and vision intermingled here...
His skittish eye patrolling where be quiet, where be rest:
Attentive becoming his condition for selfsame release herefrom...
"Must all men attend their selves for peace, for repair,
Because in the eye undistracted—" an image of the sun appeared...

*David Macaluso*

## Fly like an Eagle

Fly like an eagle so free,
over the city as high as can be.

Looking down on the world below,
gliding gracefully and often slow.

People see the beauty but not inside,
from the eyes of the eagle its on intense ride...

Seeing is believing but half only,
hearing wind that blows so cold and lonely.

Angel is the wind beneath the eagle's full wings,
silently playing the harp intertwined freely and openly sings.

The journey has just begun searching for the unknown,
now part of Mother Earth and Father Sky no longer alone.

Spreading knowledge to all who seek Great Mystery,
creating a guide that created Great Spirit - to be free!

The children smoke from the Sacred Pipe as Spirits
release and Hearts accept Eternal Peace.

Drown to a beautiful Power Place, they quietly sit,
seeking Earth Connection, gathering energy, praying for it.

Fly like an eagle so free,
so high, only blue eyes of angel can see!

*Jessica Jo Amick (Angel)*

## you ain't no friend of mine

parasitical
not an original thought in their minds, their lives
they bring nothing to the party
blinders, narrow, hateful really
they want what's yours, they want to even be you
they want your friend your cars, your jobs,
your possessions, your pets, your vacations, your television set
but they don't know it
they have their vapid smiles and eavesdrop so carefully
so afraid to say the wrong thing
occasionally they slip
they study, they read, they try way too hard
to hard to make it seem like its really who they are
it's all so easy they scream
but they check the rear view mirror, they check the liquor cabinet
they check the ash tray, they check the refrigerator
it's all in place
now everybody smile
we're such good friends, we all get along so well
aren't we lucky

*Barbara Martinelli*

## Cry For The Children

Born into a world of "selfish greed,"
Parents not striving to meet young's need.

Sent to a sitter, while a "buck" is made,
Abused, neglected with no one to aid.

Infants need guidance from wizened hand,
Youth raising children, none meets demand.

Bodies mature with delinquent mind,
Robbing, Maiming, "Mafia" designed.

Human life deleted like that of a fly,
Killing each other, "No one will cry."

Constant denial, "It's not my fault!",
Another teenager lies "dead" in a vault.

"Crack" is the "master" do not blame me,
"I assert virtue, I should go 'free.'"

Sire pleads "youth hood," shielding the bad,
"Don't accuse my child, He's just a lad."

A hand will not guide, "Lust" they will heed,
Reaping from sowing with tainted seed.

"I cry for the children."

*Arita Calley*

## Untitled

To and fro we fly in the early light of the morning,
Passing the doves who soar so slowly,
We begin our daily desires to be with the sky.
Too soon, it is day and the sound of life
Comes calling us back to our feet.
Still we fly, farther, faster, through the whole day.
The night comes at last and we go back,
Back to our homes where the birds run up and down the yard to
their food
With young behind and back again to the sky above.
Never can we go again, for the loss of day of our lives
With a gain of a lifetime of memories is far too great
For the ground that we call our jail.

*Justin Brown*

## A Call to Ministry

Years before accepting the call,
passions for writing were buried within.
Through prayer and meditating upon His Word,
His voice illuminated sharp and clear.

With pen in hand; I scribbled each word,
the ministry is His, I am His pen.
Sparks of passion ignited more flames,
burning intensely into nuggets of gold.

Now when I look back to Calvary,
I am glad I accepted my Master's call.
Obedience is such a small price to pay,
For Jesus gave His life and paid it all.

*Claudia N. Tynes*

## Kaleidoscope

Through the eyesight, I watch
patterns form as my hand evenly
turns seven years, spiralling together
the varied textures and hues of memory.

Placid blues of youth attract the eye
with longings for simplicity and
first friendship, then fade in the
sharp shadows of intricate red-orange
distractions, and are finally softened by
a wiser, reminiscing violet.

Yet, in face of their evolving colors,
the patterns themselves remain forever
constant, a beautiful quilt-work, deftly-
made and strong. I do believe it is these
patterns which bring me the most comfort
and joy, and which will keep me
adding evermore to the pending
keepsake designs.

*Darcie Rives*

## "Revolution"

It seems they move in cycles,
peace, change, and war. A leader seeking
unity-a struggle till eternity - the one who broke the mold
watch the book unfold.
Some people go insane, cowering
beneath their pain, perplexed - what is the leader saying?
Stretching out his hand - swift but with demand.
A spark flies off his mane,
the spark that lights the flame
Revolution is its name.

*Franklin Russell*

## "What I See"

What I see is a family, a nation of
people like you and me. What I see
Is dream and goals shattered, to some
people those things don't matter. What
I see is violence and war, you can't
even walk to the corner store. What I
see is self destruction instead of
creative and positive productions.
What I see is a world of hate, that's why
we have an unbelievable crime rate.
What I see is nothing but hard times,
what ever happened to those intelligent
minds? What I see is a conspiracy,
there are so many people with a lot of
hostility. What I see is a world of
anger, wake up and realize our
lives are in danger.

*Jennifer C. Lee*

## In the Night Time

In the night time,
People walk the city streets for a reason.
Crystal's fall asleep in peace, and the moon looks down feeling
A sense of security.

In the night time,
The stars are kept busy catching children's wishes and dreams.

In the night time,
Prisoners try to find a world through their guilted dreams.

In the night time,
Who are you dreaming of?
I am in the night time, waiting for the sun for the sun has never
Experienced the night time.

*Alicia Johnson*

## Problem Solved

The world wonders are coming past,
Peoples outlooks on life leaves embedded
impressions that last.
I used to think that the world and it's people
were getting better but I was foolish to see,
that comments about shades of skin makes
some people blind towards me.
Living in a world of disease and destruction
sometimes comfort of a human being are all we share,
I pray for the moment when everyone of all
races and colors sit, understand, and care.
Our children are all we have to make this dream
come true,
But in order for this to even start it must begin
with you.
I am blind toward your color for I cannot see,
I embrace the Word of God-brothers and sisters
stand by my side and be blind towards me.

*Cheryl Washington*

## A Book

Pages to turn and pages to browse and
pictures that remind me of my sadness and of love.
Oh, the joy of reading,
Watching, listening, looking for answers.
Right in my head I see the words of colors dancing in
the sky. Answers, answers floating in the wind.
The spine saying open and close.
When I let my mind clear and become part of the book
I see love and my friends becoming another
part of the book.
Why me I wonder?
The pictures let out sighs of relief.
Books open up a world that is free from hunger, pain and
poverty. I wonder will there ever be a place where I can
dry my tears and leave my weapons and my fears in a
world nothing can destroy?
The book brings my heart filled with vacant spaces.
Books make me feel like laughing,
Without them, I feel bored and alone.

*Dana Stroud*

## My Birthday Treasure

Birthdays come, and birthdays go,
But, my 61st Birthday was "Special."
Your last birthday card said,
Miss you, will be glad when you are home.
Signed your lover
Words unsaid for 38 years are now mine,
On that special card.
Rest in peace my gentle man.

*Virginia L. Hunter*

## As Day Begins

Rooted deep in the gray-brown soil, covered over by
pine needles, a slender black trunk emerges.
Large as it departs from the ground, growing thinner as
it reaches upward searching for the still non-existent
sunlight, and the beginning of still another day.

Growing in all manner of ways, small thumb-sized limbs
appear to encircle the tree, pointing in awe as they seem to
be showing off awesome mountain peaks of nearly mountains.
The slender arms become ever smaller branches tapering
gently. They too are awaiting morning's warm touch.

As a proper dressing, weightless almond-shaped petals are
molded to hold the dew for the trees thirst.  As if patiently
awaiting the dawn, tiny petals seem to balance on fragile stems.
They too quiver with excitement as the wind plays a noiseless
game of tag, as it surreptitiously winds its way westward.

Finally as the breeze begins to build, glistening leaves, wet
with moisture, begin to twinkle as the sun climbs even higher.
Suddenly light appears over the ridge, darkness is again forgotten.
Another day has begun, and the faithful tree will once more
offer a leaf-lined haven to a wandering sole.

*Janie Goeb*

## Untitled

Through music, granted the great gifts of wisdom
Placid sages muse beneath summer haze
Proposed questions, to come of age
On the night's doorway
Tired birds return to rest
These sullen stars mock and pray
How they gesture, smug and quivering
Sing me a song
Tell me a fairy tale bold and strong
A king born today the heart's great sorrow
Greater than the precarious sea
Lonely innocent child dance in your house of make believe
Awake in a rose garden
Don't you it's God's will that you'll always know a tomorrow

Let not burning passion cling with flesh
Instead pave the road of freedom with it drink no spoiled wine
For the feast is a fraud just as time

Quick to smile in the hour you greet your guest
Search for strength to power
Until his moldy seeds are discovered under the rugs of incest

*Alphonse Jagrosse III*

## Getting Rid

Span tall, extend wide
Popping a thousand rubber bands
    pulled taut over limbs
Release, grow submissive
    turn to jelly
Free the mind of its oppressive
    and imagined urgings
Close the eyes ever so gently
Slacken a trussed up mask, obligingly furrowed
    features frozen in worry and hurt
Markings of sorrow solidly burrowed
    into vulnerable skin
    in remembrance of things past
Make bold the dream and float on thin
    transparent sheets of sea
    and blue white sky
'Til there is no more feeling
    and no more memory

*Joan Ross*

## The Ungloved Hand

A.I.D.S.
Portal to the abyss.
Wasting away, bone and skin.
No strength for life,
    a mere breath
        awaiting death.
Family and friends gone,
    even the nurse would not comfort,
Nor the assistant change the sheets.
No human love or divine spark,
    until he felt the ungloved hand on his.

*Deborah Carver*

## I Turn My Troubles Over To God!

I turn my troubles over to God when I have
problems and don't know what to do.
I put my hands together, open upward, and pray,
"Lord, I turn them over to you!"

I then part my hands, turn them over, emptying
them; my mind feels at peace and more calm.
I don't understand why, but I feel a great weight
is lifted from me without a qualm.

Dear God, Lord, Father, whatever we may call Him;
maybe Savior or even Heavenly Son.
He hears and is there, no matter what we ask,
as long as we pray "Thy  will be done."

Nothing is too small or large, so turn it over
to Him!  The prayer may not be answered
as you have asked; but He will help you with
what He thinks is best, you may be assured.

It seems things start happening pretty soon,
and seem to start falling into place.
It is the Lord working His wonders, I have no
doubt.  It is His will, and by His grace.

*Ada Stein*

## Losing Innocence

The flower is closed; a tender, untried bud with petals shut tight
Protecting its heart from the harsh weather of life
Then a warm, gentle light surrounds the bud, day after day
Bringing it to a brilliant, thriving bloom
Often, rain falls, but the light is always there
And so the flower continues, gaining strength
But all too soon a cloud passes over; the bloom is cast in shadow
Angry storms toss it about; the petals strain to close
To shelter itself as it once had, yet this cannot be so; once opened
The flower is vulnerable to the unpredictable whims of life
And can never again retrieve the innocent safety of a bud
And so the flower stands
Valiantly straining to remain whole in the face of the fury
But nothing can remain unscathed against the onslaughts of life
And slowly, one by one, the bloom loses its petals
Whisked away by the strength of the winds
Until but one remains tenaciously grasping the heart
Never giving up in the face of adversity, even as its grip slips a notch
For it believes, in a naive recollection of youth
That the light will one day return

*Julie Kennepohl*

## Night Dreams

Night dreams
purple shadows
people running in the streets
senses deprived of their use
let's leave this place
go to the ocean
go to the sea
go to where we can be free
we wonder aimlessly for hours
down the rivers and highways
down forests and falls
to the land we love to hate
we'll live here until the end of our hour
night dreams
and I awake
shake the dreams from my head

*Jason McFarlane*

## "The Lightnin' Bug"

When I was young, just a little tyke; I caught lightnin' bugs,
put 'em in a jar to watch at nite.

Since then I've travelled long and muddy roads - known pain
and joy; and carried a few too many heavy loads.

And now that I near my time of rest, I pray that I have done
my best.

And as my light begins to wane, I wonder would I do it all
again, the same.

One thing I do know for quite sure, I'd cherish every moment,
Every kiss and hug; and I'd set free that wondrous lightnin' bug.

*Jackie C. Whitehead*

## Seasons

Snowflakes make people go slowly in winter;
Rabbits make shadows at dusk.
In spring, snowflakes melt into puddles,
   pussy willows pop up.
In Spring, we plant a garden.
Seeds turn into plants,
   buds turn into maple tree leaves,
   summer is about to be here.
The stars above twinkle,
   the smell of lilac is in the air,
   the magic of summer
      is certainly in the air.
Apple blossoms turn to apples,
   back to school for me.
Bears prepare for hibernation,
   the first snowfall is already here.

*Jessica Fradkin*

## Birthday Muse

Today was my birthday, my nineteenth one,
Ran to the window and smiled at the sun,
My heart was singing a song of gladness,
But way down inside I felt a touch of sadness,
The one I loved and called my very own,
He wasn't able to be at home.

In my mind's eye I pictured his smile,
Even envisioned him holding me awhile,
But that wasn't enough on this special day,
Went to that dance anyway,
Had a good time too; no time to waste,
I was only nineteen, for goodness sake!

*Elizabeth S. Smith*

## Walkabout

on the tracks
rainbows glistened in a pool of oil
under a silver white moon

from far away came rumbling
and suddenly, like an unequivocal and incisive
bolt of lightning,
a train sliced through the puddle

for a moment the scream was deafening
the oil gleamed brilliantly
with the overwhelming intensity of this encounter
the train was radiant and sure of its place

in a flash the train disappeared
crashing and roaring into its future
all the better for its brief absorption of wet, viscous colors

the puddle, cut so decisively into strands,
dispersed its own separate trails
and the little blood streams
slowly flowed along the tracks
to be accepted drop by shimmering drop
into the waiting river

*Heather Coltman*

## For Paul Wylie

The light of your eyes
rather caught me by surprise.
I couldn't for the life of me figure out why.
To find the source of that light, I certainly tried.

Then a friend gave me a devotion as she passed me by.
Reading your story, I discovered the reason why:
Christ is the source of your radiant light
for in Him you have found and take your greatest delight.

And that made me happier than happier can be,
for I've found another friend with whom I'll spend eternity.

*Christie Hayman*

## I Am Strong....

I AM STRONG....I don't need a hand to hold... and yet...you hand
reaches out to me... so strong... so warm....I catch myself wanting...
wanting to reach back...then...I remember...a hand that reaches may
just as easily be withdrawn...taking with it it's warmth...and leaving
mine cold...and empty....and grasping...
I'M STRONG..I don't need arms to hold me or to hear "I love you"..
spoken tenderly to me...and yet...you give me both...arousing
emotions
....sleeping safely inside me...."Oh please," I tell myself, "go back
to sleep. I must not feel...or believe...or hope...or dream"....
I AM STRONG... I don't need anybody...and yet....sometimes the
loneliness echoes throughout my very being...Are you for real or just
a mirage...tantalizing my mind and soul...some say that the eyes are
windows to the a soul...if that's true....then surely when you look
into mine you see... that....
I AM STRONG...really .....I AM......aren't I?

*Chelsea Rice*

## "Then And Now"

"Your first brief note was suspect.
I looked at it in fear.
Almost as if it could bite back.
Danger seemed very near.

How many tons of paper,
How many miles of words,
Have crossed the space between us,
Like a flock of homing birds?"

*Versa R. Gramines*

## Insomnia

I never have fallen asleep counting sheep,
Reading, for hours, has no powers over me.
Soft music, entrancing, is merely enhancing
to my wakefulness.
A glass of hot milk, when I can endure it,
won't cure it.
To try to relax is a tax, and a strain
on my brain.
Though not ill, with a pill, I suppose I'd instill
a brief dose.
But watching T.V. is my remedy,
particularly,
a show I await with great anxiety.

*Bobbie Goodman*

## Silent Prayer

Expectant Father feints restraint,
Ready the world to acquaint,
Not before a silent prayer.

Long days with pen in hand,
Now closing chapter for Fatal Command,
Not before....

Brush and palette held many an hour,
Now final touches to painting of awe and power,
Not before....

Tower to be, four below, sixty above,
Full throttle for first earth shove,
Not before...

Giants of industry think combine,
Handshakes, pens to sign,
Not before....

"Ashes to ashes, dust to dust,"
Pass from this earth one must,
Not before a silent prayer.

*Joseph J. Rutkowski*

## Untitled

Why is love always blind?
Realized a fraction too late,
it took us all so long to find,
we acted on fits of hate,
Now it seems you must go away,
still couldn't tell you I loved you. Your head shakes sadly,
I know you can't stay. No longer one...we are two.
Your lips brush my brow, the touch feels so tender,
what can I do now, but watch you in wonder.
Say you need time to think your thoughts out,
I'll give you as much as you need,
what is your love really about?
You come, then you go, then I bleed.
If this is the end, just tell me so,
don't leave me alone, in vain with my sorrow,
you won't be back, not today, nor tomorrow.
Perhaps I should have told you,
the feelings I hold for you,
on my heart your love's just a blister,
speak of me, tell them, "I'll miss her".

*Celina Pulelehua Nelson*

## Untitled

Pink, green,
Red, blue, and white.
Squares tiles.
Solids and stripes.
Soft lights sunlight.
Neon bright.
Horses, cars, boats and planes
Bells hums, rings, dings
Food, games books and C.D.'s.
Shampoo, clothes, pop, and T.V.'s.
Americans, negroes, spaniards, and Indians.
Talking, walking.
Stopping. Looking.
Picking, choosing, winning and losing.
Laughter. Tears.
Shouts. Fears.
Hello's
Good Byes how do you do.
SPACIOUS CROWDED
NOISY Quiet the mall.

*Deemia Romes*

## Samarobryn

Radiant river of cosmic flow
Reigning throughout from the mystic zenith
Lunar spirits traveling with gathered mist
Creating bedazzled normal mentality

Gallant auroras silently form
Throughout the noble sky
Myoclonic forces twitch mortal realms
Within tranced darkness of astral vision

Celestial ties bond as one
Forming a wholeness of awareness
Time drifting throughout portaled seconds
Upon the beamed gateways of eternity

Neutral pods sprout with gleaming array
Synthetic eyes gaze the crowded earth
Soon combining to shelter the world
With the darkness of an eclipse

Demented minds of shrouded hope
Created by the former cast of existence
Thrusting bolts portrayed by thunderous lyrics
Harvesting the seeds of all being

*James S. Hodges*

## A Love Song

Far away, when you awake,
Remember me moving between
People and ideas, trying
To solve improbable equations.
A citadel of bees
Humming with honey and venom.
Lustful as a monkey at dawn.
Tired dirty with waiting.
Untended and rebellious as a mountain goat.
Simmering always with impossible pride.
Knuckle deep in love with my own hair,
Brushing to flames. Waking up gray
And half dead of dreams in the
Can-Can morning of the
Evening of my life.

*Ellen C. Jenssen*

## I Will Hold You

As you close you eyes tonight
remember precious moments like this
are you to tuck into your dreams
to keep you warm while you sleep.
As you close your eyes tonight
remember the things that fill your world
with music, beauty, and smiles and
hold them tightly to your heart.
As you close your eyes tonight
remember that the darkness that surrounds you
is gently and the shadows are harmless;
Seek the moon and it lead you into morning.

*Candice Brister*

## Requiem For My Mother

With laughter that follows, the endless silence that remains
Remembering, the sorrows, and feelings still the same
Tears streaming down like rivers, more laughter that will come.
Down your spine you feel shivers, when you're the only one.

Like rains when they fall, the dark clouds start to form
You wait patiently for the call, its cold but never warm
Beer and drugs will never help, for stars no longer shine
You just can';t help yourself, it's not yours its not mine

And the dew that still remains, as the rains cease to pour
The burning of the pain, is what you're living for
You can sense but you're not sure, while climbing the next wall
Who you are, who you were, and why your tears must fall.

*Cindy Lee*

## Memories' Garden

In memories' garden, - long planted with care
Remembrance I still cultivate.
Not set in neat rows, - tumbled thoughts
often go - back to childhood,
foolish daydreams, - some mistakes.
And while my mind is tending, to musing,
unending, - I wonder, - if changes I'd made.
If I'd sown more carefully, - nourished
more tenderly, -
Would I now say, remembering has paid?
I nod, and surmise, - and wipe misty eyes.
Oh yes, - such reflections do pay.
There's joys I can't measure, - and
love I still treasure,
And mistakes? - I still make
them today.

*Joan Hoffman*

## My Mother; The Rose

   Her trials of life
remind me of the thorns on a rose.
Each thorn holds its painful scar
in the depths of her soul.
   The stem is her backbone
it held up the rose.
Many times her strength and courage
went untold.
   Like love honesty and moral values
helped her grow.
The roots hold firm
and nurtures the rose
   The petals are her personality and beauty within
so soft, and gentle, she's my life-long friend
this rose I see, at times her determination
and drive overwhelms me.
   I'll always love my beautiful rose
She's my mother, I hope she knows.

*Belinda Rice*

## Angels

They stood there their raiment all aglow.
Reminding me of sun sparkling on snow
I looked up and saw all in a row.
Michael and Raphael and an angel I didn't know.

Serene and majestic they waited quietly—above.
As I looked up to see them I felt surrounded by love.
Their melodious voices penetrated my mind.
The words held the secret for saving mankind.

"Please, listen once more to this message - it's clear.
We proclaim God's love for all who will hear.
Pray together, help each other, ask forgiveness of the Lord.
We give you His promise of a glorious reward."

*Frances Mundy*

## Where have All the Playgrounds Gone?

Happy voices ringing loud and clear
Replaced by guns, shootings and fear.
Violence in the schools and on the street
Change our children, fearing all they meet.

Music sings of peace and white turtle doves
Encircling us with a world full of love.
Let's start singing each day of the year
And send to the world, peace, not fear.

No more bombs, bombs and more deadly bombs
No more playgrounds turned into children's tombs
No more killing between sister and brother.

Let's start singing together of peace ahead
Giving our children a world free from dread.
All will join in harmony, singing of peace
And all shall drop guns, making bloodshed cease.

Again the playgrounds will roar with laughter
Giving children and man happiness ever after.

*Janice Irene Gildea*

## Regret In Taking For Granted

Sparkling blue eyes, like the clear Caribbean Sea,
Revealing hidden secrets - mirrors reflecting emotions,
   two eyes unmasked
The strong, proud lion with snarling teeth and raging anger,
Leaving the frightened prey in its place, helpless to the
   unavoidable predator - DEATH.
Fear erupted from those eyes; showered my heart, causing a sick ache
   inside.
And then, a burst of love made sure I knew his feelings
And remembrance etched on my mind, my heart broke;
Precious drops of pain and sorrow fell on my cheeks,
Cascades to the floor.
How could someone so strong wither like an autumn leaf in the
   merciless sun?
All of the questions that now can't be answered,.  All of the teaching
   that now can't be done.
Yet, despite everything, I regret most the fact that only once
   in our time together-
Only once
   Did I notice his blue eyes.

*Alexandra Ghosh*

## Thoughts

The Sun
Rises on the Eastern Horizon
And sends forth its life-giving brilliance
For all to share in
Plants, Animals, and Beings alike

But a cold wind blows across the land
Carrying the chilling -voices
Of hate and intolerance
From coast to coast

Dark Clouds gather in mass
Threatening to diminish
The warmth, The light,
The truth of the Sun

And as the weaken Sun
Drops below the Western Horizon
And Darkness envelopes all
All can be found awaiting

The return of the renewed Sun
Bringing new hope, new opportunity
The Dawning of a New Day!

*Douglas E. Coleman*

## If Living It Was

There he stood—if standing it was. As the crowded commuter train rolled on, his frenzied eyes darted from one curious observer to the next—so ashamed, so afraid, yet so helpless to suppress even a twitch.

The effects of some drug?...Symptoms of some terrible disease?... Manifestations of insanity?

So many questions, yet so many answers—so many clues to unravel the mystery, to help the curious spectators imagine what his frightened eyes had seen, what his crooked hands had done...if imagine they could.

Did they not see the bold insignia on his threadbare jacket? The once-proud tattoo on his once-able arm? The sunken but obtrusive scars of our delusive human sacrifice?

Producing a needle and a piece of cloth, the innocent spectacle began to sew—if sewing it was. More like chopping wood than sewing, the thick needle stabbed the ragged cloth—without form, without pattern, but not without purpose.

His frenzied eyes began to focus—needle in, needle out... His trembling hands began to steady—needle in, needle out...His shaking frame began to calm—needle in, needle out...
And the soldier was living again...if living it was.

*Adam M. Meek*

## Untitled

Lost in a day dream, I see three boys,
running and laughing and living life's joys.
As the image grows hazy and withers in time,
some choose to forget, but these memories are mine.
I can still feel the pain the separations have caused,
and the guilt in my heart for the times we have lost.
There are emotions I feel, some happy, some sad.
Yet I cherish them all, knowing now what I had.
And the boys that once played and took life by the hand,
let the years pass them by, as each grew to a man.
But fate was not kind and the memories are few,
as the three young men have now become two.

*Erenes A. Miranda*

## Paws Of Time

Paws, they stretch across the great plain,
running swiftly, softly, across rocks, that have fallen
long ago and now rest here.
Time is here, as their
ancestors once were
waiting, whispering their soft
songs, as they wait for the return of the great cats
- the Lords of love.
Running in day with sun reflecting off their glistening
coats - to their land, a place for their cubs to grow
and learn and love.

*Donna Lynn Smith*

## If I Forget Jerusalem

O Lord God, Jehovah, the One who weaves a perfect tapestry of
salvation for all humanity
Let the earth open up and swallow all my possessions
Let the flocks of sheep you have given me that feed in the lush
meadows, all die of some dreaded disease-

If I forget Jerusalem

O Father, curse me with skin as white as snow from leprosy
Cause all my teeth and hair to fall out
Make me blind as a cave bat in the noonday sun
Cause my feet to swell that I may not walk through the streets of the
beautiful City of Zion-

If I forget Jerusalem

My Lord and Master, make me a slave of my enemies
Cause them to afflict me with scourgings till my back is wounded
with deep gashes, and my blood runs free, down to the earth

And, oh, my precious Abba, when I breathe my last breath, have my
family bury me in an unmarked hole somewhere on a deserted mountain
And you. Yes, even you my Father, disinherit and forget all about me-

If I ever forget my home, Jerusalem

*A'loma D. Williams*

## Rebirth

As the slow but energetic creature crawls along the ground
endlessly
searching for food, A crazed and unfamiliar thought enters its mind.
A thought that cannot be explained by the animal itself for it has a
very a limited amount of knowledge about life.

The creature finds itself a safe and secure resting spot in
preparation
of the upcoming burial service it is about to bestow itself. As it
wraps itself in a silk-like blanket, the creature falls into a deep
sleep not knowing if it will ever see daylight again. With every
lagging day, the creature wonders what ever possessed him to do this
to himself." "Is there a greater force at work here?" the creature
ponders to itself.

As the weeks slowly roll by, suspicious feelings start
to occur within the temporary tomb. Things such as hearing
become more defined and, light begins to filter through the life
sustaining web.

It was as if the God-forsaken creature had been given another chance.
It emerged a few days later with beautiful lustrous wings protruding
from its back. The earth ridden creature no longer had to crawl on
the ground in search of food, for its wings took him higher than any
bird could go and farther than any wind would ever blow.

*Daniel Urie*

## Life

Living in this world of endless times,
searching for something we may never find.
But as this world turns on its power and speed, people are
robbing fighting and killing for things they don't need.

You will see the young getting old with bitterness in their
hearts and the old getting older and drifting farther and farther
apart.

You may ever see people who will say they're your friend,
but they will turn their back on you every now and then.
SO WHAT IS LIFE?  IS THIS WHAT IT'S ALL ABOUT?

Wouldn't it be good to live in this world and never find this
We should put trust in the one above and let him fill our
hearts and souls with LOVE.

Then we could live in this world as Sisters And Brothers,
not just for ourselves but also others.

*David McClain*

## Master's of Flight

Master's of flight in beauty and grace,
seasonal migration's without given chase,
building skyscraper's, in their tranquil place,
to better observe, we build them abodes, moulded shy of nature's trait's,
beaten, shot, their habitat's lost, approaching extinction with fevered pace,
these creature's ours to protect, slowly disappearing, without any embrace,
observe's are we, while they passes, answer's that be, to our human race!
this is my woke-up call, "let's protect", before it ends in our disgrace!

*Dorothy Hefelfinger*

## Fellowship Restored

The Lord had compassion on Adam, watching him tend his garden,
   alone.
Seeing he not only desired the perfect mate,
   but on his face it had shone.
Yet God knew that all too soon, this help meet he would create,
Would break the fellowship of God with man, and seal their mortal
   fate

For by the serpent, man's companion would be soon beguiled...
As she delighted in the pleasure's of God's "Eden" -still undefiled.
However, Satan's act of deceiving woman and thus the seem man,
would cast him down, cursed to eat the dust and to slithers upon the
   land.

The throne was room empty, the silence broken only
   by his grieving sighs.
His bosom tight and heavy, his tears tricked from his eyes.
Man chose the tree of knowledge, he must be
   "separated" from the tree of life.
And for this choice of man, the son of God would have to die.

Love is freely given, and can not be forced from man,
To choose right or wrong, this choice must be given to him.
Without free will, man would be a mere vessels of "clay" taken
   from the land.
The Lord embraces the father, and states: Now, we will enter the lamb!

This would be the penance for all sin, the ultimate redeeming act,
To forgive men for all their transgressions
   and the drawing of them back.
Purchasing their souls from the deceiver, that perpetrator of sin,
Christ paid the price to restoring fellowship of God, with men.

*Jack R. Ryder*

## My Mother

My Mother is a gift from God.
She guides me through those endless odds.
She lifts my spirits when I'm down,
Her patience and guidance are always around.
No matter what happens she still gives her love.
I firmly believe she's a gift from above.
She never hesitates to help someone in need.
She forever taught me to resist greed.
She says, "You can't always get, you have to give too,
and then one day it all come back to you.
Be kind, be gentle and most of all be humble.
God never sleeps, but hears your prayers, even when you mumble."
My mother, yes my mother, she's a gift from God above
and I want her to know that I give her my love.
I'm sure there are many mothers like mine;
if you have one, cherish her, for she is divine.

*Gloria Williams*

## Sacrifice Of A Jewel

She doesn't have much to call her own.
She has faith in all around her.
She never has a complaint.
She always smile and says "Honey, God will protect you".
She's been through a life time of sadness and loneliness
of course she had friends but still there was avoid dwelling
within her never once did she believe that God wasn't
watching without a thought her self she worried for,
Yet without a thought herself she worried her
Self near death each and everyone of those she loved.
The mst gallant this she did before her
untimely death.  Was to instill her spirit in my mother.
Who's a spit-n-image of someone.  Who I wish I
could trace places with.  So the world could see
What a priceless jewel Nadean Welch
was.  And in my heart will always be alive
forever and ever amen.
She sacrificed everything for those
she loved with the price of her life like Jesus.

*Christy Cook*

## Happy Mother's Day

Our mother is our lifeline in everything we do,
She is always there helping out showing love for you,
Her eyes sees many things we do not understand,
But mother is always there to give a helping hand.

She listens with her ears for things we may never hear,
She protects us from things that each of us may fear,
Her hands work so very hard to help us all she can,
She makes all things so easy, otherwise we don't understand.

She is on her feet each day, from morning until night,
She is washing, cleaning, cooking doing every thing in sight,
But her heart is overflowing with love for me and you,
She shows you all the love she has in all that she will do,

A mother's love is oh so great, with words we cannot tell,
But just to know that Mother's there the feeling sure is well,
So if your mother is here today, there's many things you can do,
One is give her hugs and kisses, say mother I really love you,

Now please don't forget Grandma she is there for helping out,
She is a wonderful person she teaches us what love is all about,
You should always praise Grandma, in all the things you do,
Our Grandma is our Grandma, but she is your mother's, mother too.

*Janice Robinson*

## Life's Tears

Tear drops like morning dew;
As my lifetime dreams came true,

Tears like flames of fire,
As I saw the glory tire.

Tears falling from the sky,
As my life began to die.

Tears down the window pane
As the world went insane

Tears like a spring rain
Full of joy, full of pain

Tears filled with memories
Full of failures, full of victories

Tears descending from above
My soul is at peace, like a dove . . .

**Suzanne M. Hunt**

## Perceptions

Love
Entangled in rope
Which stretches
From here to Eternity,
Engulfs me
With feeling.
I want to cry.

Rose petals
begin to fall,
as I stare
with wonder:
What makes it beautiful?
The last petal falls,
I smile.

**Suzanne I. Shea**

## The Sunset

A sunset paints the sky
Its radiance so ethereal
The sky reminds me of you
In all its beauty and amazement

I sit here waiting
Hoping it never leaves
Longing to hold it and not let go
Drinking in all its beauty

Perhaps my sunset will be kind
And stay for an eternity
Or perhaps my sunset will disappear
Wishing only to move on

For now I just enjoy it
Watching its every move
Never leaving my window—

You are my sunset
**Monty Youngblood**

## Ski Utah

White and powdery,
Skiis waiting to spray it up;
Slash and Thrash Utah Snow.

**Delbert Farley**

## The Number Game

6 feet tall to 6 feet under
9 to 5 might
Grant you 20
After 60.

20 years to walk
On 3 legs,
20 years to squint
With 4 eyes.

Imagine 60,
Years gone forever
Decaying in remorse,
As you read this paper.

6 feet tall with faith, tomorrow
1 day closer
To 6 feet under.
1 day less to wait.

**J. Michael Mills**

## Darin

He's my type
A boy I like
What does he look like
The notion I can't swipe
Don't gripe
He's ripe
So sweet
A treat
But does he have cute feet?
I call him Winnie The Pooh
Although he can't seem
To say I love you
He's my cute teddy bear
With brown eyes and brown hair
His affection is there
He just can't display
it or share, but I know he does care
But why does he just stare, or glare?
I love him, Darin, the new country I live in
now.

**Rebecca Cathers**

## A Second Thought

And from blackness opens light
a far and beauteous ocean bright
a sky of blue, an endless delight
a wind of never ending might.

Two distant shores of evermore
two wings of strength for which to soar
the sun gold a lion's roar,
this is life to which Earth bore..

My arms, I wrap you up with care
to harm you they would never dare
my life for yours, I would not spare
to me, your love 'tis only fair.

**Missy Kuhn**

## Insanity

Insanity!
It's fear.
Fear of Life,
Fear of Death,
It's fear of anything.
But then again, fear of nothing.

**Maryam Amid**

## The Refugee

I am an Arab refugee,
A female Arab refugee
I'm from Palestine you see
I was an Arab Palestinian refugee.

Where in the world is Palestine?
Show me the map while I dine.
Why is there no Palestine?
Because Israel replaced Palestine.

How is it to be a refugee?
One cannot imagine how it will be.
Losing everything you own
Not even living in your home.

What is my advice for one can do?
Except move on with little clue
What will take place in the future
Adjusting is not for every creature.

I'm now a citizen in Illinois
I'm happy with my two boys
We all did visit the Holy Land
I did move on and I'm so very glad.

**Madeleine Hoss**

## Back to Steven

You still walk ahead of me
a few giant steps, only
now you carry my bag
and open most doors.

At night we hesitate to touch
the other first, as if
the one who reaches out
will come back empty-handed.

This scene is so like married,
I keep thinking I am
bound to you
by deed and legal tender.

I have wished myself pregnant
so you would see how full I am
without you, enjoy the child in me
if the woman leaves you could.

**Marcia Bernstein**

## Back to Steven

You still walk ahead of me
a few giant steps, only
now you carry my bag
and open most doors.

At night we hesitate to touch
the other first, as if
the one who reaches out
will come back empty-handed.

This scene is so like married,
I keep thinking I am
bound to you
by deed and legal tender.

I have wished myself pregnant
so you would see how full I am
without you, enjoy the child in me
if the woman leaves you could.

**Marcia Bernstein**

## One Moment In Time

Life - Death
A gentle swing
Comes together in space
Time is but a resting place
Slowly we look at life
Where have we been?
Will others remember who we are?
So much we wanted to do
Each day went by
Then turn around moving to beyond
Remember I was there
Caring - sharing
Giving you hope
Pushing you on
We know it's hard to say GOOD-BYE
So just look at the sky
I'll be there twinkling just for you

*Susan K. White*

## Angelic Kim

I often wish that I could see
a heavenly angel fair,
and gently touch that holy robe,
and know that he is there
to guide and protect me from
sins that ensnare,
and help me to live
a holy life that is rare.

But now I find great comfort indeed
in this our human race,
for I have met a few souls
who have an angel face,
whose spirit is so calm and meek
when trouble assail the soul,
no matter how the winds may blow
or how the waves do roll.
I am here to tell you of my grand daughter
whom I know quite well.
All she needs is an angel wing
and off to the sky she would sail.

*Mattie Hershey*

## Mama

Mama? Mama?
   A little old lady
in the hospital
   called and cried.
Mama? Mama?
   A plaintive cry
that went to my heart.
Mama? Mama?
   I wondered why
she looked and called and cried,
Mama? Mama?
   I'm beginning to understand
this little old lady who called
Mama? Mama?
   She was lost
and felt need for her mama.
   Now I feel loss and need.
Mother
   I cry for you.

*Marceile Sawyer Edmundson*

## My First Lobster

I never thought that I should see
A lobster staring up at me.

Yet there he was upon my plate
His deadened eyes mere slits of hate

So big, so beautiful he lay
This noble creature's fate fulfilled
The giant claws forever stilled

No more to swim 'neath sun or rain
Along the lobster shores of Maine.

Must I take up the tools to crack
The shell of this majestic back
And pluck the morsels sweet and white
I fear I've lost my appetite.

*Thelma Z. Hoover*

## On the Road Again

You put me on the road again.

I wanted a home for you and me,
A loving and caring family,
   You hug me;
   I kiss you;
All I asked was love to sustain.
You put me on the road again!

I tried to hold you intimate,
I wanted you to penetrate,
   All of you,
   All in me.
I never thought of pain or gain
You put me on the road again!

What whorl-winds churned your mind
Never would I be able to find;
   Blank eyes,
   Deep sighs.
Have thrown my throbs and sobs in drain.
You put me on the road again!

*Rasik Pandya*

## Reality

Eternity's web
A pain in my heart
I wonder if body and soul can part?

I feel a touch
It comes from my mind
I so yearn to leave my body behind
   And
Go to the light
Feel the warmth, stay there forever
not going forth.

Forth to reality's destruction
To what we have done,
To our minds and our plane.
I wish we were one.

*Renee Lauren Hall*

## Imagination

Soaring high above the boundaries
of human constraint
Swimming through the depths
of water unknown
Carefree and boundless,
Imagination is found

*Meredith Hastings Dunton*

## Letters To 2218

Darkness of nightfall
A reminder of my loneliness
Thoughts of you
overwhelm my soul

I peer at the moon
Wondering if you are doing the same
Wishing on a star
Whispering I love you

The distance between us
Keeping me away
The one that I love
Is where I belong-with you

The letters, the phone calls
just aren't enough
I want to, need to be
embraced by only you

Soon we will be together
Feeling like an eternity
I will be waiting
Where I have always been—right here.

*Rachael A. Cove*

## Memories

A pond full of wishes,
A river immersed with dreams,
Gathered by the current,
They're scattered into streams.

A well filled with could-haves,
And a jar filled with dids.
I have shut up all my should-haves,
And forgotten all my bids.

Such things I have regretted,
Some things I forgot,
I wonder what might have been,
I wonder quite a lot.

The memories I have,
And the memories I will,
Are locked inside a half full closet,
To which I have my life to fill.

*Samantha Luterman*

## A Sad Spring

We've had
a sad
spring.

Day
by day
we'll see
what the future brings.

I pray
for a bouquet
of possibilities.

*Sue Pianalto*

## Mistakes

My heart is heavy with pain.
My eyes burn from the fallen tears.
Mistakes we make as years go by,
But heartaches never heal inside.
You may forgive
But you can never forget,
The heart you broke can never be fixed

*Peggy Smith*

## My Guardian Angel

I saw her once, I saw her twice.
A shining light in my sight.
Full of love, there she was,
shining over me, singing a song.

There she was, beautiful as a rose,
full of love like my father, ready to
pick me up and hold me close.

Caring for me every night, I hear her
voice singing her song, a song to me.
Her song that is only for me.

*Marisol Claudio*

## Summer Days

Sitting on a dock,
A temple of sorts;
Below
Another world flashes.
Above, the sun shines
As I cast,
There are only possibilities.

*Stacie Davidson*

## Believe

A smile for a smile
A tender word for a
Tender word
A helping hand for a
Helping hand
A smile
A tender word
A helping hand
These things we all need
It happens when you believe.

*Virginia A. Dannewitz*

## Behind A Mask

When I close my eyes I see the world.
A world that has never been seen.
Because our eyes are like a screen.
A screen that hides the truth from us.
But people think it not a fuss.
They see the world through deceitful eyes.
And never see the truth that lies
Behind a face or behind a mask.
Look past falsehoods is all I ask.
When you look beyond this foolish game.
You will see we're all the same.

*Michael Yuen*

## "Old Love"

All these years I have wondered
About the boy I once loved
The boy unique in his own way
Free to do what he pleased
Then one day...we drifted apart
He moved away from my heart
He exclude my being
And went with his new friends
And I was left alone
Without anyone unique to care for
Then one day he came back
He said to me:
"I knew of a person such as you once."
I wondered,
Had he really forgotten his old friend
And the girl who once loved him?

*Patricia Ferraiuolo*

## Magic Gold

This is the story that has been told
About the moon of yellow gold
The way it shined above the sea
Late one night for all to see.
And if you listen very well
I'll tell you of a magic spell
Of little people, who I am told
Come out to play when the moon is gold.
They ride the moonbeams from dusk to dawn
Laughing and singing until the dawn.
They dance and sing and play all night
But with the dawning of the light
Off they hurry to secret places
Where no one here can see their faces
To wait and watch, so I've been told
For another moon of yellow gold.

*E. M. Davis*

## Children

People lived upon on the playground
About to submit
To the cunning twinge
Of the befriended governor
Who sees the majority say
Is the popular way
That can measure to catastrophe
When the under out spoken of hardship,
But the memory of pain
Isn't enough for large parasites
To know that killing their own
Is destroying their home

*Troy D. Stanley*

## The Test Of Life

We go through life a wondering
About what's wrong and right.
Looking for the answers
Like why the day becomes the night.

Life is a long journey
That has its ups and downs.
They say it's like a circle
That always comes back around.

But to me it's like a river,
Running swiftly on its course
It has its highs and low spots
And never shows remorse.

Now look back on your own life.
Have you accomplished all your goals,
Have you lived life to its fullest,
Without breaking any rules.

And ask yourself this question
Are you living life to your best.
If the answer doesn't come easy,
You know you've failed the test.

*Todd Lee Johnson*

## Untitled

To each of us she was a best friend,
A teacher, a role model, a preacher.
In a lifetime she became a sister,
A mother, an aunt, and my grandmother.
Which one is she now that she has
been captured by Alzheimers?
I wish I could rescue her.

*Tracy Slinkard*

## Transparency

He ate a bowl of cereal for breakfast.
Abstracted it,
Played at it
Finished it.

Never concrete,
or connected to other cereal lovers
It was
a penance of alienation
which toyed with his transparency
and tugged
at his gratitude.

The bowl at hand
tested the integrity
of his entire character
and became
a dear and contentious
friend
to his memories
of smaller navigations of life.

He ate a bowl of cereal for breakfast.

*Sue Ylitalo*

## Birds In Water

They made their way
across the boardwalk
to the seaside church
with the murmuring
movement of water
touching the shore,
knowing the simplest gesture
would affect the world
around them,
breathing the fresh smell of rain
after heat,
watching the hill-shadows,
the houseboats, sea gulls, and tide,
the egrets in wet land—
They were ready
for the morning song.

*Thelma Schiller*

## How Our World Really Is

I hold the Bible in my hand
Afraid to see the pages
As our world turns around us
We can all see the traces
What has our world become
When not everyone gets along
Hand in hand we should walk
Singing only one united song
We all want our children to live
In a world full of peace
No more fighting between colors
Enough food for us to eat
Though everyone doesn't love everyone
We should still try to get along
With only kindness in our hearts
We should all try to belong
Guns are being held by a child
Crazy as it may seem
Drive by shootings do happen
Life has become a bad dream

*Lori Duval*

## Change

Like the leaves in autumn
I've fallen for you
Like the leaves fire red color
I burn for your love
And like the change of the season
I too — change

*Ramona J. Roley*

## This Is Love

Today is the day we start again
    after all we have discovered
We've learned so many things
    like broken hearts recover
We know much more from then till now
    there are so many tools to use
Our value has increased with age
    this love is too precious to lose.
We vow with the help of God above
    to treat each one with care
And walk through life together
    thru stormy days and fair
We'll have our rocky days, I know
    but the sun again will shine
I'll walk along with you with pride
    for you alone are mine.
My heart will beat with love for you, my
eyes your best will see.
Together we will build our home to stand
for eternity
And when our time on earth is done our
journey at an end
I will wait for you in heaven my only lover,
my best friend.

*Rose Howard*

## The Notebook

The notebook cried
after it had been dropped in the gutter
because a careless kid let it slip away
on a dark, gloomy and rainy day.
It cried out it contents
in clouded, disgusting water,
all the words it ever had
all the memories
ruined
forever.

*Todd Gerstenberger*

## The Warm Showers

It was a warm rainy summer
afternoon. It wasn't windy. There
was no thunder and lightning on
that day; the sky was cloudy
and gray. The streets did not
flood on that day either. I
was able to see the road very
clearly as the warm showers
fell on me from above the
sky. It rained very hard on me
for the first three minutes;
then it suddenly stopped. I
walked for a total of five minutes.
I really missed walking in the
warm showers. It felt great
all over. I sure would love
for those days to return. I
would do it all over again.

*Robert Howard Beacham*

## Aureole

A tree of loneliness
against time
your leaves have fallen
before, good harvest

Halo of Aureole
crown of fertility
she lets her hair down
in victory

Shadow of the hourglass
across my lap
love is the season
whose swell I have tapped

I can remember your leaves
flowing in the stream
the kiss of winter
whispering

Aureole,
an unfamiliar name for sunrise
for a smile
or a prayer.

*M. A. Pagan*

## A Baby Born

A baby born. A baby scorn.
Ain't the color it ought to be.
People look down at its face,
in disgrace.
Ain't the race it ought to be.
The child looks up and smiles.
The Lord looks down and grins.
Heaven wins.

*Steve (SWAGS) Wagner*

## A Growing Boy

A growing boy is such a wonder;
All arms and legs and feet.
At what he does he often blunders,
But after all he's really neat.

He stands for justice in a fight,
And if he's hurt, he will not cry.
"Gee, Mom, I fought with all my might.
You ought to see the other guy."

With small creatures he's soft-hearted.
He cannot stand to see them hurt.
If from a pet he must be parted,
He sheds hot tears into the dirt.

A growing boy is a marvelous thing;
All appetite and cracking voice.
With power to make a Mom's heart sing;
And all who watch him grow, rejoice.

*Vivienne Rae*

## Two

One perfect dream rested between two,
lovers remaining silent.
    Never to touch, never to move,
But ever in complete peace.
    Through time they stay this way.
Dreams never fading,
    love never swaying.
An eternity together they will spend,
    always at peace, but never as one.

*Shauna Lauderdale*

## Camelback

As evening sunsets fall,
All Heaven changes hues,
Looms a colossal mountain
Humped and black and tall.
Here, a palm tree's silhouette
Against a flaming tide,
there, pinpoints of light are set
Against dark mountainside.
Now rock and sky are truly one,
And with night's fullness done,
the Camelback will yet reflect
the rose-pink morning sun.

*Letitia Bellows-Temarantz*

## A Poem

A poem enables me to impart
all I feel within my heart.
It interprets what my mind perceives,
all of which my heart believes.
With who's aid I may express,
what I usually tend to suppress.
Be it the fruit of grandiose schemes
or the content of elusive dreams.
A poem is a form of literary food,
nourishing an ever changing mood.
It urges dormant thought to motion,
inviting release of ambivalent emotion.
It motivates my heart and soul,
inducing philosophic thought to flow.
Call it prose, poetry, even verse,
its a means I use to converse.
Poems bestow my psyche eternal youth,
providing faith, hope, love and truth.
Projecting what my heart is seeing,
a poem explicates my inner being.

*William H. Nelson*

## The Rainbow

The rain came pouring down
all morning long.
The sky looked dark, the wind
howled softly.
Suddenly in the afternoon the
rainbow boldly appeared.
It quickly chased away the
strong rain clouds.
It displayed a bright pretty
ring of colors.
In it you could see a beautiful
message from God for us.
To this day the rainbow is a
welcome sight.

*Mary Ann Singleton*

## The Gas Shower

I am alone
In a crowded hall,
Filled with people.

They shut the door,
And turn off the lights.
We scream.

By now we know.
It is not a shower.
It is death.

*Audrey Clark*

## Dreams Of You

As I sit in my downy bed dreaming,
All my dreams are of you.
The dreams all spent on yesterday
Come easily into view.

I could have walked with you forever
On the warm, white, salty sand,
Our shoulders gently touching,
Walking hand in hand.

The sunset, a golden splendor
And you were by my side
Tender embraces in silver moonlight..
..Ah, but it's all been in my mind.

I've spent my lifetime dreaming
Of a love that never came true,
I can't go back to yesterday,
I can't go back to you.

*Suan Angelo*

## Uncle Sidnee

Uncle Sidnee is my friend,
all my troubles he doth end,
love to see him every day
at my work and in my play.

Lovely rainbows shimmer near
playful raindrops I can hear
sizzling fireworks overhead
coloured blue and green and red.

Like a rocket I ascend
soar around a hideous bend
drifting through the spangled night
swallowed up in sheer delight.

All too soon there comes the end
back to earth I do descend
landing lightly on my feet
seeing diamonds in the street.

*Suzanne Towber*

## Iron Soul

To the west I left my splendor,
All to whom I could remember.
Encased in time
relinquished prime,
I have gone on my sojourn.

To the desert I came and slept,
The spotlight of the moon I kept.
Taking ground
All I found,
I have gone on my sojourn.

To the center I found the pole,
I fell the depth of iron soul.
Into the flame
I will remain.
I have gone on my sojourn.

*Leslie J. Apodaca*

## Love

Love is sweet and special
A thing to be showed not said.
As people deny the meaning of love
the flame between them is dead
As they rekindle their flame
It slowly dies and they
know their love has been denied.

*VeraLynn Sober*

## Alone

Alone I sit,
Alone I think,
My face not lit,
My eyes can't blink.
Feel not full.
Feel no greed.
Feel not cruel.
Just sit and bleed.
Lies I said lie alone.
Lie there like a broken phone.
Lies you said can't teach me.
Close my eyes just won't agree.
Down in shame,
All alone,
Fly away,
Don't know who from.
Will you hear me crying loud?
Will you find me in the crowd?
Are you strong to help me heal?
Be alone, just not for real.

*Maria Fourman-Lyakhovich*

## Motion Making

Moving on ahead
  Always half as far to go:
    My infinities.

Walking the right road
  So much better than running
    Rushing the wrong road.

This road we both see
  Makes itself a road for me
    If I will walk it.

Now a loss of speed
  And senses signal dropping:
    Something in my head.

Who, how?  Inertia:
  So great a problem poses.
    Unlikely Moses!

Less dense than tested
  Now I'm dancing buoyant
    Cork that couldn't sink.

*Paul M. McKowen*

## Creation!  Word Also Knowledge

With: heart, flesh and soul is
always life, life is never to
to hard live, the way we
live and life that's we lives.

My skin cleaver to my bones, that's
never tear.  Neither these or
those bones of mine are old
are broken.  Life is never full
of pain, angry, fear of shame,
Those words will never be in vain.

Days, night, darkness and light also
years that will never be
search out.  Life is never sadness
badness or nightmare when the
world turns as star as ruble
life, will never fear of death
that will never occur.

*William T. Yates*

## Empty, Crowded Room

Sitting here alone inside
an empty, crowded room
is it empty 'cause my soul is empty
and I'm doomed?

Empty while its crowded
is it crowded with my friends?
Or is it just a crowding of my thoughts
which make no sense?

Or is it empty desolate
with no one left around
and crowded 'cause I'm searching
for my life that's still unfound?

Which ever way I look at it
I'll reach an answer soon
The darkness enveloping me's
An empty, crowded room.

*Michelle Theis*

## Music In The Attic

To strum
an old guitar is fun;
to make the strings with life resound,
melody found;
the song sung out with force,
it will, of course,
bless those who hear;
they will in turn appear-
to join and sing
around the old forgotten thing.
An old guitar is fun
to strum.

*Mark D. Zubyk*

## Seasons of Love

When tender leaves are budding green
And all is new
Remember me.
I'll think of you with heavy heart,
Emotion yet unseen.
And come the summer's starry night
When roses bloom
And life is sweet in nature's womb,
I'll wish for you
Till darkness fades to light.
And when the green has turned to gold,
The leaves will fall
As tinted tears.
My soul will call across the miles
its secret love untold,
For when the earth is cold and bare
And all is white
With winter snow,
The fire's light will blaze in eyes
That whisper still "I care."

*Pamela Jeffries*

## Untitled

Deeper, dig deeper
Dear
And float lightly
On my red running river
Red, rambling love
So much red
So much for you

*Steve Dininno*

## Devotion

As Moslem turns to Mecca
And bows himself to pray,
My thought turns towards you certain
As filters forth the day.

Engaged in looming trifles
Distracting sad or droll,
Unmoved for all man's, moving,
The day rounds to a whole.

Deceit and vacant purpose
Dissolve along with light,
As moslem turns to Mecca
And a heart to you at night.

*Muriel Alexander*

## Haunted

A shadow lurks
and creeps,
Commemorating a past
I never lived,
Bliss
I never knew,
Laughter in which
I never joined.

Far worse than any
Memory of my own
It sears
With nostalgic flame,
It stabs
With every gaze
From its saddened eyes of
Forgotten times.

I, who never lived them,
Cannot forget them.

*Naomi Deardorff*

## Paintings

Today is for our generation
And generations that may come.
For we can tell what will be
Our futures' main outcome.

For we are all like artists
Who are drawing as we live.
And just how beautiful our paintings are
Depends on what we give.

For in these paintings we need
To use all of our skills.
By praying, studying, learning.
And doing the Lord's will.

For we need to grasp new opportunities
And start learning from our past.
For the painting that we leave
Forever will last and last.

*Monique Dupree*

## Windsail

Windsailers,
Sailing over the light-blue water.
Fluorescent colors,
Pink, orange, yellow, blue.
Leaving white wakes
Behind them.

*Matti Baldassari*

## Friends

He sat on the stone step
And hugged his friend's neck.
Head to chest together they
    embrace,
Two old friends with wrinkled
    face.
His words touch the dog's ear,
Gentle, hushed and soothingly
    clear.
While his toil-worn hand strokes
    the strong, stout head,
Cradled, at rest, the dog's eyes
    speak peace to the words
he's said.

*Phyllis J. Matthews*

## "She's The Angel In My Heart"

She was sweet as an angel,
and I loved her so,
We went and got married,
A long time ago,
With four little children,
Our love gave us then.
They grew up and got married,
And had little ones of ten,
We promised together,
That we'd never part,
Now she sings with the angels,
She's the angel in my heart.

*Thomas R. Collins Jr.*

## Untitled

You are standing by the window
And I only have ten fingers
So I trace your many profiles
Yet I hold this burning water.
Hide my face within the curtain
And I think I'll wait forever
With my back to your reflection
Till you move within the glass and
It is morning, it is morning
And the door is open; Leaving
Is a sweet and yellow flower
But I think I'll wait forever.

*Maria Lokshin*

## Indian Giver

I opened my heart to you
and I thought that you did the same
you came to me with open arms
I said I loved you and you said ditto
though I thought you meant it
Now you're gone you took your
love from me
you're an Indian Giver can't you see
my heart cries out for you
I still love you
but I know that I'll never
be the same
I'm not that kind of person
who plays with love
because love is no game
your name is the game
Indian Giver!

*Tonya Burge*

## Haunting Memory

I have a dream that haunts me
and it never goes away.
It's an unhappy, terrible memory
that invades my life each day.

For years and years I've had this dream
play over and over again.
The outcome never changing
and strife my only friend.

If only I could go back in time
to this day I must relive.
I would change the final outcome
and there'd be nothing to forgive.

One day I got a calling
from my Savior and my friend
He said, "Come unto me my child
and your nightmare I will end."

Forgiveness by Him I was given,
my nightmares put on a shelf.
Sometimes it sneaks back now and then
because I just can't forgive myself.

*Margaret M. Dunn*

## Go To God

When life seems so unfair
And it's really got you down
Go to God
He'll make you smile, not frown.

When you're struggling with a problem
And don't know what to do
Go to God
He'll help you work it through.

When you feel you're all alone
And no one seems to care
Go to God
He is always there.

When Satan tries to come within
And ruin a perfect day
Go to God
He will make him go away.

When you know Heaven's right for you
And Satan's hell is wrong
Go to God
That's where you belong.

*Sherry Tharp*

## Untitled

Did you ever love someone
And knew she didn't love you?
Did you ever start to cry
And wonder what good it would do?
Did you ever look in someone's eyes
And say a little prayer?
Did you ever look in someone's arms
And wish that you were there?
Don't fall in love my friend
You'll see it doesn't pay.
Although they say I love you
They'll hurt you bad someday.
And when I say don't fall in love
They'll hurt you before you're through.
Believe me baby I ought to know
I feel in love with you.

*Lisa Loiacono*

## Lunchroom Contemplations

We sit among the laughter
    and let our ears
Burn
    at the sound.

We know your gossip
    is meant to cause
Pain;
    yet, we rejoice in the knowledge
that it goes on without us...
    Still, without us, it wouldn't be.

*Sebrina Mason*

## Fathers' Day

Son we really miss you
And long to have you near
Only in our dreams
Someone so dear
The meaning of the day
Just for a hug from you
Longing as we must
All the day thru
I know we'll meet again
Its in the future plan
But how do I get thru
I guess with footprints in the sand

*Shirley Frederick*

## Irregular Scars

Moss gathers upon the stone
and mankind aims for the stars

I continue to write alone
exposing irregular scars

You won't find them searching
you will be as blind

For they are as invisible
scars upon the mind

Confusion fights to lay them bare
with aging skin and graying hair

But only conversation
and the scribbling of the pen

Can cause these scars to surface
and laid bare, slowly mend

I'll leave the moss upon the stone
laugh at man and the stars

I'll continue to write alone
exposing irregular scars

*Luella Revis*

## Whisperings

Whisper my name in dawn's half light,
and my love will waft through the air
like a wind-blown kite.

Whisper my name in the noon day sun,
and fast to your side I shall run.

Whisper my name in darkest gloom,
and my presence will fill the room.

Whisper my name in your heart,
and I'll be there
for nothing can keep us apart.

*Rudy Soriano*

## Father In Law

This man has planted from a seed
    And nurtured 'til it's grown

Into a strong and thriving tree
    A family all his own

Each branch was formed with loving care
    As it began to yield

The fruit that makes a life so whole
    A treasured, happy child

Who's then since turned
    From once a boy, into a caring man

Continuing to bear the fruit
    Which was his fathers plan

It takes a dad to show his son
    The ways of old you see

So he can pass the fruit of life
    On down the family tree.

*Muriel V. Stephens Hufman*

## Hands

One was rough with years of work
And one was soft as the petals
    of a newly opened rose.
Each yearned toward the other.
One sought strength and comfort
While the other carefully touched
    the rose petals
Sighing deeply.

*Leah Armstead*

## Suppose

Suppose the world were blind
And only you could see
Would it matter how you looked
Would you do things differently

Would that nice new car be half as great
Or that lovely dress so splendid
If only you could see it
And that was where it ended

What would we do with all our time
No more posturing and posing
There'd be no need for any of that
Of course..I'm just supposing

*Linda G. Mannix*

## Alone

Awakened by his threats
and profanity
He in his drunken stupor
sits before her like her judge
Torturous to her soul
In silence she cries
Emotionally she dies
Once thought to be her gentle lover
Like her knight is shining armor
In her dreams she'd run to him
Now in reality she runs from him
Silence fills the room
for now he sleeps
So once again
He leaves her to herself
Alone
In silence she cries.

*Mary Eustace*

## Love

On baby feet, love tiptoed in
And ran around my chair,
It teased and giggled playfully,
Then settled everywhere.

It came from every corner
And grew taller every day,
And when I tried to hide from it,
Love found me, anyway.

A world of hope, love brought to me
With gentle touch and smile.
And 'though my heart grows older
Love remains a little child.

*Virginia S. Chartrand*

## Lost Life

The soul her smirked
and ravaged by winds of time,
hath given wrath to crime
crime for lack of love.
This man's lock of bless.
The dew upon the meadow fell
While on earth
This man looked for hell.

The path for evil
And easy prey does not lay
Tormented he tine loved ones,
and who seek upon his stall.
Pacification he has none
medals of buffanery
he has won.
Time runneth out
worried be he
Worried be he
who dares to be
Man's mockery!

*Mary L. Swenson*

## Passage Of Time

Another day till sunshine, clouds,
and rusty smelled rain.
Another day to discover yourself,
and maybe someone else.

Another week till vacation,
one well deserved.
Another week of tedious work,
somewhere a paycheck lurks.

Another month till the seasons change,
mother nature's paradise.
Another month of political games,
displaying your degrees in frames.

Another year till we decide,
what to do tomorrow.
Another year of best wishes,
dreams, debts, and dishes.

The passage of time, passing
quickly...as I turn gray.

*Michael T. Hardesty*

## Home

Help me find my way back home,
And see my Mama there.
To feel her love and kindness,
To know she will always care.

To listen again to her teachings,
To hear her prayers for me.
I want to hear her singing,
The old home place to see.

I want to go out to the garden,
To hear the blue birds sing,
to feel the cooling breezes,
And to hear the church bells ring.

I'm lonesome for the old things,
I want to go back home,
I want to see the sunset,
And never more to roam.

*Orene Walters Ballard*

## Senses

As I sit before the fire,
And see the glowing blaze.
My mind begins to wander,
As though I'm in a daze.

As I sit before the fire,
And hear the crackling noise.
My mind recalls the memories,
Of sadness and joys.

As I sit before the fire,
And smell the fragrant scent.
My mind brings back each moment,
Of happy days well spent.

As I sit before the fire,
I can almost taste the flame,
My mind stands still a moment,
But it will not dwell on shame.

As I sit before the fire,
And feel the warming heat.
My mind begins to dream,
Of goals I've yet to meet.

*Roy E. Orr*

## Beach

Water splashes against the rocks
And shells wash up to the beach.
The sun sinks down into the sea
And daylight is seen no more.

Sea gulls caw into the sky,
Swooping down to the water.
Shells sit calmly on the shore.
Pink and white on the grainy beach.

The sand is brown, tanned from the sun.
Everything settles into it's place,
Just as perfect as before.
And they wait and wait and wait
For the sun to come up again.

*Megan Springer*

## Daddy

Daddy - when you comin' home? he cried.
And tears rolled down his face.
We're having cookies with our tea
and I'm saving you a place.

Daddy - when you comin' home? he cried.
Please tell me where you've been.
My teddy's getting very tired
and you have to tuck us in.

Mommie says you're visiting
in God's home we call Heaven.
But will you be comin' home again
for my birthday, when I'm seven?

Daddy - can I come with you? he cried.
Or should I stay and be a little man?
And take care of Mommie and Teddy;
I guess you'll come home when you can.

*Louise Platt*

## Life's Riches

As twilight's peeking ore the hill,
And the distant call of the whippoorwill
Mingles with the lovely sound

Of crickets chirping on the ground,
I sit and lean back in my chair
With fireflies blinking everywhere
And wonder who that man could be
Who said I'm Poor. Poor? Who, me?

*Thelma P. Williams*

## I'll Be There

When the wind won't blow,
and the moon turns to dust,
I'll be there

When the sky cracks,
and the sun won't rise,
I'll be there

When the stars fall from the heavens,
and the seas go dry,
I'll be there

I'll be there for you
through all the tragedy
that the earth may bare
for I am your love caught in despair.

*William E. Walker II*

## Wanted

I'm a full-blooded fugitive
And the streets are mine.
Why do I run?
Just for the glory,
Just for the fun,
Just for the thought,
Of being the one.
I'm a full-blooded fugitive
And behind trees I hide.
Why do I hide?
Just for the glory,
Just for the fun,
Just for the thought,
Of being the one.

*Mesha Polk*

## Modern Slavery

I will remember these days
And the words that I say
Although they're been spoken
With a heart that was broken
From a place the call jail
Trying to make our love fail
Those words are still true
When they speak about you
For someday soon I'll be out
And my heart will proudly shout
I want your love to belong tome
That's when I know I'm truly free

*Tim Carver*

## Cooperation

Two good people working great together
And they are a chain, united as one
Making the difficult work much better
And maybe making it even more fun

Beholding a lot of trust and belief
Each person reducing the job by half
May make doing the tough task a relief
And there may even be room for a laugh

Belief in each other is a great plan
And it may be worth giving a good try
It works for a woman and even a man
It will maybe bring relief by a sigh

Cooperation is the perfect tool
To make any job or any task cool

*Richard Ficarrotta*

## Reality Bites

Everybody thinks life is a game
and they kill others just for fame.

They do it for fun or on a dare
but what they don't know is life
doesn't care.

Killing all around us
people sick and dying
open up your eyes and
see the people crying

Can't we stop ourselves.
Must we ruin a world of
love and laughter for a
lifetime of hate and
destruction here after.
Gangs, riots, and war's galore
please tell me what are we fighting for?

*Natalie Mayle*

## Upon The Death Of My Sister

We talked of life, me and my Sis,
And we talked of death some, too,
The meaning of all That and This,
Who will go first, me or you,

We didn't talk enough, it seems,
It suddenly was her turn,
And now I tell my hopes and dreams
To my mantle and a Sky Blue Urn.

*B. J. Hale*

## Voice of the Flag

My heart is weak
And tonight I can sleep.
The wind is at rest
For the best of the best
Those promises I made I did keep.

I fly low in the rain
And I never complain.
The price I have paid
For my colours to fade
And the peace in the night is the same.

They mended my wholes
And patched up my soul.
That day at the fort
When they needed support
My stars flew far with my stripes.

The blood they shed was true
For my torn red, white, and blue.
I fly high in the morn'
Days after the war
I hope the soldiers can hear my voice too.

*Patrick C. Alexander*

## "Mother"

Mother, means love
and understanding -
  She's someone who loves
you no matter what you
have done.
  She's that one person you
can always turn to when you
feel alone.
  You can talk to her
because she understands and
loves you just the way you
are -
  To her you never have
to prove a thing.
  "Just be yourself."
  This makes her the
beautiful and unique Lady
she is.
  "I love you Mom."

*Virginia Raymond*

## The Lonely Way Out

Everyday's a new world
and what will tomorrow bring?
Will it be sunshine and flowers...
or gray skies and rain?

Will it embrace me with
peace, tranquility and grace?
Or will I be caught up in
societies suicidal race?

Will I speak kindly to my neighbors...
or kick them down?
Will I work for God..
or let my soul drown?

Can I stay cheerful and strong?
Can I survive the struggle...the strife?
Or will I end it all
by ending my life?

*Phyllis Wallace*

## God's Ripened Fruit

An apple seed I planted
And with faith did watch it grow.
I knew some-day there'd be a tree
With apples fit to show.

I cared for it with water
But God did all the rest.
Now I'm eating apples
That are the very  best.

Sometimes I like to think of God
As a giant apple tree;
His love out-stretched like branches
And the apples you and me.

I'd pray, "please hang on tightly Lord
And do not let us fall,
For the apples ripened on your tree
Are the sweetest ones of all."

So let plant a seed of kindness,
And with faith just watch it grow,
For God's ripened fruit of happiness
Will never cease to show.

*Marion Hanson*

## Goodbye?

I rush down the river in my canoe,
And yell to my friend, "I can't see you!"
For he's fallen in,
In a horrible way
The rush of the river,
Made the boat sway.
He fell right in
Like a bird that can't fly.
And now I can't see him,
So is this,
Goodbye?

*Russell Sprunger*

## Peace, Please

Cold war or hot,
Are we in war or not?
The bombs and death are sure
And pain and grief some did endure.

Was the man berserk or insane?
What did he feel he would gain?
Satisfaction or warped type peace,
Or simply his hatred release?

Oh God help us to see,
Hatred callouses you and me;
But love causes peace and care
For our fellowman everywhere.

May we cease to destroy our own,
And seek to ever be know
As stable, intelligent beings,
Who care about other's well being.

There's much we can accomplish here,
If we all seek to help our peer;
We'll find that we are all of worth
To help make peace on earth.

*Shirley Knight*

## Hell's Shooting Gallery

Aura of booze,
around bones with little skin,
skin pricked, prick-on-prick,
by shared needles of death,
ugly ego-centric pain, vomiting out
on all around him,
uncontrollable bowels gushing
liquid scum from demons -
on the long, long days
between his almighty "fix",
sweaty smells fowl, from terror
of his dooming, damning wait,
the stench of decaying laundry
oozing from the crack under his door.

Lighting incense and prayer,
we tried to sooth the hell
of being witness to a beautiful soul
bottom out.

*Whitefire*

## Billy Hand

There is nothing in life quite so grand,
as being in love with Billy Hand.

His ability is unsurpassed in gentility,
a one and only to last.

What else could you say about him?
He is honesty without a whim.

A pleasure is his sweetness,
light-hearted from within.

His innocent face portrays
an angelic cherubim.

*Paula Bertolino*

## The Feeling Of Need

I can remember as far back
as childhood, having that feeling
of need...

A hunger inside that one must
seek to feed...

I begin to grow older and
the feeling has become much
BOLDER!

Now I sit here embracing the
blessed title of "Woman", experiencing
that deep feeling of need.
The feeling I experienced as
a little girl.

I find myself searching...
Yea, yes indeed a "Woman"
knows the feeling of NEED...

*Rachael Ross-Miller*

## God's Beauty

It's not the color of the eyes,
It's not the tone of the skin,
It's not the look of your face,
or the condition you're in.
But, it's the love in your heart,
the submittance of your soul,
and how much of your life you
let God control.

*Maria Hernandez*

## The Wall

I'm sitting here thinking of you,
As I am, I'm wondering what to do.

You have come over my wall
The one I thought I built so tall.

You have surrounded me with love,
Just like an angel sent from above.

You have loved me and hated me
All in the same day.

So hold on tight and let God show us the
way.

*Stephen Joseph Rubio*

## Dreaming

Last night I dreamt I had died,
as I had done years before;
with your lips touching my eyes,
then I lived for evermore!
It was a glare so strange,
a sentiment so rare,
that in the midst of night
I called your name,
even though I knew
you weren't there...

*Z. Roberto Sotomayor*

## My Life Has Just Begun

Fret ye not, for I am happy
As I sit here with my Lord,
No illness is upon me
As God promised in His word.

Joy could be no better
Than the joy which I now feel,
No words can describe it
Yet the joy is oh so real.

Don't look at me and think of death
For life has just begun,
And in God's time we will again
Unite and be as one.

*Sabra Lynn Kesner*

## Untitled

We die in pieces not at once,
As many fail to see,
A day's account is measured time
And filed in history.

The children rest in yellow peace,
Adults in routine red,
All bodies sag in cyclic waves
From weight of living dead.

Like night through quiet sleep,
The eras pass imperceptibly
And added life to life they sum
The ceaseless line of immortality.

*Walter E. Smith*

## Stand And Deliver

O my child do not weep,
depression is but a passing sweep.
Somewhere out there I will keep,
the dark ocean deeps
at your feet.

*Matthia M. Onwudinjo*

## Playmates

Perhaps he doesn't see me,
As quietly as I sit and stare.
At times he looks right past me,
As if I weren't even there.

Does he know what I'm thinking?
Do you think he wants to play?
Just as I get close enough to ask him —
He quickly swims away!

*Maggie Hunter*

## An Early Frost

The chill overwhelms me,
as the illuminating cold sets in.
Fleshly tones are drained,
but life is still within.
Branches become stiff and brittle,
which once were filled with life.
As the world still around me
seems to turn to ice.
As cold as it is outside
Colder it is within.
Longing for the touch of warmth,
but frigid winds set in.
Surrounding swirling around me
echoes of silence choke me,
as an early frost sets in.

*Mark Lamb*

## Heaven And The Heartland

I heard the angels sighing,
As they waited to receive,
The souls of the innocent,
Those children we now grieve.

I felt the heavens tremble,
As Earth began to wail.
What demons live amongst us?
However did we fail?

The skies began to open.
The rain began to fall.
As God's display of sorrow,
Touched us, one and all.

'Twas some of His creation
That held up Satan's sword,
To wreak havoc and destruction
In defiance of the Lord.

What reason for their actions?
Ever so hard to understand.
They will find no mercy,
In Heaven or the Heartland.

*Mary DeSilvestri*

## The Key

If we but touch with our eyes
As we pass through the shadows
That life flashes before us,
And see the reflections of our souls
then will our destiny be fulfilled.

If we should chance
To look beyond the shadows,
And reach beyond the reflections;
Then shall we surpass destiny,
And embrace eternity.

*Phyllis Ohanian*

## Guardian

She came into my life
at a time of anguish and despair,
as the moment of darkness
dominated the air.

The words she whispered into my ear
were as soft as silk
and as strong as steel,
destroying the illusion
of space and time
created by a finite mind.

Looking through the mirror of her soul
I became the spectator
of a promise untold.

The rhythm of her drum
spoke clearly to me
that my struggle with life
was my struggle to be.

*Sandra J. Washington*

## The Beauty Of A Rose

From its heart aroma flows,
at early dawn it clings
beneath a blanket of mystic dew.
Its petals seem to smile a smile.
The miracle of fragrance
is
The beauty of a rose.

And so my dear, your face,
a sweet reflection
constantly in sight;
morning ... noon, or in
the stillness of night.
Comfort—ing, ... warm—ing
joyous, loving—ly—;
My love with-in
in quiet manner grows
as
The miracle of fragrance
is
The beauty of a rose.

*Patsy Harvey Brady*

## Listen to the Sea

I dream of the sea,
at night.
It whispers to me
Kind and soothing words.

The sounds of the sea
and the smell of the salt,
fill my dreams with hopefulness.

How I stand by the shore and listen,
While I watch the tide roll
over the sand.

The wet sand seeping through my toes,
and the cool breeze blowing
in my hair.

The sea holds many treasures
and its stores are untold.
I know them because the sea
whispers to me.

*Melissa Brackett*

## Lanterns Glow

Choice will tell where lanterns glow.
At night the still voice knows.
Light directs and feeds the soul,
And kindles living spirits whole.
Only the still voice knows.
Step in to see the lanterns glow.
At night by darkness fierce winds blow.
Be sure to know that light will fade.
By choice, deep waters, we then wade.
Only the still voice knows,
the way in which the lanterns glow.

*Monica Woods*

## Cold Sight

On an island so old
Away from the frost and the cold
The feelings were fast
With songs of the past
A night of delight
The mornings pure sight
Her shimmering skin
Caressing sheets so thin
Her flowing hair
Crimson lips so bare
Spheres of cold steel
Her eyes did reveal
That smile so wide
Not a thing did she hide

*Steven Juhasz*

## Alone

All alone I sit here thinking
back to the good old days.
We were together forever,
having the times of our lives.
Then one day when you come to me
your face looked so sad.
Then you told me you were leaving,
you didn't want to but had to.
I wanted to die that day
but I've learned to live alone.

*Melissa Breedlove*

## Cookies And Jelly Beans

I howl at the cookie jar,
Bark at the cake,
Whine at the candy dish
My what a fake.

I love to eat-that's
my favorite wish.
Be it cookies or jelly beans
or even old stale fish.

I'm a big fat Bassett Hound.
Always with my nose to the ground.
Anything that's work is not for me.

I'm a dog of luxury
And a sight to see.

*Virginia C. Thompson*

## A Loosing Battle

If you have ever heard the cries of
battle or have seen the innocent fall,
then you know that war is brutal and
will somehow affect us all.

Sending children to fight children they
strike blindly and in fear, Always
leaving someone, somewhere left
behind to shed a tear.

There is nothing worse than this man
made plague, killing millions before
there's a cure.  Nothing devastates or
takes more lives than this disease that
we call war.

Every soldier who has fought for their
country has the right to feel honor
and pride, But I don't think anyone
can afford to forget all the men and
women who have died.

*Lynn M. Wenke*

## Heaven

The sun rose on a dark side.
Beaming light like a sword,
Not stopping at the ground,
But travelling to a place of evil.
A place where sun wasn't a word,
Love never heard of,
And hate occupied every soul.
The evil took the beam of light,
Putting it into the souls of everyone.
This place is now called heaven.

*Michelle Mulvihill*

## Hands

Your hands
Beautiful hands
Soft yet strong
Tenderly caress
Surround and enfold
My heart
They are holding
My heart
Your hands
Gently massaging
Easing the pain
And healing the sadness
Of a broken child
Your hands
Are healing
My heart
You were sent to me
And I will accept you
As a gift
Of love.

*Teri Fury*

## Springtime

When spring has come,
And winter is done,
When the animals come out to play.
There is a blossom that just bloomed,
In everyone's room,
And that very flower is
    LOVE

*Whitney Cogswell*

## Beauty

In the prime, of her time
beauty feels fairer than the days
but beauty is not made of stone
Time invades, beauty fades
into wrinkles and into grays
for beauty too is flesh and bone

High and mighty, beauty is flighty
and feels no need to understand
why many strive to bask in her glory
Beauty ruses, beauty chooses
fate holds her with a kind hand
but it is not an everlasting story

Although today love falls from the sky
and you can afford to let it die
one day love will pass you by
and judge your deeds and your skin
as if there, beauty had never been
    ...and who will love you then?

*Manuel Rosa*

## My Friend

I'd like to describe my friend to you.
Because you see,
My friend is different in many ways,
From any other friend,
That any other friend, has ever had.

My friend would not question
What I say, or what I do,
Or if I lie or speak what's true,
Or if I'm moody and disagree,
Or if I'm as mean as I can be,
And I CAN BE,
My friend remains my friend to me.

And so you see,
My friend is very strange,
But too, you see,
My friend will never change.

That, is why I state with pride,
And utter happily,
My friend will always be,
MY DEAREST FRIEND to me........

*Leo J. Hatem*

## To My Child

I want to see you one more time.
Before I leave for home.
I want to tell you that I care.
I have since you were born.

I want to see your face once more.
And hold your hand in mine.
Just softly, gently say to you.
I've loved you all the time.

I'll be leaving very soon,
And please don't cry for me.
I'm going home and this I know.
With Jesus I will be.

Don't wait too long before you come.
For I may not be here.
I want to see you one more time.
Before I go up there.

*Millie Honn*

## Lord, I Miss You

When I am awake I yearn for you.
Before I sleep I praise you.
When I sleep I dream of you.
You are my caretaker.
My reason for being
I see the bright shining glow
that surrounds you
Every time I think of you I feel the
peace of the universe in that light.
But you are just out of reach
I call to you...but you do not come
One day I will be with you
I am longing for that day
I heard your voice in the breeze
But do not know from which direction
it comes... and then you're gone
again.

*Susan Caleca*

## Soon Enough

I didn't hold her hand enough
before she went away
I didn't keep her close enough
each and every day
I didn't hear her merry laugh
enough when she was near
I didn't know the time we had
was brief and very dear
I couldn't feel the pain she knew
though mine was very real
I hadn't comprehended how
this soul of mine could feel
I couldn't see the strength He'd give
when she went home to God
Now I'm sure she needn't suffer
or struggle on this sod
I'm certain I'll be with her
in a better time and place
The day will come, soon enough,
when I'll see her precious face

*Linda J. Savary*

## Goodbyes

Like a child she lay asleep
Beneath the coverlet and counterpane.
I longed to hold her in my arms
And kiss her 'til she woke again.
But sleeping beauty she was not
A kiss could not restore the glow
That only hours past had known
Tomorrow was the time to go.
When welcome comes to bitter end
And winter love has lost the sun,
The pathways find a way to bend
Away from where they had begun.
I say good bye to you my sweet
I leave you breathing soft with sleep.
We count our destinies complete
I have a rendezvous to keep.

*Van D. Olmstead Jr.*

## The Otters' Tale

The charlatans have seen their soul
beneath the forte's ungodly hole
in bristle beds of frowns and folly
fixed in wax and clay

Beneath the sounds of the otter's den
the sojourner marks the nail
misfortune hammers unto fate
a most unwelcomed tale
the cries of fortnight, late
await, to understand the faction
go bring the pales of tears from those
who hide behind these gratings
empty them amidst the place
where effort finds its' losing

O otter, mine
do send them forth
from out of that their prison
In silence let them come

*Michelle Suzette Patènte*

## The Dreamer

The dreamer sits alone,
  beneath the shady trees,
the only one who has a dream
  is soon to have the keys.

He sits and dreams all day long
  awaiting the perfect time,
when all his dreams come true
  he will no longer have to climb.

While other people are wishing,
  on falling stars and clovers,
the dreamer has accomplished his dreams
  and the wishers will start all over.

So if you want something to happen,
  don't just sit and be a wisher,
wishing is for a fairy tale,
  but succeeding is for a dreamer.

*Victoria Potter*

## Why

Bosnia, Sarajevo, Sri Lanka too,
Black smoke fills the sky,
Children missing arms and legs,
Oh Lord, my savior, why?

Earthquake, floods and fire,
Cause much of life to die,
Families torn apart by death,
Oh Lord, my savior, why?

Robbery's, rape and child abuse,
The truthful, now they lie,
The honest have begun to cheat,
Oh Lord, my savior, why?

Drive by shooting take there toll,
As mothers stand and cry,
Respect for life has disappeared
Oh Lord, my savior, why?

The world must unite in prayer,
For Gods return on high,
Then we'll have the answer
Oh Lord, my savior, why?

*Monty Skelton*

## Power Lines

Rows of crosses line
both sides of the boulevard,
so common, they're
essentially invisible, yet
  so important.
The silent T's telegraph
the transfer of energy
and information down
the street and to the rest
  of the world.
Like a spider web, black
cables remain suspended
and bow from pole to pole,
so the pattern repeats from
  street to street.

*Elias Tobias*

## Worship

Bended knee higher then flight
Bowed head raised to Thee
Silent sounds with loudest meanings
Bodies become souls
reaching immortality

*Regina Meatris*

## Waiting

Waiting is a white-filled room
Breathing curtains of intense lace
Squeaky clean tiles and tubs
And the urge that flashes
  white
  from love lost longing
Waiting is dark worn dirt
Hungry for seed
Going unplanted
Growing only need
Waiting is hopefully pink skies
Flamingos eating cotton candy
Sickness as it lies
  on early morning streets
Waiting is an endless blue
  glass of water
  force-fed
'Til waiting cries dead.

*D. Medb Duffey*

## The Sea

Swirling
Bubbling
A gray cauldron

Seething
Writhing
A foaming hysteria

Choking
Gasping
A strangling grasp

Holding me under
Pulling...
Life...
Away

*Nickie Barnes*

313

## For You My Love

For this one rose I have given you,
but a bed of them I cannot. For nor,
am I rich nor poor, I've just made
use of what life has offered me.
For the greatest gift I can offer, is
my love for you.

For there never is a man to set
foot on this earth that doesn't need
love. Love is the joy of all seasons.
For nor not the mind, nor the
body matters, but the love that is
within inside.

For with you is where my love belongs.
For you, my dear, is my love's home.
For when I'm gone, to you, it must
be known, that until I met you the
word love was not known, I am
forever yours.

*Lori Miller*

## Who's Out There?

I know someone's out there,
but are you friend or foe?

I'm the kind of person
that really has to know.

Are you from this Universe
or another?

Do you have a father
or a mother?

Some say you have a
small grey body and enormous head.

Or are you lizard like instead?

I hope my questions will
be answered soon.

Then all the skeptics
will change their tune.

*Rose Bidmead*

## Secret Admirer

He does not know my name,
But he knows that I am there.
In his mind's eye he sees,
A most passionate flare.

As a token of my love,
A single rose have I sent.
I think of him always,
My love can never be spent.

The depth of my feelings,
He will never understand.
Or know that I've dreamed,
Of our lives together planned.

He speaks to me sometimes,
And I treasure every word.
His deep voice to others unnerving,
Is the divinest music I've heard.

Soon he will be leaving me,
And never again will his love I feel.
His absence I know,
Will pierce my heart like steel.

*Sylvia Streeter*

## I Want To Say "I Love You"

I want to say I love you
But I'm so afraid you'll laugh
And if you laughed when I told you
It would break my heart in half

I want to do more things with you
Because I love you so
And if I asked you to do these things
I'd die if you said "NO"

I want you to love me
As much as I love you
And if you said you hated me
I don't know what to do

My love for you is like a stream
That runs forever true
And my stream of love
Will never dry
As long as I have you

*Melissa Coover*

## I Love You

I want to say I love you
but I'm so afraid you'll laugh
and if you laughed when I told you
it would break my heart in half.

I want to do more things with you
because I love you so
and when I ask you to do these things
I'd die if you said no.

I want you to love me
the way that I love you
and if you said you hated me
I don't know what I'd do.

My love for you is like a stream
that runs forever true
and my stream of love will never die
as long as I have you.

*Tanya FuQua*

## The Changing Poem

I walk my dog because it feels great,
But it is better to eat some cake.
I love it when I score a goal,
and dip in a nice cool pool.

When my dog learns a trick,
She often give me great big lick.
Running and playing is so such fun,
especially when you're with someone.

We like to play lots of games,
And sometimes we fly R/C planes,
When the plane is out of gas,
I am afraid it will crash.

So I must go to Shell,
Bringing gas, before the bell
When I have all I need,
I go out and do good deed.

*Michael Flanigan*

## Untitled

Reckon not with my age
  but take heed of my mentality
Merit my intelligence for what it is
  not for what you believe it to be
Understand my struggle
  and identify my pain
Toy not my emotions by your fears
  but understand my tears
Guess not at my hearts strength
  but learn the power of my soul
Now watch my inner spirit emerge
  Recognize it
    Caress it
      Never underestimate it
        Remember it is I
          And I am WOMAN

*Monique Yvette McCrae*

## Jasper

We have a funny looking puppy,
But we love him just the same.
He's beagle, basset, lab and dauchsy.
Jasper is his name.

His paws are short and tubby
Hiss body like a log
And who'd have thoughts we'd ever need
Orthodontia for a dog!

He chews holes in al the laundry
As he dashes through the house,
Eats quarters, shoes and garbage,
Oh, Please not my new blouse!

At times his traits seem human
He reminds me of a child.
He's trusting, loving, willful
And often he runs wild.

The house became to quiet
With Jasper ill one day,
And I realized that I'd miss him
If he ever went away.

*Louann Peery*

## Just A Friend Of Mine

He takes me out every evening
Buys me the rarest wine
We seem so happy together
But he's just a friend of mine

He takes me to the finest places
We have a wonderful time
I know it looks like the real thing
But he's just a friend of mine

I know what people say
When they see us together each day
But we are trying to hide
A lost love that burns deep inside

His girl left him for another
The man I thought was mine
Now we're pretending together
And he's just a friend of mine

*Lelar Marie Teasley*

## Yes Lord, We Will

Two years ago my heart was touched,
By God, that just in case,
He had a child, not born of me,
Whose spirit our lives would grace.

What nature could no longer give,
Another child for us to love,
God knew that it was in His plan,
For Him to come down from above.

We did what we could, from this Earth,
Prepared ourselves, kept up the pace,
Then finally certified to adopt,
We waited - just in case.

Two months ago, the Lord called out,
"Will you raise this child of mine?"
So we three said, "Yes Lord, we will,"
We could not decline.

Now you're here, forever ours,
And life is not the same,
We welcome you into our hearts,
And give to you our name.

*Shelli Marie Valles*

## Life

A young boy sat
By the railroad track
Waiting for the train
In the pouring rain.

Down the track
Came the train
Pass the young man
Who looked in wonder
As it passed like thunder.
Around the bend
And out of sight
The train did run
In the raining night
Past the man
Who sat and wondered.

The old man rose
From beside the track
To walk away
And never look back.

*Marcella Hinkel*

## Broken Wings, Broken Dreams

Little birds with broken wings
Can only fly so high;
Aimlessly they flutter about;
Desperately they try.

Hindered by our broken dreams,
Our goals seem far away;
We falter through the struggle,
Our efforts seem in vain.

Like broken wings, our broken dreams
Cause us to miss our mark;
But time will heal the brokenness
And also fade the scars.

With mended wings and mended dreams,
New heights and goals to attain;
We soar above the pain we've known,
Our faith renewed again.

*Mildred H. St. Clair*

## The Flight

Rain pelted against the window,
Car lights shone through the night,
The life in her eyes was fading,
And her soul was about to take flight,
Thunder filled the silence,
And lightning split the sky,
And we all sat there waiting,
Watching for her to die.

Her life was never easy,
She fought oft, to be understood,
I wonder if she would, live differently,
If she, only could,
The storm was getting closer,
It was coming to a head,
And as the lights, flickered,
We realized with some dread,
The woman we had known so well,
Had loved for all our lives,
Slowly took her final breath,
And quietly closed her eyes.

*Maralyn C. Diggin*

## The Clown

The clown has always held a
Certain fascination for me.
Once, in my lifetime, a clown,
I'd like to be.

There must be a special someone
Behind the mask,
Bringing laughter to others,
Whatever the task.

His troubles, he doesn't dwell upon,
Donning his make-up,
The show must go on!

*Rebecca Deason*

## Mom

Beg mercy
Child's sins
Giving gift
Love
Regard striking
Child's cry
Tears run
Child's sorrow
Pain inflicted
Upon loving parent
Mercy needed
Seen by child's eyes.

*Robert E. Albert II*

## Wouldn't You Agree

*Especially for William Asher
My Friend!*
Wouldn't you agree
that
creativity
is
undoubtedly
the key
indubitably
to one's identity?

*Cynthia Lynn Dalton*

## A Haunting Passion

To reveal my love with
clarity and without reservation.

To touch your belly with
my tongue as if lapping
the milk of your generosity
and purity.

Mundane rewards of life
blush with envy at the
power of connection between
my adoration and your loyalty.
But why is it secret?

With revelation comes
the helplessness of exposure
and a bond of eternal
commitment that frightens
the loins and yet promises truth.

*Marshall S. Cherkas*

## Sleepy Time

Hush little baby don't you cry
Close your eyes and I'll tell you why
Sandman's coming from the sky
It's sleepy time, right now.

Hush little baby and you will see
Why I give this love to you, from me
Close your eyes and dream you're free
It's sleepy time, right now.

Hush little baby and you will know
That with my love, you will grow
I'll be there wherever you go
It's sleepy time - good night.

*Steven R. Ballinger*

## Between Us

And thus mind did open
Colors strewn across blood red skies
Eastwardly drift cast shadows blue.
As the wind that once blew between us

Faint yet persistent breeze, cold
Exiled to this oblivion
Resting gentle sparrow gone
Silent reflections, frozen screams

Here, alone encompassing darkness
Light forbidden world imploding
Trees with heavy leaves dripping amber
Drowning breathless empty soul

Twisting and turning this torment
Can color survive this void
This world abandoned by love
Absent emotions deep they dwell

Enthralling somber night withdrew
Eyes closed, tuned from my existence
Sweeping veil, emerging hue
Gone is the breeze that we once knew

*Vincent M. Maguire*

## On Letting Go Of "Red"

Tears
Come and go
feelings
stay.
Quiet devotion
Constant turmoil
Second guessing
thoughts
happiness.  Smiles.
tears come
and go
feelings stay
and stay.

*Penny Pulver Browning*

## The Logic of Space

The day I saw the earth
come up all red
I was falling
falling, felling
through space.
No wander!  What's up
sidedown?
Too bad I didn't live
Yesterday I yell
Black.
Too bad
I had to be
a head of Earth
Turning back.

*Maisie Whiteside*

## Burst Of Life

Whispers from sweet soft sunny seas
    coming to me on a summers breeze

Blowing to me such wisdom free
    to make the earth so shine of thee

Beneath the clouds the down pour spout
    to make the earth a rainbow sprout

Of colors such to make the heart
    rejoice at what you've done so smart

To give us all some work to do
    and make the earth a place re-new.

*Larry G. Wilson*

## Mother

You nursed me
when I was young.
You fixed my hurts and
dried the tears from my eyes.
You picked me up
when I had fallen,
you lifted my spirits
when I had been let down.
You cried for me and
at times, cried at me.
You always tried to guide me
with your gentle touch.
Now I have grown and
cannot wait to see
what type of mother I will be...
Hopefully,
just like the mother
that raised me!

*Jennifer Mason*

## Graduation Wish

High school grad of ninety-five
congratulations and all that jive

'Tis a milestone to achieve
now you've earned a small reprieve

Then off to college you will go
to learn more things that you don't know

A fine young lady, fully grown
to reap rewards that you have sown

The wealth of life has no measure
may every day bring you pleasure

The future is yours to carve and mold
so don't be shy, be brave and bold

I wish you all the best of things
and all the joy that living brings

For in my book, you are the best
heads above all the rest

There's nothing more for me to say
but, happy graduation day!

*Sharon L. Terry*

## God's Precious Black Child

Categorized!
Criticized!
Genocide!
Jeopardized!
Minimized!
Mystified!
Ostracized!
Patronized!
Propagandized!

God's Precious Black Child!!

*Rosemary Dixon*

## Echoes

Echoes, Echoes in the night.
Crying winds and weeping willows,
lost hope and damp pillows.

Echoes, Echoes in the night.
Loss of joy, loss
of might.
Empty souls drifting
in the night.

Echoes of rain, echoes of pain.
Echoes of the last cry of humanity.
Man has lost most of his sanity.
Will you, may I, try
to find a reason not
to cry?

*Marcy Alexis Hemphill*

## Friends to Love

Happiness and a friend is all I asked for
But you have given me so much more
Love burned where kindles now remain
But we started a hole new flame
Hand to Hand
Heart to Heart
Our bodies are one never to part

*Tarasa Krol*

## 'Til Then

Raindrops soft on roof of tin,
Damp chill without love's warmth within,
Kerosene lamps soft shadows cast,
Happy mem'ries from the past.

Biscuits bake in iron stove black,
Kettles boil and fire woods crack,
Blackberry jam smells pure and sweet,
Scrubbed wood floors beneath bare feet.

Old wood rocker, Grandma's lap,
Safe and peaceful dreamy nap.
Rock of ages fills the air
Guardian angels everywhere.

Years long gone, but still returns
Visions dear as my heart yearns,
Small feet down a sand road race
To feel once more that dear embrace.

To look in Grandma's gold rimmed eyes
And hear her laugh in glad surprise.
That day will come, I know not when.
She lives within my heart 'til then

*Pauline Charles*

## Untitled

I was Dreaming.
Daydreaming of a canoe.
Of me and of you.

Paddled to the Island of Sin.
Wondered - did they see us
And the mood we were in.

Believed it was magic;
Caught up in your smile.
Believed you had faith
And would stay for awhile.

Maybe it was just the mood you were in.

*Stephanie McCurdy*

## Clearly Cut

High aloft pristine beauty
descended into human desecration
temple of creation no longer glorified
with mothers tender touch long ago
tossed out of the nest to make its
way in the world to prove its
worth to pay its way
O spirit of productivity
    must
        you
            cut
                so
                    deeply
into the tender skin of one so young
bearing witness of mankind
the sabers scar for all eternity
proof of its acceptance into
that which is labeled
commodity

*Wilma Ellis*

## To My Mother On Mother's Day

Grace and wisdom salute her,
Beauty stands in awe,
The kindest soul on earth
Could lend nothing to her....
*Mary Lisa Cantel*

## Dance Concert

Only for a Moment-
Did it stay in Bloom-
Glory in the Highest-
For Me- Filled the room-

The Fruits of my Labor-
Result of my Sweat-
My Life- entertainment-
My Right- due respect.

Slowly- it faded-
I clinging to its Life-
Shortlived- it withered-
My Reward for my Strife-

The remains of my work-
Which once filled me Whole-
Only my Heart remembers-
My body is left Cold.
*Meredith Messer*

## Lead

Growing up can become
difficult and tedious
We must follow our own lead
and be wise and vigorous.

To have a superior life
we must stand straight;
take a risk
before it is too late.

Be bold and valiant;
prove to them what we are made of
Do not hold back
and we will soar high above.

One day we will reminisce
to see what we have done
We should not be supercilious
through all the deserved fun.
*Shrayas Jatkar*

## Inferno

The metallic core tugging this-
Disease
Infest my thoughts.
Control-
An evil, elusive gem,
Sparkling heliotrope-
To garnish this sin
Edged in nights' lace
Deceive not my heart
Perverse deeds of control-
Purge me of your clean...soul?
If I could stop this wound,
If I could die!
If I would make you bleed,
I would stab!
If I should let you win,
I should forever lose.
*Michelle Repcik*

## Black Hand Poison

Confusion of emotion and
Distortion of perception
Shun my ability to be
First black is white and
The hand is heart
Then black is blackest and
Hand crushed heart until
Black becomes black again and
Hand becomes hand again

This ran circles in cycles but
Now the rage is regular,
Quite unspectacular, when
Confusion of emotion and
Distortion of perception
Leak into my jugular
And poison my ability to be
*Sara Sowers*

## Zing

Zing!
Dizzy dazzling sunlight,
Drizzled damp and limp.
Zonk, zonk, zonk,
Concrete concrete trucks,
Growing girth onto the earth.
Click, click, clunk-clock,
Crawling, clawing, claiming!
Conceive.
Foamy formula —
Reformulated.
Floating flotsam flung,
Zooming doom suspended,
Naughty naught.
Oozing ozone.
Whether? Whither?
Zeal my soul,
Zelous zelibacy.
So, zaxophone and zither,
Zing, yon yin will yang!
*Ray Suzan Strauz*

## Am I My Brother's Keeper?

Am I my brother's keeper?
Do I help in times of need?
Am I my brother's keeper?
Do I help him sow the seed?
Am I my brother's keeper?
Do I help him to be strong?
Am I my brother's keeper?
Do I chide him when he's wrong?

Do I lift the weary sister
When she falters on the way?
Or do I try to do for her
A kindly deed each day?

Am I the Master's servant?
Do I heed His every call?
Do I answer every muster
Thru' winter spring and fall?

There are but a few questions
To ask yourself today
If you're your brothers keeper
Don't let him go astray
*McDonald Alston Hull*

## Ongoing Fear

I look in the mirror and what
   Do I see
From head to toe the bruises
   On me

Living in fear from day
   To day
Not knowing if I want
   To stay

In a relationship of agony
   And pain
What in the world do I have
   To gain

My head bent down as I walk
   In shame
But yet I feel that I'm
   To blame

The bruises and cuts eventually
   Go away
But the fear I have inside will
   Forever stay
*Toni Lee Painter*

## Places Where Artists Work

Places where artists
do their work
where odors of paint
and solvents lurk
Where solder and acid
vapors mix

An antique clock face
some yellowing lace
a long handled brush
a rusted locke
and a marble block
unite to create
a fertile spot

A sort of mental birthing space

That's what makes the studio
my favorite place.
*Lois Richmond*

## Did You Know Christa?

Do you know her?
Do you know of laughter, joy, and peace?
Then in a way, you've known her.
This special child, my niece.

Do you know of starlight?
Of friends around a campfire's fun?
Then perhaps you saw her there.
Giggling childlike, she's the one.

Have you chanced upon a chipmunk
Scurrying through the wood?
Maybe he was returning
To a spot where she once stood.
As once she stood a tiny dot.
On life's map, a gentle spot.
Quietly confined was she.
Until an Angel set her free.

Now on great white feathered wings,
She shared the branch where the robin sings.
She laughs with the brook as it bubbles by.
And there's one more star in the Heavens High.
*Christa Schoeppner-Hebert*

317

## Time

What time is it?
Does anyone know?
The clock says three
But is it four?
Perhaps I am backward and
Two is the time.
One more change and
I'm out of my mind!
Central, standard,
Daylight savings.
Is anyone sure
What the time is saying?
Do we sleep while it's dark
And work while it's day
Or now is it turned
The other way?
Night is day and
Day is night.
I hope in time,
I'll get it right.

*Patricia Quinton*

## Pork And Beans

When you buy a can of pork and beans
Don't get your hopes to high.
You're sure to get a lot of beans
But you'll find the pork is shy.

When you open up your beans,
Whether the short can or the taller,
You night miss the pork among the beans
The pork is so much smaller.

They've cut the pork so very small,
In such little bits of fat and lean,
That one tiny pig could furnish pork
For a thousand cans of beans.

It floats alone, that little waif,
That's mostly fat and seldom lean,
A tiny, lonely, jewel of pork
Afloat on a sea of beans.

When you read the label on the can
It won't mean what it seems
Tho each can has its tiny pork
It's mostly full of beans.

*Tom Sheehy*

## Shotglass Bum

Oh Shotglass,
Don't leave me.
Don't leave me like my,
My dirty old wife!

Oh Shotglass,
You're all I have.
All my memories,
All of my life.

Oh shotglass,
Tell me...
Where are my children,
My dirty old wife?

Oh Shotglass,
Where do I wander?
From Dumpster, to Dumpster,
All my Life.

*Scott Thompson*

## Winter Scene

Mountains reaching for the sky,
Dressed in robes of white.
Loblolly pines so high,
With icicles, catching the light.

River reflecting the sun,
Drifting along, all gold,
Too frozen to really run,
Shivering in the cold.

Old log cabin, nestled in the trees;
Window panes shimmering with light.
Outside, all is deep freeze.
Land reaching out with fingers white.

Clouds gathering to storm.
Snow flakes, drifting, idly down.
Inside, all is cozy and warm.
No where, is there a sound.

*Valencia La Verne Jernigan Hall*

## Driven

Driven by this and driven by that
Driven by various standard formats
Driven by pain
Driven by gain
What is driving you today?

Driven by the lies
Driven by the cries
Driven by the gold
Or driven by the mold
What is driving you anyway?

Driven by your boss
Driven by your loss
Driven by a need
Driven by a lead
Such driving makes one lazy!

Driven by implications
Driven by explanations
Driven by common folk
Driven by different strokes
No wonder one acts so crazy!

*Sharon Noble Houdyshell*

## The Nerve of Some People

How dare you
Drop me a line..
Like some sinker
Docked out of nowhere.

A cannibal...
Still soaked
With pieces of flesh
Displaying brittle bones.

How dare you
Think of me...
As Mother, as Daughter
When I am neither...

Knowing...
That you
Only want me
As your whore.

How dare you
Speak to me
Of the past...
As if it never happened!

*Paula Schilling*

## Night And She

Escapade of night,
Drunkenness of morrow.
Sweaty sight,
Moon dropping low.
Behold her, moon!
Behold her, garden!
She is silk on your branches,
Milk upon my lips.
　Ah!
And I..die
The time of a sigh
On a pool of light
That flows from
Her sweaty forehead.

*Saad Lamouri*

## Songs

A song in my heart
Each day of my life.
A song in my heart, I pray.

A song on my lips
To cheer me along.
A song on my lips, each day.

The songs to sing
Are a gift from God
To lighten each step of my way.

A song to share
With others I meet
A song to share, so they

Will know 'twas the love
In the Savior's heart
That gave songs to brighten each day.

*Pearl Norman*

## Love

As the days go by,
Each moment you take a chance,
Hoping not to cry,
And make it through the dance.

The aspects of love
Take your heart and your soul.
But at the appearance of a dove,
you know you have paid your toll.

As you learn about love.
You may often be blue.
But when you deeply love,
You captured all that's good and true.

*Nicole Davidson*

## My Granddaughter

A smile so sweet, it makes you cry
eyes as blue as summer's sky.
Hair as Gold as Angel's wings
dimpled cheeks by God's own touch
How I love you oh so much!
You were sent to fill my life
to fill a void, to stop the strife
that I was feeling after death
took away your Grandpa's Breath.
May you grow in grace with God.
A special child, my special pride.

*B. J. Campbell*

## Change

Life it changes quickly,
Each time we blink our eyes,

From the time that we were born,
Until the time that we die,

When we were little children,
We wished to grow up fast.

But as the times goes by,
We wish that it would last.

I wish that I could tell people,
To live for life today,

And challenge tomorrow's thoughts,
With the thoughts of yesterday.

And love your friends for who they are,
Your family just the same,

Because whenever you have called them,
They're the ones who came.

Your life is what you make of it,
How hard you work each day.

So live life to the fullest,
In every little way.

*Laura Kraly*

## Childhood

Through the panes of glass
Echoes of laughter
ricochet around the walls
Time is lost
as circles complete
Glimpses of endless days
surface among the clouds
There is no standing still
no turning back
Reality is what is now
Forward the only motion
as the hours become days
become years.

*Michele Flood*

## Evolution

My first home was warmly wet.
Embryonic sofa.
I slipped out though,
when I had the chance.

I used to love to crawl
before I could walk to them.
I enjoyed walking
before I could runaway.
I spent days running
before I could drive.
But now I hate driving,
I long to fly.

I long to fly
back to them...

*Miguel Angel Delgadillo*

## Dream Stuff

This world is strange beauty
Emerald green sky
Veiled lavender Sun
Warming Meadows of
Yellow Marigolds

A faint scent of Jasmine
A teasing playful Breeze
Gently sway a tiny Hammock
Where I lay sheathed
In Moondrop's Dew

Summer Midnight Blue
Arachnean threads holding
Tiny, silvery Stars
Red Moon Illuminating
Wondrous Spider's Work

So flimsy, so fragile
Will I fall through?
Suddenly, I wake
Was I really
Never, ever There?

*Yvonne Merau-Ross*

## Picturesque Rain

Black ominous clouds
enshroud the earth
causing daylight to cease.

Across this black sky
a blinding flash scampers
illuminating all momentarily.

Sound of clashing thunder
shatters quiet calm;
silence rendered asunder.

Walls begin to shake
as if ready to fall
and all windows to break.

Water plummets to earth
with pounding driving force
filling river and valley.

Wetness readily welcomed
the dry thirsty ground
greedily absorbs to saturation.

*D. Rodger Long*

## Flight Of The Yet Alive Holy Ones

In the western sky
    envision golden translucent clouds
Swirling earthward
    encircling the saviour band,
As Jesus reaches down
    for the yet alive holy ones
And draws them upward
    on tender arms of love.
They pass through
    crimson clouds of glory,
Then enter golden gates
    of that happy home above.

*Ruby Farnham Skaggs*

## Whispering Pines

Flared nostrils on the horses
euphoric screaming wails...
into a night of terror
with lightning at their tails...

And over the torment
of the raging tide
the sound of the blistering wind...
repeats the violence of a night
where a man could lose a friend...

When I got to the land
of whispering pines...
I'll know that I'll have won
where midsummer evening
air is heard...
to the sound of the setting sun
midsummer evening
air is heard
to the sound of the setting sun...

*Lynn E. Davis*

## Beautiful Forest

Sparkling lake,
Evergreen trees,
Fresh Alpine air,
Warm Summer breeze.
Sweet wildflowers
By a gurgling brook,
Cascading down to a mirrorlike lake.
The bluebirds song so sweet,
Is echoed all around.
All around the hills and trees
And clover on the ground.
The smell of green meadows,
Still wet with morning dew,
Adds to the exquisite beauty,
Beneath the sky so blue!

*Raina Gough*

## Faces

Faces fair
faces bold
faces change
as life unfolds
faces grimace
or smile bright
or show pain and anger
after a fight
The change of face
to be sure
is a change of mind
not dirty or pure
The change of face
without a doubt
shows what's with-in
to those with-out

*Mary Wior*

## Hazy Morning

Hazy morning
dreams bounce my
heart. Where magic
bridge lilac all the
way around sharper
and sharper crooked
summer grass

*Maia Mcpherson*

## Porcelain Doll

Little girl
Fair and light
On a pedestal
For eye's delight
Chiseled smile
But paper thin
Clear glass eyes
That show nothing within
Standing still
All her task
Hidden person
Behind a mask
Blind to uniqueness
None see inside
Mocking her words
Opinions that hide
Non seeing jesters
Mocking and mean
Porcelain doll
Silent and serene.

*Nancy Trinh*

## Burning Candles

Two unlit candles
Far from each other
Wanting to be lit
Their passion to discover

Stricken by a match
Now luminaries in the dark
Seeing only each other
Creating a passionate spark

Two burning candles
Standing side by side
Flamed with great passion
And desires undefined

Getting hotter and hotter
Than the rising sun
Melting slowly together
To finally become like one

One mind, one soul
Bonding by the heart
Hardening together
Never to be apart

*Maria Rivera*

## I See You

In Skies of true blue,
dotted by a puff of white.
I See You

Across nature's horizon,
beautiful and so bright,
I See You

Watching birds sing, dogs play,
and branches sway,
I See You

Always in my thoughts,
Forever in my heart,
We can never truly part,
For as long as I see love,
I See You

*Domenick De Marco*

## Remembrances of Jimmie,
## 13 August 1994

"The laughter is much sadder now
far less bright the day,
strength decayed to weariness
since you have gone away.

I see you in the evening stars
and in the morning sun
along the ways that once were ours,
the paths that I must run.

Yet I know nor death nor hell
shall keep us two apart
for in his time God's mercy shall
unite us heart to heart.

You shall come and smile at me
as you did long ago,
I shall hold you to my heart
and say I love you so.

Grief and pain shall pass away
sorrow shall be gone
And night surrender to the day
of God's triumphant dawn."

*Robert Baldridge*

## A Son

My heart was empty
Feelings there were none
Then a miracle happened
God gave me a son.
As I stand and watch him
I know I can't get enough
What am I feeling?
It must be love, love, love.
He needs me for comfort
And him I have to hold.
He needs me for food
And shelter from the cold.
So don't take my child Lord
This is our first start
We belong together
For we are one heart
There's so much more to say
But my time is done
You see a miracle happened
God gave me a son.

*Laurie Hetrick*

## Thank You Lord

Thank you Lord, for this day.
For promised blessings all the way.

Courage to do the tasks you will,
Strength to bear the burdens wrought.
Grace and peace in trials sought.
Food for body and for thought.

Your gentle hand to guide the way,
For I am ever prone to stray.

Patience with the ones I love
Hope, the spirit, their wayward
Hearts will turn.
For rest, my weary body yearns.

For these, and other blessings
I do not deserve.
I ask one more
You Lord, another day, let me serve.

*Sarah E. Champagne*

## Just to Know

Just to know that you are waiting,
Fills my heart with tender bliss,
For I know when the day is over,
I will share a welcome kiss.

Now fate has drawn us together,
My heart is full of lilting songs,
Like the breeze that cools the summer,
Like the lapping waves on the shore.

My heart is filled with sweet yearning,
For your kind and endearing words,
Etching memories with dawn's blessings,
And this time they won't be forged.

There is love beyond comparing,
Through the stormiest weather,
No hill is too high for climbing,
For I know that you are waiting.

In the evening after sunset,
When the world is lulled to rest,
I am happy and contented,
For my dreams are at their best.

*Lilia G. Salvador*

## Consider Then The Rose

Consider then the rose,
First crimson bud it shows,
But blossomed, steeped in red,
Ripe petals soon hang dead.

Yet as when death He froze,
He'll resurrect the rose,
With thorns rung 'round its head,
It too, death leaves not dead.

'Tho petals once decay,
Buds bloom another day,
Aft' death, His nature sings,
As in new life He rings.

Still man can't fully know,
Just how the rose bud grows,
Creation's weave's so fine,
It's lost on our dull minds.

Consider then the rose,
'Midst thorns it dies, then grows;
Again touched by His light,
Its mysteries bloom bright!

*Richard Bridgford*

## No Stranger

You are a stranger, yet I know you well.
Foolish? Perhaps.
Your voice tells me all I need to know.
It is kind - it caresses.
Silly? Oh no - A voice is all.

A saddened voice.
Lonely? Often, but never alone.
Too full of love and faith to be alone.

A gentle voice, a kindly one.
The voice of a friend.

You a stranger?
No more - no more -
I know you well.

*Maxine Sherk*

## Untitled

This is just my way of saying thanks
for all that you have done.
I learned a lot about the game softball
and also had some fun.
Though I didn't always hit the ball
or catch those pop up flies.
I only have this one excuse
"The sun was in my eyes."

*Susan M. Richards*

## The Test

Life is but a test,
For better or worse things to come,
And the only way,
To have the better things,
Is to be who and what you are,
Do not let others,
Take you astray,
But if you go astray you may,
Always come back,
To the right,
For God always forgives.

*Raymond Shadley*

## Still Life

Are you still looking
For children you don't want
Who dance in the sun

Will you find them
Where you're looking now
Or are they all still inside of you

I look for them sometimes
I listen in the stillness
Their heart seems to beat
And my heart stops

But I know I'm just hearing things
Because up to now
Their heart hasn't started
And mine hasn't stopped

Are you looking for children
Do they dance in the sun
Will you find them the next time
Have you found them before

*Thomas J. McCarthy*

## The Gift of Life

If I could give you a gift
for Christmas I would give you
me. I'd wrap myself up and
have someone put me under
the tree. On Christmas morn
you'd open me up and say, "Oh
my goodness, oh my dear, this
is the gift I'd ask for year,
after year, after year." My
life is the best gift I could
ever give you.

*Sara S. Cooks*

## Just a Little "Time Spot!"

Just a little "time spot!"
    For each to find "What's the lot!"
So much here and there.
    That means nothing to the welfare.

The time here so son gone
    Used wisely or not-be unknown.
Each day of life a chance to be
    On the road that leads to thee.

It is each life that decides
    The way it's soul shall abide.
Choose friends that lead astray.
    Or choose for "your life" God's ways.

The world's way is flashy and fast.
    Nothing in it does last.
Get on God's heaven bound road —
    He will help you carry your load —
Live eternally!

*Leo Moss Fink*

## The Thrush

He has no need to rush,
for he is a thrush.
His breast is spotted;
its white is dotted.
He hops in his own time -
not cursing nor reading rime.
Why pity the thrush?
He has no need to rush.

*Pierce Stith Ketchum*

## In Time

Listen to the wind,
For once it passed by me,
Let it whisper in your ear,
And with you I shall be,

When you see the sunshine,
I shall be the sun,
Distance is far if you don't look,
Look and we are one,

When a leaf blows past you,
Please let it blow free,
For if I may be the leaf,
You shall be the tree,

If the rain should fall,
And I know some days it will,
The raindrops shall be my tears,
For the pain you feel,

If you look for me,
You shall find me each day,
Distance is only far,
If you look away

*Tina Bere*

## New Faces

She sits in a room
Filled with people
She does not know

A new life she now leads
with many new faces she now sees.

She look at all the faces
and wonders if she fits in
Is she one with them
or is she just a new face to them.

*Theresa Fernstrom*

## Invasion Of Beauty

Shame
For the one
Who walks on flowers
Upsetting
The altar
Of sweetness and kindness
On which the hope
For humanity depends

Forgiveness
The only salvation

*Marion Gillon*

## Shattered Dreams

Was marriage meant
for you and I
our future plans
now lay to die.

Our plans to be
as one for life
to be your husband
and you my wife.

But now our kids
need both of us
for them we must learn
not to fuss.

To get along
and be good friends
forgive past pains
and make amends.

I hope we can
succeed at this
fulfill our lives
to end in bliss.

*Randy I. Abrams*

## I Pledge My Love Anew

I pledge my love anew, my love,
Forever by your side.
So many years we've stood as one,
Together held the tide.

I pledge my love anew, my love,
I will not let you down.
When life seems overwhelming,
My help anew I'll vow.

Together we are awesome force.
Together we are strong.
The team of "us" 'gainst any odds
Will ever carry on.

I pledge my love anew, my love,
My heart in you will trust.
The bond that's grown twist you and me
For wholeness is a must.

*Shirley Goodrich*

## Never

NEVER! Screams into the night
Fists clinched in mortal rage
Pointing to the heavens.
The pain uncomfortable
The rage builds
Unseen lightning strikes
Unable to find the answer
Tears flow once again.

*Mark David Urton*

## Forget Not

Oh, Forget ye rascles
Forget that he is dead,
Forget that he was ever born.
Forget!  Let nothing more be said.

The nurse stood still a warm
hand placed upon his head.
She covered him with a thin
And dirty sheet for that was all
She had, his whisper came softly
Then he was dead.

Now try to forget if you think
You can, for this very soil
You are standing on is part
of the very land he ask God to
protect and to understand.

He died for you and he
died for me.
let's not forget not forget
just because we have our
victory!

*Mickey Bock*

## "Forgive"

Again dear Lord I say forgive,
Forgive me if I've hurt a friend.
Forgive so I can make amends.
Forgive each day when I fail to do
Those things that you must want me to.
Forgive if the day has passed
And I missed the chance to help a lass
Who needed me.
Forgive me too if I failed to say,
"Thank You God"
For this beautiful day.

*Mildred Clark Dahlin*

## The Dream

Once I had a dream of
freedom, laughter, rain, snow,
smiling of being a child a little girl.
Playing with a doll, riding a bike,
skipping stones across the water;
What a dream of happiness.

The sound of an alarm
clock awoke me to reality.
And what a nightmare
my life had really been.
A hurt worse than simple
scraped knees and bruised elbows.

A pain that would never heal.
A bruise that would be black forever.
A woman never having been a little girl.
And how nice to have had this dream.
But a dream that could never be.

*Susan van der Glas*

## Snow

It looks like
fluffy white clouds.
It smells like rain.
It tastes like water.
It feels like ice.
It sounds crunchy.
It must be snow.

*Shauna Lee Ireland*

## Forgotten Past

Looking beyond the present
Frightened by the unknown
Vulnerable in lonely silence
What was once suppressed is now released
Bits and pieces fall together
Secrets are revealed
Feelings intensify with time
Knowing the truth of a forgotten past
Comfort for the fragile soul
Always yearning yet never receiving
Wanting but needing to wait
Desiring but needing to words.

*Lauren Odman*

## Fallen Tear

A tear has fallen
From deep within

Shame has no place
Fear has been
Pushed aside

Anger is the beginning
Of the end

For now I
Cannot hear the
Words of reason

And in the darkness
Of the silence
I hide within my self

Rage become the blood
Hate becomes the breath
Desperation becomes the soul

In the darkness of silence
The only sound

Is that of
A fallen tear

*Lisa V. Nuñez*

## Unfair

Life was not fair,
from her chair,
saying I did not care.
But I did care
and shared in her despair.
I surely would,
do all I could.
If there was no life in jail,
there would be no reason to fail.
I hurt in a nation,
where or when life has no justification,
one must hold on and hurt.
As one nears fear,
the law is near.
So we shed many a tear.

*Lauri Kenyon*

## Untitled

Softness flows into
gentle night -
As arms enfold
one's love -

... and whispered
Thoughts come forth again -
- we touch,
And all is right.

*Thomas M. Del Nero*

## The River Of Life

From Greenland's icy mountains.
From Indian's coral stand.
Where Africa's sunny fountains.
Roll down their golden sand.
Form many an ancient river.
From many a palmy pain.
They call us to deliver.
Their though the spicy breezes.
Blow soft over Ceylon's isle.
Though every prospect pleases.
And only man is vile.
In vain with lavish kindness.
The gift of our Father are strown.
The heather is his blindness.
Bows down to wood and stone.
Can we, whose souls are lighted.
With wisdom from on high.
Can we to men benighted.
The lamp of life deny.

*Mercy Pobee Orleans*

## "Love"

Love is something I have never had,
From my Mom or my Dad,
In fact, they were never parents to me,
Something that I had wanted them to be.
Maybe someday I will find someone
Who will give me the love I never had.

Now, that I am grown,
I have a daughter of my own.
God gave me one of his Angels from above
Someone very dear to love.

*Peggy E. Turner*

## Untitled

Grand things grow
   from smallest seed.
One kind word
   fills deepest need.
Steady slow,
   it wins the race.
Chasms spanned
   by spider's lace.
Wildfires rage
   ember's start.
One swift glance
   can win a heart.

*Michael Libott*

## Arizona Sky

Always changing
From sunrise of light golden hue
to a bright clear blue.
Along comes a white fluffy cloud
To hide the sun like a shroud.
Winds blow in
Changing once again
To a bright clear blue.
Oh!  Evening sunset arrives
With it's brilliant orange glow
As the sun sinks slowly in the West
This is Arizona sky at it's best.
Always changing
Always changing

*Waneta Case*

## Glimpses Of Great Mankind

We have seen them all
From the beginning till now
Creation and destruction
Cruelty and compassion
War and peace
Hope and despair
Big strides and many pitfalls
The mankind has seen it all.

Though we explore stars and space
We are yet to conquer within ourselves
Poets and philosophers
Scholars and scientists
Explored the nature and life
And changed the course of mankind
More than this world
Much more than this universe
Beyond all boundaries seen and unseen
We have to reach out for compassion and service
Lending a hand for an ailing man
And healing a soul is above it all.

*Phani Paruchuri*

## They Dream Of Home

Have you ever walked in alone
From the heat of a summer's day,
To a house you've dreamed your own,
In the agonies of yesterday.

Have you ever stood in a hall
And felt that you'd been there before,
Or seen shadows that made you recall
Memories, that tear at you by the score.

Have you ever felt the coolness within
that cleanses the soul of all doubt,
To enter a room so lived in,
And a place where her touch is about.

Have you ever stared silently around,
Never moving or touching a thing,
As though this were forbidden ground,
And not for so earthly a being ...

Then you too, have dreamed of home
In some far off foreign hell,
And you too have come alone,
These horrors and agonies to quell.

*Sandra West*

## Intentions

Put feeling in your heart, and
from your start.
Your message, will soar in!

Be it bad, or just for fun,
no matter what you've done.
Your intentions will let you
try it over, again!

Heart, and love, seem to go together,
as was meant,
by our Lord God, above,
you can give or take,
make no mistake, easy
you don't have to give it,
a shove!

Intentions will make or break
a dream come true, especially for two.
If from the start, love is absent
from the heart.
Making it, a sin!

*Patrick Peery*

## Reunited

As the fleeting snows of winter
Gently water seeds of spring
Then our thoughts return to friendships.
And happy memories they bring.

Of the times we spent in laughter
And of other times we cried
As our hearts were twined together
Never more to be denied.

The warmth of two hands clasped together
The security of a gentle hug
Smiling eyes that say "I love you!"
Will surely give your heart a tug.

But remember one thing loved ones
We're not going far away,
We're just parting for a short time,
Waiting for that joyful day.

When we all shall meet in heaven.
There we will join heart to heart
With our loving precious Saviour
Never more we'll have to part.

*Richard L. Tinsley*

## My Reason For Living

My reason for living
God alone only knows
I prayed for an angel
Someone I could hold

He answered my prayer
When he sent me you
Your my reason for living
Without your love I'm through

Your my reason for living
Known that someone cares
Your my reason for living
Just knowing that your there

When I fill the world closing in on me
Your my reason for living
God answered my plea.

*Lynda Chaney*

## Woolly Worm Time

Woolly worm pray tell us whether
God chose you to foretell the weather;
Or, is your timely, yet endless trek
Only a trigger to our life's reflect?

Each time I see you in the way,
My thoughts go back to yesterday.
The seeds of harvest was in the sowing,
And too soon now we must be going.
When from the fields we have come in,
And it's woolly worm time again.

Yes - we will all remember
As we near our own September;
Give pause - and have our say,
Each in his own special way.

All - and for all - would we give
Aught to turn back, but to relive.
But, hark not back to the days of yore!
Save for when we gain that distant shore,
When from the fields we have come in
And it's woolly worm time again.

*B. R. Wilson*

## Untitled

I've done a lot
God know I've tried
To find the truth
I've even lied but all I know
Is down inside I'm bleeding

And crowing on this planet's face
Are we insects
Called the human race
Lost in time
Lost in space
And bleeding

Everywhere, it's been the same
Like I'm outside in the rain
Free to try to find the game
Cards for sorrow
Cards for pain
Cause I've seen more blue skies
Through the tears in my eyes
And I realize I'm going home
I'm going home

*Nathan L. Strauss*

## Gift To Mankind

Oh youthful day!
God's gift to man,
you grow old,
And fade away,
At twilight's door,
Yet every dawn,
You rise again,
Glowing,
To add your charms,
To mankind's years,
You die each day,
In nightfall's arms,
To rise again,
In glamour dressed,
Embraced by dawn,
New born, bathed, renewed,
you give mankind,
A virtuous chance,
Each day,
Of all his years.

*Maria Giddens*

## Untitled

Goddess in my bed
gold and blue against white blankets
flame red flowers around her head
as she lay dreaming
the birth of Venus
I can see her stepping from the shell
Redon's beauty in peach fire
there within reach
yet I do not
I used to have to close my eyes to see
now I need not
there lights the morning before me
with pale moon skin
and lips to kiss the day wide open
my eyes so full, drinking
thinking all that I behold and cherish
is too inside me blooming
and if she were to rise before I do
is this what she would see in me
as I lay dreaming?

*S. C. Lovell*

## Gone Away

Gone away forever.
Gone, but not forgotten.
You're forever in my heart.
So suddenly you left us,
    no time to say good-bye.
You were my life,
    my love,
I am empty without you.
You are in a far better place now,
    but I am left behind.
Oh, how I ache for you!
How I long to hold you in my arms!
I hear you whispering in the wind,
    and laughing with me in the stars.
But it will never be the same
    as when we were together.
The tears keep coming as I search,
    in vain,
For answers I will never know.

*Mary Catherine Ruhl*

## At Dark

A moist ocean breeze raises
goosebumps.
Tidewaters lick at the rocks,
refreshing my ears.
Darkness meets moonlight, my
eyes twinkle like stars.
A journey recorded, just for the
moment, the sand meets my
stride.
Revolving yet motionless, a star
in the distance, the Great Bear
rises!
Kept back from the edge, though
my mind begins to swim.

*Michael Royer*

## "Thoughts"

Sometimes when I think of my
    Grandmother during her golden years,
I remember some of the valuable
    knowledge that fell on deaf ears;
Trying to pass on her love and wisdom
    in a very special way
Only to find that quite often I
    had nothing to say.
Now that I have reached her
    time in life,
I can understand some of the
    trials and strife,
Had I only been wise enough
    to see,
She was making a loving effort
    to help - me,

*Mary D. Jones*

## Love Is Like A Tree

Love is like a tree,
    growing with the seasons.
Our love especially,
    'cause it really needs no reason,
Except you and me,
    Really need to see,
        we're in love.

*Lauren Spenla*

## Lifelines

Dwarf spider suspended in space —
    Halfway up from the terrace,
    Halfway down from a branch above —
Out of nowhere,
Defying gravity.

Where's the lifeline?

Ah, a web-thread faintly glimmers
As the creature
Safely scampers
Through the air
To the waiting bough above.

A magic act:

When we're lost in life, suspended —
    Halfway forward toward the future,
    Halfway backward toward the past —
Comes an unseen lifeline
Out of nowhere
Faintly echoing
As we're ushered safely to our waiting
boughs beyond,
Defying gravity.

*Lissa Roos Parker*

## Happiness

Happiness is a thoughtful word;
Happiness is an achievement award;
Happiness is freedom from harm;
Happiness is a comforting arm;
happiness is a good reputation;
Happiness is appreciation;
Happiness is bright and warm smiles;
Happiness is loving eyes;
Happiness is a state of mind;
Happiness is a goal of mankind.

*Margaret L. Rice*

## Simple is the Day You Make It

Simple is the day you make it.
Hard can be the night.
Sleep softly as you can, for
the day has no fright.
Don't be lonely if you can't.
Friends are more precious than gold.
Pride can be a viral demon,
Joy is the best story told.
Trust your fears and don't look back.
Steady as you go through life.
Endeavors conquered, quest no more.
Simple is sharp and straight to the
point like a knife.

*Liz McKenzie*

## An Everything Goes Wrong Day

Do you ever have a day when everything
    goes wrong?
Your alarm clock sounds like a gong?
You have no place for a song?
Your head feels like they used it for
    ping pong?
When a minute feels two hours long?
When your boss seems like King Kong?
When you feel like a ding dong?
When all this happens, just be glad
    this day is not a week long.

*Virginia Skinner*

## Long After

Long after the summer
has vanished,
Long after the flowers fall,
I will hear the sound of
your laughter,
And listen for your call.
I will wander alone
at the lakeside,
Long after the summer
has fled...
And I will be remembering many
Of the words you once said.
Long after the summer
has vanished,
Long after my tears have dried,
I will remember your promise
to return,
And that we both knew
you lied.

*Teri Chase*

## Footprints In A Foreign Land

Though you, my son,
Have left your footprints
    In the far off Saudi sand —-
While others have shed
Their blood upon
    Kuwaiti's foreign land —-

When tell-tale signs
Of each and all
    Are dispersed amidst the air —-
I wonder who
Will ever know,
    Or remember you were there?

*Mary S. Chevalier*

## Worth Of A Man

Many people
have never had
What they've wanted
If they have
what they need
it's more than most
If those same people's hearts
Were worth gold
Then the treasures
of this earth
Are there's to hold
So, don't measure him by
the threads that he wears
Clothes really don't
make you grand
but the cloth cut
from a pattern of love
can be worn
in the heart
of a man

*Sandi Kay Krueger*

## Doggerel For A Cat

Tuxedo bit my little cat
He bit her on the ear
The next time he is hungry
He better not come here!

Tuxedo bit my little cat
He chased her down the stair
Were he to perish in his sleep
I should not care!

Tuxedo bit my little cat
Tuxedo bit my kitten
Poor bleeding little bitten cat!
Poor little bitten kitten!

*Pauline French*

## Love

I love him for the things
he gives me,
My happiness and pride,
For the things I receive,
Love and appreciation,
Most of all I love him
for being himself.

*Mary Head*

## Our Refuge

The Lord Is our refuge.
He shelter us from the storms of life.
Some of us are toppled, by the storms.
Others are like the trees,
We are standing straight and tall.
Mighty God is our shelter,
During dark and stormy times.
He reminds us to take, shelter,
under his wings.
So when your life is dark and stormy
call to your creator,
He is waiting there,
don't let life toppled you.

*Mildred Swinfard*

## To Michael David

Listen to Michael
Hear how he sings
Of a life that was lost
And now has wings

Listen to Michael
For now he is wise
And oh, can't you see
The love in his eyes.

Listen to Michael
For this is his call
He sought for justice
And kindness to all.

Listen to Michael
David - who long ago
Played on his harp
To Saul in his woe.

Listen to Michael for he can heal, too,
with the help of the Angels and me - and
you.

Listen to Michael he has much to say
if only we listen he sings to this day.

*Louise McNamara*

## "Friends"

Like the sin that warms my
heart so do you.  It is nice
to know that I can count on you.

To know you're always there
for me makes feel good.  There
is nothing to compare with our
friendship.  Friends forever and ever.

You're always there when times
are rough.  Having a friend like
you is a special blessing.  I'll
carry you in my heart always.

*Valarie Brown*

## An Invitation

Come one and all
Heed to the call.
Times of rejoicing
Are at hand.
Hear the sound
Going out,
A shout.
Come to me,
Come up.
Come to me,
Let us sup
Together.
We were made
For each other.
Come away,
Hide for a while.
Look upon my smile.
I love you.
You are mine.
Come, let's dine.

*Shirley Parsell*

## My Father's Hands

Those mighty hands
    held the leather reigns
    bucked the bales of hay
    drove the sturdy team
They were a man's hands

Those big hands
    lifted the small child
    cut the breakfast egg
    tied the little shoes
They were a father's hands

Those big and mighty hands
    chose the fine switch
    held the wide strap
    struck the fierce stick
They were my father's hands

Those mighty hands
    can no longer help
    can no longer cause fear
Those big hands are now stiff and cold
    for my father's hands are old

*Sandra Henning*

## Everywhere That Mary Went

Mary was a little lamb.
Her fleece was white as snow.
Everywhere that Mary went,
her dreams were sure to go.

She traveled far and wide - the land,
to look for what - she did not know.
For everywhere that she was sent,
was meant for her to grow.

Now God has lain his holy hand,
on Grandma's heart of gold,
to tell her now, that she was meant
to join up with the fold.

Her crown and wings are oh - so grand.
From angel hair her gown was sewn.
'Tis Angelo God had heaven sent,
only this time - not on loan!

God reached out and took her home,
to a better place, we know.
Some day we will see her again,
when it becomes our turn to go.

*Peggy A. Rivera*

## A Lasting Friend

Her positive spirit always cheers me,
Her warm smile always guides me...
She tells me her feelings,
And I tell her mine.
The honesty is pure,
our trust is genuine...
Without her, I know not
Where I would be.
I love her dearly
She's like a sister to me...
When silence is present
And there's no words to share,
our feelings of comfort
will always be there...

*Rose-Anne Blossom*

## Upon This Hill

Upon these rolling,
Hills I see,
A crucifix,
Reminding me.

Of days gone by,
Which we forget,
When life did end,
To our regret.

His body hung,
Until he passed,
From this cruel world,
Into the last.

A sign of my faith,
Was given to me,
A dove flew down,
Upon my knee.

The clouds then parted,
The cross bathed in light,
My soul now redeemed,
Because he made right.

*Marie Skauge*

## Cowboys Can Cry

As she rides off in the sunset
His broken tears roll down
What he thought he'd have forever
Slipped out from his hold.

He thought he loved his rodeo
He loved the girl much more
Now she's gone and all that's left
Is a cowboy's heart so sore

They say that cowboys just don't cry
But they don't understand
A cowboy has what's in his hands
Until he loses hold

Cowboys cry more than we know
They just won't let it show
Don't beat 'em down
Don't hurt 'em more
Just let that cowboy go.

*Naomi Ross*

## Untitled

There is a man that I know
His love is more precious than gold
When I was small he gave me the song
my heart sung
He never judged me by what I'd done
He knew me before I was conceived
He believed in me when I didn't believe
He saw in me what no other man could see
He saw in me what I could be
He loved me before I was here
His heart's desire was to draw me near
He knows my days from first to last
The only thing he's forgotten is my past
He's changed me from what I used to be
Because of what he saw in me.

*Sandra D. Ferguson*

## My Love

Been thinking of you
hopin' for a chance
feeling blue
waitin' for that glance.
My mind searches
very far
My heart keeps wonderin'
where you are.
Must of been a dream;
the love which we shared.
My feelings to tell
I did not dare.
Under your spell
'Twas the look you gave
the years have passed,
yet, my heart's
still enslaved!!

*Victor Trujillo Tesco*

## Ode to the Dish Pan

The old dish pan so faithful and true,
going to hang you on the wall,
cause your working days are through.

Going to write upon your bottom,
gone but not forgotten
from the old kitchen chore.
And may you always be remembered
as the old slave of the poor.

*Lillian E. Sproul*

## I Will Sing You A Lullaby

Precious baby so sweet and dear,
How blessed I am to have you here.
You have filled my heart with joy
My life with love, my days with delight.
I've dreamed so long of the moment
I could rock you gently in my arms,
Watching over you to protect you,
And to keep you always from harm.
So sleep now my beloved child,
Dream sweet dreams and be at peace.
Hush now and dry your tiny tears,
And I will sing you a lullaby.

*Oleva Standlee*

## The True Self

How sweet when the mind opens,
How did it happen.
The quick flicker of other's eyes.
How sweet the new smell.
How I could yell.
What is it.
The true self.
How interesting.
How beautiful to behold,
The world from this level.
How will I get use to it.
The hidden self.
God's creation.
A touch of genius, a touch of greatness,
and now sorrow.
It's all gone.
I fell, I could yell.
The peace that passes all understanding.
Is that what it was, as the Bible says.
How about you?  Are you open and alone.

*Richard Albert Gay*

## When?

Dew on rainbows, dry away
How long to wait the dawning day?

Rain on windows, trickling down
How long to reach the thirsty ground?

Swells on sea caps, rising high
How long to join the infinite sky?

Snow drifts on limbs, glistening 'lone
How long to melt the arduous stone?

Tears on cheekbones, always there
How long to answer a pleading prayer?

*Susan St. Germain*

## Kissing

Like a passionate inferno,
forehead.
Wet and dreamy like a starlit sea,
lips.
Burning with lust and desire,
neck.
Hot sweat to cool the fire,
shoulders.
Innocent like a babe,
nose.

*Rene Hernandez Jr.*

## The Secret

If you must know
how love will grow
You must have sweet harmony
And you must care
enough to share
A love for eternity
But you must remember
to be sweet and tender.
And never never lie
For if you lie..
You will destroy everything
and forever you shall cry.
Don't be a fool
live by the rules
And have by togetherness
For rules and togetherness
Are the real secret
for many a happiness.

*Mary Lou Lemos*

## A Small Sacrifice

Years ago remember
how the women stayed at home
and know one ever dreamed of
leaving children all alone.

Today it's somewhat different
as we try to earn respect
and we make ourselves important
but our children we forget.

Mommy wants a new car
and Daddy wants a boat
so Mommy gets and outside job
to help him pay the note.

Our youngest goes to daycare
and our oldest has his key
is money more important now
than our children use to be?

Will our babies ever thank us
for the luxuries of life
or will they just remind us
what we chose to sacrifice?

*Tammy Herrin*

## Wolf

Wolf, oh wolf,
hunter of the wild.
Your puppy eyes and playful ways
make you seem so mild.

Wolf, oh wolf,
For much you take the blame.
They say you killed the caribou,
I know you're really tame.

Wolf, oh wolf,
You seem to be so shy.
If they're allowed to kill you off,
a part of me will die.

*Sean Spacek*

## Poem for Adam

The life that's before me
I can mold like my own
so helpless and needy
my heart I will loan
to keep my son safe
is all that I ask
to God I've assigned
this wonderful task
I hope that he knows
I love him so much
and I hope that his life
with my heart I will touch
he was given to me
through song and through prayer
to love and to hold
I'll always be there

*Michael Clary*

## My Love Forever

When I first saw you,
I couldn't believe my eyes,
My heart fell for you instantly,
I became hypnotized.
Your beauty is so special,
You're so real, so true,
And then it happened
I fell in love with you.
I picture your face in my head,
Every time I think of you,
And then I start to think,
Would I ever have a chance with you.
If I ever get that chance,
Then it would be,
One of the great blessings,
God could ever give to me.

*Maria C. Lopez*

## I Love Thee

The other day, the Lord came to me,
I did hear, but could not see.
He called my name, said "I love thee"
And there I fell, on bended knee.

Then today, the Lord called to me,
I did hear, and knew 'twas He!
Then He said, "Come follow Me."
And I cried, "Lord, Oh I love Thee!"
I said, "Yes, Lord, I'll follow Thee."

One day soon, the heavens I'll see.
The Father, Son and Spirit make three.
For Jesus said "In heaven we'll be."
And on that day, His face I'll see,
Joined together, forever be.

We all know, the Old, Old Story.
How He died, upon that tree.
He gave his life for you and me,
That we might live eternally.
And I cried, "Lord, you died for me,"
"My Lord, You know, I Love Thee!"

*Terri Callahan*

## Prayer For Friends

I said a prayer for each of you
I didn't ask for a lot
I didn't pray for youth regained
Nor a waistline almost shot

I ask God for the simple things
That serves our lives the best
Please keep our children safe from harm
And give us a good night's rest

I ask God to ease the pain
For those who need it most
And I prayed the love I feel from you
Could reach from coast to coast

I ask God to touch that heart
That's sad and feels alone
And I prayed we'd lift each other up
Till God shall call us home

*Marcine Stewart*

## Untitled

Most females
I don't understand
But hear me out girl
I want to be your man

I know I cannot give you
Everything that you deserve
But for only you
Will I honor, protect, and serve

From our relationship
I want ever story
You are very special to me
And not just some game to play

I will cherish you
With all my heart
So don't push me away
Or I will fall apart

I'm telling you what's in my heart
So you will know
How much I really
LOVE*YOU*SO

*Rafael Batain*

## Anthony

Don't leave, your life has just begun.
I don't want to let you go.
You are my father's youngest son.
I deserve to watch you grow.

There's so much that I want to do,
So much I want to say and know.
My heart aches with love for you,
But time for bade me to tell you so.

At night I pray to God for you,
Asking, begging to open your eyes,
But he hears not this prayer true,
So my dear young brother dies.

Dear brother, far brother of mine,
Fresh from the nurturing womb,
For me, this ordeal has not been kind.
You were taken from us too soon.

Prepare the heavens, and open the gates.
Receive with warmth this soul divine.
An innocent child slewn by the fates.
Dear brother, far brother of mine.

*Wayne Soto*

## The "Disease"

As the disease moves through my body,
  I feel my life ebbing away.
This thing they call cancer
  Is in my body to stay.
I'm so young, many more years left,
  I'm just not ready to die.
I've yet to see my grandchildren,
  Oh, God, all I ask is why?
Taking it all in stride,
  Has always been my style.
Although this event is hard to accept,
  I'll keep it hid all the while.

*Marcy R. Wells*

## The Secret Revealed

Engulfed in grey fog
I feel numb as a log.
The death of my child
Caused all things to turn mild.
One thought I hold dear
Is my child to be near.
There is a reason
And some day a season
When answers to why
One precious must die
Will be then unsealed,
The secret revealed, —
When that path I take, too,
And allowed to see through
The great plan on high -
Why one precious must die.

*Marilyn Brandes*

## Brightmore Blues

A long time ago
I had a special glow
Where gardens did grow
Around beauty did flow

We grew up strong
But, something went wrong

Once, where I grew
Now, there's a gang-crew

No more lemonade-lime
With a cup costing a dime
People spend their time
Instead, with street crime

Now kids throw dice
To buy crack and ice

Once where there were pleasant dreams
Now what's heard are midnight screams
No more fishing poles and streams
Just many shattered dreams, it seems

The price is too high with dues
I have the Brightmore Blues.

*Sophia C. Mack*

## The Loon

At the foot of the mountain
  I heard the loon cry
It was calling its mate
  who swam close by

On sun danced waves
I followed them around
  Rowing, rowing
  Just to hear their sound

*Terryl Esther Jensen*

## This Way To Jesus!

"This way to Jesus!"
I heard the preacher say
as he lifted his hands up high.
The choir sang softly
as he began to cry.
And his heart broke
when nobody came.

"This way to Jesus!"
the gospel tracks read
as they lay in a puddle on the ground.
Torn between the feet
that walked upon them
rejected by those
who threw them down.

"This way to Jesus!"
as the radio played
somebody finally heard
and his heart was convicted
and his soul was changed
by the beauty in the sound of the word.

*Sandra Sedgwick*

## How To Do It

I had it all planned out, you see,
I knew just what to do.
But then my neighbor happened by
And told me what he knew.

He laid it out a different way,
Contrary to my plan,
I couldn't see how it would work,
It wasn't in my span.

But then I thought, with all he knows
I should not doubt he's right.
I did as he directed me,
And it turned out all right.

Somehow it did not quite seem right,
Nor could quite pass the test.
What I had planned to carry through
Would have been the best.

I had no way of turning round,
And doing it my way
The thing was done, and that was that,
I'll try again some day.

*Marge Plantier*

## Untitled

He thinks it's all a joke
I know he does not care.
Why can't he see my sadness?
Why can't he see me there?

I can't concentrate on anything
He's always in my mind.
His love is like the sun in the rain
It is something I cannot find

Some think love is eternal happiness
Well maybe, if that is so.
Then what I'm feeling is not love
And soon now it will go.

*Marisa Rose Demanovich*

## Clothing Blues

I'm invited to a party,
I know not what to wear.
I could wear my red party dress,
But how would I wear my hair?

It is an exclusive party.
I must look my very best.
I have to make a good impression.
I could wear my blue silk vest!

But that is so simple
Oh, this is giving me the blues!
If I wore my leather miniskirt
I could wear my new suede shoes.

Oh, what a problem,
I have a closet full of clothes
You'd think of all the dresses and shirts
I could wear one of those.

To make the right impression
I must look just so.
But I know my clothes won't look right
So I simply will not go.

*Leanna Bowman*

## America

From a distant shore
I longed for more
Than Life was offering me.

I dreamt of the day
I would sail away
To the Land of Liberty.

She beckoned to me
She set me free
She gave me a home of my own.

In a country so vast
I enjoy at last
The peace I never had known.

*Mildred J. Katemopoulos*

## Susan

The banquet was addressed
I love her he professed
For her nothing but the best
My love will pass the test
Her child my own
No need to phone
My sacred home I wish to be alone
The child's body he did caress
Her mind he did possess
Secrets hidden from the rest
Away she wished to flee
The child must be set free
He did not agree
He owned her don't you see
He could not let her be
So he killed her for all to see
His wife she must always be
I don't know what happened he confessed
I must have been possessed
I loved her far above the rest

*Terry Anderson*

## Lasting Love

Of all the people I used to love
I loved you the most.

Of all the years that past by
when I fell in love with someone else
I still loved you the most.

So we grew older and wiser
and thought we found other loves
I still thought of you and loved
you the most.

When we met ten years later
we knew we were always going to
be together and love each other.

Finally the day come where we
confessed our precious love about
each other.

I told him that of all the
other loves I had, I never
forgot him and that I loved
him the most.

*Mandy Simmons*

## The Dam

Into a room, I walk.
I meet a man
of ordinary means, but extraordinary
power. Grace be his name.
Our eyes embrace
and all at once I'm faced
with a river so full, I fear
the dam will break.

I would look.
And look again.
This river, it bends.
Oh, what walls we draw upon ourselves
to house our souls within.
Why he, or I, or we
cannot be
our past will now foretell.

Without water
the flower will surely die.
So simple. Yet,
So not.

*Terri Irene Potts*

## Untitled

There was a child
I past on the street
a blank look
was all she showed to me
I turned and followed
I had to see
my heart cried out
she arrived at her house
a cardboard box
no windows
no doors
just four walls
to keep the small winds out
my world came to an end
was torn apart
can a child's begin
and be put back together again

*C. S. Runyan*

## The Widow's Defense

My love was like a red red rose;
I picked it in the bloom.
But beneath my fierce caresses
It withered much too soon.

My love was like a swelling peach
That flinched against the knife,
Sacrificed to the hunger
In a gentlewoman's life.

My love was like the perfect song
That sirens sang to ships.
I sang it once too often;
It died upon my lips.

*Linda Turzynski*

## My Pen

As my pen moves across the page
I ponder
What to write
Will it be what others can relate to
Will it save a life or make others think
I can only hope that it will be read
And understood
But I must try and hope
To touch as many lives
As possible
Yes, even with a pen

*Patricia Capley*

## Where Did He Go?

I woke up, something was wrong.
I ran downstairs, my mother was crying.
I looked at her, the pain in her eyes.
I asked her, "What?";
She said he was gone, he was gone!

I cried, my sister came down.
I told her, she went back up.
I got dressed, we headed out the door.
I saw my Baba;
She said he was gone, he was gone!

I cried again, the family was here.
I prayed, the priest came in.
I read to Dido; no response came.
I looked again;
I said he was gone, he was gone!

*Stefka Osborne*

## Home of the Superfortress

From the air I see a road
I ride this road down below
It doesn't corrode
Made from coral, very strong so
Near the north island is an airfield
Where planes would fly to war
A bunker, once providing shield
Definitely shows its scar.
A cliff lies to its southern end
Where many breathed their last
Questions asked, no truth to bend
What happened in the past?
Cargo unloaded from a pier
From an ill fated ship to be
The atomic bomb assembled here
And the ship was lost to sea.
Oh, what a superfortress tinian was.

*Walter Anthony Kenna*

## Move It

Therapists,
I salute you
Physical and occupational.
Nurturers of lifeless limbs.
Felled by a stroke,
Now I am independent,
And on the way to walking.

Miracle of motion
You taught me to work
At movement unceasing.
Lifting my morale,
Leaving no room for dejection.
Onward and upward
Toward goals I must reach.
You are indeed
Caregivers extraordinary!

*Louise Taylor*

## Vengeance

As I was walking through the park,
I saw her shadow a staring.
Her clothes were black and so was she,
but oh what she was bearing.

Moonlight was showing through the trees,
her gun it was a firing.
The first two missed, but not the third,
my side, it was a burning.

I heard her laugh as on she walked,
as I lay there dying.
Her footsteps in the distance dim,
'twas then my heart stopped beating.

It was on the first of August,
the day that we were married.
But then in May she said that she
would leave me for another.
Although I would not set her free,
it was on that day she killed me.

*Paul Gerhard*

## The Past and the Present

When I looked into the past,
I saw the future going on,
In cycles, in tours and in visits,
Synchronous with the dawn.

When I looked into the past,
I have crossed a line of bridges;
Some were sturdy, made to last,
But they broke from laborious trudges.

When I looked into the past,
I boxed, I wrestled and I loved to spar,
And when I lost, I bit the dust,
And dropped from tug of war.

When I looked into the past,
I was an astronaut,
Who flew a rocket out of chast,
To explore my very wrath.

*Parmanand Mahabir*

## Untitled

I went to see the ice capades
I saw them in the everglades
With icy blades the slender maids
cut the surface fine
Into darkness beyond the ice
A moon tossed its light into a ring
And she stood
And he
Embraced, surrendering

Perfectly
They danced entranced, romantically

So perfectly
She led him
Let go
And fell, he into darkness
And I now know
Beyond the mists and moonlit glades
I went to see the ice capades
With icy blades these slender maids
cut the surface fine.

*Richard Winder*

## Postponed Satisfaction

Yesterday
  I saw visions and dreamed dreams
That coaxed me into a struggle
  fascinating, demanding.
And now I know I never shall enjoy
The satisfaction of final triumph.
For I have toiled to build from
  contrary elements
Foundations to support
  many houses of dreams
Only to find when those were built,
My restless, scheming soul
Had painted other castles on the sky,
Larger, higher than the ones before.
So.... I hall keep on toiling
Until the day the Master
Says "Well done."
Then... I shall be satisfied!

*Ruth Gerber Copeland*

## Share

  As the wind died down,
I saw you standing there.
With a warm glow around.
Oh!  I was drawn to stare.
Your warm smile
and sweet voice,
beckoned my smile
and a hasty choice.
I want to share with you my heart,
and every part of my mind,
but yet we are far apart.
Now I'm searching hard to find
a common bridge or link
between us two.
So I can see what you think,
and to share with you.

You seem so close, but yet again so far.
I guess I'll never reach that twinkling light
that hangs in the sky called a star.
Yes, you are my every last delight.

*Travis Ian Walker*

## "A New Beginning"

When I think of a new beginning,
I see a lush emerald green forest.
The ocean water as clear as a diamond.
Animals not dying of heartless
Misery.
Child and drug abuse brought to a halt.
Innocent children aware it was
Never their fault.
A vaccine for AIDS,
Brings an effervescent smile to the
Human race.
Most of all,
A love for all mankind,
And a world of redeeming peace
and happiness.

*Nicole Rocci*

## The Window

Looking through a window
I see many things
Secrets long in hiding
And all the pain it brings

Silence slowly turning
Calmness into rage
Feeling mislead and cornered
Locked away in a cage

Some people can only feel
Sorrow for themselves
And can't see through the window
No matter how deep they delve

Some see through the window
To wishes hopes and goals
The glass is very clear to them
In is the window of the soul

*Lindsey Youtz*

## Goalposts

Goalposts,
I see them in the distance,
Far away and small.
Hut...the play starts,
The ball is handed to me.
A hole,
So big I can't believe.
I run,
Towards the goalposts.
As I pass the line,
I see the defense fall behind.
Nothing in front of me,
But grass and open sky.
As the goalposts close in.
I see how large they are,
Giant compared to me.
Goalposts,
A goal for everyone here,
Goalposts.

*Lane Martin*

## I Like This Class

I like this class,
it is nice to me.
You are sweet to me.
I like you Miss Real.
You are like an Angel,
floating right by me.
Miss Real I will miss you.

*Leah Howard*

## Class Participation

With my eyes just slightly out of focus,
I stare at my freshly doodled name
and see how it resembles
the way my mother wrote it
in the greeting card she sent today.
So I break from my idle doodling
to tell my classmates,
who have been discussing the breakdown
of the American family,
about her.

*Lisa Anderson*

## Best Friend, Mother

For you, dear mother on this day
I thank the Lord and have to say-
He knew what he was doing
When he made a woman like you.

He found this little girl with needs
That were filled by you, it's true.
God touched you with his tender hand.
And passed his love along,
To be extended unto me
Whether I did right or wrong.

But as my childhood days passed by
And my little-girl dreams were through,
God saw what the years ahead held for me,
And gave me my best friend, YOU.

*Rebecca J. Costello*

## Clouds

If God had not made a man of me,
I think a cloud I'd rather be.
Suspended always in the sky,
Sometimes low, sometimes high.

Clouds, majestic and very strange.
Some in sight, others out of range.
Radiant in colors of every hue,
Intersperse in the sky of blue.
Yes, if God had not made a man of me,
I think a cloud I'd rather be

*Marjorie A. Bauer*

## An Ode To May

An ode to May
I thought I'd write,
As spring has taken hold.
The flowers bloom,
The earth awakes,
The sky is molten gold.

The budding leaves
Show off their green
A sign that May is here.
A rainbow winks
It's palette through
The sun's so perfect sphere.

The puffed white clouds
Soar o'er the scene.
Birds sing for all they're worth
Their symphony
Of life and joy
And love of God's sweet earth.

*Mona Bertrand*

## This Time

Once again like the lamb
I walked up the ramp
Toward the slaughtering pen.
And back into your arms.

Soothing words and
Stroking hands were
My guides to the
Waiting bloodshed.

The audience waiting,
Some excited
Some afraid
Of what they will see.

I walked, I listened
To the words.
I walked, I felt
The hands.

But this time,
I opened my eyes.
Looked into yours,
And closed my heart.

*Samantha Howard*

## Florida Snow

When I woke up this morning
I was caught quite by surprise
As I stepped out to get the paper
Which was hidden from my eyes
My car had gone from black to blue
My once green lawn is white
All due to some person who
Came creeping here last night
My trees are pink and yellow
People stop to see my show
The yard does look quite pretty in
Thirty rolls of Florida Snow

*Tori M. Spear*

## Oh, Too Soon!

I remember my father's voice
I was just a child.
"Where are you little one?
Come sit with me a while."

I remember my children's laughter
The sweetness it brings.
And, "Hey Mom, I love you."
Oh, how my heart sings!

I remember as a young woman
The love in his face.
The excitement and anticipation;
It's dimmed now, but not erased.

I remember all the joys and sorrows
The fabric of my life.
And, what plans for the future!
Mother. Grandmother? Wife.

I hear my Father's voice
"Where are you little one?
I've come to take you home now.
Your work here is done."

*Linda R. McCormack*

## I Need You

Live your own life.
I was told as a child.
Growing up in the city.
Where many children ran wild

Encouraged by this assertion.
I went in search of my dream.
I surmised to need no one.
For my peace of mind I deemed.

Along the road of trials.
I discovered my need for you.
To live my own life without other's.
Was fool's paradise come true.

We are fastened linked, and corded.
We stick together like glue.
I need you, and you need me.
For solace, and support when it's due.

The world spins on its axle.
Our existence is a day to day transition.
All need help, and assistance.
During profound moments of affliction.

**Shirley Davis**

## Rope the Moon

As I walk over this world
I will never forget all the
kind things you've said.
As I walk over this world
I will never forget all the
crude things you've said.
As I crawl over this world
I have realized that
not everything you've ever
done was great.
But I will always
understand you for who you are.
The person who could
rope the Moon.
My Friend.

**Ma'shel Devey**

## Kitty Courage

If I could be any animal I wish
I would want to be a cat

I'd climb oak trees
With so much ease
And drink milk until I was fat

My fluffy black and white fur
Would swirl in the breeze
And people would say, "look at that"

I'd saunter straight and tall
And not have a worry at all
As I purred to express how I feel

I would curl up in a lap
And listen to people laugh
As they watched a funny show on T.V.

If a cat can do that
And not feel out of place
Then why am I afraid to be me?

**Margaret Leavitt**

## My Old Bible

Though it's worn and slightly tattered
I wouldn't trade for one that's new
When I think of all the burdens
That that book has seen me through.

It was there in times of sorrow
When a loved one passed away
Gave me peace in understanding
That we'd meet again one day.

It was there in my confusion
Ever was the counsel true
Gave me hope when I had fallen
Picked me up a time or two.

It was there in my temptation
Gave me strength when I had none
Then became my soul salvation
Through the body of the son.

It was the rock that I could lean on
I've kept it near me ever since
No its not the book I treasure
But what the Bible represents.

**Sherry Rust**

## Once

If I were Me, for just one moment,
I'd pound the sounds,
Receive the waves,
Allow the sand its mournful dance.

If I were Me, for just one moment,
I'd catch the sun
in burning splendor;
Glimpse a cloud, its look askance.

If I were Me, one grateful moment,
I'd light that candle
and pour the wine,
Revel in beauty; still my hands.

If I were Me, for just one moment,
I'd stop the world;
Tip my hat;
Observe today, my one last chance,

If I were Me.

**Magali Gueits Kain**

## Freedom

What does freedom mean to me?
I'll tell you if I can.
It means we all have equal rights
to live in a good land.
Of hope filled hearts,
the right to work,
and yes, the right to live,
the right to worship as we want,
the right to speak or give.
It means that we can disagree
with Presidents or Kings,
and that is why I want to say
"Please God, 'LET FREEDOM RING'

**Larie Nelson**

## Imagination

Let imagination be your guide
Illuminating the darkened sky.
Reaching out to encompass all
With wondrous memories to recall.
Capture your utmost fantasy
Dream whatever you dare to dream.
Surround yourself with strong resources
With faith as your coach
And courage your horses.

**Sharon Kavanagh Walker**

## My Fears

I'm afraid of falling in love,
I'm afraid of being alone,
I'm afraid of becoming,
The woman for which I have grown,
I'm afraid of opening my heart to you,
I'm afraid of letting you in,
I'm afraid of what I've seen in life,
I'm afraid of who I've been,
I'm afraid of leaving this world,
I'm afraid of making you cry,
I'm afraid of no one being there,
To hold my hand to say good bye,
I'm afraid of what to do,
I'm afraid of what to say,
But the biggest fear I have,
Is the fear of pushing you away.

**Lynn Harkins**

## Time Only Repeats Itself

Yesterday I was admitted, today
I'm alone.  You see I was just put
in this old folks home.  They say they
still love me and it's for the best
but what they did was lay, this old
man to rest.  They say they will come
visit each an every day, but as time
goes on we'll slip further away.  I've
seen this happen time and time again
to my loved one's an even to my friends.
At first they'll come and then they'll
get bored and then it will be, just
another chore.  But someday they
will see how wrong they were.
Because they'll be old and need
some help and they will find out,
time only repeats itself.

**Ray Austin Roth**

## Invisible

Like a swollen heart
I exploded
Virtually shattered
One million pieces
Cracking under your feet
You stepped on me
I could not breathe
You choked me
I died
Right under your feet
You did not even see me

**Rayna Starling**

## My Seven Days

On Monday I'm strong
  I'm content with decisions

By Tuesday I'm weakened
  losing all I've envisioned

On Wednesday I settle
  I accept sacrifice

By Thursday I'm wondering
  will this really suffice?

On Friday I struggle
  with sadness and guilt

On Saturday I reflect
  on this life that I've built

Come Sunday I'm drained
  I can't take one more test

God, please give me strength
  let my heart and mind rest

For each day that has passed
  I can never regain

Let me begin my next week
  with no sorrow, no pain
    *Robin S. Mormelo*

## Self Deception

I'm forgetting you
  I'm giving up the explosive joy of
  intimate closeness.

Who needs the scent
  of sweet sensuousness?
  Who wants to feel that special lift
  only you can give?

My thoughts don't
  include you anymore.

I'm thinking of beaches,
  dancing and race cars.

Occasionally chocolate chip cookies,
  downhill skiing and ice cold
  vodka martinis (shaken, not stirred).

Why is my mind racing back to passion,
  ecstasy and memories in depth?

Don't expect me to be
  thinking of you.

Because I'm
  forgetting you.
    *Richard Laulainen Wagner*

## Full Moon

Tonight the moon is full.
I see the men who risk
  their lives to visit.
What kind are they?
Fearless, adventuresome and curious
  beyond mind set.
Where do they get their courage?
I ponder on this at full moon time —
  I'll never understand.
    *Mary A. Callahan*

## Ending Life

As the old man lay dying
(I'm here to tell)
Only one matter concerned him
It wasn't heaven or hell

The old hands lay reaching
(not the final plot)
The root of all evil
Money saved was his lot.

One member kept vigil
accepting the pain
Understanding God's blessings
In all HE would reign.

Family clan came and went
as disease spread wing
Stop all this suffering
After death all would sing.

The dying man's money
would come to its end
Not to have lived life well
was the old man's sin.
    *Loraine Wojtysiak*

## O' Woods

O' Woods,
I'm speaking to you:
I am a friend of the forest,
Your friend,
I protect you.
I thought you'd do the same.
You were my garden of solace,
My garden of silence,
The soother of my soul,
The healer of my heart.
Inspiration called to me
From every stone
Every leaf
Every tree and plant I touched.
Like the sound from the rock
that taps the lightning struck trees
(Which are not dead)
There's a voice inside them.
It echoes like a drum
D A N G E R
What went wrong?
I am a friend of the forest.
I protect you.
I thought you'd do the same.
    *Lisa Leventhal*

## The Cat

Who is it sitting there,
In that cozy strait back chair?
Oh Lordy me,
I wonder if it has a flea.
What a life! I often think,
eyes always closed, nose so pink.
Not a care sitting there,
In mother's favorite satin chair.
None else would ever dare!

What does she truly know!
Does she miss us when we go?
Does she talk when she's alone?
Has she ever picked up that phone?
All I've ever heard her say,
Is, "Meow, meow come and play!"
    *Therese Fitzgerald*

## My Psalm

God will see us through
In every thing we do
Christ is our savior
He stands waiting at the door
His spirit is our guide
He is always by our side

When trouble comes to us
In thee we will always trust
When life turns hard and cold
We know you lead us to your fold
When there is no where else to turn
We rely on you to learn

When good times have returned
We were steadfast and we learned
That choice is our greatest gift
Even when Satan chose to sift
Choice of God and happiness
Makes our life on earth the best
    *Margo Carter*

## This Day

Such a beautiful day
  in front of me
I am so glad God gave
  me eyes to see
The sun so bright and
  warm upon me
Gives me appreciation
  of what's been given to me.
This day of peace and
  so very serene
Gives me time to think
  and thank mankind
My ears to hear,
  my mouth to talk and
Two strong legs to help me walk
  my arms to reach for
    the beauty around
  and my sense of smell
    of the air so pure makes
me glad I'm alive to enjoy one day more.
    *Sharlene Gagnon*

## Luscinia Luscinia

Behold Luscinia luscinia
In moonlit grove
Singing to Alhambra's
Hoary palatial trove
An anthem carried
On clarion notes
Caressing orange blossoms
In dusty coats
Echoing ancient archways
Drowsy shadowed courtyards
Keats' note-worthy "Nightingale"
Luscinia megarhynchos
Hasn't the scale
Of Luscinia luscinia
This thrush warbles
On-key every note
Megarhynchos oft-times
Emits a...CROAK!
    *J. F. Cronin*

## Mom And Dad Are Growing Old

I live across country, many miles away
In my own little world.
I didn't think of mom and dad today.
I known they are growing old, with
   hair turning gray.
But, I didn't think of mom and dad today
They cared for me when I was small
Picked me up when I would fall
Another day has passed and I didn't call
Years fly by since I've been home.
I'm just too busy to pick up the phone.
Soon they'll be gone from this earth
Mom and Dad who gave me birth
I live across country many miles away
Too far to travel to a funeral today
Too far to travel to put a flower on the
grave.
I didn't even think of Mom and Dad today.

**Linda L. Leeper**

## Life After Death

We had both gone through hell
   in our life on this earth.
We had struggled for our marriage
   and our spouses selfworth.

When we finally thought that we
   had peace at last,
Our spouses we're torn
   from our lives like a blast.

We were both so alone
   and had no where to turn,
But we had to move on
   and stop looking astern.

Then we met at a dance
   on a March's bleak day.
As we clung to each other
   we found a love that would stay.

Now we have a bright future
   and a beautiful life.
And we share it together
   as husband and wife.

**Larry Barrick**

## Memories

In mem'ry I walked
   in the glad days of yore,
The scenes of my childhood
   recaptured once more.
I saw a white cottage,
   a garden, a lane,
A rose-covered bush
   'neath the front window pane.
The brook, and the meadow
   with newly mown hay,
Heard laughter of children
   so happy and gay.
I lifted the latch
   on the old iron gate
And ran up the pathway,
   I scarcely could wait.
The most precious mem'ry
   forever will be,
The mem'ry of mother
   there praying for me.

**Louisa L. Graven**

## Passion

Flames burning forever
in the hell of despair
in the paradise of hope
under moon light
and red skies
in the midst of summer
on the waves of disguise
battling fear on backstage theater
rambling in various colors and sizes
bubbling champagne, hiding lies
Raving wild endless landscape
crystallizing moment and space
questioning life
birthing dreams and ties
rising to the moment's apocalyptic fall
to ascend greys in velvet heights

**Odile Dewar**

## Breath By Breath

There is a special place
In the lives that lovers share
A retreat safe and secure
Of gentle hands and tender care

It is a world of emotion
Finding mutual release
A house well built
And furnished with peace

Like a symphony of answers
That is carefully tuned
It is the balm of affection
That heals the wound

For those who love each other
It is their fervent prayer
This lovely palace to construct
As one united to dwell there.

So breath by breath, hand in hand
They built it strong together
And in this very special place
They will love as one ... forever

**Lee A. Pollak**

## Looking Glass

   So here I sit again looking
in the mirror wondering who
that person is.  I see the hurting
in her face and the pain on her
brow, there is a distance in
her eyes, a far away place
where no one can hurt her and
treat her like she's nothing.
   She has a heart of gold;
she loves everyone and everything,
and in this place is the only
place you'll find her.  She's
another Alice in the looking
glass and there is where she'll
stay as long as people are mean
and heartless, because she is
safe and free there, and there
is where she'll be.

**Laura Heiser**

## Will You

Will you be there
In the morning
Will you be there
Through the night

Will you be there
To take away
My fears
To wipe away
The tears
To know my happiness
To feel my joy

Will you be there
As I grow old
When my hair
Turns gray
And the wrinkles
Start to show

Will you be there
To keep me safe
From harm forever

**Tammy L. Johnson**

## Whore

Step aside for the feline fox.
In the slippery downpour
she crawls through the fevered piers
come shadows and course,
come snickering and sparks.

Step softly from the slipperiness.
While the incestuous czars
are brilliantly decked in scandal,
ruling the breaks in the black docks,
she winds behind the dagger backs.

Slam it jam it damn it on the dartboard
in the grey whiskey bar over the water.
With a vicious swish
the peace guild is broken
by the promiscuous kitty.

Sin your heart out wooer man,
Sing your heart out.

**Rachel Edman**

## The Revelation

Something is about to happen
innocent and pure
clouds are reflected
in two watery pools
the thrush of wind
is heard under wings
rejuvenation fills the air as
thunder echoes
through the valley
A baby cries
the circle continues

**Lynn Huffman**

## Musical Days

I was listening to music
It was hot and it was new.
It's fun for me and you.
Although it made me tried
So I'm no longer wired
I kind of wish I were,
Because time is passing
In a blur.

**Melissa J. St. Jean**

## Dreams

As the mind wanders
  into dreams and expectations
visualizing events and acts
  although never seen
hearing conversations held
  although never heard
    HALLUCINATIONS
fill the head
  heartbeat pulses
and the thought is gone
    Was it a dream?
but all so real
  imagination running wild
so intense and meaningful
  perceptive is the mind
that truly thinks
    What seems only a dream
is always real!

*Robert Tolar*

## AN ANGEL CAME TO ME

An angel came to me one day
  Into my heart she flew...
"Be happy, precious child of God
  For you have much to do -
The world is full of bitterness,
  Vindictiveness and greed
And I am here to help you
  To sow a kinder seed.
Don't be afraid to show the love
  You got from Mom and Dad
This love and their example
  Taught you the good from bad.
Then when you go to sleep at night
  The pleasant thoughts you bring
To all the folks who need them
  Will cause your heart to sing."
And then the angel flew away
  A 'peace' came over me -
I knew so well what I must do
  To set my spirit free!!

*Marie A. Molinari*

## "This World Of Ours"

This world of ours
is a sinful mess.
The leaders spend hours
fighting about who is best.
The States are the boss
of a gambling empire.
That doesn't have a loss.
The poor are still poor sire.
We get a good leader
of this country so fine
But the rich money lenders
and the silent majority divine
work together to burn him.
Where is God in all of this
when you can lie and spin
a tale of sure bliss
When they get under our skin
  Wake up America

*Margaret Rogers*

## "He's Coming"

Awaiting his coming
Is called "The blessed hope"
It's tough indeed, but meets a need
In our lives and hearts
  and thinking too
Even though the HOPE is nothing new

Abandon that hope
And live just for this world
You might as well dangle from a rope
Some have chosen romance and eloped
And found life to be beyond power to cope

So...lift up your heads,
sing, smile and pray
HOPE for a coming better day
I won't be long the signs all say
before you'll enter the land
OF ETERNAL DAY.

*Ben*

## Our Common Dreams

This country
is full of people
many races, colors, and creeds
different, yet the same
all striving for one thing
(or maybe two)
peace and freedom...
one day perhaps
they will come

*Melissa Willis*

## Untitled

He who is afraid of reality
Is he who needs to search his soul,
For he who is scared to face life
Will forever live in the cold.

He who is afraid of reality is not
Only scared of life and death
And in between,
But yet he is also afraid of being
A human being.

He who is afraid of reality is he
Who has to accept things the way
They are,
For he is physically so close to
Life,
But yet,
Mentally so far...

*Sharon H. Neel*

## Nonsense

All is nonsense in the eyes of one
In the eyes of one is nonsense
Nonsense is nonsense
And sense is nonsense
All in the eyes of one
Everything is nonsense
Nothing is nonsense
Nothing makes sense
In the eyes of one
One where all is nonsense.

*Tara Brooke Garwood*

## Poet's Convention

The poet's convention
is in Washington, D.C.
For "Poet of the Year"
they have nominated me.

That is quite an honor
I was thrilled to the quick
Of the thousands of poets
it was "me" they did pick.
  -but-
I have trouble with walking
and I'm way up in years
So I really shouldn't go
I say this in tears.

I'd love to say "yes" but
this old body says "no"
To the poetry convention,
well, I just don't dare go.

*Virginia Saunders*

## What Is Wealth?

What is wealth? Is it money?
Is it rubies, diamonds, or gold?
Or greenbacks stuffed in a mattress
for security when we are old?
Ah...my friends, wealth isn't money
and the treasures of life are free -
so look all around you this moment
as far as you can see.
A walk through the forest in Autumn,
the crackle of leaves 'neath our feet,
a little dog trailing behind us
as a sparrow gives us a tweet.
The sights and sounds of nature
as they waft their way to the sky -
like a symphony of beautiful music
coming from a source on high.
And don't forget your loved ones
who shower you with love so divine.
This is wealth! You can be a millionaire
when you don't even have a dime.

*Pearl Leidy*

## But Forever

Sleep unlike death
Is not contained nor
Boxed with ribbons
Of memories

Sleep is broken by reveries
Awakened by song and refrains
Of the consciousness
And conscience

Death is forever never again
It is severance from sleep
It is not retractable
Containable or contractual

It is not tangible nor acceptable
It is final not for a day
Nor for a season as a blooming flower
But forever... in mind and time.

*Mary F. Martin*

## Silver Stream

All the knowledge of man
is nothing, but a
cold, granite rock
in shallow silver water.
Echo-trickling down
through forest-filled,
granite-forged, Virginian mountains.

Compared to, the body Earth's
eternal knowledge from
billions of evolutionary years,
that fill our star-made bodies.
Their orbits collide, with
the gravity of Earth's
previous generations.
Creating life's wonder.
The big bang.
The big question, that
my spirit still
remembers.

*Nicola Calvelli*

## To Be a Thief

To be a thief
Is the lowest form of life.
To take another's belongings
Is the object of his heist.

I trust my fellow man
Until the trust undone.
Dishonesty, lying, and cheating
Are the traits of this evil one.

When you steal from another
It effects your mind all your years.
One day the thief gets caught
And all that's left are tears.

Thief, OH Thief
What crafty games you play.
There is not much time left
Before you have to pay.

The thief is the lowest form
And will strike again.
Store away your possessions
Not to tempt this evil man.  VICTIM

*Michael Tuttle*

## A Parent's Love

A parent's love is special
it is one of a kind
you can't find it on the streets
it's in your heart and mind

Parents love their children
each and every day
even if they don't agree
with what you have to say

Parents are very protective
and try to pull your strings
that is very natural
for them to do those things

Parents are very caring
but hard to understand
just give them a chance
'cause their love for you is grand...

*Rose M. Palmer*

## Breaking the Surface

I never know when it will happen,
It always comes as a surprise.
I just find myself on the dock one day,
Ready to cut all the winter ties.

Every year the desire approaches,
As unpredictable as birth.
Breaking the surface is just that;
An occasion of dithering mirth.

As I plunge into the calmness,
Unbroken for half a year,
All the air is thrown out of my lungs.
There is ringing in my ears.

The pain in my chest is unbearable.
This is the best feeling in the world.
The creek always changes something in me;
The jollity that winter masks, these brown
waters unfurl.

The gentle current sets my mind at ease,
Along with the herons graceful fuss.
A fish brushes against my foot.
I say goodbye to winter as I break the
surface.

*Laura Mills*

## Butterflies Away

it cares, it cries
it brings alive
those dormant thoughts
within our souls

yet cold I remain
as I walk these same
long black cold hard isles

and in the corner
where my karma fell
lies a shadow
as deep as death

my head is down
in the darkest sky
and it's the worst feeling
I have ever known

*Ericharleswartz*

## Prisoner

The ball of fire was almost gone,
it hung on horizon low.
The wind ebbed, a gentle breeze,
that pushed lawn to and fro.
I lay forehead, on cold iron bars.
gazing at the dance of blades.
The window open, smell of grass,
and ticking evening shades.
I softly whistled a common tune,
without much thought or care.
When it came to have council with me,
gliding on still dusk air.
It must have heard my silly song,
to have landed, oh so near!
It then proceeded to acknowledge me,
and hop close without showing fear.
We exchanged admiration for one and other,
then from deep inside, came rage.
For it had come to gloat this day,
'Twas I singing from a cage!

*William Bohley*

## "Whisper"

Can you hear my whisper?
It is calling out to you.
Can you feel my spirit?
It is trapped inside of me.
Can you see my sadness?
It is suspended between us.
Can you grasp my love?
It is calling out to you.
Can you hear my whisper?
It is trapped inside of me.
Can you feel my spirit?
It is suspended between us.
Can you see my sadness?
It is calling out to you.
Can you grasp my love?
It is trapped inside of me.
Can you hear my whisper?
It is suspended between us.

*Michelle Lee Smith*

## Sleep?

Why do I feel guilty?
"It is her time"
trying to comfort
us

Why do you have to go?
As I remember
All the years
playing

Why are your eyes so trusting?
As I put you on the table
It's better this way
I think

Why do they call it sleep?
As her eyes close, I know
They won't ever open
again

*Stephanie Banks*

## Untitled

There was a rose, a young beautiful bud;
It lifted it's face to the sun,
And saw on a bush nearby
Another young rose - only one.
They reached out to each other,
Ignoring the thorns, and cried
"We are one!  We are one!"
Together they grew
In the sun and the rain,
To maturity, full blown and strong.
They still said to the world,
"We are one!  We are one!"
But our petals are torn;
Our thorns pierce each other sometimes
In the winds and the rain and the storms,
Yet together in love we are, only one."
And again they looked up to the sun!

*Marian Earl*

## Family Tree

The family tree is ever growing,
It loves the sun;
It dreads the cold.

It lasts through hail and snow,
It grows off love;
It grows from care;

It grows throughout the year,
This tree differs from wood and leaves;
This tree will forever live.

*Marina Lynn Rush*

## Love is like a Seed

Love is like seed.
It must be panted to enable it to grow.
And love, like the seed
Must start at the smallest point.
It cannot be forced to grow.
When undisturbed, the seed
Will blossom into
A flower.
When left untouched, trust
Will flourish into lasting love.
Trust.
  Friendship.
    Communication.
The sources that keep love alive.
The sources that enable it to grow.
And love must never
Be kept imprisoned.
For when it is freed
It shall flourish
And life will find it's seed.

*Maureen Schlicker*

## Letter to a Friend

Dear Marian,
It started in Prescott
In the mountains high
We fell in love
And it would not die.

So in the courthouse
One day we were wed
Not by the preacher
But the J. P. instead.

Up hill and down dale
We went on our way
Working together
Day after day.

Happy times we shared
And sad times too
But somehow or another
We muddled thru.

Now fifty years have come
And gone on their way
But we're still together
Even today.

So I guess for the rest
Of our days we'll be
Always together
George and me.

*Naomi Appleton*

## Dark Trilogy

How very different it seemed at the time,
It was not your typical violent crime;
For the life taken was a special one,
It was the life of my only son;
They stole his watch and left him there,
Some people just don't seem to care;
But something really should be done,
To stop the deaths caused by a gun;
My husband became so sad he died,
A tragic victim of a suicide;
Oh something really must be done,
To stop the deaths caused by a gun;
At the funeral held today,
I heard a crying woman say:
Oh my God! What has she done?
Well, what I did was buy a gun.

*Lucy A. Matthews*

## Dad

As a young man of sixteen,
it was plain for all to see.
There wasn't more for me to glean,
I knew all there was to be.

Upon completing my twentieth year,
my added knowledge was apparent.
Without worry or any fear,
no help was needed from this parent.

But one thing had me feeling sad,
that bothered me no end.
My dear old foolish Dad,
never did change and didn't mend.

His daily work gained his pay,
doing things only he would.
Through grime and sweat he made his way,
while teaching us what he could.

Later, seeking answers of my own,
my questions came with open eyes.
Learning now what Dad had shown,
"Wisdom is earned," what a surprised!

*Rocco G. Mammarella*

## A Hated Virus

There is a virus that everyone hates,
(its deadly and that's true)
Once you've got it there's absolutely
nothing you can do.
  Scientists are scrambling to find
a useful cure.
They pray and pray to find one, but
but they are not for sure.
  "Don't hate someone with this
disease, or twist the facts in braids,"
  In other words, don't hate someone
because of... AIDS...

*Stacy Lea Pavey*

The loathsomeness of Winter
Is understood when one beholds,
The fertility of open fields
Entombed in pearls of snow.
Frigid months gnaw at our essence —
A malicious, unseen sting.
Yet, have hope and perseverance,
For invariably comes the Spring —
Which thaws the tomb to water,
Letting life begin again.

*E. G. Crittenden*

## The One

Reality is not a pleasant place to be.
It's full of agony and immense pain.
There is wanting; there is needing.
No fantasy in this life of rain.
So when times are tough
And you've had enough,
turn and face the sun.
Try for a while
and experience a smile
because you are the one.

Only you can make life happen
in such a way that it stops the rain.
Only you can reach for the stars
and grasp them through the pain.
A different point of view
is all that you
need to overcome
the stress in your life,
the ignorance and strife.
You are the one.

*Linda DosPassos*

## Persephone And Demeter

Maybe April is the anxious month.
It's true that April seems
to wait
upon tulip bulbs and daffodils,
returning Persephones.

But what about October
strutting her magnificence,
a Demeter who
smears colors
as if they were
children she could not control?

*Patricia Kellogg-Dennis*

## The Way I Love

The way I love is not a secret
It's written clearly on my face
It's in my blood, it's my "motto"
In my world it has a Godly place
That's the way I love, I rest my case.

Let me love my way to love
Deep in my heart, it's all I have.
Look at my face and see it glow
Spread its light, look at my eyes
They sparkle with delight.

To love is simple, so very simple
Beware, do not betray it
Do not soil it, don't you dare
Sing a song, give it feeling
The way I love belongs to you.

And never kill it, don't you dare.
Sing a melody, sing any tune
Sing to the sun, sing to the moon
Sing to our love, sing to the stars
Love, I'm so happy the way we are.

*Nick Arvanitis*

## Daffodils

Last week a boisterous jazz band
Jammed in the neighbors' back yard.

Arrayed in blue-green suits,
They lifted yellow trumpets,

And improvised a ragtime fanfare
As robins scatted in the trees —

A syncopated concert
Celebrating spring's new rhythms.

Today they huddle in the wind,
Bells pointing to the ground,

Ravaged by a killing frost,
They mourn their thinned ensemble.

*Sharon Felts*


## The Crucifixion

On a cross....
   Jesus died
Between two criminals
   At His side

A crown of thorns
   Placed on His head
....crucified....
Till He was dead

This heavy cross
   He had to bear
For all mankind
   Did He care

As He looked down
   He forgave them all
His faith in God
   Did not fall

O - how the crowd
   Cheered and lied
For on that day
   They thought He died

*Richard H. Barnard*


## After the Dream

 In the brief fleeting moments,
Just before dawn,
  Where dreams meet reality
And memories live on,
  Where the truth and the fiction
Of life are now one,
 I linger awaiting
The rise of the sun.
  For in those brief moments
Pain disappears
  And the courage is summoned
To conquer my fears.
  The phantoms of nightmares
With night fade away,
  And the heart gathers courage
To face the new day.
  For the heart that is strengthened
From dawn's growing light,
  Can persevere onward
To conquer the night.

*Sharon McCoy*


## The Spider And The Mice

The spider on the window sill
Just couldn't stand the chill
He was getting a little old
and was afraid to catch a cold.

To two mice passing near
he said:  Brr it's cold up here.
Would you know of a spot
where it is nice and hot?

The mice said:  stay where you are
the trip there is dangerous and far
the spider thought:  who needs advice
from two silly little mice?

So, off he went, across the room
When, suddenly, there came a broom
It swept him up amid the dirt
and the spider felt really hurt.

There he was on the dustpan
From there, into the garbage can
And just as the lid came down
He thought he saw the little mice frown.

*Veronique Maes-MacDonald*


## A Love Of Mine

Sometimes I feel it's hard to find
just how I should invest my time.
And thought it just might be a ploy,
I think I do what I enjoy.
Cause something says to carry on
with what I love, until it's gone.
So once I find it not so fun,
I'll know my life on Earth is done.
Before they lay me down to rest,
I'd like to make one last request.
And that request's for you to know,
something I could never show.
The love for you inside my mind,
is how I once loved to invest my time.

*Matthew L. Hoover*


## If I Should Ever Go My Child

If I should ever go my child
Keep your memory of me not
In sorrow, but alive.
Hold this on your heart my
Dear sweet child, while never
  Letting go
Whenever you need me I will
Lift you up, and place
You down as soft as a feather
That falls from the sky.
If there should ever be a time
You think of me, look up into
The deep blue sky, while the
Birds fly through the clouds.
And there I will be with open
  Arms.

*LaToya Florence*


## Requiem

Sleep, our Host of gentle sigh,
Keeps the watches of the night,
Our camp unbroke in quiet delight
Till rooster crows his morning cry;

Dawn comes with pink cloud in the sky;
Young vivacious day is bright;
Up, Soldier, to ferocious fight!
Farewell; there lies your road to hie.

Some it may be will come again
To greet our Host with weary grin;
Some it may be must lie afar,

Not missing life so much as sleep.
Fair Sirs, God rest you in His keep
And peace beneath the evening star.

*Mel Davis*


## Persian Fable

The hot, would-be lover
Knocked on the door of her.
He proudly proclaimed,
"It is I!"
No reply.

The hopeful lover, now wiser
With his Lord as advisor,
Knocked and submitted,
"I am yours."
No more doors.

Ask the Spirit for help.
Model God up above.
Learn to give self.
Only then is there love.

*Matthew Pawlikowski*


## Sea Star

A shooting star
Landed in the ocean
Dulled by the sand
As if it were sea glass
Shining, Shimmering, Sparkling

No longer able to
Blaze across the sky

Put out by
Cold water like fire

A tan skeleton with edges
Colored like a rainbow

The stars points
Like tails
Never suspecting
It was a sea creature

Knowing thousands of people
May have wished upon
This very star

And we can unlock its
M - A - G - I - C !!!!

*Steven Ronald Vanderlinden*

## Mother Oak

Mother Oak stands beside you,
Leaves fall down from old mother oak.

Mother Oak taller, taller and taller.
Acorns glide to the grass
Like a kite going down,
   Down,
    Down,
     And down.

Swish, swish goes the grass.
Mother oak's babies grow taller,
   Taller,
    and taller.

   Just like mother.
    *Michael Wilson*

## My Child

Don't judge my child,
Let him be,
for what you think,
is what you see.

Don't judge my child,
for he is deep,
his thoughts of life,
you wouldn't believe.

Don't judge my child,
for he was six,
when he said, edit it.

Don't judge my child,
for he have a beam,
oh! what a beam, deep down inside,
if you listen,
you will find he's wise.

Don't judge my child,
listen to him,
for many will miss,
a profitable encounter.
   *Mary Mann*

## Somewhere

Somewhere beyond the sunset
Lies my future still untold,
By the only one who knows it
But I know His way He will unfold.

Sometime beyond tomorrow
"So far from now," becomes today,
With all my dreams and all my sorrows
Blooming like flowers along the way.

A face once so foreign
Becomes my dearest love.
Brought to me by my Savior,
A bond sent from above.

A joy that seemed impossible
On a day I thought I'd never see,
All combine to form the life
that will some day become such a part of me.

And although some times I'm certain
That I know how things should be,
Still my God holds my future
That day by day, He'll let me see.
   *Michelle Nicholson*

## Alpha Omega

In the beginning
   light separated from darkness
In the beginning
   land separated from water
In the beginning
   tree bare fruit
In the beginning
   there was life

In the end
   no light no darkness
In the end
   no land no water
In the end
   tree bare no fruit
In the end.....
   *Tara Puglisi*

## Storm

Thunder crashes,
Lightning flashes,
Rain pours from the sky.
Are you afraid?
No, not I
Down it comes
In sheets or drops.

The sky is sad,
But why, oh why
Does it cry?

The sky is angry.
The boom of thunder,
The flash of lightning.
But why, oh why
Must you cry?
   *Wendy Isle*

## The Storm

I hear the roar of thunder
lights streak the sky
clouds appear before me
yet the ground is dry

I strain to see in darkness
sweat fills my eyes
about me people falling
I hear sobs and cries

The loudest roar of thunder
a blinding flash ahead
now all is fallen quiet
the rain is falling red
   *Patrick A. Gelardi*

## Homework

Homework...
Like a bad habit that will
never...go...away.
Bores, belittles, burdens me.
Annoying, onerous, obnoxious.
It seems that homework will
never cease!
Hated by students; loved by teachers.
Homework prevents me
from enjoying life and
from living happily ever after.
   *Mary Beth LeCroy*

## Untitled

I lay open my mind to the world outside
like a fresh book
pages crisp and still smelling of gold

Inside one is still
beating eyes pulsing heart
I still think like a child

Yet I till the soil that has been left
unbounded by the sky
I walk the earth that is dry
stepping on the cracks

And the flowers sing lullabies
unto your sweet smile
and the birds they sing too

I lay down now
heavy heart beating slow
brow creased like an old shirt

I lay down now
upon this bed of old
and I dream and I shed
   *Vivian Colodro*

## CLEAR

Cutting closer -
Like a knife,
Hubbing streams
Of city life.

Tin and steel
Of every hue,
Conflicting with
God's green and blue.

Timbers crashing,
Crushing green,
With mighty carves
Where life had been.

Steely structures
Cold and taut,
Stand where trees
Were sold and bought.
   CUT.

   *Linda J. Porter*

## He's Gone

Gone,
Like an echo in the wind
Never to be heard
The same way again.

Lost,
As when the one you love
Says he's gone
Never to return.

Gone,
Like a worn shoe
Without its sole
Feeling the hurt within.

Empty,
As a white piece of paper
Longing to be
Colored or written on.

Gone,
Like a lost petal
Of a red rose
Never to be part of its flower again.
   *Melissa Lee*

## The Old Forest

They creak and groan
like old men with little life.
They are gnarled and wrinkled,
crippled with disease.
They have lived many years,
Now discarded like trash.
Their home is a graveyard,
to which they fit right in.
The adornments are gone,
the leaves are dead,
there is nothing left.
They bend in shame,
because they are pitied.
But in the spring they bloom again,
full of life and joy.

*Steven Bond*

## Femme Naturale

He wore wingtips
linen pants
a black shirt
that matched

He danced like a fool
He sang like an angel
I was there
again
and finally

when I was in his arms
I felt
nothing
except for his back

And when he released me
I was free
and I thought
how unfortunate
It might have been magnificent

I will never know

*Lisanne Schuller*

## Untitled

Time is just people and places
Linked together by words and phrases.
Children with a young heart.
Just don't want to go apart.
Don't hide from the sun.
Young life has just begun.
Enjoy this vitality.
Soon it will be time for reality.
If you don't try you can't take a chance.
You never know what's hidden in romance.
It's the warmth in a big smile
that makes you want to stay a while.
It's the feeling that lies between.
Everything that goes unseen.
Lying together on the ground.
All you can hear is a single sound.
Just one heart that's beating.
Just an amazing feeling.
It all goes back to those nursery rhymes.
Words and phrases linked to different times.

*Shane Catt*

## Pretty

Pretty kisses and instant
lipstick. Honey flowers and
purple towers. Lovely
maiden what's your power?

Blue wild flowers, hugging
stars far and wide, free to
throw away. Even tripping
through the Milky Way,
prettier than time, costing not
one flowery dime. Matters
not pretty one, your free to go
away, even free to stay. Let
demons not decide your
mind, so have a laugh and
have some fun for now its
just begun, now I've got to
run. Bye my pretty one.....

*Terry Engen*

## My Nanny

Happy 70th birthday Nanny
Listen to all the cheers
They're cheering about the progress
You made in 70 years

You were born in November 1924
but to your life as you should know
there was a lot more.

You grew up with your brother Merv,
a sister like you he did deserve.

One year in college
you met a lovely man
and then a few years later
he became your husband

You had a baby named Ruth
you treated her very well
then you had 2 more babies
named Mike and Joel.

Listen to all the cheers,
they're saying Happy Birthday
the reason we brought you here
was to celebrate it a fun way.

*Marc Goldwein*

## Hummingbirds

Beautiful, exquisite, dynamic
    Little things,
With iridescent colors and
    Whirring wings,
Tirelessly flitting from
    Flower to flower.
Enraptured, I'm sitting there
    Hour after hour,
Amazed by the joy that it brings.

How often I wonder
    Just where they all go
When the earth here is under
    A blanket of snow.
Some place warm without
    The chill of icy winter winds.
I'll welcome that sunny
    Day in May,
When I can look out
    My window and say
"Hello" to my tiny feathered friends.

*Martha Mize*

## Journeys

Hostage to the past
Long hidden, long quiet;
Life burning
To journey to the light.

Old mystery dwells
Where two lives join,
In a quiet place,
After a long journey.

Endless journey,
Or a moment forged of years;
The fleeing now,
Or bartered eternity.

Unnoted days bewilder memory
Of mortal years;
Surprising at journey's end
The dream of venture just begun.

A far journey
To that last twilight.
Wonder!
To touch the edge of night.

*Neil Loeding*

## Blue Eyes, Brown Eyes

Blue eyes, brown eyes
look at me.
Blue eyes is one;
Brown eyes - three.

Looking, blinking
you'd think I'd see.
Eyes like mirrors
reflecting me.

Blue eyes dance
when I am glad.
Brown eyes cry
when I am mad.

Helpless children
It must be seen
Reflections in blue
and brown of me.

*Rebecca Quast*

## Moving On

While down the road of life we tread
Looking back and looking ahead
Many choices we will find
Bring back memories to our minds

Of boyish pranks and girlish hopes
Of family pets and music notes
Of choices bad and choices good
Of children in our neighborhood

Although the memories are so strong
No longer now can we belong
Prisoners shackled to the past
Hidden behind a darkened mask

We must seek out new desires
Never let the heart retire
Keep on challenging the mind
For new experiences to find

Although as seen in the past
All things don't forever last
But the sun will always dawn
And we must keep moving on

*Larry D. West*

## For Cody

As I watch you sleeping,
lost in peaceful dreams,
I make a silent plea -
a wish for the way I
hope your life will be.

A life filled with happiness and love,
and success in whatever road you choose.

I'll be right behind you,
and I'll always love you,
no matter if you win or lose.

You have filled my life
with great wonder and joy.

And in my heart you
will remain my precious little boy.

*Melissa Johnson*

## Left Behind

I've been asked if I still
love him, and my answers always no,
but in reality that's not how my
story goes.

The truth is I still love him,
and its tearing me up inside, I
know our time together is over but
my true feelings I can't hide.

He doesn't know how much he's
hurt me, because he can't see
my pain, but the fact that our love
is over is driving me insane.

I'm trying to get on with
my life, but my broken heart continues
to tear, and thing that hurts the most,
is the fact that he doesn't care.

I remember all the times we
shared, now there just memories in
my mind, and everyday I look back
on the love that was left behind.

*Mandy Hagen*

## Love Is....

Love is friendship
Love is forgiving
Love is compassion
Love is caring
Love is in our hearts.

Love is high
Love is low
Love is here
Love is there
Love is everywhere.

Love is romantic
Love is magical
Love is beyond the groom and bride
Love is wonderful feelings
Love is forever...

*Theresa Gailo*

## What Is Love

Love is you
Love is me
Love is new
Love is free

Free to feel
Free to care
You and me
Much love to share

Love is real
Naturally
Sweet to toch
Meant to be

Love is here!

*Patricia Wilson*

## Spring in the Air

Nature is blooming.
Lovely flowers grow from the ground.
Pretty birds fly in the sky.
Nature is everywhere.
The grass is green.
Flowers are colorful.
Cherry Blossoms pretty,
Blooming in the air
Flowers sprout all around.
Animals wake up and play
In the wilderness.
At last springtime is here.

*Tolani Onigbanjo*

## Untitled

Woke up lost
lured my self inside
felt the sharpness
It sat on my chest
pressing down to my belly.

Saw myself an infant on my back,
arms reaching reaching
itching for touch
collapsing back onto
sour sheets

*Ruth Lewis*

## Who Made The World

Who was it
Made the world?
The mountain peaks
That soar above
The valleys green and low......

The bird who flies
The sunlit skies
Each animal below

Who was it
Made our dreams to dance
Our thoughts aspire high?

Was it father God in heaven
In charge of all creation
Or was it Mother Nature pure
Expressing her elation?

Whether it was her
Or it was him
In whom we're mystified
Perhaps they are a synonym
And we need not decide.

*Mimi McIntosh Stuart*

## Mother's Many Shades Of Love

We ask ourselves from time to time
Mama, do you still love me -
I'm feeling really insecure today
And need to know...you see.

Cause when the world seems not to care
I need to know your love is there -
When troubles haunt my darkened night
I need to know your love's in sight.

We need her shades of nurturing love
From the moment of our conception -
We long to feel her tendered touch
Cradled safe within abundant exception.

It doesn't seem to really matter much
If we are very young or very old -
We still need our mama"s loving touch
We still hunger for shades untold.

So remember me mama, wherever you are
Remember me near or remember me afar -
Just love me mama, in your mother's way
With your many shades of love......today.

*Valerie Pryor Howard*

## Health and the Nature of Man

In matters of health,
man's irrationality is most evident.
Seeing health as Nature's gift—
and it is—man tries not much
to ensure that it continues:
like the sun that lends us warmth,
zephyrs that cool our cheeks,
and rain that returns moisture to
the furrow'd, quenchless sea,
health is taken as natural—
given no worthwhile thought.
For when health unfettered reigns
man is most concerned with
financial and sexual prowess.
But, alas, when it's abused
out of existence, only then
is health truly appreciated.
This, then is man's nature,
and this, too, his greatest folly.

*Lloyd G. S. Goodridge*

## Many Crosses

On a lamp shade in a room
Many crosses hang -
Showing children's love of God
As Christian songs they sang.
Two boys made those crosses
As a special gift for me -
Each were wrapped with colors
Bright - so all could see.
The lamp has shown more beauty
Lighting the crosses - it now bears.
The room seems much more friendly
It shows that some one cares.

*Norma Dotson Payne*

## Empty Heart

As I look into a stain glass window
many pictures, many colors
As I look into the deep blue sea,
many blues, many greens
As I look into the open sky,
so blue, so wide
As I look down deep into my heart
so gray, so black
I ask myself, how can I change
to those same examples
of color array
I ask again,
only to hear an echo say
so dark, so black
Listen for I call you to
a better way.
The way is truth,
the way is light,
with it comes many colors,
so wide, so white.

**Louis Nocki**

## Untitled

It's a simple message
    meant to reach all teens
That being the sentence,
    follow your heart.
    Believe in your dreams.
Though others you may meet
    may try to lead you astray.
Follow your insides
    or your dreams will slip away.
Some will say
    do this all others do.
Remember another phrase
To Thine Own Self One Must Be True.
You are the future.
    You will dictate what life will be.
So follow your heart
    and like the Mighty Eagle Spread Your
Wings
What you wish for will be something
    someday
    You will live, love, touch and see!

**Steve Horrigan**

## Look At Me

Look at me
    My dear child
Look with your heart.
It took years
    From my life
To let you grow
    Aside.

Look at me
    My dear child
Look with your eyes.
What do you see?
    The scars?
Please,
    "do"
        something!

**Magdalena Wojcik**

## Suicide

I look away from
my fear, but find
it bringing me nearer
I would like to just
run, unable to,
I reach for my gun
it rises to my head,
wanted to be dead,
and then I shoot it...
my wish has been fulfilled

**Tanya Kuschel**

## What Really Matters

My thoughts aren't important,
my feelings don't matter,
I am just a face in the wind,
waiting to shatter.

My hopes have fallen,
my dreams are gone,
there is almost nothing left,
waiting to be shown.

My eyes are filled with tears,
my heart is filled with sorrow,
too much to bear,
until tomorrow.

This world is dying,
just waiting to go,
yet I am left standing here,
waiting to know.

**Missy Knight**

## Losing You

For two long years
my feelings have grown
from a mere infatuation
to a love that is full blown.

Despite all of my feelings
my wants are fading away.
It seems you have found another
and it is with her that you are today.

I have tried to forget you
to ease the pain that I am feeling.
My friends say it will take time
for my heart to finish healing.

Although I have a busy life
to you my thoughts do stray.
It is as if you are a hunter
and my thoughts... they are your prey.

The love that I feel for you
is rooted deep within my flesh and bone
and when I remember that what we had is gone
I feel so all alone.

**Teri Koeller**

## Choice

I closed my mouth today
On a word
That was to be me
Afraid of this word
Being stamped on my naked role
But when given voice
Clothed in this word
Hidden,
I was free

**Marguerite Mac Farlane**

## The Past

My past is my past,
My future is yet to be told,
All I am looking forward to
Is striding towards my goal:
My goal to be happy,
To be loving, to be free
Free of all the hurt and anger,
I have caused for thee.

I am sorry if I hurt you,
I could beg and plead,
I am facing up to my problems,
Holding my head as high as the trees,
Turning all my bad mistakes,
Into something positive for me.
You may not believe it,
But you just wait and see,
I will prove myself to you,
But first I have to do it for me.

**Sara Caplinger**

## Seaview

A snow white dove flies high above
My head, its wings extended, reaching
Toward forever, circling, soaring.
Gliding—then sailing ore the golden
Dunes, bathed in twilight's hues
And disappearing as a tiny speck
against the blue.
The ocean's waves whisper, drum, and
Pound upon the shore as evening's
shadows take control.
Reds and oranges burn the twilight
Hours into the inky blackness of
the night, punctuated only by the
flirting of the stars.
The moon rolls slowly through the sky.
Another day is through.

**Willard C. Crace**

## Forgotten

To touch the sky or feel the earth
My mind seeks a quiet place
The sun burns down
The rains flood me
Snow encases me
The air is still
The pain reaches my soul
My heart beats fast
Shadows invite me within
Feelings out of reach
Unable to erase your touch
Gone from my life - no good bye
You wanted me
I needed you
I thought you cared
You used me up
You left me empty
The tears have stopped
My body aches
My mind cannot escape

**Nancy Shoaf Kupcik**

## Fishing

A warm lifting wind carries
my tiny boat along the lake.
Sparkling sprays splash as
rhythmic waves slap the shore.
The stern rises, the bow dips;
my line straightens, then falls limp.
Rap! Rap! Rap! The rod bends down.
The reel makes a whizzing sound.
I pull back, but she is gone.
Up with the anchor, time to move on.
Another chance in another place,
but the sun no longer lights my face;
I keep trying as the day gets long.

The hills are now covered
with slightly scattered shadows
as dark clouds cruise
beneath the setting sun.
The wind has turned cold—
and fishing getting old.
        *Vincent C. Ceglia*

## Love Is Near

In my mind I see him
near - every second his
voice I hear - yet I see
he's fading fast - I know
his words will never last -
his warm embrace I
long to feel - my poor
heart I know he'll steal -
does he wonder - does
he care - how can he
know of my despair -
does he long to be with
me - will he share the
dreams I see - what
are these things written
above - I think it's
something called love.
        *Megan Lawson*

## Why Me? Why You?

   I whisper your name into the
night hoping you will hear me.

   I cry out in misery wishing you
were near me.

   I care not to see you go but
who am I to say?

   I care not to be alone but with
that I may have to pray.

   I try not to love you so much
but how can I resist?

   I try not to care so much but
that does not exist.

   Now I'll say I won't fall in
love I'll hurt before its through
trust me I ought to know
   I fell in love with you.
        *Shawnna Madlock*

## I Don't Know Why

I don't know why self-hate is everywhere
no one can say, or show the way
      and no one seems to care

I don't know why so many have to die
the little dears that never hear
      an answer to their cry

I don't know why, I don't know why

I don't know why so many fail to grow
when help is there and everywhere
      and no one seems to know

I don't know why the human race is here
its not in time. its not immune
The end is coming near.
The end is almost here.
I don't know why.
        *Leif Morgan*

## Amy

Mickey was all alone now
No one to hold his ear.
The dust was piling up,
His face only showed fear.

Fear of what had happened,
To his friend the little girl.
Her sparkling crystal blue eyes,
And short cute blond curls.

All that is left now is memories.
Memories that I never knew.
Why had she left us?
Without even a "how do you do"?

I never knew my sister.
How could I feel any pain?
When the time comes I will meet her.
And a sister I will gain.
        *Maggie Collins*

## Recipe For A Christian

Take a little bit of humbleness.
No vanity or greed!
Then add some faith that equals
The size of a mustard seed.

Stir in plenty of compassion
With lots and lots of love.
And don't forget a daily prayer
To our Heavenly Father above.

Then mix with lots of bible study.
Read His each and every word.
While listening to the sacred Hymns,
The most beautiful music ever heard.

Top it off with witnessing
And souls for salvation to win.
Then you'll have a pretty good recipe
Of a wonderful Born-again Christian
        *Vivian Jean Leslie*

## End to Begin

We know not where we're going
   nor where we will end
But, we cherish each moment
   we must end to begin
—End to Begin—
Can we start it whenever?
   Still whenever we start it
Will we still be together?
—Start it together—
   Do we know how to play?
Though the rules have been broken
   are there fines we must pay?
—Fines we must pay—
Does it clear us of crime?
   Then back to the End, only
      to run out of time, to run out of time
You must start at the End, from the End you
   move backwards, from the "End you
Begin."
        *Tami Howard*

## When the Angels Sing

All along my path
Nothing seems to last
I think of you.
All along my way,
I can hear you say
"I love you too"
When the Angels sing,
in the twilight of my
dreams - I think of you
When they dance and play
All along my way, I think of you.
A touch when no -
ones there - must be
My darling Angel's hair.
I'm sure it's you.
I wake and find you gone
and in the silence of
the song. I think of you
Sleep will come and we
will share when the Angels sing.
        *Martinette Lacy*

## "My Pain"

You hurt me, you hurt me
Now leave me alone.
You hurt my feelings,
My heart was thrown.

You lied, you cheated
You played your game.
But, now it's over
Who is to blame?

After you hurt me
My heart was torn,
I cried and I cried,
All night long.

But, now it's over
And happy I'll be,
Now that I know
You're nothing to me!
        *N. L. Santarpia*

## Life's Seasons

The clock on the wall
Now says it's fall
But it wasn't always that way.

Once it was spring
I felt like a king
When I used to go out and play.

When summer came
I was seeking my fame
I wish always there I could stay.

Will winter be cold
Or will I be bold?
For only once will I pass this way.

Life goes by fast
Like a lightening blast
So enjoy it while you may.

*Ralph Breeden*

## A Silent Prayer

I sit in my chair out in the hall of my
nursing home,
waiting for someone to call,
and no one called.
And I wondered why,
I turned to God
and I started to cry,
I'd said don't cry my love,
you're not alone.
I'm with you from nite to morn
And one of these days,
I will get a call, not from one,
but from them all.

*Valetta Arsell*

## Retirement's Setting Sun

You've over come the...
Obstacles.
Tackled all the challenges
By unsurmountable odds.
Indeed you have by all means.
Touchdown..after touch down!
You've made them.
With each and every Hurdle...
You cleared.

The sun has set...
Oh, the brilliance of that setting sun,
As the day comes to an end,.
Phase one is done!
There's a new day on the...
Horizon.
As you walk down the road a piece.
New ventures.. new challenges...
Vintage...
And like a very fine wine.
Life gets better with each venture
We dare to take!

*Remick*

## Forever Young

Pave me a desert
Of an endless tomorrow
Where I can run and play

Or build me a river
Beneath the ocean
That leads to yesterday

Tell me a story
Of two young lovers
And how their lives begun

So I won't lie awake at night
And I can fall asleep
And dream of being
    forever young....

*Patrick C. Mullendore*

## Silent Sounds

Do you hear the silent sounds
of early morning bloom?
Listen as the buds unfold
heedless of earthly gloom.
The velvet colors lift
their head to the glory
of the morning warmth,
for you to share and
praise their birth in
urn or hand or earth.
Do you hear the silent
sound in mankind's clasp of hands?
Listen as loves eyes meet.
Like sounds of many bands.
Listen for those silent things.
Listen when man's heart sings.

*Marjorie Krehbiel*

## Reflections

The tree bark tears designer strips
of flesh away from my body
creating a brilliant pool of
scarlet
and
Bullfrogs jump into the water
barely eluding my young hand
creating silvery ripples on the
inky mirrored
surface
but
that was once upon a time.
When I didn't wear dresses and
my father was the biggest man alive and
my only worries were the spiders outside
my bedroom window.
When a band-aid fixed everything and
the young lived forever and
I
was indestructible

*Melanie Davis*

## "Heaven"

Heaven is a wonderful
place.
Up in the sky, so far
away.
Where people who die go,
so far away.
So far away are our
ancestors of close
and far!

*Samantha Straight*

## Living On The Street

Within the prison walls
Of her cloudy, foggy mind,
She made herself believe;
That everything's fine,

She walked the streets
From dusk to down,
Till daylight finds her,
Huddled in an abandoned barn,

As sunlight played
It's warm caressing rays,
On tear-stained cheeks;
And hair splashed with grey.

A silent tear escapes,
From eyes devoid of heat;
From seeing....and living,
Life on the street.

Yet somewhere in the distant past,
She must have been somebody's child.
Is there someone, somewhere...
Who thinks of her once in a while?

*Myntle Bailey*

## The Season Of...

To whom we thank
Of life and gift
Of thing and thought
Of hug and kiss.

Our life is gift
Of whom we know
Of homes and lands
Of thought and show.

This year is worn
Of sad and joy
Of cold and warm
Of you and I.

As we ponder
Of change and same
Of save and share
Of wonder...

*Shelley Cordes*

## Avalanche

Dripping through a fissure
of sand, rock and clay
after centuries and millennia
millions of years of wearing away
a drop finally fell
that tossed sand grain 'gainst pebble
causing rock to fall
cliff face to tumble
an avalanche to clear
all presupposing rubble.

River changes course.
The old water bed dries
under gently clearing skies.

Ignorance and decay
can cease abruptly.

*Thomas S. Loeber Jr.*

## Your Birthday

To you my dear, I speak with love
of something far so great.
For when I hear, the birds above
I remember a date.

A day of when, the birds will sing
and flowers fully bloom.
For here again, the year will bring
a date highly perfumed.

I speak with ease, I speak with pride
with love inside my chest.
Your birthday is, my darling bride
the day I love you best.

*Manuel M. Olgin*

## Hope

As my heart cries the tears,
of the time that was lost
my mind thinks of fears,
and all other cost
as I wait for the words, that
could make me whole again,
I think of past experiences
every now and then
I realize my mistakes, I hope
that you would too,
because my darling, you know
I love you
I'm ready to be the person, you
hoped one day you'll find
I know I'm just a little late,
but baby please be kind
I know that it may never work,
but baby can't we try
to capture the passion we both have,
hidden deep inside.

*Sonia Davila*

## Blue

Blue is a shy boy,
    off by himself,
    quiet as can be.
Blue is the sky behind,
    and in front of a rainbow.
Blue is sparkling water
    that fish swim in.
Blue is a fluffy blanket,
    on a cold day.
Blue is soft and peaceful
    music like "After the Rain."
The smell of blue is right
    after a rain storm —
    very intriguing to
    go play in.
The taste of blue is
    fresh and warm
    like blueberry muffins.
The touch of blue is like silk.
To me blue is this and much more.

*Shane Wenger*

## Alone

The words I heard
oh, frightened me
away I went
and I did hide

The pictures moved
so clear and slow
the hand it touched
I felt inside

Insane you say
but it was I
no hand to hold
no one but I

I looked out there
for life you see
inside my world
no one could be...

*May*

## I Am

At this moment I am the yellow sun
on a bright summer day
lazy and bright
glowing for life
always looking to spread light
black as a funeral
sad and depressed
strong and trying to survive
shielding my self from other people

*Thomas Jackson*

## Age of Innocence

Lost to myself
on a map of my life

I glare at the sky
contemplating my strife

When will it end
Daughter, lover, wife?

The answer not clear
I reach for the knife

*J. Autumn Justice*

## It's Not Too Late

Why would you want to live
on a planet with no trees?
Don't you want your children
to play in fresh raked leaves?

We are taking from a being
known as Mother Earth,
if we don't take good care of her
we will all end up in hearths.

It is obvious that we were doomed
from the very start.
It is not too late to all chip in,
and do our earned part.

*Patricia A. Thacker*

## A Trucker's Psalm

Rolling down the highway
On my way to LA.
I think of some scenes
I see alone the way

Rather I-10, I-20 or in Tennessee
It's the life for people like me,
Rather Nashville Memphis or LA
Jackson, New York or alone the way

You grab another gear,
Then look out around you,
At the best sight near,
At love warm and true

For special people we are
Watching out for that little car,
And thank God for another day
That we can honestly say.

He helped as make it through
Avoiding accidents with you,
And everyday we pray,
"Dear God Help us through another day!

*Wayne Perschbacher*

## Rain

Pitter. Patter.
On my window sill.
    All is calm.
All is still.
    It is the sound of rain.
So soothing and nice.
    And the great thing is;
We can see it for no price.
    Rain will come.
And rain will go.
    And in a couple of months;
There will be snow.

*Mary Kenny*

## Zero Gravity

When you're walking
on the moon
all that's tying you down
is yourself
here's a star for you
grab it if you can
there's nothing out here
to stop you
except the size of
your footprints
and the amount of
air in your tank

*Mark Lester*

## Nicola

You've not quite grown
    My sister, friend.
There's still so much to see
But underneath your child like ways
    Grows quiet maturity.

It won't belong before you see
The world through bigger eyes
    But don't you change,
    Stay as you are,
        Mischievous woman-child.

*Wendy P. Quas*

## The Present

It is Christmas time
Once again.
Decisions decisions
Man oh man.
The present I will get
Will never be broken or tossed.
The present I will get
Will never be scratched or lost.
The present I will get
I will see every day.
The present I will get
Will be with me until time passes away.
The present I will get
I will love and cherish.
The present I will get
Will never make me sad or embarrassed.
The present I will get
Will be the best in the world.
It will be the love that I have
From the sweetest girl.

*Timothy Thomas Archer Jr.*

## Sorrowful Skies

The moon and the sun
Once lovers and friends

Danced in the sky
Far above earths head

They were never apart
Never night nor day

But the jealous stars
Envious of their ways

Split them apart
Never to love again

And so they follow each other
Hungry for love before the end.

*Linda McDonald*

## Untitled

Love is but a moment.
Once shared
Such joy
Then it is taken away.
Love isn't meant
Forever.
There is no forever.
Capture love when you can.
Let it go when it leaves
Or love can destroy.

*Marlene Good*

## Yet, The Greatest...

Through the mist of time and change,
One bastion constant yet remains
Stalwart 'gainst these foes of life.
'Tis love eternal that I spy
That circumvents to defy,
And cuts the murky like a knife.

Ah, love; elusive, yet ever there,
Surpassing friend, foe, and forebear,
Grant to us a greater hoard
Of gentleness and caring thought,
Of kindnesses and mercies wrought,
And be our ever present Lord.

*Vincent P. Russo*

## Untitled

The movement of man and machine
one following the other
speeding down
the black ribbon of destiny
the search for freedom
that elusive phantom
that always seems to elude one's grasp
but, if one looks hard enough
into the swirling wind
just out of the corner of your eye
you may catch a fleeting glimpse
enough to sate your curiosity
or worse yet sent upon
a cat and mouse chase
out on the furthermost edges
to find and exorcise
the demons of your innermost desires

*Michael S. Markle*

## Star

There are billions of stars in the sky,
one for every girl and guy.
To wish upon, and hope it comes true,
has, everyone the right to do.
For no matter how great or small
happiness can be granted, to all.
To dream, about, and to follow through
can make all your wishes come true, for
when you wish upon, a star,
It can take you, very far.

*Richard A. Granholm*

## Life

Life is a trip,
One journey after another.
Separating paths from
your father, mother and brother.
Pain and confusion,
like you would not believe.
Always wondering
about the things you can't see.
Lovers come and go,
friends do too.
The Lord is the only one
that will always be with you.
and of coarse yourself
For I can not run from me.
So I just live life,
letting be what will be.
I know I will make it,
day by day.
For the Lord is here with me,
to say.

*Victoria Joseph*

## Lost

To be happy once more,
Pure Bliss.
For her eyes to dance again,
as they are now dead.
Dead as the joy she once knew.
When exactly did it escape her?
She wanders from place to place
never quite knowing.
Will she ever regain this
euphoria.

*Stefanie Davison*

## Two Hearts

Two hearts...
One open, one closed
One liked, one opposed
Two hearts joined
One trusting, one afraid
One moving, one delayed
Two hearts together yet apart
One the fire, one the spark
Two hearts loving
One taking one giving
One dying, one living
Two hearts searching
One for truth, one for fantasy
One is peace, the other catastrophe
Two hearts
One lives, one dies
One laughs, one cries
They share everything yet nothing at all
One has no lock, the other a wall
Two hearts...

*Wednesday Samarco*

## Summerset

Summer has gone, I saw her go
One September twilight.
I saw the gentle zephyrs blow
Her red - gold dress
That stood against the moonlight.
The ocean shone a mystic green
And sang a mournful tune;
Each lonely wavelet seemed to taunt
The early Autumn moon.

*Warren Aidan Bradley*

## I Surrender

There's one thing I am sure of,
One thing that's meant to be,
My Higher Power (whom I call God)
Has complete control of me.

I cannot run my life myself,
As I sometimes try to do,
I always make a mess of things,
I'm sure you've tried it, too.

If I try to be captain of the ship
It's surely destined to sink,
I've tried to give orders to all aboard,
But, I have failed to stop and think.

I'm not qualified to be the captain,
I'm only one of the crew,
I'll reach my destination,
I'm sure that you will, too.

If I keep one thought foremost in mind,
My ship will sail just fine,
It's steered by a power greater than I,
"THY WILL BE DONE, NOT MINE".

*Virginia De Weese*

## "Surprise!! Surprise!!"

"Who doesn't like surprises?,
Ones that bring you joy -
Especially something you've wanted,
When my wife gave birth to our boy"

"I remember the time I made a wish,
For something I wanted real bad-
My friends gave me this Phillies gem,
A Season Ticket, was I glad?"

"A birthday party that was given me,
Caught me by surprise -
A gift I've always wanted,
A new Car, parked before my eyes"

"Surprises are the best of all things,
That you least expect -
Getting that special something,
For me, that is Respect"

"You're never too old to be surprised,
You feel like a kid again -
To get what you've always wanted,
To make Love, I can't remember when"

*Marty Rollin*

## Magic

Although I never knew
Or even had a clue
That it was you,
Who would play such a part in my heart...

That would make me complete
For now when we meet,
I get a thrill
From my head to my feet...

And I know just how real
You can make me feel,
Cause when we kiss
My world is full of bliss...

And not a minute
Do I want to miss,
For I enjoy whenever
We can be together...

And don't even have a care
If others are aware,
That its with you
My time I want to share.

*Linda Askew*

## Pray

Death is a small relief
Nothing but a dim belief
that when you die it
all gets better,
something like a
floating feather.
For when the
feather is frayed away
It will not float another
day.
So with death before
me,
my eyes turn gray.
I get down on my
knees and pray.

*Maria Bonner*

## Untitled

Born under a bleak star
or perhaps it was a solar eclipse

Was I a particle
that escaped from a sucking

Black hole
mother said I was

Whelped during a tornado
a cloudy day comforts me

The oracle said I
had a dark aura

Kafka's stories excite me
you will always find

Me standing at
Wagnerian Opera

I still morn the death
of Rainer Fassbinder

And lament the ageing
of Ingmar Bergman

Who is the incarnation
of Edgar Allan Poe?

*Sophie Rivera*

## No Greater Gift

Regardless of the time in life
Or talent great or small,
There's one that does the greatest good
For families one and all.

The talent is so common place...
Easy to overlook.
It's found in women of the world,
A GOOD OLD FASHION COOK.

Her kitchen will her kingdom be:
The dining room her throne,
And homeward will her family turn...
She'll never be alone.

Her ever ready, healthy meals
Will be her guarantee
That those who feast within her home
Will never hungry be.

And as the years go surely by,
The memories will live on
Of all the great meals that she served...
Long after she is gone.

*Mary Jean Lane*

## Ordinary People

I see
ordinary people...

Like flowers.
pushing through cement cracks
Stretching toward light
of life understood
and love.

Some grow
in asphalt parking lots
and lonely spaces,
seeds tumbled into impossible places
to blossom.

No cheers for them

Just acceptance
It is an extraordinary thing!

*Pamela McClarin*

## To the End of Time

We dance!
Our feet pound out
Intricate rhythms
Circles join, separate
Then form again
We move to the music in our hearts
That beat their way
Towards total silence.

*Marla A. Taylor*

## Only To Exist

How meaningless
our purpose seems
to have no reason
with so many beliefs
to be just that
we try to understand
something uncomprehendable
hoping to make sense
of our confusion
would you look
for something
that's nowhere
to be found
occasionally I look
to see what's not there
In hopes of an answer
that has no reply

*Michael W.*

## Christina

My dear sweet young Christina
out in the dark of the night
with your friend by your side
sharing a dream and future delights

Who would of thought that God
would have called upon you this
night, with the ruffle of leaves
that fell in the night

Who would await you as I
cried in the night, with your voice
so clear I heard you call in the night

My dear sweet Christina my love,
my joy and delight, my child so bright
you soared like an eagle with my
tears and the angels at your side
Now you are our Heavenly Father's delight

*Linda Winkler*

## People

There are lots of lonely people
Out in the world today
That really goes unnoticed
When they pass our way
People have a deep desire
To feel appreciated and loved
They need a touch, a smile
A handshake or a hug.

They could be our next door neighbor
Or they could be our best friends
They could be a sister or brother
That need our helping hands
One could be a stranger on the street
That we passed today
A friendly word, and a friendly smile
Will go a long way.

*Niley Benge*

## "Time"

Time is of the essence,
    Passing quickly before our eyes.
But who has sought to realize,
    Their lives have passed them by.
When we're young we see the world,
    As only black and white.
But as we age our views do change,
    To simple shades of gray.
We take for granted many things,
    That life does have to offer.
Until we see that death is near,
    We wish to live much longer.
Once we've noticed our time has come,
    We look at death much closer.
For in our minds the seeds were planted,
    Of what is now to come.
As things grow dark around us,
    We ponder what we may.
But if we could have altered our lives,
    I wonder how many would change.

    *Rodney Miller*

## Fortified Words

Man adopted his ways of war
pertaining to the way of doing war
against his neighbor.  The last thing
on his mind is the destruction
of the valley.  A valley where man
govern there communities and
build securities
Command is the awesome ability
to bring confrontation to the valley
the command people the worker of
the earth but by far is it known
to his countryman the compassion
he has for his hero.  There for
let the true hero the worker
understand his feel to first reconciled
then recompense.

    *Richard Seiler Jr.*

## What Is Poetry?

What is poetry?
Poetry is a touch of a hand.
A gesture of love
A beautiful day in June.

A wedding tune
A romance in bloom
A colorful blue sky
Birds that fly
an orange moon.

Canary birds singing
Warbling warbling warbling
Telling us of
spring spring spring

Tell me
What's in all of this
for me for me
Is there a pot of gold
At the end of the rainbow
For me for me.

    *Mary Martha Siano*

## Winter's Mane

The onset of winter is here.
Pretentiously the morning stars
Cast their glimmering rays against
An unwelcoming abyss.

As we nestle cradle-armed, oblivious
To the beauty of dawn's colorful hues,
Knowing I cannot stop the coming chill
Nor keep the autumn leaves from falling.

So let summer skies be your headdress
And wear upon your tiny feet shoes
Whiter than a pure, fallen snow.
And tap dance my love, upon the slick,
Fierce ice of winter's mane.

As a cub and mother hibernate,
Huddled in their cavernous abode,
So wait we.  Looking.  Dreaming.
Sweetly anticipating the fresh scents
And delights of Spring budding forth
Swiftly on a twilight's wing.

    *Mary Jo Aros*

## Pets

Dogs in the kitchen,
Puddles on the floor,
It makes me so mad,
I could kick them out the door.

You let them out...
then back in again;
Well I'll be,
they did it again!

You swat their fanny,
then their nose;
What's that?
There's a pile at your toes!

Pick up this,
Wipe up that.
Why didn't we just get a cat?

    *Sharon K. Falls-Fischer*

## Cluttered Pictures

Cluttered pictures,
Quite valuable I'm sure
All cluttered together
Here and there,

Rare are the lamps and shades
Like the pillows scattered about
And statues, they too, are priceless
I'm sure,

The walls are painted white
The curtains of china red
There's no green to speak of
To make the room bright,

Like dust left untouched
And the smell of old,
That never fades away,

Yet, you can tell by the red in
The room and everything therein,

It's a house of money
But no life or happiness dwells within,
I'm sure.

    *Lovely Faison*

## Child of Hunger

Proud little angel of hope,
Reaching towards the hilly slope,
Innocent eyes full of sorrow
Awaiting the unknown 'morrow,
Rebellious in the face of despair,
Oblivious to all earth cares,
Soft belly distended,
Young soul unmended,
Sad Angel of God stands alone,
Awaiting his passage home,
Famished body torn asunder,
For He is the child of hunger.

    *Sandra Franklin*

## The Center

I joined a Senior Citizen Club
Referred to as "THE CENTER"
We play poker twice a week
And I try to come out a winner.
I've never had a ROYAL FLUSH
Although I dealt one to a member.
Perhaps I'll get one someday soon
Playing poker at "THE CENTER"!
We have parties now and then
We dance and laugh and eat.
When we go to Atlantic City
I seldom ever get beat!
It's fun to go to "THE CENTER"
There's Bingo, Poker, and Games
Or maybe you'll just sit and talk
And tell 'em about your fame!
It's nice to have a place to go
And look forward to the moment you enter.
A place to visit twice a week
A place called "THE CENTER"!!

    *William O. Purkins Jr.*

## Remember

I like to help you with your work
    Remember
I'm just a little boy
I may not always pay attention
    Remember
I'm just a little boy
I like the times you are at home
    If you remember
I'm just a little boy
I like to do the things you ask.
I try so much to please you
    Remember
I'm just a little boy
As little as I may be dad.
I really feel so sad.
A thank you job well done
Would make it not so bad
    Remember
Dad I'm still just a little boy
Remember, Dad were you ever just a little
boy

    *Louise Hodlin*

347

## The Hummingbird and the Eagle

The tiny hummingbird
Rested on the dainty twig
Contemplating
The eagle's effortless glide
"If that enormous creature
Can soar
Surely something's wrong with little me.
I flap my wings
So rapidly."

The majestic eagle
From his lofty crag
Looked down and saw
The wee hummingbird
Flit from flower to flower.
"Surely it isn't fair
To never taste of nectar sweet
O powerful me
I'll try to move my wings
More rapidly."

*Rhoda Leavitt*

## The Greatest Work Made

As collections of eons
Riddle the sky,
As the moon so vivid
In solitude high,

As the cool ocean whispers
And hushes the earth,
As the midnight remembers
In quiet rebirth,

As the world holds it's ages
Firm in her crown,
As envelopes liquid
Pour to the ground,

Indeed there is power
As wind on wings whine,
Majesty certain
A king's work divine,

Yet all of these pale
Their magic does fade,
As I stand enchanted
At the greatest work made.

*L. Barnett*

## Tie Game

Playing hockey in the street
rollerblades on my feet,
Carrying the puck with my stick
passed their defense with a trick,
Now their goalie all covered in sweat
I shot the puck right in the net,

Back at the face-off
the game is tied,
I won the face-off
their player cried,
The puck to my teammate, then to me
I shot, but missed completely

Time running out,
they cleared the zone
My defense hit it back in the zone.
Their team wanting to win
It didn't happen,
I tipped it in!

*Nick Fazio*

## Don't Say Good-Bye

Don't say good-bye to me, my love,
Say "Au revoir, aw wiedersehen"
Good-bye could be a long, long time
Or ne'er to meet my love again.

Good-bye's a word we will not speak
For to the aching heart, it reeks
Of loneliness, of emptiness
And means a road that's rough and steep.

Don't say "Good-bye" to me, sweetheart,
Keep faith triumphant as we part:
Your smile, your touch will gently start
A glow within my burdened heart.

Though far apart we well may be
From doubts our faith will keep us free
So wipe away the tears that flow
and smile for me as I must go.

And I will go remembering
The courage that your love did bring
And I will keep the vision sweet
Deep in my breast 'till again we meet.

*Mildred Karnopp*

## Untitled

Stories of plenty
saying no more

Dreams are true
but not for you

I loved you
but that's impossible

I love you
but that's a lie

I wish you loved me
okay

Just say good-bye

Life is wrong
but what is death?

To dream-
to think you've died

Just say good-bye
just say good-bye

*Paul Hankins*

## Thanksgiving

On this day, I remember
    scenes of childhood, carefree days;
azure skies that touched forever;
    rains that wept in mournful greys.
Every season leaves its mem'ries.
    Some are painful to recall.
Yet my autumn recollections
    are my favorite ones of all.
As successive summers ripen
    to the short November days
of thoughtful walks on leafy sidewalks,
    foggy dawns and evening haze,
more there is to be reflected
    from the seasons gone before,
and in gratitude, I offer thanks
    for my Creator's store
of these scenes, like consolations
    sent by those I see no more.

*Neil W. Nilsson*

## Michael

Fuzzy white-gold hair
    Scintillating light
Beneath, a watercolor face
    Shines bright.

Ten precocious fingers
    On discovery alight
And in luminescent eyes
    Curiosity ignite.

Whirligig in motion
    Bounding with delight
Radiating energy
    With sight.

Innocence of spirit
    Still unspoiled by blight
God keep him wholly pure
    And fill his heart with light.

*Laura Jenkins Boal*

## Sententious Silence

Silently she sends
    screaming messages.
Soft sweet sounds
    easily misunderstood.
Sane sententious silence,
    mutely masking internal turmoil.

Whispering soars
    to sonic dissonance;
External submissiveness
    succumbs...simmers, swells,
Shatters...her carefully guarded
    internal citadel.

Volcanic quaking quickens
    exploding synthetic silence.
Eroded stillness... penetrated!
    secret messages... exposed!
Silent, subtle, screams
    finally heard... and understood.

*Mary E. Archer*

## "Seasons Come And Seasons Go"

Like the blowing wind,
seasons come and seasons go.
The more you experience,
the more you grow.

Things never stay the same
as you go through the years.
You find a lot to smile about,
Yet you still find the tears.

When the rainy days occur,
you find a way to stay dry.
You can overcome your sorrows.
Don't just lay down and die.

You must put your trust in God.
He'll erase your feelings of doubt.
You must also believe in yourself.
You can work your problems out.

*Cody*

## Children Are Angels On Earth

Some say we don't really
see angels, but we do.
When you see a baby smile,
you'll see angels.
If you hear children laughing,
you'll hear angels.
  Anywhere you see a child no
matter what race, color, shape, or size,
you will see an angel.
    Behind the face of tears.
    Behind the door of fears.
    Behind the wall of pain.
    You can find angels.
In the eyes of a child you
will always find angels.

Children are angels on earth
**Lillie Tenney**

## Dumb As They Come!

Know-it-alls!
  See 'm
Talking a streak.

Why?
  Do they think that
  they can get away
  with,
    "NONSENSE!!!"

I believe in good, honest, truth!!!
If I don't know
  I ask. Why can't they?

Know-it-alls
  Dumb as they come!!!
**Robert J. DiGennaro**

## A New Day

Open wide thine eyes!
See the beauty of the morn,
The sparkling of the light,
The twinkling of the dew,
The whisper of the silence,
And the beauty of a dawning day.

Open wide thine eyes!
See the distance of the plains,
The far and wide expanse,
The thrill of morning sounds,
The songs of birds in flight,
And the glow of the rising sun.

Open wide thine eyes!
See the magnitude of distance,
The expanse of the far and wide,
The beauty of an early dawn,
A treasure beyond gold
To hold the wonders of a new day.
**Stella Gatewood-Wester**

## What I Feel

If my heart could speak,
You would know within a week.
What I don't and what I do,
And that I do love you.

Just as long as one and one is two,
I will always love you.
From the very depths of my heart,
Until death due us part.
**Gene Cunningham**

## Departures

Some part of me is always leaving
Seeking yet another fate
And though I may not really travel
Imagination is escape.

Each journey starts in inspiration
The need to find a point of view
And when each thought achieves fruition
Another journey starts anew.

This restless impulse keeps me moving
Toward destinations not defined
The leaving part keeps pressing forward
The stationary part's resigned

Knowing that my leaving nature
Fills some basic unmet need
To keep horizons ever changing
As summits reached and crossed recede.

These trips of pure imagination
Give the leaving part release
And calm the soul that's never settled
The heart that never finds its peace.
**William A. Polf**

## Untitled

The child whore walks the city street
selling her soul
to an aged pervert for some dough.
As he does it to her one more time,
she stifles her pain and tears
and lets him rip her open,
exposing her to another disease
and a hate.
And she pulls at his hair
and bites and tears his raw white flesh
to get out of her trap
and her life.
**Monica Clarke**

## Lotus Seeds

Unattached to outcomes
she comes out
of her very own
very private Darkness.
Into the light
with shadows in hand
he shirks the bondage of past,
ceasing to collect its clutter.
Unaccustomed to Present
she shakes
simpers and
quakes to her soul's depth
Depth surfaces
from the mire
it will require
knowing the Unknowable
and becoming unattached
to outcomes
We come out of our
private lightless places.
**G. B. Sandoval**

## Untitled

I love my Mom
she is so nice,
I cry when I look
into her eyes.
She is so kind,
and will not whine.
It seems like she's
standing on a tower for me.
Though I am bad,
I remember
that she loves me.
**Ryan Abbott**

## Angel

An angel came looking for me
She said you can be free
Free of your pain and strife
For you shall have a new life

Come with me to heaven above
And you will know God's love
God has sent me to you
This is what you must do

Just relax and come with me
And you shall be free
Of your pain and strife
For you shall have a new life

We are going to heaven above
You shall know God's love
He has sent me to you
This is what we must do

An angel came looking for me
She showed me how to be free
I am leaving all pain and strife
I am going to my new life
**L. J. Cardin**

## That Cat

That cat, that cat, that awful cat;
She sits and watches from the mat,
And conjures up her devious plan
To always keep the upper hand.

And when I go up the stairs
I look and search, no cat is there,
But suddenly to my despair
I end up flying down the stairs!

When she came into our home
I'd open the door and let her roam.
I thought she might disappear
and I would have no cat to fear.

But she would never from me stray
And at my feet she'd spend the day.
I knew that I would never be
From that cat, completely free.

When my days on earth are o'er
And I move on to the other shore,
In my casket I fear she'll hide
And meet me there on the other side.
**Martin M. Romine**

## Untitled

We are two Opposites
She talks...I'm quiet
I think...She forgets
My windows face South and West
Hers face North and East
Yet...We are Together
Together seeing in all Directions
Thinking then Forgetting...
Speaking in Silence
Together we are not Opposing...
We are Complete...

*Matthew L. Miller*

## Young Mother With Child

With economy of motion
she wings the child
into her lap,
licks her fingers,
wipes his cheek
and plants a kiss.

she doesn't seem to notice
that he looks into her eyes
as if they hold eternities
of space and time and traces
of love's central event.

he knows what his father knows:
here is the center of life,
the universe spins on this axis.
he reaches to touch her lips

and she pauses,
remarking to herself
that he has his father's eyes.

*Matthew Burns*

## Summer Sun

Summer sun
Shine on me.
Summer sun
means lots of fun.
Summer sun
stretches as far as the eye
can see.
Summer sun
please oh please
shine down on me.

*Michele Allen*

## Bright Evening Star

Bright Evening Star
Shine on my love
Make the countryside reflect
The peace of this moment

The shadows of the enemy
So quiet and serene
Makes my mind keep thinking
Of a heavenly scene

I picture God in His heaven
And Anne is nearby
So happy and content
Waiting for me to stop by

At the end of my journey
I will want to be
With God in His heaven
And Anne and me

*Lewis Latas*

## Christmas Star

Pretty star
Shining bright
In the deep
Indigo night

Through the storm
Through the strife
Lead us to
The source of life

Pretty star
Up above
Beacon of
Most perfect love

Whether near
Or afar
Steer us true
Oh pretty star

*Vickie L. Vanderhoof*

## Tears

Tears fall for everything
Showing happiness
Symbolizing sadness
Signifying need
Pouring out in love
Forming in anger
Tears sooth and scare
Tears present trust and hate
Soothing the need to show emotion
Scaring those who watch them fall
Shown to those you trust
She'd for those you hate
Tears are for everything and everyone

*Starla Richter*

## Untitled

We think of trees,
Silent friends strong and tall,
Branch and leaf in heaven-watch,
Reach up. Reach out.

Down deep and anchored roots,
Power spread in soil and rock.
Give strength. Give life.

Forests in our land and world,
Keep plain and slope in place.
Catch rain. Hold snow.

Fiber, food and refuge offered.
Animal life sustained anew.
Gifts rendered. Gifts renewed.

Nature's craft and splendid symmetry,
Break, soften harsh line and form.
Add contrast. Unite view.

Why think of trees?
He who created trees and us,
Speaks, seeks hand and mind,
"Plant trees. Tend trees."

*Michael L. Hanson*

## Untitled

I haven't seen you
since spring
and spring is almost again
and I may not see you then.

But since I met you
you have remained
and I'm at a loss as to
whether it's your choosing
or mine.

And now,
since you are away
why do you choose to stay?

*Robert Kellum*

## "Episode Of Long Ago"

Of all our episodes in life, there's
one I can't forget... It happened many
years ago but I never will Regret...
It probably was the best way for me to
move along... And though I had some
different thoughts, my life has been a
Song... I asked the Lord what I wondered
about - He gave me His answer but not
with a Shout... He soothed me with His
gentle tone and told me that I was not
my Own... He asked me to follow a Godly
Life - and then I would not have all
kinds of Strife... I'm thankful my eyes
were directed Above... Where my heart
understood and the Lord sent His Love.

*Joyce Winchell*

## Dusk

When you see the sun
set over the mountain.
It goes to a valley.
A valley of friendship, love,
and no evil. A valley called
dusk of pretty colors. Colors
of love, joy, and romance.
Never any wars.
People caring for each other.
That's the way our world
should be.

*Rae Caron*

## Cosmic Fantasy

As I lay awake late at night
My mind-eye adjust to the sight
Of the stars above so bright
Shining with all their might.

As little specks of light
Way up out of sight
Beautiful past delight
I wish with all my might.

That I could soar high
In a star ship so bright
On the cosmic winds tonight
To complete my fantasy so right.

*Shelly Kidder*

## Now That He Lives In Me

Before the Lord could enter in
I had to open the door.

All my sins are in the past
I'm not the same as before.

He changed my life, my attitude, my way of thinking as well
He saved my soul from burning in eternal hell.

I love the life I'm living, it's filled with hope and love
All of this made possible from only God above.

His bright light shines within me, everywhere I go
It never dims or darkens, there's always a special glow.

When I see people that I know and those I've never met
They seem to smile as if to say-your gleam I can't forget.

So when Jesus taps on the door of your heart
Remember, let him in
He will give you a brand new start
Where you can only win.

*Shirley L. Duffy*

## Untitled

I looked into her face and sensed the pain she was in,
I hated seeing her hurt, but I couldn't let her go,
I always knew I loved her, but never how much,
Not until I knew she wouldn't be here tomorrow.
She knew it was her time, and I knew she had to go,
And still I wasn't ready, I couldn't find a way to
say goodbye and then she slipped away,
I couldn't even say I love you,
Now she's gone and the fault is mine for never saying,
what I felt inside. If only I could have spoken up.

*S. Bruns*

## A New Residence

You can stop your weeping, I'm not in there anymore.
I have a new residence that I'm thankful for.
In this old house, my vision was always dense.
I can see now, for I have a new residence.

This old body, it was hindering my stride.
I wanted to get up, walk, and dance awhile.
I was held back. Just didn't make sense.
But that's okay, I have a new residence.

This was one move, I didn't need to pack one thing.
I left my eyeglasses, my walker, and all my financial means.
You see, my journey is spiritual. Am I making sense?
That's okay. I'm in my new residence.

I'm excited! I'm happy! I'm bursting with glee!
When it's time, you will come to be with me.
By now, I should be making sense.
Be happy for me in my new residence.

*Michele D. Burton*

## Graveyard on the Seacliffs

Standing on the seacliffs
Seacliffs with their little graveyard
Graveyard with its pretty headstones
Headstones lavishly decorated and engraved
But one stone stands out
It simply says "Baby"
Poor baby, only one day he lived
A gull cries, reminding me of my brother
A baby brother I never saw
The baby who lived only one day.

*Megan Leong*

## Daddy's Little Girl

From the day she was born
I have been committed, I have sworn
To be the best father I can
Yet still uphold myself as a man
The love for my daughter is the strength of my existence
My love could never be separated.
No matter how far of a distance
I thank God for blessing me
Sending me a beautiful girl, alive and healthy
The gateway to my soul is the key to my heart
When she entered my world, my life took a start
She's like a jewel, a precious pearl
To me, she will always be daddy's little girl.

*Santiago Torres*

## Great Grandmother

Laying in the grass so tall,
I have great memories I do recall,

My Great Grandmother used to tell stories of long ago,
Still some of them I do not know,

My Great Grandmother was so very busy,
But she always had time to tell me of her history,

With the look in her eyes telling me so,
Not to be afraid of letting go,

My Great Grandmother has gone to a richer place,
I can still remember all her love and grace.

So listen to an older person speak,
These will be memories you'll always keep,

*Nicole Hammerle*

## Oh Hypocrite

Oh church, who forever preaches modesty;
I have never seen you humble.
As you tower over man and sea;
You humble men the like's of me.
Your steeples tower top top all others
While you preach, preach, preach humility,
Equality and poverty.
Oh, you hypocrite, you're not to blame;
It's not the church, but man that's vain!

*Stephen A. Thames*

## Tides of Love

Lord,
I have opened to you the gates of my being,
and like a tide you have flowed into me.

The innocent recesses of my spirit are full
of you and all the channels of my soul are
grown sweet with your presence.

For you have brought me peace, the peace of
great tranquil waters and the quiet of the
summer sea.

Your hands are filled with peace as the noon
tide is filled with light.

Above your head is bound the eternal quiet of
the stars and in your heart dwells the calm
miracle of twilight.

I am utterly content - in all my being is no ripple
of unrest, for I have opened unto you the wide
gates of my being and like a tide you have flowed
into me.

*Monika Miranda*

## An Early Morning Visitor

Two in the morning, sometimes three;
I hear a small whimper now, who could that be?

Someone is hungry or possibly wet;
The longer I wait, the louder he'll get!

Eyes barely open, I walk down the hall;
Into his room to beckon his call.

Tummy is full, diaper is dry;
All seems just fine, why must he cry!

Looks at his mommy and gives a big grin;
Cute as a button with that double chin.

Pick up that baby and give a big hug;
Give him a kiss and hold him real snug.

Sing him a song and rock him to sleep;
Back to the crib but don't make a peep!

Tip-toe away, so softly I walk;
In only one hour it'll be five o'clock.

Five o'clock hits, the alarm chirps away;
Get myself up to start a new day.

*Marilyn Brittan (Tyler's Mommy)*

## The Gentle Remembrance

Back in the deep, dark recesses of the years
I hear the voices of yesterday;
My mind lies in the black cradle of yesterday;
The months of winter are recalled.

In a strange ancientness, a dark, shadowy, cramped time,
A coal-soft, a black-ashes memory wafts gently, but fearfully.

A child:  Back across the long years, spanning time,
Melancholy, uncapturable days;
A child:  A sweet, soft child, passing through days
Of grass and child's sunshine;
Remember, softly, the grayed, planky, uneven porch,
The grayed old house.

Sad is the gentle remembrance
Of those time-softened, time-grayed, time-melancholied
Days............................of me.

*Patricia A. Henderson*

## In Dreams

When I'm feeling down, or when I feel depressed,
I jump into my bed, in shoes and fully dressed,

There I travel the skies above or the oceans oh so low;
The sights, the sounds, the ventures; no one else could know.

I have touched a Pyramid, climbed a Sahara sand-dune.
My star ship has orbited Saturn, Jupiter, and Neptune.

I have walked amidst the stars, and those Easter Island stones.
Once, I dove for treasure, and uncovered a pirate's bones.

I have traveled throughout the past, in a magic time machine.
I have visited the future, where the alleys of L. A. were clean.

I shook hands with J.F.K., and I flew a kite with Ben,
General George surprised me, he was quite a friend.

Ol' T-Rex once chased me, and I barely escaped that deal,
I sat with a hairy cave-dude, while he tried to make a wheel.

I wrote a song for Elvis, stayed at Graceland as his guest.
I even cheered as Broadway Joe proved he was the best.

Through it all, I have enjoyed my dreams-every single one.
I wish I could sleep forever, for my dreaming is not done.

*Travis James Callaway*

## Hello Oklahoma

Hello world!  I'm born today,
I just don't know quite what to say!

Hello world!  Today I'm one,
Living is really, really fun!

Hello world!  Today I'm two,
I've heard this is a terrible year, did you?

Hello World!  Today I'm three,
Guess what?  They gave a party for me!

Goodbye World....I died today,
The bomb just sent me on my way.

But world!  God took me in His arms,
And from this day I'll see no harms.

Mommy and Daddy, please don't cry,
And please don't feel, "An Eye For An Eye."

I only hope as days go by,
The thought of me won't make you cry.

Try not to be mad or even cruel,
Try to live by the "Golden Rule."

Hello Parents!  I'm happy Today,
I just don't know quite what to say!

*Sandra L. Coker*

## Joyful Memories

I don't know why you was taken from here
I just know in my heart you will always be near
As long as the wind blows
As long as the sun shines
As long as the moon glows
I know that you are here
Your mission here has been completed
Because up above you probably was needed
As long as I breathe the breath of life
As long as memories of you appear in my mind
As long as your name comes across my mouth
I know that you are here
My father my dear I love you so
This poem I write so you would know
That no matter where your spirit goes
I know that you are here

*Michele Green*

## Untitled

I wonder how the son feels, the brother - the father or the nobody
I know how we feel - the siblings - the wife and child or the homeless
We grieve their absence - their death - their pain
      or their loss of need
The little boy dressed in green - carrying a killer's toy
homesick for mama - no ball in the backyard with Daddy
      no longer under sister's foot
The house is silent - candles are lit - one less plate at dinner
      an empty bed to make
no more boys things
that boy comes home a man
Mama's glad - daddy gets out the ball - sister looks eye to eye
this for the boy out there
his family loves him so
come home a man
whatever you become
to you the little soldier
come home as you can.

*Natalie S. Moore*

## Losing A Loved One

How painful it is to lose someone so dear,
I know in my heart she will
always be near.
A mother, a wife, an aunt, a dear friend,
Tell me dear Lord is this truly the end?
I remember her smile, her laugh,
and her tears; memories don't die;
they last through the years.
She suffered in silence; only God knew her pain the tears that she
shed were like soft falling rain.
I'll miss her sweet smile, her bright shining face; but I know in
my heart she's in a much better place.
He opened the gates and said;
"Come" - Welcome home - for now
and for always you'll not be alone.
So when I see a white cloud or a bird flying high,
my thoughts are of her and I look to the sky.
For loves everlasting, and I'm no longer sad, I remember the
good times and in my heart I feel glad.
Rest in eternal peace and love.

### *Rosemarie Zilz*

## Girl Who Burns

I wish I liked myself enough for suicide
I let myself live to let me burn, and hide
Covered in sticky lies
Thick with embarrassment of why I never killed you
I let myself live to burn inside
To hide in the dark and cry, to be crucified
Nail me to the cross above your headboard
I need to be used, I need to be abused
I live to kill myself inside
I wish I liked myself enough for suicide
I would look so beautiful lying there
All dressed up in white
The hole in my stomach would be filled with a caulking gun
Then I would not feel it churning for once
But I live to burn

### *Stacy Westfall*

## Used and Victorian

I heard the story of poppy seeds, the truth is how they grow in me.
I live with her everyday, I know her every way.
Living with her makes me sick.  I heard you say it won't forget.
Bland is the color of your eyes, the blackness of your innocent
surprise.
Your so ill, this makes yours mine and the beauty of your hologram
is looking through me.
He sighs in tea rose meadows, backs are bare, our minds are raw.
His poison flaws, the decaying sand sitting on Eves Rock - Eyes
of stone and revenge is his savior.
Elegance he does depend on, fighting for the highness-running
from his empress.
Prince of poppies send me to your world, his blond locks, I'm the
outsider in his royal box.
He's used and Victorian.
Ivory the color of his implanted seeds.
He pretends to rest in me.
In his world I am him.  In my world he is me.
The angels ignorance glaring at me.  The signs from hell coaxing me.
I see him as he is she. bleeding of the goddess laying by me.

### *Maria Eve Wise*

## Red Ribbon

I reach for the shadow of your fingertips,
I long to bask in your laughter.
What happened to the warm glow of candles,
And the whispers of forever after...

A gust and gone—the braid of us,
Lost in endless wishing wells.
Where was that unnamed hero,
Meant to save us from ourselves?

Passion's fire pulled down a path,
That now hears the footsteps of one.
And I am left with the echo of you—
A love that won't be undone.

### *Lauren Kunkler*

## Adulthood

A son will ask his father what's wrong with me?
I look at the trees and wish to cut them down.
I look at my friends and wonder how to use them for my own greed.
I want to take the land the animals share and pollute it.
When I am angered I wish to extinct a town.
I no longer have use for such weaknesses as love,
caring, understanding or sympathy.
I will be happy so long as I may condemn others
and walk away with no pity.
I beg you father answer, what is wrong with me?
The father laughed and said, you are becoming an adult.
You will look with prejudice and hate.
To save yourself you will give others fault.
You are growing up my son, it is a sad fate.

### *Michelle Martinez*

## Saying Goodbye

A million years of personhood are now between us
   I look forward, I look back; I see your face
I've been to the mountain; learned new truth
   I grab your hand to lead the way; you pull back
I am so different now; you are still the same

My pain is enormous; truth is revealed
   Our past is your present; your pain so real
Sadness engulfed me; I first realized
   There is no room for the new me in our old life

I feared of this moment for all the journey
   Moment of choice, live now or then
The dreams I now follow are forward in life
   The pain that I feel of what I can't change inside
I'll always love you and I choose to say goodbye.

### *Mary R. Ollech*

## My Mother

My mother is my pride and joy.
I love her more than any toy.
She loves me more than food and bread.
To God she always bows her head.
She always gives me hugs and love,
Learned from the Father up above.
I thank you God that she is mine.
I think she's great - I think she's fine.
I thank you Lord that she's my mother.
I'll never ask for any other.

### *Richard B. Hayner*

## You

I can't escape my feelings for you
I love you so much, what can I do?
You once said your love for me would always be true.
Now, I'm alone in the dark, feeling blue.
If you could only realize you are the only one for me,
We could share a life in holy matrimony.
The days grew cold like glaciers of ice,
All those words said just cut through my heart like a knife.
I can't escape my feelings for you,
Everyday that passes, I stop and think of you.
I was your true love, your best friend for life,
I only wanted to be your wife.
I can't escape my feelings for you.
I long for the day to hear you say, "I love you."
I just hope one day you'll appear
And let me share my life with you.

**Tina Nicole Course**

## Secrets of My Soul

Secrets I make known to none else
I make known to you, oh Lord
Because it is you, my King, that heals me
You have the powers and keys to life's cord

The enemy knows as well
How? I did not make them known to him
He uses my secrets against me
To bring me darkness and make my life grim

But to you now my soul belongs
Because you have paid for it with a price
You broke the bond that sin had on me
Defeating Satan, who gripped me like a vice

Father, allow me to be as Paul the Apostle
To be able to say that I fought a good fight
Running daily the race for that grand prize
A crown of glory and rest under your might

I am patiently waiting for you, dear Jesus
To forever be with you as my goal
So until your second coming, dear Lord
I will submit to you the secrets of my soul.

**Samuel Cordoba**

## A Vulnerable, Yet Valuable Treasure

I am the child you see before you,
I may look like any other you see, BUT I'M DIFFERENT.

I am frail, sad, bad, mad, hopeless.
I am angry, sullen, sulky, unhappy. AND I'M DIFFERENT.

I act secretive, seductive, beguiling.
I act older, aloof, lonely. YES, I'M DIFFERENT.

I try pretense, fabrication, thievery.
I try intrepidation, timidity, suppression. WHY AM I DIFFERENT?

I feel insignificant, unintelligent, insecure.
I feel violated, unloved, diminished. WHAT MAKES ME DIFFERENT?

I am, I act, I try, I feel,
Just like other children. CAN YOU SEE THAT I'M DIFFERENT?

I need your help. I need your guidance
But mostly, I need your compassion and understanding. HELP ME BE
UN-DIFFERENT!

I am the child of abuse.
I am physically, sexually, and emotionally abused.
I am neglected and abandoned.

I am the child you see before you.
I am yesterday and today.
WITH YOUR HELP, I CAN MAKE A DIFFERENCE IN TOMORROW!

**Rosemary Walls**

## Mom

Mom, you were so dear to me,
I miss you more each day.
I cannot understand just why
God came to take you away.
I guess He needed a beautiful rose
For a spot in His garden of love.
He looked at you and then He knew
You were needed in Heaven above.
But, Mom, I also needed you
You were my friend, my joy, my life!
I could always count on you
To help with problems, stress and strife.
Your prayers and Christ-like countenance
Always seemed to strengthen me.
I knew the loving Savior
Would watch over me tenderly.
So, as I think of you, dear Mom,
And remember your kind loving ways,
Through my tears, I remember those years
Spent with you: Oh, such happy days!

**Virginia C. Blaich**

## Letter To My Mother - Part I

From the first there was no love, there was only bickering and fear
I never knew just what it was but knew it wasn't there.
Small tragedies and large as well, we never talked about.
We hid our tears inside ourselves and never let them out.
Time touched us and it's passing soon left us miles apart.
We never spoke of love or loneliness, that linger in a heart
I woke one day and found myself beside your empty bed.
Trying hard to comprehend that somehow you were dead.
I tried to summon up my tears but found they all had dried
My heart was cold and empty for there was no love inside
Love does not grow naturally, it must be sown and tended
Feelings stomped and torn asunder must somehow, someway be mended.
But you are far away now, and far too late it seems.
For any mending to be done, though always you will haunt my dreams.

**Rebecca Broge**

## Good-Bye

I thank you for being my friend and my lover.
I now go on with my life knowing that
I have met and loved someone with whom
I will always be connected.
No matter how far apart we are
I will always remember in my heart
the oneness we have had.

You truly are the kindest, loving man
I'll ever know. At moments of loneliness,
I will think of you and smile and remember
the touches, the passion, the trust, the laughs
and the secrets I will take to my grave.

You accepted me for me and I thank you for that.
You let me be me and I thank you for that.
You shared your life and love with me and
I thank you for that.

I pray for your health and happiness
and wish for you the very best future.
Should we meet in another lifetime,
I will be yours.

**Regina Griffin**

## A Long Time Ago

*(Dedicated and written for the one and*
*only true love of my life, Linda Masters.)*
We fell in love a long time ago,
I once let you down, God only knows.
I constantly repeat that moment we
shared together a long time ago;
I know I made the biggest mistake
Only you and I really know.
If only it were possible to have that
time again,
I know with all my heart I
wouldn't falter as I did then,
    A long time ago.

**Raymond L. Frullo Jr.**

## The Dive

I climb the wet metal stairs, thirty feet into the sky.
I overtake the last step.
I cool zephyr of wind hits my wet back with a punch.
I step to the edge of the platform.
I'm wet.
I'm scared.
I take my last gasp of air.
I hoist up my heavy arms.
My coaches are scanning my every move.
I press through with my arms.
I launch off the platform.
I'm flipping.
I'm twisting.
One mistake, and the water turns to hard unforgiving asphalt.
I speed to terminal velocity.
The pool goes from petty to colossal.
I stretch out.
I flex my arms and legs.
I strike the water.
There is no pain.  The fear is gone.  And I can go home.

**Max Bookman**

## Reincarnation — No Way

I may be in an imperceptible reincarnation twilight phase:
I perceive the galactic Dark Holes in a visibly soft glaze.
The twilight at dusk returns at dawn to greet a new day,
and the immortal Soul sails to another Body in the same way.
I know that my inhabitants soul is destined for a sojourn,
and the Dark Holes flash:  There is no ultimate exit zone.
In this mortal world, Death is the custodian of Life,
and yet, is it not that Death too culminates in a Life?
I try to decor my life-lamp with fragrance of honor and glamour,
but forget:  The soul will bailout when I we'd be in a dust cover.
Let it have a placid sail from here to a sojourn:  Eternity,
only then it appreciates reincarnation to define its entity.
Look at the golden Daffodils:  How long will they be in a stay?
If asked, they whisper:  We go away, reincarnation - no way.
Let's look from a different angel:  Like the misty twilight,
the flowers bounce back to life, to Mother Nature's delight.
Call it reincarnation or life-recycle:  Does it really matter?
Their sojourn cycles of life and coming-back always spatter.
Please, let me recycle with the waves of life and death,
and dance with the diversity of creatures:  Soul-oriented.

**Pranab K. Sen**

## Despair

Despair is the rock on which I stand
sadness is mine, It's the only thing I own
Loneliness comes for me to hold
Everything now is getting cold
Soon there will be another rock
Then an island

**Patrick M. Borja**

## Could We

Alone, living in a crowded world,
I picture your face and wish you were near.
Surrounded, in a completely empty life,
The pain grows stronger with each passing year.
Dead, in a life that I'm forced to live,
Depression so powerful it encompasses my soul.
Alive, in a love that is now dead and gone,
Forced to play this all too painful role.
Together, in a seemingly empty world,
You would lean close to pull me near.
Alone, in a completely filled life,
You would comfort me and calm my fears.
Alive, in a life I'm loving to live,
Happiness so powerful it encompasses my soul.
Dead, to a life of depression and hate,
Loving every minute of this wonderful role.
If we could start over again.
Could we get back to the way it used to be.
Could we lose the miles that separate us,
And get back to the love between you and me.

**Stephanie Puckett**

## Prayer of Love

Now I lay me down to sleep,
I pray the Lord sends dreams of you and me.
But if I should die before I wake,
Remember I love you and in heaven I'll wait.

The love we feel is true and strong.
It is bigger than life,
Stronger than death,
And as pure as an angels song.

You make me feel powerful, like a king.
But my power lies in the feelings of joy you bring.
In your hands I am but a child,
You calm me and soothe me with your love true and wild.

Without a doubt, I love you, and you love me.
And with this love we don't need open eyes to see
That life can be wonderful once we're together
With that in mind things will only get better.

**Stephen M. Davis**

## A Plea From The Heart

    As we climb the ladder of love,
I pray to God high up above.

    That you will come back and to help guide the way,
And that I am sorry for what I might say.

    The things that have happened I didn't realize,
But my love for you is deeper than the sky's.

    I realize now I wasn't always there,
And sometimes I really wasn't too fair.

    I criticized you when you were looking out for me,
I must have been blind, I just couldn't see.

    I know I've been selfish ad I've made you blue,
But I pray our love will see this all through.

    I didn't mean to make you so miserable and make you so sad,
All I want is what we once had.

    I hate for what has happened in the long past,
But if you want to come back, we can make this all last.

    Can you forgive me, that's all I have to say,
I hope in your heart you can only find a way.

**Micheal Dwayne Erwin**

## Prayer Mysteriously Answered

A knock was heard no one is there
I quickly sent up a prayer
Knock of death is what I heard
But I was not disturbed...
Later still another knock
Like the first no one is there
As I sat rocking, a Robin came as if he was stalking...
He pecked my window three days in succession
As if He was calling me out of depression
Soon His message became clear
Death to the past for spring is here
Newness of life was the message made clear!
Rise and rejoice for the seasons of life,
   Was given to lift me from my strife
I rejoiced and gave thanks for the peace within
That only came when I trusted in him

### *Daughter of Sarah*

## Upon Finding A Black Abalone Shell

From its resting place in sand
I raised the shell, cupping my hand
Around its roughness.  Barnacles, long dead,
Raked my palms.  Small holes shed
Sand lingering in the shell
(Fine grains, caressing as they fell);
And the aurora gleam of smooth inner skin
Glowed, as though from a light within:
Fire of opal, muted by sheen
Of pearl.  This I held between
My palms.  Great beauty dares to bide
Within a rough and darkened hide.

### *Mary E. Kelly*

## How Much Is You

Explaining my need for freedom
I said walk beside me don't let me be led
Allow me choices, give me freedom
to call my soul, my own
allow me to try unknown wings
Yet, if I fail no dishonor bring
Knowing your love will cushion my fall
help me grow strong finding helping hands
words of encouragement filling my ears
no - you can't do it would I hear
knowing should I pass or fail
I'd still know the love of an unending well
that no matter how many buckets I draw
I need only seek you hear my call
allow me to thank you later it's true
when I am grown it's then I'll appreciate you
Your seeds of loving planted so well
as I pass to mine when I tell
a new generation begins anew
God alone knows How much is you

### *Nadine Smith Van Drunen*

## A Message from Grandma

G - Is for God who sent you our way.
R - Is for Rainbows each and everyday.
A - Is for Angels to watch you play.
N - Is for Nice things to come your way.
D - Is for all of your Dreams to come true.
M - Is for Memories to share with you.
A - Is for Always, I tell you true, Grandma will
   Always be there for you.
*Love Grandma, M.A.C.*

### *Mary Ann Cerio*

## Ghost

The sun came up early one morn
I saw a ghost I could have sworn
It was big and white and very see-through
It looked like an animal from a zoo
It scared the living-daylights out of me
I rubbed my eyes to make sure I could see
It went away in about a hour
At least that's what I thought until I took a shower
It came into the bathroom and started to sing
"I want to be King, I want to be king"
The ghost went away at last, at last
Hurrah, Hurrah it's now in my past
The moon came up late that night
And I tried to forget about the ghost with all my might

### *Nothan Schulman*

## Bleeding Heart

Walking by the woods on a moonless night
I saw a grisly, gory sight.
A bleeding heart, in dust it lay
And nay a whisper or word did say.
I stopped and knelt, prayer on my lips
Poor soul, no sobs, no muffles, no miffs.
From yonder heard a heartless scream
"Stranger beware this is no dream
For that bleeding heart is the devil's work
There are spirits around and death does lurk."
Looked closely, and I missed a beat
Spellbound a moment I jumped to my feet
For I heard a gentle, sobbing sound
Of God, of Man, of pain unbound.
I smiled a gentle, knowing smile
And looked out yonder beyond the mile.
Can they never quit, I seemed to say
To hunt poor souls in sad dismay?
A bleeding heart is God's design
It could happen to you, it could be mine.

### *Puneet Handa*

## Parted Souls

You and I were once friends.
I saw myself in your eyes, long before the crush of the tide.
My aching heart sought your own.  My blood rushed through your tender veins.
I loved you because you needed me.  I hungered for your smile.

We were shadows prancing in the moonlight, awaiting the gentle embrace of the day.
You and I sought to ride the changing winds hand in hand.
Together we could fly.  United we were free.
I captured your soul and nurtured your presence.

The tides have turned.   The thickened sky mocks the enslaved sun.
I cannot see me in your eyes anymore.  My light has escaped you.
You will not run away with me to our holy place.
So we cast our lines and they fall far from the rippling waves of each other.

I sit alone and listen to the echo of an ebbing tide to remember our voices, woven with grace, singing together.
You left me to begin your life.  But we were once friends.

### *Nakia Gray*

## You Say

You say reach out if you want to live.
I say reach in and continually give.
You say make the most of what you've got.
I say contentment should be sought.
You say commitments should not be made.
I say what foundation will then be laid?
You say I'm wrong in what I say?
I say you don't know unless you try my way.
You say take care of self, no one else will.
I say you'll not find peace or learn to be still
Wrapped up in self a small package you make,
You can't hide your heart for someday it will break
You say you like what you have now?  I say reach for love,
I'll show you how.  You say you've got it made where your are?
I say there's so much more beyond that star.
So look up to God he wants you to live, but his way is love
and his way is to give.  You say you don't want to change your way?
I say that's all right but hear what I say:
"SOON YOU WILL BE OLD WITH THE PASSING OF TIME,
PLEASE TELL ME THAT HERITAGE YOU'VE LEFT BEHIND?"

*Marion Windsor*

## The Church: 1994

Depression overtakes that which I fear.
   I see the church at noon, empty,
   Cathedral white in its majesty,
   Superbly unclouded by ruthless doubt

The vast expanse fails my Savior.

   A perfect unstained theatre of white,
   Yet only whiteness lives here;
   I search and my fiery eyes fill
   With the tears of long searching;
   I see with dead eyes the bright eaves
   Perched near the grooved ceiling
   Resembling a diamond- clean sea
   Undisturbed by humanity.

Tossed by a late autumn wind, I am freezing...

   Tears bear witness to these thoughts
   I may not speak in words-
   To rise above this congregation of pain
   Perching upon those solitary eaves
   Gliding away on the diamond- clean sea

And staying forever nearer to God.

*Mark Lockett*

## "Some Days I Cry"

Some times my heart is heavy and sad from the failures I feel in life.
I see the struggle in the lives of my sons, the hurt in the eyes of
my husband when he has given up hopes on a son.  Some days I cry.

I reach back to the memories of past life, the newness of love, the
excitement of the future, the wonder of a new life, the love, the
sharing, the teaching, the laughing and the crying.  For a moment
I wonder why it has to end.  Some days I cry.

The day is beautiful!  The sun shines bright, the water ripples softly
in the lake below the house, the trees stand tall, and you know,
that is the way the Lord wants his children to stand.  The day is
so good—I wonder why—This day I cry.  Not for myself I think,
but for those I love.  The far away look in the eyes of a son, a
husband, the knowing, even tho they are next to me they  are far away.

The not sharing, the trying to be a part of their life, to reach them,
to show them they are important.  The knowing as they turn from me
with the weight of their sadness showing in their eyes, I failed
I know that life can't always be easy, that the stumbling and
falling teaches one to get up and watch the road more closely,
then maybe tomorrow we only stumble, but, we must go on—-
Some days, I cry—-

*Laverne De Bruce*

## Untitled

In my vision this dark and lonely night
I see your eyes so very bright
I want to reach out, but know I can not -
Yet you're so very close; your breath, so hot
One dimension sets us apart
My life so forlorn; dark invading my heart
What can I do to ease this morbid pain?
How do I stitch my heart to stop its bloody rain?
There is no answer for me to find
Instead I'm destined always to wear this thorny bind
Time and time again you've slipped thru my fingertips
Never will I feel your touch; your warm and gentle kiss
The agony that I'm feeling has become my destined fate
For whatever reason, I was deceived — now my eyes see hate
The fiery ecstasy I once had dwindled to a mere spark
Never again will I feel passion - only pain and dark

*Shawna M. Dickerman*

## A Glimmer

When daylight ends and night begins;
   I sit and dream of a new day when;
the sun will shine and all will smile,
   As once again, we'll tread thru the miles.
And when I lay my head down, when
   Deep night has fell;
I close my eyes and say "Dear Lord",
   make sure all the family is well.
I look back thru the years that are past,
   The good times and the bad;
Some memories make me smile, some
make me laugh; but some make me so sad.
But that's the way life is, a battle
up and down the hill;
But by the grace of God, we'll make it,
   If it be his will.

*Shirley Salyer*

## Misery Chair

Yes I sit
I sit in that chair
Yes I sit in the misery chair
Thoughts going round and round in a rage
Yes I sit in the misery chair
Confined like I'm in a cage
I try to get up, or maybe try to leave
But I still sit in that chair
feeling so much pain you wouldn't believe
So I'll sit in that chair
Resting my fat behind
Yes it looks like it's gonna be me
And that misery chair until the end of time

*Vance Bonar*

## One Thousand Years

One thousand years before me stood,
One thousand men to fight a war.
One thousand swords, One thousand shields.
One thousand men stood on this field.
One thousand skulls lay on this ground.
One thousand dead.  Their blood was spilled.
One thousand years from this day,
One thousand men will stand in place.
One thousand guns, One thousand tanks.
One thousand dead.  Their blood will spill.
One thousand years, One thousand more.
It's all the same, It's all a war.

*Amy Burgoon*

## Freeways Towns and Motels

I'm a traveling man, not much of a life
I started it when I lost my wife.

I jumped in this truck and started it up
I could see it wasn't hard to tell
That it wouldn't take long, for me to belong
To these freeways, towns and motels.

Freeways, towns and motels, has become a way of life for me
Traveling from town to town, escaping all the memories.

Tomorrow I'll make Savannah, and see an old friend for a spell
Then on to Atlanta, down through Alabama
more Freeways, towns and motels.

Enjoying each new day, and happy I'm doing well
Wondering how long I'll call my home, these freeways, towns and
motels

Freeways, towns and motels has become a way of life for me
Traveling from town to town, escaping all the memories.

I bumped into her at a small cafe, traveling through Atlanta today
Her pretty smile and baby blue eyes, just swept my heart away.

It didn't take long, for me to fall in love, with that precious
    southern belle
And I knew then, that was my end, to these freeways, towns and motels

Yes, she was my end, to those freeways, towns and motels.

*Leslie Hayes*

## Anticipation

Though miles are between us
I still recall days of old, while
walking on white sand and watching day unfold
    The castles that we built, the
waves that knocked us down, the
laughter that we shared while the
sun was going down
    My memories see me through
the days that go on by, until
I am with you again, underneath
the great blue sky.

*Marlene Logue*

## Ode to Patti

In the Light of dawn with pen in hand,
I take on the impossible task of letting the world know what you
meant to me. My mother, my mentor, my friend.

For some reason, I will never know or understand,
you wanted to die alone.
What a heavy burden that must have been.
A dark and haunting specter waiting in the wings.
When all was said and done, you slowly crept away in the dark of
night. Ashes scattered to the wind.

A warm smile, a whirlwind of energy, a petite palette of pastels,
a wonderful sense of humor, a caring shoulder, an encouraging hug or
    word.
A few of your trademarks, now existing only in my memory.

Thank you for teaching me to hold on to my dreams and reach for the
sky; how to pick myself up, dust off my knees and go on with a hopeful
sigh. The courage to dare and take a chance on life.

I've taken time to cry and now it's time to say good bye.
Although I wish I could tell you all of this face to face,
I hope you hear these words whispered on the wind and floating on
    the clouds.

*V. M. Jordan-Hoffman*

## Still to Come

There is a song that is waiting to be sung
I think, I believe, as a matter of fact, I
know this will be the one

A melody is in bloom, I will hear it soon
There are words, voices will be heard

We sing a tune, beat a drum, blow a horn and play the harp
Is my song within the key of sharp?
In the scales of time on a higher rung?

*Stephanie Govan*

## Father

If someone were to ask me what a father ought to be,
I think I would compare him to the mighty old oak tree.
His bark is old and weathered from withstanding years of rain
just like a fathers dear old face, from years of stress and strain.
The oak will stand forever, his roots clinging deep within
the earth, just like a father stands by his child from
the moment of his birth.
His branches reach up tall, aiming for the sky, and little
birds nest securely there when they're too weary to fly.
The oak tree has been around since the world began,
just like a fathers great stature, forever his devotion will stand.
So fathers always remember though your job as a father may
diminish, and your hair may turn to gray, and just like the
oak, your power may fade, always give your child love and
security, and forever more you'll be compared to the mighty
old oak tree.

*Sherry Ohly*

## My Christmas Card

As I write my Christmas cards this year
I think of the Holy one, so dear.
How He came to earth that glorious night
and all around, what a wonderful sight.
As shepherds came, and wise men three,
bearing gifts for him, on bended knee.
To give thanks, to the Lord above
for showing us all, His great love.
For allowing the Holy Child, pure and sweet
to come to earth, to offer peace.
To all of us, who live on earth
who worship now, the Christ Child's birth.

*Marian B. Martin*

## Ode To Love

When the tree gives up it leaves and I see them tumbling down,
I think of you and then I think that I am like that leaf..a clown
That stumbles through the barren ground of nothingness
To come to rest alone and worm upon my world of emptiness.

And as the leaf flutters now and then, so too do I attempt to
struggle
As I lift my weary head to the light and try to juggle,
All that life has given me to do; now without your love to keep me
    strong
I flounder in the wind blowing this way then that, but not for long.

For awhile I'm carried down a river, a gleaming stream,
Past the towns, cities and ports of call but one can only dream
Of tempting treasures and wild adventures that were waiting there,
For now I wander without thought, without will, without care.

Will this river take me through its watery way of life.
Leading me to the ends of the earth in spite of all the strife?
Or will it suddenly turn about and drown me with the tide
As the leaf beginning to falter along its lonesome ride?

*Marilyn H. Waite*

## Untitled

An old man asked me what I was looking for,
I told him a dime and maybe a little love
He said that most want more, for me there's
a beginning and from there I'll look above.
He asked if I was cold and I really couldn't lie,
my skin was pale and my body shook, he told me
all you can do is wish you weren't here, all you
are is a chapter in someone's dusty book.
I asked him for a drink of water but all he
had was whiskey, he said that we all need some
crucifix to chase away the evils, as I swallowed
I felt the burn and thought of better times,
I heard him whisper that we can't dwell on earlier crimes.
   He said you're still young, don't close your eyes yet'
   you look strong, your dreams are too new to forget
He stepped away and I was left with my thoughts,
it was cold and time to go home.
I remember thinking how nice it would be
to feel a warm touch, then the wind bit
cold as my feet hit the stone.
   *Shane Hanson*

## I Did The Best I Could

Dear Son:
I tried my son the best I could without no knowledge on how I
should, the book of knowledge of how its done, I searched all
night 'til it was dawn.

Your tender smile and loving heart you always had this from the
start, I had no knowledge from my past, there was no one their
that I could ask.

I did the best I could

When your grown and become a man I hope in time you'll understand,
I learned to love and care for you, by watching all the love in you.

You'll have a son and tell him this, I'm glad your grampa got his
wish, to my son with all my heart, I pray to God we never part.

I did the best I could

   Love Daddy
   *Ralph Sarabia*

## I Write About Love

Honey when I reached out for you, you ever not there
I tried to sleep to clean my fears.  Then I began to
beaming I saw you there, reaching out you disappeared
I was so tired and weak searching for comfort
True love is so hard to find, so I write about us.

Can you imagine how I feel, like that hungry for
up on that hill reaching out for those grapes he love
to eat, his desires to have a treat, in despair when
he could not reached.  So he complain they were not
sweet.  True love is so hard to find so I write about us.

Honey I've nothing to complain about, you are natural
Sugar sweet.  The sweetest I happened to meet, so why
should I go complain on what I can't leave.  If he were
Like me he would go write  about love, and know complain
At all true love is so hard to find so go write about love

You should have seen me with the pen between my
Thumb holding it so tightly crushing it in the palm.
Of my hands, like I was holding you.  Has my hands
began to shaking, my heart began to racing so
Naturally.  True love is so hard to find so I write about us.
   *Veronica Bogle*

## Marionettes

Have you seen a puppet dancing being moved by several strings -
I used to think that being "saved" meant acting like these things.

I thought that God, the puppeteer, must move the strings just so
That no matter what you wished to do or where you cared to go,

Well, He already had it planned, your life and where it led,
And you could choose the path to take, but when all was done and said

All the choices you could make were subject to command,
For every puppet must obey the Puppet Master's hand.

And seeing how I felt this way, I guess you wonder why
I still decided, just the same, to give this life a try.

You see, I found when on my own and "with no strings attached,"
The dreams I dreamed, the plans I made, the ideas that I hatched

Still never seemed to turn out quite the way I thought they would,
And, well, no matter how I tried, I just could not be good.

It seems I got my wires all crossed, I couldn't stand upright.
So all I did when by myself was tie myself up tight!

It took the Master's expert hand to turn my life about,
To straighten all the crooked strands and get the tangles out.

And so, my fellow marionettes, let Jesus pull the strings,
For He's untwisted many souls and given wood hearts wings!
   *Patrice E. Porter*

## You!!

Sitting alone in the darkness,
I wait for you!
Wasting away in my own private Hell,
I dream about you!
Dying inside more and more each day,
I long for you!
Screaming out your name in the middle of the night,
I call to you!
Crying until the pain subsides,
I need you!

Everything I ever want and need is from you.
Everything I do or think is for you, you are a part of me and
I am a part of You!!
   *Stefanie Summer Atkinson*

## Games of Pain

I want to hate
I want to crush all those who hurt me so.

But I think "no."
I think perhaps
they're hurting worse than me.

I rationalize
A demon guide has led them through their lives;
They, whose words are brimstone's fire
And swords which cut me down.

What gargoyle
What stoney beast
Has taught them games of pain
To play so well
'Gainst gentle me
whose chance to win is nil.
   *Rebecca Williams*

## Set Free

Nightmare's dreams fantasize.
I want to see in a man's eyes,
so I know when they're lying, cheating or stealing
or when they have no meaning of love in them
that makes them so different.
They show no guilt or shame
because they always have us to blame.
Why do they play us like toys
and then throw us away as if we have broken.
We have broken our hearts that hide us away
to never be set free in a fantasy,
that shows no love because it all floats away
above where it all can disappear and never be reappeared
and that men can't throw our love again
like warriors and a spear.

*Rachel Johns*

## I Let You Go

Sadly, Deeply,
I want to take you in my arms,
Wrap you up like one of the dolls you bought me over the years.

I want to care for you as you did for me,
To feed you, to bathe you, to put you to bed.

All these things and more have been stolen
    from me by a disease that's entered your brain,
It's made you a stranger, a loner, Why you? Why me? Why did
    our lives take this turn?

Have I said all I've wanted? Have I thanked you enough?
Do you know how much I love you? How I want you to always be
there?

Yet they tell me my home is not the place for you,
You need care, you need machines, so I must let you go.

To take you away is to tear out my heart,
Dad, how I love you, but they say we must part.

I'll still be there, I'll always be there,
But now is the time I've dreaded, to place you in another's care.

With a kiss and a prayer I release my control,
Be kind, be gentle, he's my Dad you know,
    with a big part of me in his soul.

*Rita Palumbo*

## Before You

Before you came along,
I was only half a person,
an unfinished puzzle.
Then, you came and became the missing piece.
At last I was whole, vital, alive, and in love.
And then you left and a part of me went with you.
I died inside, once again.
Now, too late, I realize that you never really fit anyway.
I just shoved you in for something to fill the gap.
The missing piece was within me;
it just took someone like you
to help me find it.
I hate you for causing me pain.
I love you for helping me
to grow up and find myself,
and though it still hurts
I thank you!

*Lisa A. Hanebrink*

## "Broken Dreams"

Sitting in my newly painted rocking chair facing the window
I watch leaves waltz to the ground.

My heart is scattered amongst the red gold leaves lying on
the new frost.

Caressing the brown teddybear sitting lonely on the shelf,
I clutch to broken promises and lost dreams.

The emptiness inside of me wells up like a raging storm and
finally sobs erupt, I can't stop.

Looking back, the calendar on the wall marked with x's,
waiting for the day when you'd be born

Jumping at every phone call, shopping and anticipating your
arrival like expectant parents.

Our happiness is stopped by the lies and schemes of a
Madonna with child who stole our hearts and robbed our soul.

Looking out of the window now covered with new snow, I
tenderly clutch a teddybear and sob for broken dreams.

*Shari Milke*

## may i call you John?

on your way home
i watched from where the lights are red

about how long ago did you last walk straight
to your own home
crooked from the knee up
the left one not right
something happened

on your way home

what is it like to walk straight
on Shadford Road
scattered rocks all about
trailing ahead of you; in timeless motion
—were they not here before

greeting the air with tentative eyes and still lips
is it the wind of Blake that lessens the weight of your sparse hair
you've yet to turn around and see me
the dreary dirt is not the only concerned about your wanderings
heels that never heal, but do walk on

my own home on an unpaved road
i'd still like to know

*Quoc-Bao Do*

## The Call of the Six Million

Fifty years passed. The world keeps spinning on its axis.
I will never visit Auschwitz or Bergen Belsen
Or any other of the cursed sites.
I will not walk on my peoples grave: The blood is still wet!
I sense pain and despair in the air....
The people of the land still remember
Not with regrets but with the melancholy
Of unfulfilled expectations!
Because playing God was exhilarating!
I will not shake the hands that held the ax
Nor will I stay under God's sky with them.
In some mysterious way
I hear the call of my lost brothers,
All six million of them!
Crying for dreams lost in the dust for nothing!
In hopeless despair, I cannot find in my heart
The grandeur of forgiveness!
All I can do is remember and honor the martyrs
Who went to sleep in the gas chambers, who never awoke
And whose eternal monument will be the chimney's smoke!

*Luba Ziegler*

## The Dream

There is a man in my dream I can see and touch,
I wish he were real, I love him so much.

We were together with the same happy feeling,
that when we were near, our hearts were beating.

Then he looked at me and gave me a kiss,
that was something I just could not miss.

When our lips were together, it was the Fourth of July,
and all the rockets and stars were up in the sky.

Then he asked me to marry him and be his wife,
I said "yes" for the rest of my life.

All of a sudden I woke from my sleep,
I thought he was mine, mine to keep.

*Vicky Carey*

## When I Look At You

Sometimes when I look at you
  I wish you were a little boy of three,
Because at that tender young age
  You trustingly relied upon me.

Sometimes when I look at you
  And see you as you now are,
I stand back, filled with pride,
  To admire you from afar.

Sometimes when I look at you
  Growing up to be such a man,
I'd like to reach out and stop time
  That is fleeting by as fast as it can.

Sometimes when I look at you
  My heart fills with such great love,
For the seventeen years I've seen you grow
  I thank the good Lord above.

To see you happy, to see you blessed,
  Will make me feel grateful, too,
What else could I ever ask for
  Sometimes when I look at you?

*Venita J. Bahun*

## Jay

It's been a year since we last spoke
I wish you were here to laugh and joke

Although we were living two separate lives
the pain of your death cut through me like knives

At first I thought it was worse for me
then I saw your family

They stayed with you 'til the end
I wish I had been as good a friend

What a shame you and me
we could've raised a family

Thoughts of you are with me still
I close my eyes to ease the chill

I can't help but cry when I think of you and me
I'll leave it at this I loved you Johnny

*Ruth Boudreau*

## A Place To Go

As I thought I closed my eyes for the very last time
I woke, looking down on the body that was once mine
I could not describe the feeling I had but it was so strong
In a way it had been too powerful for something was wrong
Inside I felt completely immaculate and this felt strange
Outside I felt as if something was wrong; something had changed
I saw a bright and gleaming light and it called out my name
I felt as if it would release me of all my sorrows and pain
But then I heard my family telling me to come back to them
I promised them soon but could not tell them when
I struggled to return to them but the light was so warm
So I tried to fight it, but could not and they began to mourn
I stepped into the light and the glory of love was there
I had a beautiful feeling that for me it would always care
I looked down again and saw them mourning my new life
I tried to console them that my new life here was nice
Now I know my loved ones will pass on to a beautiful place
And I will be waiting for them with love showing on my face
They have nothing to worry about I wish they could know
I wish I could tell them that they'll always have a place to go.

*Marie-Catheline Jean-Francois*

## Bad Dreams

I was scared last night for no reason at all.
I woke up and darkness enveloped me.
Maybe I had a bad dream,
but I really can't remember.
Then I hear some crying and a door opens,
so I call out to my mother.
No one hears but that's okay.
I feel a little bit safer now.
I'm sure it was just a bad dream.
Falling back to sleep again,
I wake up in the early sun,
when I realized what I'd done.
I remember now that my mother has been dead a few years,
so why did I call out to her?
Yes they were just bad dreams or maybe nightmares.

*Serena Porter*

## My Father

Like a sage he imparts advice through stories of years past,
I wonder how many times I've listened to the days of his youth,
the places of his life, his disappointments and angry musings.

I appear interested and engaged, as if the this were the first telling,
he repeats with emphasis knowing all well that these stories are
markers and milestone of times past.

I laugh silently as he enters the grocery store-
his maroon trousers, checkered sweater and paisley shirt are
the suit of a man governed by no conventions.

Later I notice his pajamas under his pants and admire his freedom to
be...

In time the stories resume about his parentage,
I am surprised to learn new connections to the past and
questions him further-
this awakens him as he opens wider, doors of the past that
have been closed for many years.

Our shopping completed he urges me to eat again,
never able to tell me that he loved me,
I know the food is an offering for words that can not be spoken.

Not hungry I sit and eat as he begins one more
repeated tale of years past.

*Mark Villanti*

## I Am

I am like a ray of color in the rainbow of hope.
I wonder if there is such a thing as destiny.
I hear nature's warnings of destruction.
I see the world mutate before my eyes.
I want the fullest out of life.

I am like a ray of color in the rainbow of hope.
I pretend, yet I can not hide.
I feel mother earth changing the seasons around me.
I touch the soft petals on a spring time rose.
I worry that the ones I love will die before I am ready to let go.
I cry for the loved ones that are lost.

I am like a ray of color in the rainbow of hope.
I understand that to love is to care.
I say the words of my mother in utter surprise.
I dream of a world filled with clean, crisp, fruitful joy.
I try my best at all that I do.
I hope that my goals will be achieved.
I am a ray of color in the rainbow of hope.

> *Cameron Bergheer*

## The Brave Soldier

I would climb the highest mountain to reach you
    I would journey across the desert sand without shoes
        I would dive to the greatest depths to save you
            for you my whole life I would lose

I will pick you up when you fall down
    and bring you warmth when you are cold
        I will feed and sustain your hungry body
            and give you solace as you grow old

I will accept any hardship or deprivation
    I will respond to your every call
        As your loyal servant and obedient follower
            upon my knees for you I would crawl

With a shield of armor I will guard and defend you
    I will spare you at any cost
        I will shelter, preserve and secure you
            and rescue you when you are lost

Like a brave soldier in pursuit of the enemy
    I will bridge the widest ravine
        In an instant I would lay down and die for you.
            As did a man they called The Galilean

> *Peter Mastropolo*

## A Fool Like Me

What is a fool?
If a fool is me,
than a fool is who I'll be.
If I am a fool for believing in my dreams,
then call me a fool by all means.
If I am a fool for praying for the safety of others
after I slip under the covers, than a fool I'll be.
If I am a fool happy to make someone smile
If it makes a fool without denial.
If it's the cruelty of the world that gets a fool down
and makes him wish he could turn it around,
then a fool I'll always be.
Wouldn't it be nice if everyone was a fool like me?

> *Rich Maling*

## The Actor's Prayer

Let me earn your admiration with but a few words of despair.
If escape from boredom you desire,
I can take you there.

Let me dazzle you with diamonds of wit and eloquence.
Let the poetry I wield
Leave you quite without defense.

I can make you shake with laughter, and brim with happiness,
Then I'll introduce into your soul
The horror of suspense.

Let me show you joy and love, as the words roll from my tongue.
Then I'll drag your fears into the light,
To share with everyone.

I shall hear your heart rejoice in this magic that is real,
As I dance you into brand new worlds
And make you laugh, and sing, and feel.

Thoughts of things I've said
will make the tears roll down your cheeks.

'And please, God, if I'm lucky,
This show will run at least two weeks!
Amen.

> *Paula Stewart*

## The Caged Bird Sings

They say the caged bird sings because he feels he must,
If he could not express himself, his world would turn to dust.
So I must take the words I know and form from them a poem,
To tell of life's experiences or thoughts of friends and home.

But looking back across the years or at my life and world today.
I find I owe a great debt that I never can repay.
For when I write my thoughts and my feelings about life,
I take from those around me like the farmer and his wife.

The clerk down at the general store or the ladies sorting mail,
The men who build the nation's roads or the policeman down at
    the jail.
I write about their wants and needs and those which are my own,
I try to express the feelings that are not just mine alone.

So if you read a poem of mine, that's just what you want to say.
Just remember, I thank my God that He sent your thoughts my way.

> *Telva D. Bolkcom*

## Storms

Flowers wither and flowers die.
If tear drops don't fall from the sky.
People come and people go.
Some you will never get to know.
He left us on a Monday.
I knew he'd leave someday.
Why so soon.
I can always feel his presence the early noon.
So soon....
His life he took into his own hands.
Away it went with the blowing sands.
Why? Why? Why?
He was such a regular guy.
Such pain I was unable to endure.
But there was no cure.
He was so unsure.
Well, now he's gone.
Faster than a leap of a fawn.
Sadness we feel.
God made such a steal.

> *Leigh Snyder*

## Dreams

Dreams everyone has them
If we don't have dreams then where would we be
Dreams are tomorrow's future.

When I was little I had this dream
I would be a teacher
To lead children to their future.

Dreams everyone has them
If we don't have dreams then where would we be
Dreams are tomorrow's future.

When I got a little older I had this dream
I would be a T.V. star
So when people see me they would have some fun.

Dreams everyone has them
If we don't have dreams then where would we be
Dreams are tomorrow's future.

Now I dream that I will be an Olympic Swimmer
So I can represent my country with pride.

Dreams everyone has them
If we don't have dreams then where would we be
Dreams are tomorrow's future.

*Lauren Stephenson*


## Maybe

Maybe if I run fast enough, try hard enough,
I'll be somewhere else.
Maybe my dreams won't slip through my fingers,
Maybe happiness won't pass me by.
Maybe if I cry enough tears,
An ocean will form to carry me away from all
    of this heartache and pain.
Maybe if I wish on enough stars,
The sun will rise for me in a different dimension -
A universe separate from the one which currently
    imprisons me within its cold bars.
Maybe I won't have to do great,
Maybe I can just do well.
Maybe I won't have to pretend,
Maybe I can just be me.
Maybe there will be no more sleepless nights,
Maybe I can finally find rest.
And maybe if I run fast enough, try hard enough,
I'll be somewhere else.
Maybe.

*Shelbee Jarol*


## Jonathan

Dear Child, you don't know me now but someday you'll see my face.
    I'll live forever in your heart and never leave without a trace.

Sweet Child, I may not be by your side to touch and to kiss,
    I will remain in your mind constantly, and nothing of me you'll
    miss.

Pure child, you don't understand where I stand now,
    But what you need to know about me, only time will allow.

Innocent Child, my first son Jonathan, before my eyes you stand alone.
    For you I'll give all I have because you're everything I own.

Gentle Child, life is worth living when I know I can dream of you,
    And I dream, because someday my dream of being with you will come
    true.

*Norma Perez*


## For One More Day

The hardest thing I'll ever do will be telling you goodbye.
I'll put a smile upon my face.  I'll not let you see me cry.
I'll send you off, and know you're gone.
Oh sure, I know that you'll come home,
but it'll be different next time.
You'll never again be completely mine.
I'll kiss your cheek, and touch your hand.
I'll try my hardest to understand
why it must end this way.
Why you can't always stay
beside me - where I want you most.
You'll travel the world from coast to coast.
You'll learn ways I've never known.
Maybe someday, you'll travel back home.
You've joined the military, my son - you're a man.
So I'll let you go, and if I can,
I'll hold the tears as you walk away;
and wish you were my little boy - for one more day.

*Marilyn K. Combs*


## Maya......

Maya, Maya,
Illusion, veils. . .
Worlds manifested in mi-nute details.
Trees that wither.
Rivers that dry.
Mountain and man, that crumble, but why?
Where is reality?
In what domain?
Where is Eternity?
Who can explain? . . .
To find in this universe
The ETERNAL LIGHT. . .
To overcome evolution's blinded sight.
To awaken the inconscient, to its rightful bliss
Is to taste with joy,
The Divine's kiss. . .

*Rose Kupperman*


## Ode to Elisabeth

Oh beautiful baby with brown sugar eyes
I'm completely captivated and mesmerized!
Is it possible - can it truly be
That you, precious child, belong to me?

Oh beautiful baby you're nestled so new
Against my breast and when I look at you
I see a miracle - joyous gift to behold
And the love I feel can't with words be told!

Oh beautiful daughter, God's blessing of Spring,
Fragile and small - you're the song angels sing!
You've a soft rosebud mouth breathing sweet baby's breath —
Welcome to my heart, and my life, Elisabeth!

*Susan Lord Shaffer*


## The Apple

I new you could do it.
If only you would try.
For you are the apple of any one eye.
You are so full of life your never shy.
So always remember when things get ruff.
An apple a day makes any one tuff.
So be sure to keep that beautiful smile
and when you are blue once in a while.
Remember that apple a day you can be
to every one around you especially to me.

*Mary Brackin*

## I'm Fine

There's nothing whatever the matter with me,
I'm just as healthy as I can be.
I have arthritis in both my knees
And when I talk I speak with a wheeze,
But I'm awfully well for the shape I'm in.

I think my liver is out of whack
And I have a terrible pain in my back.
My hearing is poor and my eyes are dim,
Most everything seems out of trim.
But all things considered "I'm feeling fine."

Arch supports I have for both feet
Or I wouldn't be able to walk down the street.
My fingers are ugly - stiff in the joints,
My nail are impossible to keep in points.
But I'm awfully well for the shape I'm in.

Now the moral is, as this tale I unfold,
That for you and me who are growing old,
It's better to say "I'm Fine," with a grin
Than to tell everyone of the shape I'm in.

*Linda C. DiSalvo*

## My Special Place

Leaves dance, shadows sway.
I'm safe here, no one can take me away.

Waves crash, water roars.
I'm safe here, away from you, forever more.

Sun goes down, all is well.
I'm safe here, out of your hell.

Gulls cry, sea creatures swim.
I'm safe here, escaping to oblivion.

Salt water sprays, mist on my face.
I'm safe here, no longer out of place.

Huddled tight, figure in a ball.
I'm safe here, enclosed in my wall.

Night comes, all is dark.
I'm safe here, forgetting the marks.

Foam flows, water is cool.
I'm safe here, I don't play the fool.
Night is quiet, here I hide.
I'm safe here, in my own mind.

*Luzett Martinez*

## Wild Sanctuary

Across the sea of trees, happily the evening,
In a flood of cleansing light,
Announces with solemn shadow
the coming of the night.

Opposing silence of the washed out sky
Furious rapids, like dogmatic thunder, roar,
Submerging thoughts of how it could be
To flow so effortlessly free.

A breeze like summer spirit blows
Down from the glacier, down from the snow,
To waken to things worth knowing,
Things to feel yet never know.

Lost in our valleys and our forests.
Lost in silent, moving thoughts we hike
The untrespassed sanctuary of the wilderness.

*M. P. Collins*

## Crack Cocaine

Do you know me? I'm on America's most wanted list.
I'm wanted by housewives, teenagers, doctors, lawyers and
   psychologists.
I'm known all over for causing misery and pain,
Yet people still hunt for me. My name? Crack-Cocaine!

I can make a woman sell herself and a rich man sell all of his stock
Just for a chance to smoke one of my offsprings called "Little-rock".

I'm so powerful and taste so good,
I can destroy an entire family and bring down an entire neighborhood.
Please believe all that you hear about me, believe all of the hype.
I can make people sell their very souls to the devil for a rock and
   a pipe.

I can take your dignity and make you lose all track of time,
Leave you in the gutters of life and take your very mind.
I stand far above any others that you've read about in books.
After spending one night with me, you're automatically hooked.

I'm not prejudice, I cross all racial and economic lines,
Black, white, rich, or poor, I'll take you in and control your life
   and mind.
After I'm through with you and there's nothing more to crave,
What else is left? Jail, bankruptcy or the grave?

So next time you're out and feel like scrambling your brain,
You can find me in any community, ask for me! My name?
   "Crack-Cocaine.

*Patsy A. Williams*

## Images

I see images day and night,
images that often give me fright.
These images are often in my mind,
always strange and very unkind.

These images distract me when I'm
   sitting alone.
Half of them will chuckle, the other half
   will groan.

Some of them are dark and always
   faded out.
Other's are clear as day and stand
   right out.

They stand there starring,
and they never look away.
But, then they disappear,
as I reach for them and say.

"I know this is my mind,
just pulling another stunt.
But, who are you, and
what do you want?"

*Steven D. L. Hardin*

## Hurt By Love

I lay me down to sleep I pray the Lord my soul to keep.
My body is tired, my soul is weak, for love has hurt me deep.
Again in love happy as can be me, and my true love for all eternity,
until one night when I came home, only to find him not alone,
as one he was, but not with me, there in the open for my eyes to see,
as I turn to say good-bye I wipe a tear from my eye.
Once again hurt by love, if not for bad luck I would have none,
For weeks I cried, many nights I did not sleep,
Could someone please tell me how could love hurt so deep?

*Mavis M. Jones*

## Andy

You were the light of my life
in a world filled with darkness.

I watched you struggle to live from birth.
I saw you smile, when others would have cried.
I saw you care, when those around you didn't.

And I will never, never forget you.

I saw you get up from death's door so many times.

I saw you stumble, but never give up.
I saw you love, when others hated.
I saw you triumph, and fall again.

Well, Son, you are face to face with your Heavenly Father now
and I am glad and happy that you are home.

There will be no more suffering
for my beloved Son.

There will be nor more tears for you, my Angel.
Only happiness and joy forevermore.

Please know that I am the most blessed of all Mothers
for I was given by God, the care of you, my beautiful Son.
It has been my greatest privilege in this life to raise you.

Rest, my sweet Andy.

*Molly Zilliox*

## A Minute in the Mind's Doom

Crying in fear,
    in bloodshed dreams.
Running from the evil,
    I cannot see.
While dark and mourning trees,
    suspend above me,
As though having
    violent pain.
Running in fear,
    from this eccentric dream.
Crying; pleading a pass back into reality.
    Living in a mad man's tale,
Is not where my dreams should lead, and be...
    captured in fatality.

*Mayra Alejandra Suárez Chavana*

## Ha! Ha! Leaves

    I watched the leaves come down today
in Fall they have no choice
I wonder what they'd have to say
If they but had a voice
would they tell of summertime that has been and gone
or talk about the days they'll spend lounging on the lawn
    They might say don't you tread on me lying on the ground
and if I did they would protest with a crunchy crackling sound
I'd rake them high up in a pile
a place for me to dive in
or if I wanted to be alone a place for me to hide in
I'd lie beneath my colored quilt the trees made leafy light
a place where I can close my eyes pretending that it's night
I'd stay until my prankster friend
disturbed me in my bed
by jumping on the pile of leaves
and landing on my head
So standing up I'd dust myself and then I'd grab my hat
and leave the leaves right where they are
that's why they call them that

*Mark A. Forsyth*

## You To Me

On this day our God delivered you to me.
In His brilliance he could see, our destiny.
He could see you holding me,
Then he delivered you to me.

How complex; how pro found;
I'm speechless, I utter not a sound.
I think and then I understand,
He delivered you to me, and then
To you he delivered me.

Its not so hard to understand,
I tell myself, then gather 'round,
The things most precious to my mind.
The memories that only I can find.

Not just another day, to work, to eat, to play
No, a day for us to settle in,
To think about what might have been.

On this day you came to me,
Then you said, he'll come to me.
It's not hard to understand
You loved me so, and here I am.

*Robert Booth*

## Untitled

    From the other room the man sings.
In my bedroom, through my door
I hear his mournful tune.
In the darkness quietly I listen...
As he tells me so sweetly of a love long gone.
I turn beneath my sheets and bury
my head into my pillow -
as I think how I understand his loss.
Moments after I'm lulled to sleep - - - -
the radio is turned off.

*Leigh Godfrey*

## A Random Kiss

Thirty days its been, since we said "I DO"
In spite of this time, I still love you.
Its still amazing that a random kiss
Could lead to all this bliss.

I've made many mistakes in my life,
but right now, I'm glad you're my wife.
I wish I could explain my status quo,
but you are still to young to know.

The full realization that you're growing old,
perhaps, I am old, is the way it should be told.
In spite of feeling young and all that rot,
my music is still roll and rock.

I find it almost impossible to accept,
that I'm no longer a member of the rock set.
So please bear with grumpy, grouchy old me,
my disposition is more like a stormy sea.

I now have the blessing of your Coral Reef,
upon which it can crash and subside with no grief.
Crashing breakers subside to gentle waves upon the sand,
of time and only because You choose beside me to stand.

*Robert Christianson*

## Song Title

Long ago and far away
In the shade of the old apple tree
By the river of the roses, down in the valley
You and I together, Whispering
I love you truly, I don't want any one at all
I told you so, You made me love you
And then you kissed me
A lovely way to spend an evening
I'm a little on the lonely side tonight
You're in the Army now
I dream of you, tears on my pillow
The picture on the wall
It's just a memory of you
Baby won't you please come home
I'm walking the floor over you
Maybe somebody else is taking my place
Till then, I'll walk alone
I'll never smile again
You taught me how to love you
Now teach me to forget.

*Margaret R. Potts*

## My First Love

When I was sixteen years of age
In the summer of nineteen forty-seven,
I met this boy with a freckled face,
Red hair and he was five feet eleven.

We dated for about two years
Going to the drive-in picture show.
Afterwards we'd cruise the streets
In his yellow Chevrolet truck.

On a lovely June night in forty-nine
At his parents little country home.
Claude and I became husband and wife
Then we left on our honeymoon.

During our thirty years of marriage
Had three daughters and a little son.
Our daughters, they are grown and married.
Our little son, he is in heaven.

On a Sunday in March of seventy-nine.
My husband died about noon-time.
We all miss him very much.
But we know he's in heaven with his son.

*Mildred B. Smith*

## Anniversary

Forty years have passed, like a shadow in the night.
In the twinkling of an eye, on silent wings took flight.

It wasn't all that easy, you've had your share of fights.
But, with forty years behind you, the future still shines bright.

From the redness of a Ruby, her hair you watched turn grey.
Yours went from black to silver, in what seems like just a day.

The wedding band you gave her, has worn and lost its shine.
The love you shared together has stood the test of time.

Four children from this union the breath of life you gave.
The road was long and narrow and seldom ever paved.

Forty years of yesterday that passed as fast as one.
Forty years of memories, three daughters and a son.

*Nancy A. Haire*

## Portals...

I'm tryin' to defrost some years long lost
in the vault of my memory.
I think they would surge with the right kind of urge
but I can't seem to locate th' key.

The times that I seek are not that oblique
but for some unknown reason they stay
in shadows unkind somewhere in my mind,
and they won't let me in there to play.

All I ask is the chance to have one more glance
at th' days when my children were small.
These days, lost to me, I'd give all to see,
but I'm not quite as tall th' wall.

Oh, I see just enough (bits of memory's slough),
more a taunt, more a tease than reward
for the time I invest in this unfulfilled quest.
Are they buried too deep in its hoard?

Or, perhaps it's too late to beg at th' gate,
that portal of long-ago years.
If it did let me in I would run back...but then
who's to say I could see through th' tears?

*Lucius L. Bultman*

## The Two Widows

I know two widows who carry their grief
in their hunched backs—
loneliness now, a heavier weight.

The specters of their husbands remain
in reminiscent gestures,
in the downward glances I spy.
They once held their passions close as pillows.
Now, they whisper.

I almost knew these men.

Grandfather, your art hangs on my wall.
Your restless creativity drives me.
Father-in-law, I love your son.
I walked across your grave the other day.

Without permission,
your widows welcome me into your homes,
fix me dinner on the plates you shared,
weave the tales of family history.

How would it be if you were here?
Would you embrace me as well,
and love me for who I am?

*Raymond L. Rigoglioso*

## Material Things

What's happened to love and beauty it brings
In today's universe of material things?

People are looked at for what they can do,
Rather than what they are. Oh isn't this true?

What can you do for me, how much can you make?
It's enough to give any heart a clean shattering break.

Why can't we respect, and love one another
For what we all are? But I fear, dear brother,
Love is lost and beauty it brings
In today's universe of material things.

*Sonja B. Lavitt*

## What If?

What if?  You, the young ballerina
in toe-shoes found your way to the
land of the rich and famous, or just
a heartbeat away in a crowded elevator
and I never bothered to look before
getting off.

What if, you didn't walk through
the door that day?  But what if
you did and I wasn't tall enough
to look into your twilight eyes
and share your intimate smile.

Life can be awkward sometimes, because
we don't always hold up our heads to see
the things we should.  I might have seen
the birth of a new era and closed my eyes
in age never knowing our paths crossed,
never knowing how close we came.  Did I
ever thank you for not turning away?

**Rodney Drake**

## Totally Lost

I sit here in my nothingness
In total disparity
To ponder what has polarized my brain

What's pulled this shade of verticalness
Down around my mindlessness
And severed every nerve that kept me sane?

I need to try to murmurize
So I can quickly vocalize...
In words that can arise in... a vertical horizon

Or come up with a knowledgizing sound
Along the horizontalness of ground
That could eventually be verbalized...

Could in some way be transistorized
So I could be revealized
And found.

**Rodney Richard Seeley**

## George Washington and His Men Valley Forge

I visited a group of Revolutionaries
In Valley Forge at going back in time
A teacher me and them guerrillas,
of those that knew so well to fight.
I saw them coming to the fort after the battle,
With injuries, and suffering exhaustion
and I sat beside them to tell them
today's new about our Nation.
I wiped their blood on my red clean clothes
and their sweat with my white scar,
and I sat beside them to tell them
How their blood has built this great land.
Their blood never left a stain on my clothes.
Nor their sweat on my white scarf,
for our love was the same,
it was the same for our Country All.

**Sophia Demas**

## Losing My Soul

Losing my soul, as I float up to the Most
Peaceful desire, rushes my whole body,
with a pulsating fire.

This precious passionate feeling I do acquire,
with you my Best friend, who
I truly love and admire.

**Richard Finta**

## I Love Only You

If you love me, why don't you tell me?
Instead of holding back for oh so long
I can see it in your eyes baby
So please tell me before it's too late
And I'm gone

Because I love only you, and only you will ever do,
And you know, I can't ever let you go - oh no!

When I reach for you, you seem to pull away
I know you love me babe, so why don't you stay?
It's been a long long time
Since we've both been in love;
So lets take a chance, and start a romance
We've dreamed of

Because I love only you, and only you will ever do
And you know, I can't ever let you go - oh no!
Yes, I love only you, and only you will ever do
And you know, I can't ever let you go
Please don't go.

**Rebecca Demko Mefford**

## Heroes

That boy who stays homes to study,
Instead of partying and coming in late with his buddies.

The girl who scuffles to pay her way through college;
she didn't drop out.  No, she's working hard to gain more knowledge.

That kid who deals with peer pressure everyday.
Saying no to sex, drugs, and other wrong
doings while being made fun of in every way.
ARE THEY NOT HEROES?

The father who has 3 jobs, but spends his free moments with his kids
To help raise them and to show his son what a real man is.

The mother who is fighting to stay out the welfare line
Overcoming hardships and troubles while waiting to see the sun shine.
ARE THEY NOT HEROES?

Their names may not be famous, though through history it was echoed,
But they should be recognized for they are the forgotten
HEROES.

**Tandra Turner**

## Destiny

We all wonder what is in store for us in our future.....

We are all individuals with separate identities, divided
interests, and specific goals in life.  Each one of us has our own
needs, specific wants, and certain ways about us.

It is rare to meet another person who has the same dreams, whose
hopes and fears are comparable, and whose very identity adds
compliment to your own.

I believe that it was Fate that led me to you.  She heard my
prayers and granted my wish by combining our souls, turning two
into one.

No one can predict when destiny will arrive.
We know not how it will strike, or to where it will lead.  We can
only hope that it will somehow find us, and that when it does we
will heed its call.

Our destiny is here, let our future begin.

**Tammy Moschella**

## The Right of a Child

Brought into this world innocent and pure...
Into a world with AIDS and no cure.
No safety in our school or even our city...
Filled with gangs and guns, isn't it a pity.
Pictures of missing children on milk cartons in the store...
Alarms, locks and chains protect every window and door.
Because of this violence 911 had to be invented...
And in the case of drugs, DARE is here to prevent it.
Then we have the latch-key girls and boys...
Who are so afraid of every little noise.
We teach our children the difference of good touch and bad...
But can we protect them from their own Mom and Dad.
These children learn young how to be street-wise
Since car-jacking and drive-bys have been on the rise.
They can't view a street without stopping and thinking
BEWARE: someone might be driving and drinking.
Our mothers are MADD, our students are SADD
That the world we live in is getting so bad.
Please lets change this world so it's not so wild
To remain safe and secure should be the right of a child.

*Tracy Beeson*

## Where Do Memories Go?

Do they wash away like sands
into the sea?
Or do they dissolve like mist of morning
into the air?

Do they remain the same, like elements
of chemistry?
Or do they drift away like a sailing ship
on a long, endless journey?

Do they shrivel up like a dry rose
with no air or water?
Or do they return to the mind
with full force and power?

*Sameerah M. Smith*

## Coming Of Age

Coming Of Age
Is a most difficult stage

A stage of much confusion
A time of manipulative delusion

All of your friends seem to be in a race
Where peer pressure dictates the pace

And you must remain with the pack
'Cause if you don't, your reputation will come under attack

Which eventually leads you to acquire a thirst
To entertain the thought of who you'd like to be your first

Should it be a choice solely based on the heart?
Or should experience play the most important part?

You are worried about making the right decision
As well as performing your first time with romantic precision

And though, at times your feelings may cause you to waiver
You still have your intellect and morals in your favor

Trying to figure out what's in somebody's head
Can only lead to more confusion instead

And yes, it is hard to know what others may intend
But patience and understanding can only come from a friend!

*Tracy L. Mitchell*

## Happiness Corner, U.S.A.

Happiness corner, U.S.A.
Is a tiny little place, where I can go
With my dreams and spend the day.
It is so small, it isn't on the map
But is filled with ideas galore.
And always looking for many, many more.

I can dream dreams that no one
Has ever thought of before.
Now, they will appear at happiness corner
U.S.A.

Which by the way, happens to be at my door.
Those little ideas knew what to do
To fill my heart with thoughts so new.

It is like a song that has no beginning or no end
But to go on its way to happiness corner, U.S.A.
Again and again.
Without losing its way, until it gets to the end.
Because I just close my book and walk away
Even though I am still in Happiness corner, U.S.A.

*Wilma Cruise*

## Poise

They asked me: "What Is Poise?"
"Is it eyes or lips, a well-placed smile?
Or is it a white rose
leaning against a slender vase?"

Poise drifted down the aisle in church Sunday,
wearing a flowing gown
and a big green hat.
She had stars in her eyes!

Once I saw Poise limp to a bench,
mat of grey hair, blue discerning eyes.
Trousers that sat on many benches,
lips that quivered from remembrances.

Poise sauntered past my window yesterday,
head high, challenging the world
but two brown eyes darted anxiously about—
to see who was watching.

And tonight Poise sat upon the shelf
laughing derisively at me
because I paused to help a small lad
collect the fragments of his broken dream.

*Margaret Mulligan Black*

## Soul Homeward Bound?

Where is the home of my soul? Will my soul ever rest?
Is it inexhaustible, does it know it's way in this complex
universe? Is it assigned a guide, a guardian angel or two?
I feel all is yes, and much more, enlightened as understanding
comes.

My soul was created many millennia ago, out of the greatest
love known to God and unknown to man. It has since sought it's
way back to that love. Every thing else is compared to and
rejected as falling short of that love, for my soul, as others,
decline to settle for less.
Thus being the dilemma, and being lost, confused and without
that love, in another dimension; my soul yet yearns for an
unknown length of time, for that great, illusive, unconditional
love. It goes forth, (after passing through the veil) still
yearning, still seeking, homeward bound.

*S. Brownlee-Cobb*

## The Fight

Why, what did I do?
Is it punishment or just the odds?
A roll of the die or sent from God?
I didn't ask for this.
Justice it is not, not even for.
From what did it come and where?
It crashed into my life.
I had so much going, so many dreams.
It has all gone wrong. What will it mean.
The future I envisioned is shattered.
It has threatened my life and taken my freedom.
It's hard to accept this person I've become.
Do I fight or give up?
I must rely on others now. That's hard.
My mind's confused, body: internally scared.
There is no quick fix.
If I love it's a lifelong fight. No guarantees.
All the pity I can't take. What do they think of me?
I want my life back, the way things were.
Before I was told I have cancer.

*Paul A. Cox*

## Love

What is love? Is it heard or seen?
Is it red, blue, yellow or green?

What is love? Is it slow or fast?
Does it vanish? Does it last?

Some say forever, others don't know.
Is it a light does it show?

Love is every where in every heart.
Is love something thing in little Bitty parts?

Is love weak? Or is it strong?
Too love one taken is it wrong?

How can love be many miles apart?
And still affect a person's heart ?

Please tell me what is true love?
Is it all around? Is it from above?

Is love a feeling we express
   from within?
If so I'm in love again.

*Lonnie Lowry*

## His Feelings Are Hers

A word, and he left, Feelings.
Is it spring that awakens feelings?
They lay quietly all winter.
Burning hot pulsating Feelings,
Ache, for she is ready to tell him
Her feelings are smoldering within,
Constant, heavy, yearning to show him
She's eager for him, too.

If only to see clear blue gray beautiful
Eyes sparkle happiness,
Happiness for the taking
And Her giving to him;
Not mere relief from the fire
Flaming Within Her while she's Wanting Him.
Feelings? His Feelings are Hers.

*Mary Lou Wire*

## Why?

Why is there such a thing as war?
Is it the animal inside us all,
That makes us, by heart, a fighter.
Why do we need such a thing that causes countries to fall?

Maybe it's because of the way we were brought up.
We were told to fight back. But why?
Violence only leads to more, and usually war,
And causes people to die.

So why do we do it?
Why do we spread war?
Why do we think we benefit?
When it gives us no reason to soar.

There is only on thing that works.
It is a thing we can not lease,
But, if permitted, it can last forever.
It is a thing called...
   PEACE!

*Robert J. McLaughlin III*

## Who Can I Trust?

   Who can I trust, telling my story to? Seems like there
is no one, everyone is against me behind you. I'm not
lying, although I have said my share. Right now I need a
true friend, to listen and to care. I need someone to
trust, to believe my side. To make me happy when in doubt,
make me feel like there's nothing to hide. I am torn
between two worlds, one full of jealousy, hate, deceit. The
other full of happiness, love and feeling great. No matter
how hard I try, I feel that life is passing me by. I pull
to the happiness, but get stuck in between. I must have the
worst luck that anyone has ever seen! Is there an end to
his torture? Seems like this hell goes on forever! Seems
like everyone has someone that they trust but me. I want to
be part of that, and be eternally happy. Will someone
please help me find the way?

*Michelle Kreidler*

## The Pledge To Life

What, I ask of you,
Is the true definition of that
Taste?
Such foul matter emanating from Nature;
Externally magnanimous,
Internally bitter.

Now, I ask of you,
Why do you resemble such fruit of acidity?

To be forgiving is to be in love;
To trust is to enjoy the sweetness of life.
Lamentations and despise,
Oblivion is where they reside.

Embellishment lies
In the winds of humility and giving.

*Sandra Weber*

## To Natalie, My New Wife

Time drags everything
Into itself,
All is clawed into pastness,
But now its talons
Have lost their clutch,
For through your flesh
You come to me,
Holding the sun in the heavens yet high—
And rare time in place.

*Milton A. Shaham*

I am wary of those who shun paradox -
isolated, alienated from their gizzard;
unbeset by agitating nuances
and subtleties of feeling,
neat unruffled hexagons.

Your difference bravely risks unraveling
networks of contradictions and profundities.
Seemingly opposite poles
spark a deeper unity of Being
than the sterile finished square.

---

My night desert is crowded with ebonied sky.
Standing tiptoed - stroking the velvety,
warming wind-blown fingers with trembling stars -
The Dipper tips
and burns down all the cities.

*Sheila Garden*

## Pain

For we who live with pain, we build defenses.
It comes stabbing, like flashes of lightning
Before a summer storm.
I wait for medication, and I picture
That storm coming in early morning.
Clouds are rolling across the sky.
Tree tops bend beneath the wind.
Rain sweeps down, beating against the windows.
I let pain sweep over me, like pounding waves.
Little by little it eases.  A new picture forms.
I see a meadow I know, clothed in summer green.
A pond is there with a marshy growth.
There are trilling calls of meadow larks.
Red-wing blackbirds spill their liquid notes.
I see all this and relax.  The wave passes—
Until the next time.  This way I cope.

*Olive W. Howard*

## Why I Think My Thoughts

My mind is always traveling
It goes sometimes where it shouldn't
I'm always thinking of the future
Thinking of ways to do what others wouldn't

I've often been labelled "strange"
But I don't let it get to me
I just continue to think my thoughts
Believing Heaven will be my trophy

My mom has taught me good values
And I practice them everyday
She's always at the front of my mind
Wishing I could see her one more day

I have no kids of my own
No one to leave my legacy to
I just hope my nephews think ahead
And plan for their future too

Making plans for the future is smart
It seems that's all I do
I know it'll pay off one day
Maybe you should think my thoughts too

*Paula Marie Angelle*

## Grandma

*Dedicated to Mrs. Meta Porter*

I guess I'll go see Grandma,
it has been quite a while.
She probably will forget my name.
I sure do miss her smile.
I remember when she baby-sat and I sat on her knee.
She fed me fresh baked cookies,
and showed her garden to me.
She always was so busy, my Grandma worked so hard.
Maybe I could clean her house.
Or rake and mow her yard.
Or take her for a little ride,
I won't have to go too far.
My kids would like to see her.
I won't just send a card.
If soon Grandma goes to heaven, my conscience will be clear
I can say that I just saw her.
It won't have been almost a year.
I'm sure she does get lonely
and her eyes are growing weak
I guess I'll go see Grandma not put it off another week.

*Lillian McCulloch*

## Knock Knock

In the realm of my mind I perceive it again and again.
It hollers my name claiming to be a friend.
I reject its visit when it knocks night and day,
but it refuses to disperse for it's tenacious in its ways.
It named events of my past and also things I've done,
but I was still suspicious, so my trust wasn't won.

Finally it said something to convince me we're met before,
but when I opened up, it was death at my door.

*Welwyn Samuel*

## Poetry:  A Language of Love

Poetry is not just another way to communicate.
It is a fragile bridge of empathy that connects us to each other.
In it we express those nebulous feelings brought on by caring
so much...
About our fellow man that we long to heal by touch.

Not a "laying on of hands"
But an intertwining of spirits where soul to soul we meet.
And in agamic love we great the very essence of who we are
and who created us.
With our verse we whisper, shout and say
A thank you to our Father God to whom we pray.

*Patti Clifford Stewart*

## Eulogy for a Kitten

It's been hours since it was done, though
    it seems closer to an eternity.
Behind watery eyes I remember
    everything; we named you Dinero,
my wife and I, to remind us
    of the day we found you—near death,
    scared, and alone.

We nursed you back to health, and in return you
    brought a furry bundle of joy to our lives.
The sickness came quickly, only months later, taking
    your legs and sight; you were too young
to know,
    and the decision was made.

You left our little world much like
    you entered;
near death, scared,
    but not alone.

*Steven Donaldson*

## The Christmas Thought

A thought runs lightly through my mind.
It is a small and shining island in a sea that anxious boils.
While my callow craft may flail and flounder through tortured
    foaming roils,
A quiet haven there awaits.

A thought runs lightly through my day.
It is a silver buoy that homeward tolls the way.
Though with clouded eyes and errant wit I set my vagrant sail,
Its gentle call my constant guide remains.

A thought runs lightly through my life.
It is a golden river determined onward flowing.
When ports have oared uncaring by on backs of fruitless rowing,
To flowered banks it softly bears my raft.

A thought runs boldly through my heart.
It is the glory through my being streaming like the passion through
    cathedral glass.
And without its crimson glow would my soul to shattered shards
    collapse.
Rejoice my voice its sacred name:  your love!

*Thomas W. Momyer*

## Lila

For those you are required to love-
It is an act of abandonment.
    For those who are looking in-
It is a weird relationship.
    For those who do not understand-
It is a relationship they have not yet attained.
    For those who do understand-
It is a relationship to be treasured.
    For me, it is a special bond, so few have acquired-
For me, it is called your friendship.

*Mona S. Noble*

## Groundment

Grounding really stinks
It makes you stop and think
About the things you've done wrong
But I don't think grounding should be THIS long
It's been about three months or so
Only Mom and Dad really know
When is this insanity going to end?
NO phone, NO friends, there are only letters to send
Why?  Oh, why does it have to be me?
Oh my Gosh!  It's almost Christmas I see!
Maybe by New Years they'll let me off
But I've got a cold and they hear me cough
Now they'll definitely not let me out
They'll say I'm too sick to run about
I'll show them I'll run away
If they don't let me off groundment today!!!

*Lindsay Kata*

## Solitude

Again the predator is driven into darkness.
In rage, he spews his fiery bile at the world;
with crimson hands he awaits.
Shards of despair pierce him as he crouches, motionless,
his mind prowling the familiar black.
His one desire is to lash out,
but the only thing near him is the ethereal dark.
A faintly uttered growl goes unheard in the shadows.

*Matthew Mann*

## God Little Rainbow

The flower is God little rainbow in the soil -
It may grow without much toil -
A beautiful flower soft and sweet -
With stem and leaves of green.
Bending as the wind go whispering bye -
This little rainbow comes in many shapes -
Colors ranging from light to dark -
So look at the different sizes.
In a field, a meadow, are in a pot they grow -
With scents so sweet.
God little rainbow from the earth.
Spread out for miles -
Let you think of drops of rain.
A soft touch from the sun.
There's a joy in watching a flower grow.
One could bring a smile.
God little rainbow of flowers.
Any type are kind
Now pick your favorite rainbow.

*Mamie Lou G. Williams*

## Your Eyes

Within your eyes, I can hear the music of your soul;
It reaches out to me.
Moving ever so gently, it holds me to its dance of
    silence and peace.
Within your eyes, I feel your love and closeness to the earth;
Your heart opens visions to me of generations long past; of people
    toiling and laughing together, on distant hills and meadows, of
    families tending their flocks and caring for their homes.
Within your eyes, I can smell and taste colors exploding around
me, yellows and blues - greens and blacks.  All in a profusion
of shapes and form; lines forming, thoughts of mysteries and
wonder.  All centered on a perfect design.
Within your eyes, I have touched upon the fountain of tears, from
whose font only you will bathe.
Within your eyes I have gazed and upon my looking....
"I Have Seen You!".

*Manuel Ballestero*

## The Mighty Oak Tree

In my yard there stood a mighty oak tree.
It was a real beauty - a graceful sight to see.
For many years it stood straight and tall,
Passing the tests of time, surviving them all.
The oak withstood the storms, the heat, the cold,
It was tall and proud; it was very bold.
It had such beauty and strength, even when it was bare.
I loved this great tree, I really did care.
As time moved on and Mother Nature did her part,
The mighty oak tree lost its great heart.
In its massive trunk grew a very large crack,
And though it fought hard, it couldn't come back.
To me, in some ways, this tree was a mentor,
"Always stand tall - don't be a bender."
Then one quiet night at the midnight hour,
The great oak tree lost its power.
It lay its massive body slowly to the ground.
To be so big it made such a little sound.
The other trees seemed to bow their heads
For the mighty oak tree was finally dead.

*Loy Parks*

## Just One Of Them Thangs

It was gone before it came,
It was nothing before it achieve fame,
It was nameless before it receive it name,
It came and went and still it hasn't change.
Everything is everything that is what it used to be,
Everything is nothing that is what we can't see.
It all or nothing, all for me and one for all,
Me for you and you for me and God for us all.

*William Harrison*

## Little Shack In The Back

It was a cold winter night, not a star was in sight
It was OH, NO!  But I knew I had to go
I got out of the sack, for my trip to the shack, away out back
I tip-toed from the house, as quiet as a little mouse
I didn't want to wake my MOTHER or any of the other
I'm getting old and it was so very very cold
In the two hole stall with a SEARS on the wall
That was enough for all, it wasn't nice
Just like using ice, I've heard them say
On this very day, if you have plumbing
Just quit your grumblin', you never have to go stumbling
  To use the little shack
Away out in the back.

*Mildred M. Kidwell*

## Diabetes Illness Is Unpredictable

Diabetes is an illness you cannot predict,
it will attack your body and make you sick,

Diabetes is an illness just like the sun,
it goes up and down at different times.

Diabetes is an illness just like the heat,
it will attack your body and you cannot sleep.

Diabetes is an illness just like a Tornado,
it will damage your body and skip to your arteries

Diabetes is an illness just like the stars,
it strikes large, medium and seldom small.

Diabetes is an illness just like the moon,
it shines at night to keep a proper diet.

Diabetes is an illness just a hurricane,
until now no one understand.

Diabetes is an illness just like the air,
pay attention to it and give it good care.

Diabetes is an illness just like a windstorm,
it will dislocate your limbs and make you slim.

Thank God for His son the doctor and nurse too,
if it were not for them all, what will a diabetes do.

*Louise Wells*

## Fantasy Land

Sometimes I wish I could go to a fantasy land,
It would be a dream come true.
Everyone would like me for who I am,
I wouldn't worry about feeling blue.
I would always be happy in this fantasy land
No matter what I did or said
Just peace in this land and no one getting mad.
Happiness would be all around
This fantasy land would be a dream come true.

*Stephanie Due*

## Comes The Dawn

She asks what time is it?
It's 1:30 in the morning I reply
She whimpers in pain and shudders a kit
All is quite on my next trip through the door
He asks can you stay awhile and sit?
It does not matter rich or poor
Do you know the time?
It's 3:45 in the morning I reply
I pull over the covers and check the I.V line
She cries softly am I going to die?
I reassure her all is on and I sit some
She is my patient but could be...I, you, or anyone
For I am a nurse
Some would call it a curse
Caring for the terminally ill
Do you know the time sir?
Yes it is 6:00 in the morning I reply
Outside the birds start to sing and stir
The sun rise with its brilliant light
We have all made it through another night

*Stewart Steinacher*

## Untitled

I'm very tired, and I don't know what to do.
It's 9p.m.and still homework-I'm not through.
My brother is talking, again, on the phone,
He's a cool 9th grader; he thinks I'm a 7th grade drone!
I'm sick of school and growing pains,I'm tired of exhausting my
fragile brain.  It is 5/24 tomorrow -
  Alas
This poem is due in my 9a.m. class!
Forget the clock, check out the calendars,
My mind is changing to mushy lavender.
June is coming...
The end is near.
I'll forget this wretched 7th grade year!
O groan! O gosh!
8th graders tell me, gets worse!
The thought of 8th grade torture
Will end my verse!

*Mary Dow*

## Ocean Side

I'm sitting on the beach on a sunny day.
It's amazing how it makes you feel a certain way.
Like the sky above, the oceans blue,
it's like a dream, but I know its true.
The sky turns scarlet as the sun sets to sleep,
It's sinking into the ocean deep.
The moon comes up above the water as it reflects white,
This must be truly the most awesome night.
I'm hypnotized by the beauty of this sight.
All I can do is stare,
at the awesome grace.
With inner peace that I share,
it brings a smile to my face.
In my heart I know, I'll always remember this place.

*Richard Bakker*

## The Fundamental Man

He slipped upon his mist of mind and mused upon his muse;
Nothing there, he contemplated; nothing much that I can use!
And so he hides in practicals, for life is really short and dim;
Never mind the madrigals that hum their hues for him;

Limericks leaping in the soul, songs that swarm like bees.
So life goes on with usables, no grandiosities to tease
His fundamentals.  His strolls are dull, not even droll,
And so his seven stages go, from very new to very old.

*Patricia Erwin Nordman*

## My Love

How do I tell of my love for you?
It's as fresh as a flower kissed with dew
It's as large as the sky on a clear bright day
As pure as the snow falling on its way
It's as unwavering as a mountain against a storm
It will keep you always warm
It is yours to hold and forever keep tight
It will keep you company on a long cold night
It's yours to use just please don't abuse

It's undying and everlasting like time
I'm so happy I'm yours and you're mine
It's private and exciting, always inviting
It's always loving, never fighting
It's new, yet feels old like it's always been around.

Perhaps it has just waiting to be found.

*Vicky Dearinger*

## A Young Mother

I feel just like I'd like to say of may dear child just passed away.
It's body lies beneath the sod, it's spirit took it's flight to God.
It makes me heave a sigh and weep to see that baby in my sleep!
Me thinks I see, at night in bed his shining face and golden head.
His hands and face so clean and neat, the darling child did look so sweet.
It seems I hear him in the night, to say, "grandpa I want a bite."
The dear sweet babe has gone to rest, but not upon his mothers breast.
I loved him once, I love him yet, oh that sweet face I can't forget.
Oh, can it be, I heave a sigh, that Jesus loved him more than I?
Where first the babe was loaned to me, I was as proud as I could be!
It's pa and I both loved him well, how great the joy no tongue can tell.
I know now, mother, what you said, the night you laid me on the bed.
I know now, mother, what you meant when down upon your knees you went.
I know now, mother, how you felt your heart like mine, doth nearly melt.
I know now, mother, why you prayed and many blessings on me laid.
I know now, mother, why you wept while lying on your arm I slept.
It was because a mothers love, is ever on her little "dove."
I loved my babe and so did you, the doctor loved the baby too.
We'll meet him far beyond the tomb, within that lofty upper room.
And when we pass beyond the door, there time and space will be no more.

*Sandra J. Hamilton*

## Dreamland Run

Running in a cold black night
It's dark, pitch black
In the distance a light
Maybe a star or a candle
Could be a match
The beginning of a blazing fire
Perhaps the sparkle in the eye of a long lost friend

I race toward the light
Starving for air, lungs burning, blood pounding, muscles aching
The light dims
Energy levels down, drained, tapped out
I trip, stumble, fall in confusion
Struggling to my feet
Eyes opened wide this time
I climb the mountain

Back in bed—soft sweet bed
I close my eyes travel back to sleep
Picking up the pace
Racing again toward the light
In dreamland

*Mark Box*

## My Heart

Sometimes I wonder why God put me here at this place,
It's hard to get up every morning thinking everything
  is going great and that's when I wake up because it
  was all a dream and I go on with my day trying to
  hide the hurt with a smile on my face.
But, it's hard to do when I see guys with girls
  having so much fun,
I just look at them and walk by saying in my mind
  somewhere, somehow I'll find me one.
So when or if I find the right girl for me,
  the lonely weekends I've wasted for so long
  won't be so bad,
And maybe I will bump into a girl who has a heart of
  gold and is a beautiful sight to see.
Then I can love and be loved by that right someone,
  and I'll forget all about how long me and my
  feelings have been sad.
I don't know how much longer me and my heart
  can wait, before my feelings fall apart or how
  long my heart will last before it bends or till it will break.

*Stanley Marks*

## Unenlightened

The world is mine or so I'm told
It's laxity and light are all in me
With each new day, the dawn's coming reveals my soul
Yesterday I was a promise
Today I am tomorrow
In my spirit I find life
In my hands is the future
In me lies a mixture of extreme emotions
The day, in it's entirety, is brilliant
Such as that of freedom and life
The world has promised me infinity
Yet given me limits
How can the world be mine, when I am yet to be enlightened

*Pam Green*

## Smokey

The colt was born on a stormy night,
It's mother was a mustang mare, full of fight.
When wolves attacked, she put them to flight.
The colt grew up on the open range.
He was brought in from the range at the age three,
Broke by the wrangler, cowhorse to be.
He bucked and fought to be set free.
Every morning he was rode, he was center stage.

A cowboy named Clint wanted smokey for his string,
He told his boss "that horse will be the thing."
Clint and smokey were the best on the team.
Clint rode smokey for fifteen seasons.
Smokey bucked with clint everyday he was rode.
He was a good cowhorse and did what he was told.
Smokey got better and better as he grew old.
He was put out to pasture for many good reasons.

*William J. Morgan*

## Life

The flowers petals reach up for the sun.
It's life is brand new, it has just begun.
It sits among friends, in the new cool morn.
It is soft and bright, for it has just been born.
It soaks up the heat of the suns warm rays.
It will live its life here, for all of its days.
A small breeze lifts its sweet smell around.
It will flow away, never hitting ground.
A flowers doesn't live very long, before it dies.
But before it goes, it whispers its good-byes.

*Lori Wood*

## Echoes of Ecstasy

I sit beside a hillside stream and listen to
  its playful murmurings - at times I think
I hear sounds of tiny laughter and I smile.
Perhaps the stream finds me amusing, or maybe
  it shares a secret with the daffodils along its edge -
    for they tremble with childlike joy
      at something I have missed.
I gaze into the sparkling stream for I intend
  to discover the source of its gaiety - instead
I see reflected there the sunny daffodils.
But in that liquid mirror, it is no longer flowers -
  'tis fluid sunshine I behold - oh, how I long
to savor forever its warm golden sweetness.
I close my eyes, inhaling deeply the fragrant,
  sun-sweetened air - my tongue and throat tingle
  as if I'd tasted the richness of ambrosia.
Each breath I take is pure refreshment which
  exhilarates my mind and body - such delight
  blossoms in my soul that I begin to laugh
And join in nature's jubilee.
*(Copyright 1976 by Lynne K. Logan)*

    **Lynne K. Logan**

## On An Eagle's Wing

The canyon swept below me,
Its rocky wasteland stretched to infinity.
A thin, tired bison wandered freely,
Its frail posture bringing me pity.
The sun shone dim at the rim of the canyon
Illuminating the stones with a glow
The color of Indian autumn corn.

My eyes diverted.
And chasing the buffalo through the canyon
Flew the Caddo, their formation untorn
By the rapidity of the chase
Their long raven hair whipped their worn faces
As they gripped tighter the manes of their horses.
They gained on the buffalo, their spears in mid-air
The sun beat down as they held tighter the backs of their mares.

I held my breath as I saw the spear coast
And at once the tribe faded as unreal as a ghost
And suddenly — there was nothing

Save a canyon, and the sunset
Flown on an eagle's wing.

    **Sophia Naftali**

## My Home

My home is a lonely house,
Its rooms are not filled with laughter.
There is no air of family and friends,
Only hours that are longer than norm.

If you listen you can hear the creaking of
this lonely house,
As it settles in to more quiet, lonesome days
that will fade into years.

It remembers days of family gatherings,
Birthdays, reunions, visits and holidays.
With sweet aromas of food on the tables to be shared
by all.
In earlier days it heard plans of things to come,
New beginnings, new life, happiness, dreams yet to surface,
and yes of death.

It has heard a mother's heart break, a baby cry, a son's
agony and puppy's whine.
Today my lonely home hears the creaking of its
own settlement for the lonesome years to come.

    **Rosalie A. Patterson**

## The Choice Of My Heart

Two boys, one heart
It's so confusing, where do I start?
I like them both, my emotions are jumbled
The football of love I must have fumbled.
They are so different, not alike at all
Maybe I'm just setting myself up for a double fall.
One is so funny, sweet, and kind.
The other is tall, husky, and has a great mind.
One like drama, movies and stuff.
The other plays hockey, he can't get enough.
The one I pushed my heart at just pushed away.
The other put his arms around me-he was here to stay.
The one is so sweet, the apple of my eye,
Or is the other one to be my guy.
My hearts all mixed up, doesn't know where to turn
Can't figure out how it won't get burned.
The two knights are mine at least in my dreams.

    **Stephanie L. Resser**

## Reunion

Over three thousand miles, I've trekked to The Wall.
I've come to pay tribute, to you, one and all.

It's been twenty-eight years, since we stood side by side.
We served with great honor, we served with great pride.

On that cold black surface, your names are inscribed.
You died for your country, safely home I arrived.

Although you are gone, and will never return,
In the core of my heart, your spirits still burn.

I stand here in silence, reunited with friends,
My heartfelt respect, shall not come to an end.

So now I must go, but these verses I'll leave.
And for you who have fallen, I'll continue to grieve.

Farewell, My friends......

    **William Baumann**

## Our Gift from Heaven

You are our tiny rosebud nestled in my womb
I've nourished and cherished you, and soon our bud will bloom
When we knew that you were coming, we were full of pride and joy
We know we will love you, girl or boy.
We will love and protect you, and guide you on your way
We will try to make life pleasant, each and every day
We know that you will stumble, but we will not let you fall
You are our gift from Heaven, the greatest gift of all.

    **Yvonne Lovingood Lucas**

## Ethereal Vision

She seemed like a cat, dressed in black—
jacket and slacks and tight knit cap,
moving through Central Park and the streets
of New York with ease and grace and mystery.

Those of us old enough to remember know
she was really a bird, like a white dove,
flying above we mere mortals, gliding
through the air at her husband's Inaugural Ball
in flowing white chiffon over white satin.

All her fabulous and tragic life,
Jacqueline Kennedy Onasis had been flying
on the thin line of the horizon.
With one wing toward the heavenly skies
and the other toward the muddied earth,
she flew close to the clouds
or into the brilliant sun.

    **Yvonne Lubov Rusiniak**

## The Country Girl

People milled around her,
Jane had never seen such large crowds.
Yet she was never more lonely,
if someone would only say hello.
She looked at her chapped hands,
and swore never to return to the farm.

Jane had second thoughts about the city.
She noticed that nobody showed her pity.
But she was determined never to feed hogs again,
that was a job now left to her brothers.
She had left behind the farm life,
Jane wanted to be a city man's wife.

But nobody glanced her way.
She shook her head and sighed,
her parents never lied,
it was heartless city where lamps, like moons, hung on posts.
Her heart sank as the sun went down.
Jane was never more alone.
Perhaps tomorrow someone would look at her and smile.

*Rudolph Peart*

## Hay Diddle Diddle

An oval trip in Armstrong's life rotated
journey cheer, the launching site of satellite
sparked a new frontier, a romantic taste was
viewed from sound, tranquility on the sea,
Astronauts weaker by the pound from lack of
gravity.  Pearly butts in silver suits beam
with naked bloom, volcanic pits and mountain
groups on the far side of the moon, orbit flight
reflects by light, no air in which to breathe,
a temperature drop in lunar nights no wind,
no rain or cheese.
Apollo quakes in seismic form as Saturn crashed
the land, the outer crust still stiff and strong,
and the cow leaps inner man, meteors and comets
rock and roll, the surface marked from their blast,
crater hits and asteroid holes left patches of
gray colored glass.
Hay Diddle Diddle take control feed that
challenger's brain, though knowledge eliminates
danger, education promotes the change.

*Linda Lillibridge*

## The Meaning Of Easter

E  is for the Early visit to the tomb on Easter morn
    just as the shepherd traveled on the day He was born.

A  is for all the miracles He performed before He died,
    Even when He raised Lazarus from the dead, as Martha
    cried.

S  is for the Sabbath when we worship Him at church,
    The reading of the scriptures, for the truth
    we do search.

T  is for the six Trials He went through for me and you,
    Thank you Jesus for what you did and for all you do.

E  is for the Everlasting love He showed us on the cross,
    He left heavens glory to come down and suffer our loss.

R  is for the Resurrection, of the life He did freely give,
    Because of this, all who die in the Lord shall have
    another life to live.

*Linda Sue George*

## A Valentine Poem

Valentine's Day is a special day
Just as you are special in every way.
So I hope you don't think I've gone too far
Because I know you're worth it - yes you are!
So in keeping with the tradition of this day
I hope you'll receive this heart sent token
For this is the day when "I love you"
    is rightly spoken.

*Robert Mendoza*

## Meladee's Clown

When you're alone, and feeling down,
Just imagine there's this clown.
You see his face with a frown,
You think, I must turn it upside down.

You see his eyes and there's a tear,
I wonder if this clown's in fear?
Could I make him smile and cheer?
I know his special and very sincere.

He's sometimes happy, and sometimes sad,
I've never seen him ever get mad.
The children tell me he's real rad,
Inherited no doubt from his Mom and Dad.

I've claimed him as Meladee's clown,
I'm gonna him a hunting hound.
I must leave now to go to the pound,
So Meladee clown will never frown.

*Meladee L. Simpson*

## The Boundaries

Don't say you can't, before you ever begin.
Just remember if you don't ever play, you can't ever win.
If you want to play, practice hard.
If you want to be the best, practice harder.
When you step to a challenge just remember,
That you should be the one the challenger remembers.
When you practice, find your limits,
Then break through them and find new limits.

*Stacey Scarborough*

## Home, Sweet, Home

Home's not just a place to come home to
Just to eat and to sleep and to be
Home is a place where you're loved a whole lot
And that's what's important to me

Home is a place full of sunshine
A place to be happy and free,
Home is a place where you just can let go
A place where you're V.I.P.

A home is a place full of laughter and fun
Where everyone's all full of glee,
A home is a family together.
Where it's not lots of "I's" it's a "we".

So now that you understand the meaning of
    family and home
You probably think your family is great
Well, I'm sure that it is, but you'd better give up
Because mine's already won for first rate!!

*Sarah Sydlowski*

## The Animals Of The World

Horses riding into the sunset until you can't see them anymore

Pandas eating their food and getting ready to sleep

Tigers running to catch their dinner
Kangaroos caring for their young
A hundred gorillas dead by the sunset
The survivors left soaking with
    fear, anger, hatred
    towards people.
Snakes crawling to find food
You are looking in the sunset
You see the animals, wondering —

How many are dead?
How many are alive?

You think this is crummy
You think this world is mean
You just wish we could learn:
You don't have to kill them —
Learn to live peacefully with the animals of the world.

*Melony Fortier*

## Back When

Lincoln's secretary was named Kennedy.
Kennedy's secretary was named Lincoln
Both were shot on a Friday with their wives present.

Booth shot Lincoln in a theatre and hid in a warehouse
Oswald shot Kennedy from a warehouse and hid in a theatre.

Both assassins were themselves killed before their trials.
Lincoln's successor was Andrew Johnson.
Kennedy's successor was Lyndon Johnson.

Andrew Johnson was born in 1808.
Lyndon Johnson was born in 1908.
Lincoln and Kennedy - each name 7 letters

"Strange but true this goes to you."

*Margaret Krienke*

## Woman Of Color

Woman of color, why do you hold your head down?  Do you not
know freedom we have finally found?
Woman of color are you ashamed in this world you came?
Do you not like your color which you got from your mother?
Woman of color the whips that left you scars on your back do
they show in your face?  Is that why you dare not go any place?
Don't let them stop you.  They have stopped us long enough.
Now it's time to rise above and shower this world with nothing
but love.
My mother, my father, my sister, my cousin, my brother, we have
won too many battles, overcame too many wars but yet we are
far from victory.
When we have finally gotten victory we can sit back and look
at the world we were not given but the world we fought hard for.
So woman of color hold your head high as if you're gonna fly
across that beautiful, blue sky.
Woman of color, we made it through yesterday, we've made it
through today.  With God on our side you better believe we can
make it through another day.

*Shavette L. Lovemore*

## Pity the Man

Blest is the man who works with a smile,
Knowing his labour to be worthwhile,
Knowing the pleasure of building with skill
The moments fly quickly as he works with a will.

Proud in the knowledge he has part in a plan
That points to a happier life for man.
Knowing in labour he finds true wealth
For it offers him happiness, contentment and health.

But pity the man who can hardly endure,
Who labours only, his pay to secure.
Every hour is a day, each day seems a year
His eyes hold no laughter, as evening draws near.

He finds no such pleasure in building with skill,
He has neither the love, the heart, nor the will.
Finding no comfort, taking part in the plan
His life is so empty - oh, pity the man.

*Orville E. Bayes*

## If I Were In Charge Of The World...

If I were in charge of the world,
LA Gear would change their attire.
The Bulls would never trade Horace Grant,
Robert Parish would retire.

If I were in charge of the world,
High schools would have Jai Alai.
I'd go sky-diving every day,
Because it's the best way to get high.

If I were charge of the world,
You wouldn't have third trimester reports.
Teachers wouldn't give homework,
Classrooms would be basketball courts.

If I were charge of the world,
There'd be no teacher a witch.
Politicians wouldn't be such jerks,
Hilary Clinton wouldn't be such a _____.

Yes, if I were in charge of the world,
Poverty wouldn't be such a case.
Because if I were in charge of the world,
It would be a better place.

*Peter Avila*

## One Fall Day

A leaf floats to the ground
later dried, brown crumbled.
A dog brushes his tail,
a happy motion to the owner.
The leaf no longer visible.

He watches her, eyes closed,
a mutter, a groan
she's gone,
he weeps, he is left behind,
alone.

She screams as her body is ripped apart
with pain,
He is born with frustration as his warmth
is gone,
Find's her breast, everything forgiven,
She beams, pain forgotten.

Darkness a blanket with stars,
The moon watches with delight as the lights go out.

*Michelle Paton*

## Laughter

Laughter is the gift I would give the world.
Laughter lightens one's heart,
while it brings a smile to one's face.
Laughter tells the world you are happy,
that you appreciate her beauty.
Laughter says you enjoy being with others,
for others help you learn to laugh at yourself.
Laughter makes a child's tummy hurt with delight,
while it cures the loneliness of an old man.
Laughter eases tensions,
when things might be hard.
Laughter is a two-fold gift,
if you share, you will receive some in return.
Laughter brings gifts of the world to your door steps,
but I will be the one who shares my laughter first.

*Melodie Stevenson*

## Not Love Deferred

You say that I must now forbear, delay,
Lean on the morrow's frail security,
    Bask in the promise of an unborn day,
Entrust my faith to dark futurity.

You say tomorrow you might comfort me
With tidings more propitious, news less stark.
    Ah, that is well, my dear, but don't you see
The future lies behind a question mark?

Tomorrow is the second bridge from here.
How can I compass it should this one fall?
    I'd rather cinch this little moment, dear,
Than gamble for what might not come at all.

Though I demand today enormous sums,
Tomorrow owes me nothing — till it comes.

*Pervis W. Hayes*

## My Cats

Lovers come and they go. But my cats stay. Children grow up and
leave but my cats stay. Things change in life but my cats remain
the same. Loyal friends are they, years have passed and still they
stay. Been through hard times, but my cats still remain with me.
Maybe I take them for granted. The sweetness of them, for when I'm
blue it's my cats I can always turn to. They comfort me. Put their
on me as if to say, it's O.K. you have me. I will always stay and be
with you, as long as I am allowed.

*Margaret Kimmer*

## Biding Time

Just biding my own sweet time on a lonely, wooden bench.
Leaves from White Oaks softly fade to red light and fireflies:
the bleeding acorns remain in shadows of gemstone trees.

Just biding my own sweet time on steps to worn front porches -
as useless as a silver broccoli pin from Newport
or an empty symphony hall of folding, aluminum chairs.

Just biding my own sweet time in ancient inns by the sea.
Patchwork quilts and boxcar children bring odors of train stations
wreaking of unanswered letters and broken stained German glass.

Just biding my own sweet time in a long forgotten room.
My sad imagination of what should have been
lingers like dusty, unkept promises that bide my own sweet time.

*Scott B. Morgan*

## Wind

Whispery gentleness, refreshes on a summer's day.
Overbearing strength, forcefully pushes a storm on its way.
Dutifully blowing, hastens flower's pollen to stray.
Swaying leaved branches, breathe dryness where wetness lays.
Gustily rushing sails, across waters and bays.
Drying dancing garments, hanging gracefully and gay.
Soaring colorful kites, high in the sky, as children play.

*Sharon Fisher*

## Your Drinking

You may think you are not hurting anyone with your drinking,
Let me assure you, you are wrong with your thinking.

You may take a drink and be on your way,
Family and friends are the ones who have to pay.
You keep drinking like it has a use,
It is the family and friends who have to take the abuse.
Your drinking makes you loud and mad,
It makes family and friends embarrassed and sad.

When you are drinking there are things you can't discuss,
Your drinking makes you angry and you begin to fuss.

Your words cut like a knife in the heart,
From you, your family and friends stay apart.

You wake up in the morning and "your world" is alright,
Your family and friends are still suffering from last night.

You say you are sorry and for awhile it seems okay,
Later you take another drink, and it's all a replay.

Over a period of time, your body and mind it corrupts,
During the same time relationships and homes it disrupts.

What do you think family and friends are to do,
If your drinking is the most important thing to YOU?

*Vanessa Stroman*

## Suicide Missions

Crash and burn fire warriors of the sky
Let us all die close by the side of our leader
The wind is in our souls, in our heart
The final mortal sacrifice
Only we have not succumb to cowardice
Only we stand up for what we think is right
A great challenge for our enemy
for us we shall perform with ease
Watch us as we self-destruct and take down the enemy
Know how strong we are
Death is just an obstacle, fading we overcome
Instead of dying out and fading away.
Die with dignity and respect
And know that you have helped contribute
to the future of your country...

*Monica Detweiler*

## A Tour of Spring

Let's pick wild mushrooms by decayed tree stumps
Let's dig for sassafras roots with knobby bumps
Let's climb the towering, gritty sawdust pile
Let's look for asparagus by a broken stile

We're free from winter's prisonous vice
Slide down the totem pole, it's so nice!

Let's watch rabbits dally by the berry briars
Let's sing lusty songs by spirited campfires
Let's pitch our tent near some tousled stream
Let's tell macabre misdeeds under a moonbeam

We're free from winter's prisonous vice
Slide down the totem pole, it's so nice!

*Myrtle Harazin*

## Let Freedom Ring

A people proud of wars so cruel
Let's kill them all, break all the rules
Let's take their home, the wars been fought
A man, a life, it matters not

Let's get it all, take all we can
The life, the love, the precious land
Let's give to them a little plot
A man, a life, it matters not

America you're proud to be
The land of teeming liberty
But what it all sounds like to me
Is simple, plain insanity.

*Pam Zirkle*

## If You Just Believe

There's so many things going on in this world today
Let's take a little time — time out to pray
Just try it and the results you'll see
Cause all you really have to do is believe
With a little faith it's nothing that you can't do
Just watch and see and all of your dreams will come true
A happier life you will then live each day
Peace, joy and happiness will soon come your way

If you see someone and you know that they're in need
Lend a helping hand; the benefits are oh so sweet
To say a kind word to help brighten up someone else's day
Will really mean a lot when you see the smile upon their face
What we really need is something from each and every race,
Creed and nationality, to make this whole world a better place
Just remember that each and everything you do
Will always be a reflection upon you

*Lisa L. Jones*

## Destiny Within

On the southern border of our family farm
Lies, a seductive swamp, filled with ancient beauty and muddy charm
Here, wild creations, and the secret to life itself are divinely
    guarded from men
Elusive dreams of my own destiny I feel dwells within
Each year, in the month of May, I anxiously stand in a near by field
Searching the skyline, to witness what the swamp will yield
For deep inside it's interior, almost unreachable by me
Grows a special creation of God's called a cotton wood tree
Hidden beside a creek with roots anchored to the soft ground below
The tree's branches defiantly sway with the winds that blow
In season unselfishly, it releases all newly formed seeds
Bound in fluffy balls of cotton, they race with the breeze
Like snow in the summer, I watch them pass my face
I know a loving God has already prepared for them a place
So the divine lesson from the swamp emerges; yield to life's
    understanding and yield not to despair
For our Heavenly Creator will tenderly guide each of us through the
    air
Thus from the distant mist my destiny I saw and in time we will all
come to see life wildly sows us in many directions; like the seed from
the cotton wood tree.

*Robert Mitchell Pitts*

## Angel

I am an Angel that flies up above like a bird.
I watch over people so they won't get hurt.
I wear all white, with golden blonde hair.
My eyes are as blue as the ocean.
My skin is as brown as the sands at the beach.
My clothing is as white as a piece of paper.
My crown on my head is as gold as a million dollar ring.
I don't need shoes because I live on the clouds in the sky.

*Tori Blontz*

## Hands

The secret of my love
lies within the bronzed blackness of your hands.
Hands alive with pain of endless labor
Hands
Strong hands.
Overrun with callous—
aged, yellowed
thick with life's daily setbacks.
Nails
Tough nails.
Embedded and aching with inequality's grit.
Hands
Never defeated.
Never humbled.
Unconquered.
The craft of life
is perfection
engraved in every crevice of your
bitter, coarse hands.

*Lynnette C. Velasco*

## Release Yourself

Life can be a race with time,
Life can actually make you loose your mind.

With every breath that you take,
You know when you're going to make a mistake.

But you never choose to listen to yourself,
You place your conscience on a shelf.

In God our Fathers amazing grace,
You allow yourself to lose your place.

You finally see where the battle lies.
Not before but after your spirit cries,

Your spirit of joy cries quiet yet loud,
You find you're no longer happy or proud.

Your world is lost and unable to bloom,
You then remember the closet where you'd gone to groom.

You release your sorrow, grief, your shame.
You realize you're the one to blame.

You humbly kneel at gods' feet, you feel you're in a world of peace;
A wounded spirit now regained, you again remember who shared
your pain

A vow you made to the one you knew,
Would always take good care of you!

*Vivian R. Peyton*

## Washday

Past and present crowd up into a jumble
    Like a pile of dirty laundry

And there you are with the past needing to be sorted:
    Light from dark,

Remembrances in tatters thrown away, the dark and grimy
    Discarded or bleached

Until, unrecognized, they can be used again,
    The delicate

Washed separately with care and stored lovingly
    For future use.

*Margaret B. Smith*

## Life

Life is magic; but I've seen all the tricks
Life is truth; but I'm a liar
Life is a mystery; but I need answers
Life is understanding; but I'm confused
Life is reality; but I live in fantasy
Life is a high; but I'm depressed
Life is conquest; but I've only been conquered
Life is order; but I'm chaos
Life is serenity; but I'm insane
Life is standing out; but I blend in
Life is hope; but I'm hopeless
Life is pleasure; but I've only pain
Life is meaning; but I've no purpose
Life is love; but I only hate
Life is living; but I've died a thousand times
Life is faith; but I stopped believing
Life is everything; but I am nothing
Life is time; but mine is running out
Life is a struggle; but I've given up
Life is a beginning; but I've ended

*D. P. Villeneuve*

## Dismal Lightning

Lightning bright up in the sky,
light me a path so I can fly;
the night is dark - I feel alone,
but help I see when you have shown.

When you have lit and shined abright,
I get a tingling and feel delight:
but when you fade and darken out,
return it does - the same old doubt.

You give me hope that I will see,
the passage life has written for me;
but the page has blanked when again I look,
for your thunder seems to unwrite the book.

Yet, you've a sign as you roar and are gone,
'do not tarry - but ever anon'
never to strike and exalt challenge met,
no fortune is gained your way is not set.

The path I fly is not by air
'tis the wonder of things for which I stare;
your brilliance pray, please share with me,
spare me a moment for tranquility.

*Phillip de La Moll*

## Chris's Mother

She was so close I thought I knew her.
Like a fire started by a small spark,
The fire spread and spread far.
It was supposed to burn for a long time
But the fire fell short of its goal.
God's breath had blown it out.
Soon nothing was left but charred ashes of her memory.

We miss the excitement of the fire that burned.
Nothing can get it back now.
We ask ourselves, "How could it happen to someone we love?"

I don't know if I miss her the most.
They said she would have liked me if I had met her.
This makes me think of all the things I could have done—
But didn't.

*Rebecca Redels*

## Masterpieces

A little lake nestled deep in the woods
Like a mirror so calm and still,
Whose silence is broken only by the deep bellow of a bullfrog
Or the haunting cry of the whippoorwill

The fresh clean smell of the damp morning air
The dawn's first faint glimmer of golden light,
Masterpieces one and all
Painted forever in the memories of smells and sounds and sights

Dark blue violets, dogwoods, and multicolored wild wood's flowers
Water gurgling over rocks as little streams flow through deep cut
     erosions,
Large raindrops raise bubbles upon the lakes calm surface
As flashes of light precede cracks of thunderous explosions

Refreshing sweet odors follow after the rain
And drift slowly through majestic trees that have outlived our
     father's fathers,
Royal Kings of the green shaded forests
Whose time weathered faces stare back from the pale blue waters

Spellbinding, captivating, scenes to be recalled over and over
Beautiful memories that fade not with time,
Masterpieces each and every one
Painted forever upon the canvasses of the mind

*Thomas Kruger*

## The Reality of a Dreamer

Light falls on the face of a dreamer
like a whisper in someone's ear
Or a drop of water falling from a faucet on the
black pavement below
The dreamer awakens into a world where he feels like
a stranger
And yearns to be back into his dream world
Where his awful reality can be pushed away
Loneliness and damnation are his only reality
He has a death sentence for stopping a life
barely started
Oh, to be back in that dreamer world he says
to the gray walls of his cell
The walls of course don't answer back but
the cell door does, with a creek as it opens
A guard enters to bring him to his destiny
After which he can dream forever

*Theresa Journeau*

## Life Like Fireflies

The road construction signs loom ahead
like fireflies in the night
warning of impending Armageddon
with their on-off-on-off serenade.
Emotions come rushing at me from all angles.
Pain, rage, hunger, love, lust
(in no particular order),
longing, wanting, needing.
Memories, too: walks, talks, picnics, fights
(I miss those now),
hand-holding, lovemaking, hugging.
The way you left still haunts me.
No reason, no remorse, no need,
No you!
And now my life begins anew.
A brand new life — without you.
The road ahead looks dreary.
An interstate road to nowhere.
Through nowhere. From everywhere.
I had it all, and now I face nothing.

*Ryan Tuley*

## A Coward's Silent Breath

Signals bounce back and forth,
Like light rebounding between prisms.
But Fear and Pride tangle our paths,
And Uncertainly keeps us lost and off course.

Can you fell my gaze?
Inner fires strain to break free;
To melt away the barriers we've placed between us.
Yet I stray from the molten path created,
And the seconds to our meeting stretch to years, which drift away.

What do we fear so, You and I?
Primordial Instincts fighting with Pride;
We are stuck in an emotional tug of war.
First you, then I, neither falling first;
Every strategy pulled awry.

Heroes and soldiers are brave in the face of death;
Yet I shiver at the thought of possible rejection.
Thus, for warmth, I gather only fantasies,
And the hopes and fears colliding in my dreams
May gain their freedom but on a cowards's silent breath.

*Lisa Harrison*

## Promises

Promises,
   like sand castles
   were swept away with the sunset tide
Softly told,
   like smooth caresses,
   dissolving, like crests of sea foam
   sifting through my desolate soul of sand
Bathing me in salty kisses
   that slip out to sea
   in the cool of the night
Swells of your promises
   are left floating in the waves like jellyfish
   and the shore foolishly welcomes them,
   like I
who am left like scattered chips of sea shells,
   deserted on the beach

*Michelle Fleet*

## Tribute of Time

Behold' our time is fleeting fast away,
Like sifting sand day by day;
From a childhood off laughter, I grew to see
Things of the world, and the perplexity

All too soon I grew to accountability
Took steps to marriage and responsibility;
My' My' to-morrow may never be
What gift have I left for the world to see?

I must change and seek a worthy goal
That will guide me, to save my soul
Many think when this life is done, there is no more
But there is an endless life, on heavens bright shore

So the steps I take now must be true and sound
At this end I am facing, judgement ground,
As moments are flying by, day and night
I will strive to lead some one to God's gospel light

For this deed takes away, deaths dark sting,
That I may greet Christ, Our Saviour and King;
When this step is gained, great victory is given
And rewards are received, for our crowns in heaven.

*Mary Nettie Hinshaw*

## Goodbye Dad

It was a mid-spring morning when I got the call,
little did you know how it would affect us all.
We were miles apart and trying so hard,
I thought things were better till you played your last card.
I know you had pain—I could feel it from here,
we were always here for you if that was your fear.
We struggled and struggled and fought to be close,
but still at arm's length, we were kept for the most.
Hearts were broken that rainy day in the spring,
we were shocked and dismayed by this horrible thing.
We loved you Dad, I know life was hard,
the choices you made kept us all far apart.
Your grandchildren will remember their GREAT GRANDPA
WAYNE.
I will remember how you struggled with pain.
So I guess Good-bye is appropriate now,
I wish I could say it—but I'm not sure I know how!!!!!

*Tammi L. Harroun*

## Daddy's Girl

Tiny ribbons in her hair
Little fingers pointing there
Little booties colored blue
She will always be daddy's girl

Pretty pictures drawn in crayon
of a daddy and his girl
This is you, this is me here in
the picture you see, I'm daddy's girl

Those tiny ribbons now are bows
Those little fingers now wear gold
Those little booties colored blue
Now just memories she out grew

Someone ask her whose little girl are you
She said; "I'm daddy's girl;l, I'm daddy's world.
I will always be daddy's girl.

*Pauline Massingill*

## Sixty-Five Roses

*(The title of this poem relates to a true story in which a*
little girl was told by her Doctor that she had a disease called
*Cystic Fibrosis; she thought he said sixty-five roses.)*
They called it "cystic fibrosis,"
   oh, how those words used to frighten me,
Enzymes, antibiotics, postural drainage, Vitamin E,
   everyday I wished that I could be free from all these.

But as the years went by these became a part of my life,
   and I began to see that much good can come from strife.
For I began to notice that there were "roses" among the "thorns,"
   so I wiped my tears away, no longer would I mourn.

For there are so many things to be thankful for each day,
   like daffodils or snowflakes, pumpkins or summer days,
Like picnics or birthdays, or a puppy with which to play,
   like a family which truly cares, or the friends who come my way.
Yes, there are so many "roses" to be found each and everyday,
   if we will not let the "thorns" of life get within our way.

So this is how I daily live with cystic fibrosis,
   a disease of many "thorns" which also has many "roses."
Yes, this is the poems of my life, which God has given me,
   a life of caring for "sixty-five roses,"
   so they may bloom more beautifully.

*Stewart Kessinger*

## Treasured Memories

In an old run down trailer park on the west side of town
Lived a mother and her three daughters where poverty was abound
Although the single parent family lacked for material things
They had each other in which to cling
Through the thin walls of a tiny mobile home
The distant call of Christmas Bells seem to ring alone
On a top bunk close to a warn wooden ceiling
During the cold winter nights lay a young girl dreaming
Her burning desire for a more prosperous life
Gave the impoverished girl the will to survive
Years have passed and life has gone on
The little girl now has children of her own
A parking lot and a few new buildings
Simply replaced the old family dwellings
In her mind treasured moments still exist
And a once blessed childhood is greatly missed

*Tressa A. Hendrix*

## Under The Honey Moon (Song Of Cupid)

In the land where the fairies dwell,
lives a dear fellow the stories tell:

He is the author of joy supreme.
The sweetest ever a maid can dream:

His name is Cupid with bow and dart.
He seldom misses a yearning heart:

He plays no favors, treats all the same.
There is no one but can win his game.

Seeing not with eyes but with the mind,
this skillful archer is painted blind:

Since that far time when the world was young,
poets have ever his virtues sung:

So maiden list, you will hear his wings,
and whirring shaft as he gaily sings:

Come, come and sail with me far out across life's boundless sea.
Idly the ship in he harbor lies, fair is the breeze under blue starry
  skies:

Come, sail, the hours grow late, you be the captain, I'll be the mate,
under the charm of the time of June, UNDER THE HONEY
MOON:

*Marjorie Boose*

## Today

Today is like all the rest;
Living in an interstellar dream adrift in space.
No one can hear me scream.
One of a billion stars shine almost as bright.
I just think I will be long gone,
Before anyone sees my light.
Today is like yesterday;
Filled with confusion and pain.
A single snowflake in a blizzard.
Cotton candy in the rain.
One of billions of people living a life we all share
I just think I will be long gone,
Before anyone knows I was there.
Today is, as they say;
A good day to die
I wonder if I left this place.
Would any one ask why?
One in a billion;
My odds are pretty long.
I just think I will be long gone...

*Thomas A. Bigger*

## Untitled

She can't count the days that he's been gone,
long days gone by can't be remembered,
not forgotten either, unheard of son.
Left home to find his own, not to return,
travels this earth in search of his hearts wife.
Constantly looking, waiting for one turn,
for urgency he journey's, commences life.
Through love and through war his eyes stir insane,
tries not to be biocidal, thinking,
that his worries are sands with tiny grains.
Hopes to find his castle like some lost king.
  with sign's he understands how to travel far
  with call's for his maiden, pursue to embark.

*Ryan Davis*

## Hey Black Child

Hey black child what is your name?
Look at me don't turn away again
lift your head up high and tell me
what you see? An African beauty
from the mother country.

Hey black child do you see God's beauty
in me full of love for all humanity?

Hey black child don't feel intimidated
by what others might say hold fast to
your dreams and don't let them
go away. What some may see as
weakness others see as strength.

Hey black child look closely at me
not judging by what you think you see
full of potential, love, and hope this is
what you see in God's true
African beauty.

*Tasanee La'Trice Jordan*

## Look Into The Eyes

Look into the eyes of a child
Look into the eyes of wild

Look into the eyes of no worries
Look into the eyes of stories

Look into the eyes of frustrations
Look into the eyes of question

Look at me tell me what you see

Look into the eyes of teens
Look into the eyes of keen

Look into the eyes of fear
Look into the eyes that keep you near

Look into the eyes of suggest are, look into the eyes of pressure

Look at me tell me what you see

Look into the eyes of an adult, look into the eyes of fault

Look into the eyes of clever, look into the eyes of pride

Look into the eyes of fire, look into the eyes of desire

Look at me tell me what you see

Do you see man or boy, do you see gun or toy

Do you see a heart of fear, do you see a heart of tears

Look at me tell what you see

*Morial Vallot*

## Look Into Yourself

When troubles are abrewing, and you start to throwing blame.
Look into yourself, before you call a name.

If you feel sad and lonely, and the world seems out of whack.
Look into yourself, to see just what you lack.

If he does this, and she does that, and things don't seem the same.
Just go in and look and you may find.
you've been looking through eyes, that are blind.

Things are the same, it is you who have changed,
your views, on the one whom you blame.
So look into yourself, go way in deep,
and then, get on with this game.

*Pauline S. Reisdorf*

## Peace

I was sitting on the soft, green ground, staring,
looking all around.
I tilted my head way up high to look at the big,
beautiful sky.
White fluffy clouds were floating by, a burst of
blue from far and wide.
A circle of light, so bright and willing, I saw
it smiling, I saw it grinning.
A cool summer's breeze circled all around
me, it kissed my face, I hugged my knees.
I heard children playing in the distance,
I heard birds singing in the trees.
I smelled the cool country air.
I did nothing, nothing, nothing but stare.
What a moment, a precious moment.
I felt peace throughout the earth.
There was no violence, there was no hurt, no
pollution, no confusion, just graceful,
peace and harmony.

*Rachel A. Hutchison*

## No Rainbows Today

After Midnight and Magic is dead -
Looking out this motel window
To the stars overhead -
Too many memories - A network of scars -
A thousand eternities in Lovers discard -
These arms now empty - Phantoms of Love -
The yesterday's tempting - Haunting enough -
Love so sour and yet, bittersweet -
Be dead on the Morrow - Fractured/Discreet -
Sick unto madness - Rattles the brain -
Eyes just sipping this Backwash of Pain -
Lost in the a forest - A Wilderness Shame -
Smoldering Hearts - Other's to Blame -
Salt has no flavor and HERE COMES THE RAIN!
Clouds storming thru in dark angry rage -
Guess there will be....
......NO RAINBOWS TODAY!!!.......

*Michael A. Doelz*

## Our First Christmas Together

It's our very first Christmas together my dear.
I'm sure you'll agree 'twas a wonderful year.
In our garden of love there's been nothing but clover.
Your love's filled my heart, till my cup's running over.
There's love in your kisses or just in your touch,
You're easy to love and I love you so much.
So, I wish you the merriest and happiest days
With the love and respect you can cherish always.

*William V. Rush*

## The Brother

There he sat, that small nephew of mine
looking sad and glum but extremely kind

What could make those huge, beautiful brown eyes sad,

You only have to look around him to see the
circumstances and understand why he would be so mad

For this little brother of his would pester, pinch,
and fight with him only to get his own way again

So there's never a moments peace he can share alone
therefore, he must pull into a world of his own
for his little bother to have all the attention it seems,
just irks him and I know he wants to scream!

Please help him someone, he needs to excel
with his brother he can't, he'll be in hell!
For in his heart he wants a bond with his brother
but he can't do it if there's no help from others!

So he trudges along this painful, silent path
hoping that his brother grows up fast
so they can have a friendship that will last.

Maybe someday!

*Paulette Blackburn*

## Memories

Who is this man with hair of gray,
looking so tired, so old?

The face is vaguely familiar,
but the eyes are strange, distant.

Eyes that reflect dreams, winning,
losing, loving and being loved.

Memories of Lilacs in the spring,
how he loved that fragrance.

His father's flower garden in the summer.
Walks in the woods, sailing on the lake.

The wonderful smells and sounds of fall.
Leaves, colors, football, pumpkins and mums.

The excitement of the first snow.
Crisp air, turkey and Christmas trees.

Who is this man with hair of gray,
looking so tired, so old?

The face is more familiar,
but the eyes, still distant.

*Victor E. Gattuso*

## Memories

Here on this wall, I'll display all my girls,
Looking their best in ruffles and curls.

You'll see in their photos, their charm and their grace,
Their perfect complexions and smiles on their face.

You'll notice their beauty, their eyes how they glow,
With each photo added, each year how they grow.

I'll look at the photos, remembering the years,
When life was fulfilled with laughter and tears.

And many a friend will come here to call,
And pass this display upon my wall.

And they'll give not a glance from one to another,
Because photos are memories in the heart of a Mother.

*Veronica Nelson DeChausse*

## Mountains of Memories

I feel like an infant that just entered the world,
Lost and confused, without a clue.
As I walk through the vast field,
I can only see beautiful, rolling, mountains in the distance.

My heart is shattering with every step I take.
My thoughts are obscured due to the absence of my lover.

Every mountain reminds me of our great moments alone
   together.
Oh yes, that one over there brings to mind our most romantic night.
It looks alone and scared, but you can tell that it is
   adoring the precious attention and loving its surrounder.

Oh how I wish I can see him again.
It would be so nice to just hold each other until sleep has
   taken over.

As I look at the mountains I am reminded of his beauty.
Yes mountains are the most beautiful objects in the world.
   *Laura Forchelli*

## The Rose

Life is like a rose;
Lots of petals and thorns;
Lots of happiness and equal parts of sadness but in the end to hold
the rose we compromise.

Sometimes we draw blood and sometimes the fragrance;
So, sometimes we live for others, sometimes for the well-being of
our home and rarely for ourselves.

The smart one is who learns early on to enjoy both the blood and the
fragrance while others cry and get hurt.
So learn to bend in front of destiny because He who writes knows
protects and cares for you.

Live but with compromise, compromise and compromise foremost in
your mind else you will never hold the rose.
   *Shivani Sethi*

## Rules

Everywhere you look nowadays there sure are
lots of rules: No shirt, no shoes, no service!
Please, don't walk on the grass. No smoking,
because of the clean air, indoor act. No
parking in the handicapped parking spaces
...only to find that there are non-handicapped
people occupying those parking spaces, which
in turn makes the handicapped people very angry.
If your children are out and about with you and you go
in a store sometimes there will be a sign posted,
"keep an eye on your children (kids) please don't let them
run loose... or they will be sold as slaves." Well,
Mr. or Mrs. store owner; slavery went out of style
along time ago, along with the manual typewriter.
There are rules, rules, and even more rules ... did
you know that sometimes rules govern rules and that
you sometimes find yourself breaking some of the rules,
rules - even the most simplest of the rules.
I hate following rules! Because just how many
people are really following the rules the way they are suppose to!
   *Robin Marie Papworth-Walsh*

## The Light

As we see the light, a little beam filtering thru the black mist
of tomorrow radiates into a full multitude of sparkling diamonds
with each reflection bouncing from one to another then we see
the full scale of a beautiful universe engulfed in his full light
and the blackness of tomorrow has passed away.
   *Myra Sue Mann*

## Lonely Woman

The woman sat all alone on the beach
Loud noises of waves splashing on her feet.

She was all alone with no one to care
No one for her feelings to share.

Out in a distance a ship sails in the night
Up in the heaven the moon shines bright

She sat so quietly with no one around
Watching and waiting for the waves to calm down.

When the ships had sailed out of sight
The woman got up and walked into the night.

She kicked at the sand as she strolled by
And looked straight ahead and gave a sigh

She walked out into the cold dark sea
Lovely and graceful as she could be

As I gazed into the water so bright
I saw the lady war no where in sight

With the moon shining so bright in the sky
The lonely woman had just said goodbye.
   *Marita Hinson*

## Love Has Its Times

When you make it nice,
Love has pleasant  times.
People have a lot of infatuation,
When it's real love we say congratulations.
When everything works out right,
You'll have your partner every night.
You'll have your joys and sadness too,
That's all a part of love, I thought you knew.
Sometimes it is better,
Enjoying the nice weather together.
When you can talk to each other,
It makes it so that you're not a bother.
Three strikes you're out for me,
If you set them free, wait then you'll see.
That's my opinion about love and its times,
They all are surprises, but that's the end of my rhymes.
   *Monica Rose*

## My Little Love

Chelsea, my little love, you are my world.  Chelsea, my little
love, you are my girl.

I've waited so very long to hold you in my arms.  Now that you're
here, I will always hold you near.

With a handful of pretty smiles and a pocketful of dreams, you are
the sweetest thing that I have ever seen.

I wish you could know how I love you so; but some day you'll see...
you mean everything to me.

My little love, my little love, you must have come from up above.
   *Tamara Jacobson*

## A Gift For Gratitude

The grass beseech the heavens for rain,
Lightening and thunder emphasize the request,

Branches drumming to the rhythm of the wind
And birds corralling the little ones to safety;

The rain came and flowers respond with the gift
Of beauty;

Heaven acknowledges the gratitude and rejoices.
   *Myem Carpen*

## Yesterdays

Sitting there in your rocking chair
Loving hands just folded with care
Thoughts must keep your head in a whirl
While thinking back when you were a girl

High topped shoes with buttons tight
Corset pulled with all your might
Tiny waist and long, long dresses
Set off by your silken tresses

Wrapped around your shoulders lace
Cameo gently set in place
Nosegay of flowers in your hands
Held together by ribbon strands

Riding proud in your one horse carriage
While suitors begged for your hand in marriage
Sleigh bells ringing on wintry nights
Oh it must have been a sight

One that I would have loved to have seen
But alas just in my dreams
Those were the days when people cared
and what they had they gladly shared

**Nancy Iris Handford**

## The Composer's Song

Living life is performing a song,
lovingly created by a Composer,
for which an instrument is designed to play.
Inside this instrument lies music that keeps the song alive.
The music that only the Composer hears.
It may be the melody or the accompaniment,
But every type of music is important and every part is heard.
As the song begins, it flows from line to line, exploring new keys.
The instrument follows the Composer and listens for His beat.
And the song is beautiful.
But throughout the piece, wrong notes are played,
tempos become irregular, even the instrument breaks.
Yet, the song goes on, becoming wiser, sweeter.
And when it comes to its final note, it ends.
And every flaw will be remembered no more.
But the music will not die.
It may be forgotten by new awakening instruments,
But to the One who composed it,
To the One who gave up this song, for the instrument to play,
The music will be forever heard, for it is the Composer's song.

**Sara Skladal**

## Secret

A long, thin, brown string of a child
Lying in the dust of Mogadishu.
Is it you?
Covered with a rag of flies
In the nose and in the eyes.
Is it you?
Hungry child, you are so thin
The sun shines lightly through your skin.
Is it you?
No longer water in your eyes
And all your mucous has run dry
Caked and hardened on your lip,
Have you let the Secret slip?
Are you here to save us all?
Are you the One who has been sent?
Is this what the Secret meant?
Are you the one, Faithful and True?
Is it you?

**Travis of Bickley**

## The Beauty Of Maine

From snowcapped mountains to the rocky shore,
Maine offers beauty, tranquility and much, much more.

Lobsters and clam bakes and people who smile,
these things you'll find when you stay awhile.

When you're frustrated, hassled and feeling insane,
you'll find peace and serenity in the beauty of Maine.

To those who come and never leave,
so many dreams they do conceive.

Year in, year out, the seasons' change,
Each one uncovers the beauty of Maine.

Warm hearts and strong hands are offered when needed,
A call for help does not go unheeded.

Our pride fortifies like links in a chain,
For all of these things are the beauty of Maine.

**Mary Ellen Plato**

## Sitting in the Snow

I feel your words wrap around my soul,
Make me think time won't take it's toll.
So how much more time 'till were all said and done,
'Til we kill our happiness, destroy what we've won.

When I ask why and you say "I don't know,"
When you say "never" my tears fall like snow.
The snow on the ground piles up like our lies,
Covered in frozen like our sugar-coated lines.

So why does your voice ease my shivering body,
When we both know your lying when you say you love me.
Why waste our time, why wish for more
When we've both seen what's out there, seen it all before.

The rain falls on me now, my eyes so dry and red
My body aching for your arms to soothe my feverish head.
the cold coils around me and freezes my tear streaked face,
The snow thickens upon me and traps me in my place.
Like you have me trapped now, so afraid to just let go,
And just now I realize you liked me in the snow.

**Mollie Swartz**

## Only Just Began

To be with her and to laugh for awhile,
makes his eyes shine,
and God's eyes smile.

No talk, no voice, no literal interpretations
are,
in this place of wondrous vibrations.
Waking beside her, in a garden of green,
Love, in his heart,
does not go unseen.

Words go unspoken, as they weren't yet made;
emanating feelings, instead, were played.

God in paradise,
gave this splendor, divine;
bestowed upon them, resting sublime.

This was the beginning,
only just begun;
and legend in it's making,
History was on the run.

**Sue Jackson**

## Why?

Why is our skies all filled with smoke;
Making all of our children choke?
Why isn't our water crystal clear;
So we can drink it without fear?

Why is there trash lying all around?
Where is the beauty we once found?
Why can't our children go out and play
Without someone trying to take them astray?

Why are there drugs out in our schools?
Why are people taking them like fools?
What ever happened to our lands?
People have ruined them with their hands!

Together we can clean up this mess
And give us back what God did Bless!
All of those thing were gifts of Love;
Given to us from God above!

Together we can make a stand
And give our children back their land!
*Melissa Wilkes*

## My Opinion

O.J. You think you're a hero
Man look in the mirror
I am no fan of yours
No, I do not know the number on your shirt
But that's okay neither can anyone else see through all that dirt
Sitting there in court you show no shame
You are real good at shifting the blame
O.J. you haven't said a word
But the nation asks what occurred
Domestic violence is the story here
Do you remember when you and Nicole's life was so dear.
You have two small children
Now their grandparents will have to wipe away their tears
and comfort their fears
O.J., or Juice as you are known, was your love to Nicole shown?
"THE TRUTH WILL SET YOU FREE", they say
Confess O.J. is what we pray
*Lorraine MacMillan*

## Let Me Introduce My Mother

There are many beautiful things on this earth,
Many of which I'm very fond.
From the God created miracle of birth,
To each and every new day's dawn.
But one compares to no other,
"Let me introduce my Mother."

She had five of us children to take care of,
She taught us to love and fear God,
And somehow she always had enough love
And I'm sure God's head gives a nod,
When I say there'll never be another.
So, "let me introduce my Mother."

She's as fine a woman as a woman can be,
Showing others she really does care.
I'd like to show others what she means to me,
So I'll live my best so that everywhere
She'd be proud to say to everyone,
"Let me introduce my son."
*Timothy R. Fordyce*

## Night Time Climb

Have you ever climbed a mountain? It's sometimes very tall.
Many times we need some help, in case we just might fall.

Bedtime can be like a mountain, the steps are hills so tall.
And we need help to get there, if we will only call.

Our mountain climbing expert, might be our mom or dad,
But sometimes experts just like this can't be called or had.

If this ever seems to happen, there is someone who'll do.
He's your friend in play and fun, your puppy dog will do.

He comes along in fun and games, he chases toys for you.
He listens to you when you're sad, he licks your tears for you.

So after hugs and kisses, start your climb so tall.
Take along your friend with you, he'll know just what to do.

When you reach your final peak, kneel down and talk to Jesus.
Tell Him you've enjoyed your day and I'll have another if I may.

Bedtime can be an adventure, it has led to dreams.
And dreams can be the future, if we have friends, it seems.
*Mary Libroth*

## The Last Goodbye

As you go your way
May peace walk with you
Until the adjoining day

And when that day comes with morning hue
While walking upon grass beaded with drops of dew
May peace still walk with you.

O' this pain about my chest
That harbors all my wants and fears,
How I would like to tear it from my flesh
And end these painful years.

But for the hope of eternal love
Given to those completing God's task,
I can for another moment endure
This painful throb about my chest.
*Thomas Kelly Sparkman*

## Our Time

That first time I saw your face I knew I'd loved you then
Maybe another time or place I wasn't sure quite when

I loved you a long time ago but it wasn't meant to be
Our love had just begun to grow it was not time for me

So once again I've come to wait I knew you'd look for me
We found our love last time too late this time it's meant to be

I knew one day that you'd be there just like you were before
To deepen that past love we share this time there's so much more

I believe we have one love in every life we live
And if that love is deep and true it's forever there to give

Maybe it was just a dream or perhaps another life
Whether it was then or now I knew I'd be your wife
*Patricia Blais Stubbert*

## Brigadoon

Brigadoon, Brigadoon
Land of Scotland's forever.
Land of pipes skirl, and tattoo of drums.
Land of the Highland Fling
Land of the Lochs, and hideaway glens.
Land of the thistle and heather.
Land of Tartans and meaningful plaids.
Land of Scots' memories stirring.

Land that time should forget.
*Walter F. Harter*

## A School Girl's Dream

When I grow up I will be rich,
Maybe have a kid or two;
I'll have butler to answer the door,
And a maid with lots to do.

The pool will stretch across the yard,
The spa will take up half;
The Porsche will replace the Mercedes Benz,
And at bills I plan to laugh.

When I grow up I think I will,
Find my dream come true;
He'll be six feet tall and dark and have,
The biggest eyes of blue.

We'll have a second house in France,
But when the weather's bad;
We'll take the jet as a getaway,
To go see Mom and Dad.

As I lay here dreaming up my life,
The thoughts just make me smile;
But maybe I should just concentrate,
On finishing school for a while.

*Trista Hoffman*

## Life

No one ever said life was easy
Maybe it's just me
I face problems everyday
Work, school, and at play
It's true you should take one day
at a time
But also enjoy what you have
Life is short ;  stop the violence
Life is hard; take it day by day
Life is full of problems; meditate
Life is roller coaster; it has it's ups and downs
Life is not always bad; remember
the good times
Life is God's gift to us; take
care of your gift.
See people for who they really are.
  Life.....

*Megan Magnera*

## Dad

Days come and go, as weeks slip into earthly time.
Memories once strong and clear, seem locked in the cell of my heart.
They dance on my thoughts, but do not linger.
They hide from the pain of November, and belong to my best friend.
Quiet, peaceful, and lasting to eternity.
The wind and sun, of moving water and stirring pines.
Of spirits in spirit, far removed from this age.
Yet there is learning as there always can be.
Love, a decision to love, and to give beyond measure.
A love not given to fleeting anger or indifference.
Steadfast with compassion, looking through to see the truth of
  character.
Not like some quaint feeling, but of daily committed purpose.
A weary soldier who had fought the good fight.
An example for my hope.

*Neal R. Ewing*

## My Best Friend

It all started long ago on that old, rickety, brown rocking chair.
Memories were created through sweet melodies and gentle
  words read from novels and picture books.
Enlightening her mind from a very young age, she prepared
  her for the difficult tasks that life had in store.
From bottles to sack lunches, she watched her baby grow to a child.
Between girl scouts, piano lessons, and wiping runny noses,
  she still found an abundance of time to love and play
She held her hand along the way as her child discovered
  Band-Aids, homework, and other children.
When unkind words darkened the day, she was always there to pull out
  the sun and find a smile
From a child to a young woman her pride and joy had blossomed.
Never tiring she became the unacknowledged voice behind so many term
  papers and assignments.
The best of times they always had, she was her very best friend, full
  of hope and encouragement.
Lessons were taught, wisdom and knowledge were instilled, maturity
  and love had taken their toll.
The time had come to temporarily say goodbye.
With the grace and poise of her mentor, the child stepped for the
  first time to test her own wings.
She soon would return, but time had flown so fast.
She knew, however, they would always be together in heart and spirit
  for they were best friends—even better they were mother and
  daughter.

*Suzanne Forstrom*

## Homesick for New Mexico

In the streets of Salt Lake City
Mi hermana and I gathered the hardly
Verdolagas, which grew in the cracks
Of the sidewalks, in grocery bags.

Our abuelita, at my tío's home, coció frijoles
And made papas fritas y tortillas frescas
Para mi tío y la fiesta de su cumpléaños.

Several city natives stopped y nos
Preguntaron porqué estábamos juntando yerbas.
We tried without success to explain
That they were vegetables which would be part
Of a special birthday meal.

And they zoomed along tisking
And flicking nickels at my sister and me
Shaming us for celebrating
Our heritage.

*Liddie Martinez*

## Generations Of Wonder

Looking out the window, knowing not what I'll find.
Millions of thoughts race through my mind.
Why is our world so cold,
and why must every soul grow old?
Why do we fight one another,
When the American way is brother help brother?
  Why do we judge by the color of skin,
  Why don't we look for the person within?
Why don't we help the poor and the homeless,
Why, instead, are we so heartless?
  All of these thoughts race through my mind,
  Not knowing the answers I will find.
Hopefully, one day all the pain will be ended,
And all those torn souls will someday be mended.
  Maybe one day, I'll look back in regression,
  And remember today as a time of depression.

*Tina Hook*

## Gone for Good

Hendrix, Morrison, Joplin, and Cobain
Missing you causes us so much pain
Lennon, Moon, Chapin, and Eric Carr
We all remember who you are
Marvin Gaye, Mercury, and Stevie Ray Vaughn
Your music reminds us that you're gone
Presley, Holly, Valens, and Big Bopper
I remember when you were such a chart topper
Jones, Van Zant, Jon Boham, and T-Rex
Diseases, disasters, drugs, and car wrecks
Nilsson, Nelson, and Eazy-E
They each meant something to you and me
Otis Redding, Frank Zappa, Steve Clark, and Cliff Burton
Thinking of you creates such hurting
Selena, Sid Vicious, and Andy Wood
I cry when I know that you're gone for good

*Paul J. Brown*

## Living Without

I had slipped to a catastrophic low, the booze would have to be no
    more.
At first the spirits weren't greatly missed, except the physical
    cravings.
I had experienced a feeling of rebirth, a gratifying sort of sow.

Left, behind, the bars and its plasticness;
    the reckless carousing and raucousness that caused pain.
Now the world was full of possibilities.
    Light reflecting day, not neon.

But...life without euphoria was melancholy ,though I don't know why.
Without passion and risk my mind reverted to the whims of exhilaration
and glitter and yes, sin. I put away the fear of death, and dreamed of
laughter. For any feeling, no matter how tragic, was better than
    utter stoicism.

Drink was like a love affair, bad and twisted at times but gloriously
dangerous and uplifting. And like the love of a woman it's feeling of
irreplaceability is gravely missed.

The glass and its fingers held high cannot be dismissed as all
treacherous. The world is not and will never be, heaven. Drink
appears a chance better and no feeling at all can be as deadly as life
in the bottle.

*Vincent Casale*

## True Blue Love

Summer mists caress my body in waves,
More often than my man these days,

Radiant sun unleashes my love starved soul,
My man requests room, board, and toll,

Eyes come in smiling,
In an hour, Baby, see you!

My friend the sun so patient and strong,
Waits as my man and I dance sad and long,

I awaken wondering where has my man gone?

By my side my sun still dances slowly,
Off the remains of loves sad reflected glow,
My love, the sun extracts hurt deep and low,

Without this! Oh were would I be?
No sun drying tears of what will never be,
No sympathetic trees to blow my fears away,
High into the heavens, hear the echoes as I pray,

The earth sings with me sweet and low,

It may sound strange, it may seem untrue,
Nature wonders are my true lovers
Faithful, loyal and true blue.

*Leslie Maxwell Cook*

## The Sea

I stand atop a sea gulls' wing, soaring, circling
As we circle I see the mighty ocean, blue and strong,
It stretches across the horizon as far as the eye can see,
Below waves break and foam against the rocks,
Coming closer with each astride to the sandy beach,
Miles and miles of forever wonder striving to reach the shore.

*Michael W. Davis*

## Motherhood

Of all the jobs I have ever had,
Motherhood is one, I thought,
I would never have.

Nine months of morning sickness,
Preterm labor, Brethine, Bedrest and Boredom.
Braxton Hicks, Irritability, many False Alarms
and finally, the real thing... Childbirth!!

Late nights with little sleep,
crying and not knowing why.
Dirty diapers, Colic and Teething,
I wondered, was it all worth it?

With eyes full of wonder
each day a new discovery.
Babbling with delight,
as he sees his own reflection

Of all the jobs I have ever had,
Motherhood is the greatest one
I will ever have.

*Rhonda Tucker*

## Winter Snow Plows

Snow plows pushing snow so high.
mounds, and mounds,
So soft and white.
Deer, looking for grass, along the ridge.
Children seeing all this from atop a bridge.
All God's creation's soft and white.
Saying "Oh Lord" what a sight,
Seeing snow plows go out
of sight, pushing snow
so soft and white.

*Lois E. Stratton*

## "Sweeping Down The Plain"

A fresh and scented clear blue morning full of dreams and hope,
Mowers humming, children swinging from a knotted rope,
Buses growl, the children laugh; here comes the early mail.
A dentist starts a root canal, small puppies chase their tails.

Mom and Sis reveal some secrets as they drive downtown
They're looking for a place to buy a long white wedding gown.
Instantly, the world explodes. The glass and metal fly.
Oh God! My God! Oh my dear God! Why? Oh Why? Oh Why?

Bloody devastating screams pierce this now dark day.
Groans and cries within the wreckage slowly face away.
Emergency is full of dead; some dying some in comas,
A morbid silence sweeps the land, all pray for Oklahoma.

A vicious brutal spineless act inspired by hate and Satan
Diminishes and terrifies a once proud, mighty nation.
Moms hold children's photographs; Dads hold heads in hands.
Funerals and poems about footprints in the sand.

We'll bury and salute the dead; we will repay the debt,
We'll overcome the tragedy; we never will forget
About an enemy within, about the grief and pity.
about the dead and terrorized in Oklahoma City.

*Paul Henry Medina*

## Words

Words are only letters put together. Why do they hurt so
much when they are sometimes spoken? Sometimes they can make
you feel so good, so special. But other times they can make
you feel like giving up. Words can be a very cruel thing sometimes.
Words can take you up or bring you way down.
Sometimes words can weigh so much but than other times
people can take them so lightly. Words are used sometimes to
slap you in the face. Other times words are used to touch
your heart. Words were not intended to cut you like a knife.
Words were created to communicate to one another. People
should choose the words they speak with some thought before
they speak them.

*Sherry A. Wolfe*

## My Protector

I sat near a thorny bush today.
My arm tingled when in caressed the bush
Causing me to bleed.
It dripped on to the green lawn
Ah, a Christmas contrast.
Everything looks so perfect
Even with red leaking all over
I may be a rose
Sweet and beautiful
Or a thorn
Selfish only because I'm protecting my heart
My head searched for a place to rest
Finally giving up when no one offered comfort.
Dad left and I got lost.
Maybe I actually found my strength came out...
Along with my heart.
The thorns cover the bush
The thorns hide the rose
The thorns shelter me
And I should have let you leave me when you left

*Ona L. Rieder*

## My Child's Illness

Oh, God what is this love you have so great, decreed?
My child lies in a bed of death and illness, I'm so bereaved

The body may be small, but the soul is strong, within
Listen to the words that come, from this child's heart singing

Through this he'll touch the hearts and souls of all, within his reach
A glorious transformation he'll achieve, its of the soul, no one can teach
    Your heart and soul will reach the highest of all creation
As only the soul can feel and say, mere words deny, this inspiration

Your soul will reach God's door, so intense and burning true
Please heal this child of mine, for no one here can do, what you

The months and years my child has lost, jumping high so full of life
Will be replaced by our Great Lord, the mission here, is of greater
    stride
    Of all that touches mine on earth, this is of devastation
But through the pain of soul and heart, all faith comes fast, to restoration

And change the hearts and souls of all, whom, this child will touch
All intertwine with God, their lives change forever, it is besought

In the end the memories perceived, of the years gone by, of this so true
    Is not of jumping, climbing trees, but of the soul so binding
    with our Lord, assured

*Rebecca Seqovia*

## Choice

My mind, my body, my life
    My Choice

No one gives you the right
So now I'm gonna Fight
To make pro lifer's understand
That it's not abortion on demand

It's our right, our lives, our decision
    Our Choice

Not Pro-abortion nor Pro-death we say
But still you are out there day after day
Waving your signs and saying your prayers
while in the past the Fight hasn't been fair

We are pro-woman, pro-rights
    Pro-Choice

*Shawndra L. Gierman*

## Paper And Pen

Paper and pen,
My confidant, my friend.
I'm soothed by your feel,
By writing what's real,
And stories sometimes too.
I lie to myself and to you.
Well, not lie exactly,
I just don't see clearly.
It's hard to look inside,
See the pain, swallow the pride.
But pen and paper are always there
With my greatest joy or darkest despair.
I can pretend to be strong or let myself go,
And only pen and paper will know.
For pen and paper will never tell
All the secrets I hide so well,
Things hidden in verses and between the lines
But there for the finding if I take the time.
Pen and paper, paper and pen
I come to you for comfort, my dear old friend.

*Suzanne Grady*

## Her Grandfather's Eyes

I can't believe what I heard today
My dear sweet daddy has passed away.
And as the tears flowed from my eyes
I began to realize,
That my daughter has her grandfather's
Eyes.

They are deep blue and serious.
They are kind, understanding and curious.

As I look into her eyes I'm taken back
To my childhood days,
His stern concern, his understanding ways,
The deep blue grey of bygone times,
The happy eyes of bygone times.

I can't believe what I heard today
Dear daddy has passed away.
As the tears flowed from my eyes
I looked into my daughter's eyes
And smiling, I began to realize
My daughter has her grandfather's eyes.

*Susie McCann*

## Welcome Home

You arrived home early, from a trip far away -
My emotions were high as we spoke on the phone.
No words could express what my heart shouted out -
Happiness and love welling up as I said, "Welcome home."

You arrived in my life through the gift of a friend.
We've moved swiftly this month - honesty setting our tone.
We both "know" our next step on this winding path -
A lifetime together, nightly bidding each, "Welcome home."

You arrived in my soul long before time began.
With you there is a peace that I've never known.
My lover, my friend, my soul-mate, and much more -
Feeling whole and complete I can say, at last,
"WELCOME HOME!"

*Victoria Kat*

## Any Wish Come True

If I could have any wish come true,
My First wish would be to share forever with you.

Our days would be simple, our nights care free,
We'd roam over this land like a large roaring sea.

If I could have any wish come true,
I'd wish for your biggest dream to come to you.

To never have worries that cause you to frown,
To give you pleasure; more worthy than a countries crown.

If I could have any wish come true,
I would wish for your happiness to always be brand new

No ups and downs to cause you unwanted pain,
In your heart, only sunshine, not a drop of rain.

But, if I could have only one wish come true,
My one wish would be to share forever with you.

*Rhonda L. Egly*

## Untitled

As I look back at my childhood,
my fondest memories are not
Disneyland or the toys that were bought;
They are grandma's house
in the Sunflower State;
it's her rhubarb pie and fresh corn that I ate.

It's sitting in the henhouse
eating cookies she made,
running eggs to her kitchen, as fast as they were laid.
I would listen to coyotes, howling at night;
I always had dresses from her Singer Upright.

The haunted barn was the place
for my cousins and I;
From the rafters was the rope swing, each one of us would fly.
They would chase me with a locust, tied to a string
Our treehouse and stilts were never boring.

As I look back at my childhood
always with a large grin,
What I would do to be little
and at grandma's house again.

*Leanna Curry Wells*

## Stuffy The Teddy Bear

I'm lying on this shelf tattered and old
My friend has outgrown me, you see.
Not one single grudge do I hold
For I've had a life of fun and glee.

Gone from my head is my left ear
One glass eye has long disappeared,
This position n the shelf was my fear,
When that slick new red bike appeared.

It makes me feel a little lost and sad
Since this time in my friends life has come,
I remember the fun and cuddling we had,
Now I know these things are over and done.

My time has arrived, I'm sorry to say,
We all have to drink of the "aging cup"
I'm among the baby toys he has put away,
For my dear friend is growing up.

But from my shelf I'll watch my friend
As his life and growth begins to soar,
For our love of each other will never end,
And he will, take me from this shelf once more.

*Lorraine Hasson*

## The Greatest Victory

Running for years only to find
My greatest of enemies only seconds behind
Scared to stand I fall never to see
My weary self behold victory
For to win over oneself is the greatest of wins
To wipe out all blemish and be free from all sins
To stand and to triumph living for the good
To be as one could, might, must, can, and should
Deserves the highest of praise and all should acknowledge
Our real live hero whose free from self's bondage
For the one that we fight knows us and can see
That he is in I and I am in he
It is I that is selfish, it is I who is wrong
Yet it's I who has humility in my two-voiced song
And so my two selves struggle in a battle beyond degree
Still battling with strong eyes on the Greatest Victory

*Rachael Alisha McBride*

## A Cycle Of Life

As I trod along the hardened path of life
My head is not always up, but inclined down.
Instead of seeing the beauty, I only see strife.

Soon the path steepens, as the challenges grow
And my vision narrows more,
Serving only myself, with burdens in tow...
So on friend, family and God, I close the door.
Upon reaching the summit, challenges won,
I reap the rewards of my labor hard earned.
Yet the rewards are fruitless; they are none.
Revelation hits me, that upon what is greatest, I have
turned.

Now this deep chasm in my soul is filled
With faith, hope and love, that I now hoard.
I will not follow the path of man unskilled,
But the one made for me by my Lord.

*Mike Maggio*

## Final Emotion

I was running free along the edge of the ocean
My heart has never had such an emotion
As the waves crashed upon the shore
It crushed my heart and my life it tore.

I've always wanted to see a beautiful sunset
And as I watched I became upset
To know that my life people would soon forget
Yet, I know that in Heaven my life would soon be spent

I all of a sudden felt a cold breeze
Against my skin, I thought I would freeze
Yet I felt happy deep down inside
I just laid down and then I cried.

I ran along the warmest beach
The end of my life I soon would reach
I wasn't scared of what lie ahead
Because my death, I no longer did dread

And so I laid down on the warm sand
I listened closely to the angels band
Out of breath calmly I lied
Quietly on the beach I died.

*Nicole S. Kindschy*

## My Mengioma

I must have gone mad or was very tired
My life became so deeply mired.

What once was passion became a dread
I screamed in the darkness God let me be dead.

His eyes could not see his heart could not hear
He was abusing the woman he once held so dear.

Again I screamed on deaf ears and then I ran
Consumed with fear and exhaustion I was where I began.

I fell into an abyss only God and I know
I moaned for my groom. He did not come. I could not go.

He had no forgiveness and he could not see
The women he scorned was not even me.

He says guilt is within not created
What is my guilt? Nearly dying? Why am I so hated?

When love is found by fate
Only to lose it again
Makes me wonder if it is worth the wait.

This leaves me ponder 'til the day I die
All and all was it all a lie?

*Sheila LaCour*

## Streak Of Independence

I'm not a little girl stumbling out of
my own front porch.
I don't have dirt on me that you can wash.
My hair will grow as it pleases, regardless
of how much you want to fix it.
I don't wear clothes that you can straighten.
My room will be mine no matter how hard
you try to clean it up.
I don't have a voice you can sing with.
My speech will stand on its own without
your approval.
I'm not a little girl sitting on the sidewalk,
waiting for someone to help me up.

*Laurie Christenson*

## Ship

My love, my life, my ship at sea.
My rudder, my ballast, my hull are thee.
My sail, to catch, the winds that blow.
My compass, pointing, true to go.
My wheel, to steer, 'cross oceans wide.
My anchor, steadfast, 'gainst the tide.
My deck, my stand, 'bove perilous brine.
My cabin, my shelter, 'gainst rain or shine.
My hold, my galley, bunk at night.
My charts, my log, my lamps for light.
My mast, my bow, with flags hung proud.
My treasure, o'rwatched, by cannons loud.
My vessel, 'cross, the seas of life.
My ship, my love, my darling wife.

*Michael Altman*

## Lost

I lie here in total darkness
My soul finds itself alone once again.
I reach out for you though you are not there.
Nothing but pain is real now.
Still I call out your name—longing for you to answer!
So afraid to let you go.
You invade my soul.
You haunt my every thought.
My days are endless.
The nights are longer.
If I could see you for just a moment, to touch you and know you were
real
Would take away all of this hurt and erase all of the anxious
feelings, but
After that moment was gone and reality set in
I would be alone.
Alone once again.

*Meighan L. Elliott*

## Travelers

I travel by wind.
My spirit flies free.
My soul is buried deep.
My heart will no longer weep.
I travel by land.
My feet run free.
My body is buried deep.
My heart will no longer weep.
But who am I, who am I, the one
To be called your love?
Love is so much more than we ever
Can hold, only our future kingdom will ever know.

*Nicole Jordan*

## Salty Tears (Won't Irrigate the Desert)

I am the desert, My Love, that you wander in.
My words are sand, wind whipped into your eyes.
And none of the tears that dribble onto me
melt the crust of dusty dreams.

The tears, wrung from you,
should quench my thirst and nurture a garden.
But they choke me, salt sucking whatever
surviving life away, like I choke you.

You must be thirsty, but I have nothing to give.
We can't coexist. I must search for something purer
than salty tears. I wait to love
the one with the divining stick.

*Zachary Oliver*

## The Seeker

Where are the things that glimmer and glisten?
Mystery, fascination, allure, and aspiration, have all vanished.
The soul grows tired of the journey, but cannot give up the search.

Drawn at last into the forbidden,
the seeker will embark toward the darkened mist.
The dread of nothingness, greater than the danger
that lurks in the beyond.

Tread with caution.
The pilgrimage, certain to be costly,
will be taken at the price.
Those who cross over will pay with their purity and honor,
for the emerald breeze, the golden moon,
the scarlet sea, the sparkling view.
Pray that the told not be the pain of others, or the soul itself.

But, would not the Knowing be helpless
in changing the path pursued?
The inner voice will struggle with the thought,
preferring questions over the loss of peace of mind,
turning from the reflection that threatens to disclose
what lies within.

**Rochelle L. Millsap**

## Out Of Synch

Ashes of broken dreams dance sprightly on subtle,
naked breezes-newborn species of an arson's hand.

Life ebbs from a gaping gunshot wound to a child's head.
The blood forms warm, still pools on the hardened asphalt.
Eyes are open, blankly staring.
Silenced, is his voice.

A young girl-embraced by night's darkness-cries herself to sleep,
unable to erase the memory of the sweaty faces raining lustful,
smirking expressions of completion upon her as their
owners spent themselves.
The mother sits in the next room erasing her own memories.
Consumed by match, pipe and addiction, she exhales the charred essence
of a painful past and her daughters broken spirit.

In another part of the city I am in my car at a stop light,
  exchanging pleasantries with a perfect stranger.
The light turns  green.
As I pull away, I smile, though I am deeply saddened.

**J. Stuart Severo**

## I Bit of Me

  "Envy" one too many know its
name, do you know it's shame?
  Or do you use it just
to blame, how life is unfair
to only you?

  "Love" like the beauty of a dove...
do you see love as he does?  for
you say; I don't feel it, if I can't "see" it
  "Peace" a peace of mind" or a
piece of me?  Which shall it be?

  And so for "Truth" well, the
truth is "Golden" for when the
words were spoken — there was
no "truth" — there ... so why should
you care — when you change the
meaning of all my feelings?

**Tisha Whitaker**

## Untitled

The hour is now at hand.
Neither glory nor ruin
Can prevent the final outcome.
Swift death awaits us all.
Only those lucky enough
Can receive its fatal touch.

Yet we hold our heads proudly.
For now we are alive
Gambling away our lives.
In hopes of making history.
The stakes may be high but duty calls us home.
Through fighting, peace can be achieved.

Hear that, sweet cannons!
Our common foe approaches.
What match are they against our untested steel.
If might does make right,
Then fools we all must be for even trying.

Somehow we stand firm.
So to in defeat as well in victory.

**Stephen Reynolds**

## When A Petal Falls

When a single drop from a gentle rain fell upon the seed,
Nestled softly upon fertile soil, the sun began to feed.

So small and insignificant, it begins its frail ascent
Reaching upward toward the light, its desire shows no relent.

Rising to maturity, it stands delicate amidst the shower.
The seed that fell upon the ground, becomes a lovely flower.

Its beauty is beyond compare, striking sublime.
To the admiring eye, impeccable, its fragile bloom divine.
Beneath its radiance, upon the ground, lies a petal unperturbed.
Its absence, inconspicuous, the flower's beauty undisturbed.
There's so much elegance that still remains so much pleasure to extend
What it possesses, far exceeds, what lies beneath the wind.

This symbol of benevolence, has given so much to us all.
We recognize it enduring value, even when a petal falls.

**Rex Criner**

## Grace

I had never felt the sun upon my face,
never been given to or touched by
the miracle of grace.
Beneath a blanket,
wrapped in my own disgrace,
you found me.
Turn down the music and blacken the light;
signal the trumpet, and release the snare;
add a cool streak of blue to backdrop the night;
and come see, come see.
Open the window and extinguish the flare;
tighten your hold, release your fright;
you delivered me.
I had never touched the wings of the wind;
never waltzed with a dancing leaf;
or laughed until tears gave in;
from whispers to shrieks of a desperate plea,
bathed in light and cleansed of sin,
my spirit's free.

**Lisa Bowers**

## Bright Star

How many times tears drop silently in a night
Never known to anyone, never seen by sight
How many faces are seen every day
That apply the smile after tears wipe away
Oh you silent mourner, I am your brother
Though conceived by a different mother
And I know him by name, he that lurks in the still
He seeks to confuse, rob and to kill
He's the trespasser of peace, a pain in your head
That whispers in your ear of an inevitable dread
He's collected your tears to put out a flame
That will destroy him and expose his shame
He'll tell you that you're alone and all done
That no one cares and there's no where to run
He's a liar! The father of lies!
He'll disturb your soul with his preserved lullabies
But that's not who or where you are......
For you are much more, and you're held very dear
Go, tell the enemy whose child you are.....
The king of the universe, and you're his bright star

*Michael A. Billy*

## Springtime In Kentucky

Springtime in Kentucky brings
    newborn colts
    romping and kicking up their heels
    in emerald paddocks.

Watchful mares guard the frolicking colts
    out of the corner of their eyes,
    remembering the carefree days of youth
    when all the senses of life were new.

Newborn calves lie in tufts of new spring grass
    and stand on uncertain hooves
    nuzzling the warmth of their mothers' bellies
    seeking the nourishment of life.

Newborns stand against the shelter of mothers' withers
    in the winds and rains of March,
    playfully rejoice in gentle breezes,
    and breathe the fragrance of sun-soaked grass.

Life renews itself in the Bluegrass
    as the first white pear blossoms grace the landscape
    and the perfume of dark pink magnolia blossoms explodes
    upon the land, criss-crossed by sparkling springtime streams.
*(March 1995)*

*Merideth A. Hildreth*

## Trophies of Freedom

I have no home but the hills I roam
no bed but the warm, brown earth
and over my head the sky for a shed,
my range is the land of my birth.

I've no trophies to show, no goods to bestow,
when at last I have proven my worth,
with contented heart from this life I'll depart,
at peace and with happiness girth.

For, the hills I know and the vales below,
bright sheen of an inland sea,
sunrise at dawn, dew of the morn,
solitude found on the lea.

And I cannot complain that my life was in vain
tho' I've little the world can see,
for freedom is mine and the stars that shine
are trophies enough for me.

*Sara Hewitt Riola*

## In God's House

I'll not know tears or pain
No fears or shame in God's House

There will be no deaths or sorrows
no more for in God's House I'll
dwell forever more.

The joys and happiness I can't imagine,
but I'm sure I'll know when
I'm in Heaven, for this is in God's House

So for now I'll watch and I'll
Pray for soon to come that glorious day
When I'll be called up to live in
God's House

*Patty Hutchison*

## The Buckle

See this brand new buckle...I got it just today
No, I didn't buy it, and that I'm proud to say
Now you can't buy this buckle in a truckstop or
    in any old western store
Where a truckdriver or yuppy cowboy can buy the
    one they most adore
Why..you can't buy one for any amount of pay
You have to earn it..you do it the old fashioned way
Now when a cowboy wins one, he'll wear it with pride
And show the world what he's done..it makes him feel good inside
For each buckle brings back a memory and each buckle
    has it's own tale
Whether he won it on the rodeo circuit or won it on the
    endurance trail
Now my riding days are over and from competition I will quit
For every time I win a new buckle, my hat don't seem to fit

*Verlyn Gramling*

## "God Is There"

When love wreaks its bitter revenge, its taste bitter sweet
no joy within, and its friendly smiles turn to hatred's stare
do not fear for my savior is there.
When warm hugs turn to menacing screams, when loving days
alone
turn to eternal dreams, when bruises of the heart no longer
can hide, don't you give up for he lives inside.
When there is not a drop of love left, and it seems like
you're all by yourself, and you sit there empty no tears to
cry, don't despair for his love never dies.
When you can no longer find any love in his words, his apologies
for tomorrow, today have been heard, his abuse for later already
felt don't give up for his love never melts.
When it seems that there's nowhere to turn, bridges you've crossed
long been burned, apologies accepted long gone by, fall on
your knees and let God hear your cry.
And when you live that long awaited dream, your heart so happy
you no longer hear his screams. Your face glowing bright,
no more bruises to hide. Don't forget the man who gave you
back your pride.

*Talamieka McNeil*

## Time Is Short

Sun rise warmth, new day dawning,
Rooster crowing, thank you Lord, for another morning.
Afternoon rush, going and gone,
I take time to hear a bird's song.
Evening is here, time to say a prayer,
I thank the Lord, for his tender care.
Time is just a whisper in a loved one's ear,
Tell them you love them, we haven't long here.

*Laura Krigbaum*

## It's My Turn

I always tell them, "Stay on the beam."
No matter what follow your dream.

And when my own dream is too far to reach,
I often find it hard to practice what I preach.

When I find my hall is long;
that's when I'm most confident and strong.

I have always taken their ware,
and dealt with it in love and care.

But this time I'm the one that's hurting,
and there's no one here for me worrying.

I don't want to pick up the pieces this time,
I only want what is mine.

This time I want some stronger than I,
to hold me so I can just let go and cry.
*Marie S. Hernandez*

## Sunset

As I was sitting by the sea
No one around for miles but me
I wondered if I was the only one
Who saw the setting of the sun
It certainly was a glorious sight
To see the sky and sea alight
As the sun went down to meet the sea
I felt the urge to get up and flee
And yet I could not leave the shore
The selfish me said more, more, more
I hoped there would be another day
When I'd see a sunset and feel this way
Then the gentle breezes began to blow
And the lullaby of the waves was soft and low
It was as if God was putting the sun to sleep
And giving me a memory to keep
*Virginia M. Owen*

## People Never Listen

People never listen.
No one ever cares.
Tears fall down one's face,
With loneliness and disgrace.

But...People never listen.
No one ever cares.
Blood falls down one's cheek,
Flows down to the bottom of their feet.

Please listen to me, please help.
Please take care of me.
And, catch me when I fall,
Wake me when I sleep.

Tell me when I'm good.  Punish me when I'm bad.
Control me when I'm cheerful or glad.
Talk to me when I'm lonely,
Feed me when I'm bony.

All I want is a friend, a sibling.
Someone who cares.
But...People never listen.
No one ever cares.
*Tana M. Turner*

## A Single Bird

A single bird flies alone, maybe someday she'll find a home.  Far
from a place where things are bad, far from a place that makes her sad.
Maybe someday she'll find a tree, a safe little place for her to be.
Far above the Earth so high, far from a place that makes her cry.

That single bird still flies alone, maybe some day she'll find a home.
*Mellissa L. Perkins*

## For My Mother on Mother's Day

Sons write millions of cards - all thinking their love unique,
  "No one has a mother like mine," they think,
Carefully signing the card.
  "If only I could find the words to express, they think
And struggle to phrase such a love.

Older sons think of unconditional love,
  And marvel at such a sacred thing.
Younger ones take her for granted, like sun, sky, and earth.
  Older ones consider the wisdom of her reproach,
Younger ones compare their women to her.

It's one of God's eternal mysteries I am sure...
  The more I admit I am my mother's doing,
The more that I am my own man.

Sons write millions of cards - all thinking their love unique.
  "No one has a mother like mine," they think,
Carefully signing the card.
  I sign mine, and think it paltry...
Perhaps it's something better left to angels.
  Only angels whisper about a son's eternal love,
Mine for my Mother dear.
*Mark Vincent Soutor*

## All Alone

All alone in my room at night,
No one to tuck me in tonight.
All alone 'cause a stupid mistake,
How did I know that a friendship would break?
All alone in a bottomless pit,
No more, in my heart, would a place be lit.
For I've lost a good friendship, a very close one,
Now that it's gone, I'm afraid I have none.
This one little trick, this one little fear,
Which caused me to lose a friend that was dear.
Friends do not lie, friends do not shout,
I'm afraid that's not all that friendship's about:
Friendship is caring, giving, and sharing!
I guess I'll just wonder, I'll probably never know.
How long or how far this friendship would go.
For a friendship I've had and a friendship I've lost,
But I wish I didn't have to pay that cost.
Now that it's over, now that it's done,
I wish I had another chance, just one.
*Nicole C. Hronas*

## Rim Country

I need not seek the comfort of a hymn;
Nor pose in yoga form and meditate.
I slowly lift my eyes and seek the rim
That lines the heavens above this chasmic state.

I hear the distant murmur of a brook
And voice of tiny warblers singing praise.
From far below in some secluded nook
To you their songs of rapture ever raise.

Amid the arms of towering pines I stand,
And hear your voice and listen to your word.
And all around behold the splendor of your hand
Communion with your presence Mighty Lord.
*Viola A. Knauf-Kotas*

## Childhood Lost

Curled up in huddled silence I sit
  nose pressed upon cold glass.
I am
  the picture of ten-year -old simplicity
with no so ten-year-old emotions
  threatening to rise
and spill upon my cheeks,
  like the endless flow of crystal raindrops
down the frozen window
  of my soul.

*Veronique Hillmann*

## Sleepless Nights

Another sleepless night
Not a cloud in the sky,
But yet I hear the rain

Inside my mind there boils a fight
Somehow someway I must try
Try to carry on thru the pain

But for now the end is out of sight
And my soul it dose cry
So these nights of torture remain

One day my soul shall shine bright
Never more to here a bitter lie
With an end to this confusion in my brain

But still the madness becomes light
My soul shall continue to die
While slowly going insane

Oh how I wish it could end tonight
And end my hearts cry
Putting an end to this horrid pain

But alas my soul is still in flight
And the angels are out of sight
As I sit and fill the rain

*Steven Dean Sandusky*

## Untitled

I would write of a bird, an extremely wise fowl
Not a hen or a rooster, this ones an owl
That lives in Texas, a smart bird is he
He dwells in a bird-house, instead of a tree
When shadows grow long, he comes out of his house
To look for his dinner-perhaps a field mouse
Some day I am certain, that he'll have a date
With an owl that he loves, to bring home for his mate
Some night in the moonlight, he will fly to her roost
To sing songs of his love, his prestige to boost
His song will be tender, warm, happy and gay
And she'll preen her feathers, in a most feminine way
As they sit in the shadows, long before day
His song will be soothing, here's what he'll say
Everyone is in slumberland but you and me
Making love in the moonlight, happy as can be
This is my story of an owl so wise
That lives in a bird-house, neath bright Texas skies

*Phillip E. Richard*

## Philosophy of Life

Only once to trod this restless path
Of do's and don'ts and fiery wrath.
Yielding here and bullying there,
To make a place for others where
Living may be a worthwhile sport
Of happy days and days too short
To do all of the good that's in our hearts.

*Larry E. Fast*

## Threnody

Not endless sunshine or long days of gray rain -
Not all beach and glittering sand, or transcendent songs
The oscine masters sing....

Not seamless days and nights, or endless fair winds -
Or miraculous flights of fancy reshaping time and space
For an avaricious age.... Look! - and see! -

The last beluga shudders in a foul Azerbijanian sun,
Cruel hook breaking the oil-filmed jaw.
Lighter by twenty tons, the Caspian sinks and dies.

You cannot see the mountains - through haze like smoke - or hear
The last waves roaring down the strand
From the last sea, or fear the legacy of vanished trout or caviar.

A fetid silence grips the wilted lemon trees, and Dom Perignom flows
Where intellectuals take their ease... the rivers sink, without sound,
and ferry mud to the seas.  They, too, shall die....

What can be said of our fevered reign?
"They ruled with terror and with pain, ignorant of their natures,
And that which they could not fathom, destroyed...."

Time shall not mark our going - or abide our infinite vanities.  Earth
spins and spins, like a top.  Only sun and silence shall hear it stop.

*Milton E. Pharr*

## The Lost One

A lost soul along the path of life
Not belonging to anyone
Shunned away by each passerby
A wilted rose blackening with the hands of death
Blood trickling down dotting the ground
Death is but a blessing
Alone in a dank, dark well
Absorbed by the wicked, vulturous shadows
Dreams belittled, wishes stripped of hope
Nightmares devouring the night waves
Tears without a solacing hug
Chances missed
Choices made
But you only get one chance anyway
The unwanted
The unloved.

*Little L*

## A Precious Thing

I sometimes feel so worthless,
not good for anything.
Where are all my talents?
I cannot paint, dance or sing.
I know I fail You often, and I am so ashamed.
I think You must regret that "Christian" I am named.
I hang my head in shame
as tears roll down my face;
Then I think of you, Lord,
and of Your saving grace.
I think of how You died upon the cross for me.
You died the shameful death
of hanging on a tree.
You died that I might live;
the King of all the Earth.
I can no longer say,
"My life does not have worth."
You see, my Saviour lives in me.
I am a precious thing.
My body is a temple for God's Almighty King.

*Sherry J. Mosley*

## Something Lacking

no chocolate in my life
nothing sweet and stimulating
no dessert after dinner
no treat in the afternoon
nothing smooth and rich and delicious to melt in my mouth
no luscious confection consumed simply for pleasure
none of the delightful decadence that other people have
no frivolous food at all

*Sue Redding*

## Tippecanoe

William Henry Harrison gained world-wide prominence at
Tippecanoe in
    November, 1811.
By badly beating and thoroughly discouraging the Indians and securing
    a place in heaven.
He served as aide-de-camp to General "Mad Anthony" Wayne in 1793,
And, at the Battle of Fallen Timbers, he was sighted for "conspicuous
    gallantry."
As he trimmed the British at the Thames Battle in 1813,
General Harrison gained more fame on the great national scene.
The National Whig party nominated "Tippecanoe" for president in 1839.
He won by a landslide in 1840 because of Martin Van Buren's
    presidential decline.
He was inaugurated on March 4, 1841
In the cold, freezing rain, wind, and sheets of sleet but no warm sun.
The frontiersman died from pneumonia 31 days after taking office
But not before selecting Daniel Webster Secretary of State, a great
    choice.
Webster, thanks to Harrison, was destined to serve his country well
Until 1852, the year he heard the final death bell.

*Willard R. Carson Jr.*

## A Night In The City

There goes the sun
Now let's go have some fun
Let's go rob, and steal
And maybe find someone to kill
Let's go smoke, and drink
Who cares what our parents think
Come on you're wasting time
Let's go get in another bind
Let's let everyone suffer from our rain
Then laugh at their pain
So, if you think your life is really s--tty
Then come and spend a night in the city!

*Tina Eilders*

## The Harvest Home

He feels the lost of shimmering homeland green
Now that he is bound upon a shore of sand
Where scarce a blade of grass is seen.
The oily waters lapping at his feet are salt
"Are salt, are sick," the gently whispering waves repeat
And an endless wash of tears pours down his cheeks.

Yet when he walked his native verdant fields
And daily fed his Soul with sights of woodland green
And drank and washed in iridescent waters running clean
His restless mind began to scheme
How to grasp for himself a larger share
And turn nature's green to green that he could horde
And hold within a little box that he could lock
And only he would have a key.

Now he weeps as he stands upon these burning sands
The dying waters kissing at his feet.
"God help me!" he cries, arms beseeching the skies
But the key is still clutched in his hand.

*Louise Studley Stone*

## Send Me An Angel

Asleep in my haven, the door slightly creeks
Nowhere to hide, don't dare make a peep

A smell fills the air, all feeling is lost
This incident will take place, no matter the cost

My magical place where all is at rest
Appears before me, this is the test

Lord, send me an angel

Trying to understand is the hardest at times
I have caused no one harm, committed no crimes

No control over fate, my destiny looms
But out of the blackness, a light fills my room

The most radiant angel with halo above
Wraps her wings around me with compassion and love

I ask to go forever, she says I cannot stay
"There is more to life, than pain and strife
And you will know that some day"

Lord, send those an angel whose life is in need
Whose lives are entangled by perversion and greed

Let them know your kindness, your gentleness, your peace
Until the day that their anguish will solemnly cease.

*Leanne Freiberg*

## Umma

She lays limp while I rub tiger balm into her tofu flesh
occasionally letting escape a quiet moan of pain

Her once smooth yellow/brown skin is now red with agony
I put down one leg and pick up another
I scoop up more tiger balm with my index finger
and start from her rough heels up to her tired thighs

A near blasphemous thought surprises and shames me
Has she ever felt the warm trickle of arousal?
Has anything but blood and pain visited these thighs?

I put down her leg and go into the kitchen to see
if the water is boiling
I stay there a little too long My mother calls to me

I quickly wipe my eyes and blow my nose
on a rough paper towel with pink floral and goose designs
I look at my reflection in the metal kettle and see
My eyes and nose are red

I let down my hair to hide my shame
Forgetting to put on gloves
I carry the steam towels to my mother

They burn my hands.

*K. Kristianne Lee-Yahng*

## Untitled

Megan,
Oddball in a crowd,
Preliminary dancer,
Brave and determined.
Sister of a growing baby,
Daughter of two hardworking parents,
Stepdaughter of a nice woman.
Lover of peace, fantasies, and nature,
Who feels delighted with life, energetic, and unusual.
Who needs love, comfort and caring friends.
Who gives favors, compliments and attention to others,
Who fears hatred, death and most bad consequences.
Who would like to see peace, love and cooperation.
Resident of Stamford, Connecticut,
Slocum.

*Megan Slocum*

## Staid Innocence

Youthful dreams respond to beck and call
Of age required. The exuberance that
Once sparked and blazed into unquenchable
Deeds wrought, has been stilled and muted
By the serpent of the real that crushes
It and leaves it withering in apathy
Until neglect all but destroys it all.
And in this lair of the beast, imagination
No longer is the aegis that shields
Against the onslaught, but stead becomes
The shroud in which are wrapped the dead
And dying. So disdained and deterred,
The mind becomes atrophic; the heart,
So retarded, cries and yearns no more;
The soul, so ignored, can no longer be
Heard through the din. The flame, thus
Extinguished, flickers and dies, leaving
But ashes to choke and gag what is now
But a hollow shell.

*Michael Obertance*

## The Cost

It will cost an intense narrowing
of all our interest on this earth -
It will cost an immense broadening
of our interest in Jesus' birth -

It will cost extreme concentration
of our Holy God's point of view -
It will cost everything that is not
from Him that lives in me and you -

It will cost repenting - by turning from all
those things we know aren't right -
It will cost surrendering it all
letting Him take charge of our lives -

It will cost sincere humility
as we kneel before Him and pray -
"God, make me as Holy as You can make
a poor sinner saved by grace" -

*Patty J. VanSlambrouck*

## Golden Years

The, "Golden Years," bring illusions to the mind
of Dignity, Comfort and Wisdom refined,
Yet to many, "The Sunset Years," are not so kind
As this poem will try to remind.

The old man down the street is all alone
A wheeled chair has become his throne,
Past problems have long ago departed
Leaving new problems, with a course as yet, uncharted.

So it is the, "Why," of his life that for him remain
Like missing links in a chain
And call for his subtle intuition
To solve this, perhaps his final, uncharted mission.

The art of acceptance and patience finally won
Leaves his Heart and Spirit their course to run
Mysteries and problems, one by one, now being solved
For within himself they are being resolved.

*Wendell E. Hauenstein*

## "Home"

God has shown us all the way,
of how to be with Him someday.
I hear his voice; the time is near,
Why won't you listen? Why can't you hear?
Why can't you see? The signs are clear,
because to Him, we all are dear!
We had better wake up, the hour's at hand,
cause, now the fighting's, over the Holy Land.
So gather your heart and cast your vote;
Come on aboard; don't miss the boat!
The place I call "Home" is Heaven you see.
Don't you want to give in, and go Home with me?
I know where I'm going and who I'm gonna see.
Don't you want to see Him? Come, go Home with me!

*Wanda Dossey Carson*

## Crocodile Tears

Swishing and swirling through the dirt
of life that has congregated on my face,
pushing their own little paths, making their
marks in the menagerie of pain contorted
in my features.

Soothing and smooth, the mere trifles
of this once forgotten being are lost
in a torrent of waves washing over
myself in a dead set mission against
the world.

In the far outreaches of this netherworld
in which I have become lost, thoughts tug
at the outskirts of my mind, mocking voices of
long forgotten mortals seize at my most deserved
melancholy.

Here sits a being ravaged beyond recognition
she shared her thoughts, hopes, dreams, and fears,
only to be victimized back in to her asylum
to weep in the darkness of her once cherished
emotions.

*Shellei Boucher*

## Eve Of Deliverance

Of faith in man, I question some
Of motives not quite clear
In stone cold eyes, their hearts are numb
Astringent bitter tears

This fallen race, humanity
Is left to die alone
Bewildered by calamity
To reap the graves they've sown

A child's gaze of innocence
Untainted rays of hope
A symbol of man's penitence
Balanced on a tight rope

And still I weep for human kind
Souls who have fought in vain
These prayers of light we hide behind
Fail to conceal the pain

Perhaps an answer can be found
To end this seething hate
The hands of time must be rewound
Before it grows too late

*Tara Anne Bruckler*

## Web of Life

Oh, what a wondrous entangled web
of mysterious growing life we weave.
Serpents of lies intermingling our web,
as tragedies and sorrow mold its sleeve.

Brightness ever turning into darkness,
dances the harmony into the pain.
Smite injustice turns anger of larkness,
to a confusion or chaos of rain.

Let not amiss the purity of just,
or the indifference of blissful mind.
Understanding, compassion are a must,
for the detangling web of all mankind.

The answer is simple to see, my friend,
just walk to the light and see with your heart.
Behold a true angelic light to send,
it sings in glory to our heaven's heart.

*Stella Hansen*

## Dream Weaver

Thoughts of dreams beyond mists-
Of places that were.....
Times ever changing, thoughts ever taking shape
In the recesses of my mind,
Penetrating the dream mists.

Were they reality?
Or were they just dreams, dreams from the dream time,
Far beyond my thoughts?

I feel the energy of things past....
Have I lived?
Were they just dreams,
The phantoms of my mind?

Constantly moving, relentlessly changing,
Transforming time and times,
My mind has lived on,
And taken me on voyages beyond space.

Were they reality?
Were they just dreams?
Am I here?  Have I lived? .....
Or am I just a dream? ......

*Ruth Petri AKA Moon Pearl*

## A Glimpse of Heaven

Of garden blooms and sweet perfumes
of sunshine streaming through, the
butterflies in their disguise complete
the rainbows hue.
Of starlight glowing in the night
of evening's twilight calm.  The
moonbeams dance in shadows, upon
the garden wall.
Melodies so peaceful, serenade from
up above.  A whisper in his gentle
voice, reveals for us his love.
A fragrant breeze to caress the leaves
of each and every vine; carries the
hope of his promise, in a moment
untouched by time.
His mercies on the path of life
are strewn with blossoms fair.  A
glimpse of heaven for now must wait,
in the mist of daydreams here.

*Patti Benner*

## "Trip West Review"

I'm just thinking about all the things we saw,
Of the many times we stood in awe,
Of God's handiworks far and near
Our hearts full of thanksgiving and prayer

We viewed the Arch in St. Louis that first day
Then onto Rapid City continuing our way
To see one of our very special places -
Mt. Rushmore with the president's faces.

It would be difficult to forget Yellowstone Park
Where so much for so little was ours from the start
Old faithful geyser was puffing and ready to go
And before our exit, gave a second show.

Was cool in San Francisco, L. A. was spread out
We enjoyed Mann's Theatre and the footprints about
Las Vegas was great Wayne Newton and all
The MGM was beautiful where we all had a ball.

The most breathtaking and awesome territory yet
Was the Great Grand Canyon the sunrise and sunset
We crossed the Rockies and the desert too
Every day's dawning brought something new.

*Louise F. Caldwell*

## Eve,

I thank you for your friendship full of special memories
Of the times we had together seeking God among the trees

In that garden that he made for us to frolic, love and kiss
Full of wonder, full of beauty, full of love distinctly his

In the glory of his beauty we lost sight along the way
Of the things "in love" he told us and of how we must obey

I don't know what hit me cause it happened all so fast...
First the apple, then our nakedness, then God's heart rending blast

Don't you know what you have done, because my word you disobeyed?
Your lives and all your children's is the price that must be paid

As the grave opens it's mouth with an insatiable desire
And you see each other fed to both the worm and to the fire

No longer will your friendships know the joy of innocence
But of anger, malice, woe and fear and bitter arrogance

As he sent us both away, I saw a tear, I heard a sigh
I could've sworn I heard him say, I wish they didn't choose to die

I wish they hadn't chose the pain, the separation and the fear
That's around life's every corner, loss and death are always near

Now their lives are full of weeping, wailing, agony and grief
All because they listened to the lies of that deceitful thief

*Robert M. Aitken*

## Migrating Birds

The birds are flying southward for the winter.
Oh birds! can you not stay a little longer
And by your staying hold back what's to come?
They say all things in Nature are related,
Winds, rain, the tides of Ocean, sun and moon
And even the smallest things. No sparrow falls
But its descent through a few feet of space
Has some slight influence on the flight of stars.
And yet I know you cannot stay and that
There is a law which says small things cannot
Control the large but are controlled by it.
And so farewell!  Enjoy your flight and live
As birds do in perpetual summertime
While I, less favored, stay here, shivering
In my poor room, and patiently await
Your predetermined coming back next spring.

*Robert Larson*

## Grandma's Cookies

A little boy sat at the table, eager eyes, but quiet as could be
"Oh Grandma, Oh Grandma, do you have some cookies for me?"
She smiled at her grandson, and I heard her softly say
"No, I don't have any cookies, I didn't get to the store today."

"But grandma, you always told me, if I was a good little boy
There would always be milk and cookies, for me to enjoy"
You said "Comb your hair, wash your hands and your face
Your reward of good cookies, will be sure to take place."

I seem to remember, her cookies were always so sweet, so good
She always had plenty, and she said that she always would
But that was a long time ago, she is just so busy you see
I guess she forgot how to bake, those sweet cookies for me.

"I'm sorry my grandma doesn't bake, she did, but now no more
I only hope she can keep her promise, and make it to the store"
Then when I ask for a cookie, she can easily say, "Yes take two"
Now I know my grandma loves me, and I love my grandma too."

**Richard T. Rogers**

## Poetry Contest

I'm a winner! I'm a winner! They're sending me a check!
Oh, I know I'm a beginner, but I figured what the heck?!
I'll sit down and I'll write one - they're always so much fun
When the juices start to flowing and the words begin to come

It's as if the words are living and they want to run and play
So much they need to tell us, so much they have to say
"Write me down! Write me down! Use me to make a rhyme!"
Like there's only so much poetry and very little time
To get across the message and the joy they want to spread -
They can't wait to be discovered and remembered and reread

Words are personalities, like living breathing things
Some seem to move so heavily, some seem to fly on wings
How fun it is to play with them, to pick and choose a few
To arrange them all on lines and page to make a sequence new

Poetry's a game I play, somewhat like hide and seek
The words want me to find them; they'll hide but hope I'll peek
And find them fast with little thought they'll jump into my mind
And beg me to include them in a happy snappy rhyme

So, I'm a winner! I'm a winner! Thanks for your invitation!
To have my words and rhymes and poem be in your publication...

**Tracey Weingartner**

## Christmas Forever

Snow and trees,
oh the memories.
Hot cocoa and a loving smile
laughter and gentle touches
sledding and warm hugs
presents under the tree...
Our first Christmas just you and me.
Snow falls gently out our window.
As we cuddle close.
Old Christmas movie on television.
No one but you and me.
Love is in our hearts and in our first home.
I'll always remember that Christmas
just for you and me.

**Michele Turner**

## Oklahoma

Cries of despair and help,
Oklahoma cries with a yelp.
Floor two is where they would laugh and play,
As their parents would sit and work all day.
They would play with their toys and all of their friends,
Until the day it came to an end.
The day was April 26,
When all of our hearts fell like bricks.
The building blew up at 9:00 A.M.,
And then all of their dreams were at an end.

**Melissa Dudley**

## Longing to Belong

Tattered shorts
Old smelly sneakers
A stench which drew attention as he walks by.
He is a loner
He is hungry
He is tired and the world is mean towards him.

The only thing he had ever received was the gift of life.
His name is Arria and he's twelve years old.
Arria has grown to feel pain and suffering.
Unhappiness is no stranger to him either.
Fear has walked and slept with him many times.
Who can he complain to?
Is someone out there to listen?

Hope is a long way from dropping by him anytime soon or was
she standing there with him when the old lady pulled up
along side him, rolled down her window and asked,
"Son can you mow lawns?"

**Theresa McTaggart**

## The Dream

I had a dream last night, I dreamed that I was floating
on a cloud. Everything was beautiful as well as peaceful.
As I floated along very quietly, I came upon you. You
were just sitting there very peaceful and full of joy.
When You looked up and saw me, your face shined as bright
as the stars above. As I approached You, You began to
smile. I knew then that You had not forgotten me. You
took my hand and led me to a wonderful place. A place
where there are no more tears or pain. I felt that this
place had to be heaven. Then You took me by the hand
and led me up higher into the sky. You told me that you
wanted me to meet your Father, You said that He was my
Father also. Our Father looked at me and smiled. I
thought, "What a Beautiful face," so kind, so strong,
but yet gentle, Our Father spoke with a gentle voice
and said, "Welcome Home My Child."

**Vivian Smith**

## Autumn Days

Colored leaves fall to the ground-
On an Autumn Day, without sound.
They are yellow, orange, rust and red-
I'll dream of them as I go to bed.
Pumpkins, squash and Indian corn-
Decorate the house where I was born.
Out the window in which I gaze-
Goldenrod in the breeze still wave.
Birds heading south, rest from flight-
Gather near the pond - oh what a sight!
A freshly made wreath, the colors of fall-
Hangs on my door for neighbors who call.
My favorite season now is here-
I'll savor each day for another year.

**Marion Kerr-Snyder**

## Remember

Running through the vacant lot
On Benson Street
Where the sofa lays ripped free of cotton stuffing
With rusty coils naked,
Wooden arms splintered, cracked like bones,
A nest for rats;
Where the 1959 Ford's busted headlight lens,
Like a crucible, palms a white bead of sun,
Casting hot light into the air, blinding birds;
Where shattered windshields are crystal webs
That ensnare no flies, only stones;
Where last July a big-top tent
Wore a smooth brown spot in the mustard weeds;
As he walks past,
He remembers it all.

*Victor M. Sandoval*

## Touched

I was once touched by an angel yet she was an angel
on earth. A miracle sent from the heavens, this we
knew from just after birth. A child so full of
happiness, every day she brought so much joy. She
had a heart of pure love to share with any man,
woman, girl or boy. So many were touched by her
spirit, her talent to brighten everyone's day, her
ability to lift anyone's life, in only her sincere,
loving way. Cheering up a room with only one smile
or calming you with her soft, gentle touch. Making
it impossible not to realize why each person loved
her so much. Yes, I was once touched by an angel a
spirit of true neverending love. Into my life she
brought happiness and a faith in the powers above.
Though this angel was taken to heaven, that is the
place she truly belongs. Every heart that her spirit
touched has definitely felt a love that will last
life long.

*Mark Allan Lampa*

## Another Night Alone

Another night alone, with storms
on the horizon.
Remember how afraid I use to be of storms,
and how you would never leave me alone...but
always stay near.
Storms so unusual this time of year...just
as it's unusual you not being here.
Will you be looking in on me?
Somehow I feel you near.
Not just when the storms come,
But most all the time.
So often I feel your presence in many ways.
In different rooms, sometimes when I'm shopping,
In an outfit I may be wearing...a piece of jewelry
I may select.
You still seem near.
As if you know...all the plays,
I want you to direct.

*Pauline Young*

## Paranoia to One's Own Race

As I look into the past, and realize how we came
Not on our own, or by choice, but by force
It saddens my heart, to think of my own as thy enemy or thy criminal.

We rape ourselves, and beat ourselves
But "why" the one question we all ask
Because...........................
no one answers

*Leeann Williams*

## Black Light And Smoke

The black light lingers
On the smoke, seeping through my fingers

Tendrils of the smoke clutching at my mind.
Through the tortured passages they wind

Exposing my mind to a different world
A world bathed in Black Light

It's atmosphere filled with smoke
Smoke from a many fingered plant

A world peopled with vacant eyes
Eyes staring into space.

IS THIS HELL?
GODS
NO!
GOD, where am I?

*Vernes A. Collins*

## Untitled

I cried out your name last night.
Once again I felt your touch,
As you gently caressed my body.
I savored the sweetness of your lips,
As you tenderly kissed my own.
My ears listened to your soft voice,
As you whispered love words to me.
My mind was lost in a different time,
Where the only inhabitants were you and me.
My body was taken to heights,
That it will never reach again.
I came back to earth and realized,
That I had only been dreaming again.

*Sandra Lynn Ann Hargrove*

## Growing Old

There are many advantages to "growing old"
One can say anything so I've been told
'Tis rumored the elderly are slightly daft
Must be a leak in their mind shaft.
Well, the young can take a lesson from us
No need to carry on and make a fuss
For there's one thing that's abundantly clear
If you set your goals and persevere
Have faith in whatever you do
Success will surely come to you
As for me, I'm a young seventy-six
Realizing that though my past I can't fix
I can still strive for a better tomorrow
Able to cope with both pleasure or sorrow
Trying to be helpful to those I meet each day
Who enrich my life in their own special way
So if you ask me about "growing old"
Life's full of wonders as yet untold.
Face each day with a cheerful smile.
Take it from the — living's worth the while

*Ruth Stalerman*

## Untitled

Beautiful thoughts to be kept
Should be caught in their hurried flight
To be placed in one's diary of dreams
Ere they wing their way on through the night
For when once they lose their quaint phrase
Though their essence be recaptured
Their first burning innocent birth
Is lost to eternity

*E. Veril Hollins*

## One Moment There

Like early morning in the lake of dreams, my feelings;
One moment there, the next, vanished in a swirl of confusion

As elusive as the will-o-the-wisp leading weary travelers to their
lonesome destinies, my emotions;
One moment there, the next, buried in a mass of tumbling
cinderblocks

Like the hummingbird, darling from flower to flower in a blur of wing
and beak, my thoughts;
One moment there, the next, lost in the cavernous recesses of my mind

Like a crystal clear spring, bubbling in anticipation of every moment,
my laughter;
One moment there, the next, dying in a blinding explosion of lost innocent

As blind and vulnerable as a newborn kitten, my love;
One moment there, the next, spirited away on the winds of insecurity

Like a super-nova in the black void of space, my life;
One moment there, the next, disappearing in the vacuum of time

*Scott A. Elrod*

## "Bonnie - A Lady"

A, lady beautiful, gentle, sincere, smiling face.
One of a kind.
Grade A in every way.
Deep understanding and appreciation.
Excellence in character.
Filled with ever encouraging words.
Superior in kindness-unlike any other.
Our #1 Director- so cool, calm and collected
A guiding light for all to emulate.
Loves children people, animals and nature.
Soft in voice, logical, accomplished, admired and respected.
Your students adore you- you'll always be their favorite.
teacher! those happy little faces!
The fabric of our school an unbelievable history!
You're kept faith with yourself and your effort has benefited so many!
None will ever forget you!
Lady Luck is with you.  And so we crown
you, "The Lady" of the flagged bedecked school on the hill.

*Mary Lyons*

## Nature's Fireworks

A flash of light streaks across the blackened sky.
One - two - three, the rumbling thunder breaks the silence.
A storm is brewing across the lake.

The next bolt of lightning crackles and spreads across
the darkened sky.
You count again, and the thunder answer its reply.

Time and time again - first the lightning brightens the dark sky
in all its wonder,
And then the roar of the thunder sounds its call.

We see the storm as it creeps through the night toward us,
But, we are not frightened, just awed by
Nature's own fireworks, lightning and thunder.

*Lynn E. Henk*

## Untitled

Far and away - far and away
  I see the eyes of you
  is it really you or is it just the outlines
  the outlines of a man not quite whole
  but not quite incomplete
  but then I ask of myself
  can one ever be totally whole
  or can they just believe themselves to be whole.

*Lindsey M. Grieve*

## Wanted For Father's Day

Wanted - a father who will live at home
one who will teach his child right from wrong
one who will take his child out for a walk
and take a little time to sit and talk.

Wanted - a father who will go to work
come straight home when he gets his check
one who puts his family first in his life
and shows trust and love towards his wife.

Wanted - a father who is a churchgoing man
one who knows what is right and takes a stand
one who knows how to love a child,
one who is sincere and often smiles.

Wanted - a father who doesn't use crack cocaine
one who thinks to use it is a shame
one who knows how to play ball
one who is still around to watch his son grow tall.

Wanted - a father for a child to call Dad
the best friend a child ever had.
If a man like that comes your way
please send him to a child for Father's Day.

*Maureen H. Cottonham*

## No Greater Love

He was the eldest in his family
Only fifteen when his father died
Taking with him the boy's adolescence
Leaving him with no time to cry.

How would he handle such obligation?
Who would he turn to for inspiration?
He managed somehow to get through the years
Inspiring his family in getting careers.

He distinguished himself in the office he chose
And he rose to the top, as everyone knows
He's loved and respected and held in esteem
But he'll never recapture the loss of his teens.

They gathered around him in mourning once more
No longer kids,as in times of yore
Grieving for mother, saying their last goodbye
How they admired him, as they watched how he cried.

After the funeral, with bills to be paid
They all came forward, as on a crusade
He looked at his family he knew their devotion
But "Give me the Honor," he said with emotion.

*Yvette H. Gaines*

## Beyond The Realm Of Reality

In a place so far and near
Only in my mind does it seem clear
With reality only a memory I have no fear
I am so lonely in a place so far and near

Beyond the realm of reality is me
A condition brought on by LSD
When you look into my eyes is it me you really see
Or just an image of what used to be

Will I ever view you through clear eyes again
This madness seems to never end
Oh, how long has it been
Please help me if you can
Help me find myself again.

*Rory Tate*

## I Weep

I weep a tear runs down my cheek, I wipe it dry
I cry for you are gone you have departed this
great big earth I'm sure you have gone to a
better place with peace, no sorrow, no terrible
tomorrows, I weep a tear runs down my cheek I
wipe it dry...

*Lenore Osenbaugh*

## First Love

Up until now, I have been very sad
Only sitting and waiting for someone
Because without love the times would get bad
Just like the earth would be without the sun

Then there she was with her beautiful face
I did not pay attention to her color
I did not pay attention to her race
Because I knew that I had found her

She has eyes like the stars, pretty and bright
Her tender beauty is fit for a queen
She is just as important as the light
In the sky, great happiness I have seen

She is the one, that was sent from above
She is the white dove that gave me first love

*Robert Pinella*

## I'm A Ghetto Man That's Where I Stand

Strolling on the fine line
Ooops! Hanging on a spider twine
learning essences the hardest way I can
I'm a ghetto man that's where I stand

Mystical mystery's in time
wisdom picture of karma, sometimes,
are hard to understand
I'm a ghetto man that's where I stand

Broke again
lost myself accommodated a few scars and bars
moving back to the avenue
I'm a ghetto man that's where I stand

Broke again
sweet empress won't you take me in
Mr. Chance stole my pants
I'm a ghetto man that's where I stand

I'm a dreamer, gall
chasing a imaginary man
who has no patterns
I'm a ghetto man that's where I stand

*Matthew B. Love*

## Let There Be Light

Let there be light,
or a deluge let there be,
a tidal bore, a tornado, or a violent tremor,
only to make room for peace, for love,
to do away with the vices, to let in
the peace dove for peace, for love,
just as Picasso envisaged.

Let there be light,
let all the good old forces
stage a significant comeback,
to wreck the evils, to disclose the facts
and figures very much of our own.
Just to make room for peace, for love,
just as we crave for it.

*Syed M. Haque*

## The Promise Made

Was it fifty years ago when Val and Shirley wed
or it was only yesterday, like the cake cutter said.
Fifty years seems so long to others like you and me,
but fifty years went real fast for Val and Shirley.
Fifty years, the words roll off our tongue.
Some lives have finished, others have just begun.
daughters are born and grow to women.
Grandchildren arrive and gram's eyes are swimming.
Years continue to come and to go.
Val and Shirley continue to grow.
Spending the best of their lives together
because Val promised Shirley he would love her forever.
Happy 50th Anniversary!!!

*Richard F. Stout*

## If I Share My Tears

Smiles I share so easily with friends
Or loved ones or people I don't even know.
Trustless smiles protect me like armor
Deflecting words that can wound,
Deeds that can damage, emotions that can kill.
Smiles stand between you and me and touch.

Tears I save for solitude;
They're mine and I hold to them dearly.
I fear they will wash away my privacy
And expose me to your love.
Vulnerable then, shall I allow my tears
To fall into your heart?
Will you treasure them and add to them your own?

If I share my tears with you,
It must be only that I trust you
To treat them tenderly and to understand
The pain from which they flow.
If I share my tears with you,
You will know that I have entrusted with you
The most delicate portion of my soul.

*Robyn Apffel*

## Mothers Day

There was never an idle moment
Or never an idle day
That Mother didn't think of me
In every single way.
She fret and worried for my needs
Her prayers were always there
There is no way I could repay
For her loving tender care.
She was given to me by God's great love
As he put this world in space
She is borrowed to me for each passing year
Is only by his grace.
I care not for flowers she will never see
When she is laid to rest
It is now I want to show my love
For a mother whom is loved the best.

*Ruth Lohman*

## Mother

M is for the Memories you store then share
O is for the Obedience you deserve
T is for the Tender care you always give so dear
H is for the Heart you have that's made of pure GOLD
E is for Everything you are always willing to do
R is for Respect you are entitled to from each and everyone.

Put all these together and you will see just how great a MOTHER
you are.

*Verley Lloyd Boyd*

## From the Bench

From the bench on top of the hill I can look back to where I've been
or out to where I'd like to be or forward to where I'm going.
All this I can see from the bench on top of the hill.

Looking back I can see the creek
and the cabin and the well and the fireplace
and the old storage shed and the outhouse and the slate pile and the arch.
I remember each of them well: how they feel and how they sound
and how they smell and I hope they never change, though I know they
probably will.
All this I see and hope from the bench on top of the hill.

Looking out I see a valley. I've never been there before,
but I can see trees and flowers
and green and yellow and pink and blue and I hope it will stay
long enough for me to explore all of it, though I know it probably won't.
All this I see and hope from the bench on top of the hill.

Looking forward I can see the fallen tree and the hollow tree
and the tree
shaped like the IU sign. And way up ahead in the meadow I can see the
apple tree
and the tire swing and the peonies and the black raspberries and
the old wagon wheel
and I hope they have not changed, though I know they probably have.
All this I see and hope from the bench on top of the hill.

*Michelle Matheson*

## The Loss of Mother's, Ear

Where are the days when I could talk to you about anything

Hey Ma! I got my menses, hey Ma! I'm getting breasts —
Or the mother and daughter talks when that first boyfriend came
Around — wedding bells, birth, happiness, sadness and your sweet
Advice —

Your support when part of that institution collapsed
Sister, brother, grandmother and aunt being called by the
Creator (gone!)

Then old age setting in —

Gone are the days of talk and response, talk and response —
Gone are the days of that swift tongue and sharp ear —
I am also a victim of your old age —

I mourn but I also understand —
It's a path I also will take —
What I do have, is a library of your ear of yesterday —

PATIENCE — I LOVE YOU
*Patricia Washington*

## A Dream

There's nothing more pleasurable than following a dream
or trying to build your self esteem

If you remember where you've come from,
where you are and where you're going

Then you'll never forget who you were,
who you are and who you'll always be

The ultimate dream is to be free
and being free, is being whoever you want to be
Not some of the time but all of the time

*Pamela D. Howard*

## Untitled

The hues of blue,
    orange, yellow and
        crimson
fill the morning air with a fragrance
sweeter than the song of angels in heaven.

Through delicate lines and brilliant colors
    the wildflowers of Spring speak of the simpleness
        of the untold splendors of Heaven's gardens.

Wildflowers of diverse color, from diverse lands come
together
in one short burst of magnificence showing
    the beauty of the inner soul,
the vulnerability of the human heart,
    and
the strength of the human spirit.

With great expectation we await Spring in all her glory
    For Spring speaks to our souls though her grace
        and
            beauty.
    *Terri Evans*

## My Friend

With all the hours we would talk,
Others began to mock
And from that first walk
You began, my heart, to unlock

From March to September
I was a fan of your club, a member
Must you forget and not remember,
The friendship that sparked and would later become an ember

When it came time
I saw no sign
Were all those things you said a line?
And if not, may I ask my crime?

You were from beginning to end the friend I sought
And with a challenge I fought
You were my best friend, I thought
So why did you break your promise, I miss you a lot

As for me, my friendship I did lend
The smiles I did send
And even though time may mend,
I am still waiting for you, my friend

*Sara Tuma*

## Best Friends

We met, we fell in love and we married,
Our life has been a road of ups and downs,
But even tho we don't see eye to eye sometimes,
I would never think of going out of bounds.

I yell! I give you Hell!
But I love you with all my heart,
And heaven knows if you ever left me dear,
My whole life would fall apart.

We're the best of friends and always will be,
Even tho we're man and wife.
My respect and love for you will last forever,
And I'll love you all of my life.

*Luella L. Lawrence*

## Dreams Are....

Dreams are made from our thoughts,
Our minds, our souls.
They are our wanting desires,
Our feelings, our cares.

Our dreams are part of what we are,
They are our hidden life, our fantasies.
In our dreams, we can be whatever we want.
We are untouchable, undeceivable.

Dreams are a way of life,
A hidden path to a secret treasure.
But the past is always leading on,
For a path is just a dream,
And a dream is just a thought.

*Matthew A. Luers*

## Champions!

Competition is Life!  At least for today,
Our time must be focused and clear!
Today we prepare, we get better, we pay
for excellence all through the year!

Competition means learning and practice and thought
toward perfecting the things that we do,
so skills we develop from lesson we're taught
help solve problems in life, old and new!

The winners in games, as in life, show the way
to all who would do something well.
So "Champions" we call them, and follow their way,
and learn from the stories they tell!

And those who would learn from the best of our kind
take the best they have learned on the way,
correcting, perfecting the gold to be mined;
chasing clouds from their bright, shiny day,

To be "Champions" themselves, of all or a few,
or even of one, for a day!
. . And now they will lead: for, they learned and they grew!
Now, they help someone else on the way!

*William W. Oakland*

## The Pleasure Of Your Company

This morning when I awoke to the sound of birds chirping
outside my window, I remembered you.
Thanks for sending such sweet music to awaken me.

Your spirit lives within my soul and with each day
that passes you give me new things to behold.  "Just look at the
flowers", you told me one day; "the mountains, clouds, and oceans
all about - just know that I AM".

I adore your ways; how you catch me off guard and speak
with encouragement to restore my heart - Because you know man alone
cannot fill the gaps that can leave you feeling lonely; empty....

As I thumb through the pages, the Word that you speak sends comfort
and assurance - sends gratifying peace.  Thanks for speaking through
others you've sent my way when I know not the answers; when I tend
to go astray.

I know you're always there for me; near and never far.
I invite you daily, through prayer and praise, to join me - when I'm
dining or working in the garden even while driving my car.

I enjoy your presence; I delight in your company.

*Rhonda A. Williams*

## Graduation

Why, oh why does this year have to end?
Over the past year, I have made some great friends.

Fortunately, I'll be seeing two of them next year,
but I will not be seeing one friend who is so dear.

She's going to Ledyard and I to St. Bernard,
the thought makes swallowing the lump in my throat quite hard.

During the next year we will converse on the phone quite a lot.
It won't be the same, but it'll be all that we've got.

I'll miss other kids and the teachers I've had.
Although on that night, I hope to be glad,

I will be happy to leave most of those boys.
Their obnoxious behavior gets me annoyed!

For other reasons that night, I'll be joyous as well,
For a new horizon to look upon, new dreams to fulfill.

Though graduation night will cause me some pain,
I don't want to look back on it with disdain.

I will not say a very sorrowful goodbye,
because though not in class, there will be a "next time."

*Sarah Lombardo*

## Metamorphosis (Made In N.Y.)

The spring has spilled
over the stairs and turned into
a puddle.
And I'm getting lost, melting
into the everyday
transforming into a uniformed crowd.
But not giving up yet!
Feverishly grabbing for support,
rock, stone, but everything's torn down
pedestal of glass cracked,
I'm trying to awaken the sleeping multitude
I scream...shout
rescuing myself
and all those
stony words...echo...roll...
next
only a quiet moan can be heard.
Passer-by's legs crash pieces...
glass dust
of an unknown origin.

*Loreta Muskardin*

## Love Is Many Things

Love is the rose that will never wilt
Love is the perfectly balanced scale that will
never tilt
Love is the one true immortal and will never
die
Love is the bird that flies higher that anything
else in the sky
Love is the one emotion which can equal anger
and hatred
Love can't be expressed with colors or words
that can be shown or said
Love is a true emotion, one of the heart
Love is more valuable than any work of art.

*Rachel Hunt*

## To A Friend

Having ANOTHER birthday?  I know just how you feel.
  Painful corns on your toes, calluses on each heel,
Your shoulders are aching.  Your back has constant pain
  Both knees keep on buckling, your hips can't take the strain.

Your ears can't hear so well, seeing is hard, both eyes,
  Getting so forgetful, acid stomach—can't disguise.
Many teeth are missing, must survive on soup—plain.
  Can't smell the spring flowers, late hours, you must refrain.

Shaking hands, a real chore, thumbs and fingers gnarled up,
  Wrists are pretty swollen.  Hard to hold your coffee cup.
Your neck is stiff and sore, can't stand to wear a tie,
  You want to look your best, each effort a sigh

You're in a sad condition, don't worry.  It will pass.
  You'll get back to normal, your smile will be first class.
You know, I'm only kidding, for your age you do fine.
  Keep your sweet self, happy, helpful and kind.

Have a happy birthday, I pray God will bless.
  Things you do for others, may each day bring success.
Count all your blessings, you have received through the years
  Lock them deep in your heart.  Among your souvenirs.

  *Marie B. Pearson*

## The Middle of Things

There comes a time called the middle of things
past things are forgotten and gone;
new plans excite us to dream, and invite us
to spend all our thoughts dreaming on!

But, this is the time when I like to pause;
put all of my thoughts on re-wind,
then run them again - sort out lovely from pain;
something unusual I find——!

There are thank you's I need to say over again.
There are gifts, where one thank you won't do -
the love in the giving, the way it was given;
- can not cover it, simply thank you!

I must stop to say thanks, in the middle of things,
first, for blessing from God above,
then thank you for all things so many, so much,
that came from dear ones I love!

  *Phyllis J. Morgan*

## Omnipotence

There is a time and place where in the midst of violence, there is
  peace
Ironically ruled by crackling thunder and illumined streaks;
Giving reason for pause no matter what the demands,
Reminding us of the Power that surrounds, enfolds, and enwraps.

Stillness is created inside when chaos rules the outside.
We are forced to go inward, even to look inward,
Beckoned by a Force seeking humility and respect
That needs NOT ask for permission or adhere to prediction.

How sensual the sound and how bright the light
Divinely merging as one, giving birth in our hearts and in our
  homes
To an awkward, but oddly familiar silence and an eerie darkness
Forcing a renaissance of the lost art of conversation.

Hearts grow fonder in the intimidation of the hour
And soothingly, we release a binding tension...
A build-up, if you will,
As we defer our earthly controls, ambitions and "strengths"
To those of...a higher Power.

  *Pamela M. Everett*

## Booted From The List

While in the mall the other day,
People were smiling indiscreet.
I smiled and tried to meet their eyes,
But they were looking at my feet.

And so I kept on going
And in a window I did see
Someone who looked familiar.
Good Guffey!  It was me.

I kept a getting closer
And as I started looking down,
There was something strange about my boots -
One was black - the other brown.

So, I ask you Mr. Blackwell,
Have I started a new fad
Or have I made your "hit list"
by dressing like a cad?

  *Latna Mellott*

## The Ice Cream Man On Memorial Day

I stopped to talk to the ice cream man,
perched in his truck next to Memorial Park,
where he spilled from his cornucopia of sweetness
red, white and blue popsicles, chocolate bars
and mounds of ice cream—
bits of happiness in a cone—
until the last child left.

The parade was over.
The Congressman had intoned his patriotism.
The Boy Scouts had marched with the flag.
The mayor had sung praises for honored dead.

We sat in his truck, talked about selling ice cream—
long hours, little pay.
he hold me how his daughter was embarrassed
he sold ice cream.
he felt ashamed, too,
he had done no better with his life.
No, don't write about me,
Ginny would hate me, he said.

  *Marjorie Hauptman*

## On Divorce

I've reached a period in my life.
  Period.
My friend says I'm just in a (parenthesis)
[It feels more like brackets]
I keep hoping maybe it's just a comma, a brief pause,
Even a semicolon would be okay; closely connected
Or a colon:  Something will follow
Anything but the forever period.
I lived with the question mark for so long.  Isn't the period
preferable?
I worry that the exclamation points will never come again!
I dream of them in big, bold print spread majestically throughout
the pages!!!
Is this really the final chapter?  The end?  Period.
The loneliness of the sad period.  If only I could add two
friends . . . a brief interruption, more to come . . .
Please let my period emerge into this hopeful ellipsis. . .

  *Leslie Medlock*

## Untitled

Delicate trees whisper my wisdom in the wind
Philosophize, I can
Escape, I cannot
Truth to be spoken only in the rays of sun
Mystery unfolds in night
Disguised, truth comes out
Time brings no relief
Free to all who can accept
Rain falls once again
Fine weather no longer comes
The darkness sets in
Feelings are not discovered until too late
Examples are shown
Question me not, for,
Delicate trees whisper my wisdom in the wind

*Mary Jo Dailey*

## Grace

One look at me and you can see I'm just as plain as one can be.
Plain of face and overweight and with a somewhat awkward gait,
I stumble through life's daily chores hoping not to miss any open
doors that may offer up a better life, maybe not richer but with far
less strife.
    I know that my life is of my own making
    and good things are usually there for the taking.
    I know to work hard, be loving and caring,
    and I know the Lord wants us all to be sharing
    our knowledge and skills to better our world,
    not fighting and killing, trigger fingers curled.
    We share this place and we must get along
    ignoring our differences, work to be strong as a whole
    not simply one here and there.
    The plain, the strong, the meek all must share
    in making our lives the best that we can,
    and if we all start today and lend others a hand
    no one has to stumble. We can march heads held high
    through the streets of our world. Together we can fly!

*K. S. Stickler*

## Ode to My Mother

I can see my mother in the garden
planting roses.
Her hair is blowing in the wind
like a sunflower's seeds floating away.
Her touch is so golden, it fills you
up with happiness.
My mom is a rose in a field.
From a far off place you can smell her perfume
Her teeth are like white daisies in the sun.
My mom is a butterfly flying away in a sunset.
I can taste my mom's cooking right now.
My mom has a smile of happiness.
My mom has a nose of pride.
I can hear my mom's singing a mile away.
My mom is beautiful, and I love her!

*Ruben Calzada*

## Someone's Light-Bulb Idea

Backpacks, such diversity ... colors, shapes, sizes, prices
Packet so full, what do they contain?
Schoolchildren fortunate to own them
Hung by two straps over their shoulders
Occasionally over one
Watching their skip-a-long strides
I remember my first day of school
With only a pencil and a notebook
Returning home with many books
curled up in my left arm
Skipping along on my long trek home!

*Vera Kelly*

## Baby Doll

I trace its lips lined in faded red, a ghostly smile.
Plastic eyes glint and shudder,
open and close
as if on wavering hinges.
Opaque, blue pupils reflect
the dimness of the room.
Molded fingers reach out for something,
waiting.
The pink dress with its lacy trim lies on my bed,
contrasting the worn, ebony sheets.
I pick the doll up and squeeze its stuffed body
tightly.
As I turn its face towards mine,
a wrenching, mewling cry echoes from its center,
where a heart should be.
Soothingly, my fingers caress its limp hair.
I give of myself as no one has
given,
and I rock back and forth
until it sleeps.

*Nikkii Wolf*

## In Heaven, Am I

If I should die
Please do not cry
Look to the sky
For there am I
Above the mountains
I will soar high
Near wildflowers, streams and butterflies
Shall be I
Let raindrops, soft and gentle
Comfort thee
The beautiful snowflakes
Will be with me
If I should die
Please do not cry
With our Father, Peaceful, Am I
Look to the sky
In Heaven, Am I

*Patricia M. Fraser*

## Addictions

I am an addict...there's no doubt it's true.
Please let me explain what I mean to you:
Oh just please say the magic "C" word —
Not callabazoom or cilly-ja-wham
C if you can guess just what I am!
M&M, Snickers, Kit Kat...How's that?
Milky Way, Brownies, Fudge too...
Maltballs, Reeses, Yoo-Hoo!
Have you guessed? Do you know?
Shall I put on a show...about a man named Wonka?
Oh, C how I love ya! If you don't know soon,
I'll grab us some spoons for C ice cream and C topping.
If you already know, go ahead eat C snow!
You've jumped leaps and bounds, Covered cherries and Mounds.
Unsure you dare say? Oh, then I fear,
It's time to call Whitman and Three Musketeers!
Godiva, Lady of the Land, she will tell you where you stand,
Oompa Loompas to greet you and many to meet you...
Chocoholics in our Chocolate Land.

*Sharon M. Black*

## My Dolphin and Me

Flying through the air on my dolphin's back,
plunging down he and me,
around the world and across the sea.
Up and down we go again
as if the world had no end
With my dolphin following me
across the wide and open sea,
just my dolphin and me.
The bright sun set on the ocean waves.
I admire the beautiful sheet of glass,
pink and purple, yellow, and white,
Made the ocean a spectacular sight.
In the lake through the stream,
This was like a wonderful dream.
To the park, people wanted to see,
when a gunshot echoed through the shallow air.
It zipped by me and into his head.
As quick as a blink all the dolphins disappeared
with one big splash.
Think of how the world will be,
without my dolphin following me.

*Tiffany Tietz*

## "Blossoms"

Each fragile petal unfolds before me
Portraying fragrant ecstasy
Morning dew drops gently fall
Supple stems stretch out tall
No sounds are captured here
Dusk till dawn they bow, demure
Arising color clad beauties
beneath the sun
Breathtaking wonders each and every one
Busy bees supping their sweet splendor
Softly swaying on gentle breezes
they surrender
All are made from the master Artist's hand
To our delight they are, "Oh so grand!"
Blossoms...

*Sandra L. Reading*

## The Other Side of the Moon

He lay at the turn of the road,
Powerless to rise yet powerless to die,
With rustled breath from a parched throat,
Yet not a word as all passed by.
And a hollow battered mug by his side,
Echoing an effortless effervescence of hunger and thirst,
Ruthlessly revealed in unshamed delight,
By the stealthy moon of greed and lust.
He spat at her in furious rage,
At those relentless rays from high that shone,
And screamed out in helpless disgrace
To let him live and die alone.

Yet, as he looked from his cushioned bed,
Night, a three quarter old;
With labored breath and flakes of sweat,
And eyes unchained from dreams of cold.
There! there was his moon, soft as snow.
A newly wed - in spotless white;
That veiled much, yet revealed more.
He revealed in ceaseless delight.

*Shuvendu Sen*

## A Human Thunderbolt

Music so sweet to the heart, soul, and mind
Preaching the truth, always gentle and kind
Not wanting any to be left behind
Hoping through his witness, Jesus we'd find

Words of love and wisdom for all to hear
Always praying to God we would draw near
For us he has done this year after year
Always in his full 'armor of God' gear

For Christ he takes a definite stand
Mile after mile he crossed this land
A powerful and influential man
Talented, anointed, carved in God's hand

A flash of lightning from heaven above
Radically honest, but filled with love
Different, but as peaceful as a dove
Charm and charisma that fits like a glove

He's filled with spirit like a new born colt
So dynamic you see and feel the jolt
Energy so big with a mighty volt
God sent us a human thunderbolt

*Sharon E. Coursey*

## To David

Love yet untold
purifies me with a liquid fire.
strands of burning red and gold
fall from your mouth to mine
making a pentecost of passion:
if anyone knows how to speak in tongues
it is you and I...
Tufts of silken recognition fall upon me
aching revelations that ask for my touch
I am rising, rising from my sleep
needles pierce the tide of numbness that recedes
leaving in its wake
only my shivering body
and wondering heart

*Mary C. Maloof*

## After Talking To A Composer

The words came...sliver, translucent..threads of letter-symbols;
Purposeful, with meaning...no, more...with direction
Toward the inner space of wonder, imagining.

The sounds came...golden, strong..overlays of note-symbols;
Movement, with gesture...yes, even more...with growing timbre
Toward the inner space of wonder, imagining.

The queries came...copper, bright..from like minds;
Toward the next space of wonder, imagining.

The answers came...brass, shining.. with conviction;
Assurance, with more questions...yes, growing with more on- flights
Toward the inner space of wonder, imagining.

*Sally Monsour*

## Portion

Portion today, portion tomorrow. Portion in pain and in sorrow.
Portion is all that I hope for, to enjoy the beauty God has
enstore. Whether days full of pleasure or a life full of dreams.
Portion is constant and full of delight; it's all but a
Portion that I request on this night. Is it fair? Or will a
Portion be enough, oh how I wish and hope so much. Give me my
allotment and spare no justice or pity alike, all that I need
is my Portion tonight!

*I. Ishod*

## "The Other"

In my wildest of dreams, I never thought I would
pursue something so much,
As I have with you, through a glance, spoken word
or a touch;

I beg you, don't prejudge my sentiments in vain,
My feelings for you sometimes drive me insane;

My passing display of affection may be a hard thing to hide,
But, by far, not more difficult than the tears I have cried;

Life sometimes may deal us an unkind blow,
When we wake to reality and suddenly know...

Our dreams are only as vivid as the life we breathe into them,
Whatever they are, or where or when;

Through the sins, I've expected us both to commit,
I drowned in self pity, here as I sit;

Looking for forgiveness somewhere in your eyes as we meet,
Never wanting for just passion on that "dead end" street.

*Michele L. Paolini*

## House

The
quaint old
woman has lived
in isolation, nestled in the mountains
and evergreen forests of Vermont.  She has seen the
seasons cycle through over two centuries; strong, study,
and defiant against the passage of time. She has dutifully cradled and
protected families of many generations form the biting cold and silent
snow of
New England winters.  She is filled with the musty scent of
old wooden floors, now aging, and the smell and warmth of a
large fire in the hearth, with the sweet scent of the pine forest
and the thick blanket of snow she wears to keep warm.  Sit
down and stay a while; rest in her big, soft, worn chairs.
Listen to the tales she has to tell as she reads from her
journals and scrapbooks from the past two hundred years.
She is not a lonely woman.  With a cool, crisp, dancing
stream as her companion, and families that spend
Thanksgivings and Christmases with her, she happily nestles
herself and passes her years in the mountains of Vermont.

*Mark Michalowski*

## Lost Heart

Mixed feelings emerge from a heart which was once content,
Question and struggle begin to show it's eery face,
Their minds begin to wonder and question authority,
The heart cries out but is ignored,
For what's done is done and can't be changed,
The helpless soul is in mourning forever
baring the pain of a lost loved one,
Never again will their voice echo or their
face light up a dark, gloomy room,
But their presence will always dwell in
the hearts of those who truly loved them.

*Melissa Diane Claar*

## Love

Love is stars shining bright.
Love is the moon watching over us.
Love is the colors of the sunset.
Love is hearts for you and me.
Love is Moms, Dads, sisters and brothers together.
Love is the circle of life.
Love is God and his son.
Love is love for you, forever.

*Nichole Renee Sims*

## The Threads That Hold Us Together

Long strolls through the golden wheat pasture,
Quiet times under a favorite oak tree,
Wading through a shallow, crystalline stream.

Playing in a nearby hay stack in an old abandoned barn,
Talking on the phone with a good friend for hours,
Laughing at a humorous joke,
Flying over a twinkling city in a luxury plane.

Feasting with friends and family on memorable holidays,
Praising and singing in the church sanctuary,
Sitting on Grandpa's knee listening to his exhilarating stories.

Taking a long drive in your first new car,
Saying those everlasting words 'I do,'
Holding your first born child,
Cherishing time spent with loved ones.

These are the threads that weave our lives.

*Wendy Woolley*

## Grandmother

G is for God's gift from Heaven above;
R is for respected; you are admired and loved;
A is for appreciated, which you very much are;
N is for noble; you are a shining star;
D is for dearest—grandmother of all;
M is for mercy; you are good to all;
O is for optimistic; you look for the best;
T is for tender; your love stands the test;
H is for heart, which holds love and care;
E is for excellent; you are beyond compare; and
R is for radiant; you are elegant and fair.

*Rolallen Ruelo*

## Radiant Moments

Radiant love is so romantic
Radiant love is what makes me panic.
Candle light dinner, by a fire.
That is my weakness and desire.
Taking a walk in the moonlight,
and the cool breeze blows though my hair
As you hold me gently, to let me know you're there
as we go on a picnic and sit under the
shade of a tree.
Nothing else seems to exist in the world,
But you and me.
These words are just thoughts
None have yet to come true
So will you come to me,
So I can share these moments with you?

*Tiffany Dodge*

## Ode to Harrisburg

Mystical events along the susquahanna streams.
Radioactive bubbles in the American dream.
Cosmic powers in the hands of man and radioactive fall out with no
evacuation plans.
Horrific nightmares that no mind can hold.
Radioactive fallout death in thousands will toll.
Now the wizard of death emerges from his radioactive hell.
Cloaked in scientific euphemisms that will never tell about ionized
particles and gamma rays.
Changing DNA arrangements which govern heredities ways.
Investigations and cover up lies
Radioactive waste that cancerize.
The end is clear and certain but investigations tell.
That radioactive waste is a man made hell.

*Clifton-Walston*

## Liberation

From the ashes of the past
Raises a sad butterfly
Its wings tainted with pain
Searching for light

New Hope
Makes her fugitive of bad memories
With the impulse life gives
It breaks hidden iron bars
Liberating itself of the sorrow that ties

Not a cry
Not a tear
Only the shadow
Of a drop of anguish
That begins to disappear

*Lydia Walteros*

## An Oak Tree

An oak tree's branches,
reach out like arms holding a new born baby,
Its leaves flutter,
in the soft, cool spring breeze,
Its brown bark protects it,
like a dog protecting its pups,
The different color leaves,
fall to the ground,
but don't make a sound,
for they drift away,
to sweave, swirl, and sway,
in the soft, cool breeze.

*Scott Gerber*

## Bridges To Cross

Age has its merits of blessed memories for me
Recalling the love shared with a "Spirit Set Free"
Like stepping stones, through the years of her life
Many filled with joy and others with strife.

She had "Bridges To Cross" and "Many Mountains To Climb"
But her love for others always helped her to find
The answers and reasons she found in the Truth
By accepting His Word as her daily proof

No - one's an Island Unto Themselves
Nor would she be judged by her earthly wealth
To ask to be perfect was not part of her plan
Her impassioned plea was to hold to His hand.

So with loved ones beside her, He called her away
Her suffering over at "The Dawning of Day"
Finally at Peace, her last bridge was crossed
We'll be re-united some day, ALL IS NOT LOST!

*Merry M. Wortham*

## Just for a Visit

Every Sunday they whelp us out in the big room, so we can wait for our
relation and friends to come to visit us soon. We will sit and wait
and watch, then look at the big clock on the wall, that says tick
tock, tick tock. I finally dose off to sleep in my wheel chair; then
I hear some say one say, how are you today? I look up and smile, but
it's not for me. Oh! Who is that coming thro the door? That is
surely some one for me; but they went the other way. Why it's half
past four, there soon will be no more; as it's supper time and they
will take us back thru the big door. I'll be back next Sunday, to
wait and see; maybe one will come and visit me and I'll be so happy,
you wait and see.

*Maxine Huesman*

## Here At The Wrong Time

I'm standing at the window gazing out at the rain
Reflections in the water seem like a dream
They say everybody's got some special talent to share
But my life's rushing by me leaving me unaware
Contemplating my life to this point
Bewildered to where it will lead
I never seem to get it until it's to late
I'm always one step behind the pace
I find myself trying to comprehend
But it seems that I never fit in
Did you ever feel like you were here at the wrong time
Maybe your time has past or not yet begun
I think I may be here for no reason
Maybe I'm not supposed to be here at all
As I look to the future with my life in full view
I'll have to keep on struggling just to get thru
I climb another mountain of troubles and pain
Just to reach the top and fall into the valley again
Every time I think I've got a firm grip on this life
I have to start all over again

*Rick Kinkton*

## Insight

You are the heart and soul of me
Regardless of life previously lived
Of roads traveled and stopping to rest
To gain strength, fortitude, food for thought
Continuing on in the best and worst of times
Giving life everything you had
Fighting the good fight has made you the
person you are today
A person of strength, character, vision, virtue
All earned by your own endeavors
And I find this spirit as I look deep into your eyes
Deserving of undying loyalty and devotion
For the rest of the journey together
Bound hand in hand
Giving solace through trials and tribulations
A part of life when they come our way.
I will never let you down
I will always be there for you
Because you deserve only the best.
That will be me, loving you.

*Mary E. Arthur*

## Masla Viola

Masla Viola knows the pain of being rejected by patriarchy and it's
religions;
Of being relegated to second or third place behind men and their
possessions and the churches of "sports".

Her eyes reflect the anguish of being made over in the image and
likeness of man who worships at the alter of youth.

She possesses deep secrets of the soul passed on to her by powerful
goddesses before their reign of equality gave way to that of lesser "Gods."

The bloody struggles of the centuries have been her domain.
Eternal Knowledge is hers.

The shock of living shows on her face.
Yes, her mouth is open in horror and in awe; a solemn "Om" resounds.

She is the Amazon in shining armor who will free us from our suit of
enslavement.

She is wisdom incarnate and the embodiment of pain and despair.

Yet, she is the hope of the world the crone, the hag, the wise woman
within us all.

*Susan Isabel*

## "First Love"

First love don't last forever, even though they still
remain, There's no way to work things out, it only stays the same.
    The feelings hurt forever, a lifetime of destiny, still
dreaming of the dream, you know can never be.
    And to try to move on, would only get you sad, as the
pain is in your heart, right now it's not too bad.
    Yet the tears can last forever, a love beat down to the
floor, and yes you'd like to die, but sometimes you're not
too sure.
    If it's destiny you're awaiting, then the time is still
not right, it may just wear you down, but you still must
fight.
    So if you're not too sure, about the way you hold on,
then let it slip away, and soon it will be gone.
    Just tell yourself it's over, and that you'll find
someone new, and if you break down in tears, just remember
who is who.
    And though it seems so hard, still hurting while it's
there, you can't seem to give up, just don't let him know
you care.

*Lisa Kay Zeller*

## To Ma

All fallen souls with spirit broke,
    remember these words: Here I found hope.
True beyond my life's duration,
    The wish of peace for all creation.

For of Motherhood we all do live,
    May that love echo and all forgive.
In sorrow and mourning they endure,
    Then find a dawn to blossom more.

So as Mother's love was truly rare,
    And all my life she really cared:
As true to promise their heartfelt ballads,
    Neglect show none for all are valiant.

Imagine my dream: Dance once more,
    For each lullaby of joy they borne.
Chime the bells: reap God's reward,
    And forever reach to hearts ignored.

For not at all does that love cease,
    With peace for all and worldly feast.
Still never to end and forgotten not,
    My inner peace will never stop.

*Michael Lippi*

## Old Man God Knoweth All

No one knows the hurt I feel, no man will ever know unless God
reveals it to him. But old man God knoweth all. Some may think that
I'm not saved or do not have the Holy Ghost, just because of my
actions, but man looks at the outer appearance, but God looks at the
inner appearance. But no man ever know unless God reveals it to him.
But old man God knoweth all. Many times my past get in my way, but
God said in his word, old things shall pass away and behold, all things
shall become new. But no man will ever know unless God reveals it to
him. But old man God knoweth all. I traveled a long road to get to
where I am now. But I know beyond a shadow of a doubt through God's
saving grace, I've come a mighty long way. But no man will ever know
unless God reveals it to him. But old man God knoweth all. Through my
trials and tribulations, God was standing by my side. He let me know
that whatever the circumstances are or what outcome maybe I will never
walk alone. But no man will ever know unless God reveals it to him.
But old man God knoweth all. In my life God deals with me in many
was, not to man's liking, but to God's liking. There are times I
can't agree with everything that is said, but after all God is still
dealing with me. Some may not know that God does not deal with us in
the same way. But no man know ever unless God reveals it to
him...but old knoweth all.

*Marcia F. Johnson*

## My Love

My love for you is the largest river
Roaring past the trees
The tears you see running down my face
Is the fear no one ever sees

Without you my life is dark and empty
Blackened without hope
No one can bring me to safety

The rain pours down on me at night
As I stand there in dread
The lightening cracks and thunder roars
Only inches above my head

Silence makes me cry at night
So loud it hurts my ears
When stars come out and the winds are still
I will be found in tears.

*Shelly Turk*

## Take A Walk

Inward and throughout
root hairs seek out
a flower grows.

Unpainted canvas unneeded
unbeautiful unknown
skinned over wet, oil paint, rainbowed.

enfolded in pure admiration undeserving love
gentle child peering into flowers
in a field of yellow daffodils.

Childlike love so blind, so forgiving,
blemishes, chosen to be unseen,
and I so full of these.

Muscle entwined fingers tenderly drawing
my heart to You strings detaching
a tug-of-war between want-and-need.

Fear of the forsaken road begging to be tread
'walk with me' a whispering plea
alas, I hesitate.
Take my hand and leaf, dear Friend this last time I give
for, oh, forbid I should turn again.

*Shannon Dow*

## Alter and Ego

Smiling lips? Sparkling eyes?
Rosy cheeks? Bah! Paradise?
You shouldn't smile when you look in the mirror!
If anyone sees you, she'll think you're queerer
Than Ponce de Leon with his fountain of youth.
'Fess up, ego, and admit to the truth!
Look at your wrinkles; you're older than sin;
Your yellow toothed smile is a senile grin.

Go away twin alter, you old ink spot!
You make me feel ancient, but I am not.
I'm as young as I feel and I feel fine.
My mirror tells me that my eyes still shine.

*Rachel A. Preston*

## Untitled

Run away
Run far and
run away
until all you see are laughing children
and perfect four leaf clovers
lining green hills
with silver-blue pools of water
go run away to that perfect world
I will remain in my world
and we will then be separated
as you run away to something that you will never find
and as I live in a slightly imperfect world
with just one alteration needed.
you.

*Monika Verma*

## One Year In Time

In the spring of life is fun and games
Running and playing without any blame
Young and sprouting in body and mind
No cares of life at any time.

The summer of life is more sincere
In full bloom life's challenge draw near
Like the small creatures fight for their young
In this life survives only the strong.

Determine to win at this awesome quest
Sometimes struggling to do what's best
Looking back on all of the years
Can bring happiness, joy, or tears.

Midlife is like Autumn, approaches too fast
To meet it head on, forget the past
Like leaves turning colors; orange, brown, and red
Skin sags, hair greys, flesh wrinkles and spreads.

The wind of life is creeping right on
Everything is cold, silent and gone
When winter is over comes sweet peace of mind
Life only seems like one winter in time.

*Margie V. Ware*

## Rendezvous

The water clothes the earth with majestic beauty. Violently rushing waves hug the deserted shore at all sides leaving only a dark rim of mud in their wake. The sun casts a golden glow with iridescent shades of green and blue sparkling like diamonds in the distance. Glorious to behold is the splendor that embraces and enfolds a seemingly endless span. I am warmed and comforted by its resplendent hue.

Darkness gathers quickly and the radiant fireball fades beyond the ocean's rim. The blackness of the night effaced all beauty. Rushing waves with their ominous roar welcome me no longer. I hasten to escape from their sinister and grasping reach.

*Sharon L. Konschak*

## Within

As each verse becomes printed in
our life, the end of each year closes
one chapter, only to begin the next.

It's thin our pain, the strength
from within guides us thin our concerns
so we may preserve and begin to complete
our enigma.

*Lawrence Lombardo*

## "Don't Tell Me"

My son...

"Don't tell me what to do.....I'm not a baby,"
  said the toddler.

"Don't tell me what to do......I can do it myself,"
  said the child.

"Don't tell me what to do.....I'm not a child, anymore,"
  said the teenager.

"Don't tell me what to do.....I'm an adult now,"
  said my son.

My son...
  Please understand, how hard it is to let you go,
  to make your own mistakes,
  to feel your own pain.

"I won't tell you what to do.....You're an adult. Just know, I will
always be there for you,"
  said the parent.

*Linda Goins*

## One Way Street

No way to go but one.
Same feelings, nothing done.
Walking on a six inch sidewalk.
No one wants to talk.

Sun glaring in your eyes.
Maybe warning you of future bad times.
Legs start to get heavy; hands clammy.

Where in the world does this road lead;
to a castle, to the Lord or to a bad seed?

Can't change direction; it's a sin.
Anxiety, uncertainty kicking in.

No intersection in sight.
No free bird in flight.
Day is quickly turning to night.
Wherever I go I hope I get there all right.

Where in the world does this road lead;
to a castle, to the Lord, or to a bad seed?

*Michael Agiorgousis*

## I Am Tired

Lord I am tired of being bent over this
same tub as I see my mother scream
my father made to crawl as my sister's
body is being bold away my brother put
behind bars for looking and that
same man the wrong way and my
children oh yeah! My children being sent
to that far far land and only coming
back to me in a brown box Lord maybe
your head be turned and you just
can't look this way my hands are
hurting and my feet aching I cant
take no more Lord I am tired

*Veronica C. Couzzens*

## Rain Clouds

Sun runs before the shade,
Rain cloud begins the raid.
Flashed lightening
Would say it won,
yet runs shade,
before eternal sun.

*Mary Nadia Zemeske*

## Remembering A Dead Son

Listen with care, and you will hear
A quiet tune
Beneath the orchestra's discordant blare.
The perfect flute
Or the demented piano player,
Singing a song to you once he is gone ...
"Once, I was there."

*Leo Holland*

## A Little Girl So Fine

To think that only yesterday a little girl so fine,
Sat across the table her chair raised up to mine.
Her words were few and precious her life so light and free,
I thought not of the day she'd want a life for her and he.
For such days seemed so far away as distant as the moon,
And so I watched her mother feed her another spoon.
The years progressed in order till one day dark and gray,
His call divided Mom from us with I alone to stay.
One quarter century has passed since first I saw her face,
And now I see her dressed in white in satin, silk, and lace.
I give her hand most willingly to one whose name is Paul,
And pray their lives together will scan the highest wall.
I'll always have within me fine memories rich as wine.
Of one who'll always be to me a little girl so fine.

*Philip Oddo*

## Frogs and Raspberry Beer

My friend the frog
sat in a big band music playing bar
smoking a clove cigarette,
drinking a raspberry beer.

His beret slightly titled
looking to me a bit like a pistachio incense stick burning.
He hopped from his lily pad to the trench coat covered woman
I'm disappointed being brunette.

Her diamond fingers seemed to intrigue him
. . . batting blue eyes,
flipping a curl behind a hoop earring
almost catching the thread dangling from the hat upon his green head.

Long webbed fingers latching with hers
like a London bridge made in kindergarten,
both kidding, me watching. . .
wondering about all of the other frogs in their lives.

Frogs ever hopping, never satisfied . . .
always hopping, hoping . . .
never satisfied.

*Tucker-Roberts*

## A Falling Star

I sat and watched the sky above, it was an awesome sight

The stars were out in full array and glistened with their lights

I made a wish as I looked up and
saw a falling star

It fell to earth I know not where
perhaps right where you are

It could well be that you were
looking up and saw it too

Perhaps you wished upon the star,
cause, you were feeling blue

If we both wandered through the fields and walked amongst the heather
We may just find it waiting there, to bring us both together.

*Maria Febrona Williamson*

## Not a Cloud in the Sky

Not a cloud in the sky; wave one kiss before I die
Say it isn't so as I will; caught in parachuting bitter pill
All is rosy as a thorn; brothers and sisters fatally torn
Twixt the family and the self; are there only more bones on the shelf
Wake to shake the quake on my eyes; buried in mounds of festering flies
Walks past does not dare; thinks I am one who would scare
Excuses abound by the Millions; Platitudes spewed by the Trillions
Even the old Archangel can quote; that which faithful saints once
      wrote
Years of fear appear minutely; as I hear of my duty
Victims stand short of pride; daring the arrogant way too wide
Sometimes at the world I just stare, unaware I wonder if I care
'Tis it weakness to want truth; 'tis it weakness to be a ruth
Born of mother and a father; some wonder why we bother
Then nature calmly whispers; as the Spirit leads us on.

*Wade J. Bove*

## Iconic-Images Dwelling In My Mind

Images flickering endlessly; with stricken people fleeing on the screen.
Images frozen in time; showing starving children in 'stills,'
with no strength for a scream.
Glimpses of a camera-man, trapped in the snare of a film —
Steaming
through voyages, over the invisible ionosphere in a thin-film.
Sailing on currents of electricity; and on radio-waves modulated in
frequency.
Washing my senses thread-bare, with no chance for clemency.

I candidly see the terror in the eyes of those vanquished.
I clearly see the hunger in the eyes of those famished.
Pain and sorrow flood my finite mind, like a resounding Coda.
A feeling of loss overwhelms me, and drowns me into an infinite
Coma!

Barrels, do have the power to put a man in some kind of motion.
Some times they have a hole, so that bullets can fly.
Some times they have a lens, to capture fleeting images with deft
and sly!
But I thank God for sparing me; and on my couch, watching these
images I limply lie.

*Moinur Rahman*

## If Only ...

There is a human race
searching for that special place.
But along the way you best enjoy
every day in every way.
We think we know the seeds we sow
will set the roots and bear the fruits.
Milestone passed
things amassed.
We specialize in almost there
it is way too boring just being there.
The greater the drive
the harder to arrive.
I almost saw that place I used to wish to be.
It is hard to find
actually, it is a state of mind.
You move along you get further behind
You move along you change your mind.

*Will Holder*

## Limerick

This mademoiselle from Marseilles,
She labored by night and by day.
Her service was quick.
She was paid by the trick.
'Twas better than minimum pay.

*Michael Wasserman*

## Say Goodbye

You came into my dreams again
Shadows fade against the wall
I see you come for me
Never fading completely
I keep my distance, though it's hard to
How do I say goodbye
When all I can do is cry for you
It's time, It's time, It's time
My speech is paralyzed
Can't make sense of any words
I'm tryin' to leave this space I'm caught in
Take my hands and pull me in
can't help myself I'm dreamin' again
How do I get out of here
and where do I go then?
I keep my distance from you
even though it hurts to
How do I say goodbye
When all I can do is cry for you
It's time, It's time, It's time

*J. D. Rolfs*

## Footsteps Of Time

Footsteps of time keep running through my mind,
Shattering my dreams — reality can blind.
My plans for fame and riches, a life so grand
The hungry hourglass consumed the sand.

Licking at hurried feet like a forest fire,
Flames of youth and pursuit of desire.
Days like autumn leaves floated to the ground
Touching the earth with a lonesome sound.

Duties dulled the spirit, survival smothered years,
Happy times and memories diluted all the tears,
From beginning to end was such a short flight,
"Fasten your seatbelt and turn off the light."

Destiny surrendered, seduced by the wine,
There is no escape, there's no need to pine.
The teacher, the healer in pantomime
All lost to the victor — the enemy time.

*Penny Vavak*

## To Whom It May Concern

The mistress of evil
She comes out when she is called
She is dealt through the lives of many
The richest and poorest of people
She brings happiness and escape to millions
She becomes their friend; then eats away at their soul
She is beautiful and graceful; what she does, she does well
The mistress of evil
When she is done with you, she'll leave you wanting more
Yes, more of her love so she can infect your soul.
When she is gone all too often she leaves death and destruction
She is lethal, she is heartless
Her name
Cocaine

*Nicole Kelly*

## Little Girl

She couldn't walk, she couldn't crawl,
She couldn't really do much at all.
Her mumbled words when she strained to speak,
Her clumsy limbs were awkward and weak.
But still her sparkle blue smile crushed all the darkness
And all the lies.
After four years of teaching us truth,
This little girl that made each day new,
Curled up in her mothers' arms and peacefully passed away
From this life to the kingdom where all God's children
Can run and play and every tear is wiped away.
Now when the little birds sing and when the flowers bloom,
The sun looks in her empty room, the angels look in
with a cool calm breeze, the wind calls her name then
goes to sleep.

*Rick Anselme*

## The Color of Sue

I once met a girl named sue
She had six boys with skin of blue.

They were alone and shunned by the town
Skin was suppose to be white or brown.

Then one day Sue met a fellow
He had six girls with skin of yellow.

They got together because they didn't care
About the color of skin or the color of hair.

They fell in love and oh what a joy
When each girl married a boy.

Time went on and you should have seen
Their beautiful babies with skin of green.

Now they've started their own little town
Where nobody's white and nobody's brown.

You are welcome to visit if you don't care
About the color of skin or the color of hair.

*Suzie Miller*

## Nameless

When I was seven my sister took my name.
She hated hers, you see, and no one stopped her.
That is my outrage

Her fifteen years were intense, extreme.
She argued and fought with yearning and need
And hated herself and cried because
She wanted the love she thought I had.

They tried to help - but only HER because
I was silent in my grief over the loss of myself.
And she made all the noise.

I became a nobody when the I of me was taken
Along with the other things she borrowed, ruined, used.
It was a pattern, or so it seemed
To the child who had nothing...

Not even a name.

*Nancy McGlinchey*

## Smile Like A Clown

Sometimes I feel just like a clown
I have to smile to hide the pain and frown
Let me hang on Lord, just a few more miles to go
I want my journey here to be a good show

*Lorraine Vincent*

## Fire

The fire is a romantic thing.
The most beautiful thing you've ever seen.
Fire will burn and turn and turn,
Until it stops to burn.
Fire is cool but dangerous in a way,
With one you should not play.

*Topher Getz*

## Mother Earth

Nourishing her young with her flesh,
    She like a fertile cow
    gives her body to her young.

Her children created by the light of God,
    The creatures dwelling within her
    made in his image.

Unaware of the magnitude of damage being done,
    Her nurtured children destroying her body
    in the name of what they call success.

Her body withers,
    Leaving only destruction
    to those so dependent on their mother.

Their father, God, answers their prayers,
    Giving his children morals and intellect
    so that they may cherish what is theirs.

Warnings neglected or even left undetected,
    We destroy our Mother Earth
    and so have failed ourselves.

*Stephanie Santos*

## Untitled

The wind decided to play games today.
She started with one tree-
Then a second one down at the end of the yard,
but decided to double back.
I had a hard time following her.
She turned over first one leaf, then another.
The small, new tree in the middle of the yard,
Was caught up in the game.
The little tree bent with her,
But all of a sudden,
She turned to the big leaves
On the maple and oak.
As fast as she started the game, she left.

*Mary Ellen Gill*

## Black Mother

She is strong and Regal, with her head held high,
She walks with pride and authority. She is a beautiful
Black woman, passing her wisdom on down to her children.
She is of strong spirit, for she has faced many tough
times and seen many hardships, overcoming them all
With a smile on her lips, dismissing her worries with a flick
of her hand.
She works hard and asks for little. Never giving up when times
get rough. Trusting only in God, she strives on. She pushes her
children to be the best they can be, never to accept being
second rate. She is a queen among commoners; a rose among thorns.
She may not have fancy jewels like diamonds and rubies, but
She looks upon her children with love and adoration. These are
her jewels: Her precious stones, nothing is more valuable then
these, her flesh and blood. She will never die, as long as there are
those alive to share her wisdom, give her love, and mimic
her kindness and grace. Beautiful women you are everything
and more. It is with Love and admiration that these words
are given. To you, Black mother, always and forever.

*Marquita Gibson*

## Sarah

Sarah is a helpless little girl, living in a cold cruel world,
she's caught up, in the middle of a war, between her mom and dad,
They fight about things that can't control, and things they never had.
They don't even notice how it hurts her, they don't seem to care
    when she cries,
they are too busy hurting themselves, each wishing that the other
    one would die.
They don't really know how much she needs them, she needs their love
    to survive,
it takes a lot more than food and a roof, to keep a child's hopes alive.

A little girl needs a loving mommy, who will keep her safe from harm,
but she also needs her daddy, to be there, and to keep her warm.
She needs to be held and cuddled, and tucked into bed at night,
she needs them to help her say her prayers, and then turn off
    the lights.
She doesn't need to hear them screaming, and calling each other names,
She doesn't need to hear all the excuses, each saying that the other
    one's to blame.

It won't be very long, until little Sarah's grown,
and then it will be too late, to tell her what they should have shown.
the words will fall on deaf ears, when they try to tell her they care,
all that she will know, is the way they hurt her so,
when she needed them so bad, now she'll tell them to go.
And they'll have to pay the cost, for the love that they have lost,
the love of a sweet little girl, who lives in a big cruel world.

*Margaret Ronson*

## Untitled

What is time? What does matter? Why
should we care? Life is only pain
that knows but little joy or it's
so numb with pain.
That the love of mother goes by
unnoticed by one's own self greed for life.
The love of a mother for her child
is the true holy love in this wicked world.
For the love of a mother knows no
bounders, knows no stopping points.
For the love of a mother shall be
the glowing light that guides her
children through the darkest of times
for the love a mother brings us
together and makes us strong. To carry
on with ours lives, even after our
mother body has gone.
For our mother love will always
be in our body and soul

*Rusty Dean Kiser*

## The Rose

    The sun shining and the birds chirping
show the first signs of spring. Under the tree,
a lonely bush senses also that spring has come.
Feeling a need to stretch out its beauty, the
petals unravel as the arms open wide, welcoming
the season.
    The petals soft as satin lay bare, bathing in
the sun, while the purifying scent fills the air.
However, amongst all of the radiance lies the
viciousness of a thorn. Protecting from any
who dare pluck the beauty. Unless it is that one
special soul who can tend to it and treat it with the
love it deserves.
    Walking by, even a hunter glances to see the bush.
Despite the violence by which he is surrounded, he
cannot help but to stop and stare with appreciation
at the soft, gentle beauty of the rose.

*Lorraine Messner*

413

## W.B. Yeats - 1939

You died in the year,
Sick, old-aged flesh, infirmed, interred
Among the red-gold swirl of autumn leaves,
Less evocative than your soul.
Dead?  You smiled and stood upon a pine-dark shrouded knoll,
To cast an eye upon humanity that sudden stricken, grieves,
Heads bent and muffled sorrows heard......
"Wait! wait!" you cried.  "No tear!  No tear!
For I am not here in the ruin of the grave;
Do not look on and mourn this face, in death,
All white and taut,
This marble flesh,
This wax mortality.
No tear
No tear
But hear this simple epitaph:
'Remember, remember, what he spoke
And what he sought'."

*Pearl Moultrie*

## The Trapped Wolf

The trapped wolf howls with a mournful cry, of chances past which signify, a different road but passed right by, and the trapped wolf now reflects.

When he came to the crossroad, with many a thought his mind overflowed, and evil offered to carry his load, now to evil the wolf is in debt.

He never wondered if he chose wrong, so he simply trotted on, very bold and much headstrong, determined to follow his path.

Now the wolf hears the call of his master, which surely means eternal disaster, he tries to run, faster, faster, but the evil is too quick.

The wolf knows he must pay the price, of trotting on without thinking twice, he thought he lived in paradise, but now he sees the truth.

He took the path he thought was easier, partly true, he got much leisure, but he led a life much sleazier, that led to his demise.

The trapped wolf howls with a mournful cry, of chances past which signify, a different road, but passed right by, and the trapped wolf now regrets.

*Missy Steward*

## The Diver

A slow, peaceful descent into the deep blue,
Silence —
Then, like a familiar face, comes a beam of light,
Brightness -
You look around with childlike curiosity,
Wonder —
A feeling of majesty and splendor
Amazement -
Colorful life then floods your eyes,
Kaleidoscopic -
One last glimpse of beauty in the deep,
Ascend -
Dry land,
Everyday life,
True passion found in the deep blue,
Discover it -

*Lisa Williams*

## Trapped

Dreams, ability, longing to be free
But unseen chains hinder me
Bound by tradition
I'm trapped in this condition

*Shirley A. Jordan*

## Peace Inspiration

Peace is delightful love;
Silence as the bright sky above.
Calm as fresh, spring roses dangling
Joy like silver bells dangling.
Deep in the heart it cling.
till it is aroused, like flying dove wings
It spread like falling flakes of snow.
Cover troubles with its white glow.
Peace fill sad moments with tears.
But God's holy spirit heal all fears.
Look for peace, find it calmly.
Fill life with its sweet love warmly.
Look for peace, in every little place
See it in every sad and smiling face.
Oh!  How happy and cheerful all will be.
When peace rules all folk like you and me;

*Mary Leath Hall Williams*

## To Pegasus (A Tribute To A Dallas Landmark)

Majestic horse with feathered wing
Silent hooves at twilight bring
Stardust trails on moonlit night
Forever on your endless flight

How many years have you danced?
Across the night sky lightly pranced
Bringing wisdom of another world
Trapped in ancient mythic lore

Proud your image soared so high
Once far above the city sky
Your silent red immobile icon
Now dwarfed by towering glass and neon

Do children still now with you ride?
As I once did at four or five
In dreams upon your back I'd fly
From rooftop into starlit sky

Years later now I still do yearn
On passing freeways quickly turn
To catch a glimpse of days gone by
A flash of red against the sky

*Suzie Oliver*

## In Silence

The silence of the white snow falling,
Silently each green leaf starts growing,
So silently spring is in the air,
And children are singing everywhere.

Silently flowers begin to bloom,
Their sweet fragrance filling every room.
The silent beauty of each twilight,
Earthy smells fade into the soft night.

The peaceful rest of the afternoon,
Silently a lamplight fills the room,
In silence an evening star appears,
Silently a velvet night draws near.

So silently Our God enters in,
In silence freeing a heart from sin,
So silently God works in our lives,
So that everything spiritual survives.

The silent message God will impart,
To every troubled and weary heart,
Is the silence found in a quiet place,
Where one can behold God face to face.

*Rachael Johnson*

## Forever, Being

*Memories*
The fabric of life.
Silken threads woven beyond duplication,
more precious than the air we breathe.

Can we capture them?

Only as we treasure the glimpse
of a butterfly in flight.
Elusive beauty is lost,
if we dare to pin its wings.

No matter what is bound by lock and key,
hidden, never more for me to see,
All is here,
alive, and real.

I'll forever have my memories!
*Susan C. Buttimer*

## A Song For A New Year

Ring the bell, ... bell, .... bell;
sing the song, ... song, .... song;
say the word, ... word, ... word;
cry the cry, ... cry, ... cry;
  ... of peace, ... peace, ... peace.

Sing out the words
... cry loud the sounds
... ring out the songs
... say it strong ... for peace, ... peace, ... peace

Ring the bell, ... Sing the song, ... Cry the cry.

Hear ... the cries, ... cries, ... cries;
  ... the ... words, ... words, ... words;
  ... the ... songs, ... songs, ... songs;
  ... the ... bells, ... bells, ... bells; ... of peace.

Ring the bells, ... bells, ... bells.
Ring the bells long.
Ring the bells loud.
Ring the bells strong.
Ring the bells.
Ring the bell.
*William J. Zeidlik*

## If I Had A Wish

In a place that is far, far away from here
Sit a circle of children full of hunger and fear
But nobody comes, they sit all alone
They haven't a thing not even a home.
And in the back sits a child who cries
Dirty with filth and swarming with flies.
Their lives consist of no love and no fun,
Everyone talks about them but nothing is done
These children can't be saved from their fate
There's no place to go, no way to escape.

In the streets of our cities sits a man with no name
But puts up a fight for life just the same.
The cold dirty street is the place he calls home,
He hasn't a place to claim as his own.
People walk by and ignore he is there,
When his tears start to fall, nobody notices nobody cares.

If I had a wish, just one wish it would be,
For the world to open their eyes and see:
That if we open our hearts and show that we cared,
All the hurt in the world could start to be spared.
*Mindy Lavigne Burt*

## The Curse Of The Aged

A sweet little lady with a great big smile
Sits in the foyer waiting for her child
Greeting each person as they pass her by
Her eyes glued to the door just like a spy
Her eyes light up and a great big grin
When the door opens and a man walks in
A man, he may be but to her just a boy
He has given to her many years of joy
With his hands held out and a grin on his face too
Happy Birthday, Dear Mother, Happy Birthday to you!
When the visits over and the man turns to go on his way
"There goes my husband" he hears his mother say
The tears are close to coming as he goes out the door
Then he remembers all the good times they had before
How could the monster take her mind away?
And leave the love she gives to him each day
The memories are there but they seem to come and go
The curse of the aged, the old peoples foe
They call it Alzheimer's, this disease of our race
"God help us!" he cries, as the tears flow down his face.
*Mabel M. Miller*

## The Cry of a Fatherless Child

### (Who Will Make Me Whole?)

My heart aches for that paternal man,
Sitting, crying and wondering; should I understand?

Why doesn't he love me?  He doesn't even care;
not a phone call, nor a letter; is my father aware?

Why doesn't he love me?  He barely knows my name!
That paternal man; my father, does he feel ashamed?

Years of unfelt love, yearning within my soul;
does my father understand, it is he who'll make me whole?

Hi sweetie and I love you, yes!  Ringing in my ear,
Yet!  It is just another fantasy to make me feel he's near.

When I look into the mirror, who do I see;
is it an image of my father, staring at me?

Who is my father and what is his name?
It is he whom I will need, to reverse my shame.

I hunger for my father's love, deeply within my soul;
it is he, that paternal man, who will make me whole.
*Renita Patrice Edmonds*

## The Slovac-Gypsies' Polka

From the forests of "Old Bohem'ya,"
Slovac-Gypsies would come and dance;
With their tambours and golden ear-rings,
They would polka, and sing-romance.

Slovac-Gypsies would play their music,
And their fame spread across great-lands;
Soon, the Polish, and German, minstrels,
Formed their own, snappy, polka-bands.

Play the music of "Old Bohem'ya,"
Loved and cherished from Prague to France;
From the Baltic to "Old Bulgar'ya,"
Polka-partners still love to dance.

From the North Sea, to Sarajevo,
From the Danube, to Leningrad;
Polka music is loved by millions,
And it helps when we're feeling sad.

Slovac-Gypsies, we hope you're list'ning,
We are grateful for all you've done;
And, we thank you for Polka-music,
It's enjoyed by most ev'ryone.
*F. Henry McKinney*

## Life

On a cold winter day, a boy went wondering into the dark
  snow-covered forest.

There were footsteps in the snow
  and the boy followed.
At the end he came upon a single red rose glowing in
  beauty, standing all by itself in the snow-covered
  forest.

As the boy went to pick up the rose — the bright glow
  disappeared slowly and so did the rose.
  Night-time grew older as day-time wilted away.

The boy slowly walked back home in the cold darkness
  of the footsteps he had followed there...

  *Robie Hayek*

## A Sonnet For Springtime

As I walked from work to my car today,
So caught up in the problems facing me,
I near missed the pear trees along the way
Dressed in snow white blossoms for all to see.
As I drove home at too hurried a pace,
Daffodils along the side of the road
Caught my eye with their yellow, glowing grace;
And, enjoying the tiny suns, I slowed.
As I gazed through my kitchen window pane,
The forsythia shone sunny and bright,
Dispelling shadows of gloom once again
With cheerful, inspiring, radiant light.
Amazing!  So many a simple thing
Can renew a heart.  But why not?  It's Spring!

  *Rhonda Maiden*

## Dear Amber

I'm still here and so is my heart
So don't ever feel lonely even when we are apart.
I'm not close by
But I am not really gone
Because you have my heart
The heart that you won.
It took me by surprise feeling this way
It just crept into my soul never going away.
I don't want pain
I hope it is fake
Because I don't want that burning
As I feel my heart break
Losing you now will kill me for sure
Because I never had feelings that were this pure.
I love you Amber
And that scares me to death
Because if you ever left me
You would take my breath.
Now that I've said all that I feel
I hope you understand my love for you is real.

  *Robert Vigil*

## A Letter to My Father

When leaves of flame red and granny apple green
skip across the path, while whispering cool winds
chase the leaves in endless play

And gray streaked skies lonely cries are muffled by
the cloud's games of hide and seek with the stars

And old today's ride on the tails of always remembered
fragrances into today

I taste the bitter sweet that you meant life to be.

  *Roberta E. Clover*

## Love

Love is like a shining dewdrop in the morning sun.
So fragile, but yet so real.
Even at night, when you're sound asleep,
Into your dreams it will steal.
It can change your reason for living,
and changes your life so much.
It can lift you right out of your daily grind
Causing lovely thoughts to flow from your mind.
Your senses become more keen and alive,
Giving more reason to want to survive.
Love is something that can't be seen,
But one carries an aura and also a gleam.
An electric current flows through the air,
You don't push a button, but you know it's there.
Like a fortune cookie, it could crumble apart.
If the love foundation doesn't stem from the heart.

  *Ruth Jones Cliatt*

## Who Am I

Here I am at home alone with anything to do.
So I set around and watch TV until one are two.
I ask myself who am I?  Do I have a life but
yet I set and wonder why my life is just like ice?
No one knows this hurt I feel that is deep within
my soul only GOD the man up above
the one that truly knows.
He's a person just like me but yet he understands
so that's why I ask him, who am I?  So I can believe again.

  *Mary Ellen Wilson*

## A Smart Thinker

I want to know all about dope
So I won't get caught in the rope
When I grow up to be an adult
I don't wish to be found in a drug cult
Please HELP me as I try to decide
On which side I should reside

Parents and older adults, I admire
So whatever they do, I desire
And when they "do drugs", thinking its cool
I will do also, cause that's the rule
Mother, father, sister, brother
Support me, So I won't be like the others

Some folks teach me that drugs are bad
And when I see drug users, I am sad
Yet others say "getting high" is bright
Sometimes, I wonder whose right
But I know using drugs makes life harder
So I pray, God will help me to be SMARTER!

  *Meynell J. Williams*

## The Rose

  To me you are like a rose, so delicate and so beautiful.  Your
skin radiates with warmth and your lips feel like soft velvet rose
pedals glimmering with the morning's first dew.  Your aroma is so
sweet that even a bed of roses can not compete.  When you wake in
the morning, your smile blossoms like the rose waking and
reaching for the morning sun.  Every pedal that unfolds itself is
like a dream coming true.  If a rose could speak it would sound
like you, so warming and soothing with every sound.  The rose is
the symbol of beauty and love, but the rose can not even compare
to you!

  *Scott Patterson*

## An Early Good-Bye

There is pain in an early good-bye, my son
So many dreams you must put aside
So many memories to cause you pain
So many plans to change, so many feeling
You must deny so many questions unanswered
There is pain in an early good-bye
So many reasons I hope you could stay
There was so much to tell you, I loved you
Completely, so many tears to cry
I have no regrets I just wasn't ready
I'll cry a little bit, I'll die a little bit.
So if you see tears in my eves it's
the pain of an early good-bye
Heaven could of waited,
It's not easy my son, to say.
"An Early Good-Bye"

**Mary Jane Cora**

## Thread Of Life

The thread of life is sometimes a fragile one.
So many times it gets tired in knots.
Poking through the fabric of our souls.
Trying to mend so many holes.
Raveling and fraying from time to time.
But never breaking.
Weaving each of us together, like flowers in a tapestry.
It is a silk threat, glistening and shining us so bright.
But in our darkness, holds us together so tight.
Only to fail us, when we let go.

**Pamela Perkins**

## Wisdom?

The wisdom, of man, oh, makes him feel so grand.
So profound is the knowledge he has found,
he can walk so proud,
because he has accomplished so much.
Oh, how foolish man really is.
Through the deceitfulness of the price of this world,
man is blinded to he danger that shall befall him.
What do you mean? I do not understand.
Is it not man that created this society?
Look at how wonderful life has become,
because of man's self-sufficiency.
Oh, how blind has satan made thee.
Is it wonderful to kill a fellow man?
For it is written, thou shall not kill,
Is it so wonderful to take that which is not yours?
For it is written, thou shall not steal.
I sit so wonderful to hate your fellow man,
because he does not look or live up to your standards?
For it is written, to love one another.
The wisdom of man, oh, is so grand.

**Wilfred Hill Starkey Jr.**

## Alone

The night surrounds me.
Somehow I exist
My life so every changing
Alone to think and feel
The streets so quite

So Alone
A smile on my face
A tear in my eyes
Reflections of the past
I think we all feel that way sometimes alone.

**Paul Harris**

## A Really True American

We live in America the land of the free,
So we each should say, "Dear Lord, You've blessed me."
Many thanks unto God we each should give,
Especially for America, the land where we live.
The Pilgrims came to America for freedom of religion to hunt,
But now folks in America for other things want.
They still want their freedom but they also want power,
And they want to make money everyday, every hour.
They think if the flag salute with a group they can say,
Then they are a true American in many a way.
But a Really True American is one who gives thanks to God,
Who let their forefathers come and develop this sod!

**Lucille Olomon Sands**

## Too Much Smoke!

Smoking too much makes one's lungs weak...
So weak, in fact, it's hard to speak...

And, when someone has to gasp for air,
You know for sure something's wrong somewhere.

A cough is a sign of too much smoke.
It's against one's health...and one could go broke.

If it's such a problem, then, why not cease it?
But, smokers retort with, "just decrease it."

If ever a cig became a part of my hand,
I know it could send me to an other-worldly land...

And, if that were the case, then, my epitaph might read:
"She died in an oxygen tent when she lit up a weed.

**Linda Caldwell Hutchins**

## Segregation

There really is no black or white,
so why bother to fuss and fight?
We are all the same underneath,
talk what you know, practice what you preach.
There's only one God that comes
down from above, who lends a hand
and does what he does.
Evolution leads us all to one place,
which tells us there's really only one race.
People are people wherever you go;
we just speak different
languages wear different clothes.
After all the hurt we put others
through, I hope these words got
through to you.

**Leilani Haynes**

## The Right Way

We are all created equal, in his sight.
So why must we so often, fight for what is right.
Love and equality is needed by all.
We do not need someone, to make us seem small.
Instead of anger and hate, use compassion and care,
One to anther, to help us get there.
To a place where we can understand and forgive.
A place where love spurs us on to live.
We must help each other achieve this goal.
We just can't reach it, by doing it alone.
So remember when you look, into another's face,
You really are looking, into God's Grace.
So let us help each other, each and every day.
This is what is meant for us, this is the right way.

**Vija Aina Vilinskis**

## Twilight, 24 August 1770

A thing of beauty is a joy forever,
  so wrote our friend Keats in his poem to you.
Lost boy in a city bloody cruel, full of struggle and woe,
  muted by echoes of chant, scribbled lines of verse,
  an angel chalice to trumpet your name about the city.
Thomas, you were both lonely and alone with genius
  and alienation sharing your pillow.
If tear stains could speak your beautiful mind to revive
  the kindness of the human soul, I wish yours to flow fresh.
Admonish stone hearts to prune the sharp thorns embracing them,
  lest they die in spirit before the body remembers to shrivel.
To our shame and far greater pain, your rueful young life swallowed
  itself with the bitter arsenic raised to your lips.
Sleepless soul of Wordsworth's resolute mention, I pray you may
  slumber in a peace you had not here with us tainted mortals.
Sweet and gentle is she, the Lady of Redcliffe wraps you in her
  mantle to bear you to her bower where crisp Autumn never
comes.

*Raymond J. Colombaro*

## Flowers

Some flowers are like people
Some are typical, some are just some.
Some are old and ready to die
But they still reach out and cry.

They want that help that only people can produce,
Love, care, and a little bit of more.

Some are young and are called dumb and
have a smaller thumb.

But we're all together in the great pot of life.

You wonder how this may all rhyme?
Just say your mine because we're all worth more then a dime.

*Rosanne Hereford*

## Friend

Strawberry lime rickies
some Boston drink for koolaid corners.
I wouldn't have known
Except for when I met Susie.

Now I can tell stories of how I gave
Uncle Murray toilet water when I was three.
I say that sometimes even though
It happened to Susie
not really to me.

But it's like I can
because sometimes when she's holding my hand
She says she can't tell
which one belongs to who

*Wendy Barness*

## Memories

There are good ones and bad,
Some joyful and some sad.
Memories of the birthdays gone by,
And the kite I learned to fly.
Memories of basketball in hot weather,
And the good times we spent together.
Memories are the treasures no one can take,
And they don't ever break.
And when death separates two people,
Memories are all you have left.
While you can, you'd better have fun.
You can't relive your memories because
What's done is done.

*Phil Hoschouer*

## The Wig

When I look in the mirror what do I see?
Some old gal staring back at me.
Gotta do something...but what shall I do?
Maybe a face lift—that would be new!
Perhaps a blond wig—or is it too bold?
Maybe no one will notice that I'm growing old.
So I bought the wig, then went out to see
if any of my friends would recognize me.
Said Kate, "It's nice and looks great when it's new
but blond's not your color...no it's just not you!"
Then June saw it next. "I can't believe my eyes.
I should have gone with you to help and advise!"
So I asked my friend Gracie—I knew she'd be true.
"Really, Lois, I think gray would look better on you."

*Lois Blackwood*

## Fearful Trust

Some say to trust we simply must,
Some say refrain this causes pain,
Some say be careful and learn to be shrewd,
For trust has caused many to truly be fooled.

Yet others say trust will never bring pain,
nor lies or deception or sad gloomy days,

Still there are those who fear her the same,
And learned that this truly is not always kind,
Left many confused, alone and quite blind,

Now trust is a word we truly define,
With many expressions within one's own mind
And what we reveal from deep down inside,
That trust is a means we need to survive.

*Melissa (M'Stine) Persghin*

## Resigned

Some things will never ever change
Some things will never get better
It's so easy to get used to pain
But don't be resigned to never.

You see, life is too short to keep waiting
And happiness must be an endeavor
Even in misery, the hands keep ticking
So don't you be resigned to never.

Days become months, months become years
Don't make monotony a friend forever
Try not to be a slave to your fears
Or else you will become resigned to never.

If you feel weighed down, trapped, or at the end of your rope
Then the chains - you have to sever
Look inside and believe; stay strong and don't give up hope
If not - be resigned to never.

Yesterday is gone, who knows 'bout tomorrow
Today is all we've got, our last together
Because my time has come to go
And I won't be resigned to never.

*Lisa M. Kneut*

## Sounds Of Spring

List to the notes now pealing
Far from over the hill
The beauty of nature revealing
When the earth is calm and still.

*Theodora Bloomfield*

## The Day The Nation Bled

The sky is crimson over head
Someone has to count the dead
Nothing good can be said
On the day the nation bled

The people weeped and they sighed
Their pain they could not hide
Innocent young and old that day had died
On that day the nation cried

Misbegotten rage had raised its head
With little thought of human dread
Factors unknown to this point had led
To the day a nation bled

A little child's song stopped too soon
A mother's last embrace left an open wound
A once secure nation was buried in an unwanted tomb
Many fears that day lay in those ruins

Let's make this nation safe again today
Show our strengths in a new way
Hand in hand let's kneel and pray
That a new peaceful nation will arise this day

*Mike Hiltzman*

## A Guiding Shadow

I look into your eyes each day, and realize how lucky I am to have
    someone like you in my life
I remember the good times we had, and the bad, and smile at the
    thought of what came next
My memories then fade as I return to the present and face the future
    with you at my side
I face a sea of temptation, a desert of sin, and a jungle of lost
    hope that seem to swallow and consume me
But You guide me along the path and help me fight the dangers that
    I face with my head held high
When it is over, I turn to face You but thinking I will see no one
    because the battle is won,
But there I always find You, standing by my side, never leaving me
    for a moment, with love on your face.
Now, as we continue our journey through life together, the temptation
    turns wildly overcoming
Yet there is no fear but only courage, no weakness but only strength,
    for in every hurdle there is You
Not until now so I truly realize that You would die for me,
    for You have become a true friend, sincere, kind, and loving.
When people come to me and ask, "Who is it that you take refuge
    in and adore so greatly ?"
I will answer with pride, "It is the Lord, Jesus Christ,
    the Son of God."

*Pauline Isidro*

## Journey

I sat today and realized I am not the person I feel inside
something has happen, something within me
something that one or two will know and few will see
the person I am is being challenged by me
the person I may become does not exist and will never be
the person I leave behind was never there for me

The journey I have started was never planned, you see
I took one step and the next I knew I had taken three
I was the passenger and the only one to know the way
so I led myself into the unknown and I knew not the way
that is no problem... not for me because I'm not lost...
I'm just not free

The journey will continue
and I know not why, but if I should try to stop it better to die
so freely I walk, talk and play for the journey for me is the
only way

*M. Sparks Johnson*

## Will You Still Love Me?

You've always been my friend
someone on whom I could depend
Since we were just little boys,
And now that we've grown into men.

I remember when we were young
chasing women and drinking wine
I remember our first love affairs
When we couldn't get enough behind.

It now seems that I have the weight of the world
thrust upon my shoulders
While I try to counteract drugs and destruction,
I feel I'm just growing older.

Confined behind these abasing bars
There's not a whole lot more I can say
I've lost my dreams, my desires
Someone's taken my manhood away.

In the process of all I've lost
I remember what I've retained
the joy and pleasure of your friendship
Will you still love me now that I have AIDS?

*Tamera Coyne-Beasley*

## I Want ........

I want morning and afternoon delight.
Someone to hold and touch throughout the night.
Someone who loves and wants to share that love.
Someone whose heart mine fits like a glove.
Someone who loves our God above.
A man only the creator is first in his life.
Some who respects me and wants me as his wife.
Someone to sit and talk to as we grow old.
Someone who's there a part of my soul.
Someone who loves children, his and mine.
Someone who's loyal generous and kind.
A fine example in the community, an honest man.
A man of integrity who takes a strong stand.
Someone I have the affection of his thoughts even in a fight.
We both know that the other will never take to flight.
I think of the warm torrent winds of afternoon delight.
Then the cool evenings and the dawn of day, sunny and bright.
Ah!  I want a man who knows he's strong in personal might;
Knowing that he'll spend the rest of his life treating me right.

*Mary C. Brown*

## My Body

Something strange is happening to me,
Something strange in my body.

I feel like turning into a bear,
'Cause all over I'm growing hair!

My eyes really itch,
I think I'm turning into a witch!

My cheeks are turning red,
Geez, I need to go to bed!

My head is getting so big,
That I need to wear a wig!

There is something ticklish in my ear,
That's why I have trouble to hear!

My hands are so green,
Maybe that's why I'm so mean!

So this is the story of my body that's old,
For this is the first time it was ever told.

*Vanessa Ruth Carpio*

## Pain

Pain disguises itself in many shapes and forms
Sometimes buried away just deep enough
Or the reflection in a shallow pool of water
Anyone experiencing it indeed has it rough

Pain is the end of the road
The last stop on your way down
Places itself around every corner
For no apparent reason steals your crown

Pain follows no particular pattern
Leaves no trail for criminal investigation
Not a clue to be found, makes no mistakes
Seems to have its own torturous maturation

Pain has no obvious universal appeal
But somehow we can all relate
It's not restricted by language barriers
And can lead to unintended hate

Pain is the source of despair
A precursor to prolonged depression
Can put its wrath upon you effortlessly
The final chapter of one man's obsession

*Michael Whatley*

## To Die Or To Fly....

Sometimes I feel like I could die,
sometimes I feel like I could fly,
often the feeling's of death arise
but often the feeling's
are lacked of a doubt.
The doubt of feeling unable to fly,
is just so hard
in this dark gleamy sky.
It looks so blue and bright,
but in my eyes all I see is night.
The clouds are all of the same kind,
all just a big blur in my mind.
There's never a place to park,
to stop and rest so you can find your best.
Finishing the test is all just a joke,
as I began to float.
I suddenly drown
next to the place from which I jumped.

*Sarah Hanson*

## Are You Really Struggling?

Dear Lord,
Sometimes I feel so troubled, unable to stand alone,
Searching for the answer, and yet it is unknown.

Lord, so many times I wonder why I feel this way,
for deep inside my heart, I feel sorrow and dismay.

Lord, please help me to understand the reason for
it all, because, I know you will never let me fall.

Please give me strength and courage to face each struggling foe,
to reach deep within myself and find wisdom when I feel low.

Lord, help me to remember you made me from the start,
and the feeling I should have inside, is joy within my heart.

Lord, thank you for opening up my eyes,
For giving to me understanding, enough to make me wise.

Lord, please help me to remember when I'm down and feeling low,
That on the cross of calvary, you paid a price you did not owe.

*Shelley Branam*

## Friendship

Good friendships never truly die.
Sometimes they go into hibernation,
sometimes they get lost in the whirlwind of our lives,
but they never truly die.
A good friend will always be there,
no questions asked,
to offer needed help or to simply just listen.
It is a wonderful experience to renew an old friendship.
The rekindling adds a new spice,
an element of adventure,
and is usually accompanied with a self-discovery.
Talking of the past sheds new perspectives on old
and often forgotten memories,
sometimes happy, sometimes sad,
but each adding to the beauty of our lives.

*Victor L. Skukalek*

## Footprints On The Shore

The seashore calls to me each day,
Soon, I must be on my way,
To that bountiful habitat by the sea,
Where the essence of life is eternity.

Waves crest and fall with a haunting roar,
Each one a part of the one before,
Rhythmically urging the soul to enjoin
The powerful union of earth, sea and sun.

Sandpipers swoop to the surf in the breeze,
Wings tinged with silver like fluttering leaves;
Not far from shore the dolphins play,
Cavorting about in the ocean's spray.

Sea shells abound in this mystically place,
Colorful, shiny, some like hard lace;
Gulls step around with an attitude,
Then soar away in their quest for food.

Miles of beach bid you walk along,
Where warm winds hum the ocean's song;
If prints of your feet appear on the shore,
Destiny will call "come back", evermore.

*Louise Wright*

## Spring

The wind of March doth blow.
Soon these chilly days will go.
The beautiful trees will shoot forth their buds.
The scene which everyone dearly loves.

The winter is long and dreary.
Soon the days will be bright and cheery.
We can work in our garden fair.
The flowers we've dreamed of shall be there.

The joyous laughter of children sweet,
Shall be heard in every street.
Even the little birds of the air
Will be praising God for his loving care.

Many shall never see another spring.
They shall be gone from this earth to never sing.
But there is a place of beauty where we can go.
For Jesus gave himself to make it so.

We can go where summer never ends.
Where flowers bloom forever and voices blend.
There'll be no cold or rain or pain to annoy.
Nothing to harm, nor heaven's beauty destroy.

*Pauline Brown Powell*

## Tears

The stillness is unbearable,
sounds of broken hearts.
Red rimmed eyes, speak as though he's here in every part.
We know he's gone and we really want him back,
Somehow things must get back on track.

Lost in body,
Here in soul
Here's his glory know foretold

His soul floats like feathers in the wind,
be gone with yourself, he's hiding within.

He took his life among the trees, follow your heart,
you will see.

He is gone but you are here,
Say goodbye forget your fears.

Goodbyes are hard,
but the end is near,
remember him always,
for here is a tear.
*Tina Jordan*

## House Without Windows

You stand in your clean kitchen,
spatula in hand;
I look for little overtures of masculinity,
find not any.

Excusing the limp buzz buzz
conversation
thoughtfully
revamping my life.

Fireflies swell and soak the air
loudly,
luminous orbs filling all the pain
I can bear inside me

You shook all passion off as a cloak
of bright snow
shuddered, redwing to perch
dangerously,

Crazily from deck and sky,
a house without windows.
I bite my toast

The snow tearing my eyes.
*Regina Taylor*

## The Pain Of Divorce

I feel as though the wheels of my life are spinning,
spinning out of control,
while I'm stuck here in this place of despair.

On the outside I have kept control.
I seem calm, content, happy and at peace,

While inside my soul
there is anger, wrath, uncertainty, and a very deep sadness.

All of these emotions are like a whirlwind,
turning round and round inside.

Will they ever stop?
Will this pain ever go away?

How long can I keep trying,
trying to gain control?

Is there hope beyond the present,
or will tomorrow just bring more of today?
*Vanessa Lamm Williams*

## Imagination

From a red paper moon hung a blue paper star
spinning slowly in the light breeze from a window.
A child's creation,
Imagination

What as precious gift that is too soon taken
from a child when he is shaken
into adulthood
by the brutal reality of the truth
that the moon is not red, that god is dead
that a star is not blue, and most truths are untrue.

Oh, I pray for the sight of a child
to be able to see through
the brutality
of reality

And again see my moon as red, that faith is not dead
a star is blue, and love is true,
where imagination is much treasured
and each thought need not be measured.

Come back, my child. Visit me often.
I miss you.
*Michael T. Pritchett*

## Awakening

Sun rays streaming light and warmth to all it touches
Squirrels scurrying in a game of chase
New life springs forth after slumber

Dew dancing on grass blades as a diamond glitters
Gray mist envelopes the surroundings like a babe in a blanket
Tears of joy fall to refresh and quench life's thirst

Tree limbs outstretched to heaven
So gnarled and twisted, yet peaceful and serene
A robin sings to babes in her nest
Water gently rolls and splashes over rocks in its path
On its way to a final destination.
*Leesa A. Wheeler*

## The Mission

I am a soldier of love taking no prisoners is my order

The mission - To break my enemy's heart

I am the soul survivor of this bloody war
Standing above the casualties of your missiles

The mission - To fight all tears that dare to rise

I am the one who will reign over the blackness of night
Commanding the sun to come forth

The mission - To conquer the pain of your kiss

I am the woman who will stop in your very tracks
Mocking you every step of the way

The mission - To walk with my head held high and
Your memory under the feet

I am the fire that will burn your flesh
Causing you to write in torturous agony

The mission - To eliminate your existence from my mind

I am the ray of hope that shines ever brighter
Revealing the silhouette of happiness

The mission - To triumph completely over this heartache

I am the one who will never look back
Fulfilling the mission... to live on without you.
*Michelle Gracia*

## Look at Them

Look at them,
Standing in a shadow, waiting for a friendly friend.
With a frown on their face, and a cup in their hand,
Waiting for someone to think of them.
Just look at them, look at them.
News papers for blankets, scraps for clothes,
Boxes for houses, no shoes for toes.
Give them a dime or a quarter or two,
You can help them you know what to do.
Just look at them, look in their eyes,
Look at them, don't fantasize.
When you work all day, and you come home at night,
You can sleep in your bed without a fright,
And have food to eat almost every night,
But it's hard to do when you are poor.
Just look at them they count on you, look at them, you know it's true.
I know some things they do are wrong,
But if we help them they could be strong,
Just look at them, they have pain,
Look at them, it's such a shame.  Just look at them...

**Yanick Dalhouse**

## Echo of a Man's Memory

Down the shadow of despair,
Stands a man with a lighted torch,
Searching for a mystery;
The soul of a river stone.
Mornings and nights he sings only one song:
No more lilies in the plain,
No more trees in the mountain.
Roses stop blooming
To listen to his melody, to give him love.
His song transcends
The fear of his heart,
Fighting the wind of destiny,
Fighting the glamour of memory.
Beside him, by the older trees,
Younger generations take place,
Bringing to the land the echo of yesterday's hope,
Bringing to his mind the peace of tomorrow.

**Samson Denis**

## Over The Rainbow

Over the rainbow in the sky
Stands Gods Mansion way up high
The River of Life flows freely there
Waiting for someone to partake and share
The Joy of Jesus everywhere
He went home to His Father way up high
To build me a Mansion in the sky
Won't you come and share with me
The Joy of Jesus that is free
He's waiting there with His arms open wide
To bring you close and deep inside
The River of Life will not let you slide
It will bring you in with His great tide
So come along and share with me
The River of Life that is totally free
And pick out your Mansion way up high
Over the rainbow in the sky

**Mary Pepitone**

## ACCOUNTABILITY

I'm all grown up now

Though painful memories of terrible wrongs
Still invade my thoughts and my dreams
    My anger has waned
    And forgiveness is actually a part of my vocabulary

No longer can my past excuse my present
    For when all is said and done
    I do know it is I who makes my choices

And they did the best they knew how.

**Mary Lou Clever**

## Divertissement

The warmth from her body
    Still permeated the sweater
And comforted him in his
    Restless state of bewilderment.

What was he feeling?
    Of how much was she aware?
The ridiculous barrier of age
    Separated them by convention.

A spell insubstantial, evanescent,
    Seemed to hold them both,
Soothing and yet disturbing,
    Their need bringing recognition to each.

A longing for another time, another life,
    A desire to touch, to be touched,
To feel a caress from another's laughing eyes.
    A desire to respond.

**Rhoda Fear**

## Waiting Alone

The cries of the name that have been spoken me
Sting my mind over and forever and too much.
The death would take me away from the monsters,
But away from the one I love and have not forgotten
And yet so long not found,
for the curse has separated us.
With each broken footstep I take
closer and closer I am to nothing.
The voices in my soul scream mind numbing shrieks of anguish,
My tortured consciousness travels with me.
Into a field of daisy flowers I stagger and lay my breaking
bones on the thick grass,
Stitching my eyes shut I hallucinate of everything there is.

**Luke Brandyn**

## The New Black Woman

I am the new black woman, full of pride
Striving for my family, working hard to make that stride
I am the new black woman, although sometimes full of woe
From fighting to reach the top, but yet I still say go

I am the new black woman, beautiful in every way
Trying to keep my family together, even though it gets harder day by day
I am the new black woman, I have been bought for a fee
Standing by my man, though he doesn't always stand by me

I am the new black woman, educated and free
Some lessons learned by books, others are learned from the street
I am the new black woman, A vision from God's sight
I may get tired and sometimes complain, but I'll never give up the fight

I am the new black woman, stern, but yet kind
Complex, but yet simple; scarce, but not hard to find
I am the new black woman, I am here to stay
Love me, hold me, hug me, together we can go all the way

**Rhonda Moore**

## Mankind

I am MAN
Strong and mighty
Long bones, muscle and brain,
Image of God.

I am MAN
Builder of ships that laugh at the wind
Constructor of bridges over the waves,
Maker of great cities.

I am MAN
User of land to grow my food,
Destroyer of rivers, lakes, and streams,
Polluter of earth.

I am MAN
Warrior with spear, arrow and gun,
Killer, torturer of tribes, conqueror of fire.

I am MAN maker of light to chase the dark,
Explorer of heavens, moons and stars,
Dreamer of dreams.

I am MAN all these I am, all these I am.
All these I am.

*W. L. McDermit*

## Romance

Ever ponder the wonders of romance?
Such as Romeo and Juliet
Think about the lack of love stories if they never met
Cleopatra and Mark Anthony
Who knew how destructive jealously could be
Bonnie and Clyde

Would you give them a ride?
Elizabeth Taylor and Richard Burton
Look what happened when they began flirting
Kings of England and all their wives
What tales they could relate if they were still alive
Adolph Hitler and Eva Braun
They were made to pay for choices gone wrong
Madonna and Sean Penn
Perhaps they'll try marriage once again
Lastly Bogart and Bacall
Didn't they have it all?
Strange liasions are so beguiling
That's why they always leave us smiling

*Sandra Glassman*

## Untitled

Whenever I think I've finally escaped
Suddenly... flashes fly over my eyes...
Something grips me tight on the inside
My emotions slide to the bottom

Feeling from the inside out
I want to lay still for eternity
Letting my emotions flow through me
Devouring my sense of reality
My mind how it tortures me

Can I break free?
Hope dangles on a string just out of reach
That leaves me grasping at air
Falling down into a realization of question marks.

*Michelle Grafwallner*

## Window Dressing

A glint of sun softly touches the dew
suddenly revealed by a whispered breeze.

The sway of tall field grass echoes a faint swishing stir
among lofty emerald blades.

Chirps of different origin, as if in retort to one another,
continually fill the air from all directions.

A butterfly floats by, drifting as if suspended in space
as a flurry of air lightly lifts it.

The drone of a bumble bee partaking of the flower,
roars through the serenity,
steadily pumping his wings in constant flight.

The distant forest green laden limbs bow and dip
exposing glimpses of habitats sheltered there.

In fields beyond, fences separate the cows, the horses, the sheep,
only their muffled sounds drift into hearing.

Noise from a distant highway offends briefly, sporadically,
yet the scene remains unscathed, oblivious to the intrusion.

A window unmasked into heaven, a window cherished,
a window coveted on the edge of town.

*Linda M. Jones*

## Be My Valentine

Roses are red, violets are blue,
Sugar is sweet and so are you.

This little rhyme is not very new,
Nevertheless, the words are true.

For you are the sweetest man in my life
And I count it a blessing to be your wife.

Your great big smile and tender ways
Add happiness to all my days.

It means so much to know you're there
And that you love me and you care.

You make me happy every day
And I love you in every way.

As our years together come and go
I want to say "I love you so."

Here are lots of hugs and kisses,
From your one and only Mrs.

The reason for this little rhyme,
Is "Will you be my Valentine?"

*Wilma L. Freeman*

## Planet Earth

Earth Mother.
  Sky Father.
    Earth Father.
      Sky Mother.
Interchangeable (Inexhaustible) Parts.. Theology??  Religion??
  Fantasy??
Owners manual note*
  *This planet comes with no spare parts!!!
    !!!REALITY!!!
What you see is what you get!!!

*Saundra M. Aubry*

## 'The Mighty Zambezi River'

She meanders through forest patched hills,
Summoning kith and kin to join her on her way,
Promising them all the fun and thrills
And tranquillity, when they reach that yonder bay.

She gathers up momentum as she swells up in size.
Like a girl suddenly matured to a young woman
She becomes unpredictable, strong and wise,
And races to get to her destination as soon as she can.

She plummets three hundred feet down the gorge,
Making smoking thunder, shooting spray into the sky,
Dropping to the rocky bottom in utter satisfaction,
Looking up back at her incredible work of art,
Smiling and marveling at such unmatched perfection.

Deep inside, she very well knows
That not many rivers can stage such an act.
Because, as sure and as long as she still flows,
She knows she has already made an impact.
And no matter what,
There will always be only one mighty Zambezi River,
One Victoria Falls, one wonder, the world over.

*Masiye Tembo*


## Hotsprings

Gone is the dense and misty woodland where thin rays of
    sunlight penetrated, ripening gooseberries on the bush.
While in our childhood days, we ventured down where the
    orange buffalo berries hung like grapes from silvery-
    leafed trees across the river's edge.
There, sand vipers hissed as we traversed the footbridge
    to that enchanted island.  Heady odors of grapevines
    and hushed voices of nature were there.
Our small barefeet pattered on the soft damp paths to
    where the wee pink aquamarine made a net around the
    shore of a lovely pool.
There, rusty bubbles, warm and steaming, changed into
    clear blue-green water and floated us with ease.  A
    grey turtle swam curiously by.
As we dipped and splashed, the woods rang with our
    laughter.
Oh, rare and wondrous days at Hotsprings 'til old
    Missouri River changed course and turned us out
    forever from our Garden of Eden.

*Lillian Houchen*


## Outstanding Youths

Paint our faces for we are savages
Surviving in this urban jungle civilization
Putting our lives in jeopardy to attend
Schools based on intelligence deflation

When will you realize our spirits are broken
It doesn't take a genius sleuth
To deduce that this world holds no room
For our outstanding youths

You call us naive, yet you still think
That we believe all of your lies
You forget, we live in the real world
That's why we consent without looking at you in the eye

Full of potential with nowhere to go
You tell us what's right and why
However, you don't see the river of tears
From all of us who can do nothing but cry

Do you think you can threaten us
By insisting we'll wind up locked up and jailed
Well, as far as we outstanding youths are concerned
Your little life lessons have already failed

*William Delahoussaye*


## Inspiration

Inspiration, inspiration
Sweet inspiration
Still is the night which precedes the maker's dreams
Behold - the creation of pre-dawn perfection
No illusion
No fantasy
Out of darkness comes light
Out of the mist spawns you
Flawless in all of your splendor and glory
A standard of beauty by which all women are judged
You are...
The seed of passion, the fruit of love
The substance of womanhood
Eternal is your flame, motivating all seekers of truth...
Refreshing the body
Replenishing the soul
A lifetime millennium
You are...
Inspiration.

*Tyrone Blue*


## I Have Accepted Him

I feel a rush of wind in my face, knowing that the Lord has
    swept me off my feet.
Like a feather he has whirled me into a new reality.
I am at least uplifted and secure in his hands and know he is
    with me always.
His power, his grace, his beauty is abound for all who seek
    him.
I have let go of my fears and doubts and I trust in him.
My wish is that you also know not to fear or doubt, but trust
    in the Lord for He is with us always.
He is power.
He is grace.
He is beauty.
He is here now and forever.

*Lynn Field*


## What I See

What I see is a shadow in the dark moving so
swiftly, as I watch slowly.

What I see is a light, it leads to a tunnel which is
long and frightful, but still it is not so frightful cause
inside yourself is life.

What I see is streets with ugly sights,
horrible to the human eye.
People on the cold grounds starving, dirty, and tired.

What I see is a reflection in the mirror.
It steps forward as I step forward.

What I see is shapes of people in the darkness walking
in and out, but somehow they are still there.

What I see is fire burning red flame,
hot sparks, man's creation.

What I see is words in my mind turning
about as they hang on in my memory.

What I see is myself praying
to see the light of life.

*Natasha Butler*

## Swinging on a Rainbow

Swinging on a rainbow, together you and I
Swinging on a rainbow watching all our cares drift by
The sun is in his heaven, not a cloud is in the sky
Whilst we're swinging on a rainbow you and I

Swinging on a rainbow, way out in the blue
Swinging on a rainbow making all life's dreams come true
Swinging on a rainbow, you love me and I love you
Whilst we're swinging on a rainbow just we two

Swinging on a rainbow, swinging to and fro
Swinging on a rainbow, looking at the world below
Swinging on a rainbow, we'll find happiness quite soon
And go swinging on a rainbow honeymoon

*Thomas Winstanley*

## "S" is for Stu

S is for the songs you've had us to sing,
T is for Tony and all the musicians in the "gang."
U is for all of the underlying things that you do.

G is for Gloria who supports you and us choir members, too.
A is for the artists that you know, discover, and promote.
R is for remembering our purpose and aim,
D is for your devotion and work for our fame.
N is for your never-tiring to get us to our quest,
E is for your energizing us to seek to be the best.
R is for the Richmond Tri-City Mass Choir...

You're the founding father of this crew,
We love you and we'll be here all this journey through.
Happy Birthday, Stu from all of us today,
On this extra special twenty-seventh of May.

*Margery Lee Houston*

## See The Sun-Set

The next time you are honored to watch the setting sun,
  Take a few moments to absorb all the splendor the
  "King of the daily Sky" has to offer—

Notice the streams of glory that shine from it,
  Like the pinnacles of a crown, casting gentle light
  On all within reach—

Acknowledge the passionate colors that are cast across the
Horizon - the sun's domain,
  The reds, oranges, pinks, purples
  Can you not be in awe when you witness these grandiose
  Colors that are enslaved to this simple act of beauty?

As each fleeting second passes by and this mass of wonder
Symbolizes the close of yet another day,
  Encounter the subliminal, soothing effect of this settling
  giant that graces our senses
With its halo of magnificent colors that decorate the vast sky.

As you witness this metamorphosis of the sun's province,
  Give thanks to the almighty Lord for the chance to absorb
  This quiet beauty.

*Lisa Treadway*

## Realization of Dawn

In the light of dawn as every one person sees it
There is no real beauty,
But, in individuals there is something much greater
Their own dawnings

*Michelle Hickey*

## Untitled

Deep inside my soul, I know that nobody could ever
  take away my dignity.
I know who I am, and the beauty inside me, is my only
  destiny
The effort I take toward that extra step to fulfill my
  dreams, is my one soul desire
I will always be strong, and eager to make my dreams
  become higher
The dreams I dream are such an inspiration
Dreams keep me strong and open for any new creation
Having the knowledge I have makes me understand
Dreamers who have self respect and dignity, all go
  hand in hand.

*Mindi Johnson*

## Lingering Images

Softly, Sweetly, you caress me
Teasing tentacles undress me
Smoky grey, you do delude me
Blind eyes see not what eludes me
You whisper in my ear so gently
Touch my lips, your breath, fresh, mintly
But then, whoosh, you're blown away
Here one moment, but not to stay
You left me cold, and in the rain
no longer arouse me, but bring me pain
I beg, I plead, I do beseech you
Bring back the time, when I, you would woo
When sensuality was your name
Seduction was our mating game
You lead me on, and then you dropped me
You flounced away, and flaunted hotly
I'd call you back, If I remembered thee
I think I'll call you...memory

*Wendy Sue Schultz*

## I'm Lonely

I'm lonely, won't you come beside me and hold my hand,
tell me everything will get better, that the sun will shine tomorrow,
that the way I feel today will soon pass.
  I'm lonely, won't you come stand beside me,
look deep into my eyes and tell me what you see,
can you see the pain, the hurt and the emptiness inside of me,
if you touch me can you feel it too.
  I'm lonely, won't you put your arm around me,
to shelter me from the world, where I won't hurt or cause pain
to the people who mean the most to me.
  I'm lonely, won't you walk with me thru life, children,
sickness, thru death.
  I'm lonely won't you just love me?

*Linda J. Smith*

## Untitled

Darkness -
  then tenderly
    the quiet dawn
  a lone, shy harbinger reveals.
Silence -
  then softly now
    his lonely song
  a message of the season bravely peals.

*Mary Jane Williams*

## Divorce

Measure injustice for me
  tell me the dollar amount I may have
  for your unkindness and untruth

Rights and wrongs are only sides won't you agree
I forgot that's impossible for you and me

You say that you love me
  but this love I can't see
  we're too different, there's no comfort

I know you're sorry
  and I forgive you because I understand you

Why are we so cruel to each other
  Please stop talking, your words are tormenting me
  I know what I'm doing to you but what about me

It's unfortunate
  but divorce is the only way for me

Life is too short to live this miserably
  Now please let me be

The injustice we both feel now
  happened when we did agree

We married
### *Sandy Jo Roemer*

## A Prisoner Of My Own Making

The things I did in my young life
That brought me pain, misery, and strife
Cost me in my many mistakings
I was a prisoner of my own making

No one made me do it, you see
But I failed to listen to Mom and Daddy
The teacher, and the preacher, and friends I knew
Warned me and said son, it just won't do

Soon I found myself and there seemed no hope
Then I realized I had played the dope
I was raised in church from a small child
I got in with friends and I turned wild

I found myself a prisoner of my own choosing
Where I was now I found myself losing
In the night I knew prayers were prayed for me
Then, I called on God and he set me free

No longer a prisoner, no longer bound
Blind, now I see, Praise God, I'm found
Telling others, please don't go where I've been
A prisoner of my own making, a life of sin.
### *Rex E. Goodson*

## Our Wedding Poem

It is our love,
That is uniting us together today.
We each are one person becoming two.
We will participate in each others hopes, dreams and future.
In our future there will be many difficulties that arise,
And it is these difficulties that will develop our strengths.
These strengths build a foundation of trust, respect and honesty.
And we exchange these promises in our vows of love today,
Where we devote our lives to one another.
I give you this ring,
A symbol and a promise,
Of a love that will last forever,
A happiness we will share all of our lives.
So hold this love in your hopes,
And remember it in your prayers,
Today and always.
### *Sandy Dechant*

## Encouragement

Encourage and inspire,
That is my desire.
To see some good in all,
And not what comes after the fall.
To be a beacon in times of storm,
To encourage someone when they're weak and worn.
To be a ray of sunshine in the dark of night,
To give encouragement when one would give up the fight.
To be a role model for others to see,
That I truly belong to Thee.
Let a spirit of love radiate from me,
To show all that there is joy in serving Thee.
Let them see that my life is so full and complete,
Because I owe it all to Thee.
Your grace is sufficient to hear our petitions,
And grant our needed wishes.
In you we can find everything we need,
To encourage and inspire.
### *Minnie L. Brown*

## Untitled

While strolling by the park one day, I paused to watch the children
play and as I watched their labored games, recollections stirred my brain
of forgotten children from my youth—
Forgotten children I once knew.

I found myself drawn back in time to a fishing hole with friends of mine
Gathered on the sunlit banks, so filled with life and youthful pranks.
We swore that we would never part, Hope to die and cross our hearts!
The summers never seemed to end; each day was filled with many friends
And oh, the endless games we played till supper called us all away
We never missed one single day to gather in the fields and play
a game of tag or kick the can, blind man's bluff
or you're the man

We ran and swam and jumped and played
Until the day had gone away
Then guided by the fireflies' light,
We made our way back home each night.

It's here the memories gently dim; old age has found me once again,
But a friendship lost has been renewed
  With forgotten children I once knew.
### *Steven K. Bivin*

## Before The Storm

Just a shadow on the wall, simple shades of gray, not having any
meaning not meaning anything at all...the while complaining about a
power surge that dims the lights within these walls...are gray and
moving to a sound not heard above the whispers or the screeching or
above the well-intended preaching or the prodding or the constant
teaching of the self-appointed leaders of an all-consuming,
self-indulgent way to have it all.

I feel alone, abandoned, stranded, eager not to learn the price I've
paid to live at home and wander through the caverns of the times when
passage meant the walls beyond and water brings to them that wait a
higher form. Since then the world has changed. Youth seeks to
rearrange. The format is the one to blame. The icon opens doors and
danger is the illness based upon the way you play the game. These
chains of love are constant and forgiving, all the while pretending,
choosing, borrowing, bending, never really hearing and listening not at all.

Drifting deep into the dark and very small...unimportant wasted moments
time and life have rendered to the meek and timid stumbler who still
refuses to fall yet comes in peace and throws the stone unturned
by passion on the crimson steps of your front door.

Foreboding, empty, dreary, black. Give and give and only lack.
Rushing, rushing nothings right. Reach out your hand as those who
have before you done. Leave footprints in the sand and when the tides
of change have come upon, across or here among whatever is left will
just be crumbs. Your strength must always stand as one.
### *Holloman Gatti*

## Fears Hold On Us

There was an employer named Frank who only hired non-handicapped individuals
If a handicapped person applied he just told them some bunch of crap
Then one night Frank had a dream and in the dream a wise man asked him
Why didn't you hire Bob who has C.P., he would have done such a good job
That you could have bought the elegant looking camera that was in the store.
Frank answered, "If I did, my insurance rates would soar."
The wise man said "If you don't start hiring the non-handicapped,
 you are going to lose much much more.

Frank decided to ignore the wise man that appeared in the dream and go on with life
Well two young men named Paul and Jeff who had seizures really went to strife
They sued under the ADA as they didn't buy Frank's crap
The case went straight to court and one could hear the first judge's first rap

The judge listened very intensely and then ruled that Paul and Jeff
had won, but that's not all you'll both receive backpay, fines of 20,000 dollars
plus punitive damages and then one could hear the judges last rap.

Frank had to go to his bank to start paying for everything which was quite a lot
His checking, savings, and $20,000 CD quickly saw all his accounts
 that had a 0 as the blot

Well that night, the wise man appeared again in Frank's dream
The wise man said, "I warned you, but you did not listen to me,
so now you have to pay a very high fee."

*Fred Sayin*

## The Poet

The Poet sees the world we know with quite a different view; He'll
look at something very old and see it very new.  The Artist paints on
canvas, the azure sea and sky; The Poet uses only words, to brush his palette dry.

The Poet writes the hopes and dreams of those who can't express; And
so, through poems, he speaks for them, the thoughts they won't
address.  He lives his life in words of song, with verse..sometimes
astounds!  A "Don Quixote", righting wrongs.. all better for the sounds.

He writes of wars and lover's passion; romantic shores and man's new
fashion.  He writes of today and tomorrow's dreams shattered;
Inhumanity to man and lonely lives battered.  He tells o f snow and
flame and fire; and every kind of human desire.  He can make a man
into a living God, or show us footprints, where Kings have trod.

The Poet can bring to everyone, a close encounter, with God and son.
A new view of life, and inspiring goals, that make us reach inside our
souls!  He writes of man, in mirth and jest and gives us reason to
seek the best.  He dreams and writes and writes of dreams; and shows
to us our empty schemes.

He uses all manner of style and verse, to make something beautiful of
something worse!  He will, at times, such thoughts impart, to somehow
mend a broken heart.  So, please, God, bless the dreamy Poet, who
makes your wonders to enthrall!  And bless his words and keep
alive...the Poet in us all!

*Jerry Peters*

## Day By Day

Dear Lord,

Please help me somehow find peace in my life, I'm nobodies girlfriend, nobodies wife.

Please help me to understand that that's O.K.  Please give me hope it won't always be this way.

Please send me someone that I can love, to hold me and kiss me and put me above.

Please keep me busy so I won't feel the pain.  Please give me spirit, don't leave me drained.

Please hold me close when I want to cry, sometimes it hurts so bad I want to die.

Please carry me when I can go no more, lift me from water, bring me to shore.

These feelings I have are hard to explain, I no longer see sunshine, I only see rain.

There are so many things I don't understand, I need to reach out and hold your hand.

Lord, I know that your with me and you hear my prayer, I know in your own way you'll help me up there.

Please stay in my heart every step of the way, and I know things will get better day by day. Amen.

*Terri Garcia*

## A Sunny Day

I woke up very early,
One bright and sunny day;
The day was surely sunny,
In every single way.
The sun was shining brightly,
The birds were sweetly singing
A song that made me smile,
And stop and listen for a while.
If only I could sing as they,
Then I could help brighten every day!

*Julie Taylor*

## Peace

Peace, like hope, is elusive —
one moment within
 the grasp;
the next, yielding
 to the killing fields.

Like a shimmering mirage,
peace offers the illusion
 of well-being
while its adversary
 prepares its annihilation.
Yet, in those transitory interludes
 are crafted
the hopes and aspirations
 of civilizations.

*Harold Corey*

## Untitled

As I walk along the
open road, I reflect upon the past.
I question the choices I have made.
 Were may good choices?
I guess that most of them were.
 But as I reflect on the
last choice I made
I realize,
Not getting gas, four miles past
was a wrong choice made.
So now,
 I walk along the open road.

*Howard Collier*

## Passion

And if we had met as friends first
or didn't we,
Would the pain be any less
Would the emptiness before me
be filled with fond recollections
to placate the rage inside
the silence of your soul
I think not
Why can't passion be enough
to maintain the flame ablazing,
contain the gratitude of grazing
in the beauty of her pubic passion
between the annals of her thighs
so luminous in nature, so empty
of desire, to reveal the true
beauty which is hers and only hers,
to awaken in the arms of sudden showers
of compassion for the nature
of desire doesn't wait and doesn't cower
at the feet of one so sweet?

*Jorge Valadez*

## Forever Young

You will never have gray hair
  or lose your teeth.
Wrinkles will never mar your
  youthful face.
That face will sit forever,
  unchanging behind our eyes.
You will laugh and sing
  and fly freely now.
And it will always be Spring.

Although it is sometimes
  Winter in our hearts.

*Judith Rosevear*

## Once Upon A Time

Sometime in the past,
Or was it in the future?
We touched,
And in your eyes
I met a soul
Grasping mine,
In gentle hands of love.
Remembering the emptiness
Of once upon a time,
Or was it tomorrow,
My love, my love.

*Herbert T. Smith*

## Believe In Yourself

Who am I? We sometimes ask ourself,
or what can I do?
Trust me- you are "Somebody,"
Regardless of what you have been through!

People are in your corner much more
than the eye can see...
You must "first" Love yourself
and let "your heart" have its peace;
"Then" your "mind" will become free!

To have money is good, but it's not
Like "Good Health"......
Remember, Please to....
Believe in Yourself!

*Gerard Herriott*

## Tell the Good News

Spread the gospel of Jesus Christ,
our Savior and risen King.
Tell the world of His goodness,
oh, let the praises ring.
He died for the sins of you and me.
They nailed Him on a cross.
Just think how the Savior suffered,
so men would not be lost.
No greater love have I witnessed,
and this I can't deny,
so grab a hold to His nail-scarred hands
don't let Him pass you by.

*Joyce Fuller*

## Untitled

Meet Jesus in the morning
Peace will fill your soul
Each day will be a blessing
A joy beyond control

*Rose Burnham*

---

Coming home from school,
On a day I can't forget.
Being a small child,
What I heard almost killed me.
How could I live without him?

*Melanie Walker*

## In The Distance - My Destiny

I was looking at the skyline,
out there in the distance;
what did it mean to me-
could it be my destiny?
I heard the distance calling,
and I felt like I was falling,
on a breeze.
I was walking down a road,
and there were the trees,
and the birds,
and a smile;
and that carried me on my journey,
mile after mile.
And I was looking at the skyline,
way out there in the distance;
I knew what it held for me-
it was my destiny.

*James D. Sorensen*

## Quest for Knowledge

O Little Boat, on current float,
Out to the open sea,
From river wharf,
O little dwarf,
Into eternity;
From ebb and flow
Where changing tide
No longer changes man,
But glows its glow,
On earth below,
With colored rainbow span;
Go see the sea,
Seen diff'rently,
See all there is to know—
A chance to live with knowledge, more,
With still more room to grow.
So, little boat, with current—go!
The wind will blow with force,
Then may the hands of fate be kind,
And keep you right on course.

*Alice B. Paulsen*

## Monet

When shower and color
  pastel and gray
Blend in light and dance
Step back in awe
Focus, imagine
And feast your eyes on the chance
To see a distant world of them
Who rest and swarm with souls
And capture time in Renaissance
Of virgins and of gold.
Silas Marner spoke to me
Steppenwolf called my name,
I lost a light but found a peace
In swans and poets the same.

*Endsley Givhan*

---

## In Memory Of My Mother

You can only have one mother
Patient kind and true.
No other friend in all the world
be as true as you.
For all the loving kindness she
ask nothing in return,
If all the world deserts you
to your mom, you can turn.
So all we can do dear mom
Is to tend your grave,
And leave all our love to the
best mom God ever gave.
We send you a bouquet
of roses sprinkled with
million of tears,
If tear drops could build
a stairway and our hearts
could lead the way
we would climb the stairs
to heaven just to be with you today -

*Alma Williams*

## School Things

Pencil, binder, notebook, paper,
pen, gym clothes, workbook, stapler.
Pencil sharpener, chalkboard, chalk,
Reading book, gym shoes, lock.
Dictionary, flag, even some glue,
Principal, secretary, assignments to do.
Teacher, friends, ruler, desk top,
At 3:24 it's time to stop!

*Amanda Raders*

## Hill Run

The silhouettes of distant hilltops
penetrate the haze.
Clouds obscure details
lost in the pale light of sunset.

Hawks search the brush for prey.
In silent anticipation,
they circle in pairs.

I run the contours of the hills
and push the air before me.
The hawks rise - connected.
In the distance, a cloud moves.
Another hilltop reveals itself.

*James W. Wolff Jr.*

## Oklahoma

A bomb shook the ground for miles.
People were in a scare.
A building fell in piles.
The lower level was for daycare.

It was only nine o two
In the morning.
The ground still covered in dew.
Like fire, a warning spread.

Volunteers came for miles.
Children, people, under the rubble.
There were no smiles.
Rain was predicted, it was trouble.

They searched into the night.
The volunteers,
Search the rubble in fright.
Families, friends, so many tears.

*Christy Teschmacher*

## Family

Family is people who care
people who need you
and people who share

Family is helping one another
working together
and loving each other

Family can consist of many
or as few as two
they support us
in all the things we do

Family is everything we need
love them back
and you'll succeed.

*Jaimi Marie Pearson*

## Transfigured Night

Two armadillos
performing peccadilloes
among the pussy willows
sleeping upon pillows
of grasses and aloes,
on an eve all hallow'd
by candles of tallow
and moonlit shadow,
the wind in billows
of sound like violin bows
or scented boughs
of fragrant rose.....

How much do those fellows
in Cabalistic clothes
purport to know
or attempt to close
within the door of eternal woes?

*Florence E. Kline*

## In Memoriam: Amelia Earhart (1898-1937)

Soaring through arching skies,
piercing through morning mists
steering a constant course
farther and farther into the west,
In a squat monoplane
clear-eyed and fearless,
fashioned for greatness
with just one companion
armed only with courage
this god and this goddess
ended their quest.

*Barbara Lorimer*

## The Door

Open not the door my child,
Please do not turn the key.
For what is there will frighten you
As long ago it frightened me.

For long ago the key was turned,
The evil was set free.
And long ago they fought the fight,
The fight that saved both you and me.

So close your eyes my sleepy child,
And drift off with your dreams.
The evil's gone, we are alone
Just you my child, and me.

*Charis Anne Smith*

## Someone

I hear the laughter of the children
Playing in the snow
It brings back memories of the days
Not so long ago
It seems like only yesterday
We played the games they play
Dreamed the dreams of every child
To be someone someday
Now after years of dreaming
And living day to day
I find that I am someone
No matter what they say
It took me years to see it
Understand it too
that if I'm nothing more than this
I am someone to you

*Darlene Fletcher-Laliberte*

## Untitled

I am like a little girl
Playing with ribbons in the air
Spinning in the air
I am like a lost child
Hugging herself in the cold
It is always cold
I am like a used woman
Walking mindlessly, afraid
Constantly afraid
I am like a fallen angel
Scratching away at her skin
Tearing out her hair
Screaming and crying
Without making a sound.

*Deniz Perin*

## Native American

People who were hurt
proud, people strong
clear vision quest found
some confused others not
majestic, mystic- human
some are afraid of us
only because they do not
understand, we are human
live, breath, dance have a
great spirit, we look up to for
guidance, spirituality, protection
love, hate, peace, calm
we understand it all
nature, natural, mystic
majestic, cool, hot love
teachers, some not
some elders, braves and maidens
children hold the future
I am proud to be Cherokee and Irish

*Carrie Lea Handy*

## "Only One"

In this life; it's been told
Only one true love
Only one to touch the soul

Some will never know
Others will let go

Blessed are the
have and to holds.

*Joan Bishop*

## Priorities

Soft dewy petals,
pure pastel honest,
bursting with life and great joy —

No lies, no misdeeds,
pure created life,
proud creature that knows not pride —

Living and giving,
it knows nothing else.
It lives for us to enjoy.

Yet, we pass it by.
we, so full of self,
are blind to its sacrifice

*Heidi Sprow*

## My Heart

There's a special place to
put you; in my heart you go.
I'll keep you there forever,
and never let you go.
We'll love now and forever,
throughout eternity.
Together we'll show the
world, how love is meant to be!

*Debbie Hannah*

## Rain

Rain is nice,
Rain is wet,
Rain is water that
plants will get.

Rain pours light,
Rain pours hard,
Rain pours into
everyone's yard.

Rain brings water,
Rain brings spring,
Rain is good for
everything!

*Felix Hsieh*

## Raindrop

Raindrop, falling against my window pane
Raindrop, rain fall, rain drop
The sound of heavenly drop
Calling me to silence to sound there of
Playing anew instrument there of
Only a sound that rain drops can play
Giving me peace within
Dropping wherever it list
Can you hear? Can you feel?
When rain drops is falling
The understanding is so simple
I'm at peace within
As the rain continue to drop
I fall into a sleep
Rain drop, rain drop, keep falling
Never stop, never stop, raindrops

*James L. Ash*

## Say What!

Ranchers can't stand the prairie dog
Ranchers can't stand the eagle
Ranchers can't stand the buffalo —
Wolf, coyote and wild horse either.
How fussy and demanding
In country of give and take
If they can't survive with the wild
Being ranchers was their mistake.

Did they ever hear of herders
Or cowboys to watch the cows
Are they too cheap to employ them
Come tell us the story now.
We're always hearing their bawling —
About our innocent friends
Nature that's resplendent
They're in a hurry to make an end!

**Agnes Jane Sorensen**

## Self-Portrait

Still waters run deep.

Silence

whirling wind,
reflections,
sparkling stars of light.

Birds

warmth

A quietness fills the air,
And if I stand still,
I can hear my heart beat

because still waters run deep.

**Frances Brzycki**

## Special Love

While standing in roses
remembering how I fell in
love, among the butterflies
surrounded by soft breezes
the sun is glowing down on us.

The petals begin to fall
but we're destined not to.
The happiness we make
together is flawless like a
rose and shall remain.

Love is clear, like looking
through windows only
thicker than glass.
Much more precious than
a bouquet of roses.

**Betty Skoler**

## The Bather

Regretting former loves,
   she moves among the bathers
      on the banks of the Holy River.

Lamenting children lost,
   she dips into the water
      in that place of solitude.

Surrendering memory,
   she moves beyond reality
      into the arms of her beloved.

**Dorothy Lee Hansen**

## Mother...Where Are You?

Mother....were you thinking?
Reminiscing over your early years?
I was standing in front of you
and you...you were not here.

I was staring at your face
but you, mother seemed to be far away
where?... Where have you gone?
Tell me as you did
when I was your child.

Reaching for the stars into space?
Or maybe inside...of yourself.
Just now I know where you stay
looking for God...beyond the earth.

Looking for God?...talking with him?
Asking for something?...perhaps for me?

If that is the truth, you talked with God
have you asked him, about the next life?

Please....please...pray to him
I wish be there....with you...again.

**Emilia O. Garrido**

## The Magic of Love

Love is the echo of a mountain
Resounding in all its corners
Releasing a magic fountain
Bursting out with all its forces

Love is everywhere
You can find it in a star
Up there somewhere
So near, not very far

It's in the moonlight
It's in the rain
Feel all its might
Feel all its pain

There is no mystery
When love awakes
Don't give me misery
Find me a place

To stay so close to love
For he'll know why
When he wakes up above
So deep ... inside

**Jose L. Fernandez**

## To Live

Climbing, climbing, climbing,
Rocks fall,
   fall all about me,
An avalanche of moments - so harsh,
Crags of death and time.

Climbing, climbing, climbing,
With so few things to grasp.
Such little time to rest,
No chances to be found.
But to let go is to give up,
And leads to fall, to forever sleep.
No more goals to find.

To go on against a height so great,
Toward a fate unknown.
What if I slip and hit the earth?
Would I leave anything to be found?
So formidable are the mountains,
But to climb, is to be alive.
To strive! To strive! To strive!

**Eryn Nakamura**

## Autumn Jewels

Gold and garnet leaves of hardwoods
Rustle in the cooling breeze
Set among the emerald
Of the pine and cedar trees.

Rich hues to sustain
Through the long cold winter days
A reminder of nature's blessing
Reflected in the sun's deep gaze.

Many times, life seems so wintry
Without the warmth of bright sun rays
Longing for the jeweled colors
Of those velvet autumn days.

**Iris Garris Jones**

## For Sarah

The death of a mother, like no other,
Saddens, wrenches, eviscerates.
It pains.
Then time, the Great Healer, slips by.
Slowly (or sometimes quite suddenly)
The essence of her being emerges
Distilled to brightest brilliance.
And, perhaps,
As happened with the other, my mother,
The essence flows forth—
Inundates the subconscious—
Makes itself comfortable;
And resides forever
In the memory.

**Jean Grill**

## Save The Children

Open up your hearts and minds
Save the children of our time
Save the weak and save the poor
Save the slow and insecure
Give them hope and make them well
Help them lift themselves from hell
It's your decision so make the choice
Speak up right now, raise up your voice
Feed their stomachs, feed their minds
Show them that your more than kind
That you want them to succeed
That you'll help them learn to lead
They are the future of this land
Give our children a helping hand

**John Sands**

## I Have Seen an Eagle Fly

I have watched a new day dawning,
Scented woodsmoke on the breeze.
I have breathed the frosty air
And tasted water sweet and pure.
A songbird trills to greet the morning.
A coyote barks across the valley.
And in the stillness of the sunrise
The world awakens and I rejoice.
I am most blest of all mankind.
I've heard the laughter of a child.
I have seen an eagle fly.

**Bonnie Blankenship**

## Answers

Have you ever watched a tear-drop?
Seen the crystal dreams within?
Wondered at the wished there,
or the 'what could have been's'?

Can you see beyond the rainbow?
Past the yellows and the greens?
Do you listen to the melodies,
sung by first never seen?

Will you try and touch the stars?
Fly with hopes never bound?
Turn faces to the heavens.
while remaining on the ground?

Have you listened to the shadows?
Heard the tales of the past?
Will you understand the moment,
and believe that it will last?

Can you turn your eyes inward?
See the heart that beats inside?
Face the fear that blossoms there,
or do you turn, and try and hide?

**Harvest Eckert**

## Obsession

Like dancing live electric wires
Senses out of control

Fight or flight signals
From some primal source

Held captive in this modern today
A yesterday soul

Longing for sedative bliss
A drink, a drug, another love

So the mind can die, the heart can
Slow, the soul can mend

There is no shield against the pain
Of my obsessive desire

**Edward J. Cronin**

## A Poet

From the heavens God
sent beauty. And in this a
poet was born.
A poet takes this
beauty and enables a blind
man to see, and a deaf man
to hear.
A poet can make a
rich man feel the sorrow's
of a poor man, and a poor
man feel for a rich man.
Because once the pen
hits the paper the magic begins.
Once you read what
is wrote you will feel the
sorrow and the happiness
and things you otherwise
would never know.

**Jenny Shaffer**

## Still Just You And Me

Look at the sun
setting into the sea
from dawn till dusk
it's just you and me.

Finding love in this world
our chances our few
as the hours pass by
it's just me and you.

When you hold me close
my hearts filled with glee
on the white sandy beach
it's just you and me.

Moonlit kisses
passionate and true
as we snuggle together
it's just me and you.

I love you so much
now can't you see
the darkness has come and gone
and it's still just you and me.

**Jenna Gathje**

## Running Wild

Motionless images
Shadows in the clouds
Reflections in my eyes
My imagination runs wild

Walking a step behind
Thinking a step ahead
A mind full of illusions
My imagination runs wild

When I see you next
When you smile at me
When you're back in my arms
My imagination runs wild again

**David Weddel**

## Terrorist In America

The Eagle's nest
shaken twice
after dawn's first light.

The States of
New York and Oklahoma
families at work.

Bombs burst in buildings
not in air.

Gave proof
to Americans
terrorists are here.

Silent cries of dead
139 plus
gleam through
American's pride.

The Red, White, and Blue
not so bright
half mast.

The Eagle's feathered nest
is spattered with her own blood.

**Dana Jo Hopkins**

## High Society

Forlorn the moon,
She spills the wine.
Should questions be asked?
In his holy nook he waits,
In her blessed book she writes,
of blossoms and stupid songs.
Sticking like glue.
When the moon cries and
the watch lies,
'tis not or ain't?
The great chaos had no conscience,
but only moral deceit.

**Cedes Griffin**

## A Dying Rose

*Dedicated to*
*Pansy Ethel (Alderman) Campbell*

She had cancer.
She was dying, wasting away.
Her mind and body wilting away;
a rose that was never watered.
Chemotherapy,
Acid rain poisoning her fragile
existence.
Her hair, dry petals
Falling from the stem.
Her body,
a dehydrated stem
that could no longer support her.
And yet, the thorns
of her absence remain intact,
piercing the hearts
of those who love her.

**Corey Campbell**

## My Mother's Song

If my mother would sing
She would be young again,
In her light flowered cotton dresses
Her thick black wavy hair.
The songs would linger there
Resting on her shoulders
a gossamer shawl
Her songs would perfume the air
wafting from room to room.
I could sleep so soundly then
with my mother's songs covering me.

If my mother would sing
my father would turn
and look at her face
and watch her eyes.
He would see her lips soften
and remember when they parted
so willingly for him.

If my mother could remember her songs
If my mother would sing.

**Diana Linda**

## Limerick

There once was a teacher from TN.
  Who challenged each child to be,
A winner of all,
And quiet in the hall.
  This teacher was special, you see!

**Lavada Stanfill**

## Covered With Dust

When batteries aren't included
  Shelf-life matters
But that's only because of you:

The dust collecting on my crown
resembles the clarity of my thought
so far
  removed from the shelf of life
as to be recycled and born again
but
  this time as a watch
  that time as a bird
and next time as a curse.

Bless me I've sneezed my life away
always sticking my nose in
  with my two cents
  my shave and my haircut
  cutting costs when it should be free.

*James Lawrence Thibault*

## Web

White Christmas lights
Shine
As dew drops strung
Around a spider's web.
Imagine if the spider people
Were to decorate our town
With their intricately woven tapestries,
Strung from tree limbs to roof tops.
When the early morning sun
Cracked across the sky,
We would open our eyes
Breathless
Under an umbrella of
Dazzling lights.

*Jennifer Cote*

## Untitled

She appeared, so softly
silently, at noon
This woman from another
Place and time
To see what I see
To hear what I hear
Now a friend

*Chris Hopper*

## Denots

The Youth is ones mass joy.
Simplicity.
Strikes at the soil.
My arms burn.
Only a Freshman would question.
The serious smokers are in AWE.
(DuHumb!)

The reaper is nervous but can
feel the light.
Let's hope it s not a train.

Work hard - Play hard,
Always love the Ladies.

*John Parker*

## I Ricks

Jumped of a creek bank
Six feet high
Broke both my wrists
And it made me cry,
Went to the doctor
And I got them fixed;
Now I can try
Some more new tricks.

*Anthony Ortez*

## The Storm

Lovely ladies floating by
Skirts billowing toward the sky,
Ankles showing trim and firm
Petticoats blustering in a storm.

Hats askew, curls surrendering
Clouds above become impending
Squeals of laugher, glee, some frightened,
Claps of thunder; bright the lightening.

Drops of water slow at first
Then a deluge; a dam that's burst.
Soaking, dripping, all is wet.
Storm continues on as yet.

*Helen R. Kroesser*

## Tapers

You could not know what you had done
Slipping so quietly that night
  into my life
Your present-ness mirrored my past
Coloring back the years that grayed
  with time
You dotted my darkness with
  your gentle star shine
And left your light flickering
  in my soul
You touched my life with laughter
And made me whole again.

*Eileen Rhoads*

## Raining

Those thousands of
small drops falling
on the rocks and the
hard clay on the high
ground,

Gathered together here
and there, then, as more
thousands came,

Formed ever larger puddles
that flowed between the
biggest stones and all at
once;

Went running down, down
over sticks and stones,
passing logs and stumps
and even

Made tiny waterfalls but
suddenly; the rain stopped!

*Floyd A. Hoag*

## Snowboarding

Carving edge to edge,
Smooth deep powder.
Floating through the trees,
A silent hawk.

At peace with one's self,
Trees appear and diminish,
Gliding softly behind, ever so softly.

Chill bites at my face.
A rush and warmth sits deep inside.
Nature and I are one
and no one can touch me.

I feel my arousal,
insides churn
Grit my teeth.
I'm going down,
penetrating the center of the woods.
My heart soars,
Wings spread, I take flight.
This is heaven;
This is where I belong.

*James M. Adam*

## White

Today was a white day
Snow falls without an end
Trees looked white and pure
on a bitter winter day.

The snow became simple rain
the rain was falling so clear
winter went fast, and disappeared
washing all the snow away.

Memories of a snowy day
will always be in my mind
the day when the snow was white
the day when the rain was clear.

Now things have changed a lot
the winter is not as cold
the snow now rarely falls
but the rain keeps falling clear.

*Carlos M. Simancas*

## The Rosebush

Once there was a rosebush
So beautiful and blooming,
it stood out among all others.
Once there was a gardener
who took very special care
of these roses all year long.
They bloomed every summer.
No matter what the winter was like.
Every day their gardener went out
and checked on his very special bush.
Rain or shine he was always there.
Then the gardener became ill.
only once in a while he made it out.
The roses became less and less.
Finally one day the gardener died,
and the roses wept.
They knew they had lost their best friend.
One day the last rose bloomed,
it was placed on the gardener grave,
where they, once again, would be together
forever more.

*Barbara Roberts-Franco*

## Sixth Senses

Tears of sorrow are
so contagious you see,
effects others instantly.
The connection among
emotions throughout all of
we... is more powerful
then the eye can see.

We do not need our
hands to feel, the hurt
and pain from another's
ordeal, it does not take
an ear to hear, the cries
of hunger and despair...
we do not need our mouth
to speak, the loving thoughts
that are buried deep.

To let our sixth senses
kick in, will lessen the
havoc we all hold within.

*Dana Ingrahm*

## The World I Live In

The world I live in
So cruel in every way
Everyone's against you
No one is your friend
No one to trust
The world I live in
Is all but fun
The world I live in
Is full of pain
The world I live in
The world I live in

*Jenifer Hunt*

## A Tribute to Mom

She's sweet beyond measure,
So gracious and kind;
A more priceless treasure,
Would be hard to find.

Her thoughts are of others,
Instead of herself;
Her eyes are on Heaven's crown,
Not on Earth's wealth.

As nursemaid and teacher,
As chauffeur and cook;
She followed the Bible,
Not Spock's baby book.

She guided our footsteps,
With her tender care;
And kept us from straying,
Through her constant prayer.

Who is this gentle lady,
Who shines above all others?
You could call her God's masterpiece.
We simply call her Mother!

*Cathy D. Lee*

## Precious Love

So Precious is the Heart
So Pure is the Soul
The Life of a Child
The Joy is Untold

To Come Into This World
To Breathe the Air of Life
The Happiness of it All
The Tragedy is Just in Sight

The Lord's Beloved Children
Is Just a Gift to All
We Cherish What we Have
Until he Comes to Call

The Pain we Feel Inside
The Anger we Must Express
To Lose the One You Love
No One Could Ever Guess

To God we Must Accept
He Knows we Pray in Vain
Take Care of OUR Beloved Son
We'll Always Love You Blaine

*David Blische*

## Jewels of Time

I hold none but your gentle hand,
So tender and so very warm,
I hear none but your loving heart,
Whispering in the waking morn.

I see none but your tender smile,
And try to capture it as mine,
To hold with all the precious things,
As jewels in my sands of time.

I sense your very kindly thoughts,
Your wishes true and most sincere,
Delightfully they penetrate,
Through depths that we alone can hear.

I share none but your dear caress,
As you softly touch my brow,
Eternity of cares elapse,
For they hold no terror now.

I see the light at break of day,
Through your eyes for you are there,
My heart beats by the air you breathe.
Please hold it in your loving care.

*Helen Sprinner*

## Untitled

Honestly, to answer your question,
some are more beautiful it's true.
But when I see with my heart
no woman looks as good as you.
When I watch you sleep,
when I hold you near,
when I hear your voice,
then the truth is clear.
You are the one I want,
you have all I need.
The beauty that you have,
no other could exceed.
I will look no further,
my heart will never stray.
Know as you give your love,
it's a love I won't betray.

*John Fox*

## Whispers

There are whispers on the wind
    Some call the breath of life
They swirl sometimes unnoticed
    Through sadness, pain, and strife
But the sounds these whispers make
    Are always there to hear
We may just need reminders
    Someone to hold us dear
So if it seems at times
    There is no good to speak of
Let us not forget the whispers
    For they are the sounds of love

*James McCaffrey*

## Untitled

Some days seem slow,
Some days take flight,
Weeks and months and years,
All go flashing by;

Sand through an hourglass,
Night to day
And back again,
All go flashing by;

A smile, a tear,
A laugh, a cry,
The blinking of an eye,
All go flashing by;

Seconds, minutes,
A moment in a life,
Now becomes a memory,
All go flashing by.

*David Witty*

## Four Seasons in a Family

We feel the chill of autumn frost;
Some unkind word is spoken.
A goal is set as yet unmet.
Some promise made is broken.

Autumn rains may usher winter,
Gusting winds may come and go,
Reckless word may shadow sunlight,
Thoughtless deeds bring ice and snow.

Then comes a gradual warming spell
The promised hope of springtime
A planted seed, a loving deed,
A tender word at Maytime.

Early spring, late spring an summer
Starlit skies may be help to guide
Gentle words and warm sweet passions..
Stormy winds will now subside.

*Florence DeBoer Wigon*

## "Lord" We Find You

"I got to",
see what the world will be
"I got to",
see what the world will be
I got to see.
What the world will be,
without "Jesus"?
"Lord" we find you, everywhere
in the world.
That's all I got to say.

*Constance Davis*

## Mile to Smile

Somethings
Sometimes
Some memories
Some minds

Past games
Present hurts
Future resents
Left burnt

Shoved behind
Fear ahead
Rage in anger
Forgive instead

Stuck in dark
Never shine
Glow and glory
Where's mine?

Scars to prove bruises to pain
Cuts of anger will it rain?

Somethings sometimes
Some memories some minds

*Amanda Cook*

## Time

It can run and it drags
Sometimes earned
but for some, taken away.

Some have too much
Some complain, not enough
And others just wish it would stay.

It can be long or short.
Lost and found.

It's measured in multiple ways.

In seasons adjusted
2 times a year
achieved by altering days.

A topic of interest
or subject forgotten
a wasted expense
or a valuable commodity sold

But one thing that's certain
it's never enough
as we pass from youth into old

*Gena Greathouse*

## Easter Rain

On spring Sunday morning
Son day morning
Clouds shrouded
In mourning gray,
Look
To see highway crosses
Standing straight and tall
Repeating
One after another
  "Empty...
  Empty....
  Empty....
  Empty..."
Then sky shell cracks
Pouring forth its deluge:
Delinquent praise!

*Beverley A. Rogers*

## Purpose Pursuit

Mind rending
  soul tending
    truth lending
      foe fending
        mistake mending
          path bending
            blindly wending
              idea vending
                vibe sending
                  hope never-ending
                    payoff... pending

*Jaenet Renae*

## Utopia

Peace flowing gently o'er the land;
Sparkling bright is the ocean sand.
No submarine or battle ship
Must she endure within her grip.
Silence reigns throughout the night,
Not a cry or murderous sight!
No poor or needy skulking round;
No rich or haughty trodding ground.
No cry or worry for relief;
No one a God or tyrant chief.
The ruler of the land is peace!
  UTOPIA!

*Esther Weitzel Burbol*

## I'll Always Be There

I'll always be there for you,
Standing strong and true,
Willing to face any challenge
For you........

Sometimes it's something said,
Or perhaps being silent,
To meet the need of friendship
For you........

The caring and sharing and strong,
Never failing to reach,
The heart cry I'll hear,
For you........

Just need me, I say to you
Watch what happens.
When you call out to me,
I'll always be there for you.

*Barbara S. Rieth*

## Night

Darkness succeeds the daylight
Starlit decorated sky
The sun's past due
The moon's brand new
Traces of travelling clouds
Obstruct the moon
While nature's at rest
To the sounds of darkness.

*Hanesta Blango*

## Consequences

Consequences were so steep
Feelings also were so deep
I need to think before I sleep.

*Liam Bradley*

## Cycles

Galaxies spawned, planets formed
Stars decay to red giant's burn
Earth's spin brings light and dark
Seasons come, fade in turn

Green plants grew, fish swam
Prehistoric creatures far and wide
Apes and elephants did abound
Man crawled, stood, then took stride

Flowers burst forth, grow tall
Fed on earth, sunlight and rain
Beautiful 'til sting of first frost
Perennials go dormant not in vain

Lusty babies born, gain pounds
Food and drink making bones strong
Youth succeeds to adulthood
'Til old age or misfortune stills life's song

Man is gifted with ability to learn
Can exercise freewill, plan ahead
Will we care for earth and fellowman
Or will existence cease, all things dead?

*Bill Cleveland*

## Moonbeams

A silver coin thrown in the sky
Stayed with the earth
by and by.
He circled her as she circled the sun
And lit the night for everyone.
With a silvery gleam and a watery glow,
Each night he bathes the earth just so.

*Emily Burton*

## Nothing Left

This man-so old
Stood..looking

Sapling, weeds, briars, an
Old foundation of rock. A
place where a house once
stood, strong—proud.

"Raised a family here." He said
we stood a long time—quietly.
I asked if there was anything I
Could do. He didn't seem to hear.

"It's all gone-nothing left."
Tears welled in his eyes,
He slowly walked away. Leaving
Me to stand alone- to think.

Myself-suddenly old
Stood.... looking

*Agustin Acosta Jr.*

## Loneliness

If I'm by my self I'll cry.
She change my life
She loves me with all her
heart, Love it change me
it make me feel emotion
I can cry laugh, Love and
Live. If I was without
Love for a minute I'd die
Loneliness it scares me

*John E. Tracey*

## "Tuan Jim"

I can't refuse the thoughts of you
streaming mad
through the Congo
river flooding
tears of angry tribesmen
calling "Tuan Jim.."
to your starch white grin.
I'm planning to end our relations
clipping
shadows of your rosebuds
in May before your time
can reach its highest
cast down from the meridian,
up the river
again only brought
a suffering
bundle of thirsty natives
quenched by the sweat
streaming down your
countenance onto the blade.

*Bree Dean*

## Untitled

Dark leathery skin
  Stretched tight
  over the bone of skull
Withered lips pulled back
  In a grimace/smile
  to reveal
  bleached white gravestone
  nubs of teeth
Eyeballs dried into
  leftover grape skins
  In their sockets
Body splayed in the deserted street
The photographer stoops down
  to get a better angle

*Alan Choi*

## Our Nation

As I daily read the news,
Such input of varied views;
Amazes me, when I see,
So many people disagree.
No matter what our view,
One thing we should do,
Remember what is right.
Views should not start a fight.
Debate should help us know.
Thoughts can help us grow.
God's inspiration should be,
Important in society,
Why should we fear debate?
If we wait, it's too late.
Creation should be given thought,
If evolution must me taught.
Our children really must,
Know yet, in God we trust.

*Esther M. Farr*

## Untitled

Be unto me a voice of spring
And I to you shall bring
  A stone of love
  A tear of rain
  A golden drop of silver pain

*Rich Fifield*

## Sunrise

Down where trees meet the sky,
sit on ground and watch the sunrise.
Red. Orange. Fluorescent, pink,
where does the sky get
the colors the sunrise make?
The sun ignites the sky like a burning
candle, and the air warms like
a hot panhandle.

*Amanda Lombardi*

## Sunrise

Rising reaching shimmering fountain
Sunrise over snowcapped mountain
Life spreads without a single word
Stirring rabbit chirping bird
Coming alive like a living being
Great beauty but not one human seeing
Stately deer with soft brown eyes
Turns its head to see the rise
Of glowing ball of nature's power
Deep orange in this waking hour
Ascending time is finally done
Burning brightly the newly risen sun

*Jesse Beene*

## A Pilgrim's Tale

Sadness and emptiness merge
Sunset glow impending
Wandering aimlessly on the shore

Dreams and visions
Fading with the evening softness
Moving to and fro with the tide

No attachments
Seeking to find authentic self
Exploring the edge of humanity

Solitude
Searching for truth
Among the sands of change

Contemplation
Listening to the God voice
Within the shell of seclusion

Expectation
To be free
Surrendering to the motionless wave of
humanity

*Corene K. Besetzny*

## Imaginary Place

The wind blows through my hair
sunshine upon my face
I walk down the lane
to my secret hiding place

There is no place like it
its where I go and stay
to lie beneath the old oak tree
and pass the time away

To dream those special dreams
to think of what could be
my special hiding place
that no one else can see

Its my imaginary place
it has been from the start
its tucked deep inside
in my mind and in my heart

*Ellen Y. Ladd*

## Beginning at the Shore

The breezes from the ocean
surround me as I dream.
The morning fog has lifted;
From the sky
descends a sun beam.
The sea gulls fly and chatter
back and forth along the way;
the ocean starts it pounding noise,
the beginning of a new day.

I walk the beach and run
my fingers through the sand;
while across the way from me
there's a kite that zooms to land.
As the sun begins to climb
I hurry back to shore.
The waves beat out the time
as they will forever more.

*Ida W. Idomir*

## Hesitation

The best years
Sweet souvenirs,
Hopes and dreams bouquet.
It was yesterday.

The best wine
Born under sun sign
It's the oldest one.
With its magic taste and hue
It is going by years through,
As well as I do.

If a dear guest
Is appearing at my door,
I am hesitating for
What I could offer more
To do my best.

A rusty poem
Or an old wine
Heavenly tear gem,
Or both of them?

*Constantin Stoicescu*

## Tammy's Little Hands

Tammy's little hands
  Tammy's precious little hands
Busy all the day thru
  Working for Jesus working for you

Tammy's little hands
  Tammy's precious little hands
So faithful, so true
  Helping mother and daddy, too

Tammy's little hands
  Tammy's precious little hands
Trusting, loving, and gay
  Joyfully, happily at play

Tammy's little hands
  Tammy's own little hands
So tired at end of day
  Folded now to pray

*Elizabeth C. Matthews*

## A Silent Cry

Alone in the silent night
Tears that were never seen

Cries you could not hear
The privacy that was violated

Untold dark secrets,
thoughts of anguish

So innocent and young
Not understanding why

As the years past,
A childhood that was misplaced by anger

Into a silent cry...

***Elsie Nieves***

## A Real Close Friend

There's nothing better
Than a real close friend
A person you can count on
All the way to the end

To be your friend
Would be my pleasure
The kind of relationship
I would really treasure

To listen to records
Or just have a good talk
To go to the movies
Or go for a walk

Whatever we do
We'll have fun to the end
And that's the best part
Of having a real close friend

***David Storch***

## Universal Love

Our Savior's love is greater far
Than any human tongue can tell,
It's higher than the highest heaven
And deeper than the lowest hell;

It reaches earth's remotest ends,
Throughout the universe extends
To every nation, tribe and tongue
He made and loves them everyone.

He is the Shepherd, we're the sheep
Safe and secure He will us keep,
If we will follow where He leads
He will provide for all our needs.

Come, let us praise His holy name,
With thankful hearts His praise proclaim.
With matchless mercy, love and grace
He will all our sins erase.

***Bertha Lee W. Jones***

## As the Wave Is to the Ocean

As the wave is to the ocean
So we and God are one.
Each having an infinite moment
To glisten in the sun.

Sometimes mightily roaring;
Sometimes nigh asleep;
Ever, always changing,
Our final goal to keep.

***Joyce A. Truchinski***

## Who?

Who will write the poem
That brings the world to tears
After war, hate and sorrow
Might a rhyme replace our fears?

Who will sing the song
That disperses sticks and stones
To scatter clouds of darkness
Can a brilliant sun be shown?

Who will say the word
that impels the timid heart
to pour out a kindness
with the swiftness of a dart?

Who will ring the bell of love
in a tower crossing time
and draw the world to listen
to the beauty of its chime

Lift your banner high then
let your cry be known
when the heart's door is open
the shepherd's seed is sown

***Joseph F. Manning***

## One

O little you —
    that drop in the ocean,
    grain of sand thus be.
        Why wave the wind.

O small one —
    a feather in the sky
    leaf in forest, thee.
        Why rise the hills?

        "For still the earth"
        The Voice proclaims,
        "For I made thee."

Yes little you
    ocean shall play for you
    and the wind shall sing!

Yes small one
    the forest too shall dance
    and the hills shall smile!

        For and with you
            Gladness for all
        No matter how small.

***Danette Zdansky***

## The Hawthorne Tree

We went today to the "Author's House"
That sits by the ridge in the wood
And there beside the welcoming door
The Hawthorne tree still stood.

Planted with love
For his two daughters
Tenderly cared for
By sunshine and waters.

"To his Abba and Rose
With great delight"
Now half blooms pink
And half blooms white.

***Jacqueline L. Childs***

## Out Of The Money

The race I ran was badly run,
That even I could see,
I ran for love hard as I could
    But did
Place out of the money.

Really I didn't have a chance,
The odds were against me,
I ended up down in the dump
    And way,
Way out of the money.

In love you're either first or last,
Between don't mean a thing,
Only to place or even show
    You know
I'm out of the money.

I placed way out of the money,
Love turned its back on me,
My should have been sure didn't win
    Again,
I'm out of the money.

***Jess Kelly***

## Who Am I

Who am I
That He should care.
Who am I
That He should die upon a tree.
Who am I
That He should care so much for me.

Who are you
That He should care so much for you
That He should die upon a tree
That He should set you truly free.

Who are we
That He should care so much
For you and me
That He should give His life
So that we could evermore be free.

Just who are we
He knows and He cares
He is the only answer
Yes, He cares for you and me.

***Alberta A. Cox***

## My Dear

Pity is a furious thought
that others do not see
I do not feel for you my dear
for you mean the world to me
unto your eyes I cannot see
the same I cannot hear
and as for you and friends around
I call for you my dear
I thought that in a dream I saw
a tiny arrow and bow
it circled around the world my dear
and followed you quite so
tonight the sky gets black and dull
and the stars they do not shine
they know your back is turned to them
just as grief to mine
now close your eyes and rest awhile
for you day has been long my dear
and do not think of poisonous things
for hell has not come here

***Jessica Lynn Hoffer***

## Untitled

Full of doubts
That plague my brain
Flitting though
These unfiltered thoughts shed shadows
In the light
And replace blindness
With clear sight

Holding up the cloudy candle
Future's ghosts ride through
My dreams
And
Turn my certainty
Inside-out

*Emily Brown*

## A Special Gift

This is a very special gift,
That you can never see.
The reason it's so special is...
It is just for you from me.

Whenever you are lonely
Or even feeling blue,
You only have to hold this gift
And know I think of you.

You never can unwrap it
Please leave the ribbon tied.
Just hold this gift close to your heart.
It is filled with love inside

*Barbara Ann Jabs*

## Dance of the Northern Lights

It is sad to me
That you have never seen
The Northern Lights.

I try to explain Aurora Borealis
In terms a scientist would use...

But I only know
The colors of the sky
And the way I felt

When the wind blew
And how my sister laughed
Because we wore pajamas
In the middle of the park.

We lay on our backs
For hours trying to capture them
Like fireflies in a mason jar
But they raced across the sky
Like Eskimo children at play.

Take my hand and you can still see them
    faintly glowing
and know like I do.

That night they must have danced for you.

*Jessica Dawn Smith*

## Justice

As substance and shadow,
the act and the word
never meet in full embrace:
Justice is the child of promise
of conduct seeking to embrace ideals
presumed to be good.

*Ernest R. McKinney*

## Planting Flowers

We watch and assume
that the flowers are almost in bloom
It's beautiful to look at
the lovely plants just keep
your garden away from
those pesty ants.

*Jenna Fisher*

## There Is A Special Little Boy

There is a special little boy
The angels said he came
He is a loving child of God
Joshua is his name
The Lord has sent him here to earth
To learn and grow each day
With wisdom, love and a giving heart
He will know just how to pray
So give him love and guidance
As he grows stronger every day
And Jesus will love this special child
In a very special way.

*Eileen Gressi*

## Nicola

*To my baby girl, Nicola Arielle Flores*

The twinkle in your eyes
The beauty of your smile
Your gentle touch
Your warm embrace
Makes you a heavenly angel

Those ten busy fingers
Those two curious feet
Your loving coos
Your playful ways
Makes you a wonderful child

A wish upon a star
The love in my heart
A gift from God
The miracle of life
Makes you my beautiful daughter

*Gladys Pawliski-Flores*

## Who Am I?

Who am I?  I am a child of God;
the beloved child of a Father
who has given me riches beyond compare.

You give me life;
abundant life now and the promise
    of eternal life with you.

You give me love;
unconditional love that accepts me
just as I am.

You give me hope;
hope that helps me persevere through
    the doubts and difficulties of life.

You give me peace;
peace that gives a calming, restful
    center to a stressful world.

But, best of all, you give freedom;
freedom to walk and talk with you
    and to feel your awesome presence within me;
freedom to give myself to you and to let
    you softly, gently mold me to your will.

*Helen Thompson-Kramer*

## Alone

Sitting alone and scared,
The black rolling clouds
Coming closer and closer.

The smell of rain fills the air,
You imagine the smell afterwards,
About how everything will smell clean.

You can hear the rumble of thunder.
The lightning flashes through the sky,
Lighting up the city on and off.

The sky darkens,
The thunder rolls louder,
The lightning comes down in huge bolts.

The rain begins to pour,
Cleansing streets, plants and buildings.
Soon the storm is over.
You can hear the pitter-patter of raindrops
Falling from the limbs and leaves.
The thunder rolls away, the birds come out and
I'm not alone anymore.

*Elyssa Bragg*

## For Maya

Now I myself know why
the caged bird sings—
Not quite for the benefit
of its captors, really,
as much as there being
nothing else to do,
or to hope for.
But the prettiest songs in history,
the ones that leave their mark,
come from the throats
of such iron-collared birds—
As if when all else
is removed
from a life,
that Life itself
comes forth,
pure and naked,
as music.

*Catherine L. Stephens*

## Concrete Rose

How was I supposed to know
the day we were to meet
That your pretty little rose
was made of solid concrete.

You looked sweet
but your petals were hard as stone.
I'm sorry that I brought you
and your cold, cold rose into my home.

I LOVED YOU
And you said the same.
Unfortunately, I didn't play
by the rules in your game.

Many others are to come,
those I will meet.
But your pretty little rose
will always be concrete.

*Justin McClain*

437

## Keep the Faith

The race will be long
The fight will be hard
The runner will weary
The soldier will be scarred
The battle is bloody
The hurdles are high
Some will not make it
Some men will die
Losers are forgotten
The dead are left to be
Why do they do it?
What good can they see?
Why do they struggle?
Why do they fight?
It is the pride of conquering
The promise of victory in sight
It is the end that you look at
It is the faith that you keep
Though the battle is hard
And the road is too steep

*Cindy Carlson*

## The Source

From within
the fire burns.
In the dark
it lights a way.
In the cold, a warming fire.
The wood, it crackles
with an orange cherry blossom flame.
It burns steadily hotter
until I am consumed.
The flame and I merge.
I become the light.
I supply the heat
I am the fire.

*Brian Slaughter*

## The Seasons

Spring is when the flowers bloom.
The fragrance smells like nice perfume.
The night are cool, the days are warm,
A cold front brings on thunderstorms.

Summer brings the humid air,
I walk around with my feet bare.
The swimming pools, the sunburned skin,
My baseball team brings home a win.

Halloween is in the fall,
My favorite season of them all.
I dress up as a scary dude,
And try to get my favorite food.

Winter's when it snows a lot,
I stay inside and get real hot.
This is the end of a year's spell.
I hope you spent the whole year well.

*Jim Kennedy*

## Big Puffy White Clouds

If I had a spoon
As tall as the sky
I'd dip unto the clouds
As they pass by.

I'd take a taste
To my secret nook
to see are they as
Good as they look!

*Leone W. Vollmer*

## Look At The Sun

It is so bright and light
The grass is like cash
It is nice and breezy
And I am lazy

It is so bright
I am so right
I like the light
Cause it is bright

See the light
It is bright
From the sun
I have so much fun

*Alex Corona*

## Morning

Another;
The great
Forgiveness of the God

Beginning;
There
A calm dawn
Opening the morning

Dewdrops on a leaf
Gradually
Ceases the sweet dreaming

Under the graceful lightening
From the east
A snail
Crawling with the loaded sky on its back
Departing, making a long journey.

*Chun Ho Kang*

## Finding Contentment

Peace and happiness seem to be
The greatest treasures life can hold,
But finding them, we realize,
Is a hard and trying task.
We run and stumble blindly on
Working endlessly, sometimes,
Ever searching and always seeking,
Some contentment and some joy.
Why can't we just go ever onward
Finding pleasure in earth and sky,
Contented with joy or sorrow,
Just happy to be alive?
Peace, happiness and even joy,
Really can be ours, we know
As we stop and look about us,
And help another, first of all.

*Evelyn J. Lewis*

## Out of My Bedroom Window

You're the star out my window,
That shines through the night.

You're the sun in the morning
that make everything sunny bright.

You're the snow on the mountain bean
so crystal white.

God you're the love of my life
that does everything incredible right.

*Angela Davenport*

## Tenderly Junk

The room was set for conquer,
the items on display;
she would go through and pick and choose,
and most she'd throw away.

She knew the plan of action,
she was prepared to win!
But when it came down to the fight,
she threw away the bin.

She hated all the clutter,
but couldn't bear to part
with anything she'd ever owned,
for each was dear to heart.

She finally took some matchsticks
and set the place ablaze.
She couldn't stand the inner war
and burned it in a craze.

So now when she finds objects
are meaningful and dear,
she smashes them while she still can,
but sheds a bitter tear.

*Jean Marie Walker*

## Gold

The medium of exchange
the lure of lore
the means by which
all are capable
the dispatch of the needy
the hapless greed of gold
the ultimate temptation
the weakness of great men
and small women
the ziggurat of hope
an idea of necessity
born of the burden
of carrying child
innocent, transfixed
and a judgement
the retribution of pain
the punishment of hope
the balm of the wicked
the arc of the covenant

*Jeff Scott*

## My Love

The beauty that is starlight
the magnificence of the sea
the glory of a rainbow
that is my love for thee!

Heaven in all its splendor
Lilies in the fields
the pleasure that you render
crashing thunder when it peals.

The gentleness of moonbeams
the beauty of a stream
the softness of the rain drops
the dreams of you I dream.

To touch you when it's morning
to hold you through the night
your eyes are like the springtime
their sparkle  clear and bright.

My love for you is eternal
no man could ask for more
you are my love- my lady
it is you whom I adore!

*Joseph Mignone*

## "Bird On A Wire"

In the steel gray eyes of dawn
the masses stand,
as gaunt and depleted as their shadows.
Straight rows of lifelessness
whose bleeding souls cry,
while tombs of death belch
and the black snows fall.

    But lo'————-
Amid the din of fear and hatred
a pair of hungry eyes gaze
to behold a bird on a wire.
The embodiment of pure life
in the form of song and feather.
The content of memory,
a jewel of hope
from the Master of Life,
the avenger of death.
And death shall be no more;
only life eternal.

    *Jeanne Haugen*

## Picture Perfect

Picture.
The news is on the lawn once again;
Just there, with everything zen.
Perfect.
A mother loves her favorite son;
Must learn football from square one.
Picture.
A bus explodes in Jerusalem;
Should, should be called the Dead Zone.
Perfect.
Calvin fights with Hobbes, the tiger;
Makes us giggle and grin with laughter.
Picture.
You over-read this poem today;
Then let it slip into yesterday.
Perfect.
Make peace now across your land;
Turn around and shake your neighbor's
hand.

    *Jonathan Hayes*

## Dreaming Big

The dream that I think of
The one no one else has heard,
It's a dream that many have
One that is common throughout the world.

But though it is a common one
No one would think I could
Because you see I am a girl
And no one thinks girls should.

It is a dream so wonderful
A dream with power involved
If this dream comes true for me
The world will know women have evolved.

I'll give a hint to my dream
Mr. President better look out.
'Cause mighty women are on the march
Men, this is no reason to pout.

I want to work in the White House
I want to be its top resident
For wouldn't the world be better if
God made a woman president.

    *Britta Monson*

## For A Friend

Tears fall,
The pain does not.

One moment feels dull,
The next,
Feels forever.

Tears fall,
The pain does not.

A witness of mourning,
I cannot feel your pain,
Just raise my fist —

In Anger,

At the cruelty of life;
The unfairness of death.

No explanation can I make,
Nor would I even try;

But,
If death could be traded for life,
Mine for hers;

I would.

    *Daniel P. Katz*

## Life

The restlessness in thy soul
The recklessness toward our goal
The coyness in our teasing ways
Fills life throughout the live long days.

The guiding stars don't lead by hand
Into any certain kind of land
But helps to find oneself inside
Toward the way you easily glide

Wisdom is not just in legions
That Pave the way in to being
Not only in the great Religions
But in the heart of seeing

Now the day is ending
and tiding now doth go
Into the shallow waters
Of the hell on earth below...

    *Betty Harrington*

## The Road to Memory

It's a long, long way
The road to the yesteryear
Filled with happy days
And sprinkled with many a tear
Climbing the heights to the mountains -
Deep in the vales of despair
Drinking the dew from life's fountains
Seeking release from all care,
It's a long, long road
And memories grow sweeter each day,
Share another's load
Tomorrow will soon be today.
Each stone a step to eternity,
Follow your guiding star
Building a pathway to memory
Viewing the past from afar
It's a long, long way
So build for tomorrow today,
And there'll always be
A road to memory.

    *Dorothy Blanchat Armour*

## The Rocking Chair

With the motion it shares,
The rocking chair is soothing.
Every creak of its bones heard,
Sounds the promise of companionship.
Comforting, during the Christmas moment,
As the Joys of Christmases are remem-
bered.

    *Brian Pankratz*

## Shadows

At night when the room shines bright
The shadows come alive

They dance, they yell,
They celebrate
Until the morning sun rises

They go back to the dark
Until the next night
When the moon shines bright
They rise.

    *Joshua Dempsey*

## Smiles

I sit and watch
The shadows creeping in.
The trees blackened by dusk
Against a purple sky.

As I sit in solitude
I think about the day.
I wonder if I've helped someone?
I've met along the way.

Did I lift somebody's spirits?
Some one feeling blue.
Did I send a cheery smile along?
To last the whole day through?

We all have many chances
To give our smiles away.
Who knows how much that smile might
mean?
To brighten some ones day?

So if you show your love for others
Then whatever else is true.
The smiles you gladly give away.
Will all return to you.

    *Irene Hiche*

## Mount Sinai Harbor

A winding road, a narrow path
The shoreline close on hand
The Indians proceed with careful steps
on this most God blessed land.

Nonowantuck or dried up stream,
Where fish and clams abound.
A patch of land, a shallow pond,
this fertile spot they found.

Now in it's place, a lighthouse stands,
that over looks The Sound
and guards this very special place
this still most sacred ground.

The lighthouse keeps a vigilance
so that we all may know
Time has not changed, this lovely place
where the Indians used to go.

    *James H. Roden Jr.*

## Isle of Evermore

The dune-land dreams beneath the sun,
The sighing shadows come and go;
From daylight dawn 'til daylight done
The shifting sand-hills fold and flow.

The restless waves roll in to shore
Defiant of a king's decree,
Who long ago said "Nevermore
Will the waters defy me!"

The king is dead long ages past,
That like his dust so his decree
Upon the singing wind was cast,
And up the strand creeps the sea.

The gulls come there to rest and brood-
You see them so with dreaming eyes
At the place where he once stood,
And then they go with haunting cries.

The cresting waves alone remain,
And forlorn fields beyond the strand;
The dunes, the waves, and the rain-
These, and the silent sifting sand.

*E. D. Ward*

## Untitled

When mute lips speak
the silence is loud
and nothing is left unsaid
I speak my mind
you only listen quietly
I want answers
but they are not yours to give
I own them
they can't escape the silence
there is comfort in it.

*Allison Merriman*

## The In-Between

The day lost all its splendor
The sky grew dark with gloom
The fog fell like a blanket
And the flowers wouldn't bloom
Life hid well in shadows
That curled in the mist
The world was dark and dreary
Clenched in sorrow's fist
The misery was endless
Fate in reaper's hand
time stood still and waited
For sunlight on the land
The night was cold and desolate
The earth a drift with sin
For this was just the in-between
Who knows where eternity begins?

*Bonnie Eskridge*

## I Ask the Question, Why?

Why Lord, Why me?
The answer comes back softly
It's not your place to question
It's your place to wait and see.
These are things that happen.
Every season.
And for everything that happens.
There's a reason
So put your love and faith in me
I'm always with you
You will see.

*Benyl Yates Wagner*

## Untitled

Today so grey
The sun slips away
The warmth is gone
And I am alone.

The breezes chill
the winds at will
Deep in my soul and I am alone.

Fighting the tears
Feeling the years
Without a home I am alone.

Just needing you
Will never do will you go away
Or will you stay.

Will it last long
Or has your love gone
Away with the sun
Are the days done.

Today is so grey the sun slips away
The warmth is gone
And I am alone.

*Janette Bernard*

## The Night

The moon shown brightly through
the trees, casting shadows from the
leaves.
    The wind blew gently in the night,
while stars twinkled far and bright.
    The crickets sing their deep sad
song, seeming glad the day is gone.
    And now my weary mind finds
peace, as all my earthly worries cease.
    God made this time for man to
rest, so with the night was man well
blessed.

*Doloros M. Considine*

## The Ecstasy of Diamonds

The profoundness of the Heavens.
    The twinkling of the stars.
The azure of the evening skies.
    The brilliancy of Mars.
In all are quite entrancing
    And perplexing to enhance,
For they all inspire
    An essence of romance.
Yet—there is an earthly object
    That delightfully enchants
Me in a selfsame fashion
    At a fleeting glance.
It's aura's fascinating
    Even to a King,
For even they aspire to
    The spell that diamonds bring.

*Don A. Alonso*

## Deliverance

A poem
Rises...
To truth
Delivers...
The obvious
Afraid...
To speak.

*Lisa Yim Heung Moy*

## Our Game

The crack of the bat,
The umpire's call,
Will we never hear those sounds at all?

Baseball! It's our national game,
The players and owners
are putting it to shame.

Some young fans may never see at all
A world series game of baseball.

Something must be done,
But what will it be?
And who will do it?
You or me?

I will tell you who can
A forgotten group called "The Fans"!

*Elie Rosenberg*

## A Soldier's War

The strangers met, found love, then wed.
The war grew near and threatening.
He had to leave with much regret.
She stayed behind. She paid the rent.

While he was gone the first babe came
The photos traveled 'cross great lands.
She hoped he'd see the sweetness there;
resemblance, family traits and all.

He'd kiss the image and dream of days
that he'd be home, and they'd be one.
He'd watch the moon in foreign skies
and knew it's glow would shine at home.

Then came the day, guns down, flags up!
The planes flew back to family grounds.
The parents met, knew love, and wept.
Their dreams fulfilled, their family whole.

He served his land, now had his life
to prosper as his dad before.
She had more babes and with each prayed
that their lives not be touched with war.

*Judith K. Cutway*

## "At Your Feet"

You can look at life, your life,
The way it is for now
And what it has become,
Or you can look into, your life!

Be careful not to peer, too deep,
At all you have done
Or who you have touched,
There may be secrets to keep!

A push or a shove, here and there,
To look away now and then
Or to tell a small white lie,
Who can say what is honest or fair?

What of those laws, we should live by,
Some are so grand to all
And some border on a line,
Then others are clear as the sky.

The rules of life are hidden deep,
You can look almost everywhere
And someday, your dawn may come
To the answers, which laid — at your feet!

*Donald J. Hall*

## Marriage Changes Everything

If things could stay
The way they were
Than life would be
A constant blur

Of butterflies
And starry eyes
And wings that soar
Through brilliant skies

Of notes and flowers
And quiet hours
And unraised voices
With love that showers

But it always ends
And we're just the same
As the others
Who have changed their name
*Alice Hall*

## The Fence

Beyond the fence
The world is expansive and
sometimes scary.

But within the fence
It is always scary and dead.

Through the fence
Sometimes there is pain, uncertainty,
and horrible lonely darkness.

But within the fence
There is no reality.

Through life's fences, not around them,
That is the biggest risk-
to be real and feel the pain.

But certainly when the end comes
It would be awful to never have been.
*Ellen M. Quigley*

## Alone

Alone, all alone.
The world seems so distant,
and so cold.

Alone, all alone.
No one hears me,
no one understands.

Alone, all alone.
Daring thoughts all around, tempt me.
Questions build in my mind.
Doubt and hopelessness surround me.

Alone, all alone.
What is this place I'm in now?
Where is the love?
Where is the joy?

Alone, all alone.
The rain falls silently as I sit here, all alone.
With no place to call my own.

Alone, all alone.
This darkness I'm in
is now my home.
*April Ferguson*

## Through The Eyes Of A Child

Through the eyes of a child,
the world should be viewed,

There would be no more violence,
or the world so askew.

Through the eyes of a child,
the world should be seen,

More trees would be planted,
more grass in deep green.

Less concrete..less building,
less hunger is seen.

Through the eyes of a child,
the world would be great,

There would be only love.
There would be no more hate.

Through the eyes of a child,
the world should be viewed.

It would not seem so old,
it would all seem brand new.

If we'd open our eyes
and see as they do.
*Cindy Foss*

## Autumn Leaves

The leaves are turning shades of red,
Their beauty thrilling me.
They seem so proud, upon the trees,
For all the world to see.

Basking in the sunshine,
Gaining beauty with each day,
Until at last they fall to earth;
The wind sweeps them away.

Then raked into a heaping pile,
For a child's happy leap.
A run, a jump, a giggle;
The child is waist-deep.

Then soon forgotten, turning brown,
They're swept away once more.
Leaves left crispy, dull and dry,
Not pretty like before.

But come spring, with weather warm,
Bright sunshine and wet rain,
The leaves will form upon the trees;
There's beauty once again!
*Donna McGullion*

## Message From The Heart

Strangers meet,
their eyes connect,
a fire starts within their hearts.

No one knows the reason why,
but love is started,
and starts to fly.

The message is clear,
no questions asked,
for love is a mystery from the past.
*Debra A. Brown*

## Tomorrow

Love is there
Then it's gone
But you know
Tomorrow
A new day will dawn.
It may hurt
This is true
But this will pass if
Given time to
Don't give up
You must go on
Tomorrow
A new day will dawn.
Love is not over
For you, oh no
If you have the courage
To go on until
Tomorrow.
*Brandon Lee Boutwell*

## The Music Of My Love

The music of my love lingers
then spans the gamut,
leaping lightly over
outstretched fingers
to encompass all the planet.

Present, past, future telescope
into the moment.  Tones
rise from despair to hope
then fall again -
suspended cosmic drones.

Does it matter if unrequited passion
dies each day?
a romantic strain
in blood-stirring fashion
revives the deluded dream play,

(and) like some spectral avatar
the image serves to mask the plain
and naked face: our star
carries us to joy and pain
in equal place.
*Dorothy Spafard Hull*

## Untitled

Don't call me a child
there is no name for me,
tired, desperate hope
that led the dying dream astray
and shaded ground
that we
forgot to cover
in the wake
of a rageless anger
and the exhaustion
that no sleep can cure
permeates
my very breath

Fragile bones
bound in the filth
of a yesterday
that I can't let go of.
*Jenn Zimmerman*

## Echoing Three

Laughing, dancing in the sun
There's always room for everyone
Tiny hands and tiny feet
Never fearing cold or heat
Curiosity killed the cat
Splashing water with a bat
Growing, showing life's a ball
Not a care or worry at all
Asking questions constantly
For life is but a mystery
Crushing crayons in the carpet
Mommy has to tell me stop it
No, no, no is what I say
When things don't seem to go my way
Echoing those who have gone before
Sitting quietly is a chore
Now it's time to take a nap
I'll sit upon my daddy's lap
It's not easy being three!

*Darcia Parham-Parks*

## There's Only One Me

You are something special
There's only one you and one me,
There's no carbon copy and
There never will be.

All of the hoopla, virus,
AIDS, nudity and sex.
It's a fleeting moment,
no meaning, but lust!
Not like a commitment,
love, sharing and trust.

You have a choice!
Picking your partner in life!
What will it be?
A person with no morals and respect
or one who saved his,
or her virginity.

To young people, life seems endless,
but in reality it flies by.
Do something constructive,
and to help others please try.

*Catherine Rasche*

## Little Women

Mischievous little women,
These four small friends of mine are;
Who indulge in soft whispers
And those tickling small girls talk.

Adorable and all charm,
They question me unguarded;
Startled, I find no answer
And which leaves me embarrassed.

Four cute, funny little girls,
Being with them is pure joy;
They make my day uplifting
I shan't ask the day to end.

*Jennifer Ann C. Aguilon*

## Tanka

A lonely lady
Searches for tomorrows in
Yesterdays mirrors
Cracks camouflage facial lines
Drawn at the dawn of the day.

*Michael Izzo*

## When I Close My Eyes Forever

Never more to roam
These rooms and halls
Never again to hear the calls
Of love or command

Never to smell a rose
Or pick a flower
For this old body
Will have no power

I'll say goodbye
To those I love
And go to the ones I've lost
Up in heaven above

I'll go home
To be with Him
My precious Savior
And my Friend

And I'll roam
The great halls
Of my Mansion fair
And limb the golden stairs

*Freida Arnold*

## Friends

Friends are cool
They are really nice
They help you a lot
And give you advice

Some are funny
Some are smart
Some are friendly
And all good in heart

You can make a friend
In school or at home
You can be a pen pal
Or call one on the phone

So if your home alone
Saying boo hoo hoo
Make a friend
A friend for you

*Christopher Novela*

## Winter Reflections

As you can see,
They are very powerful on me.
Winters soft light,
Shines all night.
It was that cold, cold.
Wintery night when that man said
"sold", "sold"!
That man he betrayed us as slaves,
Now I work hours, maybe, days.
With no food,
How could they be so crude?
On another cold night like that
a little girl died,
right by my side.
Don't be denied,
or washed away with the tide.
Fight for your right,
to be black or white!

*Jamie Lynn Miller*

## Thoughts

Thoughts are like opinions,
They are yours alone and
Each one of us are entitled
To them.

They can be deep thoughts,
Frivolous ones, maybe
Just a penny's worth,
But they belong only to you.

You can share one or all,
Only if you please,
With whomever you please.
They are yours alone.

*Bernadette Harris*

## Why Dreams?

Dreams are like wisps in the mind;
They clog the space and use up time.
No words, No substance,
No strength, No courage.

Why dream at all,
if only just to dream?
Why try to imagine,
those things yet unseen?

Because dreams speak out
for the wondering world;
And dreams take hold
of reality yet untold!

Dreams bring strength
to faltering conviction;
And unfailing courage
to otherwise hopeless faith!

why dreams you dare to ask?
Then dare to dream and ask again!

*John Brant Smith*

## Snowmen

Snowmen are special things
they have no halo or, any wings
standing there with eyes so black
are they really looking back
children build them while at play
when they are finished they run away
it's like they put him on a shelf
and left him there all by himself
then the sun comes out one day
so the snowman goes away
we shall miss his staring eyes
and think of him when a new snow flies.

*Doyce L. Bell*

## Someone Has to Paint the Stars

Someone has to paint the stars,
they are losing shape and color.
Someone has to paint the stars,
they make the people shutter.
Someone has to paint the stars,
because now they refuse to glitter.
Someone has to paint the stars,
they seem to be turning bitter.
Someone has to paint the stars,
they could use some sharpening too.
Someone has to paint the stars,
so that they shine for you.

*Christine Malkowski*

## A Special Message

People who take drugs are bad.
They hurt themselves and make
    families sad.

When taking drugs, they know not
    what they do
But ruin their lives, this is true.

They act weird and very strange.

Their minds become a batting range.

They lose all trust and all feelings.
They must stop and start the healing.

Why they do this, I know not why.
All they do is make their families cry.

So stay away, I know you can.
Just Say NO and be a better man.

*Anthony Vitolo*

## Answers

There are answers waiting for me
They lie beneath the sea
They wait undisturbed for my commitment
They wait so patiently

Or maybe a short dark barrel
That ends in red and gray
I could have all the answer then
If I commit to Judgement Day

Commitment is a hard thing to give
Especially for answers that I seek
I'm sure I'll finally give it though
But I think I'll wait until next week

*Deborah Morgan*

## How Do They Forget The Pain

How do they forget the pain, how.
They lose a game and they are sad,
but in two minutes they are laughing.
How do they forget the pain, how,
they get smashed into the boards
by some six foot gorilla
but they just get up and skate away.
How do they forget the pain, how.
They get hit in the foot with a
rocketing slap shot.
But they just keep playing like it
was a mosquito that landed on them.
How do they forget the pain, how.
They get hit in the stomach by a bully.
But they just laugh like it didn't hurt,
but you can tell they are hurting.
How do they forget the pain, how.

*Adam Sager*

## My Song To You

I am lonely and alone!
The world is not kind to
lonely souls.
Suddenly, from afar
the wind brought a refreshing,
cool breeze.
I unfolded my soul to the
palms, and confessed how
tired and weak I feel.
They embraced, and rocked me
in the stillness and rhythm
of a song.

*Helen Petrulli*

## Gone But For Awhile

I saw them in the distance
They run closer
As if out of a fog
They materialize
Two sons
My own
Their laughter and movements
Are like the sandpiper
Darting in and out
Knowing no evil
But I can only look
Not touch
For they are no longer mine
Was it pride or foolishness
That I lost them
I will never know
But in my heart and mind they will always
Remain
For they are of my blood
And that no one can deny

*Briggs Christian Morris-Smith*

## Pain of a Child

The clouds are moving in
They seem to becoming dark
I hear know sound
It's starting to rain
The rain is pouring down
It's getting darker and darker
How long will it last
I see the light shining through
The sun will shine
I'll wait for the rain to pour down
The sun will shine once again

*Cathy D. Offenberger*

## The Zoo

We're going on a field trip today.
They're bringing us to the zoo this
day.  Orange and Black lizards are
there, teacher has one in her
hair.  Humming birds sing a sweet song,
A monkey with a tail so long.
Ostrich run so fast
Hey!  That looks like a dinosaur
from the past.

Myna bird squawking away,
elephant eating fresh hay,
prairie dog digging under ground,
ocelot just hanging around.

Well, it's time to end this nice day
I hope we come back some time in May.

*Erin Young*

## 9-23-92

  Jaws wagging...
Poison spewing lips.
  Hands pointing
from...
  those should
point to.

*Leo G. Kelly*

## God

God is the best
thing to happen to anybody in
the world.

No matter what
he's always on
your side.

He loves you very
much.

He's my best friend
I ever knew!

God

*Jamie Cross*

## Answers

Is it I, that am abnormal
Things that seem so clear to me
I am but unfamiliar

Should it have been, could it be
I find myself searching
Yet I always wonder

The purpose of all is within
Sooner than later we must know
The reality behind our imagination

To some, it is so real
For few, it is untrue

Locked away with no place to go
Forcing others to remove disbelief

I am out, watching beyond
Knowing that it could be so real
Yet no one understands the truth
Or is it, that, I am not sure

It would be intriguing
Only to find out, the answers I await
Then the truth will be revealed

*Gerald T. Hylla*

## Untitled

Think of the good things
Think of the bad
Remember all the times
That you had

Remember the pleasures
Remember the pain
It will never be
The same

Think of the dream
And the wish
That you made

If you could
Do it again
Would go
Do it the same

*Greg Hammock*

## The Future - It Came

Right now is real -
This day, this hour, this minute.
But tomorrow will come;
then it will be only memories I feel
with every second in it.

The joy, the hope, the fear, the pain;
I'll live it.
But this I cannot explain:
How, suddenly it came.

*Brenda L. Gronstal*

## Flowers

When Earthly eyes no longer see
This planet's beauties as they be
For 'tis too late, that is the key
As earthly eyes no blossoms see.

Then loving friends should send to thee
Examples of this h'venly sea
While Earthly eyes can blossoms see
This planet's beauties as they be.

*Harriet Hoevet Bennett*

## Cigarettes

Lie filed in rows
thoughts cramped
one taken- missed for minutes
but memory over whelmed
with new room to move
each cancer takes its turn
my fiter
plucked from pack-placed between lips
feels the heat
as time ticks by
in high temperatures mind remembers
those before
regret not spending more time
knowing I'll follow
shrinking in smoke and ashes
drowning in flame and sadness
nothing left for farewell
my last puff taken-
I rest

*Dustin White*

## Mudslide In California

The mountain held
through decades of storm
   and earthquake

This year the tears could not stop
too many tears that could not stop
softening
softening the mountain
   undercutting

Crushing
breaking
it all came down
transforming the familiar landscape
   forever.

Thank God.

*Jamie Andress*

## Near Me

Help me as I struggle
Through my life today.
I know that you are near me
Even when I stray.

Help me in my weakness
Give me strength to follow your way.
I know that you are near me
Even when I stumble on the path.

Help me in my trials
Illuminate my path.
So I will know that you are near
Even when I feel trapped.

Help me in my goings
And comings in this world.
I know that you are near me
Especially when I pray.

Help me now to ponder
Your marvelous ways, O God.
I can feel you near me
Giving me peace in the storm.

*Carol Kruckenberg*

## "Aunt Matilda"

I knew about Matilda
Through out my whole life long
The epic of her dilema
The coming of her freedom like a song

Resting in the mountains of Virginia
She had her long and tiresome day
Toiling long in slavery's bondage
Until freedom come her way

With scars and marks from whipping
She glistened black as night
Her skin a cloak of servitude
On her face a whip mark for fright

Proof of her defiance and hate
At the condition of her kind
She disobeyed orders given
a bravery hard to find

This ancestor you know of now
I rejoice in knowing sure
besides the taste of whip and hate
She tasted freedom, sweet and pure

*Derek Brooks*

## Outreach

Symbiotic thoughts progress
Through tests of time and mind.
The total human empathy
Brings much to Humankind.

Some bright marks are made
By those whose paths are carved
Through life, their shadows
Ever seeking those they are to serve.

The moral thread that interweaves
Those folk who seek to know,
Sealing in infinity
Their restless souls to grow.

Always upward, ever reaching
To Perfection's core,
Open to each mystic chance
And wondering evermore.

*Gloria Vogel*

## Untitled

The white rippling waves,
crashing upon the gray rocks
have a peaceful sound.

*Lydia Evans*

## Driving Rain

Thump. Slide...
Thump. Slide...

Oil paths etched in red
Spread by the blade.
Laths of bloody grime
Behind frosted pane.

Crack. Rummmm...
Crack. Rummmm...

Bell bones vibrate
In time with the flash.
Atavistic fears well
Behind tired eyes.

Bump. Splash...
Bump. Splash...

Burning muscles untie
On intimate streets.
Warmth abides
Behind tight blinds.

*Deborah L. Finn*

## Oh! Lord

Inscribe upon my heart oh! Lord,
Thy word hidden in my heart;
Engrave it in so deeply,
That from thee I never part.

Fill me with thy spirit, Lord
Let me soar as eagles upon high,
Saturate me through and through,
So that my spirit never runneth dry.

Teach me thy ways oh! Lord,
Give me a mind such as thee;
That so to myself shall I cease
For like thee I long to be.

I will wait upon thee, oh! Lord,
Yet help me to be still;
So that I may hear that still
Small voice, bidding me to thy will.

*Diana J. Burgess*

## 'Tis

'Tis good
'Tis bad

'Tis joy
'Tis sad

This right
'Tis wrong

'Tis short
'Tis long

'Tis play
'Tis pay

'Tis life's way..............'Tis!

*Francis X. Murphy*

## It Could Have Been A Code Blue

I wanted to move from the city
to a place where
a rose is still a rose
and a waste plant a dump
so I went to the mountains
of North Carolina
but there I found
new neighbors
were lawyers and doctors
who fly little planes
on weekends
and one day
when I was
watering flowers
the hose wouldn't work
so the next door neighbor said
"You've developed
an aneurysm..."
and that's when
I moved back to the city.

*Barbara Falletta*

## Man of the Fort

Oh, minute man of the fort,
to be just like you!
Courageous, brave, and ready to run
when called on any que.

Even through the worst of fights,
he always has his pride.
Even through the worst of battles,
his determination never subsides.

His body is made of copper,
His pedestal of stone.
All around him people swarm,
Yet he is all alone.

Oh minute man of the fort.
To be just like you...
Unaware of time and events,
To be only a statue.

*Emily Morrison*

## Nebraska's "Sea of Red"

What a great sensation
To be number one in the nation!
When the Stadium fills
With that "Sea of Red"
And coach Osborne and team
Flood on the scene
True blue fans all seated and ready
Their great spirit and power...
Unbelievably steady.
What strength when Nebraskan's
As a team pull together
This bond is not matched
Anywhere...ever.
So lets hear it again,
For another big win.
Come on Nebraska
We will do it again!

*Darlene Reynoldson*

## A Baby's Smile

There's nothing like a baby's smile
To brighten up your day.
A smile so warm and full of love
To send you on your way.

There's nothing like a baby's smile
To let you know how much
Of the pleasure they can give to you
By their little kiss or touch.

There's nothing like a baby's smile
To make you feel so warm,
To make you count your blessings
for the day that they were born.

There's nothing like a baby's smile,
So cheery and so bright.
It makes you want to pick them up
and hold them very tight!

There nothing like a baby's smile,
Nothing on this earth.
It's the final bit of evidence
of the miracle of birth.

*Deborah L. Brim*

## Why

Why is it so hard
To express the feelings of the heart,
When things aren't said
And in reality it's hard to grow apart.

Why does love hurt
And can make you feel so sad,
Does all this loneliness
Make it feel that all things are bad.

Why does a heartache
Cause you so much pain,
And your eyes start to burn
Before tearfully they start to rain.

And why do I love you
I guess I truly don't know,
I just know that these feelings
Make me love you so.

And why do I miss you
Now that you have gone,
When all that I need
Is your love and a chance to belong.

*Danny Payne*

## Shots In The Night

You ever lay in bed listening
to people yell?  Soon or later
Someone is gonna get hurt cause of
Shots in the night.

Once a fight involves gangs,
who ever outside, might be the
one who gets hurt too.  So many
people:  Little ones, old ones and
babies that ain't even born could
be hurt by all of the ...
shots in the night.

Cause of all the fights, we
lose one person almost every
five minutes.  Many more plead
that they can live through the
pain of someone they lost due too...
shots in the night.

*Desiree Trobaugh*

## You Are Still My Friend

Must we lose what we love,
To know how much we love it.
It is always there now,
That absence, that awful absence.

Six years today, God took your hand.
And walked with him.
We know he will be safe and happy.
Until we meet again.

Since we laughed at a joke.
Since I felt your face.
Touched by your hand, my friend.
Or give you an embrace.

At twilight, when hour draws near.
And sunset flames the sky.
We think of you often.
And the happy days gone by.

Thoughts of you come drifting back,
With in our dreams to stay.
To know that you are resting.
When twilight ends the day.

*Evelyn T. Tallman*

## Reminiscences

I feel somebody's presence
to my close up
in my sweet dreams and fancies
whose love, care and warmth,
while sharing our ideas in the dreams
takes me off into the pure heaven
but a sudden scream opens
the eyes and mind
and there is nothing else
except an album of infallible
reminiscences
of the moments spent together.

*Depinder Paul*

## Untitled

Have you ever tried as hard as you can
To reach a goal just round the bend
As yet unseen but still in mind
You pull and tug and try to find
That cup joy that's just beyond
Your right to wish it could be won
And now its yours you smile inside
It's all that you hoped you're satisfied

*Bonnie M. Wilson*

## Friends

It gives me great pleasure
to make new friends,
just to hear them say
come back again.
Get on the bus and travel so far,
making new memories, while
wishing on a star.
New adventures and pleasures
to tease your mind.
We all become one of a kind
so pack your bags and get on the bus
we would love to have you
travel with us.

*Dorothy Crotts Callahan*

## Prayer For Grace

Lord give me the grace
  to see this new day through
Despite the many things
  that I've no gift to do
Help me not to count the
  awesome failures in my life
But rather to create upon
  the wondrous things I might
Be there to guide me in my stress
  when life looms dark and cold
And all my greatest efforts
  seem too frail to keep control
Then make me ever mindful
  of your every gift to me
That I might share them great or small
  with all who pass my way
So when this day is over
  as night consumes the sun
I'll know through grace I've tended all
  that's right that should be done

### *Eileen O'Brien Balger*

## Heart And Soul.........

From the bottom of my heart,
to the depths of my soul,
my love for you will always stand bold,
my love for you is higher than the sky,
my love for you will never die,
as long as the clouds produce snow,
my love for you, will continue to flow,
so bright, loving, and it's always true,
take my love and it will stay,
so warm and joyful until my last day,
my love for you is sweeter than honey
to a bee, it will always be true,
as long as fish swim in the sea,
in my life you play a very big part,
cause you live in my soul
and stay in my heart,
so whenever you're feeling down and blue,
just remember that I love you.

### *Cicely Matrice Reed*

## Leaves

From the sky the leaves are falling.
To the ground but not to die.
Mother Earth her arms enfolds them
Safely, gently lets them lie.

Softly sleep with rains calm voices,
Merge with ground to profit all.
Life to death to life unfolding
Go the loving leaves of fall.

### *Duane A. Chaffee*

## Arranged Unhappiness

Falling from the mountain,
to the peak I am blind.
Floating like moisture,
Waiting for its return.
Spinning and bouncing through the clouds
the sun shining through me,
Now tumbling in the snow,
It begins to rain.
Why can't I stand
And taste the rain.
The rain is not pure?

### *Antonio Crespo III*

## Voice of Reason

Who are you I cried out
To the voice
Within the wind

Why, I'm the voice of reason
And I've come to help you win

You've been down too long
You've become weak, no longer strong
You must resist your opposition

I think perhaps
You've grown somewhat fond
Of your unsuitably quiet disposition

So, I'm here to lift you up again
Upon your fragile, yet sturdy feet
I will not sit here idly by
And watch you bow down to defeat

For you are truly larger than life
This fact I guarantee
And once you're standing on your own
Like the wind
You shall be free!

### *Cynthia Lynn Dalton*

## Private Noise

The darkness of memories
Too deft to describe

In darkness
Where closeness
To bodies, to pillows
Takes me back

Tears form
Knocking me awake
Your silence jolted
By my private noise

When you ask why
I cannot say

But you can
Hold me, rock me
As I hug
The darkness

That brings me
Memories
Of early losses
Forgotten joys

### *Carolyn Weisz*

## Yes

Afraid to relent,
  too tired to fight -
wanting the untouchable,
  and resisting the opportunity.
His hands awaits,
  palms open, heart, too.
Kneeling before me, he's
  bold, yet kind.

Fearing the touch,
  and eager to grasp,
too tired to fight -
  afraid to relent,
my mind will not allow,
  but opportunity will.
His hands await
  palms open....
fearing the touch,
  I grasp.

### *Diana M. Colby*

## Too Young

Hot sultry summers,
Too young for work,
Too old for games in the street;

Reading the good books,
Classics they were,
Raising the doubts in young minds;

Salinger,... Steinbeck,
Sinclair,... Orwell,
Conrad, Huxley, and Fast;

Hot sultry summers,
Too young for work,
Too old for games in the street.

### *Harry T. Roman*

## The Tulip

Brightly beaming tulip bloom
tossing to a windy tune
rooted rainbow, shades of red
bobbing like a strung balloon

Waving in a windblown arc
near enough the next to knock
berry bouncing on its stem
keeping time both tick and tock

Calling come and play with me
tulip games to gladden thee
sing along my tulip song
you can pick the melody

### *Daniel Dombrowski Jr.*

## The Tempest

Rays of the sun
Touch me as fingers
The wind sweeps me
In a seductive dance
Dark eyes meet mine
A sweet smile
A kind word
And many thoughts of you
Deliver me Lord
From this loneliness
Deliver my beloved to me
A brush on the arm
A wink, a look
Dangerous feelings
Creep into the lonely
Crevices of my being
To yield my passion
Would be so nice
But I've been bought
And for a price

### *Faye Strange*

## Undying Souls

Forever working souls
Transferring from one to another
Transfixing spirits lightly
Hanging on to pieces of each life
Changing ever so slightly
Looking for redemption
In everyday lived
Never forgetting each other
Memories of a life before
Together as always
Loving each other more and more

### *Elizabeth C. Highley*

## The Circus

Circus tigers, lions and bears,
Trapeze artists, tight rope walkers.
The clowns!

Elephants, monkeys, and horses,
The music, the sparkling costumes.
Ice cream on a stick.

The laughter and applause,
Girls twirling on rings, juggling pins.
Soft drinks and popcorn.

Beauty and joy under the big top,
Bring us to memories of childhood.
Cotton candy.

The things dreams are made of.

*Arlene J. Johnson*

## Trees

Trees are green
Trees are tall
Some are lean
Some are small!
In the springtime
Trees are full
In the fall
Trees are dull!
In the winter
They are white
In the summer
They are bright!
So plant your seeds way down low
So in years to come they will grow!

*Christine Mazzello*

## The Camps 1944

I look through the window and I see..
Triangle sunsets,
The swirling wind,
Red angered trees,
Square black flowers,
Evil branches, twigs, scratch,
Scratch, scratch, blood.
Uncensored daffodils,
Hard concrete walls,
Unmerciful bars
Imprisoned forever
Bared down, tied down, tied up,
Suffocated. Confusion. Chaos.
And one tiny tear
rolling down a tender child's cheek.
He who has no hero, no hope.
He can't feel anything anymore
Out of control, No one to love
Gone in a tiny breath,
A candle blown out, forever, always.

*Daphna Milstein*

## Blood

Blood, it runs, runs, runs,
Through the body it flows.
It drips out of your body
when it finds an opening
as if searching a way out.
Trapped in for years,
running desperately through your body,
never to disappear, never to reappear
in your body.

*Brian London*

## Love

No one can
truly define love,
and yet within our
hearts are its words.
Love can be completely
beyond our grasp,
or right in front of us.
It lives somewhere
between calm and passion,
between clarity and
obscurity, and between
music and silence.
Love is a timeless
verse of truth
and passion-words
and thoughts from
deep within us all.

*Deborah J. Vine*

## Kelly

Two bodies lay naked
twined together
like a rope of life
The rope is long
with many knots
to be tied and untied
but the greatest knot
is the knot
that will never
come loose
the knot of eternity

*Joseph R. Hodapp Jr.*

## Love Is Music

Love is music
  Two hearts hear
The magical promise
  That each holds dear
The warming smile
  The tender touch
That glance that says
  "You mean so much"

Love is the joy
  That two hearts share
That makes each moment
  Precious and rare
It's comfortable silence
  And laughter too
Love is a dream that
  Has come true.

*Dawn Patnode*

## No Better Place

Did you ever jump
Up and down
Sinking nearly
To the ground?

Then jump back up
And stretch out flat
Landing softly
On your back?

Her words proved true
When Grandma said
"There's no better place
Than a feather bed."

*Dianne Cook Miller*

## Christmas at the Flynns

Are you replete, she asked?
Two sisters had performed all
  the tasks.
Provided all the food
  and amenities.
So beautiful, so kind-
  generous and caring.
Their home so clean and bright,
Their meal so delicious
  and peaceful.
All of it so close to my nest.

I, who have been so lonely,
  negative and afraid
Left their home with
  promises made
To myself - Uplifted!

You let me go with all
  good wishes.
I left you with all
  the dishes.

*Helen D. Dunn*

## The Trunk

In the attic by the iron bed,
under the rafters, I must duck my head.

There sets an old trunk,
rusting latches, missing handles.
The contents lying in shambles.

Inside . . . a woman's hand-made sweater,
which kept her warm in balmy weather.

A book of poems and pressed inside,
dried purple heather.
Also I see a pair of mens slippers,
in dark brown leather.

Next, a cigar box, holding within,
an antique "Cameo" pin.
And . . . wedding pictures,
taken of them.

I feel that I know them,
and with tears,
I quietly closed the lid.

*Carol Moniz Haskell*

## Untitled

Father, I am growing
up, I need a man in my life.
Where did you go? I bet you're lost
Time is passing us, reach me
The sun is setting, minutes falling
You can still lift me. I am yet a child
I can't build without you. Father
Am I not yours? I can't go back
You left me, never telling me who I was
Tell me, help me, No.
I don't need you. Who are you, old man?
I am your father
I was here all along.
You are my son, you are a nation
I need to talk to you and teach you
The sun is rising again, a new day
I have lifted you, remember
I have created you, go forth
Tell all my people, that they can never.
Become a parent without first becoming a
child!

*Joseph J. Abney*

## Death Rides Mad

Death rides mad
Upon our doorstep
Yet not the winner all.
Still hard and fast
The game does play.
Ravaging,
Taking toll the very spirit.
But unconquered
We resist with equal might
Against eternal fate,
For life a little longer.

*Eleanor Guerin*

## Winter Is Around

Snow is gently falling
  Upon the cold ground.
Winter is calling
  For its all around.

Slowly the leaves are dying
  Off the big bold trees.
Most of the birds are crying
  For they are without the bees.

As the weather goes cold
  And the ground turns white.
With snowmen standing big and bold
  Winter comes as a long cold night.

*Christi Gannott*

## Untitled

Roses are red,
Violets are blue.
But come to think of it,
That's not really true.

See-apples are red,
And cherries are too,
But violets are violet,
They're not really blue.

I've figured it out,
And there's just no denying it,
It's so awfully hard,
To rhyme things with violet.

*Cody Carter*

## Roundbelly Blues

Remember black in the day...
voluptuous breast
wide hips, thick thighs were in

Picasso saw it
I am full, I am round
I am every big bone pot bellied woman
that has ever walked this land

Images shift and change
my body breaks down
holds no more weight, 225 pound me
I don't eat, I devour

Then came twiggy
no breast, tight butt
slick thighs, skinny as a rail

Sometimes now I starve myself
day-in and day-out, I live in fear
haggard, frail all washed out
looking in the mirror I cry
it wasn't always like this

Remember back in the day...

*Gayle L. Fuhr*

## Color It Glorious

Morning found the lacy cloud
Waiting for the coming sun
To spread a tint of color, proud,
Upon it's self, that boasted none,
And make it shine in any crowd,
As the night was finally done.

For awhile, all cares were lifted,
While the sky was gently brushed,
And the darkness slowly drifted,
Showing pastels, soft and hushed,
Mixed with love and finely sifted
For a sky so shy, it blushed.

Now the vision has retreated,
Making way for the new dawn,
And we sighed as it receded,
Asking what this day will spawn,
Knowing we were royally treated
By those moments-too soon gone.

*Berdyne D. Travis*

## Wonders of Nature

Nature is all around us
Waiting to be explored.
The beauty of the trees,
the glistening of the seas,
are these the call of wonder?

We look upon a rose
with tenderness and care,
Wondering if some unearthly
Creature had put it there.

Nature isn't hiding, it's there
for all to see.
If we would take time out
to discover, the world would
brighter be.

*Cynthia M. Francis*

## Love

Heart swelling, practically bursting!
Wanting, lusting, eyes only for one.
Craved for, killed for, lied for,
  Died for.
Anticipation for your next moments
Alone, no matter how short, makes your
Heart pound frantically.
Starting, dreaming, imagining
Wanted, needed, yearning deeply
  Burning.
Sacrificing all for your one.
Blinding, deceiving, world in a
  Whirl.
Confusing, mind boggling
Unconsciousness
Suspicion, jealously, tragedy,
Unbelieving assumptions.
Accusing, raging, storming, yelling,
Dying inside.
Apologies, forgiveness it's all better now.

*Becky Hesson*

## The Nightmare Land

Foggy trees shake,
warlocks creep,
swamp sounds scream,
the little children sleep.

The cold wind blows,
over the land that nobody knows,
while the sun sinks low and deep,
the nightmare land.

*Jacqueline de Segonzac*

## Things Are Alive To Me

My rocking chair
was once a tree
that grew and blossomed
now it pleasures me.

My gloves of wool
that keep my fingers from the cold
once warmed a sheep
somewhere, I am told.

My cotton blouse
was once a plant
in view of butterfly and bee
and so it goes
things are alive to me.

*Joan Gordan*

## Time to Cherish

The days we shared, were the days I
  was so happy.
I just thank God, that you were always
  there with me.
Those days were so wonderful,
  we smiled and also frowned.
And like a wave, we had our ups
  and downs.
But to do what you did, must have
  been so hard.
Why didn't you come and talk,
  that's all you had to do.
Well my friend and also my love,
  I miss you so much, with all my heart.
And to my Lord,
  Please take care of the one I love.

*Crystal K. Robledo*

## To Awake at Night

To awake at night, and
watch you in dream state.
  To wonder if your heart
is in harmony with mine.
  To share the night with you
knowing this is not special, but
shared time.
  To see you resting and
unaware of life's relenting problems
in this state of unconsciousness.
  To know how lucky I am to
feel your presence next to mine.
  How untrue to say this time
is not special, for whenever we
are together, you are my world.

*Homer F. Sloan Jr.*

## The Slug

Overturned stones;
water is seeping
into the earth,
world of the creeping

The peaceful slug,
most unsightly beast;
its life doesn't matter
nor does its peace.

Sprinkle of salt
like a sorcerers spell,
burns the slug
and it starts to melt.

Too slow to flee;
to naive to know
the God-like whim
behind the acid snow.

It writhes and suffers
because of its look.
Its unsightly body
is now unsightly gook.

*Jason Chickneas*

## Hard Times

I know you are having problems
We all have our ups and downs
Just remember you can count on me
If you need me, I can be found

Don't look at the big picture
Take things day by day
Don't give up way too soon
Happiness comes to those who wait

Have faith in what your heart says
It knows you best
And always keep one thing in mind
Make yourself happy, above the rest

Although the situation is hard
And it's tearing you apart
Strength will come from those hard times
As the light shines through the dark

Never forget my thoughts to you
They are sincere with truth and love
And remember I'm always here
With prayer for you to the Lord above

*Genia Capps*

## Truth

Like actors in a play
We all wear our make-up and masks
We play out scenes with no scripts
Limited only by the scene itself
Along with our shields
We pretend we are free
Lying to ourselves
And patronizing others
We are true to the masks
And characters we portray
but what happens when
We have to take the mask off?

*Jenni Baldwin*

## My Friend, My Mother

Many are the times,
we both laughed and cried.
Openly we talked,
about girls and their guys.
Together we hoped.
Happily we tried.
Elopement was my wedding.
Remembering you is my pride.
With every rise,
and every fall.
You've been my friend,
my mother, through it all.

*Eleanor Rainey*

## What Is Our Love?

Our love is what
    we discovered.

Our love is what
we brought into
each others lives.

Our love is when
we discovered what
is meant to be.

What is meant
    to be?

Our love is meant
    to be.

*Jessica Frazier*

## Death Sneaks Upon You

Life is short
We live to eventually die
We all blossom at our own pace
Some wilting before others
To wilt is to be apprehensive
Scared of what's to come
We all have a time
Not specific
One that comes with the wind
Unexpectedly!

*Angela Durbano*

## Time

It passes us,
We waste it.
When we need it most,
We can't find it.

It's worth more than gold,
We admire it.
It's stronger than the bold,
Can't stop it.

It makes us meditate,
We need it.
It takes a toll on our lives,
Some hate it.

When we suffer the most,
We tire of it.
When our lives are spent,
We want more of it.

If you take some time
And think of it.
You might learn something
And get the most of it.

*Irbert Luis Vega*

## Alone and Well

Alone and well,
well, alone anyway.
Here I sit,
Here I think,
Here I cry.
Alone and lonely,
Devastation,
misery loves company.
Not my own, however,
on my own,
away from home.
Home is where the heart is.
Where is my heart?
Where is my home?
Here.
Where?
Where my soul lies to rest,
Alone and well.

*Deborah Starks*

## Unite

Dope dealers of America unite.
We're in for a hell-of-a-fight.
We can't be relaxing
If legalized they'll be taxing
Our dope - till its priced out of sight.
So put down your pistols, buy a pen.
Don't shoot write to your congressman
Tell them the facts - no taxes on crack.
Or we won't vote you in......next year.

*Alma J. Perkins*

## Shade, And A Still Rain

The old ways
Were simple,
They taught us to smoke,
But only if someone handed us
The cigarette

My ancestors were
Bitter,
They thought it wise to reap the land,
But through someone else's hands

This little rain is ivory,
The end of a tear's journey,
An elephant screaming

*Christopher J. Cellini*

## Makes A Difference

You debate, I debate
What a difference
we make

In a world of democrats
who likes to debate

Issues after issues
deciding which issue
opinion, opinions
yours or mine

Listen, listen
to our speakers

In the world of debate
we can make a difference

Open your mind
and your heart
Oh yes, we can make a difference

*Jane F. Roberts*

## Hands

Have you ever stopped to think,
What a pair of hands can tell,
Hands are such a give-away.....
Tiny, little, Baby hands,
They just speak of innocence.
Hands that heal, and hands that hurt,
Hands that work, and hands that won't.
Hands that damage, hands that mend,
Hands so ruthless, they can kill.
But, thankful be, for gentle hands,
Hands that comfort, and caress.
Hands, more eloquent than speech,
For, the silent messages they speak.
Hands, are such a give-away....

*Beatrice De Silva*

## Spring

I look around me and
    what do I see?
Beautiful Rhodies and Azaleas
    attracting the bees.
They soon will leave me
    until next spring,
So I've planted Petunias, Zinnias
    and other annual things.
My vegies are being kissed
    by the warm sun,
Awaiting nurturing rain
    that always comes.
I have my sunsets with
    colors God made,
Then off to bed relaxed
    as a Babe.
There's no other place I'd
    rather be seen
Than in the Northwest
    where it's lush and green.

*Jerrine Schoenberg*

## "Help"

I am a girl crippled and sad
what have I done Lord that could be so bad
I've been this way for many years
and in these years shed many tears,
to go outside just once to play
just to use my legs would be so free,
oh Lord here my plea!

*Cathy L. Dunham*

## Me, Myself and I

We pulled in all directions.
What me wanted to do myself said no.
And I couldn't agree with either.

Now I decided to run.
Yes, I'd run away from me and myself.
I'd show them, I said run away and think.

I ran, and ran I don't know how far;
Or where I was; or where I'd end up.
But if by magic a house appeared.
All shiny and new.  It beckoned, come in.
I went inside, and there I found
The answer.  Cool, calm, and serene.

Now me, myself and I live in harmony
With one another.  The answer is, love.

*Edythe B. Rains*

## The Great Power Of The Wind

The great power of the wind
What mighty force it can send
It can cause the trees to bend
Damage can take years to mend

Seems to come from way up high
Somewhere from beyond the sky
Man has watched with a great sigh
It has caused many to die

Oh what a powerful source
Way beyond man's reach of course
It has such controlling force
Just storms through with no remorse

Seems as though it had a goal
Came so quick and played its role
And we know down in our soul
It is out of our control

*Jennifer D. Sharpe*

## Indecision

What will I say if I meet her?
What will I say and what will I do?
I have been glib, with fear and hate,
Sorrow sleeps with me of late,
But love and I have been too shy,
Stammered a greeting and looked away
Quickened our step or moved aside
When she spoke my name, I never replied
Just turned my head and hurried by.
So what will I do if I meet her?
What will I do and what will I say?
Ask her to come and walk with me
See if she'll stay and talk with me
Tell her a story that's merry and bold
Or soft and sweet as the love-tale's told
Perhaps I will say, but what will I say?
And what will I do when she walks away?

*Charles J. Hackett*

## The Death Of Elwood Jones

'Twas on a warm September's day,
when Elwood Jones, he died.
Because he disobeyed his parents,
Their teachings he defied.

He skipped school to have some fun.
And with some pals a'swimming went.
The fun was great while it did last.
then came the accident.

Elwood went soaring through the air
From off a rocky bank.
He came down in a graceful curve,
And into the water he sank.

Beneath the water's flowing crest,
there lay a jagged stone.
He met the stone, full head-on
And crushed his cranium bone.

*James E. Burke*

## Untitled

No longer in control of the winds
We ride the breeze
Only sharing fragments of a heritage
To whom we please
Speaking from the wise man's spirit
I pray thee can learn to hear it

*George Henry Croff Jr.*

## The Tree

My tree of trees
when first we met,
I was a child
and saw it planted.

As I grew,
so did my tree,
supporting me in it's arms.

    (I called down to friends,
    not quite as brave -
    and eyed by Mom,
    "Be careful, please.")

Then came the time
to leave my tree.
I would be back,
and did return,
too old to climb
protected, still
within it's shade.

*Florence Rolle*

## True Love

True love is what I see in his eyes
When he talks and doesn't tell me lies
I know it's true when he's there for me
That's the only way I could see
That God has put us together
And I could only hope it's forever.

He makes me laugh, as you can see
Because I love him and he loves me.
We talk, and talk, and talk some more,
I think this is what true love is for.

The one that I truly love
Is the one I put above.
He's the only guy I see,
That's how I know he's right for me.

The only thing I think of
Is him, my true love
He probably only thinks of me too,
but I'm not sure if his love is true.
He treats me better than any other gal
But he also treats me like a pal.

But I love him and he loves me
That's what true love is you see.

*Joanna Patafio*

## The Dance of Dreams

Come and dance with me beloved one
When the darkness falls
For now my lover the day is done
And the one who loves you calls

Close your eyes and fly with me
To dance upon the moon
For what earthly care could there be
When our spirits together swoon

Your strong, yet gentle touch I miss
Having you only in dream's embrace
But still I feel your passionate kiss
And see your smiling face

Yes, come with me to dance
This dark and lovely night
In a shared dreamer's trance
Moving as one in the pale moon light

*Elizabeth S. Scott*

## I Dream the American Dream

I dream the American Dream
When I can make my mortgage
    payments on time,
And the new car that's parked
    outside it's mine.

I dream the American Dream
When I can afford the
    best medical care,
And little school children
have all their car free.

    I dream the American Dream
When I don't need a loan
    for my college tuition,
And my children can fulfill
    their life's ambition.

I dream the American Dream
When hatred in this country
    is swallowed up in love,
And America is again
    respected by all the world.

**Esther l. Seales**

## Ache

Why does it hurt so much
When I hear him talk to her.
Why do I want it to be me
When I know it would never work.
I chose to be alone;
I like being free;
It's important to be free;
Yet there's a bone marrow ache
To be a part of someone.
Why?...
Why am I not whole as I am?

**Betty Meyer**

## Heartache

I want you to believe me
when I tell you how I feel
and take away the wall of ice
You're using as s shield

I look at you and hope to see
The warmness in your face
Instead of warmness there
Icy daggers takes its place

You saw me look in your direction
You turned and walked away
I didn't let it bother me
There'll be another day

It takes a lot of love
to melt a frozen heart
I've loved you all your life
You knew that from the start

Think of all the love I have
take away the shield
be the kind of person
I've hoped someday you will

**Hattie Mitchell**

## Home Again

It is not easy to fall asleep
when the monsoon rains upon you.

I soar through the unforgiving bush
with eyes of trees upon me.

I pass the shadows of unborn souls
and step through the rain drops.

Then suddenly, I realize
the faceless shadows are me,
on their way to your house.

**David L. Metoyer**

## You Came Into My Life

You came into my life
when things were upside down,
Now you've rearranged all problems
and announced me queen with a crown.

You came into me life
and my view of the world has changed,
You brought my joy and happiness
and now my future is arranged.

You came into my life
and showed me how to love,
Now I soar through the air with freedom
and can fly as far as a dove.

You came into my life
and showed me how to love others,
I realize we are all united
as sisters and brothers.

You came into my life
showing me a rainbow of colors but blue,
Now I can say till the end of time
I owe my love and life to you.

**Bobbi Martin**

## The Run

In the heat
when you're beat
and your body wants to cheat.

In the rain
when you're strain
and the water hits your brain.

In the snow
then you know
that the cold has chapped your nose.

When your headache wants to pop
and your legs want to stop,
never ever drop.

When you've done your very best
then you may rest,
until the next
RUN

**Greggory Erick Gibbons**

## The Room

I walk into the room
You are the only one I see
The other people milling around
Mean nothing to me

**Marjorie C. Mahaney**

## Lament of Age

How strange the light,
    when youth turns to old.

The sun shines mellow,
    never quite as bold.

The moon reigns the soul,
    when it rises full.

The spirit rages,
    but the eyes are dull.

In the mind youth lives on.
    Memories of days gone by.
But the body is not willing,
    I wonder why.

How strange the light,
    when youth turns to old.

The heart beats ever warm,
    but the blood runs cold.

Remember me for what I was,
    forever young and strong.

Loving, caring; laughing, sharing,
    throughout my whole life long.

**Charlene Madison**

## My Tree

There was a place I used to go,
Where a lively oak tree used to grow,
With fields of grass around;
Where other trees are found,
But none were as pretty as my tree.

I climbed a lot of trees back then,
And there were a lot of places I had been,
With neon lights all around,
And other places to be found,
But none were so peaceful as my tree.

I sat amidst the branches thick,
My tree was never ever sick
Of me and my prancing around.
There are so many joys to be found,
In the heart and the life of my tree.

I ran to my tree for comfort,
In mid-winter and the middle of summer,
And my tree was always around,
But, today, I looked and I found,
That reality had chopped down my tree.

**Elizabeth Waddle**

## Virgin Voyage

Along the banks of a silent stream
Where stones and sandbags lay
Prevent erosion in the fall
Which rain would wash away

A Mallard hen camouflaged
Amidst green grass and stone
Makes her nest in a hollow niche
With her down she plucked alone

She tends her eggs within her nest
Soon yellow ducklings squawking
They'll waddle down to the waters edge
And into the water plopping

**Jean Wilcox**

451

## Aging

Who is she?
Where did she come from?
Have you seen her before?

There - in the mirror -
Deep in the image,
Staring out from within -
Look beyond the gray
And the lines of age.

Could there be someone
You once knew
Staring out at you?

Not so, not so!
That old hag in there
Is not anyone I've known before!

She's just an old scold
With some troubling words:

"While you were gone,
Time in its flight
Made off with your youth
And left you this sight"!

*Frances Richmond*

## A Secret Place

I have a place inside of me,
Where I go now, and then.
To meet once more with those
I love.

I think of them, and they are there,
All laughter and good cheer
The warmth I feel, can only be
Their love.

And so although, this place is far,
And difficult to find,

It's there I know, and so are they,
The best of all my kind.

*Henry J. Meyers*

## Land of the Leprechaun

Deep in a clear cool forest
Where the grass is always green
There lives a very large family
Most people have never seen.

You've got to believe to see them
It's where the four-leaf clovers grow
And tiny "good luck" red mushrooms
It makes a fantastic show.

I was invited to visit them
What a wonderful sight to see
Among the clover, mushrooms and flowers
They romped and frolicked with glee.

Deep in this mysterious forest
Lives a king whose name is Sean
He's been their king for many years
It's in the land of the Leprechaun.

When it was time for me to leave
He told me I could take one little tyke
I picked out the one I wanted.
And I named him Little Mike.

*Colleen Scheiman*

## The View

Majestic is the viewing
Where wanting eagles fly
Where rivers run forever
And mountains meet the sky

The presence of a freedom
Death cannot take away
The joy of the beholder
Is fulfilled beyond today

The draping of a beauty
That we all hold so dear
So precious and preserving
To a dream so very near

You see the rays of sunshine
The tall and mighty trees
The chasing of the shadows
By the early morning breeze

How beautiful is this picture
I view so bright and clear
It looks so very far away
And yet it seems so very near.

*Earl Birlew*

## Thoughts Runnin Thru My Head

I'm tired! My bones ache!
Where's my energy?
Work fourteen hours a day
Just to meet the rent I pay
Got a mind and body
Of a twenty year old
Yet, I feel forty.

Guess I got some nerve expecting
A helping hand to pull me up
A nice easy ride
So that I can close my eyes
Just for a second.

Or a friendly gesture
From a strange face.
And dare to think of
A man's, big strong hands
To rub my back and say to me
"Everything's gonna be alright."

Dream on lady, dream on
One day you'll see the light.

*Donna Mason*

## My Prayer

Once a prayer is uttered
Whether aloud or in the heart
It acts just like a pebble
Dropped in a pool so dark.
The little waves increase in size
And keep the pool in motion,
Spreading blessings on their way
And whispering of devotion,
Even when they reach the shore
Their message is not spent
For earth absorbs their impact
And nourishes the blessing sent.

*Donna B. Jones*

## Love

One thing in this world
Which is the greatest thing
That could never end
And nothing comes between

That four letter word
Which makes you real nervous
Once it is said
You forget the whole purpose

Memories that are left behind
Was it worth all the pain
At least it was once real
Now nothing remains

It's all for the better
I believe that is true
Maybe I'll find somebody
Someone like you

*Carol Kirk*

## Life

Who's to say,
Which way should I choose.
It's up to me,
If I succeed or loose.
Why do you worry?
Why do you cry?
I'm not a little girl!
I'm grown now and will try!
Before we both die!

*Betty Schlick*

## Untitled

A swaying tree is brought to silence,
while a newborn child has broken through.
The silence broken, the mighty angered.
To trouble he for a minor cliche
then what about an uproar.
Is this the way it was meant to be,
the trouble and the hate?
Was this planned, step by step as
a toddler's day or was it just
a sketch?
To all who fret and wonder, yes
this is the way 'twas planned!
For if it weren't would joyous live.

*Emily Berks*

## The White Kaleidoscope

My kaleidoscope became
White as a sheet,
And died of shame,
When all her colours faded.

She passed on, as a
Rainbow in a dream,
And was reborn, at
Sunrise in a cloudless sky.

Then over seas of
Many shades of blue;
Over fields of green,
Beaches of white sand;
Over neon cities, on and on
She drifted, shouting
For her mother,
Aurora Borealis.

*Altamont A. Mills*

## Cat And Canary

I once had a bird called wing.
Who all day loved to sing,
Until his cage was open,
Which the cat was hopin'
Now "wing" can no longer swing.

*Bella Wein*

## Sonnets of the Cow

If I were a bovine beauty,
Who lazed upon the hill,
Wouldst thou love me truly?
Or wouldst thou love me nil?

If I were a bovine beauty,
Would you be mooing over me?
Would you leave me in the pasture,
Or sail steerage out to sea?

If I were bovine beauty,
Would you love me for my worth?
Would you love me for my assets?
Or love me for my girth?

Oh, to be a bovine beauty
A cow can only dream,
That one day I might grow up,
To be the Dairy Queen.

*Debbie Roth*

## A Little Birdie

There is a little birdie
Who sits on the twig and sings
The song whenever he sees me
Walking down the street.

I say to him "My little friend,
What kind of song you sing?"
And here is what he has to say
"It is a love song you love to hear."

So, I am walking down the street
waiting to hear my friend to sing,
walking faster and wondering where
is the birdie who sings so sweet.

There is my friend with another bird
they sing the love song for me,
I say to him "My little friend
who is the other bird who sings so sweet?"

And here is what he has to say "this is my
wife I love her so,
we are married and flying away and never
again to come back."

When I walk by the place I love I miss my
birdie's singing,
I wish him luck and a lot of love with his
wife he just married.

*Hedy Wolf Formanek*

## The Search

There came a time in my life
When I had to take a look
At who I was and what I've done
and where I wanted to go.

The search lead within my soul
To find the real me
And coax her out to merge her life
With all the rest of me.

*Carol Wolf*

## Native Americans

Native American are all people
 who've been born here
No matter what race or color
 we must stand up for America
And up hold our heritage that's
 our forefathers left us in
Building up our american heritage
 that's stood for over 200 years
As men fought and died to keep
 we must not let America down
As we're proud and brave Americans

*Irene Mary Larson*

## "Love, Damned Love"

Damn you, Love, where do you come from
why do we fall in your trance
everywhere I turn, there you are
How do I flee from your chains
why must you aim your arrows at us

Damn you, Love, I run from you
yet you follow you holler my name,
I pretend not to hear

Damn you, Love, can you leave me alone
for once, I wish to die
to die and never hear of you
So I do, I fall to my grave and rest
For then, death has taken his toll

Damn you, Love, you cause nothing but,
pain... misery... jealousy
A tear trickles down, I look back and see
people, filled with sorrow
because of you, Love, but yet, I too

*Eric Kaika*

## Inheriting Secrets

The pain I've felt
will die thereafter,
To him I knelt,
I'm born a bastard.

In all my life
I've never felt love,
past's dark demon's fly
casting shadows above.

Shunned from reality
a curse from the starts.
My emotional frailty
brings pain to my heart.

All of pasts lies
have now been brought forth.
My life long cries
have shown what life's worth.

One touch from the knife
as the blood trickles down,
an end to my life
my pain is now gone.

*Chris Schnee*

## Inflection/Retrospection

If I look into your eyes,
Will I go blind from the hatred I see?
Or will you mesmerize me,
And leave me cold?

If I look into your heart,
What will I find there?
Fire or stone, Marrow or bone?

If I dare love you,
Can you love me in return?
These questions, in my mind burn,
Because my heart you already have.

*Cindy Richardson*

## Old Fashioned America

Only in the Country
Will you get to see
Old fashioned America
As it use to be.

Just like Tom Sawyer
And Huckleberry Finn
When you step back in time
To how it must of been

Railroad tracks and trains
Running through town
Hobo's still jumping off
To take a look around

Things haven't changed much
And people don't care
They like it as it is
And aren't moving anywhere

Progress is for others
With their itchy feet
But people in the Country
Like shopping on Main Street!

*Adeline Fleischer*

## Whispering Souls

Souls begin to whisper,
winds begin to blow.
Lord, I really miss her,
and God you only know.
The trees will shed their leaves,
and wheels will keep on turning,
As her spirit flows in the breeze,
her soul will still be burning.
Every whisper heard,
means your soul is churning.
These whispers that I hear,
means the wheels are turning.
And Lord, you know each time
I hear a whisper,
I think of April, Lord how I miss her.

*Connie Sue Bake*

## Untitled

The love we give to children,
Will be multiplied in heaven.
For there is no greater love on earth
Than we give to our own brethren.

Let us not be so forgetful,
That one day we'll be regretful
Of the love we didn't give,
To those loved ones that we grieve.

*Jesse Castillo*

## Untitled

Sitting in a rocking chair
Winnie-the-pooh's there
Wishing for a care bear
With all my heart

Thinking that all war
Is a complete bore
Wishing that I can soar
Like an eagle

Something's wrong with the atmosphere
It is something that's not clear
It is something that you can't hear
With all your might

**Alexcia Reynolds**

## A Valley View

On a cool fall morning
　With a sky sparse of clouds
There's a valley of beauty
　Behind a low hazy shroud.
My eyes cannot focus
　On all that's before me,
Allowing my mind
　To enhance what I see,
A steeple extends
　Above the fog cloud,
A bell beckons all
　With tones soft and loud.
Inside there is peace
　With kind people and love,
An extension of grace
　From our GOD above.
A drive in the country
　Through the beautiful hills,
Gives one an assurance
　And a comforting thrill.

**Gary K. Connell**

## When Winter Is Here

The leaves on the ground
with falling snow
making a crunching sound
is the way it goes

The geese going south
flying high and vast
having no food in their mouth
cause they're on a fast

The trees are blowing
with the hard wind
the snow is slowing
while the trees bend

The children come out
playing in heavy snow
running all about
is the way it goes

As he finishes out his mission
nothing is heard
everyone is out of commission
even a bird

**Jason Weaver**

## You

The dark encircled me
with its whispers last night.
Your name echoed
through the cosmos;
a call to fatal love.
We met in the ether
...somewhere.
Was it Venus? Jupiter?
Or just a distant moon?
We embraced...
and the forces of our natures met,
intertwined, and triggered
the explosion—
a joyful noise,
heard throughout the heavens—
making the gods
... smile.

**Arvid Knudsen**

## My Body

Sacred temple that God creates
With millions of details
Incredible machine that elevates
The blood through my head and heals.

My arms, my legs, my head, my heart.
All of them are treasures
That would be difficult to replace.

I wonder as a time goes by,
What my body will be
And silently ask my God
For strength that my body needs
To walk these paths, and reach my dreams

Enjoy the song of the birds
Face up to the sky,
And let the hope fly
That diseases will delay

The fragility of my bones
I want to retard,
Please God, help me,
Help me to go that far.

**Amelia Gomez**

## The Robe

Perfect and flawless
With no visual seam
Holy and sinless
He came to redeem

Lots were cast
Unable to divide
His words would last
Not the wound in His side

Cursed by the cloth
Blessed by His death
Loudly they scoffed
While His loved ones wept.

A garment of red
The dice fell for that day
An army now dead
Their bones gone away.

Holy and sinless
He still remains
Perfect and flawless
in eternity reigns.

**Betsy Tar**

## Who Could Know

I didn't know hearts could break
with such an ache.
I didn't know I'd be left at home
all alone.
We were so happy back in 1951
when God made us one.
We said, "til death do us part"
but that was at the start.
Who could know
the time would fly by so.
The two girls were such a joy
even though we didn't have a boy.
There were many ups and downs,
many smiles and many frowns.
He was always there when I needed him
but now my eyes grow dim
for tears get in the way.
"But it will get better", they say
and some day I'll meet him at the pearly gate
where he waits.

**Carol Brookins**

## House Of None

To the House Of None
With sun and moon of blood.
Fighting off the demons haunt,
Living without love.

Not bright nor dark,
But a perfect shade of gray.
It doesn't strain your eyes or heart,
At night or in the day.

I left this place of grace,
To look for hearts so pure.
Dankness raped my eyes of cause,
And color loved to blur.

Evil is the world to be,
And in it, chaos rules.
Never leave your House Of None,
To be amongst those fools.

Here is where my soul stays,
And here I shall relate.
Here I am the god of time,
Staring unto fate.

**Jared Perrine**

## God's World

I walk in God's world
With the kiss of His breeze
On my cheeks,
The warmth of His sun
On my head,
The blue of His sky
Above me
With white fluffy clouds
Floating through.

I feel like a princess
Lovely and loved,
When I walk so.
The cares that would
Bind me to earth
pass away,
And I am as happy
as a child once more;

When I walk so
In God's world.

**Eva J. Knopp**

## Lyrics from the Dance of My Soul

Acquaint the practical mind
with the natural given senses.
Shed the mental images implanted
by mother's protective pretenses.

As the mystical lyrical poetries
of my mind sing;
I feel the notes of the blue bird,
the wind chime gently rings.

Ever present the perceptive voice
relays an urgent message:
Let truth pour forth, from
the magical soul, of a
life in time passages

*Joann Bohannon*

## Footprints

The footprints were filled
With the tears of the sea.
Tears that quenched the fire
That burned within her soul.
As the icy fingers reach out,
They consume the fragments
Of her remaining sorrow
And the sunken treasure below.

She was an open vessel
And the storms of life
Beat her beauty down.
The waves crushed her soul
Removing the tormenting pain.
The footprints in the sand
Only tell that she is now among
The sunken treasure below.

*Cynthia S. Aslaner*

## Morning Thought

I laid awake this morning
With you by my side

And as I watched you slumber
A tear came to my eye

I thought about the day we met
And the joy you brought to me

And I wondered just how long
This joy was meant to be

You gave to me happiness
A love I cherish so

You swept away the loneliness
That I use to know

And as I laid there thinking
Just what you mean to me

You turned and while still asleep
Embraced me tenderly

I held you close this morning
I whispered I love you

And although you didn't say it
You said you loved me too

*Florian Antczak*

## Lost Love

Oh! that I could great each dawn
With zestful feeling through
My empty shell; to rise and conquer
Some new horizons, or delve into
The dragonfire of hell
That rides the crest of human pawn,
And stalks the ravaged spirit; though
Once filled with some illustrious
Goal from which Fate saw fit
To crush and fell.
But, Taunting memories of days spent
In blissful, sweet content,
Forever plague my depth, and all
Beyond is banished from my view.
So, 'til I am again with you,
And feel the tender warmth and glow
Within your strong and bold embrace
I'll wait in hope to soon behold
Your sweet and loving face,
To kiss and tell

*Jean E. Sedar*

## Platonic Love

She was the lovely vista
    Within his trance
Where she flowed her tableau
    In feathery dance,

Appearing like a vision
    In midnight lace
Arraying every passion
    With silhouette grace,

But, as night began to fall
    Around his heart,
He fondled her comely beauty
    Only in his art.

*Gus Wilhelmy*

## Swale

As a race horse Swale was swell!
Won two thirds of the Triple Crown.
Worth millions, they said.
Forty to be exact.
A stud that never stood,
but should have.
A horse that ran fast,
but not the fastest.
A colt that never stopped:
just
dropped
dead!

Now his heart, his hoofs, and his head
are buried in Kentucky.
Making the grass bluer.

*June Wilson*

## Life

It's not a game
It's reality
It's not a game of cards
  or
A game of chess
It's life

*Dudley*

## Early Backwood Farms

Fedid air, a fireplace smoulder
    wood ash over all;
Dirty windows grimly floors, old
    newspaper cover the walls.
Smoke bedims each shadowed chamber
    hanging rank and stale;
Clutter, coughing, and children crying,
    want and need prevail.
Year after year they struggle
    until a backwood grave;
In their own cherished dirt
    claimed the agrarian slave.

*Edward E. Storms*

## Mountain Man Love

A mountain man coughed his life away
Working down in an old coal mine
Hardly any money, just barely getting by,
Had two kids, his wife is dying slow.
Everyday was another day of labor,
Shovelin' all that coal.
His house ain't worth a nothin';
Though he built it with his own hands,
The worthless life of a mountain man.
Although he died six years ago,
His undying love haunts the town.
Why he didn't show it,
When he was alive,
No one will ever know.
Now all that we see
Is a fading shadow,
Where the mountain man should stand.
The widow cries in silence
For she is just a mourning mortal,
Love is the only cure.

*Eva James*

## Mom's Curls

Two little curls, cute as they could be,
wound themselves about the
temple of thee.
One faced the right, the other to left
encircling, caressing, whimsically.

Foolish vanities displaced their set;
never did their essence
change — stubbornly.
Vibrant locks dazzled, isolated
aspects of their person, passionately.

Yet the curls continued tickling,
tricking, playing hard
to tame, glibly,
Communicating their differences,
enhancing woman innocently.

Be not preoccupied with the wave,
the style, the look, the do.
Curls are only hair forever changing,
challenging to you.
Gently guide the strands, tendrily...
Beautiful you!

*Barbara Palmer*

## Love

Glowing hearts
Yearning to collide,
Responsible love
We need not hide.

Embers of desire
Trickling through,
Romantic love
That's me and you.

Iridescent longing
For all to see,
Mutual love
How close can you be?

Chastised love
Leaves much sorrow,
Contained love
Grows not tomorrow.

Compatible feelings
Hard to sever,
Ageless love
Lasts forever!

*Carolis A. Shropshire*

## I Couldn't Love You More

We don't have lots of money.
Yes, at times we barely get by.
Stumbling through the piling bills,
I glanced at you and sigh!

You wear that look of helplessness;
that bleeds my heart to the core.
And it's time like these I realize,
I couldn't love you more!

I'll never have pearls and diamonds,
or gowns of satin and lace,
but in the laws of love and passion,
my riches cannot be replaced!

The warmth of your eyes penetrates me.
A touch from your hand so secure.
Your breath on my neck tantalizing.
Soft whispers your lips reassure.

We may never require a status,
or financially even the score.
but we tread the calmest waters,
of what is ideal and pure.

*Jennifer Young*

## Many Things

I am a human
yes I am
an island that is small
while all else is tall
a bird trapped in a tree
with a broken wing, let me be
a cheetah running fast
far, far from the past
a dolphin jumping high
just to reach the blue sky
the ticks very slowly
where the place might be snowy
when the sun warms
the snow will swarm
the drop on a leaf
sitting their in grief
the reflections of the untold
will be their for you to hold
one of these I may be
but myself I am meant to be

*Jose Alvarez*

## Life

You reach to touch a flaming star
Yet are not tall enough.
You stoop to pick a budding flower
yet are not small enough.

You strain to lift a rock-bound weight
yet have not strength to do it.
You see the light beyond the gate
but will not enter through it.

You follow roads that lead you on
to pointless wastes of time.
The hills o'r which you should have gone
you bother not to climb.

You upwards look to find the sun
yet close your eyes to light.
A course of life you hoped to run
yet lose your way in flight.

*Erika A. Ganswith*

## Cassandra's Tummy

Sandra is my baby
Yet every day she bothers me
Waking up and hollering
"I'm still hungry" can't you see

I feed her every morning
There's lunch and dinner too
Yet she keeps on pressing me
"I'm still hungry aren't you"

So snacks and fruit I give her
Two or three she'll eat you see
Yet shortly thereafter
That kid will pressure me

"I'm still hungry, grandmother"
Won't you please come and give me
Food for my big tummy
It won't fill up, can't you see

What can I do to help her
Fill that tummy, won't you please
Provide to me a remedy
To quell her roaring pleas.

*Geri D. Collier*

## Yesterdays Tomorrow

We're dreaming of tomorrow
Yet what about today
Wasting precious time
Just dreaming life away

Yet, yesterday is gone
And tomorrows a new day
Hoping that it's better
And someone will show the way

It used to seem so easy
We had time to waste away
Dreaming of the future
Yet forgetting about today

Because we feel so young
And life seems so long
That yesterdays tomorrows
Are already done and gone

So we need not stop dreaming
And live a solemn way
Just let's not give tomorrow
What we can have today

*Jerome M. Witt*

## If There Is Ever A Chance

If there is ever a chance
    You and I should meet
Under a different circumstance,
    Then I'd know for sure
We would be meant to be together.

On the day the wind
    Brings you to me
And knowing we were
    Finally meant to be,
Our love would last forever.

For now, I must let you go,
    But always remember even
Though pictures are nice to have,
    They can never replace the
Wonderful memories two
    People have shared a time ago.

*Jason Davidson*

## Gift

A gift is something
you appreciate.
Given freely, nothing
to negate.

Love is unconditioned.
It's supplied, not petitioned.

Through time we will
be with each other,
and not each others possession.

*Jane E. Wunderlich*

## My Daughter

You are my daughter,
You are my Child,
And I love you every day,
We've been through the storm
And through the rain,
But we have sun shining days.
A mother's love is special,
It should nourish and show you the way.
Its hurts my heart sometimes, my child,
When you go astray.
I dried your eyes when you cried,
And asked, "Momma, why must this be?"
But through it all I'm overjoyed,
Because God gave you to me.

Mom

*Irene Young*

## Untitled

On December the 7,
You went to heaven,

Even though you lived in California,
Everyone will still mourn ya.

You did a lot,
since you were a tot.

You were always in the mood
to cook lots of food.

The last time you were here,
you loved us so dear.

We will never forget
the last time we met.
Good Bye Chuck!

*Janice Ruhl*

## Our World, My World

I have wrapped myself around your world , losing sight of its
velocity. I bow head, as I can longer up with your rapidly.

How was my encounter, I do not know, for it raised to touch me, and
has succeeded to turn my world upside down. What is it worth?

I am no longer the sparkle in your eyes, as you preceded to more
until you find own star. When did the fire of passion leave our comfortable space?

I does not make sense, why start off as two and move on as one,
why start at all is my question. If I could have a chance, I
would change things, but change what, shy and how?

Our world is no longer a union, it is parting , it is disappearing...
was I kidding myself? Did I ever hear your whisper through the wind,
did I ever experience the brilliance of your soul, or did I just
imagine your immaculate in the light of the moon?

There was no world, I wanted one, but there was truly none.

Perhaps, as we part I should unravel my secret: I was wrapped
myself around your world, trying to find my own. Yet I was unsuccessful.

As I struggled to hold you, I pushed you farther. Now your departure
makes my world empty and abandoned. If I could whisper my last wish,
it would be have a chance to hear the echoing sound of your name.

*Elvanelga C. Isenia*

## The Night Is Upon Us

Switchblade in my pocket I wander the
street, carefully picking out my next victim.
But so hard to grasp, so far, I cannot reach
it.

I need it
I live on it
And with switchblade in hand I can reach it
I see him, the man the life force of my world.
I pull the jagged weapon out of my tattered
Trench coat.
Pulling over my head about to strike.
Someone screams and a bullets is heard
Through the night piercing like the
Switchblade.

*James M. Parker Jr.*

## She Is

She is female by definition, feminine in nature, color is true
Womanly qualities or characteristics that she could never lose
A state of being with a state of mind collective in thought, body, and
    soul, and even in time.
She is gentle, soft, delicate, and intriguing by the way that she moves.
All the earth is held silent, for she is soothing like an earthy jazz jazz groove.

With her eyes as bright as moon drops on a late summer's night
Lips as soft as a baby's touch, she'll love you with all her might
Her heart speaks in words that only the strongest man can understand
While her tenderness can tell a story on its own
It is written in the palm of her hands.

She can make your darkness turn to light and the coldest wind keep you
    warm through the night.
She is silky like chocolate and smooth like honey till all of her
    thoughts and aspirations flow like a calm river after the storm.
One look, and she will take your breath away,
Yet a stare will leave you speechless....

What a man would not do for her, for her spirit is wild and free,
Untaming and somewhat fierce... Yes fiercely free.
Walk beside her and find that her kind of love will keep you safe
    through the wildest storm.
It has never felt quite like this before.
Give her every drop of strength you have and she will give you more in return.
For all that she is, she is above all things a woman.
Naturally, she is.

*Archuleta A. Jackson*

## Walk On 'Till You See the Sun

We believe in you and
You are only one
To lift your spirit
Brighten your way
For each day of the year
Brings new hope in our hearts
For peace will mark the celebration
Of a unified people
A testimonial to the endurance
Of spirit walk on
The thought of God
Warms our hearts
And will bring peace
United, one for all
And all for one
God bless america
Walk on till you see
The sun up above
For every cloud has a golden lining

*Fran Krengel*

## "Death"

You have no aroma,
You cannot be seen.
Some think you're wonderful,
But others think you're cruel and mean,
The way you just grab someone,
And take them to your world.
You give us no warnings,
Or any clues.
You tear apart families,
And destroy friends and communities.
But whenever you take someone out,
You bring someone new in.

*Jolene Huelsenbeck*

## Caught in the Web

Your body sticks to the web
You just can't seem to move
Your energy is paralyzed
Stop and realize
Free yourself
Be optimistic, take action
Don't remain
Caught in the web.
(St. Albans, WV)

*Judy A. Cunningham*

## Explorer

Ever so smoothly and artfully
    you waltzed past all my defenses
Penetrating deep into the
    very center of my being.
Exposing me, the real me,
    the me that even I never knew.

Amazing, exciting and terrifying
    to suddenly feel.
Again? No, for the first time
Places in my heart that
    have been numb forever.
Emotions previously denied existence.

Wondrously divine and precious
    the gift of true love,
that binds us together in intimacy
    beyond comprehension.
Meant only to be experienced
    and enjoyed!

*Cynthia Pawl*

## A Precious Child

A special little baby boy, whose life it
seem was not going to be.
He was sent upon this earth, not knowing
he was meant for me.
Birth I did not give him, but God had
already made a decision then.
I was told he'll not be here long, then
you will have to let him go.
God looked down upon him, said I could bring
you home to me.  For now tho, that will not be,
Through stranger's arms he placed this child,
within my arms so tender and mild.
I asked God up above, did you send him
for a while because he needs so much love,
God looked down on us and smiled.  I knew then
this special gift would be with us for a while.
When the time does come and God decides an angel
he will be.  I'll get down upon my knees and thank
him for sending him to me.

**Ellen Hursh**

## Lost Gran'nie

Frail lady appeared, wandering to and fro,
Seemed apparent, not knowing where to go.
Where do you live, need help from me?
You look lonely, lost as can be.
Faltering foot-steps, head bowed low,
Glad to show the way to go.
Hair tangled, tear stained face,
Roamed away from old home place.
Hungry?  when was last time you eat?
I can tell you are tired on your feet.
Cup of coffee, smells good to me,
Made the way it should be.
Bowl of soup, crackers too,
Yes, food is good for you.
Old man hunger, thing of the past,
Each bowl filled, disappeared fast.
Knock heard on door,
We are not alone, as before.
Gran'nie lives in a home, few blocks away,
Found by this lady who cares, happy to say.

**Edith Mae Payne**

## I See Dad

"Hi Dad!" "I'm the twelfth of the children!" "So you remember?"
"Seems Dad" "Nearly ninety you be!" "I always was a contestable
young lad." "Suppose?" "Maybe?" "You knew I could spout a temper?"
"Mainly!" "Too myself and others make mad and look ever so sad!"

"And sure enough!" "There it was!"  A slice of great oak timber!"
"Across my pad seating!" "quickly planted as if too you were mad!"
"It was only all the chocolates!"  "Of the box left from the
Holiday of December." "That!" "I thought only should have had!"

"But!"  "Then I could hear the rasping of disciplines poke"
"And I knew it was you Dad!"
"Yes!"  "Because we were a house many."  "We had to share with the
other!"  "Forty some year!"  "Yes" "They've seen me  and passed all
our families Comrade!"  "The Kennedys!"  "Nixons!' "Carters!"
"Reagan's!"  "and others" "Have turned economics a structure!"

"They have changed!" "And unchanged!" "Lives and Families!" "Some
more happy!" "Some more Sad!"
"They try to pull us apart!"  "Then sew us all back together"
"I know!" "Certainly Sire!" "You!" "Your sib!" "Did align with
greater card!"  "Yes Dad!"  "We the children!"  "They the leader!"
"All bent and bowed!"  "But Now!"  "I see Dad!"

**Gary Hendershot**

## Visions of the Heart

Time passes on but my love remains
Seem's like only yesterday, my heart was singing
Love's refrains, but just like the wind are time
together was gone, and now the memories are
all I have to live on, what could have been
will never be known.  And those things will
always be a dream in the back of my mind
I hope my hasty heart will forgive me if I stop
and think of you one more time.

**Dolores J. Ney**

## The Light of a Thousand

The light outside my clear glass window,
seems to die from my glance so quick.
The darkness created for my love,
provides me the sight enough to see.
As the wind howls,
and the rains fall to ripen the bounties,
I see the light of a thousand people.
In all colors, sizes, shapes, and lives,
kissing one another's hand,
seeing every person's hidden dimensions and understanding.
And yet, I sit here in my abode,
alone, confused and hidden,
by my outside paper wrap.
To shy to touch a strangers hand,
To confused to understand private dimensions beside my own.
But, my iron door is bending and crashing,
as these people enter my domain.
My mind is carefully opened by their and my own words,
and just by their listening,
my paper wrapping is falling off for me to emerge.

**Crystal Ellerbee**

## Choices

The brightness of the room
sets my frustration afire.
In this yet still gathering place,
I steal furtive glances at the world
alive beyond the glass.

Reminded at once of a similar setting
many years ago, when first the muse
stirred in my soul.
Too green then, I did not realize
the strength of her pull on the ordinary.

To stay in her embrace seemed an elaborate choice,
one not in keeping with stronger voices and wiser minds.
Thus, I entered a world made free of muses;
void of their fancy and whim;
bereft of their music.

Today - no different from most,
the silence overwhelms me.

**Jill C. Twardy**

## Attic Dancers

Blowing dust from the cover of my faded Memory Book,
Settling in the corner of my hideaway attic nook,
I release them one by one, my emotions,
To do a little dance for me.

First gladness, then disappointment and sorrow,
Tapping out time gone by.
Then back you go.
To the business
of gathering
dust.

**Carol Robison**

## Dis-Illusion

In the twilight of a dream,
Shadows dance.
Eluding to the harmony of circumstance.
A captured moment; time and space
Rehearsed response of inner grace.
No less the cost than everything
if truly you believe.
A Mardi Gras requiring the actors guise,
Faith portrayed as fact in fabricated lies,
The hope and promise present tense,
with answers lying always hence.
so lonely is as lonely does
in serenades of Oz.

*Corrine L. Woodman*

## Pixie

Blue eyes, blond hair, complexion, so fair
She and her bow, were quite a pair
So full of pep, is a gal, named Pixie
From way down South in the heart of Dixie

She is a live wire, and a real cutie
With good shape, and natural beauty
Down to earth, a real southern bell
Who is the daughter, of Farmer Dell

You should see this Pixie milk a cow
A prize winner, who took all the bow's
Can rope a steer, and ride bare back
For this gal Pixie, does not lack

Her Pa, Farmer Dell sit's with pride
As Pixie became, a beautiful bride
She and her loved one, so very happy
As they made Farmer Dell, grandpappy

*Frances Ragsdale Boring*

## Questions

"Gaea", he asked, "Why is the sky blue?"
She answers as best she can
But the questions never end
They're been coming since the dawn...

"Gaea", he asked, "What happens if I do this ?"
She shoos him away
Tries to tell him it's naughty
He only cries and runs to pout...

"Gaea", he asked, "Do you think you can stop me?"
she chases after her little boy
As he turns the corner...
Lights the match...

"Gaea", he cries, "make it stop!"
"It's too late" she sighs.
As their home went up in flames..
All was lost.

*Erin Jatko*

## If My Thoughts Like Birds

If my thoughts, like birds, could fly to you,
Your world would be filled with the sound of their wings.
If my prayers, like the wind, could touch your soul,
You would know how my own spirit sings.
If my joy, like a fire, could warm your heart,
Your being would burn with a pure clean flame,
And if love is a bridge that can span the earth,
Your heart will hear when I speak your name.

*Joan-Marie Caldwell*

## The After Affect

The beat of the drums filled the air.
She could feel the rhythm in her soul.

Her feet glided across the ground as if it were ice.
Her arms swayed in the cool summer's breeze like the wings of an
eagle.

She was dressed in the colors of her country.
Her skin was the color of golden brown sand.

Her eyes were bright, black and soulful.
Her long slender neck was ordained with thick golden rings.

Bracelets of ivory covered her arms.
Her face had the childish look of innocence.

They called her Nandia.

Her feet shuffled across the dirt as if she had been walking forever.
Her arms laid limp at her side.

She was dressed in patched up rags.
Her skin was covered with dirt, beads of sweat dripped from her face.
Her arms were covered with welts.

She looked older than her twenty-five years.
Her eyes looked as if she was lost in something she didn't
understand and desperately wanted to find her way home again.

Her faint expression gave you the impression of years of pain and
suffering.

They called her Nandia.

*Cori Lynn Dorsey*

## A Wind Blew Through My House Last Night

On the clattering subway,
She dropped her patchwork shawl.
Alone amid the masses,
A stranger not at all.

Dark then light then dark again,
A still she gave to me.
The train strained its dogged tracks;
My chains the ones released.

Supposedly a token,
A simple smile she gave.
In exchange for treasure,
Revelation with it came.

A wind blew through my house that night,
And I knew I was not alone.
Eyes closed, what seemed like merely breath,
Seemed that which was already sewn.

Limbs sway, leaves leap, blinds rattle for sight,
And then it crawls right through our scrim.
Silence, darkness, blinding songs of light,
More spring than autumnal wind.

*Ben Caswell*

## Mismatched Feelings

How are you my friend, are you dead? Are you tired, are you
sick? Are you sad, are you mad? Are you grateful, are you good?
Are you hyper, are you happy? Are you living great?

I hope you don't take this personally, but your clothes do
not match. Your right sock is black and your left sock is
blue. Your pants are pink and your shirt is not new.

What, what did you say? You're having a bad day? Why that's
o.k. you look great! I love your pink pants and your black
and blue socks, and the shirt that is not new. Well, sorry,
mirror, I've got to go to school.

*Candace Slay*

## A White Christmas Tree

*Dedicated to my Mom, Pearl C. Racine West*

Mom, saw a white Christmas tree somewhere.
She fell in love with it because it was rare.
Mom, would go in the woods to pick her tree when Christmas was near.
It had to be a sassafras tree with layers of pretty tiers
She would do this with pride every year.
It would stand in the corner and looked so bare.
Then mom would wrap every limb with love and care.
It looks like a tree in the woods with snow on it.
People can't understand how it is done and are taking back a bit.
When it is decorated it's done with a flair.
There is a yard under it no ones aloud to touch they wouldn't dare.
It is one of the prettiest christmas trees you'll ever see.
I would never have a green christmas tree it's not for me.
Please learn how to wrap a white tree no matter what it takes.
Don't let the family tradition die for your Nanny's sake.
I would love to see this tradition carried on that's true.
Then you can be proud to pass it on to the next generation too.

### Betty West-Goodman

## Letting Go

What could she have been thinking, as she gathered reeds and sod
She formed a tiny cradle, she put her faith in God.
She took her sleeping baby, and gently placed him there,
Then set adrift this little ark, to land she knew not where.

There must have been that moment, when standing on the brink
With wild imagination, would he float or would he sink?
She held on far too tightly, but she knew he couldn't stay
She prayed that God would give her strength to push the child away.

So she trusted in the Lord and he floated safely down
A river of uncertainly, to stand on Hallowed ground...
Now we can learn this lesson, believe in God, although,
I have found the hardest part, is in the "letting go".

### Arloa L. Means

## My Lover, My Wife

With her hair brown and curled and eyes dark as coal,
she gazed in my eyes and captured my soul.
Never had I felt such a stirring within,
Until our eyes and our hearts met, our love to begin.
We talked of our dreams as if they were one,
we talked all the day until it was done.
We walked hand in hand as we talked about life,
I knew that somehow I would make her my wife.
As I sat and gazed at her beauty so timeless,
I pondered what to do, to make her say yes.
Should I promise the moon and the stars in the sky?
For without her sweat love, I surely would die.
I have searched all my life for woman so fair,
so I asked for her hand, our lives would we share.
She held me and kissed me and in a voice soft and low,
said, I have always loved you and I want you to know,
together, forever through life will we stand,
I will be your woman and you will be my man.
As we exchanged our vows and promises for life,
I thanked God for this woman, my lover, my wife.

### Gene A. Franks

## Tea Time

A lady bug came to visit me today.
Without an invitation, she arrived in time for tea.
Delighted to see her, I asked her to stay
And we spent hours talking Friday away.

### M. J. Cunningham

## The Leader's Daughter

She is the last one to receive, a treat, a badge, that extra hand
She is the last to take the lead or with the flag to stand.
She waits, not always patiently, her turn to come about,
She always seems to be the one, at which the leader shouts.
Each task that's done, each project made, she must complete it twice,
When all the other girls are stinkers, she must continue to be nice.
If she should be among the ones, to test the rules or stray,
No one recalls the other girls, but she was seen that day.
I'm sure this would not be her choice, to be last upon the chart,
How can I show her openly she is first within my heart?
There must be times, perhaps too many, she wonders is this for me?
She might have chosen a different route this one has not been easy.
And through it all she walked this path, her faith in me did not falter
I want to tell her how proud I am to claim my special
  "Leader's Daughter."

### Diane C. Epps

## To Diana, With Love

This is an ode to my Diana, who for a short time was my wife.
She is the woman who brought a new meaning to my life.
She is truly a woman that must rank up there with the best.
She has a sensuality that would make any man feather her nest.
She would not win a beauty contest or other such things.
But to be with her, you would feel touched by angel wings.
Diana must know that she is a woman through and through.
She has good and bad as we all humans do
What makes Diana so special and worthy you see,
Is the warmth that she brings to you and me.
She has such a beauty that comes from within,
That her friendship for life I must win.
One word of warning for those who would be a friend,
If you try to possess her that would be the end.
Diana, as you travel about this fair land,
I hope you realize that you are a woman most grand.

To the rest of the world whom you shall meet
They will find that as a person you are hard to beat.
So to Diana, to the real woman inside be true.
She is truly good, the real and honest you.

### Carl R. Mahaffey

## "I Want To Go To Grandma's House"

I miss my Grandma. Daddy says I can't go see her.
"She moved," he says. What does that mean?
What happens when people move?
Where do they go? Where do Grandma's go when they move?
I remember my Grandma's house. I fed the ducks there.
I got to lay in my Grandma's big bed and watch my Ninja Turtle movies.
Grandma used to let me eat my fruit loops on a tray in her bed.
She brought me juicy juice and fruit chews. Grandma read me stories.
She let me play sharks in her big bed and I could jump up and down.
Where do Grandma's go when they move? Do they go across the ocean
in a big boat? Do they go across the mountains in a big plane?

Why can't I see my Grandma anymore? I used to see my Grandma all the
time. I would go visit her and she would come visit me. I haven't
seen my Grandma in a really long time, "since she moved".

I miss my Grandma. I miss her hugs and I miss her smile.
My Grandma and I used to play games. We played with my toys and she
hugged me. I wish my Grandma hadn't "moved." It must be really far
away. Did she forget where I live? Does she remember me? Does
she remember the fun we had? I hope my Grandma doesn't forget me.

I am only four years old. I miss my Grandma. I miss the ducks and my
Ninja Turtle movies. But most of all I miss my Grandma's hugs.

### Dee Bryce

## Dilemma

I got a call from a long-time friend, we talked for quite a while.
She said her world was falling apart, and she really admired my style.
She thought I had it all together, never needed anyone;
My spouse and kids are perfect, and I even schedule time for fun.

And I thought how, in all the years gone by, I'd painted just that
   picture for my friend.
Didn't want her to know I wasn't up to par, but was often at my wit's end.
Sometimes I feel invincible, with eyes behind my head.
Sometimes I feel the weight of the world—those are the times I dread.

Cause I've been standing in my own light. I've been blocking out the
   Son.
I could barely hear Him calling, when He told me not to run.
He said "That burden is far too heavy for you to carry all alone."
But I was casting a lovely shadow, trying to do it on my own.

It's good to be independent—to stand on your own two feet,
To glory in the power of womanhood, an experience that can't be beat.
But sometimes you need a sister, a mother or a really good friend.
Trust in that urge to reach out, the sweetness will never end.

And don't be standing in your own light don't be blocking out the Son,
Or you may not hear Him calling, when He tells you not to run.
You know that burden is far too heavy for you to carry all alone,
And you'll be casting a lonely shadow, if you try to do it, don't
   try to do it, all on your own.

   *Deborah G. Halverson*


## Nursing Home Life

Our mother sits in the nursing home,
she sits in a wheel chair all alone.
She's wonderful and wise, gentle and kind,
no other like her you'll ever find.
She has her memories of childhood ways,
of life as a youngster and happier days.
Of her husband Charles, her three daughters and son,
the laughter and tears and the love she has won.
Her Christ likeness is unknown to mankind,
but God has a place where her crown jewels will shine.
If we could just market the wisdom she's earned,
it would be more valuable than all we've learned.
She sits all alone now and waits for the day,
when angels will come and take her away.

   *Dolores Wiggins*


## Please Mister, Please?

Large brown eyes looked up at me their message clear.
She struggled valiantly but could not hold back the tears.
Gently she took my hand. I knew the meaning of that plea.
She sensed that love was near and turned her eyes to me.
I held her tiny tear stained hand, gave it a gentle squeeze.
I felt the tear drops running and a weakness in my knees.
I remembered well the house with all the cupboards bare.
I couldn't understand the sorrow in mothers vacant stare.

We had so much in common, this hungry, homeless miss.
Kindred spirits we, on my cheek she sealed it with a kiss.
She shared our home, our love, our dreams and our life.
She gave the joy of motherhood to my lovely, lonely wife.
Life ended for this tiny angel so full of love and unafraid.
Angels took her at age of five with birth contracted Aids.
If I must live on sadly and forever it matters not the place.
I will not ever in life or death forget that lovely little face.

   *Fulton E. Franklin*


## My Teacher

I have an unusual teacher who juggles Jolly Ranchers.
She surrounded her desk with cacti and also some octopi.
She fixed a cake supreme covered with soda pop cream.
My teacher eats worms for lunch and served us caterpillar punch.
She gathers bats and dissects rats.
She wears seaweed and a hat of reeds.
I have a strange teacher who loves gross creatures.
During lunch break she dances with a snake.
Her desk is glass and a garbage mass.
She has blue hair that floats in air.
Her face is green and she pretends to be a queen.
She grades tests with pencils on the window sill.
My teacher is three feet tall and acts like she is not small.
With purple eyes she actually flies.
She has a tail like the stair rail.
My teacher is an alien,
She also has a good imagination.
She is a demotyphenon,
When she talks she goes on and on.
I'M PROUD OF MY TEACHER!!!

   *Emily A. Benavage*


## America Mother of the World

My country once known as the strongest nation the world has ever seen
She walked the world as a proud being
arrayed in glory and beauty
Now her glory is deteriorating and the beauty has begun
to turn into some kind of horror - in all her glory
she has attempted to feed the world, even her enemies
know of her generosity
She has build schools for the under privilege nations,
sent food, clothes, weapons, technology, she has touched all the world
Now her grate budget cuts, slashing of social programs are quite
ironic since,
she has taken care of all the world and is still attempting too-
for working america her children
may not get educated or face possible starvation -
How do we feed the world and educate them? We face the same
crisis that she so readily tries to eliminate in all the world
America what about your children?

   *James Glover*


## Untitled

I have a daughter whom I dearly love
She's not just super- she's a step above
She's made me proud in so many ways
She brings me joy and brightens my days.
I miss her so- we're so far apart
But she's always close here in my heart
I love to go visit her- she treats me so well
We have so much to share and stories to tell.
Her home is a showplace- she has such a touch
Her meals are delicious and I eat too much.
She dresses so nice and has such style
She truly is beautiful with her happy smile.
I might sound prejudiced describing this gal
For she is my daughter, my friend and my pal.
I'm one lucky Mom, you'll have to agree
God blessed me the day he gave her to me.

   *Florence Wood*

461

## Impressions!

As a flower with petals full of morning dew
shimmers in the early sunlight.
As a butterfly coming out of its cocoon
to catch the fresh breeze and to make its first flight.
As I write these words to share with you
I try to communicate.

As a diamond dances on water
in the mid afternoon sun.
While the trees bend their branches
with the help of a breeze
wetting their leaves, splashing, having fun.

As the evening settles in, bringing the night sky
filled with thousands of twinkling lights.
Another day is removed.
For me, a brief interlude.

As I finish writing these last words
I hope that I have not only created pictures for you to see
but that I have reached you in a way that needs no explanation.
Except that we have communicated.

*Julie Giddens*

## A Ring For Jenny

Waiting to find their home, icy blue facets
Shine recklessly from their velvety perch.
July 23, another beginning.  The eager mother invited
to join her man son in his breathtaking ring search.

Both silently aware that within the glittering cases
There is held the symbol about a lifetime, babies, their smiling
    faces.
He's done the hard part.  The perfect lady he did discover
Jenny with a heart of laughter gives herself; committed energy,
    devotion.  The lover.

Finally a woman trustworthy of his sensitive nature.
She's real.  A humorous beauty who adores my boy.
A woman known as Jenny
who promises only to bring him joy.

A pretty scary step.  "Will you marry me and stay loyally beside me
    forever?"
Fresh faced and earnest do any of us ever understand what those words
    mean?
Too big a concept.  It is life itself.  A blue print for the species,
    infinitely clever.

And so the hopeful young man promises to a woman known as
    Jenny, his life.
And he knows that her humor and love will fill his dreams,
    for he has finally found her, his devoted wife.

*Donna L. Friess*

## Farewell

Has it only been a day
since you told me that you were going away?
Has it only been that short while
that you gave me your farewell smile
and  said be good, and I nodded my head
that I understood?
Understood that you were leaving me
and that you again I might never see.

Oh how I wanted to tell you then
that I would miss you so,
and that I did not want you to go.
But I just nodded my head
and said that I understood,
even though I knew I never would.

*Dolores Hickman*

## Untitled

Island snow, it's showing
Shivering palm leaves blanketed, this cool white dust
A cold wet kiss on a shivering cold day only
Warms the heart beating stronger the
rotting cement city with all it's rotten worms
digging down into a s--t hole of clay
Shivering palm fronds blanketed
Death slowly seeping into then,... Island snow
Keep close to the green it's always warming
Silver hoops on my tenth gone
back to home it's owner holds a spot
Scary it's so evolving and the pain is dissolving
Captured in a cabin tortured by life turn little time
While they frolic in the Island Snow
Kicking cold white dust into my eyes
Coming to, just enough to see the palm leaves
Soaked with death fall to the ground
The only sound...
my flesh ripping open in display
the white foot trails are everywhere except near.

*Danielle Turk*

## Dream Vacation

Eleven floors up, the woman in lavender
shivers and sighs as she faces the wrinkled
brow of a dubious sea — and her own —
reflecting in this hotel window; she sees

in the glass certain darkblue shadows
which may either be deeper seas —
her husband is out there fishing —
or shadows in her own sea-colored eyes.

She has finally told them:  NO.
No thank you.  And sent them away.
For something she has always craved —
could it be time?  Or space?

By now the children — hardly children anymore —
are fine without her, playing tennis
on the 4th floor or tanning themselves
in confident exposure by the pool.  She is

shaken by this.  Shaken too by the strange
power of silence and one bold word —
that it could leave her alone, with only
a black pen and clean white sheet to love.

*Jean Lorraine Tupper*

## Keys Please Don't Drink and Drive

Back to back there's another wreck
Side-to-side another child dies
Why do you choose to drink and drive?
It wasn't your child who cruelly died, it was mine.
There's a thin line between life and death so when you drink and drive
It's like pulling a loaded gun off the shelf.

Why drink if you can't think?
Why drive if it's possible someone could lose a life?
Why play dice with other people lives?
It's not wise to drink and drive.

There is another form of being intoxicated, a liquid crack
With the monkey alcohol on your back.

Driving under the influence is like playing with an explosive
Waiting for something to happen.
Don't leave someone paralyzed or traumatized
for the rest of their lives.
And don't make families attend memorial services
for lifeless bodies in closed caskets.

Put you keys away if you've been drinking today.
Please don't drink and drive.

*Cleveland S. Barrett Sr.*

## Awakening

A blackened Sword beside my bed,
Silent and dark, seemingly dead.

The dust that covers the life within,
Is just a reminder of how it's been.

I often think back to when we were a pair.
The failures and triumphs we did share.

Then back to the present I suddenly come,
Tears in my eyes....but my heart is numb.

The longing to scrape the dust away,
Grows ever stronger with each day.

I know that I have failed to be
The soldier that you want of me.

I'm sure that I can fight and win,
But without you Lord, it's 'might have been.'

The beginning
### *Beverly Johnson*

## Memories

It's been 50 years ago today,
Since you vowed to love each other each day.

A special bond to last this long,
As perfect as a love birds song.

You've been together through thick and thin,
Your precious love will never end.

Your love will always carry you through,
A feeling to last your whole lives through.

You have the rest of your lives to share,
Each day showing how much you care.

You've had it all through the years,
Through all the love, heartaches and tears.

You have a precious kind of love,
As pure as a snow white dove.

A celebration is in the air,
All your family and friends will be there.
### *Betty J. Wagner*

## The Highest Power's Address

AMERICA, the child I favor,
sit with ME in this park that you share with your siblings.
Consider the blessings I have bestowed upon you.
  2 Behold the land,
from which you may draw the fruit of your choice.
  3 Remember the Rebellious Child and her children
you drove out of that same land
so long ago.
  4 WHO delivered you to Independence
from that Abusive Suitor?

KEEP in mind the witty invention, be it Science, Agriculture,
Government, Architecture, Artistic Endeavors of Medicine.
  2 And know that none of this would be possible
without your Father — in whom you say you trust.
  3 OR is currency your new father?
  4 Use your power to administer equal justice!
  5 Love ME and MY grandchildren as you love yourself,
Lest I favor another child.
### *Eric Bailey*

## My Little Silver Bell

In those green and shady meadows we've visited before.
Sits a silver little Church, and in it is all my love for you.
The trees that surround that little church are the words I have
stolen from your heart.  And that little silver bell that hangs
is the last honest smile you gave me when I left home, to start
my journey.  And it still hangs in that imaginary church in my mind.
It rings only when you come to visit me, through that little forest
of trees.  And it keeps on ringing till its time again for you to leave.
Then it has no need for ringing anymore.  Till I call you at home,
and your voice takes its place.
Ring-ring collect from me.
I love you till the end of time.
### *Eddie Vasquez*

## Untitled

Study Hall is over, now I have a "free"
Sitting by myself, nobody with me
What should I do?  Take out a book?
Open to the first page, take a look?
Or get a friend, play a little chess?
Found my friend James.  He said, "Yes."
The game is almost over, I am winning by a horse
He's a good player, but I always win, of course
He moves his bishop to the fourth square
The pressure is building up.  It's something I can't bear
I take my time, I'm going really slow
I do what my mind tells me, so I go with the flow
I took his Rook, I am back in the game
I am not losing now so there is no shame
The bell just rang, I hope I'm not late
Before I go I want to put him in checkmate
Nobody won, it ended in a stalemate
Now I am mad but it is because I am late
This poem is not true, I wrote it for fun
I shall be writing more poems, but as for this one, I'm done.
### *Jared Davin*

## Who Will Feed Benji Blue Jay?

Raised him from a chick, this beautiful
Sky-blue bird with big feet, powerful
Beak, and white with tan trim.  My awful
Mortgage was too much for me to pay,

So I rented an apartment a
Few blocks South of my old yellow house.
After New Year's Day, I will move out,
To a new life.  Far enough away

From my neighborhood for even this
Large, hungry bird to follow me.  Wish
I might win the Lotto, and keep Bliss
Place, my home for twelve years.  My blue jay

Eats peanuts from the shell, and wheat bread.
Every year, he and his mate, Mildred,
Raise two chicks.  Patio fence, instead
Of front yard feeder, could make them stay.

Two by six cedar fence on Jade Drive,
My new address, will feed birds just fine.
Who will feed Benji Blue Jay?  I'll try.
He's ten years old.  Ten more years, I pray.
### *Geraldine Coomes*

## A President, A First Lady

Fallen by a bullet
Slain through the head
Almighty God he is dead

Sweet little Caroline, brave little John
Your father!  He is dead
Dear Jackie so kind so true
What!  Oh What!  What now will you do?
You stood beside him when he rose to fame
You were beside him when his body was lamed
The ring from your finger you placed in his hand
Good by to your loved one till you meet again

Fallen by an illness she could no longer endure
Almighty God she, Jackie is now with you,
Her love was undying even though she was dying
And would soon be beside her loved one again
Taken from us by an illness she could no longer endure
Almighty God they are both together again, forever with you!
Our Past President John F. Kennedy and First Lady
Jacqueline are now together in Heaven with you.

*Georgia Anderson Cross*

## California

Not much left for me here anymore; those who see me turn around and
    slam the door
Where will I go?  What shall I do?
I do know I must get away from you
turn your back on me; now all I feel is free
I am free to leave now; to leave the only home I've ever known
feel like I'm in the twilight zone
feeling that there is no one there; this is a truth you'll have to bear
wanting your love, you're turning away, giving it to her everyday
Will you miss me when I'm gone?  Like the player misses his pawn?
Will you forget me, forget I'm alive?  Of your thoughts I'm deprived
turn away when I need you most; to mass depression I now am host
two-thousand miles away I'll be; from this house I must flee
Maybe you don't believe the words I say; but it's getting closer
    everyday
I need you to comfort me in my hour of need; my warnings you will not
    heed
Please, take my hand and guide me through the darkest parts of my
    life
you are who knows me best; so help me put my thoughts to rest
I do not wish to leave, but I must; for you I have lost all trust
stab me in the back; now, I'm the one on the attack
When I leave, I may never see you again
Have a good life, if you can

*Diane C. Gingrich*

## The Awakening Of An Orchestra

The sun begins to peak over the horizon,
    slowly you begin to see his smile.
Then out of no where you begin to hear pretty song,
    song by an orchestra of birds.
The smile becomes brighter and the songs become louder.
In the background you hear an instrumental,
    the sounds of a crystal clear stream flowing down the rocks into a
    enchanted pond where the fish wait to be served, listening.
Rocks begin to fall down the mountain sides,
    drums, begin, to end the beautiful sounds of the orchestra.
The wind and leaves begin to clap, as the sun beginning to curl up
    under the horizon to dream of what beautiful songs that will
    be heard when he awakes.
It was truly the awakening of an orchestra.

*Joy Weaver*

## "Winter"

I was a beautiful baby, lying
sleeping in my mother's arms!
Never a thought of dying,
never a thought of harm,
So soft, sweet, and lovely, it's Spring

Gee!  How time has swiftly flown
I am a woman now, fully grown,
Have been busy as a bee.
I am loved, and married.  Don't you see?
School days have passed so swiftly!  It's Summer.

Now all my children are grown,
And they have children of their own,
No one left at home you see,
Just my dear husband, and me;
We are lonesome as can be.  It's Fall

My husband is dead and I am here,
I'm left in this house I loved so dear
I can not stay here all alone,
I have to find another home,
with folks my age, it's Winter now.

*Hestella Oliver*

## Red Tides

Along the shore talesmen stand, eroded.
Smacked by waves of facts
countercurrents of advocacy engender.

Arguments, zealously asserted to uncover
truth beneath the ocean floor,
on balance.  Remaining asunder.

Yet, in lunar power lies an unseen cohort;
its opulent reflections of influence
skew the scales of justice, and distort,

beyond nature's force of gravity,
transforming truth into red tides,
contaminating reality.

As evidential fragments of shell
life scattered along life's shore of perception,
in memory of Pyrrhic victories.

*Claire Marie Schultz*

## Mother

As Nature endows roses to represent beauty,
So are Mothers the symbol of devotion and duty.
They are the center of the continuance of life,
They give selflessly daily as Mother and Wife.

Then there is an extra special Mother,
who stands mile-high above all other,
her sense of duty knows no border,
The needs of her family are her first order.

We are very lucky to have this mother right here,
Devotion, love, strength she gives without fear.
So with these lines we want to say,
Our thanks, our love are yours day after day.

You are the bond that holds us all.
We want to be part of you and answer your call.
Be ours to love, to hold and admire,
You are the tops, our love will not tire.

*Fred Percy*

## Missing You

When I look into your eyes,
so beautiful but so sad,
I wish an end to all goodbyes
thinking of all the lonely times we've had.

It hurts and aches within my heart,
having you so far away.
I don't feel whole when we're apart,
but we'll be together again, someday.

That someday couldn't come soon enough,
when the days seen much too long,
But it'll get here, though it may seem tough,
because our love keeps me feeling strong.

Darling, soon we'll be in each other's arms
and I'll be happier than anyone could be.
I'll feel safe from any danger or harm
and wonderful knowing you love only me.

*Camilla Ahnstrom*

## When Evening Falls

The sun is now setting behind the mountains
So breathtaking beautiful and serene.
In colors of bright red, orange and purple,
What a lovely sight for my eyes to see.
And there, in the distance over the glistening ocean,
Is rising the moon quiet and pale,
As if he was wrapped up in a whisper of silver,
To let us know that evening is here.
When in the trees the nightingale
Is singing her evening song,
And a lonely cricket loves to join in
For a happy sing-a-long.
I'm sitting here thinking, how delightful to dream,
Until the cry of a sea gull
Brings me back to reality.

*Adina H. Gabler*

## The Borrower

The Son of Man was always borrowing.

There was no room at the inn for him to be born,
    so he borrowed a stable.

He owned no bed,
    so he borrowed a piece of bare ground each night.

He was called to no pulpit,
    so he borrowed the side of a hill to preach.

He owned no cup,
    so he borrowed one to draw living fountains of water for a sinful
    woman.

He owned no bread,
    so he borrowed a small boy's lunch and fed a multitude.

He owned no beast,
    so he borrowed an ass and rode it in triumph into Jerusalem.

He owned no banquet table,
    so he borrowed an upper room and fed his disciples and us his own
    body and blood.

He committed no sin,
    so he borrowed ours and bore them in our place upon the cross.

He owned no grave,
    so his broken body was laid in a borrowed tomb.

Lord Jesus, borrow this aimless life of mine and use it to thy Glory.

*Harold W. Westover*

## Why Wait?

I think I feel a poem coming on
so I'll write this one before dawn.
Why wait until tomorrow to tell someone you care?
For tomorrow they may not be there.

So why not say "I love you"
to those we hold so dear?
Because if we wait too long
we might have to shed a tear.

So I'll tell all you folks I know
how much a friend has meant to me.
Cause it takes folks like you
to make my day feel complete.

Now, go hug your spouse and children
and put on a very large grin.
'Cause you've told them you love them,
and now life won't ever be grim

*Belle R. Clarke*

## Happy Birthday, Angel

Angels aren't born - they simply appear,
    So, it's unnecessary to speak of a year.
        There's one in my house, and one in my heart,
        And I've tried forty years to tell them apart.
            But that's what one gets, by wedding a sprite
            One moment loving the next in a fight,
At times I ponder, and wonder if can it
    Be she's mis-placed from some far away planet,
        Where the air is much sweeter, and never too chilly,
        And the ways of our world would be quite silly.
Never-the-less, when "push comes to shove."
    We realize that we're still much in love.
        And so Happy Birthday any old how.
        It may not be the day, but it's "just right" now.
            And if you'd like to hear me say so,
            I love you - you can bet your HALO!

*Bobby Joe Houser*

## Fond Memories of Mom

She was good-hearted, and quite petite,
so mannerly, and clean, and neat,
it seemed her singing was enchanted,
those things, I guess we took for granted.
Now, what stands out and makes me sigh
is my longing for her butterscotch pie.
It was made from scratch, of course,
fresh ingredients were the source.
There was no box of pudding needed,
with such perfection she succeeded,
and produced that true confection,
never hearing one objection,
surely with a magic touch
that yummy pie I crave so much!

*Ida Lillian Hobbs*

## Necrobiosis

Insanity is the necrobiosis of the mind.
    Slowly deteriorating certain sections of the brain.
In this lost brain tissue is where one will find
Memories of love and all that is kind.
    Hatred and darkness are all that remain.

It is in these catacombs of the mind
    Where madness and hatred pave the way
    For darkness to force all sources of light away.
Where the nefarious acts of all of mankind
    Are worshipped forever, through darkness and day.

*Donald G. Smith*

## Sleeping Angels

Sleeping Angels they are to me,
so peacefully they slumber.
Their energy has been put to rest,
till morning when they'll wake with zest!

As sure as the sun rises,
they greet a brand new day.
Their little eyes will "twinkle",
as they think of adventure and play.

Then, the ULTIMATE JOY...no words dare express,
their little arms close round your neck,
that small little touch, of their Angel like lips,
fills my soul with a lifetime of love.

Their eyes are so trusting,
their innocence....so pure,
then they smile with that smile....
and yes ...now I am sure!!!

That nothing in life can ever compare,
with the love of your children....
WHAT A BLESSING TO SHARE

*Bambi Forker*

## Happy To Be Nappy

Oh my crowning glory
    So thick with curly locks
It has passed from my African roots
    To the slave ships brought to this land
So versatile, so amiable
    Well groomed and clean
It's our pride, our strength
    A history of our being
We were taught that our hair was "negative"
    So we emulate what's "positive"
Which was straight.

Let's go back in history and get the record straight.

From warrior to marital status
    To ceremonies large and small
It was a status symbol to them all
    Hair twisted with mud, clay or straw
Cowrie shells or beads in braids large or small
Nonverbal communication your crown will tell all
Nappy, kinky or curly it sure feels great
Happy to be nappy that's me—let's appreciate!

*Jeannette Jones-Beebe*

## The Hero I Never Knew

I love him so much, I love him
    so true,
He is the hero that I never knew.
He was a sailor - a CPO
    snuck into the war and let nobody know.
He was so young, too, - only 16 years then
    and was killed by age 22

His death was untimely
    came after the war
On his way home
    his ship was in danger and nobody saw.
It exploded into flames
    and only one man was killed
It was he - my uncle - it was
    God's will
He was honored posthumously
    given a funeral in a military way
He's still remembered by all
    a hero to this day

*Ellen M. Cataldo*

## Old Shed

I gaze at the old shed in the field.
So visible to many, yet so concealed.
The decaying of boards, a sagging roofline,
Valiantly defying the passage of time.
Standing so proudly, yet so unsure,
The length of time, two hundred years or more.
Development and progress seen in the distance,
This antiquated shed, a symbol of resistance.
Its time remaining and the elements to endure,
Probably a few years, not much more.
Yet wavering and still standing for all to see,
One day this grand old shed will be just a memory.

*Eugene Green*

## A Woman's Thought

Once we were young
So was our idea of love
Did we even have the idea
Who's to know

Knowing is where it begins
The idea of love is appealing
To one who has yet to experience
That first feeling of love

The first feeling may last
'Til we realize that maybe it's not the right one
Then the right one comes along
And the partnership begins

In the midst of the partnership
We look back
We can't believe what time has past
The amazement overwhelms us

We then begin to ponder
And we wonder what the rest of life holds

*Ellie M. Hunley*

## Untitled

Many travel life's road looking for a star
Some cross the stage reaching for a star
Few climb a mountain to become a star
Most idle, content to gaze at a star

Stars that are lackluster and terminal

It is time to acknowledge and cleave to the
one true star. The star for which we do not
have to look nor reach. The star for which
we do not have to climb; but the star that is
worthy of our ultimate respect. The star that
willingly comes to all man kind as a baby in
a manger. Jesus, The Christ, sent by God to
shine in our lives affords us joy and peace
through salvation. The star is able to make
you shine "Brightly Everlastingly."

*Herbert L. Hildabrand*

## People's Purposes

The world is in trouble with its tongue
Some use it to go up
Some use it to go down
While others don't use it and remain on the ground
It therefore shows that men determine their fate
Some lose at the finish
Some at the gate

*Dean Francis*

466

## Walking Down The Street

One day I was walking down the street and
Someone stepped on my feet.
I yelled real loud and scared a cow.
A lady came over to see if I was alright and a
Nearby dog gave her a bite.
The lady screamed and dropped her ice cream
and that was all in my dream.
The next morning I got a call from Alanzo Mourning.
We had a long talk but it wasn't my fault.
When I hung up I took a look up and hoped to never be stuck up.

*Curtis Broidy*

## Dreams

Dreams come, tucked away in hidden consciousness—
Sometimes fleeting, as momentary reflections of life;
Sometimes transparent, visible only to the eyes of the beholder;
Sometimes locked in silence, blocked from view by the mind's steel
    grasp.
Mood swings compromise discouragement's misfortune with faith's
    fulfillment,
Transcending thoughtless absent-mindedness and abstruse consideration.
Dreams wing forth as gladness or pain—
Descending the intensity of despair; ascending new realms of
Fantasia.
Even in dreams—
Christmas magic attunes the most austere wave length in tempting
    imitations of sugar-coated fantasies;
Fairy tales quiver on the edge of the spirit's delight, abruptly
    descending into reality's vast depths;
A child's imagination mind-melts nightmares into trembling monsters,
    devoured by intrepid fathers in flannel pajamas;
A dog's hope emerges in a tail-wagging dimension of milk bones and
    "good dog" echoes, nullified by "bad dog" displeasures and
    cat-snarling idiosyncrasies.
Willing or not—
Dreams integrate into personal usefulness or neglect;
The mind the deciding beacon.

*Christine S. Webb*

## Revival

As I sit quietly in the church I adore,
Sometimes, I think it's a bore.
Counting hairs on a head,
Or dads that look dead,
Nothing's going on: just singing a song.
But, wait, as they pass the plate,
I see Brother Ben, confessing his sin.
Something is happening!!!
As the Gospel is being preached,
Souls are being bleached.
And I learn: My God is not dead.
For the Blood He shed,
He did not dread.
As on the third day he arose
And jumped to His toes,
So, only God knows,
That pain never goes.... away.
And that is why we have Easter today.
So, in church, I am not bored,
Because I love the Lord.

*Ashlee Caviness*

## Untitled

It takes a heap 'O' gruntin' in the house that we call home
Sometimes, when pa's not gruntin', I do it all alone
I grunt when I get out of bed and again when I sit down
I grunt when I am all dressed up or in my old nightgown

Is it 'cause I'm getting older and my bones don't work so well?
Or is it just my way to say "I really feel like hell?"
If I take my vitamins and drink my metamucil,
I'd forget about the gruntin' and try to be more useful.

Don't hafta act like I am old, just 'cause I'm eighty-one.
Think I'll get a perm and get out and have some fun.

*Dorothy Costello*

## The Greening of the Ghetto

The trees are budding now
Soon the barrenness outside my office will change.
The row houses with there
curtainless windows, torn roof tiles
and boarded-up doors will disappear.
I'll no longer stare back
At the emptied-eyed buildings.
The dingy, depressed zombie-like
Tombs standing in rows, waiting.
Just waiting...
Standing next to an empty lot
Wondering which will meet
The wrecker's ball next.
But people live there
among the deserted buildings.
Zombie-like, too, waiting.
Just waiting...

*Elizabeth A. Calkins*

## I'll Enjoy the Cold

The snow stops for a spell and the world seems to hold still.
Sound pauses. Clouds pause.
I close my eyes....and enjoy the cold.
A bitter breeze jolts me from my slumber and I remember the sun
coming to move time along.
There's a stale beauty in this winter
A color in its colorless wonder
and I know I'll miss it when it goes

Like taking down the Christmas tree
or watching the snowman melt away
I'll miss nights by the fireplace
I'll miss frosty wind biting at my face
I'll miss the white, pure, quiet world
I'll miss it all when it goes
I feel a shiver but instead of dreading
I enjoy the cold.

*Dana Reyes*

## Only God Knows

I hurt so deeply, in my heart and soul,
Since the death bell, for my beloved son, tolled;
The devastating pain of early grief, has faded some,
But the longing and missing him, will not succumb;
This is love, between a Mother and her child,
This love sent, from God above, does not last, for just awhile;
It goes on, from year to year, until I see, his face so dear;
Only God above, knows, the depth and purity, of
A Mother's Love.

*Elizabeth K. Crane*

## The Boy with the Laughing Eyes

First thing I noticed were his laughing eyes;
Sparkling and blue, they danced with surprise
And wonderment, as the bright red balloon
Slipped from his grasp and shot straight for the moon.
"Let's wave our farewells and be off," I said
To the boy with the laughing eyes.

Walking home, we encountered an angry young man—
Knife drawn in his trembling hand.
"What's this—a retard parade?" he asked,
Crouched low, hell-bent on his murderous task.
Suddenly mute, the steely gaze softened, transformed by
     his search for truth
From the boy with the laughing eyes.

Before I met him I used to wonder how they could survive
In a world of raging fury and all-consuming lies.
But once I saw the beauty masked behind those "sparkling blues,"
I knew I had to pass along this wealth to each of you.
For just like the young man's, my eyes were opened in Truth
By the boy with the laughing eyes.
*This poem was inspired by and is dedicated to the mentally disabled
children of REACH Center in Portland, Oregon—from whom I have
learned much.*

> *JoAnn Wilson*

## Rainy Day

Windy, rainy, scary outside
Specially, when I put my self aside
Not to mention the feelings that slide
Its not me the one who always cried.

Starred from the window looking for the bride
The one who took my heart and climbed
The mountain that I always go to hide
Its not me the one who always cried

Asked for help, nobody came to guide
Turned to the love in my heart and smiled
Cause the hope that you still here by my side
You are alright, she replied

I wish I can tell all the man kind
That I love you, and I know your not blind
As much as I carry in my heart and my mind
You are the one and the rest are behind.

> *Emad Farid Aziz*

## Real Life

You must not tell anyone, for time ticks on with unbelievable
speeds, and to look back you could see a bottomless bag of busted
dreams; dealing with devastating real-life once lived by lonely
ladies in the fast lane of unending fears, and frustrations...
we move forward making magical memories of unlived, unrehearsed,
hopes of high, healthy places, pleading to pull your pent-up
anger, and anguish out over the rainbows, rising repeatedly
to invite, install, include changes, and charges of a better,
believable, benign, beginning that will blossom in the
spring-spontaneous, spunky, special, and sought out as a
continuous, planned, careful, connection of needs filled fueled
by fluctuations in fantasy, and futures beginning to at last
love, live, and lie down to sleep, silently, and through a
complete cycle of solitude, and satisfaction-goodnight.

> *Joanie Burnap*

## Runaway

She hurries down an alley,
Splashing water about as she searches for shelter.
Nothing is found except for
The darkness at the alley's end.

A raindrop breaks upon her cheek,
Mixing with the tears;
As she looks around herself,
She begins to comprehend the fear.

She dives under a cardboard box,
Escaping from the Earth's shower;
Cramping herself tightly;
Hoping for warmth and comfort.

As the rain beats down on her fragile roof,
She sits there...shivering to herself,
And talking to no one
But herself.

She asks herself,
Is there anyone out there?
Is there anyone that cares?
The response is Silence.

> *Abbas Kermani*

## The Vase

The vase cracked in blown glass shards,
Splintered blues and glimmering pink
In uneven spirals of shattered shapes,
She piled them up in wobbly stack.

It was our wedding vase, and it
Smashed before, but glue made
Fragments adhere in new symmetry,
Until today, it smashed beyond repair.

I cupped the remnants gently,
Rocking them into slipping slivers
In the quiet of solitude, and the aftermath
Of your death, it's just an object, or so
It was and so are we, so temporal.

Your spirit was not your body,
Nor was this vase, though symbol of the past,
This splintered vase turns unique colors
To the light and shines hidden beauty
At unfinished edges, and I yearn to know you
Do this too, circling sideways turning raw
Beauty and opening broken edges to the light.
*(3/30/95)*

> *Esther Roberts*

## Tennessee Spring

Velvet and satin,
  spring nights in Tennessee.

The breeze from the window,
  open for the first time since
  the last oak leaf perched on the sill last fall,
announces its arrival by gentle rattle of the blinds,
  then flows silently across the room to greet me
as it would an old friend, with a gentle nuzzling of my cheek
  and the gift of the fragrance of lilacs and honeysuckle.

In the darkness, the muffled shuff shuff of wings glides past,
  telling miniature tales of fear and death,
    and loving provision for children of the night.
      And I close my eyes and sleep

In the velvet and satin
  spring night in Tennessee.

> *Joyce Fox*

## Insomnia

Night flights.
  Star sights.
    Lights bright.
Black ink glare
  On the skyways of the mind.

Like time-lapse photography,
Red tail lights streaking over steel bridges
In the hard stare darkness of a high-rise world.

Up high,
  Down low,
    Around and through,
      Swirled, brilliant, tiny streaks of color.

Tracks.  Fast.
Zip-zap synapse.
Thoughts flashing through steel grid tracks.

White lights smeared,
Back and forth,
Faster, faster, faster.

Sleep will never come.
I just keep driving this fast track night.

  *Carol A. Payne*


## Untitled

Sitting alone and trying to create
Staring at the paper I just meditate
A day not complete unless I produce
Like an orange that bares us no orange juice

Is it wrong for going on when you're so uninspired
Like swimming through quicksand and starting out tired
Or is there a chance to come out with real art
When starting out slowly, not feeling with heart

I think I have finished and with some success
It many not be brilliant or into excess
But this little poem has come out quite well
My own little ring of the victory bell.

  *Bob Williams*


## Silent Passage

Stars cross; two lovers sit by a spring.
Staring, not conversing, but speaking everything.
A deer frolics by as a bird sings its tune.
Quietly sharing as they stare at the moon.

He questions, "Why do you love me?"
Hesitantly she replies,
"As the sun and her moon
Light the heavenly skies.
I question not why,
And neither should you;
All I know is the heavens
Say I shall, so I do

"But, what if the heavens
Tell you fallacies, my love?"
"Who are we to be questioning
Such strong feelings from above?"

And with that, they remained there.
For all that it's worth,
True love shan't be questioned
For it's not of this Earth.

  *Joanna Adler*


## Nature

Petals of every color, leaves of every shade
stems of every width, thorns of every shape
trunks of every age, trees of every size
buds of every scent, grass of every height
nature's stunning harmony
a graceful, peaceful sight

Dark of every evening, depth of every night
rays of every morning, glow of every light
noise of every city envelops every life
yet in nearby places, quiet...peace...delight
nature's striking balance
crucial simple right

Rain from every cloud, mist from every dawn
drops on every surface, dew on every lawn
every note is equal in nature's basic song
soil...flower...human...nothing right or wrong
nature's startling message
honest, loud and strong

Nature's lucid answers
bid where we belong

  *Evelyn Maribel Cortez*


## Untitled

Venus has given her blessing.  Alas cupids arrows
Strikes only a bastion you have erected around your heart
While you have alluded to my acts of affection as pleasing
You continue to parry with a proffer of friendship unwittingly.
For friendship is that all important element to a superlative romance
History is Venus's witness that all the great love
    sonnets are bound in friendship
The  friendship you offer makes me in my heart feel as if I am
the basilisk.  To trust me as one would trust a creature
So vile can only harden a heart which will kill friendship
And all that is beautiful that would grow from it.
My words and thoughts are those of a man who knows
That when the heart is given free reign it finds love,
But never where it is forced to seek
I did not seek yet I have been smitten
By your appearance into my life.

  *Jon Jorstad*


## A Feeling Of Love

  There is a love that will always be there 'til the end,
such a relationship will grow and mend.
  A relationship so special and real,
in which, you want everyone to feel.
  A feeling of honesty and care,
something in a relationship that should always be there.
  A relationship like this could never be measured,
because it would be honored and treasured.
  This is a love that in hopes will last eternally,
within the heart and soul, you see.
  A feeling of love and trust,
something in a relationship that is a must.
  A feeling of spiritual love in the heart,
in hopes many lives never part.
  Something as special as love,
was sent from heaven above.

  *Julie Herzog*

## Day Night and Storm

Flowers swaying in a soft breeze.
Sun rays twinkling the morning dew on the green grass.
Birds chirping to announce the break of dawn.
A motor wakes the slumbering creatures to a new day.
Sunlight covers the land and sea, when a cloud sails by.
A black cloud blocks the sun's light, threatens a storm.
No more sun, just one cloud, color-dark.
Raindrops fall down-plump raindrops-onto the ground.
Falling, falling-slower and slower they fall.
No more rain, just sun, no clouds.
The grass is damp from the new rain.
Night nears, a dark night to give slumber.
Darkness covers a misty graveyard, darkening the tombstones.
Stars begin to twinkle, giving visions for dreams.
Sleep is given and accepted-the end of the day.

*Catherine Tucker*

## The Rose

As a rose awakens by a gleam of
sunlight through the meadow of dewdrops,
it broadens gracefully and expands its
radiant petals of the deepest red,
wondering what the day will bring her
if she will have to sit in an outcasted world
forever, it may look paradise, but look closer
now what do you see? She's not as powerful
as a sorcerer but like a queen that rules
the meadow.
Maybe today she can change the world
struggling fiercely she tries to stop the
pollution that's killing her and the meadow,
but it's no use, now the sun going down
over the hills, the meadow is silent.
She bows her head and prays for the
life that could be great if all the pollution
stopped and what tomorrow brings if
that will be the great day her and the
meadow can live in peace.

*Aimee Brown*

## I Pray, Oh God

Let me think only of pleasant things:
    Sweet baby sounds,
    Peach glow sunsets,
    Mockingbird wings.

Let my mind dismiss the hurts of the day:
    The tried and failed,
    That burning envy,
    The tender words I didn't say.

Are the dreams that waken me in the night:
    Your whisper,
    Your reminders,
    Your gentle smite?

Let me always know your loving care:
    Your Word,
    Your Way,
    That you are there.

*Geraldine L. Hopkins*

## Suicide

Oh death my love, I have been seduced
Take me away from all these troubles life has produced

No more pain to be felt
No more false laughs to smile
No more worries or cries
No more problems to pile

A deep secret place where no one will find me
Death to my rescue, My soul will be free

Permanent tears tattooed on my inner core
I must find and enter the universal door

Don't baffle yourself and ask each other why
Something inside of me was already starting to die

Oh God, forgive me for I know this is a sin
For maybe on the other side a new day will begin

Happiness and good times my life was then
Damage, despair and hardships I have also been

In my coffin I will celebrate and dance
I'll make sure I pick out my party dress in advance

Oh a life of despair I can no longer hide
I can only find comfort in my friend "SUICIDE"

*Chandra Lindsey*

## Words Of Love

The words of love are spoken here,
    taken to heart and held very dear,
    their meanings are never spoken in jeer,
    and sometimes they are given with a tear.

The words of love are spoken here,
    not always spoken when we are near,
    their meanings remove all doubt and fear,
    for when they are spoken they are always clear.

The words of love are spoken here,
    they fall softly on the ear,
    they are always grand and never mere,
    and they put our spirits into high gear.

The words of love are spoken here,
    listen closely and you will hear,
    they are spoken in kindness with no hint of a leer,
    for their meanings are special and to us they dear.

Yes the words of love are spoken here.

*Eileen Rocco*

## Mother's Day

My mother raised me, and taught me about life and
Taught me the knowledge that I'll need,
To become a man, that I am indeed.
Today is mother's day,
Mom, I just wanted to say;
That I love you so very much!
And I remember all of the kisses, hugs, talks and every little touch..
You taught me to be a perfectionist,
Those hugs, talks, and kisses are missed...
Mom, I know that I've made lots of mistakes in my life.
But it's all because I made myself live with strife...
I love you very much...
Happy mother's day
I love you
I'm sorry for anything,
And everything that I've done!!!

*Donald Johns Canning*

## Bad Dreams

Wide-eyed terror as only a child knows
Tear-stained pillows
Late-night cries
Sleepy feet pad across the floor
Loving hands skilled at drying eyes
Mama's been here a few times before...

Cradled in the rocking chair her mind wanders
Back across the years
Other children's tears
Nights of terror when families were torn
No mama's coming to banish their fears
Those wide-eyed children, forever alone...

*Barbara D. Crone*

## Love Me

Love me!  Love you!
Tell me how and I will!
Lean your head on my chest and hear the beat of my warm heart...
Feel it pulsating against your warm body...
Showing you love, showing you warmth...
Love me!  Love you!
Show me how and I will...
Give yourself, an I will give myself
Let's share in hearts
Two hearts too become one.
Love me!  Love you!
Tell me how and I will...

*Elizabeth Elaine Simpson*

## The Battle's New

The battle's new and now's the dying
Ten thousand charge with arrows flying
orphans young and widows crying
The battle's new and now's the dying

The battle rages to and fro
with every man trying to kill his foe
though some are valiant and lay men low
The battle rages to and fro

The battle's over and none has won
Though some would say a victory's won
The field is filled with dead and dying and
and every home has last a son...
Though some would say a victory's won

*Don Schultz*

## Mail

There's not too much in life that's better,
than getting one inspiring letter.
It really gives me one great thrill
to get a letter or a bill.

I even like the ads they send
and invitations to attend,
weddings, funerals, - I don't care,
as long as I'm invited there.

They tell me that I'm over due,
in sending my donation to-
a church or other things who say,
we need your money - right away!!!

But, still,- this doesn't bother me,
I love getting mail, as you can see
my day goes by,- I feel much better
on those days, when I get a letter.

*James E. Davis Jr.*

## Les Images De La Neige

There is no greater joy I know
than walking in fresh fallen snow
like lying on a pillow light
of softest satin pure and white

Each flake of snow a piece of lace
each one displays a special grace
like doilies on a table old
were memories have not grown cold

Trees spread their shoulders wide and high
to hold the cotton from the sky
as slaves put bales upon their backs
until the weight caused them to crack

Although they have the briefest life
they cause majestic trees such strife
for nature's greatness can be shown
she takes revenge against her own

*Jeffrey Anson*

## The Ferris Wheel

I never had a more exciting night
Than when we two were on the Ferris wheel.
While riding up and down in youth's delight
A glance, sideways glance I chose to steal.
And you so young, so young and innocent
Reached out and kissed my cheek as we went up,
While I was only waiting, heaven sent,
To take a peek as we began our drop.
I don't know why I thought to look at you
But young men's eyes can wander anywhere.
Soft skin, with lace together drew
My eager eyes to glimpse; my satan's stare.
Years later now you say you knew my tale
But slyly kept your hands upon the rail.

*Jack Lupas*

## Mother's Day And Penny Candy

Mother, this mothers day I wanted to
thank you for always being there when I've needed you.
I know you have sacrificed so much,
and growing up I took what you did for granted
I am really sorry.  I wish I could go back and
when you made each of those sacrifices let
you know right then how much I appreciate
what you had done.
   I love you very much.  I want you to know
I do recognize everyday what a wonderful
and special mother I have.  I am sorry
if I only tell you how special you are
once a year.
   I do love you and I hope you have
a wonderful Mother's Day.
I miss you.

*Elizabeth Baker*

## Beauty of the Night

Have you ever watched the sun go down and the skies grow dark and
      still?
The soft night breezes gently blowing through the trees upon the hill.
When most of the world lies down to sleep the rest of the night long,
And the crickets begin to serenade with their beautiful rhythmic song.
Then suddenly you gaze into the sky and see pretty specks of pearl,
Against a beautiful black velvet coat - then your eyes begin to whirl,
For right above your head you see the beams of the midnight moon,
And you know your time to fall asleep is coming very soon.

*Jo-Ann Barberio Tompkins*

## A Gift

At birth it is dictated by some almighty power up above,
That a blessed few should be bestowed with a special gift of love.
It is a love which cannot be earned through experience,
Nor acquired in some form of an award.
It is a gift which can never be taken,
And once given it need not be replenished nor restored.

It is a gift freely given, even before it can be truly understood,
Yet its fruits are always evidence to feelings true and good.
It is a gift which provides a shielding warmth,
And a beaming light each time it is brought to mind.
And although it is sought by many,
It is a treasure that no man can ever find.

It is a gift which should be spoken of often,
But seldom is the frequency with which it is heard.
But its pleasures are so deeply cherished,
That it is not easily put into the spoken word.

This love is special in that it must be given
From one place and no other.
It is a love originated from a sister,
And given to her younger brother.

**Jack A. Rahm**

## A Time Of Thought And Reflection The Woman She Is

Cute she is, no doubt there can be. Charm she has, no question of
that as with her personality, no debate is required or needed.
Of her tact and persuasion to produce results, the fruitful facts
are clear and plain; though not always fair and square.

With her to trifle is most unadvisable; as sly and prideful her cause
to advance she makes no attempt to conceal. Her opinion to plans and
agendas does she not in the least withhold. Her thoughts and feelings
of mind she feels most free to express on any and all matters.

Oh, no doubt of the intensity of her fervor, and how clever she is.
Not at all shy or reserved, she will let you know what the score
quickly is. So when she is about be most cautious and careful of your
mouth and step. For if out-of-line or out-of-place you should speak,
act or be; the price of infraction you will most certainly pay.

Furthermore, for your peace of mind, and enjoyment of relationship,
if possible; be kind, nice and accommodating. Say yea or nay, and
along with the game play and nothing more. In all the doings promote
harmony and tranquility as much as possible.

**Johnny L. Madden**

## The Sun

The sun is a bright fire ball
That glows in the vast blue sky.
It rises in the morning
Leaving the sky streaked with pink and orange.
Then the sun warms the earth and
Is prepared to get people motivated.
Finally, it goes beneath the earth
And leaves the sky streaked
With bright, beautiful colors
which, this time are lavender, pink,
orange, and yellow.
Then a whole new day comes about,
And the pattern of the sun's path
Begins all over again.

**Jennifer Haley**

## Twilight Hour

I dream of you at twilight dawn
    that half-wake, half-sleep time before sunrise
When leaden body and mind are adrift
    with cobwebs of sleep still upon my eyes.

You touch me, caress me with ethereal hands
    lips brushing mine are soft as a dove
I reach out with arms that are aching for you
    to hold you once more, my life, my love

But, my arms remain empty, holding naught save air,
    your presence lingers in my shadowy room
As Ariadne paints blackened sky to gray
    I awaken from my sopor, alone in dawn's gloom

**Inez Rooney**

## Help

Lord, send me where I won't go, Lord send me,
That I might help the weak to grow,
That I might help the feeble walk,
Lord, that I might help others grow,
Lord, that I might help the silent talk,
Help me to help others grow. Send me Lord, that I might grow,
Humble me Lord, that I might know, that unto Thee all glory flows.
Lord, let me stand and hold the hand of some
    child who has not seen to claim the land.
Lord, help me to help the sick lift eyes to Thee,
That they might see, the promise of eternity.
Help me Lord, to extend my hand to the lost,
    and show them that Jesus paid the cost.
Lord send me that I might grow.
Humble me Lord, that I might know, that unto Thee all glory flows.
Help me Lord to do the little things,
If a dish needs washed or water brought,
Humble me Lord, let me help.
Help me to help others grow.
And keep me mindful Lord, that to Thee, all glory flows.

**Garnetta Clark**

## Rose

As perfect as a Rose can be
that is what you are to me
Strong in the cool winter days
Healthy in the summer haze
You bloom so perfect, so gentle at ease
You're so calm and always ready to please
Your stem does not bend. It stays straight and strong
When the wind blows - it does you no wrong
Once people take a look at you
They fill as though your love is true
The fire red that you hold so bright
How it glows in the dust of the night
When you are with others, oh how you stand out
as though - happiness and love is what you're about
But in the shadow of the night
When the moon rays - shine on you - oh what a sight
You stand in this perfect pose
Just like a long stem beautiful Rose
This is what you are to me mother
A Beautiful Sweet Red Rose and nothing other

**Jacqueline Byrd**

## Untitled

But for different dress,
You've got a smile up your sleeve,
Like my little girl.

**Phyllis Sue Newnam Sand**

## True Reflection

'Tis only but equality
That makes us so profane and shallow.
We're but sculptures of prevarications
Our freedom is somewhere but here,
And only for a spare of time
In which we stand over a pond
We see our true reflection
Moving, dancing to the rhythm of our own stillness.

For this but water that moves
And we? We do too, unconsciously.
Oh, the breeze, it is the pounding of the drums
Which shakes us even more.

But we step back,
Away from the water,
Back into our apathetic quest to request
Nothing but our own foolish equality.
Returning into our
Narrow-minded, diurnal, self-being existence
Like horses with tunnel-vision.

*Eugene Farber*

## Only the Weak Survive

Glenn, you're the stronger half of our whole
That navy blue tuxedo really looks great on you
There's nothing like being as happy as a fish in water.
Glenn, this is the beginning of a new life for you, and I know
that you're extremely nervous, the sweaty palms and the constant
pacing back and forth are a dead giveaway, but you'll be just fine.
You're in the spotlight now! Mama's crying, and you give her your
silk handkerchief. God, I wish that this was all over, you screamed.
Everyone in the room thought that all you wanted to do was to get
out of that miserable monkey suit.
Instead of going through with the vows, you ceased the ceremonious
celebration by committing suicide in front of your friends, family,
and me. Blowing your brains out, in front of me, wasn't very
thoughtful, bur after five years, I understand your need to put
an end to all the internal suffering. From time to time, I still
smell the gun powder, and the sight of your face covered with
crimson red blood makes me want to throw up. You were always as
strong as an ox, at least that is how everyone saw you. I thought
only the strong survived. So if that is true, what am I, your
weaker half, still doing here — surviving?

*Jan Sandusky*

## Hourglass

And now I strike another match, warning all the spirits
That now I'm all alone and I breathe so loud they hear it
And I'm watching it glow with a shining, shimm'ring light
While all the sunlight has gone down, leaving only night
And the wax is dripping down from the stagnant, burning flame
I am holding it so close, but it never feels the same
All the inspirations fleeing on the rising smoke and heat
Without any hope to reconcile the lies I've kept discreet
All I see is melting candle, nothing stable left to see
The shrouds and cloaks have fallen on the circle all around me
With the stars against my will, and no will to back my pride
I have nothing left to lose and there's nothing left inside
The fading, blurring void that they thought was once a being
Has become an empty shell from which spirits now are fleeing
And all this hatred in me is consuming all my thought
All the fractured dreams I have, have come to be my lot
And without the reasons for myself, I have to shy away
I have to leave before I see there's no time for me to stay
The helpless, drowning, heartless words, slipping through my hand
All is slipping all away as fast as hourglass sand

*Dave Thompson*

## She

*Dedicated to Vicki Lynn Dalton*

She's a dew-drop on a rose, with a heart
That overflows, with love for me,
her love for me.

She's the apple of my eye, makes me
feel I'm ten feet high, she builds me
up, she builds me up.

She's the kind of girl that's always there
even when you're down. The kind of girl
that simply cares, she'll never fool around.

Vowed to love her all my life, when I
took her for my wife, she's good to me,
been good to me.

More than lovers were best friends,
happily the story ends with this in
mind, till the end of time, we'll love each
other so...

*David Rivera*

## Moonstone

What gentle spirit slumbered in this stone,
that plucked from beach lay in his fevered hand?
Shaped, smoothed and polished by a force unknown,
its mystic beauty now obscured by sand.

We washed it, dried it, held it to the light
where all its spectral colours came alive.
A look of wonder made his smile so bright,
it seemed both boy and moonstone were revived.

The stone was carried with him through the years
and it was with him on that fateful day
when he was lost forever with my tears.
My heart weeps; tears have nothing more to say.

What gentle spirit wakens in this stone
and in my hand tells me I'm not alone?

*Elizabeth Bigelow*

## Lost Love

My love's eyes are like ponds,
that reflect my love when I look through them.
My love's lips are like those of fire burning from a fireplace on
   a cold winter's night.
My love's skin is tear drops,
that escape my eyes when he is not there.
My love's hair is like strands of silk that fall gently upon his brow.
My love's soul is the blanket that covers our bodies at night.

Or maybe my love's eyes are really stones, that never shone for me.
And maybe my love's lips are cold as ice that never felt a ray of light.
His skin might be like the tear drops I cried because he was not mine.
Could his hair be that of dead grass,
that crumples at the ends with the slightest touch?
Can it be that my love's soul is really the darkness I hide in?

I lost a love I thought was mine,
But how could I, when His love was never mine to begin with?

*Amita Shenoy*

## To Sea No More

A cabin boy on a ship was I,
that sailed for Africa on a sea as dark as the midnight sky.

Once there the seamen would go on shore,
with ropes and chains and guns they bore.

They would return with scores of dark men,
all bound and scared, strong and thin.

Down below deck these men would be chained,
crammed side by side for weeks on end.

A certain amount of loss was expected,
when forced to lie in waste — they infected.

The cries they made, the misery, the smell,
for those poor creatures it surely was hell.

That was my only voyage you see,
a seaman's' life was not for me.

### *Elizabeth Edwards*

## Little Things

It's the little things
That tear me to pieces.
It's the things that no one else notices,
The reminders that only affect me.
It's the "If only's", "What If's" and "Why not's"
It's all the things that should be.
It's what no one else can see,
Your pictures, the nightmares
and the unfulfilled dreams.
It's those tiny feet - prints in black ink.

Little things
Like newborn babies, diaper commercials
Baby clothes and baby toys.
It's unused yellow booties, Winnie-the-Pooh and the Color Pink
Any of these things can make me cry.
Any little thing makes me want to die.
Because all these things should make life happy,
complete and full, but, instead -
Each of these things make me wish,
If only I had my little girl.

### *Gerene C. McNatt*

## Missing Uterus

I miss my uterus,
   that thing
      that seemed to want
         to bleed me dry;
Until I threw up my hands:
   "I give up," I cried,
      and let them toss it
         in the surgery bin.

My uterus had given me
   my sunshine boy,
      and my youngest,
         the rainbow, my heart song,
            many years ago.

I did not understand what this female trouble was.
I did not know that my uterus cried for me.
I could not cry my awful sorrow, my dreadful hurt;
And so my uterus wept red tears for me.

And now, when my loins quiver
   from my lover's caress,
      I miss my uterus.

### *June Engle*

## Remember

The ocean shaped my heart
that you will always remember me.

I may appear unusual in form and color,
but I am the true nature of life's creation.

A million waves brought me to you;
my strength and beauty is everlasting.

I was made for your pleasure,
your eyes can enjoy me in my natural state.

Remember where you discovered this heart.
It was on the beach,
surrounded by one of the wonder of the world.

The sea, my evolution.
Embracing me now, and forever.

### *Juanita Lee Owens*

## Words and Music

You wrote the music and I sang the song,
That's the way it was during our life long.
Often the melody was soft and sweet,
In lyrical sounds the strain would repeat.
Sometimes the score would strike a minor key,
Echoing tidings of melancholy.
Moving down the board strident chords would play,
In discordant bass notes of black and gray.
Arranging the theme for true harmony,
Our life then became a grand symphony.
The music stopped when death caused us to part,
But its muted tones linger in my heart,
Until the day when we have our rebirth,
In the soon restored Paradise on Earth,
When all the people will joyfully sing,
A never ending praise to Christ, their King.

### *Edith Stahl*

## Garbage In-Garbage Out

Computer programmers always tout
The adage: Garbage in-Garbage out.
The human mind is a living computer.
Of that there's very little doubt.
Programmed with education, ethics, and experiential time
Added to mores, philosophy, and religion
Impressed upon the human mind;
If garbage gets in there's resultant garbage out.
The particular garbage cannot collect to compost day by day,
To be spread to produce a greener field;
But remains to feed a virus of decay
Within the life it occupies
Until it's submerged in fetid stink.
That odor society cannot withstand
And gasping weaker from it shrink.
So friend, with garbage in one cannot win.
But be found refuse without a doubt
To be spewed in the end as garbage out.

### *Charles H. Thornton*

## I Wish...

I wish I had a delicate porcelain doll
that is wearing a fluffy white gown.

I wish I was a beautiful bluebird
flying among the grass.
I wish I was a black horse pounding
on the ground.
I wish I was a boat rocking like a cradle.
I wish I was a book shelf so that I
could hold books.

### *Emily Newell*

## My Boyhood Friend

'Twas dark and cold one foggy night as I was walking home,
The air was damp, my clothes were wet, it chilled me to the bone.

The sound of many crickets chirping, was eerie to the ear,
And as I walked along the trail, there suddenly appeared,

A dark and loathsome ugly shape that stood my hair on end,
That made me gasp a strangled breath, no motion did I tend.

I stood there looking, no breath expelled, the creature did not move,
My fear arose, my throat did choke, my bowels I thought I'd lose.

And just as I was sure to faint, my worries turned about,
The moon shone through a patch of fog, which raised from me a shout.

The dark and frightful thing I saw, which made a boy of me,
Was long ago my faithful friend and favorite boyhood tree.

'Twas long ago when I was young when walking down this trail,
My friends and I brought many boards, a hammer and some nails.

We built ourselves a mighty fort, way up high to glory,
So we could hide from neighbor kids and tell our scary stories.

So once again my gnarled friend, your bark is aged and gray,
You've brought to me such boyhood charm upon this cold dark day.

*James McCampbell*

## My Angel

The love of my life.
The angel that open my eyes.
God, take care of my baby.
I only wish it was me holding her and loving her.
Though my arms feel so empty,
I know my little angel will be safe with you.
Help me through these days
so that in sometime to come the world will be beautiful again.
My beautiful daughter Christina Marie the angel I love

*Donna M. Stephens*

## The Beauty of Today

What a lovely beginning for today.
The beautiful dawning seemed to say,
"Behold, not a cloud is in the sky
To cast a shadow as the day goes by."
Then comes evening with the sunset's show,
Followed by the twilight's gentle glow.
Oh! what can I do to add to the day's beauty?
Shall I seek only to do my duty?
Or shall I prayerfully and joyfully live
That joy to someone else I may give?
Oh! I believe I've found the way
To add to the beauty of today.

*Dottie Howell*

## For Emily

As I sit here looking at the shimmering light bouncing off
the duck floating on the lake...
I think of you...For duck was word one.

As I scramble around the kitchen on a harried night after
work, trying to cook and bake...
I think of you...For pots and pans were your greatest fun.

As I sit on the porch pondering the stars at night knowing
soon the world will wake...
I think of you...For those stars gave you to me.

And when life's pressures are too much to handle and I feel
one more day I cannot make...
I think of you...For you are my angel baby.

*JoAnn E. Hogenson*

## Carolina Mornings In Love

Carolina mornings in love, are best in the world by far.
The beauty of mountains without sounds of machines or cars,
Silence of a cool breeze that can be heard.
Birds are singing as we walk hand in hand, looking at
each other not saying a word.
Together we enjoy life and mother natures wonderful things.
We will trust and love, face what life brings,
The streams are long and rocky, they twist and turn.
A lot like love, as we grow older we learn.
Trees are tall, mountains are steep,
We're in love this morning, forever we'll keep.
Years are passing like clouds in the sky,
We're still loving and laughing, very seldom we cry.
Birds are sailing through the wind and gliding very slow,
As though they're saying" Carolina mornings in love,
We'll never let go".
My wife, my love, Carolina mornings and me
This is heaven on earth, with my love Beverly.

*Audley Cantrell*

## Meanderings

Spring is almost here again
the birds and geese are in their glory
the dawn has come in shades of pink
life goes on with her story

The months have passed since you have gone
the cold snow of winter has melted away
the spring rains will soon be here
to wash the chill away

But still my heart shall miss you
your warmth and love... too far away
you warm now the land of Heaven
a better place...so you must stay

Give love to all those who have gone on before
to those who's words I cannot hear
those whom I miss since they've gone on
and hold so dear...yes, hold so dear

And spring is almost here again
the birds will soar in early dawn
the sun shall shine, earth will be made warm
and life, precious love, shall go on, yes, life will still go on.

*Deanna Brown Pointon*

## The Birth Of My Son

The birth of my son is the birth of my life
The birth of my son is the birth of my marriage
The birth of my son is the birth of my manhood
The birth of my son is the birth of my love for humanity
The birth of my son is the birth of my belief in God

With my son's first touch I knew I was alive
With my son's first cry I knew I was wanted
With my son's first mess I knew I was needed
With my son's first smile I knew I was happy
With my son's first snoring I knew I was home

And now we take walks in his stroller and talk
And now we read bedtime stories together and learn
And now I lay awake listening to him breathing, praying
And now I open the doors to his dreams whispering my love
And now I know what it's like not to be selfish
And now I try to be the father my father was to me, wise

The birth of my son is the birth of my life

*Dennis E. Hackin*

## Writer

Lost in a book unfinished, gone to get the pen off the counter
the book still written with the finger of someone
Someone not seen, only heard but not by his own voice
a voice carried through air telling me what to do
Shut it out, the words are not my own: got to write the book
myself
forget those who do it for me
I hear the voice of all those, all but one, one I can't hear
listen for it, hear for your self
Lost in a book unfinished, looking for the pen to use
it can't be heard it's loud
    LOUDER, LOUDER, LOUDER
I can hear it now...........myself.

### *Christopher L. Rohe*

## Fake

This illusion is parting, bringing me down
the charade has to end.
Life is a memory of intelligent fools,
who knew better than to get involved.

I'm not who I say I am, or maybe I am
but then, you won't understand.
I'm circling around, finding myself,
but right now I'm just a fake.

Strange conversations are passing my by
but I don't have nothing to say.
Cornered and hungry, you might do anything,
but for me it's a definite fact.

Strange on the surface, stranger farther down
I'm still not sure what to do.
Born into stillness, Born into insanity
I'm just trying to understand.

### *Chris Young*

## A Timeless Day

Hear the sounds of the village on a warm spring day,
The children all about us at play,
The sound of many moccasined feet,
Going out to hunt for meat,
See the sun shine on the grass and dew,
Early in the morning when everything is new;
Women at work grinding corn,
Or mending the leggings her man has torn,
Young lovers pay no heed to what the old ones warn,
And in the tepee a child is born.

### *Gary Perkins*

## Frustrations

The color of frustration is black
the dark sky before the storm.
Never knowing when the thunder will crack
or when the lightning will begin to strike.
The heavy silence sets in
a smell of water permeates through.
The senses disturbed can not pin
Whether to be distressed, calm, or bemused.
Then the North wind begins to blow
pushing the forlorn trees around.
The rain begins to flow
tears from the confused sky.
While the lone bird stands dripping
alone and in despair,
A faint ray is peeping
letting the bird know it's still there.

### *Izabela Debkiewicz*

## "What Is Happening"

*(Dedicated to the victims of the Oklahoma City Bombing)*

The sun was shining oh so bright,
The day held opportunities and challenges,
But oh, certainly not the possibility of fright.

The children, oh so sweet and pure,
Were given over to the day care center
Where they knew their safety was secure.

The men and the women totally unprepared,
As they started their day of work they
Went about, for sure not aware....

Then tragic struck, took them all by surprise,
Now there is no feeling of peace and fear has arised,
The destruction of broken bodies, hearts and minds,
The loss of loved ones and pain all intertwine.

How do we know we'll ever again be safe,
And that once again our life's won't lay in waste.

How can this be, for do we no longer
Live in the land of the free.

### *Carolyn A. Curran*

## Last Day

This is the day
The day of the death
The day that my best friend
Took his last breath
He'd been drinking and driving
When some kids out had run
In front of the car, just to have some fun
There was little time to react
Before the bodies were thrown
But he couldn't control
The way the car rolled
The police came to the accident
And what did they see?
The bodies of small children
Thrown all over the street
My best friend had been driving
Just a little too fast but it wasn't the speeding
That had slowed his react
If he hadn't been drinking they might've had a chance
But now seeing the headstones I see the chances have passed.

### *Jennifer Waun*

## Caught in the Upbeat of Opus 5

Our whispered warmth tempered that January night.
    The first note struck true enough.
    Its bittersweet poignancy echoed —
            and re-echoed —
    and was finally silenced by the acoustics
    of time and space.

Opus 4 is over — and gone — leaving but voiceless emptiness.
    But even emptiness can retain the memory of a cadence.
    And sometimes a long-forgotten note of the flute
        picks up the beat — to whisper its original
        obbligato in a chamber of silent echoes.

Your voice may have done it — or perhaps an
    unknown drummer marks the time.
    Whatever happened, it's there.
    Shall we listen to it, Dear One?

### *Irvin W. Long*

## The Shadow Of The Moon

He walked into the desert carrying only empty memories.
The desert sun tried to drown him in waves of blistering heat.
Gasping for air, he could only stand thinking of the shadow of the
memories that had disappeared with the morning heat

The wind slapped his face, he could almost feel her hands.
The hours turned into evening lights.
He stood his ground, his face, blistered from the heat and dried blood
lay upon his cheeks.

The wind stopped and the heat turned cold and still he stood waiting
for a sign.
The full moon rose and tears came to his eyes as he reached out to her.
How can I live without you?
What would a morning cup of coffee be without you?

The moon was closer now, memories seemed to rise from the moons
surface.
He could almost see her now, etched in the shadow of the moon.
Ever so softly he could hear her voice in the twilight of the moon.

Darling I will always be with you!
Picture me at your side, let me smell the aroma of the morning coffee.
Talk to me at night, let my spirit live in your world until your
can join me in mine.

*David C. Reffert*

## The Devils Are On The Loose

The Devils are on the job, trying to see who can they rob.
The Devils are on the phone talking about me, you, Mary and Mrs.
Jones. They never stop talking to realize what they are doing is
wrong. They talk all night, and talk all day, please tell me God
when do they ever have time to pray?

The Devils are on their jobs, breaking up peoples homes by talking
so much on the mean machine called the Telephone. The Devils are
in the church, and some of the biggest Devils sit on the front seat,
clapping their hands, patting their feet trying their best to keep up
with the beat. The Devils get up in church to testify, they'll get the
church going, by making a fake cry, then wind up telling a big fat
lie. I hear people getting up in church saying,"God blessed me from
smoking," some even say, "God blessed me from taking drugs."
But I never heard anyone get up in church to say,"God blessed me
from my Telephone, because honey I know I talk too long on my
pink Telephone."

Now if you talk on the telephone, don't talk about what someone
else has seen, or what someone else has heard. Please talk about
what you know, because that "He say, She say" thing can get you dead.

*Alfred Bryant Jr.*

## Spring

Spring is weaving her magic spell,
The dogwoods with blossoms are gay,
The breezes are whispering joyful tunes,
All nature seems bent upon play.

Soft green wedding veils drape all the trees,
And the brook sings its own secret song
As it bubbles along over sandbars and rocks,
Glad that its journey is long.

The swallows are building their nests in the eves,
The sparrows are twittering near.
The songbirds are singing their own joyous lay
With notes that are fluently clear.

The bees in the clover are buzzing away,
The butterflies hover there, too.
My own heart's responding with feelings of joy
For everything's shining and new.

*Berniece MacGregor*

## Untitled

I remember the cold marble, the fragrant sea,
the dry red rock, the hot sidewalk, the inviting mountain
all that has made me, I remember
torched yells from bloody sheets, seeking solace in
the passing train noise, laying alone in the rain
of my soul, holding my still child's belly in fear
of hearing a heartbeat, looking at my blood to see
the invisible virus
all that has made me, I remember
patting your back because he was gone, barbie
pool, barbie clothes, barbie car, barbie sandra,
a song I cannot help to cry to, your love so fearful
I cannot tell the truth
all that has made me, I remember
trembling beneath an angel
coming at the sound of your breath,
feeling like a goddess every time he looks at me,
protecting him from me, feeling like an old soul healed.
All that has made me, I remember.

*Jasmine Savio*

## The Fleeting First

The first fragile violets of spring,
the first exhilarating swim of summer,
the first nipping frost of autumn,
the first downy snowflakes of winter,

The first two tiny teeth,
the first wobbly steps,
the first faint freckles,
the first day at school.

The first bite of turkey at Thanksgiving,
the first gift found under the Christmas tree,
the first loud burst of fireworks on Independence Day,
the first strains of "The Wedding March" at a wedding.

Alertly, with all of your senses
savor each fleeting detail.
Though first may come again
with each new season,
with each precious - child,
with each gay celebration,
that "ordinal one" will exist
only in your heart hereafter.

*Judi Stuart*

## I Am The Seed Of Knowledge

I am the roots of my father,
   the flower of my mother;
I am the growing seed of knowledge.
I celebrate the life that is within me
   and around me.
I breathe the clouds of immortal beauty.
I speak to the gods who helped raise me.

I remain One with the Earth, and
   transcend all thoughts that come to mind.
I may recall yesterday,
   yet I live for today.
I am Christine,
   and I am all that created me.

*Christine Klein*

## A Table Grace

Dear God, we thank you that we could hear
The food being prepared with love so dear.
And I thank you, Lord, that I am truly able
To see my friends gathered around this table.
And we thank you, Lord, that we can smell
The aroma of the food that we love so well.
And I thank you, Lord, that I can taste
This meal which wasn't prepared in haste.
And we thank you, Lord, that we can touch
This delicious food that we love so much.
And we ask you, dear God, in Jesus' name,
To bless the handicapped who can't do the same.

*Carl L. Paulun*

## A Glass Blown Ship

A glass blown ship that's known no storm but tells a story still;
The fragile sailors find no warmth to ease their weary wills.
Time has not a place on board, for those who live the sea;
The life behind is not restored, nor put to memory.
What pulls his heart to crystal capes and ports of teasing towns
To only find that life escapes, and still the sea astounds.
The glass blown ship that never sinks nor passes in the night,
And yet adventure slyly winks and lures men to the night.
With but a jolt it sails no more and lies below the sea:
Its sailors find a final shore and learn life's mystery.
So many yarns her cabins weave docked at her watery slip,
And fragile sailors all believe, who sail a glass blown ship.

*Jana Maddox*

## Sunflower Soul

The ribbon of road is long and winding.
The gnarling oak trees line the way to
My destination.
The artist's knife cuts deep across the
canvas, from time to time;
Widening the vast prairie.
A light breeze combs the fine grasses
Leading to the horizon.
The sunflowers bow their deep brown faces
And lower their weary arms;
Under the sky exploding with hues of purple,
pink and blue.
The sun slowly setting as I travel home.
I am weary like the sunflower.
In the morning my heart lifts with
The rising sun,
As I journey down the same road
I had the night before;
The sunflowers, now so fresh, unlike
They were then.

*Chris Kulinski*

## I'll Go into the Harvest

I'll go into the harvest the field's already ripe,
  The heads now are heavy, may fall er'e comes the night.
I'll rusk out now, to gather each ripe grain that I can,
  The fruit's already falling and their the souls of man.

God send me to the harvest to the fields already white,
  Help me Lord to reach them and show to them your light.
Each precious grain I gather as through this life I trod,
  Will be a precious reaper in the kingdom of our Lord.

I'll go into his harvest as he shall lead me on,
  I'll be his harvest reaper, until the he calls me home,
Till others reap the harvest among the souls of men,
  Let me gladly labor, till Jesus comes again.

*Ataka Rhodes Royse*

## My Sanctuary

Amid the soft twilight of the snowy landscape,
  the golden moon silently ebbs behind velvety clouds.
Long dangling icicles slowly reach for the earth,
  the quelling sun recedes behind snow capped peaks.
Small mountain quails fleeting swiftly amid sagebrush,
  darting about seeking meager morsels of food.
Chickadees sitting upon snow laden branches,
  fervently pecking seeds from jutting cones.
The serenity of the majestic mountain glen,
  so fully touches my soul with reverence.
My inner spirit rejuvenated by nature's grandeur,
  my yearning spirit nourished from afar.
I leave this refuge of tranquility behind,
  while thoughts linger amid snowy vista.
My soul filled by natures splendor,
  my heart instilled with love.
One day I shall return to my sanctuary,
  savoring the fullness of nature's legacy.

*Dave R. Oester*

## Children

From falling leaves through blowing snow into
the greenness of spring.
Emerged the word known through out mankind.
Moms the word equality beef.
Bulls beef and lock the gate.
Grain and gain he doesn't always know the game.
Who the one that stepped in the pie and got in the eye.
Wising up to a few words of wisdom.
Children sometimes go sour and surely floe through dollars.
With patience in the midst of uncertainly will help them flower.
Visions of violets can only happen when it's in their own time.

*John L. Thompson*

## Heartland's Heartbreak

Oh, 'tis a great pity,
The heartbreak in Oklahoma City.
From shock, anger, and disbelief;
there's no sign of relief.
A natural disaster perhaps would be better understood,
BUT A BOMB! For what possible good?
So many innocent people killed,
We know that wasn't God's will.
Jesus said "suffer the little children come to me",
Not "suffering little children to be".
Those DEATHMONGERS so cold and uncaring,
How could they be so daring:
To break so many bodies and hearts,
And split families apart.
Satan's disciples they must be,
Oh Satan we must return them to Thee.
Lord help us all understand why
So many had to die.
Oh, 'tis such a great pity....
The heartbreak in Oklahoma City!

*Aldina Collins*

## Untitled

Stepping through life a day at a time,
  the hours they pass away.

Looking ahead for what I might find,
  adventures to come my way.

Wanting for nothing and getting along,
  gleaning from life what I may.

The message is clear to the ear that will hear,
  the moment is where we most stay.

*Carl Brandon Morris*

478

## A Cowboy's Day

I get up early, I go to bed late,
The horse I ride is bucking and rank.
The day is either too cold or too hot,
I don't worry about this, a lot!
My mind is clear, my eyes are not,
I have to use them each day-a lot!
The cattle are restless, just like yesterday,
We ride through them and toss out some hay.
At noon I start fences, there's a lot to ride.
We're looking for breaks-on which there's cow hide.
I find a young calf, lonesome and cold,
I pick her up, over my saddle she goes.
Something's taken a nip out of her nose.
Line camp is coming up, overnight I'll stay.
The calf is walking, she's OK.  I start a fire for coffee and hotcake.
It's about midnight and I lay myself down,
With a smile on my face - very seldom I frown.
I'll wake up before dawn, the chores are waiting,
But the work is steady and I'll always be free,
The job is my Lady, My love, My passion - it's me.

### *James M. Stewart*

## Abuse

Abuse, verbal or physical is hurtful and degrading!
The hurt that accompanies verbal abuse is not understood by
Others because there are no visible scars.  Why can't it be
understood that constant, repeated put-downs, threats, name
calling and demeaning another does leave scars..deep seeded
emotional scars.  It hurts so bad.. especially when those you
love don't seem to care.

Physical abuse always is hurtful to those who receive it!
Hopefully when noticed..HELP will be offered by others and
love, understanding, caring and comfort will be given.

The scars that can not be seen.. hurt and need the same love,
understanding, care and comfort.

PLEASE HEAR as we speak..when we finally can.. we are hurting
and we need the comfort, understanding and love from those who
mean so very much to us.

### *Judy Kenney*

## To Have A Brother

It's hard to describe
The hurt the pain the sorrow
The shame we feel together as we try to get along
I can't describe my feeling while facing him to say
I love you
Not knowing if he'll laugh or cry to keep up his pride
Words can't describe the cold angry feeling that flood my heart
As I try to be kind while he sarcastically but playfully
Teases my mind
I can describe the feeling that comes over me when
I look deeply into his eyes
When he is showing to me a loving friendship that lies
Waiting just behind
At this time other feelings fall aside
This special moment causes me to suddenly realize
The true meaning of a brother
he's someone who at times feels just like me
So when my feelings are all I can see
I take time out to look way down deep
Then we can feel the love that there is to see

### *Debbie Land*

## "The Keeper Of Memories"

My world is so empty, my heart in despair
"The keeper of memories", it's just not fair
Am I the only one, have I the only key
That unlocks the guarded trunk, of hurtful memories
When I watch you from a distance, your face is still the same
Why has only mine changed, and darkened with such pain
The past still holds me, like a vice so tight
There's not a day with out it, and no peace for me at night
"The keeper of memories", I'm so tired and weak
When the past is so hurtful, it's pleasure that I seek
Release me dear God, from the "pain of the past"
And lighten my load, only this shall I ask...
Find a new "keeper", perhaps it's His turn
Let Him be the one, who's heart forever yearns.

### *Deborah A. Smith*

## Two New Little Angels

The new Little Angel stood at the gate, Saint Peter may I come in?
The kindly old saint looked down at her and his face broke wide
with a grin,
Come in my child, he quietly said, what's this you have a friend?
Yes, she replied and shyly reached back to pull the little boy in.
He started out ahead of me, but that really didn't matter for I
Ran fast and he crawled slow, so we would reach the gate together.
Saint Peter reach down and kissed them both and sent them on
their way.
With tear in his eye he quietly watched....two new Little
Angels play.

### *Barbara Jean Hendrick*

## Peace

Do you see the light shining there?
The light so bright and intense, yet bare?

I follow the light and pray.
I pray for peace to last through the day.

Do you see the water ripple here?
The water glistens and wets, but is only a tear?

I shed a tear and cry.
I cry for serenity to not pass me by.

Do you feel the sun's heat now?
The sun so hot and strong, but how?

I envy its strength to shine.
I'd shine for happiness to last for all time.

Do you see though the dark comes near?
The dark so deep and black, like fear?

I step back from the dark and wish.
I wish for no more to go amiss.

### *Daniela Ridley*

## Jesus Is My House

Jesus is my house for He is the foundation of my life,
The roof that covers me from the storms,
The walls that protect me from the ill winds of life,
The rooms where I rest, cleanse and feed my weary soul,
The windows through which I see God,
The steps I climb to God,
The doorway to Eternity.

Jesus is all I need.

### *Diane C. Smith-Stone*

## The Choice

Before in your womb I was allowed to dwell
The Lord said He already knew me well.
But you said over and over in a very loud voice,
"I am a woman and this is my choice.
I chose to make the decision which allowed you to be;
But whether you live or die is now up to me."
You gave me life, allowed me to form
Now don't I have the right to ask to be born?
I've heard that Heaven is a really nice place
And if you choose death, I know I'll go there due to God's grace.
But I would really like a chance on the earth to run and play,
To laugh and to grow and get bigger each day.
There are laws to protect whales and dolphins and even the big manatee
But not a single one to protect an innocent unborn babe like me.
Yes, you are a woman and like it or not you are also my mother.
If you don't want me, there are still other choices for you to discover.
Somewhere out there is a woman whose womb is empty and barren,
Just waiting for someone like me to give her a chance of caring and sharing.
So I ask you to choose carefully for me as I have no voice.
Please remember that God knew me before you made me your choice.

**Diane Bledsoe**

## Longer And Longer

When I first met you long ago
The love I knew began to grow.
My heart learned things it never knew,
How to love,
Trust,
Care,
And be true.

We have been through so very much
The tears, the laugher, the gentle touch.
Day after day our love grows stronger,
My heart wants to love you...
    Longer and Longer.

**Jackie Vavra**

## The Infinite Brains

Am I wrong, what is there?
The moor of endless time, unfrequented,
The gray, forlorn grass, stretching forever, never to be sheared,
Hair on the scalp, stirring with the ammonia thick wind,
The eyelid of cloud, the countenance eternal.

Here is the place of two brains,
Adorning the immortal contingencies,
A wealth of soil, curls of the deep,
Pounding together, a heartbeat conveyed,
The brain of day, the brain of night, the Redwood.
I elect the place of two brains,
I do not disavow the eternal eyelid,
Stretch with the immortal Redwood,
I sail with the ceaseless light,
The ceaseless dark,
The ceaseless birth,
The ceaseless death,
The immortal heartbeat.

**Christian Reed**

## Valley In Spring

The snow has melted and the grass has turned green.
Sunshine cascades down from the bright blue sky into the valley.
The daffodils and jonquils sway in the gentle breeze as it whispers
    it whispers through the trees of the valley.
Through this sea of flowers a narrow stream quietly flows.

**Alyce M. Nielson**

## Tomorrow's Dream

Tomorrow's dream do come through...
Surely the sun will come up in the morning...
It is like whispering something sweet... soft... surely...
in your ear.
It is like following the distant path of your hearts desire...
Surely the sun will come up in the morning...
Follow your dreams till tomorrow.

**Anthony Kelly**

## Love Is The Grandest Confusion

Love is the grandest of feelings,
The one that can devastate most.
Love is the greatest of problems,
To which our hearts play the hosts.
Love is the harshest of lies,
One appearing right out of our dreams.
Love is the most treacherous of tortures,
Producing the loudest of screams.
Love is the grandest illusion,
And no one can escape its spell.
Love is the grandest confusion,
The wanderlust we all know so well...

**Gloria K. Smith**

## Tales of a Broken Heart

This is a pain I cannot hide,
The pain I felt that day when you said good-bye.
You were once there and now you're gone.
All I can do now is just long,
For the happiness and love I once felt for you before.
But, now my heart is just to sore.
You will never understand the love, anger, and hurt I felt inside.
You will keep on wondering because our love has already die.
You tell me that you was never with another.
But, I'm sorry I can't help but just wonder.
You dug a deep pathway into my heart.
But, now all you're doing is just tearing me apart.
I loved you and you knew,
Now who am I to blame for losing you.
Sooner or later time will pass by,
But, I will never forget that day you said good-bye.

**Chanthy Ly**

## One Alone

My heart was broken and shattered
The pain was more than I could bear
All I lived for and all that mattered
Was gone when he said I don't care.

The heartaches were coming on fast
And loneliness in waves did sweep
For I had thought this love would last
But instead of joy now I would weep.

I cried for all that he was putting away
For his heart had turned to stone
And I begged so hard for him to stay
Cause one alone is just not a home.

So many days and nights before me
Not knowing what I would do
For I had failed somewhere you see
Now there was nothing to come home to.

But light comes after the darkness
And thank God life does go on
Thought I don't think so one day I might
Trust and love again and not be alone.

**Frances W. Pollard**

## The Final Journey

When you journey to that Country, not made with human hands;
The path is straight and narrow, and you must walk alone.
Protect your future goal with wisdom because you must prepare,
To join this wondrous Country, when earth resigns your care.
The colors of the rainbow will be flashing out their hues;
Blue depicts the sky above, yellow, stars of gold;
The ray of white is purity and green the earth below;
The opulent red brings the lightning flash that touches from afar.
Angels busy at their work hanging out the stars,
They represent all Christians who enter through the bar.
Carpets of clouds, soft and gray, harps all made of gold;
The Angels play their melodious harps to rapture up your soul.

*Elma A. Voorheis*

## Invisible Walls

How did these walls appear?  Invisible walls.
    The perfect moment in time slipped through fingers.
    The happy memories in their minds linger.

Why did these walls appear?  Invisible walls.
    One quarrel and everything left their side.
    All because of a few minutes of silence were set aside.

The invisible walls became more clear as the months swept by.
Finally, a night together, happiness formed like a sweet lullaby.

Did these walls finally fall down?
    Memories of the present or past that drown or behaved like a clown.

The walls did not fall as silence filled up the days and nights.
Words were exchanged one night, but the other didn't see the light.

The knife dug into her back deeper and harder.
Her words didn't seem to matter.

The walls were still there.  Invisible walls.
    It was time to say goodbye and go on with life.
    Now that it's over, everything can be taken with strife.

Will these walls ever fall down?  Invisible walls.

*Ericka Idler*

## Little Girl

The beauty of her sleeping, took my breath away
The picture of pure innocence, perfect in every way
Fulfillment of your young love, created in God's eyes
She looks like a cuddly toy, breathing deep with occasional sighs.

The beauty of her laughing, took my breath away
This inquisitive little girl, trying to grow up each day
With imagination and spirit, that everyone will love
Her school days proud and testing, her angel from above.

The beauty of her smiling, took my breath away
A young woman full of hope, school, work and dates each day
She won't be home now very long, it seems like yesterday
Her pure innocence was asleep, in that car seat far away.

Such beauty, love and innocence, so perfect in every way
Her skills, knowledge and independence, will carry her each day
The circle isn't quite complete, until the final bell
She'll find the same love and hope, that only time will tell.

The beauty of her sleeping, took her breath away
The cycle is full circle now, her life is full in other ways
For that little life depends on you, to grow just like a seed
You love, teach and share a life, just what every little girl needs.

*Donald R. Enders*

## May!

The glorious month of beginnings, the fulfillment of spring!  the
The promise of summer! —— May!
the time to see a tree bring forth a new leaf.

Look to the lilac tree opening it's packet
hear the faint hum of the yellow jacket!

An apple tree becomes a bouquet — it's fragrance spicy and sweet
Floats in the air — yards away.

Stars slowly dissolve as the sunrise lights the east
And like a great HALLELUJAH!  birds sing-as in a feast!

This is the teeming time-the earth abounds with the golden dust of
life dancing to new music!  — Listen for the sounds.

The leaves clothed in their new robes of purple and green sheaths
Hiding tiny hosts of flowers beneath.

Dusk brings those tiny lanterns — the Fireflies with their mysterious
messages winging thru the night —
adding a fairy-like glow with their ever wavering light.

Wild lilies of the valley, stretching thru meadows!
Forget-me-nots bordering a little stream!

THIS Glorious Season —— FLEETING, as in a dream,
But the remembered fragrances, we shall always keep, for this great
beauty is the reason "THE EARTH-THRU WINTER-HAS TO
SLEEP!"

*Jane Hanson-Harris*

## The Gothred Slayer

I was weak and he was strong, our battle lasted all night long;
The rage of mine that made it start, aimed my sword to his heart;
I was thought of as not so brave, as to lay a monster in a grave;
In a flash he snatched my sword, and in his eyes Brandy I poured;
He snarled and growled in great pain, battle advantage I now could
    gain;
I darted behind a nearby place, to hide my teary fear filled face;
Now he caught a fresh new scent, and after my stud, Triton, he went;
He then returned to make me his meal, like his last who was made of
    steel;
I thought back to his horror filled scream, as I ran fast to the
    stream;
I yelled out a bloody cry, like that of his as he die;
For when he cried out, the rocks and pebbles shifted about;
Now boulders shook and began to fall, dust and rock covered all;
Lo' I found that mashed in face, and jumped about that dreadful place;
I found my sword and cut off his head, and dragged it down that rocky
    bed;
The town sang out great shouts of joy, and some couldn't believe I,
    not a boy;
And gained a title to call my own, "The Gothred Slayer"
    who risked it alone.

*Brandy Lee Thomas*

## True Love

Very rarely one ever sees, from spring to winter snow;
The lovely enchanted face of this patient, smiling rose.
It needs not paint and diamond pins, nor gaudy folded bows;
To shine upon all who care, this single, silent rose.
When trouble storms and tears the heart, with love and care it sews;
'Til strength and hope beam bright and strong this loving, caring rose.
How it can live 'til time grows dim, no one will ever know;
Even when it feels not love, this humble, lonely rose.
If you should chance to feel it's touch, place in trust your soul;
Within the wondrous caressing of, love's beautiful, forever rose.

*James A. Marsters*

## The Light in the Midnight Sky

The light in the midnight sky was of stars dancing.
The rainbow whistled in flashing waves of dawn.
On the river bank a dual of doves sat upon a moonstone.
Singing a sweet tune of whistles, they flew through the sky
into the midnight sun. Soon they were invisible.
Coming from silver willows, their music so sweet,
a flock of golden swallows perched on a glistening tree.
In the grass, appeared a yellow bird. As tiny as a toothpick,
as thick as a yellow golf ball, it soon began to fly.
It began to sing a tune. Once it was finished, the dual
of doves had returned. Then over the clearing,
flocks of beautiful birds approached. I watched them
until the sky grew dark. Then I fell asleep. While asleep,
I dreamt a dream of a flock of doves in a silver stream.
In the distance was a purple sun. When the moon appeared,
the birds were gone. But I could still hear their sweet song.
A song of hope. A song of joy. A song that filled the heart of God.
Their song made the dark go light, made the stream turn gold.
As soon as it ended, I said to myself, This is what heaven must
hold.

**Christylyn Giunta**

## Reflection

I am what I am, but what am I?
The reflection I see in another man's eye?
Could there be more than meets the eye?
I am what I am, but what am I?

I am who I am, but who do I see?
The exact same person looking back at me?
Can the person be changed whose looking at me?
I am who I am, but who do I see?

I'm not too sure about tomorrow, but
I'm still here today. Though other things
may come and go, reflections always stay.

**David Felton**

## To End A "Being Late" Love

Walker: Do you wait for an easy path...?
the road is long, it's difficult track...
It's to wet your lips
with a bitter sip,
it's to plow the sea on raft without mast,
it's a Cleopatra searching for her asp
after loosing her precious candor..
When you never find what you're looking for.
when you have to cross the suffering line;
after feeling that... when nothing is fine...
everything fail like a broken ground...
like to tear up... like to tear down...
after feeling loosing a great real love.
the sorrow is coming... the painful is here...
And your life is sinking, you falling in tears;
together we have to cross flaccid rope,
because we are killing
this strange feeling...
This being late love...

**Antonio Jose Guerra**

## The Rose of Pain and Sorrow

I sit here and look at the rose,
The rose which reminds me so much of you, of us.
The rose that you gave me just before you left
When you told me you were mine forever.
But how can this rose remind me of you,
When a rose symbolizes love and all we had was pain?
Perhaps it's because my love for you is eternal, everlasting.
I know in my heart I'll always love you, even though I want so much to
hate you.
But, I can't.
Even though you took everything from me and gave nothing in
return.
So, now, as I sit here and think back, all the pain returns
As I realized I was just a pawn in your game of deception,
Just a conquest to be conquered.
All I wanted was your love;
Instead, I got the rose of pain and sorrow.

**Crystal Knight**

## The Creature

Slowly I approach the lair of the creature,
the same creature that has hounded me for so long.
It sleeps upon the bones of the fallen, safe and secure,
that none would dare seek it.

The walls of the narrow tunnel lead down deep,
black, dark and cold as stone under my touch.
My heart races, booming in my chest,
but carefully as a cat I take my next leap.
It sleeps upon the fallen, dreaming of its next victim.

Peering into the cavern, a dark and oppressive place,
lying upon the countless others it has claimed, I see it.
For any surprises, my mind is alert; my heart continues to race.
The creature sleeps, its cold lips curled in a satisfied smile.

But I falter, the excitement taking its toll.
The silence broken, the creature rises, its fangs bared and ready.
Its eyes dark and cold. The creature has risen.

About the creature I faced, the legends were wrong.
A cruel, deadly evil thing I thought would await.
This creature was glorious, and beautiful laird upon its throne.
The creature has risen, and I have chosen my fate.

**Earl P. Burke**

## A Garden of Flowers

A garden of flowers planted in spring, will all the joys of
the season bring. The rainbow of it's many hues, are sprinkled
well with rising dews. The Crocus has an easy grace, as it
peeps through the snow with a cheerful face. The Lilac blooms
in lavender pale, and over natures moods prevail. The Violet's
grow in purple hue, their gladness in spring again renew. The
Rose so adorned with beauty fair, is blessed with an essence
beyond compare. The snowy white of the Fleur-de-lis stands in
pristine majesty. The pansy so pensive and pretty near by, seems
both reticent and shy. The Daisy's never their secrets tell
so old in nature and loved so well. The Honeysuckle capricious
and small, climbs over the olden garden wall. The Dahlia dressed
in waxen green, seems to be the reigning queen. The Hollyhock
so slender and tall, preens her color over all. The Sunflower
nods it's heavy head, as it smiles down on the flower
bed. Delicate, precious, fragrant and fair, they charm the bees
with their sweetness rare. Soon the hummingbird so bright, sips
the nectar with delight. The butterfly with sprightly wings,
to the petals gently clings. The sunbeams shine on grass and
trees and joins the playful summer breeze.

**Fern I. Tuck**

## The Rocking-Horse Magnetic

I am:
The smile apologetic, the rocking-horse magnetic,
    the heart agoraphobic
of the murder alphabetic;

The silence unrequited, the needle uninvited,
    the echo unresponsive
of the serpent subdivided;

The answer unendowed, the question disavowed,
    the sacrificial portrait
of the domineering crowd.

*Derek Smith*

## Joshua

The smell of your hair, the smell of your baby sweet skin;
The smile that comes from your heart an lights up your blue
    eyes from within;
You are my sweet loving boy, you have given me so much joy;
I know in my heart that you are growing so fast and this
    babiness cannot last,
You are already so full of energy, a spirit so free, a precious
    life so short of a time given to me.
To protect and cherish, to love and to teach, to give to you
    what has been given to me:
Through Christ Jesus, your family and friends you will learn
    and grow and become a man.
Then you will leave and go your own way, but at least I had
    you for a little while, though it may seem only a day;
My sweet baby boy I love you, you see, so try not to grow
    too quickly for me;
You will anyway, this I know to be true, but I'll cling to my hope
    that for a little while longer with me I can keep you.
But, know in your heart, that in mine you will stay, that
    sweet baby boy God gave me that beautiful day!

*Dawn M. Jones*

## Where The Children Play

I stare in dismay at where the children play
The smog and the rubble, the broken stubble
The ooze beneath their feet, that's where I'd spend my day

Tin cans and jars, old junker cars
A place to hide, where God would cry
It's such a special treat

Acid mist and wretched odors, languished colors around the
borders
Imported toxins, complex potions
Beguile the senses, induce bad notions
I fear of whom I'll meet

Neverending, they'll climb and climb
The top they'll never reach
The spoils of success the winds will heap
A monster they cannot beat

There's not much left to say, as I heave and sigh
The leaves cannot disguise, the earth cannot hide
The fruits of labor, shown with paper
And all I can do is stare in dismay
At where the children play.

*Chit-James F. Cayton*

## King's Pawn

Game has lasted long many are dead.
The sound of bishop echoes in my head.
Two moves ago the queen was killed.
Much blood this day has been spilled.
Generals have tried best they know,
But enemy litters the board like fresh fallen snow.
Cold white faces continue to advance,
Unstoppable and persistent as an avalanche.
Skillful movement of enemies clergy,
Cut through our forces like doctors performing surgery.
King's existence is now in danger.
Fills a soul with uncontrollable anger.
Generals think and struggle to find a way.
King must escape to live another day.
To save a king they must kill a pawn.
When they order the move I'll be gone.
General's order came loud and clear.
The sound of bishop echoes in my head.
Game lasted long but now I am dead.

*Jared Brice Maloney*

## Taken for Granted

When the man meets the pretty woman's eyes,
the spark ignited an unbreakable love.
His good heart melted into a hundred dyes,
And life was like the peaceful song of a dove.

The man catches all the woman's quick glances,
and he alone can fill the vacancy in her heart.
They went everywhere, their favorite dances,
and when she cries, his soul feels like a dart.

The great love seemed to be an act of fate,
but soon the relationship began to fade.
Human nature takes for granted the good,
then the love ends like feelings never made.

They now act as though neither of them ever met,
but inside each heart, pain swells, you can bet.

*James Deasy*

## What Is Life

Life is the flower that turns it's petals to
the sun in the morning hour

Life is the breeze that blows through
the trees

Life is the bird on the wing that lifts
it's voice to sing

Life is the rain that falls from the sky
and makes the plants grow high

Life is the child that grows to a man
and tills the earth with his hand

Life is the man that at the end of his
time, he does not weep, because he
knows soon he will sleep

What is life, life is death, without one
you can not have the other, how could
you know that you live, if you did not
die

*Charles L. Call*

## Spring Awakening

The beauty of creation manifests itself in spring.
The sun sends down its warming rays to wake all sleeping things.
To walk in the woods 'neath the newly dressed bowers
Reveals newness of life in the awakening flowers.
I find hepaticas so dainty, and crocus of all shades
And Jack-in-the-pulpit as if a sermon he's made.
The carpet is the green moss speckled with brown
All of God's growing things wears a new gown.
To breathe the sweet air after one of spring's showers
Should freshen the soul from weary worn hours.
What a pity for those who look but don't see
The glories of nature as God meant it to be.

*Hilda Petterson*

## Untitled

As the day wears on and the dark creeps in,
The sun's a blaze of fire and the night is full of sin.

Young lovers free their passion, no longer is it hidden,
For in the cloak of darkness, it cannot be forbidden.

As the ball of fire descends slowly upon the sleeping earth,
A newborn child cries at the dreadful experience of its birth.

All trace of light is gone, there is blackness all around,
Nothing can be seen as your heart begins to pound.

In this land of nothingness you feebly find your way,
As suddenly you wake up and see the light of day.

*Carissa L. Guertin*

## Untitled

The sun gives a beautiful ray of which warms my face
The suns warmth gives a sunflower in a field a chance
to bloom from its embrace
The sun gives all the warmth and nurturing of a mother,
and gives the earth a chance to grow and hence gives a
life to another.
The suns beautiful rays represent a sign of peace and
gives those who are hurt a chance to let some things
go which cannot be released.
The sun gives everything a touch of beauty and makes
everything feel as if it were in a state of tranquility
The sun with all its gifts gives us a small touch of heaven,
when urges me to look up and praise and to sing with
glory, it's just as though I've read a fairy tale from a story
The sun makes me feel like a bird flying through the clouds
flying backwards, front and around.
I feel as though I can fly to heaven and back and fly to the
ends of the universe and never have to look back
The sun fills me with peace that for once I know that
happiness can now be in my reach

*Allison Napoleon*

## Sunset

Bursting through the clouds, a blazing, burning,
orange sun.
The sky masterfully painted with expertise. A
beautiful pink,
purple brush stroked across the sky. Caught in
the moment,
registering the sunsets in my memory, I awaken
out of shock.
The beauty is so awesome. I feel so small. In
awe, I stand
with my knees weak, almost falling to the
ground.
It's magnificent! I bend slowly to the ground
with my arms out -
stretched in praise.

*Emily Susz*

## High School Years

Oh what happened to those high school years
The times that brought so many tears.
A time where friends came together
And others were cast out forever.
Although I laughed through my hate
I wondered what I did to deserve this fate.
No one noticed, no one cared
To ease my pain, never bared.
No one knew what it was like to be
No one tried to find the real me.
Oh how confusing those times were
And wonder, would I ever be friends with her?
If I had only been accepted,
I might have never felt so rejected.
I'll always remember to this day
The pain and loneliness that never went away.

*Beth Warchol*

## Life

What is life? Is it the ramblings of the heart?
The trials and errors of the soul? Or, is it a
deep vortex of thought, that day after day,
we dwell upon, digging ourselves deeper and
deeper into?

Life is a play. No script; undefined. It is a
drama, a tragedy, a romance and a comedy,
all rolled into one. Actors walk on and off
the stage as people walk into and out of your
life. There are no practices, no rehearsals.

Live and act every day as if it were your last
performance. Improvise. If you act with enthusiasm, joy and
passion you will live so. Hold on to your
understudies tight. Teach them to act and to
live as you did. Teach them well; and with
love. Motivate them with the old adage; no
matter what... "The show must go on!"

*Amanda McFaul*

## I Hurt

I hurt
The trivial hurts that no one quite intends
And yet the blade of truth which cuts
Across the tissues of the mind
Can scar the smoothest skin of life's facade
It leaves its mark upon the soul and blends
Into the warp and woof of self - a hurt that never ends.

I hurt
For those whose loneliness can scarcely be endured
At times the song of life has faded
Far beyond the confines of the present mind,
And life becomes too close and stifling, tired
With thoughts of deep despair, for no one cares.

I hurt
For those whose life has sensed this cut
Incisive, deep and long,
They know the meaning, of the cross
Yet in a sense are strong.

*Frances W. Staley*

## Ode To A Vampire

The sweet caress of a vampire's kiss,
The true last sign of mortal bliss.
The last whimper of his prey
Marks the dawning of the day.
Our predator sleeps until the night
When he is wakened by the full moon's light.
Then he goes out to prey and kiss,
Truly the last sign of mortal bliss.
Then our story starts over again,
For centuries and centuries and centuries on end.
While we wake and while we sleep,
Through the dark, he does creep.
Souls he takes and souls he breaks
Souls that never ever wake.

*John Cole*

## Hope With Life

Who can say what shall be, while onward continues time;
the turn of events far beyond our control or design.
From moment to moment our existence sets on a balance,
that weighs the substance of our being, that we each are measured.

We often look towards tomorrow with memories of yesterday.
Passing moments are gone, yet lessons from then, influence today.
All through our days, we live from pleasure to pleasure;
while stored in our innermost thoughts are the causes of pain.

Through it all, breath is a festival with many spectacles.
Running our course is a test to endure a multitude of obstacles.
Yet beyond the purpose we each have meaning, to live is joyous.
As with tasting the butter with the sweet, we come to appreciate
   happiness, by overcoming suffering.

*Goo Gilmore*

## Anatomy of Fear

In amongst men, my solace I placed,
The voice within my thoughts it rejects,
For who am I among men for my trust to place,
My peace of mind, in their language I lost.

This miserable, unpredictable time,
Always my back for me to guard.
For whosoever my being to trust I put,
A good sound sleep in my time to evade.

To those all my love I give,
All those to whom my trust I placed,
Their minds my hands to anatomize,
For in this time, nobody is here but me.

Their language no more could I understand,
Their ways constantly inconsistent.
And oftentimes their smiles in my sleep I see,
But forever my senses their loyalty to ignore.

*Ayokunbi Banjo*

## Summer's Night

   Is it the summer's night and
the warm breeze that makes my heart
pound and my palms sweat?  Or is it the
stars in your eyes and the colors of your
hair.
   Is it the wine that touches my
lips, that shorten my very breath?!  Or
is it your girlish smile and the passion
in your walk.
   Could it merely be unbridled lust?..
Or is it true love.

*Author Woodruff*

## Autumn

Autumn is a special time of year,
the wind rustling through the leaves.
The multicolored shrubbery on the hillside
and the shimmering aspen trees.
The hills are just dazzling with all
the many colors, red, brown, gold and white.
Some of which are simply radiant
when they catch the sun rays just right.
The majestic colored forest is simply
marvelous with all the different colored leaves.
But the prettiest of them all seems to
be the quivering aspen trees.
A mountain stream is flowing down
toward a deep blue attractive brook.
Where some hungry trout are waiting
for some happy anglers hook.
All of the many different colors are
everywhere for everyone to see.
The trees and hills with all their
splendor and the quaking aspen trees.

*Chester C. Jackson*

## Untitled

SOMEDAY
The winds of change will blow away the silence
Tender words of interest and concern will be spoken
And my heart will sing and the sun will shine
Even tho' the day is dark and gloomy.

SOMEDAY
Two hands will clasp in fond togetherness
And eye look into eye in sweet understanding
Then my spirits will soar and the skies will be blue
Even tho' winter winds are blowing.

SOMEDAY
A warm and close embrace will signal security
And say "I love you" through words unspoken
And I will be at peace and the world will be calm
Even tho' adversity continues to knock at my door.

*Alice C. Criddle*

## Peaceful Encounter

I stand above the clouds on a mountain peak
The world far below puts me out of reach
Free from the earthly turmoils, terror and pain
For only a second I am suspended from the fast lane
I can walk among the clouds almost touch the sky
My being stretches as my soul cries
The planet moves on while the sun warms my heart
Now is my time to get a renewed start
I am now ready to surge ahead in this beautiful day
What matters how bleak and dangerous the way
I start to descend toward the dry valley below
My whole body is filled with a spiritual glow
I am running over with a happiness of hope and love
From the peaceful encounter that came from above.

*Dolores Lunsford*

## Summer Time

Cutoffs and tee-shirts and sandals and shades
The smell of salt water and sand quickly fades.
The beaches, the lifeguards, the sun and the sky
I do tennis and swimming, look at that GUY!
The pools and the ocean and all the great stores.
The shopping on streets, the relaxing on shores.
Going to camp so far, far away
Sailing on sailboats out on the bay.
No homework, no papers, God it's so cool.
A memory now, 'cause I'm still in school.

*Adrienne Wiggin Neff*

## Untitled

And here, I find myself alone.
The world goes on around me. I don't
understand why it does not stop,
though I have never controlled it.
Later, I will get into my car
the color of dusk, and drive to the coast,
after watching them from the top of the ferris wheel.
Their faces were blurred as it spun, but I saw them love;
how she held him, when he kissed her.
There, I was alone, sitting by myself next to James Dean.
Here, I am alone, but I am not sorry I made him angry.
Love has nothing to do with pure desire.
Soon, I will get into my Dusk and drive
to a revitalized life.
Until I can, I wonder:
What do these walls want with me?

*Donna May Daniels*

## On Growing Old

I am growing old.
The years are piled high, one upon the other.
They cast their shadows across my weary life.
I no longer have the options of the young.

Confined to the restrictions of an old and worn frame
I walk in vain toward the dreams that I once had
As I struggle through the fading years
And grope my way toward a semblance of my goal.

I know that life has a way of overflowing
With pain or sorrow
To thwart the joyous moments of each day
And grind away at my good intentions to prevail.

As I approach the twilight hours of my life
I wait with patience for the setting of the sun
When the gate at the end of this life's pathway
Will close behind me and I'll step into immortal time.

And yet within my heart there is no fear
Though the coming end may be near or far
Because my faith in God will take me home
And I'll spend eternity with him up there.

*Albert M. Hobbs*

## Harvest

The north wind brooms its way across
the yellow fields

The undulating sweeps making momentary
dips and long drags across the hill crests

Grasshoppers leap and fly in the torrid July sun
like helicopters wings beating in frenzied madness
against the hot dry air grasping another second of flight

The dusty earth powdered oozing between the toes
in puffs with each planted step

The hot air stifles breathing

The horizon dances in vibrancy
little blue streaks of lakes and rivers
mirage themselves

The world was 160 acres, the sun came up
it went down, food was on the table
the roof was overhead
there were 4 brothers and 4 sisters and
one set of parents

I was 10 and one with nature

Life would never be so simple again

*Frank A. Walter*

## When Death Does Come Our Family's Way, the Loss We Feel, the Grave does Seal Away

Families live and grow together, share together,
Their loss together, a treasured member of their clan.
The lives they shared, the hopes they dared; the memories that
Are retained.

The warm recalled emotions, of past experience; of happier days,
And sorrowful days, and everything in between that's done.
The blossoming of a life, the pain of sudden grief;
The molding of a family's mind; the honor to a loved one's name!

The tragic heartfelt loss, of a personage of past remembered
Family fame. The barren final emptiness,
The lonely hollow shallowness, of the pain of offsprings
Mournfulness; a bygone life has come and gone!

A familiar voice, a common gait, a studied face,
Will no more come this way again; for death's door has opened
Wide, its dark still mysteries await! The somber church bells
Toll their gloom, their gloomful brazen notes are heard.

A faint farewell, a fond adieu, a peaceful dreamless sleep is
Due. As loved ones pass by overhead, returning to their lives
Again, returning to their ways once more. Their footsteps will
Not tread this way again.

*Fredric Marsh Jr.*

## Appreciation

Thanks to your family; they included me.
Their taking me in really helped me, you see.
I feel like telling a story about happiness for many years.
Also there were times when we shed tears.
You're a mixture of sister and friend, and you will be to the very
end.
If God calls me, and it's my fate,
I'll be waiting for you at the gate,
Along with those already there to have the reunion we will share.
If God calls you before he does me,
I pray the reunion will still be.
All of us will be happy there,
And none of us will have a care.

*Gladys F. Blatchford*

## Birds Graceful Wings

Why do birds fly so gracefully with their bright colored wings?
Their wings are as bright as the morning sunshine.
Their movements are slow and look like a dancing stroke of a waltz.

Back and forth they go, up the horizon and down the stream of the
ocean.
Hear the roar of their singing.
When the flocks go migrating to find their love ones.

They're the most beautiful and enchanting creatures God has made.
Birds should be kept free and alone, to amuse their beautiful
feathers.
But when captured they're captured by those who can not see such
grace.

They're in fear.
Their feathers begin to fall apart as a symbol of such sadness and despair.
They must hide from such cruelty.

Freedom is their home,
high in the mountains and up in the sky.

*Jonathan A. Alfaro*

## The Big Bang

Quiet and calm in the vast back void
then appeared a perturbation of God's word
Time vibrated in and out of space's heart
rising and climbing in heated nought

A flaming explosion shook infinity
this was the start of sublime eternity
the star matter expanded from a single point
and this, God decided, He would anoint

Gravity laid down some tough forces
star dust formed into bright torches
the stars lit up the heavens wide
and time and space sat side by side

Four dimensions did now exist
this was God's deepest wish
the stars spread to higher heights
and soon came the birth of life
            *Allan H. Lambert*

## A Heart Reunited

My nights were long cold and rainy.
Then came the days, lost and lonely.
I'd find myself, reasons to cry.
Seeking for you, I'd try and try.
A voice, than a vision; is something there?
It's only my worries leading nowhere.
This is the time I would kneel to a prayer.
Hoping my wishes would not end in despair.
I begged the good Lord to stop all the pain,
and offer to hold you once more, once again.

I don't understand, my memory is bleak.
My thoughts of you are growing weak.
Day after day, I sense something wrong.
But something of spirit keeps me strong.
Now I'm resting at a strange place at last.
It's simple and peaceful, it came so fast.
Yes, brought together by love never lost.
Pain is now gone, my Lord rewards our cost.
My nights are forever, the days to my heart.
Our love is together and never apart.
            *Francisco Jimenez Jr.*

## "Thank You Jesus For Saving Me"

   I was lost and knew not what to do...
Then Jesus renewed my mind and open my eyes..
and brought me through!!!!
Then God told me son keep your eyes on me.....
and I will guarantee you peace.

   I've confessed my sins and ask Jesus to be Lord of my
life...So now the prison doors have opened and if it's God's Will,
I'll be blessed with a wife!!!!

   There are those who aren't physically incarcerated, because
they're not behind a bar....But they are spiritually incarcerated and
you know who you are!!!  You need to know that God
loves you so much and that's why Jesus set us free...

   Today, "Praise God Almighty "is why I'm able to
understand how blessed we are and say...
   Thank You Jesus For saving Me!!
            *Gerard Herriott*

## Icing

The flurries fly, circling, floating, aimless
then, their purpose found, they coat the open field,
embracing the empty trees once full of life's foliage,
now with barren branches reaching skyward, as if begging heaven
for sun's return to spring

The snow falls, oh how it traces a tree perfectly
poised on every branch and twig, on every bough, a
thin slice of white, a shimmering outline of beauty's stock

And it falls; covering everything like darkness
hiding lines, masking every detail, as if night, it covers all but
shape, all is coated with winter's icing in the morning stillness
laying sugary to the eye.
            *Greg Marron*

## My Angel

I screamed, you cried, and we both tried.
Then their you were,
So small, so perfect.
My angel from the sky.

Your coughs and Pox and mumps and such,
That kept us up all night.  Had me in such a fright!
Then he helped.
My Angel from the sky.

Your first date, you were late.
Had me pondering, what was your fate?
My Angel from the sky.

Your prom was just first class.
As you are lass.
My Angel from the sky.
            *Jan Martin*

## My Dream

It all started with position one, standing next to the barre.
Then, we moved on to leap and arabesque, combinations across the
room.
Finally, the big day came, my first time on stage.
The sequins on my costume shining, my hair in a braid.
Dancing the steps I learned just yesterday.
After a while, I grew and
Moved on to harder things; jete, tondu.
You were my hopes and dreams.
You were what kept me going in life.
When times were tough, I'd bouree turn to you.
I stepped on the dance floor, the music would start.
Suddenly, all my problems faded magically away.
I would soar on my feet, like a bird.
And the steps that were so difficult, seven years ago,
Came so easily now.
I was the best in the class, the teacher's pet,
   something I longed to be.
Everything came naturally, as if in a dream..
Suddenly, things got harder.
I won't give up though, not after all I've been through.
We're still together, and always will be, till the end of eternity.
            *Jennifer A. Howard*

## Butterfly Me

Butterfly me went for a swim
but I didn't see the cat
hunched just below the brim
            *Lauren De Rosa*

## Morbid Thoughts

Life is game, or so they say.
There are only two requirements, in order to play.

You must first, be born, and then you must die.
And the whole purpose of life, is to figure out why.

When you are born, you are taught how to play.
After you've learned, you are sent on your way.

At first it seems easy, it even seems fun.
Then, without warning, you loss someone.

You start searching your past, for how could it be....
That something like that, could happen to me.

You've met the requirements. Rules must be obeyed.
You'll play the game of life, until your dying day.

That's, when you realize, what you've already known.
When you play the game of life, you play it alone.

And suddenly you know it, you've figured out why.
The purpose of life, is to lean how to die.

*Bonnie K. Hills*

## Sunrise

The sun rises and sets everyday without notice.
There is a difference however, with the sun rising in the country
    or the city.

In the country the sunrise is very dramatic.
The fog starts rising and clearing out.
The trees on the hillsides and mountains appear with their splendid
    colors.
Green, red, orange and gold reaching for the sky.
The ever towering mountains coming into view.
The sun rising, demanding a fanfare.
Bellowing out, "I-have-risen!"

A city, fast paced, heavy traffic, has a quieter, subdued sunrise.
No fanfare needed here for the sun to rise.
It starts out dark with the buildings out of view.
Then the sun slowly rises.
The buildings in view as shadows.
Gradually they come into full view.
The sun is rising and saying, "Hello."

*Hope Brien*

## Permanent Tremble

There is a sudden rise in tears being produced,
There is a lack of compassion,
There is a sudden rise of aggression,
There is a lack of comfort.

Or is this the way it's always been?
I have been watching and listening,
But I haven't been paying attention.

I have been awakened to the trial of all humankind,
In celebration of the explosion, in terror, in sarcasm.
The large wooden door opening with a whistling, screeching innocent
side. With thousands of veins, muscles, and bones pushing with great
anticipation. My friends of knowledge and corners, my friends of
honor and grief. I, the great nothing, welcome you into my lack of
attention, into my lap of anger and seduction. My casket, my
throne,
my routine, and permanent tremble you hear.

*Dave Birg*

## Where Did Love Go

Where did love go! Ask the little old man? Seem as if
there is no more in the land. Look around you, what do
you see? There aren't too many people left like you and
me. Where are the ones that was so kind? God fearing in
heart, who reached out to help his fellow man.

Why is there so much hatred in the land? Woman against
woman and man against man, child against parent, which
is so sad to see, and this really hurts an old man like
me, to see the world crumbling and falling to its knee.

When I was a young man and in my prime, I never saw or
heard of so much crime. Even the baby cry out with pain
from the mother's use of cocaine in her vein. The other
day I heard a young girl say "I am so ashamed, of what
my father has done to me."

Now I'll pray for that young boy who didn't respect me,
stole my money, even raised his hand to hit me. I do
believe he enjoyed what he did as he ran away laughing
at me. But I can't find it in my heart to hate him you
know, cause then you could ask me.....WHERE DID LOVE GO!

*Dolores J. Parker*

## Have a Nice Day!

'Twas just before daybreak in a small quiet town,
there was an old man feeling so down
Complaining and cursing 'bout this and 'bout that,
nobody loved him not even his cat.
"Why does God do this?" he'd shout and he'd say,
I'm cold and neglected day after day."
Then came a voice so soft and so cool,
"If you do unto others they will do unto you."
"So stop complaining, Get off of your duff."
The good Lord was saying "Enough is Enough!"
"Don't Wallow in pity! Go out of your way.
Make someone else happy, then you'll feel that way."
Time will pass quickly skies will turn blue,
Then someone will go out of their way to see you.
It won't happen on instant, but soon on replay.
You'll smile at a friend and be happy to say.
Thank you for stopping, taking time on your way.
For yours and Gods love helped me "Have a nice Day."

*Eileen Wilcox*

## God's Garden

Beyond the sunset, flowers still bloom,
There will be no clouds to shadow the moon.
There will be no sadness to mar our days,
No tears to shed over others ways.

As we walk through God's Garden,
There is no whisper of doom.
There is beauty everywhere,
And there is no gloom.

Working for Jesus in his special place,
By the side of his Father with beauty and grace.
Bowing our heads in humble prayer,
Thanking our Father, we are all over there.

By His blessed grace he loved us all,
The great, the humble, the weak, the small.
His hand outstretched to lead us home,
Across the dark water, no more to roam.

*Evelyn Daily*

## "Think Of The Possibilities"

If I were to win a lottery ...
These things I think I'd do-
Payoff all bills -current and past due
Buy a new car-that we need so bad
And get a few things we never had!
A weeks vacation - to wet a line
Going fishing, we'd have a great time!

To set back and dream
Of the things we can do
Plan each day and don't be a fool.
Help our kids get on their feet.
A new car for each-what ever they need.

To win a lottery would be neat
Six numbers away from a grand treat
Your life would change- at the blink of an eye..
There are so many dreams that could come true.
What would you do ..If this happened to you?

Think of the possibilities...

*Clarence E. Good*

## These Three Words

These three words are so often used.
These three words are so often abused.

Said many times to capture your greatest treasure.
They mean much more than a single night's pleasure.

With these three words I promise to be there when you're in need.
I'll be there in a hurry, you'll never have to plead.

With these three words I'll give you my heart.
Not just a portion but every single part.

I promise to please you in every way.
And I'll do this each and every day.

With these three words, I'll fulfill your every desire.
From sun up to sun down, I will never, never tire.

You're the one who's made my life complete.
No one else could ever dare to compete.

Your love has made my soul soar like the birds.
This is what I'm saying, in these three words:

I Love You.

*Charles White*

## Friends Like Mine

Friends like mine are hard to find
They are constant, loyal and especially kind

The love they give touches my heart
O' please Dear Lord, don't let us part

I can feel their friendship, so true
May it last my whole life through

I'll share the love of those I know best
Until the day I am laid to rest

And as I wither away I know
My tears will somehow show
I am grieving in my state of mind
For the wonderful friends I left behind

*Arlene Pellino*

## Why Me

There are trials in life we all have to bear.
They are rarely easy and seldom seem fair.

It has occurred to me when trials befell,
If heavens's not on earth, then earth must befell.

I've looked up and asked, "My dear God, why me?"
Then slowly this answer was given to me.

God is not to blame for giving us this strife.
Good and bad things happen-it's the way of life.

I believe what God does is to truly care,
Feeding us love and strength by just being there.

But there's one thing we must do and it's not a hard task.
To receive God's help, we need only ask.

*Cheryl Quickle*

## Dreams, Hopes, Wishes And Riches

Dreams of the mind are oh so fine.
They are what the mind can see.
Faith, work and charity can make dreams a reality.

We often fall prey, a victim of incessant hope.
Not realizing there's a better way to cope.

Wishes! Yes, our heart's desire.
But not much of a satisfier.

"Living the life" doesn't have to be a dream.
We all have what it takes to have our "preaches and cream."

Yes, a price has to be paid to reach success.
But there is security in being your best.

It also takes fight to stay on top.
Better that, than being among the "have-nots".

No there's nothing wrong traveling vicariously.
But don't do it without plans, goals — you know, carelessly.

Yes, "I have a dream" is a start.
But go further, explore possibilities, play a big part.

Riches will belong to a chosen few.
However, chosen is an attitude and your attitude is you.

*Courtney R. Kelsey*

## Best Friends

Friends will be friends
They come and they go
Some are ok and some are so, so
But whatever they are
The good or the bad
Whether they make you feel sad or glad
They are your friends
Good friends indeed!
And they are what everyone, everyone needs
So be friendly and kind
And fill everyone's mind
With good not bad
And make people feel glad
With things that you do
So, You Can Be A Good Friend Too!

*Justin Reed*

## Balloons

Balloons are a pretty sight
They come in colors from red to white.

Some are big and some are small
But big or little we like them all.

They are fun at parties and at the arcade
They are fun at the zoo or in a parade.

Some look like animals or monkeys or apes
They come in all sizes, they come in all shapes.

So the next time you look way up at the moon
It almost looks like a big yellow balloon.

*Andriane G. Mallow*

## Life Isn't Fair

Life isn't fair
they say and I hear
and I bet it's not
with a slash through your eye$
or a tear on your cheek
but if seen from the death
of a strong 'gainst a meek
we'd see an equal
number of valleys and peaks
for you were low when he was high
and you were there when he decided to die

Persecuted most, but gained something more
you saw that view
but salt on the sore
No, life isn't fair
in dollars or looks
how do you size that to my joy
of catching your stare
- Life it's the only one fair.

*Jared S. Rowe*

## Ode To Jocks

Jocks think they're so cool,
They strut around campus like it's theirs to rule.
With furrowed brows above their eyes,
They turn bespectacled nerds into mincemeat pies.
Their protection is tupperware,
And with their fearsome glare,
They win stuffed animals at every fair.

Jocks think they're so cool,
They play dunk the dork in a swimming pool.
With their towering height they rise,
You would never catch them baking quiches or pies.
When you see them around and you ask to play,
But all they say is, "Look kid, go away."
With a big build and lots of hair,
They get all the girls to stare.
Jocks think they're so cool
Hey, I can't argue, I'm their stepping stool.

*Jason Dorvee*

## Dreaming

Hunting in darkness, eyes in a tree,
Sounds in a distance of things you can't see.
A test of strength from the darkness of night,
Shadows of wander-some lurking under moonlight.
Unfamiliar world dimming the sounds you hear,
Wandering at a distance, or as close as your ear.
A light comes on and your back where you were,
Frightened and alone for it was only a blur.

*Erika Hawkins*

## Why? America Why?

A trail of tears the children cry.
They want answer to their questions.
Why? America why? Did the young and the old have to die?

You can see the fear in their eye.
They too, don't understand why their friends and relatives had to die.
Why? America why?

The tragedy took the lives of innocent children, their mothers,
And their fathers.
America too had lost their sisters and their brothers.

Yesterday the children cried a trail of tears.
Today they sense what the grown-ups fear.
They have tried to understand this destruction too.
They sit in silence just like you.

With tears in their eyes, the children still ask, why?
America why?
Why did my mommy and daddy have to die?
The trail of tears, the blood stained face, it's something
That America can not erase, no matter how they try.
The questions still remain. Why? America why?

*Barb Edgerly*

## The Last Supper

The Apostles were sitting at the table with Jesus to dine,
They were breaking bread and drinking wine.

Our Lord is our Shepherd watching over the sheep,
He is our God, our Master of all, even when we sleep.

St. Jude said to Jesus 'Why do you not manifest yourself to the world?'
Jesus said 'I am doing what I was told.'

At the Last Supper Jesus also originated the Mass,
This is how everything has come to pass.

Jesus also gave the Apostles the power to continue the Holy rite,
That is why everything in church is just right.

Jesus said to his Apostles 'He who betrays me is at hand,
as we go along, you will see and understand.'

Jesus again said to his Apostles 'My time is near,
I shall have passover with you all here.

We are all together, soon we will all go in different directions.
We have to pray and teach the people and make corrections.

I will be back on the third day,
now I go ahead to make a place for you to stay.

I will wait for you - so you will not go astray."

*Frances Basile*

## Friends

Friends are so important to me they come with a lifetime guarantee,
they're always there to lend a hand and
right beside me they will stand.

To lose such a precious thing, such sadness this would bring,
I would hate to think of letting go such misery my life would show.

The way they come into your life, I thank the Lord every night.
I'll hold onto you the best I can and beside each other we will stand.

It doesn't matter what we do; I know I can always trust in you.
To be there when I need a hug or just to give on extra nudge.

I thank you for the time we share it shows me that you really care,
I hold a place deep in my heart, a place I know we'll never part.

So in parting I will ask, one final thing of you at last
Together in life we'll take a stand, just walk beside me and
hold my hand.

*Denise Erger*

## The Eyes Of The Future

When I look into the eyes of the future
They're so bright and ever so clear
They show such a deepened interest
In all things they hold dear

The eyes of the future shows an innocence
And trust that's truly rare
The eyes of the future show kindness
In children everywhere

When I look into the eyes of the future
There's beauty and strength so bold
When I look into the eyes of the future
It's indeed a sight to behold

*Ernestine Beard*

## Alas, Challenger

Alas, Challenger
Thine shining star As a supernova seen This crepe-girded winter's day.
Seven gone- seven, the ranks of Angels!
    Earth-born, we stretch To the glittering diamonds
    Strewn on the blackvelvet reaches.
We, vicarious adventurers watched In awe, as 7 thousand pounds of fire
Tightly reined, held in check By the stellar-sailors' hands Jumped
quickly on its way.
Midst mingled sighs and claps, Did any feel the touch
Of ill-intending fate, soon to show her head?
Did any know the fear death brings When amongst our ephemeral lives,
As on that bright, fateful day?
Did the angels cry in horror As we stricken mortals did,
At one minute, twelve, on thy fragile leap?
When thy harnessed fire Across the sky did fly, Lacking control of God
or Man.
Alas, Challenger,
We consign thy 7 all-too-mortal star-graspers To the grasp of God.
And as Fate again deals our quest a stunning blow, We say,
Alas, Challenger, Farewell, phoenix, sailor to the stars.

*Jo Ellen Jeweler*

## Ode to a Mule

If you ever feel sorry for what you've got
Think of the mule and consider his lot.
He is out every morning at the break of dawn.
We even complain when we mow our lawn.
He pulls the plow until his back is weak.
But we need coffee before we peak.
He asks no favors, just some feed at night.
A little bit stubborn, but a beautiful sight.
Consider the Derby, that wonderful race.
I feel that a mule should be setting the pace.
There's another fact I want you to hear
It was a mule, not a horse, under Paul Revere.
In case you feel I've broken some rules
I just want you to know how I feel about mules.

*Harold Panter*

## Choices

Life deals you choices you someday must face.
Think very carefully, set your own pace.

Hasty decisions throw your life in a spin
Until you're so confused you don't know where to begin.

Instant pleasures beyond your belief,
May turn out to be full of sorrow and grief.

Think it out carefully and then make your choice
When you realize it's the right one, your heart will rejoice.

Follow your heart and think very clear
Soon you will see that true love leads you here.

*Jodi L. Thacker*

## Nursing Home Visit

Only the lonely are the ones I went to see
Thinking I might get a smile from
Some poems I would read.

Startled and amazed for what I found inside
Was a depth of inner memories
That keeps most of them alive
They don't know the contribution
They can give to life
For just jotting down those memories
Brought poetry to new light

Don't discard those old ones
Left alone in homes
They have a multitude of memories
Each one of them a poem

*Jean McNutt*

## Imagination

A world of his own..a retreat....
This four year old, Franklin, found it "neat".
Just a big cardboard box—four feet by four feet.
But he made it, oh, so complete.  Into it he took a mat, a bat,
and a hat.  For only a moment in the box he sat.
And then...BAM!....his imagination took over...just like that.
He was in "his world" before I could say "KERSPLAT".
The hat was a ball cap and the mat his four bases.
He was pitcher, batter, umpire...all the places.
The crowd cheered for him, and he beamed up at their faces.
He hit the blooper, the bunt, and, oh, yes, the home run!
With gusto he played and had such fun.
Never discouraged....never undone.
He was the champ, the hero, NUMBER ONE!
Never once did he leave his "box retreat."
He played the game until it was complete.
Oh! To be four once more in our own little "world" sublime.
No cares, no problems, oblivious of time.
Once a day, let's try it, oh, how neat!
Our nice quiet "own world" retreat.

*Glenda Balint*

## Heartbeat

I cherish, thrilled-unaware of the thumping heartbeat!
This is my moment, my diamond,
Not to wear or spare,
But to feel within.
Exulted power of omnipotent happiness
Of coitus' delight
Merged is the Pleasant, the Good, the Beautiful,
Sense dramatically all rolled into one
Simultaneous!
Within - I sing silent and loud
I apart of the moment share the living world!
I must be here
for me - for you - for all mankind!
Yes son - aged I feel well
Were G'd to extinguish my last breath soon,
I'd shout that this and every moment is the greatest
Allowed by that majestic divinity.

*Arthur Weil*

## Wishes

I wish the world was a perfect place
where one would be accepted, no matter what race
and people were gentle, kind and true
no matter what we say or do.
Where children were granted a place of peace,
to live there innocent lives without to much amiss.
where friendship would be real and true,
and equality would be accepted too.

*Irma Leblanc*

## This life

This life, filled with its pain and sorrow
This life, filled with hope for tomorrow
this life, filled with its good and bad surprise
This life, filled with is midnights and sunrises
This life, filled with its worries and woes
This life, filled with days that come and go
This life, filled with its choices as you try to survive
This life, makes the decision whether you do or die
This life, will decide where your soul will call home
Will it be heaven or
hell
when
this life
has gone
this life

**Jewel L. Howard**

## No Warning!

The bombing captured much attention.
  This madness, difficult to mention,
Was the result of an evil invention
  For the streets of Oklahoma.

The sounds of pain, of shock, of fear,
  Were clearly audible everywhere.
Why had this bomb been planted there
  In the streets of Oklahoma.

Many hearts cried when the terror came
  Which left some dead, and many lame
From the vision which seared the brain;
  In the streets of Oklahoma!

The world saw the remaining shell
  There, in the heartland, a living hell!
The cowards gave no warning bell
  For the streets of Oklahoma!

**Billie Jo Cole**

## My Healthy Mom

Mom I'm so glad you are healthy
This means more than being wealthy
I hope this will keep
Longer than my jeep
I'm so proud of you when you stopped smoking
Now we don't have to hear all that choking
So if you could pass those genes
To my two little teens
For I myself have inherited some
Because all I do is rant, rave and hum
Of the unhealthy environment
That should be for our enjoyment
So I hope you stay that way
On every Mother's Day!

**Janet Coviello**

## A Dear Friend

Your never seen face is more noticeable to all.
Your smile is no longer smiling.
You were all alone, but no one could tell.
You never opened up to let anyone know.
You hid it so well how would we know
You could end your life in such an awful way.
So sudden and horrifying how could we live.
Thinking we could have helped if we only knew.
But in our hearts you are so very dear.
We shall never forget such a dear friend.

**Danielle Parent**

## Painting A Picture Of My Recovery

My palette of paint, the variety of addiction
This paint becomes death, without direction
And sure to come, without God's help
I'm not ashamed, or by myself
This brush I hold, in my hand
Twelve steps of recovery, written by man
This tool I shall use, will paint my new life
Freedom from pain, the old ways of strife
This brush that I'll use, will paint my own portrait
Soaked full of life and love, complete without hate
My canvass is clean, brand new and bright
Just as my future, my God is in sight
This painting will take, sometime to dry
As my recovery, I shall not lie
The horizon I'll paint will never end
the ones I've hurt, I'll make amends
my picture will be displayed, for all to see
to continue the message,
for those in need.

**Gerald E. Chase Jr.**

## Dark Glass

Grain trailing grain
those gritty sands of time
go lazily as dust
drifting low upon the winds,
the random winds of life — toneless — somnolent
until high soaring moments, each seeming endless,
come to fire our dreams, horizon to horizon,
like lightnings that flatten the walls of night.
Each leaves memories more vibrant — self renewing,
stark still loneliness easier to know
and that freezing touch of far forever nearer,
one tinge warmer — softer — less to dread.
Then each year here tumbles onward to the end
when all shall file down to an easy, ceaseless peace.

**Daniel L. Hall**

## Rite Of Passage

Oh, Come!  Let's go a-walking now to see
  Those hopping, crawling insects:  Arthropods.
  Too well we know their names (exclude the frogs):
The wasp, ant, spider, honey bee.
Suddenly, we see a butterfly
  With wings outspread, a frail and floating flower.
  She drinks the nectar from this garden bower.
Beauty was here, now gone from human eye.
How can these fragile insects go so far?
  Survive tempestuous winds through which they fly?
  Pelted by rain and snow through darkened sky?
Instinct?  It's God who lights the guiding star.
Through heartbreak, stress, and love, we suffer strife,
Enduring rite of passage in this life.

**Clara Whitney**

## Curious

Is there someone there who's calling out to me
Wondering where I am, wondering where I'll be
Someone who will care and want to love me
Show me who are so that I can see
Where is he
Why can't I see
Someone who is calling out my name
Tell me, does he feel the same
Is he near or is he far
I'm curious, as to who you are

**Jennifer L. Ariola**

## Keeper Of The Key

There is a man who loves me still today,
Though he is groping for each word to say.
His thoughts are locked inside his guarded soul,
Where many pains and sorrows thrash and roll.
His eyes are solemn and betray his smile.
They look at me with wonder, not with guile.
But what he's feeling I may never know —
The words are in a place I cannot go.
He strives to show me that I'm in his heart,
And how he wishes we would never part.
I long to free him from his 'prisoned cell,
To ease his pain and tell him all is well.
But, I am not the keeper of the key,
For he alone can set the prisoner free.

*Janet E. Falk*

## Manhattan From Newark Airport Terminal

That atom bomb is not to be denied, Walt Whitman,
(though heaven knows how we have tried!)
Except for war against some other side;
we're both to use it to restore our pride
lest Gods destroy us as we decide.

This other side we have identified.
Is always there no matter how supplied.
It comes complete in cycles that abide
as time counts down that empty space inside.

From Newark Airport Terminal Manhattan's skyline sighed
in sunlit spring across the great divide.
So brief it seemed in arrogance that lied
in aged beauty the bomb may yet deride.

*Gerald A. Somers*

## "Welcome Son"

We've waited for many a year!
Through all our prays and lots of tears.
God has given us you.
Welcome Son! Glad you're here.

Toys await you, diapers too,
But most of all our love for you.
Tears will come and so will hurt,
But Daddy's arms will ease that pain.
Welcome Son! Glad you're here.

Scrapped knees and bloody noses,
Mother's gentle touch will brush away those tears.
Our pleasure will be, singing, reading and playing with you.
Welcome Son! Glad you're here.

Baseball, football and mechanics too,
Daddy will see you through, happiness is
That you share with us, the joys of life.
Love is holding you in our arms.
Welcome Son! Glad you're here.

*Janet E. Gendron*

## The Dream

I start down steps that are sturdy and sure,
Yet somehow cloudy and obscure,
I greet familiar friends that I've never met,
As mystic animals I pet.
I look around
And find creatures that shouldn't be found.
When I learn I must leave,
In two my heart does cleave,
But as friends wave and farewell say,
I know that somehow, I'll return someday.

*Ashlee Tessier*

## Never Ending

I love spring with time ticking its way
Through fruit blossoms pinned against an azure sky,
And love fresh-birthed.

I love summer with time ticking its way
Through picnics, rainbow arches of sprinklers' spray,
And balmy nights of love.

I love fall with time ticking its way
Through falling tie-dyed autumn leaves
Making graffiti in the air,
And love warming itself in front of fires.

I love winter with time ticking its way
Through Christmas lights and carols,
Snow-dipped landscapes in pristine white,
And long nights of cuddled love.

I love life with time ticking its way
Through joy and sorrow, tomorrows after tomorrows,
Aeon after aeon,
Recycling love and generations

Forever.

*Ciwa Griffiths*

## A Vacation Package

So short our visit to this planet, with curiosity we tread
through our vacation of life.

Enjoy you stay! Come again soon! Tell all your friends it's a
sunny fun place to be.

A travel agent could sell us a ticket to this Disneyland of
fun. It's got adventure, it's expensive, yet cheap, we can
fit any budget.

One way or round trip. Will you want to go back once you
have come? Can you go back?

I'm on vacation. Here for a short visit. I want to be made
to laugh and smile. To never get fat. To be thoroughly
entertained.

A vacation is never long enough. So I'll enjoy the time that
I have, and you should too.

Odd to say the least, a vacation package called "Life"

*Deborah A. Conners*

## Light the Way

The breeze blew
   through the knight's hair:
As the waves crashed against the shore,
   the first rays of dawn
   pierced the storm's final clouds.
With the sun warming him,
   the knight's anticipation grew.
A laugh that tore his weather-worn face
   flew from his lips,
   for the first time he saw the 'stead in which he was born.
With a look back to the spectres that followed,
   the knight stepped through the door...
   And was gone.

*Anthony Liranza*

## "A Special Place To Me"

I like being in my special place,
whether its in the daytime or at night.
It makes me feel secure and at peace with myself when I'm uptight.
I can imagine being anyone I wants too be, but I liked being me.
A special place is something, that's no one can take its
felt from the heart for our own sake.

*Beverly Ann Butler Allen*

## Survival Is Only One Thought

A slow cold rain is falling
  Through the meadow of my soul,
    The wind brings the mist,
      The mist the color of pain.

I can hear the howling breezes and in their wake
  Bitter the taste in all my senses,
    While in my eyes the colors
      Fade to black and gray.

A gale of agony descends into that which is my being
  Leaving questions never answered
    As the confusion of it all takes hold.

Knowing that which is real
  And deciding on pictures of fantasy
    I resign myself to find a clearing
      In all the clouds that surround me.

I reach out from within
  And go to a place where I can weather the storm
    Which has taken the color from my face.

No matter how bleak or desolate things have become
  I have but one thought, that which is survival.

**Jesse James Johnson**

## Extremes of Desire and Torture

The sun shines through the window, giving the wall a golden tone
Through this I envision your silhouette with its divine form
I clear my mind of all thought, only to see — I'm alone
I fill the void in my mind with the memories of you — but soon
  everything goes back to the norm

Time goes by and I'm swimming in thought — thoughts of you
Will this torture ever end — this infinite loneliness
All of a sudden I'm living my life in a vacuum and the many thoughts
  are becoming few
Now, the loneliness — the wanting to be with you is becoming
  hopelessness

I close my eyes and imagine your warm body pressing against mine, but
  the image soon fades
Mentally I beg for your presence
I question, what have I done to deserve this punishment - I can not
  see you, feel you, touch you, but now you loom

I see your shadow enter the room and once again I can feel the effervescence

That one minute you were gone fertilized my desire
The torture is over and my tongue can once again be wet with your
  feeling
The temperature has been turned up and no water can quench our
  undulant fire
All the while knowing the sojourn of happiness will vanish — only for
  the cycle to repeat once again.

**James F. Jenkins Jr.**

## Life By Days

  Today, I discovered my new hands.
Time seems to fly like the hour glass's sands.
  Today, I grew hair on my head.
In my mother's womb I stay safe in bed.
  My skin is soft and pale,
but I am alive as a baby whale.
  I never hear, directed at me, my mother's voice.
She only talks to her boyfriend Royce.
  Today, I turned five weeks old.
At least, that is what I am told.
  Today, my mother had jam and tea.
It was good, but then Mommy killed me.

**Jill Moreland**

## Some Distinctions Of Life

Why do any of us wander
Through this life without a hope
To explore each and every morsel
Of life's journey's tremendous scope?
Nothing is new that we will encounter,
But each circumstance is not the same.
We must track those steps of exploration
Which may lead to our exposure to fame.
The crevices of life can make us stumble;
We should not despair, there is level footing ahead.
We must not forget to reach for the rafters,
Take hold and swing, by determination be led.
When that goal has been captured and saddled,
Take the time to reflect on the chore.
Nothing is as rewarding and as fulfilling
As the experience of life's open door.

**Debra J. Kinsey**

## Wings of Gold

He was meant to fly with wings of gold
throughout a sky of light
His love makes a passage for others to seek
The end of his journey is bright.
He left this earth for a reason,
a reason I can't understand
But I know up above he is watching me
I reach out and he gives me his hand.
I dream of Him in a peaceful spot
Where God has made him a bed.
There are roses surrounding my David tonight
It is warm where he rests his head.
As my mind drifts away, I can see him
but soon he is taken away.
Reality returns, and once more we're apart
He was never intended to stay.
As each day passes, I pray for him
Until he comes calling for me.
He'll sweep me away with his wings of gold
for that is my destiny.

**Erika Fredrick**

## Humanity

  Inanimate creatures move
throughout time, living life day by day,
not realizing the time span within the
actual limit of existence.
Fools don't ponder upon the minor
confusion, or take appreciation of
anything less than themselves.
  Ignorance hides itself within various
illusions as people hallucinate the
twisted scheme of freedom.
I sit here alone, impatiently waiting
for the release of intelligence, quietly
I fumble through the darkness in
desperate search for the winded
flicker of light - inside myself
a piercing scream murders an
innocent child's last hope for survival.

**Heather M. Corp**

## Eyes See Anew

Loveliness shows and it grows
Thru the window sill
From a room with a view of a person
That's always in solitary mood
Here arrives a good friend
Eyes through the shutters
Lovely eyes that flutter
Long walks
Apart, yet still close
A bond that comes together
Now water lilies flower
Two who devour
A friendship so close
Happiness sends smiles to each others faces
No one will stutter
When one is with the other
A window still remains
A true friend came
Making a dormant world flower

*Christopher Yanez*

## When You're Old

You care for people sometimes.  Love comes only to few.
Time is all I have, that's all that's left for you.
You think you do not love me, but time will tell it's toll.
The time I gave to you my love, will get you when you're old.

You see the many faces of friends who are like foes.
The love you'll never hold inside for you are much too cold.
Someday you will regret the day you ever made me blue,
in all our lives we have to pay for all the things we do.

And in the end, my friend, you'll see how life has passed you by
And how I didn't laugh at you but your sadness made me cry.

Let some people laugh at me and say I see thru you.
But those same people will someday be as sad and down as you.
And together you may try and fail as all fools do,
because if we don't live together as brothers we die together as fools.
So shall you.

*Carol Badger*

## Love Sonnet

Soft as spider-silk my sleep divides
   Time whispered words still linger in my soul.
The lips that made my secret dreams inside
   Speak low, so deep my walking head can hold.
Though rain can slowly melt my frozen tears
   And sunshine often keeps the pain at bay,
Nothing save your love erases fears
   And darkness without you kills every day.
To morning's pink embrace I always wake,
   Although I know, like dreams, it too will die.
My love for you shall have a different fate;
   Eternal as the deep unfathomed sky.
A life alone I could not bear to keep,
   Nor do I dare to dream of endless sleep.

*Jennie Ann Simon*

## Brasstown Bald

Oh, majestic mountain so noble to be viewed,
With sturdy hardwood forest so heavily imbued,
We attempted to ascend you in the course of half a day,
But with daylight fading quickly, your summit far away,
We realized to conquer you took heartier souls than we.
Perhaps it's for the better, and the way it's meant to be.
For we still can view your splendor at the closing of the day,
But for what it's like to scale your peak I really cannot say.

*Floyd Hopkins*

## Wondering

I watched as they carried you away,
To a place where you've never been.
I watched as they all said goodbye,
Wondering if I'd ever see you again.

Is there a heaven where you're at?
Can you hear these thoughts in my head?
Everyone here think I am so strong,
But they never see behind my eyes.

Can you see us from where you are,
Or have they taken away your memory?
Is there such a thing as reincarnation?
If so, are you the butterfly I saw today?

Sometimes I curse this love I feel for you,
For it makes me weak, as well as strong.
I wish I could say each day I'm a little better
But you always hated for me to lie

Our time didn't last long enough.
So much that we never said or did.
As the stars fade into the night,
I'm wondering if I'll ever see you again.

*Jon B. Dunham*

## As The Wild Waits

I'll forget in time, while the wild waits;
To add another memory to pasture.
A single reaction burned in so deep;
The image is seen through the shadows.
Calm wind blows eroding the pain;
Of a memory put out to dry.
The flashbacks of yesterday fade from within;
As the wild waits for it's capture.
Time, more than time, is all that I need;
To erase this unwanted memory.

*John P. Conrard*

## My Mother - Edna Mae

My Mother, a saint from heaven sent
To be with us, she was only lent.
When I was three, almost four,
She entered in at heaven's door.

Of eleven kids, I was the least.
The table was prepared for a Kingly feast.
Not much of her I can remember,
I do know her heart was tender.

A comfort on the darkest day,
Why did she have to go away?
So fond the memories here on earth,
By the ones to which she gave birth.

Time has not power to erase
Memories of her smiling face.
Many years have passed by
And in my heart I still cry.

Tears of joy replace the sad
Because I know, and I am glad,
Songs of praise she daily sings
To our Lord, God, and King.

*Frank A. Mathews*

## Untitled

Come on.  Where?
To Carmel - Why?
 Well, don't you know?
It's the first game of the year
 And Larry will go.

All dressed in their best
 Is "Mother and Dad"
With Grandmother Isley from the South -
 Neatly clad - Then
Moving slowly, the game begun
Then in they came-Bea, Marty and Granny True
 To root for The Great Grand son.

But - How about the game?
 O, the game was won,
The House just roared,
 And the crowd all left
As the rain just poured.

But - say - Who won?
 Why - Carmel - Who else.

*Joseph D. True*

## Hypocritical Value

Money's sprung out of the skies to fulfill the greedy eyes;
To compel us to waive our unadulterated values upon which our future
 relies;
Soon there will be no love or sentiments, only a material that never
 dies;
It's happening as I write my friends, I'm certain you realize;
We have deflowered our spirituality in order to win a prize;

We are born into a society that dictates our lives;
With a set of opinionated norms, folks, and hidden archives;
Simulating a set of corroded, barbed. and russet knives;
Used solely against the ethereal bond that money rives;
To leave the commonwealth with mercenary men and their insatiable
 wives;

I often gaze at people's face to beseech consciousness;
Instead, I sense hostility, recognize hypocrisy, and perceive
 meanness;
I stare into their eyes only to discover a scantiness;
Caused by a superficial way of life that lacks deepness;
Which can never be found in traits such as greed and wickedness;

*Danny Samir Haidar*

## In God's Pocket

I want to be in your pocket Lord,
To depend on the faithfulness of your Word,
I want to be what you want me to be,
That others may through me your life see.

I need to be in your pocket Lord,
To live outside, I can't afford,
In weakness, sin, strife and pain,
And never feeling your presence within.

Please keep me in your pocket Lord,
Shelter me from this cruel world;
Let your Spirit safely guide me
As you walk closely beside me.

Give me the wisdom to follow your will,
Give me the patience to wait and be still,
Give me a heart that's willing and true,
That longs to know much more about you.

I want to stay in your pocket Lord,
Strengthened each day by your Holy Word,
Clinging to you for all of my needs,
 Safe and secure as your Spirit leads.

*Evelyn R. Freeman*

## To The Light Of My Light

You are like the sunshine enlightening my day.
You are like a flower, blooming and beautiful.
You are like the water, quenching my thirst.
You are like a rainbow, coloring the sky.
You are like a spring afternoon, warning the earth.
You are like a winter snow, coating the ground.
You are like a sunrise, lighting up the day.
You are like a summer shower, cooling the day.

*Brian Marcocci*

## To My Mom

If there were only words
to describe my love for you,
I would say those words everyday,
the morning sparkling with dew.

I do not know how I could live
without you each and every day.
So, Mom,
this is what I say:

Mom, Mom, I love you so.
And I hope that you don't go.
If you and I should ever have to say good-bye.
Every day I'll cherish you and watch you in the sky.

*Bribo*

## My Last Walk

I just went to sleep for the last time
To dream my last dream
To walk my last walk
I have crossed the great divide
For I have crossed over to the other side
The side of reality
When people dream of things they never have
And lie the biggest lies
They talk a good talk
and they walk that walk
I have been there for the last time
It is time for me to go back to the other side
The side where you walk in faith, love, and joy
With God at your side.

*Emmanuel Clary*

## Life

Life can be like a child's cry but no one
to ease its woes, hopeless and helpless.

Then life can be like children's laughter,
happy, free and full of joy.

Life can be the sun without its
light, dark and worthless.

Then life can be like the sun's rays,
free, playful and priceless.

Life can be like a polluted ocean,
Lonely, fearful and of no use to anyone.

Then life can be like a sparkling sea
with white shiny diamonds reflected off its aquatic clear-
blue surface, accompanied, confident and man's greatest treasure.

Life can be like a young sapling swaying happily
in the breeze, relaxed, calm and happy.

Then life can be like an old weeping willow tree
at the end of its time, worried, depressed and sad.

Life can be anything:  the dark draw
of satan's death or the light, beauty of an angel's life.
But to any side of any life there is righteousness and there is evil.

*Jesse Thomas*

## Creation of Love

When God created men and women he gave them a purpose in life
To get along and love each other, not to argue and fight
He gave most of us children so we could love and care
and all the love that we could share

Centuries have come and centuries have past
But the love of God will always last
God put love in men's and women's heart,
And it should never part
God's love will live on, and will always remain strong

Pray to God, he will guide men and women right
Obey his commandments, read and believe in his word
He will give us strength, courage, love and some of us insight
Above all he will give us eternal life

God's love is the same when we were young, and as we grow old
God created men and women and brought them together
And he hopes we'll be with him in heaven forever and ever

*Hank Guion*

## Alienation

To create human life - sharing, loving (hopefully!)
To give birth - pain so great, so easily forgotten
just the two of you - Mother-Child
Then... the whole world rushes in-.. to help?
A number of years, preparing to separate, so
that the cycle may continue.
Hopefully, there has been nurtured a fragment
of the lovely oneness, created at conception and lasting
through the severing of the umbilical cord.
The pain of sadness, when one has failed to
nurture, in a way that brings mother and child respect,
love and understanding....
Is an ache that creates pain to the soul,
and is unequaled, in what traversed through
the birth canal...so long ago.

*Colleen Waugh Young*

## Beach House

Oh how nice it must be
To have a house down by the sea
    Where you can go to get away
From the work and hum drum of every day,
    To stroll along the miles of sand
And watch the waves as they crash and land,
    The beauty of a moonlit night
Reflecting on the sea so bright.
    All this describes a peaceful ocean,
But there's another kind of motion!
    It can be fierce down by the sea -
Then it's not a place I'd want to be
    With winds so strong, and lightning flashing
The waves so high and thunder crashing
    I'd leave my house down by the sea
And come back home and be a busy bee.

*Doris Dunevant*

## Hey, Mr. Moon

Hey, Mr. Moon you're the strangest of things,
    Up in the sky with all your rings,
One day you're over the tree the next day my house,
    Hey, Mr. Moon are we playing cat and mouse,
One of these days I'm going to figure you out but that would be a
    shame,
    For it will put an end to our little game.

*Donald Gismondi*

## Untitled

To caress the sun and moon, gently as they glow.
To hear the Angels laughing, as another gains its wings.
The flow.  Raging water, beats lovingly upon the earth.
Man child dancing in his birthday suit,
Unashamed, Rebirth.
Arms out to the heavens, with feet as light a feather,
Woman with her sensuality,
Beauty, Love, A Glow.
Offerings, for what it is they share.
God above keeps smiling, for true love it is theirs.
Man and woman together, as the ocean reaches shore.
For eternity, love remains, so it shall be forever more.
Earth changes direction, unity has its way.
Man and woman gave affection,
Peace, Love and glory, all are present today.
Sun and moon grow brighter,
Baby on a star.
And as it was meant to be,
We are.

*Jamel Gilliam*

## Let's Show Her We Love Her - All The Year

Although, each year, we set aside a day
To honor one we cherish and hold dear,
Let's make a solemn promise and let's keep it,
To show her that we love her, all the year.

Oh, sure it's fine to have a glad occasion
In this happy joyous season of the year,
And bring a lovely token of affection
To fill her Mother's Day with love and cheer.

But, other times, we're tempted to forget her
When we're weary from our toil and cares are rife
But her endless love has followed you each moment,
Since she first bestowed on you the gift of life.

It doesn't take too long to write a letter
Or visit her or call her on the phone,
Or just to pause, occasionally, and tell her
That, of all the mothers, you are glad she is your own.

So, instead of just on rare occasions
When special anniversaries appear,
Let's fill her heart with joy and peace and gladness,
By showing her we love her - all the year.

*Dottie (Dorothy M.) Wolfe*

## A Friend to Know

Ho!  How great to have a friend
To know how true his friendship has always been
To greet him when you meet again
To shake his hand, and friends always remain

A friend whom for a friend has time
A friend who waits to lend a hand
A friend sincere until the end
This friend is a friend of mine

A friend unselfish true, and fine
A friend who is good because you need him
Whom cares not who you are nor where you been
one whom has compassion for all mankind

A friend that matters not to him
Who you are nor from where you came
One who's heart is true until the end
Who waits to give it if you ever need his hand

*Ernest Pierce*

## American Lover

I fly to you Kuntsevo, open winged
to land upon a frantic dream
My feathers stroked and flattened by desire
Arrows waiting on the scene.

Searching heat that burns my inner-being
To rise above a frantic dream
Neck erect, mouth beaked in scream
Scissors gently halts my fleeing.

Kutsevo's manna paid with scrumbled feathers, cursed
To bury under a frantic dream
Clipped-winged, unarmed tells chapter, verse
Of you, smiling muse, chant your triumphant hymn.

Sail to Russia land I came from
To wander in a frantic dream
Hold me, heal me, let me rest upon
Your waves of wheat, rock cradle's golden stream.

Hold me tide upon your body
Vane sky high to search my dream
Forward, forward no returning to Kutsevo's whispered luring
Shipwrecked in my yearning, lingering sea gulls scream.

*Danja Kadenskaya*

## Thoughts On Separate Togetherness

Flora sprouts in the desert wind as floods of tears promote the bloom
to maintain a haven for fauna to meet
friendship is a mindful thing of the hearts of many that need to speak
some thoughts are shared, but souls not bared
for the bloom does fade in the arid air
the dehydrated plant does have some hope
that some future rain will provide the scene
in order to open irrigated plains requires energy
above the level of pain
however, my dear, do keep in mind
your soul to search would be a prospectors find
I opened today the door of the nave
and the beauty within was beyond
the flower I know must wilt in its way
but memory it seems makes tomorrow today
pandora's box has been opened wide
but much to my surprise I found it as
ordered as the chambered nautilus

*John A. Lynch*

## Icarus Lost

I thought this was what I wanted - this flight, this freedom -
To raise plumed arms and catch the circling streams of air,
Coasting through curves of azure sky
While the sea below shone copper in the blaze of sun.

I thought the moment of release, dangling in dizzy suspension,
Then arrowing forth with wings fanned open
Above the dwindling ground, away from those sheer stone towers,
Would be the perfect time, the two of us, unbound,
Laughing at our captors, amazed at our sharp cleverness,
New lands before us to explore.

But then that small sound - a hiss, a rustle,
The whisper of feathered wings turned to paper and ash.

He fell swiftly, wordlessly,
And the silent splash far below was like a breathless puff of smoke
Smoothed over by the ripple of the waves.

I thought this was what I wanted,
But as the winds bore me away to a new country,
A single white feather
Blew into my salt-stung eyes,
And I lost all sense of my direction.

*Ellen R. Collins*

## Concrete Widows

Concrete Widows take vengeance on lonely, outwardly speaking
to selves souls, devastate suburban shakers skim their pockets
for silver objects of liquoric delight. Spiteful memories in
mechanical magicians swipe my window's ledge, ringing in my
drums - I lose my rhythm and forget my name, instead I'm cloned
after every tree in park, every cloud in sky, every animal that
mimics my cry.
Concrete Widows spitting fire in my ears, can hear nothing but
my fears. Tragedy reaps belly beers walking cajuned strips
of land pelted with yellow stripes of demented limitations,
smashing bubble flame against putrid framed dance clubs - I lose
my sense of time fidgeting to the stagnant momentum of lost
concentration and nervous damnation.
Concrete Widows hurl magnets in the T causing me to be bumped
by-polar junkies who thrive off tense needles being shoved down
into their wallets sucking them stupid of 85 coins while stomping
on their loins made for making it on their own.
Concrete Widows want to live in padded cells made of grass,
rivers, beaches, mountains and clean air, but the s--t don't
kill fast enough.

*Adam Coben*

## Thinking of You

Through the paths of life I walk,
To sing, to laugh, to cry, to talk,
Accepting all and never balk,
    I think of you.

Through winters, frost and cold and chill,
I stay withdrawn, reserved and still,
Till spring brings forth the daffodil,
    I think of you.

Birds come back and flowers bloom,
To fill the air with sweet perfume.
Thoughts of love, of bride and groom.
    I think of you.

Through summer and humid heat,
Those children playing on the street,
Their joy and laughter, skipping feet,
    I think of you.

Autumn leaves with colors bold,
Red and purple, yellow and gold,
Surely when my time grows old,
    I'll still, think of you.
*(4-15-90)*

*John Bedner*

## To Be Loved

To rest whenever you fall in the soft grass,
To sleep in a hammock by moonlight,
To see all the colorful fish by a raft,
To run in the flowers barefoot,
To pick fruit in the fruit orchards
To play tag in the grass shaded by a tree,
To wade in the brook,
To make pies and bread with homemade butter,
To watch the fishermen catch their fish from a
    small craft.
Too peaceful
Too beautiful
To be True.

*Justine Olivia Bune*

## Untitled

The days of yesteryear have flown
  To spread their wings in time and space
And brought to naught the seed we've sown
  For God has made us run a race
To reach a destined time and place
  We live, we love, we find a peace
Beyond all human understanding
  But judgment rears it's ugly head
We feel that life is too demanding
  Its when we hear the Master's voice
That calm prevails, and we rejoice
  In knowing Christ will save the day
He says, I am the Life, the Way
  To heaven's door, where Jesus reigns
In Kingly robes, and He ordains
  Who shares this home of heavenly bliss
We live by Faith, and knowing this
  We praise the Lord, Alleluia
    *Flora Miller*

## God's Presence

Country roads beckoned, inviting me in,
To stroll their by ways once again;
I found a murmuring brook, sun-dappled, aglow,
And friendly little blue bells nodded hello.
In a shaded glen, all filled with peace,
I knew I would find the God I seek,
But when I would pray in that soft lighted place
Finding no words to pray
Strangely, a little bird perched on a limb
Warbled a little song, the prayer my dumb lips could not find.
And waiting, wafting upon the still air
Church bells were ringing out a hymn I knew,
Silvery as the tree o'er shadowing this wondrous place
Wherein God knelt with me.
    *Hazel B. Duffield*

## Save Her

A loving smile a fond embrace, thoughts brushing by the mind;
To take advantage of a virgin child is most cruel beyond unkind.
First you tell her that you love her, the only one that you'll adore;
Then you go and leave her, for one that's much more mature.
She dwells alone in solitude in a dark distorted room;
The pain in her heart is much more greater than the pain that stings
  her womb.
No longer caring she looks for many men to give them all her special
  favor;
But perhaps what she's really searching for is one that might finally
  save her.
A woman be like a fruitful tree, when picked to soon she does not
  ripen;
A man be like the serpent of Adam and Eve a belly crawling vipen.
So spare her please before you go to stab her with your flaming knife;
For when the blood be gone, her heart shall be scared for life.
    *Ginger Hawk*

## The Simple Wants of Growing Older

When you were born:
We walked, talked, and rocked to console you,
When you grew up, you became independent,
Now we are getting older;
Simply, all we want now is respect,
A hug, a kiss and love.
Back that we gave to you,

Console us now as we grow old.
    *Caroline Marie Migalski James*

## Although...In My Heart

Although I can't give a hearty applause
to the artist whose performance deserves it.
I want him to know that I was thrilled by it all,
and in my heart I applaud it.

Although I can't stand and salute our nation's flag,
while our national anthem is playing,
I'm proud of that flag and I like to brag,
and in my heart I'm standing and saluting.

Although I can't dance and swing with delightful grace
out on the dance floor,
my eyes enjoy seeing the smiles on people's faces,
and in my heart we'll join and dance forever more.

Although I can't get down on my hands and knees,
and talk with God in prayer,
I know he will answer my wants and needs,
when I sit and pray from my wheelchair.

Although my physical condition limits my way of life
and affects my attitude,
I can't let go and give up the fight,
and in my heart I can never lose...
    *Gary B. Harris Smith*

## Lost Blue

In the service of others, no life given in vain,
To the brothers and sisters who have died, or been slain;
Your memory stays with us, so true, proud and fine,
And we'll carry it with us
As we walk the thin blue line.

You're with us on the dark roads, through the rain and the sleet,
And you're standing beside us in the worst of the heat.
Your memory stays with us like a heavenly sign,
And helps to protect us
As we walk the thin blue line.

It's a long trip we're taking, at times a rough ride,
But we go where we must and we go there with pride.
Your memory stays with us, it will never confine,
And helps to direct us
As we walk the thin blue line.

The families and loved ones, their loss is so clear,
You're so far away, but you'll always be near.
Your memory stays with us, 'tho heavy hearts pine,
And we'll carry it with us—
As we walk the thin blue line.
    *Chuck and Kim Craft*

## "Falling Tree"

There she stands a figure so mighty and tall,
to wake up every morning and hear nature's call.

No one notices she's been there for years,
through the rough times and the tears.

Through the wind the rain and the snow,
yet she still stands only to blow.

You've sat under her on hot summer days,
she even protects you from the sun's evil rays.

It's a shame we mustn't see her go,
I enjoy watching her beautiful branches flow.

There she stands a figure so mighty and tall,
definitely an inspiration to us all.
    *Charles Mastromarino*

## Our Journey

You asked me to be your loving wife
To walk with you on your journey thru life
I know you love me and promise to
Stay close beside me all the way.

We can't know how long we'll be on our way
Or what will befall us before we are thru
So well ask the Lord's blessing every day
To supply our needs and keep us true.

We will ask him to walk with us every day
Just to make sure we don't lose our way
With our journey almost ended and heaven in sight,
If we've trusted in him, he will make things right.

*Helen Maas*

## Statue in the Garden

Here in this garden, I listened
to wind and pulled up weeds, uprooting
the ones that exist with
teeth and poison as my father
buried a thousand seeds; only the strongest
would raise their porcelain eyes from
the earth, yet we waited
to see them infantile and thirsty.

In the night, I watched through the fence
as they unwound in green threads and laced
the moon into the center for her light,
stars already fallen and resting, cupped
in the buds. The universe grew,
preserved in the garden walls.

I have been christened at the edge of this garden,
rooted like an immovable statue by the
black thumb of earth. What this garden was
I am; it diffuses into my palms, plants
me under the lips of the ground
and I am beneath it's surface.

*Jessica Wangsness*

## For Grandma, with Love

Today she died.
Today I cried.
I cried for the world "death"
Because it sounded so real.
Then I thought , and I started to cry again.
This time, I cried for the word "life"
Because that was more of what she was about.
She was full of Life.
She was special.
Life.
She liked that word - we all did.
She was so happy, she was getting it back.
But then, that other word, death, took her.
And we all cried.
But she wouldn't want us crying,
because we have our lives.
What she would want is for us to live our lives,
to the fullest extent possible.
To make her a part of our every day lives, would make the word
Death sound less harsh and the word Life even more precious.

*Jana Friedman*

## Svengalis

Forget my name,
tonight and tomorrow.
Surprised?
Fine. Make me lie.
But wait!
The ambient mirror
arches my veiled shift,
softens the length of your shadow;
thickens the texture of your brooding leather jacket.
Then draws envy in where the curve is blinded
and the nippled street lamp
swivels.

*Diana Steinman-Yaker*

## Gone Too Soon

In the blink of an eye you were gone,
too soon for me to cry.
I find myself asking why,
Why did you die?

The pain of memories haunt me in the night,
and they fill me full of fright.
Why did you have to go?
What did God want with you?

I cry for you now,
and I always will.
The mere thought of you gone makes me feel ill.
I can't think of anything but you.

You were my love,
my partner, and my life.
And in the blink of an eye you were gone,
Too soon for me to say good bye.

*Amber D. Weaver*

## "Judgment Call"

I know what it's like to be driven
Tossed on a path to and fro
When the pressures are probing like arrows
And daggers are piercing the soul

Knowing all eyes around you are viewing
Making measure of your good and your worth
Thru ignorance they mock your descending
And your heartache is shaded by mirth

When the battle is rampantly raging
And your flesh is consumed by the fires
And the heart knows no peace in the waking
From the dawn of the lonely desires

So hold to the hand that's unchanging
Letting faith on its wings take her flight
The same God parting water for Moses
Will give songs to you in the night

For God owes no man any answers
Of his mercies and love to sustain
As He is your King and your Master
No judgement of man shall remain

*Gail Bunch*

## "Dog Dreams"

Dreams run like wild dogs through the empty night.
Traveling in packs, and leaving a few stragglers to be captured
by the hunter.
Carrying their dangerous lives,
uninhibited until the first break of light.

Wild dogs arrive from the forests, the mountains, and from the city,
as mysterious creatures:
curious, spiteful, scary, and witty.
They hunt with total concentration for their tender prey.

Dreams resemble untamed lunatics painted colorless and gray.
They develop their own personalities.
Their patterns are unpredictable because of their liberties.
What is it that controls the lives of wild dogs and dreams?
Maybe nothing at all,
or so it seems!

### *Derek Gladding*

## The Firefly And I

Strolling along, as the dusk deepens blue, through the whispering
trees and grasses.
A cheery traveler will journey with you, and guide the route your
path is.

He'll suddenly appear in a bright orange burst, gently riding a
current of air.
His visit is brief, not directed by haste, but departing he just
isn't there.

Warmed by the light of your scurrying friend, you wander now easy
and free.
For during your trek, from start to the end, a guide Diogenes
will be.

The waxing moon will lightly brighten, as darkness fills the sky.
A pleasant walk, the wind, the night and, the Firefly and I.

### *Edward J. Borges-Silva*

## The Desolate Hot Desert Land

Land with ridges hills and rock bridges
Trees cactus cougars and bears
Coyotes and snakes to raise a man's fears
And all other scary things he hears

While trudging thru the heated sand
of the desolate hot desert land

And above the vultures circle round
sooner or later they will come down
and attack something lying on the ground
for in deaths stillness it has been found

Javelinas foraging in a pack
wary of the coyote ready to attack
in the desolate hot desert land
while trudging thru the heated desert sand

Even here if you follow the rules of the land
and watch where you walk and stand
there is beauty eventually you will see

While trudging thru the heated desert sand
in the desolate hot desert land

### *Edward David*

## Through Strife-Find Life

Many the patterns that flow through our life,
trying to reach us, touch us, or to feel our strife.
God's loving days circle was with compassion.
bringing with each day a new and wonderful sensation.

His messages, usually full of wonder and love,
sometimes confuse us and seem to be darkness from above,
Not to hurt us or mar us for life but to make us sit up and listen,
to the circle of life that was given to us the day we were christened.

Life must have its hard times to make us grow strong,
for by sharing these hard times we learn fellowship and how to belong.
Fellowship is such an important part of life that we can share,
and in giving to all we truly learn the meaning of the word care.

Wanting to show what we are all about we often get lost in self,
confining ourself to such a limited space puts important items on the
    shelf.
Ring for hours or years only to resurface when you are unaware,
they will come back to you in full bloom when you think you don't
    care.

In dark and in light we gain a chest full of treasures,
and in sharing the curves, angles and corners we find much pleasure.
If we only stop to look, listen, and feel His gentle touch,
we can realize that in giving to others He gives back so much.

### *Bernard Reuter*

## Broken Heart

My daddy owned a tractor when I was a boy
'Twas a great big one, dad said "it's no toy"
With all my heart, I loved dad's tractor
I could say three words: "Mama, dada, tractor"

It had big iron wheels much taller than I
Mama said if I fell off them, I'd surely die.
No soft rubber like the wheels on dad's car
When I'd climb upon one, I could see quite far!

My daddy would tuck me under his arm
We'd go tractoring all over dad's farm.
Oh how wonderful! it gave me great joy
To own a dad with a tractor when I was a boy!

Then, one day my dad sold the old dear
Vowed he'd buy himself a new one next year
We'll get one that is green and trimmed in yellow
In sorrow - I burrowed my head in my pillow!

### *Alpha Peterson*

## Remember Him

You remember all the bad times you
two had, but I hope you remember more of the good times.

Remember the time you and him
had that crazy idea to hold that
dance that the principal said no to.

Remember the times when he
would hit some of you girls on the
butt, and you would just laugh at him.

Remember the couple of times you
and him were a couple.  You knew you
two were better friends, but you tough
hey why not.

I hope you and I never forget him.
I know what he meant to you cause
he mean just the same to me, so please
remember him forever in your heart.

### *Heather Smith*

## Somatic Adaptation

Men with slapping hands
unable to conquer the enemy within.

With industrialized emotions
slaughter young women,
with words spewing from battery acid lips.

With their nonresponding hearts
they seek connections with their hands and feet.

Their women have become living exhibits
of black eyes and broken arms.
Busted lips that cannot kiss and ribs that are cracked.

Women parading themselves in paranoia.
Singing the same old tunes, drinking the same old drink,
the drink of pain.

Standing firm, standing strong
blaming themselves for his wrong.

Medicating their mind with hope.
Sedating their souls with lies.

Disavowing love for themselves,
mixing the witches brew.
A recipe for disaster.

*Alvin A. Sims*

## The Rock

Silently, it sits undisturbed, tranquil in its latent powers as the
unremitted palpitations of the sea slowly intensifies its
echoes—rising gracefully, forcefully, bursting ever higher,
engulfing the moist mass until it completely consumes its ever side
and suspends it in its fluid aura of refreshing loveliness.
Explosive waves powerful with vigor and life, luster and intensity,
thrust yourself upward casting your lofty exalted peaks in
overflowing exhilaration of cadence and splendor that ever so gently,
soothingly, descends down the fluid whetted edges, leaving behind soft
cool fragments glistening with enduring moonlit sparkle in timeless
  motion.
In a flickering it was as if it was existing, as if it soared in its
joy and ecstasy.
But morning's prudent renunciations again calm the
vast, powerful, deep eruptions sharpening its crags and supporting its
perennial stand.
O' ardent rock move and be stirred! Are you still
yet in your blaring silence untouched. And in your thirst, drink not
it's torrid waters.
In solitary stance, steady in form, you abide—-
filled with resounding echoes of silence.

*Joan Guastella*

## My Best Friend

I never understood how strong my feelings were
until I realized you weren't there.
My heart aches so intensely
at times it seems impossible to bear.

I dream of your beautiful eyes
a vibrant blue like the Akumal Bay,
your loving hands caressing me,
and the passionate words you always say.

My memories of our precious time together
are so apparent in my mind
I envision being held in your embrace
mesmerized by an eternal bind.

As I focus on the future
I see you as my very closest friend
life will be complete if you're by my side
knowing that our love for one another will never end.

*Carla R. Scheets*

## Odyssey to Infinity

Serenely will my longing gaze caress the awesome night
Until end of time,
For I have sailed beyond the skies of terraced earth
to climb along its curving dawn upon the moon,
So left behind my bond and every tie since birth.
Felt the breath of life suspended as though darkest space,
I crossed the bar upon a manmade silver star
and reached a place where man has never gone
To see a star in chaos born and watch the haunted
death of stars outworn.
Untold moments spanned from ions,
I was born along through loneliness that time will not erase.
But lo, I heard the music of the spheres.
And with the angels sang - to awake the coming day-
Then ventured for beyond the sun's great face
Into eternity, to go where mighty beings, fearing trod,
And in the mirrored ball of night, unspeakably inspired,
Beheld one universe entire arrayed in purest light
That fled through hallowed splendored halls
Hurled out in streams from God.

*Betty L. Sutherland*

## The Search For Cosmic Truth

Bid pulses have little pulses
Upon their backs to taunt 'em.
Little pulses have littler pulses;
Littlest of all is the quantum,

Who, physicists complain, is ultra fey,
Will do anything to spite 'em
Just 'cause it lives one quantum leap away
From the more corpulent infinitum.

Well, let's fill our cups and feel no distress!
'Tis only one great thought the less.
For suppose TRUTH did supplant surmises.
Would we like a life without surprises?

*Bob Steele*

## Untitled

I tether at the edge of my canyon.
Upwards I can see the blue sky
Filled with the song of life.
Below is the dark crevices of my canyon
Filled with the colors of my soul.

I struggle to remain on the edge
Knowing full well how easy it would be to fall below.
Even death would not come easy for it is a long fall
Filled with sharp edges—jagged,
Leaping to tear the flesh from my bruised body.

How sad it would be to fall.
The world would mourn for at least a day or so
But then I'd be forgotten.
Never to have the luxury of feeling
Even if it is only pain.

So I grasp at a stronger foothold and reach for the sky
And hope that the winds of life
Will carry me for a while.
While I gather the strength needed to hold on.
Believing that it will only be a while longer.

*Colleen Bershad*

## The Weeping Willow

Beneath the leaves of gold.
Use to be a time, love was near.
Before the autumns first frost.
The golden years leave, never again to appear.
Some branches become withered and old,
Like a heart a branch becomes bare.
The best times in life are lost.
Stress on broken branches cause them to tear.
Ripping of bark like breaking the heart.
Torn away, with such pain, wounds inside so deep.
Fractures across the grain which splinters apart.
Underlies the leaves only fond memories to keep.
Left deep roots, unearthed to see.
Nothing substitutes a feeling of loss.
Gone to soon, never again will be.
Ashes to dust as mulch is to moss.
Hollow to limb decaying from within thus lies.
A fallen branch with this family tree dies.

*John J. Alves*

## Old Timer's Disease

I have come from another world, not across
Vast space, but a span of time,
To one I do not understand, nor do I here belong.

From a world of hard men and soft women I've come,
Of courage, guts and elan,
Of grace, gentility, charm, knowing right, though often wrong,

In this strange world the men are softer, but lacking
Compassion, the women are harder
But more demanding, their speech crude, their appearance uncouth.

As in remote antiquity, they know their
Mothers but not their fathers,
They take feelings for wisdom, folklore for historic truth.

Oh, stop this world and let me off! For here no
Word I say can have meaning,
Nor any work I do have worth, here I could not belong.

I would go back where I belong, but no,
That world is gone forever.
It is buried 'neath the sand of time, coupled with my youth.

*Charles Ellison*

## The Best Of Years—The Best Of Days

Gathered here together at Blue Ridge Temple, before the preacher
Vowing your love forever, for all the world, and to each other
While his love surrounds you, and friends are gathered around you
We're wishing you in every way, wonderful years and best of days

Starting on a new life's journey, it's surely music to your ears
Adventures that promise to linger, through many countless years
And much contentment throughout, that's what it's all about
With stardust and some moonbeams, too, lighting the way for you

It's your own love story, to keep with you always, like no other
To hold deeply in your heart, and it's especially made for lovers
Making wonderful memories, that will go with you along the way
And endless times to remember, through the years and best of days

Marriage is a promise of many things, that happen through the years
Build on that forever, and like a flower it soon erases your fears
With enchanted, eternal love, and the glowing moonbeams from above
You will share in endearing ways, happy years and the best of days

There is no greater satisfaction that a person can have in this life
Than to be partners in a true love that is shared by a man and wife
And God said it best when He gave us the lasting message from above
Of all the gifts that I give to you, the greatest of these is LOVE...

*Betty Alumbaugh*

## Julie's Prayer

Julie was a precious girl—she had just turned eight
Waitin' for the bus to come—didn't wanna be late;
As it stopped she climbed inside—just thankful for the ride
Then tears came to her eyes— some things she couldn't hide;
Sunday service had been good—the invitation came
Down the isle Julie walked—nobody knew her name;
There's something she must say—asked the church for her to pray
She stood alone with tear filled eyes—as hearts turned soft that day
Said "My mother couldn't come—her face is black and blue
My daddy beat her up last night—there's nothing I could do;
My daddy's drunk most every night—the whiskey makes him fight
No matter what my mommy does—to him it's never right;
Last week one night I couldn't sleep—heard my mommy cry
She asked the Lord up above—if He'd just let her die;
So I ask you to pray for us—and make my mommy well
And pray my daddy drinks no more—before he goes to hell";
Yes, the Lord sends a child—to soften hearts made of stone
You never give a second thought—to things that you've done wrong;
No matter what the preacher says—no matter how he pleads
The Lord sends an eight-year-old—to bring you to your knees.

*Elbert Lawrence*

## Love Forever

When I think of you, I feel your love all around me, makes me feel
    warm.
From the first glance our hearts came alive resisting all odds.
From moment to moment our love grew to perfection.
I thank the stars for the time we had together as man and wife.
When you spoke, you were so romantic, that I would hang on your
    every word.
From you I've learned that love can live beyond life and death, its ok
Along life's way I am not really alone, I have your memory and love
to get me thru the good times and bad times.
And even in your death I can still feel your love direct me
in shaping the future, come what may, I can handle it.
I feel your presence comforting me when things go wrong, and
somehow it's alright in my darkest hour.
Your love was truly the best gift given to me to last thru out
    eternally.
I long for the day we will be together again as one,
    we weren't meant to be apart.

*Joanne Wells*

## What Is Love

Love is two people sharing their life together as one.  Being honest,
warm and loving to each other.

Walking arm and arm on a deserted beach in a light rainfall.  Having
a candle lit dinner for two.  Then cuddling by a roaring fire sipping
wine and talking about their future together.

Love is waking up in each other's arms as a warm spring breeze comes
through the open windows.  Listening to the birds chirping in the
trees with their dew ladened leaves dripping down upon the new
spring grass.

Love is giving a little more tenderness when one is a little under
the weather or feeling low.  Love means, when apart we think of each
other or take the time out to phone and say I Love You.

Love means when there is a problem they talk it out without shouting
at each other, because making up is the best part.

*John Byrne*

## "Getting To The Root"

It seems like only yesterday, when Grandpa
was bouncing me on his knee.

The wisdom and knowledge he instilled in me,
could have only come from our "Family Tree."
So it doesn't matter how many branches come
from that tree, whether it's Aunts, Uncles,
Cousins, or whatever it might be.

Eventually everything goes right back to the
"root" of that tree. As we reunite there
shouldn't be any bickering, but love for each
one that we see. That's why "Family Reunions"
are important for everyone like you and me.

*Charlesetta Hulon*

## About Heaven

The guy I met that day in heaven
Was-oh, I'd say just five feet-seven.
He talked, he quipped, he'd chat a bit...
A listener: a 'change' from where I sit.

He'd ask a question with respect, but curious.
The answers flowed as we bond; mysterious.
Then "yes," "you're right" I heard once more.
The strangers' interest began to soar...

A peek beneath the hurts and pain
The childhood lost; but on to gain
From books I'd read; he believed I grew...
From cherished lessons so hard, but true.

Reflecting; husband said: "I'll miss you dearly"
Meant what I did or gave sincerely,
But not the inside person - me...
The thoughts, the memories or dreams I see.

To spend some time to share what's known
From many years and kids all grown
A flight attendant who knew not why
That heaven began that day in the sky.

*Billie Hudspeth*

## Priceless Antiques

While walking around yesterday, I went into a store, junk
was scattered everywhere, everywhere..even on the floor.
I said to a lady standing nearby. "I wish this junk could speak!
She quickly answered me and said. "Why this ain't junk"
 "It's priceless antiques!".

There was an ole Heater, a pot bellied stove, these were
The best so I was told. I wonder how many came in from the
cold to warm by its heat, in days of ole.. just sitting around
the ole pot bellied stove.

I saw rugs mugs, ole clay jugs. Rings and things, hanging
from strings.. I never saw so much junk in one place!
But all of this.. brought a big S M I L E to my face.

So.. when my hair turns to gray and I've lost all my teeth.
My sight has grown dim, and my joints.. they all squeak.
With a pain here and there, I'm drawn up in a heap.
You can say, "she's not J U N K, "She's a priceless antique!"

*Frances O'Neal Williams*

## Hard Ball

The game loved by boys, presidents, and those between
was that American pastime called baseball,
Action controlled by an umpire's call.
Home run! For a ball batted over the wall.
 The aggravation of our situation, then, unforeseen.

Long ago cost was low, to pass the gate
Old uniform pants were loose,
for sliding through dust and tobacco juice.
Lusty fans roared praise and abuse.
 Revenue was adequate for players, owners, and to operate.

Rains stopped games. Fans got wet.
So, roofs, lights, and rugs became a need.
Fortunes, to players, were guaranteed.
Players now chewed sunflower seed.
 Admission skyrocketed at threat of debt.

Millionaires squabbled - wouldn't arbitrate.
 A strike followed - not at the plate.
President and Congress put to shame.
Our nation can't play - a little boy's game.

*Jack Robinson*

## Gangster Prayer

 Anger burns hotly within my soul; attitude intact.
Watch it! Don't 'Dis' me/can't take yo mess right now.
Another day, another time, I can smile at your foolishness
and walk away. But now... get out my face
or you lose yours.
 A breath of cool night air to refresh my spirit/to calm my soul.
But it's to no avail for the gangster I grew up being
in the streets, in the ghetto still lives in me...
mean/tough/strong will to survive/stand tall-erect/no
weakness/no clown/taking no mess/kissing no butt/bowing down to
no one/the gangster in me lives on.
 Please help me Lord, I pray, if this attitude's wrong.
But it's part of me - who I am. So change me - make me more
like you... Then I think about it; God ain't no sissy/don't clown -
or bow down/He's master of survival even from everlasting to
everlasting/He's tough-not mean/powerful/strong and fair in
judgement/the Almighty!
 Hey, what the deal—is this gangsters or Christ image I bear?
Bring me into balance where strength of Character is unquestionable
and the Spirit's Fruit evident.. This gangster prays.

*Jerry Johnson*

## Coincidence

My body is cold and trembling while you
Watch me with bold, unfriendly and dark eyes
That travel through me like the brisk wind too
That seeps through my old, buttonless disguise.
You stare as if we have met before now.
Did I treat you as you do me today?
Is this the reason why you won't endow
Me with change so I may be on my way?
Wait! It is becoming ever so clear.
The look from your eyes is not unfriendly
Or cold but is sheer, unexpected fear
Because your fear is of being like me.
This is why I encourage you to run
Before you realize you are my son.

*Beverly M. Drayton*

## Night

Night takes over as day goes to sleep.
Watch over the earth, it shall keep.
The stars shine bright as they twinkle in the sky.
Hoping faithfully that day will soon draw nigh.
The moon, a round sphere, stands above all.
Never letting down its guard, until at day it doesn't fall.
Now dawn creeps over the darkened sky.
And soon the sun shall be the most high.
The stars cry happily, for it is time to rest.
The moon hands over its duties, putting the sun to the test.
Now the sun must continue the legacy the moon left behind.
And In the sky, the moon you shall not find.

*Chinwe Asomugha*

## The White Dove

Sitting alone on the leafless branch,
Watching, listening, breathing the cold air.
Appearing lovely in the lifeless picture of
The world.
Waiting for his turn to go,
Observing all other souls in the darkness.
The time seems to be coming, but
It somehow flashes before his eyes, and
He can't follow through with all that
He has planned.
Suddenly, his body decides to fly off into
The pale sky and become the white dove's shadow.
He, now, can forever he that beautiful,
Waiting picture in the dense clouds of reality.

*Gillian Woods*

## Angels

Guarding me from harm: an angel,
Watching over me
Though it, I can't see.
With white wings spread high
Over a purple sky.
Tell me,
Why are angels white?
Because they carry with them light?
And why are they always so kind and good?
Because they do what the Lord says they-should?

*Barbara Baard*

## No Space to Live

Under the trees I sit or lay,
Watching the ants find their way.
There once used to be plenty to eat,
Now there is nothing but scrubs to eat.
All of our homes are falling down,
With loud crashing and thundering sounds.
Now there are sounds of mourning good-byes,
Nothing to look at from way up high.
I heard from my Momma long ago,
That things that are living just had to go.
I wish those big people would stop coming,
Taking our homes while coming and going.
Why can't they stop destroying our homes,
To make bigger and bigger ones of their own.
Now all of our families are running out,
Just to die while scurrying about.
I have a feeling that this will go on,
Until nothing is left and all is gone.

*Cathy Kim*

## As The Leaves Fall

I gaze out my window,
watching the leaves fall.
In a way they symbolize something,
My childhood; my life.
The deep grays, reds, and yellows,
are emotions and feelings,
slowly gliding into the summer-ending grass.
The gray leaves remind me of darkness
and sadness,
the death of someone I loved.
The deep reds, some shaped like hearts,
reflect the love for my family and friends,
and the love they have given to me.
The bright and pale yellow ones
show the happiness I have in my heart,
a prosperous outlook for my future.
Every year I have watched these colorful
individuals, and I will continue to do so.
For in them lies what composes my soul.

*Cynthia Zdanczyk*

## Reflections

As we travel through our journey of life,
We all should reflect on our laughter and strife.
One makes us light-hearted, enjoyable and bright.
The other makes us old and wrinkled to get things "right"

The laughter of youth, with a breeze through your hair.
The jubilant race without a care.
To hurry to maturity, so far away,
Through dating and proms and graduation day.

Our journey of life has its' many paths, up and down.
One must reflect on its' nurturing sounds.
The laugh of a child, so innocent and pure.
The crack of a bat, a home run for sure!

The path to a first day on the job brings great joy.
So, as advice, I say to you ol' boy,
Don't let the advancements and promotions pressure take their toll.
Keep in perspective your chosen goal.

For when you are reflecting back while sitting in your chair alone,
Think of the good times you so endearingly honed.
For you can't remember the contents of that last spread sheet,
But the warmth of love from family and friends can't be beat!

*Colleen Weida*

## Together Still

Let me hold your hand honey as we go over the hill.
We built our strength on love and we share it still.
It hasn't been easy to make the climb,
but the way was eased by your hand in mine.

Up yonder, there will be no shadows, neither darkness nor night.
For the Lamb of God which redeemed us shall be our Eternal Light.
There's been happy times along the way,
like a graduation or a raise in pay.

At the edge of the slope, we will stop to rest.
Look back if you wish, our lives have been blessed.
We've been spared the grief of being torn apart,
by death or divorce or of a broken heart.

The view ahead is one of the best.
Just a little bit further and we'll be able to rest.
We move more slowly now, but together still.
Let me hold your hand honey as we go over the hill.

*John M. Jipson Jr.*

## "Not Knowing You, Or Why?"

Excuse me Sir, you don't know me,
we didn't get to meet before you had to run,
see, many years ago you spent time with a woman,
and that woman gave birth to your son.

When he came back, the husband who had left her,
he apologized by giving your baby boy his name,
but this new addition did not help the marriage,
so when he left for good, it was your child he blamed.

Then after all of those years of just being me,
I accidentally learned the truth was a lie,
from that secret there came confusion and hurt,
yet for some reasons, my family can't understand why?

I'm fully responsible for the life that I live,
and I don't think I've done all that bad,
but I know from the questions that fill my heart,
I could do much better if I just knew my Dad.

So if your out there Dad, I forgive you,
still I struggle between who I was, and who I am,
I guess when it came down to being a father,
you just really weren't that much of a man.

   *James Macon*

## Lighten Up!

We believe we are good; we believe we are fair.
We do not have a clue, that the answer is there.
When we are in the dark, walls are all around us;
In our own little world, darkness surrounds us.

Fear: Our biggest problem; It may be our only one.
Fear takes on many forms, that may never see the sun.
Light is the answer, to all of our prayers.
Light, where are you? Darkness doesn't seem fair!

We think life is, the way it will be.
Ah, but we have choices, please, don't you see!
I do not like fear, but it seems to like me.
Oh yes, at times, it's so dark that I can't see!

Light is always there, when we strive to be our best!
We can be out in the light, with others as guests;
Having a picnic, and having a great time,
Enjoying the light, with fear, FAR BEHIND!

What a lovely picture, this boy can paint!
I just painted a picnic, without any ants!
Out of darkness, and into the sun;
Come out of the cave, let's have some fun!

   *Glenn A. Pustka*

## Isolation

I have feelings only I understand.
Though they may try, no one can really see.
Who ever said, "No man is an island,"
Obviously never felt like me.

I seem to have a pleasant attitude,
But that definitely is not the case.
My thoughts put me in total solitude,
Though it will never be shown by my face.

I hardly ever share the things I feel
And I may appear to be strong and brave.
My emotions are kept secret and real,
And I will bring them with me to my grave.

In life the one thing that I've always known:
In my mind I'm utterly alone.

   *Elliot Garcia*

## The Rivers that Flow!

When we arise each day, and take our first deep breath,
we don't think what life can really bring.

We open our eyes to see,
but we really don't know what's in front.
We open our mouths, but don't know what song to sing!

We travel to relieve our minds.
We take trips of nature, as we see rivers that flow.

Our minds relieve our everyday,
what we see is a reality of every tree and flower that grows!

We think in our heads, our lives are the same us rushing waters,
that crash over rocks and flow with the sounds of greatness.

In our everyday lives we rush over our obstacles and let the
beauty pass us by, only if it could be a sound of sweetness.

Let us guide ourselves to the brightness
and enjoy every breath we breathe.
We have ourselves to be drifters, as a feather that
slowly makes it down and lands softly on a leaf.

Life is like a river that flows.
We try to follow, but don't know where it goes.

Isn't Life Beautiful
   *Carrie Miller*

## Where Are The Children?

Will we wake up from our sleep someday and much to our surprise.
We hear no children playing only silence there resides?
Will we wonder why the parks and schools are empty from their songs?
The tinkle of their laughter, the pitter patter of their feet
it seems we've waited much too long to wake up from our sleep.

Where are the children?
There's a generation that is gone
They cry out from their unmarked graves, what did we do wrong?
To laugh, to play, to feel the warm of sunshine on their backs,
To want to fill their lungs with air, was that too much to ask?

God gave us a gift so precious and we've throw it in His face.
We've cast aside His children, and to His name we've brought
disgrace.

When He comes to us as King of Kings and majestic
   Lord of Lord,
With Holy fire in His eyes, with truth and justice as His sword
To gather all His people, He's forgiven for their sins
Will He ask the question we fear most?
Where? Where are my children?

   *Cynthia A. Weaver*

## Joe

When into our daughter's life you came,
we knew things would never be the same-
in just two weeks she will have your name.
As much as a parent would will,
we cannot make time stand still.
You have made good use of the duration,
with your strong will and determination.
As we let go we hope and pray - Lord knows we try,
to give to our children what money can't buy.
And then we hear Director Freeh at the ceremony
remind us character can't be bought with money.
A certain few were blessed with honesty and integrity,
those that choose to abuse this do not have pity.
Use these gifts well and use them wise and know
those who know you are filled with pride,
for you Joe are a graduate of the FBI.

   *Grace Durkin*

## Son's Day

Can it really be a year since I heard my sons say,
We hope you have a very happy father's day?
That year really went by as swift as a breeze,
I suppose other fathers have thoughts like these,
Again, a present or card I know they will being,
They want me to feel like, well what else, a king,
But before I'm made king and they put on that crown,
Maybe this day should be the other way around.
Because in all my weaknesses, they have stood by me,
And that sure wasn't easy, the way I used to be,
My work sometimes, I put way ahead of them,
I would work long and late at the slightest whim,
When I needed an excuse, I was quick with a plead,
While you two are in school, you won't have a need,
They did many things, important to them you see,
But when they looked around, they didn't see me.
Like other fathers, I wish I could do some things again,
But we know from His Work, that's not God's plan,
So I ask your forgiveness, and there's more I could say,
But for now, let me wish you a happy son's day.

*Harvey V. Taylor*

## Now And Forever

In this world of great temptation and desire
We lost, the greatest gift of all
Love that set our hearts on fire
And made us feel, ten feet tall

We were conquerors
Strengthened by love
Now we're desperados,
And desperate for love

Together, we were strong and independent
We needed no-one
Now we're frighteningly weak, and dependant
And we need ... everyone

Yet, despite all cost
You again I would love
And despite our faults
You are the only one I'll ever love

*Brenda Lowe*

## A Mother's Prayer

You sent him to us, Father, a sweet new little soul,
We loved and treasured the time he was here, and manhood was his goal.
Then, after a few short years, you called him to come home.
We trust you, God, to care for him and never let him roam,
Away from the path of righteousness he trod while he was here.
And because we miss him so much, we've shed, many a tear.
We know that you had other work for him to do over there.
There's never been a night or day we've forgotten him in prayer.

Though we have other children, and they are a joy to behold,
We'll not forget our son who's with you, He too is of our fold.
The other children miss him too, our family's just not complete.
But that's the way it'll stay, 'til the curtain parts and we meet.
Now, until that happens, Father, remember this mother's prayer;
Please keep our boy beside you in your kind, loving care.
And tell him when he gets lonely, that his family all miss him too.

We are trying to live so we all can be together again with you.

*Betty H. Pierson*

## Alone At Christmas

We live alone and like it, us formerly married folk
We manage quite nicely whether really rich or broke
But when it comes to Xmas I think of yesteryears
And my throat gets a lump and my eyes fill with tears

My thoughts go back when I was a boy
As I excitedly unwrapped each Xmas toy
And my momma and poppa watched with pleasure
As I got involved with each boyhood treasure

And then years later with children of mine
I discovered the joy of giving at Xmas time
It's now another Xmas and most are having a ball
But to be alone at Xmas is the saddest blow of all

So all you folks who think it smart
to sever relations and make a fresh start
don't burn your bridges you might still have time
cause it's mighty lonely at Xmas time
Xmas is for families they respond to the call
But to be alone at Xmas is the saddest blow of all.

*Bernard Greenspan*

## The Painter

Lost shadow in moon's silvery stream
We paint each a lover's dream
Each hath in mind this flame survives time
Our gladness be wild and troubles be few
Perennial as spring dew
Mist dances upon your lips
Our flesh doth thirst a tender kiss
Twilight sparks a lustful run
Two brushes become one
From a gentle touch new life begun
Escaping darkness into light
Her sparkling eyes are blessed with sight
Small precious package sacred and new
Shall please Him as few do
We alone shall guide her way
Setting examples day by day
Her future and spirit no one shall crush
This guarantee by the painter's brush

*Gary Maxwell*

## A New Year For Us All

Another year is dawning, we hear the strains of Auld Lang Syne
We see what we've accomplished, we reminisce in time
We are supremely grateful, for everything God has taught
And this New Year is so joyous, with the blessings He has brought

Good health, good friends, prosperity, all give a reason to cheer
An understanding and loving family, that we hold so very dear
But we should not turn our backs, on those who are not as blessed
We should make every effort to help, the downtrodden and depressed

In this forthcoming year we should do all that we can
To make our lives a better one, and to help the common man
Life is filled with these opportunities, and the New Year offers hope
With all the Lord's love and guidance, we'll have the strength to cope

So I wish you Happy New Year, to the strains of Auld Lang Syne
Don't mind me if I shed a tear, it comes with the passage of time
And with this I hope you know, you're a friend that is very dear
Lets pray, with God willing, we'll do this again next year

*Ira Fein*

## A Toast to the Future

Out of familiarity into the darkness
We walk with open hearts and open eyes.
Free of past sentiments and even older traditions,
We carry the torches with which to light our own way.

Our hopes and desires will be our guide
Through the many obstacles that will stand in our way.
And we will take comfort in knowing
That what we reach for can be attained.

There will be no one to make us promises
Or kiss away our wounds, so
We must reassure ourselves.
And when the journey seems endless,
Remember "The future is ours!"

*Cheryl LaRue*

## Great Papaw

My Great Papaw is a very old fellow
Wearing a smile and dressed in old yellow.

Hot coffee and milk he would drink sip by sip,
It would always linger in the corner of his lip.

His love for us was great and unmeasured;
A telegraph machine is among things he's treasured.

He heard the engine's whistle as he stood by the panes,
Pulled a watch from his pocket to note the time of the trains.

Precious memories remained in the back of his mind,
As he tugged on the watch stem to give it a wind.

He took off his wire-rim's and loosened his tie,
And he grew weary as the day turned to night.

Many years spent in this room with another,
He is without his wife now, and has a daughter for a mother.

Recalling the past, he begins to weep
On a pillow of feathers as he drifts off to sleep.

This is normal for this very old fellow
Wearing a frown and dressed in old yellow.

*Justin Long*

## Life's Search

One lazy summer day I sat along the river contemplating my life.
Weary from the endless search for internal peace and happiness,
I laid back and closed my eyes.
Listening, I heard the gentle rhythm of the waves as they
lapped upon the shore.
From the brush, the crickets were in serenade
and the birds above sang along in harmony.
The breeze rustled through the leaves of the trees,
cooling the sun's rays.
I opened my eyes to the sound of a fish jumping
playfully in the river.
The sky was an endless blue with wispy white clouds.
To my delight, a butterfly was fluttering about
and landed upon my knee.
Within all this splendor I realized my search was over,
as I needn't have looked any further than my own heart.
For within the calmness of my soul I found utopia.

*Barbara J. Cook*

## Paris

You said you'd take me to Paris mon premier amour
We'd share conversation stroll down by the left bank
I never make it there
You said we'd go to the opera instead of the opry
Memphis just ain't the same
You said "call in to work late, pack a small suitcase."
It's still sitting here

When did your heart stop beating my name
Your voice stopped resonating
The notes that harmonized our love
Composed a lonely ending

You said you'd take me to Paris
We'd celebrate our love
A soft vision in white on a warm Paris night
Sail our dreams down the Seine
When did your heart stop beating my name
Your voice stopped resonating
You said you'd take me to Paris
Instead you took her to Paris

*Brenda Leff*

## Seniors

'Tis the beginning of our age to know what we
were then.

To remember the "good old" days when we know
what was when.

'Tis the time of our lives to remember every
woe.

Why our children want to help?
I guess Heaven made it so!

But now is the time of Love, Faith, and Hope.
The time when we both can cope.
So; with our hearts we understand
The wants of our little clan.

The years gave us "love with heart",
And to know that we shall never part!

*Gerald R. Bloss*

## To Mama

I want to thank you for all you've done
We've said this to you quietly
We've said this to you loudly
Now where saying it to you for the last time
Thank you Mama
You raised us to be strong girls and strong women
You were very strict sometimes too strict
So we thought
But look what you made
Three strong women standing here before you today
We use to argue and fight sometimes
But with each fight and argument we became a better person
And a much more understanding daughter
As we sat with you those last hours Mama
We felt such deep love and devotion
We prayed, and we begged
Till your very last breath
Then we knew at last Mama
You had found peace with the Lord
And would feel no more pain

*Dorothy Carson*

## Amusingly Amused

What a sight I did behold;
   What a sound of deep-dark echoing;
What a taste of everlasting ice cold,
   I felt it all a part of me.

Where blue jays nestled high aloft;
   Where mountains split and shed their tears;
Where whirlwinds play in vengeful turf;
   I felt it all a part of me.

How can a word be so powerful;
   How can a Nation be so gutless;
How overnight the ants rebuild their empire;
   I felt it all a part of me.

What, Where, and How shall meet;
   What asked Where and How didn't know
What tricks, inventions, and cures we'll greet;
   I felt it all, and am quite amused.

     *Carolyn Ann Martin*

## Our Grandson

Look at him, that little boy,
What a sparkling bit of joy.
He came to visit us for awhile,
He gave us joy and many a smile.
Dad and Mom needed a break,
So Grandpa and Grandma an adventure did make.

We got out the puzzle of the rabbit and ball
And Sven started in with nary a stall.
He looked at each piece matching colors and curves,
Turning and fitting them 'til the total picture emerged.

His sturdy, dimpled, little boy hands were a joy to behold
as he worked each puzzle piece without being told.
The finished picture he held up with delight,
Saying "Look Grampy, I did it just right!"

     *June Crafton*

## Reply Of The Cross

Oh cross, who is the man you bear,
what crime had Him suspended there?
And the cross replied, "He is innocent
and yet He died!"

Oh cross, where are the clothes He has worn,
and who gave Him the crown of thorn?
"He is mercy, greed striped Him bare,
hate put the crown of the thorn in His hair,
for that He died," the cross replied.

Oh cross, who drove the nails so deep,
and why do so few people weep?
"He is justice, the nails were driven in by pride,
bigotry put the hole in His side."
For that He died, the cross replied.

O cross, who stood in judgement there,
where were His people, didn't they care?
He is hope arisen, His people are charity,
His children are love.
He must wait until they overcome, and His will be done,
for that He died, the cross replied.

     *Jane Pyrek*

## Who's In The Mirror?

As I look in the looking glass a stranger glares back at me
What happened to that little child who's eyes were full of glee?
Then there was a teenage girl full of hopes, wishes and dreams
I remember when she fell in love, how her face did beam
There was also a young woman full of pride and respect
She took her ideas out in the world hoping to reflect
Then there was a wife and she became a mother
What happened to these people? I cannot discover
I look again in the mirror, this person looks my way
I swear she's almost fifty, her hair is thin and getting gray
She's fighting the battle of the bulge
Fat's winning and she's losing
Age is showing on her face, she doesn't find it amusing
She looks at me, I look at her and it becomes quite clear
The people that I'm searching for are all from yesteryear
The years flew by so quickly, they truly went to fast
The people I am searching for are in the looking glass
I wish that I could step inside and go back and visit my past

     *Joyce Juanita Horton*

## Chance

I have
What I Believe to BE
A Natural Affinity
(A God Blessed Gift)
For Seeing and Understanding Patterns.
And
In Being, so
I also Have the Faculty
Of breaking them down
For someone else... to See how.
I also find MYSELF in Possession of a TALENT called Creativity.
In which
May Allow me to Alter THESE Patterns
Within Reason.
In this
I BELIEVE
I have the POWER OF CHANCE,
To Alter my Premonitions,
To the GREATER ADVANTAGE.

     *Jose Escalera*

## "Silent Servant"

In he back of the room he stands alone
What is now his prison was once his home

He's a silent servant his soul runs deep
His body's the prison of the mind he keeps

The voices whisper in the night
Beckoning the darkness that shuns his light

He cries out to no one there
What has happened to the man who once lived here

He's a silent servant his soul runs deep
His body's the prison of the mind the keeps

to the sun that blinds by the moon that binds
The world had forgotten his lonely kind

In the back of the room he stands alone
What is now his prison was once his home

He's a silent servant his soul runs deep
His body's the prison of the mind the keeps

In the back of the room
A silent servant
He stands alone

Silent servant

     *Heatherlynn Rivino*

509

## Reality

Why, we say, do we do these things?
What is the profit that it brings
Please consider how many creatures-
With not so many intelligent features;
Just simply do what instinct recalls-
In the different seasons-spring or fall.
But us, with our many ingrained habits
Just hop along like so many rabbits;
Without realizing, many times, the real reason
Has nothing at all to do with the season.
We use nature as an excuse, you see
To explain why we go on a shopping spree.
When, really we are compensating -
For something said, or too much waiting.
For our ship to come in or a windfall to happen
When, if we realize that we already have more than enough
The urge to have more and more will be forsaken.

*Judy Potts*

## Three Short Weeks Less

Minus half, then minus Whole,
What pain does pierce my mortal soul,
To take them both and leave me none,
But now the shocking deed is done.

Was not my choice, that they should leave,
Nor was it mine to stand and grieve,
Beside a grave so newly made,
And watch another parent laid.

But He who knows these things the best,
Has bid them Home, eternal rest,
So now they stroll on tranquil shores,
Hand in hand, they weep no more.

No pain for them, they're not apart,
Is I who have the aching heart,
Left to deal and do my best,
Until in time, I too shall rest.

It's my turn now to carry on,
And seek the way that they have gone,
To help another, as they would,
Renounce the wrong, exalt the good.

*Eva Joan Alberts*

## "Flesh And Bone"

*Dedicated to my friend...Billy Joe Sasser)*
What mysteries lie behind each face?
What secrets or forgotten place?

How much hurt can one man bare -
Until he can no longer care?

If all is lost - what's left to give?
Our life unfolds - each day we live

What place is there - to put the pain?
When we hold on - does it remain?

Can we forget - what's in our past?
Impressioned deep - and made to last?

Is there an end - to what we learn?
Can we go back - and still return?

Lost beneath the bitter tears -
Did it take months - or days - or years?

Are all these memories - carved in stone?
Or were they made by "Flesh and Bone?"

*Denise McVay Penny*

## Undecided

What is this thing I see?
What sort of object is next to me?
Could it be a puddle, or lake, or a sound?
One that is deep and perfectly round?
Or maybe something bigger, like an ocean,
With tumbling waves that are always in motion.
And what is that little dot I see?
A rowboat, or speedboat or yacht maybe?
Then again, an ocean liner would be more fun,
With a mighty captain on the run.
Waves are crashing and rain is pouring,
But come now, let's not make this picture boring.
Out comes a dolphin or shark for food.
A whale, I think, would fit this mood.
With large teeth bared, it heads for the boat.
And a scream comes from the captain's throat.
But that's not really what I see.
My eyes are playing tricks on me.
To think what I saw in a circle; do I dare?
What then, would I see in a square?

*Christine Verbit*

## Mother's Last Poem

Moma moma so great and kind you're always been there no matter what time.
You helped us come a long, long way and you always made sure that we stayed that way.
You picked us up and turn us around and you said we would no when our feet was on solid ground.
You always tried to do what right and made sure your family was together at night.
You have been though hard times and you stayed ahead and you never let dust getter around your head.
Your children are grown and they are on there on so God has ask you to let them carry on.
So you moma may come home to sit around his heavenly throng.

*Abbie Clowney*

## One Wish To Be Granted

One wish to be granted,
What would you have it be?
To achieve much wealth and fame,
Would this be your destiny?

Or, would you wish for peace?
To abide in the hearts of all mankind,
To know the joy of freedom
In this land so great and fine.

Able to help others by lending a hand,
For when we give of ourselves, serving others,
True happiness comes in the end.

So, think carefully of one special wish,
For soon you will see,
The greatest one of all,
To meet and know your Savior,
Who died at Calvary.

*Hazel Payne*

## Three Eating Meetings

I went to a breakfast meeting today.
When it was over I went on my way.
Then, after a couple of errands were run,
I completed the shopping that needed to be done.

Over lunch, our committee members set some dates
And smiled as the waiter brought our plates.
What in the world am I going to do;
For tonight's program committee is serving stew!

*Judith Elaine Christian*

## Untitled

O' Oklahoma fair city, we all grieve over the calamity,
what wrong did you do whom did you deserve, for such a misfortune
to deserve, who in the world can utter a figure of damage or cost,
for so many decent innocent life's lost, who are these insane,
that caused horror agony and so much pain, what did they attain,
let us hope their friends learned that there is nothing to gain,
and from violence abstain, harming others disdain, be rational and
do not act like Cain. The authorities and inhabitants in the
city of Oklahoma, deserve praise and a diploma, for the way they
functioned in distress after the disaster, and were able the
situation to muster, at present the task is to clean up the
clatter, and rebuild manifold better.

*Jacob Haruvi*

## Wonders of Spring

I wonder if I'll see another spring,
When flowers bloom and robins sing,
When meadows glisten from the morning dew
And all the world seems bright and new.
When sunbeams sail across the silvery stream
With little white clouds drifting in between.
When hills and woodlands come alive
With creatures great and small.

And happily my heart rejoices,
I feel the hand of God is over all.

*Hedwig Schroeder*

## The Pen

It was a long time ago
when he gave me the pen.
Oh, how he believed in me
   way back then.

The pen he gave with love and encouragement
helped me chronicle the way I felt,
sharing my words, my thoughts, my beliefs,
that could burn, freeze, and melt.

Through the years, and my changing careers,
he continued to urge, to encourage.
But I had a job to do, a family to feed.
Altruism gave way to material greed.

After years away, I'd something to say.
Picked up the pen, and saw nothing but
spilled ink and scattered pieces everywhere.
And like he, the pen he gave, was done.

It was long ago
when he gave me that pen.
They are both gone now,
leaving me only with my memories of when...

*Brian J. Kennedy*

## "The Wolf"

When he goes to sleep in the darkish night,
When he wakes up in the happier day,
To live each day he has to fight the fight,
He hunts and eats meat, not the grass or hay,
He has no play or fun, but lots of work.
He hunts the rabbit and he kills the deer.
His whole life he spends in the swampy mirk,
And he is dog like, and he has no fear
He is gray with hints of brown and of white,
He fights along side his full-blooded brother,
He is full of life and is full of might
When two years old he leaves his Mother
With his powers he is hard to engulf
If you have not guessed it, he is the wolf.

*Jonathan Hilliard*

## One Free Wish

I was walking in a meadow,
   when I saw a wish float by.
So I reached up so tenderly,
   and pulled it from the sky.
Then I took the wish so tenderly,
   and held it to my chest,
Then pondered in this mind of mine,
   how this wish would suit me best.
I thought at first of wishing,
   for a treasure of silver and gold.
And then I got to thinking,
   that happiness it would not hold.
So then I started to wonder,
   If I should wish for love.
But would love from a wish really be true love?
So then I thought I would wish, for peace throughout the land.
And then I thought if peace was wanted,
   it could be brought about through man.
And then I really started to wonder, was this wish here meant for me?
And I wondered about it one more time, then I let the wish go free.

*John Mandato*

## Still Novel In Our Hearts

Do you remember that great Tuesday evening
When I saw you first in a festival crowding?
Your cute eyes were twinkling like stars and
Sparkling like lighted candles in a church
We looked each other as if knew for all the
Past and present generations
When I made next steps to reach you
Smile shone like gems on your tender lips
Shyness beauty spread like rainbow making
Your face prettier than before
I felt like a gentle breeze that blew
Smooth on a lonely spring flower
When I whispered we would match well
You were freed of making a choice
Glittering eyes you raised to me sent
Waves of agreement signals instantly
Love grew from then, became selfless
So far no force broke it apart
We still keep those first looks novel
Deep in hearts like pots of treasures

*Jay Andrews*

## Happy Retirement

For years I've thought of that moment sublime,
when it will finally be my retirement time.
No longer will I have to jump out of bed,
rush around all day, to earn my bread.
Father Time I'll no longer need to race,
I'll now proceed at a more leisurely pace.
The date for stopping work, has now been fixed,
but I admit, to my surprise, my feelings are mixed.
Sure I'd like to travel around this land of ours,
take long walks in the woods, to pass the hours.
Catch up on some reading, get in some writing too,
take the grand kids out more often, to a museum or zoo.
Now I say to myself "You've got to beware,
how will you use time, which you have to spare?
Do something creative in those golden years,
or soon you certainly will be bored to tears."
One thing is for sure, if I want a happy retired life,
I must mind my own business, without bugging my wife.

*Isfried Neuhaus*

## Soul

O Lord, help me be true to me.
When people turn their backs to me,
  help me remember the me I am to be.
When they spew their hatred and judgment on me,
  help me realize it is not me they truly see,
  but a part of themselves they fear to face.
For if they stopped to look at me,
  they may find we are similar in kind.
When those around me point and call me names,
  help me stand true, free from shame.
Give me the strength to look deep inside,
  to feel your love and to know I am blessed by your touch.
You are the truth and the truth is in me.
To be who people say I should be,
  is to be less than I am - an image not really me.
I cannot be who they want me to be,
  without being untrue to You and me.
O Lord, I pray for my soul to fly,
  to be free and unencumbered by the mandates of humankind.
O Lord, I pray my true self to find.

  *Barbara F. Strouzas*

## Our Andrea

She chose a heavy cross to bear
When she dedicated her life to share;
To teach God's word to such as we,
And preach the story of "The Tree."

Never a single day goes by
That Jesus doesn't hear her humble cry,
Father, forgive us, and through your love
Lead us to your home above.

We've had her for such a short, short while
oh, how we will miss that lovely smile,
Thick and fast the tears will flow,
When we are forced to see her go.

But, work she must, for God and man;
And when she has done all that she can,
How I would love to be around,
When she trades that cross for her
heavenly Crown.

  *Arthur Toyne*

## A Grandmother Cries

A grandmother cries
When she hears a child dies.
Her pillow is filled with tears
And daily her broken heart shakes with fears.
Satan lies and cheats
And begs you to follow his feet.
Keep satan from your mind.
Tell him to get far behind.
His ways are mean and cruel.
He'll change you to a fool.
He comes to rob and steal.
No compassion does he feel.
He'll coax you on his side.
So run away and hide.
Join God's team of care and love.
Look only to the Father above.
A better life you will see
Than satan's filled with misery.
A wonderful world God did create
And special people with no hate.

  *Eileen McCollum*

## The Season of Spring

In the stillness of the morning,
When the birds began to sing,
The phases of your life reappear and you know
It is the beginning of Spring.
The quietness of watching nature,
Start to fill the air,
Makes the certainty God is watching
And we are so in his care.

The comfort and pleasure that you feel,
When this day began,
Will fill your heart with love to share
With your fellowman.

  *Eddie Lynne Hammonds Weise*

## A Dog Gone Life

The dogs howled at the moon at night
When the moon bowed very low
The dogs howled very loud
When the moon came up and beamed in the sky

The dogs barked and wagged their tails
And carried on by sunlight
In the shadow of the day they slept
They wagged their tails round and round

They looked at the beaming sun
And their eyes were full of light
They are looking at the world going around
They march along the winding road

Just to play and howl with the sun
Their master called and they heard his cry
Hoping to come home at supper time
They cried aloud and howled for their master's bread
Knowing somebody they will come back home again

They howl at the wind and look at the moon
Listening for their master to call
Them home at noon.

  *Clyde C. Seaton*

## Easter

I don't mind waking up so early
When the muezzin calls for prayer
Allah'u - Akbar ... voice inuring
Echoes from mosque through chapel's crannies
Trickles through heart, reverberating
With most elating words - "Our Father"...
  Ravishing sunshine is so pearly...
  Wreathed in green, the church looks grayer...
  The Gospel was so reassuring;
  It's Easter... Children carry bunnies,
  People greet priest, the other - waiting -
  Talk, and are smiling at each other...
Al-Hajjis wrapped in white attires
- Their turbans sparkle in dazzling glare -
Greet us with friendly "Go in peace"...
- Allah created all of us...
  The jacarandas' blue sapphires
  Snow on us all through breathless air...
  Salem Aleikum... will you please,
  Wake me again for morning Mass?...

  *John Gallar*

512

## Thy Self

For how does thou, comfort thy self
When thy self wards, comfort from thy self
For thou seeketh, the voice of another
While thy voice seeketh, to spend thy thoughts
How does thou seeketh, thy greatness
Thy greatness is, that thou seeketh
Where does thou find divinity
When the divine, is who searches
Where does thou, find thy love
When thou cannot see, thou is love
Thy self is where thy love, must be spent
Where does thou, find such wholeness
Could thy wholeness be, in thine own heart
Comfort, wisdom, greatness, divinity and love
Birth giveth thou these, fully
If thou cast thy petals, of pretence
Let thou seek within thy self, thy answers

*Debra Mulholland Strom*

## The Automobile

All caring, loving gentle people by our side
when we drive its Dr. Jekyll and Mr. Hyde

The signal in front blinks and blinks without a turn
all this and they cut in front as you burn

All the racist slurs emerge with a flurry
on the highways and byways as we hurry

The automobile gives us freedom so they say
none of which is found on the bus or subway

Courtesy is they say contagious
behind the wheel we are all outrageous

*John M. Rajcic*

## To Our Baby

Oh sweet little babe, lying there so silent
When we looked in your eyes
We knew you must have been heaven sent
Every morning as we awaken
We remember your precious dark eyes
They would always glisten
You're so sweet, you always gave us
a beautiful smile
We would smile also, and the feeling
would be in our hearts for awhile
Baby, you have touched everyone you knew
You had that special kind of glow
That nobody else could ever show
We will never forget you, our precious one
In our hearts you will always remain
Now, God has sent for you to be in his
pretty little rose garden
And when our lives are over down here on earth
We will see you again, up in heaven

We love you,
Mommy and Daddy

*Janice Elliott*

## Under The Stars Of Alabama

We were waltzing under the stars of Alabama
When we saw the reflection of our love in the moon
And we knew without a doubt there would be a wedding in June
Followed in a year or so by a bundle of joy.
A curly hair girl like a mom or like daddy a blue eyed boy.
And we would remember that might that you held me tight
And we waltzed under the stars of Alabama

*Ella Mae Rozell*

## My Mother is the Best

My Mom's so very special because she's always there.
When you can't get to sleep at night; when there's gum in your hair
She's there to cook you breakfast and make supper at night
She's there to help with homework or break up a fight
She works very hard to please us as she always tries her best
She'll help you with a task like sewing a button on a vest
She never has a day off or time to spend alone
But whenever you need her she'll give it all her own
She milks those cows twice a day; she feeds calves and helps make hay
And after she's done all of this she'll shoot hoops and never miss
She does so many things
But I can only name a few.
And Oh! I almost forgot one she cleans up when we have the flu
But most of all she teaches us what we need to know
And helps earn the money to buy the food we need to grow
I love her so much-way too much too ever explain
And I am positively sure she loves me just the same.

*Jenny M. Dierickx*

## 'Broken'

Do you remember when you broke away from your family?
When you did everything on your own, made your own decisions?
How did you feel in that moment?
Were you jumping for joy with a feeling of liberation,
or crying from the pain in your heart that brought you deep down
where nothing else exists
but the flames that engulf you in its smoke?
With all my heart and soul I want to go from here
but with this same force I want to stay here, in this port where
everyone protects me and everyone loves me.
And with my whole being I want to fall in love for the first time,
I want to feel myself in love and I want to be loved,
I want to live the feelings that come with this force,
with this passion!
And how can you do what I want?
I can't because they hold me back with this feeling of guilt that
does not let me do anything for myself.
I want to live MY life mixed in a little with theirs.

*Alisa A. Cataldo*

## After the Storms

Have you ever had a bad time
When you felt that life went wrong?
When all you tried to do about it
You wondered "Where I do belong."

Well we all have them now and then
As we travel down life's highway,
The way gets dark, and the storms get rough
And we look for another by-way.

If we just hold in there for a while
And don't loose sight of our goal,
We'll see the lights from heaven
That will thrill our very soul.

So hang on tight and pray a lot
No matter how dark the way;
Because God is there to help us out
It will all get better some day.

*Helen G. Wilcox*

## Where's the Love

What have we done
Where can we go
Look around see what we've done
Millions have died through war and hate
We have no right to determine others fate
The killing is done by the young and old
And innocent teenagers are killed
For what's the price we must pay
Can you solve the hateful riddle of life
Can you detour the fateful course
Hate has become the dominant race
Look into the other's face
The answer to the riddle is a struggle
Can we find enough love in our hearts
We can all do our part
If we find enough love in our hearts

*Jamie Lee Rudnicki*

## Peace

What's wrong with this world?
Where do I begin?
There are too many enemies,
and not enough friends.
Too many people who think they are right,
too many vandals roaming the night.
Too many people with nothing to eat,
too many people who live on the street.
Too many problems that never make sense.
This world is plagued with too much
violence.
Too many toxins are filling the ground.
Too many forests are being cut down.
Too many wild animals trapped in the zoo.
This world could be better but it's all up to
you.

*Jordan Hugh Lee*

## Environment

Environment, it is a total disgusting mess
Where is the government?
Is this total pollution a need?  Or is it just simple greed?
I think it is the latter, I must confess.
You see a thick brown cloud over any city.
So totally unhealthy, it is a pity.
It makes the peoples lungs aching,
and their eyes burning upon awaking.
Is the use of chemicals such a need,
to even kill a harmless simple weed.
Most all the food you eat
is chemically polluted, including meat.
You know, we can-not live without clean water,
that in itself is a very serious matter.
How are the future generations going to live?
What price will they have to pay and sacrifice to give?
So, all you out there, stop this pollution.
I know that you know, that there is a solution.
I know God made this earth for our use,
and I am very sure He does not like its abuse.

*Albert Wettstein*

## Bike Hike

One day in summer
I went biking
past the park
and came back hiking.

*Vincent Fichera age 10*

## Ode to a Lost Relationship

Sometimes life is like a charade;
　　where music boxes never are played.

Initial exchanges pass, as on parade;
　　their essence hadn't a chance to be weighed.

In our awareness years - backward
　　glances should've stayed.

Perhaps, then friendships could've
　　been made.

*Carol Ann Murphy*

## My TV And Me

O give me the comfort of my tv set
Where sex and violence I usually get
And relevant programming hasn't arrived yet
I want not to think for myself.

Where across the spectrum banality abides
On that 19-inch screen my future rides
I care less that intelligence constantly hides
I want not to think for myself.

Some call it the box, some the tube, some the telly
Doesn't matter as long as my beer's on my belly
And I'm munching on cold cuts straight out of the deli
And continue not to think for myself.

Whether reruns of Gilligan or Starsky and Hutch
Or late night movies, it's never too much
As long as that remote is safe in my clutch
I want not to think for myself.

So, change not the pattern, keep giving me more
I'll watch dusk to dawn till my eyes are sore
And look eagerly forward to what the new season has in store
Please, don't let me think for myself.

*Charles C. Washburn*

## The Quiet Room

In the quiet room of my aloneness,
where the world does not see me,
and no one knows who I am,
I may sit, wordless,
wondering about the silence I have selected,
my eyes moving slowly over
lifeless things, such as,
a bowl of silk roses on the table,
a book of proverbs on the shelf,
sunlight, piercing an amber prism near the
window, all these revealing I am
someone who has made choices.
Even the small cat, purring on the sofa indicates
choices.  Why then am I here alone,
with no one to speak to,
wondering what it was that
brought me here?

*Gloria Valenti*

## Clemency

　Tears of sadness are cried by a clown.
Your dreams have been shattered,
sorrow is where you drown.
Love is a game we all play,
never to lose and always trying to win.
You stand in a line of broken hearts,
with the memory of her face and name.
I'm the angel of mercy, for I know of this pain.
For I was this poor heartbroken man who felt
victim of the game.

*Joel Perez*

## Untitled

I knew you once, in the enchanted dream,
where we ran free and green,
discovering unicorns and elves
and giants... and ourselves.
Greener than the hills we ran;
spellbound in a magic land.
I trembled at your trembling touch, and you...
tasted fresh and green and sweeter than the dew.
And we never dreamed the dreamers grace
that blessed us in that special place.
Innocent and green
and tender as the grass,
we let the golden days slip pasts,
warm; enfolded in the Wizards dream.

*Daniel J. Dahms*

## Land Of The Unjust

The land of the unjust
Where you have very few friends you can trust
Every day a constant battle to be the best
No matter who you hurt or kill, you'll never pass the test
Everyone and everything has a price
You will never win the game by being nice.

The land of the unjust
Where you do what you must
Different people, different races
You refuse to see their faces
Prejudice and hatred cloud your sight
The anger burns, you have to fight.

The land of the unjust
We're all just creatures of dust
This land where rapist and murderers don't do time
Thanks to the courts, they don't pay for their crimes
Convenience decides the fate of unborn babies
After that it is too late for maybe
The land of the unjust
This is the world we live in, the land of the unjust.

*Jared Sommers*

## The Babies

The babies cries were loud and clear,
where's Mom and Dad, why aren't they here?
The babies lay with tears in their eyes
they couldn't run nor could they hide,
they couldn't dispute their parents lies.

They longed for attention and loving care,
but Mom and Dad, they just weren't there.
When the babies were gone and there were no more cries,
Mom stares into space and now she cries.

Where was the love I should have had?
With all those babies I should have been glad,
but no one told me I had to give love
that I was the one who had to be strong,
now they tell me, but my babies are gone.

*Carolyn Daniels*

## It Is Quiet Here

There is a nice place where we can have peace,
where there is quiet and comfort,
and sweet sleep brings release.
There are flowers around us, and our loved ones never die,
we go there often to visit and to cry.
It is the place where we all say goodbye,
We walk and tell them what we are doing down here
A cemetery is a wonderful bed,
"And found memories are always dear."

*Irene Schweinfurth*

## 70

As I reach the seventieth year of my life,
Which has been filled with much love and a bit of strife,
I am very happy to find
That there still are new interests to fill my mind.
I can take a long walk
And enjoy a good talk.
I appreciate the fact that I can still go to work
And even take pleasure from tasks I used to shirk.
I look at the foibles of my young with some disdain,
Their values, their actions, most of which don't seem sane.
Yet, truly what can I say?
I used to be much the same way.
At this age it is really funny,
Feeling good takes priority over accumulating money.

*Evelyn Eiden*

## Spring Comes in like a Lamb and Goes Out like a Lion

February went out of sight
While March brought in Spring's peaceful light.

It came in like a lamb, so soft and calm.
Almost like the silent breeze that sways the palm.

And as the weeks go
The more fearsome it will grow.
And as you will soon find out how it's going to be.
Rough. Rough like the storms on the mists of the sea.

Then in April it will start to cease,
And continue the rest of spring in ease!

*Amanda Schalk*

## A Snowfall

Soft as the down of a feather,
white as an angel's gown,
floating through the dusky Heavens
on its earthen journey bound.

Like the sparkling of brilliant diamonds
against velvet deep and dark,
so the snow lends its queenly beauty,
making the Earth a fairyland park.

There is peace in the bright still night,
and Heaven is very near.
It brings warmth and goodness to the spirit,
willing a feeling of good cheer.

*Carolyn J. Bollhoefer*

## Woe of a Wanton Woman

There will come a day, I truly hope -
When you will realize that you've been a real dope!
You will find you are unable to cope -
For "God's" sake, one would think I had a rope!
I'm not trying to tie you down -
And I'm not making you out to be a clown!
I just want to be your dancing friend -
Why can't you see that would not be such a terrible end!
To Polish music we could twirl, twist, we could even kick -
I honestly feel that I would not be such a bad pick!
We could really have a great time -
Seems to me being my dancing friend would be just fine!!??

*Connie A. McElhone*

515

## Thank You, God, For The One

Thank you, God, for the one
Who dressed me in fine laces;
She showed me how to take life
With all it's strides and paces.

Thank you God, for the one
Who taught me how to live;
She taught what was right from wrong
How to apologize and forgive.

Thank you God, for the one
Who taught me to be free;
She told me, that no matter what
My life belongs to me.

Thank you God, for the one
Who helped me when I was blue;
She gave her strength, her heart and soul
She advised me on what to do.

Thank you God, for the one
I wouldn't trade for another;
Thank you God, for the one
The one I call my Mother.

*Debora Geritano Ruiz*

## Who?

Who is the person that is so sweet?
Who is the person that puts you to sleep?
And says don't make a deep!
    IT'S YOUR MOTHER
Who is the person that sings while mopping through the house?
Who is the person that says AH! There's a mouse
And sometimes says bring me a tissue so I can clean your snout,
    IT'S YOUR MOTHER
Who is the person that likes to give hugs?
Who is the person that tucks you in bed
makes you feel snug,
And sometimes says we don't want to go to the beach
it is full of slimy slugs
    IT'S YOUR MOTHER
So I take this time on Mother's day
To say I love you in a special way
Thank you for being a wonderful Mom
Sending me through school and helping me get reading for my prom
    YOU ARE MY MOTHER
And no other could ever be like my Mother.

*Dianna Nicole Scales*

## Friends

Searching for friends
    who last a lifetime...
Cherishing the moments
    we shared together.
So far apart...
    So close in our hearts.
Fond memories of times past,
    laughing till the sun came up.
Sharing our dreams,
    giving support, love, and respect for each other,
        having someone to lean on.
Our hearts close together.
I am glad that you are here
    and I am a part of your life.
For when I leave this world
    and the angels call me,
I will know...
    that you are a friend
        who lasts a lifetime...

*Jeanne Habeck*

## For The Graduates

There is a girl not fully woman
Who lives not yet free;
There is a boy not yet man
Still sitting on momma's knee.
Both aching for that awakening,
Dutifully searching for to see
That day and hour when life affords them
The man and woman they ought to be.
Stumbling toward their futures,
They try to escape insecurity
As they see that maturity has not been rendered
When physical appearances escape the years of puberty.
But while not looking, however actively pursuing
This desired developed maturity,
Their beings quicken and they successfully achieve
The stature of the man and woman they sought to be.

*Jennifer Jennings Sanders*

## Our Rightful Place

Here was a woman
Who never hung a work of art,
(Except the church calendar)
Traveled further than Saint Louis,
(She remembered the zoo)
Or saw a Broadway show.
(She would have loved the tap dancing)
Nonetheless - based on 60 years experience
Living in Richardson County
She had two rules for life.
Number 1 Don't be high falutin.
Number 2 Our kind of people don't do that kind of thing.
"High falutin" covered thinking you were somebody.
"Our kind of people" covered being somebody.
Like deposed royalty somehow stranded in a country town,
She kept us ready to assume our rightful place.

*Barbara Armbruster*

## Unity

We celebrate the memories of those
Who sacrificed for our gain
We cry with passion
For those we have lost

Men that dreamed from within (dreamers from within)
Men that struggled from without (struggling from without)
Woven together for a singular purpose
That of freedom for all

We cannot forget men with vision that saw beyond
That left before us
For we walk with pride
Cause they walked beyond boundaries

Goal of a positive few
Transcends the indifference of others
For the gifts that they carried
Are for all of us to behold

Cherish what was given
It was for our growth
Relish the time that was
For it surely wont come again for with it, came a family

*Joe L. Dawson*

## A Love Song

'Tis true, 'tis true!  She's my dearest Trudy
Whose being combines brains and beauty.
To have a wife so sweet
Is a delightful treat.

Blessed is that wondrous day we did meet:
The fateful day our hearts as one did beat.
Destiny would roll a lucky seven:
Our love on earth would be made in heaven.

We walked and talked, fingers entwined;
The future projected in our eye's mind.
Unaware the moment the Rubicon we had crossed
Together to pursue our destiny tempest-tossed.

The years passed so fleetingly
As we happily fulfilled our destiny.
Crossing valleys and climbing mountains,
Drinking bitter-sweet from life's fountains.

Yesterday has ticked away the seconds;
Tomorrow the unknown us it beckons.
And now's the time to turn the page;
Hand in hand, to wait what the morrow will presage.

*Edward Boltuch*

## To My Father

To my Father whom I truly love.
Whose heart is as big as the sky above.
I wish we had more time to spend,
to sing and dance and make new friends.
But God is calling you to be with Him.
Though we will miss you throughout the years,
and we may cry some lonesome tears
I feel so blessed to have spent some time
with my father who was so very kind.
But we will be together again,
when our time here is at an end.
The love I feel I cannot hide,
but I'll see you on the other side.

*Daniel E. Vincent*

## Brit For Short

Hurrah!  For the dog they all called Brit!
Whose motto must have been, "Don't ever quit"!
A short haired hunting dog trained to point game;
This dog was a girl!  But she had my brother's name!

Before the show, Brit was well groomed,
One look at her and the other dogs were doomed!
To relinquish the show, ribbons and all;
To Brit!  The dog with the lucky paws!

I can still hear them yell, "GO BRIT GO"!
Bring home the blue ribbon, and win and show!
Why, I'd say my brother Brit is a man among men!
I know that I would rate him at least at ten!

To run like that and never quit!
This dog Britannia is just like my brother Brit!
Britannia has now retired from the show and the race;
With a family of ten little Brits to take her place.

One hundred and forty one shows to her credit,
And money to those who chanced to bet it!
Brit the show dog is now a mother,
And I'm so glad, they named her after my brother!

*Janie Ruth Voight*

## The Prayer

Welcome to my nightmare
Why do all of you stare
All my life and soul painted black
My anger and pain felt on this rack.

I am standing on the steps of Hell's inn
Sent down here for all my evil sin
My many punishments only one but death
Pushed me down by words under the Devil's breath.

Black pointed finger poke my back like a bed of nails
Body tossing and turning my arms they flail
His evil pompous laughter rips my heart
Like a dull sword ripping me in half and apart.

Oh God don't let me die in this horrid way
Don't turn away because of my sin listen to the way I pray
Oh God I'm on my knees begging your forgiveness
I want to live and love these are feelings that I miss.

Shed a tear of Ice cold rain on this place
It's fire and hot steam are burning my face
Take my hand in yours take me to your sky
Oh God save me I don't want to die.

*David Parker*

## "Where Is The Snow?"

Where did the long Winter go?
Why was there never any snow?
So warm the wind, so gray the skies,
but my heart couldn't feel
    the winter's cold sighs.

We long for Spring when Winter is deep,
but we're glad to experience
    the long Winter's sleep.
To everything its season,
    and the time is right
    to work by day and rest by night.

Without the Summer, the Spring loses hope,
just as Autumn, losing Summer, learns to cope.
But where is Winter when I need it so?
Did it really forget me
    by refusing me snow?

*Evelyn Dale Buck*

## What Will Happen To Me?

Sometimes when I walk I often wonder.
Will life be rosy or just full of thunder.
Will I ever love or will I ever be loved.

Will I live, will I die
    will I laugh, will I cry.

Life is filled with much
    confusion, agony and pain.

Life is also filled with so much
    love and happiness.

That's why it seems so insane!

I often ask God what do I do,
    where do I go?

In the silence I hear do what
    you want, it's your own show.

So that's why I think life is
    full of dances,

That is why we need to
    take chances.

...or we may lose the things
    we love the most....

*Bradley Urfer*

## Forever Wind

Wind is a rustling symphony that strings across the sea
Wind is a reed-like melody that passes over me
There's wind forever, though I've gone by
There's wind forever, it's there - up high
And I am here - but I am dead,
While wind lolls its vespus above my head
Why should death take me when life holds so much
And why is there wind when its substance can't be touched
Why am I dead when I've done no wrong
And yet I lie dead while wind sighs it's song

And forever and forever it's breeze shall pass
Across my grave until the last
I've known no wind for countless years
But it laughs in life, while I cry silent tears
And I am gone for death is clever
But wind is there, it's there - forever.

**Raymond Muscarello**

## January's Lament

New is the year so bright and clear;
Winter is on us, but Spring is near;
Just three months to April with flowers popping;
Birds are returning just see them hopping.

Snow has retreated from hill and tree;
Ponds are liquid and algae free;
Warm breezes begin to caress each bush;
Crocus and tulip starts their push;

Soon the warm air swirls around us;
Once again we begin to fuss;
Remembering the cool of Winter and Spring;
As you feel the menacing insect sting;

Before you know it, Fall is back;
Bright with color and asthma's hack;
All too soon the days become shorter;
And Winter, as usual, is at our border;

So take all in stride, it pays not to worry;
Of Summer's heat or Winter's flurry;
Enjoy what you can from season to season;
Not to complain, 'cause there's no reason!

**Glenn M. Auble**

## Down from the Hills

Down from the hills,
Winter's white caps over my shoulder
Are packed with water sweetened
From late spring rains.
Valley's flowered meadows' dripping heads
Suddenly face the warming sun,
A carpet of colors each asserting its own hue.
Oh, happy song - a promise of more to come!

Streams bubble their freedom,
Atoms of another time.
How can I contain myself?
This feast of senses
So long closeted in cabin fever.
I'll remember yesterday, and today is my day -
And tomorrow...
Order is remembering, and excitement in the remembrance.

**Bert G. Vilaska**

## God's Lost Child

He looked in this lost soul no one had seen,
Wiped away the tears and made me clean.
Took a broken heart (Spirit), made it smile from within;
Said, child, your life as it was has come to an end.
Accept me in your heart, I will feel your every hurt,
    and cry your tears,
Give you a love you have never known through the years.
Trust me, my child. Take my hand, for we will walk
    this life together.
For soon your reward will be you, the Son, and our
    Father forever.

**Debrah Turnbough**

## Christmas Eve

The star of bethlehem guided the way
Wise men came to have their say
The angels sang songs from heaven above
Everyone came to show Jesus their love.

The babe was lying in a manger below
The site was shinning with a huge glow
Joseph and Mary were close at his side
To watch over him with pride in their eyes.

The son of God was born on this night
What a glorious moment it was a delight
The shepherds came from a distant afar
To worship the king by only one star.

**Dee Kurczewski**

## Untitled

Standing next to the pond,
With a beautiful flower in my hand,
The smell made me float into the humid air,
While the stickers are drawing blood,
But the pain didn't get me because of beauty,
Made me think lovely thoughts,
All pain at that moment does not exist,
Once more I am greeted by the aroma,
Again lifted me higher in the sky,
The color of the flower drains down my arm,
Colored drops dripping from my arm to the dirt,
Where a similar flower sprang up quickly.

**Jeff Taylor**

## Candy Apples And Jelly Rings

All he knows is candy apples and jelly rings
With a ferries wheel, as his shield
He sits inside his room
With thoughts of you know who
He loves everyone he is with
As long as the love doesn't fit
He walks around in a daze
Looking for that purple haze
His life is but a dream
But dreams are not what they seem
When you live in between reality and a dream
Candy apples and jelly rings don't come free
But if you dream a little dream of me
I will set your fantasy's free
And then your dreams shall be of me
Cause candy apples and jelly rings are always what they seem

**Jodi Pocai**

## The Pussy Willow Tree

Off we went, my mother and me
With a slender sprig of a willow tree.
Beside the old well, out in our yard
Seemed like a good place for a tree to stand guard.
We murmured the words "grow where you're planted"
That it would grow we took for granted!
Ten years have past, it's so lovely and tall.
Each springtime she goes to the annual ball.
She dons her gown, soft tufts of grey
Too soon it's over and they go away.
I wonder if you see it, from up above,
Our tree that we planted is home to the Dove.

*Emma Lou Shadle*

## The Turkey

You never heard of the "Turkey", a minesweeper
    with a sturdy hull?
She was blessed with a drunken crew and many a gull.
Wherever she went the seas were clean as a dime.
A fighting ship, a Navy ship, she never feared a mine.

I'll never forget the night in Lake Erie, only
    twelve feet deep.
The storm was wild - the rocks would make "mama" weep.
The crew was sick with the shuddering heaves.
The helm struggled against the water and sheaves.

Me and the Captain prayed for a light,
But the rudder fixed at 45 degrees right.
Into the harbor the wooden devil sailed,
Without a crew, to safety she high tailed.

*Gordon Reeves*

## Marriage

This couple is here today, to strengthen their vows,
With blessing from family and friends,
Their love will endow.

When they first saw each other,
It was love at first sight,
They make the world shine,
They are each others light.

A family is what they dreamed for,
Two girls is what they got,
They have shared their love,
Since the day they tied the knot.

They've been through a lot in 15 years,
Yet they would never drift apart,
They will always deeply love each other,
With all of their heart.

As their love keeps growing,
And their dreams come true,
Still 'til this day, they say, "I love you."
Marriage is for lovers, that have good hearts,
They will stay together, till death do they part.

*Hollie Ranger*

## Special Kind Of Love

There he stands, a strong, handsome man,
With a brand new suit and a ring in his hand.
He strides forward with pride, heading to the altar,
his heart leading his feet, his steps will not falter.
Standing before him is his true love,
Her beauty and grace is like a white dove.
For these two souls life has just begun.
Their new life together has bring forth change,
But twenty five years later, their love remains the same.

*Dale Christenson*

## Picture of My Mother

I'd like to paint a picture of my mother
With dark eyes and soft brown hair
And I'd emphasize every wrinkle
'Cause I know what put them there

I wouldn't try to paint on her face a smile
I'd paint her as I know she is
Nothing overdone or elaborate
Just a face that has weathered the years

I'd paint her with an understanding face
The kind to which you could confess
I wouldn't try to make it just soft and white
But you'll love her none the less

For I'd paint that picture so true to life
That people would stop and stare
And some would see there a knowing look
As through they found accusations there

But others would think it a beautiful face
The kind I have always known it to be
Yes that's what I want is to paint it exactly
As I see it so all the world can see

*Irene Johnson*

## Test

I am just a boy on his way to becoming a man.
With each day I find challenges to test me.
My soul is like an angel and my wings are being tested.
Please Lord help me to come through with flying colors.
For today I cannot see so clearly. I feel so much pressure.
I am sure I won't be able to stand it much longer.
My wings are cracked. Soon they will splinter and fall.
I beg of you Lord, may I ask you to keep me from harm while
I grow a new pair of wings, for I love you.
I wish to spend all my life with you and for you while on earth.
I will seek refuge in the people that love me.
Besides my family, I have found an angel that cares for me and
my love is what she lives for and I live for hers.
I thank you for answering my prayers from yesterday.
Today I have a prayer for you to please take care of my earth angel
and allow me to live a long healthy life to please her.
And if this is not true love let it go away nice and peaceful for
I don't need rejection to be another pain in my test of life.
Please help me! Amen.

*George Thamer*

## A Legend—A Legacy

Rebecca braved the rough ocean voyage to this new land
With her husband and son and few belongings in hand.
In the New England wilderness they made a new home,
But hostile Indians chased them and caused them to roam.

Richard, his son and others had to hunt for supplies.
They soon learned that going ashore had been unwise,
For they came upon Indians—Pequots—ready for war
Who killed each and every white man that had come to the shore.

Rebecca was left in the shallop to try
To escape with the others; they did not want to die.
They settled in Rhode Island, around Newport goes the tale
Rebecca bore the first child born in R. I. who was pale.

She was a strong and stalwart woman who raised her son John
To become a loving and God-fearing sturdy young man.
John soon had a family — six children who worked hard—
And two of them became ministers — preachers of God.

They produced many offspring; these grandchildren did thrive,
All because Rebecca's courage had caused her to survive.
Though no monument is standing as a tribute to her,
Eighth great grandmother Rebecca was a heroine — pure.

*Elizabeth S. Gill*

## Life By Rote

Are we all living life by rote
With little hope to understand
All the moral principles of mankind
Just repeating them mechanically by rote

The ten commandments have been read for centuries
Study them now and compare your understanding
To the horrible realities of the world today
War, greed, racial hatred, divorce, homeless terrorism

Thy kingdom come thy will be done
An excellent example of the repetition of words
With very little attention to the power of the mind to understand
Can one find Gods kingdom on earth as it is in heaven

What are the true meaning of the phrases
Love honor and obey till death do us part
Have to many repeated them mechanically by rote
Creating the decline of family as a horrible reality

Yes the moral principles of mankind
Have become a repetition of words
With little hope for understanding
As many are living life by rote

*Arthur L. Johnston*

## Life

On May 16, 1982, I came into this world, brand new
With not a care in the world to start my life out;
I was so healthy and began running about.
Years went by of fun and joy,
I'm 13 and still a young boy.
I started chasing girls and my heart began to thump,
I thought it was love but seems to been a lump.
It passed through my heart and left a hole on depart,
that leaves no choice but to open the heart.
I will have surgery June 13th,
By two Drs.' that can't be beat.
There by my side will be angels from above,
Along with a bunch of those I love.
When I open my eyes, there will be a grin,
From Nathaniel my best friend.
God assures me he will never depart,
When the surgeons go in and open my heart.

*Brody Bogan*

## The Farmer's Loving Wife

She wishes upon the shade of the sundial
With penny-copper,
In-God-We-Trust eyes,
In the Fall season,
Beneath skies, overcast.

She shrills while reaching high,
One hand apart and one a fist
In gained regret through vows,
For the wheat to sway and bow
To her bare, white feet.

With a raindrop,
Realization bites and drools
And wheat fades from the whetted fields
Of yellow, grassy bareness;

But, in time, the rain will give way
To Fall's second cousin, Spring,
And Spring's hop-scotching child-seed,
Hope.

*Jamie Whitney*

## Just a Storm in the Night

Now he is gone to the store and he'll be back
  with roses.
Yes, it has happened once more.
And Brooke, just a kid, knows; but she won't tell.
For she fears what comes from their room;
  The screams of pain; the vicious yells.
"Help me," is the cry of the night covered by the
  winds howling just right.
Now crouched in a corner filled with pain; tears
  running down her face like the on-coming rain.
The lightning strikes hard; like his hand across
  her face.
And like his deep, furious voice, the thunder roars.
Now crouched in a corner, she wonders —
  can I take this anymore?

*Bissi*

## The Window

Through my window hence you came,
With sable hair and cloak to match,
A book of verse opened the latch.
Light from moonbeams played upon your face,
Dark forgiving eyes showed harbored grace.
While I lay, hoping to get a glance,
Of moonbeams upon which you danced.
A voice so kind spoke words of praise,
Tempting me with every phrase.
Crickets chirped a tale of woe,
I had no fear of the radiant glow.
A single touch from your cold lonely hand,
Brought me to a far enchanted land.
You come to me a tortured soul,
Once again our meeting has taken its toll.
Now, as the sun begins to appear,
I have no qualms or mortal fears.
I understand you must go as I remain,
To await your return from the mystical domain.

*Carolyn A. Winiarski*

## Ode To The Tiburon Gander

Before the dawn begins to glow,
With sightless eyes a ghost I see.
Beloved gander friend to me,
Who all my needs would know
Before I asked.
Dear love, dear life, dear eyes,
Why did the humans have to look
With envy on our happy lives?
At night I hear the brethren flying north
across the vault of heaven;
and you, an echo of their cry,
keep calling me
"Come home! Come home!"

*Francis Ingall*

## The Land I Call My Own

When the wind blows, oh when the wind blows,
Where does it take you when it flows? It
makes me flow to a land where nobody
knows, a land where everyone is reaching
out a helping hand and flowers bloom
everyday and no one is mad in any way
and children always happily play and I am
here this very day. That is the land I
call my own.

*Hillary E. Barthe*

## "Storming Of The Clouds"

That day I decided to spend my time
with the sea and its grains of summer sand.
Though the day seemed shorter because
the sun left its position and was in
the clouds, the birds began to fly, the crabs
entered their homes, and little children stopped to play.

But before I could turn around
a large roar ripped the gray sky in
half, and a large silver bent knife took aim
in the whipping water as if
it were butter.  Then silence made
every living, breathing, thing deaf around me, tame.

I watched the clouds die and the sun live again.

*Damian Bednarz*

## Friendship

After the last fallen leaves of Autumn,
With their colors of red, brown, orange and tan,
When the final snowflakes of winter
Have descend softly to the ground,
When the last flock of birds have taken flight,
To flee the cold and storm,
When the flowers of Spring
Have ceased to bloom;
And the Robin and Meadow Lark
Hushed their sweet song;
Look beyond the rainbow,
After the quiet storm,
There, blooms the summer's last rose my Love,
After the last rose has faded,
Look for me my dear,
I'll be there,
I am Friendship, I will be beside you,
Forever in your thoughts
I cannot die!!!

*Doris E. Wright*

## The Diablo Range

Your voluptuous hills,
with their tree green'd recesses,
promise hidden delights.

What kind devil
dwells upon your verdure crests,
amidst Lick Observatory's nippl'd breasts,
to reach out to time's beginning
and the 'mother of us all'?

You want a Big Bang?
I'll give you a big bang:
Feast your eyes on these evergreen slopes.

*Charles Bernstein*

## God Lives In An Eagle Eye

Christmas day, clear and cold.
Traveling north to visit a childhood home
On a stretch of road closed in by larch and pine.
Focused on the snow covered peaks ahead
A bald eagle swooped down
From his perch, from the heavens.
Matching my speed, so close
We could have touches.
He seemed to be saying.
'Look into my eye and see yourself.'
And God was there, too.

*Debra Hastings*

## The Inner Mirror

I sit and wait,

upon a shell of grapefruit
with thoughts that wonder
fresh and clear,
to strange lands to guide
my mind to search and steer,
to gaze be on the looking glass
within the inner mirror,
To wander where I've never been
with very little fear,
To see what I've been looking for
and what I've found
And gazing at the action appearing all around,
and when I want some action
I know that it is free
for all the adventure in the world is inside of me.

*John Adam*

## Premature Requiem

Beyond the cells merrily knitting the fabric of you
    within the depth of me,
    Lay a dream of "we" - you with mommy and daddy.

Then I peeked at you through sound wave images,
    you resting ragged on my inner nest - I wept!
Oh dark night, my soul fainted.
I cannot reverse your dying.
I cannot postpone your embryonic death.

Prayer seeped in all around you,
    weaving the cradle for your journey back.
As you shrink,
    my heart swells with motherly sorrow.

Christmas is here now, the steeple chimes herald the hour.
    Gesu' Bambino, baby blest,
    as I celebrate your birth memorial for the 25th year,
    I give you a most treasured gift,
        a dwindled form,
        a tiny guest swaddled in love.
    Be its natal rest.

*Judith A. Litchfield*

## One Way

Day after day, in darkness and cold,
Wondering how my life will unfold.
Will you be there to hold my hand,
And guide me through the promise land?
I think of you often, and how it could be,
Our life together, just you and me.

I'll walk in your footsteps, we'll cover the path,
Look towards tomorrow, no turning back.
I'll stand beside you, we'll come as one,
Endless nights spent, romancing the sun.

Please don't deny me, your hand in my hand.
'Till death do us part, we will walk this land.
Diamonds and pearl, could never replace,
The love that I feel, when I look at your face.
Give me a chance, that's all I ask,
to prove to you, my love will last.
And if the time comes, when we must part,
Know that you are in my heart.

*Jamie Swob*

## Dark Alleys

Through the dark alleys of time I walk.  Wondering.
Wondering of what I will do, of what I will become.

Through the dark alleys of time, I gaze, in amazement at the
success of others and wonder why I have no success of my own.

Through the dark alleys of time my life is like a dream, of hate
and wrong doings, and happiness, none.

Through the dark alleys of time I walk, I have the time to think,
and dream.  I think, and I think my life is pointless and wonder
why I am here, here in the dark alleys of time.

*Dan Vickery*

## Poets Lost In Time

If man were born of poetic verse
words of life in rhyme with time
stories and facts, a history changed
no mortals, but poets living in rhyme

Men their existence, being poetry in motion
living the sirens of ancient seas
delicate senses, tortured hearts:
are poets their eulogies etched from the tears
of everlasting love.

*G. W. Gregorio A. West*

## Another Level

To understand and express real love at this point in life
Would be attempting to capture the infinite.
I feel an inspiration of overwhelming determination that is
supported by a false sense of confidence.
Winning is my cloak of life.
Loss is experiencing a fate worse than death.
This is a day of great sorrow, today I have seen myself.

My mind is hooked, I am subject to a habit.
Addiction comes in many forms and is more vicious than
the afflictions of the cat of nine tales.
I imagine without hallucinogenics,
I am asleep without barbiturates
I spin pass reality without amphetamines.
Yesterday I saw the real me—it was a day of great sorrow.

I have been jarred by the other side of me
I have allowed myself to construct an illusion of reality.
I have verbalized a lie when my mind spoke the truth.
I have fought a battle with me, now I live in a world of caution.
Today is a day of great sorrow for now I know me.
Tomorrow will be beautiful for within I have reached another level.

*Goldia T. Brinson*

## Color World

Brown is the teddybear I hold at night
Yellow is the sun that shines so bright
Blue is the sky over my head
White is the pillow on top of my bed
Black is the pavement underneath my feet
Red is the apple I'm going to eat
Silver is the money we work for hard
Green is the grass in my backyard
Purple is the bruise upon my knee
Gold are the fish that swim in the sea
Gray is the hair on a billy goat's back
Orange is the fruit we carry in a sack
The world would never be the same
Without the colors I just named!

*Andrea Patterson*

## I Try To Live Without You

I loved you once, I loved you twice, maybe three times
would be nice, although my love is flowing strong, somehow
I felt it would be wrong, you say you love me then you
don't, I could still love you, but I won't, I'm so tired
of all those lies I've had, too many good cries, I wish for
once it would be gone, that same memory that still lives
on, so please for once leave me alone, don't try to call
me, don't try to talk to me, I need some time to be alone,
though without you there's not much left, just all those
tears I gave for you, and all those letters you send me,
just say you love me, just one last time, and that's it I'll
draw the line, good-bye my love, once and for all I will
survive without your cruel and painful heart, if I ever
see you again, you will see me with another love that I will
hold in my arms, so please stop calling me to forgive you even if
you try to convince me with all your tears, understand, I
don't want to be with you, so this is the last good-bye
for us two, but remember I never told you that I never love
you anymore.

*Carmen Anaya*

## Last Home

Heads bowed low, blank stares, smiles, a glimpse of the past.
Years ago, so vital—living, working, and loving, time went
  by much too fast.

Now, they wait quietly, some to be fed, some loudly waiting,
  some crying, some still.
Entertainment for those who are able to think.  Others lie in beds.
  Yes, time went so fast, and always will.

The halls are quiet now except for the moans; time to sleep and
  dream of homes—real homes, happy memories, families so rare,
  the smell of coffee from the kitchens, old-fashioned biscuits
  and cinnamon rolls, none can compare.
Holding back their tears, so brave, (so sad) to think of what was
  left behind.

Time to change the diapers again; almost daylight, another day begins.
  Telephones ring, nurses scurry, workers change shifts,
  some just to earn their pay and pass the day, others giving
  God's gift of tender loving care.
Precious lives, still discerning, knowing this is their last home.

*Joyce McDaniel*

## White Diamond Dandelion!

Set near favorite white peach fruit trees amused by a tiny flood,
  yet dried by the
sun greeting fragrances of lilacs
and peonys into a jubilee parade
of melody winds, it was set free!

Wet with dew, a very rare treasure of white bloom is born,
pretty as a diamond crown enhanced by the promises beyond the sea;

Array it in fame, for the best microscope finds it
wedded to prismatic sun glows, as a princess whiter flower
of dandelion glory...

Play gets dreamy to hope a better than Rembrandt oil painting
artist paints it as a giant enlarged top view bouquet attracting to it's
ancient story...

Let its exquisite beauty mated genesis from ages of time,
place its petaled gems of whiter diamond luster, into brighter
wisdoms to be...
White Diamond Dandelion!

*Aloha E. Grant*

## Disconnected Connection

We are all connected in some way or another
Yet my only blood connection is disconnected

What is a young girl to do when the blood is thin
The only way to go is away from home...far, far away

Same state, same city, same town, same blood...connected
So close so far so thin the skin...so close to the mind...disconnected

Is it possible to disconnect the child inside the mother
Why now....after we struggle for the growth does the stem break

Too many flowers to bundle, to hold, to die...to pass by
The light never seen by the red, the purple, the blue of the veins

Common thoughts, sacred vows, independent roots taken way
Accept the thorn...for it is she who bleeds most

Yet, the exception must be torn right in the middle
For sky and water without a middle would be no life

We all need a middle to be connected, so why disconnect
To have the power to fertilize, why now, why now, why

The stem so strong, the flower so bright, so connected to earth
The roots, the blood, the metamorphosis so slow to grow

Cut and destroyed under the knife of love to fertilize the seed
Now forever lay the petals...disconnected...dying...dry blood

### *Jill Leber*

## Letting Go

Waiting for this day
    yet wanting you to stay
Giving up control
    but still holding on
Standing back while you make your choices
    biting my tongue not to say
    I wouldn't do it that way
Giving you a little shove
    knowing you may stumble
    praying you won't fall
Thinking back to all I've done
    the things I'd like to change
Holding back the tears of joy
    along with tears of pain
Wondering if my mother
    also felt this way
Your life to now is embedded
    in my soul
The hardest thing I've ever done is
    letting go.

### *Debe Armstrong*

## Time Line

The lines of time entwine a rhyme
Written of the winds of scherzo.

The spiral flow constrains most to go
In endless, random dancing show.

But when the sound of your mind learns the music of time
And spins it with the rhythm of rhyme,

A pattern emerges, and then converges
With one of a synergic glow.

For your and for me the pattern burns free
In counterpoint rhythm and melody.
Love is the key.

### *Dale Johnson*

## Our Family Chain

Our family is like a chain, many links long.
You add a link at a time; longer it gets
Middle school - Pickerington, oh.:  we attended a program,
Sixth grade - blue team - title:  "Poetry Alive."
Welcome speech given by Great Grandson Jay.
He's one terrific link, only twelve, but Great!
They acted out the poems, giving title and author.
17th Great-Grandchild; one more link added.
A.M. Easter service we attended; sermon, "Very Good"!
Celebrated both Easter and 60th Anniversary at Ann's!
Earl gave the blessing; he's a born leader!
There were thirty out of forty links present.
Kenneth gave me a necklace with five birthstones.
Earl in Jan.; Elaine in June; Ann - Mother - Dad in
Dec.; Ann born on my 25th birthday; dark red hair;
Blue eyes; "a small miniature of her Dad now."
"Was he ever happy!"  "My Birthday gift!"
Our family has meant everything to us.
Children are doing the same for their families.
"By loving all siblings, it will be returned!"

### *Edna Butcher Smith*

## Function Of The Mouth

You bring happiness with your mount, you bring sadness with your mouth
You are a grouch or a saint through your mouth.
You will get along with people with your mouth,
Or you will become an our cast because of your mouth.
Your mouth speaks your mind.  Every sense in your body
is expressed through the partnership of your mind and body through
your mouth.
Your nourish yourself with your mouth, you can destroy yourself
through your mouth.
You can sing, you can speak, you say marvelous thing
Or you can curse, scream, shout, making the world miserable.
You can mimic, you can smile all with your mouth.
What an instrument that only humans can turn to so many uses
and abuses,
You can be praised, blessed, insulted or belittled by someone's mouth
You can be hurt, nagged also by someone's mouth.
If only a person would cherish his priceless possession and use it
For healing and bringing out smiles with this instruments of his
I wonder if hurricanes and volcanoes wouldn't then be influenced
and curb their missions?

### *Bella Faust*

## "Heart Of Gold"

Deeper and deeper grows this line on my face
You are gone without a trace
Leaving behind a fleeting warm embrace
Hearts of Gold, no one can take their place

You touched each of our souls
For the price of a cut, our stories told
Your struggle never revealed, a woman so bold
No stories of your plight, only of the Love of your children
A heart of Gold

Missed you are and alone we've become
We all find it hard that you are gone
Your love for life is now with God
And your cries shall now be heard
To miss you seems so absurd

Climb into the Chariot Of God and
May God take the reins
And someday, soon, may we meet again

### *Frank Cawley*

## "Children Of The World"

So far away, yet so near,
You are in our hearts, do you hear,
Speaking many languages, here in this land,
All of you are the same, do you understand,
Different costumes do you have, in this world you
must all show love,
Playing together, sharing many things,
Guarding all earth's creatures, like angels with wings,
All the rain forest of which there are few,
The future of this planet, we leave it up to you,
Settle all your differences peacefully, no wars, no hungers,
everyone living so happily,
Going to the moon, traveling into space is great,
What is more important is your world, before it is too late,
The United Nations does its share,
Promoting peace, in many ways, showing that it cares,
So children of the world, wherever you may be,
God bless you all, I mean it believe me.

*Adela Melendez*

## A Gift

You brought a little light in a room full of darkness.
You brought a little purpose in an empty wondering.
You brought a little calm in utter confusion.
You brought a little peace in a troubled soul.
You brought anticipation in anxiety.
You brought a little joy where joy was not.
You brought a little glee in lowered and empty eyes.
You brought life back where life had strayed.

   the glimmering of light
   the inkling of purpose
   the intent of calm
   the struggle of peace
   the fantasy of anticipation
   the want of joy
   the hope of glee
   the hunger of life

Thanks for the gift...

*Joyce Smith Gamble*

## Times Change as You Get Older

People say,
  you can't see the forest because of the trees,
but if you close your eyes and dream,
  you can actually feel the breeze.
People say,
  beauty is only skin deep,
but don't close your eyes and weep.
  Because if you spend you're time crying,
You will never get any sleep.
People say,
  ugly plume to the bone.
Believe this and you will be all alone.
  Beauty is in the eyes of the beholder,
You'll believe this as you get older.
  Time change, people change,
Believe this and you'll get bolder.
  So open your eyes,
and see the blue skies.
Then you will be able to see the forest,
  because of the trees.

*Cameron Gary Longanecker*

## Kindness

Kindness is just a simple gesture showing
you care —
Reaching out to someone and share.
Kindness knows not a stranger,
and it expresses no danger.

Kindness is not a deed or chore.
It is like a seed planted deeply
that continues to grow.
Kindness is humble and meek.
It knows only of "good words" to speak.

It glows like a star in the darkened sky —
for certainly it is something
of not to be shy.
Kindness has no choice of race, color, or creed
it's just doing or showing a good deed.

God shows us His kindness by blessing
us abundantly,
that we may continue to pass it on freely.
Kindness is simply showing concern.
It is a lesson each of us should learn.

*Helen Washington*

## Why Dad?

When I was a baby
  you held me in your arms.
When I was a toddler
  you protected me from harm.
When I was five
  you were always by my side.
Now that I'm older
  you're here no longer.
Is it because your love for me has died,
  that's why you're no longer at my side?

*Abigail A. R. Rutherford*

## Lost Love

I think you know I love you
you just don't know how much.
I know you love me,
but I think sometimes you
say enough is enough.

I want to make this work
I'll do the best I can.
I want a home and family maybe next to the sand.

You and Amanda are life to me...
Don't you see
Without you two there's
no need for me.

I want a fresh start with you
You are the man for me
There will be no cost for you
The price will be free.

I think you should think about this long and hard.
If you look enough you'll find its in the cards

I've learned how to say no, I'll sign it guarantee
Especially if the price is as high as you and me.

*Florence Goblisch*

## Mother, Please Don't Cry

Oh mother!  You are sweet, you are so gentle and nice,
You make my heart beat, for me you are like bread and rice.

You are like roses filled with red, with love all over,
And a brilliant head, like a purple clover.

You will be in my heart forever, even after you die,
I hope that day will never come, you clever - mother,
    please don't cry.

You are a blossom in my arm you are a piece of sweet,
That would cause no harm, you're my once in-a-life-time treat.

You're the one that fills me with joy, or sometimes grief,
Oh boy!  You are like a full grown leaf.

Your warmth to everyone, will never make me lie,
I will always be a good son - mother please don't cry.

The warmth of your touch the things that you do
You love everyone so much and we all love you.

You're one that will bring fillings within me,
Happy or sad you will always be in my heart, even if I'm bad.

I love you with my heart whole, all this not a lie,
This comes from my soul - mother please don't cry.

*Igor Norinsky*

## Ode to the Lighthouse

What if the lights went out and
    you no longer could see?
What would the world be like for you and me?
Sometimes strange shadows appear,
    and we think we can see,
    and it disappears, what now what to do?
I say to myself and cry,
    this sudden darkness will it go away?
Where do I turn, what do I do?
I turned to the Lighthouse, they helped me through.

I've learned to cope and the day is only night,
    but though I'm blind, I now have special sight.
What wonders I now perform because my heart
    has joy and peace,
And now the fear inside of me has begun to cease.
And within myself I have found my worth
And I live in simple harmony with mankind on earth.

*Hilda Kaiser*

## Morpheus And Hypnos

Everyday, I seek you out.
You, only, I desire.
I crave you, and I search for you,
But never can you be found.

Never enough of you can I get.
Satisfaction is just beyond my reach.
I am wear from the lack of your presence,
I feel as if I shall drop from exhaustion.

The search for you is endless.
A lifelong pursuit.
Every minute of every day,
I look for ways to stop.

To rest a moment and to feel you.
Your caressing effect on my body.
I desire your touch,
Your gentle fingers of tranquility.

I try to look into the future,
But there is no hope for us.
I don't think I'll ever find you,
Until the day I die.

*Crystal Philbrook*

## My Mind, All Minds

My mind, all minds, what have you done to my body and soul?
You rule me with your supremacy and power-without pity, without mercy;
You make me like a slave - bound to follow your desire;
You ruthless mind - you give me no choice.

Why did you make me hate the things I have,
And focus my desires on the things that I don't have?
You create in me a covetous heart -
Envious and jealous to the things that others have.

Why did you force me to acquire more wealth,
Power and prestige that I really don't need;
To do forced labor and go against my will,
And set up a standard that I can not fill?

My mind, all minds, why are you keeping me awake?
I do need some rest; I do need some sleep;
Why did you trouble me to conquer love, attention and praises;
And once conquered, they are just useless?

My mind, all minds, I only have a short life to live,
All the things you're dying for can't be taken to my grave;
All I need is a small space and some air for me to breath;
Will you make me happy?  Will you make me free?

*Cirilo F. Castillon Jr.*

## Mother

You went through suffering and pain to give me life
You stayed awake with me so many nights
You sang to me sweet lullabies
You read to me nursery rhymes
You would fix my hair with the prettiest bows
And you would dress me in the best of clothes
As I watched you clean and cook so many days
I always wanted to grow up and be like you in so many ways
You taught me the morals of life and the values of being
a perfect mother and good wife
You always have called me "mama's baby"
even now that I'm a grown lady
You're the mother so many wished they had,
and as I think about those that doesn't, it's really sad
I thank God everyday for blessing me with
a mother like you

*Carmen Pearson*

## Your Image

A young death a terrible world inflicted on you.
You wanted a little mercy for being there on your
Native soil, loving the sun, walking along the
Familiar path with friends and animals.

Your figure - a fragrance of Asian trees, as pure as
Asian peace and water.  This is the soil stepped by the
First man on earth, our ancestor.  Then why need mercy?

Ask whom?  Doubts, questions must be swallowed.
The answer has been tested, terribly contested
And re-defined at last by rejecting history.

Life without history?  Without calendar years?  Yes yes,
There have been no wars no holocausts no pedigree no love
No memory in Asia.  What month is it?  What century is it?

Somewhere on the familiar path, the emergence of leaves
Reminds us of the seasons with their fairies and legends.

The air is sweet
The lilac sleeps
The lilac dreams

No, you didn't die, you never forget spring,
Your image returns here wanting to live again.

*Han Misyou*

## I Love You, Grandma

You were always strong and on the go
You were always early and the first to go

I felt so close when we played our game
I hope to God you felt the same

Thanks for the traits you've given me
Without you I could never be

My only regret is our time is gone
It's gonna be hard not to feel this is wrong

I love You Grandma I don't know who's to blame
The last I remember is you calling my name

Now that you're at peace for awhile
I will always remember your pretty smile

I LOVE YOU GRANDMA
*Jessica Lillo*

## Hold On

I see you standing there with that look upon your face.
You won't even lift your eyes to look me straight in the face.
Won't you please just talk to me and tell me what's wrong.
I'll give you all my love for you to hold on.
Hold on I'll never let you go.
Just hold on tight and I'll be there through the night.
Remember all the memories, the laughter and fun.
Remember all the days we spent in the bright hot sun.
Hand in hand we'd walk with a smile on our face.
I'll give you all my love for you to hold on.
Hold on I'll never let you go,
Just hold on tight and I'll be there through the night.

*Jennifer Lynn Sanderson*

## Irving, Irving

Old man, repeating, repeating, repeating
Your anthology of anecdotes
I've heard this one forty times
One for each year you've outlived me

You pause — we're on Park Avenue — because
Someone has tossed out a Vogue magazine
You fish it up, you want it for me
Pretty me, in blond curls and mink coat

Now, on Madison Avenue,
You stop again to spit into
The gutter - I utter
"Oh, no...." Wish I were
Alone

For these ten years, on certain Saturdays
I've walked, like this, with you
On New York street and avenue
But what I can't get used to
Is how you never hurt me
Old, man, oh, friend, friend, friend

*Constance Carmody*

## Moving

You feel as if your soul just collapsed, and that
your heart never had its last beat which told you,
you were alive
and that the same eyes that once carried a magical twinkle
had now seemed to have the same warped,
hopeless identity of your former self.
The things that you would have once done had now
seemed like worthless minutes that could have been saved
just in time to hit center ground of your own
empty, confused world.
MOVE ON!!!!!!!!

*Candace Renee Simmons*

## "Accompanied By An Angel"

The anticipated time has arrived,
your essence has fully come
all that you are to be is present
among the sweet smell of morning dew,
you bring with you.

O mankind, you have declared
my little one, the odd piece in your puzzle
and that you just don't fit

But I say, that angel that has accompanied you,
has brought the healing of the Almighty
and it is you my beloved, that is God's most
prized example of his love, grace and kindness

So to all the Justins, Davids and Joshuas
your life does fit, it fits in the divine puzzle
of the Almighty's most perfect plan.

*Deborah Rutherford Abdullah*

## John F. Kennedy - Mourned

You stand there,
Your face is etched with the horror of death.
Your features glow,
Orange with excitement.
You stood tall,
Proud.
Your eyes sparkled as much as diamonds.
You spoke easily in front of crowds,
And you were always easy-going.
You were a friend to everyone in the country.
You always wore suits in front of the cameras,
To look good to the country.
I wish you had been able to finish your term as President,
To help the country even more.
I also wish you had seen the Space Program begin in 1969.
You were an awesome,
Able,
Amazing,
Individual,
And many mourned your loss.

*Joshua Stewart*

## Second Love

I just want to be next to you for I love the way you feel,
your hand in my hand.
The vibrations of our souls giving strength to one another.
I just want to be next to you to lose myself in peaceful abode.
Let me bear your pain and you can bear mine until the union
explodes into streams of joy.

I just want to be next to you until we two immerse into one.
Friendship begets love, yet ours has come hand in hand.
I feel the joy of my childhood birthdays and Christmas morn.
I feel the warmth of the sun on my face and the smell of nature on
an autumnal day.

The vitals of my body cry out that I just want to be next to you.
The pulsations of our hearts drawing love from one another and
giving love back to one another.
Uniting our lost loves, our rejections, our despair, until they
bring forth one beautiful flower of joy.
An eternal joy to last forever - I just want to be next to you.

*Ellen R. Freitag*

## Crispin

Like a brief breeze through the still air,
Your life passed swiftly by, though soothing memories linger,
A sense of relief you were here at all.
And you endure still, etched in concepts you embraced.
Seeker of self, yet seeker, too, of gentle repose.
Needful of people, eyes that blinked trust,
Enriching this earth by your capacity to love,
And that hidden spring of courage you displayed,
Such noble acceptance of each endeavor to make you whole again,
As the mass of illness descended upon you.
We fought well, you and I,
Until whatever took you overcame our wills and our resistance,
Though not your spirit's essence,
Which mocks mere mortal time.
I hear you in the rustle of the trees,
I see you in droplets of rain that fall,
As darkness comes I reach for thoughts of you.
And with these thoughts the pain abates as I now perceive
The quiet triumph of the life you led
Emerges victorious over death.

*Carolyn M. Trombe*

## Life

Hold on to the love in your heart;
your love for life, your love for others, your love for love,
and mostly your love for yourself

Accept and enjoy the present, the here and now
Don't live in the past, it's where it should be; left behind you

Don't worry about tomorrow, today is too precious and nothing will
ever repeat itself in the same fashion

Don't go looking for trouble, sooner or later it finds you
A good friend is few and far between, treasure them

Don't start something that isn't worth a ripple in the water;
here one second and gone the next

Enjoy yourself always; your time here is short
anything can happen at anytime

Remember that nothing is carved in stone, cuts do heal,
memories do last, pain does pass
Make the most of every moment, every second of everyday

Enjoy everything to its fullest
You can only go around in life once.

*Jenny Schwinghammer*

## My Lover

Your smile lights up my day.
Your sexy eyes show me the way.
I love to see your sexy walk.
I love to hear your sexy talk.
I love when you call me Baby.
So I can answer to you yes Honey.
I want to run my fingers through your hair.
And smell the breath of fresh air.
I be there to hold your hand to cross the street.
And walk you home to rub your feet.
I want to hold you tight.
In my arms all night.
I like the way you move to the funky beat.
I hope you are that good between the sheets.
We don't have to be ashamed.
To play love games.
You be my candy.
I be your brandy.
My lover my lover my lover.
Forever forever forever

*Graham Brome*

## Lizzie ("If I'm Lucky, This Time I'll Die")

You had no right to deny us
Your shimmy-shake punk rock loveliness
Sometimes that tender thoughtful maturity.
You had no right O.D. on drugs
When I want to see you, hear you
Remembering those soft puckered lips in friendly greeting.

Could I have those future years you didn't cherish
Could I give you, I tried those hopes and fantasies
You discarded; could I reverse the irrevocable.

Could I hold on to my anger, disgust, not love
For having done this and your faults remember.
What were they now? Even then so inconsequential.

How could you choose oblivion; the gradual fading of all light
To the glittering sea, the sheen of flower petals
The serene joy of sunlight?

But I grieve most selfishly perhaps
Not for your loss, but mine, Lizzie
That your fatal flickering special charm, is gone.

*Christine Fimbres*

## Untitled

Gently you show me love.
Your soft red lips touching me,
Making me give in to your wishes.
Those sky blue eyes showing kindness,
And understanding for the things that don't come easy for me.
Smooth hands that caress me,
Gently exploring my body.
The sweet, loving words that are whispered,
Making me melt in your arms.
The love you show is new to me,
Unlike anything that I've ever felt.
Quietly, I pray, that it will never end.
However, I know, deep in my soul,
I know what the morning will yield.
Silently, I wish it not to happen.
But I know it will.
Come the morning, I'll awake, alone.
Your sweet smell, still on my pillow.
Fond memories are all that are left,
To satisfy me, eternally.

*James A. Keyser*

## A Friend

You are loved,
you're a wonderful mother,
and a friend, like no other.
Sometimes we wonder,
why our lives seem hidden away
but God sees the pattern,
and this is His plan, His way!
He trims here and some there,
and we soon see something beginning,
brand new, without wrinkle or tear,
the cloth of our lives, is a beauty to view,
and looking from behind, our God sees it, too.
A new color added, by knowledge of what He sees,
and when it's complete,
we know the artist designs,
for only the elite, and as you see your life,
you'll know its His plan,
to make you complete, detached from the world,
a unique blend of His perfect love,
designed by our Father and patterned above.

*Florence C. Billings*

## Take the Time

Take the time to love one another each and every day
You're only here for a short time, don't waste it or delay

Be kind to one another, give love, and a helping hand
Live each day to the fullest, it makes life seem so grand

Yes, there will be problems, sadness, loss, despair
Just remember; God, family, friends really do care

If someone needs comfort, be the one that is there
Tell them you love them, feel for them, remember them in prayer

It may not solve the problem, but just being their is love
That's part of life too, with guidance from above

Life is much too short to fill it with hate
Love one another, it makes each moment a nicer fate

If you've been hurt; try to forget, more so to forgive
It makes both lives more pleasant to live

To sum it all up - it's love - that's easy to see
Take the time to do it, that's the key

*Herb McFarland*

## Modern Success

Your Profession brings you accolades.
You've achieved high integrity and quality.
The financial stability, respect of colleagues
And satisfaction fills your needs.

At home, another dinner thaws in the microwave.
The jig-saw puzzle got done in one day.
The pages are worn in your "Games" magazine
As music plays to take you away.

You go to exhibits, shop the malls
And stroll the pathways by the falls.
You smile at faces that keep going by,
Wondering why no one touches your life.

You laugh to yourself at the feature film,
Pretend to look interested sipping your drink.
You retire alone to your satin sheets,
Only a moist pillow gives evidence of your defeat.

*Diane Maxwell*

## Always Remember

Always remember, as long as you live,
you've always had so much to give.
Always Remember, you gave it with love,
as being our Mother and with help from above.
Always Remember, though it may not always show,
we love you dearly and are certain you know.
Always Remember, through bad or through good,
we'll stand by your side as for us you would.
Always Remember, the future, we can't see,
so we'll make each day the best that it can be.
Always Remember, if we searched the world over,
we would never find a more loving Mother.
And Always Remember, each day as it starts,
we'll love you forever from the bottom of our hearts.

*Deborah B. Dwinnell*

## To You My Love, I Wish To Say...

You are my Best Friend.
I cannot imagine my life before You.
This World would be a very lonely place without Your presence and love.

You are my Lover.
Deep within me, I long for You, desiring to touch your face, hold you.
To take You to that place where only You and I share.

You are my Wife.
The very Seed of my family rests within You.
I long to hold Your babies in my arms, watching them grow, being
with their Mother, as they mature.

You are my Soul Mate.
A Perfect Gift, made all the more special by each passing day that
we share the unfolding of Our lives.
A Perfect Gift that I can never deserve.

As we share our life together, I commit to you that GOD will be the
ruler of our household.
That our children will grow up knowing the Love of Christ.

And knowing that all Love comes from GOD, I will lift You up to Christ
in Thanksgiving each day, that my Love for You will continue to increase.

So, stay with me my precious, that I may share the experience of
growing old with the Love of my Youth.
Hold me my sweetness, and know that I shall Love you ALWAYS in ALL WAYS.
Your Husband and Lover,

*John R. Polster*

## Who Has Walked In Silence

Oh, if I were a poet
Who has walked in silence, withdrawn from the present
In deep lament from the past darkly
Perchance to hear of the aesthetic beauty plum blossom
But I walked thru centuries of my mind in silence
And with the calling from me to you, hollowed within my depths
From afar—a ring—closely; ever so—your voice
My cry—I am—with love

*Lisa Lang*

## Barnacle Dreams

I dream of you in ages unknown, filled with imaginings of what it
   will be like
when we become comrades in arms, in love, in armor,
longing to never be separated worlds gone awry.

I dream of you sitting in an office by the bay, staring through a window
and wonder are there visions of me and the world with us in it?
Or just the endless sound of the wind echoing, slipping, through the
   glass of the panes
inviting you to dip, plunge, immerse your body, your soul,
into the salty depths of the Pacific.

I gather my hopes, I gather my fears, I label them dreams, I put you
   inside them.
Will there come a day when these imaginings will give way to something real?
To the touch of your skin, silky, soft,
to the touch of your lips against mine, singing silently of love yet
   to come.

Or will I sit, forever, at the edge of these dreams swirling,
at the edge of these not so distant fears, encroaching, and wonder
how many times will I be tempted to try on that coat you left hanging
   in my closet,
as a promise of days still to come.

How I wish there could be one more week, one more glimpse of eternity,
   of you and me making love,
jungle love, beneath a roaring freeway.

*Deborah Krainin*

## Always By My Side

Life is not easy, it was never meant to be.
That is why I'm grateful my Lord watches over me.

He soothes my aching heart when peace is hard to find.
A wonderful presence brought over me that is ever so gentle and kind.

When I am hardest hit, when grief and pain take over me,
He can feel all the ailing and all my troubles He can see.

So go ahead and cry, let all your feelings come right out,
But know that not long after the hurt the healing will come about.

Be at peace and remember we have an understanding God,
And when I'm hurt the worst I know He is always by my side.

*Shelli Barnes*

## Dreams

Life is such a chasing after dreams
That lie beyond the realm of present thought,
Eluding capture, as our valiant schemes
Would weave a web wherein our dreams be caught.

And if a dream be held within our hand,
As iridescent sheen of fragile wing,
Shall thus perfection lose of hope's command,
And holding it, despair of heart shall bring.

Thus better for the heart, beyond our reach
Forever one more dream on distant shore,
Until at last eternal peace we seek,
And chase the fragile dreams of life no more.

*Rebecca Jacques Britt*

## I Tried

I tried my best not long ago to be a friend to let you know,
that life can be both harsh and cruel for princesses and kings
and fools.

I tried to tell you to beware of sleeping giants and ghosts that
glare. To be on guard for friendless friends that use you as a
means to ends.

I tried my best to hold your hand, to help you up so you could
stand, and standing now so you could run, to rainbows far beneath
the sun.

I tried my best to make you smile, to laugh and sing...to stay a
while. And talk of tales from mind and heart, forever kept when
sails depart.

But time was scarce...it was not found. Clear visions
left...there was no sound. And moments faded into night,
to chase the darkness into flight.

Yet, somewhere out there...there remains, a voice that echo's
past the pain. Beyond the still these words are cried,
"I did my best!...Oh how I tried!"

*Morgan Bays*

## First Mate

The storm rages,
waves crash against the hull
Closing my eyes I dive
Calm, just below the surface
colors dance around me, aqua-blues, greens.
Warmth comforts my soul
Looking up I see the golden glow
My heart beats like a hummingbird's wings
Love.
Lungs aching, I surface,
The storm rages on.

*Chad M. Geffert*

## A Gift that Keeps Giving

He left you with a deadly disease,
that makes you just want to leave everyone behind.
You never meant for it to happen like this.
It was just supposed to be one innocent long kiss.
In his head it was destined.
You should have used some kind of protection.
You go to see if you are pregnant,
instead you find out you are going to die,
and that something is growing inside.
You have a son, but you still know,
that you won't be able to see him grow.
You finally pass on,
as your son lives on.
But when he turns 23,
he will catch the deadly disease.

*Melinda Ishee*

## Thoughts and Feelings

I'd like to gather all the beauty
  that man has ever known
Wrap it all in a big, pretty box
  with a nice big bow
Carry it on over to where you live
  and say "here mom is how much I love you."

To be able to light up your face
To have the money to buy you a beautiful
  dress with frills of lace
To give you all world at peace

For there is nowhere to be found
  a more deserving, and loving force than you

And how I would like to give you
  back your youth
To show you all the places I've been
To see you climb my mountains
  and talk to my God

To do all these things that you may see
How much I love you mother
  and what you are to me.

*Patrick Michael Meehan*

## I Looked Out And Beyond

I looked out and beyond, I saw you sleeping,
that moment in time will never be erased.
I love you, but I must say good-bye
I shall never forget your smiling face.

Please don't shed a tear
Please promise not to cry.
You must believe that my soul is aching too.

I know I promised never to leave,
but right now it's the right thing to do.

I looked out and beyond
I heard you call out my name
how I just wanted to say I'm right here.

As I walked toward the door
My heart ached in pain, my body trembled with fear.
And in an instant tears fell from my eyes.
I can't do it. I can't leave you.
I'm afraid if I leave I'll never love like this again.
But, some how I found the strength to go
I opened the door and I walked out
That was the day my soul died. I Looked Out and Beyond

*Melissa Berger*

## "Love"

What words can my soul say
that not even my heart with each
heat can utter.  Beyond description are
feeling that even one that speaks
every language of the world can't explain
Goes as deep so the depth of the
heart of the earth can not reach!
Only God knows for he mode love
so mortal man can't tell how sweet,
how precious it feels to hold love,
touch it, feel it, live it!

*Wanda Willis*

## Ode to a Citrus Fruit

O greenish, ovate, slightly sour lime!
That puckers up my mouth with every bite
Yet thou art still a sweeter fruit; I might
Find thee (unlike thy sister orange) a rhyme.
O citrus fruit!  That grows in balmy climes!
Fluorescent pastel colors:  What a sight!
That thou can still glow under dark of night
(When coated with Chernobyl fallout slime).
And if in someone's mouth I put a lemon in
Or orange, or lime, or grapefruit fleshy red,
That taste of peeled fruit with boundless power
Will pucker up their lips (Rather unfeminine!)
...An overdose will cause imploded heads:
O citrus fruit!  Why art thou so darn SOUR.

*Tad L. Ramspott*

## Mute Words

Where do the words come from
  that say so little and mean so much,
How were the letters chosen for
  noble words and expletives?

How, possibly, can I use these words
  powerful pawns, painful puns,
To paint sentences that reach the soul
  and touch the stars in winter?

And how can mere letters and ink
  begin to describe desire or
A smiling face swinging on a
  white plank in the blonde wind of August?

Perhaps I shouldn't try.  Perhaps
  I except too much of my nimble friends,
Usually so close, skirting away as I
  wrestle phrases to coherence.

And where does this inexplicable pain of
  clay unkindled, marble unmarred,
Brushes with no paint, feelings with no words,
  find rest?

*William C. Peebles*

## Dying Inside

I'm lost, inside I feel I've lost someone.
That someone is you.
I feel as if you will never be close again.
Inside I feel as if a major part of my life
has been taken away, and it has.
My plans with you were broken, and now your gone.
Farther than you ever were before.
It seems as if I'm dying inside when your gone,
and now that your gone I'm dying.

*Sherrie Metz*

## Untitled

If beyond a doubt, there is positive proof,
that someone, acted, insanely un-couth.
Thinking the only way, to rule the world
into violent possession, they blatantly hurled.
Somehow we were betrayed because we were sad.
We would accept anything, to just feel glad.
You know you shouldn't, but you look away,
You shut out, reality, of what they say.
You'll embrace the part, that lifts you up,
you are tired of emptiness, and want a full cup.
It doesn't matter, if, it is filled with deceit,
it warms your belly, and lets you sleep.
As you close your eyes, the reaper waits,
one last moment of peace, before, you enter hell's gates.

*Maurine Fergueson*

## The Character of Color

Here is a story about Brother Red, he had an idea stuck in his head.
That the walls in his room should be painted anew, so out of his bed
  in a rush he flew.
Brush and bucket he grabbed as he ran, red is quite an industrious man
He painted the wall he painted the floor, before he went out he
  painted the door.

Here is a story about Brother Blue, Who had gotten himself a terrible flue.
So he wrapped and rolled in layers of clothes, until you could
  hardly see his nose.
He drew the curtain and locked the door, turned off all light till
  there was no more.
Covered with cushion and blanket so blue, that's how Blue takes care
  of a flu.

Come on, said Red let's go for a walk, Blue said no, let's sit here
  and talk.
They talked all day and half the night, until there hardly was any light.
Red started leaning on Blue - he was bored, as Blue kept
  pouring out all his thoughts.
The night came on so dark and deep, soon Blue had talked himself into
  sleep.
What you could see on the bench in the distance, in color it had a
  different consistence.
Blue had stopped being so verbal, together with Red he had turned into
  purple.

*Vibeke Pedersen*

## Life Moves On

Some folks like to say all things are really resolved in time,
That thought gave me inspiration to write this little rhyme.

Other folks say seriously one has to forget and bury the past.
Doing this actually brings problems that continue to last.

Life Moves On!
Still other folks say one has to learn to stay very very busy.
It is not totally helpful and only keeps one's life in a tissy.

Professionals advise one has to process the true, real pain.
That is the best way for true peace and health to regain.

Life Moves On!
One has to calculate all the losses they did in life receive,
It dismisses denial and reality is what is left to then believe.

One has to sort out belongings and discard unnecessary junk.
That's painful sorting dressers and reviewing every old trunk.

Life Moves On!
Some friends abandon us and relationships definitely do change.
It takes much courage to have so much in life to rearrange.

Life moves on from suffering to recovery and making new goals.
It has to do with finding ourselves surrounded with new roles.

Life Moves On!

*Linda Reese*

## This Place

There is this special place I know
That very few see and very few go
You'll find no flowers no grass or trees
But you'll find love and honesty
It's a place you can go when you're at wits end
It's a place you can go when you just need a friend
You can cry if you want to or laugh right out loud
You can act kind of timid or act kind of proud
No judgements are made so you need not be shy
This place is always open whenever you come by
This place can be fragile or strong as a ox
It's hard to believe it's smaller than a box
This place is my heart and I can not deny
I hope you'll stop by and give it a try

*Rhonda Nolan*

## Interview

There is a dignity in that worn face
That waits across my desk, and just a trace
Of fear or loneliness or both. His eye
Goes anxiously around the room. A sigh
Discloses weariness as if his years
Have known too much of holding back their tears,
I ask the questions slowly, knowing well
Retirement to him seems like a hell
Of empty waiting days... I see this same
Sad face a thousand times a year, the name
Is different but the hungry searching stare
Is timeless, nameless, borne as dust in air,
Whenever age, brought low by glittering youth,
Cries out in silent pain for mercy, truth...

*Leon Silin*

## The Impatient Date

I cling to every sparkling moment
That you are close to me
I live for the next time that we are close,
And wonder when that time might be?

Your eyes how they entrance me, I am caught with-in your spell.
Centuries seem to have past since I have seen you last,
And silly as it might be, I know it has only been a week
That I will see you once again, when the week has shown it's end

Patience is not my virtue,
When the only thought I have is you.
So please bear this time with me,
As the beauty of you is a joy to see
And when the beauty is so deep,
I know you were chosen from my sleep,
As that most Noble figure of a man,
The Prince who would take me in his arms
And carry me off to Fantasy Land,
I still wonder, what time will I see you again?

*Yvonne Eve Evans*

## Alone

What does it mean to be alone
You're never alone as long as you have yourself
You can fall back on your memories
Look ahead to your goals and dreams
But what happens when you're not sure
If those memories were good or bad
What will you do when your dreams and goals
Are no longer in reach or sight
Will I lose more than my mind
At that time will I really care
No one made me alone
I did it to myself
Should I care

*Jim Sullivan*

## Love

Love is a feeling you feel deep inside
That you cannot possibly hide
True love makes you leap with joy
Is something no one can destroy
True love will pass all tests, true love is for the best
Sometimes you may have to part
But you will always share a heart
If your love is going to last
You must not go to fast
Love has it's highs and lows
But that's just how it goes
So remember honey, love is not for jewels and money
It's just a wonderful feeling you feel inside
Not an act of pressure or pride
Just a feeling of deep connection and affection
Towards a special girl or guy
Love is something you cannot buy
Love is a wonderful feeling you feel deep inside
That you cannot possibly hide

*Tanya Tews*

## My Son

One year today my precious son
That you were laid to rest,
Your soul is now with God,
Your body returned to dust.

Now you are resting, my son
In our heavenly Father's arms,
No more pain or tribulations,
Eternally safe from any harm.

You filled my life with happiness,
Love for you overflowed my heart,
Sweet memories I will cherish,
From me they will never depart.

My son, forever I will love and miss you,
Close in my heart you will always stay,
In our Lord and Savior daily I trust,
He gives me strength for each new day.

*Shirley A. Wernick*

## It's So Hard

Lord, it's so hard to remember each day
That you're on my side come what may
Trials and temptations come from all sides
Saying forget about Jesus - come along for a ride
Forget your problems - trip out for a while
You know I have what makes you smile

Lord, it's so hard what will I do?
Will I submit or come running to you?
For one fleeting moment go out and sin
Then after awhile start over again
Torn between flesh and that which is good
Feeling abandoned and not understood

Lord, it's so hard and each day it seems worse
If only I would remember to put you first
So many thoughts and so many choices
And oh so many distracting voices
Trapped by memories and things in my past
Will I ever say I'm finally free at last
Oh Lord
Its so hard

*Wendy Leigh Souza*

## Yearning To Rise

The landscape out before me, I yearn to rise,
The abyss of ground below me waiting to possess,
The heavens above me, beckoning my body,
The cliff my mother made, is now my run off,
The wings I have, I am not scared to bear,
I see my brothers, flying overhead,
Pitying this wretch that is grounded instead,
My heart beating of fear and exhilaration,
I run, praying to God to survive, to take flight,
The edge is here and I spread my wings,
My shadow across the rocks below, waiting,
But my will is strong, and I do not fall,
My shadow races across the clouds below,
My wing tips dancing with the air,
At last I am free, fearing when I must return,
My mother calls, but return I won't for the air,
Yes the air is my domain now,
At last, I am at peace.

*R. Horrobin*

## The Rodeo Legend

When Sunday comes and the clowns come out
The anthem is over and the rider's mount
The crowd is yelling the clown is joking
Red rocks compelling and broncos are broken
A eight second try with rider pride.
Second guess a legend and you could die
Unleashed fury and gathering force
A cowboy's dream can be course
His back is aching with pain and his knuckles
Prizes were taken with gold in his buckle
The battle is over tonight their through
Tomorrow their thriving for something to do
Cowboys are liven with this in mind
That's how they like it and that's just fine

*Nathan J. Eckhout*

## 58,000 Dead Americans

Ricky Hill
the baby of a three-boy family
he never went to college as planned
he never married Paula Mae Williams

Vietnam
20th Anniversary of the War
American's Longest War Scream the Headlines
Only Conflict that ended in Defeat for America

Ricky Hill
he was trained at Fort Benning, Georgia
he was the first off the boat
his body was blown all over Vietnam by a mine made by people
who never called
him niggah

Ricky Hill
His soul lives at the Vietnam War Memorial
without tears or pain
in the distance Abe Lincoln sits, staring
I wonder what he is thinking?

*Lee Harris*

## Experiencing Life

There is so much beauty in God's creation,
The beaches, mountains, and deserts of our nation.

The changing of seasons, the monsoon of rains,
The fields and the valleys, the hills and the plains.

The flowers, the bushes, the trees, all with color,
The snowflakes with each one different than the other.

To travel the Earth, to see all the views,
To hear of events that are told in the news.

To experience life means to live life each day,
By enjoying God's creation as you go along your way.

Do not be burdened by life's trouble and pain,
Just breathe deep and start on your path once again.

Yes, that is the secret to experiencing life,
To make the most of your struggles and strife.

And you will see how much better life can be,
When you experience life to the fullest like me.

*Sheila W. Kearney*

## Disneyland

Look through the eyes of your children and see
The beautiful things they reveal to thee
The twirley birds flutter
The butterflies shutter
This Disneyland world for you and for me.

The clouds as they rain are lemoned ice tea
The rainbow so high and promises we see
A pot at the end,
A new life will begin
This Disneyland world of you and for me.

So look through the eyes of your children and see
The beautiful things they reveal to thee
Your days seem brighter
Your loads are lighter
This Disneyland world for you and for me.

*Linda Lue Narzisi*

## "I Love You"

I love you like the earth
The beauty of its whole
The complexity and simplicity
That connects your inner soul
I love you like the sky
Your beauty never ends
Like following a straight and simple road
That sometimes has its bends
I love you like the sea
I can see the depth of it in your eyes
It reflects your sensitivity
Unveiling no lies
I love you like the fire
There's more to you underneath
It releases itself into the night
And in the morning it lets you breathe
I love you like the wind
Your soft spokeness wisps me away
But it seems to be your calmness
That keeps me forever to stay

*T. J. Henderson*

## Patterns In Waves

A link to those who know flight.
The birds of the skies with sight so keen
Looking out for me as I have seen.

Coincidence or fascination,
Why do I see this interest in me?
This creature of freedom
Might it care about me...
Absurd, not likely, my human ego has the best of me.

And then one day, this realization
As I dove into the depths of the sea,
It were as if I were flying
Over huge crevices.
Giant summits covered with ocean.
Gaping canyons below.
As I soared, easily in the currents above
Swooping and banking, I felt so free,
Comfortable, relaxed,
Natural...this was me.

*Stephen Klatzke*

## The Words in the Wind

I was standing at the edge of the woods, when like a song playing at
the break of day, look at me, one tall tree seems to say, while
    waving its
limbs around as it gently touches its neighbor, as if to say, wake up
and listen, to the words and music in the wind, as the wind gently
swayed the branches to and fro, I know I heard music and laughter
here below, the gently breezes in the trees seemed to say, I see the
birds in their nests over there, so I will grow a foot or more, so
they will know that I protect them there.

The wind floating in and out, you can see the leaves and trees sway
around and around, as they dance among themselves, a waltz is what
you hear, If you are very still and listen, not loud, but ever so
gentle you can hear the music.
On the hill side next to some pine trees a deer lifts its head, turns
its ears and eye into the breeze, maybe it can see and hear the same as I.

Even the birds sings softly as if following an invisible
leader, as the wind caress my face. I know its the trees and limbs
and leaves that carries these without a trace. So beautiful to my
ears as if the words are carried on Angel wings. Listen and in your
minds eye, you can hear the wail of fiddles mingled with laughter,
fading into a into a whisper as you close eyes and listen to the words
in the wind.

*Ruth Padgett*

## The Wind That She Was

The flow of the wind, the wind that she was,
The breeze of summer's ebb, early autumn,
The wind of breath frosting window pane,
A wind that whispers like a child's touch,
A wind that sighs its aura of innocence.

The flow of the wind, the wind that she was,
The metaphor of her state, rarefied air,
Wind of touching force, unforeseen yet felt,
A zephyr that fills the sails, nudging the ship,
A metaphor of things existing barely, rare and radiant.

A glow in the fog, a mist diffusing
Into nothingness, barely being, tenuous
As a rose flowering by tempest-sea,
Storm-swept by waves of dark and cold menace,
Yet the frailty endures, a whisper within the thunder.

The flow of the wind, the wind that she was,
Her message mute and urgent, secret voices
Echoing through the fiords of her labyrinth past,
Her heart trembles to sounds of far-off galloping.
What utterances besiege her distant soul?

*Steven N. Rosenkrantz*

## Winter

Life is put on hold and your soul grows cold
The brightness in you seems not to shine through

The grace which is yours, soon locked behind doors
The harsh winds of change makes life seem so strange

WHEN WINTER COMES

For once you can see the defects in me
No longer can hide the traces of pride

The deepest desires, emotional liars
The frailty of will soon to be revealed

WHEN WINTER COMES

Healing of the soul, the ultimate goal
The external life comes under the knife

In times of despair, remember His Care
The pain of it all, one day to recall

WHEN WINTER COMES

*Rosita Dozier*

## A Rose

A rose is a symbol of the love I have for you.
The center is my heart from which all my love flows
    to each petal each part of my life

Each petal has a special meaning..Love -respect-honor
    Admiration-devotion, all of these I feel for you.
The leaves are my arms reaching out for you, to embrace you
    and hold you close, to me forever.
The stem is my body, my being, which supports my emotions,
    my heart and my never ending need to have you close to
me, touching me.

It is the tangible thing I have to give, that is symbol of the
    untouched but felt things I want you to have.

From me to you I give this rose. which is me.

*Rebecca S. Hunt*

## CNN Focuses On Somalia

Such a time of it they have; the heat of the day.
The chill of the night and the mosquitoes that follow.
Such is the time and they yearn for help.

Countable ribs on their concertina chest
Bones protruding as if chiseled by a sculptor's hand of famine.
Their skin pale and taut
Like a glove on the doctor's hand.
Flies clinging in clumps on their sweat scented backs.

Each day a weary pony drops,
Left for the vultures on the plains.
Each afternoon a human skeleton collapses,
Left for the time when history will tress the past.

Life ceases to be a beautiful choice.
For many you are better off dead.
For it is a life of turmoil.
A life of agitation.
A life of tormentation and a life of suppression.

Worried tense and tired, I sit in silent prayer;
God, I demand, why do you allow them to suffer so?
Not a word from him. Not a word!

*Nellie A. Obare*

## Memories

I awoke to the sights and sounds of the sea —

The lapping of waves on the sand,
The chirping and fluttering of sea gulls swooping down
For their morning feast,
The laughter of children jumping into the waves like fish.
I saw the beautiful fabrics
The colors reflected in a thousand mirrors.
I was enveloped in a sea of blue.
The sky, the sea and the perfectly matched,
Perfectly executed designs of God and man
Put together to create one of those magic moments
We mortals call "memories."
How can one thank God for life and all creation?
How can one thank one's family for its existence — its being?
How can one thank friends for friendship and the sharing
Of a special moment of whatever we have and whatever we are
With whoever we meet along the way and say;
"Where have you been all my life?"
This is called "Life," this is called "Love"
This, I believe, is what we are created for.

*Nina Spearman Reese*

## City Of Light

Paris-the city of love and the city of beauty,
The city of peace and artistical duty.
The names are a song dancing in your ear,
The sights are painting of millions of artists.
You stop for a moment...then, filled with information,
You explode!...

And you compose and you combine
All words, and notes, and color...
The gardens are drunk with green,
The Seine is drowned in blue,
And you create and do escape
This world of false and true.

Be in your own reality.
The dream just keeps on dreaming,
But watch your coming back
When rain and gray'll abound you.
Try to keep the memories alive.
Create...And they'll surround you.

*Marina C. Ionescu*

## Circle of Blue

I look up into the morning sky
The clouds have parted and there is a circle of blue

The rays of sun are shining on the clouds
Changing their grey to yellow

As I am gazing up into this sky
I am awed by the power of my Creator

This beautiful circle of blue is my vision to heaven
My true Self

I am of the same beauty, the same magic

The blue is my soul
My inner strength

The clouds that surround it are my body
Opening up to all possibilities
My creative soul is emerging

My body is opening up
Letting the light of heaven shine from inside of me
Out onto the world.

*Linda Colleen Miller*

## The Hunchback Of Cope

My Girl says I am dull, but only during the week
The clouds that hover my brain
are apparent in my speech
I tell her:
You mop some floors,
dump the trash,
make sure the toilets are clean;
Then, tell me after five days
if the teachers are very pleased.
For I am the Hunchback of Cope;
not much glamour to my game.
I work beyond midnight
I get some thanks, I get some blame.
I dream of being a musician
for all the world to listen
to a single note so sweet;
to see the faces glisten.
Maybe someday perhaps, you'll hear my song being played
on the radio station; is there anything wrong
with a dream?

*Richard Hernandez*

## Spring

The wind against your face -
  the cool breeze through your hair.

These are signs of Spring.

Daffodils, tulips, and crocuses in bloom -
  Wishing they'd last for just a while more.

The trees budding new leaves -
  and coming back to life anew.

These too, are signs of Spring.

Springtime rain which makes it all grow -
  We take it all in, and somehow -
    take it for granted.

Spring is a new beginning for nature,
  as well as for ourselves.

We can start over once again, and
  Bloom and grow within ourselves
    in mind and spirit.

*Patricia A. MacGeorge*

## Death I Love

Today the love of my life is gone,
The darkness of the world encircles me
The sorrow of my life is inescapable
I know not what to do.
I look for something
I look for something to live for.
Today the light of my life has gone.
Now the darkness has come.
For she has died and so has our love.
I know not what to do, I know not how to carry on.
For today the darkness had come
And the light is gone
The power of death is real.
The power of darkness is that of all my fears
I know not what to do, I know not how to carry on
Now that my love is gone, gone, gone..

*Shaun Reft*

534

## To You

So small and beautiful
The day you were born
I stared in wonderment
At your shining face
You grew slowly
Always bringing happiness and joy into my heart

Now you are on the threshold of being a young lady
I look at you and ask myself
Where have all the years gone?

As time passes us both
I hope that you will always realize
That I love you
You are the best parts of me

My spirit, my hopes and my dreams
Travel with you into the future
Always remember me as I will you

My Daughter
*Richard A. Manacle*

## Lonesome

I'm lonesome for the years that used to be;
The days gone by without a hint of memory.
I'm lonesome for the friends I used to know,
The fields where only wild grasses used to grow.
I'm lonesome for the innocence of childhood,
And the faith I had that everything was good.
I'm lonesome for the times when we were seldom ever sad;
The time when I believed love excluded all that's bad.
I'm lonesome for the childhood fantasies that once were mine,
And that "lived happily ever after" line.
I'm lonesome for life's vision that ignorance gave to me,
And hoping, someday it will reign here for everyone to see...

*Ra Nae N. Fausett*

## A Moment In Time

Away from entanglement of noise and light,
    The dense forest enveloped my soul.
Rounding a curve, an old wooden bridge,
    Such enchantment, I can hardly behold.

The river below bubbles with joy,
    Carving a beauty, all its own.
The change of seasons only enhance,
    The loveliness, time has sewn.

Cobwebbed, splintered, and worn with time,
    Only the language of my heart can feel,
The certain beauty in the old shackled mill,
    Hanging by a thread on the hill.

My heart stood still, for a moment in time,
    This place, to me is spiritual.
It awakens the spirit of God in me,
    Overwhelming my soul, what a miracle!

*Shirley H. Ketner*

## Beside The Sea

The salty breeze for you and me
White sea gulls fly about so close
While blue waves dance along the coast,
A lighthouse stays above so tall;
The lonely lifesaver throughout the night
Becomes a giant candlelight
For passing ships near jagged rocks;
Across, the salty path of Hope!

*E. B. Pysz*

## The Disease

There is a disease that affect us all at one point of our life.
The disease will begin in one part of the body and the slowly spread
to the other parts. There is no cure for this disease, you just have
to wait and let the disease run its course. I have caught this
disease. It is slowly taken over my body, destroying all my
strengths. It controls my thoughts, it has destroyed barriers that I
built up over time. It is only a matter of time until this disease
will take over me. I can only hope that she catches the disease too.
The future seems bleak, it is getting late and I am slowly dying.
This disease, the disease they call love, is slowly forcing me to
accept the inevitable - my love for the most beautiful creature in
this world, a woman.

*Steven A. Brooks*

## The Little Cherokee Indian Girl From Oklahoma

How can I ever be
The fair skin girl my mother wants
Cherokee Indian is what you see
When you look at me.

I stay inside
So I won't get brown.
I don't even go to town.
What can I do, I say.

I wouldn't if I could,
I couldn't if I should,
Change one thing about myself,
So for now I put it on the shelf.

*Maxine Justice Woodson*

## The Fairy Legend

The legend says:
The fairies cried
When they heard the sad news
That Jesus has died

Nailed to a cross —
    crucified
He hung there, he suffered,
He bled and he died

A ransom for poor sinners
Like you and me.

The fairies tears fell to earth —
Solidified
Into small red stained crosses

Now though you search the wide world over
You'll never find another place
Where the small red crosses are found
Save on one steep hill-side
In my own home state Virginia

*Martha Walden*

## Hold on to You

Time seems so rough,
you want to give up.
You feel like a blind man,
and you are holding the cup.
It may not always help,
but you take what you can get.
You sometimes get frustrated,
and your first thought is to quit.
When you feel that there is nothing left for you to do,
always remember to hold on to you.
Hold on to that person deep down inside,
sometimes we are forced to swallow our pride.
It will all be worth it in the end,
remember that person is your best friend.

*Jayme Russell*

## My Forest

The touch of your hand beneath my own
The feel of your heart tender and grown
My special kisses reserved just for you
Water and teardrops when I'm missing you
You're my forest because you protect my soul

Guiding my heart and keeping me whole
Everyday that I love you the sun shines for me
You are my forest protecting me by every tree
Sharing any hurt with a joke or two
I will never accept thoughts of losing you
My forest of strength, guidance, and hope
I need you I had for fertile love we are so
My daily harvest beneath our tree of life
I treasure the day when I become your wife

**Tiffanny Spears**

## The Dark Empress

The tumultuous Gemini of the universe.
The fickle, femme fatal.
The warrior who takes no concessions,
makes no excuses.
Engulfing all in her wake,
she plunders, devastates and destroys.
The philanderer of hopes.
The panderer of dreams.
Some worship, others curse,
but soon all succumb to the beauty of love.

**Randi A. Powell**

## Lummi Island

Dypaloh,
the first word of our book.
What does it mean? we asked
on the ferry to Lummi.

We found a path winding down thickets to sand.
Stones under our soles, we tested
the clear thickness of Puget Sound.
She told us she spread her husband's
ashes at Big Sur.
We paused to absorb her memory.
I once read Gray's "Elegy" to students over
graves in an English churchyard, he said.
No one ever read to me as a child.

He read to us then,
the rise and fall of his voice in
concert with the waves
where the Great Turtle rose from the sea, the Earth on its back.

Let's take our photo, she said.
We crouched together on a length of log: a clan captured by Kodak,
At our beginning

**Marilyn Lee**

## A Blessing

The clouds over head; the sun shines threw.
With it's touch of yellow and blue.
I've been blessed, Behold! The heavens I see;
I feel Gods love; Yes it he!

The mountains are a sculptures dream,
and the ocean can make a painter scream.
The valleys are so perfectly clear,
its the most beautiful thing I've ever seen.

The white and fluffy clouds just gleam!
As if it were dusted with sun beams.
As I sit watching it all just disappear,
I wish God will always be near.

**Crickit King**

## From East To West—The Flying Eagle

The fearless engineer grips the controls of his endless train—
The Flying Eagle— as it skims along from East to West. Without
sound, over invisible tracks, the sleek fast-moving transport
takes on a shiny exciting appearance in the sun rays.

With its fail-safe system for signals, switches and the train
itself, The Flying Eagle carries hundreds, perhaps thousands, of
cars for miles and miles without end.

The countless passengers, called aboard by the stern penetrating
voice of the conductor, bring their personal experiences with
them—some happy or thrilling, others sad or indifferent. As
the train crosses fields and deserts and snakes around hills and
mountains, scenic views flash in picture-windows, almost
unnoticed as memories superimpose themselves.

The engineer holds fast to the rigid itinerary—a journey's-end
for each rider. On departing from The Flying Eagle, they
off-handedly notice a black and white sign—Destination
Unknown—on the rear-car door. They find themselves in an
unfamiliar place, where time is no longer, space is without
horizon, and they now are breathing new air...Forever.

**Marguerite A. Follett**

## Freedom Preserved

Oft times we take for granted,
The freedom we so enjoy.
Of how these wonders happened,
Were taught us when we're just boys!
We owe the freedoms of this land,
To those who took a stand;
When our pride and rights were threatened,
By someone in far away lands.
From the very beginning,
Our forefathers set the tone;
That this great land we live in,
Would always be our home.
To those who have fought so bravely,
To preserve, for us, this heritage,
Known only in the American way.
To keep our proud flag waving,
For, forever and a day.
To all who have so gallantly served, a giant salute is due.
For, we walk in the paths of freedom,
All because of you, OUR Veterans!

**Sanford M. Glick**

## '10 P.M.'

there, on the bed, laid a breathless figure.
the gaze in his eyes seemed empty;
As he laid there, still.
that night-
The night I died.
i could no longer feel.
to rejoice and be happy
Were without meaning.
my soul departed the trinity,
Taking its own course.
indifference became me;
for others I had no remorse,
Compassion, love.
i, myself became a lifeless being-
Walking nowhere, seeing nothing,
Oppressed, Depressed, The Suppressor,
because of which
The rested figure's empty gaze.
that night
At 10 p.m.

**Wyneika Wilburn**

536

## The Hands Of Time

I was just twenty three when I first wished to stay
the hands of time no further to stray into the future
this was perfect to me to stay forever at age twenty three.

And then in my thirty's more children had we,
and God in his wisdom so good to me and so
many blessings he sent our way and once more
in my human the hands of times I wished to stay.

Grandmother grandfather so happy were we, to have
grandchildren play to our knee, our cup runneth
over for much love had we.

Now in our twilight year we know a peace and quiet.
A little sad and much more slow and yet.
Clear God grant more time to me to think of
the joys of an age long ago, to pass to those
younger my faith in thee, and my bits of
wisdom from age twenty three.

*Martha Sue Howard*

## I Can't Remember

I can't remember my childhood,
the happy times, nor sad times,
I'm sure there were some of both,
I can't remember the flowers,
never smelled them, nor enjoyed
their beauty and fragrance.
I can't remember the leaves,
enjoying their shade, and beautiful colors.
Where are all the birds?
Realizing they had gone south,
from the cold weather here.
I hurry to do the laundry,
so it can dry, while I do my work.
Every minute counts, but I don't
want it to end, as that will mean
a change in all our lives.
Mabee for worse, who knows

*Lilly Kirkland*

## Memories Three

I tried to think of you today, I found your memory has gone away.
The heart ache that was here to stay has finally went away,
I have finally gotten over you.
Your memory doesn't hurt no more, I will shed no tear's for you,
my pillow will never be wet no more.
It took me a long time to learn, the endless night's I stayed
awake thinking that you would soon return.
I didn't know how much I could take
But now the day has came, my heart know's where it
should be, I don't know where the relief come's from,
all I know is I am finally free.
Yes I tried to think of you today, I found your memory has gone away.
The heart ache that was here to stay has finally gone away.
Gone away to stay.

*Reede M. Doty*

## Whispers

I remember the days we once had,
your hand within mine,
walking across the beach on a warm summer day.
And as I looked into your eyes,
I knew at once,
the difference between everything and nothing,
was only a whisper away...
and it was.

*Michael A. Gluck*

## Untitled

Hope reigns in nature.
The hope of new life and health.
The joyous botanical world is ready to burst forth
It's brilliance to benefit those who need
the healing power of beauty.

The bulbs cold dark domain is now flooded with
the quickening of the life-light from above.
The mounting joy is exploding the crusty outer shell
that once protected the fragile life within,
but now seems to entrap it.

The ever increasing sense of purpose drives
the tender shoots to see what lies beyond the surface
when they experience the magnificent warmth and light
of the promised land, they reach up with open faces
in praise and worship of the One who set them free.

*Pat Stansbury*

## Empty Nest

So I am sitting, a drink in my hand,
    the house is so empty ... But do you understand?

Yes I have family, with lives of there own,
    the cup comes up empty ... When I'm here alone.

What do you do, and who can you call,
    with silence your friend ... And you're ready to fall.

Why hurt the others, with pain that you feel,
    making them suffer ... With no cards to deal.

Laughter and joy, truly all I need.
    I thought I would have it... when I planted the seed.

Come back to me, give me more time.
    It's hard to let go ... So many years you've been mine.

I know that you can't, life isn't that way.
    You make what you can ... Of every new day.

So listen now and please will you hear.
    Life is so short ... And children are dear.

Tell your young ones, what is in your heart.
    Life is so quick ... And then you must part

Go on with your life, I do understand.
    So I am sitting ... A drink in my hand.

*Terri A. Brown*

## The Pain of Loss

The pain of loss beyond any words.
The hurt which accumulates turning more inward.

How will the deceit ever be removed from the mind?
Day in, day out becoming more intertwined.

The tears at night turn with fears during day
Pain! Pain! Will it ever go away?

Day turns into night, minutes into hours
Darkness becomes an obsession keeping visions out but ours.

Silence is searched for no faces to meet
Loneliness is no longer feared but becomes a retreat.

Promises in the night words without truth
Plans and dreams in the dark become memories without proof.

*Mary Eckel*

## "Reflections"

The greatest victories are often won during
The inconspicuous moments of quiet times;
The most meaningful words spoken in a
Whispered, hushed tone.
The most appreciated works are acts of
Kindness without recompense, commotion,
Or thought of reciprocation.
The most blessed gifts are those offered
In anonymity.
The strongest person is that individual
Who is able to tame the fury of violence
And hatred into Lessons of Love.
The wisest individual welcomes time as a
Precious commodity, not to be wasted.
The seeker after Truth realizes that he is
Not the master of his own fate and his
Kinsman proclaims that God is a Friend
And truly cares;
That individual is also my Kinsman.

*Mark H. Stevens*

## The Bombing

Why? Why must it be?
The killing, the crying, all the people dying.
Why? Why must it be?
Funerals, bodies, and prayers.
Why? Why must it be?
Caring, comforting, loving, and wondering.
Why? Why must it be?
The man will be caught,
Just the way it should be.
Lives will be lost but they will move on.
Yeah, that's the way it will be.
They will clean up the place
and it will look as if
nothing ever happened.
I hope that's the way it will be.

*Sarah M. Ries*

## One Legged Raven

A cold, wistful wind blew
the last leaf off the elm tree.
You hear the cow's snobbish old moo,
reminiscent of her gayer days.
Oh! dear one-legged raven,
though unable to preen, tail feathers deprived,
your robust figure navigates well,
reaching atop the church gable to send
the hearty greetings to your flock.
I heard you raised at least two
of those two still hanging around,
you intercede their rivalry squabbles.
They try to recapture the tenderness once received.
I've watched you closely as years gone by,
while my life entwined with sufferings and light,
often submerging myself in emotional pain,
for I know of no other way.
Oh! dear raven, you casually battered and untended beauty,
you are my friend, unbeknownst to you.

*Yuriko L. Okubo*

## Where the Rainbows Cross

Where the rainbows cross and the wind is strong,
the leprechauns dance and sing their songs.

They sing of treasure, parties and gold,
they sing of people brave and bold.

They sing all day and dance all night,
where the sun and moon are always bright.

Four leaved clover lay about,
that are picked by leprechauns thin and stout.

A big black pot of shiny gold
stands in the center of the village old.

Where the rainbows cross, and the world is still,
the leprechauns wish for peace on earth and to men goodwill.

*Theresa Fitzpatrick*

## Blue Monday

I am alone.
The loneliness surrounds me like a fog,
until it almost smothers me.
Sometimes it's ok to be alone;
and sometimes it hurts so badly I feel as
though I can stand outside myself and see the pain.
Tonight, I can see the pain.
Oh, God, my heart aches for someone to care
whether I live or die, laugh or cry.
My arms hunger for someone to hold;
My body yearns to be held.
Now the tears begin to fall;
They will ease the pain a little,
Wash away some of the heartache;
And tomorrow I will awaken a little stronger.
Perhaps tomorrow there will be another
lonely person who needs to be held...
And maybe we will find each other.

*Lin Harvey Dunlap*

## Untitled

Her eyes were tinted red,
the look of Death consumed them.
The skin around her eyes seemed to
deteriorate,
whenever the sun gleamed off her face.
Her soul yearned to be free,
as her body yearned to lay limp.
She gasped and tried to hang onto
each breathe she took.
As she peered out the window to watch
as life passed her by,
the most mysterious light shined
down upon her,
like as if she was performing in front of
an audience.
She then whispered a little prayer,
and laid her head to rest.

*Tracy Gale*

## Christmas

When bells ring and children sing
When snow falls and one loves all
When enemy are friends and nations colors blend
When love and care are in the air
Then you know its Christmas

*Ryan McGlynn*

## Invocation

Come back to me darling once more in a dream
The love of your brown eyes again on me beam
I long for their brightness, their love, their light
To bring back my youth in a vision of night

I long for your hand with it's magical touch
To bring me the comfort I'm needing so much
To hold you again in a loving embrace
To see the sweet smile that would light up your face

I mourn for the days and the years that are gone
I sigh for your love, that has left me forlorn
I long for one moment, to pillow your head
Again on my breast, as before you were dead

Then come to me dear, when flowers are in bloom
When the air is laden with the sweetest perfume
Come in the stillness of a summer calm night
When the moon and the stars are shining so bright

Then down the sweet vales of dream land together
We'll wander alone - ah, could we forever
Too well I know, in the gloom of tomorrow
My heart must bear it's dark burden of sorrow

    *Matthew Henry Panton*

## "Living Colors"

Living Colors I see - and how they do glow,
The magnificent colors of a brilliant Rainbow.
The crescent shape - the red, pink, and green,
Such a beautiful sight, never have I seen.
I see violet and purple - there's orange and blue.
The beautiful sky beyond now comes into view.
All the colors of the world are there to see,
The serenity there - for you and for me.
I reach for my brush - and I meditate,
For those radiant colors, I must duplicate.
I gently dip my brush into a light blue;
Other colors I mingle to form the right hue.
Compelled with desire to preserve this great scene,
To share this tranquility with others, I dream.
How pleasing I believe, to me it would be,
To capture those colors, for all others to see.
With a stroke of my brush, and there on the wall,
Living Colors appear, oh the grandeur of it all.
So, from home to home, inspired I must go.
To leave living Colors for all, to see and to show.

    *Thomas Gaines DeWitt*

## Majestic Powers

Yesterday I saw a rainbow painted in the sky
    The memory still lingers in my mind.
Today I heard music soft and romantic
    And my heart feels tender and kind.

Last evening I smelled the lilacs
    How that fragrance took control!
Just now the touch of my grandchild's hand
    Overwhelms my sensitive soul.

Each day I taste of God's riches.
    Each day of His bounty full and free.
May I have a heart full of forgiveness
    And my life fully consecrated and committed be.

    *Lila Meyerkorth*

## The Dream!

Late last night I awakened from
The middle of my dreams
To your familiar smile!
    When I close my eyes
    I can assemble your face in my head
    Your eyes are lovely dark and deep
    There are promises you must keep
    And things we must do before we can sleep

Like the raven and the dove
Searching for its perfect love
You must have fallen from up above
Because you're what I day dream of!

    *Parish Blake*

## Autumn

When the sky is seen, in its deepest blue,
the moon at night at it's brightest hue,
the midsummer flowers, beginning to fade,
soon autumn is here, in all it's parade.

The forest green turns, to crimson and gold,
which is a beauty, for eyes to behold,
the sharp wind blows, the air chilly at night,
next morning the dew, not crystal, but white.

Then leaves come down, from their heavenly berth,
to rest in silence upon the earth,
a look at the brown meadow, which was so green,
tells us the story, another season is seen.

The birds are gathering, for their southernly flight,
the farmer is reaping, with all of his might,
fires in the homes, are all aglow,
soon the earth is covered, with a blanket of snow.

    *Wilson C. Solomon*

## In the Dark

As I lay by your side and watch you sleep
The moonbeams softly touching your face
You look like an angel long lost in sweet
dreams
I reach to caress your still body
It feels warm and gentle
Your heart beats strong against your chest
And I am taken away by its sound
I turn to embrace you and can't help but
wonder
Is this place that I am in real
As I slowly drift within your sleep
I think of each day I spend with you
Like a memory that will soon end
And like a dream that was only in my mind
That soon fades away with time

    *Tina Huntley*

## No More Leaks

I looked at the ceiling
Yes, there were water spots.
They dripped on my piano
That was crying rainy drops.
Keys that tried to run away
Because they found they couldn't play.
The repair man came and dried their parts
Joy thereof filled both our hearts.
No more leaks on the inside
For the roofer came and stemmed the tide.
Happy notes are ringing true,
Keeping dry was the thing to do.

    *Betty J. Royer*

## Untitled

You are my breath; I am your breath;
You are my flower, my rose, my heart aglow;
The wine runs pure, the honey sweet;
My one, my one, my one;
You are my day, the eternal flow.

*Rita Rigert*

## Shadows Before Dawn

She lies awake yearning for his touch.
The moons casts a light through her open window.
A slight breeze sends the curtains dancing
She clutches her left breast as though holding her aching
   heart like a wounded bird
She laughs at the sorry sight of her.
Shortly her tears turn to sorrowful ones.
Oh, how she longs to be with the one who whispers sweetness
   in her ears,
Kisses her lips so tenderly, and makes her quiver whenever he is near.
But alas! A stranger at her door.
She silently gasps at the black figure as her body trembles in fear.
The black figure leans down and kisses her lips.
The closeness of the stranger is that of her lover's.
His darkness envelopes her.
Her body shakes with spreading passion and desire.
She can feel his touch through her sheer nightgown.
She loves him as no other.
She wants him more that the lover she wept for a moment before.
As dawn approaches he kisses her for the last time.
And as the sun rises he slips away.
She is alone again.

*Melissa Morris*

## The Red Rose

Of all the different flowers
The most beautiful is the rose
It has a true significance
Which, in a verse, I will compose.

The bright red rose reminds me
Of the blood Christ shed for all,
We should think of this when about to sin
And we will seldom fall.

The thorny stems are symbolic
Of the earthly crown He wore.
Oh, how it must have made,
His sacred head so sore.

The fresh green leaves remind me
Of the new life we begin
When we have been forgiven
Of each and every sin.

*Mary Valentine Smith*

## Treasures Of Time

Bell ringing, as I enter the antique shop.
The musty smell within its confines.
Picturing old homes and attics in my mind.
A feeling I am walking through time.

Exploring the past of people lives.
Fine china placed on cabinets and tables.
Toys designed to amuse children and tools
of workers from many trades.

Listening to the bell ring once more.
I leave returning to present times.
Wondering what treasures, will be kept,
for the old antique shop.

*Pat Bordner*

## The Mystery of Man's Soul

The darkness side of one's mind is
the mystery of a soul of man.
What a man wants is the soul of
a pure and heart of a woman
who wouldn't know the mysterious dangers
of the mind soul of man.
A man who hides in the dark shadows
seeking his pried
A woman who has the heart of golden
wing's which turns into the demon of hell.
The power of man is the power of
the devil who wants to process the woman's soul
when a woman who become the body
and soul of man, she become as one.
And as time goes by than the woman
becomes the power of man with
the wisdom of fight the mysterious evil
of the mystery of a man's soul.

*Susan Teresa McCarthy*

## Untitled

I still remember deep inside of my heart
The night we were in the dark

Oh! my love we have loved one another
Now you are telling me this can go on further

Now without you, how can I laugh
Words is the only thing have left

I never have a thought
Love hurting my heart

The days, months, and years change
But my love will always be the same

I have been thinking of you all the time
My heart is waiting of you to come

No mater how long, I'm still here with my soul
Please understand I'm waiting for you

My heart is waiting and watching you
I will never what to move

Want to send my words with the wind to tell you
If you going to be mine, then you will always be cool

You and I will be mash I still want you back
I am not trying to lie I'm here to share life

*Meuy Seng Saelee*

## The Whooping Crane-Endangered

The time has come for all to hear,
   the cry we've all held most dear.
There must be something we can do
so he'll fly that sky so blue.

   The cry is calling, it's fading fast,
that we took for granted, and thought it would last.
If only we'd put aside some space,
   to keep the whooping crane's great race.

   We'll keep fighting to the end,
whether we break, whether we mend.
But, whatever happens in my heart there's pain,
for that crying call of the whooping crane.

*Tera Beth Kilbride*

## The Old One

Bare, dry branches stretched stark against the blue summer sky,
the old one stands.
Bark tattered, peeling away, a testimony to death among the
verdant woods.

How long have you stood, old one, braving the wind
and the snows?
Proud, strong, surpassing the ages of man,
what history has passed beneath your crown?

Soon you will crumble and fall, no longer a monument
of your past glory.
The armies of death shall consume you
and leave nothing to mark your place.

And so too it shall be with me,
once tall and strong; now withered and weak.
I too shall fall and be consumed
and nothing will mark my place.

The fate that awaits us can not be denied.
Our days of glory past,we stand now only
as mute testimony to what once was
and soon to what no longer will be.

*Suzanne Hare*

## Ocean Blue

When I sail the ocean blue
The only thing I can think about is you

You are the only thing on my mind
But the more I think, the more I run out of time

I will try to make it last for a while
As I think of you while I sail along the ocean blue.

The shining sun rays beaming off the ocean waves
Wash the shores for the following days

Furthermore
The waters stay cold in the midst of the night
And the fog grows thick and looks very tight

The night grows young and there is more nothing to do
Except think of you
As I sail the ocean blue.

*Tukerry Shorts*

## The Day After Death

The words "I'm sorry, we did all we could" echoed relentlessly.
The pain was all too real.
The clouds were but an ominous shadow.
Time, a tireless host,
The day after death.

Life, once warm and bright,
Now dark and cold.
The grief possessing her dreams,
No solitude of heart,
The mind growing heated,
The day after death.

The joys of Heaven spilling on earth,
Grief feeding on her restless soul
Hungry for a quiet mind she fell to her knees,
Reaching upward to a sky lit with fear,
Touching the Heavens for the first time,
The day after death.

*Reva J. Hartmann*

## Down the Path

We ambled down the path thru woods
The path made by animals and humans
It led to a pond of a nice large size
On our way down, saw several things
Different birds fluttered thru the trees
And squirrels made their way over boughs

Farther down we spotted a doe and fawn
They stared at us, then they were gone
Near the pond there was a little turtle
Crossing the path as we watched it crawl
We sat near the edge of the pond
And saw two ducks take a flight

Also watched a raccoon on the other side
Washed food every time it took a bite
Then we saw a frog dive into the pond
And we watched the minnows swim around
Soon, back up the path, we trekked
Arrived at home, sat on porch and relaxed

*Marshall N. Butler*

## A Sad Day In Oklahoma

It was a normal town it lies to the west
The people who lived there thought their town was the best

At one sad moment their was a very loud bang
A great building fell and cries of pain rang

Dust and dirt bellowed into the sky
You could hear adults scream, you could hear children cry

Sirens cried loud and fireman ran about
They did everything they could to get everyone out

A baby died in a fireman's arms, what a terrible sight
I'll pray for them both each and every night

That tragic day touched many a life
Some lost parents, some lost a wife

Some lost a friend, some lost a family member
This cruel act is something we'll always remember

Lets always remember the families of those who had to die
Lets thank the Lord for those that lived, but had to cry

Don't forget the kids in the nursery at play
They didn't ask for their lives to be taken away

*Michael D. Morris*

## My Hero

All little children have their heroes,
The Power Rangers up to  police officers.
These heroes are looked up to everyday.
But my hero is my mama!
It is not easy to raise a kid now days,
At times she could pull out her hair,
she would get so angry.
But she always remains cool and handles matters as a Christian.
She prays for both my sister and I everyday.
She would risk her own life to save my sister's or mine.
She cooks three meals a day for us,
so we never starve.
Now it is my turn to pray for her,
she's done so much for me.
I lay awake to share her pain,
that hurts so badly.
I love my mama, with all my heart!

*Tania Nicole Saxon*

## Pride In the Heartland

"Oklahoma," where the wild winds still sweep
the plains — but the sweet innocence of peace
is not there.

Is this America the Beautiful?
Where militia, mafia, street gangs and drugs
guns, drugs and violence rules???

Has someone stolen our dreams????
Is this a reality check, or just the 90's!
Where children are violated and life is wasted
where the elderly are forgotten and people
over 50 are no longer useful?

How can we continue to sing "Amazing Grace"
when the silence speaks and shouts "Why"??!!
Can you ever look at a Teddy Beat in the same way??

We will survive because God's grace is greater than
our fault and is sufficient for our needs, and he
understands our despair at this tragedy.

"America" look toward Oklahoma City and find the basic
fundamentals that are still alive in our country today.
These truths give us hope for our future, remember and be
proud of the "Heartland"

*Mary N. Dees*

## Dawn

Oh, sing of the beauty of earliest dawn;
The promise to man that the world will go on,
That proof that his hand is still firm at the helm,
And he's in command of the heavenly realm.
So, on with the day! let the sun pour its rays;
Let soft benediction of rain ease its ways.
So, honor our God for His mercy and care.
We know through the ages He'll always be there.

*Ruth E. Runion*

## Untitled

Never have I seen the horizon so grand
The reflections on the water, of the sky and of the land
I wonder if in years to come this will still hold true
For the hands of time can be so cruel, to what's now the ocean blue

If I were to be so bold, and say what's on my mind
I think that it is pitiful, how quickly we turn blind
We act as though we have no clue, why nature's falling prey
To the desecration of the land, in which we are meant to stay

I wonder if our children will see the beauty we see today
Or will time and negligence take it's toll and that beauty fade away
I would hope that we will wake up and see what's happening around us
And leave a thing of beauty for those that are our loved ones.

*Laurie Ann Elliott*

## Broken Hearts

Broken hearts, broken souls.
The peace I've sought, the peace
I've lost.  Hearts ache from love
Lost, the pain, the pain makes me
long for peace of mind and soul.
The dreams of happiness, unthinkable, unreachable.
Cold feelings are welcome to ease the pain,
The pain of a broken heart, shattered
dreams, lie at my feet.
No hope for happiness, long since past.
Forever longing for a peace to mend...
  Broken hearts

*Terrence R. Young*

## Untitled

Upon the littered path of my forsaken dreams
The remnants of hope still glow faintly,
Lighting the way into my forbidden lair
Of denial and destruction.
Walls of glass and silver
Faintly reflect the pain within,
While permitting the desirous visions
Of all that is without.
Colors fall from the sky and run down the walls,
Creating the illusion of life within,
But life lies only without.
As I press my face against the glass,
And rest my hand upon the lifeless silver trim,
I can feel only the cold within,
And long for the warmth
That is forever without.

*Mary Beth Tuerk*

## Goodbye

I failed to mention everything in it's correct way; never knowing
the right thing to say.
I'm filled with pain; now feeling weak,
losing all the strength I'd gained.
The other night, I had a dream; the salt shaker empty,
the pepper filled to the top.
And as usual, a sense of the unseen; and true clarity
for what was not.
Even while deep in sleep I connect things to my conscious life, for
I'm intent on relieving the strife.
I failed to mention everything in it's correct way; never knowing
the right thing to say.
In the dream there was one other memory; of you pleading:
"go away".
My response; never knowing the right thing to say; was:
okay.
As I awoke from that dreary night; I was filled with fright,
it was for your sake that I'd said goodbye.
Realizing my mistake, I began to cry.

*Marianne Yanosik*

## "Dogwood Days"

It's dogwood time in Southern Indiana,
The rolling hills are wreathed in pink and white,
And people come from far and wide
Just to view and enjoy the scenic sight.

The hills along the Ohio River
Are a'glow with the blooming trees -
Redbuds, dogwoods, and flowering locust -
All as pretty as you please.

If we could hold on to a season,
Could any be better than this -
Spring and all that springtime brings:
Gentle showers and vernal bliss?

When it's dogwood days in Hoosierland,
Hearts are light and full of cheer,
Lovers rendezvous, and wedding bells ring
During this special time of the year.

*Robert R. McEllhiney*

## The Schafer Reunion

Long ago and far, far away, from a foreign land across the sea,
The SCHAFER'S came to AMERICA — To be independent and FREE!!!
They left behind loved ones so dear, crossed the Mighty Ocean Blue,
To find New Land and Old Friends; make dreams of a New World come
true!!
Catherine and George came from RUSSIA, landed on ELLIS ISLAND in
late November.
'Twas the winter of nineteen-hundred eight: Just in time for the
eight clan member.
In the next ten years to come, four more were added to the clan.
Thus a total of a dozen children - - minus four In GOD'S AL-
MIGHTY PLAN
Two boys and six girls — All got married, had their share of work,
laughter and tears.
Thirty years brought many changes; hard times, but many good, good
years!!
The families populated and scattered, throughout this country so wide.
Some lost touch with one another, some passed on to the other side..
Seventy-one years have passed away, since they landed on this GREAT
SHORE:
The FIFTH GENERATION IS IN THE MAKING — Could the
SCHARFER'S ask for
anything more??

*Pauline A. Schafer Turner*

## Tree Harvest

The woods - they're in the woods! I hear them.
The screaming of saws
Disharmonize my being,
Yanking me, tearing me.
The crash of giants toppling to earth
Is a symbol of the world today -
No peace, all noise and fury,
Meaningless,
Destructive,
Wasteful.

Nature mourns. Little birds tossed out of nests
Lie on the ground
Peeping.
Softest flowers lie crushed,
Helpless beneath aged oaks,
Sent sprawling on the forest floor
By the bite of the saw -
Limbs broken, leaves torn,
Only their trunks (if straight and whole)
Thought worth the saving - after the bark is stripped.

*Ruth Myer*

## The Sea and I

As I walk beside the sea
  The sea and I are lonely
The waves break upon the shore
  Rushed on by the angry winds -
The turmoil which seethes within
  My heart is like the sea.
As the waves beat the sands in
  Futile desperation - so I try to
Maintain a sensitive love
  Can he understand my need, does he
  want to!!
Or shall I spend the remainder of my life -
  Lonely as the sea, ever searching -
Never a final resting place, just a constant
  And futile wandering of my soul.
The sea and I.......

*P. Kelemen*

## Grandmother Moon

Many winters have passed since I was a young girl
The seasons have brought both joy and sadness

I have looked into the faces of my children's children
And my heart is filled with gladness

I have brought about the visions of days past and my love in th
power of their spirits  - soon they will seek to give life to their
  visions

Know this my children
The earth, sky and moon were created and brings us the lesson of above

Know yourselves and be courageous
The north wind's winged messenger brings us strength and tenderness,
born from seasons past

Many days have been filled with the laughter of my children
When nighttime was filled with soft sounds and the air was clean and
the wind was calm and cool

I gave many thanks to my grandmother moon for she has guided me
through many long days and the love I was given showed through in
my vision

I ache for the old ways when the gentle light of the moon touched our
  hearts

Soon I will leave you and be in the vision the circle  of life — 'he
spirit of giving - I welcome the wondrous gift and gladly take  y
  place beside her — my grandmother moon.

*Theodora Campanella*

## Waterfall

Crystals of blue fall sparkling here,
The secret of peace lies breathlessly near.
Sharp needles of green rain down from above,
Their furtive wanderings are known but to the dove.
Pools of icy water linger here and there,
And of the mermaid on a rock fingering fair hair.
Rainbows dancing merrily in the depths of waters deep,
Where memories reflected abundant here to reap.
Happiness has reigned here, however, so has sadness,
There is a story of lovers, one was driven to madness.
After one was heartbroken, he came here and told all.
For not only is it beautiful, it listens—this waterfall.

*Leanna Petronella*

## Shock Waves

Of all the sadness - the unjust madness....
The shock of it all
A drowning of innocent tears
Weary eyes, young hearts, soiled cries
Our sorrow riddened hearts,
"Solemn prayers"
Go out to you
A bombs blast - the terror's path.....
As the sound waves fell cold
We heard the news, outraged with disbelief
Tears of silence, blackened skies, senseless violence
Your many strengthened efforts,
"Embracing heroes" we confide in you
The lonely news - the grim views....
Photo fixed emotional fears
Those affected - embedded in the minds of all
A community, a nation, a collective sea of
"Unified dedication"
For your pain reddened sorrow
"Eyes of a grieving nation turn to you."

*Terry L. Stokes*

## Logandale, Overton Heron

Heron, Heron standing so still watching
the sky
Your stare was so intense we
wondered why
You stood there for hours didn't Bat
An eye
Were you waiting for your mate to
come on by
The Ladies at Moapa Valley water district say
You stayed late
On your migration did your mate meet
it's fate
Or were you just scanning looking
for a date
You displayed patience and devotion in
your wait
You flew off alone we are sorry to say
Hope your persistence will somehow pay
Maybe you will find your mate another day
On the other side of the valley in another flyway

*Wilfred L. Deyo*

## The Circle

Gone is the patter of little feet
The soft breathing of a child fast asleep
Gone are the days of toys on the floor
The yelling and screaming and slams of doors
Gone are the years of school and dates
Gone are the times of hurries and waits
Gone are the laughter and the cries
God how the years have sure flown by
But life is not over it has just begun
By the marriage of your daughter and the birth of her son
It's such a joy starting over again
Your daughter is now your very best friend
You sit and talk laugh and cry
With toys on the floor you give a sigh
While holding Nana's little man on your lap
You listen to the soft breathing of his nap
With a smile on your face and a tear in your eye
You remember the times of days gone by
Your thoughts interrupted she says with a grin
By the way Mom... were having twins

*Molly Morris*

## A Walk in the Winter Woods

The day is cold.
The soft pat-pat of my snowshoes upon the snow is soothing,
Reassuring,
As if to remind me that I am still here.
For though I feel lonely,
I am not alone.
I have seen the tracks:
The large feet of the rabbit,
The delicate hoof prints of the deer;
Even the jumping prints of the squirrel.
Yes, they are there,
Though I cannot see them,
Hidden there in the crystal-like woods.
The snow falls lightly,
The day is beautiful;
The spirits are with me,
And I am not alone.

*Leslie E. McEvers*

## God's Creation

Yes, God has made so many beautiful things
  The starts, the moon, the planets with their rings,
The flowers that bloom each and every spring
  The birds that fly with outstretched wings.

He made the gentle breeze to blow;
  He made the ocean waters flow,
All the living things that grow
  All of this here below.

Mountains and hilltops all around
  Colored with nature brightly abound.
Animals who walk or crawl the ground,
  Such magnificent creatures are found.

But what is so amazing to me
  Is not His creation of land or sea,
Nor is it the beasts that came to be
  That brings me to my bent knee.

Love has given me a way
  Of saying what I have to say;
It's for you, my dear, that I pray
  Thanks to God every day.

*Teresa A. Johnson*

## Young Girl On A Bicycle

Even from my front porch I can see
the steamy air
rising up and causing her face to flush a bright red.
The sweet perfume
of those moist white flowers hanging on heavy green vines,
captures her briefly.

Biting off the ends
and spiting them out
onto my perfect green lawn
sucking them hard
to get a single succulent, sweet drop

Push, push
push, push
down the street
lets loose her feet and hands
and cruises through the dark tunnel of trees
on the cobblestone
sets up a pleasant rhythm
click, click
click, click

*Terry L. Christin*

## The Tree Sonnet

A priceless sacred treasure is the tree.
The sun and rain give seed the means to root.
Soon buds foretell the future flowers and fruit.
In time the pine, like us, mere dust will be.

The seasons signs are seen on tell tale trees:
A flowery feast becomes a branching arch;
The flaming fall gives way to snowy larch
Or ash and aspen quaking in the breeze.

In days of yore in hallowed groves of oak
The priests performed their secret holy rites:
They carved the trunk to see the sylvan sprites;
With fire and chant they prayed to heal their folk.

WITH CHRIST THE CROSS BECAME THE BLESSED TREE
WHEREON HE DIED, FROM SIN TO SET US FREE.

*Wilbur Harold Wright*

## Today and Tomorrow, the Sun Will Rise

I awake in a valley of beauty,
The sun is rising, and the path ahead looks steady,
I pick myself up from the comforting night of sleep,
In my possession is my soul, and that is all,
As I walk, I inhale life and exhale love,
I look up and see the mountain top, for that is my destination,
I see the dew on the trees, glistening like teardrops from a laughing
   pal,
I turn to look at the past, where my footsteps are set in the sand,
Head on, again, evil approaches and the sky fades to black,
Thunder yells and rain beats upon my head like a drum on a silent
   night,
I look up and can no longer see the mountain top,
Fear stabs me in the chest, for I am now lost in his fiasco called life,
The earth shakes beneath my feet and I lunge for a tree,
I feel balanced, but suddenly the tree is split in half by a bolt of lightning,
I have fallen,
While becoming steady, I slip in the mud,
I panic and tears jump from my eyes, a mist floods my view,
Wiping my eyes, I see something reflecting light,
It is the sun, bright and blooming, showing me the way, hope,
Reality has struck, and the search is over...

   *Megan Salo*

## Untitled

I look for her as silence drifts and day fades into night,
The sun rays die as the moon hangs high and glows with all its might.

Her eyes are red from the tears that fall as she continues to weep,
The abuse she takes and promises she makes are getting hard to keep.

As she rages on she still grows strong and faces the deceit
Of the nations at war, the battles at hand, the lessons of defeat.

From the homeless, the hungry, and those without a clue,
She tries desperately everyday to tell us what to do.

We listen, we hear, but do we really understand
That the world as we know it is getting out of hand.

If we turn around now it may not be to late,
We can save her poor soul from such a dreadful fate.

The myth in this rhyme is that she'll always be there,
This could be because most people don't care.

The morals are gone, we've committed a crime,
God's time clock is ticking - we're marching in time

To the beat of a drum, so different, so free,
She can dance to the music, "She's" Mother Nature, you see.

   *Nicole Ashmore*

## The Accident

In a fraction of a second a deplorable mistake was made...
   The terrorizing remembrance of a moment that refuses to fade.

The existence of my closest companions was nearly taken away
   A horrifying image of a reality I wished never to portray

And in the darkness, as my vision dims, blood is what I see
   of that dreadful instant, and the culpability that fell upon me.

Sinfulness, guilt, and shame roam about my remorseful heart
   On account of that awestricken moment, grief refuses to depart.

Over and over the situation is dramatized in my perplexed mind
   but an exact duplication of what occurred I can't find.

The pain I feel is so intense that tears exist no more
   Numb is what I am cause I carry a heart that tore.

In a fraction of a second I nearly lost my closest friend
   and in that fraction of a second, a part of me came to an end.

   *Virginia Lopez*

## Nature

The wind, the calm, the rain, and the snow.
The sun, the clouds, the stars, and the moon.
Changes occur in winter, in summer, in spring, and in fall.
All four seasons bless us with nature's beauty.

Nature blesses us with its best.
We learn and grow from nature at its worst.
Nature can be friendly and sometimes quite wicked.
It can be beautiful and a beautifier.

We experience sights, sounds, and wonderful scents.
Oh, what a wonder to watch the flowers and the trees grow.
To be able to watch the snow fall or listen to the wind whistle about.
To enjoy nature's different scents of flowers, the rain, and the new
mowed lawns.

Nature creates many opportunities for fun.
Of course, nature continuously gives us energy to enjoy all our
surroundings.
Observing the changes in nature, shows us we too can and need to
change.
Nature is a pleasure, a teacher, a friend and foe.

Nature and all of its creations are from God.
All of the nature is for nurturing our souls.
Most important, nature shows us how to change and to gain rebirth.
All of the nature, is for us to treasure and to treat with respect.

   *Pattye Probasco*

## Green

Green is...a field of flowing grass in the evening breeze,
   the taste of a crunchy apple.

Green is...a warm spring day with a book and a pillow,
   green is the son of blue and yellow.

Green is...when you are green with envy over someone you
   love, which is not good.
Green is...the beautiful sea at the beach.

Green is...the warm summer days with friends and family,
   but most of all green is LOVE.

   *Zack Shook*

## Little Old Ladies

Growing old can be very confusing.
   The things that they hear are sometimes amusing.
They can't remember what they had for lunch,
   But remember a years ago Mother's Day Brunch.
The names of their friends are hard to remember.
   They're never quite sure if it's May or December.
Shopping for clothing could last through the night.
   They can't make up their minds between purple and white.
Their shopping cart pushing can wipe off your smile,
   Slow, stop-and-go traffic down the middle of the aisle.
Accident free, they arrive hale and merrier.
   To the rest on the road, they're more often a carrier.
Since three-fourths of a century have now passed for me,
   I'm one of those Ladies from Hades, you see.

   *Ruth Spann*

## The Graduates

In their tassels and in their gowns,
   The Seniors marched without a frown.
With their heads so firm and high,
   They look like angels in the sky.
And with a silent prayer in heart,
   They wished that they would never part.
For now they know that the road is long,
   In the future where they belong.

   *Rita M. Noa*

## The Fields Could Dance

The flowers sway in the tune of the wind
The trees glide their arms so high in the sky,
and the leaves dance all through the air
The tall brown grass bend their old backs
can't you hear the cracks?
colors here
colors there
colors everywhere
The sun lights the way for all,
this way not one will fall
The sky begins to darken
Everything comes to a stop
The flowers are still.
The trees are in place
The leaves not at a pace
The tall brown grass now in line
Everything is still and quiet
For it is night,
And until the next day,
it's time to be on our way

*Rosa Lou Avella*


## "A Mother's Love"

As I hold you in my arms and look at your face
The waiting and pain, time did erase.

Your ten little fingers and ten little toes
The joy of fulfillment, only a Mother knows.

You've been sent from Heaven up above
For me to care for, cherish and love.

And now your life is in my keep
Many promises I make to you as you sleep.

I'll nurture and love you and watch you grow
The "Seeds of Life," I'll help you sow.

God's greatest gift has been sent my way
My beautiful baby daughter was born today.

*Linda Whetman*


## Never Forget!

On a fabled day in '95
The walls did collapse and the people did strive
To understand the awful mess
And ask God the victims to bless.

It happened in the morn at 9:02
And left people feeling confused, lonely, and blue.
"Why, God, why," the people did ask,
"Did someone do this terrible task?"

People murdered, one hundred sixty-seven,
Surely each of them will go to heaven.
They did not ask for this terrible fate,
Nor in their hearts did they feel hate.

From all over came rescuers too many to count.
The nine shaky stories they bravely did mount.
To pull from the wreckage those who were dead;
To search for those who couldn't have fled.

To express our pain, words are too few.
So we have talked and worked and even cried, too.
The pain is so great, and deep our regret.
April 19th's victims we will never forget!

*Russell Lambert*


## The Light

The rippling waves, the calm ocean breeze,
The water so blue, and unknowingly blind,
It can't see the damage, uncanny feeling of revenge,
Of a world it remembered to be sacred and kind.

In some ways it's lucky to not know the truth,
To not comprehend what has become of our lives,
The anger has overwhelmed our consciences and souls,
The murder, the hostility, the guns, the knives.

Can you vision the world 100 years from now?
Can you imagine a world without acrimony and hate?
You could never sketch a picture of a more horrid place,
Than the world around us, we've lived to create.

But there's always hope, although it's unseen,
You can never give in the game you must win,
It may seem you'll lose an unwinable fight,
The world of regret and countless sin.

Yet there are many shades of gray when there's no color at all,
The masterpiece is almost finished and you've come so far,
That you tend to stare at the darkest moon,
And forget the sun, our brightest star.

*J. Jones*


## Grip The Rain

Tomorrow's sun will never come and
The waves won't touch the shore.
How I wish the nights were done
but yet I crave for more.

The rainbows in the sky slowly fade away.
Tomorrow dreams will always die and
Clouds of beauty turns to gray.

Yesterday's kindness is now a mystery
Now what will be in store?
The day shows philosophy.
But the night's mist has heavenly door.

The silence has calling
for the waves to touch the shore.
And greatest wishes are falling.
How can the white dove soar?

How can I make these wonders stop and
wander from all the pain?
I only want to stand on the mountain top
and try to grip the rain.

*Michael Dusk*


## Christmas 1994

The days are short, the nights are long.
  The wind blows cold in the eaves.
We feel Father Time afoot in the land.
  He's gathering in the sheaves.

The seeds sown from Pandora's ark,
  yield a crop scarce worth the reaping
Save here and there amidst the tares
  a golden stalk is creeping.

We all cling to that golden stalk for
  beyond cruel winter's solstice
We see the New Year's Child, the promised one,
  Springtime's golden notice.

The cherub face, the chubby fists,
  The limbs all feckless flailing,
The golden hope, the world's rebirth
  that makes our toil availing.

*R. E. Andrews*

## I'm Watching You

When the mist of the dark simmers near
The wizards and witches start shifting their gears

As the shadows appear
Ya start watching your rear

The full moons the best
To fondle your prey
You better get your rest
Cause I'm here to stay

But don't get frightened
And don't never ever turn your back
Cause I'm only flying
Straight towards your track

Always remember one thing
Looks can be deceiving
And the touch of my sting
Is quite intriguing

***Linda Harris***

## Apocalism

I Heard the Bomb
The World is Going
I Closed my eyes, and it went Away
We Wanted the End of the World
So I made It Bleed, and it Cried like a dog
And I blew It apart, Ha-Ha, I blew It Apart
And We love it, So now you're Gone
And I rule The world
All of It, in my Gilded Mind Soon to be shattered
Ha-Ha, But till Then
You died First, and I'll see you Later
In the underworld, Maybe
As the seven bowls are poured in My Mouth
And the Amphetamines wear off
So take Your life and take Your World
And get the Hell out of Mine
I'm a Part of the Apocalism
Soon Derived Apocalism
Soon
Apocalism

***Michael Paul Regalado***

## New Age

While in my day I watch and see
The world's tide rise and fall before me.
From great individuals of society,
To a society of no individuality.

We are dependent now, on dependency;
For breakfast, lunch, and divinity.
Within our soul of mortality
Lies the rusted stain of individuality.

Fear does stand of fear itself
Paranoia, greed, and vanity-fair.
Filling our jails and hanging trees.
Out to kill you before you kill me.

The flag of truce between power and dark-
To embrace immorality; to receive the mark.
To gnash our teeth and loose our soul;
To fall forever down the dependence whole.

To tell you things to do about
Is not at all what I'm about.
You are you as a rose is a rose;
To rise! To fall; then decompose.

***Rob Wright***

## On the tennis court at night

The trees stand tall above me in the empty wind
their shadows black fairies fluttering around me
and I alone, pacing, prowling, pacing,
a mad woman muttering moronic matter in the moonlight.

Plotting quietly
dreaming
of a place far away
to leave Bluebeard's castle.
I have not seen the corpses
but I feel them
shimmering against my skin.
They whisper to me in the night.
"Leave," they tell me softly,
"before you join us."

***Maisie Rubinstein***

## Children Are The Music Of My Life

Their eyes sparkle like the sounds of the piano.
Their tears are heard through the wailing of the saxophones.
Their hurt through the clarinets.
Their gentleness through the flutes.
Their self-esteem through the trumpets.
Their anger through the how brass.
Their hearts thump in excitement like drums in cadence.
When they are at peace and happy
The music comes in complete harmony.

***Phoebe J. Deibert***

## Before the Mountain, the Valley

In awesome majesty the mountains rise,
Their towering peaks reaching to the skies.
Snow-capped, in breathless beauty do they stand,
A monument to God's eternal hand!
There, azure-blue lakes, and crystal-clear streams,
The sun glinting on the forest pristine.
Breath taking view, lifting the soul to God,
Because they were created by His word!

Yet no beautiful mountains e'er could be,
Except first we have crossed some wide valley.
We tread it alone, and oft' in deep pain,
God's face seems hidden, our journey in vain.
Lift up your head and His beauty behold,
Keep your eyes on Him 'til you reach your goal.
After the valley, and the night of woe,
The mountain-top glory will fill your soul.

First comes the test in the valley below,
Before the mountain-top blessing we can know.

***Mona A. Fetter***

## Roads

Isn't it funny how we all walk down the same roads
Then again the same road is different for each of us
Through our journey good and bad
There are many roads we choose along the way
Why do we let go of some
Yet cling to others
Sometimes we make the wrong choice
Other times we make the right choice
How do we know which choice to make
I wish I had the answers
Remember the right choice for some is the wrong choice for others
Just remember you can always choose another road along the way

***Laurie L. Smith***

## Pronouns

A long time ago there was ME - or was it I?
Then came YOU and changed it to WE
So, I stopped thinking about ME - or I
And concentrated on a few little THEYS.
WE watched them grow, day by day.

THEY each became an I, such as ME.
THEY each found a YOU and one found two.
THEN came the time when the Lord called YOU.
I'VE lost one pronoun, but I have all the rest.
So, come on, Lord, have I passed the test?

*Margaret E. Yaeger*

## Relationship

The moon's rays shine towards earth and all its life.
Then life is I drawn towards the moon and each other.
The wolves howl is pulled to the moon; and too, is the sea
and all its creatures.
Then— is it not rational that a man and woman will also
seek its beauty and mystery?
In doing so, they find the companionship of each other; The
power in being two, yet, remaining one.
As with the cycles of the moon - so are too - the cycles of
friendship; love; and life together.
Even though the moon fragments with its cycles and the
seasons— it always returns to its entirety, its whole!
So too, are you with each other!

*Linda Jean Dorris*

## Untitled

I fell asleep for about half an hour at your desk last night.
Then woke to see you lying there.
So beautiful in your slumber,
So peaceful in your dreams,
It was a shame to leave you like that.
Or would have been, had I.

I watched you forever, as forever I had watched for you.
And you lay.
Eyelids of glass closed to me,
Yet loving me as only your closed eyelids could know that I love
you.
Breath long and slow.
Yet loving me.
Loving me.

I saw you sleeping and knew rest.
I did not need to sleep anymore.
I wasn't tired then.
And you lay there.

I looked at your sleeping body.
I felt your sleep.
And I loved you in a moment.

*Sierra Brown*

## Black

At night I see shadows on the wall,
The dark figures make my skin crawl.
Seeing bats flutter at night,
Fearful they might swoop down and take a bite.
Under my feet I feel the lifeless ground,
Looking around I can hear my heart pound.
Faster and faster my heart begins to pound,
Sensing evil lurching around.
From far away I hear a werewolf's howl,
Afraid that the werewolf might begin to prowl.
With all these things lurching behind my back,
Why is my favorite color black?

*Patrick Shane Walker*

## Heroes Past and Now

When I look back upon my youth
there comes to light one steadfast truth

I've had some heroes who helped me see
that life holds so many opportunities

MY heroes were not people of long ago
MY heroes were "teachers" I'd come to know

They were heroes who came armed to school each day
with truth, love and understanding for all our needful ways

These heroic, "special teachers" helped mold confidence and skills
and taught us that NOTHING is impossible, if in fact it be our will

So we grew, matured and developed, moving on to achieve our dreams
and now we sit and share these thoughts with our own loving offspring

So.......to you, SPECIAL TEACHERS "Extraordinaire,"
please ponder on this coming truth

That you have been (and are) "special heroes"
to many of this decade's youth.

*Regina Allen-Wilson*

## The Man and the Hickory Tree

A young man came up the hill looking for the perfect tree,
There he found a young hickory that overlooked the sea.
He wanted to build a tree house to escape all the sadness
He found among people who showed him so much badness.
The location was so wonderful, the view stretched on forever,
But the size of the hickory was a problem he found however.
It was young and frail and thin, not much more than a sapling;
Not a major problem for which to find himself so grappling.
He would wait until it grew up into a tree so grand,
That he could build a mansion strong enough any storm to stand.
So off he went to live his life until that day would come,
When his young hickory to his many charms would succumb.
Years went by, and other things caused him to forget his tree,
But then the weights of life's struggle fell off and set him free.
He came with wood and nails and even a brand new hammer,
So finally he could build that house above life's loud clamor.
It mattered not he now was old and not many decades were left,
For with his tree he could recover those years stolen as if by theft.
Yet he was shocked to find a tree house already built up high,
And there a-playing was the cheery boy he had been in days gone by.

*Thomas C. Cross*

## I Am Your Ancestor

I am your ancestor of many years gone by
There is a resemblance no one could deny.
Our ears, our eyes, our chins are the same
We share all that and even our name.

You stand by my tombstone and wonder about me
Yet, I am only one branch on your family tree.
Your manner, your laughter, your walk is like mine
How I wish I could show you or give you a sign.

Our paths were not destined to cross, it's quite true
I'm your "Guardian Angel" and I'll watch over you.
I am your ancestor and I always will be
I am part of you, you are part of me.

*Linda S. Brenner*

## "Prelude To Spring"

The day was cold, dark and dreary,
the worth wind blew with relentless fury;
the trees were bare, no buds to be found,
no song of birds, snow covered the ground;
it seemed mother nature had turned her back on spring,
when suddenly I heard a mocking bird sing.

*Olive W. Sayers*

## Wait Upon the Lord

When life is stressful and hard to bear,
There is a source of strength and care.
When you feel faint and fear to fall,
The strength of eagles is there if you call
Upon the Lord who rules with strong arm.
He will carry you and keep you from harm.
Wait upon the Lord, who knows all your needs.
He gathers His lambs and gently leads.
Even great nations are to Him as dust,
Yet He tells us to simply trust.
Wait upon the Lord and do not faint.
Fly like an eagle within His strength!

*Shirley Thomas*

## The Door

I open the door yet I cannot see inside,
There is no hint of light within.
Though I direct light upon the doorway,
It does not penetrate.
I reach beyond the darkness and cannot touch within.
There is no heat nor is there cold,
Yet I fear to enter there and find no one to care.
In such one place before, I found pain and tears.
Of that unknown I am aware,
I seek only a candlelight within to guide my way.
Then I may not fall in pain or worse,
Break a priceless treasure there.
I remain frozen unable to enter, unable to turn away.
Will a light appear to guide me or will the door simply close,
Leaving me with emptiness outside the doorway of your heart.

*A. F. Whisper*

## Death Of A Leader

The sky is dark and smeared with the clouds.
    There is no moon today.  It's dead.
It shone upon the sleeping minds of hailing crowd
    That followed shining cold wherever led.

The mourning will be over, and the stars will pass away
    Regretful of the time when sky was silent.
The sun will rise and warm the people with the light of day,
    And they will cheer fresh erected tyrant.

*Michael Aluker*

## Welcome To The World Little One

Welcome to the world little one.
There is so much to see.
You shall live your life surrounded by love and happiness.
The world is a scary place for a child,
But as you grow,
You will learn to make the world be at your command.
There are many things to say,
But the right words are hard to find.
The main thing is to be grateful for life,
Never doubt yourself,
And stand strong on your beliefs.
Others will follow you,
For you are their leader.
"THE CHOSEN ONE."
GOD Bless Little One!

*Regina K. Robuck*

## "Lonely Shore"

There is a rapture on the lonely shore,
There is society, where none intrudes
By the deep sea, and music in it's roar;
I love not man the less, but nature more
From these our interviews, in which I steal,
From all I may be, or have been before
To mingle with the universe and yet feel
What I can never express, yet cannot conceal.

*Martha Marcia Garcia*

## My Fathers

Before I was one year, my father left my mother.
There was just she and I, no sister or brother.
Her world was filled with pain, no longer wanting to be.
She struggled to go on, because she still had me.
I was her salvation, and reason to live.
Because of me, she was forced to give.
She gave me love, and took care of me.
Soon found my step-father, and now there was three.
Birth-father was gone, only one I had.
Mom remarried, and then I had a dad.
He loved me and raised me, I loved him so.
He was the only Father, that I did know.
I grew and got married, and children came too.
Wanting my birth-father, I was sometimes blue.
Deciding to look for him, my children were grown.
I was forty-six now, and birth-father unknown.
A day came I found him, was so very glad.
I now was blessed, with a father and a dad.
My life became happier, than dreamed it could be.
I found my Father above, and now I have three.

*Marsha Heiken*

## The Answer

One day a tiny Angel decided he would go, to seek out the Creator,
    there were things he wished to know

He stood before the God-light, he felt so meek and mild, then he heard
    a gentle voice say, what do you wish my child

Dear Father, said the tiny voice, I'd like to ask you why, there is
    such sorrow on the earth, such terror from the sky

Why did you send man sickness, pestilence and war, is this the
    only reason man was created for?

My child, the God-light answered, this was not within my plan,
    I created joy and happiness then I left it up to man

The world I see is peaceful with so much love to share, I breathed my
    life into man's soul but somehow he doesn't care

Man seems to have forgotten the secrets he was taught, he used his
    will, ignored my laws now he suffers what he's wrought

I created man in my image, his spirit is divine, why would I ever
    want to hurt this creation that is mine

One day, perhaps man will discover the wonder of his fate,
    he'll use the goodness in him before it is too late

Somehow he'll find the answers I've made so plain to see, then
    he'll use his will for happiness and find his way to me.

*Maryann Simmons*

## The Gates of Heaven

Close your eyes in a gentle sleep,
There you will find a sweet, sweet peace.
Awake and find that love surrounds,
Embraced by goodness and joy abounds.
Golden splendor and cherished ones,
All of wonder has just begun.
A river flowing, never still
Grace abounding as is His will.
I won't let go, we're just apart.
Forever in His presence, always in my heart.

*Patti Joan Weber*

## Masterpiece of Love

O, my love, my one true love,
There's no one else below or above.
I try to be as graceful as a dove,
But usually doesn't matter when

it's you I'm thinking of.

I see rose petals rippling in the wind,
While I think of flowers you'll never send.

As I imagine your beautiful,
brown eyes watching me by and by,
I want to cry,
Because I know I'll never
Have you and my tears will never dry.

*Rosanna Stewart*

## Being A Woman

Being a woman can be a pain,
There's so much to lose, yet so much to gain.

When you express your feelings, they call you aggressive,
Yet when you keep them within, they say you're submissive.

Some say that a woman should never make a first move,
They say you should sit back and wait for the man to come to you.

To some extend I think that's true.
Don't let that man know he's of interest to you,
Because, if he knows, it will gas up his head.
He'll turn around and will play you instead.

But then again they could be wrong.
You could lose that man if you wait too long.

He'll think, "Maybe I failed, but at least I tried."
And you're still left standing there, holding on to your pride.

Girlfriend, all I can say is watch your back.
Be sure who you're dealing with, and know how to act.

Because, being a woman is not an easy thing.
It takes some experience and a lot of maturing.

*Suzette Francis*

## Thank You

Thank you father, for being to me so gentle and kind
Your love is constantly on my mind.
Even tho times aren't quite fair,
Its a true comfort in knowing that you are there.
I've looked long and none can compare
To the special way, that only YOU can care.
So, to you I am so thankful, so humble, so true,
As I am waiting patiently, just for you.
My holy and almighty father, you are my heart and soul
And forever being with you,
Is my only goal.

*Pamela Scott*

## I'll Walk Alone

Ich liebe dich, tu amour
These words breeze by to whisper
I love you

I walk alone into the sunset
Watching the moon rise with the evening glow
Watching the stars bring forth their glitter
To fill each moment with thoughts
I love you

I walk through the woods listening to the calm
Ripple through the silence by the rustle of the leaves
Piercing my thoughts
'Til the barrier is broken, I'll walk alone

I walk along the beach
Hearing the riptides caressing the rocks
Feeling the sand beneath my feet
The roar of the breakers echoing my thoughts
'Til I'm with you

I'll walk alone 'til you're beside me
Ich liebe dich, tu amour
And into the sunset I'll walk alone.

*Tom T. Kumagai*

## Mothers

Though our mothers might not be here but in their heavenly home,
They are always close in heart no matter where we might roam.

Our childhood years are treasured because of their loving care,
And whenever we were sick their caring hands were there.

Mothers taught us to bless our food and at bedtime say a prayer,
And they read bedtime stories with a very special flair.

Mothers taught about right and wrong so we'd know how to be
And do our very best so we'd always be trustworthy.

Then when we grew up and married and had our families,
We probably raised our children very similarly.

And now that our children are grown and have their families too,
They are no doubt doing some things that we taught them to do.

Our mothers merit the accolades that we give to them,
And we truly believe each one deserves a diadem.

*Margaret Millington King*

## The Invisible People

The Invisible People,
They are people of the night,
Strong, Proud and Vehement.

The Invisible People,
Their hearts are made of gold,
August, Majestic and Genuine.

The Invisible People,
They are giants that once stood in holes,
Oppressed, Melancholy but Not discouraged.

The Invisible People,
They built this world and continue to hold it upon their shoulders,
Durable, Industrious and Assiduous.

The Invisible People,
They never cease to exist in this world.

*Rosalind Anita Brown*

## Young Girls

Young girls are so confusing to understand
They are so beautiful and naïve and insecure
They all plot and plan, to one day land a man
Which one, I know, they're unsure
Some think older is better
Some don't know any better
Young girls, are put on earth to humble fathers
They are a father's worst nightmare
They are a father's best dream
Sometimes they can make us feel like kings
Young girls make you love and hate
Young girls make you lie in bed late at night wide awake
Eyes staring at the dark ceiling
Unseeing, unheard, silently weeping
Long after they are out of sight
Young girls teach Fathers the meaning of true undying love

*Mack H. Wysinger Jr.*

## Media Taboo

Light strands bind Libra's hands.
They are the blood vessels of the curious
Cyclops who stares, remembers, and transmits.
Pleasure demons are trapped in your house
Behind a glass ceiling.
Hear them scream and wail.
It will make you laugh at those who cry.
The Cyclops shall only
make them shed more tears.
His power is immense.
He feeds on the Republic
for which he stands.
The juice flows into him,
But some may drip free.
Only the Cyclops can strange blind
Libra, only he could free the woman who
Cut off more than she could chew...
Could make Libra's eager fingers
Look foolish and foment riots...
Could let insanity defend itself.

*Mark D. Juszczak*

## What About Your Friends?

Why do your best friends want to leave you, when
they are the ones that really need you? They put
you down when your back's turned or you're not around.
When they're all up in your face you thinking that they
are a total disgrace. If you kick them out believe
me, don't get me wrong, they won't be gone for long...
   But then they could be a friend when you're
down and out; you try not to let them turn you
out. When you try to make it work, they don't
care how much it hurt. You really want to have
a friend to walk with hand in hand, you don't
care if it's a girl or boy, man or woman.
You don't care, you just want them there
in your corner, you want them to cheer you on
until the break of dawn... Sometimes you feel
you don't want them around and they'd rather not
be down or around with you; you ask them a
question — what's wrong, sadness, you thought you have
bring... What about your friends? Will they
stand around and let you down again!!!

*Tyrhonda Statam*

## My Guests

While they are in my house, they require my respect and attention.
They belong to another kingdom; they are beautiful and strange.
Strangest of all, from the Amazon, dark and fleshy, Displeased, shuts
   up glowering, baleful red.
Another a delicate lady, fragile and slim, wearing a gentle lavender,
   a gentle perfume.
One from the desert, big, tall, insolently striding, shouting with
   color under our tamer sum.
One straight out of heaven, white wings poised for an instant in love,
   and then gone.
One bringing peace.

*Marie I. McHenry*

## My Beautiful Grandmothers

Although my beautiful grandmothers have passed away,
They bring me a source of pleasure and happiness every day,
On top of my desk are the pictures of my grandmothers,
I have a chance every day to look at their beautiful smiles and faces,
Their capacity to love and be loved was so great,
I was so lucky and so fortunate to have them as caring friends,
They had the most compassionate loving hearts,
The strong love I had for my grandmothers will always
   remain in my heart and soul,
Forever through eternity I will take my love and respect for them,
I thank God every day for my wonderful grandmothers,
They were very, very special human being.

*Steven Schachter*

## Stan

The tinkling music of dream crystals fill the hall
They dance above and around
The regal T-rex skeleton
In life, rather small and aged,
in death
Awesome, overwhelming
a glimpse of antiquity
Beyond the mere mind of man
His roars linger faintly
Elusively
Surely if all the whispers of awe
Ceased
You could hear clearly.
Are his cries for his once planned mate
Now encapsulated in eventual decay?
Or cries of a captive freed from
The bondage of the ages?
Or a warning?
T-rex was also
Master of his world.

*Nina Siefken*

## Women Bitch

Women bitch - women complain
They say the snoring is driving them insane.

They moan - they groan
They wish their children grown.

All the while they have a home
With people who love them and no desire to roam.

They want their freedom - to do what?, I ask,
To be all alone with no one to care?

Women bitch - women complain
But I must say - I think them insane!

*Susan G. Grossholz*

## Mother Is A Forever Friend

My memories flow to yesteryear.
They flood my life today.
Of my "Ole fashion" mother,
A mother that is a forever friend.
A mother that made a house a home.
A smile lit her face;
Sending a glow into every place.
So gentle and kind—others always in mind.
I can hear her voice so clear,
As it echoes in my ear.
Many times I needed a hug,
Mother was there to offer without a shrug.
If I had a special joy to share,
She was always there.
Memories of yesteryear delight my heart,
Special memories that will never part.
They cannot be erased.
Nothing can take their place.
Mother is a forever friend.

*Mary E. Hale*

## Veil

Two turtle doves fly
They fly so high, but not in the sky
They hurt, but feel no pain
They do nothing wrong, but take no shame
They cry, but shed no tears
They are involved in danger, but have no fears
They fall, but never land
They have feathers, but feel like sand
Instantly they now fail
They leave nothing behind but a white veil
I have lost them, but did not cry
My call for them can not be denied
The veil continues to fly

*Wade Carlson*

## "Hawks"

The birds flying above apologizing, for
they had not known what they had done.
Circling in the sky trying to find their nest,
but only to find a cut down tree,
in which the nest had laid.

Only the two remain, male and female,
knowing they are the only two remaining,
who can revitalize their ancestry. Following,
wherever we go are humans with eyes like
the antennae of a butterfly, or a snout of an
elephant hoping to catch a glimpse of us.

A long life ahead of us only teens flying,
far far away to a place where the fish are
plentiful, and the wingless are few. My
mate, plummets to the ground offering
feathers to the human with the talon,
without a farewell.

Now the only one left, no one to learn my
language, no one to hear my stories. Only me
to lead a lonely life and to die a sad death because of humans.

*Travis Yarlagadda*

## Heaven's Realm

The mortal wounds embodied the landscape,
They lay limp and frail inconspicuous to each other,
Each a victim, a victim of life's holocaust,
Each being, lay, opened eyed and transfixed at the sun's radiance,
The holocaust that beared the earth's eternal destruction,
A destruction that only lead to life's black hole of death,
A hole that would repel every Gods gift of nature,
The holes hunger only grew devouring every immortal being,
Laying each embodied figure in a scattered row,
The wind blew frightfully vanishing the scars that had once been tarnished on each human.
Scars that would only represent the ordeal and scorn that each being would endure during its journey through life,
a perilous travel that would only result in the joys and swifts downfalls of the worlds duration,
Whether life's existence would end in one fatal blow or continue into immortal length,
Few would know the answer, but most would cross the gate into heaven's realm...

*Stephen Salyer*

## Ouch!

Scrapes and scratches, bumps and cuts.
They make you cry, and drive you nuts!
Blood and stitches are not much fun, and you
just can't wait until they're done.

Boo-boos make you say boo ho and that
is not all they do. They make you cry
and scream and fuss. If you cry in front of
friends - you'll blush.
Doctors make you feel much better if your
sick in any weather.
I have to go now - I think I'll skip,
ooops — watch out oh no - I tripped.

*Sara Baxter*

## My Answer To River Of Dreams

Today I got a letter, it was good news for me.
They really liked my poem, and published it will be.

I can't believe someone heard, the words said from my heart.
For I know not what I'll say with pen in hand I start.

Sometimes I talk to Mom, cause she's no longer here.
She always read my verses, and kept each one so dear.

She'd smile at silly things I wrote as if she really knew.
My private thoughts I told her, on paper as I did you.

Same there to my children, or my husband, who's my life.
Or to God, that I'll be worthy to be called Mom and wife.

But, only in my secret dreams I dared wish for immortality.
Now when my life is done, someone - will - remember me.

*Z. Louise Howard*

## Without A Cry

You came into this world all rosy, so small, without a cry
You departed this world the same, leaving us to seek the why.
You left behind a twin brother, a little larger and stronger,
And he senses your passing because you cuddle him no longer.
Oh, little granddaughter, so cute, maybe you understand why,
And will come to comfort us when we feel the need to cry.
An angel in God's heaven, loved by all who went before us,
And you wish we could accept the loss without all this fuss.
Maybe as time passes, we will know and can understand why
You came so quietly, loved us a while, then left without a cry.

*Susan E. Munstedt*

## Lindy

Although he's dead he still lives on,
They say he died in old Jack's arms,
But in my mind he still lives on,
He's not around you say — it's true,
But he's not dead I'll prove to you;

Oft' times I hear him at the door,
Or at the table coaxing more,
He was so sweet so glad to mind,
The very last one of his kind;

We played together when both were small,
I still have got our first play ball,
But — alas, all I have to throw to is the wall,
Cause he don't feel like playing ball,
So we just sit — don't chase at all;

At night I hear him at my bed,
And if our Ma is not around,
He jumps in happy as a clown;

And so to you he may be dead,
But that to me is foolish dread.

*Ward E. Toner*

## Silver Wings

The Indians called him "Silver Wings"; he came back every year
They smile when they remember when "Little Gray" first appeared

She was dainty and demure as she stood by Silver's side
That he was wild about her could never be denied

He ran hissing at the other ganders if they came near his "Little Gray"
With his silver wings outstretched he flapped and shooed them all away

He helped Gray with the nesting, gave the goslings tender care
They were never left alone, "Silver" or "Gray" were always there

In the northland it's hard to find the winter's feed
And the call of the wild goose is a call that they must heed

One day something happened, a sad and painful thing
A careless hunter's arrow broke "Gray's" dainty little wing

"You must go," Gray softly whispered, "the north wind is wildly blowing."
"Good-bye my love, I long to go with you where you are going."

He wrapped his wings around her, together they hovered on the ground
Beneath the melted snow of winter Silver and Gray were found

Man could learn a lesson from "Silver Wings," that faithful goose
If you ever find a true love, hang on and don't let loose!

*Mary Kay Milam*

## Images

When images appear in sleeping dreams;
They start and end with you.
A story of old, A thought to hold,
Starting and ending with you.

Old memories of long ago,
So blue and bitter-sweet;
You hollow my thoughts,
Like an empty cave, slowly I watch,
As you quickly fade.

Settle in new scenes of silver smoke,
Misty though you may be;
I look forward to adventure,
With soft melting love;
As in dreams it was meant to be.

I awaken with dawn, searching my thoughts;
To find they have all come true.
The life I dreamed, I shared;
Still starts and ends with you.

*Patricia Naomi F. Ulrich*

## Let's Ear It

My ears have heard well o'er the years,
They survived joy, heartbreak, thunder and tears.

Suddenly my left ear went on the blink,
It's very tired of what it hears, I think.

The left ear's silence is frustrating you'll agree,
Variable noises within it are heard only by me.

The doctor has drugged it and gassed it too,
Hopefully, but slowly, just maybe 'twill be like new.

I hear in my right ear just fairly well,
Perhaps I hear things I best not tell.

My world quickly changed, but I'm trying to cope,
With my balance gone, a cane gives support and hope.

Unsure of my future, whether years, months or days,
Friends and family will celebrate when I hear sound waves.

*Ruth M. Land*

## I Like Cats

I have two cats with passions of their own.
They test themselves and me to the limit,
And of patience I have little, almost none.
I try to catch each cat's attention,
But what each cat is thinking,
I wouldn't care to mention.
Waft is female, a duchess surely born.
Max has a pedigree that is his own.
She sits disdainfully to watch
When Max heads toward the door.
She knows it's too darned cold outside.
(He seldom knows the score!!)
And yet he's smart enough and curious like his species,
Investigating every new device from hairbrush to squeegees!
Waft takes her name tag off with license number, too,
By hooking paw through collar, making my life a zoo.
I wish for every time I've released her,
Someone would give me a dollar and I'd be a millionaire!
But if I must choose a faithful friend who never loses touch
I think I'd have to select a cat. They please me so much!

*Veda Steadman*

## Vaporized Time

Out from the dust in the ground came the form we call mankind
They walked
They talked
Like li'l flecks o' dust they covered the planet earth
So busy, busy, BUSY
From goal to goal
Progress fumbled
As past the future became

Into the dust does mankind go

*Timothy J. Duffy*

## They

Who are they;
they who have taken away our freedom;
they who have taken our lives.
They are so young
and yet so angry.
Their colors, caps
and signs tell us who they are and what they stand for.
Look the other way.
Don't make eye contact.
Are they truly heartless?
Are they truly to blame?
They are our children.

*Mary Menner*

## The World of My Meadows

A leitmotif haunted my dream.
  They will take away my world before I can live in it.
  I will lose its beam.

Be brave!  Life rolled on over bumps,
  when one didn't look or notice.
  Teeny tiny feet tiptoed when an eye was open.

Tears fell on the highland meadow, I ran after empty mysteries.
  My desire had spoken.

Memory caressed my thoughts and lingered with remembrance,
  entwined with langrous hope.

Sweet meadow, oh gossamer thought,
  squeeze my heart with tightened rope.

Behind my back change was a monster who gobbled
  up idealized thought
Beauty hid behind old visions that pervaded reason
  with ideas lazily sought.

No, never, Time did not steal, I was not robbed.
Life was lived not snatched, and
  I was a stranger to this world, it was too hard and edgy
  And I too charmed by Nostalgia.  I smile sweetly at the Past.
  *Theodora Kinder*


## A Few Of Life's Little Gifts...

There are lots of good things.  More, than it seems
They're right here, right now, not just in dreams
They're here to please you, to lighten your mood
But you do have to find them or they're gone for good

...Long winding roads and highways without end...
Cards from old friends and all the love they send
...The smell of roses, of grasses, of spring...
The path of rainbows and all the joys they bring

...Long talks over coffee, conversations 'til morn...
Reflections on water, and the silence of dawn
...Hotels and showers and long drives and mist...
Dim lights and glass walls, love affairs and bliss

...Fireworks and mornings and silhouettes and smiles...
Whispers and darkness and champagnes and choirs
...The smell of winter, and the romance in June...
They're few of life's gifts which are always gone too soon
  *Marietta A. Javier*


## We Are Family

Get to know me, grow to love me.  We have one
thing in common that we share.  We are family don't you care.
Family should be like a marriage.
We should be together in sickness and in health
in poorness and in wealth.
We should not be surprised when our loved ones become ill,
we should be close so we know how we feel.
I need to know about your life and you about mine -
we should sit down and chat from time to time,
things we've disagreed upon leave them behind.
When we see each other we should not criticize.
Tell me how much you love me and you're glad I'm alive!
I'll be there for you and you for me, so when things
happen unexpectedly our conscience will be free.
Death is something we all must face.
Life is too short, we have no time to waste.
We are all here by God's good grace.
Wear this world as a loose garment and lean on your faith.
I love you and you and you, I'm telling you today so you'll
know I feel that way.... TOMORROW IS NOT PROMISED!!!!
  *Monique Sherylle LaGarde-Taylor*


## Untitled

Thoughts drift back to days gone by.
Think of lost friends and want to cry.
Drifting further my thoughts start to raise.
Memories lock on to better days.
Smiles and laughter run around my head.
Thinking of things that were said.
We will live forever and never part.
Now I can only remember with my heart.
As God as my witness I say again.
I wait for the day to once again see my friend.
  *Robert Pich*


## Just Thinking

Dying is an alone thing.
Thinking of dying too, has a lonely ring.
If we try to be pragmatic and efficient,
Someone points out deeds undone, plans deficient.
So do what needs to be done.
They mourn and grieve and try to run from tears,
Sad ending, and yet want to achieve
The calm that lasts.
Memories held fast
In corners of their mind,
And brought out
When they must find
Reasons for what happened long ago,
Remember that to go from one dimensions to another,
Requires no long goodbyes.
A treasured memory is the key, and the sadness need not stay
It only lingers on the air as perfume along the way.
  *Norma V. Yandell*


## Mother of Mine

Again I endure a sleepless night,
Thinking of things I've done wrong and right,
If only I could go back in time.
To hear her recite a nursery rhyme.

As I sit on her lap in the rocking chair,
There are happy memories, no one can share,
Just a couple of hugs, and a kiss on the cheek,
Were enough to insure a good night's sleep.

Those days of reassurance are all but through,
Just as each day of Spring brings morning dew,
The flowers with all their petals in bloom.
Are only followed by darkness and gloom.

So here I am as the years take their toll,
Praying that I've been a worthwhile soul,
Getting ready to cross the unforeseeable line,
To again feel the peace with this mother of mine.
  *Laurie Dey*


## In Touch

This is my life, let me live it.
This is my life, can you feel it?
If you have touched it, then I owe it
Not to myself alone.

We crossed paths down life's highway of time.
Your life and my life have intertwined.
This is my life.  Let me live it?
No, I must make atone.
My life was given for me to give.
All the best that you may live.
I love my life.
I love you.
My life not mine alone.
  *Peggy Major*

## Alone

As I stood there, staring into space,
thinking of what was and could have
been, I had mixed emotions. My life
flashed before my eyes. All that happened...the pain
was there, but the happiness was hidden,
deep in the corners of my twisted mind,
to far away to recall. It was all a bad
nightmare. I felt the cold metal in my
hand, remembering what it symbolized.
The fear...the horror...nobody cared. And
neither did I. I lifted the gun to my head. All
time stood still. It was just me, the gun and my
memories....I didn't care anymore. My
finger found the trigger and pulled hard.
Bright lights flew at me, forcing me down...
And now I lie in a pool of my own
selfish blood...just me...truly alone...
I don't care anymore...I don't have to.

*Sarah Rhodes*

## Come Home My Children, Come Home

Running away from a family that don't understand,
Thinking that you know the way to the Promise Land.
Fifteen years old with nowhere to go,
    Come home my children, come home.

Promises of a new life out there,
The world's full of problems, enough to share.
Where will you sleep and who will care?
    Come home my children, come home.

Beware of Kings bearing gifts.
Cocaine's out there for you to sniff.
Be careful or you'll wind up stiff
    Come home my children, come home.

You're not grown up, it's not your time,
They'll take your body, your soul, your mind.
And what of those people you leave behind,
    Come home my children, come home.

Believe in yourself and we will, too.
Believe in yourself the way we do.
Too little to gain, too much to lose,
    Come home my children, come home.

*Tanya Dashiell*

## The Death of a Child

Tender darling loving and sweet
This child playing at her mothers feet
Young and growing with eyes open wide.
To understand the complexity of the world outside
Laughter and tears comes as if one
To the new eyes of a child as they
reach for the sun.
The sparkling admiration of a proud
father be as he watched his child
grow as the trees.
Then one nite as the star are at rest
The softy and comfort of the family is
oddly at test shattered by silence
panic has come deaths cold hand
has blackened the sun
How do I tell a mother we did
all we can we just couldn't lift
that cold ugly hand
tender darling, loving and sweet
your laid to rest at your mothers feet.

*Steven R. Bartz*

## Drugs and Love

Drugs and love don't make a good match;
    this, I know for a fact.
Drugs and love are a bad combination;
    they will make you lose all communication.
They will make you forget that you have a life;
    they will cause you to leave your husband or wife.
They will turn your life upside-down;
    they will turn your smiles into frowns.
Drugs and love do not mix;
    you'll do anything for a fix.
They will blow your mind and make you a whack;
    these are all results of that drug called crack.
Drugs will take away your love and affection;
    they cause you to rehab for correction.
You don't have to be a user to be abused by this;
    they affect the victims of the one who uses it.
Whatever you do, wherever you go;
    to drugs, please say no!

*Mary K. Cochran*

## Finis

This is a poem for all the poems I won't have time to compose.
This is a poem for all the dreams I'll not be able to fulfill.
This is a poem for all the good and evil that exists within us.
This is a poem for all the love I've given and received.
This is a poem for the beauty of nature.
This is a poem for evil people that love could set right again.
This is a poem for all the sick, poor, homeless, and oppressed.
This is a poem for the woman I love.
This is a poem for those I don't understand, and vice versa.
This is a poem for all the friends and relatives that have passed
    away.
This is a poem for all the brothers and sisters I have.
This is a poem for all the good times as well as all the bad times.
This is a poem for you alone as well as the whole world.
This is a poem of life and death, this and that, yin and yang.
This is a poem that tells how we all sort a feel.
This is a poem for loneliness and pain, happiness and joy.
This is a poem for kings and peasants alike.
This is a poem about questioning and accepting.
This is a poem with no rhyme but reason.
This is a poem of what the eyes perceive and the heart senses.

*Roger B. Goldman*

## Frans Hals: Portrait of a Young Man:

## The Great Paintings

Blond, moustached, German, paint not tissue or blood
this is all that remains of him,
to the artist, this is all this young man was.

And the paint, the paint, lasts the aeons,
though the subject who sat is long since only ashes and bones.
The portrait is more alive, real, than that darker tone.

Like portraits by Rembrandt, Titian, Watteau,
art is constant, faithful, unchanging through time's changing flow.
With care, their images, in paint, retain their golden glow.

And retain the fascination of the faithful,
Who pass by them in museums, eyed by watchful guards.
Life is beautiful in life's season, but death, its end, is always
hard.

Still the paint and its beauty lingers in time, beyond time,
in an enduring season, in an unending prime,
in which the mortal becomes immortal, both human and sublime.

To the ignorant and unjust they are nothing as life is nothing.
Still, they endure as beacons in their fragile shade,
images of the human spirit, filled with light, and slow to fade.

*L. E. Ward*

## "Soldier's Song"

Hi, Mom; hi, Dad
This is me - your son.
I'm hurt, Dad.
No, don't cry, Mom.
Remember when I enlisted
in this thing they call the army?
I promised I'd come home safe...
and I'm hurt.
But then again
I'm not home yet.
I got hit with a bomb, Dad...in the leg.
No, Mom, it doesn't hurt much.
How could it now, when there isn't much left?
Yeah, Dad.
They're sending me home.
Hey, Mom...
Remember when I was little
And you told me that everyone was God's child?
Then, why do we fight the way we do?
Why do we fight in this infernal-like place?

*Susan De Vantier*

## "Dearest Dreams"

Sitting and overlooking the lake mirrored in falls splendor,
This is one of the things in which my dearest dreams are rendered.

The crisp wind blowing across my face,
My body in a warm quilt's embrace,
As look upon my children's faces, so happy and so tender.
These are some of the things in which my dearest dreams are rendered.

I sit here and I ponder how some people have to wander,
Always searching, ever grasping, for that big brass gleaming ring.
Never realizing their treasures were their family's not their things.

Some day, They'll say, "Where did time go?"
Did you notice our children are all grown?"
As they sit together most quietly
on their great financial thrones.

My husband puts his warm hand in mine and we both contentedly smile.
Our children playing happily amidst the falls great splendor,
These will be the memory's in which
Our dearest dreams are rendered.

*Mary C. Geertsema*

## After He's Gone

This is the sound of his absence, silence...
This is the size of the hurt, immense...
An indentation on his pillow
shadows a ghostly remembrance.
His scent is carelessly laundered away.
Each day's grief an accumulated burden...
Does anyone care?
My mind plays tricks...
Leaping sequences to illuminate
memories lost.
Birdsong trills me awake each dawn...
Flowers frame my window...
Roses redolent of summer
fragile receptacles of dew.
Swallows dart above new-mown hay and
The breeze ruffles hair from my face
Drying salt tears from my cheeks...
Beauty and solitude embrace my senses
while the utter peace splinters my soul.

*Sonia Lowis*

## May All, Dear God, Obey Your Law

"May all, dear God, obey your law."
This light where am I? That baby?
Who are you? What happened that boy?
I'm God - your end for serving me,
if well, in life - eternal joy.

How could I serve you well in life?
I gave to you intelligence
to learn and know the laws in strife
of nature and moral events.

The laws of nature? No comments!
Morality? Is that a song?
It's keeping all my commandments
through conscience telling right from wrong.

You're telling me the wrong and right?
I'm no stringed puppet - I will choose.
That's right - I gave free will to fight
to win heaven's reward - not lose!

You lost by stopping your unborn.
It is my body for my use.
Is it from her that I was torn?
Yes, but she'll pay for her abuse!

*Vincent Healy*

## If I Had Someone To Love Me

If I had someone to love me
This way would I be

Myself and Adam are alike
Both along with beauty in sight

I ask myself, "What shall I do?"
"Easing the pain is up to you"

Searching for her so she would hear
"You posses the remedy for the cure"

Damn! What shall I do?
This is so true

Knowing that it is only one remedy
Her love would be plenty

Without it, I'm a sure slave to loneliness
How can a man give so much power to a goddess

If I had someone to love me
Then let it be that this is a free man to be

Oh boy, I must not give up
If I want out of this rut

*Ronald J. Hill*

## My Thanks To God

My prayers have all been answered love...
Those prayers I said to God above... At least
the most important part... You want my love
within your heart... I've seen our love both
come an go... But our love will last, this
I know... It's good and strong, it's pure, not
wrong... It's built on all the smallest cares,
all our dreams, or hopes, our fears... We've
shared them all, but a few... This my love I
leaves for you... To find, to love, to keep
within... For my Darling, it'll be no sin...
He's nourished our love since it wa born...
We'll make it grow, this we've sworn... For
no one can destroy our love... For we have
faith in God Above...

*Rosemarie J. Rotonda*

## The Pine Tree

Oh what a magnificent sight it is to see,
This wonderful things we call a pine tree.

It starts at the ground and stretches high towards the sky,
And during its life watches many things parade by.

The deer, the turkey, the quail and bee,
All stop, then look and take note of the great tree.

And to the wood land creatures this tree will surrender,
Its seeds, shade, limbs and magnificent splendor.

So when the times comes for this mighty tree,
To share its bounty with you and me.

Please do not look at it as a crime, or a terrible thing
done by mankind. For in the end the tree must fall,
If any of its offspring are to survive at all.

For without the sunlight an extra space,
The smaller seedlings would die without a trace.

And the little seedling at its feet,
Would grow up short, spindly, and weak.

In the end the old tree gladly pays the supreme price,
For unto its off spring it has given life. And when you ponder the
life of the tree, it is not much different from you and me.

*R. Travis Shepherd*

## A Warm Spring Day

It is a warm spring day, the trees are in bloom, and my
thoughts are turned to you. I remember the times we shared
together walking under the moon.

You taught me so many things in my life, how to live, laugh and
love, and then on a sad cold winter day you were gone like a
beautiful dove.

Your memory lives on in my life each day of the wonderful times
we shared, and as the desert breeze blows I understand how much
you really cared.

You were not only my Grandma but also my friend so on this
warm spring day, as you look down from the heavens above there
is one thing I want to say.
  GRANDMA YOU HAVE MY LOVE!

*Tammy Morrissey*

## My Home

  I sit here in this room eight by ten,
thoughts on my mind of way back when.
  I look out my window, as far as I can see,
and wonder, how "God" could have let this happen to me.
  I know its not his fault,
I sit here in this room.
  It's the things in my past,
that caused me this doom.
  I miss the sound of the wind blowing threw the trees.
But all I hear now, is steal doors, under lock and keys.
  The people are here, for things they have done.
They have destroyed their lives, and taken away their fun.
  Their hearts filled with hate, is all you see.
But their people, just like you and me.
  Well if you know not of this place I talk of,
that sounds so grimsom.
  It's my home, they call it prison.

*Mark S. Johnson*

## Paths Of Sin

In tapestries of pain
threads of destiny asphyxiate.
Roads woven through barren abyss
and paths chosen by blinded fate.

Cackling of the Devil's whore,
lingering howls of the hounds.
What souls dance in the macabre halls,
What innocence lost in the playing grounds?

*Laljit Sidhu*

## Retirement

Today, I placed all the memories and debris of twenty-six years into
Three cardboard boxes and two shopping bags.

This was not a day for contemplating of past regrets or future
  opportunities.
It was time set aside for packing and repacking,
And I took my best friend along, since she's a much better packer than
  me.
It's nearly impossible, you know, to fit all that needless accumulation
  into
Three cardboard boxes and two shopping bags.

I completed the final papers, turned in my key, and loaded the car.
Now I'm at home; the car, packed full to the brim, in the driveway.
We amuse ourselves watching television, playing cards, munching chips,
And doing anything we can imagine rather than think about those
Three cardboard boxes and two shopping bags.

Still it's difficult to focus on our games, and our gaiety is forced.
No matter how I try, I'm not fooling anyone tonight.
Even my dog is sleeping a little away from me, not right at my feet.
It's as if she knows that part of me is still in that car, tucked into
Three cardboard boxes and two shopping bags.

*Shirley A. Barnes*

## Gramma's Glasses

You've seen true love,
Through gramma's glasses.
You've seen your children grow,
Through gramma's glasses.
You've seen times change,
Through gramma's glasses.
You've seen people rearrange.
Through gramma's glasses.
You've seen many seasons,
Through gramma's glasses.
You've seen your grandchildren born,
Through gramma's glasses.
You've seen many holidays,
Through gramma's glasses.

Well gramma it's time for us to say goodbye.
But we know that you'll live on in the our hearts forever.
There won't be a day that goes by that we won't think of you
When we lift our eyes to the sky
  Goodbye

*Terra Ralston*

## Two Windows

One window looks out on my backyard
Where I love to watch these children play.
The front one reveals friends and neighbors
Sharing pieces of life from their day.
But two lovely windows together
Show me scenes of what's blessed and whole,
For they are young eyes
And in them I can see
The wisdom and love in your soul.

*Rudy Hawkins*

## What Is Love

Love is a candle that burns bright,
Through out day through out night,
Shining, flickering and always feels right.

No this isn't true, love is a painting,
A masterpiece a portrait of you.
With lines, and shadows,
It's true, a perfect portrait, a portrait of you.

But again I'm wrong, love it is strong,
Not from the body, but from the mind,
Love is gentle, love is kind, and it's beautiful,
But always must come from the mind.

Once again I am wrong, but still I am right,
Love is a candle that burns day and night.
It is a picture, a portrait or two,
It's from the mind and the heart.  This is true.

Love is different between me and you.
My love is all these, a candle that burns,
A mind that learns, a portrait or two,
All these together, equal my love,
And my love is you.

*Lee Cavicchi*


## Stampede Oh Children Of Innocence Young

Stampede, stampede oh children of innocence young,
Through the grass of dew and green newly sprung.

Capture these times and store them away,
Deep in your heart, for tomorrow a new day.

Trace those footsteps back, back to the youth,
Of childlike mercy, and of kindness to divine truth.

But continue to run, run with full hearts content,
Keeping the pace steady, fearing tomorrow's lament.

As we slowly grow older, striving, yearning for the younger,
Stampeding, stampeding for the youth we still hunger.

*Paul Ernest*


## Richard

Seeming without effort, you soar like an eagle, slicing through the heavens.  As you dance with the clouds, you sprinkle the earth below with angel dust, bringing love and warmth.

And though you have traveled many paths, and worn many faces, our hearts have touched, and the tendrils run deep, like a mighty oak's searching roots.

You carry the sword of truth, the power within.  You are the lion and the lamb.  Like a wave, powerful, crashing , shaping the sands, yet soothing, gently caressing, as it slides back to sea.

You bring the mirrors that light the path.  And though the dragon lurks near, you are never alone.  For you are loved, for now, and always.

*Leslie Ann Rous*


## If Forever See the Rainbow

If forever see the rainbow
you've got to stand a little rain
for every love and friendship has to have a little pain.

Every love starts with blue skies
but those blue skies sometimes turn gray and it's then that I hope
it's not hard for you stay, but when those gray skies again turn blue.
If your still here I'll know you love me true.

*Paulette Cain*


## "The Smallest Light"

It matters not how dark it might be;
Through this, life's stormy sea—
If we could but grasp, within our sight,
Just a glimpse of the smallest light.

It matters not the gloom and despair,
If someone would only care,
To help us reach a higher height;
With a glimpse of the smallest light.

It matters not, though sickness came;
What hope and what health, we would regain,
With a glimpse of the smallest light.

It matters not though all alone;
And no one to call our very own,
Life would seem bright if we could grasp sight,
Of a glimpse of the smallest light.

What darkness would flee,
If we could but be,
That light within the night.

*Madelyn Yanchyshyn*


## Life's Plans

Aging is a mystery to me,
Time and years, go by fast and free,
I thank God for my (85) years,
With courage and prayers, I have no fears.

God is great, God is good,
And my great family, by me, stood;
They were their in joy and sorrow,
I thought then, there is always tomorrow.

Life to all of us, has it's ups and downs,
We meet tomorrow, doing our rounds,
So be happy and thank Him for it all,
Live life to the fullest, have a ball.

Gods plans in our life is a mystery too,
But live your life, and see it through;
The crosses you bear, are heavy and light;
Hope and courage, will make it alright.

Nobody knows their destiny
Only Gods plans, we will foresee;
So stay happy, don't be sad;
Think it over, life's not bad.

*Theresa Donnelly*


## Time Approaches

Time Approaches:
Time for Love, Joy, Happiness, and Cheer.
A new Life awaits in line,
Where I am Yours and You are Mine.
This new Life begins now and here.

Weeks away,
But quickly they dwindle, swiftly they surpass.
Our Wedding Bells begin to chime;
Our Hearts beat together in rhythm and rhyme;
Our Love and Marriage will Forever last.

Moments Pass.
I sit alone and Wonder what our Future holds,
What valleys and peaks we will climb and endure.
We will conquer them all Together for sure,
And we shall follow the path that for Us God molds.

Time Approaches:
Time for Smiles, Hugs, Kisses, and Laughter.
The nervous feelings will soon leave our Souls,
Leaving Pure Happiness, which onward rolls.
I LOVE YOU, MY BRIDE, and I shall Forever After!

*Raymond S. Bureau*

## Time for Everything

Our activities have certain allotted time.
Time for play,
Time for what we have to say,
Keep on schedule and all will be fine.

There is a time for prayer.
Most people only hear it at church
Or bedtime for others who care.
Then don't forget the thanks for food.

There are prayers that come from the heart.
Some are memorized,
Some are long,
And some are short.

A small boy, age two and one half
Attended church with his mother one sunday.
Brother Smith was called on to lead prayer.
The mother was watching the time.
After fifteen minutes the son stood up in the seat,
Saying very loud, "I believe it's time to say Amen."
This was the writer's great grandson, Chase.

*Vaudaline Thomas*

## "Mianus Gorge"

The Gorge in spring wildflowers bloom,
'Tis here a woodland orchid looms,
The trillium and the blood root, too,
You'll find them here as spring breaks through.

Mianus River runs nearby
Trout rising to a hatch of flies.
Along the river bank one finds,
Some willow brush and hemlock pines.

'Tis memories here of days gone by,
use no "Orvis" rod nor a sacred fly.
A willow stick is what it be
'Twas worms, some hooks and a line for me.

In mornings I sit by this wooded stream
to listen, relax and enjoy the scene.
White water starts not far down the glen
It sends back its echo now and then.

Mianus Gorge and its cathedral pines
What a Godly place to spend some time.
Hark!  In the evening one can hear,
A flute like song, 'tis the thrush that's near.

*Walter R. Bell*

## My Best Friend

My best friend's name used to be cocaine
To admit that now I am full of shame
My best friend used to help me to escape
If someone had recorded us, they would've had a great comedy tape
My best friend was always there when I needed her
But now all those times are just a blur
My best friend was slowly killing me
And this I was too blind to see
My best friend was actually satan in disguise
I thank God for finally making me realize
My best friend now comes from within me
For cocaine and I were never really meant to be.....

*Patricia Russo*

## Icarus' Descent

What wings of ancient plumage
To ambitious Icarus' descent
May I borrow for an hour's usage
For brief freedom in my soul's ascent?

Give to me mother a just recompense
For sorrow's unjustly rendered
Upon a child's waking innocence
To adult mayhem I resolutely surrendered

Your evasive shadow darkened the hearth
Who awaited the gingerbread man
In his wake two bittersweet morsels on earth
Were left in the rain like grains of sand

*D. M. Heffernan*

## Color Makes No Difference

A color is a nice thing to be but you have to like your color
to be one, like, Black, white light skinned and dark skinned and
you have each others color to, because if you didn't like a color
of your friend you will no have a friend at all so remember color
makes a different this is from a 10 years old girl that is in 4th
grade and her name is Shakese Monta Williams.

*Shakee Williams*

## Did You Ever Wonder?

Did you ever wonder, what it would have been worth?
To be that guardian angel who told of Jesus birth.
One sent to spread the good news all over this great earth.
Can you just imagine what a privilege it became,
To be the first one ever to say His holy name!
Did you ever wonder?
Will we ever be worthy of such an important task?
Can we ever be an angel?
Why should we even ask?
Did you ever wonder?
What this world would be today, if Jesus had not been born.
And the angel had no say.
Did you ever wonder?
Living without his love,
Sent to us each day from his angels up above.
Guiding our footsteps day after day,
Reminding us daily our need to pray.
Did you ever wonder?
What such an important part, the angel plays in each our lives,
Right from its very start.  Did you ever wonder?

*Mary E. Barnhart*

## Crimson

God is a God of brightness, therefore the God of light.
To brighten the dark days of winter, he sends the snow so white.
He is the master artist, with a full color scheme.
He can lighten life's darkest days, with a color that will gleam.

White speaks of purity, that descends from heaven above.
Offered to those who trust Him, from his heart of love.
Some days are filled with darkness, that cause us to feel sad.
Then there's the golden sunlit days, just to make us glad.

There are the brownish days of fall, when so many things turn brown.
But there is the rainbow colored springtime, to turn it all around.
Now, we all have our favorite color, that we like the best.
And we are quick to choose it, from among all the rest.

But there is one color above them all, it is the crimson red.
It represents the blood of the son of God, that on the cross was shed.
Yet Jesus Christ shed His life's blood, while hanging on the cross.
That from that day unto the end of time, no soul need be lost.

*H. Fitzgerald Durbin*

## The Dealer

Who are you anyway, LIFE
to deal ME a hand of pain?
I refuse it! I won't play!
Re-deal hand that is sane!

It is just not fair, I say to you LIFE!
Don't try and make ME understand,
How you can deal others royal flushes,
Then deal me a losing hand!

What did I do? Why me? Why me?
How did you choose your mark?
Was it done with a lot of deliberation
Or, was I a shot in the dark?

And since I may have been this shot in the dark
What makes you think I will play
This hand that is so fraught with troubles
Losing every step of the way?

Later on I think: "What exactly is fair?
And, who decides anyway?
You, LIFE, must deal the cards you have,
And I have no other choice but to play.

*Mary Ann Bryant*

## Awaken

He's here: It's time,
To expand upon my state of mind.
To open my eyes,
To sacred lies;
To see just what I'll find,
out alone,
At the edge of time:
Out across the final line.
Beyond the land of my fathers pride,
On through the land where the Goddess died:
To the secret place deep inside,
To the only place I can go to hide.

burning colours touch my soul,
filling my mind with visions of old:
And this essence of love which fills the air,
eases the heart: And lifts despair.

*Sean Stephan Sullivan*

## Amazing Cats

I walk down the narrow alley
to find what always ceased to amaze me.
I walk to the garbage can
I walk to the box across the way
I walked till I found what I was looking for
I lifted up the newspaper
And there to my amazement were seven more!
And then it looked up to me as if to say,
Have you come to care for me and my young?

*Lisa Raywood*

## Parents

Parents are our guiding light
They see us through the darkest night
When we need them they are always around
They pick us up when we fall down
Sometimes we don't listen to what they say
But it's for us that they hope and pray
When we leave, and are fully grown
It's our parents' house that we call home

*Russell McFarland*

## A Mother's Wish

If I had one wish for my daughters, what would it be?
To have them grow up and be able to see.
What the world has in store for them, for the rest of their days,
And even longer than that-it would be for always.

Being a good person inside is all I could ask,
Raising children these days is a very tedious task.
Living life to the fullest, their way always seemed right,
I don't always understand, try as I might.

After we're gone, grand babies will remember-doing their part,
To live up to the memory of their Mom straight from the heart.
So if I had one wish for my daughters, here's what it would be,
To be able to live in a world...happy, healthy, loved, and free.

*Terry A. Cook*

## Take A Moment, Hear What I Have To Say

I truly don't mean you any harm, if you would only take a moment
to hear what I have to say
What I utter sounds meaningless to you, but sounds eloquent to me
What I wear appears atrocious to you, but is complete for me
I truly don't mean you any harm, please come down and listen
My words sound ludicrous to you, but constitutional to me
The foul odor that offends you, which comes from my poorly erect
body, lets me know that I am alive
The waste I consume may appear rotten to you, but is most appropriate
and delectable for me
I don't mean you any harm, if you would only take a moment listen
The glare you see in my eyes as I stare at you, it is just the dazzle
in my eyes
My walk appears sluggish to you, but is the affliction I suffer
I truly don't mean you any harm, if only you would take a moment,
come down from your perfect world and hear what I have to say.
The way I live may seem impossible for you, but was just an
unfortunate turn in life for me. Yes, the way I live is dreadful to
you, but is survival for me.

*Tanya Mason*

## Even The Least Of These

Hark! Hark! The dogs do bark
To let all know you're there;
That's why the Animal Shelter
Is miles from anywhere!

Folks bring in moose, sometimes a goose,
Some pony that's gone astray.
A box wiggles with ferrets, kittens and parrots,
They stream in night and day.

We hope all have a license,
Guaranteeing a free call home;
So their owners will come to claim them,
And take these critters home!

Can you imagine the surprise—
We'd likely drop our cup—
What if a pet called to the Shelter,
To learn if it's person had been picked up!

*Maria Bryson*

## Why

Why am I here; why oh why
To learn how to cry, to look up and see the sky
Or maybe to feel what it's like to fly, so high; sigh
Yes, that must be it; now I can stop crying....
I'll start flying
Well, at least I'll start trying
But wait, what's that you say; I'm dying
But I've just begun to fly, to fly, to fly, to fly..........to fly
Oh..........Why

*Stephen Michael McCoy*

## Just Me

I try to live my life each day.
To let God's light shine through,
To show that I'm a child of God.
And I love you and you.
For God is love, if we show love,
In every thing, we do.
We shine his light, through day and night.
And hope to make a path for you.
And if you walk the path I walk,
You too with God will talk.

You'll feel his spirit in your soul.
And know that God has made you whole.
Someday we'll meet Him face to face.
And hear him say "come take your place.
That I've prepared for all the blest.
Come enter into perfect rest.

*Mary K. Clendenen Shumate*

## It's Up To You

It's up to you.
To live in peace and harmony.
At one with God and man.
In the land of the living.

It's up to you,
To run guns, drugs or revel in riotous living.
But this remember:
Those who live by the sword, die by the sword.

It's up to you
To make or not to make babies,
How many and at what age,
But if poverty like smoke envelopes you; blame no one.

It's up to you,
To rise up, step up and succeed against all odds
Or stumble at the familiar pit,
And swell the ranks of the condemned.

No matter your choice,
This society will move on
With or without you.
It's in your hands.

*Oladimeji Olakunle*

## The Meaning Of Life

So how hard is it to play the game of life,
To live through all its suffering and strife,
To clear its obstacles and cross its streams,
To reach its goals, the realization of your dreams.

So is life just a novel of failure and success
Consisting of winners and losers, satisfaction and distress?
Whatever happened to the simple pleasures?
Those most basic elements which we all treasure.

There is nothing more special than a picturesque sunrise,
Or reeling in a fish, no matter what the size.
And who can forget his very first kiss
Those feelings of butterflies combined with bliss.

People may think everyday is the same
When they are seeking only wealth, fortune and fame,
But the one who watches the eagles soar
His experience of life will never be poor.

If we just slow down as we run through the fields
Only then will we see what life truly yields,
And as the poppy seeds fly and the words tries to cope
We should all stop and smell the flowers of hope

*Paul Fadil*

## Untitled

In such a short time we have grown so close,
to love as one, eternally

Days filled with pleasure, nights of passion and romance
will forever be cherished

My heart yearned to be loved by someone like you,
now all my dreams have come true

Childhood fantasies of the perfect guy, only to be tromped out
by abuse, until the day I met you,
when every fantasy came true

Daydreams of things to come, a family filled with love,
our future, when we are one...

A perfect life we will lead, holding on, eternally
all of our hopes will come true, if we believe in us

Our passions will burn strong, like the flame of an everlasting
candle, until the time is right,
and we, as one, move on....

*Melissa Robinson*

## America

When I came to America, I had me a plan
to make me some money and live like a man

Here in America, the land of milk and honey
is where I had planned to make me some money

They said that America, had wealth untold
but there is so many people, on the welfare roll

Jobs were limited, so many people unemployed
computers were taking over and our dreams were destroyed

Why is there so many people, out of work?
Crime rates were so high and so many people are hurt

It seems my dream, was all a fantasy
I'm hungry for work and food, and that's a reality

They criticize communism and how bad it is
but a least in China, a poor man can live

I, thought that America, was the land of the free
but the lack of employment, had made a slave out of me

Back in the old country, we weren't very rich
and we didn't have to deal with, second hand politics

Now my plans are to return back home
until politicians in America, can correct their wrongs.

*LaDon Hall*

## My Valentine Prince

My valentine prince brings me elegant redolent flowers
to my door in the morning and sends seductive long
stem bouquets of red roses at school.
He calls me up to say he loves me and can't wait to
see me.
When his handsome brown eyes looked into mine I fell
under a spell and his well-made arms protect me as
he embraces me.
As his smooth lips touch mine I fall deeper into his
charm.
The day is almost diminished and we say our last goodbyes
and depart.
Our day of love might be gone but we will remember it
forever.

*Rosie Bradford*

## Maine

My heart yearns to return home
to oceans of blue and coastlines of rock,
to pine trees so green and winters so cold.
Sandy beaches with sea gulls singing and soaring in the air.
Starfish and crabs, blueberries and forest glades.
The roots of my beginning..........home.
Peace, serenity...
Waves crashing upon rocky coastlines
thunderous and majestic
calming and soothing.

*Laurel L. Shafer*

## A Lonely Man

My name is Sam, the lonely man

Each night I visit the bars
To pass the lonely hours

I'm gaining lots and lots of pounds
From drinking all those rounds

My name is Sam, the lonely man

All my clothes are so tight
My waist is an awesome sight

I can't dance too close
From drinking to so many toasts

My name is Sam, the lonely man

I walk my dog down the street
To see perhaps, any gal I can treat,

But they turn and walk away
Therefore, I have another discouraging day!

I would even kiss their lovely hands
But of course, they have other plans!

My name is Sam, the lonely man.

*Paul Beier*

## Only Me

Here I am inside of Mom crying to be free.
To run, to jump, to laugh and play how happy I will be!
Here I come into the world so stop and look at me.
Now my life has just begun to grow and learn you see.

Look at me Mom, I'm ten today and happy still am I,
But little do I know that someday I must die.
I want to live forever and never say good-bye,
But people have to go someday, come and tell me why.

I'm twenty one and going strong legal as can be.
I know the answer why we die, so come and learn from me.
God gives each one a life to live to do the best you see,
To do the purpose he has given to make him proud of me.

Half my life has gone away, how fast it passes by.
I still have time to do my deed before I say good-bye.
I want to live forever but can't and you know why.
But, I'll take the time that I have left to do my deed and die.

I've lived my life it's time to go. I'm happy as can be.
A tiny baby's born today to take the place of me.
I want to see the Lord thy God and make him proud of me,
Before I sleep and say good-bye please remember me.

*Rebecca Stickle*

## Ape or Adam

I went to the zoo today
to see if Darwin was right;
The story of Adam and Eve
kept me tossing in bed all night.

Darwin, Schmarwin, H. G. Wells;
Homo sapiens, chimps, anthropoidea,
N'anderthal, Schmanderthal, Ark or ape,
fact or fiction, myth, or idea?
Anthropology, evolution,
Garden of Eden, Darwinism?
Confoundment, confusion, convolution—
my brain's in a turmoil with each new schism.

The chimp I was watching and gen'rously feeding,
gathered his gifts of peanuts with glee.
He tossed them back from his cage, and I swear
he said he's descended from me.

*Victoria Hanson*

## Be Proud

If you should feel a moments shame,
To see your people walk in chains.
Forget, be proud.

When they recall the brave or bold,
Remember those that did their toil.
Be proud.

Be proud of those that nursed, that cared,
That sowed and plowed; made art and prayers.
Don't be misled, the quiet bit you see,
Were lives that shaped our destiny.
Be proud.

And in their name, those kind and mild,
Turn now and aid the buyer's child.
His memories are rotted, maimed,
Remembering his people's shame.

*Sue Willard Olivier*

## Scrapbook

Is it not fun and pleasure so
To sit and paste them in a row?
Some pretty, some ugly, while others are funny;
Some making faces when it was sunny.

There are your pictures, when young and old;
Pamphlets and clippings that you unfold
To read of yourself on newspaper print —
Of important occasions, and a certain event.

It gives you a thrill to look at a friend
And wonder if he has that same old grin.
Then come the pictures of the feminine world;
Some your friends, most others your girl.

I wonder what will happen to Bob and Jerry,
To David and Dick, and Jack and Perry.
I'll still have the pictures of Sam and Paul;
I'll turn the pages and remember them all.

*Leonard N. Bridges*

## Untitled

As the sun sets in the far west
Visions of love are at their best
As we lie on the sandy beach looking at the beautiful sea.
I can't help but wonder, what will ever be?
Will things go slow or pass us fast,
Will we go to the future or have memories of the past?
We should not go forward or back they say
because the memories of today shall fade away.

*Melissa Biro*

## Till We Meet Again

God looked around his garden and found an empty space,
When he saw there was no cure, he took you to his place.
Your golden heart stopped beating and your tired body put to rest,
You were lifted to heaven and we knew it was for the best.
Your memory will always be here in my heart,
And I know we will never part.

*Tracey Gulley*

## Talking

Talking can be so much fun to do,
To someone or an imaginary friend,
I can tell them how much they mean to me,
Over and over again.

Talking can be so much fun to do,
Especially in class at school,
I can jabber and jabber and talk a lot
Not learn and end up a fool.

Talking can be so much fun to do,
There are plenty of words to say and use,
I can gossip about places and people I know,
But my friends trust in me I'd abuse.

Talking can be so much fun to do,
By just moving the mouth on my face,
I can make friends or I can make enemies for life,
So talking like everything else has a time and a place.

*Mary J. Little*

## Untitled

In the East I see the ray of birth
To the delight of the future
and a beginning of the spirit.
To the naive it is the beginning of a right
there to take its hold
and grasp the new.
Never to look at the shadows
to see the reason.
To others it is the shadow
of the ray that gives the reason.
The glimmer that shows the hope.
Before the dawn there is a past.

*Rebecca McGowan*

## Memories Still Linger

I must go out to the fields again
To the dusty rows once plowed
To my Mom's way - and my Dad's way
Where many a dreams have died

I gaze into the open space
And ponder each day and the other
Bending and picking each boll with haste
My mind drift to many sisters and brothers

Long lasting memories still linger
With each passing day
I'll never eat certain things
No matter what anyone say

Stand up! Pick up! Stop digging in the dirt!
If you don't get busy!
We can't afford that sweater and skirt!
100—200-300—you know, that is a must
If I don't reach that figure
My—my—what a fuss!

*Stella Nash*

## Strength

I pray for strength for me
To the higher powers that be.

I pray for strength and guidance for you
Knowing God's grace will carry us through.

Sometimes my body is racked with pain
Good health and sound mind I want to regain.

Turned upside down this world is in;
Misery, violence, destruction and sin.

From within we must make a start
Standing firm together, not weak and apart.

If you see me down , help me up
Being alone can really be tough.

Be patient and kind to others
Even if they're not your sister or brother.

Ask for strength, he'll give it to you
He's always merciful, gracious and true!

*Olivia P. Graviett*

## Simple Twist of Fate

From the womb of the women,
To the light of the world, we bring together one form of life.
Babies that cry of hunger, neglect, and love,
The children that laugh and play all day,
They have no worries, know no shame.
We need to find one way to see,
The rich, the poor, the black, the white,
Bring us together, make world peace.
We hear the cry of one child's sorrow,
Putting our hands together in prayer for tomorrow.
People say the word of love,
But who really knows the meaning?
In our world, we have no love,
With love, comes happiness, with happiness comes peace.
We know not the meaning of peace,
Therefore, our true souls are not whole, nor released.

*Stephanie Sposito*

## Garden Of The Dragons

From frothy waves that tumble and roar
To the sky where crying sea gulls soar

We wash away regrets and sorrows
In the undertow of distant tomorrows.

The dragons we've hidden in our growing souls
Have weaved our pathways of destining woes.

Have we the ability to conquer these fears
That have encumbered our lives throughout the years?

We remember the age of frilly bows and red wagons
To seek our answers in the garden of the dragons.

*Laura Bloomfield*

## The Garbage Disposal

Today at work went okay,
Until almost the end of the day.
All the food looked far, far less than stunning.
Darlene had to stick her hand down the drain.
The garbage disposal had to be a pain.
It wouldn't start again.
Which should be a sin.
So we had to remove all the gunk.
And put it in the sink and remove the chunks.
This was a great ending to my union career.
So just remember that when you want to work here.

*Thelma Mendenhall*

## New Beginnings

Oh to begin, to begin anew
To try one more time when you thought you were through
To throw off old bindings that clung on like glue
And find there's a light ablaze inside you
The light that's been with you throughout all your years
But that couldn't be seen through the haze of your tears
Will now be your beacon to guide you along
To help you find right paths and sidestep the wrong
And as your life blossoms and love starts to seep in
You'll say to yourself I can do it, I can win
To give up on me would have been such a sin
Thank goodness I chose once again
To begin.

*Lizanne E. Cave*

## Silence of the Night

In the dark of the night, silence seems to scream,
To wake all those memories, which bring the tears.
And the problems which were had, and thought long gone,
Now seem so very near.

All the fear of unseen things,
Come creeping into the mind.
The doubts of past and future,
Are ten times magnified.

Time seems to be suspended,
In the silence of the night.
But with the dawning of the morning,
Everything, again, seems well and right.

*Patty J. Cutlip*

## Gone Away

My daddy's gone to heaven;
to walk the streets of gold.

To talk to all the saints;
the ones from long ago.

I know he is so happy and all the pain is gone;
We'll meet him again and it won't be very long.

He's probably helping JESUS build all the mansions there;
so everything will be ready, when He meets us in the air.

Oh, happy day, dear JESUS, when we see our loved ones there;
There isn't anything on which this can compare.

So, as we strive, dear JESUS, to do YOUR precious will
Helping us to hear YOUR sweet, sweet voice when we are quite and
   still.

Please, know how much we love YOU and all the saints with YOU;
We meditate and we pray, and YOU keep us from being blue.

Watch over us dear JESUS, and keep forever in YOUR grace;
Until that glorious day when we see YOU face to face!!!!

*Patricia G. Mize*

## A Mother's Lament

Child of mine
with flaxen hair
laugher spills unbidden from your sweet mouth
Flowers beckon and
apron strings tie us
But too soon they break and the blossoms die
and you must leave me
to discover the stars
alone

*Sharon McCormick*

## Yesterday and Tomorrow

There is no place like when we used
   to watch the sun go down.
All our family would be together, and
   that is where our happiness was found.
We never had very much, but we
   all learned to share.
No matter what was given to us we
   knew it came from lots of care,
Our older folks were funny as they
talked for hours, and what stories they would tell.
The children knew not to interrupt, and
   we knew to listen well.
They told us of old times and sometimes
   it would get late.
But one of the things we learned from
   them was to love a lot and never hate.
Times are not the same anymore and we
   sometimes have lots of sorrows?
We will try to remember what they told us
   and we will have better tomorrows.

*Louise Williams*

## The Wheel of Time

The wheel is stopped. It is but for a moment motionless —-
To weep and wail aloud for one small, minute, and microscopic bit
Of frail and mortal human flesh that only yesterday
Partook of earthly pleasures and its sunshine,
Its problems, yea, its heartaches, and its pain.

And yet — that one small piece of dust and clay
Today lies still, so still, and white, and pale;
Lifeless, we surmise; but, wait!
Hark! 'tis the sound of music!
And rustling sound of — What!

Who comes on almost quiet, but swift and shiny wings?
And why?
Ah! Methinks 'tis angels! God's own glorious creation...
Come to bear away the soul of one who lives!

True - these earthly tabernacles soon must fade and pass away.
But soul and spirit who have trusted Christ who saves from sin,
Will live forever, free from grief and pain,
Free from the chaos which possesses and imprisons Earth,
And born again to live anew with Christ — forever!!!

The Wheel of Time again resumes its turning.

*Lila C. Knight*

## Jesus I Wish

I wish I could have been there
To worship and adore you at your birth,
To feel and see the glory
That had come to bless the earth.

I wish I could have touched you
Looked deep into your baby eye
Where all the wonder of the ages glows and comes alive

I wish I could have sung to you a loving lullaby
To tell you how thankful I am
You left heaven's beautiful sky

I wish I could have watched you grow
Into the savior of man kind,
And heard your tender pleading
For their hearts and souls and mind.

I wish I could have said I love you
More than anyone or thing I know,
And will try to prove this always as thru life I go.

Yet through thee are wishes I'm sure you already know
How much you mean to me and if will always be so

*Vi Dykins*

## Mom And Dad

i went searching for the words
to write to you.
i rode the wind,
and marveled at the curious sky.
i looked and listened
in obscure woodland valleys.
i heard the whispers of the great deserts,
the roar of the pounding surf,
and the tales of meandering streams.
i surveyed the mountaintops of dreams.
The answer came in the stillness of the quest within.
my own heart beat revealed the one word.
It was and is love.
i am eternally grateful.

*Stephen M. Murillo*

## Love Is Sunshine

Love is sunshine, love is grand, love is
toes scrunched up in the sand.
Simple pleasures day by day,
fatten up our future way.
Hopes and dreams will come our way,
knowledge, wisdom, strength to pray.
Mysteries of life are everywhere, we must
show the world we care.
Rain and teardrops are the same,
earth must have its days of pain.
Listen to your voice within,
it will steer you from your sins.
Happiness is everywhere...
when we learn to give and care.

*Sally Salierno*

## Memorial Day

A nation untied that standing tall.
Together we are strong divided we fall.
As a nation we have had many wars making history.
We must keep marching on to victory.
As a nation we must honor God in every way.
Even if we are driven by sorrow and sadness on this memorial day.
Many years ago they took the bibles out of the schools.
Now it became a young violent world of fools.
Many wars has pass and gone.
Losing many love's one as time has shown.
It time for this nation to come back to God.
And many problems will be solve.
I thank the men and the women who have given their life's
For their grace and love for many to survive.

*Wayne Mosley*

## Flowers Have Great Powers

An impatien loves the shade,
too much light and it begins to fade.
A hibiscus loves the heat
and the size of the flower is hard to beat.
An iris is a spring delight
and only appears if the elements are just right.
A rose is a favorite to all
and loves to grow in spring and fall.
Sunflowers thrive in the summer
and are too numerous in number.
Petunias make a lovely accent
and can be found in an array of color and tint.
A buttercup is just the right size
for a child to pick and cherish as a prize.
Everyone knows the power
the earth gives us in a flower.

*Pamela Voyles*

## Crossroads

Heaven and earth
touch at the crossroads in our life.
The road is dusty...
and ahead we try to see without vision,
yet with our heart we can feel tomorrow.

Capture all that is wonderful,
with one glimpse of what is to be...
Blinded by our plight for perfection.
we tip toe around this beautiful planet.

When will this journey end to begin a new one...
When will we finally decide which road to take..
the dust clears and we see light.
I sorrow in what I've lost from past years of ignorance.
Please Lord, let me not mourn for one more minute lost.
For this one life of mine
is all I have...let me live it with fullness and joy.

The future is ours to shape the unknown years ahead
that illuminate high within the sky.
A memory of the never forgotten star
we had wished upon long long ago.

*Laury E. Young*

## The Beauty of Summer by the Ole Mill Stream

Our house is next to the ole mill stream, located in the center of town;
One warm summer day, I walked over and looked around;
The peace of mind, the beauty I found, had been to my unknown;
And the greatest pleasure of it all, it was just a few steps from home;
The sun kissed rocks felt warm beneath me as I sat upon the ground;
I watched a pretty yellow butterfly as he flew around;
The sun shining on the water, sparkled like diamonds everywhere;
I couldn't turn my eyes away, I had to sit and stare;
The summer sun was welcome, brought warmth and delight;
Maybe I had no time for this, but felt I earned the right;
The sweet smell of summer flowers, and a warm summer breeze;
Was enough to make me linger there, and thank God for days like
   these.

*Laura Foster Hutchinson*

## Up From the Ashes

This heart once innocent;
trusted love, believed hope, let faith, and held truth.
This heart was pure and simple.
But time matured, knowledge shone;
thus awakened self.
Fear then ruled; with shame, confused;
to lay this pearl amid the ashes.

This heart, then young;
defined love, envisioned hope, kept faith, and followed truth.
This heart was strong and sure.
But time matured, knowledge shone;
wherein, self arose.
Fear then ruled; with shame, confused;
to lay this pearl beneath the ashes.

This heart, now broken;
remembers love, recalls hope, mends faith, and grasps truth.
This heart is humbled low.
Time is full, wisdom speaks, self is ceased to be.
Christ Jesus reigns; with grace, revealed;
to raise this pearl from the ashes.

*Renee Evans*

## It Took A Long Time To Get To Know You

At first you hated me
Trying everything possible to get rid of me
But nothing worked
I, married your brother
I have seen you grow into a very gentle
    person, not so hard any more
You're always there to lend a helping hand,
    when anyone needs one
You're there to listen, when things don't
    seem right
But you have feelings and you need to show them
They are eating you up inside
Show your feelings, let them out
You know, we are not made of steel even
    though people think we are
We can be broken just like anyone else
Everyone has feelings
For some it is just harder to show
I am glad we have become better friends not enemies
If you need a shoulder I am here for you

*Ruth A. Langiewicz*

## For A Love Which Can Never Be

At times I find myself cursing the Gods.
Trying to dissect emotions and carefully separate primal instinct
    from remembrances of the soul.
Yet in the end, are they not one in the same?

An urge which thrusts me out into the open and strips me of all
    convention
Only to twist me into a helpless victim of circumstance.
Clawing my way back into the soft underbrush to lay until darkness
    descends.
And then, alone, I curse the Gods.

I beg for daylight.
To be thrown into the open and be able to react... Ah, but for
    circumstance.
The soul remembers and I must question why.

The soul which was born in a cave and has traveled through the ages
Must now bear the weight of knowing too much and of guarding it
    closely,
Keeping it away from the other tribal members.
Always doing the right thing.
And for now, cursing the Gods.

*Melissa Kent*

## A Lonely Boy...

Once upon a time there was a boy and a shattered mind,
Trying to locate the answer to the confusion he finds.
Walking down the street of a thug-lined hood,
Trying to find some answers if he could.
In a third-floor window stands a woman.
Who has always wanted to be there for him.
Never has she loved him ever more,
So she runs to the apartment's front door.
Gets to the street and yells out his name,
As if he is incorporated in some sort of fame.
The boy turns around at just the wrong time,
At the end of the day when the sun seemed to shine.
Two men with masks run out of the store,
With many people's lives they seem to ignore.
Suddenly shots are fired and the boy goes down,
On a lonely street on the wrong side of town.
The woman runs over and starts to cry,
Takes the boy in her arms were he finally dies.
All that's left to say is the lives ran out of the cat,
And all the boys hopes and dreams end just like that.

*Todd Matson*

## A Vicious Cycle

We work hard for many a year
Trying to please those who are dear.

It seems worth the effort 'cause there'll be an end
And that there is something better 'round the bend.

Retirement for some is just resting or changing pace
And forgetting about the daily rat race.

Someday we know our IRA's and 401K's will already be seen
For someday they'll actually turn into green.

So we work hard and wait for the day
When we can choose what to do, that comes our way.

Of course, when we retire, again we must worry
'Bout how to spend all that money in a hurry.

'Cause after working that hard, to leave it behind
Would seem to be a terrible grind.

So we'll try to understand when the kids don't think it's funny
When they see us spending their inheritance money.

*Merlyn Olson*

## The Sadness

Heart breaking, pounding - oozing.
Turmoil mounting, pressure building -
Waves crashing - emotion spilling, tears falling.

Fear rising:
    From the depths, from the pit,
    From the knowing.
    From the emptiness of before you,
    From the shadow of your going.

I hear your voice - from beyond the present.
We were one in life,
And still you are with me!
Someone new takes your place.
I love - he loves.
He is alive and here,
And still you are with me!
How can I end the sadness?
Emotion spilling
Tears falling
Guilt ridden
You are gone forever - goodbye.

*Sharon Young-Spano*

## A Prayer

I sought You Lord when You were not yet near
'Twas a time of questions and doubt.
A babe in the midst of confusion and fear
With trembling hands reaching out
To touch this strange power at work in my life
That eases the pain, the suffering and strife.
And though I faltered along the way
The steps become shorter with each passing day.
Hope sprang up and faith took hold
Bringing rich blessings and joy untold.
No time now for sadness nor fear of night
For me, dear Lord, there shines a great light
And I smile with those whom I hold dear
And rejoice that the time to be with you is near.
Thank you, God, for teaching me to pray
For they have now rolled the stone away.

*Lucille Moose "Miss Lucy"*

## Poem For Ireland

I flew to Ireland for a holiday.
'Twas in the splendorous month of May.
The land of Erin, 'twas as a dream.
With sky so blue, the land so green.
Everywhere my eyes did gaze, saw wonderment and beauty;
rivers, lakes and mountains, a portrait of divinity.
The Irish so gay with their laughter and singing,
'Twas never a moment my heart wasn't winging.
God's plan, my destiny, brought me there,
A bit of heaven so pure, so fair.
A place my ancestors had known,
a place they once had called their home.
All too soon I had to leave,
My heart was heavy, how it did grieve.
And pondering as I traveled to my home off afar,
I realize that Ireland, makes our earth a brighter star.

### *Patricia Greene Ciaschi*

## Joan and Kim Are 30 — Happy Birthday!

On the first of August, Nineteen Sixty-two,
Twin girls were born to the Leongs, as due.
They were cute and bright, like beams from the sun.
The parents were glad—two for the price of one!

They were named Joan Maureen and Kimberly Faye.
Identical in looks, not like night and day.
They joined brother Michael and were good babies.
Of this I vouch, and there's no maybe's.

Except for losing their dad at an early age,
You might say that their childhood was from a page
Showing family gatherings, vacations and games,
Cousins and friends, schools and occasional fames.

Most of their lives were spent on Ardenwood Way.
The years past, they grew in stature day by day.
Joan is at Davis, completing her P.H.D.
Kim moved to Denver to start a new destiny.

This year will be a milestone on their date of birth.
Three decades have passed since their arrival on earth.
May God grant them special blessings the coming year,
Along with my birthday wishes, loud and clear!

### *Victoria Leong*

## The Two Lovers

Two lovers who loved so well
Two lovers who said farewell
One of the lovers his heart fell
Straight into the murky depths of hell
This lover did indeed weep
He tossed and turned he could not sleep
Not a single solitary peep was heard
Because that would be so absurd
He decided to go after her one fine day
The big bright sun was in his way
He drove for half an hour when he found her he asked her to stay
He lays in the darkness he does not know what to say
He loved her so much he let her go
He know he had to that was so
He almost quit life except for a single deed
The existence of a friendship seed
She did not know of his love
He could only be near her through the friendship glove
He dare not show her his love
Until he saw a sign of peace, a lovely dove

### *Ryan Travis Price*

## In Memory of the Challenger Crew

Five Brave Eagles soaring so high
Two White Doves flying in the sky
All seven racing to reach out in space
Not one of them knowing they would lose their race.

But never fearing, brave to the last
They were doing their best and going so fast.
Then in a few seconds God took them home
To rest evermore, nevermore to roam.

Seven more Angels soaring so high,
In God's lovely mansion so high in the sky.
They laugh and sing all the day long,
And to their loved ones they sing this song:

Never fear dear loved ones be ever so strong,
Because we have reached the place we belong.
In God's Holy Home we are happy to say,
To us our lives were lived in the very best way.

### *Opal Hudgins Warren*

## Lifebeat

My voice echoes amongst the hills,
unanswered, unheard,
Coldness wraps her icy fingers about my throat, Suffocating me,
and loneliness, my only friend.
My lover, you are the only one who can answer my voice in the wind,
the only one who stills the pain, lingering in my mind,
amongst the harshness dispelled by my tormentor.
Empty, so empty...
Lost in a world that has not accepted me,
turned me down for lack of wisdom to their knowledge.
Blood turned to ice, for blood cannot see
the black cloak which is shielding me from my reality.
Oh, lover, can you not answer me?
My cry of pain into the dark night?
Alone in a field of dead leaves and failed light?
I cry alone, embracing myself to my knees.
Answer my prayers. Make my voice to be answered, heard,
Comfort me when I am choked with pain,
Catch the tears that fall from mine eyes,
and together we shall walk into the world with strength.

### *Lucinda B. Bebyn*

## Living in the Shadows

Shadows dancing in the trees,
under fullest of moons,
reflections of me.

Facets of opposite travel the night,
the deepest shades of darkness,
the brightest ribbons of light.

That which is evil and that which is good,
live together in the fathomless woods.
An eternal battle rages under gray shadows of night,
the evil of confusion and the goodness of true sight.

### *Tamra L. Kinzel*

## Changes

Life is but a whirlwind
We are but sand in its path.
Like the sands in the hourglass of time
The breath of life blows through.
As time flows on and life goes by
Headed toward an all too certain end,
The last grain of sand falls
To a fate that is all too true.
As it is in life so must it be in death,
Thus the whirlwind of life blows through
To take the last grain of life and begin anew.

### *Rick E. Butler*

## Don't Cry For Me

Please, don't cry for me when I'm gone
Unless they are tears of joy.
For, I've gone on to a better place.
Please, don't ne made at me for the way I've gone.
For, It was the way God intended,.
And the way I had to go.

Please, don't dwell on my death
For, it won't change the past.
And, it won't bring me back,

Please, don't forget about me
For, I loved you all
And need to be remembered

Please, don't cry for me when I'm gone
For, I'm not really gone.
I've just moved on.

*Merilyn Reed*

## Period

I've never seen a man cry
Until I saw that man die
It's only then when his past is replete
It's only then when his life is complete

Replayed memories and unsought dreams
Down his cheek one tear streams
As he realizes this sigh's his last
He's just a memory gone in the past

With this death a lesson is learned
Within time tables turn
Just a warning so beware
Trust no one and never swear

No one cries till it's too late
A tear's in sight when they meet their fate
In twelve years I have seen
Who to push and on who to lean

With this last phrase I'll leave to you
With these last days without a clue
They'll only know at a death
How things are in our last breath

*Veronica Maria Lara*

## Cascades

Hear the restless waters pounding
  Up against the rocks rebounding
Driven down by natures ceaseless surge.
  Through the endless ages boiling
Never tiring of their toiling,
  Keeping faith with times relentless urge.

From the uplands hear it crashing
  Angry white plumed cascades thrashing
Ever rushing on to meet the shore.
  Through the high walled canyons swirling
See the angry rapids twirling
  Flowing swiftly downward evermore.

To the lowlands, bubbling, churning,
  Around the bend now gently turning
Ever widening as it seeks the sea.
  Softly now a watery by-way,
Gently now a glistening highway,
  To the sea of sweet tranquility.

*William A. Jaques*

## A Country Not My Own

In the middle of the night, I faintly smell the fragrance of you
up on the wind. And the beauty of your laughter, I can hear. Those
many miles that separate you and I seem so ar at times like these,
as though the wind it self has lifted you and carried you to me.
I reach out to touch the wind to feel you close to me, and to know
peace. I search the wind to catch your smile, to hear your laughter,
to hope you're near. These endless days of longing, wishing.
to see you once again, you hair blowing in the wind to cover and then
unfold, to reveal the beauty of your face. It hurts to be a man,
to have t say goodbye, to have to leave loved ones and see them
start to cry. To go away to some far away land, away from the girl
I love, knowing how much you will miss me. I pray you well preserve
your love. I look for a letter from you each day, and when one
doesn't come. I wonder if I've lost you and tears enter my eyes.
Each morning I arise before the sun is up another day. I pray to the
Lord, Oh God please take my hand and guide me on my way, Oh God. I
love her with all my heart and soul, and here I am miles away in a
lonely land. I'm a lonely man and when that time comes to meet her,
be proud and take my hand.

*Mitchell L. Varner*

## I Am A Poet

I am a poet, A whim of fate
Upon this world I celebrate
I am conscious of the power
Beating my heart by the hour
I see the living and the dead
And know the trails they both tread
I know triumph and disaster
And what rushes time on faster
I know the country's shame and victories great
And the highest and lowest and what they rate
Life has loosened these elements for my eyes
And parted the clouds that range the skies
Bestowing hammer-strokes upon my ways
So I may pierce the night and days
No greater design could I therefore ink
Or pass the phrase that loops the link
I loom in height and haze
A movement on which the world will gaze
For I am a poet, A whim of fate
And I sing my songs from Eternity's Gate

*Shirley Fielding*

## Ascension's Wings

On Ascension's wings I rise to the summit of mankind's consciousness,
upon which the splendor of heaven breathes.

As I sit upon the rock of forgiveness, beauty stills my wings.
"Make fast" the wind whispers, "for eternal bliss is upon thee."

Watching from the corners of my eyes, glimpses of shadows untold.
There awaits my freedom - with glee, I spring forth to see!

Ah, heaven awaits no longer, my child, it has come to thee.
Be still and seek my heart, on else nothing waits.
The gifts of heaven are plenty; the gates remain open,
for upon thee I ponder - my glory for thee to see,
all heaven is about you.

On earth do I see the mysteries of heaven flood forth;
The guiles of men do not tear, for with one is the father,
The kingdom, and there is no fear.
Please remember this, my dear, with thee I will always stay,
if, from upon me, your thoughts never stray.

Aumen Aumen Aumen
*Penelope Marth*

568

## The Clothesline

The clothesline, is a long time thing of the past.
Use to show you had performed an important task.
The clothes were so beautiful drying in the sun.
It showed that the burden of washing had been won.
The Lord, gives us the same sunshine today,
But it seems no one wants, to use it that way.
The wind made the clothes so fluffy and soft.
You loved to watch the way they would toss.
But all wasn't the same when the line did break.
You knew how long washing them again would take.
In winter the clothes would freeze.
Especially, if there was a cold, cold breeze.
They would be as stiff as a board,
If they hit you, it would make you roar.
Now, the washer and dryer have caught on like mad.
And not seeing the clothesline can make you feel very sad.
Things will, just never be the same.
For today, the old clothesline is used for other things.

*Leigh Silver*

## Song To The Sparrow

I sit under the weeping willow tree
waiting for the return of the sparrow
countless long days...endless long nights...
waiting for the wind to come
and swing my grandfather's hammock.

Watching the swirling fog of winter
metamorphose into the glorious spring shades of pinks and violets
the days have slowly turned into red and yellow autumn
onto the color of sunsets in summertime
but the sparrow eluded my call...
and now lies miles away from the sorrow of my heart.

I am drowning in the endless eddy of my tears
drifting in memories muffled by the silence of the night
whispering the melody of my song to the sparrow
blown to the Far East - to feel him once more in my arms
reaching out to his warm bed of deep slumber
lulled by the whisper of the wind
and the quiet dance of my grandfather's hammock in the yard.

Still I sit...waiting,
for the sparrow to return.

*Rowena S. Mando*

## Feather Dusting

Search in the shadows and see what you find.
Walk on without thinking, leave light behind.
Ancient tongue no one will ever understand.
Whispers of the past seek the soul to command.
Do not fear the spirits much wiser that you.
When they can offer hope that before never grew.
Love is as old as the pebbles and stones of time.
What new poet comes with what new rhyme?
Nothing really changes, and little ever will.
Why run from destiny watch it find you, be still.

Tombs and graves house that bit of worthless shell.
Walk with the brave that refused their souls to sell.
Beauty beneath dust and age will be buried deep.
Whispers of life will one day bring it forth from sleep.
Earth will rise to the splendor supposed to be lost.
Why ponder of fate, stand strong no matter the cost.
Love lasts forever, not dying with the setting sun.
What greatness falls to ruin without a race been run?
Remember the glory of the ages now so long past.
When soon each babe will be a memory gone fast.

*Melanie Bunger*

## The Day You Left

I walk into the dark room and there in a box,
Was a person I once knew, but now I had lost.
There were people there, but I didn't speak,
For my mind was filled with memories,
And my thoughts were weak.
One by one they said their goodbyes,
Some glazenly stared, mostly they cried.
Then it came, I was next.
I felt my heart drop from my chest,
It had been too soon.  I can not let her go.
I wish I had an answer to why she chose this ending,
I guess I'll never know.
I walked to the box with the feeling of fear.
Seeing her for the last time, only brought more tears.
I knew I had to go, but I want to stay.
There was so much I had wanted to say.
Now it was too late so I passed on,
But her memory would never be gone.
She chose to go, I choose to stay.
She will remain with me in spirit each day.....

*Margaret C. Taylor*

## Was It Really You, or Just Another Dream?

Was it really you, or just another beautiful dream?
Was it really me, or was I in a dream?
Though it was short, it was exhilarating.
Though it was exhilarating, you left me there craving!
Oh how I craved for the touch, oh how I wandered for you.
Oh how I suffered not knowing why, I strive for you!

Admiring Picasso, some declared how he, the best artist.
Incongruently I declared, how he who created you, the best artist.

What a piece of art, quiet a creation you are;
you balance the stability and sensitivity, what a sensation you are.
Your beautiful eyes, I see rainbow and more,
your beautiful voice, I hear Beethoven and more.

Be my rainbow, and be my love song,

let it be just you and me, and nothing will go wrong!

*Nailesh A. Bhatt*

## Part of the Holocaust

The ashes from my camp fire are blown into the clear black sky that
was once a sorrowful gray.
As I look up I feel myself transported into a time where men were
punished because of their religion, and I remember the place where
the bitterness came to an extreme climax.
Auschwitz.
The place our brothers and sisters were murdered by their cousins and
friends.
Where the ovens were supplied with flesh instead of wood and coal.
Where the blankets that kept murderers warm were made of the dead's
hair.
Where the shadows that once kept many clean turned to cramped death
chambers.
Where starvation and fatigue were as well known as the beatings Nazis
put prisoners through.
Where women were separated from their husbands and children
and sent
to work, as they wondered of their loved ones fate.
Where screams were only heard by the uncaring and the wind.
As I leave the past I wonder what the five and a half million who were
murdered thought in their last moments of life.
And I wonder what the Nazis felt when they committed their
unforgivable sins.

*Linda Corlew*

## The Gift of Life

I was walking at a pace, I felt as if someone
was staring at my face
I thought it was the reflection
Of the color of my complexion

I walked a little farther then I got weak
I was standing at the edge of my own life peak
But I turned around to see
That the Lord stood before me

Tall and bright with shining gleam
It felt like a timid dream and
the Lord said to me
don't be frightened, don't be alarmed

My dear child, I'll do you no harm
Take my hand and you will see
That the gift of life stands upon me
Tell your family and your friends
The gift of life has come again

*Teia T. Boyce*

## Our Love

If your love was the ocean and mine
was the land, we'd be together until the
earth's end; Nothing could come between
us wouldn't tear us apart, we were meant
to be together from the very start.

My love is higher than the highest
peaks for you, your love is deeper than
the deepest depths for me; Your words
are like a gentle breeze that makes the
soft ocean spray, they make me feel as
warm as a sunny summer's day.

Me being a woman and you being a man,
our hearts bound as one while we walk
hand in hand; I love you with all my
soul, you love me the same, like two lions
in the jungle our love will never be tamed.

*Mary Ann Skinner*

## Enjoy Today

Enjoy today, it will not come again,
waste not the hours of thinking of tomorrow,
more than half our heartache and our sorrow
    are over what the future may contain.
The darkest doubts and worries never changed
    the color of the sky nor turned the tide,
but he whose faith burns like a light inside,
questions not the things God has arranged.
"For everything a season," every man
must journey from old to reach the new,
    discovering as he is passing through
        the desert, an oasis in the sand.
For there are dreams that really do come true,
    ... and this is all we need to understand.

*Lisamarie Priola*

## Different Side

Look beyond what you can see
You will see a different side to everything
You will find beauty abounding
Constant warmth surrounding
Light shining through
Nature in harmony with you
Everyone has this ability
So sad only few can see
You may be that one or two
Keep on searching and you will find you

*B. Keith Turner*

## With a Tear in My Eye

I stood alone with a tear in my eye,
Watching you go, hearing goodbye
Whispered softly on the wind
And I knew our time was at an end...
The roses were red covered in dew,
Reminding me so much of you,
Blooming so strong in the summer's light,
Reaching, growing with all their might...
The rain fell slowly and still they stood,
And drank the dew in the shaded wood;
Then winter came and they were gone,
Like you, they found a better home....
Buried beneath the ice and snow,
The pain was great and healing slow....
Then spring came and I saw them again,
But you couldn't return home with them,
And finally I learned to say goodbye
As I stood alone with a tear in my eye...

*Lisa Gordon*

## Migrant Worker

Fresh morning mist dripping off of green leaves
wave like a never ending sea to the
overworked laborers as they begin
their infinite day of gathering and
picking fruit with their weathered hands, sore backs
and eyes that tell a story of a time
when beautiful empires stood tall and
food was abundant, where their culture was
strong and sacred as they worshipped and danced
for the heavens above, the jungle around
them and all the gods who walked beside them.
Mayans, Opatas, Yaquis, Zapotecs
and Aztec heroes NOW kneel to the earth
NOT in sweet songs of prayer for their makers,
but to work their tired bodies, tired
souls, bowing before coarse shimmering leaves
worshipping the hands that give the green paper
wishing in their hearts to once again see
the sun rising over the pyramids
But their empires sadly stand no more.

*Sara Catalina Dorame*

## Life

Going through phases
We are herded along
Turning here, turning there
Listening to the internal song
Watching for the timely changes
As the options go on

As the options go on
And in every face I meet
A sense of exhausting determination
As their eyes pass from light to dark...dark to light
With undaunting expectation
To the next turn they seek
As their options are narrowed

As their options are narrowed
We find our mission in sight
Charging ever forward
The beam of truth never leaves their eyes
As they look skyward
Hoping to complete it before twilight
For then...our goal will be done.

*Mark Darty*

## Hindsight

When we are young,
We are told to aspire

To conquer the world
But not set it on fire
Stay out of clinics
And stay out of jail
One will make you a cynic
The other will see that you fail
Clerics devoutly say clinics are fine
Celebrities say they make us divine
If jails are to be your very last hope
The doctors will say you surely can't cope
So try to wash with a little more soap
Or else give yourself a lot more rope
The world is a party-time for the sinner
So please divest yourself if you're a winner
The devil himself awaits the second-rater
Unless, of course, you're a top headwaiter

*Richard C. Urquhart*

## The Strong Wind of the Desert

## and the Biggest Eagle of the Western

American and non-Americans sometime we need to fight
we brothers from other nations and we all end up crying.
We may fight for freedom, territory or right making our
women and children cry.
We love our brothers, it does not matter from what side
but, there are situations that we have put our men to fight.
I wrote this poem to my brothers from the Middle East, land of
Kings, Sultans and Sheikhs, people of courage and strong beings.
If, I hadn't been born in the Caribbean and God would have
asked me in which place you would like to have been born in, I would
have said The Middle East.
The Middle East is well known as the land of the Islam
those are my brothers one in their kind, people that in their
language call Allah to GOD.
Oh God Almighty!  Thanks Merciful Allah!
The Persian Gulf war is over,
our women and children don't have to cry.

*Marina R. Mendez*

## When I'm With You

When I'm with you it doesn't matter what
we do, because I'm always happy just to be
around you.

Even the dullest moments seem bright,
because you put happiness in my life.

Looking into your eyes my problems disappear,
because the shine and sparkle in them makes
me forget my fears.

Whenever we're together that brightens up
my day, because the special love we share
is with us in every way.

Whenever I'm alone and I think of you.
A special feeling comes over me,
It's the feeling I get when I'm with you.

*Nancy Kotzuba*

## Boomerang

Your shape is already known
We know what to do
You must be thrown
As hard as we can

We know it will always come back to us
Just like good friends, we throw them away
But they won't sway
They come back your way

Can't change good friends
From faithful to feigned
In the end it's all true
Through the bad and without a clue
Your friends will come through for you

Can't change their ways
Unlike clay, we can't mold them
But in the light we behold them
As the creatures they are
So virtuous and true
They'll come through for you

*Tim Ross*

## The Best Man's Toast

Adrift in a mist of desires
We live in an endless dream,
A dream which bonds us to ourselves
And is sustenance to a needing heart.

Among the mist is a path on which we traipse
In a network in which we all tread,
A network which is home to a love that is,
Twice as high as the heavens,
And thrice as loud as thunder.

As the dust rose on the path,
From the step of my foot,
I walked on blind and aimless,
Unsure of the road I was on,
Unsure of my destination,
Unsure of love.

At a crossroads we met,
And shared a breath,
and a breath became a word, a word became a touch,
And a touch became a bond, and with a shower of passion,
The dust cleared and two became one.

*Michael Fabre Jr.*

## Wild Flowers Mama and Me

We were a happy family, Mama, Daddy, two brothers and me.
We lived in a house on a hill, down in the valley was a big field;
There wild flowers did grow;  It was my favorite place to go.
Off to the field I did race, I knew wild flowers would bring a
smile to Mama's face.
Mama was sick you see and soon with Jesus she would be.
As I stood by her bed that day; I will never forget the words she
did say, "Mama's going away you see, won't you pack a bag and
come with me?
A child I was and could not understand, when Mama was so weak
she could hardly stand.
Now that I am older I can see, what Mama was trying to tell me.
She knows it was her time to go but her love for me touched her so.
I was her little girl you see and no longer could she be with me.
As I go back to those days so long ago — I see the field of wild
flowers that I loved so.
In my mind it will always be, wild flowers, Mama and me.

*Mary Bishop Dowdy*

## Hope

Your place was empty, without you there
We missed you mightily we love you dear
That smile of grace, so sweet and clear
With days getting longer and weather fair

Your health improved and smile so bright
You'll feel much better so very light
Oh! We'll rejoice that you've won the fight
There'll be prayers, and shouting to God's delight

Lift up that weary frame of flesh
Spread out the table, for "God's" the guest
For you're his child, one of the best
He tried you over, you stood the test

The task is over now, "God" be praised!
Now comes the night, and the days
The sun to shine in many ways
Your heart just bursting with things to say

Just praise the "Lord" and praise him well
I've things to say and stories to tell
About "God's" grace, how he excels
Thy voice will ring out clear as a bell

**Susan E. Wisdom**

## Untitled

We must go we must hurry for what we do not know,
we must go we must hurry cannot stop the flow.
We move faster and faster as each day goes by,
without realizing time crawls then dies.
Second by second and day by day,
we run frantic in our lives without a true way.
Efficient and swift is the route to go,
if we want to live life today not tomorrow.
Zipping by with lightning speed,
we tend to miss the things we need.
A gentle rain, sweet smell of the earth,
the virgin plains, and a child's birth.
Now stop and look at yourself and hear,
the roughness, see the stench, feel the joy of a sitting bench.
Just sit and meander thoughts of the day.
Time remains the same as we travel our way.
In the midst of sorrow a child laughs at death
with innocence and a naive smile.
This is the way life is and how life will remain
until time no longer matters and history is unknown.

**Michael D. Nix**

We worship,
  We pray,
In prayer, we give thanks.
We renew our faith and celebrate our strength.
We share our church and our temple,
our house and our rug.
We share synagogue and pagoda,
and all our love.
In silence and in meditation
In song and dance and rhyme
Call it Jesus or Buddha or Mohammed,
Confucius, Tao, yours and mine
  All different names
  For one different thing:
  Life, Love, and Light
  The One, the Supreme

**H. V. Le**

## I Know That You Are Real

Well I have never seen you, perhaps the time will never arrive, that
we shall meet. But I know that you are real, I can feel the warmth
of your heart pass over my face, as I look toward the sun.

I want to do one part in the play with you, but they tell me that you
are only a fantasy, they say that you are not real.

Then I hear your voice, and I know that you are real. You are as real
as the rain that falls. I know that you are as real as the dew on the
rose. Then I look around, and you are not there. A tear falls cause
I know the play will soon end. The actors are preparing for the final
act. Will you step forward and do one scene with me, or will you
break my heart, and we will forever be part.

**Ludema M. Garza**

## Our Beautiful Mother

Mary, how great you love,
we thank you for the many blessings.
They are like beautiful doves,
sent from heaven for our takings.
Your arms are so inviting,
the way you hold them out.
Are you trying to enlighten,
us to proclaim your goodness with a shout?
Someday dear Mother please:
meet us with your smile.
As we prepare to leave,
to travel, to heaven, our last mile.
May all your people especially your students,
be rewarded with your graces.
Bless their friends, teachers, and parents,
as they prepare to take their heavenly places.

**Rosetta Fuemmeler**

## Our Legacy

In this, our twilight years,
We together,
Study the tapestry we have woven.
Happy with the few gold and silver threads,
tokens of our minor victories'
But more than that, enthralled
With the brightly colored threads
Depicting our oneness, our love, our strength,
our joy, and laughter.
And we are pleased with the story it tells
To those of ours who follow in our footsteps.

**Marion Haycraft**

## Life

We are born into a world so strange and unfamiliar.
We travel the many highways that life has to offer
getting off which exit nobody knows.
There are those we will pass only to be seen but never heard.
With every breath of life taken in we stroll along
this road we have chosen learning to
live and living to learn from life and our existence
becoming wiser each day that passes by.
We are born to love and learn from each other
only to die, forget and repeat it all until it is all done right.

**Salvatore Conti**

## Big John Koons

Big John has gone away
we were all surprised and saddened
when we heard the news that day
Big John left so fast
We all know we cannot last
When we must leave this place someday
We all agreed that is the way BUT NOT TODAY
John played golf most every day
But when with us he had his say
Of days on the ranch at Woods Landing
Of haying, riding, roping, branding
John was there in World War II
to do his part and much more too
We hope Big John has gone aloft
Where everyday he can play golf
Where the course is always long and green
Where there will be a good trout stream
Big John has showed the way
We know some day we'll have to pay
And we will hope to go that way BUT NOT TODAY

**Myron E. Mike Kilmer**

## Why So Soon

The two of us grew up side by side for most of the time;
We would play until we were exhausted;
Share every silly secret and laugh like hyenas—
But not anymore.

We went to the same school from just about the start to the finish;
Helped each other through those bad times
And made the best of the happy times—
But not anymore.

In later years of school the events started to change,
We went our separate ways to fulfill our dreams.
Leaving each other at this point in life was difficult—
But not as difficult as the one to come later.

The years came and went and life went on;
We had our own families and were happy;
And at holiday gatherings we hugged and kissed—
But not anymore.

Then the time came for you to leave;
It was a lonely autumn morning;
I did not know it would come that fast—
Good-bye my dear friend.

**Tammy Tam**

## Carry On

When all seems distraught,
Weary and unbearable - carry on.

When all around seems bleak and the
Down brings darkness - carry on.

When the burdens are heavy and challenges
Are to heavy to bear - carry on.

Whatever the reason, while you don't understand, you are part of
A mysterious plan - so, carry on.

Carry on when the sunlight rises, through each day
As it sets, giving your all to each day's call.

**Sonja Wilson**

## Grandpa's House

They're tearing down my grandpa's house today.
We'd hoped it wouldn't happen, not in our lifetime anyway.
That spot of land will never be the same
Without grandpa's house that gave the street its name.

Time marches on; forget those days of yore,
They need the land for another warehouse store.
That's progress kids, you can't hold back the tide,
All we'll have felt are memories tucked inside.

Of times when all the family gathered there—
Cousins, aunts, uncles—relatives to spare;
We'd eat at feast spread out on grandma's table,
As much of dumplings, pies and cakes as we were able.

Then programs in the living room, and singing;
With fun and games the house was fairly ringing.
While great-grandparents' portraits on the wall
Seemed to look down and smile upon us all.

Once, long ago apple blossoms bloomed outside the door
Where soon asphalt will spread the garden o'er.
No more will it be a place where children play,
They're tearing down my grandpa's house today.

**Thelma Brisbine**

## Just Say No

You kissed me then, and said that wicked eyes
Were ever meant to kiss; what more you said
I never knew, and will not dare surmise.
And yet, I do not doubt you bent your head
And mentioned that the moon with up-turned lips
Bestowed her smile like light upon the sky:
'Tis odd I have misplaced your choicest quips
And cannot hold you to your strangest lie:
So, now that I have lost the argument,
My reason thinks to choose some other path;
At least I'll make you somewhat penitent:
Has no one ever told you in your wrath,
Yes, you, the same so greatly self-admired,
Your kisses, dear, leave much to be desired?

**Labelle Gillespie**

## The Cross And The Resurrection

The gladdest day and saddest day
    were just three days apart.
In the memory of a Christian
    these days must not depart.

They mean the victory over sin
    for every living Soul.
Eternal life with Jesus Christ,
    which is the Christian's goal.

So as we walk the path of life,
    which is the narrow way,
Take up the cross and follow me,
    we hear the Master say.

Go tell the lost of Jesus, and what He means to you.
The fields are white to harvest
    but the laborers are few.

Our work will soon be finished here.
    The toils will soon be ore.
He'll say, Well done my servant, let's go to yonder shore.

So when this life is over, and our victory is won,
we'll have a Resurrection Day and live with God's own Son.

**Ruth Daly**

## Jessie and Bill

Easy going Jessie and wild man Bill ...
  Were up to their chins with evils and ills ...

Packed up the van and gave old Joe away ...
  They headed South for lazy, sunny days ...

Purchased a single with an ocean view ...
  Of dolphins, sailboats and bikinis too ...

Alex, the cat, seemed to settle right in ...
  As did Jessie and Bill in sun kissed skin ...

Walking the beach front as the natives do ...
  Getting acquainted with the local whose who ...

Living the good life on the Emerald Coast ...
  It's what the Doc ordered they agreed with a toast ...

Ever so often homesickness slips in ...
  Thinking about the kids and the grandchildren ...

Jessie and Bill have slowed down their pace ...
  Realizing they were lucky to leave the rat race ...

Now when family visits for a few days at a time ...
  It's enjoyed, cherished and remembered in kind ...

  *C. F. Grandy*

## Live Life To Its Fullest

From the first day that we're born, to the day that we die
we've got to make the best out of life as time passes us by

No matter how bad life can be for you, you've got to remember one
thing...don't throw it away because once it's gone,
you'll never wake up to the light of dawn

Everyone has their own way of living, there are those who are taking,
and those who are giving, whether you fit any of the above
remember that you are always loved

Live life as if there were no tomorrows, bring in as much happiness
as you can, because if you live life to its fullest, you'll grow to
know and understand

Don't let the little things get you down, don't let it break your
heart, because if you come to realize, there's always a chance for a
brand new start

No matter how fast time seems to fly, never let the beating of your
heart die, life is defined by the way you live it, it's all a big test
to see if you can learn by your mistakes and hopefully not say
forget it

  *Virana V. Carpenter*

## Untitled

My darling, child of a beautiful mother
What could make you want to kill your brother?

Sweet angel, child of godless world
The innocent baby of baby girl

Little lover, not old enough to drive a car,
Feeding your baby from a stolen jar.

Young smoker, you like playing the little fool
God forbid you should ever go to school.

Slick junkie, shady dealings in a street light's beam
It's hard to believe you're only fourteen.

Mangled body, dumped by crime in an alley
Little victim, now just another for the tally.

  *Lori Biddle*

## What Was My Little Sister

An apple began a seed, a dog began a pup.
What exactly was my sister, before she grew up?
I used to watch her dribble, she'd slobber all over the place,
Was she some kind of martian, that came from outerspace?

Her head seemed quite big, because she really had no hair, she
threw her food all over the floor and sat in a really tall chair.

We shared the same bedroom, sometimes even the same bed, but
before I could go to sleep at night, her feet were usually in my head.

I never understood at all, why she'd make so much noise.
She had a lovely cradle and a bundle of wonderful toys.

I told my mom she wasn't normal; that she looked a little weird.
But mom couldn't understand me, or any of my fears.

Her nose was sort of spread, and she hadn't any teeth.
Yet, she'd always eat as much food as a monster or a beast.

I picked her up one day and realized that she was sort of cute,
But before I could even give her praise, she threw up on my boot!

My family members would always come to see my baby sister, and when
she'd spend the night with them, I guess I'd kind of miss her.

So, no matter how weird my sister looked, or how much we argue now,
I guess I'm sort of glad at times...My Mom had a second child!

  *Tawana Petty*

## Gone

Where do people go when they are no longer there?
What happens to the memories you used to share?
Left alone to dwell in my sorrow
I wonder what's left for my world tomorrow.
As he left our worlds filled with fear
beginning to shed its lonely tears.
Is the world falling apart?
Or is this pain the only thing left in my heart?
As we hugged for the first and last time in a while
Through the tears we began to smile.
But why?
How do you smile while you cry?
The lonely tears poured down.
He whispered while he looked around
"I love you, and I'll be okay.
I'll see you on a better day."
Will there ever be a better day?
One which I can share
my thoughts and fears again with someone who cares.

  *Leah Strausbaugh*

## Purpose

What is the purpose of a man's life?
What is the quest that he seeks?
Is there life forever after
Or does it lies beyond his reach?
Is man a blind and solitary sailor,
Who has been cast aimlessly to sea?
Or is he being guided to safe harbor
By a navigator who is there but cannot be seen?
These are the questions of a man's life.
That he must answer in his own way.
As he travels through life's journey
Toward his fate that lies ahead.

  *Manuel Copado*

## Through the Eye

It is through the eye, the heart and the mind that we see;
what is to be you and who is to be me.
For it through patience, feeling and love we are schooled;
in ways to share our hearts and not be fooled.
But, throughout our paths of life we see;
those beams of light that show me, me.

Without that light of guidance past, we may not know when, how to go,
or how fast.
Thank you for your heart, your love and the key;
that gave me the light that shows,

I Am Me.
*Ray L. Underwood*

## "Listen To The Wind"

It's too bad we all can't hear...
What she has been trying to say to us
It is all too clear

We're always in a hurry
We keep the bustle, always on the move
And, we don't even know what we're trying to prove

We are destroying mother nature
Because money is our number one
Forgetting the circle of life, what have we done

If only we could stop and think
And usher in the true silence
Nature is working so hard to get us in sink

To our ultimate destiny she desires
Everyday we should take some timeout
To face the conditions we have created, she crying out

Because it is all within
All the truth and enlightenment is there
Only if, we could stop and listen to the wind
*TJ*

## "Changing Times"

Growing up, my problems were few;
Whatever happened to the happy times I once knew?

Precious memories of happy times in our home;
Now, I am married with two children of my own.

One of whom could not cope with the changing time;
Who instead fell victim to a life of crime.

We tried to help; and, were always there;
But, in return, we got a cold, blank stare.

Was it peer pressure, adolescence, or what went wrong?
I know in my heart that I have to be strong.

Remembering her first word, first step and fall;
She is now confined behind her first prison wall.

It used to be a hug would always make things better;
Now, I can only do that by writing her a letter.

Who would ever think the beautiful baby in a carriage,
Would someday be the breakup of my marriage?

Oh, to be young again and problem free;
Sometimes, I feel, the victim is me!
*C. J. Sterner*

## Children To Love

My heart is so happy and so full of joy
When all around me are my children to love.

A very special feeling, a very special warmth
is when you have little children to hug and to
hold and all the time you know, they are your
children to love..

Nothing can erase the immense love in your heart
for that tender little smile or that big smooch in
your cheek.  No amount of money can ever replace
the uniqueness of children to love.

So hold them and kiss them and give them all your
love, cause soon, so soon they won't be children
anymore.
*Mary A. Macias*

## Man of the 90's

The time was in the 90's
When dating was taking a chance
To find someone whose compatible
And not out for a little romance
So out with my friends for an evening
When over the horizon I see
A great looking man of the 90's
With the hopes of him meeting me
We spent a great evening together
And seemed to get on very well
What started out as just friendship
Turned into a love we both share
So this just proves my point if you dare
Are looking for someone to share
Their's still some great men of the 90's
If you just take your time and beware
*Rita J. Forster*

## Chance

Love is loss
When hearts are tossed,
As is youth's magic
When truths seem tragic.

When the world turns cold, one dreams of
warmth; when the world turns dark, one
dreams of light, till these become a lone and
torrid, brightest shining star, far and away
in some arctic midnight sky.

Dare reach for it, lest it is found
to be merely a dream or if touched turns
to dust that sifts away through the burnt
fingers of a famished grasp so insecurely
tight that the guiding light could never
have shined finding right.
*Michael Allen Flowers*

## Tears

Life still has joy though our hearts hang heavy
We can either choose weeping or levity
I choose to hear music though the tide seems menacing

Stand tall walk sprightly
Let the tears dissipate
You can again travel life lightly

Through thick or thin you can make it in
There is still much in life to savor
If we but trust and never waiver

Life still has joy though our hearts hang heavy
*Leatrice L. Marson*

575

## The Family Cottage

Cottage, cottage by the lake,
when I get there I watch you wake.

Once the unpacking is all done,
we go out and have some fun.

During the late summer days,
we go swimming through the waves.

Then just before it gets dark,
we take a short walk to the park.

At the park we buy an ice cream,
we eat it so quickly that we scream.

Next we gather at the family bonfire,
but then we all start to tire.

After roasting marshmallows our tummies are fed,
and now it is time for us to go to bed.

*Nathaniel Bacon*

## Untitled

When all of my faith had died.
When I had hid
my face in the dark and cried.
I had no wish to live if this was all life
had to give.
When everything was dark you offered me
your heart.
A gift so rare and so kind.
It was more than
I could ever hope to find.
You helped me win back the dream, I had lost.
All of my sadness
has ended with the birth of love.
Please do not let me down.
Now I feel the soft touch of the breeze;
I hear the sighing of the seas;
Although the beauty of the earth means
a lot to me, I would give up my life on earth for you.
Your spirit young and free, you gave life back to me.
You are my hope in this world.

*Tina L. Miller*

## Death Of A Friend

This day is so sad my friend.
When I heard the sad news of your death
how your life was took away.
You were my friend from childhood and so I must say.
I hope the good Lord held your hand in your time of need
I hope the angels in Heaven were there
to receive a most precious person and friend.
You will never be forgotten.
I'll remember your laughter and your tears.
Everyone one who has ever known you, loved you
I know, so in this poem I want everyone to know.
How much I love you and I'll never forget.
I must say goodbye but you will be in our hearts and minds forever
more so where the sun shines and the winds whisper so low
we will hear your laughter ring out than we will know.
That you are with us always.

*Mildred Mann*

## Sunset

When I'm upset or to scared to go home
When I need to get away from everyone
When the times just get to rough
I go to my favorite hill
And watch the sunset.

I let my thoughts drift away
I think of all the good times we've had
I let the glorious ending of the day, start the next.

When everything seems to go wrong
And my esteem seems to be at its lowest
I let the warmth of the glorious sunset, warm my thoughts.

*Steve Perry*

## Nana

A tribute:
When I think of all the love that can exuberant
From a total being, I think of Nana.
Strength:
Always the backbone, where lay constant turmoil.
Struggles which snatched her youth, but never her spirit.
Stability:
A constant in my life; a reminder to embrace, to enhance,
To encourage, to move forward with no turning back.
Good fortune:
As to lay claim as to not what one had,
But as to what one was.
Heart:
A wisdom that belied her years, yet endowed her
To see beyond the common good.
A memory:
Heaven opened up her arms for a short niche in time,
And blessed me with an angel who shared her life with mine,
Before God took her home.
Nana.

*Toni Gopee*

## "Blink"

You say the heavens collide amongst your bed
when in the night you lie with an abrupt
of indifferent thoughts in your head
you mumble of a soul outside your window striving to get in
but you refuse to see that it is only the wind
you bloom in sigh of frightful behavior when
your blossoms decide to die then tears trickle down
the wilt to frown that only you can cry
you say you hear footsteps when in moment dark
though you cannot see that it is only the beating of your heart
as the morning wakes you create a grave and lay the blossoms
you whisper that the tears you weep will drip upon them
throughout their infinite sleep as like the heavens which collide
onto you when silently at night you dream of indifferent thoughts
that only you can think of without a meanful cause.

*Nadine Hernandez*

## Despair

When one sits and sits, so alone
When one walks and walks, to no-ones home
When one looks and looks, but no one sees
When one talks and talks, though no-one hears
When one sleep and sleeps, just to drown
the slips and slips pulling you down
Where do you turn?, where will you find?,
that relieving peace,...a piece of mind?.
For heaven's sake, there's peace above.
For goodness sake, there's hope in love.
For eternal's sake, you must not grief...
For future's sake, you simply must believe.

*Yolanda Robertson-Goetz*

## Untitled

There are times
when it's easy to rhyme
Even if you don't care to
the words go from your brain through
your pen and trail across the page
with memories from every single stage
of your life, some speak of pathos some
of humor

Many are accurate, others like a rumor
are exaggerated, but oh it can be fun
playing with words-making a pun
seeing a once blank page filled with lines
that you found in your very own mind's
secret place that sometimes grows bold
and stirs up feeling that clamor and
burst forth and unfold.

**Peg Lynch**

## Buy To The Heart

A bank book is super,
When it's got money in it, that's pure,
Specially, when you have worked all year!

Wouldn't it be nice, to have some pretty material,
It's sort of better to look at, than a plan bowl of cereal,
But, is stuff really real?

When your getting married, its nice to have some earrings
Or, would you rather have a pair of wedding rings?
Either way you look at it, bells are gonna ring!

When I go to the store, I grab a cart,
I try to buy things, that won't fall apart,
But, you can never buy, somebodies heart!

Watching trees grow,
Makes a nice little home, for a crow,
But, is that really how life goes?

**Rolanda Atkinson**

## Siesta Days

As a child I could hardly contain my glee,
When mama would say, "Let's head for the key."
The gateway to the world it would be
waiting, watching and beckoning me.
The days were long but not long enough,
especially when the tide was rough.
We'd wait and watch for just the right wave,
then sail on the crest of a Siesta day.
The sand is fine, the whitest they say,
the people there - a vast array,
Some say it's too hot but how could they know,
they've spent too much time surrounded by snow.
As time has passed, the world has changed
yet Siesta Key remains the same.
It's the same now as it was then,
the beauty of it limited by pen.
The only thing that's changed is me,
as I ready myself and head for the key,
now I'm the one who gets to say,
"Come on kids, it's a Siesta Day!

**Martha Troyer**

## Reunion Day After Abortion

There is coming reunion day,
when mother has been forgiven
and is now walking among the living
one day she will join her little son
Who lives up in heaven
she has searched so long to see
him on the road that circles the universe,
and ends at heavens throng
they will now walk hand in hand
hear God's great angel band
they will stroll down Glory Avenue
where life has been given anew

**Verna Snider**

## Where To From Here?

Puzzled is he about what is to be
when one comes to the end of the road.
All will agree where the body goes, but what about the soul?

Does it escape the body and live forever more in heaven or hell —
the abodes where angels and demons are thought to dwell?

Where is heaven and hell?
Are these real places —
or illusions that the mind embraces?

Believe as you wish.
Believe not you may.
Search for the truth along life's way
until the final Judgment Day.

Life comes and then it flees,
to where unknown by me.
Life is precious, life is free,
but can life forever be?

When the final race is over,
when the last open door is closed,
Power That Be, look down on me
and point the way to go.

**Oneale Adams**

## Alone

A tear comes to my eye and how I wish that it would fall...
when so much wells up deep inside, the inner child so small.
I turn to no one, no one there to hear my inner cry.
The child so small forms but one word, a question...only "Why?"

"Why?" she asks with innocence, my heart beats hard and fast...
I do not have the answer, tho' I seek it in my past.
For there we meet together, that small inner child and I.
I fear when I must go there, where the secrets dormant lie.

But go I must to help the child that never had a friend...
the child that never shed a tear and never did intend...
to grow up so alone, it seems, afraid to love and trust,
afraid to laugh, afraid to cry, but now she feels she must.

The secrets that have stopped a life are buried deep inside;
remembering, the hardest part...much easier to hide.
The fear is growing stronger now, the fear to overcome.
To help the child, I cannot be so cold, so dim, so numb.

A child so badly hurt it seems, she cries so I can hear.
I can't ignore the little voice, so frightened and so dear.
"I'm here for you," I say out loud, and suddenly I'm free.
I'll never be alone again, as long as I have me.

**Lisa Saul**

## Pitfalls of Human Weakness

The spirit is willing but the flesh is weak,
When the temptation of material pleasures is what we seek!

When man sees life's eternal as being forever,
"The Word of God" obeyed is the only true lever!

A spiritual being living as a mortal becomes,
Transformed from temptation's earth to eternal's everlasting from!

Temptation lures as life's temporary pleasure,
As God's everlasting values are life's lost treasure!

Sin overtakes human consciousness as habits are formed,
As transgression is the burden that has to be bourned!

Temptation into sin is the frailty of human weakness,
As blessed are those who inherit the earth in searchful seekness!

A newborn spirit desires the milk of the word,
As acts of disobedience and failure are confessed and forgiven when
   heard!

Human weakness then becomes spiritual strength saved by grace,
As pitfalls tempting the flesh are forgiven in Christ's place!

*Roger Pique*

## Seeds Of The Live Oak Tree

We have known for quite a while that this would come.
When the youthful seed of the Mother tree must be disbursed
   upon the windy currents of life.
We have shared much through the years.
Much love, much laughter, much sorrow, yet most importantly
   we have shared much love of life
And now this maternal oak is telling us that this is our
   chance to return what we have learned.
The wind is blowing harder now more impatient that before.
And before it catches us and takes us all away....
I would like for all to know, that even though
   you will go your way, and I will go mine
We will always be together, bonded for all eternity
   under the protective shade of the Live Oak Tree

*Wendie Waters*

## Somehow

Sometimes...there are sometimes
When we reach for a destination
That is beyond our limits
And we keep trying to get there
Until we finally do...sometimes!
Somedays...Yes, there are somedays
We feel like staying undercover
Forgetting the sun has risen
Looking around and not forward
To people constantly coming over...somedays!
Somehow...We must have a somehow
We must salvage our strength
Straighten the sometimes and somedays
To face each and every new trial
And wake to new meaning within...somehow!

*Rhonda Mink*

## "Walk Through The Garden"

I will walk through the garden with you.
We will laugh, we will cry
We will relive the past and see the future.
Hand in hand we will stroll.
Yet when our visit is over we will
not be saddened.
We will be at peace with our thoughts
We will be at peace with our God.

*Lacie McGlothlin*

## The Holy Spirit, My Heart's Treasure

To have the Holy Spirit is no simple thing.
When we receive it, all Heaven's angels sing.

What power we have with this precious spirit.
How could it not be, since God has given it?

Oh, the fire that burns inside!
The joy I feel, I cannot hide!

All demons must go and forever flee!
Since the Breath of the Almighty lives in me.

All fear, depression, and hatred must go!
For the love of Jesus is all I now know!

I shall rise above all worry and distress.
Nothing can take away my happiness!

Never again will I fall into sin.
Not with what I possess deep within!

Oh, the treasure I hold in my heart!
And I have the assurance He'll never depart.

That blessed assurance!  None can compare.
To know that someday, I'll meet Him up there.

To live forever as one of His own.
In that beautiful place, my eternal home.

*Nita Evans*

## The Ride Home

I am a passenger in the rear of the Metro bus
When will my stop come?
If only I knew!

With ink-covered fingertips
I rest my weary eyes on another neighborhood
But like the one before
It's not mine

With the final wave of her leather suitcase
A woman leaves the same way she came
Behind her sits an impression
In the hot sun-stained vinyl seat

I wish something would mark my exit!
Yet here in the rear, I sit

Now I find myself walking down the steps
To meet with the brisk unfamiliar air
I take it in and hold it as long as my soul will permit
which never seems to last but a moment

So with my ever-clashing face
I re-board the bus just before it pulls out again
In hopes that I'll reach home before dark

*Mary Caruso*

## "Leaving"

You would tell me to go away
Until that one day
It killed me inside to leave
I knew it was something to believe
My love for you grew stronger
And every mile between us seemed longer
I listen to your voice
I knew I had to make the choice
My heart kept on tearing
I knew I had to stop caring
I stared into your eyes
I knew it was time we had to say our good-byes

*Tamara Stewart*

578

## Mother! Mother! Mother!

You didn't even know me when you carried for nine months.
When you delivered me I could say one word.
You took care of me

MOTHER!

You have given me your life by accepted any struggle
you had taught me the right from wrong and you
have pay attention me day, and night.
You was always there for me when I need you,
and you have given courage I deserved

MOTHER!

How could I ever thank you for all work you have done for me.
I will thank you by proving your dream came true
I will be there for you wherever you need me

MOTHER!

You are wonderful woman I love most in life.
I love you more than my china doll,
wherever I be, I will always remember you.
I am all yours.

*Rufin B. Gbado*

## For A Moment

God has given mankind a clue where Heaven is.
When you listen and hear His voice, He says, "I'll show you the way."
He gives us a clue where Heaven is, when we see a rainbow after a
   thunderstorm.
For a moment God lets us observe the external planet "Alpha and Omega"
   where Heaven is.
When we see the dawn of a new day and its summer, after the calm of
   a storm.

*Paul Laffaty*

## "Dad"

Dad, did you hear me say "I Love You"
when you were dying?
Dad, did you feel my tears by your bedside?
I was crying.
Dad, did you feel my love,
as I gently touched your face?
Dad, when you opened your eyes,
I saw the pain, more than a trace.
Dad, did you feel my touch,
as I softly held you hand?
Dad, the thought of you leaving me,
I just could not stand.
Dad, did you know I was with you
when you passed?
Dad, did you now know,
that your pain was gone at last?
Dad, did you feel my tears by your bedside?
There I cried.
Dad, did you hear me say "I Love You"
when you died?

*Sharon Shrader*

## Legend Of Great Spirit's Helper

A handsome beetle with armor of blazing white
Was made Chief Starkeeper, Companion of Night.
Each evening when Father Sun slipped slowly west
To cradle down with Turquoise Woman in her nest,
White Beetle flings a canopy across the sky
Arrayed with flirting flames to charm and mystify.
Their joyous luster softly sifts to quilt the land
Bewitching ardent lovers who stroll hand in hand.
When bold and saucy dawn dares to break the day
White Beetle tenderly tucks his stars away.

*Margaret D. Youngblood*

## Perplexed

Where are we going?  When the compass of life is rusted.
Where are we going?  When our Government can't be trusted.
We've worked and paid our taxes
Until the sweat ran from our brow,
We find our backs, against the wall,
Wondering, Pondering, why?
Does anyone have the answer?
To a question asked by many,
Or should we sit back, with our lips sealed tight,
Because most in authority have plenty?
Yes!  I have the answer to the question asked by many,
We should gather up the fragments,
Of love, hope, and peace.
Turn from our wicked ways,
And from wars we should cease.
And if the masses, who are called by Jesus name.
Would humble themselves, and from sin refrain,
Trust in the Lord, and do his will,
Then all of our hopes, would be fulfilled.

*Lillie Bell Hobbs*

## I Wish...

I wish I owned a house, with lots of land...and trees,
Where birds, pets and children could be at home with me;
I wish for clouds with rainbows, pure and gentle, too;
For skies always beautiful, the blue showing through.

Only God can make flowers, trees, and butterflies...
And I know He's the one in charge of all the skies;
Whatever clouds, trials, or sunshine comes my way,
I'm confident they're exactly right for that day!

Seasons come and go, and years continue on their rounds;
Some bad things must be, but the best things still abound.
The One Who changes not is always in His place;
I wonder how He holds all the stars out in space...

I wish for land here on earth, where things freely roam,
But I may never have that place to call my own;
True, I may never have my wishes while here below;
Still, I'll have them all when on to Heaven I go!

Enough for me is that glorious promised Land,
Where He is the Light, and all is just what He's planned;
My dreams will all come true in Heaven's perfect realm;
Wishes and dreams will be perfect, too, because of Him!

*Ruth M. Peters*

## Good-Bye

She had to go, and so we cry,
where did she go, did her soul die?
Or is her soul still here, and her image went away,
Or did God take her on a mission today?
A raindrop just fell, or was it a tear?
From all the people who still wish she was here.
God took her away, she was needed up there.
We need her here too, guess life isn't fair.
Death's so confusing, where did she go?
Someday, one day, we all will know.
I wish I knew her better, before she had to die.
I knew her well enough, to give her one last kiss good-bye.
Good-bye.

*Shonna Drew*

## Alone

The lights go out and no one's around
where have they all gone, where is the sound
could it be that they are all dead
or maybe it's all in my head
somebody's here, I can just tell
maybe they'll come out if I let out a yell
what's going on here, what's wrong with me
why am I a victim of this tragedy
what brought this doomsday to my fate
always full of love, never any hate
was it the devil, made of such dread
oh God please help me, as I try to clear my head
please let my mind get back on pace
and allow me to leave this horrid place
did I do something to cause great confusion
or is it what I'm hoping a horrifying illusion

### *Will Moore*

## Maug

Where is that strange place, I hear about,
where its natural harbour has claimed heavy
anchor with its many shots of chain?
Never to be seen again.
Where Jurassic like birds greet vessels and
dive 'neath the clear, deep water for their subsistence?
Where voyagers observe in great interest,
a pre-historic view of unspoiled, clean and
verdant islands with its rich, virgin marine life.
The ancient volcano, perhaps a couple
millions of years old with its steep ridges
and inclines, inviting guest which navigate its waters.
Where is this place the world has never heard of?
Where lucky divers tell fascinating stories
about down below. Of deep drop offs and cone
shaped bottoms, which taper into the darkness
off to unimaginable depths. Of white tip sharks,
giant sea turtles, octopus, eels and many many kinds of fish.
I believe to have been to such a place.
It is called Maug, one of the fifteen chain of islands of the
Marianas.

### *Walter Anthony Kenna*

## Untitled

Today we are living in a world full of pain,
where people are only out for their own gain.
In the earlier years, we had people looking out for each other.
Now we look down upon our family, our brothers.
People worry about little things, like color.
We say they are not like, they are some other.
How do we know whose morals are right,
when the people making them want to fight.
How do we know that our lives are getting better.
We will find that mother nature will help us, if we let her.
We destroy hopes, dreams, and what not
With guns, death, decay and what not.
We have to stand up to fight those who do us harm
because they trick us with their little charms.
We all have a voice that must be heard.
Because we are not like some cow herd.
We have a lot to live for.
So keep living and you'll see what life is for.
Listen to what I have said.

Live life before you are dead.

### *Bil Terry*

## Window's Edge

Evening,
   where private displays of random violence rage like
frenzied beats about to pounce.
   Where out cries of strong emotion rest silent in
dormant wisdom.
   Where a search for the eternal mystery of butterfly
freedom exists while resisting glorious nights of slumber.
   Where hell's scream burns at the wake of nature.
   Where eyes are sweetly embedded within the sultry forest,
but intensely aware that with time a whisper will be
stolen from a child's precious lips.
   Where a treasured departure over the fence and into a
dream raises a torn curtain of midnight that reveals
faltering rocks beneath waves of tranquility.
   Like these faltering rocks we are the shadows that have
receded into a lament for the death of our seasonal love.
   Please don't wander from the road.
   We're bleeding tears.

### *Michael McCormick*

## Mountains

I long to be in yonder mountains
Where the creeks, still run free
and people are few and far between
with all things glowing, in the beauty of green

Sunlight dances on morning due
polished rocks still bring a thrill
with all trails leading to paradise
high upon, my lovely mountain

In the mountains, the air is sweet and free
the birds and beast, are all friends of mine
mountain breezes, are worth more than gold
and music plays all the day, in mountain melody

There're flowers and trees, that blow in the breeze
on the wind is the sweet scent, of the mountain
clear nights bring out the stars, for all to see
God in heaven could be no more pleased, than me on my mountain

### *Michael Ray Martin*

## Time Together

We've known each other for a short time,
Where within our presence a peace that I find,
So freely, so pure, my emotions do flow,
To one so special they so easily go.
Our eyes connect, with feelings of content,
Deep inside, that our paths were meant.
To learn each other can be easily done'
if we create the environment, in which fear is gone.
Just a glimpse at your smile makes me warm inside.
Where my heart is the pilot of feelings, I can't hide.
Not to invade your life with complexity and pain,
But to bring complete happiness and assist you,
Through the rain, in a stormy breeze and when far from home.
I will always be there, to set your heart at ease.
We must venture through our present and future.
And continue to search our lives for the precious time,
That we deserve together, to create a special bond.
And carry though the love for each other devotedly..

### *Suzette M. Mudie*

## Condemned To Die On Calvary

If it were not for the beauty of Easter
Where would sinners like you and I be?
For it was for our sins that Jesus Christ died on Calvary
By the hands of cruel, wicked, blinded men who refused to see

Before His betrayal, yes, even before His Crucifixion
His spoken promise, "In three days will be my Resurrection"
But evil men mocked and scolded Him, with ire and disbelief
As they condemned Him, and chose Barabbas, a murderer and thief

The crowd who loved and followed Him for His Power and Divine Insight
Became irate, dumb founded, very sad when they saw the awful sight
Of His swollen bloodstained hands, His bruised pierced side
The love, yet agony, on His Mother's face when she heard her Savior's
    cries

Yet, in those long dark hours of bedlam, fright and despair
He prayed, "Father forgive them their ignorance, of what I bear
I had no choice, but to drink from this bitter cup of evil and sin
So men will have a chance, through my salvation, to live and death
    will flee and end"

"It is finished," He said; bowed His head and gave up the ghost
Panic, gloom, flashes of lightning, covered the Earth from coast to
    coast
It was now apparent and plain for all to see and agree
That surely this was the Chosen Christ, who was Crucified
    to set men free.

*Willie Evelyn Squalls*


## Nostalgia

I wonder
Whether I still love you,
If I do,
Why did we have such a separation.

I wonder
Whether I hadn't loved you a long time ago,
If I hadn't
Why don't my memories fade with the lapse of time.

Recall your sweet smile,
My passions rise and fall like tidal waves,
But all of these have already passed,
Only the charming nights are as fair as before.

*Quentin Li*


## Oklahoma

One bright clear day the sky did fall.
Which broke our hearts one and all.
Some people thought it was worth the
price to take the innocent and so much life.
To you I say great pain you've wrought,
and in my opinion without one thought.
To all the lives which you have stolen.
Just because your heads are swollen
with all your complaints about the government
gives you no right to stand in judgement.
Unless you atone and pray for forgiveness,
lost are your souls for God is thy witness.
Some feel angered all still feel grief
for those who's lives are now incomplete.
To you...your pain I know is quite deep,
but now their souls are our Lord's to keep.
So live your lives well and make them proud
you'll see them again somewhere beyond the clouds.

*Tammy Williams*


## Sonnet For A Marriage

I stood, that April dawn, transfixed by sky
Which lay, it seemed to me, quite like your blue
Shawl - your scarf, perhaps - gentle and shy
Around the shoulders of the hills; it hue
The colors of your eyes. And, later, when
We knelt to bless the promises we said
In that small chapel of Saint Catherine
The slant of sky that touched your face seemed thread
To weave the fabric of each April dawn,
Of all our suns, each rose, each rain that led
Till half a hundred years - and you - were gone
Taking my heart with you as you fled.

Now, every dawn I stand and search the skies
For shawls and scarves and O, my love, your eyes.

*Rose L. Breslin Blake*


## The Secret Of My Youth

That night at his house we were all alone.
Which was a plan that I wish I would have known.
Innocent flirting pinned me to the ground;
Unable to move or make the slightest sound.
It happened so fast. He came on so strong.
I've no memory of a moment when I did something wrong.
Trapped! No way out! Pressed against the sink!
Terrified and trembling! No time to think!
I pushed him away as he grabbed my arm;
Assuring me he meant to cause no harm.
I'll always remember his aggressive brown eyes.
His innocent talk was just a disguise.
It's been a secret I have kept inside.
Flashbacks and nightmares have been hard to hide.
Flinching at his movement, frightened of his stare.
When I close my eyes, he is always there.
With no idea of price I've unwillingly paid my toll.
My pushing had no influence. His strength was in control.
I'll always be haunted by the fear inside my mind.
I entered his house with courage; but my pride I left behind.

*Melinda S. Brown*


## Hello - Goodbye

I was saying hello to a new-born babe
While someone was saying goodbye
To a dear old friend
Who had reached life's end
And was getting ready to die

One has just started his journey in life
While the other is almost through
One has known all the struggle and strife
Of trying his best to be true

Asleep in his crib lay the little boy
Who had brought to his parents their greatest joy
Indeed they were blessed for their faith and their love
Indeed they were blessed with a gift from above

Now the dear old friend
Who's wrinkled with age
Has almost turned the final page
And when it's time to close his eyes
He will awake to his surprise
And find himself in a beautiful place
Where he will see his God face to face

*Nancy C. Greco*

## What Is Never Sought Is Rarely Found

The white bright blue sunshined clouds stand in the mist.
While the glass coated birds fly high in the sky.
Looking below the gummy bear fish look for a dish to give
them a ticklish feel that makes it unreal to be in this deal.
  Down to the west the white powdered sugar stands high in the
chocolate mountains and the cinnamony mash flows out
of the mouth with a sugary ease that gives each a please
to have such a good sugary wees.
  Up to the south the flowers browse for a house to have a
pedal of medal to protect them from the pedals of bikes
from the kids on a hike that don't know a bit about the
likes of the light on which the flowers grows bright.
  Now for the east which is full of the breast that eat from the
least known increase of leaves which have the grief of the teeth
of the breast that love to eat grease from the toes of the crows
down in the holes with the moles and the lows brows of the most
unknown tolls with loads of crones
on their toes and moles on their pet crows.

**Ramon Da Silva**

## 1 Year, 28 Days, and 11 Hours

He sat in silence and thought of home
While the stillness drove him insane.
The jungle was his umbrella against the world
And cigarettes passed the time.
Sweat slowly rolled down his face
As the sound of bullets sang him to sleep.
His gun was his only lover through the nights
And fear his constant companion.
There was really no time to cry.
He was too busy trying to just keep breathing.

Now, he sits alone and thinks about the jungle.
He lingers on what he knows and where he's been
And cigarettes pass the time.
Sweat slowly rolls down his face
As the memories of bullets keep him from sleeping.
He is simply too tired to ever have a lover.
Every time he closes his eyes, he remembers.
He has come too close to death to ever be afraid.
Still, there is much for him to think about.
It is enough for him just to keep breathing.

**Michelle Suzanne Smith**

## Last Night

In a peaceful solo-sitting,
  while watching the night go by,
    I welcomed the breeze onto my face
      and the clouds into my eye.
        I pondered the sky and reasons why,
          and thought of the stuff I do.
            At first - in the clouds
              and no stars to see
                I thought only of me.
                  As the clouds went free
                    And the stars shown through,
                      I sighed -
                        and thought
                          about
                            you.

**Stinzo**

## The Song Of The Son

I showered you with granite, my son
While you showered me with silk
I gave you hot, steaming bile, my son
While you gave me sweet milk
I showed you nothing but trouble, my son
While you gave me joy
I gave you the coarse sands from Hell's beaches, my son
While you bowed and gave me exotic poi

I ask you my son, what justice is there in this world?
And you answered thus, my son:
Nothing but my love and life's splendor unfurled.

**Lin Hendler**

## Words

They can be spoken or shouted or
  whispered in your ear
They can bring happiness or sorrow or
  even induce fear.
They can be spoken as prayers to the
  Lord above
Or uttered with warmth to the one
  that you love.
Always choose them carefully, with a great
  deal of tact
For once past your lips there's no
  bringing them back.
We all have our favorites, I certainly
  do
The four words I like best are;
  "Sheryl, I Love You."

**Ralph J. McCullagh**

## Reincarnation (The Base Cannot Be Diffused)

History's revenge tugs at rampant souls
whispering to us through the tattered pages of dead men's ink
as vinegar tears preserve the spirits in a bottle cast off to sea.
Pandora's Box afloat—curse or blessing for an unsuspecting traveler;
restless images of lives since past stir the brain in unreachable
wisdom, and History does not sleep.

In those who are fortunate to be mad, it dwells,
alive, hungry, insatiable—wanting us to know the others.
It kicks and screams until we take up our pens and write,
possessed of a spirit which formed our being once, so long ago.

The specters remain in pieces
fused by the intercourse of a wild enchantress and spellbound prince
on the eve of the summer solstice

And you—you fell without a care from your mother's womb
on the day of the eclipse
refreshed and new after a centennium's sleep
there again to be touched and molded
(so they thought)
but the soul remains deliciously tainted...
deliciously tainted...

**Maria Josephine Wolff**

## Poets

What would this world be like without poets?
Who explain the events that make up our existence as no one else can?
Who would write the love poems that young lovers recite?
No one to examine the soul.
No one to record the raw emotions.
Would we live in a society of androids?
Mindless drowns who neither think nor feel.
No imagination.
No freedom of the soul.
Would this be a world without poets?

**Misty S. Hodges**

## Symbols

Petals, mature and full as a woman
White as a mountain top in winter
Leaves reaching toward the moon
Heat fills him, his heart a sun to passion.
Stem lifts a longing heart to the sky
Words are invisible, emotions unknown
This heart should no longer be left alone
Therefore mended by the figurine of dream pools.
Petals, pure as a fallen tear
White as the light in her life
Leaves reaching out towards the man
Heat fills her, her heart the moon to paradise.
Stem lifts an offering to the sky
The innocence of another left alone
Watered from the tears of yesterday
Blooming forth into the halls of beauty.
Petals, as delicate as the hearts
White as the glowing chastity of unison
Leaves combining the two to one
Heat surrounds them, their souls one for each other.

*Michael Bagley*

## Fires In California

Orange and red flames all around.
White ash falling on the ground.
A moving inferno, flames from hell'
water was needed the flames to quell.

Miles of destruction, hearts in despair.
The smell of burning on the air.
Neighborhoods evacuated during the night,
with the glow of the fire still in sight.

What should we take and what can we leave?
Only a short time to decide what to retrieve.
Birth certificates, photographs, works of art,
were placed in vehicles before the engines did start.

Down through the canyon we drove in the dark,
single file calmly, this was no lark.
The firemen so brave battling the foe,
their bodies so weary, yet they kept on the go.

Eventually, days later, the blaze it was tamed,
but homes large and small by the fire were claimed.
Friends and neighbors will remember this calamity,
the terrible consuming fire of 1993.

*M. A. Hawkings*

## Dreams

A dream gives hope to ev'ry one
    Who dare a dream to start—-
It's not a vision of the mind
    But longing of the heart.

Dreams live both in the young and old
    And keep our spirit strong—
    Dreams give direction to our life
        When things we do go wrong.

A dream is like a yellow rose
    That, given love and care,
Will blossom from a bud of hope
    And lift us from despair.

    A dream's as strong as one's belief,
        As weak as someone's doubt;
    A dream's as gentle as a breeze
        Or forceful as a shout.

Hold fast your dreams and nourish them
    With faith and love from you—
And you will find within your heart
    That all your dreams come true.

*Richard Day*

## Memories

Oh whimsy, thou old nemesis to me
    who does unkindly trip about
        in my sore mind's retreat
            and picks away at old thoughts and deeds

You, who harasses my tomorrows
    with all my yesterdays
        and points your crooked old digit my way
            and spares me not from unkinder times

Would that I could call upon some champion
    to come forth and slay thee
        and have these many times done so
            and lo you resurrect at your will

And spite my would be happy heart
    for pleasure is not your end
        but rather your cloak
            and in misty times of unprudent play

Your trenchant hand scalds
    my unawares soul
        and leaves me to weep
            in my remembrances

*J. Ellsworth Dean*

## The Forgotten Fisherman

A long time ago, I met a man
Who had rock cod scales all over his hands.

He told me of his life, and how it had been
And how he had this feeling it was about to end.

He was an old man, old and gray,
But who could see happiness in his yesterday.

This old man was brave and true,
But on his breath, I smelled a drink or two.

He had his good points and some bad ones at that.
You could sure tell from his talk, where his life had been at.

He gave his life to the sea, and ask nothing in return,
But a drink now and then, and some money to burn.

And as I walked away down the old rickety dock
I thought a lot about our little talk.

I thought about his life, free with the sea,
And now as I stare, I realize that's the life for me.

*William Clyde Forkner III*

## Ode To My Mother

You vengeful, spiteful, witch
Who has treated me like s--t
For all these years, can you now see
Why I cried those tears?
You claim to love, but I wonder why
You've forgotten the beating, which made me cry
To hurt you, like you hurt me
Is my only wish you see
So one day soon, I'll extract my revenge
And I only hope, it will make you cringe
So just keep smiling your fake smile, hiding the pain our family feels
You are the only one who's in denial, and with one look you send me
    chills
And my father, the enabler
Who always said, "I'll talk to her later."
But I won't let you get to me
I love you mother, goodbye!

*Michelle Coburn*

## Little Girl Lost

Once there was a little girl lost
who hid from the world
all the rape of her soul

She yearned for the light but on one condition
that no one would see
what little remained of her.

They had fondled her body, (how good it felt!)
and the innocence of her heart
was changed forever.

Crying in silence and wondering why;
self-hate constrained her
and punished her so.

Was it wrong to want love or a piece of the sky?
Was it selfish to need a safe place to play?

"Perhaps I am bad", she whispers to herself,
for she's learned to like touches
in her private places.

So the shame runs deep in the darkness of her night;
and the pain is overwhelming as it tears apart the remnants
of her lost, deserted soul.

*Suzanne M. Bielec*

## Moo-oo Cow

We had a moo-oo cow
Who liked to take a bow
Her hair was smooth as silk
And she gave us good milk.

My Dad fed her well
As one could easily tell
Her registry papers named her "Moo-oo Cow"
And she took another bow.

Now - my sister has many moo cows
Some on dish cloths
Some serve sugar and cream
Others on the stove —
    And how they gleam
One on the cabinet - chewing her cud
A few cows near - eating hay
Listen! and you'll hear them say
"I'm a Moo Cow - and I like to take a bow."

*Rowena Bragdon Holt*

## "The Quiet Man He Was"

There once was a man who lived in a small town,
who lived a very private life.
He was a man who seemed to walk alone,
but he knew walking beside him was his good friend the
Lord Jesus Christ.
Many wondered why he was so silent and why he never
talked to anyone anywhere.
There were many who found him to be strange,
but he was only a man full of dreams waiting to be shared.
He believed in the greatest gift,
even though he was young and there were things that he
did not know.
He did not care about what risks he might be taking.
All he cared about was finding the gift and letting it grow.
He has not yet found the gift,
but he continues to search with his heart and he hopes
someday that the gift will be in his hands
'Till that time comes he will continue to be who he is.
He will continue to be the quiet man.

*Scott Herrick*

## Who Am I?

What is this chronic pain?
Who of my fellows can place my blame?
My head upon my clasped knees
Only allows the caressing breeze
To intensify the gnawing "Why?" "Who am I?"

Reminiscing, I see my dad and mom,
My sister, and my brother Tom,
All my teachers taught me well
How to add and how to spell,
Nothing seems to be awry but, "Who am I?"

My preacher came by the other day
And said for me to kneel and pray
If my heart were sorely tried
And if these things applied,
Was I anxious and so would cry,
If I wondered, "Who am I?"

A response was flashed to me about our Christ upon a tree,
He lived His life to forgive and bless
Those in doubt and had to guess,
To point the way to heaven on high for answers to, "Who am I?"

*Lillian Havlena*

## Little Angels

They look so peaceful when they're sleeping.
Who would have known how beautiful
it could be.

She goes to sleep
holding my hand while I rock her.
She has to be touching me
and that touch is like
nothing I've ever felt before or since.

He fights sleep
but when he gives up
the overwhelming relief
shows on his face.
His gentle limp body
against his daddy's solid chest
is the picture of comfort.

Sometimes, in the middle of the night
I go to them
just to watch my angels
breathe and dream.
They look so peaceful when they're sleeping.

*Nancy Pridgen*

## Face of War

Oh!  Where go the children of each generation,
Whose innocence played at the bordering nation?
Smiles and laughter, each little face wore,
But must they change, - to the face of war?

We may dream of the hero from Trojan shore,
Or, perhaps, the Mongol in Asian lore.
Somewhere, distorted, twixt bravery and fear,
Our eyes we shut; - nothing is clear!

What gain has it been through all the tears,
Long suffering and strife for a thousand years?
And, in my mind, I hear once ore,
The banshee wail, - in the face of war.

*Lyle McLeod*

## Prejudice

Not only a word, an idea of spite,
Whose to say if it's wrong or it's right.
A feeling of hatred is loud and clear,
We don't want to believe these problems are here.

These feelings are evident, no matter how slight,
Against this we must stand and begin our fight.
A fight against bigots and racists who hate,
Don't let these ideas seal our peoples fate.

It's in our own hands, our future, our lives,
As long as we listen to these poor peoples cries.
Our prayers will be answered and end what's not right,
If we all ban together, take a stand; unite.

So start when there young and instill this one thought,
"We can all be friends with those we have fought."
So look past the differences; the color of skin,
And look at the person that lies within.

*Michael J. Betzinger Jr.*

## A Report On Our Progress Towards Self-Destruction

Time is meaningless
whose turn to throw the dart?
who knows?
it's all random
it's so anonymous
is there no God?
where art Thou?
ahh! I've known all along!

Bombs continue to fall
people are still driven to the camera
in wretched fear
in wretched pain
crying and screaming in silence
frozen in history
so... whose turn to throw the dart?
ahh!! Who cares!!

"...until tomorrow, this is Today in World News.
Have a good evening."

*Magali Olivencia*

## Unanswered Questions

What's beyond this prison cell?
Why am I subjected to hell?
How much longer will I have to stay here?
When will I stop being engulfed with fear?
Why do I even have to hide?
Will loneliness ever leave my side?
When will I feel a cool morning breeze?
Will the world ever be at ease?
Is my family alive or dead?
Why can't I sleep in my own bed?
Why am I treated as if I don't matter,
as Hitler keeps climbing his powerful ladder?
Hitler hates me because I'm a jew,
but, Hitler, what did I ever do to you?

*Rae Robertson*

## The Storm

SHE ranted and raved and threw things
HE ranted and raved and threatened
And the anger tornado spinning wildly through the room
Cut its path of destruction.

In the quiet after the storm
Stunned survivors survey the damage
Do we rebuild? Or
Do we just pick up and move on.

*Roberta Cooper*

## Undercover

I'm afraid...there are so many questions I ask myself.
Why can't I come forth from the waterfall of disguises.
and let my feelings flow from within...
Pain and pleasure make me everyday. Let love rain
upon my heart, not a broken heart full of despair...
Love me for what I am, if you don't, leave me in the
ashes of broken hearts. There my soul feelings for you
will die but the path that lies ahead will be a disembodied travel.
It's too bad that it is so hard to trust words, that's why I always
follow my heart.
I wish that I didn't have to be hooded from pain and feelings.
A glass heart,
fiery emotions
and love
passing
by like
seasons.
-Help me Lord-

*Tuscsasa Wilson*

## Blinded For Why

Why must people, pretend to care for each other?
Why can't people see, the needs for each other?

Why must they live together, acting to love one another?
Why can't they see, there's more than sex with one another?

Why must they hurt, and torment each other?
Why can't they admit, their reality to each other?

Why must they lie, within one another?
Why can't they be honest, and trusting to one another?

Why must they act, to be for each other?
Why can't they see, life no good for each other?

Why so hard for them, to truly see one another?
Why all the whys, about one another?
Why it's obvious,
They're blinded by each other!

*Ronald W. Lyons*

## "A Feeling Of Loneliness"

*Dedicated to Nicole DeNike*
I am sitting down at home.
Why do I feel so alone?
It is not very clear,
why you are there and I am here.
My mind is in total despair,
life is not very fair.
My soul continues to decay
every minute you spend away.
I know you will soon be back,
but it is then that I begin to crack.
I start to fear you will not feel the same
every precious moment I call out your name.
If our heavenly love is really true,
then you will surely remember, I will always love you!

*Vince Levigne*

## The Dark Road

Walking down the dark road
with only a cloud of white before me,
Each step, a step into the future,
Each step a mystery.
Up ahead I see the headlights of a car,
A sense of reality to an unreal situation,
and yet not.

*R. Lee Caswell*

## Restraint-Free!

Sitting in my chair, I wondered and sighed
Why does my caretaker keep me tied?

I can recall when I walked the halls free
Enjoying my life in tranquility.

Now that I've aged and become so gray,
My restraint-free life they have taken away.

"It's for your own safety," they reply
Often overlooking the fear in my eyes.

Oh, if only they would trust me again.
So what if I fall? That is no sin.

Yes, I could hurt my back, leg or arm
Or cause some other bodily harm.

But that's the price I'm willing to pay
To have the restraints removed today.

The patient safety is important, too,
But restrict our mobility they should not do.

*Priscilla Pinder*

## WHY?

Why does the world seem to turn on me?
Why is it that sometimes it is hard for me to see?
Why is it that life is so full of pain?
Why is it that life sometimes make you insane?
Sometimes I wonder, Why God put me here?
Why is it that they say resurrection day is near?
It's hard for me to understand, Why all of these
things must be, is it above my power to see?

Why does God take lives away?
Why is it that we all just can't stay?
Why is it that little girls and boys can't get along?
Why is it that in harmony and unison we all can't sing a song?
There has to be a reason for all of these Why's, maybe one day
God will answer my Why's.

*Rashawna Dominique Cooper*

## Memoriam

Has pain not quenched my old heart's fires?
Why then not those of desire?
Thoughts of my mind are often with you,
Only your image in my heart is viewed.
The fires engulf your image of stone
And your sweet face remains alone.
Still within me are my memories,
To keep or lose, I would equally grieve.
Men leave behind proof of their sins to show
Like thieves who would rob in the pure white snow.
But of our relationship, no more signs appear
Then left by fish swimming or birds flying through the air.
And between us all sweetness was had.
All nature would yield or we could add.

*Lynda L. Woolf*

## Blackness

Although my skin, my black skin is shiny like dew, my hair like
wire, and my teeth like pearls from the oyster, some think I am
not beautiful, but I have described the queen of Sheba, and KING
Solomon thought she was beautiful.
  Black is beautiful,
  Black is divine,
  Let black roll on,
O black sons, O black daughters, Why must you let the oppressors
kill you?
O black mothers of America, Listen, Listen, Listen!

*Mary E. Hightower*

## Operation: Apocalypse

When will we see the end of the world?
Will it be when an evil plan is unfurled?
Will it be by fire, bomb or flood?
Will it be because God senses our lack of love?
Will we be over-exposed to ultraviolet rays?
The ozone is already depleting in too many ways.
Is it all our fault, because of violence, of crime?
Will we all self-destruct when it comes our time?
We must change our ways, of love and of hate.
While we still have a chance, while it isn't too late.
Teenage pregnancies, murder, shootings and death.
We must step aside and let fate do the rest.
With poverty, hunger, depression and sin,
What became of the happy world we once lived in?
I say if we must go, go with dignity and pride.
Make-up for your past; go along for the ride.
Being on the same planet as all the hatred and crime
Might be punishment enough 'til we get ourselves in line,
I guess there's only one last thing I can say:
If alive we'll find out on that fateful Judgment Day.

*Sarah Lombardi*

## Rock 'N' Ivy

Candles burning brightly; leaves falling lightly.
Winds blowing softly as a whisper against my face.
Is this the heart of an embrace?

Think of us as two
When we could be as one.
Two hearts entwined clinging to catch
  hold as rock-n-ivy.
Gathered closer to my heart; tucked
  inside; stitched never to be free again.
You are in my memory and I believe in you.

By the shadow on the moon, up the stairway to nowhere
The lines of rhythm are written up; then down.
Soundlessly like a touch of the wind the flame burns out.
No longer embraced.
No longer a heart.

*Susan Mann*

## Ardor's Cafe

He offered me some sugar—
Wispy, brown hair covered a bright blue eye,
Strong, masculine jawline formed a handsome smile,
Broad shoulders,
Well-defined arms,
Solid hands that appeared to be reaching,
Just enough tanned skin showing from an unbuttoned collar,
A desirable appearance,
Offering me some sugar,
I looked at my coffee cup,
My eyes no longer lingered,
And I responded, "yes, thank you."
And he brought me some sugar,
For my coffee,
And his bright blue gaze remained,
Until he had to leave,
And I placed the sugar beside my cup,
Because I don't take sugar in my coffee.

*Toniann Wright*

586

## Rex

He was always there
With a bark and a wagging tail
His way to say; I'm glad you're back
and I hope you're here to stay"
I'm lonely when you're away"

He's there when I'm happy there when I'm sad
and tired and all alone

And he tries to say - in his doggy way
'I know how you feel' then he gives me his bone
and goes on his merry way.
I'll miss you pal, if you have to go
and then I'd worry too
suppose you're the one who is left alone
and who will explain to you
It wasn't that you weren't loved
or that you chewed the rug and chased the cat
It would just be that my time had come
Please, God, if that's how it will be
Have someone else to love him someone just like me.

*Ruth E. Merrill*

## The Dream

I sit here and watch you pass by
With a beautiful young lady at your side
She has brown hair, she's shorter than you
I can't see her eyes, but that's all right
You're both dressed very casually
As you two walk by, side by side, hand in hand
You don't notice me sitting alone, watching you
You stop and kiss her gently on the lips
As you continue to walk along
I turn my head and cry softly
You don't know this but I've loved you from afar
But how could you know, you were too busy with "other things"
An arm is gently wrapped around my shoulders
To comfort and ease my pain
My head is pulled to lay upon the chest of a strong, young man
All of my pain is exposed as I cry
I look into the eyes of the person holding me, rocking me
And I see your handsome blue eyes
And I realize it's all a dream.

*Michelle Rudloff*

## Untitled

Have you ever come near a precipice
With a conscious, sane mind?
Danger lurking everywhere,
Yet, you had wanted ... to jump.

... To be sucked into an unmeasurable void
... to feel the pain of nothingness
... to derive comfort from the touch
   of the coldest pair of hands
... to enjoy the burden of stress.

Shedding all inhibitions
You had wanted to feel
All odd sorts of thing
All evil fantasies.

Rather diabolic of you
I should say
Perhaps, sometimes
It's easier that way.

*Subarna Bhattacharyya*

## What Happened To Being Daddy's Girl

I use to be Daddy's little girl, now I am all grown up
with a family of my own and daddy doesn't want anything to do
with me. I'm not sure why but would like to know, is it because
my views are now my own? I've always wanted him to be happy
and tried to make him proud. I would do anything for my daddy.
So why does daddy now have a heart of stone to someone who was
once his clone?
   Maybe it's because Daddy has to do some growing of his
own.
   I'll love you forever Daddy...

*Tracy Reynolds*

## Nothing Like A Springtime Morning In The Mountains

I woke up this morning
with a thin fog rolling
off the mountains into
the valley.
Early to class I walked
slowly through it,
watching it curl its
fingers around me,
like a ghost.
Through the grass,
thick with dew,
enveloped by the beauty
of a springtime morning
in the mountains.
I walked alone, with no one
to share it with
but the ghost of a morning
fog.

*Stacey Lay*

## Untitled

I dreamt one day (in a wheat field pregnant
with color and expectation. Scented and hot
like freshly baked bread) of love I have not ever
done, nor been in her sweetness.
Why is this metamorphosis whispers, germinant
in my ear. Naked and

Quaking in the fierce dawn, a golden mien
shimmering like the first solo journey down the Amazon's
untamed arms. Beckoned from the first time eyes ever met
Essentially, to wrap beauteous game
outstretched on the river bank, or blanket rhythm
in my soul

And when she dances with a ruby in her navel
(curtains closed but billowing, white irish linen
in the breeze that smells like the first time every woman's
hair caught the sunlight)
Pure. Exquisite. Radiance flutters from fingertips
now mine

*Stacia Merrill*

## December Is A Special Month

December is a special month, a special time of year.
We celebrate the birth of Christ as Christmas draws so near.
With holly, and some mistletoe, and don't forget the kiss-
Christmas is a special time I'd never want to miss!
We celebrate with Santa, his reindeer, and his elves.
We mostly think of others first, and not so much ourselves.
We decorate with lots of lights around a lovely tree.
We send out cards to many friends and all our family.
Our loved ones come together, from near and far away.
We know that they can't stay long so we cherish this today.
Yes, December is a special month, so let us spread the cheer!
Christmas time is special! I'm so happy that it's here!

*Sonja Campbell*

## Waves

Crystal waves that come and go
With cotton foam, soft winds that blow
Waves rising in the ocean's depths
Revealing pirate treasure, diamonds, and sometimes death

All this and more are the waves of my poem
Waves that bring the light of life
The dream of peace, the gift of life

Through waves I feel God's creation, this gives me hope
Waves touching me softly, so softly, oh
To hear your voice, the song of the sea
In this poem, you are telling me
all that I want to know

Naked waves breaking between the rocks
Disappearing drop by drop
Will form again, so far away
To break again, day after day

So Ask me, please, to return and contemplate
Your splendor
And I will sing you a son, and will a wave,
I will send her to you, so far away

   *Norma Miller*


## Baltimore Bag Lady

She strolls the streets and only half seeing,
with her head bent low and eyes almost blind.
She talks to herself; this wretched being,
the way she behaves; no one seems to mind.
She stops near a can and glances linger,
her wrinkled hand moves so fast out and in.
Swiftly to the bag beside her fingers,
clutches it tightly like a jeweled pendant.
Weary and tired she moves along the street,
in all kinds of weather, she looks the same.
No feelings showing as she shuffles her feet,
a simple, ragged old human with no name.
Is this a mother or friend we could say,
or is this a life that is thrown away?

   *Shirley D. Davis*


## The Cat's Secret

The furry pillow lays there
with its emotionless face,
yet you could tell its feelings.

Depression, uncertainty, happiness?
Does it know something I don't?
It grins at me in a mocking way.

With ears twitching like T.V. antennas,
eyes lowered like in an old western movie,
it looks like it is uncertain of me.

Its needles twitch,
it walks away gracefully,
keeping the secret to itself.

   *Michael Cesarczyk*


## Storms

Sometimes storms come in with cheetah speed,
With an eerie cat quiet, that's quiet indeed.
Then turn so loud it sounds like a battle,
With lightning and thunder, making things rattle.
And with heavy clouds that stalk the earth
Until raindrops pounce on both river and turf,
With claw scratches of lightning across the sky,
Wind can screech and make anything fly.
Then it moves on like it never occurred,
Reminding us with the rumble of a distant purr.

   *Tara Ann Morgan*


## Epitaph

He drifted through life self centered
With just enough change in his pockets to get by
Dark and brooding; hardly ever sober
An unhappy man who had nothing to give but pain
We shed buckets of tears before he vanished in the night
He left with just the shirt on his back
He left his children emotionally scarred
Afraid of answers, he avoided questions
And carried old demons to his grave
Years would pass before learning he was gone
Consumed with guilt for not feeling guilty
Penniless and without friends, I wonder
who bid him farewell?
Who stood beside his coffin stumbling over words
that wouldn't belie hypocrisy?
Were flowers placed on his pauper's grave
to ease someone's sorrow?
No stone marks his resting place, but somewhere
on the West Coast an inconspicuous mound of dirt covers
the remains of a man abandoned by life

   *Mary F. Williams*


## Untitled

I feel very much like the weeping willow tree,
With leaves all hanging down.
She stands so strong,
although her branches just grow down.
Her life with all experiences
Gay and swiftly blow;
but in the end the melancholy is all that's left to grow.
The rain comes to nurture my weeping willow tree, the drops
like tears they flow.
I can't decide what is best about her, what you see or what
you hide.
Hidden deep within your trunk my guess, it's full of many lives,
But how would the keeper feel,
if he knew you were hollow inside.
I'd like to plant another seed, to gather around your place
in the soil,
But I know if I did you might feel betrayed, and lose your
leaves and die.

   *Michelle Patrick*


## Fargoian Number Nine

A train that made the rails sing
With memories so rich and dear
All that ever rode the train
Will remember her for many a year

Both young and old would ride the train
Waiting for the sounds of whistle and bell
So slow and smooth it would start
Moving until top speed all could tell

The conductor in the aisle asked tickets please
His friendly smile was always the same
He took my ticket asking where are you going?
Sir, I replied, Minneapolis to the baseball game

At night aboard the train heading for home
The conductor would tell stories back in time
About Jesse James robbing the trains
This same train Fargoian Number Nine

At noon I would meet the trains
Talking to the trainmen I do recall
Oh! Those were the wonderful years
When the railroad gave so much to all

   *Lewis Lee*

## My Granddaughters, My Loves

There are three little girls sitting at home,
With Mom and Dad yet all alone.
They tell them, "Babies please don't cry"'
Your Nana has had to go bye-bye.
I sit and write a letter each night.
To let my granddaughters know that I'm alright.
I tell them from a prison phone,
"One day soon, Nana will be home."
I've gone and done something wrong,
So I ask you children, "Please be strong."
Everyday I look thru these prison bars,
And pray I can heal the hurt that may leave scars.

*Sandra Sullivan*

## Eyes May Perceive

As the world opens up before you
with no limits on the depths, heights nor vision
I stand in awe of not just what I see
but mainly of what I feel.

The depths bring meaning to what arises from below
extinguishing all fear
Growing in strength to overcome the divide
proving confidence to the heart that victory is sweet.

The heights are unlimited
yet, still in reach of the heart's desire
giving courage...will....and a way
to the passion that drives the wanting heart.

The vision is you, Carole, greatly arrayed in elegance
a splendor untold...unmatched in all it's glory
and though eyes may perceive,
to comprehend seems little.

*Nelson Hoyle*

## "The Trail"

The trail is dusty and hot
   with no shade or cool spots,
the dust blows thick and dry
   and the birds no longer fly,
the longhorns move without haste
   with very little green grass to taste,
the days grow busy, roping and branding
   until no steer is left standing,
the nights are spent with tales told
   of earlier herds bought and sold,
we turn in for sleep, our stomach full of biscuits and beans
   and our slumber is filled with thoughts and dreams,
until the early morning comes
   and, as if to the beat of a drum,
we turn to the trial again.

*Ronnie Hammond*

## The Golden Years like Bells that Chime

The golden years like bells that chime so softly toll away.
Until in age we plead for time to linger in its stay.
Un-noticed by our unhappiness the moments seem to fly.
And mornings with its amber dress so quickly passed us by.
We did not know, those tender years deceived by our little heart.
But now in age regretful tears recall our happy start.
A smiling morning, a happy day, a tired child at night.
No cares to worry, or display, nor question of the right.
Some little wounds were petty things, and quickly they were healed.
And after little cuts and stings anew has friendship sealed.
O golden years, forgiven years, they could no longer remain,
Would that they might, with smiles and tears, return to us again!!!

*Robert E. Johnson*

## Death in the Trenches

War is absolute horror
With our health growing weaker and poorer.
Bullets want to embrace us soldiers.
Our fear shown through the shaking of our shoulders.
Next to me lies my friend's limp body.
It's covered with mud and his head is bloody.
He was too tired to crawl
Out of the way of it all.
When the bombs and grenades fell from the sky
"Dear God," came his cry.
He dropped in the driving rain
Never to rise again.
Why he?
It should have been me.
Airplanes fly overhead.
I can't believe Dan is dead.
When we were kids in the spring
We would laugh and play on the swing
And talk about when we were grown.
I would be famous and he would be married to Joan

*Rachel Fickling*

## Dipper Of Stars

Embrace of darkness sparks its soul
With tear-like stars that jewel its bowl,
And reach for one they can't let go
'Til all's been spilled from long ago.

All heaven turns around North Star,
The queen of all that's nebular;
There Dipper cruises cosmic lace
To catch the gleam from her bright face.

When time has turned it upside down,
And dreams are emptied from its crown,
It follows there devotedly,
Enchained to one eternally.

In silver net of night terrain,
I long for light of day again
To pour the darkness from my soul
And stop the tears I can't control!

*Leland Embert Andrews*

## Her Love Never Ends

There is a girl with heart of gold, who is of minimum size
With tiny hands, tiny feet, and the world's largest eyes

She works hard, day and night, to please the ones she loves
She seeks the need to be the best, at everything she does

She loves a man who came to her, after he was terribly used
By someone who was selfish, hard, and very much confused

The user made a mark on him, taking many years to fade
It caused him fear of someone new, no matter how she's made

This little girl came to his life, so precious and so rare
The tiny one with golden heart, and also golden hair

She also had some scars and pain, but needed to keep going
The love she felt, when she found him very soon was showing

It warmed them both thru many times, when choices were hard
The man she loves needs her more, because his heart was scared

She never stops her loving ways, in spite of dark or plight
She always has believed in him, no matter wrong or right

He had to leave, against his will, to see her face no more
He didn't make the choice this time, to open up the door

But he's still here in many ways, thru family and friends
He'll always live inside her heart, for her love never ends

*Linda Alexander*

## Standing Alone

She discovers herself in perfect silence
Withdrawing within to commune with her spirit
Stoic and rooted as an old oak tree
Branches uplifted to touch the heavens ... Standing alone

Listening for the wisdom of her inner voice
Trusting her stillness for the truth she seeks
Knowing she can withstand any obstacle of life
Answers revealed in her dream scape mind ... Subconscious
guidance

Welcoming pain as a gentle reminder
That relief will follow shortly
Learning from mistakes, continuing forward
Tears flow to her ocean of memories ... Locked away

In her aloneness she finds sanctity
The temple built by years of searching
In the beat of her heart she finds solitude
Life force flows throughout her veins ... Awakening energy

When the time arrives to leave this earth
She knows she will be released
Of cluttered thoughts, emotional baggage
No more bonds to hold her down ... Freedom once again

### *Shawna Morales*

## A Daily Prayer Just For Today

Help me Lord to live this day
Without a harmful word to say
About my neighbor though he be
With all intent to slander me

Help me Lord, just for today
To help some soul on life's highway
To lift him up not push him down
Though he be a slave or wear a crown

Help me Lord, just for today
To help someone who lost his way
Though drugs have made him heathen wild
He's still my brother, he still your child

Help me Lord, just for today
To take some hand and lead the way
To tables filled with festive meal
That he may no longer, hunger feel

Lord guide my feet just for today
Help me walk Thy Holy Way
If tomorrow thou should let me see
I'll ask again these things of thee!

### *Patricia Ross Holland*

## The Greatest Gift

To love enough to see what's needed
Without thought of repayment in any way
To understand how another's peace is prized
With the sight of happiness and love remembered
Building more memories to live on forever

To join spirits and contentment helping others
These are the most precious jewels of life
Far outweighing gold and diamonds
To live on long after the giver is gone
But the beauty of the giving heart remains

Forever remember
Forever loving
Forever thankful

### *Selma Bloomenthal Zaetz*

## Mother:  You're Special

You are the woman who born me,
Without you, I wouldn't exist
You molded me with humility and pride
Inspired me the meaning of honesty.
Who else but a mother would worry
And care about how one feels
Would want to share the hurt one is hiding
Mother, you gave me the presence of dreaming
The determination to make my ambition come true
You taught me how to be humble
To stand with heads up and on my two feet
Your advice and ever listening ears
Helped me who I am today.  A retired public teacher
You are special and meant so much to me.
So now, I have the time to say —-
"THANK YOU, MOTHER" for making me who I am today.

### *Purificacion C. Calica*

## Georgetown Bum, Not Beggar

Manny,
Woeful, distressed, yearning, yet hopeful
Relative of the streets, maybe others
Lover of hope, and his guitar
Who feels aggravated, yet strong-willed
Who needs shelter, a home, a friend
Who fears poverty, dejection, loneliness
Who gives music to the corner and hope to the weary-
Who would like to see worth, wealth, a cozy home
Resident of the city bench,
Poor thing,
Last name-
Unknown and unneeded,
Good luck and God bless.

### *Lauren Dettore*

## Thoughts

Looking at you, sometimes brings tears to my eyes
Wondering why people tell me such lies
People say mirror images aren't true
But what I see, has to be the real you

The way people act and always stare
Leads me to believe that so few care
Always wondering if I'll ever look normal or right
Feeling discouraged and crying myself to sleep at night

Am I always going to feel this way, ugly and unloved?
Or is someone going to be sent to me from up above?
Oh how I wonder how it could be,
To have someone love me, just for me.

### *J. Christy Coker*

## What's Wrong with the World?

Tell me what's wrong
with the world today?
I lay awake late at night thinking of children
in faraway places also laying awake cold and
no food in their stomach
and their parents wondering if they will be
able to feed their families?  And the rich with hearts
of stone sleeping in warmth,
sending their children to private
schools and having other people
clean their houses
while many people have no houses to clean?
What is wrong with the world?

### *Rosie Willson*

## My Mask

Can't they understand the pain I'm going through?
Won't they try just this once to see the real me.
My real self is masked behind a great gray sheet of sorrow,
That no one else can see,
They don't know who I am, they can't see the true me.
They don't know what I'm going through,
They can't feel all the hurt I feel,
They just turn and walk away.
They say I don't try hard, they say I that I'm just a pain,
They say that all my actions are all a little game.
But if they took the time to look past my troublesome mask,
They'd see in a brand new light.
They'd see a whole new person, a girl, young and bright.
A girl full of energy and love and hope and cheer,
A girl who isn't dreamy, but a girl whose mind is clear.
Someone who wants to do her best,
Someone very different from the rest.
But all they see now is the masked person,
'Cause that's just who they are,
Maybe someday they will find me, a loving, caring star.

### Raychael Frances Ettinger

## A Kind of Love

A song that's not musical
Words with meanings that are truly meaningful
Expressions of love and friendship are not easily spoken,
Only written words can relay what I truly want to say.
You have always been an inspiration to me
Your strength, your wisdom, your loyalty
I see in you the glory of ancient kings
If you were not a man I'm sure you'd have wings
You might soar on high with masterful precision
Although it is just a thought
Your flight comes in vision
For you have seen the essence of the future
From a past that would always challenge you
Here you stand like time without end
I'm so proud to be your friend.

### Pat Sweeney

## A Partial View

As raindrops fall to circles upon a still pond,
Worlds follow paths upon a preset journey.
Clear streams of thought,
Making a notion of aloneness.
Part of me cries to the heavens,
Allow me to follow the moons.

Take me to your paths of predefined locations,
Make me understand the brush of color.
A company of foot soldiers,
Marching toward an already lost battle,
Understanding the fate of loss,
I fall into the ranks.

The trails fall back onto themselves,
The starts continue to make anew.
The brush of color is but a wisp of dust,
A partial view of the impending confrontation.
Let me see the final placement,
Let me move back of the line.

### William Dale Hoffman

## Ellie at the Lake

*(A 2-year old's study of her Lake Superior retreat)*
The lake for Ellie's
worth a quarter page;
its witch's-scrawl impounds a mystic stage
with interlock of circles past our ken.
And Grandma's here depicted
now and then,
as simply G-
or has a biased eye persuaded me?
The cottage where she rested
earns one spot-
exactly that.
So comfort take, good viewer, you are not
like me-
among the others features
she forgot.

### J. S. Winston

## Walter Froom Would Not Clean Up His Room

Walter Froom
would not clean up his room.
He would take out the garbage
and he would clean up the luggage
but Walter Froom
would not clean up his room.
He would wash the dishes
and make sweet wishes,
but Walter Froom
would not clean up his room.
There were socks on the boxes,
and there were kites
hanging from lights.
But Walter Froom
still wouldn't clean up his room.
Until one day
Walter wanted to go out and play
he discovered he was locked in by a cupboard.

So from that day on Walter Froom
always cleaned up his room.

### Samantha Fought

## Le Bel Chien Sana Honte

"Oh what can ail thee, maiden fair,
    Wringing your hands in despair?
Jams and jellies are made; your pantry's well strock'd,
    So you have not a care.

"Still, you continue to frown.
What is it that does confound?"

She looked with eyes full of tears
And replied with a voice full of fears.

"I found a dog at the pound,
    Full coat of black fur—soft and shiny—
Eyes that glowed red and brown—
    Feet not at all tiny.

But now whene'er I eat he watches my ev'ry move
    Eagerly wagging his tail,
With ev'ry morsel, ev'ry chew he hopes anew
    That gravity will prevail.

"And this is why I stand here in this swale
    While displeasure does my heart impale.
For I must attend to the needs, the ev'ry want
    of le bel chien sans honte.

### Mary Elizabeth Rose

## The Race

The morning sun was up, I stood staring at the black tar
Yellow lines all the way around, Coach yelled "Warm Up."

My shoes touched the tar and I began to run
This was just the beginning.

The sun began to give more heat
My yellow uniform seemed to attract it
Would this uniform win me a trophy, a ribbon?

More and more people filled the stands
I began to shake my race was coming up.

Every five minutes it got closer to my turn
The butterflies in my stomach
Began to flutter faster and faster.

Finally my race was called
Once again my dirt brown shoes met the tar
And sweat began to run even before I did.

Standing at the line I looked at the stand
Hundreds of people had their heads turned my way.

Bang the gun went off and so did my legs
I was gasping, gasping for breath, would I make it to the end?

*Renea Merth*

## A Long Drawn Inhale

The last time I saw her she had
yellow ribbons in her hair,
and a small distant smile,
missing parts that shape the fabric
but fragile as a kiss, the light fell on.

Cotton flowers danced in the smoke colored air
like a melancholy parade
as thin memories touched your husky laughter,
wistfully mourning its cause.

As we looked through your window,
the long winter carried snow
drifting like mirrors around us,
and impressions of our family album
collected at our feet
and sang its intoxicating refrain
A long drawn inhale

I could not speak, what should have been said
or it could have been said for it was already known
that you looked smashing
even while death, holding you firm

*Tarabu Betserai Kirkland*

## Undeniable Facade

It takes so much to give it up,
Yet it does no justice to keep.

To strain and suffer the unbearable lesson,
That gives no pleasure to learn.

It draws from within a great dark passion,
So tremendous it leaves quite weary.

Yet the memories of the simple, blissful joy,
Make it to be such a throbbing felt virtue.

But, oh how it makes me wonder, what is such virtue,
To be serving some debt as unknown as it's reasons.

Yet I shall always hold so close the fruit of all,
All that is love, no, no it serves no purposes.

*Michael D. Jones*

## Momma

To me as a child, she was a most amazing Lady.
Yet Liza told me to call her Momma, and the name fit so well
That I never called her another 'til they put it on her grave.
To me she was a most amazing Lady.
She wore a great big apron with pockets big enough to put you in.
She could do men things better than most men.
It was like two people in one skin.
Why, she could throw a stone and could shoot a gun so good, it sorta
made your head kinda spin.
But she was a woman through and through.
She was warm and comfortable as a blanket, like a cashmere
sweater up
against your skin.
It was something about her I couldn't understand.
She knew what you were thinking before the thought began
Old folk's wisdom she would quote with a grin.
It was up to you if you wanted to take it in.
She could have been cranky, claiming age had made her so.
but no, she was a happy person with a twinkle in her eyes.
Momma, she was a most amazing Lady, and the impact she had on
my life
Never seems to end.

*Vernon C. Neal*

## Untitled

Justice for wicked deeds is fleeting, in this day in which we live,
Yet mercy too is lacking, toward those whom God would forgive.

The most vile deeds go unpunished, or so it seems to most,
Men with lesser sins are ruined, for just one small reproach.

This seems unfair to average folk, folk like you and me,
That very wicked people, seem to always go free.

Yet let us examine further, man's usual misdeeds,
For don't the vilest acts of men, start with tiny seeds?

As we consider his evil, what could have been the start,
Just what could have created, such a wicked heart?

Such evil does exist you know, but as we ponder why,
We find that as young boy, he was known to tell a lie.

A lie, you say, how could it be that such a common mistake,
Of which we all are guilty, could a wicked man create.

Just as seeds grow in the field, and multiply at whim,
Seeds of wickedness their fruit do yield; the outcome is always sin.

Maybe if America's mamas, will teach right from wrong again,
While hearts are ripe for seeds of love, it can be the salvation
  of man.

In our society, love and forgiveness, seem to be words of the past,
But these values along with others, must return if our
nation is to last.

*Martha Grass*

## Away We Go

Who is away why do we go
Who can wait to go I know
Then will you go away I hope
To him to see no more

Away they go only to be seen no more
Why then would you go sadly glad
Run I shall ponder no more
Have you watched them flee; go

To be hidden away; we go, see us no more
Why look, none to searched, we are vanish
Time for us, to be no more
Away we go, find us here, far away we go

*Mable Duncan*

592

## My Silent Love Song

These silent words you'll never hear
Yet they pour out love with every tear.
Our life together was a sweet, sweet song
I have the lyrics, but the setting's wrong.

The time goes on, the sun still shines
I still can't forget "For the Good Times."
Sometimes the heart beats a little fast,
When I often try to remember the past.

The mind goes 'round like the clouds above,
Yet the voice is lost in silent love.
The little feet want to dance at night;
Never does the partner fit just right.

My happy way to break silent gloom
Is to sing aloud, our old favorite tune.
I'll throw a kiss, sing "honey, so-long"
But you'll never hear "my silent love song".

*Mary L. Gonterman*

## A Borrowed Child

The years come and the years go,
Yet time seems to stand still.
I had you but for a little while, a joyous unending thrill.
Such a loving and caring child, you were a joy to be around.
People came from everywhere,
To hear your laughter and your sound.
All of a sudden your body was racked with pain,
And your soul knew it's fate.
Then the Lord called to you, "I'll meet you at the Pearly Gate".
Your physical life on Earth was over,
But your beautiful soul lives on.
So loved and admired by many,
The likes of you we're never known.
I hide all the pain and sorrow deep inside,
So no one knows I live from day to day.
And if I live a hundred years, the pain won't go away.
Thank you Lord for the time you gave to me,
With my darling daughter here on Earth.
You taught me love and how to value,
Another person's worth.

*Mary Helen LeJeune*

## Precious Friend

You are a precious friend
You always understand
You always ask..never demand
When adversity comes, it is you upon whom I depend

You are a precious friend
Because you always care
Your humor and insight you'll always share
When ill winds blow you're willing to bend

You are a precious friend
Because you are always there
With a quip, a story and a greeting to send
And last of all your opinions of me, are always fair

*Lee Hogberg*

## Autumn Jacks

Hold fast to that autumn day,
with Halloween not far away,
mid hills of rust and burnished gold,
one step ahead of winter's cold,
with Jack-o-lantern pumpkin faces,
crisp clear nights and secret places,
oh again to be a child,
and by Jack Frost still beguiled.

*Sandra Gartin Lemon*

## To Eleonore — On Her Birthday

It's only numbers, dear, and
you and I
know better than to play the numbers game.

A grain of sand will tip the scale of time,
a tick-tock flip the pages of the calendar,
a stroke of midnight wrap a decade up,
and bring the magnus annus to a close.

And yet time's flow is just the same
at day's or decade's end
as every moment of the day or night.

We'll step aside, sit
this one out.
Let others play the wretched game.
It's only numbers, dear.

*Sverre Lyngstad*

## I See You

So big, so strong,
You appear as a man,
Yet I see you -
So young, so afraid....
A little boy,
With a pocket full of masks.

Tears you never cry, rage is all you know.
Fear you never show, for hope no one will know
The scared little boy I see in you.

Push me away
So I can't love you,
Don't let me speak -
For I may offer to console -
Don't watch me cry,
For you may yearn.
Don't let me be honest...
For if I do -
You may come face to face
With the scared little boy
that I see in you.

*Metta M. Dominik*

## My Other Mother

It's hard for me to tell you how much you mean to me,
You are my other Mother - and you always will be.
I know that you are his Mother and not really mine,
But you have stood beside me - all of the time.

Thanks for sharing the laughter - for wiping away the tears,
We've had such good times together through out the years.
You always encouraged me to follow my dreams,
Even when no one else believed in me - it seems

Thanks for always being there for every one of us,
You did what you had to do - and never made a fuss.
I know that you are tired and that you long to go...
But please remember us still here who need you so.

I will always be grateful and thank God above -
For my wonderful other Mother, and all her love.
You have always guided me and it meant so much -
You who taught me to cook, sew and such.

Thanks for all you have done for the children and me,
I can never repay you, but I will always love you, you see.
You are my other Mother - and I will always care...
And when the time comes, someday I'll meet you there.

*Peggy Nichols*

## Brave Little Young One

Brave little young one
you are so strong
You told your hidden secrets out of trust
for then I told them aloud.

Everyday I hear you crying inside
It sounds like a weeping willow tree blowing in
the cruel harsh wind.
Your words shout deep, dark, gloomy depression
I am here to help you, you can put your trust into my heart
If you need a friend to talk to,
just remember I am here brave little young one.

*Sandra Rogers*

## "A Wind Of Heaven"

Before your very eyes, the wind plays catch with the trees,
You can only feel numbed at the soft touch of the breeze,
Deep inside, somehow you know,
This wind carries dreams with its soft, soothing blow,
Wishes and dreams, some searching for love,
Some of the earthly kind, some of that which comes from above.

And now you are freed, of this earthly torment,
You feel this wind, for you it was meant,
You soar freely to the sky,
Life's problems, to you no longer apply,
All you know is your feelings, though you don't understand them,
It's true,
It's the feeling called "Love", only ten times it grew,
A feeling to match any others, and more,
It is this time you'll forever adore,
But alas, you're let down, no longer can you soar,
This great breeze, for you it is no longer for,
So I can only suggest, you trust your heart, for
It's the one part of you, that glides through the air, evermore.

*Timothy Meneely*

## Live Life for Its Moments

I walk through life like a field of dreams.
You can't always see as far as you can go,
But sometimes you can fly higher than you know.
I open my mind to the sky hoping it will
fill my heart, my arms, and body.
Sometimes the sky is specially nice, and even fills my soul.
But don't let these things that fill you fool
you, we're never to full to take in another.
When I am walking through this field
I feel like an elegant piece of art that
my God has created.
And for this I am grateful and free
to live life to its fullest desire.
Walk through this field accepting
what you need and giving of what you don't,
rather than taking it for what it's worth.
So with these words I walk and
sometimes even run, kneeling down to the
highest star and reaching up for the
prettiest flower

*Nichole McConnell*

## You Passed Away

Sometime ago you passed away,
your eyes fell to the light
   of day
But your soul, it did not die,
   it went to heaven, up in the sky
Someday we will meet in that
   promised land
and go into eternity hand in hand.

*Shirley R. Crouch*

## Senseless Violence

Senseless violence, what have we here?
You cause so much pain, and so many tears
Senseless violence, cowards cause fear
Senseless violence is living here
Senseless violence, please disappear
Senseless violence, look what you've done
You teach all the children, now they all carry guns
Senseless violence, what do you solve?
It confuses the children, and helps build a wall
Senseless violence, violence is learned
We are the teachers, education is burned
Help take some bricks, help tear down the wall
The words of one man can't save us all
Start with the teachers, give them desires
Teachers from learners, it causes burners
Let's put out the fire
If the world works together we can change for the better
Let's leave all the hate and close the gate
Senseless violence, senseless violence, not welcome here

*Paul Swonger*

## The Symbol!

I don't agree with you
You don't agree with me
Let's go to war!
I'll kill some of you and
you kill some of me but,
those who are left of you
and those who are left of
me, still won't agree
Let's don't go to War!
Why?
Because children die
We'll plant a tree and
name it "tolerance"
It will be the great divide
You stay on your and I'll stay on my side
The tree will be a symbol
that, separate, we will
live in peace and harmony
Remember the tree!
Eventually, we'll learn to agree to disagree

*Penny Johnson*

## A Place In Life

You feel left out.
You don't think you fit.
No one can tell you where your place
in life is.
No matter the time.
No matter the case.
One step forward,
You'll always be ahead in the race.
To wish with one hand,
And to touch someone's heart with the other
Cash in your sorrows,
And widen your eyes,
To look into the brighter tomorrows.

*Tiffanie Bowers*

## Friends

Teddy bear, teddy bear, I hold
   you so tight,
Teddy bear, teddy bear, all
   through the night.
Teddy bear, teddy bear, when
   day comes to an end,
I go to bed with my warm, fuzzy friend.

*A. J. Matarrita*

## Was Dying For You...

The second I saw you baby
You gave me wings to fly
When the second was over baby
In tears and out loud I cried
Without your love I was all lost
My life was yours I knew it most
I wanted for love to die for you
But how could I know that I die with you
When you said bye I wanted to stay
And love is taking us both away
Love was not safe when we were in motion
And feelings drown us in dangerous ocean
When silent death I got from you
My heart knew not to blame you
Love was easy we both knew
We lost it all there are no winners
Our love was high than all beliefs
For dying souls with doing dreams

*Lado V. Goudjabidze*

## Little Boy

I'm thinking of you Little Man, and now Big Boy.
You give to all others happiness, peace and joy..

Ah! Don't you remember that very special shirt?
From one girl to another you did flit and flirt.

Isn't it just wonderful to think and recall?
First a Little Boy, then a Young Man so tall.

Oh! How the years have come and the years have gone.
And we who are left must work and pray and carry on.

But it isn't as dark and gloomy as it sometimes may appear.
For Jesus our loving Savior will surely soon be here.

Then we'll look on his lively and matchless face.
And sing that old, old story of his saving grace.

Then we'll go with Him to our heavenly home on high.
Where no one gets sick or hurt, and you never hear a sigh.

All the streets of glory are made of the purest gold.
We'll see all the things of which we have been told.

You can have Jesus as your very dearest Friend.
Then you will be just like a Little Boy again.

*Wayne Wallace*

## Is There Anybody In Their - Pain Once Removed

For, alas, I thought you understood
You had me think perhaps you would
But the bottom line is being read
Prepare your mind, prepare you head

Inspired by you, believe it or not
Some higher consciousness I sought
But life set in and then the pain
I expected more, to grow, to gain

Your mind is troubled, the labels match
But there's one thing you need to catch
That I am you and you are me
Let's help to set each other free

But please of one thing, do be sure
For pain and hurt there is a cure
The cure is love and so I've weaved
These lines for you and take my leave.

*T. F. Cavanaugh*

## The Five Senses Of The Ocean

When you lay upon the warm sands of the shore
You hear sounds you can't ignore
The waves crashing upon the beach
Just like they want to talk, but have no speech
You can taste the salty air
Since it is the mark of the beach you don't really care
You can smell the seaweed brushed onto the sand
All is you can think is you love this land
You can see the horizon and pink, purple sky
Then you take, a relaxing sigh
You can feel the coolness of the wind
And you can feel the heat coming to an end
So you pack up your things and be on your way
Unfortunately you cannot stay
So you say goodbye to the sun and its features
Then to the ocean and all its creatures
This kind of nature takes you to a relaxing place
It gives you plenty of space
All is you can do is pray
That you can come back another day

*Stephanie Brock*

## Not Greek At All

Hail Calliope!  Muse of eloquence and epic poetry.
You make us writhe beneath your touch.
Your wavelengths boil the dirges in our blood.
Your solvent negligee brushes against the carbon of our flesh
Hardening our pores.   We are diamond.

Paradoxically pliant-hard earth stained-clear muted sharp we are.
We gently coax our cutting edge against the land
    to make it bleed with golds of sand.
Hand-to-mouth we fasten arms with our farmer-kin
Thus to Demeter grain goddess we rinse bone-weary hands.

Towards the laser sky Olympian soils are flowing free
    yet painfully far from our reach
So we turn to you, O muse of songs, to sweeten our bitter nests
    with flowing longings poemed and prosed
Towards a birthright for our young to grasp and keep
    those far-off stars whose fertile ices
        shall line our guts with warm repast.

Because even Pallas Athena of Parthenon provokes the dirtiest wars
Because even Zeus, when once inflamed by beauty, changed into a bull.

*Peachy Ragasa Carmona*

## Pictures Of You

Of all the pictures of you,
you may have a lot or a few,
the one you prefer from the rest
is that picture where you look your best.
Other pictures you have, it is true,
that look more like the everyday you,
they may seem much more like you, more real,
but for you, they hold no great appeal.
And those other poor pictures, how sad,
where you look so incredibly bad,
you may think they don't look much like "me",
but that's just what the camera did see.
In life sometimes we act as we should,
or badly or just pretty good,
don't you like to recall from the rest,
Those times when you behaved at your best?

*Lewis Morgan*

## Life

Life is like an ocean always wanting to explore
you never know what's going on;
on that ocean floor.

When you travel to the bottom,
or dive inside
you might find good or evil
and that's yours to decide.

When you finally get there,
you'll probably find,
that deep inside your body
there's things you didn't take to mind.

*Tanisha Dumas*

## The Freedom of the Beach

Sitting on the beach in the quiet of the night,
You notice the beauty of it all.
The moonlight glittering like a million diamonds
  on the sea.
You watch the waves lap ashore,
Hearing the crashing of a symphony.
The sky begins to glisten as stars slowly appear.
The wind blowing the sand and the sea white with
  foam.
It's just I alone in the midst of it all,
As I feel the presence of an unknown peace,
A feeling of sensation,
And a freedom that can not be explained.

*Sherry Spindler*

## Bossy Baby-sitter

Boy you get out that mud.
You out there playing in your school clothes?
You out there playing rough with them boys?
Is that blood comin' from your nose?

You gonna get it when your mother get home.
Go to the bathroom, wash your face.
You got anything else to wear?
Good.  Go up stairs change your clothes.

Are you finished?
Did you get in between your ears?
Nope.  It's dirty back there.
Hurry back upstairs and hurry back here.

Now, that looks better,
lookin' like a young knight.
Go sit down and watch T.V.
You have ten minutes till it's time to eat.

Your mother's here, it's time to go.
Go upstairs and get your coat.
Out the door is where you go.
Have a good night I'll see you tomorrow!

*LaVere D. L. Bryant*

## Moon Gaze

All these onyx nights
With the moon upon my hair
Little specks of light illuminate the air.
I gaze up at that smiling face
And dream myself lands away
In a quiet, peaceful place
Without problems of yesterday.
This Utopia I create erases stinging pain
And all evil Fate just like the suddenness of rain.
A voice wakes me from my trance
And I face the realities of today.

*Marilyn A. Cohen*

## A Season's Theme

Ah, lovely wretch who turned my heart awry;
You own my love till all the leaves have browned,
And till my autumn's sap is thick and dry -
No other dew is light upon the ground.

Ah, vapor'd smile, please always smile for me,
And though I sleep and see no more that smile,
And though I'm gone, my spirit hovering free,
I shan't forget our love - our while.

My weary heart, as though a trembling quake,
Will beat for you so deep within my breast—
And all my love will follow in your wake.
When summer's gone my leaves turn with the rest.

Although I know, too well, that fall is here;
Dear Love, pretend for me that spring is near.

*R. Geoffrey Blackburn*

## The Game Of Life

Some say you will always win if
  you play it by yourself,
Some say you will always lose.
I say you will never know.
Life is a game,
Every step is a space on the board.
Everyone plays a different game,
Some are short and some are long,
But one thing stays the same,
In everyone's game of life,
Every space is a chance,
A chance that you and you alone must face.

*Mandy Osborn*

## "The Rose"

The rose is a flower with a beauty all of its own.
You receive it as a token, for the love you have shown.

Some say that a woman's beauty, is only skin deep.
The love that they give, is not for her lover to keep.

Your beauty is different, for it comes from your heart.
Like the rose bud, when it first gets its start.

It opens up slowly, revealing the beauty that it holds.
Reaching out to you, for your loving so bold.

A fragrance so sweet and so yearning, that it warms up your heart.
Tells of a love for her, that will always be in your thoughts.

The rose has many colors of beauty to see.
But there is only one rose, that means anything to me.

The color is "white" for the purity of our love.
It has the blessings, from God up above.

*William David Lawson*

## Sonnet I

Shall I not gaze upon thy face again?
Would not such loneliness reshroud my heart?
This feeling is but absent love and pain.
Away with pain!  Forget my loss and start
Anew.  Mind turned and leaving all behind.
All precious, pleasant thoughts of what was past.
Thine gentle eyes, thine ruby lips could find
The road to torrid souls; mine cruelly cast
From Eden's grasp to pits of hell in vain,
For all that torments lies in thine own will.
'Tis frowns that wrack my brain to fall insane.
'Tis hate from thou which pulls asunder still
My spirit, longing for a freedom's gasp
So that my life is free from love's cruel clasp.

*Tom Bui*

## A Trip To The Ozarks

Way down in the Ozarks
You see Silver Dollar City and Branson, Mo.
A quaint and musical city,
Where we sometimes like to go.

People come there from everywhere
From every state in the U.S.A.
They come to relax and be entertained
To see shows, spend money and play.

All kinds of crafts are made and sold there
The Missouri mule pulls his cart
All Nashville seems to have moved there
Have built and do their part.

It is even more beautiful and restful
Than when Harold Belle Wright wrote "Shepherd of the Hills,"
It will fill you with awe and wonder,
If you can only pay the bills.

Rev. Wright came there to write and paint pictures
Now every square inch it fills,
But the traffic and congestion
Can sometimes give you chills.

**Willie Lou Shirley**

## "The Unthinkable Task"

As I look at a star in the sky
you shine in the night's eye

You've lead us one and all
and will not let any of us fall

You've gone through a lot
even shopping at Odd Lot.

You take the "A" train a lot
but you're the train which no one can stop

You are my angel in the sky
if you're gone I think I would die

As you read this I will hope, you know
that you will always glow

And one last thing, I say to you is that
I LOVE YOU

**Tomas E. Flores**

## Nannie

You never know she's there, until she's gone.
You think she's there to stay, she always has been.
You take her for granted, but you never know it until it's too late.
After she's gone, you remember the quiet times alone with her when
   you would sit and talk for hours.
When you were small she always kissed your hurt to make it feel
   better.
So much has happened since that you've forgotten, now you remember.
You could always count on her to be there whether it was a happy or
   sad occasion.
She may not have felt like going to your graduation but she stood
   proud as you walked across the stage to receive your diploma.
She may not have told you she loved you but she did and proved it all
   the time by doing the little things only a grandmother can do.
She always praised you when you did right, but scolded for things done
   wrong.  She never played favorites, she loved us all the same.
As you look upon her for the last time things you meant to say come
   back to you.
Between sobs all that comes to mind is blurted out as if asking
   for forgiveness.
Out of habit you give her one last kiss and say your final "I Love
   You."
You realize that there's a void in your life that can never be filled.
She's gone now, and all you have left are the beautiful, priceless
memories of her, the things that not even time can take away.

**Natalie Leiphardt**

## Dreams And Destiny

Running softly through my mind,
you went on padded feet.
Silent and swift, over rivers and fields
of midwestern dreams.
I slept on.
Enjoying your periodic return.
I never followed, only delighting
in your journey, glad to see your shadow
in my mind, if too short at times the visit.
Till one day I awoke and you were still there.
This time urgent nd unrelentless
you howled your message to the moon.
I followed now our tail
through mountains and deserts,
driven to, know my dream's visitor.
Who has this creature who stirred
my dreams and woke my soul to endless searching?
Turning back, you shouted my answer
and it echoed through the canyon of my heart.
With one word you set me free- Destiny.

**Pamela Norris Fox**

## To My Father

Father,
You were a daring young boy
sailing alone in the midst of the ocean

bare handed
just armed with ambitions
no fear, no stopping

You saw
the fragments of shattered dreams
drifted away by the roaring thunder

Yet,
tougher the obstacles the stronger you became

Now, father
you have arrived at the harbor
ready to take a different path for your journey

Let lingering dreams
pause for a while,

smell the roses and listen to my whisper

how I cherish
the values you have taught me
and the enduring love you have given me.

**Ogyoun Lim Yun**

## In Sand

You - nothing of me.
Waves lap at God's fair feet
   (surely pound me to death, my friend).
I gather in faith your reflecting glass
Bloody many faces
   (of you).
Sail the sea; 'tis I.
Conquer the aisle of demon lights
   (Who haunts you?  You?)
Oh sweet ghost king, please
Caress warm salt as me.
Wring your golden fire from ungiving souls!
   (remember)
A blood shores in image your throne.

**Theresa Varner**

## Betrayal

When the world hath turned its cruel back on me,
You were always there.
Why now do thy hands so quickly withdraw from me?

When the darkest evil rose up against you,
Was I not always there for you?
Why now do thy hands strike me down with such harsh reproach?

I ask of you, why does thee betray someone so close to you
that you think of him as a brother?
Hath I not cared for thee with the utmost prestige?

Why now do you stab me with your sharp knives,
forged from the purest hatred?

I have done you no evil,
Yet you seek to kill me with a fiery hate all your own!

I loved thee as if you were my own flesh and blood,
Yet you strike at me in a frenzied attack.
Why?
I will stand my ground firmly and die with this upon my lips

It's not the slashes thrown at me physically,
But the pain of you being the person throwing them.
That my friend is what will kill me...

*Ryan Oshiro*

## To My Deceased Husband

You were my life boat on the water should I be lost at sea
You were my oasis in the desert when from the heat I could not see
You were my rainbow in the heavens that drove away my cloudy
skies

You could put a smile on my face and the twinkle back in my eyes
You were the light in the darkness that showed me where to go.
You were my warmth in the winter you were my flower blooming
the snow
You were my crutch to lean on when sometimes I could not stand.
You were my water in the desert that cooled the burning sand.
I don't question why you had to leave me I only know you are gone
I know I must accept this and live my life alone
There is no more oasis in the desert no water to cool the burning
sand
There is no crutch to lean on; I must now learn to stand.
There will be no more rainbow in the heavens
    to drive away my cloudy skies
There will be no more smile on my face
There is no more twinkle in my eyes
There is no life boat on the water if I get lost at sea
I will try not to be sad or lonely because you won't be here to
    comfort me.

*Ruby Briscoe*

## For My Mother

    Happy Birthday and Happy Mother's Day
You were out of town on Christmas
    and gone Thanksgiving too,
I'd like to see you on holidays
    but can't get hold of you
your birthday is on Mother's Day
    what else is there to say
I have a present for you
    but again you'll be away
you know I love you, Mother
    so have a wonderful time
I don't even have a card for you
    so I have to make this rhyme
Enjoy every minute
    think of me if you can
You're the greatest Mom in all the world
    and I really love you.

*Dan R. Mayes*

## Untitled

If you look closely you will see the pain in my eyes
You will see our love as it slowly dies
The glorious feelings we once shared, the babies that we made
Our wonderful dreams we had, slowly begin to fade

But my spirit is not as easily broken
As our wedding vows we had once spoken
Those were the days of innocence and love
I believed in you and in God above

Now, as I pick up the broken pieces of my heart
In this time we have spent apart
I have come to know a new self within me
That can no longer bear the pain and longs to be free

Such cruel things you used to say and do
I hope the other women never had to see the real you
I hope your children grow without the fear
That you inspired when you were near

I hope your hands never raise again in rage
I hope my heart can break free from this cage
And still sometimes, late at night - I cry
As I wish our love had not needed to die...

*Susan Behan-Almanzar*

## Happiness

I sit alone today and I am not lonely.
You wonder why.
I can look out my window
And see the beautiful blue sky.

I can see tall trees
And their leaves swaying in the breeze.
I can see a hummingbird dart by.
I surmise it wants to catch a fly.

I see a rabbit go hoping along.
It reminds me of a merry song.
I notice the colorful butterflies - so graceful they seem.
They appear as if they have come out of a dream.

Nature has included
Some gorgeous flowers for me to view.
Man has not excelled them in any way,
And I can enjoy them this very day.

And as I think of what I can see,
I am reminded of what God has given to you and to me.
He does away with our strife,
And gives us an assurances of eternal life.

*Thelma Williams LeGette*

## Someone Else

If I were somewhere else — would I see the shame
Would I feel the pain
If I were somewhere else

If I was someone else
Would I worry the same
Would I still sing
If I was someone else

What if that someone was you
Would you be me — for a day — for a dollar
Maybe a lifetime

If I were you — I'd be you
That's if I was someone else

*Sylvia P. Barnes*

## For Dairy Cows, Sent to Slaughter

Fuzzy-faced in winter
You worship the sun-
The few smiling hours-
You kick the snow in play,
Dancing in the wind.

Overgrown or ancient, but never lonely-
Warm faces buried in silage-
Eyes look wonderingly up at me.
Tongues caress me, warm and lingering-
Where will your love go when you die?

In spring, abandoned,
The field lies witness to your souls - still dancing.
The field is overrun with flowers:
    Tiny, delicate, yellow and white.
The beauty of your lives remains,
Your bodies no longer breathing.

As the ivy climbs the trellis
Your souls point towards heaven
And sing the song - eternal-
Of the sun, the moon, the wind.

**Lisa Phillip Rimland**

## Widow Of The Surviving Veteran

My heart. My soul. My husband; where have you gone?
Your eyes: such a beautiful blue do not perceive me anymore.

Your mind, so sharp and witty: a rare combination of intellect,
conscience and creativity is congested, filled with unspeakable
terror, fatigued by the weight of your losses.

Your heart: so generous, so compassionate and gentle,
is trapped in your body, broken by your losses.

Your hands so tender, so gentle; the hands that held me,
loved me, that comforted and caressed me;
that put your ring on my finger, are now violent.

You dreamed all night. You screamed all night.
You were defending your life. But it is me you choked.
And when you awoke, I held you while you cried.

There is nothing I can do. I have to leave you now.
A woman has to be safe in her own home and her husband's bed.

I asked Jesus to give you back to me. I did not care for His answer.
But I will abide, knowing later to find it superior to my request.
In heaven I find you. We can spend forever making up for lost time.
We will not have missed anything. You will always be my husband.

**Maureen Wheat**

## Journey

Like warm sunlight on a seed,
Your iridescent being beckoned to me.
Heedless of any unknown harm
I was unable to resist your charm.

Your ephemeral being touched my soul,
Commanding my spirit to unfold.
Evoking forgotten feverous desires,
This spirituous journey have you inspired.

My soul soars toward exulted heights,
Reaching for eternal heights.
My joy it is utterly astounding
Exhilaration so ever abounding.

Ceaseless searching for these treasures,
Have you given me forever.
Your guiding light shall remain with me,
Etched in my soul eternally.

**Sheila P. Wolff**

## What A Woman

What a woman you are; it is plain to see.
Your spirit possessed by inner and outer beauty.
With looks so powerful, my eyes can hardly stare.
Such a woman is special, not to mention rare.

Your walk is untainted by the rough, coarse earth.
God has surely blessed you since your day of birth.
Your body is perfect with every splendid curve.
You're truly a Goddess- whom I am to serve.

The sound of your voice fills my heart with glee.
Your eyes and smile can anyone's misery.
With hair so soft, and lips so sweet.
It's not hard to tell why you're so unique.

My sorrow id lifted by your simple presence.
What a woman you are; in every aspect, every
essence.

**Yomi R. Desalu**

## A Lady Proud And Fair

I've never wondered how it's be, I can't say when and where.
You've eft me just a legacy; you're a lady proud and fair.

I've never given any thought that you would leave me here;
And now these thoughts remain with me, you're a lady proud and fair.

So all I will do is reminisce, how you've applied your love with care.
If nothing else is said but this, you're a lady proud and fair.

So I'll say this dear mother who is grand
    that since you've left me here,
I'll always only think of you as a lady proud and fair.

Remember how you coddled me and all your grand ones too?
You're like a flower of beauty, for all of loving was you.

So I'll say it once more dear mother who's grand,
that during my time left here,
if one must know anything of you,
you're a lady proud and fair.

**Patricia E. Brown**

## Wines

I hold in my hand Tradition, Community, Nature, God and Man,
    Harmony in Cycles;
In bottled liquids pale gold, sparkling citron, blood red, light peach.

A sip,
I see great grandfather, grandfather, father, and son.

A sip,
I remember neighborhood cookouts, Fourth of July parades,
    Memorial Day.

A sip,
Behind closed eyes, I see a spider's intricate web; I hear birds'
    morning song,
the drip of a faucet, the roar and crash of a waterfall.

A sip,
I feel the joy of new life, the parting of an old one.

A sip,
I flow through all the seasons, fall, winter, spring, summer.

A sip,
I capture the Essence, the Senses, the Inner Being.

**C. A. Enin-Okut**

## The Eagle's Nest

Much is to be learned about the eagle's nest and what happens therein;
The mother eagle teaches her young how to fly, freely, in the mighty,
   rushing wind.
When the time comes, she plucks some feathers out of their soft,
   comfortable nest,
So they'll be unsettled and, yes, you guessed:
They cling to the edge and she pushes them out and they fall;
Headed straight for the jagged rocks, they hear her call;
"Mother's here," as she swops down under them and swiftly bares them
   away,
Back to the nest she takes them and there they want to stay! ! !
Can you see, christian friend, how so like the eaglet we are?
God pushes us out of the nest and we fall so very far.
He lets us "see the rocks", they're jagged and fierce,
But all of a sudden, His hand reaches out to catch us, and not by one
   are we pierced!
We're placed back in the nest, safe and secure, once more,
And we cry, "Don't do that again," I like it like it was before!
Just like the eaglet, we don't want to walk by faith every day,
We want to stay as we are, content in our own way!
Does this sound like you, christian friend?
If the answer is yes, then let's both begin:
To listen to our Master as He tells us what to do,
And step out by faith and obey what He tells us to.

   *Sandra McBroom*


## Queen Nefer

She was higher than the mountains,
She was higher than the sun,
She was Queen Nefer the Egyptian one.
She was Queen of Egypt and much more,
She was love, beauty and always perfection
She never needed one correction.
She was Queen of the Nile and the Egyptian sky,
She was Queen Nefer that's why.

   *Bianca Taylor*


## Why, Oh Why?

The placid peace is torn asunder, by the roar of the explosive thunder,
Cries of lament we do not restrain, as from death's pain is heard the
   refrain:
Why, oh why, did they die?

Oklahoma's torment resonates from door to door, equally, distantly,
   from shore to shore,
Why, oh why, did they die?

Family, neighbor, and friend seek reprieve, from sorrow that today
   offers no leave,
Why, oh why, did they die?

A bewildered nation wails in despair, wrenching people with anguish everywhere,
Why, oh why, did they die?

Young children, joy of today and hope of generations of life, their
   play transformed to death and strife,
Why, oh why, did they die?

From deaths gaping wounds is heard again and again, the refrain we
   long soon will end,
Why, oh why, did they die?

Solace is found deep within, in the grief of lost love that once had been,
Why, oh why, did they die?

In life as in death we remember we must, in God place our eternal trust,
Why, oh why, did they die?

Alas, the peace of loving care, conquers the hatred that filled the air,
Yet still echoes the mournful cry: Why, oh why, did they die?

   *Paul E. Knapp*


## Rivers

**A**llegheny,
**M**ichigan, Monongahela, Merrimack,
**E**lkdhorn,
**R**appahannock,
**I**llinois,
**C**hattahoochee, Cumberland, Columbia, Cheyenne,
**A**labama, Arkansas,
**N**iagara,

**W**abash,
**A**lbany, Attawapiskat,
**T**allahatchie, Tallahala, Tomoka,
**E**ast, Edwards,
**R**oanoke, Rio Grande,
**W**ithlacoochee, Weeki Wachee,
**A**ppomattox,
**Y**azoo, Yalobusha, Yukon,
**S**askatchewan, Santee, Suwannee,

Flowing, Winding, Meandering
Throughout America.

   *Suzanne E. Mericle*


## Marie, Mon Très Cher Et Devin Déesse

Marie, each kiss I sprinkled upon your head
Was filled with a thousand eager dreams
That you were somebody else instead;
I am not sure what I heard in your screams-
Perhaps regret words never could have said
But what your touch did that night, to me, seems
To transcend the world outside of your bed.

I can never forget what occurred
With you nor can I ever understand
But, in the simplest sense of the word
Now that I am supposedly a man,
I feel like a wounded, flightless bird
Plummeting towards the anxious land.

When I think of your in your bed, supine,
I wonder if any man could resist
Your loveliness, which is so divine;
That majestic moment when we two kissed
Has led to my heart's imminent decline.

Am I a sinner or am I a saint
Because I showed a lack of self-restraint?

   *Yousef A. Sait*


## To Sid- What Is A heart?

   The heart is an organ like a pump.
When it's well you can really jump.
   When it's weak and like a lump,
One sure feels so down in the dump.
   But have hope, keep your spirits high,
As we travel the blood circuit supply.
   Let's start with the Vena Cavas to auricle right
Through the right ventricle with a push not light.
   Now on the way to the lungs and back,
Through pulmonary arteries and veins with slack.
Now into auricle left with $O_2$ to spare,
Through the left ventricle and now we are there.
   At the Aorta that mighty tube
To all the body with life giving lube.
   So keep the rhythm with Lub-A-Dub
While we root for you with a back rub.
   And have heart, we wish you well
That soon you will dance the "Tarantelle."

   *Jack Gross*

## Musical Language

Beethoven, Handel, Schubert and Bach, Mendelssohn, Wagner, Schumann and Bloch.
Mozart and Mahler, Goethe and Gluck, Singspiel and lieder, Einstein and Bruch.
Pachelbel, Humperdinck, Telemann, Brahms, Strauss and Hoffmann, Lutheran Psalms.
Sausage und strudel, sauerkraut, beer, German und stalwart, heavy, sincere.

Purcell, Chaucer, Elgar, Hope, Sullivan Shakespeare, Tennyson, Pope,
Newton, Bacon, Bunyan and Donne, Milton, Marlowe, Dryden and Maugham.
Tallis, Lewis, Britten and Byrd, Windsor, Tudor, Richard III.
Anglo Saxon, Anglican, Blake, kidney pie, pudding, Salisbury steak.

Rossini, Puccini, Vivaldi, Torelli, Scarlatti, Respighi, Assissi, Corelli.
Monteverdi, ravioli, Pavarotti, Donizetti, Donatello, Machiavelli.
Allegro, vivace, staccato, rubato, toccata, partita, canzona, legato.
Spaghetti, spumoni, zucchini, martini, lasagna, chianti, fritatta, linguini.

Ravel, Voltaire, Hugo, Bizet, Pascal, Descartes, Saint-Saens, Dufay.
Dukas, Rousseau, Dupre, dauphin, ballet, ballade, galliard, Gauguin.
Cezanne, chanson, Fauré, Rameau, Molière, Monet, Satie, Gounod.
Dufy, Lully, Chabrier, Debussy, sauté, soufflé, chérie, mon ami.
Croissant, escargot, meringue, flambé, divan, rosé, negligee, bidet.

***Eleanor G. Nash***

## Winning

The name of the game is winning, it's the only game of feelings,
the name of the game is feelings, it's the only game of winning.

The name of the game is competing, compete to win and winning is thrill,
thrill is the game of feelings, it's the only game of winning.

The name of the game is politics, by hook or crook, by promising or lying,
promising and lying is the game of feelings, it's the only game
   of winning.

The name of the game is attitude, bad attitude means loosing and good
attitude means winning, loosing and winning are the feelings,
   it's the only game of winning.

The name of the game is respect, learning to respect yourself and others,
living with respect is the feeling, feelings of respect is the
winning, it's the only game of winning.

The name of the game is Life, living the life with sorrow and happiness,
sorrow and happiness are the feelings, life is the game and
living is the feeling, it's the only game of winning.

The name of the game is GOD, understanding the peaks of heaven and
bottoms of hell, heaven and hell are feelings, it's the only game of winning.

***D. G. Parekh***

## Queen Anne's Lace

She was born the child of a shiftless drunk, in a town that had no heart.
Annie would never fit in with the rest, and they made sure she knew from the start.
Thru a window in time my mind still recalls the first smile on Annie's sweet face.
As I pledged all the love in my six year old heart with a bouquet of Queen Anne's Lace.
Greeted with teasing and burdened by shame thru most of her sad childhood years,
Annie tried to erase all her sorrow and pain with a shower of innocent tears.
Sometimes I'd find her walking alone, with teardrops bright jewels for her face.
I'd vow that she's always be Queen of my heart, and pick her some Queen Anne's Lace.
Annie grew lovely with beauty and grace that outshone her hand-me-down clothes,
and she found that her beauty could open up doors that once had been kept firmly closed.
My heart swelled with pride as I walked by her side, the day she won First Place,
at the Country Fair Pageant for Miss Seventeen, dress trimmed in Queen Anne's Lace.
Then school days behind us we went our separate ways, me to college and Annie to life.
By our tenth reunion, I was a lawyer, and she was some millionaire's wife.
I said, "Annie, your jewels make you look like a queen," as I saw a sad look on her face.
She said, "I'd trade them for all the love of a boy, and a bouquet of Queen Anne's Lace.
My life went all right, then on my wedding night, for the last time I saw Annie's face.
'Neath a headline that read, "Millionairess Found Dead in a Room Full of Queen Anne's Lace.
Thru a window in time my mind still recalls the first smile on Annie's sweet face,
   but I misread the value she placed on that love, and the bouquet of Queen Anne's Lace.

***Karen K. Blamey***

## My August Day of the Burning Bush

Singed by your mere thought
When split into words
and heard
by voice alone
Loved

By you
reaching out
When you rustle still air
by mere voice

You touch me
stirring waters of my soul

Play me
Set me once more
Sum apart

To yearn to seek
if merely to see
through a prism

. . .

In quiet loving
All while merely
Loving You

***Remé A. Grefalda***

## The Wind

A huge white disk
floating in the sky
an eerie light around it
like a person doomed to die.

Then you hear a woosh -
all of a sudden it's gone -
you step back with a gasp
when then, a light goes on.

It's a foggy sort of light
a light that never ends,
a slice goes through it
a slice that never mends.

The slice grows steadily bigger
and the clear light of the moon peeps out,
You see that it was only the wind
And then you turn about.

***Renée Ricard***

## Heartless

The earth is still
yet I hear the cries
all the lies
you tore my soul apart
it hurt
the pain, sorrow, and fear
I cried all day, all night
never shall feel the same
I do have shame
for you my love
you have played a game
now your calling my name
for my love and forgiveness
but you missed
I will go on though you did me wrong
I am strong
never again will I belong
to such a cruel person as you
never true.

***Staphané Claus***

## U.S.A. - Red, White, And Blue

Unanimously, all Americans join hand in hand,
Symbolizing our peace and unity under One Flag, One Land.
Allegiance to our Flag, we pledge.

Red and white stripes; white stars cover a blue square background,
Each star, fifty in all, represents one of our states
Depicting our patriots' labor who proudly built our solid ground.

White House, our historic home, residence of every First Family,
House of all and each American, it was built with pride and unity.
In God we Trust, in One Glorious and Victorious Nation we believe.
True treasure, hiding our unique and precious American Heritage,
Everlasting pride we have in our great land and veterans' courage.

Always be ready to serve your Country with pride and with honour,
Never looking back, but always remember to look forward.
Dare on the Fourth of July to be patriotic, show your true colours.

Bald Eagle is our emblem.  It portrays our power and courage,
Leading and challenging our young and healthy future generations,
Under a proud, strong, and united Nation projected image,
Eyewitness of the growth of our great land and strong traditions.

*Elizabeth Balaram*

## Andy and Me

My lovey, wasn't it only a year ago we fell in love...
...and the sun was shining everywhere?

Wasn't it only a year ago our children reached up to us
with hugs and kisses...
...and the sun was shining everywhere?

Wasn't it only a year ago we packed our bags,
had cameras in hand and were ready to go...
...and the sun was shining everywhere?

Wasn't it only yesterday, or, maybe, it was a year ago,
GOD suddenly called you home?
And on that day...in that hour...minute...second...
our world ended - disappeared as if it never was.
...and the sun stopped shining everywhere.

Now, my lovey, it's today.  The sun is shining.
I guess I must find out why.

*Marilee Bogdanovs*

## Surrounded by the Mississippi

I must put flowers on the Ganges.
          There is no Ganges here.
Immeasurable mantra drops eddying
          Now in serenity.  Now in longing.
Does angst burn more once removed by the Ganges?
Is anguish less there
          coddled playfully in warm waters soothing serenity
          woven tightly in motionless temples music
               eddying.  Through space.  Saints
               Silent power.  Silence.  Presence.
Brushing the hopeful breeze blessing the water that blesses the
breeze embracing me.

I must put flowers on the Ganges.
          Lotus flowers and Tulsi.
          And Marigold and Jasmine heavy in my senses.
I shut my eyes and smell them here.
          Where there is no Ganges.
          Water is the same.  Like pain.
The deafening sound of an echo.  That started there and bellows
here. And back again.

          Trapped.
*Narveen Virdi*

## no place for a child

the heavy hand of war
     bears down upon me

these tender young lives of our three children
     forever changed

was has ultimately
     consumed the father's thoughts and presence

he's gone.  not disappeared
     although once thought dead

¡Siempre La Causa!
     his children somewhere down the line when there's time

there have been no bombings here when i live
and yet i stand naked

          challenged with the task of rebuilding my home
          nursing our wounds alone

i despise this lifestyle of war
     that threatens to one day seduce and reduce
     the futures of my sons and daughter to
     mere addicts of hatred

"war is no place for a child," a woman once said
     and she knows...for hers are all dead.

*Peggy Feltes*

## Untitled

They say that a friend is always a friend
To be true 'til your very last breath,
When your last day comes to its end.
But no friend has ever been truer
Than this friend I have found in you.
When the sun sets on my closing lids
Still I will be swearing loyalty to you, too.

*Tina Thousand*

## Sleepless

As I gaze toward the stars, perhaps to detect just one sparkle,
or even a twinkle of a star that mirrors those which emulate in
     your eyes.
I feel the darkness caressing my very being, and I am once again,
     Sleepless.

Sleepless,
pondering over the knowledge that emotions of desire, enchantment,
and sensitivity are rekindled within me.

Sleepless,
knowing that you seek love,
and the love you give in return is reflected in the aurora that
     illuminates around and through you.

Sleepless,
because in your voice, reality has betrayed you, tarnishing that which
     you so desperately seek, to be loved.

Sleepless,
refusing to dream, knowing that to dream can not fulfill that which
     is the essence and reality of your touch.

Sleepless,
because your fate and my destiny will not allow our love to flourish.

Sleepless,
acknowledging that your quest for love is within your grasp,
and that unlike me, you will sleep the sleep of one that has found
     love and tranquility.

Sleepless
*Elbert W. Jones*

## Albert Schweitzer

There is a man who fought for people's lives,
Who lost his by doing so.
A man courageous enough to seek his destiny,
He tried to make a leper colony.
He began to understand "reverence for life,"
While helping the sick colonies.
He began life as a sick young boy,
But with his Mother's hopeful tears,
Gave him the strength as he grew on
And on to strengthen his fears.
He became a strong little boy,caring a lot,
His Father was a preacher and preached
To him a lot.  Young Albert headed to school.
He went to medical school for sevens years.
He knew he wanted to serve humans for
The rest of his years.  His first leap was to set up a hospital,
In Africa where the people could go.
He spent decades with sacrifice and toil
To the Africans, we know.
That is why I admire Albert Schweitzer so.

*Ahnjené Schnase-Starkey*

## THE BIG ONE

Firemen cringed,
Mustaches singed.
Doors unhinged.
Looters binged.

Psyched-out housepets ran amok.
Shattered stucco came unstuck.
Most folks were spared by Lady Luck,
Though some could not Fate's Fickle Finger duck
And were by a plague of ruin struck.

Mere survival instant heroes made.
But unsung rescuers' roles to the hilts were played.
Ironic twists in Buck Helm's fate left many hopes betrayed,
Yet grateful flashbacks to those heroics probably won't fade.

Oh that Black Seventeenth, many were with fitting angst imbued,
When they—by buckles, cracks and jolts—-
Were in a handful of endless seconds screwed.
Still, they didn't see fit just to sit around and brood.
No, THE BIG ONE could not make those gutsy people come unglued!

*Adam Pollack*

## A Distant Light

You saw a faint glow in the distance but so far away did it seem.
That the light at the end of that tunnel could have only been but a dream.
When you glimpsed that faint dot of light, a dream began to take shape.
So you opened your mind and knew no length of time could give your dream an escape.
Each day of each year that went by would find the tunnel more and more bright.
It was with patience and trust, conviction a must, you believed in that faraway light.
Though your heart would beat softly at times at the thought of the distance to go,
You had faith and endurance to go the whole distance, a pace that you never did slow.
You believed in yourself all the way, in spite of hardship, struggle, and strife.
Knowing dreams can be real, but if only you feel, the heartbeat that brings them to life.
Now you're at the end of that tunnel in the light that was so faraway.
You can bask in the glow of an achievement bestowed to which only your heart and soul knew the way.
You knew dreams were meant to be lived.  They're a way of setting up goals.
Ones we strive to fulfill, through sometimes sheer will, to become a more complete soul.
You gave substance to something and life to a dream as difficult as that may have been.
But it was only for you and to yourself you were true and that is all that counts in the end.
It's with great pride and esteem that I write this for you to honor your achievements this way.
It's my faith in you and in all that you do and it's with love I applaud you today.

*Kristie D. Griffiths*

## Ship

my love,
my life,
   my ship at sea.

   my sail,
to catch,
   the winds that blow.

   my wheel,
to steer,
   'cross oceans wide.

   my deck,
my stand,
   'bove perilous brine.

   my hold,
my galley,
   bunk at night.

   my mast,
my bow,
   with flags hung proud.

   my vessle,
'cross,
   the seas of life.

   my rudder,
my ballast,
   my hull are thee.

   my compass,
pointing,
   true to go.

   my anchor,
steadfast,
   'gainst the tide.

   my cabin,
my shelter,
   'gainst rain or shine.

   my charts,
my log,
   my lamps for light.

   my treasure,
o'rwatched,
   by cannons loud.

   my ship,
my love,
   my darling wife.

*Michael Altman*

## Is This Life When

Your feet are all swollen
Your ankles are out of whack
Your belly is protruding
Your chin holds up a sack
Your eyes are out of focus
Your glasses do all the work
Your back is all contorted
Your out of work
Your legs are all flabby
Your muscles are all weak
Your appetite disappears
Your body can not eat
Your hands are all trembling
Your mind is confused
Your wife has left you
Your children become abused
Your sent into therapy
They tell you, you will survive
And all they ask of you - is to
Take more of their little while lies

*Donald E. Heitmiller*

## Sailor's Dream

Strength is like the world war sea.
Stretched long and wide.
The reflection of the full moon.
Still the river flows blue, gray.
So far is she.

*Riseé Shade*

## Ring Of Fire

Ring of fire, burning bright,
Sinks beneath the sea tonight,
Beyond the horizon, to opposite worlds,
Do you not ever tire?

Up every morning, you are the dawn,
Fairy circles are your lawn,
High above my head at noon,
Then sink into clouds of pink.

Burning bright, burning bright,
How I miss your warmth at night;
Save the summer, you stay awake,
Even as I drift through dreams.

*Lisa Kemmerer*

## Delight

I watched you
slip the moon
into your pocket
and wondered
how you could be so
selfish
and then
you put a bow on top
and placed it
in my hands

*Michelle Nellis*

## The Spring Season

I am walking through the arbor
Smelling fragrant flowers
With rainbows above
From the Spring showers.

Flowers are in bloom
The little birds sing
The animals are happy
And I dream of Spring.

The clouds above
The Easter bunny
The apple trees
It's all so nice and funny!

I love the Spring
The season to smile
The shiny sun glittering
I've been walking for a mile!

I like Easter egg hunts
And licking lollipops
Games of all sorts
Spring is a time for hippiti-hops!

*Pratyusha Rao Katikaneni*

## Right Where You Want Me

How you torture me so.
So beautiful are you
You up and left
Took my heart with you.

Dreaming you'll come back
Disillusioning myself
For you, by you
From you, because of you

How much more naive
Could I be
Right where you want me
Without you either way!

*Susan Hawks*

## Eternal Rest

She was like the sun,
So constant and bright.

She was like the moon
That lights my way at night.

She was like the rain
That nourishes and revives.

She was like the air I breathe,
Without which I would die.

She asked for nothing in return
And always gave her best.

Now at the end she smiles —
Welcoming her eternal rest.

*Willa Winston*

## Feelings

Feelings run so deep
So deep but yet so near
Feelings too hard to understand
The feelings that you fear

Trying to hide what feels so right
Holding in what feels wrong
Making decisions, but don't know why
Then holding out and being strong

Never knowing why you feel the way
    you do
Thinking the worst is behind you, and
    then realizing the truth
Going through the worst of times and
    getting all confused
Thinking everyone really cares, and then
    feeling so used

Blocking out the pain
But drowning in your sorrow
Trying to blow it off
And wishing for a better tomorrow...

*Mikki*

## Untitled

I want to die, I'm
    so full of pain.
I slice my wrist,
    and watch it rain.
I love you darling...
    you are that seed.
I love you baby...
    you help me bleed.
See what love did to me,
    It cut down my tree.

*Raymond Lees*

## Renewal

A slow gentle inward stir
When warmth comes from the hearth
not the sun

When your heart knows the warm love
That melts life's harsh snow.

This is my time of peace
Renewal of body and soul

Renewal through nature's sleep.

*Linda Cryer*

## "Labeled"

I've been labeled
So have you
I've been labeled "geek"
You've been labeled "popular"
Why?
You're nothing, but a conniving bitch
Pretty?
Maybe
Stupid?
For sure
Me?
Well I'm nice and smart
Pretty?
Don't think so
Stupid?
Not a chance!
So why are you better than me?
I guess I'll never know

*Stephanie Routson*

## Before the Sun Goes Down

I rise in the dark —
So many things to do
Before the sun goes down.

Where do the hours go?
The day is spent
Before it's felt,
But that's not living
And I have living to do
Before the sun goes down.

Before the sun goes down
I must climb the hill to tomorrow
And look to the future.

Before the sun goes down
I must purchase the hours of this day
To use for my life —
    My hopes —
    My dreams —
Otherwise, they will fly past me
At the speed of light
Before the sun goes down.

*Ruth Ann Leone*

## Welcome To This World

Welcome to this world,
    So much awaits for you.
The many things of old
    for you now blossom new.

May your mornings reign of sunshine,
    and your evenings burst with stars.
May you carry the rainbow's magic
    in your heart, whenever you are.

May a waterfall of happiness
    sprinkle love on all you know.
And may the world sign out in peace
    as you live and learn and grow.

May your eyes forever sparkle,
    and your smile never fade.
May your mind be full with memories
    of all the friends you've made.

Welcome to this world,
    a gift of life-so sweet and true.
May your heart be filled in joy
    with eternal love bestowed on you.

*Lori A. Hanna*

## LOST

We plan to meet,
So recently bereft of
  our loved ones
How will it go?
I feel I shall cry, will he?
Maybe we'll cry together
Longing for love now gone.
We were there, the four of us
At love's first blooming
Proud and happy days
The years took their toll
Here we will be, alone together
Groping for happy memories
Two lost souls.

*Ruby Sarty*

## "Sunny - Two"

Little Meggie Boobers,
So small and yet so big.
You have a way about you
That makes life fun to live.

The big smile in your little face,
That twinkle in your eye.
You tug at all our heart strings.
Your love's ten times your size!

The faces that you make at us,
The cute things that you do.
We're just so glad to have you here,
Our little "Sunny - Two."

The energy that you create
Just being in a room.
A hug and kiss from "Sunny - Two"
Could make an old grump swoon.

An image of your mother,
We called her "Sunny" too.
It must be her good nature,
That sparked that love in you.

*Paula Bertaud*

## Jour D'Avril (An April Day)

So dismal a day.
So somber a morning.
A drizzly curtain
Over the garden so gay.
So mourning my heart
Heavy with unshed tears
Can but sigh
Morose in my tryst.
The spectral vista of a too near morrow.
Hope folded away
This so dismal a day.
Tomorrow bring back the sun
To the garden so gay
And to my so chagrined self
Laughter anew
With its caressing
Comforting
Golden rays.

*Maria C. Derum*

## School Days

The happy days we spent in school
so swiftly passed away,
and never comes to us again
where ever we may stray.

Enjoy each day and count
the cost, before time pass away.
Treasure each moment, use them well
time wasted cannot be regained.

Learn all you can, while you can.
Days to come you will not regret.
Keep in mind your special goal,
and you will never fail to grow.
Rest if you must but never stop,
until you reach your goal.
Do your best and leave the rest
to take care of itself.

*Mavis Miller*

## Soft Side Up

Turn me over
so that I may be vulnerable
to feel, to see life,
to yank to a halt
and love.

Safety is not touching,
living, hurting.
Safety is just safe,
  Locked in a corner
    to exist.

You turned me over
to peer into me.
I'm not untouchable
  anymore:
I'm turned soft side up.

*Nancy J. Parker*

## Plato, Plato!

Man never changes
so why bother?
Only a philosopher
would understand.
Is it dear sir
for those rare moments
when man transcends
the normal
comes out of the cave
and becomes a hero?
Is that why bother?

*R. J. Lamb*

## I'm In Love With Thee

I'm in love with thee
so you have the key
You have the key to my heart
so don't you dare dare dart
but if you do remember me
and remember that I love thee
I'll love thee to my death
and I'll say with my last breath
I love thee
Then I'll flee
I'll flee to the heavens above
Like a milky white dove
And even then...
I'll love thee

*Robin Schaefer*

## The Girl

She falls like mist
    soft,... cool,
        wet against my lips.
Hair that tickles
    hush the mouth she kissed.
A dam that broke
        words flood her;
            it's best to stand away.
At night she stalks and rubs me
        like a cat begins to purr.
Her flesh, forbidden scent
        drives me like a nail,
    through our hearts and soul and love
            together -
        we will never fail.

*Rob Carlton*

## A Tear

A tear drops from the
Soft pale cheek of a
child.  The tiny pink lips
quiver with fear and
sadness.  This child has
been through so much, her
mother has reached rock
bottom her father, she
doesn't know what is to
become of him.  She knows
that happiness is to
come soon and she
is to be once again
the fun loving, talkative
girl she used to be.
She knows it will happen
soon, but for now a
tear drops upon the
soft, pale cheek of
a child.

*Nicole Jacobs*

## I Love You

Gently a touch,
Softly a kiss,
As I whispered to your heart,
The words you always wished.

Oh listen so closely,
Hear with your mind and soul,
I love you so dearly,
You are my one, my all, my whole.

Sweetly a whisper,
Strongly a caress,
I will hold you in my arms,
And I'll show you tenderness.

So look very sincerely,
Upon my heart through and through,
You will find swirling gently
Those three words, girl "I Love You."

*Mike Parnell*

## Wind

As the wind blows
The quiet sound comes over the
  town
Love is in the air

*Lindsay R. Gaken*

## Tapestries of Childhood

Winter is so cold, bleak and
solidly grey
So am I
I walk among people young
old solidly grey
I'm alone I cry
Something's gone from my being
A long ago child raped of
person and mind
I'm my parents objection and
the world was not kind
I laugh as a Jestor in some
long ago court
The clown that cries secret tears
always with an amiable retort

Yes I'm a clown, I've a fictitious a
painted face
I walk in solitude as a Loner
with no particular grace
I'm alone I cry

*Lynn Fay*

## God's Ballet

Some reach their arms to the sky,
Some bend down to the earth,
Some spread them outward to embrace
The whole of the worldly race.

As God's musician, the wind, blows;
Their dancing they begin.
They bend and sway and reach above
As a tribute to His love.

The mighty oak, the lithe willow,
And trees of ev'ry form,
Dance by the will of God on high
To the wind's musical sigh.

*Peggy Marsh Eubanks*

## I Never Thought

I never thought that I could love,
Someone as much as you.
I never thought that I could care,
For you the way I do.

I never thought that I would miss,
You're warm caress and touch.
I never thought that I would miss,
Another quite so much.

But then you came along one day,
And stole my heart away.
And now an emptiness occurs,
Each time that you're away.

So keep me close and keep me near,
Please hold me don't let go.
I love you more than you would know,
And that my dear is so.

*Warren T. Good*

## Fate

Gratefully this week has passed
With a happy ending and smiles
For the next course that will be
Served up to us by the powers of fate
Let us be ready for this
Which life is preparing
For we and thee...

*Terri L. Irwin*

## Wanderer

Looking for someone
Someone special, someone mine
But never finding

People rush around me
Like a river, always flowing
Never ending

But I am different

I wander aimlessly
Looking for a sign
Which never comes

But I continue
Hoping, Searching, Seeking
Forever Alone

*Rebecca Lysik*

## A Special Gift Of Friendship

A friendship is something special,
Something strong and bold.
It's shared between two people.
That only they can hold.
Love is found in many different places,
That only friends can find.
It is a special gift,
It's from their two hearts combined.

*Lori Roberts*

## Untitled

Like a bridge
   Spanning the world,
The communications network
   Has grown.
As a bridge
   Can decay and needs repair,
The huge network also
   Fails from time to time.

From wooden bridges
   To steel trusses
To laser optics
   The network has history.

Which history is more valid?

Has communication
   From people to people
Been productive?
   Has instant communication
Created instant understanding?
          Or....

Are wooden bridges better?

*Nancy Paciencia*

## Life

Feelings exploding inside,
Wanting to run and hide.
Looking as I go up in flames,
Playing these foolish games.

*Rebecca Elliott*

## Untitled

Perhaps I'm wasting time
(Spiraling down the serpentine)
You see, the world is
peeking in on me
and maybe it sees what I don't know
(what I should be)

Perhaps it is all settled
Holding fast all acts have meddled
There is no way
no course to curse
And I am - excuse me - non-entity
Someone holds my hand
And guides me:  In the sense
that I am being dragged and pushed
where?

*Phil Lutzak*

## Untitled

Through the windows I see a man
standing out upon the sand

Coming closer as he walks,
wondering if I should talk

Even if I tried I couldn't
I'm too scared so I guess I wouldn't

Hiding in my closed in room
wondering if he will be there soon

I can feel him breath in my ear
whispering things I don't want to hear

His strong hands are hurting me
he's taking off my vest

I try to remove his hands
that are pushing on my chest

I can hear my mom saying
we'll be out of here soon

That's when I realize
I'm in a hospital room

If they don't catch that guy someday
another rapist will have his way

*Melisa Vaughan*

## My Window-Ledge of Life

On my window-ledge of life
Stands a vase of memories,
Burnished by the sands of time
It mirrors light from centuries
Of standing undisturbed while I
Have tried to fill it faithfully
Each life I've lived upon this plane,
And locked it with a precious key
I left behind me whence I came
To safeguard for eternity.

*Marcia W. Newcomb*

## Are We?

Civilized human beings
we are, they say.
But we take our young boys
and send them away.
To pick up a gun
and kill if they can.
Then we say ...
"You've become a man."

*C. S. Dean*

## Untitled

Pale blue eyes,
Staring silently
From their secluded resting place

Outside is bleak, Weary,
Destruction is imminent
Yet it's arrival delays

This pain within
Leaves the soul cold,
Sorrow
Anger
Fear
Guilt
It builds

Comfort is a fallacy
Fear, habitual

Alone it cannot be conquered
Yet bring me
a smile,
A friend,
And I'll forget.

*Ryan P. Scott*

## Stop

Stop the motion
Stop the days
Stop the nights
And the maze.

Stop the dogs
Stop the oars
Stop the people
And the wars.

Stop the bombs
Stop the planes
Stop the thunder
And the rain.

Stop the screaming
Stop the silence
Stop the crime
And the violence.

Stop and listen
Stop and feast
Stop and say
"PREPARE FOR PEACE."

*Sean Wolf*

## Through The Jungle

I'm going to flow through the river,
swing through the trees,
run along a jungle path,
fly on the breeze.

What animals shall I meet?
Perhaps even beak to beak,
Maybe with a monkey,
Maybe with a fleet
of flying parrots,
Why I could feed them carrots!

But I'm going to flow through the river,
swing through the trees,
run along a jungle path,
fly on the breeze.

*Stephanie M. Rose*

## Promise

Life leads me down
Strange paths
In strange places,
Through city streets
And open spaces.

What magnet draws me
Ever onward?
What is it that gently
Urges me forward
Toward my destiny?

Pulled by a gravity
Unseen,
Irresistible, like a voice
In the distance, calling,
I have no choice.

I follow where it leads.
No more,
No less.
The future is promised,
Already in progress.

*Milly Simmons*

## Fir Timber And Yellow Pine

Fir timber and yellow pine,
    Sunlit shadows intertwine,
In that grove, so dear to me,
    Muted hours of ecstasy.
There mossy paths with violets strewn,
    Rival roses of the June,
Birds mating and on wing,
    Gladly usher in the spring.

*Syd A. Caplen*

## For Claudia, at a Quarter Century

Visions still filled with brightness,
Sunshine caught in mid air;
Tangled strands wildly flying,
Body air bathed and bare;
Limbs perpetually flashing,
Defiance, young bred,
And delicious embraces,
Before darkness and bed.
So young and so precious,
And mine, always, to keep,
This image of Claudia
In my heart is burned deep.
Still racing with moonbeams,
I share with the world,
Untethered and loving,
My precious young girl.
Orbits her choosing
Attract my sweet prize,
Knowing well she can rest,
In her mother's eyes.

*Rea W. Jacobs*

## Mom

You bring joy, laughter and
sunshine to a rainy day.
You bring peace, love and
harmony to an argument.
You bring light, warmth and
spirit to a shadow.
You bring color, security and
hope to a scary dream.
For all that you do,
I thank you!

*Shannon Newmyer*

## Immortal Angel

Immortal Angel shed your light on me
take my hand walk with me into the
setting sun Immortal Angel still full
of life now is your time to live
among the blessed ones with beauty
unknown to man Immortal Angel I wish
to share a secret that not too many
know Immortal Angels can not die they
only live up in the sky enjoying
all that God gave them Immortal
Angel I send you my love on the wings
of a dove you are so very immortal to
me for you live in my heart and my
soul Immortal Angels can not die
they only spread their wings and
learn to fly.

*Molly Faith*

## In Your Hands

Take my Love;
take my Heart;
place them both,
in your Hands.

I trust you with,
the most vital part,
of me; "Myself".
Hold them forever.

Cherish them everyday;
and in your hands,
my life and love.
will stay.

*Margaret Fox*

## I Forgot!

The house is ready to greet my guest
Tea is waiting in the pot -
Fancy cookies wait in plates
I know there is something I forgot! -

The clock ticks the time away
I forgot "what" in my rush?
I hope I don't talk too much
If so, I hope someone says "Hush" -

My aching feet beg me to stop
Put them up so they can rest -
They have walked with me all day.
I tell them I will "after awhile"
They mustn't, mustn't be a pest -

The door bell rings - they are here!
I hope my smile is still in place -
My hair - oh, well - it's too late -
Now, I know - I forgot to fix my face!

*Lettie O. Rogers*

## Slave

The scourge of self hatred
tears into my soul.
It would cry out in pain.
If not for the gag
that seals its lips
and renders it in vain.
Anger and depression
scarring my psyche
erodes away my mind.
Enslaved by myself
oppressor extreme
no freedom will I find.

*Mike Ursu*

## Listen To Me

When I went through my
    teenage years
I learned to cope with pain
With inward joy and
    outward grit
Moved on to each new plane,.

When I want through my
    middle years
I shared my coping skills
With children and a
    loving man
Moved on to higher hills.

Now going through my
    later years
I pray dear God to cope-
My teenage grandson's
    hardest phase
With life - with love -
    with hope
      *Shirleyanne Chase Parr*

## Untitled

Love is such a warm feeling
That blossoms from the heart.
It grows with each passing year
With much work will never depart.

Love is always challenging
Though there are moments without it.
True love continues on
Even when the heart is in doubt.
      *C. A. Crawford*

## Something

Marriage is something
That I won't experience again.
Relationship is something
That I only want with friends.
Time is something
That I hope can rush by.
Tears are something
That I never want to cry.
Pain is something
That I never want to feel.
Life is something
That I do not know how to deal.
I am something
That I never want to know.
You are something
That I must let go.
So, good-bye to all of you "somethings,"
Good-bye to you all.
No more of you- "somethings"
I am trapped inside my wall.
      *Michelle Hughes*

## Spring Love

In the morning stillness,
The air is calm and tranquil,
As the birds sing to me of
    a new day awakening.
The sun gives me its warm hello
And the wind fluffs up the trees
While the petals of newborn flowers
    open themselves to the sky.
You come to me and warm me
    with your heart.
And in your arms, I am whole.
      *Shelli J. Maher*

## Devotion

Under the red sky lies an ocean of dark;
that is what I see.

A woman's cry; that is what I hear,
in the shade beneath the willow tree.

Beneath the willow tree,
above the black sea;
Because I lurk near what
comforts me.

In the shade, the grass
colored jade;
Because I creep near the
spot he lays.

Beneath the ground,
above what is hell;
Because we had a secret I
couldn't let him tell.
      *Melissa Brickey*

## Untitled

Eyes
that make me soar
blue-tinged
    asparkle
    like crystalline water
    flowing icy
    ensnared in small pristine valleys
yet warm
    with the glow
    of fine ensniftered brandy
amusingly watching
touching
ensuring interest
      *Terry L. Rhodes*

## Summer Sounds

When I hear a Blue Jay,
That makes my day.
Every time I hear a Robin,
My heart starts a throbbin.
When I hear crickets chirping,
It's music to my ears.
Summer Sounds, Summer Sounds,
How I love thy Summer Sounds.
      *Neosha Gardiner*

## Perception

The excitement in your voice
That never ending laughter
It's that inward beauty
Natures natural glow
It permeates the core of your being
Is it real or just my perception?

Do you laugh to hide your fears
Do you laugh to hide your tears
Is this that inner beauty
Which haunts my soul
Will we merge to make me whole
Is this real or just my perception?

Living in the past
Fond memories won't last
Afraid to live
Mixed messages you give
Take a chance
You have good intentions
Is this real or just my perception?
      *Val Munroe*

## Blind

  Life is beauty
that no one seems to recognize,
    Hatred we love
love we despise.
We close our eyes
    to the beauty,
We open them
    to the ugly.
We love the demons
    and the night,
We hate the angels
    with the light.
Life is beauty
That no one sees,
The devil has your soul
    just like me.
      *Lauren Stasak*

## Outside Looking In

Everyday I pass beside a brick wall
that separates me from the world;
    looking.
I see him but yet I wonder does
he see me;
    looking
I turn and walk away, still unaware
of him;
    looking.
I stopped just to see, but as I turned
he was there with me on the outside.
He told me as I turn away that I
belonged with him on the inside
because he loved me.
    Now all of my dreams are coming
true, because I'm on the inside;
    looking out.
      *Lisa Berryhill*

## Evolution of Man

I was once a mighty rock
that settled just off shore
and when you heard the waves make noise
It was me that made them roar

Then I become a tiny pebble
Just rolling to and fro
My life had no direction
No control to where I'd go

Now finally I'm a grain of sand
Just there to fill the beach
My life has no more meaning
there's nothing left to teach

For life is like the ocean
And you are but a wave
You give until you finally crash
There's nothing left to crave
      *R. John Bolduc*

## The Poet Tree

I picked a poem from the poet tree,
To read to I, Myself and me
A simple verse, with words that rhyme.
Just to help us pass the time.

As I perused the words, so fine
And savored every thought sublime;
I marvelled that, how great it be,
Such thoughts can grow on a poet tree.
      *Margaret Kist*

## "Menard Pen"

Peering through the bars of
the cage searching for a glimpse
of hope thru the glaring haze...
Day turns tonight, night back
to day sweet Freedom is but a heart
beat away.  Day light shines brightly
bittersweet thru cell house windows
facing front street.  Menard Prison is
nowhere to be, when your out date shows
boy you'd better flee.  Sweet, sweet
liberty...

*Michael Crane*

## II

The sand ends
The cliff drops
And choices lie
In my feet
Or my wings

To pounce on air
And fall into
Or fly into
Or turn into
Or turn around

And face my desert past

*Leigh Burnham*

## The Piper's Song

The morning mist was clean and cool.
The earth embraced its frosty chill.
An autumn sun was breaking through
A wooded grove upon the hill

Below a valley came to life
As melting shadows crossed its face.
A passing breeze left in its wake
A flowing field of golden grace.

A sound emerged from somewhere far
Within the vale.  I tried to see.
A wailing sound in modal tones
Did spirit me to fantasy.

It carried 'round the valley floor
And up the jagged mountain slope.
It pleaded for a human tear
To share its agony and hope.

So plaintive was this mystic cry,
My happy heart it did invade.
'Tis now a haunting memory,
The morn the lonely piper played.

*Peggy Switzer Samii*

## The Night

As the sun sets, my eyes awaken
The evening is about to unfold

My desire can not be mistaken
My story will now be told

The bedroom seems so lonely
The T.V. is getting old

My inspiration, best friend and lover
Is somewhere miles from home
Musette, I'm lost without you
I can't express that over the phone

Just a few more days to get thru
Until then I must bare it alone

*Len Falcone*

## Dead But Still Alive

The Pain.
The fear.
No Faith.
No love.
She screamed with no sound.
She ran with blistered feet.
She cried with blood for tears.
She was tortured till
her last breath was taken.
She had the most
Unimaginable pain.
She was dead and gone
but her pain was still
very much alive.

*Nora Hall*

## Life

Life is the sound of our heartbeat,
the feeling of an unborn child,
the feeling of life within,
that will soon be born into this
world of sin.
A world of corruption, weakness,
evilness, adultery, and liar too.
But life can also be
a world of love and peace,
a body united with the soul
to have a deep affection
for someone or something
forgiving, mercy and kindness
but to obtain life,
we must live with each
the good and evil within
period of darkness between sunset
and sunrise,
life is sunshine but yet the rain in day,
life is given and then taken away.

*Mary Finley*

## Dreams

My favorite pair of old jeans
The first time I wore them,
they were right for me.
Wearing them over and over.
I hope they will always last.
Fading and
Developing new holes every day.
When I slip them on
They make me happy.
My friends encourage
While my parents discourage
the life of my beautiful jeans
And I wonder
What will become of them
In 10 or 15 years.

*Susan Hens*

## Incommunicate

To act is to interact,
what we do, tact or no tact
has results in many ways
to speed forward or delay
Good or bad another day,
So does it not make good sense
with selfishness to dispense?
Be universal in thought —
love for all thus
having sought.

*Laura A. Fontaine*

## Saved From Madness

All around me was darkness
The four walls manifested a stark mess
Destructive thoughts were unrestrained
Panic and despair caused me pain
Convinced my mind was out of control
The truth of my state began to unfold
Crippling fear ruled my world

Melancholy concealed thy message of love
Self-pity prevented healing from above
In sincere humility I cried out
The Lord did hear my shout
After the storm subsided
Calming thoughts of peace had resided
Jesus stood before the clouds

Satan kneeled down before him in defeat
Along with my burdens and sins at his feet
Jesus had conquered my fears, thus
stopping my tears
No longer did I fear the night
Because in Jesus' eyes love shone bright
The true meaning of "champion" was clear

*Linda Camacho*

## Fireside Dreams

The logs crackle, pop, and settle,
the glow warms up the night;
outside the snow flakes lightly dance,
inside it is "just right".

A flake clings to the outer pane,
inside, a steamy mug;
the blanket outside is moon white,
inside, we're curled upon the rug.

A quilt drawn up to share the warmth,
gazing beyond the trees;
getting lost in the view of the stars,
as music colors the breeze.

The majesty of winter nights,
All nature reigns above;
while within the cabin, just two,
lost in our spring of love.

Let's run back to the clouds so high,
settled among the pines;
celebrate our love again, sweet-
if only in our minds.

*R. Craig Collins*

## Land Of Liberty

The air is sweet and it is spring.
The good earth wakens at our touch
  Our thanks for much.
The beauty of a summer night
The freshness of a summer day
  For these, we pray.
A tall and flaming autumn tree
But autumn flowers are fading fast
  They cannot last.
The flags at half-mast on the street
The ending of an endless task
  "Oh why?" we ask.
Another grasps the flaming torch
For bells of freedom still must ring
  Another spring.

*Mary Simmons Carmichael*

## Nature

The sky is blue
The grass is green
On the grass there is some dew

The grass is dancing in the sun
The flowers are having such fun

When the sun is light
The flowers sing
When the sun is bright
It is a sign of spring

I see some trees
I see some land
You see some bees
You see some sand

*Nicole Desnoyers*

## MAPLE LEAVES

They shed in the autumn
the green maple's leaves
changing from yellow to gold
and then orange and brown

The fine line etchings
that are drawn in the skin
of these leaves
are like sketches of pencil art

Are like lifelines
going down some road
to eternity

Are like human veins
going everywhere
but, then nowhere.

*H. Patricia Blackshire*

## "Monetary Messiah"

The mint became its Bethlehem,
The green paper, its manger.
"Follow me" it said,
"Pay no mind to the danger."

The poor became its stewards,
Aristocracy, its bride.
"Follow me" it said,
"I bring happiness and pride".

Selling and buying became,
Its consecratory rite.
"Do this in memory of me,
The way, the truth, and the light".

Discarding all reason,
We allow its control.
"Follow me" it said,
"Perdition of the soul".

*Phillip Darrell Collins*

## Summer

Bright sun rays warm
the ground where the ocean
lay. Sand and water swish and
sway in the sailing wind.
Waves crash on the shore and
fish jump in the air. A rock
lies in the way shaped like
a chair. A boat sails it's way
to sea and a ship stops at the
pier. And I am happy and content
while I'm waiting here.

*Paige Fagala*

## Youth

When I was young, it was hard to see,
The highway of life ahead of me,
I jumped at all the easy ways,
Not caring about another day,
Or what harm I might do.
For I was young, Id always say,
I'll wait. Just one more day to change.
I laughed at all, that I was told,
How do you know? Your all to old!
And then one day, to my dismay,
I seen the sorrow that I had made.
The years they flew, I know not where,
And now, I have a child to rear.
I'll do my best for him to see,
So he won't end up sorry like me.

*Virginia Grimm*

## The Horse: A Tribute

They swept across the Russian steppes,
The horses of the Huns.
Six hundred braved Death Valley
Under fire from Russian guns.

They pulled our covered wagons
In pioneering quest,
And sped through hostile country
To open up our West.

And now, removed from battle
To save them from the kill,
They grace our shows and pastures.
With their beauty and their skill.

Teammates through both war and peace
Since the world began,
Purple hearts, blue ribbons
For the noble friend of man.

*Thomas H. Flood*

## To Him

Hi, old love, remember me?
The joys we shared, the secrets bared.

"I heard undying love", whispers
the old backyard tree.
It witnessed our kiss, heard me
say: I love the bristles
'round your sweet lips."

Separated now by time and space,
the glowing moon
reveals your face as I renew our
vow to send a message
by first star.

Although I walk at night alone,
your memory glows with
happiness we've known.

Perhaps some early morning
quiet, or gentle evening rain.
I'll look up and hear you call my name.

*Nada J. Hill*

## To Jean On New Year's Day

In the brightly lit ballroom
Under the sparkling chandeliers
A brand new song begins
As we take up our old positions
In the ancient dance

*Susan L. Daly*

## Soul's Delight

The eagles soar,
The lions roar.

New babies cry,
As elders die.

The children laugh,
As cynics chaff.

Bright flowers rise,
From laden skies.

All beauty ignites,
The soul's delight.

*Victoria Clise*

## Little Girl

I wonder if he ever knew
The love she felt inside
The secret of a little girl
Trying to catch his eye

Anything to make him smile
And please his precious heart
His gentle hugs touched her soul
She felt it from the start

Hoping it was meant to be
His presence made her weak
He always gave affection
And kissed her on the cheek

But being a little girl
Made dreams of love grow more
He consumed her every thought
She tried but couldn't ignore

I wonder if he'll ever know
Or if she'll ever tell
She loves him with all her heart
Or live on dreams to dwell

*Marnie Furniss*

## The Colored Mountains

What an earthly sight!
The mountains glowing as if on fire.
The sun's last rays of light,
Makes them look even higher.

The moon filtering slowly thru,
It will soon be dark;
Just barely a hint of blue,
Then the stars will make their mark.

Not a cloud in the sky,
The colors stretch a dazzling bouquet;
So sad to say good-bye,
To such a beautiful, perfect day.

*Melissa A. Budner*

## Love

Love is the light in a little child eyes
The purr of a kitten. A small surprise.
Love is unselfish in truth and deed
A dethronement of self - another's need
Love is the spirit of the central core
A aura of Graces - evermore.
Love is a discipline, that grows within
A seed of new life, that conquers sin.
Love is God - A spiritual rebirth
Lifting my soul above the earth.

*Ruth Enabnit Ritter*

## Morning Girl

A pristine gem,
The one the king singled out.
All his treasures were no match
This one bright,
Bright like the morning sun.
A true find.
Lancelot, the gallant one, in his quest
for the gift-stone, fell short.
The monarch himself found this gem.
Shining
Shining
The morning sun
A morning girl
A gem.

**Robert R. Sanchez**

## A Hoarse Cry

A broken man holds
The past that maimed him,
Remembers and relives it
Like a childhood summer.
He knows the echoing crack
Of the gun and the
Sound of his life screaming.
He has seen himself
Fall like a drop
From a cloudless sky.
He knows nothing else,
And endures the pain
Like the scar on his chest,
And the hoarse cry on his lips.

**Thomas Asturias**

## My Last Wish

Come walk with me
The path is slow
Cloaked in morning flowers

Come walk with me
And take my pall
The time is only ours

Come walk with me
So gently speak
Loving words that light my soul

Come walk with me
My spirit soars
My rest is on the knoll

**Nadine E. Anderberg**

## Flowers

The flowers of life are like
the people on earth.
They come in all colors and
sizes.
Just like the human bean
on earth.
The flowers wither and die
and people grow old and pass on.
But like the flower and
like the person.
The estons goes on and we
remember it with good and happy
memories.
Like the flower and the
estons of that human beans,
the memory lingers on.
For all times.

**Sasha Hernandez**

## Galveston

The sea has been your making,
The sea has been your breaking,
Galveston you have stood.

Sun, sand, sea and storm,
Victorian to art-deco,
Native son to tacky tourist,
Pirate's haven to oil platform,
A tiny strip of earth loam,
Astride a brackish bay.

Galveston in the morning light,
You look like a promise.
Galveston in high noon melt,
You look a bit anile.
Galveston in the sun's go-down,
You look like forever.

**Susan Phillippi**

## Eternal Clock

Sometimes I feel
the sea in me
as if through all
eternity
the ebb and flow
of endless tides
washed me ashore
to dwell awhile.
To wander yet
another mile
of rendezvous
with fate to keep
until again
the cradle deep
lulls me to sleep...

And this goes on
forever more.

**Sibyl McEwan Kellman**

## The Pilgrims Landing

The first time I saw plymouth Rock
The sight of it was quite a shock.
A pebble more is what I saw.
(To call it more would be a flaw)
Why, it should be against the law.

The hist'ry books, when I was small,
pictured it so big and tall;
with pilgrims standing on its crest
Flag waving; oh my, — do they jest?
One pilgrim might upon it get,
(And then, for sure, his feet be wet.)
So little is this rock, and yet....

And yet with reverence do I gaze,
My mind a wandering in the haze,
at pilgrims wading to the shore;
To change our world forevermore

**Richard C. Koch**

## You Can Fly

This time
upon a branch
his tiny feet grasped tight
until he felt secure - be brave
fledgling!

**Rebekah Parks**

## Dreams

The air is damp
The sky is gray
The day was gone
The night will stay
As we sleep
In our beds
Our minds will wonder
In our heads
We dream of love
We dream of hate
We dream of anything
Of sin and fate
Our dreams are real
Our thoughts are fake
We dream of anything
Our minds can make

**Megan Russell**

## My Dream

I had a dream last night.
The sky was all aglow,
Far brighter than the fullest moon
With Angels flying round about.
The sweetest music I did hear
Coming from the harps above.
The trumpet sound I did hear
As the Lord appeared.
"My child it is time to come home."
Great joy there was
Among the angels that were there
To have one more voice
Sing in the Heavenly choir.
But I awoke to hear
The alarm clock ringing in my ear.
How sad I was at first that this was just a dream
But now I know what joy awaits
As I wait with great anticipation
For my Lord to appear
When my dream is not a dream but a reality.

**Lillian Eck Gunnels**

## My Knight

As I close my eyes I see,
The small child of three.
Clinging tight to her doll,
The tears hot where they fall.
In her room, alone, late at night,
Happy to see the sight,
Of her Knight in shining armor,
Standing at the door.
He brushes away her tears,
Listens to her fears.

The girl now grown,
Sitting alone.
It's been over a year,
The pain still is near.
Life took him away from me,
My knight I'll never again see,
But he's still here, My Knight,
He's still in my sight.
As long as I have the memories we've made,
Not even God has taken him away.

**Lucinda Hind**

## End of an Era

The curtains are drawn
The stage stands dark
The players came and
Played their part

A certain stillness fills the air
I look around but all I see
Are memories of a time
that used to be

The players have moved on
Leaving their props behind
And an audience that
Stands still in time

Voices echo in the hallway
And down the basement steps
I thought I heard my name
I'd forgotten they all left

As I go on with my life here
I know it's not just the end
of a play
It's the end of an era.

*Laurie Ringseth-Swerrie*


## Suns Without End

Without knocking at my door
  the sun through my window
  paths its way
  brushes dust
  and gently caresses
  my awakening self.

Dazzling light
  tarnishes the milky way
  whose sparkling splendor
  was my bed partner.

Windows within and without
  open to
  the pain and joy
  of the awesome birth
  of life and death
  in a void of
  darkness and light.

Filling passions
  with the wonder
  of suns without end.

*Wilson Reid Ogg*


## In the Spring

In the spring we see
The trees and flowers bloom.
An awakening of our world
With fragrances we want to consume,
We'd like to store them
In a special hideaway room.
The hot days that will follow
Appear as an impending doom.
But the season ends quickly
And into a busy summer we zoom!

*Polly Enkoff*


## The Meadow

It is night and the moon is setting.
The wind is peaceful.
The sky is calm.
You can see the grass bend a tad, but
be real quiet, you can feel the wind
slowly moving over you.

*Scott Szelong*


## Thunderstorm

Crashing thru the night
The wind screamed it's eerie melody
Pagan stars disappeared
Into hushed, black anonymity
The growling, roaring thunder spake
Of the mighty storm's advancing wake
Scurrying squirrels screeched in fear
As all living things from far and near
Took flight
And ran and wailed
As the mighty storm
Began it's assail
The tall, trembling trees
Swayed and bowed
And to each other
Reached
Their limbs in rhythmic frenzied fear
As the raging, mighty
Thor appeared!

*Sylvia Wright Fellie*


## Predation

The moon is full
The wolves are out
Nocturnal creatures
Roam about

Predators on the prowl
Their eyes luminary
Quarries are wary
Their eyes starey

Glowing eyes
Pierce through darkness
All is quiet
In the still and starkness

The prey pursued
The wolves feast
All in a night's work
For the savage beast

*Margaret Brown*


## He

He is a ray of hope traveling
the world
  Stopping to see everything
that can be seen
  Seeing Evil makes him
shudder in fear
  Standing up to fear makes
him brave
  Yet when angry he
shows no violence
  When he cries, he
closes down
  When he is happy he
smiles

*Pam Deem*


## Peaceful Haiku

The sun slowly set
as I drifted into a
deep and peaceful sleep.

*Maritess D. Gurtiza*


## Lullaby To An Unborn Child

Stay where you are; it's warmer there.
The world outside is cold and dark;
And death awaits to doom those born
Before they partake of a part
Of Life, before they can exist.

Stay as you are, a part of me,
And I will shelter and protect
You from the world you cannot see,
Nor feel, nor hear; nothing except
Through me can you experience.

Stay how you are, small and young
And innocent, without regret;
Without a conscience, past or mind
To cloud your days. Stay there and let
Your muted world create your dreams.

*Megan Tibbits Slater*


## Watercolors

Your paintings,
Their blue-grays imprecise
As blowing mist,
Have brought sea-light,
Coastal air to inland rooms
Where I have lived.
They are my rooms' other windows,
Carry the wind's freshness
Of a day (how long ago?)
You set up near that house
At anchor on its spit of sand,
Washed in those blues,
The strokes of beach grass;
The day in drenching fog
You stopped to look at ghosts
Of houses floating in a field.
I wanted you to know
They are here still, those days,
That hour's light,
Still here.

*Marjorie Mir*


## Gone Away

Everything has its time to leave,
their candle is left burned out.
Everything has to leave, but what
happens to it after it has left?
  What has happened to it all?
Crazy some might say.
Where is the life I recognize?
It is gone away.
  I will not cry about yesterday,
I will go on. But there is another
world, I somehow have to find.
As I try to make my way,
I realize that everything is gone away.

*Shannon Siroin*

## The Sea and Land

The rust-stained rocks thrust
Their mighty shoulders against
The pounding fury of the on-rushing sea.
The jade green waters,
Flecked with whitened foam,
Swirled and curled
From the bottom of the sea.
The flotsam from the oceans' depths
Were hurled at the rocks with glee.
"Give way and let me ashore",
Says the sea.
"Swirl and curl..Break your waves
On me, but I will stand",
Says the land.

*Lee E. Herring*

## Metamorphosis

I can now fly,
There are wings everywhere.
With these wings of leather
I can soar in ecstasy.
Like smoke in a Summer's night,
I can crawl far and high
Encircling no more trees and rooftops
Only rejoicing at my metamorphosis.
I can now sing to us a new song
That I know you can dance to.
Fresh from the river
I feel cleansed and renewed.
Awash with a new reality
Enacted in vine-like embrace
I rejoice at my solemn investiture.
I shall now be free
Because even in slumber
You still can hear me sing!

*Lui Akwuruoha*

## A Silent War Going On

Stillness in the air
There is a war going on out there
We pass it by each day
By pressing a button.

But when it hits home
Like Oklahoma City
We call it National prayer day.

This war has been going on
since the 60's
Every minute someone dies
Like Vietnam
The casualties of war
Are my brothers and sisters.

You had to be twenty to enlist
Now it's ten
Playing together on the ceiling of hell.

Going out to church
Coming out pale
Talking in tongues with the holy one
Praying to God that your son doesn't have a
gun.

*Leonard F. Dixon*

## The Music Of Distrust

With passing of each year,
There is less and less time,
To overcome human fear,
And merely hope sometime,

For lessening of tension,
Leading us to forget,
How profound the reason,
To stop getting upset,

With person or thing,
Caught in the web,
Of the very sad song,
Music of distrust,

Instead of hope today,
Sending fear away,
As simple act,
The human pact,

Not arriving,
ever.

*Thomas N. Cranston*

## Future

As far as mine eyes can see
There is no tomorrow,
for change would be upon us,
instead there's only sorrow.

The grass would be greener
and the trees a little taller,
the earth a bigger and better place
instead it just gets smaller.

Our kids should be the
future of this world,
but instead they're overtaken
by violence, these boys and girls.

Tomorrow should be a change
for the better, not worse,
for this chance God has given
will be lost to Satan's curse.

*Terri Lynn Minor*

## Untitled

At twenty I was quick to sneer
    There seemed so much of folly here
And often would remark how come
    That older folks all seemed so dumb.

At twenty-five I had suffered pain
    I'd lost a goal I'd planned to gain
And though I'd ridden to a fall
    I still believed I knew it all.

At thirty I had come to see
    That life was really puzzling me
And strange opinions I could hear
    Without responding with a sneer.

At forty and no longer young
    I'd almost learned to hold my tongue
Instead of absolutely so
    I sometimes answered I don't know.

At fifty age has slowed me so
    Now at a gentler pace I go
And now I understand how come
    That older folks all seem so dumb.

*Russell Patterson*

## "The Challenge"

Some make art their life.
Therein lies the challenge:
To make life your art.
Experience and witness,
grow and learn
through your art.
One piece at a time, you must:
Create it;
experience it;
share it;
be it;
and when all is done,
set it free.....

*William D. Shroyer*

## All Grown Up

The years passed quickly,
    they are fully grown
And now they have children
    of their very own
My wonderful son and daughter
    who have brought me such pride
Now have full lives that they take
    in their stride
I've loved them so much
    for thirty six years
Through laughter and sadness
    and all of their fears
They have given me more pleasure
    than words can express
And I pray nearly daily
    for their happiness!

*Rhoda Haas*

## The Hands of a Mother

The precious hands of a mother,
They are like those of none other.
Even when throbbing with ache,
In love a new turn they take,

Though calloused and worn,
They still comfort a child torn.
When lost in this vast land,
He gropes for that gentle hand.

She cries, "Willing hands have I,
I'll be there when you cry.
My love is eternal and strong,
Even if you do many a wrong."

If a human can show such love,
How much more does God above.

*Priscilla Luke-Suneetha*

## Shelia

What makes the flowers cry,
the slicing of the hoe?
Is it fear too soon to die,
it seems that I should know?

What makes the flowers cry,
so far away the snow?
They chase away the butterfly
and yet I do not know.
What makes the flowers cry,
it isn't fear I find,
but a child who's gone they smiled upon
and they are left behind.

*Marvin V. Little*

## Nomads Of The Highway

When nomads roamed the desert...
They rode on camel backs
And Indians moved their campsites
And erased all moccasin tracks.

But the nomads of our highways
Traverse the interstate's
In motor homes with cars in tow
To avoid those motel rates.

And the "Knights of the Highway"
Transport food and much much more...
The cars we drive... the tools we use...
And goods for shop and store...

The nomads of the highway
May claim one spot for home,
But their hearts are ever yearning
For another place to roam.

There's fun and high adventure
Awaiting you somewhere...
Get in that line of traffic...
That goes from here to there.

*Oneta A. Anderson*

## A Slice Of Eternity

Choice of words is still my own
they shall sing in amber tones
of morning gladness
black opaque of silent night.
Sorrow comes with needled sharpness,
scars—then fades away again.
Joy is fleet and hangs on wing,
worlds roll over in the sky.

Even so, I live in my world.
Even so, I live 'till death
greatest word of all the words
puts me in his final sentence,
adds a period and is done
with the writing on the wall
of the stars that flame then char
to a velvet toneless ember.

*Ruth Hershey Irion*

## A Tribute to Mothers

Mothers are a blessing from above
They're full of joy, warmth, and love
They cheer you up when you are blue
And they're always there for you.
Mothers are so nice and kind
They do so much, but they don't mind.
They cook, they clean, they fix your hair
They'll take you almost anywhere.
They're full of love and full of care
Their love for you they'll always share.
They do so much in so many ways
We should give them a lot more praise.
So as you can plainly see
Mothers are a special gift, to me.
I love my mom, I truly do
And I bet you love yours
And she loves you.

*Rebecca Lynn Robinson*

## On Growing old

Time files, m'body sighs.
Things change, less range.
Mission's done.
What a run!
When'd it happen?
Was I nappin'?
Grand kids now.
So take a bow.
Go with the flow.
But take it slow.
Think new things.
Then try new wings
Like love and service.
Now, don't get nervous.
Play it cool.
You're no fool.
Older, yes
But not a mess.
Things to do.
That's the rule.

*Melvin Senator*

## Rebirth of Spring

As I look out my window
  this beautiful day
The sky so blue
  the clouds at play

The flowers are showing
  their colors so bright
While the fountain in the pond
  is dancing with delight

Birds fly by
  singing their special song
and building their nests
  for the young to belong

Spring is here
  a lovely time of year
For the beginning again
  of rebirth so dear.

*Marilyn J. Winterborne*

## Gulf Of Destiny

Beside his gulf of destiny,
This blazing strand that summoned him
To oil and war and history,
He walks alone, sweat soaked and grim.

As wavelets lap the blistered shore,
The broiling orb fires forth its flare
To parch the lifeless coast yet more
And curl the brown soil-bearded air.

The sun's kiss stings his weathered face,
He turns to look across the dunes
And sees dust dance with gritty grace
As heat haze hums its toneless tunes.

He dreams of cool drinks in the shade
Of breeze blown trees in meadows green,
Of liquid sounds small brooks had made,
Of rain washed air that can't be seen.

He longs for rustling leaves turned gold,
For frosty nights beside the fire,
For brilliant days of breathless cold,
For snowdrifts blowing ever higher.

*Lowell W. Weber II*

## The Porch

If boards could tell a story.
This grey and weathered porch,
friend and homely haven, creaking
tales of love and glory.

Watched the birds upon the wing
flying in the breath of spring.
Watched heaven drop its
rainbow with the dew.
Children's giggles wrapped
in sunburst memory.
Cares crept silently to clouds,
escaping.
Moonlight captures reason,
season after season.

We creak and groan
in harmony with life and bone.
Standing in the light of dawn
this old Porch and I.
Tomorrow's time enough to die.

*J. Von Limburg*

## Untitled

We hope you are surprised to find
  this party is for you

Your birthday means so much to us
  It's the least that we can do

Balloons and punch, a delicious cake
  with ice cream to put on top

Kahlua and cream, wine or run
  or even a soda pop

Dinner is ready for you to taste
  we hope you do enjoy

And after that you'll open your gifts
  oh boy, oh boy, oh boy

We hope that you are happy
  and know how much we care

And thank you Donna for giving us
  A birthday we can share

*Richard D. Tisue*

## And Four to Know

A banker, I will wed,
  This sweet thing said to me.
Before I die, my bed, she said,
  Will share another three!

An actor, dark and tall,
  Could have me as a wife.
We'd really have a ball,
  Through the mid-part of my life!

Then a tailor, who could dress,
  This body given me.
He must be, I will confess,
  Part of my family tree!

I'll need an undertaker,
  After I pass away
Before I meet my Maker,
  These are the words I'll say!

One was for the money, and
  Two was for the show,
Three was to get ready, man
  And four was for to go!

*Richard E. Nickel*

## A Young Warrior

Is this hell?  He asked aloud
Tho' none could really hear,
Thru' the machine gun chatter,
And exploding shells, that
Filled his young heart with fear.

The days and nights it seemed,
Brought endless cold and rain,
As he trudged and crawled thru'
Miles of mud, with his body
Wracked in pain.

With mind benumbed and body torn,
He walked like the living dead,
While tho'ts of warmth, and love,
And kin, ran wildly thru' his head.

The clouds then broke, and someone
Cried, look out!
His hand reached for his gun.
In a searing blast he fell with
Lifeless eyes — staring at the sun.

**Robert A. Smith**

## Past Presence

Rejoice in the fondest of memories
Those who have touched our hearts
Speaking to us with joy and laughter
Renewed afresh as is each day
We need not understand this happiness
We share when love is given

Yet we puzzle, in times of despair
Vainly searching the mind for answers
From there, can come no solutions
Only moments in which we are unaware

Take comfort in the soul alone
Emanating this simple wisdom
The past can not cause the present
The creation of time itself

**Rich Nick**

## The Song

Thank you for your hope
though I'm not perfect
and wrong every day.
You have given something
no one has given me
you love me
Thru the dark tunnels
of life
your love is and has been
constant and strong
never failing
always there.

**Pamela Theresa Childs Speer**

## Death

People must not waste their
time, because all we have is
each other, and time itself.
I am running out of time and
death is coming on.
But just remember one thing,
death is not the end.  It is
the beginning of sharing forever
with those who left you in life.

**Lindsay Hamrick**

## Afraid

The fear that runs
through our mind

The feeling of being alone,
facing the fear

The thoughts racing around
unaware of the outcome

Scared as we walk along
not knowing where to go

Our heart races with anxiety
crying out for help

To find that fear
is just a thought.

**Tammi Jutte**

## Through Someone Else's Eyes

Have you ever tried to see the world
  Through someone else's eye?
Have you tried to see their laughter
  Or strained to hear their cries?

Have you been there when they're lonely
  And their face contained a frown?
Or maybe when they're angry
  Or perhaps when they were down?

Have you been there to hold their hand
  Or just stand by their side
When they wanted to run away,
  To run away and hide?

Were you there when they were happy
  Or maybe when they were blue?
Or when they just need
  A friend they could talk to?

You could find a friend
  A comrade and a pal, too
If you try to look at the world
  From someone else's view.

**Melissa F. Youd**

## Flying Enchanted

Soaring
Through the dream of one young mind
Leave the sorrow well behind,
A dreamer of a different kind,
With different dreams for a dreamer
To find.

Approaching
A destiny beyond this place
As quick as light for light must chase,
To enter is as a unique race,
For it's more than a life but a
Unique face.

Entering
The world that gives a lasting crease
Of bliss the pain begins to cease,
Enchanted love the warmest fleece,
A relaxing soul which can soar warm
As peace.

**Robert Clements**

## Seeking Wildroses

Bring me no roses
tied up with strings;
gesture exposes
agenda that stings.

No gift these roses,
stifled tears brings;
"gift" presupposes—
my wounded heart wrings.

Empty each rose is,
hollow each rings;
sham here deposes
sweet red buds to things.

Shame claimed the roses,
no color still clings;
love decomposes
enstrangled by strings.

**Susan Jared**

## In My Mind's Eye

Travel, in my mind's eye
to a distant land,
a far away place
brought ever so close
through time and space.

Travel, in my mind's eye
no roads, no maps
no instruments of direction
guided only by the knowledge
of your affection.

Travel, in my mind's eye
how I long to go there
to feel your warm comfortable embrace.

Travel, in my mind's eye
I know you as we have
lived together all my life
Yet each day is a new beginning
the excitement of being there
for the very first time.

**Lolita B. Bayaua**

## Is It Really Love

We're fighting to hold on
to a love we both feel fallin'
apart but is it worth the fight,
will it survive, will we survive
what we've put each other
through, at the end will the love
we spent so long fighting for
still be there after all the time
we have been apart, is it as
strong as we both seem to believe
or are we making ourselves believe
something that's not even there,
are we fighting for something
that we won't to be or is it really
love we've spent so long fighting
for, is it really love or just a dream
we're holdin' on to and waiting
to come true so is it really
love we're fighting for.

**Sheila M. Kell**

## The Work of God's Hand

I didn't see God come down
To build a tree
Or lay a carpet of green
Over the waiting land.
I didn't see God cover
The winter earth with snow,
But this I know:
It was all the work of His hand.

I didn't see God paint the sky
At sunset or early morn,
Or build a mountain peak
Above winter fields or summer storm.
I didn't see Him place the stars high
Over a sleeping land,
But of this I'm sure:
This too was the work of His Hand.

I didn't see God send His Son
To die: To rise again for you and me-
I didn't see, nor can I fuller understand
This crowning work of His Hand.

*Norton Scott*

## Untitled

I no longer have the capacity
To deal with the catastrophe
Just when my life seems fantastic
Here comes the drastic
Death destruction
Doom and Gloom
With all this misery
There is no
Room
Room
For
Dreams
Goals
Fantasy
For
I know
Ahead
Lies
Reality

*Marianne Elizabeth Cerroni*

## Not Alone

Alone to look into my heart
To examine cracks of time
To see that they have long since healed
Leaving only scars behind

Alone to look into my mind
To bring it up to date
To discard all the unkind thoughts
Distrust and fear and hate

Alone to sort my memories
To keep the very best
To live them over in my mind
To know that I've been blest

Alone to value what I have
The one I hold most dear
The love and kindness he has shown
With every passing year

Alone, did I say alone
But that can never be
From up above my Lord looks down
He truly smiles on me.

*Lillian Crowther Deslaurier*

## A Message From Marty

It was time for me to go
to fly free with the wind
to dance the heavens
to soar the skies
to meet my destiny
I am with you always
my spirit is everywhere
in the gently whispering breeze
the glad song of the birds
the sound surf
and the soft falling snow
I am the heavens
and I am the earth
I know no bounds
I am free to roam this universe
Do not be sad for me
I've found my destiny
I am gone from you for now
but my spirit is with you always

*Mary Morrison*

## The One For Me

He goes with me
to get closer to her
They become great friends
or at least that's what I believed
He says he loves me
He tells her the same
we break up
He says I'm to blame
He goes with her
Now it's all a blur
How did it happen
were we not meant to be
Does he really love her
and only used me
I won't believe this
For it can't be true
maybe one day
he'll come back and see
that we were meant to be.

*Nancy Holmes*

## Vacation

I have a moment to ask the sun,
To leave the rain, to sing on the sea.
A lazy road to time away.

I have a moment to bless the moon,
To count the stars, to smell the rose.
A savored segment in a dutiless day.

I have a moment to climb a hill,
To read a book, a whistle a tune.
No phones to answer, no words to say.

I have a moment to close my eyes,
To smell the air, to feel the breeze.
No obligations or bills to pay.

I have a moment to gather my words,
To write them down, to capture the mood.
A scene of serenity in a wondrous play.

*Mary V. Gresik*

## 104th Congress

I wish I had some profound thoughts
To mull o'er in my mind
To pass along to those like you
And all of my mankind.

Had I as much to say right now
As you folks think you do
It'd be a darn sight easier
To communicate with you.

I'd have the answers 'fore you do
If you ever asked
I'd never miss a chance like that
To take you all to task.

I'd speak right up—cry out loud
Like all your brothers too.
And let you know I know as much
As you folks think you do.

*Robert R. Johnston*

## Dream Land

Dream Land - Is The Place We Go,
To Rejuvenate Our Spirit, Body,
Mind And Soul.

It's In This State,
That We Can See,
Our Lives - Quite Differently.

The Thoughts We Suppress,
During The Day - Come Into The Light,
And Out To Play.

Dream Land - Is A Wonderful Place
To Be - It Gives Us A Chance,
To Visit - Family And Friends
We Ordinarily Wouldn't See.

When We Awaken - We'll Realize
They're Someone We Know
In This Most Current - Lifetime.

Dream Land - Is The Place We Go,
In The Hopes To Discover
All The Many Wonders
Of Our Past, Present And Future.

*Lynne Louise Skinner*

## Untitled

It angers me
to see the pain
that divorce causes.

Mouths say "Yes,"
Hearts say "No."
Tears keep flowing;
is this the route
that we must go?

Now that you have heard
the pain of the victims,
you are hearing the pain of not only me,
but the pain of all of the masses.

*Rachel Baird*

616

## Keep Me Whole

I wish I had you
to talk to now,
I wish I could
bring you back somehow.

Your spirit has touched me,
in so many ways
I know you'll be with me
throughout the days.

When I'm all alone
and lost at night,
I know you're here,
It'll be all right.

Walk with me
through my life.
Walk with me
through sorrow and strife.

Walk with me,
soul to soul,
walk with me,
keep me whole...

*Scott Josler*

## My Friend

If I should need a companion
  To walk the extra mile,
Who's always there to greet me
  With a warm and friendly smile.

If I should need a helper
  To lift me when I'm down,
And embracing arms of friendship
  To gently turn me 'round.

If I should need a hand
  To steady my faltering ways
And eyes to see beyond myself
  In life's confusing maze.

If I should need the means
  To achieve a worthy goal,
And encouraging words of wisdom
  To calm my troubled soul.

I wouldn't need to place an ad
  Or seek somebody new:
I'd just thank God for giving me
  That kind of friend in you!

*R. Luther Sanders*

## Shadows Of Yesterday

Walking by my side,
To which I confide,
Stands my shadow,
Dancing in the wind.

Walking on the sand,
My shadow next to me,
Say good night,
Before the daylight.

Walking in the moonlight,
My shadow growing tall,
Goodbye till tomorrow,
Wipe away your sorrow.

Walking through my past,
Seeing something can't ever last,
But what the future will cast,
Is something that may last.

*Shelley Gerbig*

## Baseball in the Rain

Only fanatics sit in box seat
To watch baseball in the rain
Play ball!

Baseball caps peek out
Under brightly-colored ponchos
Anxious boys with empty mitts
Drape over dugouts
Too many empty seats
To care about numbers
Hawkers sell Bud Lite
To shivering fans
Groundskeepers stand by
To unroll tarps
Mud-stained uniforms and
Dirt-caked cleats
Jacketed umpires
Cast blind eyes skyward

Only fanatics sit in box seats
To watch baseball in the rain
Game called

*William R. Burgett*

## Who

Who teaches the spider
  to weave a web
Or the geese
  to fly in a V?
Who chooses the hues
  of aspen and oak
And wild oats that grow
  by the sea?
Who tells the robin
  when it is time
To lift its wings
  to the South?
Who fashions a snowflake
  a pattern of six
Or a snapdragon's
  wry little mouth?
Who made the heavens
  endless and deep?
Who whispers, "Crickets,
  it's time to sleep?"

*Leonora Riddering Burnet*

## Heavenly Father

You are my strength and shield
  To you I yield
My faith is in thee
  Your blessings to be
Your wisdom you give
  So I may live
Courage I get from thee
  Mine enemies I will not see
May spirit will be free
  As I serve thee
My happiness comes from you
  Knowing all things are true
In you there is peace
  Serenity will not cease
May my spirit live in you
  Knowing all things are true

*Lola Mae Blackmon*

## When Time Stands Still

If I'm standing close
to you the feeling I feel,
when time stands still.
  The world stops moving,
I'm on a cloud, but I
feel so proud.
  When you look into my
eyes, its no surprise that
feeling I feel, when time
stands still.
  I don't want it to end
that feeling I feel, when
time stands still.....

*Shelley Lynn Miller*

## Let's Keep Democracy

We are not all strangers,
Together we must be,
One for all, and all for one,
Let's keep our liberty.

We must work together,
In peace and harmony
So let's all get together,
To keep democracy.

No matter what his skin may be,
White or black or brown,
Let's all work hard and pitch right in,
In every nook and town.

We were all born free men,
As God said it must be,
So let's make a stand, in our homeland.
Let's Keep Democracy.

So let's make a stand, in our homeland.
Let's Keep Democracy.

*Nathan Rawlins*

## "Finally Home"

With his gentle touch, he
took my hand
upward to a sea of clouds

Where angels run and play
and sometimes even cry for the
people below.

And a light came for him, warm
and full of energy, he smiled
at me and told me a story
A story for a child, but meant
for man.

He had wisdom and compassion
within his words.

And when time came he gracefully
set aside a place in his home
and his heart for me.

And he told me "Son you're finally
home."

*Luis A. Arce*

## Apple "Sass"

Adam and his sons one day
Took themselves a walk
And as they passed the Garden
The sons began to talk.

Dad, what is that place over there?
All covered up with weeds?
Should we know about a place like that?
Does it hide some dark, dark deeds?

Adam sighed and said to them
Boys, as the world you roam
Remember this is where your mom
Ate us out of house and home.

Eve did into temptation fall
But, folks, let's be truly fair
She didn't do it all alone
'Cause Adam ate his share!

*Pat Straumann*

## Choices

I'm writing this poem to
try and win money
should it be sad or
should it be funny

Maybe all about the sun
or about the rain
one thing I'm sure
it will never bring me fame

Life's good times or
life's hardships we face
good things we've done
or times of disgrace

Birth of a new baby
or the death of a love one
a good job we've had
or one we got fired from

One thing for certain
there's lots of good choices
but going around in my head
there are just two many voices

*A. M. Shaver*

## Change

When you close your eyes
Try to see the world as it would be
If you could turn back the hands of time
Warn heroes of their foes
Save Anne Frank in the attic
Meet long-lost relatives
or just sit back and stare. . .
Could you have won a war
With your point of view?
Of would it ruin everything
By fiddling with fate?
Although it may sound strange to you
I'd really like to try
I'd really like to know
If I could somehow change my world
By changing the past somehow. . .

*Laura Esty*

## Walking Alone

Walking down the road of loneliness,
trying to get out of this mess,
that we have created
from all of our hatred,
quickly traveling
slowly unraveling,
the strings from our time together,
the faster I go the more that gathers.
I keep on walking as my heart grown,
and hopes for another twin,
so, I can get on a new road,
and leave behind this heavy load.
Now that I'm all alone,
my heart has time to find a new home.
I've been here before,
but I haven't learned anymore.
So, I walk this road of loneliness,
no friends, no time, no guests.
Just me, myself, and I,
walking alone until I die.

*Ruth E. Hamilton*

## The Free Cat

The graceful feline
Turns it's glowing eyes
To mine and poses regally.

Burning green embers
Like a living flame
Mystify and amaze.

She stands alone, calm.
Disdainful of me
Ears cocked to the breeze.

When I turn my back
I always feel sure
She watches me still.

Grace of a dancer
Greed of a human
Eyes of the green flame.

The graceful feline
With the green embers
Regards me quietly
And resumes her slumber.

*Witty Huang*

## Mom

My mom is the best.
You'd think she never rests.

If you need a peer,
Or just an ear,
She's always there,
With tons of care.

She listens well,
And would never tell.

Her love for me is strong.
She's like a beautiful song.
I could never go wrong.

I wouldn't take anything for this girl.
She's the best mom in the world.

*Christina M. Mitchell*

## The Scarecrow Season

Harvest your soul
under Ashen Moon.
Don't reap the sickle
Now... Too soon.

Dance around a
tender fire, cleanse
the soul of a liar.

Sing the song of
our sins, this is when
the pain begins.

October hours much
too long, seems like
days for our wrong.

Native ritual of
demise, life and death
before your eyes.

Pray to the Spirits
for their pleasin'.

HARVEST OF SOULS
IN THE SCARECROW SEASON.

*Mark S. Worlein*

## Life Unfolds

Softness and the bitter-sweet
unearthing thoughts,
of unconscious dreams,
While reaching out,
holding on,
With hopes and dreams,
Our life unfolds,
into what is now,
but was then,
While cherishing moments
with the dearest of friends.

*Mary Anne Crowe*

## My Children

My children so sweet and young,
until they are yelling at the
crack of dawn.

My children so innocent and kind,
until they are outside and begin
to whine.

My children always in a fight,
until they are tucked in for
the night.

*Lisa Robertiello*

## Our Child

God in his infinite wisdom chose
us to nurture and protect you.
He gave you into our loving care
blessing us in so many ways.
You were the most precious and
special of gifts.
On each and every day of your life
you must always remember,
you are loved more than mere
words can ever express.
Not only do we cherish every one
of the days we spend with you,
we're so fortunate to know
that you also love us too!

*Sandi Phipps*

## Little Squirrel

Whisky, frisky, hippity hop,
Up he climbs to the tree top.

Whirly, twirly, round, and round,
Watch how he dashes to the ground.

Furly, curly, twisty tail,
Long as feather, fat as snail.

Where's his a acorn dinner,
It's hiding in its shell,

Snappity, crackity,
Out it fell!

Eat up your dinner,
Crunchy, hard, and cold,

If you don't eat soon,
your food will surely mold.

**Michelle McGuinness**

## Minuet

Ah the fateful gleam of twilight,
  Upon the ocean great
The rising image of the moon,
  That glimmers o'er the waves.

The maiden of the midnight hour,
  The beauty of the moon.
Her face is with me, day nd night,
Minuet, pray go not soon.

Minuet, my love, stay by my side,
  Your face with me always abide.
Your eyes are twilights settings till,
Your face shining moon o'er the hill.

In your presence it is that my heart
  throbs yet,
Pray go not soon, my love, MINUET.

**Natalie Jean Valdez**

## Dusk

Daylight and darkness falls
  upon this earth,
As two shadows overlap
  with one another.
The brightness of the day
  and the stillness of the night,
Clash together upon the
  earth's horizon,
Thus, bringing dusk.

Sunset and clouds, magnificently
  placed by 'The Creator' himself,
Await the oncoming
  brilliant stars that
Shine across the tranquility
  of the night.
As man shares his thoughts and
  loneliness to the heavens,
Thus, comes dusk.

**Martha Lind**

## Haiku

Our kites soar on high
Billowing against the sky
Like wild geese in flight

**Mary J. Horvath**

## Friend's Forever

Friend are forever
very, very clever
helping each other
Like a sister and brother
They stick together
Like birds of a feather

Friends take up for each other
Not leaving you for another
Another person that may not be
the same color as you and me
Black, yellow, or white
They are the same in my sight

Friends take care of friends
forever till the world ends
Hoping it will not
giving it all they've got
to stay together
as friends forever
*(written at age 11)*

**Lauren Delahoussaye**

## Mama's

Just dropping in
Via U. S. mail
To tell you exactly
What my feelings entail.
I don't want to create
Some great big Trauma
Because I know "I'm"
The Best of Mama's!
But I'd like you to have
Something especially for "you"
Cause, "YOU"—"YOURSELF"
Are a GREAT MAMA too!
So enjoy "YOUR DAY"
AND
Until the time comes around
They tell you, without question
A BETTER MAMA has been found.

**Marie Garrison**

## Gretna Green

Jo measured out her days
waiting for the plaid ride
only JEOPARDY could provide

On her final ride she lay abed
marking with Mac their wedding day
and their fortieth year in America

Alex said
  ESCAPE is the category
  and the question is:
  "Where in a Northern Sea
  do eloping lovers flee
  from a jilted fiancee?"

Mac mumbled "Bowling Green"
  one contestant said "Dover"
  and Alex said "Time's over"

Jo wept aloud and arched her neck
then spread her tent upon the dross
like a penitent swan dying on a cross

**Tom Carey**

## My Little Prayer

Dear Lord thank you for today
Walk beside me all the way.
Keep me safe from all that would
cause me heartache if it could
Guard my eyes, and ears and lips,
Give me strength to come to grips
With each problem I must face
and some courage just in case
Never let my footsteps stray,
Lest perhaps I lose the way,
And whatever may befall
Keep me humble through it all
If a cross must be my share,
Make it one that I can bear
and through shadows of the night
Hold me close "till morning light".

**Irene Shaw Killen**

## Wonders

Slide down the pyramids of Egypt
Walk through the temples of Greece
Skydive in the Grand Canyon of America
Climb Mt. Everest of the Himalayas
Explore the castles of England
Enjoy the beautiful sight of Mt. Fuji
Scuba dive in the waters of Hawaii
Ride down the Amazon river
Walk on the Great Wall of China
Live in the outback of Australia
Take a cruise in the Caribbean Sea
Drink water in the Atacama Desert
Bull fight in Barcelona, Spain
Sail around the world
Hang glide off Mt. Kilimanjaro

**Michael Cove**

## Illustrations

Greed and power,
War and hate,
Do we need to illustrate?

Power corrupts,
That is known.
Why so many people,
Without a home?

This is what we need to hear,
Why do we operate under fear?

This is what I question thee,
Why can all of us not be free?

**Nicole Speed**

## Is That You?

You're the salt on my potatoes,
You're the sugar in my tea;
And it really is amazing
What you're laughter does for me.
You're the spice in my con-carne,
You're the butter on my bread,
If it wasn't for your cheer-ups
Life surely would be dead.
You're the honey on my biscuit,
You're the flavor in my stew;
If it wasn't for your teasing
I surely would be blue!
You're the topping on my pudding
You're the icing on my cake;
So lets get busy eating.
Where's the knife and fork and plate?

**Elma V. Honeycutt**

## Something To Die For

My little girl
Was four years old
Back in seventy nine.
She was quiet
A joy to me
The four years
That she was mine,
And then one day,
The good Lord came,
And took her away.
Now, I know
He's being good to her,
In his own special way.
The good book says
I will see her again,
But it don't say when,
But I sure hope
When that day comes
She will remember
Who I am.

*Robert E. Miller*

## The Storm of Life

The start of the storm
was the day I was born

Grayness covers the sky
at the sound of my cry

Thunder crashes
with each bat of my lashes

Lighting strikes
for everyone of my fights

A drop of rain
for all of my pain

The sky is clearing
for death is nearing

The clouds roll away
for I died today

*Mary E. Lehecka*

## History...

Here at one time in history
was told His story and
now is a part of history.

Children sang, "Jesus loves
me" and lives were joined in
Holy Matrimony.

People moved away, some to be
elsewhere a part of His story
and others unto glory.

In this building now vacated
once was told His story and
children sang "Jesus loves me."

The church has not failed, but
has moved elsewhere to be a part
of history, or unto glory.

*Sam L. Martin*

## November Rain

Water.
Water descends
from the black sky
above.
Drops.
Drops descend
from my eyes.
Tears.
Tear drops,
more building,
Teardrops fall.
And so
　　do
　　　you.

*Monica Wielander*

## Landfall

As we set foot on shore,
Waves crashing over fresh lava,
Glistening under moonlight
A crimson river aglow
Ravishing yonder cliffs
Down the slopes it flows.
Sounding with a loud hiss
Sulfuric steam lingers in the air.
As we climb the higher ground
Puffy clouds dot the sky
In the slight breeze sway palms
Will they last another day?
As molten earth passes through
A patch of cane explodes
Standing far above the beach
We watch our catamaran go below.

*Mark T. Migita*

## My Little World

In my own little world
way down on two
I look out my window
and throw kisses to you.

In my own little world
I am so glad you are here
for bringing me sunshine
every day of the year.

In my own little world
I give thanks to God above
for bringing me happiness
and someone to love.

*Ruth E. Scott*

## Too Late I'll Find

What is in my mind?
What tears at my heart?
Why, I ask, do I in time
Always crave what I
Seem never to find!
Ever search my soul
To hope in time
What I need so much
I'll surely find.
Only then too late
For in shadowed time
Too old I'll be,
In soul, in body, in mind!

*Merrill Hermann*

## Forgive and Forget

From the time we are born
We experience pain
That can cripple our lives
Or be counted as gain.

So much that's inside us
Has been stored from our past.
We try hard to forgive
But the memories last.

To forgive and forget
Is the right thing to do;
Not the acts done against us
But the pain we went through.

We can always remember
Experiences we've had.
When the pain's been detached
We won't see them as bad.

We will see them instead
With a new point of view,
As a witness of what
God's brought each of us through!

*Maggie Odom*

## Life

It is midnight . . .
　we see war,
　we see hate
　we see a burnt car in an
　integrated state.
　People of all kind are killed.
　Their red blood is spilled!
The sun came out ...
　kids of all colors play,
　people of all creed pray,
　and to the people, tranquility
is a key ...
　to the door of equality.
　Love is great
　in a harmonious state.
　There is no fear
　because there is no hate
why do we have to live in the
　darkness?

*Mona Al Rifai*

## "Dad"

Sometimes we get so busy
We sweep daddy under the rug;
When really he's the one
Who deserves a great big hug.

When he seems to be so tired
Nothings gone just right;
There's time to hug you
And tuck you in at night.

He worries about you
When you are sick in bed;
Works hard all week long
So you are warm and fed.

Dads love to play ball
To show how much they care;
And when you need a ride
They'd take you anywhere.

Tell dad that you love him
He's special in every way;
Give him hugs and kisses
Especially on Father's Day.

*Lola Moore*

## From The Cradle To The Grave

From the cradle, to the grave
We watch our children grow
From a child of infancy
To someone who favors me
But one day, comes a stranger
With evil on his mind
who steals the unprotected
and no one hears their cries
except the one who has taken them
for reasons, to late, unknown
if you have any heart at all
please send the children home

Screams will fill your nights
As visions fill your head
Each day will hear your prayers
That your child doesn't come back dead
Cries heard only by the who has taken them
For reasons, too late, unknown
If you have any heart at all
Please send the children home

**V. Marando**

## Elegy to a Dryad

Don't you hear that Dryad weeping,
    Weeping by that fallen tree;
Fallen with no shred of mercy
    By the hand of Mr. T?

Do you see that mother robin
    Hovering O'er her brood of three;
Lying dead, their nest all shattered
    By the hand of Mr. T?

Trees that offered shade and beauty
    Living monuments that He
Planted as a gift for mankind
    Not the axe of Mr. T.

Precious wildlife by the hundreds
    Birds that once were wild and free,
Sing no more, their voices silenced
    By that terrible Mr. T.

**Toni Poster**

## Fly United

Just think if everywhere you
Went, your lover went with you.
And every time you made a
Move, your lover made it too.

To get to where you're going
Is a problem that you share.
And in order to make the trip,
You must really go by air.

But navigation ain't your bag,
And speed and skill you lack.
And to make matters even worse,
You must fly back to back.

So you follow along the interstate
To know just where you're at,
Hoping the last thing you hear,
Is not a big loud splat.

Wishing, like you're cousin, you
Had moved into a rug.
But that ain't the way of life
For an adventuresome love bug.

**G. Bartlett Seavey**

## Colors Of People

When you look upon a man.
    What do you really see?
The colors of the skin or
    a heart like you and me.

God made us all his image
    blew breath upon our face.
He says we're all his children
    He never spoke on race.
So when you see your fellow man,
    what do you really see
The outer parts and not the heart
    then you're far from Gods reality.

**Ruth Griffith**

## Minding the Stones

Over all our life time
what have we built from the rubble,
you and I?

Stone walls against mindlessness?

The work of getting the stones in place
was done underground.
The difficulty was is remembering
that the smooth side needs to be up.

Each of us requires a constant supply
of stones
because our souls continue the labor
of transformation.

The mark on these stones
discloses where they are to be sawed.

In time each of us will find
inside one
a new name.

**Mary Louise Cox**

## Wish

What the world needs
What people take for granted
A new one leads
through hell's gates enchanted

Human greed tells
the story always told
Passion of silver bells
and blocks of solid gold

She might kill for riches
he might kill for fame
All the sons of bitches
humanity's gone lame

Sin is an illusion
to all of those who want
Nothing short of confusion
a wish is all we've got

**Ralph Chapman**

## The Butterfly

B eautiful creature sitting
U pon a hummingbird feeder
T asting it's very sweetness
T horoughly enjoying it
E ven tho it is watchful, wary
R esting there in beauty and
F leeting fragileness
L eaving with a whisper of wings to
Y onder hill and a lovely flower

**Patty Krueger**

## I Often Wonder

I often wonder
what the future holds
for you and me
will growing old be
part of our reality?
Will respect and compassion
become old-fashioned?
I hope much later
than sooner
I hope much sooner than
later we learn
war is not the answer
for hate is just a cancer
an ailment of the heart
an ailment of the mind
a disorder of the soul
love and honesty is what we need
what does the future hold
for you and me?
    I often wonder

**Larry Terry**

## Home

How wondrous is the gift of home,
Whate'er the numbers of its rooms;
Its centerpiece the Sacred Tome,
And grace to meet whatever looms,

How great it is to have homeland,
To which one always can return
From any planet's distant stand,
However much we there did learn:

How great legumes and fruits home-grown,
With cel'ry melons, beans, what not,
That grow from seeds that we have sown
In our own hard-worked garden plot:

The runner longs to reach home base;
The team plays best on its home court;
After the storms he's had to face,
The sailor longs to reach home port;

There is a realm beyond our dreams:
Life's race is won, and time is past:
Warm glowing welcome brightly gleams:
Our makers says: "You're home at last!"

**J. Carter Swaim**

## Life

What's happened to the world
What's happened to ME
Life is the flame
The blood pumping through our bodies
The world is a secret
with no one to tell it to
Life is a road that never ends
The door that opens to us
the door that sets us free
You must break the lock
clean up that big scramble in your head
Fill the cracks between the people
create yourself and not others
End the darkness and let the light in
We all go around in this world
What's Happened to the world??????

**Lily Strauss**

## Dawn

It's so early in the morn
When a new day is born.
While the dew is still lingering,
Not even a bird is singing.

Oh, the flower bed
of brown, gold and red
is very much alive;
the dampness must revive.

The night fall is far away—
Almost another day.
The morning fog must leave
A new day to receive.

From the dawn, through the sun
Until the day is done
Natures noises lingers
From its tiny little singers.

And if the fog should leave,
Soon it will retrieve,
as the sun leaves the flower bed—
A brown, gold and red—-

*Shirley M. Rhodarmer*

## Morning

How beautiful it is in the early morn
When all is hushed and still
The trees lend their majesty to
A robin on a window sill

The dew upon the primrose path
A dove rests humming in the tower
A rose is then no longer a rose
But a guest of the sunlit hours

A moth kissed lightly the goldenrod
A bee took nectar from the clover
A cathedral chimes and all is well
And then the morn is over.

*Loumanda Vinson*

## Happiness

When does happiness occur?
When does the theory take hold
In the evolved gray star stuff
Of the Cosmos?
When will it matter that Kepler
Preferred reality to more
Comforting misinterpretation?
How long once the clock is reset
Before it ticks down
To happiness?

Monday my children come to visit
Perhaps that is enough

*Mark Fowler*

## A Battered Wife

"Battered wife knows all too
well, how a boxer feels after
each round."
  Rounds (1-5) he's enraged with
anger.  Rounds (6-10) he's got
the upper hand.  Rounds (11-15)
Is the ultimate knock out!
"And what belt shall he win
the belt of courage, or the
ultimate belt of control?"

*Yulanda Tisdale*

## Poem To Takis

There was a time when life was fresh
When flowers blooming caught my eye
And as we basked in sunlight blessed
Our child laughed; he seldom cried
We struggled as we worked and learned
Together, forging bonds so firm

But, just as we were on a roll
As love prevailed, we reached our goals
Immersed in each other, heart and soul
So confident, perhaps too bold —
We didn't notice, as we loved,
Secure that life would be our "high,"
That flowers seeking azure skies
Abruptly, sere and withered, died!

Through all the seasons hot and cold
There are still flowers to behold
Yet now I just keep walking by
The sunshine perished when you died!

*Lisa Robbins-Stathas*

## A Patient Visitor

I was in my house
when I felt the wind
blow.  And I was seated in a
chair when I saw this glow.
Just then, I looked up into
the face of a ghost of a man
that I didn't know?  At this
moment, I thought to myself:
"If this is death, I'm not
ready to go!"

Then the ghost of a man
turned and walked through
the hall.  Immediately this ghostly
form walked right through the
wall!  Well the ghost of a man
he wasn't tall.  I saw a ghost
of a man; and that was all!

*Pamela C. Krystopolski*

## Where

Where do I go
  when I want
    to be alone...
A place where my
  thoughts can gather
    and my mind can roam.

Where do I go
  when I want
    to feel free...
A place of solitude
  so I can be me.

Where do I go...
  I really
    don't know!

*Pamela McPherson*

## A Time to Help an Offender

There is a time to be like a rock
When in a position you are caught
Another has given you a test
Just be strong in the Lord and rest

Feel the power He gives to you
To stand strong taking right view
The circumstance you find yourself in
In strength of Jesus you will win

Another time it may take wisdom meek
You cannot fail as Jesus you seek
To contain your feelings, but have love
Help the offender with wisdom from above

With guidance of Holy Spirit you gain
A Victory to help in Jesus Name
Helping another in God's Pathway
Keeping him in faithful walk to stay

*Susan Essler*

## Confused.......

It's funny how
when it is noisy
you want it quiet

And when it is quiet
you long for noise.

How, when it is crowded
You can't wait to be alone

And when you're lonely
  you want anyone...

*Margo M. Wright*

## Love In Green

Love in green - a heartening spell,
when nature does lean to fondly tell.
Its' lovely secret to the ear,
and for the eye it does appear.

And love is gift - among the green
a true up-lift now from the scene.
'Tis mirror of the God so true,
this emerald of forest view.

Now bloom endows the spring's fair land,
and in love I here now stand.
A love for all - yes old and new,
and all the green - that here now grew.

Love in green - a heartening spell,
when nature does lean to fondly tell.
Its lovely secret to the ear,
and for the eye it does appear.

*Mark W. Haggerty*

## Untitled

Conflict starts war.
Treaty starts peace.
Soldiers show fear.
Farmers watch geese.

War ends lives.
Peace is a dove.
Pity the wives.
Raise children with love.

*Tom Sheehan*

## Second Amendment

Two hundred years and more ago
When our country was at its source
The fastest way to communicate
Was a rider on a horse.

When Paul went on his midnight ride
To spread the word of the British plan
He utilized the latest tech
The best that was at hand.

When lawmen were remote and few
And settlers were in need
They sometimes had to defend themselves
With grit and guns and speed.

On that page in history
The second amendment made good sense
With hostiles in the hinterlands
Times could be intense.

But now near the twenty first century
Urban sprawl doesn't mix with the gun
Today if trouble you perceive
Just dial up 911.

*Roger Markle*

## Superwoman Syndrome

Who does Superwoman turn to,
when she's trapped by kryptonite?
When her lead shield is gone
and she's lost the will to fight?

Where does she find release
when Calgon no longer takes her away
and her knight in shining armor
has suddenly learned to stray?

She can't yell, "Beam me up Scotty"
and leave it all behind,
so she calls up Wonder Woman
in order to ease her mind.

For only another super hero
can really empathize
with the trials and tribulations
of a superwoman's life.

*Linda Khademol-Reza*

## Daring Kids

In the morning
When the birds fly way up high
In the sky
Daring kids wake up
Because the same they want to try.

They soon pick up a pen
And count to ten
Then get their kite
And quickly they start the flight.

Now these daring kids know
It is easy to fly up high
In the sky.

Their mothers cry
Because this is something
They never saw before
And if they become pregnant again
Boys they'll have no more.

*Vivian Dos Santos*

## Take Heed

Who will light the candles
when the children have all gone?
  All those brilliant, promising
pinpoints of light winking out...
  Enfolded, enveloped and shrouded
by the velvet black blindness of night.
  The once great clock
will still tick and chime,
  marking these times
of infinite passage thru cosmos
  crowded with vaporous voices
drifting...echoing but falling
  only on shadows of ears.
Take heed...who will light the candles
  when the children have all gone?

*Paula Slade*

## The Ocean And Me

  There's a feeling that engulfs you,
when you are near the ocean.
  Handsome boys and pretty girls,
Just going through the motion.
  But do they grasp the concept,
of the power that's within.
  They think it might be love,
Or just interpret it as sin.
  For me its a place of power, a
place of peace, a place of worship.
  When the waves rejoin the water
A never ending courtship.

*Stephenie Dean*

## U.S.

I stand in a field of dreams
Where rows of sunflowers sleep soundly
And bluebonnets dance in the dusk
A picture
Kept vivid in the minds of
The Hungry and Cold
By the constricting hands of power.

I stand in a field of hope
Where crops of corn cover the country
And sheaths of wheat whisper
Welcoming
Into her open arms of plenty
Those who travel far

We stand in a field of grace
Where God nourishes the Hungry
And shelters the Cold; Memories
Of ancestors toiling through hardships
Woven together by a common thread
A field of Hope
Tended by man and nurtured by God.

*Margaret A. Flinn*

## Dreams On Hold!

In the quiet of the day
you can hear the most
heartbeats of suffering people.
In their eyes I can see my soul.
Take their hands freedom,
Convince them -
There are still dreams left in this world
Who shall saves us?
The Cross!

*Maj-Lis R. Reese*

## Untitled

Love is a place
where the heart stands naked.
Love is a time
that can not end.
Love is a feeling:
warm and embracing.
Love is freedom,
pure and high flying.

Love is a fever
of volcanic proportion.
Love is a hunger
that yearns to be fed.
Love is a hunter,
silent and deadly.
Resistance is futile.
Surrender your soul.

*M. J. Crowley*

## Happiness

Happiness is a home
Where there is peace in your heart
And with a lot of love
They have no desire to part.

Happiness in a home
Where Jesus word is right
No one says a cruel word
And they have no fight's

Happiness is when parents
Show they love and care
Then their little children
Never have a fear

Happiness was in my old home
Our parents thought what was best
When young we wasn't allowed to roam
When we go back, there's the old home.

*Nina Pruitt*

## Untitled

i used to sit, and wonder where....
where's my Mother, doesn't she care?

i'd look here, i'd look there......
where's my Mother, doesn't she care?

why,
i thought i'd looked everywhere,
'til i stopped....
then felt behind me, someone there.

as i turned,
i was met with this loving stare.
from this woman,
my Mother.......
(i thought didn't care)

at once i sensed a peace in the air.
for, i knew in an instant....
she'd always been, (for me),
right there!

*Michael W. K. Brown*

## Masterpiece In The Making

Life is an empty canvas,
Which parents begin to paint.
Their words and deeds and actions
Sketch the character of their saint.
Family, friends, and foe alike
Are artists in the fray.
Each applies a brush of color
As they interact each day.
Colors bright and pretty
Make images of love and joy.
Colors dark and dreary
Draw shadows of sorrow and woe.
Upon the canvas of my life,
Lovely pictures someone drew.
Paint some more, my wonderful wife,
For my favorite artist is you.

*L. Melvin Roberts Jr.*

## The Heart Has Its Reasons

The heart has its reasons
Which reason does not know.
It acts in peculiar ways,
You never know where it will go.
You wish upon a falling star,
And wait for fate to come.
When you were little you dreamt so hard
Of who you would become.
The future will be full of joy
Of love and happiness.
Can you remember way back when
That boy with that first kiss?
Love is confusing
Yet wonderful and true.
When you are in love,
You'll never be blue.
The heart is a precious muscle
Full of choices of good and regret.
No matter where your heart takes you,
You'll never ever forget.

*Rebecca Lang*

## While Fireflies Fly

I shall talk with friends
While fireflies fly
And children laugh
While the world goes by

I shall remember
And not forget
What is important
And what I must do yet.

*Loralyn Reynolds*

## My Shadow

I have a little shadow,
Who follows all the day,
And everywhere I go,
He is always wanting to play.
But today I was too busy,
So I guess I made him sore,
For the next day,
When I looked out,
My shadow was no more.
I searched both high and low,
And called to him all the day,
But it was to no avail,
He wasn't meant to stay.

*Nathan Hitchcock*

## I Wonder

I wonder how a child
who has been
beat down, battered and bruised
emotionally, physically and spiritually
gets up each day?

I wonder how a child
who has been
used and abused
sexually
by friends, strangers and family
can still smile to say hello?

I wonder how a child
who has been
sworn at, yelled at and beaten verbally
still believes
life is worth living?

But more than anything,
I wonder how I
can make this child
feel loved?

*Pamela C. Benedict*

## Who Said You Are A Minority

Who said you are a minority,
    Who has the right to decree
    That you're of a lesser nature,
    Than you desire to be?

Who said you were inferior,
    Mediocre or common place,
    Trite or ordinary,
    The lesser of the human race?

Who took this word, minority,
    Placed it upon your head,
    Their opinions as a basis,
    To accept what they have said,
    To live your life on assumption,
    Thought and theory,
    By owners of a paper,
    Sometimes entitled degree?

Who said you are a minority,
    Who proclaims that they are best;
    All are created in God's image,
    How can one be more or less?

*Levi R. Raynor*

## My Hope

That, that I am, I shall never.
Who I shall be, I shall not!
Love that was, is no longer.
A man, without, I am not!

What of this love that isn't?
Live without, I could never.
Live without, I could not!

How can love lost if ever,
be found to love again?
When will a heart if broken,
find freedom of pain within?

To purify thy soul, my cure,
make end of doubt release fears hold.
In time, unknown love's truth unfold.

Where patient trust in hope remain,
the cherished prize, of love regain.

*Joshua James Owens*

## Joey

There is a little guy next door to me,
who is just about to turn three.
He is so cute and quite strong,
He won't be little very long.

The "Why is why?", he asks of me,
Seems to go on endlessly.
It seems no matter how I try,
He ends up always asking me, Why?

The "Why stage seems to have no end,
But his little mind won't bend.
"Why is this and Why is that,
Why oh why is a cat a cat?"

"Why do squirrels climb up trees,
And why do they spit down seeds?
Why do I sweep and clean the walk,"
The "why" goes on the more I talk.

I love that little guy of almost three,
And yes, you've guessed, his name is Joey,
He smiles so cute and has sparkling eyes,
He wins you over—doesn't even try.

*virginia schelosky*

## Dave Rickles Day

There once was a boy named Dave Rickles
Who liked to play with pickles
When he was done
He hadn't had much fun
So he went to play with nickels
His Dad named Salve Rickles
Asked to play with his pickles
Dave said yes
Then there was Kes
Who also wanted Dave's pickles
Dave went in fickles
And told Kes no pickles
So Kes ran and took Dave's nickels
Said trade you for the pickles
Dave said sure
Kes went into a blur
So Dave got to keep the nickels
And gave his Dad the pickles

*R. Blackburn*

## Old Man

Do you know the old man,
Who lives down the road,
Who walks with a cane,
And has a pet toad?
He gave me a present,
That I'll show you someday,
It's related to you,
But let me explain.
It's more than a box,
Its secrets hold true,
With an outside of velvet,
And an inside of blue.
But what I keep in it,
I want you to see,
It's all of the love,
That you've given to me.

*Maegan Ley*

## Help on the Road of Life

How I want to help another
Who on the road of life is lost,
But how to go about it
And not even count the cost?

I would need to have compassion
For a lost one needs some love.
But I couldn't manufacture it-
I'd get it from above.

If the lost one knows it's genuine
It sure could pave the way
For a lonely wandering traveler
To have a winning day!

*Martha Boehm*

## Where Is My Home?

Whatever happened to togetherness?
Why all this loneliness?
Whatever happened to being friends?
Why can't the hate ever end?
Whatever happened to our morals?
Why do we have all these quarrels?
Whatever happened to our youth?
Why can't we ever hear the truth?
Whatever happened to what was right?
Why does everyone have to fight?
Whatever happened to I love you?
Why can't it be like it used to?

*Tom Oman*

## Black Cat

O black cat,
why do you come to my door?

Cross my path
and my bad luck
will be yours also,
so be wise...
Though you are sleek
prowling round the corner
suspiciously precise,
your purr is annoying
and your fur a shredding mess.
But I am lonely on this night,
so I will invite you in
to nuzzle against my leg
and entertain me with your presence.
O black cat

why did you come to my door?

*Scott Counsell*

## Questing Conscience I

Who do you please?
  Why you my friend?
What if I sneeze?
  It's the living end.
And what if I cry?
  No harm to come.
And if I don't try?
  Just try some.
What if I fall?
  It's up you gain.
I'll build a wall?
  It's all in vain.
Will I find me?
  It's possible to.
What will I be?
  It's up to you.

*Noreen M. Buff*

## Abortion

Month one - me and my mommy
will have so much fun
Month two - I thought she loved me;
but what could she do?
Month three - I would have tried
hard to make her proud of me
Month four - could someone please
tell me what she did it for?
Month five - I still love her and
I'm not really alive
Month six - if she knew she didn't
want me - then why'd she have sex?
Month seven - I think I'm in a better
place now, it's HEAVEN
Month eight - I hear people say that
she did it out of hate
Month nine - she may be called a
"murder" but she was once mine

*Nicole Dillon*

## Flood

We think the rains
Will never stop.
The water has no thought
Except to spread
To living room and garden bed,
And places where cars
Have to park,
So everybody needs
An Ark,
For everywhere the world is wet.
The haven't conquered
Nature yet!

*Rilla Black*

## Untitled

Heavy heart that weighs in me
Will not let my eyes to see
The glory of each new-born day.
But here I sit, worry away.

To see my days forever doomed.
To see my nights forever gloomed.
But in my heart, I know to be.
A spark of hope I do not see.
That spark of hope will
urge me on.
Before this day forever dawns.

*Ray Wong*

## Tears of Blood

Tears of blood I cry for you,
Wishing we were never through.
I see you standing with your friends,
Will my sorrow ever end?
You said you cared, you always will,
but my heart you'd gladly kill.
Tears of blood well up inside,
They are tears that try to hide,
The pain I feel when you are near,
Through the blood I try to peer.
It's hard to see my pain and grief,
When you say you don't believe,
In true love to call your own,
Through the glass you throw the stone.
I try to move on, I try not to care,
But the memory of you is always there.
Now my feelings will never show,
and from you I'll slowly go.

*Melissa Hughes*

## The Snow Trip

Once I went on a snow trip
  with a group of friends.
We went to the top of the mountain
  a mile high.
    Then back to rent skis
But I didn't want to ski down
  the mountain side.
    So I chose some ski shoes
they were circle round with
  lacings.
I got on them and started to walk.
I could feel the crunch, crunch,
  of the snow.
    I could smell the fresh scent
of the air in the trees.
  I looked upward toward the sun
as it looked back at me.

*Linda Conover*

## The Chambered Nautilus

Satin smooth, the walls of your home
  With colors of soft pastel hue.
An architect's dream of perfect design,
  An incredible beauty to view.
If your house you outgrow,
  Its spiral design
Lets you add a new room
  In double swift time.
No grime can adhere
  To your beautiful walls.
No cold wind can blow
  Through your airtight halls.
Supremely designed
  To show God's love,
Like our heavenly homes
  Being built above.
Their beauty sublime
  We shall someday see
When He calls us home
  To eternity.

*Pauline C. Sheppard*

## Geminilibra

Your mind's a narrow room
with doors locked
Window with shades down

My mind's too open
No walls
No barriers
Or boundaries
Too many directions
Too many ways to go
No trails traveled
To the ends

Sometimes,
I envy you
Your closed up room.

*Mary Corrao*

## The Man from Mars

There once was a man from Mars
He liked to eat candy bars.
His name was Mike
He liked to ride a bike.
But he hated cars.

*Kyle Moyer*

## Spring

How good it is for spring to come
  with flowers and dainty things,

The sky is like a big smile
  bending sweetly over me.

The sunshine flickers through the
  lace of the leaves

Bringing a golden dream.
  The birds sing softly in the air
with a feeling of happiness.

  The wind comes gently o'er
the grass to whisper pretty things,

  So many friends are near
to say that spring is here.

*Naomi Okun Rhoden*

## The Damnable Waltz

The demons danced,
With fools entranced,
Held by romance,
Waiting for chance.

The spirits turned,
With souls they burned,
From flames they learned,
What pain they earned.

The chords are old,
And long since cold,
A harp of gold,
For the soul you hold.

*Michael J. Bertram*

## At Intercostal Canal

I sat on the cement pier,
with my face in the sun,
gentle breeze on my back,
waves lapping at my feet.
A barge shoved by,
sending rounded billows
pulsating to the shore
like the great heartbeat of God
surging his love
through all life's course.

*Loretto Bonfield, C. S. N.*

## Untitled

I want a gown of salt lace
with the roar of the sea
when I walk.

I want a shawl
of the sea breeze
rising before the storm.

I want shoes made of footprints
formed in the cool, wet sand-
left behind by someone
as yet unseen.

*Lois C. Neve*

## God's Grace

My life was drab and dreary
with troubles hard to bear,
but only 'til I decided
to turn to God in prayer.

For every reason God would give
to help me on my way,
Satan found a better one.
But God would always say.

"My child, you are a chosen one.
Don't lose your rightful place.
Set your sights on heaven,
and get within God's grace."

It took a lot of praying
for humbleness within.
But soon I felt the power of God
relieve the pain of sin.

He took away the guilt
built up inside of me.
And soon my life began to bloom
as flowers bloom on a tree.

*Tomi Ann Swaim*

## Untitled

I'm a strong Black woman
  with visions of where I've been
  and where I'm going.

I'm a strong Black woman
  who stands by her Black man
  in their time of need.

I'm a strong Black woman
  who teaches her Black children
  pride, strength, and dignity.

I'm a strong Black woman
  who stands stern against
  racial injustice.

I AM A STRONG BLACK WOMAN!

*Sheree M. Tilley*

## Untitled

  Mine is a dungeon
With walls of emotion
Covered with satin
Stained with the blood
Of my tears
Cried over you
  Mine is an ocean
With waves of flowers
Planted in hearts
Thorn covered bushes
Shoved ever deeper
Ready to die
  Mine is a bedroom
Without any windows
Full surrounds emptiness
Grasp it and take it
Never to drop it
Waiting to see

*Mandy Hanks*

## Our Precious Lord

You are my God
With your powerful might
I pray to you always
Morning, noon, and night

I feel you so near
When I also go through fear
You are my delight
Knowing you are here.

You bring us joy
You give us grace
Never a doubt
Of our Lord's precious face.

*MaryGrace Esposito*

## Thoughts

A special thought
withheld inside the mind
The thought glistens
through the eyes
but just won't come
across the lips
Though the thought
is still in the mind
It is not heard
because it is not spoken
But even through that
it can be felt
and absorbed
into the heart

*Lori Rechtenbaugh*

## In Gratitude

Lord, thank you for another day
Within this life of mine.
Give me the strength to live it well,
Whatever I may find.
Bestow from your abundance
Whatever I may lack.
To use the hours wisely,
For I cannot have them back.
Lord thank you for another day,
In which to make amends
For little slights or pretty words,
Inflicted on my friends.
For sometimes losing patience
With problems that I find.
For seeing faults in other's lives,
But not the ones in mine.
Lord thank you for another chance, in which to
try to be
A little more deserving of the gifts you've given me.
For yesterday is over, and tomorrow's far away,
And I remain committed to the good I do today.

*Pearl E. McIntyre*

## Yesterday

  Good morning world, I usually say
without a thought of yesterday.
But things have changed and
mornings are gray.
My best friend has gone away.
The rains came and the winds blew.
There will never be a friend like you.
We played together and we were two
now I am one and I miss you.
I pray each night that we can play
as tho we did like yesterday

*Patty Witt*

## A Lonely Heart

It bleeds
Without blood
It cries
Without tears
It feels empty
Although it is full
It breaks
Without cracking
Many of times it has wished
It did not have to feel
The pain it has felt
From being alone
It has been given to many
Yet given to none
There has not been a day
That it has not cried out
To be touch
Yet a lonely heart
Can not be held
Only loved.

***Roy Lee Tate Jr.***

## Saying Goodbye

I'm sitting here, looking at the cross
Wondering why I had this loss
I miss her so much
Why did it happen to such
No more going for walks
No more having such great talks
My mommy won't be coming home
That's why I feel all alone.

***Tammy L. Sudholtz***

## In Cambridge On Cam

Throwing your huge arms forward
wrists sharply bent and
fingers stiffly pointing-
the force softened by
your crown of silken hair
cascading down-
you seize me.

Transfixed, mesmerized,
the silent moment
pregnant
with fearsome fantasies and
dusty dreams,
I am in thrall.

You mad maestro! What
do you ask me-
how shall I escape you
weeping willow tree?

***Natalie Shainess***

## Time Will Tell

How slow is time
When suspense you wait.
It really seems a crime
That time can tell your fate.

Tenseness comes waiting,
Impatience, fear, and hating.
Time invisible as the wind
Hold it's secret till the end.

Ah, but comes at last
Time with all it's powers
Fading like the summer flowers
Into memories of the past.

***Mary P. Marshall***

## The Wizard's Redemption

It comes to mind, I've written for man,
Written many pieces, fit for a band.
Written of religion,
And a-many, troublesome decision.

Written of the times,
In humorous rhymes.
Written of plays in other days,
The way they then, would phrase—

Misfortune, suffers not, for a cause,
But is expelled from witless oz.
So foolish in His clever game,
A magician, just the same.

Though in time his twisted heart,
Will, for him depart.
So happy then he'll be,
To cast his spells lavishly.

Through the laurels lattice bough,
We can praise the wizard now,
For the redemption of his heart,
And the correction of his art.

***Ray Eugene McCormick***

## One Last Time

His face was wan and grey
Years of toil left their legacy
The good times were had by others
And his absence spoke loudly.

We met and rode together
Almost strangers in my youth
He spoke of many things past
And left nothing to remember

I saw him no more after
For his life faded away
And I mourned this man in sorrow
For I had called him father

***Lester Simon***

## Pride And Inspiration

Miracles never last—
yesterday will eventually pass.

Ignorant me does not care—
nothing matters in this time;
space has caught me in its lair.
Pride kills the meaning of this rhyme,
insults my nature;
rapes me of who I really am—
allows my soul to be captured,
takes control only to condemn.
Inspiration always hides;
only you could be so kind
never to let me lie.

Make me another soul;
admire my lonely heart—
time, I will let go;
trust tears me apart.

***Tony Manno***

## War And Balance

You may be hostile,
Yet I am full of peacefulness,
I may be tranquil,
Yet you are full of spinelessness.

You are a fighter,
Yet I am a defender,
I am an adorer,
Yet you are an antagonist.

War is balanced,
As long as both sides,
Are unchallenged,
And no one takes sides.

***Penny Rose***

## Shadow

Why won't you walk with me?
You are always behind, in front or aside.
You flitter about, and I can't see,
Whether you are here, there, or astride.
Sunshine, and you match my pace,
Cloudy, and you hide.
Sometimes we like to race,
Other times you get a free ride.
Won't you be my friend and speak?
Are you a shadow that will fade?
You are silent, and so very meek,
How I wish we could trade.

***Mildred Pumroy***

## The Song of Spring

In the song of spring
You can surely hear
The music playing -
A blue bird singing
Sweet words of love
Church bells ringing
Rain drops falling
Upon the leaves.

The leaves you see, and
The palm tree swaying
In the breeze - will promise
You many things, even bring
Some pleasant dreams...

But in your search for happiness
You, must try to understand - why!
Your lover won't take you, firmly
By the hand; as the love boat drifts
Across the sea to paradise.

***Mary Stevenson***

## Miss You

What do I do,
when the clouds roll by.
How do I live with,
that last goodbye.
I hear the birds,
that come to sing,
on my window sill,
I pray and dream
can this be true.
In my heart and mine
the sounds are you.
Miss you.

***Ruth Briffett***

## Why? (On Abortion)

I am small, and I am weak,
   You cannot even see my feet.

My, how time is going by so fast,
   and I am getting so big;
You can now see my feet and my toes,
   I wonder if mommy knows?

I've heard of a peace that's outside,
   from where I am;
I also hear it's really great,
   I'm so excited I just can't wait.

I thought mommy would be anxious
   to see me;
And to know that I'm a girl,
   And pretty as a pearl.

But I guess not;

Because, today mommy is going to kill me;
   And although I don't know why,
The little time I have left with mommy,
   I can't help but to sit here and cry.

*Rebecca Pierson*

## Just Be Nice

Lying and cheating
you don't have to accept
but honesty and kindness
is a way of respect

Fussing and fighting
is not the way to be
talking and laughing
always works for me

If you want something
without paying a price
all you have to do is...
JUST BE NICE!

*Rose Marie Palmer*

## If All Else Fails

If all else fails I'll find a place
You know the case

This place must be
For you and me

Where we can roam
And find a home.

If all else fails I'll find a place
You know the case

This place must smell like
A new nature hike

And it must have sound
For that's where I'm bound.

If all else fails I'll find a place
You know the case

This place I must see
Cause that's where I'll be

And I'm sure to stay
Not that far away

Cause

This is my place you know the case!

*Nicole Kathleen Durfee*

## Untitled

You said you'd never leave me.
You said I'd never have to cry.
You said our love was strong
That it would never die.
But when I found out that you lied
My heart was torn in two.
And when I looked back one last time
You had found someone new.
You said you'd always love me.
You said you'd always care.
Imagine all the pain I felt
When you were never there.
We had some really rough times
You said we'd make it through.
I guess you were wrong
But so was I to ever have loved you.

*Theresa Dotson*

## Reality

They stand tall and proud,
young men and women of today's world

The ones of tomorrow, which
they defend what they must

Scared to believe the honor of
real life problems

Though they must travel
down a rough and steep road
ahead of them

Bravery and courage flow in
their heart and souls

Faces of stone hide the fears
and the tears in their looks

But the eyes never lie

Days vanish and come with a blink
of an eye

tomorrow is another day,
another fight.

And yet another war.

*Lynnette K. Lamb*

## Missing In Action

I miss you.
   Your warmth,
    Your smile,
     Your touch.
That sensitive you,
   That means so much.

A simple little complement,
   About the way I wear my hair.
    A stroll in the park,
     Holding hands when we are near.
That quick little peck on the cheek.

The love in you,
   And all your loving ways.
    Your arrogance,
     Your tenderness,
The witting things you say.

A love that came ...
   Closest of them all.

I miss you.

*Viola D. Soles*

## To My Fourth Granddaughter

Precious little Angie, today is
your Birthday — the first day
of the rest of your life! My
heart is warm with love when I
look at you — such tiny features,
brown hair and fair skin!

Sleep is an elusive thing for you
at night - you'd rather sleep
when the sun shines bright — in
other words you have your "Days"
and "Nights" mixed up! It's a
"topsy turvy" world you'll say
— that is until you learn
that "Night is Night" and "Day is Day!"

May your days all be filled with
dreams come true, with happiness
and cheer — and that the joy you
know today will grow greater
every year!!!

Never was a Birthday Wish more
loving and sincere than this
wish I give to you for happiness
in the coming years!
   Love —
*Grandma Reva Marx*

## To My Loving Great Grandmother

Your unspoken words
Your gentle touch
Is what makes me
Love you so much.

You always knew when I was coming.
I guess you heard my little feet running.
Down the path and across the road
To your path that's just been mowed.

Now you are so far away,
Maybe we will see each other someday.
But for now I will stay,
And think of you every single day.

*Terra Leigh Kearney*

## Untitled

My misery is your pain
Your joy is my happiness

My dreams are your realities
Your sweetness is my compassion

My bed is your resting place
Your desires are my giving

My loneliness is your sadness
Your depression is my anxiety

My longing is your fulfilling
Your love is my life

My wondering is your knowing
Your going is my emptiness

My coming is your excitement
Your cry is my tear

My word is your strength
Your beauty is my hope

My arms are your comfort
Your kiss is my silence

My despair is your darkness
Your softness is my passion

*Russ Myers*

## LoLa

I kissed her brown wrinkled hand,
her aging face,
which shows all seventy-five years of her
bittersweet life,
curves upwards,
 forming a smile, showing her white dentured teeth
her gray hair with spots of black, reaches her sagging shoulders,
but her eyes stood out, glassy and black.
Reflecting here years she spent in Project 4,
she was a housewife, looking after nine kids,
her oldest son, father, was sent to work at fifteen.

   She took care of me when I was a child, when my mother
was taking care of the sick, and father was fixing cars.
I was always naughty, she told me stories about Aswang
tormenting disobedient little boys and girls.
Every night she would sit on her bed, saying the rosary,
every Sunday, she would dress-up and go to church asking the
Santo Niño to keep her youngest one happy in the afterlife.
LoLa lives in America now, wears American clothes, but
there is still part of her in Project 4, Quezon City, Philippines.

### *Ronnie C. San Jose*

## No More Light

   Rooting like the death of wood.
The crackling of sparks into the dark sky filled with the stars.
The evil sounds that carry through the wind make my madness compress
all of these feelings.
   I feel love from hate inside myself.
The darkness covers the sky and the blanket of stars disappear
as I watch.
I no longer see the light of the moon for evil has aroused.
A crack of light appears then disappears for I see it no longer.
I cannot see anymore evil, I can no longer see happiness for they do
not exist in my eyes.
A white wall I see and beyond the wall the light of the sun shines
bright.

### *Lisa Martineau*

## Your Face

I'm writing this poem to take up space,
So I'm writing it about your ugly face.
It's got pimples, and zits, and freckles too,
And your nose is hairy, and filled with goo.

### *Karim Dhanani*

## The Struggle Of Life

The struggle of life has yet begun by us being here we know how to win.
The struggle of being afraid, but facing the world, and people everyday.
The struggle from working all day hearing the master yell at his slaves.
The struggle that slaves march to be free, standing up for their
rights, and yet they got beat.
The struggle that one man tried to make a speech, while people look
as, they pass in the street.
The struggle as we hold hands, being afraid of what God made.
The struggle of slaves getting scraps, while others eat proper with
one another, and the rest eat in darkness of fear.
The struggle to believe in what is right, but how will the struggle
stop, if we can't come as one.
The struggle of beating one another, instead of looking for a way so
love could spread with peace through all.
The struggle of life is the world's tears for every drop is a pain we share.

### *Tara Renée Brooks*

## The Best Way of Living

Lord, help me to share
your love with others
Help me not to be selfish
and hide my light
My eyes were blinded, but
now I see for Jesus came
inside to fellowship with me.

When you have fellowship
with Jesus you are never
alone, for He abides within
If you don't have this
Fellowship, ask Him to come
in and the better life will
   begin.

### *Peggy Housley*

## Mother's Day 1993

Loving thoughts from far away
your notes and gifts impart.
It's hard to find the way to say
what's really in my heart.
So often, if I find the time,
I find the words too few.
These simple thoughts and silly rhymes,
for now, will have to do.
The days go by much faster now,
as my life becomes my own,
But memories always linger of how
you made for me a home.
I love you more than this can show
and keep you always near
And hope that you will surely know
to me you are so dear!

### *Roberta K. Young*

## Forget

I don't know how to forget.
Your pretty eyes
And soft red lips
Looking at me as I walk down the street
Kiss me again like you use to do
One more time just me and you
You can't tell me to forget
The love we had
Kiss me again
And make me laugh
It's just one thing
I want to let you know

I will never forget
how you let me go

### *Tiffany Brown*

## "Mom"

Your words of wisdom
Your sound advice

Your promise to be there
Anytime, anywhere

Your spirit's still here
I sense you're near
You've always kept your promises to me
Some not so plain to see
But I know your presence will always be
Especially in my loving Memory

### *Shasta Glasgow*

## Queen

As the leaves of Autumn descend into the Spring,
a new generation is born.
To plant new seeds in a fertile ground,
for history repeats itself.

Such a royal life is scorn,
as she walked this earth,
in a time of enslavement, she carried
the unborn future.

Her silver lined hair made of silk,
such soft ebony skin.
To endure such pain but not to notice it,
a strong legacy in her blood.

Such a young African Princess blessed upon her,
the sacrifice she cries silently.
The inheritance for generations to follow
to over some the harsh reality,
in such inner dreams.

*Stanley E. Jones*


## Closure

White dress, Roses, and Candlelight -
  A scene out of a dream.

The warm feeling of relations and friends on
  a starry autumn night.

In the house of divinity's light
  we come together to make things right.

For the last time do I make my long walk alone.

My destiny waits for me down the way, atop a round
stone staircase, for him I won't delay.

This is the closure I've dreamed of.

I make my long decent, down to the one for whom
I was meant.

I climb those steps to freedom, at last my heart is content.

Vows were said and tears were shed,
But these words will bond to the end.

A gothic mergement of kindred souls. -

They're found again, home again, in love again, and
whole again. "Forever has just begun!!"

*LeAnn Marie Walters*


## The Great Whore

She sits like a goddess on seven hills,
And drinking the blood of prophets is her thrill.
She has deceived the Christians into playing her game,
For by subtle deceit they fornicate in her name.
Her glory and fame is the Holy See,
And where the man of sin has been exposed in prophecy.
The Christian's have worshipped the Pope by choice,
For hell awaits them for heeding his voice.
The mark of the beast is clear as can be,
And Christian's have kept his commandment faithfully.
It's the righteous who have shed their innocent blood,
But only the elect have chosen to avoid the flood.
God will avenge the blood of his saints,
For he will destroy Rome and the Vatican City-State.

*R. Michael Smith*


## Superficial Offers

The water waved madly in my general direction,
And when my eyes met them I waved back.
I thought of it for a little while,
And then glanced back; the little pond said,
"Come here, little one, and play, just for a while."
I said, "Maybe I shouldn't, well, okay, but just for a while."

I walked toward it and it waved me on.
"Hurry, hurry!" It said, as it waved more harshly.
My toe touched it's tumbling, rough exterior.
It's coldness bit me and I drew back.
"Sorry." It said, as it warmed up a bit.
I stepped in, compliantly; knee deep I was.

It said, "If you jump right in, it'll feel better."
So I did, and it grabbed my ankles,
Pulled me under, and held me there until I died.
That's when I realized that it's offer was
Irresistibly Superficial...
Silly Pond!

*Evan M. Abla*


## The San-Tee

Nineteen hundred and sixty-seven, the summer of our discontent,
As we cruised by the San-Tee Motel,
The watering hole of our small-town kingdom,
Where brown-breasted town girls, our classmates,
Sat firm-legged and flat-bellied, potential purveyors of ecstasy,
Oblivious to the coming demise of innocence.
Summers often die suddenly, as do people and their places.
The San-Tee is one of them now.
Echoes of squealing teen girls and crackly-voiced
Young men were bull-dozed into the shell of the pool,
Asphalted over, and consecrated as the altar place
Of yet another burger temple.
Brown-breasted town girls, still firm-legged and
Flat-bellied, uniformed priestesses of the charbroiled cult,
Stand not so far atop the past,
Not so different from their elder sisters,
Telling us we can have it our way,
Yet by their stance and manner,
Assuring us that we'd never really have it our way
—then or now.

*Robert L. Kipps*


## Man Made Rain

At your demise the storm clouds came.
Causing perfect conditions for man made rain.

How can my heart endure such pain?
Things just won't be the same.

So many handkerchiefs I have stained.
While during this sadness, my strength has drained.

I often wonder if angels cry?
When one of God's creations has to die.

While attending the ceremony that could not soothe.
I watched your body that would not move.

Friends and loved ones, they all came.
It seems, just to watch me weep and wail in shame.

But the evidence that I loved you was a secret I could not keep.
Which caused my eyes to continually weep.

Must I look at you and remember the things we use to do?
Shall I kiss your lips while reminiscent of what we have been through?

During future visits I will refresh your flowers and
  wash the dust from your name.
For I will forever have a endless supply, of man made rain.

*Otis Wilson*

## Remembering Decoration Day

I remember, as a child, Decoration Day,
    celebrated for Veterans, alive and dead.
The setting, a cemetery, respectfully,
    the band played — a poem was read.

A man of importance gave the address,
    national and local history the theme.
This solemn holiday in our small town,
    has all but vanished from the scene.

I am wondering, in retrospect, if
    such events are missed, in some way.
If so, this might prove to be a clue,
    why respect has all but vanished, today.

So could we bow our heads, in prayer;
    remembering what THEY have given up?
And never, ever, forget, again,
    what our fighting VETS have done for us.

*Marcella Earleywine*

## Dream Deferred

The sky once shone bright with hopes and
dreams
    Each one dulled and faded a
                              w
                                a
                                  y
                                      though
Many stolen by rejection or
Torn down by ridicule
Leaving the night sky dark and dying
Only one dream remained
Hanging low and
    alone
        in the night sky
The dream that once shone bright
fell slowly to the ground
The last of its kind now lay crying in the road
Shall the dream cry forever?
Will he ever forgive me for letting him cry so long?

*Jacqlyn Schneiser*

## Lavender-Blue Purple Plum Days

In my grandmother's garden
    Floating in a sea of violets
There are flowering plum trees
Masses of mauve shaded sweet peas
Containers crammed with purple-paisley pansies
Spiraling lavender-blue foxgloves
    That catch your fancy

Purple martins harken you
To gaze at an amethyst larkspur
The smell of French lilacs so sweet
Afternoons thicken with sunshine heat

Grandmother and me
Drink raspberry-flavored tea
    And dream of far away places
Where ladies in indigo purple
    Hide their faces

A most satisfying way
To spend a lavender-blue, plum purple kind of day to

*Jacqueline Lee Davis*

## Let Your Love Show

Let your Love show,
For the opportunity may present itself,
no more.

MOM!  I can never put your Love in tow,
but always before.
Because it's your Love that gives my life its glow.

A glow with hopes of displaying the signature of Loving Hands and
the pouring out of Kind Heart,
Which embraces the guidance and
Enhances the discipline of caring and
Sharing through the years.
This is my way of saying:
MOM!  I LOVE YOU,
MORE THAN I CAN EVER SHOW.

*Jimmy D. Milton*

## July 15, 1992

White sterile walls enclosed about the
frame of one who was once so free
and now lay so still — confined I stood beside his bed
my head throbbing to the beat of the beeps
coming from the box beside his head
which was only held together by strips
of gauze and metal rods and then
I surveyed the damage and calculated the losses:
an eye...an arm...a broken leg...
all can be replaced in time but tell me
is the damage only that which I can see
or will there be another day another chance
to hear him say that he loves me
more than I will ever know
And so I stood beside his bed
clutching the hand that once held mine
as tears trickle down my cheeks
and tears to sobs as I hear the
steady beat of beeps become one long ring
and then an Angel got his wings.

*Rachel Lee Keller*

## Reborn Into Faith

To begin anew,
    fresh as a budding flower before spring.
God planted the seed inside me.

The seed grew into a plan;
    the plan grew into learning;
learning grew into maturity;
    maturity grew back into childhood;
childhood grew into spontaneity;
    spontaneity tried new things;
new things caused me to gasp;
    gasping caused silence;
silence taught patience;
    patience brought strength;
strength brought compassion;
    compassion brought peace of mind.

The Holy Spirit had entered my soul.

*Nancy Williamson*

## The First Stone

We flaunt religion in the pagan's face,
And say our way of life is sure and true;
But were the Christ to walk this earth today,
What think you we would do to Him—a Jew?

*Rita Barr*

631

## Autumn Wind

I stand outside in the night,
gazing at the silhouette of trees against the sky,
inhaling deeply, savoring the scents,
of autumn leaves as they gently rustle by.

An awesome beauty of Gods creation,
autumn arrives with a majestic air,
the woody scents, and glorious colors,
tell me that God is everywhere.

Softly whistling through the trees,
the autumn wind is gentle and warm,
carrying with it, as it brushes by,
the reality of God in another form.

Trees silhouetted against the nighttime sky,
crystal raindrops from heaven above,
the breathtaking beauty of majestic mountains,
the joy of Gods everlasting love.

Sadness sometimes overwhelms me,
when the future seems bleak and dim,
then God comes forth, giving me strength,
He lets me feel the autumn wind.

*Sandra Hender*

## Without Saying Goodbye

We cried and sighed 'cause you're gone,
Gone without a parting word to the life beyond;
Yet, within our heart we'll ever cherish
And keep your mem'ry lovingly and forever fresh.

Year after year the ideals you had died for,
Will kindle and keep burning within our shore;
For the love of your people, your country and God,
And for democratic idealism you shed your blood.

In the fields of battle you braved the perils of war,
But in peaceful Dallas, an assassin's bullet from afar
Founds its mark, and on the lap of your loving wife,
You collapsed and lay unconscious, fighting for dear life.

When came the dreadful hour, Jackie withstood bravely,
Beside your deathbed, she was there praying fervently;
With what sorrow had she suffered for your leaving!
With what pain had her heart been pierced for your parting!

It grieved us so deeply 'cause you never said goodbye,
But little John saluted readily as you silently passed by;
And when we learned of your death after tense waiting,
We kept saying, "this man died that freedom may ring."

*Andy L. Bunuan*

## The Face Of God

Wandering souls, nomadic and apart
Have forgotten the face of God,
By removing divine love from their heart.
They have forgotten how to love,
Been replaced with greed and lust
Surely, if you must
Learn life's lessons,
Consider your sustenance and progressions.
Won't you travel toward the sun?
Where all of time has begun.
Wandering souls, nomadic and apart,
Give your self a beginning,
Give your self a start.
Feel the warmth,
Electrify your senses,
Open your eye and see...
The face of God.

*Joiya Valentine Isoke*

## Destiny

Down the path I saw him, his clothes tattered and torn,
    His walk was one of defeat, his eyes were weary and worn.

Then as I drew closer, his image cleared in my eyes,
    I now knew who it was, but still I did not know why.

Why he was there, walking toward my place,
    Why that look of compassion, glowed faintly from his face.

Then his eyes lit up, as he spoke to me,
    He said a few soft words, that shook my reality.

Behind that door lies the future, here, I give you the key,
    But once you get inside the gate, you control your own destiny.

All that I call tell you, is I just went down that way,
    And the evils of life that await, are not just there to play.

So before you go on, be sure your way is planned,
    To make sure that you don't get caught, in life's unmerciful
    quicksand.

*John Garrett*

## A Walk With Myself

I like my walks in a young wood,
I appreciate them like not many could.
I look all around and up above,
For nature's simple beauty is what I love.

Like a playful child with a joyous heart
I watch the songbirds swoop and dive.
I've seen many people who know life and think they are smart,
But only when I see things like the birds, do I feel truly alive.

I wonder how some people could not feel this,
For them life is just a blur.
They need to slow down from their mad bliss,
If not, their mind will never stir.

Without the usual noise around;
That always brings me smiles.
Because I walk on not pavement, but ground,
My mind can wander miles.

As I walk beneath my tent of leaves
Where all light comes from the sky,
I could be rushing around doing so many things,
Instead I just talk to me, myself, and I.

*Craig B. Rowin*

## "My Tongue Is The Pen[cil] Of A Ready Writer"

I speak of the days long ago before pocket protectors, when
I carried my pencils there
In my right front pocket. My trousers were loose then,
But in today's tighter pants when I sit
The pencils would break -
    indeed they do.
It was always, "Millard, gimmee a pencil"; "Millard lemmee borrow
    yer pencil",
And on, and on, and until today, "Here, let me borrow a pencil,"
    and
They ALL knew they had work to do.
But only nerds carry pocket protectors with pencils in 'em.
So, where were they when Scoutmaster Louie and the Beaver Patrol
    told us to
    "Be Prepared"

*Bob Millard*

632

## Untitled

So I heard.
I heard that he loved me.  And
That I was his pet
now what?
Tell me, what do I get?

Can I be quiet?
Can I get calm?
Can I say okay, that
This is my face; these are my legs; these are my arms?
Tell me, what do I do with the rest?
Where does my heart go with this news?
Frankly I'm tired of singing the blues.
But tell me ...
Can I discard the words from decades back,
like "You're no good," and
There's so much you lack.
So now I tell you.
Dad, you did a brilliant job and it's not done yet.
But look what I got for being your pet.

### *Janice Restler*

## Untitled

As I sit in my room,
I look around at everything.
I sit and wonder, what tomorrow will bring.
Will I make it through the day,
Or will I die, will I be honest, Or will I lie.
As I sit I wonder about my life,
Will I be shot or stabbed with a knife.
This world is turning and on everyone here.
If you mind your own business, there's nothing to fear.
I mind my own business everyday, as I talk to God each night I pray.

"As I lay me down each night, help me to always do what's right.
And if someone is to do wrong, please put them where they belong."

"Keep me walking the right path, even though others may laugh.
Give me the skills to teach my friends,
To do what's right and never to sin."

"God I'm happy to walk in your shoes, with you I win, never will
loose.  Watch over my friends, my family and me,
I'll do my best just you and me...Amen

### *Crystal Walters*

## World Harmony

What a magnificent world this would be
If we could live in harmony
No more wars fought between nations
Instead the forming of caring relations.

No more sending young men to fight
To come back scarred — such a horrible sight!
Nations with greed for power and glory
Youth lost to battles — an old, old story.

No more killings of young and of old
How wonderful harmony and peace to behold
Families displaced, forsaken, forlorn
Together again with hope now reborn.

Doves of peace filling the sky
The world's song a symphony On High
It's message the end of all war and all strife
That all on earth could look forward to life.

Then love would encircle each heart and as one
Nations would no more bring wars to be won
Dark clouds of ruin would then drift away
The Brotherhood of Man would reign from that day.

### *Rose Abrams*

## The Bird

It is not as beautiful as, a swan or a dove,
In fact, to the recipient, it is something we do not love.
We see it a lot from people these days,
Flying freely in many ways.
It flies from motorists, who aren't happy with us,
Or from people who feel like taking their frustrations out on us.
The recipient becomes stunned,
Or at the most waves back.
Friends use it as a joke,
But, if you ask me, its the yoke.
It's obscene and rude,
and won't come from a nice dude.
It is a trademark from a person, I do not wish to know.
So next time you receive a bird, and don't know what to say,
Just say, thanks for telling me I'm number one today.

### *Jill Marie Raghanti*

## Doesn't Fit

Man had an idea tried it out for size
it fit backwards just like life.
Trailed on over the rugged pathway
what a waste of time it never changed his life.
In his mind he knew of trash.
Didn't have the key for a lighted door.
Didn't want the key after awhile.
Wanted an escape.
His body was a cold depressed wind
when gone the coldness left
the depression reformed.
He was the cleverest of them all
for years he declined to an ultimate low.
His idea fit backwards just like life
and now if doesn't fit at all....

### *Stan Hopkins*

## Friend

A friend is someone who is always there,
it's one who never lets you down.
It's someone who always has a smile,
even when your face wears a frown.
It's someone who will sit and listen,
or just be there if you want to cry.
It's someone who will never turn their back on you,
or if it's going to hurt you, never tell a lie.
A friend is one who will defend you, when others think you're wrong.
It's one who'll stand beside you, and help you fight
your weakness, and make it something strong.
And no matter what your illness, your body or your mind.
They'll be right there beside you, a greater friend you'll never find.
So when you find someone, who fits what I've described to you.
Don't ever lose their friendship, remember they need a friend too.

### *Thelma M. Fox*

## Homeboy

  Look at ya' walkin' down the street wit yo' pants
fallin' off your a--.  Thinkin' dat you so cool, callin'
yo' brothers niggas and yo' sistas b------s and h--s.
Thinkin' dat you such a Mac Daddy, cuz you've got some
flo' up in yo' pocket.  Whatz wrong wit you boy, you
'pose to be a preacher's son.  Sellin' rocks to younger
brothers and smokin' dough in yo' mamma's crib.  Yo' ol'
man catches yo' a-- smokin' that s--t, he'll put a
woopen to yo' backside.  Am tellin' you this homey, yo'
a-- gonna get killed one day, if you keep hangin' wit
'dem gang bangers.  They ain't yo' friends boy, they o'nt
care 'bout yo' a--.  So you best get away from 'em 'fore
it's too late.  Get what am saying HOMEY.

### *Marie N. Hall*

## The Sounds Of Nature

I sit in the sun listening to the sounds around me
It's so peaceful and quiet and I'm where I want to be
That old bullfrog down at the pond
He croaks so loud he can be heard by everyone
Those crows with that caw, caw, caw
They're really loud when they open that maw
I hear some other birds but not so loud
Look at those cardinals so bright and proud
I hear some geese flying over with a honk
Those barking dogs I'd like to give a bunk
When living in the country sounds carry far
Sometimes it's hard to figure just what they are
There must be a new calf at the neighbor's next door
It must have been it's mama that calf was bawling for
If only these sounds were all that could be heard the world over
The sounds of Peace instead of the clamors of WAR that hover

### *Imogene Hines*

## This Woman I Call Mother

For twenty seven years now,
I've been breathing, because of your choice,
    That this baby girl, you would raise somehow.
Knowing when all was said and done, you'd rejoice.

    You cared for this small child,
Day and night, year after year.
    Chasing evil away, if it dared rile.
Bravely you journeyed on, despite the fears.

    Never once did you consider giving in,
And just allow whatever - to be.
    Faithfully you held on, to all you believed in.
Knowing that one day, our every happiness we'd see.

    You were a remarkable mother to have,
Giving unselfishly, anytime I was in need.
    Always available for a hug, or to share a laugh.
Teaching me the art of love, thee sadness of greed.

    For all these things and so many more -
I wish to give thanks and credit where it's due.
    To the woman who gave me the wings to soar,
And the precious gift of her love - eternally true.

### *Teresa Helton*

## There Have Been Times

There have been times, when I've had to smile when I've wanted to cry.
I've had to make myself go on living, when I wanted to die.

There have been times, when shame has made me hide away
While I hoped and prayed for a better day.

There have been times, when I've fallen into a dark pit.
I had to fight and struggle to claw my way out of it.

There have been times, that I've been in such despair.
Hunting futility for someone to care.

There have been times, when my tortured soul was lost.
I fought for peace of mind at any cost.

There have been times, when life dealt me a hand
    I didn't know how to play.
Believe me buddy for that, I've had much to pay.

There have been times, when my being has been battered
    like a wilted flower.
Luckily I was able to put myself, in the care of a higher power.

There have been times, and there will be times
    that my faith will be put to the test.
Hopefully I'll reach within, and give it all I've got,
    to do my very best.

### *Carolyn Mitchell*

## The Country Drive

He liked driving in his car, but never too far
Just a little ways to see the cattle graze
His favorite thing of all were the crops growing tall
To see the end of harvest before the first snowfall.

He enjoyed every flower that ever grew
If he didn't know their name, he wished he knew
He'd notice the shrubs and bushes too, and comment on the birds
To him, these were the things worth putting into words

The wide open spaces is what he liked the most
To look as far as you could see
This is the best place to be he said, on the prairie.

He'd roll down the window and take it all in
The long grass in the ditches-
The golden wheat in the fields blowing in the wind.

Then the sun would start setting off to the west-
That was another thing he liked the best-
.....And then it was time to go home.

### *Roberta Davis*

## The Attic

There's a smell up here and it comforts me
Memories hang in the air waiting to be reborn
A dust-cloaked box at first holds promise
but I find I know its history
A trunk hides its secrets
and only a key long gone
can persuade it to talk
But there's a small crate in the corner
calling out for discovery
and I look into the life of a person I don't know
No dark secrets lurk but simple things surprise me, "Billy"
When was he Billy?
Second grade? First grade?
On a class assignment
long, looping strokes
struggle to stay in the lines
It reads, "I love my Dad"
I smile
Me, too

### *Robert Fouch*

## Do You Ever Miss Me?

For three years we kissed and said I love you.
Now we're apart, and I'm with someone new.
Since we've been apart, there's been a lot of screaming.
But I hold you near me every night while I'm dreaming.
Even after hateful looks or silent acts,
We both still know all the facts.
We cared so much and were in love.
A love like ours could not be let go of.
An accidental meeting, just by chance.
I forget how things are now and we exchange a glance.
As I start to reach out and call your name,
I suddenly remember, things are not the same.

And every second I wonder 'Do you ever miss me?'

Do you pretend like she is me?
Pretend it's the way it used to be?
Do you stare at us in the frame
And want to hold me like it's the same?
Do you cry when you try to close your eyes?
Or did you forget about me, break all the ties?

And every second I wonder 'Do you ever miss me?'

### *Jami Jo Paugh*

## A Hunter

His world is of forests, valleys and streams,
Of oranges and yellow, browns and greens.
His mind is of iron, his heart one of gold,
His thoughts filled with dreams which have never been told.
He lives for the wind, the dust and fresh air
And moments to sit and think out a prayer,
To hunt in the daylight, to fish in a brook,
To sit under a tree in a cool shady nook.

His world is different, beyond all you've known.
He could live in the forest and not be alone.
Just give him the mountains the hills and the green
The fish, the animals and a babbling stream.

*Constance Debo*

## The River

Roll on mighty stream, roll on, roll on,
Push on mighty currents in your bed,
Undercut and overflow your banks instead
Of trickling through those separated pools.

Join with other rivers on your way,
Until you fall relentless to the sea,
Move along your tons of land debris,
And pile it high upon the ocean shore.

Oh the pithy stories you could spin,
As tiny boats upon your bosom ply,
Looking up at dark or sunny sky,
Sweetly singing as you go your way.

From tiny source in yonder mountain chain,
You tend to make each tributary thine,
Here rapids, there eddy, here straight line,
You swiftly fall to your last rendezvous.

*Alfred E. McAdam*

## Fatherly Love

When I was young we swung and sang sonnets
Remember our favorite, "Pin Your Easter Bonnet?"

Walking alone to school you didn't mind
Because you were watching me from behind

I didn't know you were walking behind me
I thought I was alone and walking free

Always there like a knight in shining armor
You could be counted on to save my honor

Those were the times when life was carefree
And gone they are—they went so quickly

Life here will never be the same
You aren't here for the laughter and pain

And when I gazed upon your sweet face
I realized your soul was in another place

For when the soul leaves the human remain
There is nothing left—not even pain

Oh, Father dear, I miss you so much
How I would love to give your hand a touch

For now I bid you a farewell adieu
Because I know someday I will be with you

*Judi Witek*

## Eclipse

Happy times, sad times, good and bad times
seem to be a part of life,
Still we cling to each other, feeling
grateful for one another because strong
is the power of love, and the beauty of
this everlasting love cannot be stripped
away, It has chosen it's path through
rough and all and will remain through each
passing day, though saddened we are when
times comes to release a loved ones hand,
It's been described as a loving warmth
and to compare no one can, the caring
hands which reach out to cradle the surviving
soul, are the very same hands which guide
our hearts to fill the empty hole, filled
with memories both warm and clear never to
be replaced, will remain as long as we
permit, with the love in which they were based.

*Linda F. Hatch*

## I Wish I Was An Angel

I wish I was an angel,
so I could spread my wings and fly.
I wish I was an angel,
so I could sore across the deep blue sky.
I wish I was an angel,
so I could dance upon the big white clouds.
I wish I was an angel,
to sprinkle love, and happiness upon everyone.
I wish I was an angel to be close to loved ones who are gone.
I wish to be an angel after my life is done.
I hope the Lord grants me my wish,
so that one day I can sore the deep blue skies
to keep a watching eye on those I left behind.

*Jeanette L. Adams*

## A Mother Like No Other

There are dreams, visions, and hallucinations.
Some are God's own wisdom, some are the devils visitations.
I live my life now with some hesitation.
Praising God for all creation!

I saw in my mother many faults,
Those of my own; were blamed on my folks.
I would buy my mother now a many colored coat.
My feelings of love now are not so remote.

The real truth is, she never made any mistakes.
When I asked her, she made me pie instead of birthday cake.
When she was working hard, I used to skate.
And I hope she forgives me before it's too late.

*Bill Fleming*

## Rites of Spring

The bird's song of sweet melody announcing that once again spring has taken a toe hold.

Winter's somber hue of cold, dreary, and darken skies, casting a pall over all.  Now giving way to skies in various shades of blue, the warming sun, and to the gentle breezes.

While underneath the semi frozen soil, the first signs of spring manage a valiant fight and poke their tiny heads out and gently unfurls its petals in the massaging rays of the sun, a crocus now sways in the gentle breeze.  Telling all in its celebration that spring has begun.

Renewal and rebirth just adds a greater beauty to the earth, for all of us to take note in the passage of winter and the settling in of spring.

*Sandra Allen*

## Thank You For This Man

Thank you for this man
That you've given me to love;
Thank for your his life
That you've let me be part of.

With him a tiny space
Is like a mansion with any other;
A piece of bread, like a feast,
I can say that he is much
though our things are least

Though difficult times have lain hold of us
Peace comes when we hold each other;
You're gift to me in this strange land,
is my husband, my lover.

When good times come with plenty
help me not release my hold;
let our love in all circumstances be sturdy and bold.

Let us keep to the path you've lighted, your divine example of love
By which you gave of yourself, your own blood.
May our unity be a reproduction of your heart,
May our love be stronger in the end than at the very start.

*Jessica Spier*

## The Coral Isle

The thundering surf batters the slim ribbon of shore.
The beach has withstood many eons of constant war
But it is slowly losing its will to the sea.
The dull below of waves is shouting of victory.

With every pulse of every breaker, another minutiae is won.
"Another beach will soon be ours, in only a few turns of the sun.
Then on to the next lying right behind.  It hasn't got time to prepare
We'll cover the world 'ere eternity ends, and soon receive our share."

All while the thunderous war goes on, the waves grow ever more sure.
But behind the lines,
    slowly,
      silently,
        another island is born.

*Beverly G. D. Schmidt*

## Untitled

As suddenly as you thrust out of the womb
The earth will stop
Time will stop
Your alignment is perfect
The breathe sucked from your body
Thrusting you out
Taking in your new atmosphere
Looking at what is left behind
Suffering joy
The predictable
The unpredictable
What life on earth is all about go, go
Your new world awaits you
Cut loose the umbilical cord
That connects you to Mother Earth
Transcend to the ethereal skies
Remorse relinquished
It's where we're all meant to be live a little
Then die for the rest of your life forever
Transcendent beauty

*Marya Dosti*

## Morning Solitude

Some mornings I get up early
To greet the dawn of day.
The beauty of early morning
Exceeds more than words can say.

Rare fragrance from the old-fashioned rose bush
Drift by as I walk through the grass
New formed buds in their petals
Will be flowers for the graduating class.

As I meander around my garden.
With feet wet with morning dew,
I thank God for the grandeur around me
And for blessings the new day ensues.

I ask God to continue my Utopia
As I day dream and build castles in air,
May I live this day humbly and graciously
In a way that shows "I care"

*Daisy Suit*

## Lonely Dove

As a rainbow came into sight
The love from within continued to fight
So as the day began to fall
The loneliness of waiting continued to call
So the thoughts of love passed into mind
As I tried to look for the love which I hope to find
With that my love for you will continue to be tossed
And the feeling of love will forever be lost
So as the dawn started to near
The thought of you brought about a tear
As the sun rose high above
In mind I was thought to be just a lonely dove

*Christopher Schafer*

## To A Friend... "Heaven On Earth"

My eyes once captured a glimpse of rain dancing upon a distant shore
The thunder roared and the wind blew

And the rain continued to dance across the ocean

A deep, penetrating Navy painted the vast sky
As the moon's silvery light directed it's stroke

Perfectly perfect and there was I witnessing a masterpiece in creation

The moment lasted through the night and settled upon the edge of dawn
While the wave's gentle movement lulled me to sleep upon a feathery bed of white sand

I've never awakened from that night
Many rains and may days have come and gone

Yet, when the thunder roars And the wind blows
An intense emotion quickens me

Invigorated, I awake upon white sand
Captivated by rain dancing upon a distant short
Beneath and endless navy sky
Compatibly illuminated by... A sparkling crescent

And for the moment am completely delighted by pure pleasure

Beholden to nothing else as the dawn glides into sight
I ease back into a peaceful sleep without any regrets

*Maya Marisa Woolfolk*

## To My Best Friend

I give to you, a gift of words
To show you what you did for me
You made me realize
I can be anything I want to be

There is nothing I could give you
To show you how much I care
So I will wrap these words up for you
So you can carry them everywhere

I take you wherever I go
Because your always with me
Our friendship is something I cherish
More than anything, I believe

*Amy S. Reger*

## Three Gifts from Heaven

Three gifts from heaven
Three beautiful girls
Three gifts from heaven who could ask for anything more.
They are oh, so different personality wise
yet so much alike sweet, funny, and gifted
which make me very proud.
My eldest child stubborn, hot tempered, a beauty to see
The second easy going, sentimental, has eyes that
ask questions before her mouth speak.
The last one I prayed for and God answered my prayer
quiet, soft spoken, with a smile that could take her anywhere.
Every time I look in the mirror I see her
standing there.
Three gifts from heaven
Three beautiful girls
Three gifts from heaven, and I love you all.

*C. Bell Smith*

## Friends

Friends should always be there, for love and for care
through the roughest and the worst
when some begin to believe they're cursed
through happy and glad
through sad and mad

Friends should always be there, for love and for care
through the times when you wanna kill
but you know you need to chill
when all the anger bottles up inside
and you know you just can't let it slide

Friends should always be there, for love and for care
when you need a shoulder to cry upon
until the slightest crack of dawn
when the new day begins
and the old day ends

Friends should always be there, for love and for care
to hold on tight
and never lose sight
to trust and forgive,
for as long as you live

*Monica Jones*

## Draw Me A Picture

A task which
cannot
be endeavored
for a picture cannot
be drawn,
only
developed.

*Kimberly L. Rihaly*

## The Investment

I read about a mother who gave her only child
to God, a promise she meant to keep.

I know a living God who gave his only son
for man, a sacrifice that caused God to weep.

The woman invested her child in God.

God invested his son in man.

Who? Or what? Have you invested your
child in?

*Fredrico Hernandez Stewart*

## "Grandma You're The Greatest"

Grandma you're the greatest, you've always been near.
To pick me up when I had fallen and add a bit of cheer.

You'd always pick me up and say "oh darlin'! let me see"
or just pick me up with loving eyes and bounce me on your knee.

Well, now I've gotten older and the circumstances changed,
but still you've always been there and I know you'll stay the same.

You may not have diamonds or be rich like millionaires,
but without the love you give to me my life would be so bare.

You are a present from God up above,
you're a wonderful woman over-flowing with love.

I thank God daily for this gift you see,
for this wonderful gift has been given to me.

Grandma you're the greatest and I hope that you will see,
the love that fills my heart for you, is the love you gave to me.

*Kimberly R. Ramsey*

## Life

The seed falls to the ground and the life starts.
Up comes a tree with a weak trunk, but soon
The tree becomes stronger and the base stabilizes.
The limbs branch and the twigs go to the moon.
The buds, the beautiful buds blossom into leaves,
And the leaves grow strong. Sometimes they get sick and lorn
for water. Always green, but not with envy, the leaves
grow strong. Then autumn comes and the leaves morn
for their friends who whither and die away. The seas
tide roles out and you forget about the tree,
but then the tide rolls in.
The cycle keeps on going leaving memories
Etched into your mind like the prick of a thorn.

*Michael Mattler*

## Jesus Is My Comfort, I'm Not Alone

"Your loved ones are gone,
You're all alone."
That's what some people may say.
But little they know of the place
in my heart where God's love
warms and sustains me every day.

How could one forget or ever compare,
The memories that's cherished
or the love we did share.

Our love had no boundaries
tho God called you home.
But I find comfort from my heartache -
For Jesus is with me.
I'm not alone

*Voncile Ledbetter*

## Desert Secrets

He filled his suitcases with secrets, only to be
abandoned, after hours of searching through
gardens of burning peacocks, left with his
pride aflame.

Finding forgotten veils, packed away in tents of
travelers who do not lie, and who are protected
by the wind.

He would sit with them and they spoke to him,
soft, slowly of ancient lights and turning
away from that desert, his eyes dimmed only by
shadows of forgotten loves, who became
faces, shining swiftly with pain
and laughter.
Like shells collected but left behind,
to be washed out to sea again.

*Annette King*

## Manikin Ball

Come on down to the manikin ball
At your favorite department store mall
We've got access to all the latest created
We have canned music by Music, Incorporated

Come on down to the manikin ball
When the doors close, we take to the hall
We've got to stand, poised all the day
So when the doors close, we swing and sway

We've got the rhythm of steel ball bearing feet
For moving on waxed floors, our slide step is neat
And our glide step is like a clean sweep
We wear the clothes that help you compete
But when someone comes and knocks us down
We are melted back into another gown
For another very showy go round

We can pretend we're the people down the block
Or we can be a movie star in a purple smock
Dancing under a phosphorescent spray,
While dancing, dancing the nighty away.

*Ann McHen*

## Displaced In Time

I walk along the Street of the Dead
here at the place where God's once resided.
I look upon the beauty you left behind.
Your high towering temples of the Moon and the Sun,
the wind whispered that I was to late.

Come join us the ancient ruins seem to say.
The Gods were beckoning me to remain.
As the shadows grew long in this place I call home,
I stood in silence and decided to stay.
the wind whispered that I was to late.

Echoes of sorrow, sad songs from the dead,
whispers that Quetzalcoatl had sailed away.
Gone are the warriors with their magnificent plumes.
Gone are the people, the gods and the blooms
and I wondered if I was too late.

Among the shadows I searched for the man,
the king, the hungry coyote, a poet they say.
The one who walks like a pauper in order to stay.
Upon the sun's temple I see his silhouette,
then I realized that I was born 500 years too late.

*Angie L. Moore*

## Proximity of Life

Motion of the heart - achingly continuous.
Fluidity in its repetition - comforting.
Calming overwrought senses that burst on a white-hot vista
    like sunflares in a black sky.
Days rotate in cylinders of nothingness leading to egos that control
    illusions.
Spectres of grandeur straggle within and without the psyche.
Creations of uselessness left for generations to gape and gawk -
    and this was the legacy of mankind?
Creations of emotions left for generations to tend and teach -
    and these, to the beneficiaries of mankind.
Burden/relief, burden/relief, burden/relief.
Hours revolve on timepieces of infinity lending borrowed moments
    to fragile travelers.
One said, "It is the knowledge of infinity that is the reason."
Another, "No, it is knowledge of not infinity that is the reason."
The third, "It is both; the despair and the hope."
And all, "Ah yes, the planet's dream."
Inhale/exhale, inhale/exhale, inhale/exhale.
Axis, revolution, galaxy, CREATOR.

*Anna MacKenna*

## Forget

Forget his friendly smiles
forget the lovely things he said
Forget the good times you had with him.
Remember he's not yours anymore.

Forget the big heart candies he gave you.
Forget his way he showed his love.
Forget the times you had with him.
Remember, he left you for her.

Forget the red roses
Forget the way he said, "We will always
be together,"
Forget the friendly, lovely hugs he gave you.
Remember, he's not yours anymore

Forget that friendly house where you went
Forget the warm kisses
Forget the way he smiled, with those puppy eyes
Remember, he left you for her.

*Angela Ckarapetyan*

## Love Is Gone

Passionate young hearts in a merry chase,
grew together while reaching for the moon.
Life sped like a sonic boom through space,
time was short, the journey ended soon.

There was joy and laughter, now it's pain,
manifesting sadness that chases away sleep.
Fun and play turned to lost hope and disdain.
The reason for existence is now buried deep.

The stately clock chimes in the empty room.
the reading light is on, the paper un-read,
and the lounge chair sits vacant in gloom.
Nights are long, alone in a king sized bed.

Quiet is as noisy as a roaring engine,
while silence is deafening to the ears.
Loneliness race around for attention.
Oblivious - days and nights turn to years.

Love is gone, desire and hope hushed too soon,
lonely as a cloud with no occasion for rain,
embracing a comet, spinning around the moon,
passing rainbows and stars to a night of pain.

*Annie McClure*

## The Spinning Epitaph

Traveling down my bumpy road
I came to the place where buzzards meet.
As they finished their lavish meal
I saw the feast was my child.

Forgive me innocent one,
I know not why I chose to ruin us.
This vortex in my head is without escape
You are not alone, the buzzards circle us both.

*Anthony Craddock*

## I'll Forgive You Anyway

As I look at your picture,
I can see the love you had for me.
I can see how happy you were.

As I look at your picture,
I can see the pain I didn't know to be.
I'd never know it was there.

You were so brave.
Hidden was the pain.
A smile shown through.

You were so brave.
You had everything to lose and nothing to gain.
You were never blue.

If I had only known,
You wouldn't live forever.
I would have etched everything in stone.
If I had only known
I wouldn't see you each.
My memories would be known.

You went away without saying goodbye.
But I think I'll forgive you anyway.

*Amy Hymel*

## My Secret

Hey sweet thang, token of my heart,
I have a secret that I wish to tell you, but
I'm too shy.  So I'm just going too write it
down and hope you get it someday, somehow.
I've thinking of you since day
one.  I've enjoyed your smile, your voice,
your scent, your skin, and your legs even
though it belonged to someone else.
A week has passed and we've
gotten to know one another, but now I
know that there's no longer another, and
there is a lonely, broken heart waiting to be
repaired.  I just wanted to let you know if I
ever get the chance, I'll raise your heart
to an increase level next to mine an I'll
be cautious to never let it decrease.

*Annissa Hayes*

## "I Miss You"

I sit here feeling so empty and lonely,
I think of you after every minute of the day
wondering where you are and what you are doing
and crying a tear for every minute we are apart.
Somewhere in the emptiness...
Somewhere in the loneliness...
I find myself feeling very loved and realize
it's not the love that hurt's so much it's
being without you.

*Angela Bradley*

## Untitled

I know before I die I will look back through my life to my first love.
I will search among the memories that will have collect throughout the
years I have lived.
My eyes will fill with tears as I recall a smiling face that made be
feel overwhelmed with joy and I myself will smile.
Then as soon as I smile I know it would fade away leaving me with only
the knowledge that he is now only a memory.
My emotions will ache as it did when I was a young girl engulfed in
real love who knew she would have to wait for many weeks or months
to see him again although this time it would be forever.
My last moment of mortality will be of simple movement.
The rise and fall of my chest as I take in my last breath.
But, as my eyes close for one last time my only thought will be
"I love you."

*Annette Koutchak*

## Life's Deception

The effort to enjoy life is too great
If I climb out of this pit I have jumped into,
I will be too tired to laugh, too tired to love, too tired to live.
My mind is unleashing such a weight upon my heart, such a weight.

I cannot remember, so I will make myself forget.
A narrow path I must lead on the edge of a divide
Of pain...of death...of false ego.
The desire to acquire that which is memory, that which is free,
Pulls me down.

True devotion is the only route to the absolute
The guide is faint...but the guide is there.
I will go because I am shown the way.

Far beyond lies a land of incredible freedom...
Of joy, of happiness,
All I must do is turn my cheek to joy.
The peace that lies beyond is real, it will always be there —-
I just have to reach that point.

Come along, those who are in pain..yes, you,
If happiness is a burden...if life handcuffs you to the ground...
Come along, and we will be free, we will enjoy life again.

*Angie Stinnett*

## Each Of Us Has Our Worth

There are many things we each do well,
It takes but one of us to tell.
To be unselfish in our daily giving,
Has made our lives prove worth the living.

Unique we are in our individual approaches,
Distinguishes each one of us beyond reproaches,
A task to be done, you can count on us,
Even if during the interim, there comes a fuss.

But words uttered are not meant to be,
Personally inflicted by you or me.
They are signs of the strains and burdens we carry,
And we know in our hearts they will not tarry.

So as this year comes to an end,
And to each of us, we remain a friend.
A bond between us will continue to grow,
And we'll look back and say, "I told you so."

*Annie E. White*

## The Journey

Life leads us to a great many places.
We leave behind many unfilled spaces.
The search for truth persists,
the answers resist
but, only for the need to continue the journey.

The way ahead is course and unknown.
We might decide to turn, and go home.
Stripped and cheated,
our will defeated-
we vow once again to continue the journey.

Time passes within itself so readily.
We grow bemused and discontented steadily.
The allure slips away,
perseverance at bay
we no longer have the strength to continue the journey.

Desperation and despair has now passed.
The struggle for direction, gone, at last.
Acceptance becomes clear,
comfort grows dear
we realize that we are now ready to begin the journey.

*John Campbell*

## Pearl

Pearl was a place of western and untold gold,
Were people were killed as I was told.

The mountains were covered with those putting down their claim,
To warn others that it was his domain.

The school house once stood on a hill so grand,
As the echoes of lost children in their own land.

The hotel there sat as the sound of the piano went rolling on,
Now is burnt down and so much has gone.

The mill was running and now the big wheel sits and waits,
Until the day of the opening of the gates.

Now pearl is a ghost town and long lost memories are gone,
As the fever of gold won't be for long.

*Renee A. Matney*

## The Dark One

In Gaelic, they say my name means the dark one.
What does this mean?
I know I have a dark side.
I shield things from the light,
Keep it hidden, keep it dark.
I know wrong from right, know it well.
This well get me through life.
Do I know my boundaries?
I know why I love the light.
Light is key, light is good.
I don't like the dark,
For fear of the unknown and the hidden.
The dark side tempts me, though.  Why?
My free spirit will show me the light,
and when the dark side called for me again, I will not be afraid;
I welcome you, dark spirit.
Oh, hazel eyes, hazel eyes, see in the night, see the light.
Accept the dark, know the dark, be wary of the dark;
But follow the light.

*Kerry Frankland*

## Questions From A Soldier

Machine guns sing a song of death,
What is the reason I am here for?
Is glory a reason for me to die?
Why have I come to war?

My comrade lost his life in battle,
When is a soldier supposed to cry?
Two children and his wife remain,
When is a man too young to die?

I think of the family I left behind,
Why has this become a painful dream?
The enemy attacks my trench,
Can you hear the wounded scream?

Disease and starvation have joined the Allies,
Which method of victory will prevail?
A loaded revolver placed in my mouth,
Why has God sent me to hell?

*Phelon R. Taylor*

## Papa

Where are you Papa.
Where are you tonight.
Come hold me Papa.
Come hold me tonight.
I know that you hit Momma last night.
Momma says that you must fight.
Why must you fight Papa.
It gives me such fright.
Momma says that you take snow Papa.
Why do you take snow in the summer Papa.
Momma says the snow causes you to be someone else.
I do not want someone else Papa.
Where are you Papa.
Come hold me tonight.
My teddy bear will keep me warm Papa.
My teddy bear will not give me love Papa.
My Momma will give me love Papa.
But she is hurting with fright.
Who will talk to me, Papa.
Who will love me tonight.

*Peter Baldwin*

## Look Up

Sometime in your life
You may feel no joy,
Or may feel that the river of life has run dry.
But remember, my friend,
That a smile sent your way,
Can renew your faith in all men.
Yes, you may be the one
Someone is looking too,
For the hope he has felt slip away,
Give him a smile and a warm, friendly look
And it may by chance, brighten His day.

*Rose M. Rich*

## Goodbye

Even though we have to go our separate ways.
There are a few things I would like to say.
You haven't made me think any less of you.
Although you have given me many reasons to.
There are still feelings for you inside of me
But, they're not strong like they use to be.
And there's this part of me that wants to hate you.
But, that would be too easy for me to do.
But, I can't love you, that's too hard for me to do.
Now the only feelings left, are those of a friend.
With that kind of friendly love that will never end.

*Kim Harvey*

## Intimate Apparition

I stand here motionless
And wonder if it was just a dream.
Could I have ever experienced such joy?
Or, is my mind taunting me?
Painting... surreal imagery of happier times.
A memory of a place, and a moment that can
Never be again.
I see you standing before me,
Expressive eyes green as the sea,
Leave nothing to be said.
A warm summer breeze offers it's caress.
I am seduced by my own imagining's,
Amidst the deafening roar of the ocean's surf.
Thank you!  For allowing me to indulge in my delusion.
Seashore you are a fine lady,
And as always, you've been a most gracious host.
Slowly... I back away,
Mournfully... the images dissipate.
I return to my reality and bid farewell,
To my beloved "Ghost."

### *Anthony Gomez*

## Memories

Where are all the days gone by?
Buried in archives of time?
Waiting to be relived
In the imagination of the mind.
Simmering golden memories
Not quite clear; a little faded,
But there, oh yes, there for the remembering.

### *Anna Belle Leonard*

## When as a Child

I use to listen to my Mother, when as a mere child
My imagination would run wild
She would talk to my Father, when it was no bother
The stories they would tell, were spoken well
They would talk about life and its strife(s)
I was very content, because this was time well spent
My understanding of life was my interpretation, let's
say my world my imagination
Back then, I thought we could live forever?
Sometimes, well, they would talk about death me never?
When it came I would hold my eyes wide-open so I wouldn't
die, my world in my mind's eye

### *Roosevelt Hudson*

## Iodine

A latchkey spring is in gestation
while leaves leap off their trees without parachutes
and every time a shadow is out of place
I think you're still here
want to burn down the attic
so I can see the sun again
maybe it all made no more of a difference
than the eye of a madman
moving across a silent landscape...
but I cannot agree while I watch my willow die
under her own weight, staring holes in me
circles everywhere
circumference nowhere
stone against stone leaving impressions
I do not understand, a purpose by default?
And somewhere else...
there is a pasture, dotted with men standing
against blades, against blades of grass,
and the breeze is bending all alike in anger.

### *Sara Rowen*

## All About Cats

You know, I'm partial to cats and that's a fact!
Be they female or male, calico, white or black,
Skinny or fat, long-haired or short-haired
Makes no difference, that!

Cats are buddies, snuggling in your arms so tight.
They keep you warm and contented
Like big furry blankets or goosedown quilts,
Or chicken soup on a cold winter's night!

Cats are independent, I like that.
They show love when they are ready.
It trickles down on you like rain on a hot summer's day
And refreshes you on the way!

Cats bring out your best without even trying
So take off your hat, cause
I can't envision a world without cats
And that's that!

### *Angela R. Hiser*

## Just One Step

Just one step in the right direction
Can change the course of your life;
Just one step in the wrong direction,
Can lead you to a world of strife.

When you stumble you must take a look
To make sure you're on the right way;
If you discover you're on the wrong road,
He'll forgive you if you stop and pray!

When Jesus lived down here among men...
He often asked God to show him the way;
All who believe in God's Holy word,
As in the past he'll hear what they say!

Just one step in the right direction,
And you know God is on your side;
Just one step in the wrong direction—
There's no place you can run and hide!

### *Anderson Caudill*

## Terror In The Heartland

Oklahoma City was the place,
   9:02 on April 19th, the time and date.
Parents comfort their children as they cry,
   little did they know it would be their last good-bye.
As I watch from my tv,
   it still remains a mystery
Why someone would take the lives
   of fathers, brothers, sisters, wives.
Underneath all the rubble,
   lies the cities greatest trouble.
Just three days before this mess,
   families shared Easter's happiness.
But all that seems so long ago,
   families laughing with faces aglow.
All the states fears and sorrows,
   how can we make it through tomorrow?
Why does the healing take so long?
   When will we be able to move on?
Only my sympathy I can express.
   Oklahoma, may God bless!

### *Amy Holley*

## Look In That Mirror...

Wake up and look at
  yourself day by day
What do you see?
Do you see the child that
  you never were?
Do you see the adult you're
  going to be?
Or do you see yourself with
  this blank look,
Wondering who is that or
  why am I here?
Go to sleep at night and
  look at yourself in
That mirror and say
  I know who I am,
    Who are you???

***Meghan Denise Clemente***

## Love Is Like The Seasons

Why are you so glum, my sweet,
Your face so long and drear?
You look as if you've lost a friend,
As if you'll shed a tear.

The summer months have passed us by;
My love, they're all but gone.
The winter season has made its nest,
Ahead I see no dawn.

You ask me why I seem so sad,
I fear you do not know.
Summer's sunny days have faded,
All that's left is snow.

I do not wish to bring you down,
I hope you find new light.
Autumn has overcome my heart,
Good night, my love, good night.

***Jason Shettles***

## Little Angel

Little angel bow down
your ear to God
Let Him tell you when
to play the music
for His children to
come home.
Some are weary, some
have fallen by the way.
So bow down your ear
Maybe you can play today

***Margaret Wynn***

## Eagles

On a far off distant mountain peak
An eagle soars on wings widespread
Slowly his fleeting path does make
Ever looking for his brood to feed
At once his piercing eyes does see
The game he stalks so patiently
So silent is his change of flight
The one he stalks will never see
Like an arrow fast in flight
With talons stretched his foe to seek
He swoops his prey and climbs on high
To some far distant mountain peak

***Keith John Nichol***

## To Live

To live amongst your sunshine
and stroll inside your shadow.
To walk in your footprints
behind you as you travel.
To feel the feelings you do
and see life through your eyes,
Experience your love
and be the sunshine in your skies.
To feel your need to follow
and walk my shadow too,
and know you share my feelings
and see things as I do.
To think that you desire me
as I desire you,
and know you'll stand beside me
as I will stand by you.
These dreams and thoughts and feelings
and to know that you're the one,
are the reasons for my happiness
and tomorrow's rising sun.

***Karen Barnes***

## Untitled

We should love the lord with
all our heart.
Try to let nothing take us apart
I say it because
I live for him and continue
trying not to sin.
So put your faith in the Lord,
and accept His joy
which I have adored we all
have our problems
It's fair to say, but the good
Lord is with us day after day.
Knowing this
you will grow strong.
Never decreasing all your life long.
So live in the future,
die in the past, cause your a new creator
and his goodness will last.
Remember that your going to win.
Say no - go to satan and also to sin.

***Kurt Hinds***

## Untitled

I can't stop thinking of you
And all the days that past,
But this relationship we're having
is moving way too fast.
You say you really love me
How do I know that it's true?
Yet I've only know you shortly
and I know I like you too.
I wonder if love's a normal word
A word you use everyday,
a word that comes out so easily
one you always have to say.
Does it have any meaning?
One with feelings so true?
Do you really feel this for me,
or are you just saying this on cue.
I would love to say it back to you
It would make things easier to see,
But if you're sure your love is real
then later that's how'll be for me.

***Kristy Madamba***

## The Singing Road

Listen to the singing road,
And hear the different songs,
Each one according to the load
Of the vehicle without prongs,

But equipped with rubber tires,
That produce various sounds
Sometimes like singing wires,
At other times like braying hounds

If the road is black top,
The song is like a lullaby,
But if the road is cement top,
It's like the swoon of a lonesome guy.

If expansive joints in concrete are
Sometimes filled with tar,
The music is like white heat,
But different with each car.

Sometimes like rock and roll,
But depending on the load
Even tunes that sound like soul,
But all are from the singing road.

***Kenneth E. Spaulding***

## The Unmaterial Gift

You said you love me,
And I know that's true.
Because when you're near,
The gray sky turns blue.

Your smile brings rays,
Of golden sun.
I know that forever,
You're the only one.

Your eyes are the stars,
Twinkling in the sky.
When I see a tear,
I just break down inside.

You bring me joy,
In everything you do.
And in my heart,
There's many things I want to do for you.

The most important gift,
I want to give you.
Is just the gift of letting you know,
I love you too.

***Kevin Goodman***

## Snow Dance

Somersaulting snow maidens
dance spryly as spring snows
drift down from heaven's kitchen
lighting blue fire trails

Attentive tin soldiers
stand taught as strong desires
flare from flashes of alabaster skin
spilling laughter from sultry lips

Drifting cautious couples
gently caress as feelings begin
falling from lofty perches
drowning earth's screams.

***Kathleen A. Muja***

## The Thirteenth Apostle

And through the cloud of pain,
And through the hard, cold rain,
I saw a smiling face;
Lovely, calm, full of grace.

And from the Sea of Galilee,
The word of God came down to me.
It rumbled past two thousand years,
To fall at last upon my ears.

"Your body's good, your mind is whole,
Your future's saved, and so's your soul.
So go and spread my word to man,
And by my side you'll take your stand."

I'm not a Baptist, not a Priest,
I do not bow unto the East,
I love my God without a crutch;
Do you believe just half that much?

The word of God is in my mind,
The message there we soon shall find.
I feel it there; my mind release,
A single word; the word is peace.

**Kriss Overby**

## Lessons

Sometimes...things,
Are not as...they seem!
Are they...Lessons?
Or...Are they Dreams?

Knowledge...Gained
A process...it's life!
Gained In...Acceptance.
Gained In...Joy.
Gained In...Strife!
But nothing learned,
Is a wasted life.

**Kenneth Price**

## Second Sight

Sometimes at night
as I walk my dog.
moonbeams pierce the screen of dark
and veil the garden like a bride.
A solitary star blinks
lonely messages from space.

Down the road, frozen silver
in the silent night
shadowy, the house looms, sleeping
curled around the past.

And on the dew - touched grass
in the moonlight, the children dance
Acrobats and magic tricks and
lemonade - five cents.

Fountains of laughter
Fall back to earth
silent as bubbles in the quiet air.

Then, for a breathless moment
Through the barred window of the past I peer
sometimes at night as I walk my dog.

**Kitty Barr**

## "Without A Home"

Huddled in the alcove,
Barely seen by night's eye,
She trembled from the dampness,
Too cold to even cry.

Her face awash with dirt,
Her eyes a forlorn stare,
Wild brush and other stuff
Entwined her curly hair.

Garbage half-hid her body,
Thin and underfed,
Her eyelids flickered from weakness,
She looked almost near dead.

Emotion strangled my aching heart,
How she must feel so all alone...
I knelt down beside her,
Gave her my hand,
And took that sweet puppy home.

**Kim Charlton**

## Summer Is Near

Summer is near
Big trips and family
Vacations are here
Summer is near
Big water parks
And family places open up
Summer is near
And everyone can here
Everyone having fun
And playing in the sun

**Kim Smith**

## Room for Me

Our Father who art in Heaven
Can I talk with thee
You see dear Lord I'm just a cat
Is there room for me?

My owner doesn't care no more
This is plainly true
You see dear Lord, I'm just a cat
Can I be with you?

I'll lay my head upon this ground
And pray as I do weep
You see dear Lord, I'm just a cat
Please take me as I sleep.

The pain has gone as my breathing stops
And the dampness has gone away
You see dear Lord, I'm just a cat
Am I here to stay?

The smile on your face and touch of your hand
Has made me happier than I could ever be
You see dear Lord, I'm just a cat
But there really was "room for me"

**Kevin E. Leahy**

## Cruel World

I see the child that once was me.
Innocent and pure once was she.

Never exposed to hate or sin.
I think of the child I could've been.

Corrupted by a world of greed and shame.
Who do I go to? Who do I blame?

**Katara S. Simmons**

## I Am Not There

The girl I once knew,
Cries out for help
I do not hear her
I am not there
Her tears stain her face,
Her mouth open wide
I cannot see her
But she does not care
She calls out for me,
For anyone near
I do not hear her
I am not there.

**Kristy Herzog**

## The Tree In Winter

Her naked arms are outstretched,
Crooked, waiting to embrace the sky.
She stands alone, a singular gray figure
Facing the elements and seasons.

This Winter she is barren;
Her leafless branches reach to the sky,
An empty azure frame.
The sun offers little warmth.

Beams and rays of light, so far away.
The tree shivers subtlety.
Leaves lie crumpled and dead at her feet.
She waits for Spring.

Hollow and bending in the icy wind,
She stands alone, braving the cold.
Dark falls and she faces the night,
She waits for Spring and the Kiss of
Morning's Light.

**Kristin Moses**

## Solitude

I am an empty room,
dark and alone.
No one to talk to,
no happiness shown.
They cannot get in to me.

I am an entry way,
closed from inside.
No one can enter,
to see what I hide.
Therefore I am abandoned.

I am a cellar wall,
dank, wet, and cold.
No one to warm me,
and covered with mold.
They have all left me to fate.

**Kimberlee Luman**

## A Hole

There's a spot below my window,
No. A hole.
   A very distinct hole.
A wall hanging once filled that hole.
   A gift from a friend.
The gift is now gone.
   My friend is gone.
All that's left is a hole.

**Kevin T. Burtyk**

## Light!

Like sparkling sun on dancing water;
Diamonds on the ripple's crest.
Bubbling with childish laughter;
This simile describes her best.

A feather floating on the breezes;
Turning, twirling, never still.
High above dark clouds she's gliding;
Golden sun, her wings doth gild!

May she ever bless this earthbound
Dwelling of immortal soul;
She of light and golden Summer
In her mother's arms enfold.

*Kathy Floyd*

## The Living and Dying

Why God why
Do people die
Why does AIDS infect
And cancer deny

Why do people we love
seem to live and then die
some even leaving
without a goodbye

And why are they good
those people who die
ones we care for and love
sick in bed they do lie

It hurts when they leave
I mean when we part
for the love they have given us
is there from the start

I want to know who deserves to be sick
to live part of life not how they would pick

I think love and hope are what bring us together
The living and dying forever and ever

*Kathryn Romansky*

## Books

I love to read books
even about fish hooks
Books can take you places
and to meet many faces
Books can take you to the past
'Til you're home at last
Books can take you in the dark
Or to meet a shark
Books can take you to see lots of blood
Or to see a flood
So go and read a book
Even if it is about fish hooks.

*Kristina Baker*

## Dark Dreams

Dark dreams surround me,
Filling my empty soul,
Their gift is slumber,
Rest from the hectic world,
What's the point of staying awake,
When sleep's peace beacons to me.
Tempting me to close my eyes,
Never to open them again.

*Kin Feret*

## Rain

When rain falls to the ground
Flowers weep all round,
And when I sit to pray
I hope it rains everyday.
Animals sit together in threes
under the beautiful maple trees
The dark, cloudy, gray skies
Always seem to be in disguise,
Everything is dreadfully wet
So I lie down and forget
That the clear skies are very near,
I hope the sun will hide in fear
Behind the clouds so far away
I wish it would forever stay
Even though the rain has to go,
I hang my head very low,
I know it will come back soon,
As I watch the bright moon
I close my eyes and fall asleep
As I try not to weep.

*Katie Klekamp*

## A Cowgirl's Moodswings

Vanity was put on a pedestal
For everyone to admire
Ego was prominently displayed
With a sign saying "For Hire"
Greed sat on a shelf
Its need would never tire
Passion tries to rule my life
Throwing fuel onto my fire
Sex crawls across the bed
It looks to satisfy desire
Lust frolics with love
But taking any buyer
Mood lays very low
Excitement pumping it higher
They're all looking for satisfaction
Found it?
I say you're a liar!

*Kathleen E. Speer*

## Seeking

I guess I hate myself the most
    for the cowardice inside
What happened to the courage
    that previously did reside

One morning I awoke to gray
    with fears a million-fold
and nothing left to fight them with
    Just terror in my soul

If I could find a little bit
    of what I once possessed
Perhaps I could build on it
    while searching for the rest

I've looked to therapy, friends and books
    a glimmer here and there
But nothing like the boldness
    I had when I was fair

Could be I'm afraid to find it
    To give it back it's name
Because it holds responsibility
    You sometimes win the game

*Kathy Bittle*

## Who's There?

Knock — Knock
Go away!
I'm busy, leave me alone.

Tap — tap
Who's there?
Can't someone get the door?

Rap — rap
Good grief
Can't anyone get the door?

Thump — Thump
Let's see...
It's can't be, but I'm not sure...

Click — Turn
Oh no......
Who's just entered through the door?

*Kim Kadooka*

## The Pain He Caused Me

I thought,
Having a boyfriend was great.
Except when we fought,
And said things we hate,
And wanted to kill ourselves for later.

Who thought the kid I love,
Would cause me pain.
I prayed to my God above,
And wished I would gain,
His trust and love again.

Now I'm trying to forget,
Everything we did share,
And how we first met.
It's really not fair,
That he hurt me so much.

*Kimberly Adamski*

## interracial eros

two
he and I
picture his skin, like chocolate
    shining
against mine like ivory
    glistening
I writhe in ecstasy
he lies delirious
    beneath me
urging my whisper
together
we scream
in a sordid symphony

*Kate Mollohan*

## Panther

Pacing, roaming, sinewy, taut,
his limbs flexed, then outstretched,

reaching for invisible heights
beyond his inhibiting concrete lair.

Muscles ripple as he flows
upward to another rock-hard ledge.

No jungle shadows to protect, to cool.
His eyes smolder with inner fire.

His roar reverberates, echoes;
filling the man-made jungle with rage.

*Kathy Larson*

## Untitled

I have a friend, you know His Name
His love for us is always the same
And when we sin and fall away
His loving arms reach out to say,

"The blood I shed the price I've paid
Will you believe or was it all in vain?

Giving your lives to me in part
Will only make you a half-filled heart

All of you and nothing less;
This I promise, to do the rest

The time you've spent to find your needs
The pain I felt on Calvary -

To give you true life, a living way
To guide your steps each and every day

But if you decide to hide your heart
My love for you will never depart

Don't take too long to trust in Me
The hour is coming when all will see

That half-filled hearts in disbelief
can never be washed by Calvary"

*Kelly Laratonda*

## A Small Lonely Child

A small lonely child sat alone,
His mother left him to be unknown,
His frail body cold as stone.

Be a young child, he shall not dare,
Alone in the world no one to care,
For motherly love was very rare.

A small lonely child sat alone,
His mother left him to be unknown,
His frail body cold as stone.

Marks from sins were left on each limb,
His chance at a normal life seemed dim,
He asked God to shine down on him.

A small lonely child sat alone,
His mother left him to be unknown,
His frail body cold as stone.

*Kerrie Kessler*

## Betrayed!

Bereft with grief,
I beseech you,
Busy brethren,
Please beguile me
To begin to
Believe that I
Was not betrayed
By the being
Who bestows life
And its blessings!

My broken heart
Cannot brave the
Broad boundary
or bear the big
Burden brought by
Death's brutal breach
Unless buttressed
By your bounty
and befriended
Before too long!

*Kathryn Hager*

## Lonely Love

I am so confused
I don't know what to do
No matter how hard I try
I'm still missing you
No matter what the hour
life is still so sour
Thinking of our times together
good and bad
You were always there for me before
But where are you now
When It's you I'm yearning for
How many lonely hours must
I bare
Before you turn around and care
How many more tears must I cry
Just to get a simple "hi"
I don't know why
But I guess it's true
That you don't love me
But I love you!

*Karen M. Reger*

## Small Piece of Heaven

As I come to this place on the mountain.
I ponder its space, its time.
And all who came before me
Fitting into its Rhythm and Rhyme.

As the sun began its sojourn
its brightness paved the way
she unfolded her beautiful meadow.
Grander than any written play.

The dew drops she had dancing
on the tips of meadow grass.
Their prisms laughing gaily
as if no time would pass.

In the distance the fire hole river
seemed sure of its destiny, its way
For the ocean tugged its heartstrings
A part which no man could play.

But like all within her boundaries
Like many on this earth.
I had only come to honor her.
This small piece of heaven on earth.

*Kathy Mills*

## Self Portrait

When asked to write a portrait of myself,
I sat stunned at virgin page.

No paints of color to sweep canvas,
No shadows of detail for my face.

My only instrument, my pen.
Mere words to fill the page.

I began a thousand times
To find others in my place.

I began a thousand more,
Placing strangers on my stage.

And at the end of this,
The knowledge that I gained,

Was that the portrait of myself,
Left me stunned by empty page.

*Karen Lovell*

## Untitled

It would be grand
if there were a place
a cloudy land
or pearly gates
I could call your name
and see your face
I could walk through time
of forgotten days
I hurt for this
to see the past
lives I've missed
that didn't last
my life from you
without you here
where did you go
you just disappeared
it would be grand
if there were a place
I could hold your hand
and kiss your face

*Keith A. Goddard*

## Candle of Love

A single flame burns
   In the darkness of the night
The candle stands alone
   Yet it shines so bright
I like the candle
   Am alone it's true
But burning in my heart
   Are thoughts of you
I am the candle
   You are the flame
Burning together
   As one and the same
My heart burns for your love
   Day after day
As the candles glow
   Guides our way
Eternal is the flame
   Burning bright
Lonely is my heart
   Burning for you every night

*Keri*

## Summertime Days

   I love to walk
in the sand
   and have fun,
in the sun.

   I like to sit
on the patio,
   and listen to
rock and roll
   on the radio.

   I like to
drink iced tea,
   While I sit on
a large rock
   down by the sea.

*Karen Dobson*

## Untitled

We are on top of the ocean
in the ship of life.
We can row forward,
grasping each wave as we go.
There will be storms,
but we row with all our strength,
to gain control.
Each storm we row;
each wave we grasp;
builds our character,
gives us wisdom to handle the next.
Sometimes along the way
we lose something,
When the storm rages out of control.
Eventually the calming takes over;
the peace shines through;
We again are rowing forward
in the ship of life.

*Kyra J. Mason*

## Her Daydream

She dreams that she
is all alone
On a stone in her back yard.

She thinks that she will
drift away and sway in
the air so hard.

She thinks that she is
a beautiful flower
And then an indigo veil.

She dreams she is singing
in a pond and then a
Nightingale.

Then she dreams of rich
Ice cream, as yummy as can be.

Then dreams of a beautiful
Rose, as pretty as the sea.

How beautiful she looks in
the glistening sun,
And then she woke up and
Her dream was done.

*Katie Grube*

## When Will It Be My Turn

When will it be my turn?
I've been waiting for ever.
Momma and Pappa got to go,
now it's grandma's turn.
Auntie went last year,
and just the other day Rena went.
When will it be my turn?

I've been ready for along time;
Well at least I think I'm ready.
There's nothing keeping here.
Every bodies gone now.
When will it be my turn?

I wonder what it's like.
I've heard a lot of stories about it.
I bet it's nice -
so peaceful and quite.
Even if it's not,
anything has got to be better then here.
I guess I just have to wait.
But, when will it be my turn?

*Komoia S. Johnson*

## A Sister's Prayer

God, bless my brother Jerry.
Keep him safe I pray.
Not only him, but all the men
Who go to fight today.

Watch for him, dear Lord,
As he comes marching by.
He'll be the tall one over there,
With eyes that match Your sky.

Keep him near, not for my sake,
But for his father proud,
Who awaits his son's return,
And sings Your praises loud.

Let my heart rest easy
As my mother's son
Jumps off the plane, unpacks his gear,
Then reaches for his gun.

If You see fit to let him die
While he's so far away,
Give me the grace to understand
And faith enough to pray.

*Kathryn Goins*

## Thoughts About Springtime

The soft bare breasts of earth
Lie exposed
In rows and rows
Of newly plowed ground
And all around
Are signs of spring
And natures reawakening.

What will this new year bring, my Love?
Will it bring peace and happiness;
The fulfillment of all our dreams;
A new beginning,
Or will it bring grief and tears?
For Springtime for us
May never be again.
Your precious body
May lie frozen in the ground:
If you lose this round
In your fight with cancer.

*Katrina P. Davis*

## Other Days

Here I stand;
Look ahead through the haze.
Anticipating and waiting for other days.

I've always wondered
Where I would be;
What kind of life lies ahead of me.

Here I stand;
Look behind through the haze.
Afraid to let go of other days.

My family and friends...
Always on my mind.
It seems there's so much
That I'm leaving behind.

When I move on,
When I'm out on my own,
I can always go back.
I can always come home.

Here I stand, look around me,
Through all of the haze.
I will always have with me these other days.

*Kimberly Sloan*

## Still

Brown hair worn at the shoulder
looking young, not much older
than twenty-two or three,
that's my lovely Marie.

Our little girl is six or seven
next week eight, next month eleven
or so it seems that all
my dreams have come true,
since I began with you.

And when we're old and gray haired
you will know that I have cared.
When you look at the old blue eyes
and I heave love-heavy sighs
still so much in love, Marie.

*Kenneth M. Kippels*

## The Wind

The wind rushes through the willows
	making them wail and whine.

The wind reels by the windows
	wiggling the curtains and the blind.

The wind washes briskly
	over the fields and the weeds.

The wind rustles up a wild whiff
	that makes me sneeze.

Achoooooooooooo!
Whew!

*Karen R. McClellan*

## Mother's Grief

Before the pain scar
my face, my face was full
of happiness.

Before my eyes flooded with
tears my eyes had happiness
life and hope.
The best years my son, left
me with you.
Who my son will buy my
memories, the world is getting
smaller.
who will exchange my grief
with happiness.

Nobody my son, nobody because
my memories are so great that
nothing can replace them.

*Kathy Moraitis*

## Once Was and Will Never Be

I lie naked upon the silky flesh,
my hearts pounding fast as I sweat.
Soft dim light-shadows of two-
the gentle sound of music-
the touch of me to you.
The moment is intense,
a fragrance of perfume.
A look in your eye- the stars-and moon,
and never before has such  beauty arose
As I call out to her again-
and again-I am Alone.

*Kenneth L. Murphy*

## Sunset

Like a dying flower,
my petals slowly fall.
Once so beautiful and untouched,
like the picture on my wall.
As I remember how I felt,
soaking up all sunlight.
Cherishing every minute,
as if sometime it might.
Diminish within a day,
as it surely did.
Every ounce of laughter,
was taken and safely hid.
Faster my petals fall,
With all hope I had regained
Wilted and completely bare,
alone in the darkest shade.

*Kristen Hobbs*

## Reflection Of Soul

There is a world
of opposites and parallels,
A world of moonlight
on still waters.
A world of reflections,
of magical moments
caught only in dreams.

And sometimes we
wonder what our
reflection sees.
A handsome face,
a genuine smile.
Happiness or despair,
maybe they see as we do.

Either way is just
one more soul we keep,
as long as we
keep it well.

*Kevin Crowe*

## Cherish Always (Now And Forever)

To my dearest love Jerry,
Our love is a like a magical phenomenon;
Mystical as time itself!
All our years together,
Only time stands to enhance.
Each wonderful kiss by you
Brings such great delight!
Precious is our love....
I'll cherish you always!
Happy Anniversary
Now and forever,
Eveline.

*Karen Kenyatta Moody*

## Winter Moon

The swollen glow looms,
sheathed in a glaze
of fuzzy yellow frost.
Threads of light like cobwebs
sew curtains of snow over
treetops dipped in moonlight.
Violet shadows
from smooth salmon birches
drift on the golden gloss
of lacquered snow
and gather in pools
left from a fawn's
first step.

*Kevin Longacker*

## Untitled

Trudging through the grey,
Stagnant stream of my days.
Throwing the wasted memories
Into the dying flames.
Deception leading me by the hand,
Its lowly licks
Poisoning my dripping wounds.
Caressing my needy soul,
Scratching my deepest core.
Savagely raping,
Punishing thrust,
To my bad faith.

Abandoned I stumbled into the future.
Desolation shook my hand
And welcomed me
Into it's vast mansion.
Alone spells on existence:
It could have been the wind.
It blew away an ideal, and
took you in its tightening grasp.

*Kelly Ossewaarde*

## A Woman In Distress

Unjustified pain,
suffering.
Deep down pain
needed to come out.
It surfaces,
and tears flow.
But in those tears
more pain grows -
unjustified pain
not caused by me.
Suffering.
The tears that flow
are an endless stream.
To keep it inside
would cause you to rot.
Would anyone care?
Probably not.
Unjustified pain,
suffering.

*Kimberlyn Solomon*

## Death

A void, a darkness, it
Swallows up everything
No one escapes
And yet there is no torment
Just stone, quiet, earth
There is a fear of going,
entering this place.
There is sleep but
no dreams.
There is no fighting here
no racial hate
no drugs or guns.
Why is there in life?
Live your life in full
Be good, be happy.
Everything you gain,
Will leave you in the darkness
We all enter the void.
We all become the darkness.

*Kathryn Staley*

## The Ghosts Of Now

The ghosts of now
Swoop down from the sky,
And spread throughout the land.
They will bring joy and sorrow;
Health and weakness.
Yet every person
Will be affected in a different way.
And then the ghosts
Go up in triumph,
To come another time.
We wait;
Watching.
For the ghosts of now.

*Kathleen G. Owens*

## 'Will Always Be

you will always be
the
impression left
by
the touch
of
my love

*Kurt R. Daniels*

## In the Sky

When you wake up
the sky is black
and rain is pouring down
you see puddles on the ground.

You now know what is waiting for you
you do not want to go out,
but you have to
you grab your coat and hat,
and leave your home.

Then you look up
red, orange, yellow,
green, blue, and purple
shine bright in the sky.

*Kristin Flannery*

## A Wonderful Christmas

The trees are bare
The snow lay deep on the ground
The stars are everywhere
What a wonderful Christmas

Children playing with their toys
The house is cozy and warm
Families come together praying
What a wonderful Christmas

The church bells are gaily ringing
The snow is peacefully falling
There's music in the air
What a wonderful Christmas

We celebrate the birth of Jesus
With love and understanding
Knowing he will always be with us
What a wonderful Christmas

*Kathy Lockridge*

## The Veteran

A yellow ribbon,
The symbol of our support
hangs limply,
Nailed to the tree by pride.
Faded
Tattered
No longer full and glorious
it hangs forgotten,
left to the plagues of time.
The dandelions of our life
growing pale,
Carried away by the winds
until one day a storm rages,
causing new blooms,
new ribbons
bright and full
with the glory of what they are.

Then picked
and nailed to the tree
by pride.

*Kevin J. White*

## Oklahoma Stage

Think of a broadway play
then sweep away that stage,
for now we live in a more serious age,
where props are real and gone to rubble,
the faces tired, beards grown to stubble

Think of a cowboy rodeo,
that's a different kind of show,
from that place of shattered windows,
where toys lay silent, side by side,
the little ones with nowhere to hide.

Think of oozing oil rigs,
then think of what money can't buy -
nor peace, nor any understanding
of the forces that were commanding
sad minds like we see in McVeigh,
or ones who hate with what they say.

Think of forgiveness and brotherly love,
then set the stage again.
God is watching the next act
no matter what we say is fact.

*Katherine West*

## In My Heart

In this world
There is a lot of pain
As my tears fall down
Like burning rain
These tears aren't for you
They are for my soul
Because those I love
Are trying to take control
Life is hard
Can't people see
Life hurts them
As people hurt me
I don't understand
Why my heart bleeds
Don't people know
That I too, have needs
I need love from
People in my heart
Because all life is doing
Is ripping me apart

*Kandice Miller*

## I Wish I Could See You Tonight

I'm just sitting here alone
There's no one but myself
I'm staring at the phone
Because there is no one else
It appears I lost you forever
There's nothing I can do
I'm so used to being your lover
But only one of us was true
It's been close to a year now
I admit I still disagree
I only wish I knew how
To put things where they used to be
These words are not what's true
It's the meaning that they imply
It's the only thing I can do
Because I refuse to say "good-bye"
I never thought I was wrong
I only thought I was right
I haven't seen you for so long
I wish I could see you tonight.

*Kevin Caldwell*

## My Gift

Such a special gift we all possess,
    This capacity to love.
It can lead you to the lowest place
    Or to the skies above.

It can run you down a danger path,
    With troubles high and low.
It can lead you into happiness
    With all the beauty it can show.

Many times I've often wondered
    Now I know that it can be,
Of all the gifts from God on high,
    He gave this one to me.

It must have been to show His love,
    That yes, He truly cares.
With all the problems of this world,
    He is there to share.

Alone, you say, oh no I'm not,
    For He can never leave
This human spirit, a piece of Him,
    On this, I do believe.

*Kimberly Claunch*

## Untitled

Alone in the darkness
This is silence is but a tomb
The cell that's built around me
A wall of cold and doom
This shelter of terror
I now hold so close
A vault of swelling shame
I feel I must dispose
The being that dwells inside
And the voices that echo forth
Why me? Why now? Why this?
Can't be! Can't keep! Abort!

*Kendra E. Sester*

## Reflections

Oh Society, so sick, so fierce
With toothpick axes you prod and prick
The breastplate armor of mankind's soul
To maim, to hurt, to wound, and to pierce.

*Jane Benson*

## Jesus Is Waiting

As walking through,
This weary life
What can we do,
But take it in strife

There doesn't seem much,
That we can do
Oh if only we had someone,
We could look up to

But there is a hope,
Someone is out there
He's as close as His name,
And big enough for all to share

His name is Jesus,
And He's waiting for you and me
Oh people turn to Him,
So that He may set us free

A better life is waiting,
Just around the bend
Turn your life over to God,
And His love upon you will descend.

*Kimlee Hopson*

## Reflections

Reflecting back, on the
times we spent together.

Reflecting back, on the
war stories you told.

Reflecting back, on the
day I visited you for the
last time.

Reflecting back, on the
pain on your face, the tears
in your eyes, and the sorrow
you felt.

Reflecting back, on the
words you spoke to me.

Fred, you said, "I'm waiting
to hear the angels say it's
okay to come home now".

The angels came and took you
home on Sunday, June 4, 1995.

    Rest in peace, Fred.
    Your home now.

*Kimberly Elise Henry*

## Marionette

Somebody
Upstairs
is playing with my mind
and it bothers me
they'll pull one string
force one action on me
all right
I might not be who I think I am
but I'm not who you think I am
I'm staring in a mirror
and it's shattering
cutting my eyes
making you blind
forcing my hand
blacking your reaction
somebody's breaking the Puppet's will
Who's gonna stand up for it now?

*Karen McCarthy*

## Little and New

Small and black with piercing blue eyes
Can he see?
afraid on shaky legs he cries
like he knows now he depends on me

*Karyn Ross*

## Evening Shadows

Evening shadows enfold the earth
When Day is called to rest
And Night tends her wandering children.
The closing day reveals to us
The mountains standing firm and proud
And trees whose arms are lifted high
In thanksgiving at eventide.
Thus Quiet walks near ponds and streams
Where fish and foul have taken rest.
The fragrance of each morning bud
Still lingers in the heavy air
Reminding us that morning, not long past,
Is still not long to come!
And as we watch the sun's last rays
Fade calmly in the arms of Night
We hear the wind call out to God:
"All is calm; all is quiet."
And God replies: "All is peace."

*Kenneth R. Van Gilder*

## Edge Of Insanity

Everything is standing still
When I breathe it shakes the room
I wonder shall I stay with night
and await my fatal doom

My pride is pushing in
as my mind is wanting out
my adversaries everyone
And everyone's in doubt

Remarks are to slander
ones you thought have done you wrong
you try and think of how to hate
when you've known it all along

You spite and curse and promote hate
and think your soul is on a mission
your mind didn't make the boundaries
you're just a fatal vision

*Kimberly Hicks*

## Best Friends

Thoughts, dreams, love, and all;
When we have questions,
our best friends will call.
We share secrets;
our words from the heart,
we are best friends;
and we'll never grow apart.
When we're in trouble;
and we don't know what to do,
we'll talk it over;
me and you.
We'll laugh together;
We'll have tons of fun,
when we're together;
we are as one.
We all have worries;
so much doubt,
but there is one person;
you'll tell it right out.

*Kiang Bouthsy*

## Moors

The winds of Heaven roared those days
Where around the moors I used to play
And sat beneath the strong old crag
I thought of you and Socrates.

So sometimes in an empty mood
Those flickers of light so marred
You reminded me
Mere specks are we
Oh, how you quoted the Bard!

Our days of old are not yet won
To sell my soul to life's metronome
We heed the whistling of the wind
To return whence you and I begin.

*Kelly Windsor*

## Calvary's Love

For you were shamed;
who knew no shame.
For you were mocked;
without a cause.
For you were persecuted;
when you gave love.
For you were spit upon;
when you were humble.
For you were beaten and in pain;
when you have healed many.
For you were naked before
all men; so we might be
clothed in righteousness.
For your blood was shed;
so we could have life.
For you were hung on a cross;
when your heart was broken.

Thank you Lord for taking my place
and for giving the best gift - yourself.

With love to my Savior
*Kimberly S. Daley*

## Untitled

Because
    Why not?
Forget and rot!
then,
be shot
become a blot
and off
off
to Camelot.
Where?
I forgot!

*Karin Emerson*

## Colors

We are the colors of the earth
Yellow gives birth
Brown has love
White is a spiritual dove
Blue is night
Orange is happy and bright
Green is grassy and full of hope
Gray is an ivory slope
Purple's surprising
Red is uprising
Black is exceedingly fine
I want them all to be mine

*Kristin E. Jones*

## Love Hurts

You cared for me, but I did not care.
You sang to me, but I did not listen.
You told me that I would get hurt,
but I laughed.
You cried for me, but I did not know.
You called me, but I did not answer.
You loved me, but I loved someone else.

Now I want you, but you do not realize.
I cry for you, but you do not know.
I dream of you, but it's only dreams.
I call you, but you do not answer.
I speak, but you do not hear.
I answer, but you do not care.
I should have listened, but love hurts.

*Kristi Dundas*

## Father From God

On the day I was born,
You were there to see,
What life was going to be like,
As a Godfather to me.

I was so tiny,
I was so young.
You were there to see,
Just how my life had begun.

You have always been there.
Through the good and the bad,
It is really nice having,
More than one Dad.

All through the years,
You have always been in my heart,
I'm never going to let that change,
Even though now, we are apart.

It is going to be hard,
And I'll do the best I can do,
But Don, please don't forget,
How much I love you!

*Karen Day*

## Borderlene

I remember everything...
Your face twists, taunts my dreams
I scream out in utter terror
Am I awake or is this a dream?
Reality...the edges run together
The border nears...
I've been here before
Virgin heart - first love
Falling, tumbling down
Bruised, dazed - I survived
Weary but somewhat wiser!
This,....this is different
My journey's been cruel and long
Stumbling I grasp my wounded heart
Your betrayal has ripped my world apart
Alive? Dying...yet not enough to let go
This time I leap, plunging downward
My heart wildly beats, echoing the fall
Loneliness howls beside the shore
As blackness engulfs my soul,...alone.

*Kimberly Kelling-Payne*

## Venice First Encountered (1976)

Venice — do you remember
A crowded day in midsummer
The blue August sky
Thick waves that washed the boats,
Gondolas plying their trade
In the wake of the motorized corps?

Were you laughing then
Queen of cities?
No, I think you were a little sad,
Though a faint smile
Played upon your features.
Bright still were the jewels
That shone in your hair.

Nothing surprises.  It is all there
As in the photographs.
Only close she seems a faded courtesan
Still beautiful, but best seen from afar.
What was she then once
When princes mounted her
Magnificent in white and gold?

*Eve M. Gilmore*

## My Daddy's Side

She grew up in a Southern State
A naïve girl who could not wait
To be a young lady on her own
But she found herself all alone

The preachers sermons wasn't heard
She wanted love, not God's word
Fire and brimstone she didn't fear
But loneliness would bring a tear

Her daddy tells her "you're just a child.
Don't grow up like me rough and wild."
His pleading voice tears her apart
As she leaves to follow her heart

She searched the bayous of Louisianne
And found her daddy in another man
He drank, gambled, and left her alone
She felt empty but it made her strong

She learned happiness wasn't found in men
Love was her children that she felt within
Many years later and nights she cried.
Wondering why she found her daddy's side.

*Tracy K. Johnson*

## Wild Stallion

Spun gold is the mane,
Flames are the tail.
The horse is wreathed
in shining mail.

The stallion that knows
No master or name,
and pays no heed
to bit or to rein.

On jagged peaks
Of mountains high,
He stands alone
'gainst open sky.

He is a picture
of something that's wild.
An awesome creation
in the eyes of a child.

*Renee Rall*

## "To My Wife"

Honey, dear, I love you more and more
    and more and more each day.
When I'm feeling blue,
    your loving smile lightens my day.

You are the dearest friend
    that I could ever suppose.
I am the most blessed man
    from my head to my toes.

So, my love, I pledge to you
    my undying love.
We will make it through
    with grace and strength from above.

I want to learn from the past;
    but the pain, I'll forsake it.
And take the lessons into the future.
    With you, I know I'll make it!

So, remember, dear, as you read,
    I truly love you.
And I do not ever regret
    the day that I said "I do".

*Larry Wallenmeyer*

## For Andy

Waxed eyes
and pale breath
Surround the drowning girl
her cries go unheard
in the completeness of death
waxed eyes
and pale breath
scoop the melon of her head
she will go with them now
she will join the dead

*Nina Cicero*

## "Reflections"

When the sun sets o'er the mountain
And weary I seek my rest;
'Tis then that I remember
And dream of those that I loved best.

In my dreams I see a vision
That is far beyond compare;
'Tis a vision of my dear mother
Sitting in her old arm-chair.

With her children clustered 'round her,
The Bible in her hand;
She told the wondrous story
Of the "Great and Promised Land".

I'm so grateful for these memories
That have kept me through the years;
Steadfast in truth and wisdom,
And free from grief and tears.

The lessons that she taught me
Have lingered for years untold;
Though time has passed so swiftly,
The memories never grow old.

*Esther H. Kring*

## Horizon's Dawn

On the threshold of a dream
Days of futures past
Of Diamonds and rust
Moments more to go
The coming of dawn

*Karen Severino*

## Forgotten

She sits in a chair staring all day
At a picture in her wrinkled hand
Months gone and no visits anymore
Her worn body can barely stand

She doesn't begin to understand
Why she has been left all alone
Sheltered in a place for old folks
Surrounded by people never known

Though there's three meals a day
And a roof to keep away the rain
Nothing washes away the bitterness
And no one stops by to ease the pain

I know how tough it's been for her
Across the room I see her every day
She's not the only one in this old home
That has no one to ease their way

Make friends while your young
For you'll never know when you're old
If you'll have someone to care for you
Or warm your thoughts from the cold

*Al Ward*

## A Haiku Trilogy

He touched a cherry blossom
But it's petals drifted away
    with the breeze

He touched a peach blossom
But the petals descended
    like flakes of snow

He touched an apple blossom
But the petals like silk
    became butterflies

*Sebastian*

## Stone Forest

Jagged monolithic forms
Clustered, juxtaposed
like sentinels -
Once hidden from sight
eons ago!
Nature's sculptures
Submerged millions of years,
Leaving forever evocative shapes.
With receding waters,
Now revealed to human eye,
Countless huge majestic forms
Stirring the imagination
To wonderment and awe!!

*Ruth Lubin*

## Words Like "Love"

Words silence cages
from their
lofty, dizzy flight.

Words speared
into the heartwall
before they can alight.

Majestic, monumental,
sacred in ruins:
words like Babel's Tower.

Words like "love."

*Peter Wolf*

## First Love Lost

Splintered darkness, compounded night,
Dancing in the firelight.
Depths of sorrow, heart of pain,
Happiness faded and naught to gain.
Love is lost,
Upon a churning sea my heart is tossed.
Soul of blackness, sister night,
On her silent wings of flight.
Fled is Joy, her brother, Pain,
Lying in my arms again.
Who can see the pain inside,
Behind it's darkened walls I hide.
Time is lost, a thing unknown,
As heartache sits on bony throne.
A thing of darkness I have become,
Joys and fears, I have none.
All is lost and still I hide,
Melding together my shattered pride.

**Nathan Benjamin Norris**

## Winter Freeze: Self Admonition

When winter comes,
Don't dread it.
Let it happen.
Let the waters freeze over
Let the bare oaks be covered.

Don't be afraid to become numb
The bluest waters stay warm
deep down inside.
But don't look there
For fear of what can hide
Winter is the frozen wall
Around the mind.

Don't dread it-seize this season
Let it happen-savor this feeling
Closed eyes, heart slows in rate
Cold pricks the skin, as snowflakes
decorate

That is the sign
That safety is inside
Behind the frozen wall
Of the mind.

**Becca Bredholt**

## The Pitch Of Hell

When the light fades
For one last time,
It is not the night with the moon,
It is the pitch of Hell.

The darkness envelopes you
As the Reaper's cloak is thrown,
Transporting you to a place of dark;
It is the pitch of Hell.

Your feeble presence has been crushed
By the fingers of bones that possess
The power to make the world dark;
It is the pitch of Hell.

The sleekness of the crow,
Messenger of the Devil himself,
Beholds all that is black;
It is the pitch of Hell.

Before the world was formed,
All one could see
Was the darkness of the universe;
It is the pitch of Hell.

**Robert Cameron**

## It Is Everything Above

Forever true
Forever strong
Living everywhere
It cannot be wrong
Never failing in the fight
Giving each day
With all its might
Holding on to all it can
Trying to grab every man
Hoping, bearing, believing all
All these things I say to you
For one special quality
Can pull you through
Every statement said above
Is true of only. . .
Love.

**Marlene D. Parish**

## Rolling Tymes

Panties peeking out
from under an
entirely too-short
nightgown
and they hold
up the air
and pull down
the darkness
and wrap up
tightly in
the hummm
of the electric
light outside of
the tear stained
window of the
hourly-rated
hotel
the Mona Lisa
and I cry for you

**Rachel Raybourn**

## Homeward

O' wondrous night, your bright beauty
Hidden from sight,
A haven for night creatures
Winging fearlessly homeward.

Wee, common bits of contentment
Soaring gently,
O' but mysterious infinity
What is homeward?

Gentle wisps of quiet soaring sounds
O' peace, tranquility,
Twists of time going round,
Oft times in a flurry.

A wish to whisper,
To be but a bird
And when desirous
Not to be seen or heard.

Tiny creatures, hark! 'Tis but life,
To be lived, conquered, amidst much strife,
You are free to settle, to fly, to flee,
But forever, Homeward.

**Merrie L. Anderson**

## Shades

As love flickers and fades
Life turns to grey shades.
**Kyle Kirby**

## Untitled

Snowflake.
How do we
distinguish the
difference.  DO
We?  Or do we
just accept
Their individualized
beauty as a
lovely
thing.
how do
We
look upon
ourselves
the same?

**Justin Soles**

## A Forgiven Love

Don't turn away, please don't turn away.
I have to know why you hurt me so.
I love you now, I always will.
My love for you my love be still.
My dreams have faded away.
Please don't turn away
I know you were untrue
But I still love you.

Don't turn away, please don't turn away.
I have to know, why you hate me so.
I remember that day you were untrue.
But don't turn away, my love be true.
Please tell me now, you love me still
You love me now and always will.
I love you so please let me know
Why you hurt me so.

**Priscilla Garate**

## As Death Lay Before Me

As death lay before me,
I hear the painful agony
of a distant echoing cry,
that soon begins to die.

All the cries begin to fade,
and soon become a grayish shade
of darkness growing ever bleak,
as the Strong become the Weak.

Paralyzed with mortal fear,
I slowly shed a salty tear—
wondering who is at blame,
but know that we must share the shame;
because no one person is at fault,
and our society must be taught
to always abide by our own heart,
and do what's right in our own small part.

We have to learn that violence is not the key,
it will only unlock more misery;
and in the end we all will die,
as our deaths roll slowly by.

**Megan Hogan**

## Untitled

I love you mom and dad.
"I love you Tyrone! You do?"
"Yes we do Tyrone!"
I love you Mom and Dad.
I love you too, Tyrone.
Tyrone, we love you too.
I love spring!
My Mom loves spring.
My Dad loves spring.
I love spring I love spring!
Danez loves spring too.
My Mom loves it too.
I love spring!
My Dad loves spring too,
Devon loves spring too.
Maurice Mahoney loves spring too.
I love spring too!
It is fun.
Spring loves me.

*T. Bynum*

## Screaming

Running into adolescence
I waited,
I poured my life onto a lined page.
Hear me...
marching blindly into
womanhood,
I scrutinized my very existence
on a cocktail napkin.
Hear me...
Where were you? I've been
waiting for you.
Because you are filled
with the thoughts of the world,
you enter into mine
...because you are filled
with thoughts...
And the friendship that was locked
up inside my head
screaming...
has made it into my heart.

*Debbie Shields*

## Untitled

Deep inside the butters flew,
I wishing they would cease.
For tomorrow was a day anew,
filled with awful beasts.
Why must one be measured?
To suit the world's design.

*Melissa Nivens*

## Untitled

If only you could be me
If only for just a moment
To see what is me.

But only for a moment
Because me
Is not a pleasant place to be.

For you to see inside
You must enter
By earning the right to enter.

I wish for you to try
For once inside
You will see the tears I cry.

*Wendy L. Stalder*

## Left Behind

Love, please come to help me!
I'm dying in my own tears!
I thought nothing to be wrong
his leaving confirmed my fears

The way he smiled
it drove me wild
the way he left,
was like a theft

He tore all innocence from me
then stole off with my heart
even though he didn't love me
it killed me to see him part

*Lani Hoopiiaina*

## Untitled

Life
Joyful, adventurous
Exciting, moving, uplifting
Adults, children, shadows, grave
Vanishing, boring, expired
Lonely, dark
Death

*Zachary Fox*

## Lilacs

Mirrored in tables
lilacs spill perfume
over portraits of young girls
caught in silver frames
a still life
recalling mornings
when curls
laced with sun and satin
slapped at the wind

When girls in pastels
wild flowers in the grass
playing hopscotch
jump rope
blind man's buff
paused to rest
among lilacs
beneath clusters
of amethyst stars

*Patricia P. Adam*

## Untitled

Come to my land
My land of secrets
Where all lies known to everyone
We know the secrets
The ones of the moon
And sky
And stars.

The wonderful land
The land of secrets
Where all lies known to everyone
We know the stories of
Suns and
Stars and
Mystical lands.

*Brandon Baruch*

## Face

Eyes
Nose
Hair
It is a face.

Look beyond,
Farther and deeper.

You can't; you don't
     want to.
You're blind.

Scream!
Yell!
Cry!

You are still blind!

*Jennifer Shirah*

## Nightlight

Don't look now but the moon is full
Rendering life to the inearthed soul.
They arrive to posses the living
Securing your fears of night
By giving courage and fearlessness
With added extra daylight;
For those who walk in disbelief
Or subdue this eerie fright
You can just think of this moon
As your own personal nitelite.

*Robert Keith Van Wagoner*

## Plagued

I am plagued with self-doubt
self-conflict
and inner turmoil
searching
trying to escape
the life of hatred
the only life I know
trying to reach out
but failing to find anyone
I can't afford escape
I refuse to pull the trigger
and yet I seek refuge
from the storms
hovering around me
Like bombs ready to explode
I am plagued
tortured by mental torment
and agony
a manic depressive
trapped by self-doubt

*Jill Flickinger*

## Dragon

From the sky descending,
The chill of death impending,
The midnight dragon drops.
All the king's men sending
Orders for defending
The shining castletops.

Talon meets sword,
Incautious men are gored.
The battle rages on.
But the knights defend their lord,
And with a final, painful chord,
The dragon is now gone.

*J. Drelb*

## What Is White?

White is eggs,
sugar, sour cream,
clouds in the sky
and vanilla ice cream
White is milk and flour
in pancakes
White is the cold snow that
looks like mashed potatoes
White is cotton like popcorn
White is the tune of piano keys
White is your shiny teeth
White is paint and creamy
whipped cream
White is the bright daisies in the
beautiful garden
White are the stars in the
dark blue sky.

*Steph Royden*

## Untitled

The olive is picked from the branch
The apple falls, rolls on the ground
The avenues ones life will take
Will be noticed on the day of their wake

*K. Pete Peterson*

## Love

When I walk on
The Beach
And gaze at the Sea
It's your face
Mirrored in God's Wonder I see
And then
When this walk we share
Heavenly music fills the air
We are as one in tune with
God and Time

*Betty B. Broadbent*

## Clouds

Upon the crested hill
The clouds gently roll,
Gathering momentum with each swirl
As toward the east they go.

Soft as cotton candy
White as new fallen snow,
Reach out and touch them, but no
They slip out of your hand.

Gliding, twisting and rolling
They dance like dewdrops on grass,
And away they go
Far, far to the east.

Over another hill
Across the distant mountain,
They travel the sky highway
To their final destination.

*Gellia Garner Hunt*

## So Lovely Are The Lilacs

So lovely are the lilacs in early spring,
Ones lonely heart begins to sing,
What a very fragrant little thing!
Such a joy they seem to bring,
So beautiful are the lilacs in spring.

*Greg M. Ciesnicki*

## Soaring

The blue jay flies
through the air
And onto the tree

I wish I could fly
as does he

Wouldn't that be
wonderful for me

*Donzelle Finazzo*

## Time Will Tell

Time is never-ending
Time is pending
Time stands still while
Time flies by
Time is of the essence
Time is your limit
Time you start doing something with it
Time will make friends
Time will make enemies
Time will make you rich
Time will spend your pennies
Time brings fame
Time brings sorrow
But most important time brings tomorrow
Time is on your side
It's a race against the clock
Time is forever
But there is never enough
Time will tell

*Robert E. Moore III*

## Forever and Beyond

Like vines of ivy,
we are interwoven,
Entangled in our own web,
As the world falls to pieces,
at our very feet,
We are engrossed in each other

You are my life,
and I am your existence,
Together - we are one,
When we are apart,
the stars leave the sky,
And the darkness closes in on our lives

As the darkness envelopes us,
and our world caves in,
We cannot live separate lives,
Ours is one - in life or in death,
together - forever and beyond.

*Heidi Smith*

## Life Is Like.....

Life is like a box of chocolates
Not knowing what's in store
The American Dream is on our minds
Along with love ones we adore.

Life is like a flowing stream
Rough yet smooth alike
The strenuous work of a hectic day
And the peacefulness of night.

*Kristopher Gutierrez*

## Peggy's Task

Immigrant Peggy
went with children three
into
unknown territory

Laborer Peggy
worked three meals a day
rented
one room upstairs in the bay

Warrior Peggy
sent them to the country
safety
was her goal for three

Mother Peggy
brought them home again
schooled
her daughters to attain

Weary Peggy
said "I'm through
dear ones
the rest is up to you"

*K. M. Crisp*

## Untitled

As the bus pulled away, I watched
you walking down the street and
thought of the moment we just shared.
The "final farewell" the hug that in
reality last only a moment, yet
will last in our heart for a lifetime
As I remembered this moment, I wanted
to get up and scream out the
window, "I love you, Sara!  I love you!"
But instead I sat there in the cold
seat by the window and watched you.
I watched you walking down the street
with your head up and spirits high
and tried to figure out what you were
thinking.  Were you thinking like I was?
Were you thinking we promised we'd
write, visit, and call even though it
will eventually fade away?  We made it
through one summer apart.  Surely we
can make it through another.  Can't we?

*Laura Piccione*

## Walk Beside Me

Always walk beside me
You're more than just a friend
Let me feel the tenderness
Of your gentle hand

Sitting by the fire aside
Listening to the rain
If you were not beside me
It wouldn't mean a thing

Sunny days and blue skies
Flowers in full bloom
Your roses in our garden
With drops of morning dew

Fragrance of the jasmine
At night beneath full moon
Breezes softly blowing
Casting their perfume

All these times I treasure
And I want you to know
I'll always walk beside you
No matter where we go

*Holly Smith*

## Loneliness

The lady waits by
the water, day after day
as the tide rolls in
and the tide rolls out.  A
single white dove flutters
above the water where
the lady waits, the
water empty of sail,
empty of hope, empty of
love.

*Amy Hufnagel*

## "Christine"

Now that I know you're leaving
my heart cries with sadness
and in my mind I will keep you always
because you are part of me.

With your hazel eyes
and your tender lips
although they never were mine
I will kiss you in my mind
even in my dreams
when I am in my sleep.

With your little tail
that you make with your hair
I like to touch and play
with it in the air
just to keep you close
to my body in despair.

So you will go far away from me
but your essence will stay in my heart
and forever live the rest of my life
with your presence in my mind.

*Angel L. Garcia*

## Untitled

The sheets lay loose
across my flesh
   worn and soft by
   time and dreams.
You drift, silently
into the edges of consciousness
I always meet you there
my heart it hears you closer still.
Forever hold you
once my flesh
come to me thru
time and dreams
you breathe, gently
God's grace across my writing heart.
He always meets us there
and lets our hearts beat closer still.

*Angela Davis Lane*

## Lady Bengal

They never
let her out of the cage
where she paces
relentlessly,
alone.

Amber coals
glow deeply into the night
until a smoky veil
drops dreams of men
to haunt her feline heart.

Upon the infinity
of concrete she waits,
uncomprehending
mortal fears. Then
one day at feeding time

feeling rather frisky,
Lady reaches out...
leaving a Panthera tigris
calling card

on a man she just wanted to touch.

*B. A. VanderBoom*

## Flowers Say It Best

Today————I had the most wonderful time,
And I never even spent the price of a dime.

"Ah," you say, "Please, please come on here;
What did you do that caused you such cheer?"

I went back to the place where I'd worked in the past
To see old friends, converse and laugh—it was a blast!

And I passed out flowers one by one,
Passed them out, 'till all were gone.

You should have seen the smiles on their faces,
And gloom, there weren't to be found any traces.

There were all smiles, as I passed along,
And in my heart there was joy and a song.

Many of them said, "We've been expecting you."
And I am glad that I made it all come true.

I am so glad that Our Father in Heaven above,
Shines on His children through flowers of "LOVE!"

*Wayne Wallace*

# BIOGRAPHIES

**ABDULLOH, DEBORAH**
[pen.] Debbie Rutherford; [b.] June 8, 1956, Cinti, OH; [p.] Thomas and Janet Rutherford; [m.] Amin Abdulloh, July 12, 1986; [ch.] Joshua, Rachel; [ed.] Withrow High, Xavier University; [occ.] Work at home, Mom; [memb.] St. Paul A.M.E. Church - Cinti, Ohio. Serve on the Steward board, the Missionary Society and Finance Committee.; [oth. writ.] Wrote while in college, but never pursued to publish anything; [pers.] "Let your light so shine before men, that they may see your good works, and glorify your father which is in heaven." Matt. 5:16; [a.] Forest Park, OH

**ABNEY, JOSEPH J.**
[b.] August 16, 1973, Bronx, NY; [p.] Pearlie M. Abney; [ed.] Montclar High School, Oral Roberts University; [occ.] Elementary School Teacher; [hon.] Dean's List - ORU; [oth. Writ.] "I Won't Burn", "Game Over", "The Grace Of That Man"; [pers.] You must believe in yourself, when there is unbelief there is no hope, no life. I think the struggle and the fight must go on. Don't get too comfortable. We are not there yet.; [a.] Ontario, CA

**ADLER, JOANNA**
[b.] December 31, 1976, Oceanside, NY; [p.] Angela and Mark Adler; [ed.] Oceanside H.S. (graduated June 1995), presently attending Binghamton University; [occ.] Full time student; [pers.] Though just a bud on the great tree of life, my time to blossom will come with the new day.; [a.] Oceanside, NY

**AGUILON, JENNIFER ANN CUIZON**
[b.] February 9, 1956, Pasay City, Philippines; [p.] Daniel F. Aguilon and Rosetta Aguilon; [ed.] St. Mary's Academy (Philippines) Philippine School of Business Administration (Philippines); [occ.] Administrative Assistant and Bookkeeper; [oth. writ.] Several poems, unpublished; [pers.] I have an enormous belief in the goodness of mankind.; [a.] Cerritos, CA

**AHERNE, ALLEN**
[b.] September 23, 1949, Brooklyn, NY; [p.] Harriet and Robert Aherne; [m.] Eileen Aherne; [ch.] Andrew and Evan; [ed.] Masters Degree, Teachers College, Columbia University; [occ.] Teacher; [oth. writ.] Include a variety of poetry and composition; [pers.] The mind divides, the heart unites, poetry transcends; [a.] Sea Cliff, NY

**AKERS, JIMMY LEE**
[b.] June, 1961, Houston, TX; [p.] Harold and Marie Akers; [m.] Carol Akers, June 17, 1995; [ch.] Chris, Sheila, Brian; [occ.] Offshore-Drilling Rig; [pers.] The poems I write are about life and love and learning to take both hand in hand with Crist for a better today and tomorrow. I dedicate them to God and my wife Carol for without them I would never have written them.; [a.] Livingston, TX

**AKERS, GARY**
[pen.] Gary Akers; [b.] July 23, 1944, Hollywood, CA; [p.] William and Mary Akers; [ed.] Long Beach Polytechnic High School, Chouinard Art Institute, Long Beach City College, Calif. State University Fullerton; [occ.] Custodian; [memb.] Calif. Scholarship Federation 1961; [hon.] Bank America Award of Excellence in Art 1962; [pers.] Despite my troubled past I have hoped that thru art I can confront and penetrate the darkness. In a small pond we can see both the slime below and the reflection of the sky.; [a.] Anaheim, CA

**ALBERT II, ROBERT E.**
[pen.] Red Ace; [b.] December 23, 1975, Riverside, CA; [p.] Robert Albert, June Albert; [ed.] Truman High, The Joe Herndon Area Vocational-Technical School; [occ.] Unemployed; [oth. writ.] I have many

other stories and poems that have not been published yet.; [pers.] I dedicate my poem to my family and the many families out there. I write my poems from within my heart even if it's affected by my surroundings...; [a.] Independence, MO

**ALEXANDER, MURIEL W.**
[m.] Herbert Camitta (by 1st), Ralph E. Alexander; [ch.] Bruce Camitta, Hugh Douglas Camitta, Kristin Zimet Kristin Zimet; [ed.] Graduated Packer Collegiate Institute, Brooklyn, NY and Goucher College, Baltimore, MO, Poetry studies with Dr. Whalen, Goucher, A. Kreymborg, NYC and L. Speyer, Columbia University, NY; [pers.] Enjoying best of two worlds, living in Rochester, NYC and Rochester, NY. Busy with old and new friends, managing two households and trying to remember birthdays, anniversaries, zip codes and phone numbers.

**ALFARO, RICHARD**
[pen.] Rick; [b.] December 26, 1961, New York; [p.] Richard Alfaro, Ramona Alfaro; [ch.] Keith Richard; [ed.] Hicksville High School, Five Towns College, ARTI Recording Studio; [oth. writ.] Several other poems and songs but none are in publication at current time. I am hoping several more will be in publication soon.; [pers.] I write from my heart and soul on life experiences. I dedicate this insert to my first son Troy who died at birth and my second son Keith Richard who has inspired me to go on.; [a.] Bayside, NY

**ALLEN, SANDRA**
[pen.] Sand; [b.] January 7, 1953, Denver, CO; [p.] Raymond and Jean High; [m.] Fred Allen, March 6, 1971; [ch.] Barbara Jean; [ed.] Widefield High School, Colorado Mountain College; [occ.] Homemaker/Volunteer; [memb.] Central Colorado Mine, Rescue Station, Oro City-Miners; [hon.] Outstanding Service 1982, Central Colorado Mine Rescue Station, July 7th and 8th, 1988 Oro City Miners for best display and costumes, as well in 1993 write up in the Herald Democrat Feb. 24, 1995, Quiet Volunteer; [oth. writ.] 5 years friendship, published in Piera, due for release in February, 1996; [pers.] Be happy with yourself on the inside for it will show on the outside, giving you the chance to accept the flows and imperfections in yourself and others, a fair hand for yourself and others; [a.] Leadville, CO

**ALLEN, MAXINE**
[pen.] Maxine Allen; [b.] March 10, 1937, Montgomery, AL; [p.] Lylian Bernice Richardson; [ch.] Anthony, Philip, Teresa, Eric, Katherine; [ed.] Rosati Kain and Sumner High School, Forest Park Comm. College; [occ.] Writer; [hon.] Numerous awards and honors from Poetry performances; [oth. writ.] Published a small collection of poems titled, "What's Loving A Black Man"; [pers.] "Words to me are the wings of the spirit, transporting you to a higher sphere, there you meet and become acquainted with the essence of your soul and know the power that life holds."; [a.] Saint Louis, MO

**ALLISON, KRISTEN ELIZABETH**
[b.] January 30, 1982, Louisville, KY; [p.] Jim and Barbara Allison; [ed.] Barret Traditional Middle School; [memb.] Middletown United Methodist Youth Choir, Four Musketeers, Beta Club; [a.] Louisville, KY

**ALUMBAUGH, BETTY D.**
[b.] January 13, 1928, Pittsburg, KS; [p.] Lavon and Ivan Gruver; [m.] Carl Alumbaugh (Deceased), August 8, 1948; [ch.] (Daughter) Karen Lavon, (Son) Randall Lee (deceased), and Grandson Jason Lee; [ed.] Lamar MO High School Lamar, MO; [occ.] Worked for many years for Southwestern Bell Tel Co, also Michi-

gan Bell Tel Co., and Mountain States Tel Co. and Richards Gebaur Air Base; [oth. writ.] Have written many poems. Do some art work, and like music very much. Also like to read, attend church and be with friends. This poem was inspired by friends, Ruth and Glen Teters and Wedding.; [pers.] It seems there's so much violence around, that if people would listen to some good music, or poetry or do some art work, they would be much more peaceful. The arts seem to have a calming effect.; [a.] Kansas City, MO

**ALVAREZ, JOSE MANUEL**
[b.] April 22, 1980, Brooklyn, NY; [p.] Jose Alvarez, Lidia Alvarez; [ed.] Cox Highs Shool Grade 10; [occ.] Student; [memb.] Concert Band, Marching Band, YADAPP (Youth Awareness Drug Abuse Prevention Program); [hon.] 6th grade Reflections Contest, Awarded Superior Concert and Marching Band for High School; [oth. writ.] Mother's Day Letter published in Newspaper (Virginia Pilot, May 14, 1995); [pers.] Never give up, each step you take is a new beginning. It may seem helpless but keep on going for the gold.; [a.] Virginia Beach, VA

**AMES, JANICE MAURINE**
[pen.] Janice Maurine Ames; [b.] April 30, 1936, Sioux City, IA; [p.] Clara and Maurice Ames; [ed.] Kansas State College, Manhattan, Kansas; [occ.] Entertainer, Singer, Farm Manager; [memb.] United Congregational Church of Christ, I sing with the Mearl Lake Orchestra in Sioux City, Iowa Gospel Singing, T.V. shows thruout the world; [hon.] Miss Sioux City, 1st Runner up Miss Iowa, Watch For His Light, the poem in this book is also a song, Gordon James of Dallas, Texas wrote the music, I wrote the words, I sing this song in my Gospel Shows.; [oth. writ.] Over 200 poems "The Sea" in 1990, Silver Poet Award published in World Treasury of Golden Poems and "The Golden Key", Golden Poet Award in 1987, Honorable Mention in Great American Poetry Anthology, both published by John Campbell; [pers.] I've traveled the world over entertaining. I was in the Stardust Hotel Lounge with Don Cornell in Las Vegas. I've also worked many Cruise Ships and was in the Far East entertaining the military and private clubs seven different times. Everywhere I'd go I'd try to assist mankind and many times I'd be inspired to write a poem to help someone.; [a.] Sloan, IA

**AMES, JANICE MAURINE**
[b.] April 30, 1936, Sioux City, IA; [p.] Clara and Maurice Ames; [ed.] Kansas State College, Manhattan, KS; [occ.] Entertainer, Singer, Farm Manager; [memb.] United Congregational Church, I sing with the Mearl Lake Orchestra in Sioux City, IA. Gospel singing in churches various TV shows throughout the world; [hon.] Miss Sioux City, 1st Runner up Miss Iowa, Watch Forttis Light - the poem I'm sending in is also a song - Gorden James of Dallas, TX wrote the music and I write the words - I sing this song in my Gospel shows; [oth. writ.] Over 200 poems. The Sea in 1990, Silver Poet Award published in World Treasury of Golden Poems and The Golden Key Golden Poet Award in 1987, Honorable Mention in Great American Poetry Anthology - both published by John Campbell; [pers.] I've traveled the world over entertaining. I was in the Stardust Lounge with Don Cornell in Las Vegas. Also I've worked many Cruise Ships and was in the far east entertaining the military seven times. Everywhere I'd go I'd try to assist mankind and many times would be inspired to write a poem to help someone; [a.] Sloan, IA

**AMICK, JESSICA JO**
[pen.] Angel; [b.] October 16, 1977, Phoenix, AZ; [p.] Christine and Dale Amick; [occ.] Working on modeling career, and acting career; [hon.] National Physical Fit-

ness Award and Volleyball Award in School; [oth. writ.] I write alot of poems and stories; [pers.] I have always been very creative and love to share my poems for different people to interpret if differently.; [a.] Phoenix, AZ

**ANDERSON, MERRIE**
[pen.] Merrie Anderson Ayers; [b.] Hawaii; [p.] Ducat, Gordon and M. Marjorie; [m.] Widow; [ch.] Russell, Richard, Randall; [ed.] Redlands High School, Valley College; [occ.] Self-horse Breeding; [memb.] American Horse Show Association, Arabian Horse Association; [oth. writ.] First novel completed, currently working on second, numerous poems, articles; [pers.] I like to write fiction, of characters in peril with emotional conflicts and trauma, but with perseverance find their dreams do come true; [a.] San Bernardino, CA

**ANDERSON, AJA JAVAE**
[b.] April 13, 1982, Washington, DC; [p.] Mr. and Mrs. Tony and Toni Anderson; [ed.] Dwight Englewood, 8th Grade Englewood, NJ; [pers.] Poetry has always had a special place in my heart. It always will.; [a.] Teaneck, NJ

**ANDERSON, ONETA, A**
[b.] January 16, Harrold, TX; [p.] Abner C. and Grace Ashley; [m.] George W. Anderson, December 20, 1941; [ch.] Gayle Masarie, Carol Fatook, Granddaughters, Anne, Helene and Jennifer Poo, Heidi Betha Susannah Masarie; [ed.] Master's in El. Adm.; [occ.] Retired El. Prin.; [memb.] Delta Kappa Gamma; [oth. writ.] Published in 1940 and 1941 in North Texas (Student Mag. of North Texas State, Denton, TX; [a.] Saginaw, MI

**ANDERSON, MARY LOUISE**
[pen.] Louise Cooper; [b.] June 2, 1980, Waltham, MA; [p.] Roland Anderson, Carol Anderson; [ed.] Still attending Waltham High School, and have graduated from Kennedy Middle School, and T. R. Plympton Elementary School; [memb.] Member of Y.O.U. (Youth Opposed to Using), and The First Baptist Church of Waltham; [oth. writ.] Small poems that I never published or even thought of publishing.; [pers.] I try very hard to express what has happened in my life on to paper. I am a strong believer in writing about what you know about.; [a.] Waltham, MA

**ANDERSON, STAFFORD I.**
[b.] July 15, 1941, Jamaica, WI; [m.] Daphne, September 13, 1970

**ANDERSON, LISA**
[b.] October 2, 1976; [ed.] Audubon High School, Douglass College at Rutgers University in New Brunswick; [occ.] Student; [memb.] Douglass Scholar's Program; [oth. writ.] Poetry in Rutgers University Anthology; [a.] Audubon, NJ

**ANDRESS, JAMIE**
[b.] November 1, 1952, Oxnard, CA; [p.] Joann and John Danch; [m.] Widow; [ch.] Robin, Jesse, Caleb; [occ.] Mother; [pers.] I live by the grace, mercy and power of God through Jesus, my Friend, Savior and King.; [a.] Ojai, CA

**ANDREWS, JAYAN**
[pen.] Jay Andrews; [b.] November 29, 1957, Chittadi, Mundakayam, Kerala, India; [p.] V. C. Andrews and Annamma Andrews; [m.] Tissy Jayan Andrews, September 21, 1987; [ch.] Five year old daughter Punnya Ann Andrews (Pet name, Donnu); [ed.] Bachelor of Science in Electrical Engineering from Regional Engineering College, Calicut, Kerala, India. Professional Development Certificates in: 1) Project Mgmt, 2) Building Electrical Design from New York University,

New York, now doing graduate Prourm in Energy Mgmt at Nyit Old Westbury, NY; [occ.] Energy Auditor, Westchester-Putnam Affirmative Action Program, 901, N. Broadway, White Plains, NY; [memb.] 1) 'Karuna' - Non profit organization doing charity work around the world, 2) Participating member in 'Sargavedi' Literary Organization of Keralites in New York, 3) 'St. Gregorios Orthodox Church' (Malankara Syrian) Bronx, New York; [hon.] 1) Got award and first prize for best among Malayalam (Mother Tongue) poems published in Periodicals in New York conducted by Federation of Kerala Associations in N. America, 1994, 2) Second best poem in Malayalam contest conducted World Malayali Conference in NJ in 1995; [oth. writ.] Stories and poems in local newspapers, periodicals, souvenirs etc., etc.; [pers.] I like to reflect the beauty of nature and love that makes human hearts vibrant; [a.] New Rochelle, NY

**ANGELO, SUAN**
[b.] July 10, 1943, Denton City, TX; [p.] Wm. P. and Lera Shugart; [m.] A. W. Angelo, July 7, 1979; [ch.] Jana Lynn, Emily Kay; [ed.] North Texas State; [occ.] Retired from Banking after 25 years; [memb.] St. George Orthodox Church, Golfcrest Country Club; [pers.] I believe poetry is a very personal expression of emotions, some easily related, others more difficult. The format allows tenderness to passion, or love to rage, to be expressed by the writer almost as easily as an artist may use the canvas.; [a.] Pearland, TX

**APPLEGATE, ELIZABETH**
[b.] March 11, 1974, Bremerton, WA; [p.] Robert and Judith Applegate; [ed.] Ledyard High School, Wheelock College, Boston, MA; [occ.] Student, soon to be elementary teacher; [hon.] Dean's List - 3 years; [pers.] I write poetry to glorify the Lord Jesus Christ and to tell others what He has done for me. It is He who gave me the gift of poetry.; [a.] Gales Ferry, CT

**APPLETON, NAOMI**
[p.] Benjamin J. and Jane H. Johnson; [m.] H. L. Appleton, August 6, 1934; [ch.] John L. Appleton and Edna L. Jones; [ed.] High School; [occ.] Retired; [pers.] I have always loved poetry but never attempted to write any until recently. My favorite poem is "If" by Kipling.

**ARCHER JR., TIMOTHY T.**
[pen.] Taig Archer; [b.] July 13, 1977, Mobile, AL; [p.] Anne and Tim Archer; [ed.] St. Dominic's Elementary School, McGill-Toolen High School; [occ.] Foreman's Aid, Lipford Construction, Mobile; [hon.] McGill-Toolen Honor Roll; [pers.] I am influenced strongly by my fiancee, Christy, and my family. My writings reflect the love that I have for those I care about.; [a.] Mobile, AL

**ARMSTRONG, MICHAELA**
[b.] January 11, 1952, West Lafayette, IN; [p.] William and Francesca Hartnett; [ed.] Elementary Education B.S. SUNY, Plattsburgh, N.Y. (Masters of Education) M.Ed. University of Illinois, Champaign, Urbana; [occ.] Kindergarten Teacher; [memb.] Association for the Education of Young Children (National and Iowa), Smithsonian Institute, National Geographic Society, Iowa Reading Association; [oth. writ.] Curriculum writing in Science, Social Studies and Language Arts for Elementary Teachers in our school district; [pers.] One of my goals is to immerse my students in literature, highlighting the various voices and cultures of the world. We do a great deal of reading, writing and story telling in our daily lives within our community.; [a.] Iowa City, IA

**ARMSTRONG, JILL**
[b.] July 8, 1982, Muncie, IN; [p.] Loretta and Steve Armstrong; [pers.] Thank you to Mrs. Losco for getting me interested in writing poetry. Also my family for supporting me.; [a.] Muncie, IN

**ARNOLD, FREIDA LOUISE**
[b.] March 8, 1927, Charleston, WV; [p.] Clara and Ben Van Bibber; [m.] Charles M. Arnold, February 4, 1946; [ch.] Forrest Arnold, Marsha Greathouse, Katrina Kelly, Lee Arnold; [ed.] Graduated from Stonewall Jackson High in Charleston WV; [occ.] Ex-Psychiatric Aide Tech. now retired; [oth. writ.] I have over 50 poems I have written; [pers.] God gives me the inspiration to write these, I could not do it on my own.; [a.] Spencer, WV

**ARSELL, VALETTA**
[pen.] Val Arsell; [b.] July 31, 1943, Brooklyn, NY; [p.] Donald, Valetta Secor; [m.] John E. Arsell, April 11; [ch.] Tracey, Donald, Craig, Amy Arsell; [ed.] H.S., School of Nursing; [occ.] L-Practical Nurse, Working in an intermost office, 15 yrs at a nursing home; [memb.] Calvary Lutheran Church-Liny; [pers.] I strive for families, friends and relatives to understand old age loneliness and love for others at all times.

**ARSHT, EDWIN D.**
[pen.] Eda - E. D. Arsht; [b.] October 6, 1929, Philadelphia, PA; [p.] Sylvia Arsht (Nee Dick), Samuel J. Arsht; [m.] Susan E. Arsht (Nee Edelstein), February 3, 1991; [ed.] Central High School of Phila, AB 1947, Swarthmore College (PA) BA (Zoology) 1951, Thomas Jefferson Univ. Med. College (Phila) M.D. 1955 Rotating Internship and Gen'l Practice Residency, 1959; [occ.] Family Physician (M.D.) and Medical Director Harlee Manor Nursing Home; [memb.] American Medical Association, American Academy of Family Physicians, American Medical Directors Assoc., American Geriatric Society; [hon.] Certified by American Board of Family Practice, Charter Member and Diplomate, 1970, Fellow American Academy Family Physicians, 1971, Certified Medical Director, Long Term Care 1993 (AMDA); [oth. writ.] Psychological Approaches to family practice: A primary care manual, 1979 (Joint Author) Lib. of Cong. ISBN0-8391-1327-7 Rebuttal Article Bulletin Federation of State Medical Boards, 1984; [pers.] The more things change, the more they stay the same. All change is not progress for which the ultimate goal is peace...; [a.] Springfield, PA

**ARTHUR, MARY E. (HILL)**
[ed.] R.N. and college Cr. am pub. author of some short story form (poetry) service adventures "Army Basics"; "Hut Mates"; "Troop Ship"; "Troop Train"; "10th Replacement Center"; "P.O.E."; "Stainless Steel"; "Midnight Convoy"; and more; [occ.] Retired R.N. Writer S/S; [pers.] This poem is in memory of two special officers I met in service who felt this way about me by the way they treated me. One was at P.O.E. Oct. 14 '44; the other at 10th Replacement Cntr. later in England. They remain in my heart and I've kept their love letters. And have many mementos of service adventures.; [pers.] Without challenge what would life be?; [a.] Shippensburg, PA

**ARTIGA JR., FRANK**
[b.] March 24, 1972, Los Angeles; [p.] Frank and Sonia Artiga; [ed.] Cal Poly Pomona University, BSCE; [occ.] Civil Engineer; [memb.] ASCE, NSPE; [hon.] Several poetry contests (local and at school); [oth. writ.] The unaddressed letters, several local writings in paper; [pers.] With my growth in age, I have grown in wisdom. And as such I relate my views of life to all those who may share the same ideals.; [a.] Maywood, CA

**ARVANITIS, NICHOLAS P.**
[pen.] Perastikos; [b.] February 12, 1929, Greece; [p.] Panagiotis Maria; [m.] Alexia Arvanitis, November 17, 1993; [ch.] Peter, Angela, and Christ (from ex marriage); [ed.] B.S. of Mechanical Engineering; [occ.] Retired; [memb.] Ahepa Organization Greek Orthodox Church of St. Nactarios from 1962; [hon.] Charter Oak High School 1982 Advisory Council on Engineering; [oth. writ.] My Own Love, 18 Volume 250 pages each written in Greek language. 5 volume published Greece Nov. 1993 (Greek National Library). 1SBN-960-08-0025-1. One volume with 125 pages in English not published yet.; [pers.] The Book, don't doubt about anything you want to learn correct. The book is a foundation stone of knowledges which build your pyramid of life (Reach For It); [a.] Desert Hot Springs, CA

**ASH, JAMES L.**
[pen.] Martha Bush; [b.] November 5, 1949, Sanford, FL; [p.] James Johnson, Leona Johnson; [ed.] Crooms Academy, DeKalb Tech; [occ.] Junior Apprentice Mechanic, MARTA; [memb.] Chamber of Commerce, Beulah Baptist Church, America Homebase Business Association; [pers.] I love writing poetry, articles, and at the present time working on a book. I plan to write on a variety of Christian subjects. I'm a born-again believer in Jesus, my Lord.; [a.] Decatur, GA

**ASKEW, LINDA**
[pen.] Linda Loo-Loo; [b.] September 29, 1957, Pedro, OH; [p.] Dallas Carmon and Lillian Carmon; [ch.] Sheena Marie Jones and Kelli Ann Askew; [ed.] Ironton High; [occ.] Original Pancake House (Waitress); [oth. writ.] I have written over 100 unpublished poems; [pers.] From a child I have always loved poetry, therefore, my goal is to publish a book of poetry to be dedicated to my children; [a.] Deerfield Beach, FL

**ATKINSON, ROLANDO**
[b.] November 30, 1972, WI; [p.] Wayne and Donna Anderson; [m.] Aaron Francis Atkinson, September 5, 1992; [ch.] Melinda Sue Atkinson; [ed.] Graduated from Adams Friendship Aera High School, WI. year 1990; [occ.] CNA - Certified Nursing Assistant; [memb.] I belong to Trinity United Church of Christ; [oth. writ.] Where Ever You Are? and A Birth of a Baby; [pers.] I would like to dedicate this poem to all the hard workers in the world. And to my husband for his dedication to me!; [a.] Portage, WI

**AUBLE, GLENN M.**
[b.] July 20, 1936, Elgin, IL; [p.] Donald and Gladys Auble; [m.] Barbara R. Auble, August 22, 1958; [ch.] Marcus and Robin; [ed.] Univ. of Illinois Institute of Aviation grad. Graduate Realtors Institute; [occ.] Realtor; [memb.] Realtor Assoc. of the Western Suburbs, Illinois Assoc. of Realtors, National Assoc. of Realtors, Wheaton Lions Club, Wheaton Chamber of Commerce, Ambassadors Club, SPEBSQSA; [hon.] Realtor of the Year, Presidents Award, et al; [pers.] The Golden Rule is my way of life; [a.] Wheaton, IL

**AUSTIN, CLESTER**
[pen.] Chet Austin; [b.] February 21, 1948, Quincy, MA; [p.] Helen R. Austin; [ch.] Meghan S. Reeves, Christofer Bacella; [ed.] GED; [occ.] Maintenance Tech.; [oth. writ.] 25 copywritten songs; [pers.] Truth is stronger than lies. Love is stronger than fear.; [a.] Somerville, MA

**AUTHIER, JASON**
[pen.] Joseph Misael; [b.] November 29, 1977, Minot, ND; [p.] Barbara and Paul Authier; [ed.] Graduated from Cranston High School East, Cranston, RI in 1995. Currently a Freshman at Rhode Island College; [occ.] Student and Free Lance Writer; [memb.] Cranston

Mayor's Advisory Council on Substance Abuse; [hon.] 1995 CODAC Award, CCI's Cranston Volunteer of the year; [oth. writ.] Poems published in City Paper and Countless Articles in School Paper; [pers.] A large majority of my writing is from personal experience, whether it be poems, stories, or articles. Real life is the best inspiration.; [a.] Cranston, RI

**AVELLA, ROSA LOU**
[pen.] Daisy; [b.] February 21, 1982, Ridgewood, NJ; [p.] Alan M. Avella, Sr., Jo Ann L. Avella; [ed.] Saint Anne School Fair Lawn, NJ; [occ.] Student; [memb.] Choir, St. Anne Cheer leading, St. Anne; [hon.] 2nd Honors at Saint Anne School, 2nd place in the New Jersey National Competition for St. Anne cheer leaders of Fair Lawn; [a.] Fair Lawn, NJ

**AVILA, MONICA**
[pen.] Monica Rose; [b.] October 2, 1975, Lake View Terrace, San Fernando Valley, CA; [p.] Roberta Villegas; [ed.] Made to 11th, one month from completing 11th. Didn't finish. Foot Hill High, Pacific High School Sacramento; [occ.] Unemployed at this time; [hon.] Campus Verdes Child Care Center, Certificate of Appreciation, Award for participation, for people reaching out, Sacramento; [oth. writ.] Several writings none published yet; [pers.] I enjoy making people happy and laugh. I'm outgoing and understanding I just like to be myself.; [a.] San Fernando Valley, CA

**AVILA, PEDRO RESENDE**
[pen.] Pete; [b.] March 31, 1981, Brazil; [p.] Katia and Andy Avila; [ed.] Lafayette Elementary, Stanley Intermediate, Campolindo High School Freshman; [occ.] High School Student, Basketball, Soccer, Volleyball, and Waterpolo player, Swimmer, Basketball and Soccer Referee; [memb.] FIFA (Federation Internationale de Football Association); [hon.] Stanley M.H. School Scientific Excellence Award, Lafayette Elementary Georgraphy Bee Winner, Extended Awards in Basketball; [oth. writ.] Simple Poetry, Understanding the Road; [pers.] "Don't try to beat the rock, simply climb it."; [a.] Lafayette, CA

**BACON, EVELYN E.**
[b.] January 28, 1914, New Auburn, WI; [p.] Severt and Nellie Skaw; [m.] Paul A. Bacon (Deceased), May 7, 1944; [ch.] Pat, Sandra, Bob and Dorothy; [ed.] 2 years College, 1 year - Chippewa Falls, WI, 1 year Tacoma Comm. College; [occ.] Retired; [memb.] Covenant Celebration Church - Tacoma, WA; [oth. writ.] I have several other poems that I have written; [pers.] I love to read and I play piano for nursing homes. I also have a notebook of poems from magazines and newspapers; [a.] Tacoma, WA

**BAILEY, LUCILLE**
[b.] November 26, 1930, Bolyston, MA; [p.] Mr. Edward Aucoin, Mrs. Florence Aucoin (died Nov. 6, 1980); [m.] Dwight Bailey, May 26, 1951; [ch.] Stephen Bailey, Linda Taylor, I have 5 grandchildren; [ed.] High School Graduate; [occ.] Live in Care Home; [memb.] Agawam Baptist Church; [oth. writ.] 2 poems published in Springfield Newspaper in Mass. Many years ago when they accepted them while I lived in Mass.; [pers.] I reflect His faithfulness. Love to creation, His people i my poems. Our God has some surprises in the way He creates things! What a Creative God who can make anything - who knows everything!; [a.] Arcata, CA

**BAILEY, ERIC**
[b.] March 9, 1968, Newark, NJ; [p.] Allen Cooper, Betty Bailey; [ed.] Irvington High, Center for the Media Arts, School of Visual Arts; [occ.] Writer; [pers.] I would like to take the gift that God has given to me and

turn it into a gift that I could give to Him.; [a.] Orange, NJ

**BAIRD, RICHARD A.**
[pen.] Richard Anthony; [b.] August 1, 1967, Trenton, NJ; [p.] Harry James Sr., Dolores Jean; [ed.] Moses Braun School, Villanova University, St. Joseph's University (M.B.A.); [occ.] Technical Support Representative, Primavera Systems, Inc.; [pers.] Thanks to the continued support of my family and friends, this moment has been made possible. I believe if you look hard enough - you can see the true heart of every person and realize that we are all not that different from each other.; [a.] Ardmore, PA

**BAKE, CONNIE SUE**
[pen.] Connsuella Bakkola; [b.] September 14, 1975, Dover, OH; [p.] George and Twila Bake; [ed.] 1993 graduate of Conotton Valley High School, Bowerston, Ohio; [occ.] Big Bear store #71, New Philadelphia, Cashier; [memb.] Tops #1073, Carrollton, The Ohio Wagon Train 4-H - 11 years; [hon.] Honor Roll; [oth. writ.] Many other poems, none published; [pers.] Experience is the key to poetry. You can't write a real poem without feeling it in your heart first. My poetry is my way to express the goodness and the hardships experienced so far in lifetime.; [a.] Leesville, OH

**BAKER, DARLA SUE**
[b.] September 23, 1960, Fort Worth; [p.] Patsy Sue Davenport, George Baum; [m.] E. L. Baker III, June 19, 1993; [ch.] I have a 14 yr. old daughter from a previous marriage; [ed.] I'm going to College to become a Physical Therapy Assistant; [occ.] Mother, Wife, Student; [hon.] Several years ago I won a few ribbons in Toast Masters; [oth. writ.] I have a journal, I write my feeling down, sometimes they turn into poems; [pers.] I have lost several people in my life that meant alot to me, I started writing out my feelings of grief etc... and I found it to be very healing.; [a.] Fort Worth, TX

**BALDRIDGE, ROBERT LINDSEY**
[b.] August 20, 1919, Providence, RI; [p.] John Percy Baldridge, Elsie Lydia (Erickson) Baldridge; [m.] Helen (Everts) Baldridge, June 14, 1943; [ch.] Lawrence Clayton, John Preston, James Joseph (deceased), Robert Lee; [ed.] Roosevelt High School, Des Moines, Iowa, Iowa State College, Ames Iowa (BS Civil Engineering), US Army Associate Command and General Staff, College presented by Satellite School, Portland, Oregon; [occ.] Retired; [memb.] Army Engineer Association, National Association for Uniformed Services; [hon.] Best Non-Technical Article, 1949 Iowa State Engineer (Student Magazine, Iowa State College), Ames, Iowa; [oth. writ.] None published; [pers.] Christian; [a.] Portland, OR

**BALDWIN, JENNIFER**
[pen.] Jenni Baldwin; [b.] November 4, 1978, Richmond, IN; [p.] Vicki Elliott and Michael Elliott, Harry Baldwin and Jana Baldwin; [ed.] Currently Junior at Northeastern Jr. Sr. High School; [occ.] Student; [memb.] Northeastern Concert Choir, Northeastern's Drama Dept., Fountain City Softball League; [hon.] Nominated to have biography published by Who's Who Among American High School Students, received a GTE Scholarship to attend Earlham College's Explore-a-College, Nominated to attend The National Young Leaders Conference, ISSMA State Solo Contest (vocal) received II; [oth. writ.] Nothing published; [pers.] The whole world is a stage and we are all actors playing a small part in a much bigger picture, never ignore the details, for that's all we as people are.; [a.] Richmond, IN

**BALDWIN, PETER**
[occ.] Retired; [a.] Manchester, CT

**BALISINSKI, BIANKA**
[b.] February 1, 1977, Latina, Italy; [p.] Gretchen and Jerry Balisinski; [ed.] Currently enrolled at Mt. San Jacinto (Menifel Campus) transfering to Longbeach State. Hoping to get a degree in Psychology; [occ.] Manager at a Video Store; [oth. writ.] I have other poems. Two published in my High School. But mostly I write to relieve myself from trapped feelings; [pers.] "Man is great, because he is miserable."

**BALL, DARREN**
[b.] May 13, 1966, Woodland, CA; [p.] LaNell and Elwyn Ball; [m.] Tika Ball, September 26, 1992; [ch.] Jessica; [ed.] Woodland High School, various Colleges and Universities; [occ.] Computer Programmer; [oth. writ.] Several poems, all of which have not been published; [pers.] My life's philosophy can be understood by reading the poem I have written, "A Tree."; [a.] Woodland, CA

**BANKS, STEPHANIE**
[b.] November 4, 1975, Newton, KS; [p.] Donald W. and Tammy Rogers; [m.] Chris Banks, August 14, 1994; [ch.] Bryce Alan; [ed.] Newton High, Hutchinson Junior College; [occ.] Residential Support Specialist, Northview Dev. Serv.; [oth. writ.] Two other published poems; [a.] Newton, KS

**BARGAS, REBECCA**
[b.] February 26, 1968, Portland, OR; [m.] Tyler Bargas, 1987; [ch.] Nathan and Emily; [occ.] Full time Mom; [pers.] I believe that human feelings give way to creative ability. That ability is within each one of us. It is up to us to find our own means of expression, and our choice whether we allow it to be shared with others.; [a.] Troutdale, OR

**BARI, VIRGINIA**
[b.] April 12, 1949, Brooklyn, NY; [p.] Phil and Lucy Bari; [ed.] Saint John's University, BS Ed. Adelphi University, MA Early Ch. Queens College, MS Special Ed, London University Sped (summer semester); [occ.] Sp. Ed teacher, Resource Room, PS. 127 Queens NY; [memb.] Reading Reform Foundation, Orton Dyslexia Foundation Studied Phonics/LD; [hon.] Dean's List, Cum Laude, undergraduate; [pers.] I have always had a love for poetry of Keats, Emily Brontë, Emily Dickinson and feel my work reflects metaphysical qualities and embodies a love of divinity.

**BARKLEY, M. ROSE**
[b.] January 7, 1964, New Jersey; [p.] Ralph and Louise Barkley; [ed.] Pemberton Twp. High School, University of MD, Eastern Shore, (VCU) Virginia Commonwealth University; [occ.] Student; [memb.] Rho Epsilon Fraternity, Golden Key National Honor Society; [hon.] Member, Honors Program (VCU); [oth. writ.] Poems published in local, regional newspapers/magazines, poem appeared in premiere issue of Biracial Child magazine. Publication in National Library of Poetry "Edge of Twilight" collection.; [pers.] "There exists no positive vibe too insignificant to be expressed in some way."; [a.] Richmond, VA

**BARNES, LEONA L. DUNGAN**
[b.] February 22, 1915, Iowa; [p.] George and Katherine Dungan; [m.] Deceased; [ch.] William Earl, Jack Alexander, Larry Dallas, Paul Sherman, Mary Katherine; [ed.] High School Graduate which was acquired when in her seventies; [occ.] Retired; [oth. writ.] A book of poems are being put together at this time; [pers.] After having raised four boys and a girl during the depression and beyond I feel as though I have the education of the highest degree, from the university of life. My inspiration comes from daily living, others joy or heartache, friends and family and of course from my private line to my heavenly Father.; [a.] Gainesville, GA

**BARNES, SYLVIA P.**
[pen.] Susie; [b.] September 25, 1957, Franklin, VA; [p.] Roy and Mildred Barnes; [m.] Nikola Maj; [hon.] I've currently written a compilation of 42 original songs, and composed all the music. The compilations include, "Gospel", "Pop/Jazz", "Pop/Rock", R and B Jazz" and Gospel/Blues.; [oth. writ.] Writing gives words color. Therefore, words paints it's own picture and sets it in the frame of one's mind.

**BARNES, MARIA CAYENNE**
[b.] September 1, 1959, Columbus, GA; [ed.] Junior - Clayton State College; [occ.] Small service business owner aspiring writer; [hon.] National First Place winner 1989 for Best Collegiate Advertising Campaign, National First Place winner 1990 Sales and Mgmt. Competition, Board of Trustee Scholarship 1991; [oth. writ.] Children stories song lyrics. And southern stories about family ties.; [pers.] Pat Conroy says quote" I try to explain my life to myself". Abraham Lincoln say" Most people are about as happy as they make up their mind to be" - These Z quotes explain my philosophy on writing.; [a.] Decatur, GA

**BARNHART, MARY E.**
[b.] March 2, 1939, Phillippi, WV; [p.] Cletus McCauley; [m.] Alice McCauley, March 14, 1956; [ch.] Darlene, Joyce, Michael; [ed.] High School, Bridgeport, W.Va.; [occ.] Housewife; [memb.] Mt. Clare United Methodist Church, Administrative Board Worship Committee, Beech Mountain Sportman's Club Aux.; [oth. writ.] Song for Palm Sunday entitled The Little Grey Donkey, numerous poems in Church papers and bulletins; [pers.] The love of my Lord has always played a strong part in my writing. I write what I wish could happen and what I know can happen when we trust in the Lord. I write about what I see in my friends and family.

**BARNSWELL, BARRINGTON**
[b.] June 25, 1960, Jamaica; [p.] Veronica Goulbourne; [ed.] AA Business, College of Dupage; [occ.] SPU Tech, Hinsdale Hospital; [oth. writ.] Have written several humored poems since high school, covering various topics including sports, politics, religion and romance. Specialize in writing poems for special occasions.; [pers.] Poetry, at its best, is a reflection of life, that captures some aspect of man not with a brush but with a pen, not painted on canvas but composed on paper.; [a.] Hinsdale, IL

**BAROWICS, CHARLES C.**
[pen.] C. Cass Barowicz; [b.] February 2, 1967, Detroit, MI; [p.] Dennis and Juanita Barowicz; [ed.] Wadsworth High 1985, The University of Akron 1989; [occ.] Warehouse Inventory Controller; [memb.] Grace Luthern Church Usher, Volunteer High School Basketball Coach; [hon.] 3-Year Letter Winner, Men's Basketball from the University of Akron 1986-1988; [oth. writ.] I have had other poems published in magazines and in church notes; [pers.] I write so other people can see how life is seen through other's souls. Hopefully it changes how they feel towards a subject. My two biggest influences are my Savior Jesus Christ and Martin Luther.; [a.] Wadsworth, OH

**BARRELL, DAWN H.**
[b.] December 7, 1940, Chattanooga, TN; [p.] Althea and Martin Holman; [m.] John M. Barrell, October 7, 1972; [ch.] Step daughters: Janet Berman, Nan Barrell, Cynthia Olander; [ed.] 4 years University of Georgia, Degree in Marketing; [occ.] Marketing Representative, Panasonic Trade Show Representative; [memb.] Who's Who of Women 1990/1991, Administrative Board Member, Peachtree City United Methodist Church, Daughters of the American Revolution, Life Member Republican Task Force; [hon.] Phi Beta Phi, Grand Cross Order of Saint Stanislas, Dame of Justice Sovereign Order of the Oak Dame of Merit Order of St. John of Jerusalem, Governor's Staff State of Georgia, Elected Delegate State Republican Convention, 1984, 1985, 1986; [oth. writ.] 1992 - Published in Selected works of our world's Best Poets, 1993 - Published in Great Poems of Our Times, 1994 - Published in Outstanding Poets of 1994, 1995 - Best Poems of 1995; [pers.] My life would make a wonderful book - filled with travel, mystery, heartaches and happiness. Through it all, I wouldn't change a day of my life.; [a.] Peachtree City, GA

**BARRETT SR., CLEVELAND S.**
[pen.] The Ghetto Poet Hulk; [b.] January 28, 1965, Hollywood, FL; [p.] Cleveland and Jo-Ann Barrett; [m.] Karen Barrett, October 26, 1991; [ch.] Krystal Barrett, Darnisha Barrett, Cleveland Jr., Mose Barrett, Ciara Barrett Cleveland, S.C. Barrett, Martell Barrett; [ed.] Joliet East High School, Carlenshaw Institute Bolingbrook IL; [occ.] Security Officer; [memb.] Member of International Society of Poetry; [hon.] The worlds #1 greatest Ghetto poet Hulk, America's Best Selving Black author of Ghetto Poetry an Phosophy; [oth. writ.] United We Stand Divided We Fall, Can You Her My Echo, Invisible Chairs, Black Butter Fly, You Can Run But You Can't Hide Aids, Mentally In Incarcerated, Policy Brutally, A Toast From Me To You, Pipe Dreams, Forty Acres And A Mule, Black Hole, I Will Over Come; [pers.] The Ghetto Poet Hulk has just finished writing his first book tittle "Can You Hear My Echo" the Ghetto Poet covers all dimensions and topic from education, welfare, oppression, politics, politicians, famous authors, from the main stream to the Ghetto Black Hole.; [a.] Harrisburg, IL

**BARRIER, MARGUERITE V.**
[pen.] Gypsy V. Barrier; [b.] September 4, 1969, Christ Church, New Zealand; [p.] Rowena and Lawrence Barrier; [ed.] Graduated from Albany High, appentishiped under Roger Doyle to become a horse trainer; [occ.] Hunter/Jumper Trainer, Owner/Trainer of Midnight Blue and Co Training Stables, Livermore, CA; [memb.] American Horse Show Association (A.H.S.A.), Pacific Coast Horse Association (P.C.H.A.), (C.P.H.A.) California Professional Horsemen Ass.; [oth. writ.] I mostly enjoy to write about the children and their horses, how ever my poetry has a vast range of topics.; [pers.] Life is simply the karma, you bring with your laughter. Your life story is told, it's the song of your endless smile. It calls so sweetly to those who surround you. And we find we rejoice in life's little dances.; [a.] Livermore, CA

**BARTLETT, ANNE**
[b.] January 9, 1983, Oyster Bay, NY; [p.] Bryan and Mary Bartlett; [ed.] Bayville Primary School, Bayville Intermediate School; [memb.] Save The Manatee Club; [hon.] Scholastic Effort; [pers.] I try my best in everything I do. For if you try your best, you can do no better. Don't ever give up you dreams and hopes. I never have and I never will.; [a.] Bayville, NY

**BARUCH, BRANDON**
[pen.] Edward Norris; [b.] April 7, 1985, Los Angeles; [ed.] Currently Elementary Student - Los Angeles; [pers.] I have lots of feelings. Often I cannot express them in any way but my writing, ever since I discovered the art of poetry, I've been fascinated. It's like music in my ears.; [a.] Los Angeles, CA

**BASS, MONA LISA**
[b.] November 23, Birmingham, AL; [p.] R. C. Graham and Annie Graham; [m.] James Arthur Bass, May 4, 1976; [ch.] Tracey Melissa Bass, Casey Diana Bass; [ed.] Brighton High School, Alabama State University, (B.S. Degree), major: Art, minor: English; [pers.] My poems are written from the heart. They maybe real or surrealistic in content. I observe life and write from its many chapters. Especially those chapters that most would rather not know about.; [a.] Montgomery, AL

**BAUMAN, ESTELLA ANN**
[pen.] Stell Bauman; [b.] March 8, 1919, Ost., KS; [p.] Deceased; [m.] Deceased; [ch.] 2 Boys and 3 Girls; [ed.] Grade and Ged; [occ.] Retired song-writer; [memb.] BMI, Fredonia Golf Club, Sacred Heart Auto League; [hon.] Golden Poet's Award, Silver Poet's Award; [oth. writ.] School Class Reunion's Book of Poems - by Stell for family and friends; [pers.] Writing songs and music. Have my 1st song out: "How can we forget," this and poem is what I love doing most.; [a.] Fredonia, KS

**BAUMANN, THOMAS**
[b.] December 5, 1961, Roms, NY; [p.] Paul and Helen Baumann; [occ.] Programmer Intermedia Communications, Inc.; [oth. writ.] This is my first public writing; [pers.] I hope it is as fun to read as it was to write.; [a.] Palm Harbor, FL

**BAXTER, SARA MICHELLE**
[pen.] Sara B.; [b.] February 23, 1985, New Jersey; [p.] Walter and Karen Baxter; [ed.] My schooling is now at the 6th grade level. I enjoy school very much!; [hon.] I enjoy playing the piano. I've composed my own song. I've received honors at school I'm involved with the girl scouts and soccer and baseball. I've also been in charge of story horror at our library.; [oth. writ.] I'm in the process of writing my own book of poems. I like to add humor to many of my poems, it makes people feel light and I like that.; [pers.] Poetry to me is a beautiful way of expressing my feelings. I enjoy bringing happiness to others through my words. I have been greatly influenced by the author Shel Silverstein.

**BEARD, ERNESTINE**
[pen.] Sofia B.; [b.] May 29, 1939, Dongola, IL; [p.] Joe and Lucille Farr (Deceased),; [m.] Roy Lee Beard (Deceased), March 17, 1967; [ch.] Douglas (Deceased), Roy Jr., Marta, Kevin, Carla, Stephen; [ed.] Coleman Elementary Du Sable High School, Harold Washington College (Chgo.); [occ.] Teacher Assistant, John M. Smyth School Chicago IL; [oth. writ.] Numerous poems unpublished, 3 plays unpublished; [pers.] Writings and poems inspired by my children and all the children I've met throughout my lifetime.; [a.] Chicago, IL

**BEARDSLEE III, CLARK S.**
[b.] June 3, 1922, Buffalo, NY; [p.] Clark S. and Doris Beardslee; [m.] Wanda L. Beardslee, December 28, 1974; [ch.] Gary, Karen, Clark Jr., Jill; [ed.] Kenmore High School, Ohio Wesleyan Univ.; [occ.] Retired; [memb.] Elks Lodge 1415, American Legion Post 270, Our Lady of Perpetual Church, International Society of Poets; [hon.] Pilot, U.S. Army Corp. 1942-1955 - World War II Service Medal; [oth. writ.] Have been writing poems for over 50 years; [pers.] I have been blessed with the ability to put my most personal thoughts into poetic verse. It has been a great source of expression for me over the years.; [a.] Downey, CA

**BEASLEY, TAMERA COYNE**
[b.] Boston, MA; [m.] Darryl K. Beasley, June 20, 1995; [ed.] Brown University, Duke University Medical School; [occ.] Internist and Pediatrician; [memb.] Board of Directors of the Lincoln Community Health Center, Delta Sigma Theta Sorority, National Medical Association, First Calvary Baptist Church; [hon.] Robert Wood Johnson Clinical Scholar, NMA/Mead Johnson Award in Pediatrics, Ciba Geigy Community Service Award; [oth. writ.] Several published poems and articles; [pers.] My poems reflect the realities of life and love.; [a.] Durham, NE

**BEAVERS, LEE**
[b.] July 11, 1975, Winchester, VA; [p.] Roger and Wanda Beavers; [ed.] Cornerstone Christian Academy, currently a student at Bob Jones University; [occ.] Student; [memb.] Grace Independent Bible Church; [pers.] I thank God for His marvelous creation. Without it I would have nothing to write about.; [a.] The Plains, VA

**BEEBE, JEANNETTE JONES**
[b.] December 15, 1960, Brooklyn, NY; [m.] Kenneth Beebe; [ch.] Jasmine M. Kenneth J.; [ed.] St. John the Baptist, H.S., Spelman College, Atlanta Area Technical School; [occ.] Cosmetologist - part time Mother and wife - full time; [memb.] Volunteer for "Look Good Feel Better" program, Mulvey School PTA, St. Charles P.T.O., Long Island Family Support Consumer Coun.; [pers.] "Always strive to do the very best and keep your head towards the sky.";; [a.] Central Islip, NY

**BEIJAN, KEVAN S.**
[b.] August 20, 1968; [p.] Fereydoon and Christie; [ed.] Grand High School, University of North Texas; [oth. writ.] Several other poems, published and unpublished, as well as several short stories; [pers.] Although I have penned these words, it is my Heavenly Father and my earthly family with whom I credit my inspirations.; [a.] Aubrey, TX

**BELISLE, BARBARA J.**
[b.] Birmingham, AL; [p.] William and Betty Mayweather; [ch.] 3, 6 Grandchildren; [ed.] High School, Prentice High School, Montevallo, AL, B.A.: Miles College - Birmingham, AL, MA: University of Montevallo - Montevallo, AL; [occ.] High School English Teacher, Retired June 1, 1995; [memb.] Shelby County Education Assoc., Alabama Education Assoc., National Education Assoc., Presently, same associations for retired members, Shelby County Language Arts Curriculum Development Committee; [hon.] Citation for serving as President of SCEA, Citation from community for service, Golden Apple Award from governor (1st issued county), Black Achievement Award from Shelby county Democratic Conference, Tribute from Montevallo High School for service; [oth. writ.] Essay: "Teaching Japanese Poetry through Sei Shonagon's "The Pillow Book" published in The Individual and the World, 1st Story in short story collection being considered by publisher, essay, "Where's U're?" being considered by newspaper; [pers.] All people are the same, therefore, if we're sensitive to each other's joys and pain, fears and hopes, we can learn to understand and appreciate each other. I usually try to appeal to that sameness in my work.; [a.] Montevallo, AL

**BELK, JANIS EDWARDS**
[pen.] J. Me; [b.] August 1, 1948, Washington, DC; [p.] Vincent Edwards, Hattie Edwards; [ch.] Demetress Maria, Dionne Cecelia; [ed.] Univ. of the District of Columbia; [occ.] Sales Representative, Value City Furniture, New Carrollton, MD; [memb.] The National Association for Female Executives (NAFE), NAACP, Image, Inc.; [oth. writ.] Biblical teachings and poems published in area, Religious-based newsletters; [pers.] I desire that my written works will have universal appeal and inspiration during my lifetime and beyond.; [a.] Washington, DC

**BELL, KATE**
[pen.] Kate Bell; [b.] May 26, 1951, Long Island; [ch.] Hannah and Evan; [ed.] Hunter College N.Y.C., working on Masters Degree; [occ.] Teacher of young children; [hon.] Cum Laude; [oth. writ.] Book of Poem in Progress; [pers.] I began writing in my early forties. In poetry I explore my spiritual lessons and experience my soul.; [a.] Stockbridge, MA

**BENNETT, BRANDY ELAINE**
[pen.] Emily Draven; [b.] November 30, 1078, Wilmington, NC; [p.] K. G. Bennett, Belinda C. Bennett; [ed.] E. A. Laney High School; [occ.] Great American Cookie Co., Cashier, Student; [hon.] United States Achievement Academy 2 years in a row; [oth. writ.] "My Bonnie Lass", and "The Souls Shadows"; [pers.] I strive to bring out a darker mood in my poetry. It hightens the imagination and exposes a unique spirit in my work.; [a.] Wilmington, NC

**BENNETT, HARRIET HOEVET**
[pen.] Harriet Hoevet Bennett; [b.] May 19, 1930, Lowell, IN; [p.] Edward Bernice Hoevet; [m.] Divorced, March 5, 1949; [ch.] Daniel Charles; [ed.] BA Mus Ed-Olivet Nazarene Univ. M Music Ed - V of I; [occ.] Retired Teacher; [memb.] National Audubon Society, National Wildlife Federation, AARP, United Church of Christ; [hon.] Alpha Tau Delta, Indiana Girls State; [oth. writ.] "Joy", "Shall I Tell You?" musical pieces, "Rosettes" - a craft project in "New Generations"; [pers.] We are on this earth to help one another. Stretch your potential!; [a.] Hodgkins, IL

**BENTON, MARGARET N.**
[pen.] Margo; [b.] July 11, 1926, Hawkins, CO; [p.] Nelson and Fannie Hord; [ch.] Gerald A. Benton III; [oth. writ.] Unpublished meditations and poems for friends; [pers.] Asking questions of the Universe and searching for and reflecting reason for be-ing.; [a.] Kingsport, TN

**BERCAW, KENNETH W.**
[b.] May 8, 1963, Los Angeles; [p.] George E. Bercaw, Margaret M. Bercaw; [ed.] St. Bernard High School, Santa Monica College, Long Beach State; [pers.] The heart is willing and moments of inspiration are the wings.; [a.] Los Angeles, CA

**BERENSON, KENDRA JOY**
[b.] April 7, 1984, Greenbrae, CA; [p.] Robin and Douglas Berenson; [ed.] 6th grade; [occ.] Student; [hon.] 1st Place Poetry at County Fair; [oth. writ.] Several Poems and Short Stories; [pers.] I want my writing to remind people of the importance of peace and equality.; [a.] San Rafael, CA

**BERGER, MELISSA**
[pen.] Yvonne Lee; [b.] November 5, 1975, New York; [p.] Dina Jones, Kevin Nelson; [ed.] Brentwood H.S. Pace University, Virginia Union University; [occ.] A student at Virginia Union University; [memb.] Black Student Union, Student Government Association, Virginia Union University, News paper (informer); [oth. writ.] Several poems published in literary magazines as well as winning a contest for humanities for a poem I wrote for the Holocaust; [pers.] A friendship as well as a relationship that is real can not be measured by time alone, but also by what is concealed by the heart.; [a.] Richmond, VA

**BERKOVICH, CINDY DAWN**
[pen.] Misty Dawn; [b.] May 14, 1971, The Dalles, OR; [p.] Kenneth Godwin, Diana Godwin; [m.] James D. Berkovich; [ch.] December 29, 1989; [ed.] Wahtonka High, Columbia Gorge Community College, Institute of Children's Literature; [occ.] Office Automation Clerk,

Bonneville Power Administration, The Dalles, OR; [hon.] Student of the Month: History Received Certificate of Completion with The Institute of Children's Literature, a correspondence school; [oth. writ.] Write many short stories, many poems, have not had any stories published. I have also written several songs.; [pers.] As I write, the paper and ink are my closest friends. I envision another person and write what I feel they are feeling deep inside. I wish to help someone with a smile on paper, or to enlighten someone's thoughts with my writing. I have always loved the plays of Shakespeare and the poetry of Robert Frost.; [a.] The Dalles, OR

**BERRY SR., WAYNE V.**
[pen.] Joe Berry; [b.] February 6, 1944, McBee, SC; [p.] Floyd C. Berry and Dorthy; [m.] Loadeth Berry, June 27, 1971; [ch.] Wayne V. Berry Jr.; [ed.] 3 1/2 yrs. College, 2 yrs. Manhattan College, 1 1/2 yrs. Baruch N.Y.C.; [occ.] Teacher - Mechanical at N.Y.C. Tranit Authority and Postal Worker; [hon.] N.Y.C. Transit Authority - for Dedication and Teaching Ability, Air Force Award as a Missilist expert; [pers.] Wayne V. Berry Jr. was instrumental in helping many friends and co-workers, whenever they were in need of financial or personnel help. He was loved by many; [a.] Brooklyn, NY

**BERRY, RAY**
[b.] February 13, 1952; [p.] Gloria Johnson, Lee J. Berry; [ed.] Walterboro High, 1970, The University of Miami cum laude 1974, Bachelor of Fine Arts Degree (BFA), Tyler School of Art of Temple University 1976, Master's of Fine Arts, (MFAJ); [occ.] Artist, Writer; [hon.] National Gallery of Art - Smithsonian Institution, Library of Congress Chase Manhattan Bank, The Prudential, The Readers' Digest Association; [oth. writ.] Novel in Progress about New York Art World titled:, "Emotional Bingo"; [pers.] Words as a medium are very similar to colors. I try to blend words to stir one's emotions, and create rich interior landscapes framed as windows to the greater spirit.; [a.] New York, NY

**BERRYHILL, LISA M.**
[pen.] Dudette; [b.] November 16, 1979, Anniston; [p.] James D. and Wanda F. Berryhill; [ed.] Sipsey Jr. High, hoping to go on to Walker High School and then go on to Auburn University to become a lawyer; [occ.] Student at Sipsey Jr. High School; [oth. writ.] I have written several other poems. One about a girl named Misty. "My name is Misty", "Stream of Love", "I Love You", (etc.); [pers.] I am 15, and stubborn, stubbornness makes it easier to write. When I'm sad, I write about depression. When I'm hyper, I write weird. My writing expresses my true feelings.; [a.] Sumiton, AL

**BERTRAND, NONA**
[b.] March 5, 1930, Ogdensburg, NY; [p.] Elmer and Mildred Quenelle; [m.] A. John Bertrand, November 24, 1949; [ch.] Cherie Marie Johnson; [ed.] Massena High School, Massena, NY; [occ.] Retired; [memb.] Sacred Heart, Knights of Columbus Auxiliary, St. Timothy's Catholic Church; [oth. writ.] Poetry in Anthologies, articles, short stories in magazines, magazine fillers, presentation material; [pers.] Writing poetry is a way for me to express my innermost feelings and thoughts, and to artistically convey them to others.; [a.] Summerfrield, FL

**BEVANS, KATHLEEN**
[b.] October 12, 1940, New Orleans; [p.] Marion and John McNamara; [m.] Thomas J. Bevans, August 27, 1960; [ch.] Mary Kay, Tom, Beth, Allyson, Chris; [ed.] St. Mary's Dominican High, Loyola University - New Orleans, B.S. Grad., Work - U. of Houston; [occ.] Creative Writing Teacher, Memorial School of the Oaks, Houston, TX; [memb.] Hermann Hosp. Pastoral

Care Comm., Comboni Missionary League of So. California, Eucharistic Ministers - St. John Vianney Church, Houston; [hon.] Past-Pres. of Comboni Missionary League, Cardinal Key National Jesuit Honor Society, Who's Who Among America's Teachers' - 1994; [oth. writ.] Two pub. poems, one in Nat'l Library of Poetry - Where Dreams Begin - 1993, have written numerous poems, esp. to my beloved grandchildren; [pers.] I have always loved words and have felt that words must be used wisely because one's words have such power. It is a terrific privilege to be able to "Soar", so to speak, with one's written words.; [a.] Houston, TX

**BHATTACHARYYA, SUBARNA**
[b.] November 4, 1963, Calcutta, India; [p.] Sudhakar and Geeta Bhattacharyya; [ed.] Lady Brabourne College, Calcutta, India, Columbia University, New York; [occ.] Doctoral Candidate in Biological Sciences, Columbia University, New York; [pers.] Life is too short, and I try to live it with a certain flair. I have been particularly inspired, and influenced by Maya Angelou's poems.; [a.] New York, NY

**BIESTERFELD, BONNIE**
[b.] November 13, 1955, Farmingdale, NJ; [p.] Herbert and Verna Ritter; [m.] Joseph, July 6, 1974; [ch.] Stacy Laurn and Ashley Lynn; [ed.] Ocean Township High, NJ; [occ.] Homemaker and Community Volunteer; [oth. writ.] Short stories, poems and thoughts to ponder; [pers.] My work comes from within, influenced by my daily surroundings. I try to make poetry paint a picture of what we all might take for granted.; [a.] Coral Springs, FL

**BIRDWELL, IAN**
[b.] November 2, 1974, San Antonio, TX; [p.] Sandra Birdwell; [oth. writ.] Book of "Poetry" in progress; [a.] Palestine, TX

**BIVIN, STEVEN KENT**
[pen.] Stephen Kent; [b.] December 25, 1965, Lufkin, TX; [p.] Kent and Nell Bivin; [m.] Angela (Dawn) Bivin, December 6, 1995; [ch.] Brittney Raye Bivin, Chase Steven Bivin; [ed.] Hudson High, Lufkin, TX; [occ.] Service Mgr., Village Quik Lube (Lufkin, TX); [oth. writ.] Several songs published through B.M.I.; [pers.] Poetry was the key that first unlocked the doors of my imagination. As a child my favorite was called "Seein" things, but when I discovered, Kipling and Longfellow, poetry became a friend for life.; [a.] Lufkin, TX

**BLACK, CRYSTAL**
[pen.] Crystal Black; [b.] February 1, 1950, Kittanning, PA; [p.] Finley Klingensmith and Phyllis Peters; [m.] David W. Black, April 15, 1970; [ch.] Tamerin Renee - Brian Christopher; [ed.] Ambridge Area High School; [occ.] Full time mother and homemaker; [pers.] I wrote this poem for my mother's 50th birthday. A time and age of reflections.

**BLACK, MARGARET**
[b.] York, PA; [p.] Joseph Black; [ed.] York Catholic High School, York, PH, Penna State Univ., State College, PA, St. Petersbury Jr. College, Clearwater, FL; [occ.] Homemaker and Volunteer; [hon.] Public Speaking, Art; [oth. writ.] Religious writing, short plays, short stories, one poem published in college poetry magazine; [pers.] The springs of the human heart, and expressing what I feel for others and their situations.; [a.] Clearwater, FL

**BLACKBURN, GEOFFREY R.**
[pen.] Richard J. Hansen; [b.] January 24, 1947, Salt Lake City, UT; [m.] Joan A. Blackburn; [ch.] Eric Reddick, Samantha, Sabrina, and Courtney Blackburn; [occ.] Artist, Writer, Publisher, Inventor, Karater Teacher; [oth. writ.] Book: "The Future-izer Hand-

book and Goal Processor," Poetry published in us and British Anthologies, play (written in sonnet form) published in text book, and produced on stage and T.V.; [pers.] During my varied "careers" I have learned that the so-called "creative process" is truly a universe any activity by any one. How this works is the subject of my book "The Future-izer Handbook and Goal Processor".; [a.] Salt Lake City, UT

**BLACKBURN, PAULETTE**
[b.] April 22, 1948, Hartford, CO; [p.] Raymond and Julie Bonczek; [m.] Thomas Blackburn, June 7, 1969; [ch.] Tylee Robert, Benjamin Ames; [ed.] Henry James Memorial H.S., Simsbury, Ct., Chandler School for Women, Boston, Mass.; [occ.] Sales Associate for CFH Associates; [pers.] Poetry brings me great joy, and allows me to express myself and my feelings.; [a.] Mechanic Falls, ME

**BLACKBURN, TYLER R.**
[pen.] Verdelite Winters; [b.] November 25, 1974, Portland, MS; [p.] Thomas and Paulette Blackburn; [ed.] St. Domink Regional HS, Roger Williams Univ., Bristol RI; [occ.] Student; [hon.] Dean's List (3 times); [pers.] If you don't know yourself, you don't know anything.; [a.] Mechanic Falls, ME

**BLACKSHIRE, PATRICIA H.**
[b.] Chicago, IL; [p.] Mack Cornelius Blackshire and Virginia Geneva Durant Blackshire; [ch.] Mary Maxyne Reed, Sam Blackshire (Deceased), H. Patricia Blackshire, Walter James Blackshire, Susie Henning; [ed.] Robert S. Albott Elementary, Edmund Burke Elementary, Vincennes V.G. Center, Englewood High School, Illinois State Univ. (Normal, IL.); [memb.] Member of a professional legal association since 1990, Network of Christian Mem. and Women, Inc., voted by peers of the legal association as an Alternate Delegate in 1993 to NAL's 42nd Annual Meeting and Educational Conference; [oth. writ.] Submitted an, essay to the Washington Times Newspaper "My Oakwood Table" in 1993, Reed Certification and Runner-up position

**BLINDER, JASON**
[b.] August 21, 1983, Long Island, NY; [p.] Toff and Helene Blinder; [ed.] Laurel Hill School, Port Jefferson Elementary; [hon.] Played several times for the Guild and skipped the 7th Grade; [pers.] When one knows the difference between what he needs and what he wants, he shall most certainly achieve.; [a.] Port Jefferson, NY

**BLOOMFIELD, THEODORA**
[b.] August 2, 1912, Oneida, IL; [p.] Charles and Albertina Krantz; [m.] Ralph Bloomfield, May 13, 1939; [ch.] Ellis, Nancy Bottemiller, Roger and Ralph Jr.; [ed.] High School, 1 yr. training in Pediatric nursing; [occ.] Retired; [memb.] Immanuel Luth Church Wadena, International Society of Poets; [oth. writ.] I have written poems since grade school, write for my own enjoyment and for others. Have had some published.; [pers.] I love people and love to keep others. Writing poetry is my best way to express what is in my heart, I'm thankful to God for this gift.; [a.] Wadena, MN

**BLOUNT, KENNETH**
[b.] December 10, 1954, Dayton, OH; [p.] Hattie Mae Blount, Willie Blount (Deceased); [ch.] Angela Renee Blount; [ed.] Dunbar High School, G.E.D. - 1977; [occ.] Security Officer, Dayton Convention Center; [oth. writ.] A poem entitled "I Just Want To Help", which will be published soon in At Water's Edge through The National Library of Poetry, and unpublished manuscript with Carlton Press. The title was Realistic Poetry, (1974); [pers.] I write poetry about problems that affect everyone.; [a.] Dayton, OH

**BLUE, ROBERT L.**
[b.] December 12, 1954, Logansport, IN; [p.] Jerry and Mary Blue; [ed.] Carroll High, Vincennes University; [occ.] Registered Nurse; [pers.] Through prayer I have discovered and continue to perfect my God given talent. Knowing that I will someday be judged as a Christian for what I have done with my talent: "I continue to seek a depth without measure that only God can guide me to." Gregory A. Hackett, 1995.; [a.] Flora, IN

**BOCK, MAXCINE**
[pen.] Mickey; [b.] November 12, 1929, North Platte, NE; [p.] L. G. (Shonty) Page Cabbie; [m.] Ron L. Bock; [ch.] Barbara Pinney, Rod Anderson, Steve Anderson; [memb.] Am. Legion, Judge Adr., Marine Corps Aux, FRA, Emblem Club, Harwood UMC; [hon.] Raytown, MO, Chamber of Com. Chairman, Round up Days - USM Corps; [oth. writ.] Short stories and news paper articles.

**BODINE, DON**
[pen.] Hendavthor; [b.] New York; [m.] Sally; [ch.] 5; [ed.] Oregon State University, B.S., Rph., and Life; [occ.] Pres., CEO of Chain of Professional Pharmacies in Or., and Id.; [memb.] Oregon State University President's Club, Kappa Psi, VEW OR, St. Pharm. Asso., Nat. Asso. of Rental Druggists, charter member of Nat. Senatorial and Presidential Communities; [hon.] Serving my country and living free in the U.S., Earning a college Educ., with the G.I. Bill, Worshiping freely, experiencing success in what remains of the free enterprise system, living happily with a wife and being a father and time to enjoy reading and writing.; [oth. writ.] Lyrics, poems, half-completed books, media statements (mostly politically active), and numerous statements of profundity, none "Published", some printed in media; [pers.] Everyone should increase discernment and understanding of the profoundness of life, it should be a passion.; [a.] Dallas, OR

**BOGAN, BRODY**
[b.] May 16, 1982, Beaumont, TX; [p.] Karen and Wayne Bogan; [ed.] Evadale Jr. High; [memb.] Piney Woods Youth, Rodeo Assoc.; [pers.] Brody has always struggled in school. He wrote this poem at the last of the school year in 7th grade. Brody had open heart surgery June 13, 1995. He was released from ICU in record breaking time. He is doing great. He was so thrilled his poem is to be published. It truly is a Blessing; [a.] Evadale, TX

**BOGLE, DELORES VERONICA**
[b.] August 19, 1937, Kingslon LA, WI; [p.] Manlel Bogle, Finella Bogle; [ch.] Maymmie A. Seiuright, two adapted Sandra Chaplin, Valine Altha; [occ.] Home Health Aide Alpha Elementary School; [memb.] Of the L.S.P., Holey Thresa Church, St. Pratic; [hon.] I.S.P., E.CA Award; [oth. writ.] Yes personal and things that happen to me that all most drive me crazy. And weighing help me to escape so I get all the joy, peace contentment from writing.; [pers.] All my poem is me. I want to be a song writer a composer I love singing, people love to love me sing, but I am afraid of my voice in colored, that why I write my poem with lyric. I write about certain thing I get a bills, that why I enjoyed been at me.; [a.] New York, NY

**BOHLEY, WILLIAM J.**
[b.] May 17, 1960, Barberton, OH; [p.] John W. Bohley, Gwen M. Bohley; [m.] Kathy L. Grezlik, November 19, 1994; [ch.] America Bohley, Caitlin Bohley; [ed.] Walsh Jesuit H.S., Stark Tech., Institute; [occ.] Mechanic; [memb.] NRA, Holy Trinity Church; [pers.] Dedicated to all those falsely accused. Favorite poet Robert Burns.; [a.] Akron, OH

**BOLIN, RONALD ANTHONY**
[pen.] Ronald Anthony Bolin; [b.] May 18, 1957, Louisville, KY; [p.] Roy and Shirly Bolin; [ed.] Iroquois High School, Columbia School of Broadcasting, California Coast University; [occ.] Budget Analyst with the Dept of Navy; [memb.] American Society of Military Comptroller, American Legion, Lifetime member of International Society of Poets; [hon.] Numerous Military and Civilian Government Awards, Lifetime Royal Patron States with the Principality of Hutt River Province Australia; [oth. writ.] Alien observations published in "River of Dreams"; [pers.] The survivability of the human race is directly proportionate to the level of care and concern put into action by each individual of the human race!; [a.] San Diego, CA

**BOOKMAN, ROBERT MAXWELL**
[pen.] Spud Enigma; [b.] January 22, 1983, Seattle, WA; [ed.] Currently in the seventh grade at Brentwood School in Lost Angeles; [memb.] U.S. Diving Assoc., U.S. Hockey Assoc., U.S. Tennis Assoc., Rose Bowl Aguatics Diving Team, Marina Cities Ice Hockey Team; [hon.] All-State of California Junior Olympic Diving Team; [oth. writ.] Published in The Outlook to save historical landmark; [pers.] I thank my Poetry Society teacher Laurel Schmidt for inspiring me to write about the challenges that I face at diving and which mean a great deal to me.; [a.] Santa Monica, CA

**BORGES-SILVA, EDWARD J.**
[pen.] Rachel Jacobs; [b.] October 31, 1958, Vancouver, WA; [p.] Edward B. Silva, Sybil V. Borland; [m.] Amber D. Borges-Silva, April 3, 1986; [ch.] Patricia Rachel; [ed.] Adams High '77, Portland Community College Courses; [occ.] Window Craftsman; [memb.] Canby Christian Church; [oth. writ.] Social and Political essays as yet unpublished. Several editorial responses in local publications; [pers.] "Honestly, fidelity, integrity"; [a.] Portland, OR

**BOSTON, BRUCE**
[b.] September 17, 1979, Bowling Green, KY; [p.] Ed Boston, Judy Boston; [ed.] Barren County High School, Glasgow, KY (Sophomore); [occ.] Student; [hon.] Kentucky Academic Association, Governor's Cup - State Finalist (1994) - Literature, National PTA Cultural Arts Program, 'Reflections' 1992, 1st place, State Level Visual Arts; [oth. writ.] None published; [pers.] I enjoy revealing the beauty and mysteries of the night to my readers through my writings and illustrations.; [a.] Glasgow, KY

**BOUTHSY, KIANG**
[b.] May 2, 1979, Laos; [p.] Bounma and Nheune Bouthsy; [ed.] Pulaski High School; [occ.] Student; [hon.] Honor Roll, Perfect Attendance; [oth. writ.] I wrote several poems that have never been published before; [pers.] I like to write what/how I'm feeling. I like to express myself in writing and hope to achieve many goals.; [a.] Milwaukee, WI

**BOWERS, TIFFANIE**
[b.] November 4, 1981, Mt. Sinai Hospital, Milwaukee; [p.] James T. and Yvonne Bowers; [ed.] 8th Grader; [occ.] Student, Milwaukee Educational Center; [hon.] Bowling Awards, Student of the Month; [oth. writ.] Literary Press Awards; [pers.] I write poems to express feelings and emotions. If everybody would do something positive and conservative like writing poetry there'd be alot less crimes.; [a.] Milwaukee, WI

**BOWES, DANIEL**
[b.] October 26, 1978, Brooklyn, NY; [p.] Elizabeth A. Bowes, Gerald Bowes; [ed.] John Dewey HS, Brooklyn NY; [occ.] Student at John Dewey HS; [hon.] National Merit Scholarship Semi-Finalist; [oth. writ.] Academic essay is school political magazine, several poems and short stories in school literary magazine; [pers.] I haven't been writing for very long, and I'm still trying to find my voice. My influences are the noir writers (such as James M. Cain) and beat poets (i.e. Allen Ginsberg); [a.] Brooklyn, NY

**BOWKER, PATRICIA**
[b.] April 17, 1969, Oneonta; [p.] Lillian Pratt and William Wlasiok; [ed.] 2 years of Law, Sherburne-Earlville, Jr. and Sr. High School; [occ.] Quality Assurance; [hon.] Various merits awards and Editors Choice Awards; [oth. writ.] I've been published for the last 4 years in "The National Library of Poetry", and in local newspapers; [pers.] To know me, is to read my poetry: It is a reflection of my personality on the way I view everyone through my thoughts and feelings.; [a.] Sherburne, NY

**BOYCE, CHARLES**
[pen.] Charles Cemento; [b.] June 17, 1981, Brooklyn; [p.] Mr. and Mrs. B. Cemento; [ed.] Junior High Graduate, Elementary Graduate; [occ.] High School Student at Lafayette High School; [memb.] Former Boy Scout of America; [hon.] 5th Grade Scholastic Awards for Reading and Math; [oth. writ.] Personal only, none submitted; [pers.] Live positively for today. Tomorrow may never get here.; [a.] Brooklyn, NY

**BOYCE, TEIA T.**
[pen.] Kayla Summer; [b.] June 23, 1971, Greenville, SC; [pers.] I love writing. It's like a mystery within itself and inspiring to the soul.; [a.] Greenville, SC

**BOYD, VERLEY LLOYD**
[pen.] Rev. V. B.; [b.] February 20, 1951, Jamaica, West Indies; [p.] Deceased; [m.] Divorced; [ed.] Jones Town Primary, Kingston College, Jamaica Police Academy; [occ.] Loss Prevention Officer; [pers.] I was influenced by a certain woman on the job who I am deeply in love with. She is such a special person and I know she will inspire me to write more.; [a.] Hempstead, NY

**BOYER, WILLIAM S.**
[b.] April 12, 1966, Chester, PA; [p.] Bea Boyer, Faustino Ayala; [ch.] Desmond Anthony, Nichole Leigh; [ed.] J.P. McCaskey H.S.; [occ.] Courier; [memb.] Lancaster Young Men's Christian Association; [oth. writ.] Several poems soon to be published; [pers.] I was inspired to write by my wonderful wife to be, Rebecca Sweigart and greatly motivated by three other beautiful women in my life.... My sisters, Dolores, Vicki, and Precious. Thank You.; [a.] Lancaster, PA

**BRACK, LAURA DORIS SMITH**
[pen.] Laura Doris Smith; [b.] March 15, 1914, Topeka, KS; [p.] Laura Belle De Bertice La Grange; [ch.] Marjorie Louise, Raymond Gene, Martha May, James Franklin, David Louis; [ed.] high school, biographical survey of my Childhood and Early Teen Years; [occ.] Homemaker, copyrighted; [memb.] Soprano, Bethany Oratorio Society, Bethany College Lindsborg KS; [hon.] Pianist-Organist, Salvation Army Salina; [oth. writ.] To A Wild Goose - poem, Spring (poem), other poems, My Trip To The East Coast; [pers.] My creed love one another, child Evangelism Teacher; [a.] Salina, KS

**BRACKIN, MARY**
[b.] October 22, 1935, Geneva Co, AL; [p.] B. J. Hodges and Mamie; [m.] James L. Brackin; [ch.] Michael, Larry, Stephen, Stacey; [ed.] Ged - after children were adults and proud of it; [occ.] R. Nursery School Teacher; [memb.] Hartford Baptist Church, Mission Volunteer Consultant, Gideone Auxiliary, Member, other volunteer work; [a.] Hartford, AL

**BRADLEY, BETTY ANN**
[pen.] "Moonlight"; [b.] July 7, 1948, Lancaster, WI; [p.] Lawrence Bradley and Jean Elenor Mink; [ch.] William and Desiree; [oth. writ.] Poems, poems and more; [pers.] Keep your heart and soul open to God, then you should grow and become who God wants you to be, caring and sharing and good to one another with understanding and unconditioned love you will see you won't have to ask any other for God will show you the way to be loving, to be loved, to love, and you can say I am loving, I am loved, I love "Moonlight".; [a.] Dallas, TX

**BRADLEY, LIAM J.**
[b.] August 8, 1984, NY; [p.] Monica Mignone, Michael Bradley; [ed.] James Wilson Young, Middle School, Bayport, NY; [occ.] Student; [hon.] Presidential Award for Academic Excellence, Writing Award, Spelling Award; [pers.] My true individual inspirations were my mother, my 5th grade teacher, Virginia Metzendorf, and my best friend David Zwaik.; [a.] Blue Point, NY

**BRADLEY, ANGELA**
[pen.] X-Zashon; [b.] April 16, 1981, Charleston, SC; [p.] Julia Garrett, Randy Bradley; [ed.] Summerville High School (I am currently going); [hon.] I have won awards at school for my poetry; [pers.] Thanks: Harry, Julia, Grant, Jackie, Randy, Shannon, Kara, Grandma, Grandpa, and my little sister Tabitha with all the love in the world. I would also like to thank my idol Ricki Lake.; [a.] Summerville, SC

**BRADY, PATSY**
[pen.] Patsy Harvey Brady; [b.] December 11, 1937, Chicago, IL; [p.] Mrs. Alice Marie Lowe; [m.] Paul E. Brady, February 1, 1986; [ch.] One son (31 yrs. old), four step sons; [ed.] Graduated from Seminole High School, Sanford Fla., one year vocational school Mary Karl (now) Daytona Community College; [occ.] Beauty Parlor; [memb.] Osteen Bapt. Church, Member of the Choir - Assistant Pianist, Coordinator for Neighborhood Watch, served as a volunteer at Central Fla, Regional Hosp., Sanford, Fla.; [hon.] Outstanding Senior in the Seminole High School Band; [oth. writ.] I've written over a hundred poems! I wrote a few since the 5th grade, but would write one for birthdays, new births, or weddings and give them as a gift. But have really been writing them quite often on a regular basis since April '95.; [pers.] I write to express a love of nature, to reflect my love for God and His Love for all. I enjoy writing, and find it a great since of satisfaction. I love to share them with anyone that will listen.; [a.] Osteen, FL

**BRATTEN, MS. JOYCE ANN**
[pen.] Joyce A. Bratten; [b.] November 23, 1953, Girdletree, MD; [p.] James E. Sr. (deceased) and Emma L. Bratten; [ed.] Snow Hill High School, Snow Hill, MD; [occ.] Office Secretary, Wicomico County Health Dept., Salisbury, MD; [memb.] St. John Holiness Church, Stockton, MD; [oth. writ.] Poems published in local church bulletins and publications; [pers.] "I write each poem prayerfully."; [a.] Salisbury, MD

**BRECKENRIDGE, THOM E.**
[b.] April 25, 1980, Fresno, CA; [p.] Nancy and Durbin Breckenridge; [ed.] Fresno Christian Elementary, Fresno Christian Junior High, currently enrolled in Fresno Christian High School; [occ.] High School Student (Sophomore); [pers.] I can do all things though Christ who strengthen me.; [a.] Fresno, CA

**BREWER, JENNIFER L.**
[b.] April 14, 1962, Lincoln, ME; [p.] Leonard Noyes and Sandra Guyer; [ch.] Padrick Paul, Kristin Jens and Martin Casey; [ed.] Dexter Regional High School, Husson College; [occ.] Financial Consultant; [memb.]

Dr. Phillips Little League Board of Directors; [pers.] I try to draw from life experiences in my writing, hoping to help others relate to similar personal feelings.; [a.] Orlando, FL

**BREWER-BROOKS, DORIS**
[pen.] Helen Stiener Rice; [b.] October 24, 1937, New Orleans, LA; [p.] Octavia and Nathan Johnson; [m.] Separated, July 4, 1989; [ch.] Ronald, Gregory, Linda, Joseph, James, Vanessa, Stacey; [ed.] High School, Two years college, vocational school; [occ.] Retired Disability; [memb.] St. Stephens M.B.C., Choir Member, American Heart Assoc.; [hon.] Plaques, Certificates; [oth. writ.] Started Autobiography (unfinished) several speeches for speaking; [pers.] I love the words of different songs. It encourages me to think of words to write down.; [a.] Fredricksburg, VA

**BRIDOPANAK, RICHARD**
[pen.] Linda Gautes; [b.] March 24, 1960, Anaheim, CA; [p.] Allen and Gonet; [m.] Susan, June 18; [ch.] Four; [ed.] Stanford BA 82, Stanford Law, 85; [occ.] Trial Attorney; [oth. writ.] "The Cold Wind Whistles Around The Headstones Now, Easter Dawn"; [a.] Mission Viejo, CA

**BRINSON, GOLDIA**
[b.] July 20, 1919, Gary, WV; [p.] Hutchel and Rosa Tucker; [m.] Leonard Brinson (Deceased); [ch.] Carolyn, Michael, Keith Carlos, Caprice, Carmaye; [ed.] Gary High, Bluefield State College; [occ.] Retired School Teacher (Elementary); [hon.] Gene Guess Memorial Award, 4 Awards from City of Anchorage, Alaska for Outstanding Community Service; [oth. writ.] Short poems in local papers, founder of Arts Organization in Anchorage, Alaska; [pers.] I wish to convey the depth and understanding of real love, the pain and joy that true love brings. Each poem must have substance.; [a.] Federal Way, WA

**BRISCOE, RUBY**
[b.] January 30, 1933, Bigwood, KY; [p.] Buck and Lula Tackett; [m.] Lenual D. Briscoe, November 23, 1951; [ch.] Dwight D., Michael D. and Mark Briscoe; [occ.] Housewife; [oth. writ.] None that have been made public; [pers.] While thinking, should I suddenly lose my spouse on whom I have been dependent so many years. What would happen to me?; [a.] Middletown, OH

**BRISTER, CANDICE**
[b.] October 24, 1952, Orlando, FL; [p.] Claude A. Brister, Winifred C. Brister; [m.] James S. Armentrout, May 27, 1982; [ch.] Aaron McGraw; [ed.] Douglas Freeman High School, Richmond VA., Grady Memorial Hospital, School of Nursing, Atlanta Georgia, Macon College, Macon Georgia, currently enrolled in an independent self study program at Graceland College, Lamoni Iowa; [occ.] Pediatrician RN, Childrens Hospital, Richmond, VA; [oth. writ.] Only recently began writing, has authored a private collection of poems not yet submitted for publication.; [pers.] Personal growth is a lifelong process. A successful individual will not overlook his or her opportunities to learn new things about the world around them or about themselves.; [a.] Richmond, VA

**BRISTOL, BETH D.**
[pen.] Beth D. Bristol; [b.] April 20, 1939, Colorado Springs, CO; [p.] Oscar L. Grauberger, Ruth Heist Grauberger; [ch.] Dr. Terrence A. Bristol, Julie J. Bristol; [ed.] Berthoud H.S., Berthoud, CO, Penn State University, Berks Campus; [occ.] Student; [memb.] AAUW, Atonement Lutheran Ch., Friend of Berks Co. Libraries; [hon.] President, Board of Directors, The Children's Home of Reading; [pers.] I try to reflect my heritage and gratitude for the past and hope for the

future in my writing.; [a.] Wyomissing, PA

**BROADBENT, BETTY B.**
[pen.] Bet-E-Bee; [b.] February 28, 1921, Mars, PA; [p.] Russell and Kathleen Burger; [m.] Gene (Deceased), July 7, 1942; [ch.] Patricia, Kathleen, Janie, J.R. and Obie; [ed.] High School and Business College; [occ.] Retired; [memb.] Trinity Community Church, Share Club; [hon.] National Honor Society, Letter for Quill and Scroll in Journalism; [oth. writ.] Just poems for the family and friends; [pers.] Am trying to express caring and the beauty of God's blessings to all; [a.] North Fort Myers, FL

**BROCK, ANN**
[pen.] Ethelann T. Brock; [b.] June 29, 1925, North Castle, NY; [p.] Clarence and Ella Taliaferro; [m.] Vernon Brock, March 6, 1954; [ch.] Carol Gallaher - Chip Wall, Patricia Prince, Vanessa Jarmakovitz; [ed.] Katonah High, Business College; [occ.] Housewife; [memb.] Hope Community Church, Family and Community Education (F.C.E.), been on Stephens County Association Committee as Secretary and Local as President and Secretary; [oth. writ.] One story of Christmas and grandson published in local paper, The Marlow Review; [pers.] I am very close to the young and the elderly.; [a.] Marlow, OK

**BROME, GRAHAM**
[b.] October 26, 1956, Barbados; [p.] Markine Brome; [ch.] Christine; [ed.] St. Lucy Sr., and St. Lucy Sec.; [occ.] Super; [oth. writ.] Jokes and songs not published yet. (Tee-Shir Writing).; [pers.] Try to be the best at what I do, treat every body like I want to be-treated. Always have a smiling face.; [a.] Brooklyn, NY

**BROOKS, STEVEN A.**
[b.] January 5, 1974, Atlanta, GA; [p.] R. Steven and Eileen B. Brooks; [ed.] 3 yrs. at Southern Methodist University; [occ.] Student; [hon.] National Honor Society, Varsity Track Athlete; [oth. writ.] Several poems for contests in High School; [pers.] I want to express, through my poems, the emotions that a person can feel while involved in a relationship.; [a.] Dallas, TX

**BROOKS, DEREK STEPHEN**
[b.] August 11, 1951, Pittsburgh, PA; [p.] Jesse and Lucretia Brooks; [m.] Katie Springer Brooks, July 31, 1983; [ch.] Tracy Deborah Brooks, Daariat Van De Vere Brooks; [ed.] University of Pittsburgh, University of Ife, West Africa, Crown Business Institute, New York; [occ.] Banker, Chemical Bank New York, N.Y.; [memb.] Studio Museum in Harlem, Schomberg Center for Black Culture, Hansbourgh Recreational Facility; [hon.] 1991 NYCHA Art Award (Painting), 1992 NYCHA Art Award (Painting); [pers.] I write from sorrow as well as joy, striving to perfect the gifts that inhabit my human spirit.; [a.] Bronx, NY

**BROWN, DOROTHY I.**
[pen.] Dorothy I. Brown; [b.] April 24, 1929; [p.] Mr. and Mrs. A. Monroe Wehe; [m.] William C. Brown; [ch.] Kenneth, Diane, S. S. William C. Brown Jr.; [ed.] Lake Stevens High School, WA, Everett Community College, WA - Asst. Dietitian; [occ.] Retired - 35 years in Food Service. Now to travel and write; [memb.] Pearl Center For Christian Living, C.A.P, KY, Salvation Army, American Indian R.C. of So. Dakota. International Society of Poets, Preferred Writers Memberships, KY; [hon.] National Library of Poetry, International Society of Poets - for '95, "A Distinguished Few" - many Editor's Choice Awards, Tenn. TNNN - TV. Award for the "Most Distinguished Poet of 1994"; [oth. writ.] "Demo taped "Quiet Times", poems published in Sparrowgrass, W.V. Calif. and GA; [pers.] Goal is to have my book published for family and friends, "My

Life In Poetry" in '95, "44 to 94". My belief is to live each day as if it is your last, and you will be a better person for God and Country. To write is a gift from the Lord.; [a.] Mill Creek, WA

## BROWN, PAULINE

[b.] May 24, 1910, Iowa; [p.] Oscar and Ida McAninch; [m.] Clarence W. Brown, December 6, 1936; [ch.] Conrad, Benjamin, Blaine, David, Clarine, Angeln, Lorisa and Mary Ida; [ed.] Mt Ayr High School (Iowa) 1928, Northwestern Bible School, Grad. 1935, Minneapolis, Minn.; [occ.] Retired; [memb.] Baptist Church, Christian School Society; [oth. writ.] Poems in High School, articles in the local paper and a short story published in the Power for Living magazine; [pers.] Taught public school two years. Taught Piano for fifteen Years including seven years to international students in Liberia, West Africa.; [a.] Keizer, OR

## BROWN, FRED H.

[b.] December 17, 1914, Gene Autry, OK; [m.] Jessie Hodge, January 12, 1947; [ch.] Sherry Lynn Ramm (Child), Michael Jason Brown Ramm (Grandchild); [ed.] Southeastern University of Okla. Durant; [occ.] Retired as Mechanical - Design Draftsman, U.S. Navy World War II; [oth. writ.] Eternity is first poem entered in a contest.

## BROWN, PAUL J.

[b.] September 12, 1977, Stone Ham; [p.] Paul Brown Sr. and Shirley; [ed.] Whittier Vocational (and regional) Technical High School and I'm in Graphic Communications; [occ.] Crew Member of McDonald's in Haverhill; [memb.] Participated in the 1994-1995 Project Awesome Program; [hon.] Award Certificate for most improved test scores. Certificate of achievement for completing the Awesome Program; [oth. writ.] Quite a few to name but those will be for another time; [pers.] If you want your life on track, only you can do it. Only you're the one who can bring success or failure to complete your life.; [a.] Haverhill, MA

## BROWN, MARY C.

[b.] March 17, 1949, Cary, MS; [p.] Mary and C. J. Johnson; [m.] Jesse Brown Jr., January 8, 1977; [ch.] Jason, Jessica, Joi and Jeramy Brown; [ed.] Englewood High School, Chicago State University; [occ.] 5th Grade Teacher Robert H. Lawrence School for Math and Science - Chicago, Illinois; [oth. writ.] Two unpublished books of poems. "Private Thoughts"; [pers.] My writings reflect human strength and a strong since of personal values. I'm motivated and influenced by my personal relationship with my God and my family.; [a.] Gary, IN

## BROWN, ELAINE

[b.] December 18, 1930, New York City; [p.] Richard and Mae Brown; [m.] John W. Riley, April 19, 1979; [ch.] Conrad Stanley Taylor, Steven R. Taylor, Michael A. Taylor, Wm. Cobb; [ed.] Mabel Dean Beacon High, Medical Aid Training School; [occ.] Retired Nurses Aid; [memb.] Juter National Society of Poets 1994-1995, Song Writer for Majestic Records of Linden Texas, County Music; [hon.] Editors Choice Award by National Library of Poetry 1993, E.C.A. for 1995; [pers.] My writings are about feelings, thoughts and experience of my life, you can say that my personal life as well as social life can be seen in my poetry.; [a.] Fayetteville, NC

## BROWN, MARILEE ELSIE

[b.] June 14, 1946, Knoxville, TN; [p.] Arthur and Lucile George; [m.] John E., May 15, 1965; [ch.] Robert, James and Micheal; [ed.] Central High and University of Maryland; [occ.] Homemaker, but I do alot of arts and crafts; [oth. writ.] Clark Gable, If,

Midsummer Storm, King Jesus; [pers.] I wrote this poem at an English 294 class at the University in Bentwaters, England. It is not my best poem, but one of my favorites.; [a.] Greenback, TN

## BROWN, MICHAEL W. K.

[b.] January 22, 1948, Salt Lake City; [p.] Wayne and Miriam; [ch.] Michael Bryan Brown, Chelsea Heather Brown, and Sterling Michael Vicent Brown; [ed.] Bachelor of Arts, Philosophy, University of Utah; [occ.] Systems Analyst; [memb.] Air Life Line, Make A Wish Foundation, Aircraft owners and Pilots Association; [hon.] Honor Roll, Dean's List, Commercial Pilots License; [oth. writ.] I've been fortunate to have three other poems published; [pers.] "Ultimately, children are our only Resource."; [a.] Murray, UT

## BROWNING, PENNY PULVER

[b.] August 26, 1951, Plainwell, MI; [p.] Robert E. Pulver, Dolores Carruthers Pulver; [occ.] Graduated 1969, Otsego High School, Otsego, MI; [pers.] Think to me to Reed, wherever you are, and I will catch your thought, and we will drift away like wisps of smoke from Autumn's burning leaves.; [a.] Plainwell, MI

## BRUCKLER, TARA ANNE

[b.] April 10, 1974, Livingston, NJ; [p.] Richard and Helene Bruckler; [ed.] Emmaus High School, Lehigh Carbon Community College; [occ.] Department Manager; [pers.] If I am remembered for nothing else, let me be remembered as a dreamer and a romantic, for life is truly beautiful in my eyes, and it is my hope that all men may stop to reflect upon this, especially in these trying times.; [a.] Allentown, PA

## BRYANT, JANICE

[b.] November 25, 1940, South Gate, CA; [p.] Clarence Roland Goforth, Helen Leora Galpin Goforth; [m.] Divorced; [ch.] Michell, Leann, Cheri, Kathy, Connie and Mark; [ed.] Verdugo Hills High, University of Montana, Salk Lake Community College; [occ.] Full-time Student, Part-time Teleservices Specialist; [hon.] Numerous Ribbons for Ceramics and Floral artistic design and 1 Special Merchant Award for dried flowers plus ribbons in culinary, Canning and Baking; [oth. writ.] I have several poems tucked away, I am working on a Fantasy Trilogy. Locked In Chrystal is my first publication.; [pers.] Writing helps me to expand my awareness of the world as it heightens my imagination, and it can be therapeutic.; [a.] Murray, UT

## BRYANT, C. W. COUNTRY

[pen.] Country Bryant; [b.] March 25, 1922, Huff, AK; [p.] Rev. and Mrs. E. C. Bryant; [ch.] 2-Daughters Cindi and Bonita; [ed.] High School and 3 years Americana Leadership College; [occ.] Writer and Food Business; [memb.] Life Time - Tulsa Songwriters; [hon.] Some Accolades Attached - use as you see fit; [oth. writ.] Some attached use as you wish all or none UBD Judge; [pers.] The more I can know about self the better I can communicate with you; [a.] Tulsa, OK

## BRYANT, MARY ANN

[b.] Alabama; [p.] John and Laura Thomas; [m.] Hughelin; [ch.] 6 Adults; [ed.] Miller High, Wayne State U., Masters - Guidance Counselor; [occ.] Counselor, Secondary Ed Teacher - Detroit Board of Education; [memb.] St. Gregory Church, Mich Counselors Ass., Mich Humane Society; [hon.] Gold Medal - High School - Essay Contest; [oth. writ.] Several - Essay Contest "What America means to me" Newspaper Howling Dog Press - (poem); [pers.] Writing is not something one hearts, but is felts so, from the heart to the paper is sometimes a difficult task which is in itself requires another special talent.; [a.] Detroit, MI

## BRYSON, J. MARIE

[pen.] Maria Bryson; [b.] January 27, 1943, Bloomington, IL; [m.] Ralph Bryson; [ch.] Anna Raquelle, Nikki Teresa Corrinne; [ed.] Sacramento State College, School of Life; [occ.] Enjoying life, employed by Multnomah Cty., library, Portland, OR; [hon.] Two beautiful self-reliant daughters, respected friends; [oth. writ.] Many light-hearted poems shared with friends; [pers.] My poems just poke fun at life's daily adventures, a bit like Ogden Nash.; [a.] Portland, OR

## BRZYCKI, FRANCES

[pen.] Marie T. Falcon; [b.] January 23, 1972, Portland; [p.] Helen and Alfred Brzycki; [ed.] West Linn High School, Pacific NW College of Art, The Pursuit of Excellence Series; [occ.] Designer; [memb.] Context Walk Organization; [hon.] Designer of the 1993 Portland Rose Festival Collector's Series label for Oak Knoll Winery; [pers.] The most important belief to have is the belief in one's self.; [a.] West Linn, OR

## BUCK, EVELYN DALE

[b.] September 1, 1922, Parris Is., SC; [p.] Walter Edward Dale Sr., Sylvia Gertrude Smith; [m.] Paul Charles Buck (Deceased), March 20, 1953; [ed.] High School Diploma, 3 years of college and Music School: Florida State College for women, Sherwood Music School, Temple University; [occ.] Retired; [memb.] I do not belong to any clues or organizations. I was a Hospital Corps Wave in the U.S. Navy during World War II. I worked for the Federal Government for 31 years and for private industry for 12 years.; [hon.] 5 award for essay, "Preserving Democracy for America" when I was a Sophomore in High School, Certificate of appreciation from U.S. Depth. of labor just from to retirement 6-3-86; [oth. writ.] Various poems, mainly "Snow" poems, Christmas poems, and patriotic poems; [pers.] I have spent the years since my late husband's demise in caring for my health and my home, and for a darling little peke-a-poo dog, which I no longer have. I have had many creative moments when I feel the inspiration to write a poem.; [a.] Philadelphia, PA

## BUDNER, MELISSA A.

[pen.] M. A. G. Budner; [b.] December 2, 1974, Parma Hospital; [p.] Eugene R. and Joanne M. (Horvath) Budner; [ed.] Graduated Salem Senior High, June 1993, currently attending Bluffton College for Education Major; [occ.] Student; [memb.] Bluffton College Educational Organization, St. Paul Catholic Church; [hon.] Salem Foundation Scholarships, Salem Board of Education Scholarship, TEP Scholarship from Bluffton Honors Program - Bluffton College; [oth. writ.] No other published writings; [pers.] I write because it is the best way to express myself and my feelings. It is not written for the benefit at anyone, yet the enjoyment of everyone.; [a.] Salem, OH

## BULTMAN, LUCIUS LEGRANDE

[b.] January 29, 1929, Columbus, SC; [p.] Charles F. J. Bultman and Jessie M. Stulb; [m.] Mary E. Kelly, October 15, 1955; [ch.] Mary Kelly Hucko, Laura Caruso, Mollie Baney, Lucius L. Jr., F. Michael, Joseph John; [ed.] High School, Benedictine Military School, Savannah, CA., Attended 2 years, University of South Caro., did not graduate, Purdue University W. Layfayette, Indiana, 2 yrs. Insurance Course L.I.M.I., Graduated 1954; [occ.] Semi-Retired, work part-time music and magazine outlet (family owned); [hon.] God's blessings immeasurable, a loving wife, children, and friends who are true friends; [oth. writ.] Golf humor sold to golf digest in 1960's both sold without querying first-beginner's luck. "Custer's Last Shank" explanation of how battle of little big horn started as a remember guest golf tournament but developed into battle due do handicap misuse. "Ballad of Pigeon Named `T'" 34-8 line stanzas detailing the rise and fall of three hustler's efforts in trying to skin an easy mark. As narrated by T's caddie "The Shootout", published in state golf associated paper. Two trail dusty cow hands, seated atop a corral fence. Natch as the marshall (Wyatt Earp implied) tries to conduct a shootout under a new handicap system while the more knowledgable of the two tries to explain to his friend why "Why" still hasn't "Slapped Leather" even though his oppenent has fired three shots. The third one being the one that alerts the marshall to a possible "Handicap Abuse" or (Sec: Mae-B 1-2 MNY) and enables the marshall to shoot his way out of otherwise death.; [pers.] In my earlier days of writing I found serious composition to be a problem. Every start in a serious vein would invariably turn to or end up in humor. Although I have mellowed with age I still find humor the easier.; [a.] North Augusta, SC

**BUNCH, MS. GAIL**
[pen.] Gail Bunch; [b.] October 20, 1950, Jackson, MS; [p.] Paul and Sarah Sprayberry; [m.] Divorced; [ch.] Daughter - Scarlett Myers, grandson - Channing; [ed.] Secretarial College and other Technical Courses; [occ.] Secretary with M.S. State Dept. of Transportation; [oth. writ.] Poems published in "Poetry South" 1992, also in "Yarn Spinner" of MS Poetry Assn., several unpublished poems and songs. Every poem I have written was a result of a true experience.; [pers.] Enjoy playing piano and singing. Song and poems come from the innermost of our being. For many years life seems to be a race, then with the experiences of our joys and trials, it becomes a journey.; [a.] Jackson, MS

**BUNNER, BRUCE**
[b.] November 9, 1933, White Plains, NY; [p.] Edgar Bunner, Alice Bunner; [m.] Ingrid, October 13, 1962; [ch.] Edgar, Erika, Bruce J., Elke; [ed.] New York University, BA Degree; [occ.] Insurance Executive; [hon.] Honorary Doctorate from Azura Pacific University; [oth. writ.] Numerous articles for Professional Magazines related to insurance topics (e.g. Wall Street Journal, National Law Review, etc.); [pers.] That I might share the experience of Saint Paul "That I may know Christ and the power of His resurrection." Philippians 3:10; [a.] Weston, CT

**BUNUAN, ANDY L.**
[pen.] Andy L. Bunuan; [b.] October 16, 1924, Agoo, La Union, Philippines; [p.] Ciriaco and Alejandra Bunuan (Both deceased); [m.] Josie Belvis-Bunuan, April 28, 1951; [ch.] Cesar, Jun, Joy, Ed and Sue; [ed.] High School Graduate and Radio Operator Graduate, Christ the King Academy and Central Inst. of Technology; [occ.] Retired Employee, Telecom Office, Baguio City, Phils.; [memb.] Legion of Mary, Holy Name Society, Knights of Columbus, Couples for Christ - Baguio City, Philippines and Milpitas, CA, U.S.A.; [hon.] News Correspondent of the Year (1960-1968 Consistent) at Itogon, Benguet, Philippines; [oth. writ.] Several news and feature articles published in local newspapers; [pers.] My writings reflect on the realities of life to touch the inner core of the heart, mind and soul.; [a.] Milpitas, CA

**BURBOL, ESTHER M.**
[b.] February 14, 1922, Cleveland, OH; [p.] Karl L. and Orpha Scott Weitzel; [m.] Charles J. Burbol Sr., September 6, 1941; [ch.] Charles J. Jr. and Bob R. Burbo; [ed.] Graduated Brooklyn Village High School, 1940, Brooklyn Vill., Ohio, Real Estate Classes, Brokers License, Designations: Graduate of Realtors Institute and Certified Residential Specialist; [occ.] Retired January 1994; [oth. writ.] Many poems between 1934 and 1984, this poem written in High School in 1938, received "A and Par Excellence" grade on it. I also wrote my Autobiography in verse.; [pers.] "When a special

kindness is shown you, pass it on to someone else." "Be proud of that person looking back at you from the mirror." (My poem was born of all the world strife prior to WWII and is still a prior for today.); [a.] Sarasota, FL

**BURDITCH, MARYLIN GERALDINE**
[pen.] Mary Lin Burditch; [b.] July 9, 1943; [p.] Louis Stein, Shirley Lotman Stein; [m.] Nathan Burditch, September 5, 1965; [ch.] Paul Stewart Burditch, Alisa Beth Burditch, Jason Burditch-McKenzie; [ed.] Olney High, American College Art and Sciences, Villanova University, Compass Rose, Phila Mediation at Small Claims; [occ.] Paralegal/Mediator, Sales Associate, Artist, Writer, Curator; [memb.] Phila Art Museum, Franklin Institute, Hapassah, American Heart Association, Vision thru Art, Arts for Blind and Sighted; [pers.] On the stage of life I strive for am outstanding performance, meeting every challenge as my personal focus of achievement. All the while, carrying Robert Louis Stevenson in my pocket!

**BUREAU, RAYMOND SCOTT**
[pen.] R. S. Bureau; [b.] November 19, 1969, Rockville, CT; [p.] Richard L. and Mary L. Bureau; [m.] Beth L. Bureau, June 17, 1985; [ed.] Bachelor's Degree in English Education, University of North Florida, Jacksonville, FL, Clay High School, Green Cove Springs, FL; [occ.] English Teacher at Clay High School, G.C.S., FL and part-time English Teacher at Florida Community College at Jacksonville; [memb.] Ocean Park Baptist Church, Jacksonville Beach, FL, National Education Association; [hon.] High School: National Honor Society, Beta Club, Top Ten Percent; [oth. writ.] Short Story: "Line Drive", it is a short story about an aging baseball player looking for one last moment of glory before he retires. Also, "Certified", a short story mixing baseball and science fiction. I frequently write poems.; [pers.] I love sports. Therefore, my two short stories are sports-oriented. I have also announced sports for radio stations. Even more so, I love my wife. She is the inspiration for all of my poems. Philosophy: Rich men need not be wealthy.; [a.] Jacksonville, FL

**BURGE, TONYA L.**
[b.] January 11, 1978, Warren, OH; [p.] Phil and Barb Burge; [ed.] Senior in High School - plan to go to Texas State University for - Criminals Justice Degree; [occ.] Secretary at Cleveland Punch and Die; [oth. writ.] Whisper in the night you sounds outside the window, remember how precious love is mom; [pers.] "Remember nothing lasts forever".; [a.] Ravenna, OH

**BURGHER, STEPHANIE**
[pen.] Claire Isabell; [b.] September 6, 1956, Atlanta; [p.] Joel and Hope Reeves; [m.] Derick Blake Burgher, October 10, 1981; [ch.] Christopher Blake, Phillip Jorissen; [ed.] Bachelor of Fine Arts Georgia State University: Photography, Printmaket: Minor in French and Art History, Dean's List; [occ.] Artist, Mother, Wife; [hon.] 1990 Awarded 2nd place for drawing and printmaking, Stamford Festival of the Arts, Stamford, Connecticut; [oth. writ.] A few years ago I decided to stop making visual art. I picked up a pen and a journal and started writing. I am pleased that this poem is young to be published.; [pers.] There is in nature, among many things, objects like trees and stones that do not have voices but will out-run the sound of my own. Theirs will repeat into the distance of time and mine might echo into swells of rhyme and reason. Sometimes words not easily remembered are suddenly recognized in the voice of a stranger.; [a.] Wilton, CT

**BURGUN, KEVIN J.**
[b.] March 25, 1976, Pittsburgh, PA; [p.] Jerome and Clare; [ed.] Joliet Catholic Academy, Kirkwood High School, currently enrolled at Hope College; [occ.] Stu-

dent striving to become an English teacher; [memb.] Alcohol Issues Matter (on Campus alcohol awareness group), Church College Group; [oth. writ.] Several not quite finished screenplays, poem published in school paper "Infiltration"; [pers.] I am influenced by people around me, especially those I'm close to. My writing reflects people. Romans 12, Thanx Heather.; [a.] Kirkwood, MO

**BURKE, EARL PRESTON**
[pen.] Awari Dragonus; [b.] November 3, 1968, Vicksburg, MS; [p.] John H. Burke and Alice B. Burke; [m.] Theresa R. Burke, April 21, 1989; [ch.] Tamarr Elizabeth; [ed.] Vicksburg High and University of Southern Mississippi; [occ.] Student Living Advisor, Piney Woods Country Life School, Piney Woods, MS; [memb.] Alpha Phi Alpha Fraternity; [pers.] There is a little bit of the dragon in all of us. Set it free and you will soar.; [a.] Piney Woods, MS

**BURNHAM, LEIGH**
[b.] July 31, 1973, Dallas; [ed.] B.A. English from the University of Texas at Austin, currently pursuing M.A. Counseling at Amber University to be completed May 1996, intending to pursue doctoral work in Humanities; [pers.] Never underestimate humanity, never overestimate humanity.; [a.] Richardson, TX

**BURNHAM JR., JEANE W.**
[b.] March 10, 1925, Gratiot Co., MI; [p.] Jeane W. and Lyna May B.; [m.] Diana Bell Burnham, April 15, 1966; [ch.] Jacquelyn, David, Susan, Kim, Richard, Isabella, Bruce; [ed.] 1-12, Okha. A and M. 1943; [occ.] Retired January 1, 1990 Mich. Dept. of Transportation; [memb.] WW-II, VFW, American Legion, Military Order of Purple Heart, AARP, VAVS, Member of St. Aidans Episcopal, Ann Arbor; [hon.] 1994 NL of P, Editors Choice Award for the "Evergreen". First poem to be published.; [oth. writ.] The Evergreen, NL of P., after The Storm 1994., The Butterflies 1988, unpublished; [pers.] Everything is Beautiful, even the Ugly!! The Lord Jesus is my pilot.; [a.] Ann Arbor, MI

**BURTON, MICHELE D.**
[pen.] Dee-Dee; [b.] June 3, 1958, Houston, TX; [p.] John Barber and Constance Barber; [m.] Edmund T. Burton, July 18, 1987; [ch.] Jonella M. Barber (age 17), Candace L. C. Burton (age 5), Latasha C. E. Burton (age 17 - step daughter); [ed.] Institute of Children's Literature, year of graduation 1995, Massey Business College - 1977 Exec., Accounting; [occ.] Administrative Broker - Insurance; [memb.] Fruit of the Spirit Youth Ministries - Vice President and Drama Director, Ad and D PLayers Theatre: Volunteer Work; [hon.] ACSR Designation: Accredited Customer Service Repres Entative, Semi-finalist: 1995 North America Open Poetry Contest; [oth. writ.] Short plays: "A Second Chance" and "Do Not Terminate Me", short skits: "Where Ya' Gonna Run To?" and "Is It All In Vain?" All unpublished works; [pers.] I endeavor to write positive material that is balanced with truth and integrity, which will enable and assist our youth to become productive, strong and bold leaders.; [a.] Houston, TX

**BUSER, SHERI JEAN**
[b.] September 20, 1980, Pedley, CA; [p.] Gioviana, Marry Buser; [ed.] Van Buren Elem., Jurupa Middle School, Jurupa Valley High School; [occ.] High School Student; [memb.] R.O.T.C, FFA, Choir, Club Live (Sat. Night Live), Drama Club, Cheerleading; [hon.] F.F.A., Gold Scholar Award, R.O.T.C. - Cadet Sgt., NCOIC, Drill Team/Color Guard/Guide on Bearer Awards, 6 award Ribbons with Cluster leaf; [oth. writ.] Other poems that I never published; [a.] Pedley, CA

**BUSHONG JR., DOUGLAS STEPHAN**
[pen.] Douglas Stephan Bushong Jr.; [b.] January, Key West, FL; [p.] Deceased; [ed.] Hallandale High School, Broward Community College; [occ.] Baker and Confectioner; [hon.] Phi Theta Kappa, Dean's List; [oth. writ.] Various poems and Short Stories. Currently working on a screenplay entitled "The Rain Painters".; [pers.] I believe, Poetry is the constant search for understanding of the world around us. As we see it, in contrast to the way we would like to perceive it.; [a.] Fort Lauderdale, FL

**BUSS, LARRY R.**
[b.] October 28, 1934, Catasauqua, PA; [p.] Jenny Buss, Herman Buss; [m.] Fern Buss, June 14, 1958; [ch.] Bryan Donald B.; [ed.] Attended Rochester Inst. of Technology, Catasauqua High Grad.; [occ.] Retired; [memb.] Board Member - Catasauqua Public Library, Bethlehem Palette Club and Quarter Century Club; [pers.] My poetry is usually a reflection of my experiences and beliefs that can't otherwise be said.; [a.] Catasauqua, PA

**BUTLER, MARSHALL N.**
[b.] January 21, 1913, Brunswick, MD; [m.] Mildred A. Butler, April 28, 1938; [ed.] Virginia School for the Deaf and Blind, Staunton, VA; [occ.] Linotype operator at The Washington Post, Washington, D.C., Retired March, 1973; [memb.] International Society of Poets (life time), The International Society of Authors and Artists, The National Authors Registry, Winchester Deaf Fellowship, Winchester Sign Language Organization, N.A.D., F.C.A., C.T.U., V.A.D.; [hon.] Accomplishment of Merit (5), Creative Arts and Science Ent., Certificate of Poetic Achievements 1991, 1992, 1993, American Poetry Annual, Editor's Choice Awards 1993 (2), 1994 (3), 1995 (1), The National Library of Poetry, Honorable Mentions, Iliad Press and World of Poetry, Golden Poet of 1992, World of Poetry, Certificates of Publication, Iliad Press; [oth. writ.] Published by Sparrowgrass Poetry Forum; 1991 American Poetry Annual, The Amherst Society; Yes Press, Tenn.; Cader Publishing Ltd.; The National Library of Poetry; Quill Books; Creative Arts and Science Ent.; Celebrations, Cader Publishing Ltd.; Olympus, Mile High Poetry Society; Inspirations In Ink, Creative Arts and Science Ent.; Mile High Poetry Society; Cader Publishing Ltd.; Iliad Press; University Press, Va.; Hearing Hearts Magazine; Oak Leaf Newsletter, Northern Shenandoah Valley Audubon Society, Boyce Va.; Many poems printed in The Hands and Silango Newsletters, Winchester, Va., "This Is Life," Best Poems of 1995, The National Library of Poetry, 2 albums "Visions" by the Sound of Poetry, The National Library of Poetry.; [pers.] I strive to make my poems enjoyable in reading.

**BUTLER, LORRAINE E.**
[pen.] Lori Butler; [p.] Frederick and Isabel Hoelzer; [ch.] Scott F. Butler; [ed.] BA - Dowling College, MA - Adelphi University; [occ.] Second Grade Teacher, Fifth Ave Elementary School, Northport - East Northport School District, New York; [pers.] Usually, I express my deepest thoughts and feelings through painting. This is the first time I have used a palette of words.; [a.] East Northport, NY

**BUTLER, NATASHA LYNN**
[pen.] Tasha; [b.] May 28, 1982, Mount Clemens; [p.] Sanford H. Butler III (Deceased), Mitchelle M. Pawlisz; [ed.] 7 years of Elementary, 2 years of Jr. High, I'm very active in sports, Volleyball last yr., Basketball and Track this yr. 95; [hon.] I was very honored to have been selected in the Anthology of Poetry. I'm very excited about being entered in another book.; [pers.] Go for your dreams they can be pursuit.; [a.] Utica, MI

**BYRNE, JAMES**
[b.] February 16, 1962, Newton-Wellesley Hospital; [p.] James Byrne, Sarah Byrne; [ed.] Quincy High School; [occ.] Stand-up Comedian; [pers.] I believe that life is a Spiritual Journey. The more I learn about myself, the more understanding I can have for others. I have been greatly influenced by the lyrical writings of Roger Waters.; [a.] Quincy, MA

**CAIN, PAULETTE**
[pen.] Paula; [b.] May 2, 1957, Colorado, OH; [p.] Elvin and Arisona; [m.] Divorced; [ch.] James Kane, Shilo Cain; [ed.] Computers and typist; [occ.] Owner of La-Paul Cleaning Services; [hon.] Typing and Math, Typing; [oth. writ.] Do I Ever Cross Your Mind Does; [pers.] I find great comfort in my poetry. I relax when I write poetry. It ease my very soul within.; [a.] Columbus, OH

**CALLARI, BARBARA**
[b.] May 19, 1943, Boston; [p.] Helen and James Bonelli; [m.] Anthony J. Callari, March 1, 1961; [ch.] One; [ed.] High School Ed; [oth. writ.] Poems

**CALLAWAY, TRAVIS JAMES**
[b.] January 9, 1976, Seguin, TX; [p.] Jim and Lynn Callaway; [ed.] Seguin High, South West Texas State Univ. Student; [occ.] Student S.W.T.S.U. San Marcos, TX; [oth. writ.] One poem published in high school paper; [a.] Seguin, TX

**CALVELLI, NICHOLAS**
[pen.] Nicola Calvelli; [b.] March 22, 1965, Vineland, NJ; [p.] Stella and Nicola Calvelli; [m.] Divorced - Single Parent; [ch.] Dylan Francis Nicola Calvelli 3 1/2 yrs. old; [ed.] Associates Degree in Liberal Arts from Camden county College, Planning to attend Rutgers University, in Sept. 96 - Major Journalism; [occ.] Fulltime student; [hon.] Dean's list - Camden Co. College; [oth. writ.] Published in Camden County College's Literary Magazine "Bridges"; [pers.] In my writing, I want to convey to the reader emotions and a sense of a larger idea or meaning through using isolated imagery which is common, if not taken for granted by the human experience.; [a.] Pine Hill, NJ

**CAMEROTA, NIKIE**
[b.] August 17, 1978, Long Beach, CA; [p.] Robert and Christine Camerota; [ed.] Still student in Chino High School; [occ.] Still Student; [hon.] One honor I have is being a big sister to my younger brother; [oth. writ.] Poems about love, depression, and subjects because I write whatever I feel in my heart; [pers.] Most of my writings goes to Tim Grijalva to show my love for him. All my writing is influenced by my aunt who died when I was young, who also wrote poetry.; [a.] Chino, CA

**CAMPBELL, COREY L.**
[b.] July 30, 1976, Portage, WI; [p.] Susan Jewell, Stanley Campbell; [ed.] Middleton High, University of Wisconsin - Madison; [memb.] The Dollywood Foundation; [oth. writ.] Article published in local newspaper, various writings for classes; [a.] Middleton, WI

**CAMPBELL, SONJA MARIA**
[b.] March 30, 1966, Gray, IN; [p.] Jimmy James and Cleta McDow; [m.] Scott A. Campbell, September 26, 1987; [ch.] Cody Scott Campbell, Kayla Mary Campbell; [ed.] Graduated from Granbury High School in 1984 and from Tarrant County Junior College in 1987 with an Associates Degree in Applied Science; [occ.] Registered Dental Hygienist for Dr. Mitchell Walker in Granbury, TX; [memb.] Lakeside Baptise Church-I teach a Sunday School Class for 1 and 2 year olds; [oth. writ.] Personal notes and poems for family and special friends; [pers.] My writings are reflective of

my personal feelings for my family and special friends. It's how I express my love for them.; [a.] Granbury, TX

**CANTRELL, AUDREY**
[pen.] Audrey Cantrell; [b.] August 13, 1950, Pickens, SC; [p.] John and Josephine Cantrell; [m.] Beverly U. Cantrell, November 23, 1988; [ch.] Michelle Cantrell Darrington, Michael Cantrell, Ray Brown (step son); [ed.] Pickens High School; [occ.] Manager, Grant Body Shop, Inc.

**CANUTESON, PAT**
[pen.] Pat Canuteson; [b.] February 6, 19565, Clifton, TX; [p.] Oren James Canuteson Jr., Barbara Canuteson; [m.] Karen Canuteson, April 28, 1984; [ch.] Jared Layne, Joshua James, Leah Ashley, Sarah Nicole; [ed.] Clifton High School - 1973, Texas A and M University - graduated in 1977; [occ.] Civil Engineer and Executive Director, Valwood Improvement Authority; [memb.] Rotary International, Bent Tree Bible Church - Dallas Matrocrest and Farmers Branch, Chambers of Commerce, National Society of Professional Engineers, Texas Professional Engineers; [hon.] Thus far, I have written as a hobby and haven't submitted my work to receive anything except pleasure from the reader, Rotary International Paul Harris Fellow; [oth. writ.] Other poems I have written and self published locally as well as a children's book teaching a moral value (as yet unpublished) about friendship.; [pers.] I write primarily about family or about life's experiences, and I strive to teach values as well. My writing is about things I love and comes straight form the heart.; [a.] Carrollton, TX

**CAREY, TOM**
[b.] June 28, 1937, Bronx, NY; [p.] Marjorie Schraudner; [m.] Marlene Carey; [ed.] Amadeus, Candale; [pers.] Summer walks in Vienna.; [a.] Flushing, NY

**CAREY, VICKY**
[pen.] Victoria Queen; [b.] September 12, 1959, Yonkers, NY; [p.] Sonia and Frank Puglisi; [m.] Paul Carey, October 16, 1982; [ed.] Mahopac High School; [occ.] Input Analyst; [pers.] Dreams are the key to express one's soul in the search of true happiness!; [a.] Mahopac, NY

**CARLANDER, JEANETTE**
[b.] April 16, 1932, Coos Bay, OR; [p.] Jeffry and Martha Sandness; [m.] Loren Carlander, June 12, 1954; [ch.] Four; [ed.] B.A., Concordia College, Moorhead, MN; [occ.] Retired; [memb.] Christ Lutheran Church, ELCA; [oth. writ.] Anecdotal family stories; [pers.] I see no conflict between creation and evolution. I believe life is truly beyond our understanding and that God probably has his reasons.; [a.] Seattle, WA

**CARLIN, PAUL A.**
[b.] January 15, 1969, Cambridge, MA; [p.] Kenneth M. Carlin, Dianne M. Carlin; [m.] Helene A. Carlin, May 7, 1994; [ed.] Milford High School; [occ.] Travel Consultant; [pers.] Please stop the violence and help save our planet.; [a.] Milford, MA

**CARLSEN, PATRICIA J.**
[pen.] P.J.; [b.] May 26, 1950, Utica, NY; [ed.] New Hartford School Sys., MVCC College; [memb.] Int'l Test Garden Society; [oth. writ.] Several other poems and notes of feeling not yet published; [pers.] I endeavor to get in touch with my soul, and hopefully help others to do the same, through my poems.; [a.] New Hartford, NY

**CARLSON, WADE**
[b.] January 9, 1982, Chicago City, MN; [p.] Kay and Wayne Carlson; [ed.] Entering 8th Grade; [occ.] Stu-

dent; [memb.] Received the Presidential Academic Award, Honor Roll Student achieved Scouting Awards; [oth. writ.] Poems - The Eternal Rose Sunset Vision, Rivers Connect with Time, Star, Blonde, when Roses dance Love always, U.R. Secret, and I am also working on more; [a.] Chicago City, MN

**CARLSON, BILLIE**
[b.] May 11, 1949, Waverly, IA; [p.] Irvin and Gladys Renn; [m.] Divorced; [ch.] Joshua 15, A.J. 11; [ed.] Working toward A.A. Degree in Criminal Justice, Graduated from High School, Waverly-Shell Rock in 1967; [occ.] After an accident, I have become a full time student,; [memb.] St. Matthews Evangelical Lutheran Church; [oth. writ.] I have many poems and short story but have never had them published; [pers.] I have always used writing and singing as my own "self-help" therapy. Words on paper that come from a soul filled with stifled emotions, allow me to heal naturally from within.; [a.] Omaha, NE

**CARON, RAE**
[b.] January 21, 1985, Michigan; [p.] Robert E. and Paula Caron; [ed.] Birmingham Covington School District; [pers.] My poetry is what I think and see. I have Ms. Dot Feahony and Ms. Pat Parikh to thank for encouraging me.

**CARPEN, MYEM**
[b.] April 18, 1942, Guyana; [p.] Mootoo Carpen and Maharanie; [m.] Ianthe Hasler; [ch.] Ramsey, Indira Bryan; [ed.] B.B.A. Marketing; [occ.] Realtor; [pers.] Aspire to be American's uno numero mistic poet; [a.] Lindenhurst, NY

**CARPENTER, VIRANA V.**
[b.] November 15, 1970, Vientiane, Laos; [p.] Kiat and Vasana Vongthongthip; [m.] Timothy L. Carpenter, June 11, 1993; [ed.] Roosevelt High School, Portland Community College, Major: Psychology; [pers.] I wrote this poem to help myself realize the value of life and hope that it will become an inspirational for others.; [a.] Portland, OR

**CARPIO, VANESSA RUTH**
[b.] August 7, 1986, California; [p.] Gorgonio Carpio and Ruth Carpio; [ed.] Third Grade Alvarado Elementary School; [hon.] First place Martin Luther King essay contest, Participant, Young Author Faire, Young Actors' Workshop (3 stage plays), Talent Show (piano) at student in third grade; [a.] Union City, CA

**CARR, DORIS DENTON**
[b.] August 18, 1929, Hammond, IN; [ed.] Calumet City High, Art Institute of Chicago; [occ.] Artist, Writer, Clover Publishing Co.; [memb.] Life time - Membership International Clover Poetry Association - Member of Mark Press, Babylon N.Y. Center for spiritual awareness. Awareness NY, Lakemont Georgia.; [hon.] Title of Danae, International Clover, Poetry Association - Washington D.C., Who's Who in poetry raised-lansing Illinois 1978; [oth. writ.] "Beautiful the Country" (Golden Eagel Press - London England). stenciled "Spring" and "Winter Therapy", "A Prayer To A Poet:, "Marvel of Earth", "A Baby Nose", Mark Press, Bablylon N.Y.; [pers.] Keep your mind only on good in the world. It will bring you heal the happiness.; [a.] Ellijay, GA

**CARRICK, DIANE CAMPBELL**
[b.] December 28, 1930, Detroit, MI; [p.] Byron and Grace Campbell; [m.] Charles Hansford Carrick, December 15, 1973; [ch.] Hallie Christiansen, Richard Broerman; [ed.] Thornton High School, Harvey, Ill., University of Illinois, Champaign, Ill.received B.S. degree - education; [occ.] Artist; [memb.] Kappa Kappa

Gamma Sorority, Hope United Methodist Church; [hon.] National Honor Society, Quill and Scroll Journalism, Selected paintings in Juried Art Shows; [oth. writ.] Children's Book, Illustrations - books and magazines, Book of my poems, Articles - newspaper; [pers.] I enjoy expressing myself in drawing, painting and poetry.; [a.] Englewood, CO

**CARSWELL, NATHANIEL**
[pen.] Nathaniel O'Sean; [b.] May 6, 1978, Morganton, NC; [ch.] Ashely Brooke; [ed.] Freedom High, Western Piedmont Comm. College, UNC; [occ.] Chef; [memb.] Born again Christian; [hon.] MVP - Burke County Sports; [pers.] God gives talent to every one, some just have to look harder to find what it is we were placed here to do. I believe a person is what he or she does with their free-time.; [a.] Morganton, NC

**CARTER, CODY**
[pen.] C.S. Carter, Darian Qui; [b.] September 18, 1977, Garland, TX; [p.] Billy and Janet Carter; [ed.] Rockwall High School Rockwall, TX; [memb.] Literary Society, Mr Alpha Theta, Band; [oth. writ.] Published in School Literary Society book, and in local electronic magazine; [pers.] "If at first you don't succeed, erase all evidence you ever failed." Jay Little; [a.] Rockwall, TX

**CARTER, KRISHA SHAUN**
[b.] March 13, 1977, Augusta, GA; [p.] Ms. Mary E. Carter; [ed.] Augustus R. Johnson Health Science and Engineering High School, currently attending Oxford College of Emory University; [memb.] Y-Club, National Honor Society, FLAIR Foreign Language Honor Society, Literary Society; [hon.] 1st Place 4-AAA Regional Literary Competition (2 years), 1st Place Delta Sigma Theta Poetry Reading Contest (2 years) 3rd place 4-AAA State Literary Competition (2 years); [oth. writ.] Several unpublished poems, two short stories, 'Vive L'imposteur' and 'Home of the Dove'; [pers.] It is our deepest desire of the world to see us as more than our eyes allow.; [a.] Augusta, GA

**CARTER, MARGO**
[b.] February 6, 1943, Charleston, SC; [p.] France and William Brock; [m.] James Carter, April 1, 1967; [ch.] Laurey (Deceased); [ed.] Bishop England High School - Trident Tech, S.C Sampson Tech, N.C.; [occ.] Entertainer, Producer, Booking Agent, Vocalist, and Home Maintenance Engineer; [oth. writ.] Children's short stories and Few songs (words and music); [pers.] I have chosen to be happy for the rest of my life. To be better, not bitter no matter what life throws my way.; [a.] Saint Louis, MO

**CARTER, IRBY GERALDINE RIDGE**
[pen.] Irby Dean; [b.] April 30, 1907, Tampa, FL; [p.] Irene C. and Irby S. Ridge; [m.] George C. Carter (Deceased), June 25, 1949; [ch.] George C. Jr., Michael J. Katherine A. Marie T. and Paul C.; [ed.] Peabody College for Teachers, 1945-45, U.T. Nashville 1975-77; [occ.] Real Estate Investor, Lay Minister Catholic Diocese of Nashville; [memb.] Madison Chamber of Commerce, Shooting Stars, Wheel Anundess and Plus 'N More Western Square Dance Clubs, B and N Country Western Dance Club; [hon.] Recipient U.S. Dept. of Agriculture citation for meritorious service 1968, Who's Who of American Women (12th edition 1981-82); [oth. writ.] "Mini Poems", "Poems Portraits", and work in Progress "Love Storm" ( musical); [pers.] Nashville Tennessee area information person for Western Square and Round Dance clubs.; [a.] Madison, TN

**CASE, WANETA**
[b.] June 27, 1924, La Cygne, KS; [p.] John and Pauline Vail; [m.] Cdr. Earl John Case U.S.N. (Deceased),

August 26, 1942; [ch.] Cheryl Case, Vail John Case; [ed.] Buckley High School, Buckley, WA, Wilson's Business College, Seattle, WA; [occ.] Retired was a fashion model; [memb.] Presbyterian Church - DAR - Scholarship Chairman for Aqua Fria Chapter Sun City, AZ; [hon.] Hobbies - metal sculpture and oil painting; [oth. writ.] Local papers only; [pers.] Positive thinking, never look backward, always look forward.; [a.] Sun City

**CASPER, BRUCE**
[b.] July 22, 1952, Salt Lake City, UT; [p.] Lewis Dale and Helen Francis Casper; [m.] Dolores J. Chaffee-Casper, August 15, 1988; [ed.] Bonneville High School, University of Utah; [occ.] Retired; [memb.] Bayview Bible Chapel, V.F.W. USMC, U.S. Dept. of Interior, Volunteers, A.A.; [hon.] World of Poetry Press, Golden Poet's Award 1982; [oth. writ.] Who Will Care, That We Were There? (72 Post Register Press),; Laws [82 World of Poetry Press], The Unwanted Warrior (88 CC M and D Pub.), Volunteer America (Copyright March 1995), Current Project, A.A. Bible Study Guide; [pers.] This quest, this journey, this life. We are Spirituel Beings going through a human experience, not Human Beings searching for a Spiritual Experience. The Quest is Peace of Mind.; [a.] Full-Time Rivers, USA

**CASTILLO, JESSE**
[b.] January 29, 1948, Donna, TX; [p.] Julian and Eva Castillo; [ch.] Jesse Edward, Albert and Cynthia Castillo; [ed.] Donna High and Pan American College; [occ.] Manager Rental Company; [pers.] I believe that the #1 purpose in life is to make others happy.

**CASTILLO, MARYLINDA C.**
[b.] September 21, Manila, Philippines; [p.] Abe and Linda Campo; [m.] Roger, May 29, 1977; [ch.] Roger Jr. and Marianne; [ed.] Bachelor of Arts in English, Bachelor of Laws; [memb.] Philippine Association of University Women Member, Philippine Integrated Bar; [pers.] My writings reflect on man's striving for the best in life and in the essence of his earthly existence.; [a.] Mesquite, TX

**CASTILLO JR., JULIO EFRAIN**
[b.] June 1, 1972, Chicago, IL; [p.] Julio Efrain Castillo, Sr.; [m.] Laura Velazquez Castillo, July 1, 1994; [ed.] A.A.S., Graphic Arts at Robert Morris College, B.S. Political Science at Roosevelt University; [occ.] Full time student; [memb.] United We Stand America (Ross Perot) Founder; [pers.] We have but only one habitat, the world! It is the only home in which God gave us sustaining all life beyond our wildest imagination. Let us not destroy our kingdom for there is no place like home, give people a chance!; [a.] Chicago, IL

**CASTILLON JR., CIRILO F.**
[pen.] Casti Christell; [b.] September 12, 1948, Aklan, Philippines; [p.] Cirilo Castillon Sr., Victoria Fernandez; [m.] Carmelita Santos Castillon, July 19, 1970; [ch.] Claire De Lune, Cynthia May, Cyrus Jay; [ed.] Roxas Memorial School of Arts and Trades, Columban College, Baker College; [occ.] Wood Model Maker, General Motors Corporation; [memb.] Subic Bay Apprentice Alumni Assn., Kahirup Michigan, Uaw Local 160; [hon.] Dean's List; [oth. writ.] Poems, short stories for children and teenagers; [pers.] Every man's work is judged by his purpose.; [a.] Warren, MI

**CASTRO, JOHN**
[b.] Bakersfield, CA; [p.] Emilio and Jennie Castro; [ch.] Manuel and Valery Marie; [ed.] California State University at Los Angeles; [occ.] Workers Compensation Hearing Representative; [pers.] Poetry must be inspired. For me Irene Rodriguez, Eleanor Lopez and Gilbert have been that inspiration. People who really

believe in you understand that success takes time, devotion and sometimes a little disappointment.; [a.] Los Angeles, CA

**CATALDO, ALISA A.**
[b.] April 26, 1970, New York; [p.] Maria and Benedetto Cataldo; [ed.] E.L. Vandermullen H.S., Suffolk County Community College, Sunye Stony Brook; [occ.] Italian Teacher; [memb.] American Association of Teachers of Italian; [hon.] Pope Foundation Scholarship, Teachers Assistantship SUNY at Stony Brook, AAII Bursary for Seina Program; [pers.] Through my writings I try to understand myself and the things that occur in my Italian - American life.; [a.] Mount Sinai, NY

**CATALDO, ELLEN MARY**
[b.] July 25, 1957, Malden, MA; [p.] Joseph Cataldo, Jennie Cataldo; [ed.] Everett High School, Bay State College; [occ.] Head Tax Assessor for the Massachusetts Dept. of Revenue; [memb.] Volunteer - American Cancer Society; [hon.] Honor roll - Everett High School Deans's List - Bay State College; [oth. writ.] I wrote serious poems throughout High Schools although I don't know what happened to them. I'm attempting to write some new poems.; [pers.] The poem "The Hero I Never Knew" was written to honor my uncle Joseph Carideo who was killed in a ship's accident on 12-18-46. I never meet him because I was born in 1957.; [a.] Chelsea, MA

**CATT, R. SHANE**
[b.] January 21, 1976, Davies County, IN; [p.] Ronald and Connie Catt; [ed.] Grad. North Vigo High School, Terre Haute, IN. Now attending Ball State University, Muncie, IN.; [pers.] Do you have other names and address I can send poems to?

**CAVANAGH, SUSAN CARLTON SMITH**
[b.] June 30, 1923, Athens, GA; [p.] Edward Inglis Smith, Hart Wylie Smith; [m.] G.S.T. Cavanagh, October 25, 1977; [ed.] Athens High School, University of Georgia, B.S in Zoology, MFA in Drama. Various Courses at Duke University while employed there.; [occ.] Naturalist, Artist, Illustrator, Sculptor, Professional Botanical and Scientific Illustrator; [memb.] Phi Kappa Phi Honorary Society Episcopal Church, Chi Omega Sorority in college, Deans List, Puppeteers of America, Garden Club of America, National Society of Colonial Dames in the State of Ga., History of Medicine Association; [hon.] Dean's List, Thalian-Blackfriar's Scholarship, Art work chosen for permanent collection in Hunt Institute for Botanical Documentation, Carnegie-Mellon University, Printer's Institute of America Award and Graphic Arts Award for illustrations for two children's book for American Heritage Press, National Medal from Garden Club of America, Nature Sculptures on permanent exhibition at State Botanical garden of Ga; [oth. writ.] National Beta Club Short Story award in High School. Wrote and illustrated book: 3-Famous Artist Naturalist of the Colonial period. Contributed and illustrated children's book for American Heritage Press Illustrated children's books for Am. Her Press and Doubleday. Illust. appear in Wildflowers of North Carolina. Illustrated for Jack and Jill Magazine.; [pers.] As a child I realized everything is full Surprises, even the commonplace. And I continually strive to reveal often-overlooked marvels that surround us in the world of nature.; [a.] Athens, GA

**CAVE, LIZANNE EMILIA**
[b.] July 21, 1961, Brooklyn, NY; [p.] Vivian Mark Cave, Beryl Veronica Cave; [ch.] Sparkle Veronica Taylor; [a.] Brooklyn, NY

**CAVICCHI, RYAN**
[b.] November 14, 1980, Framont, CA; [ed.] Entering Manteca High, Manteca; [occ.] Student; [oth. writ.] Working on other poems and a novel; [pers.] Good writing must come both the heart and the mind, not one or the other.; [a.] Manteca, CA

**CAVINESS, ASHLEE MARIE**
[b.] November 16, 1984, Tupelo, MS; [p.] John and Lois Caviness; [occ.] Booneville Head Start Anderson Kindergarten, Anderson Elementary, R.H. Long Middle School; [occ.] Student; [memb.] Gaston Baptist Church, Children's Choir, McCoy's Auto Sales Softball Team, Booneville Life Chain, American Family Association; [hon.] Anderson Elementary Honor Roll, Student of the Week, Science Fair 2nd Place, Basketball Awards (6), Beauty Review Alternate; [oth. writ.] Write poems and songs for family and friends; [pers.] I write to put my thoughts into words, my emotions on paper and to help others understand my point of view.; [a.] Booneville, MS

**CERAR, VIRGINIA**
[pen.] Ginny; [b.] December 28, 1962, Bethany, NY; [p.] Mr. and Mrs. Daniel Buckley; [m.] Mr. Jack Cerar, September 16, 1988; [ch.] Sheena, Sadie and Aja (3 German Shepards); [ed.] Massapequa High School, Nassau Community College; [occ.] Sales Manager for K.C. Electronics; [oth. writ.] The Flight Of A Bird, Imagination, Little Girls Prayers, Remember Me I Love You, Stranger, I Caught A Cloud Today, I Really Miss My Mother, and many, many more; [pers.] I wrote this poem for my younger brother Michael. Growing up in our family was very tough at times. I took some of my anger out on my brother, and he didn't deserve it. He was so cute and is my way of saying, Michael I'm so sorry that I hurt you. I love you and may you always remember how very special you are to me I love you Michael always!; [a.] Islip Terrace, NY

**CHAFFEE, DUANE**
[b.] June 8, 1946, Klamath Falls, OR; [p.] Charles Chaffee, Dolly Chaffee; [m.] Divorced; [ch.] Charles A. and Curtis D.; [ed.] Milo Academy, Oregon Institute of Technology B.T., Texas Christian University M.S.; [occ.] Medical Technologist (Medically retired); [memb.] American Society of Clinical Pathologists; [hon.] Dean's List; [oth. writ.] Several unpublished poems; [pers.] My poetry is straight from my heart. I feel my observations can be a source of hope and courage to others.; [a.] Portland, OR

**CHAN, KALEI KRISTEN**
[b.] October 29, 1981, Hayward, CA; [p.] Steve and Cathy Chan; [ed.] 8th grade student Cesar Chavez Middle School; [occ.] Student; [hon.] Academic Excellence (New haven Schools) - Outstanding Athlete Girls' Basketball - Young Authors Faire; [pers.] I enjoy writing, and playing basketball is my passion in life. I believe they help me to maintain a good balance of my body and mind.; [a.] Union City, CA

**CHANDLER, ELEANOR**
[b.] March 29, 1914, Mount Vernon, NY; [p.] Maurice and Pauline Hayes; [m.] Paul Edgar Chandler, October 14, 1932; [ch.] Charlotte (Thomas), Maurice Paul Chandler (Deceased '95); [ed.] B.A. Fine Arts, Pratt Institute, M.A. Fine Arts in Education, Columbia University; [occ.] Writer, Weaver, Painter; [memb.] Rudolf Steiner Fellowship Community; [oth. writ.] "Cycles" A collection of my poetry from 1930-1995 A lifetime of growth; [pers.] 25 years with the Army in Europe and Africa and 60+ years teaching Arts and Crafts have taught me to honor and respect all human spiritual activity.; [a.] Chestnut Ridge, NY

**CHANDLER, WYETH**
[b.] February 21, 1930, Memphis, TN; [p.] Walter and Dorothy Chandler; [m.] Beverlyn; [ch.] John W Jr., Cathy, Laura, Bebe; [ed.] Castle Heights Mil. Acad., Memphis State Univ. - B.S. (List), Univ. of Tennessee - LL.D.; [occ.] Trial Judge State of Tennessee; [memb.] U.S. State and Local Bar Assoc., Judicial Conformer, Kolran Veteran OSMC (Air) Various Clubs and Veterans Organization; [hon.] 68-72 Council man city of Memphis, 72-82 Mayor of Memphis, Resigner To Broome Judge; [pers.] Great admirer of Shakespeare Deihens and Elgabetha poets.; [a.] Mamphis, TN

**CHANG, JANICE MAY**
[b.] May 24, 1970, Loma Linda, CA; [p.] Belden S. and Sylvia T. Chang; [ed.] B.A. in Liberal Studies, CA State U. San Bernardino, 1990, Cert. in Paralegal Studies, CSUSB, 1990, Cert. in Creative Writing, CSUSB, 1991, J.D. LaSalle University, 1993, N.D. Clayton School of Natural Healing, 1993, Ph.D., International Univ., 1994; [occ.] D.O. Anglo-Am Inst. of Drugless Therapy, 1994., General Counsel, JMC Enterprises, Inc., 1993, Adjunct Professor, LaSalle University, 1994; [memb.] American College and Legal Medicine, American Naturopathic Medical Association, American Psychological Association, American Society of Law, Medicine, and Ethics, Association of Trial Lawyers of America, National Authors Registry, International Society of Poets; [hon.] Editor's Choice Award, 1994, 1995, President's Award for Literary Excellence 1995, Golden Certificate Award, 1995. Listed in: Who's Who in American LawRegistry, International Society of Poets. Editor's Choice Award, 1994, 1995, President's Award for Literary Excellence 1995, Golden Registry, International Society of Poets. Editor's Choice Award, 1994, 1995, President's Award for Literary Excellence 1995, Golden Certificate Award, 1995. Listed in: Whos' Who in American Law, 1996-7, Who's Who in Writers, Editors, and Poets, 1995-6, Who's Who in California, 1995, National Honor Society, Alpha Gamma Sigma-Mu, Delta Theta Phi Law Fraternity; [oth. writ.] Writingscapes: Insights and Approaches to Creative Writing, 1991, "Lighthouse Bloom", "Ocean Love:, "Journey Into Nightfall", Approaches to Psychological Counseling, 1993; [per.] Poetry is the most expressive form of revealing ourselves. It captivates the inherent beauty and speaks truthfully about our world.; [a.] Loma Linda, CA

**CHAPMAN, RALPH**
[pen.] Edward Lloyd; [b.] August 27, 1977, Ponten Plains, NJ; [p.] John S. Chapman Jr., Lauca A. Chapman; [ed.] Apopka High; [occ.] Student, Johnson and Whales University, N. Miami, Florida; [memb.] Marine Corps Reserves; [hon.] High School Band, Directors Award for Excellence, Who's Who Among America High School Students Award; [oth. writ.] Several Unpublished Poems and Short Stories; [pers.] Writing brings out the deepest and sometimes darkest thoughts and ideas in the far corners of my mind.; [a.] Apopka, FL

**CHARLES, DAPHNE**
[b.] December 2, 1983, Miami Beach, FL; [p.] Marie G. Charles and Fritz Charles; [ed.] 6th Grader; [occ.] Student; [memb.] I am a member of the student advisory council at Oak Grove Elementary; [hon.] 5th Grade Science Bowl Award for 5th Grade 1st, 4th, and 1st Place, Hall of Fame award, on Principal's 5th Grade Hono roll 6 times; [a.] North Miami Beach, FL

**CHARLES, PAULINE**
[b.] January 24, 1925, Indiana; [p.] John and Catherine Harbison; [m.] Verlin Charles, March 4, 1947; [ch.] Merry Kay, Waneta Charline, Larry Verlin, Chris Edward; [ed.] Middletown High School; [occ.] Homemaker; [memb.] Hillcrest Baptist Church, Carlisle, Ohio

(Sunday School Teacher) Market Place Craft Mall, Springboro, Ohio; [hon.] Various Art Awards; [oth. writ.] Several unsubmitted poems and articles written for the Joy of expression. This is my first experience as a contestant.; [pers.] To share with others treasures of the heart.; [a.] Carlisle, OH

**CHASE, TERESA**
[pen.] Teri Chase; [b.] October 25, 1972, Wabasha, MN; [p.] Kenneth Chase, JoAnn Chase; [ed.] Stevens Point Area Senior High, Mid-State Technical College-Stevens Point and Mashfield Campuses; [occ.] Word Processor I, Sentry Insurance, Stevens Point, WI; [memb.] Business Professionals of America; [hon.] Placed 6th in Medical Concepts test at State Competition; [oth. writ.] Had a poem published in Catholic Newspaper, article for The Cougar (a school newspaper); [pers.] I try to touch the hearts and lives of people through my poetry by personalizing them in a special way.; [a.] Junction City, WI

**CHEVALIER, MARY SMITHHART**
[pen.] Mary S. Chevalier; [b.] November 3, 1929, Manning, TX; [p.] Bertha Cox and Auzy Smithhart; [m.] Robert Aubrey Chevalier, June 28, 1946; [ch.] Robert David, Alice Denise, Donna Lynn, Stephen Daniel; [ed.] Joaquin High School, Panola Junior College, School of Nursing; [occ.] Homemaker - Licensed Vocational Nurse - Retired; [memb.] First Presbyterian Church, Joaquin - Former member and officer in Daughters of the Republic of Texas; [hon.] Valedictorian 1946 Joaquin High School - Many Nursing Awards over a period of 15 years - W.O.P. Certificate of Merit awards (6) - W.O.P. Honorable Mentions (7) W.O.P. Golden Poet Awards (5) - W.O.P Gold Medal of Honor 1992 - W.O.P. silver Poetry 1990 - WOP Who's Who in Poetry 1990 - NLP Editor's Choice Award 1995 Semi-finalist NLP 1995 N. American open; [oth. writ.] Poetry Contest - Published in NLP's 1995 "Windows Of The Soul" - Published in W.O.P's "The Great American Anthology" 1988. Published article in Rodale's Organic Gardening 1986 - Published in NLP's Anthology "Outstanding Poets of 1994" - Selected for "The Sound of Poetry tape, 1994-1995 - Published NLP's "Best Poems of 1995" Associate Member I.S.P. 1994-1995.; [pers.] My Poetry is simple and inspired by events that have touched my life, either by my immediate family or through personal observations. In my poetry, I hope to show my love for God, my family and fellow man - as well as the universe around me.; [a.] Joaquin, TX

**CHIN, GRACE**
[pen.] Me Pine - Grove Hermiet; [b.] November 8, 1924, Peking, China; [p.] T. L. Ko and Y. C. Yang; [m.] Ming L. Chin, October, 1951; [ch.] Leslie, Lydia; [ed.] M.I.T. School of Architecture, Oberlin College, grad., School Euf Litt., Peking Univ. undergrad. Eug Litt.; [occ.] Retired architect, Active in Arts and Letters; [memb.] National League of American Pen Woman, M.I.T. Wamli's Club; [hon.] Listed in "Who's Who Among Asian Americans" 94-85 for achievement in Architecture. Won many awards in painting.; [oth. writ.] Sculpture and photography since retirement. Many poems (in classical chinese) were published in C.T. Univ. Monthly Semi-Finalist in '94-95 N. Amer. open poetry contest sponsored by Nat. Library of Poetry.; [pers.] Sond by Nat. Library of Poetry.; [a.] New York, NY

**CHITTY, ALVEN L.**
[b.] April 18, 1940, Ray City, GA; [p.] Lawson and Ava Lou Chitty; [m.] Louise Geruntino Chitty, October 20, 1962; [ch.] Michael, Renee, Marc; [ed.] Pasco High School, Dade City, FL; [occ.] Mason; [memb.] Richmond East Moose, VA; [oth. writ.] Poems of friend and relatives and some short stories not published; [pers.] I

love writing about friend, family and personal experiences.; [a.] Highland Springs, VA

**CHOI, IRENE FELICIA**
[b.] May 12, 1977, Bronx, NY; [p.] Joon H. Choi, KaeSun Choi; [ed.] Charles E. Gordon HS, NY, Michigan State University; [occ.] Student at Michigan State; [memb.] National Honor Society; [oth. writ.] Editorial in local newspaper, several poems in high school literary magazines, several poems in Comell Summer College literary newspaper and one short story; [pers.] Writers may state the greatest lies or the greatest truths. Thankfully, the writer is not always obligated to tell which is which in her writing.; [a.] Bronxville, NY

**CHRISTENSEN, PHILLIP**
[pen.] Phillip Christensen; [b.] August 17, 1957, Portland, OR; [p.] Frank J. Margaret; [m.] Mitzi, October 3, 1977; [ch.] Philip, Stefan and Dylan; [ed.] Multnomah Bible College, Mt Hood Community College; [occ.] Instructor and writer; [hon.] 1994 and 1995 Portland Music Association Award winning song writer; [pers.] Everything beautiful bares the fingerprints of God.

**CHRISTIAN, JUDITH E.**
[b.] September 17, 1937, Minnesota, MN; [p.] John and Marjorie Jacobson; [m.] David M. Christian, Jr. (Deceased), March 27, 1957; [ch.] David III, Robert, Joan Wallace, M. Lynn Frazier, Susan Bendingfield; [ed.] Bessemer High School, University of Alabama-Tuscaloosa, University of Alabama-Hunstville, Samford Extension Center Hunstville; [occ.] Grandmother to 17, Alabama Dir. Disaster relief emergency, Child Care, Teacher, English as a Second Language; [memb.] Board Member and Office of Hunstville Association for Pastoral Care, University Baptist Church, Teacher of English as a Second Language, North Alabama Crafters Association, ALA WMU Conference Leader, American Red Cross Disaster Relief Worker, National Fellowship of Baptist Educators, Hallelujah Choir; [oth. writ.] Forty years of poetry for fun and inspiration; [pers.] Where there is no vision the people perish, therefore, I wish to encourage, inspire enrich, and minister beyond my bounds.; [a.] Hunstville, AL

**CHUBB, JOAN E.**
[b.] November 3, 1947, British Columbia, Canada; [p.] Matt and Viola Hill; [ed.] James Monroe High School, U.S.C. - California; [occ.] Independent Corporate Consultant (Paralegal); [oth. writ.] I have been writings poetry since I was 16. This is the first poem to be published.; [pers.] My poetry has always reflected my inner most thoughts, personal feelings and experiences. I write to let out my emotions and feeling and to search for a higher awareness of myself.; [a.] Playa Del Rey, CA

**CIASCHI, PATRICIA GREENE**
[b.] Ithaca, NY; [occ.] Registered Nurse; [oth. writ.] I write mainly for personal enjoyment and find it very relaxing; [pers.] My personal philosophy is to live simply in loving kindness, and to see beauty and good in all of God's creation. This particular poem I submitted reflects my feeling of love and joy that I felt on a recent trip to Ireland.; [a.] Ithaca, NY

**CICILLINI, GIOVANIA**
[pen.] J. Minutolo Cicillini; [b.] September 14, 1949, Italy; [p.] Amedeo, Assunta Minutolo; [m.] Vincent Cicillini, November 28, 1970; [ch.] Julie, Anthony and Vinnie Jr.; [ed.] Magistrali in Italy and Bachelor of Arts (in Comm.) at William Paterson College; [occ.] Professor of Italian and own Ad. Agency; [memb.] Sylvia Sammartino Lodge of Wayne, Vita, The Center for Italian and Italian-American Culture, Inc.; [oth. writ.] Several poems published in Il Pungolo Verde, articles

for W.P.C. Beacon and Independent News Poetry Book "Sogni di Gioveufu" and "Stefanie and La Sua Bambolo Sprevibile" and Children book.

**CILLUFFO, KIMBERLY**
[b.] November 7, 1979, Fontana, CA; [p.] Anthony and Patricia Cilluffo; [ed.] Currently in 11th grade at Aquinas High School in San Bernardino, CA; [occ.] Student; [hon.] Honor Roll; [oth. writ.] Several other unpublished poems; [pers.] "I want to live my life fully and take everything one day at a time".; [a.] Rialto, CA

**CIOFFI, DIANE**
[b.] June 28, 1964, New York City; [p.] Helen and Edward McCabe; [m.] Daniel Cioffi, April 9, 1983; [ch.] Scott, Shaun, Michael, and Renee; [ed.] High School, Tottenville H.S., Staten Island NY; [occ.] Housewife and Mother; [pers.] I enjoy writing poetry even though this is my first publication. I have been writing since High School. I write what I feel.; [a.] Lake Ariel, PA

**CLAIBORNE JR., ALBERT EARL**
[pen.] Al Claiborne Jr.; [b.] April 11, 1963, Torrance, CA; [p.] Albert and Ersula Claiborne; [ed.] High School, Elmira High School, Elmine Oregon; [occ.] Engineers Program at Southern Pacific Railroad; [memb.] The Free Arts Foundation For Abused Children; [oth. writ.] Love like try, If life was a painting, Mindy, Drowning in my tears, A place called love, a poets pen, Harvest time, The Fisherman; [pers.] If rain should fall upon the ground a poet would convey that puddles turn to rivers bound to oceans far away. I believe a poet is an instrument of angels.; [a.] Long Beach, CA

**CLARK, JAMES M.**
[b.] November 15, 1927, Saint Claire, MI; [m.] Lydie G. Clark, August 30, 1949; [ch.] Denise, Devin and James Jr. and 5 grandchildren; [ed.] Masters degree in Education Eleons Univ. of Miami (Florida); [occ.] Retired early, because of Parkinson's disease (PD); [memb.] Heads a support group for PD patients and care givers in Central Chicago; [hon.] Past President of local chapter of Parkinson Association; [oth. writ.] Several articles in local newspapers and newsletters on coping with PD; [pers.] Call me "old-fashioned" but I prefer the more traditional forms of poetry, with adherance to rules of rhyme and meter and plain language.; [a.] Chicago, IL

**CLARK, AUDREY**
[b.] April 21, 1982, Alexandria, VA; [p.] Bronna Zlochiver and Tim Clark; [ed.] Kindergarten, Elementary School, Middle School. (Pre-K-7); [memb.] Potomac Appalachian Trail Club, Whale Adoption Project; [hon.] Principals Scholar, Regional Spelling Bee Contestant, Japan/America Art Exchange; [pers.] Be free.; [a.] Falls Church, VA

**CLARK JR., BERTRAM CLARENCE**
[pen.] Bertram Clark; [b.] August 5, 1948, Louisville, KY; [p.] Bertram Sr. and Elizabeth Clark; [ed.] Vista College - Berkeley, CA. - A.A. Degree, University of San Francisco - San Francisco, CA., Bachelor of Public Administration (Also working toward a master of public administration at U.S.F.); [occ.] Tax Consultant; [memb.] Toastmasters International, Terri Simmons with Renewed Faith Gospel Group, Allen Temple Baptist Church United Men's Alliance and Choir; [hon.] Toast Master's Success Leadership Award - 1991, Federal Public Service Employee Award - 1990 Volunteer Income Tax Assistance Awards from 1988 to 1993; [oth. writ.] I have written many poems and essays that are currently unpublished; [pers.] The soul of my existence is reflected in my poetry. My poems articulate and many encounters in this life. I am inspired by every

thing and every body that I experience.; [a.] Oakland, CA

**CLAUDIO, MARISOL**
[b.] November 5, 1980, Chicago, IL; [p.] Angelina Claudio and Angel Luis Claudio; [ed.] St. Helen School, second year at Josephium High School; [occ.] Student; [memb.] Young Chicago Authors Program; [hon.] (Freshmen Year), First Semester - First Honors in Religion I, second Semester - First Honor in English I, "B" Honor Roll; [oth. writ.] One poem "Little Rag Doll" published in Anthology of Poetry 1994; [pers.] Everybody has talent hidden talent, if you look deep in your heart you will find the hidden talent, inside of you.; [a.] Chicago, IL

**CLAUNCH, KIMBERLY**
[b.] April 14, 1960, Weatherford, TX; [p.] Rochelle and Perry Claunch, Glen Rose, Texas; [ed.] Presently involved in pursuing a career in medicine; [memb.] Phi Theta Kappa, Dean's List; [oth. writ.] Staff writer for college newspaper; [pers.] I believe that there are no meaningless details in this world. No matter what your position, your actions and words do make a difference to others. I strive to make that experience a positive one.; [a.] Cleveland, OH

**CLEVER, MARY LOU**
[pen.] Mary Clever; [b.] January 23, 1942, San Francisco, CA; [m.] William Clever; [ch.] Four grown sons; [ed.] Attended San Jose State College - Major: Television Production Hertnell College (Salinas, CA): Early Childhood Education; [occ.] Day Care Direction; [memb.] Monterey Co. Family Day Care Asso.; [hon.] Past President Monterey Co. Family Day Care Asso., Music Director Salinas Valley Church of Religious Science, Sang for Pres. of the U.S. (Clinton) with Woodie Guthrieis "American Song" Cast, Coalition for quality Children's Video "Kid's First" endorsement For children's music video... Songs and Finger plays for Little Ones."; [oth. writ.] "Letting Go" (prose) Working on 2 children's books. Always writing - music, poetry, stories.; [pers.] We are who we are...before we remember what we already know...and after. If I can inspire others to find the good in themselves and those around them...To remember what they already know...I am happiest.; [a.] Salinas, CA

**CLINKENBEARD, EVERYL**
[p.] Thomas and Gladys Dean; [m.] Tom Clinkenbeard, March 20, 1957; [ch.] Tom Jr., Glenn, Darrell, Mark Terry; [occ.] Manager - Information Systems; [memb.] First Church of the Nazarene AARP; [pers.] I find beauty and wonder in each and every aspect of God's creation and would like to help others recognize the wonders of this universe.; [a.] Terre Haute, IN

**CLOVER, ROBERTA**
[pen.] Bert; [b.] May 3, 1951, Camden, NJ; [p.] Mr. and Mrs. Ernest Clover; [ch.] Naivasha Salim and Antar Salim; [ed.] Michigan State University; [pers.] I have been blessed in this lifetime with an unconditional love from my grandfather (PopPop) and my uncle Earl.; [a.] Southfield, MI

**COBB, CISSIE**
[b.] March 7, 1955, Kalamazoo, MI; [occ.] Songwriter; [oth. writ.] "Born Bad" a song in the movie "Natural Born Killers."; [pers.] After I was beaten nearly to death by the man I loved, it was as though part of me died only to rebirth into a more spiritual being. I have found a new path for the rest of my journey. Lookout world...here I come!; [a.] Venice Beach, CA

**COBURN, MICHELLE**
[pen.] Michelle Coburn; [b.] November 23, 1980, Azusa, CA; [p.] James and Laura Coburn; [ed.] El Camino Real High School; [occ.] Student; [pers.] Beware of Religion, Blame Society, Broaden the boundaries.; [a.] West Hills, CA

**COCHRAN, GEORGE E.**
[b.] August 31, 1944, Albany, CA; [p.] Claude A. and Leahbelle Cochran; [ch.] George E. Scott Cochran; [ed.] High School and JC; [occ.] Engineer; [oth. writ.] Several poems and song lyrics; [pers.] My writings are of things I have seen, places I have been, and thoughts that have crossed my mind. As I looked back on my writings, I am reminded of where I have been, who I am and the life I have lived.; [a.] Vancouver, WA

**COCKFIELD, BESSIE L.**
[pen.] Lucy; [b.] April 13, 1925, Wars Shoals, SC; [pers.] Since coming down with Cancer in 1990 and given six months to live, I no longer have Cancer anywhere in my body. I praise the Lord and thank Him from the bottom of my heart for restoring my health. Also, for providing me with the best doctors and nurses to care for me. Thanks to them all, I'm now in my sixth year. I would like to say a very special thanks to Dr. W. Larry Gluck, he is my main Doctor that's cared for me through all of this illness. Dr. Gluck is the best, most kind and caring person and doctor I have ever known. He's been a friend to me since the first day we met. I can not Praise the Lord enough for what he has done for me. Neither can I say thanks to Dr. Gluck enough for the care he's given me. God Bless him. He is the best.

**COFFEY, NANCY**
[b.] October 31, 1951, Brooklyn, NY; [p.] Elizabeth Caraichner and James Barton; [m.] Divorced; [ch.] Elaine Marie Coffey; [ed.] Walt Whitman High School, Long Islawa; [occ.] Cook - P.S. 39 Elementary School, Stated Islawa, N.Y.; [pers.] To me, writing is like freedom, a place without boundaries.; [a.] Staten Islawa, NY

**COGSWELL, WHITNEY**
[b.] March 2, 1986, Marietta, OH; [p.] Russ and Traci Cogswell; [ed.] Reno Elementary through third grade level; [occ.] Student; [memb.] Kelly School of Dance and Reno Flag Corps; [hon.] Tag Program for Gifted Students; [pers.] I thought of this poem when I was looking out of my window and since it was Spring I named my poem Springtime.; [a.] Marietta, OH

**COIN, JEANNIE**
[b.] January 27, 1950, Artisia, NM; [p.] Nina Lyde; [m.] Divorced; [ch.] Three boys, Jimmy, Jeremy, Jason, Four grandchildren Dayton, Taylor, Logan, Mason; [ed.] Graduated from Denton High 1968; [occ.] Disabled; [oth. writ.] I have a lot of poems I have written over the years; [pers.] My poems are about the Good Lord his mercy and grace. I owe him my everything. He has keep me alive. I am a brittle diabetic. He has brought me out of acoma many times. He has also healed my eyes. I was legally blind today I have 20/30 vision all because of Him.; [a.] Denton, OH

**COLBY, DIANA M.**
[pen.] Twila Sue Colby; [b.] November 20, 1975, Murray, UT; [p.] Orrin and JoAnn J. Colby Jr.; [ed.] Granite High School; [occ.] Student at Utah State University; [memb.] The Church of Jesus Christ of Latter-Day Saints; [oth. writ.] Several poems published in my High School Literary Magazines; [pers.] To experience life is to gain knowledge, but to be knowledgeable enough to learn from others experiences is the intellectual way to safely satisfy human desire. And what better way than through the art of the written word.; [a.] South Salt Lake City, UT

**COLE, JONATHAN H.**
[pen.] Earendil / Aethelwulf; [b.] August 28, 1971, Tuscaloosa, AL; [p.] Jimmy Cole and June Cole; [ed.] Muscle Shoals High; Mississippi University for Women BS in Biology; [occ.] Graduate Student / Instructor; [memb.] Society for the Study of Amphibians & Reptiles; [hon.] Beta Beta Beta; National Dean's List (several times); [oth. writ.] Poem published in elementary school newspaper; article published in undergraduate school newspaper; junior author on unpublished reptile behavior research; [pers.] "Never wear a dance belt that's fits too tightly..." JHC; [a.] Muscle Shoals, AL

**COLE III, JAMES W.**
[b.] August 1, 1947, Baytown, TX; [p.] Bill and Colleen; [ed.] BA English University Houston; [occ.] Mill Worker; [pers.] Anyone who wishes to correspond with me about his or her poetry or anyone else's may write me.; [a.] Baytown, TX

**COLLIER, GERI**
[pen.] G. Dial Collier; [b.] November 1, 1942, Detroit, MI; [p.] Haste Dial, Zephreana Pearson; [m.] Widowed; [ch.] Tracie and Kimberlie, Three Grandchildren Shaunn, Cassandra and Bryanna; [ed.] Grad. Studies, Instructional Technology, Wayne State University, B.A. Business Administration; [occ.] Program Liaison, University of Michigan; [memb.] ASTD; [oth. writ.] Middle Passage (A poem written in two voices); [pers.] Life Cassandra's Tummy, I write for children, I also write poems about love and poems about nature. The bulk of my writings, however, are of motivation and inspiration to person of color.; [a.] Southfield, MI

**COLLINS, PHILLIP DARRELL**
[b.] February 10, 1974, Springfield, OH; [p.] Linda Collins; [ed.] Graduate of Horizon High Sch. Brighton, Colorado, 1993. Attended Front Range Community College, Westminster, Colorado. Clark State, Springfield, Ohio.; [occ.] Restaurant Employee; [memb.] Phi Theta Kappa National Honor Society; [hon.] "Best Drama Student of the year" - 1992-93, Horizon High Sch. Brighton, Colorado., Poetry published in the 1992 Literary Edition of the "Library of Congress."; [oth. writ.] Story published in Front Range Community College Literacy Publication. "Night of the Raven" - short story in Chrysalis "Seeds of Apathy" - poem in Chestnut Poetry Forum Compilation; [pers.] The conformist is nice and neat. The idealist is messy and untidy. We could settle for the crystalline purity of emotional suppression. I, however, will chose the cacophony of free will.; [a.] Medway, OH

**COLTMAN, HEATHER**
[b.] November 16, 1958, Zambia; [p.] Peter and Felicity Coltman; [ch.] Christopher Paul Staves; [ed.] Doctor of Musical Arts, Master of Music, Bachelor of Music; [occ.] Assistant Professor of Music and Director of keyboard studies at Florida Atlantic University; [memb.] African Wildlife Foundation Children International many musical organizations, Phi Kappa Phi; [hon.] Numerous awards in International Piano competitions in USA and Europe - extensive career as concert pianist across 3 continents; [oth. writ.] 2 collections of love poems, other poetry; [pers.] My poems reflect personal and compelling moments of my journey towards truth, depth, and meaning in human relationships.; [a.] Delray Beach, FL

**COLVIN, SHARON**
[b.] July 31, 1944, Joliet, IL; [p.] Thomas and Flossie Dwyer; [m.] Ralph R. Colvin, November 21, 1981; [ch.] Thomas (Deceased), Richard Karensue, Robert and David; [ed.] Graduate of Manhattan Public Grade School, Manhattan, IL, Graduate of Lincoln Way High, New Lenox, IL, 1/2 Semester Interior Decorating, Louis

College, Lockport, IL; [occ.] Currently doing Clerical Work; [hon.] Received Award for Sales Recognition at Hallmark; [oth. writ.] Have written poems for Weddings, birthdays, graduations, funerals, new businesses and births - shower and engagements; [pers.] I have had a poetic mind since childhood. I love to just sit and think of life for me it has always been one of my most important wishes - to "publish my work" and my feelings.; [a.] Crest Hill, IL

**CONLIN, DAN**
[b.] August 12, 1979, Saint Louis, MO; [p.] Bud and Jeanne Conlin; [ed.] Sault Area High School; [occ.] Student; [memb.] Key Club (Kiwanis), H.S. Swim Team, Sault Competitive Aquatics Team, H.S. Quiz Bowl; [hon.] Michigan Summer Institute: Archeology, Hugh O'Brien Leadership Conference; [pers.] I wrote this poem as a tribute to my grandfather who served in WW II and Korea.; [a.] Sault Sainte Marie, MI

**CONNER, ERIKA LORENA**
[b.] March 27, 1987, Los Angeles, CA; [p.] Eddie C. Conner, Andrea L. Conner; [ed.] 3rd Grade student at Baldwin Hills Elementary School; [occ.] Student; [memb.] Girl Scouts of America, Jack and Jill of America, Inc.; [hon.] Student of the Month, Spelling Bee Champion 1995, Academic Honor roll 1994, 1st Place Relay Track Meet; [pers.] I give special thanks to my grandmother, Lois Wallace and my 2nd grade teacher Ms. Sklavenit for influence and support.; [a.] Los Angeles, CA

**CONOVER, LINDA**
[b.] Long Beach, CA; [p.] Shirley and Edward Well; [m.] Divorced; [ch.] Randy James Conover; [ed.] San Marcos High School, AA Degree Santa Barbara City College; [occ.] Volunteer at various places; [memb.] California Federation of Chaprral poets, Fris of Christian Church of Santa Barbara; [hon.] Poet of the Month, Happy Publishers, T.V. Interviewer Certificate for Reading Poetry; [oth. writ.] Eleven Poems published in anthologies by Happy Publishers, remembering collection of poems; [pers.] I feel everyone is unique and has their own special talents and they should use them to the best of their ability.; [a.] Santa Barbara, CA

CONROY, DOUGLAS
[pers.] To create an atmosphere for young high school students to realize, while they are there, the overwhelming power structure of conformity—via corporate advertising, politics, modern technology, sensationalized T.V., etc. Conformity is a nonthreatened tool used handily by healthy mid to upper class white men—a bureaucracy, in which we need more people to refuse their business until they are no more! I wish to establish education reform in high school English, History, and (if there are any) Philosophy classes, so young people don't have to pay a lot of money for what they'd learn in college what they could easily learn in high school. I would like to teach high school English, always continue writing, open solely community-funded hospitality houses and recreation centers, be a social worker, sustain my sense of humor, and always encourage, no, DEMAND, always, that people always ask 'Why?'!; [a.] Poughkeepsie, NY

**CONWAY, DWIGHT**
[b.] August 2, 1952, Dallas, TX; [p.] Earlice White; [m.] Bernice Conway, December 16, 1989; [ed.] 2 yrs. College; [occ.] Parking Lot Attendant; [oth. writ.] Book of Poetry (True Life Poetry); [pers.] I was burned in Dallas and educated with two years of College and began writing poetry about people which helped me when buying a home. After which, every time I'd see something that struck attention I'd jot notes down and later put it together.; [a.] Dallas, TX

**COOK, DARRELL WAYNE**
[b.] February 14, 1952, Portland, IN; [p.] George O. Cook - Ruth E. Cook; [m.] Divorced; [ch.] Sabrina - Daniel - Kristi; [ed.] H.S. graduate with 8 yrs. of Technical Training in Mechanical and Electrical; [occ.] Skilled Tradesman with United Auto Workers; [memb.] Halfway Lodge F and AM; [hon.] Various Military Awards including the Bronze Star during Viet Nam; [oth. writ.] I have several hundred poems not yet submitted to anyone. They are all filed away in a safe place.; [a.] Redkey, IN

**COOK, LESLIE MAXWELL**
[pen.] Blue Gums; [b.] May 9, 1958, Detroit, MI; [p.] Carrie B. Maxwell, Melvin L. Maxwell; [m.] Tim Cook, April 30, 1994; [ed.] Mumford High, Univ. of Michigan, Laney Cosmetology School; Computer Learning Center; Diablo Valley College/Environmental Engineering Dept.; [occ.] Environmental Field Technician; [memb.] Member of Glide Methodist Espiscopal Church, San Francisco, CA; National Cosmetology Assoc./ Platinum Member (since 1989); Look Good...Feel Better, Program (since 1991); Cancer Makeover Program; [hon.] Burgandy and Blue Honors Club (Mumford High School - 1976); [oth. writ.] Extensive Collection of poems focusing on; joy, peace, life, suffering of mankind and womankind and humanity and also poems from personal experience and survival.; [pers.] I pray for continued grace and mercy from God, while living a life filled with passions that create, "A boil that cannot be stirred down."

**COOKE, BARBARA J.**
[b.] May 7, 1943, Pipestone, MN; [p.] Russell Hall, Mildred Peterson; [m.] Jeffrey Hirsch (Lifetime Partner); [ch.] Brandy McLaughlin Wall; [ed.] Univ of Cols, Naropa Institute Boulder, Cols, Monterrey College of Law, Monterrey, CA - will receive J.D. June 2, 1996; [occ.] Law Student, Innkeeper; [memb.] Pi Beta Phi, Delta Theta Phi; [a.] Monterrey, CA

**COOMES, GERALDINE SAWYER**
[pen.] G. Coomes; [b.] March 20, 1935, San Francisco, CA; [p.] Albert P. and Margaret Bird Sawyer; [m.] Joseph Earl Coomes, Jr., June 17, 1955, (Divorced); [ch.] Bryan Joseph (1960), Harlan Stephen (1961), Grandson Scott Harlan (1986); [ed.] A.A. Santa Rosa J.C. 1954, AB with Honors, Sacramento State College 1960, Univ. of LaVerne 1981, Institute of Children's Literature, Conn. 1987-88, 95-96. (Corres.) Attended UC Berkeley 1954-55.; [occ.] Substitute Teacher, Retired. Recently worked at United Artists Theatre Circuit, Inc. and Burger King.; [memb.] College Greens Swim and Racquet Club. The International Society of Poets, Free Associate Member. SMART Kids, Sacramento Metropolitan Area Reading Tutoring for Kids. Sierra Club. National Wildlife Association.; [hon.] 3rd Place, Named Miss Personality, Miss Sonoma County competition, 1953. 3 College Scholarships. World of Poetry Golden Poet 1985, 86, 87, 92, Silver Poet 1990. The National Library of Poetry, Editor's Choice Award 1994-95. Listed in Who's Who in California.; [oth. writ.] Federal copyright Paul 1-859-446, 12/06/93 for R and B song, "My Girlfriend Hates To Cook and Clean". Copyright pending for country song, "A New Father, Like A Night Pilot." Cassette album release soon for country song, "He's a 1995 Man. "Write own greeting card verses.; [pers.] Robert Frost, Carl Sandburg, and Elizabeth Barrett Browning are my poetic influences. I believe that each person is doing the best that they can do, within the framework of her or his life events.; [a.] Sacramento, CA

**COOPER, RASHAWNA DOMINIQUE**
[b.] May 18, 1979, Newport News, VA; [p.] Mary L. Ruffin; [ed.] Currently a junior at Rocky Mount Senior High School; [occ.] High school student; [memb.] Y.V.O.T.C. (Youth Voices of the City), Future Homemakers of America (FHA), Future Business Leaders of America (FBLA); [hon.] Outstanding Achievement Award from Rocky Mount Alumnae Chapter Delta Sigma Theta Sorority, Inc., President of Study Body and FHA in 9th grade, Honor Roll 9th and 10th, 2nd place 2 yrs running in the Citywide Martin Luther King Oratorical Contest; [oth. writ.] Students Taking Action Reaching Solutions (STARS), The Killer, Stress, "Promoting Unity..... The Dream Lives On"; [pers.] Do unto others as you would have them do unto you.; [a.] Rocky Mount, NC

**COPADO, MANUEL**
[b.] July 28, 1948, Detroit, MI; [p.] Eugenia and Manuel Copado; [m.] Susan Joanne Copado, May 5, 1979; [ch.] Jason; [ed.] B.A. Wayne State Univ. Detroit, Michigan; [oth. writ.] Currently Completing a compilation of poems and lyrics. I began writing in 1969. Recently began writing an Auto Biographical Book titled Journeys; [pers.] My life and writing has been influenced by Harry Chapin, one of our greatest "Story Tellers" and Humanitarians. For the past two years I have been I involved in a personal battle against cancer.; [a.] Madison Heights, MI

**CORDOBA, SAMUEL**
[pen.] Samuel Cordoba; [b.] July 13, 1967, Allentown, PA; [p.] Pedro F. and Ramona Q. Cordoba; [ch.] Samantha Marie Cordoba Born and Died May 30, 1995; [ed.] Personal experience; [occ.] Witness for Christ; [memb.] God's Family; [hon.] Heir of God through Christ; [oth. writ.] His Journey Home - Your Love For Me; [pers.] I love you Tressa, mind, body, and soul. - Flash; [a.] Allentown, PA

**CORN, JANIE W.**
[b.] June 24, 1937, Marietta, GA; [p.] Rev. Herbert and Lena Williams; [m.] Harold G. Corn, December 31, 1953; [ch.] Sheila Adams, Sharon Holloman, Jim H. Corn; [ed.] High School; [occ.] Personal Banker; [oth. writ.] I have several things that I have written but this is my first writing to be published.; [pers.] Raised in a Christian home, I grew up with a very strong belief in God and always a caring heart for others.

**CORTES, KRISTA**
[b.] July 4, 1981, Franklin County; [p.] Gildardo and Linda Cortes; [occ.] Student at North Henderson Christian School; [pers.] I think everyone has a talent you just have to look deep inside yourself to find it.; [a.] Henderson, NC

**COSTELLO, MARY AGNES**
[b.] September 22, 1916, San Francisco, CA; [p.] Andrew and Mary Scully; [m.] Edward Martin Costello, October 3, 1936; [ch.] Edward M. Jr. (Ted) - Beverly Ann - Andrea Mary; [ed.] St. Paul's High School, Healds Bus. College; [occ.] Retired Office Clerk; [memb.] Arthritis Foundation, St. Paul Alumnae Assoc., Several Religious Organizations, Calif. Pacific Med. Center; [hon.] Doing volunteer work at Calif., Pacific Medical Center and Arthritis Foundation. Received Awards of Appreciation at above and from Recreation Center for the Handicapped Inc.; [oth. writ.] This is my first to be published; [pers.] Wrote this poem after the death of my loving husband as part of grieving process. Got the idea after a stranger who cared for my husband one day wrote a beautiful poem to me (about me).; [a.] San Francisco, CA

**COTE, JENNIFER**
[b.] June 4, 1969, Los Angeles, CA; [p.] Peter and Gai Jarrett; [ed.] The Art Institute of Fprt Lauderdale - Photography, The Atlanta Apt. Assoc. - CAM; [occ.]

Assistant Property Manager; [memb.] 7 Stages Theatre in Atlanta. Choi Kwang-do Mrtial Arts; [pers.] When I write poetry, it is usually because I am struck by, or like to bring forth the beautiful simplicity in something I have seen or felt.; [a.] Acworth, GA

### COTTONHAM, MAUREEN H.
[b.] April 22, 1930, Homer, LA; [p.] Wesley and Mattie Pace Harper; [m.] Ernest L. Cottonham Jr.; [ch.] Anthony, Cedric, Greta; [ed.] B.A. Concentrated in Sociology, Chicago State University, Licensed Practical Nurse; [occ.] Retired L.P.N.; [memb.] mount Earia C.M.E. Church, Stewardess, Missionary, Choir Member, Sunday School Supt.; [hon.] Poem book recently published "Song of Life" published in local Newspaper; [oth. writ.] Working on second poem book; [pers.] I thank God that He allowed my talent to stay with me until I had the time to write.; [a.] Jonesboro, LA

### COUNTER, JENY
[b.] June 26, 1976, Iron Mountain, MI; [p.] Pam Counter and Bob Counter; [ed.] Florence High School, Bay de Woc. Community College; [occ.] Manager of Wendy's and Home Health Care Aide (TLC); [hon.] Dean's list; [pers.] No one actually inspires me to write I just find it within myself. My ability to write has given me the opportunity to explore my own feelings.; [a.] Florence, WI

### COVE, MICHAEL
[b.] June 16, 1982, Los Angeles; [p.] Sherry Cove, Wayne P. Cove; [ed.] La Mesa Jr. High; [occ.] Jr. High Student; [oth. writ.] Several private poems; [pers.] I continue my dreams in my writings.; [a.] Canyon Country, CA

### COX, PAUL A.
[b.] March 24, 1970, Dublin, TX; [p.] Suella Shaner and Ken Cox; [m.] Julie Williams Cox, February 5, 1994; [ed.] Marton B.A. in Psychology and English and University of Texas and Austin. Few graduate classes; [occ.] P.T. Bookstore Mgr., Plane. TX; [memb.] Phi Kappa Psi, AMA, FBCN; [oth. writ.] Working Progress: Autobioloy; [pers.] While not every one is blessed enough are for each person to believe they are among these that are.; [a.] Dallas, TX

### CRANE, ELIZABETH
[pen.] Liz Klinner; [b.] October 26, 1950, Selma, AL; [p.] Robert and Mary Klinner; [m.] Wayne Crane, April 26, 1969; [ch.] Paul Anthony, Wayne Derrick "Bo" Sean Evan, Amanda Nicole; [ed.] Dallas Co. High; [occ.] Homemaker; [memb.] Compassionate Friends; [oth. writ.] My other poems and this one published in local newspaper; [pers.] The poems I have written, were a gift to me, from my Lord Jesus. They are in loving memory of Wayne Derrick "Bo", my second born son. Born September 10, 1972, Died May 29, 1992; [a.] Selma, AL

### CRAWFORD, CINDY
[pen.] CA Crawford; [b.] October 5, 1964; [p.] Robert Crawford and Willa Scott; [ed.] Hudson Valley Community College, A.A.S. Accounting in 1986; [occ.] Unemployed-data entry operator; [memb.] Sierra Club, World Wildlife Fund; [oth. writ.] None as of yet; [pers.] Poems never go out of style.; [a.] Walden, NY

### CREE, HOBART JAMES
[b.] March 13, 1918, (Deceased, May 18, 1994); [pers.] This poem was found after your passing. Hopefully will give others the same joy it has given me. A tribute to my father and my best friend. You're missed very much. Ronald Ross Cree.

### CRITIENDEN, ELISHA G.
[b.] December 9, 1969, Tallahassee, FL; [p.] Charles Critienden, Faith Jackson Critienden, Joel Kelman (Stepfather); [ed.] Granada Hills High, Granada Hills, Ca, University of California, Los Angeles, University of California, Hastings College of the Law; [occ.] Full time Law Student, aspiring Federal Prosecutor; [memb.] Hastings Constitutional Law Quarterly, UCLA Alumni Association; [hon.] Dean's List, Phi Beta Kappa, Golden Key National Honors Society, Pi Gamma MV; [oth. writ.] Other unpublished poems, short stories, and the draft of a novel several unpublished pieces for piano; [pers.] I find the most important philosophy of life is found in Antoine de St. Exupery's "The Little Prince", Ch. 21.; [a.] Woodland Hills, CA

### CROSS, JAMIE MARIE
[b.] January 9, 1984; [p.] Connie Gibson and Giovanni Smith; [ed.] I am in sixth grade; [occ.] Student; [hon.] I received Bowling Awards and Writing Certificates; [a.] Eminence, MO

### CROSSWAIT, HELEN G. MOORHOUSE
[pen.] Paleface; [b.] November 19, 1930, Rosebud Indian Reservation, SD; [p.] Florence and Albert Moorhouse; [ch.] Constance of Woming, Mark of Montana; [ed.] Bachelors Degree in the Arts University of Newsbraska, Lincoln 1985; [occ.] Performing Storyteller and Writer; [hon.] Hon. Mention, Natl. Literary Contest, Am. Mothers, 1995 (held NYC June 95) 2nd Place - Nebraska - Essay Div. Am Mothers Lit. Cont. 1995 Previous Honors Natl. Libr. of Poetry; [oth. writ.] Published: South Dakota Magazine Husker Magazine Self Published: (2 books) Riot in a Parrott Shoppe and Other Eruptions and Reflections of a Paleface from the Rosebud; [pers.] My writing reflects the prairie and its people. My spiritual strength is gained from my close ties to the west and its rich traditional historical and colorful characters, Native Americans, Homesteaders, Ranchers etc.; [a.] Chadron, NE

### CRUISE, WILMA
[b.] August 27, 1897, Buffalo Co, NE; [p.] Charles and Ada Day; [m.] Ray Cruise (Deceased), March, 1919; [ch.] Robert Virgil Cruise, Warren Douglas Cruise; [ed.] Grade School, High School, Graduated 1915, Normal School, Graduated 1918, taught School 1 year; [occ.] Retired Homemaker; [memb.] D.A.R. 35 years; [oth. writ.] Short Stories, Poetry, Children Stories, 2 Books—Family Histories, "This is my Story", "Bits and Bits and Pieces"; [pers.] I spent around forty years in Genealogy, which was really my first priority.; [a.] Pleasanton, NE

### CRUSE, VIRGINIA
[pen.] Virginia Cruse; [b.] July 21, 1927, Pinola, MS; [p.] J. W. Boggan, Winna Miller; [m.] Benny Cruse, December 29, 1946; [ch.] Dan and Chuck; [ed.] 3 years College, Northeast LA State University; [occ.] Retired Bookkeeper; [memb.] Grayson Bpt. church, Caldwell Parish Garden Club, Grayson Beautification Committee, Republican Nat'l. Committee; [hon.] Valedictorian High School; [oth. writ.] Poems published in local Newspaper. 2nd Place in State on poem entered in State Cultural Events of Senior Olympics.; [pers.] My poems reflect my love for God and His love for humankind.

### CULBERTSON, DEVIN
[b.] June 26, 1981, Portland, OR; [p.] Kim Culbertson, Elijah Sims; [ed.] Lincoln High School (Sophomore); [hon.] Talented and gifted Students program, international studies center program; [oth. writ.] A collection of poems in which this is one; [pers.] I write my feelings not my thoughts, my pen is just trying to keep up with my mind.; [a.] Portland, OR

### CUMMINGS, CLARA EVELYN CLARK
[b.] December 15, 1912, Viginia; [p.] Willard and Helen (Nellie) Clark; [m.] James Patrick Cummings, January 8, 1940; [ch.] Walter James; [ed.] High School, Business College and Washington Bible College; [occ.] Retired WU Telegraph operator; [memb.] Teacher and Deaconess Baptist Church. Active in Missions and Senior Citizens; [oth. writ.] Published in local paper since 1929 on various occasions also in Nat'l Society of Poets and World Poetry; [pers.] A real joy are our three grandchildren Richard, Karen and Amy who keep us in touch with the current generation. I graduated in VA. Husband and Son were born in New York City. Active in MD. for 35 years where our son graduated from U.S.N.A.

### CUNNINGHAM, MRS. JO
[pen.] Mrs. Jo Cunningham; [b.] December 1, 1914, Wichita, KS; [m.] Joe R. Keith, May 5, 1956; [occ.] Retired - I am 80 yrs old.

### CURRAN, CAROLYN A.
[b.] June 29, 1943, Hazel Park, MI; [p.] Kenneth and the late Florence Curran; [m.] Divorced; [ch.] Six sons and four grandsons; [ed.] High School; [occ.] Homemaker, Write poetry and short stories; [hon.] 2 Editors choice awards; [oth. writ.] I have had 2 others poems published 1 in Best of 95 and 1 in East of the Sunrise (95) I have wrote over 70 poems; [pers.] I enjoy writing poems about life's happenings. And expressions of the heart.; [a.] Troy, MI

### CURRY, JULIE
[pen.] Julie B.; [b.] October 22, 1962, Newark, NJ; [p.] Terry and Otis Robinson; [m.] Single; [ch.] Son names Ashanti who is 16 years; [ed] Plainfield High School, Plainfield, NJ; Essex College, Newark; [occ.] Sales Clerk, Medical Student; [memb.] Urban Womens Writing Club; [oth. writ.] Unknown screen plays, Let's Chill! and Glory Bee!; [pers.] I write for arts sake, I write for the people, I write because I love it. I was influenced by my mother who gave me my first book.; [a.] Somerville, NJ

### CURTIS, SARAH DIANE
[b.] November 15, 1980, Anniston, AL; [p.] David Curtis, Dennise Curtis; [ed.] Johnston Elementary, Anniston Middle School, Pleasant Valley High; [occ.] Student; [memb.] Pleasent Valley Marching Band, United States Tae Kwon Do Alliance, Future Homemakers of America, New Liberty Baptist Church; [hon.] Young Author's Conference; [oth. writ.] Our father God, published in Anthology of Poetry by Young Americans 1992 Edition One Snowy Morning; [a.] Wellington, AL

### CURTIS JR., GLENN
[pen.] Glenn Curtis Jr.; [b.] December 17, 1981, Atlanta, GA; [ed.] Currently 9th grade; [occ.] Student 9th grade; [memb.] U.S. Chess Federation; [oth. writ.] Many unpublished poems of my own currently in my personal books "Look What I Made"; [pers.] Life is a poem to be enjoys and learned from. It is usually also short.; [a.] Decatur, GA

### CZERWINSKI, ANNA J.
[pen.] Anna MacKenna; [b.] January 14, 1947, Buffalo, NY; [ed.] Kensington H.S., State Univ. College at Buffalo, N.Y.; [occ.] English Teacher, Writing Specialist LA Salle Sr. High School, Niagara Falls, N.Y.; [memb.] Twin Cities Camera Club, Myrddin Writers' Group, W.N.Y. GTO Club, Inc., Foothills Trail Club; [hon.] Teacher of the Year - LSHS - 1981, Gold Medal - Ice Dancing; [oth. writ.] Poems in local publication, Articles for Original Muscle and The Legend; [pers.] As I write I look to the Author of Light to lead me to truth

and reality and hope. Favorite Poets: Thomas Hardy, Robinson Jeffers.; [a.] Niagara Falls, NY

**DAHMS, DANIEL JOSEPH**
[pen.] Daniel Joseph Dahms; [b.] January 18, 1942, Benton Harbor, MI; [p.] George William Dahms, Frances Lucille Frazier; [m.] Dixie E. Dahms, November 20, 1965; [ch.] Darin Andrew Joseph, Derek Anthony; [ed.] Penn High School, Indiana University at South Bend; [occ.] Sales Representative, Whitehead Electronics; [memb.] Ancient Order of Hibernians in America INC., IUSB Alumni Associations Knights of Colombus, Veteran: United States Air Force, Indiana Army National Guard; [hon.] Phi Alpha Theta; [oth. writ.] Several poems and articles published in local and business publications; [pers.] The membership of the Penn High School Class of 1960 enjoyed and I hold deep feelings for each of them. My poems included in this volume is about and for those wonderful individuals.; [a.] Mishawaka, IN

**DALY, RUTH HATCHER**
[pen.] Ruth Marie Daly; [b.] October 19, 1907, Jacksonville, FL; [p.] George and Ida Hatcher; [m.] Alexander M. Daly, December 23, 1923; [ch.] Robert F., Doris M., A.M., Jr., Jacqueline E., Charles F.; [ed.] Duval Co. High; [occ.] Retired - Full-time mother and wife for 60 yrs.; [memb.] Old Capitol United Methodist Church, Corydon, Indiana - AARP; [hon.] Godly Woman! Reared 4 children of strong values. (First son died at 9 years of age). Has 11 grand and 18 great grands. Could there be greater honor?; [oth. writ.] Numerous writings in church papers and senior publications.; [pers.] Mom's writings were based on her strong faith in God's word. Our life would contain a full gamut of human emotions and experiences. These gave us a full storehouse of memories as we pressed on in the race of life.; [a.] Corydon, IN

**DANDRIDGE, EULA B.**
[pen.] "Judy" Dandridge; [b.] March 3, 1924, Illinois; [p.] Nannie and John Dandridge (Both Deceased); [ed.] Augusta Tilghman High School and Business College, Paducah, KY; [occ.] Retired Office employee of Studio Transportation Drivers, Teamsters Local 399 for Motion Picture Industry or no Hollywood, CA; [memb.] International Society of Poets - Retired Member of Teamsters Studio Union #399 No. Hollywood, CA, GULLS - Women's Luncheon Club in Oxward, CA - Benefiting Various Charities; [hon.] National Honor Society - From Graduation - High School - American Legion Scholarship Award. Editor's Choice Awards, in at days end and edge of twilight 1994 - the National Library of Poetry; [oth. writ.] Two poems printed in at days end and edge of twilight - the National Library of Poetry - one poem printed in best poems of 1995 - National Library of Poetry - one poem printed in newspaper (Dolores Star - Dolores, Colorado) in 1993.; [pers.] Special interest - music of all kinds - sang with opera chorus in 1956 with Los Angeles, conservatory of music. Poetry, Tennis, Dancing. At age 5 moved to Paducahi, KY with mother and family of one brother three sisters mother, nannie, died at age 96, 2-8-92 loved to make rhymes. Moved to Los Angeles, CA, age 20, resides now in Oxnard, CA. Since March 1990, Ancestor - Martha Dandridge Custis Washington - wife of George Washington.; [a.] Oxnard, CA

**DANIELS, DONNA MAY**
[b.] January 9, 1976, Illinois; [p.] David and Diana Daniels; [ed.] Streamwood High, Elgin Community College; [occ.] Snack Shop Attendant, Streamwood Lanes, Streamwood, IL; [oth. writ.] Several poems published in high school literary magazine; [pers.] A great amount of my writing depicts James Dean's America, the wonder, the confusion, the pureness of the

heart. Here's to you, Jimmie. And to Pat Bellanger - thanks, you're the man.; [a.] Carol Stream, IL

**DARNER, ROBERT J.**
[pen.] Robert McHenry; [b.] May 25, 1970, Greenville, OH; [p.] David Darner, Paulo Smith; [ed.] Greenville Sr. High School; [memb.] Business Professionals of America; [oth. writ.] Tragedy, a friend says goodbye; [pers.] You need a goal to have a purpose. "Let love shine through the hearts of all men, and forget those you have loved".; [a.] Greenville, OH

**DARTY, MARK**
[b.] November 2, 1974, Jackson, TN; [p.] Jim and Carolyn Darty; [ed.] Palm Bay High School, Junior at the University of Central Florida in Orlando (Psychology BS); [occ.] U.C.F. Psychology Undergraduate Research Assistant; [memb.] Co-President and Lead Community Service, Advocate of Phi Eta Sigma National Honor Society; [hon.] President's List, National Dean's List, Dean's List, Freshman Honors Award; [oth. writ.] Work in progress: A book with two plays; [pers.] Look into yourself to find the meaning of yours and of mankind; [a.] Orlando, FL

**DASHIELL, TANYA AURELIA**
[pen.] Margaret; [b.] February 21, 1959, Washington, DC; [p.] Bobby Gray Taylor; [m.] Donald J. Dashiell Jr., December 27, 1985; [ch.] Candies Nicole Dashiell, Donald J. Dashiell III; [ed.] Cardozo High School University of MA Eastern Shore; [occ.] Pharmacy Dept, Giant Food; [memb.] Sisters United, Salisbury Writers Club and PTA; [oth. writ.] Children's stories, "Scooby's Dragon," true stories, Dort go up stairs," Fiction, "Stranded", Educational Pre-teen" What every Preteen wants to know"; [pers.] "Writing is an art that is filled with adventure that will touch your spirit." My writings are filled with the experiences of life. Allow yourself to re-live them again and again.; [a.] Salisbury, MD

**DAVENPORT, ANGELA**
[pen.] Angie; [b.] June 13, 1968, Cuyahoga Falls, OH; [p.] Druscilla Davenport; [ed.] Redlands Senior High School; [hon.] Awards of merit certificate. Several poems published in local newspapers.; [pers.] First, I'm thanking all mighty himself, God. For giving me the strength to do another poem. My mother Druscilla Davenport, my baby sis Monica, for loving me. Thanks to the whole Davenports Family and Manuel, Earl, Freeman; [a.] Highland, CA

**DAVIN, JARED**
[b.] June 11, 1979, Bronx, NY; [p.] William and Laura Davin; [ed.] Fordham Preparatory High School; [occ.] Student; [pers.] I really love poetry.

**DAVIS JR., JAMES E.**
[pen.] James E. Davis Jr.; [b.] October 15, 1926, Philadelphia, PA; [p.] Edith May and James E. (Deceased); [m.] Nancy Lou Davis, August 14, 1994 (2nd Marriage); [ch.] Two from 1st marriage; [ed.] High School, The Institute Of Children's Literature; [occ.] Retired; [oth. writ.] I've written over 150 poems in the past year. Several of my poems were publishes in local paper. Presently getting a book of poems together.; [pers.] I try to love humor in my writing. Through the years I've found humor to be the thing that makes life pleasant and joyful.; [a.] Schwenksville, PA

**DAVIS, SHIRLEY D.**
[b.] October 30, 1934, California; [p.] Walter and Ruth Thompson; [m.] Leland Davis, April 20, 1985; [ch.] Patricia, Shirley, Howard, Stuart and Kelly; [ed.] Essex Community College, Baltimore, MD; [occ.] Public Records Specialist, Lee County Government; [memb.] Auxiliaries of the V.F.W. and American Legion; [pers.]

Day by day issues that concerns so many people often reflects in my writings and feelings.; [a.] Cape Coral, FL

**DAVIS, CONSTANCE**
[b.] September 10, 1951, Atlanta, GA; [p.] Mrs. Queen Esther Grier; [ch.] Phillip Larita, Gary Corey, Drayton, Malu; [ed.] S.H. Archer High, Atlanta Archer Tech; [hon.] The Editor's Choice Award (3) by the National Library of Poetry; [oth. writ.] Many poems unpublished, and 5 poems published by the National Library of Poetry; [pers.] "A Couple of days ago I didn't hear it anywhere, "Jesus lives.".; [a.] Atlanta, GA

**DAY, HALLETTE DAWSON**
[pen.] Hallette Dawson; [b.] July 22, 1947, Atlanta, GA; [p.] Harris Dawson Jr. and Evelyn Dawson; [m.] David Allen Day, July 20, 1991; [ch.] Emily Juliana Dawson; [ed.] Frankfort American High School, Frankfort, Germany, Schillar College Stuttgart, Germany, Gulf Park College, Long Beach, Mississippi; [occ.] Housewife and Mother; [pers.] I do my best writing late at nite, when my family is asleep, and all of the hectic world is quite.; [a.] Herndon, VA

**DE SOUZA, ANTOINE**
[b.] November 2, 1936, Brazil; [p.] Francisco and Carmen; [m.] Sonia S. De Souza, September 21, 1986; [ch.] Tyler and Tiffany; [ed.] Oswaldo Cruz College - Brazil, Temple School of Communications; [occ.] Cosmetologist; [oth. writ.] Metaplus-a screen play, poems of lvoe parody, poems Potpourri, music translations of foreigner origin into English and vice-versa; [pers.] All my writings are to reflect: The beauty of simplicity, The sensuous of the soul, The awareness of the non obvious, The wisdom, dept and cynicism of human kind.; [a.] Norristown, PA

**DE VASTEY, YVONNE WATLINGTON VANCE**
[b.] November 14, 1931, Philadelphia, PA; [p.] Susie Banker and Joseph Watlington; [m.] Jean De Vastey, November 24, 1987; [ch.] Guy Vance and Dean Vance; [ed.] Girls High, Phila, Temple University (Tyler School of Fine Arts-BFA), Antioch University (M.Ed); [occ.] Community and Organizational Consultant, Bodywork Therapist; [memb.] Frat Mt. Air Neighbors, Rainbow Women Network; [hon.] Chapel of the Four Chaplaine Award; [oth. writ.] Several articles published in local newspaper and many published poems; [pers.] I aim to approached day with great focus, expressing that which works in my heart into my writing.; [a.] Philadelphia, PA

**DE SOUZA, ANTOINE**
[b.] November 2, 1936, Brazil; [p.] Francisco and Carmen; [m.] Sonia S. De Souza, September 21, 1986; [ch.] Tyler and Tiffany; [ed.] Oswaldo Cruz College - Brazil Temple School of Communications; [occ.] Cosmetologist; [oth. writ.] Metaplus - a screen play poems of love parody, Poems potpourri, Music translations of foreigner origin into English and Vice-Versa; [pers.] All my writing are to reflect: The beauty of simplicity, The senses of the soul, The awareness of the non obvious, The wisdom, dept and cynicism of human kind.; [a.] Norristown, PA

**DE SILVESTRI, MARY**
[b.] April 8, 1944, NY; [p.] Alfred and Mary Calvaruso; [m.] Joseph De Silvestri, Sr., June 30, 1963; [ch.] Alfred John, Joseph Alexander Jr.; [ed.] In Business Administration; [occ.] Vice President - Contract Sales, Propper MFC. Co., New York; [memb.] President - Cathedral Preparatory Seminary Parent's Association, Member - Northside Women's Democratic Association; [hon.] Occupational Awards: Sales Achievement Award - 1992, Outstanding Achievement Award - 1994; [oth. writ.] Several poems, children's play for elemen-

tary school presentation; [pers.] Poetry is the music of the world, the expression of the heart and the communication of the soul.; [a.] Corona, NY

**DE PAULA, HENRIQUE**
[pen.] Sorcerer; [b.] December 12, 1928, Sao Paulo, Brazil; [p.] Antonio De Paula, Amalia Salgado; [m.] Maria Luiza De Castor De Paula, May 31, 1958; [ch.] Julio Cesar and Carlos Alberto, Valerie and Celia (In Laws); [ed.] First and Commercial Schools; [occ.] Construction Laborer, (In Brazil I was a sales manager); [memb.] International Society of Poets; [hon.] Five Awards from The National Library of Poetry. Books: In the Desert Sun-1993, Dance on the Horizon, Tears of Fire and Edge of Twilight-1994. Best Poets of 1995.; [oth. writ.] Many articles published about sports in the newspaper "Noticias Populares, on Sao Paulo-Brazil and many poems printed in brazilians and portuguese-american newspapers, in Newark-N. J. and somerville-MA. The magazine Ponto de Contro, Elizabeth-N J. also print my poems.; [pers.] I write about everything. In tragic but sometimes the humorous too. My book about the humanity, God religions, governments and so on is almost ready to be printed. Title of my book: God, THE OUTRIGHT LIE.; [a.] Newark, NJ

**DE LUCCIA, GERTRUDE M.**
[b.] December 28, 1916, Scotland; [p.] Agnes MacKee-Duncan MacLenan; [ch.] Jeffrey, Nancy, Gail; [ed.] Newton High, Business College; [hon.] Tem Perance Award for Thesis, Reader's Digest - Humours Saying; [oth. writ.] I am writing a book about veteran's; [pers.] I am act to write emotional poems. Also romantic ones. Due to my own life, I strive to bring out in my writing, the grief, laughter and episodes, that I have experienced.; [a.] Saint Petersburg, FL

**DEARDORFF, NAOMI R.**
[b.] January 18, 1974, WV; [p.] Oliver and Barbara Hogue; [m.] Robert Deardorff, June 12, 1992; [ed.] Teays Valley Christian School, West Virginia State College; [occ.] Day Care Teacher; [pers.] I prefer reading and writing poetry that denotes places of the heart. I greatly admire the poetry of Edgar Allen Poe.; [a.] Scott Depot, WV

**DEBBAN, GLENN L.**
[b.] June 3, 1973, Holbrook, NE; [p.] Wilma F. and William L. Debban; [ed.] AA Degree in Marketing from San Diego Evening College, and classes at San Diego State University, majoring in Marketing Management. I also hold an instructors LIC in Cosmetology.; [occ.] Accounting Technician For the US Navy, at Naval Station S.D.; [memb.] Grace Lutheran Church, San Diego; [oth. writ.] Numerous poems and song lyrics, "Life Journey" is the first one to be published; [pers.] Debban, Glenn L. Born June 3rd 1937, twenty minutes after my twin brother Gary L. Debban, in Holbrook, Nebraska moved to Greeley, Colorado, at the age of 13, and attended High School there. Enlisted and spent four years in the Air Force. Move to California in 1969, where I attended College. My talent and love for writing has been recently discovered. I have written a number of song lyrics, as well as poetry.; [a.] San Diego, CA

**DECKARD, LYNN**
[pen.] Lynn Ramirez (Wade); [b.] December 10, 1961, Abilene, TX; [p.] Ben Wade, Barbara Helms; [m.] Douglas A. Deckard, November 30, 1991; [ch.] Christina Lee Ramirez, Ryan Allen Deckard, Matthew Arnold Deckard; [ed.] Technical School, Licensed Practical Nurse; [occ.] LPN; [memb.] Deca in High School; [hon.] Certificate of Merit on Poem Blossom, and Dual Heartbeat; [oth. writ.] Blossom, Dual Heartbeat, Wrong Direction, Angel; [pers.] My family is my greatest joy,

My children are my world.; [a.] Lexington, KY

**DEIBERT, PHOEBE**
[b.] September 7, 1951, Aberdeen, WA; [p.] Marguerite Marshall, Ogden Jhanson; [m.] William J. Deibert Sr., November 11, 1969; [ch.] Bill Jr., Jerod, Tawnya; [ed.] ITT Peterson School of Business (Seattle, WA), Elma High School; [occ.] Instructional Aide and Library Assistant and Color Guard Advisor; [memb.] PSE; [oth. writ.] I have many I've kept in my personal book; [pers.] Young children become the mirror images of people whom they idolize. Are you giving your admirer the kind of image you desire?; [a.] Elma, WA

**DELOACH, CYNTHIA MORRIS**
[pen.] Cynthia Morris DeLoach; [b.] March 31, 1960, Claxton, GA; [p.] David Morris Sr., Linda Morris; [m.] John C. DeLoach, December 2, 1978; [ch.] Heidi Melinda; [ed.] Humpty Dumpty Kindergarten, Evans County Public Schools, and The Institute of Children's Literature; [occ.] Self-employed; [memb.] American Red Cross, St. Jude Family Circle, and Eastside Baptist Church; [hon.] Who's Who Among American High School Students, and presently serving as 1995-1996 Co-Youth Chairperson for the Evans County Chapter of the American Red Cross, 1995-1996 of Directors of Evans County Chapter of the American Red Cross; [oth. writ.] None published at present; [pers.] Through my writing I attempt to make the reader think with their heart and act with their soul.; [a.] Claxton, GA

**DeMARCO, DOMENICK C.**
[b.] October 12, 1962, Port Chester, NY; [p.] Armando DeMarco, anna DeMarco; [ed.] Blind Brook High, Pace University-Lubin School of Business; [occ.] Financial Coordinator, Mitsubishi Imaging Inc., Rye, NY; [memb.] National Asthma Center, Pace University Alumni Assoc., The Sine-Aid Society, The Vestibular Disorders Assoc.; [hon.] Blind Brook Occupational Education Award, Dean's List; [oth. writ.] Several non-published poems and songs; [pers.] Being a romantic at heart, my writings reflect the sentiments of those who won or lost love.; [a.] Rye Brook, NY

**DERR II, CHARLES RAYMER**
[pen.] Carlos Derr; [b.] October 1, 1942; [p.] Charles Raymer Derr, Jean Kerns Derr; [m.] Trisha Kane Derr; [ch.] Tara Derr Rodgers, Ethan Appleby (Derr); [oth. writ.] Andalusia of Weeping, a novel; [a.] Reston, VA

**DEVANEY, DOROTHY**
[b.] July 7, 1917, Iowa; [p.] Clair and Mary Waters; [m.] Francis DeVaney (Deceased), 1936; [ch.] Monty, Stanley, Helen; [ed.] Graduated from high school in Iowa; [occ.] 25 years in Cafe 20 years in apple shed now retired; [oth. writ.] I have written a lot of poems just for my own amusement and for friends.; [pers.] My husband and I were young teenagers during the depression. We ran off and get married. We went to Idaho then to Wash. He built this house I wrote about.; [a.] Waterville, WA

**DIETRICH, HELEN**
[b.] April 14, 1921, Campell, NY; [p.] Clarence and Mable Stanton; [m.] Louis J. Paulauski Sr., October 15, 1938; [ch.] Alvina Paulauski and Louis Paulauski Jr.; [ed.] 10th Grade Completed; [occ.] Retired; [memb.] Easter Star Chapter Felicitas #500; [pers.] My husbands death inspired me to write this poem to know one can feel the assurance of the Lords promise for eternal life.; [a.] Williamsport, PA

**DIGIACOMO, DONNA**
[b.] February 23, 1976, Philadelphia, PA; [p.] Mary Ann and Donald DiGiacomo; [ed.] Community College of Philadelphia, Little Flower Catholic High School for girls, Visitation BVM Elementary School; [occ.]

Student, Journalist; [memb.] Editor-in-chief of Community College, of Philadelphia's Student newspaper, Student Vaneyard Student at the Institute for Children's Literature in West Redding, Conn.; [oth. writ.] Held Sports Column in neighborhood paper in 1994, nearly 100 letters to the editor published in local newspapers an national magazines.; [pers.] Reading is the best form of meditation.; [a.] Philadelphia, PA

**DIGIOVANNI, SHANE**
[b.] August 8, 1978, Camp Hill, PA; [p.] Lizetta DiGiovanni; [ch.] Leigh, Rory, Shane; [ed.] Continuing in High School; [occ.] Sales and Advertising; [memb.] Volunteer fire company Station 6- Dover, PA; [pers.] These poems are dedicated to Mom, who passed away April 12, 1995. You always encourage me to write from the heart. Here it is, Mom.; [a.] Dover, PA

**DILLENBECK, LEILANI**
[b.] November 17, 1962, Michigan; [p.] Marie S. Dillenbeck; [ed.] B.S. Physical Education, University of Southern Mississippi; [occ.] Kroger's; [oth. writ.] Currently unpublished; [pers.] If first we can recognize the many sides and internal conflicts of ourselves and humanity, perhaps we can overcome our learned biases. When I write I hope to make people think about their differences and look for a solution that brings everyone together as one group - the human species.; [a.] Cookville, TN

**DIXON JR., LEONARD**
[pen.] Leonard Dixon Jr.; [b.] February 11, 1978, Brooklyn, NY; [p.] Gwen Dixon and Leonard Dixon Sr.; [m.] Charlene, Keisha and Rodney; [ed.] Mamaroneck High School; [occ.] Student; [memb.] F.B.L.A Further Business Leaders of America; [oth. writ.] Several poems published in local school magazines and newspapers; [pers.] In the essence of human kind I strive to tell the reality in our society and to make people think about our world being I have been greatly influenced by Langton Hughes.; [a.] Larchmont, NY

**DOBSON, CLIFTON M.**
[b.] January 24, 1964, New York; [p.] Rayney and Priscilla Dobson; [ed.] New York Education; [occ.] E-Prom Programmer for Motorola, Arlington Heights, IL; [pers.] When I write, it's from the soul, and that will never change.; [a.] Chicago, IL

**DODGE, TIFFANY**
[pen.] Poettic-with 2 T'S; [b.] April 6, 1980, Billings, MT; [p.] Paul and Tammy Dodge; [ed.] Finished freshman year of high school will be attending sophomore year this coming fall; [occ.] Summer job at Job Service West a Clerk General; [hon.] Last year you (National Library of Poetry). Published my poem on AIDS.; [oth. writ.] I write short stories, but have never gotten any them published.; [pers.] I can write about any subject, but my greatest ability is on the subject romance.; [a.] Billings, MT

**DOMBROWSKI JR., DANIEL D.**
[pen.] Daniel D. Dombrowski Jr.; [b.] April 30, 1968, Buffalo, NY; [p.] Marlene Dombrowski, Daniel Dombrowski Sr.; [ed.] Lake Shore Central Senior High, Erie Community College North, Buffalo State College; [occ.] Office Manager, Build-All Corporation, Lancaster, NY; [hon.] V.F.W. Post 5798 Essay Competition winner; [oth. writ.] Poetry published in Buffalo's Art Voice. Contributing Editor to the portrait magazine of Buffalo State College.; [pers.] Those who keep their distance from the world are often the ones with the best view.; [a.] Lancaster, NY

**DOMBROWSKI, THOMAS**
[pen.] "TJ"; [b.] January 27, 1965, Chicago, IL; [p.] Thomas and Marge Dombrowski; [ed.] Forest View

High School, Arlington Heights, IL; [occ.] Writer, Seeker and Adventurer; [oth. writ.] "Endless Love", "Follow the Rainbow", "I Love the Rain", "Divination"," Speaking of the Wigs", "Listen to the Wind", "Say it all", "Love and life", "Listen to within"; [pers.] Life is like a pond. Everything we do is like throwing a rock into the pond and creating ripples in the water. We all are in some way or another interconnected. So what we do affect us all. So start with love at the core spreading outwards. What a wonderful world it would be!; [a.] Elk Grove, IL

**DOMINIK, METTA MENZONI**
[b.] June 16, 1966, Vineland; [p.] Florance B. Mahoney and Peter J. Menzoni; [m.] Joshua M. Dominik, December 24, 1994; [ch.] Melissa and Heather Mazzarella Amanda and Carley McCloskey; [occ.] Child daycare Owner, operator; [oth. writ.] Several other poems; [pers.] I write what I feel inside and what I see in the eyes of those who surround me.; [a.] Landsville, NJ

**DONALDSON, CLIFFORD**
[b.] August 25, 1957, CA; [p.] Mom and Dad; [ch.] Kevin Dren, Jennifer Kayliegh; [ed.] High School; [occ.] U.S. Navy; [oth. writ.] A lot, but nothing published this is my first; [pers.] I just put on paper where I've been and. And remember those people I have met, I don't forget anyone.; [a.] Lemoore, CA

**DONALDSON, STEVEN EDWIN**
[b.] August 17, 1972, Sacramento, CA; [p.] Charles Donaldson, Vicki Donaldson; [m.] Amelia Perry, June 10, 1995; [ed.] Hiram Johnson High School, Sacramento City College; [hon.] 2nd Place, Opinion Story, Journalism Association of Community Colleges, California Northern Section 1994; [oth. writ.] Several articles published in college and local papers; [pers.] Writing is more than putting words on paper-its painting a picture with words. The key is to read. I have never read a book that I haven't gotten something out of.; [a.] Sacramento, CA

**DONATO, GINA**
[b.] April 2, 1986, Fort Lauderdale, FL; [p.] Steve and Neyda Donato; [ed.] St. Clements School; [oth. writ.] Has written over 75 poems started writing at 5 years old.; [a.] Fort Lauderdale, FL

**DONSEY, CORI LYNN**
[b.] April 23, 1978, East Chicago, IN; [p.] Adrian Jenkins, Abraham Donsey; [ed.] Chicago Central High School; [occ.] Senior High School; [memb.] African American Studies Committee; [oth. writ.] Unpublished poems: They took your freedom, Are we not the same, I knew a place, You don't know; [pers.] 'I have been influenced African-American and Native History. I desire for my writings to reflect those emotions; [a.] East Chicago, IN

**DORAME, SARA CATALINA**
[b.] July 4, 1975, Santa Rosa, CA; [p.] Gilbert and Jo Dorame; [ed.] Ursuline High, currently attending Santa Rosa Junior College; [occ.] College Student; [oth. writ.] Several poems in local Newspaper, Santa Rosa Press Democrat. A poem in the Anthology "The Poets" published by the Cera Foundation.; [pers.] I wish more people learn about their History and try to understand one another's differences. I am quiet influenced by my mixed Heritage, including European, Mexican, and Native American Blood.; [a.] Santa Rosa, CA

**DORVEE, JASON RICHARD**
[b.] November 24, 1979, Glens Falls, NY; [p.] Barbara Dorvee, Louis Caterina; [ed.] Guajome Park Academy, Roosevelt Middle School, Mission Montessori Carlsbad Montessori; [occ.] Student; [memb.] Junior Honor So-

ciety, Peer Assistant Leader, Academic Team, Black Belt Club of the Oriental Martail Arts College; [hon.] Various Academic Achievement Awards; [oth. writ.] Several poems and short stories printed in the school publications; [pers.] "Knowledge, and the ability to interpret and apply that knowledge is power. Through knowledge and the understanding of that knowledge comes enlightenment."; [a.] Carlsbad, CA

**DOS SANTOS, VIVIAN**
[pen.] Baby; [b.] August 22, 1987, Boston, MA; [p.] Jovelino Dos Santos, Mrs. Judite Tavares; [pers.] I am influenced by my Daddy who likes to write about many things he sees. He says we can become happier if we are able to express ourselves through writing. Then I decided to write the poem I sent you.; [a.] Cambridge, MA

**DOS SANTOS, JOVELINO**
[pen.] Daddy Gold; [b.] November 13, 1954, Brazil; [p.] Julianio Dos Santos, Ms. Nair Torres; [m.] Ex-spouse Ms. Judite Tavares never lived together but married; [ch.] Vivian Dos Santos, Melissa Dos Santos; [ed.] University Degree; [occ.] Teacher in the Boston Public Schools; [pers.] I prefer to write about women, mainly about the ones I do not like. But, if it happens that I write about a woman that I like, I do it on a rainy day, because, for me, it seems that the rain can wash away my suffering.; [a.] Boston, MA

**DOSPASSOS, LINDA**
[b.] July 7, 1995; [ed.] Cardinal Dougherty High School, La Roche College, Wesley College; [occ.] Student at Wesley College; [hon.] President's List, Wells Scholarship, Editor-in-Chief of The Whestone; [oth. writ.] Several poems in other anthologies and two poems on audio cassettes; [pers.] A poem without feeling is like a bird without wings. I encompass all I have into every word I write in order to relay my life's struggles and future hopes to the reader.; [a.] Philadelphia, PA

**DOUCET, DAISY J.**
[b.] June 25, 1953, Houston, TX; [p.] Herman and Mariam Davis; [m.] Sam Winston Jr., June 5, 1993; [ch.] Larry, Levar and Robert grandchildren - Shaina and Larry III; [ed.] John C. Fremont Occidental College Prep Courses Upward Bound Student (2 yrs); [occ.] Stock Broker Assistant at Dean Witter Reynolds, Inc.- Malibu; [hon.] High School Essay Contest Winner - Reading is a Mind Expander-1970; [oth. writ.] Can You Imagine-Children's book My Country, Wake Up America, You People-Picture book; [pers.] The greatest gift to give to anyone in LOVE-Love never hurts.; [a.] Los Angeles, CA

**DOW, MARY KATHRYN**
[pen.] Mary Dow; [b.] November 3, 1981, Boston, MA; [p.] Kathryn and Philip; [ed.] 8th Grade in 95-96 Blessed Sacrament School; [occ.] Student; [hon.] Honor Student

DOWLEN, RULYE H.
[p.] Charlie T. Hale and Sallie Moss Hale; [m.] Percy B. Dowlen, 1967; [ch.] Norris Stephen, Staci Hale Dowlen Cruse; [ed.] High School, Business School, School of Cosmetology; [occ.] Shop Owner 25 years Hair Dresser; [memb.] Nashville Hair Dressers Assoc.; [hon.] Salutatorian High School (12th), Rayette Specialist Award in Field of Cosmetology, Class Poet 12th Grade. Semi-finalist, not Library of Poetry.; [oth. writ.] 8 songs have ben recorded by Music Publishing Companies.; [pers.] "Best likely to succeed" "Best all around girl".; [a.] Ashland City, IN

**DOWNS, BETTY LAVON**
[pen.] Lavonne; [b.] April 4, 1931, Winslow, AR; [p.] Oleta Pearl, James Ross Smith; [ch.] Lisa Rene Parks,

Amber Lenee (Adopted); [ed.] Fayeteville High, Fayetteville, AR. 12 years, 1 year Prophecy, H Smith under Jr. Kesner Ph.D, 1 1/2 years Missionary Baptist Seminary Little Rock, AR; [occ.] Preparing for missionary to Puerto Rico, Housewife; [memb.] Lifetime member UFW, Retired Fire Ladies, RB President 1974, Belonged to Missionary Baptist Church 43 years taught all Sunday class; [hon.] Woman of the Year 1978, Redondeo Beach, worked round table and helped city with Disability grants, Dial-a-ride, helping neighbor, fed. grants project steady, project touch, homeless, burned out families. Half way house for others throw away children adolescent 13-18 between 12-18.; [oth. writ.] Small articles in newspapers and Readers Digest; [pers.] I'm striving to reflect Jesus in my writings through Christian ideals, morals, and concepts. Early president and their devotion to God have given me the inspiration to write.; [a.] Redondo Beach, CA

**DRAKE, GLENDON F.**
[pen.] Glen Drake; [ed.] Ph.D University of Michigan, BA Miami University Oxford, OH; [occ.] Writer; [memb.] Several unrelated to poetry; [oth.] Several but all irrelevant to poetry; [oth. writ.] One book, 13 articles or chapters in books. Poetry written, but unsubmitted and, therefore, before now unpublished. About 40 public presentations.; [pers.] The poem contained here in broke, my attempt at the word's longest poetical writing book in the Guineas book of records. Many more poems have followed and await critical eyes.; [a.] Forestville, CA

**DRAYTON, BEVERLY MICHELLE**
[p.] Queenie and Calvin Singleton; [ed.] Howard University; [occ.] Desk/Production Assistant, WRC-TV, Washington, DC; [hon.] Dean's List; [a.] Clinton, MD

**DRIEGERT, JANET H**
[b.] March 25, 1946, Indiana; [ch.] Two, self-sufficient sons; [ed.] B.A. from H. Sophie Newcomb College Of Tulane University; [occ.] Administrative Assistant; [memb.] US Masters Swimming, Easter Seas Society, Volunteer Guild, Richardson Children Theatre; [hon.] Have been an active volunteer in many organizations throughout my life; [oth. writ.] A Children play published in Southern Living; [pers.] Quit making excuses and "just do it." Give something back to your community.; [a.] Plano, TX

**DRINNON, JANIS BOLTON**
[b.] July 28, 1922, Pineville, KY; [p.] Clyde Herman and Violet Hendrickson Bolton; [m.] Kenneth C. Drinnon, June 13, 1948; [ch.] Dena Drinnon Foulk, M. David E. Foulk, Grandchildren - Bethany Erah Foulk, Jonathan David Foulk, Julia Elizabeth Foulk; [ed.] Middlesboro, KY High School, Journalism classes at Lincoln Memorial University, Commercial Art Certificate from Art Instruction School, Correspondence courses with Newspaper Institute of America, Drama instruction and Singing lessons with private teachers; [occ.] Homemaker; [memb.] New Hopewell Baptist Church, Knoxville, TN, International Society of Poets; [hon.] Editors Choice Awards by The National Library of Poetry for two poems - "When Our Purpose Here Is Done" published in The Dark Side Of The Moon in 1994 and "Blessings" published in The Best Poems Of 1995. Nominated for Poet Of Year for 1995 by The International Society of Poets.; [oth. writ.] While attending college, wrote articles for local newspaper. Recently had some poems published in Anthologies.; [pers.] I have always enjoyed the finer things of life and nature, especially those that are spiritually uplifting and bring beauty to the soul. I have never been much for organizations, preferring to be a doer rather than a participant.; [a.] Knoxville, TN

**DUDLEY, JESSYCA**
[b.] August 26, 1984, Chicago, IL; [p.] Jesse B. Virginia Dudley; [ed.] Francis W. Parker (F.W.P) 6th Grade; [memb.] USIA US Tennis Assoc., Joel Hall Dancers; [a.] Chicago, IL

**DUFFIELD, HAZEL BELT**
[pen.] Jeri Duffield; [b.] July 14, 1913, Lambtown Hardin Country, IL; [p.] Willis Howard Belt; [m.] Arizona Taylor Belt, Charles Lawrence Duffield, August 18, 1938; [ed.] High School, Some College; [occ.] Retired. When I worked head of Duro Chrome Corporation, St. Louis, MO.; [memb.] Harahan Christian church, Harahan Louisiana; [hon.] First runner up in the Louisiana Power and Light Cook Off, also honorable mention another year for one of my recipes; [oth. writ.] Other religious poems published by The Tico Times, San Jose, Costa Rica, CA, when I lived there for 18 years.; [pers.] I like cooking, am an avid reader, prefer classical music, sang in my church choir, and did volunteer work for the Salvation Army, the women's club of Costa Rica, very active in church work. Have done quiet a bit of traveling.; [a.] Tarzana, CA

**DUFFY, TIMOTHY J.**
[b.] February 24, 1950, Teaneck, NJ; [ch.] Sean Robert, Ryan Timothy; [ed.] H.S. - Bergen Catholic, B.A. - William Paterson College, M.A. - Rutgers University (third book pending.), M.I.M. - American Graduate School (Thunderbird); [occ.] Writer, Poet; [memb.] Vagabond Poetry (also, local readings); [hon.] Phi Zeta Kappa, 3rd Place Poetry Contest winner Editor's Choice Awards, President's Award, one of outstanding poets, Anthology entries, Newspaper entries; [oth. writ.] Have been writer and editor. Author of two poetry books.; [a.] Monmouth Beach, NJ

**DUJMOVIC, LORETA MUSKARDIN**
[b.] February 20, 1958, Riteka, Croatia; [p.] Anton and Nikoleta Muskardin; [m.] Dean Dujmovic, June 16, 1993; [ed.] School for Economics and Hotel Management - Dpatita, Croatia; [occ.] Hotel Manager; [hon.] Golden Poet 1991, World of Poetry, Sacramento, CA, published in World of Poetry Anthology 1991; [oth. writ.] 19 poems published in the magazine for culture and literature "Rival" in Rijeka, Croatia No. 1/1991; [pers.] This poem is dedicated to my parents Anton and Nikoleta, with love and respect and to my husband Dean who brings laughter and fun in everyday life.; [a.] New York City, NY

**DULEY, ROBERT L.**
[b.] July 12, 1954, Louisville, KY; [p.] Robert E. and Marlene A.; [ed.] Providence High School and Governor Mifflin High School, Indiana University Southeast College; [occ.] Plant Manager; [hon.] Dean's List, etc.; [oth. writ.] Several on a variety of Topics none published; [pers.] I'm not a philosophical person but I honestly believe that there is a majority of people who think and live unealistically. And that a vast majority of people live afraid to say what they mean or how they feel because of uncertain inevitable consequences. I'm definitely not once of those people.; [a.] Floyds Knobs, IN

**DUNAWAY, KELLI LYNN**
[b.] November 15, 1974, Evansville, IN; [p.] Nancy Dunaway and Eddie Dunaway; [ed.] Eldorado High School, Southeastern Illinois College, Southern Illinois University at Carbondale; [occ.] Student - (History/Pre-law major); [hon.] Dean's list, National Young Leader Alumni; [oth. writ.] Several unpublished poems; [pers.] Dream to reach the stars and live to reach your dreams, and remember if the people lead, the leaders will follow.; [a.] Eldorado, IL

**DUNCAN, MABLE T.**
[pen.] M. Duncan; [b.] May 21, Florida; [p.] Mrs. Katie Jones; [m.] James Duncan, July 2, 1982; [ch.] Milton Garey, Miles Garey, Michelle Garey; [ed.] Attended Dbcc, BCC, grad. Sheridan-Voc. School, grad. International Seminary; [occ.] Retired Nurse 27 yrs. of Practice; [memb.] Founder of the S.A.V.E. Women Society. Members of Christian Fellowship Soc., Sigma Gamma RHO A.O.H. Church of God, Volunteer "Way out Hopefuls"; [hon.] "The most well rounded." (Nursing School Student) "Miss 11th Grade Sweetheart" "Compassionate and Kind Nurse", Nursing School; [oth. writ.] Biographical Reading of Introductions. I entered other poets in 1984-85 not a winner then.; [pers.] I enjoy writing poets to express thoughts of life, soul and employment of ideals.; [a.] Daytona Beach, FL

**DUNEVANT, DORIS**
[b.] April 29, 1924, London, England; [p.] William and Emma Dwan; [m.] J. Clifton Dunevant, July 12, 1947; [ch.] Paul, Lindsey, Angelina, Deborah and Cindy; [occ.] Retired Homemaker; [memb.] West Albemarle Baptist Church, American Heart Association; [hon.] Mother of the year 1980 of West Albemarle Baptist Church; [oth. writ.] Devotionals and speechless for church programs; [a.] Albemarle, NC

**DUNHAM, JON B.**
[pen.] Spencer Crawford; [b.] October 12, 1968, Portsmouth, OH; [p.] Bill O. Dunham and Mary Alice Dunham; [ed.] Portsmouth West High School, Senior at Shawnee St. University Major in History; [memb.] Quad Squad (Basketball Team) Actively involved in Portsmouth Little Theatre, and Shawnee State Theatre Department; [hon.] Dean's List; [oth. writ.] Tough Love - a poem that was turned into a song for "Music of America," A cassette of fun known song writers and singers. Had a column college newspaper.; [pers.] I use writing as a form of therapy, with each word coming from my heart and soul.; [a.] Portsmouth, OH

**DUNN, ZELLA J.**
[b.] November 15, 1960, Bellamy, AL; [p.] Mrs. Lillie Mae Dunn; [ch.] Lillian Dunn, Thomas Dunn and Michael Dunn; [ed.] Sumter Co. High, York, AL, City College of San Francisco, San Francisco, CA; [memb.] First Union Baptist Church of San Francisco, CA; [hon.] City College of San Francisco, "Business Olympics," Essay Contests Scholarships from City College of San Francisco, Poetry Contest held by City College of San Francisco; [pers.] I begin writing poetry in High School, and all the words I express are straight from the heart.; [a.] San Francisco, CA

**DUNN, MARGARET**
[pen.] Margaret Mary Dunn; [b.] August 1, 1961, Coaldale; [p.] Patrick Kane, Betty (Wertman) Kane; [m.] James Matthew Dunn, May 22, 1982; [ch.] Deanna Laura and Justin Patrick; [ed.] Panther Valley High School, Lehigh Carbon Comm. College; [occ.] Cert. Nurses Aide, Studying to be respiratory Therapist; [memb.] Several; [oth. writ.] Poem "A Special Game" published in a delicate balance (spring 1996); [pers.] My writing is inspired by personal experiences and emotions. I write from the heart and use writing as an outlet.; [a.] Lansford, PA

**DUNN, FRANCES**
[b.] February 23, 1941, Lisman, AL; [p.] Bettie and T. J. Graham; [ch.] Carolyn Curtis; [ed.] Stillin School; [occ.] House Work; [oth. writ.] For The Clover Drive, School Newspaper. At Great Neck, NY; [pers.] I always try to do the best I can in what ever I do. I want my poem to make people happy. I would like to continue writing poem.; [a.] Great Neck, NY

**DURHAM, BONNIE IDA**
[pen.] Clarida Potter; [b.] February 25, 1913, OK; [p.] Mr. and Mrs. Charles Walker; [m.] Alton H. Durham (Deceased), January 2, 1933; [ch.] Thomas Keeler Durham; [occ.] Retired; [memb.] Motor Corp, American Red Cross, World War II, Delta Rho Delta National Sorority Theta Chapter (Business Women Sorority); [oth. writ.] Religious Poems published in church Bulletin, and for friends who are ill or have lost a loved one; [pers.] I am a private person and this is my first attempt to really publish. I do volunteer work in hospitals, nursing homes - my heart goes out to lonely people.; [a.] Palm Beach, FL

**DWINNELL, DEBORAH B.**
[b.] September 16, 1953, Anderson, SC; [p.] Neil Brown, Jo Makos; [ch.] Tiffany Leigh, Danny Ray, Brandon Christopher; [ed.] Ben L. Smith High, Florida Community College Jacksonville; [occ.] Secretary; [memb.] Woodmen of the World Society; [pers.] My first dedicated to my Mom from her children, Debbie, Butch, Sheila, Rodney and Jimmy. Through my writings, I hope to stress the importance of living each day to it's fullest and to always show the love and appreciation we feel for those dearest to us.; [a.] Yulee, FL

**EADS, MISS PAMELA MICHELE**
[pen.] "Pale Moon Singing"; [b.] July 28, 1955, Marion, VA; [p.] India and William Eads; [ch.] Erick Christian, Rebekah Lyn Meliher; [ed.] Rootstown High School, Rootstown OH Columbia Bible College; [occ.] Secretary; [memb.] New Milford Baptist Church; [hon.] Arion Award, Best Vocalist; [oth. writ.] "Rebekah (a mothers story)," "Mother," "Erick," "Embrace," Duty's Call, "My Love," "Seekfull Eyes," "Christmas" "Angela Friend"; [pers.] Poetry is a picture of words painted on a canvas of wood for all to enjoy and be refreshed. It says, look through my eyes and feel the essence of life.; [a.] Ravena, OH

**EARLEYWINE, MARCELLA**
[b.] June 18, 1923, Hutsonville, IL; [p.] Tony Sankey and Helen Sankey; [m.] Ted Earleywine, November 22, 1942; [ch.] T. Michael and Tony Earleywine; [ed.] Hutsonnille High, Terre Haute Commercial College; [occ.] Secretary Retired, Housewife; [memb.] Hutsonville First Christian Church Affiliate, Thursday Afternoon Thimble Club, est. early 1900's, Hutsonville H.S. Alumni Association, Bi-monthly Bridge Group; [oth. writ.] Several poems for church specials as well as poems for friends marking special occasions.; [pers.] I have found that a poem will, in general fit most situations, be it happy or solemn, and I try to create just the "right one."; [a.] Hutsonville, IL

**ECKEL, MARY**
[b.] August 2, 1951, Wood County, OH; [p.] Herbert and Margaret Thatcher; [ch.] Kelly (17), Susie (16), and Norman (13); [ed.] B.S. Bowling Green State University, Working on Master; [occ.] Special Education Teacher; [memb.] Phi Kappa Phi, Kappa Delta Pi, St. Thomas Moore; [oth. writ.] Darkness, Foolish Heart; [pers.] Writing poetry gives me the opportunity to express my deepest feelings.; [a.] Bowling Green, OH

**EDMOND, JEFF**
[occ.] Choreogeorapher/Pap and Jazz Dance Teacher; [memb.] Screen Actors Guild, AFTRA, Eavity; [hon.] Cleo Award for Best Actor in Phoenix House Commercial; [oth. writ.] Off-Off Broadway Musical "Bugout" Original Music Video, "I Want To Get A Head"; [a.] Bronx, NY

**EDMONDS, RENITA P.**
[pen.] B. T. L; [b.] April 2, 1961, Phoenix City, MD; [p.] Alveta Edmonds and Robert Williams; [ed.] Pershing

High, Central State University, Faith College of Bible Knowledge Holly Ghost Full Gospel's School of the Prophets; [occ.] Special Education Teacher, Webber Middle School Detroit; [hon.] The National Dean's List 1980-1981; [pers.] What a man thinkest, so is he. I have been greatly influenced by my dear mother, Alveta Edmonds, and my Pastor and Spiritual Mom Dr. Corletta Harris Vaughn.; [a.] Detroit, MI

**EDWARDS, KIM E.**
[b.] February 10, 1956, Saint Louis, MO; [p.] Deceased; [m.] Charles D.A. Edwards, July 9, 1985; [ch.] Keenan, Jewell, Lashanda, Keisha and April; [ed.] Sumner High St. Louis, Forest Park Comm., St. Louis, Mc Kendree Coll., Radcliff, KY; [occ.] U.S. Army, Food Server; [oth. writ.] Several short stories, poems; [pers.] Take Chances, Enjoy Life, Don't Miss A Beat; [a.] Vine Grove, KY

**EDWARDS, KATINA J.**
[b.] January 31, 1980, Greenville, OH; [p.] Ron and Marianna Edwards; [ed.] Currently a Sophomore at Greenville High School, Greenville, Ohio; [memb.] 2nd year member of Greenville Color Guard and a member of the Future Homework of America; [a.] Greenville, OH

**EISZELE, CRAIG M.**
[b.] January 7, 1954, San Diego, CA; [p.] Ruth D.; [m.] Debra A., December 26, 1987; [ch.] Heather Ashley and Cody Craig; [ed.] Estancia H.S, Orange Coast J.C., Cal-State University Fullerton-B.A.; [occ.] Real Estate Broker; [memb.] C.S.U.F. Alumni Assoc., The Surf Rider Assoc., Calif. Assoc. of Realtors, National Assoc. of Realtors, North Country San Diego Assoc. of Realtors; [oth. writ.] Many poems - unpublished, songs unpublished, starting a novel; [pers.] I try to express what I and my family would rather be doing and how beautiful the earth could be.; [a.] Oceanside, CA

**ELLIS, EDNA T.**
[pen.] Edna Trout; [b.] September 5, 1913, Mahaxxey, PA; [p.] Lewis Trout and Eleanor Trout; [m.] Frank Ellis; [ch.] Eleanor Harrison, John Ellis, and David Ellis; [ed.] Mahaxxey High; [occ.] Retired (23 yrs. Acct. Dept. - Sun Sentinel; [memb.] Sentinel Graphics Federal Credit Union; [pers.] I live each day by the Golden Rule - I have a strong will to maintain a positive attitude-very fond of animals.; [a.] Plantation, FL

**ELLIS, JUDY D.**
[b.] February 6, 1945, Kansas City, MO; [p.] Ruth Bodenhamer; [m.] John Ellis, March 6, 1982; [ch.] Mike, Steven, Sheri, Shannon and Sara; [ed.] 2 yrs. College - Maple Woods Com. College, KCMO; [occ.] Food Show Coordinator - Setup Food Shows Across USA; [memb.] Englewood Baptist Church; [oth. writ.] Published poems to Reader's Digest and Army Magazine several years ago; [pers.] Our decisions we make indeed reflect the way we live. From an individual to corporation and countries. Therefore individually and collectively, we can make a difference!; [a.] Castle Rock, CO

**ELROD, SCOTT A.**
[b.] March 16, 1965, Newark, OH; [p.] Sharon and Steven Rackmill; [ed.] Cooper City High, Broward Community College; [occ.] Cardiac Assistant, Auto Transfusion Technician; [memb.] International Thespian Society; [oth. writ.] Numerous Writings not Published, Songs and Lyrics; [pers.] My writing is a reflection of my views on personal and or response to specific events in my life.; [a.] Hollywood, FL

**ENGLE, JUNE**
[b.] June 12, 1952, Barbados; [p.] Samuel and Flo

Gibbons; [m.] Divorced, July 15, 1979; [ch.] Two Boys ages 15 and 10; [ed.] B.S. - Nutrition and Chemistry, M.S. Nutrition and Statistics, Curnell University, MD - Stanford Medical School; [occ.] Physician, Women's Health; [pers.] I do this for fun and as a way to express feelings that pop up from my unconscious - I never plan my poetry.

**ENGLISH, AMBER**
[b.] November 7, 1978, Marion, OH; [p.] Ron and Betty English; [ed.] Junior at Harding High School; [memb.] French Club, Yearbook Staff, Varsity Tennis Team, active member of Youth Fellowship and Epworth United Methodist Church; [hon.] Honor Roll (class rank 18 out of 452), JV Tennis Award in 1994-95; [a.] Marion, OH

**ERDELL, PROFESSOR JOHN BUCKLAND**
[b.] October 3, 1916; [p.] Charles W. Erdell and Lillian Schmidt; [m.] Paquita de Leon, June 21, 1947; [ed.] Graduate - The Art School - Pratt Institute, Brooklyn, NY.B.S. M.A. Professional Diploma, Teachers College, Columbia Unity, New York School of Photography, Schools in Photography in Germany, Brooklyn Museum Art School; [occ.] Professor Emeritus; [memb.] Kappa Delta Pi Honorable Society in Education-Louise Bogan Poetry Society - International Poetry Society. Honors: Five US Patents in Photography, One Patent Reveals Producing 10,000 or more Colors on Paper Film, Winner of Hall of Education Award, New York World's Fair 1963, I have taught and Practiced Art and Design all my Life; [hon.] American Anthology, Who's Who in Poetry, 1989, Great Poems of the Western World, Fourteen Editor's Choice Awards Distinguished Poets of America, The National Library of Poetry, I have taught thousands of Students young and old on many levels of art and design, in my retirement due to accident I confined my Activities to Creative Poetry, The National Library of Poetry has been Main Channel of Expression; [a.] New York, NY

**ERGLE, JESSICA D.**
[b.] July 13, 1980, Snellville, GA; [p.] Virgil and Debbie Ergle; [ed.] Now attending 9th grade at Brookwood High School; [occ.] Student; [hon.] Honor Roll, Jr. Beta Club, "Presidential Academic Achievement" Award; [pers.] Always remember the past. It will help you to not made the same mistakes in the future.; [a.] Lilburn, GA

**ERICKSON, JOAN**
[b.] January 25, 1933, New York; [p.] Rose and Walter Hebold; [m.] Frederick Erickson, July 26, 1952; [ch.] Rose, Linda, Frederick Jr. and William; [ed.] Flushing High School, NY; [occ.] Retired; [pers.] Do not dwell on material things for happiness. Reach out to others. Keep love paramount and you will be rich in love.; [a.] West Babylon, NY

**ERKER, ERIC SCOTT ALEXANDER**
[b.] June 15, 1979, New York City, NY; [p.] Joseph Erker and Diane Sinno Erker; [ed.] Fordham Preparatory High School 1993, will graduate in June 1997; [occ.] Student; [memb.] On Staff of Rampart, School Newspaper; [hon.] Two Scholarships Awarded from Fordham Preparatory School, Certificate of Merit in National Latin Exam-1994; [oth. writ.] Poem- The River Man, Publish in the National Poetry Society's National High School Anthology-1995; [pers.] The foundation of man's accomplishments is his ability to express himself through the written word.; [a.] Bronx, NY

**ERLANGER, MICHAEL C.**
[b.] April 8, 1915, New York City, NY; [m.] Mary Erlanger, March 12, 1949; [ch.] Amy Folhman, David Erlanger; [ed.] 4 Years College; [occ.] Retired; [memb.]

Explorer's Club; [oth. writ.] Silence in Haven - At Heaven, Mindy Lindy May Surprise - Random House 4 backs poster - privately printed 1, 2, 3, 4, 5 (short stories privately printed); [pers.] I write far me in delighted when makes contact with someone else.; [a.] Athens, GA

**ESPOSITO, MARYGRACE**
[pen.] MaryGrace Esposito; [b.] May 15, 1956, Hollis Queens, NY; [p.] Marilyn Foutz Phillips and Ralph Esposito; [m.] Divorced; [ch.] None, but do volunteer work with children; [ed.] West Babylon High School, No College; [occ.] Life Model; [memb.] Sacred Heart Church; [oth. writ.] Three poems in methodist place where I live, echoes of yesterday, after the storm, best poems of 1995. A poem at children's volunteer work.; [pers.] The Lord helps those who help themselves.; [a.] Tampa, FL

**ESTRADA, MAY**
[pers.] My only thought is to thank the person that inspired my words to pen. To my dear friend Kathy, thank you for believing in me. Love, May; [a.] San Pedro, CA

**EUBANKS, PEGGY MARSH**
[b.] December 2, 1947, Loveland, OH; [p.] Ralph and Nettibel Marsh; [m.] Robert Eubanks; [ch.] Dawn, Bob and Terri; [ed.] 1 High School Diploma from Clearmont Northeastern High School, Owensville, OH; [occ.] Chief Statement Analyst; [memb.] National Assoc. of Insurance Women; [hon.] Silver Poet Award, Poem "Dawn" published in "Best Poems of 1994", and "Transposition" published in "Best Poems of 1995"; [oth. writ.] Numerous unpublished poems and songs; [pers.] I strive to find the good in all situations. I find there's usually something that can be used to your advantage if you look hard enough.; [a.] Lakeside Park, KY

**EUSTACE, MARY**
[b.] November 27, 1957, Albuquerque, NM; [p.] Ben and Felicita Eustace; [m.] Divorced; [ch.] Angelo and Michelle Ortega; [ed.] Valley High School; [occ.] Jeweler-Inventor Artist; [hon.] I invited an earring called the Eartwirl. I've achieved my Design Patent to it; [pers.] In my shoes. I walk through this life with God in mind. I do believe in the ripple effect, whether good or evil. It sure goes a long way.; [a.] Albuquerque, NM

**EVANS, NITA**
[b.] March 10, 1957, Ardmore, OK; [p.] Herman and Eva Lee Connel; [m.] Phil Evans, August 6, 1977; [ch.] Kyle Edward and Jenny Beth; [ed.] Healdton High 1 yr. and East Central University; [occ.] Housewife and Mother; [memb.] 1st Baptist Church; [hon.] Dean's Honor Role, ECU; [oth. writ.] "Message from Heaven" published in "Precious Memories", Collection of poems about Oklahoma City bombing in April 1995; [pers.] Most of my poems are God-inspired. Hopefully, you can sense my love for Him in every line.; [a.] Elk City, OK

**EVANS, KELLY**
[b.] October 30, 1977, Cooperstown, NY; [p.] Beverly and Robert Evans; [ed.] 1995 Graduate of Richfield Springs Central. Attending Herkimer Country Community College in the Fall to Study English; [hon.] Rotary Incentive Scholarship, Andy Wilde Memorial Scholarship, Margaret Bolton Award; [oth. writ.] A poem published in local newspaper for a young student with cancer and A poem in my senior yearbook written in memory of a classmate.; [pers.] If I can influence just one person to go after what they want, as I have by being published, then I have accomplished what means most to me-teaching others that you can make dreams come true.; [a.] Richfield Springs, NY

**EVANS, CATHERINE V.**
[b.] August 2, 1959, Clinton, MO; [p.] William Allred and Catherine Allred; [ch.] Melissa J. Evans; [ed.] Wichita West High, Wichita Area Vocational Technical; [occ.] Purchasing Assistant for Wichita Public Schools (USD #259); [oth. writ.] Several poems; [pers.] My poetry comes from feelings and emotions in my heart, it really does speak to you.; [a.] Wichita, KS

**EVANS, YVONNE EVE**
[pen.] Eve Evans; [b.] November 30, Washington, NC; [p.] Mr. and Mrs. Leamon H. Ingalls; [ed.] RJR High - Private Coaches (voice, acting, modeling); [occ.] Q.C Technician, Singer/Song Writer (Country Gospel); [memb.] NASMP; [hon.] Cover Story, Model in Several Magazine (One even published one of my poems.) several (poems published also in local publications (N.C.) (also beauty queen-actresses and singer) Did some acting roles and commercials- was cohort and singer for a hollywood showcase.; [oth. writ.] Several of my poems have been published in quite a few publications planning a book or books for the future.; [pers.] I am romantic in every way. I know it shows in my writings. I feel that poetry and music as well as art, are expressions of one's soul.; [a.] Charlotte, NC

**EVERETT, PAMELA MICHELLE**
[pen.] Pamela Michelle Everett; [b.] October 16, 1963, Atlanta, LA; [p.] Quinton and Dorothy Everett; [ed.] Bachelor in Journalism, University of Georgia 1985; [occ.] Self-employed, Full-time Doctoral Student in Psychology; [memb.] Atlanta Lawn, Tennis Association, Delta Sigma Theta Sorority, St. Anthony's Catholic Church; [hon.] National Merit Scholar (1981), Deans's List (1981, 1982, 1983, 1985), Award for Highest G.P.A. among 1985 graduating black females from U.G.A., "Employee of the Year" Award (1991) out of 8000 Employees; [oth. writ.] Wrote a bi-monthly newsletter entitled "Action" from 1989-1995 (focus was on environmental education): Wrote an article for UGA campus newspaper entitled "Law School Semester: Switch Should Aid Students" (Spring, 1985), also article for Athens Banner Herald, "Soaps have become examples of life "(6-9-84); [pers.] I live today as through I will die tomorrow, I plan tomorrow as though I will live forever.; [a.] Atlanta, GA

**FAHEY, DENNIS MICHAEL**
[b.] December 7, 1947, Newark, NJ; [p.] Raymond and Jacqueline Fahey; [m.] Linda (Savage) Fahey, 1977; [ch.] Geoffrey P. (1980), Christopher J. (1983); [ed.] Our Lady of Lourdes, West Orange NJ, Immaculate Conception H.S., Montclair NJ., St. Joseph's College, Philadelphia, PA; [occ.] Industrial Purchasing Mgmt.; [oth. writ.] Various poems, stories, a novel underway. Began writing personal poetry in college. Learned about real poetry from Francis Burch SJ, and St. Joseph's.; [pers.] A practical idealist with a strong sense of right and wrong. (Too serious for my own good.) The poem, "Boo's Secret Song" refers to Boo Radby, the silent hero who saves Jem and Scout Finch, in "To Kill a Mockingbird," by Harper Lee.

**FALLETTA, BARBARA A.**
[b.] December 1, 1943, Akron, OH; [ed.] Kent State University, University of Miami, Florida Atlantic University; [occ.] University Professor and Museum Lecturer - Art History; [memb.] Phi Delta Kappa and Phi Kappa Phi Honor Societies; [oth. writ.] Publication in professional journals, wrote and presented a series of Art History Lecturers for Public Television.; [pers.] The goal of my profession and writing is to teach and share a part of myself with others.; [a.] Pompano Beach, FL

**FARMER, BRENDA J.**
[b.] July 10, 1963, Springfield, TN; [p.] Jerry and Dorothy Porter; [m.] Mark Farmer, January 29, 1988; [ch.] Amy Jo, Jenny Lou, and Joey Wayne; [ed.] Springfield HS, P/T Vol State University; [occ.] Full time Mom; [memb.] Greenfield Missionary Baptist Church; [oth. writ.] This is first time I've ever submitted, but I've written many other poems and short stories.; [pers.] I write what I see, what I hear, what I feel. Some people say I have talent, a few think I'm just very strange.; [a.] Springfield, TN

**FAULCONER, CHAPIN R.**
[b.] August 4, 1972, Charlottesville, VA; [p.] P. Hunter and Phillipa R. Faulconer; [ed.] St. Anne's Belfield 1975-1991, University of Virginia 1992-1996; [occ.] Student; [memb.] Kappa Alpha Theta Sorority, Co-Chair - Independence for Student's with Disabilities - Omicron Delta Kappa - Leadership Society; [a.] Charlottesville, VA

**FAUST, BELLA**
[b.] Poland; [p.] Syma and Gdala Katz; [m.] Isidor Faust (Deceased), 1945; [ch.] Two Sons; [ed.] High School; [occ.] Sculpting, Writing; [memb.] Met. Museum of Art, Westside Art Coalition, Write Ups in Artspeak, Dorot (Generations Helping Generations); [hon.] Awards from International Center - Camp Cummings for Retarded Children, Senior Center Vol, Artwork given to Cancer Society and New York Hospital; [oth. writ.] I am currently writing Autobiography - short stories poetry for senior centre magazine.; [pers.] Best to develop talent, even in later years. I want to better this world. I want to better this world. Legalize drugs. This will decriminalize drug use and will make law enforcement more efficient. This would stop killings and save money.; [a.] New York City, NY

**FAY, LYNN**
[pen.] "Lynn"; [b.] January 18, 1945, Fresno, CA; [p.] Laverne Johnson Taggert; [m.] Divorced; [ch.] Scott Scheidt, Dana Scheidt, Laurel Scheidt, Duke Joseph and Brit; [ed.] 2 Years College; [occ.] Writer; [memb.] North Shore Animal League; [oth. writ.] Book pending "Mirror Image" a personal insight to an anorexics struggle and eventual triumph.; [pers.] A personal thank you to a daughter and son who have made my life a sunny personal haven away from life's repetitive storms.; [a.] Fresno, CA

**FEATHEROFF, AUTUMN**
[b.] August 20, 1980, Lancaster, OH; [p.] Kim and Dwayne Featheroff; [ed.] Currently a Sophomore at Fairfield Union High School, after graduation I am planning to attend college (unknown) to pursue a career in the field of Physical Therapy; [memb.] New Life Christian Center's Pura Power Youth Group, Fairfield Unions, FFA, Chorus, Spanish Club, Reserve Softball Team, Football and Basketball Cheerleading Squads and Fellowship of Christian Students, and LGSA (Lancaster Girls Softball Association); [hon.] Fairfield Union's Outstanding Chorus Member, Several Trophies from the Participation in Softball; [oth. writ.] A variety of different poems ranging from dreams to love. A few have been published in school newspapers and Christian magazines.; [pers.] I am trying to reach a great level of peace in my writings. Not just in the soul but in the surroundings of ones life. I feel all people should work together to make an overpowering love that can only be felt in this place we call earth!; [a.] Rushville, OH

**FEE, LINDA**
[pen.] Billie; [b.] April 30, 1952, Cleveland, OH; [p.] J. Ernest and Lois Legare; [m.] Dannie Fee, June 12, 1970; [ch.] Moria Lynn Fee; [ed.] Mentor High; [occ.] Home Maker - Bar Manager and Volunteer for Lake Metro Parks; [memb.] AMVETS Post 40 Auxiliary, Past Madam Pres. of Mentor Eagles #3605 Auxiliary; [oth. writ.] Few poems published in local flyers.; [pers.] Many of my writings has to do with nature and romance since both have much influence in my life.; [a.] Mentor, OH

**FEIN, HELEN SHIRLEY POLINSKY**
[b.] January 13, 1927, Norwich, CT; [p.] Pauline Allen Polinsky, Samuel Polinsky; [m.] Arnold E. Fein, March 11, 1956; [ch.] Tina Debra Fein-Dinitz; [ed.] Griswold High School in Jewett City, CT, St. Peter's College, N.J. (Graduated 6/5/82 - Cum Laude); [occ.] Writing, Developing Arts Programs, currently Chair of Sarasota Co. Arts Council, Arts Day "Showcase"; [memb.] Theta Alpha Kappa, Sarasota County Arts Council, Ringling Museum Numerous Charity Organizations; [hon.] St. Peter's College, Dean's List, College Cum Laude Graduate, American Legion Medal Recipient in High School, County Wide Recognition for Volunteer work for Arts Organizations; [oth. writ.] Will have article in Anthology to be published in Anthology to be published by E.P. Dutton late in 1995 (Marlene Adler Marks, Editor), Newspaper Articles. Presently compiling book of Family Memoirs and Essays, titled "Dear Nathan-Family Matters."; [pers.] With my writing and poetry, I am trying to recapture, for today's generation, the closeness of family ties that have been dissipated - to a large extent mainly due to our mobile society.; [a.] Longboat Key, FL

**FEIN, IRA J.**
[b.] November 5, 1952, New York City, NY; [p.] Robert and Ida Fein; [ed.] Long Island City High School; [occ.] United States Postal Worker, New York City; [oth. writ.] Various Birthday, Valentines Day, Poems that have been used for greeting cards. "A Christmas Prayer" soon to be published for syndicated distribution.; [pers.] Our time on earth is way too short, make the best of it! I have been greatly influenced by the writings of Kahlil Gibran, especially "The Prophet" a beautiful work.; [a.] Carle Place, NY

**FELDON, GARY**
[b.] February 13, 1982, Pasadena, CA; [ed.] K.L. Carver Elementary School, San Marino, CA, H.E. Huntington Middle School, San Marino, CA; [occ.] Student; [hon.] 1995: Second place All-League Wrestler California Age Group Wrestling Association, 1994: All-California Fifth Place Wrestler, USA Wrestling Association, Second Place All-League Wrestler, California Age Group Wrestling Association, 1993: First Place All-League Wrestler, California Age Group Wrestling Association; [pers.] You are not who you think you are. You are not who other people think you are. You are who you think other people think you are.; [a.] Pasadena, CA

**FELDON, GARY**
[b.] February 13, 1982, San Marino, CA; [p.] Diane and Steve Feldon; [ed.] Carver Elementary, Huntington Junior High; [occ.] Student; [hon.] 5th in CA, USA State Finals, 2 time League Runner-up (CAGWA), 1 time CAGWA League Champion (all wrestling honors); [pers.] You aren't who you think you are, you aren't who other people think you are. You are who you think other people think you are.; [a.] San Marino, CA

**FELLHAUER, RUTH L.**
[pen.] Ruth Fellhauer; [b.] November 11, 1932, Chicago, IL; [p.] Agnes M. and Earl P. Lewis; [m.] Jay L. Fellhauer, May 21, 1955; [ch.] Beth Ellen, Paul Richard, Kim Eileen, and Tracy Lynn; [ed.] High School by G.E.D. Diploma, AA Degree, Johnson County Comm. Coll., Bachelor's (1987) and Masters (1989) in Social Work - Univ. of Kansas, Licensed in the State of Kansas by the BSRB; [occ.] Semi-Retired, Volunteer Activities; [memb.] (NASW) National Assoc. of Social Workers; [hon.] Advanced Standing Master's Program; [oth.

writ.] Current Project: Self publishing a book of a Literative Poetry.; [pers.] I have read poetry all my life...and I draw on my life experiences in my writing. Classic poetry helped me become the person I am today!; [a.] Emporia, KS

**FELTES, PEGGY**
[b.] March 10, 1963, Aurora, IL; [p.] Laurie and Herbert Feltes; [m.] Divorce; [ch.] Three; [ed.] East Aurora High School, Kishwaukee College (current) (Nursing Program); [occ.] Single Parent, Student; [memb.] Unitarian Universalist; [pers.] It is my intent to write with such clarity that my own experiential expressions brings forth the bittersweet of life to my reader.; [a.] Dekalb, IL

**FERET, KIN**
[b.] August 21, 1980, Ashland, OR; [p.] Stan Feret, Myra Feret; [ed.] Sophomore - Plainfield, High School - Plainfield, CT; [oth. writ.] Many short horror stories none published, many other poems none published.; [pers.] I write what I feel at the time.; [a.] Wauregan, CT

**FERGUESON, MAURINE**
[b.] February 9, 1938, Park City, UT; [p.] Oren J. and Marie Anderson; [m.] Ernest R. Fergueson, December 19, 1967; [ch.] David Wayne, Linda Marie, Connie Nelda, Robert Clair, Judith Lynn, Norma Jean; [ed.] High School (Davis), Bookkeeping Night School; [occ.] Owner/Manager Mobile Homes/Corporation MJN Inc.; [memb.] Layton Chamber, Neighborhood Watch Leader, Military Affairs (Hill Field, Utah), Northern Utah Apartment Association, Davis County Domestic Violence Volunteer; [hon.] Lifetime Membership NSP Profile in Park City Record; [oth. writ.] Local Paper Apartment Assoc. Magazine (pamphlets) "Parenting in the Nineties" "Control your Life" poems in six different books in NLP.; [pers.] I started writing poetry seriously in 1990. I found I could say what I felt if I wrote a poem. Sometimes God puts the words in my head and I write them down.; [a.] Layton, UT

**FERNANDEZ, JOSE**
[pen.] Joe Fernandez; [b.] July 6, 1933, Ponce, PR; [p.] Jose Fernandez and Lydia Rios; [m.] Regina Pietri; [ch.] Jose Luis, Jose Ivan and Gloribelle; [ed.] Ponce High School and Catholic University of Ponce, PR; [occ.] Retired - Management Consultant; [memb.] American Legion; [hon.] 1986 - Honor Award by Catholic University of Ponce PR to my poems in Spanish, several US President's mentions for the poem "America It's You"; [oth. writ.] Several poems in Spanish published in local newspapers.; [pers.] If I could undo the things of the past and abide by the laws of the present I would be the happiest man of the future.; [a.] Ponce, PR

**FERNSTROM, THERESA JOHNENNE**
[b.] July 23, 1978, Fairfield, CA; [p.] Bill and Christine Fernstrom; [ed.] Senior at Modesto High School; [memb.] Livingwater, Bible Church, Active in Local Health Club; [hon.] A Who's Who Among American High School Students 1993-1994 also a Purple Belt in Taekwondo; [oth. writ.] I have also have written a young girl falling it was published in A Far Off Place and There One Minute published in Best Poems of 1995.; [pers.] Do not give up and never listen to people that say you can not do something because you can if you set your mind to it.; [a.] Modesto, CA

**FERRAIUOLO, PATRICIA**
[b.] July 21, 1981, Bronx, NY; [p.] Francine and Thomas Ferraiuolo; [ed.] St. Francis Xavier Elementary, St. Catharine Academy, High School; [occ.] Student; [hon.] 1991 and 1993 Sen. Guy J. Nelella Reading Contest Winner, St. Francis Xavier Class of 1995, Literature Award, 1995 First Honors Elementary, High School Honors Society; [oth. writ.] Article published in

Bronx Times Reporter, several poems published in Elementary School Newspaper.; [pers.] All my writings have come from a part of me and my experiences so far in life. When you read one of my poems, you are reading a part of me. I've been greatly influenced by my surroundings.; [a.] Bronx, NY

**FERRARO, SANDRA OLIVER**
[pen.] Alyssandra Oliver; [b.] July 21, 1954, Salt Lake City, UT; [p.] Charles and Alice Oliver; [m.] Daniel Ferraro, February 2, 1980; [ch.] Jenny, Heather, Adam, Bretton, Nicholas; [ed.] Graduated - Viewmont High School, B.S. Degree - Brigham Young University; [occ.] Elementary Teacher J.A. Taylor Elementary, Centerville, UT; [memb.] Daughters of the American Revolution; [oth. writ.] Poems, children's stories and a novel yet to be published.; [pers.] My hope is to always write something that is thoughtful or that in some way inspires the human heart.; [a.] Kaysville, UT

**FERRELL, KRISTIE E.**
[b.] March 3, 1954, IN; [p.] Marie L. and Jack E. (Deceased); [m.] John Ferrell, June 11, 1977; [ed.] Taylor High School - Center, Indiana; [occ.] Housewife (or Domestic Goddess! Ha! Ha!); [memb.] Women of the Moose Chapter 1379; [hon.] Three Honorable Mentions in the International Scholastic Art Competition, several 1st Place and 1 Best of Show Ribbons at Dixon Mayfair for Baking, Paintings and Drawings, in different mediums; [oth. writ.] Several poems that have yet to be published an two that were published and two that were published in the news letters of different places of employment.; [pers.] I write about my life situations ups and downs, usually things that people can relate to at some point and time. This particular poem I dedicate to my husband John.; [a.] Fairfield, CA

**FIEBIG, MARGIE**
[b.] August 2, 1935, French Camp, MI; [p.] Henry Casey Tyler and Mattie Moore Tyler; [m.] Joseph Robert Fiebig Sr., August 31, 1953; [ch.] Elinor Snow, Joseph Jr., Edward, Jerry, Joyce Carson, Christopher; [ed.] High School Diploma, Some College, H.S. - Ackerman High School; [occ.] Assistant Librarian, Art Instructor - Ackerman Elem. School have been there 25 years; [memb.] Methodist, Choctaw Fair Committee, Parent/Teacher Org., Discipline Committee, Illustrator for Teacher Materials; [hon.] A write up in our Co. paper on the Art Murals that I have done in the School; [oth. writ.] Articles in various newspaper - I am in process writing a children's book and doing the illustrations. I have written a number of poems, this is my first to submit for a contest.; [pers.] God gifted me with talents that I feel he wants me to share - there is so much beauty to write and share and tell - I can reach the children through art that otherwise would be passed along and lost somewhere on the wayside.; [a.] Ackerman, MS

**FIELDS, EVELYN SOLOMON**
[pen.] Evelyn Solomon Fields; [b.] October 23, 1937, Lawrence, MA; [p.] Said and Rachel Solomon; [ed.] St. Mary's and Lawrence High Schools, Lawrence Massachusetts (CLVS); [occ.] Sales Assoc.; [memb.] Volunteer in Vacuna Program also, had Poetry Reading in a Nursing Home for 2 yrs. 11 months; [hon.] Golden Poet Award, 1988 World of Poetry Award of Merit Honorable Mention World of Poetry February 1, 1988, Honorable Mention Award of Merit] November 21, 1987 by World of Poetry, Honorable Mention Award of Merit March 15, 1988, World of Poetry Silver Poet Award 1990, World of Poetry Papers; [pers.] I feel anything written from the heart. Will be good.; [a.] Methven, MA

**FIFIELD, RICH**
[b.] May 20, 1946, Memphis, TN; [p.] Stiles R. Fifield (Deceased), and Helen Pope; [m.] Susan Whiteheart Fifield, September 22, 1990; [ch.] Stiles R. Fifield III; [ed.] A.B. History UNC, Chapel Hill, NC '69; [occ.] Sales Executive Alliance Display and Packaging, Winston-Salem, NC; [a.] Greensboro, NC

**FINAZZO, DONZELLE**
[b.] April 24, 1941, Auburn, NY; [p.] Donald and Phoebe Bibbens; [m.] Joseph Finazzo, August 19, 1967; [ed.] Weedsport Central School graduated 1959, Auburn Community College 1975; [occ.] Housewife; [memb.] Order of Eastern Star, Brutus Chapter, Weedsport NY; [hon.] Honor Society Weedsport Central School, Hon. Mention National Physical Handicapped; [pers.] I enjoy writing poems, but have never had any published. I don't write stories.; [a.] Auburn, NY

**FINKEL, ROSALIE LOCURTO**
[b.] February 22, 1938, Brooklyn, NY; [p.] Dominick LoCurto and Angela LoCurto; [m.] Gerald B. Finkel, December 30, 1984; [ch.] Laura Ann Colassano and Jeanine Ann D'Ottavio; [ed.] Lafayette High School; [occ.] Secretary; [pers.] I hope my writings will influence all people to love each other and unite as one family as God wants it to be.; [a.] Brooklyn, NY

**FINTA, RICHARD HARDIN**
[pen.] Rich Finta; [b.] June 11, 1956, Oakland, AR; [p.] Betty Johnson; [m.] Bert Johnson, February 6, 1993; [ch.] Troy (6) and Brandin (2); [ed.] Piedmont United School Dist.; [occ.] Head Eastodian, Piedmont Middle School, Piedmont; [memb.] CSEA, California Certified School Ass., DASS Ass.,; [hon.] Superior Workmanship in Cerean 1967 for Superior Workmanship for assisting, Custodian Ratings Consistently #3 in Cal. Rich Cerean/phsc. for Piedmont for poem (Handicap Kids); [oth. writ.] Being Handicap, Earthquake, Being Here, Yearbook Poems; [pers.] Believe in yourself and don't give up, on you're goals! Picture what you want in mind and go for them.

**FISCHER, SHARON K. FALLS**
[b.] December 3, 1956, Enid, OK; [p.] Bob Falls, Jolene Falls; [m.] Bruce Fischer, October 30, 1990, (renewed vows 10-27-95); [ch.] Joseph Jay, Jacob Anthony, Nicole Louise; [ed.] Enid High School, Enid, Okla.; [occ.] Domestic Engineer; [pers.] My writings come from personal experiences. My inspiration come from my memories with my sister Janna and my children. Like my family, memories have a way of perfecting themselves with time.; [a.] Enid, OK

**FISHER, AIMEE**
[b.] October 11, 1980, Pompton Plains, NJ; [p.] Ernest and Zofia Fisher; [ed.] 9th or 10th when poem was written: 9th Grade when book will be published I will be in 10th Grade; [hon.] High Honor Roll in School; [pers.] I hope that my poem, which I wrote at 14, will shows kids, as well as adults, anywhere, no matter what others think, that nothing should stand in the way of who they really are and their goals.; [a.] Pompton Lakes, NJ

**FISHER, HAROLD**
[pen.] "Pickles"; [b.] October 18, 1924, New York, NY; [p.] Mr. and Mrs. David Fisher; [ed.] 1 year and a half of college; [occ.] Semi Retired Jones Beach State Employee; [memb.] Freeport Rec. Association for Swimming; [hon.] Many Medals for Swimming Awards 1st and 2nd Place; [oth. writ.] Many other poems, I have written and short stories.; [pers.] Harold Fisher, born on October 18, 1924 in NYC. Went to Dewitt Clinton HS in Bronx 1 1/2 yrs college, 3 yrs Army '43-46 2 yrs in Pacific. Hope to contribute at this late stage to world and humankind in general. Life for me is juts beginning

and am looking forward to many goals I hope to achieve.; [a.] New York City, NY

**FISHER, DAVID C.**
[b.] November 19, 1969, Aurora, IL; [p.] David and Lois Fisher; [ed.] Associates Degree in Criminal Justice, Background in Business Waubonsee Junior College; [occ.] Police Officer; [hon.] Dean's List; [oth. writ.] Several poems shared only with close friends or family. None published.; [pers.] I use poems as a stress reliever and as a means of communicating what's on my mind at a particular time.; [a.] Hinckley, IL

**FITZGERALD, RACHEL**
[b.] October 6, 1981, Philadelphia, PA; [p.] Barbara Fitzgerald and Roger Fitzgerald; [ed.] 8th Grade Germantown Friends School; [occ.] Student; [hon.] Equestrian Awards; [a.] Philadelphia, PA

**FITZPATRICK, KELLY**
[b.] November 22, 1977, CA; [p.] Kerry and Randy Fitzpatrick; [ed.] High School - Westford Academy; [pers.] There is much I have to learn and much I have to experience before I can become the poet I wish to be.; [a.] Westford, MA

**FITZSIMONS, MICHAEL**
[pen.] Gooffus; [b.] March 27, 1981, Dodgeville, WI; [p.] Dale and Jeanne Fitzsimons; [ed.] Freshman at Mineral Point High School; [occ.] Student; [memb.] World Wildlife Federation, National Audubon Society; [hon.] Presidential Academic Award, Math Team Award, Honor Roll; [oth. writ.] Fnar Fen Fnoogin Fever, A New World; [pers.] "It's better to keep your mouth shut and appear stupid than to open it and remove all doubt." A quote by Mark Twain.; [a.] Mineral Point, WI

**FLACK, KAREN M.**
[pen.] K. Flack, K. M. Flack; [b.] February 15, 1950, Nanticoke, PA; [p.] Andrew and Shirley Gall; [m.] Harry (Bud) L. Flack, May 9, 1971; [ch.] Corey (daughter); [ed.] Belfast Central School, Belfast, NY, Technical Writing and Engineering at various area colleges in NY State; [occ.] Technical Specialist; [hon.] Copywriter of the Month, Special Honors for Technical Efforts, Special Honors for Creative Writing; [oth. Writ.] Freelance For Local Publications, Wild Game Recipe Book, Editor Of Various Company And Professional Newsletters, Political Campaigns, Radio Copy Writing.; [pers.] I'd like my words to move people, whether it be to laugh, cry, get angry, or experience whatever I'm seeing or feeling. I believe there is beauty in everything around us.; [a.] Caneadea, NY

**FLEMING, MARJORIE FOSTER**
[pen.] Marjorie Foster Fleming; [b.] September 12, 1920, Cheltenham, PA; [p.] Major B. and Helen V. Foster; [m.] Paul S. Fleming, May 6, 1961; [ch.] John and David Hundermark; [ed.] Oak Lane Country Day School - Cheltenham High School - Ursinus College 42 - Attended Temple Univ. (advertising) - Pierce Business College - Arthur Murry, Dancing - Cheltenham Twsp. Art Center Painting, Photography, Claywork, Creative Writing, Cheltenham Adult School, 8 yrs. Private Piano Lessons, on the Job Training Radio and T.V. Script Writing, in the Home Training, Song Writing and Poetry; [occ.] Homemaker, Writer, Painter, Sculptures, Musician, Collect Sheet Music all kinds; [memb.] Lifetime member of Cheltenham Twsp. Art Center, "Distinguished" Member International Society of Poet's Great Books Club; [hon.] WW II Army - Navy "E" Award with Philco Corp. - Red Cross Award for Occupational Therapy WW II (Valley Forge Army Hospital), Stage Door Canteen Hostess (regular) and "Special Duty" Stage Door Gant Hostess (for members of the Purple Heart Society) in Philadelphia Navy Hosp. private

homes, and Conventional Hall - special award from Major Samuel of Phila. for contribution to "4th of July Celebration" as member of special Events Dept. of Philadelphia Evening Bulletin (largest Evening Newspaper in the Nation) "Miss Eifrith Alley" (oldest still occupied street in America Chair person, coordinator, and honored quest at 100th Year Anniversary Celebration of the Philadelphia Evening Bulletin in College: President of Dormitory, Treas. and Chaplain Omega Chi Sorority; [oth. writ.] Short - short stories and short stories (children and adults). College May Pageants (2nd place), play, Cartoon - illustrations, assisted writing scripts for TV and Radio, and Theater with Bennett Productions 1948-49. Editor of House Organ (Cheltenham Twsp. Art Center) proof reading make up, writing-articles, reports, and stories. Auto-Biography and poems in progress. Song lyrics and Essays.; [pers.] I believe God has given us a purpose to fulfill which may or may not be revealed. I think that if we are able to use our experiences with both "Good" and "Bad" toward enhancing our spiritual growth, and if we then, act for "Good" with "Love" we will be "Happy." Vola! We have one step up on the stairway to Heaven.; [a.] Crystal, IL

**FLORES, TOMAS**
[b.] January 4, 1980, Dominican Republic; [p.] Zoila G. Diaz de Flores; [ed.] Dwight Englewood School (Sophomore); [occ.] Student; [pers.] You're not insane, you're sane in an insane world and writing is the way to sanity.; [a.] Fort Lee, NJ

**FLOYD, KATHY**
[b.] Atlanta, GA; [p.] Marjorie Scott and F.M. Vandegriff; [m.] Robert W. Floyd, April 28, 1963; [ch.] Bonny (My Grandchildren: Chrystal and Kara Frey), Angi (My Grandchildren Samantha and Savannah Ford); [memb.] My husband and I are members of Rock Cut Baptist Church as well as several Pro-Family Organizations; [pers.] This poem was written especially for my granddaughter, Samantha - I have written poems for my daughters as well as my other three grandchildren. I believe my inspiration is my faith in God and my love of family.

**FOGARTY, BRENDA**
[b.] June 13, 1966, Glencoe, MN; [p.] Charles and Rosemary Weber; [m.] Patrick E. Fogarty, November 25, 1983; [ch.] Jessica Lee, Felicia Mary, Colin Patrick; [ed.] Howard Lake - Waverly High School, Wright Vocational Center; [occ.] Para - Educator; [oth. writ.] Leisure poem writings; [pers.] I've always enjoyed reading and writing poetry. Personal tragedy's bring out the best of my poetic writings. This poem is a reflection of my grandmother's death.; [a.] Silver Lake, MN

**FORD III, JEROLD E.**
[b.] April 10, 1963, Saint Joseph, IL; [p.] Jerold and Rhonda Ford; [m.] Anna L. Ford, March 22, 1986; [ch.] Jason David, Samantha Kay, Jared Ellis, Annette Sharee; [ed.] Trenton High School; [occ.] Warehouseman; [pers.] Alan Ashley Pitt's poem "No Creativity" says it all.; [a.] Saint Joseph, MO

**FORKER, BAMBI**
[b.] January 4, 1958, MN; [p.] Duane and Gertrude O'Connor; [m.] Duane Forker, July 18, 1981; [ch.] Joshua, Daniel, Adam Levi, Travis Tanner, Trevor Joseph, Kaili Lynn and Korbi Lynn; [ed.] High School Graduate, School of Life, raised 9 children and lost 3 babies... 4 teenagers at once... what college teaches that?; [occ.] Mother, Homemaker, Author, Photographer; [memb.] Maple Grove United Methodist Church; [hon.] "Miss New Buffalo" 1975, Coached Little League Baseball, Runner-up Poetry Contest; [oth. writ.] Many not yet published, several pictures and stories in local

newspapers and the Chicago Tribune.; [pers.] As a mother of 6 and step-mother to 3 (raised 9 children), "Children are our Future," "Love is the Golden Key," "Treat other's as you want to be Treated," "True Faith in God."; [a.] Three Oaks, MI

**FORSTER, RITA J.**
[b.] March 15, RI; [p.] Joseph and Rose Corriveau; [m.] James J. Forster, December 19, 1990; [ch.] Dawn, Cheryl and Todd; [ed.] Central Falls High, H&R Block Tax School; [occ.] Tax Preparer and Co-owner/J&R Tax Service; [memb.] Associate Member of the NCO Open Mess; [oth. writ.] James and love of a lifetime.; [pers.] My love for poetry along with the support and love I receive from my husband that someday I will publish a book of poems.

**FORSYTH, MARK A.**
[pen.] Red Panther; [b.] May 30, 1959, Harrisburg, PA; [p.] James T. and Marion B. Forsyth; [ed.] Graduated Norview High Norfolk VA in '70, Traveled US and Canada gathering material for poems; [occ.] Various Truck Driving Operations; [memb.] An Avid Outdoors Man Involved in Hunting, Fishing, Trapping, Camping, Outdoor Photography; [hon.] Honorable Mention Award from World of Poetry Contest for Poem "Fishing in the Spring." Special Award Received for Catch and Release of Trophy Muskie from N.Y. State Save the St. Lawrence River Foundation; [oth. writ.] (Unpublished) Native North, When Yellow Creeps into the Green, Oh the Sky, The Road Not Yet Traveled, Precious Sister, Mountains in the Mist, Fishing in the Spring, Two Pals in Pike Time, The Mental Lost and Found, etc.; [pers.] Extensive research into mohawk ancestry and iroquois culture at akwesasne reserve. The earth is an entity with heart and soul, the universe is round, life is a circle, there are spirits in stones, i am related to everything.; [a.] Windsor, VA

**FORTIN, CHRISTOPHER**
[b.] August 26, 1976; [p.] Richard Fortin, Mary Fortin; [ed.] Algonquin Regional High School; [occ.] Student, Westfield State College; [memb.] WSKB; [hon.] Dean's List; [oth. writ.] Several poems published in Sachem, Kleider and Personae; [pers.] My writings are influenced by social and religious issues and current events. I have turned many of my poems into songs.; [a.] Northborough, MA

**FOSTER, MARSHA D.**
[pen.] Gloria Forester; [b.] December 3, 1976, San Antonio, TX; [p.] Kay and John Foster; [ed.] Plano East Senior High School, University of North Texas at Denton; [occ.] Student; [memb.] Classic Learning Core Honors Program; [hon.] Who's Who Among High School Students, National Merit Commended Scholar, Editor of Aurora Literary Magazine; [oth. writ.] Several poems published in School Literary Magazine, several unpublished short stories and poems.; [pers.] Published in a real book? Wow! Thank you Mr. Donne and Mr. Browning.; [a.] Plano, TX

**FOSTER, ADAM**
[b.] September 26, 1979, Amarillo, TX; [p.] Kathy Foster, Michael Foster; [ed.] Student at Sanford - Fritch High School; [memb.] Red Cross; [a.] Canyon, TX

**FOUCH, ROBERT**
[b.] September 4, 1969, Kingwood, WV; [p.] William Fouch, Jodi Fouch; [ed.] Bachelor of Liberal Arts degree in Journalism from Marshall University in Huntington, WV; [occ.] Copy editor at Newsday on Long Island; [memb.] Society of Professional Journalists; [pers.] I write because it gives me pleasure. I hope my writing ultimately gives others pleasure, too.; [a.] Central Islip, NY

## FOUGHT, SAMANTHA

[b.] July 10, 1981, Lindsay, CA; [p.] Scott and Shelly Fought; [ed.] Elementary thru Jr. High; [memb.] Lindsay Christian Church; [hon.] Honor Roll Student, I'm also a straight a Student; [pers.] I enjoy camping and being outdoors. I love to read and write, and be involved with my Church.; [a.] Lindsay, CA

## FOX, DESIREE L.

[b.] March 11, 1975, Ventura, CA; [p.] Barbara J. Fox, Donnie L. Fox; [ed.] Saint Bonaventure High, Ventura College; [occ.] Student (Biology / Pre-Pharmacy major); [hon.] Dean's list, National Honor California Scholastic Federation; [a.] Ventura, CA

## FOX, JOHN

[b.] September 20, 1966, Boaz, AL; [p.] Richard Fox and Judy Woodard; [ed.] Alexander City Junior College, Snead State Junior College, St. Leo College, Georgia South Western College; [occ.] English Teacher, KFLI, Inchon, Korea; [pers.] My goal in writing is to express feelings that are honest and clear. I seek to share what I see, hear, and feel.; [a.] Albertville, AL

## FOX, MARGARET D. HARTER

[pen.] Margaret Fox; [b.] April 18, 1953, Lebanon, MO; [p.] Robert L. and Joyce L. Harter; [m.] Kenneth M. Fox, April 12, 1994; [ch.] Shona L. Nabarro, Joyce M. Dailey; [ed.] G.E.D.; [occ.] Housewife; [hon.] My highest honor in life has been, to be a mother to my two children and grandmother to my two granddaughter Ashley Megan and Paige Nicole and a very special honor of having my poem chosen.; [pers.] I try to treat people fairly and justly. As I expect to be treated. I respect life and try to live it to my fullest everyday. I try to live as God wants us all to live.; [a.] Cookeville, TN

## FRANCES, KRENGEL

[pen.] Fraceska Kren; [b.] December 2, 1925, Belgium; [p.] Maurice and Regina Krengel; [ed.] HS Graduate - R. Stevenson Julia Richard 1 yr. Columbia; [occ.] Retired; [memb.] Israel Binds Emuna - Ort. Jasa Art Assoc. Cancer; [pers.] Poetry is good for the soul am pleased that you chose my poems (2) and very honored that they will be in the urbanry in Washington.; [a.] Lakewood, NJ

## FRANCIS, SUZETTE

[pen.] Dimples, Ladybug, Princess; [b.] December 26, 1974, New York, NY; [p.] daphne Toomer and Veniel Anderson; [m.] O'Niel Francis, March 17, 1994; [ed.] Graduated: Erasmus Hall High School, spent 2 years at New York University currently attending Fayetteville State University; [occ.] Student, Fayetteville State University, NC; [hon.] National Holocaust Remembrance Award, Excellence in Gymnastics, National Dean's List; [oth. writ.] (Poems) "I Believe in You," "So Far Yet So Near," "Testimony," "My Deepest Secrets," "Holier Than Thou," "Losing You," "Words from the Heart," "The Key to My Heart," "Let's Stay Together," "Time After Time," "Pondering Love."; [pers.] I strive for excellence in all things that I do, and I know that I can only achieve excellence when I put God first and foremost in my life.; [a.] Fayetteville, NC

## FRANCOIS, MARIE CATHELINE JEAN

[b.] July 30, 1974, Brooklyn, NY; [p.] Phinelie and Jeveille Jean-Francois; [ed.] The Mary Louis Academy, Hofstra University; [occ.] Full time Student; [memb.] International Society of Poets, Hofstra Literary Magazine Club; [hon.] Dean's List, Editor's Choice Awards (95 and 94), Eugene Schneider Prose Award; [oth. writ.] Poems published in Best Poems of 1995 and After the Storm including other anthologies by NCP, short stories including "Respect" which won Eugene Schneider Prose Award.; [pers.] In my poetry, I try to

attack very real and painful issues we all face and portray them through a positive light.; [a.] Hollis, NY

## FRASER, PATRICIA M.

[b.] September 15, 1951, Billings, MT; [p.] William H. Long, Helen Long; [m.] Steven J. Fraser, December 29, 1976; [ch.] Kristopher John, Amy Nicole; [ed.] Libby Sr. High School, Murphy - Griffin Business College; [occ.] Homemaker; [a.] Billings, MT

## FREEDLINE, REBECCA

[b.] February 2, 1984, Cleveland, OH; [p.] James and Marina Freedline; [ed.] Entering 6th Grade, St. Francis Xavier School in Medina, OH; [occ.] Student; [pers.] My best poetry is that which comes from my heart. It expresses my feelings and beliefs and is easiest to write.; [a.] Lodi, OH

## FREEMAN, EVELYN R.

[pen.] E. Rhunette Freeman/Rhunette; [b.] December 4, 1921, Jax, FL; [p.] Ruben and Fannie Daughtry; [m.] Divorced, January 31, 1940; [ch.] Roderick J., Paul L., Raymond K., Diann C. Primus, Vanorian R. Williamson, Carol Y. Emerson, Barbara P. and Leslie D.; [ed.] Graduate Edward Waters College, High School Department 1939; [occ.] Retired; [memb.] Turner Chapel A.M.E. Church; [hon.] Salutatorian of Graduating Class, Bahamian American Federation, Zeta Phi Beta Sorority, Inc. INZ Chapter (both for community service); [oth. writ.] Messages of Love in Poetry Rhunette Poets; [pers.] God's grace is sufficient to develop my God-given potential to the fullest to His glorification and to encourage my senior (others) fellowman.; [a.] Marietta, GA

## FREITAG, ELLEN R.

[pen.] Ellen Reilly; [b.] January 4, 1943, East Orange, NJ; [p.] Ruth Reilly and Walter Reilly; [m.] Bruce Freitag, March 16, 1991; [ch.] Ruth Ellen, Elizabeth and Peter; [ed.] Our Lady of the Valley HS - Orange NJ, Seton Hall University - Bachelor of Science William Paterson College - Masters Degree in Elementary Education in English Literature; [occ.] Substitute Secondary English Teacher; [memb.] St. Elizabeth's RC Church, Valley Hospital Auxiliary, New Jersey Education Association, Sigma Theta Sigma Sorority, Cystic Fibrosis Foundation; [hon.] Scholarship Award by the Soroptimist Club of Newark Partial Scholarship to Seton Hall University Awarded by Our Lady of the Valley High School Miss Seton Hall, Dean's List - Seton Hall University Various Athletic Medals Including two New York Marathon Medals; [oth. writ.] Children's Book - Peter Searns What Love Is, various poems Master's Thesis entitled "Color Symbolism and other methods in the Literature of Bronte and Crane."; [pers.] Poetry releases the thoughts of the heart and puts reflections into words.; [a.] North Haledon, NJ

## FRIESS, DONNA L.

[pen.] Donna L. Friess; [b.] January 16, 1943, LA; [m.] Kenneth E. Friess, June 20, 1964; [ch.] Rick, Julie, Dan; [ed.] Ph.D. Human Behavior; [occ.] Professor of Psycho of Relationship; [memb.] 1. Nat'l Writers Club, 2. Mother's Against Sexual Abuse, 3. Nat'l Coalition Against Sexual Abuse, 4. International Porcelain Artists; [hon.] 1. Recognized by Nat'l Kidney Assoc. for writing 1994, 2. Recognition Award by United States Office of Justice for Efforts to Stop Child Abuse April 1995, 3. 1994 and 1995 Univ. of Calif at Irvine Honored for Writing by Friends and the Library, 4. Outstanding Dissertation - United States Int'l Univ. 1993; [oth. writ.] Cry Thru Darkness - Heath Comm. Inc. Deerfield, Florida 1993. Autobiography, 2. Just Between Us - Healing Guide for survivors of childhood Trauma. 1995 (H.I.H. Public S.JC. CA), 3. Circle of Love! Secret to Successful Relationships 1995 (H.I.H. Pub).; [pers.] "Protect the children."

## FRULLO JR., RAYMOND L.

[pen.] Linray; [b.] February 5, 1944, Waltham, MA; [p.] Raymond Frullo, Tina Frullo; [ed.] St. Mary's High, Bentley College; [occ.] Marketing and Sales Consultant; [pers.] Dedicated and written for the one and only true love of my life "Linda Masters.";  [a.] Brewster, MA

## FURNISS, MARIAN BEERY

[b.] June 16, 1978, Lancaster, OH; [p.] John F. Furniss Jr., and Judith Groff; [ed.] Lancaster High School (Sr.); [occ.] High School Student (Sr.); [memb.] The Names Project Foundation; [pers.] Poetry is my way of expressing every emotion and feeling I have. It helps me understand myself as well as others.; [a.] Lancaster, OH

## GAGNON, SHARLENE

[pen.] Sharlene Gagnon; [b.] February 21, 1942, Smyrna Mills, ME; [p.] Ruby Marquis and Leo; [m.] Divorced; [ch.] Philip Gagnon, Tony Gagnon, Kristen Gagnon; [ed.] East Hampton High, East Hampton Connecticut; [occ.] Housewife; [memb.] Our Lady of Snows Catholic Organization in Belleview - Illinois; [hon.] In School Essays and Art Drawings; [oth. writ.] One Legged Seagull - A Snowflake from Heaven - About a dear brother who died of Aids - Lost Loves and New Found Loves; [pers.] I write to ease my heart of hurt over my life time and people who have been very close and dear to me. I wrote a small book about my brother who died of aids.; [a.] Myrtle Beach, SC

## GAINES, YVETTE H.

[pen.] Lolly; [b.] August 5, 1908, New Orleans, LA; [p.] Emily Sarpy and Alexander Harris; [m.] Charles R. Gaines, August 12, 1929; [ch.] Yvette G. Gagnet, 3 grandchildren - 6 great grandchildren; [ed.] High School - Ursuline Academy; [pers.] I started writing poetry in my early sixties and they depict my experiences and observations of life.

## GAKEN, LINDSAY R.

[pen.] Lindsay R. Gaken; [b.] June 1, 1977, Ann Arbor, MI; [p.] Lawrence and Mary Gaken; [ed.] Graduated from Chelsea High in 1995, and currently attending Washtenaw Community College; [occ.] Studying to be an Athletic Trainer; [hon.] Won the strive Scholarship; [oth. writ.] I write other poems, stories and songs but this is first publication.; [pers.] In my poetry I try to reflect the true feelings of ones heart. My influences are the people that surround me every day.; [a.] Chelsea, MI

## GALEWALER, SEAN

[b.] November 15, 1977, Denton, TX; [p.] John Edward and Susan Galewaler; [ed.] Junior year in High School; [pers.] Better days are dead and gone greater times are yet to come they all run together like a quills on a feather. I admire Walt Whitman and his style of poetry.; [a.] Whitesboro, TX

## GALLOF, SANDRA A.

[b.] October 2, 1947, New York; [p.] Paul and Lenore Lieberman; [m.] Irwin Gallof, April 21, 1968; [ch.] Brian, Scott, Phillip; [ed.] James Madison H.S., Farmingdale University; [occ.] Para-Teacher, B.O.C.E.S., East Bway; [memb.] Trustee - Temple Beth Sholom Ctr. "One in Nine" Breast Cancer Coalition; [hon.] Essay Award Winner: Green Mountain Pet Products; [oth. writ.] Essays, poems and short stories.; [a.] Massapequa, NY

## GALUSZKA, FRANCIS J.

[b.] October 4, 1968, Queens, NY; [p.] Michael Galuszka, Theresa Galuszka; [ed.] Lindenhurst, H.S.; [occ.] United States Postal Worker/Freelance Artist; [hon.] Editor in Chief of L'Ateiler (H.S. Art/Poetry Magazine), Proclamation of Dedication from County

Legislature; [pers.] I would like to dedicate the poem "Ode" to my dear friend Mr. Daniel Sanchez, for whom this poem was written for and inspired by.; [a.] Lindenhurst, NY

**GAMBLE, LAURA**
[pen.] Laura Gamble; [b.] July 5, 1947, South Buffalo Township, PA; [p.] Clarence and Hannah Fennell; [m.] Dennis Gamble (Deceased), February 6, 1978; [ch.] Amy Vantine, Gregory Beer; [ed.] Freeport Area High School, Career Training Academy; [occ.] (I am in-between jobs, but am trained for Medical Admin. Assistant; [memb.] Church of God, International; [oth. writ.] This is my first; [pers.] I have a great love for the writings of King David in his Psalms of the Bible. Also am a romanticist at heart.; [a.] Kittanning, PA

**GARATE, PRISCILLA PHILLIPS**
[b.] January 7, 1945, Dalton, GA; [p.] Carlton Phillips and Nellie Phillips; [m.] Roger H. Garate, August 15, 1964; [ch.] Sherry Marie Evans, Roger C. Garate; [ed.] Miami Norland High, Miami FL, Some College Courses; [occ.] Office Manager Harblock; [oth. writ.] Tips for experts for local newspaper.; [a.] Douglasville, GA

**GARCIA, ELLIOT**
[b.] November 18, 1980, New York City, NY; [p.] Gilbert Garcia, Eliana Garcia; [ed.] Iona Preparatory School, Class of 1998; [occ.] Student; [memb.] Spanish National Honors Society; [hon.] Spanish National Honors Society, Latin National Honors Society; [pers.] I firmly believe that the only true solitude anyone can find is within their own mind, and I express this belief in my writing.; [a.] Yonkers, NY

**GARCIA, ANGEL L.**
[pen.] Papo, Coco, Che; [b.] October 18, 1960, Puerto Rico; [p.] Angel Luis Garcia, Luz P. Flores; [m.] Sonia Noemi Gonzalez, October 3, 1986; [ch.] Joshua A. Garcia, Soannel Garcia; [ed.] Jose S. Alegria High, 2 yrs. Inter American University; [oth. writ.] El Sonador (The Dreamer) love poems; [pers.] A moment in life its a lifetime in your mind.; [a.] Dorado, PR

**GARDEN, SHEILA**
[b.] June 26, 1922, Mount Vernon, NY; [p.] Anna Wolf and Joseph Weber; [m.] Divorced from Hyman A. Getoff; [ch.] Peter Getoff, Tova Getoff; [ed.] A.B. Davis High School, New York University, University Southern CA - Graduate School Social Work; [occ.] Almost Retired MSW/LCSW; [memb.] Amnesty International, War Resisters League; [hon.] High School Graduation, English Prize; [oth. writ.] High School Year Book Editor, Poetry in Year Book, Essays and Letters - local and National small newspaper; [pers.] I am passionate about continuous self development, and fulfillment of Humankind's potentialities and drive for freedom.; [a.] New York, NY

**GARRETT, JOHN**
[b.] February 9, 1981, Stonybrook, NY; [p.] John B. Garrett, Catherine Ardle; [ed.] First through Eight Grade; [hon.] National Junior Honor Society, Graduated Middle School Honors, Excellence in Academics for Creative Writing and Health, President's Academical Fitness Award; [oth. writ.] Several poems printed in School Poetry and Song Anthology; [pers.] The key to tomorrow is how you live today.; [a.] Hauppauge, NY

**GARRISON, EVELYN C.**
[pen.] Ev; [b.] April 21, 1937, Banner Elk, NC; [p.] Bessie and William Carpenter; [m.] Gene Garrison, November 26, 1987; [ch.] Gina Parker, Daniel Pittman; [ed.] Crossnore High, Crossnore, NC; [occ.] Operate Elderly Care Facility; [pers.] My poems are based on personal experiences in my life. I call them "Poems

from the Heart."; [a.] Deltona, FL

**GARVIN, PEGGY ANN**
[b.] July 6, 1947, Kansas City, Missouri; [p.] Charles Leon Wade, Sr. and Nelle Chris Wade; [m.] W. Franklin Garvin, September 6, 1980; [ch.] Robert Thomas Blackburn (son); Michele Deanne Blackburn (daughter); [ed.] Graduated from Lord De La Warr High School, New Castle, Delaware and Goldey-Beacon Jr. College, Wilmington, Delaware; attended Aiken Technical College, Aiken, SC; [occ.] Graphic artist at Savannah River Site, Aiken, SC; [hon.] My first romance novel was nominated for four awards at the Tunnel Con III convention in Las Vegas, NV (7/94) and again for 2 awards at a distant shore convention in Los Angeles, CA (7/95). One of my poems won third place at the LA Convention. (8/95) I received the Editor's Choice Award by the National Library of Poetry; [oth. writ.] I have had 46 poems published in various fazine's from 1992 through the present. I have also written two romance novels published by Dream Weavers, Montmorenci, SC; Parallel World's Within the City and I Shall But Love Thee Better...; [pers.] I have always written poetry to express my deepest feelings. My first book was written during a particularly dark time in my life. Escaping into the lives of my characters enabled me to survive the harshness of reality. I discovered that for me, writing enhances the quality of life!; [a.] Aiken, SC

**GARWOOD, TARA B.**
[b.] May 31, 1976, Washington, DC; [p.] Richard and Nancy Garwood; [ed.] Quince Orchard High School, Jacksonville University; [occ.] Student, Musical, Theatre Major; [memb.] Thespian Troupe #4444, American Federation of Television and Radio Artists, and Screen Actor's Guild; [hon.] Received scholarship from MD Distinguished Scholar Program, Talent in the Arts, MD All-State Thespian, Honor Roll and Dean's List; [a.] Gaithersburg, MD

**GAY, RICHARD**
[b.] May 21, 1937, Boston, MA; [ch.] Three; [ed.] High School; [occ.] Painter; [memb.] Full Gospel Business, Men's Fellowship International; [hon.] Archery; [pers.] I would like people to explore the Christian life.; [a.] Weymouth, MA

**GAZDAGH, LORI**
[pen.] Little L; [b.] March 27, 1971, Cleveland, OH; [ch.] My little Bunny; [ed.] Nordonia High, pursuing a degree in Psychology at the University of Akron; [occ.] Student; [hon.] Psi Chi - National Honors Society in Psychology, Dean's List; [pers.] Love is a precious gift, so if you get the chance to receive it then treasure it always, because life without love is no life at all. Thank you J. and S.; [a.] Sagamore Hills, OH

**GBADO, RUFIN B.**
[pen.] Rufin B. Gbado; [b.] April 21, 1972, Benin; [p.] Gabriel Gbado, Anntoinett; [ed.] High School, Godomey Cotonou Benin (West Africa), Computer Operator; [occ.] Student at York College; [pers.] I believe if there is tomorrow, there is always another chance for a dream to become reality.; [a.] Jamaica, NY

**GEFFERT, CHAD M.**
[b.] March 17, 1969, Warwick, RI; [p.] John and Darlene Geffert; [ed.] Milford High, Community College U.S.A.F., University of Anchorage Alaska, Dean College; [occ.] Self-employed; [pers.] I'm thinking of you.; [a.] Milford, MA

**GEORGE, LINDA SUE**
[b.] August 9, 1950, Cleveland, TN; [p.] James Blair, Essie Blair; [ch.] Yolanda Cooper, Chris George, Clarissa George; [ed.] College Hill High, Cleveland

High School; [occ.] Linens - American Uniform CO; [memb.] Church of God, Sanc.; [oth. writ.] Several poems written for family and friends obituaries.; [pers.] To always write a poem for the enjoyment and uplifting of others. To remember that this is a gift from the Lord and use it wisely.; [a.] Cleveland, TN

**GERBER, SCOTT**
[b.] August 31, 1983, State Island, NY; [p.] Ellen and Kevin Gerber; [ed.] Graduated from Public School April 1994. Currently attending Paulo Intermediate School 75; [occ.] Student/Writer/Author/Journalist; [memb.] Paulo Star Member, Honor Society Member 1995, Staff Member of Paulo Paw Prints (newspaper); [hon.] Published poet in Bibliomania V/1995, Published and appeared in S.I. News, Arista Society, Presidential Award, Student in Focus Award, Excellence in Communication Arts, Honorable mention/Paulo Writing Project/Poetry Contest; [oth. writ.] Articles published in Paulo Paw Prints. Poem published in Bibliomania V. Currently writing science-fiction novel entitled "Alien Invasion."; [pers.] Being an author is only one of my many goals. I'm somewhat like the oak tree in my poem because I'm prosperous in the writing field. I hope to be a talented author/poet/writer. I was influenced by Bruce Coville to write my latest novel. "Alien Invasion" and I hope it gets published.; [a.] Staten Island, NY

**GERHARD, PAUL W.**
[b.] March 1, 1951, Sellersville, PA; [p.] Clifford Gerhard, Mabel (Geiger) Gerhard; [m.] Cynthia (Hagey) Gerhard, December 22, 1973; [ch.] Nora Diane Gerhard, Aaron William Gerhard; [ed.] Souderton Area High School; [occ.] Metal Crafter Knoll International East Greenville, PA; [oth. writ.] Several songs written for guitar; [pers.] Enjoy writing songs and poems about life.; [a.] Salford, PA

**GERSTENBERGER JR., TODD**
[b.] September 27, 1982, Santa Barbara, CA; [p.] Christine Klos-Gerstenberger, Todd Gerstenberger; [ed.] Pacific Elementary School; [occ.] Student

**GETTRY, JOAN E.**
[b.] Jamaica, WI; [p.] Irene and Sylvester Grant (Deceased); [m.] Martin D. Gettry (Deceased); [ch.] None - except for my loving 8 yr. old English Springer Spaniel Dog; [ed.] Presently attending La Guardia Comm. College, Future: Hunter College; [occ.] Homemaker and Student; [memb.] Women's Auxiliary - N.Y. Medical Center of Queens, International Society of Poets; [hon.] Dean's List; [oth. writ.] Enrollment in Institute of Children's Literature; [pers.] I look on each day as a brand new miracle, and a privilege, because it gives me an opportunity in discovering another facet to my life, which did not exist the previous day, and in effect, it has become a glorious learning process.; [a.] Beechhurst, NY

**GIBBONS, GREGG E.**
[b.] January 11, 1975; [p.] Kevin and Barbara Gibbons; [ed.] Currently attending Joliet Jr. College; [a.] Bolingbrook, IL

**GIDDENS, MARIA**
[m.] A. C. Giddens; [ch.] Three; [oth. writ.] About 200 unpublished poems; [pers.] Many of my poems, have been written thru tears, for life is beautiful in joy. Ignited by a spirit, having learned "Joyful Illumination through sadness."; [a.] Los Angeles, CA

**GIDDENS, JULIE DELABRUE**
[pen.] Raven; [b.] July 14, 1961, WI; [p.] Ronald and Alma Delabrue; [m.] George W. Giddens Jr., January 15, 1994; [ed.] High School and 2 yrs. college, Univ. of

Wis., Oshkosh; [hon.] Honor Student (nomination) award (Menominee Indian High School); [oth. writ.] Won various 1st place poetry contests in High School!; [pers.] Always listen and believe in thy true self, for no one knows other than you!!; [a.] Alva, FL

**GIERMAN, SHAWNDRA**
[b.] June 22, 1975, Lansing, MI; [p.] Kathy and Steve Smith, Jeff and Cheryl Gierman; [ed.] Haslett High School, Lancing Community College; [occ.] Assistant Manager Prestige Fragrance and Cosmetics; [pers.] Reading and writing poetry is a wonderful release. It is very soothing for the mind, body and soul.; [a.] Okemos, MI

**GILLIAM, KELI**
[b.] August 2, 1974, Muskogee, OK; [p.] Jim and Beth Welch; [m.] Wes Gilliam, March 19, 1994; [ed.] Hilldale High School, Senior at Northeastern State University studying to be an Elementary Education Teacher; [occ.] Salesperson at Zales Jewelry; [memb.] Muskogee Church of Christ; [hon.] President's Honor Roll; [pers.] God is the source of my inspiration, without him, I would be nothing.; [a.] Muskogee, OK

**GILLON, MARION L.**
[b.] February 25, 1945, Birmingham, AL; [p.] Marion and Kathryn Gillon; [ed.] Hayes High School, Birmingham, AL, Tougalou College, Mississippi Harvard University, Cambridge; [occ.] Educator; [memb.] Board of Directors, Greater Boston Regional, Youth Council; [oth. writ.] An Angel Named David, City Nights, For Gloria, On The Imaginations of a Poet; [pers.] I wrote my first poem after hearing Maya Angelou read at Clinton's Inauguration, and after 47 years I discovered the joy of putting my feelings in poetry.; [a.] Cambridge, MA

**GILMORE JR., WILLIAM**
[pen.] Goo Gilmore; [b.] December 25, 1953, Seoul, Korea; [p.] Martello Gilmore and Lawanda Kursh; [ch.] Creusa, William III, and Myole Gilmore and Amon Churchill; [ed.] Riverside Community College and Columbia University; [occ.] Telecommunications Technician; [memb.] Rialto Golden State Basketball League - President, Iron Horse Ridge Community Association - President, NAACP - Secretary, and Youth Basketball Coach School Volunteer Teacher; [hon.] Certificate of Appreciation Calif. State Assembly, Several Coaching Awards and Administrative Awards; [oth. writ.] Poems published in "World of Poetry" and "Black Poetry"; [pers.] Though there's simplicity with our lives, our unique experiences often become the events for which we individually have purpose. I try to convey this meaning to our existence in my writings.; [a.] Colton, CA

**GINGRICH, DIANE C.**
[b.] December 5, 1974, Sellerville, PA; [p.] John and Gerry Gingrich; [ed.] Pennridge High School, Penn State University; [occ.] Office Clerk; [hon.] I was awarded Editor's Choice Award for my poem, "Reason," in the National Library of Poetry's Song on the Wind; [oth. writ.] "Reason" (poem), various unpublished works. Currently working on my first novel.; [pers.] I would, first like to thank Ken R. and my family for all of their support. I never intended for my work to be published, it was just a way to vent my feelings. Gradually my writing got better and I decided to submit. At first, I was embarrassed that people were reading my innermost thoughts and feelings. I realized, though, that people can relate and I may possibly help someone out, therefore, it's all worth it to me.; [a.] Sellersville, PA

**GIVENS, JACLYN RENEE**
[b.] October 18, 1979, McCall, ID; [p.] Wanda Givens,

Mike Givens; [ed.] 10th Grade this year 1995-1996; [occ.] Student Germantown High School, (10th grade) Germantown, TN; [memb.] French Club, Drama Club; [oth. writ.] Poems printed in High School Newspaper (Meridian High School - Meridian, Idaho); [pers.] Anyone can write a poem, but it takes a truly special person to write poetry.; [a.] Germantown, TN

**GLADE, JESSICA**
[b.] March 22, 1984, Des Moines, IA; [p.] Mr. and Mrs. Thomas Glade; [ed.] Guthrie Center, Iowa School; [occ.] Student; [hon.] Student of the Month in May 1995. County Fair Guthrie Center Production Classson-a-Ray, 1995 Swine Grand Champion; [a.] Guthrie Center, IA

**GLASSMAN, SANDRA**
[pen.] "Melodee"; [b.] August 27, 1940, Brooklyn, NY; [p.] Joseph, Rebecca Gruber; [m.] Stewart, December 27, 1958; [ch.] Marrah, Lee; [ed.] High School; [occ.] Piano Teacher; [memb.] A.B.I., ISP Distinguished Member, ACM - American College of Musicians; [hon.] Four Editor's Choice Awards from "National Library of Poetry for 1993-94-95, 2 poems in Holocaust Museum Archives in Washington, DC; [oth. writ.] Composed music for book "Take Care of Josette" by J. Wolf.; [a.] Oceanside, NY

**GLUCK, MICHAEL**
[b.] June 7, 1970, Amitville, NY; [p.] David and Ellen Gluck; [ed.] Sachem High, Suffolk Community College; [occ.] Deputy Sheriff, Suffolk Country Sheriff's Dept; [hon.] Pi Alpha Sigma, Dean's List; [pers.] I write for myself, all the virtuous feels and their outdated ideals, those idealists that grasp at the straws to keep from falling off the cliff.; [a.] Miller Place, NY

**GOBLISCH, FLORENCE**
[pen.] Florence Goblisch; [b.] December 10, 1965, Oak Lawn, IL; [p.] Robert and Carol Goblisch; [ch.] Amanda Noa; [ed.] Valparaiso University; [occ.] Babysitting/ Manager of Country Court; [memb.] First Church of Nazareen/Volunteer Work; [hon.] Evergreen Park, High School Honor Roll; [pers.] I was influenced to write this poem, because of an emotional time in my life. Now I am very happy and furthering my education at VU to become a social worker for children I care deeply for my stepdaughter Amanda.; [a.] Valparaiso, IN

**GOEB, JANIE A.**
[pen.] Janie A. Goeb; [b.] February 8, 1936, San Diego, CA; [p.] Andrew and Margaret Chamberlain; [m.] Julian Goeb, December 26, 1954; [ch.] Sheryl Lynn, Julie Anne, Steven Andrew; [ed.] A.A. Nursing; [occ.] Registered Nurse; [memb.] A.A.C.N. (American Assoc. of Critical Cou Nurses), American Cancer Society, National Wildlife Federation, The Yosemite Fund; [oth. writ.] Nothing published; [pers.] Grandmother of 6, great-grandmother of 1 love nature, best - God's greatest gift to us is our world and the treasure in it - it is our keepsake.; [a.] San Diego, CA

**GOINS, KATHRYN A.**
[b.] March 26, 1941, Independence, MO; [p.] Sidney Jones, Kathryn Jones; [m.] Robert A. Goins, September 9, 1968; [ch.] David, Dan, Dale, Sid, Jenifer and Robin; [ed.] St. Ann's Elementary, Van Horn High; [occ.] I work part time as a deli worker, it's fun; [memb.] Past Pres. Belton Lioness Club, Belton, MO, Member of Coleman Baptist Church Peculiar, MO; [hon.] Blue Ribbon Winner of Cakes and Breads - Raymore, MO, Grandma of 16 children - nine girls and seven boys; [oth. writ.] Many poems and short stories unpublished at least 10 songs of praise and worship.; [pers.] It is in each of us to be happy, a choice I make each day.; [a.] Raymore, MO

**GOLDMAN, ROGER B.**
[b.] August 4, 1965, Spokane, WA; [p.] Lloyd and Bernice Goldman; [ed.] 1 yr. University of GA, 1 yr. Dekalb Community College completed certificate in Prof. Cooking Techniques U.C.L.A. extension; [occ.] Fast Food Manager; [oth. writ.] Eat Brains, Odes, and Out Cry, and "Story Teller"; [pers.] I attempt to stimulate vivid pictures in the mind as well as evoke some form of emotion from the reader, be it positive or negative. I like to make people think and discuss those thoughts I evoke.; [a.] Nashville, TN

**GOMEZ, AMELIA A.**
[b.] November 28, 1941, Ricardo Flores Magon Dgo, Mexico; [p.] Francisco Alvarez, Aurelia Alvarez; [m.] Mariano A. Gomez; [ch.] Mario Gomez Jr., Gabriela Gomez; [ed.] Elementary, Mexico 2 years, C.A.I (California Air Craft Institute; [occ.] Work, Part Time, Student, Part Time, Volunteer; [memb.] Sacred Heart; [hon.] C.N.A., Air Craft Institute (Certificates), Pin and Badget (Volunteer Certificate of C.N.A.; [oth. writ.] Poems in Spanish My First Language - and plan to write more and publish a small book with my own poems or small pieces of writings.; [pers.] Respect all human being and help anyone who need my assistance, for better condition of life.; [a.] Prescott, AZ

**GOOD, MARGARET**
[b.] February 4, 1933, Torrance County, NM; [p.] Claude and Bertha (Crider) Brown; [m.] Paul W. Good; [ch.] Dena Sue Roberts, Edward F. and Steven W.; [ed.] Ewing School, Torrance County, NM, Estancia High School, Torrance Co. NM, Harding University, Searcy, Ark. (2 yrs); [occ.] Retired Secretary; [memb.] Church of Christ, International Society of Poets; [hon.] New Mexico Girls State 1950, High School Salutatorian, Scholarship to Harding College, published in anthologies: High School 2 Years and Sermons in Poetry College 1 Year Famous Poets Society, Hollywood, CA; [oth. Writ.] Today's Great Poems Famous Poems To Day, At Days End best Poems of 1995 Reflections Of Light East Of The Sunrise At Water's Edge Sparkles In The Sand and 3 poems in "Vessels," A Christian Paper For Women By Women.; [pers.] I credit my 6, 7, 8th grade teacher, Eulah Watson, now deceased, for getting me started writing poetry. My writings generally consist of things with which I am familiar, specific events, people and religion.; [a.] Stephenville, TX

**GOODMAN, BETTY WEST**
[b.] January 1, 1937, Media, PA; [p.] Norman and Pearl West; [m.] Richard Goodman, April 9, 1955; [ch.] Rhonda, Journa and Jensine (three daughters); [occ.] Homemaker; [memb.] Women of the Moose 530 Chapter; [hon.] Editor's Choice Award 1994, Editor's Choice 1995; [oth. writ.] Fourth of July, What is a Daughter, Mother's Day, Love and a White Christmas Tree; [pers.] I love to write poems for the ones I love it makes me feel good to see my words down on paper. I hope my family enjoys the poems that I write. I write after losing love ones it helps with the grief.

**GOODSON, REX EDWARD**
[b.] April 16, 1931, Wylie, TX; [p.] Rex Odel Goodson; [m.] Joseph (Hass) Goodson, February 4, 1953; [ch.] Three boys and two girls; [occ.] Retired through Mary Kay Cos. Co.; [oth. writ.] Published once a month in tutor St. Mission (Church) in Paris, Tex., other poems sent out several states to hundreds of people.; [pers.] To help lift people who are down and place a little joy in their hearts. I have been blessed by other writer poems. I have written 400 poems and around 200 gospel songs.; [a.] Garland, TX

**GORSE, PETER F.**

[b.] November 16, 1915, Attlebough, MA; [p.] Peter and Bessie Gorse; [m.] Marion Cardin Gorse, April 17, 1943; [ch.] Margaret Gorse Sullivan, Peter F. Gorse Jr., Michael P. Gorse, 13 grandchildren, 2 great grandchildren so far

## GOTTSCHALK, KELLYANNA TAYLOR

[b.] November 26, 1967; [p.] George and Marianne Taylor; [m.] Bruce; [ed.] Lakewood High School, Cleveland State University; [memb.] International Society of Poets, Cleveland State Univ. Alumni Assoc.; [hon.] 3rd prize 1994/95 North American Open Poetry Contest for "Winter Warrior" as published in After The Storm by the National Library of Poetry Editor's Choice Award for "Winter Warrior"; [oth. writ.] I am to be published in the Best of 1996 for "Watching the Dawn" as published by the National Library of Poetry, plus many poems, short stories, and children's stories.; [pers.] I am so pleased to be published now for the 3rd time by the National Library of Poetry. I hope to continued writing and submitting, it is my greatest joy to write of the things I love!; [a.] Brunswick, OH

## GOUDJABIDZE, LADO V.

[b.] August 28, 1945, Republic of Georgia; [p.] Michael and Angelica Goudjabidze; [m.] Shake Goudjabidze, July 20, 1968; [ch.] Marina Goudjabidze and Iris Goudjabidze; [ed.] Academia of Fine Art; [occ.] Artist, Sculptor, Painter, and Designer; [memb.] Nassau County Art League, Flushing Council of the Fine Art, and Knickerbocker Art Association; [hon.] Gold Medal, Knickerbocker Artist Exhibition (1981), Flushing Council of Art Award (1985), International Humanitarian Award (1985), Queens Child Guidance Center Award (1987), The Veno Royal Museum Award - Japan (1990); [oth. writ.] Collection of short stories and poems - none currently published.; [pers.] Everything created with care and love is truly art.; [a.] Flushing, NY

## GOULD, EILEEN CANDY

[pen.] Eileen Candy Gould; [b.] November 20, 1932, Grants Pass, OR; [p.] Mr. and Mrs. F. W. Cooper; [m.] William H. Gould, December 2, 1960; [ch.] John W. Gould - 27 yrs. old, Thomas F. Candy Ph.D. - 45 yrs. old (first marriage); [ed.] (In full High School 2 years Jr. College), Cert. Dent. Nurse (Ortho. Tech, Dent. Tech., X-ray Tech.), CNA (2) with Sp. Aid Addition; [occ.] Retired with disability in 1988; [memb.] I'm a member of the S.D.A. Church, and I do all I can for God, a lot of my poems are Christian work, the SDA conference love my poems, but I've never sent work anywhere; [hon.] I don't know how much honor it is, but I draw and write the Christian poem in our cards we send our many friends; [oth. writ.] I have written many poems, enough to fill a good sized book. I also draw. I have just completed a children's book doing all my own drawings, in the book. I also write for our Church Paper.; [pers.] I love to write poems and short stories I love to draw. With CTC in my arms and hands I can't do it very long at a time but I do it.; [a.] Edmonds, WA

## GOVAN, STEPHANIE

[pen.] Yolanda Mossman; [b.] October 10, 1935, Jamaica W.I.; [p.] Catherine Howard Ritchie; [m.] Divorced; [ch.] Donna Yvette Mossman; [ed.] Elementary School Jamaica, WI; Junior High and High School - United States of America; [occ.] Medical Records Coder certificate - SUNY - Down State Medical Center, Brooklyn, NY; [pers.] I am proud to be a national citizen of the United States of America; [a.] Brooklyn, NY

## GRACE, WILLARD C.

[b.] November 6, 1932, Bel Air, MD; [p.] Charles Everett and Ruby D. Grace; [m.] Mary Lou Grace, November 23, 1956; [ch.] Willard C. Grace Jr., Sarah Anne Milligan; [ed.] Eastern Nazarene College, A.B.,

Lincoln University, B.D., Lancaster Theological Seminary M.R.E.; [occ.] Clergyman United Methodist Church; [memb.] Dicken's Fellowship, International Free-lance Photographers Organization, American Image News Service, member and holder of Readers Credentials of the Society of Preserve and Encourage Rado Drama, Variety, and Comedy; [oth. writ.] "The England of John Wesley" Video "The London of John Wesley," published poetry; [pers.] I'm attempting to merge modern media with historical data and thereby preserve for future generations information both visual and written. This is mostly being accomplished in England.; [a.] Mount Joy, PA

## GRAMLING, VERLYN

[b.] June 7, 1942, Hickory Flat, GA; [p.] Ides Gramling, Doris Gramling; [m.] Janice (Markel), April 12, 1963; [ch.] Mylon, Scott, Tracy, Tina, 6 Grandchildren; [ed.] South Cobb High; [occ.] Retired from Building and Landscaping Career; [hon.] NATRC 1977 Top Horseman of the Year - Chief Joseph Award - Numerous Other Award for Competitive and Endurance Trail Riding Events; [oth. writ.] Several other poems in the "Cowboy Poetry" style; [pers.] I try to reflect my appreciation of the Western lifestyle and nature as well as God's handiwork in my poetry.; [a.] Douglasville, GA

## GRASS, MARTHA

[b.] March 8, 1961, Muncie, IN; [p.] Reverend and Mrs. Ronald Drown; [m.] Kenneth Grass; [ch.] Mother of 5 beautiful, gifted children; [memb.] GulfCoast Faith Fellowship, Vocalist - Praise and Worship Team; [oth. writ.] I enjoy singing and writing "Inspirational" music.; [pers.] I am often moved to write about painful experiences or political and moral issues. God is my source.; [a.] Cape Coral, FL

## GRAVES, COURTNEY ANNE

[b.] March 9, 1983, Farmington, NM; [p.] John A. Graves, Lisa Graves; [ed.] Will be attending 7th grade at Manassas Park Intermediate; [occ.] Babysitting during summer vacation; [hon.] President's Education, Award for Academics 1995, Outstanding Student 1995, Conner Elementary, Outstanding Reader and Writer 1995, Conner Elem.; [oth. writ.] This poem published Manassas Journal Messenger May 11, 1995; [pers.] I get inspiration from nature, surroundings and feelings.; [a.] Manassas Park, VA

## GRAY, NAKIA

[b.] November 23, 1976, Baltimore, MD; [p.] James Gray, Carol Gray; [ed.] The Hockaday School in Dallas, TX, The University of Texas at Austin; [occ.] Student at Ut-Austin Field of Study, Biology-Pre-Med; [memb.] The Black Health Professions Organization, The Health Professions Council, NAACP, The Good Street Baptist Church; [hon.] Alpha Lambda Delta, Phi Eta Sigma, Dean's List, National Commended Scholar, The College Board, National Young Leadership Award, National Young Leaders Conference - Washington, D.C.; [oth. writ.] Features Editor of High School Newspaper, The Fourcast.; [pers.] I strive to reflect truth by allowing myself to feel.; [a.] Dallas, TX

## GREEN, BOBBY

[b.] May 5, 1968, Goslen, NY; [p.] Joan and David Smith; [ed.] Monroe Woodbury High, Nassau Community College, C.W. Post - Long Island University; [occ.] Personal Trainer; [oth. writ.] Several poems never shown to anyone before.; [pers.] The material that I write comes deep from my soul and at times it yearns to be heard throughout the world.; [a.] Westbury, NY

## GREFALDA, REME A.

[b.] June 11, 1941, Victoria, Hong Kong; [p.] Jose Grefalda and Remy G. Cabacungan; [ed.] St. Paul

College, Manila Philippines, Farleigh Dickinson University, NJ, Shakespeare Theatre Inst., CT; [occ.] Legal Assistant; [memb.] Philippine Educational Theater Association; [hon.] Poetry award in college, Dean's List, Photography Awards; [oth. writ.] Short stories and poems published in local newspapers, scripts plays for stage and TV, poetry included in photography exhibit. 1996 Release - Book of Poems "Baring More Than Soul" Dorrance Publishing Co.; [a.] Arlington, VA

## GREINER, LISA

[pen.] Lisa Greiner; [b.] December 20, 1957, Columbus, OH; [p.] Andrew and Jean Greiner; [ch.] Ryan Padget; [ed.] North Eugene High, Winn Watts High, Lane Community College; [occ.] Cook and Gardener; [oth. writ.] Several poems and short stories, none published.; [pers.] Lisa strived for peace and a happy place in the world. She loved old books and collected and read them, history of Indian Love, and Early Settlers. Lisa was in a fatal car crash on January 27, 1995. Her writings will keep her with us forever.; [a.] Marcola, OR

## GRIFFITHS, CIWA

[b.] February 1, 1911, Fiji Island; [p.] Jennie Scott Griffiths and Arthur George Griffiths; [ed.] B.A., San Francisco State, M.S. University of Massachusetts Ed.D., Univ. of Southern Calif.; [occ.] Retired now Founder, HEAR Center, 1954; [memb.] Writers Club of Leisure World, Guild of HEAR Center, College Club Audio-Verbal International; [hon.] Outstanding Service Achievement Award, Calif. Federation of Women 1970, G.H. Bollinger Humanitarian Award 1979, Who's Who American Women, 1977-78 The World's Who's Who Women, 1978 Teacher of the Year Award, A.G. Assoc., 1991 Leisure World or a Month, July 1993, 1st Prize, Writer Club Prose Contest, '93 Honoree 40th Anniversary HEAR Center 1994; [oth. Writ.] HEAR - A Four - Letter Word Conquering Childhood Deafness - One Out of Ten - Patterns, 'til Forever Is Past.

## GRONSTAL, BRENDA

[b.] June 8, 1946, Dallas, TX; [p.] Doyal McGowen, Mattie McGowen; [m.] Philip Gronstal (Deceased), June 14, 1969; [ch.] Kurtis Randal, Kendyl Ryan; [ed.] Castleberry High School, North Texas State University; [pers.] I find must aspects of living worth reading and writing about, and I am especially fascinated by the subject of time.; [a.] Lucas, TX

## GRUBE, KATHLEEN

[pen.] Katie Grube; [b.] November 25, 1982, Pensacola, FL; [p.] Steven Grube; [ed.] Attends Fort Clarke Middle School, Gainesville, Florida; [occ.] Middle School Student; [memb.] National Junior Beta Club Student Government; [hon.] Most Outstanding Student in Reading, Most Outstanding Student in Language Arts, Most Outstanding Student in Mathematics, Mebane Middle School (1995); [pers.] Medicine interests me very much, but in the future I do wish to make writing a hobby or even and then profession in addition to being a doctor.; [a.] Gainesville, FL

## GUENTHER, CHARLES

[b.] April 29, 1920, Saint Louis, MO; [p.] Charles R. Guenther and Hulda C. Guenther; [m.] Esther (Klund) Guenther, April 11, 1942; [ch.] Charles Jr., Cecile, Christine; [ed.] Ph.D. Fellow, Saint Louis Univ., 1976-79, LHD, So. Ill. Univ. - Edwardsville, 1979 BA, MA, Webster University AA, Harris Teachers College; [occ.] Freelance Writer; [memb.] Poetry Society of America (Midwest Regional Vice-Pres. 1976-90), Academy of American Poets, Missouri Writer's Guild (past pres.), St. Louis Writer's Guild (past pres.), St. Louis Poetry Center (past pres.), Special Libraries Assn. (past pres., Greater St. Louis Chapter), American Literary Translators Assn., Sigma Delta Pi, American Rose Society; [hon.] Order of Merit of th Italian Republic, 1973, James Joyce Award, 1974 and Witter Bynner Poetry Translation grant 1979, Poetry Society of America, French American Bicentennial Medal, 1976, Missouri Writer's Guild Poetry Award, 1983, 1986, 1993, Walter Williams Award, 1987, 1995, Doctor of Humane Letters (LHD), So. Ill. Univ. - Edwardsville, 1979; [oth. writ.] Author of ten books incl. Phrase/Paraphrase (1970), The Hippopotamus, Selected Translations (1986), and Moving the Seasons, Selected Poems (1994). Contributor to 300 magazines worldwide. Book reviewer, St. Louis Post-Dispatch since 1953. Book reviewer (1972-82) for the St. Louis Globe-Democrat (now defunct).; [pers.] A poet's relation to his time is complex and mutable. His temperament, attitudes and sense of the function of poetry are all changeable and conflict with one another throughout his life. The spirit of poetry, its essence or "duende" is forever renewed by the magic spring-like force of each new age. (From "The Pluralism of Poetry" by the author, Charles Guenther).; [a.] Saint Louis, MO

**GUERIN, ELEANOR**
[b.] December 7, 1942, Battle Creek, MI; [p.] Vincent C. Guerin, Helen Guerin; [m.] Joseph F. Jackson, September 27, 1987; [ed.] Southern Illinois Univ., Washington State Univ.; [occ.] Retired from Broadcast, Film, Advertising Profession; [memb.] Board Member, Friends of the Gilkey Center for Graphic Arts - Portland Art Museum; [oth. writ.] Lifelong Diary and Journal Keeping, this is a first published work.; [a.] Portland, OR

**GUNN, ANDREA L.**
[pen.] Andrea Solomon; [b.] October 3, 1948, Los Angeles, CA; [p.] Charles Solomon, Elizabeth Solomon; [sib.] brother Douglas L. Solomon; [ch.] Barbara Lynn Bennett, Brian Jay Bennett; [m.] March 21, 1987; [ed.] Gardena High, El Camino College, Cal State University; Psychology Major, Business, Design Arts Minor; LifeSpring: Personal Awareness Trainer; [hon.] Pedragal School: Special service award - Teaching; Special Olympics: Outstanding service award; [occ.] Management Consultant; [pers.] Everything in life has value and in that value lies a messge. My writings are a vehicle for those messages.; [a.] Torrance, CA

**GUNNELS, LILLIAN ECK**
[b.] August 21, 1928, Meno, OK; [p.] Joseph Eck and Eva Koehn; [m.] Charles W. Gunnels, September 17, 1949; [ch.] George, Grace, Ginnette and Glenn; [ed.] High School, Ringwood, OK; [occ.] Retired; [hon.] Editor's Choice Award from the National Library of Poetry; [oth. writ.] Children stories for my grandchildren poems for myself for my own enjoyment.; [pers.] Writing is my way of expressing my inner feelings.

**GURTIZA, MARITESS**
[b.] June 23, 1978, San Diego, CA; [p.] Domingo Gurtiza, Asteria Gurtiza; [occ.] High School Student; [a.] San Diego, CA

**GUTHRIE, MELISSA M.**
[pen.] Lisa Guthrie; [b.] July 27, 1964, Newman, GA; [p.] Mike and Valeta Mills; [m.] Steven W. Guthrie, August 31, 1990; [ch.] Jessica Amber Kierbow (8), Taylor Mills Guthrie (3); [ed.] Flint River Academy, Columbus College; [occ.] Insurance Agent, Mills Insurance Agency; [memb.] President - Elect of the Manchester - Warm Springs Pilot Club; [hon.] Delta Kappa Gamma, Dean's List, Winner of Logo Contest for Roosevelt National Arts Society; [oth. writ.] Several poems published by Famous Poets Society in California, local newspapers, and read on the radio station the Joy FM (93.3).; [a.] Woodbury, GA

**GUTIERREZ, KRISTOPHER S.**
[pen.] K. Gutz, Gola; [b.] August 2, 1977, Dallas, TX; [p.] Oscar and Peggy Gutierrez; [ed.] Lewisville High School, Southern Nazarene University; [occ.] Student; [memb.] Lewisville Soccer Alumni, Storm Soccer Club, SNU Soccer; [hon.] Soccer Scholarship; [oth. writ.] Various Lewisville Texas Publications; [pers.] I enjoy expressing my feelings while entertaining readers with my writings.; [a.] Lewisville, TX

**GUTTMANN, MARION**
[b.] October 5, 1927, Pensacola, FL; [p.] Louis and Abella Guttmann; [m.] Evelyn Johnson Guttmann, January 18, 1956; [ch.] Michael, Stephen and Rodney Guttmann; [ed.] U.S. Army Leadership School; [occ.] Real Estate; [memb.] St. Mary's Catholic Church; [pers.] "Daddy's Little Girl", was written about my son and his love for his daughter Angela Michelle Guttmann and his spouse Susan and their other children Jennifer and Samantha.; [a.] Pensacola, FL

**HACKETT, CHARLES J.**
[b.] New York City, NY; [p.] Winfield and Kate; [m.] Mary-Ellen Ryan, January 1995; [ch.] Peter; [ed.] Brooklyn College, Columbia University Hospital Administration; [occ.] Consultant, Hospital Administration; [memb.] Reserve Officers Association International Chiefs of Police, Officers Club USMMA, Turf and Field Club, American College of Healthcare Executives; [hon.] Hofstra University Man of the Year 1980; [oth. writ.] The last happy hour, a novel, double day 1976. The anatomy of survival (in progress) G.I. Book of verse published in England.; [pers.] The art of being wise is the art of knowing what to overlook, William James.; [a.] New York, NY

**HACKIN, DENNIS E.**
[b.] June 3, 1945, Laveen, AZ

**HAGEDORN, JOSEPH A.**
[b.] August 7, 1963, Los Angeles, CA; [p.] Michael, Eleanor Hagedorn; [ed.] Saint Louise High, University of Hawaii, College of Engineering; [occ.] Design Engineer, Artist; [memb.] Hawaii Forest Industry Association, Hawaii Craftsmen; [pers.] I must only attempt to describe a process that is not driven by external information, implying a slowing-down sense and concentrating thought so that the act of deciphering and interpreting is also seen as information albeit an internal one.; [a.] Kailua, HI

**HAGEN, MANDY**
[b.] June 30, 1981, Vallejo, CA; [p.] Turrie Johnson, David Hagen; [ed.] Two Harbors High School; [occ.] Student; [a.] Two Harbors, MN

**HAGER, KATHRYN A.**
[pen.] Katie Hager; [b.] June 27, 1956, Brooklyn, NY; [p.] William M. Hager and Erna C. Hager; [ed.] Saint Thomas Apostle Grammar School, the Saint Mary Louise Academy, Molly College, C.W. Post University; [occ.] Special Education Elementary Teacher at Henry Viscardi School in Albertson, NY; [memb.] Adirondack Council, Alzheimer's Association, American Museum of Natural History, Center of Marine Conservation, Defenders of Wildlife, the Environmental Defense Fund, the Gorilla Foundation, the Jane Goodall Institute, The Marine Mammal Center, the Policy Board of Herricks Teacher Consortium, Mountain Lion Preservation Foundation, the National Audubon Society, the National Geographic Society, North Shore Animal League, North Wind Undersea Institute, NYZS the Wildlife Conservation Society, Plaza Playhouse, National Multiple Sclerosis Society, Special Olympics. Sierra Club, Theodore Roosevelt Sanctuary the Whaling Museum, the Wilderness Soci-

ety, World Wildlife Fund; [hon.] Certificate of Appreciation for 15 years of dedicated service at Henry Viscardi School, December 14, 1994, Molloy Colleges Alumni Award, June 7, 1981, Alpha Mu Gamma, Delta Epsilon Sigma, Omicron Alpha Zeta. Psi Chi, Full Scholarship to Molloy College, NYS Regent Scholarship, the Mary Louis Award, Jamaica Rotary Club's Student of the Year Award; [oth. writ.] 150 unpublished poems, on poems published in Molloy Forum while I was Senior there, "First Flight" in Songs on the Wing, "Dewdrop At Dawn" in The Garden of Life," "Icy Sentinel" in at Water's Edge, and "A Croft of Crocuses" in Mists of Enchantment through the National of Poetry.; [pers.] I strive to convey universal concerns and emotions in my poems. I am greatly influenced by deep faith In God, a passion for nature and theater, my personal experiences, and an appreciation for the power of language. They are constant themes in my poems.; [a.] Williston Park, NY

**HAIDAR, DANNY**
[pen.] Cedar Lebchrist; [b.] October 4, 1973, Lebanon; [p.] Samir and Noha Haidar; [ed.] Currently pursuing a Bachelor of Science in Accounting; [memb.] Columbia House Video Club, Columbia House Music Club, BMG Music Club; [oth. writ.] Many academic essays. Other poems and songs that are yet to be published. Through various media.; [pers.] Never underestimate the powerbroker within.; [a.] Manchester, NH

**HALES, RUTH**
[b.] August 11, 1923, Iuka, MS; [p.] Charlie Grisham and Mamie Gardner Grisham; [m.] Tip Hales, March 8, 19047; [ch.] Mike, Randy, Melba; [ed.] High School; [oth. writ.] Many other, not published.; [pers.] I spent my life caring for my husband and raising my children. It has been very rewarding. As ford my writing, it was for personal enjoyment and occasionally a message to a friend or family member.

**HALL, KARL**
[b.] August 27, 1977, Fort Bragg, NC; [p.] Ted Hall, Sue Hall; [ed.] Oswego High School; [occ.] Student; [hon.] American Legion Award Winner, Illinois State Scholar, National Honor Society, Who's who in American High School Students; [pers.] I write as a hobby. It is enjoyable and comes rather easy to me.; [a.] Montgomery, IL

**HALL, MARIE NADIA**
[b.] July 11, 1995, Haiti Port; [p.] William Hall and Louise Borgelin; [ed.] Middle School Graduate and High School Student; [memb.] Florida Business Leader of America, Engineering Magnet, Student Council, and Vice President of Sophomore Board of Formal High School; [oth. writ.] Other personal poets that has not been published.; [pers.] I write poems referring to the environment around me, how young black brother and sister treats one another. I have written a couple of romantic poets.; [a.] Miami, FL

**HALL, DONALD J.**
[pen.] Coyote; [b.] September 5, 1950, Chicago, IL; [p.] Gerald and Elvira Hall; [m.] Linda S. Hall, May 6, 1972; [ch.] Ryan and Season Hail (two); [ed.] High School (A.A. Szagg), College (Moraine Valley, C.C.), Philosophy (Arch International); [occ.] Metal Refinisher, Professional Parent; [memb.] Arch International, N.K.J.U. Karate Association; [hon.] Blackbelt, Kyokushinkai Style; [pers.] Everyone should think on life, and be a philosopher on their life's meaning. My poetry is my philosophy, my wisdom - a gift given to me, thought. Maybe some day, I will get lucky - someone will notice.; [a.] Palos Hills, IL

**HAMILTON, ELIZABETH M.**
[b.] November 27, 1981, Boston; [p.] William and Jeanne Hamilton; [ed.] Blessed Sacrament School; [occ.] Intern H.M.S. Systems; [pers.] You never know what you can achieve till you take a chance. So why the hell not!; [a.] Walpole, MA

**HAMILTON, KRISTI**
[b.] October 26, 1967, Seattle, WA; [p.] Richard L. Rinker and Gwenlyn J. Benson; [m.] Douglas R. Hamilton, April 27, 1989; [ch.] Ryan Douglas, Tyler James; [ed.] Pendleton High School - Pendleton OR, Brigham Young University - Provo, UT; [occ.] Homemaker - I am also employed as a Substitute Teacher for Elementary Grades, Pendleton, OR; [memb.] I am currently serving as the Young Women's President in The Church of Jesus Christ of Latter-Day Saints; [hon.] National Honor Society, Citizenship Cup Winner (High School); [oth. writ.] I love to express my feelings and emotions through the medium of poetry writing. This is the first time something I have written has been published.; [pers.] I like to write about people and/or things I love and care about.; [a.] Pendleton, OR

**HANDFORD, NANCY IRIS**
[pen.] Nancy Iris Handford; [b.] Port Talbot, South Wales; [p.] John Handford, Anne Handford; [ch.] Allan J. Dingman, Nancy A. Dingman; [oth. writ.] Several poems published in local newspaper.; [a.] Bronson, FL

**HANDY, CARRIE LEA**
[pen.] Chero Wind; [b.] October 21, 1974, Romney, WV; [ed.] Hampshire High, Romney, WV; [pers.] I strive to reflect the feelings of the Cherokee and other native Americans that have been persecuted in the past and even to this day and age. And the people who need a voice and have none.; [a.] Paw Paw, WV

**HANSEN, STELLA**
[b.] July 10, 1953, Oakland, CA; [p.] Jack Kilpi, Elaine Kilpi; [m.] John C. Hansen, April 10, 1982; [ch.] John J. Hansen, Brian D. Hansen, Jennifer R. Hansen; [ed.] Petaluma High, Santa Rosa Junior College; [occ.] Housewife; [memb.] American D.diabetes Association; [hon.] Secretarial A.A. degree; [pers.] it is threw my own personal soul searching, in seeking the meaning and purpose in life, that I am drawn to writing. It is my wish to somehow make a difference.; [a.] Santa Rosa, CA

**HANSON, SHANE D.**
[b.] December 24, 1975, Merrill, WI; [p.] Jim Hanson, Linda Sparby; [ed.] Merrill Sr. High 1994; [pers.] Thank you.; [a.] Merrill, WI

**HANSON, RANDI**
[pen.] Randi Hanson; [b.] February 22, 1981, Grant, NE; [p.] Kent and Jo Ann Hanson; [ed.] Wheatland High School; [occ.] Student; [memb.] New Life Fellowship Church; [hon.] Lettered Two Years In Wheatland High School Marching Band; [pers.] In my writing I have tried to show what things look like from a teenagers point of view. I have also tried to make people understand things look different through our eyes.; [a.] Elsie, NE

**HAQUE, SYED M.**
[pen.] Anupam Haque; [b.] January 1, 1951, Bangladesh; [m.] Supti Haque; [ch.] Nausheen Haque, and Naureen Haque; [ed.] B.S. (Elect., Engg.), Dhaka, Bangladesh, M.S. (Comp. Science), City College, New York; [occ.] NYC Transit Authority; [memb.] Institute of Engineers, Dhaka, Bangladesh; [oth. writ.] Published 3 books in Bengali. Published several poems, short stories in local news papers.; [pers.] I love all the beauteous things. I seek and adore them.; [a.] Bronx, NY

**HARLING, REBECCA**
[b.] October 30, 1961, Memphis, TN; [p.] Mother Deceased; [m.] David Harling, February 28, 1987; [ch.] Adam Harling (6), Brian White (16); [ed.] Frasier High School - Memphis, TN, San Jacinto Jr. College - Houston, TX; [occ.] Senior Human Resource Generalist; [pers.] I was an orphan at the age of 2 and have had an extremely difficult life including losing a three-year old son. However, I am a firm believer in beating the odds and becoming successful and fulfilled.; [a.] Houston, TX

**HARRIS, LEE**
[b.] December 30, 1941, Bryan, TX; [m.] Lois Harris, August 14, 1964; [ch.] Mason Harris, (son 25 years old); [ed.] BA Journalism, CA State Los Angeles; [occ.] Electronic Editor, Los Angeles Times; [a.] Los Angeles, CA

**HARRIS, NEIKETA**
[b.] April 30, 1978, Atlanta, GA; [p.] Joyce Heard; [ed.] Southside High School; [occ.] Student; [memb.] Future Force, Student Government Association, Future Business Leaders of American, Band (Majorette), Barbizon Modeling Agency; [pers.] I write for inspiration that reflect on day to day experiences.; [a.] Atlanta, GA

**HARRIS, KIRK D.**
[b.] October 20, 1960, Benton Harbor, MI; [p.] Golden and Yvonne Harris; [m.] Arleen Harris, February 16, 1991; [ch.] Southwestern Michigan College; [ed.] Computer Systems Specialist; [pers.] I believe that nature and man's soul are in perfect harmony with each other. If you close attention to the wonders of nature, you can hear it talk to your soul.; [a.] La Puente, CA

**HARTER, WALTER FAY**
[b.] November 26, 1907, Newark, OH; [p.] Clarence and Lorena Lou Harter; [m.] Dawn Irene, September 15, 1930; [ch.] Dawn Adana and Richard Ellis; [ed.] High School, 2 Years Business College, 5 - ICS Courses; [occ.] Retired Accountant; [memb.] Free and Accepted Masons, Columbus Chippers, Mifflin Presbyterian Church, National Association of Woodearvers; [hon.] Scoutmaster Key; [oth. writ.] have written 25 other poems (not published) 5 short stories and 5 novel write (also not published).; [pers.] Have loved and read poetry ever since I started to read. Wrote nothing until after joining Se. Cit class last far on creative writing.

**HARTMAN, SHANNON DAVETTE**
[pen.] DaVette Jackson; [b.] Boise, ID; [p.] David M. Jackson and Renee Helen, Irene Abbott; [m.] Deceased; [ch.] Patrick and Shawna M. Stroup; [occ.] Singer, Writer, Supervisor, Ace Parking Management Inc.; [pers.] If we all touched the heart of one being a day, our soul would radiate enough light to rid the world of darkness.; [a.] Portland, OR

**HARTMANN, REVA**
[b.] May 10, 1959, PA; [pers.] Never regret things you've done, regret, only those things you didn't do.; [a.] New Port Richey, FL

**HARTNEY, ART HOWARD**
[pen.] Art Howard; [b.] June 25, 1955, Chicago; [m.] Valerie Powers Hartney; [oth. writ.] Three as yet unpublished novels co-authored with Valerie (a direct descendent of Pocahontas), entitled, The Hamburger God, Bend Down Moon, and Hard, powerfully dramatic work of dark humored fiction realism. What they're saying about these novels: "Brilliant. When I finished I felt less alone." "Enthralled. I couldn't put it down." "Definitely not for the shy or timid thinker." "It's raw!; [a.] Novato, CA

**HARTUNG, ADELAIDE**
[b.] April 13, 1941, NJ; [ed.] BA and ED; [occ.] Mom, Reliever and Social Force; [pers.] When I write I am usually driven by an idea - words will just flow either influenced by what I feel or view. I never develop or search for an idea.; [a.] Philadelphia, PA

**HARTZ, JENNIFER LEAH**
[b.] April 30, 1981, Port Townsend, WA; [p.] Harold William Hartz, Nancy Leah Hartz; [ed.] Currently enrolled in Chimacum High School; [occ.] Freshman Student; [memb.] Port Townsend Church of Christ; [hon.] Miss American Co-ed Pageant, numerous ribbons in Jefferson County Fair, Participant in Kiwanis Stars of Tomorrow Talent Show; [oth. writ.] I write short stories, songs, many poems and plays. I am now working on a book.; [pers.] Everything I write comes from the heart, and it wouldn't be there if God hadn't put it there. If my past was any different, I don't know if my life would be as happy as it is now. "Thanks" to God, Hannah, my friends and my parents.; [a.] Port Hadlock, WA

**HARVEY, KIM**
[b.] May 30, 1979, Greenville, MS; [p.] Gary Harvey and Ellen Harvey; [ed.] Pascagoula High, Greenville High, T.L. Weston; [memb.] Temple Baptist Church, High School Band; [hon.] Principal's List; [oth. writ.] Several poems not published.; [pers.] I write to go express my feelings. Experiences in my life have influenced me to write poetry.; [a.] Greenville, MS

**HARVEY, ALACIA**
[pen.] GT Ali; [b.] December 7, 1963, Guyana, SA; [p.] Michael Connell and Alexis Connell; [m.] Carlyle Harvey, September 5, 1992; [ch.] Tesfa, Michael, Makeda Ayana, Mandisa Eintou; [ed.] Eastern District High, New York City Technical College; [occ.] Parent Leadership Group Community School 21; [pers.] Give to the world, in God's name, the best you have and the best will come back to you.; [a.] Brooklyn, NY

**HATCH, ARTHUR S.**
[b.] April 6, 1920, Orange, MA; [p.] Mr. and Mrs. Chales Hatch; [m.] Virginia Anderson Hatch, July 3, 1940; [ch.] Jan Athur Hatch; [ed.] High School; [occ.] Retired; [oth. writ.] Poems and random thoughts.; [pers.] When thoughts come to my head, I like to put them in poems or saying, and hang them on the refrigerator for family and friends to reach.; [a.] Orange, MA

**HAUGEN, JEANNE MARIE**
[pen.] Re Hewson or Re Haugen; [b.] March 19, 1957, Baudette, MN; [p.] Harold T. and Grace K. Frazier; [m.] Kelly Haugen, October 8, 1983; [ch.] Kristina Marie; [ed.] High School Graduate, 1 Semester College, Eng. Comp. presently Enrolled with Ins. for Children Lit.; [occ.] Counter Help and Coffee House; [hon.] Achievement Award in Writing and Directing, Kennedy Sr., High 1975; [oth. writ.] Book (novel) "Dove in a window," two short Christmas stories accumulation of approx., 60 poems. All unpublished as yet.; [pers.] the written word has many stories to tell, but I believe the greatest story os one of hope and inspiration. My greatest satisfaction would be that hearts and souls of my readers.; [a.] Richfield, MN

**HAUPTMAN, MARJORIE L.**
[pen.] Marge Leahy; [b.] August 31, 1938, Jackson, TN; [m.] Jack Hauptman; [ch.] James, Laura, Jack, Skye, Tara And Kyle; [ed.] Syracuse University, candidate for M.A. in English at State University of New York at Stony Brook; [occ.] Presidents, Corporate Editions, Inc.; [memb.] National Writers Union, Westchester Fairfield Local; [hon.] Who's Who of America Women, 14th thru 19th (1984-1996) Editions; [oth. writ.] Currently, mostly business/newsletter writing, articles pub-

lished as staff writer for Rome (N.Y) Daily Sentinel and Westchester - Rockland Newspapers.; [pers.] Words - whether in newspapers, fiction,poetry or business - have a power and utility that amazes, their use demands responsibility.; [a.] Bellport, NY

**HAWK, GINGER**
[b.] February 16, 1957, Philadelphia, PA; [p.] Nellie and Albert Umfer; [m.] Peter Hawk, July 2, 1983; [ch.] William Merritt Jr.; [occ.] Office Manager, W. Baczek DDS Parksley VA; [pers.] To my sister Elaine Merritt thank you forever urging me to display my talent it took years but I am glad I finally listened your the best.; [a.] Parkley, VA

**HAWKS, SUSAN DIANE**
[b.] January 27, 1963, Wilmington, DE; [p.] Joy kidd; [ch.] Manuel (13), and Daniel (12); [oth. writ.] Many more waiting for others to read, one book in the works.; [pers.] As is with the man I love anything worth having is worth waiting for.; [a.] Euless, TX

**HAYES, WANDA DIANE**
[b.] May 31, 1953, Long View, TX; [p.] Lunnie and Ella Johnson; [m.] Vincent Hayes Jr., November 24, 1984; [ch.] Deonnah Nicole Hayes and Vincent Nathaniel Hayes; [ed.] Point Loma High School, Mesa College; [occ.] Principal Clerk, County of San Diego, Public Work Department; [memb.] Highland Park Church; [pers.] I am inspired by my never ending love for my friend and husband, Vincent Hayes Jr., and our two children Deonnah and Nathan Hayes.; [a.] San Diego, CA

**HEADLEY, PHILLIP**
[pen.] Phil; [b.] May 29, 1953, West Salem, IL; [p.] Bill and Dorothy Headley; [ed.] 12 years; [oth. writ.] The Gift, The Tomb of Jesus The Master, Unnatural Death, many, many others.; [pers.] It should be counted a blessedness for all of us to be loved by such a loving Heavenly Father. May we all strive to live for him.; [a.] Olney, IL

**HEANEY, MARY BRUST**
[b.] May 12, 1933, Philadelphia, PA; [p.] Raymond Brust, Mary Feely Brust; [m.] Joseph A. Heaney, June 25, 1955; [ch.] Joseph III, Kathleen, Steven M.D., Clare, Michael, Patrick; [ed.] B.A. Degree, M.D., Rosemont College, High School, School of the Holy Child, Sharon; [occ.] Freelance Writer; [memb.] Holy Child Alumnae Assoc. Rosemont College Alumnae Association National Alliance for the Mentally Ill, Irish American Club, St. Paul, MN; [oth. writ.] Essays and poems published in Wisconsin, Psychiatric Association Bulletin, Essays in Local Newspapers, Articles in Sports and Ski Magazines and Medical Journals; [pers.] I write to share all the joys, pains, insights, hilarity and tragedy of my life's experience.; [a.] Cumberland, WI

**HEARN, CHARLES V.**
[b.] September 4, 1930, Indiana; [p.] Forrest V., and Emma F. Hearn; [m.] 1st Divorced - 2nd Died, I'm a widower, 1st - 1953; [ch.] By 1st Married: Debra Lynn, Charles Gregory, Martin Curtis; [ed.] Fairmount High School (Indiana), Thomas A. Edison U. Ph.D. (72), University of Kentucky College of Medicine, Certified in Rational Behavior Therapy (78); [occ.] Behavioral Scientist in Pprivate Practice, and President of the American Ministerial Association; [memb.] Diplomate the American Board of Examiners in Psychotherapy. Fellow the American of Behavioral Science. Board of Examiners in Pastoral Counseling. Certified Specialist in Behavioral Science. Fellow the Meninger Foundation (Charter Member) International Council of Sex Education and Parenthood of, the American University, Washington D.C.; [hon.] Commendations: Los Ange-

les County Board of Supervisors. The City of Santa Monica, U.S. Army Korean War, Bronze Star (50-53); [oth. writ.] Many articles in various publications pertaining to Human Behavior and Psychotherapy.; [pers.] "The first step to being in control is, knowing when you are not." I'm not perfect, God isn't finished with me yet, He's in control.; [a.] Santa Monica, CA

**HEBERT, KEVIN**
[pen.] Kevin; [b.] June 23, 1961, New Iberia, LA; [p.] Daniel and Bernice Hebert; [m.] Ginger Hebert, July 14, 1990; [ch.] Katherine Hebert (girl); [ed.] 2 1/2 Years of College at North Western State University; [occ.] Sales Manager, Daily Advertiser; [oth. writ.] Short stories and other poems, but this is the first one I've ever entered for competition.; [pers.] There are far too many complainers in the world, so I make a conscious effort to be happy and to be genuinely nice to people. It seems to work just fine.; [a.] New Iberia, LA

**HEFFERNAN, DONNA MARIE**
[pen.] DM Heffernan; [b.] Brooklyn; [ed.] Fordham University, Our Lady Of Perpetual Help High School; [occ.] Graphic Artist; [memb.] National Audubon Society, and Claidheamh Soluis; [hon.] The New York Times Essay Scholarship; [oth. Writ.] "My Triumphant Return To Earth," (a collection of short STORIES), Sports Editor, The Observer.; [pers.] "Let us be like a China cups - with no hands to collect anything but ourselves..." Marie to Hugo, in "China Cups."; [a.] New York, NY

**HEIKEN, MARSHA**
[b.] December 23, 1946, Marshaltown, IA; [p.] All Goosey, and Virginia Haskell, Ora Haskell (Stepfather); [m.] Kent Heiken, November 6, 1965; [ch.] Kim Hejda, Ami Garman, Hayley Condran; [ed.] Washington High; [occ.] Motel Owner, Manager; [memb.] First Church of the Open Bible; [oth. writ.] A published poem in an Anthology Seasons to come receiving an editor choice award I have wrote many poems for years.; [pers.] My 9th cousin was Robert Frost and my Mother Maiden name was Frost. Also a distant cousin is Robert Burns. My aunt, my daughter and niece also write poems.; [a.] Cedar Rapids, IA

**HELSEL, ELIZABETH E.**
[b.] December 10, 1966, Pontiac, MI; [p.] Charles and Patricia Helsel; [occ.] Assistant Service Mgr., Anderson Honda, Bloomfield Hills, MI; [oth. writ.] Novel in progress as yet, untitled.; [pers.] All goals can be realized, all dreams achieved, through persistence, hard work and kindness to others.; [a.] Clarkston, MI

**HELTON, TERESA W.**
[b.] February 10, 1968, Tryon, NC; [p.] Joyce McEntyre, Floyd Wilhelm; [ch.] Ashley Nicole (July 11, 1985); [ed.] Tryon Elementary, Tryon, NC., Tryon High, Tryon, NC., Isothermal Community College Tryon and Columbus, NC; [occ.] Mother, Writer, Sales Person; [memb.] Moose Lodge; [hon.] Honorary Mention for poem. Published in "Great Poems of Our Time", published, but not sure of book title.; [oth. writ.] "I Lay Me Down To Rest", "Leave The Wind Crying", plus many others - unpublished.; [pers.] I write about my life, thoughts, feelings and emotions. As a mother, and daughter, I've learned to appreciate every aspect of life. We are not guaranteed another minute, so let the world and those you love know the real you.; [a.] Canyon Country, CA

**HENDER, SANDRA**
[b.] Febraury 2, 1952, Ridgway, PA; [p.] Pasquale Cancilla, Cancilla-Boardway (Deceased); [m.] Charles E. Hender III, December 19, 1981; [ch.] Currently sponsor child in the Philippines, 8 years old boy "Rene";

[ed.] Kenmore West Senior High Bryant and Stratton Business Inst.; [occ.] Analyst-Mercy Hospital Health Information/Records Department, Buffalo, NY; [memb.] Children International; [oth. writ.] A multitude of other poetry and prose unpublished just recently finished a non-fiction manuscript entitled "Inside Myself" also unpublished. I'm in the process of illustrating this book.; [pers.] My writings are based on true experiences, and deep heartfelt feelings, such as those that occur with the changing of the seasons. The autumn is the most incredible of all the seasons, and in my opinion, the most magnificent, is the beauty and wonder of nature that inspires me, and the love of God. He is the purest love of all. I tried to convey this in "Autumn Wind."; [a.] Buffalo, NY

**HENDERSON, PATRICIA A.**
[b.] January 26, 1949, Murfreesboro, TN; [p.] Lucille S. Allen, John T. Allen; [ed.] Central High School, Middle Tennessee State University; [occ.] Provide Social Work Services at Alvin C. York V.A.M.C.; [memb.] Mid Cumberland Council of Health Care Social Workers, A.H.N.A.; [hon.] Dean's List; [a.] Murfreesboro, TN

**HENDERSON, LONNA**
[b.] October 3, 1969, Houston, TX; [p.] Kay and Lonnie Henderson, Nick Salem (step-dad); [ed.] BFA from University of North Texas, also attended Texas Tech. University and attended The Royal College of Art in London; [occ.] Art Director at McKone Advertising; [memb.] 1. Dallas Society of Visual Communicators (DSVC), 2. Planet Funk Dancer (Cardio Funk, Hip Hop Dance); [hon.] In 1988 from Cy-Fair High School, 1. Scholarship from the Virginia Rinn Poe Artistic Achievement, 2. Scholarship in Dance from the Brigade Booster Club, 3. Gaddy Award for Best Overall Campaign, Television Spot, Radio and Print Ad from University of North Texas 1991, 4. Nominated Outstanding Portfolio in Art Direction from U of North Texas 1992; [pers.] To draw on my source of God to fulfill my true potential.; [a.] Dallas, TX

**HENDLER, LIN**
[pers.] "Happy the man, and happy he alone, he who call today his own: He who, secure within, can say: Tomorrow do thy worst, for I have lived today." Horace, "Life's prison bars maybe as beautiful as hope or as ugly as greed, but they will always hold you the same." Lin Hendler.; [a.] Los Angeles, CA

**HENDRIX, TRESSA ANN**
[b.] December 26, 1956, Beebe, AR; [p.] Anna Odean Griffen (Ellis); [m.] Edward R. Hendrix, June 4, 1984; [ch.] Randall (17), Edward Jr. (10), and Jessica (7); [ed.] 29 Sem. Hrs. Nursing, 50 Qh. Early Childhood Ed. Class; [occ.] Assistant Manager of Shoneys; [hon.] Exceptional performance awards for SY 1989/90, 1990/91 Academic Award; [oth. writ.] From Daze To Fear, Division of Hearts, A Sister's Love and Faded Dreams; [pers.] If you want something in life then it's worth waiting for.; [a.] Austin, AR

**HENK, LYNN E.**
[b.] March 25, 1945, Evanston, IL; [p.] Anne and Walter Seidel; [m.] Charles W. Henk, March 14, 1970; [ch.] I had one son (Roy), but he died; [ed.] Evanston Township High School, Evanston, IL, Parsons College, Fairfield, IA, Evanston Business College, Evanston, IL; [occ.] Clerk typist for Lions Club International, Oak Brook, IL; [memb.] International Society of Poets, Business and Professional Women's Club of Evanston; [hon.] Paul Harris Fellow from the Rotary Foundation of Rotary International, several Editor's Choice Awards for poems from the National Library of Poetry; [oth. writ.] "Love in America" in U.S. in Clover '76, "A Holly Wish" in our 20th Centuries Greatest Poems and

The Space Between, "It's In The Star" in The Coming of the Dawn, "To My Son Roy" in After The Storm, "Memories Of My Time Up At The Cottage" in Best Poems of 1995, and "A Sailor's Observation" in Mists of Enchantment.; [pers.] The poems that I write are a part of me and my life, and the lives of the people that are close to me.; [a.] Cicero, IL

**HENKEL, DONALD G.**
[pen.] Donald G. Henkel; [b.] December 5, 1930, Middlebranch, OH; [p.] Hilda Fry Henkel - Herbert Henkel; [ch.] Denise Barnhart, Mark B. Henkel, Donald B. Henkel; [ed.] Greentown High School, Greentown, Ohio, Journey-man Carpenter, Journey-man Machinist; [occ.] Architectual Brick Sales, Detroit, Michigan, Game Inventor; [memb.] Flat Rock First United Methodist Church Part of a Mission Team to Costa Rica; [oth. writ.] The Rules, Instruction and Description of games invented "Call Pitch Baseball" "Word List" Poems, "Sentimental Treasures," "Take Time," "Family," "Friendly Advice," "Promise to Ed Dolan"; [pers.] Live one day at a time and fill it with faith, hope and charity along with the Golden Rule.; [a.] Trenton, MI

**HERMANN, MERRILL**
[b.] August 7, 1937, Chicago, IL; [p.] Harvey and Lorraine Hermann; [m.] Marsha, July 11, 1959; [ed.] Northern Illinois University; [occ.] Retired; [hon.] Editor's Choice Award 1995; [pers.] I'm constantly amazed about what goes on around me and more specifically what I feel are the mysteries of life. I believe my poetry reflects that search for life's meaning.; [a.] Darien, IL

**HERNANDEZ, NADINE**
[b.] June 7, 1978, Downey, CA; [p.] Gamaliel Hernandez, and Carmen H.; [ed.] Home Studies; [occ.] Home studies; [oth. writ.] Various poems have been published in local magazines: "Little Dizzy Spells" an "The Circle."; [pers.] Strange... how can we think of nothing, and how the reasonless means of nothing can make you think.; [a.] Pomona, CA

**HERNANDEZ, CARLOS**
[pen.] Carlos De Hernandez; [b.] May 30, 1976, Chicago, IL; [p.] Maria and Joaquin Hernandez; [pers.] As a first generation Mexican - American I have experienced both the strength of a traditional loving family and the struggle of living in a harsh urban environment. My poetry is the part of me that I wish to share.; [a.] Chicago, IL

**HERNANDEZ, LINDA**
[b.] November 1, 1949, Santa Monica, CA; [p.] Vern and Virginia Maynard; [m.] David Hernandez, April 12 1986; [ch.] Tina Marie Nett; [ed.] Rolling Hills High School, San Diego Mesa College, Los Angeles Harbor College; [occ.] Writer, Secretary, Singer, Songwriter; [hon.] Best-Supporting Actress, Scripps Ranch Community Theater 1985-86, Director of Christian Education, Valley Community Church; [pers.] I strive to reflect love and encouragement through the written word. Love has to be shared in order for it to be love. Not to mention that I adore my sister!; [a.] Tujunga, CA

**HERNANDEZ, MARIE S.**
[pen.] Marie S. Hernandez; [b.] November 6, 1958, Longview, TX; [p.] Milton C. and Lovonig Owings; [ch.] Robert P. Martines II, Sarah Marie Martines, Michael S. Hendrie, Alexander S. Hernandez; [ed.] Complete High School 2 Yrs. College; [oth. Writ.] When Life Hands your a Blow, Yesina, my Prayer, STNG, The Wind Carries Our Hearts Desire, There Must Be a Way, Arsenio Hall, Billy the kid, Diamond, My First Love, Screen Plays: Aquilis, Satan Son; [pers.] If you restrict your dreams, you will restrict your

life.; [a.] Dallas, TX

**HERNDON, BILLIE G.**
[b.] January 15, 1931, Small Mining, WV; [m.] Lewis E. Herndon, February 24, 1948; [ch.] Patricia Ann Thompson Hodges, Grandson: Timothy Todd Thompson; [occ.] Retired Nurse, Husband is a retired DuPont Chemical Plant Operator; [hon.] Of all of my accomplishments, I am most proud of my daughter, Pat and my Grandson, Tim Thompson; [oth. writ.] Changing Season, When - Will I Stop Loving You? Someone cares.; [pers.] My poetry maybe attributed to my ancestry. My father was Irish and my mother was the daughter of a Cherokee Indian Princess. You can't mix these two without getting explosive results.; [a.] Belle, WV

**HERRICK, SCOTT**
[b.] August 28, 1976, Seaford, DE; [p.] Blaire and Gwendolyn Herrick; [ed.] Seaford High, Delaware Technical and Community College; [occ.] College Student; [pers.] Writing is my way of expressing my feelings towards life and the gifts that it gives to all.; [a.] Seaford, DE

**HERRING, LEE E.**
[pen.] A Gently Ames; [b.] February 18, 1921, LaFayette, CA; [p.] Lee and Ruby Herring; [m.] Helen Louise Herring, November 24, 1940; [ch.] Michelle Lee Herring (son), Suzanne Michelle Herring Macaully (daughter), Carrie Christine Macaully (granddaughter); [ed.] Graduated from High School - 1983 was Student Body President, my Senior year, plus 57 years in the School of Hard Knocks former owner of Tigard Automotive Supply Co. a NAPA Auto Parts Store; [occ.] Retired since 1980; [memb.] I have been a Mmember of Newberg Lodge 104 AF and AM Masonic - I joined the Lodge in 1947 and now a Life Member. In 1995 I donated a copy of my poems - some people can write poetry - some people can write rose to the Lodge and they have printed a new poem every two months in the lodge trestle board. I have been a member of the Junior Chamber of Commerce. And other membership over. The years in community projects, but after retirement. I have stopped, other than still trying to write. Bits and pieces of life down.; [hon.] Editors choice award from the National Library of Poetry - (1993) I have enjoyed the association with the National Society of Poets. Elizabeth Barnes had informed me for the last 4 years, that I have been. Nominated for membership in the society of poets. If my health and fiances ever improve, I hope to join the society, but I do enjoy still being able to submit. My poems to your programs and really appreciate having same of my work published; [oth. writ.] I have written a few stories, non published, I have written letters, over the years to Senator Mark Hatfield of Oregon and my own personal opinion to other Senator and Congressman over the years. Some day I hope to write an one man's opinion and several subjects, politics, abortion, religion, mankind, peace-world peace wars, my own opinion on the reporter writers like George Wills, Mike Royko, William Saffire, and people like Rush Limbaugh, Howard Stern, E. Gordon Liddy, New Grindwhich and such.; [pers.] Live and let live, we can dream of a world at peace. I believe someday, we must believe in ourselves and believe in each to protect our future. We should try to see the good in everybody we may meet each day. I likes to think of myself as a Franklin Delano Roosevelt. Middle of the Road Democrat Roosevelt was the First President, I ever voted, voted for, when I was 21 years old.; [a.] Newberg, OR

**HERRIOTT, GERARD**
[b.] April 26, 1954, McKeesport, PA; [p.] Gertrude Herriott, Gerard Herriott Sr.; [m.] La Verne Herriott, September 24, 1995; [ch.] Jose and Gerard III Herriott;

[ed.] Graduated from McKeesport High School and went to College and Cooking School did 3 years in Army; [occ.] Chef at Warm Daddy's! Owner of ZZB; [memb.] I.S.P Member City Wide Youtharama Board of Director's Member; [hon.] Award of merit from I.S.P award for poet of month in City News Paper! Tribune published news also published in moment papers. In time, in National Library of Poetry Book! West side weekly Newspaper Published in Milestone Magazine Greeting; [oth. writ.] Bookmarks, cards, pictures from size poems on 8 1/2 by 14 paper!; [pers.] I enjoy writing I attended the I.S.P convention, I don't think I got fair recognition! The poem I used was "Our Young Need Love"!; [a.] Philadelphia, PA

**HESSON, REBECCA SUE**
[pen.] Becky Hesson; [b.] June 7, 1979, San Diego, CA; [p.] Steven M. Hesson, and Karen A. Hesson; [ed.] Cox High School, 9th grade; [occ.] Student; [memb.] Girl Scouts of America; [pers.] My goal in life is to express, myself through my writings. I try to make it surge from my heart and soul.; [a.] Virginia, VA

**HETRICK, LAURIE**
[b.] June 23, 1963, Lawton, OK; [p.] Linda Habhegger and Bill Hetrick; [ch.] Cameron Joseph Hetrick; [ed.] Sparta High School, now attending WITH in Rice Lake, Wisc.; [occ.] Waitress; [hon.] My Biggest Honor is my Son; [oth. writ.] This poem is the first to be published.; [pers.] I believe that no matter how bad you think your life is. Good things can happen, if you let them. Thank you very much.; [a.] Rice Lake, WI

**HEWITT, CRAIG RICHARD**
[b.] March 31, 1970, Moline, IL; [p.] James Hewitt, Joyce Metcalf; [m.] Deborah Focazio, June 22, 1996 (to be); [ed.] Saguaro High School Scottdale, AZ, Arizona State University Tampa, AZ; [occ.] Promotional Director, ACC, Student, ASU; [hon.] Honors English, Excellence in Philosophy; [pers.] I believe our compassion is the principle to our humanity. By writing I wish to touch those true of heart. To evoke an emotion is to change the world. Dedicated in loving memory of August Claeys.; [a.] Scottsdale, AZ

**HICKMAN, CHRISTINE**
[pen.] Chris Conway; [b.] August 1, 1965, Rockville Center, NY; [p.] James F. Conway Jr. and Patricia Conway; [m.] Charles David Hickman, December 8, 1989; [ch.] Sarah Marie, Grace Anne, Jesse James, and John David; [ed.] Bishop Kelley High School Tulsa, O.K., Tulsa Junior College, Tulsa, OK; [occ.] Homemaker; [hon.] This is the first poem published; [oth. writ.] I have many other poems that have not been published. I hope not been published. I hope to have them published soon.; [pers.] Share a smile. It may make someone's day or even their life. I have been greatly influenced by Helen Stiener Rice. My favorite by he is "Pathways.".; [a.] Madison, MO

**HICKMAN, DAVID ERIC**
[b.] June 7, 1964, South Jersey; [p.] Bill and Regina Hickman; [ed.] High School Graduate; [occ.] Auto Body Man; [pers.] Don't let your thoughts escape you, share them with the masses and receive immortality in Black and White.; [a.] Mayslanding, NJ

**HICKMOND, JEROME**
[b.] November 17, 1951, New Brunswick, NJ; [ed.] Somerset High School, City College, San Diego; [occ.] Hospital Assistant; [pers.] Writing should be based on truth and reflect the human condition.; [a.] San Diego, CA

**HICKS, DEBORAH MARTINEZ**
[b.] November 5, 1961, Wilmington, DE; [p.] Esther Martinez Michelson, John Simpson Hicks; [ed.] B.A.

English and Psychology with honors, University of Rochester, M.A. and M.Ed., Teachers College, Columbia University, M.A. University of Santa Monica in Applied Psychology; [occ.] Educator/Counselor/Creative Artist/Writer; [memb.] 1. Movement of Spiritual Inner Awareness, 2. Institute for Individual and World Peace, 3. Educare Foundation; [hon.] Kappa Delta P - Education Honor Society, Graduated all Universities with Honors (Cumb Laude), Dean's List, University of Rochester and Columbia University; [oth. writ.] Journals of poetry (not yet published), original song-writer (with songs used in video and short films), writer and editor for University of Santa Monica Alumni Newsletter (1994-95); [pers.] All of my writings are the forms through which spirit speaks to me, teaches and guides me. My wish is that the spirit in the writing will touch the hearts of all who read it, to serve as a reminder that peace is always present - in our hearts.; [a.] Santa Monica, CA

**HIGHTOWER, MARY E.**
[b.] December 5, 1927, Glenno, VA; [p.] Eugene and Peachie Jones; [m.] John A. Hightower, January 7, 1975; [ch.] Five; [ed.] High School, Saluda, VA, Business School 1 - Glen High 45 Years Cashier Work Experience; [occ.] Retired, Former Seamstress and Craft Design; [hon.] Union Organization for better Wages - 1955, Recreation Advisory Council Society; [oth. writ.] Open letter to local newspaper published and nativity scene drawing published.; [pers.] I have always loved writing poetry, and short stories and drawing or painting pictures.; [a.] Philadelphia, PA

**HILDRETH, MERIDETH ALISON**
[b.] February 12, 1966, Lubbock, TX; [p.] Dr. C. Earl and Gene Malore Hildreth; [ed.] 1987 B.A. History Texas Tech University, M.A. University of Akron (1991) Urban Studies/Urban Planning; [occ.] Urban Planner; [memb.] Toastmasters International, Business and Professional Women, Vintage Dance Society, American Planning Association, American Farmland Trust, National Trust for Historic Preservation; [hon.] Steamboat Toastmasters President's Award (1994); [oth. writ.] Reflections: A collection of poems and memories (1994), not published.; [pers.] Experience is the essence of life.

**HILL, JOHN**
[pen.] Euclid (occasionally); [b.] February 5, 1972, Phoenix, AZ; [p.] Sharon Johnson and Larry Hill; [ed.] High School, Cedaredge High School; [occ.] Fishing; [memb.] Columbus Evangelical Free Church; [oth. writ.] Many others pomes on varying subject matter.; [pers.] My poems reflect the way I feel, and visualize life at the time of their writing. My inspiration stem from many different things: A colour, a world, a smell, or a feeling.; [a.] Grand Junction, CO

**HILL, MERRELL G.**
[b.] January 9, 1933, Lineville, AL; [p.] Marion F. (Deceased) and Onelda W. Hill; [m.] Ann Hill (Deceased), November 29, 1958; [ch.] (2 sons) Jeffrey Glenn Hill and Michael Lin Hill; [ed.] B.S., Elementary Education, Southeastern Oklahoma State University; [occ.] Retired U.S. Air Force, Supervisor of Inventory, Alabama Cooperative Extension Service, Auburn University, AL; [hon.] Air Force Meritorious Service Award; [pers.] I enjoy writing for the enjoyment of others. My poems are written for specific individuals, and their joy and excitement from receiving them is my reward.; [a.] Auburn, AL

**HILL, RONALD JEROME**
[pen.] Mann; [b.] August 31, 1970, Laurel, MS; [p.] Jaguline Hill and Ronald McNeil; [ed.] Provine H.S., Jackson State University, University of Southern, MS; [occ.] Self-employed; [hon.] Dean's List (JSU); [pers.]

Everybody has to try different things and meet different people in order to become a better person.; [a.] Hattiesburg, MS

**HINDS, KURT A.**
[b.] April 7, 1960, Rose; [p.] Don Hinds and Lily Hinds; [ed.] High School in Westchester; [occ.] Poet, Freelance Poet; [memb.] The National Library of Poetry, Minister of Prayer; [hon.] I recently attended the International Society of Entered my First Poetry Convention and Received, Plaque and had a lot of fun, I have written many poems in Churches that were Published; [oth. writ.] I wrote a soap commercial, and many poems about many things.; [pers.] Honesty is the best greatness policy, and greediness is worth nothing.; [a.] Bill Garden, CA

**HINES, WILLIAM**
[b.] May 23, 1962, Balston, Spa; [p.] William Hines, Ann Dewidis; [ch.] Jesse Lennon Charbonneau (15), Michael Anthony Hines (7); [ed.] Albany High School; [occ.] Clef; [pers.] As we approach Armageddon and holocaust I pray that man will find the good in himself that is there in all of us and fight against the evil that drives us to self-destruction. We are basically a good people. We are just easily mislead.; [a.] Troy, NY

**HINSHAW, MARY**
[b.] March 24, 1916, Winchester, IN; [p.] Roy and Effie Mosier; [m.] Cecil Hinshaw, December 9, 1972; [ch.] Franklin, Rodric, Paul; [ed.] Lincoln High; [occ.] Housewife; [memb.] Dunkirk Friends Church Central Early Meeting of Friends; [oth. writ.] I have written two small poems books one titled "Deep Soul Food" the other one "Golden Roots." I have read some poems in public, and sold a few poems books to friends. Another friend made the books for me. Mostly so I could keep them.; [pers.] I write sometimes as I receive different request, as one man wanted a poems about the flag. A bride wanted a poem about her new steps in married life. A girl a confirmation prayer for Church. I write by requests for occasions for the others.; [a.] Winchester, IN

**HINTON, LAWARREN**
[pen.] Speedy; [b.] June 9, 1978, Raleigh, NC; [p.] Judith C. Hinton; [ed.] Currently Junior in Clayton High School, Clayton, N.S.; [occ.] After School Job with my Uncle Micheal; [hon.] Sports Awards for Soccer and Baseball; [oth. writ.] High School Paper; [pers.] This is for my best friend in the world... Donald Lamont Armstrong. I see ya.; [a.] Raleigh, NC

**HOAG, FLOYD A.**
[b.] November 11, 1924, Port Huron, MI; [p.] Albert and Gladys Hoag; [m.] Betty Jane Bland (Deceased) April 19, 1944, Diana Lynn Losey, September September 19, 1981; [ch.] Valorie, Elizabeth and David; [ed.] I Attended Local Schools but Finished High School under the G.I. Bill. Also have Two Sem. at our Junior College; [occ.] I have work on many different Jobs, I retired from the I.S.D. Schools in 1990 where I had worked as a Janitor; [oth. writ.] I have three small poetry books printed locally to sell at art and craft shows and have copyrights on all of them. Almost ready for the third. You have printed two of my poems and I have an "Editors choice" award for both! At this time, I have written over 5,400 poems and I am still writing. At this time I am putting together about washington D.C.; [pers.] "Do as much as you can everyday be joyful and keep a song in your heart!"; [a.] Port Huron, MI

**HOBBS, IDA LILLIAN**
[pen.] Ida Lou; [b.] December 20, 1917, Owosso, MI; [p.] Etta and Elmer Johnson (Both Deceased); [m.] Walter E. Hobbs (Deceased 1989), April 17, 1942; [ed.] Lansing Eastern High School, B.A. Eastern Michi-

gan University, Michigan State University, University of Denver, Colorado State University, Greeley, University of Maryland; [occ.] Retired Teacher; [memb.] Life Member International Society of Poets, National Retired Teachers Association, Retired Senior Volunteer Persons, Life Member Alpha Delta Kappa, AARP; [hon.] High School Honor Roll, Quill and Scroll Society, College Newspaper Staff Reporter, Chairman-Editor of Spanish Handbook for Teachers, Alpha Delta Kappa International Honorary Sorority for Women Teachers, Delegate to ADK Convention, Vice-President, President, Chaplain, Historian, of ADK Theta Chapter Englewood-Denver, Colorado, The International Society of Poets, International Poet of Merit Award, 1994, The National Library of Poetry Editor's Choice Awards for Outstanding Achievement in Poetry, 1994, 1995, Cash Award for Winning in Top Ten, for entry at ISP Convention Contest, 1994, Recognized in "From The Poet's Corner", Lansing State Journal, 1995; [oth. writ.] Poems for Senior Citizens Newsletters, (Teen-Age Years, High School Paper, Easterner, and Lansing State Journal), National Library of Poetry Anthologies, Dark Side of the Moon, and Best Poems of 1995, The International Society of Poets Audio Tape, Expressions, and the National Library of Poetry Audio Tape, The Sound of Poetry, Entry in World's Largest Poem for Peace, "Hurrah for the 4th of July."; [pers.] I enjoy painting in all mediums and I like to "paint" in my poetry. I trust in the Lord, believing that things happen for a reason. I see things as they are and strive to think positive. Don't ever give up. You won't know if you can do something unless you try.; [a.] Holt, MI

**HODGES, JAMES**
[pen.] Eagle Swanson; [b.] May 8, 1975, Reidsville, NC; [p.] Donald and Rachel Hodges; [ed.] Graduated From Class of 1993 At Rockingham County Senior High; [occ.] Machine Operator; [memb.] Member of the International Society of Poets; [hon.] Two Editors Choice Awards in Poetry, The International Poet of Merit Award; [oth. writ.] "Blood" published in Echoes of Yesterday. "Stone Gathering" published in Best poems of 1995. "Everlasting Glisten" published in East of the Sunrise.; [pers.] Be true to your heart mountain will crumble river will part.; [a.] Reidsville, NC

**HOFFER, JESSICA**
[b.] August 25, 1980, Latrobe, PA; [p.] Terri Hoffer; [ed.] Donegal Elementary School - Now entering 10th grade at Mt. Pleasant Jr. High; [memb.] Mt. Pleasant Drama Club, Mt. Pleasant Swim Team, Mt. Pleasant Sr. High Yearbook, Mt. Pleasant Tower of Power Marching Band, Gamma Omega Society; [hon.] 1st Place - Pennsylvania Child Abuse Poem Contest, Presidential Academic Fitness Award; [oth. writ.] Poems in Mt. Pleasant Jr. High Yearbook, articles for the outlook.; [pers.] As a young writer I am still trying to form my identity. And the thought I remember is: Even a fool knows we cannot touch the stars, but the wise man knows on trying.; [a.] Donegal, PA

**HOFFMAN, WILLIAM DALE**
[b.] October 18, 1956, Colorado Springs, CO; [p.] Earl Hoffman, Barbara Hoffman; [m.] Pete Moreno, February 1, 1994; [ch.] Levi Hoffman; [ed.] Widefield HS, University of Colorado; [occ.] Network Analyst; [pers.] In a world where we are each fragile, we have to live with a full spirit and work to fully express our feelings.; [a.] San Leandro, CA

**HOFFMAN, JOAN**
[pen.] Joan Hoffman; [b.] November 24, 1933, Brazil, IN; [p.] William T. Coward and Mabel E. Coward; [m.] James W. Hoffman, January 26, 1957; [ch.] Bill, Sheryl (Deceased), Ben and Rebecca Joan; [ed.] High School Graduate, 1951; [occ.] Now Retired - from a Officework,

I'm now a "full-time" House Wife; [memb.] Active as a Member of Jehovah's Witnesses Faith; [hon.] Music awards (for voice) 1950 (3rd place) and 1951, (1st place); [oth. writ.] Have written a lot of poetry and some lyrics for songs.; [pers.] I've written and enjoyed reading and poetry since I was a teen. It seems what I feel inside, is best expressed on paper. I hope to pass on my feelings for others and life itself in this way (even in a small way).; [a.] Terre Haute, IN

**HOLDMAN, SHANNON SPANGLER**
[b.] August 13, 1970, Chattanooga, TN; [p.] Ernest and Sarah Spangler; [m.] Troy C. Holdman, August 9, 1991; [ch.] None now, praying for a lot, from our Lord; [ed.] High School, Tax School, Asst. Nursing Aid, Classes; [occ.] Asst. Nursings Aide; [memb.] I am a proud Member of Denny Hill Baptist Church in Harrison, TN; [oth. writ.] Two children's books not published. Alex and the bad secret And Alex learns about heaven. Also other poetry not published.; [pers.] Walk through life by faith not sight. Because what you see may make you loose your destiny.; [a.] Harrison, TN

**HOLLAND, PATRICIA ROSS**
[b.] July 26, 1956, Kings Mountain Hospital; [p.] Harold Edward Ross, Helen Barrett Ross; [m.] George Thomas Holland Jr., April 13, 1977; [ch.] Amanda J. Mitchem, Nathan Thomas Holland; [ed.] Bessemer City Jr. High; [occ.] Housewife/Creator; [memb.] Carson Memorial Baptist Church; [oth. writ.] My book, not yet published. Victory, eternally, and poetry a testimony of life.; [pers.] I yearn to reach a lost world with my testimony, my poetry, and with help from God, through the words of God! It's quite possible this book could become a movie. There's a miracle in the making.; [a.] Bessemer City, NC

**HOLLEY, AMY**
[b.] November 17, 1980, Panama City, FL; [p.] Richard and Ronda Holley; [ed.] I am presently attending a Crawford Mosley High School in Panama City, Florida, where I am in 9th grade, but when this poem was written, I attended Mowat Middle School in Lynn Haven, Florida at the present time, I plan to continue my Education by going to College and getting my degree in the Medical Field; [hon.] Recieved Laura Marien Award at Mowat Middle School; [a.] Lynn Haven, FL

**HOLMES, NANCY**
[b.] November 2, 1981, Nashville, TN; [p.] Roy Holmes and Bobbie Davis, David (step-father); [ed.] Watauga Elementary Greenbrier Middle, Currently 8th Grader; [occ.] Student, Greenbrier Middle School; [memb.] American Heart Association (through School) American Red Cross (through School) 5 years in 4-H 2 years in FCA; [hon.] David Deaton Karate School won a Bronze Metal for 2nd place sparring in 1993 am currently a Mascot for Greenbrier Middle School; [oth. writ.] Won 3rd place in a 100 word essay on "Why to Stay in School"; [pers.] I would like to thank Regina Holmes for inspiring this poem, and Mr. Steve Weaver for being a great poetry teacher.; [a.] Nashville, TN

**HOLMES, ELLEN**
[pen.] Ellen Holmes; [b.] June 5, 1925, Alater, MO; [p.] Clifford and Tillie Holmes; [m.] Deceased, August 14, 1949; [ch.] Richard Wiseman, James Wiseman, Bob Wiseman and Ronald Wiseman; [ed.] Slater High School, Missouri Valley College, Elementary Education Major, Current Retired; [occ.] Elementary Ed. Teacher and Floral Designer; [memb.] Fairlville Extension Club, Slater Garden Club, Federated Club, First Baptist Church, AARP, Marshall Monday Club, Sec - Marshall Senior Citizens Board, Vice Pres. AARP; [hon.] Program Chairperson for Study Club, Program Chairperson for A.A.R.P. Blue Ribbon Floral Designs,

Blue and Red Ribbons for dress designing; [oth. writ.] How to design a wreath, lets decorate or paint a shirt. Steps to a basic Floral design, make and design you wardrobe.; [pers.] If you think you can, you can. When one door closes another opens let your mistakes be pillows to success. Remember God Loves You.; [a.] Slater, MO

**HOLT, ROWENA**
[pen.] Rowena Bragdon Holt and Robert Endicott Bragdon; [b.] October 29, 1914, Merom, IN; [p.] Ralph Emerson Bragdon and Mayme Lowe; [m.] Louis Jewel Holt, January 4, 1936; [ch.] Fern Yvonne Holt, Bonnie Ruth McDonald and Julie McDonald (grandchild); [ed.] High School Correspondence Courses in Health and Interior Decorating, Music and Voice Lessons; [occ.] Retired Sec. now a Homemaker and Write Poetry; [memb.] First Christian Church Telephone 88 Class; [hon.] Charter life time member of ISP. Best Ppoems of 1995 National Library of Poets. Who's Who in Ppoetry - Our World's Favorite Poems by National Library of Poetry, Editor's Choice Award by National Library of Poetry Published in many Anthologies; [oth. writ.] Working on a poetry book.; [pers.] "A Merry Heart Doeth Good Like A Medicine." A disability can be used to help someone in need maybe a ministry in poetry.; [a.] Camden, AR

**HONN, MILLIE**
[pen.] Millie Honn; [b.] October 1, 1930, Ambia, TN; [p.] Maynard and Melissa DeWitt; [m.] Lloyd Honn, September 24, 1977; [ch.] Richard Whaley, Ridgley Whaley and Angela Hamptom DeMarr; [ed.] High School Graduate; [occ.] Funeral Home Attendant; [memb.] Crossroads Christian Church, Psi Sorority, Bell Choir, Soft Shoe Aerobics Class, Play Trombone in Community Band; [oth. writ.] I have written poems and short stories over 50 years. I have had some poems published in local newspapers. I sent alot of poems to friends on their birthdays.; [pers.] This particular poems was written for a friend who is terminally ill. Her son was not coming to visit her so, she asked me to write that she could sent to him. He is now visiting her.; [a.] West LaFayette, IN

**HOOPIIAINA, LANI**
[pen.] Lani Hoopiiaina; [b.] March 9, 1982, Modesto, CA; [p.] Judith Chism and Tom Hoopiiaina; [ed.] Elementary Junior High School; [occ.] Student, Poet, Story Writer; [hon.] Excellent Author Awards Upstanding Achievement Awards; [oth. writ.] Hundred of poems and short stories one book in progress.; [pers.] "It doesn't matter who wins because there is a winner in all of us."; [a.] Woodlake, CA

**HOPKINS, DANA JO**
[pen.] Dana Jo Hopkins; [b.] November 26, 1951, Myrtle Point, OR; [p.] Mr. and Mrs. Lester Bradshaw; [m.] Richard D. Hopkins, December 24, 1995; [ch.] Jeff, Lisa and Jason; [ed.] Eagle Point High School Eagle Point, Oregon; [occ.] Custodian at Southwestern Oregon Communication College, Coos Bay OR; [oth. writ.] "Cowgirls Don't Cry," published in "The Beacon," a literary magazine of Southwestern Oregon, Communication College. "Spelling" published in "Coos County R.S.V.P. volunteer" news letter.; [pers.] Life is a series of cycles, which contain positive and negative and negative events. I use pure innocent love to create a positive result.; [a.] Coquille, OR

**HOPPER, CHRIS FARLEY**
[pen.] Chris Farley; [b.] November 12, 1923, Harris, MO; [p.] Fern and Albert Farley; [m.] Deceased, June 23, 1945; [ed.] Trenton MO, High School, Long Beach State College (no degree) many (Writing and Language Course); [occ.] Realtor/Gift Shop; [memb.] Kauai

Historical Society, NPT-WAR Art Museum, Talents Organization County; [hon.] Citizen of Year, Salesman of Year, Awards from Hoag, Hospital Misc. Awards Citizen of Year Npt., Bch.; [oth. writ.] The day I became invisible.; [pers.] If I've lived to 72 through our past I can do anything. Don't give up, keep trying.; [a.] Corona Delmar, CA

**HORIGAN, JAMES P.**
[b.] July 5, 1966, Elmira, NY; [p.] J. Michael and Elizabeth Horigan; [m.] Lynne Horigan, April 29, 1995; [ed.] Corning College; [occ.] AT&T Product Specialist; [pers.] Living is the easiest thing to do, but life, is the hardest to achieve!; [a.] Omaha, NE

**HORROBIN, ROB**
[b.] October 13, 1978, Clinton, NJ; [p.] Bea Moser, R.G. Horrobin; [ed.] Attending Proctors Academy in Andover, NH, Starting Junior Year in September, 1995; [occ.] Student; [memb.] Guitar Player in Contemporary Style, Lacrosse Player, Football Player, Avid Skier (all of the above I will play competitively in '95-'96); [hon.] Highest C.P.A. for '94-'95, at Valley View School (9th-10th grades) and Elaine Grace Award for Achievement 1995-1996 School Year; [pers.] Every one has creativity, but some people have a friendship with it. These people are the makers of art, and the dreamers of dreams.; [a.] Hopewell, NJ

**HORTON, JOYCE JUANITA**
[pen.] Joyah Karstairs; [b.] August 19, 1943; [m.] Joseph Edward Horton, October 25, 1964; [ch.] Jeffrey Todd Horton and Michael Shannon Horton, Dog - Prince Charming; [ed.] Temple University Business School, Germantown High School, Roosevelt Jr. High School, Eleanor Coke Emlen School; [occ.] Loving wife and mother, writer of poems, articles and short stories. Worked for Internal Revenue until birth of first son; [memb.] 1994-1995, Member in Good Standing - the International Society of Poets, Saint James Church; [hon.] December 15, 1991, Merit Certificate from the World of Poetry. Poem "The World Around Me." Published best poems of 1995 volume 1, poem "No Definition." Editors choice award 1995 poem "No Definition," Semi-finalist 1995 North American Open Poetry Contest. Poem "Who's In The Mirror?" Also entered into final competition winter 1995/96, recited two poems on WMZQ Radio's talking Christmas card 12/94, and 6/95 recited poem "Lightning Bug Love" on WMZQ Radio; [oth. writ.] Article, "Bring Back The Good Old Days," on file with aim Magazine for future use.; [pers.] If the words from my pen that I impart can reach another's mind or touch a heart if I can bring to the face of man, woman or child the slightest resemblance of a smile the time I spend writing make my life worthwhile.; [a.] Leesburg, VA

**HOSCHOUER, PHILIP C.**
[b.] February 18, 1981, Union City, IN; [p.] Donald and Linda Hoschouer; [ed.] Completed Junior High at Mississinawa Valley; [occ.] Student; [hon.] Kim Gilbert Memorial Award, A-B Honor Roll, President's Education Award

**HOSKINS, N. THERESE**
[pen.] Therese Hoskins; [b.] May 14, 1952, Denver, CO; [p.] Daniel Hoskins, Norris Hoskins; [m.] Divorced; [ch.] Matthew James; [ed.] East High, Colorado Mountain College; [occ.] Bookkeeper; [hon.] Certificate of Merit Communications/Humanities Colorado Mtn College; [a.] Denver, CO

**HOUCHEN, LILLIAN**
[b.] Platte, SD; [p.] John and Lillian (Baer) Hugg; [m.] William E, June 10, 1961; [ed.] Studies include Art (Watercolor, Oil and China Painting), Writing and

Business; [occ.] Retired; [pers.] Having a lifelong interest in art, music, poetry and rockhounding, I find that there is never enough time to do all that one wants to do. My mother, a schoolteacher, wrote poetry for her pupils to recite. She inspired my own interest in writing.; [a.] Carson, CA

**HOUSER, BOBBY JOE**
[pen.] B. J. Houser; [b.] August 26, 1922, Paducah, KY; [p.] Robert and Lorena Houser; [m.] Madeline Brewer, December 23, 1949; [ch.] Kathryn Renee, Patricia Lee, Robert James; [ed.] B.A. in Science and Mathematics, Master's Degree in Adult and Supervision; [occ.] Retired Coordinator of Adult Education Polk Co. Fla; [memb.] (Former) Lions Club, City Environmental Board, Church of Christ, Lambda Chi Alpha, Latin Club; [oth. writ.] "Death on the Runaway," "The Assassin," "Tell Me, Spider," "The Rose," "Perplexity," "Mindtree"; [a.] Plant City, FL

**HOUSTON, MARGERY LEE**
[pen.] Mallory Houston, M. Lee Houston; [b.] December 1, 1950, Prince George, VA; [p.] Oscar Lee, Hortense Lee; [m.] Lawrence R. Houston, March 9, 1991; [ch.] Nedra Lee Mallory; [ed.] John Marshall High School, Virginia Union University, Richmond, Virginia; [occ.] Teacher - Whitcomb Model Elementary School, Richmond, VA; [memb.] John W. Barco Chapter Alumni Association, National Education Assoc./Virginia Education Assoc./Richmond Education Assoc., Richmond Tri City Mass Choir; [hon.] Dr. Dorothy Cowling Award, G.O. Chiles Scholarship; [oth. writ.] Several poems published in "The Good News Herald", a local newspaper.; [pers.] My writing seeks to inspire, praise, comfort or cheer the reader or recipient. People, life experiences and the concerns of society influence my writing.; [a.] Richmond, VA

**HOWARD, ZELMA LOUISE**
[pen.] Z. Louise Howard; [b.] January 9, 1935, Leadwood, MO; [p.] Sylvester and Jessie Watson; [m.] David A. Howard Sr.; [ch.] (4 children) Wanda, Patricia, Paul and Bill, (2 step children) Carla and David; [ed.] High School, some College, Licensed. Professional, retired auto Worker; [occ.] Part time beautician in Health Care Host for the aged; [memb.] UAW, Retiree; [hon.] It's a honor to be published in this fourth book from National Library of Poetry. My "Tribute to Auto Workers" was also published in UAW., Union Paper, also Editor's Choice Award; [oth. writ.] Tribute Auto Workers in River of Dreams. "Dear Mother" in Best Poems of 1995 also. This poem will be in. "A Delicate Balance."; [pers.] I strive to reflect the love, I have for my family, with. These words from my heart. That I may be remembered in the same way as I do. Those who are no longer with me.; [a.] Ballwin, MO

**HRONAS, NICOLE C.**
[b.] July 10, 1982; [p.] James Hronas and Maria Hronas; [ed.] Holly Avenue Elementary School, Richard Henry Dana Middle School; [hon.] Principal's Honor Roll; [pers.] Writing is just the mind on papers: The mind has no limits. I'd like to thank all my supporters.; [a.] Arcadia, CA

**HUBER, KATHERINE**
[pen.] Katherine Kroeger; [b.] March 20, 1914, New York; [p.] Dorothea and George Kroeger; [m.] Arthur Huber, January 16, 1949; [ch.] Susan Loralee; [ed.] High School Graduate, Various Business Courses; [occ.] Retired; [memb.] "WELCA" Women of the Evangelical Lutheran Church in America Past Member "Friends of the Library" Treasurer, Mtvle, Garden Club Paramus N.J. Treasurer; [hon.] Girl Scout Award to Audubon Soc. 3 wk. Nature Training on Island off Maine; [oth. writ.] "A Halo For Poochie" (Short Humorous Story)

Lovable Mutt. All true happenings enjoyed by school children and adults, not published; [pers.] The most wasted day of all is that on which you have not laughed.

**HUDDLESTON, LISA DENEISE**
[b.] May 7, 1962, Glasgow, KY; [p.] Morris Guffey and Shirley Guffey; [m.] Ken Huddleston, November 16, 1977; [ch.] "Mandy" Huddleston, Carrie, Abbie Huddleston; [ed.] Monticello High School, Parkland Junior College; [occ.] Personal Business Coordinator; [hon.] Honorable Mention Oak Brig Contest 10-94; [oth. writ.] "I Hope You Smelled The Roses," "Milestone Road," "Jessie Malone," "Freedom Land."; [pers.] Writing is like life, you must live for the moment. We never knew what is around the corner, so we must live life to the fullest.; [a.] Monticello, IL

**HUDSON, ADRIENNE ANNETTE**
[b.] September 2, 1977, Tuscaloosa, OK; [p.] Leonard Hudson and Sherrie Hudson; [ed.] Gordo High School, Shelton State College; [occ.] Student; [memb.] Sand Springs United Methodist Church; [hon.] Mu Alpha Theta, Torch Invitation Scholarship (Bevill), Presidential Scholarship (Berill State), Academic Scholarship (Shelton State), Certificate of Achievement; [pers.] Everyone needs to escape from reality, need an answer to a problem, or definition to the emotions they feel. I used my poems as a way to put my feelings in perspective and a sort of silent shoulder to lean on. No one likes to feel alone and when I write, it's as if my pen is silent friend that knows exactly how I feel.; [a.] Gordo, AL

**HUDSON, RANDY**
[b.] July 26, 1952, Cleveland, OH; [ed.] J.F. Rhodes High, Florida Southern College; [memb.] Peachtree United Methodist Church, Stephens Ministry, Choir; [pers.] The love and inspiration for these words came from somewhere else. I was just being me and being real. Thanks for the gift.; [a.] Peachtree, GA

**HUDSON, RUTH STRONG**
[b.] July 3, 1910, Cleveland, OH; [p.] Gladys Mosher Strong, Herbert William Strong; [m.] Charles Lowell Hudson, September 29, 1937; [ch.] Judith, Charles Lowell Jr., Mary; [ed.] B.A. Vassor College, 1932-1935 M.A. Western Reserve (now case Western Reserve) University, 1947 Ph.D. at Western Reserve; [occ.] Retired School Teacher; [memb.] Numerous; [hon.] Belle Skinner Fellow of Vassar College, 1932-37, Phi Beta Kappa, George M. Ryland and James Kendrick Fellow, Vassor College, 1993-34; [oth. writ.] Three Magazine Articles, Co-author of the First Hundred Years hare away Brown School, 1876-1976, essay in Bourgeois, San Culottes and others Frenchmen, Wilfrid Laurier Press, 1981, the Minister from Frances Conrad Alexandre Gerard, 1729-90, Lutz Printing Publishing Co., 1994.; [a.] Bainbridge Township, OH

**HUDSPETH, BILLIE**
[b.] April 1, 1937, White Earth, MN; [m.] Bill Hudspeth; [ch.] 5 Grown and Successful Adult Children - Youngest Attending Columbia Law School; [ed.] Variety of College, Writing Courses, Workshops and Poetry Readings; [occ.] Flight Attendant, Northwest Airlines, Pt-Time Realtor; [pers.] Belief that simplicity and basics begin, create and complete our lives.; [a.] Kingston, WA

**HUELSENBECK, JOLENE**
[pen.] Jo; [b.] September 2, 1981, New Jersey; [p.] Robin Huelsenbeck-Sportell (Mother); [ed.] Currently attending the "Marine Academy of Science and Technology" (M.A.S.T.), I look in the New Jersey to get into this School you must very Hard Tests, Interviews, etc.; [memb.] Girl Scouts; [hon.] All throughout school I have been in "Above average" classes. These are classes for the Academic Gifted Students; [oth. writ.]

This is my first publishing and I'm only 13 years old. This is my first poem I ever submitted to any kind of contest, etc.; [pers.] "You only live once, so live your life to the fullest."; [a.] Freehold, NJ

**HUESMAN, MAXINE**
[pen.] Maxine E. Elliott; [b.] July 23, 1914, Independence, KS; [p.] Mr. and Mrs. Harry E. Elliott; [m.] Separated; [ch.] Manis Bell, Virginia Robison and Ralph Garland (two girls and one boy, all married); [ed.] 11th grade; [occ.] Retired; [memb.] Methodist Church in Independence, Kansas; [pers.] Grandma and grandpa keller come to Independence, Kansas in 1902, lived on truck farm mother, Olive Adline Keller met and married dad Harry Elliot at a small cement plant North of Independence called Le-Hunt they were both 24 when married, there were 3 girl, Maxime oldest, lucille 3 year younger and baby sister Fannie in 3 years. They are all deceased now only me left I ran a family restaurant for 10 years, then ended up as (nurse aid, taking care of old folks after they came home from hospital, I love old folks after Dad died in 1965, mother lived on her own in small town, she finally had to go in to a Nursing home for 10 years, as her mind got all mixed up. I went everyday and took her for rides and visited her every sunday and most of week days. That is where I got the idea to write this poem as I would fix and sacks of popcorn for mother and they all seen me to this for her and I ended up fixing 25-30 sacks for the other wheelchair patients as each sunday the all wheelchairs out in lobby and wait for me, and I could see the longing and hurt in their eyes for some one to visit them. Mother passed away in 1978, so that ended that in my nursing career I have seen so many lovely old folks, all just waiting for a visit.

**HUFMAN, MURIEL VIRGINIA**
[pen.] Muriel V. Stephens Hufman; [b.] June 17, 1956, Fairbanks, AK; [p.] Stewart C. "Steve" Stephens and Laura B. "Babe" Stephens; [m.] Joseph Dean Hufman, March 23, 1987; [ch.] Blake Edwards Vermeulen Hufman (12), Haley Allison Hufman (7,) Laurel Belle Hufman (2); [ed.] Austin E. Lathrop High School, University Of Alaska - Fairbanks, AK; [occ.] Mother/ Writer/Author Artist; [memb.] A member of God's eternal family - through Jesus Christ, Our Lord. John 3:16; [hon.] Granddaughter to Laura Belle Wright, Famous Eskimo Woman and Founder Laura Wright Parkas; [oth. writ.] Over 1,200 poems authored a book to be published the diary of a mother. An intimate walk with God - Book of Poetry/Personal poems illustrated and framed.; [pers.] All poetic material prayerful inspired and written from the tablet of my heart to yours. In gracious praise to my loving parents where their time and encouragement has been a blessing to me.; [a.] Anchorage, AK

**HUFNAGEL, AMY**
[b.] September 22, 1982, Magee Womens Hospital; [p.] Mr. and Mrs. Patrick Hufnagel; [ed.] Gastonville Elementary School, current 7th grade student at Madonna Catholic Middle School; [memb.] Tri M Honor Society; [hon.] Presidential Academic Fitness Award, Monvalley Lincoln Academic Award; Presidential Education Award; [a.] Eighty Four, PA

**HUGHES, JOSEPH G.**
[pen.] J.G. Hughes or Uriah; [b.] July 20, 1943, OH; [p.] Mr. and Mrs. M. K. Hughes; [ed.] 2 Years, Electrical Engineering, University of Dayton, Ohio; [occ.] Studio Electrical Lighting Technician; [memb.] S.A.G., A.F.T.R.A., I.A.T.S.E., (Locals 728); [oth. writ.] Poems; [pers.] I believe in peace, love and light, forever.; [a.] Los Angeles, CA

**HULON, CHARLESETTA**
[b.] El Paso, TX; [p.] James and Betty Hulon; [ed.] Southeastern High, Wayne County Community College; [occ.] City of Detroit; [memb.] WODCA, Police Community Relations Council; [hon.] Payroll Conversion Team Study, AFSCME, American Red Cross; [oth. writ.] Written poems for family and friends for special occasions.; [pers.] Having Christ in my life, has made me to be become a stronger individual. Without him I could not have accomplish my goals.; [a.] Detroit, MI

**HUNLEY, ELLIE**
[pen.] Ellen Hunley; [b.] December 1, 1965, Exeter, NH; [p.] Virginia Cowing and Carl Goodwin; [m.] James Hunley Jr., May 2, 1987 in HI; [ch.] James R. Hunley III, Carlton J. Hunley; [ed.] 3 Years College; [occ.] Housewife

**HUNT, DIXIE L.**
[b.] January 26, 1942, Kansas City, KS; [p.] Edward and Lois Reynolds; [m.] Marlon L. Hunt, February 14, 1985; [ch.] Dion Quinn, Connie O'Neil, Warren, Stone, Eric Stone, Cassandra Enoch and Brian Reynolds and 8 Grandchildren; [ed.] La Puente High Attended Chaffey Community College; [occ.] Homemaker; [memb.] Past PTA Board Member, Pat Boy Scout Committee Member, Past Fontana Karate Club Board Member and Past Literacy of America Volunteer; [hon.] Dean's List; [oth. writ.] None sent in for publishing before.; [pers.] This poem was a gift from the Lord.; [a.] Fontana, CA

**HUNT, KATHY**
[pen.] Kay Hunt; [b.] October 3, 1951, Granbury, TX; [p.] Jimmie D. Lemens and Patricia Lemens; [m.] Scott Hunt, September 2, 1987; [ch.] Tiffany Hunt; [ed.] Carl Albert High School, Oscar Rose Jr. College; [occ.] Title Insurance Agent, Southwest Title and Trust Company; [pers.] The bombing of the Federal Building in Oklahoma City, April 19, 1995, justs 3 short blacks up at the street from our companies building - was the inspiration of many poems. This poem was for my co-workers.; [a.] Choctau, OK

**HUNTER, DARLENE DENISE**
[b.] November 26, 1956, Middletown; [p.] Ulysee and Anna Hunter; [ed.] Middletown High School, Miami University (Middletown), Southern Ohio College; [occ.] Home Health Care Provider; [memb.] Bethlehem Temple, Apostolic Missionary Outreach Committee; [pers.] I love children and enjoy teaching Sunday School (Ages 9-12 years). Morals and Christian values are very important to me. I take pleasure in reading spiritual poetry and children's novels.; [a.] Middletown, OH

**HUNTER, VIRGINIA L.**
[pen.] Virginia L. Hunter; [b.] April 24, 1918, Cleveland, OH; [p.] Catherine and Steven A. Grosse; [m.] Howard C. Hunter (Deceased), December 27, 1941; [ch.] Sandra-Lynn Hunter, (Deceased); [ed.] St. Mary's - West 30th. St. Cleveland, Ohio, Catholic School, Grammar and High School Graduate, some courses in Business Semester College Introduction to Psychology; [occ.] Homemaker (The Business World I worked in also 10 1/2 years in the Medical Office) of Ophthalmology Drs.; [hon.] I am very proud of my typing pins in High School (1933); [pers.] In the third grade - I had the lead role of being the old lady who lived in the shoe (being the mother - I loved doing the role.) I also said poetry in High School - I love the theatre the arts - good music - made many ceramic items - do my own landscaping - my yard is my carefree time.; [a.] Cleveland, OH

**HUNTLEY, TINA**
[pen.] Tina Huntley; [b.] May 10, 1960, Newton, KS; [p.] Lydia Owens; [ed.] Newton High, 3 Years College for Art and Computers Design; [occ.] Motorola Inc.,

Chandler, AZ; [memb.] Emergency Respond Team American Heart Association; [oth. writ.] Placed in local poetry contests, school newspapers, and published in local women's magazine.; [pers.] The poems I write come from within me. Through experiencing of life and guidance from above. I write what I feel.; [a.] Gilbert, AZ

**HURSH, ELLEN F. L. S.**
[b.] September 25, 1943, Mansfield, OH; [m.] Gerald Hursh, September 30, 1967; [ch.] Rob Sherry Pam, Skip Margaret "Chuckie," foster child; [hon.] Poems Publish in Two Pther Books; [oth. writ.] "Forever and Always," "Desert Sheild Son"; [pers.] As stated this was written and dedicated to our foster son, "Chuckie" who is now 6. Thanks to Children Services of Richland county for him.; [a.] Mansfield, OH

**HUSTED III, GLENN LELAND**
[b.] June 13, 1960, New London, CT; [p.] Glenn L. Husted Jr. and Hazel Y. Husted; [m.] Lynn R. Husted, July 26, 1980; [ch.] Amanda Anne, Travis Leland; [ed.] Ledyard High; [occ.] Senior Armor Instructor; [memb.] Hattiesburg Kriegspieler, National Rifle Association; [hon.] 26 Military Decorations, U.S. Army Mastergunner Graduation; [pers.] This poem was written aboard a troop ship during the exodus from Somalia in March, 1994. "If any many have an ear, let him hear "Revelations 13:9.; [a.] Sumrall, MS

**HUTCHISON, RACHEL ANNE**
[pen.] Rachel Anne Hutchison; [b.] November 3, 1982, Shelby, OH; [p.] Mike and Donna Hutchison; [ed.] Richmond Elementary, Willard Jr. High School, Willard, Ohio 44890; [occ.] Student; [memb.] Willard Jr. High Band, Jr. High Majorette, Member of the Red Marauder Baton and Competition Corp. for 9 Years; [hon.] Several Artistic Blue Ribbons, Trophyiest Medals for Baton Twirling Competitions, Twirl's Yearly at A.Y.O.P. (America's Youth On Parade), held at Notre Dame University; [pers.] I try my best to write how I feel from my heart!; [a.] Willard, OH

**HYLER, KELLY**
[pen.] Susie Rae; [b.] December 13, 1956, Greenbrae, CA; [p.] Forrest and Comoretta Brandon; [m.] David Hyler, September 30, 1985; [ch.] Shanna Deanne, Dimen John; [ed.] Kingsburg High, Santa Rosa Junior College; [occ.] Property Manager, Santa Rose, California; [memb.] Humane Society, American Society for the Prevention of Cruelty to Animals, Christian Coalition Church, Assemblies of God Church North Shore Animal League; [oth. writ.] Never published until now, but I am currently working on 1 short story, 2 manuscripts and more poems.; [pers.] As a writer, I hope to help and inspire readers. To encourage, enlighten, and motivate. To try to embrace people's emotions and stimulate them to try to make a difference in today's world.; [a.] Santa Rosa, CA

**HYMEL, AMY ELIZABETH**
[b.] October 12, 1977, Thibodaux, LA; [p.] Bruce Hymel and Iris Hymel; [ed.] Thibodaux High School, Nichollos State University; [oth. writ.] Many other poems in a collection at home.; [pers.] I miss you, grandad.; [a.] Thibodaux, LA

**HYSONG, BARBARA S.**
[pen.] Barbara S. Rieth; [b.] August 22, 1941, Stanford, CT; [p.] Louise C. Caputo (Sestito) and Salvatore A. Sestito; [m.] Thurman L. Hysong, August 6, 1993; [ch.] Denise Lynne, Wayne Robert, Robyn Anne, Glenn Micheal; [ed.] Sarasota High High, Omega Real Estates School; [occ.] Self-employed, B&T Specialist-Wholesale; [memb.] Fellowship of Believers Church; [hon.] Honorable Mention in National Art Contest; [oth. writ.] Several poems published in local newspa-

pers.; [pers.] The heart of man is the core and balance of his existence. All issues begin and end there.; [a.] Sarasota, FL

**IBARBIA, EXPEDITO A.**
[b.] April 19, 1934, Philippines; [p.] Agaton Ibarbia, Petra Ibarbia; [m.] Rita Adolfo Ibarbia, December 20, 1958; [ch.] Linda Ibarbia, Maria Ifft, Joel Ibarbia, Ester Soria; [ed.] Washington State Univ., Univ. of Rhode Island, Univ. Philippines, (Ph.D., M.S., B.S.A.); [occ.] Agric. Biologist, Consulting Horticulturist; [memb.] American Society of Horticultural Science; [hon.] Phi Sigma Society, Society of the Sigma Xi, Alpha Zeta, Post-Doctoral Fellowship; [oth. writ.] Newspaper Columnist, Editorships of College and High School papers, Publications in Scientific Journals.; [pers.] Humanity is the eternal puzzle.; [a.] Salinas, CA

**IMIG, ALICE M.**
[pen.] Alice Marie Imig; [b.] December 31, 1914, Muskegon, MI; [p.] Hans J. Nielsen and Karen S. (Hamsen) Nielsen; [ch.] Janet M. Thuesen - Kroeger, Richard J. Thuesen (adopted); [ed.] Muskegon H.S. and Community College; [occ.] Retired (was co-owner of Bakery with 1st husband (a Danish Baker) also - a Real Estate sales person, a secretary, and a spanish and danish and literary tutor); [memb.] Active in Church Organizations, (Muskegon - local lodge, (Also Mich. State President) and a Past Presidential of Danish Sisterhood of America; [hon.] Church Award from Central Lutheran Church - Muskegon, Mich. and Literary Volunteer Certificates from - Muskegon, States of MI and IL; [oth. writ.] Other songs and poems and articles in church publications and articles in Muskegon, MI "Chronicle." Several articles in National "Danish Sisterhood News."; [pers.] With all 4 grandparents from Denmark, I'm a 3rd generation danish american very proud of and interested in my danish heritage. I read, write, and speak danish fluently and have tutored in Danish, Spanish, and English as a second language.; [a.] Joliet, IL

**INGALL, FRANCIS HERMAN BARCLAY**
[pen.] Francis Ingall; [b.] October 24, 1908, England; [p.] Francis Drew Ingall and Lillias Barclay Ingall; [m.] Margaret Ingall, November 22, 1957; [ch.] Francis Drew, Carola M. and Ivor CT Ingall (previous marriage); [ed.] Hurstpierpoint College UK, Royal Military College, Sandhurst UK, Military Staff College, Quetta, India, US Citizen Since 1968; [occ.] Writer/ Publisher Ret Military Officer, also Prof Actor Retired; [memb.] Actors Equity, SAG, AFTRA Cavalry and Guards Club, London, Indian Cavalry Officers Assn. UK, President R. British Legion CA, President the Queen's Club SF, Consul Genl. Emeritus, Pakistan; [hon.] Distinguished Service Order for Gallantry WWII Name sent to King Geo VI for gallantry WWII. Officer Order British Empire, for services to Pakistan, as Founder their "West Point" 1947 Knight Comd. Polonia Restituto (for services Polish Forces WWII), author/pub, Autobio, "The Last of the Bengal Lancers" 1989, also "Uncle Ham" children's stories and taped recordings, "Daniel in Lions Den etc.; [pers.] I was last British Officer to Comd my Regt, "6th Duke of Connaught's Own Lancers" when an Armored Regt vs the German Army, Italy WWII I had joined that Bengal Lancer Regt when they were horsed Cavalry 1930 in India.; [a.] Sonoma, CA

**INGRAHM, DANA**
[b.] September 23, 1961, Twentynine Palms; [p.] Ross and Jan Branch; [m.] Jack Ingrahm, September 9, 1985; [ch.] Curtis, Jessie, Ryan; [occ.] Housewife; [oth. writ.] Wrote and published book of poems titled (In Memory To All) also poem published in Tomorrow never knows.; [pers.] I try to take nothing for granted, I thank Gid everyday for my health, happiness and un-

conditional loving family and friends. Through my poetry I hope I give something back.; [a.] National City, CA

**IONESCU, MARINA**
[pen.] Maris; [b.] August 26, 1978, Tg-Jiu, Romania; [p.] Ernest and Marina; [occ.] High School Senior, preparing for College, for Piano Performance; [memb.] Member of National Honor Society,; [hon.] Honor Musician at New England Music Group, Scored 30 on ACT (34 in English), Honorable Mention in the Sarah Tarp of Writing Contest; [oth. writ.] Many other poems in English, French and Romanian.; [pers.] I believe in true colors (how colors influence perception), true love (reciprocated love), and someone up there (who's who over me).; [a.] East Lansing, MI

**ISENIA, ELVANELGA C.**
[b.] January 28, 1963, Curacao; [p.] Cesar, Cecilia Isenia; [ed.] BA in Economics, Boston Univ, MBA Simmons College; [occ.] Management Trainee; [oth. writ.] Poem published in a special edition dedicated to the 20th Anniversary of GSM - Simmons College in Boston; [a.] Brighten, MA

**ISIDRO, PAULINE ELIZABETH NAGAR**
[b.] March 12, 1984, Los Angeles, CA; [p.] Dr. Romeo L. Isidro, Mrs. Elizabeth N. Isidro; [ed.] Currently in 6th Grade at St. Bernardine of Siena School; [occ.] Student - 6th Grade; [hon.] Consistent First Honor Student at St. Bernardine of Siena School; [a.] Bell Canyon, CA

**ISOKE, JOIYA**
[b.] April 20, Seattle, WA; [ed.] Student of Creative Writing Philosophy and Psychology; [occ.] Writer - in Waiting and Student, Barber by Trade; [oth. writ.] Currently working on a book of poetry and prose titled "Desert Soul" which embodies my life experience in New Mexico.; [pers.] Writing is my way of expressing my soul. My goal is to be a voice for those souls whose voice has been stifled and unheard.; [a.] Albuquerque, NM

**JACKSON, EMILY M.**
[b.] October 13, 1979, CA; [p.] Judge Frank Y. and Joni Jackson; [ed.] I am a Junior at Bethel High School in Lancaster CA; [occ.] Student; [pers.] I love writing poetry and short stories. I would like to pursue a career in writing.; [a.] Lancaster, CA

**JACKSON, MARC**
[b.] March 14, 1974, Watseka, IL; [p.] Ed and Joanne Jackson; [ed.] Graduated from Benton Central High School in 1992; [occ.] Factory Worker at Schumacher's in Hoopeston, Illinois; [pers.] I strive to be the best in everything I do.; [a.] Williamsport, IN

**JACKSON, SUE**
[b.] October 27, 1949, Peoria, IL; [m.] Robert J. Jackson, September 11, 1982; [ch.] Pam, Debra, Kelly and Lisa Carrington; [oth. writ.] Several groups of poetry and prose, freelance articles for special interests; [pers.] My collections reflect a wide spectrum of personal observation and experience, from humorous to deeply spiritual.; [a.] Peoria, IL

**JACKSON, THOMAS H.**
[b.] April 11, 1980, Monterey, CA; [p.] Janie W. Montgomery and James H. Jackson; [ed.] 10th Grade; [occ.] Student, Cox High School, Virginia Beach, VA; [a.] Virginia Beach, VA

**JACKSON, VALERIE**
[b.] September 27, 1963, Lufkin, TX; [p.] Clara & McKinley Jackson; [ed.] Woodville High School,

Stephen F. Austin State University; [occ.] Elementary Teacher; [oth. writ.] Poems in book Golden Moments. My first book of poems, anticipating publication.; [pers.] I want the readers to feel what I write. My favorite poet is Maya Angelou.; [a.] Woodville, TX.

**JAGROSSE III, ALPHONSE**
[b.] February 12, 1968, New Haven, CT; [p.] Alphonse and Patricia Ann Jagrosse; [ed.] High School Diploma Graduated from Technical School; [hon.] Honors thru school graduation with honors; [oth. writ.] Outlines for plays, poems, some lyrics misc. all original unpublished; [pers.] I believe art, books, music are keys to the subconscious that can free and make us more aware of ourselves. What Impossibly? Questions a God.; [a.] West Haven, CT

**JAHN, SARAH V.**
[b.] March 11, 1981; [p.] Wayne and Wanda Jahn; [ed.] Currently attending Missouri School for the Blind; [occ.] Student; [memb.] Secretary/Treasurer of Student Council; [hon.] Honor Roll, Outstanding Cheerleader Award in 7th Grade; [pers.] Three years ago I was diagnosed with a brain tumor. It was removed, but I am now legally blind. I am a Freshman in High School. I sing, play piano, and love to read and write.; [a.] Saint Louis, MO

**JALBERT, KEITH A.**
[b.] October 20, 1974, Waterville, IA; [p.] Jacqueline and Gerard Jalbert; [ed.] Current Writing Major at University of Maine at Farmington; [occ.] College Student; [memb.] Save the Tiger project at Hornocker Research Institute, College Radio; [oth. writ.] Local newspaper; [pers.] Death is a door which we all must open. Do it with an open mind and a clear heart.; [a.] Lewiston, ME

**JAMES, CAROLINE M.**
[b.] February 26, 1942, Scranton, PA; [p.] Thaddeus and Caroline Migalski; [m.] Ronald D. James, May 28, 1966; [ch.] Allan R. James (28), Esther C. James (25); [ed.] Scranton Central High School, Antone's Costomology School; [occ.] Leave of Absence; [memb.] St. John Newmann RCIA Program; [pers.] Believe in a positive attitude. It helped me through my cancer therapy and my husband's cerebal hemorrhage all in one year 1994.; [a.] Lancaster, PA

**JAMES, JENNIFER**
[pen.] Jenny J.; [b.] April 1, 1974, Bronx; [p.] Fitz James, Dorreth James; [ch.] Jasmin Alejandra Rosales; [ed.] Uniondale High School, Nassau Community College; [occ.] Bank Teller; [memb.] Community of Concerned Adolescents, Newspaper Staff Writer, Latin American Club Member, and Multi-Cultural Club; [hon.] Principal's Achievement Award, Reading Award, English Award, Student Council Member, Honor Society Member, and Honor Roll; [per.] Anything is possible in life as long as you are determined it can happen. And through my writings my heart and soul is delivered throughout.; [a.] Uniondale, NY

**JANTZ, KIMBERLY**
[b.] February 23, 1979, Garden City, KS; [p.] Joanice and David Jantz; [ed.] Currently a Junior at Syracuse Junior/Senior High School; [oth. writ.] Many more poems, this is the first to be published; [pers.] My poems are from personal experiences or from my friends personal experiences. They mean a lot to me and to my friends. I hope that anyone who reads them feels the same.; [a.] Syracuse, KS

**JANVIER, CAROL I.**
[b.] October 15, 1961, Jamaica, WI; [p.] Phyllis Forbes and Gerald Forbes; [m.] Jacques Janvier, August 1,

1992; [ch.] Camille Burke, Jamilah Janvier and Jacques Janvier Jr.; [ed.] Dorchester High School, Quincy College; [pers.] This poem is dedicated to my husband Jacques Janvier. I am very proud to know that I am blessed with the ability to write and impress someone. I hope my writing will influenced others to write.; [a.] Randolph, MA

**JATKAR, SHRAYAS ARUN**
[b.] March 12, 1980, Goshen, NY; [p.] Shobha Jatkar, Arun Jatkar; [ed.] 10th Grade at Gateway Senior High School (95-96); [occ.] Tele-Marketer for the Pittsburgh-Post Gazette (newspaper); [memb.] Marching Band, Karate, Track and Field, Basketball, Science Club, Junior Volunteer at Forbes Regional Hospital, Volunteer - Monroeville Parks and Recreation Program - Basketball Asst. Coach, Camp Counselor - Music Camp; [hon.] Won many trophies in Karate Tournaments, Black Belt in Karate, Letterman for Track and Field (1995 season), Honors Band, Section Leader in Marching Band, Apprenticeship for International Studies, Won Medals in Chess Tournaments; [a.] Monroeville, PA

**JAVIER, MARIETTA ANTOINETTE**
[pen.] Moondance; [b.] August 23, 1979, Bulacan, Philippines; [p.] Antonio Javier, Africa Javier; [ed.] Fairfax High School; [occ.] Student; [memb.] Fairfax High Volleyball; [hon.] Certificates of Citizenship and Excellence from Fairfax U.S.; [oth. writ.] Poems to be published in Iliad Press Anthology; [pers.] My writings are souvenirs from experiences of watching the world from a distance. I believe in the gently of emotions brought out by solitude and maturity, and the art of the expression of them.; [a.] Los Angeles, CA

**JENKINS, ASHLET ANNETT**
[b.] September 26, 1985, Chevrolet, MD; [p.] James and Paterica Jenkins; [ed.] Fifth Grade; [occ.] Student; [hon.] Honor Roll Awards School Writing and Math Award; [oth. writ.] Short stories when have not been publish and other poems; [pers.] One should set the highest standards for themselves and work toward achieving it.; [a.] Fort Washing, MD

**JENKINS, CASEY MORINAGA**
[b.] December 13, 1984, Torrance, CA; [p.] Sue Morinaga and Don Jenkins; [ed.] Southwood Preschool, Seaside Elementary; [occ.] 5th Grade Student; [memb.] Girl Scouts; [hon.] GATE (Gifted and Talented Education) 1994-1995, 1st Place Science Award 1995, Literature Award 1991; [oth. writ.] The Pilgrim's First Christmas; [pers.] I wrote "I Am The Desert" to show that nature has it's own life. So let's keep it clean so it can live.; [a.] Torrance, CA

**JENNINGS, ALPHA HENRY**
[b.] June 21, 1914, Mapleton, KS; [p.] Logan and Gracie Jennings; [m.] Kathleen M. Jennings, June 6, 1953; [ch.] Lyndon, Jeannine and Carol; [occ.] Machinist for GM, Farmer; [memb.] He held the position of Priest in the Reorganized Church of Jesus Christ of Latter Day Saints; [pers.] My father passed away 1-25-95. He was loved and respected by all who knew him. He was always ready to help anyone, no matter what. He had true Christian Charity and always turned the other cheek.; [a.] Fort Scott, KS

**JENNINGS, CHARLOTTE J.**
[b.] August 29, 1969, Chicago, IL; [p.] Charlotte Chandler, Roy Chandler; [ch.] David Lee, Amber Marie, Amanda Lynn, Raymond William; [ed.] Wilmont High, Gateway Tech. College, University of Wisconsin Parkside; [occ.] Full Time Student, Volunteer VW, Parkside Volunteer Center; [pers.] I hope to touch the hearts of others through my writing.; [a.] Kenosha, WI

**JENSSEN, ELLEN C.**
[pen.] Ellen Clarke Jenssen; [b.] August 5, 1914, Arendal, Norway; [p.] Olga and Oscar B. Jenssen; [m.] 1st August 15, 1943, Divorced 1949, 2nd January 20, 1951, August 1969 Divorced; [ch.] Clarke A. Olsen (1st marriage), Tana E. Klugherz and Alice J. Klugherz; [ed.] G.C. High School 4 years, 1 year Pratt Inst., both in Brooklyn NY; [occ.] Painter - Fleischer, Studio - Now Retired; [memb.] I.A.T.S.E. Local 644, Greenpeace, Sierra, Irregular Church Goer; [oth. writ.] One poem "Village Voice," three short (Humor) pieces in "Saturday Review," one poem in "Look," poems in H.S. Paper Humor in Fleischer House Organ; [pers.] I am interested in the marvelous, sometimes grotesque, influence of nature of man and the reverse. My favorite poets are Whitman, Housman and Dickinson.; [a.] Great Barrington, MA

**JOHNSON, ARLENE J.**
[b.] July 5, 1939, Livingston, MT; [p.] Michael and Faye Ricci; [m.] Roger D. Johnson, September 12, 1958; [ch.] Steven, Rebecca, Eric; [memb.] Museum of the Rockies International Society of Poets; [hon.] Three Editors Choice Awards, The National Library of Poetry. Certificate of Acknowledgement as a Famous Poet for 1995, from Famous Poets Society; [oth. writ.] Several poems published in anthologies by the National Library of Poetry and Famous Poets Society. Funeral cards, book "Potpourri from the soul."; [a.] Bozeman, MT

**JOHNSON, BETTY J. GARNER**
[pen.] Abby Brown; [b.] April 18, 1945, Winston Salem, NC; [p.] Cordella Garner, Luther Jackson; [m.] George E. Johnson (Deceased), March 9, 1982; [ch.] Sean I. Garner, Artessa M. Garner; [ed.] Carver High School, Nurse Aide Training, Unity Secretary Training, Forsyth Tech. College; [occ.] House Keeper at Winston Salem State University; [oth. writ.] Looking in the Mirror, Married Man, The Shadow, The Bottom of the Barrell, Cry Silently, A Beautiful Ache, Pain, Little Mind, I'm Not Worthy of Your Love, The Greatest Artist etc.; [pers.] Even the lowest of people can come forth with genius work, if their is a will.; [a.] Winston Salem, NC

**JOHNSON, DALE**
[b.] January 4, 1948, Reading, PA; [p.] Clymer and Marion Johnson; [m.] Patricia F. Johnson, February 19, 1971; [ed.] BS Chem. Drexea University, MS Polymer Science, LeHigh University; [occ.] Development Manager, Elf Atochem North America; [memb.] American Chemical Society; [oth. writ.] Technical Papers; [pers.] My wonderful wife Patti has been my inspiration. All of my poems have been written to and for her.; [a.] Reading, PA

**JOHNSON, JOY**
[pen.] C.J.C.J.; [b.] May 23, 1955, Newark, NJ; [p.] Michael Cifelli, Marion Cifelli; [m.] Christopher B. Johnson, December 29, 1990; [ch.] Zachary Michael Johnson; [ed.] Upsala College - BA, Fairleigh Dickinson - M.A.I.; [occ.] Teacher of English as a Second Language, Basic Skills and G.E.D.; [hon.] Dean's List, Belinne Award for Community Service Awarded by Fairleigh Dickinson University; [oth. writ.] Poems on various topics; [pers.] I try to communicate the ideas of peace and brotherhood by focusing on human similarities and disregarding human differences.; [a.] Boonton Township, NJ

**JOHNSON, KIMBERLY ANN**
[pen.] Kimberly Ann Johnson; [b.] February 12, 1971, Nyack, NY; [p.] Robert and Sandra Johnson; [ed.] Nyack High School, Delhi College, St. Thomas Aquinas College; [occ.] Counselor - Volunteer counseling service New City, NY and Studio Eleven, Nyack, NY;

[memb.] Valley Cottage Fire Dept. Ladies Auxiliary, Volunteer Counseling Service; [hon.] Dean's List; [oth. writ.] My own private collection, perhaps one day to be seen; [pers.] If you give me the wings - I shall fly.; [a.] Valley Cottage, NY

**JOHNSON, MARCIA F.**
[b.] September 19, 1952, Tigrett, TN; [p.] Eugene Johnson, Frances E. Johnson; [ch.] Kenyona Johnson, Timothy W. Wilson Jr., LaShunda M. Wilson; [ed.] Dyersburg High School, Career Academy (for typing), Sinclair Community College; [occ.] Credit Research Specialist, Flagship Financial, Inc.; [memb.] Deliverance Temple Church; [hon.] Dean's List; [pers.] I am striving to be an inspiration to others, and to express my own emotions, feelings and ideas. Also for healing and growing, to become a stronger person and to strengthen my values.; [a.] Dayton, OH

**JOHNSON, MARY JANE**
[b.] February 1, 1918, Minneapolis, KS; [p.] Bernadina and George Palmer; [m.] Ed Johnson (Deceased); [ch.] Five children, eight grandchildren, one son missing 25 years; [ed.] B.A. Univ. of Mn. MacAlester College - St. Paul MN Mankato State College, Kindergarten - Elementary School and Special Ed. Teaching; [occ.] Senior Citizen Retired; [oth. writ.] "Book How to Own and Operate a Successful Preschool and Day Care Service" self published and have them at a publishers now but have not heard from them for 4 months; [pers.] If everyone would love one another - this world would be a better place.; [a.] Seattle, WA

**JOHNSON, MINDI A.**
[b.] December 25, 1975, CA; [p.] Janel Schultz; [ed.] High School Highland High School, Palmdale, CA; [oth. writ.] I love to express my feelings on paper I have lots of poems. But this will be my first one ever published.

**JOHNSON, PENNY**
[pen.] Penny Johnson; [b.] July 1, 1940, Danville, KY; [p.] Irene Sebastian and Buford Carr; [m.] William E. Johnson, July 15, 1958; [ch.] William E. Johnson Jr., Robert Anthony Johnson; [ed.] Graduate Famous Writer's School, Westport Conn., Graduate - Newspaper Institute of America, NY; [occ.] Free-lance Writer, Poet; [memb.] International Society of Poets - National Writer's Club - Kentucky Association Gifted Education - American Biography Institute - Deputy Governor - Peale Center Christian; [hon.] Honorary Doctor of Letters, London, England International Woman of the Year from International Biography Centre, Cambridge England, Most Admired Woman of the Decade - A.B.I.; [oth. writ.] Published poetry in several national and Worldwide Anthologies poems, "Everlasting Freedom," "Light in the Night," "The Symbol," "Surprise," "My Husband - My Sons."; [pers.] I am bi-lingual English is my first language - poetry is my second - people worldwide understand me when I speak my second language.; [a.] Lexington, KY

**JOHNSON, ROBERT E.**
[b.] May 12, 1926, Vermillion, SD; [p.] Ragna Whaples and Eric Johnson (Both deceased); [m.] Callie C. Johnson, July 6, 1971; [ch.] David K., Johnson, Ramona Johnson; [ed.] Sacramento CA High School, University of California, Berkeley, CA, M.A. Degree Finance, Certified Public Accountant; [occ.] Retired; [pers.] At present time writing a 3rd person novel on my many years of experience in motion picture industry as chief financial officer of major studio for 22 years. Giving detail of what went on behind the scene during contract negotiations.; [a.] South Lake Tahoe, CA

**JOHNSON, TERESA**
[b.] July 29, 1967, Franklin, IN; [p.] Bobby and Shirley Coley; [m.] Rick Johnson, August 29, 1987; [ch.] Christopher Joe and Jaimie Lee; [ed.] Greenwood Community High; [occ.] Manufacturing Technician Alpine Electronics; [memb.] Color Guard 1983-85; [hon.] Honor Roll 1979-1980, Volleyball State Champs in 1981; [oth. writ.] Poems published in local newspaper; [pers.] I want to personally thank you my friend Barb for helping me to believe in myself and for inspiring me to write again. Your friendship has meant so much.; [a.] Greenwood, IN

**JOHNSON, TRACY KAYE**
[b.] October 7, 1963, New Orleans, LA; [p.] Donna DeJaynes and Edward DeJaynes, Isaac Johnson; [m.] Wesley Lee Spahr; [ch.] Jessica Armstrong (11), Christian Spahr 20 months; [ed.] Associates Degree in Art, Carl Sandbury College; [occ.] Full time mother and aspiring writer; [hon.] Certificate of Recognition, Sandburg Scholars Graduate, Dean's List, 3rd Place in Pencil Drawing Contest; [oth. writ.] I am currently working on a novel, my life story. Also, we are planning on incorporating excerpts into the Sociology and Psychology books throughout the College Curriculum. My interview of poet in College Newspaper.; [pers.] I hope my personal experiences will enlightened others to reach for their dreams. Philosophically, I believe there is good in evil, and evil in good.; [a.] Wataga, IL

**JOHNSON JR., CARL L.**
[b.] March 26, 1961, New York, NY; [ed.] BA in English Queens College CUNY 1994, MA in English Queens College CUNY 1996; [hon.] Dean's List; [pers.] The written and possesses a trail the spoken word never can, it has a permanence and cannot be whisked away by a gust of word nor fall upon deaf ears.

**JOHNSTON, ROBERT R.**
[b.] March 6, 1926, Mount Vernon, IL; [p.] Edward and Jewel Johnston; [m.] Doris A. Johnston, September 27, 1935; [ch.] Linda Johnston Smith, Richard E. Johnston; [ed.] Dreber High School (Columbia, South Carolina), University of Illinois (Urbana), University of Miami (Florida), Washington University; [occ.] Geologist; [memb.] Tau Kappa Epsilon, American Association of Petroleum Geologists, Institute of Certified Record Managers; [hon.] American Association of Petroleum Geologists, 1988 Distinguished Service Award; [oth. writ.] Various poems and essays; [pers.] I preferentially compose around current events.; [a.] Pleasant Hill, CA

**JONES, IRIS**
[pen.] Iris Eileen Jones; [b.] May 8, 1933, Kenosha, WI; [p.] Ralph R. Wyman and Elva Tate Wyman; [m.] Glenn Harvey Jones, April 18, 1953; [ch.] Glenda Lynn, Glenora Jean, Jennifer, Lee, Jeffrey Alan, Benjamin Mark, Annette Elva; [ed.] Mary D. Bradford High School, Kenosha, WI, Community College Anchorage, AK, clerical skills training Anchorage, AK; [occ.] El Tovar Hotel Retail, Grand Canyon, AZ; [memb.] American Poetry Association, Poetry Academy Inc.; [hon.] Various awards for poems, songs and paintings and merit awards, medallion received, received medallion award from Milton Beryl at Poetry Academy at the Beverly Hills Hilton Hollywood; [oth. writ.] American Poetry Anthology, National Library of Poetry; [pers.] I continually strive to please God and bless those who read my poems or hear my songs. My greatest inspiration is the Lord!; [a.] Grand Canyon, AZ

**JONES, JACK E.**
[b.] July 11, 1929, Tulsa, OK; [p.] Harvey M. and Jewel J. Jones; [m.] Patricia S. Jones, December 21, 1955; [ch.] Candace, Cheryl, Jerry Lynn, Paul; [ed.] Central High School, Tulsa, Okla. - Oklahoma State,

Tulsa University - University of Dallas - (not a graduate); [occ.] Retired - Freight Industry; [memb.] Family Place Church Promise Keepers; [pers.] A happy Christian who loves his country and his fellowmen.; [a.] Irving, TX

## JONES, LISA L.

[pen.] LiSay; [b.] October 23, 1963, Richmond, VA; [p.] Donald and Ann Jones; [ed.] B.S. Bus. Education, Hampton Univ., Hampton, VA, Charles City Public Scholar and Bruton High, Williamsburg, VA; [occ.] Customer Service Administrator; [hon.] 1993 Mid - Atlantic Songwriting Contest - Finalist; [oth. writ.] I am songwriter as well as a poet and I write songs for other individuals as well as for myself.; [pers.] Because it seems that in this world we live in we are constantly reminded of all the "sad and negativity" that exists and surrounds us each day, I choose to write about uplifting and inspirational subjects hopefully providing words of encouragement.; [a.] New Carrollton, MD

## JONES, WINNIEFRED A.

[b.] February 12, 1938, New Orleans, LA; [p.] Rev. and Mrs. Lloyd J. Armour Sr.; [m.] Rev. Johnny Jones Jr., December 19, 1959; [ch.] Adriene, Valerie, Johnny and Christopher; [ed.] J.S. Clark High School, Dillard University, Bachelor of Science in Nursing, Emory Univ. - Master of Nursing; [occ.] Assistant Professor of Nursing; [memb.] National League for Nursing, Southern Nursing Research Society, Dillard Univ. Prof. Org. of Nurses, Sigma Gamma Rho Sorority, Academy of Medical - Surgical Nurses, Free Mission Baptist Church; [hon.] Sigma Theta Tau, International Nursing Honor Society, Alpha Kappa Mu Honor Society, One of the Great 100 Nurses for 1995 in Louisiana; [oth. writ.] (None for publication at this time - some are in progress); [pers.] The ability to communicate is necessary for the continued peaceful existence of mankind. I strive to use any of the talents that God has given me to serve others. This poem is my way of communication the need to recognize the need to recognize that all children are different and mature at different eyes.; [a.] New Orleans, LA

## JONES JR., JOSEPH TIMOTHY

[pen.] Timothy Jones; [b.] September 7, 1955, Atlanta, GA; [p.] Joseph T. Jones and Evelyn Freeman; [ch.] Joseph Lee Jones; [ed.] I graduated from South West High, attended Bruton Parker College for two years; [occ.] Horticulture Landscaping; [memb.] Mt. Vernon Baptist Church of Christ; [hon.] I have certifications that includes, communications, pastoral studies, theater appreciation, carpentry horticulture, and baking; [oth. writ.] I have been writing poems for twenty years, I am compiling them into a book for publication.; [pers.] I strive to be altruistic, because I love people. I want to serve them with what's lacking in the world today, and that's love. Love is the beginning, the middle and the end of everything in creation. I want to love like Christ did.; [a.] Atlanta, GA

## JORDAN, SHIRLEY A.

[b.] May 12, 1948, Los Angeles, CA; [p.] Eunice and Hanson Henry Sr.; [m.] Divorced; [ch.] Dawn Smith and Christina Jordan; [ed.] Fremont High School, Los Angeles City College; [occ.] Postal Clerk; [memb.] Bethany Community Church; [hon.] 2 Superiority Awards Forensic League, Drama and Chorus Awards; [oth. writ.] Published songwriter and gospel I wrote and co-produced a play "Good News?" Numerous poems and songs and skies for Church and school.; [pers.] I'd like to enlighten and inspire others with my writings. To God be the glory.; [a.] Los Angeles, CA

## JORDAN, TASANEE

[b.] October 11, 1982, Hollywood, FL; [p.] Everett and Jordan; [ed.] Junior High; [occ.] Student; [hon.] Honor Roll Science Award, Band, Art, Bible and Student Association; [pers.] Always be, best you can be in whatever you do.

## JOSLER, SCOTT

[b.] September 24, 1971, Lebanon, NH; [p.] William and Sally Josler; [ed.] Hartford High, Johnson State College, College for Lifelong Learning; [occ.] Tank Maintenance Manager for a Propane Company; [memb.] National Propane Gas Association; [oth. writ.] Various poems, song lyrics, and 2 novels in the works; [pers.] I write everything from a heart felt, personal perspective which hopefully will instill some sort of an emotion from the reader.; [a.] White River Junction, VT

## JUDKINS, RENEE MICHELLE

[b.] March 10, 1962, Detroit, MI; [p.] Marie Therese Zemke and Jerry B. Judkins; [m.] Divorced; [ch.] William Jason Thomas (12), Melanie Rose Mignon (2); [ed.] Associate Degree in Electronics Technology; [occ.] Nutritional Health and Weight Loss Consultant and Marketing Director; [memb.] Our Lady of Refuge Catholic Church, Boy Scouts of America (served four years as an adult leader), Supporters of Scamp, Supporter of Right to Life; [hon.] 1994 Top Sales Volume - 2nd Place, 1993 Sponsorama Winner - 6th place both awards from First Fitness International Inc. also, Qualified Marketing Director, November 20, 1993, also for FFI, Inc.; [oth. writ.] A compilation of poetry I've written over the past 20 years, all unpublished; [pers.] All of my poetry consists of feelings and emotions taken from within my heart and written on paper. When reading my poetry, the readers can feel my joy, my pain, my excitement, etc. and relate it to experiences in their own lives.; [a.] Keego Harbor, MI

## JUHASZ, STEVEN

[pen.] Steven Juhasz; [b.] February 22, 1946, Mezotur, Hungary; [p.] Paul and Elizabeth S. Zath Mary; [ed.] 11th Grade; [occ.] Utility/Camera Person F&F Productions.

## JUSTICE, JESSICA AUTUMN

[pen.] Poetic Justice and J. Autumn Justice; [b.] October 7, 1978, Fort Wayne, IN; [p.] Joseph Justice and Judy Spieth-Justice; [ed.] Leo High School; [memb.] National Honors Society, SADD, Leo Drama Club, In The Wings Club; [pers.] I'd like to recognize these enigmatic teenage years for the inspiration and courage to verbalize my emotions. As for my generation and those to come, we will strive to remember and cherish Martin Luther King Jr., Hiroshema, the '60's, Kurt David Cobain, my so called life, both Woodstocks, Summers at LJCA, nights at Azar's, and the Brady Bunch.; [a.] Grabill, IN

## JUTTE, TAMMI

[b.] May 17, 1972, Spring, TX; [p.] Jan M. Jutte; [ed.] Tumwater High School, Pierce College, Multnomah Bible College, Central Washington University; [occ.] Commercial Fishing, Receptionist; [memb.] Gold's Gym, United Way; [oth. writ.] Poem published in "Echoes from the Silence"; [pers.] Strive to be the best you can be, for your happiness comes from within.; [a.] Olympia, WA

## KANG, CHUN HO

[pen.] Chun; [b.] June 30, 1938, Korea; [p.] Kum Yung Kang, Joung Sook Lee; [m.] Joung Ja Kang, March 15, 1969; [ch.] Michael S. Kang, Steven S. Kang; [ed.] Seoul National University (BA Physics), Cal. State University of L.A. (Graduate School); [occ.] Test - Technician "A" (S Calif. Edison CO.); [oth. writ.]

Several poems and articles have been published in local newspaper and "Modern Praxis."; [pers.] I constantly think and try to get in Touch with the Aspects of Human pain and suffering.; [a.] Los Angeles, CA

## KARAPETYAN, ANGELA

[b.] February 23, 1981, Armenia; [p.] Sirvard and Oganes Karapetyan; [ed.] 9th Grade in Hoover High School; [hon.] I Achievement Awards 2 Cope 4 Life Awards, Doggers Diamond Geography, 2 Awards from We Care... for Youth, Dare, a Top Raisin Readers Award; [oth. writ.] Several poems published in school newspaper.; [a.] Glendale, CA

## KARIDES, DOLORES

[b.] February 2, 1927, Brookfield, IL; [p.] Norma and Louis Klikas; [m.] Nicholas Karides, June 8, 1947; [ch.] Constance Stuckey, Louis Nicholas Karides; [ed.] Private and Public School in Brookfield, Illinois and Chicago, Illinois, English Major at Sinclair College, Dayton, Ohio; [occ.] None—Hobby: Writing; [memb.] Member of Greek Orthodox Christian Church, Past Officer of Philoptochos Society, Former President of the American Field Service for Fairmont High School, Kettering, Ohio, Former PTA President, Member of Arthritis Foundation; [hon.] Selected to Receive Awards in New York and in California with TV Spot Reading my Poetry, but declared due to Disabling Arthritis; [oth. writ.] Wrote a weekly Column for the Kettering-Oakwood Newspaper in Kettering, Ohio for 2 years, and have had many Anthologies, Religious and Fraternal Organizations; [pers.] If I can give some small measure of comfort and happiness to other, some words of inspiration to help build strength and hope, then my life will not have been in vain. The enrichment of someone else's life makes my own worthwhile.; [a.] Springboro, OH

## KATZ, DANIEL P.

[pen.] Marge Simpson; [b.] December 1966, Mount Vernon, NY; [p.] Wonderful people; [ch.] Belmont; [ed.] Either too much or not enough — I'm not sure yet; [occ.] President of Computer Software Firm; [memb.] Avoid them — although I belong to a Gym; [hon.] Hon. Mention Short Story Contest and Jack Nicklaus Golf Hole Design Contest, Runner up in Club Championship (4 and 3 after 36 holes); [oth. writ.] Many, but few ever read.; [pers.] I write when inspired. Unfortunately, inspiration often comes during the worst times in your life. I wrote this poem for one and rededicate it to two, PJH and DMK, ILUBAAW.; [a.] Philadelphia, PA

## KAYS, ROGER B.

[b.] March 16, 1947, Akron, OH; [m.] July 19, 1969; [ch.] Greg (21), Brian (17); [ed.] B.S. Political Science, Univ. of Calif, Davis, 1969, M.A. Management, Univ of Redlands, Redlands, CA 1987; [occ.] Transportation Systems Consultant, Trans Systems Operations Mgr.; [memb.] National Defense Transportation Association, Association of the U.S. Army, The Retired Officer Association, Delta Nu Alpha Transportation Fraternity, Calif. Public Parking Assoc., National Parking Assoc., Institutional and Municipal Parking Congress, VFW, Amer. Legion; [hon.] Poem "Suppose" read at dedication ceremony for Bronze Statue of 3 Soldiers and Vietnam War Memorial, Wash., D.C.; [oth. writ.] Several poems published in local newspapers, free publications and church bulletins and community information pamphlets.; [pers.] God's grace and love rescued me from a disaster and His inspiration has helped me write over fifty poems and songs in the past 11 months. I hope others find inspiration in my poem "Wings" and yet realize that God, as in all things, was the true inspiration and author—I merely held the pen.; [a.] La Habra, CA

**KEARNEY, TERRA LEIGH**
[pen.] Terraleigh; [b.] June 1, 1981, Goldsboro, NC; [p.] Debra S. Yates and Walter H. Kearney; [ed.] Nahunta Elementary School, Norwayne Middle School, I am a Freshman at Charles B. Aycock; [memb.] Beta Club; [hon.] 1st Place Wayne Collection; [oth. writ.] Friendship - Wayne Collection; [pers.] This poems is dedicated to my great Grandmother. She was a very special person and always will be remembered and loved in our hearts. Atha Edmundson loved her family as they loved her.; [a.] Pikeville, NC

**KEASTER, K.**
[b.] September 5, 1913, Miami, TX; [p.] Glenn Goffee and Rose English; [m.] Floyd Keaster, November 13, 1975; [ch.] Paul (Stannert), Rosemary (Melling), Suzanne (Felt), Lisa Teeper (deceased), Thaeve Lyons, James Stannert, Candace Harris all we Stannert; [ed.] High School, Amarillo, Texas; [occ.] Retired; [oth. writ.] I am going my memoirs under the title go Recollections and Reflections, I have a small booklet of poems called Incidents and Illusions.; [pers.] Goray but: The big discovery of my life is how powerful are truth and love just a pitch can go more than all the military and legal strengths in the whole world, truly...; [a.] Pedro Woolley, WA

**KEENE, FAYE**
[b.] July 12, 1918, Jackson, KY; [p.] James and Linnie Duff; [m.] Buford "Pete" Keene, December 25, 1936; [ch.] Judith Slack, Susan Timberlake; [ed.] High School Diploma; [occ.] Retired; [oth. writ.] Wrote weekly news column for Hartsville vidette newspaper for 2 years in Hartsville, TN, write interview column for Westminster windows (a monthly publication in Rock Hill, SC).; [pers.] I have written poetry since the age of 12. Am now a retired widow and find that my personal writings have been a wonderful way to vent my emotions.; [a.] Rock Hill, SC

**KEEWER, CHARLIE**
[pen.] LC; [b.] August 4, 1961, Shreveport, LA; [p.] Russel and Ethlene; [ch.] Joseph; [ed.] Ashland High School, Polk Community College; [occ.] Keener Fence Ashland OH; [oth. writ.] A book that needs to be published, called Words From A Heart.; [pers.] I write to speak my heart, to speak words very few know.; [a.] Ashland, OH

**KELLER, RACHEL LEE**
[b.] January 4, 1969, Long Beach, CA; [p.] Edward and Karen Keller; [ed.] Valley Christian High; [occ.] Full-time Student Part-time Bank Teller (Wells Fargo); [hon.] Dean's List, Ebell Scholarship, President's Scholarship; [oth. writ.] Poetry published in University publication "West Wind" Working on children's stories for Future Publication.; [pers.] The soul will heal faster when it unites with a pen and paper. (And it's cheaper than therapy!); [a.] Lakewood, CA

**KELLEY, KIM L.**
[b.] June 11, 1957, New York; [p.] Lee and Jody Kelly; [ed.] West Islys High School Graduate, Completed a 2 year Braille Course and Averaged an A; [memb.] Committee to Reach all Suffolk Handicapped, Past Member of the Suffolk Seagulls, participated in the National Games for the Cerebral Palsied; [hon.] Won a Scholarship at Graduation from the West Islip Teachers Association; [oth. writ.] Wrote, produced and directed two plays, in which I also performed.; [pers.] Remember, you have to keep God first. You can do nothing without him.; [a.] Brookhaven, NY

**KELLMAN, SIBYL M.**
[b.] November 19, 1927, Albany, NY; [p.] Mr. and Mrs. Marion William McEwan; [ch.] Donna Baumann,

Kathryn Diamond; [ed.] New Lebanon High School, Albany Business College, Institute of Children's Literature - Currently on Advanced Course; [occ.] Retired; [oth. writ.] Poetry published in various newspapers and magazine.; [pers.] It's all in the genes. Some of my ancestors in Scotland were bards or minstrels to the other clans.; [a.] Galway, NY

**KELLUM, ROBERT**
[pen.] Bobby; [b.] March 20, 1937, Thorpe, WV; [p.] James C. Sr. and Mary Ann Kellum; [ed.] City College, NYC B.A. Degree; [occ.] Mental Health, Admin.

**KELLY, ANTHONY**
[b.] December 23, 1957, Jamaica, WI; [p.] Trevor Vassell, Audrey Vassell; [m.] Drusilla Scott-Kelly, August 5, 1987; [ch.] Ashley Ann and Jillian Kelly; [ed.] Deer Park High School, Fashion Institute of Technology; [occ.] Photographer; [pers.] With my thoughts on paper when writing poems, I hope it will captive the reader's Imagination. I strive for success by harmonizing with one another, and bringing love to mankind.; [a.] Wyandanch, NY

**KELLY, JEFFRY T.**
[b.] June 3, 1963, WA; [ed.] Skogit Valley College, North Seattle Comm. College; [occ.] Nurse; [memb.] SPEBSQSA, Seattle Chapter; [hon.] Sound of America Tour-1982, All-State Choir-1982, 2 Scholarships; [oth. writ.] Won two poetry competitions in Elementary and High School.; [pers.] I write all types, poetry is a form of listening to yourself.; [a.] Seattle, WA

**KELLY, KAREN**
[b.] February 23, 1971, Brigeton, MA; [p.] John and Norma Kelly; [a.] Medford, MA

**KELLY, MARY E.**
[b.] November 18, 1926, Portland, OR; [p.] John and Mabel Eggink; [m.] Mark W. Kelly, April 3, 1946; [ch.] Mary Kathleen, John Michael, Ann Maureen; [ed.] BA in Education, Teaching Credential, Post-Grad. Work Toward M.A. (incomplete) San Jose St. Univ. San Jose, CA and Santa Clara Univ. Santa Clara CA; [occ.] Retired Teacher and Writer and Musician; [memb.] Pine Cone Performers, Pine Mt. Lake aviation Assoc.; [hon.] None that amount too much; [oth. writ.] Four self-published poetry books, short stories published in children's magazine, published articles on birds, guest editorials in local new papers, many poems, stories, articles yet to see publication.; [pers.] We must continue to grow as long as we live, full maturity is rarely realized until we die. History is our greatest teacher.; [a.] Groveland, CA

**KELLY, VERA**
[b.] May 12, 1924, Hawthorne, NJ; [p.] Catterina and Victor Siletti; [m.] Thomas; [ch.] John and Jessica kelly and Jacqueline Galka; [ed.] Hawthorne High School; [occ.] Housewife; [memb.] A.A.R.P.; [hon.] Poem "Ice and Snow" in Anthology Seasons to Come/Poem "The Old Three-Wheeler Bike" In Anthology After The Storm/ Poem "Apple Picking Country" In best poems of 1995. First and second prizes in Art - watercolor in Senior contest Passaic Country. Honorable mention in Pen and Ink in all ages Contest; [oth. writ.] Poem "Rummage Sale" in Hawthorne Press, Poems "A Lick and A Promise" and "I talk to the Plants" in Senior Bulletin.; [pers.] Receiving and honor is fun, fun, fun! In this world today, creative skills are alive and flourishing! Hi to all who jump in and Try!; [a.] Hawthorne, NJ

**KENNA, WALTER ANTHONY**
[b.] August 21, 1962, Frankfort, West Germany; [p.] Hendryk and Rita Kenna; [ed.] Associates of Arts,

Jacksonville FL 1986, Aviation Mmaintenance Technology, Riverside School of Aeronautics, 1993, Utica, NY; [occ.] Aircraft Powerplant and Airframe Mechanic; [memb.] American Legion, Marine Corps League, Shortwave Listeners Club; [hon.] Expert Rifleman (USMC) Student Achievement Award at Riverside School of Aeronautics; [pers.] Travel, you will grow in knowledge and perspective.; [a.] Saipan, MP

**KENNEDY, JIM**
[b.] May 28, 1981, Cincinnati, OH; [p.] Jim and Barlo Kennedy; [ed.] Summit Country Day, Middle School, Summit Country Day High School; [memb.] Boy Scouts of America; [oth. writ.] Others poems and stories in class. None of them have been published. She made reading and writing interesting to me.; [pers.] I owe everything that I ever wrote that was any good to Kay Ryan, Literature teacher.; [a.] Cincinnati, OH

**KENNEDY, MAYDRA JANE PENISSON**
[pen.] J.P. Kennedy; [b.] August 31, 1938, New Orleans, LA; [p.] Clare Elda Walter Penisson and Charles Christopher Penisson Jr.; [m.] Jacob L. Kennedy Jr., July 17, 1974; [ch.] Wendy Jane Kennedy; [ed.] The Public School System - McDonogh #26 Elementary School, Gretna High School and West Jefferson High School; [occ.] Housewife; [memb.] The International Society of Poets; [hon.] "Peaceful Reflections along the Mississippi" took third Place in 1991's Competition; [oth. writ.] Poems - Peaceful Reflections Along The Mississippi, A Martyr, Inspiration, True Friendship, Peace; [pers.] This poems, now on your own, was written to release my feelings and reassure my daughter of how I felt about the major decision she was making by leaving home and furthering he education in the university of her choice.; [a.] Gretna, LA

**KENT, MELISSA YARNELL**
[b.] February 16, 1953, Springfield, MO; [p.] Duane and Patsi Yarnell; [ch.] Gregory Travis; [hon.] Silver Poet Award; [oth. writ.] Several poems used for wedding and anniversary invitations. Many writings including poetry, essays and short stories.; [pers.] I write from the core of my soul. Whether it be about life and love or something humorous, I attempt to write that which will be felt by someone needing the piece.; [a.] Branson, MO

**KESSLER, ESPREE DEVORA**
[pen.] Espree Devora; [b.] March 2, 1979, Los Angeles, CA; [p.] Joseph Kessler, Hermine Hilton (Kessler); [ed.] Warner Elementary, Emerson Jr. High, University High; [occ.] High School Student; [memb.] California Polytechnic Journalism workshop; [hon.] 1. Principal's Award Elementary School Essay Contest, 2. Emerson Jr. High Graduation Speaker, 3. California Scholastic Press Association Award (High School); [oth. writ.] 1. Feature editor of High School newspaper "The Warrior," 2. Literary editor of Annual magazine "Indian", 3. Illustrator for parent, child book "Tongue ticklers for To Adults."; [pers.] "Life is philosophy. Without philosophy we would mentally die."; [a.] Los Angeles, CA

**KETCHUM, PIERCE STITH**
[ed.] Graduate from an University about 13-14 years after graduating from High School; [oth. writ.] Originator of a new form of writing named limnid (acronymic derivation), lists including (in progress) Life List of Pierce Stith Ketchum.; [pers.] There are three states pertaining to dependability in people. A person may be, in general dependable or belatedly dependable or undependable.

**KIENLE, ROSEMARY IDA**
[pen.] Roe Kienle; [b.] Piqua, OH; [p.] Pauline and Carl Kienle; [ch.] Matt Popham and Susan Wetherill; [ed.]

Miami University, BFA Wright State University, MAE; [occ.] Freelance Artist and Potter, Art Teacher, Secondary Ed.; [memb.] Western Ohio Christian Writers; [hon.] For Color Pencil Drawing and Fabric Design - Stenciling; [oth. writ.] Poetry Published in "Selah" the journal of the Western Ohio Christian Writers.; [a.] Piqua, OH

**KIENOSKI, VANESSA**
[b.] June 11, 1984, Hayward; [p.] John and Donna Kienoski; [ed.] 6th Grade of Elementary School; [hon.] Honor Roll at Treeview School; [oth. writ.] Some other poems that have not been seen by the Public but by teachers and friends.; [pers.] I love reading poems from other ages like B.C.'s and also love reading quotations. I hope every one likes my poems.; [a.] Hayward, CA

**KILGORE, DAWN M.**
[b.] December 28, 1966, North Carolina; [p.] John and Betty Van Arnum; [m.] Brian T. Kilgore, October 2, 1993; [ed.] Leto High School, St. Pete Junior College, University South Florida; [occ.] Student; [memb.] Christ our Redeemer Lutheran Church, International Society of Poets; [oth. writ.] Four other poems published in anthologies working on a novel.; [a.] Tampa, FL

**KILLEN, IRENE SHAW**
[b.] July 28, 1909, Boaz, AL; [p.] Franklin and Salina Rodgers Shaw; [m.] Rev. William Horace Killen, May 20, 1927; [ch.] 7 children, 11 grandchildren, 11 great grandchildren; [ed.] Greenhill, Alabama; [occ.] Substitute Teacher, Sales Clerk (Died January 2, 1994); [memb.] Held various offices within the United Methodist Women; [pers.] Dear wife and mother, her life was one of service and unselfish love to God and family and all who knew her.

**KILLINGBECK, JESSIE**
[pen.] Killy (sometimes); [b.] April 21, 1910, Walla Walla, WA; [p.] Ivy Steven, Austin G. Gilliland; [m.] Frank B. Rehdonf 1931 - Cecil D. Killingbeck, May 26, 1931; [ch.] Five, 4 sons, 1 daughter, Charles, Jessie Lee, Frank, Fredrick, William; [ed.] 1 yr. San Jose State College 3 yrs. College at the Redwoods Ant. English - Majors; [occ.] Retired (Artist); [memb.] Redwood Ant Assoc. Poetry Club, San Jose Ca. AR.R.P. Chap 1799 Luke Tahoe Presbyterian Church Tahoe Ant League; [hon.] Compliments Outstanding, Poems in Ideals Magazine; [oth. writ.] Essay, short stories on local papers Personal memories more unpublished poems.; [pers.] I enjoy writing my own experiences, also those of other people's experiences, and to share with friends family.; [a.] South Lake Tahoe, CA

**KILPATRICK, STEPHEN**
[b.] August 26, 1958, Dungannon, NI; [p.] James, Maureen Kilpatrick; [ch.] Elsa Teresa and Mary Kilpatrick; [ed.] St. Patrick's College Armagh, St. Patrick's Secondary Cookstown; [occ.] Maintenance Contractor; [memb.] Disabled American Vets, National Geographic World Wildlife Fund, Whale Watch; [oth. writ.] Poems published in Dungannon observer Tyrone Democrat, Ulster Herald. Poems published in "Northern Ireland Poets" - (Anthology).; [pers.] We praise and remember the ancient Architects of poetry but continuing to peruse their words through the centuries, poetry is the restless spirit of the mind.; [a.] Queens, NY

**KINDER, CARLA**
[b.] November 13, 1963, Stillwater, OK; [ch.] Travis and Zachary; [ed.] Perkins High School, Indian Meridian Tech. School; [occ.] Admin. Assistant; [hon.] Who's Who in Amer. H.S., Voice of Democracy Essay; [oth. writ.] This is my 1st.; [pers.] Always believe in yourself and never lose sight of your dreams, because you are the only one who make them come true.; [a.] Perkins, OK

**KINDER, THEODORA**
[pen.] Theodora Kinder; [b.] September 13, 1931, Los Angeles; [p.] Jack Kinder and Gisela Kinder; [m.] George Murray, December 21, 1957; [ch.] Rachel Karen Murray, David William Murray; [ed.] Los Angeles High School, George Washington University, UCLA University of California at Los Angeles, B.A. 1973 History and Art History; [occ.] Director Monticello Interiors Architectural Design - Real Estate; [memb.] Society of Architectural Historians National Trust for Historic Preservation American Cinematheque - Show Coalition Los Angeles Country Museum of Art; [hon.] Phi Alpha Theta, History Honor Society, under the name of Marilyn Kinder Murray Award Winner - All City Shakespeare Festival; [oth. writ.] I am working on an epistolary novel.; [pers.] I've always been charmed by nostalgia, drawn to the past. In my early 20's I joined the Diplomatic Foreign Service and went to Turkey (where I met my husband). Every day I become more in love with Thomas Jefferson and his ideas, than ever. I've been to Monticello 3 times and lived a week at the Univ. of VA.; [a.] Los Angeles, CA

**KINDSCHY, NICOLE**
[pen.] Shea; [b.] November 25, 1976, Bishop, CA; [p.] Lowell and Susan Kindschy; [ed.] Graduated from Hesperia High School, I am now going to Cal. State to get a Bachelors in Criminal Administration; [occ.] Assistant Manager at Long John Silvers; [oth. writ.] I have alot of poems which are not published which I would like to get published someday.; [pers.] I strive for my goals because my goals are all I have - one day I will reach these goals.; [a.] Apple Valley, CA

**KING, ANITA D.**
[b.] December 18, 1958, Jackson, TN; [p.] Manuel and Juanita Williamson; [m.] Donnie King, June 11, 1988; [ch.] Jeremy Spencer; [ed.] JCM High School, Lambuth University, LaSalle University; [occ.] Education Assistant, Entrepreneur; [hon.] Poetry Contest, Lambuth Univ. 1st and 2nd Prize plus Honorable Mention; [pers.] To enhance the African-American experience thru poetry that captures the mind.; [a.] Jackson, TN

**KING, DONNA S.**
[b.] August 27, 1957, Loran, OH; [p.] Hobert and Enda White; [ch.] Megan King, Bradly King; [ed.] Franklin High; [occ.] Secretary; [pers.] I dedicate my poems to (God) for he put the (Word's) in my heart, so other's could comprehend the pain and to an, attorney who was three for (me) though the hard time of my life. Three, feel me through the hardiest time of my life.; [a.] Franklin, OH

**KING, LISA**
[b.] July 21, 1969, Silver Spring, MD; [p.] Mary Mayhew, Robert Nichols; [m.] Michael King, November 11, 1991; [ch.] One on the way; [ed.] St Mary's High in Colorado, Mount St. Mary's College, University of MD in Baltimore Country; [occ.] Camp Director; [memb.] Sierra Club; [oth. writ.] Several articles published in College Newspaper, the Mountain Echo, of which I was features editor.; [pers.] The most important thing I've learned is respect of self and all other living things. I try to convey this any my writing.; [a.] Dearborn, MI

**KINKTON, RICK**
[b.] April 29, 1955, Louisville, KY; [p.] Gerald and Zelma Kinkton; [m.] Sharon Kinkton, October 1, 1994; [ed.] Trinity H.S., Eastern KY Univ., Richland College; [occ.] Manufacturing, Engineer; [oth. writ.] Several Songs written and copyrighted but not yet published.; [pers.] My leisure time is spent playing guitar and writing songs. My desire is to be a songwriter.; [a.] Garland, TX

**KIRKLAND, JANETTE**
[b.] October 19, 1934, Westover, TX; [p.] William and Maxine Campbell; [m.] Douglas E. Kirkland, March 18, 1955; [ch.] Mark, Kerry, Jeff, Annette and Stephen; [ed.] Eastern Oregon College of Ed. LaGrande, Oregon, David Lipscomb College Nashville, Tennessee; [occ.] Secretary and Clerical Statistician at Roseburg Forest Products Co. for the past 20 years, beginning 4-25-75; [pers.] I have always believed that Earth is a school where we come to learn life's lessons. Although we may all be in different grades, races, countries and religions - I feel we will all graduate with honors in time.; [a.] Glendale, OR

**KIRKLAND, TARABU BETSERAI**
[b.] November 17, 1949, Buffalo, NY; [p.] Mamie and Albert Kirkland; [m.] Nobuko Miyamoto, August 25, 1986; [ch.] Kamau Ayubbi; [ed.] BA. History - Canisius College Buffalo, NY, Bennen High School Buffalo, NY; [occ.] Playwright, Poet, Independent Consultant; [oth. writ.] Poems published in local poetry magazine. Griot Anthology, plays produced in Oakland, CA and Los Angeles.; [a.] Los Angeles, CA

**KIST, MARGARET**
[b.] September 16, 1942, Sault Ste. Marie, MI; [p.] Orval Heaton, Grace Tominac; [m.] Joseph X. Kist Sr., March 27, 1962; [ch.] Joseph X. Jr., Frank A. (deceased), Jenny G.; [ed.] To 1 yr. College; [occ.] Homemaker; [memb.] National Society of Tole and Decorative Painters, Cambria Co. Penn., Historical Society; [pers.] An appreciation of God, nature, family and everyday life, inspire my poetry. It's my way of saying thank you.; [a.] Woodhaven, MI

**KIVETT, KATHERINE RUTH**
[pen.] Katherine Ruth Kivett; [b.] September 25, 1949, Indianapolis, IN; [p.] Silas C. Kivett, Ruth S. Kivett; [m.] Divorced; [ch.] Erik David, Ingrid Elizabeth; [ed.] B.A. in Journalism U. of Minnesota, M.A. Counseling and Psychological Services, St. Mary's College, Mpls, MN; [occ.] Therapist; [memb.] Am. Assoc. of University Women, Kappa Kappa Gamma Member, National Assoc. of Investors Member, Institute of Poetic Sciences Founder, Woman Supporting Women in Business, Member, Junior League; [oth. writ.] Currently self - published a book of essays on self healing and transformation.; [pers.] I firmly believe that when we as individuals are physically, emotionally, intellectually and spiritually healthy we can personally transform our own life and help those around unimprove their lives.; [a.] Boulder, CO

**KLATZKE, STEPHEN**
[b.] September 8, 1966, New York, NY; [p.] A. Alan and Michaelle; [oth. writ.] My writings are meant to expose our universe. I want to give the reader a new perspective, seeing through the surface, looking deeply at the universe to perceive its truth. As we are bound to our planet hurling through space, we should realize that we will not be bound forever. The dynamic and limitless universe persists. The human race resists. Next....; [a.] San Diego, CA

**KLEIN, HEATHER**
[pen.] Heather Klein; [b.] December 28, 1982, San Francisco, CA; [p.] Deborah and Curtis Klein; [ed.] I'm a 6th Grader at Ophir School in Oroville, CA; [occ.] Student; [memb.] Oroville Youth Soccer, Girl Scouts and Oroville Gymnastics; [hon.] Honor Roll Student; [oth. writ.] A book written in 1994 called Nightmare Mountain, a book written in 1995 called Heather's story.; [pers.] I would like to give special thanks to my 5th grade teacher, Mr. John Vaugh, because he assigned a color poem to write. I would also like to give thanks to my parents who suggested that I enter my poem.; [a.]

Oroville, CA

## KLINE, FLORENCE E.
[ed.] A.B. Cum Laude, Cornell University, M.A. in Romance Studies Cornell University, C. Phil. in Romance Languages and Literatures, Univ. of California, Berkeley; [occ.] Translator of Foreign Languages; [memb.] Northern CA translator Assoc., Medieval Academy of America, Philological Assoc. of Pacific Coast, Medieval assoc of Pacific, Society Rencesvals, Modern Language Associations, American Symphony Orchestra League, National Flute Association, Assoc. of California Symphony Orchestras, Kensington Symphony Orchestra, Principal Flute and President, Board of Directors; [hon.] Ford Scholar's Fellowship, Alpha Lambda Delta and Alpha Mu Gamma (honor societies), Cornell Research Grant, Univ. of California Regents Grant, Prize for excellence in teaching at the University of California, Berkeley; [oth. writ.] I have translated numerous articles which have appeared in European Journals.; [a.] Berkeley, CA

## KLOTZ, FRIEDA D.
[b.] October 23, 1959, Fairbanks, AK; [ed.] Austin E. Lathrop High School, Fairbanks, AK, University of Alaska, Fairbanks, AK; [hon.] Cum Laude, University of Alaska, Fairbanks, AK; [oth. writ.] Other poems published in local West Michigan papers.; [pers.] To me, there is nothing more magnificent, more awe-inspiring than the natural wonders of creation and the human spirit. If by my talents, I have shared these treasures, touched your heart and rekindled your spirit, then I have succeeded in my goal.; [a.] Zeeland, MI

## KLUMP, FRANK A.
[pen.] C.D. Lee; [b.] Paterson, NJ; [p.] Frank B. Klump, Carmela "Millie" Klump; [m.] Lisa Klump, May 26, 1979; [ch.] Melissa Lynn, Frankie Andrew; [ed.] Clifton Senior High School, Rutgers University, William Paterson College, New Jersey Dental School; [occ.] Dental Insurance Executive Delta Dental Plan JN, Parsippany NJ; [memb.] Omicron Kappa Upsilon, New Jersey Dental Association. Academy of General Dentistry, American dental Association, American Association of Dental Consultants the Three Stooges Fan Club, The Andy Griffith Show Rerun Watchers Club; [hon.] Fellow in the Academy of General Dentistry, Former 10 years member of Mensa, Summa cum Laude graduate of William Paterson College, Wayne NY; [oth. writ.] None published. I have written poetry as ab gift to friends and family only.; [pers.] My writings reflect a side of me and my nature that is not normally evident in everyday life. The poetry that I create comes in all different forms and varieties an is influenced by any type of convention or popular trends.; [a.] Sparta, NJ

## KNAPP, PAUL E.
[p.] Donald Knapp, Janet Knapp; [ed.] Nova High, Ft. Lauderdale, FL, B.S., M.E., University of Florida; [occ.] Health Physicist, U.S. Nuclear Regulatory Commission; [memb.] Certified Health Physicist, American Academy of Health Physics; [hon.] Rotary International Group Study Exchange to India 16th World Scout Jamboree Staff 1988 Who's who in America; [oth. writ.] Poems, "4WD Poet" and "Ballet Boy" in the Southern Writer, novel-False Positive (Winston-Derek, 1991), essay - "Half-life and Eternal Life" in Beyond Dualism (Presbyterian Church, U.S.A.) and "Aaron" in the Southern Writer, lyrics "Hikers Prayer", Music 70 Publishers, arranged by R. Sowash 1995.; [pers.] Poetry is the inspiration that grows from life, and the yearning that transcends life.; [a.] Chattanooga, TN

## KNIGHT, MILDRED L.
[pen.] Millie Knight; [b.] July 10, 1935, Oklahoma; [p.] William and Ada Hines; [ch.] John Edwin, Linda

Sue, Cheryl Jean, Lori Lavonne; [ed.] Burroughs High; [occ.] Homemaker; [oth. writ.] I have written several poems to my children, Grandson Jason friends for weddings and funerals.; [pers.] This is my first publication I'm inspired by my love for my kids and I speak from the heart in poems.; [a.] RidgeCrest, CA

## KNIGHT, LILA C.
[b.] April 11, 1931, Chattanooga, TN; [p.] William H. and Anna Bonine Cucksee; [ch.] David, Jonathan, Paul, and Joel Knight and Sheryl Knight Carlock; [ed.] Rossville Public Schools, Rossville, GA, Edmondson Jr. College, Chattanooga, TN, Secretarial Diploma January 1951, Life Underwriters Training Council I, Chattanooga, TN, 1986, attended Univ. of GA; [occ.] Gwinnett Co. (GA) Public Schools - Special Ed. Bus Driver; [memb.] Nat'l. Ass'n. for Female Executives, Nat'l. Trust for Historic Preservation, Nat'l. Committee to Preserve Social Security and Medicare (NCPSSM), International Biographical Ass'n (IBA), American Ass'n of Retired Persons, Library of Congress, Amazing Grace Baptist Church; [hon.] Honorary Citizen of Boys Town, Professional Insurance Agent Award, Sales and Persistency Award, in Insurance, having my poems published by the National Library of Poetry, including, AARP - Chapter 4065, "A Friend," in River of Dreams, "How Swiftly Gone", in Season to Come; [oth. writ.] "Today is Mine," in Best Poems of 1995, Vol. II, several poems not yet published: "The Wheel of Time," to be in Windows of the Soul, "MY Navajo Home," and others. Biog. sketch in many Who's Who books and Personality books.; [pers.] Jeremiah Gilbi... ask for the old paths, where is the good way, and walk therein, and ye shall find rest for your souls. Romans 12:18.. as much as lieth in you, live peaceably with all men. I Timothy 4:14: Neglect not the gift that is in thee.; [a.] Lawrenceville, GA

## KNUDSEN, ARVID
[b.] Queens, NYC; [p.] Arvid Knudsen, Helga Marken Knudsen; [ch.] David Knudsen, Nancy Knudsen, Carolyn knudsen Adams; [ed.] B.F.A. Cooper Union, NY, Post Graduate Work: Literature, Children's Literature, Film Production, TV Production; [occ.] Book Producer - Consultation to Publishing Industry; [memb.] American Institute of Graphic Art. American Association of Book Producers; [hon.] 2 American Institute of Graphic Arts "50 Best Books of the year" Awards, plus more than 20 other Major Editorial, Art and Design, and Book Production Honors, Awards and Citations given in the Field; [oth. writ.] Ten children's books.; [pers.] I relish the truth in an old Indian Legend, the past is old and dead. The future is new and unborn. The only time is now!"; [a.] Santa Monica, CA

## KONSCHAK, SHARON L.
[b.] September 11, 1947, Bridgeton, NJ; [p.] Frank and Gloria Prichett; [m.] Paul J. Konschak, June 22, 1968; [ch.] Paul Edward Konschak; [ed.] Millville Sr. High School, Cumberland Co. College; [occ.] Homemaker; [memb.] St. Paul's Lutheran Church Spirit Committee, South Jersey Lupus Assoc. Great Books Reading Club; [hon.] Quill and Scroll Honorary who in American Jr. College, Who's Who American Woman; [oth. writ.] Write for church publication and local newspaper (club and organization items).; [pers.] My writing expresses my personal feelings and ideals. I enjoy many modern day women authors.; [a.] Millville, NJ

## KOTAS, VIOLA KNAUF
[p.] Arthur Knauf, Dolores Knauf; [m.] Leland D. Kotas; [ch.] Leann, Laura and Donald; [ed.] St. Charles High School, Southwestern Secretary; [occ.] Retired Insurance Secretary; [pers.] I began writing poetry at the age of 10. I never submitted any for Publication. I have always enjoyed the poetry of the great poets of the

19th Century-Longfellow, Emerson and others.; [a.] San Diego, CA

## KOUTCHAK, ANNETTE
[pen.] Matthew Palmer; [b.] February 28, 1981, Anchorage, AK; [p.] Janet Koutchak; [ed.] Unalakleet Elementary and Middle School; [occ.] Student; [memb.] National Junior Honor Society; [hon.] Most creative in Eighth Grade; [oth. writ.] Many stories and other Free style poems.; [pers.] I'm thankful to have a gift of writing. Because I know I can accomplish my dreams with it. This gift is something no one else can ever touch.; [a.] Unalakleet, AK

## KOUTSIS, JOANNA
[pen.] Joanna Koutsis; [b.] January 16, 1973, Denver, CO; [p.] George Koutsis, Vasiliki Koutsis; [ed.] Thomas Jefferson High, University of Colorado - Boulder (Recent Graduate, B.S. Finance); [memb.] American Hellenic Educational Progressive Association, Hellenic - American Culture Association; [oth. writ.] Various poems, short stories - unpublished.; [pers.] The soul can dance, but not without difficulty under the weight of human flesh, or in the confines of a pen.; [a.] Denver, CO

## KOZACZUK, JONATHAN A.
[pen.] J.A. Kozaczuk; [b.] April 10, 1985, Hayward; [p.] Tony and Ester Kozaczuk; [ed.] 5th grade; [occ.] Student; [hon.] Principals List, Salvation Army Honor Camper Jr. (Music Camp), ACSI Solo Festival - Superior, ACSI Speech Meet, ACSI short story contest, Piano Examination - Distinction; [oth. writ.] The Stowaway; [pers.] Seek ye first the kingdom of God and His right esouness.; [a.] Hayward, CA

## KRESS, LOUISE M.
[b.] October 17, 1948, NJ; [ed.] North Plainfield High School, Ann May School of Nursing, Neptune, NJ; [occ.] Registered Nurse; [memb.] Minnesota Nurses Assoc., American Nurses Assoc., Minneapolis and National Multiple Sclerosis Society; [hon.] Poem, Prelude, Published in the National Library of Poetry Anthology Dark Side of the Moon; [oth. writ.] Poetry and short stories.; [pers.] All writing begins in my heart as I attempt to express human experience through the medium of words.; [a.] Minneapolis, MN

## KUBA, JOSEPH MICHAEL
[pen.] Joey Kuba; [b.] January 5, 1984, Marysville, OH; [p.] Ricky T. Kuba, Sheila K. Kuba; [ed.] Elementary and Jr. High; [hon.] Creative Writing, Essay Contest 1st Place Presented by Modern Woodmen of America; [pers.] A person's perception makes them Unique. I express mine through writing.; [a.] East Liberty, OH

## KULINSKI, CHRISTINE
[pen.] Chris Kulinski; [b.] February 15, 1962, Chicago; [p.] Richard and Joyce Jensen; [m.] Frank A. Kulinski; [ch.] Jeff Micheal and Lisa; [ed.] Elkgrove High, IL William Rainey Harper Palatne IL Diploma, Institute of Children's Literature and current enrolled at ISC; [occ.] Discount Designer Clothing Store; [memb.] Transfiguration Church of Wauconda IL; [pers.] This poem is dedicated to my family and Joanne Reobock my empositor teach who said I had potential and E.A.P.; [a.] McHenry, IL

## KUREK, LILLIAN J.
[b.] April 1, 1954, Huntington, NY; [p.] Paul and Frances Schuster; [m.] Dwight E. Kurek, December 17, 1983; [ch.] Rebecca and Alexander; [ed.] Sacred Heart Academy, Nassau Community College; [occ.] Retail Buyer; [memb.] Sodality of Our Lady of Perpetual Help; [hon.] President Cup from Gamma Tau Gamma, Dean's List; [a.] Fountain Hills, AZ

**KUSCHEL, TANYA**
[b.] March 31, 1995, Janesville, WI; [p.] Fred and Kathy Kuschel; [ed.] Lincoln Elementary, Milton East, Northside Intermediate, Milton Middle School; [occ.] Student; [memb.] VFW (Veterans of Foreign War) Junior Girls; [hon.] Honors 3rd grade through 7th grade, 2nd Place Trophy in Bowling, also came in 2nd in VFW Poppy Sales; [oth. writ.] Very few unpublished writings that I wrote couple years back.; [pers.] I think poetry writing is a way to express your feelings through words, when you are unable speak.; [a.] Janesville, WI

**KUSMIREK, JOHN**
[b.] May 11, 1959, Poland; [ed.] Curie High, American Academy of Art, and School of the Art Institute of Art; [occ.] Freelance Artist; [hon.] United Insurance Calendar Award, Printer of Month Award, Graphic Designer of the Month, and Wiebotts Gold Key Award; [a.] Fort Collins, CO

**LA SALA, CAROLANN M.**
[b.] April 25, 1957, New York; [ch.] Lisa Michelle, Gina Maria; [ed.] M. S., Ed. - Long Island Univ., N. Y. B. A. - Adelphi Univ., Garden City N. Y. Herricks High School, New Hyde Pk, N. Y.; [occ.] Professor of Education, Long Island. University C. W. Post Campus Brookville, N. Y. Add'l - Educational Consultant; [memb.] American Assoc. of University Women, National Council of Teachers of Mathematics, Mental Health Assoc. Educators of Nassau Cty, New York, Museum of Natural History Educators, American Cancer Society; [hon.] Dean's List Education Grants; [oth. writ.] Prisms, Adelphi Univ.., 1977 (several poems); [pers.] Our words are meaningful and powerful, and can never be taken back. Therefore, we must use them wisely.; [a.] Westbury, NY

**LACY, ANITA**
[pen.] Anita Laisure Lacy; [b.] November 18, 1947, Newark, OH; [p.] Vince and Mabel Laisure; [m.] Carl W. Lacy, April 10, 1966; [ch.] Brian Keith, Troy William and Christopher Matthew, (1 grandson) Scott Anthony; [ed.] High School Graduate; [occ.] Home Maker; [oth. writ.] Several poems, am working on two other projects, 1. A Children's Book, 2. A Mystery; [pers.] I am inspired every day by my family and friends around me. Their love, devotion, endurance and courage through bad times as well as the good, have enabled me to capture my emotions on paper.; [a.] Newark, OH

**LAHIJANI, NAZANIN**
[pen.] YSL; [b.] August 16, 1975, Fullerton, CA; [p.] Nasser and Linda Lahijani; [ed.] University High School UCLA (currently attending) as English Major; [occ.] Student; [memb.] Persian Cultural Club (UCLA)-Treasurer, Co-founder Iranian Student Group (UCLA)-Treasurer, Hillel Jewish Youth Organization, Iranian-American Literature Club (UCLA), Co-founder; [hon.] Two time Winner of outstanding Academic Achievement Presidential Award, Who's Among Senior High Writers Award, Graduated High School in High Honors, Nat'l. Deans List, College Honors; [oth. writ.] Several poems published in contest anthology and UCLA's Iranian-American Literature Magazine, children's stories written for my siblings, news articles written for voice of America during Washington D.C internship.; [pers.] Rene Descartes-I am thinking I exist Nazanin Lahijani-I am writing therefore I exist. Thank you Mommy, Daddy and Grandma. Without your support where would I be without your inspiration what I would do?; [a.] Los Angeles, CA

**LAKER, MARILYN**
[b.] September 2, 1947, Waimea, Kauai, Hawaii; [ed.] Waimea High School, Waimea, Hawaii, New Mexico State University, Las Cruces, N Mex.; [occ.] Corporate Officer; [pers.] I have always enjoyed writing short essays and poems. Last summer, with the untimely death of my youngest son at age 15, I became my refuge, it allowed me away to express my sorrow and to recall the happy and wonderful memories that my son left behind.

**LAMBERT, RUSSELL G.**
[b.] July 2, 1995, Manchester, TN; [p.] James and Nell Lambert (deceased); [m.] Linda Carole Lambert, June 17, 1994; [ch.] Joshua Stephen and Jonathan Samuel; [ed.] B.S.Ed., Southwest Texas State University, Currently pursuing M.Ed. at University of Central OK; [occ.] Secondary Science Teacher; [memb.] American Federation of Teacher's, Trinity American Lutheran Church Council; [hon.] Kappa Delta Pi, Dean's List; [oth. writ.] Several unpublished, some published in my schools anthology.; [pers.] This poem reflects my feelings on the April 19th OKC bombing. The final death toll was 168 instead of 167. All my poetry is a reflection of my feelings about something personal, good or bad.; [a.] Oklahoma City, OK

**LAMEIRO, JUAN A. M.D.**
[pen.] J.A.L.A.-MD; [b.] January 5, 1955, Cagwas, PR; [p.] Alodia Aguayo and Ambrosio Lameiro; [m.] Sonia E. Caro, August 27, 1979; [ch.] Veronica, Juan Alejandro and Gabriel; [ed.] University of Puerto Rico School of Medicine and Affiliation Hospitals Neurosurgery; [occ.] Neurosurgery; [memb.] Southern Medical Association; [hon.] National Defence Service Medal, Armed Forces Expeditionary Medal, Humanitarian Service Medal, Joint Meritorious Unit Award, Army Service Ribbon; [oth. writ.] Unpublished poems and songs.; [pers.] As a neurosurgeon with the army's 86th evaluation hospital at Mogadishu, Somalia, during operation restore hope. I realized the consequences of a war and the suffering of children in a devastated country as this, therefore "I pray for the war to end.";
[a.] Stevensville, MI

**LAMOURI, SAAD**
[b.] May 26, 1971, Marrakesh, Morocco; [p.] Ghani Lamouri and Souad Rkha; [ed.] San Diego State University, College of Engineering; [occ.] Electrical Engineer; [hon.] Dean's List; [oth. writ.] Many poems and song lyrics that are yet to be chanted.; [pers.] Poetry is for me away to explore my own depths. The more I write, the more enlightened I become.; [a.] San Diego, CA

**LANE, ROBIN S.**
[b.] September 10, 1962, Elizabeth, NJ; [ch.] Jodi Lynn - age 12, Tommy Ryan - age 8; [pers.] I have always found writing down my thoughts and emotions to be very therapeutic. It helps to unclutter the mind. Initially my writings were simply of the events that occurred in my day to day life; how I felt about something or someone or perhaps something I may have wanted to say to someone, but didn't. Never intending to write poetry, I suddenly noticed the words in my writings often seemed to flow into poetic verses. As I shared those verses with people close to me, I found I was getting such a positive reaction whether my poems were "up" or "down," people were expressing how I touched them on their thoughts and emotions. I put into words what they felt inside. Knowing that others felt as I did and knowing that it helped them to read my poems was in itself - therapy for me. Submitting my poem to the National Library of Poetry was my first step towards gaining enough confidence in myself to put together a book of my poems that I hope to someday share with those who may feel their alone out there. Maybe by reading one of my poems, they will realize they're not!; [a.] Boca Raton, FL

**LANSFORD, DOLORES**
[pen.] Lee Barbaree; [b.] March 8, 1931, Oklahoma; [p.] Jack and Lucille Barbaree; [m.] R.A. Lansford, June 9, 1941; [ch.] Four children; [ed.] Carlsbad High School Graduated; [occ.] Housewife and Mother and Grandmother; [pers.] I feel personal happiness when I know I have given all I can of myself to bring laughter and kindness and love to the people around me and faraway.; [a.] Cave Creek, AZ

**LARON, VERONICA MARIA**
[pen.] Maria; [b.] January 19, 1983, Queens, NY; [p.] Ilarion Lara and Azra Lara; [ed.] LES Enfantes Montessori School, Our Lady of Mount Carmel Catholic School, Forrest Elementary School, Memorial Middle School; [occ.] Student; [hon.] Honor Student, Principal/Dean's List; [oth. writ.] Many more poems, never tried publishing.; [pers.] A while ago I realized it was very necessary that I get a more realistic approach to life, it was this realization that inspired me the most.; [a.] Fairlawn, NJ

**LARSON, IRENE MARY**
[b.] September 19, 1921, Lynd, MN; [p.] Andrew and Mary Larson

**LARSON, ROBERT**
[b.] September 27, 1909, Los Angeles, CA; [p.] Gustave and Alma Larson; [m.] Frances (deceased), March 17, 1989; [ch.] November 11, 1942; [ed.] Los Angeles High School, Chovinard Art School, Otis Art Institute; [occ.] Artist and Writer; [memb.] I am a convert to Catholicism; [hon.] I attended Otis Art Institute on a Scholarship; [oth. writ.] In 1954 I edited and wrote the foreword to A 4-Volume Life of Christ I have had numerous articles published, including one in American Heritage, April 1966.; [pers.] I have been a mural painter, a theatre scene designer, a journalist and publicist for an Archaeological Society, "Migrating Birds" is the first of my poems to be published.; [a.] Los Angeles, CA

**LAWRENCE, ELBERT**
[b.] December 2, 1944, Winnfield, LA; [p.] Coy Lawrence and Bertie Lawrence; [m.] Linda Lawrence, August 14, 1964; [ch.] Todd Lawrence and Tony Lawrence; [ed.] Sikes High - Business School; [occ.] Machinist - Riverwood International, West Monroe, LA; [memb.] Louisiana Songwriter's Association; [oth. writ.] Have had several songs recorded-demos.; [pers.] Can write about many subjects. Being exposed to and witnessing life's problems makes writing possible-with God's help.; [a.] West Monroe, LA

**LAZER, HELEN**
[pen.] Helen Lazer; [b.] August 5, 1923, Paterson, NJ; [p.] Sarah Jacob Weinberg; [m.] Jack; [ch.] Jonnele Caro and Jill Rosen; [ed.] Still studying from N.J., N.Y, NYC, at present Fau Bocaraton, FL; [occ.] Writer/Lecturer, Interior Designer; [memb.] Former Pres. of Art-Teacher-Activities for Human Rights-(Too many to list); [hon.] Jaycees Humanitarian Award-Ort Award for outstanding service-etc.; [oth. writ.] Children Book "The Most Important Journey You Will Ever Take" "The Deception" "The Reality" The Dream" A Book for all time."; [pers.] The process for raising human consciousness lies in "The Road To Seldom." That road although hard travelled since the age of 25, is my greatest achievement. As consciousness grows, the miracle becomes self evident!; [a.] Pompano Beach, FL

**LE, H.V.**
[b.] December 29, 1934; [p.] Can D. Le and Doa T. Vo; [m.] Phuong Van Le, January 22, 1962; [ch.] 4 Children; [ed.] Bachelor in Law/Economic, Master Degree in Finance; [occ.] Sr. Accountant; [hon.] Received honor at the contest of "Prizes of Economic Works, 1960.";

[oth. writ.] Had translated various poems and had written about literature and philosophy of the chinese culture.; [pers.] I have greatly influenced by confucianism and Tang's Poems.; [a.] San Francisco, CA

**LE VAULT, IRIS MARIE**
[b.] September 22, 1939, Sesser, IL; [p.] Wanda and Orval Piper; [m.] Richard Gale LeVault, June 9, 1957; [ch.] Todd Le Vault and Toni-LeVault Morket; [ed.] Goods-Barren Twp. High School, Sesser, Ill.; [occ.] Housewife; [hon.] 1994 Editors Choice Award from The National Library of Poetry; [oth. writ.] Poem, To My Son, published in Journey of the Mind by the National Library of Poetry.; [pers.] Writing helps to free the mind and is quite comforting to the soul. I try to express in my writing only the feeling within my heart.; [a.] Sesser, IL

**LEAHY, KEVIN E.**
[b.] October 29, 1955, Ridgway; [m.] Lorrie Ann Leahy, January 20, 1984; [ch.] Jacob Michael Leahy, Elysha Mary Leahy; [ed.] Ridgway High School, Houghton College; [occ.] Husband and Father; [memb.] American Heart Association; [hon.] Two Beautiful Children and an Beautiful Wife; [oth. writ.] Numerous poems to my Kids and wife.; [pers.] Writing is one of the few things that give me a sense of purpose in life, next to my wife and kids.; [a.] Ridgway, PA

**LEAVITT, MARGARET**
[pen.] Grit Barker; [b.] April 8, 1960, Akron, OH; [p.] Shirley And Vincent Dannemiller; [ch.] Andrea Leavitt, Samantha and Nicholas Leavitt; [ed.] 1978 Stow High School Graduate; [occ.] Senior Receptionist; [memb.] Streetsboro Junior Baseball Coach - A Handicapped League, Former Member of Toastmaster; [pers.] I am a child from a family of 12. I strived to write poems that reflect success through personal growth.; [a.] Cuyahoga Falls, OH

**LEE, LEWIS**
[pen.] Lewis Lee; [b.] May 14, 1923, Staples, MN; [p.] Edwin and Teresa Lee; [m.] Ruby Lee, July 26, 1947; [ch.] 4 boys, 2 girls; [ed.] Staples High School, Minnesota Business School; [occ.] Retired; [memb.] American Legion, Veterans of Foreign Wars; [oth. writ.] Wrote music and lyrics to the following songs, "Jesus Tells," "Could It Be Love, Ruby," "Christmas Love," "Say That You'll Mine," and "State of Arizona," songs on commercial records and taps, one of my poems was published in local newspapers.; [pers.] My parents were professional musicians, they gave me encouragement to write songs and poetry.; [a.] Yuma, AZ

**LEGASSIE, HELEN**
[b.] December 1, 1913, Maine; [p.] John and Helen Sullivan; [m.] Deceased, December 22, 1958; [ch.] 1 son, 1 grandchildren from former marriage (my first marriage); [ed.] Parochial School; [occ.] Housewife or Homemaker; [oth. writ.] I have another poem the poem about.; [pers.] My daughter was 4 yrs. and 7 months. A beautiful little girl blond and blue eyed and a sweet nature.; [a.] Berlin, NY

**LEIPHARDT, NATALIE**
[b.] September 17, 1968, Wagoner, OK; [p.] Chuck and Edna Leiphardt; [ch.] Jolean Leiphardt; [ed.] Sophomore Year of College; [occ.] Student at Eastern Oklahoma State College in Wilburton, Oklahoma; [hon.] Made the President's Honor Roll the Spring Semester of 1995, and I won several Trophies at Speech Tournaments during High School; [oth. writ.] Several poems published in other Anthologies.; [pers.] I have found that if I put the really troubling feelings down on paper so I can study them then I can better deal with my sadness or grief. If I'm able to help someone in the

process of helping myself then I have accomplished something great.; [a.] Crowder, OK

**LENNON, PAUL J.**
[b.] November 16, 1943, Dublin, Eire; [p.] Jack Lennon and Christina O'Connor; [ed.] High School, Dublin, Ireland: Spanish in Salamanca, Spain, Lic. Philosophy, and S.T.L. degrees Gregorian Uni. Rome, Italy, M.Ed. C.U.A., Washington, D.C.; [occ.] Community Development Specialist (Social Worker) with immigrant (mostly Hispanic) neighborhood community, Falls Church, VA; [memb.] Am. Ass. Marriage and family Therapy WPAS, AFI (American Film Institute Subscribe to common Boundary magazine covenant house, Shalem Spiritual Whitman Walker Clinic Institute; [oth. writ.] Other poems in English in Spanish: "Cantos de jacob" (spiritual) "Viaje hacia la Pascua" (erotic): "Diarios de Amor" and "Cartas"; [pers.] Missionary priest (R.C.) Mexico 1971-84. Left priesthood '89 first poetic writings 1978 on falling in love. Write when occasionally feel "inspired," mostly lyrical, sometimes quimsical. Presently studying Post Masters in Marriage and Family Therapy, VA Tech.; [a.] Alexandria, VA

**LEVIGNE, VINCE**
[b.] March 3, 1978, Detroit, MI; [p.] Vince and JoAnn Levigne; [ed.] I am a student at Henry Ford 11 High School in Sterling Hts, Michigan; [occ.] Student; [memb.] German club, SADD, National Tae Kwon Do Association, Varsity Football, Varsity Wrestling, Varsity Track, St. Therese of Lisieux Youth Group; [hon.] All Academic Football, All-Academic Wrestling; [oth. writ.] I have written other poems and short stories. I have had two poems published. ("A Far off Place" and "Best Poems of 95'"); [pers.] Life should not be taken for granted. I believe in setting goals and working hard to achieve them.; [a.] Sterling Heights, MI

**LEWIS, BRANDON D.**
[b.] January 31, 1982, Livonia, MI; [p.] Vickie A. Lewis and Dale P. Lewis; [ed.] 8th Grade Student; [occ.] Student and Artist; [memb.] Boy Scouts of America Troop 865; [hon.] National Geographic Society School Champion, Honor Roll, Presidential Academic Achievement Award; [pers.] Tolkien is King! J.R.R. Tolkien's Hobbit and the Lord of the rings have greatly influenced the way I write.; [a.] Westland, MI

**LILES, JO ANNE**
[pen.] Jo Anne Posey Liles; [b.] October 23, 1933, Red Level, AL; [p.] Crayton and Vinnie Posey; [m.] Curtis Bryan Liles (deceased), May 23, 1952; [ch.] 3 boys and 6 girls, 12 grandchildren; [ed.] Graduated from Red Level High School; [occ.] Retired; [memb.] Member and Music Director of Fairmount Baptist Church in Red Level, AL. Active Member of Beta Club in High School; [hon.] Salutatorian of class of 1952 at Red Level High School; [oth. writ.] Love Makes A Away, Anniversary, My Strong Box Of Treasures, Be Still and know, For This He Came, Amazing Love.; [pers.] Poetry, like any other God, given talent, should be for the benefit of its readers-whether for comfort, encouragement, or just simple pleasure.; [a.] Red Level, AL

**LILIBRIDGE, LINDA**
[b.] September 17, 1945, Griswold, CT; [p.] George and Odelle Lillibridge; [ch.] Erin Lee Cholewa; [ed.] Griswold High School, Mohegan Community College Eastern Connecticut State University; [occ.] State of Conn.; [oth. writ.] David's Whiskers, A Man, Curves; [a.] Lisbon, CT

**LIND, MARTHA**
[b.] January 18, 1947, Port Arthur, TX; [p.] Arva and Katielee Collins; [ed.] Charles R. Lind, Jr. and April Marie Lind; [occ.] Thomas Jefferson High, Lon Morris

Jr. College-Jacksonville, TX and Sam Houston State Univ. Huntsville, TX; [memb.] St. Cyprians Episcopal - Lufkin (Choir member); [pers.] In my expressions through pen and paper, I achieve to grasp all the meaning of life by only my senses God so graced upon me.; [a.] Lufkin, TX

**LIPSCOMB, JASON PAUL**
[pen.] Jason Paul Lipscomb; [b.] September 19, 1975, Gaffney, SC; [p.] William and Robin Lipscomb; [ed.] Jupiter High School, Jupiter, FL.-Clemson University-Clemson, S.C.; [occ.] Student and Equip Manager-Clemson Soccer Team; [hon.] Dean's List-Clemson, President List-Clemson, Boy Scout Awards-Tennis Trophies-Baseball Trophies-All Star Baseball Team 8 yrs.; [oth. writ.] Several poems published in Jupiter High School Magazine. Also published for a family book. Local newspaper publications.; [pers.] This poem along with several others where written in memory of my cousin, who was killed in a car accident. Others were written because I feel I am my own person with different out look in life.; [a.] Gaffney, SC

**LIRANZA, ANTHONY JOSEPH**
[pen.] Adren Lupine; [b.] January 31, 1980, San Diego, CA; [p.] G. Gisela Liranza (mother); [ed.] Ynez Elementary, (Sophomore) Arroyo High; [occ.] Student (Arroyo High School); [oth. writ.] Several poems published by "The Quill," a poetry/short story book published by student volunteers at Arroyo High.; [pers.] I like believe that our world is beautiful but I have never forsaken, forgotten it's darkness. My poetry is a reflection of the world and of myself.; [a.] Temple City, CA

**LITTLE, MARVIN V.**
[pen.] Maveli; [b.] October 17, 1938, Washington Co., IL; [p.] Leonard and Velma Little; [ed.] Marissa Township High School, Lincoln Land Community College; [occ.] Maintenance - King's Daughters Home for Women; [pers.] With imagination as the only leaven, I love to knead the mass of words and, childlike, am always amazed at the creation that rises, seemingly by a will of its own.; [a.] Springfield, IL

**LLOYD, FIDELITA NINA**
[pen.] Ninie Clemente; [b.] December 18, 1953, Bronx, NY; [p.] Bonifacio Clemente and Catalina Medina Solis; [m.] James Lloyd, August 26, 1972; [ch.] James Lloyd Jr. and Anthony Richard Lloyd; [ed.] Jane Addams V.H.S. (1971-1974), Pace University (1976-1978), Empire Technical School (1985), Hostoss Community College (1989-1992); [occ.] Student, Lehman College (Fall 1995); [memb.] Phi-Theta Kappa, Nation Wide Honor, Society (Permanent Member); [hon.] High School (3 yrs), Honor Society (Gold Merit Seal), Pace University-Private School Teachers (licence) All credit requirements achieved to teach Hairdressing and cosmetology, Empire Technical School-received a (Gold Merit Diploma) Honor Student in computer programming and data processing. Grade average=100, Hostoss Community College-3 yrs. in the (Honor Society) Dean's List plus Phi-Theta Kappa (Degree A.A); [oth. writ.] Published poems in another contest I entered - The Library of Congress (Washington D.C.) Anthology book "Diamonds and Rust" Poem tittle "Bag Lady, Bag Lady," Ware Do You Rome?; [pers.] I'm a good humanitarian. I am a licensed Professional Hairdresser and Cosmetologist (21 yrs). I earned an (Associate Degree in Liberal Arts) major (Psychology). I'm recently working on a B.A. Degree major: Psychology, minor: Sociology.; [a.] Bronx, NY

**LOCKETT, MARK ALLAN**
[b.] September 20, 1974, Clearfield, PA; [p.] Dennis Lockett, Cynthia McKarkle; [ed.] Clearfield Alliance Christian High School, Messiah College; [occ.] Stu-

dent; [hon.] Dean's List all Semesters of College, High School Valedictorian; [oth. writ.] Several poems, a few published in the magazine poetic justice.; [pers.] I often try to depict the struggle of mankind in m writings - as well as the hopes that we may or may not ever accomplish. Influenced by Yeats, Auden, Faulkner and O'Connor.; [a.] Clearfield, PA

**LOGAN, FANNIE ETTA WEST**
[pen.] Etta Asbell; [b.] June 19, 1937, Morven, GA; [p.] Sallie Etta and William McKinley Asbell; [m.] Roy West, June 22, 1954; [ch.] Randy West; [pers.] Feelings I have about God.

**LOGGINS, NANCY VIRGINIA**
[b.] April 20, 1940, Murrayville, GA; [p.] Jim and Nancy M. Smallwood; [m.] Cliff Loggins, July 3, 1956; [ch.] Bobby Sue, Joann, Gail, Jimmy, Patty, Becky; [occ.] Fieldale Farms

**LOHMAN, RUTH**
[b.] March 10, 1919, Driscoll, ND; [p.] Charles Young, Clara Young; [m.] Joe Lohman, July 7, 1944; [ch.] Eldon Lohman, Sharon Lawrence; [ed.] Tuttle High School, Tuttle ND, Bismarck Commercial College Bismarck ND; [occ.] Retired Secretary; [memb.] First Baptist Church of Seattle Wash. also Choir Member, First Baptist Church of Poway CA, World War II Veterans Men and Women's Club Enumclaw WA, Professional Business Men and Women Fellowship Enumclaw WA; [hon.] Ruby Pin Achievement Award for Highest Sale work for Avon CO, Pasadena, CA; [oth. writ.] Many poems in a note book entitled poems for all occasion. My poem "There Never Was an Idle Moment" is in it.; [pers.] All my writings are from my heart. I believe we sometimes fail to recognize our many blessing, and to love one another - the need of the world today.; [a.] Poway, CA

**LOMBARDI, AMANDA**
[pen.] Elizabeth, Nestie; [b.] March 17, 1985; [p.] Cathy Zacher and Dave Lombardi; [ed.] Working on Fifth Grade; [occ.] Elementary School; [memb.] Girl Scouts, Guyasuta Cheerleading, the Royal Order of Deweyism Community Swim Club

**LOMBARDO, LAWRENCE**
[b.] April 5, 1960, Owens, NY; [p.] Kenneth and Prudence Bagtlett; [m.] Nydia Lombardo, October 25, 1986; [ch.] Allison Justine Lombardo; [ed.] B.A. Sociology Claw and Criminal Justice/Suny-old Westbury, N.Y.C. Police and Correction Academy; [occ.] Retired Sergeant N.Y.C. Transit Police; [memb.] Executive Assistant, N.Y.C., Retired Transit Police Association, Lynbrook Citizens Party, Lynbrook Civic Assoc.; [hon.] Cop of the Mouth-12188, Dedication Award N.Y.C. Transit Police, Dedication Award N.Y.C., transit Police Columbia Assoc. 2 Letters of Merit, Transit Police; [oth. writ.] I have other poems published with the National Library of Poetry N.Y.C. Daily News, Newsdey Lynbrook U.S.A, Lynbrook Herald; [pers.] We must never focus of the men and women who paid the ultimate sacrifice for our being.; [a.] Lynbrook, NY

**LOMBARDO, SARAH ROBBINS**
[b.] April 19, 1981, New London, CT; [p.] Melissa Robbins and Michael Lombardo; [ed.] Presently a Freshman at St. Bernard High School Uncasville, CT; [occ.] Student; [a.] Norwich, CT

**LONG, ALICE LOUISE**
[b.] July 1, Grand Island, NE; [p.] Jake G. Long, Dee Ivez Graten; [ed.] Dunipton Public School, Kemney Stake College, San Francisco State, The New School; [occ.] Writer; [pers.] I dedicate this and all my poetry to Jake and Bill. Both are my daily inspiration.; [a.] New

York, NY

**LOPEZ, VIRGINIA**
[pen.] Virgy; [b.] November 30, 1968, New Jersey; [m.] Javier Lopez, September 24, 1994; [ed.] Union Hill HS, Bergen Community; [occ.] Dental Hygienist; [hon.] Deans List, Honor Roll, Distinguished Academic Achievement Awards; [oth. writ.] Several unpublished poems.; [pers.] I dedicate this poem to my friends, Anixa, Nerys, and my sister Marly.; [a.] New Jersey

**LORIMER, BARBARA**
[b.] Portland, OR; [p.] Wilfred and Anne Lorimer; [ed.] U of Portland College of Nursing, BSN, BA in History, Boston University, Main Ed, NYU. R.N.; [occ.] Student - MA in English Program PSU Portland State University; [memb.] Served as Peace Corps Vol. in Sabah, Malaysia-2 years-served as cadet in US Army Cadet Nurse program 3 yrs.; [pers.] I wish to thank my writing teachers-past-present and future for contributing to my knowledge and skill in writing in life.; [a.] Portland, OR

**LOVEMORE, SHAVETTE LAFAYETTE**
[b.] March 15, 1979, Kington, JA; [p.] Toby Lovemore and Lorna Lovemore; [ed.] Junior, Seton Academy; [occ.] Student; [memb.] Christ Universal Church, Student Council, Volunteer for Women United to save our Families; [oth. writ.] Personal collections of poems and short stories.; [pers.] Through my writings I like to show people, especially young people that if you believe in yourself and in god all your dreams can become reality.; [a.] Chicago, IL

**LOWRY, LONNIE**
[pen.] Big L. Lowry; [b.] April 20, 1932, Lorena, TX; [p.] Mr and Mrs. Jack Lowry; [m.] September 27, 1952; [ch.] Six sons-three Daughters; [ed.] 11th High School, G.E.D. - 2 yrs. Oklahoma State Tech, Okmulgee Okla.; [occ.] Retired; [memb.] 1st Baptist Church-Robinson TX. WACO Singles Square Dance Club, WACO TX; [hon.] Dean Honor Roll at Okla.. State Tech.; [oth. writ.] Many other poems-unpublished by choice.; [pers.] Treat each person as if they were you.; [a.] Riesel, TX

**LUBIN, RUTH**
[b.] May 22, 1911, Saint Louis; [p.] Anne and Harry Shapiro; [m.] Deceased, June 29, 1930; [ch.] Barbara Berger, Mardene Conrad; [ed.] A.A. Pasadena Junior College 1938 - B.A. UCLA 1953, M.F.A. H.S.C. 1960; [occ.] Art Teacher in Continuing Ed. at Pasadena City College; [memb.] C.T.A NE.A American Association of University Women A.A.U.W. University of Southern CA Volunteer at Andrus School of Gerontology also an Andrus Associate; [hon.] Sculpture Award at Chicago Art Institute, Exhibited at Pasadena Museum of Los Angeles County Museum, Won the Award of Ms. Senior California in 1994, also was selected in the top ten in the Nation in 1994, Won Award in poetry 1990-1994; [oth. writ.] At present time writing a book "Transform Thru Visualization."; [pers.] Life begins at 80! Life is a challenge!! Good health is the key to fully enjoy it at any age. To line creatively with purpose using imagination to its fullest degree in all aspects of life makes you a participant not just an onlooker. Life your life with joys, laughter to enable you to react for bliss!; [a.] Arcadia, CA

**LUCERO, EDITH**
[pen.] Dee Dee; [b.] July 2, 1969, Los Angeles, CA; [p.] Maria G. Lucero and Edward C. Lucero; [ed.] Rosemead High School, Pasadena City College, and California Business Institute; [occ.] Nurse; [oth. writ.] Several other poems written by myself, which I have never submitted and shared. In which I intend to, such as:

"The Trials of Life" and "Tears From a Broken Heart."; [pers.] Through my writing, I try to interact reality in terms of personal experience and my values. I hope it will broaden the way people think and behave toward each other. Thank you for your inspiration Mom and Sister Sylvia.; [a.] Rosemead, CA

**LUTZAK, PHIL**
[b.] June 4, 1954, New York City, NY; [p.] Helen and Walter Lutzak; [m.] A. Sclafane; [pers.] My life is a string of calms and storms, no different than yours and no more important, not like yours today and just like it tomorrow.; [a.] Brooklyn, NY

**LYNCH, JOHN A.**
[b.] April 7, 1935, Flint, MI; [ed.] Bachelor of Science, Michigan State University, Master Teacher of Science College of William and Mary; [occ.] Retired-Teacher Flint Community Schools; [memb.] UTF-MEA-NEA, NSIA-PDK; [pers.] I feel that every one should be express the opportunity to express themselves.; [a.] Clio, MI

**LYONS, RONALD W.**
[b.] April 26, 1953, Saint Louis, MO; [p.] Lois Collen Lester; [m.] Jamie L. Lyons, September 25, 1993; [ch.] Ronald D. Lyons, Patricia C. Lyons and Lawrence L. Lyons; [ed.] GED; [occ.] Woodcrafter; [hon.] UNESCO Bronz Metal for bookplate design 1990; [oth. writ.] Numerous poems over the years of life.; [pers.] The essence of the soul sometimes find their release through pen in hand.; [a.] Saint Louis, MO

**MACGEORGE, PATRICIA A.**
[b.] June 17, 1954, Detroit, MI; [m.] Glenn C. MacGeorge, October 10, 1975; [ch.] Eric; [ed.] Associates Degree of Science. Henry Ford Community College, Dearborn, MI; [oth. writ.] As a member of a local church choir, I had an opportunity to write 2 verses to a popular hymn.; [pers.] As I grow older, I've come to realize, it's the little things in life which bring me the most happiness. A true friend, a kiss, a hug, a wagging dog's tail, a smile, a thank you, or I'm sorry, flowers in my yard, music, song, these are my "cup of tea."; [a.] Wyandotte, MI

**MACK, SOPHIA C.**
[pen.] Sophia C. Johnides/Mack; [b.] January 20, 1948, Detroit, MI; [p.] George Johnides, Irene A. Fite, Both Deceased; [m.] Divorced; [ch.] Angela Marie Attard, Noel Anthony Valade; [ed.] Kimball High, Specs Howard School of Broadcast Arts, Russel Schools for Real Estate; [occ.] Store Manager, Minnesota Fabrics Grand Rapids, MI, Representative for Exect'; [memb.] St. Nicolas Greek Orthodon Church, Bally's Vic Tanny; [hon.] Million Dollar Sales Awards in Real Estates, Numerous Top Sales Awards in Avon; [oth. writ.] Have complied over 70 poems into a book called "Sophia's scruples and Internal thoughts in poetry ready for publication; [pers.] Ultimately, it is my belief, that we all strive for happiness which leads us to success, only to be accounted for no matter how great or small they may appear to be. Never theless, each of us determines and answer to our selves, our loved us ones, those who we care about the most and desire to share and surrounds our lives with.; [a.] Kentwood, MI

**MACY, ANGELA**
[b.] August 31, 1977, OH; [p.] Ronald and Theresa Macy; [ch.] Carol Amanda, Jennifer Marie; [ed.] Nancy Hill Elementary, Jefferson Middle School, West Aurora High School; [occ.] Student; [oth. writ.] Published in my school literary magazine "Muses"; [pers.] No one has influenced me taught me how to write. It's simply come from deep down inside of me. Poetry try is the one thing in my life I feel I am good at and now I know for

sure. This has been dream of mine for a while and now it has come true! Praise God!; [a.] Aurora, IL

**MADDEN, JOHNNY L.**
[b.] December 16, 1953, Breckenridge, TX; [p.] Mr. and Mrs. Paul Madden; [ed.] A.A., Eastern Oklahoma State Course, B.A., Oklahoma Baptist University, M.S., Northeastern State University; [occ.] Field Supervisor, Sgt (8), Security; [memb.] The Amherst Society the National authors registry; [hon.] Certificate of Poetic Achievement; [oth. writ.] Various poems being published in several anthologies, I.E., American Poetry Annual, Inspirations, Endless Harmony and Treasured Poems of America; [pers.] I assign poetry a place above the finest bottle of wine, the finest cigar or the finest peace of music.; [a.] Little Rock, AR

**MADLOCK, SHAWNNA**
[pen.] Maddog; [b.] June 17, 1979, Alaska; [p.] Dagmar Stranak; [occ.] Student; [pers.] I wish for the one's I love to realize how much I care and love then in so many words.; [a.] Wasilla, AK

**MAEDER, GREGORY J.**
[b.] December 30, 1954, Minneapolis; [p.] James J. and Ann D. Maeder; [m.] Patricia G. Maeder, July 31, 1981; [ch.] Samuel G. Maeder, Rebecca A. Maeder; [ed.] Charles A. Lindbergh High School Grad. Control Data Inst. Certificate - Computer Programming.; [occ.] Owner of Twin Star Electronics, Inc. Printed Circuit Board Manufacturer.; [memb.] US Chess Federation; [pers.] "Be Ye Kind" Ephesians 4:32; [a.] Crystal, MN

**MAES-MACDONALD, VERONIQUE**
[b.] November 10, 1961, Belgium; [p.] Rene and Blanche Maes; [m.] Bill MacDonald, May 7, 1988; [ch.] Kelly Jayme, Michelle; [ed.] Royal Atheneum, Welteren (Belgium), Regent College New York; [occ.] Mother, student, Co-owner of Fotamac, Scenic Photography; [pers.] I believe that poetry can be a wonderful tool to reach and teach children. We can all remember a poem or two all remember a poem or two our from our childhood and the lessons they contained.; [a.] Santa Barbara, CA

**MAGGIO, F. MICHAEL**
[ed.] US Airforce Academy '90; [occ.] Law Student University of Houston Law Center; [a.] Houston, TX

**MAGUIRE, VINCENT M.**
[b.] May 26, 1972, Van Nuys, CA; [p.] Teresa and Brian Hallum; [occ.] Accountant's Assistant, Agoura Hills, California; [pers.] If tomorrow is anything like yesterday, why did I have to have today?; [a.] Granada Hills, CA

**MAHONEY-COX, MARY LOUISE**
[b.] October 7, 1925, Bismarck, ND; [m.] John Lyman Cox II, October 17, 1958; [ch.] six; [ed.] BA - Lake Forest via Sarah Lawrence - Manhattanville College Ed D not complete - Teachers College Columbia Univ.; [occ.] Writer and counselor; [memb.] Committee on Crime and Delinquency; The Labyrinth Project of CT.; [oth. writ.] Published Images of a Voice and Color; essays; [pers.] I believe that each life is a poem. By writing down the words we hear inwardly we become students of own lives. We see more clearly, where we have been and where we wish to go.

**MAJOR, PEGGY MCLAUGHLIN**
[pen.] Evangelist Major; [b.] April 15, 1938, Durham, NC; [p.] Pearl and Lee Winston McLaughlin Sr.; [m.] Deceased; [ch.] Colay Major Jr., Mayrice Major and deborah Major, Antra and Dominique; [ed.] CCB of Balto. College Grad.; [occ.] SSA, Metro West, Computer Operator SOS, Dos; [memb.] Gospel Tabernacle

Apostolic Church, Asst. Supt of Sunday School, adult Teacher. National Sunday School President of P.F.O.J.C.; [hon.] LIC. Evangelist/Dist. Elder W. Murray - Pastor. Social Security Performance Awards; [oth. writ.] Personal Pleasure writings, children book, play and other poems (unpublished) Jingle contest won cash award from the Steger's Maryland Fresh Exp Inc.; [pers.] For every accomplishment in my life I give all the glory and honors to Jesus Christ.; [a.] Baltimore, MD

**MALLOW, ADRIANE GRACE**
[b.] February 28, 1983, Winchester, VA; [p.] Robert Mallow, June Fletcher Mallow; [ed.] 6th Grade student age 12; [occ.] Student; [memb.] Gifted and talented Spectra; [pers.] I have two brother, Lucas who is 14 and Justin who is 10. I enjoy all sports and reading Sinclair Smith and R.L. Stine books.; [a.] Flintstone, MD

**MANACLE, RICHARD A.**
[b.] April 16, 1948, New York City; [p.] Edward and Estelle Manacle; [ch.] Richard, Michael Sean and Teresa Marie; [ed.] St. Augustine High School; [occ.] Security Officer Roberto Clemente Middle School Montgomery County, MD. District of Columbia Retired Police Officers Association; [oth. writ.] Several poems published in local papers.; [pers.] After working as a Police officer for 22 years in Washington, D.C. and seeing both the good and evil of humanity, I have tried to use the emotions we all have experienced in my writings.; [a.] Germantown, MD

**MANDO, ROWENA SALVA**
[pen.] Wina; [b.] February 24, 1963, Philippines; [p.] Augusto Salva and Mabel Torres Salve; [ch.] Regina, Ragika, Rika and Rania; [ed.] St. Scholastica's College AB Management; [occ.] Freelance writer; [hon.] National Secondary Schools Press Conference, Second Place - Sports Reporting, Fourth Place - Feature Writing St. Theresa's Academy Artist of the Year-H.S Graduation; [pers.] The words from deep inside my heart spews forth because love is all around me. Laotzu was right - 'A journey of a thousand miles must indeed begin with a single step.'; [a.] Sunnyvale, CA

**MANDUCA, FRANCIS J.**
[pen.] F. J. M.; [ed.] M.S. Ed. Univ. of Maine; [occ.] Musician, Educator; [memb.] American Federation of Musicians; [oth. writ.] Music, Prose, Poetry; [pers.] I enjoy integrating emotions and intellectuality to create improvisational expression. "I seldom have a poem to write but when I do, it springs in sight full bloom, and eager to relay the thoughts I'd probably never say, if I took time to do it right!; [a.] Ocean Park, ME

**MANN, MARY**
[b.] Alabama; [p.] Mr. and Mrs. Charlie Dunklin; [m.] Edmon Mann; [ch.] Shaftone, Daniel, Antony; [ed.] Robert L. Austin High Kellogg Community College A.A. Spring Arbor College B.A.; [occ.] Educator; [memb.] Arc Michigan American BBWA; [hon.] Certification of appreciation mea; [oth. writ.] Essay published in class anthology at spring Arbor College, Other poem published.; [pers.] I thank God how he speaks to my heart. When I write I write from the heart. When my audience read I want it to minister to their hearts, and leave a lasting impact.; [a.] Albion, MI

**MANN, MATTHEW**
[b.] June 15, 1971; [a.] Louisville, KY

**MANNIX, YARDLEY**
[b.] December 17, 1985, New York; [p.] Gary and Cathy Mannix; [ed.] Oak Creek School 4th Grade; [occ.] Student - IN, 4th-Grade; [memb.] Girl Scouts; [hon.] Picture and poems in the Arizona Republic Newspaper winner of poetry twice in school districts; [pers.]

I am a Christian! And I love Jesus!; [a.] Cornville, AZ

**MANNO, ANTHONY PAUL**
[pen.] Tony Manno; [b.] January 1, 1973, Charleston, IL; [ed.] Currently attending Marian College in Fond Du Lac, Wisconsin; [occ.] I currently work in a grocery store; [hon.] Dean's list at Marian College. Also Received Presidential Scholarship; [oth. writ.] Several poems published in school publications. Have a column in school newspaper.; [pers.] 1. What does a peace of literature mean? Nothing if you do not read it. 2. All people are equal; [a.] Mt. Prospect, IL

**MANZANO, JOAN A.**
[b.] Trinidad; [p.] Lorna Olivier; [m.] Leo Manzano; [ch.] Perry Gince Vanessa Lisa, Don, Sophia, Natasha, Alicia Charise, Tisschya; [ed.] Nelson St. Girls R.C Primary School. St Joseph's Convent, St Joseph, High School Trinidad.; [occ.] Housewife; [oth. writ.] Poems (3) and one short story published in the Trinidad Express Newspapers in Trinidad; [pers.] I would like to raise man's consciousness through my writings as to the tragedies and sufferings all over the world, that we could all strive to make it a betters world. To dream is a reality it can come through at any age.; [a.] Brooklyn, NY

**MAPLES, AMANDA KAY**
[b.] February 17, 1987, Manassas, VA; [p.] Sharon Kay Maples, Ben W. Maples; [ed.] I'm in third grade this year; [occ.] Full time kid and loving daughter; [memb.] Student at Oakcrest Elementary School honor student; [hon.] Excellent grades two time first place winner of broken arrow art contest, most creative student award 2988 Baby contest - Manassas, VA; [pers.] I like writing about flowers and nature. I wrote "sweet like honey" for my mommy because I Love Her. I always want to be writing and drawing.; [a.] Broken Arrow, OK

**MARGULIES, ROBERT A.**
[pen.] Robert Alan; [b.] April 28, 1932, Manchester, England; [p.] John and Betty Margulies; [m.] Holly Brooke Margulies, January 10, 1987; [ch.] Keith Alan, Kevin Drew, Kraig Denton Thomas Wyatt (Stepson), Joanne Brooke (Stepdaughter); [ed.] Woodrow Wilson High (Wash, D.C.) University of Maryland: BS (College Park, MD) California State University Long Beach: MBA (Long Beach, CA); [occ.] Senior Principal Specialist, Mc Donnell Douglas; [memb.] Society of Competitive Intelligence Professionals: SCIP, McDonnell Douglas Long Beach Management Club, 1st Pressbyterian Church of Westminster President; [hon.] Phi Kappa Phi National Honor Fraternity, Man of the year Y's men Club Mcdonnell Douglas Long Beach Management Clubs, Society of Competitive Intelligence Professionals Fellows Award; [oth. writ.] 1st Published poem. Have shared my poems with others at social gathering; [pers.] Poetry allows me express my experiences observations, and perceptions about the past, present, and future; [a.] Westminster, CA

**MARRON, GREG P.**
[b.] March 23, 1969, San Francisco, CA; [p.] Don and Margarita Marron; [ed.] Canutillo High, Bachelor Equivalent Electronic-El Paso Technical School; [occ.] Minister, Full-time volunteer at Watchtower-World Headquarters of Jehovah's Witnesses, Data Communications; [pers.] Life provides us with inspirations. Poetry helps to express that and hopefully to move others, to tell someone we care, to make another laugh. We write at times because we feel strongly about something, whether it be happy or sad. If we used poetry to hide behind, then we find ourselves trapped in art. Poetry for the most part was meant to be shared.; [a.] Brooklyn, NY

**MARS, HOWARD T.**
[b.] January 11, 1926, NY; [p.] I should hope so Benjamin and Frances Mars; [occ.] Retired; [memb.] American Chemical Society Halt, Smithsonin; [hon.] I never won a Nobel Prize; [oth. writ.] Volumnist, Bowie Times, poem published in "On threshold of a dream"; [pers.] The world is flat. Stay away from the edges.; [a.] Bowie, MD

**MARSH, FREDRIC**
[pen.] Fredric Marsh, Jr.; [b.] February 16, 1948, Madison, WI; [p.] Fred and Thelma Marsh (Deceased); [ed.] High School College Preparatory.; [occ.] Photographer; [hon.] Silver medal 3000 Meter race walk, masters division, 93, 94. Finalist in photographer's forum annual photo competition, work published in their Best of Photography Annual Featured poet in the Amherst; [oth. writ.] Society's Annual Poetry Competition Title" Pastoral Setting's". This poem was only the third poem that I had produced when I first was inspired to take up poetry in October of 1994.; [pers.] In my poetry, I attempt to strive for a state of poetic uniqueness, harmony, balance, and rhythmic flow. My poem's are inspired by my dream's, supernatural, and life experiences, and scientific knowledge acquisition.; [a.] Stoughton, WI

**MARSH, JENNY CATHERINE**
[b.] November 10, 1982, Newark, NY; [p.] Cynthia and James Marsh; [occ.] 8th Grade Student; [hon.] High Honor roll two years in a row, Math Olympiad award, art award, student of the month award; [oth. writ.] 1 other poem published in book inspirations; [a.] Chapel Hill, NC

**MARSHALL, CAROL ANN**
[b.] September 7, 1932, Hermosa Beach, CA; [ch.] Mother of 4 children, 1 granddaughter, 7 grandsons; [ed.] Santa Ana College, AA - Liberal Arts and English - CSUF; [occ.] Semi-retired; [pers.] Discovering my individual strength and power as a woman has moved me and my writings to reach higher and deeper for my authentic voice.; [a.] Orange, CA

**MARSHALL, GLORIA L. WILLIAMS**
[pen.] Gloria L. Williams; [b.] August 7, 1964, Shelby County; [p.] Willie and Maggi Williams; [m.] Landis Cepeda Marshall, August 4, 1995; [ch.] Aaron, Synoya, Otero, Victoria and Landis Jr.; [ed.] Graduated from Montevallo High School and attended the University of Montevallo for one and a half years.; [occ.] Clerk Typist I with the State of Alabama; [memb.] Member of the NAACP Birmingham Chapter; [oth. writ.] Remembrance, A Nation Of Color, We are A People, No Man's Land, Mama; [pers.] To wait patiently is ones faith in that which he believes, but to hurry is ones faith that only he can succeed.; [a.] Montevallo, AL

**MARSTERS, JAMES A.**
[b.] April 8, 1942, Kalamazoo, MI; [p.] Jewell and James (Deceased); [m.] Jean M. Marsters, November 5, 1957; [ch.] James, Timothy and Kim; [ed.] H.S.; [occ.] Press Operator; [memb.] U.S. Chess Federation unofficial rating (expert); [hon.] Black Belt (Karate), television Repair, Radio - Teletype specialist; [oth. writ.] Fragments - Published by Winston Derek, 1993 - various individual poems published over the years.; [pers.] Man's evil manners live in brass, their virtues we write in water. (by someone else)

**MARTH, PENELOPE LINN**
[pen.] Penelope Marth; [b.] March 23, 1964, Independence, MD; [p.] John and Virginia Marth; [ed.] Independence Christian School, B.F.A. Kansas City Art Institute, Advertising/Display Art Joe Herndon Technical School; [occ.] Freelance Artist

**MARTIN, ALBERTA**
[b.] April 7, 1919, North SC; [p.] Deceased; [ed.] William Penn H.S. Phila PA. B.S. and M.S. in Education from University of Pennsylvania R.N. graduated from Mercy Douglas Hospital School of Nursing Phila. PA; [occ.] Retired Professor of Nursing (Temple University); [memb.] American Red Cross Alpha Kappa Alpha Sorority United Methodist Women of Zoar U. M. Church; [hon.] Theta Chapter Chi Eta Phi Sorority Inc. for outstanding chapel of four Chaplains for outstanding services to all people nominated twice by Nursing faculty/students for Linbach's Award for outstanding teaching; [oth. writ.] Several nursing articles and nursing books reviews published in professional nursing journals; [pers.] I search out the good in others, especially young people and encourage them to develop both mentally and intellectually. As a consequence I do volunteer tutoring in Math, science and reading.; [a.] Philadelphia, PA

**MARTIN, DARA LEE**
[b.] October 29, 1973, Renton, WA; [p.] Darrell and Ann Martin; [ed.] Liberty High; [pers.] I would hope to have all my writings be a reflection in my mothers memory; [a.] Renton, WA

**MARTIN, MICHAEL RAY**
[pen.] Michael Ray Martin; [b.] June 26, 1950, Detroit, MI; [p.] Millard and Donya Martin; [m.] Cynthia Lynn Martin, March 29, 1969; [ch.] Michael Ray Martin II; [ed.] Allen Park High, Macomb College, Highland Park College; [occ.] Auto Mechanic, with G.M.; [memb.] International Society of Poets; [hon.] Nominated as Poet of the year for 1995 by International Society of Poets; [oth. writ.] Beauty Of The Flower - In The Garden Of Life, A Cold Winters Day - In Between The Raindrops, Shadows - best poems of 1996; [pers.] Poems I believe come from the heart and soul. Yet, they're only words till they touch another's heart and soul, then and only then do they become a poem.; [a.] Warren, MI

**MARTINDALE, CHAD**
[b.] September 2, 1979, Denton, TX; [p.] Danny and Shirlee Martindale; [ed.] Sophomore at Valley View High School in Valley View, Texas; [memb.] Valley View FFA, Hillcrest Church of Christ Valley View Athletics; [hon.] Honor Roll Scholar Athlete. Parliamentary Procedure - District Champs - Dairy Cattle Judging Team - State Finalist; [oth. writ.] Several Other poems that I am trying to get published.; [a.] Valley View, TX

**MARTINEAU, LISA**
[b.] July 16, 1979; [p.] Judy and Paul Martineau; [ed.] Chinook Middle School Bellevue High School; [occ.] Student; [hon.] Honor Society (High School) Golden Bear (Middle School); [pers.] Writing poems to me is like magic. I feel like no one can tell me I'm wrong because when I write what I feel no one change that. I hope someday to publish my poems when I write the last poem will be never.; [a.] Bellevue, WA

**MARTINELLI, BARBARA**
[b.] 1953, California; [p.] Ernest and Betty Martinelli; [m.] Charlie Winton, September 7, 1979; [ch.] Two; [ed.] Stanford University (Graduate); [occ.] Script Supervisor, Script Writer, Mother; [a.] Barkley, CA

**MARTINEZ, JOSE F.**
[pen.] Jose Francisco; [b.] July 7, 1935, El Gauche; [p.] Felipe and Rita Martinez; [m.] Fabiola Gonzales, November 22, 1958; [ch.] Joseph, Janice, Lloyd Jonathan, Jacqueline, Jeanette, Judy; [ed.] Espanola High, St.

Micheals College. Industrial Training Institute US army; [occ.] Electronic Technician A; [memb.] Knights of Columbus Legion of Mary; [hon.] Good Conduct Medal; [oth. writ.] My dreams Float across the sea. La cata beso con sabor. Me sento como un rey contigo.

**MASON, JENNIFER A.**
[b.] November 4, 1980, OH; [p.] Jim and Arletla Mason; [ed.] Carroll Christian High School, Heritage Preparatory High School; [occ.] Student; [hon.] National honor society, who's who in American History, who's who among American, High school student.; [oth. writ.] I try to write the feelings of my heart. I try to dedicate each poem I write to someone special. Find that poetry is a great way to let your feeling show.; [pers.] Orlando, FL

**MASON, KARRIE**
[pen.] Karrie Pace; [b.] March 13, 1978, Orlando, FL; [p.] Dezman and Christina Mason; [ed.] High School - (Divine Christian Academy); [occ.] Newspaper; [memb.] National piano guild society; [hon.] 4 Kawanis Medal's; [oth. writ.] Time to rest, Blue Valley; [pers.] Whoever may read this in the future may they know it came from a human heart.; [a.] Clovis, NM

**MASON, KYRA JO**
[b.] March 4, 1956, Aurora, MO; [p.] Emma Gene Mason; [ed.] Some College - Miller High School - Southwest MO. State; [occ.] Sales Representative Missouri State - Lottery; [memb.] National Association Female Executives; [pers.] Everyone can play a masquerade people are so complicated, I go to depths and search for the true being that lies within. My poems reflect the masquerade in the way I think they fell underneath the surface; [a.] Eldorado Springs, MO

**MASTROPOLO, PETER**
[b.] August 23, 1946, New York City, NY; [p.] John (M.D.) Deceased, Mary (Teacher) ret.; [ed.] Archbishop Stepinac H.S. White Plains, NY Manhattan College, Riverdale NY (BS) Iona Grad. School, New Rochelle, NY (M.S. Bio.); [occ.] Asst. Golf Pro, H.S. Bio. Teacher Currently working full time as an Asst. Golf Pro.; [memb.] Distinguish Member International Society of Poets; [hon.] Editors Choice Award 1995 National Library of Poetry, Deans List 1967, Manhattan College; [oth. writ.] "Grieve not for me" (After The Storm) "The Forest Deep" (At Waters Edge) "Myth, Man and Mind" - not published (Copyright Lib. of Congress); [pers.] Through my writing I wish to express the beauty of Science and Nature; [a.] Lake Worth, FL

**MASUCCI, JENNA**
[pen.] Dragon Tears; [b.] September 27, 1981, Queens, NY; [p.] Robert and Charlene Masucci; [ed.] K-8 St. Martins of tours school 9-12 Academy of St. Joseph; [occ.] High School Student; [memb.] Jr. Tennis League School Literary Magazine; [hon.] Other poetry has been published in the up coming fall anthology of poetry of treasure poems of America, 1st place '95 school oratorical contest; [oth. writ.] Escape, published in treasured poems of America Fall '95 Edition.; [pers.] I love writing. I am an aspiring novelist and think of Stephen King and Rod Serling as my role models. I want all the world to know how I feel; [a.] Amityville, NY

**MATARRITA, A. J.**
[b.] August 7, 1985, Miami, FL; [p.] Pamela Matarrita, Alexis Matarrita; [ed.] 5th grade student at Alexander D. Goode Elementary School York, PA.; [memb.] Cub Scouts; [hon.] Pome published in local newspaper; [a.] York, PA

**MATHERS, BILL**
[b.] July 30, 1948, Utica, NY; [p.] Bill Mathers Sr., Doris Mathers; [m.] Katie, September 25, 1993; [ch.]

Karleen Alena, Jessica Leslie, and Jason William; [ed.] BSBA Syracuse University - 1976; [occ.] Human Resource Director; [memb.] Board member Junior Achievement, Toastmasters Int., Society for Human Resource Management; [hon.] Graduated College Cum Laude, Dean's list, Alpha Sigma Lambda, National Honor Society-past president; [oth. writ.] Many other poems; [pers.] To be a work of art, poetry should not only reflect the intellect of the mind, but should also reveal the emotion of the heart and richness of the soul.; [a.] Grapevine, TX

**MATHEWS, TRACEY ALEXIS**
[pen.] Tracey Shadle Mathews; [b.] January 11, 1954, Richmond, IN; [p.] Richard and Emmalou Shadle; [m.] David E. Mathews, May 16, 1974; [ch.] Christopher Allen, Laura Kelly; [ed.] Graduated Hagerstown High School 1972, Indiana Business College 2 yrs.; [occ.] Machine Operator Plastic Injection Mold Corp.; [memb.] Voluntary Optometric service to humanity (V.O.S.H) North Shore Animal League; [hon.] Certificates for contributing time and knowledge on mission to: Haiti, Guatamala, Honduras for Vosh International; [oth. writ.] Published in 1995 sparrow grass poetry contest Poem: Sunrise; [pers.] I am a dreamer, as a dreamer one falls in love with all of lifes treasures, we seldom take time to explore. The world around us has much to offer, if only we take time to inhale her beauty...; [a.] Chuckey, TN

**MATHEWS, VIVIAN**
[b.] November 24, 1910, Waterloo, WI; [p.] Charles Archie, Architect, Amanda Hinitz Archie-Vocalist; [m.] Dr. Willis W. Mathews, February 21, 1942; [ch.] Charles, Willis A. Monie; [ed.] B.S., BA, MA, PHD Un. of Wisconsin Taught of Wisconsin Un. Wayne State.; [occ.] Retired; [memb.] Eastern Star, St Clair Shores Art Club, Sigma Psi (graduate honey) Sigma Delta Epsilon (Women's Honorary); [hon.] Quilting Oil Painting Teaching; [oth. writ.] Amanda Archie Cookbook Archie Clay (genealogy) Histology and Development History of the Ovartestics of Lymnea Stagnalis; [pers.] Do you best, help others do their best, and help to extend love to all mankind.; [a.] St Clair Shores, MI

**MATHEWS SR., FRANK A.**
[pen.] "Buddy" Frank Mathews; [b.] June 18, 1947, Michigan; [p.] James T. and Edna Mae Mathews; [m.] Patricia A. Mathews, March 19, 1966; [ch.] Angel Rickard, Frank A. Mathews Jr.; [ed.] Graduate Waverly Central High; [occ.] Operator with E.I. Dupont; [memb.] Humphrey Co Laity Club Glenwood United Methodist Church; [hon.] My F Awards softball MVP Awards Editor's Choice Award; [oth. writ.] Poetic voices of America - Sunor and Fall and Spring 94 and 95, after the storm-95; [pers.] To write so people will enjoy reading to write for God.; [a.] Waverly, TN

**MATTHEWS, ELIZABETH C.**
[pen.] Leila Elizabeth Curry; [b.] March 16, 1919, Denver, CO; [p.] Franklin and Helen Curry; [m.] Deceased - Elijah Matthews, April 5, 1942; [ch.] Evelyn Elizabeth Matthews; [ed.] 12th grade graduate Business school Graduate; [occ.] Retired from Accounting; [memb.] Shaw neighbor Assn., American Diabetes Assn., American Heart Assn., Lafayette Park United Methodist Church; [hon.] Top Honors - Spelling grade school, Top honors typing - High School; [oth. writ.] Several poems not yet published.; [pers.] My poems try to express the purity of Jesus, and the purity and beauty of my subject, and how the life of Jesus can influence the cleanliness of our life.; [a.] St. Louis, MS

**MATTLER, MICHAEL**
[pen.] Michael Mattler; [b.] March 19, 1979, Detroit; [p.] Henry Mattler, Patricia Mattler; [ed.] Going into 3rd year high school at West Bloomfield High School;

[occ.] Student Captain Golf Caddie Valet Parking Attendant; [memb.] High School Varsity Football High School Varsity Track And Field; [hon.] Earned letter for athletics in track and football nickname "Maddogg" for tenacity on the field. High School Honor Roll; [pers.] Life is short, so live everyday to its fullest because you can't change the past.; [a.] West Bloomfield, MI

**MAXWELL, DIANE**
[pen.] Diane Isaacson; [b.] September 21, 1952, Long Beach, CA; [m.] Divorced for 13 yrs; [ch.] Scott Dean, Stephanie and Sandra Isaacson all grown; [ed.] Bachelor of Science in Nursing from Regents College, University of New York.; [occ.] Emergency Dept. Charge Nurse Gulf Coast Medical Center Wharton, TX; [memb.] Distinguished member if the International Society of Poets; [hon.] Diamond Homer Award from the Famous poets Society, Certificates of merit for poetry. Listed in the 1989 who's who in America poets.; [oth. writ.] Poems in "Distinguished poets of America" "Best Poems of 1995 " " The Best Poems of the 90's" "American poetry Anthology" and 1989 Anthology of midwester poetry".; [pers.] As human beings, we have so many feelings that don't even have names. As poets, we put those feelings into words. I'm flattered and grateful that people are relating to my words.; [a.] Wharton, TX

**MAY, JANE**
[b.] May 30, 1945, Keene, NH; [m.] Victor W. May Jr., June 1, 1964; [ch.] Charlene, Sandra, Victor, Corrine and Fred; [ed.] Keene High and Monadnock Regional; [occ.] Care giver and Cashier; [memb.] Woman's International Bowling Congress; [oth. writ.] Several poems non published; [pers.] My writings are to express feelings left unsaid. Maybe someday they will help others deal with hard spots in their lives.; [a.] Marlow, NH

**MAYHEW, MARY**
[pen.] Marilyn Michaels; [b.] October 15, 1940, Pennsylvania; [p.] Dorothy Redinger; [m.] Single; [ch.] Jack Gregory, Michael Gregory, Lori Boettinger, Lisa King, Tamara Mayhew; [ed.] UCLA; [occ.] Writer and photographer; [memb.] The American Film Institute, Society of Children's Book writers and Illustrators; [hon.] Presidential Award, Photographic Awards; [oth. writ.] Articles Published in local newspapers.; [pers.] Life is a mystery not be taken too seriously. Love it, enjoy it, bath in its beauty, then leave it behind with warm remembrance and to peacefully on.; [a.] Canoga Park, CA

**MAYO, EMMA FAITH**
[b.] May 4, 1953, Washington, DC; [p.] Thomas and Lois Mayo; [ch.] Landen Hughes Mayo; [occ.] Entrepreneur; [hon.] Editor's Choice Award (National Library of Poetry), and Poet of Merit Award ) International Society of Poets; [oth. writ.] Untitled poem, "Where dreams lie still.." published in the anthology, "Songs on the Wind", The National Library of Poetry, 1995; [pers.] Though life has not been kind, I have been fortunate to discern its wonders and beauty. I believe with all I have became because (and inspite) of my suffering that the poetic voice reverberating through me is the chant of countless others. My desire is that through God's gift of words, I may lend a rhythmic voice to souls like myself who may feel alone and unheard.; [a.] Washington, DC

**McADAM, ALFRED E.**
[b.] October 25, 1921, Palmer, MA; [p.] Henry J. and Margaret McAdam; [m.] Ruth M. McAdam, June 7, 1952; [ch.] Margaret E. Reeves; [ed.] Palmer High School 1939 Moody Bible Institute 1952, Taylor University 1954, Fuller Seminary 1954, Butler University 1963; [occ.] Retired was public school teacher; [memb.] Colonial Hills Baptist Church; [oth. writ.] I have com-

piled 7 booklets of poems. There are 35 poems in each booklet (unpublished); [pers.] fear thou not, for I am with thee, Be not dismayed, for I am they God, I will strengthen thee, yea, I will help thee, yea, I will uphold thee with the right hand of my righteousness.; [a.] Indianapolis, IN

**McAULIFF, PATRICIA F.**
[pen.] Patricia, F. McAuliff; [b.] April 10, 1955, Bryn Mawr, PA; [p.] Earl and Emilie Forte; [m.] Steve McAuliff, April 7, 1978; [ch.] Matthew (13) and Katie (10); [ed.] B.A. in English from Rollins College, H.S. Degree from Conestoga High School; [occ.] Writer and Storyteller; [hon.] Dean's List (twice, graduated Cum Laude; [oth. writ.] 25 Children's Stories (unpublished), 30 poems (2 published), one short story (unpublished); [pers.] I enjoy writing to express my emotions, or create pictures and feelings with words.; [a.] Dallas, TX

**McCAMPBELL, JAMES**
[b.] March 12, 1958, Kent, WA; [p.] Jack and Barbara McCampbell; [m.] Cathy, June 11, 1981; [ch.] Robert, Deborah, Jennifer; [ed.] Grad. Cass City High School Taking Courses In Engineering At Various Community College.; [occ.] Manufacturing Tech.; [memb.] The Church of Jesus Christ of Latter Day Saints Scout Master B.S.A; [hon.] Honor Society In High School, Received the Harold Ferguson Award for Top Bald Member in High School, Awards from the Detroit news for Mechanical Engineering Drawings; [oth. writ.] Several poems given to church publications; [pers.] I'd like to thank my mother wife and children to write when the spirit dictates.; [a.] Waterford, MI

**McCANTS, MONTGOMERY LAMARR**
[b.] December 29, 1958, Detroit, MI; [p.] Theresa and Kermit McCants; [m.] Stella Mae McCants, February 17, 1995; [ch.] Iesha Montgomery Jr,. John Sasha, Kyra, Devin, Kita, Otis; [ed.] Graduated 6/76 from Northern High School in Detroit, Mi - Attended Austin Peay State University from 9/79 to 8/81; [hon.] Honorably Discharged from the U.S. Army in 1979 Serve from 1976-1979; [pers.] A special thanks to my wife. Family, and friends for their continued support and belief in me ( I Love You All).; [a.] Elkhart, IN

**McCARTHY, JEROLINE D.**
[pen.] Jerry McCarthy; [b.] September 23, 1942, New York, NY; [p.] Rufus and Clara Coaxum; [m.] Louis McCarthy, July 22, 1967; [ch.] Christopher and Andrew; [ed.] Washington Irving High Bronx Community College; [occ.] Managerial Secretary on Hiatus.; [memb.] The African-American Cultural Society, Various Church Groups; [oth. writ.] "His miracles when they came" ran at the local church, past editor for the hartfords newsletter, "7 YI".; [pers.] Hope kicks in by the human spirit connecting with divine power. It is that power I allude to for our survival.; [a.] Palm Coast, FL

**McCARTY, CHRISTOPHER**
[b.] November 30, 1984, Ohio; [p.] Tommy and Sharon Appell; [ch.] I have 3 brothers and 2 sisters Kam, Pat, Nick, Krista, Justin,; [ed.] I'm in fifth grade; [occ.] Child student; [memb.] I'm a member of the first Pentecostal Church on Dakota Avenue and I go to West Franklin Elementary; [hon.] Jack Hannah from the Columbus zoo sent an autographed; [oth. writ.] Picture, tell me how much he enjoyed my poems.; [pers.] When I grow up I want to write poems like my mom, and save the manatees from extinction. I love my mom, poetry and the manatees.; [a.] Columbus, OH

**McCLAIN, HOWARD ROMANCE**
[pen.] Romance; [b.] Chicago, IL; [p.] William and Annie McClain; [m.] Mary L., February 18, 1961; [ch.] Howard Scott, Michael Lamont; [ed.] Marshall High

School, Crane College; [occ.] Retired (U.S. Postal Service); [hon.] Gammon Untied Methodist Church Choir, Olivet United Methodist Church Choir, U.S. Postal Service; [pers.] I want to be like a cool summer breeze that soothes every heart in it's path.; [a.] Chicago, IL

**McCLAIN, JUSTIN**
[pen.] Lud; [b.] January 7, 1978, Paducah, KY; [p.] Ronnie and Donna McClain; [ed.] Senior in High School; [oth. writ.] A small collection of previously unreleased, original writing and songs; [pers.] "Trust" us very similar to an illegal narcotic. In that, if you indulge and encourage it, it will eventually consume you and be the major cause of your downfall.

**McCLURE, ANNIE**
[b.] April 28, 1925, Navarro Co. TX; [p.] J.H. Rivers (Both Deceased) Ida Williams; [m.] Dean McClure (Deceased), June 4, 1943; [ch.] Renee' Anne McClure; [ed.] Ennis High, Mountain View Jr. College Dallas, Associates Degree (Arts and Sciences); [occ.] Retired; [memb.] WIBC, Dallas 600 Club; [hon.] TAAF Silver Medal Dean's List, Outstanding Achievement Award; [oth. writ.] Family History World War II, Several poems published; [pers.] Dedication to each endeavor. Words hold a special magic to stir the imagination and cleanse the soul.; [a.] Duncanville, TX

**McCLURE, MURIEL LANDRUM**
[pen.] Miss E. F. Aunt Muriel; [b.] March 30, 1034, Home; [p.] Deceased; [m.] Deceased, December 24, 1944; [ch.] 5 Sons; [ed.] 11 grade some college; [occ.] Retired Nurse Aide; [memb.] The National Library of Poetry - and the poet's voice of 602 Elizabeth St. of Wiggins, Miss, 39577; [a.] Wiggins, MI

**McCOLLOUGH, JESSICA N.**
[pen.] Jessica N. McCollough; [b.] February 23, 1982, Riverside, CA; [p.] Kathy Bianonte, Mac McCollough; [ed.] Currently attending Terra Cotta Middle School. I'm in 8th grade; [occ.] School and friends; [memb.] National Geographic, Science Club, Jr. Marine Corps. Club, Sailing Club, Art Club, Drama Club, California Jr. Scholarship Club.; [hon.] Straight A's Student; [pers.] I intend to be a marine biologist when I grow up.

**McCORMICK, MICHAEL P.**
[b.] May 2, 1970, St Louis, MO; [ed.] B.A. from Missouri Baptist College in English; [oth. writ.] Other writings have been published on Missouri Baptist College literary magazines.; [pers.] Poetry, to me is a psychological diagnosis of manic depression. In a sentence one can be taken from the exhalation of existence to the doldrums of the abyss. In a word lies freedom and death, sex violence. The limitations are unbound. You see?; [a.] St. Louis, MO

**McCORMICK, SHARON L.**
[b.] November 1, 1942, Oakland, CA; [oth. writ.] Former SF Chronicle Newspaper Reporter; [pers.] Poem written in memory of my son Terry who died of AIDS in 1990.; [a.] Alameda, CA

**McCOY, SHARON**
[b.] March 30, 1978, Ft. Worth, TX; [p.] Judy and Leon McCoy; [ed.] Southside Hide School; [occ.] Student; [memb.] American Diabetes Association Key Club; [hon.] Duke University Talent Identification Program, regional creative writing contests; [oth. writ.] Other poems published in local school magazine (Menagerie); [pers.] I write to express emotions with in myself that otherwise I could not convey. I also like to make connections with others through my writings who understand such feelings.; [a.] Gadsden, AL

**McCOY, STEPHEN MICHAEL**
[pen.] Michael; [b.] September 27, 1947, Portland, OR; [m.] Lynne Taylor-McCoy; [ed.] AA, BA, Work towards MA, the Baillie School, Lane Community College, Fort wright College, Eastern Washington University; [occ.] Veterans Counselor, State of Virginia Employment commission; [memb.] Various Groups and Organizations to preserve and restore the planet, and protect and recognize the equal rights of its non-human inhabitants to be here as equals with us.; [hon.] Who's who in American Colleges and Universities, Dean's Lists; [oth. writ.] Articles of various length for professional submissions, speeches and presentations for various groups and organizations; [pers.] Let us never forget that truly, the pen in still mightier than the sword, and that it's also easier to 'right' with.; [a.] Portsmouth, VA

**McELLHINEY, ROBERT R.**
[b.] September 22, 1927, Princeton, IN; [p.] Ross and Myrtle Staser McEllhiney; [m.] Theresa Hessig McEllhiney, February 23, 1952; [ch.] Karen Paris, Mona McGregor, Ross McEllhiney, Loretta McEllhiney; [ed.] B.S. - Purdue University, MBA - Indiana University; [occ.] Professor Emeritus - Kansas State University; [memb.] Masons, Scottlin Rite, Shrine, Eastern Star, Beta Theta P., Alpha Zeta, Alpha Mu, American Legion, American Society of Agricultural Engineer.; [hon.] Who's who in the West, who's who in International Engineering, Who's Who in the Midwest, Who's Who in American Education and five other Who's Whos. Am. Feed Industry Assn. Distinguished secure Award, Democracy Cross of Honor Legion of honor; [oth. writ.] 262 Published Articles or chapters in trade magazines and books, "Truck Management" (Book) "Feed manufacturing Technology II "(Book) "Feed Manufacturing Technology IV" (a book), nine other poems in eight anthologies, "Kansas - A view from the flint hills" and "The Land and Star" (Booklet) poetry and essays.; [pers.] I consider myself a "Situation" poet. My best effort have involved retirement. Deaths, masonic event and people, and significant human and natural events and conditions.; [a.] Manhattan, KS

**McGLOIN, JEAN**
[b.] April 4, 1977, New York, NY; [p.] Ethel and Thomas McGloin; [ed.] Wayne Valley High School, attending Bryn Mawr College; [occ.] College Student; [hon.] National Honor Society, Who's Who of American High School Students, PTO Scholarship

**McGLYNN, R. RYAN**
[b.] March 25, 1983, New York; [p.] William and Phyllis McGlynn; [ed.] Completed the 6th grade K-6 Oak Knoll School of the Holy Child, Summit New Jersey will attend Delbarton in Morris Township New Jersey. Entering the 7th grade.; [hon.] Mathematical Olympiads Awards 1993-95, National Current Events League Award 1993-95, Certificate of Achievement - Ciba Geigy Science Awards 1993-95 Presidents Environmental Youth Award 1992-95; [pers.] Education is like walking it will take you anywhere you want to go.

**McGOWAN, REBECCA LYNN**
[b.] August 25, 1972, Danbury, CT; [p.] Deborah J. and William McGowan; [ed.] Currently a student at Southern Connecticut State University; [a.] Cheshire, CT

**McHALE, KRISTEN MARGARET**
[b.] June 26, 1980, New Brunswick, NJ; [p.] William and Pamela McHale; [ed.] Matawan Regional High School (Sophomore); [occ.] Student; [memb.] Girl scouts, Key Club, Student Council, Youth Choir, Youth Club; [hon.] Dr. Norman Field Student Achievement Award, Who's Who among American High School Students, music honor society; [pers.] Success is a journey, not a destination.; [a.] Matawan, NJ

**McKENZIE, ELIZABETH ANN**
[pen.] Liz McKenzie; [b.] March 30, 1960, Washington, DC; [p.] Robert Leo, Mary McLane Powers; [m.] James Marvin McKenzie; [ch.] Sara Marie Powers age 18 attending A.C.C. College; [ed.] 12 years Be all Jr. Sr. High school - self taught pianonist, key board artist composer of songs, lyricist and poet 10 years Nursing Asst.; [occ.] Domestic Engineer; [memb.] Maple hurst Swim Team 1967, 1968, 1969, 1970. Frostbury Moose #348 Member. St Michaels Church; [hon.] Swimming Trophies for racing, diving. Honorable mention in Art class. I also have performed publicly in a band, singing and playing the keyboards for 2 years.; [oth. writ.] I've written hundreds of poems and songs. I' have been writing and composing since the age of 5 years. Publicly performing 2 of my original songs, in 1989 1900 in Western Maryland W. VA.; [pers.] Life and love in general have greatly influenced my writing I have always written from my heart and mind. Sometimes it comes so fast to me, I have to hurry to put it on paper.; [a.] Frostburg, MD

**McKINNEY, DARYLYN**
[pen.] Darylyn McKinney Rose II; [b.] June 16, 1962, Neptune, NJ; [p.] Everett and Ida L. Moore; [ch.] Megan Rose and Evan Patrick McKinney; [occ.] Nursing Tech.; [oth. writ.] 300 Poems and short stories.; [pers.] To life in this world, with a gentle spirit, we must not only love, but always's try to forgive the past, that may hinder us from our future. Love in Christ always.; [a.] Sacramento, CA

**McKINNEY, DEBBIE SUE**
[b.] June 9, 1961, Sault Ste Marie, MI; [p.] W. Michial McKinney and Patricia Marie McKinney; [m.] divorced; [ch.] I've been single, with my child 13 years. Brandon Patrick Elkins age 14, Raysha Rene Smith McKinney age 6; [ed.] Graduate of Elkhart Central High 1979; [occ.] Executive Secretary/Office Manager of S&S Siding Applicator's Inc. (Employed there for 8 years); [memb.] I am involved with 2 POW/MIA groups, I am involved with issues concerning all veterans.; [hon.] Being published in this book is my highest honor thus far.; [oth. writ.] I have my own personal collection. I was published in Eugene Field-An Anthology in Memoriam I have had several letters and writings in local newspaper.; [pers.] "Look further-beyond what you see" I am humbled, and jubilant. I feel as tho the Lord has reached down through the clouds and touched me, that the secret words of my soul may touch someone else.; [a.] Elkhart, IN

**McKINNEY, FREDRICK HENRY**
[pen.] F. Henry McKinney; [b.] April 17, 1941, Pontica, MI; [p.] Mr. and Mrs. Bert McKinney; [m.] Beverly Sue (Speer) McKinney, November 9th 1962; [ch.] Laura Jean (Nevins) 32 and Keith Edward McKinney, 29; [ed.] Rochester Public Schools, 4th and Wilcox, Freed-Hardeman College, North-West Airlines Training Center, McConnell Airline School (Minneapolis, MN); [occ.] Wholesale Distributor of Gift Shoppe Merchandise; [memb.] International Society of Poets ASCAP (Song-Writers) Composer; [hon.] Golden Poet Award 1987 and 1991-92 Interlochen Music Camp - (Scholarship) Honorable Discharge (United States Navy); [oth. writ.] Record-Album (Sunrise Record Company) Song Lyrics/Music Religious and Secular; [pers.] A Poet dedicated and trained by Masters of Perfect Metrel Perfect Rhyme; [a.] Bay City, MI

**McLEOD, BRIAN**
[pen.] Ian Locke; [b.] September 25, 1961, Boston; [p.] Kenneth McLeod, Tamara McLeod; [ed.] B.S. Eastern Ct. University, Enfield High School Computer Processing Institute, Connecticut School of Broadcasting; [occ.]

Data Processing; [memb.] Bally's Health Club; [hon.] Graduated with Honors from High School; [pers.] I write to capture a moment in time as seen through multi-colored glasses. Writing is therapy for me I hope to compare songs eventually.; [a.] Enfield, CT

### McLEOD, LYLE
[b.] February 18, 1948, San Diego, CA; [p.] Harold C. McLeod (Deceased), and Loretta Metzer; [m.] Single; [ed.] Hoover High School San Diego State Univ.; [occ.] Saddle Maker and Leather artisan; [memb.] Leather makers guild. International society of poets distinguished member; [hon.] San Diego historical Society - Gen'l. Gatchell Mem. Award, Ft. Guijarros Museum Foundation award - Military History, Several Awards for Poetry that has been published; [oth. writ.] "History of San Diego Militias from 1847-1917." SD Hist. Soc. Nat. Lib. of Poetry: "Common Soldier", "The Cutting Word" Famous poets society: "Wishing Wells"; [pers.] With the friends I love, - I'm rich with good health, horses and dogs, fortunate. Living with mountains, rivers, and wildlife lucky. These are God's gift to me. What I do with them is my gift to God.; [a.] Ilfeld, NM

### McNEIL, TALAMIEKA WANNETTE
[pen.] Talamieka McNeil; [b.] August 11, 1980, Grenada, MS; [p.] Miss Thelma Hardiman; [ed.] I am currently a sophomore at Montgomery County High School; [occ.] At this present moment I am unemployed due to age.; [memb.] I am a member of The National Honor Roll Society, Litter Quitter and Me Too Detective Club; I am a former member of the Girl Scout Club; [hon.] I have received the United States Achievement Award, the eighth grade English Award, World Book Achievement Award and medal, President Award for Educational Excellence for 4 consecutive years.; [oth. writ.] I have written several other poem's but, have never had the courage to send one in until now.; [pers.] I was created by a teardrop from whence came the sea. Many have doubted my power and so abused me. Yet throughout my trials, many tears and so much bitter pain, you look to the sky and still wonder why I reign.; [a.] Kilmichael, MS

### McNUTT, JEAN
[b.] May 20, 1925, Mich; [p.] Don and Beatrice Irwin; [m.] Harvey Mcnutt, April 10, 1952; [ch.] Roger, Barry, Douglas, Elaina; [ed.] 12th; [occ.] Retired; [memb.] Lifetime member ISP American Legion Aux current President of Paper and Pen Poetry Club; [hon.] Award and Merit ISP. Editors choice 1994 and 1995 Nat' Library of poetry Honorable Mention Iliad Press; [oth. writ.] Books poems to ponder and peons to ponder #2 unpublished 10 poems published in anthologies; [pers.] My poems date back to 1958 I try to write in as simple language any age group can enjoy. Poetry to me ie the language and love I intend to spread it around.; [a.] Saranac, MI

### McPHERSON, JUDY
[b.] June 9, 1960, Seattle; [p.] David Knight, Dorothy Knight; [m.] Ray McPherson, July 16, 1983; [ch.] Celia Kristine, Traia Janette; [ed.] Mt. Rainier High, Carolyn Hansen Fashion College; [occ.] Housewife; [pers.] I'm trying to make my mark in life, no matter how subjective life is a lot like that though isn't it? Some like it some don't.; [a.] Glendale, AZ

### McRAE, DAVID MICHAEL
[b.] April 6, 1935, San Diego; [p.] John and Hank McRae; [m.] Mary Margaret Wittman, June 11, 1960; [ch.] Douglas, Lynne and Laurie; [ed.] A.B San Diego State College (1957), M.D. University of California S.F. (1962); [occ.] Retired Pathologist (teacher); [memb.] ASCP Int'l Academy of Path., Pacific Dermatological Association; [a.] Orange, CA

### McTAGGART, THERESA DIANA
[b.] October 31, 1972, Jamaica, West Indies; [p.] Arthur McTaggert, Viola McTaggart; [ed.] St. Catherine High School Westchester Community College; [occ.] Bookkeeper, Cashier, Student. Pathmark, Mt. Vernon; [memb.] Wilson Center Associates; [hon.] Medal for Outstanding Achievement in Biology. Presidents list; [pers.] Happy thoughts are good thoughts. It takes less to smile than to frown.; [a.] Mount Vernon, NY

### MEADOWS, DELLA A. R.
[pen.] Della A. R. Meadows; [b.] April 1, 1919, A Diamond Ranch Kelvin, AZ; [p.] Phil and Rose Hall, Deceased; [m.] Redondo Phil Meadows, June 15, 1950; [ch.] Son, Phil R. B. 6-1-51, Killed in plane crash 7-18-1982; [ed.] Continues. Perpetual student; [occ.] Retired but active First Presbyterian Church, etc.; [memb.] Life. Pinal Co Hist. Soc., Life: Fraternal Order of Police, Life: Pro Rodeo Hist. Soc. Soc., Inc. Member: McFarland State Park - Fl., etc. Have dropped most others.; [hon.] Most recent honor June 7, 1994, an 800-bed $53,000,000.00 Prison named for me by Dept. of Corrections; [oth. writ.] Book 1: "Good Morning in the Dawn, Dear Son," (all proceeds, annually to Shriners 'Crippled Childrens' Hospitals. Book 2: "Manna From Heaven" recipe book written for First Presbyterian Church, Book 3: "Where Two of Three Are Gathered" History of First Presbyterian Church's first 100 years— written for the Church.; [pers.] "Do what you can, where you are, with what you have." Not original but my philosophy. Have enjoyed books and study, classical music, world travel, etc.; [a.] Florence, AZ

### MEDLOCK, LESLIE
[b.] January 23, 1947, Louisville, KY; [p.] Dorothy Mason; [m.] Divorced; [ch.] Alison Taylor, Brad Medlock; [ed.] A.S. Enterprise Jr. College. B.A. Columbus College, M.Ed. Columbus College; [occ.] English Instructor, Troy State University; [hon.] Cum Laude Graduate, Lambda Iota Tan Honor Society; [oth. writ.] Poems published many years ago in local papers and college and high school paper.; [pers.] I have not written in over 20 years and now find myself wanting very much to express my emotions on paper as a means of release.; [a.] Enterprise, AL

### MEEK, ADAM M.
[b.] April 3, 1965, Chicago; [p.] Marcellus R. Meek, Cynthia B. Thompson; [m.] Gretchen D. Binhammer, April 22, 1994; [ed.] A.B. Univ. of Michigan, J. D. Northwestern University; [occ.] Attorney at Law; [memb.] Chicago Bar Assoc. Ill - state Bor Assoc., American Bor Assoc.; [hon.] Phi Eta Sigma (Nat Hon. Society), James B. Angell Scholar (U. of M.), Dean List, graduated U. of M. with High Distinction; [pers.] I hope that writing will be a step toward fulfilling my responsibility to make a constructive contribution to society by enhancing peoples' awareness, understanding and compassion for one another.; [a.] Chicago, IL

### MELENDEZ, ADELA
[pen.] Adela Melendez Parmele; [b.] January 20, 19401, San Salvador, El Salvador, CO; [p.] Guillermo Melendez Blanco and Lydia Parmele Sanders; [ch.] One Giannina Maria Melendez; [ed.] (Colegio "La Asuncion" San Salvador, El Salvador C.A.), SF - St. Joseph's - St. James (Boarding-School) Presidio Jr. High, William McKinley and George Washington High School, (I did not graduate); [occ.] Taking care of my three grandchildren - Michael, Ray and Alexia; [oth. writ.] I have written about ele-poems in El Salvador. But I left them there. I never had them published. However, I shall get in touch with the person who I left them with. And may be I'll be lucky and have them publish also.; [pers.] "I say to you all, who ever you are, wherever you may be,

we have a united nations, together, let's all try to make it a united world."; [a.] El Sobrante, CA

### MELLAS, BARBARA R.
[b.] March 16, 1945, Flushing, NY; [p.] Herbert and Ruth Jones; [m.] James P. Mellas, June 22, 1989; [ch.] Kimberly; [ed.] Southhold High School; [occ.] Retired Maintenance Administrator, from 31 years with Nynex, working with flowers at present; [hon.] "Extra Step" Award from Nynex for outstanding service to the customers; [oth. writ.] "For You Blue" Published in the Suffolk Times local paper for my husbands retirement; [pers.] I am a very spiritual person and my message is to give others faith and inspiration; [a.] Smithtown, NY

### MELLO, MARY H.
[b.] December 25, 1949, Dunkirk, NY; [p.] Mr. and Mrs. John Bemis; [m.] Manuel C. Mello Jr., February 14, 1991; [ch.] Dana, Jennifer and Stephanie; [ed.] Currently in Community College of Rhode Island, working toward bachelor's in Health and Science with Nursing Background; [occ.] Nursing Assistant at Hopkins Manor in No. Providence R.I; [hon.] 4.0 Student in CCRI that will get nursing degree and then Bachelors in Health and Science at the University of Rhode Island.; [oth. writ.] Personal Collection of poems and short stories short story published in children's magazine; [pers.] The way to deal with the cynical attitude of the people you encounter is to kill them with kindness and always treat others with the same respect that you would like yourself.; [a.] Cranton, RI

### MELLOTT, LATNA
[b.] August 30, 1942, Cincinnati, OH; [p.] William C. and Golden Gibbs; [m.] David Vincent Mellott, April 15, 1965; [ch.] Mark; [ed.] Albany High School, Ohio University; [occ.] Mellott Distributing Willoughby, Ohio (Vice-Pres.); [pers.] My writing usually reflects the comedy and poignancy of everyday life.; [a.] Mentor, OH

### MELVIN, DAWN
[b.] April 1, 1975, Fayetteville, NC; [p.] Mildred C. Melvin; [ed.] Methodist College 2nd year student (Communications); [pers.] I mostly express my feelings in my writings. Subjects that I feel strongly about, and that make people want to search deep into their soul.

### MENDENHALL, THELMA SUE
[b.] August 10, 1976, Columbus, OH; [p.] Wayne and Carolyn Mendenhall; [ed.] Graduate of Kenton Senior High School in 1994. Attended Bowling State University for one year. Now attending Lima Technical College for Executive Secretarial; [occ.] Cleaning Personnel; [memb.] Church of Christ, National Honor Society.; [hon.] Top 3% for my poem what's it called when 10 other poems published by Poetry Press.; [oth. writ.] 103 other poems, 8 short stories, many essays; [pers.] Dream, follow your dreams and never give up or them.; [a.] Kenton, OH

### MENDOZA, ROBERT
[b.] March 15, 1961, East Chicago, IN; [p.] Lupe Vela and Adrian Mendoza; [ed.] George Washington High School, Purdue University Calumet; [occ.] Electronics Engineer Kelly Air Force Base, San Antonio, TX; [memb.] Purdue University Alumni Assoc.; [oth. writ.] Several poems still unpublished or made public.; [pers.] To my dear friends Mollie A. B. Kennedy and Renee C. Brooks to whom I love deeply and share this poem with. You are both very dear to me, I share this poem with you and others, so be it (S.B.I.).; [a.] San Antonio, TX

### MERRILL, RUTH E.
[b.] November 19, 1911, Providence, RI; [p.] Charles - Lora Chester; [m.] Warren (Deceased), February 2,

1927; [ch.] Ann Grace; [ed.] High School; [occ.] Retired.

**MERRILL, STACIA**
[pers.] The author lives and plays in Western Massachusetts with her 4 years old son Zack

**MERSING, HEATHER**
[b.] August 29, 1977, Torrance, CA; [p.] Walter and Bonnie Mersing; [ed.] Graduated from Palos Verdes Peninsula High School June 95; [occ.] College Student; [memb.] Mount OLive Lutheran Church; [oth. writ.] Poem the Drifter; [pers.] You are always someone, but you need to believe in yourself so you will know it too; [a.] Rancho Palos Verdes, CA

**MESSNER, LORRAINE**
[pen.] Lorraine C. Messner; [b.] August 20, 1979, Sacramento CA; [p.] James and DeLanie; [ed.] Junior in High School, hoping to attend University of Southern California with a major in Theatre; [occ.] Student; [oth. writ.] Other unpublished poems; [pers.] As I get older I realize life is very precious and it goes by very fast. We all must make the best of it. But waiting around for something to happen won't do. You must work at what you want, and sooner or later it will pay off.; [a.] Raleigh, NC

**METCALFE, MICHELLE MARIE**
[pen.] Mikki; [b.] December 26, 1980, Clark AFB, Philippines; [p.] Brad and Anita Metcalfe; [ed.] I am currently a sophomore at Nashville High School; [memb.] National Honor Society; [hon.] Academic Honors in every year of schooling; [oth. writ.]; [pers.] My poems tend to portray confusion frustration, and hurt. Writing is like revealing a secret that is burning up inside. Once you reveal your secret, its like a weight has been lifted off your shoulder and you have a sense of relied and fulfillment. Writing is a way for me to release stress and to mark memorable moments in my life.; [a.] Niceville, FL

**MEYER III, BRAYTON L.**
[pen.] Elroy Meyer; [b.] August 16, 1967, Bronxville, NY; [p.] Brayton L. Meyer Jr. and Mary Meyer; [ed.] East Aurora High School; [occ.] Machine Operator; [oth. writ.] This is my first published work.; [pers.] I would like to thank my family, friends, and higher power for all the love I have been given.; [a.] East Aurora, NY

**MIGNONE, JOSEPH MICHAEL**
[b.] May 21, 1943, Jersey, City, NJ; [p.] Generoso and Micheline Mignone; [m.] Christina Mignone, May 13, 1967; [ch.] Diane Mignone, Christopher Mignone; [ed.] Holy Family High School Union City New Jersey, Fairleigh Dickinson University (2 yrs.) Teaneck, New Jersey; [occ.] Benefits Mgr. and sportwriter and the Wall Herald; [memb.] Knights of Columbus Cantor in Church Choir Executive Board of Local Little League Organization.; [hon.] KOFC Family of the year '91-92 and '92-93 and Knight of the year '93-94; [oth. writ.] Many featured articles in addition to regular weekly sports coverage in the Wall Herald. Numerous poems written and presented to church and civil designatories on special occasions.; [pers.] I enjoyed a special relationship with my father and have been inspired by his deeply, moving poetry. Like him writings are centered upon the people I love the beauty of nature and our Lord who has created them.; [a.] Brick, NJ

**MIHELIS, HRISOULA**
[b.] January 18, 1974, Athens, Greece; [p.] Anastasios and Athanasia Mihelis; [ed.] Long Island City HS Lagaurdia Community College; [occ.] Receptionist; [hon.] A Vassar/Laguardia Exploring Transfer Program Nominee at Laguardia Community College.; [a.] Astoria, NY

**MILKE, SHARON J.**
[pen.] Shari Milke; [b.] August 14, 1952, Tala Bluff, IL; [p.] Virginia Eills Nee Milkbrandt; [m.] Marten, September 26, 1992; [ch.] In process of adopting our first child; [ed.] Wheeling High School Oakton Community College; [occ.] Kennel Manager Preir Animal Hospital; [memb.] Member of trinely Lutheran Church,; [hon.] Editors Choice Award 1995; [oth. writ.] Contemporary poets of Britain and America 1993, songs on the wind 1994; [pers.] My poems are about my life and the loved ones that surround me. I'm blessed me have family and wonderful friends; [a.] Des Plaines, IL

**MILLER, DIANNE COOK**
[ed.] B.A. in education - Anderson University, Anderson, Indiana, M.A. in Education - Ball State University, Muncie Indiana; [occ.] Elementary School Teacher - Fairmount, Indiana; [a.] Alexandria, IN

**MILLER, IDA MAE GURLEY**
[b.] June 29, 1934, New Albany, MS; [p.] Eugene and Hattie Gurley; [m.] Widowed; [ch.] Gerald Wayne Calhoun, Linda Joyce Calhoun; [ed.] U.C.T.S. - B.F. Ford High School, New Albany, MS, Kennedy-King and Harold Washington Colleges, Chicago, IL; [occ.] Clerk-Typist; [memb.] Berean Baptist Church Choir and Sunday school; [hon.] Good Citizenship Award upon graduation from high school, received plaque for length of service, cited for perfect attendance, good job performance and won first place in an oratorical contest at places of employment.; [oth. writ.] A few writings published in in-and out-of-town newspapers, church bulletins, keep family journal, have two articles ready for publication (short stories).; [pers.] I write to record and preserve memories. Recently, after writing a short story of dear friends who have past on the poem, "Departed Friends" was born.; [a.] Chicago, IL

**MILLER, KANDICE**
[b.] April 21, 1980, Oregon; [p.] Donita Miller, David, Miller; [ed.] Tumwater High School; [occ.] Student; [pers.] My inner feelings come out through my poems; [a.] Tumwater, WA

**MILLER, LORI LEA**
[b.] December 10, 1969, Valdosta, GA; [p.] Melba and Johnny Miller; [occ.] Assistant Head Cashier; [pers.] True happiness lies within ourselves. We can't be happy with the rest of the world until we're truly happy with ourselves.; [a.] Valdosta, GA

**MILLER, MAVIS**
[b.] Jamaica; [p.] Evelyn Miller, Herbert Miller; [ed.] Northern Academy High J.W.I. Browns Town Community College, Claremont Elementary School Jamaica West Indies; [occ.] Eligibility Specialist Human Resources Administration; [memb.] New Testament Church Of God; [hon.] A - Student; [pers.] I would like to encourage children to stay in school and decrease the drop-out rate.; [a.] New York, NY

**MILLER, RACHAEL ROSS**
[pen.] Rae Robinson; [b.] August 18, 1906, Philadelphia; [p.] Marlene and Robert Ross; [m.] Richard Miller Sr., July 11, 1986; [ch.] One wonderful son, born September 26, 1988 (Jr.); [ed.] High School 2 yrs. Community College Several Vocational school related to Nursing CEU; [occ.] LPN - Charge Nse Supervisor; [memb.] Acorn Community Grd. Nse. Service Organ; [hon.] Several Awards for Academics to perfect attendance while in schools publications in High School poetry Society.; [oth. writ.] One poem published while in high school. There are other writing that I keep close

to my heart and soul!; [pers.] My pen is lead by my winner spirit. My writings are for women of all ages. There is a sisterhood!; [a.] Philadelphia, PA

**MILLER, ROBERT E.**
[pers.] This poem is a tribute to my daughter Angela Marie, killed by a drunk driver on Halloween night Oct. 31, 1979; [a.] Louisville, KY

**MILLER, TAMMY K.**
[pen.] Kaye Deming; [b.] January 20, 1970, TX; [p.] Winfred Miller and Janice Ashcraft; [ed.] University of Houston - Criminal Justice Major, New Boston High School; [occ.] Paralegal; [memb.] Houston Legal Assistants' Assoc.; [hon.] Who's Who Among American High School Students; Dean's list; [oth. writ.] Unpublished personal poetry and journals; [pers.] In life what is seen through the soul may not be seen with the eye. Yet, the eyes are a pathway to the soul.; [a.] Houston, TX

**MILLER, TINA LAMARR**
[b.] August 18, 1970, Florida; [m.] Ray Lewis; [ch.] Gordon Miller, Ravaughan and Demetrius Lewis; [ed.] Mansfield school of business - admin. Asst.; [occ.] Cook; [pers.] I would like to dedicate this and all of my poems to Mr. Mary Sellers (mom) for always encouraging me to keep striving to do and be the best that I can; [a.] Jax, FL

**MILLS, ALTAMONT**
[b.] July 25, 1930, Kingston, Jamaica; [p.] J.B, Mills (Dec'd), A.E.D. Myers (Dec'd); [m.] Enid B.(Nee Vaughan), December 15, 1962; [ch.] Suzanne A.; [ed.] Excelsior School Kingston, Jamaica, Council of Legal Education, London, England; [occ.] Retired; [oth. writ.] Unpublished; [pers.] Some people have lived their entire lives on mountains, and never once have seen the stars; [a.] Tampa, FL

**MILLS, KATHRYN**
[b.] March 2, 1953, Pocatello, ID; [p.] Robert and Roberta Neeley; [m.] Robert, December 16, 1972; [ch.] Robert and Rachel; [ed.] High School con't Medical Education; [occ.] Health Unit coordinator, mother, wife.; [memb.] National Parks and Conservation Assoc., Defenders of Wildlife, Green Peace, World Wildlife Fun.; [hon.] National Wildlife federation, Backyard Wildlife Habitat Achievement. Motherhood; [oth. writ.] This is my first.; [pers.] Protect mother earth and all her inhabitants, she is all we have.; [a.] Glenwood, IA

**MILLSAP, ROCHELLE L.**
[ch.] Christy Jo and Joseph Austin; [ed.] University of Wisconsin Milwaukee. Bachelor of Science.; [hon.] Graduated Cum Laude with class of 1977.; [oth. writ.] I have several pieces written, but have never sought publication.; [pers.] My writings are an effort to express the soul's journey. I believe that it is only by seeing through our veiled realities and suffering the anxiety of change that we become "real".; [a.] Nashville, TN

**MILTON, JIMMY DEWAYNE**
[pen.] J. D. Milton; [b.] April 24, 1955, Edgewood, TX; [p.] Dortha Rene Lewis, Marzell Milton; [m.] Regina Denise Milton, June 6, 1981; [ch.] Crystal Denetta Milto, Marisa Dawn Milton; [ed.] Edgewood High Edgewood, TX B.S. Computer Science East Texas State University, Commerce, TX; [occ.] Sr. Quality Engineer (Software); [memb.] Omega Psi Phi Fraternity, Inc. Delta Xi Chapter, Association of old crow; [hon.] Who's who among students in American Universities and Colleges; [oth. writ.] Several poems published in Fraternity's News; [pers.] Discord the word "can't because when used you have already accepted defeat. We all need to take time out and give thanks to

those who help us.; [a.] Garland, TX

**MINOR, TERRI**
[b.] November 18, 1965, Hartsville, SC; [p.] Mildred and Gary Arthur; [m.] Cedric Minor, September 15, 1988; [ch.] Warren Kelvin, Cedric Lance II; [ed.] Hartsville, Sr. High, Cochise College, Central Texas College equipment record and parts special (U.S. Army); [occ.] Student; [hon.] National Defense Service Medal, Army Good Conduct Medal, Army service Ribbon Markmanship Badge Rifle; [oth. writ.] Several poems that have not been submitted.; [pers.] My poems reflect the way I see the world and the changes to be made.; [a.] Ft. Hood, TX

**MINZBERG, JANE G.**
[pen.] Jane G. Minzberg; [b.] February 18, 1903, Lithvania; [p.] Julius and Julia Goldstein; [m.] Isaac David Minzberg, March 4, 1929; [ch.] Deborah Pincus (daughter) Caroline Joy Pincus (Granddaughter); [ed.] Teacher's Degree; [occ.] Poet and Artist; [memb.] Life member of Hadassah and National Retired Teacher's Assoc.; [hon.] The painting for which I won first place, was of the tree which inspired me to write the poems. "My Inspiration" 1st Prize Senior Citizen Art Contest; [oth. writ.] Collection of poems.; [pers.] You cannot write poetry without genuine emotion. Poetry is the distilled essence of one's thoughts and feelings.; [a.] Elizabeth, NJ

**MIRANDA, BRENDA MARIE**
[b.] July 17, 1979, Mt. View, CA; [p.] Al and Martha Miranda; [ed.] Starting High School 9/95; [occ.] P/T Waitress, vacations; [memb.] Member of Church of Christ; [pers.] Loves animals and wants to be Marine Veterinarian; [a.] Seaside, CA

**MIRANDA III, ERENES A.**
[b.] October 17, 1965, Columbus, GA; [p.] Erenes Miranda Jr. and Doris Miranda; [m.] Cheryl Miranda, March 30 1990; [ch.] Richard Martin, Erin Alexandria; [pers.] Would like to dedicate "Lost in A Day Dream" to my late brother Robert, and younger brother John.; [a.] Fresno, CA

**MITCHELL, CAROLYN MCDONALD**
[b.] September 18, 1953, Waycross, GA; [p.] Walter McDonald Alta McDonald; [m.] David L. Mitchell, December 1987; [ch.] Arthur Robinson 22, Ashle Collier 15, David and Michael, Mitchell (twins) 7; [ed.] Associate Degree Thomas College 1982, Presently working on B.S. Degree; [memb.] Good Shepherd Episcopal Church; [hon.] Who's Who in College Students 1982 CMA License 1982; [pers.] One must never give up. I have suffered with Bi Polar disorder (laymen terms-Manic depression) for 20 yrs. Triumph over my person conflict has inspired my writing.; [a.] Thomasville, GA

**MITCHELL, TRACY**
[pen.] Legacy; [b.] September 21, 1965, New York; [p.] Robert and Artie Mitchell; [m.] Single; [ed.] Norman Thomas Commercial H.S. New York University (NYU); [occ.] International Accountant; [memb.] National blood drive National Honor Society, Tri-State Intern Alliance; [hon.] National Honor Society Salutatorian in Jr. High School Math Champion in East Side division in High School (NYC), District Award for Musical Excellence in Jr. High School; [oth. writ.] Two poems published in Jr. High School newspaper and several unpublished works.; [pers.] I believe poetry is the ultimate way to express feelings you have inside that you find difficult to utter orally!!!; [a.] Bronx, NY

**MIZE, PATRICIA**
[pen.] Patricia Mize; [b.] January 7, 1940, Birmingham, AL; [p.] Luther and Jewell Pilkington; [m.] Jo-

seph and Mize September 3, 1955; [ch.] Terri Mize Shugart, Lisa Mize Templin, son-in-law Willard Shugart Johnny Templin-Granddaughter-Stacey Shugart; [occ.] Housewife

**MIZLOCK, COLETTA L.**
[b.] January 31, 1948, Medina, OH; [p.] Mable and Earl Flagg; [m.] John Mizlock, May 15, 1992; [ed.] Shaw High, Finlay College A.B.W.A. Scholarship.; [occ.] Domestic Engineer; [hon.] Deans list. B.S. in education 15 hrs towards masters at Lake Erie College 3 Achievement Awards in Deaf Sign Language; [oth. writ.] For pleasure I write poetry about nature, children and spiritual.; [pers.] Nature and the love in the heart of man reflects the light of Christ within us all is the potential to share, care, be patient kind and forgiving.; [a.] Willowick, OH

**MOLINARI, MARIE A.**
[b.] April 3, 1926, Philadelphia; [p.] Joseph Molinari, Anne Molinari; [ed.] High School South High School for girls; [occ.] Retired - Tax Analyst; [memb.] Holy Cross Prayer Group Amateur Theater Groups; [oth. writ.] Many poems published in local newspapers, several songs, music and lyrics, used in amateur threate productions. Among them, "They Call Me Lucky", "Polk Dot Panda", and "The Situations Sad"; [pers.] I wish to encourage the goodness of mankind by way of example.; [a.] Clifton Heights, PA

**MOLL, PHIL**
[pen.] Phillip Dela Moll; [b.] February 3, 1948, Pinkney Ville, IL; [occ.] Firefighter; [oth. writ.] "And a nation weeps" published in local and Oklahoma newspaper "To life" "A rhythm and a reason", etc.; [pers.] I feel poetry should 'embolden the world yet make it comprehensible; [a.] Barrington, IL

**MOMYER, THOMAS**
[pen.] Momyer; [b.] December 26, 1947, Mt. Pleasant, PA; [p.] Meredith Momyer; [m.] Pamela Momyer, May 22, 1988; [ed.] B.A., Univ. of Miami Coral Gables - English, Mass Communications Tulane University - Chemical Engineering; [occ.] Systems Analyst; [oth. writ.] Columnist for Database Management Magazine, "The Travails of knorft" weekly political satire in the New Pittsburgh Sun.; [pers.] 1. Art is for Art's sake, 2. Work hard, party harder!; [a.] Matawan, NJ

**MONHOLLEN, VIRGINIA A.**
[pen.] Jenny Shaffer; [b.] March 22, 1959, Somerset, PA; [p.] George Shaffer, Gerry Homer; [m.] Robert T. Monhollen, June 30, 1995; [ch.] Cory Jo Micheal Shaffer, Shawna Marie Shaffer, Thad and Christina Monhollen; [ed.] Payne Elementary and Jr. High, Wayne Trace High School; [occ.] Housewife; [hon.] Volunteer Award for drawing pictures for head start program; [pers.] I would like to dedicated my Grandma Nancy Breslin for telling me to keep writing because you never know what will come of it.; [a.] Grover Hill, OH

**MONTBLANC, GINNY**
[pen.] Virginia Marcelene Montblanc; [b.] December 18, 1932, Dubuqur, IA; [p.] Alphonse Schmidt, Clara Schmidt; [m.] 1st Thomas Allen, 2nd Robert Montblanc, February 19, 1997; [ch.] Thomas Michael Patrick Edward, Julie Mar, Margaret Clare, Peter Joseph, Mark Matthew (All Allens) and 10 stepchildren; [ed.] Visitation Academy, Adrian College, Life and Great Parents.; [occ.] Homemaker - editor of newcomers Newsletter; [memb.] Not Pertinent - Mostly Social and Sport; [hon.] Volunteer of the Year Award Croswell Opera House 16 Children (This is #1); [oth. writ.] Histories - Croswell Opera House, newspaper and pamphlet, St. Francis History, paperback book, newspaper articles; [pers.] To touch the heart, to open the eye of the soul.; [a.] Rogers, AR

**MONTGOMERY, KIMBERLY ANN**
[b.] December 10, 1964, Hinsdale, IL; [p.] Joyce Hauge and Thomas Jernigan Sr.; [m.] Mark Lyle Montegomery, October 17, 1981; [ch.] Allison Marie, Ashley Elizabeth; [ed.] Downers Grove South High D-G, Ill, College of Dupage - Napersville, IL; [occ.] Office Manager Telecommunications Dispatcher; [memb.] Bolingbrook Trojans Cheer leader (Coach); [hon.] Coaching in cheerleading, cheerleading and Pon Poms - in school - Secretary of the year Award - "1986"; [oth. writ.] I have several poems I have written but this is the only time one has been released to any public member. Never in any contest. Always within the family.; [pers.] Writing was always my pass time - I wrote all my feelings down about everything because of an accident in 1981 I lost alot of my writings - so warning to anyone who likes to write - keep coping in safe place - It's so easy to write feelings down if you can't say them my daughter Allison is 13 yrs. and she also loves to write.

**MOON, SUSAN**
[pen.] S. C. Moon; [b.] May 30, 1950, Hawaii; [p.] Thelma Hall, George Hall; [m.] K. G. Kuster; [ch.] Kajal 9, Michael 8, Rohini 6; [ed.] CSULB; [occ.] Home schooling 3 children; [memb.] KCRW, Greenpeace; [pers.] What fascinates me about writing poetry is the sharing with others of our most personal selves; [a.] Long Beach, CA

**MOORE, ANGELINA L.**
[b.] June 15, 1956, Laredo, TX; [p.] Norma and Arturo Leal; [m.] Bruce W. Moore, May 26, 1979; [ch.] Christopher L. Moore, Jessica L. Moore; [ed.] Bachelor of Science from the University of North Texas; [occ.] Quality Assurance Specialist, Images-on-call, Dallas, Texas; [pers.] One day I hope to enthral readers with writing as so many others have done for me.; [a.] Garland, TX

**MOORE, NATALIE**
[b.] June 5, 1974, Dallas; [p.] Lindsay Angelo - Stan Moore; [ed.] 2 years Baylor undergrad. 1/2 semester England - Lit. studies SMU - JR year, 1992 - graduated I first Baptist Acad.; [occ.] Full-time Student; [hon.] Working on Southern Methodist University School Paper; [oth. writ.] Short Stories and poems recognized in schools.; [a.] Dallas, TX

**MOORHE, RICK**
[pen.] Decker; [ed.] Mendel High, Chicago State U. cable television.; [oth. writ.] Hundreds of poems written for an ex-girl friend and two unpublished and unedited graphic novels written for my best friends, L. Isbell.; [pers.] When the world around us becomes too much of a burden, laugh. Laugh insanely, madly, furiously. Shout to Heaven itself! Or, just lie down and take a nap.; [a.] Chicago, IL

**MOOSE, LUCILLE BLACK**
[pen.] Miss Lucy; [b.] May 18, 1905, Flatwoods, TN; [p.] Thomas and Josephine Black; [m.] Ralph Moose, May 22, 1941; [ed.] High School B.S. Degree Memphis University.; [occ.] Retired Teacher Primary Grades; [memb.] The Presbyterian Church Alpha Delta Kappa Honorary Sorority for Women Educators. Order of the Eastern Star American Heart Association Mary Bryan Book Club.; [hon.] For Retired Teacher of the year in Tipton County a plaque for service in the Church as Choir Director one of Bush's Thousand Points of Light; [oth. writ.] Poems for the Pine Cane of official magazine for Kirby Pines Estates. Articles for the official County paper the Covington Leader.; [pers.] I consider myself an optimist by nature I only ash far a "faith that smiles" most of my writing both prose and poetry is rather light reading.; [a.] Memphis, TN

**MORAITIS, KATHY**
[b.] January 24, 1948, Greece; [p.] Antipas, Sotirios and Helen; [m.] Eleftherios Moraitis, July 7, 1968; [ch.] Constantinos Moraitis and Theoula Moraitis; [ed.] Diploma of High School received in Greece.; [occ.] Disabled. I worked in Atlantic Bank at New York investigator.; [memb.] Before my illness (cancer), I was an active member in St. Demetrios Greek Orthodox Church.; [hon.] Received outstanding awards in PTO for Greek School. Received honor awards for being an active member in St. Demetrios Orthodox Church; [oth. writ.] I have written over 70 poems dedicated to my son, Constantinos Moraitis, who was a victim of crime. My beloved son was robbed and murdered two years ago.; [pers.] Refer to the back of this sheet.; [a.] Jersey City, NS

**MORAN, KATE TAYLOR**
[b.] February 14, 1949, Evanston, IL; [p.] Gil and Marion Moran; [ch.] Joseph Taylor; [ed.] M.A. in Special Education 1980, U of Colorado Teacher for Denver Public schools, artist, observer; [occ.] Teacher; [hon.] M.A. U of Colo. Peach Cobler, 1967, Fall Festival, Downers Grove, Illinois Dean's List President List; [oth. writ.] Storied, poems newspaper articles.; [pers.] Skydive! Go for it anyway; [a.] Denver, CO

**MORETT, JAMES**
[pen.] James Lightning; [b.] March 4, 1968, Bryn Mawr, PA; [p.] James J. Morett and Mary Wright Morett; [occ.] Framing Carpenter; [hon.] 1st Prize Pegasus Literary Magazine Spring 1993; [oth. writ.] I remember it well; [pers.] Writing bears the difficulty of finding the laxed, unconscious feelings of our perceptions and inspirations, and to then have the relentless conscious precision to put it all together and add our own culturally refined touch, which still may never be enough. But I will never give up.; [a.] West Chester, PA

**MORGAN, DEBORAH**
[b.] November 7, 1954, Keywest, Fl; [p.] Robert and Ivy Pierce; [m.] David, May 21, 1994; [ch.] Robert Shaw 22 yrs.; [ed.] Presently attending Broward Community College major - Education 3. 92 GPA; [occ.] Student; [memb.] Pet Aid League; [oth. writ.] Novels in progress; [pers.] Since life isn't always sweet, my poems express the other side of the coin.; [a.] Hallandale, FL

**MORGAN, JASON M.**
[pen.] Sue Denim; [b.] July 18, 1977, New Orleans; [ed.] University of Tennessee at Chattanooga; [pers.] Artsy, Candelabras, Moan, Voraciously, Midnight, Devour; [a.] Chattanooga, TN

**MORGAN, SCOTT B.**
[b.] December 27, 1969, Ft. Watton Beach, FL; [p.] Dr. and Mrs. H. B. Morgan; [ed.] B.A. in Psychology Varterbilt, University J.D. Hemline University school of Law; [hon.] Magna Cum Laude - Varderbitt, Dean's Scholarship - Hemline; [pers.] You do what you know, until you know better and then you do better.; [a.] St. Paul, MN

**MORGAN, TARA ANN**
[b.] March 10, 1982, St. Louis, MO; [p.] Edward and Edna Morgan; [ed.] Student in 8th grade, Visitation Academy; [occ.] Student; [a.] St. Louis, MO

**MORRIS, DORIS LYNNE**
[b.] July 28, 1946, Oregon; [p.] Arnold and Ruby Quigley; [m.] Jesse E. Morris, June 7, 1969; [ch.] Jeffrey (18), 5 step-children, 14 great grandchildren; [ed.] Corrallis High School, BA. from Cascade College, M.A.T from Lewis and Clark Coll. Correspondence course from In St. of childrens Literature; [occ.] Past teacher, now self employed and assistant hospital chaplain; [memb.] Lincoln Park Christian Church, Gideon's

International Aux. Puget Sound Poetry Connection; [hon.] Honor society in High School Dean's List in College Magna Cum Laude (.A.A.T degree; [oth. writ.] Self-published collection of poems, entitled Apples of Gold; [pers.] Through nearly 30 years of diabetes and its completions (amputation of bath legs, impaired vision, kidney failure) God's presence, He's love, and faithfulness have sustained me.; [a.] Tacuma, WA

**MORRIS, FRANCES**
[b.] January 14, 1941, Rocky Mt., NC; [p.] Raymond and Minnie Winstead; [m.] Wayne T. Morris, February 22, 1957; [ch.] Mike, Robbin, Jefferson, Julie, Jonathan and Mindy; [ed.] High School Eq.; [occ.] Homemaker; [oth. writ.] I have written about 7 volumes of personal journals, short stories childhood memoirs, lots of poetry. Never tried to have any published before, but enjoy writing.; [pers.] I have been greatly influenced by my large family and childhood experiences, as the daughter of a tobacco share cropper farming in North Carolina.; [a.] Layton, UT

**MORRIS, JULIE**
[pen.] Julie Atlee; [b.] December 14, 1945, Pasadena, CA; [m.] Divorced; [ch.] Margaret, Molly and Neil; [ed.] Attended University of Southern California Southern Oregon College; [occ.] Struggling, single parent; [oth. writ.] Several articles in local newspaper. 1st poem ever written in 3rd grade was published in PTA compilation; [pers.] I believe in honesty at all costs and that love is the reason for life.; [a.] Rancho Santa Margaret, CA

**MORRIS, MICHAEL D.**
[pen.] Michael D. Morris; [b.] November 23, 1958, Montgomery, WV; [p.] Madelyn and Julian Morris; [m.] Kelly Adair Morris, August 26, 1978; [ed.] Valley High School Carver Vo-Tech; [occ.] Carpet Installer; [oth. writ.] Gifts From God, A Man Named, Thank You Lord, The Greatest Peoples This Side Of Heaven, A Prayer, Love, My Grandmother, Two Special People; [pers.] I strongly believe that everything I have in life is because of God. Everything I am able to do is because of God. If I live the way God says, some day I'll live in heaven with him; [a.] Kimberly, WV

**MORRIS, SHIRLEY REICHARD**
[b.] September 2, 1942, Arkoma, OK; [p.] Ernest and Clara Reichard; [m.] Widow of Charles H. Morris, September 29, 1967; [ch.] Andrew J. Greenwood, Donna G. Kinne, Robyn D. Long; [ed.] Spiro High School graduate of Mellies Beauty College; [occ.] Stockroom attendant for James Rivers corp at FT. Smith, Arkansas; [memb.] Calvary Missionary Baptist Church Delightful Doll Society; [oth. writ.] Several poems published in newspaper; [pers.] I strive to express the feelings of my heart in my writings.; [a.] Van Buren, AR

**MORRIS-WIDSOM, SUSAN E.**
[b.] May 9, 1930, Princess Anne, MD; [p.] Samuel and Isadora Morris; [m.] Herman L. Wisdom (divorced); [ch.] Robert, Herman Jr. Vincent, Robert Sorden, Herman Jr., Vincent Derrick, Lloyd, John, Linda, Josephine, Eugene Venable; [ed.] Gained GED, 2 yrs. college (EDD) Medical Assistant, Surgical Tech. ECC (Essex County College); [occ.] None - retired; was security guard last 6 yrs.; [memb.] Buelah Baptist Church, (Senior Chorus, Sunday School Teacher correspondent secretary); [hon.] Honorable mention in another poetry contest; Pres. Honor Roll ECC - Liberal Arts; [oth. writ.] Day in the Life of a Boy, What is the Color of Your soul, Hope; [pers.] For all whose lives I touch in passing, may they be better and much richer for the experience.; [a.] Newark, NJ

**MORRISON, GARY**
[b.] December 12, 1941, Detroit, MI; [p.] John Morrison, Bertha Stephens; [m.] Divorced from Author Gayce Morrison, August 31, 1963; [ch.] Jennifer Roshan, Kevin Alexander; [ed.] Ed.D., University of Massachusetts, M.A., Yale University (Southeast Asia Studies) B.A., High Honors, University of California Santa Barbara, Newport Harbor High School; [occ.] Secretary - General, Hawaii Bahai Community.; [memb.] United Nations Association - Hawaii friends of the East-West Center, Honolulu Institute for the healing of racism, World Watch Institute, Pacific and Asian Affairs Council (PAAC), National Association for the study of Education; [hon.] Woodrow Wilson Fellow, University of California Regents Scholar, National Defense Foreign Language Fellowship. Fullbright-Hays Fellowship; [oth. writ.] More than 25 Articles and reviews published in various journals including World Order Magazine, Herald of the Sough (Australia), Roteiro (Brazil), Journal of Research and development in education, and one one-act play produced.; [pers.] Influenced by modern existentialist writers, personal recovery processes, and the universal principles of the Bahai faith, my writing attempts to illuminate and transform inner states of psychic pain and to bear witness to personal and public Trauma to arrive at soulful moments of oneness, unity and wholeness; [a.] Kaneohe, HI

**MORRISON, MARY**
[a.] Portland, OR

**MOULDER, DEBRA WILDER**
[pen.] Debra Wilder Moulder; [b.] June 5, 1960, Kansas, City; [p.] Lora and Richard Morris; [m.] Phillip Moulder, May 22, 1992; [ch.] None 1 cat, 1 dog; [ed.] ULLA; [occ.] Marketing Sales; [memb.] Chambers of Commerce; [oth. writ.] I am currently working in a children book and am in search of a published; [pers.] I am inspired when I quiet down long enough to listen to my inner self - she guides me through my writings to explore myself and work around me I believe I am touched creatively by the spirit of my great great Aunt nobelist Laura Ingall Wilder of Little House In Prairie series

**MOULTRIE, PEARL**
[p.] Ned Moultrie, Mary Moultrie; [m.] Divorce; [ch.] Mary D. Blair, Donzetta M. Blair; [ed.] Pima College, University of Phoenix, Stephens College; [occ.] Co-ower of American cottage, an interior decorating company and writer; [memb.] New Testament Baptist Church; [hon.] Phi Theta Kappa Dean's List, honors in English at Pima College in Arizona recognitions for outstanding service in pimat country Juvenile system; [oth. writ.] Poems: "No worse place" "visions" and "A poem for Easter" Currently working on a book titled, It's A Long Road: Scenes and Philosophy from the Life of a Black Woman; [pers.] As a spiritual person and a black woman I seek through my writing to find "the road less traveled by".; [a.] Miami, FL

**MOWRY, AUDREY**
[b.] August 1959, WV; [m.] Joe Mowry; [ch.] Daughter - Taylor Sons - Joey and Spencer; [ed.] Master's from West Virginia University; [occ.] Mother, Teacher; [memb.] Girl Scouts of America Troop Leader; [hon.] Summa Cum Laude, Delivered Dean's Address, Dean's List. Golden Key National Honor Society; [oth. writ.] Research articles written for a published in the Journal of Fluency Disorders; [pers.] I believe that when we are able to look within our individual sorrows and hurts and achieve peace, all mankind gains a greater sense of gentle integrity through our efforts.; [a.] Mill Run, PA

**MUDIE, SUZETTA DOREEN MARGARET**
[pen.] Suze, Susie D. Cheese Chucky; [b.] February 22, 1971, Trinidad, West Indies; [p.] Preston and Doreen Mudie; [ch.] Christopher Joseph Mudie; [ed.] Vessigny Secondary School, Trinidad West Indies, Fayetteville State University, North Carolina; [occ.] Food service specialist in United States Air Force; [pers.] Feelings of the heart, are not meant to be lock away but better expressed on paper for the words to experience. My mother is was always the inspiration for my poetic creations. Thanks Mom; [a.] Norvenich Airbase, Germany

**MUHAMMAD, MARYAM E.**
[b.] April 18, 1936, Detroit, MI; [p.] Edward J. Dew Sr. and Catherine Roland; [ch.] Ricardo Ware, Mary K, Sameerah, Wahad, Rahaman and Rahim Muhammad; [ed.] Microcomputer Training-Wayne Community College, MSC Skill Center, Lic. Beauty Operator; [occ.] Retired Disabled Worker (State of MI-DSS.); [memb.] Sera-DAC for retired State of MI employees. Block Club, Neighborhood Watch/Public and Private Schools, Parents Organizations; [hon.] Outstanding services Western High School, Humanitarian-MYC Chicago, IL. Huuron Valley Women's Facility Community Service Neighbor Watch-City of Detroit. Outstanding Service (Sis Clara Muhammad School-Chicago, IL.; [oth. writ.] Reflect upon the Whirl of Emotions (book of 40 poems. Bible Commentary for Reference a muslim is humble.; [pers.] "Our destiny depends on how we live"; [a.] Detroit, MI

**MUJA, KATHLEEN A.**
[b.] June 24, 1965, Denver; [p.] Thomas R. and Bridget C. Cramer; [ch.] Thomas age 7; [ed.] BBA General Business University of Denver; [occ.] Labor and Employment Specialist; [pers.] Seeking correspondence from poets to discuss art, life etc.

**MULLENDORE, PATRICK**
[b.] September 24, 1964, Smithville, MO; [p.] Clinton and Donna Mullendore; [m.] Mitchie Mullendore, September 30, 1989; [ch.] Dax Alexander; [ed.] North Platte High School, Currently in Medical Program at Penn Valley College in Kansas City, MO.; [occ.] Musician, Student; [hon.] Arion Award for music, toured Europe with American Musical Ambassadors Symphony, various music Awards Local as well as National.; [pers.] I have a very wild and broad imagination. I write what I feel and try to keep it interesting. Simple as that!; [a.] Kansas City, MO

**MUNDY, FRANCES**
[b.] November 18, 1924, Philadelphia, PA; [p.] Margaret Sullivan Haley and Thomas Haley; [m.] Bill Mundy, November 5, 1949; [ch.] Barbara, Margaret, Kathleen and Bill Jr.; [occ.] Retired; [oth. writ.] Poems published in the hook "Dark Side of the Moon" and best poems of 1995; [pers.] My faith in God is the most important part of my philosophy. I also feel a sense of humor and common sense will see you through most difficulties.; [a.] North Forth Myers, FL

**MUNIZ, JACOB**
[b.] December 31, 1968 Los Angeles, CA; [m.] Donna Muniz, November 23, 1990; [ch.] Sean R. Munix, Tre A. Muniz; [p.] Roosevelt High; [occ.] Teacher's Assistant, Prairie Correctional Facility/Appleton, MN; [pers.] You should appreciate the time you spend with you're children and not take it for granted

**MUNSON, GEORGIA**
[b.] February 22, 1950, Buffalo, NY; [p.] Nicholas and Della Munson; [m.] Ronald Munson, September 2, 1968; [ch.] Ronda Lee, Robin Lynn, Rachel; [ed.] Calif. High School Fullerton J. College; [occ.] Dept. Mgr.; [oth.

writ.] Several poems still unsubmitted; [pers.] Sara Teasdale influenced my romantic style. But life and love gave me the words.; [a.] Laguna Hills, CA

**MUNSTEDT, SUSAN E.**
[b.] February 19, 1927, TX; [p.] Deceased; [m.] Deceased; [ch.] Christine Reynolds, Judy Cameron; [ed.] High School, College; [occ.] Legal Secretary Data Entry Clerk; [pers.] 6 great grand children, 1 grand child

**MYER, RUTH**
[pen.] Ruth Myer; [b.] March 17, 1925, Covert, NY; [p.] Clara Bossett Wilson, Earl S. Wilson; [m.] LeConte Myer, March 4, 1950; [ch.] Beverly, Cynthia, John, Jim, Annette, Denise, Joseph, Micheal; [ed.] Interlaken High, fredonia State Teachers College; [occ.] Farm housewife,organist and choir director, piano and organ teacher; [memb.] Interlaken reformed Church, The American Guild of Organists, Women's Aglow. Reformed Church Women's Ministries.; [oth. writ.] A poem, "Black berrying", published. A book published "A Farm Girl In The Great Depression", (1995), windswept Press.; [pers.] I have a great love of nature and this is often reflected in my writings. Not less that this is my faith in God which often finds its way into my writing.; [a.] Ovid, NY

**MYERS, RUSS**
[b.] May 1, 1945, Reading, PA; [ed.] BA-Art, AAS-Respiratory Care; [occ.] Respiratory therapist; [oth. writ.] Numerous screen plays and stage plays. Yet unperformed; [pers.] Raised a ministers son I saw the "World" from another dimension. Glass houses are no refuge.; [a.] Lilburn, GA

**MYRICK, JUSTIN**
[pen.] Myrick; [b.] October 10, 1979, Atlanta, GA; [p.] Sandy Akins, Mike Myrick; [ed.] Gilmer County High School; [memb.] Gilmer High School Football Team, Basketball Team, and Track Team. Also a member of the Junior Beta Club.; [hon.] Awarded football letter jacket as a Freshman in high school; [pers.] I believe that if someone strives, for a goal and lets nothing get in its's way, then that goal shall be accomplished.; [a.] East Ellijay, GA

**NAKAMURA, ERYN A.**
[b.] January 17, 1978, Honolulu, HI; [p.] Philip and Gert Nakamura; [ed.] Currently a high school student at Hawaii Baptist Academy; [occ.] Student; [hon.] Language School- Japanese Speech Awards June 1993. Principal's Honor Roll - 4 years; [oth. writ.] Mothers Day Poem - 1988; [pers.] I wrote this poem to tell people that even tho' the rocks may fall and we are tempted to quit, we cannot and should not. We have to strive on in life if not for ourselves, for the future of all the children in this world. We have to leave something behind for them to build on. We cannot let go of life as the easy way out, because every step we take can make our mountains a little easier to climb and every little step we take brings us all closer to the top.; [a.] Kaneohe, HI

**NAPOLEON, ALLISON**
[b.] October 3, 1977, Bethel; [p.] Francine Heitt, Harold Napoleon; [ed.] Grace Christian School; [occ.] Full-time student; [memb.] Amnesty International; [hon.] Who's Who Among American High School Students high Honor Roll; [pers.] The poetry that I write comes from my heart and reflects my feelings.; [a.] Bethel, AK

**NARZISI, LINDA L.**
[b.] November 3, 1956, Delta, UT; [p.] Glen S. Taylor, Verna LaRae Taylor; [m.] Frank E. Narzisi, February 20, 1994; [ch.] Thure (T.J) Johnson, John Glen Johnson, Frank W. Narzisi; [ed.] Delta High School UVCC;

[occ.] Roller in Steel Mill; [pers.] I try to see the beauty of life through my boys. I try to see myself and the things. I do through their eyes.; [a.] Riverton, UT

**NASH, ELEANOR G.**
[pen.] Ele Nash; [b.] September 22, 1936, Butler, PA; [p.] Arthur Preston George, Emma Purveyance Haines; [m.] Manuel Gimenez Jr., November 22, 1961, James F. Nash, February 16, 1985; [ch.] Sean Gimenez (son), Kelly Sanford (daughter); [ed.] Butler High Pennsylvania School of Business College of Notre Dame, Belmont, CA; [occ.] Organist/Choir Director; [memb.] American Guild of organists Phi Beta; [hon.] Dean's List; [oth. writ.] Several poems published in literary journals in Eugene, OR; [pers.] My love affair with language began with hearing music in the words.; [a.] Bothell, WA

**NASH, STELLA RILEY**
[b.] November 3, 1942, Gould, AR; [ch.] Chad Jereme Nash; [ed.] Gould High School, University of AR- Pine Bluff, (B.S.) New York University (M.A.) 18hrs Rural Sociology - The Penn State University - University Parks, PA; [occ.] Regional Nutrition Director - USDA/FCS/MPRO; [memb.] American Dietetic Association United Church of Montbello Place M.S. PTA Far Northeast Denver Neighborhood Assoc. Montbello Optimist Delta Sigma Theta Sorority; [hon.] Valedictorian - High School Outstanding Educator of America 1973, Outstanding Young Women of America 1974, Who's Whom the West 1994, Who's Who in the World 1996, Cum Laude (UA-PB); [oth. writ.] 1 - Journal article, 1 newspaper article and many newsletter articles; [pers.] "Yesterday is but a dream tomorrow a vision of hope. Today well lived - makes every yesterday a day of happiness and every tomorrow a vision of hope".; [a.] Denver, CO

**NASON, TRACY**
[pen.] Tracy Nason; [b.] October 24, 1979, Portland, ME; [p.] Susan and Ralph Nason; [ed.] Sophomore at Deering High School; [memb.] Book Club, yearbook Breccia (Literary magazine); [hon.] Honor roll, Spelling; [oth. writ.] "Cove's Tide" The Space Between, "Unfinished Lives" Best Poems of 1995, "Infinite" Breccia; [pers.] I love writing poetry as much as I love life. That's an important aspect. Life is worth living only no one knows the meaning of it.; [a.] Portland, ME

**NEAL, MELISSSA WALKER**
[pen.] Shoelace; [b.] June 16, 1972, Hot Spring, AR; [p.] Johnny and Brenda Walker; [m.] Chuck Neal, January 11, 1991; [ch.] Christopher Lee 3, Emily Renea 5 months; [ed.] Magnet Cove High; [occ.] Full time mom; [oth. writ.] High School year book, advertisement in local newspaper and on local radio for the country garden,; [pers.] I love children, shoes and fishing. My writings come from within and gently tug at me to be released.; [a.] Bismarch, AR

**NECESITO, RODOLFO I.**
[b.] June 21, 1940, Philippines; [p.] Leocadio and Felicidad Necesito; [m.] Estrella S. Tatlonghari, November 27, 1971; [ch.] Abigail; [ed.] Litt. B in Journalism, University of Santo Tomas, Manila; [occ.] Civil Service Employee; [memb.] Board Member, Asingan Association of Northern California, Inc.; [hon.] Plaque of Appreciation from the above-mentioned association; [oth. writ.] Wrote several features and new stories for Filipino newspapers both in San Francisco and Manila over span of 30 years; [pers.] Every person has the blood of a poet running in his/her vain.; [a.] San Francisco, CA

**NELLIS, MICHELLE**
[b.] August 1, 1976, Charoleston, SC; [p.] Kathleen Nellis; [ed.] Chamblee High School, University of Geor-

gia; [occ.] Student Sophomore of UGA; [memb.] Member of Community Theatrical group A.C.T., cast member of "The music man", "Chris Cross", "S.S. Broadway", Robin Hood", "The Sound of Music". Cocaptain of Intramural Soccer team of UGA; [hon.] Won state wide strong contest for Illinois in 1985, included in Who's Who Among American High School Students and the Deans List which recognizes outstanding College students; [oth. writ.] Published in high school newspaper and literary magazine, included in CERA's Anthology of Poetry, and the National Library of Poetry's Mists Enchantment.; [a.] Atlanta, GA

**NELMS, JACQUELINE EVON**
[pen.] Bear; [b.] April 10, 1961, GA; [p.] Marth Ann Tyson, Johnson Thoms Tyson; [m.] Michael Lee Nelms Sr., May 1, 1982; [ch.] Michael Nelms (11), Lanita Nelms (9), Ashley Nelms (8), Abe Faust (5), Tyrone Faust (3); [ed.] Flower Dryve Athens GA, Clarne Middle Athens GA,Ely High Pompano Beach Fla; [occ.] House wife; [oth. writ.] Several poems wrote, none published before. First time trying; [pers.] Life it self is not worth nothing with out "Jesus" you got to have faith in all that you do and say! And never never ever give up.; [a.] Athens, GA

**NELSON, EMILY**
[pen.] Emily Nelson; [b.] Loma Linda, CA; [p.] David and Beverly Nelson; [occ.] Coaches Assistant at Pasadena Ice Skating Center; [memb.] United States Figure Skating Association. (USFSA); [oth. writ.] One poem published in Anthology of Poetry By young Americans; [pers.] "Life is journey not a destination, and time is a guide that heels all. I try my best to live and not just exist". "No one's life is worth living unless he has something worth dying for."; [a.] Glendale, CA

**NEMBHARD JR., GUY S.**
[pen.] Guy S. Nembhard Jr.; [b.] June 14, 1973, Fayettville, NC; [p.] Guy Nembhard, Renee Verrett; [m.] Charlene "Rosebud" Mitchell, tent. July 7, 1996; [ed.] West Indies College High, JA, Glendale Adventist Academy, CA, Columbia Union College, MD; [occ.] Student, Resident Asst. in Dorm, Security Guard on weekends.; [memb.] National Collegiate Athletic Association (NCAA), Contributing Writer for Columbia Journal, Member of Varsity Volleyball and Basketball teams.; [hon.] Member of National Honors Society, Highest GPA for Freshman and Sophomores (wich), was able to sing lead role in the Gilbert and Sullivan play Pirates of Penzance. (Frederick).; [oth. writ.] A complete history of Jamaica, many poems and short stories published in school newspapers and journals, few writings in Vallejo Drive Vingette.; [pers.] In my opinion there is an inherent level of talent in all people. One can tap into it through life's experiences and discover his/her dreams and excite personal development.; [a.] Takoma Park, MD

**NEUBAUER, GEORGE E.**
[pen.] George, Edward Neubauer; [b.] November 17, 1910, Buffalo, NY; [p.] Joseph J., Martha K. Neubauer; [m.] Florence Angeline, September 4, 1933, Saint John Gualbert Church; [ch.] Sandra Carole; [grnd. ch.] Brian J., Kelly L., Jeff T. Styles; [ed.] Fosaick Masten High School dropout, La Salle University Correspondence - - (My reason for school dropout, help parents, support family of eleven which I loved and respected dearly.); [occ.] Employed E. I. DuPont De Ne Mours - retired 1972 after 43 years as manufacturer New Products Production Planning and Scheduling Coordinator; [memb.] Senior Citizen Organizations Saint Benedict Holy Name Society, Health Care Giver Assoc., Entertainment Weekly Giving Me and Family Daily Knowledge and Amusement.; [hon.] To my role models, parents -- top priority and education; Wife - Ever lasting

happiness and love; Steve Allen - his humor, books "Reflections"; Rush Limbaugh - Truth in politics also his books, etc.; Geo. E. Neubauer - always, straightforward.; [pers.] Every day I awake I have a solio faith in God, guiding me in all ventures. Decisions and activities for every human being alive, regardless of creed, color, (or) race.; [a.] Amherst, NY

**NEUENDORF, GAIL M.**
[pen.] Damiette, Panther; [b.] December 5, 1967, Queens, NY; [p.] Hans P. and Loretta V. Neuendorf; [m.] Ray Montanez (Divorced), March 2, 1985; [ch.] John Montanez, Edwin Cruz, Loretta Cruz, Eric Shaw, Janel Shaw; [ed.] Touro College; [occ.] Aspiring writer, tore of all trades; [hon.] Published in community bulletins; [oth. writ.] Born Again, Little Girl, Lost; [pers.] I'd like to thank my mother for blessing me and passing her talent on to me. I'd like to thank my family, my father, Helen, John, Paul, Elsie, Dominic, Mark and Cindy for supporting and encouraging my works. My children and Sachen "Marco" Bhanoe singh for shining the light.; [a.] Brooklyn, NY

**NEWCOMB, MARCIA W.**
[b.] December 10, 1908, Philadelphia, PA; [p.] Alice Gibbs Wilt and Maurice Davidson Wilt; [m.] Capt. Mervyn C. Stone, April 24, 1936, San Francisco, CA, C. Leonard Newcomb, February 14, 1978, Sonoma, CA (Deceased); [ch.] Susan Stone Trumbull, Novato, CA. Peter Clement Stone, (deceased); [ed.] Germantown Friends School, Philadelphia. Ogantz School, Philadelphia Art School, Philadelphia; [occ.] Retired; [memb.] Sonoma Valley Historical Society, DAR Life Membership Native American Heritage Assoc. Various Environmental Organizations; [oth. writ.] Several short stories, one novel, a book of poems, as yet unpublished; [pers.] Many of my poems were in some way connected with the sea or with my philosophy on life in the 1930's. Creation seemed to be a biological need ... when my children arrived the need to create poetry dissolved.; [a.] Novato Marin County, CA

**NEWMYER, SHANNON**
[b.] November 1, 1976, Bellflower, CA; [p.] Terry and Karen Newmyer; [ed.] High school graduate attending College; [occ.] Full time student; [oth. writ.] Unpublished poetry; [pers.] Writing poetry is an enjoyment as well as a full-fillment for myself. I wish to continue writing in my spare time.; [a.] La Habra, CA

**NICHOL, KEITH JOHN**
[b.] November 2, 1927, New Sharon, IA; [p.] Mabel and Paul Nichol; [m.] Judith Nichol, August 19, 1964; [ed.] Four C's Business College; [occ.] Deceased, October 14, 1993; [hon.] Editor's Choice Awards 1994 The International Poet Society Merit Award 1994, Diamond Homer Trophy 1995; [oth. writ.] Several poems published by Mile High Poetry Society and Sparrow grass Poetry Forum; [pers.] This poem and eight others were discovered after his death. All nine poems, the only ones he ever wrote, were written just before or right after his second brain tumor surgery in April of 1993.; [a.] Estes Park, CO

**NICHOLS, PEGGY**
[pen.] Libby Pease; [b.] September 25, 1941, Farmington, ME; [p.] Bertelle and Eva Sibbly Pease; [m.] Divorced; [ch.] Susan Powers, Philip, Michael, Rebecca and Bill Nichols; [ed.] Central H.S. N.N. Portland Me. Class of 59 Student - Institute of Childrens Literature 1994-95; [occ.] Preservation Tech Bath Iron Works (ship building); [memb.] Presbyterian Church; [oth. writ.] The Stranger In The Dark Side Of The Moon - Newspaper columns and features, heritage booklets - Newsletter at work; [pers.] Poems help me work through emotions.; [a.] West Bath, ME

**NICHOLSON, ICHELLE**
[b.] June 15, 1982, Houston, TX; [p.] Lori Nicholson; [ed.] I'm in the eight grade at Watkins Jr. High School; [oth. writ.] A poetry collection called "Insights"; [pers.] Any dream can come true. Any obstacle can be overcome. Any star can be touched.; [a.] Houston, TX

**NICKERSON, JEAN D.**
[b.] January 29, 1943, Woodbridge, England; [p.] Douglas and Doris Orford; [m.] William J. Nickerson, January 11, 1986; [ch.] Kevin - Gary and Lee; [oth. writ.] 2 poems, My Best Friend, Ode To A Brother-in-law.

**NIX, PATRICIA CAROLYNNE**
[pen.] Niki Lyn Nix Niki Bird Nixie; [b.] May 17, 1941, Kleberg Co, TX; [p.] Paul and Estelle Tracy Nix; [m.] Donald Eugene Bird Jr., May 1, 1985; [ch.] Tracy Junel and Cynthia Lorraine; [ed.] A.A.S. (Registered nurse) West Ark College Ft Smith AR, B.A. Psychology - St Leo College, Fla. Post Graduate Work-Education-Stetson U. Dland, Fla. First grade H.M. King High School - Kingsville, TX; [occ.] Registered Nurse - Bee Ville Independent School Dist, Beeville, TX; [memb.]; [hon.] Phi Theta Kappa, Kappa Delta Pi, Deans Lists; [oth. writ.] Nature's Little Guys - Pub. The Guide (a series of Nature Stories). A Spot Forever - unpublished family (S.Tex) History. Nixies Song - unpublished collection of poetry. A Lifetime of Personal Journals-unpublished hope someday to make publishable!; [pers.] Pv 25:11 "Like golden apples in silver settings, so is a word spoken at the right time." (God's Word). I seek for that wisdom.; [a.] Mineral, TX

**NOBLE, BETTIE NORMAN**
[b.] August 22, 1932, Downers Grove, IL; [p.] Emmett (Doc) and Marie Norman; [m.] Delbert J. (Del) Noble (Deceased), February 13, 1954; [ch.] David W. Noble, Son Diane Marie Noble Lincoln, Daughter; [ed.] Graduated form the Downers Grove Community High School Class 1950; [occ.] Mother, Grandmother of 4, unemployed at the moment but will start soon as an aide for Bright Ideas Child Care; [hon.] Married to a wonderful man for 40 years. Mother to two wonderful children; [pers.] The past year and a half have been so very sad to me, and my family, since my husband and very best friend died unexpectedly. In my writing I am trying to show that others share my sadness and their love helps me to get on with my life and I try to do the same for them.; [a.] Morris, IL

**NOBLE, MONA SABINO**
[b.] June 25, 1964, Lanai; [p.] Benjamin and Yonora Noble; [ed.] Hilo High School; [occ.] Pastry Cook at Desert Flours Breadery and Bistro; [pers.] I believe that the world is my school, I can learn from it, take what is rightfully mine, respect it, but, most importantly - Live it!; [a.] Sedona, AR

**NOSHIRVANI, MAHSHID**
[b.] January 29, 1951, Teheran; [p.] Mohammada Azam Farahmand; [m.] Vahid Noshirvani, November 15, 1975; [ch.] Narguess (Daughter) and Sohrab (Son); [ed.] Suny Purchase; [occ.] Photographer; [a.] Dobbs Ferry, NY

**NUGENT, J. W.**
[b.] November 14, 1948, Pittsburgh; [p.] Joseph and Mercedes Nugent; [m.] Karen Nugent, March 9, 1973; [ch.] Shaun Joseph, January 19 1978; [ed.] Mining Engineering Technology, Mine Management Fire Science Technology; [occ.] Engineer Mine Rescue Coordinator; [memb.] Society of Mining Engineers, Institution of Mining Engineers, National Fire Protection Asso., National Mine Rescue Association, People to People International; [hon.] Chartered Engineer UK,

European Reciprocity, Who's Who in Government 1990 Bronze Star of Army Accommodation Kentucky Colonel tribute to Veterans; [oth. writ.] "Tour of Duty" an anthology. "A Long Journey Home" writing s of the Vietnam War; [pers.] Language is the music by which we can communicate. Poetry is the dance by which we celebrate.; [a.] Littleton, CO

**NUNES, VICTORIA**
[pen.] Victoria Nunes; [b.] June 6, 1983, Venezuela; [p.] Emidio Nunes, Mireya Nunes; [ed.] La Salle Elementary School (Venezuela), Knapp Elementary School, Kulp Elementary School and Oak Park Elementary School; [occ.] Student and part-time babysitter; [hon.] Several school awards; [oth. writ.] Books published at school. The Rainbow, The Lady Bug That Could, My Old Friend Martha and an article published by The Reporter (Local newspaper); [pers.] I have been inspired to write because of personal experiences. I like to write to show people things in my point of view. I am a sentimental person and I like to write my feelings down on paper.; [a.] Lansdale, PA

**NUNNELEE, JEARL BURT**
[pen.] Jearl Nunnelee; [b.] June 18, 1924, Caulksville, AK; [p.] Jerry Bed and Gertrude Nunnelee; [m.] Cynthia Nunnelee, December 27, 1980 (second marriage); [ch.] Four children by former marriage - all grown now; [ed.] B.A. University of Kansas in English Literature, M.A. Western State of Colorado Ed S University of Northern Colorado; [occ.] Photographer - own studio in Elizabeth, CO. Retired from 30 years as public school teacher and administrator; [oth. writ.] Two unpublished novels, an unpublished parent handbook, and several poems in various stages of completion; [pers.] I have wanted to be a writer a far as I can remember, but only since I retired from public school work have I had time to work at writing seriously.; [a.] Elizabeth, CO

**O'BRIEN, DORRIS M.**
[b.] June 12, 1939, Chicago, IL; [ch.] Four Children, Six Grandchildren; [ed.] College Graduate-Nursing Degree; [occ.] Nurse-Specialty Nutrition; [oth. writ.] "Nanans Silly Poems" Poems written for and about my Grandchildren (non-published - as yet) "Feelings" (non-published as yet); [pers.] Most of my poems are inspired from events shared with and unforgettable statements made by my Grandchildren. Recording these special events in poem keeps the memories alive.

**O'CANNOR, KAREN L.**
[pen.] Karen Wilcox O'Connor; [b.] May 27, 1956, Elmira, NY; [p.] James V. and Anne M. Wilcox; [m.] Mark C. O'Connor, June 13, 1981; [ch.] Jonathan E. O'Connor, Michael J. O'Connor; [ed.] Elmira Free Academy, The College of the Holy Cross (B.A.), Suffolk University (M.B.A.); [occ.] Director OVMS Finance Digital Equipment Corporation; [pers.] My goal in writing is not to be self serving but to be deserving of the time others give to reading my work.; [a.] Medfield, MA

**O'NEAL, ADELLA DARDEN**
[b.] November 1, 1938, Wilson, NC; [p.] William Darden, Ethel Darden; [m.] Freddie L. O'Neal, June 27, 1981; [ch.] Veronica R. Grace, Arvis R. Grace; [ed.] Key West High Sch., Queens borough Comm. College, Lynn University; [occ.] Registered Nurse, Licensed Funeral Director; [memb.] Rocky Branch United C.O.C., Rocky Branch Womens Fellowship; [hon.] Several Awards for Poetry, Certificates for Outstanding Achievement in Mission Work; [oth. writ.] Poem published in Anthology: The Coming Of Dawn, poem published in Local Newspaper, Short Plays unpublished, One Hundred poems unpublished; [pers.] I am inspired to write on subjects that are spiritual, educational and motivating. I endeavor to spread the "Mes-

sage of Hope" to God's people.; [a.] Wilson, NC

**O'SHEA, MARIAN KELLY**
[pen.] Marian Kelly O'Shea; [b.] March 23, 1932, Glascow, Scotland; [p.] Rose Ann Keigthron Kelly, John Kelly (Both Deceased); [m.] Joseph O'Shea (Deceased), January 17, 1953; [ed.] Culinary Grad. 1948, Lyons Sch. of Catering, Varied Certs. 1967, Johnson and Wales, Col. of Bus., Arts/Features Grad. 1989, Newspaper Inst. Am, Radio/TV Production Grad. 1993, Sawyer Sch.; [occ.] Editor, Writer, Nurse Asst. Clerk-Steno, Engrg. Brown Unive. Prov., RI 1969-70, Charge of Criminal Stats and Confidential Dossier/ Criminal, RI 1969-69, Data Entry Clerk, RI Health Dept., AIDS Resch. 1992, Data Entry Clerk, NACB, Providence, RI 1992-93; [memb.] Museum of Women in Arts, Charter Mbr. 1987-89, AM Poetry Societies, Nat'l. 1985-93, Nat. Trust for Historic Preservation, Hon. Mbr. 1990; [hon.] Hon. Mention, Free Verse, Anaheim, Calif. 1988, Virginia Baldwin Awd. Lyrics, 1989. Hon. roll Cert. Sawyer 1993.; [oth. writ.] Am Poetry Anthologies 1985-90; [pers.] My interest in poetry has been stimulated by relatives, and a natural instinct. I write what I see in Landscape-and Emotions of Life.; [a.] Providence, RI

**OAKLAND, WILLIAM WAYNE**
[pen.] Bill Oakland; [b.] July 4, 1942, Seattle, WA; [p.] Ruth S. Oakland, Westcliff Colo; [m.] Phyllis K. Oakland, September 22, 1961; [ch.] Phyllis Toebes, Bonny Smajda, Liza Arden, Lori Boots; [ed.] Kailua HS, Hawaii, Central Michigan U., Upper Iowa U., USAF pilot training ad Fighter Upgrade, 11 years Fighter Pilot, 13 years Transport Pilot; [occ.] Airline Pilot retired USAF and Ang Lt/Col; [memb.] Alpa, (Air Line Pilots Assn) United States Amateur Contest - Roller skating Americans Fighter Pilots Assn. National Guard Assn.; [hon.] Top Gun 113rd TFW 1974 (Fighter Pilot) National Champion Figure Skater 1982, 1994 Silver and Bronze Medalist 5 times 1983-93, Marathon and Ultra-Marathon finisher, Meritorious Service Medal, Air Force Commendatory Medal, District of Clororism Distinguished Service Medal. National Guard "Minuteman" Award; [oth. writ.] 330 Poems - including "I am Hubble", published in Hubble newsletter ad several newspapers. Poems about skating and competition, published in "Skate" Magazine. Expression of appreciation published in Westcliff, Co. newspaper.; [pers.] I write to honor achievements and commemorate events-for people!; [a.] Upper Marlboro, MD

**OBARE, NELLY ATIANO**
[b.] October 21, 1969, Kenya; [p.] Mr. Calleb Obare, Mrs. Edwina Obare; [ed.] (B.A) Economics from MS University of Baroda, India; [occ.] Direct Care Counselor, St. Jude I.A.H.D; [pers.] A bird sits on my car, - it sings its sweetest old song. Suddenly, a car pulls nearby and scares it off "As civilization advances, poetry disappears." It shouldn't be so.; [a.] Peekskill, NY

**OBOT, OTU A.**
[pen.] Adjudicator; [b.] April 28, 1949, Nigeria; [p.] Asuquo Obot, Iqun Obot; [m.] Carol O. Obot, August 20, 1974; [ch.] Nsedu Obot, Ekaette OBot, Otu A. Obot II; [ed.] Valparaiso University, Illinois Institute Technology, Purdue University, Canisius College, Marst College, Buffalo State College; [occ.] President/CEO, Emerald International Holdings, Ltd.; [memb.] Cal Communicators, Toastmasters, The Resicrucious Order, Amorc, The Better Life Club, American Entrepreneurs of Factoring Professionals; [hon.] Volunteer of the Year Award - Jay Cee's. Numerous Awards from the New York State Correctional Olympics Committee. Several Fraternity Awards.; [oth. writ.] Several prose and poetry published in local newspaper, New York Correspondent for the Better Life News, Freelance

Publications in local papers.; [pers.] If everyone of us took the time to recognize each other as a product of Cosmic Manifestation, and accordingly, we will all be that much better off.; [a.] Amhers, NY

**ODILE, DELXIAR COLOMB**
[pen.] Colomb Adele; [b.] January 29, 1959, Madagascar; [p.] Maurice Colomb, Colette Colomb; [ed.] Sorbonne University (BA in French and Russian Lit.), Second BA in Social Work (France, Paris), Teaching (Redential V.CI) America, U.C.S.B. "MA" in French Culture and Language; [occ.] French and Russian Teacher, Laguna Beach High School; [memb.] President of a French Conversation Club at the Sutton Place Hotel (Newport Beach) California Member of Steve Mellow's Reader Theatre in Orange County; [hon.] Deans's Honors List (Sorbonne University), Award on Outstanding Thesis for Social Work Diploma (Selected by the French Ministry of Health) 1984, Outstanding Student Teacher Award (U.C.I.) 1989; [oth. writ.] Several French Poems, French Thesis on "Juvenile Delinquency and the Justice System" Short Anecdotic Stories (1984) used in Stand Up Comedy Routined performed at Private Parties (Orange County) 1992-1993; [pers.] I was greatly influenced by BAudelaire and Dorothy Parker. Poetry is the heart of life. Without poetry one would not paint colors on cavasses, write symphonies, perform "Pas de Deux", build Cathedrals. Poetry creates Magic among isolated words and ideas to enlighten bare pages and make them fly!; [a.] Laguna Beach, CA

**OHANIAN, PHYLLIS**
[pen.] Dianne Hall; [b.] March 13, 1945, Corbin, KY; [p.] Theodore and Mary Lambert; [m.] Divorced; [ch.] Lynn - Erika, Grandson - Joshua; [ed.] Central High Parker Institute of Technology; [occ.] Ground crew employee for major airline; [memb.] Swan Pond Baptist Church. I am Labor Union.; [hon.] Several Commendations at work including 9 years perfect attendance; [oth. writ.] Several poems (unpublished) working on novel (fiction); [pers.] I am an avid reader. A seeker of knowledge and spiritual fulfillment. My writing, during inspirational periods, is influenced by life's experiences; [a.] Detroit, MI

**OKUBO, YURIKO L.**
[b.] August 8, 1937, Tokyo, Japan; [m.] Deceased, 11-23-79; [ch.] Three; [ed.] Pasadena City College (AA Degree) - 1961; [occ.] Probation Dept. Orange Cnty., CA; [pers.] A gypsy family inherited a crow from their grandfather who died at age 80; he raised this crow as a young boy; so after a few years of life in Basque, this crow is at least 80 years old. He stays with the family whole day and protected in his cage in the night. I hope my friend raven will live a long life.; [a.] Anaheim, CA

**OLAR, AMY**
[b.] January 6, 1976, Mansfield; [p.] John and Susan Olar; [ed.] Ontario High, NCTC (North Central Technical College); [occ.] Bankteller; [pers.] My goal is to show hope towards those who are struggling with various alcohol and drug related addictions and to courage not only them, but their parents as well. My poetry reflects upon past experience through my teenage years.; [a.] Mansfield, OH

**OLEJNIK, CAROL MARIE**
[b.] October 14, 1943, Rosebud, TX; [p.] Edwin and Juanita Marek; [m.] Larry Olejnik, August 17, 1963; [ch.] Diane Olejnik; [ed.] Rosebud High School, Oakland Community College, member of Dean's College, Southern Illinois University; [occ.] Owner of Carol's New Creations—writing, designing and marketing framed Christian art.; [oth. writ.] Christian creeds. i.e., WOMAN OF WORTH, MAN OF INTEGRITY, and other inspirational prose.; [pers.] My writing is meant to

inspire others to be the best they can be.; [a.] Houston, TX

**OLIVENCIA, MS. MAGALI**
[b.] May 9, 1961; [p.] Wilson and Alba Olivencia; [ed.] Currently attending County College of Morris in Randolph, NJ currently majoring in Humanities/Arts; [occ.] Undergraduate student at County College of Morris; [memb.] International Society of Poets, Phi Theta Kappa Honor Society; [hon.] Phi Theta Kappa Honor Student, Editors Choice Award 1994 and 1995 from National Library of Poetry; [oth. writ.] "Familiar Patter, published in At Day's End by the National Library of Poetry 1994. "The River of Forgotten Souls", published in Best Poems of 1995 by National Library of Poetry.; [pers.] I am greatly influenced by environmental and social issues of today. how these forces shape and influence the individual and social society; [a.] Long Valley, NJ

**OLSEN, ANGELA MARIE**
[pen.] A. M. O.; [b.] December 6, 1968; [p.] Patricia S. and Jerry E. Olsen; [ed.] Hong Kong International School - H.S., Hamilton College - B.A., Georgetown University and Catholic University - MS; [memb.] International Society of Poets; [hon.] Editor's Choice Awards, "The Rosebud" and "The Raven's Rape"; [oth. writ.] The Rosebud published in Journey of the Mind, The Raven' Rape published in At Water's Edge and East of the Sunrise, The Temple of Lily published in Best Poets of 1996; [pers.] I have been greatly influenced by my studies of thought progression and style in Asian literature, and moved in motion through my analysis of Shakespearean symbolism.; [a.] Falls Church, VA

**OLSON, VELYN C.**
[b.] July 13, 1925, Milwaukee, WI; [p.] Lorenzo and Margarita Farino; [m.] Clarence F. Olson, 1950; [ch.] Kathleen Gunta and Jeanette Olson (Three Grandsons); [ed.] St. Rose of Lima and West Division High School, Milwaukee, WI. Trained as a Dental Technician at Austenal Laboratories, Chicago, IL; [occ.] Dental Technician and Homemaker; [memb.] International Society of Poets, St. Raphael Catholic Church V.F.W. and American Legion Auxiliaries; [hon.] Editors Choice Award; [oth. writ.] Numerous poems and several humorous children's poems depicting good health and hygiene (Unpublished).; [pers.] I am inspired by the writings of the early Greek and Italian Poets and Philosophers. Some of my poetry reflects my husband's forty-two years of Military Service. My children's stories are based on the experiences of my children, nieces, nephews and grandsons.; [a.] Madison, WI

**ONION, JANICE D.**
[b.] June 18, 1911, GA; [p.] Bessie and William Dunagan; [m.] Oliver L. Onion, April 2, 1936; [ed.] Agness Scott; [occ.] Home-maker; [memb.] Washington Restaurant Association - Administrative Assistant (retired); [oth. writ.] Unpublished poems, essays in "Window of the Soul"; [a.] Bogart, GA

**ONWUDINJO, MATTHIA M.**
[b.] June 29, 1972, Toledo, OH; [p.] Dr. Adolphus C. Onwudinjo and Ms. Paula L. Onwudinjo; [ed.] Our Lady of Apostles Secondary School - Lagos, Nigeria Bergen Community College - Paramus, NJ, Rutgers The State University of NJ, New York University; [occ.] Student, artist (Fine); [hon.] Honors' List, Dean's List; [oth. writ.] Several unpublished poems, lyrics, short stories.; [pers.] "Reality Bites, Escapism Relieves" I write about myself and myself being in the shoes of others. I try to feel what others go through at any given level and cry out foul or fine!; [a.] Englewood, NJ

**ORTEZ, ANTHONY**
[b.] April 30, 1982, Dallas, TX; [p.] Jan and Richard Ortez; [ed.] 7th Grade

**OSBORN, MANDY**
[b.] November 21, 1980, Aurora, CO; [p.] Burton Osborn, Elizabeth Osborn; [ed.] Elizabeth Grade Schools; [occ.] Part time cashier at a local restaurant; [memb.] Girl Scouts, Trood 897; [oth. writ.] I am trying to publish a book, but this poem is the only one ever published; [pers.] I write my poetry from the heart. Inspired by all things and events in this world I write all kinds of poetry. I dedicated my poetry to mom and dad and Lisa. Also to my friends and family.; [a.] Elizabeth, CO

**OSBORNE, HELEN A.**
[b.] November 20, 1925, Goodman, WI; [p.] Harry and Lilian Petersen; [m.] Bruce H. Osborne, September 1, 1948; [ch.] David Osborne, Karen Farmer; [ed.] Goodman High, Business Institute of Milwaukee; [occ.] Retired; [memb.] Girl Scouts, Republican Women's Clubs; [hon.] Various certificates and plaques for efforts in precinct work.; [oth. writ.] Number of other poems. Book manuscript.; [pers.] It is my belief that all talent is God given. How it is used is up to the individual. My love for poetry was instilled at an early age by a Mother who appreciated its worth.; [a.] Phoenix, AZ

**OSENBAUGH, LENORE R.**
[pen.] Ellie; [b.] January 25, 1951; [p.] Mr. and Mrs. Juan Gomez; [m.] Howard Osenbaugh; [occ.] Nursing Assistant; [oth. writ.] Growing old - on the thresh-hold of a dream.; [pers.] This poem I dedicate to my father who passed away January 1, 1994 New Years Day will never be the same. Oh! What a shame.

**OSMERA JR., LYNN**
[b.] December 24, 1968, Lincoln, NB; [p.] Lynn and Gale Osmera; [ed.] B.S. in Marketing from University of Nevada, Las Vegas; [occ.] Sales, Marketing; [hon.] Louis Armstrong Jazz Award - 1987; [oth. writ.] Deja-Vu (a collection of songs/poems that I've written).; [pers.] I enjoy writing pieces that evoke an emotion or a feeling. If I can touch someone simply with words, then that is my reward for writing. I like to write in both the Gothic and New Romantic styles.; [a.] Athens, GA

**OSTROM, NASTASHA**
[pen.] Sasha; [b.] October 25, 1985, Mesa, AZ; [p.] Donavon and Vanessa Ostrom; [ed.] Presently a 4th grader at Bustoz Elementary School in Tempe, Arizona.; [pers.] Nastasha strives to be a better writer and loves to draw.; [a.] Mesa, AZ

**OVEN, JOSEPH J.**
[pen.] Jason Gunter; [b.] September 5, 1970, Hartford, CT; [p.] Joe and JoAnn Oven; [m.] Fiancee and Laura Dempsey; [ed.] Hanover - Horton High, Auburn University; [occ.] Exercise Physiologist at East Alabama Medical Center; [memb.] National Strength and Conditioning Association, Green peace, Environmental Defense Fund; [hon.] Dean's List, Who's Who Among Students in American Junior Colleges; [oth. writ.] Numerous unpublished scripts (short stories and movies), long and short form of poems.; [pers.] To unite people by putting into words the emotions that all of us feel.; [a.] Auburn, AL

**OWENS, JUANITA**
[b.] July 8, 1946, Sacramento, CA; [ed.] BA, MA, MA, and Ed.D. University of San Francisco; [occ.] Community College Counselor; [hon.] S.F. Police Commissioner, Chair, San Francisco Commission on the Status of Women, Commissioner Board of Permits and Appeals; [pers.] The poem I write express my deepest

feeling of moments in my life. My writings started in my later years when I became more in touch with those feelings. I hope my writings touch the souls of all people.; [a.] San Francisco, CA

**PAGAN, M. A.**
[pen.] M. A. Pagan; [b.] December 11, 1954, New York City; [p.] Mr. and Mrs. M. Pagan; [m.] Marsha L. Berry Pagan, October 1, 1994; [ch.] Newborn Pagan; [ed.] Theodore Roosevelt High School, Ithaca College 1977, B.S., New York University 1990, M.A.; [occ.] Documentary Producer and Writer; [memb.] Internation Telivision Assoc., Association of Independent Film and Video Producers, Association For Research and Enlightenment, Emergency Volunteer; [hon.] Student Gov't President, Boy Scouts of America, Ithaca College Scholarship Award, New York City, Laurente Medal and Award Directors Service Award 1993, Directors Service Award 1994; [oth. writ.] Poems published in: The Creation Cornell University Press, The Kinanza Edition, Plays The Miracle Box, To Dream of Tea, and other short stories.; [pers.] To read and write poetry is to share the divine experience.; [a.] Flushing, NY

**PAGE, LAURA G.**
[b.] December 20, 1930, Kansas City, KS; [p.] Elmer and E. Veril Hollins; [ch.] 5- Andre, Robin, Darrye, Maste and Tamara; [ed.] 12th Grade, Acctg courses at UCLA Extension; [memb.] BMI; [oth. writ.] Song written at age 15 named "Why Don't You Write Me"; [pers.] I have been influenced by my love for Jesus Christ and the gift of writing that he gave me.; [a.] Los Angeles, CA

**PALMER, MILDRED G.**
[pen.] Millie Palmer; [b.] March 17, 1946, Curacao, Antilles, Netherlands; [oth. writ.] A collection of poems entitled, Conversations With The Soul, published in 1992 by Guyasuta Publisher, Pittsburg, Pa., now Sterling House Publisher.; [pers.] It is grace alone that moves my life and its because of grace that I write.; [a.] Rego Park, NY

**PAMIN, DIANA DOLHANCYK**
[pen.] Diana Dolhancyk; [b.] December 13, Cleveland, OH; [p.] Peter Dolhancyk, Diana Dribus Dolhancyk; [m.] Leonard Pamin; [ch.] Louis Peter, Diana Anne; [ed.] West Tech. High, Titus College of Cosmetology; [memb.] Arthritis foundation, International Society of Poets, and I've sponsored a young girl in India for 15 yrs.; [hon.] "Editors Choice Award" for outstanding achievement in poetry, for "The Parting" in Journey of the Mind, published by the N.L.O.P. "Editors Choice Award" for "Stormy" in Songs on the Wind.; [oth. writ.] "Shadow Side" published in At Waters Edge, and now Best Poems of 1996. "The Parting" published in East of the Sunrise and the SUN STAR Newspaper.; [pers.] Always give someone a smile, you'll never known whose heart you might lighten. I strive to see beauty in all things. I wrote my first poem at the age of 12. I wanted to be a singer, dancer, writer, in the arts, anything creative.; [a.] North Royalton, OH

**PARDEL, CARMEN**
[b.] October 4, 1974, Midland, MI; [p.] Linda and Stanley Pardel; [pers.] Live long, die old, by and by. But die.; [a.] Midland, MI

**PARKER, BROOK SUSAN**
[occ.] Actress, working also writer. Currently coming out in two films in "96". "Stronger Days" and "Driven".; [oth. writ.] Screen play - "Under The Sun", poetry - currently working on a novel.; [pers.] It is merely by the grace of God the beauty and life still shine... Thanks so much for allowing me to be apart of your contest.; [a.] Los Angeles, CA

**PARKER, DOROTHY R.**
[b.] 1927, New Jersey; [ch.] Three sons; [ed.] B.A. Univ. of Cal., Berk., 1969, Ph.D, University of New Mexico 1988; [occ.] Assoc. Prof. of History, Eastern New Mexico Univ.; [memb.] Board of Directors, Hist. Soc. of New Mexico, Western Hist. Assoc.; [oth. writ.] Singing an Indian Song, A biog. of D'Arcy McNickle Univ. of Neb. Press, 1992 publ. Phoenix Indian High School for the Nat'l. Park Service, 1993 publ. Articles and Book Reviews.; [pers.] I have been a non-traditional for many years student, and believe that education, both formal and informal, is a lifelong responsibility, vocational, and privilege.; [a.] Portales, NM

**PARKER JR., JAMES M.**
[pen.] James M. Parker Jr.; [b.] July 12, 1980, Chicago, IL; [p.] Kathy and James Sr.; [ed.] High School Sophomore; [occ.] Student; [hon.] Award for Signature poem "Childs Play" April 18, 1991; [oth. writ.] Childs Play, A Dark Night, A Ripple In Time, Down On His Luck, Inner City Life; [pers.] Life is not a party!; [a.] Stickney, IL

**PARKS, LOY,**
[b.] February 20, 1938, Dahlonega, GA; [p.] Howard and Bonnelle Parks; [m.] Mary Gleave Parks, December 27, 1973; [ch.] Matthew Parks, Lolita Parks; [ed.] Dahlonega Elm. School Ged; [occ.] Lead Press Operator, Avery-Dennison Flowery Branch GA.; [memb.] Mt. Sinai Bpts. Church, Masonic Org.; [oth. writ.] Company news letter poem in local newspaper. (Several); [pers.] I write many poems for my friends who have problems, or want to say something special to their love ones. I seldom use my own name, therefore they get the credit, I get the satisfaction of helping someone on life's journey.; [a.] Gainesville, GA

**PARR, SHIRLEYANNE CHASE**
[pen.] S. Faust-Chase Parr; [b.] May 24, Chicago, IL; [p.] Frank and Lillian Chase; [m.] Ralph L. Parr (Deceased), May 30, 1957, James C. Cartledge, Sr., March 7, 1970; [ch.] Sherrye, Kevin, Lori and (Stepchildren) Bernice, Marti, Jerry, Mike; [ed.] Morton High, Columbia College, Morton Jr. College, University of Illinois (B.S.) University of Central Florida (M.A.); [occ.] Communication Counselor, Writer; [memb.] New Hope Covenant Church, Volunteer Association, PTA, Winter Park Memorial Hospital Assn. Women in Military Service Memorial, Peale Center for Christian Living, Florida Sheriff's Association (Youth Ranches).; [hon.] National Honor Society, Theta Sigma Phi, Plague of Appreciation (Tuskaville School), Morton Junior College, Golden Honor Scroll, Dean's List.; [oth. writ.] Creative Communication, Colossus, various radio scripts, two books in process of copyrighting, Elements Affecting Foreign Students' Attitudes Toward American Television.; [pers.] My writings reflect the deep feelings I have involving intra- and interpersonal relationship. Poetry adds the music.; [a.] Goldenrod, FL

**PARSELL, SHIRLEY**
[b.] April 28, 1942, Leicester, England; [p.] Gladys Peake Pratt, Wilfred Gordon Peake; [m.] Ivan L. Parsell, March 9, 1963; [ch.] Leslie Ivana, Stuart Graham, Kyle James. Grandchildren: Nichole and Mark; [ed.] Rushey Mead Girls School Leicester England. Certified by Ohio for Home Health Aide; [occ.] Housewife; [memb.] World Harvest Church. Columbus, Ohio; [oth. writ.] Several poems published in the Titus Touch a publication of mothers touch, an outreach of the family life department of World Harvest Church Columbus Ohio. Also forthcoming 50 poems ready for publication in a book. To be called Hidden Treasures, two poetic, illustrated children books, called Cats and Hidden Treasure.; [pers.] I feel that the poetry I write comes from the overflow of my heart after spending much time reading and reflecting on the precious jewels found in the hidden

treasures of Gods word to mankind. I also recognize and acknowledge the importance of much encouragement and support of family and friends. Given to me along the way.; [a.] Wharton, OH

**PARSONS, JAMIE BAKER**
[b.] January 2, 1963, North Carolina; [p.] Harold and Carolyn Baker; [ch.] Casey Anne, Christa Elisabeth; [ed.] South Stokes High; [occ.] Student; [memb.] Medows Baptist Church; [pers.] Writing allows me to express feeling and emotion that can not be spoken. My desire is to share with others the perspective and balance that I have experienced in my life through writing.; [a.] Walnut Cove, NC

**PARUCHURI, PHANI K.**
[pen.] Anweshi; [b.] June 2, 1959, Nramabad, India; [p.] Koteswara and Vanaja Devi; [m.] Vijaya Sree, February 7, 1993; [ch.] Venkata Kalyan, (11 months); [ed.] MD.; [occ.] Anaesthesiology, Pain Management; [memb.] American Society of Anaesthesiology, American Academy of Pain Management.; [hon.] Literary and Poetry Awards for Indian Magazines.; [oth. writ.] Several poems, stories, essays, published in Indian magazines, one poetry book "Kavya Sudha" (Nector of Poetry.) Won poetry award. Now in the process of writing a book on philosophical outlook on Human History.; [pers.] I try to make a word which can truth every human being and bring out good to the mankind.; [a.] Southfield, MI

**PASTERNACK, JEFFREY**
[b.] May 4, 1968, Cincinatti, OH; [p.] Stefan and Gail Pasternack; [ed.] University of Maryland, BA in Criminology and Criminal Justice Studies; [occ.] Health care Consultant; [memb.] Delta Chi Fraternity, UMD, Alpha Delta Chi Fraternity, Frostburg; [hon.] Gold Key Honor Society; [pers.] Intention. Nothing else matters.; [a.] Boca Raton, FL

**PASTOR, ERIC**
[pen.] Five; [b.] August 6, 1971, Oahu, HI; [ch.] Daughter, Kiani Paster age 4; [occ.] Colormatcher, Utleys Inc.; [memb.] MR; [oth. writ.] I have others but are yet to be heard.; [pers.] If there is anything that is real in life it's pain. Influenced by Edgar Allen Poe.; [a.] South Bronx

**PASTORE, BEN**
[b.] February 26, 1975, Patchogue, NY; [p.] Robert Pastore, Maria Pastore; [ed.] Patchogue Medford High School, Brookhaven Technical School; [occ.] Graphic Artist/Full time Minister of Jehovah's Witnesses; [oth. writ.] A collection of poems called the Gardens of Sirverity; [pers.] The submitted poem is one of several, intended to capture the lessons learned by coming of age, as well as the paradox, reality has proven to be.; [a.] Medford, NY

**PATENTE, MICHELLE SUZETTE**
[pen.] Maigret Jensin; [b.] February 21, 1949, Philadelphia; [p.] Rose and Robert Marcel Patente; [ed.] George Washington High, The Jay Dash School of Dance/ Certificate of Teaching, The Community College of Philadelphia, Associate Degree in Library Science.; [occ.] Free-lance story-writer and performing artist; [memb.] Twenty-seven year member of nichiren shoshu of America, a Buddist organization for valve creation and human revolution.; [hon.] Royalties for drug and alcohol rehabilitation in America, especially street alcoholism, prison system reconstitution, child prostitution and teenage runaways quididem, seven lyric myths (major works).; [oth. writ.] Umbrians Poetica, Poetry and Lyric Myth, The Guards Of Matilde, Selected Poems, My Father was a Frenchman, Jesefca and other stories, Selected stories.; [pers.] I continue to live my

work. Classical literature and the victorian poets are my past times. My cellist and I use the Back Suites for our performances, at which time I read to an audience and she accompanies me on her musical cello. At that time John Sebastian's presence can be deeply felt and the audience forms a beautiful soul of its own.; [a.] Philadelphia, PA

**PATINO, MARY A. MACIAS**
[pen.] Tina Patino; [b.] October 10, 1942, El Paso, TX; [p.] Flavio and Margaret Patino; [m.] Divorced; [ch.] Grace, Corina, Yvonne, Annette, Gilbert, Leopold III and Luis Anthony.; [ed.] Garfield H.S., East Los Angeles, CA, College: USCLA. 2 yrs.; [occ.] Nursing in Geriatric Home Care for Visiting Nurse, Ass.; [memb.] American Heart Medical Association, Public Notary, Medical Board Member for NEC. Bryman Campus, member: American Medical Assist, Ass., Lic: Medical Technician, San Gabriel Mission Catholic Church; [hon.] V.NA July 95, Customer Service Excellence Award; [pers.] As a hobby I write, my thoughts as I feel at the time. I love life and am grateful for this gift. I say "Enjoy, feel and be happy today and for all given thee for tomorrow may not come.; [a.] Monterey Park, CA

**PATTERSON, JUANITA JOYCE**
[b.] June 29, 1946, Madera; [p.] Lewis Earl Patterson, Joyce Marjorie Patterson; [m.] Divorced, March 7, 1964; [ch.] Roger Lee Boyett, John Lee Boyett; [ed.] Chowchilla High School, Merced Jr. College "Criminal Justice".; [occ.] Currently Training for Correctional Officer.; [hon.] I have won "Numerous Contest", working for "God".; [oth. writ.] "God's garden not yet published. Inspired one and one half hr. before my father died.; [pers.] God is the originator of my ability to be inspired, and I give him all the credit for this gift. I vowed to God I would tell others about this gift which I also memories for others.; [a.] Chowchilla, CA

**PATTERSON, ROSALIE ANN**
[b.] February 20, 1938, Oklahoma; [p.] Mr. and Mrs. Clyde W. Maness; [m.] Johnny W. Patterson, March 21, 1956; [ch.] 2 children, 4 grandchildren and 1 great grandchild; [ed.] Southeast High School, Valley Brook Grade School; [occ.] Wife, Mother, Grandmother, Help Part Time at my Husbands Business, Business Jet Design, in Shawnee, Oklahoma. Where we do paint and interiors airplanes.; [oth. writ.] Have been writing poems since 1967. I have about 30 other poems written thru the years. At different stages of my life.; [pers.] My honors and awards are my dearly loved children. My very special grandchildren and my husband of thirty-nine years. My mother and my memories of my very beloved daddy, who departed this life many years ago.; [a.] Choctaw, OK

**PAUGH, JAMI JO**
[b.] November 4, 1977, Independence, KS; [p.] Michael Paugh, Sharon Paugh; [ed.] Independence High School (Senior); [occ.] Student; [hon.] SAC president of KS, Regents Honor Academy 1995, National Honors Society, ELP Gifted Program; [a.] Independence, KS

**PAULUN, CARL L.**
[b.] August 14, 1937, Guernsey, OH; [m.] Grace M. Paulun, December 16, 1989; [memb.] International Society of Poets; [hon.] Editor's Choice Award (twice), two poets in the semi-finals in The 1995 Open Poetry Competition. All from The National Library of Poetry.; [oth. writ.] I had a book published in 1994 entitled, "Let's Be Friends" which contained some poetry. I also write song-poems.; [pers.] I write because I enjoy it, if I make any money on it, that just adds to the enjoyment.; [a.] New Philadelphia, OH

715

**PAVEY, STACY**
[b.] November 24, 1983, Bedford, IN; [p.] Michele and Westly Jones; [ed.] I'm in grade school (6); [hon.] In the news paper, published Rainbow in a Rainforest in Dusting Off Dreams (Quail Books); [pers.] I write what I feel. Encouraged by family, friend, and fourth grade teacher (Jackie Robbins).; [a.] Bedford, IN

**PAYNE, DANNY K.**
[b.] March 4, 1948, Fulton, MO; [p.] Charles Leroy and Minnie Pearl Payne; [m.] August 1978, Divorced, November 1994; [ch.] Darrin K.Payne, David N. Payne; [ed.] Fulton High School, Fulton MO. 65251; [occ.] Disabled with MS, Since November 1989,; [hon.] American Defense, Medal while in service 1965.; [oth. writ.] Over 100 poems written. 2 poems published in songs but not released. Poem -"Where are we now" printed in several newspapers and sent to white house in March 1995; [pers.] My goal is to eventually have all my poems published into a book. Viet Nam Era Veteran.; [a.] Fulton, MO

**PAYNE, NORMA DOTSON**
[b.] January 22, 1918, Forest, IL; [p.] Emeryl and Elizabeth Elder Doston; [m.] Jess Willard Payne; [ch.] Daughter - Teri Ann Payne-Nunnally, two grandchildren - Daniel And Matthew Nunnally; [ed.] Decatur High School, Decatur Illinois - Millikin University - B.S. Northwestern University - Grad Work Chicago University - Master's Degree University of Illinois.; [occ.] Retired School Teacher and Guidance Counselor; [memb.] American Legion - Alpha Chi Omega - Women's Study Club - Van Buren Golf Club.; [hon.] Am Red Cross Overseas Service by Harry Thuman, 1971 Leaders of Am. Secondary Ed. 1973 - Cat of Recog. Mo Dept of Ed for work n Ed-Occupational Decision Making - 1975, Who's Who in Mo Ed., 1976-1977, Personalities of West - Mid West - 1978, Who's Who in the World of Women - 1978 Edition 1979, Honor by Winona High School Students on retirement, reporter for Dee Run Golf Course; [oth. writ.] I have write poetry since I was in high school sending many of my friends a poem on occasion - of birth - illness - and death - also notes of friendship.; [pers.] I have been fortunate to work with some of the Top Professionals in the field of education. Although I have been retired from the Educational field since 1979 - I have been active in Community Activities. Play golf daily.; [a.] Van Buren, MO

**PAYNE, HILDA J.**
[pen.] Hilda Gaw, Hilda Gaw Payne; [b.] June 22, 1940, Hilham, TN; [p.] Carlie and Ola Gaw; [m.] Everly C. Payne, June 14, 1986; [ch.] Pamela Wells, Jama Landreth, Paul Harmon; [ed.] Anderson High, Tucker Career Center; [occ.] Pre-School Teacher, Heritage Christian Schools Lodi, NJ; [memb.] Community Baptist Church; [oth. writ.] "Dream Date" (published) in 7th grade, "My Lord Knew", "100% Dividends", "Blueprint on File", "Grandpa Loved Me", "Grandmom's Prayer", "Lifted Like The Wind", "Master Controller" and others.; [pers.] I would like my Lord and Savior Jesus Christ to be honoured in everything I write. Most of my writings are from personal experiences.; [a.] Garfield, NJ

**PEARSON, JAIMI MARIE**
[b.] April 25, 1979; [p.] Paul and Karen Pearson; [ed.] Union Hill Elementary School and Nevada Union High School; [occ.] Student, (Junior in High School); [pers.] For Casey, Patches, and Mickey: you make true additions to my family and, of course, to everyone who consists in and contributes to my never ending family. Love Jaimi.; [a.] Nevada City, CA

**PEDERSEN, VIBEKE SHARUP**
[b.] April 27, 1958; [occ.] Teachers of Arts and Crafts; [oth. writ.] Master's thesis on handworks history and it's importance for our well being; [pers.] An artistic expression serves as a window to our soul, I strive to help children speak through their window.; [a.] New York, NY

**PEERY, PATRICK H.**
[pen.] Patrick H. Peery; [b.] June 5, 1948, Liberal, KS; [p.] Amos and Ruth Peery; [m.] (Ex-spouse) Betty Peery, October 5, 1981; [ch.] (son) Patrick Joe Peery; [ed.] High School; [occ.] "Disability" "Retired"; [memb.] "American Legion" First Baptist Church; [hon.] "Golden Poet 1990", "Golden Poet 1991", "Award of Merit Certificate 1990", "Award of Merit Certificate 1990"; [pers.] Each time I write a poem. It's with the "Hoper", that I might be able to help another "Person on People" in this world, find an "Answer or Solution" to the one thing we all have, Trouble.

**PELES, GIL**
[b.] August 3, 1978, Corona, CA; [p.] Noga Peles, Amit Peles; [ed.] Norco High School, Norco, CA (currently enrolled); [occ.] Student; [memb.] Mock Trial, Marching Band, Concert Band; [hon.] Who's Who Among American High School Students, Multiple Year Award, California State Science Fair Finalist; [a.] Corona, CA

**PELTON, TINA**
[pen.] Tina Pelton; [b.] June 17, 1975, West Plains, MO; [p.] Herbert and Elleen Walker; [m.] Kevin Pelton, June 22, 1991; [ch.] Michael, Kimberly; [ed.] High School 10th Grade, GED; [occ.] House Wife; [pers.] Like most of my poems I reflect the pain and confusion of life and death. But never allow to control me only strengthen me.; [a.] Saint Clair, MO

**PENN, DEBORAH**
[b.] May 6, 1978, Indianapolis, IN; [p.] Ross M. Penn Jr. and Joyce Penn; [ed.] Southport High; [occ.] Cashier, Marsh Supermarkets, Student; [pers.] I write poetry to reflect what is happening in my life. I was greatly influenced by the sonnets and plays of shakespeare.; [a.] Indianapolis, IN

**PERKINS, GARY PAUL**
[pen.] Gary Perkins; [b.] August 20, 1951, Rochester, NY; [p.] Harold and Jeanne; [m.] Michelle, May 28, 1989; [ch.] Colin and Abby; [ed.] High School; [occ.] Antique and Art Dealer; [oth. writ.] Nothing published; [pers.] There is no justification for the destruction of the very elements that support human existence.; [a.] Tempe, AZ

**PERSEGHIN, MELISSA MCSTINE**
[pen.] Melissa McStine Perseghin; [pers.] Words are the bond that connect us with one another, whether silent or verbal when we try to understand them we learn acceptance of each other.

**PESCE, KRISTEN MARIA**
[pen.] Kristie Pesce; [b.] March 9, 1979, Laurinburg, NC; [p.] Sam and Vickie Pesce; [ed.] Junior at Scotland High School in Laurinburg, NC; [occ.] Student; [memb.] Anchor Club, Publications Club, Drafting Club, Drama Club, German Club; [hon.] Honor roll student, Cheerleader, Model, Tap, Ballet, Jazz, Lyrical, Dancer; [oth. writ.] No others submitted; [pers.] Poetry allows me to express the inner most thoughts and fears.; [a.] Laurinburg, NC

**PETERSEN, KAREN K.**
[pen.] Kayo; [b.] October 1, 1962, Eau Claire, WI; [p.] Robert and Arlene Bogstad; [m.] Arthur A. Petersen, June 27, 1992; [ch.] Dennis Best, Nathaniel Best, Benjamin Best; [ed.] Graduated Mondovi Public Schools

1981 / Assoc. Degree with honors in Marketing at Chippewa Valley Technical College, Eau Claire, WI; [occ.] Full-time student with Lakeland College for Bachelors Degree in Business Administration; [memb.] OW-Jaycees, Nazereth Lutheran Church Choir, Chippewa Valley Technical College Alumni Assoc.; [hon.] Outstanding Female Marketing Student of the year (DECA) 1990-91; Awards - State, Regional and National DECA; [oth. writ.] Poetry published in college newspaper as well as assigned articles.; [pers.] My poetry is a reflection of my life and beliefs. With my writings I hope to "touch a cord" in someone else's heart as they relate personally to the poem.; [a.] Owen, WI

**PETERSON, ANTOINE P.**
[pen.] Antoine Peterson; [b.] October 23, 1970, Atlanta, GA; [p.] Ms. Beatrice S. Peterson; [ed.] Northside High, Southern Tech (Smyrna, GA); [occ.] Walt Disney World Entertainment; [hon.] First place blue ribbon in High School Poetry Fair; [oth. writ.] Published in local literary magazine in 1988; [pers.] I love my mother with all my heart, she is my inspiration. Never wish on tomorrow and let today fade away.; [a.] Orlando, FL

**PETERSON, JUDY**
[b.] June 25, 1949, Sheboygun, WI; [p.] Milton Federer, Frances Federer; [m.] Douglas Peterson, June 2, 1989; [ch.] Joel Thomas, James Matthew, Jody Lynn, Mark Nathan, Joni Marie; [ed.] Lakeland College - B.S. Elementary Ed., Defense Language Institute - Russian Grace Theological Seminary - Master of Divinity; [occ.] Home schooling mother of five children - ages 10, 8, 7, 7, 4, Freelance Writer; [memb.] Concerned Women for America; [hon.] Dean's List, Magna Cum Laude (Grace Theological Seminary), Army Commendation Medal Good Conduct Medal,; [oth. writ.] Lyrics for two songs currently in production with Hilltop Records; [pers.] I have always enjoyed the power of words to sway and excite both hearts and minds. I love to discover and reflect the profound through simplicity. I owe a great deal to such writers as John Steinbeck and Robert Frost.; [a.] APO New York, NY

**PETRI, RUTH L.**
[pen.] Moon Pear / Branwen; [b.] July 14, 1926, Chicago, IL; [p.] Appalonia and James Strange; [m.] Harry H. Petri, January 21, 1946; [ch.] Michael and Mario Petri; [ed.] Morton High School; Palomar College - Cosmetology, graphic arts - porcelains and ceramics; graduate of Basic and Graduate Course 1970-'72 of Silva Mind Control; [occ.] Retired; [memb.] AARP - National Committee to preserve Soc. Sec. and Medicare; The Philosophical Library and Life Enrichment Cntr. Escondido, CA was given to me for over 22 yrs. (and still going) of volunteer work; [hon.] Life Membership Award with Philosophical Library - Awards in Hair-styling and coloring from Clairol and Revlon; [oth. writ.] Poetry - Dream (Real) Stories; [pers.] When one takes the time to reflect on the past and dream of the future, take pen and paper and start writing. You will surprise yourself on what you can share with others.; [a.] Escondido, CA

**PETRULLI, HELEN**
[b.] April 25, 1908, Kiev, Russia; [p.] Henry and Dora Schulner; [m.] Nicholas Petrulli, January 1950; [ch.] Rebecca Heskes; [ed.] Junior High School Educational (self-taught); [occ.] Retired, Writer of own autobiography, started own business (making health candies, without sugar); [hon.] I won awards for recipes and fancy commercial gift boxes of my dried fruit candies. I won honors in fancy natural foods preparations!; [oth. writ.] Poetry and auto-biographical stories.; [pers.] I was a teenager when my mother and four children arrived in America from the Soviet Union! I graduated Junior High in Chicago and started working-we were poor.

However, I continued to go to evening school and improve myself. I was creative in foods and wrote recipes.; [a.] Los Angeles, CA

**PETTEE, DOROTHY V.**
[b.] Toledo, OH; [p.] Thelma and Arthur Ashford; [m.] Francis W. Pettee (Deceased); [ch.] Denis A., David W., Michael R., Stephen F., John L., Joseph L., Maria C., Laura A.; [ed.] Bachelor of Arts and Master of Arts, University of Toledo; [occ.] Academic Adviser and Adjunct Instructor, Humanities; [memb.] Christ the King Catholic Church, Intercollegiate Advisers Committee, University Womens Commission, National Academic Advising Assn.; [hon.] The Outstanding Adviser of the Year Award at The University of Toledo in 1992; [pers.] Being able to see life through rainbows, to feel with such intensity that words race out of my mind and fingers, and to think so fiercely that time often seems to stand at attention force me to write. This is the first time that I have entered a contest. Courage at last.; [a.] Toledo, OH

**PEYSSON, MICHELE**
[pen.] Michele Peysson; [b.] February 6, 1970, Long Island, NY; [p.] William Peysson, Maureen Peysson; [occ.] Manuscript Clerk, West Publishing; [oth. writ.] Children's short stories, adult short stories, none published yet.; [pers.] My writing is influenced by a wide variety of works, from Shakespeare to Anne Rice. I can appreciate and reflect anything that is deep or twisted, or both.; [a.] Bethpage, NY

**PEYTON, VIVIAN R.**
[b.] October 8, 1961, Bethesda, MD; [p.] Grant Byrd and Doris Byrd; [m.] Everett E. Peyton Jr., August 8, 1987; [ch.] Terrina Vivianese, Terrell Eugene, TaLee'a Evette; [ed.] Walt Whitman, The Institute of Children's Literature; [occ.] Homemaker; [pers.] Be happy, hopeful, peaceful and patient, Life is a gift so take good care. Whatever you do, do in love.; [a.] Oxon Hill, MD

**PFAEHLER, CHRISTEN LEE**
[b.] August 4, 1971, Eagleville, PA; [p.] Richard and Gale Pfaehler; [ed.] Twin Valley High School, East Stroudsburg University; [occ.] Weight Management, Program Director; [memb.] World Wildlife Fund, Berks Aids Network, National Rehabilitation Association; [hon.] Academic Dean's List, Field Hockey Scholarships, Alpha Gullable Shits; [oth. writ.] All of my poems were written for a select few to view except this one, so I never attempted to publish any of my work before.; [pers.] To create an image, arouse emotion, and feel passionate, all in one moment-is poetry. Carpe Diem Baby.; [a.] Elverson, PA

**PHARR, MILTON E.**
[b.] January 25, Gastonia, NC; [p.] Robert William and Edna Higgin Botham Pharr; [m.] Felicia Ciuro Pharr, December 1, 1968; [ch.] Devinson Ciuro Pharr, Kerina Ciuro Pharr; [ed.] B.A. DePauw University, M.A. Columbia University, H.S. Highland High, Gastonia, NC; [occ.] District Manager, Social Security Admin., Pittsfield, MA,; [memb.] Smithsonian; [hon.] Graduated Columbia Univ., High Honors; [oth. writ.] Short Story, "Sunday In town", Published in the Southwest Review; [pers.] My principal themes are the environment and space, and they hopes for peace and brotherhood among all peoples.; [a.] Williamstown, MA

**PHILPITT, EDWARD T.**
[b.] November 15, 1926, Washington, DC; [p.] Isabel and Richard Philpitt; [ed.] Graduate of Benjamin Franklin Univ., Wash., DC 1952; [occ.] Poet; [memb.] The International Society of Poets; [pers.] Thinking is the ground work needed for growth. The secret of life - "continuous growth". To lighten the load, change

thoughts when necessary. It's through individual thoughts that we can entertain the stardom within.; [a.] Washington, DC

**PICKELSIMER, EVELYN**
[pen.] "Pickel"; [b.] October 14, 1942, Atalanta, GA; [p.] Curtis and Winnie Mae Clotfelter; [m.] Floyd David Pickelsimer Jr., August 5, 1966; [ch.] Dina Marie Swearing; [ed.] Clarkston High School, Clarkston, GA.; [occ.] Communication Director; [oth. writ.] "The Children Did Not Cry", What Really Matters"", "Cabin Night", "I Love Being Lost In You", "It Should Be Me", Several Home Poems For business paper; [pers.] "To see anyone crack a smile".; [a.] East Point, GA

**PICKENS, JULIE M.**
[pen.] Julie M. Pickens; [b.] July 29, 1980; [p.] Dolores A. Lawrence; [ed.] Powell High, 9th grade.; [occ.] Student; [memb.] Powell Pep Club; [oth. writ.] Others but not as good.; [a.] Powell, TN

**PIERSON, REBECCA**
[pen.] Dimples; [b.] May 20, 1979, Lake Wales, FL; [p.] Wayne and April Pierson; [ed.] I attend Lake Region High School in Eagle Lake, FL; [memb.] I'm a flute player in my High School band; [oth. writ.] I've wrote many other poems. One of my favorites is called: A River Runs Through Us. It's the 1st poem I ever wrote.; [pers.] I love writing poems. They express all my thoughts and feelings in so many ways. Paper and pen: always my friend.; [a.] Winter Haven, FL

**PINO, CARLOS R.**
[b.] October 24, 1950, San Juan, PR; [p.] Dominga C. and Juan N. Pino; [m.] Anna M. Pino; [ch.] Carlos P. Jr., Elaine V., Juan C., Marianna R., Gabriel A.; [ed.] Dr. Cadilla H.S., Arecibo, PR, Columbia College, MO; [occ.] Employment Services Representative; [memb.] International Association of Personnel in Employment Security, Vietnam Veterans of America, Vice President Borger Kiwanis Club; [hon.] Military Decorations: Joint Serv. Commendation Medal, J/S Achievement Medal, Army Commendation Medal, w/ 1st Oak Leaf, Rep. of Vietnam Gallantry Cross, Combat Infantry Badge. Vietnam Service, Vietnam Campaign with 3 Battle Stars, National Defense Service Medal with Gold Star.; [pers.] Passion, Panache, and substance are indeed, the bare essence of life.; [a.] Borger, TX

**PIONK, JULI ANN**
[b.] February 3, 1948; [p.] Wm. and Virginia McCarthy; [ch.] Frank Pando, William Pando, Christine Pionk, Lea Pionk and Grandson Joshua Miles Pionk; [ed.] St. Philip Neni High, Macomb College; [occ.] Inventory Control Analyst, Cadillac Rubber and Plastics, Cadillac, MI; [pers.] Ben's Den is a reflection of the beginning of a nine year relationship with my best friend Ben Stewart, Marine City, MI. It is hard work and practice that allows one to recognize and label inner feelings, but it is God's gift that enables the literary reflection of these feelings.; [a.] Cadillac, MI

**PIPER, JOANN CHASE**
[pen.] Jo Piper; [b.] April 5, 1929, Lake City, IA; [p.] Ella and Wilber Chase; [m.] Charles M. Piper, March 23, 1951; [ch.] Steven, Kevin, Alan; [ed.] BA Education (English) at UNI, Rebuilding Seminars, C of C Workshops, Workshops on Aging, Writing with J. Webb; [occ.] Writer, Volunteer for Aging, Homemaker, Crafts; [memb.] University Honors Societies, Pi Tau Phi Sorority, International Society of Poets, RSUP, Church of Christ; [hon.] 5 Editors Choice from NLP, Distinguished member of ISP, Volunteer Awards, College Honors; [oth. writ.] "Grandma's Psalm", "Intruder", "A Daughter Writes Home", "Retirement Recipe", "Tribute", "Love Letter", "Equinox", "Prodigal Found",

"The Word"; [pers.] I am very blessed and still feel humble to have the talent to write. I encourage others in the golden years to use any creative talents they have.; [a.] Loveland, CO

**PIQUE, ROGER**
[pen.] Roger O Pique; [b.] February 1, 1941, Detroit, MI; [p.] Oliver and Eleanor; [m.] Mary Edith, August 26, 1973; [ch.] Roger, Robert, Kipp; [ed.] Fulton City High School, Colorado State University, Dale Carnegie Course; [occ.] Retired Insurance Executive; [memb.] National Honor Society, Quill and Scroll Society High School, Kentucky Iden (Involvement in Drug Education Against Abuse); [hon.] Citizen of Year 1976, Salesman of Years 1973-1977 Combined Insurance Company of America.; [oth. writ.] All poems God's Eternal News, Blood and Honor, Life's River, The Moon Follows Me, One Winter's Night, Dedication Life, My I.C. Journey, My Lit'l' Boy, Reflections At There Grave, What is Forgiveness?; [pers.] I emphasize camouflaging your problems costs you the price of common sense, self discipline, long range physical and mental harm and spiritual desecration.; [a.] Fulton, KY

**PITTS, HERBERT L.**
[b.] October 1, 1949, Baltimore, MD; [ch.] Alexandria Nefertiti (9), and Zulekha Monique (7); [ed.] Graduate Faculty Center of the New School for Social Research (M.A.), Corwell University (B.S.); [occ.] Diversity, Multicultural Consultant; [hon.] Educational Achievement Award from Coalition of 100 Black Women 1994, YMCA Black Achievers of Business and Education Award 1985; [oth. writ.] Essays and poems have been published in Black View Newspaper, Rainy Day, Okike, Eclipse, Watu, and we speak as liberators: Young Black Poets; [a.] Elgin, IL

**PITTS, ROBERT M.**
[b.] December 15, 1950, Florence; [p.] Mr. and Mrs. R. L. Pitts; [m.] Kimberly Dawn Pitts, October 10, 1975; [ch.] Alar and Anna Pitts; [ed.] B.S. Francis Marior College; [occ.] Farm Manager for Pee Dee Reseach Center; [pers.] Being raised on a southern farm, I was exposed to hard work, close family relationship, tradition and God's gift of imagination. Created in me an eagerness to offer through writing, life in different view.; [a.] Florence, SC

**PLATO, MARY E.**
[b.] February 15, 1955, Gardiner, ME; [ed.] High School - currently pursuing a degree through University of Maine; [occ.] Field Advisor and Examiner for Dept. of Labor - Unemployment Comp. Tax; [memb.] I.A.P.E.S. (International Association of Personnel in Employment Security.), World Wildlife Foundation; [oth. writ.] I have written mostly for friends, family and for retirement parties. I also write children's stories - unpublished; [pers.] I truly believe that each phase of our lives should be viewed as new chapters in a book, filled with new adventures and challenges.; [a.] Augusta, ME

**PLAYER, GALE L.**
[b.] June 30, 1935, Rochester, NY; [p.] Berton J. and Erma L. Patterson; [m.] Divorced; [ch.] Joanne, Jeanne, Jacquelyn, James; [ed.] Spencerport Central School Attended Rochester Business Institute, Moody Bible Institute (May 1994 graduate of External Studies Department); [occ.] Department Secretary/Administrative Assistant, Department of Communication, SUNY College at Brockport. Also church organist (since 1965); [memb.] Civil Service Employees Association; [hon.] Adele Catlin Secretarial Award, SUNY Brockport, NY (1988), Editors Choice Awards: "Power to Kill" (in At Day's End 1994), "Alone" (in best poems of 1995/1995), Alpha Iota Honor Sorority/RBI, Dean's List.;

[oth. writ.] Numerous articles and poems included in local newspapers and national magazines. The National Library of Poetry. "Power to Kill" (At Day's End, 1994), "Alone" (Best Poems of 1995), "At the Close of Day" (Windows Of The Soul, 1996).; [pers.] I am very active in all areas of church work. I have been church organist since 1965. Studied piano/organ for many years at the Eastman School of Music, Rochester, NY. I enjoy all areas of writing but available time prohibits doing as much as I'd like. Grandmother of 13, great grandmother of 2.; [a.] Spencerport, NY

**POLF, WILLIAM A.**
[pers.] A poet who lives in Manhatta, and also works for a living.

**POLIZZI, JOSEPH**
[b.] September 5, 1916, Philadelphia; [p.] Giuseppe Polizzi; [m.] Concetta Di Bella Polizzi, 1950; [ch.] Ronald Polizzi; [ed.] Finished 7 grade Furness Junior High School; [occ.] Retired 1967 from Phila., Police Dept.; [pers.] Summer. One Summer day as it was really hot, the earth was like in a boiling pot I dreaded to go to work that day but read and sleepy on the lofty hay.

**POLLAK, LEE**
[pen.] Lee Pollak; [b.] September 2, 1950, Upland, CA; [p.] William and Florence Pollak; [m.] Gayle Susan Pollak, March 10, 1973; [ch.] Layne, Eric, Joanna; [ed.] Chaffey High School, Ontario, California; [occ.] Auto Interior and Exterior Restorations; [oth. writ.] I've written hundreds of poems, but have never offered them for publication before.; [pers.] If it is alive, capture it in your heart and learn all you can from it so as to enhance your own life and pleasure in living.; [a.] Oceanside, CA

**PORTER, BONNIE**
[b.] July 19, 1976, Auburn, WA; [p.] Douglas Porter, Cheri Porter; [ed.] Studying to become a message Therapist, Graduated from Federal Way High School June of 1994.; [occ.] Entrepreneur; [memb.] Sponsors a Native American child through save the children, The Nature Consonancy, Center for Marine Conservation, HSUS, World Wildlife Fund, etc; [oth. writ.] Poetry plus a monthly publication full of poems quotes short stories song lyrics and black and white drawings, and more. Submission with cover letter and S.A.S.E. accepted.; [pers.] Let's share poems son! Send your work with S.A.S.E. as many un-used US poster stamps as you send to: Bonnie Porter PO Box 3796 Federal Way, WA 98063-3796.

**PORTER JR., GEORGE E.**
[pen.] "Geo"; [b.] December 19, 1952, Los Angeles, CA; [p.] George Porter Sr., Tyree Porter; [ed.] Mount Carmel H.S. and 4 years college; [occ.] Businessman; [oth. writ.] I have been writing poetry since I was a child; [pers.] As a son of God, I know that what ever creative gifts that I am blessed with come from my Father!; [a.] Los Angeles, CA

**POTENZA, LAURA BROWN FONTAINE**
[pen.] Laura Brown Fontaine Potenza; [b.] November 22, 1923, Oxford, NC; [p.] King and Ellie Wall Brown; [m.] Nicholas Potenza, October 1, 1992; [ch.] Anita Fontaine, Gray Alisha Fontaine, Leonard Fontaine, Daren Fontaine; [ed.] College, Vocal lessons, New York City, Art lessons, Palm Beach Community College, Computer lessons - PB Community College; [occ.] Retired; [hon.] National Honor Society Scholarship for best all round student in College, best affirmative debate team in NC, (high school) James A. Gray High School, Winston Salem, NY.; [oth. writ.] Poems published in college, Meredith College, Raleigh, NC; [pers.] To own is admired, to share is divine.; [a.] Greenacres, FL

**POTTS, JUDITH K.**
[pen.] Jodie Paul; [b.] February 8, 1939, Terre Haute; [p.] Kenneth and Edith Jones; [m.] Harold C. Potts, June 14, 1974; [ch.] Cheryl (36), Linda (33), Bill (32), Christy (18); [ed.] High School and Associate Degree from Ivy Tech. State College in Medical Assist. And Medical Transcription; [occ.] Private Duty Nurse, Self-Employed; [memb.] National Association of Medical Assistants. American Association of Retired People, (Anyone over 55 can belong regardless of employment or retirement); [hon.] First Place in speaking - oral dissertation on Allergies for Associate Degree at Ivy Tech. State; [oth. writ.] Poems published in National High School Anthology, Magazine Articles all rejected; [pers.] I believe you should follow that "Still Small Voice" that comes within if you only listen with your conscience and intuition.

**POULSON, ERIN**
[b.] June 25, 1985, San Jose; [p.] James and Sheryl Poulson; [ed.] Entering the 5th grade Fall of 1995; [occ.] Student; [pers.] I love to write books and poems. I hope to someday be a famous writer. This is the first time I've actually had something of mine published. This is a great reward to me.; [a.] Los Gatos, CA

**POUR, KIMBERLY**
[b.] October 4, 1956, Blue Island, IL; [p.] Russell and Naomi Moennick; [ed.] Washington High School, several college classes including Creative Writing.; [occ.] Bookkeeper - Shilo Inn Hotel and Home Business "The Gift Basket"; [oth. writ.] Several stories and poetry written for friends and family; [pers.] Poetry is universal. You will find it in the painters brush, the musicians instrument and a child's smile. Without it we are lost. It is the heart and soul of life.; [a.] Portland, OR

**POWELL, CHRISTINE**
[pen.] Esther Davidson; [b.] October 22, 1961, DeKalb, IL; [p.] Evlyn and Allan Jones; [ed.] San Diego State University, B.A. in Psychology, Masters of Social Workers; [occ.] Psychotherapist; [memb.] National Association of Social Workers; [oth. writ.] Chrysalis, Healing from Abuse through spirituality; [pers.] I hope to bring the healing love of God to wounded people through poetry.; [a.] San Diego, CA

**POWELL, RANDI A.**
[pen.] Desiree Rand; [b.] March 3, 1967, Denver, CO; [p.] Quinton and Normal Powell; [ch.] Jordan (daughter); [ed.] George Washington High, The France - American Institute, C.V. Denver International Correspondence Schools and The Alliance Francaise; [occ.] Intake Coordinator The Adoption Center; [memb.] Colorado Black Women for Political Action and The Alliance Francaise; [pers.] Obtain happiness by embracing truth.; [a.] Denver, CO

**POWELL, VIOLET PAULINE B.**
[b.] June 20, 1918, Knoxville, TN; [p.] Mr. and Mrs. Fred R. Brown (Deceased); [m.] Charle T. Powell Sr., November 30, 1935 (Divorced); [ch.] C. T. Jr., Sarah, Billy, Barbara, Fred, Lee, Nancy; [occ.] Retired; [oth. writ.] In process of writing a book "White Sandy Path" I have authored approximately one (100) hundred poems.

**POYNTER, RAY E.**
[pen.] Top; [b.] March 16, 1924, Sachse, TX; [p.] Fay and Fred Poynter; [m.] Wanda Jeane Poynter (Jeane), October 11, 1946; [ch.] David, Stephen, Paul, Jennifer, Cynthia, and Timothy, 12 grandchildren; [ed.] 2 years of college and many army schools besides Agriculture and Conservation College graduate.; [occ.] I made the U.S. Army my career, I am now retired. I spent 25.3 years in the Infantry and am one of about 300 to receive the Combat Infantry Badge for 3 wars; [memb.] DAV

Life member, Born again Christian; [hon.] 21 Metals from 25.3 years in the Military service. Including four Bronze Stars and the Purple Heart, Long Rifle Award in Scouting, the Freedom "Foundation Award" Many 21 metals from WW11, Korea, and two tours in Vietnam; [oth. writ.] I have a collection of poems some have been published that I have written. Mostly about my War days and Vietnam services, I won a Freedom Foundation Award for an Essay on "What I can do for Freedom".; [pers.] I take pride in youth activities and have been a youth guidance for many years. I won the "Long Rifle Award" in Scouting advisor when I had three of my boys in scouting.; [a.] Berryville Arbuses, AR

**PRATT, CAROLE**
[b.] May 9, 1953, Hollywood, CA; [p.] Lloyd and Mildred Springer; [m.] Thomas Pratt, August 6, 1977; [ch.] Jennifer Ray, James Lloyd, Sarah Diane (all Pratt's); [ed.] College Fresno State U; [occ.] Mother, selfemployed; [memb.] Alders gate United Methodist Church, Girl Scouts of America PTA; [pers.] I have been writing poems for about 5 years. This is the first I've shared outside of my immediate family. Would like to study poetry.; [a.] Irvine, CA

**PRESTON, RACHEL A. WHITE**
[pen.] Rachel A. Preston; [b.] July 30, 1908, Dunn, NC; [p.] Charles B. and Katie S. Aycock; [m.] C. Howard White, December 31, 1931, White J. Preston, July 22, 1990; [ch.] Howard White, Jr., Katherine A. White, and Hannah E. White; [ed.] After graduation of High School in 1925, I entered U.N.C. at Greensboro, N.C. and was graduated in 1929. Further studies at N.C. State and U.N.C. Chapel Hill; [occ.] Rejoicing in the Lord who keeps me on a light bash; [memb.] At this stage in life, I've outgrown a bunch of educational and social organizations. I belong to community Presbyterian Church and a few bridge groups; [hon.] Being the mother of 3 fine children, the grandmother of 9 grands, and the great grandmother of 3 and 2 great grandsons; [oth. writ.] Children's Chapel Programs and Children's stories and poems.; [pers.] Wisdom is more important than power. A wise person can find joy everyday if she wants too. Laughter helps the grief stricken with less weight and more love than unasked for advice.; [a.] Whispering Pines, NC

**PRICE, JOANN DENISE DELUGT**
[p.] Dorothea T. Delugt-Collins and Henry J. Delugt Jr.; [m.] Walter J. Price; [pers.] I pray for every reader that this poem cause the love, power and truth of Jesus, (The Anointed Messiah) to be made known. All glory and praise belongs to God who is the creator and posses or of Heaven and Earth.; [a.] Chandler, AZ

**PRICE, RYAN TRAVIS**
[b.] July 14, 1978, Hastings, NE; [p.] Bruce Price, Susan Price; [ed.] Senior at Hastings High; [memb.] Ecology Club; [hon.] Eagle Scout, National Forensic League Member, President of Ecology Club; [pers.] Life has poetic motion.; [a.] Hastings, NE

**PRIOLA, LISAMARIE MAGRAS**
[pen.] Lisamarie Magras; [b.] March 9, 1965, Saint Thomas, VI; [p.] Gene and Theresa Magras; [m.] George C. Priola Jr., August 2, 1990; [ch.] Theresa, Jessica and Michael; [ed.] Curtis H.S. and S.I. College.; [occ.] Vice President of family owned business.; [memb.] Real Estate Association, Boy scouts of America Association, Working Womens Association; [hon.] Boy scouts of America, Mother of the Year. This is my first contest and I'm very proud and honored to be a part of your book.; [oth. writ.] I've worked so hard on my poetry. I hardly have the time for myself but when I do I spend most of it writing.; [a.] Staten Island, NY

**PRITCHETT, MICHAEL T.**
[b.] February 28, 1938, Dyer Co, TN; [p.] H. Quinn Pritchett; [ed.] Air Command and Staff College, USAF, 1984, MA Journalism, University of Missouri, 1970, B.S. Journalism, University of Tennessee, 1960; [occ.] Unemployed; [memb.] American Association of University Professors, AAUP, 1995, National Council for Excellence in Critical Thinking, 1993-1995, American Personnel Guidance Association, South Atlantic Modern Language Association, 1992-1995; [hon.] Published in Lyricist, 1995, Published in Iliad, 1995, Who's Who Among America's Teachers, 1994, Honorable Mention for Poetry in North Carolina, The Lyricist, 1994, Published twice in New South Writer, 1995, Published by The National Library of Poetry, Windows of the Soul, 1995, Semi-finalist in North American Poetry Contest, 1995, Letters of Commendation 1985-1986, Quality Salary Increase, (USAF) 1984, Outstanding Performance Awards, 1975, 1976, 1977, (USAF), Internal Revenue Special Service Awards, 1973-1974 (BIA); [pers.] No one can live in fear, he can only exist.; [a.] Sylva, NC

**PRUDHOMME, BARBARA**
[b.] November 23, 1949, Casper, WY; [p.] Bob and Betty Harshman; [m.] Al Prudhomme, November 26, 1982; [occ.] Sales Representative for PM Group Life Ins. Co.; [pers.] I enjoy running, painting and writing. My husband and I enjoy hiking and backpacking in Yosemite. It's the beauty and peacefulness of the mountains that inspires me the most.; [a.] Dallas, TX

**PRUITT, NINA S.**
[b.] October 17, 1916, NC; [p.] Deceased; [m.] Clarence H. Pruitt, November 13, 1939; [ch.] Robert L. Pruitt, Dora Gina Pruitt; [ed.] 7 Grade; [occ.] House Wife, I was raised on a farm; [memb.] Local Baptist Church; [hon.] Poems Only, Best Poems 1994-1995; [oth. writ.] I love to write poem for a hobby and for the love of the Lord; [pers.] I am a Born Again Christian I have had cancer and the Lord Healed me, is why I praise him in the poems.; [a.] Forest Hill, MD

**PUSTKA, GLENN A.**
[ed.] St. Paul High, Shiner, Texas, (currently) Texas Lutheran College, Seguin, Texas; [occ.] Produce clerk in grocery store chain; [pers.] Looking forward to more life and education.

**PUTZ, PHYLLIS E.**
[b.] February 15, 1922, Minneapolis, MN; [p.] Howard Fjersta and Stella Himle; [m.] Carl (Deceased), September 6, 1946; [ch.] Linda, Michael, Teresa; [ed.] Austin High School, Registrar Mayo Clinic, Then Radiological Technician and started writing in teens and started oil painting classes; [occ.] From European Teachers, (artists in oils); [memb.] Womens Aglow Int'l, International Society of Poets Sons of Norway, Artists Asia (oil Painting); [hon.] National Library Editors Choice, Merit Award; [oth. writ.] Several writings on cards, artistic ass'n in Areas where I have lived. I strive to put my poems to have the feeling that arises from a great painting on display on a white clear wall; [pers.] I have been influenced by the greatness of the early 40's, 50's Classics, and the early years of my family history, The Classics.; [a.] Gross Valley, CA

**QUADIR, AMREEN FATEEMA**
[b.] June 25, 1985, New Hyde Park, NY; [p.] Dr. Abul Quadir, Dr. Layla Quadir; [ed.] Signal Hill Elementary School; [occ.] Student; [hon.] N.Y.S.S.M. A gold medal, several Student of the Month Awards and writing awards.; [oth. writ.] Poems and short stories for school.; [pers.] My poems are influenced by the beauty of nature and living things.; [a.] Dix Hills, NY

**QUAST, REBECCA**
[b.] August 24, 1964, Orlando, FL; [p.] Reese Thomas, Barbara Thomas; [m.] Gary Quast, May 5, 1990; [ch.] Cassandra Jean, Kathryn Marie; [ed.] Libertyville High School, College of Lake County, Northern Illinois University; [occ.] Mother, Homemaker; [oth. writ.] Personal poem collection; [a.] Chatsworth, GA

**QUINCAN, TERENCE E.**
[pen.] The Fox, J. D. Tealman; [b.] December 13, 1940, Hamilton Ontario, Canada; [p.] Mr. and Mrs. James Quinlan (Deceased); [m.] Single; [ed.] Senior Matriculation complete (grade 13 in the Province of Ontario) Canada Nine Honours, 72% year average; [occ.] Writer; [memb.] None to speak of in the last few months of 1959 in Guelph, Ontario it was studying to be a Jesuit priest. In March 1989, here in London, I became an Anglican.; [hon.] Only in high school in my hometown, Brantford, Ontario. My family moved from Hamilton to Brantford when I was three years old. God did not want me to become a priest. I accepted His will I'm happy.; [oth. writ.] I have had several poems published in various papers in Southern Ontario, including 16 short poems in the Toronto sun the poets corner newspaper, Toronto, Ontario.; [pers.] I have always a bided by a quotation from Hamlet- quote. "To there own self be true and it must follow as the night the day, thou can't not there he false to sigman-unquote.; [a.] London Ontario, Canada

**QUINTAMILLA, JULIANA II**
[b.] May 1, 1981, Victoria, TX; [p.] Felipe Quintanilla, Juliana Quintanilla; [ed.] Mercedes High School for Health Professions; [occ.] Student passing to the 10th grade level.; [memb.] HOSA (Maybe this year I'll get in it again.); [hon.] Best Student in 8th grade, Music Award, A&B year round Honor Roll Award.; [oth. writ.] Just school work writing papers, and personal poems kept in my home.; [pers.] One who tries to succeed in life, will eventually succeed. I want to thank my parents for everything they're done for me. I love you mom and dad.; [a.] Penitas, TX

**RAASCH, EDWARD R.**
[b.] October 14, 1914, Indianapolis, IN; [p.] Deceased; [m.] Grace K. Raasch, September 26, 1937; [ch.] Mrs. Stacy (Janice) Schronk Mr. Douglas L. Raasch; [ed.] Manual High Indiana University Del Mar College; [occ.] Retired; [memb.] First methodist church Kiwanu Club Lumber Assoc. (Local, State and National); [hon.] Past Pres. Kiwanis, past Pres. Lumber Assoc. State Lumber Director Several awards in news broadcasting in Kiwanis clubs Radio and TV commercials plus voice overs. Past member board of adjustment in Corpus Christi; [oth. writ.] Plays, short stories working on a book. (Willing to work to get published); [pers.] As a business man, I had many challenges, but at retirement time, I accepted (reluctantly) another challenge, how to operate a washing machine, dishwasher, sweepers, making a bed properly, etc - Oh joy!! I love to write, that's a legacy I can leave to my children and grandchildren.; [a.] Corpus Christi, TX

**RAGHANTI, JILL M.**
[pen.] J. R. Wayland; [b.] June 17, 1976, Youngstown; [p.] David and Cindy Raghanti; [m.] Single; [ed.] Boardman High School, 1994. Kent State University (Trumbull Campus) Working toward B.A. in Communications.; [occ.] Assistant manager of M&P Coney Island, in both Warren and Boardman.; [memb.] Member of the National Forensic League, Ruby Standing. Also The Quill and Scroll Society.; [hon.] Achieved the highest gem in the National Forensic League, a Ruby. Won Third place in the Tri-County Journalism Festival. Became a member of the Quill and Scroll Society, after one year on news staff. State qualifier in Speech. Third place in the Italian Lang.; [oth. writ.] Sports editor for my school paper, and currently a staff writer for my college paper.; [pers.] Smile and laugh at life, it is the only way to survive. It does not matter what we gain in the end of our journeys, it is what we learn along the way that makes life meaningful.; [a.] Youngstown, OH

**RALL, RENEE ANNE**
[b.] December 18, 1982; [p.] Ron and Alison Rall; [ed.] I have been home-schooled all of my life.; [pers.] I enjoy writing about horses especially and I have been influenced by the writings of C.S. Lewis.; [a.] Mansfield, OH

**RAMAGE, ERIN**
[b.] December 27, 1980; [p.] Bonnie Ramage, William Ramage; [ed.] Boardman Glennwood Middle School, Bigelow Middle School (precious year); [memb.] A.S.P.C.A., World Wildlife fund, Peta (People for the Etheal Treatment of Animals); [pers.] There is more to be learned from darker things like wolves than from any faithless fascination. Religion is falser than hatred for good. True faith is rare.; [a.] Boardman, OH

**RAMSEY, JANEEL A.**
[b.] September 25, 1972, Silverspring, MO; [p.] Oscar and Alice Ramsey; [ed.] 1995 Graduate of the University of Maryland College of Business Accounting; [occ.] Daycare Substitute/ Aide; [memb.] Active member of the church of the Nazarene; [hon.] Received a gold medal at a church talent festival for the poem "By the sea".; [oth. writ.] Various poems.; [a.] Bowie, MD

**RAMSEY, KIMBERLY R.**
[pen.] Renee Luv; [b.] February 22, 1973, Little Rock, AR; [p.] Brenda L. Spears and Alvin L. Ramsey; [ed.] Joe T. Robinson High school, Baptist Schools of Nursing and Allied Health.; [occ.] Nursing Student, Nanny.; [memb.] American Red Cross Association; [hon.] National Honor Society, National Beta Club; [oth. writ.] "Will you miss me when I'm gone" "Love me for Me" "My one and Only"; [pers.] I feel my writings are so touching, because I take emotions that I feel inside and express them on paper for others to share. I have been inspired by situations in my life. This is dedicated to my Grandmother "I'm a Faye Ramsey" with all my love.; [a.] Van Nuys, CA

**RANGER, HOLLIE DEE**
[b.] April 19, 1983, Philippines; [p.] Danny and Diane Ranger; [ed.] Attending Caesar Rodney Junior High 7th Grade; [hon.] Student Council, Honor roll, Citizenship Award; [oth. writ.] Positive attitude, relationship, peace, aids, violence, we do not; [pers.] If you practice and get better you've made a start. The end only comes when you quit.; [a.] Camden, DE

**RANSOM, MILDRED J.**
[b.] May 18, 1932, Statesbury, WV; [p.] Geo and Clara Keaton Murdock; [m.] Loyd Franklin Ransom Sr., February 11, 1955; [ch.] Pam Hedrick, Loyd F. Ransom Jr., Christina Davis; [ed.] Shady Spring High (1950) one yr. Beckley College; [occ.] Grocery Store Clerk, husband owner Ransom's Mkt. 36. yrs; [memb.] Daniels Bible Church; [oth. writ.] Many Writing's (none published) this is my first entry.; [pers.] Writing helps me to sort my thoughts and encourages me there is hope in this world which seem's so troubled I pray others will be encouraged as they read my writing. There is pleasure to be found with power and pen.; [a.] Daniels, WV

**RASCHE, CATHERINE A.**
[pen.] Kitty; [b.] January 28, 1930, Dale, IN; [p.] Mr. and Mrs. Gilbert Gogel; [m.] Al J. Rasche (deceased), October 1950; [ch.] Nine children; [ed.] High School, Insurance School Life and Health continuous Educa-

tion; [occ.] Insurance sales; [hon.] Beeline Fashions Sales Consultant, won new car 1964 for sales; [oth. writ.] Have several, I will send you!; [pers.] Love to help people! Help people and there will be somebody to help you.; [a.] Evansville, IN

**RAVENELL JR., JAMES**
[b.] September 17, 1974, Brooklyn, NY; [p.] Denise Spring Moore, J. Ravenell Sr.; [ed.] Canarsie High, NY Institute of Technology; [memb.] Alpha Phi Alpha Fraternity Incorporated, National Society of Black Engineers; [hon.] NYIT - Dean's list, Canarsie High Fencing M.V.P.; [pers.] Continue to hold up the Light....; [a.] Brooklyn, NY

**RAYNOR, LEVI R.**
[b.] January 9, 1955, North Carolina; [p.] Roosevelt and Lucille Raynor; [m.] Margie Raynor, April 25, 1981; [ch.] T'Chall D. Raynor, JoCosta M. Raynor; [ed.] High School Graduate; [occ.] Residential Instructor; [memb.] International Society of Poets; [hon.] 1995 International Society of Poets Merit Award: Nominated for 1995, ISP poet of the year: 1995 North American Open Poetry semi-finalist: Poems published in through paradise Anthology, windows of the soul, Premier edition of Who's Who in New poets Anthology, Nominated for who's who in new poets 1996 year award, Poem published on "Impressions" Audio by the ISP and "The Sound of Poetry" Audio by the National Library of poetry; [oth. writ.] A collection of poems for publication titled: "Freedom of the Mind."; [pers.] My poetry and artistic talent is a gift from God bestowed unto me, as such it is my desire and purpose to share this gift with others so that others may become positively aware, inspired and motivated.; [a.] Middletown, CT

**RAZ, ED**
[b.] Manila, Phil; [p.] Constantina and Sinforiana Raz; [ed.] Rowland High, Mt. San Antonio College, Cal Poly Pomona; [oth. writ.] First published poem, but this is only the last part of a four part poem.; [pers.] Finding beauty in everything I see and how we all must find our own truth is what I try to convey in my writing; [a.] Chino Hills, CA

**RAZIEL, MICHAEL**
[b.] May 1, 1946, New York, NY; [ed.] A.A L. Beril Arts Colorado Mountain College, B.S Geology Ft. Lewis Cutlose; [occ.] Self-employed company ("Magma Minerals") Miner, Jevueller and Ruh Carver.; [pers.] Poetry is on expression of my inner most trives and needs, the interface where my shadow can come out to play.

**READING, SANDRA LEE**
[pen.] Saskia Hle; [b.] January 17, 1948, Brighton, MI; [p.] Clare and Shirley Reading Jr.; [ch.] David D. Reading and wife Linda and Aaron R. Richman; [ed.] High school grad., Oakland Community College SE Campus; [occ.] Deputy Clerk Country and Professional Clown; [memb.] World Clown Assoc. Clowns of America International Church of God Zolfo Springs, Fl; [hon.] Golden Poet awards 1989, 1990 World Poetry Press, 1995 Poetic Voices of America Award, Editor of School Paper Award for active participation as recruiter's wife for US Army; [oth. writ.] Column in newspaper, poems in local newspapers, Legislation for National Child Safety Awareness Week in Congressional record May 1992; [pers.] God is inspiration and my life and writings reflects his power, grace, love and mercy and most assuredly, His majesty.....; [a.] Wauchula, FL

**REARDON SR., CHARLES E.**
[b.] August 2, 1946, New York, NY; [m.] Marie Reardon, August 8, 1987; [ch.] Charles E. Reardon Jr.,

Jeanine McCarthy; [ed.] Newfield H.S. N.Y., Suffolk Comm. College, N.Y., Edison Comm. College, Fl.; [occ.] Electric Utility - Materials Management Sect.; [memb.] Emmaus Community; [oth. writ.] Poetry as a hobby; [pers.] I love my wife Marie more than any words could ever say. I thank the Lord for his Love.; [a.] Cape Coral, FL

**RECHTENBAUGH, LORI**
[b.] March 5, 1969; [p.] Mr. and Mrs. Donald Rechtenbaugh; [ch.] Jacob Lee; [ed.] Freehold Boro High, Brookdale Community College; [occ.] Certified Home Health Aide; [pers.] I try to express love, hope and survival through my poetry.; [a.] Freehold, NJ

**REDDY, KUCHAKULL S.**
[b.] February 15, 1954, India; [p.] M. Ranga Reddy, M. Vasantha; [m.] K. R. Reddy; [ch.] Two; [ed.] M.A. and Ph.D. (One Semester); [occ.] Professor English Dept. and E.S.L.; [memb.] N. Women's Organization; [hon.] Golden Poet-Award Winner, N.R. Author; [oth. writ.] Published many poems.; [pers.] "Was I made for the world of poetry or the world of poetry was made for me?"

**REDELS, REBECCA DAWN**
[b.] October 6, 1981, Corpus Christi, TX; [p.] S. Lynn and Jane Redels; [ed.] 7 years in the Corpus Christi Public School System's, Gifted and Talented Program.; [occ.] Student; [memb.] Church of Christ, Baker Middle School Choir, 4 Year member of the Corpus Christi Chapter National Piano Playing Auditions; [hon.] Two time representative of the Texas Music Teachers Association's State Convention, Silver Medalist in the Corpus Christi Vocal Solo and Ensemble Contest, Baker Middle School Choir Award for Outstanding Female Student.; [oth. writ.] "Becky" "The Piano", "Time", "Chris's Mother; [pers.] The things that motivate me to write my poems are music and Mother's teachings.; [a.] Corpus Christi, TX

**REED, MERILYN RENEE**
[b.] February 2, 1976, Yakima, WA; [p.] Richard and Lorene Reed; [ed.] Lake Worth Community High School (G.E.D.); [occ.] Cosmetition; [oth. writ.] Other poems (unpublished); [pers.] In loving memory of Heather Hanna Hussy.; [a.] West Palm Beach, FL

**REESE, MAJ-LIS RUTH**
[b.] Sweden; [ch.] One daughter; [ed.] Fashion design and Illustration public health; [occ.] University part of fund raising; [oth. writ.] A collection of poems; [pers.] I was born and raised in Sweden, in the province of Vaermland, known for legends and poetry through such writers as Selma, Lagerloff and Gustav froding. I now live in; [a.] California

**REESE, NINA SPEARMAN**
[b.] Pampa, TX; [p.] Ruth Spearman and Late John R. Spearman; [m.] Jay Rodney Reese; [ch.] Jay Reese Jr., Sharon Reese; [ed.] B.S. in Education Texas Tech University Graduate School - SMU; [occ.] Artist, Decorator writer; [memb.] Tri Delta Alumnae, Mortar Board Alumnae, Dallas Museum Associates Dallas Museum League the shakespeare study club women's board Dallas Civic Opera Les Femme Du Monde Committee; [hon.] Who's who in American Colleges and Universities Who's Who on tech campus, outstanding woman student, all College Nina Reese Counselling Center named in my honor Editor's choice award 1995. The National Library of Poetry; [oth. writ.] "Thou Souls And The Sea" published in: A Moment in Time; [pers.] I seek truth honor and beauty in all things.; [a.] Dallas, TX

**REEVES, GORDON**
[b.] September 14, England; [p.] Mary and Edward; [m.] Delores, October 15, 1945; [ch.] Marc, Thomas, Walter, Laura, Eileen, Mary Deborah; [ed.] Two years Brooklyn College 12 years Navy; [occ.] Retired; [hon.] Purple heart, Philippine presidential citation; [oth. writ.] Poems

**REFT, SHAUN**
[b.] April 1, 1979, Kooiak, AK; [p.] Deette and Alberta Reft; [ed.] Currently a Junior at St. Mary's High School in Stockton California.; [occ.] Student; [hon.] Honor role at St. Mary's High School; [oth. writ.] Several Poems Published in St. Mary's Literary Magazine inscape; [a.] Stockton, CA

**REGALADO, MICHAEL**
[pen.] Paul Luevano; [b.] September 30, 1978, Montebello, CA; [p.] Richard Regalado, Rose Marie Regalado; [ed.] Don Bosco Technical Institute High School; [occ.] Student; [hon.] Who's Who among American High School students, National Honor Society, Dean Principals List; [oth. writ.] My own personal poems. Many on subjects on "Self" and "Destiny".; [pers.] By advancing too fast, we expose ourselves. Try to find your destiny in yourself, not among others.; [a.] Pomona, CA

**REGAN, KELLI**
[b.] May 11, 1969, Bayshore, NY; [p.] James Regan, Patricia Regan; [m.] Mike Stevenson; [ch.] Alyssa Jean; [ed.] Sachem High School; [pers.] I write what I feel in my heart. My only influence is everyday life. This particular poem was written in loving memory of my brother, James Regan, who was murdered.; [a.] Pembroke Pines, FL

**RENAE, JAENET**
[pen.] Eve October, Avaye Noor; [b.] September 30, KC, MO; [occ.] Artist, Singer, Designer, Owner of apparel accessories company.; [oth. writ.] Published essays, poetry.; [a.] Los Angeles, CA

**RENDON, REGGIE**
[pen.] "Tint"; [b.] August 23, 1959, Robstown; [p.] Regulo Sr. and Eva Rendon; [ch.] Priscilla Rae Rendon, 5 yrs old (now in kinder); [ed.] Robstown High School 4 yrs a few college courses.; [occ.] Refinery Worker; [memb.] International Society of Poets, 82nd Airborne Assoc.; [hon.] Editors choice award by National Library of Poetry. Selected for Best Poems of 1996 By The National Library Of Poetry, two poems to appear in one anthology, one poem to appear in two different anthologies.; [oth. writ.] I have just finished producing two of my own anthologies, under the auspice of A.M. MGMT. (Owner) Santos Medina, writing two more different books.; [pers.] "Whatever you do in life son you be there Prior." My first sargent the day I left the army, serving in the mighty 82nd Airborne Division.; [a.] Robstown, TX

**REYNOLDS, STEPHEN R.**
[pen.] Andrew Cobbs; [b.] August 11, 1971, Aknon; [p.] Gilbert and Dorothy Reynolds; [ed.] University of Houston 1994-present, Kent State 1990-94, Nortor High School Grad 1990; [occ.] Student; [memb.] Thesbians Society; [oth. writ.] Some poems published in high school newspapers, working on novel entitled The Heartless; [pers.] I hope one day to be able to write so I, can hopefully bring to others what literature has brought me.; [a.] Houston, TX

**REZA, LINDA KHADEMOL**
[b.] July 14, 1953, Dallas, TX; [m.] Mojtaba Khademol Reza, October 20, 1973; [ch.] Leila, Laudan; [occ.] Physician; [memb.] American College Obstetrics and

Gynecology, Dubuque Medical Society, central Association of obstetrics and gynecology, girl scouts; [a.] Dubuque, IA

**RHODARMER, SHIRLEY**
[b.] May 6, 1950, Jackson, NC; [m.] Seby Rhodarmer, August 23, 1968; [ch.] One son, Charles; [ed.] High School Camp Lab, Cullowhee, NC; [occ.] Christmas tree farmer; [oth. writ.] Have written hundreds of poems and country and gospel songs. Never tried to have anything published.; [pers.] Writing is my way of talking. I feel no one understands my feelings, but paper. I got extra credits in school for poems and stories.; [a.] Waynesville, NC

**RHODEN, NAOMI OKUN**
[b.] October 5, 1948, Clarksdale, MS; [p.] Rheta and Nat Okun; [m.] Louis A. Rhoden, February 14, 1973; [ch.] Bette Caren, and Andrew Ivan; [ed.] Clarksdale High School; [occ.] Housewife, volunteer cookbook editor and speaker for Clarksdale Public Schools; [memb.] Beth Israel Temple; [hon.] Certificate of appreciation for outstanding and dedicated service to the public schools; [oth. writ.] An illustrated drawing for king features syndicate, cookbooks: "Heidelburger", "Pot-Luck", and "Cooking to the beat"; [pers.] Happiness to me is doing for others.; [a.] Clarksdale, MS

**RHODES, SARAH ANN**
[pen.] Sarah Rhodes; [b.] January 14, 1982, Portland, OR; [p.] Jon and Darla Rhodes; [ch.] John, Daniel, Joshua; [ed.] Seventh Grade Sunrise Jr. High Clackamas, OR; [occ.] Student; [memb.] St. Pauls Episcopal Church.; [hon.] Achievement Award from Johns Hopkins University, (SAT scores) 4.0 GPA 94/95 school year Principles honor roll 94/95 yr.; [oth. writ.]; [pers.] Never give up on what you know in your heart is right.; [a.] Clackamas, OR

**RHODES, TERRY L.**
[b.] September 7, 1940, Pawhuska, OK; [p.] Raymond and Ozell Rhodes; [m.] Patrica (deceased) December 18, 1960; [ch.] Erin and Christopher; [ed.] Cleveland, OK High, Glendale Community College, College of Alameda; [occ.] Air Traffic Controller; [oth. writ.] Hundreds of poems, but I have submitted anything for publication since my days in college; [pers.] I write mainly for my own enjoyment about whatever topic occurs to me at the time; [a.] Reno, NV

**RHUDY, CYNTHIA**
[pen.] Cynthia Chambers Rhudy; [b.] January 23, 1947, Winston-Salem, NC; [p.] Herbert and Oreon Chambers (adoptive parents) and Dorothy Kestler; [ch.] Tanya Watkins, Crista Stephenson and Ty Rhudy; [ed.] RJ Reynolds, Winston-Salem, NC; [occ.] Receptionists at Smith Helms Mulliss & Moore, Charlotte, NC; [memb.] Florence Crittenton Auxiliary and past Pres. Florence Crittenton Auxiliary, member of Calvary Church and coordinator of Street Ministry of Calvary Church since '82; [hon.] Awarded Volunteer of Year from George Shinn Shelter '87; Volunteer Group of Year '92-'93-'94; received award from Foundation of Carolinas (for work with homeless) in '94; awarded the Fourth Place Editor's Choice Award from The National Library of Poetry for publishing of "Lord Help Us to Be Just Like Him" Sept. '95; [oth. writ.] Several writings published in Calvary Life of Calvary Church, NC; [pers.] Been greatly influenced by the writings about my best friend, the Lord Jesus Christ, and by authors Amanda Bradley, Helen Steiner Rice, C.S. Lewis and Maya Angelou. I pray my writings can be a reflection of hope and encouragement to others as the Lord has truly been a source of strength, hope and encouragement to me.; [a.] Charlotte, NC

**RICARD, RENEE A.**
[b.] February 6, 1985, Eugene, OR; [p.] F. Craig and Gail E. Ricard; [ed.] Currently in 5th grade at Pleasant Hill Elementary School, Pleasant Hill, OR; [occ.] Student; [hon.] Third place Regional Odyssey Of The Mind Tournament, May 1995 Oregon writing festival, 1995 Blue Ribbon Science fair, 1994-1995 honor roll P.H. Elementary; [pers.] Poetry is fun, it describes many feelings in may different ways.; [a.] Pleasant Hill, OR

**RICE, CHELSEA GAIL**
[b.] August 29, 1957, Asheville, NC; [p.] Callie Alene, Rollins and Zola Carnel Rice (Father); [ch.] James Steven Jones, Jeffrey Scott Jones; [occ.] Home Maker; [memb.] Church of the Incarnation; [oth. writ.] Article for "Woman's World" - Several Articles published in local newspaper; [pers.] I am greatly influenced by hardship but inspired and enabled by God.; [a.] Asheville, NC

**RICHMOND, LOIS E.**
[b.] October 31, 1941, Louisiana; [m.] Jim Richmond, 1963; [ch.] Russell Richmond; [ed.] Klamath Union High In Klamath Falls, Oregon-1959, B.A. Louisiana College-1964 1967-Ma. Louisiana State Univ.; [occ.] Administer Richmond Scholarship Foundation; [memb.] Calif. Assoc. of Retired Teachers San Diego Writers' Guild; [oth. writ.] Articles for teens and parents of teens- published in the Adolescent Counselor; [pers.] For me, poetry is the essence of Language; [a.] San Marcos, CA

**RIEDER, ONA LEE**
[b.] April 24, 1974, Santa Cruz, CA; [p.] Dan and Donna Rieder; [ed.] I am currently a student at Ventura College and will be transferring this January to a school in Northern California.; [occ.] I am studying to become an Elementary School teacher with an emphasis in English and Social Work.; [memb.] P.E.T.A., Friends of the Ocean, Surfrider Foundation, H.I.V. - A.I.D.S. Peer Educator.; [hon.] Carmen Camarillo Award, Deans List.; [oth. writ.] I have written several poems which are stored in the depths of my room and have been shared only with my family and close friends.; [pers.] You meet each person in life for a reason. I'd like to thank the most important people in mine - my mom, dad, sister and grandma. And the extended members, Lesley, Carrie, Mandy, Dipu and Jenny. Thank you to my most influential teachers, Kevin and Margo Buddhu and Barret Culmback. You've made such a difference!; [a.] Camarillo, CA

**RIEDER, WILLIAM MCCANE**
[pen.] Will Rieder; [b.] 1866, Ohio; [m.] Blanche Martin Rieder, 1910; [ch.] Marjorie E. Rieder Boose (1908), Ralph Rider (1911); [ed.] He graduated from college in Ohio and taught School for awhile; [occ.] He owned and operated the first bike; [memb.] Shop and Movie Theatre in Niles-Mich. The theatre was called the "Strand". A silent movie house of the turn of the Century; [hon.] I'm sure but no information available at this time. There is a copy (printed) write-melody market of Niles MI; [oth. writ.] "Is there really a God?" (1950) dedicated to grand daughter a Lullaby -(1942) and other, the lullaby was written also for (Sandra Sue Boose Anderson in the Land of the Fairies"; [pers.] He wrote this in 1922 or close to that year. He left poetry to family members to read after he was gone he passed away at the age of 92.; [a.] Niles, MI

**RIGHTER, ELIZABETH**
[pen.] Shawnee Tree; [b.] October 19, 1937, New York City; [p.] Mr. and Mrs. Bukk G. Carleton; [ch.] Amy Laura, Daphne Brewster, Tracey Dana; [ed.] Radcliffe College, Radcliffe Graduate School, University of Hawaii, Bryn Mawr College; [occ.] Archaeologist-Government of the Virgin Islands; [memb.] Society of Pro-

fessional Archaeologists, St. Thomas Historical Trust, St. Thomas, St. John Arts Council, Society for Historical Archaeology, National Association of State Archaeologists.; [hon.] Graduated Cum Laude, NEH grant awards (2); [oth. writ.] Poetry read at Arts Council meetings, College Anthology of Poetry, Natural History, CRM Bulletin, reports and articles.; [pers.] While I believe that there is an overall plan and wisdom that guides our spiritual lives, I like to see the fun and absurdity in the ego of mankind.; [a.] St. Thomas, USVI

**RITCHIE, JULIE**
[b.] June 25, 1981, Lima, OH; [p.] Barbara, Michael Ritchie; [ed.] St. Charles School; [occ.] Student; [memb.] Youth choir, School choir, student senate, tumbling, cheer leading, track, field, volleyball, hand bells, and server; [hon.] School honor roll gymnastics 9 trophies (1 vault state title) 1 plaque 17 medals (6 gold, 5 silver, 6 bronze); [oth. writ.] "What If" "The Spellbinder" "Crazy Enough" "The Seasons Go By" "Rough to the Edge" "Far Enough to Die"; [pers.] I think you can do anything if you put all of you into it. Just do it!...; [a.] Lima, OH

**RIVERA, DAVID TIMOTHY**
[pen.] Daniel Nathanial Hart; [b.] December 17, 1953, New York City, NY; [p.] Tony and Santa R.; [ed.] Saint Lukes Parochial (elementary) School (8yrs.) Rice High (4yrs.) Parochial School; [occ.] Handyman - Aspiring Poet and Songwriter; [memb.] American Legion Post # 1945; [oth. writ.] Have several poem - songs (compositions) with the hope of sharing them with this blue, blue world.; [pers.] I live to be the poet, to rhyme the world. To make its every recess a colorful place to live, to laugh, to cry happy, to cry sad.; [a.] Astoria, NY

**ROBERTIELLO, LISA**
[b.] November 22, 1965; [p.] Paul and Eileen Kovolesky; [m.] James Robertiello, January 28, 1989; [ch.] Bevin 6, James 4 1/2, Nicholas 3 1/2, Joseph 2 1/2; [occ.] Homemaker; [pers.] Thanks to my children, for without them I could not have written this poem.; [a.] Lincoln Park, NJ

**ROBERTS, ESTHER M.**
[pen.] Esther M. Roberts; [b.] March 10, 1959, Fort Worth, TX; [p.] Will J and Marie Roberts; [ed.] M.S. in Critical Care Nursing, UCSF, CA., B.S. in Nursing, Oklahoma Bapt. University, Rift Valley Academy, High School, Kenya East Africa; [occ.] Staff Nurse in a Critical Care Unit at a Medical Center; [memb.] 1. American Assoc. of Critical Care Nurses (Also local chapter) 2. Prior secretary with Local Unit Council of Calif. Nurses Assoc.; [hon.] 1. Advanced Cardiac Life Support Certification, 2. Critical Care Registered Nurse Certification (CCRN), 3. Cited Twice in "Who's Who Among Young American Professionals"; [oth. writ.] Published twice in University of California. S.F. Newspaper "Synapse"; [pers.] Cutting to the chase and describing life with authenticity is my goal. I write out of my experience, but also attempt to portray the human experience as I see it.; [a.] San Francisco, CA

**ROBERTS, GAVIN G.**
[b.] February 12, 1985, Grand Prairie, TX; [p.] Guy and Kirsty Roberts; [ed.] Lichen Elem. School (K-5); [occ.] Student (5th Grade); [memb.] YMCA Indian Guide Program (Father/Son), The Black Belt Club; [hon.] Honor roll student, Accepted in G.A.T.E., (Gifted and Talented Education Program); [oth. writ.] "My Dream" and "Time for Bed"-short stories; [a.] Citrus Heights, CA

**ROBERTS, TERRENCE J.**
[b.] December 3, 1941, Little Rock; [p.] William and Margaret Roberts; [m.] Rita J. Roberts, March 8, 1962;

[ch.] Angela Rayschel, Rebecca Darlene; [ed.] Los Angeles High School Cal State Univ LA - BA, Sociology UCLA - MSW So. Illinois Univ. - Psychology, Ph.D.; [occ.] Chair, Master's in Psychology, Antioch University; [memb.] American Psych Assn. Board Member 1. Eisenhower World Affairs Institute, 2. Economic Resources Corp., 3. Infina Technologies; [hon.] Southern Christian Leadership Council's Drum Major for Justice Award, 1995, NAACP Spingarn Medal, 1957; [oth. writ.] "Managing Trial Stress" in trial handbook for California lawyers, 1987; [pers.] In all ways and at all times I strive to be an engaged and involved citizen of the universe.; [a.] Pasadena, CA

**ROBINSON, DAVID LAWRENCE**
[b.] March 30, 1964, NM; [p.] Paul D. Robinson, Phyllis Ross; [ed.] G.E.D. and the University of life; [occ.] Photo Copier Technician; [oth. writ.] I've written many poems of different thoughts and feelings, but have given most away to the person whole inspired them.; [pers.] I would like to give glory to Christ Jesus for the change He's made in my life. God is very real and His word is true. For even if a man did not believe but lived by the principals of the bible the world would be a better place.; [a.] Albuquerque, NM

**ROBINSON, JACK K.**
[pen.] Jack Robinson; [b.] September 1; [a.] Bellingham, WA

**ROBINSON II, HILTON CLIFTON**
[pen.] Btovn; [b.] April 22, 1977, Loma Linda, CA; [p.] J. Condel Robinson, Barbara J. Robinson; [ed.] Clairbourn Elementary, and Flintridge Preparatory School, and Franklin and Marshall College, Class of 1999.; [occ.] College Student; [memb.] American Field Service, member and Returnee (France, 1993); [hon.] Creative writing student of the year, 1993, Athlete of the year, 1995, MVP Cross Country and track, 94-95, National Honor Society, Calif. Scholastic Fed. Bronze Medal, National Hispanic Scholar, Honorable Mention and Marshall Scholar, 1995-99.; [oth. writ.] A short story and several poems in Folio.; [pers.] I am currently influenced by Jack Kerouac's is writing and other authors of his generation; [a.] Arcadia, CA

**ROBISON, FRANK A.**
[b.] October 7, 1916, Newark, OH; [p.] T. G. and Florence Robison; [m.] Helen K. Robison, May 2, 1942; [ch.] Two, Patricia and Joseph; [ed.] Newark High School, Ohio State University '38 BA, Ohio State University '41 JD; [occ.] Retired Attorney; [memb.] Ohio State University, Alumni Association, Hound Builders Country Club, Licking County Historical Society, Licking County Genealogical Society, Circus Fans Association; [pers.] Poetry should provide a pleasant experience to the reader; [a.] Newark, OH

**ROBLYER, JOHN SCOTT**
[b.] September 23, 1959, Vermont; [p.] Wallace L. Barbra S.; [m.] Esther J. Roblyer, March 3, 1990; [ed.] Paralegal, College courses for business and Religion.; [occ.] Student; [oth. writ.] What is black and white? Man see's... poem the world; [pers.] Life is not easy, but with the Lord, it set's easier.; [a.] York, PA

**ROCK, KAREN M.**
[b.] October 23, 1963, Pittsfield, MA; [p.] Joseph and Lorraine Rock; [ed.] Lee High School; [occ.] Reservations Sales Agent - Delta Air Lines; [oth. writ.] Several poems which remain unpublished.; [pers.] Writing poetry for me is therapeutic. It enables me to solidify my inner-most feelings.; [a.] Arlington, TX

**RODRIGUES, CLAUDIA**
[b.] January 26, 1953, Hayward, CA; [p.] Alma and Carl Rodrigues; [ch.] 3 Danette Rodrigues, Deanna Marino Steve Marino; [ed.] Graduated from San Leandro High School; [occ.] Work with the elderly volunteer work for a magazine (media service); [oth. writ.] Several poems, but all unpublished.; [pers.] I try to reflect each truth, as it unfolds on the spiritual path. As we move ahead, the kingdom within, unleashes the gifts and qualities, that lie within us all.; [a.] San Leandro, CA

**RODRIGUEZ, BILLY**
[b.] September 18, 1975, San Diego, CA; [p.] Richard and Anna Rodriguez; [ed.] Cibola High School two years at Arizona Western College; [occ.] Currently enlisted in USAF; [pers.] Expand the mind explore the unknown challenge destiny; [a.] Yuma, AZ

**RODRIGUEZ, MELANIE**
[b.] May 24, 1973, NC; [m.] Paul Jansen; [ch.] Ryan, Miranda; [ed.] On-going; [occ.] Full-time student; [pers.] Thanks for the fairy tale Paul, all my love, Melanie; [a.] Denver, CO

**ROEMER, SANDY JO**
[pen.] Rochelle Radimer; [b.] August 26, 1952, Binghamton, NY; [p.] Hedwig Pecka, John Austin Roemer; [ch.] Stephanie Ann Marie Phelps Chad Allen Schulze; [ed.] Lebanon Valley High School Harrisburg Area Community College; [occ.] Self employed real estate agent/broker/auctioneer; [memb.] Central Susquehanna Valley Board of Realtors Pennsylvania Auctioneers Association; [hon.] 1970 Miss Travelers Protection Association 1st Runner up 1970 Miss Lebanon Valley Pageant, 1993 Editor's choice award presented by the National Library of poetry.; [oth. writ.] Poem published in the National Library of Poetry anthology titled The Coming Of Dawn. To date 167 poems to be published in a book titled Without A Dime; [pers.] To my son I never really understood the complexity of living until I started writing then my dreams became reality and my "soul" was exposed in every poem.; [a.] Lovelle, PA

**ROGERS, MARGARET**
[b.] November 9, 1924, Jackson, CO; [p.] Orville and Hazel Bradley; [m.] Ernest Rogers, April 17, 1954; [ch.] Bradley Rogers age 40, Torrest Rogers age 32; [ed.] High School; [occ.] Retired; [memb.] First United Methodist Church, Duquoin, IL; [pers.] Home delivered meals on wheels for about ten years but no award I'm worried about the way our country is in; [a.] Duquoin, IL

**ROGERS, MRS. T. J.**
[pen.] Lettie O. Rogers; [b.] April 21, 1922, Mullins, SC; [p.] W. F. Orr - Ethel S. Orr; [m.] T. J. Rogers, March 3, 1946; [ch.] Martha Ellen (Brown), Nancy Marie (Ward) Anita Louise (Byrd) Jim Rogers Mullins; [ed.] High School; [occ.] Retired - Farmers Home Administration.; [memb.] Macedonia Methodist Church Past President - Secretary - (Teacher) Green thank garden club - now chaplain order of Eastern Star - Clemson Extension Club - Spivey Prayer Group.; [oth. writ.] Short songs stories - never sent to publisher - I have had several poems printed in local newspaper - garden Club Eastern Star Programs year book x-programs also in church Bulletins - (Poems and Song); [a.] Mullins, SC

**ROMES, DEEMIA ELIZABETH-ANNE**
[b.] February 3, 1971, Adrian, MI; [p.] Adrienne And Larry Limbacher; [ch.] Victoria Paige Romes

**RONEY, ALEXA JOY**
[b.] November 8, 1982, Stuart, FL; [p.] Jack and Emily Roney; [ed.] K - 8th; [occ.] Student; [hon.] (PTA) Local Reflections literary awards - 3 years 93-94-95; [pers.] "Act as if it is impossible to fail"; [a.] Decatur, AL

**RONSON, MARGARET**
[pen.] M. Ronson; [b.] October 16, 1959, Birmingham, AL; [occ.] Office Manager Music City Auto Care Products Inc.; [oth. writ.] Numerous others unpublished; [pers.] I hope other adults will take this writing to heart and consider the turmoil we bring to the lives of the children we love.; [a.] Nashville, TN

**ROSA, MANUEL**
[b.] June 28, 1961, Pico, Azores, Portugal; [p.] Francisco and Margarida; [ed.] Most Important things were learned by trial and error.; [occ.] Digital graphic, artist, drummer; [memb.] Lifetime membership in the human race; [hon.] Boston globe's "Art Merit Award 1977" "Love Awry" published in "a delicate balance". "Amor, Amor" music album publish in Portugal by "MSG"; [oth. writ.] "Beauty" was inspired by the most beautiful little girl in the world. It's an honor and a pleasure to have her in my life to love and to hold. Only God could have made such a work of art.; [a.] Somerville, MA

**ROSENBAUM, JENNY LENORE**
[b.] Paterson, NJ; [p.] Della Spark and David Rosenbaum; [ed.] Barnard College (Columbia University), B.A.; graduate studies in English and Comparative Literature, Indiana University; [occ.] Writer and Editor; [oth. writ.] Articles on travel and culture published in the Los Angeles times, The Christian Science Monitor, the San Francisco Examiner, the San Francisco Chronicle, Asia Pacific Travel, Tours and Resorts, The New Renaissance, and other publications.; [pers.] My literary inspirations have ranged from Borges, Marquez, Allende, and Durrell to Lorca, Donne, Joyce, St. John of the Cross, and Homer. Spiritually and philosophically, Buddhist, Sufi and Taoist texts / wisdom have influenced me. Such cinematic artists as Fellini, Bertolucci, Bergman, Kurosawa, Ozu, and Satyajit Ray have also deeply affected my sensibilities. A desire for heightened spiritual awareness -- as well as simple wanderlust -- have triggered my travels to Asia, Mexico, and the Mediterranean world. Journeying represents, for me, an opportunity to evolve a haunting communion with antiquity and the exhilarating contemporary unfoldings of the ancient worlds. The notion of finding spiritual homes -- that one can feel a profound kinship with cultures far from one's native soil -- has been an ongoing catalyst to my travels and writing.; [a.] San Francisco, CA

**ROSETTA, AMANDA ANNE**
[b.] December 12, 1980, Plano, TX; [p.] Richard and Ann Rosetta; [ed.] Amanda is a home schooler in the 9th grade.; [occ.] Home school student; [oth. writ.] A one act play entitled Geography. A motion picture film script entitled Pootsie.; [pers.] I am a seeker.; [a.] Portland, OR

**ROTH, LEA MICHAEL**
[a.] Greensboro, NC

**ROTH, RAY AUSTIN**
[pen.] Ray Austin Roth; [b.] July 1, 1956, Jacksonville, FL; [p.] C.H. (Boot's) Roth, Vera Roth; [ed.] Maranatha Academy; [occ.] Work for Relocation Company; [oth. writ.] Have written several other poems, but none Published; [pers.] I would like to dedicate this poem to my sisters, Shirley Manning and Sandra Gresham, God has truly blessed me with two Loving and caring sisters to whom, I owe much in life. I love you both and thanks; [a.] Jacksonville, FL

**ROTHSCHILD, CYNTHIA S.**
[pen.] Cynthia S. Rothschild; [b.] September 1, 1960, Bronx, NY; [p.] Robert and Jean Rothschild; [pers.] "This poem is dedicated to my special friends who have helped me to overcome the difficult obstacles of my life"; [a.] Jackson, NJ

**ROUS, LESLIE ANN**
[b.] November 19, 1958, Glendale, CA; [p.] Bucky Rous, Mildred Rous; [ed.] Agoura High School, California State University Northridge; [occ.] Legal Office Manager; [hon.] Dean's List, Cum Laude; [pers.] The true joys of being human are found only with an open heart and love for all.; [a.] Agoura Hills, CA

**ROUTSON, STEPHANIE**
[b.] May 17, 1984, Atlanta, GA; [p.] Donna and Tom Routson; [ed.] Starting sixth grade at Bayshore middle school, Belford, New Jersey.; [occ.] Student; [hon.] Outstanding Academic Achievement, Honor Student; [oth. writ.] "A Deep Rage." "The World." "A Dogs Life", "Everything I wish for", I won't" "I Don't Care", "Kisses", "Spoiled Brats", "Now", "Stars," "Blood"; [pers.] Let people live the way they want to live.; [a.] Belford, NY

**ROWEN, SARA**
[b.] May 1, 1976, Albany, NY; [p.] Albert Rowen, Drane Rowen; [ed.] Guilderland High School, currently attending Russell Sage, Junior College of Albany; [occ.] Upper Hudson Valley Writers Guild; [hon.] Poetry Award at JCA Honors convocation in spring of 1995... (2nd place in second semester of first year at Sage JCA.); [pers.] The primary influence in anything I've written comes from having a strong sense of intuition and colorful emotions, my writing, like the heart, speaks independently and has reasons of it's own.; [a.] Albany, NY

**ROWIN, CRAIG B.**
[pen.] Craig Burnham Rowin; [b.] June 14, 1981, Farmington, CT; [p.] Gary A. Rowin, Cynthia B. Rowin; [ed.] Freshman in East Lyme High School, (k to 8th grade Salem Elementary School), Salem, Ct; [memb.] Marching Band and Concert Band, Sailing; [hon.] Johns Hopkins CTY (Center for Talented Youth) Baltimore, MD attended summer of 1994. Young authors Award first place June 1994.; [oth. writ.] Short stories; [pers.] "The quieter you are, the more you hear"; [a.] Salem, CT

**ROWLAND, JANICE L.**
[p.] Richard Osborne and Betty Osborne; [m.] James Rowland, September 25, 1987; [ch.] Rebecca Lynn; [ed.] Oak Ridge High School, Orlando Valencia Jr. College, Orlando; [oth. writ.] Seeking publication for children's books she was written.; [pers.] Work hard to realize your dreams it is better to attempt and fail then to regret never trying.; [a.] Orlando, FL

**ROYER, MICHAEL ALAN**
[b.] November 7, 1978, Newport News, VA; [p.] James Earl Royer, Christine Mumford Royer; [ed.] W.T. Woodson, H.S., Class of 97'; [occ.] Student; [memb.] Sign language club, W.T. Woodson H.S.; [oth. writ.] Varsity letter in swimming as Manager of swim team.; [pers.] "At Dark" is my first attempt at publishing. I greatly enjoy poetry, after graduation from High School I intend to pursue a 4 year degree in forestry.; [a.] Alexandria, VA

**ROYSE, ATAKA RHODES**
[pen.] Ataka Rhodes Royse; [b.] February 17, 1925, Florence, AL; [p.] William Henry and Myrtle South Rhodes; [m.] Ralph Royse, June 6, 1987; [ch.] Mark, Adam and Paul Arron; [ed.] High School and Nursing; [occ.] House-Wife, Paster's Wife, Missions Dir.;

[memb.] Independent Fellowship; [hon.] Hosp. Corp. Of America, Humanitarian Award, Distinguished Serve Award, Nazarene, Spotlighted News Papers, Radio and T.V. Distinguished Member of International Society of Poets; [oth. writ.] Poem in Golden Ann. School Book, Several pub, by National Library Of Poetry, special tributes, dedications, award services.; [pers.] I strive to beauty, hope and praise in my writings. My Mother was my early mentor, I learned to love and deliver with oral protection from. Her I have been blessed with many mentors. I am indebted to the poets who have gone before me.; [a.] Tulsa, OK

**RUBIO, STEPHEN JOSEPH**
[b.] June 8, 1951, Austin, MN; [p.] Luis Jacento Rubio, Mary Ann O'Malley Rubio; [ch.] Robert Joseph Rubio; [occ.] Master Carpenter Edens Realty - Columbia, SC; [hon.] Veteran of United States Coast Guard-Vietnam Era; [oth. writ.] Wrote many poetic notes and letters to his fiancee; [pers.] Believed in Jesus Christ as his personal Saviours. His writings reflect his belief in the Trinity.

**RUDD, LUCY**
[b.] June 5, 1940, Salyersville, KY; [p.] Harmon McCarty and Mary McCarty; [m.] Emery Cletis Rudd, September 15, 1956; [ch.] Lola Delois, Cathy Ann, and Tabitha Michal; [occ.] Stocker at Wal Mart Cynthiana, Ky.; [oth. writ.] Poems for local Newspaper songs I have recorded about my self and other people a song I wrote about my job at Wal-Mart I also wrote an item for true confession; [pers.] I thank God for my talent and will always try to be a blessing to others through writing and poetry; [a.] Falmouth, KY

**RUHL, JANICE**
[b.] December 27, 1981, Joliet, IL; [p.] Linda and James Ruhl; [ed.] 8th Grade At Martino Jr. High in New Lenox.; [memb.] Girl Scouts and National Junior Honor Society; [hon.] Presidential Academic Award; [pers.] I wrote this poem after my Uncle Chuck died.; [a.] New Lenox, IL

**RUIZ, DEBORA GERITANO**
[pen.] Debbie Geritano Ruiz; [b.] June 9, 1958, Brooklyn, NY; [p.] Matty and Millie Geritano; [m.] Jose "Joe" Ruiz, December 9, 1983; [ch.] Joseph 11, Matthew 8, Steven 2; [ed.] John Jay High School; [memb.] American Wildlife Federal Wish Foundation, American Museum Association; [pers.] Sometimes in life the Mountains seem high. Keep your Faith and keep your chin up. No matter what never forget to say "Thank you, God."; [a.] Brooklyn, NY

**RUSH, MARINA LYNN**
[b.] October 22, 1971, Danville; [p.] Don and Judy Miller; [m.] Robert Rush, May 21, 1994; [ed.] Paxton High School, Parkland Junior College; [occ.] Welder, Eagle Wings Industries.; [hon.] Musical and athletic awards in High-School; [oth. writ.] A poem for my sister as a wedding gift. Other personal poems; [pers.] I try to release my emotions on paper, rather than verbally toward people.; [a.] Danville, IL

**RUSSELL, JAYME JOLOR**
[b.] September 15, 1977, Omaha, NE; [p.] Jeanne Kay Rehfeldt; [ed.] Graduated from Thomas Jefferson High School, Council Bluffs, Iowa. Now attending Bellevue University, Bellevue, Nebraska.; [occ.] Receptionist at Ranney Chiropractia; [memb.] Member of Deca, Student council, and Pom Pon at Thomas Jefferson High School. Now a member of the Bellevue University Dance Team.; [hon.] Received a leadership award, Scholarship as an entering Freshman at Bellevue University; [oth. writ.] With approximately 35 other poems I have written, 3 of which were written for my mother,

1 has been published in the "Jacket Journal" at Thomas Jefferson High School.; [pers.] "Hold on to you" was written for my cousin Kenny Joseph Franks. Facing some hardships in his life I felt he needed to be reminded that he is a good person who is loved very much. He needed to know it was too soon to give up.; [a.] Council Bluffs, IA

**RUSSELL, FRANKLIN**
[b.] January 31, 1979, Santa Monica, CA; [p.] Etta and Richard Russell; [ed.] Park School, Brookline 7-9 grades. Tosiah Quincy School 3 and 4 grades 5 Home School 6th Gardner Street School, LA 10th home school; [occ.] Student; [pers.] Life is what you make it, I am still searching, life is the undefinable, the answers cannot be found by thinking about them, seek to love life while you live yours; [a.] Roxbury Boston, MA

**RUSSELL, PATRICIA LEE**
[pen.] Patricia Lee Russell; [b.] October 15, 1942, Glendale, CA; [p.] Clarence Pounds, Nita Pounds; [m.] Richard G. Russell, December 14, 1991; [ed.] Hoover High, Glendale, Calif.; [occ.] M.P.S.C. (Motion Picture Screen Cartoonist) Animation Painter; [pers.] For me poems and sculpting are very personal expressions bath which I deadly love to do and it is extremely satisfying to find that the piece gives pleasure to someone else.; [a.] Mount Vernon, OR

**RUTKOWSKI, JOSEPH J.**
[b.] April 6, 1910; [p.] Stanley and Bernice; [m.] Rae, April 23, 1936; [ch.] Geoffrey; [a.] Santa Barbara, CA

**SAFRANS, JAMES DEREK**
[b.] December 9, 1963, Bellflower, CA; [p.] Marian Safrans, Gerald Safrans; [ed.] H.S. grad., Trade School; [occ.] Musician-Drummer, chef; [oth. writ.] Many others none published yet!

**SAIT, YOUSAF A.**
[b.] June 9, 1978, Washington, DC; [pers.] My poetry would be nothing without blind boy grant, Allen Ginsberg, thin women, and fourth period. The very last thing that I want to do is write these words to jealous scorpions in the dust.

**SALLMAN, WALTER C.**
[pen.] Walter C. Sallman; [b.] November, Scania, KS (deceased); [p.] Frank and Amelia Sallman; [m.] Esther Varnick; [ch.] Lenora, Charla, Vivian, Frank, Eva, Larry, Gary, Rita, Karl, Melisa; [ed.] 8th grade attended a small country school in Republic County; [occ.] Was a carpenter in Concordia, KS area; [memb.] Luthern Church, Carpenters' Union; [hon.] A wonderful wife still living - Esther Sallman Horting (83 years young) and ten children and tons of grandchildren! Four sons who followed in his footsteps; [oth. writ.] "Little Sailor Boy"; "Julius Ceaser"; "Looking for Santa" published in school paper in Stillwater Oklahoma; [pers.] His philosophy was "Life is like a flower - first we bloom then we die, 'cause other blossoms take our place and that is the reason why. I'll go with the wind and in nature I'll be - look all around and you will see me."; [a.] Concordia, KS

**SAMUEL, WELWYN**
[b.] November 13, 1971, Antigua; [p.] Eugene and Georgian S.; [m.] Ava Samuel, October 8, 1994; [ed.] Bayside High, Queens Borough Community College; [occ.] Martial Arts Instructor, Kyodai Karate Do; [pers.] I give thanks to God for blessing me with the talent to write from within. And I give thanks to my wife for pointing out this talent.; [a.] Harriman, NY

## SANCHEZ, ROBERT R.

[b.] March 12, 1948, Santa Fe, NM; [p.] Bob and Sally Sanchez; [ch.] Christopher, Candice, and Jamie Sanchez; [ed.] University of New Mexico; [occ.] Teacher-Arroyo Del Oso Elementary School; [memb.] Albuquerque Teachers Federation, Risen Savior Church Lectors; [pers.] I believe a single poem can reveal volumes about a person.; [a.] Albuquerque, NM

## SANCHEZ, VELVET JONES

[b.] September 23, 1964, Brooklyn, NY; [p.] James Burnidene Jones; [m.] Albert Sanchez Sr., September 22, 1990; [ch.] Savannah Rain, Stepkids, Jeremiah P. Albert Jr.; [ed.] Sheepshead Bay HS., J. Sargent Reynolds CC., Devry Tech, School of Hard knocks; [occ.] Clerical Worker at Brokerage Firm; [oth. writ.] Published in the amherst societies anthology the American Poetry Annual.; [pers.] My greatest goal on life is to raise my daughter to be open-minded to different people and situations. Hopefully readers of my poetry will do the same.; [a.] Brooklyn, NY

## SAND, PHYLLIS SUE NEWNAM

[b.] February 12, 1931, Epworth, ND; [p.] Zelnoe Jackson Newnam, Susie Ella Lindley Newnam; [m.] Shirley S. Sand, August 24, 1952; [ch.] Thomas Richard Sand, James Waldow Sand, Catherine Roberta Sand, Nielsen Constance Renae Sand Bellomy; [ed.] 1971 MEd. UND-Grand Forks, ND, 1970-B.S. in education-(New School) UND, 1952-Minot State Teachers College, AA (2 yrs.); [occ.] Retired (self-employed), Teacher of Learning disabled; [memb.] NEA (life), ND Edn. Assn. (life), ND Ret. Tchrs. Assn., Greater Grand Forks Sr. Citizens Assn., Dav Aux., North Star Quilters Guild (charter). Minnkota Genealogical Soc., Rho Chapter Delta Kappa Gamma, United Methodist; [oth. writ.] For my own pleasure; [pers.] I've always enjoyed poetry and remember some that I memorized as a child in school.; [a.] Grand Forks, ND

## SANDERS, BOB

[b.] August 21, 1962, Columbus, GA; [p.] Cary Sanders, Kathy Sanders; [m.] Mary Sanders, July 4, 1986; [ch.] Courtney Sanders; [ed.] Dothan High School, U.S. Navy; [occ.] System Analyst; [memb.] Promise Keepers, King George Quarterback Club, Oakland Baptist Church Brotherhood Director; [hon.] Navy Letter of Commendation, Navy Expeditionary Medal; [oth. writ.] Several poems written for close friends and local publications.; [pers.] I strive to reflect the goodness and love of God in my writing. I hope others are uplifted and encouraged by my poetry.; [a.] King George, VA

## SANDERS, DAVID JOE

[pen.] David Joe Sanders; [b.] September 26, 1946, Sylva, NC; [p.] David and Katy Sanders; [m.] Brenda L. Sanders, September 17, 1975; [ch.] David Joe Sanders Jr.; [ed.] Western Carolina University, Winston-Salem State University, Major: English, Minor: Speech and Theatre; [occ.] Retired, Free-lance writer; [memb.] AMVETS; [hon.] Alpha Psi Omega; [oth. writ.] National High School Poetry Anthology, The western Carolinian, The Nomad, National College Poetry Anthology, Pegasus; [a.] Emerald Isle, NC

## SANDERS, JENNIFER LYNETTE

[pen.] Jennifer Jennings; [b.] March 6, 1970, Dallas; [p.] Otis and Lillie Kathryn Jennings; [m.] David Odell Sanders Jr., July 9, 1994; [ed.] University of Notre Dame, 1992; [occ.] Accountant; [pers.] Parents-in-law: Rev. and Mrs. David Odell Sanders

## SANDERS SR., ROBERT LUTHER

[pen.] Luther; [b.] May 18, 1992, Emma, KY; [p.] T.M. and Bell Sanders (Deceased); [m.] Helen Elizabeth (Deceased), April 8, 1945; [ch.] Brenda Spruill, Robert Luther Sanders, Jr.; [ed.] 5 1/2 years of College; [occ.] Pastor North Zulch, Free Will Baptist Church; [memb.] Free will Baptist Church, Rotary Club; [hon.] The greatest honor was when my dear wife agreed to marry me. (She went to be with the Lord 3 1/2 months ago) citation and advancement in rate for conduct in action in World War II.; [oth. writ.] Several poems, two commentaries on books of the Bible. Romans and Hebrews, and articles for magazines, etc.; [pers.] Do right!; [a.] College Station, TX

## SANDOVAL, GRETCHEN BAUMGARDNER

[pen.] GB Sandoval; [b.] September 19, 1956, Huntington, WA; [p.] Fredric and Barbara Salter Baumgardner; [m.] Fredrick Sandoval, August 27, 1989; [ch.] Stepdaughters Jennifer and Estrella Sandoval, son Sky "Cielo" Sandoval; [ed.] Piedmont Virginia Community College, BA-English and Social work New Mexico Highlands University, MSW-New Mexico Highlands (NMHU); [memb.] Association Humanistic Psychology, member National Ass'n of Social Workers, Co-op America, The town of Cochiti Lake Assembly elected member 1995.; [hon.] Nominated Who's Who in Social Work 1989. Los Trabajadores dela Raza Estudiantiles, member and president. Nominated for Board Diplomats Status as social worker; [oth. writ.] Series of Haiku and nature poems, collection of free form poems.; [pers.] I need poetry-it is as food to my spirit, since the age of 12 when I first began to write it has been the expression my soul requires.

## SANDOVAL, VICTOR M.

[b.] October 16, 1945, Los Angeles; [p.] Henrietta Sandoval, Manuel Sandoval; [m.] Pamela Luisada-Sandoval; [ch.] Christopher, Chedly, Manuel; [hon.] U.C.L.A. Writing Project Fellow; [oth. writ.] Short story: Hail the Champ, Novel: Free Fall; [pers.] I believe that life experiences are memories that need to be passed on.; [a.] San Gabriel, CA

## SANDRIDGE, CLARA

[b.] September 14, 1930, Endicott, VA; [p.] Mrs. Wm. Ingrom-Calliestone, Wm. Lutter Ingrom; [m.] February 5, 1952; [ed.] 12th yrs. self taught; [memb.] B.M.I. International Society of Poet affiliated with Chapel Recording Co. Jeff Roberts Publishers, Magic Keege Productions top records.; [hon.] Army recognition for song. (3) Editors Choice Awards. Numerous honorable mentions published for years 29 songs wrote from tragedy, Awards of Merit accepted for Emotions of Love - vol. III Magic Keye; [oth. writ.] Your favorite GI Joe. Family Tragedy Rides in the Big Shiny Automobile, Love in a Nut Shell. Parteneron I am Your Little Girl.; [pers.] Hello world! To be accepted internationally is a great honor is a great honor thank you. Look for me.; [a.] Danville, VA

## SANDS, CAMIE

[pen.] Camie Sands; [b.] October 2, 1955, Seattle, WA; [p.] Marilyn and Terry Fenton; [m.] Larry Sands, December 10, 1983; [ed.] Plenty; [occ.] Owner-Ad Agency; [memb.] "All-Girls Book Club", Sunrise Rotary, Sunrise Toastmasters, St. Patricks Church; [hon.] 2nd Grade: "Keep WA Green" Poster Contest, High School: Scholarship to Summer School for poets and Cornish School of Allied Arts in Settle, Industry awards, for Creativity in Advertising; [oth. writ.] TV and radio ads, brochures, print ads; [pers.] I want to capture concrete, concise images in poetry so the reader recognizes the experience, from that point I like to move to the shadows of metaphysical where intuition and hearts connect; [a.] Tacoma, WA

## SANDSTEAD, AURIEL J.

[pen.] Auriez Sanchez; [b.] June 6, 1923, Keota, CO; [p.] Charles F. and Fae Stanley Oram; [m.] Willard W. Sandstead, March 16, 1946; [ch.] Vicki Jo, Margo, Shauna; [ed.] Stoneham High School, University of Denver, University of Northern Colorado (UNC); [occ.] Retired teacher and social worker; [memb.] NU chapter-Alpha Delta Kappa, Sigma Kappa, Colorado Quilting Council, National Education Assn., South Platte Valley Historical Society, Folk Art, Women in the Arts.; [hon.] 1964-(AAHPER) American Assn. of Health, Physical Education and Recreation-the National Award to a Junior College for best program implements for girls and women. 1978-Steering Committee for state organization, Colorado Quilting Council. 1979-Charter President of Colorado Quilting Council. 1988-First Quilter-Historian entered in Colorado Quilting Council Hall of Fame. 1992-Honorary Lifetime member of High Plains Heritage Quilters of Colorado.; [oth. writ.] Numerous human interest articles published in The Fence Post. Also a couple in the American Quilt Study Group newsletter.; [pers.] Brighten the corner where you are.; [a.] Sterling, CO

## SANDUSKY, STEVE

[b.] October 22, 1957, Louisville, KY; [ed.] Computer Science A.S. (but still learning); [memb.] ISOP, American Legion; [pers.] God can only love those who love themselves so love yourselves and we can love each other; [a.] Louisville, KY

## SANTARPIA, NANCY

[pen.] Anita Lynn; [b.] February 18, 1981, Brooklyn, NY; [p.] Teresa and Fred Santarpia; [ed.] Freshman, Fontbonne Hall Academy; [occ.] Student; [hon.] U.F.T. Scholarship Bond Award, Excellence in Communication Arts, Peace Essay Finalist; [oth. writ.]; [pers.] Feelings and thoughts can be expressed in many different ways for me it's poetry.; [a.] Brooklyn, NY

## SAUL, LISA

[pen.] Lisa Allison Saul; [b.] January 18, 1957, New York, NY; [p.] Abraham and Marjorie Saul; [m.] Claudio Alessandro, March 13, 1975; [ed.] University of Miami, B.A. in English (Creative Writing); [occ.] Creative Director, American Bankers Insurance Group; [memb.] Acorns Theatre Company; [hon.] Dean's List, Cum Laude; [pers.] I truly believe in the power of positive energy. What we see...what we believe, happens first in our minds, then manifests on a physical plane.; [a.] Miami, FL

## SAUNDERS, MARGARETTEE COMBS

[b.] October 3, 1925, Atlanta, GA; [p.] Deceased; [m.] Alfred Saunders (Deceased), January 10, 1943; [ch.] Two adult sons, Don and Mark; [ed.] Undergraduate study: Cambridgeshire (England) Tech. College, E. Washington State Univ., Post grad. study: Cal. State U., Los Angeles, Coll. of Notre Dame, Belmont, CA; [occ.] English teacher (retired); [hon.] Undergraduate honor student, recipient of three gold and one silver award in poetry, associate editor, Calif. English magazine. Coordinator of the Montclair (Calif.) Honors English program.; [oth. writ.] At Eastern Washington U. I had a short story, "Mix up," published.; [pers.] I believe the peaceful coexistance can become a reality if we look for the GOOD in others rather than for the weaknesses.; [a.] Pacifica, CA

## SAVAGE, JACKIE

[pen.] Diamond, Amethyst; [b.] Trenton; [p.] Margret C. Brown, Mildred Savage (foster-mother); [ch.] Derrick D. Savage; [ed.] Trenton Central High School, Community College of Phila, Benjamin Franklin Adult Evening School, Phila. Training Center, Temple University PASCEP Program; [occ.] Unemployed, retired

Correctional Officer; [memb.] Commonwealth of Pennsylvania Policemen's Benevolent Assoc. Inc. Cepa Int' Inc., Mayor's Iteracy Assoc., Urban League of Phila., American Diabetic Assoc.; [hon.] Phila Training Center Dean's List, two Honor Roll Certs., Temple University PASCEP Program, two Certs. for Completion of Courses and Achievements. The National Library of Poetry. Editors Choice Award for 1995. International Society of Poets Award for Society Principles for 1994-1995; [oth. writ.] Three of my poems have been selected to be published in three different books by The National Library of Poetry.; [pers.] I believe in equality and justice for all. My poems are written from life experiences. I was greatly influenced by Mr. Ed Coleman; [a.] Trenton, Philadelphia

**SAVARY, LINDA J.**
[b.] May 25, 1959, Adams, MA; [p.] Raymond Luscier, Norma Luscier (Deceased); [m.] Kevin Savary, November 4, 1978; [ch.] Michael, Daniel, Jeffrey, Rebecca; [ed.] Hoosac Valley High; [occ.] Homemaker; [memb.] Evangelical Free Church Board of Missions Chairperson Board of Directors, Cheshire Little League; [oth. writ.] Several poems regarding Mother's death. Several Humorous Poems. Many Personal Poems written for Friends and Family; [pers.] Writing is a form of therapy for me. When I'm grieving I put it all down on paper. When I am feeling especially joyous, I share that feeling by writing for friends and family.; [a.] Cheshire, MA

**SAVINO, JAMES P.**
[pen.] Beno; [b.] April 13, 1966, Baldwin, NY; [p.] Joseph and Diane Savino; [m.] Maureen Savino, December 16, 1995; [ch.] Gina Marie Savino; [oth. writ.] The love for Maureen and the love of my family; [pers.] I just didn't lose my Dad I lost my best friend, I love you and miss you everyday.; [a.] Coram, NY

**SAVINON, V. ROSELYN**
[b.] January 8, 1963, New York City; [ch.] One daughter; [ed.] Some college-Philosophy and Sociology courses greater Hartford Comm. Coll; [occ.] Administrative Asst. for an executive search firm; [memb.] Health Crisis Network Buddy Volunteer Program, Project LEAD (Literacy for Every Adult in Dade) Volunteer, Laubach Literacy Action Member; [oth. writ.] I have written several poems that were published in my high school paper. I have also written several stories and skirts which I've never attempted to publish.; [pers.] I believe that the world is better off when people care for and love each other, thus I strive to touch people with love whenever I am able to do so.; [a.] Miami, FL

**SAYIN, FRED H.**
[pen.] Paul K. Radar; [b.] March 13, 1966, Seaford, DE; [p.] Ahmet N. and Angela C. Sayin; [ed.] BA Psychology 1988, working on Elem. Ed., Teaching Certificate Completed a UYO Course in 1994; [occ.] Bakery Asst. and Independent Distributor of Homeopathing drugs Rexall; [memb.] National Eagle Scout Assoc., Singles Keeping the Face Church Group Emmaus #12 Young Adult Church Group; [hon.] Employee of Month-1994, Famous Poet-1995, Earned Eagle Scout Award in Boy Scouts, highest rank in 1984 in Boy Scouts which is highest rank - 1984; [oth. writ.] Poem "The Sign of Spring" in reflections 1992. An unproduced play called "The Idiot Kid" high school sports writer college sports trivia writer and a poem called "Guilts Hold Us"; [pers.] Developed minor and psychomotor (temporal lobe) seizures at age 22. Had for seven years. "Everybody has a specific talent or skill even the disabled, if adults don't show respect to the disabled don't expect main streaming to work."; [a.] Winter Park, FL

**SCADUTO, JANICE DAWN**
[b.] October 20, 1961, Brooklyn, NY; [p.] William, Marilyn Chapman; [m.] Thomas J. Scaduto July 18th, 1981; [ch.] Thomas L. Jr., Chris, Jonathan; [ed.] Canarsie High School graduate 1979 / major English Literature I.C.S. Grad Child Day Care 1992; [occ.] Child Day Care; [memb.] Humane Society, Earth Institute (Save the Whale), National Wildlife Federation, A.S.P.C.A.; [hon.] Parents Volunteer Award 1987-1992; Switchboard Volunteer Award; Girl's Tracke Team Captain Trophy; [oth. writ.] "Never" published in **Edge of Twilight** by The National Library of Poetry; [pers.] I always wanted to write poetry, but it perfects itself with each draft, so never give up, there will be an acceptance one day!! Now, my inspiration comes from my three sons, and husband Thomas-Joseph of fourteen years, he is my inspiration!!; [a.] Brooklyn, NY

**SCALES, DIANNA NICOLE**
[b.] July 30, 1983; [ed.] Tabernacle Christian Academy; [oth. writ.] My Autobiography (Fiction); [a.] Chicago, IL

**SCALES, JOYCE W.**
[b.] September 30, 1934, Winston-Salem, NC; [p.] Elcy and Ilene Walker; [m.] Lester E. (Gene) Scales, June 8, 1951; [ch.] Cindy Underdal, Cathy Durham; [occ.] Housewife; [memb.] Pine Chapel Moravian Church, Women's Fellowship; [oth. writ.] Several poems and story written for our Church newsletter.; [pers.] I write poems to bring comfort to the sick, peace to the sorrow and God's love to everyone.; [a.] Winston-Salem, NC

**SCHAEFER, ROBIN**
[b.] February 13, 1980, Cincinnati; [p.] Donna and Jack Schaefer; [ed.] Home School; [occ.] Volunteer at the Cincinnati Museum of Natural History; [oth. writ.] This is my first publication; [pers.] I write what I feel; [a.] Cincinnati, OH

**SCHALK, AMANDA MARIE**
[b.] September 18, 1984, Toledo, OH; [p.] Paul and JoAnn Schalk; [ed.] Haggerty Elementary Belleville, Michigan; [memb.] Girl Scouts-Junior level 4H Student Council Drama Club "A" Honor Roll - Grade 1-5; [hon.] Principal's Award; [pers.] I became interested in poems after my grandmother read some to me. I like animals and would like to be veterinarian someday.; [a.] Belleville, MI

**SCHEFFER, MARGARET ANN**
[b.] April 2, 1943, Graceville, FL; [p.] Lawrence and Ann (Mitchell) Balkcom; [m.] Roy D. Scheffer, June 26, 1966; [ch.] Roy Allen Scheffer, Melinda Ann Scheffer; [ed.] Graduate of Graceville High School, Chipola Junior College, Florida State University; [occ.] Working family Business (automotive parts); [memb.] First Methodist Church Marianna, Florida, Florida State Alumni Association; [hon.] Dean's List Chipola and Florida State University; [oth. writ.] Poems short stories; [pers.] I try to reflect the need for the soft and gentle elements of life, with awareness of man's dependence on God, somebody bigger than you and I.; [a.] Marianna, FL

**SCHIELY, SUE ANN**
[pen.] Sue Ann Schiely; [b.] January 12, 1971, Bedford Heights; [p.] Norman Schiely, Jeanette Schiely; [ed.] Bedford High School, Cuyahoga Community College (Associate's Degree in Applied Business Management); [occ.] Accounting Clerk, Flexalloy, Inc.; [memb.] The LGP Drama Group, The Walden Woods Project, HSUS, PPFA The Sierra Club; [hon.] Dean's List, Volunteer Appreciation Award from Reach Out Counseling Center; [oth. writ.] Poem published in the Offerings Poetry Quarterly, July 1995, short story entered in the Writer's Digest 1995 competition, personal essay pending publication in the Reach Out's Volunteer News.; [pers.] "Every aspect of your life was meant to be, so let go of the past, grasp today with diligence, and share your future with faith!"; [a.] Bedford Heights, OH

**SCHLICK, BETTY JO B.**
[pen.] Jo; [b.] August 12, 1960, Pensacola, FL; [p.] Thomas, Arlene Schlick; [m.] Lawrence Schlick, April 21, 1979; [ch.] Lance, James, Jason; [ed.] Island Trees High Levittown, Longisland, NY; [occ.] Domestic Engineer; [memb.] National Parks and Conservation Association National Wildlife Federation The Cousteau Society; [oth. writ.] Several Poems; [pers.] We should never under estimate our creator. "We all have a hidden talent".; [a.] Brentwood, NY

**SCHLICKER, MAUREEN**
[b.] April 11, 1959, Roslyn, NY; [p.] John T. and Maryellen Crawford; [m.] Warren F. Schlicker August 27, 1983; [ch.] Krystie Alburda, Lindsay Ann; [ed.] holy Trinity H.S. Nassau Community College; [occ.] Physical Therapist Assistant, Lymphedema Therapy; [memb.] Arthritis Foundation National Geographic Society; [a.] Lake Grove, NY

**SCHLICKMAN, NITA D.**
[b.] December 16, 1920, Des Moines, IA; [p.] Mr. Mrs. James and Mildred Donelan; [m.] Willie B. Winsett, April 3, 1994; [ch.] Kenneth G. Schlickman; [ed.] South High School graduate; [occ.] Learning to live life to its fullest every day!; [memb.] AZ State Poetry; [hon.] Golden and Silver award for my poem "Eve"; [oth. writ.] Poems and short stories printed in Senior Paper in Colo. (a poem in the Sunday Supplement); [pers.] I enjoy writing about life. I thank God for any ability I have. I'm thankful for teachers who encouraged me, inspite of my poor spelling and lack of education. To my family and friends I'm indebted. I believe the best things in life are free.; [a.] Green Valley, AZ

**SCHMIDT, KELLY MCINTIRE**
[b.] April 17, 1967, Keywest, FL; [p.] Charles and Dolores McIntire; [m.] Anthony Schmidt, May 2, 1994; [ed.] U.S. Navy Mid State College (Auburn, ME) Attending St. Leo College; [occ.] Full time student (Sociology major); [oth. writ.] Several private poems; [pers.] As a veteran, my heart feels a great love and pride towards our military members who devoted their lives to save our freedom.; [a.] Virginia Beach, VA

**SCHNEE, CHRISTOPHER N.**
[pen.] Chris or Schled; [b.] January 22, 1976, Portsmouth, VA; [p.] Steve and Wendy Schnee; [ed.] Graduated Sultan High School 1995, Jan. Main studies were English and art. Attending Saddleback College majoring in English.; [occ.] Independent Contractor; [hon.] Awards from the English department in school. And my poetry was published in the local newspaper; [oth. writ.] About 50 other poetry writings and short stories.; [pers.] Re: But even with it's powerful thrashing it crumbles helplessly into white ashes of foam. Just before it's death was complete you realize it's destiny... It was born to die... A thought, ponder. Imagine yourself... think.; [a.] Mission Viejo, CA

**SCHNEIDER, PATRICIA ANNE**
[pen.] Patricia Clunen Schneider; [b.] March 23, 1952, Alliance, OH; [p.] Wilbur and Margaret Clunen; [pers.] My writings are a mirror that reflects my life. The agony and the ecstasy. It's been a journey, thou at times bitter sweet I find I must share it in my poetry.; [a.] Granada Hills, CA

**SCHOLL, COLIN**
[b.] May 17, 1974, Newburg, NY; [p.] Dennis Scholl-Josephine Scholl; [pers.] This and other poems that I have produced where written during my incarceration in LA county jail. There is no limit to the good we can do if we don't care who gets the credit.; [a.] Los Angeles, CA

**SCHOONMAKER, RICKEY R.**
[pen.] Rickey Ray; [b.] May 17, 1948, Detroit; [p.] Louise Schoonmaker; [m.] Grace Schoonmaker, May 16, 1968; [ch.] Rickey II and Tammy; [ed.] Northern High School; [occ.] CNC operator; [memb.] VAW; [hon.] Outstanding Community Service from Lewis College of Business. Spirit of Detroit Award from City Council Detroit.; [a.] Detroit, MI

**SCHUCKMAN, BARBARA J.**
[b.] Morristown, NJ; [p.] John and Helen Coolock; [ed.] Hanover Park High; [occ.] Substitute Secretary for the Livingston Board of Education; [memb.] Hunterdon Hills Colline Club, Morris Hills Dog Training Club, Livingston Art Assoc., Northfield Baptist Church, African Violet Society; [hon.] Juried art shows, received Honorable Mentions for all my poem and received 2 for sound.; [oth. writ.] A poem "Washington Crossing Pa., was published in hounds a Hunting magazine. Some art work was published in Colonial Homes magazine; [pers.] I write and have written storied I would like to see published for children.; [a.] Livingston, NJ

**SCHURMANN, CAROLYN HULL**
[pen.] Carolyn Hull Schurmann; [b.] April 21, 1932, Parsons, WV; [p.] Monzel and Verona Hull; [m.] Richard Schurmann, June 21, 1958; [ch.] Brett, Ann, Mark; [ed.] Fort Hill High (Cumberland, MD) Frostburg State Univ. (Frostbury, MD). CCC - AA in Nursing; [occ.] Retired; [memb.] Audubon Society Sierra Club. Good time singers. ECC; [pers.] My interest from childhood have been music, (I sing) art (I paint) and as of late writing poems and songs (I compose). Without these I am lost; [a.] Catonsville, MD

**SCIARABBA JR., VINCENT N.**
[b.] March 19, 1963, Washington, DC; [p.] Vincent and Sylvia Sciarabba; [m.] Divorced; [ch.] Evening Star Sciarabba; [ed.] Diploma from Swansboro High School; [occ.] Construction Forman (Carpenter); [oth. writ.] Personal writings that coincide with my life.; [pers.] I love all aspects of yourself unconditionally and becoming one with the universe. All knowledge, emotional strength, and creativity is accessible!!; [a.] Santa Fe, NM

**SCOLLON, ELIZABETH**
[b.] January 21, 1956, New York City, NY; [p.] John Rastetter, Antoinette Rastetter; [m.] Edward J. Scollon, April 7, 1979; [ch.] Jennie Louise Scollon; [ed.] St. Jean Baptiste HS, Queens College, NYU; [occ.] Teacher, Brandeis H.S., New York, NY; [memb.] D. A. Sokol; [a.] Westfield, NJ

**SCOTT, PAMELA**
[pen.] Pamela Scott; [b.] September 3, 1968, Meade, MD; [p.] Frank and Constance Day; [m.] Major Scott, May 23, 1994; [ch.] Michael Scott; [ed.] Meade Senior High and Anne Arundel Cun College.; [memb.] Kingdom Builders COGIC Hanover Md Vice President of the Pastor Aid Committee for Pastor Elder Kenneth Fowlkes; [hon.] Spanish awards from High School; [oth. writ.] Feelings in poetry relationship in poetry poetry emotions, spirits of poetry poems by the spirit; [pers.] Praises and Glory and Honour to God the father Jesus Christ for blessing me this way my love and gratitude to all my sisters and brothers of kingdom builders COGIC; [a.] Hanover, MD

**SCOTT, RYAN**
[b.] July 13, 1978, Clarks Summit, PA; [p.] Ann and Paul Scott; [ed.] Liberty High School; [hon.] Keystone Award for 1st place, feature writing in journalism awarded by Pennsylvania School Press Association; [oth. writ.] Articles for school newspaper; [pers.] Writing is my one true outlet for my feelings, and my writings are a true reflection of my inner self.; [a.] Bethlehem, PA

**SCROGGIN, CHERYL KINNEY**
[b.] February 4, 1962, Boston, MA; [p.] Wayne and Norma Kinney; [m.] Tom Scroggin, September 1, 1991; [ch.] Christopher, Cassie, Kristina; [ed.] Dos Pueblos High School, SB City College; [occ.] Full-time mother former preschool teacher; [memb.] S.B. Foursquare Church; [pers.] The Kinney family goes back 200 yrs. There were other poets in the family tree. I come from a new heritage the first Kinney was Israel. Kinney and they all were missionaries.; [a.] Santa Barbara, CA

**SEAGRAVES, GRETCHEN**
[b.] February 8, 1980, Dayton, OH; [p.] Bill and Karen Seagraves; [ed.] Tri-County North High; [occ.] Student; [memb.] Foreign Language Club, Drama Club, and Band; [hon.] Advanced English and Honors Courses; [oth. writ.] Several other poems for church and school.; [pers.] My writing is inspired by some events and people in my life such as my parents, my friends, and my English teachers thanks!; [a.] Lewisburg, OH

**SEALES, REV. ESTHER L.**
[b.] September 5, Warthen, GA; [p.] Deceased; [ed.] B.S. in Secondary Education from Fort Valley State College, B.S. in Bible from Philadelphia College of Bible, Masters of Divinity from the Lutheran Theological Seminary at Philadelphia; [occ.] Manager; [memb.] Alpha Kappa Mu National Honor Society, Newspaper Institute of America, United States Achievement Academy ordained elder in the African Methodist Episcopal Church; [hon.] Who's Who Among Students in American Universities and Colleges, U.S. Achievement Academy Alpha Mu Gamma Foreign Language Honor Society; [oth. writ.] Many short stories, plays, poetry and sermons; [pers.] "Seek ye first the kingdom of God and his righteousness, and all these things shall be added unto you." Matthew 6:33; [a.] Elkins Park, PA

**SEATON, CLYDE S.**
[pen.] Clyde C. Seaton; [b.] January 13, 1943; [p.] Roy and Thelma Seaton; [m.] Sadie D. Seaton, March 7, 1976; [ch.] Jermaine Tyrone Seaton; [ed.] Buniwick High School and P.S. 3.; [occ.] Clerk; [memb.] Trinity Community Assemble of God; [hon.] Berean College Police Department, Trinity Community Assembly of God; [oth. writ.] One happy big family and other; [pers.] I love to write poetry to bring peace and contentment to humans soul.; [a.] Bronx, NY

**SEDAR, JEAN E.**
[b.] October 10, 1920, Ohio; [p.] Edward and Sadle Hawn (Deceased); [m.] Joseph W. Sedar (Deceased), October 12, 1939; [ch.] M. Lynne, Joseph W. and Richard H.; [ed.] Central High School, Palomar College, Mt. San Antonio College, Mt. San Jacinto College.; [occ.] Retired but keeping busy; [oth. writ.] Poems and short stories (many yet unpublished); [pers.] I try to seek the deeper feelings that portray the emotional undercurrent of human lives, and the beauty of nature.; [a.] San Jacinto, CA

**SEDGWICK, SANDRA L. J.**
[pen.] Sandii; [b.] January 9, 1954, Fort Camp, KY; [p.] Geneva and Ben Johnson; [m.] Divorced 1987; [ch.] Demond, Brandon, Jamel, Donnell and Ben Sedgwick; [ed.] Graduated from Warwick High School

1972. First female in ROTC at Tuskgee Institute 2nd year student at Victory Life Bible Training Center, Hampton, VA; [occ.] Service Coordinator for Boddie Noel Ent Kiln Creek Tebb, VA; [memb.] Member of Sigma Gamma Rho Epsilon Theta Chapter of Tuskgee Inst. Alc. Member of Le Sprit De Corps Black Pearl Honor Soro Tuskgee Inst.; [hon.] Quill and Scroll Journalism Award, First place in the BNE Mission 2000 Ralley 1994 Mission, Public Speaking Awards; [oth. writ.] Editor in Chief for "The Epistle" newsletter, various publications in the Tacoma Facts magazine Tacoma Wash, published in various anthologies and self published "A Different Direction"; [pers.] You can know the love of family, friends and even special men or women. But if you don't know Jesus love, you're missing the greatest love of all.; [a.] Newport News, VA

**SEK, BEATA ANNA**
[b.] March 31, 1975, Ridgewood, NJ; [p.] Maria and Kazimierz Sek; [ed.] Mahwah High School, Ramaro College of New Jersey; [occ.] Teller at IBNJ Bank; [memb.] International Student Organization, Culture Club, College Cheerleading; [hon.] Student Leadership Award, Spirit Award; [pers.] With all of life's personal difficulties, I have cried, laughed, and learned through many hardships. I have strived and continue to strive, but with only the help of my love, T-Bear.; [a.] Mahwah, NJ

**SENATOR, MELVIN**
[b.] May 14, 1937, Brooklyn, NY; [p.] Inuwig, Esther; [m.] Rochelle Senator, January 25, 1958; [ch.] Laura, Susan; [ed.] B.A. Brooklyn College M.S. Long Island University C.A.S. University of Bridgeport; [occ.] Writer/retired high school house master; [memb.] Phi Delta Kappa Ct. Assn Secondary Principals; [hon.] Phi Delta Kappa Recognition award (1995 and 1984), Veterans of foreign wars award, John Hay Academic Fellowship, Field Associate/Master Teacher Award - University of Bridgeport; [oth. writ.] Novel of the 1950's, Travel Articles, School Conically Guides; [a.] Norwalk, CT

**SHAKOOR, SAYED**
[pen.] Mike Shakoor; [b.] September 11, 1974, Afghanistan; [ch.] Noori Shakoor; [ed.] High School Grad. presently on College Microcomputer management; [occ.] Cook; [oth. writ.] A collection of poetry along with stories for young adults.; [pers.] In oder to find a path that you can walk around the sun and not get burned, listen to what your heart whispers.; [a.] Schenectady, NY

**SHANAHAN, KARIM**
[b.] February 12, 1981, New York, NY; [p.] Steven Shanahan, Naima Shanahan; [ed.] St. Margaret's Of Cortona Iona Prep; [hon.] Headmaster's List Academic Olympics-first place; [a.] Bronx, NY

**SHARP, BENJAMIN BUCK**
[pen.] "Ben"; [b.] March 13, 1927, Turnerville, NJ; [p.] Joseph Franklin Sharp, Della Beatrice Pierson Sharp; [m.] Catherine Miriam Luss, December 26, 1948; [ch.] Stephen Dwight, Colleen Faith, David William; [ed.] Public Schools Camden and Gloucester City, NJ Haddonfield and Glassboro HS, Peirce School Bus. Adm. '47, '48 Philadelphia Coll Bible 50-53, Nyack Miss. College '53-'56 Nyack, NY 10960; [occ.] Retired postal worker September 30, 1988; [memb.] Ordained Minister Christian and Missionary Alliance September '58, Free Methodist N.A. July 4, 1959, Con. Cong. Christ Conf. '66, member: UMC Wildwood Crest, NJ '94; [hon.] Was awarded small plaque for solving parcel post problem Rockland, MA 02370 o/a 1985; [oth. writ.] 2 religious pcs. daily. None published except short piece on "Revival" by Inter-varsity several yrs ago. Dozens of manuscripts extant. Many were lost

in the moving process.; [pers.] I write for the glory of God and praise of Jesus Christ with aid of Holy Spirit. I advertise my counseling services 24 hrs. day in Cape May City "Trading Post"; [a.] Wildwood, NJ

## SHARPE, JENNIFER D.
[b.] March 21, 1954, Sullivan, IN; [p.] Dale Smith and Betty Smith; [m.] Michael F. Sharpe, February 1, 1986; [ch.] Keri R. Sharpe; [ed.] North Central High School; [occ.] Quality Control Analyst, Columbia House, Terre Haute, IN; [a.] Terre Haute, IN

## SHAW, DENISE A.
[b.] July 17, 1953, San Bernardino, CA; [p.] Harry Brock, Barbara McGrew Brock; [m.] Robert Shaw, December 4, 1982; [ed.] Pacific High, Sand Diego State University; [occ.] Banking; [pers.] I have a great appreciation for the important of family in ones life. I receive great joy and pleasure from the memories I have from my childhood. I believe that a person legacy is based on what he or she gives to others throughout their lifetime.; [a.] San Diego, CA

## SHELTON, TYANNA YALONDA
[pen.] Ms. Ann; [b.] December 28, 1979, Battle Creek, MI; [p.] Joyce Annette Butler, Sylvester Fayette Shelton; [ed.] Sophomore at Battle Creek Central High School; [memb.] Emmanuel Temple Apostolic Church "The Church where the impossible becomes possible through Jesus Christ. Greater Battle Creek Kellogg Community College Upward Bounds.; [pers.] I dare the people of this world to help me discover this place!; [a.] Battle Creek, MI

## SHERFEY, IRIS ROSE
[b.] March 26, 1922, Sawyerville, IL; [p.] Albert Rose and Ivy Russell; [m.] Charles R. Sherfey, June 12, 1946; [ch.] Eva, Jackye, Charles, George, Charlene, James, Kelly; [ed.] Northwestern High School; [occ.] Retired; [memb.] RLDS Church; [hon.] I am honored daily by my seven children, seventeen grandchildren, and four great grandchildren; [oth. writ.] Several inspirational poems and short stories that are used in church programs.; [pers.] After many years of devoting my time to home and family, finally, at the age of 73 I have the time to minister and share the love of Jesus Christ with others. The Lord has blessed me with this gift of creative writing as my way of reaching out.; [a.] Bellingham, WA

## SHIELDS, DEBBIE
[m.] Michael Shields, July 18, 1992; [ch.] Joshua and Emileigh; [ed.] Burbank High School Class of 1980, Southern California College and California State University at Northridge; [occ.] Assistant Preschool Director; [memb.] National Association for the Education of Young Children, Southern California Association for the Education of Young Children; [hon.] BA in Journalism; [pers.] I try to bring an intimacy to my poetry that evokes emotion from the reader, or sometimes just myself.; [a.] CA

## SHROPSHIRE, CAROLIS ANNETTE
[b.] Chattanooga, TN; [p.] Willie Clyde Simmons; [ed.] St. Leo College working towards BA Psychology; [occ.] United States Marine Corps, Administrative Chief; [memb.] Women in the Military, Washington, DC; [hon.] International Society of Poets, Int'l Poet of Merit; [oth. writ.] Time Passage; A Break in the Clouds, Livin' by the Grace of God, recorded by Music AD; The Gift, written for City of Norfolk, VA, Adopt a Family Program; [pers.] 1994 was a rough year, full of disappointments. However, hope springs eternal.; [a.] Chesapeake, VA

## SHROYER, WILLIAM D.
[pen.] Dion Janu Shore; [b.] December 28, 1971, Johnstown, PA; [p.] David and Brenda Shroyer; [ed.] Greater Johnstown Vo-Tech, with a degree in Business Data Processing.; [occ.] Residential Program Worker (also called "houseparent") for the mentally retarded.; [hon.] Previous award from the Laurel Arts (of Somerset, PA) poetry contest, and the wonderful honor of having the parents and the circle of friends that I do.; [oth. writ.] "A New Generation," a poem published as part of a local collection of few years ago. I have written many of my works for personal enjoyment and expression, and have just recently decided to bring them out to the public.; [pers.] The Supreme Being is a cosmic scout-master: It weaved the tangled web of life in a most complex knot, not to be undone, but to be studied, understood, and maybe someday, reproduced by us, loyal scouts.; [a.] Somerset, PA

## SIDLOW, JEFF
[b.] January 30, 1971, Detroit, MI; [p.] Victor and Darlene Liss; [ed.] Friends Central School University of Miami; [occ.] Artist-Actor; [memb.] Alpha Epsilon Pi Fraternity; [oth. writ.] I've been writing poetry and song lyrics for only two years (by the time of this publication) but have over 100 completed works.; [pers.] I get most of my inspiration from songs.; [a.] Coconut Grove, FL

## SIFUENTES, JENNIFER A.
[b.] November 21, 1971, Tyler, TX; [p.] Art and Jeanette; [ed.] Concord High, B.A. in English and Psychology at the University of Delaware (1994); [occ.] Community Relations Coordinator for Borders Books and Music; [hon.] Golden Key Nat'l Honor Society (1993), Woman of Promise Certificate of Distinction (1993), Sigma Tau Delta (English Honor Society-1993), Psi Chi (Psychology Honor Society-1994); [pers.] I am a staunch supported of animal rights and strive to make a career in public relations for the environmental protection movement. My work is influenced by my love for the natural world and romantic poetry.; [a.] Bear, DE

## SIKES, MARY KATHERINE
[pen.] Kathy; [b.] March 6, 1959, Savannah, GA; [p.] Mr. and Mrs. Herman F. Gold Jr.; [m.] Raymond Marvin Sikes, February 23, 1985; [ch.] Raymond Bryan Sikes; [ed.] Savannah High School (graduated in 1977) (some vocational and College); [occ.] Housewife; [memb.] I joined the newspaper staff at my high school as literary feature editor.; [hon.] I received a Certificate of Service from my school newspaper, The Blue and White in 1975. I was awarded a Certificate of Merit from the World of Poetry in 1990 and the Golden Poet Award from the same society in 1991 for one of my poems, Jesus. It was ranked honorable mention. I also had a short story published in a local newspaper, back in 1974.; [oth. writ.]; [pers.] My Jr. high school teacher was my greatest influence for me to become a writer. We (his class) kept a journal and that's how I got my start. That was twenty one years ago and since then I've always loved to write.; [a.] Savannah, GA

## SILFIES, PATRICIA
[pen.] Patricia Silfies; [b.] March 27, 1940, Bethlehem, PA; [m.] Terry J. Silfies, August 26, 1956; [ch.] Terence, Martin, Steven; [ed.] Liberty High School; [occ.] Travel Counselor; [memb.] Christ UCC Church Faith at Work; [oth. writ.] Many poems not published not shared with friends; [pers.] This is my gift from God I use it to express my feelings of encouragement to others that is my gift to God.; [a.] Bethlehem, PA

## SIMANCAS, CARLOS M.
[b.] October 7, 1972, Havana, Cuba; [p.] Andres and Miriam Simancas; [ed.] Wakefield High School; [occ.]

Medical Assistant; [hon.] Future Business Leader of America, 3rd Place Winner in North Virginia Region for writing "Job Description Manual"; [oth. writ.] Other poems includes: "Time", "Trees and leaves", "Friendship Like a Flower," "Stay After All" and many more.; [pers.] I write base on my own personal experiences. I have been greatly influenced by the work of Robert Frost.; [a.] Arlington, VA

## SIMMONS, CANDACE R.
[b.] July 16, 1982, Washington, DC; [p.] Richard and Mildred Simmons; [ed.] Eugene Burroughs Middle School; [occ.] Student; [memb.] Eugene Burroughs Middle School Band, St. Barnabas Episcopal Church; [hon.] Honor Roll, President's Academic Fitness Award; [oth. writ.] Several poems and short and stories; [pers.] I try to stay real.; [a.] Ft. Washington, MD

## SIMMONS, KATARA
[b.] August 3, 1977, Lake Wales, FL; [p.] Thomas and Betty Simmons; [ed.] Still in High School (senior); [occ.] Student; [memb.] Yearbook Staff, Church; [hon.] 10th grade: first place in county-wide Anthology Contest, 11th grade: second place in county-wide anthology contest.; [oth. writ.] Several poems, writings published in local newspaper and county-wide book of Anthology.; [a.] Sebring, FL

## SIMMONS, MARYANN
[pen.] MaryAnn Simmons; [b.] April 20, 1933, Brooklyn, NY; [p.] George and Marie Joseph; [m.] Billy, January 3, 1953; [ch.] Michael, Scott, Tracy Allan and Sheri-Lyn; [ed.] High School-College credits in Government and Religion; [occ.] Area Director for Direct Sales Company; [memb.] Church of Today Have been too busy for membership in clubs.; [oth. writ.] There are many. Some have been put together in a collection called Poems from the Heart.; [pers.] My poems are a reflection of my observations of life. Each poem has a happening behind it.; [a.] Rochester Hills, MI

## SINGLETON, KEISHA
[b.] December 12, 1978, Washington, DC; [p.] Calvin and Queenie Singleton; [ed.] Senior-Surrattsville High School, Clinton, MD; [occ.] Student; [memb.] Pep Club, Female Coalition, Students High on Prevention, Student Government Association and National Honor Society; [hon.] 1st place in Alan Campbell Essay Contest, Honor Roll, Maryland Distinguished Scholar; [a.] Clinton, MD

## SKAGGS, RUBY
[pen.] Ruby Farnham Skaggs; [b.] January 16, 1912, Commercial Point, OH; [p.] Pearl and Alice (Green) Farnham; [m.] William Pleasant Skaggs, November 21, 1935; [ch.] David, Keith, Kenneth Wayne, Elaine, Maxine, Nancy and Joy; [ed.] 10th yr. High School; [occ.] Homemaker; [memb.] Churches of Christian Christian Union Church. (Happy Valley) National Library of Poetry, Quill Poetry, Nashville Top Records Music Co.; [hon.] Poems published in 8 different anthologies by National Library of Poetry. Poems published in 4 Quill Poetry Books poems chosen for tapes entitled Best Poets of 94 and 95 read by Ira Westrich. Charter member of lifetime member of International Society of Poets Recognition for many of my oil paintings.; [pers.] Writing poetry has been a great source of enjoyment to me. I need to write poetry as a fulfillment. When I meditate about certain things then I often feel a compelling to write in rhyme.; [a.] Chillicothe, OH

## SKINNER, MARY ANN
[b.] April 27, 1966, Kansas City, MO; [p.] Frank and Mary Draper; [ch.] Logan Leon, Ceaira Davoe; [occ.] Excavation Sub-Contractor; [oth. writ.] Several poems not published; [pers.] I say my talent is a God given.

Everybody has one, you just have to find yours. What appears easy for some, may not come as easily for others. But if you enjoy it whatever it may be, don't give up. Develop it.; [a.] Lees Summit, MO

**SKOLER, BETTY K.**
[b.] October 18, 1950, Hartsville, SC; [p.] Reginald and Dorothey Kea; [m.] Jim Skoler, July 19, 1985; [ch.] Amanda, Jason; [ed.] High School; [occ.] Order Processing Assistant; [pers.] Poetry is something beautiful and I've never written a lot but do believe I could do a great deal of it.; [a.] Florence, SC

**SLADE, PAULA**
[b.] Oak Park, IL; [p.] Samuel Cinman, Elsie Jeske Cinman; [m.] Barry J. Gillogly, June 24, 1984; [ch.] Samantha Alexandra; [ed.] University of Chicago, Roosevelt University, American Conservatory, Art Institute of Chicago, Niles West High School, Skokie, Ill.; [occ.] Writer; [memb.] Screen Actors guild, American Federation of Television and Radio Artist, Actors Equity; [hon.] Various award for writing and art while in school; [oth. writ.] Co-wrote with husband for Radio, Television and Newspaper in Southern California.; [pers.] I have always found the act of writing and reading poetry to be the most loving way with words. it's the delicate tethering of heart and mind to soul that binds us all.; [a.] Martha's Vineyard Island, MA

**SLAUGHTER, JEAN**
[pen.] Jean Slaughter; [b.] March 7, 1937, IN; [p.] Dorothy and Wilbur Sheffer; [ch.] Susan and Daniel Slaughter; [ed.] Earlham College, Ball State University; [occ.] Writer, poet, story teller, living history actress and teacher (20 yrs); [memb.] The Writers Center, The Nature Conservancy, Nat'l Parks Wildlife Federation, Nat'l Wildflower Research Center, Methodist and Church, The Nat'l League of American Penwomen; [hon.] The Nat'l League of Penwomen: Midwest Writer's Workshop Fiction and 1975 Advance Fiction (Winner 2 yrs) Midwest Scholarship 1975-76 Family Circle (2) writing contests Indiana Press Women's Scholarship; [oth. writ.] Non-Fiction Grant Assistant Creative Arts writer BSU, Script writer: published in state and national publications.; [pers.] I have a strong urge to write words not by chance or choice but by my nature. A phenomena in my life and maybe in the after times a piece of me will be left.; [a.] Muncie, IN

**SLOAN, ELDRIN**
[pen.] Squeaky Sloan; [b.] July 24, 1954, Spalding County, CA; [p.] Edmond and Rosanna Sloan; [m.] Patsy Ann Sloan, August 14, 1975; [ch.] Carlos A. Sloan, Laytonya A. Sloan; [ed.] High School, Act Travel School; [occ.] Disabled, work for Delta Airlines 19 yrs. 3 months; [memb.] Cleveland Chapel, AME Church, Jerry Lewis Muscular Dystrophy Association; [pers.] I strive to let people with a disability know that even if you have a disability you still can achieve. Even though I have limb-girdle dystrophy I play piano, water paint, write poems and I'm writing music anybody can still achieve.; [a.] Hampton, GA

**SLOAN JR., HOMER F.**
[b.] November 5, 1948, Savannah; [ch.] Two; [ed.] High School; [occ.] Millwright; [oth. writ.] Twenty on so; [pers.] To enchanted memories and meetings of the heart; [a.] Savannah, GA

**SLOCUM, MEGAN**
[b.] March 23, 1983, Stamford; [p.] Elaine Slocum, Kieran O'Connell; [ed.] Julia A. Stark Elementary School, Current Student at Walter P. Dolan Middle School; [occ.] Student; [hon.] 2 Consecutive citizenship awards, 4 consecutive honor roll awards, presiden-

tial achievement award, certificate of Merit for an outstanding entry in conflict resolution writings.; [a.] Stamford, CT

**SMALL, JANET**
[pen.] Janet Small; [b.] January 13, 1956, Minneapolis, MN; [p.] Lloyd and Margaret Small; [m.] Randy Stark; [ch.] Jason, Randi Lynn, Jacob; [ed.] Some College; [occ.] Writing my book of poems; [memb.] St. Olaf Lutheran Church; [oth. writ.] I'm getting my poems. I've wrote over the years together and hoping too publish them in a book, I'm hoping to write a book too; [pers.] Every one who dies I know and love I write a poem and read at there funeral I feel it adds a special touch; [a.] North Minneapolis, MN

**SMITH, ANN MARIE**
[pen.] A.M.S.; [b.] December 1, 1950, Germany; [p.] Deceased; [m.] Deceased; [ch.] Chayzee and Tanya Smith; [occ.] LPN; [hon.] Poet Society National Poems, American Society of Poetry; [oth. writ.] Madame Rue Treasure, Poems for All Season, That Place, Their Time Will Come; [pers.] If its a thought write it or it will be gone people find themselves in many ways mine is threw my writing.; [a.] Indianapolis, IN

**SMITH, DONALD G.**
[pen.] The Wizard; [b.] August 14, 1976, Dayton, OH; [p.] Phil Smith, Peggy Smith; [ed.] Milton-Union High School Miami Valley Career Technology Center; [occ.] Host, Pearson House Restaurant; [hon.] Honor Student at Miami Valley Career Technology Center. Tech. Prep. Scholarship for Sinclair Community College; [oth. writ.] Several poems and short stories which have never been published.; [pers.] Love and hatred are the strongest of emotions, I choose to write about the one that I know best.; [a.] West Milton, OH

**SMITH, DONNA LYNN**
[pen.] Donna Lynn Smith; [b.] June 24, 1972, Danbury, CT; [p.] Roger Smith, Mary Smith; [ed.] Bethel High; [occ.] Veterinary Technician; [pers.] Thru my poetry I attempt to portray images and emotions I have been greatly inspired by my mothers strength and perseverance.; [a.] Brookfield, CT

**SMITH, ELLEN M.**
[pen.] El Lion!; [b.] January 3, 1934, Guymon, OK; [ed.] Pre doctored student in curriculum and instruction at USC - Columbia, SC; [occ.] Educator; [memb.] Phi Delta Kappa Fraternity; The Delta Kappa Gamma Society International; [hon.] Who's Who in Elementary Ed; Honorary Educational Fraternity; Phi Delta Kappa; The Delta Kappa Gamma Society International; Scholarship - $5,000 Doctoral studies; The Delta Kappa Gamma Society International; [oth. writ.] Article for local newspaper - "A Characterization"; a collection of poems which I presented with appropriate slides; children stories; [pers.] I write to honor people and celebrate the beauty of creation. I love intricate and unique uses of language.; [a.] West Columbia, SC

**SMITH, GARY B. HARRIS**
[pen.] Gary B. Harris Smith; [b.] July 27, 1955, Saint Louis; [p.] Martha Harris, R. B. Smith; [ed.] B.A. History, M. A. in Secondary Ed. Guidance and Counseling Murray St. University; [occ.] Kentucky Tech. Instructor; [memb.] "Honorable order of KY Colonels" N.E.A. (National Education Assoc.); [hon.] Governor appointed position in the Executive Committee on the Advisory Board for Vocational Rehabilitation, Melbourne Mills, KY, Handicap Achievement Award and runner up in KY's "KY. Tech. Teacher of the Year"; [oth. writ.] Golden Poet of the Year "Best Morning Start"-Silver Poet of the Year "Sterling Spar-

rows" and other published poems, short stories; [pers.] I never take the little insigne, figant things in life for granted, because if you lose them, they will become your greatest desires.; [a.] Eddyville, KY

**SMITH, GEORGE**
[b.] July 3, 1942, New London, CT; [p.] Ernest Smith, Frances Smith; [m.] Ann B. Smith, December 30, 1972; [ch.] Shawn William, Erin Kathleen; [ed.] Stonington High, Mohegan Community College; [occ.] Administrative Assistant; [memb.] Board member of the Local Commission on Aging; [oth. writ.] Multi-subject editorials published in local newspapers. Also, many other (unpublished) poems I've read to local poetry classes.; [pers.] I admire the poetic masters, emulate none, and wish for my writings to evoke fond readings.; [a.] Pawcatuck, CT

**SMITH, GLORIA KATHERINE**
[pen.] Gloria K. Burnett; [b.] June 25, 1966, Mooretown, NJ; [p.] Henry Sr., and Gloria M, Burnett; [m.] Steven J. Smith, November 11, 1991; [ch.] Samantha Leighann 8, Taylor Anne 2; [ed.] Moorestown H.S. 1984, Bradford School 1985 ICS - Law Enforcement present Bartending Course; [occ.] Unemployed; [hon.] Shorthand Award 130 Words per minute academic 3.9 gpa Certificate of Appreciation US Army 1991 Golden Poet - World of Poetry, 1990 Award of Merit honorable mention; [oth. writ.] "The Silver Shore" many unpublished poems. Currently working on a novel.; [pers.] I am proud of who I am and all I have, for which I thank God. My philosophy is that I would rather be hated for who I am than loved for what I am not.; [a.] Columbus, GA

**SMITH, HEIDI MARIE**
[b.] November 25, 1979, Emmett, ID; [p.] Lori and Bryan Douglas Smith; [ed.] LA Grande High School, Young Authors Convention; [occ.] Student at La Grande High School; [hon.] 4.0 GPA; [oth. writ.] Several poems, written at various times, none yet published. Other writings such as a myth and short stories.; [pers.] Poetry is an emotion that is expressed in a symbolic form with words. My poetry is a reflection of my inner thoughts and emotions. Yet, it can be interpreted many different ways. That is the beauty of it. Poetry is a mirror of one's self, and not only writing it, but reading other people's gives me pleasure.; [a.] La Grande, OR

**SMITH, JANICE**
[b.] July 15, 1981, Passaic, NJ; [p.] Daniel Smith and Rosemary Smith; [ed.] St. Anne School; [occ.] Student (8th Grade); [hon.] Creative Writing and award and Poet of the Year; [oth. writ.] Several poems published in other books and magazines such as: "Children's Digest", "Anthology of Poetry by Young Americans"; [pers.] My babysister inspired me to write this poem because we almost lost her at birth. The point of my poem was to convince someone to save the life of their little baby that could bring so much joy into the world.; [a.] Rochelle Park, NJ

**SMITH, JOHN B.**
[b.] November 20, 1953, Fayetteville, NC; [p.] Carl and Louella Smith; [m.] Penny A. Smith; [ch.] Edwin, Matthew; [ed.] Warner Southern College; [occ.] Technician; [pers.] My philosophy is to always consider the "source". Good or bad, you will have a better insight to the situations in your life.; [a.] Winter Haven, FL

**SMITH, MICHELLE LEE**
[b.] March 30, 1980, Albany, NY; [p.] Carol Ann and John V. Smith; [ed.] Completed 9th grade; [occ.] Sophomore at Union Endicott High School; [memb.] JV Basketball Cheerdale, Peer Mediation, Union Prebysterian Church and Youth Group, Miss Judy's Art of Dance; [hon.] Presidential Academic Fitness

Award, High School Roll 3 consecutive yrs, Best of show IBM Scimatech fair 1994; [oth. writ.] Published in poetry and The Children: State University of New York at Binghamton, in June 1992 and May 20, 1994; [pers.] I possess a great passions for writing. I am able to express myself liberally and unconfined. It also gives me the opportunity to reflect on the past, relate to the present and aspire to the future; [a.] Endicott, NY

**SMITH, MICHELLE SUZANNE**
[b.] June 20, 1970, Lake Charles, LA; [p.] Ken and Alice Fay Smith; [ed.] Sulphur High School, Louisiana State University - Bachelor of Arts in English - Creative Writing; [occ.] High School English Teacher; [memb.] Alum of Zeta Tau Alpha; [hon.] Dean's List, most spirited teacher; [oth. writ.] Writes Poetry and Short stories; [pers.] I am very interested in writing about mankind's ability to overcome obstacles and to survive. It is the people who survive in spite of everything that are the most fascinating.; [a.] Lake Charles, LA

**SMITH, R. MICHAEL**
[b.] October 3, 1961, Cincinnati, OH; [ed.] Western Brown High School, United States Army Military Intelligence Analyst.; [occ.] Author-Poet; [memb.] International Society of Poets; [hon.] Appointed to West Point Military Academy; [oth. writ.] Unpublished Author of "Plaques of the 1990's."; [pers.] I dedicated this poem "The Great Whore" to the fulfillment of the prophecy in II Thessalonians Chapter 2. The Pope of the Roman Catholic Church has been revealed as the "man of sin."; [a.] Cleveland, TN

**SMITH, ROBERT A.**
[b.] January 20, 1930, Monroe, LA; [p.] Jewel Smith, Alpha Smith; [m.] Francisca Alvina, July 19, 1975; [ch.] Mary Ann, Linda Sue, Jewel Steven, Robert A. Jr., John Francis; [ed.] Barkdull Faulk Elementary Neville High, El Paso Community Col.; [occ.] Retired; [oth. writ.] Wake up!! Heart of Dreams, An Anthology Flowing With Emotion. Ed. Tina Fina. Mineral Wells, TX: Creative Poetry Assiates, 1994. 280. The Challenge, A Collection of Poems and Short Stories (unpub). Plus five Novels.; [pers.] Perfection of beauty belongs only to God. Only the eyes of the soul can see the perfection of beauty in words, painting, music, or people, for beauty is not of the visible thing, but of the indiscernable heart and soul.; [a.] El Paso, TX

**SMITH, ROBERT R.**
[b.] December 5, 1954, Pineville, LA; [p.] Robert C. and Norma Smith; [ed.] Alexandria Senior High; [occ.] Resident Counselor Teen Challange St. Louis; [oth. writ.] Many, many more poems and short stories... none published; [pers.] I have seen and been a participant in hell, I have also tasted of the fruits of heaven, forgiveness, grace, mercy and love... Utopia and Oblivion have one thing in common, neither truly exist.; [a.] Sanford, FL

**SMITH, SHIRLEY L.**
[pen.] Shirl; [b.] July 18, 1944, Lyes, VA; [p.] Abraham and Rose Newman; [m.] Decease; [ch.] Peggy Ann, Grover Jr, George Howard; [ed.] Ambler High School; [occ.] "Sample Maker"; [memb.] Zion Bapth Church, YMCA; [oth. writ.] Several poems not published yet; [pers.] I strive to reflect the way I feel in my writing about my sorrow and joy.; [a.] Lansdale, PA

**SMITH, TAYLOR PEGGY**
[pen.] Flossie Bloomgarden; [b.] January 14, 1936, Kittanning, PA; [p.] Cleo and George Taylor; [m.] Edward J. Smith (Deceased), October 23, 1953; [ch.] Edward Ann, Amy, Dorinda, Edward, Shaun; [ed.] High School graduate, attended Cosmetology School; [occ.] Certified Nursing Assistant; [memb.] Nurse Aide Registry of

PA, A.A.R.P.; [pers.] I have been inspired by the beauty of nature, and Helen Steiner Rice's writings.; [a.] Chicora, PA

**SNEED, LAUREL ELIZABETH**
[pen.] Lolli Rose; [b.] July 16, 1952, Pueblo, CO; [p.] Mrs. Frank S. Rose; [ch.] Donald Dillon Sneed, Margaret Megan Rose Sneed; [ed.] Alvin High School, Sam Houston State University Masters Degree; [occ.] Kindergarten Teacher A. Davis Ford Elementary Spring TX; [memb.] TSTA, RAGT, Woodlands United Methodist Church; [hon.] Kappa Delta Pi, Deans's List, Teacher of the year; [oth. writ.] A collection of my poems and songs, this is the first time I have submitted any for publication.; [pers.] I write as a means of understanding and healing. It is a some what spiritual experience for me. Writing allows me "to let my inside out so I can let the outside in". It is cathartic and clarifying. I hope it helps others.; [a.] Spring, TX

**SNOW, AMY**
[b.] April 11, 1972, Ware, MA; [p.] Mary Ellen Snow and Mark Snow; [ed.] Quaboag Regional high UMASS - Amherst; [occ.] English teacher; [memb.] Mass teacher's Association; [hon.] Golden Key National Honor Society Dean's List; [oth. writ.] Currently working on a coming of age novel; [pers.] Each person creates and is responsible for their own destiny I try to write about and reflect on the struggles to reach that destiny, Maya Angela is an inspiration poet for me; [a.] Amherst, MA

**SPANG, BETH**
[b.] October 5, 1979, Meridian, MS; [p.] Jeff Spang, Deb Bain; [ed.] I am in 10th grade at Putnam City North High School in Oklahoma City, OK.; [occ.] Student; [hon.] 4.0 + Grade point average maintained; [oth. writ.] Poems published in local newspaper and writing contest publication.; [pers.] Always look on the bright side in life.; [a.] Oklahoma City, OK

**SPIRES, JEAN E.**
[pen.] Jean Barlow Spires; [b.] February 6, 1925, Grand Forks, ND; [p.] Henry, Dena Barlow; [m.] November 14, 1943, spouse deceased; [ch.] Four, six grandchildren, one great-grandchild; [ed.] High School, psychology, manager - choir, writing - school band; [occ.] Counselor - youth leader; [memb.] Home Economics Club, Alfa Tau Sorority, Secretary, President PTA of Jackson Twp. School; [hon.] Valedictorian - 8th Grade and High School; sang on radio in N D - Winner of County Recital - ND; 1st Prize essay contest; started 1st Emergency Home Care for 3 children - 8yrs. alone; earned degree in psychology; [oth. writ.] "What Home is to Me," newspaper reporter, have several poems and short stories; 8 years voice lessons; editor for magazine; [pers.] "God will not give you a Cadillac, if you can only ride a bicycle!" I do not believe in the word "can't." Nothing is impossible. Believe in God and yourself.; [a.] Mt. Sterling, OH

**SOLES, JUSTIN**
[b.] October 1, 1977, Joplin, MO; [p.] Paul and Becky Soles; [ed.] Senior 95' Galena High School; [occ.] Student; [memb.] Tennessee Prarie Friends Church Assoc. of Christian Athletes Member High School Yearbook Comm.; [oth. writ.] School newspaper; [a.] Galena, KS

**SOLES, VIOLA D.**
[pen.] Gibski; [b.] September 29, 1946; [p.] Willie and Iola Gibbs (Deceased); [m.] Deceased; [ed.] Master of Arts, Health Care Management, State University of NY at Buffalo; [memb.] People United for Justice-Buffalo, National Assoc. For Female Exec., NY State Civil Service Emp. Assoc., Officer, Political Action Commit-

tee, and Women's Committee. Buffalo Quarters Historical Society; [oth. writ.] Book of Poetry-unpublished, Country Chicken short story-unpublished; [pers.] In this "life learning cycle," my philosophy is to elevate my level of consciousness to the highest spiritual realm possible while sharing that knowledge with others.; [a.] Buffalo, NY

**SOLOMON, CAROLE HELLER**
[b.] April 22, 1941, Cleveland. OH; [ch.] Tony Solomon 28, Robby Solomon and Mendonza Solomon 26; [ed.] B.A. in English from UCLA J.D. from Loyola Law School; [memb.] California State Bar Association, Los Angeles County Bar Association; [oth. writ.] The Real Estate Sales Organizer published in 1985 and marketed through 1992. An Anthology of Spiritual Poetry, a work in progress.; [pers.] I have always longed for compassionate justice for myself and others in a world of peace and opportunity for all. Since my recent studies with master meditators on a spiritual level, I am in the process of developing a more universal perspective from which to live my personal life. Pursuant to this philosophy, I have been concentrating on bringing more spirituality, in the form of compassion and understanding along with inner peace and serenity, into my everyday life, since I be live world peace can only be achieved when individuals find inner peace for themselves and practice compassion for others.

**SOLOMON, KIMBERLYN E.**
[pen.] Kimberlyn; [b.] Pittsburgh, PA; [p.] Rich and Bette Sandora; [m.] Scott R. Solomon; [ch.] Michael, Samuel Amber; [ed.] Keystone Oaks High Broward Community College; [occ.] Public Supermarkets. Inc. FT. Laud. Fla; [memb.] Honor society high German Club, modern dance cheer leading, creative writing disable veteran assoc. Leukemia Society special Olympics; [hon.] High Honor Grad. in High School (W.I.N.G.S. Program) Broward Comm. College; [oth. writ.] Enjoy writing poetry and short storied I my thoughts; [pers.] That the only person you really need to fear is the one in the mirror, that sometimes we truly are, our own worst enemy, but changes does come of you don't give up.; [a.] Ft. Laud, FL

**SORENSON, CHRISTOPHER**
[b.] June 14, 1986, Aurora, CO; [p.] Dayna and Brent Boynton; [ed.] Attended K-3rd grade at Laredo Elementary School in Aurora, CO. Now attending home school; [pers.] My 3rd grade teacher, Mrs. Nancy Johnson, got me interested in poetry. I tried to write enough poems in 3rd grade to fill a book. I really like poetry and I hope to get more poems published. This has been a neat experience for me.; [a.] Aurora, CO

**SORENSEN, ROBERT L.**
[b.] November 15, 1953, Chicago; [p.] John and Betty Sorensen; [ed.] BS in Geography at Northern Ill. University 1975, 3 minors; [occ.] Unemployed Construction engineer; [memb.] The Geography fraternity and Geographic Society Church older in Lutheran Church; [hon.] National Merit Scholarship Society Magna Cum Laude graduate Worked on Federal programs in Construction 'Joe' Children book 1971; [oth. writ.] Have written as hobby books in Sociology and Science fiction and several hundred poems subject love movie review column for MU newspaper in 1971 local movie and TV scripts-Wheaton, Ill for Capiviaco; [pers.] Let is a building process until the finished product and an artist can be found in any discipline and so can an artistic subject. And communication of this can go a long way to inspire life and create love all around; [a.] Martin, TN

**SOTOMAYOR, Z. ROBERTO**
[b.] Puerto Rico; [p.] Zoilo and America Sotomayor; [ed.] University High School, University of Puerto

Rico, BS. School of Medicine, University of Buffalo New York, MD 1st Lieutenant USA Army Organization and Medical School; [occ.] Doctor in Medicine; [memb.] American Medical Association, American College of Physician, American Assoc. of Internal Medicine, Puerto Rico Medical Association, Puerto Rico Assoc. of Internal Medicine; [hon.] Bronze Star Medal, Korean Conflict Commendation Ribbon with metal pendant Korean, Korean Conflict; [oth. writ.] Several poems writing about; [pers.] Never say it can not be done with perseverance anything can be done.; [a.] Rio Piedra, PR

**SOUTOR, MARK**
[pen.] Mark Soutor; [b.] December 15, 1956, Minnesota; [p.] Dan and Lois Soutor; [ed.] B.S. Univ. of Minnesota Henning High School, Henning, MN; [occ.] Consultant, writer; [memb.] Colorado Youth at Risk, Advisory Board Member; [hon.] A number of awards for volunteer work in Denver, CO; [oth. writ.] A novel on growing up in rural Minnesota "From Fields Where Glory Does Not Stay"; [pers.] I am committed to individual spiritual transformation and strive to reflect that in my poetry and writing; [a.] Denver, CO

**SOUZA, WENDY L.**
[pen.] Sunshine; [b.] November 23, 1968, Long Beach, CA; [p.] Thomas and Janice Brom; [ed.] Jordan High School, Long Beach City College; [occ.] Data Entry Operator; [hon.] California Scholarship Federation, graduated with high honors. Being selected as a semifinalist in this contest.; [oth. writ.] Nothing published yet but hopefully as I grow in my writing things will improve.; [pers.] In my writing I try to reflect that people must see that there is a God and that what they sow they will eventually reap. Usually when they least expect it.; [a.] Gloucester, VA

**SPANN, KAREN YVETTE**
[pen.] K'san; [b.] December 29, 1974, Fort Gaines, GA; [p.] Catherine Jenkins and Johnny Jenkins Jr.; [ed.] Abbeville Public Schools (Abbeville, AL), Alabama State University (Junior, Montgomery, AL); [occ.] Full-time Student; [memb.] Alabama Democratic Conference, Phi Eta Sigma, Britain/DuBois History-Sociology Society (ASU); [hon.] Dean's List (College of Business Administration at Alabama State University), National Dean's List, Presidential Scholar (ASU); [oth. writ.] Over 300 poems, songs, and short stories; [pers.] "God grant me the serenity to accept the things I cannot change, the ability to change the things I can, and the wisdom to know the difference."; [a.] Abbeville, AL

**SPANO, SHARON YOUNG**
[b.] September 30, 1953, Burbank, CA; [p.] Mickey Dowding, Bill Young; [m.] Joe Spano, November 26, 1994; [ch.] Marie Hale Chavez; [ed.] Indio High School; [occ.] Office Manager, HRM Machine, Inc.; [oth. writ.] Unpublished books of poems Entitled "Heart Songs" various other poems published in poets review. "Rusty" published in your anthology "Dark Side of the Moon"; [pers.] My poems are simply my way of communicating my feelings, my desire is for others to relate to them.; [a.] Costa Mesa, CA

**SPARKMAN, THOMAS KELLY**
[b.] March 22, 1950, Sparta, TN; [p.] Mr. and Mrs. Tommie H. Sparkman; [occ.] Retired Army Sergeant and Corrections Officer; [pers.] Written after visiting the Vietnam Veterans Memorial and seeing the names of nine (9) buddys. This was my last goodbye.; [a.] Blythe, CA

**SPAULDING, KENNETH E.**
[pen.] Ken Spaulding; [b.] December 31, 1917, Rome, NY; [p.] Forest Dayle and Corinne Gertrude (Bolten);

[m.] Lois Beightol, January 8, 1950; [ch.] Ernest Neil, Suzanne Elaine; [ed.] Santa Ana Evening High, Religious Science Practitioner (RScP), Religious Science Ministerial (RScM); [occ.] Semi-retired insurance broker, Religious Science Practitioner; [memb.] Book publicists of So, Cal. National Writers Club, Glendale Church of Religious Science; [hon.] Top Star Member, Pac. Mut. 1947, 48, Big Tree Member, Pacific Mut. Life 1949, 51, 54 Nat. Quality Awd. Nat. Assn. of Life underwriters 1955; [oth. writ.] Book-Simple I Ching, poems-Billboards vs. Trees, The Mystical Connection, What Price Peace!; [pers.] I believe we are all visitors to earth, and custodians of what we have. In that vein, should all be good custodians, and we will have all our needs and wants taken care of.; [a.] Glendale, CA

**SPEAR, TORI M.**
[b.] September 30, 1966, Indiana; [p.] Preston, Jane Spear; [ed.] Largo Senior High School, St. Petersburg Junior College; [occ.] Customer Service-Cigna Healthcare, Inc.; [hon.] 1st prize ($75.00) in local Elks Club Essay Contest-1985; [pers.] My favorite quote (originator unknown) "The reason you were always a failure in life is because you were always to afraid to try." Never be afraid to try to make your dreams come true.

**SPEARS, CAROL E.**
[b.] May 13, 1933, Clinton Co., OH; [p.] C.H. and Marjorie Brose; [m.] L.T. Spears, July 12, 1952; [ch.] Nancy Spears Long and James D. Spears; [ed.] Martinsville (Ohio) High School; [occ.] Retired Homemaker; [memb.] Mayfair Church of Christ, Huntsville, AL; [pers.] I started writing to pass time and to entertain grandchildren during a period that I was bedfast, limited activities allow time to write for friends and family amusement.; [a.] Madison, AL

**SPEED, NICOLE**
[pen.] Castra Lia, Cat, Panther; [b.] July 2, 1981, Fresno, CA; [p.] John Speed, Debra Speed; [occ.] Student; [oth. writ.] Several poems none published; [pers.] I write for my own satisfaction, but enjoy it when other people appreciate it.; [a.] Santa Rosa, CA

**SPIER, JESSICA**
[b.] July 30, 1971, New Orleans; [p.] Roger and Sallie McIlwain; [m.] Scott Spier, August 17, 1991; [ed.] Louisiana Tech University Bachelor of Arts in child life and family studies; [occ.] Audio visual librarian The School of Tomorrow H.Q., Lewisville, TX; [pers.] I would like to thanks God for the gift of being able to write poetry. My prayer is that my poetry will touch the lives of those that read it in a special way, even if it is only to bring a smile to their faces.; [a.] Coppell, TX

**SPRUNGER, RUSSELL**
[pen.] Russell Sprunger; [b.] March 5, 1981, Pasadena, CA; [p.] Maureen and Richard Sprunger; [ed.] Completed Huntington Middle School. Entering San Marino High School, fall 1995.; [occ.] High School student; [memb.] California Junior Scholarship Federation; [hon.] Silver Medallion for Academic Achievement, Athletic Letters in Football, Cross Country, Volleyball, GATE (Gifted And Talented Education); [oth. writ.] Other poems published in school publication, "In Our Own Words."; [a.] San Marino, CA

**SQUALLS, WILLIE E.**
[b.] Leesburg, FL; [p.] Rev. Napoleon W. and Mary Bagley (Deceased); [m.] Ralph (Deceased); [ch.] Norma G., Ronald C. (Deceased); [ed.] High School graduate; [occ.] Retired; [memb.] St. Stephen A.M.E., Zion Church, other auxiliaries of above church; [oth. writ.] Creative writing, other poems, but of longer than twenty lines. I started a corresponding course in writing for

children, but didn't complete, the course.; [pers.] To God give the glory for His gift. I receive many congratulations, from people who hear the poems, but the praise is given to God for His blessings and words.; [a.] Asbury Park, NJ

**ST. GERMAIN, SUSAN**
[pen.] Sue Tacy LaPointe; [b.] August 15, 1946, Springfield, MA; [p.] Jerry and Helen Benoit; [m.] Roger St. Germain, March 20, 1993; [ed.] Cathedral High School Springfield, MA, Bay Path College, Longmeadow, MA; [occ.] Writer; [memb.] Fedhaven VFW Memorial Post 7361 Auxiliary-Sr. Vice Fedhaven Women's Club-President; [oth. writ.] Poem-Once in a Lifetime-On Threshold of a Dream-(Sue Tacy LaPointe) (page 325), Triple Cross Trilogy-novels (in progress), Return to Ludlow-novel (in progress), several newspaper articles for view post 7361; [pers.] Writing is an escape! However, in escaping I have found myself, re-enlightened, over and over again.; [a.] Fedhaven, FL

**ST. JEAN, MELISSA M.**
[b.] January 13, 1984, Anchorage, AK; [occ.] Currently in the 5th grade at Griswold Int. School; [memb.] Member of Smithsonian Institute, and Audubon Society; [hon.] First place winner in a school wide essay contest; [pers.] I think women, men, and all living things should be treated with respect.

**STALDER, WENDY**
[b.] January 3, 1964, Canton, OH; [ed.] East Canton High School, 1982, New Mexico State University 1988; [occ.] Teacher, Coach El Paso, Texas; [memb.] Texas Association of Basketball Coaches. Texas Girls Coaches Association; [hon.] High School All American Athlete, all State Athlete (OH), Intercollegiate Athlete of the year.; [a.] El Paso, TX

**STALEY, FRANCES W.**
[b.] November 19, 1908; [p.] Agnes and William Cuthill; [m.] Dean Staley (second marriage), September 24, 1971; [ch.] Stan Pederson; [ed.] B.A. U. of Wisconsin Madison, Wis.; [occ.] Retired; [memb.] University Women Church Deacon, PTA, Woman's Club; [hon.] Valedictorian in high school, American Chemical Award, One of 6 chemistry in State of N. Dak. in 1927; [oth. writ.] AAUM book of poems published

**STANAWAY, KERRY J.**
[b.] New Zealand; [m.] Theresa; [ch.] Five Children; [ed.] University of Aukland; [occ.] Geologist and enjoy writing verses.; [oth. writ.] Have written articles in industry and scientific journals on Geology and Mineral prospecting.

**STANFIELD, ANDY**
[b.] December 12, 1969, Gadshen, AL; [p.] Don Stanfield; [ed.] Southside High Jacksonville State University BA English and History; [oth. writ.] I write songs, poems and I'm currently finishing my first novel.; [pers.] Nietzschean Taoist; [a.] Rainbow City, AL

**STANLEY, TROY D.**
[pen.] Roger Holland; [b.] August 26, 1973, St. Petersburg, FL; [p.] Richard Stanley and Susan Stanley; [pers.] Love your neighbor; [a.] Columbus, OH

**STANSBURY, PAT**
[b.] July 23, 1960, New Jersey; [m.] Paul Stansbury; [ch.] Sandra Leigh, Paul Charles, Thomas James, Joel David; [pers.] In my careful pursuit to share the hope I've found in God through Christ I find encouragement from His own lips. Psalm 45:1 "My tongue is the pen of a ready writer."; [a.] Ballwin, MO

**STARLING, RAYNA**
[b.] June 2, 1979, Phoenix, AZ; [p.] Raymond (Deceased) and Glenda Starling; [ed.] Solano Elementary School, Challenger Middle School, and currently a junior at Greenway High School; [occ.] Student and habilitation technician with physically and mentally challenged children; [memb.] Girl Scouts, Swim Team, Science Club, Yearbook Staff, French Club band and Children International Sponsor; [hon.] Honor Roll, bowling, swimming and twirling trophies, Arizona Junior Solar Sprint-third place best design math awards and spelling bees.; [oth. writ.] Several other poems. One published in school newsletter. A book in the making.; [pers.] The power I felt reading works from Edgar Allan Poe led me believe that I had that kind of strength inside and only had to find it. To anyone who has a dream, make individual goals and step by step make your way to the top.; [a.] Phoenix, AZ

**STEINACHER, STEWART A.**
[pen.] Bear Cub Steinacher; [b.] May 27, 1966; [p.] William A. Steinacher, Helen Carol Bubenheimer; [ed.] H.S. grad. 1984, United States Marine Corps 84-88, Tooling and Machining 89-91, Nursing 93-95; [occ.] Nurse at Good Samaritan Hospital, West Islip, NY; [memb.] Wolverine Hunting and Fishing Club Inc. Owner, member New England Bone Marrow Donorship. Veteran of U.S.M.C.; [hon.] Meritorious Mast U.S.M.C., Handball Champion, U.S.M.C., Infantry Weapon Specialist U.S.M.C. and U.S. Army Ordnance Center Graduate, Infantry Weapons-Refresher Course Graduate, Nuclear, Biological, Chemical Warfare School Grad.; [pers.] If mankind continues at it's present rate of consumption and waste. The planet will surely be depleted of all its resources. We have to realize the planet is not ours, its alive and we must care for it.; [a.] Dix Hills, NY

**STERN, GUADALUPE Q.**
[pen.] Lupe; [b.] May 1, 1957, Acapulco; [p.] Catalina and Cano Ochoa; [m.] Phillip Earl Stern, June 4, 1977; [ch.] Louie Cruz, Phillip Stern, Catherine Stern; [ed.] Roosevelt High School also other training in the medical field.; [occ.] Heavy Equip. Operator in the University California, LA; [memb.] Red Cross, Lost Angeles Mission, Children's International; [oth. writ.] Several poems some published, in local newspaper, and songs still in process; [pers.] Life itself and my family has been the number one influence in my songs and poetry writing; [a.] Bell Gardens, CA

**STEVENS, MARK H.**
[b.] October 5, 1948, Cleveland, OH; [p.] Ben Stevens, Anne Stevens; [m.] Amy Stevens, October 17, 1987; [ed.] B.A.-California State University, Northridge. M.A.-Kent State University, Ph.D.-The Claremont Graduate School; [occ.] Legal Assistant; [oth. writ.] M.A. Thesis: "The Federal Butions To Early Radio's Growth in America." Ph.D. Dissertation: "Meyer Lissner and the Politics of Progressive Municipal Reform in the City of Los Angeles 1906-1913."; [pers.] As a born-again Christian, I believe God can transform lives, giving inspiration to the love of the Lord Jesus Christ through expressions of the Heart, that others might also be touched and, in so doing, believe.; [a.] Los Angeles, CA

**STEWART, JAMES M.**
[b.] September 24, 1942, TX; [p.] Claudia and J. D. Stewart; [m.] Bonnie J. Stewart, November 11, 1985; [ch.] Melissa Stewart, Daniel Stewart; [ed.] B.A. U of Texas M.S. Sociology Texas A and MU P.H. D Psychology Texas A and MU; [occ.] Self Employed Psychologist; [memb.] A.P.A., A.S.P.C., "Time Common" Texas War on Drugs Ass.; [hon.] Medal of Service Award D.A.R.T, St Matthews Church Founding Mem-

ber; [oth. writ.] "Common Reasons for mental awareness" (essay) "The Buffalo" (poem), "Rivers of thought" (poem) "Smile" (poem); [pers.] Was on Jeopardy The game show lost!!, "A smile will beat clinical depression"; [a.] Houston, TX

**STINNETT, ANGIE**
[pen.] Angie Stinnett; [b.] May 3, 1979, Omaha, NE; [p.] Valorie and Jerry Smith; [ed.] High School Sophomore; [hon.] 1993 National Honor Society; [oth. writ.] Several poems published in local newspaper and school books; [a.] Omaha, NE

**STINSON, PATRICIA ASHLEY**
[pen.] P. A. Stinson, Ashley Stinson; [b.] April 15, 1978, Atlanta, GA; [p.] Pam and David Fuller; [ed.] Lovejoy Middle School, Lovejoy High School; [memb.] French Club, Chorus and Literary Magazine at Lovejoy High School; [pers.] I have been strongly influenced by my parents, grandparents, close friends, and teachers. I would especially like to thank my mother for being supportive of everything I do.; [a.] Jonesboro, GA

**STONE, JENNIFER**
[b.] August 22, 1984, Flint MI; [p.] Wojtek Stone, Bozena Stone; [ed.] George F. Robert's Elementary School; [occ.] Student in 6th grade; [oth. writ.] Books wrote in Elementary school. The cat and dog who went to Florida, Friends Forever, The Old Tool Shed Mystery, A Tiger named Ziara.; [pers.] This is my first time writing poetry so other people can read it.; [a.] Utica, MI

**STORCH, DAVID**
[b.] September 16, 1960, Canton, OH; [p.] Gary and Florence Storch; [ed.] Jupiter High; Palm Beach Jr. College; University of South Florida; [occ.] Sales - Avon Park Chevy, Olds, Geo; [pers.] My writing comes from life experiences and people who have touched my life.; [a.] Sebring, FL

**STORMS, EDWARD E.**
[b.] May 5, 1930, Christian, CO; [p.] Barney Edward and Ophliea Bennett Storms; [m.] Billie Carter Storms, February 25, 1954; [ch.] Judy Ann, Edward Eugene II, Marcella Ruth, Michael Schyuler; [ed.] Eight years one room School, High School GED; [occ.] US Army Retired; [memb.] First Baptist Church Dawson Springs, KY. Lifetime member VFW, Thirty year member lodge of Free and Accepted Masonry; [oth. writ.] Numerous poems, none published. None ever submitted before.; [pers.] I write mostly about the early years, growing up in Southwestern Kentucky on a remote backwood farm. Of a people held cultural captives of the land they loved. Of Agrarian Pastoral Primitiveness.; [a.] Dawson Springs, KY

**STOVALL, JEAN MARIE**
[b.] May 21, 1970, Rockford, IL; [p.] Deniss and Carol Stovall; [ch.] Necie, Brennitta; [ed.] West High School, Rockford, IL. grad. 1989; [occ.] Homemaker, Crafter, Aunt and Sister; [memb.] Wildlife and International Wildlife Fed., Jeh. Wit.; [hon.] Who's Who Among American High School Students, High School Diploma, High School Chief Ad Editor; [oth. writ.] Published articles in West High School newspaper 1988-1989 publish poems in local paper; [pers.] One must believe in oneself to succeed at what ever one wants to do in life. The journey one takes in life has mary roads, which road one takes depends on him or her.; [a.] Rockford, IL

**STRAUSBAUGH, LEAH**
[b.] February 14, 1980, Fairborn, OH; [p.] Jon and Belinda Strausbaugh; [ed.] Sophomore at Frank W. Cox High School Virginia Beach, VA; [occ.] Student at Frank W. Cox High School VA Bch, VA; [a.] Virginia Beach, VA

**STRAUSS, RAY SUZAN**
[pen.] Ray Suzan Strauz; [b.] June 3, 1930, Sweden; [p.] Herman and Golda Welssberger; [ch.] Rachel M. Catlin, Daniel I. Strauss; [ed.] Hunter College, NY, Art Student League, NY; [occ.] Real Estate Investor; [memb.] United National of U.S.A. Pacific Coast Chapter Inspector of my Local Election Precinct Member S. T. Temple.; [hon.] Dean's List, Citizenship Medal from daughters of the American Revolution Honorable mention in two competitions; [oth. writ.] Magic Spell 1, Magic Spell 2, Magic Spell 3, (Spelling textbooks for grades 1, 2 and 3); [pers.] Expansion of Ecology into various areas. Modernizations of morality let's self control become imposed ny parent and educators; [a.] Los Angeles, CA

**STROM, DEBRA MULHOLLAND**
[pen.] Debra Mulholland Strom; [b.] August 15, 1956, Syracuse, NY; [m.] Richard Strom, November 18, 1970; [ch.] Ritchie, Tina; [ed.] N.Y. G.E.D. Kent State Univ. Psych Major; [occ.] Student-Writer Rochester, NY; [oth. writ.] About to publish my 1st two books. Called: My Promise and My Promise The Forgiving Child. Over 1,000 pages of poems.; [pers.] My first two books are my autobiography in poetry. Due out in 1996.; [a.] Fairport, NY

**SUBECKI, JOHN F.**
[occ.] President-CEO Comwell-Consultants to Management; [oth. writ.] Several articles published in Business Publications; [pers.] Favorite Quote "On the day of judgment we will not be asked what we have read, but what we have done, not how will we have discoursed, but how I've have lived." The Imitation of Christ, Thomas A. Kempis; [a.] Flanders, NJ

**SULLIVAN, DANIEL**
[b.] March 7, 1928, Springfield, MA; [p.] Daniel R. and Kathryn B. Sullivan; [m.] Lorraine Sullivan, October 29, 1952; [ch.] Kathryn, Michael, Sharon and Stephen; [ed.] BS Chemical Engineering Univ. of Massachusetts, MS Chem. Eng. U of Mass., BA. Russian Language Syracuse, Univ.; [occ.] Pres. Sullivan Engineering Co. Chesterfield, MO; [memb.] Soc. of Automotive Engineers, Soc. of Plastics Engineers, American Chemical Society, National Right to Life Committee; [hon.] One year academic leave and seven promotions by Monsanto Co., Chair of symposium of Amer. Chem Soc., Chair of St. Louis Soc. of Plastics Eng'rs, Education Committee. Two terms on school board. Listed in "American Men of Science"; [oth. writ.] Published articles and patents on various polymer technologies. Contributor to "Light Quarterly", Chicago Numerous "portfolio" poems.; [pers.] "Who is like unto God?" What do I have that He did not give me? What could he take that I do not owe Him?; [a.] Chesterfield, MO

**SULLIVAN, SEAN**
[pen.] David Lister; [b.] January 12, 1968, Boston, MA; [p.] Eileen and William Sullivan; [m.] Michelle, November 9, 1994; [ed.] Boston and Quincy Public Schools G.E.D.; [occ.] Paper-Handler, Boston Globe Press room, Boston Newspaper Company; [memb.] Graphics Communications Int. Pressman Union Local #3N; [hon.] The first of Hopefully many is being published in "Windows Of The Soul." Thanks - B.S.C. - S.S.C.; [oth. writ.] Sean Sullivan Vol. One (The Final Dance) not published; [pers.] The journey is its own reward.; [a.] Hingham, MA

**SUSZ, EMILY ANNE**
[b.] August 23, 1978; [p.] Mark and Mary Susz; [ed.] Leawood Middle School, Kansas City Academy of Learning High School; [occ.] Student-11th grade; [oth. writ.] Several poems published in "The Phoenix Sound"

(a monthly literary publication) and one poem in the Anthology of Poetry by Young Americans.; [pers.]strive to reflect my personal feelings so that the lonely don't feel lonely anymore.; [a.] Leawood, KS

**SWANSON, MS. GLADYS I.**
[pen.] Ms. Gladys I. Swanson; [b.] February 22, 1922, Hammond, MN; [p.] Charles E. and Mary Julia Young; [m.] Carroll E. Swanson, May 29, 1949; [ch.] Kalvin Carroll, Caryl Robert and Cinda Marie Swanson Mack; [ed.] High School, Mpls Business College; [occ.] Retired - City Engineers Public World Mpls. 30 years; [memb.] Zeta Beta Chi Sorority Past Pres and Also Past Pres of Solo Club Mt Olivet Lutheran Church; [hon.] Past Editor "Line from nine" publications for 6 yrs. (monthly) Writers Workshop award; [oth. writ.] Write children's Stories article on poems in NE Sun newspaper. American Poetry Anthology American contemporary poems "Love Line of Life" poems - 50 poems; [pers.] My poems are written from the soul and from experience and observation and on - going faith.; [a.] Richfield, MN

**SWARTZ, MOLLIE**
[b.] April 9, 1980; [p.] Isabel Lark and Sam Swartz III; [ed.] Warwick High School-1 yr. tutor US Learning Center Lancaster; [occ.] Student; [a.] Lititz, PA

**SWENSON, CARRIE ANN GREER**
[b.] December 26, 1959, Rockford, IL; [p.] Judith Ibarra, Norman Swenson; [ch.] Nathan Andrew, Andrew Christopher; [ed.] Auburn High School with some adult education courses; [occ.] Cashier, CUB Foods, Rockford, IL; [oth. writ.] Several poems, and short stories but this is my first to be published. Hopefully the first of many.; [pers.] Much of my life has been hindered because, I didn't believe in myself. With lots of therapy and encouragement, I think, I'm finally getting it. Keep on believing in yourself.; [a.] Rockford, IL

**SWENSON, MARY L.**
[pen.] Maria Antonia Leone; [b.] February 18, 1913, Italy; [p.] Maria-Guissepez Leone, Nicole Leone; [m.] Sterner Swenson, June 28, 1958; [ch.] Alex Clemente - Deceased and Antoinee Clemente; [ed.] Two years High School and 30 years business woman restaurant manager; [occ.] Retired Housewife and Teacher of Italian; [memb.] "Church Women United St. Thomas Aquinas Church University of North Dakota; [oth. writ.] Cook book and poetry book; [pers.] Lectured to university student. Taught Italian to students, at home. Took English Art courses attended Lectures at University (by experts); [a.] Grandforks, ND

**SWIERINGA, GEORGE R.**
[b.] July 12, 1934, Milwaukee, WI; [m.] George and Emma; [m.] Gloria, December 31, 1965; [ch.] 20 Children includes many who were adopted; [ed.] B.S. in Education and 61 years of living; [occ.] Working with Disabled adults; [memb.] I'm a non-joiner; [hon.] A few 1 mile and 10 k trophies; [oth. writ.] I've written some newspaper articles on home maintenance; [pers.] Peace is the answer; [a.] Fort Washington, MD

**SWONGER, PAUL SHAWN**
[b.] March 26, 1979, Edina, MN; [p.] Peggy Swonger (mother); [ed.] Paul attends Pro-teen High School in St. Louis Park MN, He is entering the 11th grade; [hon.] Certified Mediator (Ramsey Co) family recognition Award-Wilder Foundation; [oth. writ.] Several other poems none published yet. Also writes song lyrics and music: Baby Don't Leave, "One More Try", "Eat Fly", "Senseless Violence"; [pers.] Everyone has the right to live without fear. The greatest catastrophe we face as people, is that we rise up against each other.; [a.] Richfield, MN

**SZORI, CORINA**
[pen.] Corina Szori; [b.] June 18, 1967, Romania; [p.] Augustin and Nastasia, Nastase; [m.] Laszlo Szori, July 1, 1991; [ed.] High School, Second year at Lorian County Community College; [occ.] Waitress at Farmer Boy Restaurant; [hon.] Dean's List 3rd place in the poetry contest of L.C.C.C. in 1994; [oth. writ.] Had poems published in College's publication.; [pers.] I come from a country which was covered in darkness for a long, long time. My heart goes out to all the people who had been suffering either from love or from oppression. "VIVAT LA LIBERTY!"; [a.] Elyria, OH

**TALBERT, BARBARA**
[pen.] Barbara Talbert; [b.] November 23, 1937, Boston, MA; [p.] Robert Morey, Hazel Morey; [ch.] David Henry, Diane Marie, Cynthia Joan, Christopher Andrew; [ed.] Newton High School, Boston University LGE '57; [occ.] Business Owner, Talbert's Office Plus; [memb.] Better Business Bureau, Write Your Congressman, Medina Chamber of Commerce; [pers.] The current and passing scene is a motivation for my work.; [a.] Medina, OH

**TALLMAN, EVELYN**
[b.] November 13, 1922, South Westerlo, NY; [p.] Mrs. Hazel F. Mabie; [m.] Deceased, January 23, 1940; [ch.] One; [ed.] Greenville Central High School National Baking School, 835 Diversey Parkway, Chicago, Illinois; [occ.] Retired and Write; [memb.] Social Service by Albany Co., Social Security Benefits; [oth. writ.] International Society of Poets

**TAM, TAMMY Y.**
[b.] June 11, 1978, San Francisco; [p.] Kar and Celine Tam; [ed.] Saint Ignatius College, Preparatory; [occ.] Student; [pers.] Good is good, Bad is bad, but that is not always the case so believe in what you see and hear for yourself.; [a.] Millbrae, CA

**TAYLOR, AMANDA**
[b.] December 5, 1981, Houston, TX; [p.] John and Marilyn Taylor; [ed.] Jr. High; [occ.] Cheerleading, Student Council, Basketball, Volleyball, and Track; [memb.] (NJHS) National Junior Honors Society; [oth. writ.] What to do "Love Is a Word", If Dreams Come True; [pers.] God chooses what we go through, but we choose how we go through it.; [a.] Georgetown, TX

**TAYLOR, BIANCA**
[b.] January 23, 1982; [p.] Ralph and Diane Taylor; [ed.] Junior High School 204 District 30; [pers.] I write to reflect, uniqueness upon mankind. The visions of my writing and blind to ethnicity by open to the soul.; [a.] Long Island City, NY

**TAYLOR, BRIDGETTE JANETTE**
[b.] July 27, 1971, Yakima, WA; [p.] Kenneth and Kathleen Huard; [m.] Michael Lee Taylor, August 21, 1993; [ch.] Jackson Lee, McCarns Taylor; [ed.] Graduated as Salutatorian from East Valley High School in 1989. Graduated as Honor Student from Yakima Valley Community College in 1991.; [occ.] Student, Mother, Writer, Artist; [hon.] Most outstanding writer, Senior English 1989. Dean's List and President's List from 1989-1991. Junior Masonic Achievement Award - best essay 1988.; [pers.] I write purely from emotional and personal experience. The poem in this book dealt with my grief over losing my brother and how difficult it has been to overcome.; [a.] Fayetteville, NC

**TAYLOR, IRMA M.**
[b.] November 23, 1957, Winston Salem, NC; [p.] Charles and Doris Morrison; [m.] Divorced; [ch.] Erica Y. Taylor, Jason L. Taylor; [ed.] Currently studying at High Point University seeking degree in Media Com-

munications; [occ.] Administrative representative with major airline.; [hon.] Certified teacher of Africentric "rites of passage" "United Collective"; [oth. writ.] Book review column published monthly in local periodical, "AC Phoenix"; [pers.] Goals of reaching potential understanding self, and attaining spiritual atonement with the Universe is my aim through the written word for others as well a myself; [a.] Winston Salem, NC

**TAYLOR, JULIE CHRISTINE**
[b.] December 9, 1984, Fanwood, NJ; [p.] Douglas and Elizabeth Taylor; [ed.] Shallowford Falls Elementary School Marietta, GA; [occ.] 5th Grader. Age 10 1/2 years old; [memb.] Shallowford Falls Writing Club; [hon.] Won writing fair in third grade; [oth. writ.] No other published writings; [pers.] Thanks a whole bunch to Mrs. Joan Stommen and Mr. Kim Puckett for introducing this contest to me and for inspiring and encouraging me to write this poem.; [a.] Marietta, GA

**TAYLOR, LOUISE E.**
[pen.] Louise Taylor; [b.] November 28, 1921, Cleveland, OH; [p.] Alexander and Anne Erdey; [m.] Edward Winthrop Taylor Jr., September 12, 1953; [ch.] Mary Lou, Mark and Paul; [ed.] Cleveland College Western Reserve University, John Adams High (Cleveland) UCLA Extension; [occ.] Admin. Asst. Pacific Clinics; [memb.] Jane Austen Society Oblate of St. Andrews Abbey Arroyo League (service group), World Community for Christian Meditation; [hon.] Pius X Medal (for teaching); [oth. writ.] Misc. Articles Annual Historian Reports (Arroyo League) Past feature written on staff of the tidings official archdiocen newspaper; [pers.] Having been felled by a stroke, my rehabilitation has been aided by the diligent efforts of many dedicated therapists; [a.] Los Angeles, CA

**TAYLOR, MARJORIE**
[b.] December 26, 1941, Highland Park, MI; [p.] Taylor and Leona Moss; [m.] Robert E. Taylor, March 16, 1958; [ch.] Paul and Diane Roberta, Vickie; [ed.] High School Ged College, Journalism and Art - no degree; [occ.] Freelance Writer; [memb.] International Poetry National - Poetry Society; [hon.] Don't call me sinner flowers need ground, wind stands for a lady. Cobweb cradles; [oth. writ.] (Rain Crow), (Glass Cradle), (The Baby Sitter Green), Bell Tree (The Window Diane), Golden Crown Rose), (The Inn), (Broken Angels) Little Corn - Little Baskets), (Happy Ending) The Five and (Dime Palace), (Lonely Is Wind's Companion) (Baby Shirley Temple) Society/What's Round Becomes A Crown; [pers.] (Ho-bo Angel) (White Cap Mountains) (Henrietta Brown) Ain't Nothing Like the Real Thing (Madam Sin) Woo Singwood (Wild Flower Fences) I believe for every drop of rain a flower grows. And all the stars are mine and their all yours to, and it cost not a penny. Amen.; [a.] Aurora, IL

**TAYLOR, MARLA A.**
[b.] April 5, 1961, Boston, MA; [p.] Bernard and Gloria Taylor; [m.] James E. Goodwin, August 8, 1991; [ed.] Thomas Woolton High, Montgomery College; [occ.] Office Manager; [pers.] My writing Usually reflects the common bond that all people share. All of us wish and work for a measure of happiness and are equally deserving of it! Take what you need and leave some for others.; [a.] Gaithersburg, MD

**TAYLOR, MONIQUE SHERYLLE LAGARDE**
[pen.] Nique; [b.] Michigan; [p.] Leonard and Theodosia LaGarde; [m.] Bradley K. Taylor, April 25, 1986; [ch.] Tenisha Montae, Bradley Leonard, MonteSha Sade Lenora, Brandon Amos, Montez, and Monique Amaris; [ed.] Shrine of the Little flower High School - Royal Oak MI - College-Wayne State University Detroit, MI "Senior"; [occ.] Domestic Engineer; [memb.] Precious

Blood Church-former member of Detroit Jaycees-Member of Parental Volunteers-MBS Training Center-Oak Park MI; [hon.] Honor Student at Shrine High, President of The Kiswahili Club at Wayne State University; [oth. writ.] Several other writings-written for special occasions - specialize in personalizing poetry for any given situation or event. Locally known for writing talent.; [pers.] For all that I have - I give thanks to God who is above. The real blessing is to realize that it is he who gives you talent and unconditional love.; [a.] Oak Park, MI

**TAYLOR, PHELON R.**
[b.] January 20, 1977, Columbia, SC; [p.] Robert L. and Patricia B. Taylor; [ed.] 1995 Graduate Elkins High School Missouri City, Texas; [occ.] Student; [memb.] DECA, Fort Bend County Teen Court; [oth. writ.] A book of poetry titled "From the Inside Looking Out", currently unpublished; [pers.] I would like to thank God for the gift, my parents, and my teachers at the progressive High School, especially Mr. Vernon Rusher and Kathryn Raeke, I wrote "Questions from a Soldier" for a 10th grade History Class.; [a.] Missouri City, TX

**TAYLOR, TAMIKO SHUNTA WILLIAMS**
[pen.] Mickey; [b.] June 4, 1968, Chicago, IL; [p.] Willie T. Williams and Mary D. Williams; [m.] Mitchell D. Taylor, August 1, 1990; [ch.] Nyisha Nichol, Sharonda Shawayne, Jonathon Mathew, Josef Donte, Jamia Cassara, and Shakiela Maryanna.; [ed.] John D. Shoop, Roseland Community High.; [occ.] Artist, homemaker; [memb.] Greater Bethany Church of Los Angeles Writer's Guild.; [oth. writ.] Several poems and songs and children's melodies with some poems written in Christian news letters and pamphlets.; [pers.] I strive to touch the world with the flavor of feeling. I am greatly influenced by songwriters a poets of old, and I get my inspiration from God. I reach deep with in me to pour out to others the things God put in my heart that we all can discover.; [a.] Long Beach, CA

**TEASDALE, STEPHANIE**
[b.] June 7, 1980, Plattsburgh, NY; [p.] Matthew and Valerie Teasdale; [ed.] Presently in 10th grade; [hon.] Young Author's Contest in Elementary School. (1st place); [oth. writ.] Numerous poems; [pers.] I wrote this poem after my mother died of cancer 1 week before my 15th birthday. She was truly one of the greatest woman alive to deal with a terminal illness and me at the same time. This poem is dedicated in her memory.; [a.] Helotes, TX

**TEMBO, MASIYE**
[pen.] Masiye Faiton Tembo; [b.] April 16, 1959, Bulawayo, Zimbabwe; [p.] Fainess Gumbo and Faiton Tembo; [m.] Dorcas Dube Tembo; [ch.] David, Chelesile, Shayne and Yuyani Tembo; [ed.] Mpopoma High School, Bulawayo, Zimbabwe; [occ.] Residential Counselor, Vinfen Corporation, Somerville MA; [oth. writ.] Several unpublished poems, 'Wrath of the Evil Spirit' - Novel just recently finished, not yet forwarded to publishers.; [pers.] My writings are aimed at reflecting my feelings and experiences I've had with people and mother nature. My wife, Dorcas, has been my greatest inspiration.; [a.] Chelsea, MA

**TERRILL, JACEY**
[b.] December 28, 1981, Iowa City; [p.] Tate and Deborah Terrill; [ed.] West Middle School 8th grade; [occ.] Volunteer at Bethesda Care Center; [memb.] YWCA; [oth. writ.] None that have been published.; [a.] Muscatine, IA

**TERRY, LARRY**
[pen.] Larry Terry; [b.] August 8, 1968; [p.] Laurence and Pearl Terry; [ed.] Berklee College of Music Professional Music Composition; [occ.] Musician/Songwriter; [hon.] VW-Greenbay Jazz Festival, National Cultural Afro-Academic Technological and Scientific Olympics, Berklee College Scholarship, Black Youth Achievement Award Library of Poetry/Congress Publications; [oth. writ.] Songs When We Met We're Much The Same, If We Care, Drives Me Crazy, I Just Think About You, I Don't Even Know Your Name; [pers.] Regardless of our status or position in life, we're all much the same. There's so much to share with and learn from each other.; [a.] Cambridge, MA

**TEVOROGER, EILEEN BONNIE**
[b.] February 2, 1945, Bronx, NY; [p.] Lila and Edward Valentine; [m.] Bruce Frederick Two-Roger, June 26, 1977; [ed.] Rancho High School Graduate Las Vegas, NV, West LA College, Mt. San Antonio College. Walnut Calif. Dale Carnegie Graduate; [occ.] Housewife; [memb.] F.O.T.O. (Member Friends of the (Griffith) Observatory). National Audubon Society.; [hon.] High School Grad. Diploma Dale Carnegie Graduate Diploma, second place for "Titus and Ondronicus" Rancho High School "Miss Better Posture" Miss Lake Mead 92, one of 12 Runners up in Miss Teen age America 1960; [oth. writ.] "The Sea of Fantasy", "My Love is Like the Rain", "I Touched Your Lightning Rod", "Ever So Gently", "I Can't Give if You Won't Take It"; [a.] Burbank, CA

**THACKER, BEULAH A.**
[b.] March 24, 1907, Belington, WV; [p.] Francis and Roberta Thacker; [m.] Single; [ed.] Free School, Buckhannon High, West Virginia Wesleyan College, Buckhannon, W.V. Post Graduate Work at Catholic U., Washington, D.C.; [occ.] Retired Teacher; [memb.] Catholic Church Md. and W.V. Retired Teachers Assn. WV Artists and Craftsmans Guild Barbour County Retired School Employs W.V. Historical Society, A.A.R.P. National Library of Poetry; [hon.] Diplomas - Certificates Pins from Catholic Secular Society and ISP Membership; [oth. writ.] Hester - Libretto based on Scarlet Letter, Children's stories on Nature—"Woolly Bear's Sleeping Bag." House hunting Honey Bees, Sneaky Slinkeys" Breakfast, more stories - several poems and meditations.; [pers.] My children's stories, are may way to help the little ones to enjoy nature. We must love nature and God's way of creating. I spend much time in hand weaving for new designs and reproduce old patterns.; [a.] Philippi, WV

**THAMES, STEPHEN A.**
[pen.] Andrew James; [b.] June 25, 1955, Cortland, NY; [p.] Ray C. and Mary B. Thames; [occ.] Unemployed Musician/Writer.; [oth. writ.] One Record Album and a non-published book of poems.

**THOMAS, BARBARA**
[pen.] Otoe-Missourian Tribe; [b.] February 5, 1936, Fort Yuma, CA; [p.] Mr. and Mrs. Melvin Stanley; [m.] Marvin D. Thomas, April 4, 1973; [ch.] Cheryl Clark, Valerie Clark, Dereck Clark, Kevin Clark, Cyleste Clark; [ed.] 12th grade and self taught; [occ.] Minerpick and Shovel, Retired-Occupation above; [memb.] Mining organization, people for the West N.I.A. and Mother Lode; [hon.] Several, Awards World of Poetry, Honorable Mention, Motorcyle-Enjoy-20 years Mostly in World Poetry, Songs in Progress with Ramsey Kearney; [oth. writ.] The National Library of Poetry World of Poetry Mountain Messenger-Article Poem, Songs Composer, Hollywood Artists Record Hilltop Records, Mountain Messenger Song Writer.; [pers.] If I can touch a Persons heart with one word what a wonderful world in sharing poetry. Inspired by

Shakespere.; [a.] Downieville, CA

**THOMAS, KATHLEEN W.**
[b.] August 24, 1894, Georgia; [p.] John and Creasy Williams; [m.] Willis Franklin Thomas, July 3, 1910; [ch.] Eleven - raised ten grown; [ed.] Common School, 7th Grade; [memb.] Baptist Church, Council on Aging.; [hon.] Oldest in my Church- Their charter member and 1st Pianist 8 yrs.; [oth. writ.] We were married 62 years, lived thru 2 World Wars and the Great depression raising a family at same time, next week - unable to do any

**THOMAS, PAULINE**
[pen.] Pauline Hamilton; [b.] April 16, 1962, Jamaica, WI; [p.] Daisy and Fredrick Sealey; [ed.] Bayridge High School; [occ.] Hair Dresser; [oth. writ.] Several Poem's but none have been published; [pers.] Hold on to your dream and keep believing in your self. Because dream do come true if you hold to that dream

**THOMAS, SHIRLEY A.**
[b.] November 25, 1935, B'ham, AL; [p.] Willis and Macie Wordell; [m.] Bruce Thomas, July 7, 1954; [ch.] Connie, Kelly, Terry; [ed.] BA Birmingham Southern College MS Samford University; [occ.] Kindergarten Teacher - Pleasant Grove Elementary; [memb.] Alpha Lambda Delta Hon Soc. Phi Sigma - Honor Society Kappa Delta Epsilon - Prof. Ed. Soc. Kappa Delta Pi - Honor Society Kappa Delta Pi Honor Society Kappa Phi Kappa - Honor Society Alpha Delta Kappa - Honorary Sorority for women educators; [hon.] Summa Cum Laude - B'Ham Southern Col. Outstanding Graduate Student - Samford U.; [oth. writ.] Poems, songs, none published; [pers.] My poetry comes from my heart based on my life experiences.; [a.] Pleasant Grove, AL

**THOMAS JR., JESSE**
[pen.] Jess, Jay, Jacob; [b.] November 7, 1982, Dunkirk, NY; [p.] Bernice and Jesse Thomas Sr.; [ed.] E.C.C. #36 (Kiato-2nd qt.) H.B.B.A. #76 (3-8th) (present education); [memb.] Buffalo pred. search F.H.A. (Community Service Club) Medic Club, President of Student Govt., class president, student representative on (School) sire-based Management Team, Treasures of, N.J.H.S; [hon.] More honor Roll every marking period, Highest 7th average Highest math S.A.T., F.H.A. award (Community Service Award), elected in to (N.J.H.S.) National Junior Honor Society; [oth. writ.] Black American, Beautiful (in Ehallenger), Freedoms Journey (short story) poems, End of Time, Life, Love, Forest, and Butterfly; [pers.] I worked hard to accomplish my goals and regret a good head on my shoulders, to do this you must have a good attitude and personality which established by emotional expressions. I feel through poems people can express feelings.; [a.] Buffalo, NY

**THOMPSON, DAVE**
[b.] October 10, 1978, Red Wing, MN; [p.] Stuart and Michelle Thompson; [ed.] Junior at Hastings Senior High School; [memb.] Thespian, Youth Planning Council; [oth. writ.] Hastings Raider's Digest Las Printed some of my poems.; [pers.] People should show their true selves because it's better for other to accept you for who you are then who you pretend to be.; [a.] Hastings, MN

**THOMPSON, JANA**
[b.] September 12, 1978, Columbus, OH; [p.] Ray and Barbara Thompson; [ed.] Bexley High School my Last year - yeh!; [occ.] Student; [memb.] Eastern Paralyzed Veterans Association Cantor at Saint Catherine's Parish - Columbus Youth Chorale; [hon.] Who's Who Among American High School, Students member of Carnegie Hall Collegiate Choral-Omea state convention Superior violin soloist Chicago's Consortium Hon-

ors Choir Soloist; [oth. writ.] Published every year in school's Lamplight magazine poems published also in Illiad Press Inspirations and 1992 Anthology of poetry by young Americans.; [pers.] Music, Art, and Literature should move a people so deeply they are disoriented and enchanted all at once.; [a.] Bexley, OH

**THOMPSON, JOSEPH M.**
[b.] March 26, 1946, Mesa, AZ; [p.] Bill Thompson and Barbara Western Thompson; [m.] Marilyn Miller Thompson, April 23, 1971; [ch.] Joseph, Jared, Lisa, Matthew, Tamma, Aaron; [ed.] A.S.U.; [occ.] Cannery Field Representative L.D.S. Welfare Services S.L.C. Utah; [oth. writ.] Introduction to republished edition of "The Strength of Being Clean" by David Starr Jordan.; [pers.] I am not a poet. I merely listened to the spirit and recorded its whisperings.; [a.] South Jordan, UT

**THORNBURG, GINGER COOPER**
[b.] June 24, 1962, Welch, WV; [p.] Harry and Mary Cooper; [m.] Timothy P. Thornburg, June 18, 1994; [ed.] Mt. View High School, Welch, WV Bluefield State College, Bluefield, WV Central Piedmont Comm. College, Charlotte, NC; [occ.] Inventory Control Clerk; [memb.] Women's Auxiliary of (VFW) Veterans of Foreign Wars Mecklenburg Public Library, Charlotte, NC Union County Public Library, Monroe, NC; [oth. writ.] Several poems published in my high school paper.; [pers.] I make myself take one day at a time. There is no such a thing as luck, everything is in God's hands.; [a.] Indian Trail, NC

**THORPE, JENNIFER IRENE**
[pen.] Jenny Irene; [b.] October 31, 1978, Cincinnati, OH; [p.] Shawn and Debbie Thorpe; [ed.] Ridgedale High School Marion Ohio; [occ.] High School Student; [memb.] SADD, Spanish Club, FFA 4-H, Student Council, Fellowship of Christian Athletes.; [hon.] Academic Honor Roll, Governors Award-Litter Prevention, FFA Greenhand Award, "Who's Who Among American High School Student's", Second Team all Conference in Cross Country.; [oth. writ.] Non-Published; [a.] Marion, OH

**THOUSAND, TINA MARIE DRAKE**
[b.] October 13, 1972; [p.] Melvin and Rebecca Drake; [m.] Christopher Thousand, June 27, 1992; [ch.] Jonathan Joshua Thousand; [pers.] This poem was inspired by a lifelong friendship with my best friend, Melissa Reynolds; [a.] Pulaski, NY

**THURMAN, RUTH H.**
[pen.] Ruth Charlton, Ruth Richey, Ruth Thurman; [b.] March 30, 1920, Washington, AK; [p.] William and Emma Rust; [m.] Donald Thurman (Deceased), Wm. Richey (Deceased), Donald Thurman (Deceaded), 1940, 1966, 1973; [ch.] Pamela Charlton (Deceased); [ed.] Commerce High School, Portland, OR, Williams-Tholen Music School; [occ.] Former member of Advertising and Sales Promotion Dept., Hyster Co., Executive Secretary, Paul Hayden Kirk, FAIA, Court Secretary, King County Superior Court (Seattle), Edgar Freed, Atty., Portland, Retired-To Sun City, Arizona; [memb.] Legal Secretaries, Women in Construction, Presbyterian Church of Laurelhurst Program Committee, YMCA Cardiac Program; [hon.] Various Piano Competitions AT&T Competition with women in Construction - Slogan Winner; [oth. writ.] Poems published in church publications, also Hyster House Organ; [pers.] Writing is my lifeline; [a.] Sun City, AZ

**TIBBITS, DAN**
[b.] February 15, 1967, San Bernardino, CA; [p.] Jack and Jean Tibbitts; [m.] (Engaged) Roseann Black; [ed.] Sierra High School; [occ.] Ceramic Tile Setter; [oth. writ.] Several other poems, this is the first I've had

published.; [pers.] It's an honor to share my innermost feelings through my poetry

**TICE, BRADLEY S.**
[b.] October 6, 1959, Palo Alto, CA; [p.] L. T. Tice and Paula N. Tice; [ed.] B. A. History (1987) San Jose State University.; [occ.] Director of Research Pacific Language Institute; [memb.] The Japan Association of Language Teachers. International Society of Poets 1994-1995.; [hon.] Editors's Choice Award 1995. Citation and 3 Honorable Mentions in "Poet's at Work".; [oth. writ.] Chapbook titled "Suburban White" The Plowman Ministries, (Ontario, Canada).; [pers.] Poetry is the bridge to the human soul.; [a.] Cupertino, CA

**TILLMAN, JOHN**
[pen.] John Tillman; [b.] February 27, 1965, Chicago, IL; [p.] Bedie Tillman, Sonny Anderson; [ed.] Manley High, Saint Louis University; [occ.] Theatre actor, Rizing Stars Ensemble, Chicago, Ill.; [memb.] Amnesty International J.C. Productions; [hon.] Betta Gamma Beta; [oth. writ.] A completed screenplay, a stage play that's currently in production.; [pers.] I strive to employ subtle imagery and crisp language to paint a rich canvas of feelings and experiences in my writing.; [a.] Chicago, IL

**TLUCEK, JENNIFER**
[pen.] Fer; [b.] February 2, 1982, Dallas, TX; [p.] Ronald and Michelle Tlucek; [ed.] Seagoville Middle School Student (8th grade); [memb.] Student Council President, As I gymnastics, Highland oaks church of Christ; [hon.] Sports, Softball, bowling and soccer. Also, A.B. Honor roll all year award.; [pers.] This poem was my first I've ever written and I wanted to dedicate it to jody cash. He is my first love.; [a.] Seagoville, TX

**TOMAN, TERRY JOHN**
[b.] April 23, 1952, Louisville, KY; [p.] John and Ruoelle Toman; [ed.] B.S. University of Illinois 1974; [occ.] Real Estate Consultant; [memb.] Appraisal Institute (MAI) University of Illinois contributing Dawn; [a.] Newport Beach, CA

**TOOLEY, JEWEL I.**
[pen.] Jean; [b.] Hillview, IL; [p.] John and Anita Baze; [m.] John Tooley, April 16, 1938; [ch.] Three children; [occ.] Retired Nurse; [oth. writ.] I have been honored for the care and time spent on the comforts of others in my work.; [oth. writ.] One published song - fifteen poems; [pers.] When my days work is done and I have time to pick up my pen, I thank the higher powers that gave me this small gift of putting words together.; [a.] Decatur, IL

**TORRES, SANTIAGO**
[b.] January 15, 1964, New York, NY; [p.] Eva Gali and Santiago Torres Sr.; [ch.] Shana Geneva Torres; [occ.] Paraprofessional; [pers.] I try to write about love a lot. In this crazy world it seems like a lot of people have forgotten about it. Be it love for your child, spouse, parents or oneself.; [a.] Bronx, NY

**TOULSON, CHRISTINA**
[pen.] Molly Faith; [b.] October 5, 1974, Virginia; [m.] Ryan R. Anderson; [ed.] Woodstown High School 1993 Salem Community College 1994, Wilma Boyd Career School 1995.; [occ.] Freelance Writer, Reinesaunce Faire, Student; [memb.] International Society of Poets; [hon.] Lonely field National Library of Poetry Best Poets 95; [oth. writ.] Forever Love, Nat'l Lib of Poetry, Tree Salem Sunbeam, Dawn, Sparrowgrass Poetry Forum "Poetic voices of America Summer 1995"; [pers.] Those who step back from life make their dreams come true, so step back and tell me what you see. This Poem "Immortal Angel" is in memory of my grand father my

muse forever. Captain Harry Toulson may your ferry boat in Heaven glide on smooth waters, I love you!; [a.] Alloway, NJ

**TOWBER, SUZANNE M.**
[b.] October 23, 1939, NYC; [p.] Easter McQueen, C. M. Overmiller; [ch.] Samuel, Mary, Margaret; [ed.] H. S. Grad.; [occ.] Packer of Envelopes; [memb.] St. Cecelia's R.C. Church, AARP; [oth. writ.] I have been writing and composing since childhood! This is the first time I have submitted anything for publication; [pers.] I am inspired by the muse of poetry. She dictates and I write down.; [a.] Coatesville, PA

**TRAVIS, MR. BERDYNE D.**
[pen.] Bernie Travis; [b.] November 30, 1919, Michigan; [p.] Grover and Etta Travis; [m.] Helena M., August 16, 1964; [ch.] Daniel and Daniel Marlene, Carolyn, Barbara; [occ.] Retired: Formerly was Director of Purchases for Frigidaire; [oth. writ.] 110 poems but none submitted for publishing until 'Windows of the Soul'. Many of my verse have a humorous trend. We need smiles.; [pers.] A veteran of WW II in Africa and Italy.; [a.] Argyle, TX

**TRIPLETT, JORY SHEPHERD**
[pen.] Jori St. Claire; [b.] February 2, 1970, Purlear, NC; [p.] John and Judy Triplett; [m.] Patrick Wayne Triplett, September 3, 1988; [ch.] Jamie Nicole Triplett; [ed.] West Wilkes High School; [occ.] Administrative Assistant Carolina Mirror Company, N. Wilkesboro, NC; [pers.] Having been raised in the midst of God's splendor in the heart of the Blue Bridge Mountains, the natural beauty that surrounds me is my greatest inspiration.; [a.] Purlear, NC

**TROBAUGH, DESIREE L.**
[b.] April 16, 1978, Saint Paul, MN; [p.] Ric Trobaugh and Barb Trobaugh; [ed.] Richfield Sr. High School, Roseville Area High School.; [occ.] Student.; [hon.] This is an Honor and Award to me in my life.; [oth. writ.] Several poems unpublished and many letters.; [pers.] I would like to thank my father who believed in me. To my grandpa, Uncle Kipp and Godfather Jack, who showed me a great friendship. I don't know where I would be today, if it wasn't for all of them. To all of the people who had someone close die, I know what your going through. Keep your heads up!; [a.] Roseville, MN

**TROUPE, DEBORAH L.**
[b.] April 13, 1954, Aberdeen, MD; [p.] Beverly McAfoose and David A. Vord; [m.] Thomas R. Troupe, October 20, 1990; [ch.] Kristi Lee Waterloo, Michael Robert Waterloo, Ryan Thomas Troupe; [ed.] Kiski Arca High School, Franco Beauty Academy; [occ.] Mother Homemaker, Recording Secretary Hawthorn Area Water Authority; [oth. writ.] Personal poetry for members of my family. A Children's Story written for my oldest son, none of which have been published as of yet.; [pers.] I am drawn to especially write about relationships, particularly about my family members, as a tribute to their unconditional love and acceptance of my self and each other"; [a.] Fairmount City, PA

**TROYER, MARTHA**
[pen.] Marti Troyer; [b.] August 7, 1967, Marysville, OH; [p.] Andrew and Barbara Kurtz; [m.] Joe Troyer, March 10, 1990; [ch.] Paige Nicole; [ed.] Riverview High School, Manatee Community College; [occ.] Office Manager; [memb.] Ashton Mennonite Church; [oth. writ.] Song lyrics, a short story submitted for publication; [pers.] Thank you to my family for their belief in me and encouragement; [a.] Sarasota, FL

**TRUJILLO, VICTOR**
[pen.] Tesco; [b.] January 1, 1976, NYC; [ed.] West Side High, City College of N.Y.; [occ.] Poet, Student, Stock Invester.; [memb.] M.R.; [hon.] Head of Student Gov't., Dean's List, Mediator.; [oth. writ.] Many more poems to be published soon.; [pers.] You'll always have a yesterday, so make today worth it. A man who doesn't spend time with his family, isn't a man.; [a.] Bronx, NY

**TUCKER, CATHERINE**
[pen.] Celeste Montgomery; [b.] November 19, 1982, Summit, NJ; [p.] Tony Tucker, Maisie Tucker; [ed.] Rutgers Preparatory School; [occ.] Student; [hon.] Math, English, Science, History, Spanish, Latin (Honor Roll); [oth. writ.] Various, unpublished poems and short stories; [pers.] Everything's I write comes from my heart. Nothing that I write contains violence of any sort; [a.] Bridgewater, NJ

**TUCKER, RHONDA**
[b.] December 25, 1962, Little Rock, AR; [p.] Ronald and Pat Morris; [m.] Glenn Tucker, August 18, 1990; [ch.] Samuel Morris Tucker; [ed.] Lee County Senior High School Sanford, North Carolina Sandhills Community College Pinehurst NC; [occ.] Medical Laboratory Technician; [oth. writ.] Wrote poems in school - never published; [pers.] Life's greatest treasures are children. My treasure is Sam; [a.] Jacksonville, NC

**TUCKER JR., CHARLES D.**
[pen.] Charles D. Tucker Jr.; [b.] November 2, 1963, Sarasota, FL; [p.] Bert and Ginger Black Welder; [m.] Lisa Ann Tucker, June 3, 1994; [ch.] 3 Step Sons Jacob, Josh, and Travis; [ed.] Grad. Ft. Meade High Sch. 1 year vocational school auto body. 6 years National Guard-Track Vehicle Mechanic. Every minute of every day.; [occ.] Self-employed deck and Residential Framer, Custom, Aluminum Installer.; [oth. writ.] None published.; [pers.] If you were only here, so I could show you what a man you made out of me. Daddy! Rest in Peace Herbert Albritti Sr.; [a.] Fort Meade, FL

**TULLY, JACK**
[b.] February 22, 1960, Queens; [p.] Thomas and Ruth Tully; [ed.] Brentwood High Suffolk County Community College; [occ.] Technician for Nortel Communication Systems; [pers.] Try every thing, even if think you can't, try anyway. Go everywhere, talk to a stranger, learn. Participate. Live life, remove "hate" from your vocabulary and love all things.; [a.] Smithtown, NY

**TUPPER, JEAN LORRAINE**
[b.] October 19, 1938, Boston, MA; [p.] Arnold and Dorothea Schaier; [m.] Russel Tupper, August 23, 1964; [ch.] Nancy Lincoln; [ed.] Norwood High, B.S. Simmons College MA. Central Ct. State Univ.; [occ.] Poet, Writer; [memb.] Ct. Poetry Society Mass. State Poetry Soc. Member of Woodthrush poets (8 published poets - present poems in libraries, bookstores, schools, around new England); [hon.] Listed in a directory of American poets and fiction writers featured on "Art space" a local TV show and guest speaker for book local clubs published in southern poetry rev, The Worcester Review, Blue Unicorn, and other Literary Journals; [pers.] My poetry is people-oriented if poetry can be compared with painting, I am more into "portraits" than Landscapes.; [a.] Wrentham, MA

**TURNBULL, TARA ANN**
[b.] July 8, 1980, Overland Park, KS; [p.] Danial and Cheryl Turnbull; [ed.] Ed Tech Academy - Olathe, Kansas Grade 9; [occ.] Student; [pers.] I would like to acknowledge Kelley Freund, my English teacher, for introducing me to Poetry, and encouraging me to submit this poem. This poem is dedicated to Kelley Freund.; [a.] Lenexa, KS

**TURNER, PATRICIA A. MCALPIN**
[b.] February 10, 1958, Fort Worth, TX; [p.] W. H. and Laura McAlpin; [m.] Chris S. Turner, August 5, 1989; [ed.] Duncanville High School Duncanville, Texas graduated 1976, Mt. View Community College-Dallas, Tex. 1977-79 Assoc. In Arts and Sciences, U.T. Arlington-Music performance Maj. Music Educ. 1979-83; [occ.] Private flute and piano instructor, also employed at Morton H. Meyerson Symphony Center in Dallas, Texas Asst. in Dallas Sym. Music Library; [memb.] Tau Beta Sigma National Honorary Band Sorority Texas Bandmasters Association, Texas Music Educ. Assoc. 1st United Methodist Church of Denton TX. Chancel Choir Denton Community Band, Texas Flute Society; [hon.] Music Scholarships to U.T. Arlington and Dallas Baptist University (1976-77) played for Dallas Federation of Music Teachers, Honors Day Recitals of Comm. Collose, sang with the Dallas symphony orchestra, winner of all District Music Competition for Dallas County Community Coll. Distin. 1983; [oth. writ.] Wrote articles for Jr. Hi and Hi School Newspapers, Article printed in Dallas Morning News (1995); [pers.] We Need to seek the beauty and good in those around us. Race, religion and other beliefs should be respected and those things that make us unique should be cherished because life is short and should not be wasted.; [a.] Sanger, TX

**TURNER, PAULINE A.**
[b.] March 28, 1912, Rocky Ford, CO; [p.] George and Catherine Schafer; [m.] Carl E. Turner, March 17, 1933; [ch.] Norman, Loretta, Carol, Jack, Larry and Elma; [ed.] Swink High School graduate of 1932. I've been in to 3 class reunions in Colo. in 1985-87 and 89.; [occ.] Retired and Volunteer at H. Louis Lake Senior Center; [memb.] Orange County R.S.V.P. A.A.R.P. #1639, Nat. and Garden Grove, CA I've done volunteer work at H. L. Lake Senior Ctr Ing. G. for 18 years and earned my 5000 hrs pin and disc. June 28, 1994; [hon.] Earned many pins and awards certificates from H.L. Lake Sr. Ctr. and R.S.V.P. in the last 18 yrs. I also formed a Chorale Singing Group in 1985 known as the "Young at Heart Singers". Also first 3 entries sent to the National Library of Poetry; [oth. writ.] "The Tiny Little Stranger", "Dance on the Horizon", As the Train Passed By" in "After the Storm", "Song of Eternal Praise" in "Best Poems of 1995", "Long Ago and Far Away" in "Windows of the soul" Thank you!; [pers.] I'm honored in life "Be True to Yourself" and "Follow the Golden Rule". I was encouraged by my 7 and 8th grade teacher (Lucinda Lauth) she was a great poet and influenced my life.; [a.] Garden Grove, CA

**TURZYNSKI, LINDA J.**
[b.] July 20, 1957, New Jersey; [p.] Stephen Turzynski, Jean Turzynski; [ch.] Mark Samuel; [ed.] Rutgers University; [oth. writ.] Critical Studies of Lucky Aikin, Chretien De Troyes, Wolfram Von Eschenbach, John Webster; [a.] North Brunswick, NJ

**TWARDY, JILL C.**
[b.] October 8, 1967, Albany, NY; [p.] Carole and Frederick Twardy; [ed.] B.A. - Fordham College of Fordham University Graduate School of Arts and Sciences; [occ.] Communications Assistant for the Albany Colonie Regional Chamber of Commerce; [memb.] Children, Green peace, Wolf Haven International; [hon.] Presidential Scholar, Phi Beta Kappa, Phi Kappa Phi, Deans List; [oth. writ.] Unpublished poems and short stories.; [pers.] Poetry truly is a window of the soul. Thanks to Miss Newton for bringing out the writer in me and allowing the light to shine through.; [a.] Waterford, NY

**TYNES, CLAUDIA N.**
[b.] September 30, 1950, Surry, VA; [p.] Edgar (Deceased) and Shirley Newby; [m.] James P. Tynes, February 27, 1971; [ch.] Rodney D. Tynes; [ed.] Westside High School, LOGOS International Bible College Institute of Children's Literature; [occ.] Freelance Writer, Staff (Free Gospel Deliverance Temple); [memb.] Literature Ministry Prayer, Fellowship (Ethel Herr), Free Gospel Deliverance Temple (Dr. Ralph Green), Church Writing Group (Amy Foundation); [hon.] Special Achievement and Performance Awards (Federal Gov't.); [oth. writ.] Several articles published in church newsletter (The Apostolic Voice). Devotions (The Upper Room) under consideration for publication. Writer for Local Church Ministry, Poem published in Yearbook Christian Academy.; [pers.] I came to "Serve" My duty is to "serve." In order to be like Jesus I must "serve".; [a.] Clinton, MD

**UHANE, NANCY**
[pen.] Whitefire; [b.] Phila, PA; [ed.] St. Mary's Academy (high school) Gwynedd Mercy College; [occ.] Personal Manager to Rock Guitarist Jimmie King, Stress Management Counselor for Women.; [hon.] Twice from World of Poetry in 1980's; [oth. writ.] In World of Poetry Anthology "Great Poems of The Western World."; [a.] Doylestown, PA

**UMEDA, JON**
[pen.] J. T. Umeda; [b.] August 9, 1965, Montebello, CA; [p.] James and Eloise Umeda; [ed.] Cal State University, Los Angeles Institute of Children's Literature; [occ.] Accountant, Los Angeles Fire Dept; [memb.] Los County Asian - American Association; [hon.] Third place 8th Grade Book Writing Contest; [pers.] Write what you see, without the sugar coating. Follow no one but yourself.; [a.] San Gabriel, CA

**URFER, BRADLEY A.**
[b.] May 11, 1969; [p.] Tex and Constance Urfer; [ed.] Belleville High School UW - Stevens Point MATC Madison WI; [occ.] Service Tech. Dolphin Pools and Spas; [a.] Belleville, WI

**URQUHART, RICHARD C.**
[b.] October 12, 1928, Kooskia, ID; [p.] Mr. J. C. Urquhart, Mrs. Frances MacDorman Urquhart; [ed.] Bachelor of Arts in Journalism University of Montana 1952; [occ.] Retired; [memb.] Commanders Club of the Disabled American Veterans The American Legion American Assoc. Retired Persons; [a.] Milwaukie, OR

**VALENTINE, BEVERLY**
[b.] April 25, 1942, Lafayette, IN; [p.] Clarence (Jack) and Marjorie Green; [m.] James B. Valentine; [ch.] 3 daughters; [ed.] County College of Morris Randolph, NJ., California State University; [occ.] Hypotherapist; [memb.] Poetry Society of New Hampshire, National Guild of Hypnotists, American Council Hypnotists Examiners; [oth. writ.] Several others poems; [pers.] Poetry is the result of my mind listening to my heart and soul. It is an expression of harmony my body, mind and spirit.; [a.] Nashua, NH

**VALLIERE, DENNIS P.**
[b.] May 24, 1956, Methven, MA; [p.] June and Bernard Valliere; [m.] Denise Marion, August 2, 1982; [ch.] David and Joshua; [occ.] Computer Support Specialist; [a.] Pelham, NH

**VALLOT, MORIAL BRICE**
[b.] December 16, 1982, Abbeville, LA; [p.] William and Norma Vallot; [ed.] 7th Grade Student Earth Middle School, Earth, LA; [occ.] Helps out on weekends on his (father's) sugar cane farm; [memb.] St. Therese's Church Altar server vice president-student council 7th grade, 4

year - piano student (Marilyn's Studio) School Band E.M.S., Vermillion Parish Youth Basketball, Geographic World; [hon.] Student of the year Bath School and Parish, Elocution, Science Social Studies, Louisiana Music Teachers Association - All Superior 4 yrs. - piano, poem "Daylight" published in The American Academy of Poetry School's young author's winner, honor band, 6 yr. honor student; [oth. writ.] Poem "Daylight" 1st place young author's contest, also published in the American Academy of Poetry. "Fishing" 3rd place young author's "Math" 2nd place young author's "God Everybody's Friend"; [pers.] I write because I have been influenced by the joys in life, the fears of life and the understanding of life. When write poetry I feel part of that is life.; [a.] Earth, LA

**VALQUETTE, MARIE**
[pen.] August 20, 1945, Joplin, MO; [m.] John S. Lear, Jr., December 18, 1993; [ch.] Marc A. Jeffers, Michael F. Jeffers; [ed.] Yorktown High, N.O.V.A. College; [occ.] Astrologer/writer; [memb.] The University of Science and Philosophy of Swannonoa; [hon.] Dean's List, Scholarship; [oth. writ.] Novel's Catalyst for Evil, The Spiral Stairs, Compilation of Poems, The Book of Destiny; [pers.] In my writings I attempt to portray that when laws of man fail to bring justice, universal Law will prevail.; [a.] Reston, VA

**VAN WAGONER, ROBERT**
[b.] November 4, 1961, Tucson, AZ; [p.] Dan and Sharon Van Wagoner; [ch.] Elizabeth Van Wagoner; [ed.] Rineon High School; [occ.] Pressman State of the Art Graphics Escondido, CA; [memb.] North County Alano Club Oside, CA; [pers.] One day at a time; [a.] Oside, CA

**VANCE, ELAINE I.**
[pen.] Lane; [b.] November 15, 1941, Georgia; [p.] George Thornton Vance, Inez Vance Wingard; [m.] Divorced; [ch.] Elaena M. Faraino, Berryman Allen Meherg Jr., Mark Chadler, Meherg; [ed.] A. L. Miller H. S. for girls and Wesleyan College for Women in Macon, GA; [occ.] Office Manager with Quick stop, Inc. Volunteer for Hospice, First United Methodist Church; [pers.] Poetry answers my need to verbalize my reflection of my journey to myself using God's gift to me.; [a.] Fayette, AL

**VANDER BOOM, BEVERLY**
[pen.] Randi Rivers; [b.] August 25, 1959, Jacksonville, FL; [p.] Harold and Frances Wilson; [ch.] Rachel 4 years, Jeremiah 2 years; [ed.] Currently attending College of Southern Idaho Studying prerequisites for Registered Nursing; [occ.] Full-time student and mother; [memb.] 94/95 President of Omicron Xi-CSI Chapter of Phi Theta Kappa. Member of National Student Nurse's Association. Idaho Writers' League.; [hon.] CSI President's List, National Dean's List; [oth. writ.] This is my first widely published work. I also have a song at the Idaho Historical Society Museum:" Idaho, Let's Celebrate" - Centennial Song Contest.; [pers.] I have recently focused my writing on what I love: the unusual and the macabre. My greatest influences: Edgar Allan Poe and Sylvia Plath.; [a.] Twin Falls, ID

**VANDER SCHAAF JR., DEREK J.**
[pen.] Vandy; [b.] December 7, 1968, Alexandria, VA; [p.] Derek Vander Schaaf Sr. and Karen Vander Schaaf; [ed.] JEB Stuart High, University Of South Dakota; [occ.] Editorial Assistant Business Publishers Inc.; [pers.] I don't believe in sugar-coating things in my writing. Some may call me a pessimist but I simply try to call 'em like I see 'em.; [a.] Falls Church, VA

**VANDERHOOF, VICKIE L.**
[b.] April 10, 1954, Indiana, PA; [p.] Russell James Vanderhoof, Myra Bell Lowry Vanderhoof; [ed.] University of Pittsburgh B. A. Major Speech Theatre Arts, Minor English Lit., Tri-state Business Institute-diploma, Computer Programing, Operations; [occ.] Parental caretaker, Freelance Clerical, Writer, Crafter; [memb.] Distinguished Member of the International Society of Poets; [oth. writ.] Poetry published by the National Library of Poetry - Anthologies, At Water's Edge, Beyond the Stars, Windows of the Soul, Best Poems of 1996; [pers.] Life is tough, Love is tougher, Faith is the toughest of all, God makes it worth it!; [a.] Fairview, PA

**VANDERLINDEN, STEVEN RONALD**
[b.] July 26, 1983, New Jersey; [p.] Ronald and Lynnaire Vanderlinden; [ed.] 7th grade at Tenafly Middle School, Tenafly, NJ; [occ.] Student; [oth. writ.] This is his first published work; [pers.] Steven is involved in many extra-curricular sports and music activities, and in between enjoys reading and writing poetry.; [a.] Tenafly, NJ

**VAUGHAN, BERNIECE M.**
[b.] January 24, 1913, Missouri; [p.] Clarence and Elsa Miller; [m.] George Vaughan (Deceased), August 12, 1935; [ch.] Elsa Rae Pearce, Rosemary Andersen; [ed.] B.A. - Park College, MO MA in Educational Administration - Univer. of Pacific, Stocklon, CA; [occ.] Retired School administrator; [oth. writ.] "Heritage Guest", Mary Ann, a Pioneer Woman, What Makes You You, "Reminisce", "Old Essex", "Sex Education in 20s" and others

**VEGA, IRBERT LUIS**
[b.] April 20, 1978, Ponce, PR; [p.] Alberto Vega, Irma Vega; [ed.] Caribbean School; [occ.] Student; [memb.] National Honor Society, Genesis Literary Magazine, Student Council, C.A.R.E. Environmental Group; [hon.] Second place in "Tibes" Story Competition, Honorary Mention in "Semana de la Lengua" Story Competition; [oth. writ.] El Pitirre y el Guaraguao, El Canaveral (Spanish) The Unknown Soldier (English); [pers.] I am a born again Christian that enjoys and is interested in a wide variety of literary forms but whose real inspiration comes from Jesus Christ.; [a.] Juana Diaz, PR

**VELASCO, LYNNETTE C.**
[b.] August 30, 1950, New York City; [p.] Ralph and Gloria Velasco; [ed.] Graduate of Hampton University majored in English; [occ.] Dir. of Development for youth organization, Kid's 'n U located in New York City, Freelance writer for Amsterdam News; [memb.] New York Assoc. of Journalists, Black Woman in Publishing, Poetry Society of America; [pers.] A brush stroke to ink can help, can hurt, can heal...will reveal, will dream. I have been fortunate in that I have been able to make my living writing. A writer must be eclectic, carefully study a subject, and most of all write well. I hope that my words will touch, renew, give sustenance, create peace, and act as a spirited force against injustice.

**VERA, BERNARDITA F.**
[pen.] B. F. Vera; [b.] February 17, 1948, Philippines; [p.] Deceased; [m.] Francisco M. Vera, May 16, 1978; [ch.] Allan, Christopher; [ed.] Zamboanga City High School Zamboanga A. E. Colleges Zamboanga General Hospital School of Nursing (Philippines); [occ.] Registered Nurse at Naval Medical Center, Portsmouth (Virginia); [oth. writ.] Several poems published in the school organ during my college days; [pers.] Poetry is an extension of self, that self is influenced by the people I meet, sounds I hear and most of all love! The innermost feelings of one's heart could be expressed thru poetry!

**VERBIT, CHRISTINE**
[pen.] C. M. Verbit; [b.] March 30, 1981, Michigan; [p.] Joe Verbit, Debra Verbit; [ed.] Freshman at Cousins High School, Honor Roll Students, Principal's List; [oth. writ.] I am currently writing a young adult novel; [pers.] I am only as good as I think I am, as others think I think I am.; [a.] Warren, MI

**VINCENT, LAWRENCE**
[b.] June 15, 1968, Cheboygan, MI; [m.] Donna Vincent, December 23, 1995; [ed.] Bachelor of Accounting. Currently working on Bachelor degree in English will graduate in Dec. 95; [occ.] Student at Northern Michigan University; [oth. writ.] Published in University Literary magazine and brochure of the downtown Marquette area; [pers.] Conciseness; [a.] Marquette, MI

**VINE, DEBORAH J.**
[b.] May 1, 1982, Germany; [p.] Anthony J. Vine, JoLynn Vine; [ed.] Estrella Junior High School; [a.] Phoenix, AZ

**VINSON, LOUMANDA**
[b.] September 10, 1929, Georgia; [ed.] BA and MA from Wayne State University, took course in Children's Lit. - under Frank Donoven; [occ.] Retired school teacher; [oth. writ.] I wrote two novels and five children's stories; I have two songs on the Hilltop label; [pers.] I do not have an agent for my stories.; [a.] Akron, OH

**VIRDI, NARVEEN**
[b.] September 30, 1948, India; [p.] Maj. Rattan Singh, Mrs. Rattan Singh; [m.] Dr. Prem S. Virdi, October 9, 1970; [ch.] Manisha Virdi; [ed.] M. A. in English Lit., B. Education; [occ.] Own a cultural center Business Woman; [memb.] Rotary International Q. C. World Affairs Organization, Broadway Theatre League, Boy and Girls Club; [hon.] Distinctions in Teaching, Awards YL Art; [oth. writ.] A play "The Soirec" highlighting the power of ritual in our lives; [pers.] The maturity of immigration evolving into avenue and worlds I never know existed. Who am I? I do not know I live in existential bliss. And I learning, learning, learning. I believe: as Helen Keller was asked "Is there anything worse than no sight?" "Oh, yes" she answered, "A person with sight and no vision."; [a.] Moline, IL

**VITIELLO, TOVA CAROL IRNA**
[b.] November 2, 1944, Newark, NJ; [p.] Armand and Florence Vitiello; [ed.] MA, MSW and PhD - all degrees from the University of Iowa, Iowa City, IA; [occ.] Professor of Psychology and Therapist in Clinical practice; [oth. writ.] Agnes Samuelson: A profile and analysis of the administrative career of an Iowa educator, altering behavior, cognitive restructuring, changing homorphobic attitude, poems published in Dana review and ain't I a woman?; [a.] Iowa City, IA

**VOIGT, DENNIS E.**
[b.] August 28, 1960, Little Falls, MN; [p.] Leonard Voigt and Lorraine Voigt; [m.] Judy Voigt, August 29, 1992; [ch.] Joshua Eric, Savannah Rae, Treyton Myles; [ed.] Milaca High School, Milaca, MN St. Cloud Technical College, St. Cloud, MN; [occ.] Graphic Artist/ Coordinator, St. Cloud Public School, St. Cloud, MN; [hon.] Journalism Award-1978, Quill and Scroll Award - 1978, Division of School media Specialists (DSMS) Presidential Award for outstanding Graphic Design 1985; [a.] Saint Cloud, MN

**VOYLES, PAMELA K.**
[b.] February 5, 1965, Corpus Christi, TX; [p.] Mr. and Mrs. L. Wallace and R. Raymond; [m.] Robert Voyles, December 27, 1987; [ch.] Katherine Voyles; [ed.] Bach-

elor of Science; [occ.] Teacher; [pers.] This poem was written for my dad and his love for flowers; [a.] Corpus Christi, TX

**WADDLE, ELIZABETH**
[b.] October, 21, 1981, Dallas, TX; [p.] Judy and Tommy Waddle; [ed.] Starting 9th Grade; [occ.] Student; [hon.] National Junior Honor Society; [oth. writ.] 39 other Poems none published; [a.] DeSoto, TX

**WADDLETON, JAMES F.**
[pen.] James F. Waddleton; [b.] May 30, 1971, Jersey City, NJ; [p.] William and Judith Waddleton; [ed.] St. Anne's grammar Hudson Catholic High School St. Peters College; [occ.] Student; [memb.] The Pavan school literary magazine; [oth. writ.] 3 poems published in the Pavan school magazine; [pers.] A poets words come from the heart therefore those words must be an art. (probably stated before?); [a.] Jersey City, NJ

**WADE, DEBORAH HAHN**
[pen.] Deborah Hahn-Wade; [b.] May 7, 1951, Bethesda, MD; [p.] Gloria Vidal; [m.] William Lanny Wade, January 1, 1994; [ch.] William Shane, Aimee Lynn; [ed.] St Anthony's High School for Girls, Ottawa University and Arizona State University.; [occ.] Credit Consultant, US West communications; [memb.] Telephone Pioneers of America, US West Fitness Club membership Chairman, Served on early childhood education and health at my Calvary Lutheran Church; [hon.] Several Poems and short story published in local newspapers.; [oth. writ.] I have always enjoyed writing and I hope to write more poetry that allow people to "Visualize" themselves in the settings I weave.; [pers.] Phoenix, AZ

**WAGENBLAST, JOAN**
[pen.] Joan Arrivee Wagenblast; [b.] August 21, 1920, Mondak, MT; [p.] Charles L. Arrivee Sr. and Florence Lebkicher Arrivee; [m.] G. Elden Wagenblast Jr., September 28, 1946; [ch.] Debra, David, Lucinda; [ed.] Wolf Point, Mt. High, Montana State College, Bozeman, U of M., Missoula, MT. (B.A. Eng.); [occ.] Retired-Housewife; [memb.] Sigma Kappa (Life), Beta Sigma Phi (Life), Aglow, Geneol. Soc. Emblem Club, Eagles Aux, Wasco Co., Hist. Soc. and Pioneers; [hon.] Alpha Lambda Delta (MSC) Kappa Tau, grad. with Honors (UofM), Wasco C. Farm Family—1976, 1st place poetry and 2nd place short story, Beta Sigma Phi International contests; [oth. writ.] Western play musical comedy, "The Wind Blows West," Poetry books, "Centennial Coins-1959" and "Flora's Song", 1953, poetry in local and state newspapers, anthologies, newspaper reporter, and columnist; [pers.] Am writing local and family history, own collection of poetry, learning computer, playing picochle and bridge. Words Speak of Life!; [a.] The Dalles, OR

**WAGNER, RICHARD LAULSINEN**
[b.] Oregon; [ch.] Richard Travis Wagner; [ed.] A.B. San Diego State University, former instructor, University of California, San Diego Extension; [occ.] Economist; [memb.] Kappa Sigma Fraternity, Confederate Air Force (Colonel) San Diego State Varsity Club, Old Mission Beach Athletic Club (COMBAC); [hon.] President, Whaley House Museum, San Diego California; [oth. writ.] Book of Poetry "To A Woman In Ascension" published 1978, Library of Congress Catalog number 78-69982

**WAGNER, STEVEN ROBERT**
[pen.] Swags; [b.] September 20, 1960, Iron Mountain, MI; [p.] Robert and Ruth Wagner; [m.] Tina Wagner; [ch.] Stacee and Schollin Wagner; [ed.] North Diekinson High School; [occ.] Carpenter; [memb.] Union Local 958, Nordic Ambulance EMT Volunteer, Jr Fun league

and T-Ball coach; [oth. writ.] Unpublish stories and poems; [pers.] I wish we all would judge people for what they are inside and not for what they look like on the outside, also I would like to thank my family for my life; [a.] Foster City, MI

**WAINSCOTT, SHEILA**
[b.] June 20, 1948, England; [p.] Elizabeth Fitzgerald and Michael Frain; [m.] Darrell Wainscott, Deceased Veteran, 1975-94; [ch.] Chad J. Wainscott, Mark R. Wainscott; [ed.] Putman's College, Miramar Mesa Colleges USD; [occ.] Consultant/ Laws (1990-95); [memb.] Early childhood and World Peace Associations; [hon.] Nomination not competition (elementary school), Recepient (Colleges) National Essay Competition; [oth. writ.] (Unpublished) fairytales and poetry, edited a Church Newsletter (early teens), Edited and childhood Assoc. Newsletter (1988-91); [pers.] I tend to reflect the evasive desires of the prophets for humanity, justice and world peace that, goodness equals peace (I am an admirer of R. W. Emerson, H. J. Thoneau, the transcend chatalists); [a.] San Diego, CA

**WALDEN, MARTHA LENA**
[b.] October 18, 1896, King and Queen Co, VA; [ed.] Westhampton College of the University of Richmond, 1920, WMU Baptist Training School, Southern Seminar, Louisville, KY; [occ.] Retired teacher and First Dir. of Public Welfare Essex Co.; [memb.] MOWA Band of Choctaw Indians, Mr Vernon, Alabama to whom she was a teacher and missionary 1921-1924; [hon.] Taught Sunday School many years at Ephesus Baptist Church Dunnsville, VA; [oth. writ.] Many unpublished poems and stories. First poems published, 1995 in the Poet's Domain, "The Other Side of Time"; [pers.] Miss Walden has lived a good Christian Life of service to others. She loved gardening and flowers, and handwork. She took up painting in her retirement.; [a.] Gloucester, VA

**WALINSKI, MARIA ELIZABETH**
[p.] Fr. and Mrs. F. Stephen Walinski; [ed.] Grinnell College '92; [pers.] "It isn't whether you win or lose - it's what you symbolize".; [a.] Omaha, NE

**WALKER, JEAN MARIE**
[pen.] Jean Marie Walker; [b.] July 29, 1976, Independence, MO; [p.] James and Lois Jean Walker; [ed.] Wichita High School East Northern Arizona University; [occ.] Data Entry, Accounts Receivable; [hon.] "2" in Piano Contest, First Place in Statewide Math Contest; [oth. writ.] 2 poems published in local periodical, grade school poems published in newspaper; [pers.] Pen and paper is my bread and water, piano is my air - I hope that my vital entertainments are as enjoyed by others in the years to come as they have been by me.; [a.] Flagstaff, AZ

**WALKER, MELANIE**
[b.] July 13, 1979, Perth Anboy; [p.] Catherine Walker; [ed.] Rahway High School; [occ.] Cashier at CVS; [memb.] Columbia House; [hon.] I won 3 track awards, 2 gold medals and 1 bronze; [pers.] I write what matters to me. If I feel strong about something my words just write themselves.; [a.] Rahway, NJ

**WALKER, PATRICK SHANE**
[b.] January 12, 1984, Lubbock, TX; [p.] Atty. Pat N. Walker and Carlina Walker RN.; [ed.] Six Grader, Bennett Intermediate School. Frenship District.; [memb.] Member of the Gifted and Talented, Frenship School District, Principals Advisory Committee, "A" Honor Roll, Royal Ambassadors; [hon.] Yearly Academic Excellence, Gold Medallist and Excellence in Math. Olympics, Gold Medallist in Speech Competition, First Place in 1995 Frenship District Annual In-

vention/Convention; [oth. writ.] Several school publications and others published in the Anthology of Poetry by Young Americans; [pers.] I constantly strive for perfection. My father says, my goal in this life should be to leave this world a better place than I found it. Thanks to my Mom and Dad, I have a wonderful life.; [a.] Lubbock, TX

**WALL, DAVID JOHN**
[b.] June 23, 1950, Leaith, Scotland; [p.] John Wall, Margaret Wall; [ed.] Farmingdale H.S., Nassua Community College, USCG; [occ.] Army Corps of Engineers; [memb.] B.P.O.E.; [hon.] Army Idea's of Incentive (Twice); [oth. writ.] My Story of Growing Old, A Cruel Gift, The Waters Edge Trapped in Flight, Life, I Loved You My Life, Re-entry, I Know What I Would Do, Sonny, Nine A Day in the Life; [pers.] I think my story's and prose reflect the pain and the happiness we all feel in the fact that we are alive, even if we don't know why.; [a.] Ridge Field, CT

**WALSH, ROBIN MARIE PAPWORTH**
[pen.] Robin Marie Papworth; [b.] December 23, 1957, Albuquerque, NM; [p.] Bryant Robinson, Eleanor Jane Papworth; [m.] Jeffrey Alan Walsh, November 23, 1993; [ed.] Cottonwood High School in 1976 (graduated), University of Utah major in Sociology; [occ.] Daytime Security Guard (Brasher's Salt Lake Auto Auction); [memb.] DAR (Daughter of the American Revolution); [oth. writ.] This is the first time that I have written anything that has been accepted for publication - I am very excited!; [pers.] New Mexico was the backdrop for my getting involved not only in English but also in the culture, people and architecture - at an early age. I can remember when my mother used to use the children's symphony at Pope Joy Hall at the University of New Mexico as the sitter. I remember when my 3rd grade teacher read "Little Women" to us, at that explorative age....and then picking up the how's and the why's within the written language, at the college level, where I have had to learn balance, style and rhythm to have some control over our own writings, and where I am in charge of what I write. The combination of an early symphony influence and later college course writing helped to form my style.; [a.] West Valley City, UT

**WALSTON, CLIFTON**
[b.] August 10, 1935, Jersey City; [p.] Arvella-Clifton-Louis; [ed.] Saint-Peters-College Jersey City NJ, Associate in Applied Science Bachelor-Science Dickinson high night school, Jersey City NJ.; [occ.] Port of Authority of New York and New Jersey; [memb.] Co-Founder of spirit of life cultural center-at the miller branch library of JC NJ; [hon.] Jersey City NJ. Certificates of appointment to the city spirit resource panel. By Paul T. Jordan M.D. Mayor Honored for distinguished service to the arts by St. John's arts. of J.C. N.J.; [oth. writ.] Vocalist and song writer spirit of life ensemble Inspirations-CD- make the world know we'll also be free-the vision and no money samba, (Skyscrapers); [pers.] Life on this planet will depend on how mankind uses his technology.; [a.] Jersey, NJ

**WALTEROS, LYDIA**
[b.] March 31, 1947, Puerto Rico; [p.] Guillermina and Benjamin Toro; [ch.] Mariza, Lizette, Edgar and Julio; [ed.] High School, Partial credits in Hoffra University; [occ.] Benefit claim examiner for the District Council Health Fund; [memb.] First Baptist Church of Flushing; [oth. writ.] Several Spanish Poems, short stories.; [a.] Queens, NY

**WALTERS, CRYSTAL LYNN**
[b.] December 17, 1979, Stockton, CA; [p.] Robert and Robin Walters; [ed.] Entering 10th grade; [occ.] Student - part time Coramic Worker; [hon.] 2 young au-

thors fair awards.; [oth. writ.] Innocent (not published) untitled (not published); [pers.] Anyone can do anything they want to if they set their mind to it.; [a.] Stockton, CA

**WALTERS, LE ANN MARIE**
[pen.] Lisa M.; [b.] November 3, 1977, Kingston, Jamaica; [p.] Marcia and Dennis Walters; [ed.] Attended Irving School and Lincoln Elementary School from 1982 through 1988, Derby upper school from 1984 though 1991, Then graduated this June 14, 1995; [occ.] A cashier at T.J. Maxx ("For now!"); [memb.] The North Shore animal league; [hon.] Honorable mention in my highschool art show., Choir sward 2 student Council medals, Gold star music sward, Honors in 1984 and honors in 1990.; [oth. writ.] An article in a student newspapers based in massachusetts called the 21st. Century. The name of the article is compromise not confrontation.; [pers.] "Nothing's impossible... improbable, unlikely but never impossible!"; [a.] Derby, CT

**WANGLER, BOB**
[b.] March 29, 1916, Royal Oak, MI; [p.] Albert and Anna Wangler; [m.] Catherine Wangler, November 15, 1950; [ch.] Frank and Richard; [ed.] Royal Oak Senior High - Now called Dondero High, 1 year Wayne Univ.; [occ.] Retired; [oth. writ.] Several hundred letters to the editor. Four books of poetry, self printed, concentrating on the inner beauty of people.; [pers.] Since we have all been created by God to possess something different from every person ever born, we should consider ourselves to be one in spirit; [a.] Lemon Grove, CA

**WANGSNESS, JESSICA**
[b.] September 2, 1977, St Paul; [p.] John and Mary Wangsness; [ed.] I will be a Senior at Visitation School, then I hope to attend Carlston College (not yet applied); [occ.] Student; [memb.] Lost Writing Center; [hon.] A - honor roll at school, top 5% of American Night school Students by "Who's Who in American Highschool Student's several Equestrian Championships.; [oth. writ.] Poem entitled "Inherittance" published in Poetry Novel, 4 poems published in school literary magazine put out once/year.; [pers.] Perhaps the most beautiful aspect of writing is, for me, its ability to awaken the eye and heighten observation.; [a.] Saint Paul, MN

**WARD, MICHELLE RENE**
[b.] August 23, 1977, Pueblo, CO; [p.] Kathy L. and Delbert D. Ward; [ed.] Palo Duro High School, Amarillo College; [hon.] Who's Who of American High School Student's for four years past, Graduated 6th in class of 264, numerous college scholarships.; [oth. writ.] None published; [a.] Amarillo, TX

**WARD, SHIRLEY**
[b.] April 11, 1937, Illinois; [p.] Jacob and Dorothy Lawrence; [m.] Paul Ward, October 11, 1953; [ch.] Paul Jr., Christaine, Jenice, and Russell, Ward; [ed.] Galesburg High School, Galesburg, Illinois taking a (literature) at DBCC of Florida; [occ.] Supervisor in Cleaing Service; [memb.] Cancer Society Ronald McDonald House, Fraternal Order of Police; [hon.] Many reading awards and spelling awards from school; [pers.] I was influenced by the poet, Joyce Kilmer my favorite poem is tree's I hope to be as great a poet as her some day.; [a.] Ormond Beach, FL

**WARD-WYMAN, KIMBERLY**
[b.] May 18, 1959, Rolla, MO; [p.] George and Barbara Ward; [ch.] Michael Wyman, Ashley Wyman; [ed.] William Chrisman, KC Art Inst Park College; [occ.] Product development and designer.; [memb.] Member of the theosophical society Dir. of Visions of life; [hon.] Gold Metal Skater State and National Art Awards;

[pers.] My writings are for me, a journey of the soul. A living bridge of consciousness moving through quality into oneness. An interrogation of spirit. For all people's, all colors and all races.; [a.] Lees Summit, MO

**WARE, MARGIE V.**
[pen.] Virginia Bell; [b.] March 22, 1943, Columbus, GA; [p.] Orelia Johnson and T.Z. Johnson; [m.] Theodore Ware, September 12, 1984; [ch.] Tracy D. Bell, Wesley S. Bell, Angel Ware; [ed.] Spencer High School, Columbus, GA, graduated. Attended College Preparatory School at age 33, at the Equal Opportunity Center in Hempstead, NY, graduated. Attended Nassau Community College, graduated with an Associates of Science degree in nursing.; [occ.] Registered Nurse; [memb.] American Nurse's Association. Christian Joy Fellowship Church.; [hon.] $250 Scholarship for Academic Excellence, 1978, E.O.C. Dean's List, N.C.C., 1979.; [pers.] I have always had the desire to write both poetry and song lyrics, but have never had anything published before. Two of the writers that have inspired me over the years are Edgar Allen Poe, and Helen Steiner Rice.; [a.] Hempstead, NY

**WARNER, SADIE**
[b.] November 18, 1979, Moab, UT; [p.] David Warner and Becky Paterson; [ed.] K-9th Grade; [occ.] Student; [pers.] They are more than just words to me. This isn't poetry. I'm not a poet. This is a piece of me. I'm not a writer I'm a human being.; [a.] Moab, UT

**WASHBURN, CHARLES C.**
[b.] May 1, 1938, Memphis, TN; [ch.] Lindsey Catherine, Logan Charles; [ed.] Booker T. Washington High, Kentucky State University, Milwaukee Institute of Technology, Syracuse University; [memb.] Directors Guild of America, Writers Guild of America, Pacific Pioneer Broadcasters; [oth. writ.] Poems, song lyrics, motion picture and television scripts, magazine articles; [pers.] In this world of dog-eat-dog we must take time-out to chill look for the light behind the fog to lead you over the hill.; [a.] Woodland Hills, CA

**WASHBURN, WADE S.**
[b.] June 15, 1971, San Leandro, CA; [p.] Mary and Larry Washburn; [ed.] Graduate of Ripon High School, Ripon, CA; [occ.] Quatermaster, United States Navy; [pers.] For whom do we live, ourselves or He who is in all?; [a.] Manteca, CA

**WASHINGTON, SANDRA JONES**
[b.] March 29, 1953, Denver, CO; [p.] Walter and Mazie Jones; [m.] James Washington; [ch.] Qimmah and Benjamin; [ed.] Manual high, University of Colorado; [occ.] Artist (painter); [memb.] National Museum of Women in the arts (D.C.); [hon.] Honorable mention-Dusable Museum, Chicago, IL.; [oth. writ.] Have written several poems, this is the first to be submitted for publication.; [pers.] I would like to thank all who believed and encouraged me to pursue my creative endeavors.; [a.] Silver Spring, MD

**WASSERMAN, MICHAEL**
[b.] July 17, 1910, Montreal; [p.] Benjamin and Lena Wasserman; [m.] Helen Wasserman, April 3, 1910; [ch.] Janet Tuchinsky, Arthur Wasserman; [ed.] B.A. College of the City of NY 1932, Classical Languages C.P.A. California; [occ.] Retired (C.P.A.); [pers.] Have a hobby, the Collection of Latin mottoes appearing on various insignia. Have listings of 40,000, and reproductions of about 20,000.; [a.] Los Angeles, CA

**WATKINS, CLARKE A.**
[pen.] Black Tornado; [b.] March 25, 1948, LaGrange, KY; [p.] Beatrice and Clarke; [m.] Dena, September 12, 1981; [ch.] Marlon, Ariesa; [ed.] B.A. Machine

Tool Assoc. Metalurgy and Chemistry; [occ.] Const. Contractor; [oth. writ.] Hell to Serenity, Better-Half, Reality Bites, Sweet D. Object of Desire, Bathwater, Imagination The Ultimate High, Rage, and The Master Blaster; [pers.] Discover God's love. Appreciate your specialness. Accept your humaness. Ask for help. Trust enough to take. Have the courage to change. Accept the unchangeable, be patient keep promises. Open your heart.; [a.] Elizabethtown, KY

**WATSON, BRADFORD LANCE**
[pen.] Lance Watson; [b.] March 2, 1953, Trenton, NJ; [p.] Deceased; [m.] Sonia Ivette, February 15, 1978; [ch.] Bradford Lance Watson Jr., Julian Gabriel Watson; [ed.] BA Rutgers College New Brunswick, NJ; [occ.] Claims Adjudicator; [oth. writ.] Many poems, hentofore strictly private, solely son immediate family enjoyment.; [pers.] My gift is from God, to serve his purpose, to edify, to warn. To creatively assist the National mind to grasp supernatural realities.; [a.] North Brunswick, NJ

**WATSON, JOAN D.**
[pen.] Joan Leach; [b.] November 26, 1928, Key West, FL; [p.] WMT and Josephine P. Doughtry; [m.] Ray S. Watson, January 4, 1978; [ch.] Sandra Schaeffer, Robert Leach, Sharon Fleita, Pamela Kelly; [ed.] BA and Med. - University of Florida; [occ.] Lead Case Manager Jefferson Sr. Citizens Center; [memb.] United Methodist Church, Key West, FL.; [oth. writ.] Sheltered (Novel); [pers.] Retired after 26 yrs. Teaching Elementary and Bi-Lingual Students to love learning.; [a.] Monticello, FL

**WEATHERMAN, GLENDA JUNE**
[pen.] Glenda June Weatherman; [b.] November 13, 1950, Marietta, GA; [p.] Mattie Lou Hollis, Lloyd Hollis; [m.] Billy C. Weatherman, September 13, 1971; [ch.] Jerri Marie, Tammy Lou, Billie Jean and James Clarence; [ed.] Van Horn High School; [occ.] Fifteen Years past Government service, presently unemployed; [memb.] Being a 'Mother' is the most important role in my life; [hon.] Received an award for 30 days Volunteer Service during Hurricane Andrew Recovery, also, several Performance and Suggestion Awards; [oth. writ.] Articles in Employee News at my former job, US Army Corps of Engineers. Also in the late sixties, a published poem in Dallas New Era Newspaper, Dallas, GA; [pers.] My dream has always been to put into words the feelings from the abuse and neglect from my mother. I want to show the importance of 'Love' to parents. Also, to provide hope and dreams to abuse victims.; [a.] East Lynne, MO

**WEAVER, BARBARA**
[b.] September 28, 1960, Murray, UT; [p.] Blaine and Dolores Anderson; [m.] Virgil Weaver, June 5, 1982; [ch.] RJ Weaver, Holly Weaver, Long Weaver; [ed.] Thunderbird and Galt High Schools; [occ.] Special Education High School Aid; [memb.] President of the Holy Rosary Alter Society, Treasurer of the Women in Timber, Treasurer of the Grizzly Club Parents Club, CCD Teacher; [hon.] Graduated top 10% of class of Thunderbird High, Best Character Actress award in High School, my name was in the Most Distinguished High School Students Book, 2nd place poetry award in 8th grade; [pers.] I hope to touch and maybe help a person who might be going through something similar to what I'm going through.; [a.] Loyalton, CA

**WEAVER, JASON SCOTT**
[b.] April 20, 1979, Seymour, IN; [p.] Jerome D. Weaver, Peggy L. McClintic; [ed.] Currently a sophomore at Zionsville High School in Zionsville, IN; [occ.] Student; [memb.] Member of R/C Car racing; [hon.] National Junior Honor Society, Northwestern University Midwest Talent Search, High Honor Roll, Honors Program; [a.] Zionsville, IN

**WEAVER, JONATHAN M.**
[pen.] J.M. Davis; [b.] July 21, 1983, Tampa, FL; [p.] Donna and Daniel Weaver; [ed.] Blake 7th Grade I want to be in journalism band, chorus and computer technology also sports.; [occ.] Student; [memb.] Senior Baseball Interbay little League Pitcher and all infield.; [hon.] Special mentions on all of my book report; [oth. writ.] Book reports and other poems; [pers.] I do my best writing on rainy days because it's quiet and usually it's calm and the ideas flow through my mind and on to my paper.; [a.] Tampa, FL

**WEAVER III, MD. FRED**
[pen.] Fred Weaver III, MD.; [b.] July 19, 1927, Wheeling, WV; [p.] Fred II and Martha; [m.] Divorced; [ch.] Freddy, Wanda B. Milton Woody; [ed.] Completed Psychiatric trng - UCLA., M.D. Meharry Nashville Tenn., B.S. Central N.C.U. Durham, N.C.; [occ.] Psychiatrist; [memb.] International Social, Psychiatry Assn., AMERSA; [hon.] International Social Psychiatry Congress: Lifetime Achievement Award, Chas Drew U of Med and Science a number of honors for professional work (8); [oth. writ.] Numerous professional papers on "The Creative Process" 2 other poems published - book "creative self discovery" due out June '96 Dorrence Publishing Co.; [pers.] Life's creative process, sets the stage for the creative: visual, performing and written arts and human development; [a.] Marina Del Rey, CA

**WEBB, CHRISTINE S.**
[pen.] Christine Webb; [b.] February 8, 1950, Salt Lake City, UT; [p.] Courtland and Phoebe Starr; [m.] Melvin W. Webb, December 28, 1973; [ch.] Kirsten Marie, Ryan Wendell, Tirzah Anne, Serena Rae; [ed.] Skyline High School, University of Utah, Brigham Young University, Utah State University; [occ.] Second Grade Teacher, Rosecrest Elementary, Salt Lake City, UT; [memb.] Director: Rosecrest Elementary Chorus, Member: Sons of Utah Pioneers, Voluntary Church Organizations (director, organist, teacher); [hon.] Kennecott Scholarship, Honors at Entrance Scholarship, graduated Summa Cum Laude and Brigham Young University, Phi Kappa Phi Honors Society, Utah Writing Project, Gifted Endorsement, Excel Educator Finalist; [oth. writ.] Poems published: Salt Lake Tribune and L.D.S. Church Magazine, Story: Utah Writing Project Summer 1990, Book: Adam Named the Animals, Desert Book Co. 1983; [pers.] I believe that the most effective writers draw from their own personal experiences in life. My parents and family have been the most positive motivating factors influencing my writings.; [a.] Salt Lake City, UT

**WEBB, DORTHY L.**
[b.] June 29, 1934, NE; [p.] Mildred and Simon Knudtson; [m.] Arnold L. Webb, February 21, 1954; [ch.] Jerome Lee Webb, Alinda Webb Wiarda and Patricia Webb Mitchell; [ed.] Highmore Highschool graduate; [occ.] Farmwife and caregiver; [memb.] United methodist church member and Board Sec., Order of the Eastern Star, Harrold Steakettes, National Cattle women organization, and antique auto club, 4-H and sunday school teacher for many year; [hon.] 4-H leader ship trip to Washington D.C. Alpha Xi Delta Mother's pin silver clover pin for 4-H Leader; [oth. writ.] Poem - "Teacher May I Ask You" for P+A program and other poems for social events in area.; [pers.] Life is precious, live, each moment to its fullest, spread your love to others like fresh butter on warm bread.; [a.] Harrold, SD

**WEBBER, LINDA E.**
[b.] November 11, 1950, Montclair, NJ; [occ.] Teacher Assistant in the Paterson Public School System.; [pers.] Being proud to be of the human race, and become wiser

and appreciate what life offers. We have only one life to live. Life is short, enjoy every moment and share feelings of love towards others.

**WEIL, ARTHUR**
[pen.] Arthur Weil; [b.] September 4, 1925, Hanover, Germany; [p.] Siegfred Weil; [m.] Lillian Weil, June 22, 1953; [ch.] Jeffrey Weil, Judy Weil-Steinhourn; [ed.] BA Roosevelt Univ. Chicago, Education and Pol. 5., MBA Pe Paul Univ. grad Magna Cum Laude, Phd Candidate 4 C. Berkeles did-corner not finish thesis; [occ.] Own Real State Brokerage Company Art Realty; [memb.] Kiwanas, Oaklahoma Board of Realtor Cal. Asson. of Realtor Lakeview Club California Teach. AM. Smitonian Oaklahoma Simple Ad. Mam many other.; [hon.] MBA-History and German Magna Cum Laude 1953 many letter to the editor and come poem pub. Chicago newspaper and chicago tribunal Sergeant Combat Engineer in WW II; [oth. writ.] I thought public school-most Junior and Sr. High S-wrote student skits, and have lifetime teach, California Lic from Elem. School through Junior College credential; [pers.] Everyday is grand at NY command, Templed, tarlea are the hours after I awake I do my work, I share, I dare Ingratitude, here in this place I care long after sunset in the mirror I see reflection mastered challenges, this day a treat alive, my satisfaction.; [a.] Piedmont, AL

**WEIMER, ALEASHA M.**
[b.] February 4, 1982, Cobleskill, NY; [p.] Ms. Margaret Weimer; [ed.] K-8; [occ.] 8th grade student; [memb.] FHA; [hon.] Music and Home and Careers Awards

**WELCH, DANA**
[b.] March 9, 1954, Plant City, FL; [p.] J.T. and Virgie Rogers; [ch.] Erin and Jayme Welch; [ed.] Turkey Creek High School presently a part time student at Hillsborough Community College; [occ.] Part time student, hair stylist, actress, temporary agency, and full time mom; [memb.] Turkey Creek First Baptist Church Hillsborough County Historical Society; [hon.] Short story contest through College, 3rd place "Forebearance", Honorable Mention for poetry "Certain Times" in the Hillsborough Community College magazine "Galeria" Dean's list; [oth. writ.] Short Story "What We Became"; [pers.] Through my writing I try to compellingly express emotions experienced by ordinary people.; [a.] Plant City, FL

**WELLS, DEL**
[pen.] Del Wells; [b.] 1910, Spencer, SD; [p.] George and Kresenthia; [m.] Lou Vena, 1932; [ch.] Thomas, William, Mary, Carol; [ed.] Studied Law at Home, California, Road Very Unusual.; [occ.] Retired, Attorney; [memb.] State Bar of Calif. Member of the Bahai Faith, Burbank Calif. Universal Justice Language; [hon.] Member of the local spiritual assembly bahai, 37 years Burbank Calif. I am 85 years and a little shakey.; [oth. writ.] The camphor Cup. The books Poems Being reprinted. Not sold given to friends.; [pers.] I believe that by the end of this Century will be an end to war and the beginning of a world languages.

**WELLS, JOANNE**
[pen.] J.C.; [b.] January 27, 1948, Buffalo; [p.] Kathleen and Alfred Weishaupt; [m.] Ralph J. Wells, June 21, 1975; [ch.] Dawn M. Wells, Robert J. Wells, David L. Wells; [ed.] South Park High School Plus Art Teacher grade 1-6 for a short time.; [occ.] Nurse Aide; [memb.] American Heart Association threw husbands work place; [hon.] Art awards for art work in high school. Awards as Nursing Aide; [oth. writ.] Just writing as a hobby, drink think they were good enough to publish sent a poem to see how good it is.; [pers.] I love God's children I would like to share the love I feel for God. And maybe they can find spiritual help from reading my poems and

I have all this talent because of the love I have in Jesus Christ my Lord.; [a.] Buffalo, NY

**WELLS, LOUISE**
[b.] April 12, 1938, Thomas Co, GA; [p.] Leroy and Maggie McCaskill; [m.] Nathaniel Wells, Sr., August 11, 1956; [ch.] Shirley E. Wells-McArthur, Nathaniel Wells, Jr., Lenoris J. Wells, Eric L. Wells, Allen R. Wells, Debra C. Wells-Barnes, Charlene D. Wells, Belinda U. Wells; [ed.] Boston High School Boston, GA 31626; [occ.] Retired Southwestern State Hosp./ Health Service Tech.; [memb.] Benevolent Society; [hon.] Outstanding Citizen Award, Certificate of Recognition Award; [oth. writ.] Several Poems published in local newspaper (Thomasville Times) Several poems written for church clubs.; [a.] Boston, GA

**WENTWORTH, DEBORAH DAWN**
[b.] January 11, 1980, Holloman AFB, NM; [p.] Dick W. Wentworth and Cynthia S. Wentworth; [ed.] Class of '97, Alamogordo High School, wishes to attend Washington University, St Louis Missouri with a Major in English and Minor in Music; [occ.] Student, Alamogordo High School, Alamogordo, New Mexico; [hon.] National Junior Honor Society, Rotary Club Award in Writing; [pers.] Poetry is my way of expressing what is in my heart. I am greatly indebted to my English teacher, Mrs Keehne, for her support and encouragement.; [a.] Alamogordo, NM

**WERNICK, SHIRLEY A.**
[b.] December 24, 1938, Caruthersville, MO; [p.] Robert (Deceased) and Flossie Odom; [m.] Gerald E., February 14, 1986; [ch.] Kathryn, Douglas (Deceased); [ed.] Caruthersville High; [occ.] Payroll Specialist Hazelwood School District; [pers.] Each poem that I write has a special meaning to me, and every word is from my heart.; [a.] Florissant, MO

**WEST, GREGORIO A.**
[pen.] The Lonesome Soldier; [b.] January 26, 1948, Panama; [p.] Ruperto and Naomi West; [m.] Marva S. West, April 24, 1985; [ch.] Charlene, McCormick; [ed.] 2 yrs. College Central Texas College, Primary Leadership Course, NCO Basic Course NCO Advanced Course, Administration Course, Sanitation Course.; [occ.] Retire Military, Presently employed as a correctional officer for the state of Texas.; [hon.] The Bronze Star Medal while in Combat Meritorious Service Medal Army commendation Medal with 1 Oak loaf cluster, Army Achievement Medal with 1 Oak Leaf cluster good conduct medal (5th award) National of Defense Medal overseas service ribbon numeral and export badge rifle, valorous unit award Shriner, Knight Temple Southwest Asia Service Medal with 3 Bronze Service Stars/ Kuwait Liberation Medal NCO Professional Development Ribbon; [oth. writ.] Songs, not published; [pers.] I am a sentimental person, I strive to portray myself as some one willing to be successful

**WESTGATE, ELEANOR OBERT**
[b.] July 19, 1915, Southwest City, MO; [p.] Mr. and Mrs. Albert Obert; [m.] Charles R. Westgate, May 25, 1940; [ch.] JoAnn, John, Vicki; [ed.] From age 6 to 18 attended public school at Southwest City, MO attended the University of Okla. 5 years to attain a Bachelors Degree.; [occ.] Retired School Secretary except in summers where I am a Camp secretary at Camp Mishawaka, Grand Rapids, MN; [memb.] Ex-Opera Chorus, Presently singing in a Women's Chorus and Jr. College Chorus. Sang 5 years in Okla. University Women's Choral Club. Was a charter member of a Business Fraternity (Pi Omega Pi); [hon.] I am currently the Recording Secretary of the Hyechka Music Club - Tulsa. The oldest music organization in Oklahoma and which has 300-400 members. I received "A's" under

Dr. Jewel Wurtzbaugh at O.U. who encouraged me to write. I have a suitcase full of poems, essays and biographical sketches which I hope to get out and submit someday!; [pers.] This is only the second time I have entered a contest. In about 1960 I entered a Borden's Limerick Contest and won a free meal for each member of the family! My home, my husband, my family, singing and composing songs have taken a great deal of my time.; [a.] Tulsa, OK

**WETTSTEIN, ALBERT**
[b.] August 16, 1930, Switzerland; [m.] Sophie, January 31, 1953; [ch.] Linda and James; [ed.] Eight grade (swiss) graduate of horticultural school of Geneva, Switzerland; [occ.] Semi Ret. Machinist.; [oth. writ.] Article in the P.A. Land Owner Publ. Numerous Articles in local paper on the environment.; [pers.] I grew up one vegetable farm in Switzerland. Have been an environmentalist all my life. I am afraid for future generations, at the present mate of pollution.; [a.] Bath, PA

**WHEAT-STIBICH, MAUREEN**
[pers.] If Post Traumatic Stress Disorder does not mean anything to you as a reader, then the after-effects of those who protect you are unaccounted for in Your Life's Book of Poetry.; Maureen Wheat was fortunate to find David Stibich in this life. David served his country and ultimately paid with his life. I could not provide him with children, so I offer a poor substitute of words.; [a.] Saint Louis, MO

**WHITE, BRYAN**
[b.] May 9, 1967, Granada Hills, CA; [p.] William and Anita White; [ed.] Pierce College, Associations Arts Degree, Cal State Fresno, B.A. of English; [occ.] Writer of Life; [memb.] Brother in Sigma NU Fraternity ZK 547; [hon.] Honor these poems; [oth. writ.] Have been published numerous times in the school newspapers; [pers.] Inspiration finds you at different times. It is a matter of how you use that inspiration that makes you a writer. Write now! Write all the time!; [a.] Mesa, AZ

**WHITE, DOLORES M.**
[b.] May 18, 1929, Buffalo, NY; [p.] Lucille and Emanuel Martin; [m.] Robert M. White, June 10, 1951; [ch.] Quidon White, Maceo White, Portia White, Muhammad; [ed.] M.A. in Special Education and Elementary Education; [occ.] Part time teacher (retired) Program director (Community Center); [memb.] First Unitarian Church National Education Ass., N.A.A.C.P., African Am. Health Ed. Leadership Ex. Director of Genesis Arts/KY. Inc. Lou. Urban League Guild; [hon.] KY Colonel Af. Am. Women's Literary Gp. Kuumba Award Bell Award (94); [oth. writ.] The Ninth Hour (play), Time Brings About Change (play) Living Madonna (play), other poems; [pers.] Writing is a wholistic experience, you write as you dance, with your head, your body, your emotions and your heart.; [a.] Louisville, KY

**WHITE, DUSTIN R.**
[b.] May 12, 1975, Saratoga Springs, NY; [p.] Dan and Sandy White; [m.] Carol Cares-White; [oth. writ.] Currently compiling poems and short stories for publication; [pers.] Stop existing, start living.; [a.] Millington, TN

**WHITE, KEVIN**
[b.] April 26, 1965, Midland, MI; [p.] Edward and Deloris White; [m.] Teri White, August 9, 1986; [ch.] Cassi Lynn, Garrett Marshall; [ed.] Saginaw Valley State University, BA in Education; [occ.] Teacher, Nokomis Challenge Center, Prudenville, MI; [a.] Gladwin, MI

**WHITEHEAD, JACKIE CONLEY OGLETREE**
[b.] January 28, 1951, Athens, GA; [p.] Bobby E. Conley and Jeannette C. Jones; [m.] Frank Richard Ogletree (Deceased), August 23, 1968; [ch.] Tess O. Bray, Candy O. Day; [ed.] Madison County High School; [occ.] Administrative services supervisor, overhead door corporation; [pers.] My children and grandchildren have and will always be the light of my life. I strive to always make beautiful memories with them and the other special people I love.; [a.] Winterville, GA

**WHITNEY, JAMIE**
[b.] October 19, 1971, Lebanon, NH; [p.] James Sr. and Kathleen Whitney; [ed.] Lebanon High School Playmouth State College; [hon.] Dean's List, President's List, German Achievement Award, International Foreign Language Honor Society; [oth. writ.] Several unpublished poems.; [pers.] Poetry's an eternal element, like a spirit or faith. Life's mixed with sorrow and happiness, all feelings, yet poetry seizes our attention momentarily, to provide existence lacking perfection a soothing instance of realized contentment. Poetry-eternal should be praised. It's everything known and unknown.; [a.] Lebanon, NH

**WHITNEY, JUDITH LEE**
[pen.] J. Leopold Gilbrunski; [b.] May 2, 1924, Dorset, VT; [p.] Huntington and Lee Gilbert; [m.] Leonard Grant Whitney, August 30, 1974; [ch.] Thomas Huntington, Geoffrey Neal, and Andrea Lee Gilbert; [ed.] Burr and Burton Seminary, University of Vermont (1941-43), Arizona State University (BA-1959) (MA-1963); [occ.] Retired (1987) High School Teacher (Eng. and French); [memb.] AARP, UVM Alumni Assoc., ASU Alumni Assoc. Senior songbirds (Volunteer Group), Retirees of Tempe Assoc., Ariz. State Retirees, Nat'l Wildlife Assoc.; [hon.] BA-1959 "With Distinction" (Liberal Arts) GPAWP: Greater Phoenix Area-Writing Project (1980), "Golden Pen Award": Arizona Republic and Phoenix Gazette Newspaper, 1987 (August); [oth. writ.] A book of 50 Haiku poems titled From The Heart, unpublished, a collection of 20 sketches of Vermont characters, untitled and unpublished.; [pers.] From Robert Frost: "They will not find me changed from him they knew, only more sure of what I thought was true."; [a.] Tempe, AZ

**WICK, KARI ANNE**
[pen.] A. K. Wiley; [b.] April 12, 1968, Hayward, CA; [p.] Roald and Rosella Wick; [m.] John Breshears, April 1, 1995; [ed.] Castro Valley High School - Castro Valley, CA Chabot College - Hayward, CA Liberal Arts San Francisco State - Junior (part of transferred to California year), State University, Hayward (CSUH) Currently Senior Status; [occ.] Student on Medical Sabbatical; [memb.] Past Honored Queen, Job's Daughters Sons of Norway, California Scholarship Federation, Alpha Gamma Sigma - Chabo College; [hon.] Upper 10 percent of High School Graduating Class, Dean's List - Chabot College Peder P. Johnsen Scholarship Recipient; [oth. writ.] A short story, "The Void," was published in the calstate Hayward Newspaper The Pioneer.; [pers.] Question - Always question. Learn and you will understand. Look and you will see that what you thought was only for others was there for you and me. Find peace, the greatest strength, and you will find yourself. Your mind is your freedom. To all those or who flew from the maze: What is destiny to the dreamer who flies without wings?!; [a.] Hayward, CA

**WICKS, BEVERLEY W.**
[b.] November 7, 1944, Petersburg, VA; [p.] Mary L. and John Walker; [m.] Divorced; [ch.] Mary Elizabeth Beasley and Son-in-Law, James D. Beasley; [ed.] Midway High School, John Tyler Community College, Associate of Arts Virginia commonwealth University,

Bachelor of Arts, Religious Studies; [occ.] Director of program/youth ministries, first united methodist church of fox hill, hampton; [memb.] Certified Lay Speakers-The United Methodist Church, First United Methodist Church of Fox Hill, Christian Educators Fellowship, VA. Conference; [hon.] National Honor Society and Citizenship Award-High School, Phi Theta Kappa Honor Society, Dean's list, Who's Who Among Students in American Junior Colleges Laurel's Honor Society-VCU; [oth. writ.] Poems published in community college literary magazine, "Sherwood Forest"; [a.] Newport News, VA

**WICKWIRE, CHERI**
[b.] August 1, 1944, Corry, PA; [m.] Bob Wickwire, September 2, 1962; [ch.] Shawn Nobele, Shane David, Erin Dawn; [occ.] Bank Teller, First Interstate Bank, Elcason, CA; [memb.] Epsilon Sigma Alpha, First United Methodist Church; [hon.] California State Poetry Award, Epsilon Sigma Alpha; [oth. writ.] Numerous Poetry Publications in News Papers, church magazines.; [pers.] My poetry is the "Window to my soul". My words reflect my thoughts as swiftly as the pen is put to paper.; [a.] Jamul, CA

**WIDAWSKI, EVA**
[b.] June 10, 1926, Malkay Bernard Winkler; [m.] Sam Widawski, August 16, 1952; [ch.] Margie-Lana-Gail; [ed.] Self educated; [occ.] Homemaker; [oth. writ.] Several poems in another language.; [pers.] Our lives are full of dramatic changes to perceive... and we must come to terms with.; [a.] Los Angeles, CA

**WIDEMAN, DALE**
[pen.] Denise Mitchell; [b.] February 3, 1954, Wilmington, DE; [p.] Mary Mitchell, Willie Mitchell; [m.] Brian Wideman, October 26, 1984; [ch.] Cory Mitchell, Whitney Lee; [ed.] DeLa Warr High School Ashland College Wilmington College; [occ.] Payroll Secretary, Christina School District; [memb.] NEA, Betherl A.M.E. Church; [oth. writ.] A large collection of short stories and poetry written over the years, mostly for personal and family and friend enjoyment.; [pers.] I love to write! When I am inspired it's like a song trying to burst forth- a purging of my soul in words - a ferer that needs to run it's course. When the poem or story is down on paper, I feel much better!; [a.] Bear, DE

**WIGGINS, DOLORES**
[b.] March 12, 1945, Bemidji, MN; [p.] Ben and Dorothy Weis; [m.] Charles Wiggins, July 3, 1982; [ch.] Barbie and Gary; [ed.] Mount St. Benedict Academy for High School and Bemidji State University for two years of College; [occ.] Accountant for Beltrami County Highway Department; [memb.] Ridgewood Baptist Church Poet's Guild, National Authors Registry Distinguished member of the International Poet's Society; [hon.] Accomplishment of Merit from Creative Arts and Science Ent., Poet of Merit Award from the International Society of Poets - nominated for Poet of the Year in 1995.; [oth. writ.] In the process of having a book published of poetry called "Grandma's Reflections" and am working on a second book.; [pers.] Most of my poems are of a spiritual nature. I also like to write about animals and nature.; [a.] Bemidji, MN

**WILCOX, CHERYL A.**
[b.] December 2, 1964, Lawrence, MA; [m.] Fred Wilcox, August 14, 1992; [ed.] Attended Northern Essex, Haverhill, MA; [occ.] Classified Advertising Manager at the Star in Marion, Ohio; [hon.] Dean's List student; [oth. writ.] Other poetry published in magazines over the years.; [pers.] My writing goal is to paint pictures and feelings with words.; [a.] Marion, OH

**WILCOX, GENEVA CHELETTE**
[pen.] Geneva Chelette Wilcox; [b.] November 30, 1938, Colfax, LA; [p.] Deceased; [m.] Jean M. Wilcox, February 7, 1982; [ch.] Wayne, Kenneth, Hershel, Jowers one stepson Alan Wilcox; [ed.] Confax, LA. Elementary School GED, High School until 10th grade.; [occ.] House wife; [memb.] Precinct #3 Judge for Upshur County, TX, Church Faith Baptist member of science fiction Book Club, Home Sewer, for crafters; [hon.] Blue Ribbon for Art Painting, original recipes contest winner-4 times; [oth. writ.] None, always wrote poems for my own feeling at-the-time.; [pers.] Help the people you can and love them every one and pray for the others.; [a.] Gilmer, TX

**WILHELMY, GUS**
[b.] February 17, 1935, Saint Paul, MN; [p.] George Wilhelm, Emily Wegner; [m.] Mary Rose Vallely, September 1, 1990; [ch.] Rochelle, Rebecca Todd; [ed.] Good Counsel High, Passionist Academic Inst., Univ. of MI, Univ. of WI.; [occ.] Fund Raising Consultant; [memb.] National Society of Fund Raising Executives, American Marketing Assoc, American Management Assoc, Chicago Assoc of Technical Assistance Providers; [hon.] Outstanding Young Man of America, Martin Luther King Community Leadership, Man of Year: Headstart; [oth. writ.] Our Sunday Visitor, Horizons: University of Indiana Business School, Spirit Magazine of Poetry, Louisville Courrier Journal; [pers.] I feel poetry touches deeply the innermost self and allows a poet to reveal his unique, tragically wonderful self; [a.] Chicago, IL

**WILKES, MELISSA**
[b.] April 15, 1960, Huntington, WV; [p.] Earl Dean and JoyceAnn Patterson; [m.] Timothy Wilkes, November 28, 1989; [ch.] Patty, George, Kevin, Michael; [ed.] High C-K School and the School of everyday life.; [occ.] House wife and Mother with pride; [memb.] International Society of Poets.; [hon.] Editor's Choice Award, Poet of Merit 1995, Nominee for poet of the year 1995. Published in three wonderful Anthology's; [oth. writ.] Mommy's girl in Reflections of light. Treasure's of life in best of 1996. Why in Windows of the soul. I also have a book called everyday windows in which I'm trying to get published. Who's, who in new poets; [pers.] I would like to thank my mother and father for giving me my wonderful gift of life. Our richness came from our hearts. I can only hope everyone feels the richness with their own hearts.; [a.] Catlettsburg, KY

**WILKINS, KEN**
[b.] January 31, 1927, Chicago, IL; [m.] Mabel Elizabeth, September 9, 1950; [ch.] Kathleen, Timothy, David; [ed.] BA Wheaton College, MA Cal.-State Los Angeles, BD Fuller Seminary; [occ.] Retired Science Teacher, Navy Photographer WW II; [memb.] So. Calif. Academy of Sciences, Calif. Writers Club, Grace Community Church, Int'l. Society of Poets, American Academy of Poets, Society of Children's Book Writers and Illustrators, Gopher Flats Sportsman Club; [hon.] Several Photo awards; [oth. writ.] Detectiverse-Ellery Queen Mystery Magazine, several Anthologies; [pers.] My life verse is found in Matthew 6:33 of the New Testament.; [a.] Northridge, CA

**WILKINSON, EUGENE**
[pen.] Wilkinson Eugene; [b.] September 11, 1944, Fruita, CO; [p.] Cecil and Lona Wilkinson; [m.] Judy Benjamin, October 30, 1992; [ch.] Russel and Aaron; [ed.] High School, College; [occ.] Company Manager; [hon.] Scouting; [oth. writ.] At this time I am publishing my own book of poetry.; [pers.] My poems are based on the events and emotions that have made up my life.; [a.] Tucson, AZ

**WILKINSON, MARGUERITE**
[b.] December 12, 1922, Pasadena, CA; [p.] Robert A. and Margaret I. Roberts; [m.] Vernon R. Wilkinson, December 6, 1943; [ch.] Mitchell R. Wilkinson; [ed.] Pasadena Junior College and Pasadena Business College in Pasadena, CA; [occ.] Rancher, Homemaker, Writer; [memb.] Riverside and Landowners Protection Coalition, Inc.; [oth. writ.] Three unpublished books; [pers.] In my poetry I strive to reflect a true image of the furred and feathered creatures observed on our ranch in Menard County, TX; [a.] San Angelo, TX

**WILLIAMS, A'LOMA DELORIS PAYNE**
[pen.] A'loma; [b.] November 23, 1943, Middleburg, VA; [p.] Ernest Payne and Annie Bell Payne; [m.] Deceased; [ch.] Pendleton, II David, I; [occ.] Retail sales and service; [pers.] Through writing situations, thoughts, poems, short stories, and songs, I desire to demonstrate how much we need God's salvation. His Word inspires me.; [a.] Falls Church, VA

**WILLIAMS, ANDY RENAULT**
[pen.] Andy R. Williams; [b.] February 12, 1968, Nashville, NC; [p.] Lorraine Williams; [ed.] Northern Nash Senior High, North Carolina State University; [occ.] Nash Hospitals, Inc. Systems Coordinator, Newspaper Correspondent; [memb.] Union Hill Baptist Church Humanitarian Committee, Nash Community College Transfer, Advisory Board; [hon.] North Carolina Press Association Award, Who's Who; [oth. writ.] Articles for The Rocky Mount Evening Telegram; [pers.] My motto is: We can all succeed at the best of things if we do not fail trying for the worst.; [a.] Nashville, NC

**WILLIAMS, BARBARA M.**
[pen.] Trudy; [b.] December 7, 1964, Stamford, CT; [m.] David B. Williams, May 6, 1995; [ed.] 2 ys. of College Herbert H. Lehman; [occ.] Customer Service Representative; [pers.] I strive to reflect reality in my writing.; [a.] Danbury, CT

**WILLIAMS, EDWARD DEAN**
[pen.] Eddie Williams; [b.] April 16, 1950, Littlerock, AR; [p.] Estella and Ray Williams; [m.] Rita Williams, February 25, 1975; [ch.] Shunleo, Edward and Demond Williams, Japtha Gates; [ed.] Tech. High, Metro Tech. College; [occ.] Finisher, Plastrglas; [memb.] Y.M.C.A., Tabernacle of Faith Church; [hon.] Track Runner 1st Place Winner at Franklin Elementary School 1962; [pers.] I try to get God's message through in my writing.; [a.] Omaha, NE

**WILLIAMS, GLORIA**
[b.] March 5, 1957, Panama; [p.] George Taitt (Deceased), Valerie Taitt; [m.] Divorced; [ch.] Lavette Williams, George Williams; [ed.] Midwood High School, Borough of Manhattan Community College, Fashion Institute of Technology (Fashion Design); [occ.] Police Administrative Aide with New York City Police Dept. 94th Precinct; [hon.] Won a contest over the air with a Radio Station (CD 101.9 FM), wrote a rendition for the "Cheers" Tune also sang it over the air.; [oth. writ.] Written: Poetry, Plays (working with youth groups), speeches working within my church and various organizations.; [pers.] Trust in God, believe in yourself, always strive to progress. With a good heart you will always succeed in life.; [a.] Brooklyn, NY

**WILLIAMS, JENNIFER K.**
[b.] December 22, 1977, Springfield, MO; [p.] Debra L. Williams; [ed.] Republic High School (graduation 1996), Future plans: Oklahoma Christian University of Science and Arts; [occ.] Student; [memb.] Spanish Club East Sunshine Church of Christ Youth Group; [hon.] Who's Who Among American High School Students 29th Edition; [pers.] I wrote this poem for my sophomore year English class.; [a.] Republic, MO

**WILLIAMS, MARY H.**
[pen.] "Mayzie"; [b.] September 6, 1913, Louisa Co, VA; [p.] Mr. and Mrs. John Marion Hall Sr.; [m.] Leonard F. William, June 8, 1940; [ed.] Graduated from Apple Grove High School 1933 other special courses several evening schools.; [occ.] Retired; [memb.] National Library of Poetry Previous in World of Poetry, Fifty years in Order of Eastern Star "Class of 1933". Member of Westereso Baptist Church.; [hon.] Won golden Award in 1989-World of Poetry-Several others also.; [pers.] I hope my words send a message of Joy and hope to others. That peace will overcome all.; [a.] Richmond, VA

**WILLIAMS, MARY LOUISE**
[pen.] Louise Williams; [b.] November 8, 1927, Simpson County, MS; [p.] Mr. and Mrs. George C. Toney; [m.] James B. Williams, November 7, 1948; [ch.] James B. Williams, Jr.; [ed.] High School lots of work experience in my office.; [occ.] Own Oil Co with husband; [memb.] Miss National Golf Club, Simpson County Golf, Simpson County Writers Group; [oth. writ.] Lots of poems published in your Library of Poetry Several poems in local newspaper.; [pers.] I have always put on paper the things I want to remember, and write to get frustration settled.

**WILLIAMS, PATRICIA**
[pen.] Laura; [b.] February 14, 1948, Philadelphia, PA; [p.] Lucretia and Abel; [m.] Divorced (twice); [ch.] William Bennett Jr. III, Wanda Anita-Gail Bennett; [ed.] Overbrook High School - some college courses; [occ.] Administrative Support Assistant/Office Manager - Nat'l Wy Serv. (Federal Government); [oth. writ.] Several poems not published; [pers.] I love to love and be loved, remember love has no walls, just a swinging gate.; [a.] Pine Hill, NJ

**WILLIAMS, PATSY A.**
[pen.] Ashanti; [b.] May 21, 1960, Houston, TX; [p.] Wendell and Miley Henry; [m.] Herman Williams Jr., July 25, 1987; [ed.] Elem. T.L. Marsalis (Dallas) Jr. High-Atwell (Dallas) High-David W. Carter (Dallas) College-Jarvis Christian College-Hawkins, TX; [occ.] 4th grade teacher at (W.B. Miller Elem. School) Dallas TX; [memb.] Sigma Tau Delta National English Honor Society; [hon.] 1985-Teacher of the Year Nominee; [oth. writ.] I have written many poems for my school's oratorical contest.; [pers.] In life treat everyone the way you want to be treated. Do all the good you can for as long as you can for you will never pass this way again.; [a.] Mesquite, TX

**WILLIAMS, RICHARD D.**
[pen.] Weldon Faulmann; [b.] May 23, 1939, San Francisco, CA; [p.] Manuel Reposa, Grace Faulmann; [m.] Margaret J. Williams, January 31, 1975; [pers.] Weldon Faulmann has written a small collection of poems in which he expresses his feelings as he found his anima reflected both in nature and in other people

**WILLIAMS, RHONDA A.**
[pen.] Alexa DuBose; [b.] March 16, 1956, Columbus, GA; [p.] Clarence Williams, Annie Brown; [ch.] Sean; [ed.] Columbus High, Meadows Business College; [occ.] Adm. Secretary, Georgia State University; [memb.] World Changers Ministry-choir Riverdale Middle School-PTA; [oth. writ.] Poem the Gift; [pers.] Without a vision, you become stagnated. Poetry to me is a stepping stone to greater heights, I plan to write books for children and juveniles.; [a.] Riverdale, GA

**WILLIAMS, SHAKESE**
[pen.] Kesha; [b.] April 7, 1985, Fresno; [p.] Regina Maxey, Raymond Williams; [ch.] Brittney Duckworth; [ed.] Centennial she a 5th grader; [hon.] 4x100 mile relay-gold medal student of month June "95", 400 yard dash 1st 2nd places medal; [pers.] She enjoy writing, she likes to makes poems and runs cross-country, writing interested her because she makes them up herself.; [a.] Fresno, CA

**WILLIAMS, THELMA P.**
[b.] September 29, 1934, Hunt, AR; [p.] Dan Parker, Anna Parker; [m.] J.C. McClelland (deceased), February 12, 1951; [ch.] Ricky Charles, William Frank, Paula Ann, Donna Gail; [ed.] Ozark High School, Moler Barber College Tacoma, WA, Art Instruction School Minneapolis, MN; [occ.] Laborer Cargill Turkey Processing; [pers.] My Poetry reflects my deep appreciation for our true gifts which God has bestowed upon us. With these things I am truly wealthy; [a.] Ozark, AR

**WILLIAMS, VANESSA LAMM**
[b.] September 20, 1970, Gwinnett Co, GA; [p.] Billy Ray and Omie Lee Puckett; [m.] James Robert Williams, June 24, 1995; [ch.] Monica Lamm, Trevor Williams-stepson; [ed.] JB Hunt High School Wilson Technical College International Correspondence School; [occ.] Secretary at Ethridge Associates, Inc., Wilson, NC; [memb.] Member of Wildwood Free will Baptist Church; [oth. writ.] Personal collection of poems and writings I do for self enjoyment; [pers.] Through my writings the Lord allows me to release my inner emotions. I owe all my blessings to Christ, who is my strength.; [a.] Wilson, NC

**WILLIAMS SR., CARL R.**
[pen.] Carl R. Williams Sr.; [b.] December 12, 1927, West Palm Beach, FL; [p.] James E. and Eunice T. Williams; [m.] Carol J. Williams, January 16, 1954; [ch.] Linda, Carl Jr., Carrie, James; [ed.] High School Graduate, and numerous Military and Law Enforcement courses; [occ.] Retired (State Trooper); [memb.] 32 degree Mason and other Masonic Bodies, American Legion, V.F.W., DAV, 40 and 8, Military Reunion Organizations, AARP, American Cancer Society; [hon.] Military and Law Enforcement; [oth. writ.] Program writings for Masonic and Veteran organizations, numerous poetry for same organizations, have numerous poems written over a period of time on file.; [pers.] I am a Member of the Baptist Faith Veteran (WW II, Korean Conflict, U.S.M.C.) Retired State Trooper (41 years law enforcement). My hobbies are wood working and writing poetry. I strive to reflect God and Country in my writing.; [a.] Perry, FL

**WILLIAMSON, JOHN BEDINGER**
[pen.] John Bedinger Williamson; [b.] July 18, 1949, Kingsport, TN; [p.] Robert (deceased) and Miriam Williamson; [m.] One marriage annuled; [ed.] A.A. Montreat-Anderson College (1969) in Montreat, NC and B.A. in Journalism from Memphis-State University (1972) in Memphis, TN; [occ.] President of Mega Games, Inc. manufacturer of family boardgames in Houston, TX; [hon.] Top Teacher Award in Fred Astaire Studios (1975), taught ballroom dancing for 4 years; [oth. writ.] Pretribulation Vs Prewrath a book n the Second Coming of Christ, includes the order of events concerning the Rapture of the church (the church will have to endure the Great Tribulation with the scriptural prooftexts to back it up); [pers.] The rivers of truth shall search you out and drown you, except you be in truth, then you will float and ride the waves of eternity.; [a.] Houston, TX

**WILLIAMSON, MARIA**
[pen.] Febrona; [b.] February 13, 1924, Brooklyn; [p.] Maria and Salvatore Pallotta; [m.] William, June 3, 1950; [ch.] 4 Children; [ed.] High School 2yrs, Commercial Art. Presently doing all Paintings and selling also doll maker; [occ.] Volunteer in Local Hosp.; [memb.] Pasco Art Guild; [oth. writ.] Short Stories and Column in local newspaper; [pers.] Enjoy meeting people and hope someday to be on t.v. commercials and to have a book of poems of my own printed so others can enjoy them.; [a.] Hudson, FL

**WILLIAMSON, NANCY**
[b.] September 4, 1959, Seattle, WA; [ed.] Tacoma Community College Entrepreneurial Studies, American Council on Exercise, Ace Personal Trainer/Fitness Tech. Education Continuing.; [occ.] Owner/Fit Bodies Personal Training Services Independent contractor-International sales and marketing IDN. International. (Interior Design Nutritional).; [hon.] Famous Poet. Famous Poets Society Hollywood CA., Inducted Homer Honor Society of International Poets 1995. Disney Land. Award-Diamond Homer Trophy.; [oth. writ.] Anthology (1995) Published-Famous Poems of Today-Poem - 'Life Trek'; [pers.] Imagination gives us the energy to transform our dreams into reality, to follow our hearts. To reach our human potential. To give life. To be a part of creation. Preserving Mother Earth.; [a.] Carlsbad, CA

**WILLIS, WANDA**
[b.] September 24, 1939, Ft Blackmore, VA; [p.] Calvin and Edith Thompson; [m.] James Willis Sr., November 16, 1956; [ch.] Marcella, Carolyn, Danny, Christine, James Jr.; [ed.] Ketron High Kingsport, Tenn.; [occ.] Homemaker; [oth. writ.] Have written many Gospel songs and poems of all subjects.; [pers.] My writings are feelings that come from the heart.; [a.] Rockledge, FL

**WILSON, ALEXIS**
[b.] October 13, 1965, The Netherland's; [p.] Sonja Van Beers and Billy Wilson; [ed.] Professional Children's School, Ballet Training, The New York School Of Ballet, Carnegie-Mellon University, Bachelor of Fine Arts Degree in Drama.; [occ.] Casting Agent; [memb.] Dance Theater Of Harlem; [oth. writ.] Co-writing a musical script with songs and lyrics, novel.

**WILSON, BARNETT R.**
[b.] June 27, 1929, Clarkesville, GA; [m.] Sarah Ann; [ed.] Georgia State College; [occ.] Sales; [oth. writ.] Personal Narrative Korean War, Trilogy of Historical Essays on Southern Appalachian History. An Historical Capsule - Genealogy; [pers.] A person and/or nation not knowing their history has no future.; [a.] Charlotte, NC

**WILSON, JOHN A.**
[pen.] Jack Wilson; [b.] August 13, 1928, Parkersburg, WV; [p.] Ralph Wilson and Helen Rice; [m.] Arlene Kaiser, June 12, 1993; [ch.] Melanie Wilson, John Jesse Wilson; [ed.] B.S. West Virginia U. 1952, San Francisco Theological Seminary Master Divinity 1957, M.A. Counseling and guidance San Jose State Ministry Univ. 1970; [occ.] Retired Teacher; [memb.] Journaliers-Journalism society, Naval Reserve Association, Marine Corps Retired Officers Association Santa, Clara County Sheriffs. Dept. Search and Rescue Mounted Posse, Sigma Nu Fraternity; [hon.] Tau Delta Phi Scholastic Honorary-San Jose State Univ. Journaliers-Journalism Honorary W.V.A. Univ, Life Member PTA CA, Jaycees Outstanding young men of America; [oth. writ.] Collection of poetry written during last tree years, privately published.; [pers.] Just as the human body regenerates itself, I belief in constant intellectual and spiritual regeneration to maintain a youthful being.

**WILSON, JUNE**
[pen.] June Wilson; [b.] July 12, 1946, Somerville, NJ; [p.] Marie and Irving Wilson; [m.] Samuel Annitto, November 19, 1977; [ed.] 1972 Pratt Institute, Brooklyn, NY, BA (honors) 1968 Monmouth College, West Long Branch, NJ, (Drama) 1964-65 Ithaca College, Ithaca, NY; [occ.] Artist/Painter/Adjunct Asst. Professor, Ocean County College, NJ; [memb.] (Modern Dancer) "Deakin Dance Ensemble", Red Bank, NJ (1975-1992); [hon.] Grants: 1985 N.J. State Council on the Arts/painting, 1981 N.J. State Council on the Arts (mixed media), Who's Who In American Art

**WILSON, REGINA ALLEN**
[b.] December 10, 1948, Chicago, IL; [p.] Frederick and Dorothy; [m.] Donald; [ch.] Tracy, Nicole; [ed.] Wendell Phillips High school, Olive Harvey Jr. College, Purdue University (School of Marketing Management); [occ.] Human Resources Management; [memb.] HR Association, National Association of Female Executives, Chicago URBAN League, National Thespian Society, Working in Benefits Association, Distinguished member in International Society of Poets.; [hon.] 1987 Achievement award by "Who's Who in Executive and Professional Women, 1986 thru 1990-Chicago Mayor's office of employment Award.; [oth. writ.] Over 100 poems written in my book "The Love Inside Me" (still pending publication, several writings published in local school and area newspapers and/or articles.; [pers.] I believe each person has their own unique gifts and talents to share with the world. If we use these talents for the good of all, our talents grow and so do we!; [a.] Matteson, IL

**WILSON, RICK**
[pen.] Rick Wilson; [b.] Brooklyn, NY; [p.] Mary Eieteenth Albert Wilson; [m.] Dorothy Mary, September 14, 1963; [ch.] Dori, Richard, Jean and Kathleen Mary; [ed.] Brooklyn College, Boston University; [oth. writ.] Several poems and short stories published; [pers.] This poem was written to dedicate the memory of my late wife. Without her constant help and inspiration, I would not have continued writing; [a.] Kings Park, NY

**WILSON, SONJA**
[pen.] Sonieux; [b.] March 28, 1938; [p.] Albert R. and Annelia Deville Molless; [m.] Howard Brooks Wilson, November 12, 1982; [ch.] William, Dwayne, Rachelle, Devon, Lisa and Rick Williams, step: Yvonne and Howard Wilson; [ed.] BS Education Development, Southern Illinois Un., Carbondale 1995. AA Social and Behavioral Sciences, MT. San Jacinto Coll. 1992 Designated Subj. Credential, UC San Bernardino, 1982. Apple Computers Certificate Graduate Manual Arts H.S. 1956.; [occ.] Retired Business Ed. Teacher, Substitute Teacher, Poet; [memb.] California School Board Assoc., National School Board Assoc., Nat. Coalition Black School Bd. Assoc., Calif. Coalition Black School Bd. Assoc., Chamber of Commerce Lake Elsinore, Black Art and Social Club, Eta Phi Beta Sorority, Inc. - Gamma Alpha Chapter, Community Action Plan - Madcap Group, AARP, PTSA, NCNW, The American Biographic Institute, BPAC.; [hon.] 2000 Notable Am. Women Hall of Fame 1995. The Am. Bio. Inst., Women of the year 1995. The Nat'l. Lib. of Poetry, Outstanding Poets 1994, 1995. Bethel AME Honoree in Field of Education 1995. Comm. Action Prog. Award, Exemplary Service 1994. County of Riv. Proclamation. City of Lake Elsinore Proclaim. CSBA Master of Boardmanship Award 1989. Who's Who in the West, California, America, World CSBA Outstanding Service to Children and Youth of State of Cal. 1990. Eta Phi Beta, Inc. Dedication and Leadership. FFA for support. State Supt. Bill Honig plaque for Services and to Children, Eth. Adv. Tri-Council. Etc. Poetry fetuared in Arcadia Poetry Anthology Spring 1993, Arcadia

Poetry Press. Valley News writer 1974. California Schools Employees Assoc, President's Column 1974-78. Poetry featured in Betty Ford Magazine. Poetry featured in PTSA Newsletter 1994. Collection of Poems gift to Elsinore HS.; [pers.] Life is such joy with all its challenges, hurdles, surprises, learnings, experiences, relationships if we but remember all is to our utmost growth.; [a.] Lake Elsinore, CA

**WILSON, TUSCASA**
[b.] August 25, 1978, Los Angeles, CA; [p.] Adele and Edward Wilson; [ed.] Junior at Daniel Murphy High School in Los Angeles; [occ.] Data entry, Modeling, student.; [oth. writ.] A number of other poems published in school papers.; [pers.] There is much I want to accomplish in this lifetime. I think that if you truly want to do something, you need two key things: devotion and desire to do it.; [a.] Los Angeles, CA

**WILSON, WILMA**
[b.] May 14, 1920, Taunton, MA; [p.] Martin and Lena Johnson (Deceased); [m.] Harvey W. Wilson Jr., April 24, 1948; [ch.] William, Patricia, JoAnne, Bonnie Terri and Jones; [occ.] Housewife; [memb.] Member of N. Taunton Baptist Church Charity Donations, MADD (Mothers Against Drunk Driving), Special Olympics (disabled Children); [hon.] Honorable Mention Award of Merit Certificate - for Poem "Washday Observation's" from World of poetry contest, sacramento California Awarded 1st Prize for 1992 Valentine Poem in local news paper; [oth. writ.] I have had many other Poems published in our local newspaper the Taunton Daily Gazette; [pers.] My Poems reflect on my personal life, growing up on a country farm, and the pleasure of leaving these precious memories to my family and future generations.; [a.] Taunton, MA

**WINDER, RICHARD**
[b.] May 8, 1956, Baltimore, MD; [p.] Jack and Kathryn Winder; [ed.] University of South Fla.: Literature; [occ.] Artist; [pers.] I am presently preparing to write and illustrate a children's book for adults and looking for a modest patronage.; [a.] Englewood, FL

**WINKLER, LINDA E.**
[b.] June 17, 1959, Maryland; [p.] Otis Franklin and Mary Nell Gibson; [m.] Divorced after 17 yrs. of marriage; [ch.] Naomi Elizabeth, Faith Nicole, Christina Angela (Deceased), Joshua Aaron Winkler; [ed.] High School Grad.; [occ.] Print Shop Folder Operator; [pers.] Charish the minutes you have with your loved one's, for life is to short.; [a.] Sterling, VA

**WINTERBOURNE, MARILYN I.**
[b.] May 13, 1925, Long Beach, CA; [ch.] Marlys Sams, Long Beach, CA, Diane Dixon, Santa Fe, NM, Darrell Winterbourne, Cornelius, OR; [ed.] B.A. Art-School of Arts M.S. Vocational Education School of Agriculture California State Polytechnic University, Pomona; [occ.] Retired Professor, California State Polytechnic University; [memb.] California Assn. of Nurserymen F.T.D. (Florists Transworld Delivery) California State Polytechnic University Alumni Naples Island Garden Club, Long Beach, CA, Gamma, Sigma, Delta Honor Society Alpha Zeta Society; [hon.] FFA (Future Farmers of America) President California Polytechnic University Los Angeles County Heart Association Lecture Emerita California State Poly. Univ. Orchid in the International Registry named "Marilyn Winterbourne"; [oth. writ.] Floral Design Certificate program for Long Beach City College, Floral Design Option in Ornamental Horticulture for California State Polytechnic at Pomona Numerous poems for a large variety of occasions.; [pers.] My poems are the reflection of the joy, hope and love I derive from my many friends and experiences.; [a.] Forest Grove, OR

**WIRE, MARY LOU**
[pen.] Mary Lou Wire; [b.] March 22, 1933, Paradise Twp, York Co, PA; [p.] Edith Evelyn Lines, Roy H. Mummert; [m.] Robert J. Wire, Jr., March 31, 1970; [ch.] Robert Joseph Wire, III, 1973; [ed.] West York H.S., Steno Inst., Wash. D.C. Hospital Univ of PA - Nursing Associate Arts Degree Penn State Univ. 2LAS May, 1992; [occ.] Encoder - Remote Barcoding GMF, MN, USPS (Dyncorp Postal Operations); [memb.] The Woman's Club of York White Rose Duplicate Bridge Club; [hon.] Five Grown Sons: David Calhoun - Cellist, NYC (Showboat, etc.), Scott D. Calhoun - Attorney, Atlanta, GA, Michael Calhoun - Willis Carroon (Airline Ins.), Joseph Calhoun - Marketing, Bobby, III, Naval Airman, Gulf War Vet College Student; [oth. writ.] Unpublished Poems Short Stories; [pers.] Poetry leaves some mystery and tells part of a story. I like for my poems to create an impressionistic vision. Essentially, I want to show the true essence of an emotion, a friendship, or a special place. It is then rewarding the therapeutic in it discovery for my having shared it. My shining example whose work merits study is Marianne Moore.; [a.] York, PA

**WISE, MARIA EVE**
[b.] February 19, 1980, Port, OR; [p.] Janet Davidson and Rick Wise; [ed.] Student at Evergreen high school and participates in classes at alternative learning Center-Vanc, Wash.; [occ.] Student 10th grade.; [hon.] Presidential academic Fitness award for recognition of extraordinary effort to achieve academic excellence. 1992; [oth. writ.] Currently working on a feminist (riot girl) fanzine. (underground newspapers).; [pers.] My writing initially evolved in attempt to distract my self from painful chronic everyday headaches, it is my way to escape in the midst of depression and pain. Poetry is the only world I know.; [a.] Portland, OR

**WISEMAN, JOYCE AMBROSE**
[pen.] Joyce Ambrose Wiseman; [b.] October 2, 1952, Ohio Co, KY; [p.] Herman and Florence Ambrose; [m.] Harold Wiseman, October 8, 1976; [ch.] Stephanie and Tracy; [ed.] High School, some college classes in human relations; [occ.] House wife; [memb.] National Humane Society, I am are avid animal lover.; [oth. writ.] Several poems published in university of Kentucky's Skylark Magazine some in Local Newspapers.; [pers.] I strive to reflect the deeper emotional side of my self in my writing would evolve, when I am intense and feeling with my heart.; [a.] Reynolds Station, KY

**WITT JR., JEROME M.**
[pen.] J.M. Witt; [b.] July 10, 1966, Hayward, CA; [p.] Jerome and Roberta Witt; [ed.] Bachelor of Science (B.S.) degree in Economics and Business Administration at Saint Mary's College of Moraga, CA.; [occ.] Owner of Marketing and Distribution Company.; [memb.] Trinity Lutheran Church, Various business associations.; [hon.] Academic Scholarships and sports awards; [oth. writ.] Various unpublished poems; [pers.] I hope that through my writhings, which are from my experiences and perceptions of things, that I can inspire someone or make them reflect and apply and apply them to their lives in order to better themselves.; [a.] Pleasanton, CA

**WOJCIK, MAGDALENA**
[b.] March 5, 1946, Krakow, Poland; [p.] Genowefa Leichardt, Eugeniusz Leichardt; [ch.] Lechoslaw Simon Wojcik, Malgorzata Wojcik; [ed.] Krakow Polytechnic, Faculty of Architecture - Krakow, Poland; [occ.] Architect and AutoCAD Operator; [a.] New York, NY

**WOLF, CAROL SUE**
[b.] March 18, 1941, Buffalo, NY; [m.] Richard A., November 14, 1959; [ch.] Richard, Kenneth; [occ.] Director of Development Highgate Medical Group, PC; [memb.] V.P. Buffalo Council of Churches, Chairperson of Evangelism and Outreach in the Niagara Area Baptist Assoc.; [oth. writ.] Author of Journey Into Prayer, articles in Baptist leader, share various others; [pers.] Writes and leads retreats and workshops.; [a.] Buffalo, NY

**WOLF, SEAN**
[pen.] August Raine; [b.] August 10, 1979, Portsmouth, VA; [p.] Thomas G. and Lorraine L. Wolf; [ed.] Currently a Junior at Samuel Clemens High School; [occ.] School; [memb.] CYO, BSA, TX-82 AFJ ROTC; [oth. writ.] None published; [pers.] Everyone has something to say, Just, not everyone listens. Hear ones point of view just as much as you want them to.; [a.] Schertz, TX

**WOLFE, DOTTIE**
[pen.] Dottie Wolfe or Preferred, just Dottie; [b.] Beatrice, NE; [p.] Effie May Day, John Mischinick; [m.] Raymond Peters (Deceased), Remarried Dr. Roger Wolfe, May 2, 1992; [ch.] Rosalie, Anita, Judy, Rita; [ed.] Beatrice High School, Further Business and Medical Education; [occ.] Retired Medical Sec'y, Part time entertainer and speaker.; [memb.] "Name" (National Assoc. of Miniature Enthusiasts), Monday Club, Christian Women's Club, Warblers (singing and entertainment group, Bethlehem Lutheran Church, give musical programs with original songs, (play autoharp) and poems for Senior Centers, church groups, Women's clubs, window decorating.; [hon.] Represented home town in "Ms. Senior" contest. Scholarship awards in grade and high school. Speaker at seminars.; [oth. writ.] In various church and club papers, newspapers, Miniature magazine, funeral memorial enclosures, publication of poetry book, "Kaleidoscope" in 1994.; [pers.] To dwell on the past never does any good. It's as futile as resawing yesterday's wood. As sawdust can never be made whole again, the calendar never turns backward, my friend. But God can erase all our errors away, and each dawning brings another new day. When I come to the end of my final day, may I have so lived that no one can say, "While seeking a fortune, the whole world o'er, she passed up the treasure around her own door".; [a.] Red Oak, IA

**WOOD, MARTIN TYRON**
[b.] October 18, 1971, St Vincent; [p.] Irish Charles, Stephen Wood; [m.] Marialyn Wood, December 6, 1991; [ed.] Layou Government School and St. Martin's Secondary High School St. Vincent. Then Berk Trade School NY, New York; [occ.] US Sailor Electrician's Mate; [hon.] Honor graduate Service School Command Great Lake IL Class 95150; [oth. writ.] Poems to my wife. Also to friends to help them get through rough times; [pers.] Thanks to mom and dad who taught me anything worth doing must be done right the first time. And to my beloved late great grand mother Mapeggy "education is the power needed to improve standard of living."; [a.] Norfolk, VA

**WOODLEY, JOHN WALSH**
[pen.] Jay Walsh W; [b.] May 8, 1928, St. Louis, MO; [p.] Theresa Woodley, Ralph Woodley; [m.] Divorced, June 23, 1951; [ch.] Mary, John, Mike, Ilsa, Carol, Cathy, Elizabeth, Margaret; [ed.] Thru Sophomore year, School of Liberal Arts, St. Louis University; [occ.] Advertising Sales Rep.; [oth. writ.] A weekly newspaper column in the 60's "The World's a Stage", a trade magazine column in the 80's "At The Coffee Machine" and my personal anthology of poems "Wind Track's".; [pers.] I hope to make common things uncommon, to exercise cataracts me call cliches, to contrast "believ-

ing" in a culture "believing not" and last but foremost, to sensitize that soul spot in all of us touched by the wind tracks of a personal God.; [a.] Lincoln Park, MI

## WOODMAN, MARTHA-MAY
[b.] May 26, 1924, Duluth, MN; [p.] Gertrude Catherine Apland Upthegrove, Richard Upthegrove; [m.] Robert Roy Woodman, January 20, 1945; [ch.] Maryella Woodman, Rob Roy Woodman Martha Lopata, Roy Carl Woodman, Robin Woodman; [ed.] U of Calif. AA, College of San Mateo, AA/RN; [occ.] Staff Nurse; [memb.] Calif. Nurses Ass. Sons of Norway; [pers.] We were in Pushkin Russia in the spring of 1994 teaching English. The surprising size and beauty of the lowly dandelion demanded a voice of appreciation hence this poem.

## WOODSON, MAXINE JUSTICE
[pen.] Justice Maxine; [b.] May 7, 1925, Chouteau, OK; [p.] Albert and Alice Justice; [m.] Paul Woodson, July 14, 1942; [ch.] Tom Woodson Sr., Carolyn Woodson Stephens; [ed.] High School and post graduate course in nursing, also taught cake decorating lessons, and sewing classes; [occ.] Retired and have a green house; [memb.] Evangelistic Temple Church Tulsa, OK; [hon.] Won gold medal award on Great Literature I have 6 certificates of award for Bible Advanced Study, (Christian Literature) Award from oral Roberts U. for Personality; [oth. writ.] My mother was Irish, from the house of Ulster, Ireland my father's father was full blood Cherokee Indian; [pers.] I am 1/4 Cherokee Indian. I'm very proud of my Heritage, I studied Cherokee language 2 years, I found it very hard. I can sing in Cherokee. I love our people; [a.] Chelsea, OK

## WRIGHT, JANICE JUANITA
[b.] March 14, 1974, NJ; [p.] Bea and Jerry Phillips; [m.] William E. Wright, May 11, 1993; [ch.] Rachel Ann Wright; [ed.] 1992 graduate Caesar Rodney Sr. High School 1994, grad. Wilma Boyd Travel and Career School; [occ.] Poet, sister, mother, daughter, and wife; [hon.] Authors Merit Award, Achievement Award 1994; [oth. writ.] ("At Days End"), "Until the Ends of Time", ("Between the Raindrops"), "Scattered Dreams", (Windows of the Soul), "Endless Nights", and (Best Poems 1995) ("Untitled"); [pers.] I believe this world would be a happier place if we would all be ourselves and except others for who they are or what they want to be. Encourage is the key to friendship.; [a.] Fort Knox, KY

## WRIGHT, JULIA
[b.] February 27, 1979, Jamaica; [p.] Moses and Daisy Wright; [ed.] Ely High School; [occ.] Student; [memb.] National Geographic Society; [oth. writ.] Miscellaneous poems; [pers.] True tranquillity knows do aggravation.; [a.] Lauderdale Lakes, FL

## WRIGHT, ROB
[b.] October 31, 1940, Houston; [p.] Robert Downes Wright; [m.] Mary Jean Cobb Wright, January 18, 1974; [ch.] Kathy-Sara-Michael-Timothy-Robert-Sean; [ed.] Schreimer Military Institute Kerrville, Texas, H.S. 1959, Whartom Country Jr. College - Whartom, Texas, 1959-1963; [occ.] Carpenter; [memb.] The National Library of Poetry-Owings Mills, Maryland.; [hon.] Distinguished member National Library of Poetry - Editor's Choice Award - 1995 National Library of Poetry-Honorable memories 1991-1993 National Library of Poetry-Cassette reading "The Last Ontlaw" Best poems of 1995; [oth. writ.] "The Parade" 1959-Kerrville, Texas-four poems-world of poetry 1991-1993, "The Television" and "Wild Grass Fire" Both received Honorable mention respectively; [pers.] Strive never to miss one stop-sign on this experience of flying

at expectation.; [a.] Uano, TX

## WRIGHT, ROCHELLE A.
[b.] September 17, 1933, Florida; [p.] Ben Aplin, Nina Aplin; [ch.] David G. Wright, Susan E. Wright, Sherri B. Lang, I. L. Wright Jr.; [ed.] Sopchoppy High, College Courses; [occ.] Day Care (Home); [oth. writ.] Several Articles published in magazines, company newsletter editor, 2 short books; [pers.] I admire writings of Laura Ingalls Wilder, and Janette Oke. Want to write to cause readers to reminisce, to laugh, to remember their roots, to find joy.; [a.] Winter Haven, FL

## WRIGHT, TAMMY LYNN
[b.] October 2, 1970, Ann Arbor, MI; [p.] Lillian and James Finnegan; [m.] Peter Michael Wright, June 17, 1989; [ch.] Crystal Marie Wright, Robert Allen Wright; [ed.] G.E.D. Whitmore Lake High, Whitmore Lake, MI; [occ.] Homemaker; [hon.] A+B honor roll in 7th grade; [oth. writ.] "I Still Stand Tall" and several others not published at all.; [pers.] Dedicated to my deceased daughter Jennifer Lynn Wright. I write poems as events unfold in my life and hope my poem's will someday help another persons in a similar situation.; [a.] San Antonio, TX

## WUNDERLICH, JANE E.
[pen.] Tia; [b.] August 11, 1958, Alexandria, MN; [p.] Robert Dyke, Loyis Dyke; [m.] Robert Wunderlich, July 2, 1990; [ed.] Glenwood Spgs High; [occ.] Jewelry Maker-Artist; [memb.] People for the West, Volunteer local Civic Organizations; [pers.] I reflect to the world the beauty we all hold inside, to tap the simplicity of our souls, to bring calm to chaos.; [a.] Patagonia, AZ

## WYNN, JAMES MARION
[pen.] J. M. Penn; [b.] November 2, 1918, Mira, LA; [p.] William D. and Jenetta Wynn; [m.] Katie Evelyn Womack Wynn, January 19, 1940; [ch.] Margaret Evelyn and James W. Wynn; [sib.] BA, East Texas Baptist College, now, University, Marshall, Texas.; [occ.] Retired Baptist Minister.; [memb.] Masonic Lodge, International Society of Poets, OES, and Caddo Prairie Baptist Church, Hosston, LA.; [hon.] Two awards from the Louisiana Baptist Convention for services in South Louisiana. International Society of Poets have awarded me with The Distinguished and of Merit award.; [oth. writ.] I have had one poem published by The National Library of Poetry and two others accepted for publication. I have two volumes of unpublished poems.; [pers.] My personal philosophy is: If one can find a good enough reason for doing a thing, he, or she can do it. My interest and views seek to find expression in such things as: faith, honesty, love, home, family and related subjects.; [a.] Vivian, LA

## WYSINGER JR., MACK H.
[b.] March 2, 1943, Broken Bow, OK; [p.] Mack and Beatrice Wysinger; [m.] Dorothy M. Wysinger, February 6, 1982; [ch.] Mack III, Athony, James Wysinger, Tia George, Tina Thomas; [ed.] Victor Valley H.S. Graduate; [occ.] Security Assistant V.V.H.S.D. Adelanto Middle School, Adelanto, CA; [memb.] Disabled American Veterans Church of the Valley, Presbyterian Apple Valley, CA; [pers.] I wrote this poem after listening to my daughter Tia now 23 years old telling me she wished she had needed my warning about boys and men. The next day at school Patrisia Parra, a 13 yr. old student whom I love so much cut school with a boy 18 yrs. old I could see it (history) repeating itself.; [a.] Apple Valley, CA

## YAHNG, K. KRISTIANNE LEE
[b.] February 19, 1970, South Korea; [m.] T. Kamen Lee-Yahng, April 11, 1993; [ed.] BA: University of California, Santa Barbara, currently pursuing Ph.D. in

English Literature at the University of Southern California; [memb.] Toni Morrison Society, Popular Culture Society, National Association for African-American Studies; [hon.] Graduate Merit Fellowship at the Univ. of So. Calif., Golden Key Honors Society, Motar Board Honors Society, Dean's List, College of Letters and Sciences Honors and Distinction in the Major; [oth. writ.] Poems, essays, and literary criticisms; [pers.] I hope to write poems which appeal to the intellectual as well as the emotional, as exemplified by: Cathy Song, Li-Young Lee, Maya Angelou, and Bidart.; [a.] Los Angeles, CA

## YAKER, DIANA STEINMAN
[b.] Lost Angeles, CA; [m.] Widow; [ed.] Beverly Hills High School, University of Southern California (U.S.C.), Writing-private group with Kate Braverman, author; [occ.] Art Dealer; [oth. writ.] Several poems, short shorts and essays, unpublished.; [pers.] I am fueled by a need to consider the implications of a life shaped by intensity and excess without resolution, the journey of a young widow, the unexpected sensual inventory of L.A., nostalgia and existential speculation.

## YANCHYSHYN, MADELYN
[b.] August 16, 1939, Mt. Holly, NJ; [p.] Frank Panico, Anna Panico; [m.] John Yanchyshyn; [ch.] Denise, Daryla, Jacob, Rochelle; [ed.] Burlington High, Philadelphia Modeling, Rancocas Valley, BCI Tech.; [occ.] Poet, author, and homemaker; [memb.] AARP, Deborah Heart and Lung Foundation, International Society of Poets, Song Writers Club of America; [hon.] Golden Poet Award 1986, Editor Choice Award, 1994-1995. Poet of Merit 1994, 1995, Award of Merit 1989; [oth. writ.] Author of "Sorrow and Doom Hovering America", published poems The Space Between 1994, Best poems of 1995, Treasured Poem of America 1994, Life's Inspirational poems 1995 and Window of The Soul, National Library of Poetry; [pers.] We restrict, deny and limit ourselves from tranquility, abundance of life and living by prison bars of "Time limits". Time does not exist, just state of being. Time is eternal.; [a.] Roebling, NJ

## YANEZ, CHRISTOPHER
[pen.] Sunday Driver; [b.] January 14, 1970, LA; [p.] Mary Yanez; [ed.] H.S. Diploma attending Vocational College; [occ.] Clerk; [memb.] M.O.C.A. Art Museum. Huntington Botanical Gardens, Silver Lake poets, soon to be the Founder of the Lilidom; [hon.] C.A.S.L. Skate Boarding Competitions I walked home from a poetry recital arrived home at 5:00 a.m.; [oth. writ.] Several poems published in Art Zines, The Morrizine, Dreaming of Oscar, various poetry pamphlets.; [pers.] Ink on paper creators, tingle the crowds hearts with verse.; [a.] Los Angeles, CA

## YAP, BETTE ANNE
[b.] October 18, 1982, Manila, Philippines; [p.] Betty (Deceased); [m.] Guardian-Spencer Yap; [ed.] Elementary-St. Paul College, March 1995; [occ.] Student-High School; [memb.] Scrabble Association; [hon.] Gold medalist-Legend Writing Contest of School 1994; [oth. writ.] Some other poems; [pers.] I have no specific inspiration. Everything inspires me like: my family, friends, nature, pets.... For everything is special in its own way.; [a.] Manila, Philippines

## YARLAGADDA, TRAVIS
[b.] April 28, 1979, Stillwater, OK; [p.] Rao Yarlagadda, Marceil Yarlagadda; [ed.] Junior at Stillwater High School; [occ.] Student; [memb.] Sunnybrook Christian Church, USTA (United States Tennis Assoc.), Latin Club; [hon.] Varsity Scholar, Magna Cum Laude award on National Latin exam; [pers.] I basically wrote his poem to criticize the flaws of mankind. Reading Herman

Melville's, "What Redburn saw in Launcelot's Hey", and other short stories of his influenced me in my poem, "Hawks."; [a.] Stillwater, OK

**YATES, WILLIAM**
[pen.] Greasy; [b.] September 30, 1945, Wake; [ed.] I have 16 year of schooling also two years of vocational training; [occ.] I do skill work hospital, common labor, salesman also plumber; [memb.] I am a life time member of Senior Citizen Club, also life time member of International Society of Poets. Also outstanding; [pers.] I strive for victory that never end or victory that never dies.

**YAUCH, ANNA C.**
[pen.] Anna Larson; [b.] August 3, 1936, Chicago, IL; [p.] Arthur and Corine Larson; [m.] Roy Yauch, September 6, 1980; [ch.] Thomas Scott, Cynthia Ann, Lori Lynn; [ed.] Lakeview High School; [occ.] Retired; [pers.] This is my first attempt at writing. I feel a new world has opened for me. There is so much to say about so many things.; [a.] North Fort Myers, FL

**YEARGIN, TIMOTHY GUY**
[pen.] Timothy Yeargin; [b.] February 26, 1966, Charlotte, NC; [p.] Guy Yeargin, Lillian Yeargin; [m.] Ludene Yeargin, July 4, 1986; [ch.] Brandon Lamar and Nicholas Alexander Yeargin, Stepson Adrian Robinson; [ed.] Hunter Huss High School, Musicians Institute of Technology, U.S. Army National Guard NC; [occ.] Landscaping, Musician; [oth. writ.] Sonic Underdog, Method to Madness, Hey Ole' Man, Eyes, Word of a Thousand Pictures, Ghost Stories I, Faces, Hiding Behind Belief.; [pers.] Writing is a passion for me, reflecting ideas and emotions and soul. I am greatly influenced by Neil Peart-a modern day genius.; [a.] Gastonia, NC

**YETTO, LINDA A.**
[pen.] Linda A. Yetto; [b.] August 16, 1949, Long Island, NY; [p.] Joseph Armstrong, Louise Armstrong; [m.] Anthony D. Yetto Jr., 1969; [ch.] Joseph, Tina; [ed.] St. Thomas Aquinas H.S., Fort Lauderdale, FL; [occ.] Telephone Company Directory Assistance Operator; [memb.] St. Stephen's Catholic Community, Ultre, International Society of Poetry, Telephone Pioneers of America; [hon.] World of Poetry Award, (6) Telephone Pioneer Hobby Show Ribbons Awards; [oth. writ.] Personal tributes to friends and even strangers. Also faith motivated poems on any subject.; [pers.] Everyone is special and unique in their own way and I try to see that and give testament to them in the form of poetry.; [a.] Casselberry, FL

**YLITALO, SUE**
[b.] January 25, 1949, Hibbing, MN; [p.] Dr. and Mrs. William Ylitalo; [ed.] B.S. University of Wisconsin; [occ.] Baker, Clerical work, teacher; [oth. writ.] Tears of the Rainbow, The Wisdom Of Understanding, The Injury of Understanding, The Wisdom Of Injury; [pers.] I owe my inspiration to Richard Allen, to all black friends and to friends from all cultures. I hope to show the beauty of tears, the beauty of truth, the beauty of integrity and the beauty of heartbreak.; [a.] Lincoln, NE

**YOSHIDA, AMANDA**
[pen.] Amanda T. Yoshida; [b.] September 20, 1982, Portland, OR; [p.] Junki and Linda Yoshida; [ed.] Jr. High School (Dexter McCarty Jr. High-Gresham, OR); [occ.] Student; [hon.] Second place award in the "Danny Glover Read and Ride Contest". (Essay Contest) 4 pt. Student Award; [oth. writ.] Presently working on a poetry collection.; [pers.] "Always write from the heart."; [a.] Troutdale, OR

**YOUNG, CHRISTOPHER**
[b.] July 5, 1979, St. Louis, MO; [p.] Ronald Young,

Karen Young; [ed.] Alton High School; [occ.] Student; [memb.] The International Thespian Society; [pers.] A wise man once said, "In Life there are many paths to be taken." I simply take the one the least traversed.; [a.] Alton, IL

**YOUNG, VICTOR**
[b.] February 23, 1961, Chicago, IL; [ed.] Quigley South High School, A.A.S. Triton College, B.S. Chicago State University; [occ.] Inspection Supervisor, Chicago Dept. of Health; [oth. writ.] Poetry-Hallowed Be Thy Name, Thy Will Be Done, The Cribs. Novels-Till Kingdom Come, Through The Fire, At The Crack of Dawn, Ashes to Dust; [pers.] I work with grim determination to express the romance and historical antagonisms of our time in Till Kingdom Come, Through the Fire, At The Crack of Dawn, and Ashes to Dust, epic novels.; [a.] Chicago, IL

**YOUNGBLOOD, MONTY L.**
[ed.] Tarrant County Junior College, Assoc. of Arts - Psychology, Assoc. of Applied Science - Office Systems Technology.; [occ.] Federal Aviation Administration - SW Region; [pers.] Kepp writing and, sooner or later, you will get noticed.; [a.] Ft. Worth, TX

**YOUTZ, LINDSEY**
[b.] March 14, 1981, Boise, ID; [p.] Jeff Youtz, Tina Youtz; [ed.] Les Bois Junior High; [occ.] Student; [pers.] You can't invite inspiration unless there's an open mind to receive it.; [a.] Boise, ID

**YU, CELIA**
[b.] March 10, 1931, Shanghai, China; [p.] Y. A. and K. C. Wu; [m.] Jimmy Yu, June 30, 1956; [ch.] Caroline Fijan, Cynthia Kvemann, Michael Yu and Sharon Ziesemer; [ed.] National Taiwan University, 1952 B.A. Miami University, Oxford, OH 1956, MA; [occ.] Homemaker; [memb.] Evangelical Presbyterian Church of Annapolis, MD; [pers.] I am an evangelical Christian in my faith. I am a conservative in political and social issues (as presented by Bill Buckley). I like Chinese classic poetry, J.R.R. Tolkien, C.S. Lewis, A.E. Hourmau, W.B. Yates and some romantic poets.; [a.] Annapolis, MD

**YUEN, MICHAEL**
[b.] August 25, 1978, Adrian, MI; [p.] Wylie and Louise Yuen; [ch.] Christopher James; [ed.] Saint Joseph's Academy, Springbrook Middle School, Adrian High School; [occ.] Student; [memb.] Adrian High School Ski Club, Member of the Alumni Association of Saint Joseph Academy; [hon.] Presidential Academic Fitness Award (2 consecutive times), Young Author's Award, Adrian High School Academic Excellence Award.; [oth. writ.] Invisible, My Peace, The Special Gift, Danger on the High Seas; [pers.] In my writings, I try to reflect the many colors of human emotion. I would like to dedicate all my work to Angie DeLine.; [a.] Adrian, MI

**ZAETZ, SELMA B.**
[pen.] Selma Bloomenthal Zaetz; [b.] April 6, 1913, Burlington, VT; [p.] Jacob L. and Francis M. Bloomenthal; [m.] Late Saul P. Zaetz, February 7, 1931; [ch.] Sonya Z. Hackel, Jay Lewis Zaetz; [ed.] Graduate at Burlington High School and University of Vermont, class of 1933; [occ.] Retired now writing historical background of my family; [memb.] National League of American Pen Women Green Mountain Div.; [oth. writ.] "Who Is So Good As My Mother", "Night Of Rest", Book-YWCA of Burlington, VT presents your met International by Selma Zaetz, Selma Zaetz is Favorite Ethnic recipes; [pers.] Now widowed and living with my companion Samuel Kablin in Mass. Visit Burlington, VT often to touch base with my son

and daughter-in-law and grandsons also Nashue, NH-to visit daughter and family return to Tucson, AZ for meeting my 3 brothers and friends - brothers: Dr. Sanford Bloomenthal-San Juan Capastrano retired Ophthalmologist California, Harold S. Bloomenthal-Denver, CO author many Law Books, Howard P. Bloomenthal-Tucson, AZ retired Editor New York Daily News; [a.] Denver, CO

**ZAMMITO, JOANIE**
[pen.] Joanie Mark; [b.] April 23, 1942, Berkeley, CA; [p.] Henrietta Moore, Charles Asnicar; [m.] Ronald A. Zammito, November 1, 1983; [ch.] Eugene Landers III, William Landers and Reno Hughes; [ed.] Napa High School, Napa Jr. College; [occ.] Professional Ballroom Teacher; [memb.] Our Lady Of Angels Catholic Church; [hon.] Bronze, Silver and Gold Awards, Ballroom Dance, American Style. T.V. Show "Dance Magic"; [oth. writ.] Fate Magazine and Book "4 of Cups."; [pers.] I believe my poems are spiritual, and a gift from God.; [a.] Foster City, CA

**ZDANCZYK, CYNTHIA**
[b.] October 31, 1979, Villa Park, IL; [p.] Jim and Cheryl Zdanczyk; [ed.] Willowbrook High School, Class of 1997; [hon.] National Honor Society; [pers.] I believe in the statements "Live life to the fullest" and "strive for what you want to achieve"; [a.] Villa Park, IL

**ZETTL, ERIKA**
[b.] February 3, 1926, Germany; [p.] Walter and Ella Tronicke; [m.] Herbert Zettl, July 18, 1953; [ch.] Renee Zettl, Alexander Zettl; [ed.] M.A. English, 1951 (comp. lit) postgraduate studies: UCLA and UC Berkeley Calif. Standard Teaching Credentials K-12 (Elementary through High School) Administrative Cred. K-12; [occ.] Retired teacher and principal, Bolinas-Stinson School District, CA; [hon.] Europ. Honors Exchange Fellowship (Switzerland). U.S Govn't, Scholarship for Graduate Study.; [pers.] I believe that our world is filled with beauty and wonders. Let's take it all in and share our thoughts with others, and, in turn, let others share theirs with us. Such sharing will expand and deepen our senses and mind. Our lives will inevitably gain in wisdom, understanding, and love.; [a.] Forest Knolls, CA

**ZICCARELLI, ANDREA MARIE**
[pen.] Andrea Ziccarelli; [b.] September 10, 1977, Kenosha, WI; [p.] Kathleen Ziccarelli, Frank Ziccarelli; [ed.] Carlsbad High School, Carlsbad, CA, California Polytechnic State University, San Luis Obispo, CA; [occ.] Student majoring in Environment Engineering; [memb.] Society of Women Engineers, California Scholarship Federation; [hon.] Highest of High Honors for Mathematics and Science from the Society of Women Engineers, American Legion Auxiliary Award, San Diego Building Association Award, Honor Roll; [oth. writ.] Various poems published in the Carlsbad High School newspapers; [pers.] Dreams are merely figments of the imagination to some, but each day I strive to make my dreams reality, and so far, I have succeeded.; [a.] Carlsbad, CA

**ZIELINSKI, JEANENE**
[b.] March 4, 1959, Abilene, TX; [p.] A.J. and Marie Harrell; [m.] Russell J. Zielinski, April 28, 1989; [ch.] Melissa M. Bell, Jarod J. Bell; [ed.] Graduate Peru Central School currently going to College; [occ.] Salon Owner and Cosmetologist; [memb.] International Society of Poets, Peru Central School Alumni Assoc.; [hon.] Recently won a third prize award from the National Library of Poetry for poem titled "Breakdown the Walls", which is being published in "The Garden of Life" anthology. Library of congress ISBN-1-56167-269-6; [oth. writ.] "Reflections of Light" anthology poem title "Life's Storms" Library of congress ISBN-1-

56167-264-5, "Best Poems 1996" anthology in progress poem title "Alexander and Michael" Library of Congress ISBN-1-56167-284-4

**ZIEMANN, DOREEN**
[pen.] Doreen Ziemann; [b.] October 8, 1981, San Dimas, CA; [p.] Joseph and Shelley Ziemann; [ed.] Leadergrove and Valley Elementary Schools, Park View Middle School Yucaipa Junior High; [occ.] Freshman at Yucaipa Junior High, CA; [memb.] CJSF-California Junior Scholastic Federation 94-95, 95-96; [hon.] Rotary Club, 2nd place Speech Contest 4.0 GPA 94-95, 93-94, 92-93 Presidential Award for Academic and Physical Fitness 1992; [a.] Yucaipa, CA

**ZUBYK, MARK D.**
[b.] April 25, 1974, San Mateo, CA; [p.] Francisco Zubyk, Anne Zubyk; [ed.] Hillsdale High School, The Master's College; [occ.] Student and Sales Counselor; [hon.] Bank of America, Industrial Arts Award, AWANA Clubs Citation Award; [pers.] I like to think of myself as a realist. My poetry and writings tend to reflect on the things which really make life worth living.; [a.] Belmont, CA

**ZWART, ERMA M.**
[b.] July 27, 1916, Murray Co, MN; [p.] W.W. and Irene (Kingsbury) Steven; [m.] William M. Zwart, February 20, 1935; [ch.] Roger, Marla, Judith, Joyce, Boyd, Sherry, Terry; [ed.] 12th Grade Edgerton High; [occ.] Homemaker; [memb.] The United Presbyterian Church in the United States of America recognizes Erma Zwart as an honory member. In recognition of Christian service given by United Women of first Presbyterian Church, Edgerton, MN; [oth. writ.] "Mom's Clovers"; [pers.] I believe: Love brings for the concern. Concern leads to care. Care is love in action. Actions prove the relationship.; [a.] Edgerton, MN

# INDEX